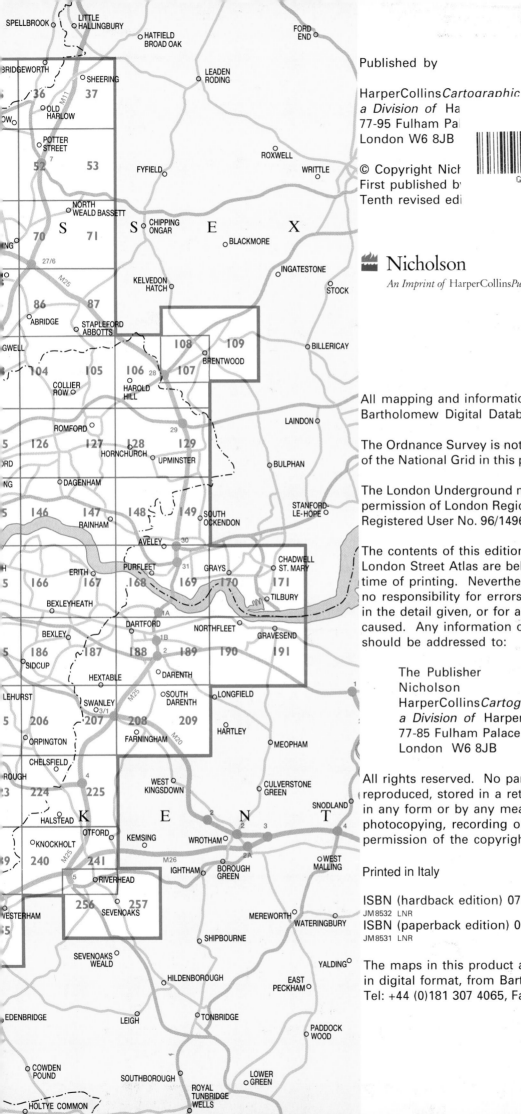

Published by

HarperCollins Cartographic
a Division of Ha
77-95 Fulham Pa
London W6 8JB

© Copyright Nich
First published b
Tenth revised edi

Nicholson
An Imprint of HarperCollins Publishers

All mapping and information is generated from the
Bartholomew Digital Databases.

The Ordnance Survey is not responsible for the accuracy
of the National Grid in this publication.

The London Underground map is reproduced by
permission of London Regional Transport - LRT
Registered User No. 96/1496

The contents of this edition of the Nicholson Greater
London Street Atlas are believed to be correct at the
time of printing. Nevertheless the publisher can accept
no responsibility for errors or omissions, or for changes
in the detail given, or for any expense or loss thereby
caused. Any information or queries relating to this atlas
should be addressed to:

The Publisher
Nicholson
HarperCollins Cartographic
a Division of HarperCollins Publishers
77-85 Fulham Palace Road
London W6 8JB

Printed in Italy

ISBN (hardback edition) 07028 3143 3
JM8532 LNR
ISBN (paperback edition) 0 7028 3142 5
JM8531 LNR

The maps in this product are also available for purchase
in digital format, from Bartholomew Data Sales
Tel: +44 (0)181 307 4065, Fax: +44 (0)181 307 4813

NICHOLSON
GREATER LONDON STREET ATLAS

CONTENTS

M25 LONDON ORBITAL MOTORWAY

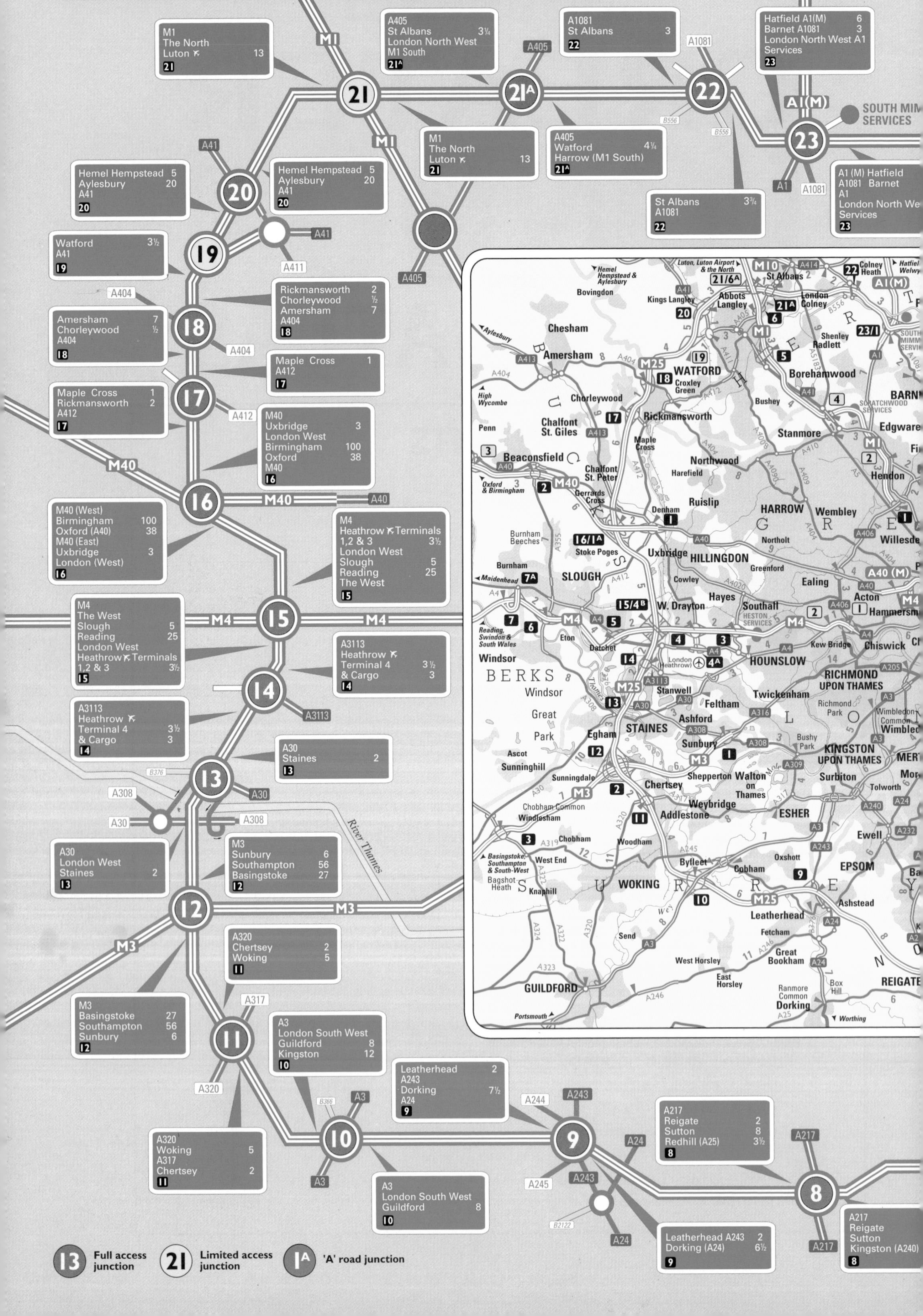

M1
The North
Luton ✈ 13
21

A405
St Albans 3¼
London North West
M1 South
21ᴬ

A1081
St Albans 3
22

A1081

Hatfield A1(M) 6
Barnet A1081 3
London North West A1
Services
23

SOUTH MIM
SERVICES

A41

Hemel Hempstead 5
Aylesbury 20
A41
20

Hemel Hempstead 5
Aylesbury 20
A41
20

M1
The North
Luton ✈ 13
21

A405
Watford 4¼
Harrow (M1 South)
21ᴬ

B556

St Albans 3¾
A1081
22

A1 (M) Hatfield
A1081 Barnet
A1
London North We
Services
23

A1
A1081

Watford 3½
A41
19

A411

A404

Rickmansworth 2
Chorleywood ½
Amersham 7
A404
18

Amersham 7
Chorleywood ½
A404
18

A404

Maple Cross 1
A412
17

A412

Maple Cross 1
Rickmansworth 2
A412
17

M40
Uxbridge 3
London West
Birmingham 100
Oxford 38
M40
16

M40

A40

M40 (West)
Birmingham 100
Oxford (A40) 38
M40 (East)
Uxbridge 3
London (West)
16

M4
Heathrow ✈ Terminals
1,2 & 3 3½
London West
Slough 5
Reading 25
The West
15

M4
The West
Slough 5
Reading 25
London West
Heathrow ✈ Terminals
1,2 & 3 3½
15

M4

A3113
Heathrow ✈
Terminal 4 3½
& Cargo 3
14

A3113
Heathrow ✈
Terminal 4 3½
& Cargo 3
14

A3113

A30
Staines 2
13

B376

A308

A30

A308

A30
London West
Staines 2
13

River Thames

M3
Sunbury 6
Southampton 56
Basingstoke 27
12

M3

A320
Chertsey 2
Woking 5
11

A317

M3
Basingstoke 27
Southampton 56
Sunbury 6
12

A3
London South West
Guildford 8
Kingston 12
10

A320

B366
A3

Leatherhead 2
A243
Dorking 7½
A24
9

A244
A243

A217
Reigate 2
Sutton 8
Redhill (A25) 3½
8

A217

A320
Woking 5
A317
Chertsey 2
11

10

A3

A3
London South West
Guildford 8
10

A245
A243

9

A24

B2122

Leatherhead A243 2
Dorking (A24) 6½
9

A217
Reigate
Sutton
Kingston (A240)
8

A217

Map detail

Luton, Luton Airport
& the North

Hemel
Hempstead &
Aylesbury

M10

A414

21/6ᴬ

St Albans 2

22 Colney Hatfie
Heath Welwy

A1(M)

Bovingdon

Kings Langley

Abbots
Langley

London
Colney

Chesham

A41

20

21ᴬ

6

Shenley
Radlett

23/1

Amersham 8

A413

M25

WATFORD

18 Croxley
Green

Borehamwood

BARN

SCRATCHWOOD
SERVICES

High
Wycombe

A404

19

Chorleywood

Rickmansworth

A41

Bushey

Stanmore

4

Edgware

A40

Penn

Chalfont
St. Giles

17

A413

Maple
Cross

Northwood

A410

HARROW

G

E

Wembley

Willesde

3

Beaconsfield

A412

Chalfont
St. Peter

Harefield

Ruislip

R

A406

2

Oxford
& Birmingham

A40

2

M40

Denham

1

Gerrards
Cross

Northolt

Greenford

E

Hendon

Burnham
Beeches

A355

Stoke Poges

16/1ᴬ

Uxbridge

HILLINGDON

Ealing

Acton

A40(M)

Burnham

15/4ᴮ

W. Drayton

Cowley

Hayes

Southall

A406

2

Hammersm

Maidenhead

7ᴬ

SLOUGH

A412

A4020

HESTON
SERVICES

M4

Kew Bridge

Chiswick

7

6

M4

4

3

4

4

A4

Reading,
Swindon &
South Wales

Eton

Datchet

14

London
(Heathrow)

4ᴬ

HOUNSLOW

A205

A4

Windsor

A3113

Stanwell

A30

13

M25

Feltham

Twickenham

RICHMOND
UPON THAMES

A3

BERKS

Windsor

Great
Park

Egham

STAINES

A308

Ashford

A316

L

Richmond
Park

Wimbledon
Common

Wimbled

Ascot

Sunninghill

12

Sunbury

1

A308

Bushy
Park

KINGSTON
UPON THAMES

MERT

Sunningdale

M3

Chertsey

Shepperton

Walton
on
Thames

A309

Surbiton

Tolworth

Mor

Chobham Common

Windlesham

2

Weybridge

ESHER

A240

A24

Addlestone

3

Chobham

11

Woodham

Byfleet

Cobham

Oxshott

9

Ewell

A243

EPSOM

Ba

Basingstoke,
Southampton
& South-West

West End

A319

12

10

WOKING

R

Leatherhead

Ashtead

Bagshot
Heath

Knaphill

U

E

Fetcham

A24

Send

A324

A322

A320

8

11

A24

Great
Bookham

GUILDFORD

A323

West Horsley

East
Horsley

M25

Box
Hill

N

REIGATE

Portsmouth

A246

Ranmore
Common

Dorking

A25

Worthing

Legend

13 Full access
junction

21 Limited access
junction

1ᴬ 'A' road junction

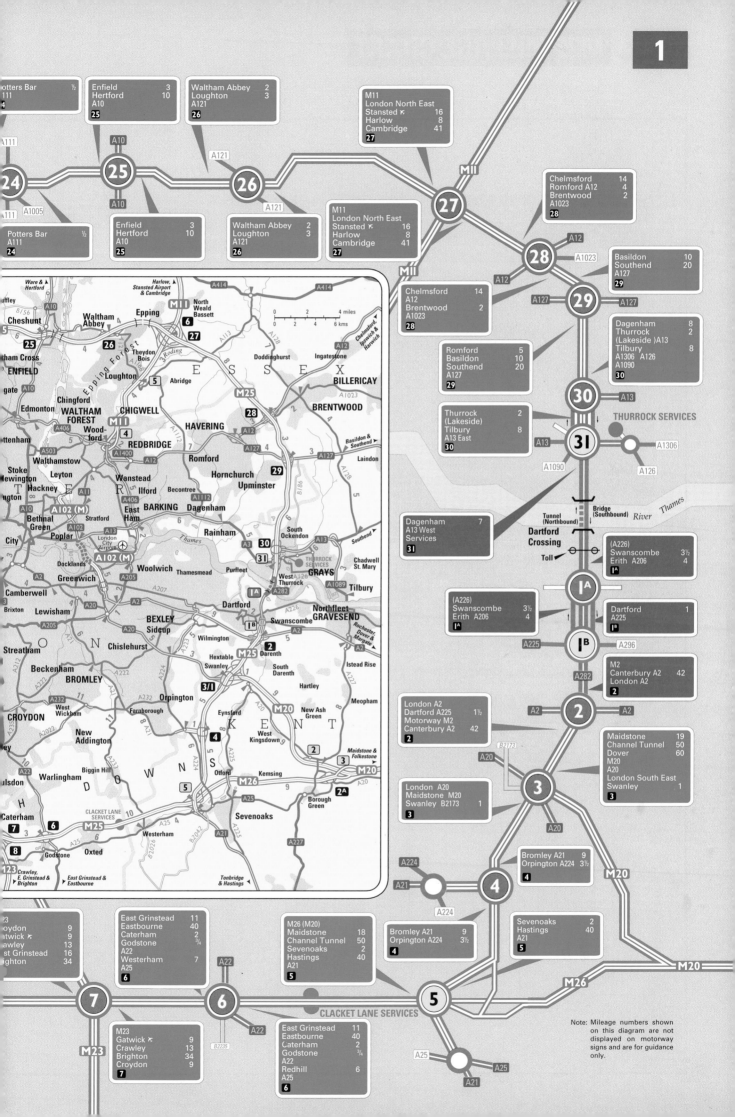

JUNCTION OF EXIT

JUNCTION OF ENTRY

Junction	No.	1	2	3	4	5	6	7	8	9	10	11	12	13	14	15	16	17	18	19	20	21	22	23	24	25	26	27	28	29	30	31
DARTFORD	1		1	4	8	12	22	25	28	35	41	46	48	51	53	55	59	53	52	49	48	45	40	37	34	28	25	21	13	10	5	4
A2	2	1		3	7	11	21	24	27	34	40	45	47	50	52	54	58	54	53	50	49	46	41	38	35	29	26	22	14	11	6	5
M20	3	4	3		4	8	18	21	24	31	37	42	44	47	49	51	55	57	56	53	52	49	44	41	38	32	29	25	17	14	9	8
A21	4	8	7	4		4	14	17	20	27	33	38	40	43	45	47	51	57	58	57	56	53	48	45	42	36	33	29	21	18	13	12
M26	5	12	11	8	4		10	13	16	23	29	34	36	39	41	43	47	53	54	57	58	57	52	49	46	40	37	33	25	22	17	16
A22	6	22	21	18	14	10		3	6	13	19	24	26	29	31	33	37	43	44	47	48	51	56	59	56	50	47	43	35	32	27	26
M23	7	25	24	21	17	13	3		3	10	16	21	23	26	28	30	34	40	41	44	45	48	53	56	59	53	50	46	38	35	30	29
REIGATE	8	28	27	24	20	16	6	3		7	13	18	20	23	25	27	31	37	38	41	42	45	50	53	56	56	53	49	41	38	33	32
LEATHERHEAD	9	35	34	31	27	23	13	10	7		6	11	13	16	18	20	24	30	31	34	35	38	43	46	49	55	58	56	48	45	40	39
A3	10	41	40	37	33	29	19	16	13	6		5	7	10	12	14	18	24	25	28	29	32	37	40	43	49	52	56	54	51	46	45
CHERTSEY	11	46	45	42	38	34	24	21	18	11	5		2	5	7	9	13	19	20	23	24	27	32	35	38	44	47	51	59	56	51	50
M3	12	48	47	44	40	36	26	23	20	13	7	2		3	5	7	11	17	18	21	22	25	30	33	36	42	45	49	57	58	53	52
A30	13	51	50	47	43	39	29	26	23	16	10	5	3		2	4	8	14	15	18	19	22	27	30	33	39	42	46	54	57	56	55
HEATHROW 4	14	53	52	49	45	41	31	28	25	18	12	7	5	2		2	6	12	13	16	17	20	25	28	31	37	40	44	52	55	58	57
M4, HEATHROW 1-3	15	55	54	51	47	43	33	30	27	20	14	9	7	4	2		4	10	11	14	15	18	23	26	29	35	38	42	50	53	58	59
M40	16	59	58	55	51	47	37	34	31	24	18	13	11	8	6	4		6	7	10	11	14	19	22	25	31	34	38	46	49	54	55
RICKMANSWORTH	17	53	54	57	57	53	43	40	37	30	24	19	17	14	12	10	6		1	4	5	8	13	16	19	25	28	32	40	43	48	49
A404	18	52	53	56	58	54	44	41	38	31	25	20	18	15	13	11	7	1		3	4	7	12	15	18	24	27	31	39	42	47	48
WATFORD	19	49	50	53	57	57	47	44	41	34	28	23	21	18	16	14	10	4	3		1	4	9	12	15	21	24	28	36	39	44	45
A41	20	48	49	52	56	58	48	45	42	35	29	24	22	19	17	15	11	5	4	1		3	8	11	14	20	23	27	35	38	43	44
M1	21	45	46	49	53	57	51	48	45	38	32	27	25	22	20	18	14	8	7	4	3		5	8	11	17	20	24	32	35	40	41
ST. ALBANS	22	40	41	44	48	52	56	53	50	43	37	32	30	27	25	23	19	13	12	9	8	5		3	6	12	15	19	27	30	35	36
A1 (M)	23	37	38	41	45	49	59	56	53	46	40	35	33	30	28	26	22	16	15	12	11	8	3		3	9	12	16	24	27	32	33
A111	24	34	35	38	42	46	56	59	56	49	43	38	36	33	31	29	25	19	18	15	14	11	6	3		6	9	13	21	24	29	30
A10	25	28	29	32	36	40	50	53	56	55	49	44	42	39	37	35	31	25	24	21	20	17	12	9	6		3	7	15	18	23	24
EPPING	26	25	26	29	33	37	47	50	53	58	52	47	45	42	40	38	34	28	27	24	23	20	15	12	9	3		4	12	15	20	21
M11	27	21	22	25	29	33	43	46	49	56	56	51	49	46	44	42	38	32	31	28	27	24	19	16	13	7	4		8	11	16	17
A12	28	13	14	17	21	25	35	38	41	48	54	59	57	54	52	50	46	40	39	36	35	32	27	24	21	15	12	8		3	8	9
A127	29	10	11	14	18	22	32	35	38	45	51	56	58	57	55	53	49	43	42	39	38	35	30	27	24	18	15	11	3		5	6
A13	30	5	6	9	13	17	27	30	33	40	46	51	53	56	58	58	54	48	47	44	43	40	35	32	29	23	20	16	8	5		1
A13	31	4	5	8	12	16	26	29	32	39	45	50	52	55	57	59	55	49	48	45	44	41	36	33	30	24	21	17	9	6	1	

Mileage Clockwise

Mileage AntiClockwise

Note: This chart shows the shortest distance between junctions. The colours indicate whether the distance is clockwise or anticlockwise. The total distance around the M25 is approximately 117 miles.

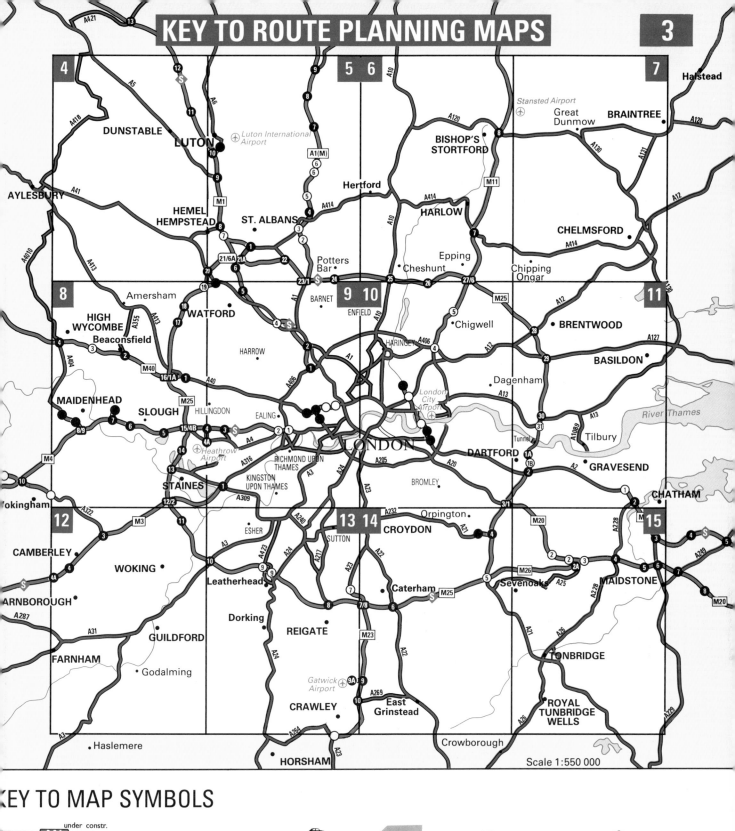

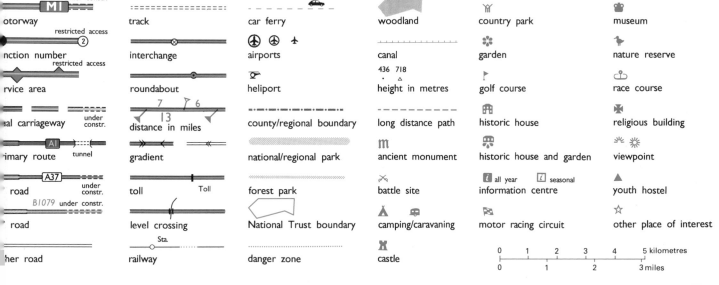

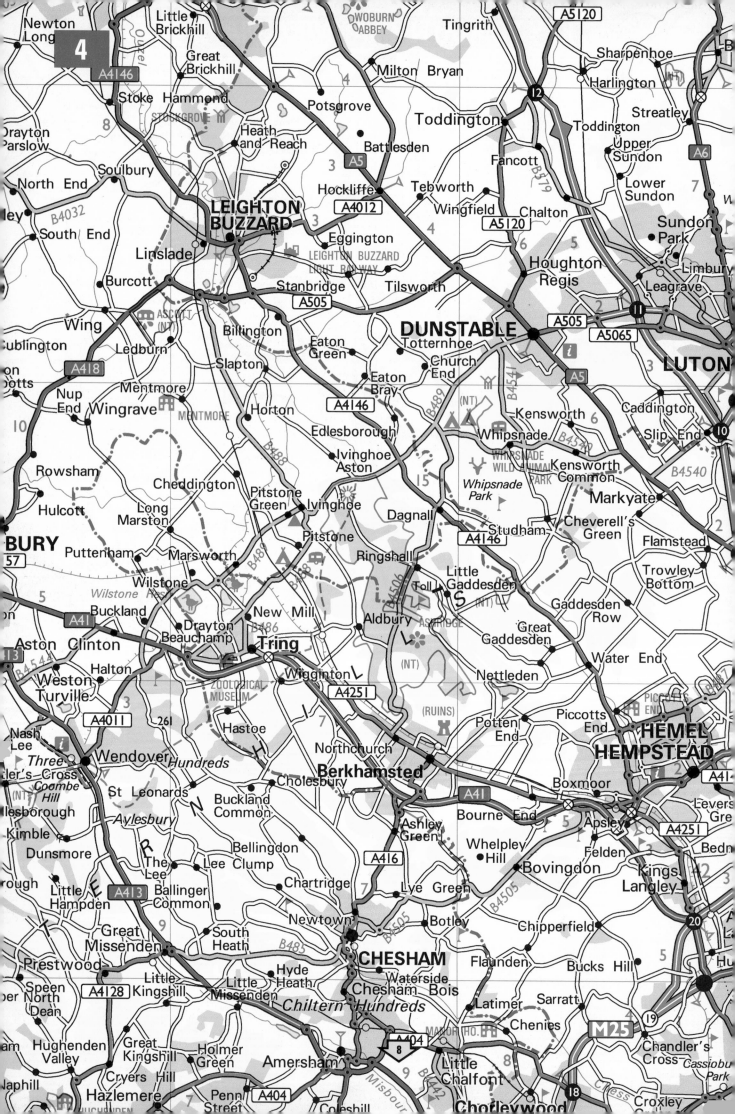

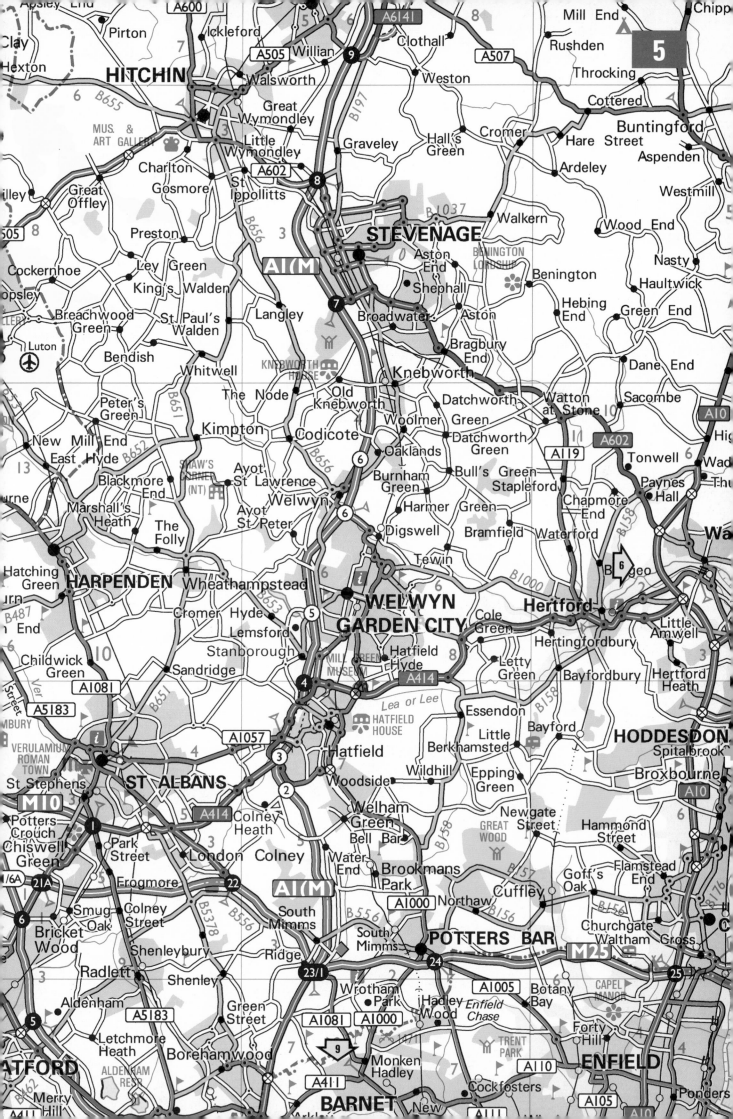

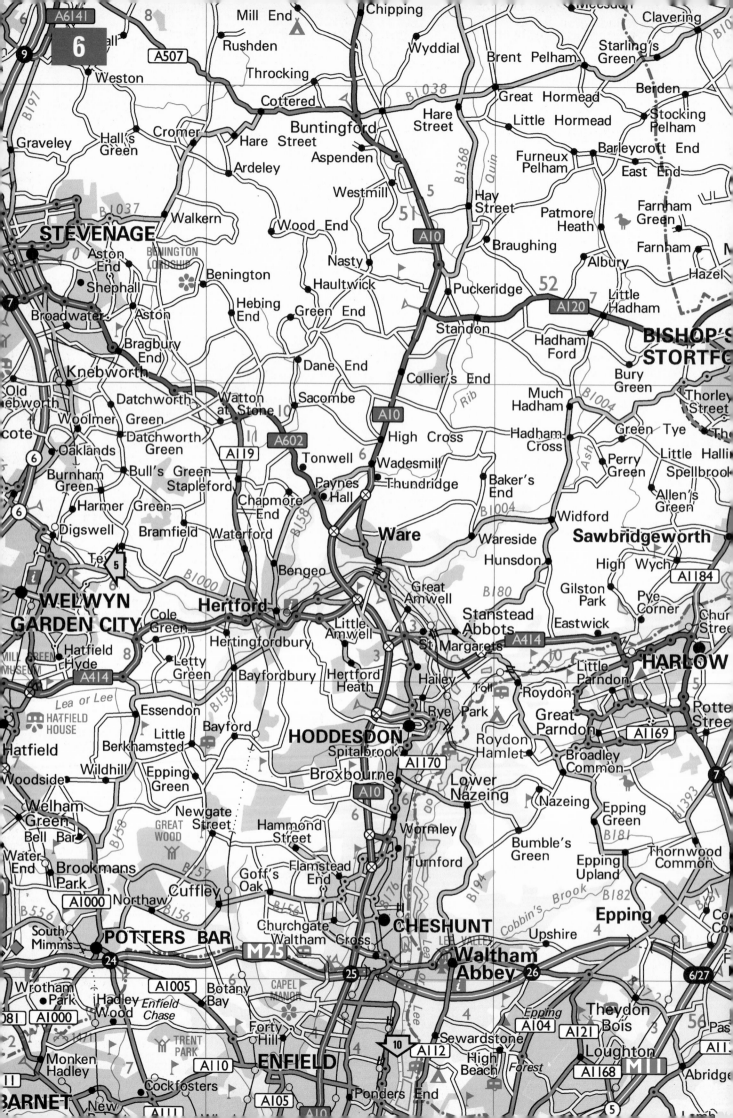

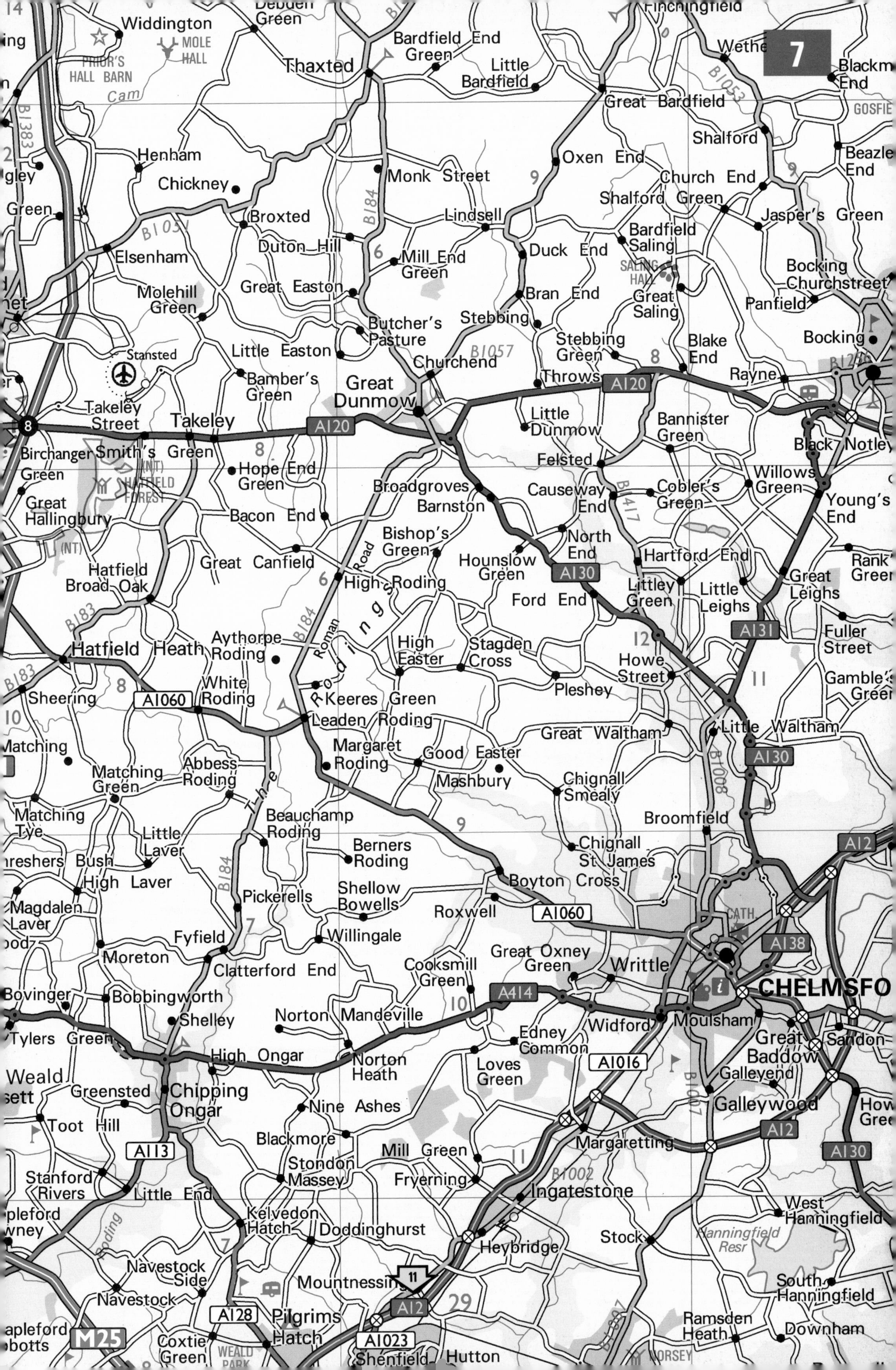
Widdington
MOLE HALL
PRIOR'S HALL BARN
Cam
Debden Green
Thaxted
Bardfield End Green
Little Bardfield
Finchingfield
Wethe
Blackm End
Great Bardfield
GOSFIE
Shalford
Beazle End
Henham
Chickney
Monk Street
Oxen End
Church End
Shalford Green
Jasper's Green
Broxted
Lindsell
Bardfield Saling
Elsenham
Duton Hill
Mill End Green
Duck End
SALING HALL
Bocking Churchstreet
Molehill Green
Great Easton
Bran End
Great Saling
Panfield
Butcher's Pasture
Stebbing
Stebbing Green
Blake End
Bocking
Stansted
Little Easton
Churchend
Throws
Rayne
Bamber's Green
Great Dunmow
Takeley Street
Takeley
Little Dunmow
Bannister Green
Black Notley
Birchanger
Smith's Green
Felsted
Green
Hope End Green
Broadgroves
Willows Green
HATFIELD FOREST
Causeway End
Cobler's Green
Young's End
Great Hallingbury
Barnston
Bacon End
Bishop's Green
North End
Hatfield Broad Oak
Great Canfield
Hounslow Green
Hartford End
Rank Green
Great Leighs
High Roding
Littley Green
Little Leighs
Ford End
Roman Road
The Rodings
Fuller Street
Hatfield Heath
Aythorpe Roding
High Easter
Stagden Cross
Howe Street
Gamble's Green
Sheering
White Roding
Pleshey
Keeres Green
Leaden Roding
Little Waltham
Great Waltham
Matching
Margaret Roding
Good Easter
Matching Green
Abbess Roding
Mashbury
Chignall Smealy
Matching Tye
Beauchamp Roding
Broomfield
Little Laver
Berners Roding
Chignall St James
Threshers Bush
High Laver
Boyton Cross
Magdalen Laver
Pickerells
Shellow Bowells
Roxwell
CATH
Fyfield
Willingale
Moreton
Clatterford End
Great Oxney Green
Cooksmill Green
Writtle
CHELMSFO
Bovinger
Bobbingworth
Norton Mandeville
Moulsham
Shelley
Widford
Edney Common
Great Baddow
Sandon
Tylers Green
High Ongar
Norton Heath
Loves Green
Galleyend
Weald
Chipping Ongar
Greensted
Nine Ashes
Galleywood
Toot Hill
Blackmore
Margaretting
Stondon Massey
Mill Green
Stanford Rivers
Fryerning
Little End
Ingatestone
West Hanningfield
Kelvedon Hatch
Doddinghurst
Stock
Hanningfield Resr
Heybridge
Navestock Side
Navestock
Mountnessing
South Hanningfield
Pilgrims Hatch
Ramsden Heath
Downham
Coxtie Green
WEALD PARK
Shenfield
Hutton
A120
A130
A131
A1060
A12
A138
A414
A1016
A113
A128
A1023
M25
B1383
B1051
B184
B1057
B183
B1417
B1008
B1007
B1002
B1053
B1256
Roding
8
9
6
11
12
10
7
29

KNOW NICHOLSON KNOW LONDON

NICHOLSON, the specialist London publisher, has an excellent range of maps and atlases to cater for your every need. Renowned for their accuracy and clarity, **NICHOLSON** maps and atlases make sure you get the most out of London.

Nicholson London Streetfinder

Paperback	£3.99
Spiral	£4.99
Paperback	£6.99
Spiral (large)	£7.99

Nicholson London Street Atlas

Mini	£3.25
Paperback	£3.75
Spiral	£4.25
Spiral (large)	£6.99
Vinyl (large)	£7.99

PREFERRED BY · LONDON · CAB DRIVERS

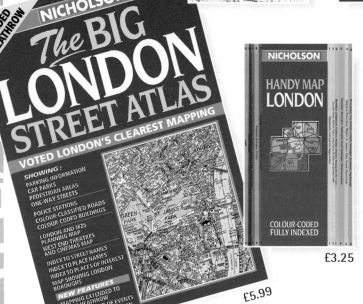

£5.99

£3.25

£3.50

£2.50

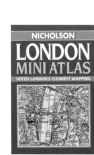

£1.50

£3.25

£3.50

All titles are available from good bookshops or call
HarperCollins Mail Order Department on 0141 306 3349 quoting code 93X.
For a list of the complete range from HarperCollins*Cartographic*,
write to: 77-85 Fulham Palace Road, Hammersmith, London, W6 8JB.

A Division of HarperCollins*Publishers.*

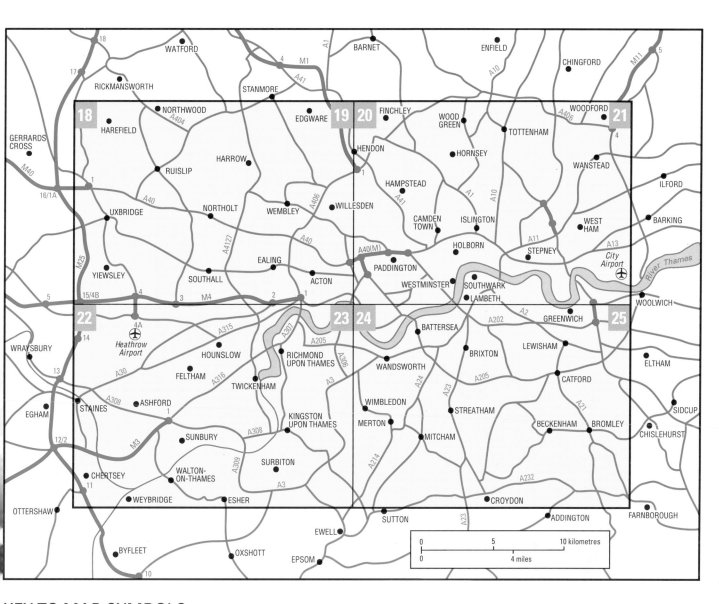

KEY TO MAP SYMBOLS

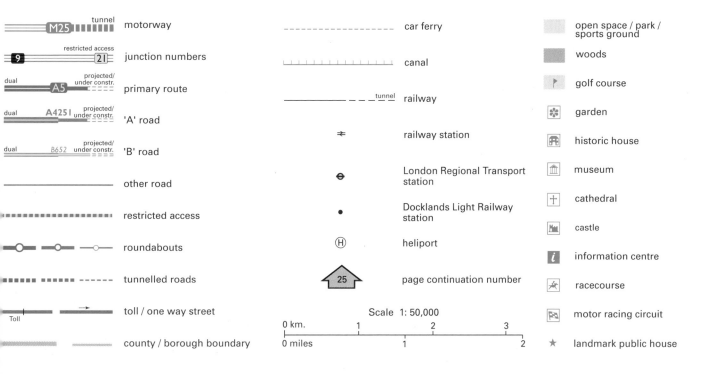

motorway	car ferry
junction numbers	canal
primary route	railway
'A' road	railway station
'B' road	London Regional Transport station
other road	Docklands Light Railway station
restricted access	heliport
roundabouts	page continuation number
tunnelled roads	
toll / one way street	open space / park / sports ground
county / borough boundary	woods

golf course

garden

historic house

museum

cathedral

castle

information centre

racecourse

motor racing circuit

★ landmark public house

Scale 1: 50,000

0 km.   1   2   3
0 miles   1   2

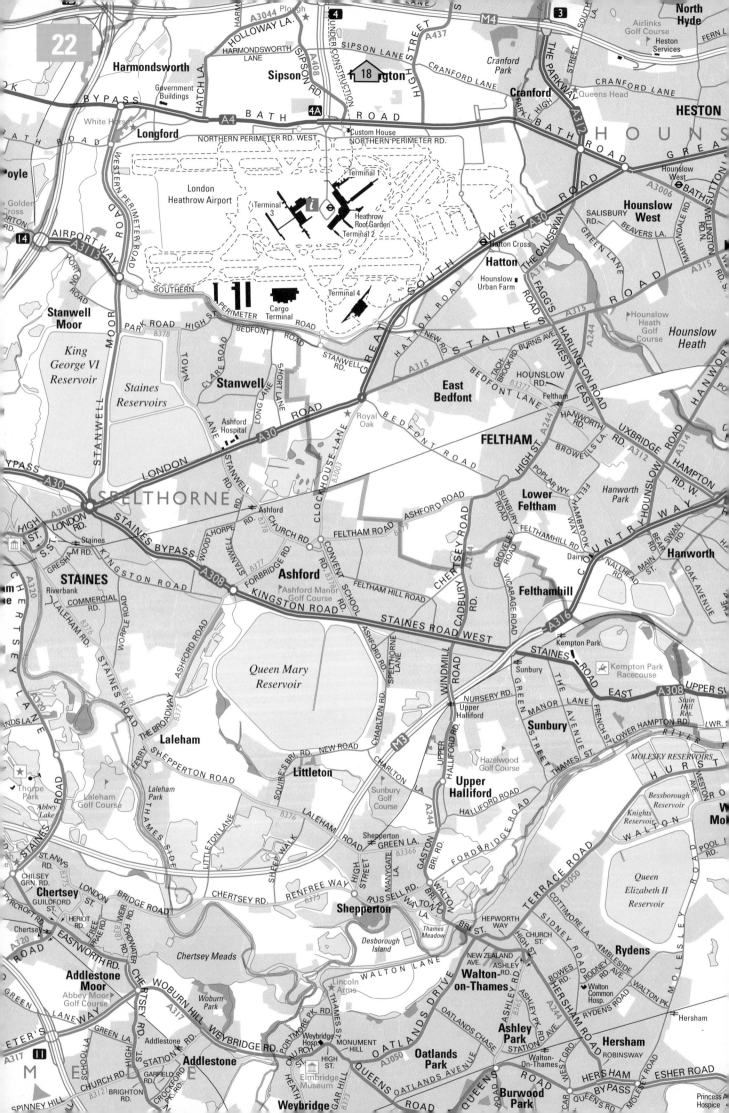

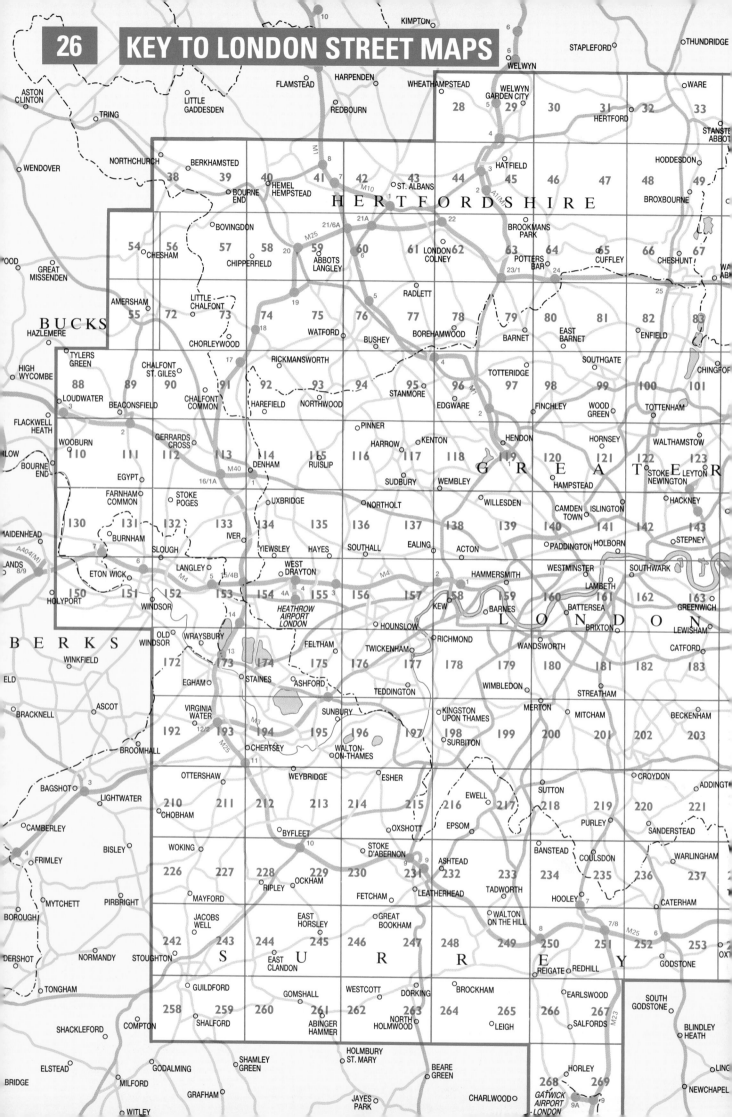

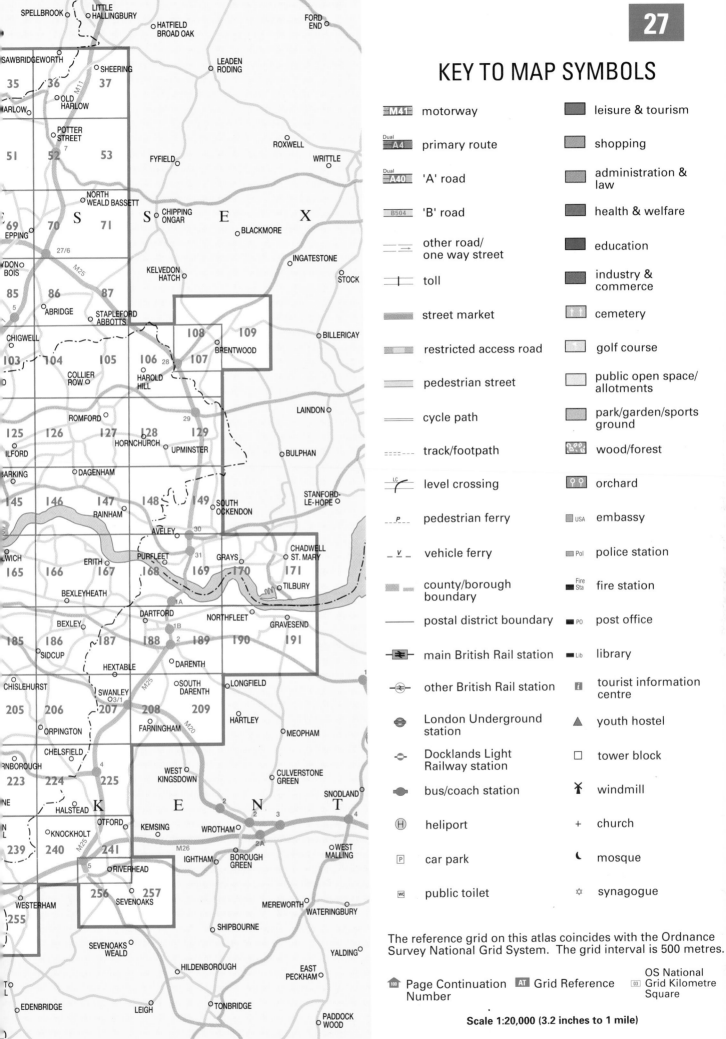

KEY TO MAP SYMBOLS

M41	motorway		leisure & tourism
Dual A4	primary route		shopping
Dual A40	'A' road		administration & law
B504	'B' road		health & welfare
	other road/ one way street		education
	toll		industry & commerce
	street market		cemetery
	restricted access road		golf course
	pedestrian street		public open space/ allotments
	cycle path		park/garden/sports ground
	track/footpath		wood/forest
LC	level crossing		orchard
P	pedestrian ferry	USA	embassy
V	vehicle ferry	Pol	police station
	county/borough boundary	Fire Sta	fire station
	postal district boundary	PO	post office
	main British Rail station	Lib	library
	other British Rail station	i	tourist information centre
	London Underground station	▲	youth hostel
	Docklands Light Railway station	□	tower block
	bus/coach station	✕	windmill
H	heliport	+	church
P	car park	☾	mosque
WC	public toilet	✿	synagogue

The reference grid on this atlas coincides with the Ordnance Survey National Grid System. The grid interval is 500 metres.

🡑100 Page Continuation Number   AT Grid Reference   03 OS National Grid Kilometre Square

Scale 1:20,000 (3.2 inches to 1 mile)

0	0.25	0.50	0.75	1 kilometre
0	¼		½ mile	

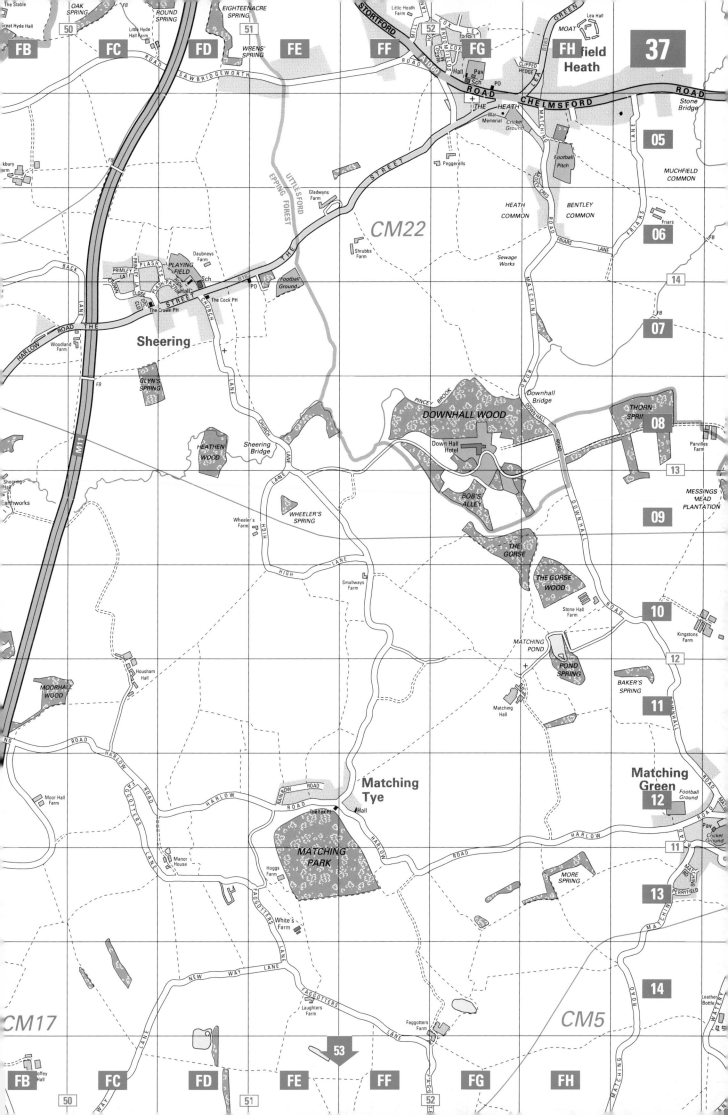

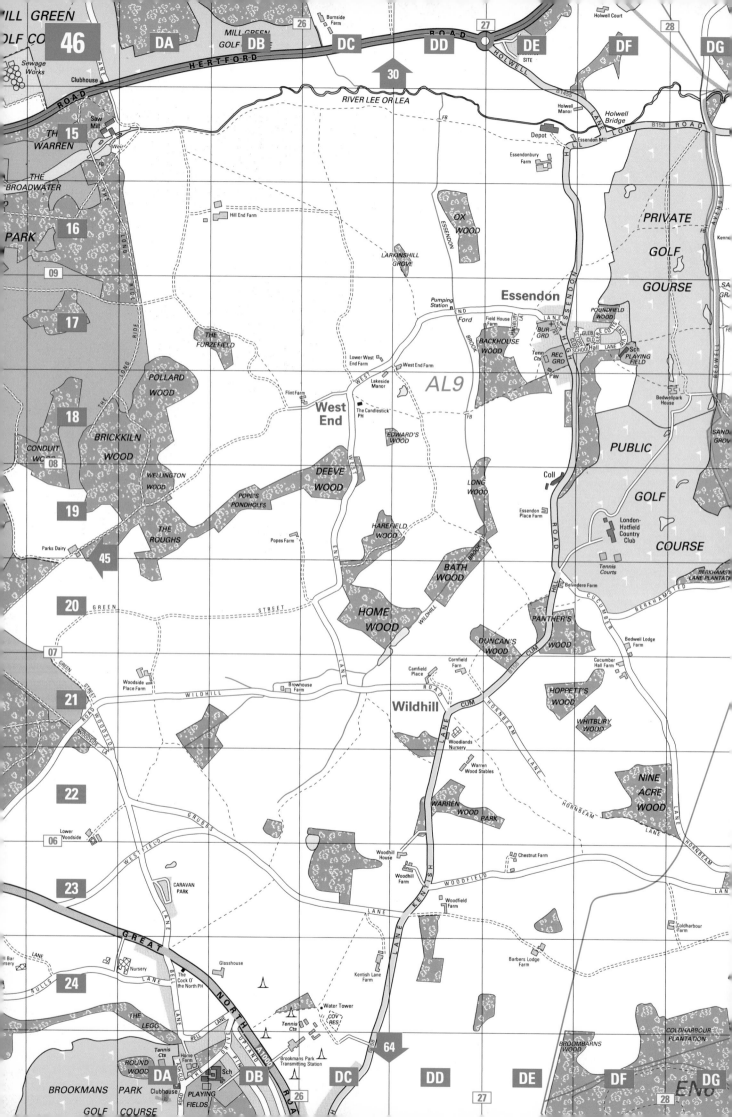

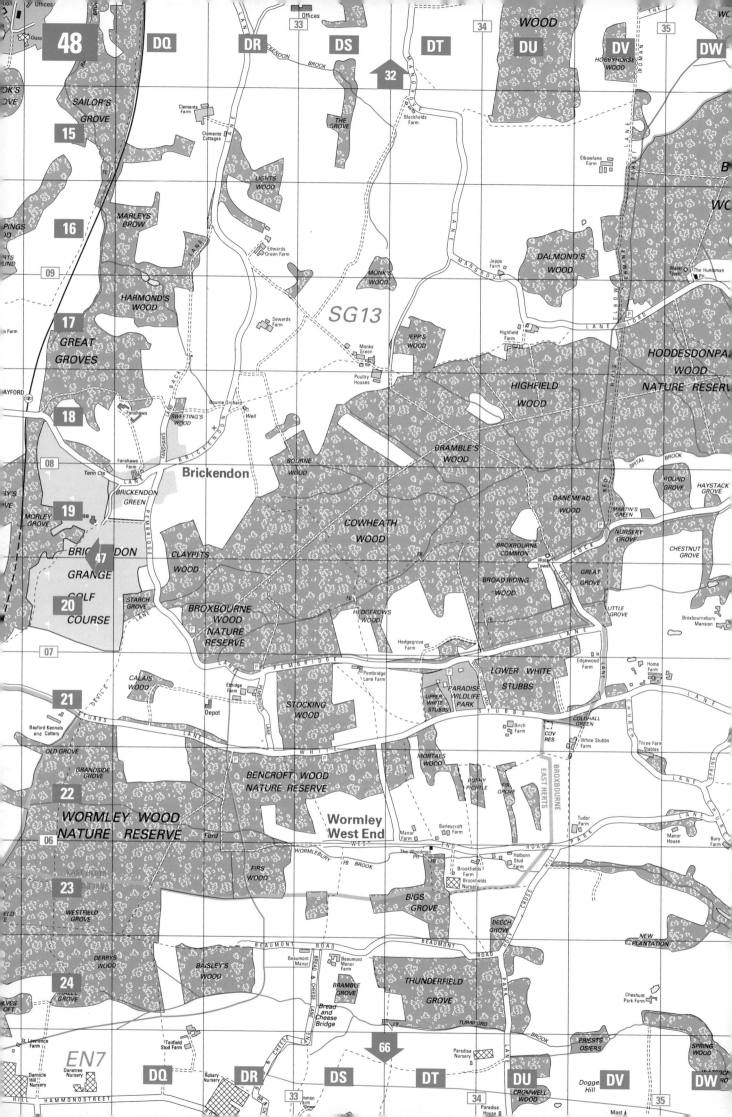

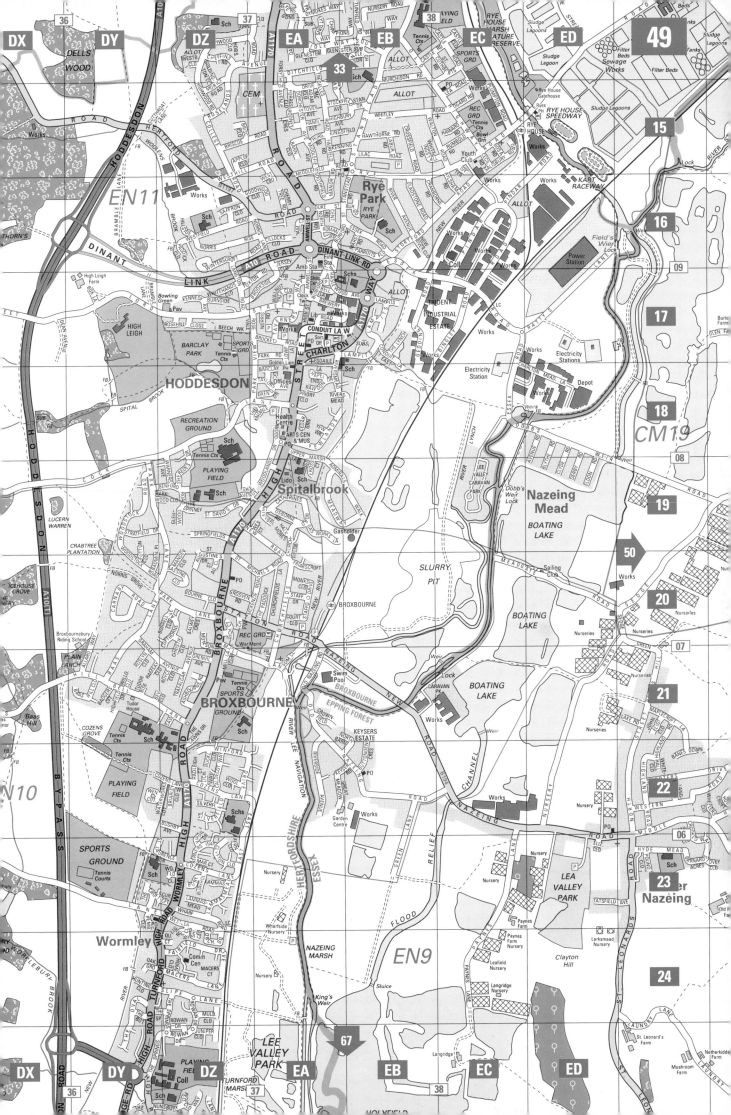

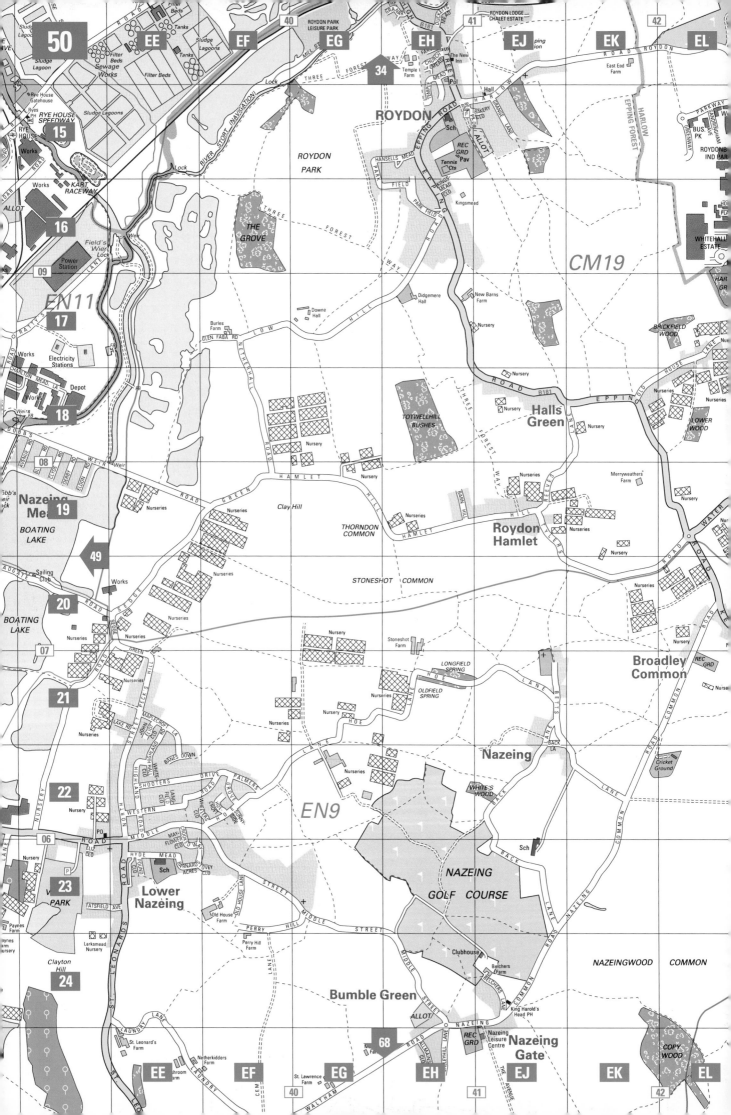

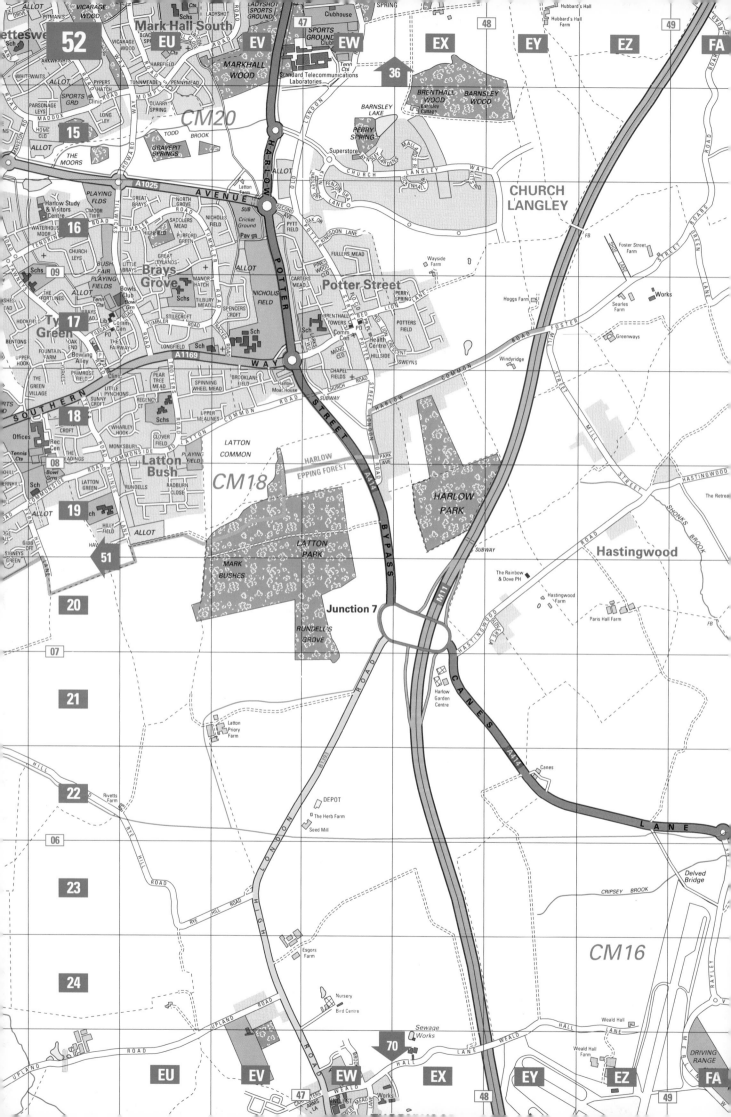

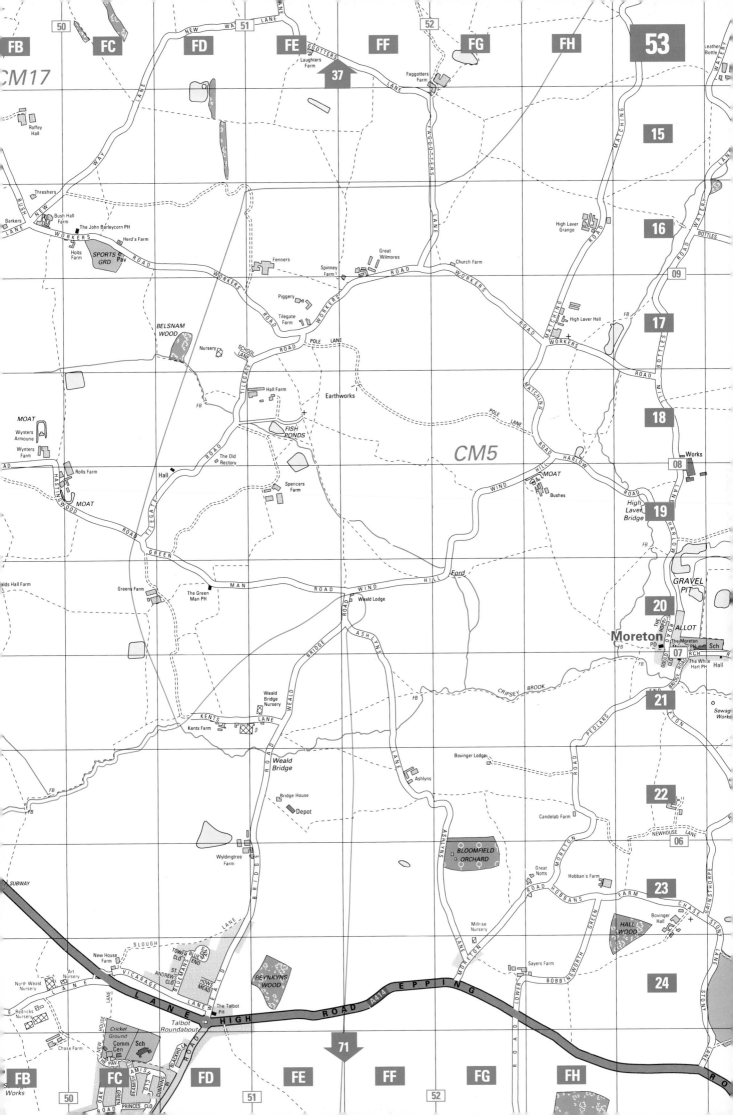

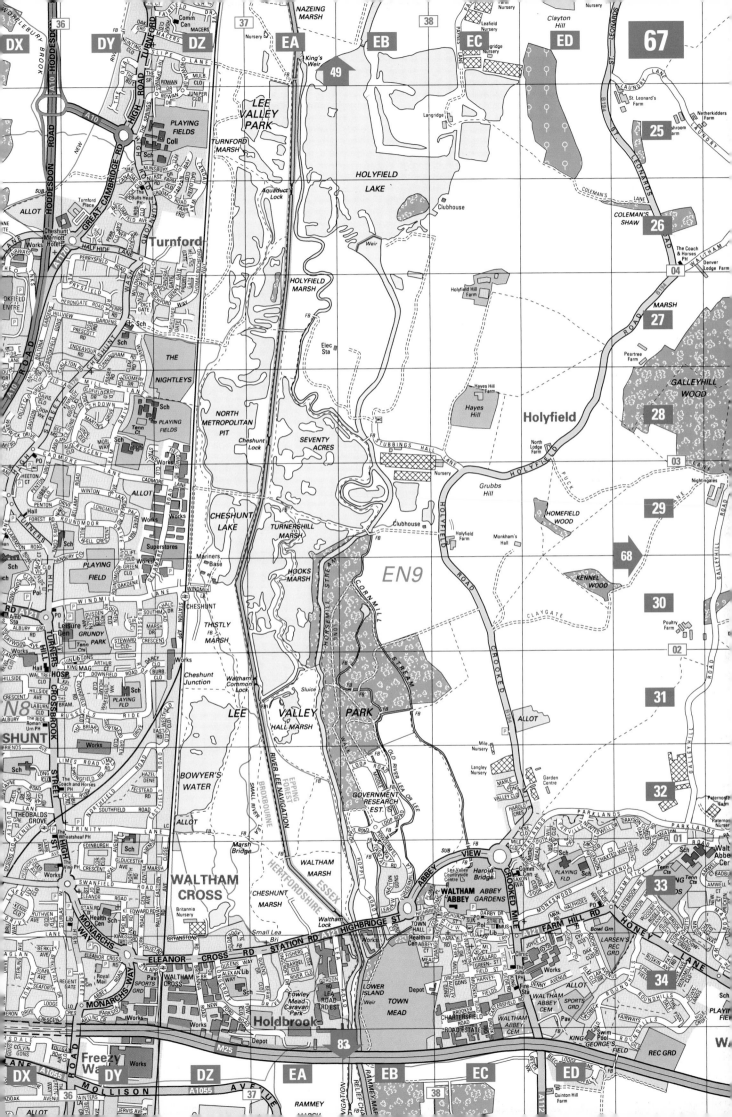

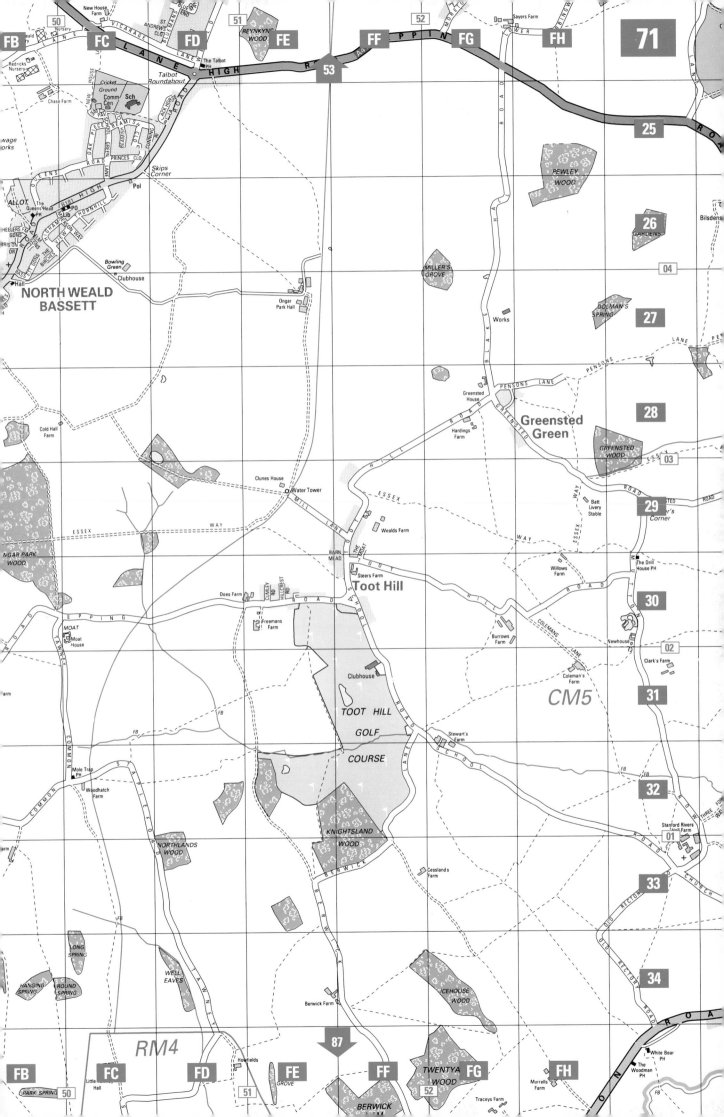

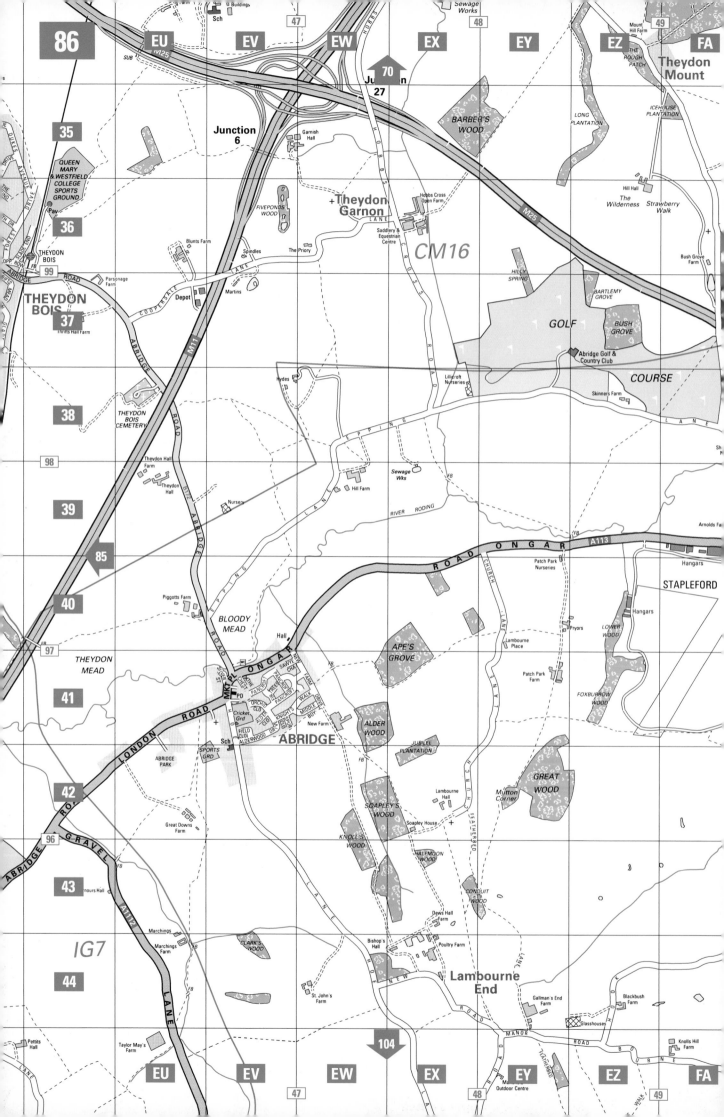

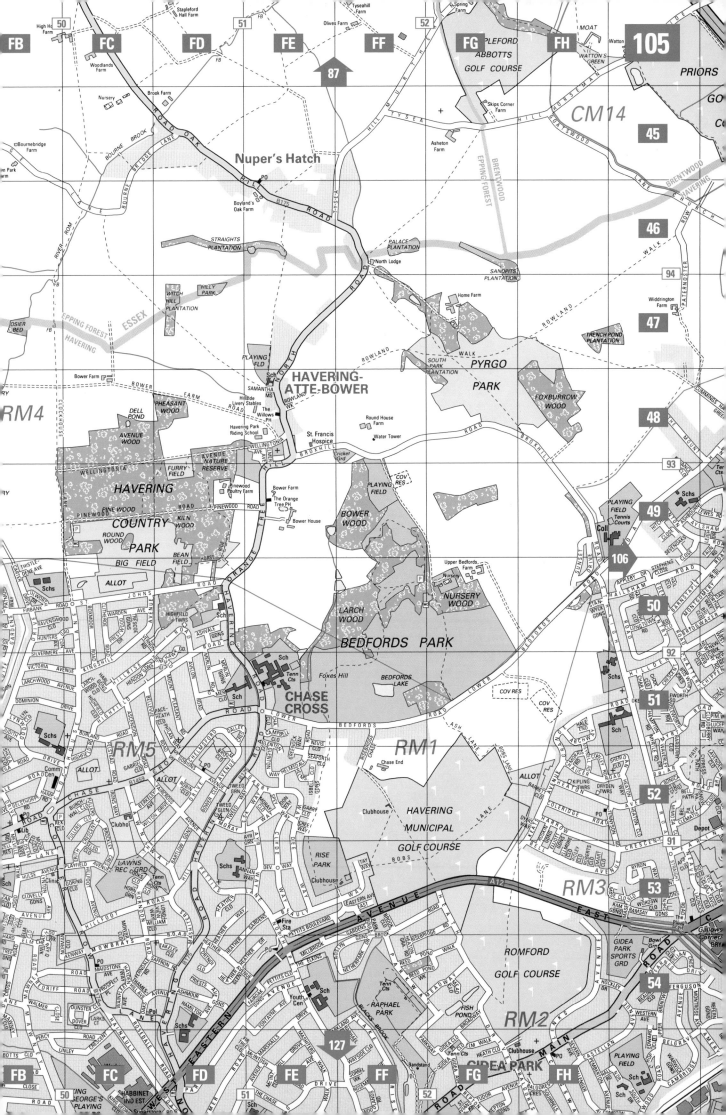

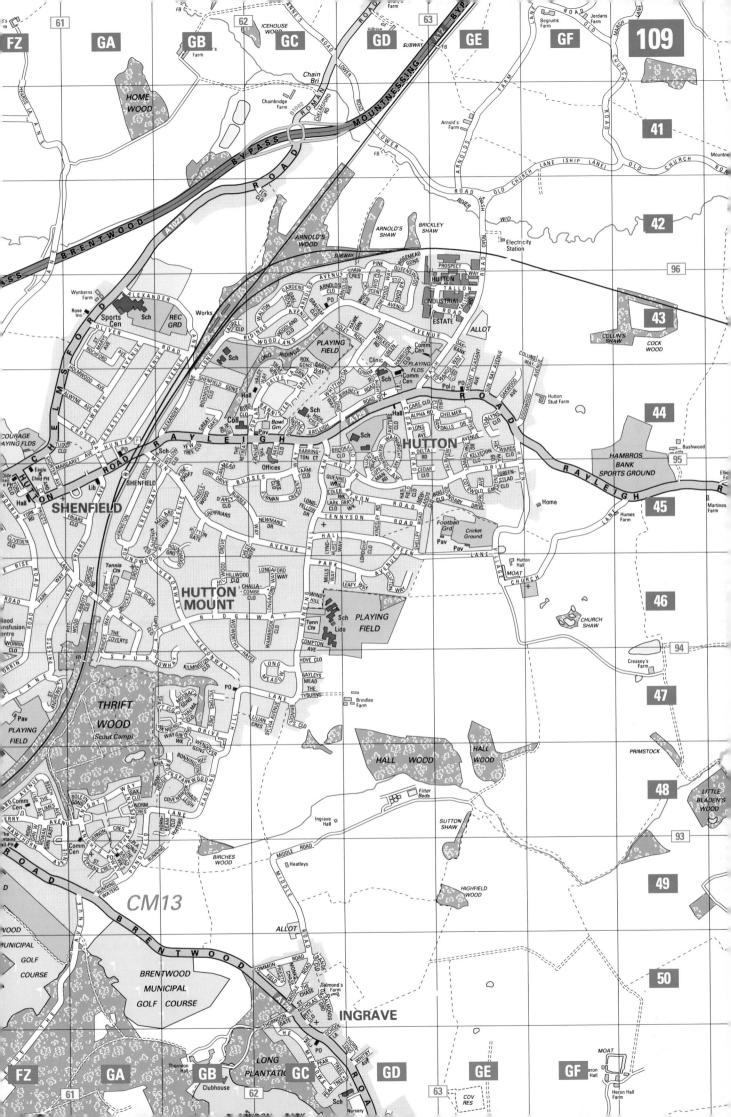

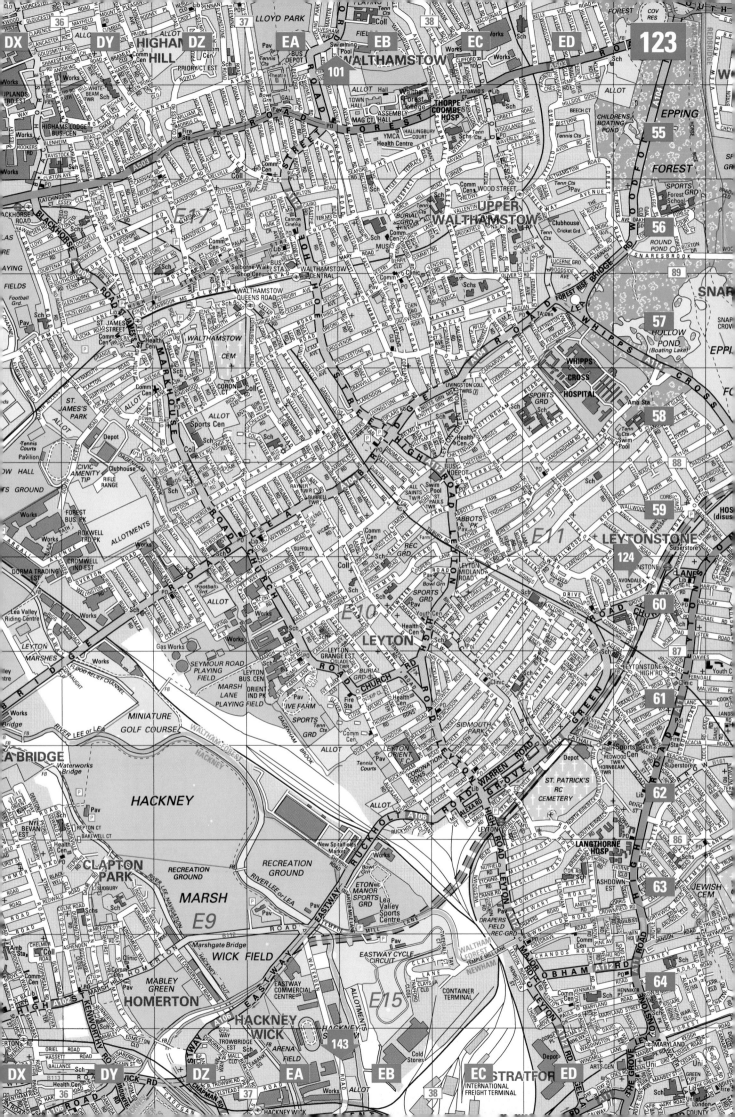

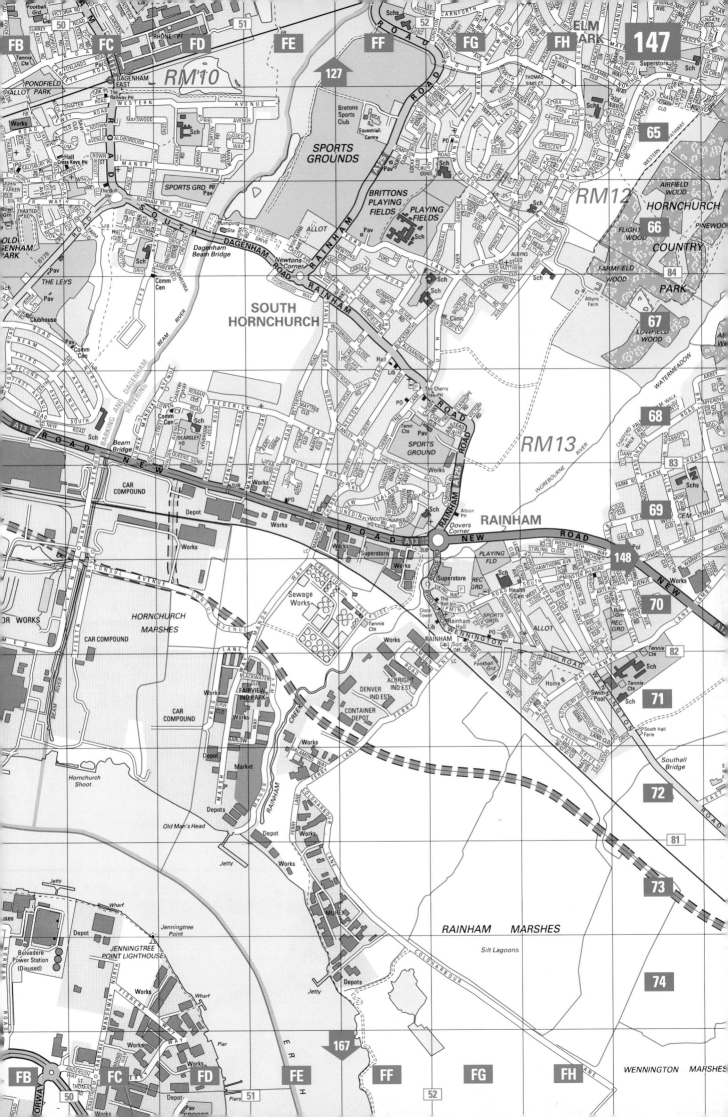

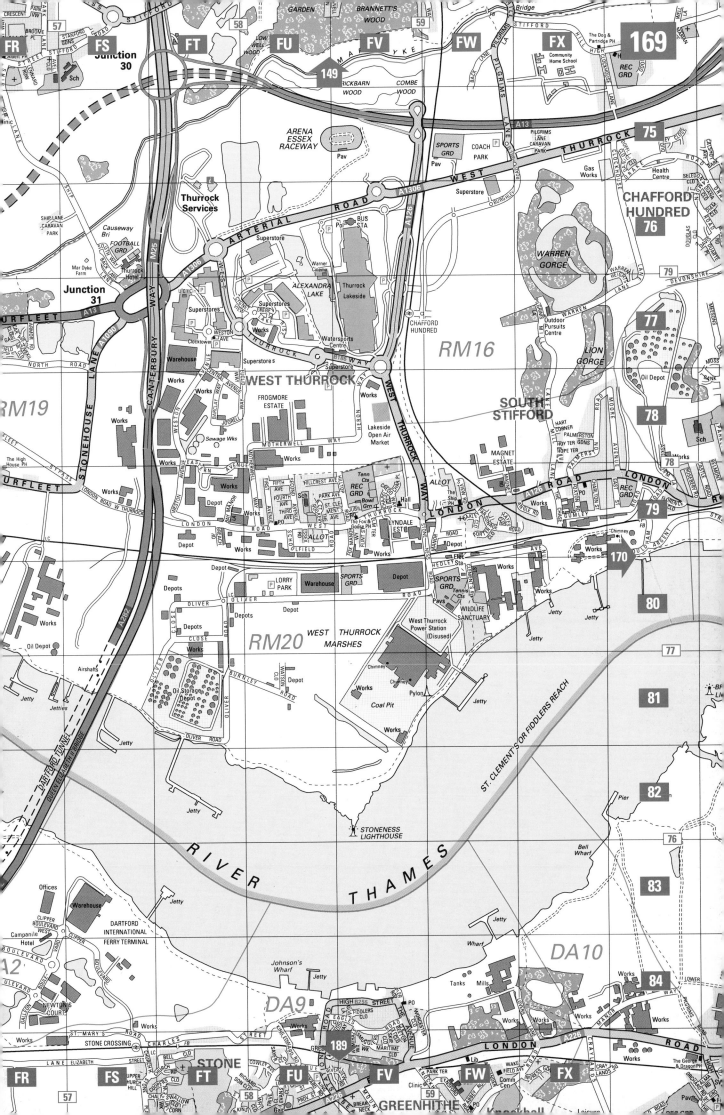

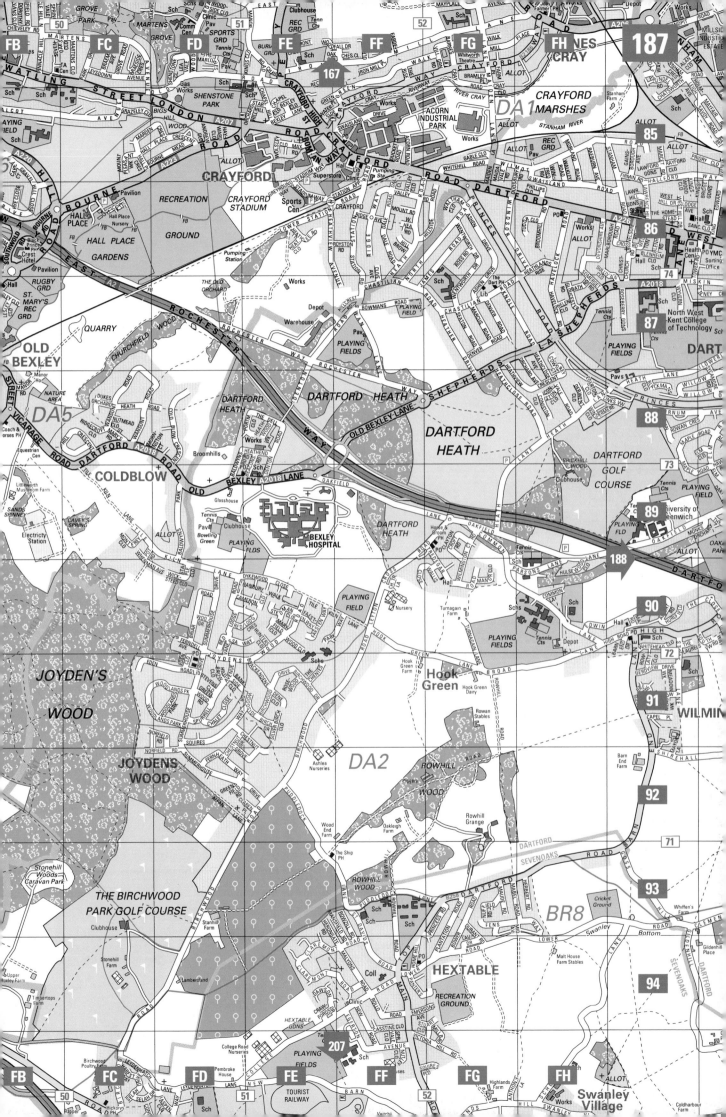

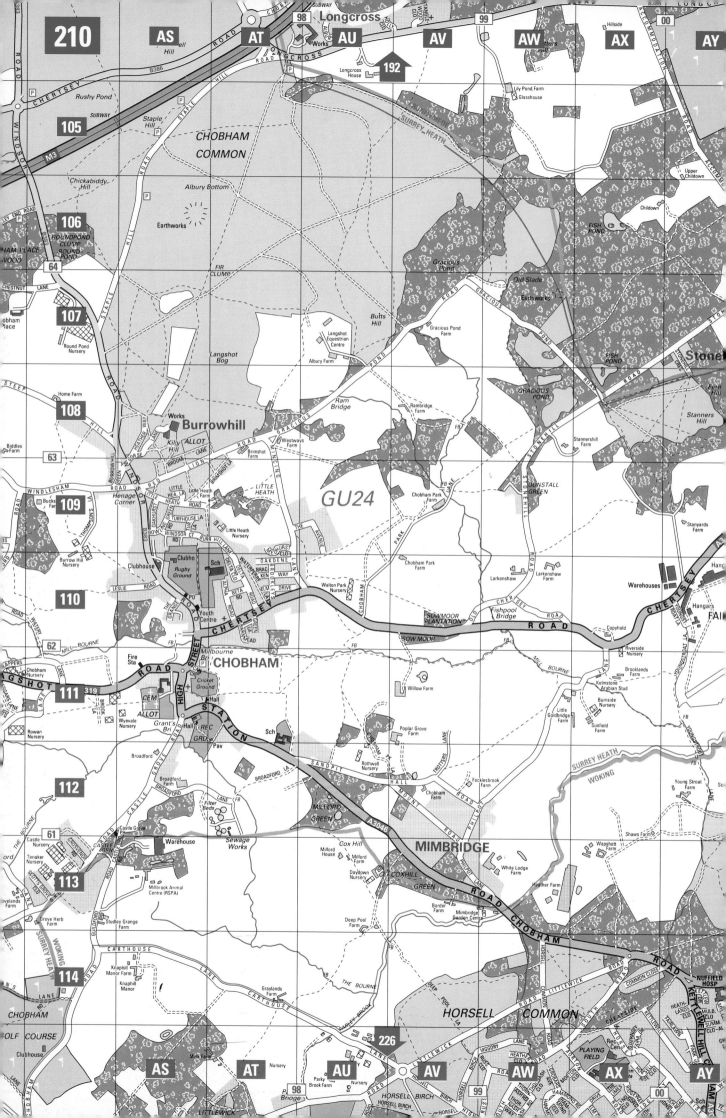

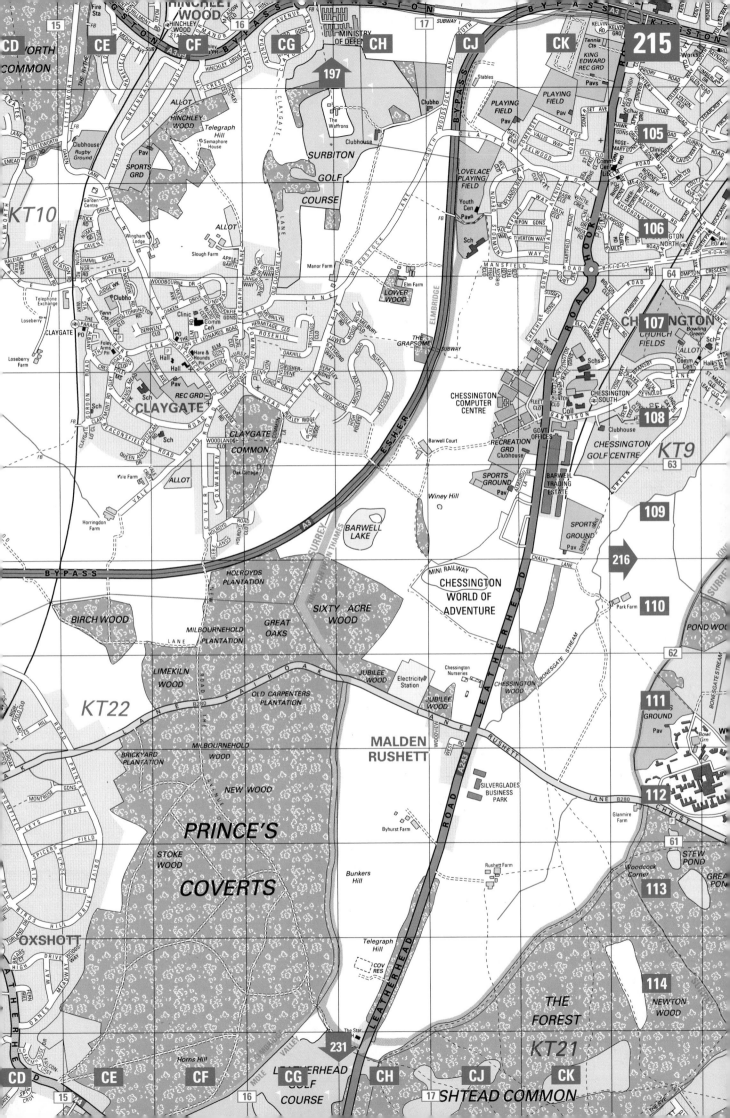

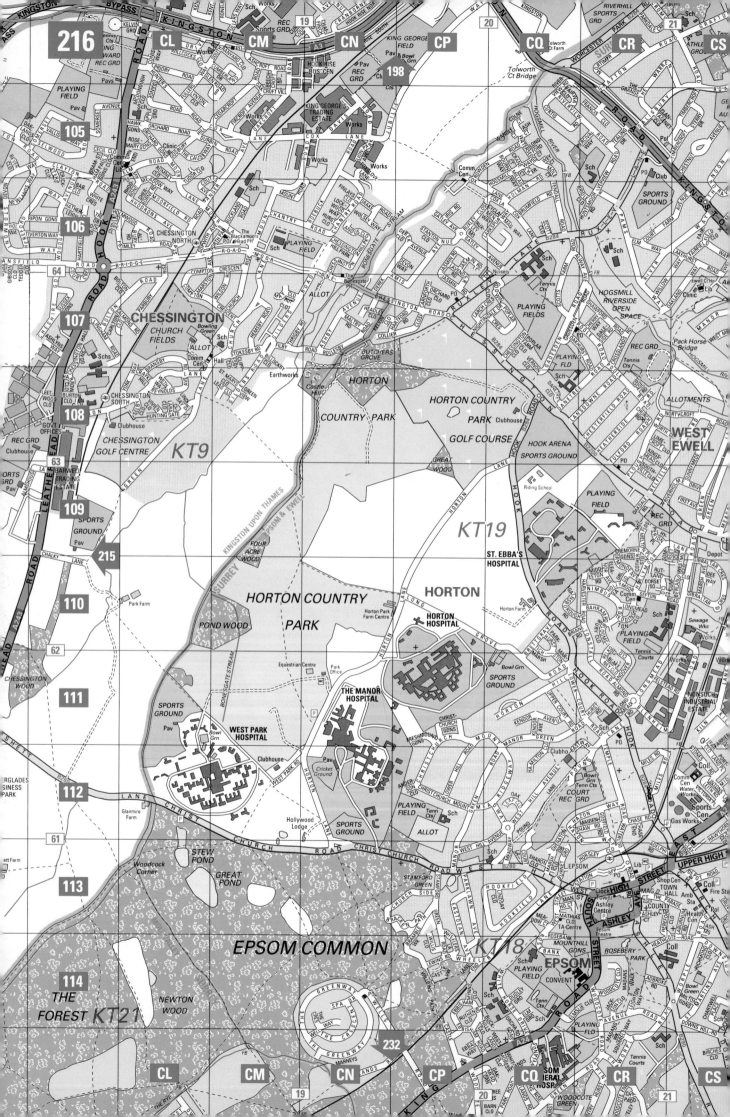

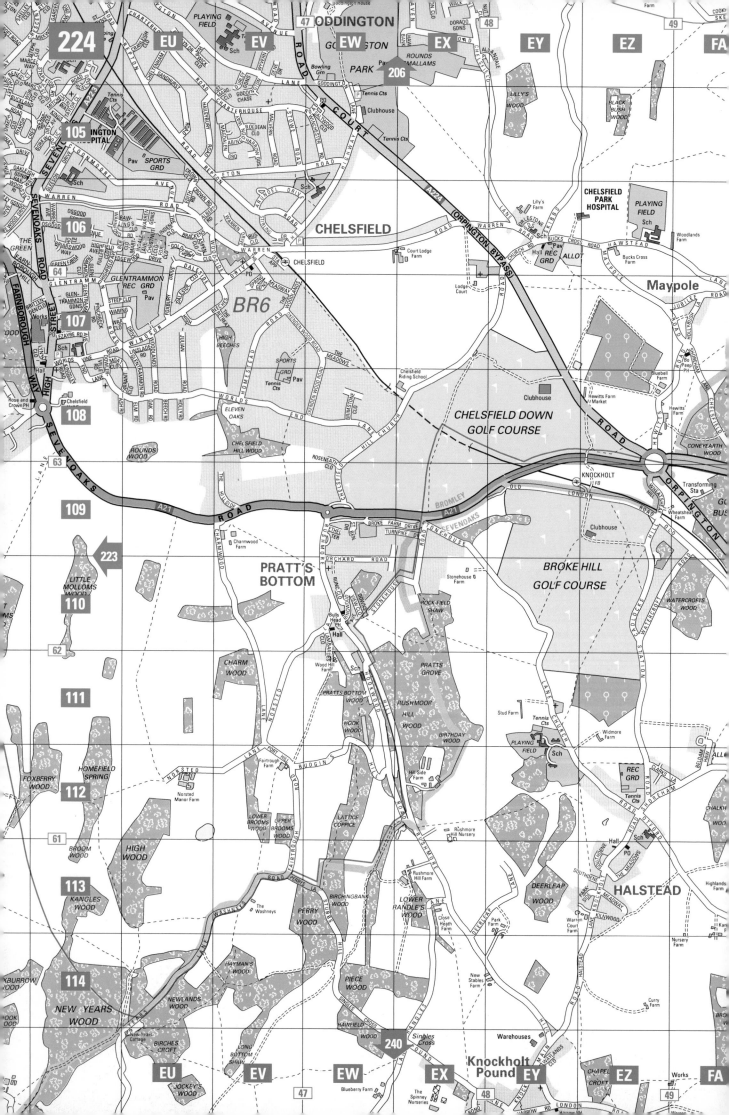

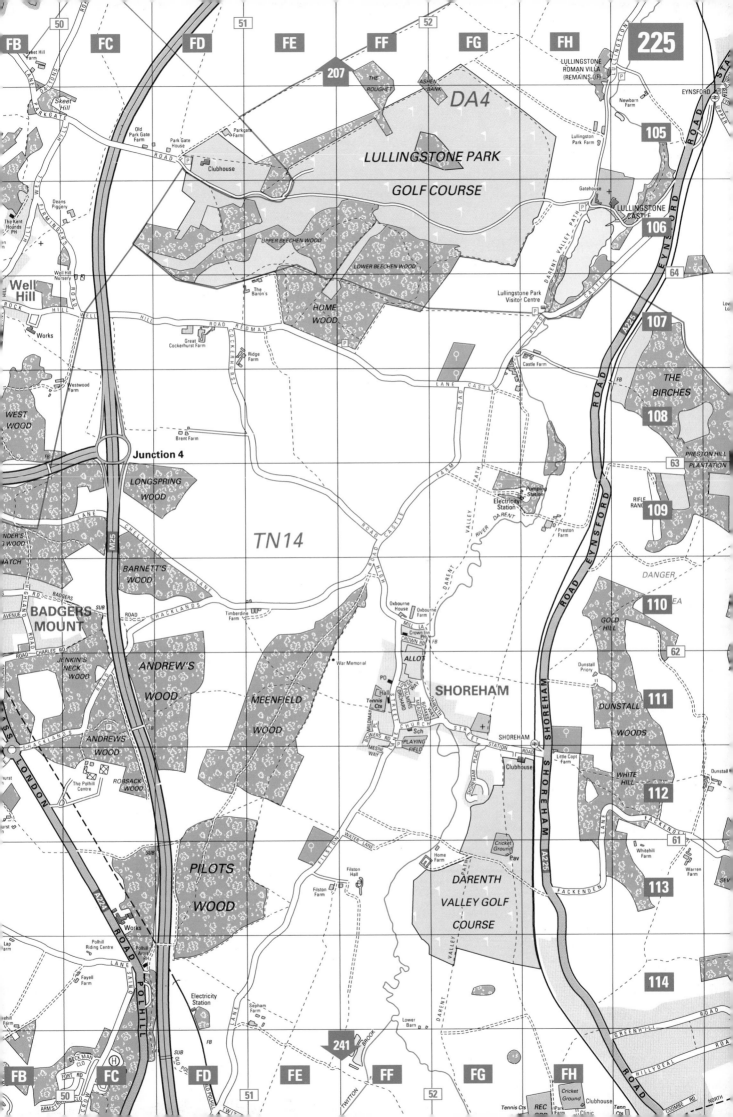

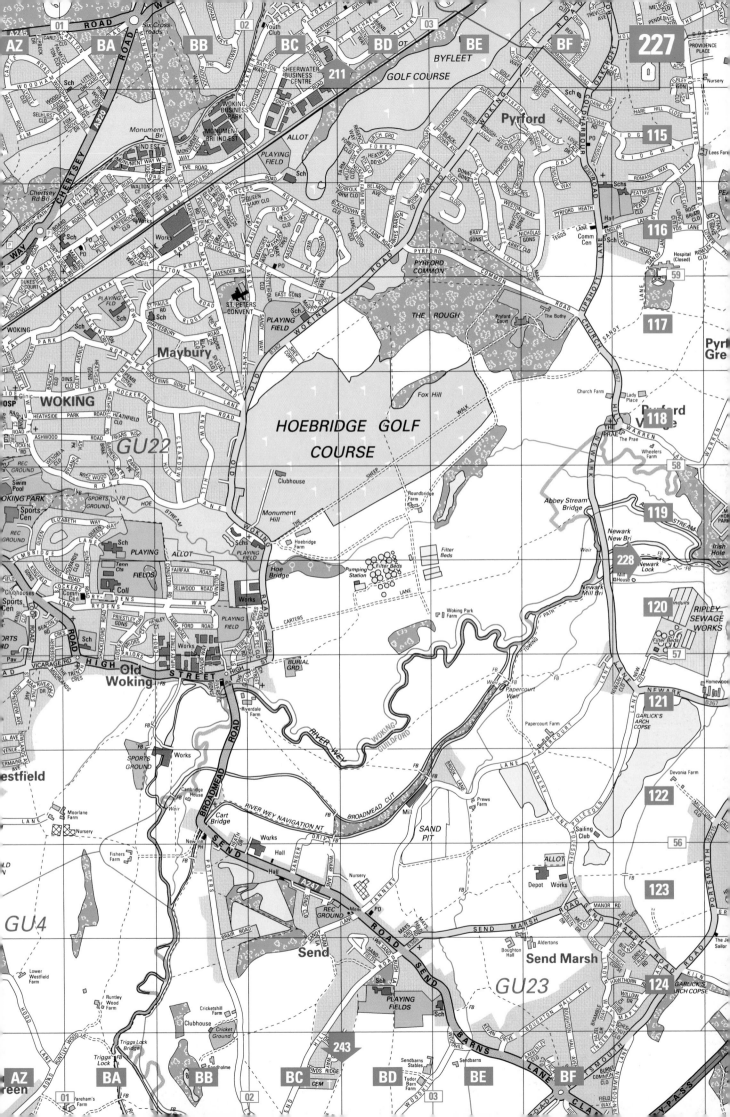

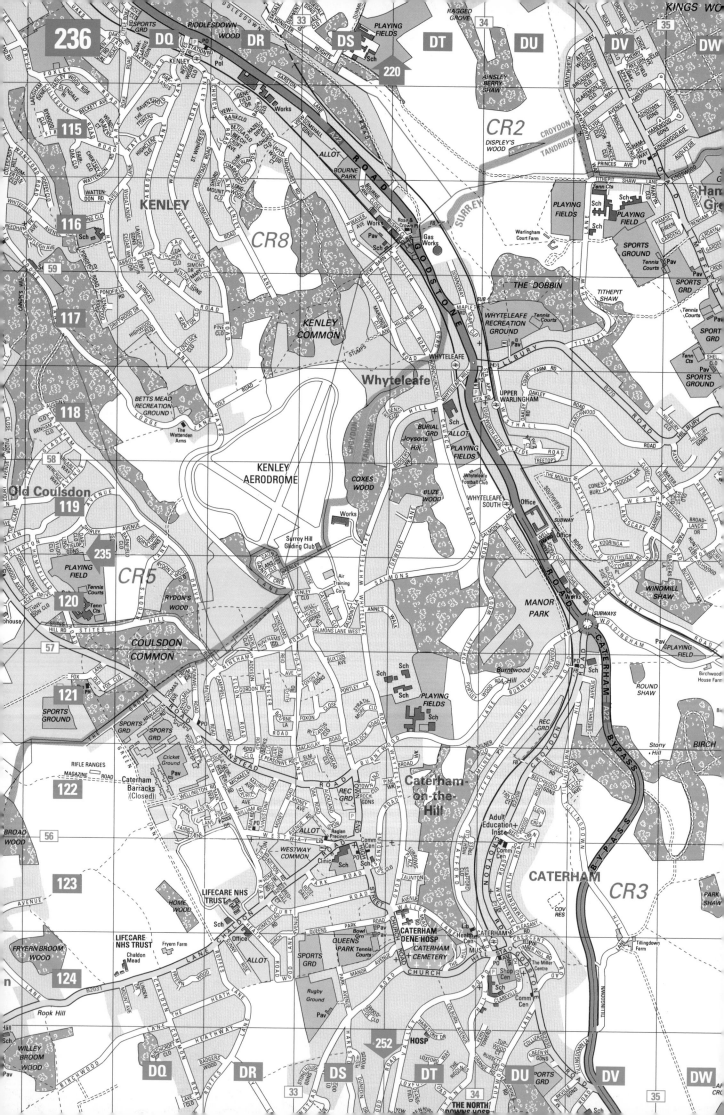

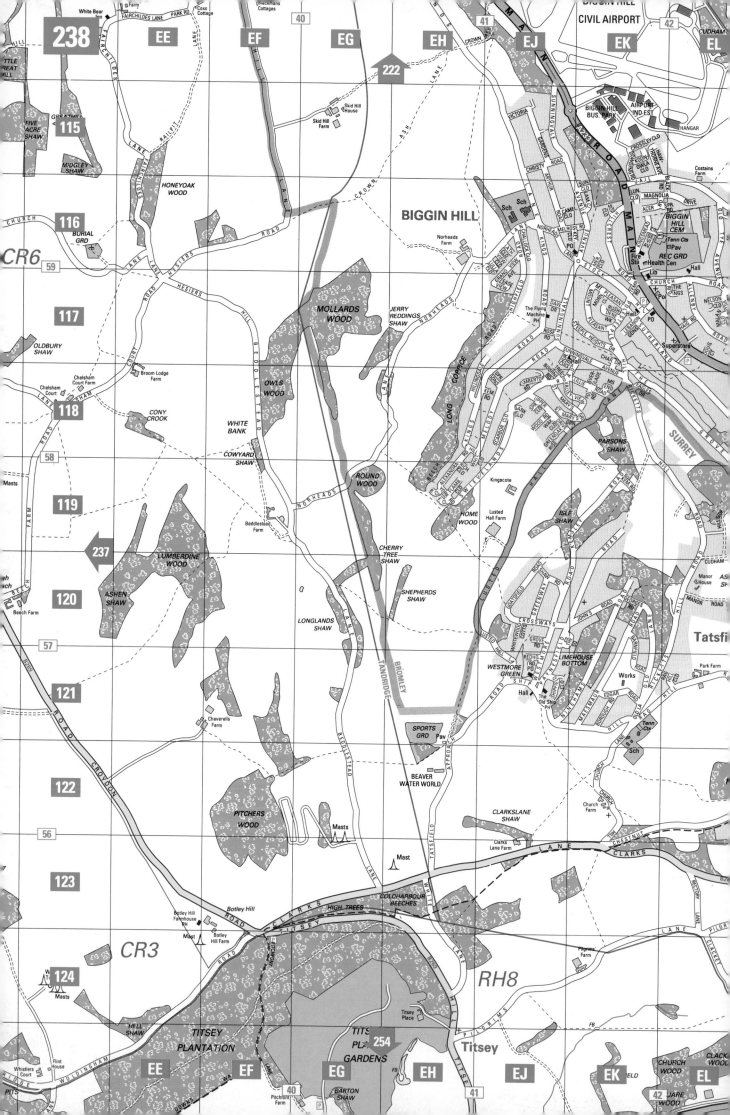

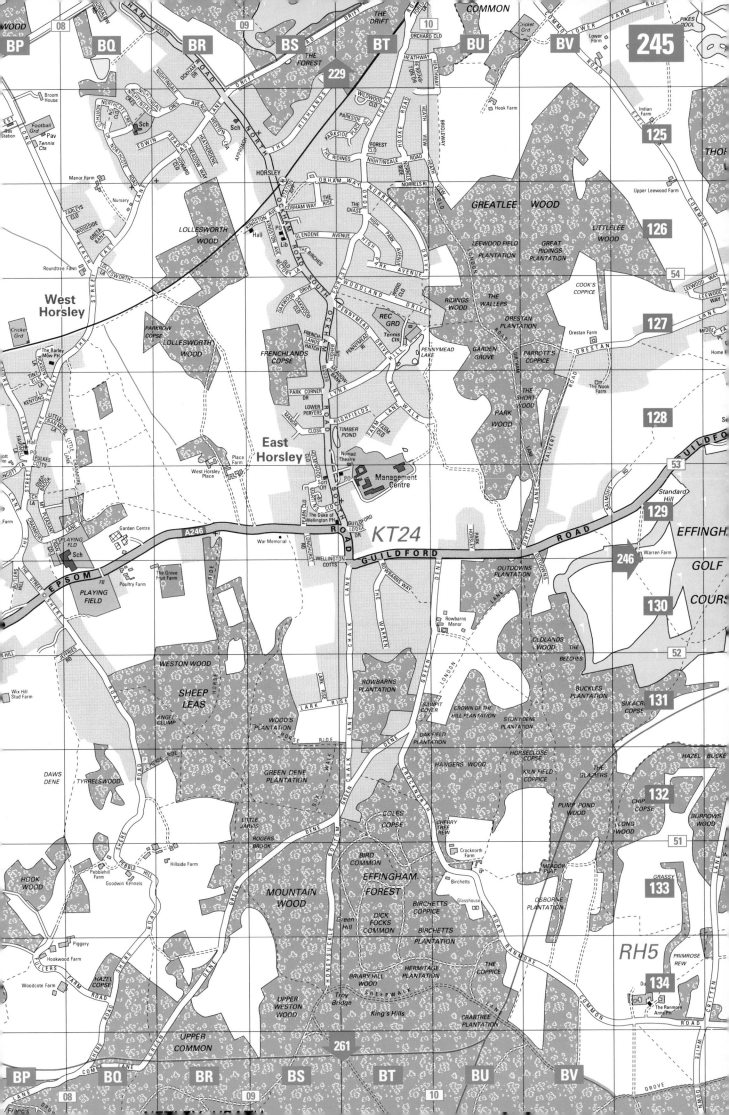

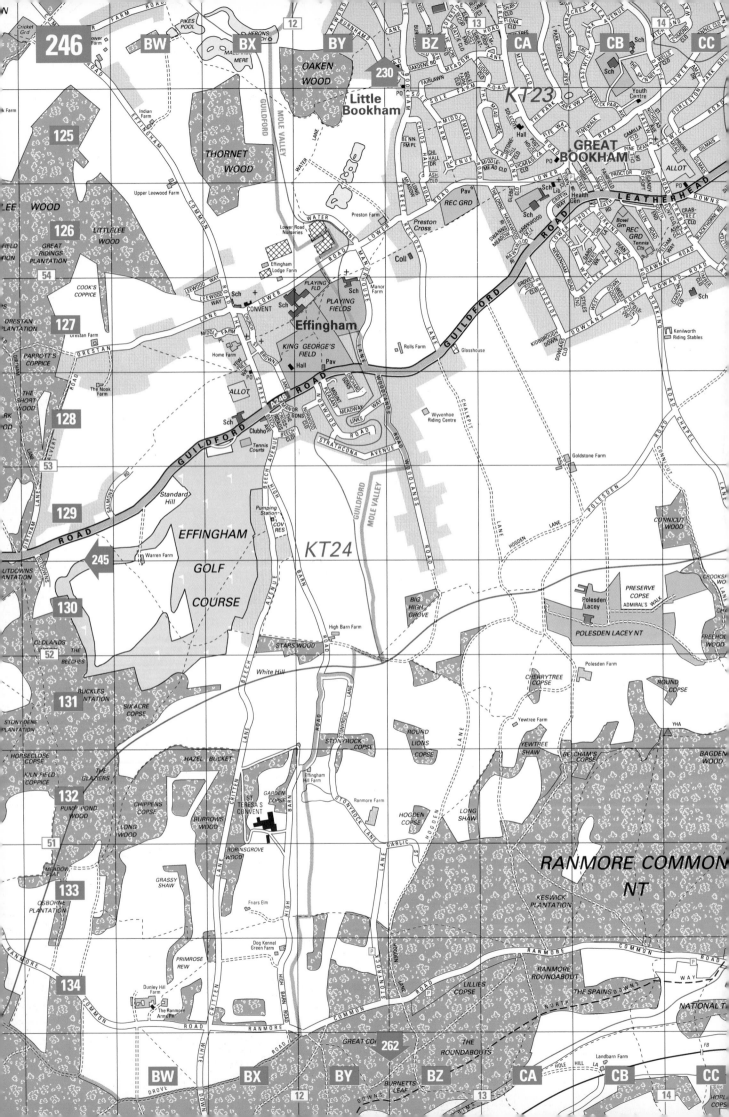

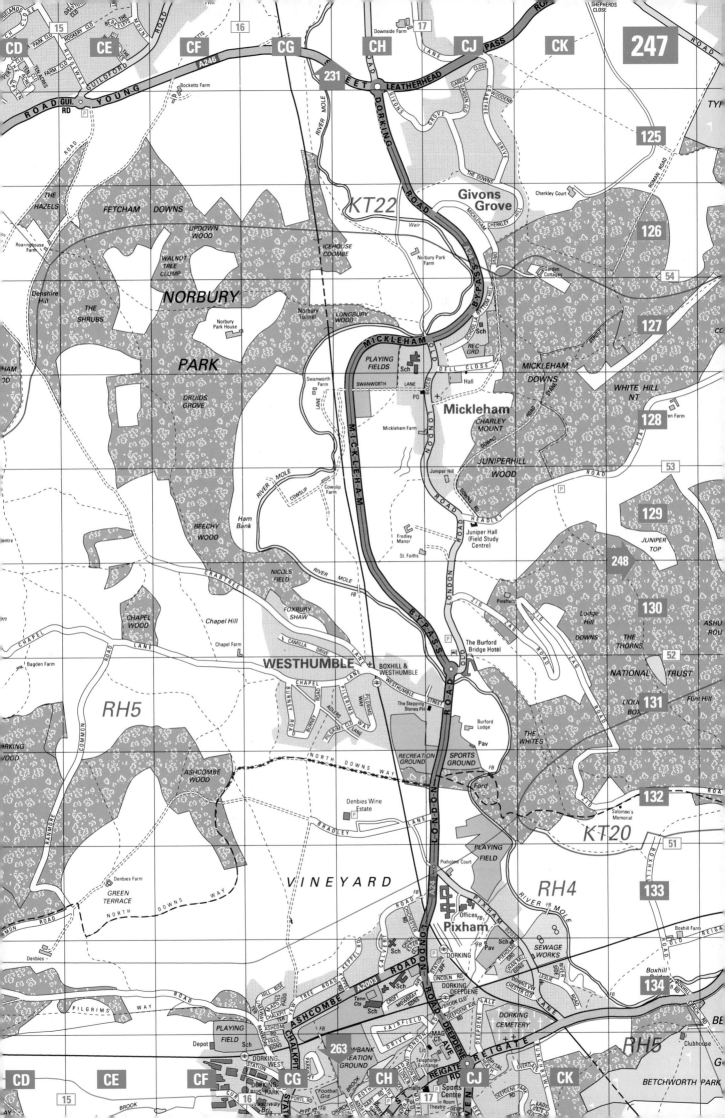

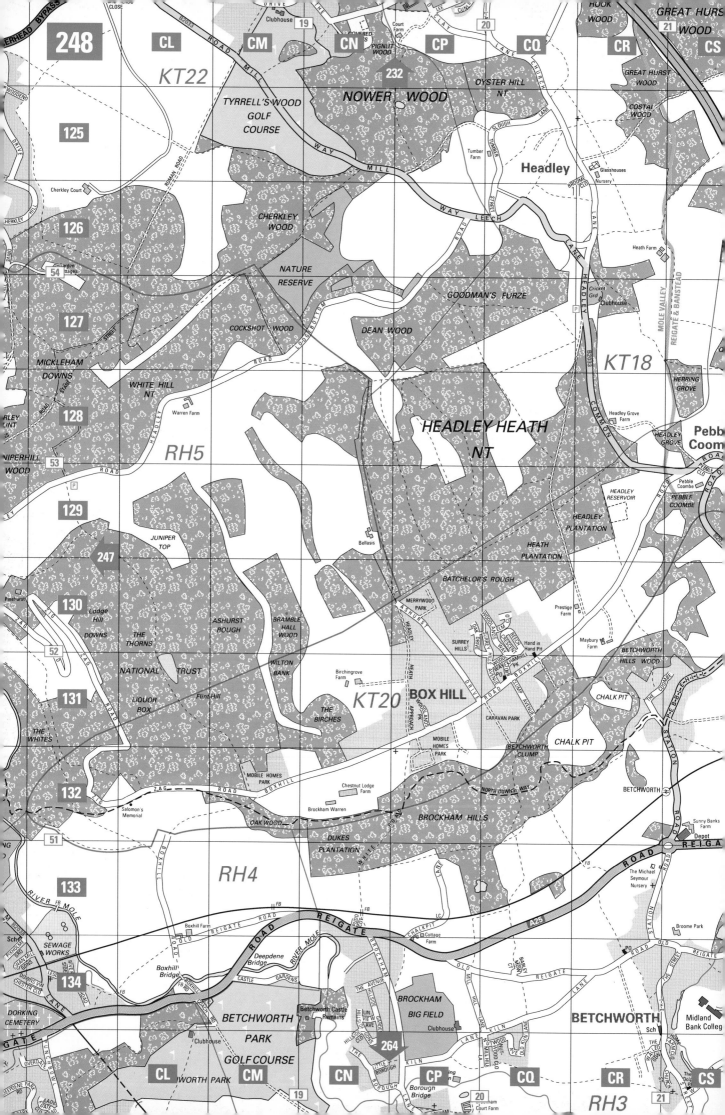

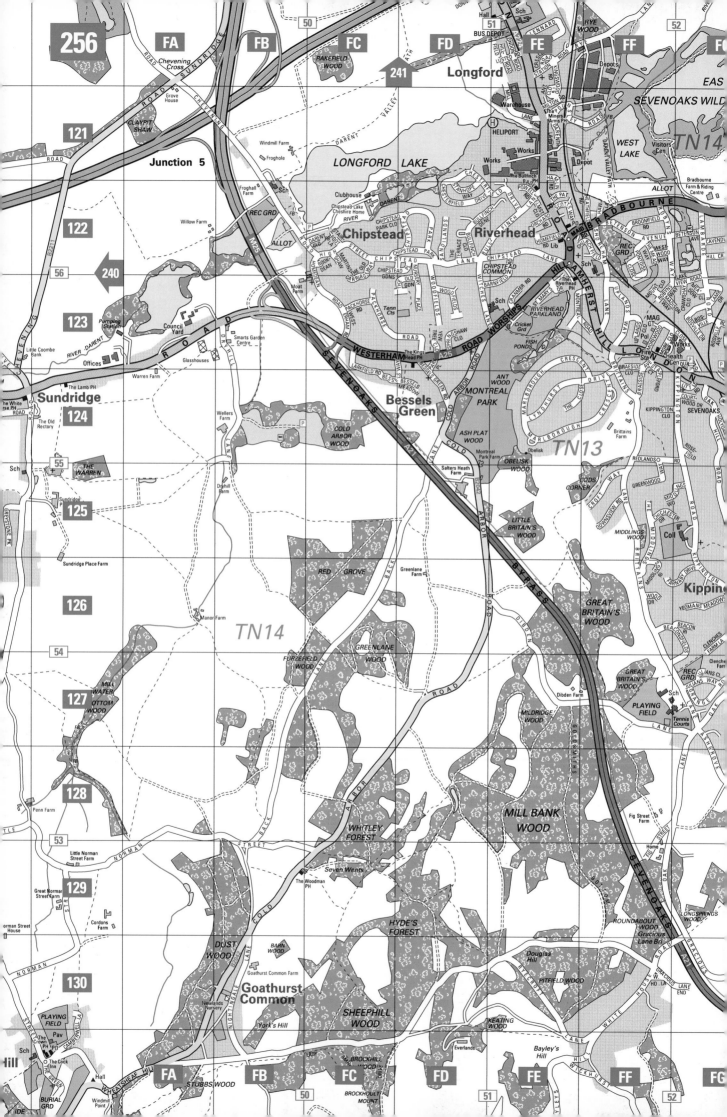

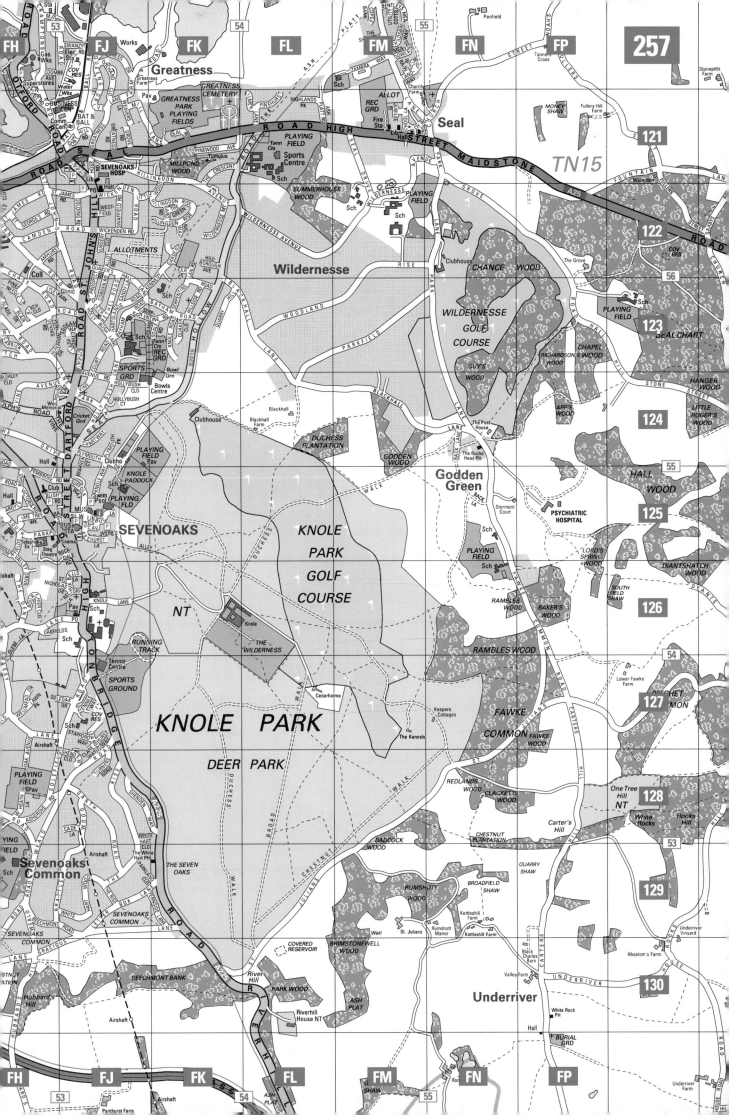

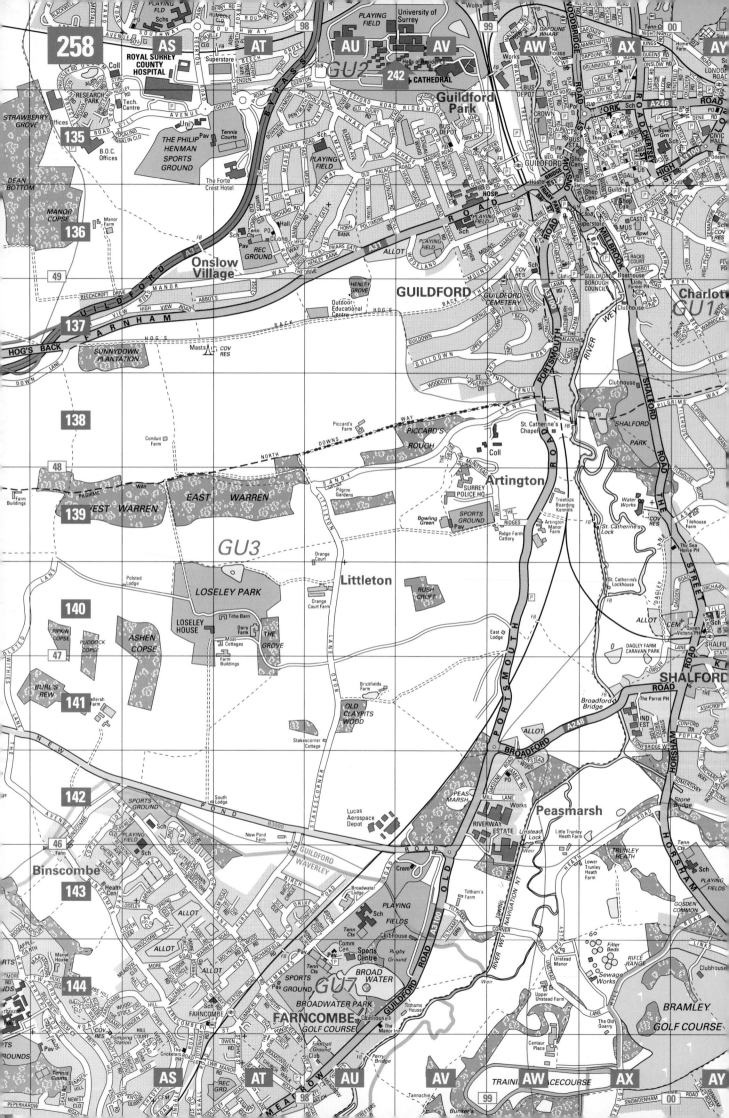

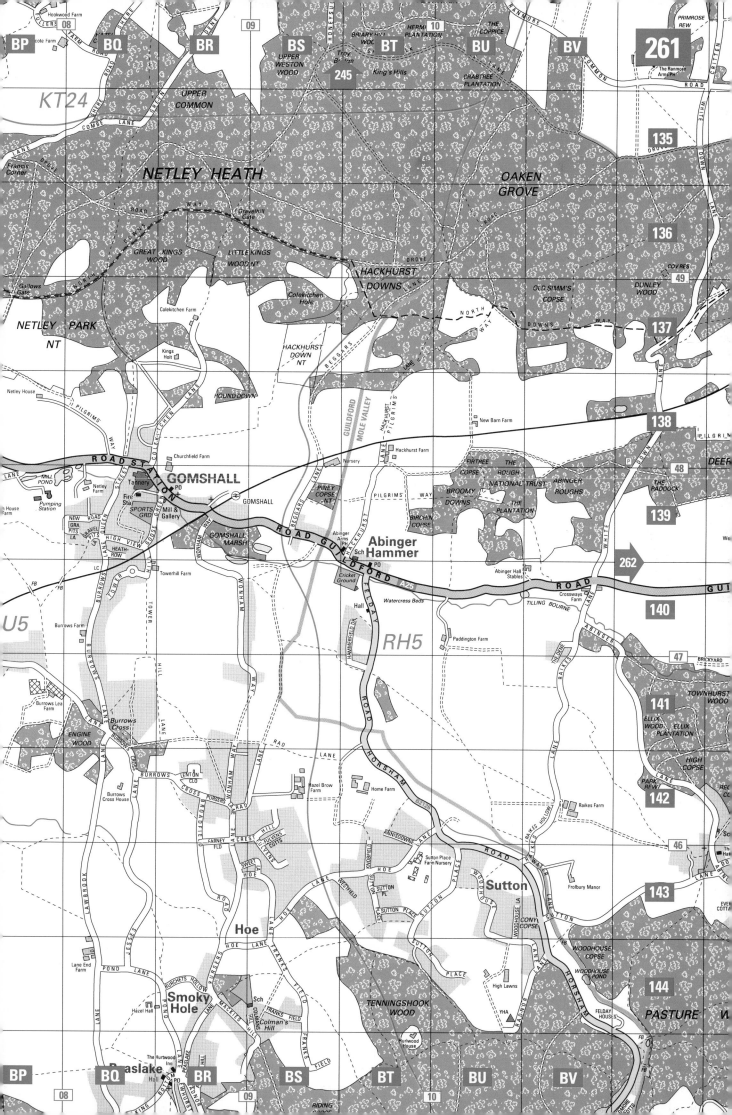

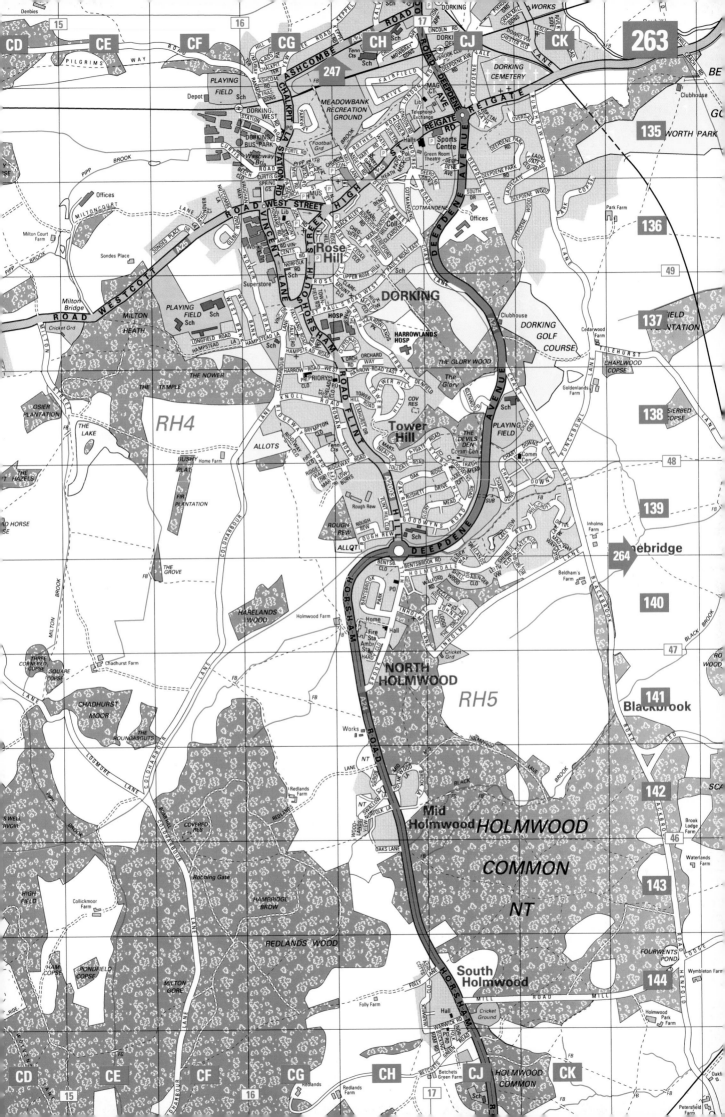

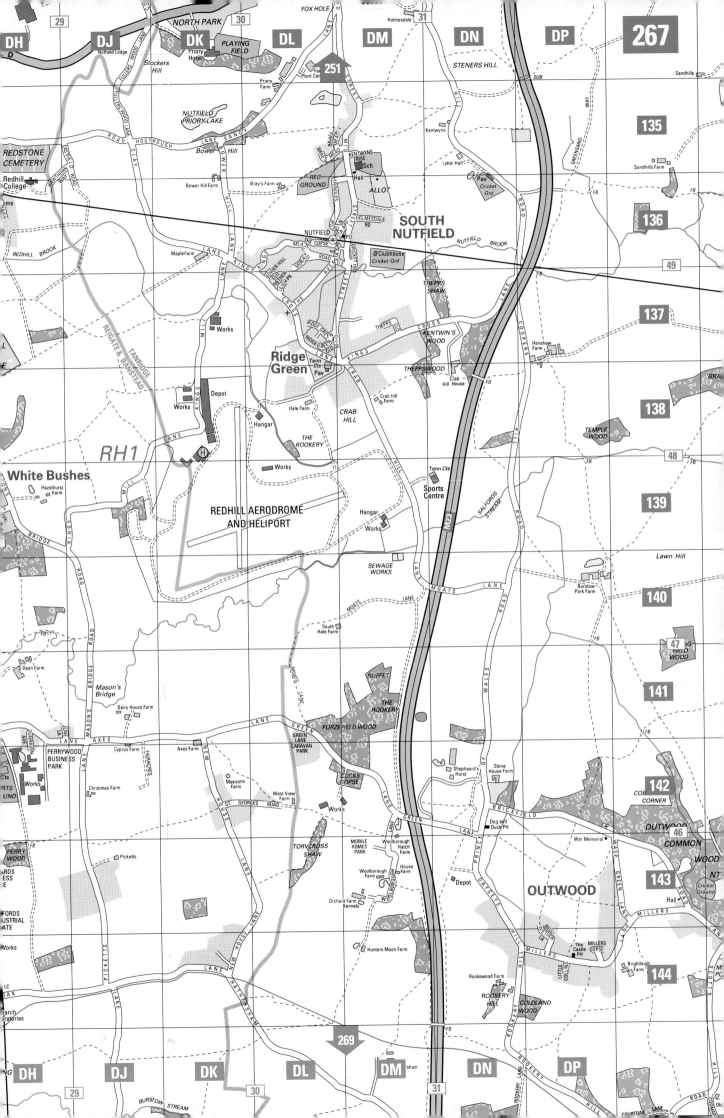

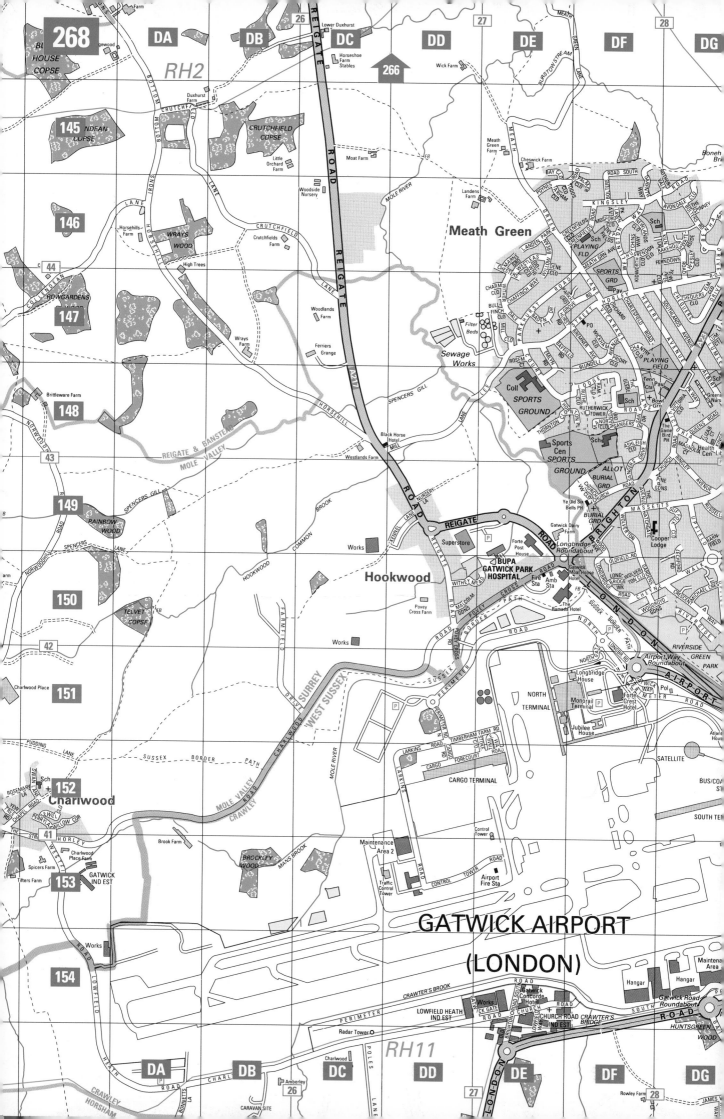

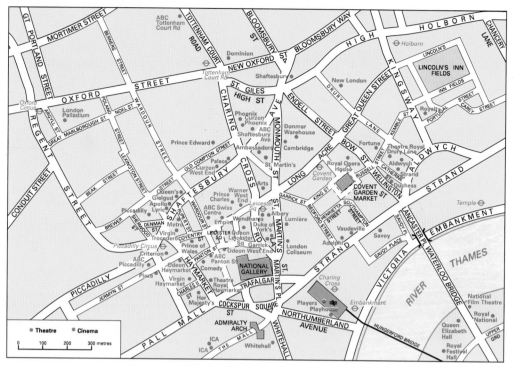

THEATRES

Adelphi 0171 334 0055
Albery 0171 369 1730
Aldwych 0171 416 6003
Ambassadors 0171 836 1171
Apollo 0171 494 5070
Arts 0171 836 2132
Cambridge 0171 494 5054
Comedy 0171 369 1731
Criterion 0171 369 1747
Dominion 0171 580 8845
Donmar Warehouse 0171 867 1150
Duchess 0171 494 5075
Duke of York's 0171 836 5122
Fortune 0171 836 2238
Garrick 0171 494 5085
Gielgud 0171 494 5065
Her Majesty's 0171 494 5400
ICA 0171 930 3647
London Coliseum 0171 632 8300
London Palladium 0171 494 5020
Lyric 0171 494 5045
New London 0171 405 0072
Palace 0171 434 0909
Phoenix 0171 369 1733
Piccadilly 0171 369 1734
Players 0171 839 1134
Playhouse 0171 839 4401
Prince Edward 0171 734 8951
Prince of Wales 0171 839 5987
Queen Elizabeth Hall
    0171 928 3002
Queen's 0171 494 5041
Royal Festival Hall
    0171 928 8800
Royal National 0171 928 2252
Royal Opera House
    0171 304 4000
Royalty 0171 494 5090
St. Martin's 0171 836 1443
Savoy 0171 836 8888
Shaftesbury 0171 379 5399
Strand 0171 930 8800
Theatre Royal, Drury Lane
    0171 494 5062
Theatre Royal, Haymarket
    0171 930 8800
Vaudeville 0171 836 9987
Whitehall 0171 369 1735
Wyndhams 0171 369 1736

CINEMAS

ABC Panton St 0171 930 0631
ABC Piccadilly 0171 437 3561
ABC ShaftesburyAvenue
    0171 836 6279
ABC Swiss Centre
    0171 439 4470
ABC Tottenham Court Rd
    0171 636 6148
Curzon Phoenix 0171 369 1721

Curzon West End 0171 369 1722
Empire 0171 437 1234
ICA 0171 930 3647
Lumière 0171 836 0691
Metro 0171 437 0757
National Film Theatre
    0171 928 3232
Odeon Haymarket
    01426 915353
Odeon Leicester Sq
    01426 915683

Odeon Mezzanine
(Odeon Leicester Sq)
    01426 915683
Odeon West End
    01426 915574
Plaza 0171 437 1234
Prince Charles 0171 437 8181
Virgin Haymarket 0171 839 1527
Virgin Trocadero 0171 434 0031
Warner West End 0171 437 4347

WEST END SHOPPING

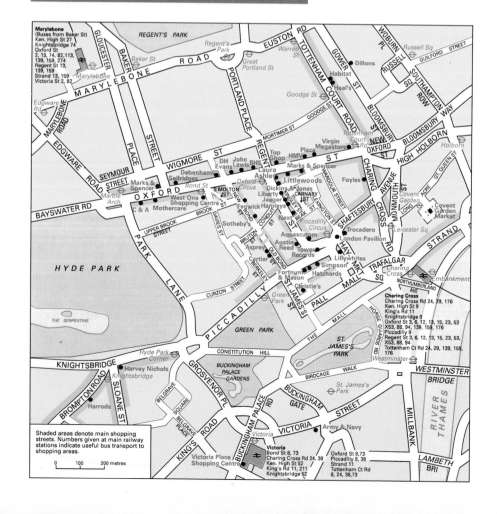

SHOPS

Aquascutum 0171 734 6090
Army & Navy 0171 834 1234
Asprey 0171 493 6767
Austin Reed 0171 734 6789
BHS (Oxford St) 0171 629 2011
C & A 0171 629 7272
Cartier 0171 493 6962
Christie's 0171 839 9060
Covent Garden Market 0171 836 9137
DH Evans 0171 629 8800
Debenhams 0171 580 3000
Dickins & Jones 0171 734 7070
Dillons 0171 636 1577
Fenwick 0171 629 9161
Fortnum & Mason 0171 734 8040
Foyles 0171 437 5660
Habitat (Tottenham Court Rd)
    0171 631 3880
Hamleys 0171 734 3161
Harrods 0171 730 1234
Harvey Nichols 0171 235 5000
Hatchards 0171 439 9921
Heal's 0171 636 1666
HMV 0171 631 3423
Jaeger 0171 200 4000
John Lewis 0171 629 7711
Laura Ashley (Regent St) 0171 355 1363
Liberty 0171 734 1234
Lillywhites 0171 930 3181
Littlewoods 0171 629 7847
London Pavilion 0171 437 1838
Marks & Spencer
    (Marble Arch) 0171 935 7954
Marks & Spencer (Oxford St)
    0171 437 7722
Mothercare 0171 580 1688
Next (Regent St) 0171 434 2515
Plaza on Oxford St 0171 637 8811
Selfridges 0171 629 1234
Simpson 0171 734 2002
Sotheby's 0171 493 8080
Top Shop & Top Man 0171 636 7700
Tower Records 0171 439 2500
Trocadero 0171 439 1791
Victoria Place Shopping Centre 0171 931 8811
Virgin Megastore 0171 580 5822

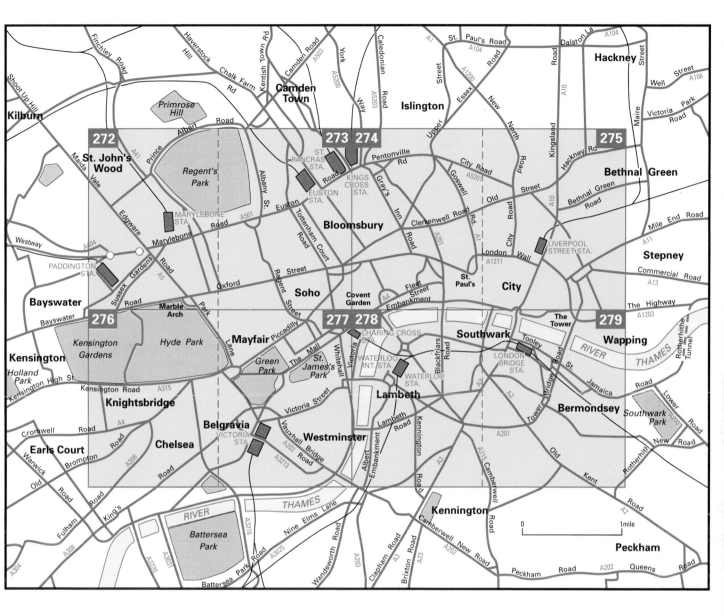

KEY TO MAP SYMBOLS

A40(M)	motorway
Dual A 4	primary route
Dual A40	'A' road
B504	'B' road
	other road/ one way street
	street market
	pedestrian street
	access restriction
	track/footpath
	ferry
CITY	borough boundary

EC2	postal district boundary
	main British Rail station
	other British Rail station
	London Underground station
	Docklands Light Railway station
	bus/coach station
P	car park
i	tourist information centre
	theatre
	major hotel
USA	embassy
10	grid reference

POL	police station
Fire Sta	fire station
PO	post office
Lib	library
	cinema
+	church
	mosque
	synagogue
Mormon	other place of worship
WC	public toilet
	tower block
274	page continuation number

	leisure and tourism
	shopping
	administration and law
	health and welfare
	education
	industry and commerce
	public open space
	park/garden/sports ground
	cemetery

Scale 1 : 10,000 (6.3 inches to 1 mile)

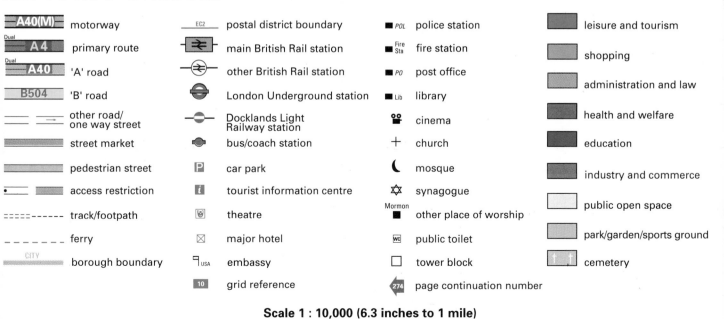

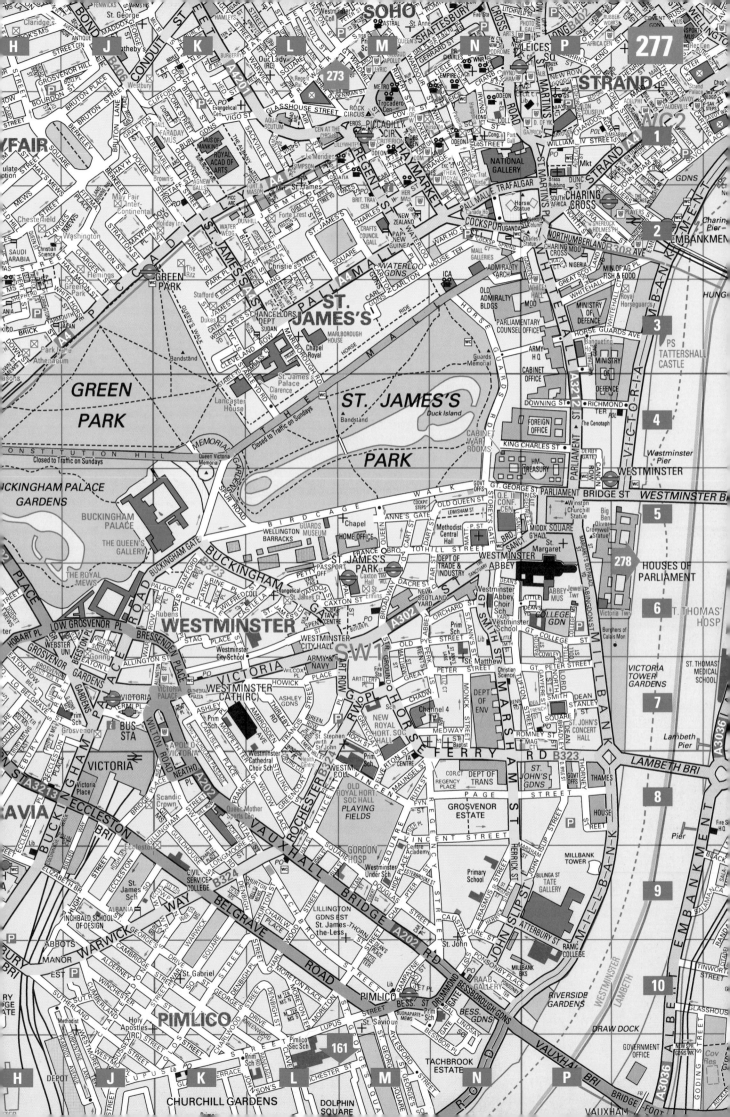

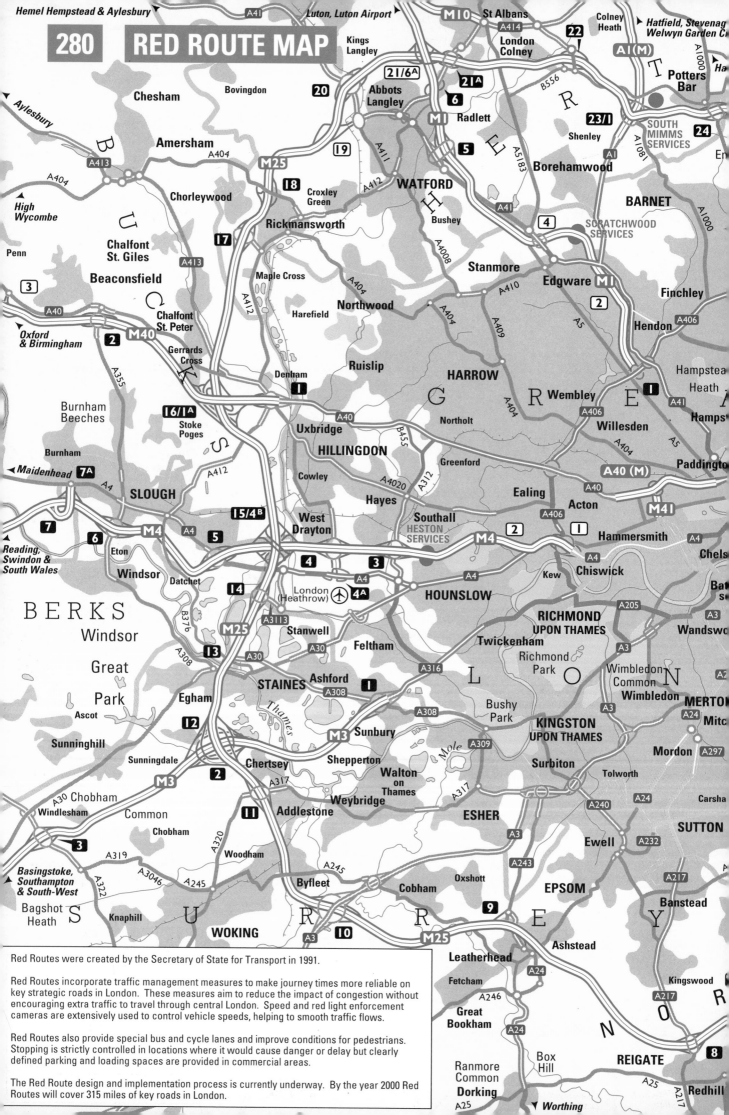

280 RED ROUTE MAP

The following is a comprehensive listing of the places of interest which appear in this atlas. Bold references can be found within the Central London enlarged scale section (pages 272-279).

George Inn, Borough High St.	279	K3	London Bridge	279	L2
Gipsy Moth IV	163	EC79	London Central Mosque	272	C3
Golders Hill Park NW11	120	DA61	London Diamond Centre	273	J9
Goldsmiths' Hall	275	H8	London Dungeon	279	L3
Gorhambury House, near St. Albans	42	BW19	London Palladium	273	K9
Gray's Inn	274	C6	London Peace Pagoda, Battersea Park	160	DF79
Great Bookham Common	230	BZ121	London Silver Vaults	274	D7
Green Park	277	J4	London Stone	275	K10
Greenwich Park	163	ED80	London Toy and Model Museum, Craven Hill	140	DC73
Greenwich Pier	163	EC79	London Transport Museum, Covent Gdn.	274	A10
Grocers' Hall	275	K8	London Zoo	140	DG68
Guildford Cathedral	242	AV134	Lord's Cricket Ground and Museum	272	A2
Guildhall, The	275	K8	Loseley House, Guildford	258	AS140
Gunnersbury Park, Ealing	158	CM77	Loseley Park, Guildford	258	AS140
H.M. Treasury	277	P4	Lullingstone Park, Eynsford, Kent	225	FG107
H.M.S. 'Belfast'	279	N2	Lullingstone Roman Villa	207	FH104
H.M.S. 'President'	274	E10	Madame Tussaud's	272	F5
Haberdashers' Hall	275	J8	Mall Galleries	277	N2
Hackney Marshes	123	DY62	Mansion House	275	K9
Haggerston City Farm	142	DU68	Marble Arch	272	E10
Hainault Forest	104	EW47	Marble Hill House, Twickenham	177	CJ87
Ham House	177	CJ88	Marlborough House	277	L3
Hamleys	273	K10	Master Mariners' Hall, H.Q.S. 'Wellington'	278	D1
Hampstead Heath	120	DD61	Mercers' Hall	275	J9
Hampton Court Palace	197	CE97	Merchant Taylors' Hall	275	M9
Harrods	276	D6	Methodist Central Hall	277	N5
Harrow School	117	CE60	Middlesex Guildhall	277	P5
Hatchlands Park, Clandon, Surrey	244	BM131	Millbank Tower	277	P9
Hatfield House	45	CX18	Millwall Football Club	162	DW78
Hay's Galleria	279	M2	Milton's Cottage	90	AV48
Hayward Gallery	278	C2	Ministry of Agriculture, Fisheries and Food	277	P2
Headley Heath, near Dorking	248	CP128	Ministry of Defence	277	P3
Heathrow Airport (London)	155	BP81	Monument, The	275	L10
Heinz Gallery, R.I.B.A.	272	F8	Moor Park Golf Club	92	BM47
Hogarth's House, Hogarth La.	158	CS79	Morden College	164	EG82
Holland Park	159	CZ75	Mosquito Aircraft Museum	62	CP29
Home Office	277	M5	Museum of Garden History	278	B7
Horniman Museum	182	DV88	Museum of Instruments, Royal College of Music	160	DD76
Horse Guards Parade, Horse Guards Rd.	277	N3	Museum of London	275	H7
Hospital Museum, Royal Hospital Chelsea	160	DG78	Museum of Mankind, Burlington Gdns.	277	K1
Hounslow Heath	176	BY86	Museum of the Moving Image (M.O.M.I.)	278	C2
Household Cavalry Museum, Combermere Barracks, Windsor	151	AQ83	Museum of the Royal Pharmaceutical Society of Great Britain (R.P.S.G.B.)	278	B8
Houses of Parliament	278	A6	Music Information Centre	272	G9
Hyde Park	276	B2	Musical Museum, High St., Brentford	158	CL79
Hyde Park Corner	276	G4	National Army Museum	160	DF79
Imperial College, University of London	160	DD76	National Gallery	277	N1
Imperial War Museum	278	E7	National Maritime Museum	163	ED79
Institute of Contemporary Arts	277	N2	National Portrait Gallery	277	N1
Ironmongers' Hall	275	H7	National Postal Museum	274	G8
Ismaili Centre	276	A8	National Westminster Tower	275	M8
Jack Straw's Castle P.H.	120	DC62	Natural History Museum	160	DD76
Jewel Tower, Houses of Parliament	277	P6	Nelson's Column	277	P2
Jewish Museum	273	N4	New Covent Garden Market	161	DK80
Jordans Meeting House	90	AS52	New Scotland Yard	277	M6
Jubilee Gardens	278	B4	North Woolwich Station Museum	165	EN75
Keats House, Hampstead	120	DE63	Northern Ireland Tourist Board	277	J2
Kempton Park Racecourse	176	BW94	Northolt Aerodrome	135	BS65
Kensington Gardens	140	DC74	Notting Hill Carnival, Ladbroke Gro.	139	CY72
Kensington Palace	140	DB74	Old Admiralty Buildings (M.o.D.)	277	N3
Kenwood House, Hampstead	120	DE60	Old County Hall	278	B4
Kew Bridge Steam Museum	158	CM78	Old Curiosity Shop	274	B8
Kew Gardens	158	CL80	Old Deer Park, Richmond	158	CJ82
Kew Observatory	157	CH83	Olympia	159	CY76
Kings Road, Chelsea	160	DD79	Operating Theatre Museum	279	L3
Knole House, Sevenoaks	257	FL126	Orleans House Gallery, Twickenham	177	CH88
Knole Park, Sevenoaks	257	FK127	Oscar Wilde's House, Paradise Wk.	160	DF79
Lambeth Palace	278	B7	Osterley Park House	156	CC78
Lancaster House	277	K4	Oval, The (Cricket Ground)	161	DM79
Langley Park, Slough	133	BA70	Oxford Circus	273	K9
Le Palais, Hammersmith	159	CW77	Oxford Street	272	F9
Leadenhall Market	275	M9	Oxshott Heath	214	CB112
Lee Valley Park	67	DZ31	P.S. 'Tattershall Castle'	278	A3
Leicester Square	277	N1	Pall Mall	277	L3
Leighton House, Holland Park Rd.	159	CZ76	Passmore Edwards Museum	144	EF65
Lesnes Abbey (ruins)	166	EX77	Passport Office	277	L6
Leyton Orient Football Club	123	EB62	Patent Office	274	D8
Liberty	273	K9	Percival David Foundation of Chinese Art, Gordon Sq.	273	N5
Limpsfield Common	254	EH130			
Lincoln's Inn	274	C8	Peter Pan Statue	140	DD74
Linley Sambourne House, Stafford Ter.	160	DA75	Petticoat Lane (Market)	275	N7
Little Venice (Waterbuses)	140	DC71	Petts Wood	205	ER97
Livesey Museum	162	DV79	Photographers' Gallery, Great Newport St.	273	P10
Lloyds of London	275	M9	Piccadilly Circus	277	M1
London Brass Rubbing Centre, St. Martin-in-the-Fields Church	277	P1	Piccotts End, Hemel Hempstead	40	BJ16
			Planetarium	272	F5

The following is a comprehensive listing of all named places which appear in this atlas. Bold references can be found within the Central London enlarged scale section (pages 272-276). Postal information is in either London postal district or non-London post town form. For an explanation of post town abbreviations please consult page 289.

Place	Page	Ref
Dulwich SE21	182	DS87
Dunton Green, Sev.	241	FC119
Ealing W5	137	CJ73
Earls Court SW5	159	CZ78
Earlsfield SW18	180	DC88
Earlswood, Red.	266	DF136
East Acton W3	138	CS73
East Barnet, Barn.	80	DE44
East Bedfont, Felt.	175	BS88
East Burnham, Slou.	131	AN67
East Clandon, Guil.	244	BL131
East Dulwich SE22	182	DU86
East Ewell, Sutt.	217	CX110
East Finchley N2	120	DD56
East Ham E6	144	EL68
East Horsley, Lthd.	245	BS128
East Molesey, E.Mol.	197	CD97
East Sheen SW14	158	CR84
East Wickham, Well.	186	EU90
Eastbury, Nthwd.	93	BS49
Eastcote, Pnr.	116	BW58
Eastcote Village, Pnr.	115	BV57
Eastwick, Harl.	35	EP11
Eden Park, Beck.	203	EA99
Edgware, Edg.	96	CP50
Edmonton N9	100	DU49
Effingham, Lthd.	246	BY127
Egham, Egh.	173	BA93
Egham Hythe, Stai.	173	BE93
Egham Wick, Egh.	172	AU94
Egypt, Slou.	111	AQ63
Ellenbrook, Hat.	44	CR19
Elm Corner, Wok.	228	BN119
Elm Park, Horn.	127	FH64
Elmers End, Beck.	203	DX97
Elmstead, Chis.	184	EK92
Elstree, Borwd.	77	CK44
Eltham SE9	184	EK86
Emerson Park, Horn.	128	FL58
Enfield, Enf.	82	DT41
Enfield Highway, Enf.	82	DW40
Enfield Lock, Enf.	83	DZ37
Enfield Town, Enf.	82	DR40
Enfield Wash, Enf.	83	DX38
Englefield Green, Egh.	172	AV92
Epping, Epp.	69	ET32
Epping Green, Epp.	51	EN24
Epping Green, Hert.	47	DK21
Epsom, Epsom	216	CQ114
Erith, Erith	167	FD79
Esher, Esher	214	CC105
Essendon, Hat.	46	DE17
Eton, Wind.	151	AQ80
Eton Wick, Wind.	151	AL77
Ewell, Epsom	217	CU110
Eynsford, Dart.	208	FL103
Fairmile, Cob.	214	BZ112
Falconwood, Well.	165	ER83
Farleigh, Warl.	221	DZ114
Farley Green, Guil.	260	BK144
Farnborough, Orp.	223	EP106
Farncombe, Gdmg.	258	AT144
Farnham Common, Slou.	131	AQ65
Farnham Royal, Slou.	131	AQ68
Farningham, Dart.	208	FM100
Fawkham Green, Long.	209	FV103
Felden, Hem.H.	40	BG24
Feltham, Felt.	175	BU89
Felthamhill, Felt.	175	BT92
Fetcham, Lthd.	231	CD123
Fiddlers Hamlet, Epp.	70	EW32
Fifield, Maid.	150	AD81
Finchley N3	98	DB53
Finsbury EC1	**274**	**E2**
Finsbury Park N4	121	DN60
Flaunden, Hem.H.	57	BB33
Fleetville, St.Alb.	43	CG20
Forest Gate E7	124	EG64
Forest Hill SE23	183	DX88
Forestdale, Croy.	221	DZ109
Forty Green, Beac.	88	AH50
Forty Hill, Enf.	82	DS37
Freezy Water, Wal.Cr.	83	DY35
Friday Hill E4	101	ED47
Friern Barnet N11	98	DE49
Froghole, Eden.	255	ER133
Frogmore, St.Alb.	61	CE28
Fulham SW6	159	CX81
Fullwell Cross, Ilf.	103	ER53
Fulmer, Slou.	112	AX63
Furzedown SW17	180	DG92
Gadebridge, Hem.H.	39	BF18
Gants Hill, Ilf.	125	EN57
Ganwick Corner, Barn.	80	DB35
Garston, Wat.	76	BW35
Gatton, Reig.	250	DF128
George Green, Slou.	132	AX72
Gerrards Cross, Ger.Cr.	112	AX58
Gidea Park, Rom.	127	FG55
Givons Grove, Lthd.	247	CJ126
Goathurst Common, Sev.	256	FB130
Godden Green, Sev.	257	FN125
Goddington, Orp.	206	EW104
Godstone, Gdse.	252	DV131
Goffs Oak, Wal.Cr.	66	DQ29
Golders Green NW11	120	DA59
Goldsworth Park, Wok.	226	AU117
Gomshall, Guil.	261	BR139
Goodley Stock, West.	255	EP130
Goodmayes, Ilf.	126	EV61
Gospel Oak NW5	120	DG63
Grange Hill, Chig.	103	ER51
Grange Park N21	81	DP43
Gravesend, Grav.	191	GJ85
Grays, Grays	170	GA78
Great Amwell, Ware	33	DZ10
Great Bookham, Lthd.	246	CB125
Great Hivings, Chesh.	54	AP27
Great Parndon, Harl.	51	EP17
Great Warley, Brwd.	107	FU53
Green Street, Borwd.	78	CP37
Green Street Green, Dart.	189	FU93
Greenford, Grnf.	136	CB69
Greenhithe, Green.	189	FV85
Greensted Green, Ong.	71	FH28
Greenwich SE10	163	ED79
Grove Park SE12	184	EG89
Grove Park W4	158	CQ80
Grovehill, Hem.H.	40	BL16
Guildford, Guil.	258	AV137
Guildford Park, Guil.	258	AV135
Gunnersbury W4	158	CP77
Hackbridge, Wall.	201	DH103
Hackney E8	142	DV65
Hackney Wick E9	123	DZ64
Hacton, Rain.	128	FM64
Hadley, Barn.	79	CZ40
Hadley Wood, Barn.	80	DD38
Haggerston E2	142	DT68
Hainault, Chig.	103	ET49
Hale End E4	101	ED51
Hall Grove, Welw.G.C.	30	DB11
Halls Green, Harl.	50	EJ18
Halstead, Sev.	224	EZ113
Ham, Rich.	177	CJ90
Hammerfield, Hem.H.	40	BH20
Hammersmith W6	159	CW78
Hammond Street, Wal.Cr.	66	DR26
Hampstead NW3	120	DD63
Hampstead Garden Suburb N2	120	DC57
Hampton, Hmptn.	196	CB95
Hampton Hill, Hmptn.	177	CD93
Hampton Wick, Kings.T.	197	CH95
Hamsey Green, Warl.	236	DW116
Handside, Welw.G.C.	29	CV10
Hanwell W7	137	CF74
Hanworth, Felt.	176	BX91
Hare Street, Harl.	51	EP16
Harefield, Uxb.	92	BL53
Harlesden NW10	138	CS68
Harlington, Hayes	155	BQ79
Harlow, Harl.	51	ER15
Harmondsworth, West Dr.	154	BK79
Harold Hill, Rom.	106	FM50
Harold Park, Rom.	106	FN52
Harold Wood, Rom.	106	FL54
Harringay N8	121	DN57
Harrow, Har.	117	CD59
Harrow on the Hill, Har.	117	CE60
Harrow Weald, Har.	95	CE53
Hastingwood, Harl.	52	EZ19
Hatch End, Pnr.	94	BY52
Hatfield, Hat.	45	CV17
Hatfield Garden Village, Hat.	29	CU14
Hatfield Hyde, Welw.G.C.	29	CZ12
Hatton, Felt.	155	BT84
Havering Park, Rom.	104	FA50
Havering-atte-Bower, Rom.	105	FE48
Hawley, Dart.	188	FM92
Hayes, Brom.	204	EH101
Hayes, Hayes	135	BS72
Hayes End, Hayes	135	BQ71
Hayes Town, Hayes	155	BS75
Headley, Epsom	248	CQ125
Headstone, Har.	116	CC56
Hedgerley, Slou.	111	AR60
Hemel Hempstead, Hem.H.	40	BK21
Hendon NW4	119	CV56
Herne Hill SE24	182	DQ85
Heronsgate, Rick.	91	BD45
Hersham, Walt.	214	BX107
Hertford, Hert.	31	DP10
Hertford Heath, Hert.	32	DW12
Hertingfordbury, Hert.	31	DL10
Heston, Houns.	156	BZ80
Hextable, Swan.	187	FG94
High Barnet, Barn.	79	CX40
High Beach, Loug.	84	EG39
Higham Hill E17	101	DY54
Highams Park E4	101	ED50
Highbury N5	121	DP64
Higher Denham, Uxb.	113	BC59
Highfield, Hem.H.	40	BL18
Highgate N6	121	DH59
Highwood Hill NW7	97	CU47
Hill End, Uxb.	92	BJ51
Hillingdon, Uxb.	134	BM69
Hilltop, Chesh.	54	AR28
Hinchley Wood, Esher	197	CF104
Hither Green SE13	184	EE86
Hoddesdon, Hodd.	49	DZ18
Hoe, Guil.	261	BR143
Hogpits Bottom, Hem.H.	57	BA31
Holborn WC2	**274**	**B8**
Holdens, Welw.G.C.	30	DA06
Holders Hill NW4	97	CX54
Holland, Oxt.	254	EG134
Holloway N7	121	DL63
Holmethorpe, Red.	251	DH132
Holtspur, Beac.	88	AF54
Holyfield, Wal.Abb.	67	ED28
Holywell, Wat.	75	BS44
Homerton E9	123	DY64
Honor Oak SE23	182	DW86
Honor Oak Park SE4	183	DZ86
Hook Green, Dart.	187	FG91
Hook Green, Grav.	190	FZ93
Hook Heath, Wok.	226	AV120
Hookwood, Horl.	268	DC150
Hooley, Couls.	234	DG122
Horley, Horl.	269	DH146
Hornchurch, Horn.	128	FJ61
Horns Green, Sev.	239	ES117
Hornsey N8	121	DM55
Horsell, Wok.	226	AY116
Horton, Epsom	216	CP110
Horton, Slou.	153	BA83
Horton Kirby, Dart.	209	FR98
Hosey Hill, West.	255	ES127
Hounslow, Houns.	156	BZ84
Hounslow West, Houns.	156	BX83
Hoxton N1	**275**	**M1**
Hulberry, Swan.	207	FG103
Hunsdon, Ware	34	EJ06
Hunsdonbury, Ware	34	EJ08
Hunton Bridge, Kings L.	59	BP33
Hurst Green, Oxt.	254	EG132
Hutton, Brwd.	109	GD44
Hutton Mount, Brwd.	109	GB46
Hyde, The NW9	119	CT57
Hythe End, Stai.	173	BB90
Ickenham, Uxb.	115	BQ62
Ilford, Ilf.	125	EQ62
Ingrave, Brwd.	109	GC50
Irons Bottom, Reig.	266	DA142
Isleworth, Islw.	157	CF83
Istead Rise, Grav.	190	GE94
Iver, Iver	133	BF72
Iver Heath, Iver	133	BD69
Ivy Chimneys, Epp.	69	ES32
Jacobs Well, Guil.	242	AY129
Jersey Farm, St.Alb.	43	CK15
Jordans, Beac.	90	AT52
Joydens Wood, Bex.	187	FC92
Katherines, Harl.	51	EM18
Kenley, Ken.	236	DQ116
Kennington SE11	161	DN79
Kensal Green NW10	139	CW69
Kensal Rise NW6	139	CX68
Kensal Town W10	139	CX70
Kensington W8	139	CZ74
Kent Hatch, Eden.	255	EP131
Kentish Town NW5	141	DJ65
Kenton, Har.	117	CH57
Kew, Rich.	158	CN79
Kidbrooke SE3	164	EJ82
Kilburn NW6	139	CZ68
King's Cross N1	141	DK67
Kings Farm, Grav.	191	GJ90
Kings Langley, Kings L.	58	BM30
Kingsbury NW9	118	CP58
Kingsmoor, Harl.	51	EQ20
Kingston upon Thames, Kings.T.	198	CL96
Kingston Vale SW15	178	CS91
Kingswood, Tad.	233	CZ123
Kingswood, Wat.	59	BV34
Kippington, Sev.	256	FG126
Kitt's End, Barn.	79	CY37
Knockhall, Green.	189	FW85
Knockholt, Sev.	240	EU116
Knockholt Pound, Sev.	240	EY116
Knotty Green, Beac.	88	AJ48
Ladywell SE13	183	EA85
Laleham, Stai.	194	BJ97
Lambeth SE1	**278**	**C6**
Lambourne End, Rom.	86	EX44
Lamorbey, Sid.	185	ET88
Lampton, Houns.	156	CB81
Lane End, Dart.	189	FR92
Langley, Slou.	153	BA76
Langley Vale, Epsom	232	CR119
Latimer, Chesh.	72	AY36
Latton Bush, Harl.	52	EU18
Layter's Green, Ger.Cr.	90	AV54
Lea Bridge E5	123	DX62
Leatherhead, Lthd.	231	CF121
Leatherhead Common, Lthd.	231	CF119

Seven Kings, Ilf.	125	ES59
Sevenoaks, Sev.	257	FJ125
Sevenoaks Common, Sev.	257	FH129
Sewardstone E4	83	EC39
Sewardstonebury E4	84	EE42
Shacklewell N16	122	DT63
Shadwell E1	142	DW73
Shalford, Guil.	258	AX141
Sheering, B.Stort.	37	FC07
Sheerwater, Wok.	211	BC113
Shenfield, Brwd.	109	FZ45
Shenley, Rad.	62	CN33
Shepherd's Bush W12	139	CW74
Shepperton, Shep.	195	BP101
Shere, Guil.	260	BM139
Sherrardspark, Welw.G.C.	29	CV07
Shirley, Croy.	203	DX104
Shooter's Hill SE18	165	EQ81
Shoreditch E1	**275**	**P5**
Shoreham, Sev.	225	FG111
Shortlands, Brom.	204	EE97
Shreding Green, Iver	133	BC72
Sidcup, Sid.	185	ET91
Sidlow, Reig.	266	DB141
Silvertown E16	164	EJ75
Single Street, West.	239	EN115
Singlewell, Grav.	191	GK93
Sipson, West Dr.	154	BN79
Slough, Slou.	132	AS74
Smallfield, Horl.	269	DP149
Smallford, St.Alb.	44	CP19
Smoky Hole, Guil.	261	BR144
Snaresbrook E11	124	EE57
Sockett's Heath, Grays	170	GD76
Soho W1	**273**	**M10**
Somers Town NW1	**273**	**N1**
South Acton W3	158	CP76
South Beddington, Wall.	219	DK107
South Chingford E4	101	DZ50
South Croydon, S.Croy.	220	DQ107
South Darenth, Dart.	209	FR95
South Hackney E9	142	DW67
South Hampstead NW6	140	DB66
South Harefield, Uxb.	114	BJ56
South Harrow, Har.	116	CB62
South Hatfield, Hat.	45	CU20
South Holmwood, Dor.	263	CJ144
South Hornchurch, Rain.	147	FE67
South Kensington SW7	160	DB76
South Lambeth SW8	161	DL81
South Merstham, Red.	251	DJ130
South Mimms, Pot.B.	63	CT32
South Norwood SE25	202	DT97
South Nutfield, Red.	267	DM136
South Ockendon, S.Ock.	149	FW70
South Oxhey, Wat.	94	BW48
South Park, Reig.	266	DA138
South Ruislip, Ruis.	116	BW63
South Stifford, Grays	169	FX78
South Street, West.	239	EM119
South Tottenham N15	122	DS57
South Weald, Brwd.	108	FS47
South Wimbledon SW19	180	DA94
South Woodford E18	102	EF54
Southall, Sthl.	136	BX74
Southborough, Brom.	205	EM100
Southend SE6	183	EC91
Southfields SW18	180	DA88
Southfleet, Grav.	190	GB93
Southgate N14	99	DJ47
Southlea, Slou.	152	AV82
Southwark SE1	**278**	**G3**
Spitalbrook, Hodd.	49	EA19
Spring Grove, Islw.	157	CE82
Staines, Stai.	174	BG93
Stamford Hill N16	122	DT60
Stanborough, Welw.G.C.	29	CT12
Stanmore, Stan.	95	CG50
Stanstead Abbots, Ware	33	ED11
Stanwell, Stai.	174	BL87
Stanwell Moor, Stai.	174	BG85
Stapleford Abbotts, Rom.	87	FC43
Stapleford Tawney, Rom.	87	FC37
Stepney E1	142	DW71
Stewards, Harl.	51	ER19
Stockwell SW9	161	DK83
Stoke D'Abernon, Cob.	230	BZ116
Stoke Green, Slou.	132	AU70
Stoke Newington N16	122	DS61
Stoke Poges, Slou.	132	AT66
Stone, Green.	189	FT85
Stonebridge NW10	138	CP67
Stonebridge, Dor.	264	CL139
Stonehill, Cher.	210	AY107
Stoneleigh, Epsom	217	CU106
Stoughton, Guil.	242	AU131
Strand WC2	**273**	**P10**
Stratford E15	143	EC65
Strawberry Hill, Twick.	177	CE90
Streatham SW16	181	DL91
Streatham Hill SW2	181	DM88
Streatham Park SW16	181	DJ91
Streatham Vale SW16	181	DK94

Strood Green, Bet.	264	CP138
Stroud Green N4	121	DM58
Stroude, Vir.W.	193	AZ96
Sudbury, Wem.	117	CG64
Summerstown SW17	180	DB91
Sumners, Harl.	51	EN19
Sunbury, Sun.	195	BV97
Sundridge, Brom.	184	EJ93
Sundridge, Sev.	240	EZ124
Sunnymeads, Wind.	152	AY84
Surbiton, Surb.	198	CL101
Sutton, Dor.	261	BU143
Sutton, Sutt.	218	DA107
Sutton at Hone, Dart.	188	FN94
Sutton Green, Guil.	243	AZ125
Swanley, Swan.	207	FE98
Swanley Village, Swan.	207	FH95
Swanscombe, Swans.	190	FZ86
Swillet, The, Rick.	73	BB44
Sydenham SE26	182	DV92
Tadworth, Tad.	233	CV122
Tandridge, Oxt.	253	EA133
Taplow, Maid.	130	AE70
Tatling End, Ger.Cr.	113	BB61
Tatsfield, West.	238	EL120
Tattenham Corner, Epsom	233	CV118
Teddington, Tedd.	177	CG93
Tewin, Welw.	30	DE05
Thames Ditton, T.Ditt.	197	CG101
Thamesmead SE28	146	EU74
Thamesmead North SE28	146	EX72
Thamesmead West SE18	165	EQ76
Theydon Bois, Epp.	85	ET37
Theydon Garnon, Epp.	86	EW36
Theydon Mount, Epp.	70	FA34
Thorney, Iver	154	BH76
Thornton Heath, Th.Hth.	201	DP98
Thornwood, Epp.	70	EW25
Thorpe, Egh.	193	BC97
Thorpe Green, Egh.	193	BA98
Thorpe Lea, Egh.	173	BB93
Tilbury, Til.	171	GG81
Titsey, Oxt.	254	EH125
Tokyngton, Wem.	138	CP65
Tolworth, Surb.	198	CN103
Toot Hill, Ong.	71	FF30
Tooting Graveney SW17	180	DE93
Tottenham N17	100	DS53
Tottenham Hale N17	122	DU55
Totteridge N20	97	CY46
Tower Hill, Dor.	263	CH138
Townsend, St.Alb.	43	CD17
Tufnell Park N7	121	DK63
Tulse Hill SE21	182	DQ88
Turnford, Brox.	67	DZ26
Twickenham, Twick.	177	CG89
Twitton, Sev.	241	FE116
Tye Green, Harl.	51	ET17
Tylers Causeway, Hert.	47	DK22
Tyler's Green, Gdse.	252	DV129
Tyrrell's Wood, Lthd.	232	CM123
Tyttenhanger, St.Alb.	44	CL23
Underhill, Barn.	80	DA43
Underriver, Sev.	257	FN130
Upminster, Upmin.	128	FQ62
Upper Clapton E5	122	DV60
Upper Edmonton N18	100	DU50
Upper Elmers End, Beck.	203	DZ99
Upper Halliford, Shep.	195	BS97
Upper Holloway N19	121	DJ62
Upper Norwood SE19	182	DR94
Upper Sydenham SE26	182	DU91
Upper Tooting SW17	180	DE90
Upper Walthamstow E17	123	EC56
Upshire, Wal.Abb.	68	EJ32
Upton E7	144	EH66
Upton, Slou.	152	AU76
Upton Park E6	144	EJ67
Upton Park, Slou.	152	AT76
Uxbridge, Uxb.	134	BK66
Uxbridge Moor, Iver	134	BG67
Uxbridge Moor, Uxb.	134	BG67
Vauxhall SW8	161	DK79
Virginia Water, Vir.W.	192	AW97
Waddon, Croy.	201	DN103
Walham Green SW6	160	DB80
Wallington, Wall.	219	DJ106
Waltham Abbey, Wal.Abb.	84	EF35
Waltham Cross, Wal.Cr.	67	DZ33
Walthamstow E17	101	EB54
Walton on the Hill, Tad.	249	CT125
Walton-on-Thames, Walt.	195	BT103
Walworth SE17	**279**	**H10**
Wandsworth SW18	179	CZ85
Wanstead E11	124	EG59
Wapping E1	142	DU74
Ware, Ware	33	DZ06
Warley, Brwd.	108	FV50
Warlingham, Warl.	237	DX118
Warners End, Hem.H.	39	BE19
Warwick Wold, Red.	251	DN129
Water End, Hat.	63	CV26
Waterford, Hert.	31	DM05

Waterside, Chesh.	54	AR32
Watford, Wat.	75	BU41
Watford Heath, Wat.	94	BX46
Wealdstone, Har.	117	CF55
Welham Green, Hat.	45	CV23
Well End, Borwd.	78	CR38
Well Hill, Orp.	225	FB107
Welling, Well.	166	EU83
Welwyn Garden City, Welw.G.C.	29	CX10
Wembley, Wem.	118	CL64
Wembley Park, Wem.	118	CM61
Wennington, Rain.	148	FK73
Wentworth, Vir.W.	192	AS100
West Barnes, N.Mal.	199	CV98
West Brompton SW10	160	DA79
West Byfleet, W.Byf.	212	BH113
West Clandon, Guil.	244	BH129
West Drayton, West Dr.	154	BK76
West Dulwich SE21	182	DR90
West End, Esher	214	BZ107
West End, Hat.	46	DC18
West Ewell, Epsom	216	CS108
West Green N15	122	DQ56
West Ham E15	144	EF66
West Hampstead NW6	120	DB84
West Harrow, Har.	116	CC59
West Heath SE2	166	EX79
West Horsley, Lthd.	245	BP127
West Kilburn W9	139	CZ69
West Molesey, W.Mol.	196	BZ98
West Norwood SE27	182	DQ90
West Thurrock, Grays	169	FU78
West Tilbury, Til.	171	GL79
West Watford, Wat.	75	BU42
West Wickham, W.Wick.	203	EC103
Westbourne Green W2	140	DA71
Westcott, Dor.	262	CC138
Westcourt, Grav.	191	GL89
Westerham, West.	255	EQ126
Westfield, Wok.	227	AZ122
Westhumble, Dor.	247	CG131
Westminster SW1	**277**	**K6**
Weston Green, T.Ditt.	197	CF102
Wexham Street, Slou.	132	AW67
Weybridge, Wey.	212	BN105
Wheathampstead, St.Alb.	28	CL06
Whelpley Hill, Chesh.	56	AX26
Whetstone N20	98	DB47
White Bushes, Red.	267	DH139
Whitechapel E1	142	DU72
Whiteley Village, Walt.	213	BS110
Whitton, Twick.	176	CB87
Whyteleafe, Cat.	236	DS118
Widmore, Brom.	204	EJ97
Wildernesse, Sev.	257	FL122
Wildhill, Hat.	46	DD21
Willesden NW10	139	CT65
Willesden Green NW10	139	CV66
Wilmington, Dart.	188	FJ91
Wimbledon SW19	179	CY93
Wimbledon Park SW19	179	CZ90
Winchmore Hill N21	99	DM45
Winchmore Hill, Amer.	88	AJ45
Windmill Hill, Grav.	191	GG88
Windsor, Wind.	152	AS81
Wisley, Wok.	228	BL116
Woking, Wok.	227	AZ118
Woldingham, Cat.	237	EB122
Woldingham Garden Village, Cat.	237	DY121
Wombwell Park, Grav.	190	GD89
Wonersh, Guil.	259	BB144
Wooburn, H.Wyc.	110	AD58
Wooburn Green, H.Wyc.	110	AF56
Wood Green N22	99	DL53
Woodbridge Hill, Guil.	242	AU132
Woodcote, Epsom	232	CQ116
Woodcote, Pur.	219	DK111
Woodford, Wdf.Grn.	102	EH51
Woodford Bridge, Wdf.Grn.	103	EM52
Woodford Green, Wdf.Grn.	102	EG50
Woodford Wells, Wdf.Grn.	102	EH48
Woodhall, Welw.G.C.	29	CY11
Woodham, Add.	211	BF111
Woodhatch, Reig.	266	DC137
Woodlands, Islw.	157	CE82
Woodmansterne, Bans.	234	DE115
Woodside, Croy.	202	DT100
Woodside, Wat.	59	BU33
Woolwich SE18	165	EM78
Worcester Park, Wor.Pk.	199	CT103
World's End, Enf.	81	DN41
Wormley, Brox.	49	DY24
Wormley West End, Brox.	48	DS22
Wotton, Dor.	262	BZ139
Wraysbury, Stai.	173	AZ86
Wrythe, The, Cars.	200	DE103
Yeading, Hayes	135	BV69
Yiewsley, West Dr.	134	BL74

General Abbreviations

All	Alley	Comm	Community	Fm	Farm	Mkt	Market	Shop	Shopping
Allot	Allotments	Conv	Convent	Gall	Gallery	Mkts	Markets	Sq	Square
Amb	Ambulance	Cor	Corner	Gar	Garage	Ms	Mews	St	Street
App	Approach	Cors	Corners	Gdn	Garden	Mt	Mount	St.	Saint
Arc	Arcade	Coron	Coroners	Gdns	Gardens	Mus	Museum	Sta	Station
Ave	Avenue	Cotts	Cottages	Govt	Government	N	North	Sts	Streets
Bdy	Broadway	Cov	Covered	Gra	Grange	PH	Public House	Sub	Subway
Bldgs	Buildings	Crem	Crematorium	Grd	Ground	Par	Parade	Swim	Swimming
Boul	Boulevard	Cres	Crescent	Grn	Green	Pas	Passage	TA	Territorial Army
Bowl	Bowling	Ct	Court	Grns	Greens	Pav	Pavilion	Tenn	Tennis
Bri	Bridge	Ctyd	Courtyard	Gro	Grove	Pk	Park	Ter	Terrace
C of E	Church of England	Dep	Depot	Gros	Groves	Pl	Place	Thea	Theatre
Cath	Cathedral	Dr	Drive	Ho	House	Prec	Precinct	Trd	Trading
Cem	Cemetery	Dws	Dwellings	Hos	Houses	Prom	Promenade	Twr	Tower
Cen	Central, Centre	E	East	Hosp	Hospital	Pt	Point	Vill	Villas
Cft	Croft	Ed	Education	Ind	Industrial	Quad	Quadrant	Vw	View
Cfts	Crofts	Elec	Electricity	Junct	Junction	RC	Roman Catholic	W	West
Ch	Church	Emb	Embankment	La	Lane	Rd	Road	Wd	Wood
Chyd	Churchyard	Est	Estate	Las	Lanes	Rds	Roads	Wds	Woods
Cin	Cinema	Ex	Exchange	Lo	Lodge	Rec	Recreation	Wf	Wharf
Circ	Circus	FB	Footbridge	Lwr	Lower	Res	Reservoir	Wk	Walk
Clo	Close	FC	Football Club	Mag	Magistrates	Ri	Rise	Wks	Walks
Co	County	Fld	Field	Mans	Mansions	S	South	Yd	Yard
Coll	College	Flds	Fields	Meml	Memorial	Sch	School		

Post Town Abbreviations

Abb.L.	Abbots Langley	Chig.	Chigwell	Hert.	Hertford	Rain.	Rainham	Twick.	Twickenham
Add.	Addlestone	Chis.	Chislehurst	Hmptn.	Hampton	Red.	Redhill	Upmin.	Upminster
Amer.	Amersham	Cob.	Cobham	Hodd.	Hoddesdon	Reig.	Reigate	Uxb.	Uxbridge
Ash.	Ashtead	Couls.	Coulsdon	Horl.	Horley	Rich.	Richmond	Vir.W.	Virginia Water
Ashf.	Ashford	Craw.	Crawley	Horn.	Hornchurch	Rick.	Rickmansworth	W.Byf.	West Byfleet
B.End	Bourne End	Croy.	Croydon	Houns.	Hounslow	Rom.	Romford	W.Mol.	West Molesey
B.Stort.	Bishop's Stortford	Dag.	Dagenham	Ilf.	Ilford	Ruis.	Ruislip	W.Wick.	West Wickham
Bans.	Banstead	Dart.	Dartford	Islw.	Isleworth	S.Croy.	South Croydon	Wal.Abb.	Waltham Abbey
Bark.	Barking	Dor.	Dorking	Ken.	Kenley	S.le H.	Stanford le Hope	Wal.Cr.	Waltham Cross
Barn.	Barnet	E.Mol.	East Molesey	Kes.	Keston	S.Ock.	South Ockendon	Wall.	Wallington
Beac.	Beaconsfield	Eden.	Edenbridge	Kings L.	Kings Langley	Saw.	Sawbridgeworth	Walt.	Walton-on-Thames
Beck.	Beckenham	Edg.	Edgware	Kings.T.	Kingston upon Thames	Sev.	Sevenoaks	Warl.	Warlingham
Belv.	Belvedere	Egh.	Egham	Long.	Longfield	Shep.	Shepperton	Wat.	Watford
Berk.	Berkhamsted	Enf.	Enfield	Loug.	Loughton	Sid.	Sidcup	Wdf.Grn.	Woodford Green
Bet.	Betchworth	Epp.	Epping	Lthd.	Leatherhead	Slou.	Slough	Well.	Welling
Bex.	Bexley	Felt.	Feltham	Maid.	Maidenhead	St.Alb.	St. Albans	Welw.	Welwyn
Bexh.	Bexleyheath	Gat.	Gatwick	Mitch.	Mitcham	Stai.	Staines	Welw.G.C.	Welwyn Garden City
Borwd.	Borehamwood	Gdmg.	Godalming	Mord.	Morden	Stan.	Stanmore	Wem.	Wembley
Brent.	Brentford	Gdse.	Godstone	N.Mal.	New Malden	Sthl.	Southall	West Dr.	West Drayton
Brom.	Bromley	Ger.Cr.	Gerrards Cross	Nthlt.	Northolt	Sun.	Sunbury-on-Thames	West.	Westerham
Brox.	Broxbourne	Grav.	Gravesend	Nthwd.	Northwood	Surb.	Surbiton	Wey.	Weybridge
Brwd.	Brentwood	Green.	Greenhithe	Ong.	Ongar	Sutt.	Sutton	Whyt.	Whyteleafe
Buck.H.	Buckhurst Hill	Grnf.	Greenford	Orp.	Orpington	Swan.	Swanley	Wind.	Windsor
Cars.	Carshalton	Guil.	Guildford	Oxt.	Oxted	Swans.	Swanscombe	Wok.	Woking
Cat.	Caterham	H.Wyc.	High Wycombe	Pnr.	Pinner	T.Ditt.	Thames Ditton	Wor.Pk.	Worcester Park
Ch.St.G.	Chalfont St. Giles	Har.	Harrow	Pot.B.	Potters Bar	Tad.	Tadworth		
Cher.	Chertsey	Harl.	Harlow	Pur.	Purley	Tedd.	Teddington		
Chesh.	Chesham	Hat.	Hatfield	Purf.	Purfleet	Th.Hth.	Thornton Heath		
Chess.	Chessington	Hem.H.	Hemel Hempstead	Rad.	Radlett	Til.	Tilbury		

Notes

A strict word-by-word alphabetical order is followed in the index whereby generic terms such as Avenue, Close, Gardens etc., although abbreviated, are ordered in their expanded form. So, for example, Abbot St. comes before Abbots Ave., and Abbots Ri. comes before Abbots Rd.

Street names preceded by a definite article (i.e. The) are indexed from their second word onwards with the article being placed at the end of the name,
e.g. Avenue, The, or Long Walk, The

The alphabetical order extends to include postal information so that where two or more streets have exactly the same name, London post town references are given first in alpha-numeric order and are followed by non-London post town references in alphabetic order,
e.g. Abbey Gdns. NW8 is followed by Abbey Gdns. W6 and then Abbey Gdns., Chertsey.

In some cases there are two or more streets of the same name in the same postal area. In order to aid correct location, extra information will be given in brackets,
e.g. High St., Epsom and High St. (Ewell), Epsom.

The street name and postal district or post town of an entry is followed by the page number and grid reference on which the name will be found, e.g. Abbey Road SW19 will be found on page 180 and in square DC94. Likewise, Norfolk Crescent, Sidcup will be found on page 185 and in square ES87 (within postal district DA15).

All streets within the Central London enlarged-scale section (pages 272-279) are shown in **bold type** when named in the index, e.g. **Abbey St. SE1** will be found on page **279** and in square **N6**. Certain streets may also be duplicated on parts of pages 140-142 and 160-162. In these cases the Central London section reference is always given first in bold type, followed by the same name in standard type, e.g.

Abbey Orchard St. SW1 277 M6
Abbey Orchard St. SW1   161   DK76

The index also contains some roads for which there is insufficient space to name on the map. The adjoining, or nearest named thoroughfare to such roads is shown in *italics*, and the reference indicates where the unnamed road is located off the named thoroughfare,
e.g. Oyster Catchers Close E16 is off *Freemasons Road* and is located off this road on page 144 in square EH72.

A.C. Ct., T.Ditt. 197 CG100
Harvest La.
A1(M) Business Pk., Hat. 45 CW23
Abberley Ms. SW4 161 DH83
Cedars Rd.
Abberton Wk., Rain. 147 FE66
Ongar Way
Abbess Clo. E6 144 EL71
Oliver Gdns.
Abbess Clo. SW2 181 DN88
Abbeville Rd. N8 121 DK56
Barrington Rd.
Abbeville Rd. SW4 181 DJ86
Abbey Ave., St.Alb. 42 CA23
Abbey Ave., Wem. 138 CL68
Abbey Clo., Hayes 135 BV74
Abbey Clo., Nthlt. 136 BZ69
Invicta Gro.
Abbey Clo., Pnr. 115 BV55
Abbey Clo., Rom. 127 FG58
Shaftesbury Rd.
Abbey Clo., Slou. 131 AL73
Abbey Clo., Wok. 227 BE116
Abbey Ct., Wal.Abb. 67 EB34
Abbey Cres., Belv. 166 FA77
Abbey Dr. SW17 180 DG92
Church La.
Abbey Dr., Abb.L. 59 BU32
Langley La.
Abbey Dr., Stai. 194 BJ97
Abbey Gdns. NW8 140 DC68
Abbey Gdns. SE16 162 DU77
Southwark Pk. Rd.
Abbey Gdns. W6 159 CY79
Abbey Gdns., Cher. 194 BG100
Abbey Grn., Cher. 194 BG100
Abbey Gro. SE2 166 EV77
Abbey La. E15 143 EC68
Abbey La., Beck. 183 EA94
Abbey Manufacturing Est., Wem. 138 CM67
Abbey Ms. E17 123 EA57
Leamington Ave.
Abbey Mill End, St.Alb. 42 CC21
Abbey Mill La., St.Alb. 42 CC21
Abbey Mills, St.Alb. 42 CC21
Abbey Orchard St. SW1 277 M6
Abbey Orchard St. SW1 161 DK76
Abbey Par. W5 138 CM69
Hanger La.
Abbey Pk., Beck. 183 EA94
Abbey Pk. La., Slou. 111 AL61
Abbey Rd. E15 143 ED68
Abbey Rd. NW6 140 DB66
Abbey Rd. NW8 140 DB67
Abbey Rd. NW10 138 CP68
Abbey Rd. SE2 166 EX77
Abbey Rd. SW19 180 DC94
Abbey Rd., Bark. 145 EP66
Abbey Rd., Belv. 166 EX77
Abbey Rd., Bexh. 166 EY84
Abbey Rd., Cher. 194 BH101
Abbey Rd., Croy. 201 DP104
Abbey Rd., Enf. 82 DS43
Abbey Rd., Grav. 191 GL88
Abbey Rd., Green. 189 FW85
Abbey Rd., Ilf. 125 ER57
Abbey Rd., Shep. 194 BN102
Abbey Rd., S.Croy. 221 DX110
Abbey Rd., Vir.W. 192 AX99
Abbey Rd., Wal.Cr. 67 DY34
Abbey Rd., Wok. 226 AW117
Abbey Rd. Est. NW8 140 DB67
Abbey St. E13 144 EG70
Abbey St. SE1 279 N6
Abbey St. SE1 162 DT76
Abbey Ter. SE2 166 EW77
Abbey Vw. NW7 97 CT48
Abbey Vw., Wal.Abb. 67 EB33
Abbey Vw., Wat. 76 BX36
Abbey Vw. Rd., St.Alb. 42 CC20
Abbey Wk., W.Mol. 196 CB97
Abbey Way SE2 166 EX75
Wolvercote Rd.
Abbey Wf. Ind. Est., Bark. 145 ER68
Abbey Wd. La., Rain. 148 FK68
Abbey Wd. Rd. SE2 166 EV77
Abbeydale Clo., Harl. 52 EW16
Kiln La.
Abbeydale Rd., Wem. 138 CN67
Abbeyfield Est. SE16 162 DW77
Abbeyfield Rd.
Abbeyfield Rd. SE16 162 DW77
Abbeyfields Clo. NW10 138 CN69
Abbeyhill Rd., Sid. 186 EW89
Abbot Clo., Stai. 174 BK94
Abbot Clo., W.Byf. 212 BK110
Abbot Rd., Guil. 258 AX136
Abbot St. E8 142 DT65
Abbots Ave., St.Alb. 43 CE23
Abbots Ave. W., St.Alb. 43 CD23
Abbots Clo. N1 142 DQ65
Alwyne Rd.
Abbots Clo., Brwd. 109 GA46
Abbots Clo., Guil. 258 AS137
Abbots Clo., Orp. 205 EQ102
Abbots Clo., Rain. 148 FJ68
Abbots Clo., Ruis. 116 BX62
Abbots Clo., Uxb. 134 BK71
Abbots Cres., Enf. 81 DP40
Abbots Dr., Har. 116 CA61
Abbots Dr., Vir.W. 192 AW98
Abbots Fld., Grav. 191 GJ93
Ruffets Wd.
Abbots Gdns. N2 120 DD56
Abbots Gdns. W8 160 DB76
St. Mary's Pl.
Abbots Grn., Croy. 221 DX107
Abbots La. SE1 279 N3
Abbots La., Ken. 236 DQ116
Abbots Manor Est. SW1 277 H10
Abbots Pk. SW2 181 DN88
Abbots Pk., St.Alb. 43 CF22
Abbot's Pl. NW6 140 DB67
Abbots Ri., Kings L. 58 BM26
Abbots Ri., Red. 250 DG132
Ladbroke Rd.
Abbots Ri., Ware 33 ED11
Abbot's Rd. E6 144 EK67
Abbots Rd., Abb.L. 59 BQ31
Abbots Rd., Edg. 96 CQ52
Abbots Ter. N8 121 DL58
Abbots Tilt, Walt. 196 BY104
Abbots Vw., Kings L. 58 BM27
Abbots Wk. W8 160 DB76
St. Mary's Pl.
Abbots Wk., Cat. 236 DU122
Tillingdown Hill
Abbots Way, Beck. 203 DY99
Abbots Way, Guil. 243 BD133
Abbotsbury Clo. E15 143 EC68
Abbotsbury Clo. W14 159 CZ75
Abbotsbury Rd.
Abbotsbury Gdns., Pnr. 116 BW58
Abbotsbury Ms. SE15 162 DW83
Abbotsbury Rd. W14 159 CY75
Abbotsbury Rd., Brom. 204 EF103
Abbotsbury Rd., Mord. 200 DB99
Abbotsford Ave. N15 122 DQ56
Abbotsford Clo., Wok. 227 BA117
Onslow Cres.
Abbotsford Gdns., Wdf.Grn. 102 EG52
Abbotsford Lo., Nthwd. 93 BS50
Abbotsford Rd., Ilf. 126 EU61
Abbotshall Ave. N14 99 DJ48
Abbotshall Rd. SE6 183 ED88
Abbotsleigh Clo., Sutt. 218 DB108
Abbotsleigh Rd. SW16 181 DJ91
Abbotsmede Clo., Twick. 177 CF89
Abbotstone Rd. SW15 159 CW83
Abbotsweld, Harl. 51 ER18
Abbotswell Rd. SE4 183 DZ85
Abbotswood, Guil. 243 AZ132
Abbotswood Clo., Belv. 166 EY76
Coptefield Dr.
Abbotswood Clo., Guil. 243 AZ131
Abbotswood Dr., Wey. 213 BR110
Abbotswood Gdns., Ilf. 125 EM55
Abbotswood Rd. SW16 181 DK90
Abbotswood Way, Hayes 135 BV74
Abbott Ave. SW20 199 CX95
Abbott Clo., Hmptn. 176 BY93
Abbott Clo., Nthlt. 136 BZ65
Abbott Rd. E14 143 EC72
Abbotts Clo. SE28 146 EW73
Woodpecker Rd.
Abbotts Clo., Rom. 127 FB55
Abbotts Clo., Swan. 207 FG98
Abbotts Cres. E4 101 ED49
Abbotts Dr., Wal.Abb. 68 EG33
Abbotts Dr., Wem. 117 CH61
Abbotts Pk. Rd. E10 123 EC59
Abbotts Pl., Chesh. 54 AQ28
Abbotts Rd., Barn. 80 DB42
Abbotts Rd., Mitch. 201 DJ98
Abbotts Rd., Sthl. 136 BY74
Abbotts Rd., Sutt. 217 CY105
Abbotts Vale, Chesh. 54 AQ28
Abbotts Wk., Bexh. 166 EX80
Abbotts Wk., Wind. 151 AL82
Abbotts Way, Slou. 131 AK74
Abbotts Way, Ware 33 ED11
Abbs Cross Gdns., Horn. 128 FJ60
Abbs Cross La., Horn. 128 FJ63
Abchurch La. EC4 275 L10
Abchurch La. EC4 142 DR73
Abchurch Yd. EC4 275 K10
Abdale Rd. W12 139 CV74
Abel Clo., Hem.H. 40 BN20
Abenberg Way, Brwd. 109 GB47
Abenglen Ind. Est., Hayes 155 BR75
Aberavon Rd. E3 143 DY69
Abercairn Rd. SW16 181 DJ94
Aberconway Rd., Mord. 200 DB97
Abercorn Clo. NW7 97 CY52
Abercorn Clo. NW8 140 DC69
Abercorn Clo., S.Croy. 221 DX112
Abercorn Cres., Har. 116 CB61
Abercorn Gdns., Har. 117 CK59
Abercorn Gdns., Rom. 126 EV58
Abercorn Gro., Ruis. 115 BR56
Abercorn Pl. NW8 140 DC69
Abercorn Rd. NW7 97 CY52
Abercorn Rd., Stan. 95 CJ52
Abercorn Way SE1 162 DU78
Abercorn Way, Wok. 226 AU118
Abercrombie Dr., Enf. 82 DU39
Carterhatch La.
Abercrombie St. SW11 160 DE82
Abercrombie Way, Harl. 51 EQ17
Aberdale Gdns., Pot.B. 63 CY32
Aberdare Clo., W.Wick. 203 EC103
Aberdare Gdns. NW6 140 DB66
Aberdare Gdns. NW7 97 CX52
Aberdare Rd., Enf. 82 DW42
Aberdeen Ave., Slou. 131 AN73
Aberdeen La. N5 122 DQ64
Aberdeen Par. N18 100 DV50
Angel Rd.
Aberdeen Pk. N5 122 DQ64
Aberdeen Pk. Ms. N5 122 DQ63
Aberdeen Pl. NW8 140 DD70
Aberdeen Rd. N5 122 DQ63
Aberdeen Rd. N18 100 DV50
Aberdeen Rd. NW10 119 CT64
Aberdeen Rd., Croy. 220 DQ105
Aberdeen Rd., Har. 95 CF54
Aberdeen Ter. SE3 163 ED82
Aberdour Rd., Ilf. 126 EV62
Aberdour St. SE1 279 M8
Aberdour St. SE1 162 DS77
Aberfeldy St. E14 143 EC72
Aberford Gdns. SE18 164 EL81
Aberford Rd., Borwd. 78 CN40
Aberfoyle Rd. SW16 181 DK93
Abergeldie Rd. SE12 184 EH86
Abernethy Rd. SE13 164 EE84
Abersham Rd. E8 122 DT64
Abery St. SE18 165 ES77
Abingdon Clo. NW1 141 DK65
Camden Sq.
Abingdon Clo. SE1 162 DT77
Bushwood Dr.
Abingdon Clo. SW19 180 DC93
Abingdon Clo., Uxb. 134 BM67
Abingdon Clo., Wok. 226 AV118
Abingdon Pl., Pot.B. 64 DB32
Abingdon Rd. N3 98 DC54
Abingdon Rd. SW16 201 DL96
Abingdon Rd. W8 160 DA76
Abingdon St. SW1 277 P6
Abingdon St. SW1 161 DL76
Abingdon Vill. W8 160 DA76
Abingdon Way, Orp. 224 EV105
Abinger Ave., Sutt. 217 CW109
Abinger Clo., Bark. 126 EU63
Abinger Clo., Brom. 204 EL97
Abinger Clo., Dor. 263 CJ140
Abinger Clo., Wall. 219 DL106
Abinger Common Rd., Dor. 262 BY144
Abinger Dr., Red. 266 DE136
Pendleton Rd.
Abinger Gdns., Islw. 157 CE83
Sussex Ave.
Abinger Gro. SE8 163 DZ79
Abinger La., Dor. 261 BV140
Abinger Ms. W9 140 DA70
Warlock Rd.
Abinger Rd. W4 158 CS76
Abinger Way, Guil. 243 BB129
Ablett St. SE16 162 DW78
Abney Gdns. N16 122 DT61
Stoke Newington High St.
Aboyne Dr. SW20 199 CU96
Aboyne Est. SW17 180 DD90
Aboyne Rd. NW10 118 CR62
Aboyne Rd. SW17 180 DD90
Abridge Clo., Wal.Cr. 83 DX35
Abridge Gdns., Rom. 104 FA51
Abridge Pk. (Abridge), Rom. 86 EU42
Abridge Rd., Chig. 85 ER44
Abridge Rd., Epp. 85 ES36
Abridge Rd. (Abridge), Rom. 86 EU39
Abridge Way, Bark. 146 EV68
Abyssinia Clo. SW11 160 DE84
Cairns Rd.
Acacia Ave. N17 100 DR52
Acacia Ave., Brent. 157 CH80
Acacia Ave., Hayes 135 BT72
Acacia Ave., Horn. 127 FF61
Acacia Ave., Mitch. 201 DH96
Acacia Ave., Ruis. 115 BU60
Acacia Ave., Shep. 194 BN99
Acacia Ave., Stai. 152 AY84
Acacia Ave., Wem. 118 CL64
Acacia Ave., West Dr. 134 BM73
Acacia Ave., Wok. 226 AX120
Acacia Clo. SE20 202 DU96
Selby Rd.
Acacia Clo., Add. 211 BF110
Acacia Clo., Orp. 205 ER99
Acacia Clo., Stan. 95 CE51
Acacia Clo., Wal.Cr. 66 DS27
Acacia Ct., Berk. 38 AV20
Acacia Dr., Add. 211 BF110
Acacia Dr., Bans. 217 CX114
Acacia Dr., Sutt. 199 CZ102
Acacia Dr., Upmin. 128 FN62
Acacia Gdns. NW8 140 DD68
Acacia Rd.
Acacia Gdns., Upmin. 129 FT59
Acacia Gdns., W.Wick. 203 EC103
Acacia Gro. SE21 182 DR89
Acacia Gro., N.Mal. 198 CS97
Acacia Ms., West Dr. 154 BK79
Acacia Pl. NW8 140 DD68
Acacia Rd. E11 124 EE61
Acacia Rd. E17 123 DY58
Acacia Rd. N22 99 DN53
Acacia Rd. NW8 140 DD68
Acacia Rd. SW16 201 DL95
Acacia Rd. W3 138 CQ73
Acacia Rd., Beck. 203 DZ97
Acacia Rd., Dart. 188 FK88
Acacia Rd., Enf. 82 DR39
Acacia Rd., Green. 189 FS86
Acacia Rd., Guil. 242 AX134
Acacia Rd., Hmptn. 176 CA93
Acacia Rd., Mitch. 200 DG96
Acacia Rd., Stai. 174 BH92
Acacia St., Hat. 45 CU21
Acacia Wk., Swan. 207 FD96
Walnut Way
Acacia Way, Sid. 185 ET88
Academy Gdns., Croy. 202 DT102
Academy Gdns., Nthlt. 136 BX68
Academy Pl. SE18 165 EM81
Academy Rd. SE18 165 EM81
Acanthus Dr. SE1 162 DU78
Acanthus Rd. SW11 160 DG83
Accommodation La., West Dr. 154 BG81
Accommodation Rd. NW11 119 CZ59
Accommodation Rd., Cher. 192 AX104
Acer Ave., Hayes 136 BY71
Jollys La.
Acer Ave., Rain. 148 FK69
Acer Rd., West. 238 EK116
Acers, St.Alb. 60 CC28
Acfold Rd. SW6 160 DB81
Achilles Clo. SE1 162 DU78
Achilles Clo., Hem.H. 40 BM18
Achilles Pl., Wok. 226 AW117
Achilles Rd. NW6 120 DA64
Achilles St. SE14 163 DY80
Achilles Way W1 276 G3
Acklam Rd. W10 139 CZ71
Portobello Rd.
Acklington Dr. NW9 96 CS53
Ackmar Rd. SW6 160 DA81
Ackroyd Dr. E3 143 DZ71
Ackroyd Rd. SE23 183 DX87
Ackworth Clo. N9 100 DW45
Turin Rd.
Acland Clo. SE18 165 ER80
Clothworkers Rd.
Acland Cres. SE5 162 DR84
Acland Rd. NW2 139 CV65
Acme Rd., Wat. 75 BU38
Acol Cres., Ruis. 115 BV64
Acol Rd. NW6 140 DA66
Aconbury Rd., Dag. 146 EV67
Acorn Clo. E4 101 EB50
The Lawns
Acorn Clo., Chis. 185 EQ92
Acorn Clo., Enf. 81 DP39
Acorn Clo., Horl. 269 DJ147
Middlefield
Acorn Clo., Stan. 95 CH52
Acorn Ct., Ilf. 125 ES58
Acorn Gdns. SE19 202 DT95
Acorn Gdns. W3 138 CR71
Acorn Gro., Hayes 155 BT80
Acorn Gro., Ruis. 115 BT63
Acorn Gro., Tad. 233 CY124
Warren Lo. Dr.
Acorn Gro., Wok. 226 AY121
Old Sch. Pl.
Acorn Ind. Pk., Dart. 187 FG85
Acorn La. (Cuffley), Pot.B. 65 DL29
Acorn Par. SE15 162 DV80
Carlton Gro.
Acorn Pl., Wat. 75 BU37
Acorn Rd., Dart. 187 FF85
Acorn Rd., Hem.H. 40 BN21
Acorn St., Ware 34 EK08
Acorn Wk. SE16 143 DY74
Acorn Way SE23 183 DX90
Acorn Way, Orp. 223 EP105
Acorns, The, Chig. 103 ES49
Acorns, The, Horl. 269 DP148
Redehall Rd.
Acorns Clo., Hmptn. 176 CB93
Acorns Way, Esher 214 CC106
Acre La. SW2 161 DL84
Acre La., Cars. 218 DG105
Acre La., Wall. 218 DG105
Acre Pas., Wind. 151 AR81
Acre Path, Nthlt. 136 BY65
Arnold Rd.
Acre Rd. SW19 180 DD93
Acre Rd., Dag. 147 FB66
Acre Rd., Kings.T. 198 CL95
Acre Vw., Horn. 128 FL56
Acre Way, Nthwd. 93 BT53
Acre Wd., Hem.H. 40 BL20
Acrefield Rd., Ger.Cr. 112 AX55
Acres End, Amer. 55 AS39
Acres Gdns., Tad. 233 CX119
Acrewood Way, St.Alb. 44 CM20
Acris St. SW18 180 DC85
Acton Clo. N9 100 DU47
Acton Clo. (Cheshunt), Wal.Cr. 67 DY31
Acton La. NW10 138 CQ69
Acton La. W3 158 CQ75
Acton La. W4 158 CQ77
Acton Ms. E8 142 DT67
Acton Pk. Ind. Est. W3 158 CR75
Acton St. WC1 274 B3
Acton St. WC1 141 DM69
Acuba Rd. SW18 180 DB88
Acworth Clo. N9 100 DW45
Turin Rd.
Ada Gdns. E14 143 ED72
Ada Gdns. E15 144 EF67
Ada Pl. E2 142 DU67
Ada Rd. SE5 162 DS80
Ada Rd., Wem. 117 CJ62
Ada St. E8 142 DV67
Adair Clo. SE25 202 DV97
Adair Rd. W10 139 CY70
Adair Twr. W10 139 CY70
Appleford Rd.
Adam & Eve Ct. W1 273 L8
Adam & Eve Ms. W8 160 DA76
Adam Clo., Slou. 131 AN74
Telford Dr.
Adam Ct. SW7 160 DC77
Gloucester Rd.
Adam Pl. N16 122 DT61
Stoke Newington High St.
Adam Rd. E4 101 DZ51
Silver Birch Ave.
Adam St. WC2 278 A1
Adam St. WC2 141 DL73
Adam Wk. SW6 159 CW80
Adams Clo. N3 98 DA52
Falkland Ave.
Adams Clo. NW9 118 CP61
Adams Clo., Surb. 198 CM100
Adams Ct. EC2 275 L8
Adams Gdns. Est. SE16 162 DW75
St. Marychurch St.
Adams Pl. E14 143 EB74
North Colonnade
Adams Pl. N7 121 DM64
George's Rd.
Adams Rd. N17 100 DR54
Adams Rd., Beck. 203 DY99
Adams Row W1 276 G1
Adams Row W1 140 DG73
Adams Sq., Bexh. 166 EY83
Regency Way
Adams Way, Croy. 202 DT100
Adamsfield, Wal.Cr. 66 DT26
Adamson Rd. E16 144 EG72
Adamson Rd. NW3 140 DD66
Adamsrill Clo., Enf. 82 DR43
Adamsrill Rd. SE26 183 DY91
Adare Wk. SW16 181 DM90
Adastral Est. NW9 96 CS53
Adcock Wk., Orp. 223 ET105
Borkwood Pk.
Adderley Gdns. SE9 185 EN91
Adderley Gro. SW11 180 DG85
Culmstock Rd.
Adderley Rd., Har. 95 CF53
Adderley St. E14 143 EC72
Addington Border, Croy. 221 DY110
Addington Clo., Wind. 151 AN83
Addington Ct. SW14 158 CR83
Addington Dr. N12 98 DC51
Addington Gro. SE26 183 DY91
Addington Heights, Croy. 221 EC111
Cleves Cres.
Addington Rd. E3 143 EA69
Addington Rd. E16 144 EE70
Addington Rd. N4 121 DN58
Addington Rd., Croy. 201 DN102
Addington Rd., S.Croy. 220 DU112
Addington Rd., W.Wick. 221 EC105
Addington Sq. SE5 162 DR79
Addington St. SE1 278 C5
Addington Village Rd., Croy. 221 DZ107
Addis Clo., Enf. 83 DX39
Addiscombe Ave., Croy. 202 DU101
Addiscombe Clo., Har. 117 CJ57
Addiscombe Ct. Rd., Croy. 202 DS102
Addiscombe Gro., Croy. 202 DS103
Addiscombe Rd., Croy. 202 DS103
Addiscombe Rd., Wat. 75 BV42
Addison Ave. N14 81 DH44
Addison Ave. W11 139 CY74
Addison Ave., Houns. 156 CC81
Addison Bri. Pl. W14 159 CZ77
Addison Clo., Cat. 236 DR122
Addison Clo., Nthwd. 93 BU53
Addison Clo., Orp. 205 EQ100
Addison Cres. W14 159 CY76
Addison Dr. SE12 184 EH85
Eltham Rd.
Addison Gdns. W14 159 CX76
Addison Gdns., Grays 170 GC77
Palmers Dr.
Addison Gdns., Surb. 198 CM98
Addison Gro. W4 158 CS76
Addison Pl. W11 139 CY74
Addison Pl., Sthl. 136 CA73
Longford Ave.
Addison Rd. E11 124 EG58
Addison Rd. E17 123 EB57
Addison Rd. SE25 202 DU98
Addison Rd. W14 159 CY76
Addison Rd., Brom. 204 EJ99
Addison Rd., Cat. 236 DR121
Addison Rd., Chesh. 54 AQ29
Addison Rd., Enf. 82 DW39
Addison Rd., Guil. 258 AY135
Addison Rd., Ilf. 103 EQ53
Addison Rd., Tedd. 177 CH93
Addison Rd., Wok. 227 AZ117
Chertsey Rd.
Addison Way NW11 119 CZ56
Addison Way, Hayes 135 BU72
Addison Way, Nthwd. 93 BT53
Addison's Clo., Croy. 203 DZ103
Addle Hill EC4 274 G9
Addle St. EC2 275 J7
Addlestone Moor, Add. 194 BJ103
Addlestone Pk., Add. 212 BH106
Addlestone Rd., Add. 212 BL105
Adecroft Way, W.Mol. 196 CC97
Adela Ave., N.Mal. 199 CV99
Adela St. W10 139 CY70
Kensal Rd.
Adelaide Ave. SE4 163 DZ84
Adelaide Clo., Enf. 82 DS38
Adelaide Clo., Slou. 151 AN75
Amerden Way
Adelaide Clo., Stan. 95 CG49
Adelaide Cotts. W7 157 CF75
Adelaide Gdns., Rom. 126 EY57
Adelaide Gro. W12 139 CU74
Adelaide Pl., Wey. 213 BR105
Adelaide Rd. E10 123 EC62
Adelaide Rd. NW3 140 DD66
Adelaide Rd. SW18 180 DA85
Putney Bri. Rd.
Adelaide Rd. W13 137 CG74
Adelaide Rd., Ashf. 174 BK92
Adelaide Rd., Chis. 185 EP92
Adelaide Rd., Houns. 156 BY81
Adelaide Rd., Ilf. 125 EP61
Adelaide Rd., Rich. 158 CM84
Adelaide Rd., Sthl. 156 BY77
Adelaide Rd., Surb. 198 CL99
Adelaide Rd., Tedd. 177 CF93
Adelaide Rd., Til. 171 GF81
Adelaide Rd., Walt. 195 BU104
Adelaide Sq., Wind. 151 AR82
Adelaide St. WC2 277 P1
Adelaide St., St.Alb. 43 CD19
Adelaide Ter., Brent. 157 CK78
Adelaide Wk. SW9 161 DN84
Sussex Wk.
Adelina Gro. E1 142 DW71
Adelina Ms. SW12 181 DK88
King's Ave.
Adeline Pl. WC1 273 N7
Adeline Pl. WC1 141 DK71
Adelphi Cres., Hayes 135 BT69
Adelphi Cres., Horn. 127 FG61
Adelphi Gdns., Slou. 152 AS75
Adelphi Rd., Epsom 216 CR113
Adelphi Ter. WC2 278 A1
Adelphi Ter. WC2 141 DL73
Adelphi Way, Hayes 135 BT69
Aden Gro. N16 122 DR63
Aden Rd., Enf. 83 DY42
Aden Rd., Ilf. 125 EP59
Aden Ter. N16 122 DR63
Adeney Clo. W6 159 CX79
Adenmore Rd. SE6 183 EA87
Adeyfield Gdns., Hem.H. 40 BM19
Adeyfield Rd., Hem.H. 40 BK19
Adhern Ct., St.Alb. 43 CJ22
Adie Rd. W6 159 CW76
Adine Rd. E13 144 EH70
Adler St. E1 142 DU72
Adlers La., Dor. 247 CG131
Adley St. E5 123 DY63
Adlington Clo. N18 100 DS50
Plowman Clo.
Admaston Rd. SE18 165 EQ79
Admiral Pl. SE16 143 DY74
Admiral Seymour Rd. SE9 165 EM84
Admiral Sq. SW10 160 DC81
Admiral St. SE8 163 EA81
Admiral St., Hert. 32 DU09
Admiral Way, Berk. 38 AT17
Tortoiseshell Way
Admirals Clo. E18 124 EH56
Admirals Clo., St.Alb. 44 CS23
Admirals Ct., Guil. 243 BB133
Admiral's Rd., Lthd. 247 CD126
Admirals Wk. NW3 120 DC62
Admiral's Wk., Dor. 246 CB130
Admirals Wk., Green. 189 FV85
Admirals Wk., Hodd. 49 EA19
Admirals Wk., St.Alb. 43 CG23
Admiral's Wk., The, Couls. 235 DM120
Goodenough Way
Admirals Way E14 163 EA75
Admiralty Rd., Tedd. 177 CF93
Adnams Wk., Rain. 147 FF65
Lovell Wk.
Adolf St. SE6 183 EB91
Adolphus Rd. N4 121 DP61
Adolphus St. SE8 163 DZ80
Adomar Rd., Dag. 126 EX62
Adpar St. W2 140 DD71
Adrian Ave. NW2 119 CV60
North Circular Rd.
Adrian Clo., Uxb. 92 BK53
Adrian Ms. SW10 160 DB79
Adrian Rd., Abb.L. 59 BS31
Adrienne Ave., Sthl. 136 BZ69
Adstock Ms., Ger.Cr. 90 AX53
Church La.
Adstock Way, Grays 170 FZ77
Advance Rd. SE27 182 DQ91
Advice Ave., Grays 170 GA75
Adys Rd. SE15 162 DT83
Aerodrome Rd. NW4 119 CU55
Aerodrome Rd. NW9 119 CT55
Aerodrome Way, Houns. 156 BW79
Aeroville NW9 96 CS54
Affleck St. N1 274 C1
Afghan Rd. SW11 160 DE82
Aftab Ter. E1 142 DV70
Tent St.
Afton Dr., S.Ock. 149 FV72
Agamemnon Rd. NW6 119 CZ64
Agar Clo., Surb. 198 CM103
Agar Gro. NW1 141 DJ66
Agar Gro. Est. NW1 141 DJ66
Agar Pl. NW1 141 DJ66
Agar St. WC2 277 P1
Agar St. WC2 141 DL73
Agars Plough, Slou. 152 AU79
Agate Clo. E16 144 EK72
Agate Rd. W6 159 CW76
Agates La., Ash. 231 CK118
Agatha Clo. E1 142 DV74
Prusom St.
Agaton Rd. SE9 185 EQ89
Agave Rd. NW2 119 CW63

Agdon St. EC1 274 F4
Agdon St. EC1 141 DP70
Agincourt Rd. NW3 120 DF63
Agister Rd., Chig. 104 EU50
Agnes Ave., Ilf. 125 EP63
Agnes Clo. E6 145 EN73
Agnes Gdns., Dag. 126 EX63
Agnes Rd. W3 139 CT74
Agnes Scott Ct., Wey. 195 BP104
Palace Dr.
Agnes St. E14 143 DZ72
Agnesfield Clo. N12 98 DE52
Agnew Rd. SE23 183 DX87
Agraria Rd., Guil. 258 AV135
Agricola Pl., Enf. 82 DT43
Aidan Clo., Dag. 126 EY63
Aileen Wk. E15 144 EF66
Devenay Rd.
Ailsa Ave., Twick. 177 CG85
Ailsa Rd., Twick. 177 CH85
Ailsa St. E14 143 EC71
Ainger Ms. NW3 140 DF66
Ainger Rd.
Ainger Rd. NW3 140 DF66
Ainsdale Clo., Orp. 205 ER102
Ainsdale Cres., Pnr. 116 CA55
Ainsdale Rd. W5 137 CK70
Ainsdale Rd., Wat. 94 BW48
Ainsdale Way, Wok. 226 AU118
Ainsley Ave., Rom. 127 FB58
Ainsley Clo. N9 100 DS46
Ainsley St. E2 142 DV69
Ainslie Wk. SW12 181 DH87
Balham Gro.
Ainslie Wd. Cres. E4 101 EB50
Ainslie Wd. Gdns. E4 101 EB50
Ainslie Wd. Rd. E4 101 EA50
Ainsty Est. SE16 163 DX75
Needleman St.
Ainsworth Clo. NW2 119 CU62
Ainsworth Rd. E9 142 DW66
Ainsworth Rd., Croy. 201 DP103
Ainsworth Way NW8 140 DC67
Aintree Ave. E6 144 EL67
Aintree Clo., Grav. 191 GH90
Aintree Clo., Slou. 153 BE81
Aintree Clo., Uxb. 135 BP72
Craig Dr.
Aintree Cres., Ilf. 103 EQ54
Aintree Est. SW6 159 CY80
Dawes Rd.
Aintree Gro., Upmin. 128 FM62
Aintree Rd., Grnf. 137 CH68
Aintree St. SW6 159 CY80
Air St. W1 277 L1
Air St. W1 141 DJ73
Airdrie Clo. N1 141 DM66
Airdrie Clo., Hayes 136 BY71
Glencoe Rd.
Aire Dr., S.Ock. 149 FV70
Airedale, Hem.H. 40 BL17
Airedale Ave. W4 159 CT77
Airedale Ave. S. W4 159 CT78
Netheravon Rd. S.
Airedale Clo., Dart. 188 FQ88
Airedale Rd. SW12 180 DF87
Airedale Rd. W5 157 CJ76
Airey Neave Ct., Grays 170 GA75
Orchard Dr.
Airfield Way, Horn. 147 FH65
Airlie Gdns. W8 140 DA74
Campden Hill Rd.
Airlie Gdns., Ilf. 125 EP60
Airlinks Est., Houns. 156 BW78
Airport Ind. Est., West. 238 EK115
Airport Way, Gat. 268 DG151
Airport Way, Stai. 153 BF84
Airthrie Rd., Ilf. 126 EV61
Aisgill Ave. W14 159 CZ78
Aisher Rd. SE28 146 EW73
Aislibie Rd. SE12 164 EE84
Aitken Clo. E8 142 DU67
Pownall Rd.
Aitken Clo., Mitch. 200 DF101
Middleton Rd.
Aitken Rd. SE6 183 EB89
Aitken Rd., Barn. 79 CW43
Ajax Ave. NW9 118 CS55
Ajax Ave., Slou. 131 AP73
Ajax Rd. NW6 119 CZ64
Akabusi Clo., Croy. 202 DU100
Akehurst La., Sev. 257 FJ125
Akehurst St. SW15 179 CU86
Akeman Clo., St.Alb. 42 BZ22
Meautys
Akenside Rd. NW3 120 DD64
Akerman Rd. SW9 161 DP82
Akerman Rd., Surb. 197 CJ100
Akers La., Rick. 73 BD44
Alabama St. SE18 165 ER80
Alacross Rd. W5 157 CJ75
Alamein Clo., Brox. 49 DY21
Baas Hill
Alamein Gdns., Dart. 189 FR87
Alamein Rd., Swans. 189 FX86
Alan Clo., Dart. 168 FJ84
Alan Dr., Barn. 79 CY44
Alan Gdns., Rom. 126 FA59
Alan Hocken Way E15 144 EE68
Manor Rd.
Alan Rd. SW19 179 CY92
Alan Way, Slou. 132 AY72
Alandale Dr., Pnr. 93 BV54
Alanthus Clo. SE12 184 EF85
Alaska St. SE1 278 D3
Alba Clo., Hayes 136 BX70
Ramulis Dr.
Alba Gdns. NW11 119 CY58
Alba Pl. W11 139 CZ72
Portobello Rd.
Albacore Cres. SE13 183 EB86
Albain Cres., Ashf. 174 BL89
Alban Ave., St.Alb. 43 CD18
Alban Cres., Borwd. 78 CN39
Alban Cres. (Farningham), Dart. 208 FN102
Alban Highwalk EC2 142 DQ71
London Wall
Alban Ind. Pk., St.Alb. 44 CN20
Alban Pk., St.Alb. 44 CM20
Alban Way, Hat. 44 CR19
Alban Way, St.Alb. 43 CD22
Cottonmill La.
Albans Vw., Wat. 59 BV33
Albany, The W1 277 K1
Albany, The, Wdf.Grn. 102 EF49
Albany Clo. N15 121 DP56
Albany Clo. SW14 158 CP84
Albany Clo., Bex. 186 EW87
Albany Clo., Esher 214 CA109
Albany Clo., Reig. 250 DA131
Albany Clo., Uxb. 114 BN64
Albany Clo. (Bushey), Wat. 77 CD44
Albany Ct. E4 83 EB44
Chelwood Clo.
Albany Ct., Epp. 69 ET30
Albany Ctyd. W1 277 L1
Albany Cres., Edg. 96 CN52
Albany Cres., Esher 215 CE107
Albany Gate, Chesh. 54 AP30
Bellingdon Rd.
Albany Mans. SW11 160 DE80
Albert Bri. Rd.
Albany Ms. N1 141 DN66
Barnsbury Pk.
Albany Ms. SE5 162 DQ79
Albany Rd.
Albany Ms., Brom. 184 EG93
Avondale Rd.
Albany Ms., Kings.T. 177 CK93
Albany Ms., St.Alb. 60 CA27
North Orbital Rd.
Albany Ms., Sutt. 218 DB106
Camden Rd.
Albany Pk., Slou. 153 BD80
Albany Pk. Ave., Enf. 82 DW39
Albany Pk. Rd., Kings.T. 177 CK93
Albany Pk. Rd., Lthd. 231 CG119
Albany Pas., Rich. 178 CM85
Albany Pl. N7 121 DN63
Benwell Rd.
Albany Pl., Brent. 158 CL79
Albany Pl., Egh. 173 BB91
Albany Quay, Ware 33 DY06
Albany Rd. E10 123 EA59
Albany Rd. E12 124 EK63
Albany Rd. E17 123 DY58
Albany Rd. N4 121 DM58
Albany Rd. N18 100 DV50
Albany Rd. SE5 162 DR79
Albany Rd. SW19 180 DB92
Albany Rd. W13 137 CH73
Albany Rd., Belv. 166 EZ79
Albany Rd., Bex. 186 EW87
Albany Rd., Brent. 157 CK79
Albany Rd., Brwd. 108 FV44
Albany Rd., Chis. 185 EP92
Albany Rd., Enf. 83 DX37
Albany Rd., Horn. 127 FG60
Albany Rd., N.Mal. 198 CR98
Albany Rd., Rich. 178 CM85
Albert Rd.
Albany Rd., Rom. 126 EZ58
Albany Rd., Walt. 214 BW105
Albany Rd., Wind. 151 AQ82
Albany Rd. (Old Windsor), Wind. 172 AU85
Albany St. NW1 141 DH68
Albany Ter. NW1 141 DH70
Marylebone Rd.
Albany Vw., Buck.H. 102 EG46
Albatross Gdns., S.Croy. 221 DX111
Albatross St. SE18 165 ES80
Albatross Way SE16 163 DX75
Needleman St.
Albemarle SW19 179 CX89
Albemarle App., Ilf. 125 EP58
Albemarle Ave., Pot.B. 64 DB33
Albemarle Ave., Twick. 176 BZ88
Albemarle Ave. (Cheshunt), Wal.Cr. 66 DW28
Albemarle Clo., Grays 170 GA75
Albemarle Gdns., Ilf. 125 EP58
Albemarle Gdns., N.Mal. 198 CR98
Albemarle Pk., Stan. 95 CJ50
Albemarle Rd., Barn. 98 DE45
Albemarle Rd., Beck. 203 EB95
Albemarle St. W1 277 J1
Albemarle St. W1 141 DH73
Albemarle Way EC1 274 F5
Albeny Gate, St.Alb. 43 CD21
Alberon Gdns. NW11 119 CZ56
Albert Ave. E4 101 EA49
Albert Ave. SW8 161 DM80
Albert Ave., Cher. 194 BG97
Albert Bri. SW3 160 DE79
Albert Bri. SW11 160 DE80
Albert Bri. Rd. SW11 160 DE80
Albert Carr Gdns. SW16 181 DL92
Albert Clo. E9 142 DV67
Northiam St.
Albert Clo. N22 99 DK53
Albert Clo., Grays 170 GC76
Albert Clo., Slou. 152 AT76
Albert St.
Albert Ct. SW7 160 DD75
Albert Cres. E4 101 EA49
Albert Dr. SW19 179 CY89
Albert Dr., Wok. 211 BD114
Albert Embk. SE1 161 DL78
Albert Gdns. E1 143 DX72
Albert Gdns., Harl. 52 EX16
Kiln La.
Albert Gate SW1 160 DF75
South Carriage Dr.
Albert Gro. SW20 199 CX95
Albert Hall Mans. SW7 160 DD75
Kensington Gore
Albert Mans. SW11 160 DF81
Albert Bri. Rd.
Albert Ms. W8 160 DC76
Victoria Gro.
Albert Murray Clo., Grav. 191 GJ87
Armoury Dr.
Albert Pl. N3 98 DA53
Albert Pl. N17 122 DT55
High Rd.
Albert Pl. W8 160 DB75
Albert Pl. (Eton Wick), Wind. 151 AN78
Common Rd.
Albert Rd. E10 123 EC61
Albert Rd. E16 144 EL74
Albert Rd. E17 123 EA57
Albert Rd. E18 124 EH55
Albert Rd. N4 121 DM60
Albert Rd. N15 122 DS58
Albert Rd. N22 99 DJ53
Albert Rd. NW4 119 CX56
Albert Rd. NW6 139 CZ68
Albert Rd. NW7 97 CT50
Albert Rd. SE9 184 EL90
Albert Rd. SE20 183 DX93
Albert Rd. SE25 202 DU98
Albert Rd. W5 137 CH70
Albert Rd., Add. 194 BK104
Albert Rd., Ashf. 174 BM92
Albert Rd., Ash. 232 CM118
Albert Rd., Barn. 80 DD42
Albert Rd., Belv. 166 EZ78
Albert Rd., Bex. 186 FA86
Albert Rd., Brom. 204 EK99
Albert Rd., Buck.H. 102 EK47
Albert Rd., Chesh. 54 AQ31
Albert Rd., Dag. 126 FA60
Albert Rd., Dart. 188 FJ90
Albert Rd., Egh. 172 AX93
Albert Rd., Epsom 217 CT113
Albert Rd., Hmptn. 176 CC92
Albert Rd., Har. 116 CC55
Albert Rd., Hayes 155 BS76
Albert Rd., Horl. 268 DG148
Albert Rd., Houns. 156 CA84
Albert Rd., Ilf. 125 EP62
Albert Rd., Kings.T. 198 CM96
Albert Rd., Mitch. 200 DF97
Albert Rd., N.Mal. 199 CT98
Albert Rd., Orp. 224 EU106
Albert Rd. (St. Mary Cray), Orp. 206 EV100
Albert Rd., Red. 251 DJ129
Albert Rd., Rich. 178 CL85
Albert Rd., Rom. 127 FF57
Albert Rd., Sthl. 156 BX76
Albert Rd., Sutt. 218 DD106
Albert Rd., Swans. 190 FZ86
Albert Rd., Tedd. 177 CF93
Albert Rd., Twick. 177 CF88
Albert Rd., Warl. 237 DZ117
Albert Rd., West Dr. 134 BL74
Albert Rd., Wind. 151 AR83
Albert Rd. Est., Belv. 166 EZ78
Albert Rd. N., Reig. 249 CZ133
Albert Rd. N., Wat. 75 BV41
Albert Rd. S., Wat. 75 BV41
Albert Sq. E15 124 EE64
Albert Sq. SW8 161 DM80
Albert St. N12 98 DC50
Albert St. NW1 141 DH67
Albert St., Brwd. 108 FW50
Albert St., St.Alb. 43 CD21
Albert St., Slou. 152 AT76
Albert St., Wind. 151 AP81
Albert Ter. NW1 140 DG67
Albert Ter. NW10 138 CR67
Albert Ter., Buck.H. 102 EK47
Albert Ter. Ms. NW1 140 DG67
Regents Pk. Rd.
Albert Wk. E16 165 EN75
Pier Rd.
Alberta Ave., Sutt. 217 CY105
Alberta Dr., Horl. 269 DN148
Alberta Est. SE17 278 G10
Alberta Est. SE17 161 DP78
Alberta Rd., Enf. 82 DT44
Alberta Rd., Erith 167 FC81
Alberta St. SE17 278 F10
Alberta St. SE17 161 DP78
Albertine Clo., Epsom 233 CV116
Rose Bushes
Albion Ave. N10 98 DG53
Albion Ave. SW8 161 DK82
Albion Bldgs. EC1 142 DQ71
Bartholomew Clo.
Albion Clo. W2 272 C10
Albion Clo., Hert. 32 DS08
Albion Clo., Rom. 127 FD58
Albion Clo., Slou. 132 AU74
Albion Cres., Ch.St.G. 90 AV48
Albion Dr. E8 142 DT66
Albion Est. SE16 162 DW75
Albion Gdns. W6 159 CV77
Albion Gro. N16 122 DS63
Albion Hill SE13 163 EC82
Lewisham Rd.
Albion Hill, Loug. 84 EJ43
Albion Ho., Slou. 153 BB78
Albion Ms. N1 141 DN66
Albion Ms. NW6 139 CZ66
Kilburn High Rd.
Albion Ms. W2 272 C10
Albion Ms. W2 140 DE72
Albion Par. N16 122 DR63
Albion Rd.
Albion Par., Grav. 191 GK86
Canal Rd.
Albion Pk., Loug. 84 EK43
Albion Pl. EC1 274 F6
Albion Pl. EC1 141 DP71
Albion Pl. SE25 202 DU97
High St.
Albion Pl. W6 159 CV77
Galena Rd.
Albion Rd. E17 123 EC55
Albion Rd. N16 122 DR63
Albion Rd. N17 100 DU54
Albion Rd., Bexh. 166 EZ84
Albion Rd., Ch.St.G. 90 AV47
Albion Rd., Grav. 191 GJ87
Albion Rd., Hayes 135 BS72
Albion Rd., Houns. 156 CA84
Albion Rd., Kings.T. 198 CQ95
Albion Rd., Reig. 266 DC135
Albion Rd., St.Alb. 43 CF20
Albion Rd., Sutt. 218 DD107
Albion Rd., Twick. 177 CE88
Albion Sq. E8 142 DT66
Albion St. SE16 162 DW75
Albion St. W2 272 C9
Albion St. W2 140 DE72
Albion St., Croy. 201 DP102
Albion Ter. E8 142 DT66
Albion Ter., Grav. 191 GJ86
Albion Vill. Rd. SE26 182 DW90
Albion Way EC1 275 H7
Albion Way SE13 163 EC84
Albion Way, Wem. 118 CP62
North End Rd.
Albion Yd. E1 142 DV71
Whitechapel Rd.
Albright Ind. Est., Rain. 147 FF71
Albrighton Rd. SE22 162 DS83
Albuhera Clo., Enf. 81 DN39
Albury Ave., Bexh. 166 EY82
Albury Ave., Islw. 157 CF80
Albury Ave., Sutt. 217 CW109
Albury Clo., Cher. 192 AU104
Albury Clo., Hmptn. 176 CA93
Albury Dr., Pnr. 94 BW53
Albury Gro. Rd. (Cheshunt), Wal.Cr. 67 DX30
Albury Heath, Guil. 260 BK141
Albury Ms. E12 124 EJ60
Albury Pk., Guil. 260 BL140
Albury Ride (Cheshunt), Wal.Cr. 67 DX31
Albury Rd., Chess. 216 CL106
Albury Rd., Guil. 259 AZ135
Albury Rd., Red. 251 DJ129
Albury Rd., Walt. 213 BS107
Albury St. SE8 163 EA79
Albury Wk. (Cheshunt), Wal.Cr. 66 DW30
Albyfield, Brom. 205 EM97
Albyn Rd. SE8 163 EA81
Albyns Clo., Rain. 147 FG66
South End Rd.
Alcester Cres. E5 122 DV61
Alcester Rd., Wall. 219 DH105
Alcock Clo., Wall. 219 DK108
Alcock Rd., Houns. 156 BX80
Alcocks Clo., Tad. 233 CY120
Alcocks La., Tad. 233 CY121
Alconbury, Welw.G.C. 30 DE09
Alconbury Rd. E5 122 DU61
Alcorn Clo., Sutt. 200 DA103
Alcott Clo. W7 137 CF71
Westcott Cres.
Alcuin Ct., Stan. 95 CJ51
Aldborough Rd., Dag. 147 FC65
Aldborough Rd., Upmin. 128 FM61
Aldborough Rd. N., Ilf. 125 ET57
Aldborough Rd. S., Ilf. 125 ES60
Aldborough Spur, Slou. 132 AS72
Aldbourne Rd. W12 139 CT74
Aldbourne Rd., Slou. 130 AH71
Aldbridge St. SE17 279 N10
Aldbridge St. SE17 162 DS78
Aldburgh Ms. W1 272 G8
Aldbury Ave., Wem. 138 CP66
Aldbury Clo., St.Alb. 43 CJ15
Sandringham Cres.
Aldbury Clo., Wat. 76 BX36
Aldbury Gro., Welw.G.C. 30 DB09
Aldbury Ms. N9 100 DR45
Aldbury Rd., Rick. 91 BF45
Aldebert Ter. SW8 161 DL80
Aldeburgh Clo. E5 122 DV61
Southwold Rd.
Aldeburgh Pl., Wdf.Grn. 102 EG49
Aldeburgh St. SE10 164 EG78
Alden Ave. E15 144 EF70
Alden Vw., Wind. 151 AK81
Aldenham Ave., Rad. 77 CG36
Aldenham Dr., Uxb. 135 BP70
Aldenham Gro., Rad. 61 CG34
Aldenham Rd., Borwd. 77 CG41
Aldenham Rd., Rad. 77 CG35
Aldenham Rd., Wat. 76 BX44
Aldenham Rd. (Bushey), Wat. 76 BY44
Aldenham Rd. (Letchmore Heath), Wat. 77 CE39
Aldenham St. NW1 273 L1
Aldenham St. NW1 141 DJ68
Aldenholme, Wey. 213 BS107
Aldensley Rd. W6 159 CV76
Alder Ave., Upmin. 128 FM63
Alder Clo. SE15 162 DT79
Alder Clo., Egh. 172 AY92
Alder Clo., St.Alb. 60 CB28
Alder Clo., Slou. 131 AM74
Alder Cft., Couls. 235 DM116
Alder Dr., S.Ock. 149 FW70
Laburnum Gro.
Alder Gro. NW2 119 CU61
Alder Ind. Est., Hayes 155 BR75
Alder Ms. N19 121 DJ61
Bredgar Rd.
Alder Rd. SW14 158 CR83
Alder Rd., Iver 133 BD68
Glaisyer Way
Alder Rd., Sid. 185 ET90
Alder Rd., Uxb. 134 BJ65
Alder Wk., Wat. 75 BV35
Aspen Pk. Dr.
Alder Way, Swan. 207 FD96
Alderbourne La., Iver 113 AZ64
Alderbourne La., Slou. 112 AX63
Alderbrook Rd. SW12 181 DH86
Alderbury Rd. SW13 159 CU79
Alderbury Rd., Slou. 153 AZ75
Alderbury Rd. W., Slou. 153 AZ75
Aldercombe La., Cat. 252 DS127
Aldercroft, Couls. 235 DM116
Aldergrove Gdns., Houns. 156 BY82
Bath Rd.
Aldergrove Wk., Horn. 148 FJ65
Airfield Way
Alderholt Way SE15 162 DT80
Daniel Gdns.
Alderley Ct., Berk. 38 AV20
Alderman Ave., Bark. 146 EU69
Alderman Clo., Hat. 45 CW24
Alderman Judge Mall, Kings.T. 198 CL96
Eden St.
Aldermanbury EC2 275 J8
Aldermanbury EC2 142 DQ72
Aldermanbury Sq. EC2 275 J7
Aldermans Hill N13 99 DL49
Alderman's Wk. EC2 275 M7
Aldermary Rd., Brom. 204 EG95
Aldermoor Rd. SE6 183 DZ90
Alderney Ave., Houns. 156 CB80
Alderney Gdns., Nthlt. 136 BZ66
Alderney Rd. E1 143 DX70
Alderney Rd., Erith 167 FG80
Alderney St. SW1 277 J10
Alderney St. SW1 161 DH77
Alders, The N21 81 DN44
Alders, The, Felt. 176 BY91
Alders, The, Houns. 156 BZ79
Alders, The, W.Wick. 203 EB102
Alders Ave., Wdf.Grn. 102 EE51
Alders Clo. E11 124 EH61
Aldersbrook Rd.
Alders Clo. W5 157 CK76
Alders Clo., Edg. 96 CQ50
Alders Ct., Welw.G.C. 30 DA09
Alders Gro., E.Mol. 197 CD99
Esher Rd.
Alders Rd., Edg. 96 CQ50
Alders Rd., Reig. 250 DB132
Aldersbrook Ave., Enf. 82 DS40
Aldersbrook Dr., Kings.T. 178 CM93
Aldersbrook La. E12 125 EM62
Aldersbrook Rd. E11 124 EH61
Aldersbrook Rd. E12 124 EH61
Aldersey Gdns., Bark. 145 ER65
Aldersey Rd., Guil. 243 AZ134
Aldersford Clo. SE4 183 DX85
Aldersgate St. EC1 275 H6
Aldersgate St. EC1 142 DQ71
Aldersgrove, Wal.Abb. 68 EE34
Roundhills
Aldersgrove Ave. SE9 184 EJ90
Aldershot Rd. NW6 139 CZ67
Aldershot Rd., Guil. 242 AT132
Alderside Wk., Egh. 172 AY92
Aldersmead Ave., Croy. 203 DX100
Aldersmead Rd., Beck. 183 DY94
Alderson Pl., Sthl. 136 CC74
Alderson St. W10 139 CY70
Kensal Rd.
Alderstead Heath, Red. 235 DK124
Alderstead La., Red. 251 DK125
Alderton Clo. NW10 118 CR62
Alderton Clo., Brwd. 108 FV43
Alderton Clo., Loug. 85 EN42
Alderton Cres. NW4 119 CV57
Alderton Hall La., Loug. 85 EN42
Alderton Hill, Loug. 84 EL43
Alderton Ri., Loug. 85 EN42
Alderton Rd. SE24 162 DQ83
Alderton Rd., Croy. 202 DT101
Alderton Way NW4 119 CV57
Alderton Way, Loug. 85 EM43
Alderville Rd. SW6 159 CZ82
Alderwick Dr., Houns. 157 CD83
Alderwood Clo., Cat. 252 DS125
Alderwood Clo., Rom. 86 EV41
Alderwood Dr., Rom. 86 EV41
Alderwood Rd. SE9 185 ER86
Alford St. W1 276 F2
Alford St. W1 140 DG74
Aldgate EC3 275 P9
Aldgate EC3 142 DS72
Aldgate Ave. E1 275 P8
Aldgate High St. EC3 275 P9
Aldgate High St. EC3 142 DT72
Aldin Ave. N., Slou. 152 AU75
Aldin Ave. S., Slou. 152 AU75
Aldine Ct. W12 139 CW74
Aldine St.
Aldine Pl. W12 139 CW74
Uxbridge Rd.
Aldine St. W12 139 CW74
Aldingham Ct., Horn. 127 FG64
Easedale Dr.
Aldingham Gdns., Horn. 127 FG64
Aldington Clo., Dag. 126 EW59
Aldington Rd. SE18 164 EK76
Aldis Ms. SW17 180 DE92
Aldis St.
Aldis St. SW17 180 DE92
Aldock, Welw.G.C. 30 DA12
Aldred Rd. NW6 120 DA64
Aldren Rd. SW17 180 DC90
Aldrich Cres., Croy. 221 EC109
Aldrich Gdns., Sutt. 199 CZ104
Abbotts Rd.
Aldrich Ter. SW18 180 DC89
Lidiard Rd.
Aldriche Way E4 101 EC51
Aldridge Ave., Edg. 96 CP48
Aldridge Ave., Enf. 83 EA38
Aldridge Ave., Ruis. 116 BX61
Aldridge Ave., Stan. 96 CL53
Aldridge Ri., N.Mal. 198 CS101
Aldridge Rd. Vill. W11 139 CZ71
Aldridge Wk. N14 99 DL45
Aldridge Way, Slou. 131 AN70
Aldrington Rd. SW16 181 DJ91
Aldsworth Clo. W9 140 DB70
Aldwick, St.Alb. 43 CH22
Aldwick Clo. SE9 185 ER90
Aldwick Rd., Croy. 201 DM104
Aldworth Gro. SE13 183 EC86
Aldworth Rd. E15 144 EE66
Aldwych WC2 274 B10
Aldwych WC2 141 DM73
Aldwych Ave., Ilf. 125 EQ56
Aldwych Clo., Horn. 127 FG61
Aldykes, Hat. 45 CT18
Alers Rd., Bexh. 186 EX85
Aleston Beck Rd. E16 144 EK72
Fulmer Rd.
Alexa Ct. W8 160 DA77
Lexham Gdns.
Alexander Ave. NW10 139 CV66
Alexander Clo., Barn. 80 DD42
Alexander Clo., Brom. 204 EG102
Alexander Clo., Sid. 185 ES86
Alexander Clo., Sthl. 136 CC74
Alexander Clo., Twick. 177 CF89
Alexander Ct., Wal.Cr. 67 DX30
Alexander Evans Ms. SE23 183 DX88
Sunderland Rd.
Alexander Godley Clo., Ash. 232 CM119
Alexander La., Brwd. 109 GB44
Alexander Ms. W2 140 DB72
Alexander St.
Alexander Pl. SW7 276 B8
Alexander Pl. SW7 160 DE77
Alexander Rd. N19 121 DL62
Alexander Rd., Bexh. 166 EX82
Alexander Rd., Chis. 185 EP92
Alexander Rd., Couls. 235 DH115
Alexander Rd., Egh. 173 BC92
Alexander Rd., Green. 189 FW85
Alexander Rd., Hert. 31 DN09
Alexander Rd., Reig. 266 DA137
Alexander Rd., St.Alb. 61 CJ25
Alexander Sq. SW3 276 B8
Alexander Sq. SW3 160 DE77
Alexander St. W2 140 DA72
Alexander St., Chesh. 54 AQ30
Alexanders Wk., Cat. 252 DT126
Alexandra Ave. N22 99 DK53
Alexandra Ave. SW11 160 DG81
Alexandra Ave. W4 158 CR80
Alexandra Ave., Har. 116 BZ60
Alexandra Ave., Sthl. 136 BZ73
Alexandra Ave., Sutt. 200 DA104
Alexandra Ave., Warl. 237 DZ117
Alexandra Clo., Ashf. 175 BR94
Alexandra Rd.
Alexandra Clo., Grays 171 GH75
Alexandra Clo., Har. 116 CA62
Alexandra Ave.
Alexandra Clo., Stai. 174 BK93
Alexandra Clo., Swan. 207 FE96
Alexandra Clo., Walt. 195 BU103
Alexandra Cotts. SE14 163 DZ81
Alexandra Ct. N14 81 DJ43
Alexandra Ct., Ashf. 175 BR93
Alexandra Rd.
Alexandra Ct., Wem. 118 CM63
Alexandra Cres., Brom. 184 EF93
Alexandra Dr. SE19 182 DS92

Alexandra Dr., Surb. 198 CN101
Alexandra Est. NW8 140 DB67
Alexandra Gdns. N10 121 DH56
Alexandra Gdns. W4 158 CS80
Alexandra Gdns., Cars. 218 DG109
Alexandra Gdns., Houns. 156 CB82
Alexandra Gro. N4 121 DP60
Alexandra Gro. N12 98 DB50
Alexandra Ms. N2 120 DF55
Fortis Grn.
Alexandra Ms. SW19 180 DA93
Alexandra Rd.
Alexandra Palace Way N22 121 DJ56
Alexandra Pk. Rd. N10 99 DH54
Alexandra Pk. Rd. N22 99 DJ53
Alexandra Pl. NW8 140 DC67
Alexandra Pl. SE25 202 DR99
Alexandra Pl., Croy. 202 DS102
Alexandra Rd.
Alexandra Pl., Guil. 259 AZ136
Alexandra Rd. E6 145 EN69
Alexandra Rd. E10 123 EC62
Alexandra Rd. E17 123 DZ58
Alexandra Rd. E18 124 EH55
Alexandra Rd. N8 121 DN55
Alexandra Rd. N9 100 DV45
Alexandra Rd. N10 99 DH53
Alexandra Rd. N15 122 DR57
Alexandra Rd. NW4 119 CX56
Alexandra Rd. NW8 140 DC66
Alexandra Rd. SE26 183 DX93
Alexandra Rd. SW14 158 CR83
Alexandra Rd. SW19 179 CZ93
Alexandra Rd. W4 158 CR75
Alexandra Rd., Add. 212 BK105
Alexandra Rd., Ashf. 175 BR94
Alexandra Rd., Borwd. 78 CR38
Alexandra Rd., Brent. 157 CK79
Alexandra Rd., Brwd. 108 FW48
Alexandra Rd., Croy. 202 DS102
Alexandra Rd., Egh. 172 AW93
Alexandra Rd., Enf. 83 DX42
Alexandra Rd., Epsom 217 CT113
Alexandra Rd., Erith 167 FF79
Alexandra Rd., Grav. 191 GL87
Alexandra Rd., Hem.H. 40 BK19
Alexandra Rd., Houns. 156 CB82
Alexandra Rd., Kings L. 58 BN29
Alexandra Rd. (Chipperfield), Kings L. 58 BG30
Alexandra Rd., Kings.T. 178 CN94
Alexandra Rd., Mitch. 180 DE94
Alexandra Rd., Rain. 147 FF67
Alexandra Rd., Rich. 158 CM82
Alexandra Rd., Rick. 74 BG36
Alexandra Rd., Rom. 127 FF58
Alexandra Rd. (Chadwell Heath), Rom. 126 EX58
Alexandra Rd., St.Alb. 43 CE20
Alexandra Rd., Slou. 151 AR76
Alexandra Rd., T.Ditt. 197 CF99
Alexandra Rd., Til. 171 GF82
Alexandra Rd., Twick. 177 CJ86
Alexandra Rd., Uxb. 134 BK68
Alexandra Rd., Warl. 237 DY117
Alexandra Rd., Wat. 75 BU40
Alexandra Rd., West. 238 EH119
Alexandra Rd., Wind. 151 AR82
Alexandra Sq., Mord. 200 DA99
Alexandra St. E16 144 EG71
Alexandra St. SE14 163 DY80
Alexandra Ter., Guil. 258 AY135
Alexandra Wk. SE19 182 DS92
Alexandra Way, Wal.Cr. 67 DZ34
Alexandria Rd. W13 137 CG73
Alexis St. SE16 162 DU77
Alfan La., Dart. 187 FD92
Alfearn Rd. E5 122 DW63
Alford Clo., Guil. 243 BB131
Alford Grn., Croy. 221 ED107
Alford Pl. N1 275 J1
Alford Rd. SW8 161 DK81
Alford Rd., Erith 167 FC78
Alfoxton Ave. N15 121 DP56
Alfred Gdns., Sthl. 136 BY73
Alfred Ms. W1 273 M6
Alfred Ms. W1 141 DK71
Alfred Pl. WC1 273 M6
Alfred Pl. WC1 141 DK71
Alfred Pl., Grav. 191 GF88
Alfred Prior Ho. E12 125 EN63
Alfred Rd. E15 124 EF64
Alfred Rd. SE25 202 DU99
Alfred Rd. W2 140 DA71
Alfred Rd. W3 138 CQ74
Alfred Rd., Belv. 166 EZ78
Alfred Rd., Brwd. 108 FX47
Alfred Rd., Buck.H. 102 EK47
Alfred Rd., Dart. 188 FL91
Alfred Rd., Felt. 176 BW89
Alfred Rd., Grav. 191 GH89
Alfred Rd., Kings.T. 198 CL97
Alfred Rd., S.Ock. 148 FQ74
Alfred Rd., Sutt. 218 DC106
Alfred St. E3 143 DZ69
Alfred St. E16 144 EF73
Alfred St., Grays 170 GC79
Alfreda St. SW11 161 DH81
Alfred's Gdns., Bark. 145 ES68
Alfreds Way, Bark. 145 EQ69
Alfreds Way Ind. Est., Bark. 146 EU67
Alfreton Clo. SW19 179 CX90
Alfriston Ave., Croy. 201 DL101
Alfriston Ave., Har. 116 CA58
Alfriston Clo., Surb. 198 CM99
Alfriston Rd. SW11 180 DF85
Algar Clo., Islw. 157 CG83
Algar Rd.
Algar Clo., Stan. 95 CF50
Algar Rd., Islw. 157 CG83
Algarve Rd. SW18 180 DB88
Algernon Rd. NW4 119 CU58
Algernon Rd. NW6 140 DA67
Algernon Rd. SE13 163 EB83
Algers Clo., Loug. 84 EK43
Algers Mead, Loug. 84 EK43
Algers Rd., Loug. 84 EK43
Algiers Rd. SE13 163 EA84
Alibon Gdns., Dag. 126 FA64
Alibon Rd., Dag. 126 EZ64
Alice Gilliatt Ct. W14 159 CZ78
Alice La. E3 143 DZ67
Alice La., Slou. 130 AH70
Alice Ms., Tedd. 177 CF92
Luther Rd.
Alice Ruston Pl., Wok. 226 AW119
Alice St. SE1 279 M7
Alice St. SE1 162 DS76
Alice Thompson Clo. SE12 184 EJ89
Alice Walker Clo. SE24 161 DP84
Shakespeare Rd.
Alice Way, Houns. 156 CB84
Alicia Ave., Har. 117 CH56
Alicia Clo., Har. 117 CJ56
Alicia Gdns., Har. 117 CH56
Alie St. E1 142 DT72
Alington Cres. NW9 118 CQ60
Alington Gro., Wall. 219 DJ109
Alison Clo. E6 145 EN72
Alison Clo., Croy. 203 DX102
Shirley Oaks Rd.
Alison Clo., Wok. 210 AY114
Aliwal Rd. SW11 160 DE84
Alkerden La., Green. 189 FW86
Alkerden La., Swans. 189 FX86
Alkerden Rd. W4 158 CS78
Alkham Rd. N16 122 DT60
All Hallows Rd. N17 100 DS53
All Saints Clo. N9 100 DU47
All Saints Clo., Chig. 104 EV48
All Saints Clo., Swans. 190 FZ85
High St.
All Saints Cres., Wat. 60 BX33
All Saints Dr. SE3 164 EE82
All Saints Dr., S.Croy. 220 DT112
All Saints La., Rick. 74 BN44
All Saints Ms., Stan. 95 CE51
Uxbridge Rd.
All Saints Pas. SW18 180 DB85
Wandsworth High St.
All Saints Rd. SW19 180 DC94
All Saints Rd. W3 158 CQ76
All Saints Rd. W11 139 CZ72
All Saints Rd., Grav. 191 GF88
All Saints Rd., Sutt. 200 DB104
All Saints St. N1 141 DM68
All Saints Twr. E10 123 EB59
All Souls Ave. NW10 139 CV68
All Souls Pl. W1 273 J7
Allan Barclay Clo. N15 122 DT58
High Rd.
Allan Clo., N.Mal. 198 CR99
Allan Way W3 138 CQ71
Allanbrooke, Grav. 191 GJ87
Allandale, Hem.H. 40 BK19
Allandale, St.Alb. 42 CB23
Allandale Ave. N3 119 CY55
Allandale Cres., Pot.B. 63 CZ32
Allandale Pl., Orp. 206 EX104
Allandale Rd., Enf. 83 DX36
Allandale Rd., Horn. 127 FF59
Allard Clo., Orp. 206 EW101
Allard Clo. (Cheshunt), Wal.Cr. 66 DT27
Allard Cres. (Bushey), Wat. 94 CC46
Allard Gdns. SW4 181 DK85
Allard Way, Brox. 49 DY21
Allardyce St. SW4 161 DM84
Allbrook Clo., Tedd. 177 CE92
Allcot Clo., Felt. 175 BT88
Allcroft Rd. NW5 120 DG64
Alldicks Rd., Hem.H. 40 BM22
Allen Clo. SW16 201 DJ95
Leonard Rd.
Allen Clo., Rad. 62 CL32
Porters Pk. Dr.
Allen Clo., Sun. 195 BV95
Allen Ct., Dor. 263 CH136
High St.
Allen Ct., Grnf. 117 CF64
Allen Ct., Hat. 45 CV20
Travellers La.
Allen Edwards Dr. SW8 161 DL81
Allen Ho. Pk., Wok. 226 AW120
Allen Pl., Twick. 177 CG88
Church St.
Allen Rd. E3 143 DZ68
Allen Rd. N16 122 DS63
Allen Rd., Beck. 203 DX96
Allen Rd., Croy. 201 DM102
Allen Rd., Lthd. 246 CB126
Allen Rd., Rain. 148 FJ69
Allen Rd., Sun. 195 BV95
Allen St. W8 160 DA76
Allenby Ave., S.Croy. 220 DQ109
Allenby Clo., Grnf. 136 CA69
Allenby Cres., Grays 170 GB78
Allenby Dr., Horn. 128 FL60
Allenby Rd. SE23 183 DY90
Allenby Rd., Sthl. 136 CA69
Allenby Rd., West. 238 EL117
Allendale Ave., Sthl. 136 CA72
Allendale Clo. SE5 162 DR81
Daneville Rd.
Allendale Clo. SE26 183 DX92
Allendale Clo., Dart. 189 FR88
Princes Rd.
Allendale Rd., Grnf. 137 CH65
Allende Ave., Harl. 35 EQ12
Allens Rd., Enf. 82 DW43
Allensbury Pl. NW1 141 DK66
Allenswood Rd. SE9 164 EL83
Allerds Rd., Slou. 131 AM67
Allerford Ct., Har. 116 CB57
Allerford Rd. SE6 183 EB90
Allerton Clo., Borwd. 78 CM38
Allerton Rd. N16 122 DQ61
Allerton Rd., Borwd. 78 CL38
Allerton Wk. N7 121 DM61
Durham Rd.
Allestree Rd. SW6 159 CY80
Alleyn Cres. SE21 182 DR89
Alleyn Pk. SE21 182 DR89
Alleyn Pk., Sthl. 156 CA78
Alleyn Rd. SE21 182 DR90
Alleyndale Rd., Dag. 126 EW61
Allfarthing La. SW18 180 DB86
Allgood Clo., Mord. 199 CX100
Allgood St. E2 142 DT68
Allhallows La. EC4 279 K1
Allhallows Rd. E6 144 EL71
Allhusen Gdns., Slou. 112 AY63
Alderbourne La.
Alliance Clo., Wem. 117 CK63
Milford Gdns.
Alliance Rd. E13 144 EJ70
Alliance Rd. SE18 166 EU79
Alliance Rd. W3 138 CP70
Allied Ind. Est. W3 158 CS75
Allied Way W3 158 CS75
Larden Rd.
Allingham Clo. W7 137 CF73
Allingham Ct., Gdmg. 258 AT144
Summers Rd.
Allingham Rd., Reig. 266 DA137
Allingham St. N1 142 DQ68
Allington Ave. N17 100 DS51
Allington Clo. SW19 179 CX92
High St. Wimbledon
Allington Clo., Grav. 191 GM88
Farley Rd.
Allington Clo., Grnf. 136 CC66
Allington Ct. SW19 179 CX92
High St. Wimbledon
Allington Ct., Enf. 83 DX43
Allington Ct., Slou. 132 AT73
Myrtle Cres.
Allington Rd. NW4 119 CV57
Allington Rd. W10 139 CY68
Allington Rd., Har. 116 CC57
Allington Rd., Orp. 205 ER103
Allington St. SW1 277 J7
Allington St. SW1 161 DH76
Allison Clo. SE10 163 EC81
Dartmouth Hill
Allison Clo., Wal.Abb. 68 EG33
Allison Gro. SE21 182 DS88
Allison Rd. N8 121 DN57
Allison Rd. W3 138 CQ72
Allitsen Rd. NW8 272 B1
Allitsen Rd. NW8 140 DE68
Allmains Clo., Wal.Abb. 68 EH25
Allnutt Way SW4 181 DK85
Allnutts Rd., Epp. 70 EU33
Alloa Rd. SE8 163 DY78
Alloa Rd., Ilf. 126 EU61
Allonby Dr., Ruis. 115 BP59
Allonby Gdns., Wem. 117 CJ60
Allotment La., Sev. 257 FJ122
Alloway Clo., Wok. 226 AV118
Inglewood
Alloway Rd. E3 143 DY69
Allsop Pl. NW1 272 E5
Allsop Pl. NW1 140 DF70
Allum Clo., Borwd. 78 CL42
Allum Gro., Tad. 233 CV121
Preston La.
Allum La., Borwd. 77 CK43
Allum Way N20 98 DC46
Allwood Clo. SE26 183 DX91
Allwood Rd., Wal.Cr. 66 DT27
Allyn Clo., Stai. 173 BF93
Penton Rd.
Alma Ave. E4 101 EC52
Alma Ave., Horn. 128 FL63
Alma Clo., Wok. 226 AS118
Alma Ct., Borwd. 78 CM38
Belford Rd.
Alma Cres., Sutt. 217 CY106
Alma Cut, St.Alb. 43 CE21
Alma Gro. SE1 162 DT77
Alma Pl. NW10 139 CV69
Harrow Rd.
Alma Pl. SE19 182 DT94
Church Rd.
Alma Pl., Th.Hth. 201 DN99
Alma Rd. N10 99 DH52
Alma Rd. SW18 160 DC84
Alma Rd., Berk. 38 AS17
Alma Rd., Cars. 218 DE106
Alma Rd., Chesh. 54 AQ29
Alma Rd., Enf. 83 DY41
Alma Rd., Esher 197 CE102
Alma Rd., Orp. 206 EX103
Alma Rd., Reig. 250 DB133
Alma Rd., St.Alb. 43 CE21
Alma Rd., Sid. 186 EU90
Alma Rd., Sthl. 136 BY73
Alma Rd., Swans. 190 FZ85
Alma Rd., Wind. 151 AQ82
Alma Rd. (Eton Wick), Wind. 151 AM77
Alma Row, Har. 95 CD53
Alma Sq. NW8 140 DC69
Alma St. E15 143 ED65
Alma St. NW5 141 DH65
Alma Ter. SW18 180 DD87
Almack Rd. E5 122 DW63
Almeida St. N1 141 DP66
Almer Rd. SW20 179 CU94
Almeric Rd. SW11 160 DF84
Almington St. N4 121 DL60
Almners Rd., Cher. 193 BA102
Almond Ave. W5 158 CL76
Almond Ave., Cars. 200 DF103
Almond Ave., Uxb. 115 BP62
Almond Ave., West Dr. 154 BN76
Almond Ave., Wok. 226 AX121
Almond Clo. SE15 162 DU82
Almond Clo., Brom. 205 EN101
Almond Clo., Egh. 172 AV93
Almond Clo., Grays 171 GG76
Almond Clo., Guil. 242 AX130
Almond Clo., Hayes 135 BS73
Almond Clo., Ruis. 115 BT62
Roundways
Almond Clo., Shep. 195 BQ96
Almond Clo., Wind. 151 AP82
Almond Dr., Swan. 207 FD96
Almond Gro., Brent. 157 CH80
Almond Rd. N17 100 DU52
Almond Rd. SE16 162 DV77
Almond Rd., Dart. 188 FQ87
Almond Rd., Epsom 216 CR111
Almond Rd., Slou. 130 AH68
Almond Wk., Hat. 45 CU21
Southdown Rd.
Almond Way, Borwd. 78 CP42
Almond Way, Brom. 205 EN101
Almond Way, Har. 94 CB54
Almond Way, Mitch. 201 DK99
Almonds, The, St.Alb. 43 CH24
The Poplars
Almonds Ave., Buck.H. 102 EG47
Almons Way, Slou. 132 AV71
Almorah Rd. N1 142 DR66
Almorah Rd., Houns. 156 BX81
Alms Heath, Wok. 229 BP121
Almshouse La., Chess. 215 CJ109
Almshouse La., Enf. 82 DV37
Alnwick Gro., Mord. 200 DB98
Bordesley Rd.
Alnwick Rd. E16 144 EJ72
Alnwick Rd. SE12 184 EH87
Alperton La., Grnf. 137 CK68
Alperton La., Wem. 137 CK68
Alperton St. W10 139 CY70
Alpha Clo. NW1 272 C3
Alpha Ct., Whyt. 236 DU118
Alpha Gro. E14 163 EA75
Alpha Pl. NW6 140 DA68
Alpha Pl. SW3 160 DE79
Alpha Rd. E4 101 EA48
Alpha Rd. N18 100 DU51
Alpha Rd. SE14 163 DZ81
Alpha Rd., Brwd. 109 GD44
Alpha Rd., Croy. 202 DS102
Alpha Rd., Enf. 83 DY42
Alpha Rd., Surb. 198 CM100
Alpha Rd., Tedd. 177 CD92
Alpha Rd., Uxb. 135 BP70
Alpha Rd., Wok. 227 BB116
Alpha Rd. (Chobham), Wok. 210 AT110
Alpha St. SE15 162 DU82
Alpha St. N., Slou. 152 AU75
Alpha St. S., Slou. 152 AT76
Alpha Way, Egh. 193 BC95
Alphabet Gdns., Cars. 200 DD100
Pershore Gro.
Alphabet Sq. E3 143 EA71
Hawgood St.
Alphea Clo. SW19 180 DE94
Courtney Rd.
Alpine Ave., Surb. 198 CQ103
Alpine Clo., Croy. 202 DS104
Alpine Copse, Brom. 205 EN96
Alpine Rd. SE16 162 DW77
Alpine Rd., Red. 250 DG131
Alpine Rd., Walt. 195 BU101
Alpine Vw., Sutt. 218 DE106
Alpine Wk., Stan. 95 CE47
Alpine Way E6 145 EN71
Alresford Rd., Guil. 258 AU135
Alric Ave. NW10 138 CR66
Alric Ave., N.Mal. 198 CS97
Alroy Rd. N4 121 DN59
Alsace Rd. SE17 279 M10
Alsace Rd. SE17 162 DS78
Alscot Rd. SE1 162 DT77
Alscot Way SE1 279 P8
Alscot Way SE1 162 DT77
Alsford Wf., Berk. 38 AW18
Castle St.
Alsike Rd. SE2 166 EX76
Alsike Rd., Erith 166 EY76
Alsom Ave., Wor.Pk. 217 CT105
Alston Clo., Surb. 197 CH101
Alston Rd. N18 100 DV50
Alston Rd. SW17 180 DD91
Alston Rd., Barn. 79 CY41
Alston Rd., Hem.H. 40 BG21
Alt Gro. SW19 179 CZ94
St. George's Rd.
Altair Clo. N17 100 DT51
Altair Way, Nthwd. 93 BT50
Altash Way SE9 185 EM89
Altenburg Ave. W13 157 CH76
Altenburg Gdns. SW11 160 DF84
Alterton Clo., Wok. 226 AU117
Altham Gro., Harl. 35 ET12
Altham Rd., Pnr. 94 BY52
Althea St. SW6 160 DB82
Althorne Gdns. E18 124 EF56
Althorne Rd., Red. 266 DG136
Althorne Way, Dag. 126 FA61
Althorp Rd. SW17 180 DF88
Althorp Rd., St.Alb. 43 CE19
Althorpe Gro. SW11 160 DD81
Westbridge Rd.
Althorpe Ms. SW11 160 DD81
Westbridge Rd.
Althorpe Rd., Har. 116 CC57
Altmore Ave. E6 145 EM66
Alton Ave., Stan. 95 CF52
Alton Clo., Bex. 186 EY88
Alton Clo., Islw. 157 CF82
Alton Ct., Stai. 193 BE95
Alton Gdns., Beck. 183 EA94
Alton Gdns., Twick. 177 CD86
Alton Rd. N17 122 DR55
Alton Rd. SW15 179 CU88
Alton Rd., Croy. 201 DN104
Alton Rd., Rich. 158 CL84
Alton St. E14 143 EB71
Altona Rd., H.Wyc. 88 AD52
Altona Way, Slou. 131 AP72
Altwood Clo., Slou. 131 AL71
Burnham La.
Altyre Clo., Beck. 203 DZ99
Altyre Rd., Croy. 202 DR103
Altyre Way, Beck. 203 DZ100
Aluric Clo., Grays 171 GH77
Alva Way, Wat. 94 BX47
Alvanley Gdns. NW6 120 DB64
Alverstoke Rd., Rom. 106 FL52
Alverston Gdns. SE25 202 DS99
Alverstone Ave. SW19 180 DA89
Alverstone Ave., Barn. 98 DE45
Alverstone Gdns. SE9 185 EQ88
Alverstone Rd. E12 125 EN63
Alverstone Rd. NW2 139 CW66
Alverstone Rd., N.Mal. 199 CT98
Alverstone Rd., Wem. 118 CM60
Alverton, St.Alb. 42 CC17
Green La.
Alverton St. SE8 163 DZ78
Alveston Ave., Har. 117 CH55
Alvey Est. SE17 279 M9
Alvey St. SE17 279 M10
Alvey St. SE17 162 DS78
Alvia Gdns., Sutt. 218 DC105
Alvington Cres. E8 122 DT64
Alvista Ave., Maid. 130 AH72
Alway Ave., Epsom 216 CQ106
Alwen Gro., S.Ock. 149 FV71
Alwold Cres. SE12 184 EH86
Alwyn Ave. W4 158 CR78
Alwyn Clo., Borwd. 78 CM44
Alwyn Clo., Croy. 221 EB108
Alwyn Gdns. NW4 119 CU56
Alwyn Gdns. W3 138 CP72
Alwyne Ave., Brwd. 109 GA44
Alwyne Ct., Wok. 226 AY116
Alwyne La. N1 141 DP66
Alwyne Vill.
Alwyne Pl. N1 142 DQ65
Alwyne Rd. N1 142 DQ66
Alwyne Rd. SW19 179 CZ93
Alwyne Rd. W7 137 CE73
Alwyne Sq. N1 142 DQ65
Alwyne Vill. N1 141 DP66
Alwyns Clo., Cher. 194 BG100
Alwyns La.
Alwyns La., Cher. 193 BF100
Alyngton, Berk. 38 AS16
Alyth Gdns. NW11 120 DA58
Alzette Ho. E2 143 DX68
Mace St.
Amalgamated Dr., Brent. 157 CG79
Amanda Clo., Ilf. 103 ER51
Amanda Ct., Slou. 152 AX76
Amazon St. E1 142 DV72
Hessel St.
Ambassador Clo., Houns. 156 BY82
Ambassador Gdns. E6 145 EM71
Ambassador Sq. E14 163 EB77
Ambassador's Ct. SW1 277 L3
Amber Ave. E17 101 DY53
Amber Gro. NW2 119 CX60
Prayle Gro.
Amber St. E15 143 ED65
Salway Rd.
Ambercroft Way, Couls. 235 DP119
Amberden Ave. N3 120 DA55
Ambergate St. SE17 278 G10
Ambergate St. SE17 161 DP78
Amberley Clo., Orp. 223 ET106
Warnford Rd.
Amberley Clo., Pnr. 116 BZ55
Amberley Clo., Wok. 243 BF125
Amberley Ct., Maid. 130 AC69
Amberley Ct., Sid. 186 EW92
Amberley Dr., Add. 211 BF110
Amberley Gdns., Enf. 100 DS45
Amberley Gdns., Epsom 217 CT105
Amberley Gro. SE26 182 DV92
Amberley Gro., Croy. 202 DT101
Amberley Rd. E10 123 EA59
Amberley Rd. N13 99 DM47
Amberley Rd. SE2 166 EX79
Amberley Rd. W9 140 DA71
Amberley Rd., Buck.H. 102 EJ46
Amberley Rd., Enf. 100 DT45
Amberley Rd., Slou. 131 AL71
Amberley Way, Houns. 176 BW85
Amberley Way, Mord. 199 CZ101
Amberley Way, Rom. 127 FB56
Amberley Way, Uxb. 134 BL69
Amberry Ct., Harl. 35 ER14
Amberwood Ri., N.Mal. 198 CS100
Amblecote, Cob. 214 BY112
Amblecote Clo. SE12 184 EH90
Amblecote Meadows SE12 184 EH90
Amblecote Rd. SE12 184 EH90
Ambler Rd. N4 121 DP62
Ambleside, Brom. 183 ED93
Ambleside, Epp. 70 EU31
Ambleside Ave. SW16 181 DK91
Ambleside Ave., Beck. 203 DY99
Ambleside Ave., Horn. 127 FH64
Ambleside Ave., Walt. 196 BW102
Ambleside Clo. E9 122 DW64
Churchill Wk.
Ambleside Clo. E10 123 EB59
Clyde Pl.
Ambleside Clo., Red. 267 DH139
Ambleside Cres., Enf. 83 DX41
Ambleside Dr., Felt. 175 BT88
Ambleside Gdns., Ilf. 124 EL56
Ambleside Gdns., S.Croy. 221 DX109
Ambleside Gdns., Sutt. 218 DC107
Ambleside Gdns., Wem. 117 CK60
Ambleside Rd. NW10 139 CT66
Ambleside Rd., Bexh. 166 FA82
Ambleside Way, Egh. 173 BB94
Ambrey Way, Wall. 219 DK109
Ambrooke Rd., Belv. 166 FA76
Ambrosden Ave. SW1 277 L7
Ambrosden Ave. SW1 161 DJ76
Ambrose Ave. NW11 119 CY59
Ambrose Clo. E6 144 EL71
Lovage App.
Ambrose Clo., Dart. 167 FF84
Iron Mill La.
Ambrose Clo., Orp. 205 ET104
Stapleton Rd.
Ambrose Ms. SW11 160 DF82
Abercrombie St.
Ambrose St. SE16 162 DV77
Ambrose Wk. E3 143 EA68
Malmesbury Rd.
Amelia St. SE17 279 H10
Amelia St. SE17 161 DP78
Amen Cor. EC4 274 G9
Amen Cor. SW17 180 DF93
Amen Ct. EC4 274 G8
Amerden Clo., Maid. 130 AD72
Amerden La.
Amerden La., Maid. 130 AD74
Amerden Way, Slou. 151 AN75
America Sq. EC3 275 P10
America St. SE1 279 H3
Amerland Rd. SW18 179 CZ85
Amersham, Rick. 73 BA39
Amersham Ave. N18 100 DR51
Amersham Bypass, Amer. 55 AL38
Amersham Clo., Rom. 106 FM51
Amersham Dr., Rom. 106 FL51
Amersham Gro. SE14 163 DZ80
Amersham Pl., Amer. 72 AW39
Amersham Rd. SE14 163 DZ81
Amersham Rd., Amer. 89 AP46
Amersham Rd. (Chesham Bois), Amer. 55 AP35
Amersham Rd. (Little Chalfont), Amer. 72 AX39
Amersham Rd., Beac. 89 AM53
Amersham Rd., Ch.St.G. 72 AU43
Amersham Rd., Chesh. 54 AQ32
Amersham Rd., Croy. 202 DQ100
Amersham Rd., Ger.Cr. 90 AX49
Amersham Rd., Rick. 73 BB39
Amersham Rd., Rom. 106 FL51
Amersham Vale SE14 163 DZ80
Amersham Wk., Rom. 106 FM51
Amersham Rd.
Amersham Way, Amer. 72 AX39
Amery Gdns. NW10 139 CV67
Amery Gdns., Rom. 128 FK55
Amery Rd., Har. 117 CG61
Ames Rd., Swans. 190 FY86
Amesbury, Wal.Abb. 68 EG32
Amesbury Ave. SW2 181 DL89
Amesbury Clo., Epp. 69 ET31
Amesbury Rd.
Amesbury Clo., Wor.Pk. 199 CW102
Amesbury Dr. E4 83 EB44
Amesbury Rd., Brom. 204 EK97
Amesbury Rd., Dag. 146 EX66
Amesbury Rd., Epp. 69 ET31
Amesbury Rd., Felt. 176 BX89
Amethyst Rd. E15 123 ED63
Amey Dr., Lthd. 230 CC124
Amherst Ave. W13 137 CJ72
Amherst Clo., Orp. 206 EU98
Amherst Dr., Orp. 205 ET98
Amherst Hill, Sev. 256 FE122
Amherst Rd. W13 137 CJ72
Amherst Rd., Sev. 257 FH122
Amhurst Gdns., Islw. 157 CF81
Amhurst Par. N16 122 DT59
Amhurst Pk.

Amhurst Pk. N16 122 DR59
Amhurst Pas. E8 122 DU64
Amhurst Rd. E8 122 DV64
Amhurst Rd. N16 122 DT63
Amhurst Ter. E8 122 DU63
Amhurst Wk. SE28 146 EU74
Pitfield Cres.
Amidas Gdns., Dag. 126 EV63
Amiel St. E1 142 DW70
Amies St. SW11 160 DF83
Amina Way SE16 162 DU76
Yalding Rd.
Amis Ave., Add. 212 BG110
Amis Ave., Epsom 216 CN107
Amis Rd., Wok. 226 AS119
Amity Gro. SW20 199 CW95
Amity Rd. E15 144 EF67
Ammanford Gdn. NW9 118 CS58
Ruthin Clo.
Amner Rd. SW11 180 DG86
Amoco Ho. W5 138 CL69
Amor Rd. W6 159 CW76
Amott Rd. SE15 162 DU83
Amoy Pl. E14 143 EA72
Ampere Way, Croy. 201 DM101
Ampleforth Rd. SE2 166 EV75
Ampthill Sq. Est. NW1 273 L1
Ampton Pl. WC1 274 B3
Ampton Pl. WC1 141 DM69
Ampton St. WC1 274 B3
Ampton St. WC1 141 DM69
Amroth Clo. SE23 182 DV88
Amstel Way, Wok. 226 AT118
Amsterdam Rd. E14 163 EC76
Amwell Clo., Enf. 82 DR43
Amwell Clo., Wat. 76 BY35
Phillipers
Amwell Common, Welw.G.C. 30 DB10
Amwell Ct., Hodd. 49 EA16
Amwell Ct., Wal.Abb. 68 EE33
Amwell Ct. Est. N4 122 DQ60
Amwell End, Ware 33 DX06
Amwell Hill, Ware 33 DZ08
Amwell La., Ware 33 EA09
Amwell St. EC1 274 D2
Amwell St. EC1 141 DN69
Amwell St., Hodd. 49 EA16
Amy La., Chesh. 54 AP32
Amy Rd., Oxt. 254 EE129
Amy Warne Clo. E6 145 EM71
Evelyn Denington Rd.
Amyand Cotts., Twick. 177 CH86
Amyand Pk. Rd.
Amyand La., Twick. 177 CH87
Marble Hill Gdns.
Amyand Pk. Gdns., Twick. 177 CH87
Amyand Pk. Rd.
Amyand Pk. Rd., Twick. 177 CG87
Amyruth Rd. SE4 183 EA85
Anatola Rd. N19 121 DH61
Dartmouth Pk. Hill
Ancaster Cres., N.Mal. 199 CU100
Ancaster Ms., Beck. 203 DX97
Ancaster Rd.
Ancaster Rd., Beck. 203 DX97
Ancaster St. SE18 165 ES80
Anchor & Hope La. SE7 164 EJ77
Anchor Boul., Dart. 168 FQ84
Anchor Clo. (Cheshunt), Wal.Cr. 67 DX28
Anchor Dr., Rain. 147 FH69
Anchor La., Hem.H. 40 BH22
Anchor Ms. SW12 181 DH86
Hazelbourne Rd.
Anchor St. SE16 162 DV77
Anchor Yd. EC1 275 J4
Anchorage Clo. SW19 180 DA92
Ancill Clo. W6 159 CY79
Ancona Rd. NW10 139 CU68
Ancona Rd. SE18 165 ER78
Andace Pk. Gdns., Brom. 204 EJ95
Andalus Rd. SW9 161 DL83
Ander Clo., Wem. 117 CK63
Andermans, Wind. 151 AK81
Anderson Clo. W3 138 CR72
Anderson Clo., Epsom 216 CP112
Anderson Clo., Uxb. 92 BG53
Anderson Dr., Ashf. 175 BQ91
Anderson Ho., Bark. 145 ER68
The Coverdales
Anderson Pl., Houns. 156 CB84
Anderson Rd. E9 143 DX65
Anderson Rd., Rad. 62 CN33
Anderson Rd., Wey. 195 BR104
Anderson Rd., Wdf.Grn. 124 EK55
Anderson St. SW3 276 D10
Anderson St. SW3 160 DF78
Anderson Way, Belv. 167 FB75
Anderton Clo. SE5 162 DR83
Andover Ave. E16 144 EK72
King George Ave.
Andover Clo., Epsom 216 CR111
Andover Clo., Felt. 175 BT88
Westmacott Dr.
Andover Clo., Grnf. 136 CB70
Ruislip Rd.
Andover Clo., Uxb. 134 BH68
Andover Pl. NW6 140 DB68
Andover Rd. N7 121 DM61
Andover Rd., Orp. 205 ES103
Andover Rd., Twick. 177 CD88
Andre St. E8 122 DU64
Andrea Ave., Grays 170 GA75
Hogg La.
Andrew Borde St. WC2 273 N8
Andrew Clo., Bex. 187 FD85
Andrew Clo., Dart. 187 FD85
Andrew Clo., Ilf. 103 ER51
Andrew Hill La., Slou. 111 AQ60
Andrew Pl. SW8 161 DK81
Cowthorpe Rd.
Andrew St. E14 143 EC72
Andrewes Gdns. E6 144 EL72
Dunnock Rd.
Andrewes Ho. EC2 142 DQ71
Fore St.
Andrews Clo. E6 144 EL72
Linton Gdns.
Andrews Clo., Buck.H. 102 EJ47
Andrews Clo., Epsom 217 CT114
Andrews Clo., Har. 117 CD59
Bessborough Rd.
Andrews Clo., Hem.H. 40 BK18
Church St.
Andrews Clo., Orp. 206 EX97
Andrews Clo., Wor.Pk. 199 CW103
Andrews Crosse WC2 274 D9
Andrews La. (Cheshunt), Wal.Cr. 66 DS28
Andrews Pl. SE9 185 EP86
Andrew's Rd. E8 142 DV67
Andrews Wk. SE17 161 DP79
Dale Rd.
Andrews Way, Slou. 131 AK73
Andrewsfield, Welw.G.C. 30 DC09
Andwell Clo. SE2 166 EV75
Anelle Ri., Hem.H. 40 BM24
Great Elms Rd.
Anerley Gro. SE19 182 DT94
Anerley Hill SE19 182 DT93
Anerley Pk. SE20 182 DU94
Anerley Pk. Rd. SE20 182 DV94
Anerley Rd. SE19 182 DU94
Anerley Rd. SE20 182 DU94
Anerley Sta. Rd. SE20 202 DV95
Anerley St. SW11 160 DF82
Anerley Vale SE19 182 DT94
Anfield Clo. SW12 181 DJ87
Belthorn Cres.
Angas Ct., Wey. 213 BQ106
Angel All. E1 142 DU72
Whitechapel Rd.
Angel Clo. N18 100 DT50
Angel Ct. EC2 275 L8
Angel Ct. SW1 277 L3
Angel Ct. SW17 180 DF91
Angel Gate, Guil. 258 AX135
High St.
Angel Hill, Sutt. 200 DB104
Sutton Common Rd.
Angel Hill Dr., Sutt. 200 DB104
Angel La. E15 143 ED65
Angel La., Hayes 135 BR71
Angel Ms. N1 274 E1
Angel Ms. N1 141 DN68
Angel Pas. EC4 279 K1
Angel Pl. N18 100 DU50
Angel Clo.
Angel Pl. SE1 279 K4
Angel Rd. N18 100 DU50
Angel Rd., Har. 117 CE58
Angel Rd., T.Ditt. 197 CG101
Angel Rd. Wks. N18 100 DW50
Angel Sq. EC1 141 DN68
Torrens St.
Angel St. EC1 275 H8
Angel St. EC1 142 DQ72
Angel Wk. W6 159 CW78
Angel Way, Rom. 127 FE57
Angelfield, Houns. 156 CB84
Angelica Dr. E6 145 EN71
Angelica Gdns., Croy. 203 DX102
Angelica Rd., Guil. 242 AU130
Angell Pk. Gdns. SW9 161 DN83
Angell Rd. SW9 161 DN83
Angerstein La. SE3 164 EF81
Angle Clo., Uxb. 134 BN67
Angle Grn., Dag. 126 EW60
Burnside Rd.
Angle Pl., Berk. 38 AU19
Angle Rd., Grays 169 FX79
Anglefield Rd., Berk. 38 AU19
Anglers Clo., Rich. 177 CJ91
Locksmeade Rd.
Angler's La. NW5 141 DH65
Angles Rd. SW16 181 DL91
Anglesea Ave. SE18 165 EP77
Anglesea Cen., Grav. 191 GH86
New Rd.
Anglesea Pl., Grav. 191 GH86
Clive Rd.
Anglesea Rd. SE18 165 EP77
Anglesea Rd., Kings.T. 197 CK98
Anglesea Rd., Orp. 206 EW100
Anglesea Ter. W6 159 CV76
Wellesley Ave.
Anglesey Clo., Ashf. 174 BN91
Anglesey Ct. Rd., Cars. 218 DG107
Anglesey Dr., Rain. 147 FG70
Anglesey Gdns., Cars. 218 DG107
Anglesey Rd., Enf. 82 DV42
Anglesey Rd., Wat. 94 BW50
Anglesmede Cres., Pnr. 116 BY55
Anglesmede Way, Pnr. 116 BY55
Anglia Clo. N17 100 DV52
Park La.
Anglia Ho. E14 143 DY72
Anglia Wk. E6 145 EM67
Napier Rd.
Anglian Clo., Wat. 76 BW40
Reeds Cres.
Anglian Ind. Est., Bark. 146 EU71
Atcost Rd.
Anglian Rd. E11 124 EE62
Cathall Rd.
Anglo Rd. E3 143 DZ68
Angrave Ct. E8 142 DT67
Angrave Pas. E8 142 DT67
Haggerston Rd.
Angus Clo., Chess. 216 CN106
Angus Dr., Ruis. 116 BW63
Angus Gdns. NW9 96 CR53
Angus Rd. E13 144 EJ69
Angus St. SE14 163 DY80
Anhalt Rd. SW11 160 DE80
Ankerdine Cres. SE18 165 EP81
Ankerwycke Priory, Stai. 172 AY88
Anlaby Rd., Tedd. 177 CE92
Anley Rd. W14 159 CX75
Anmersh Gro., Stan. 95 CK53
Ann La. SW10 160 DD80
Ann Moss Way SE16 162 DW76
Lower Rd.
Ann St. SE18 165 EQ78
Anna Clo. E8 142 DT67
Anna Neagle Clo. E7 124 EG63
Dames Rd.
Annabel Clo. E14 143 EB72
Annalee Gdns., S.Ock. 149 FV71
Annalee Rd., S.Ock. 149 FV71
Annan Way, Rom. 105 FD53
Annandale Gro., Uxb. 115 BQ62
Thorpland Ave.
Annandale Rd. SE10 164 EF78
Annandale Rd. W4 158 CS78
Annandale Rd., Croy. 202 DU103
Annandale Rd., Guil. 258 AV136
Annandale Rd., Sid. 185 ES87
Anne Boleyn's Wk., Kings.T. 178 CL92
Anne Boleyn's Wk., Sutt. 217 CX108
Anne Case Ms., N.Mal. 198 CR97
Sycamore Gro.
Anne of Cleves Rd., Dart. 188 FK85
Anne St. E13 144 EG70
Anne Way, Ilf. 103 EQ51
Anne Way, W.Mol. 196 CB98
Anners Clo., Egh. 193 BC97
Anne's Wk., Cat. 236 DS120
Annesley Ave. NW9 118 CR55
Annesley Clo. NW10 118 CS62
Annesley Dr., Croy. 221 DZ105
Annesley Rd. SE3 164 EH81
Annesley Wk. N19 121 DJ61
Macdonald Rd.
Annett Clo., Shep. 195 BS98
Annett Rd., Walt. 195 BU101
Annette Clo., Har. 95 CE54
Spencer Rd.
Annette Cres. N1 142 DQ66
Essex Rd.
Annette Rd. N7 121 DM62
Annie Besant Clo. E3 143 DZ67
Annifer Way, S.Ock. 149 FV71
Anning St. EC2 275 N4
Annington Rd. N2 120 DF55
Annis Rd. E9 143 DY65
Annisdowne, Dor. 261 BT142
Ann's Clo. SW1 276 E5
Ann's Pl. E1 275 P7
Annsworthy Ave., Th.Hth. 202 DR97
Grange Pk. Rd.
Annsworthy Cres. SE25 202 DR96
Grange Rd.
Ansculf Rd., Slou. 131 AN69
Ansdell Rd. SE15 162 DW82
Ansdell St. W8 160 DB76
Ansdell Ter. W8 160 DB76
Ansdell St.
Ansell Gro., Cars. 200 DG102
Ansell Rd. SW17 180 DE90
Ansell Rd., Dor. 263 CH135
Anselm Clo., Croy. 202 DT104
Park Hill Ri.
Anselm Rd. SW6 160 DA79
Anselm Rd., Pnr. 94 BZ52
Ansford Rd., Brom. 183 EC92
Ansleigh Pl. W11 139 CX73
Ansley Clo., S.Croy. 220 DV114
Anslow Gdns., Iver 133 BD68
Anslow Pl., Slou. 130 AJ71
Anson Clo., Hem.H. 57 AZ27
Lancaster Dr.
Anson Clo., Ken. 236 DR120
Anson Clo., Rom. 105 FB54
Anson Clo., St.Alb. 43 CH22
Anson Rd. N7 121 DJ63
Anson Rd. NW2 119 CV64
Anson Ter., Nthlt. 136 CB65
Blenheim Rd.
Anson Wk., Nthwd. 93 BP49
Anstead Dr., Rain. 147 FG68
Anstey Rd. SE15 162 DU83
Anstey Wk. N15 121 DP56
Anstice Clo. W4 158 CS80
Anstridge Path SE9 185 ER86
Anstridge Rd.
Anstridge Rd. SE9 185 ER86
Antelope Ave., Grays 170 GA76
Antelope Rd. SE18 165 EM76
Anthony Clo. NW7 96 CS49
Anthony Clo., Sev. 256 FE121
Anthony Clo., Wat. 94 BW46
Anthony La., Swan. 207 FG95
Anthony Rd. SE25 202 DU100
Anthony Rd., Borwd. 78 CM40
Anthony Rd., Grnf. 137 CE68
Anthony Rd., Well. 166 EU81
Anthony St. E1 142 DV72
Commercial Rd.
Anthony Way, Slou. 131 AK73
Anthonys, Wok. 211 BA112
Anthorne Clo., Pot.B. 64 DB31
Anthus Ms., Nthwd. 93 BS52
Antigua Clo. SE19 182 DR92
Salters Hill
Antigua Wk. SE19 182 DR92
Salters Hill
Antill Rd. E3 143 DY69
Antill Rd. N15 122 DU56
Antill Ter. E1 143 DX72
Antlands La., Horl. 269 DK153
Antlands La. E., Horl. 269 DM153
Antlands La. W., Horl. 269 DL153
Antlers Hill E4 83 EB42
Antoinette Ct., Abb.L. 59 BT29
Anton Cres., Sutt. 200 DA104
Anton Rd., S.Ock. 149 FV71
Anton St. E8 122 DU64
Antoneys Clo., Pnr. 94 BX54
Antonine Gate, St.Alb. 42 CA21
Antrim Gro. NW3 140 DF65
Antrim Mans. NW3 140 DF65
Antrim Rd.
Antrim Rd. NW3 140 DF65
Antrobus Clo., Sutt. 217 CZ106
Antrobus Rd. W4 158 CQ77
Anugraha Conference Cen., Egh. 172 AU91
Anvil Ct., Slou. 153 BA77
Blacksmith Row
Anvil La., Cob. 213 BU114
Anvil Rd., Sun. 195 BU98
Anworth Clo., Wdf.Grn. 102 EH51
Anyards Rd., Cob. 213 BV113
Apeldoorn Dr., Wall. 219 DL109
Aperdele Rd., Lthd. 231 CG118
Aperfield Rd., Erith 167 FF79
Aperfield Rd., West. 238 EL117
Apers Ave., Wok. 227 AZ121
Apex Clo., Beck. 203 EB95
Apex Clo., Wey. 195 BR104
Apex Cor. NW7 96 CR49
Apex Twr., N.Mal. 198 CS97
Apley Rd., Reig. 266 DA137
Aplin Way, Islw. 157 CE81
Apollo Ave., Brom. 204 EH95
Rodway Rd.
Apollo Ave., Nthwd. 93 BU50
Apollo Clo., Horn. 127 FH61
Apollo Pl. E11 124 EE62
Cathall Rd.
Apollo Pl. SW10 160 DD80
Riley St.
Apollo Way SE28 165 ER76
Broadwater Rd.
Apollo Way, Hem.H. 40 BM18
Apostle Way, Th.Hth. 201 DP96
Windsor Rd.
Apothecary St. EC4 274 F9
Appach Rd. SW2 181 DN85
Apple Cotts., Hem.H. 57 BA27
Apple Garth, Brent. 157 CK77
Apple Gro., Chess. 216 CL105
Apple Gro., Enf. 82 DS41
Apple Mkt., Kings.T. 197 CK96
Eden St.
Apple Orchard, The, Hem.H. 40 BM18
Highfield La.
Apple Rd. E11 124 EE62
Cathall Rd.
Apple Tree Ave., Uxb. 134 BM72
Apple Tree Ave., West Dr. 134 BM72
Apple Tree Yd. SW1 277 L2
Appleby Clo. E4 101 EB51
Appleby Clo. N15 122 DR57
Appleby Clo., Twick. 177 CD89
Appleby Dr., Rom. 106 FJ50
Appleby Gdns., Felt. 175 BT88
Appleby Grn., Rom. 106 FJ50
Appleby Dr.
Appleby Rd. E8 142 DU66
Appleby Rd. E16 144 EF72
Appleby St. E2 275 P1
Appleby St. E2 142 DT68
Appleby St. (Cheshunt), Wal.Cr. 66 DR25
Applecroft, Berk. 38 AS17
Applecroft, St.Alb. 60 CB28
Applecroft Rd., Welw.G.C. 29 CV09
Appledore Ave., Bexh. 167 FC81
Appledore Ave., Ruis. 116 BW62
Appledore Clo. SW17 180 DF89
Appledore Clo., Brom. 204 EF99
Appledore Clo., Edg. 96 CN53
Appledore Clo., Rom. 106 FJ53
Appledore Cres., Sid. 185 ES90
Appledown Ri., Couls. 235 DJ115
Applefield, Amer. 72 AW39
Appleford Clo., Hodd. 49 DZ15
Appleford Rd. W10 139 CY70
Applegarth, Croy. 221 EB108
Applegarth, Esher 215 CF106
Applegarth Dr., Dart. 188 FM89
Powder Mill La.
Applegarth Dr., Ilf. 125 ET56
Applegarth Rd. SE28 146 EV74
Applegarth Rd. W14 159 CX76
Applegate, Brwd. 108 FT43
Appleshaw Clo., Grav. 191 GG92
Appleton Clo., Amer. 72 AV40
Appleton Gdns., N.Mal. 199 CU100
Appleton Rd. SE9 164 EL83
Appleton Rd., Loug. 85 EP41
Appleton Sq., Mitch. 200 DE95
Appleton Way, Horn. 128 FK60
Appletree Clo. SE20 202 DV95
Jasmine Gro.
Appletree Ct., Guil. 243 BD131
Old Merrow St.
Appletree Gdns., Barn. 80 DE42
Appletree La., Slou. 152 AW76
Appletree Wk., Chesh. 54 AR34
Cresswell Rd.
Appletree Wk., Wat. 59 BV34
Applewood Clo. N20 98 DE46
Applewood Clo. NW2 119 CV62
Appold St. EC2 275 M6
Appold St. EC2 142 DS71
Appold St., Erith 167 FF79
Apprentice Way E5 122 DV63
Clarence Rd.
Approach, The NW4 119 CX57
Approach, The W3 138 CR72
Approach, The, Enf. 82 DV40
Approach, The, Lthd. 230 BY123
Maddox La.
Approach, The, Orp. 205 ET103
Approach, The, Pot.B. 63 CZ32
Approach, The, Upmin. 128 FP62
Approach Clo. N16 122 DS64
Cowper Rd.
Approach Rd. E2 142 DW68
Approach Rd. SW20 199 CW96
Approach Rd., Ashf. 175 BQ93
Approach Rd., Barn. 80 DC42
Approach Rd., Maid. 130 AC72
Approach Rd., Pur. 219 DP112
Approach Rd., St.Alb. 43 CE21
Approach Rd., W.Mol. 196 CA99
Appspond La., St.Alb. 41 BV23
Aprey Gdns. NW4 119 CW56
April Clo. W7 137 CE73
April Clo., Ash. 232 CM117
The Marld
April Clo., Felt. 175 BU90
April Clo., Orp. 223 ET106
Briarswood Way
April Glen SE23 183 DX90
April St. E8 122 DT63
April Wd. Clo., Add. 211 BF111
Apsfield Row, Hem.H. 40 BH18
Apsledene, Grav. 191 GK93
Miskin Way
Apsley Clo., Har. 116 CC57
Apsley Gra., Hem.H. 58 BL25
London Rd.
Apsley Mill Retail Pk., Hem.H. 40 BL24
Apsley Rd. SE25 202 DV98
Apsley Rd., N.Mal. 198 CQ97
Apsley Way NW2 119 CU61
Apsley Way W1 276 G4
Aquarius Way, Nthwd. 93 BU50
Aquila Clo., Lthd. 232 CL121
Aquila St. NW8 140 DD68
Aquinas St. SE1 278 E3
Aquis Ct., St.Alb. 42 CC20
Arabella Dr. SW15 158 CS84
Arabia Clo. E4 101 EC45
Arabin Rd. SE4 163 DY84
Araglen Ave., S.Ock. 149 FV71
Aragon Ave., Epsom 217 CV109
Aragon Ave., T.Ditt. 197 CF99
Aragon Clo., Brom. 205 EM102
Seymour Dr.
Aragon Clo., Croy. 222 EE110
Aragon Clo., Enf. 81 DM38
Aragon Clo., Hem.H. 41 BQ15
Aragon Clo., Loug. 84 EL44
Roding Rd.
Aragon Clo., Rom. 105 FB51
Aragon Clo., Sun. 175 BT94
Aragon Dr., Ilf. 103 EQ52
Aragon Dr., Ruis. 116 BX60
Aragon Ms. E1 142 DU74
Thomas More St.
Aragon Rd., Kings.T. 178 CL92
Aragon Rd., Mord. 199 CX100
Aragon Wk., W.Byf. 212 BM113
Godley Rd.
Aran Ct., Wey. 195 BR103
Mallards Reach
Aran Dr., Stan. 95 CJ49
Aran Heights, Ch.St.G. 90 AV49
Arandora Cres., Rom. 126 EV59
Arbery Rd. E3 143 DY69
Arbor Clo., Beck. 203 EB96
Arbor Ct. N16 122 DR61
Lordship Rd.
Arbor Rd. E4 101 ED48
Arborfield Clo., Slou. 152 AS76
Arbour, The, Hert. 32 DR11
Arbour Clo., Brwd. 108 FW50
Arbour Clo., Lthd. 231 CF123
Arbour Rd., Enf. 83 DX42
Arbour Sq. E1 143 DX72
Arbour Vw., Amer. 72 AV39
Arbour Way, Horn. 127 FH64
Arbroath Grn., Wat. 93 BU48
Arbroath Rd. SE9 164 EL83
Arbrook Clo., Orp. 206 EU97
Arbrook La., Esher 214 CC107
Arbury Ter. SE26 182 DV90
Oaksford Ave.
Arbuthnot La., Bex. 186 EY86
Arbuthnot Rd. SE14 163 DX82
Arbutus Clo., Red. 266 DC137
Arbutus Rd., Red. 266 DC136
Arbutus St. E8 142 DT67
Arcade, The EC2 275 M7
Arcade, The, Hat. 45 CV17
Kennelwood La.
Arcade Pl., Rom. 127 FE57
Arcadia Ave. N3 98 DA53
Arcadia Clo., Cars. 218 DG105
Devonshire Rd.
Arcadia St. E14 143 EA72
Arcadian Ave., Bex. 186 EY86
Arcadian Clo., Bex. 186 EY86
Arcadian Gdns. N22 99 DM52
Arcadian Rd., Bex. 186 EY86
Arcany Rd., S.Ock. 149 FV70
Arch Rd., Walt. 196 BX104
Arch St. SE1 279 H7
Arch St. SE1 162 DQ76
Archangel St. SE16 163 DX75
Archates Ave., Grays 170 GA76
Archbishops Pl. SW2 181 DM86
Archdale Pl., N.Mal. 198 CP97
Kingston Rd.
Archdale Rd. SE22 182 DT85
Archel Rd. W14 159 CZ79
Archer Clo., Kings L. 58 BM29
Archer Clo., Kings.T. 178 CL94
Archer Ho. SW11 160 DD81
Vicarage Cres.
Archer Ms., Hmptn. 176 CC93
Windmill Rd.
Archer Rd. SE25 202 DV98
Archer Rd., Orp. 206 EU99
Archer St. W1 273 M10
Archer Ter., West Dr. 134 BL73
Yew Ave.
Archer Way, Swan. 207 FF96
Archers, Harl. 51 EP20
Archers Clo., Hert. 32 DQ08
Archers Ct., S.Ock. 149 FV71
Archers Dr., Enf. 82 DW40
Archers Fld., St.Alb. 43 CF18
Archers Ride, Welw.G.C. 30 DB11
Archers Wk. SE15 162 DT81
Exeter Rd.
Archery Clo. W2 272 C9
Archery Clo. W2 140 DE72
Archery Clo., Har. 117 CF55
Archery Rd. SE9 185 EM85
Arches, The SW6 159 CZ82
Munster Rd.
Arches, The WC2 278 A2
Arches, The, Har. 116 CB61
Archfield, Welw.G.C. 29 CY06
Archibald Ms. W1 277 H1
Archibald Ms. W1 140 DG73
Archibald Rd. N7 121 DK63
Archibald Rd., Rom. 106 FN53
Archibald St. E3 143 EA70
Archway, Rom. 105 FH51
Archway Clo. N19 121 DJ61
St. Johns Way
Archway Clo. SW19 180 DB91
Archway Clo., Wall. 201 DK104
Archway Mall N19 121 DJ61
Magdala Ave.
Archway Ms., Dor. 263 CG135
Chapel Ct.
Archway Pl., Dor. 263 CG135
Archway Rd. N6 120 DF57
Archway Rd. N19 121 DJ60
Archway St. SW13 158 CS83
Arcola St. E8 122 DT64
Arctic St. NW5 120 DG64
Gillies St.
Arcus Rd., Brom. 184 EE93
Ardbeg Rd. SE24 182 DR85
Arden Clo., Har. 117 CD62
Arden Clo., Hem.H. 57 BA28
Arden Clo., Reig. 266 DB138
Arden Clo. (Bushey), Wat. 95 CF45
Arden Ct. Gdns. N2 120 DD58
Arden Cres. E14 163 EA77
Arden Cres., Dag. 146 EW66
Arden Est. N1 275 M1
Arden Est. N1 142 DS68
Arden Gro., Orp. 223 EP105
Arden Ms. E17 123 EB57
Wingfield Rd.
Arden Mhor, Pnr. 115 BV56
Arden Rd. N3 119 CY55
Arden Rd. W13 137 CJ73
Ardens Way, St.Alb. 43 CK17
Ardent Clo. SE25 202 DS97
Ardesley Wd., Wey. 213 BS105
Ardfern Ave. SW16 201 DN97
Ardfillan Rd. SE6 183 ED88
Ardgowan Rd. SE6 184 EE87
Ardilaun Rd. N5 122 DQ63
Ardingly Clo., Croy. 203 DX104
Ardleigh Clo., Horn. 128 FK55
Ardleigh Ct., Brwd. 109 FZ45
Ardleigh Gdns., Brwd. 109 GE44
Fairview Ave.
Ardleigh Gdns., Sutt. 200 DA101
Ardleigh Grn. Rd., Horn. 128 FK58
Ardleigh Ho., Bark. 145 EQ67
St. Ann's
Ardleigh Ms., Ilf. 125 EP62
Bengal Rd.
Ardleigh Rd. E17 101 DZ53

Ardleigh Rd. N1 142 DS65
Ardleigh Ter. E17 101 DZ53
Ardley Clo. NW10 118 CS62
Ardley Clo. SE6 183 DY90
Ardley Clo., Ruis. 115 BQ59
Ardley Cres., 37 FH05
Bishop's Stortford
Ardlui Rd. SE27 182 DQ89
Ardmay Gdns., Surb. 198 CL99
Ardmere Rd. SE13 183 ED86
Ardmore Ave., Guil. 242 AV132
Ardmore La., Buck.H. 102 EH45
Ardmore Pl., Buck.H. 102 EH45
Ardmore La.
Ardmore Rd., S.Ock. 149 FV70
Ardmore Way, Guil. 242 AV132
Ardoch Rd. SE6 183 ED89
Ardra Rd. N9 101 DX48
Ardross Ave., Nthwd. 93 BS50
Ardrossan Clo., Slou. 151 AQ79
Canterbury Ave.
Ardrossan Gdns., Wor.Pk. 199 CU104
Ardshiel Clo. SW15 159 CX83
Bemish Rd.
Ardshiel Dr., Red. 266 DE136
Fairlawn Dr.
Ardwell Ave., Ilf. 125 EQ57
Ardwell Rd. SW2 181 DL89
Ardwick Rd. NW2 120 DA63
Arena Ind. Est., Enf. 83 DZ38
Argall Ave. E10 123 DX59
Argent Clo., Egh. 173 BC93
Pooley Grn. Rd.
Argent St. SE1 278 G4
Argent St., Grays 170 GA79
Argenta Way NW10 138 CP66
Argles Clo., Green. 189 FU85
Cowley Ave.
Argon Ms. SW6 160 DA80
Argosy Gdns., Stai. 173 BF93
Argosy La., Stai. 174 BK87
Argus Clo., Rom. 105 FB53
Argus Way W3 158 CP76
Argus Way, Nthlt. 136 BY69
Argyle Ave., Houns. 176 CA86
Argyle Clo. W13 137 CG70
Argyle Gdns., Upmin. 129 FR61
Argyle Pas. N17 100 DT53
Argyle Rd.
Argyle Pl. W6 159 CV77
Argyle Rd. E1 143 DX70
Argyle Rd. E15 124 EE64
Argyle Rd. E16 144 EH72
Argyle Rd. N12 98 DA50
Argyle Rd. N17 100 DU53
Argyle Rd. N18 100 DU49
Argyle Rd. W13 137 CG71
Argyle Rd., Barn. 79 CW42
Argyle Rd., Grnf. 137 CF69
Argyle Rd., Har. 116 CB58
Argyle Rd., Houns. 176 CB85
Argyle Rd., Ilf. 125 EN61
Argyle Rd., Sev. 257 FH125
Argyle Rd., Tedd. 177 CE92
Argyle Sq. WC1 274 A2
Argyle Sq. WC1 141 DL69
Argyle St. WC1 273 P2
Argyle St. WC1 141 DL69
Argyle Wk. WC1 273 P3
Argyll Ave., Slou. 131 AN73
Argyll Ave., Sthl. 136 CB74
Argyll Clo. SW9 161 DM83
Dalyell Rd.
Argyll Gdns., Edg. 96 CP54
Argyll Rd. W8 160 DA75
Argyll Rd., Grays 170 GA78
Argyll Rd., Hem.H. 40 BL15
Argyll St. W1 273 K9
Argyll St. W1 141 DJ72
Arica Rd. SE4 163 DY84
Ariel Clo., Grav. 191 GM91
Ariel Rd. NW6 140 DA65
Ariel Way W12 139 CW74
Ariel Way, Houns. 155 BV83
Arisdale Ave., S.Ock. 149 FV71
Aristotle Rd. SW4 161 DK83
Ark Ave., Grays 170 FZ76
Arkell Gro. SE19 181 DP94
Arkindale Rd. SE6 183 EC90
Arkley Ct., Hem.H. 41 BP15
Arkley Rd.
Arkley Cres. E17 123 DZ57
Arkley Dr., Barn. 79 CU42
Arkley La., Barn. 79 CU41
Arkley Rd. E17 123 DZ57
Arkley Rd., Hem.H. 41 BP15
Arkley Vw., Barn. 79 CV42
Arklow Ms., Surb. 198 CL103
Vale Rd. S.
Arklow Rd. SE14 163 DZ79
Arkwright Rd. NW3 120 DC64
Arkwright Rd., Slou. 153 BE82
Arkwright Rd., S.Croy. 220 DT110
Arkwright Rd., Til. 171 GG82
Arkwrights, Harl. 35 ET14
Arlesey Clo. SW15 179 CY86
Lytton Gro.
Arlesford Rd. SW9 161 DL83
Arlingford Rd. SW2 181 DN85
Arlington N12 98 DA48
Arlington Ave. N1 142 DQ67
Arlington Clo., Sid. 185 ES87
Arlington Clo., Sutt. 200 DA103
Arlington Clo., Twick. 177 CJ86
Arlington Ct., Hayes 155 BR78
Shepiston La.
Arlington Ct., Reig. 250 DB132
Oakfield Dr.
Arlington Cres., Wal.Cr. 67 DY34
Arlington Dr., Cars. 200 DF103
Arlington Dr., Ruis. 115 BR58
Arlington Gdns. W4 158 CQ78
Arlington Gdns., Ilf. 125 EN60
Arlington Gdns., Rom. 106 FL53
Arlington Lo. SW2 161 DM84
Arlington Lo., Wey. 213 BP105
Arlington Ms., Twick. 177 CH86
Arlington Rd.
Arlington Pl. SE10 163 EC80
Greenwich S. St.
Arlington Rd. N14 99 DH47
Arlington Rd. NW1 141 DH67
Arlington Rd. W13 137 CH72
Arlington Rd., Ashf. 174 BM92
Arlington Rd., Rich. 177 CK89
Arlington Rd., Surb. 197 CK100
Arlington Rd., Tedd. 177 CF91
Arlington Rd., Twick. 177 CJ86
Arlington Rd., Wdf.Grn. 102 EG52
Arlington Sq. N1 142 DQ67
Arlington St. SW1 277 K2
Arlington St. SW1 141 DJ74
Arlington Way EC1 274 E2
Arlington Way EC1 141 DN69
Arliss Way, Nthlt. 136 BW67
Arlow Rd. N21 99 DN46
Armada Ct. SE8 163 EA79
Watergate St.
Armada Ct., Grays 170 GA76
Antelope Ave.
Armada St. SE8 163 EA79
Armada Way E6 145 EQ73
Armadale Clo. N17 122 DV56
Armadale Rd. SW6 160 DA80
Armadale Rd., Felt. 175 BU85
Armadale Rd., Wok. 226 AU117
Armagh Rd. E3 143 DZ67
Armand Clo., Wat. 75 BT38
Armfield Clo., W.Mol. 196 BZ99
Armfield Cres., Mitch. 200 DF96
Armfield Rd., Enf. 82 DR39
Arminger Rd. W12 139 CV74
Armitage Clo., Rick. 74 BK42
Armitage Rd. NW11 119 CY60
Armitage Rd. SE10 164 EF78
Armor Rd., Purf. 169 FR77
Armour Clo. N7 141 DM65
Roman Way
Armoury Dr., Grav. 191 GJ87
Armoury Rd. SE8 163 EB82
Armoury Way SW18 180 DA85
Armstead Wk., Dag. 146 FA66
Armstrong Ave., 102 EE51
Wdf.Grn.
Armstrong Clo. E6 145 EM72
Porter Rd.
Armstrong Clo., Dag. 126 EX60
Palmer Rd.
Armstrong Clo., Pnr. 115 BU58
Armstrong Clo., Sev. 241 FB115
Armstrong Clo., Walt. 195 BU100
Sunbury La.
Armstrong Cres., Barn. 80 DD41
Armstrong Gdns., Rad. 62 CL32
Armstrong Pl., Hem.H. 40 BK19
High St.
Armstrong Rd. SW7 160 DD76
Armstrong Rd. W3 139 CT74
Armstrong Rd., Egh. 172 AW93
Armstrong Rd., Felt. 176 BY92
Armstrong Way, Sthl. 156 CB75
Armytage Rd., Houns. 156 BX80
Arnal Cres. SW18 179 CY87
Arndale Cen., The SW18 180 DB86
Arndale Wk. SW18 180 DB85
Garratt La.
Arndale Way, Egh. 173 BA92
Church Rd.
Arne Gro., Horl. 268 DE146
Arne Gro., Orp. 205 ET104
Arne St. WC2 274 A9
Arne St. WC2 141 DL72
Arne Wk. SE3 164 EF84
Arnett Clo., Rick. 74 BG44
Arnett Sq. E4 101 DZ51
Silver Birch Ave.
Arnett Way, Rick. 74 BG44
Arneway St. SW1 277 N7
Arneways Ave., Rom. 126 EX56
Arnewood Clo. SW15 179 CU88
Arnewood Clo., Lthd. 214 CB113
Arney's La., Mitch. 200 DG100
Arngask Rd. SE6 183 ED87
Arnhem Ave., S.Ock. 148 FQ74
Arnhem Dr., Croy. 221 ED111
Arnhem Way SE22 182 DS85
East Dulwich Gro.
Arnison Rd., E.Mol. 197 CD98
Arnold Ave. E., Enf. 83 EA38
Arnold Ave. W., Enf. 83 DZ38
Arnold Circ. E2 275 P3
Arnold Circ. E2 142 DT69
Arnold Clo., Har. 118 CM59
Arnold Cres., Islw. 177 CD85
Arnold Dr., Chess. 215 CK107
Mansfield Rd.
Arnold Est. SE1 162 DT75
Arnold Gdns. N13 99 DP50
Arnold Pl., Til. 171 GJ81
Kipling Ave.
Arnold Rd. E3 143 EA69
Arnold Rd. N15 122 DT55
Arnold Rd. SW17 180 DF94
Arnold Rd., Dag. 146 EZ66
Arnold Rd., Grav. 191 GK89
Arnold Rd., Nthlt. 136 BX65
Arnold Rd., Stai. 174 BJ94
Arnold Rd., Wok. 227 BB115
Arnolds Ave., Brwd. 109 GC43
Arnolds Clo., Brwd. 109 GC43
Arnolds Fm. La., Brwd. 109 GE41
Arnolds La. 188 FM93
(Sutton at Hone), Dart.
Arnos Gro. N14 99 DK49
Arnos Rd. N11 99 DJ50
Arnott Clo. SE28 146 EW73
Applegarth Rd.
Arnott Clo. W4 158 CR77
Fishers La.
Arnould Ave. SE5 162 DR84
Arnsberg Way, Bexh. 166 FA84
Arnside Gdns., Wem. 117 CK60
Arnside Rd., Bexh. 166 FA81
Arnside St. SE17 162 DQ79
Arnulf St. SE6 183 EB91
Arnulls Rd. SW16 181 DN93
Arodene Rd. SW2 181 DM86
Arragon Gdns. SW16 181 DL94
Arragon Gdns., W.Wick. 203 EB104
Arragon Rd. E6 144 EK67
Arragon Rd. SW18 180 DA88
Bodmin St.
Arragon Rd., Twick. 177 CG87
Arran Clo., Erith 167 FD79
Arran Clo., Hem.H. 41 BQ22
Arran Clo., Wall. 219 DJ105
Arran Dr. E12 124 EK60
Arran Ms. W5 138 CM74
Arran Rd. SE6 183 EB89
Arran Wk. N1 142 DQ66
Arran Way, Esher 196 CB103
Arranmore Ct. 76 BY42
(Bushey), Wat.
Bushey Hall Rd.
Arras Ave., Mord. 200 DC99
Arretine Clo., St.Alb. 42 BZ22
Arrol Rd., Beck. 202 DW97
Arrow Rd. E3 143 EB69
Arrowscout Wk., Nthlt. 136 BY69
Argus Way
Arrowsmith Clo., Chig. 103 ET50
Arrowsmith Path, Chig. 103 ES50
Arrowsmith Rd., Chig. 103 ES50
Arrowsmith Rd., Loug. 84 EL41
Arsenal Rd. SE9 165 EM82
Artemis Clo., Grav. 191 GL87
Arterberry Rd. SW20 179 CW94
Arterial Ave., Rain. 147 FH70
Arterial Rd. N. Stifford, 170 FY75
Grays
Arterial Rd. Purfleet, Purf. 168 FN76
Arterial Rd. 169 FT76
W.Thurrock, Grays
Artesian Clo. NW10 138 CR66
Artesian Clo., Horn. 127 FF58
Artesian Rd. W2 140 DA72
Artesian Wk. E11 124 EE62
Cathall Rd.
Arthingworth St. E15 144 EE67
Arthur Ct. W2 140 DB72
Queensway
Arthur Gro. SE18 165 EQ77
Arthur Henderson Ho. 159 CZ82
SW6
Arthur Rd. E6 145 EM68
Arthur Rd. N7 121 DM63
Arthur Rd. N9 100 DT47
Arthur Rd. SW19 179 CY92
Arthur Rd., Kings.T. 178 CN94
Arthur Rd., N.Mal. 199 CV99
Arthur Rd., Rom. 126 EX58
Arthur Rd., St.Alb. 43 CH20
Arthur Rd., Slou. 151 AR75
Arthur Rd., West. 238 EJ115
Arthur Rd., Wind. 151 AP81
Arthur St. EC4 275 L10
Arthur St., Erith 167 FF80
Arthur St., Grav. 191 GG87
Arthur St., Grays 170 GC79
Arthur St. (Bushey), 76 BX42
Wat.
Arthur St. W., Grav. 191 GG87
Arthurdon Rd. SE4 183 EA85
Arthur's Bri. Rd., Wok. 226 AX117
Artichoke Dell, Rick. 73 BE43
Artichoke Hill E1 142 DV73
Pennington St.
Artichoke Pl. SE5 162 DR81
Camberwell Ch. St.
Artillery Clo., Ilf. 125 EQ58
Horns Rd.
Artillery La. E1 275 N7
Artillery La. E1 142 DS71
Artillery La. W12 139 CU72
Du Cane Rd.
Artillery Pas. E1 142 DS71
Sandy's Row
Artillery Pl. SE18 165 EM77
Artillery Pl. SW1 277 M7
Artillery Rd., Guil. 242 AX134
Artillery Row SW1 277 M7
Artillery Row SW1 161 DK76
Artillery Row, Grav. 191 GJ87
Artillery Ter., Guil. 242 AX134
Artington Clo., Orp. 223 EQ105
Artington Wk., Guil. 258 AW137
Artisan Clo. E6 145 EP72
Ferndale St.
Artisan Cres., St.Alb. 42 CC19
Oysterfields
Artizan St. E1 275 N8
Arundel Ave., Epsom 217 CV110
Arundel Ave., Mord. 199 CZ98
Arundel Ave., S.Croy. 220 DU110
Arundel Clo. E15 124 EE63
Arundel Clo. SW11 180 DE85
Chivalry Rd.
Arundel Clo., Bex. 186 EZ86
Arundel Clo., Croy. 201 DP104
Arundel Clo., Hmptn. 176 CB92
Arundel Clo., Hem.H. 41 BP19
Arundel Clo. 66 DV28
(Cheshunt), Wal.Cr.
Arundel Ct. N12 98 DE51
Arundel Ct., Har. 116 CA63
Arundel Ct., Slou. 152 AX77
Arundel Dr., Borwd. 78 CP43
Arundel Dr., Har. 116 BZ63
Arundel Dr., Orp. 224 EV106
Arundel Dr., Wdf.Grn. 102 EG52
Arundel Gdns. N21 99 DN46
Arundel Gdns. W11 139 CZ73
Arundel Gdns., Edg. 96 CR52
Arundel Gdns., Ilf. 126 EU61
Arundel Great Ct. WC2 274 C10
Arundel Gro. N16 122 DS64
Arundel Pl. N1 141 DN65
Arundel Rd., Barn. 80 DE41
Arundel Rd., Croy. 202 DR100
Arundel Rd., Dart. 168 FJ84
Arundel Rd., Dor. 263 CG136
Arundel Rd., Houns. 156 BW83
Arundel Rd., Kings.T. 198 CP96
Arundel Rd., Rom. 106 FM52
Arundel Rd., Sutt. 217 CY108
Arundel Rd., Uxb. 134 BH68
Arundel Sq. N7 141 DN65
Arundel St. WC2 274 C10
Arundel St. WC2 141 DM73
Arundel Ter. SW13 159 CV79
Arundell Gro., St.Alb. 43 CD16
Arundell Rd., Abb.L. 59 BU31
College Rd.
Arvon Rd. N5 121 DN64
Ascalon St. SW8 161 DJ80
Ascension Rd., Rom. 105 FC51
Ascham Dr. E4 101 EB52
Rushcroft Rd.
Ascham End E17 101 DY53
Ascham St. NW5 121 DJ64
Aschurch Rd., Croy. 202 DT101
Ascot Clo., Borwd. 78 CN43
Ascot Clo., Ilf. 103 ES51
Ascot Clo., Nthlt. 136 CA65
Ascot Gdns., Enf. 82 DW37
Ascot Gdns., Horn. 128 FL63
Ascot Gdns., Sthl. 136 BZ70
Ascot Ms., Wall. 219 DJ109
Ascot Rd. E6 145 EM69
Ascot Rd. N15 122 DR57
Ascot Rd. N18 100 DU49
Ascot Rd. SW17 180 DG93
Ascot Rd., Felt. 174 BN89
Ascot Rd., Grav. 191 GH90
Ascot Rd., Orp. 205 ET98
Ascot Rd., Wat. 75 BS43
Ascots La., Hat. 29 CY14
Ascots La., Welw.G.C. 29 CY14
Ascott Ave. W5 158 CL75
Ash Clo. SE20 202 DW96
Ash Clo., Abb.L. 59 BR32
Ash Clo., Brwd. 108 FT43
Ash Clo., Cars. 200 DF103
Ash Clo., Edg. 96 CQ49
Ash Clo., Hat. 64 DA25
Ash Clo., N.Mal. 198 CR96
Ash Clo., Orp. 205 ER99
Ash Clo., Red. 251 DJ130
Ash Clo., Rom. 105 FB52
Ash Clo., Sid. 186 EV90
Ash Clo., Slou. 153 BB76
Ash Clo., Stan. 95 CG51
Ash Clo., Swan. 207 FC96
Ash Clo., Uxb. 92 BK53
Ash Clo., Wat. 75 BV35
Cedar Wd. Dr.
Ash Clo., Wok. 226 AY120
Ash Clo. (Pyrford), Wok. 228 BG115
Ash Copse, St.Alb. 60 BZ31
Ash Ct., Epsom 216 CQ105
Ash Dr., Hat. 45 CU21
Ash Dr., Red. 267 DH136
Ash Grn., Uxb. 134 BH65
Ash Gro. E8 142 DV67
Ash Gro. N13 100 DQ48
Ash Gro. NW2 119 CX63
Ash Gro. SE20 202 DW96
Ash Gro. W5 158 CL75
Ash Gro., Amer. 55 AN36
Ash Gro., Enf. 100 DS45
Ash Gro., Felt. 175 BS88
Ash Gro., Guil. 242 AU134
Ash Gro., Hayes 135 BR73
Ash Gro., Hem.H. 40 BM24
Ash Gro., Houns. 156 BX81
Ash Gro., Slou. 132 AT66
Ash Gro., Sthl. 136 CA71
Ash Gro., Stai. 174 BJ93
Ash Gro., Uxb. 92 BK53
Ash Gro., Wem. 117 CG63
Ash Gro., West Dr. 134 BM73
Ash Gro., W.Wick. 203 EC103
Ash Gros., Saw. 36 FA05
Ash Hill Clo. (Bushey), Wat. 94 CB46
Ash Hill Dr., Pnr. 116 BW55
Ash Island, E.Mol. 197 CD97
Ash La., Croy. 219 DP105
Ash La., Horn. 128 FN56
Southend Arterial Rd.
Ash La., Rom. 105 FG51
Ash La., Wind. 151 AK82
Ash Ms., Epsom 216 CS113
Ash Platt, The, Sev. 257 FL121
Ash Platt Rd., Sev. 257 FL121
Ash Ride, Enf. 81 DN35
Ash Rd. E15 124 EE64
Ash Rd., Croy. 203 EA103
Ash Rd., Dart. 188 FK88
Ash Rd. (Hawley), Dart. 188 FM91
Ash Rd., Grav. 191 GJ91
Ash Rd., Orp. 223 ET108
Ash Rd., Shep. 194 BN98
Ash Rd., Sutt. 199 CY101
Ash Rd., West. 255 ER125
Ash Rd., Wok. 226 AX120
Ash Row, Brom. 205 EN101
Ash Tree Clo., Croy. 203 DY100
Ash Tree Clo., Surb. 198 CL102
Ash Tree Dell NW9 118 CR57
Ash Tree Fld., Harl. 35 EN13
Ash Tree Rd., Wat. 75 BV36
Ash Tree Way, Croy. 203 DY99
Ash Vale, Rick. 91 BD50
Ash Vw. Clo., Ashf. 174 BL93
Ash Vw. Gdns., Ashf. 174 BL92
Ash Vw. Mobile Home Pk., 59 BQ28
Kings L.
Ash Wk. SW2 181 DM88
Ash Wk., Wem. 117 CJ62
Ashan Ct., Ashf. 175 BS94
Ashbeam Clo., Brwd. 107 FW51
Canterbury Way
Ashbourne Ave. E18 124 EH56
Ashbourne Ave. N20 98 DF47
Ashbourne Ave. NW11 119 CZ57
Ashbourne Ave., Bexh. 166 EY80
Ashbourne Ave., Har. 117 CD61
Ashbourne Clo. N12 98 DB49
Ashbourne Clo. W5 138 CN71
Ashbourne Clo., Couls. 235 DJ118
Ashbourne Ct. E5 123 DY63
Daubeney Rd.
Ashbourne Gro. NW7 96 CR50
Ashbourne Gro. SE22 182 DT85
Ashbourne Gro. W4 158 CS78
Ashbourne Ri., Orp. 223 ER105
Ashbourne Rd. W5 138 CM70
Ashbourne Rd., Brox. 49 DZ21
Ashbourne Rd., Mitch. 180 DG93
Ashbourne Rd., Rom. 106 FJ49
Ashbourne Sq., Nthwd. 93 BS51
Ashbourne Ter. SW19 180 DA94
Ashbourne Way NW11 119 CZ57
Ashbourne Ave.
Ashbridge Rd. E11 124 EE59
Ashbridge St. NW8 272 B5
Ashbridge St. NW8 140 DE70
Ashbrook Rd. N19 121 DK60
Ashbrook Rd., Dag. 127 FB62
Ashbrook Rd., Wind. 172 AV87
Ashburn Gdns. SW7 160 DC77
Ashburn Pl. SW7 160 DC77
Ashburnham Ave., Har. 117 CF58
Ashburnham Clo. N2 120 DD55
Ashburnham Clo., Sev. 257 FJ127
Fiennes Way
Ashburnham Clo., Wat. 93 BU48
Ashburnham Dr.
Ashburnham Dr., Wat. 93 BU48
Ashburnham Gdns., Har. 117 CF59
Ashburnham Gdns., 128 FP60
Upmin.
Ashburnham Gro. SE10 163 EB80
Ashburnham Pk., Esher 214 CC105
Ashburnham Pl. SE10 163 EB80
Ashburnham Retreat 163 EB80
SE10
Ashburnham Rd. NW10 139 CW69
Ashburnham Rd. SW10 160 DC80
Ashburnham Rd., Belv. 167 FC77
Ashburnham Rd., Rich. 177 CH89
Ashburton Ave., Croy. 202 DV102
Ashburton Ave., Ilf. 125 ES63
Ashburton Clo., Croy. 202 DU102
Ashburton Ct., Pnr. 116 BX55
Ashburton Gdns., Croy. 202 DU103
Ashburton Gro. N7 121 DN63
Ashburton Rd. E16 144 EG72
Ashburton Rd., Croy. 202 DU103
Ashburton Rd., Ruis. 115 BU61
Ashburton Ter. E13 144 EG68
Grasmere Rd.
Ashbury Clo., Hat. 44 CS18
Ashbury Cres., Guil. 243 BC132
Ashbury Dr., Uxb. 115 BP61
Ashbury Gdns., Rom. 126 EX57
Ashbury Rd. SW11 160 DF83
Ashby Ave., Chess. 216 CN107
Ashby Clo., Horn. 128 FN60
Holme Rd.
Ashby Gdns., St.Alb. 43 CD24
Ashby Gro. N1 142 DQ66
Ashby Ms. SE4 163 DZ82
Ashby Rd. N15 122 DU57
Ashby Rd. SE4 163 DZ82
Ashby Rd., Wat. 75 BU38
Ashby St. EC1 274 G3
Ashby Wk., Croy. 202 DQ100
Ashby Way, West Dr. 154 BN80
Ashchurch Gro. W12 159 CU76
Ashchurch Pk. Vill. W12 159 CU76
Ashchurch Ter. W12 159 CU76
Ashcombe, Welw.G.C. 29 CY05
Ashcombe Ave., Surb. 197 CK101
Ashcombe Gdns., Edg. 96 CN49
Ashcombe Pk. NW2 118 CS62
Ashcombe Rd. SW19 180 DA92
Ashcombe Rd., Cars. 218 DG107
Ashcombe Rd., Dor. 247 CG134
Ashcombe Rd., Red. 251 DJ127
Ashcombe Sq., N.Mal. 198 CQ97
Ashcombe St. SW6 160 DB82
Ashcombe Ter., Tad. 233 CV120
Ashcroft, Guil. 258 AY141
Ashcroft, Pnr. 94 CA51
Ashcroft Ave., Sid. 186 EU86
Ashcroft Ct., Brox. 49 DZ22
Winford Dr.
Ashcroft Ct., Slou. 130 AH68
Ashcroft Cres., Sid. 186 EU86
Ashcroft Dr., Uxb. 113 BF58
Ashcroft Pk., Cob. 214 BY112
Ashcroft Ri., Couls. 235 DL116
Ashcroft Rd. E3 143 DY69
Ashcroft Rd., Chess. 198 CM104
Ashcroft Sq. W6 159 CW77
King St.
Ashdale, Lthd. 246 CC126
Ashdale Clo., Stai. 174 BL89
Ashdale Clo., Twick. 176 CC87
Ashdale Gro., Stan. 95 CF51
Ashdale Rd. SE12 184 EH88
Ashdale Way, Twick. 176 CC87
Ashdale Clo.
Ashdales, St.Alb. 43 CD24
Ashdene SE15 162 DV81
Carlton Gro.
Ashdene, Pnr. 116 BW55
Ashdene Clo., Ashf. 175 BQ94
Ashdon Clo., Brwd. 109 GC44
Poplar Dr.
Ashdon Clo., Wdf.Grn. 102 EH51
Ashdon Rd. NW10 139 CT67
Ashdon Rd. (Bushey), Wat. 76 BX41
Ashdown Clo., Beck. 203 EB96
Ashdown Clo., Bex. 187 FC87
Wansunt Rd.
Ashdown Clo., Reig. 266 DB138
Ashdown Cres. NW5 120 DG64
Queens Cres.
Ashdown Cres. 67 DY28
(Cheshunt), Wal.Cr.
Ashdown Dr., Borwd. 78 CM40
Ashdown Gdns., S.Croy. 236 DV115
Ashdown Rd., Enf. 82 DW41
Ashdown Rd., Epsom 217 CT113
Ashdown Rd., Kings.T. 198 CL96
Ashdown Rd., Reig. 266 DB138
Ashdown Rd., Uxb. 134 BN68
Ashdown Wk. E14 163 EA77
Charnwood Gdns.
Ashdown Wk., Rom. 105 FB54
Ashdown Way SW17 180 DG89
Ashdown Way, Amer. 55 AR36
Chestnut La.
Ashen E6 145 EN72
Downings
Ashen Dr., Dart. 187 FG86
Ashen Gro. SW19 180 DA90
Ashen Vale, S.Croy. 221 DX109
Ashenden Rd. E5 123 DY64
Ashenden Rd., Guil. 242 AT134
Ashenden Wk., Slou. 111 AR63
Ashendene Rd., Hert. 47 DL20
Asher Way E1 142 DU74
Asheridge Rd., Chesh. 54 AM28
Ashfield Ave., Felt. 175 BV88
Ashfield Ave. (Bushey), 76 CB44
Wat.
Ashfield Clo., Beck. 183 EA94
Brackley Rd.
Ashfield Clo., Rich. 178 CL88
Ashfield La., Chis. 185 EQ93
Ashfield Par. N14 99 DK46
Ashfield Rd. N4 122 DQ58
Ashfield Rd. N14 99 DJ48
Ashfield Rd. W3 139 CT74
Ashfield Rd., Chesh. 54 AR29
Ashfield St. E1 142 DV71
Ashfields, Loug. 85 EM40
Ashfields, Wat. 75 BT35
Ashford Ave. N8 121 DL56
Ashford Ave., Ashf. 175 BP93
Ashford Ave., Brwd. 108 FV48
Ashford Ave., Hayes 136 BX72
Ashford Clo. E17 123 DZ58
Ashford Clo., Ashf. 174 BL91
Ashford Cres., Ashf. 174 BL90
Ashford Cres., Enf. 82 DW40
Ashford Gdns., Cob. 230 BX116
Ashford Grn., Wat. 94 BX50
Ashford Ind. Est., Ashf. 175 BQ91
Ashford La., Maid. 150 AG75
Ashford La., Wind. 150 AH75
Ashford Rd. E6 145 EN65
Ashford Rd. E18 102 EH54
Ashford Rd. NW2 119 CX63
Ashford Rd., Ashf. 175 BP94
Ashford Rd., Felt. 175 BR91
Ashford Rd., Iver 133 BC67
Ashford Rd., Stai. 194 BK95
Ashford St. N1 275 M2
Ashgrove Rd., Ashf. 175 BQ92
Ashgrove Rd., Brom. 183 ED93
Ashgrove Rd., Ilf. 125 ET60

Ashgrove Rd., Sev. 256 FG127
Ashingdon Clo. E4 101 EC48
Ashington Rd. SW6 159 CZ82
Ashlake Rd. SW16 181 DL91
Ashland Pl. W1 272 F6
Ashland Pl. W1 140 DG71
Ashlar Pl. SE18 165 EP77
Masons Hill
Ashlea Rd., Ger.Cr. 90 AY54
Ashleigh Ave., Egh. 173 BC94
Ashleigh Clo., Amer. 55 AS39
Ashleigh Clo., Horl. 268 DF148
Ashleigh Cotts., Dor. 263 CH144
Ashleigh Gdns., Sutt. 200 DB103
Ashleigh Gdns., Upmin. 129 FR62
Ashleigh Rd. SE20 202 DV97
Ashleigh Rd. SW14 158 CS83
Ashley Ave., Epsom 216 CR113
Ashley Ave., Ilf. 103 EP54
Ashley Ave., Mord. 200 DA99
Chalgrove Ave.
Ashley Cen., Epsom 216 CR113
Ashley Clo. NW4 97 CW54
Ashley Clo., Lthd. 246 BZ125
Ashley Clo., Pnr. 93 BV54
Ashley Clo., Sev. 257 FH124
Ashley Clo., Walt. 195 BS102
Ashley Clo., Welw.G.C. 29 CW07
Ashley Ct., Epsom 216 CR113
Ashley Ct., Hat. 45 CV17
Ashley Cres. N22 99 DN54
Ashley Cres. SW11 160 DG83
Ashley Dr., Bans. 218 DA114
Ashley Dr., Borwd. 78 CQ43
Ashley Dr., H.Wyc. 88 AC45
Ashley Dr., Islw. 157 CE79
Ashley Dr., Twick. 176 CB88
Ashley Dr., Walt. 195 BU104
Ashley Gdns. N13 100 DQ49
Ashley Gdns. SW1 277 L7
Ashley Gdns., Guil. 259 AZ141
Kings Rd.
Ashley Gdns., Orp. 223 ES106
Ashley Gdns., Rich. 177 CK89
Ashley Gdns., Wem. 118 CL61
Ashley Grn. La., Chesh. 54 AR27
Ashley Grn. Rd., Chesh. 54 AR27
Ashley Gro., Loug. 84 EL41
Staples Rd.
Ashley La. NW4 97 CW54
Ashley La., Croy. 219 DP105
Ashley Pk. Ave., Walt. 195 BT103
Ashley Pk. Cres., Walt. 195 BT102
Ashley Pk. Rd., Walt. 195 BU103
Ashley Pl. SW1 277 K7
Ashley Pl. SW1 161 DJ76
Ashley Ri., Walt. 213 BT105
Ashley Rd. E4 101 EA50
Ashley Rd. E7 144 EJ66
Ashley Rd. N17 122 DU55
Ashley Rd. N19 121 DL60
Ashley Rd. SW19 180 DB93
Ashley Rd., Dor. 262 CC137
Ashley Rd., Enf. 82 DW40
Ashley Rd., Epsom 216 CR113
Ashley Rd., Hmptn. 196 CA95
Ashley Rd., Hert. 31 DN10
Ashley Rd., Rich. 158 CL83
Jocelyn Rd.
Ashley Rd., St.Alb. 43 CJ20
Ashley Rd., Sev. 257 FH124
Ashley Rd., T.Ditt. 197 CF100
Ashley Rd., Th.Hth. 201 DM98
Ashley Rd., Uxb. 134 BH68
Ashley Rd., Walt. 195 BU102
Ashley Rd., Wok. 226 AT118
Ashley Wk. NW7 97 CW52
Ashleys, Rick. 91 BF45
Ashlin Rd. E15 123 ED63
Ashling Rd., Croy. 202 DU102
Ashlone Rd. SW15 159 CW83
Ashlyn Clo. (Bushey), Wat. 76 BY41
Ashlyn Gro., Horn. 128 FK55
Ashlyns Ct., Berk. 38 AV20
Ashlyns La., Ong. 53 FF20
Ashlyns Pk., Cob. 214 BY113
Ashlyns Rd., Berk. 38 AV20
Ashlyns Rd., Epp. 69 ET30
Ashlyns Way, Chess. 215 CK107
Ashmead N14 81 DJ43
Ashmead Dr., Uxb. 114 BG61
Ashmead Gate, Brom. 204 EJ95
Ashmead La., Uxb. 114 BG61
Ashmead Rd. SE8 163 EA82
Ashmead Rd., Felt. 175 BU88
Ashmeads Ct., Rad. 62 CL32
Porters Pk. Dr.
Ashmere Ave., Beck. 203 ED96
Ashmere Clo., Sutt. 217 CW106
Ashmere Gro. SW2 161 DL84
Ashmill St. NW1 272 B6
Ashmill St. NW1 140 DE71
Ashmole Pl. SW8 161 DM79
Ashmole St. SW8 161 DM79
Ashmore Ct., Houns. 156 CA79
Wheatlands
Ashmore Gdns., Hem.H. 41 BP21
Ashmore Gro., Well. 165 ER83
Ashmore La., Kes. 222 EJ111
Ashmore Rd. W9 139 CZ68
Ashmount Rd. N15 122 DT57
Ashmount Rd. N19 121 DJ59
Ashmount Ter. W5 157 CK77
Murray Rd.
Ashmour Gdns., Rom. 105 FD54
Ashneal Gdns., Har. 117 CD62
Ashness Gdns., Grnf. 137 CH65
Ashness Rd. SW11 180 DF85
Ashridge Clo., Har. 117 CJ58
Ashridge Clo., Hem.H. 57 BA28
Ashridge Cres. SE18 165 EQ80
Ashridge Dr., St.Alb. 60 BY30
Ashridge Dr., Wat. 93 BV50
Ashridge Gdns. N13 99 DK50
Ashridge Gdns., Pnr. 116 BY56
Ashridge Ri., Berk. 38 AT18
Ashridge Rd., Chesh. 56 AW31
Ashridge Way, Mord. 199 CZ97
Ashridge Way, Sun. 175 BU93
Ashtead Gap, Lthd. 231 CG116
Kingston Rd.
Ashtead Rd. E5 122 DU59
Ashtead Wds. Rd., Ash. 231 CJ116
Ashton Clo., Sutt. 218 DA105
Ashton Clo., Walt. 213 BV107
Ashton Gdns., Houns. 156 BZ84
Ashton Gdns., Rom. 126 EY58
Ashton Rd. E15 123 ED64
Ashton Rd., Enf. 83 DY36
Ashton Rd., Rom. 106 FK52
Ashton Rd., Wok. 226 AT117
Ashton St. E14 143 EC73
Ashtree Ave., Mitch. 200 DD96
Ashtree Clo., Orp. 223 EP105
Broadwater Gdns.
Ashtree Ct., St.Alb. 43 CF20
Granville Rd.
Ashtree Way, Hem.H. 40 BG21
Ashurst Clo. SE20 202 DV95
Ashurst Clo., Dart. 167 FF83
Ashurst Clo., Ken. 236 DR115
Ashurst Clo., Nthwd. 93 BS52
Ashurst Dr., Ilf. 125 EP58
Ashurst Dr., Shep. 194 BL99
Ashurst Dr., Tad. 248 CP130
Ashurst Rd. N12 98 DE50
Ashurst Rd., Barn. 80 DF43
Ashurst Rd., Tad. 233 CV121
Ashurst Wk., Croy. 202 DV103
Ashvale Dr., Upmin. 129 FS61
Ashvale Gdns., Rom. 105 FD50
Ashvale Gdns., Upmin. 129 FS61
Ashvale Rd. SW17 180 DF92
Ashville Rd. E11 123 ED61
Ashwater Rd. SE12 184 EG88
Ashwell Clo. E6 144 EL72
Northumberland Rd.
Ashwell St., St.Alb. 43 CD19
Ashwells Way, Ch.St.G. 90 AW47
Ashwin St. E8 142 DT65
Ashwindham Ct., Wok. 226 AT118
Raglan Rd.
Ashwood, Warl. 236 DW120
Ashwood Ave., Rain. 147 FH69
Ashwood Ave., Uxb. 134 BN72
Ashwood Gdns., Croy. 221 EB107
Ashwood Gdns., Hayes 155 BT77
Cranford Dr.
Ashwood Pk., Lthd. 230 CC123
Ashwood Pk., Wok. 227 BA118
Ashwood Rd. E4 101 ED48
Ashwood Rd., Egh. 172 AV93
Ashwood Rd., Pot.B. 64 DB33
Ashwood Rd., Wok. 227 AZ118
Ashworth Clo. SE5 162 DR82
Denmark Hill
Ashworth Pl., Guil. 242 AT134
Ashworth Pl., Harl. 52 EX15
Church Langley Way
Ashworth Rd. W9 140 DB69
Aske St. N1 275 M2
Askern Clo., Bexh. 166 EX84
Askew Cres. W12 159 CT75
Askew Fm. La., Grays 170 FY79
Askew Rd. W12 139 CT74
Askew Rd., Nthwd. 93 BR47
Askham Ct. W12 139 CU74
Askham Rd. W12 139 CU74
Askill Dr. SW15 179 CY85
Keswick Rd.
Askwith Rd., Rain. 147 FD69
Asland Rd. E15 143 ED67
Aslett St. SW18 180 DB87
Asmar Clo., Couls. 235 DL115
Asmara Rd. NW2 119 CY64
Asmuns Hill NW11 120 DA57
Asmuns Pl. NW11 119 CZ57
Aspasia Clo., St.Alb. 43 CF21
Aspdin Rd., Grav. 190 GD90
Aspen Clo. N19 121 DJ61
Hargrave Pk.
Aspen Clo. W5 158 CM75
Aspen Clo., Cob. 230 BY116
Aspen Clo., Guil. 243 BD131
Aspen Clo., Orp. 224 EU106
Aspen Clo., St.Alb. 60 BY30
Aspen Clo., Slou. 131 AP71
Birch Gro.
Aspen Clo., Stai. 173 BF90
Aspen Clo., Swan. 207 FD95
Aspen Clo., West Dr. 134 BM74
Aspen Copse, Brom. 205 EM96
Aspen Dr., Wem. 117 CG63
Aspen Gdns. W6 159 CV78
Aspen Gdns., Mitch. 200 DG99
Aspen Grn., Erith 166 EZ76
Aspen Gro., Upmin. 128 FN63
Aspen La., Nthlt. 136 BY69
Aspen Pk. Dr., Wat. 75 BV35
Aspen Sq., Wey. 195 BR104
Oatlands Dr.
Aspen Way E14 143 ED73
Aspen Way, Bans. 217 CX114
Aspen Way, Enf. 83 DX35
Aspen Way, Felt. 175 BV90
Aspenlea Rd. W6 159 CX79
Aspern Gro. NW3 120 DE64
Aspinall Rd. SE4 163 DX83
Aspinden Rd. SE16 162 DV77
Aspley Rd. SW18 180 DB85
Aspley Way NW2 119 CU61
Asplins Rd. N17 100 DU53
Asquith Clo., Dag. 126 EW60
Crystal Way
Ass Ho. La., Har. 94 CB49
Assam St. E1 142 DU72
White Ch. La.
Assata Ms. N1 141 DP65
St. Paul's Rd.
Assembly Pas. E1 142 DW71
Assembly Wk., Cars. 200 DE101
Assher Rd., Walt. 196 BY104
Assheton Rd., Beac. 89 AK51
Assurance Cotts., Belv. 166 EZ78
Heron Hill
Astall Clo., Har. 95 CE53
Sefton Ave.
Astbury Rd. SE15 162 DW81
Aste St. E14 163 EC75
Astell St. SW3 276 C10
Astell St. SW3 160 DE78
Asteys Row N1 141 DP66
River Pl.
Asthall Gdns., Ilf. 125 EQ56
Astle St. SW11 160 DG82
Astleham Rd., Shep. 194 BL97
Astley, Grays 170 FZ79
Astley Ave. NW2 119 CW64
Astley Rd., Hem.H. 40 BJ20
Aston Ave., Har. 117 CJ59
Aston Clo., Ash. 231 CJ118
Aston Clo., Sid. 186 EU90
Aston Clo., Wat. 76 BW40
Reeds Cres.
Aston Clo. (Bushey), Wat. 76 CC44
Chiltern Ave.
Aston Grn., Houns. 156 BW82
Aston Mead, Wind. 151 AL81
Aston Ms., Rom. 126 EW59
Reynolds Ave.
Aston Rd. SW20 199 CW96
Aston Rd. W5 137 CK72
Aston Rd., Esher 215 CE106
Aston St. E14 143 DY72
Aston Way, Epsom 233 CT116
Aston Way, Pot.B. 64 DD32
Astons Rd., Nthwd. 93 BQ48
Astonville St. SW18 180 DA88
Astor Ave., Rom. 127 FC58
Astor Clo., Add. 212 BK105
Astor Clo., Kings.T. 178 CP93
Astoria Wk. SW9 161 DN83
Astra Clo., Horn. 147 FH65
Astra Dr., Grav. 191 GL92
Astrop Ms. W6 159 CW76
Astrop Ter. W6 159 CW75
Astwick Ave., Hat. 45 CT15
Astwood Ms. SW7 160 DB77
Asylum Arch Rd., Red. 266 DF137
Asylum Rd. SE15 162 DV80
Atalanta Clo., Pur. 219 DN110
Atalanta St. SW6 159 CX81
Atbara Ct., Tedd. 177 CH93
Atbara Rd., Tedd. 177 CH93
Atcham Rd., Houns. 156 CC84
Atcost Rd., Bark. 146 EU71
Atheldene Rd. SW18 180 DC87
Athelney St. SE6 183 EA90
Athelstan Clo., Rom. 106 FM54
Athelstan Rd.
Athelstan Rd., Kings.T. 198 CM98
Athelstan Rd., Rom. 106 FM53
Athelstan Wk. N., Welw.G.C. 29 CY10
Athelstan Wk. S., Welw.G.C. 29 CX10
Athelstane Gro. E3 143 DZ68
Athelstane Ms. N4 121 DN60
Stroud Grn. Rd.
Athelstone Rd., Har. 95 CD54
Athelstone Rd., Hem.H. 40 BM23
Athena Clo., Har. 117 CE61
Byron Hill Rd.
Athena Pl., Nthwd. 93 BT53
The Dr.
Athenaeum Pl. N10 121 DH55
Fortis Grn. Rd.
Athenaeum Rd. N20 98 DC46
Athenlay Rd. SE15 183 DX85
Athens Gdns. W9 140 DA70
Elgin Ave.
Atherden Rd. E5 122 DW63
Atherfield Rd., Reig. 266 DC137
Atherfold Rd. SW9 161 DL83
Atherley Way, Houns. 176 BZ87
Atherstone Ms. SW7 160 DC77
Atherton Clo., Guil. 258 AY140
Atherton Clo., Stai. 174 BK86
Atherton Ct. (Eton), Wind. 151 AR80
Meadow La.
Atherton Dr. SW19 179 CX91
Atherton Gdns., Grays 171 GJ77
Atherton Heights, Wem. 137 CJ65
Atherton Ms. E7 144 EF65
Atherton Pl., Har. 117 CD55
Atherton Pl., Sthl. 136 CB73
Longford Ave.
Atherton Rd. E7 144 EF65
Atherton Rd. SW13 159 CU80
Atherton Rd., Ilf. 102 EL54
Atherton St. SW11 160 DE82
Athlon Rd., Wem. 137 CK68
Athlone, Esher 215 CE107
Athlone Clo. E5 122 DV63
Goulton Rd.
Athlone Clo., Rad. 77 CG36
Athlone Rd. SW2 181 DM87
Athlone Sq., Wind. 151 AQ81
Alma Rd.
Athlone St. NW5 140 DG65
Athol Clo., Pnr. 93 BV53
Athol Gdns., Pnr. 93 BV53
Athol Rd., Erith 167 FC78
Athol Sq. E14 143 EC72
Athol Way, Uxb. 134 BN69
Athole Gdns., Enf. 82 DS43
Atholl Rd., Ilf. 126 EU59
Atkins Clo., Wok. 226 AU118
Greythorne Rd.
Atkins Dr., W.Wick. 203 ED103
Atkins Rd. E10 123 EB58
Atkins Rd. SW12 181 DK87
Atkinson Clo., Orp. 224 EU106
Martindale Ave.
Atkinson Rd. E16 144 EJ71
Atlanta Boul., Rom. 127 FE58
Atlantic Rd. SW9 161 DN84
Atlas Gdns. SE7 164 EJ77
Atlas Ms. E8 142 DT65
Tyssen St.
Atlas Ms. N7 141 DM65
Atlas Rd. E13 144 EG68
Atlas Rd. NW10 138 CS69
Atlas Rd., Dart. 168 FM83
Cornwall Rd.
Atlas Rd., Wem. 118 CQ63
Atley Rd. E3 143 EA67
Atlip Rd., Wem. 138 CL67
Atney Rd. SW15 159 CY84
Atria Rd., Nthwd. 93 BU50
Atterbury Clo., West. 255 ER126
Atterbury Rd. N4 121 DN58
Atterbury St. SW1 277 P9
Atterbury St. SW1 161 DL77
Attewood Ave. NW10 118 CS62
Attewood Rd., Nthlt. 136 BY65
Attfield Clo. N20 98 DD47
Attimore Clo., Welw.G.C. 29 CV10
Attimore Rd., Welw.G.C. 29 CV10
Attle Clo., Uxb. 134 BN68
Attlee Clo., Hayes 135 BV69
Attlee Clo., Th.Hth. 202 DQ99
Kynaston Ave.
Attlee Ct., Grays 170 GA76
Lucas Rd.
Attlee Dr., Dart. 188 FN85
Attlee Rd. SE28 146 EV73
Attlee Rd., Hayes 135 BU69
Attlee Ter. E17 123 EB56
Attneave St. WC1 274 D3
Attwood Clo., S.Croy. 220 DV114
Atwater Clo. SW2 181 DN88
Atwell Clo. E10 123 EB58
Belmont Pk. Rd.
Atwell Rd. SE15 162 DU82
Rye La.
Atwell's Yd., Uxb. 134 BK66
George St.
Atwood, Lthd. 230 BY124
Atwood Ave., Rich. 158 CN82
Atwood Rd. W6 159 CV77
Aubert Pk. N5 121 DP63
Aubert Rd. N5 121 DP63
Aubretia Clo., Rom. 106 FL53
Aubrey Ave., St.Alb. 61 CJ26
Aubrey Pl. NW8 140 DC68
Violet Hill
Aubrey Rd. E17 123 EA55
Aubrey Rd. N8 121 DL57
Aubrey Rd. W8 139 CZ74
Aubrey Wk. W8 139 CZ74
Aubreys Rd., Hem.H. 39 BE20
Aubyn Hill SE27 182 DQ91
Aubyn Sq. SW15 159 CU84
Auckland Ave., Rain. 147 FF69
Auckland Clo. SE19 202 DT95
Auckland Clo., Enf. 82 DV37
Auckland Clo., Til. 171 GG82
Auckland Gdns. SE19 202 DS95
Auckland Hill SE27 182 DQ91
Auckland Ri. SE19 202 DS95
Auckland Rd. E10 123 EB62
Auckland Rd. SE19 202 DT95
Auckland Rd. SW11 160 DE84
Auckland Rd., Cat. 236 DS122
Auckland Rd., Ilf. 125 EP60
Auckland Rd., Kings.T. 198 CM98
Auckland Rd., Pot.B. 63 CX32
Auckland St. SE11 161 DM78
Kennington La.
Auden Pl. NW1 140 DG67
Manley St.
Audleigh Pl., Chig. 103 EN51
Audley Clo. N10 99 DH52
Sydney Rd.
Audley Clo. SW11 160 DG83
Audley Clo., Add. 212 BH106
Audley Clo., Borwd. 78 CN41
Audley Ct. E18 124 EF56
Audley Ct., Pnr. 94 BW54
Audley Dr., Warl. 236 DW115
Audley Firs, Walt. 214 BW105
Audley Gdns., Ilf. 125 ET61
Audley Gdns., Loug. 85 EQ40
Audley Gdns., Wal.Abb. 67 EC34
Audley Pl., Sutt. 218 DB108
Audley Rd. NW4 119 CU58
Audley Rd. W5 138 CM71
Audley Rd., Enf. 81 DP40
Audley Rd., Rich. 178 CM85
Audley Sq. W1 276 G2
Audley Wk., Orp. 206 EW100
Audrey Clo., Beck. 203 EB100
Audrey Gdns., Wem. 117 CH61
Audrey Rd., Ilf. 125 EP62
Audrey St. E2 142 DU68
Audric Clo., Kings.T. 198 CN95
Audwick Clo. (Cheshunt), Wal.Cr. 67 DY28
Augur Clo., Stai. 173 BF92
Augurs La. E13 144 EH69
August End, Slou. 132 AY72
August La., Guil. 260 BK144
Augusta Clo., W.Mol. 196 BZ97
Freeman Dr.
Augusta Rd., Twick. 176 CC89
Augusta St. E14 143 EB72
Augustine Clo., Slou. 153 BE83
Augustine Rd. W14 159 CX76
Augustine Rd., Grav. 191 GJ87
Augustine Rd., Har. 94 CB53
Augustine Rd., Orp. 206 EX97
Augustus Clo., Brent. 157 CK80
Augustus Clo., St.Alb. 42 CA22
Augustus La., Orp. 206 EU103
Augustus Rd. SW19 179 CX88
Augustus St. NW1 273 J1
Augustus St. NW1 141 DH68
Aulton Pl. SE11 161 DN78
Milverton St.
Aultone Way, Cars. 200 DF104
Aultone Way, Sutt. 200 DB103
Aurelia Gdns., Croy. 201 DM99
Aurelia Rd., Croy. 201 DL100
Auriel Ave., Dag. 147 FD65
Auriga Ms. N16 122 DR64
Auriol Clo., Wor.Pk. 198 CS104
Auriol Pk. Rd.
Auriol Dr., Grnf. 137 CD66
Auriol Dr., Uxb. 135 BP65
Auriol Pk. Rd., Wor.Pk. 198 CS104
Auriol Rd. W14 159 CY77
Aurum Clo., Horl. 269 DH149
Austell Gdns. NW7 96 CS48
Austen Clo. SE28 146 EV74
Austen Clo., Green. 189 FW85
Austen Clo., Loug. 85 ER41
Austen Clo., Til. 171 GJ82
Coleridge Rd.
Austen Gdns., Dart. 168 FM84
Keyes Rd.
Austen Ho. NW6 140 DA69
Austen Rd., Guil. 259 AZ135
Austen Rd., Har. 116 CB61
Austenway, Ger.Cr. 112 AY55
Austenwood Clo., Ger.Cr. 90 AW54
Austenwood La., Ger.Cr. 90 AX54
Austin Ave., Brom. 204 EL99
Austin Clo. SE23 183 DZ87
Austin Clo., Couls. 235 DP118
Austin Clo., Twick. 177 CJ85
Austin Ct. E6 144 EJ67
Kings Rd.
Austin Friars EC2 275 L8
Austin Friars EC2 142 DR72
Austin Friars Pas. EC2 275 L8
Austin Friars Sq. EC2 275 L8
Austin Rd. SW11 160 DG81
Austin Rd., Grav. 191 GF88
Austin Rd., Hayes 155 BT75
Austin Rd., Orp. 206 EU100
Austin St. E2 275 P3
Austin St. E2 142 DT69
Austin Waye, Uxb. 134 BJ67
Austin's La., Uxb. 115 BQ62
Austins Mead, Hem.H. 57 BB28
Austins Pl., Hem.H. 40 BK19
St. Mary's Rd.
Austral Clo., Sid. 185 ET90
Austral Dr., Horn. 128 FK59
Austral St. SE11 278 F8
Austral St. SE11 161 DP77
Australia Rd. W12 139 CV73
Australia Rd., Slou. 132 AV74
Austyn Gdns., Surb. 198 CP102
Autumn Clo., Enf. 82 DU39
Autumn Clo., Slou. 131 AM74
Autumn Dr., Sutt. 218 DB109
Autumn Glades, Hem.H. 41 BQ22
Autumn Gro., Welw.G.C. 30 DB11
Autumn St. E3 143 EA67
Auxiliaries Way, Uxb. 113 BF57
Avalon Clo. SW20 199 CY96
Whatley Ave.
Avalon Clo. W13 137 CG71
Avalon Clo., Enf. 81 DN40
Avalon Clo., Orp. 206 EX104
Avalon Clo., Wat. 60 BY32
Avalon Rd. SW6 160 DB81
Avalon Rd. W13 137 CG70
Avalon Rd., Orp. 206 EV103
Avard Gdns., Orp. 223 EQ105
Isabella Dr.
Avarn Rd. SW17 180 DF93
Ave Maria La. EC4 274 G9
Ave Maria La. EC4 141 DP72
Avebury, Slou. 131 AN74
Avebury Ct. N1 142 DR67
Poole St.
Avebury Ct., Hem.H. 40 BN18
Avebury Pk., Surb. 197 CK101
Avebury Rd. E11 123 ED60
Southwest Rd.
Avebury Rd. SW19 199 CZ95
Avebury Rd., Orp. 205 ER104
Avebury St. N1 142 DR67
Poole St.
Aveley Bypass, S.Ock. 148 FQ73
Aveley Clo., S.Ock. 149 FR74
Aveley Rd., Rom. 127 FD56
Aveley Rd., Upmin. 148 FP65
Aveline St. SE11 161 DN78
Aveling Clo., Pur. 219 DM113
Aveling Pk. Rd. E17 101 EA54
Avelon Rd., Rain. 147 FG67
Avelon Rd., Rom. 105 FD51
Avenell Rd. N5 121 DP62
Avening Rd. SW18 180 DA87
Brathway Rd.
Avening Ter. SW18 180 DA86
Avenons Rd. E13 144 EG70
Avenue, The E4 101 ED51
Avenue, The (Leytonstone) E11 124 EF61
Avenue, The (Wanstead) E11 124 EH58
Avenue, The N3 98 DA54
Sylvan Ave.
Avenue, The N8 121 DN55
Avenue, The N10 99 DJ54
Avenue, The N11 99 DH50
Avenue, The N17 100 DS54
Avenue, The NW6 139 CX67
Avenue, The SE7 164 EJ80
Avenue, The SE10 163 ED80
Avenue, The SW4 180 DG85
Avenue, The SW11 180 DF87
Bellevue Rd.
Avenue, The SW18 180 DE87
Avenue, The W4 158 CS76
Avenue, The W13 137 CH73
Avenue, The, Add. 212 BG110
Avenue, The, Amer. 55 AQ38
Avenue, The, Barn. 79 CY41
Avenue, The, Beck. 203 EB95
Avenue, The, Bet. 248 CN134
Avenue, The, Bex. 186 EX86
Avenue, The, Brwd. 109 FZ50
Avenue, The, Brom. 204 EK97
Avenue, The, Cars. 218 DG108
Avenue, The, Couls. 235 DK115
Avenue, The, Croy. 202 DS104
Avenue, The, Egh. 173 BB91
Avenue, The, Epsom 217 CV108
Avenue, The, Esher 215 CE107
Avenue, The, Grav. 191 GG88
Avenue, The, Green. 169 FV84
Avenue, The, Guil. 242 AS127
Avenue, The, Hmptn. 176 BZ93
Avenue, The, Har. 95 CF53
Avenue, The, Hem.H. 39 BE19
Avenue, The, Hert. 31 DP07
Avenue, The, Hodd. 49 DZ19
Avenue, The, Horl. 268 DF149
Avenue, The, Horn. 128 FJ61
Avenue, The, Houns. 176 CB85
Avenue, The (Cranford), Houns. 155 BU81
Avenue, The, Islw. 157 CD80
Jersey Rd.
Avenue, The, Kes. 204 EK104
Avenue, The, Lthd. 215 CF112
Avenue, The, Loug. 84 EK44
Avenue, The, Maid. 130 AC69
Avenue, The, Nthwd. 93 BQ51
Avenue, The, Orp. 205 ET103
Avenue, The (St. Paul's Cray), Orp. 186 EV94
Avenue, The, Pnr. 116 BZ58
Avenue, The (Hatch End), Pnr. 94 BZ51
Avenue, The, Pot.B. 63 CZ30
Avenue, The, Rad. 61 CG33
Avenue, The, Red. 267 DL137
Avenue, The, Rich. 158 CM82
Avenue, The, Rom. 127 FD56
Avenue, The, Slou. 111 AP63
Avenue, The (Datchet), Slou. 152 AV81
Avenue, The, Stai. 194 BH95
Avenue, The (Sunnymeads), Stai. 152 AX83
Avenue, The, Sun. 195 BV95
Avenue, The, Surb. 198 CM100
Avenue, The, Sutt. 217 CY109
Avenue, The (Cheam), Sutt. 217 CV108
Avenue, The, Tad. 233 CV122
Avenue, The, Twick. 177 CH85
Avenue, The (Cowley), Uxb. 134 BK70
Avenue, The (Ickenham), Uxb. 114 BN63
Avenue, The, Wal.Abb. 68 EJ25
Avenue, The, Wat. 75 BU40
Avenue, The (Bushey), Wat. 76 BZ42
Avenue, The, Wem. 118 CL60
Avenue, The, West Dr. 154 BL76
Avenue, The, W.Wick. 203 EC101
Avenue, The, West. 239 EM122
Avenue, The, Whyt. 236 DU119
Avenue, The, Wind. 172 AV85
Avenue, The, Wok. 210 AT109

Balmoral Rd., Wor.Pk. 199 CV104
Balmoral Way, Sutt. 218 DA110
Balmore Cres., Barn. 80 DG43
Balmore St. N19 121 DH61
Balmuir Gdns. SW15 159 CW84
Balnacraig Ave. NW10 118 CS63
Balniel Gate SW1 277 N10
Balniel Gate SW1 161 DK78
Balouhain Clo., Ash. 231 CK117
Balsams Clo., Hert. 32 DR11
Baltic Clo. SW19 180 DD94
Baltic Ct. SE16 163 DX75
Timber Pond Rd.
Baltic St. E. EC1 142 DQ70
Golden La.
Baltic St. W. EC1 142 DQ70
Goswell Rd.
Baltimore Pl., Well. 165 ET82
Balvernie Gro. SW18 179 CZ87
Bamber Ho., Bark. 145 EQ67
St. Margarets
Bamborough Gdns. W12 159 CW75
Bamford Ave., Wem. 138 CM67
Bamford Ct. E15 123 EB64
Clays La.
Bamford Rd., Bark. 145 EQ65
Bamford Rd., Brom. 183 EC92
Bamford Way, Rom. 105 FB50
Bampfylde Clo., Wall. 201 DJ104
Bampton Rd. SE23 183 DX90
Bampton Rd., Rom. 106 FL52
Bampton Way, Wok. 226 AU118
Banavie Gdns., Beck. 203 EC95
Banbury Ave., Slou. 131 AM71
Banbury Clo., Enf. 81 DP39
Holtwhites Hill
Banbury Ct. WC2 273 P10
Banbury Ct., Sutt. 218 DA108
Banbury Enterprise Cen., Croy. 201 DP103
Factory La.
Banbury Rd. E9 143 DX66
Banbury Rd. E17 101 DY52
Banbury St. SW11 160 DE82
Banbury St., Wat. 75 BU43
Banbury Wk., Nthlt. 136 CA68
Brabazon Rd.
Banchory Rd. SE3 164 EH80
Bancroft Ave. N2 120 DE57
Bancroft Ave., Buck.H. 102 EG47
Bancroft Clo., Ashf. 174 BN92
Feltham Hill Rd.
Bancroft Ct., Nthlt. 136 BW67
Bancroft Ct., Reig. 250 DB134
Bancroft Gdns., Har. 94 CC53
Bancroft Gdns., Orp. 205 ET102
Bancroft Rd. E1 143 DX69
Bancroft Rd., Har. 94 CC53
Bancroft Rd., Reig. 250 DA134
Band La., Egh. 173 AZ92
Banders Ri., Guil. 243 BC133
Bandon Ri., Wall. 219 DK106
Banes Down, Wal.Abb. 50 EE22
Bangalore St. SW15 159 CW83
Bangor Clo., Nthlt. 116 CB64
Bangors Clo., Iver 133 BE72
Bangors Rd. N., Iver 133 BD67
Bangors Rd. S., Iver 133 BE69
Banim St. W6 159 CV77
Banister Rd. W10 139 CX69
Bank, The N6 121 DH60
Cholmeley Pk.
Bank Ave., Mitch. 200 DD96
Bank Ct., Dart. 188 FL86
High St.
Bank Ct., Hem.H. 40 BJ21
Marlowes
Bank End SE1 279 J2
Bank End SE1 142 DQ74
Bank La. SW15 178 CS85
Bank La., Kings.T. 178 CL94
Bank Ms., Sutt. 218 DA111
Sutton Ct. Rd.
Bank Mill, Berk. 38 AY19
Bank Mill La., Berk. 38 AY20
Bank Pl., Brwd. 108 FW47
High St.
Bank Rd., H.Wyc. 88 AC47
Bank St., Grav. 191 GH86
Bank St., Sev. 257 FH125
Bankfoot, Grays 170 FZ78
Bankfoot Rd., Brom. 184 EE91
Bankhurst Rd. SE6 183 DZ87
Banks La., Bexh. 166 EZ84
Banks La., Epp. 70 EY33
Bank's La., Lthd. 229 BV122
Banks Rd., Borwd. 78 CQ40
Banks Spur, Slou. 151 AP75
Cooper Way
Banks Way, Guil. 243 AZ131
Banksia Rd. N18 100 DW50
Banksian Wk., Islw. 157 CE81
The Gro.
Bankside SE1 279 H1
Bankside SE1 142 DQ73
Bankside, Enf. 81 DP39
Bankside, Grav. 190 GC86
Bankside, S.Croy. 220 DT107
Bankside, Sthl. 136 BX74
Bankside, Wok. 226 AV118
Wyndham Rd.
Bankside Ave., Nthlt. 135 BU68
Townson Ave.
Bankside Clo., Bex. 187 FD91
Bankside Clo., Cars. 218 DE107
Bankside Clo., Islw. 177 CF85
Twickenham Rd.
Bankside Clo., West. 238 EJ118
Bankside Dr., T.Ditt. 197 CH102
Bankside Way SE19 182 DS93
Lunham Rd.
Bankton Rd. SW2 161 DN84
Bankwell Rd. SE13 164 EE84
Bann Clo., S.Ock. 149 FV73
Banner Clo., Purf. 169 FR77
Brimfield Rd.
Banner St. EC1 275 J5
Banner St. EC1 142 DQ70
Bannerman Ho. SW8 161 DM79
Banning St. SE10 164 EE78
Bannister Clo. SW2 181 DN88
Ewen Cres.
Bannister Clo., Grnf. 117 CD64
Bannister Clo., Slou. 152 AY75
Bannister Dr., Brwd. 109 GC44
Bannister Gdns., Orp. 206 EW97
Main Rd.
Bannister Ho. E9 123 DX64
Homerton High St.
Bannister's Rd., Guil. 258 AT136
Bannockburn Rd. SE18 165 ES77
Banstead Gdns. N9 100 DS48
Banstead Rd., Bans. 217 CX112
Banstead Rd., Cars. 218 DE107
Banstead Rd., Cat. 236 DR122
Banstead Rd., Epsom 217 CV110
Banstead Rd., Pur. 219 DN111
Banstead Rd. S., Sutt. 218 DC111
Banstead St. SE15 162 DW83
Banstead Way, Wall. 219 DL106
Banstock Rd., Edg. 96 CP51
Banton Clo., Enf. 82 DV40
Central Ave.
Bantry St. SE5 162 DR80
Banwell Rd., Bex. 186 EX86
Woodside La.
Banyard Rd. SE16 162 DV76
Southwark Pk. Rd.
Banyards, Horn. 128 FL56
Bapchild Pl., Orp. 206 EW98
Okemore Gdns.
Baptist Gdns. NW5 140 DG65
Queens Cres.
Barandon Wk. W11 139 CX73
Whitchurch Rd.
Barb Ms. W6 159 CW76
Barbara Brosnan Ct. NW8 140 DD68
Grove End Rd.
Barbara Clo., Shep. 195 BP99
Barbara Hucklesby Clo. N22 99 DP54
Russell Ave.
Barbauld Rd. N16 122 DS62
Barbel Clo., Wal.Cr. 67 EA34
Barber Clo. N21 99 DN45
Barberry Clo., Rom. 106 FJ51
Barberry Rd., Hem.H. 40 BG20
Barber's All. E13 144 EH69
Barbers Rd. E15 143 EB68
Barbican, The EC2 275 H6
Barbican, The EC2 142 DQ71
Barbican Rd., Grnf. 136 CB72
Barbon Clo. WC1 274 A6
Barbot Clo. N9 100 DU48
Barchard St. SW18 180 DB85
Barchester Clo. W7 137 CF74
Barchester Clo., Uxb. 134 BJ70
Barchester Rd., Har. 95 CD54
Barchester Rd., Slou. 153 AZ75
Barchester St. E14 143 EB71
Barclay Clo. SW6 160 DA80
Barclay Clo., Hert. 32 DV11
Barclay Clo., Lthd. 230 CB123
Barclay Clo., Wat. 93 BU45
Moor Vw.
Barclay Ct., Hodd. 49 EA18
Barclay Ct., Slou. 151 AQ75
Barclay Oval, Wdf.Grn. 102 EG49
Barclay Path E17 123 EC57
Barclay Rd.
Barclay Rd. E11 124 EE60
Barclay Rd. E13 144 EJ70
Barclay Rd. E17 123 EC57
Barclay Rd. N18 100 DR51
Barclay Rd. SW6 160 DA80
Barclay Rd., Croy. 202 DR104
Barclay Way SE22 182 DU87
Lordship La.
Barclay Way, Grays 169 FT78
Barcombe Ave. SW2 181 DL89
Barcombe Clo., Orp. 206 EU97
Bard Rd. W10 139 CX73
Barden Clo., Uxb. 92 BJ52
Barden St. SE18 165 ES80
Bardeswell Clo., Brwd. 108 FW47
Bardfield Ave., Rom. 126 EX55
Bardney Rd., Mord. 200 DB98
Bardolph Ave., Croy. 221 DY109
Bardolph Rd. N7 121 DL63
Bardolph Rd., Rich. 158 CM83
St. Georges Rd.
Bardon Wk., Wok. 226 AV117
Bampton Way
Bards Cor., Hem.H. 40 BH19
Laureate Way
Bardsey Pl. E1 142 DW71
Bardsey Wk. N1 142 DQ65
Marquess Est.
Bardsley Clo., Croy. 202 DT104
Bardsley La. SE10 163 EC79
Bardwell Ct., St.Alb. 43 CD21
Bardwell Rd., St.Alb. 43 CD21
Barfett St. W10 139 CZ70
Barfield (Sutton at Hone), Dart. 188 FP94
Barfield Ave. N20 98 DF47
Barfield Rd. E11 124 EF60
Barfield Rd., Brom. 205 EN97
Barfields, Loug. 85 EN42
Barfields, Red. 251 DP133
Barfields Gdns., Loug. 85 EN42
Barfields
Barfields Path, Loug. 85 EN42
Barfolds, Hat. 45 CW23
Dixons Hill Rd.
Barford Clo. NW4 97 CU53
Barford St. N1 141 DN67
Barforth Rd. SE15 162 DV83
Barfreston Way SE20 202 DV95
Bargate Clo. SE18 165 ET78
Bargate Clo., N.Mal. 199 CU101
Barge Ho. Rd. E16 165 EP75
Barge Ho. St. SE1 278 E2
Barge Wk., E.Mol. 197 CD97
Barge Wk., Kings.T. 197 CK96
Barge Wk., Walt. 196 BW97
Bargery Rd. SE6 183 EB88
Bargrove Ave., Hem.H. 40 BG21
Bargrove Clo. SE20 182 DU94
Bargrove Cres. SE6 183 DZ89
Elm La.
Barham Ave., Borwd. 78 CM41
Barham Clo., Brom. 204 EL102
Barham Clo., Chis. 185 EP92
Barham Clo., Grav. 191 GM88
Barham Clo., Rom. 105 FB54
Barham Clo., Wem. 137 CH65
Barham Clo., Wey. 213 BQ105
Barham Rd. SW20 179 CU94
Barham Rd., Chis. 185 EP92
Barham Rd., Dart. 188 FN87
Barham Rd., S.Croy. 220 DQ105
Baring Clo. SE12 184 EG89
Baring Cres., Beac. 88 AJ52
Baring Rd. SE12 184 EG87
Baring Rd., Barn. 80 DD42
Baring Rd., Beac. 88 AJ52
Baring Rd., Croy. 202 DU102
Baring St. N1 142 DR67
Bark Burr Rd., Grays 170 FZ75
Bark Hart Rd., Orp. 206 EV102
Bark Pl. W2 140 DB73
Barker Dr. NW1 141 DJ66
Barker Ms. SW4 161 DH84
Victoria Ri.
Barker Rd., Cher. 193 BE101
Barker St. SW10 160 DC79
Barker Wk. SW16 181 DK90
Mount Ephraim Rd.
Barker Way SE22 182 DU88
Dulwich Common
Barkham Rd. N17 100 DR52
Barking Ind. Pk., Bark. 145 ET67
Barking Rd. E6 144 EK68
Barking Rd. E13 144 EG70
Barking Rd. E16 144 EE71
Barkis Way SE16 162 DV78
Egan Way
Barkston Gdns. SW5 160 DB77
Barkston Path, Borwd. 78 CN37
Walshford Way
Barkway Ct. N4 122 DQ62
Queens Dr.
Barkwood Clo., Rom. 127 FC57
Barkworth Rd. SE16 162 DV78
Credon Rd.
Barlborough St. SE14 163 DX80
Barlby Gdns. W10 139 CX70
Barlby Rd. W10 139 CW71
Barle Gdns., S.Ock. 149 FV72
Barlee Cres., Uxb. 134 BJ71
Barley Clo. (Bushey), Wat. 76 CB43
Barley Cft., Harl. 51 ES19
Barley Cft., Hem.H. 41 BQ20
Barley Cft., Hert. 32 DR07
Barley Flds., H.Wyc. 110 AE55
Barley La., Ilf. 126 EU59
Barley La., Rom. 126 EV56
Barley Mow Ct., Bet. 248 CQ134
Barley Mow La., St.Alb. 44 CL23
Barley Mow Pas. EC1 274 G7
Barley Mow Pas. W4 158 CR78
Heathfield Ter.
Barley Mow Rd., Egh. 172 AW91
Barley Mow Way, Shep. 194 BN98
Barley Ponds Clo., Ware 33 DZ06
Barley Ponds Rd., Ware 33 DZ06
Barleycorn Way E14 143 DZ73
Barleycorn Way, Horn. 128 FM58
Barleycroft Grn., Welw.G.C. 29 CW09
Barleycroft Rd., Welw.G.C. 29 CW10
Barleyfields Clo., Rom. 126 EV58
Barleymead, Horl. 269 DH147
Oatlands
Barlow Clo., Wall. 219 DL107
Cobham Clo.
Barlow Pl. W1 277 J1
Barlow Rd. NW6 139 CZ65
Barlow Rd. W3 138 CP74
Barlow Rd., Hmptn. 176 CA94
Barlow St. SE17 279 L9
Barlow Way, Rain. 147 FD71
Barmeston Rd. SE6 183 EB89
Barmor Clo., Har. 94 CB54
Barmouth Ave., Grnf. 137 CF68
Barmouth Rd. SW18 180 DC86
Barmouth Rd., Croy. 203 DX103
Barn Clo., Ashf. 175 BP92
Barn Clo., Bans. 234 DD115
Barn Clo., Epsom 232 CQ115
Barn Clo., Hem.H. 40 BM23
Barnfield
Barn Clo., Nthlt. 136 BW68
Barn Clo., Rad. 77 CG35
Barn Clo., Slou. 111 AP63
Barn Clo., Welw.G.C. 29 CW09
Barn Cres., Pur. 220 DR113
Barn Cres., Stan. 95 CJ51
Barn Elms Pk. SW15 159 CW82
Barn End Dr., Dart. 188 FJ90
Barn End La., Dart. 188 FJ93
Barn Hill, Harl. 50 EH19
Barn Hill, Wem. 118 CN60
Barn Lea, Rick. 92 BG46
Barn Mead, Epp. 85 ES36
Barn Mead, Harl. 51 ER17
Barn Mead, Ong. 71 FE29
Barn Meadow La., Lthd. 230 BZ124
Barn Ms., Har. 116 CA62
Barn Ri., Wem. 118 CN60
Barn St. N16 122 DS62
Stoke Newington Ch. St.
Barn Way, Wem. 118 CN60
Barnabas Ct. N21 81 DN43
Cheyne Wk.
Barnabas Rd. E9 123 DX64
Barnaby Clo., Har. 116 CC61
Barnaby Pl. SW7 160 DD77
Barnaby Way, Chig. 103 EN48
Barnacre Clo., Uxb. 134 BK72
New Peachey La.
Barnacres Rd., Hem.H. 58 BM25
Barnard Acres, Wal.Abb. 50 EE23
Barnard Clo. SE18 165 EN76
Barnard Clo., Chis. 205 ER95
Barnard Clo., Sun. 175 BV94
Oak Gro.
Barnard Clo., Wall. 219 DK108
Alcock Clo.
Barnard Ct., Wok. 226 AS118
Raglan Rd.
Barnard Gdns., Hayes 135 BV70
Barnard Gdns., N.Mal. 199 CU98
Barnard Grn., Welw.G.C. 29 CZ10
Barnard Gro. E15 144 EF66
Vicarage La.
Barnard Hill N10 99 DH53
Barnard Ms. SW11 160 DE84
Barnard Rd. SW11 160 DE84
Barnard Rd., Enf. 82 DV40
Barnard Rd., Mitch. 200 DG97
Barnard Rd., Warl. 237 EB119
Barnard Way, Hem.H. 40 BL22
Barnardo Dr., Ilf. 125 EQ56
Civic Way
Barnardo St. E1 143 DX72
Devonport St.
Barnard's Inn EC1 274 D8
Barnards Pl., S.Croy. 219 DP109
Barnato Clo., W.Byf. 212 BL112
Viscount Gdns.
Barnby Sq. E15 144 EE67
Barnby St.
Barnby St. E15 144 EE67
Barnby St. NW1 273 L2
Barnby St. NW1 141 DJ69
Barncroft Clo., Loug. 85 EM43
Barncroft Clo., Uxb. 135 BP71
Harlington Rd.
Barncroft Grn., Loug. 85 EN43
Barncroft Rd., Berk. 38 AT20
Barncroft Rd., Loug. 85 EN43
Barncroft Way, St.Alb. 43 CG21
Barndicott, Welw.G.C. 30 DC09
Barnehurst Ave., Bexh. 167 FC81
Barnehurst Ave., Erith 167 FC81
Barnehurst Clo., Erith 167 FC81
Barnehurst Rd., Bexh. 167 FC82
Barnes All., Hmptn. 196 CC96
Hampton Ct. Rd.
Barnes Ave. SW13 159 CU80
Barnes Ave., Chesh. 54 AQ30
Barnes Ave., Sthl. 156 BZ77
Barnes Bri. SW13 158 CS82
Barnes Bri. W4 158 CS82
Barnes Clo. E12 124 EK63
Barnes Ct. E16 144 EJ71
Ridgwell Rd.
Barnes Ct., Wdf.Grn. 102 EK50
Barnes Cray Cotts., Dart. 187 FG85
Maiden La.
Barnes Cray Rd., Dart. 167 FG84
Barnes End, N.Mal. 199 CU99
Barnes High St. SW13 159 CT82
Barnes Ho., Bark. 145 ER67
St. Marys
Barnes La., Kings L. 58 BH27
Barnes Ri., Kings L. 58 BM27
Barnes Rd. N18 100 DW49
Barnes Rd., Gdmg. 258 AS143
Barnes Rd., Ilf. 125 EQ64
Barnes St. E14 143 DY72
Barnes Ter. SE8 163 DZ78
Barnes Wallis Dr., Wey. 212 BL111
Barnes Way, Iver 133 BF73
Barnesbury Ho. SW4 181 DK86
Barnesdale Cres., Orp. 206 EU100
Barnet Bypass, Barn. 78 CS39
Barnet Dr., Brom. 204 EL103
Barnet Gate La., Barn. 79 CT44
Barnet Gro. E2 142 DU69
Barnet Hill, Barn. 79 CZ42
Barnet Ho. N20 98 DC47
Barnet La. N20 97 CZ46
Barnet La., Barn. 80 DA44
Barnet La., Borwd. 77 CK44
Barnet Rd. (Arkley), Barn. 78 CR44
Barnet Rd., Pot.B. 64 DB34
Barnet Rd., St.Alb. 62 CL27
Barnet Row, Guil. 242 AX129
Barnet Trd. Est., Barn. 79 CZ41
Barnet Way NW7 96 CR48
Barnet Wd. Rd., Brom. 204 EH103
Barnett Clo., Erith 167 FF82
Barnett Clo., Guil. 259 BC143
Barnett Clo., Lthd. 231 CH119
Barnett La., Guil. 259 BB144
Barnett St. E1 142 DV72
Cannon St. Rd.
Barnett Wd. La., Ash. 231 CJ118
Barnett Wd. La., Lthd. 231 CH120
Barnetts Shaw, Oxt. 253 ED127
Barney Clo. SE7 164 EJ78
Barnfield, Bans. 218 DB114
Sutton La.
Barnfield, Epp. 70 EU28
Barnfield, Hem.H. 40 BM23
Barnfield, Horl. 268 DG149
Barnfield, Iver 133 BE72
Barnfield, N.Mal. 198 CS100
Barnfield, Slou. 131 AK74
Barnfield Ave., Croy. 202 DW103
Barnfield Ave., Kings.T. 178 CL92
Barnfield Ave., Mitch. 201 DH98
Barnfield Clo. N4 121 DL59
Crouch Hill
Barnfield Clo. SW17 180 DC90
Aboyne Rd.
Barnfield Clo., Couls. 236 DQ119
Barnfield Clo., Hodd. 49 EA15
Barnfield Clo., Swan. 207 FC101
Barnfield Clo., Wal.Abb. 50 EF22
Hoe La.
Barnfield Gdns. SE18 165 EP79
Plumstead Common Rd.
Barnfield Gdns., Kings.T. 178 CL92
Barnfield Pl. E14 163 EA77
Barnfield Rd. SE18 165 EP79
Barnfield Rd. W5 137 CJ70
Barnfield Rd., Belv. 166 EZ79
Barnfield Rd., Edg. 96 CQ53
Barnfield Rd., Orp. 206 EX97
Barnfield Rd., St.Alb. 43 CJ17
Barnfield Rd., Sev. 256 FD123
Barnfield Rd., S.Croy. 220 DS109
Barnfield Rd., Welw.G.C. 29 CY11
Barnfield Rd., West. 238 EK120
Barnfield Way, Oxt. 254 EG133
Barnfield Wd. Clo., Beck. 203 ED100
Barnfield Wd. Rd., Beck. 203 ED100
Barnham Rd., Grnf. 136 CC69
Barnham St. SE1 279 N4
Barnham St. SE1 162 DS75
Barnhill, Pnr. 116 BW57
Barnhill Ave., Brom. 204 EF99
Barnhill La., Hayes 135 BV70
Barnhill Rd., Hayes 135 BV70
Barnhill Rd., Wem. 118 CQ62
Barnhurst Path, Wat. 94 BW50
Barningham Way NW9 118 CR58
Barnlea Clo., Felt. 176 BY89
Barnmead, Wok. 210 AT110
Barnmead Gdns., Dag. 126 EZ64
Barnmead Rd., Beck. 203 DY95
Barnmead Rd., Dag. 126 EZ64
Barns Ct., Harl. 51 EN20
Barnsbury Clo., N.Mal. 198 CQ98
Barnsbury Cres., Surb. 198 CP102
Barnsbury Est. N1 141 DN67
Barnsbury Rd.
Barnsbury Gro. N7 141 DM65
Barnsbury La., Surb. 198 CP103
Barnsbury Pk. N1 141 DN66
Barnsbury Rd. N1 141 DN68
Barnsbury Sq. N1 141 DN66
Barnsbury St. N1 141 DN66
Barnsbury Ter. N1 141 DM66
Barnscroft SW20 199 CV97
Barnsdale Ave. E14 163 EB77
Barnsdale Clo., Borwd. 78 CM39
Barnsdale Rd. W9 139 CZ70
Barnsfield Pl., Uxb. 134 BJ67
Barnside Ct., Welw.G.C. 29 CW09
Barnsley Rd., Rom. 106 FM52
Barnsley St. E1 142 DV70
Barnstaple Path, Rom. 106 FJ50
Barnstaple Rd.
Barnstaple Rd., Rom. 106 FJ50
Barnstaple Rd., Ruis. 116 BW62
Barnston Wk. N1 142 DQ67
Popham St.
Barnston Way, Brwd. 109 GC43
Barnsway, Kings L. 58 BL28
Barnway, Egh. 172 AW92
Barnwell Rd. SW2 181 DN85
Barnwell Rd., Dart. 168 FM83
Barnwood Clo. W9 140 DB70
Barnwood Clo., Guil. 242 AS132
Barnwood Clo., Ruis. 115 BR61
Lysander Rd.
Barnwood Ct. E16 144 EG74
North Woolwich Rd.
Barnwood Rd., Guil. 242 AS133
Barnyard, The, Tad. 233 CU124
Baron Gdns., Ilf. 125 EQ55
Baron Gro., Mitch. 200 DE98
Baron Rd., Dag. 126 EX60
Baron St. N1 274 D1
Baron St. N1 141 DN68
Baron Wk. E16 144 EF71
Malmesbury Rd.
Baron Wk., Mitch. 200 DE98
Baroness Rd. E2 142 DT69
Diss St.
Baronet Gro. N17 100 DU53
St. Paul's Rd.
Baronet Rd. N17 100 DU53
Barons, The, Twick. 177 CH86
Barons Ct., Wall. 201 DK104
Whelan Way
Barons Ct. Rd. W14 159 CY78
Barons Gate, Barn. 80 DE44
Barons Hurst, Epsom 232 CQ116
Barons Keep W14 159 CY78
Barons Mead, Har. 117 CE56
Barons Pl. SE1 278 E5
Barons Pl. SE1 161 DN75
Barons Wk., Croy. 203 DY100
Barons Way, Egh. 173 BD93
Barons Way, Reig. 266 DA138
Baronsfield Rd., Twick. 177 CH86
Baronsmead Rd. SW13 159 CU81
Baronsmede W5 158 CM75
Baronsmere Rd. N2 120 DE56
Barque Ms. SE8 163 EA79
Watergate St.
Barr Rd., Grav. 191 GM89
Barr Rd., Pot.B. 64 DC33
Barra Clo., Hem.H. 41 BP23
Barra Hall Circ., Hayes 135 BS72
Barra Hall Rd., Hayes 135 BS73
Barrack La., Wind. 151 AR81
Barrack Path, Wok. 226 AT118
Barrack Rd., Guil. 242 AU132
Barrack Rd., Houns. 156 BX84
Barrack Row, Grav. 191 GH86
Barracks Hill, Amer. 89 AM45
Barracks La., Barn. 79 CY41
High St.
Barrards Way, Beac. 89 AQ51
Barratt Ave. N22 99 DM54
Barratt Ind. Pk., Sthl. 156 CA75
Barratt Way, Har. 117 CD55
Tudor Rd.
Barrenger Rd. N10 98 DF53
Barrens Brae, Wok. 227 BA118
Barrens Clo., Wok. 227 BA119
Barrens Pk., Wok. 227 BA118
Barrett Clo., Rom. 105 FH52
Barrett Rd. E17 123 EC56
Barrett Rd., Lthd. 231 CD124
Barrett St. W1 272 G9
Barrett St. W1 140 DG72
Barretts Grn. Rd. NW10 138 CQ69
Barretts Gro. N16 122 DS64
Barretts Rd., Sev. 241 FD120
Barrhill Rd. SW2 181 DL89
Barricane, Wok. 226 AV119
Barrie Clo., Couls. 235 DJ115
Barrie Est. W2 140 DD73
Craven Ter.
Barrie Twr. W3 158 CQ75
Barriedale SE14 163 DY82
Barrier App. SE7 164 EK76
Barringer Sq. SW17 180 DG91
Barrington Clo. NW5 120 DG64
Grafton Rd.
Barrington Clo., Ilf. 103 EM53
Hurstleigh Gdns.
Barrington Clo., Loug. 85 EQ42
Barrington Rd.
Barrington Ct., Brwd. 109 GC44
Barrington Ct., Dor. 263 CG137
Barrington Rd.
Barrington Grn., Loug. 85 EQ42
Barrington Lo., Wey. 213 BQ106
Barrington Pk. Gdns., Ch.St.G. 90 AX46
Barrington Rd. E12 145 EN65
Barrington Rd. N8 121 DK57
Barrington Rd. SW9 161 DP83
Barrington Rd., Bexh. 166 EX82
Barrington Rd., Dor. 263 CG137
Barrington Rd., Loug. 85 EQ42
Barrington Rd., Pur. 219 DJ112
Barrington Rd., Sutt. 200 DA102
Barrington Vill. SE18 165 EN81
Barrow Ave., Cars. 218 DF108
Barrow Clo. N21 99 DP48
Barrow Grn. Rd., Oxt. 253 EA130
Barrow Hedges Clo., Cars. 218 DE108
Barrow Hedges Way, Cars. 218 DE108
Barrow Hill, Wor.Pk. 198 CS103
Barrow Hill Clo., Wor.Pk. 198 CS103
Barrow Hill
Barrow Hill Rd. NW8 272 B1
Barrow Hill Rd. NW8 140 DE68
Barrow La. (Cheshunt), Wal.Cr. 66 DT30
Barrow Pt. Ave., Pnr. 94 BY54
Barrow Pt. La., Pnr. 94 BY54
Barrow Rd. SW16 181 DK93
Barrow Rd., Croy. 219 DN106
Barrow Wk., Brent. 157 CJ78
Glenhurst Rd.
Barrow Way N7 121 DM62
Barrowdene Clo., Pnr. 94 BY54
Paines La.
Barrowell Grn. N21 99 DP47

Barrowfield Clo. N9	100	DV48
Barrowgate Rd. W4	158	CQ78
Barrows Rd., Harl.	51	EM15
Barrowsfield, S.Croy.	220	DT112
Barrs Rd. NW10	138	CR66
Barry Ave. N15	122	DT58
Craven Pk. Rd.		
Barry Ave., Bexh.	166	EY80
Barry Ave., Wind.	151	AQ80
Barry Clo., Grays	171	GG76
Barry Clo., Orp.	205	ES104
Barry Clo., St.Alb.	60	CB25
Barry Rd. E6	144	EL72
Barry Rd. NW10	138	CQ66
Barry Rd. SE22	182	DU86
Bars, The, Guil.	258	AX135
Barset Rd. SE15	162	DW83
Barson Clo. SE20	182	DW94
Barston Rd. SE27	182	DQ89
Barstow Cres. SW2	181	DM88
Bartel Clo., Hem.H.	41	BR22
Bartelotts Rd., Slou.	131	AK70
Barter St. WC1	**274**	**A7**
Barter St. WC1	141	DL71
Barters Wk., Pnr.	116	BY55
High St.		
Barth Rd. SE18	165	ES77
Bartholomew Clo. EC1	**275**	**H7**
Bartholomew Clo. EC1	142	DQ71
Bartholomew Clo. SW18	160	DC84
Bartholomew Dr., Rom.	106	FK54
Bartholomew La. EC2	**275**	**L9**
Bartholomew Pl. EC1	**275**	**H7**
Bartholomew Rd. NW5	141	DJ65
Bartholomew Sq. E1	142	DV70
Coventry Rd.		
Bartholomew Sq. EC1	**275**	**J4**
Bartholomew Sq. EC1	142	DQ70
Bartholomew St. SE1	**279**	**L7**
Bartholomew St. SE1	162	DR76
Bartholomew Vill. NW5	141	DJ65
Bartholomew Way, Swan.	207	FE97
Bartle Ave. E6	144	EL68
Bartle Rd. W11	139	CY72
Bartlett Clo. E14	143	EA72
Bartlett Ct. EC4	**274**	**E8**
Bartlett Rd., Grav.	191	GG88
Bartlett Rd., West.	255	EQ126
Bartlett St., S.Croy.	220	DR106
Bartletts Mead, Hert.	32	DR06
Bartlow Gdns., Rom.	105	FD53
Barton, The, Cob.	214	BW112
Barton Ave., Rom.	127	FB60
Barton Clo. E6	145	EM72
Brandreth Rd.		
Barton Clo. E9	122	DW64
Churchill Wk.		
Barton Clo. SE15	162	DV83
Kirkwood Rd.		
Barton Clo., Add.	212	BG107
Barton Clo., Bexh.	186	EY85
Barton Clo., Chig.	103	EQ47
Barton Clo., Shep.	195	BP100
Barton Grn., N.Mal.	198	CR96
Barton Meadows, Ilf.	125	EP56
Barton Rd. W14	159	CY78
Barton Rd. (Sutton at Hone), Dart.	188	FP94
Barton Rd., Guil.	259	BA144
Barton Rd., Horn.	127	FG60
Barton Rd., Sid.	186	EY93
Barton Rd., Slou.	153	AZ75
Barton St. SW1	**277**	**P6**
Barton Way, Borwd.	78	CN40
Barton Way, Rick.	75	BP43
Bartons, The, Borwd.	77	CK44
Bartonway NW8	140	DD68
Queen's Ter.		
Bartram Clo., Uxb.	135	BP70
Lees Rd.		
Bartram Rd. SE4	183	DY85
Bartrams La., Barn.	80	DC38
Barville Clo. SE4	163	DY84
St. Norbert Rd.		
Barwell Trd. Est., Chess.	215	CK109
Barwick Rd. E7	124	EH63
Barwood Ave., W.Wick.	203	EB102
Basden Gro., Felt.	176	CA89
Basedale Rd., Dag.	146	EV66
Baseing Clo. E6	145	EN73
Basford Way, Wind.	151	AK83
Bashley Rd. NW10	138	CR70
Basil Ave. E6	144	EL68
Basil Gdns., Croy.	203	DX102
Primrose La.		
Basil St. SW3	**276**	**D6**
Basil St. SW3	160	DF76
Basildene Rd., Houns.	156	BX83
Basildon Ave., Ilf.	103	EN53
Basildon Clo., Sutt.	218	DB109
Basildon Rd. SE2	166	EU78
Basildon Rd., Bexh.	166	EY82
Basildon Sq., Hem.H.	40	BM16
Basin S. E16	145	EQ74
Woolwich Manor Way		
Basing Clo., T.Ditt.	197	CF101
Basing Ct. SE15	162	DT81
Basing Dr., Bex.	186	EZ86
Basing Hill NW11	119	CZ60
Basing Hill, Wem.	118	CM61
Basing Ho., Bark.	145	ER67
St. Margarets		
Basing Ho. Yd. E2	**275**	**N2**
Basing Pl. E2	**275**	**N2**
Basing Rd., Bans.	217	CZ114
Basing Rd., Rick.	91	BF46
Basing St. W11	139	CZ72
Basing Way N3	120	DA55
Basing Way, T.Ditt.	197	CF101
Basingdon Way SE5	162	DR84
Basingfield Rd., T.Ditt.	197	CF101
Basinghall Ave. EC2	**275**	**K7**
Basinghall Ave. EC2	142	DR71
Basinghall Gdns., Sutt.	218	DB109
Basinghall St. EC2	**275**	**K8**
Basinghall St. EC2	142	DQ71
Basire St. N1	142	DQ67
Baskerville Rd. SW18	180	DE87
Basket Gdns. SE9	184	EL85
Baslow Clo., Har.	95	CD53
Baslow Wk. E5	123	DX63
Overbury St.		
Basnett Rd. SW11	160	DG83
Basque Ct. SE16	163	DX75
Poolmans St.		
Bassano St. SE22	182	DT85
Bassant Rd. SE18	165	ET79
Bassein Pk. Rd. W12	159	CT75
Basset Clo., Add.	212	BH110
Basset Ho., Dag.	146	EV67
Bassett Clo., Sutt.	218	DB109
Bassett Gdns., Epp.	71	FB26
Bassett Gdns., Islw.	156	CC80
Bassett Rd. W10	139	CX72
Bassett Rd., Uxb.	134	BJ66
New Windsor St.		
Bassett Rd., Wok.	227	BC116
Bassett St. NW5	140	DG65
Bassett Way, Grnf.	136	CB72
Bassett Way, Slou.	131	AL70
Pemberton Rd.		
Bassetts Clo., Orp.	205	EP104
Bassetts Way, Orp.	223	EP105
Bassil Rd., Hem.H.	40	BK21
Bassingbourne Clo., Brox.	49	DZ20
Bassingburn Wk., Welw.G.C.	29	CZ10
Bassingham Rd. SW18	180	DC87
Bassingham Rd., Wem.	137	CK65
Bassishaw Highwalk EC2	142	DQ71
London Wall		
Basswood Clo. SE15	162	DV83
Linden Gro.		
Bastable Ave., Bark.	145	ES68
Bastion Highwalk EC2	142	DQ71
London Wall		
Bastion Ho. EC2	142	DQ71
London Wall		
Bastion Rd. SE2	166	EU78
Baston Manor Rd., Brom.	204	EH104
Baston Rd., Brom.	204	EH102
Bastwick St. EC1	**275**	**H4**
Bastwick St. EC1	142	DQ70
Basuto Rd. SW6	160	DA81
Bat & Ball Rd., Sev.	257	FJ121
Batavia Clo., Sun.	196	BW95
Batavia Ms. SE14	163	DY80
Goodwood Rd.		
Batavia Rd. SE14	163	DY80
Batavia Rd., Sun.	195	BV95
Batchelor St. N1	141	DN68
Batchelors Way, Amer.	55	AR39
Batchelors Way, Chesh.	54	AP29
Batchwood Dr., St.Alb.	42	CB19
Batchwood Gdns., St.Alb.	43	CD17
Batchwood Grn., Orp.	206	EU97
Batchwood Vw., St.Alb.	42	CC18
Batchworth Heath Hill, Rick.	92	BN49
Batchworth Hill, Rick.	92	BM48
Batchworth La., Nthwd.	93	BP50
Batchworth Roundabout, Rick.	92	BK46
Bate St. E14	143	DZ73
Three Colt St.		
Bateman Clo., Bark.	145	EQ65
Glenny Rd.		
Bateman Ho. SE17	161	DP79
Otto St.		
Bateman Rd. E4	101	EA51
Bateman Rd., Rick.	74	BN44
Bateman St. W1	**273**	**M9**
Bateman's Bldgs. W1	**273**	**M9**
Bateman's Row EC2	**275**	**N4**
Bateman's Row EC2	142	DS70
Bates Clo., Slou.	132	AY72
Bates Cres. SW16	181	DJ94
Bates Cres., Croy.	219	DN106
Bates Rd., Rom.	106	FN52
Bates Wk., Add.	212	BJ107
Bateson St. SE18	165	ES77
Gunning St.		
Bateson Way, Wok.	211	BC114
Batford Clo., Welw.G.C.	30	DB10
Waterford Grn.		
Bath Clo. SE15	162	DV80
Asylum Rd.		
Bath Ct. EC1	**274**	**D5**
Bath Ho. Rd., Croy.	201	DL102
Bath Pas., Kings.T.	197	CK96
St. James Rd.		
Bath Pl. EC2	142	DS69
Rivington St.		
Bath Pl., Barn.	79	CZ41
Bath Rd. E7	144	EK65
Bath Rd. N9	100	DV47
Bath Rd. W4	158	CS77
Bath Rd., Dart.	187	FH87
Bath Rd., Hayes	155	BS81
Bath Rd., Houns.	156	BX82
Bath Rd., Maid.	130	AC72
Bath Rd., Mitch.	200	DD97
Bath Rd., Rom.	126	EY58
Bath Rd., Slou.	131	AK72
Bath Rd. (Colnbrook), Slou.	153	BB79
Bath Rd. (Poyle), Slou.	153	BE81
Bath Rd., West Dr.	154	BK81
Bath St. EC1	**275**	**J3**
Bath St. EC1	142	DQ69
Bath St., Grav.	191	GH86
Bath Ter. SE1	**279**	**H7**
Bath Ter. SE1	162	DQ76
Bathgate Rd. SW19	179	CX90
Baths Rd., Brom.	204	EK98
Bathurst Ave. SW19	200	DB95
Brisbane Ave.		
Bathurst Clo., Iver	153	BF75
Bathurst Gdns. NW10	139	CV68
Bathurst Ms. W2	**272**	**A10**
Bathurst Rd., Hem.H.	40	BK17
Bathurst Rd., Ilf.	125	EP60
Bathurst St. W2	**272**	**A10**
Bathurst St. W2	140	DD73
Bathurst Wk., Iver	153	BE75
Bathway SE18	165	EN77
Batley Clo., Mitch.	200	DF101
Middleton Rd.		
Batley Pl. N16	122	DT62
Batley Rd. N16	122	DT62
Stoke Newington High St.		
Batley Rd., Enf.	82	DR39
Batman Clo. W12	139	CV74
Baton Clo., Purf.	169	FR77
Brimfield Rd.		
Batoum Gdns. W6	159	CW76
Batson St. W12	159	CU75
Batsworth Rd., Mitch.	200	DD97
Batten Ave., Wok.	226	AS119
Batten Clo. E6	145	EM72
Savage Gdns.		
Batten St. SW11	160	DE83
Battenburg Wk. SE19	182	DS92
Brabourne Clo.		
Batterdale, Hat.	45	CW17
Battersby Rd. SE6	183	ED89
Battersea Bri. SW3	160	DD80
Battersea Bri. SW11	160	DE80
Battersea Bri. Rd. SW11	160	DE80
Battersea Ch. Rd. SW11	160	DD81
Battersea High St. SW11	160	DD81
Battersea Pk. SW11	160	DF80
Battersea Pk. Rd. SW8	161	DH81
Battersea Pk. Rd. SW11	160	DE82
Battersea Ri. SW11	180	DD85
Battersea Sq. SW11	160	DD81
Battersea High St.		
Battery Rd. SE28	165	ES75
Battis, The, Rom.	127	FE58
Waterloo Rd.		
Battishill Gdns. N1	141	DP66
Waterloo Ter.		
Battishill St. N1	141	DP66
Waterloo Ter.		
Battle Bri. La. SE1	**279**	**M3**
Battle Bri. La. SE1	142	DS74
Battle Bri. Rd. NW1	**273**	**P1**
Battle Bri. Rd. NW1	141	DL68
Battle Clo. SW19	180	DC93
North Rd.		
Battle Rd., Belv.	167	FC77
Battle Rd., Erith	167	FC77
Battlebridge La., Red.	251	DH130
Battledean Rd. N5	121	DP64
Battlefield Rd., St.Alb.	43	CF18
Battlemead Clo., Maid.	130	AC68
Battlers Grn. Dr., Rad.	77	CE37
Batts Hill, Red.	250	DE132
Batts Hill, Reig.	250	DD132
Batty St. E1	142	DU72
Baudwin Rd. SE6	184	EE89
Baugh Rd., Sid.	186	EW92
Baulk, The SW18	180	DA87
Bavant Rd. SW16	201	DM96
Bavaria Rd. N19	121	DL61
Bavent Rd. SE5	162	DQ82
Bawdale Rd. SE22	182	DT85
Bawdsey Ave., Ilf.	125	ET56
Bawtree Clo., Sutt.	218	DC110
Bawtree Rd. SE14	163	DY80
Bawtree Rd., Uxb.	134	BK65
Bawtry Rd. N20	98	DF48
Baxendale N20	98	DC47
Baxendale St. E2	142	DU69
Baxter Ave., Red.	250	DE134
Baxter Clo., Uxb.	135	BP69
Baxter Rd. E16	144	EJ72
Baxter Rd. N1	142	DR65
Baxter Rd. N18	100	DV49
Baxter Rd. NW10	138	CS70
Baxter Rd., Ilf.	125	EP64
Bay Clo., Horl.	268	DE145
Bay Ct. W5	158	CL76
Popes La.		
Bay Manor La., Grays	169	FT79
Bay Tree Clo., Brom.	204	EJ95
Bay Tree Wk., Wat.	75	BT38
Bayards, Warl.	236	DW118
Baydon Ct., Brom.	204	EF97
Bayeaux, Tad.	233	CX122
Heathcote		
Bayes Clo. SE26	182	DW92
Bayfield Rd. SE9	164	EK84
Bayfield Rd., Horl.	268	DE147
Bayford Clo., Hem.H.	41	BQ15
Bayford Clo., Hert.	32	DQ11
Bayford Grn., Hert.	47	DN17
Bayford La., Hert.	31	DM14
Bayford Ms. E8	142	DV66
Bayford St.		
Bayford Rd. NW10	139	CX69
Bayford St. E8	142	DV66
Bayham Pl. NW1	141	DJ67
Bayham Rd. W4	158	CR76
Bayham Rd. W13	137	CH73
Bayham Rd., Mord.	200	DB98
Bayham Rd., Sev.	257	FJ123
Bayham St. NW1	141	DJ67
Bayhorne La., Horl.	269	DJ150
Bayhurst Dr., Nthwd.	93	BT51
Bayley Cres., Slou.	130	AG71
Bayley St. WC1	**273**	**M7**
Bayley St. WC1	141	DK71
Bayley Wk. SE2	166	EY78
Woolwich Rd.		
Bayleys Mead, Brwd.	109	GC47
Baylie Ct., Hem.H.	40	BL19
Baylie La.		
Baylie La., Hem.H.	40	BL19
Baylin Rd. SW18	180	DB86
Garratt La.		
Baylis Par., Slou.	132	AS72
Oatlands Dr.		
Baylis Rd. SE1	**278**	**D5**
Baylis Rd. SE1	161	DN75
Baylis Rd., Slou.	131	AR73
Bayliss Ave. SE28	146	EX73
Bayly Rd., Dart.	188	FN86
Baymans Wd., Brwd.	109	FZ47
Bayne Clo. E6	145	EM72
Savage Gdns.		
Bayne Hill, Beac.	89	AR52
Bayne Hill Clo., Beac.	89	AR52
Baynes Clo., Enf.	82	DU39
Baynes Ms. NW3	140	DD65
Belsize La.		
Baynes St. NW1	141	DJ66
Baynham Clo., Bex.	186	EZ86
Bayonne Rd. W6	159	CY79
Bayshill Ri., Nthlt.	136	CB65
Bayston Rd. N16	122	DT62
Bayswater Rd. W2	140	DB73
Baythorne St. E3	143	DZ71
Baytree Clo., Sid.	185	ET88
Baytree Clo., Wal.Cr.	66	DT27
Baytree Ct., Slou.	130	AJ69
Baytree Rd. SW2	161	DM84
Baywood Sq., Chig.	104	EV49
Bazalgette Clo., N.Mal.	198	CR99
Bazalgette Gdns., N.Mal.	198	CR99
Bazely St. E14	143	EC73
Bazile Rd. N21	81	DN44
Beach Gro., Felt.	176	CA89
Beacham Clo. SE7	164	EK78
Beachborough Rd., Brom.	183	EC91
Beachcroft Rd. E11	124	EE62
Beachcroft Way N19	121	DK60
Beachy Rd. E3	143	EA66
Beacon Clo., Bans.	233	CX116
Beacon Clo., Ger.Cr.	90	AY52
Beacon Clo., Uxb.	114	BK64
Beacon Dr., Dart.	189	FV90
Beacon Gate SE14	163	DX82
Kitto Rd.		
Beacon Gro., Cars.	218	DG105
Beacon Hill N7	121	DL64
Beacon Hill, H.Wyc.	88	AD48
Beacon Hill, Purf.	168	FP78
Beacon Hill, Wok.	226	AV119
Beacon Ri., Sev.	256	FG126
Beacon Rd. SE13	183	ED86
Beacon Rd., Erith	167	FH80
Beacon Rd., Houns.	174	BN86
Beacon Rd., Ware	33	EA05
Beacon Way, Bans.	233	CX116
Beacon Way, Rick.	92	BG45
Beaconfield Ave., Epp.	69	ET29
Beaconfield Rd., Epp.	69	ET29
Beaconfield Way, Epp.	69	ET29
Beaconfields, Sev.	256	FF126
Beacons, The, Loug.	85	EN38
Beacons Clo. E6	144	EL71
Oliver Gdns.		
Beaconsfield Clo. N11	98	DG50
Beaconsfield Clo. SE3	164	EG79
Beaconsfield Clo. W4	158	CQ78
Beaconsfield Clo., Hat.	45	CW17
Beaconsfield Common La., Slou.	111	AQ58
Beaconsfield Pl., Epsom	216	CS112
Beaconsfield Rd. E10	123	EC61
Beaconsfield Rd. E16	144	EF70
Beaconsfield Rd. E17	123	DZ58
Beaconsfield Rd. N9	100	DU48
Beaconsfield Rd. N11	98	DG48
Beaconsfield Rd. N15	122	DS56
Beaconsfield Rd. NW10	139	CT65
Beaconsfield Rd. SE3	164	EF80
Beaconsfield Rd. SE9	184	EL89
Beaconsfield Rd. SE17	162	DR79
Beaconsfield Rd. W4	158	CR76
Beaconsfield Rd. W5	157	CJ75
Beaconsfield Rd., Bex.	187	FD89
Beaconsfield Rd., Brom.	204	EK97
Beaconsfield Rd., Croy.	202	DR100
Beaconsfield Rd., Enf.	83	DX37
Beaconsfield Rd., Epsom	232	CR119
Beaconsfield Rd., Esher	215	CE108
Beaconsfield Rd., Hat.	45	CW17
Beaconsfield Rd., Hayes	136	BW74
Beaconsfield Rd., N.Mal.	198	CR96
Beaconsfield Rd., St.Alb.	43	CE20
Beaconsfield Rd., Slou.	131	AQ68
Beaconsfield Rd., Sthl.	136	BX74
Beaconsfield Rd., Surb.	198	CM101
Beaconsfield Rd., Twick.	177	CH86
Beaconsfield Rd., Wok.	227	AZ120
Beaconsfield Ter., Rom.	126	EX58
Beaconsfield Ter. Rd. W14	159	CY76
Beaconsfield Wk. E6	145	EN72
East Ham Manor Way		
Beaconsfield Wk. SW6	159	CZ81
Parsons Grn. La.		
Beacontree Ave. E17	101	ED53
Beacontree Rd. E11	124	EF59
Beadles La., Oxt.	253	ED130
Beadlow Clo., Cars.	200	DD100
Olveston Wk.		
Beadman Pl. SE27	181	DP91
Norwood High St.		
Beadman St. SE27	181	DP91
Beadnell Rd. SE23	183	DX88
Beadon Rd. W6	159	CW77
Beadon Rd., Brom.	204	EG98
Beads Hall La., Brwd.	108	FV42
Beaford Gro. SW20	199	CY97
Beagle Clo., Felt.	175	BV91
Beagle Clo., Rad.	77	CF37
Beagles Clo., Orp.	206	EX103
Beak St. W1	**273**	**L10**
Beak St. W1	141	DJ73
Beal Clo., Well.	166	EU81
Beal Rd., Ilf.	125	EN61
Beale Clo. N13	99	DP50
Beale Pl. E3	143	DZ68
Beale Rd. E3	143	DZ67
Beales La., Wey.	194	BN104
Beales Rd., Lthd.	246	CB127
Bealings End, Beac.	89	AK50
Beam Ave., Dag.	147	FB67
Beam Way, Dag.	147	FD66
Beaminster Gdns., Ilf.	103	EP54
Beamish Clo., Epp.	71	FC25
Beamish Dr. (Bushey), Wat.	94	CC46
Beamish Rd. N9	100	DU46
Beamish Rd., Orp.	206	EW101
Bean La., Dart.	189	FV89
Bean Rd., Bexh.	166	EX84
Bean Rd., Green.	189	FV85
Beanacre Clo. E9	143	DZ65
Beane Rd., Hert.	31	DP09
Beanshaw SE9	185	EN91
Beansland Gro., Rom.	104	EY54
Bear All. EC4	**274**	**F8**
Bear Clo., Rom.	127	FB58
Stanford Clo.		
Bear Gdns. SE1	**279**	**H2**
Bear Gdns. SE1	142	DQ74
Bear La. SE1	**278**	**G3**
Bear La. SE1	141	DP74
Bear Rd., Felt.	176	BX92
Bear St. WC2	**273**	**N10**
Beard Rd., Kings.T.	178	CM92
Beardell St. SE19	182	DT93
Beardow Gro. N14	81	DJ44
Beard's Hill, Hmptn.	196	CA95
Beard's Hill Clo., Hmptn.	196	CA95
Beard's Hill		
Beards Rd., Ashf.	175	BS93
Beardsfield E13	144	EG67
Valetta Gro.		
Beardsley Way W3	158	CR75
Bearfield Rd., Kings.T.	178	CL94
Bearing Clo., Chig.	104	EU49
Bearing Way, Chig.	104	EU49
Bears Den, Tad.	233	CZ122
Bearstead Ri. SE4	183	DZ85
Bearstead Ter., Beck.	203	EA95
Copers Cope Rd.		
Bearswood End, Beac.	89	AL51
Bearwood Clo., Add.	212	BG107
Ongar Pl.		
Bearwood Clo., Pot.B.	64	DD31
Beasley's Ait La., Sun.	195	BT100
Beasleys Yd., Uxb.	134	BJ66
Warwick Pl.		
Beatrice Ave. SW16	201	DM96
Beatrice Ave., Wem.	118	CL64
Beatrice Clo. E13	144	EG70
Chargeable La.		
Beatrice Clo., Pnr.	115	BU56
Reid Clo.		
Beatrice Ct., Buck.H.	102	EK47
Beatrice Ct., Wem.	118	CM63
Beatrice Gdns., Grav.	190	GE89
Beatrice Pl. W8	160	DB76
Beatrice Rd. E17	123	EA57
Beatrice Rd. N4	121	DN59
Beatrice Rd. N9	100	DW45
Beatrice Rd. SE1	162	DU77
Beatrice Rd., Oxt.	254	EE129
Beatrice Rd., Rich.	178	CM85
Albert Rd.		
Beatrice Rd., Sthl.	136	BZ74
Beatson Wk. SE16	143	DY74
Beattie Clo., Lthd.	230	BZ124
Beattock Ri. N10	121	DH56
Beatty Ave., Guil.	243	BA133
Beatty Rd. N16	122	DS63
Beatty Rd., Stan.	95	CJ51
Beatty St. NW1	141	DJ68
Beattyville Gdns., Ilf.	125	EN55
Beauchamp Clo. W4	158	CQ76
Church Path		
Beauchamp Gdns., Rick.	92	BG46
Beauchamp Pl. SW3	**276**	**C6**
Beauchamp Pl. SW3	160	DE76
Beauchamp Rd. E7	144	EH66
Beauchamp Rd. SE19	202	DR95
Beauchamp Rd. SW11	160	DE84
Beauchamp Rd., E.Mol.	196	CB99
Beauchamp Rd., Sutt.	218	DA105
Beauchamp Rd., Twick.	177	CG87
Beauchamp Rd., W.Mol.	196	CB99
Beauchamp St. EC1	**274**	**D7**
Beauchamp Ter. SW15	159	CV83
Dryburgh Rd.		
Beauclare Clo., Lthd.	231	CK121
Hatherwood		
Beauclerc Rd. W6	159	CV76
Beauclerk Clo., Felt.	175	BV88
Florence Rd.		
Beaudesert Ms., West Dr.	154	BL75
Beaufort E6	145	EN71
Newark Knok		
Beaufort Ave., Har.	117	CG56
Beaufort Clo. E4	101	EB51
Higham Sta. Ave.		
Beaufort Clo. SW15	179	CV87
Beaufort Clo. W5	138	CM71
Beaufort Clo., Epp.	70	FA26
Beaufort Clo., Grays	170	FZ76
Clifford Rd.		
Beaufort Clo., Reig.	249	CZ133
Beaufort Clo., Rom.	127	FC56
Beaufort Clo., Wok.	227	BC116
Beaufort Ct., Rich.	177	CJ91
Beaufort Rd.		
Beaufort Dr. NW11	120	DA56
Beaufort Gdns. NW4	119	CW58
Beaufort Gdns. SW3	**276**	**C6**
Beaufort Gdns. SW3	160	DE76
Beaufort Gdns. SW16	181	DM94
Beaufort Gdns., Houns.	156	BY81
Beaufort Gdns., Ilf.	125	EN60
Beaufort Ms. SW6	159	CZ79
Lillie Rd.		
Beaufort Pk. NW11	120	DA56
Beaufort Pl., Maid.	150	AD75
Beaufort Rd. W5	138	CM71
Beaufort Rd., Kings.T.	198	CL98
Beaufort Rd., Reig.	249	CZ133
Beaufort Rd., Rich.	177	CJ91
Beaufort Rd., Ruis.	115	BR61
Lysander Rd.		
Beaufort Rd., Twick.	177	CJ87
Beaufort Rd., Wok.	227	BC116
Beaufort St. SW3	160	DD79
Beaufort Way, Epsom	217	CU108
Beauforts, Egh.	172	AW92
Beaufoy Rd. N17	100	DS52
Beaufoy Wk. SE11	**278**	**C9**
Beaufoy Wk. SE11	161	DM77
Beaulieu Ave. SE26	182	DV91
Beaulieu Clo. NW9	118	CS55
Beaulieu Clo. SE5	162	DR83
Beaulieu Clo., Houns.	176	BZ85
Beaulieu Clo., Mitch.	200	DG95
Beaulieu Clo., Slou.	152	AV81
Beaulieu Clo., Twick.	177	CK86
Beaulieu Clo., Wat.	94	BW46
Beaulieu Dr., Pnr.	116	BX58
Beaulieu Gdns. N21	100	DQ45
Beaulieu Pl. W4	158	CQ76
Rothschild Rd.		
Beauly Way, Rom.	105	FE53
Beaumanor Gdns. SE9	185	EN91
Beanshaw		
Beaumaris Dr., Wdf.Grn.	102	EK52
Beaumayes Clo., Hem.H.	40	BH21
Beaumont Ave. W14	159	CZ78
Beaumont Ave., Har.	116	CB58
Beaumont Ave., Rich.	158	CM83
Beaumont Ave., St.Alb.	43	CH18
Beaumont Ave., Wem.	117	CJ64
Beaumont Clo., Kings.T.	178	CN94
Beaumont Clo., Rom.	106	FJ54
Beaumont Cres. W14	159	CZ78
Beaumont Cres., Rain.	147	FG65
Beaumont Dr., Ashf.	175	BR92
Beaumont Dr., Grav.	190	GE87
Beaumont Dr., St.Alb.	43	CE18
Beaumont Gdns. NW3	120	DA62
Beaumont Gdns., Brwd.	109	GC44
Bannister Dr.		
Beaumont Gate, Rad.	77	CH35
Shenley Hill		
Beaumont Gro. E1	143	DX70
Beaumont Ms. W1	**272**	**G6**
Beaumont Pk. Rd., Harl.	50	EH15
Beaumont Pl. W1	**273**	**L4**
Beaumont Pl. W1	141	DJ70
Beaumont Pl., Barn.	79	CZ39
Beaumont Pl., Islw.	177	CF85
Beaumont Ri. N19	121	DK59
Beaumont Rd. E10	123	EB59
Beaumont Rd. E13	144	EH69
Beaumont Rd. SE19	182	DQ93
Beaumont Rd. SW19	179	CY87
Beaumont Rd. W4	158	CQ76
Beaumont Rd., Brox.	48	DR24
Beaumont Rd., Orp.	205	ER100
Beaumont Rd., Pur.	219	DN113
Beaumont Rd., Slou.	131	AR70
Beaumont Rd., Wind.	151	AQ82
Beaumont Sq. E1	143	DX70
Beaumont St. W1	**272**	**G6**
Beaumont St. W1	140	DG71
Beaumont Vw. (Cheshunt), Wal.Cr.	66	DR26
Beaumont Wk. NW3	140	DF66

Beaumonts, Red. 266 DF142
Beauvais Ter., Nthlt. 136 BX69
Beauval Rd. SE22 182 DT86
Beaver Clo. SE20 182 DU94
Lullington Rd.
Beaver Clo., Hmptn. 196 CB95
Beaver Gro., Nthlt. 136 BY69
Jetstar Way
Beaver Rd., Ilf. 104 EW50
Beaverbank Rd. SE9 185 ER88
Beavers Clo., Guil. 242 AS133
Beavers Cres., Houns. 156 BX84
Beavers La., Houns. 156 BW82
Beavers La. Camp, Houns. 156 BW83
Beaverwood Rd., Chis. 185 ES93
Beavor La. W6 159 CU77
Bebbington Rd. SE18 165 ES77
Bebletts Clo., Orp. 223 ET106
Bec Clo., Ruis. 116 BX62
Beccles Dr., Bark. 145 ES65
Beccles St. E14 143 DZ73
Beck Clo. SE13 163 EB81
Beck Ct., Beck. 203 DX97
Beck La., Beck. 203 DX97
Beck River Pk., Beck. 203 EA95
Rectory Rd.
Beck Rd. E8 142 DV67
Beck Way, Beck. 203 DZ97
Beckenham Gdns. N9 100 DS48
Beckenham Gro., Brom. 203 ED96
Beckenham Hill Rd. SE6 183 EC92
Beckenham Hill Rd., Beck. 183 EB92
Beckenham La., Brom. 204 EE96
Beckenham Pl. Pk., Beck. 183 EB94
Beckenham Rd., Beck. 203 DX95
Beckenham Rd., W.Wick. 203 EB101
Beckenshaw Gdns., Bans. 234 DD115
Beckers, The N16 122 DU62
Rectory Rd.
Becket Ave. E6 145 EN69
Becket Clo. SE25 202 DU100
Becket Clo., Brwd. 107 FW51
Becket Fold, Har. 117 CF57
Courtfield Cres.
Becket Rd. N18 100 DW49
Becket St. SE1 279 K6
Beckets Sq., Berk. 38 AU17
Bridle Way
Beckett Ave., Ken. 235 DP115
Beckett Clo. NW10 138 CR65
Beckett Clo. SW16 181 DK89
Beckett Clo., Belv. 166 EY76
Tunstock Way
Beckett Wk., Beck. 183 DY93
Becketts, Hert. 31 DN10
Becketts Ave., St.Alb. 42 CC17
Becketts Clo., Felt. 175 BV86
Becketts Clo., Orp. 205 ET104
Becketts Pl., Kings.T. 197 CK95
Beckford Dr., Orp. 205 ER101
Beckford Pl. SE17 162 DQ78
Walworth Rd.
Beckford Rd., Croy. 202 DT100
Beckingham Rd., Guil. 242 AU133
Beckings Way, H.Wyc. 110 AC56
Becklow Gdns. W12 159 CU75
Becklow Rd.
Becklow Rd. W12 159 CT75
Beckman Clo., Sev. 241 FC115
Becks Rd., Sid. 186 EU90
Beckton Retail Pk. E6 145 EN71
Beckton Rd. E16 144 EF71
Beckway Rd. SW16 201 DK96
Beckway St. SE17 279 M9
Beckway St. SE17 162 DR77
Beckwith Rd. SE24 182 DR86
Beclands Rd. SW17 180 DG93
Becmead Ave. SW16 181 DK91
Becmead Ave., Har. 117 CH57
Becondale Rd. SE19 182 DS92
Becontree Ave., Dag. 126 EV63
Bective Pl. SW15 159 CZ84
Bective Rd.
Bective Rd. E7 124 EG63
Bective Rd. SW15 159 CY84
Becton Pl., Erith 167 FB80
Bedale Rd., Enf. 82 DQ38
Bedale Rd., Rom. 106 FN50
Bedale St. SE1 279 K3
Bedale St. SE1 142 DR74
Bedale Wk., Dart. 188 FP88
Princes Ave.
Beddington Fm. Rd., Croy. 201 DL101
Beddington Gdns., Cars. 218 DG107
Beddington Gdns., Wall. 219 DH107
Beddington Grn., Orp. 205 ET95
Beddington Gro., Wall. 219 DK106
Beddington La., Croy. 201 DJ99
Beddington Path, Orp. 205 ET95
Beddington Rd., Ilf. 125 ET59
Beddington Rd., Orp. 205 ES95
Beddington Trd. Pk. W., Croy. 201 DL102
Beddington Fm. Rd.
Beddlestead La., Warl. 238 EF117
Bede Clo., Pnr. 94 BX53
Bede Rd., Rom. 126 EW58
Bedenham Way SE15 162 DT80
Daniel Gdns.
Bedens Rd., Sid. 186 EY93
Bedfont Clo., Felt. 175 BQ86
Bedfont Clo., Mitch. 200 DG96
Bedfont Ct., Stai. 154 BH84
Bedfont Ct. Est., Stai. 154 BG83
Bedfont Grn. Clo., Felt. 175 BQ88
Bedfont La., Felt. 175 BS87
Bedfont Rd., Felt. 175 BQ88
Bedfont Rd., Stai. 174 BL86
Bedford Ave. WC1 273 N7
Bedford Ave. WC1 141 DK71
Bedford Ave., Amer. 72 AW39
Bedford Ave., Barn. 79 CZ43
Bedford Ave., Hayes 135 BV72
Bedford Ave., Slou. 131 AM72
Bedford Clo. N10 98 DG52
Bedford Clo., Rick. 73 BB38
Bedford Cor. W4 158 CS77
The Ave.
Bedford Ct. WC2 277 P1
Bedford Cres., Enf. 83 DY35
Bedford Dr., Slou. 111 AP64
Bedford Gdns. W8 140 DA74
Bedford Gdns., Horn. 128 FJ61
Bedford Hill SW12 181 DH88
Bedford Hill SW16 181 DH88
Bedford Ho. SW4 161 DL84
Bedford Pk., Croy. 202 DQ102
Bedford Pk. Rd., St.Alb. 43 CE20
Bedford Pas. SW6 159 CY80
Dawes Rd.
Bedford Pl. WC1 273 P6
Bedford Pl. WC1 141 DL71
Bedford Pl., Croy. 202 DR102
Bedford Rd. E6 145 EN67
Bedford Rd. E17 101 EA54
Bedford Rd. E18 102 EG54
Bedford Rd. N2 120 DE55
Bedford Rd. N8 121 DK58
Bedford Rd. N9 100 DV45
Bedford Rd. N15 122 DS56
Bedford Rd. N22 99 DL53
Bedford Rd. NW7 96 CS47
Bedford Rd. SW4 161 DL83
Bedford Rd. W4 158 CR76
Bedford Rd. W13 137 CH73
Bedford Rd., Dart. 188 FN87
Bedford Rd., Grav. 191 GF89
Bedford Rd., Grays 170 GB78
Bedford Rd., Guil. 258 AW135
Bedford Rd., Har. 116 CC58
Bedford Rd., Ilf. 125 EP62
Bedford Rd., Nthwd. 93 BQ48
Bedford Rd., Orp. 206 EV103
Bedford Rd., Ruis. 115 BT63
Bedford Rd., St.Alb. 43 CE21
Bedford Rd., Sid. 185 ES90
Bedford Rd., Twick. 177 CD90
Bedford Rd., Wor.Pk. 199 CW103
Bedford Row WC1 274 C6
Bedford Row WC1 141 DM71
Bedford Sq. WC1 273 N7
Bedford Sq. WC1 141 DK71
Bedford St. WC2 273 P10
Bedford St. WC2 141 DL73
Bedford St., Berk. 38 AX19
Bedford St., Wat. 75 BV39
Bedford Ter. SW2 181 DL85
Lyham Rd.
Bedford Way WC1 273 N5
Bedford Way WC1 141 DK70
Bedfordbury WC2 277 P1
Bedgebury Gdns. SW19 179 CY89
Bedgebury Rd. SE9 164 EK84
Bedivere Rd., Brom. 184 EG90
Bedlow Way, Croy. 219 DM105
Bedmond Grn., Abb.L. 59 BT27
Bedmond La., St.Alb. 42 BZ22
Bedmond La. (Potterscrouch), St.Alb. 42 BW24
Bedmond Rd., Abb.L. 59 BT29
Bedmond Rd., Hem.H. 41 BQ21
Bedonwell Rd. SE2 166 EY79
Bedonwell Rd., Belv. 166 EY79
Bedonwell Rd., Bexh. 166 EZ81
Bedser Clo. SE11 161 DM79
Harleyford Rd.
Bedser Clo., Th.Hth. 202 DQ97
Norbury Ave.
Bedser Dr., Grnf. 117 CD64
Bedster Gdns., W.Mol. 196 CB96
Bedwardine Rd. SE19 182 DS94
Bedwell Ave., Hat. 46 DG18
Bedwell Ave., Hert. 46 DG17
Bedwell Clo., Welw.G.C. 29 CY10
Bedwell Gdns., Hayes 155 BS78
Bedwell Rd. N17 100 DS53
Bedwell Rd., Belv. 166 FA78
Bedwin Way SE16 162 DV78
Catlin St.
Beeby Rd. E16 144 EH71
Beech Ave. N20 98 DE46
Beech Ave. W3 138 CS74
Beech Ave., Brent. 157 CH80
Beech Ave., Brwd. 109 FZ48
Beech Ave., Buck.H. 102 EH47
Beech Ave., Enf. 81 DN35
Beech Ave., Lthd. 246 BX128
Beech Ave., Rad. 61 CG33
Beech Ave., Ruis. 115 BV60
Beech Ave., Sid. 186 EU87
Beech Ave., S.Croy. 220 DR111
Beech Ave., Swan. 207 FF98
Beech Ave., Upmin. 128 FP62
Beech Ave., West. 238 EK119
Westmore Rd.
Beech Bottom, St.Alb. 43 CD17
Beech Clo. N9 82 DU44
Beech Clo. SE8 163 DZ79
Clyde St.
Beech Clo. SW15 179 CU87
Beech Clo. SW19 179 CW93
Beech Clo., Ashf. 175 BR92
Beech Clo., Cars. 200 DF103
Beech Clo., Cob. 214 CA112
Beech Clo., Dor. 263 CG135
Beech Clo., Hat. 45 CU19
Beech Clo., Horn. 127 FH62
Beech Clo., Lthd. 246 BX128
Beech Clo., Stai. 174 BK87
St. Marys Cres.
Beech Clo., Sun. 196 BX96
Harfield Rd.
Beech Clo., Walt. 214 BW105
Beech Clo., Ware 33 DX08
Beech Clo., W.Byf. 212 BL112
Beech Clo., West Dr. 154 BN76
Beech Clo. Ct., Cob. 214 BZ111
Beech Copse, Brom. 205 EM96
Beech Copse, S.Croy. 220 DS106
Beech Ct. E17 123 ED55
Beech Ct. SE9 184 EL86
Beech Ct., Ilf. 125 EN62
Riverdene Rd.
Beech Cres., Tad. 248 CQ130
Beech Dell, Kes. 223 EM105
Beech Dr. N2 98 DF54
Beech Dr., Berk. 38 AW20
Beech Dr., Borwd. 78 CM40
Beech Dr., Reig. 250 DD134
Beech Dr., Saw. 36 EW07
Beech Dr., Tad. 233 CZ122
Beech Dr., Wok. 228 BG124
Beech Fm. Rd., Warl. 237 EC120
Beech Gdns. W5 158 CL75
Beech Gdns., Dag. 147 FB66
Beech Gdns., Wok. 226 AY115
Beech Gro., Add. 212 BH105
Beech Gro., Amer. 55 AQ39
Beech Gro., Cat. 252 DS126
Beech Gro., Croy. 221 DY110
Beech Gro., Epsom 233 CV117
Beech Gro., Guil. 242 AT134
Beech Gro., Ilf. 103 ES51
Beech Gro., Mitch. 201 DK99
Beech Gro., N.Mal. 198 CR97
Beech Gro., S.Ock. 148 FQ74
Beech Gro., Wok. 226 AX123
Beech Hall Cres. E4 101 ED52
Beech Hall Rd. E4 101 EC52
Beech Hill, Barn. 80 DD38
Beech Hill, Wok. 226 AX123
Beech Hill Ave., Barn. 80 DC39
Beech Hill Ct., Berk. 38 AX18
Beech Hill Gdns., Wal.Abb. 84 EH37
Beech Holt, Lthd. 231 CJ122
Beech Ho., Croy. 221 EB107
Beech Ho. Rd., Croy. 202 DR104
Beech Hyde La., St.Alb. 28 CM07
Beech La., Beac. 90 AS52
Beech La., Buck.H. 102 EH47
Beech La., Guil. 258 AW137
Beech Lawns N12 98 DD50
Beech Lo., Stai. 173 BE92
Beech Pk., Amer. 72 AV39
Beech Pl., Epp. 69 ET31
Beech Pl., St.Alb. 43 CD17
Beech Rd. N11 99 DL51
Beech Rd. SW16 201 DL96
Beech Rd., Dart. 188 FK88
Beech Rd., Epsom 233 CT115
Beech Rd., Felt. 175 BS87
Beech Rd., Orp. 224 EU108
Beech Rd., Red. 251 DJ126
Beech Rd., Reig. 250 DA131
Beech Rd., St.Alb. 43 CE17
Beech Rd., Sev. 257 FH125
Victoria Rd.
Beech Rd., Slou. 152 AY75
Beech Rd., Wat. 75 BU37
Beech Rd., West. 238 EH118
Beech Rd., Wey. 213 BR105
Beech Row, Rich. 178 CL91
Beech St. EC2 275 H6
Beech St. EC2 142 DQ71
Beech St., Rom. 127 FC56
Beech Tree Glade E4 102 EF46
Forest Side
Beech Wk. NW7 96 CS51
Beech Wk., Dart. 167 FG84
Beech Wk., Epsom 217 CU111
Beech Wk., Hodd. 49 DZ17
Beech Way NW10 138 CR66
Beech Way, Epsom 233 CT115
Beech Way, S.Croy. 221 DX113
Beech Way, Twick. 176 CA90
Beech Waye, Ger.Cr. 113 AZ59
Beechall, Cher. 211 BC108
Beechcroft, Ash. 232 CM119
Beechcroft, Chis. 185 EN94
Beechcroft Ave. NW11 119 CZ59
Beechcroft Ave., Bexh. 167 FD81
Beechcroft Ave., Har. 116 CA59
Beechcroft Ave., Ken. 236 DR115
Beechcroft Ave., N.Mal. 198 CQ95
Beechcroft Ave., Rick. 75 BQ44
Beechcroft Ave., Sthl. 136 BZ74
Beechcroft Clo., Houns. 156 BY80
Beechcroft Clo., Orp. 223 ER105
Beechcroft Gdns., Wem. 118 CM62
Beechcroft Manor, Wey. 195 BR104
Beechcroft Rd. E18 102 EH54
Beechcroft Rd. SW14 158 CQ83
Elm Rd.
Beechcroft Rd. SW17 180 DE89
Beechcroft Rd., Chesh. 54 AN30
Beechcroft Rd., Chess. 216 CM105
Beechcroft Rd., Orp. 223 ER105
Beechcroft Rd. (Bushey), Wat. 76 BY43
Beechdale N21 99 DM47
Beechdale Rd. SW2 181 DM86
Beechdene, Tad. 233 CV122
Beechen Cliff Way, Islw. 157 CF81
Henley Clo.
Beechen Gro., Pnr. 116 BZ55
Beechen Gro., Wat. 75 BV41
Beechen La., Tad. 249 CZ125
Beechenlea La., Swan. 207 FG98
Beeches, The, Amer. 55 AN36
Woodfield Pk.
Beeches, The, Bans. 234 DB116
Beeches, The, Beac. 88 AH54
Beeches, The, Brwd. 108 FV48
Beeches, The, Guil. 259 AZ144
Beeches, The, Lthd. 231 CE124
Beeches, The, Rick. 73 BF43
Beeches, The, St.Alb. 61 CD27
Beeches, The, Til. 171 GH82
Beeches Ave., Cars. 218 DE108
Beeches Clo. SE20 202 DW95
Genoa Rd.
Beeches Clo., Tad. 234 DA123
Beeches Ct., Brom. 184 EG93
Avondale Rd.
Beeches Dr., Slou. 111 AP63
Beeches Pk., Beac. 89 AK53
Burkes Rd.
Beeches Rd. SW17 180 DE90
Beeches Rd., Slou. 111 AP64
Beeches Rd., Sutt. 199 CY102
Beeches Wk., Cars. 218 DD109
Beeches Way, B.End 110 AD61
Harvest Hill
Beeches Wd., Tad. 234 DA122
Beechfield, Bans. 218 DB113
Beechfield, Hodd. 33 EA13
Beechfield, Kings L. 58 BM30
Beechfield, Saw. 36 EZ05
Beechfield Cotts., Brom. 204 EJ96
Widmore Rd.
Beechfield Gdns., Rom. 127 FC59
Beechfield Rd. N4 122 DQ58
Beechfield Rd. SE6 183 DZ88
Beechfield Rd., Brom. 204 EJ96
Beechfield Rd., Erith 167 FE80
Beechfield Rd., Hem.H. 40 BH21
Beechfield Rd., Ware 33 DZ05
Beechfield Rd., Welw.G.C. 29 CY10
Beechfield Wk., Wal.Abb. 83 ED35
Beechhill Rd. SE9 185 EN85
Beechlawn, Guil. 259 AZ135
Beechmeads, Cob. 214 BX113
Beechmont Ave., Vir.W. 192 AX99
Beechmont Clo., Brom. 184 EE92
Beechmont Rd., Sev. 257 FH129
Beechmore Gdns., Sutt. 199 CX103
Beechmore Rd. SW11 160 DF81
Beechmount Ave. W7 137 CD71
Beecholme, Bans. 217 CY114
Beecholme Ave., Mitch. 201 DH95
Beecholme Est. E5 122 DV62
Prout Rd.
Beecholme Ms., Wal.Cr. 67 DX28
Beechpark Way, Wat. 75 BS37
Beechtree Ave., Egh. 172 AV93
Beechtree Clo., Stan. 95 CJ50
Beechtree Pl., Sutt. 218 DB106
St. Nicholas Way
Beechvale Clo. N12 98 DE50
Beechway, Bex. 186 EX86
Beechway, Guil. 243 BB133
Beechway, S.Croy. 221 DX113
Beechwood Ave. N3 119 CZ55
Beechwood Ave., Amer. 72 AW38
Beechwood Ave., Couls. 235 DH115
Beechwood Ave., Grnf. 136 CB69
Beechwood Ave., Har. 116 CB62
Beechwood Ave., Hayes 135 BR73
Beechwood Ave., Orp. 223 ES106
Beechwood Ave., Pot.B. 64 DB33
Beechwood Ave., Rich. 158 CN81
Beechwood Ave., Rick. 73 BB42
Beechwood Ave., Ruis. 115 BT61
Beechwood Ave., St.Alb. 43 CH18
Beechwood Ave., Stai. 174 BH93
Beechwood Ave., Sun. 175 BU93
Beechwood Ave., Tad. 234 DA121
Beechwood Ave., Th.Hth. 201 DP98
Beechwood Ave., Uxb. 134 BM72
Beechwood Ave., Wey. 213 BS105
Beechwood Clo. N9 100 DU47
Winchester Rd.
Beechwood Clo. NW7 96 CR50
Beechwood Clo., Amer. 72 AW39
Beechwood Clo., Hert. 32 DT09
Beechwood Clo., Surb. 197 CK101
Beechwood Clo. (Cheshunt), Wal.Cr. 66 DS26
Beechwood Clo., Wey. 213 BS105
Beechwood Clo., Wok. 226 AS117
Beechwood Ct., Cars. 218 DF105
Beechwood Ct., Sun. 175 BU93
Beechwood Cres., Bexh. 166 EX83
Beechwood Dr., Cob. 214 CA111
Beechwood Dr., Kes. 222 EK105
Beechwood Dr., Wdf.Grn. 102 EF50
Beechwood Gdns. NW10 138 CM69
St. Annes Gdns.
Beechwood Gdns., Cat. 236 DU122
Beechwood Gdns., Har. 116 CB62
Beechwood Gdns., Ilf. 125 EM57
Beechwood Gdns., Rain. 147 FH71
Beechwood Gdns., Slou. 152 AS75
Beechwood Gro. W3 138 CS73
East Acton La.
Beechwood Gro., Surb. 197 CJ101
Beechwood La., Warl. 237 DX119
Beechwood Manor, Wey. 213 BS105
Beechwood Ms. N9 100 DU47
Winchester Rd.
Beechwood Pk. E18 124 EG55
Beechwood Pk., Hem.H. 39 BF24
Beechwood Pk., Lthd. 231 CJ123
Beechwood Ri., Chis. 185 EP91
Beechwood Ri., Wat. 75 BV36
Beechwood Rd. E8 142 DT65
Beechwood Rd. N8 121 DK56
Beechwood Rd., Beac. 88 AJ53
Beechwood Rd., Cat. 236 DU122
Beechwood Rd., Slou. 131 AR71
Beechwood Rd., S.Croy. 220 DS110
Beechwood Rd., Vir.W. 192 AU101
Beechwood Rd., Wok. 226 AS117
Beechwood Vill., Red. 266 DG144
Beechwoods Ct. SE19 182 DT92
Crystal Palace Par.
Beechworth Clo. NW3 120 DA61
Beecot La., Walt. 196 BW103
Beecroft Rd. SE4 183 DY85
Beehive Clo., Borwd. 77 CK44
Beehive Clo., Uxb. 134 BM66
Honey Hill
Beehive Grn., Welw.G.C. 30 DA11
Beehive La., Ilf. 125 EM57
Beehive La., Welw.G.C. 30 DA12
Beehive Pas. EC3 275 M9
Beehive Pl. SW9 161 DN83
Beehive Rd., Stai. 173 BF92
Beehive Rd. (Cheshunt), Wal.Cr. 65 DP28
Beehive Way, Reig. 266 DB138
Beeken Dene, Orp. 223 EQ105
Isabella Dr.
Beel Clo., Amer. 72 AW39
Beeleigh Rd., Mord. 200 DB98
Beesfield La. (Farningham), Dart. 208 FN101
Beeston Clo. E8 122 DU64
Ferncliff Rd.
Beeston Clo., Wat. 94 BX49
Beeston Dr., Wal.Cr. 67 DX27
Beeston Pl. SW1 277 J7
Beeston Pl. SW1 161 DH76
Beeston Rd., Barn. 80 DD44
Beeston Way, Felt. 176 BW86
Beethoven Rd., Borwd. 77 CJ44
Beethoven St. W10 139 CY69
Beeton Clo., Green. 189 FV85
Beeton Clo., Pnr. 94 CA52
Begbie Rd. SE3 164 EJ81
Beggars Bush La., Wat. 75 BR43
Beggars Hill, Epsom 216 CS107
Beggars Hollow, Enf. 82 DR37
Beggars La., Dor. 261 BS139
Beggars La., West. 255 ER125
Beggars Roost La., Sutt. 218 DA107
Begonia Clo. E6 145 EM71
Evelyn Denington Rd.
Begonia Pl., Hmptn. 176 CA93
Gresham Rd.
Begonia Wk. W12 139 CT72
Du Cane Rd.
Beira St. SW12 181 DH87
Beken Ct., Wat. 76 BW35
Bekesbourne St. E14 143 DY72
Ratcliffe La.
Bekesbourne Twr., Orp. 206 EX102
Belcher Rd., Hodd. 49 EA16
Amwell St.
Belchers La., Wal.Abb. 50 EJ24
Belcroft Clo., Brom. 184 EF94
Hope Pk.
Beldam Haw, Sev. 224 FA112
Beldham Gdns., W.Mol. 196 CB97
Belfairs Dr., Rom. 126 EW59
Belfairs Grn., Wat. 94 BX50
Heysham Dr.
Belfast Ave., Slou. 131 AQ72
Belfast Rd. N16 122 DT61
Belfast Rd. SE25 202 DV98
Belfield Gdns., Harl. 52 EW16
Kiln La.
Belfield Rd., Epsom 216 CR109
Belfont Wk. N7 121 DL63
Belford Gro. SE18 165 EN77
Belford Rd., Borwd. 78 CM38
Belfort Rd. SE15 162 DW82
Belfry Ave., Uxb. 92 BG53
Belfry La., Rick. 92 BJ46
Belgrade Rd. N16 122 DS63
Belgrade Rd., Hmptn. 196 CB95
Belgrave Ave., Rom. 128 FJ55
Belgrave Ave., Wat. 75 BT43
Belgrave Clo. N14 81 DJ43
Prince George Ave.
Belgrave Clo. W3 158 CQ75
Avenue Rd.
Belgrave Clo., Orp. 206 EW98
Belgrave Clo., St.Alb. 43 CJ16
Belgrave Clo., Walt. 213 BV105
Belgrave Cres., Sun. 195 BV95
Belgrave Dr., Kings L. 59 BQ28
Belgrave Gdns. N14 81 DK43
Belgrave Gdns. NW8 140 DB67
Belgrave Gdns., Stan. 95 CJ50
Copley Rd.
Belgrave Manor, Wok. 226 AY119
Belgrave Ms., Uxb. 134 BK70
Belgrave Ms. N. SW1 276 F5
Belgrave Ms. N. SW1 160 DG76
Belgrave Ms. S. SW1 276 G6
Belgrave Ms. S. SW1 160 DG76
Belgrave Ms. W. SW1 276 F6
Belgrave Ms. W. SW1 160 DG76
Belgrave Pl. SW1 276 G6
Belgrave Pl. SW1 160 DG76
Belgrave Pl., Slou. 152 AV75
Clifton Rd.
Belgrave Rd. E10 123 EC60
Belgrave Rd. E11 124 EG61
Belgrave Rd. E13 144 EJ69
Belgrave Rd. E17 123 EA57
Belgrave Rd. SE25 202 DU98
Belgrave Rd. SW1 277 K9
Belgrave Rd. SW1 161 DH77
Belgrave Rd. SW13 159 CT80
Belgrave Rd., Houns. 156 BZ83
Belgrave Rd., Ilf. 125 EM60
Belgrave Rd., Mitch. 200 DD97
Belgrave Rd., Slou. 132 AS73
Belgrave Rd., Sun. 195 BV95
Belgrave Sq. SW1 276 F6
Belgrave Sq. SW1 160 DG76
Belgrave St. E1 143 DX71
Belgrave Ter., Wdf.Grn. 102 EG48
Belgrave Wk., Mitch. 200 DD97
Belgrave Yd. SW1 277 H7
Belgravia Gdns., Brom. 184 EE93
Belgravia Ho. SW4 181 DK86
Belgravia Ms., Kings.T. 197 CK98
Belgrove St. WC1 274 A2
Belgrove St. WC1 141 DL69
Belham Rd., Kings L. 58 BM28
Belham Wk. SE5 162 DR81
D'Eynsford Rd.
Belhaven Ct., Borwd. 78 CM39
Belinda Rd. SW9 161 DP83
Belitha Vill. N1 141 DM66
Bell Ave., Rom. 105 FH53
Bell Ave., West Dr. 154 BM76
Bell Bri. Rd., Cher. 193 BF102
Bell Clo., Abb.L. 59 BT27
Bell Clo., Beac. 89 AM53
Bell Clo., Green. 189 FT85
Bell Clo., Pnr. 94 BW54
Bell Clo., Ruis. 115 BT62
Bell Clo., Slou. 132 AV71
Bell Common, Epp. 69 ES32
Bell Ct., Surb. 198 CP103
Barnsbury La.
Bell Cres., Couls. 235 DH121
Maple Way
Bell Dr. SW18 179 CY87
Bell Fm. Ave., Dag. 127 FC62
Bell Gdns., Orp. 206 EW99
Bell Gate, Hem.H. 40 BL17
Bell Grn. SE26 183 DZ90
Bell Grn., Hem.H. 57 BB27
Bell Grn. La. SE26 183 DZ92
Bell Hill, Croy. 202 DQ104
Surrey St.
Bell Ho. Rd., Rom. 127 FC60
Bell Inn Yd. EC3 275 L9
Bell La. E1 275 P7
Bell La. E1 142 DT71
Bell La. E16 144 EG74
Bell La. NW4 119 CW56
Bell La., Abb.L. 59 BT27
Bell La., Amer. 72 AV39
Bell La., Berk. 38 AS18
Bell La., Brox. 49 DY21
Bell La., Enf. 83 DX38
Bell La., Hat. 46 DA24
Bell La., Hert. 32 DR09
Bell La., Hodd. 49 EA17
Bell La., Lthd. 231 CD123
Bell La., St.Alb. 62 CL29
Bell La., Twick. 177 CG88
The Embk.
Bell La., Wem. 117 CK61
Magnet Rd.
Bell La. (Eton Wick), Wind. 151 AM77
Bell La. Clo., Lthd. 231 CD123
Bell Mead, Saw. 36 EY05
Bell Meadow SE19 182 DS91
Dulwich Wd. Ave.
Bell Meadow, Gdse. 252 DV132
Hickmans Clo.
Bell Par., Wind. 151 AM82
St. Andrews Ave.
Bell Rd., E.Mol. 197 CD99
Bell Rd., Enf. 82 DR39
Bell Rd., Houns. 156 CB83
Bell St. NW1 272 B6
Bell St. NW1 140 DE71
Bell St., Reig. 250 DA134
Bell St., Saw. 36 EY05
Bell Vw., Wind. 151 AM83
Bell Vw. Clo., Wind. 151 AM82
Bell Wk., Saw. 36 EY05
London Rd.
Bell Water Gate SE18 165 EN76
Bell Wf. La. EC4 275 J10
Bell Yd. WC2 274 D9
Bell Yd. WC2 141 DN72
Bellamy Clo. W14 159 CZ78
Aisgill Ave.

Bellamy Clo., Edg. 96 CQ48
Bellamy Clo., Uxb. 114 BN62
Bellamy Clo., Wat. 75 BU39
Bellamy Dr., Stan. 95 CH53
Bellamy Rd. E4 101 EB51
Bellamy Rd., Enf. 82 DR40
Bellamy Rd. (Cheshunt), Wal.Cr. 67 DY29
Bellamy St. SW12 181 DH87
Bellasis Ave. SW2 181 DL89
Bellclose Rd., West Dr. 154 BL75
Belle Staines Pleasaunce E4 101 EA47
Belle Vue, Grnf. 137 CD67
Belle Vue Clo., Stai. 194 BG95
Belle Vue Est. NW4 119 CW56
Belle Vue La. (Bushey), Wat. 95 CD46
Belle Vue Rd. E17 101 ED54
Belle Vue Rd. NW4 119 CW56
Bell La.
Belle Vue Rd., Orp. 223 EN110
Standard Rd.
Belle Vue Rd., Ware 33 DZ06
Bellefield Rd., Orp. 206 EV99
Bellefields Rd. SW9 161 DM83
Bellegrove Clo., Well. 165 ET82
Bellegrove Rd., Well. 165 ES82
Bellenden Rd. SE15 162 DT83
Belleville Rd. SW11 180 DE85
Bellevue Ms. N11 98 DG50
Bellevue Rd.
Bellevue Par. SW17 180 DE88
Bellevue Rd.
Bellevue Pk., Th.Hth. 202 DQ97
Bellevue Pl. E1 142 DW70
Bellevue Pl., Slou. 152 AT76
Albert St.
Bellevue Rd. N11 98 DG49
Bellevue Rd. SW13 159 CU82
Bellevue Rd. SW17 180 DE88
Bellevue Rd. W13 137 CH70
Bellevue Rd., Bexh. 186 EZ85
Bellevue Rd., Horn. 128 FM60
Bellevue Rd., Kings.T. 198 CL97
Bellevue Rd., Rom. 105 FC51
Bellew St. SW17 180 DC90
Bellfield, Croy. 221 DZ108
Bellfield Ave., Har. 95 CD50
Bellfields Ct., Guil. 242 AW130
Oak Tree Dr.
Bellfields Rd., Guil. 242 AX132
Bellflower Clo. E6 144 EL71
Sorrel Gdns.
Bellflower Path, Rom. 106 FJ52
Bellgate Ms. NW5 121 DH62
York Ri.
Bellhouse La., Brwd. 108 FS43
Bellingdon Rd., Chesh. 54 AP30
Bellingham Grn. SE6 183 EA90
Bellingham Rd. SE6 183 EC90
Bellman Ave., Grav. 191 GL88
Bellmarsh Rd., Add. 212 BH105
Bellmount Wd. Ave., Wat. 75 BS39
Bello Clo. SE24 181 DP87
Bellot Gdns. SE10 164 EE78
Christchurch Way
Bellot St. SE10 164 EE78
Bellring Clo., Belv. 166 FA79
Bells All. SW6 160 DA82
Bells Gdn. Est. SE15 162 DU80
Buller Clo.
Bells Hill, Barn. 79 CX43
Bells Hill, Slou. 132 AU67
Bells Hill Grn., Slou. 132 AU66
Bells La., Slou. 153 BB83
Bellswood La., Iver 133 BB71
Belltrees Gro. SW16 181 DM92
Bellweir Clo., Stai. 173 BB89
Bellwether La., Red. 267 DP143
Bellwood Rd. SE15 163 DX84
Belmarsh Rd. SE28 165 ES75
Western Way
Belmont, Slou. 131 AN71
Belmont Ave. N9 100 DU46
Belmont Ave. N13 99 DL50
Belmont Ave. N17 122 DQ55
Belmont Ave., Barn. 80 DF43
Belmont Ave., Guil. 242 AT131
Belmont Ave., N.Mal. 199 CU99
Belmont Ave., Sthl. 156 BY76
Belmont Ave., Upmin. 128 FM61
Belmont Ave., Well. 165 ES82
Belmont Ave., Wem. 138 CM67
Belmont Circle, Har. 95 CH54
Kenton La.
Belmont Clo. E4 101 ED50
Belmont Clo. N20 98 DB46
Belmont Clo. SW4 161 DJ83
Belmont Clo., Barn. 80 DF42
Belmont Clo., Uxb. 134 BK65
Belmont Clo., Wdf.Grn. 102 EH49
Belmont Ct. NW11 119 CZ57
Belmont Gro. SE13 163 ED83
Belmont Hall Ct. SE13 163 ED83
Belmont Gro.
Belmont Hill SE13 163 EC83
Belmont Hill, St.Alb. 43 CD21
Belmont La., Chis. 185 ER92
Belmont La., Stan. 95 CJ52
Belmont Pk. SE13 163 ED84
Belmont Pk. Clo. SE13 163 ED84
Belmont Pk.
Belmont Pk. Rd. E10 123 EB58
Belmont Ri., Sutt. 217 CZ107
Belmont Rd. N15 122 DQ56
Belmont Rd. N17 122 DQ55
Belmont Rd. SE25 202 DV99
Belmont Rd. SW4 161 DJ83
Belmont Rd. W4 158 CR77
Belmont Rd., Beck. 203 DZ96
Belmont Rd., Chesh. 54 AP28
Belmont Rd., Chis. 185 EP92
Belmont Rd., Erith 166 FA80
Belmont Rd., Grays 170 FZ79
Belmont Rd., Har. 117 CF55
Belmont Rd., Hem.H. 40 BL24
Belmont Rd., Horn. 128 FK62
Belmont Rd., Ilf. 125 EQ62
Belmont Rd., Lthd. 231 CG122
Belmont Rd., Reig. 266 DC135
Belmont Rd., Sutt. 218 DA110
Belmont Rd., Twick. 177 CD89
Belmont Rd., Uxb. 134 BK66
Belmont Rd., Wall. 219 DH106
Belmont Rd. (Bushey), Wat. 76 BY43
Belmont St. NW1 140 DG66
Belmont Ter. W4 158 CR77
Belmont Rd.
Belmor, Borwd. 78 CN43
Belmore Ave., Hayes 135 BU72
Belmore Ave., Wok. 227 BD116
Belmore La. N7 121 DK64
Belmore St. SW8 161 DK81
Beloe Clo. SW15 159 CU83
Belper Ct. E5 123 DX63
Pedro St.
Belsham St. E9 142 DW65
Belsize Ave. N13 99 DM51
Belsize Ave. NW3 140 DD65
Belsize Ave. W13 157 CH76
Belsize Clo., Hem.H. 40 BN21
Belsize Clo., St.Alb. 43 CJ15
Belsize Cres. NW3 120 DD64
Belsize Gdns., Sutt. 218 DB105
Belsize Gro. NW3 140 DE65
Belsize La. NW3 140 DD65
Belsize Ms. NW3 140 DD65
Belsize La.
Belsize Pk. NW3 140 DD65
Belsize Pk. Gdns. NW3 140 DE65
Belsize Pk. Ms. NW3 140 DD65
Belsize La.
Belsize Pl. NW3 140 DD65
Belsize La.
Belsize Rd. NW6 140 DB67
Belsize Rd., Har. 95 CD52
Belsize Rd., Hem.H. 40 BN21
Belsize Sq. NW3 140 DD65
Belsize Ter. NW3 140 DD65
Belson Rd. SE18 165 EM77
Belswains Grn., Hem.H. 40 BL23
Belswains La.
Belswains La., Hem.H. 40 BL23
Beltana Dr., Grav. 191 GL91
Beltane Dr. SW19 179 CX90
Belthorn Cres. SW12 181 DJ87
Beltinge Rd., Rom. 106 FM54
Belton Rd. E7 144 EH66
Belton Rd. E11 124 EE63
Belton Rd. N17 122 DS55
Belton Rd. NW2 139 CU65
Belton Rd., Berk. 38 AU18
Belton Rd., Sid. 186 EU91
Belton Way E3 143 EA71
Beltona Gdns. (Cheshunt), Wal.Cr. 67 DX27
Beltran Rd. SW6 160 DB82
Beltwood Rd., Belv. 167 FC77
Belvedere Ave. SW19 179 CY92
Belvedere Ave., Ilf. 103 EP54
Belvedere Bldgs. SE1 278 G5
Belvedere Clo., Esher 214 CB106
Belvedere Clo., Grav. 191 GJ88
Belvedere Clo., Guil. 242 AV132
Belvedere Clo., Tedd. 177 CE92
Belvedere Clo., Wey. 212 BN106
Belvedere Ct. N2 120 DD57
Belvedere Dr. SW19 179 CY92
Belvedere Gdns., St.Alb. 60 CA27
Belvedere Gdns., W.Mol. 196 BZ99
Belvedere Gro. SW19 179 CY92
Belvedere Ho., Felt. 175 BU88
Belvedere Ind. Est., Belv. 167 FC76
Crabtree Manorway S.
Belvedere Ms. SE15 162 DW83
Belvedere Pl. SE1 278 G5
Belvedere Rd. E10 123 DY60
Belvedere Rd. SE1 278 C4
Belvedere Rd. SE1 161 DM75
Belvedere Rd. SE2 146 EX74
Belvedere Rd. SE19 182 DT94
Belvedere Rd. W7 157 CE76
Belvedere Rd., Bexh. 166 EZ83
Belvedere Rd., Brwd. 108 FT48
Belvedere Rd., West. 239 EM118
Belvedere Sq. SW19 179 CY92
Belvedere Strand NW9 97 CT54
Belvedere Way, Har. 118 CL58
Belvoir Clo. SE9 184 EL90
Belvoir Rd. SE22 182 DU87
Belvue Clo., Nthlt. 136 CA66
Belvue Rd., Nthlt. 136 CA66
Bembridge Clo. NW6 139 CY66
Bembridge Ct., Slou. 152 AT76
Park St.
Bembridge Gdns., Ruis. 115 BR61
Bemerton Est. N1 141 DL66
Bemerton St. N1 141 DM67
Bemish Rd. SW15 159 CX83
Bempton Dr., Ruis. 115 BV61
Bemsted Rd. E17 123 DZ55
Ben Hale Clo., Stan. 95 CH49
Ben Jonson Rd. E1 143 DX71
Ben Smith Way SE16 162 DU76
Jamaica Rd.
Ben Tillet Clo. E16 145 EM74
Newland St.
Ben Tillett Clo., Bark. 146 EU66
Benares Rd. SE18 165 ET77
Benbow Clo., St.Alb. 43 CH22
Benbow Rd. W6 159 CV76
Benbow St. SE8 163 EA79
Benbow Waye, Uxb. 134 BJ71
Benbrick Rd., Guil. 258 AU135
Benbury Clo., Brom. 183 EC92
Bence, The, Egh. 193 BB97
Bench Fld., S.Croy. 220 DT107
Bench Manor Cres., Ger.Cr. 90 AW54
Benchleys Rd., Hem.H. 39 BF21
Bencombe Rd., Pur. 219 DN114
Bencroft (Cheshunt), Wal.Cr. 66 DU26
Bencroft Rd. SW16 181 DJ94
Bencroft Rd., Hem.H. 40 BL20
Bencurtis Pk., W.Wick. 203 ED104
Bendall Ms. NW1 272 C6
Bendemeer Rd. SW15 159 CX83
Bendish Rd. E6 144 EL66
Bendmore Ave. SE2 166 EU78
Bendon Valley SW18 180 DB87
Bendysh Rd. (Bushey), Wat. 76 BY41
Benedict Clo., Belv. 166 EY76
Tunstock Way
Benedict Clo., Orp. 205 ES104
Benedict Dr., Felt. 175 BR87
Benedict Rd. SW9 161 DM83
Benedict Rd., Mitch. 200 DD97
Benedict Way N2 120 DC55
Benedictine Gate, Wal.Cr. 67 DY27
Benenden Grn., Brom. 204 EF99
Benenstock Rd., Stai. 173 BF85
Benets Rd., Horn. 128 FN60
Benett Gdns. SW16 201 DL96
Benfleet Clo., Cob. 214 BY112
Benfleet Clo., Sutt. 200 DC104
Benford Rd., Hodd. 49 DZ19
Bengal Ct. EC3 142 DR72
Birchin La.
Bengal Rd., Ilf. 125 EP63
Bengarth Dr., Har. 95 CD54
Bengarth Rd., Nthlt. 136 BX67
Bengeo Meadows, Hert. 32 DR06
Bengeo Ms., Hert. 32 DQ06
Bengeo St.
Bengeo St., Hert. 32 DQ06
Bengeworth Rd. SE5 162 DQ83
Bengeworth Rd., Har. 117 CG61
Benham Clo. SW11 160 DD83
Benham Clo., Chesh. 54 AP29
Benham Clo., Chess. 215 CJ107
Mansfield Rd.
Benham Clo., Couls. 235 DP118
Benham Gdns., Houns. 156 BZ84
Benham Rd. W7 137 CE71
Benhams Clo., Horl. 268 DG146
Benhams Dr., Horl. 268 DG146
Benhams Pl. NW3 120 DC63
Holly Wk.
Benhill Ave., Sutt. 218 DB105
Benhill Rd. SE5 162 DR80
Benhill Rd., Sutt. 200 DC104
Benhill Wd. Rd., Sutt. 218 DC105
Benhilton Gdns., Sutt. 200 DB104
Benhurst Ave., Horn. 127 FH63
Benhurst Clo., S.Croy. 221 DX110
Benhurst Ct. SW16 181 DN92
Benhurst Gdns., S.Croy. 220 DW110
Benhurst La. SW16 181 DN92
Benin St. SE13 183 ED87
Benison Ct., Slou. 152 AT76
Osborne St.
Benjafield Clo. N18 100 DV49
Brettenham Rd.
Benjamin Clo. E8 142 DU67
Benjamin Clo., Horn. 127 FG58
Benjamin St. EC1 274 F6
Benjamin St. EC1 141 DP71
Benledi St. E14 143 ED72
Benn St. E9 143 DY65
Bennerley Rd. SW11 180 DE85
Bennet's Hill EC4 274 G10
Bennetsfield Rd., Uxb. 135 BP74
Bennett Clo., Cob. 213 BU113
Bennett Clo., Kings.T. 197 CJ95
Bennett Clo., Nthwd. 93 BT52
Bennett Clo., Well. 166 EU82
Bennett Clo., Welw.G.C. 29 CZ13
Bennett Gro. SE13 163 EB81
Bennett Pk. SE3 164 EF83
Bennett Rd. E13 144 EJ70
Bennett Rd. N16 122 DS63
Bennett Rd., Rom. 126 EY58
Bennett St. SW1 277 K2
Bennett St. W4 158 CS79
Bennett Way, Dart. 189 FR91
Bennett Way, Guil. 244 BG129
Bennetts, Chesh. 54 AR30
Bennetts Ave., Croy. 203 DY103
Bennetts Ave., Grnf. 137 CE67
Bennetts Castle La., Dag. 126 EW63
Bennetts Clo. N17 100 DT51
Bennetts Clo., Mitch. 201 DH95
Leonard Rd.
Bennetts Clo., St.Alb. 44 CR23
Meadway
Bennetts Clo., Slou. 131 AN74
Bennetts Copse, Chis. 184 EL93
Bennetts End Clo., Hem.H. 40 BM22
Bennetts End Rd., Hem.H. 40 BM21
Bennetts Fm. Pl., Lthd. 246 BZ125
Bennetts Gate, Hem.H. 40 BN23
Bennetts End Rd.
Bennetts Way, Croy. 203 DY103
Bennetts Yd. SW1 277 N7
Benning Clo., Wind. 151 AK83
Benningholme Rd., Edg. 96 CS51
Bennington Rd. N17 100 DS53
Bennington Rd., Wdf.Grn. 102 EE52
Bennions Clo., Horn. 148 FK65
Franklin Rd.
Bennison Dr., Rom. 106 FK54
Benn's Wk., Rich. 158 CL84
Rosedale Rd.
Benrek Clo., Ilf. 103 EQ53
Bensbury Clo. SW15 179 CW87
Bensham Clo., Th.Hth. 202 DQ98
Bensham Gro., Th.Hth. 202 DQ96
Bensham La., Croy. 201 DP101
Bensham La., Th.Hth. 201 DP98
Bensham Manor Rd., Th.Hth. 202 DQ98
Bensington Ct., Felt. 175 BR86
Benskin Rd., Wat. 75 BU43
Benskins La. (Havering-atte-Bower), Rom. 106 FK46
Bensley Clo. N11 98 DF50
Benson Ave. E6 144 EJ68
Benson Clo., Houns. 156 CA84
Benson Clo., Slou. 132 AU74
Benson Clo., Uxb. 134 BL71
Benson Quay E1 142 DW73
Garnet St.
Benson Rd. SE23 182 DW88
Benson Rd., Croy. 201 DN104
Benson Rd., Grays 170 GB79
Bentfield Gdns. SE9 184 EJ90
Aldersgrove Ave.
Benthal Rd. N16 122 DU61
Benthall Gdns., Ken. 236 DQ116
Bentham Ave., Wok. 227 BC115
Bentham Rd. E9 143 DX65
Bentham Rd. SE28 146 EV73
Bentham Wk. NW10 118 CQ64
Bentinck Clo., Ger.Cr. 112 AX57
Bentinck Ms. W1 272 G8
Bentinck Pl. NW8 272 B1
Bentinck Rd., West Dr. 134 BK74
Bentinck St. W1 272 G8
Bentinck St. W1 140 DG72
Bentley Dr., Harl. 52 EW16
Kiln La.
Bentley Dr., Ilf. 125 EQ58
Bentley Dr., Wey. 212 BN109
Bentley Heath La., Barn. 79 CZ35
Bentley Pk., Slou. 131 AK68
Bentley Rd. N1 142 DS65
Tottenham Rd.
Bentley Rd., Hert. 31 DL08
Bentley Rd., Slou. 131 AN74
Bentley St., Grav. 191 GJ86
Bentley Way, Stan. 95 CG50
Bentley Way, Wdf.Grn. 102 EG48
Benton Rd., Ilf. 125 ER60
Benton Rd., Wat. 94 BX50
Bentons, Hart. 51 ES17
Bentons La. SE27 182 DQ91
Bentons Ri. SE27 182 DR92
Bentry Clo., Dag. 126 EY61
Bentry Rd., Dag. 126 EY61
Bentsbrook Clo., Dor. 263 CH140
Bentsbrook Pk., Dor. 263 CH140
Bentsbrook Rd., Dor. 263 CH140
Bentsley Clo., St.Alb. 43 CJ16
Bentworth Rd. W12 139 CV72
Benwell Ct., Sun. 195 BU95
Benwell Rd. N7 121 DN63
Benwick Clo. SE16 162 DV77
Benworth St. E3 143 DZ69
Benyon Path, S.Ock. 149 FW68
Benyon Rd. N1 142 DR67
Southgate Rd.
Beomonds Row, Cher. 194 BG101
Berber Rd. SW11 180 DF85
Berberis Clo., Guil. 242 AW132
Berberis Wk., West Dr. 154 BL77
Berceau Wk., Wat. 75 BS39
Bercta Rd. SE9 185 EQ89
Berdens La., Brwd. 129 FT55
Bere St. E1 143 DX73
Cranford St.
Berecroft, Harl. 51 ER20
Beredens La., Brwd. 129 FT55
Berefield, Hem.H. 40 BK18
Berenger Wk. SW10 160 DD80
Blantyre St.
Berens Rd. NW10 139 CX69
Berens Rd., Orp. 206 EX99
Berens Way, Chis. 205 ET98
Beresford Ave. N20 98 DF47
Beresford Ave. W7 137 CD71
Beresford Ave., Slou. 132 AW73
Beresford Ave., Surb. 198 CP102
Beresford Ave., Twick. 177 CJ86
Beresford Ave., Wem. 138 CM67
Beresford Dr., Brom. 204 EL97
Beresford Dr., Wdf.Grn. 102 EJ49
Beresford Gdns., Enf. 82 DS42
Beresford Gdns., Houns. 176 BZ85
Beresford Gdns., Rom. 126 EY57
Beresford Rd. E4 102 EE46
Beresford Rd. E17 101 EB53
Beresford Rd. N2 120 DE55
Beresford Rd. N5 122 DR64
Beresford Rd. N8 121 DN57
Beresford Rd., Dor. 263 CH136
Beresford Rd., Grav. 190 GE87
Beresford Rd., Har. 117 CD57
Beresford Rd., Kings.T. 198 CM95
Beresford Rd., N.Mal. 198 CQ98
Beresford Rd., Rick. 91 BF46
Beresford Rd., St.Alb. 43 CH21
Beresford Rd., Sthl. 136 BX74
Beresford Rd., Sutt. 217 CZ108
Beresford Sq. SE18 165 EP77
Beresford St. SE18 165 EP76
Beresford Ter. N5 122 DQ64
Berestede Rd. W6 159 CT78
Bergen Sq. SE16 163 DY76
Norway Gate
Berger Clo., Orp. 205 ER100
Berger Rd. E9 143 DX65
Berghem Ms. W14 159 CX76
Blythe Rd.
Berghers Hill, H.Wyc. 110 AF59
Bergholt Ave., Ilf. 124 EL57
Bergholt Cres. N16 122 DS59
Bergholt Ms. NW1 141 DJ66
Rossendale Way
Bericot Way, Welw.G.C. 30 DC09
Bering Wk. E16 144 EK72
Berisford Ms. SW18 180 DC86
St. Ann's Cres.
Berkeley Ave., Bexh. 166 EX81
Berkeley Ave., Chesh. 54 AM28
Berkeley Ave., Grnf. 137 CE65
Berkeley Ave., Houns. 155 BU81
Berkeley Ave., Ilf. 103 EN54
Berkeley Ave., Rom. 105 FC52
Berkeley Clo., Abb.L. 59 BT32
Berkeley Clo., Borwd. 78 CN43
Berkeley Clo., Chesh. 54 AN30
Berkeley Ave.
Berkeley Clo., Horn. 128 FP61
Berkeley Clo., Kings.T. 178 CL94
Berkeley Clo., Orp. 205 ES101
Berkeley Clo., Pot.B. 63 CY32
Berkeley Clo., Ruis. 115 BU62
Berkeley Clo., Stai. 173 BD89
Berkeley Clo., Ware 32 DW05
Berkeley Ct. N14 81 DJ44
Berkeley Ct., Guil. 242 AY134
London Rd.
Berkeley Ct., Wall. 201 DJ104
Berkeley Ct., Wey. 195 BR103
Berkeley Cres., Barn. 80 DD43
Berkeley Cres., Dart. 188 FM88
Berkeley Dr., Horn. 128 FN60
Berkeley Gdns. N21 100 DR45
Berkeley Gdns. W8 140 DA74
Brunswick Gdns.
Berkeley Gdns., Esher 215 CG107
Berkeley Gdns., Walt. 195 BT101
Berkeley Gdns., W.Byf. 211 BF114
Berkeley Ho. E3 143 EA69
Wellington Way
Berkeley Ms. W1 272 E9
Berkeley Pl. SW19 179 CX93
Berkeley Pl., Epsom 232 CR115
Berkeley Rd. E12 124 EL64
Berkeley Rd. N8 121 DK57
Berkeley Rd. N15 122 DR58
Berkeley Rd. NW9 118 CN56
Berkeley Rd. SW13 159 CU81
Berkeley Rd., Uxb. 135 BQ66
Berkeley Sq. W1 277 J1
Berkeley Sq. W1 141 DH73
Berkeley St. W1 277 J2
Berkeley St. W1 141 DH74
Berkeley Wk. N7 121 DM61
Durham Rd.
Berkeley Waye, Houns. 156 BX80
Berkeleys, The, Lthd. 231 CE124
Berkely Rd., H.Wyc. 88 AC53
Berkhampstead Rd., Belv. 166 FA78
Berkhampstead Rd., Chesh. 54 AQ30
Berkhamsted Ave., Wem. 138 CM65
Berkhamsted Bypass, Berk. 38 AV21
Berkhamsted Bypass, Hem.H. 39 BB23
Berkhamsted Hill, Berk. 38 AY17
Berkhamsted La., Hat. 46 DF20
Berkhamsted La., Hert. 47 DJ19
Berkhamsted Pl., Berk. 38 AW17
Berkhamsted Rd., Hem.H. 39 BD17
Berkley Ave., Wal.Cr. 67 DX34
Berkley Clo., St.Alb. 43 CJ16
Berkley Ct., Berk. 38 AW18
Mill St.
Berkley Ct., Guil. 242 AY134
London Rd.
Berkley Ct., Rick. 75 BR43
Mayfare
Berkley Dr., W.Mol. 196 BZ97
Berkley Gro. NW1 140 DF66
Berkley Rd.
Berkley Rd. NW1 140 DF66
Berkley Rd., Beac. 89 AK49
Berkley Rd., Grav. 191 GH86
Berks Hill, Rick. 73 BC43
Berkshire Ave., Slou. 131 AP72
Berkshire Clo., Cat. 236 DR122
Berkshire Gdns. N13 99 DN51
Berkshire Gdns. N18 100 DV50
Berkshire Rd. E9 143 DZ65
Berkshire Sq., Mitch. 201 DL98
Berkshire Way
Berkshire Way, Horn. 128 FN57
Berkshire Way, Mitch. 201 DL98
Bermans Clo., Brwd. 109 GB47
Hanging Hill La.
Bermans Way NW10 118 CS63
Bermondsey Sq. SE1 279 N6
Bermondsey St. SE1 279 M3
Bermondsey St. SE1 162 DS75
Bermondsey Wall E. SE16 162 DU75
Bermondsey Wall W. SE16 162 DU75
Bermuda Rd., Til. 171 GG82
Bernal Clo. SE28 146 EX73
Haldane Rd.
Bernard Ashley Dr. SE7 164 EH78
Bernard Ave. W13 157 CH76
Bernard Cassidy St. E16 144 EF71
Bernard Gdns. SW19 179 CZ92
Bernard Rd. N15 122 DT57
Bernard Rd., Rom. 127 FC59
Bernard Rd., Wall. 219 DH106
Bernard St. WC1 273 P5
Bernard St. WC1 141 DL70
Bernard St., Grav. 191 GH86
Bernard St., St.Alb. 43 CD19
Bernards Clo., Ilf. 103 EQ52
Bernato Clo., W.Byf. 212 BL112
Viscount Gdns.
Bernays Clo., Stan. 95 CJ51
Bernays Gro. SW9 161 DM84
Berne Rd., Th.Hth. 201 DP99
Bernel Dr., Croy. 203 DZ104
Berners Clo., Slou. 131 AL73
Berners Dr. W13 137 CG72
Berners Dr., Brox. 49 DZ23
Berners Way
Berners Dr., St.Alb. 43 CE23
Berners Ms. W1 273 L7
Berners Ms. W1 141 DJ71
Berners Pl. W1 273 L8
Berners Pl. W1 141 DJ72
Berners Rd. N1 141 DN67
Berners Rd. N22 99 DN53
Berners St. W1 273 L7
Berners St. W1 141 DJ71
Berners Way, Brox. 49 DZ23
Bernersmede SE3 164 EG83
Blackheath Pk.
Berney Rd., Croy. 202 DR101
Bernice Clo., Rain. 148 FJ70
Bernville Way, Har. 118 CM57
Kenton Rd.
Bernwell Rd. E4 102 EE48
Berridge Grn., Edg. 96 CP52
Berridge Rd. SE19 182 DS92
Berries, The, St.Alb. 43 CG16
Berriman Rd. N7 121 DM62
Berrington Dr., Lthd. 229 BT124
Berriton Rd., Har. 116 BZ60
Berry Ave., Wat. 75 BU36
Berry Clo. N21 99 DP46
Berry Clo. NW10 138 CS66
Berry Clo., Horn. 128 FJ64
Airfield Way
Berry Clo., Rick. 92 BH45
Berry Ct., Houns. 176 BZ85
Berry Fld. Pk., Amer. 55 AP37
Berry Gro. La. (Bushey), Wat. 76 BY38
Berry Hill, Maid. 130 AD70
Berry Hill, Stan. 95 CK49
Berry La. SE21 182 DR91
Berry La., Rick. 92 BH45
Berry Meade, Ash. 232 CM117
Berry Pl. EC1 274 G3
Berry St. EC1 274 G4
Berry St. EC1 141 DP70
Berry Wk., Ash. 232 CM119
Berry Way W5 158 CL76
Berry Way, Rick. 92 BH45
Berrybank Clo. E4 101 EC47
Greenbank Clo.
Berrydale Rd., Hayes 136 BY70
Berryfield, Slou. 132 AW72
Berryfield Clo. E17 123 EB56
Berryfield Clo., Brom. 204 EL95
Berryfield Rd. SE17 278 G10
Berryfield Rd. SE17 161 DP78
Berryhill SE9 165 EP84
Berryhill Gdns. SE9 165 EP84
Berrylands SW20 199 CW97
Berrylands, Orp. 206 EW104
Berrylands, Surb. 198 CM100
Berrylands Rd., Surb. 198 CM100
Berryman Clo., Dag. 126 EW62
Bennetts Castle La.
Berrymans La. SE26 183 DX91
Berrymead, Hem.H. 40 BM18
Berrymead Gdns. W3 158 CQ75
Berrymede Rd. W4 158 CR76
Berrys Grn. Rd., West. 239 EP115
Berrys Hill, West. 239 EP115
Berrys La., W.Byf. 212 BK111
Berryscroft Ct., Stai. 174 BJ94
Berryscroft Rd.
Berryscroft Rd., Stai. 174 BJ94
Bersham La., Grays 170 FZ77
Bert Rd., Th.Hth. 202 DQ99
Bertal Rd. SW17 180 DD91

Berther Rd., Horn. 128 FK59
Berthon St. SE8 163 EA80
Bertie Rd. NW10 139 CU65
Bertie Rd. SE26 183 DX93
Bertram Cotts. SW19 180 DA94
Hartfield Rd.
Bertram Rd. NW4 119 CU58
Bertram Rd., Enf. 82 DU42
Bertram Rd., Kings.T. 178 CN94
Bertram St. N19 121 DH61
Bertram Way, Enf. 82 DT42
Bertrand St. SE13 163 EB83
Bertrand Way SE28 146 EV73
Berwick Ave., Hayes 136 BX72
Berwick Ave., Slou. 131 AP72
Berwick Clo., Beac. 89 AP54
Berwick Clo., Stan. 95 CF52
Gordon Ave.
Berwick Clo., Wal.Cr. 67 EA34
Berwick Cres., Sid. 185 ES86
Berwick La., Ong. 71 FE33
Berwick Pond Clo., Rain. 148 FK68
Berwick Pond Rd., Rain. 148 FM68
Berwick Pond Rd., Upmin. 148 FM66
Berwick Rd. E16 144 EH72
Berwick Rd. N22 99 DP53
Berwick Rd., Borwd. 78 CL38
Berwick Rd., Rain. 148 FK68
Berwick Rd., Well. 166 EV81
Berwick St. W1 273 L8
Berwick St. W1 141 DJ72
Berwick Way, Orp. 206 EU102
Berwick Way, Sev. 257 FH121
Berwyn Ave., Houns. 156 CB81
Berwyn Rd. SE24 181 DP88
Berwyn Rd., Rich. 158 CP84
Beryl Ave. E6 144 EL71
Beryl Rd. W6 159 CX78
Berystede, Kings.T. 178 CP94
Besant Ct. N1 122 DR64
Newington Grn. Rd.
Besant Rd. NW2 119 CY63
Besant Wk. N7 121 DM61
Newington Barrow Way
Besant Way NW10 118 CQ64
Besley St. SW16 181 DJ94
Bessborough Gdns. SW1 277 N10
Bessborough Gdns. SW1 161 DK78
Bessborough Pl. SW1 277 M10
Bessborough Pl. SW1 161 DK78
Bessborough Rd. SW15 179 CU88
Bessborough Rd., Har. 117 CD60
Bessborough St. SW1 277 M10
Bessborough St. SW1 161 DK78
Bessels Grn. Rd., Sev. 256 FD123
Bessels Meadows, Sev. 256 FD124
Bessels Way, Sev. 256 FC124
Bessemer Rd. SE5 162 DQ82
Bessemer Rd., Welw.G.C. 29 CY05
Bessie Lansbury Clo. E6 145 EN72
Bessingby Rd., Ruis. 115 BV61
Bessingham Wk. SE4 163 DX84
Frendsbury Rd.
Besson St. SE14 162 DW81
Bessy St. E2 142 DW69
Roman Rd.
Bestobell Rd., Slou. 131 AQ72
Bestwood St. SE8 163 DX77
Beswick Ms. NW6 140 DB65
Lymington Rd.
Beta Rd., Wok. 227 BB116
Beta Rd. (Chobham), Wok. 210 AT110
Beta Way, Egh. 193 BC95
Betam Rd., Hayes 155 BR75
Betchworth Clo., Sutt. 218 DD106
Turnpike La.
Betchworth Rd., Ilf. 125 ES61
Betchworth Way, Croy. 221 EC109
Betenson Ave., Sev. 256 FF122
Betham Rd., Grnf. 137 CD69
Bethany Waye, Felt. 175 BS87
Bethecar Rd., Har. 117 CE57
Bethel Rd., Sev. 257 FJ123
Bethel Rd., Well. 166 EW83
Bethell Ave. E16 144 EF70
Bethell Ave., Ilf. 125 EN59
Bethersden Clo., Beck. 183 DZ94
Bethnal Grn. Rd. E1 275 P4
Bethnal Grn. Rd. E1 142 DT70
Bethnal Grn. Rd. E2 142 DT70
Bethune Ave. N11 98 DF49
Bethune Rd. N16 122 DR59
Bethune Rd. NW10 138 CR70
Bethwin Rd. SE5 161 DP80
Betjeman Clo., Couls. 235 DM117
Stanley Clo.
Betjeman Clo., Pnr. 116 CA56
Betjeman Clo., Wal.Cr. 66 DU28
Rosedale Way
Betjeman Way, Hem.H. 40 BH18
Betley Ct., Walt. 195 BV104
Betony Clo., Croy. 203 DX102
Primrose La.
Betony Rd., Rom. 106 FK51
Cloudberry Rd.
Betoyne Ave. E4 102 EE49
Betsham Rd., Erith 167 FF80
Betsham Rd., Grav. 189 FX92
Betsham Rd., Swans. 190 FY87
Betstyle Rd. N11 99 DH49
Betterton Dr., Sid. 186 EY89
Betterton Rd., Rain. 147 FE69
Betterton St. WC2 273 P9
Betterton St. WC2 141 DL72
Bettles Clo., Uxb. 134 BJ68
Westcott Way
Bettons Pk. E15 144 EE67
Bettridge Rd. SW6 159 CZ82
Betts Clo., Beck. 203 DY96
Kendall Rd.
Betts La., Wal.Abb. 50 EJ21
Betts Ms. E17 123 DZ58
Queen's Rd.
Betts Rd. E16 144 EH73
Victoria Dock Rd.
Betts St. E1 142 DV73
The Highway
Betts Way SE20 202 DV95
Betts Way, Surb. 197 CH102
Betula Clo., Ken. 236 DR115
Betula Wk., Rain. 148 FK69
Between Sts., Cob. 213 BU114
Beulah Ave., Th.Hth. 201 DM98
Beulah Rd.
Beulah Clo., Edg. 96 CP48
Beulah Cres., Th.Hth. 202 DQ96
Beulah Gro., Croy. 202 DQ100
Beulah Hill SE19 181 DP93
Beulah Path E17 123 EB57
Addison Rd.
Beulah Rd. E17 123 EB57
Beulah Rd. SW19 179 CZ94
Beulah Rd., Epp. 70 EU29
Beulah Rd., Horn. 128 FJ62
Beulah Rd., Sutt. 218 DA105
Beulah Rd., Th.Hth. 202 DQ97
Beulah Wk., Cat. 237 DY120
Beult Rd., Dart. 167 FG83
Bev Callender Clo. SW8 161 DH83
Daley Thompson Way
Bevan Ave., Bark. 146 EU66
Bevan Clo., Hem.H. 40 BK22
Bevan Ct., Croy. 219 DN106
Bevan Hill, Chesh. 54 AP29
Bevan Pl., Swan. 207 FE98
Bevan Rd. SE2 166 EV78
Bevan Rd., Barn. 80 DF42
Bevan St. N1 142 DQ67
Bevan Way, Horn. 128 FM63
Bevans Clo., Green. 189 FW86
Johnsons Way
Bevenden St. N1 275 L2
Bevenden St. N1 142 DR69
Bevercote Wk., Belv. 166 EZ79
Osborne Rd.
Beveridge Rd. NW10 138 CS66
Curzon Cres.
Beverley NW8 272 B3
Beverley Ave. SW20 199 CT95
Beverley Ave., Houns. 156 BZ84
Beverley Ave., Sid. 185 ET87
Beverley Clo. N21 100 DQ46
Beverley Clo. SW11 160 DD84
Maysoule Rd.
Beverley Clo. SW13 159 CT82
Beverley Clo., Add. 212 BK106
Beverley Clo., Brox. 49 DY21
Beverley Clo., Chess. 215 CJ105
Beverley Clo., Enf. 82 DS42
Beverley Clo., Epsom 217 CW111
Beverley Clo., Horn. 128 FM59
Beverley Clo., Wey. 195 BS103
Beverley Cotts. SW15 178 CR91
Kingston Vale
Beverley Ct. N14 99 DJ45
Beverley Ct. SE4 163 DZ83
Beverley Ct., Slou. 152 AV75
Dolphin Rd.
Beverley Cres., Wdf.Grn. 102 EH53
Beverley Dr., Edg. 118 CN55
Beverley Gdns. NW11 119 CY59
Beverley Gdns. SW13 159 CT83
Beverley Gdns., Horn. 128 FM59
Beverley Gdns., St.Alb. 43 CK16
Beverley Gdns., Stan. 95 CG53
Beverley Gdns. (Cheshunt), Wal.Cr. 66 DT30
Beverley Gdns., Welw.G.C. 30 DC09
Beverley Gdns., Wem. 118 CM60
Beverley Gdns., Wor.Pk. 199 CU102
Green La.
Beverley Heights, Reig. 250 DB132
Beverley La. SW15 179 CT90
Beverley La., Kings.T. 178 CS94
Beverley Ms. E4 101 ED51
Beverley Rd.
Beverley Path SW13 159 CT82
Beverley Rd. E4 101 ED51
Beverley Rd. E6 144 EK69
Beverley Rd. SE20 202 DV96
Wadhurst Clo.
Beverley Rd. SW13 159 CT83
Beverley Rd. W4 159 CT78
Beverley Rd., Bexh. 167 FC82
Beverley Rd., Brom. 204 EL103
Beverley Rd., Dag. 126 EY63
Beverley Rd., Kings.T. 197 CJ95
Beverley Rd., Mitch. 201 DK98
Beverley Rd., N.Mal. 199 CU98
Beverley Rd., Ruis. 115 BU61
Beverley Rd., Sthl. 156 BY77
Beverley Rd., Sun. 195 BT95
Beverley Rd., Whyt. 236 DS116
Beverley Rd., Wor.Pk. 199 CW103
Beverley Way SW20 199 CT95
Beverley Way, N.Mal. 199 CT95
Beversbrook Rd. N19 121 DK62
Beverston Ms. W1 140 DF71
Upper Montagu St.
Beverstone Rd. SW2 181 DM85
Beverstone Rd., Th.Hth. 201 DN98
Bevil Ct., Hodd. 33 EA14
Molesworth
Bevill Allen Clo. SW17 180 DF92
Bevin Clo. SE16 143 DY74
Bevin Ct. WC1 141 DN69
Holford St.
Bevin Rd., Hayes 135 BU69
Bevin Way WC1 274 D2
Bevington Rd. W10 139 CY71
Bevington Rd., Beck. 203 EB96
Bevington St. SE16 162 DU75
Bevis Clo., Dart. 188 FQ86
Bevis Marks EC3 275 N8
Bevis Marks EC3 142 DS72
Bewcastle Gdns., Enf. 81 DL42
Bewdley St. N1 141 DN66
Bewick St. SW8 161 DH82
Bewley Clo. (Cheshunt), Wal.Cr. 67 DX31
Bewley St. E1 142 DV73
Bewlys Rd. SE27 181 DP92
Bexhill Clo., Felt. 176 BY89
Bexhill Rd. N11 99 DK50
Bexhill Rd. SE4 183 DZ86
Bexhill Rd. SW14 158 CQ83
Bexhill Wk. E15 144 EE68
Mitre Rd.
Bexley Clo., Dart. 187 FE85
Bexley Gdns. N9 100 DR48
Bexley Gdns., Rom. 126 EV57
Bexley High St., Bex. 186 FA87
Bexley La., Dart. 187 FE85
Bexley La., Sid. 186 EW91
Bexley Rd. SE9 185 EP85
Bexley Rd., Erith 167 FC80
Bexley St., Wind. 151 AQ81
Beyers Gdns., Hodd. 33 EA14
Beyers Prospect, Hodd. 33 EA14
Beyers Ride, Hodd. 33 EA13
Beynon Rd., Cars. 218 DF106
Bianca Ho. N1 142 DS68
Crondall St.
Bianca Rd. SE15 162 DT79
Bibsworth Rd. N3 97 CZ54
Bibury Clo. SE15 162 DS79
Bicester Rd., Rich. 158 CN83
Bickenhall St. W1 272 E6
Bickenhall St. W1 140 DF71
Bickersteth Rd. SW17 180 DF93
Bickerton Rd. N19 121 DJ61
Bickley Cres., Brom. 204 EL98
Bickley Pk. Rd., Brom. 204 EL97
Bickley Rd. E10 123 EB59
Bickley Rd., Brom. 204 EK96
Bickley St. SW17 180 DE92
Bicknell Rd. SE5 162 DQ83
Bickney Way, Lthd. 230 CC122
Bicknoller Clo., Sutt. 218 DB110
Bicknoller Rd., Enf. 82 DS39
Bicknor Rd., Orp. 205 ES101
Bidborough Clo., Brom. 204 EF99
Bidborough St. WC1 273 P3
Bidborough St. WC1 141 DL69
Biddenden Way SE9 185 EN91
Biddenden Way, Grav. 190 GE94
Biddenham Turn, Wat. 76 BW35
Bidder St. E16 144 EE71
Biddestone Rd. N7 121 DM63
Biddulph Rd. W9 140 DB69
Biddulph Rd., S.Croy. 220 DQ109
Bideford Ave., Grnf. 137 CH68
Bideford Clo., Edg. 96 CN53
Bideford Clo., Felt. 176 BZ90
Bideford Clo., Rom. 106 FJ53
Bideford Gdns., Enf. 100 DS45
Bideford Rd., Brom. 184 EF90
Bideford Rd., Enf. 83 DZ38
Bideford Rd., Ruis. 115 BV62
Bideford Rd., Well. 166 EV80
Bideford Spur, Slou. 131 AP69
Bidhams Cres., Tad. 233 CW121
Bidwell Gdns. N11 99 DJ52
Bidwell St. SE15 162 DV81
Big Common La., Red. 251 DP133
Big Hill E5 122 DV60
Bigbury Clo. N17 100 DR52
Weir Hall Rd.
Bigbury Rd. N17 100 DS52
Barkham Rd.
Biggerstaff Rd. E15 143 EC67
Biggerstaff St. N4 121 DN61
Biggin Ave., Mitch. 200 DF95
Biggin Hill SE19 201 DP95
Biggin Hill Clo., Kings.T. 177 CK92
Dukes Ave.
Biggin La., Grays 171 GH79
Biggin Way SE19 181 DP94
Bigginwood Rd. SW16 181 DP94
Biggs Row SW15 159 CX83
Felsham Rd.
Bigland St. E1 142 DV72
Bignell Rd. SE18 165 EP78
Bignold Rd. E7 124 EG63
Bigwood Rd. NW11 120 DB57
Biko Clo., Uxb. 134 BJ72
Sefton Way
Bill Hamling Clo. SE9 185 EM89
Billet Clo., Rom. 126 EX55
Billet La., Berk. 38 AU18
Billet La., Horn. 128 FK60
Billet La., Iver 133 BB69
Billet La., Slou. 133 BB69
Billet Rd. E17 101 DX53
Billet Rd., Rom. 126 EV56
Billet Rd., Stai. 174 BG90
Farnell Rd.
Billing Pl. SW10 160 DB80
Billing Rd. SW10 160 DB80
Billing St. SW10 160 DB80
Billingford Clo. SE4 163 DX84
Billington Rd. SE14 163 DX80
Billiter Sq. EC3 275 N9
Billiter St. EC3 275 N9
Billiter St. EC3 142 DS72
Billockby Clo., Chess. 216 CM107
Billson St. E14 163 EC77
Billy Lows La., Pot.B. 64 DA31
Bilsby Gro. SE9 184 EK91
Bilton Clo., Slou. 153 BE82
Bilton Rd., Erith 167 FG80
Bilton Rd., Grnf. 137 CG67
Bilton Way, Enf. 83 DY39
Bilton Way, Hayes 155 BV75
Bina Gdns. SW5 160 DC77
Bincote Rd., Enf. 81 DM41
Binden Rd. W12 159 CT76
Bindon Grn., Mord. 200 DB98
Bayham Rd.
Binfield Rd. SW4 161 DL81
Binfield Rd., S.Croy. 220 DT106
Binfield Rd., W.Byf. 212 BL112
Bingfield St. N1 141 DL67
Bingham Clo., S.Ock. 149 FV72
Bingham Dr., Stai. 174 BK94
Bingham Dr., Wok. 226 AT118
Bingham Pl. W1 272 F6
Bingham Rd., Croy. 202 DU102
Bingham Rd., Slou. 130 AG71
Bingham St. N1 142 DR65
Bingley Rd. E16 144 EJ72
Bingley Rd., Grnf. 136 CC70
Bingley Rd., Hodd. 49 EC17
Bingley Rd., Sun. 175 BU94
Binney St. W1 272 G9
Binney St. W1 140 DG72
Binns Rd. W4 158 CS78
Binns Ter. W4 158 CS78
Binns Rd.
Binscombe Cres., Gdmg. 258 AS144
Binsey Wk. SE2 166 EW75
Binyon Cres., Stan. 95 CF50
Birbeck Gdns., Wdf.Grn. 102 EF47
Birbetts Rd. SE9 185 EM89
Birch Ave. N13 100 DQ48
Birch Ave., Cat. 236 DR124
Birch Ave., West Dr. 134 BM72
Birch Circle, Gdmg. 258 AT143
Birch Clo. E16 144 EE71
Birch Clo. N19 121 DJ61
Hargrave Pk.
Birch Clo. SE15 162 DU82
Birch Clo., Add. 212 BK109
Birch Clo., Amer. 55 AS37
Birch Clo., Brent. 157 CH80
Birch Clo., Buck.H. 102 EK48
Birch Clo., Dart. 208 FK104
Birch Clo., Rom. 127 FB55
Birch Clo., Sev. 257 FH123
Birch Clo., Tedd. 177 CG92
Birch Clo., Wok. 226 AW119
Birch Clo. (Send Marsh), Wok. 243 BF125
Birch Copse, St.Alb. 60 BY30
Birch Ct., Nthwd. 93 BQ51
Rickmansworth Rd.
Birch Cres., Horn. 128 FL56
Birch Cres., S.Ock. 149 FX69
Birch Cres., Uxb. 134 BM67
Birch Dr., Hat. 45 CU19
Birch Dr., Rick. 91 BD50
Birch Gdns., Dag. 127 FC62
Birch Grn. NW9 96 CS52
Clayton Fld.
Birch Grn., Hem.H. 39 BF19
Birch Grn., Hert. 31 DJ11
Hatfield Rd.
Birch Grn., Stai. 173 BF90
Birch Gro. E11 124 EE62
Cathall Rd.
Birch Gro. SE12 184 EF87
Birch Gro. W3 138 CN74
Birch Gro., Cob. 214 BW114
Birch Gro., Pot.B. 64 DA32
Birch Gro., Shep. 195 BS96
Birch Gro., Slou. 131 AP71
Birch Gro., Tad. 233 CY124
Birch Gro., Well. 166 EU84
Birch Gro., Wind. 151 AK81
Birch Gro., Wok. 227 BD115
Birch Hill, Croy. 221 DX106
Birch La., Hem.H. 57 BB33
Birch La., Pur. 219 DL111
Birch Leys, Hem.H. 41 BQ15
Hunters Oak
Birch Mead, Orp. 205 EN103
Birch Pk., Har. 94 CC52
Birch Pl., Green. 189 FS86
Birch Rd., Felt. 176 BX92
Birch Rd., Gdmg. 258 AT143
Birch Rd., Rom. 127 FB55
Birch Row, Brom. 205 EN101
Birch Tree Ave., W.Wick. 222 EF106
Birch Tree Clo., Chesh. 56 AV30
Birch Tree Wk., Wat. 75 BT37
Birch Tree Way, Croy. 202 DV103
Birch Vale, Cob. 214 CA113
Birch Vw., Epp. 70 EV29
Birch Wk., Borwd. 78 CN39
Grove Rd.
Birch Wk., Erith 167 FC79
Birch Wk., Mitch. 201 DH95
Birch Wk., W.Byf. 212 BG112
Birch Way, Chesh. 54 AR29
Birch Way, Hat. 45 CV16
Crawford Rd.
Birch Way, St.Alb. 61 CK27
Birch Way, Warl. 237 DY118
Birch Wd., Rad. 62 CN34
Birchall La., Hert. 30 DD11
Birchall La., Welw.G.C. 30 DD11
Birchall Wd., Welw.G.C. 30 DC10
Bircham Path SE4 163 DX84
St. Norbert Rd.
Birchanger Rd. SE25 202 DU99
Birchcroft Clo., Cat. 252 DQ125
Birchdale, Ger.Cr. 112 AX60
Birchdale Clo., W.Byf. 212 BJ111
Birchdale Gdns., Rom. 126 EX59
Birchdale Rd. E7 124 EJ64
Birchdene Dr. SE28 146 EU74
Birchen Clo. NW9 118 CR61
Birchen Gro. NW9 118 CR61
Birchend Clo., S.Croy. 220 DR107
Sussex Rd.
Bircherley Ct., Hert. 32 DR09
Priory St.
Bircherley St., Hert. 32 DR09
Railway St.
Birches, The N21 81 DM44
Birches, The SE7 164 EH79
Birches, The, Brwd. 108 FY48
Birches, The, Epp. 71 FB26
Birches, The, Hem.H. 39 BF23
Birches, The, Lthd. 245 BS126
Birches, The, Orp. 223 EN105
Birches, The, Swan. 207 FE96
Birches, The (Bushey), Wat. 76 CC43
Birches, The, Wok. 227 AZ118
Heathside Rd.
Birches Clo., Epsom 232 CS115
Birches Clo., Mitch. 200 DF97
Birches Clo., Pnr. 116 BY57
Birchfield Clo., Add. 212 BH105
Birchfield Clo., Couls. 235 DM116
Birchfield Gro., Epsom 217 CW110
Birchfield Rd. (Cheshunt), Wal.Cr. 66 DV29
Birchfield St. E14 143 EA73
Birchgate Ms., Tad. 233 CW121
Bidhams Cres.
Birchin La. EC3 275 L9
Birchin La. EC3 142 DR72
Birchington Clo., Bexh. 167 FB81
Birchington Clo., Orp. 206 EW102
Hart Dyke Rd.
Birchington Rd. N8 121 DK58
Birchington Rd. NW6 140 DA67
Birchington Rd., Surb. 198 CM101
Birchington Rd., Wind. 151 AN82
Birchlands Ave. SW12 180 DF87
Birchmead, Wat. 75 BT38
Birchmead Ave., Pnr. 116 BW56
Birchmead Clo., St.Alb. 43 CD17
Birchmere Row SE3 164 EF82
Birchmore Wk. N5 122 DQ62
Highbury Quad.
Birchville Ct. (Bushey), Wat. 95 CE46
Heathbourne Rd.
Birchway, Hat. 45 CV16
Crawford Rd.
Birchway, Hayes 135 BU74
Birchway, Red. 267 DH136
Birchwood, Wal.Abb. 68 EE34
Roundhills
Birchwood Ave. N10 120 DG55
Birchwood Ave., Beck. 203 DZ98
Birchwood Ave., Hat. 45 CU16
Birchwood Ave., Sid. 186 EV89
Birchwood Ave., Wall. 200 DG104
Birchwood Clo., Brwd. 107 FW51
Canterbury Way
Birchwood Clo., Hat. 45 CU16
Birchwood Clo., Horl. 269 DH147
Birchwood Clo., Mord. 200 DB98
Birchwood Ct. N13 99 DP50
Birchwood Ct., Edg. 96 CQ54
Birchwood Dr. NW3 120 DB62
Birchwood Dr., Dart. 187 FE91
Birchwood Dr., W.Byf. 212 BG112
Birchwood Gro., Hmptn. 176 CA93
Birchwood La., Cat. 251 DP125
Birchwood La., Esher 215 CD109
Birchwood La., Lthd. 215 CF110
Birchwood La., Sev. 240 EZ115
London Rd.
Birchwood Pk. Ave., Swan. 207 FE97
Birchwood Rd. SW17 181 DH92
Birchwood Rd., Dart. 187 FD93
Birchwood Rd., Orp. 205 ER98
Birchwood Rd., Swan. 207 FC95
Birchwood Rd., W.Byf. 212 BG112
Birchwood Ter., Swan. 207 FC95
Birchwood Rd.
Birchwood Way, St.Alb. 60 CB28
Bird in Bush Rd. SE15 162 DU80
Bird La., Brwd. 129 FW55
Bird La., Upmin. 129 FR57
Bird La., Uxb. 92 BJ54
Bird St. W1 272 G9
Bird Wk., Twick. 176 BZ88
Bird-in-hand La., Brom. 204 EK96
Bird-in-hand Pas. SE23 182 DW89
Dartmouth Rd.
Birdbrook Clo., Brwd. 109 GB44
Birdbrook Clo., Dag. 147 FC66
Birdbrook Rd. SE3 164 EJ83
Birdcage Wk. SW1 277 L5
Birdcage Wk. SW1 161 DJ75
Birdcage Wk., Harl. 35 EQ14
Birdcroft Rd., Welw.G.C. 29 CX10
Birdham Clo., Brom. 204 EL99
Birdhouse La., Orp. 239 EN115
Birdhurst Ave., S.Croy. 220 DR105
Birdhurst Gdns., S.Croy. 220 DR105
Birdhurst Ri., S.Croy. 220 DS106
Birdhurst Rd. SW18 160 DC84
Birdhurst Rd. SW19 180 DE93
Birdhurst Rd., S.Croy. 220 DS106
Birdie Way, Hert. 32 DV08
Birdlip Clo. SE15 162 DS79
Birds Clo., Welw.G.C. 30 DB11
Birds Fm. Ave., Rom. 105 FB53
Birds Hill Dr., Lthd. 215 CD113
Birds Hill Ri., Lthd. 215 CD113
Birds Hill Rd., Lthd. 215 CD112
Birdsfield La. E3 143 DZ67
Birdswood Dr., Wok. 226 AS120
Birdwood Clo., S.Croy. 220 DW111
Birdwood Clo., Tedd. 177 CE91
Birfield Rd., H.Wyc. 88 AC53
Birkbeck Ave. W3 138 CQ73
Birkbeck Ave., Grnf. 136 CC67
Birkbeck Gdns., Wdf.Grn. 102 EF47
Birkbeck Gro. W3 158 CR75
Birkbeck Hill SE21 181 DP89
Birkbeck Ms. E8 122 DT64
Sandringham Rd.
Birkbeck Pl. SE21 182 DQ88
Birkbeck Rd. E8 122 DT64
Birkbeck Rd. N8 121 DL56
Birkbeck Rd. N12 98 DC50
Birkbeck Rd. N17 100 DT53
Birkbeck Rd. NW7 97 CT50
Birkbeck Rd. SW19 180 DB92
Birkbeck Rd. W3 138 CR74
Birkbeck Rd. W5 157 CJ77
Birkbeck Rd., Beck. 202 DW96
Birkbeck Rd., Brwd. 109 GD44
Birkbeck Rd., Enf. 82 DR39
Birkbeck Rd., Ilf. 125 ER57
Birkbeck Rd., Rom. 127 FD60
Birkbeck Rd., Sid. 186 EU90
Birkbeck St. E2 142 DV69
Cambridge Heath Rd.
Birkbeck Way, Grnf. 136 CC67
Birkdale Ave., Pnr. 116 CA55
Birkdale Ave., Rom. 106 FM52
Birkdale Clo., Orp. 205 ER101
Birkdale Gdns., Croy. 221 DX105
Birkdale Gdns., Wat. 94 BX48
Birkdale Rd. SE2 166 EU77
Birkdale Rd. W5 138 CL70
Birken Ms., Nthwd. 93 BP50
Birkenhead Ave., Kings.T. 198 CM96
Birkenhead St. WC1 274 A2
Birkenhead St. WC1 141 DL69
Birkett Way, Ch.St.G. 72 AX41
Birkhall Rd. SE6 183 ED88
Birkheads Rd., Reig. 250 DA133
Birklands La., St.Alb. 43 CH24
Birklands Pk., St.Alb. 43 CH24
Birkwood Clo. SW12 181 DK87
Birley Rd. N20 98 DC47
Birley Rd., Slou. 131 AR72
Birley St. SW11 160 DG82
Birling Rd., Erith 167 FD80
Birnam Clo., Wok. 228 BG124
Birnam Rd. N4 121 DM61
Birse Cres. NW10 118 CS63
Birstall Grn., Wat. 94 BX49
Birstall Rd. N15 122 DS57
Birtley Path, Borwd. 78 CL39
Darrington Rd.
Biscay Rd. W6 159 CX78
Biscoe Clo., Houns. 156 CA79
Biscoe Way SE13 163 ED83
Bisenden Rd., Croy. 202 DS103
Bisham Clo., Cars. 200 DF101
Bisham Gdns. N6 120 DG60
Bishop Butt Clo., Orp. 205 ET104
Stapleton Rd.
Bishop Duppa's Pk., Shep. 195 BR101
Bishop Fox Way, E.Mol. 196 BZ98
Bishop Ken Rd., Har. 95 CF54
Bishop Kings Rd. W14 159 CY77
Bishop Rd. N14 99 DH45
Bishop Sq., Hat. 44 CS17
Bishop St. N1 142 DQ67
Bishop Way NW10 138 CS66
Bishop Wilfred Wd. Clo. SE15 162 DU82
Moncrieff St.
Bishop's Ave. E13 144 EH67
Bishop's Ave. SW6 159 CX82
Bishops Ave., Borwd. 78 CM43
Bishops Ave., Brom. 204 EJ96
Bishops Ave., Nthwd. 93 BS49
Bishops Ave., Rom. 126 EW58
Bishops Ave., The N2 120 DD59
Bishops Bri. W2 140 DC71
Bishops Bri. Rd. W2 140 DB72
Bishops Clo. E17 123 EB56
Bishops Clo. N19 121 DJ62
Wyndham Cres.
Bishops Clo. SE9 185 EQ89

Bishops Clo., Barn. 79 CX44
Bishop's Clo., Couls. 235 DN118
Bishops Clo., Enf. 82 DV40
Central Ave.
Bishops Clo., Hat. 45 CT18
Bishops Clo., Rich. 177 CK90
Bishops Clo., St.Alb. 43 CG16
Bishops Clo., Sutt. 200 DA104
Bishops Clo., Uxb. 134 BN68
Bishop's Ct. EC4 274 F8
Bishop's Ct. WC2 274 D8
Bishops Ct., Green. 189 FS85
Chalice Way
Bishops Dr., Felt. 175 BR86
Bishops Dr., Nthlt. 136 BY67
Bishops Fm. Clo., Wind. 150 AH82
Bishops Garth, St.Alb. 43 CG16
Bishops Clo.
Bishops Gro. N2 120 DD58
Bishops Gro., Hmptn. 176 BZ91
Bishop's Hall, Kings.T. 197 CK96
Bishops Hall Rd., Brwd. 108 FV44
Bishops Hill, Walt. 195 BU101
Bishops Mead, Hem.H. 40 BH22
Bishops Orchard, Slou. 131 AP69
Bishop's Pk. Rd. SW6 159 CX82
Bishops Pk. Rd. SW16 201 DL95
Bishops Ri., Hat. 45 CT18
Bishops Rd. N6 120 DG58
Bishops Rd. SW6 159 CY81
Bishops Rd. W7 157 CE75
Bishops Rd., Croy. 201 DP101
Bishops Rd., Hayes 135 BQ71
Bishops Rd., Slou. 152 AU75
Bishops Ter. SE11 278 E8
Bishops Ter. SE11 161 DN77
Bishops Wk., Chis. 205 EQ95
Bishops Wk., Croy. 221 DX106
Bishops Wk., H.Wyc. 110 AE58
Bishop's Wk., Pnr. 116 BY55
High St.
Bishops Way E2 142 DV68
Bishops Way, Egh. 173 BD93
Bishops Wd., Wok. 226 AT117
Bishopsfield, Harl. 51 ER18
Bishopsford Rd., Mord. 200 DC101
Bishopsgate EC2 275 N7
Bishopsgate EC2 142 DS72
Bishopsgate Arc. EC2 275 N7
Bishopsgate Chyd. EC2 275 M8
Bishopsgate Rd., Egh. 172 AT90
Bishopsmead Clo., Lthd. 245 BS128
Ockham Rd. S.
Bishopsmead Dr., Lthd. 245 BS129
Ockham Rd. S.
Bishopsmead Par., Lthd. 245 BS129
Ockham Rd. S.
Bishopsthorpe Rd. SE26 183 DX91
Bishopswood Rd. N6 120 DF59
Biskra, Wat. 75 BU39
Bisley Clo., Wal.Cr. 67 DX33
Bisley Clo., Wor.Pk. 199 CW102
Bispham Rd. NW10 138 CM69
Bisson Rd. E15 143 EC68
Bisterne Ave. E17 123 ED55
Bitchet Rd., Sev. 257 FP127
Bittacy Clo. NW7 97 CX51
Bittacy Hill NW7 97 CX51
Bittacy Pk. Ave. NW7 97 CX51
Bittacy Ri. NW7 97 CW51
Bittacy Rd. NW7 97 CX51
Bittams La., Cher. 211 BD105
Bittern Clo., Hayes 136 BX71
Willow Tree La.
Bittern St. SE1 279 H5
Bitterne Dr., Wok. 226 AT117
Bittoms, The, Kings.T. 197 CK97
Bixley Clo., Sthl. 156 BZ77
Black Acre Clo., Amer. 55 AS39
Black Boy La. N15 122 DQ57
Black Boy Wd., St.Alb. 60 CA30
Black Cut, St.Alb. 43 CE21
Black Eagle Clo., West. 255 EQ127
Black Fan Clo., Enf. 82 DQ39
Black Fan Rd., Welw.G.C. 30 DA08
Black Friars Ct. EC4 274 F10
Black Friars La. EC4 274 F10
Black Friars La. EC4 141 DP72
Black Gates, Pnr. 116 BZ55
Church La.
Black Horse Ave., Chesh. 54 AR33
Black Horse Clo., Wind. 151 AK82
Black Horse Ct. SE1 279 L6
Black Lake Clo., Egh. 193 BA95
Black Lion Ct., Harl. 36 EW11
Black Lion Hill, Rad. 62 CL32
Black Lion La. W6 159 CU77
Black Pk. Rd., Slou. 132 AY68
Black Path E10 123 DX59
Black Prince Clo., W.Byf. 212 BM114
Black Prince Rd. SE1 278 A9
Black Prince Rd. SE1 161 DM77
Black Prince Rd. SE11 278 C9
Black Prince Rd. SE11 161 DM77
Black Rod Clo., Hayes 155 BT76
Black Swan Ct., Ware 33 DX06
Baldock St.
Black Swan Yd. SE1 279 M4
Black Thorne Rd., West. 238 EK115
Blackacre Rd., Epp. 85 ER37
Blackall St. EC2 275 M4
Blackberry Clo., Guil. 242 AV131
Rowan Clo.
Blackberry Clo., Shep. 195 BS98
Cherry Way
Blackberry Fm. Clo., Houns. 156 BY80
Blackbird Hill NW9 118 CQ61
Blackbird Yd. E2 142 DT69
Ravenscroft St.
Blackbirds La., Wat. 77 CD35
Blackborne Rd., Dag. 146 FA65
Blackborough Clo., Reig. 250 DC134
Blackborough Rd., Reig. 266 DB135
Blackbridge Rd., Wok. 226 AX119
Blackbrook La., Brom. 205 EN97
Blackbrook Rd., Dor. 263 CK140
Blackburn, The, Lthd. 230 BZ124
Little Bookham St.
Blackburn Rd. NW6 140 DB65
Blackburn Trd. Est., Stai. 174 BM86
Blackburne's Ms. W1 272 F10
Blackburne's Ms. W1 140 DG73
Blackbury Clo., Pot.B. 64 DC31
Blackbush Ave., Rom. 126 EX57
Blackbush Clo., Sutt. 218 DB108
Blackbush Spring, Harl. 36 EU14
Blackdale (Cheshunt), Wal.Cr. 66 DU27
Blackdown Ave., Wok. 227 BE115
Blackdown Clo. N2 98 DC54
Oak La.
Blackdown Clo., Wok. 227 BC116
Blackett Clo., Stai. 193 BE96
Blackett St. SW15 159 CX83
Blacketts Wd. Dr., Rick. 73 BB43
Blackfen Rd., Sid. 185 ES86
Blackford Clo., S.Croy. 219 DP109
Blackford Rd., Wat. 94 BX50
Blackford's Path SW15 179 CU87
Roehampton High St.
Blackfriars Bri. EC4 278 F1
Blackfriars Bri. EC4 141 DP73
Blackfriars Bri. SE1 278 F1
Blackfriars Bri. SE1 141 DP73
Blackfriars Pas. EC4 274 F10
Blackfriars Rd. SE1 278 F2
Blackfriars Rd. SE1 141 DP74
Blackhall La., Sev. 257 FK123
Blackheath Ave. SE10 163 ED80
Blackheath Gro. SE3 164 EF82
Blackheath Gro., Guil. 259 BB143
Blackheath Hill SE10 163 EC81
Blackheath La., Guil. 259 BB143
Blackheath Pk. SE3 164 EF83
Blackheath Ri. SE13 163 EC82
Blackheath Rd. SE10 163 EB81
Blackheath Vale SE3 164 EE82
Blackheath Village SE3 164 EF82
Blackhills, Esher 214 BZ109
Blackhorse Clo., Amer. 72 AT38
Blackhorse Cres., Amer. 55 AS38
Blackhorse La. E17 123 DX56
Blackhorse La., Croy. 202 DU101
Blackhorse La., Epp. 71 FD25
Blackhorse La., Reig. 250 DB129
Blackhorse Ms. E17 123 DX55
Blackhorse Rd.
Blackhorse Rd. E17 123 DX56
Blackhorse Rd. SE8 163 DY78
Blackhorse Rd., Sid. 186 EU91
Blackhorse Rd., Wok. 226 AS122
Blacklands Dr., Hayes 135 BQ70
Blacklands Mead, Red. 251 DL133
Blacklands Rd. SE6 183 EC91
Blacklands Ter. SW3 276 D9
Blacklands Ter. SW3 160 DF77
Blackley Clo., Wat. 75 BT37
Blackmans Clo., Dart. 188 FJ88
Blackmans La., Warl. 222 EE114
Blackmoor La., Wat. 75 BQ44
Blackmore Ave., Sthl. 137 CD74
Blackmore Clo., Grays 170 GB78
Blackmore Ct., Wal.Abb. 68 EG33
Blackmore Cres., Wok. 211 BC114
Blackmore Rd., Buck.H. 102 EL45
Blackmore Way, Uxb. 134 BK65
Blackmores, Harl. 51 EP15
Blackmores Gro., Tedd. 177 CG93
Blackness La., Kes. 222 EK108
Blackness La., Wok. 226 AY119
Blacknest Rd., Vir.W. 192 AT97
Blackpond La., Slou. 131 AP65
Blackpool Gdns., Hayes 135 BS70
Blackpool Rd. SE15 162 DV82
Blacks Rd. W6 159 CW77
Queen Caroline St.
Blackshaw Pl. N1 142 DS66
Hertford Rd.
Blackshaw Rd. SW17 180 DC91
Blackshots La., Grays 170 GD75
Blacksmith Clo., Ash. 232 CM119
Rectory La.
Blacksmith Clo., Rom. 126 EW58
Blacksmith Clo., Ware 33 DZ08
Blacksmith La., Guil. 259 BC139
Blacksmith Row, Slou. 153 BA77
Blacksmiths Hill, S.Croy. 220 DU113
Blacksmiths La., Cher. 194 BG101
Blacksmiths La., Orp. 206 EW99
Blacksmiths La., Rain. 147 FF67
Blacksmiths La., St.Alb. 42 CB20
Blacksmiths La., Stai. 194 BH97
Blacksmiths La., Uxb. 113 BC61
Blackstock Ms. N4 121 DP61
Blackstock Rd.
Blackstock Rd. N4 121 DP61
Blackstock Rd. N5 121 DP61
Blackstone Clo., Red. 266 DE135
Blackstone Est. E8 142 DU66
Blackstone Hill, Red. 250 DE134
Blackstone Rd. NW2 119 CW64
Blackthorn Ave., West Dr. 154 BN77
Blackthorn Clo., Reig. 266 DC136
Blackthorn Clo., St.Alb. 43 CJ17
Blackthorn Clo., Wat. 59 BV32
Blackthorn Ct., Houns. 156 BY80
Blackthorn Dell, Slou. 152 AW76
Blackthorn Gro., Bexh. 166 EY83
Blackthorn Rd., Reig. 266 DB136
Blackthorn Rd., Welw.G.C. 30 DA10
Blackthorn St. E3 143 EA70
Blackthorn Way, Brwd. 108 FX50
Blackthorne Ave., Croy. 202 DW102
Blackthorne Clo., Hat. 45 CT21
Blackthorne Dr. E4 101 ED49
Blackthorne Rd., Lthd. 246 CC126
Blackthorne Rd., Slou. 153 BE83
Blacktree Ms. SW9 161 DN83
Blackwall La. SE10 164 EE78
Blackwall Tunnel E14 143 ED74
Blackwall Tunnel App. SE10 164 EE75
Blackwall Tunnel Northern App. E3 143 EA68
Blackwall Tunnel Northern App. E14 143 EC70
Blackwall Way E14 143 EC73
Blackwater Clo. E7 124 EF64
Tower Hamlets Rd.
Blackwater Clo., Rain. 147 FD71
Blackwater La., Hem.H. 41 BS23
Blackwater Rd., Sutt. 218 DB105
High St.
Blackwater St. SE22 182 DT85
Blackwell Clo. E5 123 DY63
Blackwell Clo., Har. 95 CD52
Blackwell Dr., Wat. 76 BW44
Blackwell Gdns., Edg. 96 CN48
Blackwell Hall La., Chesh. 72 AT35
Blackwell Rd., Kings L. 58 BN29
Blackwood Clo., W.Byf. 212 BJ112
Blackwood St. SE17 279 K10
Blackwood St. SE17 162 DR78
Blade Ms. SW15 159 CZ84
Deodar Rd.
Bladen Clo., Wey. 213 BR107
Blades Clo., Lthd. 231 CK120
Bladindon Dr., Bex. 186 EW87
Bladon Clo., Guil. 243 BA133
Bladon Gdns., Har. 116 CB58
Blagdens Clo. N14 99 DJ47
Blagdens La. N14 99 DK47
Blagdon Rd. SE13 183 EB86
Blagdon Rd., N.Mal. 199 CT98
Blagdon Wk., Tedd. 177 CJ93
Blagrove Rd. W10 139 CY71
Blair Ave. NW9 118 CS59
Blair Ave., Esher 196 CC103
Blair Clo. N1 142 DQ65
Blair Clo., Hayes 155 BU77
Wyre Gro.
Blair Clo., Sid. 185 ES85
Blair Dr., Sev. 257 FH123
Blair Rd., Slou. 132 AS74
Blair St. E14 143 EC72
Blairderry Rd. SW2 181 DL89
Blairhead Dr., Wat. 93 BV48
Blake Ave., Bark. 145 ES67
Blake Clo. W10 139 CW71
Blake Clo., Cars. 200 DE101
Blake Clo., Rain. 147 FF67
Blake Clo., St.Alb. 43 CG23
Blake Clo., Well. 165 ES81
Blake Gdns. SW6 160 DB81
Blake Gdns., Dart. 168 FM84
Blake Hall Cres. E11 124 EG60
Blake Hall Rd. E11 124 EG59
Blake Hall Rd., Ong. 71 FG27
Blake Ho., Beck. 183 EA93
Blake Rd. E16 144 EF70
Blake Rd. N11 99 DJ52
Blake Rd., Croy. 202 DS103
Blake Rd., Mitch. 200 DE97
Blake St. SE8 163 EA79
Watergate St.
Blakeborough Dr., Rom. 106 FL54
Blakeden Dr., Esher 215 CF107
Blakehall Rd., Cars. 218 DF107
Blakeley Cotts. SE10 163 ED75
Tunnel Ave.
Blakemere Rd., Welw.G.C. 29 CX07
Blakemore Rd. SW16 181 DL90
Blakemore Rd., Th.Hth. 201 DM99
Blakemore Way, Belv. 166 EY76
Blakeney Ave., Beck. 203 DZ95
Blakeney Clo. E8 122 DU64
Ferncliff Rd.
Blakeney Clo. N20 98 DC46
Blakeney Clo. NW1 141 DK66
Rossendale Way
Blakeney Clo., Epsom 216 CR111
Blakeney Rd., Beck. 203 DZ95
Blakenham Rd. SW17 180 DF91
Blaker Ct. SE7 164 EJ80
Fairlawn
Blaker Rd. E15 143 EC67
Blakes Ave., N.Mal. 199 CT99
Blakes Ct., Saw. 36 EY05
Church St.
Blake's Grn., W.Wick. 203 EC102
Blakes La., Guil. 244 BL132
Blakes La., Lthd. 244 BN131
Blakes La., N.Mal. 199 CT99
Blakes Rd. SE15 162 DS80
Blakes Ter., N.Mal. 199 CU99
Blakes Way, Til. 171 GJ82
Coleridge Rd.
Blakesley Ave. W5 137 CJ72
Blakesley Wk. SW20 199 CZ96
Kingston Rd.
Blakesware Gdns. N9 100 DR45
Blakewood Clo., Felt. 176 BW91
Blanch Clo. SE15 162 DW80
Culmore Rd.
Blanchard Clo. SE9 184 EL90
Blanchard Way E8 142 DU65
Blanchards Hill, Guil. 242 AY126
Blanche La., Pot.B. 63 CU32
Blanche St. E16 144 EF70
Blanchedowne SE5 162 DR84
Blanchland Rd., Mord. 200 DB99
Blanchmans Rd., Warl. 237 DY118
Bland St. SE9 164 EK84
Blandfield Rd. SW12 180 DG86
Blandford Ave., Beck. 203 DY96
Blandford Ave., Twick. 176 CB88
Blandford Clo. N2 120 DC57
Blandford Clo., Croy. 201 DL104
Wandle Rd.
Blandford Clo., Rom. 127 FB56
Blandford Clo., Slou. 152 AX76
Blandford Clo., Wok. 227 BB117
Blandford Ct., Slou. 152 AX76
Blandford Rd. S.
Blandford Cres. E4 101 EC45
Blandford Rd. W4 158 CS76
Blandford Rd. W5 157 CK75
Blandford Rd., Beck. 202 DW96
Blandford Rd., St.Alb. 43 CG20
Blandford Rd., Sthl. 156 CA77
Blandford Rd., Tedd. 177 CD92
Blandford Rd. N., Slou. 152 AX76
Blandford Rd. S., Slou. 152 AX76
Blandford Sq. NW1 272 C5
Blandford Sq. NW1 140 DE70
Blandford St. W1 272 E8
Blandford St. W1 140 DF72
Blandford Waye, Hayes 136 BW72
Blaney Cres. E6 145 EP69
Blanford Rd., Reig. 266 DC135
Blanmerle Rd. SE9 185 EP88
Blann Clo. SE9 184 EK86
Blantyre St. SW10 160 DD80
Blantyre Wk. SW10 160 DD80
Blantyre St.
Blashford NW3 140 DF66
Blashford St. SE13 183 ED87
Blasker Wk. E14 163 EA78
Blattner Clo., Borwd. 77 CK43
Allum La.
Blawith Rd., Har. 117 CE56
Blaydon Clo. N17 100 DV52
Blaydon Clo., Ruis. 115 BS59
Blaydon Wk. N17 100 DV52
Blays Clo., Egh. 172 AW93
Blays La., Egh. 172 AV94
Bleak Hill La. SE18 165 ET79
Blean Gro. SE20 182 DW94
Bleasdale Ave., Grnf. 137 CG68
Blechynden St. W10 139 CX73
Bramley Rd.
Bleddyn Clo., Sid. 186 EW86
Bledlow Clo. SE28 146 EW73
Bledlow Ri., Grnf. 136 CC68
Bleeding Heart Yd. EC1 274 E7
Blegborough Rd. SW16 181 DJ93
Blencarn Clo., Wok. 226 AT116
Blendon Dr., Bex. 186 EX86
Blendon Path, Brom. 184 EF94
Hope Pk.
Blendon Rd., Bex. 186 EW86
Blendon Ter. SE18 165 EQ78
Blendworth Way SE15 162 DS80
Daniel Gdns.
Blenheim Ave., Ilf. 125 EN58
Blenheim Clo. N21 100 DQ46
Elm Pk. Rd.
Blenheim Clo. SW20 199 CW97
Blenheim Clo., Dart. 188 FJ86
Blenheim Clo., Grnf. 137 CD68
Leaver Gdns.
Blenheim Clo., Rom. 127 FC56
Blenheim Clo., Saw. 36 EW07
Blenheim Clo., Slou. 133 AZ74
Blenheim Clo., Upmin. 129 FS60
Blenheim Clo., Wall. 219 DJ108
Blenheim Clo., Wat. 94 BX45
Blenheim Clo., W.Byf. 211 BF113
Madeira Rd.
Blenheim Ct. N19 121 DL61
Marlborough Rd.
Blenheim Ct., Sid. 185 ER90
Blenheim Cres. W11 139 CY73
Blenheim Cres., Ruis. 115 BR61
Blenheim Cres., S.Croy. 220 DQ108
Blenheim Dr., Well. 165 ET81
Blenheim Gdns. NW2 139 CW65
Blenheim Gdns. SW2 181 DM86
Blenheim Gdns., Kings.T. 178 CP94
Blenheim Gdns., S.Croy. 220 DU112
Blenheim Gdns., S.Ock. 148 FP74
Blenheim Gdns., Wall. 219 DJ107
Blenheim Gdns., Wem. 118 CL62
Blenheim Gdns., Wok. 226 AV119
Blenheim Gro. SE15 162 DU82
Blenheim Pk. Rd., S.Croy. 220 DQ109
Blenheim Pas. NW8 140 DC68
Blenheim Ter.
Blenheim Ri. N15 122 DT56
Talbot Rd.
Blenheim Rd. E6 144 EK69
Blenheim Rd. E15 124 EE63
Blenheim Rd. E17 123 DX55
Blenheim Rd. NW8 140 DC68
Blenheim Rd. SE20 182 DW94
Maple Rd.
Blenheim Rd. SW20 199 CW97
Blenheim Rd. W4 158 CS76
Blenheim Rd., Abb.L. 59 BU32
Langley La.
Blenheim Rd., Barn. 79 CX41
Blenheim Rd., Brwd. 108 FU44
Blenheim Rd., Brom. 204 EL98
Blenheim Rd., Dart. 188 FJ86
Blenheim Rd., Epsom 216 CR111
Blenheim Rd., Har. 116 CB58
Blenheim Rd., Nthlt. 136 CB65
Blenheim Rd., Orp. 206 EW103
Blenheim Rd., St.Alb. 43 CF19
Blenheim Rd., Sid. 186 EW88
Blenheim Rd., Slou. 152 AX77
Blenheim Rd., Sutt. 200 DA104
Blenheim St. W1 273 H9
Blenheim Ter. NW8 140 DC68
Blenheim Way, Epp. 70 FA27
Blenheim Way, Islw. 157 CG81
London Rd.
Blenkarne Rd. SW11 180 DF86
Blenkin Clo., St.Alb. 42 CC16
Bleriot Rd., Houns. 156 BW80
Blessbury Rd., Edg. 96 CQ53
Blessington Clo. SE13 163 ED83
Blessington Rd. SE13 163 ED84
Bletchingley Clo., Red. 251 DJ129
Bletchingley Clo., Th.Hth. 201 DP98
Bletchingley Rd., Gdse. 252 DU131
Bletchingley Rd. (Bletchingley), Red. 251 DN133
Bletchingley Rd. (South Merstham), Red. 251 DJ129
Bletchley Ct. N1 275 K1
Bletchley St. N1 275 J1
Bletchley St. N1 142 DQ68
Bletchmore Clo., Hayes 155 BR78
Bletsoe Wk. N1 142 DQ68
Cropley St.
Bligh Rd., Grav. 191 GG86
Blighs Rd., Sev. 257 FH125
Blinco La., Slou. 132 AY72
Blincoe Clo. SW19 179 CX89
Blind La., Bans. 234 DE115
Blind La., Bet. 264 CQ137
Wheelers La.
Blind La., H.Wyc. 110 AC56
Blind La., Loug. 84 EE40
Blind La., Wal.Abb. 68 EJ33
Blindman's La. (Cheshunt), Wal.Cr. 67 DX30
Bliss Cres. SE13 163 EB82
Coldbath St.
Blissett St. SE10 163 EC81
Blisworth Clo., Hayes 136 BY70
Braunston Dr.
Blithbury Rd., Dag. 146 EV65
Blithdale Rd. SE2 166 EU77
Blithfield St. W8 160 DB76
Blockhouse Rd., Grays 170 GC79
Blockley Rd., Wem. 117 CH61
Bloemfontein Ave. W12 139 CV74
Bloemfontein Rd. W12 139 CV73
Blomfield Rd. W9 140 DB71
Blomfield St. EC2 275 L7
Blomfield St. EC2 142 DR71
Blomfield Vill. W2 140 DB71
Blomville Rd., Dag. 126 EY62
Blondel St. SW11 160 DG82
Blondell Clo., West Dr. 154 BK79
Blondin Ave. W5 157 CJ77
Blondin St. E3 143 EA68
Bloom Gro. SE27 181 DP90
Bloom Pk. Rd. SW6 159 CZ80
Bloomburg St. SW1 277 L9
Bloomfield Clo., Wok. 226 AS118
Bloomfield Cres., Ilf. 125 EP58
Bloomfield Pl. W1 273 J10
Bloomfield Rd. N6 120 DG58
Bloomfield Rd. SE18 165 EP78
Bloomfield Rd., Brom. 204 EK99
Bloomfield Rd., Kings.T. 198 CL98
Bloomfield Ter. SW1 276 G10
Bloomfield Ter. SW1 160 DG78
Bloomfield Ter., West. 255 ES125
Bloomhall Rd. SE19 182 DR92
Bloomsbury Clo. W5 138 CM73
Bloomsbury Clo., Epsom 216 CR110
Bloomsbury Ct. WC1 274 A7
Bloomsbury Ct., Guil. 259 AZ135
Warren Rd.
Bloomsbury Ct., Pnr. 116 BZ55
Bloomsbury Ho. SW4 181 DK86
Bloomsbury Pl. SW18 180 DC85
Fullerton Rd.
Bloomsbury Pl. WC1 274 A6
Bloomsbury Sq. WC1 274 A7
Bloomsbury Sq. WC1 141 DL71
Bloomsbury St. WC1 273 N7
Bloomsbury St. WC1 141 DK71
Bloomsbury Way WC1 273 P8
Bloomsbury Way WC1 141 DL71
Blore Clo. SW8 161 DK81
Thessaly Rd.
Blore Ct. W1 273 M10
Blossom Clo. W5 158 CL75
Almond Ave.
Blossom Clo., Dag. 146 EZ67
Blossom Clo., S.Croy. 220 DT106
Melville Ave.
Blossom La., Enf. 82 DQ39
Blossom St. E1 275 N5
Blossom St. E1 142 DS70
Blossom Way, Uxb. 134 BM66
Blossom Way, West Dr. 154 BN77
Blossom Waye, Houns. 156 BY80
Blount St. E14 143 DY71
Bloxam Gdns. SE9 184 EL85
Bloxhall Rd. E10 123 DZ60
Bloxham Cres., Hmptn. 176 BZ94
Bloxworth Clo., Wall. 201 DJ104
Blucher Rd. SE5 162 DQ80
Blucher St., Chesh. 54 AP31
Blue Anchor All., Rich. 158 CL84
Kew Rd.
Blue Anchor La. SE16 162 DU77
Blue Anchor La., Til. 171 GL77
Blue Anchor Yd. E1 142 DU73
Blue Ball La., Egh. 173 AZ92
Blue Ball Yd. SW1 277 K3
Blue Barn La., Wey. 212 BN111
Blue Cedars, Bans. 217 CX114
Bluebell Ave. E12 124 EL64
Warwick Rd.
Bluebell Clo. SE26 182 DT91
Bluebell Clo., Hem.H. 39 BE21
Sundew Rd.
Bluebell Clo., Hert. 32 DU09
Bluebell Clo., Orp. 205 EQ103
Bluebell Clo., Wall. 201 DH102
Bluebell Ct., Wok. 226 AX119
Bluebell Dr., Abb.L. 59 BT27
Bedmond Grn.
Bluebell La., Lthd. 245 BS129
Ockham Rd. S.
Bluebell Way, Ilf. 125 EP64
Uphall Rd.
Blueberry Clo., St.Alb. 43 CD16
Blueberry Gdns., Couls. 235 DM116
Blueberry La., Sev. 240 EW116
Bluebridge Ave., Hat. 63 CY27
Bluebridge Rd., Hat. 63 CY26
Bluecoat Yd., Ware 33 DX06
Bluecoats Ave., Hert. 32 DR09
Bluefield Clo., Hmptn. 176 CA92
Bluegates, Epsom 217 CU108
Bluehouse Hill, St.Alb. 42 CA20
Bluehouse La., Oxt. 254 EE128
Bluehouse Rd. E4 102 EE48
Bluemans, Epp. 53 FD24
Bluemans End, Epp. 53 FD24
Bluett Rd., St.Alb. 61 CK27
Blumfield Ct., Slou. 131 AK71
Blumfield Cres., Slou. 131 AK70
Blundel La., Cob. 230 BZ116
Blundell Ave., Horl. 268 DF147
Blundell Clo., St.Alb. 43 CD16
Blundell Rd., Edg. 96 CR53
Blundell St. N7 141 DL66
Blunden Clo., Dag. 126 EW60
Blunesfield, Pot.B. 64 DD31
Blunt Rd., S.Croy. 220 DR106
Blunts Ave., West Dr. 154 BN80
Blunts La., St.Alb. 42 BX24
Blunts Rd. SE9 185 EN85
Blurton Rd. E5 122 DW63
Blyth Clo. E14 163 ED77
Manchester Rd.
Blyth Clo., Borwd. 78 CM39
Blyth Clo., Twick. 177 CF86
Grimwood Rd.
Blyth Rd. E17 123 DZ59
Blyth Rd. SE28 146 EW73
Blyth Rd., Brom. 204 EF95
Blyth Rd., Hayes 155 BS75
Blyth Wk., Upmin. 129 FS58
Blythe Clo. SE6 183 DZ87
Blythe Clo., Iver 133 BF72
Blythe Hill SE6 183 DZ87
Blythe Hill, Orp. 205 ET95
Blythe Hill La. SE6 183 DZ87
Blythe Rd. W14 159 CX76
Blythe Rd., Hodd. 49 ED19
Blythe St. E2 142 DV69
Blythe Vale SE6 183 DZ88
Blythswood Rd., Ilf. 126 EU60
Blythway, Welw.G.C. 29 CZ06
Blythwood Rd. N4 121 DL59
Blythwood Rd., Pnr. 94 BX53
Blyton Clo., Beac. 89 AK51
Boades Ms. NW3 120 DD63
New End
Boadicea St. N1 141 DM67
Copenhagen St.
Boakes Clo. NW9 118 CQ56
Roe Grn.
Boakes Meadow, Sev. 225 FF111
Boar Clo., Chig. 104 EU50
Board Sch. Rd., Wok. 227 AZ116
Boardman Ave. E4 83 EB43
Boardman Clo., Barn. 79 CY43
Mays La.
Boarlands Clo., Slou. 131 AM73
Boarlands Path, Slou. 131 AM73
Brook Path
Boar's Head Yd., Brent. 157 CK80
Brent Way
Boars Rd., Harl. 52 FA16
Boat Lifter Way SE16 163 DY77
Sweden Gate

Boathouse Wk. SE15 162 DT80
Boathouse Wk., Rich. 157 CK81
Kew Rd.
Bob Anker Clo. E13 144 EG69
Chesterton Rd.
Bob Marley Way SE24 161 DN84
Mayall Rd.
Bobbin Clo. SW4 161 DJ83
Bobs La., Rom. 105 FF53
Bocketts La., Lthd. 231 CF124
Bockhampton Rd., Kings.T. 178 CM94
Bocking St. E8 142 DV67
Boddicott Clo. SW19 179 CY89
Bodell Clo., Grays 170 GB75
Bodiam Clo., Enf. 82 DR40
Bodiam Rd. SW16 181 DK94
Bodle Ave., Swans. 190 FY87
Bodley Clo., Epp. 69 ET30
St. John's Rd.
Bodley Clo., N.Mal. 198 CS99
Bodley Manor Way SW2 181 DN87
Papworth Way
Bodley Rd., N.Mal. 198 CR100
Bodmin Ave., Slou. 131 AN71
Bodmin Clo., Har. 116 BZ62
Bodmin Gro., Mord. 200 DB98
Bodmin St. SW18 180 DA88
Bodnant Gdns. SW20 199 CV97
Bodney Rd. E8 122 DV64
Bodwell Clo., Hem.H. 40 BG19
Boeing Way, Sthl. 155 BV76
Boevey Path, Belv. 166 EZ78
Orchard Ave.
Bogey La., Orp. 223 EM108
Bognor Gdns., Wat. 94 BW50
Bowring Grn.
Bognor Rd., Well. 166 EX81
Bohemia, Hem.H. 40 BL19
Bohemia Pl. E8 142 DW65
Bohun Gro., Barn. 80 DE44
Boileau Rd. SW13 159 CU80
Boileau Rd. W5 138 CM72
Bois Ave., Amer. 55 AP36
Bois Hall Rd., Add. 212 BK106
Bois Hill, Chesh. 54 AS34
Bois La., Amer. 55 AR36
Bois Moor Rd., Chesh. 54 AQ33
Boissy Clo., St.Alb. 44 CL21
Bolden St. SE8 163 EB82
Bolderwood Way, W.Wick. 203 EB103
Boldmere Rd., Pnr. 116 BW59
Boleyn Ave., Enf. 82 DV39
Boleyn Ave., Epsom 217 CU110
Boleyn Clo. E17 123 EA56
Boleyn Clo., Grays 170 FZ76
Clifford Rd.
Boleyn Clo., Hem.H. 41 BQ15
Parr Cres.
Boleyn Clo., Loug. 84 EL44
Roding Rd.
Boleyn Clo., Stai. 173 BE92
Chertsey La.
Boleyn Ct., Brox. 49 DY21
Bell La.
Boleyn Ct., Buck.H. 102 EG46
Boleyn Dr., Ruis. 116 BX61
Boleyn Dr., St.Alb. 43 CD22
Boleyn Dr., W.Mol. 196 BZ97
Boleyn Gdns., Brwd. 109 GA48
Boleyn Gdns., Dag. 147 FC66
Boleyn Gdns., W.Wick. 203 EB103
Boleyn Gro., W.Wick. 203 EC103
Boleyn Rd. E6 144 EK68
Boleyn Rd. E7 144 EG66
Boleyn Rd. N16 122 DS64
Boleyn Wk., Lthd. 231 CF120
Boleyn Way, Barn. 80 DC41
Boleyn Way, Ilf. 103 EQ51
Boleyn Way, Swans. 190 FY87
Bolina Rd. SE16 162 DW78
Bolingbroke Gro. SW11 180 DF86
Bolingbroke Rd. W14 159 CX76
Bolingbroke Wk. SW11 160 DD81
Bolingbroke Way, Hayes 135 BR74
Bolingbrook, St.Alb. 43 CG16
Bolliger Ct. NW10 138 CQ70
Park Royal Rd.
Bollo Bri. Rd. W3 158 CP76
Bollo La. W3 158 CP75
Bollo La. W4 158 CQ77
Bolney St. SW8 161 DM80
Bolney Way, Felt. 176 BY90
Bolsover Gro., Red. 251 DL129
Bolsover St. W1 273 J5
Bolsover St. W1 141 DH70
Bolstead Rd., Mitch. 201 DH95
Bolt Cellar La., Epp. 69 ES30
Bolt Ct. EC4 274 E9
Bolters La., Bans. 217 CZ114
Bolters Rd., Horl. 268 DG146
Bolters Rd. S., Horl. 268 DF146
Boltmore Clo. NW4 119 CX55
Bolton Ave., Wind. 151 AR83
Bolton Clo. SE20 202 DU96
Selby Rd.
Bolton Clo., Chess. 215 CK107
Bolton Cres. SE5 161 DP79
Bolton Cres., Wind. 151 AQ83
Bolton Gdns. NW10 139 CX68
Bolton Gdns. SW5 160 DB78
Bolton Gdns., Brom. 184 EF93
Bolton Gdns., Tedd. 177 CG93
Bolton Gdns. Ms. SW10 160 DB78
Bolton Rd. E15 144 EF65
Bolton Rd. N18 100 DT50
Bolton Rd. NW8 140 DB67
Bolton Rd. NW10 138 CS67
Bolton Rd. W4 158 CQ80
Bolton Rd., Chess. 215 CK107
Bolton Rd., Har. 116 CC56
Bolton Rd., Wind. 151 AQ83
Bolton St. W1 277 J2
Bolton St. W1 141 DH74
Bolton Wk. N7 121 DM61
Durham Rd.
Boltons, The SW10 160 DC78
Boltons, The, Wem. 117 CF63
Boltons, The, Wdf.Grn. 102 EG49
Boltons Clo., Wok. 228 BG116
Boltons La., Hayes 155 BQ81
Boltons La., Wok. 228 BG116
Boltons Pl. SW10 160 DC78
The Boltons
Bombay St. SE16 162 DV77
Bombers La., West. 239 ES120
Grays Rd.
Bomer Clo., West Dr. 154 BN80
Bomore Rd. W11 139 CY73
Bon Marche Ter. SE27 182 DS91
Gipsy Rd.
Bonar Pl., Chis. 184 EL94
Sundridge Ave.
Bonar Rd. SE15 162 DU80
Bonaventure Ct., Grav. 191 GM91
Bonchester Clo., Chis. 185 EN94
Bonchurch Clo., Sutt. 218 DB108
Bonchurch Rd. W10 139 CY71
Bonchurch Rd. W13 137 CH74
Bond Clo., Sev. 240 EX115
Bond Clo., West Dr. 134 BM72
Bond Ct. EC4 275 K9
Bond Gdns., Wall. 219 DJ105
Bond Rd., Mitch. 200 DE96
Bond Rd., Surb. 198 CM102
Bond Rd., Warl. 237 DX118
Bond St. E15 124 EE64
Bond St. W4 158 CS77
Chiswick Common Rd.
Bond St. W5 137 CK73
Bond St., Egh. 172 AV92
Bond St., Grays 170 GC79
Bondfield Rd. E6 144 EL71
Lovage App.
Bondfield Rd., Hayes 135 BU69
Bondfield Wk., Dart. 168 FM83
Joyce Grn. La.
Bonding Yd. Wk. SE16 163 DY76
Finland St.
Bonds La., Dor. 263 CH142
Bondway SW8 161 DL79
Bone Mill La., Gdse. 253 DY134
Eastbourne Rd.
Bonehurst Rd., Horl. 268 DG146
Bonehurst Rd., Red. 266 DG142
Boneta Rd. SE18 165 EM76
Bonfield Rd. SE13 163 EC84
Bonham Gdns., Dag. 126 EX61
Bonham Rd. SW2 181 DM85
Bonham Rd., Dag. 126 EX61
Bonheur Rd. W4 158 CR75
Bonhill St. EC2 275 L5
Bonhill St. EC2 142 DR70
Boniface Gdns., Har. 94 CB52
Boniface Rd., Uxb. 115 BP62
Boniface Wk., Har. 94 CB52
Bonks Hill, Saw. 36 EX06
Bonner Hill Rd., Kings.T. 198 CM97
Bonner Rd. E2 142 DW68
Bonner St. E2 142 DW68
Bonner Wk., Grays 170 FZ76
Clifford Rd.
Bonners Clo., Wok. 227 AZ122
Bonnersfield Clo., Har. 117 CF58
Bonnersfield La., Har. 117 CF58
Bonneville Gdns. SW4 181 DJ86
Bonney Gro. (Cheshunt), Wal.Cr. 66 DU30
Bonney Way, Swan. 207 FE96
Bonnington Rd., Horn. 128 FK64
Bonnington Sq. SW8 161 DM79
Bonnington Twr., Brom. 204 EL100
Bonningtons, Brwd. 109 GB48
Bonny St. NW1 141 DJ66
Bonny's Rd., Reig. 265 CX135
Bonser Rd., Twick. 177 CF89
Bonsey Clo., Wok. 226 AY121
Bonsey La., Wok. 226 AY121
Bonseys La., Wok. 211 AZ109
Bonsey's Yd., Uxb. 134 BK66
George St.
Bonsor Dr., Tad. 233 CY122
Bonsor St. SE5 162 DS80
Bonville Gdns. NW4 119 CU56
Handowe Clo.
Bonville Rd., Brom. 184 EF92
Book Ms. WC2 273 N9
Booker Clo. E14 143 DZ71
Wallwood St.
Booker Rd. N18 100 DU50
Bookham Ct., Lthd. 230 BZ123
Church Rd.
Bookham Gro., Lthd. 246 CB126
Lower Shott
Bookham Ind. Pk., Lthd. 230 BZ123
Bookham Rd., Cob. 230 BW119
Boone Ct. N9 100 DW48
Boone St. SE13 164 EE84
Boones Rd. SE13 164 EE84
Boord St. SE10 164 EE76
Boot St. N1 275 M3
Boot St. N1 142 DS69
Booth Clo. SE28 146 EV73
Booth Dr., Stai. 174 BK93
Booth Rd. NW9 96 CR54
Booth Rd., Croy. 201 DP103
Waddon New Rd.
Boothby Rd. N19 121 DK61
Booths Clo., Hat. 45 CX24
Booth's Pl. W1 273 L7
Bordars Rd. W7 137 CE71
Bordars Wk. W7 137 CE71
Borden Ave., Enf. 82 DR44
Border Cres. SE26 182 DV92
Border Gdns., Croy. 221 EB105
Border Rd. SE26 182 DV92
Bordergate, Mitch. 200 DF95
Borders La., Loug. 85 EN42
Borderside, Slou. 132 AU72
Bordesley Rd., Mord. 200 DB98
Bordon Wk. SW15 179 CU87
Boreas Wk. N1 274 G1
Boreham Ave. E16 144 EG72
Boreham Clo. E11 123 EC60
Hainault Rd.
Boreham Holt, Borwd. 78 CM42
Boreham Rd. N22 100 DQ54
Borehamwood Ind. Pk., Borwd. 78 CR40
Borer's Pas. E1 275 N8
Borgard Rd. SE18 165 EM77
Borkwood Pk., Orp. 223 ET105
Borkwood Way, Orp. 223 ES105
Borland Clo., Green. 189 FU85
Steele Ave.
Borland Rd. SE15 162 DW84
Borland Rd., Tedd. 177 CH93
Born Wk., Slou. 130 AH69
Bornedene, Pot.B. 63 CY31
Borneo St. SW15 159 CW83
Borough, The, Bet. 264 CN135
Borough High St. SE1 279 J5
Borough High St. SE1 162 DQ75
Borough Hill, Croy. 201 DP104
Borough Rd. SE1 278 G6
Borough Rd. SE1 161 DP76
Borough Rd., Islw. 157 CE81
Borough Rd., Kings.T. 198 CN95
Borough Rd., Mitch. 200 DE96
Borough Rd., West. 238 EK121
Borough Sq. SE1 279 H5
Borough Way, Pot.B. 63 CY32
Borrell Clo., Brox. 49 DZ20
Borrett Clo. SE17 162 DQ78
Penrose St.
Borrodaile Rd. SW18 180 DB86
Borrowdale Ave., Har. 95 CG54
Borrowdale Clo., Egh. 173 BB94
Derwent Rd.
Borrowdale Clo., Ilf. 124 EL56
Borrowdale Clo., S.Croy. 220 DT113
Borrowdale Ct., Enf. 82 DQ39
Borrowdale Ct., Hem.H. 40 BL17
Borrowdale Dr., S.Croy. 220 DT112
Borthwick Ms. E15 124 EE63
Borthwick Rd.
Borthwick Rd. E15 124 EE63
Borthwick Rd. NW9 119 CT58
West Hendon Bdy.
Borthwick St. SE8 163 EA78
Borwick Ave. E17 123 DZ55
Bosanquet Clo., Uxb. 134 BK70
Bosanquet Rd., Hodd. 49 EC15
Bosbury Rd. SE6 183 EC90
Boscastle Rd. NW5 121 DH62
Bosco Clo., Orp. 223 ET105
Strickland Way
Boscobel Pl. SW1 276 G8
Boscobel Pl. SW1 160 DG77
Boscobel St. NW8 272 A5
Boscobel St. NW8 140 DD70
Boscombe Ave. E10 123 ED59
Boscombe Ave., Grays 170 GD77
Boscombe Ave., Horn. 128 FK60
Boscombe Clo. E5 123 DY64
Boscombe Clo., Egh. 193 BC95
Boscombe Gdns. SW16 181 DL93
Boscombe Rd. SW17 180 DG93
Boscombe Rd. SW19 200 DA95
Boscombe Rd. W12 139 CU74
Boscombe Rd., Wor.Pk. 199 CW102
Bosgrove E4 101 EC46
Boss St. SE1 279 P4
Bostal Row, Bexh. 166 EZ83
Harlington Rd.
Bostall Heath SE2 166 EV78
Bostall Hill SE2 166 EU78
Bostall La. SE2 166 EV78
Bostall Manorway SE2 166 EV77
Bostall Pk. Ave., Bexh. 166 EY80
Bostall Rd., Orp. 186 EV94
Boston Gdns. W4 158 CS79
Boston Gdns. W7 157 CG77
Boston Gro., Ruis. 115 BQ58
Boston Gro., Slou. 131 AQ72
Boston Manor Rd., Brent. 157 CH77
Boston Pk. Rd., Brent. 157 CJ78
Boston Pl. NW1 272 D5
Boston Pl. NW1 140 DF70
Boston Rd. E6 144 EL69
Boston Rd. E17 123 EA58
Boston Rd. W7 137 CE74
Boston Rd., Croy. 201 DM100
Boston Rd., Edg. 96 CQ52
Boston St. E2 142 DU68
Audrey St.
Boston Vale W7 157 CG77
Bostonthorpe Rd. W7 157 CE75
Bosville Ave., Sev. 256 FG123
Bosville Dr., Sev. 256 FG123
Bosville Rd., Sev. 256 FG123
Boswell Clo., Orp. 206 EW100
Killewarren Way
Boswell Ct. WC1 274 A6
Boswell Path, Hayes 155 BT77
Croyde Ave.
Boswell Rd., Th.Hth. 202 DQ98
Boswell St. WC1 274 A6
Boswell St. WC1 141 DL71
Bosworth Clo. E17 101 DZ53
Bosworth Cres., Rom. 106 FJ51
Bosworth Rd. N11 99 DK51
Bosworth Rd. W10 139 CY70
Bosworth Rd., Barn. 80 DA41
Bosworth Rd., Dag. 126 FA62
Botany Bay La., Chis. 205 EQ96
Botany Clo., Barn. 80 DE42
Crescent Rd.
Botany Way, Purf. 168 FP78
Boteley Clo. E4 101 ED47
Botery's Cross, Red. 251 DP133
Botha Rd. E13 144 EH71
Botham Clo., Edg. 96 CQ52
Pavilion Way
Bothwell Clo. E16 144 EF71
Bothwell Rd., Croy. 221 EC110
Bothwell St. W6 159 CX79
Delorme St.
Botley La., Chesh. 56 AU30
Botley Rd., Chesh. 54 AR30
Botley Rd., Hem.H. 40 BN15
Botolph All. EC3 275 M10
Botolph La. EC3 275 M10
Botsford Rd. SW20 199 CY96
Bott Rd., Dart. 188 FM91
Bottom Ho. Fm. La., Ch.St.G. 89 AR47
Bottom La., Beac. 89 AP51
Bottom La., Chesh. 56 AT34
Bottom La., Kings L. 74 BH35
Bottrells Clo., Ch.St.G. 90 AT47
Bottrells La., Amer. 89 AP46
Bottrells La., Ch.St.G. 90 AT47
Botts Ms. W2 140 DA72
Chepstow Rd.
Botts Pas. W2 140 DA72
Chepstow Rd.
Botwell Common Rd., Hayes 135 BR73
Botwell Cres., Hayes 135 BS72
Botwell La., Hayes 135 BS73
Boucher Clo., Tedd. 177 CF92
Boucher Dr., Grav. 191 GF90
Bouchier Wk., Rain. 147 FG65
Deere Ave.
Boughton Ave., Brom. 204 EF101
Boughton Hall Ave., Wok. 227 BF124
Boughton Rd. SE28 165 ES76
Boughton Way, Amer. 72 AW38
Boulcott St. E1 143 DX72
Boulevard, The SW17 180 DG89
Balham High Rd.
Boulevard, The, Pnr. 116 CA56
Pinner Rd.
Boulevard, The, Wat. 75 BR43
Boulevard, The, Welw.G.C. 29 CZ07
Boulmer Rd., Uxb. 134 BJ69
Boulogne Rd., Croy. 202 DQ100
Boulter Gdns., Rain. 147 FG65
Boulters Clo., Maid. 130 AC70
Boulters Clo., Slou. 151 AN75
Amerden Way
Boulters Ct., Maid. 130 AC70
Boulters Gdns., Maid. 130 AC70
Boulters La., Maid. 130 AC70
Boulthurst Way, Oxt. 254 EH132
Boulton Ho., Brent. 158 CL78
Boulton Rd., Dag. 126 EY62
Boultwood Rd. E6 145 EM72
Bounce, The, Hem.H. 40 BK18
Bounce Hill (Navestock), Rom. 87 FH38
Mill La.
Bounces La. N9 100 DV47
Bounces Rd. N9 100 DV47
Boundaries Rd. SW12 180 DF89
Boundaries Rd., Felt. 176 BW88
Boundary Clo. SE20 202 DU96
Haysleigh Gdns.
Boundary Clo., Ilf. 125 ES63
Loxford La.
Boundary Clo., Kings.T. 198 CP97
Boundary Clo., Sthl. 156 CA78
Boundary Ct., Welw.G.C. 29 CZ13
Boundary La.
Boundary Dr., Brwd. 109 GE45
Boundary Dr., Hert. 32 DR07
Boundary La. E13 144 EK69
Boundary La. SE17 162 DQ79
Boundary La., Welw.G.C. 29 CY12
Boundary Par. N8 121 DL58
Boundary Pas. E2 275 P4
Boundary Pl., H.Wyc. 110 AD55
Boundary Rd. E13 144 EJ68
Boundary Rd. E17 123 DZ59
Boundary Rd. N9 82 DW44
Boundary Rd. N22 121 DP55
Boundary Rd. NW8 140 DC67
Boundary Rd. SW19 180 DD93
Boundary Rd., Ashf. 174 BJ92
Boundary Rd., Bark. 145 ER67
Boundary Rd., Cars. 218 DG108
Boundary Rd., Ger.Cr. 90 AX52
Boundary Rd., H.Wyc. 88 AC54
Boundary Rd., Maid. 130 AE70
Boundary Rd., Pnr. 116 BX59
Boundary Rd., Rom. 127 FG58
Boundary Rd., St.Alb. 43 CE18
Boundary Rd., Sid. 185 ES85
Boundary Rd., Upmin. 128 FN62
Boundary Rd., Wall. 219 DH107
Boundary Rd., Wem. 118 CL62
Boundary Rd., Wok. 227 BA116
Boundary Row SE1 278 F4
Boundary St. E2 275 P3
Boundary St. E2 142 DT70
Boundary St., Erith 167 FF80
Boundary Way, Croy. 221 EA106
Boundary Way, Hem.H. 41 BQ17
Boundary Way, Wat. 59 BV32
Boundary Way, Wok. 227 BA115
Boundary Yd., Wok. 227 BA116
Boundary Rd.
Boundfield Rd. SE6 184 EE90
Bounds Grn. Rd. N11 99 DJ51
Bounds Grn. Rd. N22 99 DL52
Bourchier Clo., Sev. 257 FH126
Bourchier St. W1 273 M10
Bourdon Pl. W1 273 J10
Bourdon Rd. SE20 202 DW96
Bourdon St. W1 277 H1
Bourdon St. W1 141 DH73
Bourke Clo. NW10 138 CS65
Mayo Rd.
Bourke Clo. SW4 181 DL86
Bourke Hill, Couls. 234 DF119
Bourlet Clo. W1 273 K7
Bourn Ave. N15 122 DR56
Bourn Ave., Barn. 80 DD43
Bourn Ave., Uxb. 134 BN70
Bournbrook Rd. SE3 164 EK83
Bourne, The N14 99 DK46
Bourne, The, Hem.H. 57 BA27
Bourne, The, Ware 33 DX05
Bourne Ave. N14 99 DL47
Bourne Ave., Cher. 194 BG97
Eastern Ave.
Bourne Ave., Hayes 155 BQ76
Bourne Ave., Ruis. 116 BW64
Bourne Ave., Wind. 151 AQ84
Bourne Bri. La., Rom. 104 EZ45
Bourne Clo., Brox. 49 DZ20
Bourne Clo., Guil. 259 BB140
Hornhatch
Bourne Clo., Ware 33 DX05
Bourne Clo., W.Byf. 212 BH113
Bourne Ct., Ruis. 115 BV64
Bourne Dr., Mitch. 200 DD96
Bourne End, Horn. 128 FN59
Bourne End La., Hem.H. 57 BA25
Bourne End Rd., Maid. 110 AD63
Bourne End Rd., Nthwd. 93 BS49
Bourne Est. EC1 274 D6
Bourne Est. EC1 141 DN71
Bourne Gdns. E4 101 EB49
Bourne Gro., Ash. 231 CK119
Bourne Hill N13 99 DM47
Bourne Hill Clo. N13 99 DM47
Bourne Hill
Bourne Ind. Pk., Dart. 187 FE85
Bourne Rd.
Bourne La., Cat. 236 DR121
Bourne Mead, Bex. 187 FC85
Bourne Meadow, Egh. 193 BB98
Bourne Pk. Clo., Ken. 236 DS116
Bourne Pl. W4 158 CR78
Dukes Ave.
Bourne Rd. E7 124 EF62
Bourne Rd. N8 121 DL58
Bourne Rd., Berk. 38 AT18
Bourne Rd., Bex. 187 FB87
Bourne Rd., Brom. 204 EK98
Bourne Rd., Dart. 187 FD85
Bourne Rd., Gdmg. 258 AT144
Bourne Rd., Grav. 191 GM89
Bourne Rd., Red. 251 DJ130
Bourne Rd., Slou. 151 AQ75
Bourne Rd., Vir.W. 192 AX99
Bourne Rd. (Bushey), Wat. 76 CA43
Bourne St. SW1 276 F9
Bourne St. SW1 160 DG77
Bourne St., Croy. 201 DP103
Waddon New Rd.
Bourne Ter. W2 140 DB71
Bourne Vale, Brom. 204 EF102
Bourne Vw., Grnf. 137 CF65
Bourne Vw., Ken. 236 DR115
Bourne Way, Add. 212 BJ106
Bourne Way, Brom. 204 EE103
Bourne Way, Epsom 216 CQ105
Bourne Way, Sutt. 217 CZ106
Bourne Way, Swan. 207 FC97
Bourne Way, Wok. 227 BA115
Bourne Way (Mayford), Wok. 226 AX122
Bournebridge Clo., Brwd. 109 GE45
Bournefield Rd., Whyt. 236 DT118
Godstone Rd.
Bournehall Ave. (Bushey), Wat. 76 CA43
Bournehall La. (Bushey), Wat. 76 CA44
Bournehall Rd. (Bushey), Wat. 76 CA44
Bournemead Ave., Nthlt. 135 BU68
Bournemead Clo., Nthlt. 135 BU69
Bournemead Way, Nthlt. 135 BV68
Bournemouth Rd. SE15 162 DU82
Bournemouth Rd. SW19 200 DA95
Bourneside, Vir.W. 192 AU101
Bourneside Cres. N14 99 DK46
Bourneside Gdns. SE6 183 EC92
Bourneside Rd., Add. 212 BK105
Bournevale Rd. SW16 181 DL91
Bournewood Rd. SE18 166 EU80
Bournewood Rd., Orp. 206 EV101
Bournville Rd. SE6 183 EA87
Bournwell Clo., Barn. 80 DF41
Bourton Clo., Hayes 135 BU74
Avondale Dr.
Bousfield Rd. SE14 163 DX82
Bousley Ri., Cher. 211 BD107
Boutflower Rd. SW11 160 DE84
Bouverie Gdns., Har. 117 CK58
Bouverie Ms. N16 122 DS61
Bouverie Rd.
Bouverie Pl. W2 272 A8
Bouverie Pl. W2 140 DD72
Bouverie Rd. N16 122 DS60
Bouverie Rd., Couls. 234 DG118
Bouverie Rd., Har. 116 CC58
Bouverie St. EC4 274 E9
Bouverie St. EC4 141 DN72
Bouverie Way, Slou. 152 AY78
Bouvier Rd., Enf. 82 DW38
Boveney Clo., Slou. 151 AN75
Amerden Way
Boveney New Rd. (Eton Wick), Wind. 151 AL77
Boveney Rd. SE23 183 DX87
Boveney Rd., Wind. 150 AJ77
Boveney Wd. La., Slou. 110 AJ62
Bovey Way, S.Ock. 149 FV71
Bovill Rd. SE23 183 DX87
Bovingdon Ave., Wem. 138 CN65
Bovingdon Clo. N19 121 DJ61
Junction Rd.
Bovingdon Cres., Wat. 60 BX34
Bovingdon Grn. La., Hem.H. 57 AZ28
Bovingdon La. NW9 96 CS53
Bovingdon Rd. SW6 160 DB81
Bovingdon Sq., Mitch. 201 DL98
Leicester Ave.
Bow Arrow La., Dart. 188 FN86
Bow Bri. Est. E3 143 EB68
Bow Chyd. EC4 275 J9
Bow Common La. E3 143 DY70
Bow Ind. Est. E15 143 EB66
Bow La. EC4 275 J9
Bow La. EC4 142 DQ72
Bow La. N12 98 DC52
Bow La., Mord. 199 CY100
Bow Rd. E3 143 DZ69
Bow St. E15 124 EE64
Bow St. WC2 274 A9
Bow St. WC2 141 DL72
Bowater Clo. NW9 118 CR57
Bowater Clo. SW2 181 DL86
Bowater Pl. SE3 164 EH80
Bowater Ridge, Wey. 213 BR110
Bowater Rd. SE18 164 EK76
Bowden Clo., Felt. 175 BS88
Bowden Dr., Horn. 128 FL60
Bowden St. SE11 278 E10
Bowden St. SE11 161 DN78
Bowditch SE8 163 DZ78
Bowdon Rd. E17 123 EA59
Bowen Dr. SE21 182 DS90
Bowen Rd., Har. 116 CC59
Bowen St. E14 143 EB72
Bowens Wd., Croy. 221 DZ109
Bower Ave. SE10 164 EE81
Bower Clo., Nthlt. 136 BW68
Bower Clo., Rom. 105 FD52
Bower Ct., Epp. 70 EU32
Bower Ct., Wok. 227 BB116
Princess Rd.
Bower Fm. Rd. (Havering-atte-Bower), Rom. 105 FC48
Bower Hill, Epp. 70 EU32
Bower Hill Clo., Red. 267 DL137
Bower Hill La., Red. 267 DK135
Bower La. (Eynsford), Dart. 208 FL103
Bower Rd., Swan. 187 FG94
Bower St. E1 143 DX72
Bower Ter., Epp. 70 EU32
Bower Hill
Bower Vale, Epp. 70 EU32
Bower Way, Slou. 131 AL73
Bowerdean St. SW6 160 DB81
Bowerman Ave. SE14 163 DY79
Bowerman Rd., Grays 171 GG77
Bowers Ave., Grav. 191 GF91
Bowers Clo., Guil. 243 BA130
Cotts Wd. Dr.
Bowers Fm. Dr., Guil. 243 BA130
Bowers La., Guil. 243 BA129
Bowers Rd., Sev. 225 FF111
Bowers Wk. E6 145 EM72
Northumberland Rd.
Bowes Clo., Sid. 186 EV86
Bowes Rd. N11 99 DH50
Bowes Rd. N13 99 DL50
Bowes Rd. W3 138 CS73
Bowes Rd., Dag. 126 EW63
Bowes Rd., Stai. 173 BE92
Bowes Rd., Walt. 195 BV103
Bowes-Lyon Clo., Wind. 151 AQ81
Alma Rd.
Bowfell Rd. W6 159 CW79
Bowford Ave., Bexh. 166 EY81

Bowgate, St.Alb. 43 CE19
Bowhay, Brwd. 109 GA47
Bowhill Clo. SW9 161 DN80
Bowie Clo. SW4 181 DK87
Bowland Rd. SW4 161 DK84
Bowland Rd., Wdf.Grn. 102 EJ51
Bowland Yd. SW1 276 E5
Bowlers Orchard, Ch.St.G. 90 AU48
Bowles Grn., Enf. 82 DV36
Bowles Rd. SE1 162 DU79
Old Kent Rd.
Bowley Clo. SE19 182 DT93
Jasper Rd.
Bowley La. SE19 182 DT92
Bowley Rd. SE19 182 DT93
Farquhar Rd.
Bowling Ct., Wat. 75 BU42
Bowling Grn. Clo. SW15 179 CV87
Bowling Grn. Ct. EC2 275 N5
Bowling Grn. Ct. EC2 142 DS70
Bowling Grn. La. EC1 274 E4
Bowling Grn. La. EC1 141 DN70
Bowling Grn. Pl. SE1 279 K4
Bowling Grn. Pl. SE1 162 DR75
Bowling Grn. Rd., Wok. 210 AS109
Bowling Grn. Row SE18 165 EM76
Samuel St.
Bowling Grn. St. SE11 161 DN79
Bowling Grn. Wk. N1 275 M2
Bowling Rd., Ware 33 DY06
Bowls, The, Chig. 103 ES48
Bowls Clo., Stan. 95 CH50
Bowman Ave. E16 144 EF73
Bowman Ms. SW18 179 CZ88
Bowmans Clo. W13 137 CH74
Bowmans Clo., Pot.B. 64 DD32
Bowmans Clo., Slou. 130 AH67
Bowmans Ct., Hem.H. 40 BK18
Bowmans Grn., Wat. 76 BX36
Bowmans Lea SE23 182 DW87
Bowmans Meadow, Wall. 201 DH104
Bowmans Ms. E1 142 DU72
Hooper St.
Bowmans Ms. N7 121 DL62
Seven Sisters Rd.
Bowmans Pl. N7 121 DL62
Holloway Rd.
Bowmans Rd., Dart. 187 FF87
Bowman's Trd. Est. NW9 118 CM55
Westmoreland Rd.
Bowmead SE9 185 EM89
Bowmont Clo., Brwd. 109 GB44
Bowmore Wk. NW1 141 DK66
St. Paul's Cres.
Bown Clo., Til. 171 GH83
Bowness Clo. E8 142 DT65
Beechwood Rd.
Bowness Cres. SW15 178 CS92
Bowness Dr., Houns. 156 BY84
Bowness Rd. SE6 183 EB87
Bowness Rd., Bexh. 167 FB82
Bowness Way, Horn. 127 FG64
Bowood Rd. SW11 180 DG85
Bowood Rd., Enf. 83 DX40
Bowring Grn., Wat. 94 BW50
Bowrons Ave., Wem. 137 CK66
Bowry Dr., Stai. 173 AZ86
Bowsprit, The, Cob. 230 BW115
Bowstridge La., Ch.St.G. 90 AW48
Bowyer Clo. E6 145 EM71
Bowyer Cres., Uxb. 113 BF58
Bowyer Dr., Slou. 131 AL74
Bowyer Pl. SE5 162 DQ80
Bowyer St. SE5 162 DQ80
Bowyers, Hem.H. 40 BK18
Bowyers Clo., Ash. 232 CM118
Box La., Bark. 146 EV68
Box La., Hem.H. 39 BE24
Box La., Hodd. 49 DY17
Box Ridge Ave., Pur. 219 DM112
Box Tree Clo., Chesh. 54 AR33
Box Wk., Lthd. 245 BS132
Boxall Rd. SE21 182 DS86
Boxfield, Welw.G.C. 30 DB12
Boxford Clo., S.Croy. 221 DX112
Boxgrove Ave., Guil. 243 BA132
Boxgrove La., Guil. 243 BA133
Boxgrove Rd. SE2 166 EV75
Boxgrove Rd., Guil. 243 BA133
Boxhill, Hem.H. 40 BK18
Boxhill Rd., Dor. 248 CL133
Boxhill Rd., Tad. 248 CM132
Boxhill Way, Bet. 264 CP138
Boxley Rd., Mord. 200 DC98
Boxley St. E16 144 EH74
Boxmoor Rd., Har. 117 CH56
Boxmoor Rd., Rom. 105 FC50
Boxoll Rd., Dag. 126 EZ63
Boxted Clo., Buck.H. 102 EL46
Boxted Rd., Hem.H. 39 BE18
Boxtree La., Har. 94 CC53
Boxtree Rd., Har. 95 CD52
Boxtree Wk., Orp. 206 EX102
Eldred Dr.
Boxwell Rd., Berk. 38 AV19
Boxwood Clo., West Dr. 154 BM75
Hawthorne Cres.
Boxwood Way, Warl. 237 DX117
Boxworth Gro. N1 141 DM67
Richmond Ave.
Boyard Rd. SE18 165 EP78
Boyce Clo., Borwd. 78 CL39
Boyce St. SE1 278 D3
Boyce Way E13 144 EG70
Boycroft Ave. NW9 118 CQ58
Boyd Ave., Sthl. 136 BZ74
Boyd Clo., Kings.T. 178 CN94
Crescent Rd.
Boyd Rd. SW19 180 DD93
Boyd St. E1 142 DU72
Boydell Ct. NW8 140 DD66
St. John's Wd. Pk.
Boyfield St. SE1 278 G5
Boyfield St. SE1 161 DP75
Boyland Rd., Brom. 184 EF92
Boyle Ave., Stan. 95 CG51
Boyle Fm. Rd., T.Ditt. 197 CG100
Boyle St. W1 273 K10
Boyne Ave. NW4 119 CX56
Boyne Rd. SE13 163 EC83
Boyne Rd., Dag. 126 FA62
Boyne Ter. Ms. W11 139 CZ74
Boyseland Ct., Edg. 96 CQ47
Boyson Rd. SE17 162 DR79
Boythorn Way SE16 162 DV78
Credon Rd.
Boyton Clo. E1 143 DX70
Stayner's Rd.
Boyton Clo. N8 121 DL55
Boyton Rd. N8 121 DL55
Brabant Ct. EC3 275 M10
Brabant Rd. N22 99 DM54
Brabazon Ave., Wall. 219 DL108
Brabazon Rd., Houns. 156 BW80
Brabazon Rd., Nthlt. 136 CA68
Brabazon St. E14 143 EB72
Brabourn Gro. SE15 162 DW82
Brabourne Clo. SE19 182 DS92
Brabourne Cres., Bexh. 166 EZ79
Brabourne Heights NW7 96 CS48
Brabourne Ri., Beck. 203 EC99
Bracewell Ave., Grnf. 137 CG65
Bracewell Rd. W10 139 CW71
Bracewood Gdns., Croy. 202 DT104
Bracey Ms. N4 121 DL61
Bracey St.
Bracey St. N4 121 DL61
Bracken, The E4 101 EC46
Hortus Rd.
Bracken Ave. SW12 180 DG86
Bracken Ave., Croy. 203 EA104
Bracken Clo. E6 145 EM71
Bracken Clo., Lthd. 230 BZ124
Bracken Clo., Slou. 111 AR63
Bracken Clo., Sun. 175 BT93
Cavendish Rd.
Bracken Clo., Twick. 176 CA87
Hedley Rd.
Bracken Clo., Wok. 227 AZ118
Bracken Dr., Chig. 103 EP51
Bracken End, Islw. 177 CD85
Bracken Gdns. SW13 159 CU82
Bracken Hill Clo., Brom. 204 EF95
Bracken Hill La.
Bracken Hill La., Brom. 204 EF95
Bracken Ind. Est., Ilf. 103 ET52
Bracken Ms. E4 101 EC46
Hortus Rd.
Bracken Ms., Rom. 127 FB58
Bracken Path, Epsom 216 CN113
Bracken Way, Guil. 242 AS132
Bracken Way, Wok. 210 AT110
Brackenbridge Dr., Ruis. 116 BX62
Brackenbury Gdns. W6 159 CV76
Brackenbury Rd. N2 120 DC55
Brackenbury Rd. W6 159 CV76
Brackendale N21 99 DM47
Brackendale, Pot.B. 64 DA33
Brackendale Clo., Houns. 156 CB81
Brackendale Gdns., Upmin. 128 FQ63
Brackendene, Dart. 187 FE91
Brackendene, St.Alb. 60 BZ30
Brackendene Clo., Wok. 227 BA115
Brackenfield Clo. E5 122 DV63
Tiger Way
Brackenforde, Slou. 152 AW75
Brackenhill, Cob. 214 CA111
Brackens, The, Enf. 100 DS45
Brackens, The, Hem.H. 40 BK19
Heather Way
Brackens, The, Orp. 224 EU106
Brackens Dr., Brwd. 108 FW50
Brackenside, Horl. 269 DH147
Brackenwood, Sun. 195 BU95
Brackley, Wey. 213 BR106
Brackley Clo., Wall. 219 DL108
Brackley Rd. W4 158 CS78
Brackley Rd., Beck. 183 DZ94
Brackley Sq., Wdf.Grn. 102 EK52
Brackley St. EC1 275 J6
Brackley Ter. W4 158 CS78
Bracklyn Clo. N1 142 DR68
Parr St.
Bracklyn Ct. N1 142 DR68
Wimbourne St.
Bracklyn St. N1 142 DR68
Bracknell Clo. N22 99 DN53
Bracknell Gdns. NW3 120 DB63
Bracknell Gate NW3 120 DB64
Bracknell Pl., Hem.H. 40 BM16
Bracknell Way NW3 120 DB63
Bracondale, Esher 214 CC107
Bracondale Rd. SE2 166 EU77
Brad St. SE1 278 E3
Bradbery, Rick. 91 BD50
Bradbourne Pk. Rd., Sev. 256 FG123
Bradbourne Rd., Bex. 186 FA87
Bradbourne Rd., Grays 170 GB79
Bradbourne Rd., Sev. 257 FH122
Bradbourne St. SW6 160 DA82
Bradbourne Vale Rd., Sev. 256 FF122
Bradbury Clo., Borwd. 78 CP39
Bradbury Clo., Sthl. 156 BZ77
Bradbury Gdns., Slou. 112 AX63
Bradbury Ms. N16 122 DS64
Bradbury St.
Bradbury St. N16 122 DS64
Braddock Clo., Islw. 157 CF82
St. John's Rd.
Braddon Rd., Rich. 158 CM83
Braddyll St. SE10 164 EE78
Braden St. W9 140 DB70
Shirland Rd.
Bradenham Ave., Well. 166 EU84
Bradenham Clo. SE17 162 DR79
Bradenham Rd., Har. 117 CH56
Bradenham Rd., Hayes 135 BS69
Bradenhurst Clo., Cat. 252 DT125
Bradfield Clo., Guil. 243 BA131
Bradfield Clo., Wok. 226 AY118
Bradfield Dr., Bark. 126 EU64
Bradfield Rd. E16 164 EG75
Bradfield Rd., Ruis. 116 BY64
Bradford Clo. SE26 182 DV91
Coombe Rd.
Bradford Clo., Brom. 205 EM102
Bradford Dr., Epsom 217 CT107
Bradford Rd. W3 158 CS75
Warple Way
Bradford Rd., Ilf. 125 ER60
Bradford Rd., Rick. 91 BC45
Bradford Rd., Slou. 131 AN72
Bradgate (Cuffley), Pot.B. 65 DK27
Bradgate Clo. (Cuffley), Pot.B. 65 DK28
Bradgate Rd. SE6 183 EA86
Brading Cres. E11 124 EH61
Brading Rd. SW2 181 DM87
Brading Rd., Croy. 201 DM100
Bradiston Rd. W9 139 CZ69
Bradleigh Ave., Grays 170 GB76
Bradley Clo. N7 141 DM65
Sutterton St.
Bradley Gdns. W13 137 CH72
Bradley La., Dor. 247 CG132
Bradley Ms. SW17 180 DF88
Bellevue Rd.
Bradley Rd. N22 99 DM54
Bradley Rd. SE19 182 DQ93
Bradley Rd., Enf. 83 DY37
Bradley Rd., Slou. 131 AR73
Bradley Stone Rd. E6 145 EM71
Tollgate Rd.
Bradley's Clo. N1 141 DN68
White Lion St.
Bradman Row, Edg. 96 CQ52
Pavilion Way
Bradmead SW8 161 DH80
Bradmore Grn., Couls. 235 DM118
Coulsdon Rd.
Bradmore Grn., Hat. 63 CY26
Bradmore Ho. E1 142 DW71
Jamaica St.
Bradmore La., Hat. 63 CW27
Bradmore Pk. Rd. W6 159 CV77
Bradmore Way, Couls. 235 DL117
Bradmore Way, Hat. 63 CY26
Bradshaw Clo., Wind. 151 AL81
Bradshaw Rd., Wat. 76 BW39
Bradshawe Waye, Uxb. 134 BL71
Bradshaws, Hat. 45 CT22
Bradshaws Clo. SE25 202 DU97
Bradstock Rd. E9 143 DX65
Bradstock Rd., Epsom 217 CU106
Bradwell Ave., Dag. 126 FA61
Bradwell Clo. E18 124 EF56
Bradwell Clo., Horn. 147 FH65
Bradwell Grn., Brwd. 109 GC44
Bannister Dr.
Bradwell Ms. N18 100 DU49
Lyndhurst Rd.
Bradwell Rd., Buck.H. 102 EL46
Bradwell St. E1 143 DX69
Brady Ave., Loug. 85 EQ40
Brady St. E1 142 DV70
Bradymead E6 145 EP72
Warwall
Braemar Ave. N22 99 DL53
Braemar Ave. NW10 118 CR62
Braemar Ave. SW19 180 DA89
Braemar Ave., Bexh. 167 FC84
Braemar Ave., S.Croy. 220 DQ110
Braemar Ave., Th.Hth. 201 DN97
Braemar Ave., Wem. 137 CK66
Braemar Gdns. NW9 96 CR53
Braemar Gdns., Horn. 128 FN58
Braemar Gdns., Sid. 185 ER90
Braemar Gdns., Slou. 151 AN75
Braemar Gdns., W.Wick. 203 EC102
Braemar Rd. E13 144 EF70
Braemar Rd. N15 122 DS57
Braemar Rd., Brent. 157 CK79
Braemar Rd., Wor.Pk. 199 CV104
Braes Mead, Red. 267 DL135
Braes St. N1 141 DP66
Braeside, Add. 212 BH111
Braeside, Beck. 183 EA92
Braeside Ave. SW19 199 CY95
Braeside Ave., Sev. 256 FF124
Braeside Clo., Pnr. 94 CA52
The Ave.
Braeside Clo., Sev. 256 FF123
Braeside Cres., Bexh. 167 FC84
Braeside Rd. SW16 181 DJ94
Braesyde Clo., Belv. 166 EZ77
Brafferton Rd., Croy. 220 DQ105
Braganza St. SE17 161 DP78
Bragmans La., Hem.H. 57 BB34
Bragmans La., Rick. 57 BD33
Braham St. E1 142 DT72
Braid, The, Chesh. 54 AS30
Braid Ave. W3 138 CS72
Braid Clo., Felt. 176 BZ89
Braidwood Rd. SE6 183 ED88
Braidwood St. SE1 279 M3
Brailsford Clo., Mitch. 180 DE94
Brailsford Rd. SW2 181 DN85
Brain Clo., Hat. 45 CV17
Brainton Ave., Felt. 175 BV87
Braintree Ave., Ilf. 124 EL56
Braintree Rd., Dag. 126 FA62
Braintree Rd., Ruis. 115 BV63
Braintree St. E2 142 DW70
Braithwaite Ave., Rom. 126 FA59
Braithwaite Gdns., Stan. 95 CJ53
Braithwaite Rd., Enf. 83 DZ41
Brakefield Rd., Grav. 190 GB93
Brakey Hill, Red. 252 DS134
Brakynbery, Berk. 38 AS16
Brallings La., Ger.Cr. 91 BA49
Bramah Grn. SW9 161 DN81
Bramalea Clo. N6 120 DG58
Bramall Clo. E15 124 EF64
Idmiston Rd.
Bramber Ct. W5 158 CL77
Sterling Pl.
Bramber Ct., Slou. 131 AN74
Bramber Rd. N12 98 DE50
Bramber Rd. W14 159 CZ79
Bramble Ave., Dart. 189 FW90
Bramble Banks, Cars. 218 DG109
Bramble Clo., Cat. 236 DS122
Burntwood La.
Bramble Clo., Croy. 221 EA105
Bramble Clo., Guil. 242 AS132
Bramble Clo., Red. 266 DG136
Bramble Clo., Shep. 195 BR98
Halliford Clo.
Bramble Clo., Stan. 95 CK52
Bramble Clo., Uxb. 134 BM71
Bramble Clo., Wat. 59 BU34
Bramble Cft., Erith 167 FC77
Bramble Down, Stai. 194 BH95
Bramble Gdns. W12 139 CT73
Wallflower St.
Bramble La., Amer. 55 AS41
Bramble La., Hmptn. 176 BZ93
Bramble La., Hodd. 49 DY16
Bramble La., Sev. 257 FH128
Bramble La., Upmin. 148 FQ67
Bramble Mead, Ch.St.G. 90 AU48
Bramble Ri., Cob. 214 BW114
Bramble Ri., Harl. 35 EQ14
Bramble Rd., Hat. 44 CR18
Bramble Wk., Epsom 216 CP114
Bramble Way, Wok. 227 BF124
Brambleacres Clo., Sutt. 218 DA108
Bramblebury Rd. SE18 165 EQ78
Brambledene Clo., Wok. 226 AW118
Brambledown Clo., W.Wick. 204 EE99
Brambledown Rd., Cars. 218 DG108
Brambledown Rd., S.Croy. 220 DS108
Brambledown Rd., Wall. 219 DH108
Bramblefield Clo., Long. 209 FX97
Brambles, The, Chig. 103 EQ51
Brambles, The, St.Alb. 43 CD22
Brambles, The, Wal.Cr. 67 DX31
Brambles, The, West Dr. 154 BK77
Brambles Clo., Cat. 236 DS122
Burntwood La.
Brambles Clo., Islw. 157 CH80
Brambles Fm. Dr., Uxb. 134 BN69
Brambletye Pk. Rd., Red. 266 DF136
Bramblewood, Red. 251 DH129
South Clo. Grn.
Bramblewood Clo., Cars. 200 DF102
Brambling Clo., Wat. 76 BY42
Brambling Ri., Hem.H. 40 BL17
Bramblings, The E4 101 ED49
Bramcote Ave., Mitch. 200 DF98
Bramcote Gro. SE16 162 DW78
Bramcote Rd. SW15 159 CV84
Bramdean Cres. SE12 184 EG88
Bramdean Gdns. SE12 184 EG88
Bramerton Rd., Beck. 203 DZ97
Bramerton St. SW3 160 DE79
Bramfield, Wat. 60 BY34
Garston La.
Bramfield Ct. N4 122 DQ61
Queens Dr.
Bramfield Ct., Hert. 31 DN08
Windsor Dr.
Bramfield La., Hert. 31 DL05
Bramfield Rd. SW11 180 DE86
Bramfield Rd., Hert. 31 DL06
Bramford Ct. N14 99 DK47
Bramford Rd. SW18 160 DC84
Bramham Gdns. SW5 160 DB78
Bramham Gdns., Chess. 215 CK105
Bramhope La. SE7 164 EH79
Bramlands Clo. SW11 160 DE83
Bramleas, Wat. 75 BT42
Bramley Ave., Couls. 235 DJ115
Bramley Clo. E17 101 DY54
Bramley Clo. N14 81 DH43
Bramley Clo., Cher. 194 BH102
Bramley Clo., Grav. 191 GF94
Bramley Clo., Hayes 135 BU73
Orchard Rd.
Bramley Clo., Orp. 205 EP102
Bramley Clo., Red. 266 DE136
Pendleton Rd.
Bramley Clo., S.Croy. 219 DP106
Bramley Clo., Stai. 174 BJ93
Bramley Clo., Swan. 207 FE98
Bramley Clo., Twick. 176 CC86
Bramley Ct., Wat. 59 BV31
Orchard Ave.
Bramley Ct., Well. 166 EV81
Bramley Cres. SW8 161 DK80
Pascal St.
Bramley Cres., Ilf. 125 EN58
Bramley Gdns., Wat. 94 BW50
Bramley Hill, S.Croy. 219 DP106
Bramley Pl., Dart. 167 FG84
Bramley Rd. N14 81 DH43
Bramley Rd. W5 157 CJ76
Bramley Rd. W10 139 CX73
Bramley Rd., Sutt. 218 DD106
Bramley Rd. (Cheam), Sutt. 217 CX109
Bramley Shaw, Wal.Abb. 68 EF33
Bramley Wk., Horl. 269 DJ148
Carlton Tye
Bramley Way, Ash. 232 CM117
Bramley Way, Houns. 176 BZ85
Bramley Way, W.Wick. 203 EB103
Brammas Clo., Slou. 151 AQ76
Brampton Clo. E5 122 DV61
Brampton Clo. (Cheshunt), Wal.Cr. 66 DU28
Brampton Gdns. N15 122 DQ57
Brampton Rd.
Brampton Gdns., Walt. 214 BW106
Brampton Gro. NW4 119 CV56
Brampton Gro., Har. 117 CG56
Brampton Gro., Wem. 118 CM60
Brampton La. NW4 119 CW56
Brampton Pk. Rd. N22 121 DN55
Brampton Rd. E6 144 EK70
Brampton Rd. N15 122 DQ57
Brampton Rd. NW9 118 CN56
Brampton Rd. SE2 166 EW79
Brampton Rd., Bexh. 166 EX83
Brampton Rd., Croy. 202 DT101
Brampton Rd., St.Alb. 43 CG19
Brampton Rd., Uxb. 135 BP68
Brampton Rd., Wat. 93 BU48
Brampton Ter., Borwd. 78 CN38
Bramsham Gdns., Wat. 94 BX50
Bramshaw Ri., N.Mal. 198 CS100
Bramshaw Rd. E9 143 DX65
Bramshill Clo., Chig. 103 ES50
Tine Rd.
Bramshill Gdns. NW5 121 DH62
Bramshill Rd. NW10 138 CS68
Bramshot Ave. SE7 164 EG79
Bramshot Way, Wat. 93 BU47
Bramston Clo., Ilf. 103 ET51
Bramston Rd. NW10 139 CU68
Bramston Rd. SW17 180 DC90
Bramwell Clo., Sun. 196 BX96
Bramwell Ms. N1 141 DM67
Matilda St.
Brancaster Dr. NW7 97 CU52
Longfield Ave.
Brancaster La., Pur. 220 DQ110
Brancaster Pl., Loug. 85 EM41
Church Hill
Brancaster Rd. E12 125 EM63
Brancaster Rd. SW16 181 DL90
Brancaster Rd., Ilf. 125 ER58
Brancepeth Gdns., Buck.H. 102 EG47
Branch Clo., Hat. 45 CW16
Branch Hill NW3 120 DC62
Branch Pl. N1 142 DR67
Branch Rd. E14 143 DY73
Branch Rd., Ilf. 104 EV50
Branch Rd., St.Alb. 61 CD27
Branch Rd. (Park St.), St.Alb. 42 CB19
Brancker Clo., Wall. 219 DL108
Brown Clo.
Brancker Rd., Har. 117 CK55
Brancroft Way, Enf. 83 DY39
Brand St. SE10 163 EC80
Brandlehow Rd. SW15 159 CZ84
Brandon Clo., Grays 170 FZ75
Bark Burr Rd.
Brandon Clo. (Cheshunt), Wal.Cr. 66 DS26
Brandon Est. SE17 161 DP79
Brandon Gros. Ave., S.Ock. 149 FW69
Brandon Ms. EC2 142 DR71
Moor La.
Brandon Rd. E17 123 EC55
Brandon Rd. N7 141 DL66
Brandon Rd., Dart. 188 FM87
Brandon Rd., Sthl. 156 BZ78
Brandon Rd., Sutt. 218 DB105
Brandon St. SE17 279 J9
Brandon St. SE17 162 DQ77
Brandon St., Grav. 191 GH87
Brandram Rd. SE13 164 EE83
Brandreth Rd. E6 145 EM72
Brandreth Rd. SW17 181 DH89
Brandries, The, Wall. 201 DK104
Brands Rd., Slou. 153 BB79
Brandsland, Reig. 266 DB138
Brandville Gdns., Ilf. 125 EP56
Brandville Rd., West Dr. 154 BL75
Brandy Way, Sutt. 218 DA108
Branfield Clo. SW17 180 DC90
Branfill Rd., Upmin. 128 FP61
Brangbourne Rd., Brom. 183 EC92
Brangton Rd. SE11 161 DM78
Brangwyn Cres. SW19 200 DC96
Branksea St. SW6 159 CY80
Branksome Ave. N18 100 DT51
Branksome Clo., Hem.H. 40 BN19
Branksome Clo., Walt. 196 BX103
Branksome Rd. SW2 161 DL84
Branksome Rd. SW19 200 DA95
Branksome Way, Har. 118 CL58
Branksome Way, N.Mal. 198 CQ95
Bransby Rd., Chess. 216 CL108
Branscombe Gdns. N21 99 DN45
Branscombe St. SE13 163 EB83
Bransdale Clo. NW6 140 DB67
West End La.
Bransell Clo., Swan. 207 FC100
Bransgrove Rd., Edg. 96 CM53
Branston Cres., Orp. 205 ER102
Branstone Rd., Rich. 158 CM81
Branton Rd., Green. 189 FT86
Brants Wk. W7 137 CE70
Brantwood Ave., Erith 167 FC80
Brantwood Ave., Islw. 157 CG84
Brantwood Clo. E17 123 EB55
Brantwood Clo., W.Byf. 212 BG113
Brantwood Gdns.
Brantwood Dr., W.Byf. 211 BF113
Brantwood Gdns., Enf. 81 DL42
Brantwood Gdns., Ilf. 124 EL56
Brantwood Gdns., W.Byf. 211 BF113
Brantwood Rd. N17 100 DT51
Brantwood Rd. SE24 182 DQ85
Brantwood Rd., Bexh. 167 FB82
Brantwood Rd., S.Croy. 220 DQ109
Brantwood Way, Orp. 206 EW97
Brasher Clo., Grnf. 117 CD64
Lilian Board Way
Brass Tally All. SE16 163 DX75
Middleton Dr.
Brassey Clo., Felt. 175 BT88
Westmacott Dr.
Brassey Rd. NW6 139 CZ65
Brassey Rd., Oxt. 254 EF130
Brassey Sq. SW11 160 DG83
Brassie Ave. W3 138 CS72
Brasted Clo. SE26 182 DW91
Brasted Clo., Bexh. 186 EX85
Brasted Clo., Orp. 206 EU103
Brasted Clo., Sutt. 218 DA110
Brasted Hill Rd., Sev. 240 EU120
Brasted Hill Rd., West. 240 EV121
Brasted La., Sev. 240 EU119
Brasted Rd., Erith 167 FF78
Brasted Rd., West. 255 ER126
Brathway Rd. SW18 180 DA87
Bratley St. E1 142 DU70
Weaver St.
Brattle Wd., Sev. 257 FH129
Braund Ave., Grnf. 136 CB70
Braundton Ave., Sid. 185 ET88
Braunston Dr., Hayes 136 BY70
Bravington Clo., Shep. 194 BM99
Bravington Pl. W9 139 CZ70
Bravington Rd.
Bravington Rd. W9 139 CZ69
Brawne Ho. SE17 161 DP79
Hillingdon St.
Braxfield Rd. SE4 163 DY84
Braxted Pk. SW16 181 DM93
Bray NW3 140 DE66
Bray Clo., Borwd. 78 CQ39
Bray Clo., Maid. 150 AC75
Bray Rd.
Bray Ct., Maid. 150 AC77
Bray Cres. SE16 163 DX75
Marlow Way
Bray Dr. E16 144 EF73
Bowman Ave.
Bray Gdns., Wok. 227 BE116
Bray Pas. E16 144 EF73
Bowman Ave.
Bray Pl. SW3 276 D9
Bray Pl. SW3 160 DF77
Bray Rd. NW7 97 CX52
Bray Rd., Cob. 230 BY116
Bray Rd., Guil. 258 AV135
Bray Rd., Maid. 150 AC75
Brayards Rd. SE15 162 DV82
Brayards Rd. Est. SE15 162 DV82
Brayards Rd.
Braybank, Maid. 150 AC75
Braybourne Clo., Uxb. 134 BJ65
Braybourne Dr., Islw. 157 CF80
Braybrook St. W12 139 CT71
Braybrooke Gdns. SE19 182 DT94
Fox Hill
Brayburne Ave. SW4 161 DJ82
Braycourt Ave., Walt. 195 BV101
Braydon Rd. N16 122 DU59
Brayfield Rd., Maid. 150 AC75
Brayfield Ter. N1 141 DN66
Lofting Rd.
Brayford Sq. E1 143 DY72
Summercourt Rd.
Brays Mead, Harl. 51 ET17
Brayton Gdns., Enf. 81 DK42
Braywood Ave., Egh. 173 AZ93
Braywood Rd. SE9 165 ER84
Braziers Fld., Hert. 32 DT09

Brazil Clo., Croy. 201 DL101
Breach La., Dag. 146 FA69
Breach La., Hert. 47 DJ18
Breach Rd., Grays 169 FT79
Bread & Cheese La. (Cheshunt), Wal.Cr. 48 DS24
Bread St. EC4 275 J10
Bread St. EC4 142 DQ73
Breakfield, Couls. 235 DL116
Breakmead, Welw.G.C. 30 DB11
Bushey Ley
Breakneck Hill, Green. 189 FV85
Breaks Rd., Hat. 45 CV17
Breakspear Ave., St.Alb. 43 CF21
Breakspear Rd., Ruis. 115 BP59
Breakspear Rd. N., Uxb. 92 BJ53
Breakspear Rd. S., Uxb. 114 BM62
Breakspear Way, Hem.H. 41 BQ20
Breakspeare Clo., Wat. 75 BV38
Breakspeare Rd., Abb.L. 59 BS31
Breakspears Dr., Orp. 206 EU95
Breakspears Rd. SE4 163 DZ83
Bream Clo. N17 122 DV56
Bream Gdns. E6 145 EN69
Bream St. E3 143 EA66
Breamore Clo. SW15 179 CU88
Breamore Rd., Ilf. 125 ET61
Bream's Bldgs. EC4 274 D8
Bream's Bldgs. EC4 141 DN72
Breamwater Gdns., Rich. 177 CH90
Brearley Clo., Edg. 96 CQ52
Pavilion Way
Brearley Clo., Uxb. 134 BL65
Breasley Clo. SW15 159 CV84
Brechin Pl. SW7 160 DC77
Rosary Gdns.
Brecknock Rd. N7 121 DK64
Brecknock Rd. N19 121 DJ63
Brecknock Rd. Est. N7 121 DJ63
Brecon Clo., Mitch. 201 DL97
Brecon Clo., Wor.Pk. 199 CW103
Cotswold Way
Brecon Rd. W6 159 CY79
Brecon Rd., Enf. 82 DW42
Brede Clo. E6 145 EN69
Bredgar Rd. N19 121 DJ61
Bredhurst Clo. SE20 182 DW93
Bredon Rd. SE5 162 DQ83
Bredon Rd., Croy. 202 DT101
Bredune, Ken. 236 DR115
Church Rd.
Bredward Clo., Slou. 130 AH69
Breech La., Tad. 233 CU124
Breer St. SW6 160 DB83
Breezers Hill E1 142 DU73
Pennington St.
Brember Rd., Har. 116 CC61
Bremer Rd., Stai. 174 BG90
Bremner Ave., Horl. 268 DF147
Bremner Clo., Swan. 207 FG98
Bremner Rd. SW7 160 DC76
Queen's Gate
Brenchley Ave., Grav. 191 GH92
Brenchley Clo., Brom. 204 EF100
Brenchley Clo., Chis. 205 EN95
Brenchley Gdns. SE23 182 DW86
Brenchley Rd., Orp. 205 ES95
Brenda Rd. SW17 180 DF89
Brendans Clo., Horn. 128 FL60
Brende Gdns., W.Mol. 196 CB98
Brendon Ave. NW10 118 CS63
Brendon Clo., Erith 167 FE81
Brendon Clo., Esher 214 CC107
Brendon Clo., Hayes 155 BQ80
Brendon Ct., Rad. 61 CH34
The Ave.
Brendon Dr., Esher 214 CC107
Brendon Gdns., Har. 116 CB63
Brendon Gdns., Ilf. 125 ES57
Brendon Gro. N2 98 DC54
Oak La.
Brendon Rd. SE9 185 ER89
Brendon Rd., Dag. 126 EZ60
Brendon St. W1 272 C8
Brendon St. W1 140 DE72
Brendon Way, Enf. 100 DS45
Brenley Clo., Mitch. 200 DG97
Brenley Gdns. SE9 164 EK84
Brennan Rd., Til. 171 GH82
Brent, The, Dart. 188 FN87
Brent Clo., Bex. 186 EY88
Brent Clo., Dart. 188 FP86
Brent Cres. NW10 138 CM68
Brent Cross Gdns. NW4 119 CX58
Haley Rd.
Brent Cross Shop. Cen. NW4 119 CW59
Brent Grn. NW4 119 CW57
Brent Grn. Wk., Wem. 118 CQ62
Brent La., Dart. 188 FM87
Brent Lea, Brent. 157 CJ80
Brent Pk. NW10 118 CR64
Brent Pk. Rd. NW4 119 CV59
Brent Pk. Rd. NW9 119 CV59
Brent Pl., Barn. 80 DA43
Brent Rd. E16 144 EG71
Brent Rd. SE18 165 EP80
Brent Rd., Brent. 157 CJ79
Brent Rd., S.Croy. 220 DV109
Brent Rd., Sthl. 156 BW76
Brent St. NW4 119 CW56
Brent Ter. NW2 119 CW60
Brent Vw. Rd. NW9 119 CU58
Brent Way N3 98 DA51
Brent Way, Brent. 157 CK80
Brent Way, Dart. 188 FP86
Brent Way, Wem. 138 CP65
Brentcot Clo. W13 137 CH70
Brentfield NW10 138 CP66
Brentfield Clo. NW10 138 CR65
Normans Mead
Brentfield Gdns. NW2 119 CX59
Hendon Way
Brentfield Rd. NW10 138 CR65
Brentfield Rd., Dart. 188 FN86
Brentford Business Cen., Brent. 157 CJ80
Brentford Clo., Hayes 136 BX70
Brenthall Twrs., Harl. 52 EW17
Brentham Way W5 137 CK70
Brenthouse Rd. E9 142 DW65
Brenthurst Rd. NW10 139 CT65
Brentlands Dr., Dart. 188 FN88
Brentmead Clo. W7 137 CE73
Brentmead Gdns. NW10 138 CM68
Brentmead Pl. NW11 119 CX58
North Circular Rd.
Brenton St. E14 143 DY72
Brentside, Brent. 157 CJ79
Brentside Clo. W13 137 CG70
Brentside Executive Cen., Brent. 157 CH79
Brentvale Ave., Sthl. 137 CD74
Brentvale Ave., Wem. 138 CM67
Brentwick Gdns., Brent. 158 CL77
Brentwood Bypass, Brwd. 108 FS49
Brentwood Clo. SE9 185 EQ88
Brentwood Ct., Add. 212 BH105
Brentwood Ho. SE18 164 EK80
Shooter's Hill Rd.
Brentwood Pl., Brwd. 108 FX46
Brentwood Rd., Brwd. 109 GA49
Brentwood Rd., Grays 171 GH77
Brentwood Rd., Rom. 127 FF58
Brereton Ct., Hem.H. 40 BL22
Brereton Rd. N17 100 DT52
Bressenden Pl. SW1 277 J6
Bressenden Pl. SW1 161 DH76
Bressey Ave., Enf. 82 DU39
Carterhatch La.
Bressey Gro. E18 102 EF54
Bretlands Rd., Cher. 193 BE103
Brett Clo. N16 122 DS61
Yoakley Rd.
Brett Clo., Nthlt. 136 BX69
Broomcroft Ave.
Brett Ct. N9 100 DW47
Brett Cres. NW10 138 CR66
Brett Gdns., Dag. 146 EY66
Brett Ho. Clo. SW15 179 CX86
Putney Heath La.
Brett Pas. E8 122 DV64
Kenmure Rd.
Brett Pl., Wat. 75 BU37
The Harebreaks
Brett Rd. E8 122 DV64
Brett Rd., Barn. 79 CW43
Brettell St. SE17 162 DR78
Merrow St.
Brettenham Ave. E17 101 EA53
Penrhyn Ave.
Brettenham Rd. E17 101 EA54
Brettenham Rd. N18 100 DU49
Brettgrave, Epsom 216 CQ111
Brevet Clo., Purf. 169 FR77
Brew Ho. Rd., Bet. 264 CQ138
Tanners Meadow
Brewer St. W1 273 L10
Brewer St. W1 141 DJ73
Brewer St., Red. 252 DQ131
Brewer's Fld., Dart. 188 FJ91
Brewer's Grn. SW1 277 L6
Brewers Hall Gdns. EC2 275 J7
Brewers La., Rich. 177 CK85
George St.
Brewery Clo., Wem. 117 CG64
Brewery La., Sev. 257 FJ125
High St.
Brewery La., Twick. 177 CF87
Brewery La., W.Byf. 212 BL113
Brewery Rd. N7 141 DL66
Brewery Rd. SE18 165 ER78
Brewery Rd., Brom. 204 EL102
Brewery Rd., Hodd. 49 EA17
Brewery Rd., Wok. 226 AX117
Brewery Sq. SE1 142 DT74
Horselydown La.
Brewhouse La. E1 142 DV74
Brewhouse La., Hert. 32 DQ09
St. Andrew St.
Brewhouse Rd. SE18 165 EM77
Brewhouse St. SW15 159 CY83
Brewhouse Wk. SE16 143 DY74
Brewhouse Yd. EC1 274 F4
Brewhouse Yd., Grav. 191 GH86
Queen St.
Brewood Rd., Dag. 146 EV65
Brewster Gdns. W10 139 CW71
Brewster Ho. E14 143 DZ73
Brewster Rd. E10 123 EB60
Breycaine Ind. Est., Wat. 76 BX37
Brian Ave., S.Croy. 220 DS112
Brian Clo., Horn. 127 FH63
Brian Rd., Rom. 126 EW57
Briane Rd., Epsom 216 CQ110
Briant St. SE14 163 DX81
Briants Clo., Pnr. 94 BZ54
Briar Ave. SW16 181 DM94
Briar Banks, Cars. 218 DG109
Briar Clo. N2 98 DB54
Briar Clo. N13 100 DQ48
Briar Clo., Berk. 39 BA16
Briar Clo., Buck.H. 102 EK47
Briar Clo., Hmptn. 176 BZ92
Briar Clo., Islw. 177 CF85
Briar Clo., Maid. 130 AH72
Briar Clo. (Cheshunt), Wal.Cr. 66 DW29
Briar Clo., W.Byf. 212 BH111
Briar Ct., Sutt. 217 CW105
Briar Cres., Nthlt. 136 CB65
Briar Gdns., Brom. 204 EF102
Briar Gro., S.Croy. 220 DU113
Briar Hill, Pur. 219 DL111
Briar La., Cars. 218 DG109
Briar La., Croy. 221 EB105
Briar Pas. SW16 201 DL97
Pollards Cres.
Briar Pl. SW16 201 DM97
Briar Rd.
Briar Rd. NW2 119 CW63
Briar Rd. SW16 201 DL97
Briar Rd., Bex. 187 FD90
Briar Rd., Har. 117 CJ57
Briar Rd., Rom. 106 FJ52
Briar Rd., St.Alb. 43 CK17
Briar Rd., Shep. 194 BM99
Briar Rd., Twick. 177 CE88
Briar Rd., Wat. 59 BU34
Briar Rd., Wok. 227 BB123
Briar Wk. SW15 159 CV84
Briar Wk. W10 139 CY70
Droop St.
Briar Wk., Edg. 96 CQ52
Briar Wk., W.Byf. 212 BG112
Briar Way, Berk. 38 AW20
Briar Way, Guil. 243 BB130
Briar Way, Slou. 131 AQ71
Briar Way, West Dr. 154 BN75
Briarbank Rd. W13 137 CG72
Briarcliff, Hem.H. 39 BE19
Briardale Gdns. NW3 120 DA62
Briarfield Ave. N3 98 DB54
Briarleas Gdns., Upmin. 129 FS59
Briarley Clo., Brox. 49 DZ22
Briars, The, Hert. 32 DU09
Briars, The, Rick. 74 BH36
Briars, The, Slou. 153 AZ78
Briars, The (Cheshunt), Wal.Cr. 67 DY31
Briars, The (Bushey), Wat. 95 CE45
Briars Clo. N17 100 DV52
Briars Clo., Hat. 45 CU18
Briars Ct., Lthd. 215 CD114
Briars La., Hat. 45 CU18
Briars Rd., Maid. 130 AH72
Briars Wk., Rom. 106 FM54
Briars Wd., Hat. 45 CT18
Briars Wd., Horl. 269 DJ147
Briarswood Way, Orp. 223 ET106
Briarwood Clo. NW9 118 CQ58
Briarwood Clo., Felt. 175 BS90
Briarwood Dr., Nthwd. 93 BU54
Briarwood Rd. SW4 181 DK85
Briarwood Rd., Epsom 217 CU107
Briary Clo. NW3 140 DE66
Fellows Rd.
Briary Ct., Sid. 186 EV92
Briary Gdns., Brom. 184 EH92
Briary Gro., Edg. 96 CP54
Briary La. N9 100 DT48
Brick, The, Ware 32 DV05
Brick Ct. EC4 274 D9
Brick Fm. Clo., Rich. 158 CP81
Brick Kiln Clo., Wat. 76 BY44
Haydon Rd.
Brick Kiln La., Oxt. 254 EJ131
Brick Knoll Pk., St.Alb. 43 CJ21
Brick La. E1 142 DT70
Brick La. E2 142 DT69
Brick La., Enf. 82 DV40
Brick La., Stan. 95 CK52
Honeypot La.
Brick St. W1 277 H3
Brick St. W1 141 DH74
Brick Wall Clo., Welw. 29 CU07
Brickcroft, Brox. 67 DY26
Bricken Clo., St.Alb. 43 CG16
Brickenden Ct., Wal.Abb. 68 EF33
Brickendon La., Hert. 32 DQ12
Bricket Rd., St.Alb. 43 CD20
Brickett Clo., Ruis. 115 BQ57
Brickfield, Hat. 45 CU21
Brickfield Ave., Hem.H. 41 BP21
Brickfield Clo., Brent. 157 CJ80
Brickfield Cotts. SE18 165 ET79
Brickfield Fm. Gdns., Orp. 223 EQ105
Brickfield La., Barn. 79 CT44
Brickfield La., Hayes 155 BR79
Brickfield La., Slou. 130 AG66
Brickfield Rd. SW19 180 DB91
Brickfield Rd., Epp. 70 EX29
Brickfield Rd., Red. 267 DN142
Brickfield Rd., Th.Hth. 201 DP95
Brickfields, Har. 117 CD61
Brickfields La., Epp. 70 EX29
Brickfield Rd.
Brickfields Way, West Dr. 154 BM76
Porters Way
Bricklayer's Arms SE1 279 N8
Brickmakers La., Hem.H. 41 BP21
Brickwall La., Ruis. 115 BS60
Brickwood Clo. SE26 182 DV90
Brickwood Rd., Croy. 202 DS103
Brickyard La., Dor. 262 BW141
Bride Ct. EC4 274 F9
Bride La. EC4 274 F9
Bride St. N7 141 DM65
Brideale Clo. SE15 162 DT80
Colegrove Rd.
Bridewain St. SE1 279 P6
Bridewain St. SE1 162 DT76
Bridewell Pl. E1 142 DV74
Brewhouse La.
Bridewell Pl. EC4 274 F9
Bridford Ms. W1 273 J6
Bridge, The, Har. 117 CF56
Bridge App. NW1 140 DG66
Bridge Ave. W6 159 CV78
Bridge Ave. W7 137 CD71
Bridge Ave., Upmin. 128 FN61
Bridge Barn La., Wok. 226 AW117
Bridge Clo. W10 139 CX72
Kingsdown Clo.
Bridge Clo., Brwd. 109 FZ49
Bridge Clo., Enf. 82 DV40
Bridge Clo., Rom. 127 FE58
Bridge Clo., Slou. 131 AM73
Bridge Clo., Walt. 195 BT101
Bridge Clo., W.Byf. 212 BM112
Bridge Clo., Wok. 226 AW117
Bridge Cotts., Upmin. 129 FU64
Bridge Dr. N13 99 DM49
Bridge End E17 101 EC53
Bridge Gdns., Ashf. 175 BQ94
Bridge Gdns., E.Mol. 197 CD98
Bridge Gate N21 100 DQ45
Ridge Ave.
Bridge Hill, Epp. 69 ET33
Bridge Ho. Quay E14 143 EC74
Prestons Rd.
Bridge La. NW11 119 CY56
Bridge La. SW11 160 DE81
Bridge La., Vir.W. 192 AY99
Bridge Meadows SE14 163 DX79
Mercury Way
Bridge Pk. SW18 180 DA85
Bridge Pk. St., Slou. 153 BD80
Bridge Pl. SW1 277 J8
Bridge Pl. SW1 161 DH77
Bridge Pl., Amer. 55 AS38
Bridge Pl., Croy. 202 DR102
Bridge Pl., Wat. 76 BX43
Bridge Rd. E6 145 EM66
Bridge Rd. E15 143 ED67
Bridge Rd. E17 123 DZ59
Bridge Rd. N9 100 DU48
The Bdy.
Bridge Rd. N22 99 DL53
Bridge Rd. NW10 138 CS65
Bridge Rd., Beck. 183 DZ94
Bridge Rd., Bexh. 166 EY82
Bridge Rd., Cher. 194 BH101
Bridge Rd., Chess. 215 CK106
Bridge Rd., Croy. 202 DQ104
Duppas Hill Rd.
Bridge Rd., E.Mol. 197 CD99
Bridge Rd., Epsom 217 CT112
Bridge Rd., Erith 167 FF82
Bridge Rd., Grays 170 GB79
Bridge Rd., Houns. 157 CD83
Bridge Rd., Islw. 157 CD83
Bridge Rd., Kings L. 59 BQ33
Bridge Rd., Orp. 206 EV100
Bridge Rd., Rain. 147 FG70
Bridge Rd., Sthl. 156 BZ75
Bridge Rd., Sutt. 218 DB107
Bridge Rd., Twick. 177 CH86
Bridge Rd., Uxb. 134 BJ67
Bridge Rd., Wall. 219 DH106
Bridge Rd., Welw.G.C. 29 CW08
Bridge Rd., Wem. 118 CN62
Bridge Rd., Wey. 212 BM105
Bridge Rd. E., Welw.G.C. 29 CY08
Bridge Row, Croy. 202 DR102
Cross Rd.
Bridge St. SW1 277 P5
Bridge St. SW1 161 DL75
Bridge St. W4 158 CR77
Bridge St., Berk. 38 AX19
Bridge St., Guil. 258 AW135
Bridge St., Hem.H. 40 BJ21
Bridge St., Lthd. 231 CG122
Bridge St., Pnr. 116 BY55
Bridge St., Rich. 177 CK85
Bridge St., Slou. 153 BD80
Bridge St., Stai. 173 BE91
Bridge St., Walt. 195 BS102
Bridge Ter. E15 143 ED66
Bridge Vw. W6 159 CW78
Bridge Way N11 99 DJ48
Pymmes Grn. Rd.
Bridge Way NW11 119 CZ57
Bridge Way, Cob. 213 BT113
Bridge Way, Couls. 234 DE119
Bridge Way, Twick. 176 CC87
Bridge Way, Uxb. 115 BP64
Bridge Way, Wem. 138 CL66
Bridge Wf., Cher. 194 BJ102
Bridge Wf. Rd., Islw. 157 CH83
Church St.
Bridge Wks. Ind. Est., Uxb. 134 BJ70
Bridge Yd. SE1 279 L2
Bridgefield Clo., Bans. 233 CW115
Bridgefield Rd., Sutt. 218 DA107
Bridgefields, Welw.G.C. 29 CZ08
Bridgefoot SE1 161 DL78
Bridgefoot La., Pot.B. 63 CX33
Bridgeham Clo., Wey. 212 BN106
Mayfield Rd.
Bridgeham Way, Horl. 269 DP148
Bridgehill Clo., Guil. 242 AU132
Bridgeland Rd. E16 144 EG73
Bridgeman Dr., Wind. 151 AN82
Bridgeman Rd. N1 141 DM66
Bridgeman Rd. W4 158 CQ76
Bridgeman Rd., Tedd. 177 CG93
Bridgeman St. NW8 272 B1
Bridgeman St. NW8 140 DE68
Bridgen Rd., Bex. 186 EY86
Bridgend Rd. SW18 160 DC84
Bridgend Rd., Enf. 82 DW35
Bridgenhall Rd., Enf. 82 DT39
Bridgeport Pl. E1 142 DU74
Kennet St.
Bridger Clo., Wat. 60 BX33
Bridges Ct. SW11 160 DD83
Bridges Dr., Dart. 188 FP85
Bridges La., Croy. 219 DL105
Bridges Ms. SW19 180 DB93
Bridges Rd.
Bridges Pl. SW6 159 CZ81
Bridges Rd. SW19 180 DB93
Bridges Rd., Stan. 95 CF50
Bridges Rd. Ms. SW19 180 DB93
Bridges Rd.
Bridgetown Clo. SE19 182 DS92
St. Kitts Ter.
Bridgeview Ct., Ilf. 103 ER51
Bridgewater Clo., Chis. 205 ES97
Bridgewater Ct., Slou. 153 BA77
Bridgewater Gdns., Edg. 96 CM54
Bridgewater Rd., Berk. 38 AU17
Bridgewater Rd. (Northchurch), Berk. 38 AT16
Bridgewater Rd., Ruis. 115 BU63
Bridgewater Rd., Wem. 137 CJ65
Bridgewater Rd., Wey. 213 BR107
Bridgewater Sq. EC2 275 H6
Bridgewater St. EC2 275 H6
Bridgewater Ter., Wind. 151 AR80
Bridgewater Way (Bushey), Wat. 76 CB44
Bridgeway, Bark. 145 ET66
Bridgeway St. NW1 273 L1
Bridgeway St. NW1 141 DJ68
Bridgewood Clo. SE20 182 DV94
Bridgewood Rd. SW16 181 DK94
Bridgewood Rd., Wor.Pk. 199 CU104
Bridgford St. SW18 180 DC90
Bridgwater Clo., Rom. 106 FK50
Bridgwater Rd. E15 143 EC67
Bridgwater Rd., Rom. 106 FJ50
Bridgwater Wk., Rom. 106 FK50
Bridle Clo., Enf. 83 DZ37
Bridle Clo., Epsom 216 CR106
Bridle Clo., Hodd. 33 EA13
Bridle Clo., Kings.T. 197 CK98
Bridle Clo., St.Alb. 43 CE18
Bridle Clo., Sun. 195 BU97
Forge La.
Bridle End, Epsom 217 CT113
Bridle La. W1 273 L10
Bridle La., Cob. 230 CB115
Bridle La., Lthd. 230 CC115
Bridle La., Rick. 74 BJ41
Bridle La., Twick. 177 CH86
Crown Rd.
Bridle Path, Croy. 201 DL104
Bridle Path, Wat. 75 BV40
Station Rd.
Bridle Path, Wdf.Grn. 102 EE52
Bridle Path, The, Epsom 217 CV110
Bridle Rd., Croy. 203 EA104
Bridle Rd., Epsom 217 CT113
Bridle Rd., Esher 215 CH107
Bridle Rd., Pnr. 116 BW58
Bridle Rd., The, Pur. 219 DL110
Bridle Way, Berk. 38 AU17
Bridle Way, Croy. 221 EA106
Bridle Way, Hodd. 33 EA14
Bridle Way, Orp. 223 EQ105
Bridle Way, Ware 33 EA09
Bridle Way, The, Croy. 221 DY110
Bridle Way, The, Wall. 219 DJ105
Bridle Way N., Hodd. 33 EA13
Bridle Way S., Hodd. 33 EA14
Bridlepath Way, Felt. 175 BS87
Bridleway Clo., Epsom 217 CW110
Bridlington Clo., West. 238 EH119
Bridlington Rd. N9 100 DV45
Bridlington Rd., Wat. 94 BX48
Bridlington Spur, Slou. 151 AP75
Scarborough Way
Bridport Ave., Rom. 127 FB58
Bridport Pl. N1 142 DR67
Bridport Rd. N18 100 DS50
Bridport Rd., Grnf. 136 CB67
Bridport Rd., Th.Hth. 201 DN97
Bridport Ter. SW8 161 DK81
Wandsworth Rd.
Bridport Way, Slou. 131 AP70
Bridstow Pl. W2 140 DA72
Talbot Rd.
Brief St. SE5 161 DP81
Brier Lea, Tad. 249 CZ126
Brier Rd., Tad. 233 CV120
Henbit Clo.
Brierley, Croy. 221 EB107
Brierley Ave. N9 100 DW46
Brierley Clo. SE25 202 DU98
Brierley Clo., Horn. 128 FJ58
Brierley Rd. E11 123 ED63
Brierley Rd. SW12 181 DJ89
Brierly Clo., Guil. 242 AU132
Brierly Gdns. E2 142 DW68
Royston St.
Briery Ct., Hem.H. 40 BN19
Briery Fld., Rick. 74 BG42
Briery Way, Amer. 55 AS37
Briery Way, Hem.H. 40 BN18
Brig Ms. SE8 163 EA79
Watergate St.
Brigade Clo., Har. 117 CD61
Brigade St. SE3 164 EF82
Royal Par.
Brigadier Ave., Enf. 82 DQ38
Brigadier Hill, Enf. 82 DQ38
Briggeford Clo. E5 122 DU61
Geldeston Rd.
Briggs Clo. SW16 201 DJ95
Leonard Rd.
Bright Clo., Belv. 166 EX77
Bright Hill, Guil. 258 AX136
Bright St. E14 143 EB72
Brightfield Rd. SE12 184 EF85
Brightlands, Grav. 190 GE91
Brightlands Rd., Reig. 250 DC132
Brightling Rd. SE4 183 DZ86
Brightlingsea Pl. E14 143 DZ73
Brightman Rd. SW18 180 DD88
Brighton Ave. E17 123 DZ57
Brighton Clo., Add. 212 BJ106
Brighton Clo., Uxb. 135 BP66
Brighton Dr., Nthlt. 136 CA65
Brighton Gro. SE14 163 DY81
New Cross Rd.
Brighton Rd. E6 145 EN69
Brighton Rd. N2 98 DC54
Brighton Rd. N16 122 DS63
Brighton Rd., Add. 212 BJ105
Brighton Rd., Bans. 233 CZ116
Brighton Rd., Couls. 235 DH121
Brighton Rd., Horl. 268 DF149
Brighton Rd., Pur. 219 DN111
Brighton Rd., Red. 266 DF135
Brighton Rd., S.Croy. 220 DQ106
Brighton Rd., Surb. 197 CJ100
Brighton Rd., Sutt. 218 DC108
Brighton Rd., Tad. 233 CY122
Brighton Rd., Wat. 75 BU38
Brighton Spur, Slou. 131 AP70
Brighton Ter. SW9 161 DM84
Brighton Ter., Red. 266 DF135
Hooley La.
Brights Ave., Rain. 147 FH70
Brightside, The, Enf. 83 DX39
Brightside Ave., Stai. 174 BJ94
Brightside Rd. SE13 183 ED86
Brightview Clo., St.Alb. 60 BY29
Brightwell Clo., Croy. 201 DN102
Sumner Rd.
Brightwell Cres. SW17 180 DF92
Brightwell Rd., Wat. 75 BU43
Brigstock Rd., Belv. 167 FB77
Brigstock Rd., Couls. 235 DH115
Brigstock Rd., Th.Hth. 201 DN99
Brill Pl. NW1 273 N1
Brill Pl. NW1 141 DK68
Brim Hill N2 120 DC56
Brimfield Rd., Purf. 169 FR77
Brimpsfield Clo. SE2 166 EV76
Brimsdown Ave., Enf. 83 DY40
Brimsdown Ind. Est., Enf. 83 DZ40
Brimshot La., Wok. 210 AT109
Brimstone Clo., Orp. 224 EW108
Brimstone La., Dor. 264 CM142
Lodge La.
Brindle Gate, Sid. 185 ES88
Brindles, Horn. 128 FL56
The Russetts
Brindles, The, Bans. 233 CZ117
Brindles Clo., Brwd. 109 GC47
Brindley Clo., Bexh. 167 FB83
Brindley St. SE14 163 DZ81
Brindley Way, Brom. 184 EG92
Brindley Way, Sthl. 136 CB73
Brindwood Rd. E4 101 DZ48
Brinkburn Clo. SE2 166 EU77
Brinkburn Clo., Edg. 96 CP54
Brinkburn Gdns., Edg. 118 CN55
Brinkley Rd., Wor.Pk. 199 CV103
Brinklow Cres. SE18 165 EP80
Brinklow Ho. W2 140 DB71
Brinkworth Rd., Ilf. 124 EL55
Brinkworth Way E9 143 DZ65
Brinley Clo. (Cheshunt), Wal.Cr. 67 DX31
Brinsdale Rd. NW4 119 CX55
Brinsley Rd., Har. 95 CD54
Brinsley St. E1 142 DV72
Watney St.
Brinsmead (Park St.), St.Alb. 61 CD27
Brinsmead Rd., Rom. 106 FN54
Brinsworth Clo., Twick. 177 CD88
Brinton Wk. SE1 278 F3
Brion Pl. E14 143 EC71
Brisbane Ave. SW19 200 DB95
Brisbane Ct. N10 99 DH52
Sydney Rd.
Brisbane Rd. E10 123 EB61
Brisbane Rd. W13 157 CG75
Brisbane Rd., Ilf. 125 EP59
Brisbane St. SE5 162 DR80
Briscoe Clo. E11 124 EF61
Briscoe Clo., Hodd. 49 DZ15
Briscoe Rd. SW19 180 DD93

Street Name	District	Page	Grid
Briscoe Rd., Hodd.		49	DZ15
Briscoe Rd., Rain.		148	FJ68
Briset Rd. SE9		164	EK83
Briset St. EC1		**274**	**F6**
Briset Way N7		121	DM61
Brisson Clo., Esher		214	BZ107
Bristol Clo., Stai.		174	BL86
Bristol Gdns. W9		140	DB70
Bristol Ms. W9		140	DB70
Bristol Gdns.			
Bristol Pk. Rd. E17		123	DY56
Hervey Rd.			
Bristol Rd. E7		144	EJ65
Bristol Rd., Grav.		191	GK90
Bristol Rd., Grnf.		136	CB67
Bristol Rd., Mord.		200	DC99
Bristol Way, Slou.		132	AT74
Briston Gro. N8		121	DL58
Briston Ms. NW7		97	CU52
Longfield Ave.			
Bristow Rd. SE19		182	DS92
Bristow Rd., Bexh.		166	EY81
Bristow Rd., Croy.		219	DL105
Bristow Rd., Houns.		156	CB83
Britannia Clo. SW4		161	DK84
Bowland Rd.			
Britannia Clo., Nthlt.		136	BX69
Britannia Dr., Grav.		191	GM92
Britannia La., Twick.		176	CC87
Britannia Rd. E14		163	EA77
Britannia Rd. N12		98	DC48
Britannia Rd. SW6		160	DB80
Britannia Rd., Brwd.		108	FW50
Britannia Rd., Chesh.		54	AQ29
Britannia Rd., Ilf.		125	EP62
Britannia Rd., Surb.		198	CM101
Britannia Rd., Wal.Cr.		67	DZ34
Britannia Row N1		141	DP67
Britannia St. WC1		**274**	**B2**
Britannia Wk. N1		141	DM69
Britannia Wk. N1		**275**	**K2**
Britannia Way NW10		138	CP70
Britannia Way SW6		160	DB81
Britannia Rd.			
Britannia Way, Stai.		174	BK87
British Gro. W4		159	CT78
British Gro. Pas. W4		159	CT78
British Gro. S. W4		159	CT78
British Gro. Pas.			
British Legion Rd. E4		102	EF47
British St. E3		143	DZ69
Briton Clo., S.Croy.		220	DS111
Briton Cres., S.Croy.		220	DS111
Briton Hill Rd., S.Croy.		220	DS110
Brittain Rd., Dag.		126	EY62
Brittain Rd., Walt.		214	BX106
Brittains La., Sev.		256	FF123
Britten Clo. NW11		120	DB60
Rodgers Clo.			
Britten Dr., Sthl.		136	CA72
Britten St. SW3		160	DE78
Brittenden Clo., Orp.		223	ES107
Brittens, Guil.		242	AU129
Britten's Ct. E1		142	DV73
The Highway			
Britton Av., St.Alb.		43	CD20
Britton Clo. SE6		183	EC87
Brownhill Rd.			
Britton St. EC1		**274**	**F5**
Britton St. EC1		141	DP70
Britwell Rd., Slou.		130	AJ69
Brixham Cres., Ruis.		115	BU60
Brixham Gdns., Ilf.		125	ES64
Brixham Rd., Well.		166	EX81
Brixham St. E16		145	EM74
Brixton Est., Edg.		96	CP54
Brixton Hill SW2		181	DL87
Brixton Hill Pl. SW2		181	DL87
Brixton Hill			
Brixton Oval SW2		161	DN84
Brixton Rd. SW9		161	DN83
Brixton Rd., Wat.		75	BV39
Brixton Sta. Rd. SW9		161	DN83
Brixton Water La. SW2		181	DN85
Broad Acre, St.Alb.		60	BY30
Broad Acres, Gdmg.		258	AS143
Broad Clo., Walt.		196	BX104
Broad Ct. WC2		**274**	**A9**
Broad Ct., Welw.G.C.		29	CY09
Broad Ditch Rd., Grav.		190	GC94
Broad Grn., Hert.		47	DM15
Broad Grn. Ave., Croy.		201	DP101
Broad Grn. Wd., Hert.		47	DM15
Broad Highway, Cob.		214	BX114
Broad La. EC2		**275**	**M7**
Broad La. EC2		142	DS71
Broad La. N8		121	DM57
Tottenham La.			
Broad La. N15		122	DT56
Broad La., Beac.		110	AH55
Broad La., Dart.		187	FG89
Broad La., Hmptn.		176	BZ94
Broad La., H.Wyc.		110	AF60
Broad Lawn SE9		185	EN89
Broad Mead, Ash.		232	CM117
Broad Oak, Wdf.Grn.		102	EH50
Broad Oak Clo. E4		101	EA50
Royston Ave.			
Broad Oak Clo., Dart.		188	FN93
Broad Oak Clo., Orp.		206	EU96
Broad Platts, Slou.		152	AX76
Broad Ride, Egh.		192	AU96
Broad Rd., Swans.		190	FY86
Broad Sanctuary SW1		**277**	**N5**
Broad Sanctuary SW1		161	DK75
Broad St., Chesh.		54	AQ31
Broad St., Dag.		146	FA66
Broad St., Hem.H.		40	BK19
Broad St., Tedd.		177	CF93
Broad St. Ave. EC2		**275**	**M7**
Broad St. Pl. EC2		**275**	**L7**
Broad Vw. NW9		118	CN58
Broad Wk. N21		99	DM47
Broad Wk. NW1		140	DG67
Outer Circle			
Broad Wk. SE3		164	EJ82
Broad Wk. W1		**276**	**F2**
Broad Wk. W1		140	DG74
Broad Wk., Cat.		236	DT122
Broad Wk., Couls.		234	DG123
Broad Wk., Epsom		232	CS117
Chalk La.			
Broad Wk.		233	CX119
(Burgh Heath), Epsom			
Broad Wk., Harl.		35	ER14
Broad Wk., Houns.		156	BX81
Broad Wk., Orp.		206	EX104
Broad Wk., Rich.		158	CM80
Broad Wk., Sev.		257	FL128
Broad Wk., The W8		140	DC74
Broad Wk., The, E.Mol.		197	CF98
Broad Wk. La. NW11		119	CZ59
Broad Wk. N., The, Brwd.		109	GA48
Knight's Way			
Broad Wk. S., The, Brwd.		109	GA49
Churchill Dr.			
Broad Yd. EC1		**274**	**F5**
Broadacre, Stai.		174	BG92
Broadacre Clo., Uxb.		115	BP62
Broadacres, Guil.		242	AS132
Broadacres, Hat.		45	CT15
Broadbent Clo. N6		121	DH60
Broadbent St. W1		**273**	**H10**
Broadberry Rd. N18		100	DV51
Alston Rd.			
Broadbridge Clo. SE3		164	EG80
Broadbridge La., Horl.		269	DN148
Broadcoombe, S.Croy.		220	DW108
Broadcroft, Hem.H.		40	BK18
Broadcroft Ave., Stan.		95	CK54
Broadcroft Rd., Orp.		205	ER101
Broadfield, Harl.		35	ES14
Broadfield Clo. NW2		119	CW62
Broadfield Clo., Croy.		201	DM103
Progress Way			
Broadfield Clo., Rom.		127	FF57
Broadfield Clo., Tad.		233	CW120
Broadfield Ct. (Bushey), Wat.		95	CE47
Broadfield La. NW1		141	DL66
Broadfield Pl., Welw.G.C.		29	CV10
Broadfield Rd. SE6		184	EE87
Broadfield Rd., Guil.		261	BR142
Broadfield Rd., Hem.H.		40	BM20
Broadfield Sq., Enf.		82	DV40
Broadfield Way, Buck.H.		102	EJ48
Broadfields, E.Mol.		197	CD100
Broadfields, Har.		94	CB53
Broadfields, Saw.		36	EV06
Broadfields (Cheshunt), Wal.Cr.		65	DP29
Broadfields Ave. N21		99	DN45
Broadfields Ave., Edg.		96	CP49
Broadfields Heights, Edg.		96	CP49
Broadfields La., Wat.		93	BV46
Broadfields Way NW10		119	CT64
Winchmore Hill Rd.			
Broadford La., Wok.		210	AS112
Broadford Rd., Guil.		258	AW141
Broadgate E13		144	EJ68
Broadgate EC2		142	DS71
Liverpool St.			
Broadgate, Wal.Abb.		68	EF33
Broadgate Circle EC2		**275**	**M6**
Broadgate Rd. E16		144	EK72
Fulmer Rd.			
Broadgates Ave., Barn.		80	DB39
Broadgates Rd. SW18		180	DD88
Ellerton Rd.			
Broadham Grn. Rd., Oxt.		253	ED132
Broadhead Strand NW9		97	CT53
Broadheath Dr., Chis.		185	EM92
Broadhinton Rd. SW4		161	DH83
Broadhurst, Ash.		232	CL116
Broadhurst Ave., Edg.		96	CP49
Broadhurst Ave., Ilf.		125	ET63
Broadhurst Clo. NW6		140	DC65
Broadhurst Gdns.			
Broadhurst Clo., Rich.		178	CM85
Lower Gro. Rd.			
Broadhurst Gdns. NW6		140	DB65
Broadhurst Gdns., Chig.		103	EQ49
Broadhurst Gdns., Reig.		266	DB137
Broadhurst Gdns., Ruis.		116	BW61
Broadhurst Wk., Rain.		147	FG65
Tuck Rd.			
Broadlake Clo., St.Alb.		61	CK27
Broadlands, Grays		170	FZ78
Bankfoot			
Broadlands, Horl.		269	DJ147
Broadlands, The, Felt.		176	BZ90
Broadlands Ave. SW16		181	DL89
Broadlands Ave., Chesh.		54	AQ30
Broadlands Ave., Enf.		82	DV41
Broadlands Ave., Shep.		195	BQ100
Broadlands Clo. N6		120	DG59
Broadlands Clo. SW16		181	DL89
Broadlands Clo., Enf.		82	DW41
Broadlands Clo., Wal.Cr.		67	DX34
Broadlands Dr., Warl.		236	DW119
Broadlands Rd. N6		120	DF59
Broadlands Rd., Brom.		184	EH91
Broadlands Way, N.Mal.		199	CT100
Broadlawns Ct., Har.		95	CF53
Broadley Rd., Harl.		51	EM19
Broadley St. NW8		**272**	**A6**
Broadley Ter. NW1		**272**	**C5**
Broadmark Rd., Slou.		132	AV73
Broadmayne SE17		**279**	**K10**
Broadmead SE6		183	EA90
Broadmead, Horl.		269	DJ147
Broadmead Ave., Wor.Pk.		199	CU101
Broadmead Clo., Hmptn.		176	CA93
Broadmead Clo., Pnr.		94	BY52
Broadmead Est., Wdf.Grn.		102	EJ52
Broadmead Rd., Hayes		136	BY70
Broadmead Rd., Nthlt.		136	BY70
Broadmead Rd., Wok.		227	BB122
Broadmead Rd., Wdf.Grn.		102	EG51
Broadmeads, Ware		33	DX06
Broadmeads, Wok.		227	BB122
Broadoak, Slou.		131	AQ70
Broadoak Ave., Enf.		83	DX35
Broadoak Clo., Slou.		131	AQ70
Broadoak Rd., Erith		167	FD80
Broadoaks, Epp.		69	ET32
Broadoaks, Surb.		198	CP102
Broadoaks Cres., W.Byf.		212	BH113
Broadoaks Way, Brom.		204	EF99
Broadstone Pl. W1		**272**	**F7**
Broadstone Rd., Horn.		127	FG61
Broadstrood, Loug.		85	EN38
Broadview Ave., Grays		170	GD75
Broadview Est., Stai.		174	BN86
Broadview Rd. SW16		181	DK94
Broadview Rd., Chesh.		54	AP27
Broadwalk E18		124	EF55
Broadwalk, Croy.		221	DY111
Broadwalk, Har.		116	CA57
Broadwall SE1		**278**	**E2**
Broadwall SE1		141	DN74
Broadwater, Berk.		38	AW18
Broadwater, Pot.B.		64	DB30
Broadwater Clo., Stai.		173	AZ87
Broadwater Clo., Walt.		213	BU106
Broadwater Clo., Wok.		211	BD112
Broadwater Cres., Welw.G.C.		29	CX10
Broadwater Gdns., Orp.		223	EP105
Broadwater Gdns., Uxb.		114	BH56
Broadwater La., Uxb.		114	BH56
Broadwater Pk., Maid.		150	AC78
Broadwater Ri., Guil.		259	BA135
Broadwater Rd. N17		100	DS53
Broadwater Rd. SE28		165	EQ76
Broadwater Rd. SW17		180	DE91
Broadwater Rd., Welw.G.C.		29	CY10
Broadwater Rd. N., Walt.		213	BT106
Broadwater Rd. S., Walt.		213	BT106
Broadway E15		143	ED66
Broadway, Bark.		145	EQ66
Broadway, Bexh.		166	EY84
Broadway, Grays		170	GC79
Broadway, Grnf.		136	CC70
Broadway, Rain.		147	FG70
Broadway, Rom.		105	FG54
Broadway, Stai.		174	BH90
Broadway, Surb.		198	CP102
Broadway, Swan.		207	FC100
Broadway, Til.		171	GF82
Broadway, Wok.		227	AZ117
Broadway, The E4		101	EC51
Broadway, The E13		144	EH68
Broadway, The N8		121	DL58
Broadway, The N9		100	DU48
Broadway, The N14		99	DK46
Winchmore Hill Rd.			
Broadway, The N22		99	DN54
Broadway, The NW7		96	CS50
Broadway, The SW13		158	CS82
The Ter.			
Broadway, The SW19		180	DA94
Broadway, The W5		137	CK73
Broadway, The W7		137	CE74
Broadway, The W13		137	CG74
Broadway, The, Add.		212	BG110
Broadway, The, Chesh.		54	AP31
Broadway, The, Croy.		219	DL105
Croydon Rd.			
Whalebone La. S.			
Broadway, The, Epsom		217	CU106
Broadway, The, Har.		95	CE54
Broadway, The, Hat.		45	CW17
Broadway, The, Horn.		127	FH63
Broadway, The, Loug.		85	EQ42
Broadway, The, Pnr.		94	BZ52
Broadway, The, Sthl.		136	BX73
Broadway, The, Stai.		194	BJ97
Broadway, The, Stan.		95	CJ50
Broadway, The, Sutt.		217	CY107
Broadway, The, T.Ditt.		197	CE102
Hampton Ct. Way			
Broadway, The, Wat.		76	BW41
Broadway, The, Wem.		118	CL62
East La.			
Broadway, The, Wdf.Grn.		102	EH51
Broadway Ave., Croy.		202	DR99
Broadway Ave., Harl.		36	EV11
Broadway Ave., Twick.		177	CH86
Broadway Clo., Amer.		55	AP40
Broadway Clo., S.Croy.		220	DV114
Broadway Clo., Wdf.Grn.		102	EH51
Broadway Ct. SW19		180	DA93
The Bdy.			
Broadway Ct., Amer.		55	AP40
Broadway E., Uxb.		114	BG59
Broadway Gdns., Mitch.		200	DE98
Broadway Mkt. E8		142	DV67
Broadway Mkt. Ms. E8		142	DU67
Brougham Rd.			
Broadway Ms. E5		122	DT59
Broadway Ms. N13		99	DM50
Elmdale Rd.			
Broadway Ms. N21		99	DP46
Compton Rd.			
Broadway Par. N8		121	DL58
Broadway Pl. SW19		179	CZ93
Hartfield Rd.			
Broadwick St. W1		**273**	**L10**
Broadwick St. W1		141	DJ72
Broadwood, Grav.		191	GH92
Broadwood Ave., Ruis.		115	BS58
Broadwood Ter. W8		159	CZ77
Singlewell Rd.			
Brocas Clo. NW3		140	DE66
Fellows Rd.			
Brocas St. (Eton), Wind.		151	AR80
Brock Grn., S.Ock.		149	FV72
Cam Grn.			
Brock Pl. E3		143	EB70
Brock Rd. E13		144	EH71
Brock St. SE15		162	DW83
Evelina Rd.			
Brock Way, Vir.W.		192	AW99
Brockdish Ave., Bark.		125	ET64
Brockenhurst, W.Mol.		196	BZ100
Brockenhurst Ave., Wor.Pk.		199	CS102
Brockenhurst Clo., Wok.		211	AZ114
Brockenhurst Gdns. NW7		96	CS51
Brockenhurst Gdns., Ilf.		125	EQ64
Brockenhurst Rd., Croy.		202	DV101
Brockenhurst Way SW16		201	DK96
Brocket Clo., Chig.		103	ET50
Burrow Rd.			
Brocket Pk., Welw.G.C.		28	CR10
Brocket Rd., Grays		171	GG76
Brocket Rd., Hodd.		49	EA17
Brocket Rd., Welw.G.C.		29	CT11
Brocket Way, Chig.		103	ES50
Brockham Clo. SW19		179	CZ92
Brockham Cres., Croy.		221	ED110
Brockham Dr. SW2		181	DM87
Fairview Pl.			
Brockham Dr., Ilf.		125	EP58
Brockham Grn., Bet.		264	CP135
Brockham La., Bet.		248	CN134
Brockham Pk., Bet.		264	CQ139
Brockham St. SE1		**279**	**J6**
Brockham St. SE1		162	DQ76
Brockhamhill Pk., Tad.		248	CQ131
Brockhamhurst Rd., Bet.		264	CN141
Brockhurst Clo., Stan.		95	CF51
Brockhurst Rd., Chesh.		54	AQ29
Brockill Cres. SE4		163	DY84
Brocklebank Ct., Whyt.		236	DU118
Hillside Rd.			
Brocklebank Rd. SE7		164	EH77
Brocklebank Rd. SW18		180	DC87
Brockles Mead, Harl.		51	EQ19
Brocklesby Rd. SE25		202	DV98
Brockley Ave., Stan.		96	CL48
Brockley Clo., Stan.		96	CL49
Brockley Combe, Wey.		213	BR105
Brockley Cres., Rom.		105	FC52
Brockley Cross SE4		163	DY83
Endwell Rd.			
Brockley Footpath SE15		162	DW84
Brockley Gdns. SE4		163	DZ82
Brockley Gro. SE4		183	DZ85
Brockley Gro., Brwd.		109	GA46
Brockley Hall Rd. SE4		183	DY85
Brockley Hill, Stan.		95	CJ46
Brockley Ms. SE4		183	DY85
Brockley Pk. SE23		183	DY87
Brockley Ri. SE23		183	DY87
Brockley Rd. SE4		163	DZ83
Brockley Vw. SE23		183	DY87
Brockley Way SE4		183	DX85
Brockleyside, Stan.		96	CL49
Brockman Ri., Brom.		183	ED91
Brocks Dr., Sutt.		199	CY104
Brockshot Clo., Brent.		157	CK78
Brocksparkwood, Brwd.		109	GB48
Brockswood La., Welw.G.C.		29	CU08
Brockton Clo., Rom.		127	FF56
Brockway Clo. E11		124	EE61
Brockway Clo., Guil.		243	BB133
Brockway Ho., Slou.		153	BB78
Brockwell Clo., Orp.		205	ET98
Brockwell Pk. Gdns. SE24		181	DN87
Brockworth Clo. SE15		162	DS79
Broderick Gro., Lthd.		246	CA126
Lower Shott			
Brodewater Rd., Borwd.		78	CP40
Brodia Rd. N16		122	DS62
Brodie Rd. E4		101	EC46
Brodie Rd., Enf.		82	DQ38
Brodie Rd., Guil.		258	AY135
Brodie St. SE1		162	DT78
Coopers Rd.			
Brodlove La. E1		143	DX73
Brodrick Gro. SE2		166	EV77
Brodrick Rd. SW17		180	DE89
Brograve Gdns., Beck.		203	EB96
Broke Ct., Guil.		243	BC131
Speedwell Clo.			
Broke Fm. Dr., Orp.		224	EX109
Broke Wk. E8		142	DU67
Marlborough Ave.			
Broken Furlong (Eton), Wind.		151	AQ78
Broken Wf. EC4		**275**	**H10**
Brokes Cres., Reig.		250	DA132
Brokes Rd., Reig.		250	DA130
Brokesley St. E3		143	DZ69
Bromar Rd. SE5		162	DS83
Bromborough Grn., Wat.		94	BW50
Brome Rd. SE9		165	EM83
Bromefield, Stan.		95	CJ53
Bromefield Ct., Wal.Abb.		68	EG33
Bromehead Rd. E1		142	DW72
Commercial Rd.			
Bromell's Rd. SW4		161	DJ84
Bromet Clo., Wat.		75	BT38
Hempstead Rd.			
Bromfelde Rd. SW4		161	DK83
Bromfelde Wk. SW4		161	DL82
Bromfield St. N1		141	DN68
Bromford Clo., Oxt.		254	EG133
Bromhall Rd., Dag.		146	EV65
Bromhedge SE9		185	EM90
Bromholm Rd. SE2		166	EV76
Bromleigh Clo. (Cheshunt), Wal.Cr.		67	DY28
Martins Dr.			
Bromley, Grays		170	FZ79
Bromley Ave., Brom.		184	EE94
Bromley Common, Brom.		204	EJ98
Bromley Cres., Brom.		204	EF97
Bromley Cres., Ruis.		115	BT63
Bromley Gdns., Brom.		204	EF97
Bromley Gro., Brom.		203	ED96
Bromley Hall Rd. E14		143	EC71
Bromley High St. E3		143	EB69
Bromley Hill, Brom.		184	EE93
Bromley La., Chis.		185	EQ94
Bromley Pl. W1		**273**	**K6**
Bromley Rd. E10		123	EB58
Bromley Rd. E17		101	EA54
Bromley Rd. N17		100	DT53
Bromley Rd. N18		100	DR48
Bromley Rd. SE6		183	EB89
Bromley Rd., Beck.		203	EB96
Bromley Rd., Brom.		203	EB96
Bromley Rd. (Downham), Brom.		183	ED91
Bromley Rd., Chis.		205	EP95
Bromley St. E1		143	DX71
Brompton Arc. SW3		**276**	**D5**
Brompton Clo. SE20		202	DU96
Selby Rd.			
Brompton Clo., Houns.		176	BZ85
Brompton Dr., Erith		167	FH80
Brompton Gro. N2		120	DE56
Brompton Pk. Cres. SW6		160	DB79
Brompton Pl. SW3		**276**	**C6**
Brompton Pl. SW3		160	DE76
Brompton Rd. SW1		**276**	**D5**
Brompton Rd. SW1		160	DF75
Brompton Rd. SW3		**276**	**B8**
Brompton Rd. SW3		160	DE77
Brompton Rd. SW7		**276**	**B7**
Brompton Rd. SW7		160	DE76
Brompton Sq. SW3		**276**	**B6**
Brompton Sq. SW3		160	DE76
Bromwich Ave. N6		120	DG61
Bromyard Ave. W3		138	CS73
Bromyard Ho. SE15		162	DV80
Commercial Way			
Bromycroft, Slou.		131	AN69
Brondesbury Ct. NW2		139	CX65
Brondesbury Ms. NW6		140	DA66
Willesden La.			
Brondesbury Pk. NW2		139	CW66
Brondesbury Pk. NW6		139	CX66
Brondesbury Rd. NW6		139	CZ68
Brondesbury Vill. NW6		139	CZ68
Bronsart Rd. SW6		159	CY80
Bronson Way, Lub.		113	BF61
Bronson Rd. SW20		199	CX96
Bronte Clo. E7		124	EG63
Bective Rd.			
Bronte Clo., Ilf.		125	EN56
Bronte Clo., Til.		171	GJ82
Bronte Clo., Dart.		168	FM84
Bronte Ho. NW6		140	DA69
Bronte Vw., Grav.		191	GJ88
Bronti Clo. SE17		162	DQ78
Bronze St. SE8		163	EA80
Brook Ave., Dag.		147	FB66
Brook Ave., Edg.		96	CP51
Brook Ave., Wem.		118	CN62
Frith Ct.			
Brook Clo. SW20		199	CV97
Brook Clo. W3		138	CN74
West Lo. Ave.			
Brook Clo., Borwd.		78	CP41
Brook Rd.			
Brook Clo., Chis.		205	EN95
Brook Clo., Dor.		247	CJ134
Brook Clo., Rom.		105	FF53
Brook Clo., Ruis.		115	BS59
Brook Clo., Stai.		174	BM87
Brook Cres. E4		101	EA49
Brook Cres. N9		100	DV49
Brook Cres., Slou.		131	AL72
Brook Dr. SE11		**278**	**E7**
Brook Dr. SE11		161	DN76
Brook Dr., Har.		116	CC56
Brook Dr., Rad.		61	CF33
Brook Dr., Ruis.		115	BS58
Brook Dr., Sun.		175	BS92
Chertsey Rd.			
Brook End, Saw.		36	EX05
Brook Fm. Rd., Cob.		230	BX115
Brook Gdns. E4		101	EB49
Brook Gdns. SW13		159	CT83
Brook Gdns., Kings.T.		198	CQ95
Brook Gate W1		**276**	**E1**
Brook Grn. W6		159	CW76
Brook Hill, Guil.		260	BK143
Brook Hill, Oxt.		253	EC130
Brook Ind. Est., Hayes		136	BX74
Brook La. SE3		164	EH82
Brook La., Berk.		38	AV18
Brook La., Bex.		186	EX86
Brook La., Brom.		184	EG93
Brook La., Dor.		263	CH142
Brook La., Guil.		260	BL142
Brook La., Saw.		36	EX05
Brook La., Wok.		227	BE122
Brook La. N., Brent.		157	CK78
Brook Mead, Epsom		216	CS107
Brook Meadow N12		98	DB48
Brook Meadow Clo., Wdf.Grn.		102	EE51
Brook Ms. N. W2		140	DD73
Craven Ter.			
Brook Par., Chig.		103	EP48
High Rd.			
Brook Pk. Clo. N21		81	DP44
Brook Path, Slou.		131	AM73
Brook Pl., Barn.		80	DA43
Brook Ri., Chig.		103	EN48
Brook Rd. N8		121	DL56
Brook Rd. N22		121	DM55
Brook Rd. NW2		119	CT61
Brook Rd., Borwd.		78	CN39
Brook Rd., Brwd.		108	FT48
Brook Rd., Buck.H.		102	EG47
Brook Rd., Epp.		70	EU33
Brook Rd., Grav.		190	GE88
Brook Rd., Guil.		259	BC140
Brook Rd., Ilf.		125	ES58
Brook Rd., Loug.		84	EL42
Brook Rd., Red.		266	DF135
Brook Rd. (Merstham), Red.		251	DJ129
Brook Rd., Rom.		105	FF53
Brook Rd., Saw.		36	EX06
Brook Rd., Surb.		198	CL103
Brook Rd., Swan.		207	FD97
Brook Rd., Th.Hth.		202	DQ98
Brook Rd., Twick.		177	CG86
Brook Rd., Wal.Cr.		67	DZ34
Brook Rd. S., Brent.		157	CK79
Brook St. N17		100	DT54
High Rd.			
Brook St. W1		**273**	**H10**
Brook St. W1		140	DG73
Brook St. W2		**272**	**A10**
Brook St. W2		140	DD73
Brook St., Belv.		167	FB78
Brook St., Brwd.		107	FR50
Brook St., Erith		167	FB79
Brook St., Kings.T.		198	CL96
Brook St., Wind.		151	AR82
Brook Wk. N2		98	DD53
Brook Wk., Edg.		96	CR51
Old Fm. Rd.			
Brook Wk., Chig.		103	EN48
Brook Way, Lthd.		231	CG118
Brook Way, Rain.		147	FH71
Brookbank, H.Wyc.		110	AC60
Brookbank Ave. W7		137	CD71
Brookbank Rd. SE13		163	EA83
Brookdale N11		99	DJ49
Brookdale Ave., Upmin.		128	FN62
Brookdale Clo., Upmin.		128	FP62
Brookdale Rd. E17		123	EA55
Brookdale Rd. SE6		183	EB86
Brookdale Rd., Bex.		186	EY86
Brookdene Av., Wat.		93	BV45
Brookdene Dr., Nthwd.		93	BT52
Brookdene Rd. SE18		167	ET77
Brooke Ave., Har.		116	CC62
Brooke Clo. (Bushey), Wat.		94	CC45
Brooke Rd. E5		122	DU62
Brooke Rd. E17		123	EC56
Brooke Rd. N16		122	DT62
Brooke Rd., Grays		170	GA78
Brooke St. EC1		**274**	**D7**
Brooke St. EC1		141	DN71
Brooke Way (Bushey), Wat.		94	CC45
Richfield Rd.			

Buckner Rd. SW2 161 DM84
Bucknills Clo., Epsom 216 CQ114
Buckrell Rd. E4 101 ED47
Bucks All., Hert. 47 DK19
Bucks Ave., Wat. 94 BY45
Bucks Clo., W.Byf. 212 BH114
Bucks Cross Rd., Grav. 191 GF90
Bucks Cross Rd., Orp. 224 EY106
Bucks Hill, Kings L. 58 BJ33
Buckstone Clo. SE23 182 DW86
Buckstone Rd. N18 100 DU50
Buckters Rents SE16 143 DY74
Buckthorne Ho., Chig. 104 EV49
Buckthorne Rd. SE4 183 DY86
Buckton Rd., Borwd. 78 CM38
Budd Clo. N12 98 DB49
Buddcroft, Welw.G.C. 30 DB08
Buddings Circ., Wem. 118 CQ62
Budd's All., Twick. 177 CJ85
Arlington Clo.
Budebury Rd., Stai. 174 BG92
Budge La., Mitch. 200 DF101
Middleton Rd.
Budge Row EC4 275 K10
Budgen Dr., Red. 250 DG131
Budge's Wk. W2 140 DD73
Budgin's Hill, Orp. 224 EV112
Budich Ct., Ilf. 126 EU61
Budleigh Cres., Well. 166 EW81
Budoch Dr., Ilf. 126 EU61
Buer Rd. SW6 159 CY82
Buff Ave., Bans. 218 DB114
Buffins, Maid. 130 AE69
Bug Hill, Warl. 237 DX120
Bugsby's Way SE7 164 EG77
Bugsby's Way SE10 164 EF77
Bulbourne Clo., Berk. 38 AT17
Bulbourne Clo., Hem.H. 40 BG21
Bulganak Rd., Th.Hth. 202 DQ98
Bulinga St. SW1 277 P9
Bulinga St. SW1 161 DK77
Bulkeley Ave., Wind. 151 AP83
Bulkeley Clo., Egh. 172 AW92
Bull All., Well. 166 EV83
Welling High St.
Bull Clo., Grays 170 FZ75
Bull Hill, Lthd. 231 CG121
Bull Inn Ct. WC2 278 A1
Bull La. N18 100 DS50
Bull La., Chis. 185 ER94
Bull La., Dag. 127 FB62
Bull La., Ger.Cr. 112 AX55
Bull Plain, Hert. 32 DR09
Bull Rd. E15 144 EF68
Bull Stag Grn., Hat. 45 CW16
Bull Wf. La. EC4 275 J10
Bull Yd. SE15 162 DU81
Peckham High St.
Bull Yd., Grav. 191 GH86
High St.
Bullace Clo., Hem.H. 40 BG19
Bullace La., Dart. 188 FL86
High St.
Bullace Row SE5 162 DQ81
Camberwell Rd.
Bullards Pl. E2 143 DX69
Bullbanks Rd., Belv. 167 FC77
Bullbeggars La., Berk. 39 AZ20
Bullbeggars La., Wok. 226 AV116
Bullbeggars Rd., Gdse. 252 DW132
Bullen St. SW11 160 DE82
Bullens Grn. La., St.Alb. 44 CS23
Buller Clo. SE15 162 DU80
Buller Rd. N17 100 DU54
Buller Rd. N22 99 DN54
Buller Rd. NW10 139 CX69
Chamberlayne Rd.
Buller Rd., Bark. 145 ES66
Buller Rd., Th.Hth. 202 DR96
Bullers Clo., Sid. 186 EY92
Bullers Wd. Dr., Chis. 185 EM94
Bullescroft Rd., Edg. 96 CN48
Bullfinch Clo., Horl. 268 DE147
Bullfinch Clo., Sev. 256 FD122
Bullfinch Dene, Sev. 256 FD122
Bullfinch La., Sev. 256 FD122
Bullfinch Rd., S.Croy. 221 DX110
Bullhead Rd., Borwd. 78 CQ40
Bullied Way SW1 277 J9
Bullivant Clo., Green. 189 FU85
Cowley Ave.
Bullivant St. E14 143 EC72
Bullocks La., Hert. 32 DQ11
Bullrush Clo., Hat. 45 CV19
Bullrush Gro., Uxb. 134 BJ70
Bull's All. SW14 158 CR82
Bulls Bri. Ind. Est., Sthl. 155 BV76
Bulls Bri. Rd., Sthl. 155 BV76
Bulls Cross, Enf. 82 DU37
Bulls Cross Ride, Wal.Cr. 82 DU35
Bulls Gdns. SW3 276 C8
Bull's Head Pas. EC3 275 M9
Bulls La., Hat. 45 CX24
Bullsbrook Rd., Hayes 136 BW74
Bullsland Gdns., Rick. 73 BB44
Bullsland La., Ger.Cr. 91 BB45
Bullsland La., Rick. 73 BB44
Bullsmoor Clo., Wal.Cr. 82 DW35
Bullsmoor Gdns., Wal.Cr. 82 DV35
Bullsmoor La., Enf. 82 DW35
Bullsmoor La., Wal.Cr. 82 DU35
Bullsmoor Ride, Wal.Cr. 82 DW35
Bullsmoor Way, Wal.Cr. 82 DV35
Bullwell Cres. (Cheshunt), Wal.Cr. 67 DY29
Bulmer Gdns., Har. 117 CK59
Bulmer Ms. W11 140 DA73
Ladbroke Rd.
Bulmer Pl. W11 140 DA74
Bulmer Wk., Rain. 148 FJ68
Bulow Est. SW6 160 DB82
Broughton Rd.
Bulstrode Ave., Houns. 156 BZ82
Bulstrode Ct., Ger.Cr. 112 AX58
Heathfield Way
Bulstrode Gdns., Houns. 156 BZ83
Bulstrode La., Hem.H. 58 BG27
Bulstrode La., Kings L. 57 BE29
Bulstrode Pl. W1 272 G7
Bulstrode Rd., Houns. 156 CA83
Bulstrode St. W1 272 G8
Bulstrode St. W1 140 DG72
Bulstrode Way, Ger.Cr. 112 AX57
Bulwer Ct. Rd. E11 123 ED60
Bulwer Gdns., Barn. 80 DC42
Bulwer Rd.
Bulwer Rd. E11 123 ED59
Bulwer Rd. N18 100 DS49
Bulwer Rd., Barn. 80 DB42
Bulwer St. W12 139 CW74
Bumbles Grn. La., Wal.Abb. 68 EH25
Waltham Rd.
Bunbury Way, Epsom 233 CV115
Bunby Rd., Slou. 132 AT66
Bunce Common Rd., Reig. 264 CR141
Buncefield La., Hem.H. 41 BQ17
Bunces Clo. (Eton Wick), Wind. 151 AP78
Bunces La., Wdf.Grn. 102 EF52
Bundys Way, Stai. 173 BF93
Bungalow Rd. SE25 202 DS98
Bungalow Rd., Wok. 229 BQ124
Bungalows, The SW16 181 DH94
Bungalows, The, Wall. 219 DH106
Bunhill Row EC1 275 K4
Bunhill Row EC1 142 DR70
Bunhouse Pl. SW1 276 F10
Bunhouse Pl. SW1 160 DG78
Bunkers Hill NW11 120 DC59
Bunkers Hill, Belv. 166 FA77
Bunkers Hill, Sid. 186 EZ90
Bunkers La., Hem.H. 58 BN25
Bunning Way N7 141 DL66
Bunns La. NW7 96 CS51
Bunn's La., Chesh. 56 AT34
Bunnsfield, Welw.G.C. 30 DC08
Bunsen St. E3 143 DY68
Kenilworth Rd.
Bunten Meade, Slou. 131 AP74
Bunting Clo. N9 101 DX46
Bunting Clo., Mitch. 200 DF99
Buntingbridge Rd., Ilf. 125 ER57
Bunton St. SE18 165 EN76
Creton St.
Bunyan Ct. EC2 142 DQ71
Beech St.
Bunyan Rd. E17 123 DY55
Bunyard Dr., Wok. 211 BC114
Bunyons Clo., Brwd. 107 FW51
Essex Way
Buonaparte Ms. SW1 277 M10
Burbage Clo. SE1 279 K7
Burbage Clo. SE1 162 DR76
Burbage Clo. (Cheshunt), Wal.Cr. 67 DY31
Burbage Rd. SE21 182 DR87
Burbage Rd. SE24 182 DQ86
Burberry Clo., N.Mal. 198 CS96
Burbridge Rd., Shep. 194 BN98
Burbridge Way N17 100 DT54
Burch Rd., Grav. 191 GF86
Burcham St. E14 143 EB72
Burcharbro Rd. SE2 166 EX79
Burchell Ct. (Bushey), Wat. 94 CC45
Catsey La.
Burchell Rd. E10 123 EB60
Burchell Rd. SE15 162 DV81
Burchets Hollow, Guil. 261 BR144
Burchett Way, Rom. 126 EZ58
Burchetts Way, Shep. 195 BP100
Burchwall Clo., Rom. 105 FC52
Burcote, Wey. 213 BR107
Burcote Rd. SW18 180 DD87
Burcott Gdns., Add. 212 BJ107
Burcott Rd., Pur. 219 DN114
Burden Clo., Brent. 157 CJ78
Burden Way E11 124 EH61
Brading Cres.
Burden Way, Guil. 242 AV129
Burdenshot Hill, Guil. 242 AU125
Burdenshott Ave., Rich. 158 CP84
Burdenshott Rd., Guil. 242 AU125
Burdenshott Rd., Wok. 226 AU124
Burder Clo. N1 142 DS65
Burder Rd. N1 142 DS65
Balls Pond Rd.
Burdett Ave. SW20 199 CU95
Burdett Clo., Sid. 186 EY92
Burdett Ms. NW3 140 DD65
Belsize Cres.
Burdett Ms. W2 140 DB72
Hatherley Gro.
Burdett Rd. E3 143 DY70
Burdett Rd. E14 143 DZ71
Burdett Rd., Croy. 202 DR100
Burdett Rd., Rich. 158 CM82
Burdett St. SE1 278 D6
Burdetts Rd., Dag. 146 EZ67
Burdock Clo., Croy. 203 DX102
Burdock Rd. N17 122 DU55
Burdon La., Sutt. 217 CY108
Burdon Pk., Sutt. 217 CZ109
Burfield Clo. SW17 180 DD91
Burfield Clo., Hat. 45 CU16
Burfield Dr., Warl. 236 DW119
Burfield Rd., Rick. 73 BB43
Burfield Rd., Wind. 172 AU87
Burford Clo., Dag. 126 EW62
Burford Clo., Ilf. 125 EQ56
Burford Clo., Uxb. 114 BL63
Burford Gdns. N13 99 DM48
Burford Gdns., Hodd. 49 EB16
Burford La., Epsom 217 CW111
Burford Pl., Hodd. 49 EA16
Burford St.
Burford Rd. E6 144 EL69
Burford Rd. E15 143 ED66
Burford Rd. SE6 183 DZ89
Burford Rd., Brent. 158 CL78
Burford Rd., Brom. 204 EL98
Burford Rd., Sutt. 200 DA103
Burford Rd., Wor.Pk. 199 CT101
Burford St., Hodd. 49 EA17
Burford Wk. SW6 160 DB80
Cambria St.
Burford Way, Croy. 221 EC107
Burgate Clo., Dart. 167 FF83
Burge St. SE1 279 L7
Burges Clo., Horn. 128 FM58
Burges Ct. E6 145 EN66
Burges Gro. SW13 159 CV79
Trinity Ch. Rd.
Burges Rd. E6 144 EL66
Burges Way, Stai. 174 BG92
Burgess Ave. NW9 118 CR58
Burgess Clo., Felt. 176 BY91
Burgess Ct., Borwd. 78 CM38
Belford Rd.
Burgess Hill NW2 120 DA63
Burgess Rd. E15 124 EE63
Burgess Rd., Sutt. 218 DB105
Burgess St. E14 143 EA71
Burgess Wd. Rd., Beac. 88 AH53
Burgess Wd. Rd. S., Beac. 110 AH55
Burgett Rd., Slou. 151 AP76
Burgh Heath Rd., Epsom 216 CS114
Burgh Mt., Bans. 233 CZ115
Burgh St. N1 141 DP68
Burgh Wd., Bans. 233 CY115
Burghfield, Epsom 233 CT115
Burghfield Rd., Grav. 191 GF94
Burghill Rd. SE26 183 DY91
Burghley Ave., Borwd. 78 CQ43
Burghley Ave., N.Mal. 198 CR95
Burghley Pl., Mitch. 200 DF99
Burghley Rd. E11 124 EE60
Burghley Rd. N8 121 DN55
Burghley Rd. NW5 121 DH63
Burghley Rd. SW19 179 CX91
Burghley Rd., Grays 169 FW76
Arterial Rd. W. Thurrock
Burghley Twr. W3 139 CT73
Burgon St. EC4 274 G9
Burgos Gro. SE10 163 EB81
Burgoyne Hatch, Harl. 36 EU14
Mompies Rd.
Burgoyne Rd. N4 121 DP58
Burgoyne Rd. SE25 202 DT98
Burgoyne Rd. SW9 161 DM83
Burgoyne Rd., Sun. 175 BS93
Burgundy Cft., Welw.G.C. 29 CZ11
Burgwood Gro., Beac. 88 AH53
Burham Clo. SE20 182 DW94
Maple Rd.
Burhill Gro., Pnr. 94 BY54
Burhill Rd., Walt. 213 BV109
Burke Clo. SW15 158 CS84
Burke St. E16 144 EF72
Burkes Clo., Beac. 110 AH55
Burkes Cres., Beac. 89 AK53
Burkes Rd., Beac. 110 AJ55
Burland Rd. SW11 180 DF85
Burland Rd., Brwd. 108 FX46
Burland Rd., Rom. 105 FC51
Burlea Clo., Walt. 213 BV106
Burleigh Ave., Sid. 185 ET85
Burleigh Ave., Wall. 200 DG104
Burleigh Clo., Add. 212 BH106
Burleigh Gdns. N14 99 DJ46
Burleigh Gdns., Ashf. 175 BQ92
Burleigh Ho. W10 139 CX71
St. Charles Sq.
Burleigh Mead, Hat. 45 CW16
Burleigh Pk., Cob. 214 BY112
Burleigh Pl. SW15 179 CX85
Burleigh Pl., Mitch. 200 DF99
Burleigh Rd., Add. 212 BH106
Burleigh Rd., Enf. 82 DS42
Burleigh Rd., Hem.H. 41 BQ21
Burleigh Rd., Hert. 32 DU08
Burleigh Rd., St.Alb. 43 CH20
Burleigh Rd., Sutt. 199 CY102
Burleigh Rd., Uxb. 135 BP67
Burleigh Rd. (Cheshunt), Wal.Cr. 67 DY32
Burleigh St. WC2 274 A10
Burleigh Wk. SE6 183 EC88
Muirkirk Rd.
Burleigh Way, Enf. 82 DR41
Church St.
Burleigh Way (Cuffley), Pot.B. 65 DL30
Burley Clo. E4 101 EA50
Burley Clo. SW16 201 DK96
Burley Hill, Harl. 52 EX16
Kiln La.
Burley Orchard, Cher. 194 BG100
Burley Rd. E16 144 EJ71
Burlingham Clo., Guil. 243 BD132
Gilliat Dr.
Burlings La., Sev. 239 ET118
Burlington Arc. W1 277 K1
Burlington Ave., Rich. 158 CN81
Burlington Ave., Rom. 127 FB58
Burlington Ave., Slou. 152 AS75
Burlington Clo. E6 144 EL72
Northumberland Rd.
Burlington Clo. W9 139 CZ70
Burlington Clo., Felt. 175 BR87
Burlington Clo., Orp. 205 EP103
Burlington Gdns. W1 277 K1
Burlington Gdns. W1 141 DJ73
Burlington Gdns. W3 138 CQ74
Burlington Gdns. W4 158 CQ78
Burlington Gdns., Rom. 126 EY59
Burlington La. W4 158 CS80
Burlington Ms. W3 138 CQ74
Burlington Pl. SW6 159 CY82
Burlington Rd.
Burlington Pl., Wdf.Grn. 102 EH48
Burlington Ri., Barn. 98 DE46
Burlington Rd. N10 98 DG54
Tetherdown
Burlington Rd. N17 100 DU53
Burlington Rd. SW6 159 CY82
Burlington Rd. W4 158 CQ78
Burlington Rd., Enf. 82 DR39
Burlington Rd., Islw. 157 CD81
Burlington Rd., N.Mal. 199 CT98
Burlington Rd., Slou. 130 AH70
Burlington Rd., Th.Hth. 202 DQ96
Burma Ms. N16 122 DR63
Burma Rd. N16 122 DR63
Burma Rd., Wok. 192 AT103
Burman Clo., Dart. 188 FQ87
Burmester Rd. SW17 180 DC90
Burn Clo., Add. 212 BK105
Burn Side N9 100 DW48
Burn Wk., Slou. 130 AH69
Wilmot Rd.
Burnaby Cres. W4 158 CQ79
Burnaby Gdns. W4 158 CP79
Burnaby Rd., Grav. 190 GE87
Burnaby St. SW10 160 DC80
Burnbrae Clo. N12 98 DB51
Burnbury Rd. SW12 181 DJ88
Burncroft Ave., Enf. 82 DW40
Burne Jones Ho. W14 159 CZ77
Burne St. NW1 272 B6
Burne St. NW1 140 DE71
Burnell Ave., Rich. 177 CJ92
Burnell Ave., Well. 166 EU82
Burnell Gdns., Stan. 95 CK53
Burnell Rd., Sutt. 218 DB105
Burnell Wk. SE1 162 DT78
Cadet Dr.
Burnell Wk., Brwd. 107 FW51
Burnels Ave. E6 145 EN69
Burness Clo. N7 141 DM65
Roman Way
Burness Clo., Uxb. 134 BK68
Whitehall Rd.
Burnet Ave., Guil. 243 BB131
Woodruff Ave.
Burnet Clo., Hem.H. 40 BL21
Burnet Gro., Epsom 216 CQ113
Burnett Clo. E9 122 DW64
Burnett Pk., Harl. 51 EP20
Burnett Rd., Erith 168 FK79
Burnett Sq., Hert. 31 DM08
Burnetts Rd., Wind. 151 AL81
Burney Ave., Surb. 198 CM99
Burney Clo., Lthd. 246 CC125
Burney Dr., Loug. 85 EP40
Burney Rd., Dor. 247 CG131
Burney St. SE10 163 EC80
Burnfoot Ave. SW6 159 CY81
Burnfoot Ct. SE22 182 DV88
Burnham NW3 140 DE66
Burnham Ave., Beac. 111 AN55
Burnham Ave., Uxb. 115 BQ63
Burnham Clo. NW7 97 CU52
Longfield Ave.
Burnham Clo. SE1 162 DT77
Cadet Dr.
Burnham Clo., Enf. 82 DS38
Burnham Clo., Har. 117 CG56
Burnham Clo., Wind. 151 AK82
Burnham Ct. NW4 119 CW56
Burnham Cres. E11 124 EJ56
Burnham Cres., Dart. 168 FJ84
Burnham Dr., Reig. 250 DA133
Burnham Dr., Wor.Pk. 199 CX103
Burnham Gdns., Croy. 202 DT101
Burnham Gdns., Hayes 155 BR76
Burnham Gdns., Houns. 155 BV81
Burnham La., Slou. 131 AL70
Burnham Rd. E4 101 DZ50
Burnham Rd., Dag. 146 EV66
Burnham Rd., Dart. 168 FJ84
Burnham Rd., Mord. 200 DB99
Burnham Rd., Rom. 127 FD55
Burnham Rd., St.Alb. 43 CG20
Burnham Rd., Sid. 186 EY89
Burnham St. E2 142 DW69
Burnham St., Kings.T. 198 CN95
Burnham Wk., Slou. 111 AN64
Halse Dr.
Burnham Way SE26 183 DZ92
Burnham Way W13 157 CH77
Burnhams Rd., Lthd. 230 BY124
Burnhill Rd., Beck. 203 EA96
Burnley Clo., Wat. 94 BW50
Burnley Rd. NW10 119 CT64
Burnley Rd. SW9 161 DM82
Burnley Rd., Grays 169 FT81
Burns Ave., Felt. 175 BU86
Burns Ave., Rom. 126 EW59
Burns Ave., Sid. 186 EU86
Burns Ave., Sthl. 136 CA73
Burns Clo. SW19 180 DD93
North Rd.
Burns Clo., Erith 167 FF81
Burns Clo., Hayes 135 BT71
Burns Clo., Well. 165 ET81
Burns Dr., Bans. 217 CY114
Burns Pl., Til. 171 GH81
Burns Rd. NW10 139 CT67
Burns Rd. SW11 160 DF82
Burns Rd. W13 157 CH75
Burns Rd., Wem. 138 CL68
Burns Way, Brwd. 109 GD45
Burns Way, Houns. 156 BX82
Burnsall St. SW3 276 C10
Burnsall St. SW3 160 DE78
Burnside, Ash. 232 CM118
Burnside, Hert. 31 DN10
Burnside, Hodd. 49 DZ17
Burnside, St.Alb. 43 CH22
Burnside, Saw. 36 EX05
Burnside Ave. E4 101 DZ51
Silver Birch Ave.
Burnside Clo. SE16 143 DX74
Burnside Clo., Barn. 80 DA41
Burnside Clo., Hat. 45 CU15
Homestead Rd.
Burnside Clo., Twick. 177 CG86
Burnside Cres., Wem. 137 CK67
Burnside Rd., Dag. 126 EW61
Burnside Ter., Harl. 36 EZ12
Hobbs Cross Rd.
Burnt Ash Hill SE12 184 EF86
Burnt Ash La., Brom. 184 EG94
Burnt Ash Rd. SE12 184 EF85
Burnt Common Clo., Wok. 243 BF125
Burnt Fm. Ride, Enf. 65 DP34
Burnt Fm. Ride, Wal.Cr. 65 DP31
Burnt Mill, Harl. 35 EQ13
Elizabeth Way
Burnt Oak Bdy., Edg. 96 CP52
Burnt Oak Flds., Edg. 96 CQ53
Burnt Oak La., Sid. 186 EU89
Burntcommon La., Wok. 244 BG125
Burnthouse La., Dart. 188 FL91
Burnthwaite Rd. SW6 159 CZ80
Burntmill Cor., Harl. 35 EQ11
Eastwick Rd.
Burntmill La., Harl. 35 EQ12
Burntwood, Brwd. 108 FW48
Gerrard Cres.
Burntwood Ave., Horn. 128 FK58
Burntwood Clo. SW18 180 DD88
Burntwood Clo., Cat. 236 DU121
Burntwood Gra. Rd. SW18 180 DD88
Burntwood Gro., Sev. 257 FH127
Burntwood La. SW17 180 DC90
Burntwood La., Cat. 236 DS122
Burntwood Rd., Sev. 257 FH128
Burntwood Vw. SE19 182 DT92
Bowley La.
Burnway, Horn. 128 FL59
Buross St. E1 142 DV72
Commercial Rd.
Burpham La., Guil. 243 BA130
Burr Clo. E1 142 DU74
St. Katharine's Way
Burr Clo., Bexh. 166 EZ83
Burr Clo., St.Alb. 62 CL27
Burr Hill La., Wok. 210 AS109
Burr Rd. SW18 180 DA88
Burrage Gro. SE18 165 EQ77
Burrage Pl. SE18 165 EP78
Burrage Rd. SE18 165 EQ77
Burrard Rd. E16 144 EH72
Burrard Rd. NW6 120 DA64
Burrell, The, Dor. 262 CC137
Burrell Clo., Croy. 203 DY100
Burrell Clo., Edg. 96 CP47
Burrell Row, Beck. 203 EA96
High St.
Burrell St. SE1 278 F2
Burrell St. SE1 141 DP74
Burrell Twr. E10 123 EA59
Burrells Wf. Sq. E14 163 EB78
Burrfield Dr., Orp. 206 EX99
Burritt Rd., Kings.T. 198 CN96
Burroughs, The NW4 119 CV56
Burroughs Gdns. NW4 119 CV56
Burrow Clo., Chig. 103 ET50
Burrow Rd.
Burrow Grn., Chig. 103 ET50
Burrow Rd., Chig. 103 ET50
Burrow Wk. SE21 182 DQ87
Rosendale Rd.
Burroway Rd., Slou. 153 BB76
Burrowfield, Welw.G.C. 29 CX11
Burrowfield Ind. Est., Welw.G.C. 29 CX12
Burrows Clo., Guil. 242 AT133
Burrows Clo., H.Wyc. 88 AC45
Burrows Clo., Lthd. 230 BZ124
Burrows Cross, Guil. 261 BQ141
Burrows Hill Clo., Houns. 154 BJ84
Burrows Hill La., Houns. 154 BH84
Burrows La., Guil. 261 BQ140
Burrows Ms. SE1 278 F4
Burrows Rd. NW10 139 CW69
Bursdon Clo., Sid. 185 ET89
Burses Way, Brwd. 109 GB45
Bursland Rd., Enf. 83 DX42
Burslem Ave., Ilf. 104 EU51
Burslem St. E1 142 DU72
Burstead Clo., Cob. 214 BX112
Burstock Rd. SW15 159 CY84
Burston Dr., St.Alb. 60 CC28
Burston Rd. SW15 179 CX85
Burston Vill. SW15 179 CX85
St. John's Ave.
Burstow Rd. SW20 199 CY95
Burt Rd. E16 144 EJ74
Burtenshaw Rd., T.Ditt. 197 CG101
Burtley Clo. N4 122 DQ60
Burton Ave., Wat. 75 BU42
Burton Clo., Chess. 215 CK108
Burton Clo., Horl. 268 DG149
Burton Ct. SW3 160 DF78
Franklin's Row
Burton Gdns., Houns. 156 BZ81
Burton Gro. SE17 162 DR78
Portland St.
Burton La. SW9 161 DN82
Burton La. (Cheshunt), Wal.Cr. 66 DS29
Burton Ms. SW1 276 G9
Burton Pl. WC1 273 N3
Burton Rd. E18 124 EH55
Burton Rd. NW6 139 CZ66
Burton Rd. SW9 161 DP82
Burton Rd., Kings.T. 178 CL94
Burton Rd., Loug. 85 EQ42
Burton St. WC1 273 N3
Burton St. WC1 141 DK69
Burton Way, Wind. 151 AL82
Burtonhole Clo. NW7 97 CX49
Burtonhole La. NW7 97 CW50
Burtons La., Ch.St.G. 72 AW40
Burtons La., Rick. 73 BA43
Burtons Rd., Hmptn. 176 CB91
Burtons Way, Ch.St.G. 72 AW40
Burtwell La. SE27 182 DR91
Burwash Ct., Orp. 206 EW99
Rookery Gdns.
Burwash Ho. SE1 279 L5
Burwash Rd. SE18 165 ER78
Burway Cres., Cher. 194 BG97
Burwell Ave., Grnf. 137 CE65
Burwell Clo. E1 142 DV72
Bigland St.
Burwell Rd. E10 123 DY60
Burwell Wk. E3 143 EA70
Burwood Ave., Brom. 204 EH103
Burwood Ave., Ken. 219 DP114
Burwood Ave., Pnr. 115 BV57
Burwood Clo., Guil. 243 BD133
Burwood Clo., Reig. 250 DD134
Burwood Clo., Surb. 198 CN102
Burwood Clo., Walt. 214 BW107
Burwood Gdns., Rain. 147 FF69
Burwood Pk. Rd., Walt. 213 BV105
Burwood Pl. W2 272 C8
Burwood Pl. W2 140 DE72
Burwood Rd., Walt. 213 BS108
Bury Ave., Hayes 135 BS68
Bury Ave., Ruis. 115 BQ58
Bury Clo. SE16 143 DX74
Rotherhithe St.
Bury Clo., Wok. 226 AX116
Bury Ct. EC3 275 N8
Bury Grn., Hem.H. 40 BJ19
Bury Grn. Rd. (Cheshunt), Wal.Cr. 66 DU31
Bury Gro., Mord. 200 DB99
Bury Hill, Hem.H. 40 BH19
Bury Hill Clo., Hem.H. 40 BJ19
Bury Holme, Brox. 49 DZ23
Bury La., Chesh. 54 AP31
Bury La., Epp. 69 ER28
Bury La., Rick. 92 BK46
Bury La., Wok. 226 AW116
Bury Meadows, Rick. 92 BK46
Bury Pl. WC1 273 P7
Bury Pl. WC1 141 DL71
Bury Ri., Hem.H. 57 BD25
Bury Rd. E4 84 EE42
Bury Rd. N22 121 DN55
Bury Rd., Dag. 127 FB64
Bury Rd., Epp. 69 ES31
Bury Rd., Harl. 36 EW11
Bury Rd., Hat. 45 CW17
Bury Rd., Hem.H. 40 BJ19
Bury St. EC3 275 N9
Bury St. EC3 142 DS72
Bury St. N9 100 DT45
Bury St. SW1 277 K2
Bury St. SW1 141 DJ74
Bury St., Guil. 258 AW136
Bury St., Ruis. 115 BQ57
Bury St. W. N9 100 DR45
Bury Wk. SW3 276 B9
Bury Wk. SW3 160 DE77
Burycroft, Welw.G.C. 29 CY06
Burydell La., St.Alb. 61 CD27
Buryfields, Guil. 258 AW136
Busbridge Ho. E14 143 EA71
Brabazon St.
Busby Ms. NW5 141 DK65
Busby Pl. NW5 141 DK65
Busby St. E2 142 DT70
Chilton St.

Cam–Car This index reads in the sequence: Street Name / Postal District or Post Town / Map Page Number / Grid Reference

Cambridge Clo. NW10 118 CQ62
Cambridge Clo. SW20 199 CV95
Cambridge Clo., Houns. 156 BY84
Cambridge Clo. (Cheshunt), Wal.Cr. 66 DW29
Cambridge Clo., West Dr. 154 BK79
Cambridge Clo., Wok. 226 AT118
Bingham Dr.
Cambridge Cotts., Rich. 158 CN79
Cambridge Cres. E2 142 DV68
Cambridge Cres., Tedd. 177 CG92
Cambridge Dr. SE12 184 EG85
Cambridge Dr., Pot.B. 63 CX31
Cambridge Dr., Ruis. 116 BX61
Cambridge Gdns. N10 98 DG53
Cambridge Gdns. N13 99 DN50
Cambridge Gdns. N17 100 DR52
Great Cambridge Rd.
Cambridge Gdns. N21 100 DR45
Cambridge Gdns. NW6 140 DA68
Cambridge Gdns. W10 139 CX72
Cambridge Gdns., Enf. 82 DU40
Cambridge Gdns., Grays 171 GG77
Cambridge Gdns., Kings.T. 198 CN96
Cambridge Gate NW1 273 J4
Cambridge Gate Ms. NW1 273 J4
Cambridge Grn. SE9 185 EP88
Cambridge Gro. SE20 202 DV95
Cambridge Gro. W6 159 CV77
Cambridge Gro. Rd., Kings.T. 198 CN97
Cambridge Heath Rd. E1 142 DV70
Cambridge Heath Rd. E2 142 DW70
Cambridge Mans. SW11 160 DF81
Cambridge Rd.
Cambridge Par., Enf. 82 DU39
Great Cambridge Rd.
Cambridge Pk. E11 124 EG59
Cambridge Pk., Twick. 177 CJ86
Cambridge Pk. Rd. E11 124 EF59
Cambridge Pl. W8 160 DB75
Cambridge Rd. E4 101 ED46
Cambridge Rd. E11 124 EF58
Cambridge Rd. NW6 140 DA69
Cambridge Rd. SE20 202 DV97
Cambridge Rd. SW11 160 DF81
Cambridge Rd. SW13 159 CT82
Cambridge Rd. SW20 199 CV95
Cambridge Rd. W7 157 CF75
Cambridge Rd., Ashf. 175 BQ94
Cambridge Rd., Bark. 145 EQ66
Cambridge Rd., Beac. 88 AJ53
Cambridge Rd., Brom. 184 EG94
Cambridge Rd., Cars. 218 DE107
Cambridge Rd., Hmptn. 176 BZ94
Cambridge Rd., Harl. 36 EW09
Cambridge Rd., Har. 116 CA57
Cambridge Rd., Houns. 156 BY84
Cambridge Rd., Ilf. 125 ES60
Cambridge Rd., Kings.T. 198 CN96
Cambridge Rd., Mitch. 201 DH97
Cambridge Rd., N.Mal. 198 CR98
Cambridge Rd., Rich. 158 CN80
Cambridge Rd., St.Alb. 43 CH21
Cambridge Rd., Sid. 185 ES91
Cambridge Rd., Sthl. 136 BZ74
Cambridge Rd., Tedd. 177 CF91
Cambridge Rd., Twick. 177 CK86
Cambridge Rd., Uxb. 134 BK65
Cambridge Rd., Walt. 195 BV100
Cambridge Rd., Wat. 76 BW42
Cambridge Rd., W.Mol. 196 BZ98
Cambridge Rd. Est., Kings.T. 198 CN96
Cambridge Rd. N. W4 158 CP78
Cambridge Rd. S. W4 158 CP78
Oxford Rd. S.
Cambridge Row SE18 165 EP78
Cambridge Sq. W2 272 B8
Cambridge Sq. W2 140 DE72
Cambridge St. SW1 277 J10
Cambridge St. SW1 161 DH77
Cambridge Ter. N13 99 DN50
Cambridge Ter. NW1 273 H3
Cambridge Ter., Berk. 38 AX19
Cambridge Ter. Ms. NW1 273 J3
Cambus Clo., Hayes 136 BY71
Cambus Rd. E16 144 EG71
Camdale Rd. SE18 165 ET80
Camden Ave., Felt. 176 BW89
Camden Ave., Hayes 136 BX73
Camden Clo., Chis. 205 EQ95
Camden Clo., Grav. 190 GC88
Springhead Rd.
Camden Clo., Grays 171 GH77
Camden Est. SE15 162 DT81
Camden Gdns. NW1 141 DH66
Kentish Town Rd.
Camden Gdns., Sutt. 218 DB106
Camden Gdns., Th.Hth. 201 DP97
Camden Gro., Chis. 185 EP93
Camden High St. NW1 141 DH67
Camden Hill Rd. SE19 182 DS93
Camden La. N7 141 DK65
Camden Lock Pl. NW1 141 DH66
Chalk Fm. Rd.
Camden Ms. NW1 141 DJ66
Camden Pk. Rd. NW1 141 DK65
Camden Pk. Rd., Chis. 185 EM94
Camden Pas. N1 141 DP67
Camden Rd. E11 124 EH58
Camden Rd. E17 123 DZ58
Camden Rd. N7 121 DL63
Camden Rd. NW1 141 DJ66
Camden Rd., Bex. 186 EY88
Camden Rd., Cars. 218 DF105
Camden Rd., Grays 170 FZ76
Camden Rd., Sev. 257 FH122
Camden Rd., Sutt. 218 DA106
Camden Row SE3 164 EE82
Camden Sq. NW1 141 DK65
Camden Sq. SE15 162 DT81
Exeter Rd.
Camden St. NW1 141 DJ66
Camden Ter. NW1 141 DK65
North Vill.
Camden Wk. N1 141 DP67
Camden Way, Chis. 185 EM94
Camden Way, Th.Hth. 201 DP97
Camdenhurst St. E14 143 DY72
Camel Gro., Kings.T. 177 CK92
Dukes Ave.
Camel Rd. E16 144 EK74
Camelford Wk. W11 139 CY72
Lancaster Rd.
Camellia Clo., Rom. 106 FL53
Columbine Way
Camellia Ct., Wdf.Grn. 102 EE52
Bridle Path
Camellia Pl., Twick. 176 CB87
Camellia St. SW8 161 DL80
Camelot Clo. SE28 165 ER75
Camelot Clo. SW19 180 DA91
Camelot Clo., West. 238 EJ116
Camelot St. SE15 162 DV80
Bird in Bush Rd.
Camera Pl. SW10 160 DD79
Cameron Clo. N18 100 DV49
Cameron Clo. N20 98 DE47
Myddelton Pk.
Cameron Clo., Bex. 187 FD90
Cameron Clo., Brwd. 108 FX49
Cameron Clo., Ware 33 DX05
Crib St.
Cameron Dr., Wal.Cr. 67 DX34
Cameron Pl. E1 142 DV72
Varden St.
Cameron Rd. SE6 183 DZ89
Cameron Rd., Brom. 204 EG98
Cameron Rd., Chesh. 54 AQ30
Cameron Rd., Croy. 201 DP100
Cameron Rd., Ilf. 125 ES60
Cameron Sq., Mitch. 200 DE95
Camerton Clo. E8 142 DT65
Buttermere Wk.
Camfield, Welw.G.C. 29 CZ13
Camgate Est., Stai. 174 BM86
Camilla Clo., Lthd. 246 CB125
Camilla Clo., Sun. 175 BS93
Camilla Dr., Dor. 247 CG130
Camilla Rd. SE16 162 DV77
Camille Clo. SE25 202 DU97
Camlan Rd., Brom. 184 EF91
Camlet St. E2 275 P4
Camlet St. E2 142 DT70
Camlet Way, Barn. 80 DA40
Camlet Way, St.Alb. 42 CB19
Camley St. NW1 141 DK66
Camm Ave., Wind. 151 AL83
Camm Gdns., Kings.T. 198 CM96
Church Rd.
Camm Gdns., T.Ditt. 197 CE101
Camomile Ave., Mitch. 200 DF95
Camomile St. EC3 275 M8
Camomile St. EC3 142 DS72
Camp End Rd., Wey. 213 BR110
Camp Rd. SW19 179 CV92
Camp Rd., Cat. 237 DY120
Camp Rd., Ger.Cr. 112 AW58
Camp Rd., St.Alb. 43 CF20
Camp Vw. SW19 179 CV92
Camp Vw. Rd., St.Alb. 43 CH21
Campana Rd. SW6 160 DA81
Campbell Ave., Ilf. 125 EP56
Campbell Ave., Wok. 227 AZ121
Campbell Clo. SE18 165 EN81
Moordown
Campbell Clo. SW16 181 DK92
Campbell Clo. (Havering-atte-Bower), Rom. 105 FE51
Campbell Clo., Ruis. 115 BU58
Campbell Clo., Twick. 177 CD89
Campbell Ct. N17 100 DT53
Campbell Cft., Edg. 96 CN50
Campbell Dr., Beac. 88 AJ50
Campbell Gordon Way NW2 119 CV63
Campbell Rd. E3 143 EA69
Campbell Rd. E6 144 EL67
Campbell Rd. E15 124 EF63
Trevelyan Rd.
Campbell Rd. E17 123 DZ56
Campbell Rd. N17 100 DT53
Campbell Rd. W7 137 CE73
Campbell Rd., Cat. 236 DR121
Campbell Rd., Croy. 201 DP101
Campbell Rd., E.Mol. 197 CF97
Hampton Ct. Rd.
Campbell Rd., Grav. 191 GF88
Campbell Rd., Twick. 177 CD88
Campbell Rd., Wey. 212 BN108
Campbell Wk. N1 141 DL67
Outram Pl.
Campdale Rd. N7 121 DK62
Campden Cres., Dag. 126 EV63
Campden Cres., Wem. 117 CH62
Campden Gro. W8 160 DA75
Campden Hill W8 160 DA75
Campden Hill Gdns. W8 140 DA74
Campden Hill Pl. W11 139 CZ74
Holland Pk. Ave.
Campden Hill Rd. W8 140 DA74
Campden Hill Sq. W8 139 CZ74
Campden Ho. Clo. W8 160 DA75
Hornton St.
Campden Rd., S.Croy. 220 DS106
Campden Rd., Uxb. 114 BM62
Campden St. W8 140 DA74
Campen Clo. SW19 179 CY89
Queensmere Rd.
Camperdown St. E1 142 DT72
Leman St.
Campfield Rd. SE9 184 EK87
Campfield Rd., Hert. 31 DP09
Campfield Rd., St.Alb. 43 CG21
Camphill Ct., W.Byf. 212 BG112
Camphill Ind. Est., W.Byf. 212 BH111
Camphill Rd., W.Byf. 212 BG113
Campine Clo. (Cheshunt), Wal.Cr. 67 DX28
Welsummer Way
Campion Clo. E6 145 EM73
Campion Clo., Croy. 220 DS105
Campion Clo., Grav. 190 GE91
Campion Clo., Har. 118 CM58
Campion Clo. (Denham), Uxb. 114 BG62
Lindsey Rd.
Campion Clo. (Hillingdon), Uxb. 134 BM71
Campion Clo., Wat. 59 BU33
Campion Ct., Grays 170 GD79
Campion Dr., Tad. 233 CV120
Waterfield
Campion Pl. SE28 146 EV74
Campion Rd. SW15 159 CW84
Campion Rd., Hem.H. 39 BE21
Campion Rd., Islw. 157 CF81
Campion Ter. NW2 119 CX63
Campions, Epp. 70 EU28
Campions, Loug. 85 EN38
Campions, The, Borwd. 78 CM38
Campions Clo., Borwd. 78 CP37
Campions Ct., Berk. 38 AU19
Cample La., S.Ock. 149 FU73
Camplin Rd., Har. 118 CL57
Camplin St. SE14 163 DX80
Campsbourne, The N8 121 DL56
Rectory Gdns.
Campsbourne Rd. N8 121 DL55
Campsey Gdns., Dag. 146 EV66
Campsey Rd., Dag. 146 EV66
Campsfield Rd. N8 121 DL55
Campsbourne Rd.
Campshill Pl. SE13 183 EC85
Campshill Rd.
Campshill Rd. SE13 183 EC85
Campus, The, Welw.G.C. 29 CX08
Campus Rd. E17 123 DZ58
Camrose Ave., Edg. 96 CM54
Camrose Ave., Erith 167 FB79
Camrose Ave., Felt. 175 BV91
Camrose Clo., Croy. 203 DY101
Camrose Clo., Mord. 200 DA98
Camrose St. SE2 166 EU78
Can Hatch, Tad. 233 CY118
Canada Ave. N18 100 DQ51
Canada Ave., Red. 266 DG138
Canada Cres. W3 138 CQ70
Canada Dr., Red. 266 DG138
Canada Est. SE16 162 DW76
Canada Fm. Rd. (South Darenth), Dart. 209 FU98
Canada Fm. Rd., Long. 209 FV99
Canada Gdns. SE13 183 EC85
Monument Gdns.
Canada La., Brox. 67 DY25
High Rd. Turnford
Canada Rd. W3 138 CQ71
Canada Rd., Cob. 214 BW113
Canada Rd., Erith 167 FG80
Slade Grn. Rd.
Canada Rd., Slou. 152 AV75
Canada Rd., W.Byf. 212 BK111
Canada Sq. E14 143 EB74
Canada St. SE16 163 DX75
Canada Way W12 139 CV73
Canada Yd. S. SE16 163 DX76
Canadas, The, Brox. 67 DY25
Canadian Ave. SE6 183 EB88
Canadian Memorial Ave., Egh. 192 AS96
Canal App. SE8 163 DY78
Canal Basin, Grav. 191 GK86
Canal Clo. E1 143 DY70
Canal Clo. W10 139 CX70
Canal Way
Canal Gro. SE15 162 DU79
Canal Head SE15 162 DU81
Peckham High St.
Canal Path E2 142 DT67
Laburnum St.
Canal Rd. E3 143 DY70
Canal Rd., Grav. 191 GJ86
Canal St. SE5 162 DR79
Canal Wk. N1 142 DR67
Canal Wk. SE26 182 DW92
Canal Wk., Croy. 202 DS100
Canal Way NW1 140 DG67
Regents Pk. Rd.
Canal Way NW10 138 CR68
Canal Way W10 139 CX70
Canal Way, Wem. 138 CM67
Canal Way Wk. W10 139 CY70
Kensal Rd.
Canal Wf., Slou. 153 BA75
Canary Wf. E14 143 EA74
Canberra Clo. NW4 119 CU55
Canberra Clo., Dag. 147 FD66
Canberra Clo., Horn. 128 FJ63
Canberra Clo., St.Alb. 43 CF16
Canberra Cres., Dag. 147 FD66
Canberra Dr., Nthlt. 136 BW69
Canberra Rd. E6 145 EM67
Barking Rd.
Canberra Rd. SE7 164 EJ79
Canberra Rd. W13 137 CG74
Canberra Rd., Bexh. 166 EX79
Canberra Rd., Houns. 154 BN83
Canberra Sq., Til. 171 GG82
Canbury Ave., Kings.T. 198 CM95
Canbury Ms. SE26 182 DU90
Wells Pk. Rd.
Canbury Pk. Rd., Kings.T. 198 CL95
Canbury Pas., Kings.T. 197 CK95
Canbury Path, Orp. 206 EU97
Cancell Rd. SW9 161 DN81
Candahar Rd. SW11 160 DE82
Cander Way, S.Ock. 149 FV73
Candlefield Clo., Hem.H. 40 BN23
Candlefield Rd.
Candlefield Rd., Hem.H. 40 BN23
Candlefield Wk., Hem.H. 40 BN23
Candlefield Rd.
Candlemas La., Beac. 89 AL53
Candlemas Mead, Beac. 89 AL53
Candler St. N15 122 DR58
Candover Clo., West Dr. 154 BK80
Candover Rd., Horn. 127 FH60
Candover St. W1 273 K7
Candy Cft., Lthd. 246 CB125
Candy St. E3 143 DZ67
Cane Clo., Wall. 219 DL108
Kingsford Ave.
Cane Hill, Rom. 106 FK54
Bennison Dr.
Caneland Ct., Wal.Abb. 68 EF34
Canes La., Epp. 52 FA22
Canes La., Harl. 52 EX21
Canewdon Clo., Wok. 226 AY119
Guildford Rd.
Caney Ms. NW2 119 CX61
Claremont Rd.
Canfield Dr., Ruis. 115 BV64
Canfield Gdns. NW6 140 DB66
Canfield Pl. NW6 140 DC65
Canfield Gdns.
Canfield Rd., Rain. 147 FF67
Canfield Rd., Wdf.Grn. 102 EL52
Canford Ave., Nthlt. 136 BY67
Canford Clo., Enf. 81 DN40
Canford Dr., Add. 194 BH103
Canford Gdns., N.Mal. 198 CS100
Canford Rd. SW11 180 DG85
Cangels Clo., Hem.H. 39 BF22
Canham Rd. SE25 202 DS97
Canham Rd. W3 158 CS75
Canmore Gdns. SW16 181 DJ94
Cann Hall Rd. E11 124 EE63
Canning Cres. N22 99 DM53
Canning Cross SE5 162 DS82
Canning Pas. W8 160 DC75
Victoria Rd.
Canning Pl. W8 160 DC76
Canning Pl. Ms. W8 160 DC76
Canning Pl.
Canning Rd. E15 144 EE68
Canning Rd. E17 123 DY56
Canning Rd. N5 121 DP62
Canning Rd., Croy. 202 DT103
Canning Rd., Har. 117 CE55
Cannington Rd., Dag. 146 EW65
Cannizaro Rd. SW19 179 CW92
Cannon Clo. SW20 199 CW97
Cannon Clo., Hmptn. 176 CB93
Hanworth Rd.
Cannon Cres., Wok. 210 AS111
Cannon Dr. E14 143 EA73
Cannon Gro., Lthd. 231 CE122
Cannon Hill N14 99 DK48
Cannon Hill NW6 120 DA64
Cannon Hill Clo., Maid. 150 AC77
Cannon Hill La. SW20 199 CY97
Cannon La. NW3 120 DD62
Cannon La., Pnr. 116 BY57
Cannon Mill Ave., Chesh. 54 AR33
Cannon Pl. NW3 120 DC62
Cannon Pl. SE7 164 EL78
Cannon Rd. N14 99 DL48
Cannon Rd., Bexh. 166 EY81
Cannon Rd., Wat. 76 BW43
Cannon St. EC4 275 H9
Cannon St. EC4 142 DQ72
Cannon St., St.Alb. 43 CD19
Cannon St. Rd. E1 142 DV72
Cannon Wk., Grav. 191 GJ87
Cannon Way, Lthd. 231 CE121
Cannon Way, W.Mol. 196 CA98
Cannonbury Ave., Pnr. 116 BX58
Cannons Meadow, Welw. 30 DE05
Cannonside, Lthd. 231 CE122
Canon Ave., Rom. 126 EW57
Canon Beck Rd. SE16 162 DW75
Canon Hill, Couls. 235 DN118
Canon Mohan Clo. N14 81 DH44
Farm La.
Canon Rd., Brom. 204 EJ97
Canon Row SW1 277 P4
Canon Row SW1 161 DL75
Canon St. N1 142 DQ67
Canon Trd. Est., The, Wem. 118 CP63
Canonbie Rd. SE23 182 DW87
Canonbury Cres. N1 142 DQ66
Canonbury Gro. N1 142 DQ66
Canonbury La. N1 141 DP66
Canonbury Pk. N. N1 142 DQ65
Canonbury Pk. S. N1 142 DQ65
Canonbury Pl. N1 141 DP65
Canonbury Rd. N1 141 DP65
Canonbury Rd., Enf. 82 DS39
Canonbury Sq. N1 141 DP66
Canonbury St. N1 142 DQ66
Canonbury Vill. N1 141 DP66
Canonbury Yd. N1 142 DQ67
New N. Rd.
Canons Brook, Harl. 51 EN15
Canons Clo. N2 120 DD59
Canons Clo., Edg. 96 CM51
Canons Clo., Rad. 77 CH35
Canons Clo., Reig. 249 CZ133
Canons Cor., Edg. 96 CL49
Canons Dr., Edg. 96 CL51
Canons Gate, Harl. 35 EN13
Canons Hatch, Tad. 233 CY118
Canon's Hill, Couls. 235 DN118
Canons La., Tad. 233 CY118
Canons Rd., Ware 32 DW05
Canons Wk., Croy. 203 DX104
Canonsleigh Rd., Dag. 146 EV66
Canopus Way, Nthwd. 93 BU49
Canopus Way, Stai. 174 BL87
Canrobert St. E2 142 DV69
Cantelowes Rd. NW1 141 DK65
Canterbury Ave., Ilf. 124 EL59
Canterbury Ave., Sid. 186 EW89
Canterbury Ave., Slou. 131 AQ70
Canterbury Ave., Upmin. 129 FT60
Canterbury Clo. E6 145 EM72
Harper Rd.
Canterbury Clo., Amer. 55 AS39
Canterbury Clo., Beck. 203 EB95
Canterbury Clo., Chig. 103 ET48
Canterbury Clo., Dart. 188 FN87
Canterbury Clo., Grnf. 136 CB72
Canterbury Clo., Nthwd. 93 BT51
Canterbury Cres. SW9 161 DN83
Canterbury Gro. SE27 181 DN91
Canterbury Par., S.Ock. 149 FW69
Canterbury Pl. SE17 278 G9
Canterbury Pl. SE17 161 DP77
Canterbury Rd. E10 123 EC59
Canterbury Rd. NW6 139 CZ68
Canterbury Rd., Borwd. 78 CN40
Canterbury Rd., Croy. 201 DN101
Canterbury Rd., Felt. 176 BY90
Canterbury Rd., Grav. 191 GJ89
Canterbury Rd., Guil. 242 AT132
Canterbury Rd., Har. 116 CB57
Canterbury Rd., Mord. 200 DB101
Canterbury Rd., Wat. 75 BV40
Canterbury Ter. NW6 140 DA68
Canterbury Way, Brwd. 107 FW51
Canterbury Way, Grays 169 FS78
Canterbury Way, Rick. 75 BQ41
Cantley Gdns. SE19 202 DT95
Cantley Gdns., Ilf. 125 EQ58
Cantley Rd. W7 157 CG76
Canton St. E14 143 EA72
Cantrell Rd. E3 143 DZ70
Cantwell Rd. SE18 165 EP80
Canute Gdns. SE16 163 DX77
Canvey St. SE1 278 G2
Cape Clo., Bark. 145 EQ65
North St.
Cape Rd. N17 122 DU55
High Cross Rd.
Cape Rd., St.Alb. 43 CH20
Cape Yd. E1 142 DU74
Asher Way
Capel Ave., Wall. 219 DM106
Capel Clo. N20 98 DC48
Capel Clo., Brom. 205 EM102
Capel Ct. EC2 275 L9
Capel Ct. SE20 202 DW95
Melvin Rd.
Capel Gdns., Ilf. 125 ET63
Capel Gdns., Pnr. 116 BZ56
Capel Pl., Dart. 188 FJ91
Capel Pt. E7 124 EH63
Capel Rd. E7 124 EH63
Capel Rd. E12 124 EK63
Capel Rd., Barn. 80 DE44
Capel Rd., Enf. 82 DV36
Capel Rd., Wat. 76 BY44
Capel Vere Wk., Wat. 75 BS39
Capell Ave., Rick. 73 BC43
Capell Rd., Rick. 73 BD43
Capell Way, Rick. 73 BD43
Capella Rd., Nthwd. 93 BT49
Capener's Clo. SW1 276 F5
Capern Rd. SW18 180 DC88
Cargill Rd.
Capital Business Cen., Wem. 137 CK67
Capital Interchange Way, Brent. 158 CN78
Capital Pl., Croy. 219 DM106
Stafford Rd.
Capital Pl., Harl. 51 EN16
Capitol Ind. Est. NW9 118 CQ55
Capitol Way NW9 118 CQ55
Capland St. NW8 272 A4
Capland St. NW8 140 DD70
Caple Rd. NW10 139 CT68
Capon Clo., Brwd. 108 FV46
Caponfield, Welw.G.C. 30 DB11
Cappell La., Ware 33 EC09
Capper St. WC1 273 L5
Capper St. WC1 141 DJ70
Caprea Clo., Hayes 136 BX71
Triandra Way
Capri Rd., Croy. 202 DT102
Capstan Clo., Rom. 126 EV58
Capstan Ct., Dart. 168 FQ84
Capstan Ride, Enf. 81 DN40
Crofton Way
Capstan Rd. SE8 163 DZ77
Capstan Sq. E14 163 EC75
Capstan Way SE16 143 DY74
Capstan's Wf., Wok. 226 AT118
Capstone Rd., Brom. 184 EF91
Captain Cook Clo., Ch.St.G. 90 AV49
Captains Clo., Chesh. 54 AN27
Captains Wk., Berk. 38 AX20
Capthorne Ave., Har. 116 BY60
Capuchin Clo., Stan. 95 CH51
Capworth St. E10 123 EA60
Caractacus Cottage Vw., Wat. 93 BU45
Caractacus Grn., Wat. 75 BT44
Caradoc Clo. W2 140 DA72
Caradoc St. SE10 164 EE78
Caradon Clo. E11 124 EE61
Brockway Clo.
Caradon Clo., Wok. 226 AV118
Caradon Way N15 122 DR56
Caravan La., Rick. 92 BL45
Caravel Clo. E14 163 EA76
Tiller Rd.
Caravel Clo., Grays 170 FZ76
Caravel Ms. SE8 163 EA79
Watergate St.
Caravelle Gdns., Nthlt. 136 BX69
Javelin Way
Caraway Pl., Guil. 242 AU129
Caraway Pl., Wall. 201 DH104
London Rd.
Carberry Rd. SE19 182 DS93
Carbery Ave. W3 158 CM75
Carbis Clo. E4 101 ED46
Carbis Rd. E14 143 DZ72
Carbone Hill, Hert. 65 DL25
Carbone Hill (Cuffley), Pot.B. 65 DJ27
Carbuncle Pas. Way N17 100 DU54
Carburton St. W1 273 J6
Carburton St. W1 141 DH71
Carbury Clo., Horn. 148 FJ65
Cardale St. E14 163 EC76
Plevna St.
Cardamon Clo., Guil. 242 AU130
Carde Clo., Hert. 31 DM08
Carden Rd. SE15 162 DV83
Cardiff Rd. W7 157 CG76
Cardiff Rd., Enf. 82 DV42
Cardiff Rd., Wat. 75 BV44
Cardiff St. SE18 165 ES80
Cardiff Way, Abb.L. 59 BU32
Langley La.
Cardigan Clo., Wok. 226 AS118
Bingham Dr.
Cardigan Gdns., Ilf. 126 EU61
Cardigan Rd. E3 143 DZ68
Cardigan Rd. SW13 159 CU82
Cardigan Rd. SW19 180 DC93
Haydons Rd.
Cardigan Rd., Rich. 178 CL86
Cardigan St. SE11 278 D10
Cardigan St. SE11 161 DN78
Cardigan Wk. N1 142 DQ66
Ashby Gro.
Cardinal Ave., Borwd. 78 CP41
Cardinal Ave., Kings.T. 178 CL92
Cardinal Ave., Mord. 199 CY100
Cardinal Bourne St. SE1 279 L7
Cardinal Bourne St. SE1 162 DR76
Cardinal Clo., Chis. 205 ER95
Cardinal Clo., Mord. 199 CY100
Cardinal Clo. (Cheshunt), Wal.Cr. 66 DT26
Adamsfield
Cardinal Clo., Wor.Pk. 217 CU105
Cardinal Cres., N.Mal. 198 CQ96
Cardinal Dr., Ilf. 103 EQ51
Cardinal Dr., Walt. 196 BX102
Cardinal Gro., St.Alb. 42 CB22
Cardinal Pl. SW15 159 CX84
Cardinal Rd., Felt. 175 BV88
Cardinal Rd., Ruis. 116 BX60
Cardinal Way, Har. 117 CE55
Wolseley Rd.
Cardinal Way, Rain. 148 FK68
Cardinals Wk., Hmptn. 176 CC94
Cardinals Wk., Maid. 130 AJ72
Cardinals Wk., Sun. 175 BS93
Cardinals Way N19 121 DK60
Cardine Ms. SE15 162 DV80
Cardingham, Wok. 226 AU117
Cardington Sq., Houns. 156 BX84
Cardington St. NW1 273 L2
Cardington St. NW1 141 DJ69
Cardozo Rd. N7 121 DL64
Cardrew Ave. N12 98 DD50
Cardrew Clo. N12 98 DD50
Cardross St. W6 159 CV76
Cardwell Rd. N7 121 DL63
Cardwell Rd. SE18 165 EM77

Cardwells Keep, Guil. 242 AU131
Stoughton Rd.
Cardy Rd., Hem.H. 40 BH20
Carew Clo. N7 121 DM61
Carew Clo., Couls. 235 DP119
Carew Rd. N17 100 DU54
Carew Rd. W13 157 CJ75
Carew Rd., Ashf. 175 BQ93
Carew Rd., Mitch. 200 DG96
Carew Rd., Nthwd. 93 BS51
Carew Rd., Th.Hth. 201 DP97
Carew Rd., Wall. 219 DJ107
Carew St. SE5 162 DQ82
Carey Clo., Wind. 151 AP83
Carey Ct., Bexh. 187 FB85
Carey Gdns. SW8 161 DJ81
Carey La. EC2 275 H8
Carey Pl. SW1 277 M9
Carey Rd., Dag. 126 EY63
Carey St. WC2 274 C9
Carey St. WC2 141 DM72
Carey Way, Wem. 118 CQ63
Fourth Way
Careys Cft., Berk. 38 AU16
Careys Wd., Horl. 269 DP148
Carfax Pl. SW4 161 DK84
Holwood Pl.
Carfax Rd., Hayes 155 BT78
Carfax Rd., Horn. 127 FF63
Carfree Clo. N1 141 DN66
Bewdley St.
Cargill Rd. SW18 180 DB88
Cargo Forecourt Rd., Gat. 268 DD152
Cargo Rd., Gat. 268 DD152
Cargreen Pl. SE25 202 DT98
Cargreen Rd.
Cargreen Rd. SE25 202 DT98
Carholme Rd. SE23 183 DZ88
Carisbrook Ave., Wat. 76 BX39
Carisbrook Clo., Stan. 95 CK54
Carisbrook Rd., St.Alb. 60 CB26
Carisbrooke Ave., Bex. 186 EX88
Carisbrooke Clo., Enf. 82 DT39
Carisbrooke Clo., Horn. 128 FN60
Carisbrooke Ct., Slou. 132 AT73
Carisbrooke Gdns. SE15 162 DT80
Commercial Way
Carisbrooke Rd. E17 123 DY56
Carisbrooke Rd., Brwd. 108 FV44
Carisbrooke Rd., Brom. 204 EJ98
Carisbrooke Rd., Mitch. 201 DK98
Carker's La. NW5 121 DH64
Carl Ekman Ho., Grav. 190 GD87
Carlbury Clo., St.Alb. 43 CH21
Guildford Rd.
Carleton Ave., Wall. 219 DK108
Carleton Clo., Esher 197 CD102
Carleton Pl. (Horton Kirby), Dart. 208 FQ98
Carleton Rd. N7 121 DK64
Carleton Rd., Dart. 188 FN87
Carleton Rd. (Cheshunt), Wal.Cr. 67 DX27
Carlile Clo. E3 143 DZ68
Carlina Gdns., Wdf.Grn. 102 EG50
Harts Gro.
Carlingford Gdns., Mitch. 180 DF94
Carlingford Rd. N15 121 DP55
Carlingford Rd. NW3 120 DD63
Carlingford Rd., Mord. 199 CX100
Carlisle Ave. EC3 275 P9
Carlisle Ave. W3 138 CS72
Carlisle Ave., St.Alb. 43 CD18
Carlisle Clo., Kings.T. 198 CN95
Carlisle Gdns., Har. 117 CK59
Carlisle Gdns., Ilf. 124 EL58
Carlisle La. SE1 278 C7
Carlisle La. SE1 161 DM76
Carlisle Ms. NW8 272 A6
Carlisle Ms. NW8 140 DD71
Carlisle Pl. N11 99 DH49
Carlisle Pl. SW1 277 K7
Carlisle Pl. SW1 161 DJ76
Carlisle Rd. E10 123 EA60
Carlisle Rd. N4 121 DN59
Carlisle Rd. NW6 139 CY67
Carlisle Rd. NW9 118 CQ55
Carlisle Rd., Dart. 188 FN86
Carlisle Rd., Hmptn. 176 CB94
Carlisle Rd., Rom. 127 FG57
Carlisle Rd., Slou. 131 AR73
Carlisle Rd., Sutt. 217 CZ106
Carlisle St. W1 273 M9
Carlisle Wk. E8 142 DT65
Laurel St.
Carlisle Way SW17 180 DG92
Carlos Pl. W1 272 G10
Carlos Pl. W1 140 DG73
Carlow St. NW1 141 DJ68
Arlington Rd.
Carlton Ave. N14 81 DK43
Carlton Ave., Felt. 176 BW86
Carlton Ave., Green. 189 FS86
Carlton Ave., Har. 117 CH57
Carlton Ave., Hayes 155 BS77
Carlton Ave., S.Croy. 220 DS108
Carlton Ave. E., Wem. 117 CK61
Carlton Ave. W., Wem. 117 CH61
Carlton Clo. NW3 120 DA61
Carlton Clo., Borwd. 78 CR42
Carlton Clo., Chess. 215 CK107
Carlton Clo., Edg. 96 CN50
Carlton Clo., Upmin. 128 FP61
Carlton Clo., Wok. 211 AZ114
Carlton Ct. SW9 161 DP81
Carlton Ct., Ilf. 125 ER55
Carlton Ct., Uxb. 134 BK71
Carlton Cres., Sutt. 217 CY105
Carlton Dr. SW15 179 CX85
Carlton Dr., Ilf. 125 ER55
Carlton Gdns. SW1 277 M3
Carlton Gdns. SW1 141 DK74
Carlton Gdns. W5 137 CJ72
Carlton Grn., Red. 250 DE131
Carlton Gro. SE15 162 DV81
Carlton Hill NW8 140 DB68
Carlton Ho. Ter. SW1 277 M3
Carlton Ho. Ter. SW1 141 DK74
Carlton Par., Orp. 206 EV101
Carlton Par., Sev. 257 FJ122
St. John's Hill
Carlton Pk. Ave. SW20 199 CX96
Carlton Pl., Felt. 175 BT87
Carlton Pl., Nthwd. 93 BP50
Carlton Rd. E11 124 EF60
Carlton Rd. E12 124 EK63
Carlton Rd. E17 101 DY53
Carlton Rd. N4 121 DN59
Carlton Rd. N11 98 DG50
Carlton Rd. SW14 158 CQ83
Carlton Rd. W4 158 CR75
Carlton Rd. W5 137 CJ73
Carlton Rd., Erith 167 FB79
Carlton Rd., Grays 170 GE75
Carlton Rd., N.Mal. 198 CS96
Carlton Rd., Red. 250 DE131
Carlton Rd., Reig. 250 DD132
Carlton Rd., Rom. 127 FF57
Carlton Rd., Sid. 185 ET92
Carlton Rd., Slou. 132 AV73
Carlton Rd., S.Croy. 220 DR107
Carlton Rd., Sun. 175 BT94
Carlton Rd., Walt. 195 BV101
Carlton Rd., Well. 166 EV83
Carlton Rd., Wok. 211 BA114
Carlton Sq. E1 143 DX70
Argyle Rd.
Carlton St. SW1 277 M1
Carlton Ter. E11 124 EH57
Carlton Ter. N18 100 DR48
Carlton Ter. SE26 182 DW90
Carlton Twr. Pl. SW1 276 E6
Carlton Twr. Pl. SW1 160 DF76
Carlton Tye, Horl. 269 DJ147
Carlton Vale NW6 140 DA68
Carlton Vill. SW15 179 CW85
St. John's Ave.
Carlwell St. SW17 180 DE92
Carlyle Ave., Brom. 204 EK97
Carlyle Ave., Sthl. 136 BZ73
Carlyle Clo. N2 120 DC58
Carlyle Clo. NW10 138 CR67
Carlyle Clo., W.Mol. 196 CB96
Carlyle Gdns., Sthl. 136 BZ73
Carlyle Pl. SW15 159 CX84
Carlyle Rd. E12 124 EL63
Carlyle Rd. SE28 146 EV73
Carlyle Rd. W5 157 CJ77
Carlyle Rd., Croy. 202 DU103
Carlyle Rd., Stai. 173 BF94
Carlyle Sq. SW3 160 DD78
Carlyon Ave., Har. 116 BZ63
Carlyon Clo., Wem. 138 CL67
Carlyon Rd., Hayes 136 BW71
Carlyon Rd., Wem. 138 CL68
Carmalt Gdns. SW15 159 CW84
Carmalt Gdns., Walt. 214 BW106
Carmarthen Gdn. NW9 118 CS58
Snowdon Dr.
Carmarthen Rd., Slou. 132 AS73
Carmel Clo., Wok. 226 AY118
Carmel Ct. W8 160 DB75
Holland St.
Carmel Ct., Wem. 118 CP61
Carmelite Clo., Har. 94 CC53
Carmelite Rd., Har. 94 CC53
Carmelite St. EC4 274 E10
Carmelite St. EC4 141 DN73
Carmelite Wk., Har. 94 CC53
Carmelite Way, Har. 94 CC54
Hampden Rd.
Carmen Ct., Borwd. 78 CM38
Belford Rd.
Carmen St. E14 143 EB72
Carmichael Clo. SW11 160 DD83
Darien Rd.
Carmichael Clo., Ruis. 115 BU63
Carmichael Ms. SW18 180 DD86
Heathfield Rd.
Carmichael Rd. SE25 202 DU98
Carminia Rd. SW17 181 DH89
Carnaby Rd., Brox. 49 DY20
Carnaby St. W1 273 K9
Carnaby St. W1 141 DJ72
Carnac St. SE27 182 DR91
Carnach Grn., S.Ock. 149 FV73
Carnanton Rd. E17 101 ED53
Carnarvon Ave., Enf. 82 DT41
Carnarvon Dr., Hayes 155 BQ77
Carnarvon Rd. E10 123 EC58
Carnarvon Rd. E15 144 EF65
Carnarvon Rd. E18 102 EF54
Carnarvon Rd., Barn. 79 CY41
Carnation St. SE2 166 EV78
Carnbrook Rd. SE3 164 EK83
Carnecke Gdns. SE9 184 EL85
Carnegie Clo., Surb. 198 CM103
Fullers Ave.
Carnegie Pl. SW19 179 CX90
Carnegie Rd., St.Alb. 43 CD16
Carnegie St. N1 141 DM67
Carnforth Clo., Epsom 216 CP107
Carnforth Gdns., Horn. 127 FG64
Carnforth Rd. SW16 181 DK94
Carnie Lo. SW17 181 DH90
Manville Rd.
Carnoustie Dr. N1 141 DM66
Carnwath Rd. SW6 160 DA83
Caro La., Hem.H. 40 BN22
Carol St. NW1 141 DJ67
Carolina Clo. E15 124 EE64
Maryland St.
Carolina Rd., Th.Hth. 201 DP96
Caroline Clo. N10 99 DH54
Alexandra Pk. Rd.
Caroline Clo. SW16 181 DM91
Caroline Clo. W2 140 DB73
Bayswater Rd.
Caroline Clo., Croy. 220 DS105
Brownlow Rd.
Caroline Clo., Islw. 157 CE80
Caroline Clo., West Dr. 154 BK75
Caroline Ct., Ashf. 175 BP93
Caroline Ct., Stan. 95 CG51
The Chase
Caroline Gdns. SE15 162 DV80
Caroline Pl. SW11 160 DG82
Caroline Pl. W2 140 DB73
Caroline Pl., Hayes 155 BS80
Caroline Pl., Wat. 76 BY44
Capel Rd.
Caroline Pl. Ms. W2 140 DB73
Orme La.
Caroline Rd. SW19 179 CZ94
Caroline St. E1 143 DX72
Caroline Ter. SW1 276 F9
Caroline Ter. SW1 160 DG77
Caroline Wk. W6 159 CY79
Laundry Rd.
Carolyn Clo., Wok. 226 AT119
Carolyn Dr., Orp. 206 EU104
Caroon Dr., Rick. 74 BH36
Carpenders Ave., Wat. 94 BY48
Carpenter Clo., Epsom 217 CT109
West St.
Carpenter Gdns. N21 99 DP47
Carpenter St. W1 277 H1
Carpenter Way, Pot.B. 64 DC33
Carpenters Arms La., Epp. 70 EV25
Carpenters Ct., Twick. 177 CE89
Carpenters Path, Brwd. 109 GD43
Carpenters Pl. SW4 161 DK84
Carpenters Rd. E15 143 EA65
Carpenters Rd., Enf. 82 DW36
Carpenters Wd. Dr., Rick. 73 BB42
Carr Gro. SE18 164 EL77
Prospect Vale
Carr Rd. E17 101 DZ54
Carr Rd., Nthlt. 136 CA65
Carr St. E14 143 DY71
Carrara Wk. SW9 161 DN84
Somerleyton Rd.
Carriage Dr. E. SW11 160 DG80
Carriage Dr. N. SW11 160 DF80
Carriage Dr. S. SW11 160 DF81
Carriage Dr. W. SW11 160 DF80
Carriageway, The, Sev. 240 EW124
Carrick Dr., Ilf. 103 EQ53
Carrick Dr., Sev. 257 FH123
Carrick Gdns. N17 100 DS52
Flexmere Rd.
Carrick Gate, Esher 196 CC104
Carrick Ms. SE8 163 EA79
Watergate St.
Carriden Ct., Hert. 31 DM07
The Ridgeway
Carrill Way, Belv. 166 EX77
Carrington Ave., Borwd. 78 CP43
Carrington Ave., Houns. 176 CB85
Carrington Clo., Barn. 79 CU43
Carrington Clo., Borwd. 78 CQ43
Carrington Clo., Croy. 203 DY101
Carrington Clo., Kings.T. 178 CQ92
Coombe Pk.
Carrington Clo., Red. 250 DF133
Dome Way
Carrington Gdns. E7 124 EH63
Woodford Rd.
Carrington Pl., Esher 214 CB106
Esher Pk. Ave.
Carrington Rd., Dart. 188 FM86
Carrington Rd., Rich. 158 CN84
Carrington Rd., Slou. 132 AS73
Carrington Sq., Har. 94 CC52
Carrington St. W1 277 H3
Carrol Clo. NW5 121 DH63
Carroll Ave., Guil. 243 BB134
Carroll Clo. E15 124 EF64
Carroll Hill, Loug. 85 EM41
Carron Clo. E14 143 EB72
Carronade Pl. SE28 165 EQ76
Carroun Rd. SW8 161 DM80
Carrow Rd., Dag. 146 EV66
Carrow Rd., Walt. 196 BX104
Kenilworth Dr.
Carroway La., Grnf. 137 CD69
Cowgate Rd.
Carrs La. N21 82 DQ43
Carshalton Gro., Sutt. 218 DD105
Carshalton Pk. Rd., Cars. 218 DF107
Carshalton Pl., Cars. 218 DG105
Carshalton Rd., Bans. 218 DF114
Carshalton Rd., Cars. 218 DE106
Carshalton Rd., Mitch. 200 DG98
Carshalton Rd., Sutt. 218 DC106
Carsington Gdns., Dart. 188 FK89
Carslake Rd. SW15 179 CW86
Carson Rd. E16 144 EG70
Carson Rd. SE21 182 DQ89
Carson Rd., Barn. 80 DF42
Carstairs Rd. SE6 183 EC90
Carston Clo. SE12 184 EF85
Carswell Clo., Brwd. 109 GD44
Carswell Clo., Ilf. 124 EK56
Roding La. S.
Carswell Rd. SE6 183 EC87
Cart La. E4 101 ED45
Cart Path, Wat. 60 BW33
Cartbridge Clo., Wok. 227 BB123
Send Rd.
Cartel Clo., Purf. 169 FR77
Carter Clo., Rom. 105 FB52
Carter Clo., Wall. 219 DK108
Hermes Way
Carter Clo., Wind. 151 AN82
Carter Ct. EC4 141 DP72
Carter La.
Carter Dr., Rom. 105 FB52
Carter La. EC4 274 G9
Carter La. EC4 141 DP72
Carter Pl. SE17 162 DQ78
Carter Rd. E13 144 EH67
Carter Rd. SW19 180 DD93
Carter Rd., Slou. 131 AL73
Carter St. SE17 162 DQ79
Carter Wk., H.Wyc. 88 AC47
Carteret St. SW1 277 M5
Carteret St. SW1 161 DK75
Carteret Way SE8 163 DY77
Carterhatch La., Enf. 82 DT38
Carterhatch Rd., Enf. 82 DW39
Carters Clo., Wor.Pk. 199 CX103
Carters Cotts., Red. 266 DE136
Kings Ave.
Carters Hill, Sev. 257 FP127
Carters Hill Clo. SE9 184 EJ88
Carters La. SE23 183 DY89
Carters La., Epp. 51 EP24
Carters La., Wok. 227 BC120
Carters Mead, Harl. 52 EV17
Carters Rd., Epsom 233 CT115
Carters Row, Grav. 191 GF88
Carters Yd. SW18 180 DA85
Wandsworth High St.
Cartersfield Rd., Wal.Abb. 67 EC34
Cartersfield Rd. Est., Wal.Abb. 67 EC34
Cartersmeade Clo., Horl. 269 DH147
Wheatfield Way
Carthew Rd. W6 159 CV76
Carthew Vill. W6 159 CV76
Carthouse La., Wok. 210 AT114
Carthusian St. EC1 275 H6
Carthusian St. EC1 142 DQ71
Cartier Circle E14 143 EB74
Carting La. WC2 278 A1
Carting La. WC2 141 DL73
Cartmel Clo. N17 100 DV52
Heybourne Rd.
Cartmel Clo., Reig. 250 DE133
Cartmel Rd., Bexh. 166 FA81
Cartmell Gdns., Mord. 200 DC99
Carton St. W1 272 E8
Cartwright Gdns. WC1 273 P3
Cartwright Gdns. WC1 141 DL69
Cartwright Rd., Dag. 146 EY66
Cartwright St. E1 142 DT73
Cartwright Way SW13 159 CV79
Trinity Ch. Rd.
Carve Ley, Welw.G.C. 30 DB10
Carver Rd. SE24 182 DQ86
Carville Cres., Brent. 158 CL77
Cary Rd. E11 124 EE63
Cary Wk., Rad. 61 CG34
The Dr.
Carysfort Rd. N8 121 DK57
Carysfort Rd. N16 122 DR62
Casband Ct., Abb.L. 59 BS31
Cascade Ave. N10 121 DJ56
Cascade Clo., Buck.H. 102 EK47
Cascade Rd.
Cascade Clo., Orp. 206 EW97
Cascade Rd., Buck.H. 102 EK47
Cascades, Croy. 221 DZ110
Caselden Clo., Add. 212 BJ106
Casella Rd. SE14 163 DX80
Casewick Rd. SE27 181 DN92
Casimir Rd. E5 122 DV62
Casino Ave. SE24 182 DR85
Caspian St. SE5 162 DR80
Caspian Wk. E16 144 EK72
King George Ave.
Cassandra Clo., Nthlt. 117 CD63
Cassandra Gate, Wal.Cr. 67 DZ27
Casselden Rd. NW10 138 CR66
Cassidy Rd. SW6 160 DA80
Cassilda Rd. SE2 166 EU77
Cassilis Rd., Twick. 177 CH85
Cassio Rd., Wat. 75 BV41
Cassiobridge Rd., Wat. 75 BS42
Cassiobury Ave., Felt. 175 BT86
Cassiobury Ct., Wat. 75 BT40
Cassiobury Dr., Wat. 75 BS38
Cassiobury Pk. Ave., Wat. 75 BS41
Cassiobury Rd. E17 123 DY57
Cassis Ct., Loug. 85 EQ42
Torrington Dr.
Cassland Rd. E9 143 DX66
Cassland Rd., Th.Hth. 202 DR98
Casslee Rd. SE6 183 DZ87
Cassocks Sq., Shep. 195 BR101
Casson St. E1 142 DU71
Casstine Clo., Swan. 187 FF94
Castalia Sq. E14 163 EC75
Roserton St.
Castalia St. E14 163 EC75
Plevna St.
Castano Ct., Abb.L. 59 BS31
Castell Rd., Loug. 85 EQ39
Castellain Rd. W9 140 DB70
Castellan Ave., Rom. 127 FH55
Castellane Clo., Stan. 95 CF52
Daventer Dr.
Castello Ave. SW15 179 CW85
Castelnau SW13 159 CU81
Castelnau Pl. SW13 159 CV79
Castelnau
Castelnau Row SW13 159 CV79
Lonsdale Rd.
Casterbridge NW6 140 DB67
Casterbridge Rd. SE3 164 EG83
Casterton St. E8 142 DV65
Wilton Way
Castile Rd. SE18 165 EN77
Castillon Rd. SE6 184 EE89
Castlands Rd. SE6 183 DZ89
Castle Ave. E4 101 ED50
Castle Ave., Epsom 217 CU109
Castle Ave., Rain. 147 FE66
Castle Ave., Slou. 152 AU79
Castle Ave., West Dr. 134 BL73
Castle Baynard St. EC4 274 G10
Castle Clo. E9 123 DY64
Swinnerton St.
Castle Clo. SW19 179 CX90
Castle Clo., Brom. 204 EE97
Castle Clo., Hodd. 33 EC14
Castle Clo., Red. 252 DQ133
Castle Clo., Reig. 266 DB138
Castle Clo., Rom. 106 FJ48
The Mt.
Castle Clo., Sun. 175 BS94
Mill Fm. Ave.
Castle Clo. (Bushey), Wat. 76 CB44
Castle Ct. EC3 275 L9
Castle Ct. SE26 183 DY91
Champion Rd.
Castle Dr., Horl. 269 DJ149
Castle Dr., Ilf. 124 EL58
Castle Dr., Reig. 266 DA138
Castle Fm. Rd., Sev. 225 FF109
Castle Gdns., Dor. 248 CM134
Castle Gate Way, Berk. 38 AW17
Castle Grn., Wey. 195 BS104
Castle Gro. Rd., Wok. 210 AS112
Castle Hill, Berk. 38 AW17
Castle Hill, Guil. 258 AX136
Castle Hill, Long. 209 FX99
Castle Hill, Wind. 151 AR81
Castle Hill Ave., Berk. 38 AW18
Castle Hill Ave., Croy. 221 EB109
Castle Hill Clo., Berk. 38 AV18
Castle Hill Rd., Egh. 172 AV90
Castle La. SW1 277 K6
Castle La. SW1 161 DJ76
Castle Mead, Hem.H. 40 BH22
Castle Ms. N12 98 DC50
Castle Rd.
Castle Ms. NW1 141 DH65
Castle Rd.
Castle Par., Epsom 217 CU108
Ewell Bypass
Castle Pl. NW1 141 DH65
Castle Rd.
Castle Pl. W4 158 CS77
Windmill Rd.
Castle Pt. E6 144 EJ68
Castle Rd. N12 98 DC50
Castle Rd. NW1 141 DH65
Castle Rd., Couls. 234 DE120
Castle Rd., Dag. 146 EV67
Castle Rd., Dart. 225 FH107
Castle Rd., Enf. 83 DY39
Castle Rd., Epsom 216 CP114
Castle Rd., Grays 170 FZ79
Castle Rd., Hodd. 33 EC14
Castle Rd., Islw. 157 CF82
Castle Rd., Nthlt. 136 CB65
Castle Rd., St.Alb. 43 CH20
Castle Rd., Sev. 225 FG108
Castle Rd., Sthl. 156 BZ76
Castle Rd., Swans. 190 FZ86
Castle Rd., Wey. 195 BR104
Castle Rd., Wok. 211 AZ114
Castle Sq., Guil. 258 AX136
Castle Sq., Red. 252 DQ133
Castle St. E6 144 EJ68
Castle St., Berk. 38 AW19
Castle St., Green. 189 FU85
Castle St., Guil. 258 AX136
Castle St., Hert. 32 DQ10
Castle St., Kings.T. 198 CL96
Castle St., Red. 251 DP133
Castle St., Slou. 152 AT76
Castle St., Swans. 190 FZ86
Castle Vw., Epsom 216 CP114
Castle Vw. Rd., Wey. 213 BP105
Castle Wk., Reig. 250 DA134
High St.
Castle Wk., Sun. 196 BW97
Elizabeth Gdns.
Castle Way SW19 179 CX90
Castle Way, Epsom 217 CU109
Castle Ave.
Castle Way, Felt. 176 BW91
Castle Yd. N6 120 DG59
North Rd.
Castle Yd. SE1 278 G2
Castle Yd., Rich. 177 CK85
Hill St.
Castlebar Hill W5 137 CH71
Castlebar Ms. W5 137 CJ71
Castlebar Pk. W5 137 CH70
Castlebar Rd. W5 137 CJ72
Castlecombe Dr. SW19 179 CX87
Castlecombe Rd. SE9 184 EL91
Castledine Rd. SE20 182 DV94
Castlefield Rd., Reig. 250 DA134
Castleford Ave. SE9 185 EP88
Castlegate, Rich. 158 CM83
Castlehaven Rd. NW1 141 DH66
Castleleigh Ct., Enf. 82 DR43
Castlemaine Ave., Epsom 217 CV109
Castlemaine Ave., S.Croy. 220 DT106
Castlemaine Twr. SW11 160 DF82
Castlereagh St. W1 272 C8
Castleton Ave., Bexh. 167 FD81
Castleton Ave., Wem. 118 CL63
Castleton Clo., Bans. 234 DA115
Castleton Clo., Croy. 203 DY100
Castleton Dr., Bans. 234 DA115
Castleton Gdns., Wem. 118 CL62
East La.
Castleton Rd. E17 101 ED54
Castleton Rd. SE9 184 EK91
Castleton Rd., Ilf. 126 EU60
Castleton Rd., Mitch. 201 DK98
Castleton Rd., Ruis. 116 BX60
Castletown Rd. W14 159 CY78
Castleview Gdns., Ilf. 124 EL58
Castleview Rd., Slou. 152 AW77
Castlewood Dr. SE9 165 EM82
Castlewood Rd. N15 122 DU58
Castlewood Rd. N16 122 DU59
Castlewood Rd., Barn. 80 DD41
Castor La. E14 143 EB73
Cat Hill, Barn. 80 DF43
Cater Gdns., Guil. 242 AT132
Caterham Ave., Ilf. 103 EM54
Caterham Bypass, Cat. 236 DV120
Caterham Clo., Cat. 236 DS120
Caterham Ct., Wal.Abb. 68 EF34
Shernbroke Rd.
Caterham Dr., Couls. 235 DP118
Caterham Rd. SE13 163 EC83
Catesby St. SE17 279 L9
Catesby St. SE17 162 DR77
Catford Bdy. SE6 183 EB87
Catford Hill SE6 183 DZ88
Catford Ms. SE6 183 EB87
Holbeach Rd.
Catford Rd. SE6 183 EA87
Cathall Rd. E11 123 ED61
Catham Clo., St.Alb. 43 CH22
Cathay St. SE16 162 DV75
Cathay Wk., Nthlt. 136 CA68
Brabazon Rd.
Cathcart Dr., Orp. 205 ES103
Cathcart Hill N19 121 DJ62
Cathcart Rd. SW10 160 DB79
Cathcart St. NW5 141 DH65
Cathedral Clo., Guil. 258 AV135
Cathedral Ct., St.Alb. 42 CB22
Cathedral Pl. EC4 275 H8
Cathedral St. SE1 279 K2
Cathedral St. SE1 142 DR74
Cathedral Vw., Guil. 242 AT134
Catherall Rd. N5 122 DQ62
Catherine Clo. SE16 143 DX74
Rotherhithe St.
Catherine Clo., Brwd. 108 FU43
Catherine Clo., Grays 170 FZ75
Bark Burr Rd.
Catherine Clo., Hem.H. 41 BP15
Parr Cres.
Catherine Clo., W.Byf. 212 BL114
Catherine Ct. N14 81 DJ43
Conisbee Ct.
Catherine Dr., Rich. 158 CL84
Cedar Ter.
Catherine Dr., Sun. 175 BT93
Catherine Gdns., Houns. 157 CD84
Catherine Gdns., Loug. 85 EM44
Roding Rd.
Catherine Griffiths Ct. EC1 274 E4
Catherine Gro. SE10 163 EB81
Catherine Howard Ct., Wey. 195 BP104
Old Palace Rd.
Catherine Pl. SW1 277 K6
Catherine Pl. SW1 161 DJ76
Catherine Rd., Enf. 83 DY36
Catherine Rd., Rom. 127 FH57
Catherine Rd., Surb. 197 CK99
Catherine St. WC2 274 B10
Catherine St. WC2 141 DM73
Catherine St., St.Alb. 43 CD19
Catherine Wheel All. E1 275 N7
Catherine Wheel Rd., Brent. 157 CK80
Catherine Wheel Yd. SW1 277 K3
Catherine's Clo., West Dr. 154 BK76
Money La.
Cathles Rd. SW12 181 DH86
Cathnor Hill Ct. W12 159 CV76

This index reads in the sequence: Street Name / Postal District or Post Town / Map Page Number / Grid Reference

Chase Side N14 80 DG43
Chase Side, Enf. 82 DQ41
Chase Side Ave. SW20 199 CY96
Chase Side Ave., Enf. 82 DQ40
Chase Side Cres., Enf. 82 DQ39
Chase Side Pl., Enf. 82 DQ41
Chase Side
Chase Sq., Grav. 191 GH86
Princes St.
Chase Way N14 99 DH47
Chasefield Clo., Guil. 243 BA131
Chasefield Rd. SW17 180 DF91
Chaseley Dr. W4 158 CP81
Wellesley Rd.
Chaseley Dr., S.Croy. 220 DR110
Beech Ave.
Chaseley St. E14 143 DY72
Chasemore Clo., Mitch. 200 DF101
Middleton Rd.
Chasemore Gdns., Croy. 219 DP106
Thorneloe Gdns.
Chaseside Clo., Rom. 105 FE51
Chaseside Gdns., Cher. 194 BH101
Chaseville Pk. Rd. N21 81 DL43
Chaseways, Saw. 36 EW07
Chasewood Ave., Enf. 81 DP40
Chastilian Rd., Dart. 187 FF87
Chatelet Clo., Horl. 269 DH147
Chatfield, Slou. 131 AN71
Chatfield Ct., Cat. 236 DR122
York Gate
Chatfield Dr., Guil. 243 BC132
Kingfisher Dr.
Chatfield Rd. SW11 160 DC83
Chatfield Rd., Croy. 201 DP102
Chatham Ave., Brom. 204 EF101
Chatham Clo. NW11 120 DA57
Chatham Clo., Sutt. 199 CZ101
Chatham Hill Rd., Sev. 257 FJ121
Chatham Pl. E9 142 DW65
Chatham Rd. E17 123 DY55
Chatham Rd. E18 102 EF54
Grove Hill
Chatham Rd. SW11 180 DF86
Chatham Rd., Kings.T. 198 CN96
Chatham Rd., Orp. 223 EQ106
Chatham St. SE17 279 K8
Chatham St. SE17 162 DR77
Chatsfield, Epsom 217 CU110
Chatsfield Pl. W5 138 CL72
Chatsworth Ave. NW4 97 CW54
Chatsworth Ave. SW20 199 CY95
Chatsworth Ave., Brom. 184 EH92
Chatsworth Ave., Sid. 186 EU88
Chatsworth Ave., Wem. 118 CM64
Chatsworth Clo. NW4 97 CW54
Chatsworth Clo., Borwd. 78 CN41
Chatsworth Clo., W.Wick. 204 EF103
Chatsworth Ct. W8 160 DA77
Pembroke Rd.
Chatsworth Cres., Houns. 157 CD84
Chatsworth Dr., Enf. 100 DU45
Chatsworth Est. E5 123 DX63
Elderfield Rd.
Chatsworth Gdns. W3 138 CP74
Chatsworth Gdns., Har. 116 CB60
Chatsworth Gdns., N.Mal. 199 CT99
Chatsworth Pl., Lthd. 214 CC112
The Warren
Chatsworth Pl., Mitch. 200 DF97
Chatsworth Pl., Tedd. 177 CG91
Chatsworth Ri. W5 138 CM70
Chatsworth Rd. E5 122 DW62
Chatsworth Rd. E15 124 EF64
Chatsworth Rd. NW2 139 CX65
Chatsworth Rd. W4 158 CQ79
Chatsworth Rd. W5 138 CM70
Chatsworth Rd., Croy. 220 DR105
Chatsworth Rd., Dart. 188 FJ85
Chatsworth Rd., Hayes 135 BV70
Chatsworth Rd., Sutt. 217 CX106
Chatsworth Way SE27 181 DP90
Chatteris Ave., Rom. 106 FJ51
Chattern Hill, Ashf. 175 BP91
Chattern Rd., Ashf. 175 BQ91
Chatterton Rd. N4 121 DP62
Chatterton Rd., Brom. 204 EK98
Chatto Rd. SW11 180 DF85
Chaucer Ave., Hayes 135 BU71
Chaucer Ave., Houns. 155 BV82
Chaucer Ave., Rich. 158 CN83
Chaucer Ave., Wey. 212 BN108
Chaucer Clo. N11 99 DJ50
Chaucer Clo., Bans. 217 CY114
Chaucer Clo., Berk. 38 AT18
Chaucer Clo., Til. 171 GJ82
Chaucer Ct. N16 122 DS63
Chaucer Ct., Guil. 258 AW137
Lawn Rd.
Chaucer Dr. SE1 162 DT77
Chaucer Gdns., Sutt. 200 DA104
Chaucer Grn., Croy. 202 DW101
Chaucer Pk., Dart. 188 FM87
Chaucer Rd. E7 144 EG65
Chaucer Rd. E11 124 EG58
Chaucer Rd. E17 101 EC54
Chaucer Rd. SE24 181 DN85
Chaucer Rd. W3 138 CQ74
Chaucer Rd., Ashf. 174 BL91
Chaucer Rd., Grav. 190 GD90
Chaucer Rd., Rom. 105 FH52
Chaucer Rd., Sid. 186 EW88
Chaucer Rd., Sutt. 218 DA105
Chaucer Rd., Well. 165 ET81
Chaucer Way SW19 180 DD93
Chaucer Way, Add. 212 BG107
Chaucer Way, Dart. 168 FN84
Chaucer Way, Hodd. 33 EA13
Chaulden Ho. Gdns., Hem.H. 39 BF21
Chaulden La., Hem.H. 39 BD22
Chaulden Ter., Hem.H. 39 BF21
Chauncey Clo. N9 100 DU48
Chauncy Ave., Pot.B. 64 DC33
Chaundrye Clo. SE9 184 EL86
Chauntler Clo. E16 144 EH73
Victoria Dock Rd.
Chauntler Rd. E16 144 EH73
Victoria Dock Rd.
Chauntry Clo., Maid. 130 AC73
Chave Rd., Dart. 188 FL90
Chaworth Rd., Cher. 211 BC107
Cheam Clo., Tad. 233 CV121
Waterfield
Cheam Common Rd., Wor.Pk. 199 CV103
Cheam Mans., Sutt. 217 CY108
Cheam Pk. Way, Sutt. 217 CY107
Cheam Rd., Epsom 217 CU110
Cheam Rd., Sutt. 217 CZ107
Cheam Rd. (East Ewell), Sutt. 217 CX110
Cheam St. SE15 162 DV83
Evelina Rd.
Cheapside EC2 275 H9
Cheapside EC2 142 DQ72
Cheapside, Wok. 210 AX114
Cheapside La., Uxb. 113 BF62
Chedburgh, Welw.G.C. 30 DD08
Cheddar Rd., Houns. 154 BN82
Cromer Rd.
Cheddar Waye, Hayes 135 BV72
Cheddington Rd. N18 100 DS48
Chedworth Clo. E16 144 EF72
Hallsville Rd.
Cheelson Rd., S.Ock. 149 FW68
Cheeseman Clo., Hmptn. 176 BY93
Cheesemans Ter. W14 159 CZ78
Cheffins Rd., Hodd. 33 DZ14
Chelford Rd., Brom. 183 ED92
Chelmer Cres., Bark. 146 EV68
Chelmer Dr., Brwd. 109 GE44
Chelmer Rd. E9 123 DX64
Chelmer Rd., Grays 171 GG78
Chelmer Rd., Upmin. 129 FR58
Chelmsford Ave., Rom. 105 FD52
Chelmsford Clo. E6 145 EM72
Guildford Rd.
Chelmsford Clo. W6 159 CX79
Chelmsford Clo., Sutt. 218 DB109
Homeland Dr.
Chelmsford Dr., Upmin. 128 FM62
Chelmsford Gdns., Ilf. 124 EL59
Chelmsford Rd. E11 123 ED60
Chelmsford Rd. E17 123 EA58
Chelmsford Rd. E18 102 EF53
Chelmsford Rd. N14 99 DJ45
Chelmsford Rd., Bishop's Stortford 37 FH05
Chelmsford Rd., Brwd. 109 FZ44
Chelmsford Rd., Hert. 31 DN10
Chelmsford Sq. NW10 139 CW67
Chelsea Bri. SW1 161 DH79
Chelsea Bri. SW8 161 DH79
Chelsea Bri. Rd. SW1 276 F10
Chelsea Bri. Rd. SW1 160 DG78
Chelsea Cloisters SW3 160 DE77
Lucan Pl.
Chelsea Clo. NW10 138 CR67
Winchelsea Rd.
Chelsea Clo., Edg. 96 CN54
Chelsea Clo., Hmptn. 176 CC93
Chelsea Embk. SW3 160 DE79
Chelsea Gdns., Sutt. 217 CY105
Chelsea Harbour SW10 160 DD81
Chelsea Harbour Dr. SW10 160 DC81
Chelsea Manor Gdns. SW3 160 DE78
Chelsea Manor St. SW3 160 DE78
Chelsea Pk. Gdns. SW3 160 DD79
Chelsea Sq. SW3 276 A10
Chelsea Sq. SW3 160 DD78
Chelsea Wf. SW10 160 DD80
Lots Rd.
Chelsfield Ave. N9 101 DX45
Chelsfield Gdns. SE26 182 DW90
Chelsfield Grn. N9 101 DX45
Chelsfield Ave.
Chelsfield Hill, Orp. 224 EW109
Chelsfield La., Orp. 224 FA108
Chelsfield La. (Chelsfield), Orp. 206 EX101
Chelsfield La., Sev. 225 FC109
Chelsfield Rd., Orp. 206 EW100
Chelsham Clo., Warl. 237 DY118
Limpsfield Rd.
Chelsham Common Rd., Warl. 237 EA117
Chelsham Ct. Rd., Warl. 237 ED118
Chelsham Rd. SW4 161 DK83
Chelsham Rd., S.Croy. 220 DR107
Chelsham Rd., Warl. 237 DZ118
Chelsing Ri., Hem.H. 41 BQ21
Chelston App., Ruis. 115 BU61
Chelston Rd., Ruis. 115 BU60
Chelsworth Clo., Rom. 106 FM53
Chelsworth Dr.
Chelsworth Dr. SE18 165 ER79
Chelsworth Dr., Rom. 106 FL53
Cheltenham Ave., Twick. 177 CG87
Cheltenham Clo., Grav. 191 GJ92
Goodwood Cres.
Cheltenham Clo., N.Mal. 198 CQ97
Northcote Rd.
Cheltenham Clo., Nthlt. 136 CB65
Cheltenham Gdns. E6 144 EL68
Cheltenham Gdns., Loug. 84 EL44
Cheltenham Pl. W3 138 CP74
Cheltenham Pl., Har. 118 CL56
Cheltenham Rd. E10 123 EC58
Cheltenham Rd. SE15 162 DW84
Cheltenham Rd., Orp. 206 EU104
Cheltenham Ter. SW3 276 E10
Cheltenham Ter. SW3 160 DF78
Cheltenham Vill., Stai. 173 BF86
Chelverton Rd. SW15 159 CX84
Chelveston, Welw.G.C. 30 DD08
Chelwood Ave., Hat. 45 CU16
Chelwood Clo. E4 83 EB44
Chelwood Clo., Epsom 217 CT112
Chelwood Clo., Nthwd. 93 BQ52
Chelwood Gdns., Rich. 158 CN82
Chelwood Wk. SE4 163 DY84
Chenappa Clo. E13 144 EG69
Chenduit Way, Stan. 95 CF50
Chene Dr., St.Alb. 43 CD18
Cheney Rd. NW1 273 P1
Cheney Rd. NW1 141 DL68
Cheney Row E17 101 DZ53
Cheney St., Pnr. 116 BW57
Cheneys Rd. E11 124 EE62
Chenies, The, Dart. 187 FE91
Chenies, The, Orp. 205 ES100
Chenies Ave., Amer. 72 AW39
Chenies Ct., Hem.H. 41 BP15
Datchet Clo.
Chenies Hill, Hem.H. 57 BB34
Chenies Ms. WC1 273 M5
Chenies Par., Amer. 72 AW40
Chenies Pl. NW1 141 DK68
Chenies Rd., Rick. 73 BD40
Chenies St. WC1 273 M6
Chenies St. WC1 141 DK71
Chenies Way, Wat. 93 BS45
Cheniston Clo., W.Byf. 212 BG113
Madeira Rd.
Cheniston Gdns. W8 160 DB76
Chennells, Hat. 45 CT19
Chepstow Ave., Horn. 128 FL62
Chepstow Clo. SW15 179 CY86
Lytton Gro.
Chepstow Cres. W11 140 DA73
Chepstow Cres., Ilf. 125 ES58
Chepstow Gdns., Sthl. 136 BZ72
Chepstow Pl. W2 140 DA72
Chepstow Ri., Croy. 202 DS104
Chepstow Rd. W2 140 DA72
Chepstow Rd. W7 157 CG76
Chepstow Rd., Croy. 202 DS104
Chepstow Vill. W11 139 CZ73
Chepstow Way SE15 162 DT80
Exeter Rd.
Chequer St. EC1 275 J5
Chequer St., St.Alb. 43 CD20
Chequer Tree Clo., Wok. 226 AS116
Chequers, Hat. 29 CX13
Chequers, Welw.G.C. 29 CX12
Chequers Clo., Horl. 268 DG147
Chequers Clo., Orp. 205 ET98
Chequers Clo., Tad. 249 CU125
Chequers Dr., Horl. 268 DG147
Chequers Fld., Welw.G.C. 29 CX12
Chequers Gdns. N13 99 DP50
Chequers Hill, Amer. 55 AR40
Chequers La., Dag. 146 EZ71
Chequers La., Tad. 249 CU125
Chequers La., Wat. 60 BW30
Chequers Orchard, Iver 133 BF72
Chequers Par. SE9 185 EM86
Eltham High St.
Chequers Pl., Dor. 263 CH136
Chequers Rd., Brwd. 106 FM46
Chequers Rd., Loug. 85 EN43
Chequers Rd., Rom. 106 FL47
Chequers Sq., Uxb. 134 BJ66
High St.
Chequers Wk., Wal.Abb. 68 EF33
Chartwell Clo.
Chequers Way N13 99 DP50
Chequers Yd., Dor. 263 CH136
Chequers Pl.
Cherbury Clo. SE28 146 EX72
Cherbury Ct. N1 142 DR68
Cherbury St.
Cherbury St. N1 275 L1
Cherbury St. N1 142 DR68
Cherchefelle Ms., Stan. 95 CH50
Cherimoya Gdns., W.Mol. 196 CB97
Kelvinbrook
Cherington Rd. W7 137 CF74
Cheriton Ave., Brom. 204 EF99
Cheriton Ave., Ilf. 103 EM54
Cheriton Clo. W5 137 CJ71
Cheriton Clo., Barn. 80 DF41
Chalk La.
Cheriton Clo., St.Alb. 43 CK16
Cheriton Ct., Walt. 196 BW102
St. Johns Dr.
Cheriton Dr. SE18 165 ER80
Cheriton Sq. SW17 180 DG89
Cherkley Hill, Lthd. 247 CJ126
Cherries, The, Slou. 132 AV72
Cherry Acre, Ger.Cr. 90 AX49
Cherry Ave., Brwd. 109 FZ48
Cherry Ave., Slou. 152 AX75
Cherry Ave., Sthl. 136 BX74
Cherry Ave., Swan. 207 FD97
Cherry Bounce, Hem.H. 40 BK18
Cherry Clo. E17 123 EB57
Eden Rd.
Cherry Clo. SW2 181 DN87
Tulse Hill
Cherry Clo. W5 157 CK76
Cherry Clo., Bans. 217 CX114
Cherry Clo., Cars. 200 DF103
Cherry Clo., Mord. 199 CY98
Cherry Clo., Ruis. 115 BT62
Roundways
Cherry Cres., Brent. 157 CH80
Cherry Cft., Welw.G.C. 29 CX05
Cherry Dr., Beac. 88 AH51
Cherry Gdn. St. SE16 162 DV75
Cherry Gdns., Dag. 126 EZ64
Cherry Gdns., Nthlt. 136 CB66
Cherry Garth, Brent. 157 CK78
Cherry Grn. Clo., Red. 267 DH136
Cherry Gro., Hayes 135 BV74
Cherry Gro., Uxb. 135 BP71
Cherry Hill, Barn. 80 DB44
Cherry Hill, Har. 95 CE52
Elms Rd.
Cherry Hill, Rick. 74 BH41
Cherry Hill, St.Alb. 60 CA25
Cherry Hill Gdns., Croy. 219 DM105
Cherry Hollow, Abb.L. 59 BT31
Cherry La., West Dr. 154 BM77
Cherry Laurel Wk. SW2 181 DM86
Beechdale Rd.
Cherry Orchard, Amer. 55 AS37
Cherry Orchard, Ash. 232 CP118
Cherry Orchard, Hem.H. 40 BG18
Cherry Orchard, Slou. 132 AV66
Cherry Orchard, Stai. 174 BG92
Cherry Orchard, West Dr. 154 BL75
Cherry Orchard Clo., Orp. 206 EW99
Cherry Orchard Gdns., Croy. 202 DR103
Oval Rd.
Cherry Orchard Gdns., W.Mol. 196 BZ97
Cherry Orchard Rd., Brom. 204 EL103
Cherry Orchard Rd., Croy. 202 DR103
Cherry Orchard Rd., W.Mol. 196 BZ97
Cherry Ri., Ch.St.G. 90 AX47
Cherry Rd., Enf. 82 DW38
Cherry St., Rom. 127 FD57
Cherry St., Wok. 226 AY118
Cherry Tree Ave., Guil. 242 AT134
Cherry Tree Ave., St.Alb. 61 CK26
Cherry Tree Ave., Stai. 174 BH93
Cherry Tree Ave., West Dr. 134 BM72
Cherry Tree Clo., Grays 170 GD79
Cherry Tree Clo., Rain. 147 FG68
Cherry Tree Clo., Wem. 117 CF63
Cherry Tree Ct. NW9 118 CQ56
Cherry Tree Ct., Couls. 235 DM117
Cherry Tree Dr. SW16 181 DL90
Cherry Tree Grn., Hert. 31 DM07
Cherry Tree Grn., S.Croy. 220 DV114
Cherry Tree La., Dart. 187 FF90
Cherry Tree La., Hem.H. 41 BQ15
Cherry Tree La., Pot.B. 64 DB34
Ashwood Rd.
Cherry Tree La., Rain. 147 FE69
Cherry Tree La., Rick. 91 BC46
Cherry Tree La., Slou. 133 AZ65
Cherry Tree Ri., Buck.H. 102 EJ49
Cherry Tree Rd. E15 124 EE63
Wingfield Rd.
Cherry Tree Rd. N2 120 DF56
Cherry Tree Rd., Beac. 110 AH55
Cherry Tree Rd., Hodd. 49 EA16
Cherry Tree Rd., Slou. 131 AQ66
Cherry Tree Rd., Wat. 75 BV36
Cherry Tree Wk. EC1 275 J5
Cherry Tree Wk., Beck. 203 DZ98
Cherry Tree Wk., Chesh. 54 AR29
Cherry Tree Wk., W.Wick. 222 EF105
Cherry Tree Way, H.Wyc. 88 AC46
Cherry Tree Way, Stan. 95 CH51
Cherry Wk., Brom. 204 EG102
Cherry Wk., Grays 171 GG76
Cherry Wk., Rain. 147 FF68
Cherry Wk., Rick. 74 BJ40
Cherry Way, Epsom 216 CR107
Cherry Way, Hat. 45 CU21
Cherry Way, Shep. 195 BR98
Cherry Way, Slou. 153 BC83
Mill La.
Cherry Wd. Clo., Beac. 89 AR50
Cherry Wd. Way W5 138 CN71
Hanger Vale La.
Cherrycot Hill, Orp. 223 ER105
Cherrycot Ri., Orp. 223 EQ105
Cherrycroft Gdns., Pnr. 94 BZ52
Westfield Pk.
Cherrydale, Wat. 75 BT42
Cherrydown Ave. E4 101 DZ48
Cherrydown Clo. E4 101 DZ48
Cherrydown Rd., Sid. 186 EX89
Cherrydown Wk., Rom. 105 FB54
Cherrytree La., Ger.Cr. 90 AX54
Cherrytree La., Iver 134 BG67
Cherrywood Ave., Egh. 172 AV94
Cherrywood Clo., Kings.T. 178 CN94
Cherrywood Dr. SW15 179 CX85
Cherrywood Dr., Grav. 190 GE91
Cherrywood La., Mord. 199 CY98
Cherston Gdns., Loug. 85 EN42
Cherston Rd.
Cherston Rd., Loug. 85 EN42
Chertsey Bri. Rd., Cher. 194 BK101
Chertsey Clo., Ken. 235 DP115
Chertsey Cres., Croy. 221 EC110
Chertsey Dr., Sutt. 199 CY103
Chertsey La., Cher. 193 BF97
Chertsey La., Stai. 173 BE92
Chertsey Rd. E11 123 ED61
Chertsey Rd., Add. 194 BH103
Chertsey Rd., Ashf. 175 BR94
Chertsey Rd., Felt. 175 BS92
Chertsey Rd., Ilf. 125 ER63
Chertsey Rd., Shep. 194 BK101
Chertsey Rd., Sun. 175 BR94
Chertsey Rd., Twick. 177 CF86
Chertsey Rd., W.Byf. 212 BK111
Chertsey Rd., Wok. 227 AZ116
Chertsey Rd. (Chobham), Wok. 210 AT110
Chertsey St. SW17 180 DG92
Chertsey St., Guil. 258 AX135
Cherubs, The, Slou. 131 AQ65
Chervil Clo., Felt. 175 BU90
Chervil Ms. SE28 146 EV74
Cherwell Clo., Rick. 74 BN43
Cherwell Clo., Slou. 153 BB79
Tweed Rd.
Cherwell Ct., Epsom 216 CQ105
Cherwell Gro., S.Ock. 149 FU73
Cherwell Way, Ruis. 115 BQ58
Cheryls Clo. SW6 160 DB81
Cheselden Rd., Guil. 258 AY135
Cheseman St. SE26 182 DV90
Chesfield Rd., Kings.T. 178 CL94
Chesham Ave., Orp. 205 EP100
Chesham Clo. SW1 276 F7
Chesham Clo., Rom. 127 FD56
Chesham Clo., Sutt. 217 CY110
Chesham Ct., Nthwd. 93 BT51
Frithwood Ave.
Chesham Cres. SE20 202 DW96
Chesham La., Ch.St.G. 90 AY48
Chesham La., Ger.Cr. 90 AY49
Chesham Ms. SW1 276 F6
Chesham Ms. SW1 160 DG76
Chesham Ms., Guil. 259 AZ135
Chesham Rd.
Chesham Pl. SW1 276 F7
Chesham Pl. SW1 160 DG76
Chesham Rd. SE20 202 DW96
Chesham Rd. SW19 180 DD92
Chesham Rd., Amer. 55 AQ36
Chesham Rd., Berk. 38 AV21
Chesham Rd., Chesh. 54 AL32
Chesham Rd., Guil. 259 AZ135
Chesham Rd., Hem.H. 56 AY27
Chesham Rd., Kings.T. 198 CN96
Chesham St. NW10 118 CR62
Chesham St. SW1 276 F7
Chesham St. SW1 160 DG76
Chesham Ter. W13 157 CH75
Chesham Way, Wat. 75 BS44
Cheshire Clo. SE4 163 DZ82
Cheshire Clo., Cher. 211 BD107
Cheshire Clo., Horn. 128 FN57
Cheshire Clo., Mitch. 201 DL97
Cheshire Ct., Slou. 152 AV75
Clements Clo.
Cheshire Gdns., Chess. 215 CK107
Cheshire Rd. N22 99 DM51
Cheshire St. E2 142 DT70
Chesholm Rd. N16 122 DS62
Cheshunt Pk. (Cheshunt), Wal.Cr. 66 DV26
Cheshunt Rd. E7 144 EH65
Cheshunt Rd., Belv. 166 FA78
Cheshunt Wash (Cheshunt), Wal.Cr. 67 DY27
Chesil Ct. E2 142 DW68
Bonner Rd.
Chesil Way, Hayes 135 BT69
Chesilton Rd. SW6 159 CZ81
Chesley Gdns. E6 144 EK68
Cheslyn Gdns., Wat. 75 BT37
Nascot Wd. Rd.
Chesney Cres., Croy. 221 EC108
Chesney St. SW11 160 DG81
Chesnut Est. N17 122 DT55
Chesnut Rd.
Chesnut Gro. N17 122 DT55
Chesnut Rd.
Chesnut Rd. N17 122 DT55
Chess Clo., Chesh. 72 AX36
Chess Clo., Rick. 74 BK42
Chess Hill, Rick. 74 BK42
Chess La., Rick. 74 BK42
Chess Vale Ri., Rick. 74 BM44
Chess Valley Wk., Chesh. 54 AR33
Chess Valley Wk., Rick. 73 AZ37
Chess Way, Rick. 74 BG41
Chessbury Rd., Chesh. 54 AN32
Chessfield Pk., Amer. 72 AY39
Chessholme Ct., Sun. 175 BS94
Scotts Ave.
Chessholme Rd., Ashf. 175 BQ93
Chessington Ave. N3 119 CY55
Chessington Ave., Bexh. 166 EY80
Chessington Clo., Epsom 216 CQ107
Chessington Ct., Pnr. 116 BZ56
Chessington Hall Gdns., Chess. 215 CK108
Chessington Hill Pk., Chess. 216 CN106
Chessington Lo. N3 119 CZ55
Chessington Rd., Epsom 216 CP107
Chessington Way, W.Wick. 203 EB103
Chessmount Ri., Chesh. 54 AR33
Chesson Rd. W14 159 CZ79
Chesswood Way, Pnr. 94 BX54
Chester Ave., Rich. 178 CM86
Chester Ave., Twick. 176 BZ88
Chester Ave., Upmin. 129 FS61
Chester Clo. SW1 277 H5
Chester Clo. SW1 161 DH75
Chester Clo. SW13 159 CV83
Chester Clo., Ashf. 175 BR92
Chester Clo., Dor. 247 CJ134
Chester Clo., Guil. 242 AT132
Canterbury Rd.
Chester Clo., Loug. 85 EQ39
Chester Clo., Pot.B. 64 DB29
Chester Clo., Sutt. 200 DA103
Broomloan La.
Chester Clo., Uxb. 135 BP72
Dawley Ave.
Chester Clo. N. NW1 273 J2
Chester Clo. S. NW1 273 J3
Chester Cotts. SW1 276 F9
Chester Ct. NW1 273 J2
Chester Ct. SE5 162 DR80
Chester Cres. E8 142 DT65
Ridley Rd.
Chester Dr., Har. 116 BZ58
Chester Gdns. W13 137 CH72
Chester Gdns., Enf. 82 DV44
Chester Gdns., Mord. 200 DC100
Chester Gate NW1 273 H3
Chester Gate NW1 141 DH69
Chester Grn., Loug. 85 EQ39
Chester Ms. SW1 277 H6
Chester Ms. SW1 161 DH76
Chester Path, Loug. 85 EQ39
Chester Pl. NW1 273 H2
Chester Rd. E7 144 EK66
Chester Rd. E11 124 EH58
Chester Rd. E16 144 EE70
Chester Rd. E17 123 DX57
Chester Rd. N9 100 DV46
Chester Rd. N17 122 DR55
Chester Rd. N19 121 DH61
Chester Rd. NW1 272 G3
Chester Rd. NW1 140 DG69
Chester Rd. SW19 179 CW93
Chester Rd., Borwd. 78 CQ41
Chester Rd., Chig. 103 EN47
Chester Rd., Houns. 155 BV83
Chester Rd. (Heathrow), Houns. 154 BN83
Chester Rd., Ilf. 125 ET60
Chester Rd., Lthd. 245 BV129
Dirtham La.
Chester Rd., Loug. 85 EP40
Chester Rd., Nthwd. 93 BS52
Chester Rd., Sid. 185 ES85
Chester Rd., Slou. 131 AR72
Chester Rd., Wat. 75 BU43
Chester Row SW1 276 F9
Chester Row SW1 160 DG77
Chester Sq. SW1 276 G8
Chester Sq. SW1 160 DG77
Chester Sq. Ms. SW1 277 H7
Chester St. E2 142 DU70
Chester St. SW1 276 G6
Chester St. SW1 160 DG76
Chester Ter. NW1 273 H2
Chester Way SE11 278 E9
Chester Way SE11 161 DN77
Chesterfield Clo., Orp. 206 EX98
Chesterfield Dr., Dart. 187 FH85
Chesterfield Dr., Esher 197 CG103
Chesterfield Dr., Sev. 256 FD122
Chesterfield Gdns. N4 121 DP57
Chesterfield Gdns. SE10 163 ED80
Crooms Hill
Chesterfield Gdns. W1 277 H2
Chesterfield Gdns. W1 141 DH74
Chesterfield Gro. SE22 182 DT85
Chesterfield Hill W1 277 H2
Chesterfield Hill W1 141 DH74
Chesterfield Ms. N4 121 DP57
Chesterfield Gdns.
Chesterfield Rd. E10 123 EC58
Chesterfield Rd. N3 98 DA51
Chesterfield Rd. W4 158 CQ79
Chesterfield Rd., Ashf. 174 BL91
Chesterfield Rd., Barn. 79 CX43
Chesterfield Rd., Enf. 83 DY37
Chesterfield Rd., Epsom 216 CR108
Chesterfield St. W1 277 H2
Chesterfield St. W1 141 DH74
Chesterfield Wk. SE10 163 ED81
Chesterfield Way SE15 162 DW80
Chesterfield Way, Hayes 155 BU75
Chesterford Gdns. NW3 120 DB63
Chesterford Ho. SE18 164 EK80
Shooter's Hill Rd.

Chesterford Rd. E12 125 EM64
Chesters, Horl. 268 DE146
Chesters, The, N.Mal. 198 CS95
Chesterton Clo. SW18 180 DA85
Ericcson Clo.
Chesterton Clo., Chesh. 54 AP29
Milton Rd.
Chesterton Clo., Grnf. 136 CB68
Chesterton Dr., Red. 251 DL128
Chesterton Dr., Stai. 174 BM88
Chesterton Grn., Beac. 89 AL52
Chesterton Rd. E13 144 EG69
Chesterton Rd. W10 139 CX71
Chesterton Ter. E13 144 EG69
Chesterton Ter., Kings.T. 198 CN96
Chesterton Way, Til. 171 GJ82
Chesthunte Rd. N17 100 DQ53
Chestnut All. SW6 159 CZ79
Lillie Rd.
Chestnut Ave. E7 124 EH63
Chestnut Ave. N8 121 DL57
Chestnut Ave. SW14 158 CR83
Thornton Rd.
Chestnut Ave., Brent. 157 CK77
Chestnut Ave., Brwd. 108 FS45
Chestnut Ave., Buck.H. 102 EK48
Chestnut Ave., Chesh. 54 AR29
Chestnut Ave., E.Mol. 197 CF97
Chestnut Ave., Edg. 96 CL51
Chestnut Ave., Epsom 216 CS105
Chestnut Ave., Esher 197 CD101
Chestnut Ave., Grays 170 GB75
Chestnut Ave., Guil. 258 AW137
Chestnut Ave., Hmptn. 176 CA94
Chestnut Ave., Horn. 127 FF61
Chestnut Ave., Nthwd. 93 BT54
Chestnut Ave., Rick. 74 BG43
Chestnut Ave., Slou. 152 AY75
Chestnut Ave., Tedd. 197 CF96
Chestnut Ave., Vir.W. 192 AT98
Chestnut Ave., Walt. 213 BS110
Chestnut Ave., Wem. 117 CH64
Chestnut Ave., West Dr. 134 BM73
Chestnut Ave., W.Wick. 222 EE106
Chestnut Ave., West. 238 EK123
Chestnut Ave., Wey. 213 BQ108
Chestnut Ave. N. E17 123 EC56
Chestnut Ave. S. E17 123 EC56
Chestnut Clo. N14 81 DJ43
Chestnut Clo. N16 122 DR61
Lordship Gro.
Chestnut Clo. SE6 183 EC92
Chestnut Clo. SW16 181 DN91
Chestnut Clo., Add. 212 BK106
Chestnut Clo., Amer. 55 AR37
Chestnut Clo., Ashf. 175 BP91
Chestnut Clo., Berk. 39 BB17
Chestnut Clo., Buck.H. 102 EK48
Chestnut Clo., Cars. 200 DF102
Chestnut Clo., Egh. 172 AW93
Chestnut Clo., Ger.Cr. 91 AZ53
Chestnut Clo., Grav. 191 GF86
Burch Rd.
Chestnut Clo., Hayes 135 BS73
Chestnut Clo., Horn. 128 FJ63
Lancaster Dr.
Chestnut Clo., Orp. 224 EU106
Chestnut Clo., Red. 267 DH136
Haigh Cres.
Chestnut Clo., Sun. 175 BT93
Chestnut Clo., Tad. 234 DA123
Chestnut Clo., Ware 34 EK06
Chestnut Clo., West Dr. 155 BP80
Chestnut Clo., Wok. 228 BG124
Chestnut Copse, Oxt. 254 EH132
Chestnut Ct. SW6 159 CZ79
North End Rd.
Chestnut Ct., Amer. 55 AR37
Chestnut Dr. E11 124 EG58
Chestnut Dr., Berk. 38 AX20
Chestnut Dr., Bexh. 166 EX83
Chestnut Dr., Egh. 172 AX93
Chestnut Dr., Har. 95 CF52
Chestnut Dr., Pnr. 116 BX58
Chestnut Dr., St.Alb. 43 CH18
Chestnut Dr., Wind. 151 AL84
Chestnut Glen, Horn. 127 FG61
Chestnut Gro. SE20 182 DV94
Hawthorn Gro.
Chestnut Gro. SW12 180 DG87
Chestnut Gro. W5 157 CK76
Chestnut Gro., Barn. 80 DF43
Chestnut Gro., Brwd. 108 FW47
Chestnut Gro., Dart. 187 FD91
Chestnut Gro., Ilf. 103 ES51
Chestnut Gro., Islw. 157 CG84
Chestnut Gro., Mitch. 201 DK99
Chestnut Gro., N.Mal. 198 CR97
Chestnut Gro., S.Croy. 220 DV108
Chestnut Gro., Stai. 174 BJ93
Chestnut Gro., Wem. 117 CH64
Chestnut Gro., Wok. 226 AY120
Chestnut La. N20 97 CY46
Chestnut La., Amer. 55 AR36
Chestnut La., Sev. 257 FH124
Chestnut La., Wey. 213 BP106
Chestnut Manor Clo., Stai. 174 BH92
Chestnut Mead, Red. 250 DE133
Oxford Rd.
Chestnut Ri. SE18 165 ES78
Chestnut Ri. (Bushey), Wat. 94 CB45
Chestnut Rd. SE27 181 DP90
Chestnut Rd. SW20 199 CX96
Chestnut Rd., Ashf. 175 BP91
Chestnut Rd., Beac. 88 AH54
Chestnut Rd., Dart. 188 FK88
Chestnut Rd., Enf. 83 DY36
Chestnut Rd., Guil. 242 AX134
Chestnut Rd., Horl. 269 DH146
Chestnut Rd., Kings.T. 178 CL94
Chestnut Rd., Twick. 177 CE89
Chestnut Wk., Epp. 51 EP24
Epping Rd.
Chestnut Wk., Ger.Cr. 90 AY52
Chestnut Wk., Sev. 257 FL129
Chestnut Wk., Shep. 195 BS99
Chestnut Wk., Walt. 213 BS109
Octagon Rd.
Chestnut Wk., Wat. 75 BU37
Chestnut Wk., W.Byf. 212 BL112
Royston Rd.
Chestnut Wk., Wdf.Grn. 102 EG50
Chestnut Way, Felt. 175 BV90
Chestnuts, Brwd. 109 GB45
Chestnuts, The, Hem.H. 39 BF24
Chestnuts, The, Hert. 32 DR09
Chestnuts, The, Horl. 269 DH146
Chestnuts, The, Rom. 86 EV41
Chestnuts, The, Walt. 195 BU103
Cheston Ave., Croy. 203 DY103
Chestwood Gro., Uxb. 134 BM66
Cheswick Clo., Dart. 167 FF84
Chesworth Clo., Erith 167 FE81
Chettle Clo. SE1 279 K6
Chettle Ct. N8 121 DN58
Chetwode Dr., Epsom 233 CX118
Chetwode Rd. SW17 180 DF90
Chetwode Rd., Tad. 233 CW119
Chetwood Wk. E6 144 EL71
Oliver Gdns.
Chetwynd Ave., Barn. 98 DF46
Chetwynd Dr., Uxb. 134 BM68
Chetwynd Rd. NW5 121 DH63
Cheval Pl. SW7 276 C6
Cheval Pl. SW7 160 DE76
Cheval St. E14 163 EA76
Cheveley Clo., Rom. 106 FM53
Chelsworth Dr.
Cheveley Gdns., Slou. 130 AJ68
Chevely Clo., Epp. 70 EX29
Cheveney Wk., Brom. 204 EG97
Marina Clo.
Chevening La., Sev. 240 EY116
Chevening Rd. NW6 139 CX68
Chevening Rd. SE10 164 EF78
Chevening Rd. SE19 182 DR93
Chevening Rd., Sev. 240 EZ119
Chevenings, The, Sid. 186 EW90
Cheverton Rd. N19 121 DK60
Chevet St. E9 123 DY64
Kenworthy Rd.
Chevington Way, Horn. 128 FK63
Cheviot Clo., Bans. 234 DB115
Cheviot Clo., Bexh. 167 FE82
Cheviot Clo., Enf. 82 DR40
Cheviot Clo., Hayes 155 BR80
Cheviot Clo., Sutt. 218 DD109
Cheviot Clo. (Bushey), Wat. 76 CC44
Cheviot Gdns. NW2 119 CX61
Cheviot Gate NW2 119 CY61
Cheviot Rd. SE27 181 DN92
Cheviot Rd., Horn. 127 FG59
Cheviot Rd., Slou. 153 BA78
Cheviot Way, Ilf. 125 ES56
Cheviots, Hat. 45 CU21
Cheviots, Hem.H. 40 BM17
Chevron Clo. E16 144 EG72
Chevy Rd., Sthl. 156 CC75
Chewton Rd. E17 123 DY56
Cheyham Gdns., Sutt. 217 CX110
Cheyham Way, Sutt. 217 CY110
Cheyne Ave. E18 124 EF55
Cheyne Ave., Twick. 176 BZ88
Cheyne Clo. NW4 119 CW58
Cheyne Wk.
Cheyne Clo., Amer. 55 AR36
Cheyne Clo., Brom. 204 EL104
Cedar Cres.
Cheyne Clo., Ger.Cr. 112 AY60
Cheyne Clo., Ware 33 DX05
Cheyne Ct. SW3 160 DF79
Flood St.
Cheyne Ct., Bans. 234 DB115
Park Rd.
Cheyne Gdns. SW3 160 DE79
Cheyne Hill, Surb. 198 CM98
Cheyne Ms. SW3 160 DE79
Cheyne Wk.
Cheyne Path W7 137 CF72
Copley Clo.
Cheyne Pl. SW3 160 DF79
Royal Hospital Rd.
Cheyne Rd., Ashf. 175 BR93
Cheyne Row SW3 160 DE79
Cheyne Wk. N21 81 DP43
Cheyne Wk. NW4 119 CW58
Cheyne Wk. SW3 160 DE79
Cheyne Wk. SW10 160 DD80
Cheyne Wk., Chesh. 54 AR31
Cheyne Wk., Croy. 202 DU103
Cheyne Wk., Horl. 268 DF150
Cheyne Wk., Long. 209 FX97
Cavendish Sq.
Cheyney Rd., Ashf. 175 BR93
Cheyneys Ave., Edg. 95 CK51
Chichele Gdns., Croy. 220 DT105
Brownlow Rd.
Chichele Rd. NW2 119 CX64
Chichele Rd., Oxt. 254 EE128
Chicheley Gdns., Har. 94 CC52
Chicheley Rd., Har. 94 CC52
Chicheley St. SE1 278 C4
Chicheley St. SE1 161 DM75
Chichester Ave., Ruis. 115 BR61
Chichester Clo. E6 144 EL72
Chichester Clo. SE3 164 EJ81
Chichester Clo., Dor. 247 CH134
Chichester Clo., Hmptn. 176 BZ93
Maple Clo.
Chichester Clo., S.Ock. 148 FQ74
Chichester Ct., Epsom 217 CT109
Chichester Ct., Slou. 152 AV75
Chichester Ct., Stan. 118 CL55
Chichester Dr., Pur. 219 DM112
Chichester Dr., Sev. 256 FF125
Chichester Gdns., Ilf. 124 EL59
Chichester Ms. SE27 181 DN91
Chichester Rents WC2 274 D8
Chichester Ri., Grav. 191 GK91
Chichester Rd. E11 124 EE62
Chichester Rd. N9 100 DU47
Chichester Rd. NW6 140 DA68
Chichester Rd. W2 140 DB71
Chichester Rd., Croy. 202 DS104
Chichester Rd., Dor. 247 CH133
Chichester Rd., Green. 189 FT85
Chichester Row, Amer. 55 AR38
Chichester St. SW1 161 DJ78
Chichester Way E14 163 ED77
Chichester Way, Felt. 176 BW87
Chichester Way, Wat. 60 BY33
Chicksand St. E1 142 DT71
Chiddingfold N12 98 DA48
Chiddingstone Ave., Bexh. 166 EZ80
Chiddingstone Clo., Sutt. 218 DA110
Chiddingstone St. SW6 160 DA82
Chieftan Dr., Purf. 168 FM77
Chieveley Rd., Bexh. 167 FB84
Chiffinch Gdns., Grav. 190 GE90
Chignell Pl. W13 137 CG74
The Bdy.
Chigwell Hill E1 142 DV73
Pennington St.
Chigwell Hurst Ct., Pnr. 94 BX54
Chigwell La., Loug. 85 EQ42
Chigwell Pk. Dr., Chig. 103 EN48
Chigwell Ri., Chig. 103 EN47
Chigwell Rd. E18 124 EH55
Chigwell Rd., Wdf.Grn. 102 EK52
Chigwell Vw., Rom. 104 FA51
Lodge La.
Chilberton Dr., Red. 251 DJ130
Chilbrook Rd., Cob. 229 BU118
Chilcot Clo. E14 143 EB72
Grundy St.
Chilcote La., Amer. 72 AV39
Chilcott Rd., Wat. 75 BS36
Childebert Rd. SW17 181 DH89
Childeric Rd. SE14 163 DY80
Childerley St. SW6 159 CX81
Fulham Palace Rd.
Childers, The, Wdf.Grn. 103 EM50
Childers St. SE8 163 DY79
Childs Ave., Uxb. 92 BJ54
Childs Clo., Horn. 128 FJ58
Childs Cres., Swans. 189 FX86
Childs Hall Clo., Lthd. 246 BZ125
Childs Hall Rd.
Childs Hall Dr., Lthd. 246 BZ125
Childs Hall Rd., Lthd. 246 BZ125
Childs Hill Wk. NW2 119 CZ62
Church Wk.
Childs La. SE19 182 DS93
Westow St.
Child's Pl. SW5 160 DA77
Child's St. SW5 160 DA77
Child's Wk. SW5 160 DA77
Child's Pl.
Childs Way NW11 119 CZ57
Childwick Ct., Hem.H. 40 BN23
Rumballs Rd.
Chilham Clo., Bex. 186 EZ87
Chilham Clo., Grnf. 137 CG68
Chilham Clo., Hem.H. 40 BL21
Old Crabtree La.
Chilham Rd. SE9 184 EL91
Chilham Way, Brom. 204 EG101
Chillerton Rd. SW17 180 DG92
Chillingworth Gdns., Twick. 177 CF90
Tower Rd.
Chillingworth Rd. N7 121 DN64
Liverpool Rd.
Chilmans Dr., Lthd. 246 CB125
Chilmark Gdns., N.Mal. 199 CT101
Chilmark Gdns., Red. 251 DL129
Chilmark Rd. SW16 201 DK96
Chilsey Grn. Rd., Cher. 193 BE100
Chiltern Ave., Amer. 55 AR38
Chiltern Ave., Twick. 176 CA88
Chiltern Ave. (Bushey), Wat. 76 CC44
Chiltern Clo., Berk. 38 AT18
Chiltern Clo., Bexh. 167 FE81
Cumbrian Ave.
Chiltern Clo., Borwd. 78 CM40
Chiltern Clo., Croy. 202 DS104
Chiltern Clo., Uxb. 114 BN61
Chiltern Clo. (Cheshunt), Wal.Cr. 65 DP27
Chiltern Clo. (Bushey), Wat. 76 CB44
Chiltern Clo., Wok. 226 AW122
Chiltern Clo., Wor.Pk. 199 CW103
Cotswold Way
Chiltern Dene, Enf. 81 DM42
Chiltern Dr., Rick. 91 BF45
Chiltern Dr., Surb. 198 CN100
Chiltern Gdns. NW2 119 CX62
Chiltern Gdns., Brom. 204 EF98
Chiltern Gdns., Horn. 128 FJ62
Chiltern Hill, Ger.Cr. 90 AY53
Chiltern Hills Rd., Beac. 88 AJ53
Chiltern Par., Amer. 55 AQ37
Chiltern Pk. Ave., Berk. 38 AU17
Chiltern Rd. E3 143 EA70
Knapp Rd.
Chiltern Rd., Amer. 55 AP35
Chiltern Rd., Grav. 190 GE90
Chiltern Rd., Ilf. 125 ES56
Chiltern Rd., Pnr. 116 BW57
Chiltern Rd., St.Alb. 43 CJ15
Chiltern Rd., Slou. 130 AH71
Chiltern Rd., Sutt. 218 DB109
Chiltern St. W1 272 F6
Chiltern St. W1 140 DG71
Chiltern Vw. Rd., Uxb. 134 BJ68
Chiltern Way, Wdf.Grn. 102 EG48
Chilterns, Berk. 38 AT17
Chilterns, Hat. 45 CU21
Chilterns, Hem.H. 40 BL18
Chilterns, The, Sutt. 218 DB109
Gatton Clo.
Chilthorne Clo. SE6 183 DZ87
Ravensbourne Pk. Cres.
Chilton Ave. W5 157 CK77
Chilton Clo., H.Wyc. 88 AC45
Chilton Ct., Hert. 31 DM07
The Ridgeway
Chilton Ct., Walt. 213 BU105
Chilton Grn., Welw.G.C. 30 DC09
Chilton Gro. SE8 163 DX77
Chilton Rd., Chesh. 54 AQ29
Chilton Rd., Edg. 96 CN51
Manor Pk. Cres.
Chilton Rd., Grays 171 GG76
Chilton Rd., Rich. 158 CN83
Chilton St. E2 142 DT70
Chiltonian Ind. Est. SE12 184 EF86
Chiltons, The E18 102 EG54
Grove Hill
Chiltons Clo., Bans. 234 DB115
High St.
Chilver St. SE10 164 EF78
Chilwell Gdns., Wat. 94 BW49
Chilwick, Slou. 131 AM69
Chilworth Ct. SW19 179 CX88
Chilworth Gdns., Sutt. 200 DC104
Chilworth Ms. W2 140 DD72
Chilworth Rd., Guil. 260 BG139
Chilworth St. W2 140 DC72
Chimes Ave. N13 99 DN50
Chinbrook Cres. SE12 184 EH90
Chinbrook Rd.
Chinbrook Est. SE9 184 EK90
Chinbrook Rd. SE12 184 EH90
Chinchilla Dr., Houns. 156 BW82
Chindit Clo., Brox. 49 DY21
Baas Hill
Chindits La., Brwd. 108 FW50
Chine, The N10 121 DJ56
Chine, The N21 81 DP44
Chine, The, Dor. 263 CH135
High St.
Chine, The, Wem. 117 CH64
Ching Ct. WC2 273 P9
Ching Way E4 101 DZ51
Silver Birch Ave.
Chingdale Rd. E4 102 EE48
Chingford Ave. E4 101 EA48
Chingford Hall Est. E4 101 DZ51
Chingford Ind. Est. E4 101 DY50
Chingford La., Wdf.Grn. 102 EE49
Chingford Mt. Rd. E4 101 EA49
Chingford Rd. E4 101 EA51
Chingford Rd. E17 101 EB53
Chingley Clo., Brom. 184 EE93
Chinnery Clo., Enf. 82 DT39
Garnault Rd.
Chinnor Cres., Grnf. 136 CB68
Chinthurst La., Guil. 258 AY141
Chinthurst Pk., Guil. 258 AY142
Chip St. SW4 161 DK84
Prescott Pl.
Chipka St. E14 163 EC75
Chipley St. SE14 163 DY79
Nynehead St.
Chipmunk Gro., Nthlt. 136 BY69
Argus Way
Chippendale All., Uxb. 134 BK66
Chippendale Waye
Chippendale St. E5 123 DX62
Chippendale Waye, Uxb. 134 BK66
Chippenham Ave., Wem. 118 CP64
Chippenham Clo., Pnr. 115 BT56
Chippenham Clo., Rom. 106 FK50
Chippenham Rd.
Chippenham Gdns. NW6 140 DA69
Chippenham Gdns., Rom. 106 FK50
Chippenham Ms. W9 140 DA70
Chippenham Rd. W9 140 DA70
Chippenham Rd., Rom. 106 FK51
Chippenham Wk., Rom. 106 FK51
Chippenham Rd.
Chipperfield Clo., Upmin. 129 FS60
Chipperfield Rd., Hem.H. 40 BJ24
Chipperfield Rd. (Bovingdon), Hem.H. 57 BB27
Chipperfield Rd., Kings L. 58 BJ30
Chipperfield Rd., Orp. 206 EU95
Chipping Clo., Barn. 79 CY41
St. Albans Rd.
Chippingfield, Harl. 36 EW12
Chipstead Ave., Th.Hth. 201 DP98
Chipstead Clo. SE19 182 DT94
Chipstead Clo., Couls. 234 DG116
Chipstead Clo., Ger.Cr. 90 AW53
Chipstead Clo., Red. 266 DG136
St. John's Rd.
Chipstead Clo., Sutt. 218 DB109
Chipstead Ct., Wok. 226 AS117
Creston Ave.
Chipstead Gdns. NW2 119 CV61
Chipstead Gate, Couls. 235 DJ119
Woodfield Clo.
Chipstead La., Couls. 234 DB124
Chipstead La., Sev. 256 FC122
Chipstead La., Tad. 249 CZ125
Chipstead Pk., Sev. 256 FD122
Chipstead Pk. Clo., Sev. 256 FC122
Chipstead Pl. Gdns., Sev. 256 FC122
Chipstead Rd., Bans. 233 CZ117
Chipstead Rd., Erith 167 FE80
Chipstead Rd., Houns. 154 BN83
Chipstead St. SW6 160 DA81
Chipstead Valley Rd., Couls. 234 DG116
Chipstead Way, Bans. 234 DF115
Chirk Clo., Hayes 136 BY70
Braunston Dr.
Chirton Wk., Wok. 226 AU118
Shilburn Way
Chisenhale Rd. E3 143 DY68
Chisholm Rd., Croy. 202 DS103
Chisholm Rd., Rich. 178 CM86
Chisledon Wk. E9 143 DZ65
Trowbridge Est.
Chislehurst Ave. N12 98 DC52
Chislehurst Rd., Brom. 204 EK96
Chislehurst Rd., Chis. 204 EK96
Chislehurst Rd., Orp. 205 ES100
Chislehurst Rd., Rich. 178 CL85
Chislehurst Rd., Sid. 186 EU92
Chislet Clo., Beck. 183 EA94
Abbey La.
Chisley Rd. N15 122 DS58
Chiswell Ct., Wat. 76 BW38
Chiswell Grn. La., St.Alb. 60 BY25
Chiswell Sq. SE3 164 EH82
Brook La.
Chiswell St. EC1 275 K6
Chiswell St. EC1 142 DR71
Chiswick Bri. SW14 158 CQ82
Chiswick Bri. W4 158 CQ82
Chiswick Clo., Croy. 201 DM104
Chiswick Common Rd. W4 158 CR77
Chiswick Ct., Pnr. 116 BZ55
Chiswick Gdns. W4 158 CQ81
Hartington Rd.
Chiswick High Rd. W4 158 CN78
Chiswick High Rd., Brent. 158 CN78
Chiswick Ho. Grds. W4 158 CR79
Chiswick La. W4 158 CS78
Chiswick La. S. W4 159 CT78
Chiswick Mall W4 159 CT79
Chiswick Mall W6 159 CU78
Chiswick Quay W4 158 CQ81
Chiswick Rd. N9 100 DU47
Chiswick Rd. W4 158 CQ77
Chiswick Sq. W4 158 CS79
Hogarth Roundabout
Chiswick Staithe W4 158 CQ81
Chiswick Village W4 158 CP79
Chiswick Wf. W4 159 CT79
Chittenden Cotts., Wok. 228 BL116
Chitterfield Gate, West Dr. 154 BN80
Chitty St. W1 273 L6
Chitty St. W1 141 DJ71
Chittys Common, Guil. 242 AT130
Chitty's La., Dag. 126 EX61
Chittys Wk., Guil. 242 AT130
Chivalry Rd. SW11 180 DE85
Chivenor Gro., Kings.T. 177 CK92
Richmond Rd.
Chivers Rd. E4 101 EB49
Choats Manor Way, Bark. 146 EV70
Renwick Rd.
Choats Rd., Bark. 146 EW68
Renwick Rd.
Choats Rd., Dag. 146 EY69
Chobham Clo., Cher. 211 BB107
Chobham Gdns. SW19 179 CX89
Chobham La., Wok. 192 AT104
Chobham Pk. La., Wok. 210 AU110
Chobham Rd. E15 123 ED64
Chobham Rd., Cher. 211 BA108
Chobham Rd., Wok. 226 AY115
Chobham Rd. (Horsell), Wok. 210 AW113
Choir Grn., Wok. 226 AS117
Semper Clo.
Cholmeley Cres. N6 121 DH59
Cholmeley Pk. N6 121 DH60
Cholmley Gdns. NW6 120 DA64
Fortune Grn. Rd.
Cholmley Rd., T.Ditt. 197 CH100
Cholmondeley Ave. NW10 139 CU68
Cholmondeley Wk., Rich. 177 CJ85
Choppins Ct. E1 142 DV74
Wapping La.
Chopwell Clo. E15 143 ED66
Bryant St.
Chorleywood Bottom, Rick. 73 BD43
Chorleywood Clo., Rick. 92 BK45
Chorleywood Cres., Orp. 205 ET96
Chorleywood Rd., Rick. 74 BG42
Choumert Gro. SE15 162 DU82
Choumert Rd. SE15 162 DT83
Choumert Sq. SE15 162 DU82
Chow Sq. E8 122 DT64
Arcola St.
Chrislaine Clo. (Stanwell), Stai. 174 BK86
High St.
Chrisp St. E14 143 EB71
Christ Ch. Ave., Erith 167 FD79
Christ Ch. Rd. SW14 178 CP85
Christ Ch. Rd., Beck. 203 EA96
Fairfield Rd.
Christ Ch. Rd., Epsom 216 CL112
Christ Ch. Rd., Surb. 198 CM101
Christchurch Ave. N12 98 DC51
Christchurch Ave. NW6 139 CX67
Christchurch Ave., Har. 117 CF56
Christchurch Ave., Rain. 147 FF68
Christchurch Ave., Tedd. 177 CG92
Christchurch Ave., Wem. 138 CL65
Christchurch Clo. SW19 180 DD94
Christchurch Clo., St.Alb. 42 CC19
Christchurch Cres., Grav. 191 GJ87
Christchurch Rd.
Christchurch Cres., Rad. 77 CG36
Christchurch Gdns., Epsom 216 CP111
Christchurch Gdns., Har. 117 CG56
Christchurch Grn., Wem. 138 CL65
Christchurch Hill NW3 120 DD62
Christchurch Ind. Cen., Har. 117 CF56
Christchurch La., Barn. 79 CY40
Christchurch Mt., Epsom 216 CP112
Christchurch Pk., Sutt. 218 DC108
Christchurch Pas. NW3 120 DD62
Christchurch Hill
Christchurch Pas., Barn. 79 CY41
Christchurch La.
Christchurch Rd. N8 121 DL58
Christchurch Rd. SW2 181 DM88
Christchurch Rd. SW19 200 DD95
Christchurch Rd., Dart. 188 FJ86
Christchurch Rd., Grav. 191 GJ88
Christchurch Rd., Hem.H. 40 BK19
Christchurch Rd., Houns. 154 BN82
Christchurch Rd., Ilf. 125 EP60
Christchurch Rd., Pur. 219 DP110
Christchurch Rd., Sid. 185 ET91
Christchurch Rd., Til. 171 GG81
Christchurch Rd., Vir.W. 192 AU97
Christchurch Sq. E9 142 DW67
Victoria Pk. Rd.
Christchurch St. SW3 160 DF79
Christchurch Ter. SW3 160 DF79
Christchurch St.
Christchurch Way SE10 164 EE78
Christchurch Way, Wok. 227 AZ117
Church St. E.
Christian Ct. SE16 143 DZ74
Christian Flds. SW16 181 DN94
Christian Flds. Ave., Grav. 191 GJ91
Christian Sq., Wind. 151 AQ81
Alma Rd.
Christian St. E1 142 DU72
Christie Clo., Brox. 49 DZ21
Christie Dr., Croy. 202 DT100
Christie Gdns., Rom. 126 EV58
Christie Rd. E9 143 DY65
Christies Ave., Sev. 224 FA110
Christina Clo. N4 121 DP60
Adolphus Rd.
Christina Sq. N4 121 DP60
Adolphus Rd.
Christina St. EC2 275 M4
Christmas La., Slou. 111 AQ62
Christopher Ave. W7 157 CG76
Christopher Clo. SE16 163 DX75
Christopher Clo., Horn. 128 FK63
Chevington Way
Christopher Clo., Sid. 185 ET85
Christopher Clo., Tad. 233 CW123
High St.
Christopher Ct., Hem.H. 40 BK23
Seaton Rd.
Christopher Ct., Tad. 233 CW123
Christopher Gdns., Dag. 126 EX64
Wren Rd.
Christopher Pl. NW1 273 N3
Christopher Pl., St.Alb. 43 CD20
Market Pl.
Christopher Rd., Sthl. 155 BV77
Christopher St. EC2 275 L5

Christopher St. EC2 142 DR70
Christopher's Ms. W11 139 CY74
Penzance St.
Christy Rd., West. 238 EJ115
Chryssell Rd. SW9 161 DN80
Chrystie La., Lthd. 246 CB126
Chubworthy St. SE14 163 DY79
Chucks La., Tad. 233 CV124
Chudleigh Cres., Ilf. 125 ES63
Chudleigh Gdns., Sutt. 200 DC104
Chudleigh Rd. NW6 139 CX66
Chudleigh Rd. SE4 183 DZ85
Chudleigh Rd., Rom. 106 FL49
Chudleigh Rd., Twick. 177 CE86
Chudleigh St. E1 143 DX72
Chudleigh Way, Ruis. 115 BU60
Chulsa Rd. SE26 182 DV92
Chumleigh St. SE5 162 DS79
Chumleigh Wk., Surb. 198 CM98
Church All., Croy. 201 DP101
Handcroft Rd.
Church All., Wat. 76 CC38
Church App. SE21 182 DR90
Church App., Egh. 193 BC97
Church App., Sev. 239 EQ115
Cudham La. S.
Church App., Stai. 174 BK86
Church Ave. E4 101 ED51
Church Ave. NW1 141 DH65
Kentish Town Rd.
Church Ave. SW14 158 CR83
Church Ave., Beck. 203 EA95
Church Ave., Nthlt. 136 BZ66
Church Ave., Pnr. 116 BY58
Church Ave., Ruis. 115 BR60
Church Ave., Sid. 186 EU92
Church Ave., Sthl. 156 BY76
Church Clo. N20 98 DE48
Church Clo. W8 160 DB75
Kensington Ch. St.
Church Clo., Add. 212 BH105
Church Clo., Edg. 96 CQ50
Church Clo., Hayes 135 BR71
Church Clo., Hert. 47 DJ19
Goddards Clo.
Church Clo., Lthd. 231 CD124
Church Clo., Loug. 85 EM40
Church Clo., Nthwd. 93 BT52
Church Clo. (Cuffley), Pot.B. 65 DL29
Church Clo., Rad. 77 CG36
Church Clo., Stai. 194 BJ97
The Bdy.
Church Clo., Tad. 249 CZ127
Buckland Rd.
Church Clo., Uxb. 134 BH68
Church Clo., West Dr. 154 BL76
Church Clo., Wind. 151 AR79
Church Clo., Wok. 226 AX116
Church Ct., Reig. 250 DB134
Church Ct., Rich. 177 CK85
George St.
Church Cres. E9 143 DX66
Church Cres. N3 97 CZ53
Church Cres. N10 121 DH56
Church Cres. N20 98 DE48
Church Cres., St.Alb. 42 CC19
Church Cres., Saw. 36 EZ05
Forebury Ave.
Church Cres., S.Ock. 149 FW69
Church Dr. NW9 118 CR60
Church Dr., Har. 116 BZ58
Church Dr., Maid. 150 AC75
Church Dr., W.Wick. 204 EE104
Church Elm La., Dag. 146 FA65
Church End E17 123 EB56
Church End NW4 119 CV55
Church End, Harl. 51 EN17
Church Entry EC4 141 DP72
Carter La.
Church Fm. Clo., Swan. 207 FC100
Church Fm. La., Sutt. 217 CY107
Church Fld., Dart. 188 FK89
Church Fld., Epp. 70 EU29
Church Fld., Rad. 77 CG36
Christchurch Cres.
Church Fld., Sev. 256 FE122
Church Gdns. W5 157 CK75
Church Gdns., Dor. 263 CG135
Church Gdns., Wem. 117 CG63
Church Gate SW6 159 CY83
Church Grn., Hayes 135 BT72
Church Grn., St.Alb. 43 CD19
Hatfield Rd.
Church Grn., Walt. 214 BW107
Church Gro. SE13 163 EB84
Church Gro., Amer. 72 AY39
Church Gro., Kings.T. 197 CJ95
Church Gro., Slou. 132 AW71
Church Hill E17 123 EA56
Church Hill N21 99 DM45
Church Hill SE18 165 EM76
Church Hill SW19 179 CZ92
Church Hill, Abb.L. 59 BT26
Church Hill, Cars. 218 DF106
Church Hill, Cat. 236 DT124
Church Hill, Dart. 188 FK90
Church Hill (Crayford), Dart. 167 FE84
Church Hill, Epp. 70 EU30
Church Hill, Green. 189 FS85
Church Hill, Guil. 260 BN139
Church Hill, Har. 117 CE60
Church Hill, Hert. 32 DV11
Church Hill, Loug. 85 EM41
Church Hill, Orp. 206 EU101
Church Hill, Pur. 219 DL110
Church Hill (Merstham), Red. 251 DH126
Church Hill (Nutfield), Red. 251 DM133
Church Hill, Sev. 239 EQ115
Church Hill, Uxb. 114 BJ55
Church Hill, West. 238 EK122
Church Hill (Horsell), Wok. 226 AX116
Church Hill (Pyrford), Wok. 227 BF117
Church Hill Rd. E17 123 EB56
Church Hill Rd., Barn. 80 DE44
Church Hill Rd., Surb. 198 CL99
Church Hill Rd., Sutt. 217 CX105
Church Hill Wd., Orp. 206 EU99
Church Hollow, Purf. 168 FN78
Church Hyde SE18 165 ES79
Old Mill Rd.
Church Island, Stai. 173 BD91
Church La. E11 124 EE60
Church La. E17 123 EB56
Church La. N2 120 DC55
Church La. N8 121 DM56
Church La. N9 100 DU47
Church La. N17 100 DS53
Church La. NW9 118 CQ58
Church La. SW17 181 DH92
Church La. SW19 199 CZ95
Church La. W5 157 CJ75
Church La. (Nork), Bans. 233 CX117
Reigate Rd.
Church La., Berk. 38 AW19
Church La., Bishop's Stortford 37 FD07
Church La. (Hutton), Brwd. 109 GE46
Church La., Brom. 204 EL102
Church La., Brox. 48 DV21
Church La., Cat. 235 DN123
Church La., Chess. 216 CM107
Church La., Chis. 205 EQ95
Church La., Couls. 234 DG122
Church La., Dag. 147 FB65
Church La., Enf. 82 DR41
Church La., Epp. 71 FB27
Church La., Epsom 233 CX117
Reigate Rd.
Church La. (Headley), Epsom 232 CQ124
Church La., Ger.Cr. 90 AX53
Church La., Gdse. 253 DX132
Church La., Guil. 260 BH139
Church La. (Worplesdon), Guil. 242 AS127
Church La., Har. 95 CF53
Church La., Hat. 45 CW18
Church La., Hem.H. 57 BB27
Church La., Hert. 47 DM17
Church La., Horl. 269 DL153
Church La., Kings L. 58 BN29
Church La., Loug. 85 EM41
Church La., Maid. 150 AC75
Church La., Oxt. 253 ED130
Church La., Pnr. 116 BY55
Church La., Pot.B. 64 DG30
Church La., Purf. 168 FN78
London Rd. Purfleet
Church La. (Wennington), Rain. 148 FK72
Church La., Red. 252 DR133
Church La., Rich. 178 CL88
Petersham Rd.
Church La. (Mill End), Rick. 92 BG46
Church La. (Sarratt), Rick. 73 BF38
Church La., Rom. 127 FE56
Church La. (Abridge), Rom. 86 EY40
Church La. (Stapleford Abbotts), Rom. 87 FC42
Church La., St.Alb. 44 CP22
Church La. (Stoke Poges), Slou. 132 AT70
Church La. (Wexham), Slou. 132 AV70
Church La., Tedd. 177 CF92
Church La., T.Ditt. 197 CF100
Church La., Twick. 177 CG88
Church La., Upmin. 129 FV64
Church La., Uxb. 134 BH68
Church La., Wall. 201 DK104
Church La. (Cheshunt), Wal.Cr. 66 DV29
Church La., Warl. 237 DX117
Church La. (Chelsham), Warl. 237 EB117
Church La., Wat. 76 CB38
Church La., West. 238 EK122
Church La., Wind. 151 AR81
Church La. (Send), Wok. 243 BB126
Church La. Ave., Couls. 235 DH122
Church La. Dr., Couls. 235 DH122
Church Langley Way, Harl. 52 EW15
Church Leys, Harl. 51 ET16
Church Manor Est. SW9 161 DN80
Vassall Rd.
Church Manorway SE2 166 EU78
Church Manorway, Erith 167 FD76
Church Mead, Harl. 34 EH14
Church Meadow, Surb. 197 CJ103
Church Ms., Ware 33 DX06
Church St.
Church Mt. N2 120 DD57
Church Pas. EC2 142 DQ72
Gresham St.
Church Pas., Barn. 79 CZ42
Wood St.
Church Pas., Surb. 198 CL99
Adelaide Rd.
Church Path E11 124 EG57
Church Path E17 123 EB56
St. Mary Rd.
Church Path N12 98 DC50
Church Path N17 100 DS52
White Hart La.
Church Path N20 98 DC49
Church Path NW10 138 CS66
Church Path SW14 158 CR83
North Worple Way
Church Path SW19 199 CZ96
Church Path W4 158 CQ76
Church Path W7 137 CE74
Station Rd.
Church Path, Cob. 213 BU114
Church Path, Couls. 235 DN118
Canon's Hill
Church Path, Croy. 202 DQ103
Keeley Rd.
Church Path, Grav. 190 GC86
Church Path, Grays 170 GA79
Church Path, Green. 189 FT86
London Rd.
Church Path, Hert. 32 DR10
Church Path, Maid. 150 AC75
Church Path, Mitch. 200 DE97
Church Path, Sthl. 156 BZ76
Church Path, Ware 33 DZ09
Church Path, Wok. 227 AZ117
High St.
Church Pl. SW1 277 L1
Church Pl. W5 157 CK75
Church Pl., Mitch. 200 DE97
Church Pl., Twick. 177 CH88
Church St.
Church Pl., Uxb. 115 BQ62
Austin's La.
Church Ri. SE23 183 DX89
Church Ri., Chess. 216 CM107
Church Rd. E10 123 EA60
Church Rd. E12 124 EL64
Church Rd. E17 101 DY54
Church Rd. N6 120 DG58
Church Rd. N17 100 DS53
Church Rd. NW4 119 CV56
Church Rd. NW10 138 CS66
Church Rd. SE19 202 DS95
Church Rd. SW13 159 CT82
Church Rd. (Wimbledon) SW19 179 CY92
Church Rd. W3 138 CQ74
Church Rd. W7 137 CD73
Church Rd., Add. 212 BG106
Church Rd., Ashf. 174 BM90
Church Rd., Ash. 231 CK117
Church Rd., Bark. 145 EQ65
Church Rd., Beac. 89 AR51
Church Rd., Berk. 39 BB16
Church Rd., Bexh. 166 EZ83
Church Rd., B.End 110 AD62
Church Rd., Brom. 204 EG96
Church Rd. (Shortlands), Brom. 204 EE97
Church Rd., Buck.H. 102 EH46
Church Rd., Cat. 236 DT123
Church Rd. (Woldingham), Cat. 237 DX122
Church Rd., Craw. 268 DE154
Church Rd., Croy. 201 DP103
Church Rd. (Sutton at Hone), Dart. 188 FL94
Church Rd., E.Mol. 197 CD98
Church Rd., Egh. 173 AZ92
Church Rd., Enf. 82 DW44
Church Rd., Epsom 216 CS112
Church Rd. (West Ewell), Epsom 216 CR108
Church Rd., Erith 167 FC78
Church Rd., Esher 215 CF107
Church Rd., Felt. 176 BX92
Church Rd., Grav. 191 GJ94
Church Rd., Green. 189 FS85
Church Rd., Guil. 258 AX135
Church Rd., Harl. 52 EW18
Church Rd., Hayes 135 BT74
Church Rd., Hem.H. 41 BQ21
Church Rd., Hert. 32 DQ08
Church Rd. (Little Berkhamsted), Hert. 47 DJ19
Church Rd. (Penn), H.Wyc. 88 AD47
Church Rd., Horl. 268 DF149
Church Rd. (Smallfield), Horl. 269 DN152
Church Rd. (Cranford), Houns. 155 BV78
Church Rd. (Heston), Houns. 156 CA80
Church Rd., Ilf. 125 ES58
Church Rd., Islw. 157 CD81
Church Rd., Iver 133 BC69
Church Rd., Ken. 236 DR115
Church Rd., Kes. 222 EK108
Church Rd., Kings.T. 198 CM96
Church Rd., Lthd. 231 CH122
Church Rd. (Bookham), Lthd. 230 BZ123
Church Rd., Loug. 84 EG41
Church Rd., Mitch. 200 DD97
Church Rd., Nthlt. 136 BX68
Church Rd., Nthwd. 93 BT52
Church Rd., Orp. 224 EW108
Church Rd. (Farnborough), Orp. 223 EQ106
Church Rd., Pot.B. 64 DA30
Church Rd., Pur. 219 DL110
Church Rd., Red. 266 DE136
Church Rd., Reig. 266 DA136
Church Rd., Rich. 158 CL84
Church Rd. (Ham), Rich. 177 CK91
Church Rd. (Harold Wd.), Rom. 106 FN53
Church Rd. (Havering-atte-Bower), Rom. 106 FJ46
Church Rd. (Halstead), Sev. 224 EY111
Church Rd. (Seal), Sev. 257 FM121
Church Rd., Shep. 195 BP101
Church Rd., Sid. 186 EU91
Church Rd., Slou. 131 AQ69
Church Rd., Sthl. 156 BZ76
Church Rd., Stan. 95 CH50
Church Rd., Surb. 197 CJ102
Church Rd., Sutt. 217 CY107
Church Rd., Swan. 208 FK95
Church Rd. (Crockenhill), Swan. 207 FD101
Church Rd., Swans. 190 FZ86
Church Rd., Tedd. 177 CE91
Church Rd., Til. 171 GF81
Church Rd. (West Tilbury), Til. 171 GL79
Church Rd. (Cowley), Uxb. 134 BK70
Church Rd. (Harefield), Uxb. 114 BJ55
Church Rd., Wall. 201 DJ104
Church Rd., Warl. 237 DX117
Church Rd., Wat. 75 BU39
Church Rd., Well. 166 EV82
Church Rd., Welw.G.C. 29 CX09
Church Rd., W.Byf. 212 BL114
Church Rd., West Dr. 154 BK76
Church Rd. (Biggin Hill), West. 238 EK117
Church Rd. (Brasted), West. 240 EV124
Church Rd., Whyt. 236 DT118
Church Rd., Wind. 172 AV85
Church Rd. (Horsell), Wok. 226 AY115
Church Rd. (St. John's), Wok. 226 AU119
Church Rd., Wor.Pk. 198 CS103
Church Rd. Ind. Est., Craw. 268 DE154
Church Rd. Merton SW19 200 DD95
Church Row NW3 120 DC63
Church Row, Chis. 205 EQ95
Church Row Ms., Ware 33 DX06
Church St.
Church Side, Epsom 216 CP113
Church Sq., Shep. 195 BP101
Church St. E15 144 EE68
Church St. E16 145 EP74
Church St. N9 100 DT47
Church St. NW8 272 A6
Church St. NW8 140 DD71
Church St. W2 272 A6
Church St. W2 140 DD71
Church St. W4 159 CT79
Church St., Amer. 55 AP40
Church St., Bet. 264 CS135
Church St., Chesh. 54 AP31
Church St., Cob. 229 BV115
Church St., Croy. 201 DP104
Church St., Dag. 147 FB65
Church St., Dor. 263 CG136
Church St., Enf. 82 DQ41
Church St., Epsom 216 CS113
Church St. (Ewell), Epsom 217 CU109
Church St., Esher 214 CB105
Church St., Grav. 191 GH86
Church St. (Southfleet), Grav. 190 GA92
Church St., Grays 170 GC79
Church St., Hmptn. 196 CC96
Church St., Hat. 45 CW18
Church St. (Essendon), Hat. 46 DE17
Church St., Hem.H. 40 BK18
Church St. (Bovingdon), Hem.H. 57 BB27
Church St., Hert. 32 DR09
Church St., Islw. 157 CH83
Church St., Kings.T. 197 CK96
Church St., Lthd. 231 CH122
Church St. (Effingham), Lthd. 246 BX127
Church St., Reig. 250 DA134
Church St., Rick. 92 BL46
Church St., St.Alb. 43 CD19
Church St., Saw. 36 EY05
Church St. (Seal), Sev. 257 FN121
Church St. (Shoreham), Sev. 225 FF111
Church St., Slou. 152 AT75
Church St. (Burnham), Slou. 130 AJ70
Church St. (Chalvey), Slou. 151 AQ75
Church St., Stai. 173 BE91
Church St., Sun. 195 BU97
Church St., Sutt. 218 DB106
High St.
Church St., Twick. 177 CG88
Church St., Wal.Abb. 67 EC33
Church St., Walt. 195 BU102
Church St., Ware 33 DX06
Church St., Wat. 76 BW42
Church St., Wey. 212 BN105
Church St., Wind. 151 AR81
Castle Hill
Church St., Wok. 227 AZ117
Church St. E., Wok. 227 AZ117
Church St. Est. NW8 272 A5
Church St. Est. NW8 140 DD70
Church St. N. E15 144 EE67
Church St. Pas. E15 144 EE67
Church St.
Church St. W., Wok. 226 AY117
Church Stretton Rd., Houns. 176 CC85
Church Ter. NW4 119 CV55
Church Ter. SE13 164 EE83
Church Ter. SW8 161 DK82
Church Ter., Rich. 177 CK85
Church Ter., Wind. 151 AL82
Church Vale N2 120 DF55
Church Vale SE23 182 DW89
Church Vw., Brox. 49 DZ20
Church Vw., S.Ock. 168 FQ75
Church Vw., Swan. 207 FD97
Lime Rd.
Church Vw., Upmin. 128 FN61
Church Vw. Clo., Horl. 268 DF149
Church Vill., Sev. 256 FE122
Church Fld.
Church Wk. N6 120 DG62
Swains La.
Church Wk. N16 122 DR63
Church Wk. NW2 119 CZ62
Church Wk. NW4 119 CW55
Church Wk. NW9 118 CR61
Church Wk. SW13 159 CU81
Church Wk. SW15 179 CV85
St. Margarets Cres.
Church Wk. SW16 201 DJ96
Church Wk. SW20 199 CW97
Church Wk., Brent. 157 CJ79
Church Wk., Cat. 236 DU124
Church Wk., Cher. 194 BG100
Church Wk., Dart. 188 FK90
Church Wk., Grav. 191 GK88
Church Wk., Hayes 135 BS72
Church Wk., Horl. 268 DF149
Woodroyd Ave.
Church Wk., Lthd. 231 CH122
The Cres.
Church Wk., Red. 252 DQ133
Church Wk., Reig. 250 DB134
Chart La.
Church Wk., Rich. 177 CK85
Red Lion St.
Church Wk., Saw. 36 EZ05
Church Wk., Slou. 130 AH70
Church Wk., T.Ditt. 197 CF100
Church Wk., Walt. 195 BU102
Church Wk., Wey. 195 BP103
Beales La.
Church Way N20 98 DD48
Church Way, Barn. 80 DF42
Mount Pleasant
Church Way, Edg. 96 CN51
Station Rd.
Church Way, Oxt. 254 EF132
Church Way, S.Croy. 220 DT110
Churchbury Clo., Enf. 82 DS40
Churchbury La., Enf. 82 DR41
Churchbury Rd. SE9 184 EK87
Churchbury Rd., Enf. 82 DR40
Churchcroft Clo. SW12 180 DG87
Endlesham Rd.
Churchdown, Brom. 184 EE91
Churchfield, Harl. 36 EV13
Churchfield Ave. N12 98 DC51
Churchfield Clo., Har. 116 CC56
Churchfield Clo., Hayes 135 BT73
West Ave.
Churchfield Ms., Slou. 132 AU72
Churchfield Path (Cheshunt), Wal.Cr. 66 DW29
Churchfield Rd. W3 138 CQ74
Churchfield Rd. W7 157 CE75
Churchfield Rd. W13 137 CH74
Churchfield Rd., Ger.Cr. 90 AX53
Churchfield Rd., Reig. 249 CZ133
Churchfield Rd., Walt. 195 BU102
Churchfield Rd., Well. 166 EU83
Churchfield Rd., Welw. 30 DC06
Churchfield Rd., Wey. 212 BN105
Churchfields E18 102 EG53
Churchfields SE10 163 EC79
Roan St.
Churchfields, Brox. 49 EA20
Churchfields, Guil. 243 BA130
Burpham La.
Churchfields, Loug. 84 EL42
Churchfields, W.Mol. 196 CA97
Churchfields, Wok. 226 AY116
Churchfields Ave., Felt. 176 BZ90
Churchfields Ave., Wey. 213 BP105
Churchfields La., Brox. 49 EA20
Churchfields Rd., Beck. 203 DX96
Churchfields Rd., Wat. 75 BT36
Leggatts Way
Churchgate (Cheshunt), Wal.Cr. 66 DV30
Churchgate Gdns., Harl. 36 EZ11
Sheering Rd.
Churchgate Rd. (Cheshunt), Wal.Cr. 66 DV29
Churchgate St., Harl. 36 EY11
Churchill Ave., Har. 117 CH58
Churchill Ave., Uxb. 135 BP69
Churchill Clo., Dart. 188 FP88
Churchill Clo., Felt. 175 BT88
Westmacott Dr.
Churchill Clo., Lthd. 231 CE123
Churchill Clo., Uxb. 135 BP69
Churchill Clo., Warl. 236 DW117
Churchill Ct. W5 138 CM70
Churchill Ct., Nthlt. 116 CA64
Churchill Ct., Stai. 174 BJ93
Churchill Cres., Hat. 45 CW23
Dixons Hill Rd.
Churchill Dr., Beac. 88 AJ50
Churchill Dr., Wey. 195 BQ104
Churchill Gdns. SW1 161 DJ78
Churchill Gdns. W3 138 CN72
Churchill Gdns. Rd. SW1 161 DH78
Churchill Ms., Wdf.Grn. 102 EF51
High Rd.
Churchill Pl. E14 143 EB74
Churchill Pl., Har. 117 CE56
Sandridge Clo.
Churchill Rd. E16 144 EJ72
Churchill Rd. NW2 139 CV65
Churchill Rd. NW5 121 DH63
Churchill Rd. (Horton Kirby), Dart. 208 FQ98
Churchill Rd., Edg. 96 CM51
Churchill Rd., Grav. 191 GF88
Churchill Rd., Grays 170 GD79
Churchill Rd., Guil. 258 AY135
Churchill Rd., Horl. 269 DP148
Churchill Rd., St.Alb. 43 CG18
Churchill Rd., Slou. 153 AZ77
Churchill Rd., S.Croy. 220 DQ109
Churchill Ter. E4 101 EA49
Churchill Wk. E9 122 DW64
Churchill Way, Brom. 204 EG97
Ethelbert Rd.
Churchill Way, Sun. 175 BU92
Churchill Way, West. 238 EK115
Churchley Rd. SE26 182 DV91
Churchmead Clo., Barn. 80 DE44
Churchmead Rd. NW10 139 CU65
Churchmore Rd. SW16 201 DJ95
Churchside Clo., West. 238 EJ117
Churchview Rd., Twick. 177 CD88
Churchway NW1 273 N2
Churchway NW1 141 DK69
Churchwell Path E9 142 DW65
Morning La.
Churchyard Row SE11 278 G8
Churston Ave. E13 144 EH67
Churston Clo. SW2 181 DP88
Tulse Hill
Churston Dr., Mord. 199 CX99
Churston Gdns. N11 99 DJ51
Churton Pl. SW1 277 L9
Churton St. SW1 277 L9
Churton St. SW1 161 DJ77
Chusan Pl. E14 143 DZ72
Commercial Rd.
Chuters Clo., W.Byf. 212 BL112
Chuters Gro., Epsom 217 CT112
Chyne, The, Ger.Cr. 113 AZ57
Chyngton Clo., Sid. 185 ET90
Cibber Rd. SE23 183 DX89
Cicada Rd. SW18 180 DC86
Cicely Rd. SE15 162 DU81
Cillocks Clo., Hodd. 49 EA16
Cimba Wd., Grav. 191 GL91
Cinder Path, Wok. 226 AW119
Cinderford Way, Brom. 184 EE91
Cinema Par. W5 138 CM70
Ashbourne Rd.
Cinnamon Clo., Croy. 201 DL101
Therapia La.
Cinnamon Gdns., Guil. 242 AU129
Cinnamon Row SW11 160 DC83
Cinnamon St. E1 142 DV74
Cintra Pk. SE19 182 DT94
Cippenham Clo., Slou. 131 AM73
Cippenham La., Slou. 131 AM73
Circle, The NW2 118 CS62
Circle, The NW7 96 CR50
Circle, The, Til. 171 GG81
Toronto Rd.
Circle Gdns. SW19 200 DA96
Circle Gdns., W.Byf. 212 BM112
High Rd.
Circle Rd., Walt. 213 BS110
Circuits, The, Pnr. 116 BW56
Circular Rd. N17 122 DT55
Circular Way SE18 165 EM79
Circus Ms. W1 272 D6
Circus Pl. EC2 275 L7
Circus Rd. NW8 140 DD69
Circus St. SE10 163 EC80
Cirencester St. W2 140 DB71
Cirrus Cres., Grav. 191 GL92
Cissbury Ring N. N12 97 CZ50
Cissbury Ring S. N12 97 CZ50
Cissbury Rd. N15 122 DR57
Citadel Pl. SE11 278 B10
Citizen Rd. N7 121 DN62
Citron Ter. SE15 162 DV83
Nunhead La.
City Gdn. Row N1 274 G1
City Gdn. Row N1 141 DP68
City Rd. EC1 274 F1

City Rd. EC1	141	DP68
Civic Clo., St.Alb.	43	CD20
Civic Offices, St.Alb.	43	CD20
Civic Sq., Til.	171	GG82
Civic Way, Ilf.	125	EQ56
Civic Way, Ruis.	116	BX64
Clabon Ms. SW1	**276**	**D7**
Clabon Ms. SW1	160	DF76
Clack St. SE16	162	DW75
Clacket La., West.	238	EL124
Clacton Rd. E6	144	EK69
Clacton Rd. E17	123	DY58
Clacton Rd. N17	100	DT54
Sperling Rd.		
Claigmar Gdns. N3	98	DB53
Claire Ct. N12	98	DC48
Claire Ct., Pnr.	94	BZ52
Westfield Pk.		
Claire Ct., Wat.	95	CD46
Claire Pl. E14	163	EA76
Clairvale, Horn.	128	FL59
Clairvale Rd., Houns.	156	BX81
Clairview Rd. SW16	181	DH92
Clairville Gdns. W7	137	CE74
Clairville Pt. SE23	183	DX90
Clammas Way, Uxb.	134	BJ71
Clamp Hill, Stan.	95	CD49
Clancarty Rd. SW6	160	DA82
Clandon Ave., Egh.	173	BC94
Clandon Clo. W3	158	CP75
Avenue Rd.		
Clandon Clo., Epsom	217	CT107
Clandon Gdns. N3	120	DA55
Clandon Pk., Guil.	244	BG130
Clandon Rd., Guil.	258	AY135
Clandon Rd. (West Clandon), Guil.	244	BG128
Clandon Rd., Ilf.	125	ES61
Clandon Rd., Wok.	243	BF125
Clandon St. SE8	163	EA82
Clandon Way, Wok.	243	BF125
Clandon Rd.		
Clanfield Way SE15	162	DS80
Diamond St.		
Clanricarde Gdns. W2	140	DA73
Clap La., Dag.	127	FB62
Clapgate Rd. (Bushey), Wat.	76	CB44
Clapham Common N. Side SW4	160	DF84
Clapham Common S. Side SW4	181	DH86
Clapham Common W. Side SW4	160	DF84
Clapham Cres. SW4	161	DK84
Clapham High St. SW4	161	DK84
Clapham Junct. Est. SW11	160	DE84
Clapham Manor St. SW4	161	DJ83
Clapham Pk. Est. SW4	181	DK86
Clapham Pk. Rd. SW4	161	DK84
Clapham Rd. SW9	161	DL83
Clapham Rd. Est. SW4	161	DK83
Claps Gate La. E6	145	EP70
Royal Docks Rd.		
Claps Gate La., Bark.	145	EP70
Royal Docks Rd.		
Clapton App., H.Wyc.	110	AD55
Clapton Common E5	122	DT59
Clapton Pk. Est. E5	123	DY63
Blackwell Clo.		
Clapton Pas. E5	122	DW64
Lower Clapton Rd.		
Clapton Sq. E5	122	DW64
Clapton Ter. N16	122	DU60
Oldhill St.		
Clapton Way E5	122	DU63
Clara Pl. SE18	165	EN77
Clare Clo. N2	120	DC55
Thomas More Way		
Clare Clo., Borwd.	78	CM44
Clare Clo., W.Byf.	212	BG113
Clare Cor. SE9	185	EP87
Clare Cotts., Red.	251	DP133
Clare Ct., Cat.	237	EA123
Clare Ct., Nthwd.	93	BS50
Clare Cres., Lthd.	231	CG119
Clare Dr., Slou.	111	AP63
Clare Gdns. E7	124	EG63
Clare Gdns. W11	139	CY72
Westbourne Pk. Rd.		
Clare Gdns., Bark.	145	ET65
Clare Gdns., Egh.	173	BA92
Mowbray Cres.		
Clare Gdns., Stan.	95	CJ50
Clare Hill, Esher	214	CB107
Clare La. N1	142	DQ66
Clare Lawn Ave. SW14	178	CR85
Clare Mkt. WC2	**274**	**B9**
Clare Ms. SW6	160	DB80
Waterford Rd.		
Clare Pk., Amer.	55	AS40
Clare Pl. SW15	179	CT86
Minstead Gdns.		
Clare Rd. E11	123	ED58
Clare Rd. NW10	139	CU66
Clare Rd. SE14	163	DZ82
Clare Rd., Grnf.	137	CD65
Clare Rd., Houns.	156	BZ83
Clare Rd., Maid.	130	AJ72
Clare Rd., Stai.	174	BK88
Clare St. E2	142	DV68
Clare Way, Bexh.	166	EY81
Clare Way, Sev.	257	FJ128
Clare Wd., Lthd.	231	CH118
Claredale, Wok.	226	AY119
Claremont Ave.		
Claredale St. E2	142	DV68
Claremont, St.Alb.	60	CA31
Claremont (Cheshunt), Wal.Cr.	66	DT29
Claremont Ave., Esher	214	BZ107
Claremont Ave., Har.	118	CL57
Claremont Ave., N.Mal.	199	CV99
Claremont Ave., Sun.	195	BV95
Claremont Ave., Walt.	214	BX105
Claremont Ave., Wok.	226	AY119
Claremont Clo. E16	145	EN74
Claremont Clo. N1	**274**	**D1**
Claremont Clo. N1	141	DN68
Claremont Clo. SW2	181	DL88
Streatham Hill		
Claremont Clo., Grays	170	GC76
Premier Ave.		
Claremont Clo., Orp.	223	EN105
Hilda Vale Rd.		
Claremont Clo., S.Croy.	236	DV115
Claremont Clo., Walt.	214	BW106
Claremont Ct., Dor.	263	CH137
Claremont Cres., Dart.	167	FE84
Claremont Cres., Rick.	75	BQ43
Claremont Dr., Esher	214	CB108
Claremont Dr., Shep.	195	BP100
Claremont Dr., Wok.	226	AY119
Claremont End, Esher	214	CB107
Claremont Gdns., Ilf.	125	ES61
Claremont Gdns., Surb.	198	CL99
Claremont Gdns., Upmin.	129	FR60
Claremont Gro. W4	158	CS80
Edensor Gdns.		
Claremont Gro., Wdf.Grn.	102	EJ51
Claremont La., Esher	214	CB105
Claremont Pk. N3	97	CY53
Claremont Pk. Rd., Esher	214	CB107
Claremont Pl., Grav.	191	GH87
Cutmore St.		
Claremont Rd. E7	124	EH64
Claremont Rd. E11	123	ED62
Claremont Rd. E17	101	DY54
Claremont Rd. N6	121	DH59
Claremont Rd. NW2	119	CW59
Claremont Rd. W9	139	CZ68
Claremont Rd. W13	137	CG71
Claremont Rd., Barn.	80	DD37
Claremont Rd., Brom.	204	EL98
Claremont Rd., Croy.	202	DU102
Claremont Rd., Esher	215	CE108
Claremont Rd., Har.	95	CE54
Claremont Rd., Horn.	127	FG58
Claremont Rd., Red.	250	DG131
Claremont Rd., Stai.	173	BD92
Claremont Rd., Surb.	198	CL100
Claremont Rd., Swan.	187	FE94
Claremont Rd., Tedd.	177	CF92
Claremont Rd., Twick.	177	CH86
Claremont Rd., W.Byf.	212	BG112
Claremont Rd., Wind.	151	AQ82
Claremont Sq. N1	**274**	**D1**
Claremont Sq. N1	141	DN68
Claremont St. E16	145	EN74
Claremont St. N18	100	DU51
Claremont St. SE10	163	EB79
Claremont Way NW2	119	CW60
Claremount Clo., Epsom	233	CW117
Claremount Gdns., Epsom	233	CW117
Clarence Ave. SW4	181	DK87
Clarence Ave., Brom.	204	EL98
Clarence Ave., Ilf.	125	EN58
Clarence Ave., N.Mal.	198	CQ96
Clarence Ave., Upmin.	128	FN61
Clarence Clo., Walt.	213	BV105
Clarence Clo. (Bushey), Wat.	95	CF45
Clarence Ct., Egh.	173	AZ93
Clarence St.		
Clarence Ct., Horl.	269	DK147
Clarence Way		
Clarence Cres. SW4	181	DK86
Clarence Cres., Sid.	186	EV90
Clarence Cres., Wind.	151	AQ81
Clarence Dr., Egh.	172	AW91
Clarence Gdns. NW1	**273**	**J3**
Clarence Gdns. NW1	141	DH69
Clarence La. SW15	178	CS86
Clarence Ms. E5	122	DV64
Clarence Ms. SE16	143	DX74
Rotherhithe St.		
Clarence Pas. NW1	**273**	**P1**
Clarence Pl. E5	122	DV64
Clarence Pl., Grav.	191	GH87
Clarence Rd. E5	122	DV63
Clarence Rd. E12	124	EK64
Clarence Rd. E16	144	EE70
Clarence Rd. E17	101	DX54
Clarence Rd. N15	122	DQ57
Clarence Rd. N22	99	DL52
Clarence Rd. NW6	139	CZ66
Clarence Rd. SE9	184	EL89
Clarence Rd. SW19	180	DB93
Clarence Rd. W4	158	CN78
Clarence Rd., Berk.	38	AW19
Clarence Rd., Bexh.	166	EY84
Clarence Rd., Brwd.	108	FV44
Clarence Rd., Brom.	204	EK97
Clarence Rd., Croy.	202	DR101
Clarence Rd., Enf.	82	DV43
Clarence Rd., Grays	170	GB78
Clarence Rd., Red.	266	DD137
Clarence Rd., Rich.	158	CM81
Clarence Rd., St.Alb.	43	CF20
Clarence Rd., Sid.	186	EV90
Clarence Rd., Sutt.	218	DB105
Clarence Rd., Tedd.	177	CF93
Clarence Rd., Wall.	219	DH106
Clarence Rd., Walt.	213	BV105
Clarence Rd., West.	239	EM118
Clarence Rd., Wind.	151	AN81
Clarence Row, Grav.	191	GH87
Clarence St., Egh.	173	AZ93
Clarence St., Kings.T.	198	CL96
Clarence St., Rich.	158	CL84
Clarence St., Sthl.	156	BX76
Clarence St., Stai.	173	BE91
Clarence Ter. NW1	**272**	**E4**
Clarence Ter., Houns.	156	CB84
Clarence Wk. SW4	161	DL82
Clarence Wk., Red.	266	DD137
Clarence Way NW1	141	DH66
Clarence Way, Horl.	269	DK147
Clarence Way Est. NW1	141	DH66
Clarenden Pl., Dart.	187	FE92
Clarendon Clo. W2	**272**	**B10**
Clarendon Clo., Orp.	206	EU97
Clarendon Ct., Slou.	132	AV73
Clarendon Cres. W11	139	CY73
Clarendon Rd.		
Clarendon Cres., Twick.	177	CD90
Clarendon Cross W11	139	CY73
Portland Rd.		
Clarendon Dr. SW15	159	CW83
Clarendon Gdns. NW4	119	CU55
Clarendon Gdns. W9	140	DC70
Clarendon Gdns., Dart.	189	FR87
Clarendon Gdns., Ilf.	125	EM60
Clarendon Gdns., Wem.	117	CK62
Clarendon Grn., Orp.	206	EU97
Clarendon Gro. NW1	**273**	**M2**
Clarendon Gro., Mitch.	200	DF97
Clarendon Gro., Orp.	206	EU98
Clarendon Ms. W2	**272**	**B10**
Clarendon Ms., Bex.	187	FB88
Bexley High St.		
Clarendon Ms., Borwd.	78	CN41
Clarendon Rd.		
Clarendon Path, Orp.	206	EU97
Clarendon Pl. W2	**272**	**B10**
Clarendon Pl. W2	140	DE73
Clarendon Ri. SE13	163	EC83
Clarendon Rd. E11	123	ED60
Clarendon Rd. E17	123	EB58
Clarendon Rd. E18	124	EG55
Clarendon Rd. N8	121	DM55
Clarendon Rd. N15	121	DP56
Clarendon Rd. N18	100	DU51
Clarendon Rd. N22	99	DM54
Clarendon Rd. SW19	180	DE94
Clarendon Rd. W5	138	CL70
Clarendon Rd. W11	139	CY73
Clarendon Rd., Ashf.	174	BM91
Clarendon Rd., Borwd.	78	CN41
Clarendon Rd., Croy.	201	DP103
Clarendon Rd., Grav.	191	GJ86
Clarendon Rd., Har.	117	CE58
Clarendon Rd., Hayes	155	BT75
Clarendon Rd., Red.	250	DF133
Clarendon Rd., Sev.	256	FG124
Clarendon Rd., Wall.	219	DJ107
Clarendon Rd. (Cheshunt), Wal.Cr.	67	DX29
Clarendon Rd., Wat.	75	BV40
Clarendon St. SW1	**277**	**J10**
Clarendon St. SW1	161	DH78
Clarendon Ter. W9	140	DC70
Lanark Pl.		
Clarendon Wk. W11	139	CY72
Lancaster Rd.		
Clarendon Way N21	82	DQ44
Clarendon Way, Chis.	205	ET97
Clarendon Way, Orp.	206	EU97
Clarens St. SE6	183	DZ89
Claret Gdns. SE25	202	DS98
Clareville Gro. SW7	160	DC77
Clareville Rd., Cat.	236	DU124
Clareville Rd., Orp.	205	EQ103
Clareville St. SW7	160	DC77
Clarewood Wk. SW9	161	DN84
Somerleyton Rd.		
Clarges Ms. W1	**277**	**H2**
Clarges Ms. W1	141	DH74
Clarges St. W1	**277**	**J2**
Clarges St. W1	141	DH74
Claribel Rd. SW9	161	DP82
Clarice Way, Wall.	219	DL109
Claridge Rd., Dag.	126	EX60
Clarina Rd. SE20	183	DX94
Evelina Rd.		
Clarissa Rd., Rom.	126	EX59
Clarissa St. E8	142	DT67
Clark Clo., Erith	167	FG81
Forest Rd.		
Clark St. E1	142	DV71
Clark Way, Houns.	156	BX80
Clarke Grn., Wat.	75	BU35
Clarke Path N16	122	DU60
Braydon Rd.		
Clarke Way, Wat.	75	BU35
Clarkebourne Dr., Grays	170	GD79
Clarkes Ave., Wor.Pk.	199	CX102
Clarkes Dr., Uxb.	134	BL71
Clarke's Ms. W1	**272**	**G6**
Clarkes Rd., Hat.	45	CV17
Clarkfield, Rick.	92	BH46
Clarkhill, Harl.	51	ES19
Clarks La., Epp.	69	ET31
Clarks La., Sev.	224	EZ112
Clarks La., Warl.	238	EF123
Clarks La., West.	238	EJ123
Clarks Mead (Bushey), Wat.	94	CC45
Clarks Pl. EC2	**275**	**M8**
Clarks Pl. EC2	142	DS72
Clarks Rd., Ilf.	125	ER61
Clarkson Rd. E16	144	EF72
Clarkson St. E2	142	DV69
Clarksons, The, Bark.	145	EQ68
Classon Clo., West Dr.	154	BL75
Claston Clo., Dart.	167	FE84
Iron Mill La.		
Claude Rd. E10	123	EC61
Claude Rd. E13	144	EH67
Claude Rd. SE15	162	DV82
Claude St. E14	163	EA77
Claudia Jones Way SW2	181	DL86
Claudia Pl. SW19	179	CY88
Claudian Pl., St.Alb.	42	CA21
Claudian Way, Grays	171	GH76
Claughton Rd. E13	144	EJ68
Claughton Way, Brwd.	109	GD44
Clauson Ave., Nthlt.	116	CB64
Clave St. E1	142	DV74
Cinnamon St.		
Clavell St. SE10	163	EC79
Claverdale Rd. SW2	181	DM87
Claverhambury Rd., Wal.Abb.	68	EF29
Clavering Ave. SW13	159	CV79
Clavering Clo., Twick.	177	CG91
Clavering Rd. E12	124	EK60
Clavering Way, Brwd.	109	GC44
Poplar Dr.		
Claverings Ind. Est. N9	101	DX47
Claverley Gro. N3	98	DB53
Claverley Vill. N3	98	DB52
Claverley Gro.		
Claverton Clo., Hem.H.	40	BK19
Claverton St. SW1	161	DJ78
Claxton Gro. W6	159	CX78
Clay Acre, Chesh.	54	AR30
Clay Ave., Mitch.	201	DH96
Clay Hill, Enf.	81	DP37
Clay La., Edg.	96	CP47
Clay La., Epsom	232	CP124
Clay La., Guil.	243	BA129
Clay La., Red.	267	DJ135
Clay La., Stai.	174	BM87
Clay La. (Bushey), Wat.	95	CE45
Clay Rd., The, Loug.	84	EK39
Clay St. W1	**272**	**E7**
Clay St., Beac.	88	AJ48
Clay Tye Rd., Upmin.	129	FW64
Claybank Gro. SE13	163	EB83
Algernon Rd.		
Claybourne Ms. SE19	182	DS94
Church Rd.		
Claybridge Rd. SE12	184	EJ91
Claybrook Clo. N2	120	DD55
Long La.		
Claybrook Rd. W6	159	CX79
Clayburn Gdns., S.Ock.	149	FV73
Claybury (Bushey), Wat.	94	CB45
Claybury Bdy., Ilf.	124	EL55
Claybury Rd., Wdf.Grn.	102	EL52
Claycroft, Welw.G.C.	30	DB08
Claydon Dr., Croy.	219	DL105
Claydon End, Ger.Cr.	112	AY55
Claydon La., Ger.Cr.	112	AY55
Claydon Rd., Wok.	226	AU116
Clayfarm Rd. SE9	185	EQ89
Clayfields, H.Wyc.	88	AC45
Claygate Clo., Horn.	127	FG63
Claygate Cres., Croy.	221	EC107
Claygate La., Esher	197	CG104
Claygate La., T.Ditt.	197	CG102
Claygate La., Wal.Abb.	67	EC30
Claygate Lo. Clo., Esher	215	CE108
Claygate Rd. W13	157	CH76
Claygate Rd., Dor.	263	CH139
Clayhall Ave., Ilf.	124	EL55
Clayhall La., Reig.	265	CX138
Clayhall La., Wind.	172	AT85
Clayhanger, Guil.	243	BC132
Kingfisher Dr.		
Clayhill, Surb.	198	CN99
Clayhill Clo., Reig.	265	CU141
Clayhill Cres. SE9	184	EK91
Clayhill Rd., Reig.	264	CS143
Claylands Pl. SW8	161	DN80
Claylands Rd. SW8	161	DM79
Claymill Ho. SE18	165	EQ78
Claymore, Hem.H.	40	BL16
Claymore Clo., Mord.	200	DA101
Claypit Hill, Wal.Abb.	84	EJ36
Claypole Dr., Houns.	156	BY81
Vicarage Fm. Rd.		
Claypole Rd. E15	143	EC68
Clayponds Ave., Brent.	158	CL77
Clayponds Gdns. W5	157	CK77
Clayponds La., Brent.	158	CL78
Clays La. E15	123	EB64
Clay's La., Loug.	85	EN39
Clays La. Clo. E15	123	EB64
Clayside, Chig.	103	EQ50
Clayton Ave., Upmin.	128	FP64
Clayton Ave., Wem.	138	CL66
Clayton Clo. E6	145	EM72
Brandreth Rd.		
Clayton Cres., Brent.	157	CK78
Clayton Cft. Rd., Dart.	187	FG89
Clayton Dr., Guil.	242	AT131
Clayton Fld. NW9	96	CS52
Clayton Ms. SE10	163	ED81
Hyde Vale		
Clayton Rd. SE15	162	DU81
Clayton Rd., Chess.	215	CJ105
Clayton Rd., Epsom	216	CS113
Clayton Rd., Hayes	155	BS75
Clayton Rd., Islw.	157	CE83
Clayton Rd., Rom.	127	FC60
Clayton St. SE11	161	DN79
Clayton Ter., Hayes	136	BX71
Jollys La.		
Clayton Wk., Amer.	72	AW39
Clayton Way, Uxb.	134	BK70
Claywood Clo., Orp.	205	ES101
Claywood La., Dart.	189	FX90
Clayworth Clo., Sid.	186	EV86
Cleall Ave., Wal.Abb.	67	EC34
Quaker La.		
Cleanthus Clo. SE18	165	EP81
Cleanthus Rd.		
Cleanthus Rd. SE18	165	EP81
Clearbrook Way E1	143	DX72
West Arbour St.		
Cleardene, Dor.	263	CH136
Cleardown, Wok.	227	BB118
Clears, The, Reig.	249	CY132
Clearwater Ter. W11	159	CX75
Lorne Gdns.		
Clearwell Dr. W9	140	DB70
Cleave Ave., Hayes	155	BS77
Cleave Ave., Orp.	223	ES107
Cleave Prior, Couls.	234	DE119
Cleaveland Rd., Surb.	197	CK99
Cleaver Sq. SE11	**278**	**E10**
Cleaver Sq. SE11	161	DN78
Cleaver St. SE11	**278**	**E10**
Cleaver St. SE11	161	DN78
Cleaverholme Clo. SE25	202	DV100
Cleeve, The, Guil.	243	BA134
Cleeve Ct., Felt.	175	BS88
Kilross Rd.		
Cleeve Hill SE23	182	DV88
Cleeve Pk. Gdns., Sid.	186	EV89
Cleeve Rd., Lthd.	231	CF120
Clegg St. E1	142	DV74
Prusom St.		
Clegg St. E13	144	EG68
Cleland Path, Loug.	85	EP39
Cleland Rd., Ger.Cr.	90	AX54
Clem Attlee Ct. SW6	159	CZ79
Clem Attlee Par. SW6	159	CZ79
Clem Attlee Ct.		
Clematis Clo., Rom.	106	FJ52
Clematis Gdns., Wdf.Grn.	102	EG50
Harts Gro.		
Clematis St. W12	139	CU73
Clemence St. E14	143	DZ71
Clement Ave. SW4	161	DK84
Clapham High St.		
Clement Clo. NW6	139	CW66
Clement Clo. W4	158	CR77
Acton La.		
Clement Clo., Pur.	235	DP116
Croftleigh Ave.		
Clement Gdns., Hayes	155	BS77
Clement Rd. SW19	179	CY92
Clement Rd., Beck.	203	DX96
Clement Rd. (Cheshunt), Wal.Cr.	67	DY27
Clement St., Swan.	188	FJ93
Clement Way, Upmin.	128	FM62
Clementhorpe Rd., Dag.	146	EW65
Clementina Rd. E10	123	DZ60
Clementine Clo. W13	157	CH75
Balfour Rd.		
Clements Ave. E16	144	EG73
Clements Clo., Slou.	152	AV75
Clements Ct., Houns.	156	BX84
Clement's Inn WC2	**274**	**C9**
Clement's Inn WC2	141	DM72
Clement's Inn Pas. WC2	**274**	**C9**
Clements La. EC4	**275**	**L10**
Clements La. EC4	142	DR73
Clements La., Ilf.	125	EP62
Clements Mead, Lthd.	231	CG119
Clements Pl., Brent.	157	CK78
Clements Rd. E6	144	EL66
Clements Rd. SE16	162	DU76
Clements Rd., Ilf.	125	EP62
Clements Rd., Rick.	73	BD43
Clements Rd., Walt.	195	BV103
Clements St., Ware	33	DY06
Clenches Fm. La., Sev.	256	FG126
Clenches Fm. Rd., Sev.	256	FG126
Clendon Way SE18	165	ER77
Polthorne Gro.		
Clennam St. SE1	**279**	**J4**
Clensham La., Sutt.	200	DA103
Clenston Ms. W1	**272**	**D8**
Clephane Rd. N1	142	DQ65
Clere St. EC2	**275**	**L4**
Clerics Wk., Shep.	195	BR100
Gordon Rd.		
Clerkenwell Clo. EC1	**274**	**E4**
Clerkenwell Clo. EC1	141	DN70
Clerkenwell Grn. EC1	**274**	**E5**
Clerkenwell Grn. EC1	141	DN70
Clerkenwell Rd. EC1	**274**	**D5**
Clerkenwell Rd. EC1	141	DN70
Clerks Cft., Red.	252	DR133
Clerks Piece, Loug.	85	EM41
Clermont Rd. E9	142	DW67
Cleve Rd. NW6	140	DA66
Cleve Rd., Sid.	186	EX90
Clevedon, Wey.	213	BR106
Clevedon Clo. N16	122	DT62
Smalley Clo.		
Clevedon Gdns., Hayes	155	BR76
Clevedon Gdns., Houns.	155	BV81
Clevedon Rd. SE20	203	DX95
Clevedon Rd., Kings.T.	198	CN96
Clevedon Rd., Twick.	177	CK86
Clevehurst Clo., Slou.	132	AU65
Cleveland, Hem.H.	41	BP18
Cleveland Ave. SW20	199	CZ96
Cleveland Ave. W4	159	CT77
Cleveland Ave., Hmptn.	176	BZ94
Cleveland Clo., H.Wyc.	110	AE55
Wootton Way		
Cleveland Clo., Walt.	195	BV104
Cleveland Cres., Borwd.	78	CQ43
Cleveland Dr., Stai.	194	BH96
Cleveland Gdns. N4	122	DQ57
Cleveland Gdns. NW2	119	CX61
Cleveland Gdns. SW13	159	CT82
Cleveland Gdns. W2	140	DC72
Cleveland Gdns., Wor.Pk.	198	CS103
Cleveland Gro. E1	142	DW70
Cleveland Way		
Cleveland Ms. W1	**273**	**K6**
Cleveland Pk., Stai.	174	BL86
Northumberland Clo.		
Cleveland Pk. Ave. E17	123	EA56
Cleveland Pk. Cres. E17	123	EA56
Cleveland Pl. SW1	**277**	**L2**
Cleveland Ri., Mord.	199	CX101
Cleveland Rd. E18	124	EG55
Cleveland Rd. N1	142	DR66
Cleveland Rd. N9	100	DV45
Cleveland Rd. SW13	159	CT82
Cleveland Rd. W4	158	CQ76
Antrobus Rd.		
Cleveland Rd. W13	137	CG71
Cleveland Rd., Ilf.	125	EP62
Cleveland Rd., Islw.	157	CG84
Cleveland Rd., N.Mal.	198	CS98
Cleveland Rd., Uxb.	134	BK68
Cleveland Rd., Well.	165	ET82
Cleveland Rd., Wor.Pk.	198	CS103
Cleveland Row SW1	**277**	**K3**
Cleveland Row SW1	141	DJ74
Cleveland Sq. W2	140	DC72
Cleveland St. W1	**273**	**J5**
Cleveland St. W1	141	DH70
Cleveland Ter. W2	140	DC72
Cleveland Way E1	142	DW70
Cleveley Clo. SE7	164	EK77
Cleveley Cres. W5	138	CL68
Cleveleys Rd. E5	122	DV62
Cleverley Est. W12	139	CU74
Cleves Ave., Epsom	217	CV109
Cleves Clo., Cob.	213	BV114
Cleves Clo., Loug.	84	EL44
Roding Rd.		
Cleves Ct., Wind.	151	AM83
Cleves Cres., Croy.	221	EC111
Cleves Rd. E6	144	EK67
Cleves Rd., Hem.H.	41	BP15
Cleves Rd., Rich.	177	CJ90
Cleves Wk., Ilf.	103	EQ52
Cleves Way, Hmptn.	176	BZ94
Cleves Way, Ruis.	116	BX60
Cleves Way, Sun.	175	BT93
Cleves Wd., Wey.	213	BS105
Clewer Ave., Wind.	151	AN82
Clewer Ct. Rd., Wind.	151	AN80
Clewer Cres., Har.	95	CD53
Clewer Flds., Wind.	151	AQ81
Clewer Hill Rd., Wind.	151	AL82
Clewer New Town, Wind.	151	AN82
Clewer Pk., Wind.	151	AN80
Clichy Est. E1	142	DW71
Clifden Rd. E5	122	DW64
Clifden Rd., Brent.	157	CK79
Clifden Rd., Twick.	177	CF88
Cliff End, Pur.	219	DP112
Cliff Pl., S.Ock.	149	FX69
Cliff Rd. NW1	141	DK65
Cliff Ter. SE8	163	EA82
Cliff Vill. NW1	141	DK65
Cliff Wk. E16	144	EF70
Cliffe Rd., S.Croy.	220	DR106
Cliffe Wk., Sutt.	218	DC106
Turnpike La.		
Clifford Ave. SW14	158	CP83
Clifford Ave., Chis.	185	EM93
Clifford Ave., Ilf.	103	EP53
Clifford Ave., Wall.	219	DJ105
Clifford Clo., Nthlt.	136	BY67
Clifford Dr. SW9	161	DP84
Clifford Gdns. NW10	139	CW68
Clifford Gro., Ashf.	174	BN91
Clifford Manor Rd., Guil.	258	AY138
Clifford Rd. E16	144	EF70
Clifford Rd. E17	101	EC54
Clifford Rd. N9	82	DW44
Clifford Rd. SE25	202	DU98
Clifford Rd., Barn.	80	DB41
Clifford Rd., Grays	170	FZ76
Clifford Rd., Houns.	156	BX83
Clifford Rd., Rich.	177	CK89
Clifford Rd., Wem.	137	CK67
Clifford St. W1	**277**	**K1**
Clifford St. W1	141	DJ73
Clifford Way NW10	119	CT63
Clifford's Inn Pas. EC4	**274**	**D9**
Cliffview Rd. SE13	163	EA83

Clifton Ave. E17 123 DX55
Clifton Ave. N3 97 CZ53
Clifton Ave. W12 159 CT75
Clifton Ave., Felt. 176 BW90
Clifton Ave., Stan. 95 CH54
Clifton Ave., Sutt. 218 DB111
Clifton Ave., Wem. 138 CM65
Clifton Clo., Add. 194 BH103
Clifton Clo., Cat. 236 DR123
Clifton Clo., Orp. 223 EQ106
Clifton Clo. (Cheshunt), Wal.Cr. 67 DY29
Clifton Ct. NW8 140 DD70
Edgware Rd.
Clifton Cres. SE15 162 DV80
Clifton Est. SE15 162 DV81
Consort Rd.
Clifton Gdns. N15 122 DT58
Clifton Gdns. NW11 119 CZ58
Clifton Gdns. W4 158 CR77
Chiswick High Rd.
Clifton Gdns. W9 140 DC70
Clifton Gdns., Enf. 81 DL42
Clifton Gdns., Uxb. 135 BP68
Clifton Gro. E8 142 DU65
Clifton Gro., Grav. 191 GH87
Clifton Hill NW8 140 DB68
Clifton Lawns, Amer. 55 AQ35
Clifton Marine Par., Grav. 191 GF86
Clifton Pk. Ave. SW20 199 CW96
Clifton Pl. SE16 162 DW75
Canon Beck Rd.
Clifton Pl. W2 272 A9
Clifton Pl. W2 140 DD72
Clifton Pl., Bans. 234 DA116
Court Rd.
Clifton Ri. SE14 163 DY80
Clifton Ri., Wind. 151 AK81
Clifton Rd. E7 144 EK65
Clifton Rd. E16 144 EE71
Clifton Rd. N3 98 DC53
Clifton Rd. N8 121 DK58
Clifton Rd. N22 99 DJ53
Clifton Rd. NW10 139 CU68
Clifton Rd. SE25 202 DR98
Clifton Rd. SW19 179 CX93
Clifton Rd. W9 140 DC70
Clifton Rd., Amer. 55 AP35
Clifton Rd., Couls. 235 DH115
Clifton Rd., Grav. 191 GG86
Clifton Rd., Grnf. 136 CC70
Clifton Rd., Har. 118 CM57
Clifton Rd., Horn. 127 FG58
Clifton Rd., Ilf. 125 ER58
Clifton Rd., Islw. 157 CD82
Clifton Rd., Kings.T. 178 CM94
Clifton Rd., Loug. 84 EL42
Clifton Rd., Sid. 185 ES91
Clifton Rd., Slou. 152 AV75
Clifton Rd., Sthl. 156 BY77
Clifton Rd., Tedd. 177 CE91
Clifton Rd., Wall. 219 DH106
Clifton Rd., Wat. 75 BV43
Clifton Rd., Well. 166 EW83
Clifton St. EC2 275 M6
Clifton St. EC2 142 DS70
Clifton St., St.Alb. 43 CE19
Clifton Ter. N4 121 DN61
Clifton Vill. W9 140 DC71
Clifton Wk. E6 144 EL71
Tollgate Rd.
Clifton Wk., Dart. 188 FP86
Osbourne Rd.
Clifton Way SE15 162 DW80
Clifton Way, Borwd. 78 CN39
Clifton Way, Brwd. 109 GD46
Clifton Way, Wem. 138 CL67
Clifton Way, Wok. 226 AT117
Cliftons La., Reig. 249 CX133
Cliftonville, Dor. 263 CH137
Climb, The, Rick. 74 BH44
Clinch Ct. E16 144 EG71
Brent Rd.
Cline Rd. N11 99 DJ51
Cline Rd., Guil. 259 AZ136
Clinger Ct. N1 142 DS67
Pitfield St.
Clink St. SE1 279 K2
Clink St. SE1 142 DQ74
Clinton Ave., E.Mol. 196 CC98
Clinton Ave., Well. 166 EU84
Clinton Cres., Ilf. 103 ES51
Clinton End, Hem.H. 41 BQ20
Clinton Rd. E3 143 DY69
Clinton Rd. E7 124 EG63
Clinton Rd. N15 122 DR56
Clinton Rd., Lthd. 231 CJ123
Clipper Boul., Dart. 169 FS83
Clipper Boul. W., Dart. 169 FR83
Clipper Clo. SE16 163 DX75
Kinburn St.
Clipper Cres., Grav. 191 GM91
Clipper Way SE13 163 EC84
Clippesby Clo., Chess. 216 CM107
Clipstone Ms. W1 273 K5
Clipstone Ms. W1 141 DJ71
Clipstone Rd., Houns. 156 CA83
Clipstone St. W1 273 J6
Clipstone St. W1 141 DH71
Clissold Clo. N2 120 DF55
Clissold Ct. N4 122 DQ61
Clissold Cres. N16 122 DR63
Clissold Rd. N16 122 DR62
Clitheroe Ave., Har. 116 CA60
Clitheroe Gdns., Wat. 94 BX48
Clitheroe Rd. SW9 161 DL82
Clitheroe Rd., Rom. 105 FC50
Clitherow Ave. W7 157 CG76
Clitherow Pas., Brent. 157 CH78
Clitherow Rd.
Clitherow Rd., Brent. 157 CH78
Clitterhouse Cres. NW2 119 CW60
Clitterhouse Rd. NW2 119 CW60
Clive Ave. N18 100 DU51
Claremont St.
Clive Ave., Dart. 187 FF86
Clive Clo., Pot.B. 63 CZ31
Clive Ct. W9 140 DC70
Maida Vale
Clive Ct., Slou. 151 AR75
Clive Pas. SE21 182 DR90
Clive Rd.
Clive Rd. SE21 182 DR90
Clive Rd. SW19 180 DE93
Clive Rd., Belv. 166 FA77
Clive Rd., Brwd. 107 FW52
Clive Rd., Enf. 82 DU42
Clive Rd., Esher 214 CB105
Clive Rd., Felt. 175 BU86
Clive Rd., Grav. 191 GH86
Clive Rd., Rom. 127 FH57
Clive Rd., Twick. 177 CF91
Clive Way, Enf. 82 DU42
Clive Way, Wat. 76 BW39
Cliveden Clo. N12 98 DC49
Woodside Ave.
Cliveden Clo., Brwd. 109 FZ45
Cliveden Pl. SW1 276 F8
Cliveden Pl. SW1 160 DG77
Cliveden Pl., Shep. 195 BQ100
Cliveden Rd. SW19 199 CZ95
Cliveden Rd., Maid. 130 AD69
Clivedon Ct. W13 137 CH71
Clivedon Rd. E4 102 EE50
Clivedon Rd., Slou. 110 AE64
Clivesdale Dr., Hayes 135 BU74
Cloak La. EC4 275 K10
Cloak La. EC4 142 DQ73
Clock Ho. La., Sev. 256 FG123
Lambarde Rd.
Clock Ho. Mead, Lthd. 214 CB114
Clock Ho. Rd., Beck. 203 DY97
Clock Twr. Ms. N1 142 DQ67
Arlington Ave.
Clock Twr. Pl. N7 141 DL65
Clock Twr. Rd., Islw. 157 CF83
Clockhouse Ave., Bark. 145 EQ67
Clockhouse Clo. SW19 179 CW90
Clockhouse Clo., W.Byf. 212 BM112
Clockhouse La., Ashf. 174 BN91
Clockhouse La., Felt. 175 BP90
Clockhouse La., Grays 170 FY75
Clockhouse La., Rom. 105 FB52
Clockhouse La. E., Egh. 173 BB94
Clockhouse La. W., Egh. 173 BA94
Cloister Clo., Rain. 147 FH70
Cloister Clo., Tedd. 177 CH92
Cloister Gdns. SE25 202 DV100
Cloister Gdns., Edg. 96 CQ50
Cloister Garth, Berk. 38 AW19
Cloister Garth, St.Alb. 43 CE24
Cloister Rd. NW2 119 CZ62
Cloister Rd. W3 138 CQ71
Cloister Wk., Hem.H. 40 BK18
Townsend
Cloisters, The SW9 161 DN81
Cloisters, The, Rick. 92 BL45
Cloisters, The (Bushey), Wat. 76 CB44
High St.
Cloisters, The, Welw.G.C. 29 CX09
Cloisters, The, Wok. 227 BB121
Cloisters Ave., Brom. 205 EM99
Cloisters Mall, Kings.T. 197 CK96
Union St.
Clonard Way, Pnr. 94 CA51
Clonbrock Rd. N16 122 DS63
Cloncurry St. SW6 159 CX82
Clonmel Clo., Har. 117 CD61
Clonmel Rd. SW6 159 CZ80
Clonmel Rd., Tedd. 177 CD91
Clonmel Way, Slou. 130 AH69
Clonmell Rd. N17 122 DR55
Clonmore St. SW18 179 CZ88
Cloonmore Ave., Orp. 223 ET105
Clorane Gdns. NW3 120 DA62
Close, The E4 101 EC52
Beech Hall Rd.
Close, The N14 99 DK47
Close, The N20 97 CZ47
Close, The SE3 163 ED82
Heath La.
Close, The, Barn. 80 DF44
Close, The, Beck. 203 DY98
Close, The, Bet. 264 CP138
Close, The, Bex. 186 FA86
Close, The, Brwd. 108 FX48
Close, The, Cars. 218 DE109
Close, The, Dart. 188 FJ90
Close, The, Grays 170 GC75
Close, The, Guil. 259 BB144
Close, The, Har. 94 CC54
Harrow Vw.
Close, The, Hat. 63 CY26
Close, The, Horl. 269 DJ150
Close, The, Islw. 157 CD82
Close, The, Iver 133 BC69
Close, The, Mitch. 200 DF98
Close, The, N.Mal. 198 CQ96
Close, The, Orp. 205 ES100
Close, The (Eastcote), Pnr. 116 BW59
Close, The (Rayners La.), Pnr. 116 BZ59
Close, The, Pot.B. 64 DA32
Close, The (Pampisford Rd.), Pur. 219 DP110
Close, The (Russell Hill), Pur. 219 DM110
Close, The, Rad. 61 CF33
Close, The, Reig. 266 DB135
Close, The, Rich. 158 CP83
Close, The, Rick. 92 BJ46
Mount Vw.
Close, The, Rom. 126 EY58
Close, The, Sev. 256 FE124
Close, The, Sid. 186 EV91
Close, The, Slou. 131 AK73
St. George's Cres.
Close, The, Sutt. 199 CZ101
Close, The, Uxb. 134 BL66
Close, The (Hillingdon), Uxb. 134 BN67
Close, The, Vir.W. 192 AX99
Close, The, Ware 33 DY06
Close, The (Bushey), Wat. 76 CB43
Close, The (Barnhill Rd.), Wem. 118 CQ62
Close, The (Lyon Pk. Ave.), Wem. 138 CL65
Close, The, W.Byf. 212 BG113
Closemead Clo., Nthwd. 93 BQ51
Cloth Ct. EC1 274 G7
Cloth Fair EC1 274 G7
Cloth Fair EC1 141 DP71
Cloth St. EC1 275 H6
Clothier St. E1 142 DS72
Cutler St.
Clothworkers Rd. SE18 165 ER80
Cloudberry Rd., Rom. 106 FK51
Cloudesdale Rd. SW17 181 DH89
Cloudesley Pl. N1 141 DN67
Cloudesley Rd. N1 141 DN67
Cloudesley Rd., Bexh. 166 EZ81
Cloudesley Rd., Erith 167 FF81
Cloudesley Sq. N1 141 DN67
Cloudesley St. N1 141 DN67
Clouston Clo., Wall. 219 DL106
Clova Rd. E7 144 EF65
Clove Cres. E14 143 ED73
Clove Hitch Quay SW11 160 DC83
Cotton Row
Clove St. E13 144 EG70
Barking Rd.
Clovelly Ave. NW9 119 CT56
Clovelly Ave., Uxb. 115 BQ63
Clovelly Ave., Warl. 236 DV118
Clovelly Clo., Pnr. 115 BV55
Clovelly Clo., Uxb. 115 BQ63
Clovelly Ct., Horn. 128 FM61
Clovelly Gdns. SE19 202 DT95
Clovelly Gdns., Enf. 100 DS45
Clovelly Gdns., Rom. 105 FB53
Clovelly Rd. N8 121 DK56
Clovelly Rd. W4 158 CR75
Clovelly Rd. W5 157 CJ75
Clovelly Rd., Bexh. 166 EY79
Clovelly Rd., Houns. 156 BZ82
Clovelly Way E1 142 DW72
Jamaica St.
Clovelly Way, Har. 116 BZ61
Clovelly Way, Orp. 205 ET100
Clover Clo. E11 123 ED61
Clover Ct., Grays 170 GD79
Churchill Rd.
Clover Ct., Wok. 226 AX118
Clover Fld., Harl. 52 EU18
Clover Hill, Couls. 235 DH121
Clover Lea, Gdmg. 258 AS143
Clover Leas, Epp. 69 ET30
Clover Ms. SW3 160 DF79
Dilke St.
Clover Rd., Guil. 242 AS133
Clover Way, Hem.H. 40 BH19
Gadebridge Rd.
Clover Way, Wall. 200 DG102
Cloverdale Gdns., Sid. 185 ET86
Cloverfield, Welw.G.C. 29 CZ06
Cloverland, Hat. 45 CT21
Cloverleys (Park Hill), Loug. 84 EK43
Clovers, The, Grav. 190 GE91
Clowders Rd. SE6 183 DZ90
Clowser Clo., Sutt. 218 DC106
Turnpike La.
Cloyster Wd., Edg. 95 CK52
Cloysters Grn. E1 142 DU74
Thomas More St.
Club Gdns. Rd., Brom. 204 EG101
Club Row E1 275 P4
Club Row E1 142 DT70
Club Row E2 275 P4
Club Row E2 142 DT70
Clump, The, Rick. 74 BG43
Clump Ave., Tad. 248 CQ131
Clumps, The, Ashf. 175 BR91
Clumps, The, Felt. 175 BR91
Clunas Gdns., Rom. 128 FK55
Clunbury Ave., Sthl. 156 BZ78
Clunbury St. N1 275 L1
Clunbury St. N1 142 DR68
Cluny Est. SE1 279 M6
Cluny Ms. SW5 160 DA77
Cluny Pl. SE1 279 M6
Cluse Ct. N1 142 DQ68
Dame St.
Clutterbucks, Rick. 74 BG36
Clutton St. E14 143 EB71
Clydach Rd., Enf. 82 DT42
Clyde Ave., S.Croy. 236 DV115
Clyde Circ. N15 122 DS56
Clyde Clo., Red. 250 DG133
Clyde Ct., Red. 250 DG133
Clyde Clo.
Clyde Cres., Upmin. 129 FS58
Clyde Pl. E10 123 EB59
Clyde Rd. N15 122 DS56
Clyde Rd. N22 99 DK53
Clyde Rd., Croy. 202 DT103
Clyde Rd., Hodd. 49 ED19
Clyde Rd., Stai. 174 BK88
Clyde Rd., Sutt. 218 DA106
Clyde Rd., Wall. 219 DJ107
Clyde Sq., Hem.H. 40 BM15
Clyde St. SE8 163 DZ79
Clyde Ter. SE23 182 DW89
Clyde Ter., Hert. 32 DU09
Clyde Vale SE23 182 DW89
Clyde Way, Rom. 105 FE52
Clyde Way, Stai. 193 BE95
Clydesdale, Enf. 83 DX42
Clydesdale Ave., Stan. 117 CK55
Clydesdale Clo., Borwd. 78 CR43
Clydesdale Clo., Islw. 157 CF82
St. John's Rd.
Clydesdale Gdns., Rich. 158 CP84
Clydesdale Rd. W11 139 CZ72
Clydesdale Rd., Horn. 127 FF59
Clydesdale Wk., Brox. 67 DZ25
Tarpan Way
Clydon Clo., Erith 167 FE79
Clyfford Rd., Ruis. 115 BT63
Clyfton Clo., Brox. 49 DZ23
Clymping Dene, Felt. 175 BV87
Clyston Rd., Wat. 75 BT44
Clyston St. SW8 161 DJ82
Clyve Way, Stai. 193 BE95
Coach All., H.Wyc. 110 AF60
Coach & Horses Yd. W1 273 K10
Coach Ho. La. N5 121 DP63
Highbury Hill
Coach Ho. La. SW19 179 CX91
Coach Ho. Ms. SE23 182 DW86
Coach Ho. Yd. SW18 160 DB84
Ebner St.
Coach Rd., Bet. 248 CL134
Coach Rd., Cher. 211 BC107
Coachhouse Ms. SE20 182 DV94
Coachlands Ave., Guil. 242 AT134
Coal Rd., Grays 171 GL77
Coal Wf. Rd. W12 159 CX75
Shepherds Bush Pl.
Coaldale Wk. SE21 182 DQ87
Lairdale Clo.
Coalecroft Rd. SW15 159 CW84
Coalport Clo., Harl. 52 EX16
Kiln La.
Coast Hill, Dor. 262 BZ139
Coast Hill La., Dor. 262 CA138
Coat Wicks, Beac. 89 AQ51
Coate St. E2 142 DU68
Coates Dell, Wat. 60 BY33
Coates Hill Rd., Brom. 205 EN96
Coates Rd., Borwd. 95 CK45
Coates Wk., Brent. 158 CL78
Burford Rd.
Coates Way, Wat. 60 BX32
Cob Mead, Hat. 45 CV16
Cobb Clo., Borwd. 78 CQ43
Cobb Clo., Slou. 152 AX81
Cobb Grn., Wat. 59 BV32
Cobb Rd., Berk. 38 AT19
Cobb St. E1 275 P7
Cobb St. E1 142 DT71
Cobbett Clo., Enf. 82 DW36
Larmans Rd.
Cobbett Rd. SE9 164 EL83
Cobbett Rd., Guil. 242 AT133
Cobbett Rd., Twick. 176 CA88
Cobbett St. SW8 161 DM80
Cobbetts Ave., Ilf. 124 EK57
Cobbetts Clo., Wok. 226 AV117
Cobbetts Hill, Wey. 213 BP107
Cobbins, The, Wal.Abb. 68 EE33
Cobbins Orchard, Harl. 36 EY11
Cobbinsend Rd., Wal.Abb. 68 EK29
Cobblers Clo., Slou. 131 AP68
Cobblers Wk., E.Mol. 197 CH95
Cobblers Wk., Hmptn. 196 CC95
High St.
Cobblers Wk., Kings.T. 197 CG95
Cobblers Wk., Tedd. 177 CD94
Cobbles, The, Brwd. 108 FY47
Cobbles, The, Upmin. 129 FT59
Cobblestone Pl., Croy. 202 DQ102
Oakfield Rd.
Cobbold Est. NW10 139 CT65
Cobbold Rd. E11 124 EF62
Cobbold Rd. NW10 139 CT65
Cobbold Rd. W12 159 CT75
Cobb's Ct. EC4 141 DP72
Carter La.
Cobb's Rd., Houns. 156 BZ84
Cobden Clo., Uxb. 134 BJ67
Cobden Hill, Rad. 77 CH36
Cobden Rd. E11 124 EE62
Cobden Rd. SE25 202 DU99
Cobden Rd., Orp. 223 ER105
Cobden Rd., Sev. 257 FJ123
Cobham, Grays 170 GB75
Cobham Ave., N.Mal. 199 CU99
Cobham Clo. SW11 180 DE86
Cobham Clo., Brom. 204 EL101
Cobham Clo., Sid. 186 EV86
Park Mead
Cobham Clo., Wall. 219 DL107
Cobham Gate, Cob. 213 BV114
Cobham Ho., Bark. 145 EQ67
St. Margarets
Cobham Pk. Rd., Cob. 229 BV117
Cobham Pl., Bexh. 186 EY85
Cobham Rd. E17 101 EC53
Cobham Rd. N22 121 DP55
Cobham Rd., Cob. 230 CA117
Cobham Rd., Houns. 156 BW80
Cobham Rd., Ilf. 125 ES61
Cobham Rd., Kings.T. 198 CN96
Cobham Rd., Lthd. 230 CC121
Cobham Rd., Ware 33 DZ05
Cobham St., Grav. 191 GG87
Cobham Way, Lthd. 245 BS126
Cobill Clo., Horn. 128 FJ56
Cobland Rd. SE12 184 EJ91
Coborn Rd. E3 143 DZ69
Coborn St. E3 143 DZ69
Cobourg Rd. SE5 162 DT79
Cobourg St. NW1 273 L3
Cobourg St. NW1 141 DJ69
Cobs Way, Add. 212 BJ110
Cobsdene, Grav. 191 GK93
Miskin Way
Coburg Clo. SW1 277 L8
Coburg Cres. SW2 181 DM88
Coburg Gdns., Ilf. 102 EK54
Coburg Rd. N22 121 DM55
Cochrane Ms. NW8 272 A1
Cochrane Rd. SW19 179 CZ94
Cochrane St. NW8 272 A1
Cochrane St. NW8 140 DD68
Cock Grn., Harl. 51 EP17
Cock Hill E1 275 N7
Cock La. EC1 274 F7
Cock La. EC1 141 DP71
Cock La., Brox. 48 DU20
Cock La., Hodd. 49 DY19
Cock La., Lthd. 230 CC122
Cockayne Way SE8 163 DY77
Windlass Pl.
Cockbush Ave., Hert. 32 DU08
Cocker Rd., Enf. 82 DW36
Cockerhurst Rd., Sev. 225 FD107
Cockett Rd., Slou. 152 AY76
Cockfosters Rd., Barn. 80 DF41
Cockle Way, Rad. 62 CL32
Porters Pk. Dr.
Cockmannings La., Orp. 206 EX102
Cockmannings Rd., Orp. 206 EX101
Cockpit Steps SW1 277 N5
Cockpit Yd. WC1 274 C6
Cockrobin La., Harl. 35 EN08
Cockrobin La., Ware 35 EN05
Cocks Cres., N.Mal. 199 CT98
Cock's Yd., Uxb. 134 BJ66
Bakers Rd.
Cocksett Ave., Orp. 223 ES107
Cockshot Hill, Reig. 266 DB136
Cockshot Rd., Reig. 266 DB135
Cockspur Ct. SW1 277 N2
Cockspur St. SW1 277 N2
Cockspur St. SW1 141 DK74
Cocksure La., Sid. 186 FA90
Code St. E1 142 DT70
Codham Hall La., Brwd. 129 FV56
Codicote Dr., Wat. 60 BX34
Codicote Rd., St.Alb. 28 CL05
Codicote Row, Hem.H. 40 BN15
Codicote Ter. N4 122 DQ61
Green Las.
Codling Clo. E1 142 DU74
Torrington Pl.
Codling Way, Wem. 117 CK63
Codmore Cres., Chesh. 54 AS30
Codmore Wd. Rd., Chesh. 56 AX33
Codrington Ct., Wok. 226 AS118
Raglan Rd.
Codrington Cres., Grav. 191 GJ92
Codrington Gdns., Grav. 191 GK92
Codrington Hill SE23 183 DY87
Codrington Ms. W11 139 CY72
Blenheim Cres.
Cody Clo., Har. 117 CK55
Cody Clo., Wall. 219 DK108
Alcock Clo.
Cody Rd. E16 144 EE70
Coe Ave. SE25 202 DU100
Coe Spur, Slou. 151 AP75
Coe's All., Barn. 79 CY42
Wood St.
Cofers Circle, Wem. 118 CP62
Coftards, Slou. 132 AW72
Cogan Ave. E17 101 DY53
Coin St. SE1 278 D2
Coin St. SE1 141 DN74
Coity Rd. NW5 140 DG65
Coke St. E1 142 DU72
Cokers La. SE21 182 DR88
Perifield
Coke's Fm. La., Ch.St.G. 72 AV41
Coke's La., Amer. 72 AX40
Coke's La., Ch.St.G. 72 AW41
Colas Ms. NW6 140 DA67
Birchington Rd.
Colbeck Ms. SW7 160 DB77
Colbeck Rd., Har. 116 CC59
Colberg Pl. N16 122 DS59
Colborne Way, Wor.Pk. 199 CW104
Colbrook Ave., Hayes 155 BR76
Colbrook Clo., Hayes 155 BR76
Colburn Ave., Cat. 236 DT124
Colburn Ave., Pnr. 94 BY51
Colburn Cres., Guil. 243 BA131
Sutherland Dr.
Colburn Way, Sutt. 200 DD104
Colby Rd. SE19 182 DS92
Colby Rd., Walt. 195 BU102
Winchester Rd.
Colchester Ave. E12 125 EM62
Colchester Dr., Pnr. 116 BX57
Colchester Rd. E10 123 EC59
Colchester Rd. E17 123 EA58
Colchester Rd., Edg. 96 CQ52
Colchester Rd., Nthwd. 93 BU54
Colchester Rd., Rom. 106 FK53
Colchester St. E1 142 DT72
Braham St.
Colcokes Rd., Bans. 234 DA116
Cold Arbor Rd., Sev. 256 FB129
Cold Blow Cres., Bex. 187 FD88
Cold Blow La. SE14 163 DX80
Cold Blows, Mitch. 200 DF97
Cold Harbour E14 163 EC75
Coldbath Sq. EC1 274 D4
Coldbath St. SE13 163 EB81
Coldershaw Rd. W13 137 CG74
Coldfall Ave. N10 98 DF54
Coldham Gro., Enf. 83 DY37
Coldharbour Clo., Egh. 193 BC97
Coldharbour La. SE5 162 DQ83
Coldharbour La. SW9 161 DN84
Coldharbour La., Dor. 263 CE142
Coldharbour La., Egh. 193 BC97
Coldharbour La., Hayes 155 BT75
Coldharbour La., Pur. 219 DN110
Russell Hill Rd.
Coldharbour La., Rain. 147 FE72
Coldharbour La., Red. 252 DT134
Coldharbour La. (Bushey), Wat. 76 CB44
Coldharbour La., Wok. 227 BF115
Coldharbour Pl. SE5 162 DQ82
Denmark Hill
Coldharbour Rd., Croy. 219 DN106
Coldharbour Rd., Grav. 190 GE89
Coldharbour Rd., Harl. 51 EM16
Coldharbour Rd., W.Byf. 211 BF114
Coldharbour Rd., Wok. 227 BF115
Coldharbour Way, Croy. 219 DN106
Coldmoreham Yd., Amer. 55 AN39
Coldshott, Oxt. 254 EG133
Coldstream Gdns. SW18 179 CZ86
Cole Clo. SE28 146 EV74
Cole Gdns., Houns. 155 BU80
Cole Grn. Bypass, Hert. 30 DF13
Cole Grn. La., Welw.G.C. 29 CY11
Cole Grn. Way, Hert. 30 DF13
Cole Pk. Gdns., Twick. 177 CG86
Cole Pk. Rd., Twick. 177 CG87
Cole Pk. Vw., Twick. 177 CG86
Hill Vw. Rd.
Cole Rd., Twick. 177 CG86
Cole Rd., Wat. 75 BV39
Stamford Rd.
Cole St. SE1 279 J5
Cole St. SE1 162 DQ75
Colebeck Ms. N1 141 DP65
Colebert Ave. E1 142 DW70
Colebrook, Cher. 211 BD107
Colebrook Clo. SW15 179 CX87
West Hill
Colebrook Gdns., Loug. 85 EP40
Colebrook Ho. E14 143 EB72
Brabazon St.
Colebrook La., Loug. 85 EP40
Colebrook Path, Loug. 85 EP40
Colebrook La.
Colebrook Pl., Cher. 211 BC108
Guildford Rd.
Colebrook Rd. SW16 201 DL95
Colebrook Way N11 99 DH50
Colebrooke Ave. W13 137 CH72
Colebrooke Dr. E11 124 EH59
Colebrooke Pl. N1 141 DP67
St. Peters St.
Colebrooke Ri., Brom. 204 EE96
Colebrooke Rd., Red. 250 DE132
Colebrooke Row N1 274 F1
Colebrooke Row N1 141 DP68
Coleby Path SE5 162 DR80
Harris St.
Coledale Dr., Stan. 95 CJ53
Coleford Rd. SW18 180 DC85
Colegrave Rd. E15 123 ED64
Colegrove Rd. SE15 162 DT79
Coleherne Ct. SW5 160 DB78
Coleherne Ms. SW10 160 DB78
Coleherne Rd. SW10 160 DB78
Colehill Gdns. SW6 159 CY82
Fulham Palace Rd.
Colehill La. SW6 159 CY81
Colekitchen La., Guil. 261 BQ138
Coleman Clo. SE25 202 DU96
Warminster Rd.
Coleman Flds. N1 142 DQ67
Coleman Grn. La., St.Alb. 28 CM10
Coleman Rd. SE5 162 DS80
Coleman Rd., Belv. 166 FA77
Coleman Rd., Dag. 146 EY65

Coleman St. EC2 275 K8
Coleman St. EC2 142 DR72
Colemans Heath SE9 185 EN90
Colemans La., Ong. 71 FH30
Coleman's La., Wal.Abb. 67 ED26
Colenorton Cres. (Eton Wick), Wind. 151 AL77
Colenso Rd. E5 122 DW63
Colenso Rd., Ilf. 125 ES60
Colepits Wd. Rd. SE9 185 ER85
Coleraine Rd. N8 121 DN55
Coleraine Rd. SE3 164 EF79
Coleridge Ave. E12 144 EL65
Coleridge Ave., Sutt. 218 DE105
Coleridge Clo. SW8 161 DH82
Coleridge Clo. (Cheshunt), Wal.Cr. 66 DT27
Peakes La.
Coleridge Cres., Slou. 153 BE81
Coleridge Gdns. NW6 140 DC66
Fairhazel Gdns.
Coleridge La. N8 121 DL58
Coleridge Rd.
Coleridge Rd. E17 123 DZ56
Coleridge Rd. N4 121 DN61
Coleridge Rd. N8 121 DK58
Coleridge Rd. N12 98 DC50
Coleridge Rd., Ashf. 174 BL91
Coleridge Rd., Croy. 202 DW100
Coleridge Rd., Dart. 168 FN84
Coleridge Rd., Rom. 105 FH52
Coleridge Rd., Til. 171 GJ82
Coleridge Sq. W13 137 CG72
Berners Dr.
Coleridge Wk. NW11 120 DA56
Coleridge Wk., Brwd. 109 GC45
Coleridge Way, Hayes 135 BU72
Coleridge Way, Orp. 206 EU100
Coleridge Way, West Dr. 154 BL77
Coles Cres., Har. 116 CB61
Coles Grn., Loug. 85 EN39
Coles Grn. (Bushey), Wat. 94 CC46
Coles Grn. Ct. NW2 119 CU61
Coles Grn. Rd. NW2 119 CU60
Coles Hill, Hem.H. 40 BG18
Coles La., West. 240 EW123
Colesburg Rd., Beck. 203 DZ97
Colescroft Hill, Pur. 235 DN115
Colesdale (Cuffley), Pot.B. 65 DL30
Coleshill La., Amer. 88 AJ45
Coleshill Rd., Tedd. 177 CE93
Colesmead Rd., Red. 250 DF131
Colestown St. SW11 160 DE82
Colet Clo. N13 99 DP51
Colet Gdns. W14 159 CX78
Colet Rd., Brwd. 109 GC43
Colets Orchard, Sev. 241 FH116
Coley Ave., Wok. 227 BA118
Coley St. WC1 274 C5
Coley St. WC1 141 DM70
Colfe Rd. SE23 183 DY88
Colgrove, Welw.G.C. 29 CW10
Colham Ave., West Dr. 134 BL74
Colham Grn. Rd., Uxb. 134 BN71
Colham Mill Rd., West Dr. 154 BK75
Colham Rd., Uxb. 134 BM70
Colin Clo. NW9 118 CS56
Colin Clo., Croy. 203 DZ104
Colin Clo., Dart. 188 FP86
Colin Clo., W.Wick. 204 EF104
Colin Cres. NW9 119 CT56
Colin Dr. NW9 119 CT57
Colin Gdns. NW9 119 CT57
Colin Pk. Rd. NW9 118 CS55
Colin Rd. NW10 139 CU65
Colin Rd., Cat. 236 DU123
Colin Way, Slou. 151 AP76
Colina Ms. N15 121 DP57
Harringay Rd.
Colina Rd. N15 121 DP57
Colindale Ave. NW9 118 CR55
Colindale Ave., St.Alb. 43 CF21
Colindale Business Pk. NW9 118 CQ55
Colindeep Gdns. NW4 119 CU57
Colindeep La. NW4 119 CU56
Colindeep La. NW9 118 CS55
Colinette Rd. SW15 159 CW84
Colinswood Rd., Slou. 111 AP61
Colinton Rd., Ilf. 126 EV61
Coliston Pas. SW18 180 DA87
Coliston Rd.
Coliston Rd. SW18 180 DA87
Collamore Ave. SW18 180 DE88
Collapit Clo., Har. 116 CB58
Collard Ave., Loug. 85 EQ40
Collard Grn., Loug. 85 EQ40
Collard Ave.
College App. SE10 163 EC79
College Ave., Egh. 173 BB93
College Ave., Epsom 217 CT114
College Ave., Grays 170 GB77
College Ave., Har. 95 CE53
College Ave., Slou. 152 AS76
College Clo. E9 122 DW64
Median Rd.
College Clo. N18 100 DT50
College Clo., Add. 194 BK104
College Clo., Grays 170 GC77
College Clo., Har. 95 CE52
College Clo., Twick. 177 CD88
Meadway
College Clo., Ware 33 DX07
College Ct. (Cheshunt), Wal.Cr. 66 DW30
College Cres. NW3 140 DD65
College Cres., Red. 250 DG131
College Cres., Wind. 151 AP82
College Cross N1 141 DN66
College Dr., Ruis. 115 BU59
College Gdns. E4 101 EB45
College Gdns. N18 100 DT50
College Gdns. SE21 182 DS88
College Gdns. SW17 180 DE89
College Gdns., Enf. 82 DR39
College Gdns., Ilf. 124 EL57
College Gdns., N.Mal. 199 CT99
College Gate, Harl. 51 EQ15
College Grn. SE19 182 DS94
College Gro. NW1 141 DK67
St. Pancras Way
College Hill EC4 275 J10
College Hill Rd., Har. 95 CE52
College La. NW5 121 DH63
College La., Hat. 44 CS20
College La., Wok. 226 AW119
College Ms. SW1 277 P6
College Ms. SW18 180 DB85
St. Ann's Hill
College Pk. Clo. SE13 163 ED84
College Pk. Rd. N17 100 DT51
College Rd.
College Pl. E17 124 EE56
College Pl. NW1 141 DJ67
College Pl. SW10 160 DC80
Hortensia Rd.
College Pl., St.Alb. 42 CC20
College Pt. E15 144 EF65
Wolffe Gdns.
College Rd. E17 123 EC57
College Rd. N17 100 DT51
College Rd. N21 99 DN47
College Rd. NW10 139 CW68
College Rd. SE19 182 DT92
College Rd. SE21 182 DS87
College Rd. SW19 180 DD93
College Rd. W13 137 CH72
College Rd., Abb.L. 59 BT31
College Rd., Brom. 204 EG95
College Rd., Croy. 202 DR103
College Rd., Enf. 82 DR39
College Rd., Epsom 217 CU114
College Rd., Grav. 190 GB85
College Rd., Grays 170 GC77
College Rd., Guil. 258 AX135
College Rd. (Harrow on the Hill), Har. 117 CE58
College Rd. (Harrow Weald), Har. 95 CE53
College Rd., Hert. 32 DW13
College Rd., Hodd. 49 DZ15
College Rd., Islw. 157 CF81
College Rd., St.Alb. 43 CH21
College Rd., Slou. 131 AM74
College Rd., Swan. 207 FE95
College Rd. (Cheshunt), Wal.Cr. 66 DW30
College Rd., Wem. 117 CK60
College Rd., Wok. 227 BB116
College Row E9 123 DX64
Homerton High St.
College Slip, Brom. 204 EG95
College St. EC4 275 K10
College St., St.Alb. 43 CD20
College Ter. E3 143 DZ69
College Ter. N3 97 CZ54
Hendon La.
College Vw. SE9 184 EK88
College Wk., Kings.T. 198 CL96
Grange Rd.
College Way, Ashf. 174 BM91
College Way, Nthwd. 93 BR51
College Way, Welw.G.C. 29 CX08
College Yd. NW5 121 DH63
College La.
Collent St. E9 142 DW65
Coller Cres., Dart. 189 FS91
Colless Rd. N15 122 DT57
Collet Clo. (Cheshunt), Wal.Cr. 67 DX28
Collet Gdns. (Cheshunt), Wal.Cr. 67 DX28
Collet Clo.
Collett Rd. SE16 162 DU76
Collett Rd., Hem.H. 40 BJ20
Collett Rd., Ware 33 DX05
Collett Way, Sthl. 136 CB74
Colley Hill La., Slou. 112 AT62
Colley La., Reig. 249 CY133
Colley Manor Dr., Reig. 249 CX133
Colley Way, Reig. 249 CY131
Colleyland, Rick. 73 BD42
Collier Clo. E6 145 EP72
Ferndale St.
Collier Clo., Epsom 216 CN107
Collier Dr., Edg. 96 CN54
Collier Row La., Rom. 105 FB52
Collier Row Rd., Rom. 104 FA53
Collier St. N1 274 B1
Collier St. N1 141 DM68
Collier Way, Guil. 243 BD132
Colliers, Cat. 252 DU125
Colliers Clo., Wok. 226 AV117
Colliers Shaw, Kes. 222 EK106
Colliers Water La., Th.Hth. 201 DN99
Collindale Ave., Erith 167 FB79
Collindale Ave., Sid. 186 EU88
Collingbourne Rd. W12 139 CV74
Collingham Gdns. SW5 160 DB77
Collingham Pl. SW5 160 DB77
Collingham Rd. SW5 160 DB77
Collings Clo. N22 99 DM51
Whittington Rd.
Collington Clo., Grav. 190 GE87
Beresford Rd.
Collingtree Rd. SE26 182 DW91
Collingwood Ave. N10 120 DG55
Collingwood Ave., Surb. 198 CQ102
Collingwood Clo. SE20 202 DV95
Collingwood Clo., Horl. 269 DH147
Collingwood Clo., Twick. 176 CA87
Collingwood Cres., Guil. 243 BA133
Collingwood Dr., St.Alb. 61 CK25
Collingwood Pl., Walt. 195 BU104
Collingwood Rd. E17 123 EA58
Collingwood Rd. N15 122 DS56
Collingwood Rd., Mitch. 200 DE96
Collingwood Rd., Sutt. 199 CZ104
Collingwood Rd., Uxb. 135 BP70
Collingwood St. E1 142 DV70
Collins Ave., Stan. 96 CL54
Collins Dr., Ruis. 116 BW61
Collins Meadow, Harl. 51 EP15
Collins Rd. N5 122 DQ63
Collins Sq. SE3 164 EF82
Tranquil Vale
Collins St. SE3 164 EE82
Collins Way, Brwd. 109 GE43
Collin's Yd. N1 141 DP67
Islington Grn.
Collinson St. SE1 279 H5
Collinson Wk. SE1 279 H5
Collinwood Ave., Enf. 82 DW41
Collinwood Gdns., Ilf. 125 EM57
Colls Rd. SE15 162 DW81
Collum Grn. Rd., Slou. 111 AR62
Collyer Ave., Croy. 219 DL105
Collyer Pl. SE15 162 DU81
Peckham High St.
Collyer Rd., Croy. 219 DL105
Collyer Rd., St.Alb. 61 CJ27
Colman Clo., Epsom 233 CW117
Colman Rd. E16 144 EJ71
Colman Way, Red. 250 DE132
Colmans Hill, Guil. 261 BS144
Colmar Clo. E1 143 DX70
Alderney Rd.
Colmer Pl., Har. 95 CD52
Colmer Rd. SW16 201 DL95
Colmore Ms. SE15 162 DV81
Colmore Rd., Enf. 82 DW42
Colnbridge Clo., Stai. 173 BE91
Clarence St.
Colnbrook Bypass, Slou. 153 BB79
Colnbrook Bypass, West Dr. 154 BH80
Colnbrook Clo., St.Alb. 62 CL27
Barnet Rd.
Colnbrook Ct., Slou. 153 BF81
Colnbrook St. SE1 278 F7
Colnbrook St. SE1 161 DP76
Colndale Rd., Slou. 153 BE82
Colne Ave., Rick. 92 BG47
Colne Ave., Wat. 75 BV44
Colne Ave., West Dr. 154 BJ75
Colne Bank, Slou. 153 BC83
Colne Ct., Epsom 216 CQ105
Colne Dr., Rom. 106 FM51
Colne Dr., Walt. 196 BX104
Colne Gdns., St.Alb. 62 CL27
Colne Ho., Bark. 145 EP65
Colne Mead, Rick. 92 BG47
Uxbridge Rd.
Colne Orchard, Iver 133 BF72
Colne Pk. Caravan Pk., West Dr. 154 BJ77
Colne Reach, Stai. 173 BF85
Colne Rd. E5 123 DY63
Colne Rd. N21 100 DQ45
Colne Rd., Twick. 177 CE88
Colne St. E13 144 EG69
Grange Rd.
Colne Valley, Upmin. 129 FS58
Colne Way, Hem.H. 40 BM15
Colne Way, Stai. 173 BB89
Colne Way, Wat. 76 BY37
Colnedale Rd., Uxb. 114 BK64
Colney Hatch La. N10 98 DG52
Colney Hatch La. N11 98 DF51
Colney Heath La., St.Alb. 44 CL20
Colney Rd., Dart. 188 FM86
Cologne Rd. SW11 160 DD84
Colomb St. SE10 164 EE78
Colombo Rd., Ilf. 125 EQ60
Colombo St. SE1 278 F3
Colombo St. SE1 141 DP74
Colonels La., Cher. 194 BG100
Colonels Wk., Enf. 81 DP41
The Ridgeway
Colonial Ave., Twick. 176 CC85
Colonial Rd., Felt. 175 BS87
Colonial Rd., Slou. 152 AU75
Colonial Way, Wat. 76 BW39
Colonnade WC1 274 A5
Colonnade WC1 141 DL70
Colonnade Wk. SW1 277 H9
Colonnades, The W2 140 DB72
Porchester Rd.
Colonsay, Hem.H. 41 BQ22
Colridge Cres., Slou. 153 BE81
Colson Gdns., Loug. 85 EP42
Colson Rd.
Colson Path, Loug. 85 EN42
Colson Rd., Croy. 202 DS103
Colson Rd., Loug. 85 EN42
Colson Way SW16 181 DJ91
Colsterworth Rd. N15 122 DT56
Colston Ave., Cars. 218 DE105
Colston Clo., Cars. 218 DF105
West St.
Colston Cres. (Cheshunt), Wal.Cr. 65 DP27
Colston Rd. E7 144 EK65
Colston Rd. SW14 158 CQ84
Colt Hatch, Harl. 35 EP14
Hobtoe Rd.
Coltishall Rd., Horn. 148 FJ65
Coltness Cres. SE2 166 EV78
Colton Gdns. N17 122 DQ55
Colton Rd., Har. 117 CE57
Coltsfoot, Welw.G.C. 30 DB11
Coltsfoot, The, Hem.H. 39 BE21
Coltsfoot Ct., Grays 170 GD79
Coltsfoot Dr., Guil. 243 BA131
Coltsfoot Dr., West Dr. 134 BL72
Coltsfoot Path, Rom. 106 FK51
Columbia Ave., Edg. 96 CP53
Columbia Ave., Ruis. 115 BV60
Columbia Ave., Wor.Pk. 199 CT101
Columbia Ctyd. E14 143 EA74
West India Ave.
Columbia Rd. E2 275 P2
Columbia Rd. E2 142 DT69
Columbia Rd. E13 144 EF70
Columbia Sq. SW14 158 CQ84
Upper Richmond Rd. W.
Columbia Wf. Rd., Grays 170 GA79
Columbine Ave. E6 144 EL71
Columbine Ave., S.Croy. 219 DP108
Columbine Way SE13 163 EC82
Columbine Way, Rom. 106 FL53
Columbus Ct. SE16 142 DW74
Rotherhithe St.
Columbus Gdns., Nthwd. 93 BU53
Columbus Sq., Erith 167 FF79
Colva Wk. N19 121 DH61
Chester Rd.
Colvestone Cres. E8 122 DT64
Colview Ct. SE9 184 EK88
Mottingham La.
Colville Est. N1 142 DS67
Colville Gdns. W11 139 CZ72
Colville Hos. W11 139 CZ72
Colville Ms. W11 139 CZ72
Lonsdale Rd.
Colville Pl. W1 273 L7
Colville Rd. E11 123 EC62
Colville Rd. E17 101 DY54
Colville Rd. N9 100 DV46
Colville Rd. W3 158 CP76
Colville Rd. W11 139 CZ72
Colville Sq. W11 139 CZ72
Colville Ter. W11 139 CZ72
Colvin Clo. SE26 182 DW92
Colvin Gdns. E4 101 EC48
Colvin Gdns. E11 124 EH56
Colvin Gdns., Ilf. 103 EQ53
Colvin Gdns., Wal.Cr. 83 DX35
Colvin Rd. E6 144 EL66
Colvin Rd., Th.Hth. 201 DN99
Colwall Gdns., Wdf.Grn. 102 EG50
Harts Gro.
Colwell Rd. SE22 182 DT85
Colwick Clo. N6 121 DK59
Colwith Rd. W6 159 CW79
Colwood Gdns. SW19 180 DD94
Colworth Gro. SE17 279 J9
Colworth Rd. E11 124 EE58
Colworth Rd., Croy. 202 DU102
Colwyn Ave., Grnf. 137 CF68
Colwyn Clo. SW16 181 DJ92
Colwyn Cres., Houns. 156 CC81
Colwyn Grn. NW9 118 CS58
Snowdon Dr.
Colwyn Rd. NW2 119 CV62
Colyer Clo. SE9 185 EP89
Colyer Rd., Grav. 190 GC89
Colyers Clo., Erith 167 FD81
Colyers La., Erith 167 FC81
Colyers Wk., Erith 167 FE81
Colyers La.
Colyton Clo., Well. 166 EX81
Colyton Clo., Wem. 137 CJ65
Bridgewater Rd.
Colyton Clo., Wok. 226 AW118
Colyton Rd. SE22 182 DV85
Colyton Way N18 100 DU50
Combe Ave. SE3 164 EF80
Combe Bank Dr., Sev. 240 EY122
Combe La., Guil. 260 BM138
Combe La., Walt. 213 BT109
Combe Lea, Brom. 204 EL97
Combe Lo. SE7 164 EJ79
Elliscombe Rd.
Combe Ms. SE3 164 EF80
Combe Rd., Gdmg. 258 AT143
Combe Rd., Wat. 75 BT44
Combe St., Hem.H. 40 BJ20
Combedale Rd. SE10 164 EG78
Combemartin Rd. SW18 179 CY87
Comber Clo. NW2 119 CV62
Comber Gro. SE5 162 DQ80
Combermere Rd. SW9 161 DM83
Combermere Rd., Mord. 200 DB99
Comberton Rd. E5 122 DV61
Combeside SE18 165 ET80
Combwell Cres. SE2 166 EU76
Comely Bank Rd. E17 123 EC57
Comeragh Clo., Wok. 226 AU119
Comeragh Ms. W14 159 CY78
Comeragh Rd.
Comeragh Rd. W14 159 CY78
Comerford Rd. SE4 163 DY84
Comet Clo. E12 124 EK63
Whitta Rd.
Comet Clo., Purf. 168 FN77
Comet Clo., Wat. 59 BT34
Comet Pl. SE8 163 EA80
Comet Rd., Hat. 45 CT17
Comet Rd., Stai. 174 BK87
Comet St. SE8 163 EA80
Comet Way, Hat. 44 CS19
Comforts Fm. Ave., Oxt. 254 EF133
Comfrey Ct., Grays 170 GD79
Commerce Rd. N22 99 DM53
Commerce Rd., Brent. 157 CJ79
Commerce Way, Croy. 201 DM103
Commercial Pl., Grav. 191 GJ86
Commercial Rd. E1 142 DU72
Commercial Rd. E14 143 DY72
Commercial Rd. N17 100 DS51
Commercial Rd. N18 100 DS50
Commercial Rd., Guil. 258 AX135
Commercial Rd., Stai. 174 BG93
Commercial St. E1 275 P5
Commercial St. E1 142 DT70
Commercial Way NW10 138 CP68
Commercial Way SE15 162 DT80
Commercial Way, Wok. 226 AY117
Commerell St. SE10 164 EE78
Commodity Quay E1 142 DT73
East Smithfield
Commodore Sq. SW10 160 DC81
Commodore St. E1 143 DY70
Common, The W5 138 CL73
Common, The, Berk. 39 AZ17
Common, The, Guil. 258 AY141
Common, The (Wonersh), Guil. 259 BB143
Common, The, Hat. 45 CU17
Common, The, Kings L. 58 BG32
Common, The, Rich. 177 CK90
Common, The, Sthl. 156 BW77
Common, The, Stan. 95 CE47
Common Clo., Wok. 210 AX114
Common Grn., Berk. 39 BB17
Common La., Add. 212 BJ109
Common La., Dart. 187 FG89
Common La., Esher 215 CG108
Common La., Kings L. 58 BM28
Common La., Rad. 77 CF37
Common La., Slou. 111 AK62
Common La., Wat. 77 CE39
Common La. (Eton), Wind. 151 AR78
Common Rd. SW13 159 CU83
Common Rd., Brwd. 109 GC50
Common Rd., Esher 215 CG107
Common Rd., Lthd. 230 BY121
Common Rd., Red. 266 DF136
Common Rd., Rick. 73 BD42
Common Rd., Slou. 110 AH61
Common Rd. (Langley), Slou. 153 BA77
Common Rd., Stan. 95 CD48
Common Rd., Wal.Abb. 50 EL21
Common Rd., Wind. 150 AJ77
Common Rd. (Eton Wick), Wind. 151 AN77
Common Wd., Slou. 111 AQ63
Common Wd. La., H.Wyc. 88 AD46
Commondale SW15 159 CW83
Commonfield La. SW17 180 DE92
Tooting Gro.
Commonfield Rd., Bans. 218 DA114
Commonfields, Harl. 35 ES14
Commongate Rd., Rick. 73 BD43
Commonmeadow La., Wat. 60 CB33
Commons, The, Welw.G.C. 30 DA12
Commons La., Hem.H. 40 BL19
Commonside, Epsom 232 CN115
Commonside, Harl. 51 ES19
Fern Hill La.
Commonside, Kes. 222 EJ105
Commonside, Lthd. 230 CA122
Commonside Clo., Sutt. 218 DB111
Brighton Rd.
Commonside E., Mitch. 200 DG97
Commonside Rd., Harl. 51 ES19
Commonside W., Mitch. 200 DF97
Commonwealth Ave. W12 139 CV73
Commonwealth Ave., Hayes 135 BR72
Commonwealth Rd. N17 100 DU52
Commonwealth Rd., Cat. 236 DU123
Commonwealth Way SE2 166 EV78
Commonwood La., Kings L. 58 BH34
Community Clo., Houns. 155 BV81
Community Clo., Uxb. 115 BQ62
Community Rd. E15 123 ED64
Community Rd., Grnf. 136 CC67
Como Rd. SE23 183 DY89
Como St., Rom. 127 FD57
Compass Hill, Rich. 177 CK86
Compayne Gdns. NW6 140 DB66
Comport Clo., Croy. 222 EE112
Comport Grn., Croy. 222 EE112
Compton Ave. E6 144 EK68
Compton Ave. N1 141 DP65
Compton Ave. N6 120 DE59
Compton Ave., Brwd. 109 GC46
Compton Ave., Rom. 127 FH55
Compton Clo. E3 143 EA71
Compton Clo. NW1 273 J3
Compton Clo. W13 137 CG72
Compton Clo., Edg. 96 CQ52
Pavilion Way
Compton Clo., Esher 214 CC106
Compton Ct. SE19 182 DS92
Victoria Cres.
Compton Ct., Slou. 131 AL72
Brook Cres.
Compton Cres. N17 100 DQ52
Compton Cres. W4 158 CQ79
Compton Cres., Chess. 216 CL107
Compton Cres., Nthlt. 136 BX67
Compton Gdns., Add. 212 BH106
Monks Cres.
Compton Gdns., St.Alb. 60 CB26
Compton Pas. EC1 274 G4
Compton Pl. WC1 273 P4
Compton Pl., Erith 167 FF79
Compton Pl., Wat. 94 BY48
Compton Ri., Pnr. 116 BY57
Compton Rd. N1 141 DP65
Compton Rd. N21 99 DN46
Compton Rd. NW10 139 CX69
Compton Rd. SW19 179 CZ93
Compton Rd., Croy. 202 DV102
Compton Rd., Hayes 135 BS73
Compton St. EC1 274 F4
Compton St. EC1 141 DP70
Compton Ter. N1 141 DP65
Comreddy Clo., Enf. 81 DP39
Comus Pl. SE17 279 M9
Comus Pl. SE17 162 DS77
Comyn Rd. SW11 160 DE84
Comyne Rd., Wat. 75 BT36
Comyns, The (Bushey), Wat. 94 CC46
Comyns Clo. E16 144 EF71
Comyns Rd., Dag. 146 FA66
Conant Ms. E1 142 DU73
Back Ch. La.
Conaways Clo., Epsom 217 CU110
Concanon Rd. SW2 161 DM84
Concert Hall App. SE1 278 C3
Concert Hall App. SE1 141 DM74
Concord Clo., Nthlt. 136 BX69
Britannia Clo.
Concord Rd. W3 138 CP70
Concord Rd., Enf. 82 DV43
Concorde Clo., Houns. 156 CB82
Lampton Rd.
Concorde Clo., Uxb. 134 BL68
Concorde Dr. E6 145 EM71
Concorde Dr., Hem.H. 40 BK20
Concorde Way, Slou. 151 AQ75
Concourse, The N9 100 DU47
New Rd.
Concourse, The NW9 97 CT53
Long Mead
Condell Rd. SW8 161 DJ81
Conder St. E14 143 DY72
Conderton Rd. SE5 162 DQ83
Condor Ct., Guil. 258 AW136
Millmead Ter.
Condor Path, Nthlt. 136 CA68
Brabazon Rd.
Condor Rd., Stai. 194 BH97
Condor Wk., Horn. 147 FH66
Heron Flight Ave.
Condover Cres. SE18 165 EP80
Condray Pl. SW11 160 DE80
Conduit Ct. WC2 273 P10
Conduit La. N18 100 DW50
Conduit La., Croy. 220 DU106
Conduit La., Enf. 83 DY44
Morson Rd.
Conduit La., Slou. 152 AY78
Conduit La., S.Croy. 220 DU106
Conduit La. E., Hodd. 49 EB17
Conduit La. W., Hodd. 49 EA17
Conduit Ms. W2 140 DD72
Conduit Pas. W2 140 DD72
Conduit Pl.
Conduit Pl. W2 140 DD72
Conduit Rd. SE18 165 EP78
Conduit St. W1 273 J10
Conduit St. W1 141 DH73
Conduit Way NW10 138 CQ66
Conegar Ct., Slou. 132 AS74
Conewood St. N5 121 DP62
Coney Acre SE21 182 DQ88
Coney Burrows E4 102 EE47
Wyemead Cres.
Coney Clo., Hat. 45 CV19
Coney Gro., Uxb. 134 BN69
Coney Hill Rd., W.Wick. 204 EE103
Coney Way SW8 161 DM79
Coneyberry, Reig. 266 DD138
Coneybury, Red. 252 DS134
Coneybury Clo., Warl. 236 DV119
Coneydale, Welw.G.C. 29 CX07
Coneygrove Path, Nthlt. 136 BY65
Arnold Rd.
Conference Clo. E4 101 EC47
Greenbank Clo.
Conference Rd. SE2 166 EW77
Conford Dr., Guil. 258 AY141

Congleton Gro. SE18 165 EQ78
Congo Rd. SE18 165 ER78
Congress Rd. SE2 166 EW77
Congreve Rd. SE9 165 EM83
Congreve Rd., Wal.Abb. 68 EE33
Congreve St. SE17 279 M9
Congreve St. SE17 162 DS77
Congreve Wk. E16 144 EK71
Fulmer Rd.
Conical Cor., Enf. 82 DQ40
Coniers Way, Guil. 243 BB131
Conifer Ave., Rom. 105 FB50
Conifer Clo., Orp. 223 ER105
Conifer Clo., Reig. 250 DA132
Conifer Clo., Wal.Cr. 66 DT29
Conifer Dr., Brwd. 108 FX50
Conifer Gdns. SW16 181 DL90
Conifer Gdns., Enf. 82 DR44
Conifer Gdns., Sutt. 200 DB104
Conifer La., Egh. 173 BC92
Conifer Way, Hayes 135 BU73
Conifer Way, Swan. 207 FC95
Conifer Way, Wem. 117 CJ62
Conifers, Wey. 195 BS104
Conifers, The, Hem.H. 39 BF23
Conifers, The, Wat. 76 BW35
Conifers Clo., Tedd. 177 CJ94
Coniger Rd. SW6 160 DA82
Coningesby Dr., Wat. 75 BS39
Coningham Ms. W12 139 CU74
Percy Rd.
Coningham Rd. W12 139 CV74
Coningsby Bank, St.Alb. 42 CC24
Coningsby Clo., Hat. 45 CX24
Coningsby Cotts. W5 157 CK75
Coningsby Rd.
Coningsby Dr., Pot.B. 64 DD33
Coningsby Gdns. E4 101 EB51
Coningsby La., Maid. 150 AC81
Coningsby Rd. N4 121 DP59
Coningsby Rd. W5 157 CK75
Coningsby Rd., S.Croy. 220 DQ109
Conington Rd. SE13 163 EB82
Conisbee Ct. N14 81 DJ43
Conisborough Cres. SE6 183 EC90
Coniscliffe Rd. N13 100 DQ48
Conista Ct., Wok. 226 AT116
Roundthorn Way
Coniston Ave., Bark. 145 ES66
Coniston Ave., Grnf. 137 CH69
Coniston Ave., Upmin. 128 FQ63
Coniston Ave., Well. 165 ES83
Coniston Clo. N20 98 DC48
Coniston Clo. SW13 159 CT80
Lonsdale Rd.
Coniston Clo. SW20 199 CX100
Coniston Clo. W4 158 CQ80
Coniston Clo., Bark. 145 ES66
Coniston Ave.
Coniston Clo., Bexh. 167 FC81
Coniston Clo., Dart. 187 FH88
Coniston Clo., Erith 167 FE80
Coniston Clo., Hem.H. 41 BQ21
Coniston Gdns. N9 100 DW46
Coniston Gdns. NW9 118 CR57
Coniston Gdns., Ilf. 124 EL56
Coniston Gdns., Pnr. 115 BU56
Coniston Gdns., Sutt. 218 DD107
Coniston Gdns., Wem. 117 CJ60
Coniston Ho. SE5 162 DQ80
Wyndham Rd.
Coniston Rd. N10 99 DH54
Coniston Rd. N17 100 DU51
Coniston Rd., Bexh. 167 FC81
Coniston Rd., Brom. 183 ED93
Coniston Rd., Couls. 235 DJ116
Coniston Rd., Croy. 202 DU101
Coniston Rd., Kings L. 58 BM28
Coniston Rd., Twick. 176 CB86
Coniston Rd., Wok. 227 BB120
Coniston Wk. E9 122 DW64
Clifden Rd.
Coniston Way, Chess. 198 CL104
Coniston Way, Egh. 173 BB94
Coniston Way, Horn. 127 FG64
Coniston Way, Reig. 250 DE133
Conistone Way N7 141 DL66
Conlan St. W10 139 CY70
Conley Rd. NW10 138 CS65
Conley St. SE10 164 EE78
Pelton Rd.
Connaught Ave. E4 101 ED45
Connaught Ave. SW14 158 CQ83
Connaught Ave., Ashf. 174 BL91
Connaught Ave., Barn. 98 DF46
Connaught Ave., Enf. 82 DS40
Connaught Ave., Grays 170 GB75
Connaught Ave., Houns. 176 BY85
Connaught Ave., Loug. 84 EK42
Connaught Bri. E16 144 EK73
Connaught Clo. E10 123 DY61
Connaught Clo. W2 272 B9
Connaught Clo., Enf. 82 DS40
Connaught Clo., Hem.H. 40 BN18
Connaught Clo., Sutt. 218 DD107
Connaught Clo., Uxb. 135 BQ70
New Rd.
Connaught Dr. NW11 120 DA56
Connaught Dr., Wey. 212 BM110
Eyston Dr.
Connaught Gdns. N10 121 DH57
Connaught Gdns. N13 99 DP49
Connaught Gdns., Berk. 38 AT16
Connaught Gdns., Mord. 200 DC98
Connaught Hill, Loug. 84 EK42
Connaught La., Ilf. 125 ER61
Connaught Rd.
Connaught Ms. SE18 165 EN78
Woolwich New Rd.
Connaught Ms. W2 272 D9
Connaught Ms., Ilf. 125 ER61
Connaught Rd.
Connaught Pl. W2 272 D9
Connaught Pl. W2 140 DF73
Connaught Rd. E4 102 EE45
Connaught Rd. E11 123 ED60
Connaught Rd. E16 144 EK74
Connaught Bri.
Connaught Rd. E17 123 EA57
Connaught Rd. N4 121 DN59
Connaught Rd. NW10 138 CS67
Connaught Rd. SE18 165 EN78
Connaught Rd. W13 137 CH73
Connaught Rd., Barn. 79 CX44
Connaught Rd., Har. 95 CF53
Connaught Rd., Horn. 128 FK62
Connaught Rd., Ilf. 125 ER61
Connaught Rd., N.Mal. 198 CS98
Connaught Rd., Rich. 178 CM85
Albert Rd.
Connaught Rd., St.Alb. 42 CC18
Connaught Rd., Slou. 152 AV75
Connaught Rd., Sutt. 200 DD103
Connaught Rd., Tedd. 177 CD92
Connaught Sq. W2 272 D9
Connaught Sq. W2 140 DF72
Connaught St. W2 272 C9
Connaught St. W2 140 DE72
Connaught Way N13 99 DP49
Connell Cres. W5 138 CM70
Connemara Clo., Borwd. 78 CR44
Percheron Rd.
Connicut La., Lthd. 246 CB128
Connington Cres. E4 101 ED48
Conniston Cres., Slou. 130 AJ71
Connop Rd., Enf. 83 DX38
Connor Rd., Dag. 126 EZ63
Connor St. E9 143 DX67
Lauriston Rd.
Conolly Rd. W7 137 CE74
Conquerors Hill, St.Alb. 28 CL07
Conquest Rd., Add. 212 BG106
Conrad Clo., Grays 170 GB75
Conrad Dr., Wor.Pk. 199 CW102
Conrad Gdns., Grays 170 GA75
Conrad Ho. N16 122 DS64
Cons St. SE1 278 E4
Consfield Ave., N.Mal. 199 CU98
Consort Clo., Brwd. 108 FW50
Consort Ms., Islw. 177 CD85
Consort Rd. SE15 162 DV81
Consort Way, Horl. 268 DG148
Consort Way, Uxb. 113 BF58
Constable Clo. NW11 120 DB58
Constable Clo., Hayes 135 BQ69
Charville La.
Constable Cres. N15 122 DU57
Constable Gdns., Edg. 96 CN53
Constable Gdns., Islw. 177 CD85
Constable Rd., Grav. 190 GE90
Constable Wk. SE21 182 DT90
Ferrings
Constance Cres., Brom. 204 EF101
Constance Rd., Croy. 201 DP101
Constance Rd., Enf. 82 DS44
Constance Rd., Sutt. 218 DC105
Constance Rd., Twick. 176 CB87
Constance St. E16 144 EL74
Albert Rd.
Constantine Rd. NW3 120 DE63
Constitution Hill SW1 277 H4
Constitution Hill SW1 161 DH75
Constitution Hill, Grav. 191 GJ88
Constitution Hill, Wok. 226 AY119
Constitution Ri. SE18 165 EN81
Consul Ave., Dag. 147 FC70
Consul Gdns., Swan. 187 FG93
Princess Rd.
Content St. SE17 279 J9
Content St. SE17 162 DQ77
Contessa Clo., Orp. 223 ES106
Control Twr. Rd., Gat. 268 DD153
Control Twr. Rd., Houns. 154 BN83
Convair Wk., Nthlt. 136 BX69
Kittiwake Rd.
Convent Clo., Beck. 183 EC94
Foxgrove Rd.
Convent Gdns. W5 157 CJ77
Convent Gdns. W11 139 CZ72
Kensington Pk. Rd.
Convent Hill SE19 182 DQ93
Convent La., Cob. 213 BS111
Seven Hills Rd.
Convent Rd., Ashf. 174 BN92
Convent Rd., Wind. 151 AN82
Convent Way, Sthl. 156 BW77
Conway Clo., H.Wyc. 88 AC53
Conway Clo., Rain. 147 FG66
Conway Clo., Stan. 95 CG51
Conway Cres., Grnf. 137 CE68
Conway Cres., Rom. 126 EW58
Conway Dr., Ashf. 175 BQ93
Conway Dr., Hayes 155 BQ76
Conway Dr., Sutt. 218 DB107
Conway Gdns., Enf. 82 DS38
Conway Gdns., Grays 170 GB80
Conway Gdns., Mitch. 201 DK98
Conway Gdns., Wem. 117 CJ59
Conway Gro. W3 138 CR71
Conway Ms. W1 273 K5
Conway Rd. N14 99 DL48
Conway Rd. N15 121 DP57
Conway Rd. NW2 119 CW61
Conway Rd. SE18 165 ER77
Conway Rd. SW20 199 CW95
Conway Rd., Felt. 176 BX92
Conway Rd., Houns. 176 BZ87
Conway Rd. (Heathrow), Houns. 155 BP83
Conway Rd., Maid. 130 AH72
Conway St. E13 144 EG70
Conway St. W1 273 K5
Conway St. W1 141 DJ70
Conway Wk., Hmptn. 176 BZ93
Fearnley Cres.
Conybeare NW3 140 DE66
King Henry's Rd.
Conybury Clo., Wal.Abb. 68 EG32
Conyer St. E3 143 DY68
Conyers, Harl. 35 EQ13
Conyers Clo., Walt. 214 BX106
Conyers Clo., Wdf.Grn. 102 EE51
Conyers Rd. SW16 181 DK92
Conyers Way, Loug. 85 EP41
Cooden Clo., Brom. 184 EH94
Plaistow La.
Cooderidge Clo. N17 100 DT51
Brantwood Rd.
Cook Ct. SE16 142 DW74
Rotherhithe St.
Cook Rd., Dag. 126 EW64
Ripple Rd.
Cook Sq., Erith 167 FF80
Cooke Clo. E14 143 EA74
Cabot Sq.
Cookes Clo. E11 124 EF61
Cookes La., Sutt. 217 CY107
Cookham Cres. SE16 163 DX75
Marlow Way
Cookham Dene Clo., Chis. 205 ER95
Cookham Hill, Orp. 206 FA104
Cookham Rd., Sid. 206 FA95
Cookham Rd., Swan. 206 FA95
Cookhill Rd. SE2 166 EV75
Cooks Clo., Rom. 105 FC53
Cook's Hole Rd., Enf. 81 DP38
Cooks Mead (Bushey), Wat. 76 CB44
Cook's Rd. E15 143 EB68
Cooks Rd. SE17 161 DP79
Cooks Spinney, Harl. 36 EU13
Cooks Vennel, Hem.H. 40 BG18
Cooks Way, Hat. 45 CV20
Travellers La.
Cool Oak La. NW9 118 CS59
Coolfin Rd. E16 144 EG72
Coolgardie Ave. E4 101 ED50
Coolgardie Ave., Chig. 103 EN48
Coolgardie Rd., Ashf. 175 BQ92
Coolhurst Rd. N8 121 DK58
Coomassie Rd. W9 139 CZ70
Bravington Rd.
Coombe, The, Bet. 248 CR131
Coombe Ave., Croy. 220 DS105
Coombe Ave., Sev. 241 FH120
Coombe Bank, Kings.T. 198 CS95
Coombe Clo., Edg. 96 CM54
Coombe Clo., Houns. 156 CA84
Coombe Cor. N21 99 DP46
Coombe Cres., Hmptn. 176 BY94
Coombe Dr., Add. 211 BF107
Coombe Dr., Kings.T. 178 CR94
Coombe Dr., Ruis. 115 BV60
Coombe End, Kings.T. 178 CR94
Coombe Gdns. SW20 199 CU96
Coombe Gdns., Berk. 38 AT18
Coombe Gdns., N.Mal. 199 CT98
Coombe Heights, Kings.T. 178 CS94
Coombe Hill Glade, Kings.T. 178 CS94
Coombe Hill Rd., Kings.T. 178 CS94
Coombe Hill Rd., Rick. 92 BG45
Coombe Ho. Chase, N.Mal. 198 CR95
Coombe La. SW20 199 CT95
Coombe La., Croy. 220 DV106
Coombe La. W., Kings.T. 198 CP95
Coombe Lea, Brom. 204 EL97
Coombe Neville, Kings.T. 178 CR94
Coombe Pk., Kings.T. 178 CR92
Coombe Ridings, Kings.T. 178 CQ92
Coombe Ri., Brwd. 109 FZ46
Coombe Ri., Kings.T. 198 CQ95
Coombe Rd. N22 99 DN54
Coombe Rd. NW10 118 CR62
Coombe Rd. SE26 182 DV91
Coombe Rd. W4 158 CS78
Coombe Rd. W13 157 CH76
Northcroft Rd.
Coombe Rd., Croy. 220 DQ105
Coombe Rd., Grav. 191 GJ89
Coombe Rd., Hmptn. 176 BZ93
Coombe Rd., Kings.T. 198 CN95
Coombe Rd., N.Mal. 198 CS96
Coombe Rd., Rom. 128 FM55
Coombe Rd. (Bushey), Wat. 94 CC45
Coombe Vale, Ger.Cr. 112 AY60
Coombe Wk., Sutt. 200 DB104
Coombe Way, W.Byf. 212 BM112
Coombe Wd. Hill, Pur. 220 DQ112
Coombe Wd. Rd., Kings.T. 178 CQ92
Coombefield Clo., N.Mal. 198 CS99
Coombehurst Clo., Barn. 80 DF40
Coombelands La., Add. 212 BG107
Coomber Way, Croy. 201 DK101
Coombermere Clo., Wind. 151 AP82
Coombes Rd., Dag. 146 EZ67
Coombes Rd., St.Alb. 61 CJ26
Coombewood Dr., Rom. 126 FA58
Coombfield Dr., Dart. 189 FR91
Coombs St. N1 274 G1
Coombs St. N1 141 DP68
Coomer Ms. SW6 159 CZ79
Coomer Pl.
Coomer Pl. SW6 159 CZ79
Coomer Rd. SW6 159 CZ79
Coomer Pl.
Cooms Wk., Edg. 96 CQ53
East Rd.
Cooper Ave. E17 101 DY53
Cooper Clo. SE1 278 E5
Cooper Clo., Green. 189 FS85
Cooper Clo., Horl. 269 DN148
Broadbridge La.
Cooper Ct. E15 123 EB64
Clays La.
Cooper Cres., Cars. 200 DF104
Cooper Rd. NW10 119 CU64
Cooper Rd., Croy. 219 DP105
Cooper Rd., Guil. 258 AY136
Cooper St. E16 144 EF71
Lawrence St.
Cooper Way, Slou. 151 AP76
Cooperage Clo. N17 100 DT51
Brantwood Rd.
Coopers Clo. E1 142 DW70
Coopers Clo., Chig. 104 EV47
Coopers Clo., Dag. 147 FB65
Blackborne Rd.
Coopers Clo. (South Darenth), Dart. 209 FR95
Coopers Clo., Stai. 173 BE92
Coopers Cres., Borwd. 78 CQ39
Coopers Grn. La., Hat. 28 CR14
Coopers Grn. La., St.Alb. 44 CL17
Coopers Grn. La., Welw.G.C. 29 CU12
Coopers Hill La., Egh. 172 AW90
Coopers Hill Rd., Red. 251 DM133
Coopers La. E10 123 EB60
Coopers La. NW1 273 N1
Coopers La. NW1 141 DK68
Cooper's La. SE12 184 EH89
Coopers La., Pot.B. 64 DD31
Coopers La. Rd., Pot.B. 64 DE31
Coopers Rd. SE1 162 DT78
Coopers Rd., Grav. 190 GE88
Coopers Rd., Pot.B. 64 DC30
Cooper's Row EC3 275 P10
Coopers Row, Iver 133 BD70
Coopers Shaw Rd., Til. 171 GK80
Coopers Wk. (Cheshunt), Wal.Cr. 67 DX28
Cooper's Yd. SE19 182 DS93
Westow Hill
Coopersale Clo., Wdf.Grn. 102 EJ52
Navestock Cres.
Coopersale Common, Epp. 70 EX28
Coopersale La., Epp. 86 EU37
Coopersale Rd. E9 123 DX64
Coopersale St., Epp. 70 EW32
Coote Gdns., Dag. 126 EZ62
Nicholas Rd.
Coote Rd., Bexh. 166 EZ81
Coote Rd., Dag. 126 EZ62
Cope Pl. W8 160 DA76
Cope St. SE16 163 DX77
Copeland Dr. E14 163 EA77
Copeland Rd. E17 123 EB57
Copeland Rd. SE15 162 DU82
Copeman Clo. SE26 182 DW92
Copeman Rd., Brwd. 109 GD45
Copenhagen Gdns. W4 158 CR75
Copenhagen Pl. E14 143 DZ72
Copenhagen St. N1 141 DL67
Copenhagen Way, Walt. 195 BV104
Copers Cope Rd., Beck. 183 DZ94
Copeswood Rd., Wat. 75 BV39
Copford Clo., Wdf.Grn. 102 EL51
Copford Wk. N1 142 DQ67
Popham St.
Copinger Wk., Edg. 96 CP53
North Rd.
Copland Ave., Wem. 117 CK64
Copland Clo., Wem. 117 CJ64
Copland Ms., Wem. 138 CL65
Copland Rd.
Copland Rd., Wem. 138 CL65
Copleigh Dr., Tad. 233 CY120
Copleston Ms. SE15 162 DT82
Copleston Rd.
Copleston Pas. SE15 162 DT82
Copleston Rd. SE15 162 DT83
Copley Clo. SE17 161 DP79
Hillingdon St.
Copley Clo. W7 137 CF70
Copley Clo., Red. 250 DE132
Copley Clo., Wok. 226 AS119
Copley Dene, Brom. 204 EK95
Copley Pk. SW16 181 DM93
Copley Rd., Stan. 95 CJ50
Copley St. E1 143 DX71
Stepney Grn.
Copley Way, Tad. 233 CX120
Copmans Wick, Rick. 73 BD43
Copnor Way SE15 162 DS80
Diamond St.
Coppard Gdns., Chess. 215 CJ107
Mansfield Rd.
Copped Hall SE21 182 DR89
Glazebrook Clo.
Coppelia Rd. SE3 164 EF84
Coppen Rd., Dag. 126 EZ59
Copper Beech Clo. NW3 140 DD65
Daleham Ms.
Copper Beech Clo., Grav. 191 GK87
Copper Beech Clo., Hem.H. 39 BF23
Copper Beech Clo., Ilf. 103 EN53
Copper Beech Clo., Orp. 206 EW99
Rookery Gdns.
Copper Beech Clo., Wind. 151 AK81
Copper Beech Clo., Wok. 226 AV121
Copper Beech Ct., Loug. 85 EN39
Copper Beech Rd., S.Ock. 149 FW69
Copper Beeches, Islw. 157 CD81
Eversley Cres.
Copper Clo. SE19 182 DT94
Copper Mead Clo. NW2 119 CW62
Copper Mill Dr., Islw. 157 CF82
Copper Mill La. SW17 180 DC91
Copper Ridge, Ger.Cr. 91 AZ50
Copper Row SE1 142 DT74
Horselydown La.
Copperas St. SE8 163 EB79
Copperbeech Clo. NW3 120 DD64
Akenside Rd.
Copperdale Rd., Hayes 155 BU75
Copperfield, Chig. 103 ER50
Copperfield App., Chig. 103 ER51
Copperfield Ave., Uxb. 134 BN71
Copperfield Clo., S.Croy. 220 DQ111
Copperfield Ct., Lthd. 231 CG121
Kingston Rd.
Copperfield Ct., Pnr. 116 BZ56
Copperfield Dr. N15 122 DT56
Copperfield Gdns., Brwd. 108 FV46
Copperfield Ms. N18 100 DS50
Copperfield Ri., Add. 211 BF106
Copperfield Rd. E3 143 DY70
Copperfield Rd. SE28 146 EW72
Copperfield St. SE1 278 G4
Copperfield St. SE1 161 DP75
Copperfield Way, Chis. 185 EQ93
Copperfield Way, Pnr. 116 BZ56
Copperfields, Beac. 89 AL50
Copperfields, Lthd. 230 CC122
Copperfields, Welw.G.C. 30 DC10
Forresters Dr.
Copperfields Way, Rom. 106 FK53
Coppergate Clo., Brom. 204 EH95
Copperkins Gro., Amer. 55 AP36
Copperkins La., Amer. 55 AM35
Coppermill La. E17 122 DW58
Coppermill La., Rick. 91 BE52
Coppermill La., Uxb. 91 BE52
Coppermill Rd., Stai. 173 BB86
Copperwood, Hert. 32 DT09
Coppetts Clo. N12 98 DE52
Coppetts Rd. N10 98 DF52
Coppice, The, Ashf. 175 BP93
School Rd.
Coppice, The, Beac. 89 AR51
School La.
Coppice, The, Enf. 81 DP42
Coppice, The, Hem.H. 41 BP19
Coppice, The, Wat. 76 BW44
Coppice, The, West Dr. 134 BL72
Coppice Clo. SW20 199 CW97
Coppice Clo., Hat. 45 CT22
Coppice Clo., Ruis. 115 BR58
Coppice Clo., Stan. 95 CF51
Coppice Dr. SW15 179 CU86
Coppice Dr., Stai. 172 AX87
Coppice End, Wok. 227 BE116
Dean Clo.
Coppice Fm. Rd., H.Wyc. 88 AC45
Coppice La., Reig. 249 CZ132
Coppice Path, Chig. 104 EV49
Coppice Row, Epp. 85 EN36
Coppice Wk. N20 98 DA48
Coppice Way E18 124 EF56
Coppice Way, Slou. 111 AR61
Coppies Gro. N11 99 DH49
Copping Clo., Croy. 220 DS105
Tipton Dr.
Coppings, The, Hodd. 33 EA14
Danemead
Coppins, The, Croy. 221 EB107
Coppins, The, Har. 95 CE51
Coppins Clo., Berk. 38 AS19
Coppins La., Iver 133 BF71
Coppock Clo. SW11 160 DE82
Coppsfield, W.Mol. 196 CA97
Hurst Rd.
Copse, The E4 102 EF46
Copse, The, Amer. 55 AQ38
Copse, The, Beac. 88 AJ51
Copse, The, Cat. 252 DU126
Tupwood La.
Copse, The, Hem.H. 39 BE18
Copse, The, Hert. 32 DU09
Copse, The, Lthd. 230 CB123
Copse, The, Red. 267 DL136
Copse Ave., W.Wick. 203 EB104
Copse Clo. SE7 164 EH79
Copse Clo., Guil. 259 BC140
Copse Clo., Nthwd. 93 BQ54
Copse Clo., West Dr. 154 BK76
Copse Edge Ave., Epsom 217 CT113
Copse Glade, Surb. 197 CK102
Copse Hill SW20 199 CU95
Copse Hill, Harl. 51 EP18
Copse Hill, Pur. 219 DL113
Copse Hill, Sutt. 218 DB108
Copse La., Beac. 90 AS52
Copse La., Horl. 269 DJ147
Copse Rd., Cob. 213 BV113
Copse Rd., Red. 266 DC136
Copse Rd., Wok. 226 AT118
Copse Vw., S.Croy. 221 DX109
Copse Way, Chesh. 54 AN27
Copse Wd., Iver 133 BD67
Copse Wd. Ct., Reig. 250 DE132
Green La.
Copse Wd. Way, Nthwd. 93 BP53
Copsem Dr., Esher 214 CB107
Copsem La., Esher 214 CB107
Copsem La., Lthd. 214 CC111
Copsem Way, Esher 214 CC107
Copsen Wd., Lthd. 214 CC111
Stokesheath Rd.
Copsleigh Ave., Red. 266 DG141
Copsleigh Clo., Red. 266 DG140
Copsleigh Way, Red. 266 DG140
Copsleigh Ave.
Copt Hill La., Tad. 233 CY120
Coptefield Dr., Belv. 166 EX76
Coptfold Rd., Brwd. 108 FW47
Copthall Ave. EC2 275 L8
Copthall Ave. EC2 142 DR72
Copthall Bldgs. EC2 275 L8
Copthall Clo. EC2 275 K8
Copthall Clo., Ger.Cr. 91 AZ52
Copthall Cor., Ger.Cr. 90 AY52
Copthall Dr. NW7 97 CU52
Copthall Gdns. NW7 97 CU52
Copthall Gdns., Twick. 177 CF88
Copthall La., Ger.Cr. 90 AY52
Copthall Rd. E., Uxb. 114 BN61
Copthall Rd. W., Uxb. 114 BN61
Copthall Way, Add. 211 BF110
Copthorn Clo., Shep. 195 BQ100
Copthorne Ave. SW12 181 DK87
Copthorne Ave., Brom. 205 EM103
Copthorne Ave., Brox. 49 DZ20
Copthorne Ave., Ilf. 103 EP51
Copthorne Chase, Ashf. 174 BM91
Ford Rd.
Copthorne Clo., Rick. 74 BM43
Copthorne Gdns., Horn. 128 FN57
Copthorne Ms., Hayes 155 BS77
Copthorne Ri., S.Croy. 220 DR113
Copthorne Rd., Lthd. 231 CH120
Copthorne Rd., Rick. 74 BM44
Coptic St. WC1 273 P7
Coptic St. WC1 141 DL71
Copwood Clo. N12 98 DD49
Coral Clo., Rom. 126 EW55
Coral Row SW11 160 DC83
Gartons Way
Coral St. SE1 278 E5
Coral St. SE1 161 DN75
Coraline Clo., Sthl. 136 BZ69
Coralline Wk. SE2 166 EW75
Corals Mead, Welw.G.C. 29 CX10
Broadwater Cres.
Coram Clo., Berk. 38 AW20
Coram Grn., Brwd. 109 GD44
Coram St. WC1 273 P5
Coram St. WC1 141 DL70
Coran Clo. N9 101 DX45
Corban Rd., Houns. 156 CA83
Corbar Clo., Barn. 80 DD39
Corbet Clo., Wall. 200 DG102
Corbet Ct. EC3 275 L9
Corbet Pl. E1 275 P6
Corbet Rd., Epsom 216 CS110
Corbets Ave., Upmin. 128 FP64
Corbets Tey Rd., Upmin. 128 FP63
Corbett Clo., Croy. 221 ED112
Corbett Gro. N22 99 DL52
Bounds Grn. Rd.
Corbett Ho., Wat. 94 BW48
Corbett Rd. E11 124 EJ58
Corbett Rd. E17 123 EC55
Corbetts La. SE16 162 DW77
Rotherhithe New Rd.
Corbetts Pas. SE16 162 DW77
Rotherhithe New Rd.
Corbicum E11 124 EE59
Corbiere Ct. SW19 179 CX93
Thornton Rd.
Corbiere Ho. N1 142 DS67
Corbins La., Har. 116 CB62
Corbridge Cres. E2 142 DV68
Corby Clo., Egh. 172 AW93
Corby Dr.
Corby Clo., St.Alb. 60 CA25
Corby Cres., Enf. 81 DL42
Corby Dr., Egh. 172 AV93
Corby Rd. NW10 138 CR68
Corby Way E3 143 EA70
Knapp Rd.

Corbylands Rd., Sid. 185 ES87
Corbyn St. N4 121 DL60
Corcorans, Brwd. 108 FV44
Cord Way E14 163 EA76
Mellish St.
Corde Way, Slou. 151 AQ75
Cordelia Clo. SE24 161 DP84
Cordelia Gdns., Stai. 174 BL87
Cordelia Rd., Stai. 174 BL87
Cordelia St. E14 143 EB72
Cordell Clo. (Cheshunt), Wal.Cr. 67 DY28
Corder Clo., St.Alb. 42 CA23
Corderoy Pl., Cher. 193 BE100
Cording St. E14 143 EB71
Chrisp St.
Cordingley Rd., Ruis. 115 BR61
Cordons Clo., Ger.Cr. 90 AX53
Cordova Rd. E3 143 DY69
Cordrey Gdns., Couls. 235 DL115
Cordwainers Wk. E13 144 EG68
Clegg St.
Cordwell Rd. SE13 184 EE85
Corelli Rd. SE3 164 EL81
Corfe Ave., Har. 116 CA63
Corfe Clo., Ash. 231 CJ118
Corfe Clo., Hayes 136 BW72
Lulworth Waye
Corfe Clo., Hem.H. 40 BL21
Old Crabtree La.
Corfe Gdns., Slou. 131 AN73
Avebury
Corfe Twr. W3 158 CQ75
Corfield Rd. N21 81 DM43
Tresilian Ave.
Corfield St. E2 142 DV69
Corfton Rd. W5 138 CL72
Coriander Ave. E14 143 ED72
Coriander Cres., Guil. 242 AU129
Cories Clo., Dag. 126 EX61
Green La.
Corinium Clo., Wem. 118 CM63
Corinium Gate, St.Alb. 42 CA22
Corinne Rd. N19 121 DJ63
Corinth Par., Hayes 135 BT71
Corinthian Manorway, Erith 167 FD77
Corinthian Rd., Erith 167 FD77
Cork Sq. E1 142 DV74
Smeaton St.
Cork St. W1 277 K1
Cork St. W1 141 DJ73
Cork St. Ms. W1 277 K1
Cork Tree Way E4 101 DY50
Corker Wk. N7 121 DM61
Corkran Rd., Surb. 197 CK101
Corkscrew Hill, W.Wick. 203 EC103
Corlett St. NW1 272 B6
Cormongers La., Red. 251 DJ134
Cormont Rd. SE5 161 DP81
Cormorant Clo. E17 101 DY52
Banbury Rd.
Cormorant Rd. E7 124 EF64
Cormorant Wk., Horn. 147 FH65
Heron Flight Ave.
Corn Cft., Hat. 45 CV16
Corn Mead, Welw.G.C. 29 CW06
Corn Mill Dr., Orp. 206 EU101
Corn Way E11 124 EE62
Cathall Rd.
Cornbury Rd., Edg. 95 CK52
Cornelia Pl., Erith 167 FE79
Queen St.
Cornelia St. N7 141 DM65
Cornell Clo., Sid. 186 EY93
Cornell Way, Rom. 104 FA50
Corner, The, W.Byf. 212 BG113
Old Woking Rd.
Corner Grn. SE3 164 EG82
Corner Hall, Hem.H. 40 BJ22
Corner Hall Ave., Hem.H. 40 BK22
Corner Ho. St. WC2 277 P2
Corner Mead NW9 97 CT52
Corner Vw., Hat. 45 CW24
Dixons Hill Rd.
Cornerfield, Hat. 45 CV15
Corners, Welw.G.C. 30 DA07
Cornerside, Ashf. 175 BQ94
Corney Rd. W4 158 CS79
Cornfield Clo., Uxb. 134 BK68
The Greenway
Cornfield Rd., Reig. 266 DC135
Cornfield Rd. (Bushey), Wat. 76 CB42
Cornfields, Gdmg. 258 AU143
Cornfields, Hem.H. 40 BH21
Cornflower La., Croy. 203 DX102
Cornflower Ter. SE22 182 DV86
Cornflower Way, Rom. 106 FL53
Cornford Clo., Brom. 204 EG99
Cornford Gro. SW12 181 DH89
Cornhill EC3 275 L9
Cornhill EC3 142 DR72
Cornhill Clo., Add. 194 BH103
Cornish Ct. N9 100 DV45
Cornish Gro. SE20 202 DV95
Cornish Ho. SE17 161 DP79
Otto St.
Cornish Ho., Brent. 158 CM78
Cornmill, Wal.Abb. 67 EB33
Cornmill La. SE13 163 EC83
Cornmow Dr. NW10 119 CU63
Cornshaw Rd., Dag. 126 EX60
Cornsland, Brwd. 108 FX48
Cornsland Ct., Brwd. 108 FV48
Cornthwaite Rd. E5 122 DW62
Cornwall Ave. E2 142 DW69
Cornwall Ave. N3 98 DA52
Cornwall Ave. N22 99 DL53
Cornwall Ave., Esher 215 CF108
The Causeway
Cornwall Ave., Slou. 131 AQ70
Cornwall Ave., Sthl. 136 BZ71
Cornwall Ave., Well. 165 ES83
Cornwall Ave., W.Byf. 212 BM114
Cornwall Clo., Bark. 145 ET65
Cornwall Clo., Horn. 128 FN56
Cornwall Clo., Wal.Cr. 67 DY33
Cornwall Clo. (Eton Wick), Wind. 151 AL78
Cornwall Cres. W11 139 CY72
Cornwall Dr., Orp. 186 EW94
Cornwall Gdns. NW10 139 CV65
Cornwall Gdns. SW7 160 DB76
Cornwall Gdns. Wk. SW7 160 DB76
Cornwall Gdns.
Cornwall Gate, Purf. 168 FN77
Fanns Ri.
Cornwall Gro. W4 158 CS78
Cornwall Ms. S. SW7 160 DC76
Cornwall Ms. W. SW7 160 DB76
Cornwall Gdns.
Cornwall Rd. N4 121 DN59
Cornwall Rd. N15 122 DR57
Cornwall Rd. N18 100 DU50
Fairfield Rd.
Cornwall Rd. SE1 278 D2
Cornwall Rd. SE1 141 DN74
Cornwall Rd., Brwd. 108 FV43
Cornwall Rd., Croy. 201 DP103
Cornwall Rd., Dart. 168 FM83
Cornwall Rd., Esher 215 CF108
Common Rd.
Cornwall Rd., Har. 116 CC58
Cornwall Rd., Pnr. 94 BZ52
Cornwall Rd., Ruis. 115 BT62
Cornwall Rd., St.Alb. 43 CE22
Cornwall Rd., Sutt. 217 CZ108
Cornwall Rd., Twick. 177 CG87
Cornwall Rd., Uxb. 134 BK65
Cornwall Rd., Wind. 172 AU86
Cornwall St. E1 142 DV73
Watney St.
Cornwall Ter. NW1 272 E5
Cornwall Ter. Ms. NW1 272 E5
Cornwall Way, Stai. 173 BE93
Cornwallis Ave. N9 100 DV47
Cornwallis Ave. SE9 185 ER89
Cornwallis Clo., Erith 167 FF79
Cornwallis Gro. N9 100 DV47
Cornwallis Rd. E17 123 DX56
Cornwallis Rd. N9 100 DV47
Cornwallis Rd. N19 121 DL61
Cornwallis Rd., Dag. 126 EX63
Cornwallis Sq. N19 121 DL61
Cornwallis Rd.
Cornwallis Wk. SE9 165 EM83
Cornwell Ave., Grav. 191 GJ90
Cornwood Clo. N2 120 DD57
Cornwood Dr. E1 142 DW72
Cornworthy Rd., Dag. 126 EW64
Corona Rd. SE12 184 EG87
Coronation Ave. N16 122 DT62
Victorian Rd.
Coronation Ave., Slou. 132 AY71
Coronation Ave., Wind. 152 AT82
Coronation Clo., Bex. 186 EX86
Coronation Clo., Ilf. 125 EQ56
Coronation Dr., Horn. 127 FH63
Coronation Hill, Epp. 69 ET30
Coronation Rd. E13 144 EJ69
Coronation Rd. NW10 138 CM69
Coronation Rd., Hayes 155 BT77
Coronation Rd., Ware 33 DX05
Coronation Wk., Twick. 176 CA88
Coronet, The, Horl. 269 DJ150
Balcombe Rd.
Coronet St. N1 275 M3
Coronet St. N1 142 DS69
Corporation Ave., Houns. 156 BY84
Corporation Row EC1 274 E4
Corporation Row EC1 141 DN70
Corporation St. E15 144 EE68
Corporation St. N7 121 DL64
Corral Gdns., Hem.H. 40 BM19
Corran Way, S.Ock. 149 FV73
Corrance Rd. SW2 161 DL84
Corri Ave. N14 99 DK49
Corrib Dr., Sutt. 218 DE106
Corrie Gdns., Vir.W. 192 AW101
Corrie Rd., Add. 212 BK105
Corrie Rd., Wok. 227 BC120
Corrigan Ave., Couls. 218 DG114
Corringham Ct. NW11 120 DB59
Corringham Rd.
Corringham Ct., St.Alb. 43 CF19
Lemsford Rd.
Corringham Rd. NW11 120 DA59
Corringham Rd., Wem. 118 CN61
Corringway NW11 120 DB59
Corringway W5 138 CM71
Corsair Clo., Stai. 174 BK87
Corsair Rd., Stai. 174 BL87
Corscombe Clo., Kings.T. 178 CQ92
Corsehill St. SW16 181 DJ93
Corsham St. N1 275 L3
Corsham St. N1 142 DR69
Corsica St. N5 141 DP65
Corsley Way E9 143 DZ65
Trowbridge Est.
Cortayne Rd. SW6 159 CZ82
Cortis Rd. SW15 179 CV86
Cortis Ter. SW15 179 CV86
Corunna Rd. SW8 161 DJ81
Corunna Ter. SW8 161 DJ81
Corve La., S.Ock. 149 FV73
Corvette Sq. SE10 163 ED79
Feathers Pl.
Corwell Gdns., Uxb. 135 BQ72
Corwell La., Uxb. 135 BQ72
Cory Dr., Brwd. 109 GB45
Cory Wright Way, St.Alb. 28 CL06
Coryton Path W9 139 CZ70
Ashmore Rd.
Cosbycote Ave. SE24 182 DQ85
Cosdach Ave., Wall. 219 DK108
Cosedge Cres., Croy. 219 DN106
Cosgrove Clo. N21 100 DQ47
Cosgrove Clo., Hayes 136 BY70
Kingsash Dr.
Cosmo Pl. WC1 274 A6
Cosmur Clo. W12 159 CT76
Cossall Wk. SE15 162 DV81
Cosser St. SE1 278 D6
Cosser St. SE1 161 DN76
Costa St. SE15 162 DU82
Costead Manor Rd., Brwd. 108 FV46
Costell's Meadow, West. 255 ER126
Coston Wk. SE4 163 DX84
Frendsbury Rd.
Costons Ave., Grnf. 137 CD69
Costons La., Grnf. 137 CD69
Cosway St. NW1 272 C6
Cosway St. NW1 140 DE71
Cotall St. E14 143 EA72
Coteford Clo., Loug. 85 EP40
Coteford Clo., Pnr. 115 BU57
Coteford St. SW17 180 DF91
Cotelands, Croy. 202 DS104
Cotesbach Rd. E5 122 DW62
Cotesmore Gdns., Dag. 126 EW63
Cotesmore Rd., Hem.H. 39 BE21
Cotford Rd., Th.Hth. 202 DQ98
Cotham St. SE17 279 J9
Cotherstone, Epsom 216 CR110
Cotherstone Rd. SW2 181 DM88
Cotland Acres, Red. 266 DD136
Cotlandswick, St.Alb. 61 CJ25
Cotleigh Ave., Bex. 186 EX89
Cotleigh Rd. NW6 140 DA66
Cotleigh Rd., Rom. 127 FD58
Cotman Clo. NW11 120 DC58
Cotman Clo. SW15 179 CW86
Westleigh Ave.
Cotman Gdns., Edg. 96 CN54
Cotmandene, Dor. 263 CH136
Cotmandene Cres., Orp. 206 EU96
Cotmans Clo., Hayes 135 BU74
Coton Rd., Well. 166 EU83
Cotsford Ave., N.Mal. 198 CQ99
Cotswold, Hem.H. 40 BL17
Mendip Way
Cotswold Ave. (Bushey), Wat. 76 CC44
Cotswold Clo., Bexh. 167 FE82
Cotswold Clo., Kings.T. 178 CP93
Cotswold Clo., St.Alb. 43 CJ15
Chiltern Rd.
Cotswold Clo., Slou. 151 AQ76
Cotswold Clo., Stai. 174 BG92
Cotswold Clo., Uxb. 134 BJ67
Cotswold Ct. N11 98 DG49
Holly Pk. Rd.
Cotswold Gdns. E6 144 EK69
Cotswold Gdns. NW2 119 CX61
Cotswold Gdns., Brwd. 109 GE45
Cotswold Gdns., Ilf. 125 ER59
Cotswold Gate NW2 119 CY60
Cotswold Gdns.
Cotswold Grn., Enf. 81 DM42
Cotswold Way
Cotswold Ms. SW11 160 DD81
Battersea High St.
Cotswold Ri., Orp. 205 ET100
Cotswold Rd., Grav. 190 GE90
Cotswold Rd., Hmptn. 176 CA93
Cotswold Rd., Rom. 106 FM54
Cotswold Rd., Sutt. 218 DB110
Cotswold St. SE27 181 DP91
Norwood High St.
Cotswold Way, Enf. 81 DM41
Cotswold Way, Wor.Pk. 199 CW103
Cotswolds, Hat. 45 CU20
Cottage Ave., Brom. 204 EL102
Cottage Clo., Cher. 211 BC107
Cottage Clo., Rick. 74 BM44
Scots Hill
Cottage Clo., Ruis. 115 BR60
Cottage Clo., Wat. 75 BT40
Cottage Fm. Way, Egh. 193 BC97
Green Rd.
Cottage Fld. Clo., Sid. 186 EW88
Cottage Grn. SE5 162 DR80
Cottage Gro. SW9 161 DL83
Cottage Gro., Surb. 197 CK100
Cottage Homes NW7 97 CU49
Cottage Homes Chalet Est. NW7 97 CU49
Cottage Pk. Rd., Slou. 111 AR61
Cottage Pl. SW3 276 B7
Cottage Pl. SW3 160 DE76
Cottage Rd., Epsom 216 CR108
Cottage St. E14 143 EB73
Cottage Wk. N16 122 DT62
Smalley Clo.
Cottage Wk. SE15 162 DT80
Sumner Est.
Cottenham Dr. NW9 119 CT55
Cottenham Dr. SW20 179 CV94
Cottenham Par. SW20 199 CV96
Durham Rd.
Cottenham Pk. Rd. SW20 199 CV95
Cottenham Pl. SW20 179 CV94
Cottenham Rd. E17 123 DZ56
Cotterells, Hem.H. 40 BJ21
Cotterells Hill, Hem.H. 40 BJ20
Cotterill Rd., Surb. 198 CL103
Cottesbrook St. SE14 163 DY80
Nynehead St.
Cottesbrooke Clo., Slou. 153 BD81
Cottesloe Ms. SE1 161 DN76
Pearman St.
Cottesmore Ave., Ilf. 103 EN54
Cottesmore Gdns. W8 160 DB76
Cottimore Ave., Walt. 195 BV102
Cottimore Cres., Walt. 195 BV101
Cottimore La., Walt. 195 BV101
Cottimore Ter., Walt. 195 BV101
Cottingham Chase, Ruis. 115 BU62
Cottingham Rd. SE20 183 DX94
Cottingham Rd. SW8 161 DM80
Cottington Clo. SE11 278 F9
Cottington Clo. SE11 161 DP77
Cottington Rd., Felt. 176 BX91
Cottington St. SE11 278 E10
Cottle St. SE16 162 DW75
St. Marychurch St.
Cotton Ave. W3 138 CR72
Cotton Dr., Hert. 32 DV08
Cotton Fld., Hat. 45 CV16
Cotton Hill, Brom. 183 ED91
Cotton La., Dart. 188 FQ86
Cotton La., Green. 188 FQ85
Cotton Rd., Pot.B. 64 DC31
Cotton Row SW11 160 DD83
Cotton St. E14 143 EC73
Cottongrass Clo., Croy. 203 DX102
Cornflower La.
Cottonmill Cres., St.Alb. 43 CD21
Cottonmill La., St.Alb. 43 CD22
Cottons App., Rom. 127 FD57
Cottons Ct., Rom. 127 FD57
Cottons Gdns. E2 275 N2
Cottons La. SE1 279 L2
Cotts Wd. Dr., Guil. 243 BA129
Couchmore Ave., Esher 197 CE103
Couchmore Ave., Ilf. 103 EM54
Coulgate St. SE4 163 DY83
Coulsdon Ct. Rd., Couls. 235 DM116
Coulsdon La., Couls. 234 DF119
Coulsdon Pl., Cat. 236 DR122
Coulsdon Ri., Couls. 235 DL117
Coulsdon Rd., Cat. 236 DQ121
Coulsdon Rd., Couls. 235 DM115
Coulser Clo., Hem.H. 40 BG17
Coulson Clo., Dag. 126 EW59
Coulson St. SW3 276 D10
Coulson St. SW3 160 DF78
Coulson Way, Slou. 130 AH71
Coulter Clo. (Cuffley), Pot.B. 65 DK27
Coulter Rd. W6 159 CV76
Coulton Ave., Grav. 190 GE87
Coultree Clo., Hayes 136 BY70
Berrydale Rd.
Council Ave., Grav. 190 GC86
Councillor St. SE5 162 DQ80
Counter Ct. SE1 279 K3
Counter St. SE1 279 M3
Counters Clo., Hem.H. 40 BG20
Countess Clo., Uxb. 92 BJ54
Countess Rd. NW5 121 DJ64
Countisbury Ave., Enf. 100 DT45
Countisbury Gdns., Add. 212 BH106
Addlestone Pk.
Country Way, Felt. 175 BV93
Country Way, Sun. 175 BU94
County Gdns., Bark. 145 ES68
River Rd.
County Gate SE9 185 EQ90
County Gate, Barn. 80 DB44
County Gro. SE5 162 DQ81
County Rd. E6 145 EP71
County Rd., Th.Hth. 201 DP96
County St. SE1 279 J7
County St. SE1 162 DQ76
Coupland Pl. SE18 165 EQ78
Courage Clo., Horn. 128 FJ58
Courage Wk., Brwd. 109 GD44
Wainwright Ave.
Courcy Rd. N8 121 DN55
Courland Gro. SW8 161 DK82
Courland Rd., Add. 194 BH104
Courland St. SW8 161 DK81
Course, The SE9 185 EN90
Coursers Rd., St.Alb. 62 CN27
Court, The, Ruis. 116 BY63
Court, The, Warl. 237 DY118
Court Ave., Belv. 166 EZ78
Court Ave., Couls. 235 DN118
Court Ave., Rom. 106 FN52
Court Bushes Rd., Whyt. 236 DU119
Court Clo., Har. 117 CK55
Court Clo., Maid. 150 AC77
Court Clo., Twick. 176 CB90
Court Clo., Wall. 219 DK108
Court Clo. Ave., Twick. 176 CB90
Court Cres., Chess. 215 CK106
Court Cres., Slou. 131 AR72
Court Cres., Swan. 207 FE98
Court Downs Rd., Beck. 203 EB96
Court Dr., Croy. 219 DM105
Court Dr., Maid. 130 AC68
Court Dr., Stan. 96 CL49
Court Dr., Sutt. 218 DE105
Court Dr., Uxb. 134 BM67
Court Fm. Ave., Epsom 216 CR106
Court Fm. Ind. Est., Stai. 174 BM86
Court Fm. Rd. SE9 184 EK89
Court Fm. Rd., Nthlt. 136 CA66
Court Fm. Rd., Warl. 236 DU118
Court Gdns., The N5 141 DN65
Highbury Cor.
Court Grn. Heights, Wok. 226 AW119
Court Haw, Bans. 234 DE115
Court Hill, Couls. 234 DE118
Court Hill, S.Croy. 220 DS112
Court Ho. Gdns. N3 98 DA51
Court La. SE21 182 DS86
Court La., Epsom 216 CQ113
Court La., Iver 134 BG74
Court La., Slou. 131 AK69
Court La., Wind. 150 AG76
Court La. Gdns. SE21 182 DS87
Court Lawns, H.Wyc. 88 AC46
Court Lo. Rd., Horl. 268 DE147
Court Mead, Nthlt. 136 BZ69
Court Par., Wem. 117 CH62
Court Rd. SE9 185 EM86
Court Rd. SE25 202 DT96
Court Rd., Bans. 234 DA116
Court Rd., Cat. 236 DR123
Court Rd., Dart. 189 FS92
Court Rd., Gdse. 252 DW131
Court Rd., Maid. 130 AC69
Court Rd., Orp. 206 EV101
Court Rd., Sthl. 156 BZ77
Court Rd., Uxb. 115 BP64
Court St. E1 142 DV71
Durward St.
Court St., Brom. 204 EG96
Court Way NW9 118 CS56
Court Way W3 138 CQ71
Court Way, Ilf. 125 EQ55
Court Way, Rom. 106 FL54
Court Way, Twick. 177 CF87
Court Wd. Dr., Sev. 256 FG124
Court Wd. Gro., Croy. 221 DY111
Court Wd. La., Croy. 221 DZ110
Court Yd. SE9 185 EM86
Courtauld Clo. SE28 146 EU74
Pitfield Cres.
Courtauld Rd. N19 121 DK60
Courtaulds, Kings L. 58 BH30
Courtenay Ave. N6 120 DE59
Courtenay Ave., Har. 94 CC52
Courtenay Ave., Sutt. 218 DA109
Courtenay Dr., Beck. 203 ED96
Courtenay Gdns., Har. 94 CC54
Courtenay Gdns., Upmin. 128 FQ61
Courtenay Ms. E17 123 DY57
Courtenay Pl.
Courtenay Pl. E17 123 DY57
Courtenay Rd. E11 124 EF62
Courtenay Rd. E17 123 DX56
Courtenay Rd. SE20 183 DX94
Courtenay Rd., Wem. 117 CK62
Courtenay Rd., Wok. 227 BA116
Courtenay Rd., Wor.Pk. 199 CW104
Courtenay Sq. SE11 161 DN78
Courtenay St.
Courtenay St. SE11 278 D10
Courtenay St. SE11 161 DN78
Courteney Dr., Grays 170 FY76
Clifford Rd.
Courtens Ms., Stan. 95 CJ52
Courtfield W5 137 CJ71
Courtfield Ave., Har. 117 CF57
Courtfield Clo., Brox. 49 EA20
Stafford Dr.
Courtfield Cres., Har. 117 CF57
Courtfield Gdns. SW5 160 DB77
Courtfield Gdns. W13 137 CG72
Courtfield Gdns., Ruis. 115 BT61
Courtfield Gdns., Uxb. 114 BG62
Courtfield Ms. SW5 160 DB77
Courtfield Gdns.
Courtfield Ri., W.Wick. 203 ED104
Courtfield Rd. SW7 160 DC77
Courtfield Rd., Ashf. 175 BP93
Courthill Rd. SE13 163 EC84
Courthope Rd. NW3 120 DF63
Courthope Rd. SW19 179 CY92
Courthope Rd., Grnf. 137 CD68
Courthope Vill. SW19 179 CY94
Courthouse Rd. N12 98 DB51
Courtland Ave. E4 102 EF47
Courtland Ave. NW7 96 CR48
Courtland Ave. SW16 181 DM94
Courtland Ave., Ilf. 125 EM61
Courtland Dr., Chig. 103 EP48
Courtland Gro. SE28 146 EX73
Courtland Rd. E6 144 EL67
Harrow Rd.
Courtlands, Rich. 178 CN85
Courtlands Ave. SE12 184 EH85
Courtlands Ave., Brom. 204 EE102
Courtlands Ave., Esher 214 BZ107
Courtlands Ave., Hmptn. 176 BZ93
Courtlands Ave., Rich. 158 CP82
Courtlands Ave., Slou. 152 AX77
Courtlands Clo., Ruis. 115 BT59
Courtlands Clo., S.Croy. 220 DT110
Courtlands Clo., Wat. 75 BS35
Courtlands Cres., Bans. 234 DA115
Courtlands Dr., Epsom 216 CS107
Courtlands Dr., Wat. 75 BS37
Courtlands Rd., Surb. 198 CN101
Courtleas, Cob. 214 CA113
Courtleet Dr., Erith 167 FB81
Courtleigh Ave., Barn. 80 DD38
Courtleigh Gdns. NW11 119 CY56
Courtman Rd. N17 100 DQ52
Courtmead Clo. SE24 182 DQ86
Courtnell St. W2 140 DA72
Courtney Clo. SE19 182 DS93
Courtney Cres., Cars. 218 DF108
Courtney Pl., Croy. 201 DN104
Courtney Rd.
Courtney Rd. N7 121 DN64
Bryantwood Rd.
Courtney Rd. SW19 180 DE94
Courtney Rd., Croy. 201 DN104
Courtney Rd., Grays 171 GJ75
Courtney Rd., Houns. 154 BN83
Courtrai Rd. SE23 183 DY86
Courtside N8 121 DK58
Courtway, Wdf.Grn. 102 EJ50
Courtway, The, Wat. 94 BY47
Courtyard, The E1 142 DV73
Courtyard, The N1 141 DM66
Barnsbury Ter.
Courtyards, The, Slou. 153 BA75
Waterside Dr.
Cousin La. EC4 279 K1
Cousins Clo., West Dr. 134 BL73
Couthurst Rd. SE3 164 EH79
Coutts Ave., Chess. 216 CL106
Coutts Cres. NW5 120 DG62
Coval Gdns. SW14 158 CP84
Coval La. SW14 158 CP84
Coval Rd. SW14 158 CP84
Coveham Cres., Cob. 213 BU113
Covelees Wall E6 145 EP72
Warwall
Covenbrook, Brwd. 109 GB48
Covent Gdn. WC2 274 A10
Covent Gdn. WC2 141 DL73
Coventry Clo. E6 145 EM72
Harper Rd.
Coventry Clo. NW6 140 DA67
Kilburn High Rd.
Coventry Cross E3 143 EC70
Gillender St.
Coventry Rd. E1 142 DV70
Coventry Rd. E2 142 DV70
Coventry Rd. SE25 202 DU98
Coventry Rd., Ilf. 125 EP61
Coventry St. W1 277 M1
Coventry St. W1 141 DK73
Coverack Clo. N14 81 DJ44
Coverack Clo., Croy. 203 DY101
Coverdale, Hem.H. 40 BL17
Coverdale Clo., Stan. 95 CH50
Coverdale Ct., Enf. 83 DY37
Raynton Rd.
Coverdale Gdns., Croy. 202 DT104
Park Hill Ri.
Coverdale Rd. NW2 139 CX66
Coverdale Rd. W12 159 CV75
Coverdale Way, Slou. 131 AL70
Coverdales, The, Bark. 145 ER68
Coverley Clo. E1 142 DU71
Coverley Clo., Brwd. 107 FW51
Wilmot Grn.
Covert, The, Nthwd. 93 BQ52
Covert, The, Orp. 205 ES100
Covert Rd., Chig. 103 ET51
Covert Rd., Esher 215 CF109
Covert Way, Barn. 80 DC40
Coverton Rd. SW17 180 DE92
Coverts, The, Brwd. 109 GA46
Covet Wd. Clo., Orp. 205 ET100
Lockesley Dr.
Covington Gdns. SW16 181 DP94
Covington Way SW16 181 DM93
Cow La., Grnf. 137 CD68
Oldfield La. S.
Cow La., Wat. 76 BW36
Cow Leaze E6 145 EN72
Downings
Cowan Clo. E6 144 EL71
Oliver Gdns.
Cowbridge, Hert. 32 DQ09
Cowbridge La., Bark. 145 EP66
Cowbridge Rd., Har. 118 CM56
Cowcross St. EC1 274 F6
Cowcross St. EC1 141 DP71
Cowden Rd., Orp. 205 ET101
Cowden St. SE6 183 EA91
Cowdenbeath Path N1 141 DM67
Bingfield St.
Cowdray Rd., Uxb. 135 BQ67
Cowdray Way, Horn. 127 FF63
Cowdrey Clo., Enf. 82 DS40
Cowdrey Ct., Dart. 187 FH87
Cowdrey Rd. SW19 180 DB92
Cowdry Rd. E9 143 DY65
Wick Rd.
Cowen Ave., Har. 116 CC61
Cowgate Rd., Grnf. 137 CD68
Cowick Rd. SW17 180 DF91
Cowings Mead, Nthlt. 136 BY65
Cowland Ave., Enf. 82 DW42
Cowleaze Rd., Kings.T. 198 CL95
Cowles (Cheshunt), Wal.Cr. 66 DT27

Cowley Ave., Cher.	193	BF101
Cowley Ave., Green.	189	FU85
Cowley Clo., S.Croy.	220	DW109
Cowley Cres., Uxb.	134	BJ71
Cowley Cres., Walt.	214	BW105
Cowley Hill, Borwd.	78	CP37
Cowley La. E11	124	EE62
Cathall Rd.		
Cowley La., Cher.	193	BF101
Cowley Mill Rd., Uxb.	134	BH68
Cowley Pl. NW4	119	CW57
Cowley Rd. E11	124	EH57
Cowley Rd. SW9	161	DN81
Cowley Rd. SW14	158	CS83
Cowley Rd. W3	139	CT74
Cowley Rd., Ilf.	125	EM59
Cowley Rd., Rom.	105	FH52
Cowley Rd., Uxb.	134	BJ67
Cowley St. SW1	**277**	**P6**
Cowling Clo. W11	139	CY74
Wilsham St.		
Cowlins, Harl.	36	EX11
New Rd.		
Cowper Ave. E6	144	EL66
Cowper Ave., Sutt.	218	DD105
Cowper Ave., Til.	171	GH81
Cowper Clo., Brom.	204	EK98
Cowper Clo., Cher.	193	BF100
Cowper Clo., Well.	186	EU85
Cowper Ct., Wat.	75	BU37
Cowper Cres., Hert.	31	DP07
Cowper Gdns. N14	81	DH44
Cowper Gdns., Wall.	219	DJ107
Cowper Rd. N14	99	DH46
Cowper Rd. N16	122	DS64
Cowper Rd. N18	100	DU50
Cowper Rd. SW19	180	DC93
Cowper Rd. W3	138	CR74
Cowper Rd. W7	137	CF73
Cowper Rd., Belv.	166	FA77
Cowper Rd., Berk.	38	AV19
Cowper Rd., Brom.	204	EK98
Cowper Rd., Chesh.	54	AP29
Cowper Rd., Hem.H.	40	BH22
Cowper Rd., Kings.T.	178	CM92
Cowper Rd., Rain.	147	FG70
Cowper Rd., Slou.	131	AN70
Cowper Rd., Welw.G.C.	29	CZ11
Cowper St. EC2	**275**	**L4**
Cowper St. EC2	142	DR70
Cowper Ter. W10	139	CX71
St. Marks Rd.		
Cowslip Clo., Uxb.	134	BL66
Cowslip La., Dor.	247	CG129
Cowslip La., Wok.	226	AU115
Carthouse La.		
Cowslip Rd. E18	102	EH54
Cowslips, Welw.G.C.	30	DC10
Cowthorpe Rd. SW8	161	DK81
Cox Clo., Rad.	62	CL32
King Charles Rd.		
Cox La., Chess.	216	CL105
Cox La., Epsom	216	CP105
Coxdean, Epsom	233	CW119
Coxfield Clo., Hem.H.	40	BL21
Toms Cft.		
Coxley Ri., Pur.	220	DQ113
Coxmount Rd. SE7	164	EK78
Cox's Wk. SE21	182	DU88
Coxson Pl. SE1	**279**	**P5**
Coxwell Rd. SE18	165	ER78
Coxwell Rd. SE19	182	DS94
Coxwold Path, Chess.	216	CL108
Garrison La.		
Cozens La. E., Brox.	49	DZ22
Cozens La. W., Brox.	49	DY22
Cozens Rd., Ware	33	DZ06
Crab Hill, Beck.	183	ED94
Crab Hill La., Red.	267	DM138
Crab La., Wat.	76	CB35
Crabbe Cres., Chesh.	54	AR29
Crabbs Cft. Clo., Orp.	223	EQ106
Ladycroft Way		
Crabtree Ave., Rom.	126	EX56
Crabtree Ave., Wem.	138	CL68
Crabtree Clo. E2	142	DT68
Dunloe St.		
Crabtree Clo., Beac.	88	AH54
Crabtree Clo., Hem.H.	40	BK22
Crabtree Clo., Lthd.	246	CC126
Crabtree Clo. (Bushey),	76	CB43
Wat.		
Crabtree Ct. E15	123	EB64
Clays La.		
Crabtree Dr., Lthd.	247	CJ125
Crabtree La. SW6	159	CX80
Crabtree La., Dor.	247	CF130
Crabtree La., Hem.H.	40	BK22
Crabtree La., Lthd.	246	CC126
Crabtree Manorway N.,	167	FC75
Belv.		
Crabtree Manorway S.,	167	FC76
Belv.		
Crabtree Rd., Egh.	193	BC96
Crabtree Wk. SE15	162	DT81
Lisford St.		
Crace St. NW1	**273**	**M2**
Crackley Meadow,	41	BP15
Hem.H.		
Craddock Rd., Enf.	82	DT41
Craddock St. NW5	140	DG65
Prince of Wales Rd.		
Craddocks Ave., Ash.	232	CL117
Craddocks Par., Ash.	232	CL117
Cradhurst Clo., Dor.	262	CC137
Cradley Rd. SE9	185	ER88
Cragg Ave., Rad.	77	CF36
Craig Dr., Uxb.	135	BP72
Craig Gdns. E18	102	EF54
Craig Mt., Rad.	77	CH35
Craig Pk. Rd. N18	100	DV50
Craig Rd., Rich.	177	CJ91
Craigavon Rd., Hem.H.	40	BM16
Craigdale Rd., Horn.	127	FF58
Craigen Ave., Croy.	202	DV102
Craigerne Rd. SE3	164	EH80
Craigholm SE18	165	EN82
Craiglands, St.Alb.	43	CK16
Craigmore Twr., Wok.	226	AY119
Guildford Rd.		
Craigmuir Pk., Wem.	138	CM67
Craignair Rd. SW2	181	DN87
Craignish Ave. SW16	201	DM96
Craigs Ct. SW1	**277**	**P2**
Craigs Wk.	67	DX28
(Cheshunt), Wal.Cr.		
Davison Dr.		
Craigton Rd. SE9	165	EM84
Craigweil Clo., Stan.	95	CK50

Craigweil Dr., Stan.	95	CK50
Craigwell Ave., Felt.	175	BU90
Craigwell Ave., Rad.	77	CH35
Craigwell Clo., Stai.	193	BE95
Craik Ct. NW6	139	CZ68
Carlton Vale		
Crail Row SE17	**279**	**L9**
Crakell Rd., Reig.	266	DC135
Cramer St. W1	**272**	**G7**
Crammerville Wk., Rain.	147	FH70
Baillie Clo.		
Cramond Clo. W6	159	CY79
Cramond Ct., Felt.	175	BR88
Kilross Rd.		
Crampshaw La., Ash.	232	CM119
Crampton Rd. SE20	182	DW93
Crampton St. SE17	**279**	**H9**
Cramptons Rd., Sev.	241	FH120
Cranberry Clo., Nthlt.	136	BX68
Parkfield Ave.		
Cranberry La. E16	144	EE70
Cranborne Ave., Sthl.	156	CA77
Cranborne Clo., Pot.B.	63	CY31
Cranborne Cres., Pot.B.	63	CY31
Cranborne Gdns.,	128	FP61
Upmin.		
Cranborne Ind. Est.,	63	CY30
Pot.B.		
Cranborne Rd., Bark.	145	ER67
Cranborne Rd., Hat.	45	CV17
Cranborne Rd., Hodd.	49	EB16
Cranborne Rd., Pot.B.	63	CY31
Cranborne Rd.	67	DX32
(Cheshunt), Wal.Cr.		
Cranborne Waye, Hayes	135	BV72
Cranbourn All. WC2	**273**	**N10**
Cranbourn St. WC2	**273**	**N10**
Cranbourn St. WC2	141	DK73
Cranbourne Ave. E11	124	EH56
Cranbourne Ave., Surb.	198	CN104
Cranbourne Ave., Wind.	151	AM82
Cranbourne Clo. SW16	201	DL97
Cranbourne Clo., Hert.	32	DQ12
Cranbourne Clo., Horl.	269	DH146
Cranbourne Clo., Slou.	131	AQ74
Cranbourne Dr., Hodd.	33	EB13
Cranbourne Dr., Pnr.	116	BX57
Cranbourne Gdns. NW11	119	CY57
Cranbourne Gdns., Ilf.	125	EQ55
Cranbourne Gdns.,	29	CZ10
Welw.G.C.		
Cranbourne Rd. E12	124	EL64
High St. N.		
Cranbourne Rd. E15	123	EC63
Cranbourne Rd. N10	99	DH54
Cranbourne Rd., Nthwd.	115	BT55
Cranbourne Rd., Slou.	131	AQ74
Cranbrook Clo., Brom.	204	EG100
Cranbrook Dr., Esher	196	CC102
Cranbrook Dr., Rom.	127	FH56
Cranbrook Dr., St.Alb.	44	CL20
Cranbrook Dr., Twick.	176	CB88
Cranbrook Est. E2	143	DX68
Cranbrook Ms. E17	123	DZ57
Cranbrook Pk. N22	99	DM53
Cranbrook Pt. E16	144	EG74
Cranbrook Ri., Ilf.	125	EM58
Cranbrook Rd. SE8	163	EA81
Cranbrook Rd. SW19	179	CY94
Cranbrook Rd. W4	158	CS78
Cranbrook Rd., Barn.	80	DD44
Cranbrook Rd., Bexh.	166	EZ81
Cranbrook Rd., Houns.	156	BZ84
Cranbrook Rd., Ilf.	125	EN57
Cranbrook Rd., Th.Hth.	202	DQ96
Cranbrook St. E2	143	DX68
Roman Rd.		
Cranbury Rd. SW6	160	DB82
Crane Ave. W3	138	CQ73
Crane Ave., Islw.	177	CG85
Crane Clo., Dag.	146	FA65
Crane Clo., Har.	116	CC62
Eastcote La.		
Crane Ct. EC4	**274**	**E9**
Crane Ct., Epsom	216	CQ105
Crane Gdns., Hayes	155	BT77
Crane Gro. N7	141	DN65
Crane Lo. Rd., Houns.	155	BV79
Crane Mead SE16	163	DX77
Crane Mead, Ware	33	DY07
Crane Pk. Rd., Twick.	176	CB89
Crane St. SE10	163	ED78
Park Row		
Crane Way, Twick.	176	CC87
Cranebrook, Twick.	176	CC89
Manor Rd.		
Craneford Clo., Twick.	177	CF87
Craneford Way, Twick.	177	CF87
Cranell Grn., S.Ock.	149	FV74
Cranes Dr., Surb.	198	CL98
Cranes Pk., Surb.	198	CL98
Cranes Pk. Ave., Surb.	198	CL98
Cranes Pk. Cres., Surb.	198	CM98
Cranes Way, Borwd.	78	CQ43
Craneswater, Hayes	155	BT80
Craneswater Pk., Sthl.	156	BZ78
Cranfield Clo. SE27	182	DQ90
Dunelm Gro.		
Cranfield Ct., Wok.	226	AU118
Martindale Rd.		
Cranfield Cres.	65	DL29
(Cuffley), Pot.B.		
Cranfield Dr. NW9	96	CS52
Cranfield Dr., Wat.	60	BY32
Cranfield Rd. SE4	163	DZ83
Cranfield Rd. E., Cars.	218	DG109
Cranfield Rd. W., Cars.	218	DF109
Cranfield Row SE1	**278**	**E6**
Cranford Ave. N13	99	DL50
Cranford Ave., Stai.	174	BL87
Cranford Clo. SW20	179	CV94
Cranford Clo., Pur.	220	DQ113
Downs Ct. Rd.		
Cranford Clo., Stai.	174	BL87
Canopus Way		
Cranford Cotts. E1	143	DX73
Cranford St.		
Cranford Ct., Hert.	31	DM07
The Ridgeway		
Cranford Dr., Hayes	155	BT77
Cranford La., Hayes	155	BR79
Cranford La. (Cranford),	155	BT81
Houns.		
Cranford La.	155	BT83
(Hatton Cross), Houns.		

Cranford La. (Heston),	155	BV80
Houns.		
Cranford Pk. Rd., Hayes	155	BT77
Cranford Ri., Esher	214	CC106
Cranford Rd., Dart.	188	FL88
Cranford St. E1	143	DX73
Cranford Way N8	121	DM57
Cranham Rd., Upmin.	129	FS60
Cranham Rd., Horn.	127	FH58
Cranhurst Rd. NW2	119	CW64
Cranleigh Clo. SE20	202	DV96
Cranleigh Clo., Bex.	187	FB86
Cranleigh Clo., Orp.	206	EU104
Cranleigh Clo., S.Croy.	220	DU112
Cranleigh Clo.	66	DU28
(Cheshunt), Wal.Cr.		
Cranleigh Dr., Swan.	207	FE99
Cranleigh Gdns. N21	81	DN43
Cranleigh Gdns. SE25	202	DS97
Cranleigh Gdns., Bark.	145	ER66
Cranleigh Gdns., Har.	118	CL57
Cranleigh Gdns.,	178	CM93
Kings.T.		
Cranleigh Gdns., Loug.	85	EM44
Cranleigh Gdns.,	220	DU112
S.Croy.		
Cranleigh Gdns., Sthl.	136	BZ72
Cranleigh Gdns., Sutt.	200	DB103
Cranleigh Ms. SW11	160	DE82
Cranleigh Rd. N15	122	DQ57
Cranleigh Rd. SW19	199	CZ97
Cranleigh Rd., Esher	196	CC102
Cranleigh Rd., Felt.	175	BT91
Cranleigh Rd., Guil.	259	BB144
Cranleigh St. NW1	**273**	**L1**
Cranleigh St. NW1	141	DJ68
Cranley Clo., Guil.	243	BA134
Cranley Dene Ct. N10	121	DH56
Cranley Dr., Ilf.	125	EQ59
Cranley Dr., Ruis.	115	BT61
Cranley Gdns. N10	121	DH56
Cranley Gdns. N13	99	DM48
Cranley Gdns. SW7	160	DC78
Cranley Gdns., Wall.	219	DJ108
Cranley Ms. SW7	160	DC78
Cranley Par. SE9	184	EL91
Beaconsfield Rd.		
Cranley Pl. SW7	160	DD77
Cranley Rd. E13	144	EH71
Cranley Rd., Guil.	243	AZ134
Cranley Rd., Ilf.	125	EQ58
Cranley Rd., Walt.	213	BS106
Cranmer Ave. W13	157	CH76
Cranmer Clo., Mord.	199	CX100
Cranmer Clo., Pot.B.	64	DB30
Cranmer Clo., Ruis.	116	BX60
Cranmer Clo., Stan.	95	CJ52
Cranmer Clo., Warl.	237	DY117
Cranmer Clo., Wey.	213	BR108
Cranmer Ct. SW3	**276**	**C9**
Cranmer Ct. SW4	161	DK83
Cranmer Ct., Hmptn.	176	CB92
Cranmer Rd.		
Cranmer Fm. Clo.,	200	DF98
Mitch.		
Cranmer Gdns., Dag.	127	FC63
Cranmer Gdns., Warl.	237	DY117
Cranmer Rd. E7	124	EH63
Cranmer Rd. SW9	161	DN80
Cranmer Rd., Croy.	201	DP104
Cranmer Rd., Edg.	96	CP48
Cranmer Rd., Hmptn.	176	CB92
Cranmer Rd., Hayes	135	BR72
Cranmer Rd., Kings.T.	178	CL92
Cranmer Rd., Mitch.	200	DF98
Cranmer Rd., Sev.	256	FE123
Cranmer Ter. SW17	180	DD92
Cranmore Ave., Islw.	156	CC80
Cranmore Cotts., Lthd.	245	BP129
Cranmore Ct., St.Alb.	43	CF19
Cranmore La., Lthd.	245	BP129
Cranmore Rd., Brom.	184	EF90
Cranmore Rd., Chis.	185	EM92
Cranmore Way N10	121	DJ56
Cranston Clo., Houns.	156	BY82
Cranston Clo., Reig.	266	DB135
Cranston Clo., Uxb.	115	BR61
Cranston Est. N1	142	DR68
Cranston Est. N1	**275**	**L1**
Cranston Gdns. E4	101	EB50
Cranston Pk. Ave.,	128	FP63
Upmin.		
Cranston Rd. SE23	183	DY88
Cranstoun Clo., Guil.	242	AT130
Cranswick Rd. SE16	162	DV78
Crantock Rd. SE6	183	EB89
Cranwell Clo. E3	143	EB70
Cranwell Gro., Shep.	194	BM98
Cranwell Rd., Houns.	155	BP82
Cranwich Ave. N21	100	DR45
Cranwich Rd. N16	122	DR59
Cranwood St. EC1	**275**	**L3**
Cranwood St. EC1	142	DR69
Cranworth Cres. E4	101	ED46
Cranworth Gdns. SW9	161	DN81
Craster Rd. SW2	181	DM87
Crathie Rd. SE12	184	EH86
Crathorn St. SE13	163	EC83
Loampit Vale		
Cravan Ave., Felt.	175	BU89
Craven Ave. W5	137	CJ73
Craven Ave., Sthl.	136	BZ71
Craven Clo., Hayes	135	BU72
Craven Gdns. SW19	180	DA92
Craven Gdns., Bark.	145	ES68
Craven Gdns., Ilf.	103	ER54
Craven Gdns.	104	FA50
(Collier Row), Rom.		
Craven Gdns.	106	FQ51
(Harold Wd.), Rom.		
Craven Hill W2	140	DC73
Craven Hill Gdns. W2	140	DC73
Craven Hill Ms. W2	140	DC73
Craven Ms. SW11	160	DG83
Taybridge Rd.		
Craven Pk. NW10	138	CS67
Craven Pk. Ms. NW10	138	CS67
Craven Pk. Rd. N15	122	DT58
Craven Pk. Rd. NW10	138	CS67
Craven Pas. WC2	**277**	**P2**
Craven Rd. NW10	138	CR67
Craven Rd. W2	140	DC72
Craven Rd. W5	137	CJ73
Craven Rd., Croy.	202	DV102
Craven Rd., Kings.T.	198	CM95
Craven Rd., Orp.	206	EX104
Craven St. WC2	**277**	**P2**
Craven St. WC2	141	DL74
Craven Ter. W2	140	DC73

Craven Wk. N16	122	DU59
Cravens, The, Horl.	269	DN148
Crawford Ave., Wem.	117	CK64
Crawford Ave., Islw.	157	CE82
Crawford Compton Clo.,	148	FJ65
Horn.		
Crawford Est. SE5	162	DQ82
Crawford Gdns. N13	99	DP48
Crawford Gdns., Nthlt.	136	BZ69
Crawford Ms. W1	**272**	**D7**
Crawford Pas. EC1	**274**	**D5**
Crawford Pl. W1	**272**	**C8**
Crawford Pl. W1	140	DE72
Crawford Rd. SE5	162	DQ81
Crawford Rd., Hat.	45	CU16
Crawford St. W1	**272**	**C7**
Crawford St. W1	140	DF71
Crawfords, Swan.	187	FE94
Crawley Dr., Hem.H.	40	BM16
Crawley Rd. E10	123	EB60
Crawley Rd. N22	100	DQ54
Crawley Rd., Enf.	100	DS45
Crawshaw Ct. SW9	161	DN81
Eythorne Rd.		
Crawshaw Rd., Cher.	211	BD107
Crawshay Clo., Sev.	256	FG123
Crawthew Gro. SE22	162	DT84
Cray Ave., Ash.	232	CL116
Cray Ave., Orp.	206	EV100
Cray Clo., Dart.	167	FG84
Cray Riverway, Dart.	187	FF85
Cray Rd., Belv.	166	FA79
Cray Rd., Sid.	186	EW94
Cray Rd., Swan.	207	FB100
Cray Valley Rd., Orp.	206	EU99
Craybrooke Rd., Sid.	186	EV91
Crayburne, Grav.	190	FZ92
Craybury End SE9	185	EQ89
Craydene Rd., Erith	167	FF81
Crayfield Rd. N3	97	CZ53
Crayford Clo. E6	144	EL71
Neatscourt Rd.		
Crayford High St., Dart.	187	FE85
Crayford Rd. N7	121	DK63
Crayford Rd., Dart.	187	FE85
Crayford Way, Dart.	187	FF85
Crayke Hill, Chess.	216	CL108
Craylands, Orp.	206	EW97
Craylands La., Swans.	189	FX85
Craylands Sq., Swans.	189	FX85
Crayle St., Slou.	131	AN69
Craymill Sq., Dart.	167	FG83
Norris Way		
Crayonne Clo., Sun.	195	BS95
Crayside Ind. Est., Dart.	167	FH84
Thames Rd.		
Crealock Gro., Wdf.Grn.	102	EF50
Crealock St. SW18	180	DB86
Creasey Clo., Horn.	127	FH61
St. Leonards Way		
Creasy Clo., Abb.L.	59	BT31
Creasy Est. SE1	**279**	**M7**
Crebor St. SE22	182	DU86
Credenhall Dr., Brom.	205	EM102
Lower Gravel Rd.		
Credenhill St. SW16	181	DJ93
Crediton Hill NW6	120	DB64
Crediton Rd. E16	144	EG72
Pacific Rd.		
Crediton Rd. NW10	139	CX67
Crediton Way, Esher	215	CG106
Credo Way, Grays	169	FV79
Credon Rd. E13	144	EJ68
Credon Rd. SE16	162	DV78
Cree Way, Rom.	105	FE52
Creechurch La. EC3	**275**	**N9**
Creechurch La. EC3	142	DS72
Creechurch Pl. EC3	**275**	**N9**
Creed La. EC4	**274**	**G9**
Creek, The, Grav.	190	GB85
Creek, The, Sun.	195	BU99
Creek Rd. SE8	163	EA79
Creek Rd. SE10	163	EB79
Creek Rd., Bark.	145	ET69
Creek Rd., E.Mol.	197	CE98
Creekside SE8	163	EB80
Creekside, Rain.	147	FE70
Creeland Gro. SE6	183	DZ88
Catford Hill		
Crefeld Clo. W6	159	CX79
Creffield Rd. W3	138	CM73
Creffield Rd. W5	138	CM73
Creighton Ave. E6	144	EK68
Creighton Ave. N2	120	DE55
Creighton Ave. N10	98	DF54
Creighton Ave., St.Alb.	43	CD24
Creighton Rd. N17	100	DS52
Creighton Rd. NW6	139	CX68
Creighton Rd. W5	157	CK76
Cremer St. E2	142	DT68
Cremer St. E2	**275**	**P1**
Cremorne Est. SW10	160	DD79
Milman's St.		
Cremorne Gdns., Epsom	216	CR109
Cremorne Rd. SW10	160	DC80
Cremorne Rd., Grav.	191	GF87
Crescent, The E17	123	DY57
Crescent, The EC3	**275**	**P10**
Crescent, The N11	98	DG49
Crescent, The NW2	119	CV62
Crescent, The SW13	159	CT82
Crescent, The SW19	180	DA90
Crescent, The W3	138	CS72
Crescent, The, Abb.L.	59	BT30
Crescent, The, Ashf.	174	BM92
Crescent, The, Barn.	80	DB41
Crescent, The, Beck.	203	EA95
Crescent, The, Bex.	186	EW87
Crescent, The, Cat.	237	EA123
Crescent, The, Cher.	194	BG97
Western Ave.		
Crescent, The, Croy.	202	DR99
Crescent, The, Egh.	172	AY93
Crescent, The, Epp.	69	ET32
Crescent, The, Epsom	216	CN114
Crescent, The, Grav.	191	GJ89
Crescent, The, Green.	189	FW85
Crescent, The, Guil.	242	AU133
Crescent, The, Harl.	36	EW09
Crescent, The, Har.	116	CC60
Crescent, The, Hayes	155	BQ80
Crescent, The, Horl.	268	DG150
Crescent, The, Ilf.	125	EN58
Crescent, The, Lthd.	231	CH122
Crescent, The, Loug.	84	EK43
Crescent, The, N.Mal.	198	CQ96
Crescent, The, Reig.	250	DB134
Chartway		
Crescent, The, Rick.	75	BP44
Crescent, The, St.Alb.	60	CA30

Crescent, The, Sev.	257	FK121
Crescent, The, Shep.	195	BT101
Crescent, The, Sid.	185	ET91
Crescent, The, Slou.	152	AS75
Crescent, The, Sthl.	156	BZ75
Crescent, The, Surb.	198	CL99
Crescent, The, Sutt.	218	DD106
Crescent, The	218	DA111
(Belmont), Sutt.		
Crescent, The, Upmin.	129	FS59
Crescent, The, Wat.	76	BW42
Crescent, The	94	CB47
(Aldenham), Wat.		
Crescent, The, Wem.	117	CG61
Crescent, The, W.Mol.	196	CA98
Crescent, The, W.Wick.	204	EE100
Crescent, The, Wey.	194	BN104
Crescent Ave., Horn.	127	FF61
Crescent Cotts., Sev.	241	FE120
Crescent Dr., Brwd.	108	FY46
Crescent Dr., Orp.	205	EP100
Crescent E., Barn.	80	DC38
Crescent Gdns. SW19	180	DA90
Crescent Gdns., Ruis.	115	BV59
Crescent Gdns., Swan.	207	FC96
Crescent Gro. SW4	161	DJ84
Crescent Gro., Mitch.	200	DE98
Crescent La. SW4	161	DJ84
Crescent Pl. SW3	**276**	**B8**
Crescent Pl. SW3	160	DE77
Crescent Ri. N22	99	DK53
Crescent Ri., Barn.	80	DE43
Crescent Rd. E4	102	EE45
Crescent Rd. E6	144	EJ67
Crescent Rd. E10	123	EB61
Crescent Rd. E13	144	EG67
Crescent Rd. E18	102	EJ54
Crescent Rd. N3	97	CZ53
Crescent Rd. N8	121	DK58
Crescent Rd. N9	100	DU46
Crescent Rd. N11	98	DF49
Crescent Rd. N15	121	DP55
Carlingford Rd.		
Crescent Rd. N22	99	DK53
Crescent Rd. SE18	165	EP78
Crescent Rd. SW20	199	CX95
Crescent Rd., Barn.	80	DE42
Crescent Rd., Beck.	203	EB96
Crescent Rd., Brwd.	108	FV49
Crescent Rd., Brom.	184	EG94
Crescent Rd., Cat.	236	DU124
Crescent Rd., Dag.	127	FB62
Crescent Rd., Enf.	81	DP42
Crescent Rd., Erith	167	FF79
Crescent Rd., Hem.H.	40	BK20
Crescent Rd., Kings.T.	178	CN94
Crescent Rd., Red.	252	DQ133
Crescent Rd., Reig.	266	DA136
Crescent Rd., Shep.	195	BQ99
Crescent Rd., Sid.	185	ET90
Crescent Rd., S.Ock.	168	FQ75
Crescent Row EC1	**275**	**H5**
Crescent Stables SW15	159	CY84
Upper Richmond Rd.		
Crescent St. N1	141	DM66
Crescent Vw., Loug.	84	EK43
Crescent Vw., S.Ock.	168	FQ75
Crescent Way N12	98	DE51
Crescent Way SE4	163	EA83
Crescent Way SW16	181	DM93
Crescent Way, Horl.	268	DG150
Crescent Way, Orp.	223	ES106
Crescent Way, S.Ock.	149	FR74
Crescent Wd. Rd. SE26	182	DU90
Cresford Rd. SW6	160	DB81
Crespigny Rd. NW4	119	CV58
Cress End, Rick.	92	BG46
Springwell Ave.		
Cress Rd., Slou.	151	AP75
Cressage Clo., Sthl.	136	CA70
Cressall Clo., Lthd.	231	CH120
Cresset Clo., Ware	33	EC12
Cresset Rd. E9	142	DW65
Cresset St. SW4	161	DK83
Cressfield Clo. NW5	120	DG64
Cressida Rd. N19	121	DJ60
Cressingham Gro., Sutt.	218	DC105
Cressingham Rd. SE13	163	EC83
Cressingham Rd., Edg.	96	CR51
Cressington Clo. N16	122	DS64
Wordsworth Rd.		
Cresswell Gdns. SW5	160	DC78
Cresswell Pk. SE3	164	EF83
Cresswell Pl. SW10	160	DC78
Cresswell Rd. SE25	202	DU98
Cresswell Rd., Chesh.	54	AR34
Cresswell Rd., Felt.	176	BY91
Cresswell Rd., Twick.	177	CK86
Cresswell Way N21	99	DN45
Cressy Ct. E1	142	DW71
Cressy Pl.		
Cressy Ct. W6	159	CV76
Cressy Pl. E1	142	DW71
Cressy Rd. NW3	120	DF64
Crest, The N13	99	DN49
Crest, The NW4	119	CW57
Crest, The, Saw.	36	EX05
Crest, The, Surb.	198	CN99
Crest, The (Cheshunt),	65	DP27
Wal.Cr.		
Orchard Way		
Crest Ave., Grays	170	GB80
Crest Clo., Sev.	225	FB111
Crest Dr., Enf.	82	DW38
Crest Gdns., Ruis.	116	BW62
Crest Hill, Guil.	261	BR142
Crest Pk., Hem.H.	41	BQ19
Crest Rd. NW2	119	CT62
Crest Rd., Brom.	204	EF101
Crest Rd., S.Croy.	220	DV108
Crest Vw., Green.	169	FU84
Woodland Way		
Crest Vw., Pnr.	116	BX56
Crest Vw. Dr., Orp.	205	EP99
Cresta Dr., Add.	211	BF110
Crestbrook Ave. N13	99	DP48
Crestfield St. WC1	**274**	**A2**
Crestfield St. WC1	141	DL69
Cresthill Ave., Grays	170	GC77
Creston Ave., Wok.	226	AS116
Creston Way, Wor.Pk.	199	CX102
Crestway SW15	179	CU86
Crestwood Way, Houns.	176	BZ85
Creswick Ct., Welw.G.C.	29	CX10
Creswick Rd. W3	138	CP73
Creswick Wk. E3	143	EA69
Malmesbury Rd.		

Creswick Wk. NW11 119 CZ56
Crete Hall Rd., Grav. 190 GD86
Creton St. SE18 165 EN76
Crew Curve, Berk. 38 AT16
Crewdson Rd. SW9 161 DN80
Crewdson Rd., Horl. 269 DH148
Crewe Pl. NW10 139 CT69
Crewe's Ave., Warl. 236 DW116
Crewe's Clo., Warl. 236 DW117
Crewe's La., Warl. 236 DW117
Crews St. E14 163 EA77
Crewys Rd. NW2 119 CZ61
Crewys Rd. SE15 162 DV82
Crib St., Ware 33 DX05
Crichton Ave., Wall. 219 DK106
Crichton Rd., Cars. 218 DF108
Cricket Fld. Rd., Uxb. 134 BK67
Cricket Grn., Mitch. 200 DF97
Cricket Grd. Rd., Chis. 205 EP95
Cricket Hill, Red. 267 DM136
Cricket La., Beck. 183 DY92
Cricket Way, Wey. 195 BS103
Cricketers Arms Rd., Enf. 82 DQ40
Cricketers Clo. N14 99 DJ45
Cricketers Clo., Chess. 215 CK105
Cricketers Clo., Erith 167 FE78
Cricketers Clo., St.Alb. 43 CE19
Stonecross
Cricketers Ct. SE11 278 F9
Cricketers Ter., Cars. 200 DE104
Wrythe La.
Cricketfield Rd. E5 122 DV63
Cricketfield Rd., West Dr. 154 BJ77
Cricklade Ave. SW2 181 DL89
Cricklade Ave., Rom. 106 FK51
Cricklewood Bdy. NW2 119 CW62
Cricklewood La. NW2 119 CX63
Cricklewood Trd. Est. NW2 119 CY62
Cridland St. E15 144 EF67
Church St.
Crieff Ct., Tedd. 177 CJ94
Crieff Rd. SW18 180 DC86
Criffel Ave. SW2 181 DK89
Crimp Hill Rd., Egh. 172 AU90
Crimp Hill Rd., Wind. 172 AT87
Crimscott St. SE1 279 N7
Crimscott St. SE1 162 DS76
Crimsworth Rd. SW8 161 DK81
Crinan St. N1 141 DL68
Cringle St. SW8 161 DJ80
Cripplegate St. EC2 275 H6
Crisp Rd. W6 159 CW78
Crispe Ho., Bark. 145 ER68
Dovehouse Mead
Crispen Rd., Felt. 176 BY91
Crispian Clo. NW10 118 CS63
Crispin Clo., Ash. 232 CM118
Crispin Clo., Croy. 201 DL103
Harrington Clo.
Crispin Cres., Croy. 201 DK103
Crispin Rd., Edg. 96 CQ51
Crispin St. E1 275 P7
Crispin St. E1 142 DT71
Crispin Way, Slou. 111 AR63
Criss Cres., Ger.Cr. 90 AW54
Criss Gro., Ger.Cr. 90 AW54
Cristowe Rd. SW6 159 CZ82
Criterion Ms. N19 121 DK61
Fairbridge Rd.
Critten La., Dor. 246 BX134
Crockenhall Way, Grav. 190 GE94
Crockenhill La., Dart. 208 FJ102
Crockenhill La., Swan. 207 FG101
Crockenhill Rd., Orp. 206 EX99
Crockenhill Rd., Swan. 206 EZ100
Crockerton Rd. SW17 180 DF89
Crockery La., Guil. 244 BL129
Crockford Clo., Add. 212 BJ105
Crockford Pk. Rd., Add. 212 BJ106
Crockham Way SE9 185 EN91
Crocknorth Rd., Lthd. 245 BT132
Crocus Clo., Croy. 203 DX102
Cornflower La.
Crocus Fld., Barn. 79 CZ44
Croffets, Tad. 233 CX121
Croft, The NW10 139 CT68
Croft, The W5 138 CL71
Croft, The, Barn. 79 CY42
Croft, The, Brox. 49 DY23
Croft, The, Houns. 156 BY79
Croft, The, Loug. 85 EN40
Croft, The, Pnr. 116 BZ59
Rayners La.
Croft, The, Ruis. 116 BW63
Croft, The, St.Alb. 60 CA25
Croft, The, Swan. 207 FC97
Croft, The, Welw.G.C. 29 CZ12
Croft, The, Wem. 117 CJ64
Croft Ave., Dor. 247 CH134
Croft Ave., W.Wick. 203 EC102
Croft Clo. NW7 96 CS48
Croft Clo., Belv. 166 EZ78
Croft Clo., Chis. 185 EM91
Croft Clo., Hayes 155 BQ80
Croft Clo., Kings L. 58 BG30
Croft Clo., Uxb. 134 BN66
Croft End Rd., Kings L. 58 BG30
Croft Fld., Hat. 45 CU18
Croft Fld., Kings L. 58 BG30
Croft Gdns. W7 157 CG75
Croft Gdns., Ruis. 115 BS60
Croft La., Kings L. 58 BG30
Croft Lo. Clo., Wdf.Grn. 102 EH51
Croft Meadow, Kings L. 58 BG30
Croft Ms. N12 98 DC48
Woodside La.
Croft Rd. SW16 201 DN95
Croft Rd. SW19 180 DC94
Croft Rd., Brom. 184 EG93
Croft Rd., Cat. 237 DZ122
Croft Rd., Enf. 83 DY39
Croft Rd., Ger.Cr. 90 AY54
Croft Rd., Sutt. 218 DE106
Croft Rd., Ware 32 DW05
Croft Rd., West. 255 EP126
Croft St. SE8 163 DY77
Croft Wk., Brox. 49 DZ23
The Cft.
Croft Way NW3 120 DA63
Ferncroft Ave.
Croft Way, Sev. 256 FF125
Croft Way, Sid. 185 ES90
Croftdown Rd. NW5 120 DG62
Crofters, The, Wind. 172 AU86
Crofters Clo., Islw. 177 CD85
Ploughmans End
Crofters Ct. SE8 163 DY77
Crofters Mead, Croy. 221 DZ109
Crofters Rd., Nthwd. 93 BS49
Crofters Way NW1 141 DK67
Crofthill Rd., Slou. 131 AP70
Croftleigh Ave., Pur. 235 DP116
Crofton, Ash. 232 CL118
Woodfield La.
Crofton Ave. W4 158 CQ80
Crofton Ave., Bex. 186 EX87
Crofton Ave., Orp. 205 EQ103
Crofton Ave., Walt. 196 BW104
Crofton Clo., Cher. 211 BC108
Crofton Gro. E4 101 ED49
Manor Way
Crofton La., Orp. 205 ER103
Crofton Pk. Rd. SE4 183 DZ86
Crofton Rd. E13 144 EH70
Crofton Rd. SE5 162 DS81
Crofton Rd., Grays 170 GE75
Crofton Rd., Orp. 205 EN104
Crofton Ter. E5 123 DY64
Studley Clo.
Crofton Ter., Rich. 158 CM84
Crofton Way, Barn. 80 DB44
Wycherley Cres.
Crofton Way, Enf. 81 DN40
Croftongate Way SE4 183 DY85
Crofts, The, Hem.H. 41 BP21
Crofts, The, Shep. 195 BS98
Crofts Path, Hem.H. 40 BN22
Crofts Rd., Har. 117 CG58
Crofts St. E1 142 DU73
Croftway NW3 120 DA63
Croftway, Rich. 177 CH90
Crogsland Rd. NW1 140 DG66
Croham Clo., S.Croy. 220 DS108
Croham Manor Rd., S.Croy. 220 DS108
Croham Mt., S.Croy. 220 DS108
Croham Pk. Ave., S.Croy. 220 DS106
Croham Rd., S.Croy. 220 DR106
Croham Valley Rd., S.Croy. 220 DT107
Croindene Rd. SW16 201 DL95
Cromartie Rd. N19 121 DK59
Cromarty Rd., Edg. 96 CP47
Crombie Clo., Ilf. 125 EM57
Crombie Rd., Sid. 185 ER88
Cromer Clo., Uxb. 135 BQ72
Dawley Ave.
Cromer Hyde La., Welw.G.C. 28 CR11
Cromer Pl., Orp. 205 ER102
Andover Rd.
Cromer Rd. E10 123 ED58
James La.
Cromer Rd. N17 100 DU54
Cromer Rd. SE25 202 DV97
Cromer Rd. SW17 180 DG93
Cromer Rd., Barn. 80 DC42
Cromer Rd., Horn. 128 FK59
Cromer Rd., Houns. 154 BN83
Cromer Rd., Rom. 127 FC58
Cromer Rd. (Chadwell Heath), Rom. 126 EY58
Cromer Rd., Wat. 76 BW38
Cromer Rd., Wdf.Grn. 102 EG49
Cromer Rd. W., Houns. 154 BN83
Cromer St. WC1 274 A3
Cromer St. WC1 141 DL69
Cromer Ter. E8 122 DU64
Ferncliff Rd.
Cromer Vill. Rd. SW18 179 CZ86
Cromford Clo., Orp. 205 ES104
Cromford Path E5 123 DX63
Overbury St.
Cromford Rd. SW18 180 DA85
Cromford Way, N.Mal. 198 CR95
Cromlix Clo., Chis. 205 EP96
Crompton St. W2 140 DD70
Cromwell Ave. N6 121 DH60
Cromwell Ave. W6 159 CV77
Cromwell Ave., Brom. 204 EH97
Cromwell Ave., N.Mal. 199 CT99
Cromwell Ave. (Cheshunt), Wal.Cr. 66 DU30
Cromwell Clo. E1 142 DU74
Vaughan Way
Cromwell Clo. N2 120 DD56
Cromwell Clo. W3 138 CQ74
High St.
Cromwell Clo., Brom. 204 EH98
Cromwell Clo., Ch.St.G. 90 AW48
Cromwell Clo., St.Alb. 43 CK15
Cromwell Clo., Walt. 195 BV102
Cromwell Cres. SW5 160 DA77
Cromwell Dr., Slou. 132 AS72
Cromwell Gdns. SW7 276 A7
Cromwell Gdns. SW7 160 DD76
Cromwell Gro. W6 159 CW76
Cromwell Gro., Cat. 236 DQ121
Cromwell Ind. Est. E10 123 DY60
Cromwell Ms. SW7 276 A8
Cromwell Ms. SW7 160 DD77
Cromwell Pl. N6 121 DH60
Cromwell Ave.
Cromwell Pl. SW7 276 A8
Cromwell Pl. SW7 160 DD77
Cromwell Pl. SW14 158 CQ83
Cromwell Pl. W3 138 CQ74
Grove Pl.
Cromwell Rd. E7 144 EJ66
Cromwell Rd. E17 123 EC57
Cromwell Rd. N3 98 DC54
Cromwell Rd. N10 98 DG52
Cromwell Rd. SW5 160 DB77
Cromwell Rd. SW7 160 DB77
Cromwell Rd. SW9 161 DP81
Cromwell Rd. SW19 180 DA92
Cromwell Rd., Beck. 203 DY96
Cromwell Rd., Borwd. 78 CL39
Cromwell Rd., Brwd. 108 FV49
Cromwell Rd., Cat. 236 DQ121
Cromwell Rd., Croy. 202 DR101
Cromwell Rd., Felt. 175 BV88
Cromwell Rd., Grays 170 GA77
Cromwell Rd., Hayes 135 BR72
Cromwell Rd., Hert. 32 DT08
Cromwell Rd., Houns. 156 CA84
Cromwell Rd., Kings.T. 198 CL95
Cromwell Rd., Red. 250 DF133
Cromwell Rd., Tedd. 177 CG93
Cromwell Rd. (Cheshunt), Wal.Cr. 66 DV28
Cromwell Rd., Walt. 196 BW102
Cromwell Rd., Ware 33 DZ05
Cromwell Rd., Wem. 138 CL68
Cromwell Rd., Wor.Pk. 198 CR104
Cromwell St., Houns. 156 CA84
Cromwell Twr. EC2 142 DQ71
Whitecross St.
Cromwell Wk., Red. 250 DF134
Cromwells Mere, Rom. 105 FD51
Havering Rd.
Crondace Rd. SW6 160 DA81
Crondall St. N1 275 M1
Crondall St. N1 142 DR68
Cronks Hill, Red. 266 DC136
Cronks Hill, Reig. 266 DC136
Cronks Hill Clo., Red. 266 DD136
Cronks Hill Rd.
Cronks Hill Rd., Red. 266 DD136
Crook Log, Bexh. 166 EX83
Crooke Rd. SE8 163 DY78
Crooked Billet SW19 179 CW93
Woodhayes Rd.
Crooked Billet Roundabout E17 101 EA52
Crooked Billet Yd. E2 142 DS69
Kingsland Rd.
Crooked La., Grav. 191 GH86
Crooked Mile, Wal.Abb. 67 EC33
Crooked Usage N3 119 CY55
Crooked Way, Wal.Abb. 50 EE22
Crookham Rd. SW6 159 CZ81
Crookhams, Welw.G.C. 30 DA07
Crookston Rd. SE9 165 EN83
Croombs Rd. E16 144 EJ71
Crooms Hill SE10 163 EC80
Crooms Hill Gro. SE10 163 EC80
Crop Common, Hat. 45 CV16
Cropley Ct. N1 142 DR68
Cropley St.
Cropley St. N1 142 DR68
Croppath Rd., Dag. 126 FA63
Cropthorne Ct. W9 140 DC69
Maida Vale
Crosby Clo., Beac. 111 AM55
Crosby Clo., Felt. 176 BY91
Crosby Ct. SE1 279 K4
Crosby Rd. E7 144 EG65
Crosby Rd., Dag. 147 FB68
Crosby Row SE1 279 K4
Crosby Row SE1 162 DR75
Crosby Sq. EC3 275 M9
Crosby Wk. E8 142 DT65
Laurel St.
Crosby Wk. SW2 181 DN87
Crosier Rd., Uxb. 115 BQ63
Crosier Way, Ruis. 115 BS62
Crosland Pl. SW11 160 DG83
Taybridge Rd.
Cross Ave. SE10 163 ED79
Cross Deep, Twick. 177 CF90
Cross Deep Gdns., Twick. 177 CF89
Cross Keys Clo. W1 272 G7
Cross Keys Clo., Sev. 256 FG127
Brittains La.
Cross Keys Sq. EC1 275 H7
Cross Lances Rd., Houns. 156 CB84
Cross La. EC3 279 M1
Cross La. N8 121 DM55
Cross La., Beac. 111 AM55
Cross La., Bex. 186 EZ87
Cross La., Cher. 211 BB107
Chobham Rd.
Cross La., Hert. 31 DP09
Cross La. E., Grav. 191 GH89
Cross La. Footpath, Cher. 211 BB107
Cross La. W., Grav. 191 GH89
Cross Las., Ger.Cr. 91 AZ50
Cross Las., Guil. 243 AZ134
Cross Las. Clo., Ger.Cr. 91 AZ50
Cross Las.
Cross Meadow, Chesh. 54 AM29
Cross Oak, Wind. 151 AN82
Cross Oak Rd., Berk. 38 AU20
Cross Rd. E4 102 EE46
Cross Rd. N11 99 DH50
Cross Rd. N22 99 DN52
Cross Rd. SE5 162 DS82
Cross Rd. SW19 180 DA94
Cross Rd., Brom. 204 EL103
Cross Rd., Croy. 202 DR102
Cross Rd., Dart. 188 FJ86
Cross Rd. (Hawley), Dart. 188 FM91
Cross Rd., Enf. 82 DT42
Cross Rd., Felt. 176 BY91
Cross Rd., Grav. 191 GF86
Cross Rd., Har. 117 CD56
Cross Rd. (South Harrow), Har. 116 CB62
Cross Rd. (Wealdstone), Har. 95 CG54
Cross Rd., Hert. 32 DQ08
Cross Rd., Kings.T. 178 CM94
Cross Rd., Orp. 206 EV99
Cross Rd., Pur. 219 DP113
Cross Rd., Rom. 126 FA56
Cross Rd. (Chadwell Heath), Rom. 126 EW59
Cross Rd., Sid. 186 EV91
Sidcup Hill
Cross Rd., Sutt. 218 DD106
Cross Rd. (Belmont), Sutt. 218 DA110
Cross Rd., Tad. 233 CW122
Cross Rd., Uxb. 134 BJ66
New Windsor St.
Cross Rd., Wal.Cr. 67 DY33
Cross Rd., Wat. 76 BY44
Cross Rd., Wey. 195 BR104
Cross Rd., Wdf.Grn. 103 EM51
Cross Rds., Loug. 84 EH40
Cross St. N1 141 DP67
Cross St. SW13 158 CS82
Cross St., Erith 167 FE78
Bexley Rd.
Cross St., Hmptn. 176 CC92
Cross St., Harl. 51 ER15
Cross St., St.Alb. 43 CD20
Spencer St.
Cross St., Uxb. 134 BJ66
Cross St., Ware 33 DY06
Cross St., Wat. 76 BW41
Cross Way, Pnr. 93 BV54
Cross Way, The, Har. 95 CE54
Cross Ways, Hem.H. 41 BP20
Crossacres, Wok. 227 BE116
Crossbow Rd., Chig. 103 ET50
Crossbrook, Hat. 44 CS19
Crossbrook Rd. SE3 164 EL82
Crossbrook St. (Cheshunt), Wal.Cr. 67 DX31
Crossett Grn., Hem.H. 41 BQ22
Crossfell Rd., Hem.H. 41 BQ22
Crossfield Clo., Berk. 38 AT19
Crossfield Pl., Wey. 213 BP108
Crossfield Rd. N17 122 DQ55
Crossfield Rd. NW3 140 DD65
Crossfield Rd., Hodd. 49 EB15
Crossfield St. SE8 163 EA80
Crossfields, Loug. 85 EP43
Crossfields, St.Alb. 42 CB23
Crossford St. SW9 161 DL82
Crossgate, Edg. 96 CN48
Crossgate, Grnf. 137 CH65
Crossing Rd., Epp. 70 EU32
Crossland Rd., Red. 250 DG134
Crossland Rd., Th.Hth. 201 DP99
Crosslands, Cher. 211 BE105
Crosslands Ave. W5 138 CM74
Crosslands Ave., Sthl. 156 BZ78
Crosslands Rd., Epsom 216 CR107
Crosslet St. SE17 279 L8
Crosslet Vale SE10 163 EB81
Blackheath Rd.
Crossley Clo., West. 238 EK115
Crossley St. N7 141 DN65
Crossleys, Ch.St.G. 90 AW49
Crossmead SE9 185 EM88
Crossmead, Wat. 75 BV44
Crossmead Ave., Grnf. 136 CA69
Crossmount Ho. SE5 162 DQ80
Bowyer St.
Crossness La. SE28 146 EX73
Bayliss Ave.
Crossness Rd., Bark. 145 ET69
Crossoak La., Red. 266 DG144
Crossoaks La., Borwd. 78 CR35
Crossoaks La. (South Mimms), Pot.B. 62 CS34
Crosspath, The, Rad. 77 CG35
Crossroads, The, Lthd. 246 BX128
Crossthwaite Ave. SE5 162 DR84
Crosswall EC3 275 P10
Crosswall EC3 142 DT73
Crossway N12 98 DD51
Crossway N16 122 DS64
Crossway N22 99 DP52
Crossway NW9 119 CT56
Crossway SE28 146 EW72
Crossway SW20 199 CW98
Crossway, Chesh. 54 AS30
Crossway, Dag. 126 EW62
Crossway, Enf. 100 DS45
Crossway, Hayes 135 BU74
Crossway, Orp. 205 ER98
Crossway, Ruis. 116 BW63
Crossway, Walt. 195 BV103
Crossway, Welw.G.C. 29 CW05
Crossway, Wdf.Grn. 102 EJ49
Crossway, The SE9 184 EK89
Crossway, The W13 137 CG70
Crossway, The, Uxb. 134 BM68
Crossways N21 82 DQ44
Crossways, Beac. 89 AM54
Crossways, Berk. 38 AT20
Crossways, Brwd. 109 GA44
Crossways, Egh. 173 BD93
Crossways, Lthd. 246 BX127
The St.
Crossways, Rom. 127 FH55
Crossways, S.Croy. 221 DY108
Crossways, Sun. 175 BT94
Crossways, Sutt. 218 DD109
Crossways, West. 238 EJ120
Crossways, The, Couls. 235 DM119
Crossways, The, Guil. 258 AT136
Crossways, The, Houns. 156 BZ80
Crossways, The, Red. 251 DJ130
Crossways, The, Wem. 118 CN61
Crossways Boul., Dart. 168 FQ84
Crossways Business Pk., Dart. 168 FQ84
Crossways La., Reig. 250 DC128
Crossways Rd., Beck. 203 EA98
Crossways Rd., Mitch. 201 DH97
Crosswell Clo., Shep. 195 BQ96
Crosthwaite Way, Slou. 131 AK71
Croston St. E8 142 DU67
Crothall Clo. N13 99 DM48
Crouch Ave., Bark. 146 EV68
Crouch Clo., Beck. 183 EA93
Abbey La.
Crouch Cft. SE9 185 EN90
Crouch End Hill N8 121 DK59
Crouch Hall Rd. N8 121 DK58
Crouch Hill N4 121 DL59
Crouch Hill N8 121 DL58
Crouch La. (Cheshunt), Wal.Cr. 66 DQ28
Crouch Oak La., Add. 212 BJ105
Crouch Rd. NW10 138 CR66
Crouch Rd., Grays 171 GG78
Crouch Valley, Upmin. 129 FR59
Crouchfield, Hem.H. 40 BH21
Crouchfield, Hert. 32 DQ06
Crouchman's Clo. SE26 182 DT90
Crow Clo., Warl. 237 DY118
Crow Dr., Sev. 241 FC115
Crow Grn. La., Brwd. 108 FU43
Crow Grn. Rd., Brwd. 108 FT43
Crow La., Rom. 126 EZ59
Crow Piece La., Slou. 131 AM66
Crowborough Dr., Warl. 237 DY118
Crowborough Path, Wat. 94 BX49
Prestwick Rd.
Crowborough Rd. SW17 180 DG93
Crowden Way SE28 146 EW73
Crowder St. E1 142 DV73
Crowhurst Clo. SW9 161 DN82
Crowhurst Mead, Gdse. 252 DW130
Crowhurst Way, Orp. 206 EW99
Crowland Ave., Hayes 155 BS77
Crowland Gdns. N14 99 DL45
Crowland Rd. N15 122 DT57
Crowland Rd., Th.Hth. 202 DR98
Crowland Ter. N1 142 DR66
Crowland Wk., Mord. 200 DB100
Crowlands Ave., Rom. 127 FB58
Crowley Cres., Croy. 219 DN106
Crowline Wk. N1 142 DR65
Clephane Rd.
Crowmarsh Gdns. SE23 182 DW87
Tyson Rd.
Crown Arc., Kings.T. 197 CK96
Union St.
Crown Ash Hill, West. 222 EH114
Crown Ash La., West. 238 EG116
Crown Clo. E3 143 EA67
Crown Clo. NW6 140 DB65
Crown Clo. NW7 97 CT47
Crown Clo., Bishop's Stortford 37 FC07
Crown Clo., Hayes 155 BT75
Station Rd.
Crown Clo., Orp. 224 EU105
Crown Clo., Walt. 196 BW101
Crown Ct. EC2 275 J9
Crown Ct. SE12 184 EH86
Crown Ct. WC2 274 A9
Crown Ct., Brom. 204 EK99
Victoria Rd.
Crown Dale SE19 181 DP93
Crown Gate, Harl. 51 ER15
Crown Heights, Guil. 258 AY137
Crown Hill, Croy. 202 DQ103
Crown Hill, Epp. 69 EN34
Crown Hill, Wal.Abb. 68 EL33
Crown La. N14 99 DJ46
Crown La. SW16 181 DN92
Crown La., Brom. 204 EK99
Crown La., Chis. 205 EQ95
Crown La., H.Wyc. 88 AF48
Crown La., Mord. 200 DA97
Crown La., Slou. 131 AN67
Crown La., Vir.W. 192 AX100
Crown La. Gdns. SW16 181 DN92
Crown La.
Crown La. Spur, Brom. 204 EK100
Crown Meadow, Slou. 153 BB80
Crown Ms. E13 144 EJ67
Waghorn Rd.
Crown Ms. W6 159 CU77
Crown Office Row EC4 274 D10
Crown Par., Hayes 135 BT71
Crown Pas. SW1 277 L3
Crown Pas., Wat. 76 BW42
The Cres.
Crown Pl. NW5 141 DH65
Kentish Town Rd.
Crown Pt. Par. SE19 181 DP93
Beulah Hill
Crown Ri., Cher. 193 BF102
Guildford Rd.
Crown Ri., Wat. 60 BW34
Crown Rd. N10 98 DG52
Crown Rd. N17 100 DU52
Crown Rd., Borwd. 78 CN39
Crown Rd., Enf. 82 DV42
Crown Rd., Grays 170 GA79
Crown Rd., Ilf. 125 ER56
Crown Rd., Mord. 200 DA98
Crown Rd., N.Mal. 198 CQ95
Crown Rd., Orp. 224 EU106
Crown Rd., Ruis. 116 BX64
Victoria Rd.
Crown Rd., Sev. 225 FF110
Crown Rd., Slou. 153 BB80
Crown Rd., Sutt. 218 DA105
Crown Rd., Twick. 177 CH86
Crown Rd., Vir.W. 192 AW100
Crown Sq., Wok. 227 AZ117
Commercial Way
Crown St. SE5 162 DQ80
Crown St. W3 138 CP74
Crown St., Brwd. 108 FW47
Crown St., Dag. 147 FC65
Crown St., Egh. 173 BA91
Crown St., Har. 117 CD60
Crown Ter., Rich. 158 CM84
Crown Wk., Uxb. 134 BJ66
Oxford Rd.
Crown Wk., Wem. 118 CM62
Crown Way, West Dr. 134 BM74
Crown Wds. La. SE9 165 EQ82
Crown Wds. La. SE18 165 EP82
Crown Wds. Way SE9 185 ER85
Crown Yd., Houns. 156 CC83
High St.
Crowndale Rd. NW1 141 DJ68
Crownfield, Brox. 49 EA21
Crownfield Ave., Ilf. 125 ES58
Crownfield Rd. E15 123 ED63
Crownfields, Sev. 257 FH125
Crownhill Rd. NW10 139 CT67
Crownhill Rd., Wdf.Grn. 102 EL52
Crownmead Way, Rom. 127 FB56
Crownstone Rd. SW2 181 DN85
Crowntree Clo., Islw. 157 CF79
Crows Rd. E15 143 ED69
Crows Rd., Epp. 69 ET30
Crowshott Ave., Stan. 95 CJ54
Crowstone Rd., Grays 170 GC75
Crowther Ave., Brent. 158 CL77
Crowther Rd. SE25 202 DU98
Crowthorne Clo. SW18 179 CZ88
Crowthorne Rd. W10 139 CX72
Croxdale Rd., Borwd. 78 CM40
Croxden Clo., Edg. 118 CM55
Croxden Wk., Mord. 200 DC100
Croxford Gdns. N22 99 DP52
Croxford Way, Rom. 127 FD60
Horace Ave.
Croxley Clo., Orp. 206 EV96
Croxley Grn., Orp. 206 EV95
Croxley Rd. W9 139 CZ69
Croxley Vw., Wat. 75 BS44
Croxted Clo. SE21 182 DQ87
Croxted Rd. SE21 182 DQ87
Croxted Rd. SE24 182 DQ87
Croyde Ave., Grnf. 136 CC69
Croyde Ave., Hayes 155 BS77
Croyde Clo., Sid. 185 ER87
Croydon Flyover, The, Croy. 219 DP105
Duppas Hill Rd.
Croydon Gro., Croy. 201 DP102
Croydon La., Bans. 218 DB114
Croydon La. S., Bans. 218 DB114
Croydon Rd. E13 144 EF70
Croydon Rd. SE20 202 DV96
Croydon Rd., Beck. 203 DY97
Croydon Rd., Brom. 204 EJ104
Croydon Rd., Cat. 236 DU122
Croydon Rd., Croy. 219 DH105
Croydon Rd., Houns. 155 BP82
Croydon Rd., Kes. 205 EM104
Croydon Rd., Mitch. 200 DG98
Croydon Rd., Reig. 250 DB134
Croydon Rd., Wall. 219 DH105
Croydon Rd., Warl. 237 EC119
Croydon Rd., W.Wick. 204 EE104
Croydon Rd., West. 239 EM123
Croyland Rd. N9 100 DU46
Croylands Dr., Surb. 198 CL101
Croysdale Ave., Sun. 195 BU97
Crozier Dr., S.Croy. 220 DV109
Crozier Ter. E9 123 DX64
Crucible Clo., Rom. 126 EV58
Crucifix La. SE1 279 M4

Daltons Rd., Orp. 225 FB105
Daltons Rd., Swan. 207 FC102
Dalwood St. SE5 162 DS81
Daly Ct. E15 123 EC64
Clays La.
Dalyell Rd. SW9 161 DM83
Damascene Wk. SE21 182 DQ88
Lovelace Rd.
Damask Cres. E16 144 EE70
Cranberry La.
Damask Grn., Hem.H. 39 BE21
Dame St. N1 142 DQ68
Damer Ter. SW10 160 DC80
Tadema Rd.
Dames Rd. E7 124 EG62
Dameswick Vw., St.Alb. 60 CA27
Damien St. E1 142 DV72
Damigos Rd., Grav. 191 GM88
Damon Clo., Sid. 186 EV90
Damphurst La., Dor. 262 BZ139
Sheephouse La.
Damson Ct., Swan. 207 FD98
Damson Gro., Slou. 151 AQ75
Damson Way, Cars. 218 DF108
Kings Ave.
Damsonwood Clo., Sthl. 156 CA76
Dan Leno Wk. SW6 160 DB80
Britannia Rd.
Danbrook Rd. SW16 201 DL95
Danbury Clo., Brwd. 108 FT43
Danbury Clo., Rom. 126 EX55
Danbury Ms., Wall. 219 DH105
Danbury Rd., Loug. 102 EL45
Danbury Rd., Rain. 147 FF67
Danbury St. N1 141 DP68
Danbury Way, Wdf.Grn. 102 EJ51
Danby St. SE15 162 DT83
Dancer Rd. SW6 159 CZ81
Dancer Rd., Rich. 158 CN83
Dancers Hill Rd., Barn. 79 CW36
Dancers La., Barn. 79 CW35
Dando Cres. SE3 164 EH83
Dandridge Clo. SE10 164 EF78
Dandridge Clo., Slou. 152 AX77
Dandridge Dr., B.End 110 AC60
Millside
Dane Clo., Amer. 72 AT41
Dane Clo., Bex. 186 FA87
Dane Clo., Orp. 223 ER106
Dane Ct., Hert. 32 DS09
Dane Ct., Wok. 227 BF115
Dane Pl. E3 143 DY68
Roman Rd.
Dane Rd. N18 100 DW49
Dane Rd. SW19 200 DC95
Dane Rd. W13 137 CJ74
Dane Rd., Ashf. 175 BQ93
Dane Rd., Ilf. 125 EQ64
Dane Rd., Sev. 241 FE117
Dane Rd., Sthl. 136 BY73
Dane Rd., Warl. 237 DX117
Dane St. WC1 274 B7
Danebury, Croy. 221 EB107
Danebury Ave. SW15 178 CS86
Daneby Rd. SE6 183 EB90
Danecourt Gdns., Croy. 202 DT104
Danecroft Rd. SE24 182 DQ85
Danehill Wk., Sid. 186 EU90
Hatherley Rd.
Danehurst Gdns., Ilf. 124 EL57
Danehurst St. SW6 159 CY81
Daneland, Barn. 80 DF43
Danemead, Hodd. 33 EA14
Danemead Gro., Nthlt. 116 CB64
Danemere St. SW15 159 CW83
Danes, The, St.Alb. 60 CC28
Danes Clo., Grav. 190 GC90
Danes Clo., Lthd. 214 CC114
Danes Ct., Wem. 118 CP62
Danes Gate, Har. 117 CE55
Danes Hill, Wok. 227 BA118
Danes Rd., Rom. 127 FC59
Danes Way, Brwd. 108 FU43
Danes Way, Lthd. 215 CD114
Danesbury Pk., Hert. 32 DR08
Danesbury Rd., Felt. 175 BV88
Danescombe SE12 184 EG88
Winn Rd.
Danescourt Cres., Sutt. 200 DC103
Danescroft NW4 119 CX57
Danescroft Ave. NW4 119 CX57
Danescroft Gdns. NW4 119 CX57
Danesdale Rd. E9 143 DY65
Danesfield SE5 162 DS79
Albany Rd.
Daneshill, Red. 250 DE133
Daneshill Clo., Red. 250 DE133
Danesrood, Guil. 259 AZ135
Lower Edgeborough Rd.
Daneswood Ave. SE6 183 EC90
Daneswood Clo., Wey. 213 BP106
Danethorpe Rd., Wem. 137 CK65
Danetree Clo., Epsom 216 CQ108
Danetree Rd., Epsom 216 CQ108
Danette Gdns., Dag. 126 EZ61
Daneville Rd. SE5 162 DR81
Dangan Rd. E11 124 EG58
Daniel Bolt Clo. E14 143 EB71
Uamvar St.
Daniel Clo. N18 100 DW49
Daniel Clo. SW17 180 DE93
Daniel Clo., Grays 171 GH76
Daniel Clo. 170 FY75
(Chafford Hundred), Grays
Daniel Gdns. SE15 162 DT80
Daniel Pl. NW4 119 CV58
Daniel Rd. W5 138 CM73
Daniel Way, Bans. 218 DB114
Daniells, Welw.G.C. 30 DA08
Daniels La., Warl. 237 DZ116
Daniels Rd. SE15 162 DW83
Danses Clo., Guil. 243 BD132
Dansey Pl. W1 273 M10
Dansington Rd., Well. 166 EU84
Danson Cres., Well. 166 EV83
Danson La., Well. 166 EU84
Danson Mead, Well. 166 EW83
Danson Pk., Bexh. 166 EW84
Danson Rd., Bex. 186 EX85
Danson Rd., Bexh. 186 EX85
Dante Pl. SE11 278 G9
Dante Rd. SE11 278 F8
Dante Rd. SE11 161 DP77
Danube St. SW3 276 C10
Danvers Rd. N8 121 DK56
Danvers St. SW3 160 DD79
Danyon Clo., Rain. 148 FJ68
Danziger Way, Borwd. 78 CQ39
Dapdune Ct., Guil. 242 AW134
Dapdune Rd., Guil. 242 AX134
Dapdune Wf., Guil. 242 AW134
Daphne Gdns. E4 101 EC48
Gunners Gro.
Daphne St. SW18 180 DC86
Daplyn St. E1 142 DU71
Hanbury St.
D'Arblay St. W1 273 L9
D'Arblay St. W1 141 DJ72
Darby Clo., Cat. 236 DQ122
Fairbourne La.
Darby Cres., Sun. 196 BW96
Darby Dr., Wal.Abb. 67 EC33
Darby Gdns., Sun. 196 BW96
Darcy Ave., Wall. 219 DJ105
Darcy Clo. N20 98 DD47
D'Arcy Clo., Brwd. 109 GB45
Darcy Clo., Couls. 235 DP119
Darcy Clo. (Cheshunt), 67 DY31
Wal.Cr.
D'Arcy Dr., Har. 117 CK56
Darcy Gdns., Dag. 146 EZ67
D'Arcy Gdns., Har. 118 CL56
D'Arcy Pl., Ash. 232 CM117
Darcy Rd. SW16 201 DL96
D'Arcy Rd., Ash. 232 CM117
Darcy Rd., Islw. 157 CG81
London Rd.
D'Arcy Rd., Sutt. 217 CX105
Dare Gdns., Dag. 126 EY62
Grafton Rd.
Darell Rd., Rich. 158 CN83
Darent Mead 208 FP95
(Sutton at Hone), Dart.
Darent Valley Path, 188 FM89
Dart.
Darent Valley Path, Sev. 256 FC121
Darenth Clo., Sev. 256 FC122
Darenth Gdns., West. 255 ER126
Quebec Ave.
Darenth Hill, Dart. 188 FP92
Darenth La., Sev. 256 FE121
Darenth La., S.Ock. 149 FU72
Darenth Rd. N16 122 DT59
Darenth Rd., Dart. 188 FM87
Darenth Rd. (Darenth), 188 FP91
Dart.
Darenth Rd., Well. 166 EU81
Darenth Way, Horl. 268 DF145
Darenth Way, Sev. 225 FG111
Darenth Wd. Rd., Dart. 189 FS90
Darfield Rd. SE4 183 DZ85
Darfield Rd., Guil. 243 BA131
Darfield Way W10 139 CX72
Darfur St. SW15 159 CX83
Dargate Clo. SE19 182 DT94
Chipstead Clo.
Darien Rd. SW11 160 DD83
Dark La., Brwd. 108 FT50
Dark La., Guil. 260 BM139
Dark La. (Cheshunt), 66 DU31
Wal.Cr.
Dark La., Ware 33 DY05
Darkes La., Pot.B. 63 CZ32
Darkhole Ride, Wind. 150 AG84
Darlan Rd. SW6 159 CZ80
Darlaston Rd. SW19 179 CX94
Darley Clo., Add. 212 BJ106
Darley Clo., Croy. 203 DY100
Darley Dr., N.Mal. 198 CR96
Darley Gdns., Mord. 200 DC100
Darley Rd. N9 100 DT46
Darley Rd. SW11 180 DF86
Darling Rd. SE4 163 EA83
Darling Row E1 142 DV70
Darlington Clo., Amer. 55 AR38
King George V Rd.
Darlington Gdns., Rom. 106 FK50
Darlington Path, Rom. 106 FK50
Darlington Gdns.
Darlington Rd. SE27 181 DP92
Darlton Clo., Dart. 167 FF83
Darmaine Clo., S.Croy. 220 DQ108
Churchill Rd.
Darndale Clo. E17 101 DZ54
Priory Ct.
Darnets Fld., Sev. 241 FF117
Darnhills, Rad. 77 CF35
Darnicle Hill 65 DM25
(Cheshunt), Wal.Cr.
Darnley Ho. E14 143 DY72
Camdenhurst St.
Darnley Pk., Wey. 195 BP104
Darnley Rd. E9 142 DW65
Darnley Rd., Grav. 191 GG86
Darnley Rd., Grays 170 GB79
Stanley Rd.
Darnley Rd., Wdf.Grn. 102 EG53
Darnley St., Grav. 191 GG87
Darnley Ter. W11 139 CY74
St. James Gdns.
Darns Hill, Swan. 207 FC101
Tylers Grn. Rd.
Darrell Clo., Slou. 153 AZ77
Darrell Rd. SE22 182 DU85
Darren Clo. N4 121 DM59
Darrick Wd. Rd., Orp. 205 ER103
Darrington Rd., Borwd. 78 CL39
Darris Clo., Hayes 136 BY70
Darrs La., Berk. 38 AS17
Darsley Dr. SW8 161 DL81
Dart, The, Hem.H. 40 BN15
Dart Clo., Slou. 153 BB79
Dart Clo., Upmin. 129 FR58
Dart Grn., S.Ock. 149 FV72
Dart St. W10 139 CY69
Dartfields, Rom. 106 FK51
Dartford Ave. N9 82 DW44
Dartford Bypass, Dart. 188 FJ90
Dartford Ind. Trd. Est., 188 FM89
Dart.
Dartford Rd., Bex. 187 FC88
Dartford Rd. 208 FM100
(Farningham), Dart.
Dartford Rd. 187 FG86
(The Brent), Dart.
Dartford Rd. 187 FH93
(Wilmington), Dart.
Dartford Rd., Sev. 257 FJ124
Dartford St. SE17 162 DQ79
Dartford Tunnel, Dart. 169 FR82
Dartford Tunnel, Grays 169 FR82
Dartford Tunnel App., 169 FR82
Grays
Dartford Tunnel App. Rd., 188 FP86
Dart.
Dartmoor Wk. E14 163 EA77
Charnwood Gdns.
Dartmouth Ave., Wok. 211 BC114
Dartmouth Clo. W11 140 DA72
Dartmouth Grn., Wok. 211 BD114
St. Michael's Rd.
Dartmouth Gro. SE10 163 EC81
Dartmouth Hill SE10 163 EC81
Dartmouth Pk. Ave. NW5 121 DH62
Dartmouth Pk. Hill N19 121 DH60
Dartmouth Pk. Hill NW5 121 DJ62
Dartmouth Pk. Rd. NW5 121 DH63
Dartmouth Path, Wok. 211 BD114
Dartmouth Ave.
Dartmouth Pl. SE23 182 DW89
Dartmouth Rd.
Dartmouth Pl. W4 158 CS79
Dartmouth Rd. E16 144 EG72
Fords Pk. Rd.
Dartmouth Rd. NW2 139 CX65
Dartmouth Rd. NW4 119 CU58
Dartmouth Rd. SE23 182 DW89
Dartmouth Rd. SE26 182 DV90
Dartmouth Rd., Brom. 204 EG101
Dartmouth Rd., Ruis. 115 BU62
Dartmouth Row SE10 163 EC81
Dartmouth St. SW1 277 N5
Dartmouth St. SW1 161 DK75
Dartmouth Ter. SE10 163 ED81
Dartmouth Hill
Dartnell Ave., W.Byf. 212 BH112
Dartnell Clo., W.Byf. 212 BH112
Dartnell Cres., W.Byf. 212 BH112
Dartnell Keep, W.Byf. 212 BH112
Dartnell Pk. Rd., W.Byf. 212 BH112
Dartnell Pl., W.Byf. 212 BH112
Dartnell Rd., Croy. 202 DT101
Dartrey Wk. SW10 160 DD80
World's End Est.
Dartview Clo., Grays 170 GE77
Darvell Clo., Wok. 226 AU116
Darvell Dr., Chesh. 54 AN29
Darville Rd. N16 122 DT62
Darvills La., Slou. 151 AR75
Darwell Clo. E6 145 EN68
Darwin Clo. N11 99 DH48
Darwin Clo., Orp. 223 ER106
Darwin Clo., St.Alb. 43 CE16
Darwin Dr., Sthl. 136 CB72
Darwin Gdns., Wat. 94 BW50
Neave Cres.
Darwin Rd. N22 99 DP53
Darwin Rd. W5 157 CJ78
Darwin Rd., Slou. 153 AZ75
Darwin Rd., Til. 171 GF81
Darwin Rd., Well. 165 ET83
Darwin St. SE17 279 L8
Darwin St. SE17 162 DR77
Daryngton Dr., Grnf. 137 CD68
Daryngton Dr., Guil. 243 BB134
Dashes, The, Harl. 35 ES14
Dashwood Clo., Bexh. 186 FA85
Dashwood Clo., Slou. 152 AW77
Dashwood Clo., W.Byf. 212 BJ112
Dashwood Rd. N8 121 DM58
Dashwood Rd., Grav. 191 GG89
Dassett Rd. SE27 181 DP92
Datchelor Pl. SE5 162 DR81
Datchet Clo., Hem.H. 41 BP15
Datchet Pl., Slou. 152 AV81
Datchet Rd. SE6 183 DZ90
Datchet Rd., Slou. 152 AT77
Datchet Rd. (Horton), 153 AZ83
Slou.
Datchet Rd., Wind. 151 AR80
Datchet Rd. 152 AU84
(Old Windsor), Wind.
Datchworth Ct. N4 122 DQ62
Queens Dr.
Datchworth Turn, 41 BQ20
Hem.H.
Date St. SE17 162 DQ78
Daubeney Gdns. N17 100 DQ52
Daubeney Rd. E5 123 DY63
Daubeney Rd. N17 100 DQ52
Daubeney Twr. SE8 163 DZ77
Dault Rd. SW18 180 DC86
Davema Clo., Chis. 205 EN95
Davenant Rd. N19 121 DK61
Davenant Rd., Croy. 219 DP105
Duppas Hill Rd.
Davenant St. E1 142 DU71
Davenham Ave., Nthwd. 93 BT49
Davenport Clo., Tedd. 177 CG93
Davenport Rd. SE6 183 EC86
Davenport Rd., Sid. 186 EX89
Daventer Dr., Stan. 95 CF52
Daventry Ave. E17 123 EA57
Daventry Clo., Slou. 153 BF81
Daventry Gdns., Rom. 106 FJ50
Daventry Rd.
Daventry Grn., Rom. 106 FJ50
Hailsham Rd.
Daventry Rd., Rom. 106 FJ50
Daventry St. NW1 272 B6
Daventry St. NW1 140 DE71
Davern Clo. SE10 164 EF77
Davey Clo. N7 141 DM65
Davey Rd. E9 143 EA66
White Post La.
Davey St. SE15 162 DT79
David Ave., Grnf. 137 CE69
David Clo., Hayes 155 BR80
David Dr., Rom. 106 FN51
David Ms. W1 272 F6
David Rd., Dag. 126 EY61
David Rd., Slou. 153 BF82
David St. E15 143 ED65
Davidge St. SE1 278 G5
Davidge St. SE1 161 DP75
Davids Rd. SE23 182 DW88
David's Way, Ilf. 103 ES52
Davidson Gdns. SW8 161 DL80
Davidson La., Har. 117 CF59
Grove Hill
Davidson Rd., Croy. 202 DS102
Davidson Way, Rom. 127 FE58
Davies Clo., Croy. 202 DT100
Davies Clo., Rain. 148 FJ69
Davies La. E11 124 EE61
Davies Ms. W1 273 H10
Davies St. W1 273 H10
Davies St. W1 141 DH73
Davies St., Hert. 32 DS09
Davies Way, H.Wyc. 88 AC54
Davington Gdns., Dag. 126 EV64
Davington Rd., Dag. 146 EV65
Davinia Clo., Wdf.Grn. 103 EM51
Deacon Way
Davis Ave., Grav. 190 GE88
Davis Clo., Sev. 257 FJ122
Golding Rd.
Davis Rd. W3 139 CT74
Davis Rd., Chess. 216 CN105
Davis Rd., Grays 170 FZ76
Davis Rd., S.Ock. 149 FR74
Davis Rd., Wey. 212 BM110
Eyston Dr.
Davis St. E13 144 EH68
Davison Clo., Wal.Cr. 67 DX28
Davison Dr. (Cheshunt), 67 DX28
Wal.Cr.
Davisville Rd. W12 159 CU75
Davos Clo., Wok. 226 AY119
Davys Clo., St.Alb. 28 CL08
Davys Pl., Grav. 191 GL93
Dawell Dr., West. 238 EJ117
Dawes Ave., Horn. 128 FK62
Dawes Ave., Islw. 177 CG85
Dawes Clo., Chesh. 54 AP32
Dawes Clo., Green. 189 FU85
Cowley Ave.
Dawes Ct., Esher 214 CB105
Dawes E. Rd., Slou. 130 AJ70
Dawes Ho. SE17 279 K9
Dawes La., Rick. 73 BE37
Dawes Moor Clo., Slou. 132 AW72
Dawes Rd. SW6 159 CY80
Dawes Rd., Uxb. 134 BL68
Dawes St. SE17 279 L10
Dawes St. SE17 162 DR78
Dawley, Welw.G.C. 29 CZ06
Dawley Ave., Uxb. 135 BQ72
Dawley Ct., Hem.H. 40 BN16
Dawley Grn., S.Ock. 149 FU72
Dawley Par., Hayes 135 BQ73
Dawley Rd.
Dawley Ride, Slou. 153 BE81
Dawley Rd., Hayes 135 BQ73
Dawlish Ave. N13 99 DL49
Dawlish Ave. SW18 180 DB89
Dawlish Ave., Grnf. 137 CG68
Dawlish Dr., Ilf. 125 ES63
Dawlish Dr., Pnr. 116 BY57
Dawlish Dr., Ruis. 115 BU61
Dawlish Rd. E10 123 EC60
Dawlish Rd. N17 122 DU55
Dawlish Rd. NW2 139 CX65
Dawlish Wk., Rom. 106 FJ53
Neave Cres.
Dawn Clo., Houns. 156 BY83
Dawn Redwood Clo., 153 BA83
Slou.
Dawnay Gdns. SW18 180 DD89
Dawnay Rd. SW18 180 DC89
Dawnay Rd., Lthd. 246 CB126
Dawpool Rd. NW2 119 CT61
Daws Hill E4 83 EC40
Daws La. NW7 97 CT50
Dawson Ave., Bark. 145 ET66
Dawson Ave., Orp. 206 EV96
Dawson Clo. SE18 165 EQ77
Dawson Clo., Hayes 135 BR71
Dawson Clo., Wind. 151 AN82
Dawson Dr., Rain. 147 FH66
Dawson Dr., Swan. 187 FE93
Dawson Gdns., Bark. 145 ET66
Dawson Ave.
Dawson Heights Est. SE22 182 DU87
Dawson Pl. W2 140 DA73
Dawson Rd. NW2 119 CW64
Dawson Rd., Kings.T. 198 CM97
Dawson Rd., W.Byf. 212 BK111
Dawson St. E2 142 DT68
Dax Ct., Sun. 196 BW97
Thames St.
Day Spring, Guil. 242 AV130
Daybrook Rd. SW19 200 DB96
Daye Mead, Welw.G.C. 30 DB12
Daylesford Ave. SW15 159 CU84
Daylop Dr., Chig. 104 EV48
Daymer Gdns., Pnr. 115 BV56
Daymerslea Ridge, Lthd. 231 CJ121
Days Acre, S.Croy. 220 DT110
Days Clo., Hat. 45 CT18
Days La., Brwd. 108 FU42
Days La., Sid. 185 ES87
Days Mead, Hat. 45 CT18
Daysbrook Rd. SW2 181 DM89
Dayseys Hill, Red. 267 DN143
Dayton Dr., Erith 168 FK78
Dayton Gro. SE15 162 DW81
De Barowe Ms. N5 121 DP63
Leigh Rd.
De Beauvoir Cres. N1 142 DS67
De Beauvoir Est. N1 142 DR67
De Beauvoir Rd. N1 142 DS67
De Beauvoir Sq. N1 142 DS66
De Bohun Ave. N14 81 DH44
De Brome Rd., Felt. 176 BW88
De Burgh Pk., Bans. 234 DB115
De Crespigny Pk. SE5 162 DR82
De Frene Rd. SE26 183 DX91
De Havilland Ave., Hat. 44 CS17
De Havilland Clo., Hat. 45 CT17
De Havilland Ct., Rad. 62 CL32
Armstrong Gdns.
De Havilland Dr., Wey. 212 BL111
De Havilland Rd., Edg. 96 CN54
De Havilland Rd., 156 BW80
Houns.
De Havilland Rd., Wall. 219 DL108
De Havilland Way, 59 BT32
Abb.L.
De Havilland Way, Stai. 174 BK86
De Lapre Clo., Orp. 206 EX101
De Lara Way, Wok. 226 AX118
De Laune St. SE17 161 DP78
De Luci Rd., Erith 167 FC78
De Lucy St. SE2 166 EV77
De Montfort Rd. SW16 181 DL90
De Morgan Rd. SW6 160 DB83
De Quincey Rd. N17 100 DR53
De Ros Pl., Egh. 173 BA93
Wesley Dr.
De Salis Rd., Uxb. 135 BQ70
De Tany Ct., St.Alb. 43 CD21
De Vere Cotts. W8 160 DC76
Canning Pl.
De Vere Gdns. W8 160 DC75
De Vere Gdns., Ilf. 125 EM61
De Vere Ms. W8 160 DC76
Canning Pl.
De Vere Wk., Wat. 75 BS40
De Walden St. W1 272 G7
Deacon Clo., Cob. 229 BV119
Deacon Clo., Pur. 219 DL109
Deacon Clo., St.Alb. 43 CD24
Creighton Ave.
Deacon Fld., Guil. 242 AV133
Middleton Rd.
Deacon Ms. N1 142 DR66
Deacon Rd. NW2 119 CU64
Deacon Rd., Kings.T. 198 CM95
Deacon Way SE17 279 H8
Deacon Way SE17 162 DQ77
Deacon Way, Wdf.Grn. 103 EM52
Deacons Clo., Borwd. 78 CN42
Deacons Clo., Pnr. 93 BV54
Deacons Hill, Wat. 76 BW44
Deacon's Hill Rd., Borwd. 78 CM42
Deacons Leas, Orp. 223 ER105
Deacons Wk., Hmptn. 176 BZ91
Bishops Gro.
Deaconsfield Rd., 40 BK23
Hem.H.
Deadfield La., Hert. 30 DF13
Deadhearn La., Ch.St.G. 90 AY46
Deadman's Ash La., 74 BH36
Rick.
Deakin Clo., Wat. 93 BS45
Chenies Way
Deal Ave., Slou. 131 AM72
Deal Porters Way SE16 162 DW76
Deal Rd. SW17 180 DG93
Deal St. E1 142 DU71
Deal's Gateway SE10 163 EB81
Blackheath Rd.
Dealtry Rd. SW15 159 CW84
Dean Ave., Hodd. 49 DX17
Dean Bradley St. SW1 277 P7
Dean Bradley St. SW1 161 DL76
Dean Clo. E9 122 DW64
Churchill Wk.
Dean Clo. SE16 143 DX74
Surrey Water Rd.
Dean Clo., Uxb. 134 BM66
Dean Clo., Wind. 151 AK83
Dean Clo., Wok. 227 BE115
Dean Ct., Wem. 117 CH62
Dean Dr., Stan. 96 CL54
Dean Farrar St. SW1 277 N6
Dean Farrar St. SW1 161 DK76
Dean Fld., Hem.H. 57 BA27
Dean Gdns. E17 123 ED56
Dean Gdns. W13 137 CH74
Northfield Ave.
Dean La., Red. 235 DH123
Dean Oak La., Reig. 265 CW144
Dean Rd. NW2 139 CW65
Dean Rd., Croy. 220 DR105
Dean Rd., Hmptn. 176 BZ92
Dean Rd., Houns. 176 CB85
Dean Ryle St. SW1 277 P8
Dean Ryle St. SW1 161 DL77
Dean Stanley St. SW1 277 P7
Dean Stanley St. SW1 161 DL76
Dean St. E7 124 EG64
Dean St. W1 273 M8
Dean St. W1 141 DK72
Dean Trench St. SW1 277 P7
Dean Wk., Edg. 96 CQ51
Deansbrook Rd.
Dean Wk., Lthd. 246 CB126
Dean Way, Ch.St.G. 90 AU48
Dean Way, Sthl. 156 CB75
Dean Wd. Rd., Beac. 89 AR52
Deanacre Clo., Ger.Cr. 90 AY51
Deancroft Rd., Ger.Cr. 90 AY51
Deancross St. E1 142 DW72
Deane Ave., Ruis. 115 BV64
Deane Cft. Rd., Pnr. 116 BW58
Deane Way, Ruis. 115 BV58
Deanery Clo. N2 120 DE56
Deanery Ms. W1 276 G2
Deanery Rd. E15 144 EE65
Deanery Rd., Eden. 255 EQ134
Deanery St. W1 276 G2
Deanery St. W1 140 DG74
Deanhill Rd. SW14 158 CP84
Deans Bldgs. SE17 279 L9
Deans Bldgs. SE17 162 DR77
Deans Clo. W4 158 CP79
Deans Clo., Abb.L. 59 BR32
Deans Clo., Amer. 72 AT37
Park Rd.
Dean's Clo., Croy. 202 DT104
Deans Clo., Edg. 96 CQ51
Deans Clo., Slou. 132 AV67
Deans Clo., Tad. 233 CV124
Deans La.
Deans Ct. EC4 274 G9
Deans Dr. N13 99 DP51
Deans Dr., Edg. 96 CR50
Deans Gdns., St.Alb. 43 CG16
Dean's Gate Clo. SE23 183 DX90
Deans La., Edg. 96 CQ51
Deans La., Red. 251 DN133
Deans La., Tad. 233 CV124
Deans Ms. W1 273 J8
Dean's Pl. SW1 277 M10
Dean's Pl. SW1 161 DK78
Deans Rd. W7 137 CF74
Deans Rd., Brwd. 108 FV48
Deans Rd., Red. 251 DJ130
Deans Rd., Sutt. 200 DB104
Deans Wk., Couls. 235 DN118
Deans Way, Edg. 96 CQ50
Dean's Yd. SW1 277 N6
Deansbrook Clo., Edg. 96 CQ51
Deansbrook Rd., Edg. 96 CP52
Deanscroft Ave. NW9 118 CQ61
Deansfield, Cat. 252 DT125
Deansway N2 120 DD56
Deansway N9 100 DS48
Deansway, Chesh. 54 AP29
Deansway, Hem.H. 40 BM23
Dearn Gdns., Mitch. 200 DE97
Dearne Clo., Stan. 95 CG50
Dearsley Ho., Rain. 147 FD68
Deason St. E15 143 EC67
High St.
Debden Clo., Kings.T. 177 CK92
Dukes Ave.
Debden Clo., Wdf.Grn. 102 EK52
Debden Ind. Group, Loug. 85 ER42
Debden La., Loug. 85 EP38
Debden Rd., Loug. 85 EP38
Debden Wk., Horn. 147 FH65
Tangmere Cres.
Debenham Rd. 66 DV27
(Cheshunt), Wal.Cr.
Debnams Rd. SE16 162 DW77
Rotherhithe New Rd.
Deborah Clo., Islw. 157 CE81
Deborah Cres., Ruis. 115 BR59
Debrabant Clo., Erith 167 FD79
Deburgh Rd. SW19 180 DC94
Decies Way, Slou. 132 AU67
Decima St. SE1 279 M6
Decima St. SE1 162 DS76

Deck Clo. SE16 163 DX75
Thame Rd.
Decoy Ave. NW11 119 CY57
Dedswell Dr., Guil. 244 BG129
Dedworth Dr., Wind. 151 AM81
Dedworth Rd., Wind. 150 AJ82
Dee, The, Hem.H. 40 BM15
Dee Clo., Upmin. 129 FS58
Dee Rd., Rich. 158 CM84
Dee St. E14 143 EC72
Dee Way, Epsom 216 CS110
Dee Way, Rom. 105 FE52
Deeley Rd. SW8 161 DK81
Deena Clo. W3 138 CM72
Deena Clo., Slou. 131 AL73
Deep Acres, Amer. 55 AN36
Deep Fld., Slou. 152 AV80
Deep Pool La., Wok. 210 AV114
Deepdale SW19 179 CX91
Deepdale Ave., Brom. 204 EE98
Deepdene W5 138 CM70
Deepdene, Pot.B. 63 CX31
Deepdene Ave., Croy. 202 DT104
Deepdene Ave., Dor. 263 CH139
Deepdene Ave. Rd., Dor. 247 CJ134
Deepdene Clo. E11 124 EG56
Deepdene Ct. N21 81 DP44
Deepdene Dr., Dor. 263 CJ135
Deepdene Gdns. SW2 181 DM87
Deepdene Gdns., Dor. 263 CH135
Deepdene Pk. Rd., Dor. 263 CJ135
Deepdene Path, Loug. 85 EN42
Deepdene Rd. SE5 162 DR84
Deepdene Rd., Loug. 85 EN42
Deepdene Rd., Well. 166 EU83
Deepdene Vale, Dor. 263 CJ135
Deepdene Wd., Dor. 263 CJ136
Deepfield Way, Couls. 235 DL116
Deepfields, Horl. 268 DF146
Deepwell Clo., Islw. 157 CG81
Deepwood La., Grnf. 137 CD69
Cowgate Rd.
Deer Pk., Harl. 51 EN18
Deer Pk. Clo., Kings.T. 178 CP94
Deer Pk. Gdns., Mitch. 200 DD97
Deer Pk. Rd. SW19 200 DB96
Deer Pk. Wk., Chesh. 54 AS28
Deer Pk. Way, W.Wick. 204 EE103
Deerbarn Rd., Guil. 242 AV133
Deerbrook Rd. SE24 181 DP88
Deerdale Rd. SE24 162 DQ84
Deere Ave., Rain. 147 FG65
Deerfield Clo., Ware 33 DX05
Deerhurst Clo., Felt. 175 BU91
Deerhurst Cres., Hmptn. 176 CC93
High St.
Deerhurst Rd. NW2 139 CX65
Deerhurst Rd. SW16 181 DM92
Deerings Dr., Pnr. 115 BU57
Deerings Rd., Reig. 250 DB134
Deerleap Gro. E4 83 EB43
Deerleap La., Sev. 224 EX113
Deerleap Rd., Dor. 262 CB137
Deers Fm. Clo., Wok. 228 BL116
Deerswood Ave., Hat. 45 CV20
Deerswood Clo., Cat. 236 DU124
Crescent Rd.
Deeside Rd. SW17 180 DD90
Deeves Hall La., Pot.B. 62 CS32
Defiance Wk. SE18 165 EM76
Antelope Rd.
Defiant Way, Wall. 219 DL108
Defoe Ave., Rich. 158 CN80
Defoe Clo. SE16 163 DZ75
Vaughan St.
Defoe Clo. SW17 180 DE93
Defoe Clo., Erith 167 FE81
Selkirk Dr.
Defoe Ho. EC2 142 DQ71
Beech St.
Defoe Par., Grays 171 GH76
Defoe Rd. N16 122 DS61
Defoe Way, Rom. 104 FA51
Degema Rd., Chis. 185 EP92
Dehar Cres. NW9 119 CT59
Deimos Dr., Hem.H. 40 BN17
Dekker Rd. SE21 182 DS86
Delabole Rd., Red. 251 DL129
Delacourt Rd. SE3 164 EH80
Old Dover Rd.
Delafield Rd. SE7 164 EH78
Delafield Rd., Grays 170 GD78
Delaford Clo., Iver 134 BG72
Delaford Rd. SE16 162 DV78
Delaford St. SW6 159 CY80
Delagarde Rd., West. 255 EQ126
Delahay Ri., Berk. 38 AV17
Delamare Rd. (Cheshunt), Wal.Cr. 67 DY30
Delamere Cres., Croy. 202 DW100
Delamere Gdns. NW7 96 CR51
Delamere Rd. SW20 199 CX95
Delamere Rd. W5 138 CL74
Delamere Rd., Borwd. 78 CP39
Delamere Rd., Hayes 136 BX73
Delamere Rd., Reig. 266 DB138
Delamere Ter. W2 140 DB71
Delancey Pas. NW1 141 DH67
Delancey St.
Delancey St. NW1 141 DH67
Delaporte, Epsom 216 CS112
Delargy Clo., Grays 171 GH76
Delaware Rd. W9 140 DB70
Delawyk Cres. SE24 182 DQ86
Delcombe Ave., Wor.Pk. 199 CW102
Delderfield, Lthd. 231 CK120
Delfcroft, Ware 32 DW05
Delft Way SE22 182 DS85
East Dulwich Gro.
Delhi Rd., Enf. 100 DT45
Delhi St. N1 141 DL67
Delia St. SW18 180 DB87
Delius Clo., Borwd. 77 CJ44
Delius Gro. E15 143 ED68
Gay Rd.
Dell, The SE2 166 EU78
Dell, The SE19 202 DT95
Dell, The, Bex. 187 FE88
Dell, The, Brent. 157 CJ79
Dell, The, Brwd. 107 FV51
Dell, The, Felt. 175 BV87
Harlington Rd. W.
Dell, The, Ger.Cr. 90 AY51
Dell, The, Hert. 32 DQ12
Dell, The, H.Wyc. 88 AC46
Dell, The, Horl. 269 DH147
Dell, The, Nthwd. 93 BS47
Dell, The, Pnr. 94 BX54
Dell, The, Rad. 77 CG36
Dell, The, Reig. 250 DA133
Dell, The, St.Alb. 43 CG18
Dell, The, Tad. 233 CW121
Dell, The, Wem. 117 CH64
Dell, The, Wok. 226 AW118
Dell, The, Wdf.Grn. 102 EH48
Dell Clo. E15 143 ED67
Dell Clo., Dor. 247 CJ127
Dell Clo., Lthd. 231 CE123
Dell Clo., Slou. 111 AQ64
Dell Clo., Wall. 219 DJ105
Dell Clo., Wdf.Grn. 102 EH48
Dell Fm. Rd., Ruis. 115 BR57
Dell La., Epsom 217 CU106
Dell Lees, Beac. 89 AQ51
Dell Meadow, Hem.H. 40 BL24
Belswains La.
Dell Ri., St.Alb. 60 CB26
Dell Rd., Enf. 82 DW38
Dell Rd., Epsom 217 CU107
Dell Rd., Grays 170 GB77
Dell Rd., Wat. 75 BU37
Dell Rd., West Dr. 154 BM76
Dell Side, Wat. 75 BU37
The Harebreaks
Dell Wk., N.Mal. 198 CS96
Dell Way W13 137 CJ72
Della Path E5 122 DV62
Napoleon Rd.
Dellbow Rd., Felt. 175 BV85
Central Way
Dellcott Clo., Welw.G.C. 29 CW08
Dellcut Rd., Hem.H. 40 BN18
Dellfield, Chesh. 54 AN29
Dellfield, St.Alb. 43 CG21
Dellfield Ave., Berk. 38 AV17
Dellfield Clo., Beck. 183 EC94
Foxgrove Rd.
Dellfield Clo., Berk. 38 AU17
Dellfield Clo., Rad. 77 CE35
Dellfield Clo., Wat. 75 BU40
Dellfield Cres., Uxb. 134 BK70
Dellfield Par. (Cowley), Uxb. 134 BJ70
High St.
Dellfield Rd., Hat. 45 CU18
Dellmeadow, Abb.L. 59 BS30
Dellors Clo., Barn. 79 CX43
Dellow Clo., Ilf. 125 ER59
Dellow St. E1 142 DV73
Dells, The, Hem.H. 41 BP21
Dells Clo. E4 101 EB45
Dell's Ms. SW1 277 L9
Dells Wd. Clo., Hodd. 33 DZ14
Highwood Rd.
Dellside, Uxb. 114 BJ57
Dellsome La., Hat. 45 CV23
Dellsome La., St.Alb. 44 CS23
Dellwood, Rick. 92 BH46
Dellwood Gdns., Ilf. 125 EN55
Delmar Ave., Hem.H. 41 BR21
Delmare Clo. SW9 161 DM84
Brighton Ter.
Delme Cres. SE3 164 EH82
Delmeade Rd., Chesh. 54 AN32
Delmey Clo., Croy. 202 DT104
Radcliffe Rd.
Deloraine St. SE8 163 EA81
Delorme St. W6 159 CX79
Delta Bungalows, Horl. 268 DG150
Michael Cres.
Delta Clo., Wok. 210 AT110
Delta Clo., Wor.Pk. 199 CT104
Delta Ct. NW2 119 CU61
Delta Dr., Horl. 268 DG150
Cheyne Wk.
Delta Gain, Wat. 94 BX47
Delta Gro., Nthlt. 136 BX69
Delta Rd., Brwd. 109 GD44
Delta Rd., Wok. 227 BA116
Delta Rd. (Chobham), Wok. 210 AT110
Delta Rd., Wor.Pk. 198 CS104
Delta St. E2 142 DU69
Wellington Row
Delta Way, Egh. 193 BC95
Delvan Clo. SE18 165 EN80
Ordnance Rd.
Delvers Mead, Dag. 127 FC63
Delverton Rd. SE17 161 DP78
Delves, Tad. 233 CX121
Heathcote
Delvino Rd. SW6 160 DA81
Demesne Rd., Wall. 219 DK105
Demeta Clo., Wem. 118 CQ62
Dempster Clo., Surb. 197 CJ101
Dempster Rd. SW18 180 DC85
Den Clo., Beck. 203 ED97
Den Rd., Brom. 203 ED97
Denberry Dr., Sid. 186 EV90
Denbigh Clo. NW10 138 CS66
Denbigh Clo. W11 139 CZ73
Denbigh Clo., Chis. 185 EM93
Denbigh Clo., Hem.H. 40 BL21
Old Crabtree La.
Denbigh Clo., Horn. 128 FN56
Denbigh Clo., Ruis. 115 BT61
Denbigh Clo., Sthl. 136 BZ72
Denbigh Rd.
Denbigh Clo., Sutt. 217 CZ106
Denbigh Dr., Hayes 155 BQ75
Denbigh Gdns., Rich. 178 CM85
Denbigh Ms. SW1 277 K9
Denbigh Pl. SW1 277 K10
Denbigh Pl. SW1 161 DJ78
Denbigh Rd. E6 144 EK69
Denbigh Rd. W11 139 CZ73
Denbigh Rd. W13 137 CH73
Denbigh Rd., Houns. 156 CB82
Denbigh Rd., Sthl. 136 BZ72
Denbigh St. SW1 277 K9
Denbigh St. SW1 161 DJ77
Denbigh Ter. W11 139 CZ73
Denbridge Rd., Brom. 205 EM96
Denby Gra., Harl. 52 EY15
Church Langley Way
Denby Rd., Cob. 214 BW112
Dendridge Clo., Enf. 82 DV37
Dene, The W13 137 CH71
Dene, The, Croy. 221 DX105
Dene, The, Dor. 261 BV141
Dene, The, Sev. 257 FH126
Dene, The, Sutt. 217 CZ111
Dene, The, Wem. 118 CL63
Dene, The, W.Mol. 196 BZ99
Dene Ave., Houns. 156 BZ83
Dene Ave., Sid. 186 EV87
Dene Clo. SE4 163 DY83
Dene Clo., Brom. 204 EF102
Dene Clo., Couls. 234 DE119
Outwood La.
Dene Clo., Dart. 187 FE91
Dene Clo., Guil. 243 BB132
Dene Clo., Horl. 268 DE146
Dene Clo., Wor.Pk. 199 CT103
Dene Dr., Orp. 206 EV104
Dene Gdns., Stan. 95 CJ50
Dene Gdns., T.Ditt. 197 CG103
Dene Holm Rd., Grav. 190 GD90
Dene Path, S.Ock. 149 FU72
Dene Pl., Wok. 226 AV118
Dene Rd. N11 98 DF46
Dene Rd., Ash. 232 CM119
Dene Rd., Buck.H. 102 EK46
Dene Rd., Dart. 188 FM87
Dene Rd., Guil. 258 AY135
Dene Rd., Nthwd. 93 BQ51
Dene St., Dor. 263 CH136
Dene St. Gdns., Dor. 263 CH136
Denecroft Cres., Uxb. 135 BP67
Denecroft Gdns., Grays 170 GD76
Denefield Dr., Ken. 236 DR115
Denehurst Gdns. NW4 119 CW58
Denehurst Gdns. W3 138 CP74
Denehurst Gdns., Rich. 158 CN84
Denehurst Gdns., Twick. 177 CD87
Denehurst Gdns., Wdf.Grn. 102 EH49
Denewood, Barn. 80 DC43
Denewood Clo., Wat. 75 BT37
Denewood Rd. N6 120 DF58
Denfield, Dor. 263 CH138
Dengie Wk. N1 142 DQ67
Basire St.
Denham Ave., Uxb. 113 BF61
Denham Clo., Hem.H. 40 BN15
Denham Clo., Uxb. 114 BG62
Denham Clo., Well. 166 EW83
Park Vw. Rd.
Denham Ct. Rd., Uxb. 114 BG63
Denham Cres., Mitch. 200 DF98
Denham Dr., Esher 215 CG106
Denham Dr., Ilf. 125 EQ58
Denham Grn. Clo., Uxb. 114 BG59
Denham Grn. La., Uxb. 113 BE57
Denham La., Ger.Cr. 90 AY50
Denham Rd. N20 98 DF48
Denham Rd., Egh. 173 BA91
Denham Rd., Epsom 217 CT112
Denham Rd., Felt. 176 BW86
Denham Rd., Iver 133 BD67
Denham St. SE10 164 EG78
Denham Wk., Ger.Cr. 91 AZ51
Denham Way, Bark. 145 ES67
Denham Way, Borwd. 78 CQ39
Denham Way, Rick. 91 BE52
Denham Way, Uxb. 114 BG62
Denholm Gdns., Guil. 243 BA131
Denholme Rd. W9 139 CZ69
Denholme Wk., Rain. 147 FF65
Ryder Gdns.
Denison Clo. N2 120 DC55
Denison Rd. SW19 180 DD93
Denison Rd. W5 137 CJ70
Denison Rd., Felt. 175 BT91
Deniston Ave., Bex. 186 EY88
Denleigh Gdns. N21 99 DN46
Denleigh Gdns., T.Ditt. 197 CE100
Denman Dr. NW11 120 DA57
Denman Dr., Ashf. 175 BP93
Denman Dr. N. NW11 120 DA57
Denman Dr. S. NW11 120 DA57
Denman Rd. SE15 162 DT81
Denman St. W1 277 M1
Denmark Ave. SW19 179 CY94
Denmark Ct., Mord. 200 DA99
Denmark Gdns., Cars. 200 DF104
Denmark Gro. N1 141 DN68
Denmark Hill SE5 162 DR81
Denmark Hill Dr. NW9 119 CT56
Denmark Hill Est. SE5 162 DR84
Denmark Pl. WC2 273 N8
Denmark Rd. N8 121 DN56
Denmark Rd. NW6 139 CZ68
Denmark Rd. SE5 162 DQ81
Denmark Rd. SE25 202 DU99
Denmark Rd. SW19 179 CX93
Denmark Rd. W13 137 CH73
Denmark Rd., Brom. 204 EH95
Denmark Rd., Cars. 200 DF104
Denmark Rd., Guil. 258 AY135
Denmark Rd., Kings.T. 198 CL97
Denmark Rd., Twick. 177 CD90
Denmark St. E11 124 EE62
High Rd. Leytonstone
Denmark St. E13 144 EH71
Denmark St. N17 100 DV53
Denmark St. WC2 273 N9
Denmark St. WC2 141 DK72
Denmark St., Wat. 75 BV40
Denmark Wk. SE27 182 DQ91
Denmead Clo., Ger.Cr. 112 AY59
Denmead Ho. SW15 179 CT86
Highcliffe Dr.
Denmead Rd., Croy. 201 DP102
Denmead Way SE15 162 DT80
Pentridge St.
Dennan Rd., Surb. 198 CM102
Denne Ter. E8 142 DT67
Denner Rd. E4 101 EA47
Dennett Rd., Croy. 201 DN102
Dennetts Gro. SE14 163 DX82
Dennetts Rd.
Dennetts Rd. SE14 162 DW81
Dennettsland Rd., Eden. 255 EQ134
Denning Ave., Croy. 219 DN105
Denning Clo. NW8 140 DC69
Denning Clo., Hmptn. 176 BZ93
Denning Rd. NW3 120 DD63
Dennington Clo. E5 122 DV61
Detmold Rd.
Dennington Pk. Rd. NW6 140 DA65
Denningtons, The, Wor.Pk. 198 CS103
Dennis Ave., Wem. 118 CM64
Dennis Clo., Ashf. 175 BR93
Dennis Clo., Red. 250 DE132
Dennis Gdns., Stan. 95 CJ50
Dennis La., Stan. 95 CH48
Dennis Pk. Cres. SW20 199 CY95
Dennis Reeve Clo., Mitch. 200 DF95
Dennis Rd., E.Mol. 196 CC98
Dennis Rd., Grav. 191 GG90
Dennis Way SW4 161 DK83
Gauden Rd.
Dennis Way, Slou. 131 AK73
Dennises La., S.Ock. 149 FU66
Dennises La., Upmin. 149 FR67
Dennison Pt. E15 143 EC66
Denny Ave., Wal.Abb. 67 ED34
Denny Clo. E6 144 EL71
Linton Gdns.
Denny Cres. SE11 278 E10
Denny Gdns., Dag. 146 EV66
Canonsleigh Rd.
Denny Gate, Wal.Cr. 67 DZ27
Denny Rd. N9 100 DV46
Denny Rd., Slou. 153 AZ77
Denny St. SE11 278 E10
Denny St. SE11 161 DN78
Dennys La., Berk. 38 AT21
Densbridge Ind. Est., Uxb. 134 BJ65
Densham Rd. E15 144 EE67
Densley Clo., Welw.G.C. 29 CX07
Densole Clo., Beck. 203 DY95
Kings Hall Rd.
Densworth Gro. N9 100 DW47
Dent Clo., S.Ock. 149 FU72
Denton Clo., Barn. 79 CW43
Denton Clo., Red. 266 DG139
Denton Ct. Rd., Grav. 191 GL88
Denton Gro., Walt. 196 BX103
Denton Rd. N8 121 DM57
Denton Rd. N18 100 DS49
Denton Rd., Bex. 187 FD89
Denton Rd., Dart. 187 FF87
Denton Rd., Twick. 177 CK86
Denton Rd., Well. 166 EW80
Denton St. SW18 180 DB86
Denton St., Grav. 191 GL87
Denton Ter., Bex. 187 FE89
Denton Rd.
Denton Way E5 123 DX62
Denton Way, Wok. 226 AT118
Dents Gro., Tad. 249 CZ128
Dents Rd. SW11 180 DF86
Denvale Wk., Wok. 226 AU118
Denver Clo., Orp. 205 ES100
Denver Ind. Est., Rain. 147 FF71
Denver Rd. N16 122 DS59
Denver Rd., Dart. 187 FG87
Denyer St. SW3 276 C9
Denyer St. SW3 160 DE77
Denzil Rd. NW10 119 CT64
Denzil Rd., Guil. 258 AV135
Denziloe Ave., Uxb. 135 BP69
Deodar Rd. SW15 159 CY84
Deodara Clo. N20 98 DE48
Depot Rd., Epsom 216 CS113
Depot Rd., Houns. 157 CD83
Deptford Bri. SE8 163 EA81
Deptford Bdy. SE8 163 EA81
Deptford Ch. St. SE8 163 EA79
Deptford Ferry Rd. E14 163 EA77
Deptford Grn. SE8 163 EA79
Deptford High St. SE8 163 EA79
Deptford Strand SE8 163 DZ77
Deptford Wf. SE8 163 DZ77
Derby Arms Rd., Epsom 233 CT117
Derby Ave. N12 98 DC50
Derby Ave., Har. 95 CD53
Derby Ave., Rom. 127 FC58
Derby Ave., Upmin. 128 FM62
Derby Clo., Epsom 233 CV119
Derby Ct. E5 123 DX63
Overbury St.
Derby Est., Houns. 156 CA84
Derby Gate SW1 277 P4
Derby Hill SE23 182 DW89
Derby Hill Cres. SE23 182 DW89
Derby Rd. E7 144 EK66
Derby Rd. E9 143 DX67
Derby Rd. E18 102 EF53
Derby Rd. N18 100 DW50
Derby Rd. SW14 158 CP84
Derby Rd. SW19 180 DA94
Russell Rd.
Derby Rd., Croy. 201 DP103
Derby Rd., Enf. 82 DV43
Derby Rd., Grays 170 GB78
Derby Rd., Grnf. 136 CB67
Derby Rd., Guil. 242 AT134
Derby Rd., Hodd. 49 ED19
Derby Rd., Houns. 156 CB84
Derby Rd., Surb. 198 CN102
Derby Rd., Sutt. 217 CZ107
Derby Rd., Uxb. 134 BJ68
Derby Rd., Wat. 76 BW41
Derby Rd. Bri., Grays 170 GB79
Derby Stables Rd., Epsom 232 CS117
Derby St. W1 276 G3
Derbyshire St. E2 142 DU69
Dereham Pl. EC2 275 N3
Dereham Rd., Bark. 145 ET65
Derehams Ave., H.Wyc. 88 AC52
Derehams La., H.Wyc. 88 AC53
Derek Ave., Epsom 216 CN107
Derek Ave., Wall. 201 DH104
Derek Ave., Wem. 138 CP66
Derek Clo., Epsom 216 CP106
Derek Walcott Clo. SE24 181 DP85
Shakespeare Rd.
Derham Gdns., Upmin. 128 FQ62
Deri Ave., Rain. 147 FH70
Dericote St. E8 142 DU67
Derifall Clo. E6 145 EM71
Bedfont Rd.
Deridene Clo., Stai. 174 BL86
Dering Pl., Croy. 220 DQ105
Dering Rd., Croy. 220 DQ105
Dering St. W1 273 H9
Dering St. W1 141 DH72
Dering Way, Grav. 191 GM88
Derinton Rd. SW17 180 DF91
Derley Rd., Sthl. 156 BW76
Dermody Gdns. SE13 183 ED85
Dermody Rd. SE13 183 ED85
Deronda Rd. SE24 181 DP88
Deroy Clo., Cars. 218 DF107
Derrick Ave., S.Croy. 220 DQ110
Derrick Gdns. SE7 164 EJ77
Anchor & Hope La.
Derrick Rd., Beck. 203 DZ97
Derry Ave., S.Ock. 149 FU71
Derry Downs, Orp. 206 EW100
Derry Rd., Croy. 201 DL104
Derry St. W8 160 DB75
Derrydown, Wok. 226 AW121
Dersingham Ave. E12 125 EM63
Dersingham Rd. NW2 119 CY62
Derwent Ave. N18 100 DR50
Derwent Ave. NW7 96 CR51
Derwent Ave. SW15 178 CS91
Derwent Ave., Barn. 98 DF46
Derwent Ave., Pnr. 94 BY51
Derwent Ave., Uxb. 114 BN61
Derwent Clo., Add. 212 BK106
Derwent Clo., Amer. 72 AV39
Derwent Clo., Dart. 187 FH88
Derwent Clo., Esher 215 CE107
Derwent Clo., Felt. 175 BT88
Derwent Cres. N20 98 DC48
Derwent Cres., Bexh. 166 FA82
Derwent Cres., Stan. 95 CJ54
Derwent Dr. NW9 118 CS57
Derwent Dr., Hayes 135 BS71
Derwent Dr., Orp. 205 ER101
Derwent Dr., Pur. 220 DR113
Derwent Dr., Slou. 130 AJ71
Derwent Gdns., Ilf. 124 EL56
Derwent Gdns., Wem. 117 CJ59
Derwent Gro. SE22 162 DT84
Derwent Par., S.Ock. 149 FU72
Derwent Ri. NW9 118 CS58
Derwent Rd. N13 99 DM49
Derwent Rd. SE20 202 DU96
Derwent Rd. SW20 199 CX100
Derwent Rd. W5 157 CJ76
Derwent Rd., Egh. 173 BB94
Derwent Rd., Hem.H. 41 BQ21
Derwent Rd., Sthl. 136 BZ72
Derwent Rd., Twick. 176 CB86
Derwent St. SE10 164 EE78
Derwent Wk., Wall. 219 DH108
Derwent Way, Horn. 127 FH64
Derwent Yd. W5 157 CJ76
Northfield Ave.
Derwentwater Rd. W3 138 CQ74
Desborough Clo., Hert. 32 DQ06
Desborough Clo., Shep. 194 BN102
Desborough St. W2 140 DB71
Cirencester St.
Desenfans Rd. SE21 182 DS86
Desford Ct., Ashf. 174 BM89
Desford Way
Desford Ms. E16 144 EE70
Desford Rd.
Desford Rd. E16 144 EE70
Desford Way, Ashf. 174 BM89
Desmond Rd., Wat. 75 BT36
Desmond St. SE14 163 DY79
Despard Rd. N19 121 DJ60
Detillens La., Oxt. 254 EG129
Detling Clo., Horn. 128 FJ64
Detling Rd., Brom. 184 EG92
Detling Rd., Erith 167 FD80
Detling Rd., Grav. 190 GD88
Detmold Rd. E5 122 DW61
Deva Clo., St.Alb. 42 CA22
Devalls Clo. E6 145 EN73
Devana End, Cars. 200 DF104
Devas Rd. SW20 199 CW95
Devas St. E3 143 EB70
Devenay Rd. E15 144 EF66
Devenish Rd. SE2 166 EU75
Deventer Cres. SE22 182 DS85
East Dulwich Gro.
Devereaux Rd., Grays 170 FZ76
Deverell St. SE1 279 K7
Deverell St. SE1 162 DR76
Devereux Ct. WC2 274 D9
Devereux Dr., Wat. 75 BS38
Devereux La. SW13 159 CV79
Trinity Ch. Rd.
Devereux Rd. SW11 180 DF86
Devereux Rd., Wind. 151 AR82
Deverill Ct. SE20 202 DW95
Deveron Gdns., S.Ock. 149 FU71
Deveron Way, Rom. 105 FE53
Devey Clo., Kings.T. 178 CS94
Beverley La.
Devils La., Egh. 173 BC93
Devil's La., Hert. 47 DP21
Devils La., Stai. 173 BD94
Devitt Clo., Ash. 232 CN116
Devizes St. N1 142 DR67
Poole St.
Devoil Clo., Guil. 243 BB130
Devoke Way, Walt. 196 BX103
Devon Ave., Slou. 131 AQ72
Devon Ave., Twick. 176 CC88
Devon Bank, Guil. 258 AW137
Portsmouth Rd.
Devon Clo. N17 122 DT55
Devon Clo., Buck.H. 102 EH47
Devon Clo., Grnf. 137 CJ67
Devon Clo., Ken. 236 DS116
Devon Ct., Dart. 208 FP95
Devon Ct., St.Alb. 43 CE21
Devon Cres., Red. 250 DD134
Devon Gdns. N4 121 DP58
Devon Ri. N2 120 DD56
Devon Rd., Bark. 145 ES67
Devon Rd. (Sutton at Hone), Dart. 208 FP95
Devon Rd., Red. 251 DJ130
Devon Rd., Sutt. 217 CY109
Devon Rd., Walt. 214 BW105
Devon Rd., Wat. 76 BX39
Devon St. SE15 162 DV79
Devon Way, Chess. 215 CJ106
Devon Way, Epsom 216 CP106
Devon Way, Uxb. 134 BM68
Devon Waye, Houns. 156 BZ80
Devoncroft Gdns., Twick. 177 CG87
Devonia Gdns. N18 100 DQ51
Devonia Rd. N1 141 DP68
Devonport Gdns., Ilf. 125 EM58
Devonport Ms. W12 139 CV74
Devonport Rd.
Devonport Rd. W12 159 CV75
Devonport St. E1 143 DX72
Devons Est. E3 143 EB69
Devons Rd. E3 143 EA71
Devonshire Ave., Amer. 55 AP37
Devonshire Ave., Dart. 187 FH86
Devonshire Ave., Sutt. 218 DC108
Devonshire Ave., Wok. 211 BC114
Devonshire Clo. E15 124 EE63
Devonshire Clo. N13 99 DN48
Devonshire Clo. W1 273 H6
Devonshire Clo. W1 141 DH71
Devonshire Clo., Amer. 55 AQ37
Devonshire Clo., Slou. 131 AP68
Devonshire Cres. NW7 97 CX52
Devonshire Dr. SE10 163 EB80
Devonshire Dr., Surb. 197 CK103
Devonshire Gdns. N17 100 DQ51
Devonshire Gdns. N21 100 DQ45
Devonshire Gdns. W4 158 CQ80
Devonshire Gdns., Slou. 131 AP68
Devonshire Gro. SE15 162 DV79

Devonshire Hill La. N17 99 DP51
Devonshire Ms. W4 158 CS78
Glebe St.
Devonshire Ms. N. W1 273 H6
Devonshire Ms. S. W1 273 H6
Devonshire Ms. S. W1 141 DH71
Devonshire Ms. W. W1 273 H5
Devonshire Ms. W. W1 140 DG70
Devonshire Pas. W4 158 CS78
Duke Rd.
Devonshire Pl. NW2 120 DA62
Devonshire Pl. W1 272 G5
Devonshire Pl. W1 140 DG70
Devonshire Pl. W4 158 CS78
Devonshire Pl. W8 160 DB76
St. Mary's Pl.
Devonshire Pl. Ms. W1 272 G5
Devonshire Rd. E15 124 EE63
Janson Rd.
Devonshire Rd. E16 144 EH72
Devonshire Rd. E17 123 EA58
Devonshire Rd. N9 100 DW46
Devonshire Rd. N13 99 DM49
Devonshire Rd. N17 100 DQ51
Devonshire Rd. NW7 97 CX52
Devonshire Rd. SE9 184 EL89
Devonshire Rd. SE23 182 DW88
Devonshire Rd. SW19 180 DE94
Devonshire Rd. W4 158 CS78
Devonshire Rd. W5 157 CJ76
Devonshire Rd., Bexh. 166 EY84
Devonshire Rd., Cars. 218 DG105
Devonshire Rd., Croy. 202 DR101
Devonshire Rd., Felt. 176 BY90
Devonshire Rd., Grav. 191 GH88
Devonshire Rd., Grays 170 FY77
Devonshire Rd., Har. 117 CD58
Devonshire Rd., Horn. 128 FJ61
Devonshire Rd., Ilf. 125 ER59
Devonshire Rd., Orp. 206 EU101
Devonshire Rd. (Eastcote), Pnr. 116 BW58
Devonshire Rd. (Hatch End), Pnr. 94 BZ53
Devonshire Rd., Sthl. 136 CA71
Devonshire Rd., Sutt. 218 DC108
Devonshire Rd., Wey. 212 BN105
Devonshire Row EC2 275 N7
Devonshire Row Ms. W1 273 J5
Devonshire Sq. EC2 275 N7
Devonshire Sq., Brom. 204 EH98
Devonshire St. W1 272 G6
Devonshire St. W1 141 DH71
Devonshire St. W4 158 CS78
Devonshire Ter. W2 140 DC72
Devonshire Way, Croy. 203 DY103
Devonshire Way, Hayes 135 BV72
Dewar St. SE15 162 DU83
Dewberry Gdns. E6 144 EL71
Dewberry St. E14 143 EC71
Dewey Rd. N1 141 DN68
Dewey Rd., Dag. 147 FB65
Dewey St. SW17 180 DF92
Dewgrass Gro., Wal.Cr. 83 DX35
Dewhurst Rd. W14 159 CX76
Dewhurst Rd. (Cheshunt), Wal.Cr. 66 DV29
Dewlands, Gdse. 252 DW131
Dewlands Ave., Dart. 188 FP87
Dewsbury Clo., Pnr. 116 BY58
Dewsbury Clo., Rom. 106 FL51
Dewsbury Ct. W4 158 CQ77
Chiswick Rd.
Dewsbury Gdns., Rom. 106 FK51
Dewsbury Gdns., Wor.Pk. 199 CU104
Dewsbury Rd. NW10 119 CU64
Dewsbury Rd., Rom. 106 FK51
Dewsbury Ter. NW1 141 DH67
Camden High St.
Dexter Clo., Grays 170 GA76
Dexter Rd., Barn. 79 CX44
Dexter Rd., Uxb. 92 BJ54
Deyncourt Gdns., Upmin. 128 FQ61
Deyncourt Rd. N17 100 DQ53
Deynecourt Gdns. E11 124 EJ56
D'Eynsford Rd. SE5 162 DR81
Diadem Ct. W1 273 M9
Dial Clo., Green. 189 FX85
Knockhall Rd.
Dial Wk., The W8 160 DB75
Palace Ave.
Diamedes Ave., Stai. 174 BK87
Diameter Rd., Orp. 205 EP101
Diamond Clo., Dag. 126 EW60
Diamond Clo., Grays 170 FZ76
Diamond Rd., Ruis. 116 BX63
Diamond Rd., Slou. 152 AU75
Diamond Rd., Wat. 75 BU38
Diamond St. SE15 162 DS80
Diamond Ter. SE10 163 EC81
Diana Clo. E18 102 EH53
Diana Clo., Grays 170 FZ76
Diana Clo., Slou. 153 AY72
Diana Gdns., Surb. 198 CM103
Diana Ho. SW13 159 CT81
Diana Pl. NW1 273 J4
Diana Pl. NW1 141 DH70
Diana Rd. E17 123 DZ55
Dianna Way, Barn. 80 DE43
Dianthus Clo. SE2 166 EV78
Carnation St.
Dianthus Clo., Cher. 193 BE101
Dianthus Ct., Wok. 226 AX118
Diban Ave., Horn. 127 FH63
Dibden Hill, Ch.St.G. 90 AW49
Dibden La., Sev. 256 FE126
Dibden Row SE1 161 DN76
Gerridge St.
Dibden St. N1 142 DQ67
Dibdin Clo., Sutt. 200 DA104
Dibdin Rd., Sutt. 200 DA104
Diceland Rd., Bans. 233 CZ116
Dicey Ave. NW2 119 CW63
Dick Turpin Way, Felt. 155 BT84
Dickens Ave. N3 98 DC53
Dickens Ave., Dart. 168 FN84
Dickens Ave., Til. 171 GH81
Dickens Ave., Uxb. 135 BP72
Dickens Clo., Hayes 155 BS77
Croyde Ave.
Dickens Clo., Rich. 178 CL89
Dickens Clo., St.Alb. 43 CD19
Dickens Clo., Wal.Cr. 66 DU26
Dickens Ct., Hat. 45 CV16
Ground La.
Dickens Dr., Add. 211 BF107
Dickens Dr., Chis. 185 EQ93
Dickens Est. SE1 162 DT75
Dickens Est. SE16 162 DT75
Dickens La. N18 100 DS50
Dickens Ri., Chig. 103 EP48
Dickens Rd. E6 144 EK68
Dickens Rd., Grav. 191 GL88
Dickens Sq. SE1 279 J6
Dickens Sq. SE1 162 DQ76
Dickens St. SW8 161 DH82
Dickenson Clo. N9 100 DU46
Croyland Rd.
Dickenson Rd. N8 121 DL59
Dickenson Rd., Felt. 176 BX92
Dickenson St. NW5 141 DH65
Dalby St.
Dickensons La. SE25 202 DU99
Dickensons Pl. SE25 202 DU100
Dickerage La., N.Mal. 198 CQ97
Dickerage Rd., Kings.T. 198 CQ95
Dickerage Rd., N.Mal. 198 CQ95
Dickinson Ave., Rick. 74 BN44
Dickinson Sq., Rick. 74 BN44
Dickson (Cheshunt), Wal.Cr. 66 DT27
Dickson Fold, Pnr. 116 BX56
Dickson Rd. SE9 164 EL83
Didsbury Clo. E6 145 EM67
Barking Rd.
Dig Dag Hill (Cheshunt), Wal.Cr. 66 DT27
Digby Cres. N4 122 DQ61
Digby Gdns., Dag. 146 FA67
Digby Pl., Croy. 202 DT104
Digby Rd. E9 123 DX64
Digby Rd., Bark. 145 ET66
Digby St. E2 142 DW69
Digby Wk., Horn. 148 FJ65
Pembrey Way
Digby Way, W.Byf. 212 BM112
High Rd.
Digdens Ri., Epsom 232 CQ115
Dighton Ct. SE5 162 DQ79
Hillingdon St.
Dighton Rd. SW18 180 DC85
Digswell Clo., Borwd. 78 CN38
Digswell Hill, Welw.G.C. 29 CX08
Digswell Ho., Welw.G.C. 29 CX05
Digswell Ho. Ms., Welw.G.C. 29 CX05
Monks Ri.
Digswell La., Welw.G.C. 29 CZ05
Digswell Ri., Welw.G.C. 29 CX07
Digswell Rd., Welw.G.C. 29 CY06
Digswell St. N7 141 DN65
Holloway Rd.
Dilhorne Clo. SE12 184 EH90
Dilke St. SW3 160 DF79
Dillwyn Clo. SE26 183 DY91
Dilston Clo., Nthlt. 136 BW69
Yeading La.
Dilston Gro. SE16 162 DW77
Abbeyfield Rd.
Dilston Rd., Lthd. 231 CG119
Dilton Gdns. SW15 179 CV88
Dimes Pl. W6 159 CV77
King St.
Dimmock Dr., Grnf. 117 CD64
Dimmocks La., Rick. 74 BH36
Dimond Clo. E7 124 EG63
Dimsdale Dr. NW9 118 CQ60
Dimsdale Dr., Enf. 82 DU44
Dimsdale Dr., Slou. 111 AM64
Dimsdale St., Hert. 32 DQ09
Dimsdale Wk. E13 144 EG67
Stratford Rd.
Dimson Cres. E3 143 EA70
Wellington Way
Dinant Link Rd., Hodd. 49 DY16
Dingle, The, Uxb. 135 BP69
Dingle Clo., Barn. 97 CT44
Dingle Gdns. E14 143 EA73
Dingle Rd., Ashf. 175 BP92
Dingley La. SW16 181 DK89
Dingley Pl. EC1 275 J3
Dingley Pl. EC1 142 DQ69
Dingley Rd. EC1 275 H3
Dingley Rd. EC1 142 DQ69
Dingonhill Clo., Hayes 135 BV73
Dingwall Ave., Croy. 202 DQ103
Dingwall Gdns. NW11 120 DA58
Dingwall Pl., Croy. 202 DR103
Dingwall Rd.
Dingwall Rd. SW18 180 DC87
Dingwall Rd., Cars. 218 DF109
Dingwall Rd., Croy. 202 DR102
Dinmont St. E2 142 DV68
Coate St.
Dinmore, Hem.H. 57 AZ28
Dinsdale Clo., Wok. 227 BA118
Dinsdale Gdns. SE25 202 DS99
Dinsdale Gdns., Barn. 80 DB43
Dinsdale Rd. SE3 164 EF79
Dinsmore Rd. SW12 181 DH87
Dinton Rd. SW19 180 DD93
Dinton Rd., Kings.T. 178 CM94
Dione Rd., Hem.H. 40 BM17
Saturn Way
Diploma Ave. N2 120 DE56
Dirdene Clo., Epsom 217 CT112
Dirdene Gdns., Epsom 217 CT112
Dirdene Gro., Epsom 217 CT112
Dirleton Rd. E15 144 EF67
Dirtham La., Lthd. 245 BV129
Disbrowe Rd. W6 159 CY79
Discovery Wk. E1 142 DV74
Wapping La.
Dishforth La. NW9 96 CS53
Disney Ms. N4 121 DP57
Chesterfield Gdns.
Disney Pl. SE1 279 J4
Disney St. SE1 279 J4
Dison Clo., Enf. 83 DX39
Disraeli Clo. SE28 146 EW74
Disraeli Clo. W4 158 CR77
Acton La.
Disraeli Ct., Slou. 153 BB79
Sutton Pl.
Disraeli Gdns. SW15 159 CZ84
Fawe Pk. Rd.
Disraeli Pk., Beac. 89 AK51
Disraeli Rd. E7 144 EG65
Disraeli Rd. NW10 138 CR68
Disraeli Rd. SW15 159 CY84
Disraeli Rd. W5 137 CK74
Diss St. E2 275 P2
Diss St. E2 142 DT69
Distaff La. EC4 275 H10
Distaff La. EC4 142 DQ73
Distillery La. W6 159 CW78
Fulham Palace Rd.
Distillery Rd. W6 159 CW78
Distillery Wk., Brent. 158 CL79
Pottery Rd.
Distin St. SE11 278 D9
District Rd., Wem. 117 CH64
Ditch All. SE10 163 EB81
Ditchburn St. E14 143 EC73
Ditches La., Couls. 235 DL120
Ditchfield Rd., Hayes 136 BY70
Ditchfield Rd., Hodd. 33 EA14
Dittisham Rd. SE9 184 EL91
Ditton Clo., T.Ditt. 197 CG101
Ditton Gra. Clo., Surb. 197 CK102
Ditton Gra. Dr., Surb. 197 CK102
Ditton Hill, Surb. 197 CJ102
Ditton Hill Rd., Surb. 197 CJ102
Ditton Lawn, T.Ditt. 197 CG102
Ditton Pk. Rd., Slou. 152 AY79
Ditton Pl. SE20 202 DV95
Hartfield Gro.
Ditton Reach, T.Ditt. 197 CH100
Ditton Rd., Bexh. 186 EX85
Ditton Rd., Slou. 153 AZ79
Ditton Rd. (Datchet), Slou. 152 AX81
Ditton Rd., Sthl. 156 BZ78
Ditton Rd., Surb. 197 CK103
Divis Way SW15 179 CV86
Dover Pk. Dr.
Divot Pl., Hert. 32 DV08
Dixon Clark Ct. N1 141 DP65
Canonbury Rd.
Dixon Clo. E6 145 EM72
Brandreth Rd.
Dixon Dr., Wey. 212 BM110
Eyston Dr.
Dixon Pl., W.Wick. 203 EB102
Dixon Rd. SE14 163 DY81
Dixon Rd. SE25 202 DS97
Dixon's All. SE16 162 DV75
West La.
Dixons Hill Clo., Hat. 63 CV25
Dixons Hill Rd., Hat. 63 CU25
Dobbin Clo., Har. 95 CG54
Dobb's Weir Rd., Hodd. 49 EC18
Dobell Rd. SE9 185 EM85
Dobree Ave. NW10 139 CV66
Dobson Clo. NW6 140 DD66
Dobson Rd., Grav. 191 GL92
Dock Hill Ave. SE16 163 DX75
Dock Rd. E16 144 EF73
Dock Rd., Brent. 157 CK80
Dock Rd., Grays 170 GD79
Dock Rd., Til. 170 GE81
Dock St. E1 142 DU73
Dockers Tanner Rd. E14 163 EA77
Dockett Eddy La., Shep. 194 BM102
Dockhead SE1 162 DT75
Dockland St. E16 145 EN74
Dockley Rd. SE16 162 DU76
Dockwell Clo., Felt. 155 BU84
Doctor Johnson Ave. SW17 181 DH90
Doctors Clo. SE26 182 DW92
Doctors Commons Rd., Berk. 38 AV19
Doctors La., Cat. 235 DN123
Docwra's Bldgs. N1 142 DS65
Dod St. E14 143 EA72
Dodbrooke Rd. SE27 181 DN90
Doddinghurst Rd., Brwd. 108 FW44
Doddington Gro. SE17 161 DP79
Doddington Pl. SE17 161 DP79
Dodd's Cres., W.Byf. 212 BH114
Dodds La., Ch.St.G. 90 AU47
Dodds La., Hem.H. 40 BJ16
Dodd's La., Wok. 212 BG114
Dodds Pk., Bet. 264 CP136
Doddsfield Rd., Slou. 131 AN69
Dodsley Pl. N9 100 DW48
Dodson St. SE1 278 E5
Dodson St. SE1 161 DN75
Dodwood, Welw.G.C. 30 DB10
Bushey Ley
Doebury Wk. SE18 166 EU79
Prestwood Clo.
Doel Clo. SW19 180 DC94
Dog Kennel Hill SE22 162 DS83
Dog Kennel Hill Est. SE22 162 DS83
Dog Kennel La., Hat. 45 CU17
Dog Kennel La., Rick. 73 BF43
Dog La. NW10 118 CS63
Doggets Ct., Barn. 80 DE43
Doggett Rd. SE6 183 EA87
Doggetts Fm. Rd., Uxb. 113 BC59
Doggetts Way, St.Alb. 42 CC22
Doggetts Wd. Clo., Ch.St.G. 72 AV42
Doggetts Wd. La., Ch.St.G. 72 AV41
Doghurst Ave., Hayes 155 BP80
Doghurst Dr., West Dr. 155 BP80
Doghurst La., Couls. 234 DF120
Dognell Grn., Welw.G.C. 29 CV08
Dogwood Clo., Grav. 191 GF91
Doherty Rd. E13 144 EG70
Dolben St. SE1 278 G3
Dolben St. SE1 141 DP74
Dolby Ct. EC4 142 DQ73
Garlick Hill
Dolby Rd. SW6 159 CZ82
Dolland St. SE11 161 DM78
Dollis Ave. N3 97 CZ53
Dollis Brook Wk., Barn. 79 CY44
Dollis Cres., Ruis. 116 BW60
Dollis Hill Ave. NW2 119 CV62
Dollis Hill Est. NW2 119 CU62
Dollis Hill La. NW2 119 CT63
Dollis Ms. N3 97 CZ53
Dollis Pk.
Dollis Pk. N3 97 CZ53
Dollis Rd. N3 97 CY53
Dollis Rd. NW7 97 CY52
Dollis Valley Grn. Wk. N20 98 DC47
Totteridge La.
Dollis Valley Grn. Wk., Barn. 79 CY44
Leeside
Dollis Valley Way, Barn. 79 CZ43
Dolman Clo. N3 98 DC54
Avondale Rd.
Dolman Rd. W4 158 CR77
Dolman St. SW4 161 DM84
Dolphin App., Rom. 127 FF56
Dolphin Clo. SE16 163 DX75
Kinburn St.
Dolphin Clo. SE28 146 EX72
Dolphin Clo., Surb. 197 CK100
Dolphin Ct. NW11 119 CY58
Dolphin Ct., Slou. 152 AV75
Dolphin Rd.
Dolphin Ct., Stai. 174 BG90
Bremer Rd.
Dolphin Est., The, Sun. 195 BS95
Dolphin La. E14 143 EB73
Dolphin Rd., Nthlt. 136 BZ67
Dolphin Rd., Slou. 152 AV75
Dolphin Rd., Sun. 195 BS95
Dolphin Rd. N., Sun. 195 BS95
Dolphin Rd. S., Sun. 195 BR95
Dolphin Rd. W., Sun. 195 BS95
Dolphin Sq. SW1 161 DJ78
Dolphin Sq. W4 158 CS80
Dolphin St., Kings.T. 198 CL95
Fife Rd.
Dolphin Yd., St.Alb. 43 CD20
Dolphin Yd., Ware 33 DX06
East St.
Dombey St. WC1 274 B6
Dombey St. WC1 141 DM71
Dome Hill, Cat. 252 DS127
Dome Hill Pk. SE26 182 DT91
Dome Hill Peak, Cat. 252 DS126
Dome Way, Red. 250 DF133
Domett Clo. SE5 162 DR84
Domfe Pl. E5 122 DW63
Rushmore Rd.
Domingo St. EC1 275 H4
Dominion Dr., Rom. 105 FB51
Dominion Rd., Croy. 202 DT101
Dominion Rd., Sthl. 156 BY76
Dominion St. EC2 275 L6
Dominion Way, Rain. 147 FG69
Domonic Dr. SE9 185 EP91
Domville Clo. N20 98 DD47
Don Phelan Clo. SE5 162 DR81
Don Way, Rom. 105 FE52
Donald Dr., Rom. 126 EW57
Donald Rd. E13 144 EH67
Donald Rd., Croy. 201 DM100
Donaldson Rd. NW6 139 CZ67
Donaldson Rd. SE18 165 EN81
Doncaster Dr., Nthlt. 116 BZ64
Doncaster Gdns. N4 122 DQ58
Stanhope Gdns.
Doncaster Gdns., Nthlt. 116 BZ64
Doncaster Grn., Wat. 94 BW50
Doncaster Rd. N9 100 DV45
Doncaster Way, Upmin. 128 FM62
Doncel Ct. E4 101 ED45
Donegal St. N1 274 C1
Donegal St. N1 141 DM68
Doneraile St. SW6 159 CX82
Dongola Rd. E13 144 EH69
Dongola Rd. N17 122 DS55
Dongola Rd. W. E13 144 EH69
Balaam St.
Donington Ave., Ilf. 125 EQ57
Donkey All. SE22 182 DU87
Donkey La. (Farningham), Dart. 208 FP103
Donkey La., Dor. 262 BX143
Donkey La., Enf. 82 DU40
Donkey La., Horl. 269 DK153
Donnay Clo., Ger.Cr. 112 AX58
Donne Ct. SE24 182 DQ86
Burbage Rd.
Donne Gdns., Wok. 227 BE115
Donne Pl. SW3 276 C8
Donne Pl. SW3 160 DE77
Donne Pl., Mitch. 201 DH98
Donne Rd., Dag. 126 EW61
Donnefield Ave., Edg. 96 CL52
Donnington Rd. NW10 139 CV66
Donnington Rd., Har. 117 CJ57
Donnington Rd., Sev. 241 FD120
Donnington Rd., Wor.Pk. 199 CU103
Donnybrook Rd. SW16 181 DJ94
Donovan Ave. N10 121 DH55
Donovan Clo., Epsom 216 CR110
Nimbus Rd.
Doods Pk. Rd., Reig. 250 DC133
Doods Rd., Reig. 250 DC133
Doods Way, Reig. 250 DC133
Doon St. SE1 278 D2
Doone Clo., Tedd. 177 CG93
Doone Gdns., Wok. 227 BE115
Dora Rd. SW19 180 DA92
Dora St. E14 143 DZ72
Dorado Gdns., Orp. 206 EX104
Doral Way, Cars. 218 DF106
Doran Dr., Red. 250 DD134
Doran Gdns., Red. 250 DD134
Doran Gro. SE18 165 ES80
Doran Mans. N2 120 DF57
Great N. Rd.
Doran Wk. E15 143 EC66
Dorcas Ct., St.Alb. 43 CE21
Dorchester Ave. N13 100 DQ49
Dorchester Ave., Bex. 186 EX88
Dorchester Ave., Har. 116 CC58
Dorchester Ave., Hodd. 49 EA15
Dorchester Clo., Dart. 188 FM87
Dorchester Clo., Nthlt. 116 CB64
Dorchester Clo., Orp. 186 EU94
Grovelands Rd.
Dorchester Ct. N14 99 DH45
Dorchester Ct. SE24 182 DQ85
Dorchester Ct., Rick. 75 BR43
Mayfare
Dorchester Ct., Wok. 227 BA116
Dorchester Dr. SE24 182 DQ85
Dorchester Dr., Felt. 175 BS86
Dorchester Gdns. E4 101 EA49
Dorchester Gdns. NW11 120 DA56
Dorchester Gro. W4 158 CS78
Dorchester Ms., N.Mal. 198 CR98
Elm Rd.
Dorchester Ms., Twick. 177 CJ87
Sandycombe Rd.
Dorchester Rd., Grav. 191 GK90
Dorchester Rd., Mord. 200 DB101
Dorchester Rd., Nthlt. 116 CB64
Dorchester Rd., Wey. 195 BP104
Dorchester Rd., Wor.Pk. 199 CW102
Dorchester Way, Har. 118 CM58
Dorchester Waye, Hayes 135 BV72
Dorcis Ave., Bexh. 166 EY82
Dordrecht Rd. W3 138 CS74
Dore Ave. E12 125 EN64
Dore Gdns., Mord. 200 DB101
Doreen Ave. NW9 118 CR60
Dorell Clo., Sthl. 136 BZ71
Doria Dr., Grav. 191 GL90
Doria Rd. SW6 159 CZ82
Dorian Rd., Horn. 127 FG60
Doric Dr., Tad. 233 CZ120
Doric Way NW1 273 M2
Doric Way NW1 141 DK69
Dorien Rd. SW20 199 CX96
Dorincourt, Wok. 227 BE115
Doris Ave., Erith 167 FC81
Doris Rd. E7 144 EG66
Doris Rd., Ashf. 175 BR93
Dorking Business Pk., Dor. 263 CG135
Dorking Clo. SE8 163 DZ79
Dorking Clo., Wor.Pk. 199 CX103
Dorking Gdns., Rom. 106 FK50
Dorking Glen, Rom. 106 FK49
Dorking Ri., Rom. 106 FK49
Dorking Rd., Epsom 232 CN116
Dorking Rd., Guil. 259 BD140
Dorking Rd., Lthd. 247 CH125
Dorking Rd. (Bookham), Lthd. 246 CB126
Dorking Rd., Rom. 106 FK49
Dorking Rd., Tad. 233 CX123
Dorking Wk., Rom. 106 FK49
Dorkins Way, Upmin. 129 FS59
Dorlcote Rd. SW18 180 DE87
Dorling Dr., Epsom 217 CT112
Dorly Clo., Shep. 195 BS98
Dorma Trd. Est. E10 123 DX60
Dorman Pl. N9 100 DU47
Balham Rd.
Dorman Wk. NW10 118 CR64
Garden Way
Dorman Way NW8 140 DD67
Dormans Clo., Nthwd. 93 BR52
Dormay St. SW18 180 DB85
Dormer Clo. E15 144 EF65
Dormer Clo., Barn. 79 CX43
Dormers Ave., Sthl. 136 CA72
Dormers Ri., Sthl. 136 CB73
Dormers Wells La., Sthl. 136 CA72
Dormie Clo., St.Alb. 42 CC18
Dormywood, Ruis. 115 BT57
Dornberg Clo. SE3 164 EG80
Dornberg Rd. SE3 164 EH80
Banchory Rd.
Dorncliffe Rd. SW6 159 CY82
Dornels, Slou. 132 AW72
Dorney NW3 140 DE66
Dorney End, Chesh. 54 AN30
Dorney Gro., Wey. 195 BP103
Dorney Reach Rd., Maid. 150 AF76
Dorney Ri., Orp. 205 ET98
Dorney Way, Houns. 176 BY85
Dorney Wd. Rd., Slou. 110 AJ62
Dornfell St. NW6 119 CZ64
Dornford Gdns., Couls. 236 DQ119
Dornton Rd. SW12 181 DH89
Dornton Rd., S.Croy. 220 DR106
Dorothy Ave., Wem. 138 CL66
Dorothy Evans Clo., Bexh. 167 FB84
Dorothy Gdns., Dag. 126 EV63
Dorothy Rd. SW11 160 DF83
Dorrell Pl. SW9 161 DN84
Brixton Rd.
Dorriens Cft., Berk. 38 AT16
Dorrington Ct. SE25 202 DS96
Dorrington Gdns., Horn. 128 FK60
Dorrington Pt. E3 143 EB69
Bromley High St.
Dorrington St. EC1 274 D6
Dorrington St. EC1 141 DN71
Dorrit Cres., Guil. 242 AS132
Dorrit Ms. N18 100 DS50
Dorrit Way, Chis. 185 EQ93
Dorrofield Clo., Rick. 75 BQ43
Dors Clo. NW9 118 CR60
Dorset Ave., Hayes 135 BS69
Dorset Ave., Rom. 127 FD56
Dorset Ave., Sthl. 156 CA77
Dorset Ave., Well. 165 ET84
Dorset Bldgs. EC4 274 F9
Dorset Clo. NW1 272 D6
Dorset Clo., Berk. 38 AT18
Dorset Clo., Hayes 135 BS69
Dorset Cres., Grav. 191 GL91
Dorset Dr., Edg. 96 CM51
Dorset Dr., Wok. 227 BB117
Dorset Est. E2 142 DT69
Dorset Gdns., Mitch. 201 DM98
Dorset Ms. N3 98 DA53
Princes Ave.
Dorset Ms. SW1 277 H6
Dorset Pl. E15 143 ED65
Dorset Pl. SW1 277 M10
Dorset Ri. EC4 274 F9
Dorset Ri. EC4 141 DP72
Dorset Rd. E7 144 EJ66
Dorset Rd. N15 122 DR56
Dorset Rd. N22 99 DL53
Dorset Rd. SE9 184 EL89
Dorset Rd. SW8 161 DL80
Dorset Rd. SW19 200 DA95
Dorset Rd. W5 157 CJ76
Dorset Rd., Ashf. 174 BK90
Dorset Rd., Beck. 203 DX97
Dorset Rd., Har. 116 CC58
Dorset Rd., Mitch. 200 DE96
Dorset Rd., Sutt. 218 DA110
Dorset Rd., Wind. 151 AQ82
Dorset Sq. NW1 272 D5
Dorset Sq. NW1 140 DF70
Dorset Sq., Epsom 216 CR110
Dorset St. W1 272 E7
Dorset St. W1 140 DF71
Dorset St., Sev. 257 FH125
High St.
Dorset Way, Twick. 177 CD88
Dorset Way, Uxb. 134 BM68
Dorset Way, W.Byf. 212 BK110
Dorset Waye, Houns. 156 BZ80
Dorville Cres. W6 159 CV76
Dorville Rd. SE12 184 EF85
Dothill Rd. SE18 165 ER80
Douai Gro., Hmptn. 196 CC95
Doubleday Rd., Loug. 85 EQ41
Doug Siddons Ct., Grays 170 GC79
Elm Rd.
Doughty Ms. WC1 274 B5
Doughty Ms. WC1 141 DM70
Doughty St. WC1 274 B4
Doughty St. WC1 141 DM70
Douglas Ave. E17 101 EA53
Douglas Ave., N.Mal. 199 CV98
Douglas Ave., Rom. 106 FL54
Douglas Ave., Wat. 76 BX37
Douglas Ave., Wem. 138 CL66
Douglas Clo., Grays 170 FY76
Davis Rd.
Douglas Clo., Guil. 242 AX128

Douglas Clo., Stan. 95 CG50
Douglas Clo., Wall. 219 DL107
Douglas Ct., Cat. 236 DQ122
Fairbourne La.
Douglas Ct., West. 238 EL117
Douglas Cres., Hayes 136 BW70
Douglas Dr., Croy. 203 EA104
Douglas Gdns., Berk. 38 AT18
Douglas La., Stai. 173 AZ85
Douglas Ms. NW2 119 CY62
Cricklewood La.
Douglas Pl. E14 163 EC78
Manchester Rd.
Douglas Rd. E4 102 EE45
Douglas Rd. E16 144 EG71
Douglas Rd. N1 142 DQ66
Douglas Rd. N22 99 DN53
Douglas Rd. NW6 139 CZ67
Douglas Rd., Add. 194 BH104
Douglas Rd., Esher 196 CB103
Douglas Rd., Horn. 127 FF58
Douglas Rd., Houns. 156 CB83
Douglas Rd., Ilf. 126 EU59
Douglas Rd., Kings.T. 198 CP96
Douglas Rd., Reig. 250 DA133
Douglas Rd., Slou. 131 AR71
Douglas Rd., Stai. 174 BK86
Douglas Rd., Surb. 198 CM103
Douglas Rd., Well. 166 EV81
Douglas Rd. N. N1 142 DQ65
St. Paul's Rd.
Douglas Sq., Mord. 200 DA100
Douglas St. SW1 277 M9
Douglas St. SW1 161 DK77
Douglas Ter. E17 101 EA53
Douglas Ave.
Douglas Way SE8 163 DZ80
Douglas Way, Welw.G.C. 30 DC09
Doulton Ms. NW6 140 DB65
Lymington Rd.
Doultons, The, Stai. 174 BG94
Dounesforth Gdns. SW18 180 DB88
Dounsell Ct., Brwd. 108 FU44
Ongar Rd.
Douro Pl. W8 160 DB76
Douro St. E3 143 EA68
Douthwaite Sq. E1 142 DU74
Torrington Pl.
Dove App. E6 144 EL71
Dove Clo., Nthlt. 136 BX70
Wayfarer Rd.
Dove Clo., S.Croy. 221 DX111
Dove Ct. EC2 275 K9
Dove Ct., Beac. 89 AK52
Dove Ct., Hat. 45 CU19
Dove Ho. Cres., Slou. 131 AL69
Dove Ho. Gdns. E4 101 EA47
Dove La., Pot.B. 64 DB34
Dove Ms. SW5 160 DC77
Dove Pk., Pnr. 94 CA52
Dove Pk., Rick. 73 BB44
Dove Rd. N1 142 DR65
Dove Row E2 142 DU67
Dove Wk. SW1 276 F10
Dove Wk., Horn. 147 FH65
Heron Flight Ave.
Dovecot Clo., Pnr. 115 BV57
Dovecote Ave. N22 121 DN55
Dovecote Clo., Wey. 195 BP104
Dovecote Gdns. SW14 158 CR83
Avondale Rd.
Dovecott Gdns. SW14 158 CR83
North Worple Way
Dovedale Ave., Har. 117 CJ58
Dovedale Ave., Ilf. 103 EN54
Dovedale Clo., Guil. 243 BA131
Weylea Ave.
Dovedale Clo., Uxb. 92 BJ54
Dovedale Clo., Well. 166 EU81
Dovedale Ri., Mitch. 180 DF94
Dovedale Rd. SE22 182 DV85
Dovedale Rd., Dart. 188 FQ88
Dovedon Clo. N14 99 DL47
Dovehouse Cft., Harl. 36 EU13
Mistley Rd.
Dovehouse Grn., Wey. 213 BR105
Rosslyn Pk.
Dovehouse Mead, Bark. 145 ER68
Dovehouse St. SW3 276 B10
Dovehouse St. SW3 160 DD78
Doveney Clo., Orp. 206 EW97
Dover Clo. NW2 119 CX61
Brent Ter.
Dover Clo., Rom. 105 FC54
Dover Flats SE1 162 DS77
Old Kent Rd.
Dover Gdns., Cars. 200 DF104
Dover Ho. Rd. SW15 159 CU84
Dover Pk. Dr. SW15 179 CV86
Dover Rd. E12 124 EJ61
Dover Rd. N9 100 DW47
Dover Rd. SE19 182 DR93
Dover Rd., Grav. 190 GD86
Dover Rd., Rom. 126 EY58
Dover Rd., Slou. 131 AM72
Dover Rd. E., Grav. 190 GE87
Dover St. W1 277 J1
Dover St. W1 141 DH73
Dover Way, Rick. 75 BQ42
Dover Yd. W1 277 J2
Dovercourt Ave., Th.Hth. 201 DN99
Dovercourt Est. N1 142 DR65
Balls Pond Rd.
Dovercourt Gdns., Stan. 96 CL50
Dovercourt La., Sutt. 200 DC104
Dovercourt Rd. SE22 182 DS86
Doverfield, Wal.Cr. 66 DQ29
Doverfield Rd. SW2 181 DL86
Doverfield Rd., Guil. 243 BA131
Doveridge Gdns. N13 99 DP49
Doversgreen Rd., Reig. 266 DB139
Doversmead, Wok. 226 AS116
Doves Clo., Brom. 204 EL103
Doveton Rd., S.Croy. 220 DR106
Doveton St. E1 142 DW70
Malcolm Rd.
Dowanhill Rd. SE6 183 ED88
Dowdeswell Clo. SW15 158 CS84
Dowding Pl., Stan. 95 CG51
Dowding Rd., Uxb. 134 BM66
Dowding Rd., West. 238 EK115
Dowding Wk., Grav. 190 GE90
Dowding Way, Horn. 147 FH66
Dower Ave., Wall. 219 DH109
Dower Clo., Beac. 88 AJ50
Dower Pk., Wind. 151 AL84
Dowgate Hill EC4 275 K10
Dowgate Hill EC4 142 DR73
Dowland St. W10 139 CY69
Dowlans Clo., Lthd. 246 CA127
Dowlans Rd., Lthd. 246 CB127
Dowlas Est. SE5 162 DS80
Dowlas St.
Dowlas St. SE5 162 DS80
Dowlerville Rd., Orp. 223 ET107
Dowling Ct., Hem.H. 40 BK23
Dowman Clo. SW19 200 DB95
Nelson Gro. Rd.
Down Clo., Nthlt. 135 BV68
Down Hall Rd., Kings.T. 197 CK95
Down Pl. W6 159 CV78
Down Pl., Wind. 150 AG79
Down Rd., Guil. 243 BB134
Down Rd., Tedd. 177 CH93
Down St. W1 277 H3
Down St. W1 141 DH74
Down St., W.Mol. 196 CA99
Down St. Ms. W1 277 H3
Down Way, Nthlt. 135 BV69
Downage NW4 119 CW55
Downage, The, Grav. 191 GG89
Downalong (Bushey), Wat. 95 CD46
Downbank Ave., Bexh. 167 FD81
Downbarns Rd., Ruis. 116 BX62
Downbury Ms. SW18 180 DA86
Merton Rd.
Downderry Rd., Brom. 183 ED90
Downe Ave., Sev. 223 ER112
Downe Clo., Horl. 268 DE146
Downe Clo., Well. 166 EW80
Downe Rd., Kes. 222 EK109
Downe Rd., Mitch. 200 DF96
Downe Rd., Sev. 223 EQ114
Downedge, St.Alb. 42 CB19
Downend SE18 165 EP80
Moordown
Downer Dr., Rick. 74 BG36
Downer Meadow, Gdmg. 258 AS143
Downers Cotts. SW4 161 DJ84
The Pavement
Downes Clo., Twick. 177 CH86
St. Margarets Rd.
Downes Ct. N21 99 DN46
Downes Rd., St.Alb. 43 CH16
Downfield, Wor.Pk. 199 CT102
Downfield Clo. W9 140 DB70
Downfield Rd., Hert. 32 DW09
Downfield Rd. (Cheshunt), Wal.Cr. 67 DY31
Downfields, Welw.G.C. 29 CV11
Downhall Rd., Bishop's Stortford 37 FH08
Downhall Rd., Harl. 37 FH08
Downham Clo., Rom. 104 FA52
Downham La., Brom. 183 ED92
Downham Way
Downham Rd. N1 142 DR66
Downham Way, Brom. 183 ED92
Downhills Ave. N17 122 DR55
Downhills Pk. Rd. N17 122 DQ55
Downhills Way N17 100 DQ54
Downhurst Ave. NW7 96 CR50
Downing Ave., Guil. 258 AT135
Downing Clo., Har. 116 CC55
Downing Dr., Grnf. 137 CD67
Downing Path, Slou. 131 AL70
Downing Rd., Dag. 146 EZ67
Downing St. SW1 277 P4
Downing St. SW1 161 DL75
Downings E6 145 EN72
Downings Wd., Rick. 91 BD50
Downland Clo. N20 98 DC46
Downland Clo., Couls. 219 DH114
Downland Clo., Epsom 233 CV118
Downland Gdns., Epsom 233 CV118
Downland Way, Epsom 233 CV118
Downlands, Wal.Abb. 68 EE34
Downlands Rd., Pur. 219 DL114
Downleys Clo. SE9 184 EL89
Downman Rd. SE9 164 EL83
Downs, The SW20 179 CX94
Downs, The, Harl. 51 ES15
Downs, The, Hat. 45 CU20
Downs, The, Lthd. 247 CJ125
Downs Ave., Chis. 185 EM92
Downs Ave., Dart. 188 FN87
Downs Ave., Epsom 216 CS114
Downs Ave., Pnr. 116 BZ58
Downs Bri. Rd., Beck. 203 ED95
Downs Ct. Rd., Pur. 219 DP112
Downs Hill, Beck. 183 ED94
Downs Hill, Grav. 190 GC94
Downs Hill Rd., Epsom 216 CS114
Downs Ho. Rd., Epsom 233 CT118
Downs La. E5 122 DV63
Downs Rd.
Downs La., Lthd. 231 CH123
Downs Pk. Rd. E5 122 DU64
Downs Pk. Rd. E8 122 DT64
Downs Rd. E5 122 DU63
Downs Rd., Beck. 203 EB96
Downs Rd., Couls. 235 DJ118
Downs Rd., Enf. 82 DS42
Downs Rd., Epsom 216 CS114
Downs Rd., Grav. 190 GD91
Downs Rd., Pur. 219 DP111
Downs Rd., Slou. 152 AX75
Downs Rd., Sutt. 218 DB110
Downs Rd., Th.Hth. 202 DQ95
Downs Side, Sutt. 217 CZ111
Downs Vw., Dor. 247 CJ134
Downs Vw., Islw. 157 CF81
Downs Vw., Tad. 233 CV121
Downs Vw. Rd., Lthd. 246 CC126
Downs Way, Epsom 233 CT116
Downs Way, Lthd. 246 CC126
Downs Way, Orp. 223 ES106
Southlands Ave.
Downs Way, Oxt. 254 EE127
Downs Way, Tad. 233 CV121
Downs Way Clo., Tad. 233 CU121
Downs Wd., Epsom 233 CV117
Downsbury Ms. SW18 180 DA85
Merton Rd.
Downsell Rd. E15 123 EC63
Downsfield, Hat. 45 CV21
Sandfield
Downsfield Rd. E17 123 DY58
Downshall Ave., Ilf. 125 ES58
Downshire Hill NW3 120 DD63
Downside, Cher. 193 BF102
Downside, Epsom 216 CS114
Downside, Hem.H. 40 BL19
Downside, Sun. 195 BU95
Downside, Twick. 177 CF90
Downside Bri. Rd., Cob. 213 BV114
Downside Clo. SW19 180 DC93
Downside Common Rd., Cob. 229 BV118
Downside Cres. NW3 120 DE64
Downside Cres. W13 137 CG70
Downside Orchard, Wok. 227 BA117
Park Rd.
Downside Rd., Cob. 229 BV116
Downside Rd., Guil. 259 BB135
Downside Rd., Sutt. 218 DD107
Downside Wk., Nthlt. 136 BZ69
Invicta Gro.
Downsland Dr., Brwd. 108 FW48
Downsview Ave., Wok. 227 AZ121
Downsview Clo., Orp. 224 EW110
Downsview Clo., Swan. 207 FF97
Downsview Ct., Guil. 242 AW130
Hazel Ave.
Downsview Gdns. SE19 182 DQ94
Downsview Rd. SE19 182 DQ94
Downsview Rd., Sev. 256 FF125
Downsway, Guil. 243 BE134
Downsway, Orp. 223 ES106
Southlands Ave.
Downsway, S.Croy. 220 DS111
Downsway, Whyt. 236 DT116
Downsway, The, Sutt. 218 DC109
Downswood, Reig. 250 DE131
Downton Ave. SW2 181 DL89
Downtown Rd. SE16 163 DY75
Downview Clo., Cob. 229 BV119
Downway N12 98 DE52
Dowrey St. N1 141 DN67
Richmond Ave.
Dowry Wk., Wat. 75 BT38
Dowsett Rd. N17 100 DT54
Dowson Clo. SE5 162 DR84
Doyce St. SE1 279 H4
Doyle Clo., Erith 167 FE81
Doyle Gdns. NW10 139 CU67
Doyle Rd. SE25 202 DU98
Doyle Way, Til. 171 GJ82
Coleridge Rd.
D'Oyley St. SW1 276 F8
D'Oyley St. SW1 160 DG77
Doynton St. N19 121 DH61
Draco St. SE17 162 DQ79
Dragmire La., Mitch. 200 DD98
Dragon La., Wey. 212 BN110
Dragon Rd., Hat. 45 CT16
Dragoon Rd. SE8 163 DZ78
Dragor Rd. NW10 138 CQ70
Drake Ave., Cat. 236 DQ122
Drake Ave., Slou. 152 AX77
Drake Ave., Stai. 173 BF92
Drake Clo. SE16 163 DX75
Middleton Dr.
Drake Clo., Brwd. 108 FX50
Drake Ct. SE19 182 DT92
Drake Ct., Har. 116 BZ60
Drake Cres. SE28 146 EW72
Drake Ms., Horn. 147 FG66
Fulmar Rd.
Drake Rd. SE4 163 EA83
Drake Rd., Chess. 216 CN106
Drake Rd., Croy. 201 DM101
Drake Rd., Grays 170 FY75
Drake Rd., Har. 116 BZ61
Drake Rd., Horl. 268 DE148
Court Lo. Rd.
Drake Rd., Mitch. 200 DG100
Drake St. WC1 274 B7
Drake St., Enf. 82 DR39
Drakefell Rd. SE4 163 DY83
Drakefell Rd. SE14 163 DX82
Drakefield Rd. SW17 180 DG90
Drakely Ct. N5 121 DP63
Highbury Hill
Drakes Clo., Esher 214 CA106
Drakes Clo. (Cheshunt), Wal.Cr. 67 DX28
Drakes Ctyd. NW6 139 CZ66
Kilburn High Rd.
Drakes Dr., Nthwd. 93 BP53
Drakes Dr., St.Alb. 43 CH23
Drakes Rd., Amer. 55 AS39
Drakes Wk. E6 145 EN68
Talbot Rd.
Drakes Way, Hat. 45 CV20
Travellers La.
Drakes Way, Wok. 226 AX122
Drakewood Rd. SW16 181 DK94
Draper Clo., Belv. 166 EZ77
Drapers Rd. E15 123 ED63
Drapers Rd. N17 122 DT55
Drapers Rd., Enf. 81 DP40
Drappers Way SE16 162 DU77
St. James's Rd.
Drawdock Rd. SE10 143 ED74
Drawell Clo. SE18 165 ES78
Drax Ave. SW20 179 CU94
Draxmont SW19 179 CY93
Dray Gdns. SW2 181 DM85
Draycot Rd. E11 124 EH58
Draycot Rd., Surb. 198 CN102
Draycott Ave. SW3 276 C8
Draycott Ave. SW3 160 DE77
Draycott Ave., Har. 117 CH58
Draycott Clo., Har. 117 CH58
Draycott Ms. SW6 159 CZ82
New Kings Rd.
Draycott Pl. SW3 276 D9
Draycott Pl. SW3 160 DF77
Draycott Ter. SW3 276 E9
Draycott Ter. SW3 160 DF77
Drayford Clo. W9 139 CZ70
Draymans Way, Islw. 157 CF82
St. John's Rd.
Drayside Ms., Sthl. 156 BZ75
Kingston Rd.
Drayson Clo., Wal.Abb. 68 EE32
Drayson Ms. W8 160 DA75
Drayton Ave. W13 137 CG73
Drayton Ave., Loug. 85 EM44
Drayton Ave., Orp. 205 EP102
Drayton Ave., Pot.B. 63 CY32
Drayton Bri. Rd. W7 137 CF73
Drayton Bri. Rd. W13 137 CG72
Drayton Clo., Houns. 176 BZ85
Bramley Way
Drayton Clo., Ilf. 125 ER60
Drayton Clo., Lthd. 231 CE124
Drayton Gdns. N21 99 DP45
Drayton Gdns. SW10 160 DC78
Drayton Gdns. W13 137 CG73
Drayton Gdns., West Dr. 154 BK75
Drayton Grn. W13 137 CG73
Drayton Grn. Rd. W13 137 CH73
Drayton Gro. W13 137 CG73
Drayton Pk. N5 121 DN64
Drayton Pk. Ms. N5 121 DN64
Drayton Pk.
Drayton Rd. E11 123 ED60
Drayton Rd. N17 100 DS54
Drayton Rd. NW10 139 CT67
Drayton Rd. W13 137 CG73
Drayton Rd., Borwd. 78 CN42
Drayton Rd., Croy. 201 DP103
Drayton Waye, Har. 117 CH58
Dreadnought St. SE10 164 EE76
Drenon Sq., Hayes 135 BT73
Dresden Clo. NW6 140 DB65
Dresden Rd. N19 121 DJ60
Dresden Way, Wey. 213 BQ106
Dressington Ave. SE4 183 EA86
Drew Ave. NW7 97 CY51
Drew Gdns., Grnf. 137 CF65
Drew Meadow, Slou. 111 AQ63
Drew Rd. E16 144 EL74
Drews Pk., Beac. 88 AH49
Drewstead Rd. SW16 181 DK89
Drey, The, Ger.Cr. 90 AY50
Driffield Rd. E3 143 DY68
Drift, The, Brom. 204 EK104
Drift Rd., Lthd. 229 BR124
Drift Rd., Wind. 150 AD84
Drift Way, Rich. 178 CM88
Drift Way, Slou. 153 BC81
Driftway, The, Bans. 233 CW115
Driftway, The, Hem.H. 40 BM20
Driftway, The, Lthd. 231 CH123
Downs La.
Driftway, The, Mitch. 200 DG95
Driftwood Ave., St.Alb. 60 CA26
Driftwood Dr., Ken. 235 DP117
Drill Hall Rd., Cher. 194 BG101
Drinkwater Rd., Har. 116 CB61
Drive, The E4 101 ED45
Drive, The E17 123 EB55
Drive, The E18 124 EG56
Drive, The N3 98 DA52
Drive, The N6 120 DF57
Fordington Rd.
Drive, The N11 99 DJ51
Drive, The NW10 139 CT67
Longstone Ave.
Drive, The NW11 119 CY59
Drive, The SW6 159 CY82
Fulham Rd.
Drive, The SW16 201 DM97
Drive, The SW20 179 CW94
Drive, The W3 138 CQ72
Drive, The, Amer. 55 AR38
Drive, The, Ashf. 175 BR94
Drive, The, Bans. 233 CY117
Drive, The, Bark. 145 ET66
Drive, The, Barn. 79 CY41
Drive, The (New Barnet), Barn. 80 DC44
Drive, The, Beck. 203 EA96
Drive, The, Bex. 186 EW86
Drive, The, Brwd. 108 FW50
Drive, The, Buck.H. 102 EJ45
Drive, The, Chesh. 72 AX36
Drive, The, Chis. 205 ET97
Drive, The, Cob. 214 BY114
Drive, The, Couls. 219 DL114
Drive, The, Edg. 96 CN50
Drive, The, Enf. 82 DR39
Drive, The, Epsom 217 CT107
Drive, The (Headley), Epsom 232 CP124
Drive, The, Erith 167 FB80
Drive, The, Esher 196 CC102
Drive, The, Felt. 176 BW87
Drive, The, Ger.Cr. 90 AY52
Drive, The, Grav. 191 GK91
Drive, The, Guil. 242 AT134
Beech Gro.
Drive, The (Artington), Guil. 258 AV138
Drive, The (Onslow Village), Guil. 258 AT136
Drive, The, Harl. 35 ES14
Drive, The, Har. 116 CA59
Drive, The, Hat. 64 DA25
Drive, The, Hert. 32 DQ07
Drive, The (Newgate St.), Hert. 47 DL24
Drive, The, Hodd. 49 EA15
Drive, The, Horl. 269 DH149
Drive, The, Houns. 156 CC82
Drive, The, Ilf. 124 EL58
Drive, The, Islw. 157 CD82
Drive, The, Kings.T. 178 CQ94
Drive, The, Lthd. 232 CL123
Drive, The (Fetcham), Lthd. 231 CE122
Drive, The, Loug. 84 EL41
Drive, The, Mord. 200 DC99
Drive, The, Nthwd. 93 BS54
Drive, The, Orp. 205 ET103
Drive, The, Pot.B. 63 CZ33
Drive, The, Rad. 61 CG34
Drive, The, Rick. 74 BH43
Drive, The, Rom. 105 FC53
Drive, The (Harold Wd.), Rom. 106 FL53
Drive, The, St.Alb. 61 CG25
Drive, The, Saw. 36 EY05
Drive, The, Sev. 257 FH124
Drive, The, Sid. 186 EV90
Drive, The, Slou. 152 AY75
Drive, The (Datchet), Slou. 152 AV81
Drive, The, Stai. 172 AX85
Drive, The, Surb. 198 CL101
Drive, The, Sutt. 217 CZ112
Drive, The, Th.Hth. 202 DR98
Drive, The, Uxb. 114 BL63
Drive, The, Vir.W. 193 AZ99
Drive, The, Wall. 219 DJ110
Drive, The (Cheshunt), Wal.Cr. 65 DP28
Drive, The, Wat. 75 BS37
Drive, The, Wem. 118 CQ61
Drive, The, W.Wick. 203 ED101
Drive, The, Wok. 226 AV120
Drive Mead, Couls. 219 DL114
Drive Rd., Couls. 235 DM119
Drive Spur, Tad. 234 DA121
Driveway, The E17 123 EB58
Hoe St.
Driveway, The (Cuffley), Pot.B. 65 DL28
Drodges Clo., Guil. 259 AZ143
Droitwich Clo. SE26 182 DU90
Dromey Gdns., Har. 95 CF52
Dromore Rd. SW15 179 CY86
Dronfield Gdns., Dag. 126 EW64
Droop St. W10 139 CY70
Drop La., St.Alb. 60 CB30
Dropmore Rd., Slou. 130 AJ67
Drove Rd., Dor. 262 BW135
Drove Rd., Guil. 260 BG136
Drove Way, Loug. 85 EP40
Drove Way, The, Grav. 190 GE94
Drover La. SE15 162 DV80
Drovers Pl. SE15 162 DV80
Drovers Rd., S.Croy. 220 DR106
Drovers Way, Beac. 89 AQ51
Drovers Way, Hat. 45 CV15
Drovers Way, St.Alb. 43 CD20
Druce Rd. SE21 182 DS86
Drudgeon Way, Dart. 189 FV90
Druid St. SE1 279 N4
Druid St. SE1 162 DS75
Druids Clo., Ash. 232 CM120
Druids Way, Brom. 203 ED98
Drum St. E1 142 DT72
Whitechapel High St.
Drumaline Ridge, Wor.Pk. 198 CS103
Drummond Ave., Rom. 127 FD56
Drummond Clo., Erith 167 FE81
Drummond Cres. NW1 273 M2
Drummond Cres. NW1 141 DK69
Drummond Dr., Stan. 95 CF52
Drummond Gate SW1 277 N10
Drummond Gate SW1 161 DK78
Drummond Pl., Rich. 158 CL84
Drummond Pl., Twick. 177 CH87
Drummond Rd. E11 124 EJ58
Drummond Rd. SE16 162 DV76
Drummond Rd., Croy. 202 DQ103
Drummond Rd., Guil. 242 AX134
Drummond Rd., Rom. 127 FE56
Drummond St. NW1 273 K4
Drummond St. NW1 141 DJ70
Drummonds, The, Buck.H. 102 EH47
Drummonds, The, Epp. 70 EU30
Drummonds Pl., Rich. 158 CL84
Drury Cres., Croy. 201 DN103
Drury Ind. Est. NW10 118 CQ64
Drury La. WC2 274 A8
Drury La. WC2 141 DL72
Drury La., Ware 34 EK06
Drury Rd., Har. 116 CC59
Drury Way NW10 118 CR64
Dryad St. SW15 159 CX83
Dryburgh Gdns. NW9 118 CN55
Dryburgh Rd. SW15 159 CV83
Drycroft, Welw.G.C. 29 CY12
Drydell La., Chesh. 54 AL30
Dryden Ave. W7 137 CF72
Dryden Clo., Ilf. 103 ET51
Dryden Ct. SE11 278 E9
Dryden Pl., Til. 171 GH81
Fielding Ave.
Dryden Rd. SW19 180 DC93
Dryden Rd., Enf. 82 DS44
Dryden Rd., Har. 117 CF63
Dryden Rd., Well. 165 ES81
Dryden St. WC2 274 A9
Dryden Twrs., Rom. 105 FH52
Dryden Way, Orp. 206 EU102
Lych Gate Rd.
Dryfield Clo. NW10 138 CQ65
Dryfield Rd., Edg. 96 CQ51
Dryfield Wk. SE8 163 EA79
New King St.
Dryhill La., Sev. 256 FB123
Dryhill Rd., Belv. 166 EZ79
Dryland Ave., Orp. 223 ET105
Drylands Rd. N8 121 DL58
Drynham Pk., Wey. 195 BS104
Drysdale Ave. E4 101 EB45
Drysdale Clo., Nthwd. 93 BS52
Northbrook Dr.
Drysdale Pl. N1 275 N2
Drysdale St. N1 275 N2
Drysdale St. N1 142 DS69
Du Burstow Ter. W7 157 CE75
Du Cane Clo. W12 139 CW72
Du Cane Rd.
Du Cane Ct. SW17 180 DG88
Du Cane Rd. W12 139 CT72
Du Cros Dr., Stan. 95 CK51
Du Cros Rd. W3 138 CS74
The Vale
Duarte Pl., Grays 170 FZ76
Dublin Cres. E8 142 DU67
Dubrae Clo., St.Alb. 42 CA22
Ducal St. E2 142 DT69
Brick La.
Duchess Gro., Buck.H. 102 EH47
Knighton La.
Duchess Ms. W1 273 J7
Duchess of Bedford's Wk. W8 160 DA75
Duchess St. W1 273 J7
Duchess St. W1 141 DH71
Duchess Wk., Sev. 257 FK128
Duchy Rd., Barn. 80 DD38
Duchy St. SE1 278 E2
Duchy St. SE1 141 DN74
Ducie St. SW4 161 DM84
Duck La. W1 273 M9
Duck La., Epp. 70 EW26
Duck Lees La., Enf. 83 DY42
Duckett Ms. N4 121 DP58
Duckett Rd.
Duckett Rd. N4 121 DN58
Duckett St. E1 143 DX70
Ducketts Mead, Harl. 34 EH14
Ducketts Rd., Dart. 187 FF85
Ducking Stool Ct., Rom. 127 FE56
Duckling La., Saw. 36 EY05
Vantorts Rd.
Ducks Hill, Nthwd. 92 BN54
Ducks Hill Rd., Nthwd. 93 BP54
Ducks Hill Rd., Ruis. 93 BP54
Ducks Wk., Twick. 177 CJ85
Dudden Hill La. NW10 119 CT63
Duddington Clo. SE9 184 EK91
Dudley Ave., Har. 117 CJ55
Dudley Ave., Wal.Cr. 67 DX32
Dudley Clo., Add. 194 BJ104
Dudley Clo., Grays 170 FY75
Dudley Clo., Hem.H. 57 BA27
Dudley Ct. NW11 119 CZ56
Dudley Ct., Slou. 152 AU76
Upton Rd.
Dudley Dr., Mord. 199 CY102

Dudley Dr., Ruis. 115 BV64
Dudley Gdns. W13 157 CH75
Dudley Gdns., Har. 117 CD60
Dudley Gdns., Rom. 106 FK51
Dudley Rd.
Dudley Gro., Epsom 216 CQ114
Dudley Rd. E17 101 EA54
Dudley Rd. N3 98 DB54
Dudley Rd. NW6 139 CY68
Dudley Rd. SW19 180 DA93
Dudley Rd., Ashf. 174 BL92
Dudley Rd., Felt. 175 BQ88
Dudley Rd., Grav. 190 GE87
Dudley Rd., Har. 116 CC61
Dudley Rd., Ilf. 125 EP63
Dudley Rd., Kings.T. 198 CM97
Dudley Rd., Rich. 158 CM82
Dudley Rd., Rom. 106 FK51
Dudley Rd., Sthl. 156 BX75
Dudley Rd., Walt. 195 BU100
Dudley St. W2 140 DD71
Harrow Rd.
Dudlington Rd. E5 122 DW61
Dudmaston Ms. SW3 276 A10
Dudsbury Rd., Dart. 187 FG86
Dudsbury Rd., Sid. 186 EV93
Dudset La., Houns. 155 BU81
Duff St. E14 143 EB72
Dufferin Ave. EC1 275 K5
Dufferin St. EC1 275 J5
Dufferin St. EC1 142 DQ70
Duffield Clo., Grays 170 FY75
Duffield Clo., Har. 117 CF57
Duffield Dr. N15 122 DT56
Copperfield Dr.
Duffield La., Slou. 132 AT65
Duffield Pk., Slou. 132 AU69
Duffield Rd., Tad. 233 CV124
Duffins Orchard, Cher. 211 BC108
Dufour's Pl. W1 273 L9
Dugdale Hill La., Pot.B. 63 CY33
Dugdales, Rick. 74 BN42
Duke Gdns., Ilf. 125 ER56
Duke Rd.
Duke Hill St. SE1 279 L2
Duke Humphrey Rd. SE3 164 EE81
Duke of Cambridge Clo., Twick. 177 CD86
Duke of Edinburgh Rd., Sutt. 200 DD103
Duke of Wellington Pl. SW1 276 G4
Duke of Wellington Pl. SW1 160 DG75
Duke of York St. SW1 277 L2
Duke of York St. SW1 141 DJ74
Duke Rd. W4 158 CR78
Duke Rd., Ilf. 125 ER56
Duke Shore Pl. E14 143 DZ73
Narrow St.
Duke St. SW1 277 L2
Duke St. SW1 141 DJ74
Duke St. W1 272 G8
Duke St. W1 140 DG72
Duke St., Hodd. 49 EA16
Duke St., Rich. 177 CK85
Duke St., Sutt. 218 DD105
Duke St., Wat. 76 BW41
Duke St., Wind. 151 AP80
Duke St., Wok. 227 AZ117
Dukes Ave. N3 98 DB53
Dukes Ave. N10 121 DJ55
Dukes Ave. W4 158 CR78
Dukes Ave., Edg. 96 CM51
Dukes Ave., Epp. 85 ES35
Dukes Ave., Grays 170 GA75
Dukes Ave., Har. 116 BZ58
Dukes Ave. (Wealdstone), Har. 117 CE56
Dukes Ave., Houns. 156 BY84
Dukes Ave., Kings.T. 177 CJ91
Dukes Ave., N.Mal. 199 CT97
Dukes Ave., Nthlt. 136 BY66
Dukes Ave., Rich. 177 CJ91
Dukes Clo., Ashf. 175 BQ91
Dukes Clo., Epp. 71 FB27
Dukes Clo., Ger.Cr. 112 AX60
Dukes Clo., Hmptn. 176 BZ92
Dukes Clo., Kings.T. 177 CK91
Dukes Ct. E6 145 EN67
Dukes Ct., Wok. 227 AZ117
Dukes Dr., Slou. 111 AM64
Dukes Grn. Ave., Felt. 175 BU85
Dukes Hill, Cat. 237 DY120
Dukes Kiln Dr., Ger.Cr. 112 AW60
Dukes La. W8 160 DB75
Dukes La., Ger.Cr. 112 AY60
Dukes Lo., Nthwd. 93 BS50
Eastbury Ave.
Duke's Meadows W4 158 CQ82
Great Chertsey Rd.
Dukes Ms. N10 121 DH55
Dukes Ave.
Duke's Ms. W1 272 G8
Dukes Orchard, Bex. 187 FC88
Duke's Pas. E17 123 EC55
Marlowe Rd.
Dukes Pl. EC3 275 N9
Dukes Pl. EC3 142 DS72
Dukes Ride, Dor. 263 CK139
Dukes Ride, Ger.Cr. 112 AY60
Dukes Ride, Uxb. 114 BL63
The Dr.
Dukes Rd. E6 145 EN67
Dukes Rd. W3 138 CN70
Duke's Rd. WC1 273 N3
Duke's Rd. WC1 141 DK69
Dukes Rd., Walt. 214 BX106
Dukes Valley, Ger.Cr. 112 AV61
Dukes Way, Berk. 38 AU17
Dukes Way, W.Wick. 204 EE104
Dukes Wd. Ave., Ger.Cr. 112 AY59
Dukes Wd. Dr., Ger.Cr. 112 AX60
Duke's Yd. W1 272 G10
Dukesthorpe Rd. SE26 183 DX91
Dulas St. N4 121 DM60
Everleigh St.
Dulford St. W11 139 CY73
Dulka Rd. SW11 180 DF85
Dulverton Rd. SE9 185 EQ89
Dulverton Rd., Rom. 106 FK51
Dulverton Rd., Ruis. 115 BU60
Dulverton Rd., S.Croy. 220 DW110
Dulwich Common SE21 182 DS88
Dulwich Common SE22 182 DT88
Dulwich Lawn Clo. SE22 182 DT85
Melbourne Gro.
Dulwich Oaks, The SE21 182 DT90
Dulwich Rd. SE24 181 DN85
Dulwich Village SE21 182 DS86
Dulwich Way, Rick. 74 BN43
Dulwich Wd. Ave. SE19 182 DS91
Dulwich Wd. Pk. SE19 182 DS91
Dumbarton Ave., Wal.Cr. 67 DX34
Dumbarton Rd. SW2 181 DL86
Dumbleton Clo., Kings.T. 198 CP95
Gloucester Rd.
Dumbreck Rd. SE9 165 EM84
Dumfries Clo., Wat. 93 BT48
Dumont Rd. N16 122 DS62
Dumpton Pl. NW1 140 DG66
Gloucester Ave.
Dunally Pk., Shep. 195 BR101
Dunbar Ave. SW16 201 DN96
Dunbar Ave., Beck. 203 DY98
Dunbar Ave., Dag. 126 FA62
Dunbar Clo., Hayes 135 BU71
Dunbar Clo., Slou. 132 AU72
Dunbar Ct., Sutt. 218 DD106
Dunbar Ct., Walt. 195 BV103
Dunbar Gdns., Dag. 126 FA64
Dunbar Rd. E7 144 EG65
Dunbar Rd. N22 99 DN53
Dunbar Rd., N.Mal. 198 CQ98
Dunbar St. SE27 182 DQ90
Dunblane Clo., Edg. 96 CP47
Tayside Dr.
Dunblane Rd. SE9 164 EL82
Dunboe Pl., Shep. 195 BQ101
Dunboyne Rd. NW3 120 DF64
Dunbridge St. E2 142 DU70
Duncan Clo., Barn. 80 DC42
Duncan Clo., Welw.G.C. 29 CY10
Duncan Dr., Guil. 243 BA133
Duncan Gro. W3 138 CS72
Duncan Rd. E8 142 DV67
Duncan Rd., Rich. 158 CL84
Duncan Rd., Tad. 233 CY119
Duncan St. N1 141 DP68
Duncan Ter. N1 274 F1
Duncan Ter. N1 141 DP68
Duncan Way (Bushey), Wat. 76 BZ40
Duncannon Cres., Wind. 151 AK83
Duncannon St. WC2 277 P1
Duncannon St. WC2 141 DL73
Dunch St. E1 142 DV72
Watney St.
Duncombe Clo., Amer. 55 AS38
Duncombe Clo., Hert. 32 DQ07
Duncombe Ct., Stai. 173 BF94
Duncombe Hill SE23 183 DY87
Duncombe Rd. N19 121 DK60
Duncombe Rd., Berk. 38 AS17
Duncombe Rd., Hert. 32 DQ08
Duncrievie Rd. SE13 183 ED86
Duncroft SE18 165 ES80
Duncroft, Wind. 151 AM83
Duncroft Clo., Reig. 249 CZ133
Dundalk Rd. SE4 163 DY83
Dundas Gdns., W.Mol. 196 CB97
Dundas Rd. SE15 162 DW82
Dundee Rd. E13 144 EH68
Dundee Rd. SE25 202 DV99
Dundee Rd., Slou. 131 AM72
Dundee St. E1 142 DV74
Dundela Gdns., Wor.Pk. 217 CV105
Dundonald Clo. E6 144 EL72
Northumberland Rd.
Dundonald Rd. NW10 139 CX67
Dundonald Rd. SW19 179 CY94
Dundrey Cres., Red. 251 DL129
Dunedin Dr., Cat. 252 DS125
Dunedin Rd. E10 123 EB62
Dunedin Rd., Ilf. 125 EQ60
Dunedin Rd., Rain. 147 FF69
Dunedin Way, Hayes 136 BW70
Dunelm Gro. SE27 182 DQ91
Dunelm St. E1 143 DX72
Dunfee Way, W.Byf. 212 BL112
Dunfield Gdns. SE6 183 EB92
Dunfield Rd. SE6 183 EB92
Dunford Rd. N7 121 DM63
Dungarvan Ave. SW15 159 CU84
Dungates La., Bet. 249 CU133
Dunheved Clo., Th.Hth. 201 DN100
Dunheved Rd. N., Th.Hth. 201 DN100
Dunheved Rd. S., Th.Hth. 201 DN100
Dunheved Rd. W., Th.Hth. 201 DN100
Dunholme Grn. N9 100 DT48
Dunholme La. N9 100 DT48
Dunholme Rd.
Dunholme Rd. N9 100 DT48
Dunkeld Rd. SE25 202 DR98
Dunkeld Rd., Dag. 126 EV61
Dunkellin Gro., S.Ock. 149 FU72
Dunkellin Way
Dunkellin Way, S.Ock. 149 FU72
Dunkery Rd. SE9 184 EK91
Dunkin Rd., Dart. 168 FN84
Dunkirk Clo., Grav. 191 GJ92
Christian Flds. Ave.
Dunkirk St. SE27 182 DQ91
Waring St.
Dunlace Rd. E5 122 DW63
Dunleary Clo., Houns. 176 BZ87
Dunley Dr., Croy. 221 EB108
Dunlin Clo., Red. 266 DE139
Dunlin Ho. W13 137 CF70
Dunlin Ri., Guil. 243 BD132
Dunlin Rd., Hem.H. 40 BL15
Dunloe Ave. N17 122 DR55
Dunloe St. E2 142 DT68
Dunlop Pl. SE16 162 DT76
Spa Rd.
Dunlop Pt. E16 144 EG74
Dunlop Rd., Til. 171 GF81
Dunmail Dr., Pur. 220 DS114
Dunmore Pt. E2 275 P3
Dunmore Rd. NW6 139 CY67
Dunmore Rd. SW20 199 CW95
Dunmow Clo., Felt. 176 BX91
Dunmow Clo., Loug. 84 EL44
Dunmow Clo., Rom. 126 EW57
Dunmow Dr., Rain. 147 FF67
Dunmow Ho., Dag. 146 EV67
Dunmow Rd. E15 123 ED63
Dunmow Wk. N1 142 DQ67
Popham St.
Dunn Mead NW9 97 CT52
Field Mead
Dunn St. E8 122 DT64
Dunnale Cres. SE16 163 DX77
Plough Way
Dunnents, Wok. 226 AS117
Dunning Clo., S.Ock. 149 FU72
Dent Clo.
Dunningford Clo., Horn. 127 FF64
Dunnock Clo. N9 101 DX46
Dunnock Clo., Borwd. 78 CN42
Siskin Clo.
Dunnock Rd. E6 144 EL72
Dunns Pas. WC1 274 A8
Dunny La., Kings L. 57 BE32
Dunnymans Rd., Bans. 233 CZ115
Dunollie Pl. NW5 121 DJ64
Dunollie Rd.
Dunollie Rd. NW5 121 DJ64
Dunoon Rd. SE23 182 DW87
Dunottar Clo., Red. 266 DD136
Dunraven Ave., Red. 267 DH141
Dunraven Dr., Enf. 81 DN40
Dunraven Rd. W12 139 CU74
Dunraven St. W1 272 E10
Dunsany Rd. W14 159 CX76
Dunsborough Pk., Wok. 228 BJ120
Dunsbury Clo., Sutt. 218 DB109
Nettlecombe Clo.
Dunsdon Ave., Guil. 258 AV135
Dunsfold Ri., Couls. 219 DK113
Dunsfold Way, Croy. 221 EB108
Dunsford Way SW15 179 CV86
Dover Pk. Dr.
Dunsmore Clo., Hayes 136 BY70
Kingsash Dr.
Dunsmore Clo. (Bushey), Wat. 77 CD44
Dunsmore Rd., Walt. 195 BV100
Dunsmore Way (Bushey), Wat. 77 CD44
Dunsmure Rd. N16 122 DS60
Dunspring La., Ilf. 103 EP54
Dunstable Clo., Rom. 106 FK51
Dunstable Rd.
Dunstable Ms. W1 272 G6
Dunstable Rd., Rich. 158 CL84
Dunstable Rd., Rom. 106 FK51
Dunstable Rd., W.Mol. 196 BZ98
Dunstall Grn., Wok. 210 AW109
Dunstall Rd. SW20 179 CV93
Dunstall Way, W.Mol. 196 CB97
Dunstalls, Harl. 51 EN19
Dunstan Clo. N2 120 DC55
Thomas More Way
Dunstan Rd. NW11 119 CZ60
Dunstan Rd., Couls. 235 DK117
Dunstans Gro. SE22 182 DV86
Dunstans Rd. SE22 182 DU87
Dunster Ave., Mord. 199 CX102
Dunster Clo., Barn. 79 CX42
Dunster Clo., Rom. 105 FC54
Dunster Clo., Uxb. 92 BH53
Dunster Ct. EC3 275 M10
Dunster Cres., Horn. 128 FN61
Dunster Dr. NW9 118 CQ60
Dunster Gdns. NW6 139 CZ66
Dunster Gdns., Slou. 131 AN73
Avebury
Dunster Way, Har. 116 BY62
Dunsters Mead, Welw.G.C. 30 DA11
Dunsterville Way SE1 279 L5
Dunston Rd. E8 142 DT67
Dunston Rd. SW11 160 DG83
Dunston St. E8 142 DT67
Dunton Clo., Surb. 198 CL102
Dunton Rd. E10 123 EB59
Dunton Rd. SE1 279 P9
Dunton Rd. SE1 162 DT77
Dunton Rd., Rom. 127 FE56
Duntshill Rd. SW18 180 DB88
Dunvegan Clo., W.Mol. 196 CB98
Dunvegan Rd. SE9 165 EM84
Dunwich Rd., Bexh. 166 EZ81
Dunworth Ms. W11 139 CZ72
Portobello Rd.
Duplex Ride SW1 276 E5
Dupont Rd. SW20 199 CX96
Dupont St. E14 143 DY71
Maroon St.
Duppas Ave., Croy. 219 DP105
Violet La.
Duppas Clo., Shep. 195 BR99
Green La.
Duppas Hill La., Croy. 219 DP105
Duppas Hill Rd.
Duppas Hill Rd., Croy. 219 DN105
Duppas Hill Ter., Croy. 201 DP104
Duppas Rd., Croy. 201 DN104
Dupre Clo., Grays 170 FY76
Camden Rd.
Dupre Cres., Beac. 89 AP54
Dupre Wk., H.Wyc. 110 AD59
Stratford Dr.
Dupree Rd. SE7 164 EH78
Dura Den Clo., Beck. 183 EB94
Durand Clo., Cars. 200 DF102
Durand Gdns. SW9 161 DM81
Durand Way NW10 138 CQ66
Durands Wk. SE16 163 DY75
Salter Rd.
Durant Rd., Swan. 187 FG93
Durant St. E2 142 DU69
Durants Pk. Ave., Enf. 83 DX42
Durants Rd., Enf. 82 DW42
Durban Gdns., Dag. 147 FC66
Durban Rd. E15 144 EE69
Durban Rd. E17 101 DZ53
Durban Rd. N17 100 DS51
Durban Rd. SE27 182 DQ91
Durban Rd., Beck. 203 DZ96
Durban Rd., Ilf. 125 ES60
Durban Rd. E., Wat. 75 BU42
Durban Rd. W., Wat. 75 BU42
Durbin Rd., Chess. 216 CL105
Durdans Rd., Sthl. 136 BZ72
Durell Gdns., Dag. 126 EX64
Durell Rd., Dag. 126 EX64
Durfold Dr., Reig. 250 DC134
Durford Cres. SW15 179 CV88
Durham Ave., Brom. 204 EF98
Durham Ave., Houns. 156 BZ79
Durham Ave., Rom. 128 FJ56
Durham Ave., Slou. 131 AM72
Durham Ave., Wdf.Grn. 102 EK50
Durham Clo. SW20 199 CV96
Durham Rd.
Durham Clo., Guil. 242 AT132
Durham Clo., Saw. 36 EW06
Durham Clo., Ware 33 EB10
Durham Hill, Brom. 184 EF91
Durham Ho. St. WC2 278 A1
Durham Pl. SW3 160 DF78
Smith St.
Durham Pl., Ilf. 125 EQ63
Eton Rd.
Durham Ri. SE18 165 EQ78
Durham Rd. E12 124 EK63
Durham Rd. E16 144 EE70
Durham Rd. N2 120 DE55
Durham Rd. N7 121 DM61
Durham Rd. N9 100 DU47
Durham Rd. SW20 199 CV95
Durham Rd. W5 157 CK76
Durham Rd., Borwd. 78 CQ41
Durham Rd., Brom. 204 EF97
Durham Rd., Dag. 127 FC64
Durham Rd., Felt. 176 BW87
Durham Rd., Har. 116 CB57
Durham Rd., Sid. 186 EV92
Durham Row E1 143 DY71
Durham St. SE11 161 DM78
Durham Ter. W2 140 DB72
Durham Wf., Brent. 157 CJ80
High St.
Durham Yd. E2 142 DV69
Teesdale St.
Duriun Way, Erith 167 FG80
Slade Grn. Rd.
Durleston Pk. Dr., Lthd. 246 CC125
Durley Ave., Pnr. 116 BY59
Durley Gdns., Orp. 224 EV105
Durley Rd. N16 122 DS59
Durlston Rd. E5 122 DU61
Durlston Rd., Kings.T. 178 CL93
Durndale La., Grav. 190 GE91
Durnell Way, Loug. 85 EN41
Durnford St. N15 122 DS57
Durnford St. SE10 163 EC79
Greenwich Ch. St.
Durning Rd. SE19 182 DR92
Durnsford Ave. SW19 180 DA89
Durnsford Rd. N11 99 DK53
Durnsford Rd. SW19 180 DA89
Durrant Pl., Chesh. 54 AN27
Hivings Hill
Durrant Way, Orp. 223 ER106
Durrant Way, Swans. 190 FY87
Durrants Clo., Rain. 148 FJ68
Durrants Dr., Rick. 75 BQ41
Durrants Hill Rd., Hem.H. 40 BK23
Durrants La., Berk. 38 AS19
Durrants Rd., Berk. 38 AT18
Durrell Rd. SW6 159 CZ81
Durrell Way, Shep. 195 BR100
Durrington Ave. SW20 199 CW95
Durrington Pk. Rd. SW20 199 CW95
Durrington Rd. E5 123 DY63
Dursley Clo. SE3 164 EJ82
Dursley Gdns. SE3 164 EK81
Dursley Rd. SE3 164 EJ82
Durward St. E1 142 DV71
Durweston Ms. W1 272 E6
Durweston St. W1 272 E7
Dury Falls Clo., Horn. 128 FM60
Dury Rd., Barn. 79 CZ40
Dutch Barn Clo., Stai. 174 BK86
Dutch Elm Ave., Wind. 152 AT80
Dutch Gdns., Kings.T. 178 CP93
Windmill Ri.
Dutch Yd. SW18 180 DA85
Wandsworth High St.
Duthie St. E14 143 EC73
Dutton St. SE10 163 EC81
Dutton Way, Iver 133 BE72
Duxberry Clo., Brom. 204 EL99
Southborough La.
Duxford Clo., Horn. 147 FH65
Duxons Turn, Hem.H. 41 BP19
Maylands Ave.
Dwight Ct. SW6 159 CY82
Burlington Rd.
Dwight Rd., Wat. 93 BR45
Dye Ho. La. E3 143 EA67
Dyer's Bldgs. EC1 274 D7
Dyers Fld., Horl. 269 DP148
Dyers Hall Rd. E11 124 EE61
Dyers La. SW15 159 CV84
Dyers Way, Rom. 105 FH52
Dyke Dr., Orp. 206 EW102
Dykes Path, Wok. 227 BC115
Bentham Ave.
Dykes Way, Brom. 204 EF97
Dykewood Clo., Bex. 187 FE90
Dylan Clo., Borwd. 95 CK45
Coates Rd.
Dylan Rd. SE24 161 DP84
Dylan Rd., Belv. 166 FA76
Dylan Thomas Ho. N8 121 DM56
Dylways SE5 162 DR84
Dymchurch Clo., Ilf. 125 EN55
Dymchurch Clo., Orp. 223 ES105
Dymes Path SW19 179 CX89
Queensmere Rd.
Dymock St. SW6 160 DB83
Dymoke Grn., St.Alb. 43 CG16
Dymoke Rd., Horn. 127 FF59
Dymokes Way, Hodd. 33 EA14
Dymond Est. SW17 180 DE90
Glenburnie Rd.
Dyne Rd. NW6 139 CY66
Dyneley Rd. SE12 184 EJ91
Dynevor Rd. N16 122 DT62
Dynevor Rd., Rich. 178 CL85
Dynham Rd. NW6 140 DA66
Dyott St. WC1 273 N8
Dyott St. WC1 141 DK72
Dyrham La., Barn. 79 CU36
Dysart Ave., Kings.T. 177 CJ92
Dysart St. EC2 275 M5
Dyson Clo., Wind. 151 AP83
Dyson Rd. E11 124 EE58
Dyson Rd. E15 144 EF65
Dysons Clo., Wal.Cr. 67 DX33
Dysons Rd. N18 100 DV50

E

Eade Rd. N4 122 DQ59
Eagans Clo. N2 120 DE55
Market Pl.
Eagle Ave., Rom. 126 EY58
Eagle Clo. SE16 162 DW78
Varcoe Rd.
Eagle Clo., Enf. 82 DW42
Eagle Clo., Horn. 147 FH65
Eagle Clo., Wall. 219 DL107
Mollison Dr.
Eagle Clo., Wal.Abb. 68 EG34
Eagle Ct. EC1 274 F6
Eagle Ct. EC1 141 DP71
Eagle Ct., Hert. 32 DV08
Eagle Dr. NW9 96 CS54
Eagle Hill SE19 182 DR93
Eagle La. E11 124 EG56
Eagle Ms. N1 142 DS65
Tottenham Rd.
Eagle Pl. SW1 277 L1
Eagle Pl. SW7 160 DC78
Old Brompton Rd.
Eagle Rd., Guil. 242 AX134
Eagle Rd., Wem. 137 CK66
Eagle St. WC1 274 B7
Eagle St. WC1 141 DM71
Eagle Ter., Wdf.Grn. 102 EH52
Eagle Way, Brwd. 107 FV51
Eagle Way, Grav. 190 GA85
Eagle Way, Hat. 45 CU20
Eagle Wf. Rd. N1 142 DQ68
Eagles Dr., West. 238 EK118
Eagles Rd., Green. 169 FU84
Eaglesfield Rd. SE18 165 EP82
Ealdham Sq. SE9 164 EJ84
Ealing Clo., Borwd. 78 CR39
Ealing Downs Ct., Grnf. 137 CG69
Perivale La.
Ealing Grn. W5 137 CK74
Ealing Pk. Gdns. W5 157 CJ77
Ealing Rd., Brent. 157 CK77
Ealing Rd., Nthlt. 136 CA67
Ealing Rd., Wem. 138 CL65
Ealing Village W5 138 CL72
Eamont Clo., Ruis. 115 BP59
Allonby Dr.
Eamont St. NW8 140 DE68
Eardemont Clo., Dart. 167 FF84
Eardley Cres. SW5 160 DA78
Eardley Pt. SE18 165 EP77
Wilmount St.
Eardley Rd. SW16 181 DJ92
Eardley Rd., Belv. 166 FA78
Eardley Rd., Sev. 257 FH124
Earl Ri. SE18 165 ER77
Earl Rd. SE1 279 P10
Earl Rd. SE1 162 DT78
Earl Rd. SW14 158 CQ84
Elm Rd.
Earl Rd., Grav. 190 GE89
Earl St. EC2 275 L6
Earl St. EC2 142 DR71
Earl St., Wat. 76 BW41
Earldom Rd. SW15 159 CW84
Earle Gdns., Kings.T. 178 CL94
Earleswood, Cob. 214 BX112
Earlham Gro. E7 124 EF64
Earlham Gro. N22 99 DM52
Earlham St. WC2 273 N9
Earlham St. WC2 141 DK72
Earls Ct. Gdns. SW5 160 DB77
Earls Ct. Rd. SW5 160 DA77
Earls Ct. Rd. W8 160 DA77
Earls Ct. Sq. SW5 160 DB78
Earls Cres., Har. 117 CE56
Earls La., Pot.B. 62 CS32
Earl's Path, Loug. 84 EJ40
Earls Ter. W8 159 CZ76
Earls Wk. W8 160 DA76
Earls Wk., Dag. 126 EV63
Earls Way, Orp. 205 ET103
Station Rd.
Earlsbrook Rd., Red. 266 DF136
Earlsdown Ho., Bark. 145 ER68
Wheelers Cross
Earlsferry Way N1 141 DM66
Earlsfield, Maid. 150 AC77
Earlsfield Rd. SW18 180 DC88
Earlshall Rd. SE9 165 EM84
Earlsmead, Har. 116 BZ63
Earlsmead Rd. N15 122 DT57
Earlsmead Rd. NW10 139 CW69
Earlsthorpe Ms. SW12 180 DG86
Earlsthorpe Rd. SE26 183 DX91
Earlstoke St. EC1 274 F2
Earlston Gro. E9 142 DV67
Earlswood Ave., Th.Hth. 201 DN99
Earlswood Clo. SE10 164 EE78
Earlswood St.
Earlswood Gdns., Ilf. 125 EN55
Earlswood Rd., Red. 266 DF136
Earlswood St. SE10 164 EE78
Early Ms. NW1 141 DH67
Arlington Rd.
Earnshaw St. WC2 273 N8
Earnshaw St. WC2 141 DK72
Earsby St. W14 159 CY77
Easby Cres., Mord. 200 DB100
Easebourne Rd., Dag. 126 EW64
Easedale Dr., Horn. 127 FG64
Easedale Ho., Islw. 177 CF85
Easington Pl., Guil. 259 AZ135
Maori Rd.
Easington Way, S.Ock. 149 FU71
Easley's Ms. W1 272 G8
East Acton La. W3 138 CS73
East Arbour St. E1 143 DX72
East Ave. E12 144 EL66
East Ave. E17 123 EB56
East Ave., Hayes 155 BT75
East Ave., Sthl. 136 BZ73
East Ave., Wall. 219 DM106
East Ave., Walt. 213 BT110
Octagon Rd.
East Bank N16 122 DS59
East Barnet Rd., Barn. 80 DD42
East Burnham La., Slou. 131 AN67
East Burrow Fld., Welw.G.C. 29 CX11
East Churchfield Rd. W3 138 CR74
East Clo. W5 138 CN70
East Clo., Barn. 80 DG42
East Clo., Grnf. 136 CC68
East Clo., Rain. 147 FH70
East Clo., St.Alb. 60 CB25
East Common, Ger.Cr. 112 AY58
East Ct., Wem. 117 CJ61
East Cres. N11 98 DF49
East Cres., Enf. 82 DS43
East Cres., Wind. 151 AM81
East Cres. Rd., Grav. 191 GJ86
East Cross Route E3 143 DZ66
East Dene Dr., Rom. 106 FK50
East Dr., Cars. 218 DE109
East Dr., Nthwd. 93 BS47
East Dr., Orp. 206 EV100
East Dr., St.Alb. 44 CL19
East Dr., Saw. 36 EY06
East Dr., Slou. 132 AS69
East Dr., Vir.W. 192 AV100
East Dr., Wat. 75 BV35

East Dulwich Gro. SE22 182 DS85
East Dulwich Rd. SE15 162 DU84
East Dulwich Rd. SE22 162 DT84
East End Rd. N2 120 DB55
East End Rd. N3 97 CZ54
East End Way, Pnr. 116 BY55
East Entrance, Dag. 147 FB68
East Ferry Rd. E14 163 EB77
East Flint, Hem.H. 39 BF19
East Gdns. SW17 180 DE93
East Gdns., Wok. 227 BC117
East Gate, Harl. 35 ER14
East Gorse, Croy. 221 DY112
East Grn., Hem.H. 58 BM25
East Hall La., Rain. 148 FK72
East Hall Rd., Orp. 206 EY101
East Ham Ind. Est. E6 144 EK70
East Ham Manor Way E6 145 EN72
East Harding St. EC4 274 E8
East Heath Rd. NW3 120 DC62
East Hill SW18 180 DB85
East Hill, Dart. 188 FM87
East Hill (South Darenth), Dart. 208 FQ95
East Hill, Oxt. 254 EE129
East Hill, S.Croy. 220 DS110
East Hill, Wem. 118 CN61
East Hill, West. 238 EH118
East Hill, Wok. 227 BC116
East Hill Dr., Dart. 188 FM87
East Hill Rd., Oxt. 254 EE129
East Holme, Erith 167 FD81
East Holme, Hayes 135 BU74
East India Dock Rd. E14 143 EA72
East India Dock Wall Rd. E14 143 ED73
East Kent Ave., Grav. 190 GC86
East La. SE16 162 DU75
East La., Abb.L. 59 BT28
East La., Kings.T. 197 CK97
East La., Lthd. 245 BQ126
East La., Wem. 117 CH62
East Lo. La., Enf. 81 DK36
East Mascalls SE7 164 EJ79
Mascalls Rd.
East Mead, Ruis. 116 BX62
East Mead, Welw.G.C. 30 DB12
East Meads, Guil. 258 AT135
East Mill, Grav. 191 GF86
Clifton Marine Par.
East Milton Rd., Grav. 191 GK87
East Mimms, Hem.H. 40 BL19
East Mt. St. E1 142 DV71
East Pk., Harl. 36 EW12
East Pk., Saw. 36 EY06
East Pk. Clo., Rom. 126 EX57
East Pas. EC1 275 H6
East Pier E1 142 DV74
Wapping High St.
East Pl. SE27 182 DQ91
Pilgrim Hill
East Poultry Ave. EC1 274 F7
East Ramp, Houns. 155 BP81
East Ridgeway (Cuffley), Pot.B. 65 DL28
East Rd. E15 144 EG67
East Rd. N1 275 L2
East Rd. N1 142 DR69
East Rd. SW19 180 DC93
East Rd., Barn. 98 DG46
East Rd., Edg. 96 CP53
East Rd., Enf. 82 DW38
East Rd., Felt. 175 BR87
East Rd., Harl. 36 EV11
East Rd., Kings.T. 198 CL95
East Rd., Reig. 249 CZ133
East Rd. (Chadwell Heath), Rom. 126 EY57
East Rd. (Rush Grn.), Rom. 127 FD59
East Rd., Well. 166 EV82
East Rd., West Dr. 154 BM77
East Rd., Wey. 213 BR108
East Rochester Way SE9 165 ER84
East Rochester Way, Bex. 186 EX86
East Rochester Way, Sid. 165 ER84
East Row E11 124 EG58
East Row W10 139 CY70
East Shalford La., Guil. 258 AY139
East Sheen Ave. SW14 178 CR85
East Smithfield E1 142 DT73
East St. SE17 279 J10
East St. SE17 162 DQ78
East St., Bark. 145 EQ66
East St., Bexh. 166 FA84
East St., Brent. 157 CJ80
East St., Brom. 204 EG96
East St., Cher. 194 BG101
East St., Chesh. 54 AP32
East St., Epsom 216 CS113
East St., Grays 170 GC79
East St. (South Stifford), Grays 170 FY79
East St., Hem.H. 40 BK20
East St., Lthd. 246 CB125
East St., Ware 33 DX06
East Surrey Gro. SE15 162 DT80
East Tenter St. E1 142 DT72
East Ter., Grav. 191 GJ86
East Thurrock Rd., Grays 170 GB79
East Twrs., Pnr. 116 BX57
East Vw. E4 101 EC50
East Vw., Barn. 79 CZ40
East Vw., Hat. 46 DF17
East Wk. NW7 97 CU52
Northway
East Wk., Barn. 98 DG45
East Wk., Harl. 35 ER14
East Wk., Hayes 135 BU74
East Wk., Reig. 250 DB134
East Way E11 124 EH57
East Way, Beac. 88 AG54
East Way, Brom. 204 EG101
East Way, Croy. 203 DY103
East Way, Guil. 242 AT134
East Way, Hayes 135 BU74
East Way, Ruis. 115 BU60
East Woodside, Bex. 186 EY88
Maiden Erlegh Ave.
Eastbank Rd., Hmptn. 176 CC92
Eastbourne Ave. W3 138 CR72
Eastbourne Gdns. SW14 158 CQ83
Eastbourne Ms. W2 140 DC72
Eastbourne Rd. E6 145 EN69
Eastbourne Rd. E15 144 EE67
Eastbourne Rd. N15 122 DS58
Eastbourne Rd. SW17 180 DG93
Eastbourne Rd. W4 158 CQ79
Eastbourne Rd., Brent. 157 CK78
Eastbourne Rd., Felt. 176 BX89
Eastbourne Rd., Gdse. 253 DY134
Eastbourne Rd., Slou. 131 AM72
Eastbourne Ter. W2 140 DC72
Eastbournia Ave. N9 100 DV48
Eastbridge, Slou. 132 AV74
Victoria Rd.
Eastbrook Ave. N9 100 DW45
Eastbrook Ave., Dag. 127 FC63
Eastbrook Clo., Wok. 227 BA116
Eastbrook Dr., Rom. 127 FE62
Eastbrook Rd. SE3 164 EH81
Eastbrook Rd., Wal.Abb. 68 EE33
Eastbrook Way, Hem.H. 40 BL20
Adeyfield Rd.
Eastbury Ave., Bark. 145 ES67
Eastbury Ave., Enf. 82 DS39
Eastbury Ave., Nthwd. 93 BS50
Eastbury Clo., Nthwd. 93 BT50
Eastbury Ave.
Eastbury Ct., Bark. 145 ES67
Eastbury Ct., St.Alb. 43 CF19
Eastbury Gro. W4 158 CS78
Eastbury Ho., Bark. 145 ET67
Eastbury Pl., Nthwd. 93 BT50
Eastbury Ave.
Eastbury Rd. E6 145 EN70
Eastbury Rd., Kings.T. 178 CL94
Eastbury Rd., Nthwd. 93 BS50
Eastbury Rd., Orp. 205 ER100
Eastbury Rd., Rom. 127 FD58
Eastbury Rd., Wat. 93 BV45
Eastbury Sq., Bark. 145 ET67
Eastbury Ter. E1 143 DX70
Eastcastle St. W1 273 K8
Eastcastle St. W1 141 DJ72
Eastcheap EC3 275 L10
Eastcheap EC3 142 DR73
Eastchurch Rd., Houns. 155 BS82
Eastcombe Ave. SE7 164 EH79
Eastcote, Orp. 205 ET102
Eastcote Ave., Grnf. 137 CG65
Eastcote Ave., Har. 116 CB61
Eastcote Ave., W.Mol. 196 BZ99
Eastcote High Rd., Pnr. 115 BU58
Eastcote La., Har. 116 BY63
Eastcote La., Nthlt. 116 BZ64
Eastcote La. N., Nthlt. 136 BZ65
Eastcote Rd., Har. 116 CC62
Eastcote Rd., Pnr. 116 BX57
Eastcote Rd., Ruis. 115 BS59
Eastcote Rd., Well. 165 ER82
Eastcote St. SW9 161 DM82
Eastcote Vw., Pnr. 116 BW56
Eastcroft, Slou. 131 AP70
Eastcroft Rd., Epsom 216 CS108
Eastdean Ave., Epsom 216 CP113
Eastdown Pk. SE13 163 ED84
Easter Gate, Beac. 88 AJ51
Eastern Ave. E11 124 EH58
Eastern Ave., Cher. 194 BG97
Eastern Ave., Grays 169 FT78
Eastern Ave., Ilf. 125 EP58
Eastern Ave., Pnr. 116 BX59
Eastern Ave., Rom. 126 EW56
Eastern Ave., S.Ock. 148 FQ74
Eastern Ave., Wal.Cr. 67 DY33
Eastern Ave. E., Rom. 127 FD55
Eastern Ave. W., Rom. 126 EY56
Eastern Dr., B.End 110 AC59
Eastern Ind. Est., Erith 166 EZ75
Eastern Pathway, Horn. 148 FK65
Eastern Perimeter Rd., Houns. 155 BS82
Eastern Rd. E13 144 EH68
Eastern Rd. E17 123 EC57
Eastern Rd. N2 120 DF55
Eastern Rd. N22 99 DL53
Eastern Rd. SE4 163 EA84
Eastern Rd., Grays 170 GD77
Eastern Rd., Rom. 127 FE57
Eastern Vw., West. 238 EJ117
Eastern Way SE2 146 EY74
Eastern Way SE28 166 EU75
Eastern Way, Erith 146 EY74
Eastern Way, Grays 170 GA79
Easternville Gdns., Ilf. 125 EQ58
Eastfield Ave., Wat. 76 BX39
Eastfield Clo., Slou. 152 AU76
St. Laurence Way
Eastfield Ct., St.Alb. 43 CK17
Southfield Way
Eastfield Gdns., Dag. 126 FA63
Eastfield Par., Pot.B. 64 DD32
Eastfield Rd. E17 123 EA56
Eastfield Rd. N8 121 DL55
Eastfield Rd., Brwd. 108 FX47
Eastfield Rd., Dag. 126 EZ63
Eastfield Rd., Enf. 83 DX38
Eastfield Rd., Red. 267 DJ135
Eastfield Rd., Slou. 130 AG71
Eastfield Rd., Wal.Cr. 67 DY32
Eastfields, Pnr. 116 BW57
Eastfields Rd. W3 138 CQ71
Eastfields Rd., Mitch. 200 DG96
Eastgate, Bans. 217 CZ114
Eastgate Clo. SE28 146 EX72
Eastgate Gdns., Guil. 258 AY135
Eastglade, Nthwd. 93 BT50
Eastglade, Pnr. 116 BZ55
Eastham Clo., Barn. 79 CY43
Hammond Clo.
Eastham Cres., Brwd. 109 GA49
Eastholm NW11 120 DB56
Eastlake Rd. SE5 162 DQ82
Eastlands Clo., Oxt. 253 ED127
Eastlands Way
Eastlands Cres. SE21 182 DT86
Eastlands Way, Oxt. 253 ED127
Eastlea Ave., Wat. 76 BY37
Eastleigh Ave., Har. 116 CB61
Eastleigh Clo. NW2 118 CS62
Eastleigh Clo., Sutt. 218 DB108
Eastleigh Rd. E17 101 DZ54
Priory Ct.
Eastleigh Rd., Bexh. 167 FC82
Eastleigh Rd., Houns. 155 BT83
Cranford La.
Eastleigh Wk. SW15 179 CU87
Alton Rd.
Eastleigh Way, Felt. 175 BT88
Westmacott Dr.
Eastman Rd. W3 158 CR75
Eastman Way, Hem.H. 40 BN17
Eastmead, Wok. 227 BA116
Eastmead Ave., Grnf. 136 CB69
Eastmead Clo., Brom. 204 EL96
Eastmearn Rd. SE21 182 DQ89
Eastmont Rd., Esher 197 CF103
Eastmoor Pl. SE7 164 EK76
Eastmoor St.
Eastmoor St. SE7 164 EK76
Eastney Rd., Croy. 201 DP102
Eastney St. SE10 163 ED78
Eastnor, Hem.H. 57 BA28
Eastnor Rd. SE9 185 EQ88
Eastnor Rd., Reig. 266 DA136
Easton Gdns., Borwd. 78 CR42
Easton St. WC1 274 D3
Eastor, Welw.G.C. 30 DA06
Eastry Ave., Brom. 204 EF100
Eastry Rd., Erith 166 FA79
Eastside Rd. NW11 119 CZ56
Eastview Ave. SE18 165 ES80
Eastville Ave. NW11 119 CZ58
Eastway E9 143 DZ65
Eastway E10 123 EA63
Eastway, Epsom 216 CQ112
Eastway, Mord. 199 CX99
Eastway, Wall. 219 DJ105
Eastwell Clo., Beck. 183 DY94
Eastwick Cres., Rick. 91 BF47
Eastwick Dr., Lthd. 230 CB122
Eastwick Hall La., Harl. 35 EN09
Eastwick Pk. Ave., Lthd. 230 CB124
Eastwick Rd., Harl. 35 EP11
Eastwick Rd., Lthd. 246 CB125
Eastwick Rd., Walt. 213 BV106
Eastwick Rd., Ware 34 EF12
Eastwick Row, Hem.H. 40 BN21
Eastwood Clo. E18 102 EG54
The Viaduct
Eastwood Clo. N17 100 DV52
Northumberland Gro.
Eastwood Ct., Hem.H. 40 BN19
Eastwood Dr., Rain. 147 FH72
Eastwood Rd. E18 102 EG54
Eastwood Rd. N10 98 DG54
Eastwood Rd., Guil. 259 AZ144
Eastwood Rd., Ilf. 126 EU59
Eastwood St. SW16 181 DJ93
Eastworth Rd., Cher. 193 BF102
Eatington Rd. E10 123 ED57
Eaton Clo. SW1 276 F9
Eaton Clo. SW1 160 DG77
Eaton Clo., Stan. 95 CH49
Eaton Ct., Guil. 243 BA132
Eaton Dr. SW9 161 DP84
Eaton Dr., Kings.T. 178 CN94
Eaton Dr., Rom. 105 FB52
Eaton Gdns., Dag. 146 EY66
Eaton Gate SW1 276 F8
Eaton Gate SW1 160 DG77
Eaton Gate, Nthwd. 93 BQ51
Eaton La. SW1 277 J7
Eaton La. SW1 161 DH76
Eaton Ms. N. SW1 276 F7
Eaton Ms. N. SW1 160 DG76
Eaton Ms. S. SW1 277 H7
Eaton Ms. S. SW1 160 DG77
Eaton Ms. W. SW1 276 G8
Eaton Ms. W. SW1 160 DG77
Eaton Pk., Cob. 214 BY114
Eaton Pk. Rd. N13 99 DN47
Eaton Pk. Rd., Cob. 214 BY114
Eaton Pl. SW1 276 F7
Eaton Pl. SW1 160 DG76
Eaton Ri. E11 124 EJ57
Eaton Ri. W5 137 CJ71
Eaton Rd. NW4 119 CW57
Eaton Rd., Enf. 82 DS41
Eaton Rd., Hem.H. 41 BP17
Eaton Rd., Houns. 157 CD84
Eaton Rd., St.Alb. 43 CH20
Eaton Rd., Sid. 186 EX89
Eaton Rd., Sutt. 218 DD107
Eaton Rd., Upmin. 129 FS61
Eaton Row SW1 277 H7
Eaton Row SW1 161 DH76
Eaton Sq. SW1 276 G8
Eaton Sq. SW1 160 DG77
Eaton Sq., Long. 209 FX97
Bramblefield Clo.
Eaton Ter. SW1 276 F8
Eaton Ter. SW1 160 DG77
Eaton Ter. Ms. SW1 276 F8
Eaton Wk. SE15 162 DT80
Sumner Est.
Eatons Mead E4 101 EA47
Eatonville Rd. SW17 180 DF89
Eatonville Vill. SW17 180 DF89
Eatonville Rd.
Ebbas Way, Epsom 232 CP115
Ebberns Rd., Hem.H. 40 BL23
Ebbisham Clo., Dor. 263 CG136
Nower Rd.
Ebbisham Dr. SW8 161 DM79
Ebbisham La., Tad. 233 CU123
Ebbisham Rd., Epsom 216 CP114
Ebbisham Rd., Wor.Pk. 199 CW103
Ebbsfleet Ind. Est., Grav. 190 GA85
Ebbsfleet Rd. NW2 119 CY64
Ebbsfleet Wk., Grav. 190 GB86
Ebdon Way SE3 164 EH83
Ebenezer St. N1 275 K2
Ebenezer St. N1 142 DR69
Ebenezer Wk. SW16 201 DJ95
Meopham Rd.
Ebley Clo. SE15 162 DT79
St. Georges Way
Ebner St. SW18 180 DB85
Ebor St. E1 275 P4
Ebor St. E1 142 DT70
Ebrington Rd., Har. 117 CJ58
Ebsworth Clo., Maid. 130 AC68
Ebsworth St. SE23 183 DX87
Eburne Rd. N7 121 DL62
Ebury App., Rick. 92 BK46
Ebury Bri. SW1 277 H10
Ebury Bri. SW1 161 DH78
Ebury Bri. Est. SW1 277 H10
Ebury Bri. Est. SW1 161 DH78
Ebury Bri. Rd. SW1 160 DG78
Ebury Clo., Kes. 204 EL104
Ebury Clo., Nthwd. 93 BQ50
Ebury Ms. SE27 181 DP90
Ebury Ms. SW1 277 H8
Ebury Ms. SW1 161 DH77
Ebury Ms. E. SW1 277 H7
Ebury Rd., Rick. 92 BK46
Ebury Rd., Wat. 76 BW41
Ebury Sq. SW1 276 G9
Ebury Sq. SW1 160 DG77
Ebury St. SW1 276 G9
Ebury St. SW1 160 DG77
Ebury Way, The, Rick. 92 BL46
Skidmore Way
Ebury Way, The, Wat. 93 BT45
Vicarage Rd.
Eccles Hill, Dor. 263 CJ140
Eccles Rd. SW11 160 DF84
Ecclesbourne Clo. N13 99 DN50
Ecclesbourne Gdns. N13 99 DN50
Ecclesbourne Rd. N1 142 DQ66
Ecclesbourne Rd., Th.Hth. 202 DQ99
Eccleston Bri. SW1 277 J8
Eccleston Bri. SW1 161 DH77
Eccleston Clo., Barn. 80 DF42
Eccleston Clo., Orp. 205 ER102
Eccleston Cres., Rom. 126 EU59
Eccleston Ms. SW1 276 G7
Eccleston Ms. SW1 160 DG76
Eccleston Pl. SW1 277 H8
Eccleston Pl. SW1 161 DH77
Eccleston Rd. W13 137 CG73
Eccleston Sq. SW1 277 J9
Eccleston Sq. SW1 161 DH77
Eccleston Sq. Ms. SW1 277 J9
Eccleston St. SW1 276 G7
Eccleston St. SW1 161 DH77
Ecclestone Ct., Wem. 118 CL64
St. John's Rd.
Ecclestone Ms., Wem. 118 CL64
Ecclestone Pl., Wem. 118 CM64
Echelforde Dr., Ashf. 174 BN91
Echo Heights E4 101 EB46
Mount Echo Dr.
Echo Pit Rd., Guil. 258 AY138
Echo Sq., Grav. 191 GJ89
Old Rd. E.
Eckersley St. E1 142 DU70
Buxton St.
Eckford St. N1 141 DN68
Eckstein Rd. SW11 160 DE84
Eclipse Rd. E13 144 EH71
Ecob Clo., Guil. 242 AT130
Ecton Rd., Add. 212 BH105
Ector Rd. SE6 184 EE89
Edbrooke Rd. W9 140 DA70
Eddiscombe Rd. SW6 159 CZ82
Eddy Clo., Rom. 127 FB58
Eddy St., Berk. 38 AU18
Eddystone Rd. SE4 183 DY85
Eddystone Wk., Stai. 174 BL87
Clare Rd.
Ede Clo., Houns. 156 BZ83
Eden Clo. W8 160 DA76
Adam & Eve Ms.
Eden Clo., Add. 212 BH110
Eden Clo., Bex. 187 FD91
Eden Clo., Slou. 153 BA78
Eden Clo., Wem. 137 CK67
Eden Grn., S.Ock. 149 FV71
Bovey Way
Eden Gro. E17 123 EB57
Eden Gro. N7 121 DM64
Eden Gro. Rd., W.Byf. 212 BL113
Eden Ms. SW17 180 DC90
Huntspill St.
Eden Pk. Ave., Beck. 203 DY98
Eden Pl., Grav. 191 GH87
Lord St.
Eden Rd. E17 123 EB57
Eden Rd. SE27 181 DP92
Eden Rd., Beck. 203 DY98
Eden Rd., Bex. 187 FC91
Eden Rd., Croy. 220 DR105
Eden St., Kings.T. 197 CK96
Eden Wk., Kings.T. 198 CL96
Eden St.
Eden Way, Beck. 203 DZ99
Eden Way, Warl. 237 DY118
Edenbridge Clo., Orp. 206 EX98
Edenbridge Rd. E9 143 DX66
Edenbridge Rd., Enf. 82 DS44
Edencourt Rd. SW16 181 DH93
Edencroft, Guil. 259 AZ144
Edendale Rd., Bexh. 167 FD81
Edenfield Gdns., Wor.Pk. 199 CT104
Edenhall Clo., Hem.H. 41 BR21
Edenhall Clo., Rom. 106 FJ50
Edenhall Glen, Rom. 106 FJ50
Edenhall Rd., Rom. 106 FJ50
Edenham Way W10 139 CZ71
Elkstone Rd.
Edenhurst Ave. SW6 159 CZ83
Edenside Rd., Lthd. 230 BZ124
Edensor Gdns. W4 158 CS80
Edensor Rd. W4 158 CS80
Edenvale Rd., Mitch. 180 DG94
Edenvale St. SW6 160 DB82
Ederline Ave. SW16 201 DM97
Edgar Clo., Swan. 207 FF97
Edgar Rd. E3 143 EB69
Edgar Rd., Houns. 176 BZ87
Edgar Rd., Rom. 126 EX59
Edgar Rd., S.Croy. 220 DR110
Edgar Rd., West Dr. 134 BL73
Edgar Rd., West. 238 EK121
Edgarley Ter. SW6 159 CY81
Edgars Ct., Welw.G.C. 29 CY10
Edgbaston Dr., Rad. 62 CL32
Edgbaston Rd., Wat. 93 BV48
Holmside Ri.
Edge Clo., Wey. 212 BN108
Edge Hill SE18 165 EP79
Edge Hill SW19 179 CX94
Edge Hill Ave. N3 120 DA56
Edge Hill Ct. SW19 179 CX94
Edge St. W8 140 DA74
Kensington Ch. St.
Edgeborough Way, Brom. 184 EK94
Edgebury, Chis. 185 EP91
Edgebury Wk., Chis. 185 EQ91
Edgehill Rd.
Edgecombe Ho. SW19 179 CY88
Edgecoombe, S.Croy. 220 DW108
Edgecoombe Clo., Kings.T. 178 CR94
Edgecot Gro. N15 122 DR57
Oulton Rd.
Edgecote Clo. W3 138 CQ74
Cheltenham Pl.
Edgefield Ave., Bark. 145 ET66
Edgefield Clo., Dart. 188 FP89
Edgefield Clo., Red. 266 DG139
Edgehill Ct., Walt. 196 BW102
St. Johns Dr.
Edgehill Gdns., Dag. 126 FA63
Edgehill Rd. W13 137 CJ71
Edgehill Rd., Chis. 185 EQ90
Edgehill Rd., Mitch. 201 DH95
Edgehill Rd., Pur. 219 DN110
Edgel St. SW18 160 DB84
Ferrier St.
Edgeley, Lthd. 230 BY124
Edgeley La. SW4 161 DK83
Edgeley Rd.
Edgeley Rd. SW4 161 DK83
Edgell Clo., Vir.W. 193 AZ97
Edgell Rd., Stai. 173 BF92
Edgepoint Clo. SE27 181 DP92
Knights Hill
Edgewood Dr., Orp. 223 ET106
Edgewood Grn., Croy. 203 DX102
Edgeworth Ave. NW4 119 CU57
Edgeworth Clo. NW4 119 CU57
Edgeworth Clo., Whyt. 236 DU118
Edgeworth Cres. NW4 119 CU57
Edgeworth Rd. SE9 164 EJ84
Edgeworth Rd., Barn. 80 DE42
Edgington Rd. SW16 181 DK93
Edgington Way, Sid. 186 EW94
Edgware Ct., Edg. 96 CN51
Cavendish Dr.
Edgware Rd. NW2 119 CV60
Edgware Rd. NW9 96 CQ54
Edgware Rd. W2 140 DD70
Edgware Way, Edg. 96 CM49
Edgwarebury Gdns., Edg. 96 CN50
Edgwarebury La., Borwd. 96 CL45
Edgwarebury La., Edg. 96 CN47
Edinburgh Ave., Rick. 74 BG44
Edinburgh Ave., Slou. 131 AN71
Edinburgh Clo. E2 142 DW68
Russia La.
Edinburgh Clo., Uxb. 115 BP63
Edinburgh Ct. SW20 199 CX99
Edinburgh Cres., Wal.Cr. 67 DY33
Edinburgh Dr., Abb.L. 59 BU32
Langley La.
Edinburgh Dr., Rom. 127 FC56
Eastern Ave. W.
Edinburgh Dr., Stai. 174 BK93
Edinburgh Dr. (Denham), Uxb. 113 BF58
Edinburgh Dr. (Ickenham), Uxb. 115 BP63
Edinburgh Gdns., Wind. 151 AR82
Edinburgh Gate SW1 276 D5
Edinburgh Gate SW1 160 DF75
Edinburgh Ho. W9 140 DB69
Edinburgh Ms., Til. 171 GH82
London Rd.
Edinburgh Pl., Harl. 36 EU11
Edinburgh Rd. E13 144 EH68
Edinburgh Rd. E17 123 EA57
Edinburgh Rd. N18 100 DU50
Edinburgh Rd. W7 157 CF75
Edinburgh Rd., Sutt. 200 DC103
Edinburgh Way, Harl. 35 ER12
Edington Rd. SE2 166 EV76
Edington Rd., Enf. 82 DW40
Edis St. NW1 140 DG67
Edison Ave., Horn. 127 FF60
Edison Clo., Horn. 127 FF60
Edison Ave.
Edison Dr., Sthl. 136 CB72
Edison Gro. SE18 165 ET80
Edison Rd. N8 121 DK58
Edison Rd., Brom. 204 EG96
Edison Rd., Enf. 83 DZ40
Edison Rd., Well. 165 ET81
Edith Cavell Clo. N19 121 DK59
Hornsey Ri. Gdns.
Edith Gdns., Surb. 198 CP101
Edith Gro. SW10 160 DC79
Edith Rd. E6 144 EK66
Edith Rd. E15 123 ED64
Chandos Rd.
Edith Rd. N11 99 DK52
Edith Rd. SE25 202 DR99
Edith Rd. SW19 180 DB93
Edith Rd. W14 159 CY77
Edith Rd., Orp. 224 EU106
Edith Rd., Rom. 126 EX58
Edith Row SW6 160 DB81
Edith St. E2 142 DT68
Queensbridge Rd.
Edith Ter. SW10 160 DC80
Edith Turbeville Ct. N19 121 DL59
Hillrise Rd.
Edith Vill. W14 159 CZ78
Edith Yd. SW10 160 DC80
World's End Est.
Edithna St. SW9 161 DL83
Edlyn Clo., Berk. 38 AT18
Edmansons Clo. N17 100 DS53
Bruce Gro.
Edmeston Clo. E9 143 DY65
Edmonds Ct., W.Mol. 196 CB98
Avern Rd.
Edmonton Grn. N9 100 DV47
Hertford Rd.
Edmund Rd., Mitch. 200 DE97
Edmund Rd., Orp. 206 EW100
Edmund Rd., Rain. 147 FE68
Edmund Rd., Well. 166 EU83
Edmund St. SE5 162 DR80
Edmund Way, Slou. 132 AV71
Edmunds Ave., Orp. 206 EX97
Edmunds Clo., Hayes 136 BW71
Edmunds Clo., Hert. 31 DM08
Edmunds Twr., Harl. 51 EQ15
Edmunds Wk. N2 120 DE56
Edna Rd. SW20 199 CX96
Edna St. SW11 160 DE81
Edric Rd. SE14 163 DX80
Edrich Ho. SW4 161 DL81
Edrick Rd., Edg. 96 CQ51
Edrick Wk., Edg. 96 CQ51
Edridge Clo., Horn. 128 FK64
Edridge Clo. (Bushey), Wat. 76 CC43
Edridge Rd., Croy. 202 DQ104
Edulf Rd., Borwd. 78 CP39
Edward Amey Clo., Wat. 76 BW36
Edward Ave. E4 101 EB51
Edward Ave., Mord. 200 DD99
Edward Clo. N9 100 DT45
Edward Clo., Abb.L. 59 BT32
Edward Clo., Hmptn. 176 CC92
Edward Rd.
Edward Clo., Nthlt. 136 BW68
Edward Clo., Rom. 128 FJ55
Edward Clo., St.Alb. 43 CF21
Edward Ct. E16 144 EG71
Alexandra St.

Elm Rd., Pur. 219 DP113
Elm Rd., Red. 250 DE134
Elm Rd., Rom. 105 FB54
Elm Rd., Sid. 186 EU91
Elm Rd., S.Ock. 148 FQ74
Elm Rd., Th.Hth. 202 DR98
Elm Rd., Wall. 200 DG102
Elm Rd., Warl. 237 DX117
Elm Rd., Wem. 118 CL64
Elm Rd., West. 255 ES125
Elm Rd., Wind. 151 AP83
Elm Rd., Wok. 226 AX118
Elm Rd. (Horsell), Wok. 227 AZ115
Elm Rd. W., Sutt. 199 CZ101
Elm Row NW3 120 DC62
Elm St. WC1 274 C5
Elm St. WC1 141 DM70
Elm Ter. NW2 120 DA62
Elm Ter. NW3 120 DE63
Constantine Rd.
Elm Ter. SE9 185 EN86
Elm Ter., Grays 169 FV79
Elm Ter., Har. 95 CD53
Elm Tree Ave., Esher 197 CD101
Elm Tree Clo. NW8 140 DD69
Elm Tree Clo., Ashf. 175 BP92
Convent Rd.
Elm Tree Clo., Cher. 193 BE103
Green La.
Elm Tree Clo., Horl. 268 DG147
Elm Tree Clo., Nthlt. 136 BZ68
Elm Tree Rd. NW8 140 DD69
Elm Wk. NW3 120 DA61
Elm Wk. SW20 199 CW98
Elm Wk., Orp. 205 EM104
Elm Wk., Rad. 77 CF36
Elm Wk., Rom. 127 FG55
Elm Way N11 98 DG51
Elm Way NW10 118 CS63
Elm Way, Brwd. 108 FU49
Elm Way, Epsom 216 CR106
Elm Way, Rick. 92 BH46
Elm Way, Wor.Pk. 199 CW104
Elmar Grn., Slou. 131 AN69
Elmar Rd. N15 122 DR56
Elmbank Ave., Barn. 79 CW42
Elmbank Ave., Egh. 172 AV93
Elmbank Ave., Guil. 258 AU135
Elmbank Way W7 137 CD71
Elmbourne Dr., Belv. 167 FB77
Elmbourne Rd. SW17 180 DG90
Elmbridge, Harl. 36 EZ12
Elmbridge Ave., Surb. 198 CP99
Elmbridge Clo., Ruis. 115 BU58
Elmbridge Dr., Ruis. 115 BT57
Elmbridge La., Wok. 227 AZ119
Elmbridge Rd., Ilf. 104 EU51
Elmbridge Wk. E8 142 DU66
Wilman Gro.
Elmbrook Clo., Sun. 195 BV95
Elmbrook Gdns. SE9 164 EL84
Elmbrook Rd., Sutt. 217 CZ105
Elmcote Way, Rick. 74 BM44
Elmcourt Rd. SE27 181 DP89
Elmcroft, Lthd. 230 CA124
Elmcroft Ave. E11 124 EH57
Elmcroft Ave. N9 82 DV44
Elmcroft Ave. NW11 119 CZ59
Elmcroft Ave., Sid. 185 ET87
Elmcroft Clo. E11 124 EH56
Elmcroft Clo. N8 121 DM57
Elmcroft Clo. W5 137 CK72
Elmcroft Clo., Chess. 198 CL104
Elmcroft Clo., Felt. 175 BT86
Elmcroft Cres. NW11 119 CX59
Elmcroft Cres., Har. 116 CA55
Elmcroft Dr., Ashf. 174 BN92
Elmcroft Dr., Chess. 198 CL104
Elmcroft Gdns. NW9 118 CN57
Elmcroft Rd., Orp. 206 EU101
Elmcroft St. E5 122 DW63
Elmdale Rd. N13 99 DM50
Elmdene, Surb. 198 CQ102
Elmdene Ave., Horn. 128 FM57
Elmdene Clo., Beck. 203 DZ99
Elmdene Rd. SE18 165 EP78
Elmdon Rd., Houns. 156 BX82
Elmdon Rd. 155 BT83
(Hatton Cross), Houns.
Elmer Ave. 105 FE48
(Havering-atte-Bower), Rom.
Elmer Clo., Enf. 81 DM41
Elmer Clo., Rain. 147 FG66
Elmer Cotts., Lthd. 231 CG123
Elmer Gdns., Edg. 96 CP52
Elmer Gdns., Islw. 157 CD83
Elmer Gdns., Rain. 147 FG66
Elmer Ms., Lthd. 231 CG122
Elmer Rd. SE6 183 EC87
Elmers Dr., Tedd. 177 CH93
Kingston Rd.
Elmers End Rd. SE20 202 DW96
Elmers End Rd., Beck. 202 DW96
Elmers Rd. SE25 202 DU101
Elmerside Rd., Beck. 203 DY98
Elmfield, Lthd. 230 CA123
Elmfield Ave. N8 121 DL57
Elmfield Ave., Mitch. 200 DG95
Elmfield Ave., Tedd. 177 CF92
Elmfield Clo., Grav. 191 GH88
Elmfield Clo., Har. 117 CE61
Elmfield Clo., Pot.B. 63 CY33
Elmfield Pk., Brom. 204 EG97
Elmfield Rd. E4 101 EC47
Elmfield Rd. E17 123 DX57
Elmfield Rd. N2 120 DD55
Elmfield Rd. SW17 180 DG89
Elmfield Rd., Brom. 204 EG97
Elmfield Rd., Pot.B. 63 CY32
Elmfield Rd., Sthl. 156 BY76
Elmfield Way W9 140 DA71
Harrow Rd.
Elmfield Way, S.Croy. 220 DT109
Elmgate Ave., Felt. 175 BV90
Elmgate Gdns., Edg. 96 CR50
Elmgrove Cres., Har. 117 CF57
Elmgrove Gdns., Har. 117 CG57
Elmgrove Rd., Croy. 202 DV101
Elmgrove Rd., Har. 117 CF57
Elmgrove Rd., Wey. 212 BN105
Elmhurst, Belv. 166 EY79
Elmhurst Ave. N2 120 DD55
Elmhurst Ave., Mitch. 180 DG94
Elmhurst Ct., Guil. 259 AZ135
Lower Edgeborough Rd.
Elmhurst Dr. E18 102 EG54
Elmhurst Dr., Dor. 263 CH138
Elmhurst Dr., Horn. 128 FJ60
Elmhurst Gdns. E18 102 EH53
Elmhurst Rd. E7 144 EH66
Elmhurst Rd. N17 100 DS54
Elmhurst Rd. SE9 184 EL89
Elmhurst Rd., Enf. 82 DW37
Elmhurst Rd., Slou. 153 BA76
Elmhurst St. SW4 161 DK83
Elmhurst Way, Loug. 103 EM45
Elmington Clo., Bex. 187 FB86
Elmington Est. SE5 162 DR80
Elmington Rd. SE5 162 DR81
Elmira St. SE13 163 EB83
Elmlea Dr., Hayes 135 BS71
Grange Rd.
Elmlee Clo., Chis. 185 EM93
Elmley Clo. E6 144 EL71
Northumberland Rd.
Elmley St. SE18 165 ER77
Elmore Clo., Wem. 138 CL68
Elmore Rd. E11 123 EC62
Elmore Rd., Couls. 234 DF121
Elmore Rd., Enf. 83 DX38
Elmore St. N1 142 DR66
Elmores, Loug. 85 EN41
Elmpark Gdns., S.Croy. 220 DW110
Elmroyd Ave., Pot.B. 63 CZ33
Elmroyd Clo., Pot.B. 63 CZ33
Elms, The SW13 159 CT83
Elms, The, Hert. 32 DU09
Vixen Dr.
Elms Ave. N10 121 DH55
Elms Ave. NW4 119 CX57
Elms Ct., Wem. 117 CG63
Elms Cres. SW4 181 DJ86
Elms Fm. Rd., Horn. 128 FJ64
Elms Gdns., Dag. 126 EZ63
Elms Gdns., Wem. 117 CG63
Elms Ind. Est., Rom. 106 FP52
Elms La., Wem. 117 CG62
Elms Ms. W2 140 DD73
Elms Pk. Ave., Wem. 117 CG63
Elms Rd. SW4 181 DJ85
Elms Rd., Ger.Cr. 90 AY52
Elms Rd., Har. 95 CE52
Elms Rd., Ware 33 EA05
Elms Wk. SE3 164 EF84
Elmscott Gdns. N21 82 DQ44
Elmscott Rd., Brom. 184 EE92
Elmscroft N8 121 DM57
Tottenham La.
Elmscroft Gdns., Pot.B. 63 CZ32
Elmsdale Rd. E17 123 DZ56
Elmshaw Rd. SW15 179 CU85
Elmshorn, Epsom 233 CW116
Elmshott La., Slou. 131 AL73
Elmshurst Cres. N2 120 DC56
Elmside, Croy. 221 EB107
Elmside, Guil. 258 AU135
Elmside Rd., Wem. 118 CN62
Elmsleigh Ave., Har. 117 CH56
Elmsleigh Cen., The, Stai. 173 BF91
Thames St.
Elmsleigh Rd., Stai. 173 BF92
Thames St.
Elmsleigh Rd., Twick. 177 CD89
Elmslie Clo., Epsom 216 CQ114
Elmslie Clo., Wdf.Grn. 103 EM51
Gwynne Pk. Ave.
Elmslie Pt. E3 143 DZ71
Ackroyd Dr.
Elmstead Ave., Chis. 185 EM92
Elmstead Ave., Wem. 118 CL60
Elmstead Clo. N20 98 DA47
Elmstead Clo., Epsom 216 CS106
Elmstead Clo., Sev. 256 FE122
Elmstead Cres., Well. 166 EW79
Elmstead Gdns., Wor.Pk. 199 CU104
Elmstead Glade, Chis. 185 EM93
Elmstead La., Chis. 184 EL94
Elmstead Rd., Erith 167 FE81
Elmstead Rd., Ilf. 125 ES61
Elmstead Rd., W.Byf. 212 BG113
Elmstone Rd. SW6 160 DA81
Elmsway, Ashf. 174 BM92
Elmswood, Lthd. 230 BZ124
Elmsworth Ave., Houns. 156 CB82
Elmton Way E5 122 DU62
Rendlesham Rd.
Elmtree Clo., W.Byf. 212 BL113
Elmtree Hill, Chesh. 54 AP30
Elmtree Rd., Tedd. 177 CE91
Elmwood, Saw. 36 EZ06
Elmwood, Welw.G.C. 29 CV10
Elmwood Ave. N13 99 DL50
Elmwood Ave., Borwd. 78 CP42
Elmwood Ave., Felt. 175 BU89
Elmwood Ave., Har. 117 CG57
Elmwood Clo., Ash. 231 CK117
Elmwood Clo., Epsom 217 CU108
Elmwood Clo., Wall. 200 DG103
Elmwood Ct., Ash. 231 CK117
Elmwood Clo.
Elmwood Ct., Wem. 117 CG62
Elmwood Cres. NW9 118 CQ56
Elmwood Dr., Bex. 186 EY87
Elmwood Dr., Epsom 217 CU107
Elmwood Gdns. W7 137 CE72
Elmwood Pk., Ger.Cr. 112 AY60
Elmwood Rd. SE24 182 DR85
Elmwood Rd. W4 158 CQ79
Elmwood Rd., Croy. 201 DP101
Elmwood Rd., Mitch. 200 DF97
Elmwood Rd., Red. 250 DG130
Elmwood Rd., Slou. 132 AV73
Elmworth Gro. SE21 182 DR89
Elnathan Ms. W9 140 DB70
Shirland Rd.
Elphinstone Rd. E17 101 DZ54
Elphinstone St. N5 121 DP63
Avenell Rd.
Elrick Clo., Erith 167 FE79
Elrington Rd. E8 142 DU65
Elrington Rd., Wdf.Grn. 102 EG50
Harts Gro.
Elruge Clo., West Dr. 154 BK76
Elsa Rd., Well. 166 EV82
Elsa St. E1 143 DY71
Elsdale St. E9 142 DW65
Elsden Ms. E2 142 DW68
Old Ford Rd.
Elsden Rd. N17 100 DT53
Elsdon Rd., Wok. 226 AU118
Elsenham Rd. E12 125 EN64
Elsenham St. SW18 179 CZ88
Elsham Rd. E11 124 EE62
Elsham Rd. W14 159 CY75
Elsham Ter. W14 159 CY75
Elsie Rd. SE22 162 DT84
Elsiedene Rd. N21 100 DQ45
Elsiemaud Rd. SE4 183 DZ85
Elsinge Rd., Enf. 82 DV36
Elsinore Ave., Stai. 174 BL87
Elsinore Gdns. NW2 119 CY61
Purley Ave.
Elsinore Rd. SE23 183 DY88
Elsinore Way, Rich. 158 CP83
Lower Richmond Rd.
Elsley Rd. SW11 160 DF83
Elspeth Rd. SW11 160 DF84
Elspeth Rd., Wem. 118 CL64
Elsrick Ave., Mord. 200 DA99
Chalgrove Ave.
Elstan Way, Croy. 203 DY101
Elsted St. SE17 279 L9
Elsted St. SE17 162 DR77
Elston La., Sev. 241 FF117
Elstow Clo. SE9 185 EN85
Elstow Clo., Ruis. 116 BX59
Elstow Gdns., Dag. 146 EY67
Elstow Rd., Dag. 146 EY66
Elstree Gdns. N9 100 DV46
Elstree Gdns., Belv. 166 EY77
Elstree Gdns., Ilf. 125 EQ64
Elstree Hill, Brom. 184 EE94
Elstree Hill N., Borwd. 77 CK44
Elstree Hill S., Borwd. 95 CJ45
Elstree Rd., Borwd. 77 CH44
Elstree Rd. (Bushey), Wat. 95 CD45
Elstree Way, Borwd. 78 CP41
Elswell Ct., Hert. 31 DM08
Elswick Rd. SE13 163 EB82
Elswick St. SW6 160 DC82
Elsworth Clo., Felt. 175 BS88
Elsworthy, T.Ditt. 197 CE100
Elsworthy Ri. NW3 140 DE66
Elsworthy Rd. NW3 140 DD67
Elsworthy Ter. NW3 140 DE66
Elsynge Rd. SW18 180 DD85
Eltham Grn. SE9 184 EJ85
Eltham Grn. Rd. SE9 164 EJ84
Eltham High St. SE9 185 EM86
Eltham Hill SE9 184 EK85
Eltham Palace Rd. SE9 184 EJ86
Eltham Pk. Gdns. SE9 165 EN84
Eltham Pl., Guil. 242 AT132
Canterbury Rd.
Eltham Rd. SE9 184 EJ85
Eltham Rd. SE12 184 EG85
Elthiron Rd. SW6 160 DA81
Elthorne Ave. W7 157 CF75
Elthorne Ct., Felt. 176 BW88
Elthorne Pk. Rd. W7 157 CF75
Elthorne Rd. N19 121 DK61
Elthorne Rd. NW9 118 CR59
Elthorne Rd., Uxb. 134 BK68
Elthorne Way NW9 118 CR58
Elthruda Rd. SE13 183 ED86
Eltisley Rd., Ilf. 125 EP63
Elton Ave., Barn. 79 CZ43
Elton Ave., Grnf. 137 CE65
Elton Ave., Wem. 117 CH64
Elton Clo., Kings.T. 177 CJ94
Elton Ho. E3 143 DZ67
Elton Pk., Wat. 75 BV40
Elton Pl. N16 122 DS64
Elton Rd., Hert. 32 DQ08
Elton Rd., Kings.T. 198 CM95
Elton Rd., Pur. 219 DJ112
Elton Way (Bushey), Wat. 76 CB40
Eltringham St. SW18 160 DC84
Elvaston Ms. SW7 160 DC76
Elvaston Pl. SW7 160 DC76
Elveden Clo., Wok. 228 BH117
Elveden Pl. NW10 138 CN68
Elveden Rd. NW10 138 CN68
Elvedon Rd., Cob. 213 BV111
Elvendon Rd. N13 99 DL51
Elver Gdns. E2 142 DU68
St. Peter's Clo.
Elverson Rd. SE8 163 EB82
Elverton St. SW1 277 M8
Elverton St. SW1 161 DK77
Elvet Ave., Rom. 128 FJ56
Elvington Grn., Brom. 204 EF99
Elvington La. NW9 96 CS53
Elvino Rd. SE26 183 DX92
Elvis Rd. NW2 139 CW65
Elwell Clo., Egh. 173 BA92
Mowbray Cres.
Elwick Rd., S.Ock. 149 FW72
Elwill Way, Beck. 203 EC98
Elwin St. E2 142 DU69
Elwood, Harl. 52 EY16
Kiln La.
Elwood Rd., Beac. 88 AH54
Elwood St. N5 121 DP62
Elwyn Gdns. SE12 184 EG87
Ely Ave., Slou. 131 AQ71
Ely Clo., Amer. 55 AS39
Ely Clo., Erith 167 FF82
Ely Clo., Hat. 45 CT17
Ely Clo., N.Mal. 199 CT96
Ely Ct. EC1 274 E7
Ely Gdns., Borwd. 78 CR43
Ely Gdns., Dag. 127 FC62
Ely Gdns., Ilf. 124 EL59
Canterbury Ave.
Ely Pl. EC1 274 E7
Ely Pl., Guil. 242 AT132
Canterbury Rd.
Ely Pl., Wdf.Grn. 103 EN51
Ely Rd. E10 123 EC59
Ely Rd., Croy. 202 DR99
Ely Rd. 155 BT82
(Heathrow Airport), Houns.
Eastern Perimeter Rd.
Ely Rd. (Hounslow W.), 156 BW83
Houns.
Ely Rd., St.Alb. 43 CH21
Elyne Rd. N4 121 DN58
Elysian Ave., Orp. 205 ES100
Elysium Pl. SW6 159 CZ82
Fulham Pk. Gdns.
Elysium St. SW6 159 CZ82
Fulham Pk. Gdns.
Elystan Clo., Wall. 219 DH109
Elystan Pl. SW3 276 C10
Elystan Pl. SW3 160 DE78
Elystan St. SW3 276 B9
Elystan St. SW3 160 DE77
Elystan Wk. N1 141 DN67
Cloudesley Rd.
Emanuel Ave. W3 138 CQ72
Emanuel Dr., Hmptn. 176 BZ92
Emba St. SE16 162 DU75
Embankment SW15 159 CX82
Embankment, The, Stai. 172 AW87
Embankment, The, Twick. 177 CG88
Embankment Gdns. SW3 160 DF79
Embankment Pl. WC2 278 A2
Embankment Pl. WC2 141 DL74
Embassy Ct., Sid. 186 EV90
Embassy Ct., Well. 166 EV83
Ember Clo., Add. 212 BK106
Ember Clo., Orp. 205 EQ101
Ember Fm. Ave., E.Mol. 197 CD100
Ember Fm. Way, E.Mol. 197 CD100
Ember Gdns., T.Ditt. 197 CE101
Ember La., E.Mol. 197 CD100
Ember La., Esher 197 CD101
Ember Rd., Slou. 153 BB76
Embercourt Rd., T.Ditt. 197 CE100
Emberson Way, Epp. 71 FC26
Emberton SE5 162 DS79
Albany Rd.
Embleton Rd. SE13 163 EB84
Embleton Rd., Wat. 93 BU48
Embleton Wk., Hmptn. 176 BZ93
Fearnley Cres.
Embley Pt. E5 122 DV63
Tiger Way
Embry Clo., Stan. 95 CG49
Embry Dr., Stan. 95 CG51
Embry Way, Stan. 95 CG49
Emden St. SW6 160 DB81
Emerald Clo. E16 144 EL72
Emerald Ct., Slou. 152 AS75
Emerald Gdns., Dag. 126 FA60
Emerald St. WC1 274 B6
Emerald St. WC1 141 DM71
Emerson Dr., Horn. 128 FK59
Emerson Gdns., Har. 118 CM58
Emerson Rd., Ilf. 125 EN59
Emerson St. SE1 279 H2
Emerson St. SE1 142 DQ74
Emersons Ave., Swan. 187 FF94
Emerton Clo., Bexh. 166 EY84
Emerton Ct., Berk. 38 AS16
Emerton Garth
Emerton Garth, Berk. 38 AS16
Emerton Rd., Lthd. 230 CC120
Emery Hill St. SW1 277 L7
Emery Hill St. SW1 161 DJ76
Emery St. SE1 278 E6
Emes Rd., Erith 167 FC80
Emily Jackson Clo., Sev. 257 FH124
London Rd.
Emily Pl. N7 121 DN63
Emley Rd., Add. 194 BG104
Emlyn Gdns. W12 158 CS75
Emlyn La., Lthd. 231 CG122
Emlyn Rd. W12 158 CS75
Emlyn Rd., Horl. 268 DE147
Emlyn Rd., Red. 266 DG136
Emma Rd. E13 144 EF68
Emma St. E2 142 DV68
Emmanuel Clo., Guil. 242 AU131
Emmanuel Clo., Nthwd. 93 BT52
Emmanuel Rd.
Emmanuel Lo., Wal.Cr. 66 DW30
Emmanuel Rd. SW12 181 DJ88
Emmanuel Rd., Nthwd. 93 BT52
Emma's Cres., Ware 33 EB11
Emmaus Way, Chig. 103 EN50
Emmetts Clo., Wok. 226 AX117
Emmott Ave., Ilf. 125 EQ57
Emmott Clo. E1 143 DY70
Emmott Clo. NW11 120 DC58
Emms Pas., Kings.T. 197 CK96
High St.
Emperor Clo., Berk. 38 AT16
Springfield Rd.
Emperor's Gate SW7 160 DB76
Empire Ave. N18 100 DQ50
Empire Cen., Wat. 76 BW39
Empire Ct., Wem. 118 CP62
Empire Rd., Grnf. 137 CH67
Empire Vill., Red. 266 DG144
Empire Way, Wem. 118 CM63
Empire Wf. Rd. E14 163 ED77
Empire Yd. N7 121 DL62
Holloway Rd.
Empress Ave. E4 101 EB52
Empress Ave. E12 124 EJ61
Empress Ave., Ilf. 125 EM61
Empress Ave., Wdf.Grn. 102 EF52
Empress Dr., Chis. 185 EP93
Empress Pl. SW6 160 DA78
Empress Rd., Grav. 191 GL87
Empress St. SE17 162 DQ79
Empson St. E3 143 EB70
Emsworth Clo. N9 100 DW46
Emsworth Rd., Ilf. 103 EP54
Emsworth St. SW2 181 DL89
Emu Rd. SW8 161 DH82
Ena Rd. SW16 201 DL97
Enborne Grn., S.Ock. 149 FU71
Elan Rd.
Enbrook St. W10 139 CY69
End Way, Surb. 198 CN101
Endale Clo., Cars. 200 DF103
Endeavour Rd. 67 DY27
(Cheshunt), Wal.Cr.
Endeavour Way SW19 180 DB91
Endeavour Way, Bark. 146 EU68
Endeavour Way, Croy. 201 DK101
Endell St. WC2 273 P8
Endell St. WC2 141 DL72
Enderby St. SE10 164 EE78
Enderley Clo., Har. 95 CE53
Enderley Rd., Har. 95 CE53
Endersby Rd., Barn. 79 CW43
Endersleigh Gdns. NW4 119 CU56
Endlebury Rd. E4 101 EC47
Endlesham Rd. SW12 180 DG87
Endsleigh Clo., S.Croy. 220 DW110
Endsleigh Gdns. WC1 273 M4
Endsleigh Gdns. WC1 141 DK70
Endsleigh Gdns., Ilf. 125 EM61
Endsleigh Gdns., Surb. 197 CJ100
Endsleigh Gdns., Walt. 214 BW106
Endsleigh Pl. WC1 273 N4
Endsleigh Pl. WC1 141 DK70
Endsleigh Rd. W13 137 CG73
Endsleigh Rd., Red. 251 DJ129
Endsleigh Rd., Sthl. 156 BY77
Endsleigh St. WC1 273 N4
Endsleigh St. WC1 141 DK70
Endwell Rd. SE4 163 DY82
Endymion Ct., Hat. 45 CW17
Endymion Rd.
Endymion Ms., Hat. 45 CW17
Endymion Rd.
Endymion Rd. N4 121 DN59
Endymion Rd. SW2 181 DM86
Endymion Rd., Hat. 45 CW17
Enfield Clo., Uxb. 134 BK68
Villier St.
Enfield Rd. N1 142 DS66
Enfield Rd. W3 158 CP75
Enfield Rd., Brent. 157 CK78
Enfield Rd., Enf. 81 DL42
Enfield Rd., Houns. 155 BS82
Eastern Perimeter Rd.
Enfield Wk., Brent. 157 CK78
Enfield Rd.
Enford St. W1 272 D6
Enford St. W1 140 DF71
Engadine Clo., Croy. 202 DT104
Engadine St. SW18 179 CZ88
Engate St. SE13 163 EC84
Engayne Gdns., Upmin. 128 FP60
Engel Pk. NW7 97 CW51
Engineer Clo. SE18 165 EN79
Engineers Way, Wem. 118 CN63
Englands La. NW3 140 DF65
Englands La., Loug. 85 EN40
Englefield Clo., Croy. 202 DQ100
Queen's Rd.
Englefield Clo., Enf. 81 DN40
Chase Ridings
Englefield Clo., Orp. 205 ET98
Englefield Cres., Orp. 205 ET98
Englefield Grn., Egh. 172 AW91
Englefield Path, Orp. 206 EU98
Englefield Rd. N1 142 DR66
Englefield Rd., Orp. 206 EU98
Engleheart Dr., Felt. 175 BT86
Engleheart Rd. SE6 183 EB87
Englehurst, Egh. 172 AW93
St. Jude's Rd.
Englewood Rd. SW12 181 DH86
Engliff La., Wok. 227 BF116
English Gdns., Stai. 172 AX85
English Grds. SE1 279 M3
English St. E3 143 DZ70
Enid Clo., St.Alb. 60 BZ31
Enid St. SE16 162 DT76
Enmore Ave. SE25 202 DU99
Enmore Gdns. SW14 178 CR85
Enmore Rd. SE25 202 DU99
Enmore Rd. SW15 159 CW84
Enmore Rd., Sthl. 136 CA70
Ennadale Cres., Slou. 130 AJ71
Ennerdale Ave., Horn. 127 FG64
Ennerdale Ave., Stan. 117 CJ55
Ennerdale Clo., Felt. 175 BT88
Ennerdale Clo., St.Alb. 43 CH22
Ennerdale Clo. 217 CZ105
(Cheam), Sutt.
Ennerdale Dr. NW9 118 CS57
Ennerdale Gdns., Wem. 117 CJ60
Ennerdale Ho. E3 143 DZ70
Ennerdale Rd., Bexh. 166 FA81
Ennerdale Rd., Rich. 158 CM82
Ennersdale Rd. SE13 183 ED85
Ennis Rd. N4 121 DN60
Ennis Rd. SE18 165 EQ79
Ennismore Ave. W4 159 CT77
Ennismore Ave., Grnf. 137 CE65
Ennismore Ave., Guil. 243 AZ134
Ennismore Gdns. SW7 276 B6
Ennismore Gdns. SW7 160 DE75
Ennismore Gdns., T.Ditt. 197 CE100
Ennismore Gdns. Ms. SW7 276 B6
Ennismore Gdns. Ms. 160 DE76
SW7
Ennismore Ms. SW7 276 B6
Ennismore Ms. SW7 160 DE76
Ennismore St. SW7 276 B6
Ennismore St. SW7 160 DE76
Ensign Clo., Pur. 219 DN110
Ensign Clo., Stai. 174 BL88
Ensign Dr. N13 100 DQ48
Ensign St. E1 142 DU73
Ensign Way, Stai. 174 BK88
Enslin Rd. SE9 185 EN87
Ensor Ms. SW7 160 DD78
Cranley Gdns.
Enstone Rd., Enf. 83 DY41
Enstone Rd., Uxb. 114 BM62
Enterdent Rd., Gdse. 252 DW134
Enterprise Clo., Croy. 201 DN102
Enterprise Way NW10 139 CU69
Enterprise Way SW18 160 DA84
Enterprise Way, Tedd. 177 CF92
Enterprize Way SE8 163 DZ77
Epirus Ms. SW6 160 DA80
Epirus Rd.
Epirus Rd. SW6 159 CZ80
Epping Clo. E14 163 EA77
Epping Clo., Rom. 127 FB55
Epping Glade E4 83 EC44
Epping Grn., Hem.H. 40 BN15
Epping La., Rom. 86 EV40
Epping New Rd., 102 EG48
Buck.H.
Epping New Rd., Loug. 84 EJ41
Epping Pl. N1 141 DN65
Liverpool Rd.
Epping Rd., Epp. 85 EM35
Epping Rd. 51 EP24
(Epping Grn.), Epp.
Epping Rd. 70 EW28
(North Weald Bassett), Epp.
Epping Rd., Harl. 50 EH15
Epping Rd., Ong. 53 FF24
Epping Rd. (Toot Hill), Ong. 71 FC30
Epping Rd., Wal.Abb. 50 EL19
Epping Way E4 83 EB44
Epple Rd. SW6 159 CZ81
Epsom Clo., Bexh. 167 FB83
Epsom Clo., Nthlt. 116 BZ64
Epsom Downs, Epsom 233 CT118
Epsom Gap, Lthd. 231 CH115
Kingston Rd.
Epsom La. N., Epsom 233 CV118
Epsom La. S., Tad. 233 CW121
Epsom Rd. E10 123 EC58
Epsom Rd., Ash. 232 CM118
Epsom Rd., Croy. 219 DN105
Epsom Rd., Epsom 217 CT111
Epsom Rd., Guil. 258 AY135
Epsom Rd. 244 BH132
(East Clandon), Guil.
Epsom Rd., Ilf. 125 ET58
Epsom Rd., Lthd. 231 CH121
Epsom Rd. 245 BP130
(West Horsley), Lthd.
Epsom Rd., Mord. 200 DA100
Epsom Rd., Sutt. 199 CZ101
Epsom Sq., Houns. 155 BT82
Eastern Perimeter Rd.
Epsom Way, Horn. 128 FM63
Epstein Rd. SE28 146 EU74
Epworth Rd., Islw. 157 CH81

Epworth St. EC2 275 L5
Epworth St. EC2 142 DR70
Equity Sq. E2 142 DT69
Shacklewell St.
Erasmus St. SW1 277 N9
Erasmus St. SW1 161 DK77
Erconwald St. W12 139 CT72
Eresby Dr., Beck. 203 EA102
Eresby Pl. NW6 140 DA66
Eric Clo. E7 124 EG63
Eric Rd. E7 124 EG63
Eric Rd. NW10 139 CT65
Church Rd.
Eric Rd., Rom. 126 EX59
Eric Steele Ho., St.Alb. 60 CB27
Eric St. E3 143 DZ70
Erica Clo., Slou. 131 AL73
Erica Ct., Swan. 207 FE98
Azalea Dr.
Erica Ct., Wok. 226 AX118
Erica Gdns., Croy. 203 EA104
Erica St. W12 139 CU73
Ericcson Clo. SW18 180 DA85
Eridge Grn. Clo., Orp. 206 EW102
Petten Gro.
Eridge Rd. W4 158 CR76
Erin Clo., Brom. 184 EE94
Erindale SE18 165 ER79
Erindale Ter. SE18 165 ER79
Eriswell Cres., Walt. 213 BS107
Eriswell Rd., Walt. 213 BT105
Erith Ct., Purf. 168 FN77
Thamley
Erith Cres., Rom. 105 FC53
Erith High St., Erith 167 FE78
Erith Rd., Belv. 166 FA78
Erith Rd., Bexh. 167 FB84
Erith Rd., Erith 167 FC81
Erkenwald Clo., Cher. 193 BE101
Erlanger Rd. SE14 163 DX81
Erlesmere Gdns. W13 157 CG76
Ermine Clo., Houns. 156 BW82
Ermine Clo., St.Alb. 42 CA21
Ermine Clo. (Cheshunt), Wal.Cr. 66 DV31
Ermine Ho. N17 100 DT52
Ermine Rd. N15 122 DT58
Ermine Rd. SE13 163 EB84
Ermine Side, Enf. 82 DU43
Ermine St., Hert. 48 DV16
Ermington Rd. SE9 185 EQ89
Ermyn Clo., Lthd. 231 CK121
Ermyn Way, Lthd. 231 CK121
Ernald Ave. E6 144 EL68
Ernan Clo., S.Ock. 149 FU71
Ernan Rd., S.Ock. 149 FU71
Erncroft Way, Twick. 177 CF86
Ernest Ave. SE27 181 DP91
Ernest Clo., Beck. 203 EA99
Ernest Gdns. W4 158 CP79
Ernest Gro., Beck. 203 DZ99
Ernest Richards Twr. E17 123 DZ59
Colchester Rd.
Ernest Rd., Horn. 128 FL58
Ernest Rd., Kings.T. 198 CP96
Ernest Sq., Kings.T. 198 CP96
Ernest St. E1 143 DX70
Ernle Rd. SW20 179 CV94
Ernshaw Pl. SW15 179 CY85
Carlton Dr.
Erpingham Rd. SW15 159 CW83
Erridge Rd. SW19 200 DA96
Erriff Dr., S.Ock. 149 FT71
Errington Clo., Grays 171 GH76
Cedar Rd.
Errington Dr., Wind. 151 AN81
Errington Rd. W9 139 CZ70
Errol Gdns., Hayes 135 BV70
Errol Gdns., N.Mal. 199 CU98
Errol St. EC1 275 J5
Errol St. EC1 142 DQ70
Erroll Rd., Rom. 127 FF56
Erskine Clo., Sutt. 200 DE104
Erskine Cres. N17 122 DV56
Erskine Hill NW11 120 DA57
Erskine Ms. NW3 140 DF66
Erskine Rd.
Erskine Rd. E17 123 DZ56
Erskine Rd. NW3 140 DF66
Erskine Rd., Sutt. 218 DD105
Erskine Rd., Wat. 94 BW48
Oxhey Dr.
Erwood Rd. SE7 164 EL78
Esam Way SW16 181 DN92
Escombe Dr., Guil. 242 AV129
Escot Way, Barn. 79 CW43
Escott Gdns. SE9 184 EL91
Escott Pl., Cher. 211 BC107
Escreet Gro. SE18 165 EN77
Esdaile Gdns., Upmin. 129 FR59
Esdaile La., Hodd. 49 EA17
Esher Ave., Rom. 127 FC58
Esher Ave., Sutt. 199 CX104
Esher Ave., Walt. 195 BU100
Esher Bypass, Chess. 215 CJ105
Esher Bypass, Cob. 213 BU112
Esher Bypass, Esher 215 CH108
Esher Clo., Bex. 186 EY88
Esher Clo., Esher 214 CB106
Esher Cres., Houns. 155 BS82
Eastern Perimeter Rd.
Esher Gdns. SW19 179 CX89
Esher Grn., Esher 214 CB105
Esher Ms., Mitch. 200 DF97
Esher Pk. Ave., Esher 214 CC105
Esher Pl. Ave., Esher 214 CA105
Esher Rd., E.Mol. 197 CD100
Esher Rd., Ilf. 125 ES62
Esher Rd., Walt. 214 BX106
Esk Rd. E13 144 EG70
Esk Way, Rom. 105 FD52
Eskdale, St.Alb. 62 CM27
Eskdale Ave., Chesh. 54 AQ30
Eskdale Ave., Nthlt. 136 BZ67
Eskdale Clo., Dart. 188 FQ88
Eskdale Clo., Wem. 117 CK61
Eskdale Ct., Hem.H. 40 BL17
Lonsdale
Eskdale Gdns., Pur. 220 DR114
Eskdale Rd., Bexh. 166 FA82
Eskdale Rd., Uxb. 134 BH68
Eskley Gdns., S.Ock. 149 FV71
Eskmont Ridge SE19 182 DS94
Esmar Cres. NW9 119 CU59
Esme Ho. SW15 159 CT84
Ludovick Wk.
Esmeralda Rd. SE1 162 DU77
Esmond Clo., Rain. 147 FH66
Dawson Dr.
Esmond Rd. NW6 139 CZ67
Esmond Rd. W4 158 CR77
Esmond St. SW15 159 CY84
Esparto St. SW18 180 DB87
Essenden Rd., Belv. 166 FA78
Essenden Rd., S.Croy. 220 DS108
Essendene Clo., Cat. 236 DS123
Essendene Rd., Cat. 236 DS123
Essendine Rd. W9 140 DA69
Essendon Gdns., Welw.G.C. 29 CZ09
Essendon Hill, Hat. 46 DE17
Essendon Rd., Hert. 46 DG15
Essex Ave., Islw. 157 CE83
Essex Ave., Slou. 131 AQ71
Essex Clo. E17 123 DY56
Essex Clo., Add. 212 BJ105
Essex Clo., Mord. 199 CX101
Essex Clo., Rom. 127 FB56
Essex Clo., Ruis. 116 BX60
Essex Ct. EC4 274 D9
Essex Ct. SW13 159 CT82
Essex Gdns. N4 121 DP58
Essex Gdns., Horn. 128 FM57
Essex Gro. SE19 182 DR93
Essex Ho. E14 143 EB72
Giraud St.
Essex La., Kings L. 59 BR33
Essex Pk. N3 98 DB51
Essex Pk. Ms. W3 138 CS74
Essex Pl. W4 158 CQ77
Essex Rd. E4 102 EE46
Essex Rd. E10 123 EC58
Essex Rd. E12 124 EL64
Essex Rd. E17 123 DY58
Essex Rd. E18 102 EH54
Essex Rd. N1 141 DP67
Essex Rd. NW10 138 CS66
Essex Rd. W3 138 CQ73
Essex Rd. W4 158 CR77
Belmont Rd.
Essex Rd., Bark. 145 ER66
Essex Rd., Borwd. 78 CN41
Essex Rd., Chesh. 54 AQ29
Essex Rd., Dag. 127 FC64
Essex Rd., Dart. 188 FK86
Essex Rd., Enf. 82 DR42
Essex Rd., Grav. 191 GG88
Essex Rd., Grays 169 FU79
Essex Rd., Hodd. 49 EB16
Essex Rd., Long. 209 FX96
Essex Rd., Rom. 126 FA56
Essex Rd. (Chadwell Heath), Rom. 126 EW59
Essex Rd., Wat. 75 BU40
Essex Rd. S. E11 123 ED59
Essex St. E7 124 EG64
Essex St. WC2 274 D10
Essex St., St.Alb. 43 CE19
Essex Twr. SE20 202 DV95
Essex Vill. W8 160 DA75
Essex Way, Brwd. 107 FW51
Essex Way, Epp. 70 EV32
Essex Way, Ong. 71 FF29
Essex Wf. E5 122 DW61
Essian St. E1 143 DY71
Essoldo Way, Edg. 118 CM55
Estate Way E10 123 DZ60
Estcourt Rd. SE25 202 DV100
Estcourt Rd. SW6 159 CZ80
Estcourt Rd., Wat. 76 BW41
Este Rd. SW11 160 DE83
Estella Ave., N.Mal. 199 CV98
Estelle Rd. NW3 120 DF63
Esterbrooke St. SW1 277 M9
Esterbrooke St. SW1 161 DK77
Esther Clo. N21 99 DN45
Esther Rd. E11 124 EE59
Estreham Rd. SW16 181 DK93
Estridge Clo., Houns. 156 CA84
Eswyn Rd. SW17 180 DF91
Etchingham Pk. Rd. N3 98 DB52
Etchingham Rd. E15 123 EC63
Eternit Wk. SW6 159 CW81
Etfield Gro., Sid. 186 EV92
Ethel Rd. E16 144 EH72
Ethel Rd., Ashf. 174 BL92
Ethel St. SE17 279 J9
Ethel Ter., Orp. 224 EW109
Ethelbert Clo., Brom. 204 EG97
Ethelbert Gdns., Ilf. 125 EM57
Ethelbert Rd. SW20 199 CX95
Ethelbert Rd., Brom. 204 EG97
Ethelbert Rd., Dart. 188 FL91
Ethelbert Rd., Erith 167 FC80
Hengist Rd.
Ethelbert Rd., Orp. 206 EX97
Ethelbert St. SW12 181 DH88
Fernlea Rd.
Ethelburga Rd., Rom. 106 FM53
Ethelburga St. SW11 160 DE81
Ethelden Rd. W12 139 CV74
Etheldene Ave. N10 121 DJ56
Ethelred Clo., Welw.G.C. 29 CZ10
Etheridge Grn., Loug. 85 EQ41
Etheridge Rd.
Etheridge Rd. NW2 119 CW59
Etheridge Rd., Loug. 85 EP40
Etherley Rd. N15 122 DQ57
Etherow St. SE22 182 DU86
Etherstone Grn. SW16 181 DN91
Etherstone Rd.
Etherstone Rd. SW16 181 DN91
Ethnard Rd. SE15 162 DV79
Ethorpe Clo., Ger.Cr. 112 AY57
Ethorpe Cres., Ger.Cr. 112 AY57
Ethorpe Clo.
Ethronvi Rd., Bexh. 166 EY83
Etloe Rd. E10 123 EA61
Etna Rd., St.Alb. 43 CD19
Eton Ave. N12 98 DC52
Eton Ave. NW3 140 DD66
Eton Ave., Barn. 80 DE44
Eton Ave., Houns. 156 BZ79
Eton Ave., N.Mal. 198 CR99
Eton Ave., Wem. 117 CH64
Eton Clo., Slou. 152 AU79
Eton College Rd. NW3 140 DF65
Eton Ct. NW3 140 DD66
Eton Ave.
Eton Ct., Stai. 173 BF92
Richmond Rd.
Eton Ct., Wem. 117 CJ63
Eton Ave.
Eton Ct. (Eton), Wind. 151 AR80
Eton Garages NW3 140 DE65
Lambolle Pl.
Eton Gro. NW9 118 CN55
Eton Gro. SE13 164 EE83
Eton Hall NW3 140 DF65
Eton College Rd.
Eton Pl. NW3 140 DG66
Haverstock Hill
Eton Ri. NW3 140 DF65
Eton College Rd.
Eton Rd. NW3 140 DF66
Eton Rd., Hayes 155 BT80
Eton Rd., Ilf. 125 EQ64
Eton Rd., Orp. 224 EV105
Eton Rd., Slou. 152 AT78
Eton Sq. (Eton), Wind. 151 AR80
Eton St., Rich. 178 CL85
Eton Vill. NW3 140 DF65
Eton Way, Dart. 168 FJ84
Eton Wick Rd. (Eton Wick), Wind. 151 AL77
Etta St. SE8 163 DY79
Etton Clo., Horn. 128 FL61
Ettrick St. E14 143 EC72
Etwell Pl., Surb. 198 CM100
Euclid Way, Grays 169 FT78
Eugene Clo., Rom. 128 FJ56
Eugenia Rd. SE16 162 DW77
Eunice Gro., Chesh. 54 AR33
Eureka Rd., Kings.T. 198 CN96
Washington Rd.
Europa Pk. Rd., Guil. 242 AW133
Europa Pl. EC1 275 H3
Europa Rd., Hem.H. 40 BM17
Jupiter Dr.
Europe Rd. SE18 165 EM76
Eustace Rd. E6 144 EL69
Eustace Rd. SW6 160 DA80
Eustace Rd., Guil. 243 BD132
Eustace Rd., Rom. 126 EX59
Euston Ave., Wat. 75 BT43
Euston Cen. NW1 141 DJ70
Triton Sq.
Euston Gro. NW1 273 M3
Euston Gro. NW1 141 DK69
Euston Rd. N1 141 DH70
Euston Rd. NW1 273 J5
Euston Rd. NW1 141 DH70
Euston Rd., Croy. 201 DN102
Euston Sq. NW1 273 M3
Euston Sq. NW1 141 DK69
Euston Sta. Colonnade NW1 273 M3
Euston St. NW1 273 L3
Euston St. NW1 141 DJ69
Eva Rd., Rom. 126 EW59
Evandale Rd. SW9 161 DN82
Evangelist Rd. NW5 121 DH63
Evans Ave., Wat. 75 BT35
Evans Clo. E8 142 DT65
Buttermere Wk.
Evans Clo., Green. 189 FU85
Evans Clo., Rick. 74 BN43
New Rd.
Evans Gro., Felt. 176 CA89
Evans Gro., St.Alb. 43 CJ16
Evans Rd. SE6 184 EE89
Evansdale, Rain. 147 FF69
New Zealand Way
Evanston Ave. E4 101 EC52
Evanston Gdns., Ilf. 124 EL58
Eve Rd. E11 124 EE63
Eve Rd. E15 144 EE68
Eve Rd. N17 122 DS55
Eve Rd., Islw. 157 CG84
Eve Rd., Wok. 227 BB115
Evelina Rd. SE15 162 DW83
Evelina Rd. SE20 183 DX94
Eveline Lowe Est. SE16 162 DU76
Eveline Rd., Mitch. 200 DF95
Evelyn Ave. NW9 118 CR55
Evelyn Ave., Ruis. 115 BT59
Evelyn Clo., Twick. 176 CB87
Evelyn Clo., Wok. 226 AX120
Evelyn Ct. N1 275 K1
Evelyn Cres., Sun. 195 BT95
Evelyn Denington Rd. E6 145 EM71
Evelyn Dr., Pnr. 94 BX52
Evelyn Fox Ct. W10 139 CW71
Evelyn Gdns. SW7 160 DD78
Evelyn Gdns., Gdse. 252 DW130
Evelyn Gdns., Rich. 158 CL84
Kew Rd.
Evelyn Gro. W5 138 CM74
Evelyn Gro., Sthl. 136 BZ72
Evelyn Rd. E17 123 EC56
Evelyn Rd. SW19 180 DB92
Evelyn Rd. W4 158 CR76
Evelyn Rd., Barn. 80 DF42
Evelyn Rd., Rich. 158 CL83
Evelyn Rd. (Ham), Rich. 177 CJ90
Ham St.
Evelyn Sharp Clo., Rom. 128 FK55
Amery Gdns.
Evelyn St. SE8 163 DY78
Evelyn Ter., Rich. 158 CL83
Evelyn Wk. N1 275 K1
Evelyn Wk. N1 142 DR68
Evelyn Wk., Brwd. 107 FW51
Wilmot Grn.
Evelyn Way, Cob. 230 BZ116
Evelyn Way, Sun. 195 BT95
Evelyn Way, Wall. 219 DK105
Evelyn Yd. W1 273 M8
Evelyns Clo., Uxb. 134 BN72
Evening Hill, Beck. 183 EC94
Evenwood Clo. SW15 179 CY85
Everard Ave., Brom. 204 EG102
Everard Ave., Slou. 152 AS75
Everard Clo., St.Alb. 43 CD22
Everard La., Cat. 236 DU122
Tillingdown Hill
Everard Way, Wem. 118 CL62
Everatt Clo. SW18 179 CZ86
Amerland Rd.
Everdon Rd. SW13 159 CU79
Everest Clo., Grav. 190 GE90
Everest Ct., Wok. 226 AS116
Langmans Way
Everest Pl. E14 143 EC71
Everest Pl., Swan. 207 FD98
Everest Rd. SE9 185 EM85
Everest Rd., Stai. 174 BK87
Everest Way, Hem.H. 40 BN19
Everett Clo., Pnr. 115 BT55
Wiltshire La.
Everett Clo., Wat. 95 CE46
Windmill St.
Everett Wk., Belv. 166 EZ78
Osborne Rd.
Everglade, West. 238 EK118
Everglade Strand NW9 97 CT53
Evergreen Ct., Stai. 174 BK87
Evergreen Oak Ave., Wind. 152 AU83
Evergreen Wk., Hem.H. 40 BL22
Redwood Dr.
Evergreen Way, Hayes 135 BT73
Evergreen Way, Stai. 174 BK87
Everilda St. N1 141 DM67
Evering Rd. E5 122 DU62
Evering Rd. N16 122 DU62
Everington Rd. N10 98 DF54
Everington St. W6 159 CX79
Everitt Rd. NW10 138 CR69
Everlands Clo., Wok. 226 AY118
Everlasting La., St.Alb. 42 CC18
Everleigh St. N4 121 DM60
Eversfield Gdns. NW7 96 CS51
Eversfield Rd., Reig. 250 DB134
Eversfield Rd., Rich. 158 CM82
Evershed Wk. W4 158 CR76
Acton La.
Eversholt St. NW1 141 DJ68
Evershot Rd. N4 121 DM60
Eversleigh Gdns., Upmin. 129 FR60
Eversleigh Rd. E6 144 EK67
Eversleigh Rd. N3 97 CZ52
Eversleigh Rd. SW11 160 DF83
Eversleigh Rd., Barn. 80 DC43
Eversley Ave., Bexh. 167 FD82
Eversley Ave., Wem. 118 CN61
Eversley Clo. N21 81 DM44
Eversley Cres. N21 81 DM44
Eversley Cres., Islw. 157 CD81
Eversley Cres., Ruis. 115 BS61
Eversley Cross, Bexh. 167 FE82
Eversley Mt. N21 81 DM44
Eversley Pk. SW19 179 CV92
Eversley Pk. Rd. N21 81 DM44
Eversley Rd. SE7 164 EH79
Eversley Rd. SE19 182 DR94
Eversley Rd., Surb. 198 CM98
Eversley Way, Croy. 221 EA105
Eversley Way, Egh. 193 BC96
Everthorpe Rd. SE15 162 DT83
Everton Bldgs. NW1 273 K3
Everton Dr., Stan. 118 CM55
Everton Rd., Croy. 202 DU102
Evesham Ave. E17 101 EA54
Evesham Clo., Grnf. 136 CB68
Evesham Clo., Reig. 249 CZ133
Evesham Clo., Sutt. 218 DA108
Evesham Grn., Mord. 200 DB100
Evesham Rd. E15 144 EF66
Evesham Rd. N11 99 DJ50
Evesham Rd., Felt. 176 BW87
Sparrow Fm. Dr.
Evesham Rd., Grav. 191 GK89
Evesham Rd., Mord. 200 DB100
Evesham Rd., Reig. 249 CZ134
Evesham Rd. N., Reig. 249 CZ133
Evesham St. W11 139 CX73
Evesham Wk. SE5 162 DR82
Love Wk.
Evesham Wk. SW9 161 DN82
Evesham Way SW11 160 DG83
Evesham Way, Ilf. 125 EN55
Evreham Rd., Iver 133 BE72
Evry Rd., Sid. 186 EW93
Ewald Rd. SW6 159 CZ82
Ewan Rd., Rom. 106 FK54
Ewanrigg Ter., Wdf.Grn. 102 EJ50
Ewart Gro. N22 99 DN53
Ewart Pl. E3 143 DZ68
Ewart Rd. SE23 183 DX87
Ewe Clo. N7 141 DL65
Ewelands, Horl. 269 DJ147
Ewell Bypass, Epsom 217 CU107
Ewell Ct. Ave., Epsom 216 CS106
Ewell Downs Rd., Epsom 217 CU111
Ewell Ho. Gro., Epsom 217 CT110
Ewell Pk. Way, Epsom 217 CU107
Ewell Rd., Surb. 198 CL99
Ewell Rd. (Long Ditton), Surb. 197 CH101
Ewell Rd., Sutt. 217 CX108
Ewellhurst Rd., Ilf. 102 EL54
Ewelme Rd. SE23 182 DW88
Ewen Cres. SW2 181 DN87
Ewer St. SE1 279 H3
Ewer St. SE1 142 DQ74
Ewhurst Ave., S.Croy. 220 DT109
Ewhurst Clo., Sutt. 217 CW109
Ewhurst Ho. E1 142 DW71
Jamaica St.
Ewhurst Rd. SE4 183 DZ86
Exbury Rd. SE6 183 EA89
Excel Ct. WC2 277 N1
Excelsior Clo., Kings.T. 198 CN96
Washington Rd.
Excelsior Gdns. SE13 163 EC82
Exchange Arc. EC2 275 N6
Exchange Arc. EC2 142 DS71
Exchange Bldgs. E1 142 DS72
Cutler St.
Exchange Ct. WC2 278 A1
Exchange Pl. EC2 275 M6
Exchange Pl. EC2 142 DS71
Exchange Rd., Wat. 75 BV41
Exchange Sq. EC2 275 M6
Exchange Sq. EC2 142 DS71
Exchange St., Rom. 127 FE57
Exeforde Ave., Ashf. 174 BN91
Exeter Clo. E6 145 EM72
Harper Rd.
Exeter Clo., Wat. 76 BW40
Reeds Cres.
Exeter Gdns., Ilf. 124 EL60
Exeter Ho. SW15 179 CW86
Putney Heath
Exeter Ms. NW6 140 DB65
West Hampstead Ms.
Exeter Pl., Guil. 242 AT132
Exeter Rd. E16 144 EG71
Exeter Rd. E17 123 EA57
Exeter Rd. N9 100 DW47
Exeter Rd. N14 99 DH46
Exeter Rd. NW2 119 CY64
Exeter Rd. SE15 162 DT81
Exeter Rd., Croy. 202 DS101
Exeter Rd., Dag. 147 FB65
Exeter Rd., Enf. 83 DX41
Exeter Rd., Felt. 176 BZ90
Exeter Rd., Grav. 191 GK90
Exeter Rd., Har. 116 BY61
Exeter Rd., Well. 165 ET82
Exeter St. WC2 274 A10
Exeter St. WC2 141 DL73
Exeter Way SE14 163 DZ80
Exford Gdns. SE12 184 EH88
Exford Rd. SE12 184 EH89
Exhibition Clo. W12 139 CW73
Exhibition Rd. SW7 276 A6
Exhibition Rd. SW7 160 DD75
Exmoor Clo., Ilf. 103 EQ53
Exmoor St. W10 139 CX71
Exmouth Mkt. EC1 274 D4
Exmouth Mkt. EC1 141 DN70
Exmouth Ms. NW1 273 L3
Exmouth Pl. E8 142 DV66
Exmouth Rd. E17 123 DZ57
Exmouth Rd., Brom. 204 EH97
Exmouth Rd., Grays 170 GB79
Exmouth Rd., Hayes 135 BS69
Exmouth Rd., Ruis. 116 BW62
Exmouth Rd., Well. 166 EW81
Exmouth St. E1 142 DW72
Commercial Rd.
Exning Rd. E16 144 EF70
Exon St. SE17 279 M9
Exon St. SE17 162 DS77
Explorer Ave., Stai. 174 BL87
Explorer Dr., Wat. 93 BQ46
Tolpits La.
Express Dr., Ilf. 126 EV60
Exton Cres. NW10 138 CQ66
Exton Gdns., Dag. 126 EW64
Exton St. SE1 278 D3
Exton St. SE1 141 DN74
Eyebright Clo., Croy. 203 DX102
Primrose La.
Eyhurst Ave., Horn. 127 FG62
Eyhurst Clo. NW2 119 CU61
Eyhurst Clo., Tad. 233 CZ123
Eyhurst Spur, Tad. 233 CZ124
Eylewood Rd. SE27 182 DQ92
Eynella Rd. SE22 182 DT87
Eynham Rd. W12 139 CW72
Eynsford Clo., Orp. 205 EQ101
Eynsford Cres., Bex. 186 EW88
Eynsford Rd., Green. 189 FW85
Eynsford Rd., Ilf. 125 ES61
Eynsford Rd., Sev. 225 FH110
Eynsford Rd., Swan. 207 FD100
Eynsham Dr. SE2 166 EU77
Eynswood Dr., Sid. 186 EV92
Eyot Gdns. W6 159 CT78
Eyot Grn. W4 159 CT79
Chiswick Mall
Eyre Clo., Rom. 127 FH56
Eyre Ct. NW8 140 DD68
Finchley Rd.
Eyre St. Hill EC1 274 D5
Eyston Dr., Wey. 212 BN110
Eythorne Rd. SW9 161 DN81
Eywood Rd., St.Alb. 42 CC22
Ezra St. E2 142 DT69

F

Faber Gdns. NW4 119 CU57
Fabian Rd. SW6 159 CZ80
Fabian St. E6 145 EM70
Fackenden La., Sev. 225 FH113
Factory La. N17 100 DT54
Factory La., Croy. 201 DN102
Factory Path, Stai. 173 BE91
Mustard Mill Rd.
Factory Pl. E14 163 EB78
Factory Rd. E16 144 EL74
Factory Rd., Grav. 190 GC86
Factory Sq. SW16 181 DL93
Factory Yd. W7 137 CE74
Uxbridge Rd.
Faesten Way, Bex. 187 FE90
Faggotters La., Harl. 37 FC12
Faggotters La., Ong. 53 FG16
Faggotts Clo., Rad. 77 CJ35
Faggs Rd., Felt. 175 BU85
Fagnall La., Amer. 88 AJ45
Fagus Ave., Rain. 148 FK69
Faints Clo., Wal.Cr. 66 DT29
Goffs La.
Fair Acres, Brom. 204 EG99
Fair Clo. (Bushey), Wat. 94 CB45
Claybury
Fair Grn., Saw. 36 EY05
The Sq.
Fair La., Couls. 250 DC125
Fair Leas, Chesh. 54 AN29
Fair St. SE1 279 N4
Fair St., Houns. 156 CC83
High St.
Fairacre, Hem.H. 40 BM24
Oakdene Rd.
Fairacre, N.Mal. 198 CS97
Fairacres SW15 179 CU85
Fairacres, Cob. 214 BX112
Fairacres, Croy. 221 DZ109
Fairacres, Ruis. 115 BT59
Fairacres, Tad. 233 CW121
Fairacres, Wind. 151 AK82
Fairacres Clo., Pot.B. 63 CZ33
Fairbairn Clo., Pur. 219 DN113
Fairbairn Grn. SW9 161 DN81
Fairbank Ave., Orp. 205 EP103
Fairbanks Rd. N17 122 DT55
Fairborne Way, Guil. 242 AU131
Stoughton Rd.
Fairbourne, Cob. 214 BX113
Fairbourne Clo., Wok. 226 AU118
Abercorn Way
Fairbourne La., Cat. 236 DQ122
Fairbourne Rd. N17 122 DS55
Fairbridge Rd. N19 121 DK61
Fairbrook Clo. N13 99 DN50
Fairbrook Rd. N13 99 DN51
Fairburn Clo., Borwd. 78 CN39
Fairburn Ct. SW15 179 CY85
Mercier Rd.
Fairby Rd. SE12 184 EH85
Fairchild Clo. SW11 160 DD82
Wye St.
Fairchild Pl. EC2 275 N5
Fairchild St. EC2 275 N5
Fairchildes Ave., Croy. 221 ED112
Fairchildes La., Warl. 221 ED114
Fairclough St. E1 142 DU72
Faircroft, Slou. 131 AP70
Faircross Ave., Bark. 145 EQ65
Faircross Ave., Rom. 105 FD52
Faircross Way, St.Alb. 43 CG18
Fairdale Gdns. SW15 159 CV84
Fairdale Gdns., Hayes 155 BU75
Fairdene Rd., Couls. 235 DK118
Fairey Ave., Hayes 155 BT77
Fairfax Ave., Epsom 217 CV110

Fairfax Ave., Red. 250 DE133
Fairfax Clo., Walt. 195 BV102
Fairfax Gdns. SE3 164 EJ81
Fairfax Ms., Amer. 55 AN40
Fairfax Pl. NW6 140 DC66
Fairfax Rd. N8 121 DN56
Fairfax Rd. NW6 140 DC66
Fairfax Rd. W4 158 CS76
Fairfax Rd., Grays 170 GB78
Fairfax Rd., Hert. 32 DT08
Fairfax Rd., Tedd. 177 CG93
Fairfax Rd., Til. 171 GF81
Fairfax Rd., Wok. 227 BB120
Fairfax Way N10 98 DG52
Cromwell Rd.
Fairfield App., Stai. 172 AX86
Fairfield Ave. NW4 119 CV58
Fairfield Ave., Edg. 96 CP51
Fairfield Ave., Horl. 268 DG149
Fairfield Ave., Ruis. 115 BQ59
Fairfield Ave., Slou. 152 AW80
Fairfield Ave., Stai. 173 BF91
Fairfield Ave., Twick. 176 CB88
Fairfield Ave., Upmin. 128 FQ62
Fairfield Ave., Wat. 94 BW48
Fairfield Clo. N12 98 DC49
Fairfield Clo., Dor. 247 CH134
Fairfield Dr.
Fairfield Clo., Enf. 83 DY42
Scotland Grn. Rd. N.
Fairfield Clo., Epsom 216 CS106
Fairfield Clo., Hat. 45 CW15
Fairfield Clo., Horn. 127 FG60
Fairfield Clo., Mitch. 180 DE94
Fairfield Clo., Nthwd. 93 BP50
Thirlmere Gdns.
Fairfield Clo., Rad. 77 CE37
Fairfield Clo., Sid. 185 ET86
Fairfield Clo., Slou. 152 AX80
Fairfield Cotts., Lthd. 246 CB125
Fairfield Ct. NW10 139 CU67
Fairfield Cres., Edg. 96 CP51
Fairfield Dr. SW18 180 DB85
Fairfield Dr., Brox. 49 DZ24
Fairfield Dr., Dor. 247 CH134
Fairfield Dr., Grnf. 137 CJ67
Fairfield Dr., Har. 116 CC55
Fairfield Dr., Slou. 130 AJ69
Fairfield E., Kings.T. 198 CL96
Fairfield Gdns. N8 121 DL57
Elder Ave.
Fairfield Gro. SE7 164 EK79
Fairfield Ind. Est., Kings.T. 198 CN97
Fairfield La., Slou. 131 AP68
Fairfield N., Kings.T. 198 CL96
Fairfield Pk., Cob. 214 BX114
Fairfield Path, Croy. 202 DR104
Fairfield Pl., Kings.T. 198 CL97
Fairfield Ri., Guil. 242 AT133
Fairfield Rd. E3 143 EA68
Fairfield Rd. E17 101 DY54
Fairfield Rd. N8 121 DL57
Fairfield Rd. N18 100 DU49
Fairfield Rd. W7 157 CG76
Southdown Ave.
Fairfield Rd., Beck. 203 EA96
Fairfield Rd., Bexh. 166 EZ82
Fairfield Rd., Brwd. 108 FW48
Fairfield Rd., Brom. 184 EG94
Fairfield Rd., Croy. 202 DS104
Fairfield Rd., Epp. 70 EV29
Fairfield Rd., Hodd. 49 EA15
Fairfield Rd., Ilf. 145 EP65
Fairfield Rd., Kings.T. 198 CL96
Fairfield Rd., Lthd. 231 CH121
Fairfield Rd., Orp. 205 ER100
Fairfield Rd., Sthl. 136 BZ72
Fairfield Rd., Stai. 172 AX86
Fairfield Rd., Uxb. 134 BK65
Fairfield Rd., West Dr. 134 BL73
Fairfield Rd., Wdf.Grn. 102 EG51
Fairfield S., Kings.T. 198 CL97
Fairfield St. SW18 180 DB85
Fairfield Wk., Lthd. 231 CH121
Fairfield Rd.
Fairfield Wk. (Cheshunt), Wal.Cr. 67 DY28
Martins Dr.
Fairfield Way, Barn. 80 DA43
Fairfield Way, Couls. 219 DK114
Fairfield Way, Epsom 216 CS106
Fairfield W., Kings.T. 198 CL96
Fairfields, Cher. 194 BG102
Fairfields, Grav. 191 GL92
Fairfields Clo. NW9 118 CQ57
Fairfields Cres. NW9 118 CQ57
Fairfields Rd., Houns. 156 CC83
Fairfolds, Wat. 76 BY35
Fairfoot Rd. E3 143 EA70
Fairford Ave., Bexh. 167 FD81
Fairford Ave., Croy. 203 DX99
Fairford Clo., Croy. 203 DX99
Fairford Clo., Reig. 250 DC132
Fairford Clo., Rom. 106 FP51
Fairford Way
Fairford Clo., W.Byf. 211 BF114
Fairford Gdns., Wor.Pk. 199 CT103
Fairford Way, Rom. 106 FP51
Fairgreen, Barn. 80 DF41
Fairgreen E., Barn. 80 DF41
Fairgreen Rd., Th.Hth. 201 DP99
Fairham Ave., S.Ock. 149 FU73
Fairhaven, Egh. 173 AZ92
Fairhaven Ave., Croy. 203 DX100
Fairhaven Cres., Wat. 93 BU48
Fairhaven Rd., Red. 250 DG130
Fairhazel Gdns. NW6 140 DB65
Fairhill, Hem.H. 40 BM24
Fairholme, Felt. 175 BR87
Fairholme Ave., Rom. 127 FG57
Fairholme Clo. N3 119 CY56
Fairholme Cres., Ash. 231 CJ117
Fairholme Cres., Hayes 135 BT70
Fairholme Gdns. N3 119 CY55
Fairholme Gdns., Upmin. 129 FT59
Fairholme Rd. W14 159 CY78
Fairholme Rd., Ashf. 174 BL92
Fairholme Rd., Croy. 201 DN101
Fairholme Rd., Har. 117 CF57
Fairholme Rd., Ilf. 125 EM59
Fairholme Rd., Sutt. 217 CZ107
Fairholt Clo. N16 122 DS60
Fairholt Rd.
Fairholt Rd. N16 122 DR60
Fairholt St. SW7 276 C6
Fairkytes Ave., Horn. 128 FK60
Fairland Rd. E15 144 EF65
Fairlands Ave., Buck.H. 102 EG47
Fairlands Ave., Sutt. 200 DA103
Fairlands Ave., Th.Hth. 201 DM98
Fairlands Ct. SE9 185 EN86
North Pk.
Fairlawn SE7 164 EJ79
Fairlawn, Lthd. 230 BZ124
Fairlawn Ave. N2 120 DE56
Fairlawn Ave. W4 158 CQ77
Fairlawn Ave., Bexh. 166 EX82
Fairlawn Clo. N14 81 DJ44
Fairlawn Clo., Esher 215 CF107
Fairlawn Clo., Felt. 176 BZ91
Fairlawn Clo., Kings.T. 178 CQ93
Fairlawn Dr., Red. 250 DE134
Fairlawn Dr., Wdf.Grn. 102 EG52
Fairlawn Gdns., Sthl. 136 BZ73
Fairlawn Gro. W4 158 CQ77
Fairlawn Gro., Bans. 218 DD113
Fairlawn Pk. SE26 183 DY92
Fairlawn Pk., Wind. 151 AL84
Fairlawn Pk., Wok. 210 AY114
Fairlawn Rd. SW19 179 CZ94
Fairlawn Rd., Cars. 218 DC111
Fairlawns, Add. 211 BF111
Fairlawns, Brwd. 108 FU48
Fairlawns, Horl. 269 DH149
Fairlawns, Pnr. 94 BW54
Elm Pk. Rd.
Fairlawns, Sun. 195 BU97
Fairlawns, Twick. 177 CJ86
Fairlawns, Wat. 75 BT38
Langley Rd.
Fairlawns, Wey. 213 BS106
Fairlawns Clo., Horn. 128 FM59
Fairlawns Clo., Stai. 174 BH93
Fairlea Pl. W5 137 CJ71
Fairley Way (Cheshunt), Wal.Cr. 66 DV28
Fairlie Gdns. SE23 182 DW87
Fairlie Rd., Slou. 131 AN72
Fairlight Ave. E4 101 ED47
Fairlight Ave. NW10 138 CS68
Fairlight Ave., Wind. 151 AR82
Fairlight Ave., Wdf.Grn. 102 EG51
Fairlight Clo. E4 101 ED47
Fairlight Clo., Wor.Pk. 217 CW105
Fairlight Dr., Uxb. 134 BK65
Fairlight Rd. SW17 180 DD91
Fairlop Clo., Horn. 147 FH65
Fairlop Gdns., Ilf. 103 EQ52
Fairlop Rd. E11 123 ED59
Fairlop Rd., Ilf. 103 EQ54
Fairmark Dr., Uxb. 134 BN65
Fairmead, Brom. 205 EM98
Fairmead, Surb. 198 CP102
Fairmead, Wok. 226 AW118
Fairmead Clo., Brom. 205 EM98
Fairmead Clo., Houns. 156 BX80
Fairmead Clo., N.Mal. 198 CR97
Fairmead Cres., Edg. 96 CQ48
Fairmead Gdns., Ilf. 124 EL57
Fairmead Rd. N19 121 DK62
Fairmead Rd., Croy. 201 DM102
Fairmead Rd., Loug. 84 EH43
Fairmead Side, Loug. 84 EJ43
Fairmeads, Cob. 214 BZ113
Fairmeads, Loug. 85 EP40
Fairmile Ave. SW16 181 DK92
Fairmile Ave., Cob. 214 BY114
Fairmile La., Cob. 214 BX112
Fairmile Pk. Copse, Cob. 214 BZ112
Fairmile Pk. Rd., Cob. 214 BZ113
Fairmont Clo., Belv. 166 EZ78
Lullingstone Rd.
Fairmount Rd. SW2 181 DM86
Fairoak Clo., Ken. 235 DP115
Fairoak Clo., Lthd. 215 CD112
Fairoak Clo., Orp. 205 EP101
Fairoak Dr. SE9 185 ER85
Fairoak Gdns., Rom. 105 FE54
Fairoak La., Chess. 215 CH111
Fairoak La., Lthd. 214 CC113
Fairs Rd., Lthd. 231 CG119
Fairseat Clo. (Bushey), Wat. 95 CE47
Hive Rd.
Fairstead Wk. N1 142 DQ67
Popham Rd.
Fairstone Ct., Horl. 269 DH147
Tanyard Way
Fairthorn Rd. SE7 164 EG78
Fairtrough Rd., Orp. 224 EV113
Fairview, Epsom 217 CW111
Fairview, Erith 167 FF80
Guild Rd.
Fairview, Pot.B. 64 DB29
Hawkshead Rd.
Fairview Ave., Brwd. 109 GE45
Fairview Ave., Rain. 148 FK68
Fairview Ave., Wem. 137 CK65
Fairview Ave., Wok. 227 AZ118
Fairview Clo. E17 101 DY53
Fairview Clo., Chig. 103 ES49
Fairview Clo., Wok. 227 AZ118
Fairview Ave.
Fairview Ct., Ashf. 174 BN92
Fairview Cres., Har. 116 CA60
Fairview Dr., Chig. 103 ES49
Fairview Dr., Orp. 223 ER105
Fairview Dr., Shep. 194 BM99
Fairview Dr., Wat. 75 BS36
Fairview Gdns., Wdf.Grn. 102 EH53
Fairview Ind. Pk., Rain. 147 FD71
Fairview Pl. SW2 181 DM87
Fairview Rd. N15 122 DT57
Fairview Rd. SW16 201 DM95
Fairview Rd., Chig. 103 ES49
Fairview Rd., Enf. 81 DN39
Fairview Rd., Epsom 217 CT111
Fairview Rd., Grav. 190 GD94
Fairview Rd., Maid. 130 AG72
Fairview Rd., Slou. 131 AM70
Fairview Rd., Sutt. 218 DD106
Fairview Way, Edg. 96 CN49
Fairwater Ave., Well. 166 EU84
Fairwater Dr., Add. 212 BK109
Fairway SW20 199 CW97
Fairway, Bexh. 186 EY85
Fairway, Cars. 218 DC111
Fairway, Cher. 194 BH102
Fairway, Guil. 243 BD134
Fairway, Hem.H. 40 BM24
Fairway, Orp. 205 ER99
Fairway, Saw. 36 EY05
Fairway, Vir.W. 192 AW100
Fairway, Ware 32 DW07
Fairway, Wdf.Grn. 102 EJ50
Fairway, The N13 100 DQ48
Fairway, The N14 81 DH44
Fairway, The NW7 96 CR48
Fairway, The W3 138 CS72
Fairway, The, Abb.L. 59 BR32
Fairway, The, Barn. 80 DB44
Fairway, The, Brom. 205 EM99
Fairway, The, Grav. 191 GG89
Fairway, The, Harl. 51 ET17
Fairway, The, H.Wyc. 110 AC56
Fairway, The, Lthd. 231 CG118
Fairway, The, N.Mal. 198 CR95
Fairway, The, Nthlt. 136 CC65
Fairway, The, Nthwd. 93 BS49
Fairway, The, Ruis. 116 BW63
Fairway, The, Slou. 130 AJ69
Fairway, The, Upmin. 128 FQ59
Fairway, The, Uxb. 134 BM69
Fairway, The, Wem. 117 CH62
Fairway, The, W.Mol. 196 CB97
Fairway, The, Wey. 212 BN111
Fairway Ave. NW9 118 CP55
Fairway Ave., Borwd. 78 CP40
Fairway Ave., West Dr. 134 BJ74
Fairway Clo. NW11 120 DC59
Fairway Clo., Croy. 203 DY99
Fairway Clo., Epsom 216 CQ105
Fairway Clo., Houns. 176 BW85
Fairway Clo., St.Alb. 60 CC27
Fairway Clo., West Dr. 134 BK74
Fairway Ave.
Fairway Clo., Wok. 226 AV119
Fairway Ct. NW7 96 CR48
The Fairway
Fairway Ct., Hem.H. 40 BM24
Fairway
Fairway Dr., Dart. 188 FP87
Fairway Dr., Grnf. 136 CB66
Fairway Est., Grnf. 136 CC66
Fairway Gdns., Beck. 203 ED100
Fairway Gdns., Ilf. 125 EQ64
Fairways, Ashf. 175 BP93
Fairways, Ken. 236 DQ117
Fairways, Stan. 96 CL54
Fairways, Tedd. 177 CK94
Fairways, Wal.Abb. 68 EE34
Fairways, Wal.Cr. 67 DX26
Fairweather Clo. N15 122 DS56
Fairweather Rd. N16 122 DU58
Fairwell La., Lthd. 245 BP128
Fairwyn Rd. SE26 183 DY91
Fakenham Clo. NW7 97 CU52
Longfield Ave.
Fakenham Clo., Nthlt. 136 CA65
Goodwood Dr.
Fakruddin St. E1 142 DU70
Falaise, Egh. 172 AY92
Falcon Ave., Brom. 204 EL98
Falcon Ave., Grays 170 GB80
Falcon Clo. SE1 278 G2
Falcon Clo. W4 158 CQ79
Sutton La. S.
Falcon Clo., Dart. 188 FM85
Falcon Clo., Hat. 45 CU20
Falcon Clo., Nthwd. 93 BS52
Falcon Clo., Saw. 36 EW06
Falcon Clo., Wal.Abb. 68 EG34
Kestrel Rd.
Falcon Ct., Wok. 211 BC114
Blackmore Cres.
Falcon Cres., Enf. 83 DX43
Falcon Dr., Stai. 174 BK86
Falcon Gro. SW11 160 DE83
Falcon Ho. W13 137 CF70
Falcon La. SW11 160 DE83
Falcon Ms., Grav. 190 GE88
Vale Rd.
Falcon Ridge, Berk. 38 AW20
Falcon Rd. SW11 160 DE82
Falcon Rd., Enf. 83 DX43
Falcon Rd., Guil. 258 AX135
Falcon Rd., Hmptn. 176 BZ94
Falcon St. E13 144 EF70
Falcon Ter. SW11 160 DE83
Falcon Trd. Est. NW10 118 CS63
Falcon Way E11 124 EG56
Falcon Way E14 163 EB77
Falcon Way NW9 96 CS54
Falcon Way, Felt. 175 BV85
Falcon Way, Har. 118 CL57
Falcon Way, Horn. 147 FG66
Falcon Way, Sun. 195 BS96
Falcon Way, Wat. 60 BY34
Falcon Way, Welw.G.C. 29 CY07
Falconberg Ct. W1 273 N8
Falconberg Ms. W1 273 M8
Falconer Rd., Ilf. 104 EV50
Falconer Rd. (Bushey), Wat. 76 BZ44
Falconer Wk. N7 121 DM61
Newington Barrow Way
Falconers Pk., Saw. 36 EX06
Falconhurst, Lthd. 231 CD115
Falcons Cft., H.Wyc. 110 AE55
Watery La.
Falconwood, Egh. 172 AY92
Tite Hill
Falconwood, Lthd. 229 BT124
Forest Rd.
Falconwood Ave., Well. 165 ER82
Falconwood Par., Well. 165 ES84
Falconwood Rd., Croy. 221 DZ109
Falcourt Clo., Sutt. 218 DB106
Falkirk Clo., Horn. 128 FN60
Falkirk Gdns., Wat. 94 BX50
Blackford Rd.
Falkirk Ho. W9 140 DB69
Falkirk St. N1 275 N1
Falkirk St. N1 142 DS68
Falkland Ave. N3 98 DA52
Falkland Ave. N11 98 DG49
Falkland Gdns., Dor. 263 CG137
Harrow Rd. W.
Falkland Gro., Dor. 263 CG137
Falkland Pk. Ave. SE25 202 DS97
Falkland Pl. NW5 121 DJ64
Falkland Rd.
Falkland Rd. N8 121 DN56
Falkland Rd. NW5 121 DJ64
Falkland Rd., Barn. 79 CY40
Falkland Rd., Dor. 263 CG137
Fallaize Ave., Ilf. 125 EP63
Riverdene Rd.
Falling La., West Dr. 134 BL73
Falloden Way NW11 120 DA56
Fallow Clo., Chig. 103 ET50
Fallow Ct. Ave. N12 98 DC52
Fallow Flds., Loug. 84 EJ44
Fallowfield, Stan. 95 CG49
Fallowfield, Welw.G.C. 29 CZ06
Fallowfield Clo., Uxb. 92 BJ53
Fallowfield Ct., Stan. 95 CG48
Stanmore Hill
Fallowfield Wk., Hem.H. 40 BG17
Tollpit End
Fallowfield Way, Horl. 269 DH147
Fallowfields Dr. N12 98 DE52
Fallows Clo. N2 98 DC54
Tarling Rd.
Fallsbrook Rd. SW16 181 DH93
Falmer Rd. E17 123 EB55
Falmer Rd. N15 122 DQ57
Falmer Rd., Enf. 82 DS42
Falmouth Ave. E4 101 ED50
Falmouth Clo. N22 99 DM52
Truro Rd.
Falmouth Clo. SE12 184 EF85
Falmouth Gdns., Ilf. 124 EK56
Falmouth Rd. SE1 279 J7
Falmouth Rd. SE1 162 DQ76
Falmouth Rd., Slou. 131 AN72
Falmouth Rd., Walt. 214 BW105
Falmouth St. E15 123 ED64
Falstaff Gdns., St.Alb. 42 CC23
Falstaff Ms., Hmptn. 177 CD92
Hampton Rd.
Falstone, Wok. 226 AV118
Fambridge Clo. SE26 183 DZ91
Fambridge Rd., Dag. 126 FA60
Famet Ave., Pur. 220 DQ113
Famet Clo., Pur. 220 DQ113
Famet Wk., Pur. 220 DQ113
Fane St. W14 159 CZ79
North End Rd.
Fanhams Rd., Ware 33 DY05
Fann St. EC1 275 H5
Fann St. EC1 142 DQ70
Fann St. EC2 275 H5
Fann St. EC2 142 DQ70
Fanns Ri., Purf. 168 FN77
Fanshaw St. N1 275 M2
Fanshaw St. N1 142 DS69
Fanshawe Ave., Bark. 145 EQ65
Fanshawe Cres., Dag. 126 EY64
Fanshawe Cres., Horn. 128 FK58
Fanshawe Cres., Ware 32 DW05
Fanshawe Rd., Grays 171 GG76
Fanshawe Rd., Rich. 177 CJ91
Fanshawe St., Hert. 31 DP08
Fanshaws La., Hert. 48 DQ18
Fanthorpe St. SW15 159 CW83
Far End, Hat. 45 CV21
Faraday Ave., Sid. 186 EU89
Faraday Clo. N7 141 DM65
Bride St.
Faraday Clo., Slou. 131 AP71
Faraday Clo., Wat. 75 BR44
Faraday Rd. E15 144 EF65
Faraday Rd. SW19 180 DA93
Faraday Rd. W3 138 CQ73
Faraday Rd. W10 139 CY71
Faraday Rd., Slou. 131 AP71
Faraday Rd., Sthl. 136 CB73
Faraday Rd., Well. 166 EU83
Faraday Rd., W.Mol. 196 CA98
Faraday Way SE18 164 EK76
Faraday Way, Croy. 201 DM102
Ampere Way
Faraday Way, Orp. 206 EV98
Fareham Rd., Felt. 176 BW87
Fareham St. W1 273 M8
Farewell Pl., Mitch. 200 DE95
Faringdon Ave., Brom. 205 EN101
Faringdon Ave., Rom. 106 FJ53
Faringford Clo., Pot.B. 64 DD31
Faringford Rd. E15 144 EE66
Farington Acres, Wey. 195 BR104
Faris Barn Dr., Add. 211 BF112
Faris La., Add. 211 BF111
Farjeon Rd. SE3 164 EK81
Farland Rd., Hem.H. 41 BP20
Farleigh Ave., Brom. 204 EF100
Farleigh Border, Croy. 221 DX112
Farleigh Ct. Rd., Warl. 221 DZ114
Farleigh Dean Cres., Croy. 221 EB111
Farleigh Pl. N16 122 DT63
Farleigh Rd.
Farleigh Rd. N16 122 DT63
Farleigh Rd., Add. 212 BG111
Farleigh Rd., Warl. 237 DX118
Farleton Clo., Wey. 213 BR107
Farley Dr., Ilf. 125 ES60
Farley Heath, Guil. 260 BJ144
Farley La., West. 255 EP127
Farley Nursery, West. 255 EQ127
Westbury Ter.
Farley Pk., Oxt. 253 ED130
Farley Pl. SE25 202 DU98
Farley Rd. SE6 183 EC87
Farley Rd., Grav. 191 GM88
Farley Rd., S.Croy. 220 DU108
Farleycroft, West. 255 EQ126
Farleys Clo., Lthd. 245 BQ126
Farlington Pl. SW15 179 CV87
Roehampton La.
Farlow Clo., Grav. 191 GF90
Farlow Rd. SW15 159 CW83
Farlton Rd. SW18 180 DB87
Farm Ave. NW2 119 CY62
Farm Ave. SW16 181 DL91
Farm Ave., Har. 116 BZ59
Farm Ave., Swan. 207 FC97
Farm Ave., Wem. 137 CJ65
Farm Clo., Amer. 72 AX39
Farm Clo., Barn. 79 CV43
Farm Clo., Borwd. 77 CK38
Farm Clo., Brwd. 109 GC45
Farm Clo., Buck.H. 102 EJ48
Farm Clo., Cher. 193 BA100
Farm Clo., Couls. 234 DF120
Doghurst La.
Farm Clo., Dag. 147 FC66
Farm Clo., Guil. 242 AX131
Waterside Rd.
Farm Clo., Harl. 34 EH14
Farm Clo., Hert. 31 DN09
Farm Clo. (East Horsley), Lthd. 245 BT128
Farm Clo. (Fetcham), Lthd. 231 CD124
Farm Clo., Maid. 150 AC78
Farm Clo. (Cuffley), Pot.B. 65 DK27
Farm Clo., Shep. 194 BN101
Farm Clo., Sthl. 136 CB73
Farm Clo., Stai. 173 BE92
Farm Clo., Sutt. 218 DD108
Farm Clo., Uxb. 115 BP61
Farm Clo., Wall. 219 DJ110
Farm Clo. (Cheshunt), Wal.Cr. 66 DW30
Farm Clo., Welw.G.C. 29 CW09
Farm Clo., W.Byf. 212 BM112
Farm Clo., W.Wick. 204 EE104
Farm Ct. NW4 119 CU55
Farm Cres., Slou. 132 AV71
Farm Dr., Croy. 203 DZ103
Farm Dr., Pur. 219 DK112
Farm End E4 84 EE43
Farm End, Nthwd. 93 BP53
Drakes Dr.
Farm Fld., Wat. 75 BS38
Farm Flds., S.Croy. 220 DS111
Farm Gro., Beac. 88 AJ50
Farm Hill Rd., Wal.Abb. 67 ED33
Farm Ho. Clo., Wok. 227 BD115
Farm La. N14 80 DG44
Farm La. SW6 160 DA79
Farm La., Add. 212 BG107
Farm La., Ash. 232 CN116
Farm La., Beac. 89 AR52
Farm La., Cars. 218 DF108
Kings Ave.
Farm La., Croy. 203 DZ103
Farm La., Epsom 232 CP120
Farm La., Hodd. 49 EC15
Rye Rd.
Farm La., Lthd. 245 BT128
Farm La., Pur. 219 DJ110
Farm La., Rick. 74 BH41
Farm La., Slou. 131 AR73
Whitby Rd.
Farm La., Wok. 227 BC123
Farm Lea, H.Wyc. 110 AF56
Farm Pl. W8 140 DA74
Uxbridge St.
Farm Pl., Berk. 38 AT18
Farm Pl., Dart. 167 FG84
Farm Rd. N21 100 DQ46
Farm Rd., Edg. 96 CP51
Farm Rd., Esher 196 CB102
Farm Rd., Grays 171 GF75
Farm Rd., Houns. 176 BY88
Farm Rd., Maid. 130 AG72
Farm Rd., Mord. 200 DB99
Farm Rd., Nthwd. 93 BQ50
Farm Rd., Rain. 148 FJ69
Farm Rd., Rick. 73 BA42
Farm Rd., St.Alb. 43 CH19
Farm Rd., Sev. 257 FJ121
Farm Rd., Stai. 174 BH93
Farm Rd., Sutt. 218 DD108
Farm Rd., Warl. 237 DY119
Farm Rd., Wok. 227 BB120
Farm St. W1 277 H1
Farm St. W1 141 DH73
Farm Vale, Bex. 187 FB86
Farm Wk. NW11 119 CZ57
Farm Wk., Guil. 258 AT136
Wilderness Rd.
Farm Wk., Horl. 268 DF148
Court Lo. Rd.
Farm Way, Buck.H. 102 EJ49
Farm Way, Horn. 127 FH63
Farm Way, Nthwd. 93 BS49
Farm Way, Stai. 173 BF86
Farm Way (Bushey), Wat. 76 CB42
Farm Way, Wor.Pk. 199 CW104
Farm Yd., Wind. 151 AR80
Farman Gro., Nthlt. 136 BX69
Wayfarer Rd.
Farmborough Clo., Har. 117 CD59
Pool Rd.
Farmcote Rd. SE12 184 EG88
Farmcroft, Grav. 191 GG89
Farmdale Rd. SE10 164 EG78
Farmdale Rd., Cars. 218 DE108
Farmer Rd. E10 123 EB60
Farmer St. W8 140 DA74
Uxbridge St.
Farmers Clo., Wat. 59 BV33
Farmers Ct., Wal.Abb. 68 EG33
Winters Way
Farmers Rd. SE5 161 DP80
Farmers Rd., Stai. 173 BE92
Farmers Way, Beac. 89 AQ51
Farmfield Dr., Horl. 268 DB150
Farmfield Rd., Brom. 184 EE92
Farmhouse Clo., Brox. 67 DZ25
Farmhouse La., Hem.H. 40 BN18
High St. Grn.
Farmhouse Rd. SW16 181 DJ94
Farmilo Rd. E17 123 DZ59
Farmington Ave., Sutt. 200 DD104
Farmland Wk., Chis. 185 EP92
Farmlands, Enf. 81 DN39
Farmlands, Pnr. 115 BU56
Farmlands, The, Nthlt. 136 CA65
Moat Fm. Rd.
Farmleigh N14 99 DJ45
Farmleigh Gro., Walt. 213 BS106
Farmstead Rd. SE6 183 EB91
Farmstead Rd., Har. 95 CD53
Farmview, Cob. 230 BX116
Farmway, Dag. 126 EW62
Farnaby Dr., Sev. 256 FF126
Farnaby Rd. SE9 164 EJ84
Farnaby Rd., Brom. 183 ED94
Farnan Ave. E17 101 EA54
Farnan Rd. SW16 181 DL92
Farnborough Ave. E17 123 DY55
Farnborough Ave., S.Croy. 221 DX108
Farnborough Clo., Wem. 118 CP61
Chalkhill Rd.
Farnborough Common, Orp. 205 EM104
Farnborough Cres., Brom. 204 EF102
Saville Row
Farnborough Cres., S.Croy. 221 DY109
Farnborough Hill, Orp. 223 ER106
Farnborough Way SE15 162 DS80
Daniel Gdns.
Farnborough Way, Orp. 223 EP106
Farnburn Ave., Slou. 131 AP71
Farncombe St. SE16 162 DU75
Farncombe St., Gdmg. 258 AS144
Farndale Ave. N13 99 DP48
Farndale Cres, Grnf. 136 CC69
Farnell Ms. SW5 160 DB78
Earls Ct. Sq.
Farnell Rd., Islw. 157 CD84
Farnell Rd., Stai. 174 BG90
Farnes Dr., Rom. 106 FJ54

Farney Fld., Guil.	261	BR142
Farnham Clo. N20	98	DC45
Farnham Clo., Hem.H.	57	BA28
Farnham Clo., Saw.	36	EW06
Farnham Gdns. SW20	199	CV96
Farnham La., Slou.	131	AL69
Farnham Pk. La., Slou.	131	AQ66
Farnham Pl. SE1	**278**	**G3**
Farnham Rd., Guil.	258	AS137
Farnham Rd., Ilf.	125	ET59
Farnham Rd., Rom.	106	FK50
Farnham Rd., Slou.	131	AQ71
Farnham Rd., Well.	166	EW82
Farnham Royal SE11	161	DM78
Farningham Cres., Cat.	236	DU123
Commonwealth Rd.		
Farningham Hill Rd. (Farningham), Dart.	208	FJ99
Farningham Rd. N17	100	DU52
Farningham Rd., Cat.	236	DU123
Farnley, Wok.	226	AT117
Farnley Rd. E4	102	EE45
Farnley Rd. SE25	202	DR98
Farnol Rd., Dart.	188	FN85
Faro Clo., Brom.	205	EN96
Faroe Rd. W14	159	CX76
Farorna Wk., Enf.	81	DN39
Farquhar Rd. SE19	182	DT92
Farquhar Rd. SW19	180	DA90
Farquhar St., Hert.	32	DQ08
Farquharson Rd., Croy.	202	DQ102
Farr Ave., Bark.	146	EU68
Farr Rd., Enf.	82	DR39
Farraline Rd., Wat.	75	BV42
Farrance Rd., Rom.	126	EY58
Farrance St. E14	143	EA72
Farrans Ct., Har.	117	CH59
Farrant Ave. N22	99	DN54
Farrant Clo., Orp.	224	EU108
Farrant Way, Borwd.	78	CL39
Farrell Ho. E1	142	DW72
Devonport St.		
Farren Rd. SE23	183	DY89
Farrer Ms. N8	121	DJ56
Farrer Rd.		
Farrer Rd. N8	121	DJ56
Farrer Rd., Har.	118	CL57
Farriday Clo., St.Alb.	43	CE16
Farrier Clo., Sun.	195	BU98
Farrier Rd., Nthlt.	136	CA68
Farrier St. NW1	141	DH66
Farrier Wk. SW10	160	DC79
Fulham Rd.		
Farriers, Ware	33	EA09
Farriers Clo., Epsom	216	CS112
Farriers Clo., Grav.	191	GM88
Lower Higham Rd.		
Farriers Ct., Wat.	59	BV32
Farriers End, Brox.	67	DZ26
Farriers Rd., Epsom	216	CS111
Farriers Way, Borwd.	78	CR43
Farringdon La. EC1	**274**	**E5**
Farringdon La. EC1	141	DN70
Farringdon Rd. EC1	**274**	**D4**
Farringdon Rd. EC1	141	DN70
Farringdon St. EC4	**274**	**F8**
Farringdon St. EC4	141	DP71
Farringford Clo., St.Alb.	60	CA26
Farrington Ave., Orp.	206	EV97
Farrington Pl., Chis.	185	ER94
Farrins Rents SE16	143	DY74
Farrow La. SE14	162	DW80
Farrow Pl. SE16	163	DY76
Ropemaker Rd.		
Farthing All. SE1	162	DU75
Wolseley St.		
Farthing Clo., Dart.	168	FM84
Trevithick Dr.		
Farthing Flds. E1	142	DV74
Raine St.		
Farthing Grn. La., Slou.	132	AU68
Farthing St., Orp.	223	EM108
Farthingale Ct., Wal.Abb.	68	EG34
Farthingale La., Wal.Abb.	68	EG34
Farthingale Wk. E15	143	ED66
Great Eastern Rd.		
Farthings, Wok.	226	AS116
Farthings, The, Hem.H.	40	BH20
Farthings, The, Kings.T.	198	CN95
Brunswick Rd.		
Farthings Clo. E4	102	EE48
Farthings Clo., Pnr.	115	BV58
Farwell Rd., Sid.	186	EV90
Farwig La., Brom.	204	EF95
Fashion St. E1	142	DT71
Fashoda Rd., Brom.	204	EJ98
Fassett Rd. E8	142	DU65
Fassett Rd., Kings.T.	198	CL98
Fassett Sq. E8	142	DU65
Fassnidge Way, Uxb.	134	BJ66
Oxford Rd.		
Fauconberg Rd. W4	158	CQ79
Faulkner Clo., Dag.	126	EX59
Faulkner St. SE14	162	DW81
Faulkner's All. EC1	**274**	**F6**
Faulkners Rd., Walt.	214	BW106
Fauna Clo., Rom.	126	EW58
Faunce St. SE17	161	DP78
Harmsworth St.		
Favart Rd. SW6	160	DA81
Faverolle Grn., Wal.Cr.	67	DX28
Faversham Ave. E4	102	EE46
Faversham Ave., Enf.	82	DR44
Faversham Clo., Chig.	104	EV47
Faversham Rd. SE6	183	DZ87
Faversham Rd., Beck.	203	DZ96
Faversham Rd., Mord.	200	DB100
Fawcett Clo. SW11	160	DD82
Fawcett Est. E5	122	DU60
Fawcett Rd. NW10	139	CT66
Fawcett Rd., Croy.	202	DQ104
Fawcett Rd., Wind.	151	AP81
Fawcett St. SW10	160	DB79
Fawcus Clo., Esher	215	CF107
Dalmore Ave.		
Fawe Pk. Rd. SW15	159	CZ84
Fawe St. E14	143	EB71
Fawke Common Rd., Sev.	257	FN126
Fawkes Ave., Dart.	188	FM89
Powder Mill La.		
Fawkham Grn. Rd. (Fawkham), Long.	209	FV104
Fawkham Rd., Long.	209	FX98
Fawkon Wk., Hodd.	49	EA18
Charlton Way		
Fawley Rd. NW6	120	DB64
Fawn Ct., Hat.	45	CW16
Fawn Rd. E13	144	EJ68
Fawn Rd., Chig.	103	ET50
Fawnbrake Ave. SE24	181	DP85
Fawns Manor Clo., Felt.	175	BQ88
Fawns Manor Rd., Felt.	175	BR88
Fawood Ave. NW10	138	CR66
Fawsley Clo., Slou.	153	BE80
Fawters Clo., Brwd.	109	GD44
Fay Grn., Abb.L.	59	BR33
Fayerfield, Pot.B.	64	DD31
Faygate Cres., Bexh.	186	FA85
Faygate Rd. SW2	181	DM89
Fayland Ave. SW16	181	DJ92
Faymore Gdns., S.Ock.	149	FU72
Feacey Down, Hem.H.	40	BH18
Fearn Clo., Lthd.	245	BS129
Fearney Mead, Rick.	92	BG46
Fearnley Cres., Hmptn.	176	BY92
Fearnley Rd., Welw.G.C.	29	CW10
Fearnley St., Wat.	75	BV42
Fearns Mead, Brwd.	108	FW50
Bucklers Ct.		
Fearon St. SE10	164	EG78
Feather Dell, Hat.	45	CT18
Featherbed La., Abb.L.	59	BV26
Sergehill La.		
Featherbed La., Croy.	221	DZ108
Featherbed La., Hem.H.	58	BG25
Featherbed La., Rom.	86	EX42
Featherbed La., Warl.	221	EB111
Feathers La., Stai.	173	BA89
Feathers Pl. SE10	163	ED79
Featherstone Ave. SE23	182	DV89
Featherstone Clo., Pot.B.	64	DD32
Featherstone Gdns., Borwd.	78	CQ42
Featherstone Ind. Est., Sthl.	156	BY75
Featherstone Rd. NW7	97	CV51
Featherstone Rd., Sthl.	156	BY76
Featherstone St. EC1	**275**	**K4**
Featherstone St. EC1	142	DR70
Featherstone Ter., Sthl.	156	BY76
Featley Rd. SW9	161	DP83
Federal Rd., Grnf.	137	CJ68
Federal Way, Wat.	76	BW39
Federation Rd. SE2	166	EV77
Fee Fm. Rd., Esher	215	CF108
Feenan Highway, Til.	171	GG80
Felbridge Ave., Stan.	95	CG53
Felbridge Clo. SW16	181	DN91
Felbridge Clo., Sutt.	218	DB109
Felbrigge Rd., Ilf.	125	ET61
Felcott Clo., Walt.	196	BW104
Felcott Rd., Walt.	196	BW104
Felday Hos., Dor.	261	BV144
Felday Rd. SE13	183	EB86
Felday Rd., Dor.	261	BT140
Felden Clo., Pnr.	94	BY52
Felden Clo., Wat.	60	BX34
Felden Dr., Hem.H.	40	BG24
Felden La., Hem.H.	40	BG24
Felden Rd., Hem.H.	39	BF23
Felden St. SW6	159	CZ81
Feldman Clo. N16	122	DU60
Oldhill St.		
Felgate Ms. W6	159	CV77
Felhampton Rd. SE9	185	EP89
Felhurst Cres., Dag.	127	FB63
Felicia Way, Grays	171	GH77
Felipe Rd., Grays	169	FW77
Arterial Rd. W. Thurrock		
Felix Ave. N8	121	DL58
Felix Dr., Guil.	244	BG128
Felix La., Shep.	195	BS100
Felix Rd. W13	137	CG73
Felix Rd., Walt.	195	BU100
Felix St. E2	142	DV68
Hackney Rd.		
Felixstowe Rd. N9	100	DU48
Felixstowe Rd. N17	122	DT55
Felixstowe Rd. NW10	139	CV69
Felixstowe Rd. SE2	166	EV76
Fell Rd., Croy.	202	DQ104
Fell Wk., Edg.	96	CP53
East Rd.		
Felland Way, Reig.	266	DD138
Fellbrigg Rd. SE22	182	DT85
Fellbrigg St. E1	142	DV70
Headlam St.		
Fellbrook, Rich.	177	CH90
Fellowes Clo., Hayes	136	BX70
Paddington Clo.		
Fellowes La., St.Alb.	44	CR23
Fellowes Rd., Cars.	200	DE104
Fellows Ct. E2	**275**	**P1**
Fellows Rd. NW3	140	DD66
Felltram Way SE7	164	EG77
Felmersham Clo. SW4	161	DK84
Haselrigge Rd.		
Felmingham Rd. SE20	202	DW96
Felmongers, Harl.	36	EV13
Fels Clo., Dag.	127	FB62
Fels Fm. Ave., Dag.	127	FC62
Felsberg Rd. SW2	181	DL86
Felsham Rd. SW15	159	CX83
Felspar Clo. SE18	165	ET78
Felstead Ave., Ilf.	103	EN53
Felstead Clo., Brwd.	109	GC44
Bannister Dr.		
Felstead Gdns. E14	163	EC78
Ferry St.		
Felstead Rd. E11	124	EG59
Felstead Rd., Epsom	216	CR111
Felstead Rd., Loug.	102	EL45
Felstead Rd., Orp.	206	EU103
Felstead Rd., Rom.	105	FC51
Felstead Rd., Wal.Cr.	67	DY32
Felstead St. E9	143	DZ65
Felsted Rd. E16	144	EK72
Feltham Ave., E.Mol.	197	CE98
Feltham Hill Rd., Ashf.	175	BP92
Feltham Rd., Ashf.	175	BP91
Feltham Rd., Mitch.	200	DF96
Feltham Rd., Red.	266	DF139
Feltham Wk., Red.	266	DF139
Felthambrook Ind. Est., Felt.	175	BV90
Felthambrook Way, Felt.	175	BV90
Felthamhill Rd., Felt.	175	BU91
Felton Clo., Borwd.	78	CL38
Felton Clo., Brox.	67	DZ25
Felton Clo., Orp.	205	EP100
Felton Gdns., Bark.	145	ES67
Sutton Rd.		
Felton Lea, Sid.	185	ET92
Felton Rd. W13	157	CJ75
Camborne Ave.		
Felton Rd., Bark.	145	ES68
Sutton Rd.		
Felton St. N1	142	DR67
Fen Clo., Brwd.	109	GC42
Fen Ct. EC3	**275**	**M10**
Fen Gro., Sid.	185	ET86
Fen La., Upmin.	149	FW65
Fen St. E16	144	EF73
Victoria Dock Rd.		
Fencepiece Rd., Chig.	103	EQ50
Fencepiece Rd., Ilf.	103	EQ51
Fenchurch Ave. EC3	**275**	**M9**
Fenchurch Ave. EC3	142	DS72
Fenchurch Bldgs. EC3	**275**	**N9**
Fenchurch Pl. EC3	**275**	**N10**
Fenchurch St. EC3	**275**	**M10**
Fenchurch St. EC3	142	DS73
Fendall Rd., Epsom	216	CQ106
Fendall St. SE1	**279**	**N7**
Fendall St. SE1	162	DS76
Fendt Clo. E16	144	EF73
Bowman Ave.		
Fendyke Rd., Belv.	166	EX76
Fenelon Pl. W14	159	CZ77
Fengates Rd., Red.	250	DE134
Fenham Rd. SE15	162	DU80
Fenman Ct. N17	100	DV53
Shelbourne Rd.		
Fenman Gdns., Ilf.	126	EV60
Fenn Clo., Brom.	184	EG93
Fenn St. E9	122	DW64
Fennel Clo. E16	144	EE70
Cranberry La.		
Fennel Clo., Croy.	203	DX102
Primrose La.		
Fennel Clo., Guil.	243	BB131
Fennel St. SE18	165	EN79
Fennells Mead, Epsom	217	CT109
Fennels, Harl.	51	EQ20
Fenner Clo. SE16	162	DV77
Layard Rd.		
Fenner Ho., Walt.	213	BU105
Fenner Rd., Grays	169	FV77
Arterial Rd. W. Thurrock		
Fenner Sq. SW11	160	DD83
Thomas Baines Rd.		
Fenning St. SE1	**279**	**M4**
Fennings, The, Amer.	55	AR36
Fenns Way, Wok.	226	AY115
Fennycroft Rd., Hem.H.	39	BF17
Fens Way, Swan.	187	FG93
Fensomes All., Hem.H.	40	BK19
Queensway		
Fenstanton Ave. N12	98	DD51
Fenswood Clo., Bex.	186	FA86
Rochester Dr.		
Fentiman Rd. SW8	161	DL79
Fentiman Way, Horn.	128	FL60
Fenton Ave., Stai.	174	BJ93
Fenton Clo. E8	142	DT65
Laurel St.		
Fenton Clo. SW9	161	DM82
Fenton Clo., Chis.	185	EM92
Fenton Clo., Red.	250	DG134
Fenton Gra., Harl.	52	EW16
Fenton Rd. N17	100	DQ52
Fenton Rd., Red.	250	DG134
Fentons Ave. E13	144	EH68
Fentum Rd., Guil.	242	AU132
Fenwick Clo. SE18	165	EN79
Ritter St.		
Fenwick Clo., Wok.	226	AV118
Fenwick Gro. SE15	162	DU83
Fenwick Path, Borwd.	78	CM38
Berwick Rd.		
Fenwick Pl. SW9	161	DL83
Fenwick Rd. SE15	162	DU83
Ferdinand Pl. NW1	140	DG66
Ferdinand St.		
Ferdinand St. NW1	140	DG66
Fergus Rd. N5	121	DP64
Calabria Rd.		
Ferguson Ave., Grav.	191	GJ91
Ferguson Ave., Rom.	106	FJ54
Ferguson Ave., Surb.	198	CM99
Ferguson Clo. E14	163	EA77
Mast Ho. Ter.		
Ferguson Clo., Brom.	203	ED97
Ferguson Ct., Rom.	106	FK54
Ferguson Ave.		
Ferguson Dr. W3	138	CR72
Ferme Pk. Rd. N4	121	DM59
Ferme Pk. Rd. N8	121	DL57
Fermor Rd. SE23	183	DY88
Fermoy Rd. W9	139	CZ70
Fermoy Rd., Grnf.	136	CB70
Fern Ave., Mitch.	201	DK98
Fern Clo., Brox.	49	DZ23
Fern Clo., Erith	167	FH81
Slade Grn. Rd.		
Fern Clo., Warl.	237	DY118
Fern Dells, Hat.	45	CT19
Fern Dene W13	137	CH71
Templewood		
Fern Dr., Hem.H.	40	BL21
Fern Gro., Felt.	175	BV87
Fern Gro., Welw.G.C.	29	CX05
Fern Hill, Lthd.	215	CD114
Fern Hill La., Harl.	51	ES19
Fern La., Houns.	156	BZ78
Fern Leys, St.Alb.	43	CJ17
Fern Rd., Maid.	130	AH72
Fern St. E3	143	EA70
Fern Twrs., Cat.	252	DU125
Fern Wk., Ashf.	174	BK92
Ferndale Rd.		
Fern Way, Wat.	75	BV35
Fernbank, Buck.H.	102	EH46
Fernbank Ave., Horn.	128	FJ63
Fernbank Ave., Walt.	196	BY101
Fernbank Ave., Wem.	117	CF63
Fernbank Rd., Add.	212	BG106
Fernbrook Ave., Sid.	185	ES85
Blackfen Rd.		
Fernbrook Cres. SE13	184	EE86
Fernbrook Rd.		
Fernbrook Dr., Har.	116	CB59
Fernbrook Rd. SE13	184	EE86
Ferncliff Rd. E8	122	DU64
Ferncroft Ave. N12	98	DE51
Ferncroft Ave. NW3	120	DA62
Ferncroft Ave., Ruis.	116	BW61
Ferndale, Brom.	204	EJ96
Ferndale, Guil.	242	AS132
Ferndale Ave. E17	123	ED57
Ferndale Ave., Cher.	193	BE104
Ferndale Ave., Houns.	156	BY83
Ferndale Ct. SE3	164	EF80
Ferndale Cres., Uxb.	134	BJ69
Ferndale Rd. E7	144	EH66
Ferndale Rd. E11	124	EE61
Ferndale Rd. N15	122	DT58
Ferndale Rd. SE25	202	DV99
Ferndale Rd. SW4	161	DM84
Ferndale Rd. SW9	161	DL84
Ferndale Rd., Ashf.	174	BK92
Ferndale Rd., Bans.	233	CZ116
Ferndale Rd., Enf.	83	DY36
Ferndale Rd., Grav.	191	GH89
Ferndale Rd., Rom.	105	FC54
Ferndale Rd., Wok.	227	AZ116
Ferndale St. E6	145	EP73
Ferndale Ter., Har.	117	CF56
Ferndale Way, Orp.	223	ER106
Ferndell Ave., Bex.	187	FD90
Fernden Ri., Gdmg.	258	AS144
Fernden Way, Rom.	127	FB58
Fernene, St.Alb.	60	BZ31
Fernene Rd. SE24	162	DQ84
Ferndown, Horl.	268	DF146
Ferndown, Horn.	128	FM58
Ferndown, Nthwd.	93	BU54
Ferndown Ave., Orp.	205	ER102
Ferndown Clo., Guil.	259	BA135
Ferndown Clo., Pnr.	94	BY52
Ferndown Clo., Sutt.	218	DD107
Ferndown Ct., Guil.	242	AW133
Ferndown Gdns., Cob.	214	BW113
Ferndown Rd. SE9	184	EK87
Ferndown Rd., Wat.	94	BW48
Fernecroft, St.Alb.	42	CC23
Fernery, The, Stai.	173	BE92
Fernes Clo., Uxb.	134	BJ72
Ferney Ct., W.Byf.	212	BK112
Ferney Rd.		
Ferney Meade Way, Islw.	157	CG82
Twickenham Rd.		
Ferney Rd., Barn.	98	DG45
Ferney Rd., W.Byf.	212	BK112
Fernhall Dr., Ilf.	124	EK57
Fernhall La., Wal.Abb.	68	EK31
Fernham Rd., Th.Hth.	202	DQ97
Fernhead Rd. W9	139	CZ69
Fernheath Way, Dart.	187	FD92
Fernhill, Harl.	51	ES19
Fernhill Clo., Wok.	226	AW120
Fernhill Ct. E17	101	ED54
Fernhill Gdns., Kings.T.	177	CK92
Fernhill La., Wok.	226	AW120
Fernhill Pk., Wok.	226	AW120
Fernhill Rd., Horl.	269	DK152
Fernhill St. E16	145	EM74
Fernhills, Kings L.	59	BR34
Fernholme Rd. SE15	183	DX85
Fernhurst Clo., Beac.	89	AM53
Fernhurst Gdns., Edg.	96	CN51
Fernhurst Rd. SW6	159	CY81
Fernhurst Rd., Ashf.	175	BQ91
Fernhurst Rd., Croy.	202	DU101
Fernie Clo., Chig.	104	EU50
Fernie Way, Chig.	104	EU50
Fernihough Clo., Wey.	212	BN111
Fernlands Clo., Cher.	193	BE104
Fernlea, Lthd.	230	CB124
Fernlea Rd. SW12	181	DH88
Fernlea Rd., Mitch.	200	DG96
Fernleigh Clo., Croy.	219	DN105
Stafford Rd.		
Fernleigh Ct., Har.	94	CB54
Fernleigh Ct., Wem.	118	CL61
Fernleigh Rd. N21	99	DN47
Ferns, The, Beac.	89	AM54
Ferns Clo., Enf.	83	DY36
Ferns Clo., S.Croy.	220	DV110
Ferns Rd. E15	144	EF65
Fernsbury St. WC1	**274**	**D3**
Fernsham Wk., Slou.	111	AQ64
Fernshaw Rd. SW10	160	DC79
Fernside NW11	120	DA61
Finchley Rd.		
Fernside, Buck.H.	102	EH46
Fernside Ave. NW7	96	CR48
Fernside Ave., Felt.	175	BV91
Fernside La., Sev.	257	FJ129
Fernside Rd. SW12	180	DF88
Fernsleigh Clo., Ger.Cr.	90	AY51
Fernthorpe Rd. SW16	181	DJ93
Ferntower Rd. N5	122	DR64
Fernville La., Hem.H.	40	BK20
Midland Rd.		
Fernways, Ilf.	125	EP63
Cecil Rd.		
Fernwood, Croy.	221	DY109
Fernwood Ave. SW16	181	DK91
Fernwood Ave., Wem.	117	CJ64
Bridgewater Rd.		
Fernwood Clo., Brom.	204	EJ96
Fernwood Cres. N20	98	DF48
Ferny Hill, Barn.	80	DF38
Ferranti Clo. SE18	164	EK76
Ferraro Clo., Houns.	156	CA79
Ferrers Ave., Wall.	219	DK105
Ferrers Ave., West Dr.	154	BK75
Ferrers Rd. SW16	181	DK92
Ferrestone Rd. N8	121	DM56
Ferriby Clo. N1	141	DN66
Bewdley St.		
Ferrier Pt. E16	144	EH71
Forty Acre La.		
Ferrier St. SW18	160	DB84
Ferriers Way, Epsom	233	CW118
Ferring Clo., Har.	116	CC60
Ferrings SE21	182	DS89
Ferris Ave., Croy.	203	DZ104
Ferris Rd. SE22	162	DU84
Ferro Rd., Rain.	147	FG70
Ferron Rd. E5	122	DV62
Ferry App. SE18	165	EN76
Ferry Ave., Stai.	173	BE94
Ferry La. N17	122	DV56
Ferry La. SW13	159	CT79
Ferry La., Brent.	158	CL79
Ferry La., Cher.	194	BG100
Ferry La., Guil.	258	AW138
Portsmouth Rd.		
Ferry La., Rain.	147	FE72
Ferry La., Rich.	158	CM79
Ferry La., Shep.	194	BN102
Ferry La. (Hythe End), Stai.	173	BB89
Ferry La. (Laleham), Stai.	194	BJ97
Ferry Pl. SE18	165	EN76
Woolwich High St.		
Ferry Rd. SW13	159	CU80
Ferry Rd., Maid.	150	AC75
Ferry Rd., Tedd.	177	CH92
Ferry Rd., T.Ditt.	197	CH100
Ferry Rd., Til.	171	GG83
Ferry Rd., Twick.	177	CH88
Ferry Rd., W.Mol.	196	CA97
Ferry Sq., Brent.	157	CK79
Ferry Sq., Shep.	195	BP101
Ferry St. E14	163	EC78
Ferryhills Clo., Wat.	94	BW48
Ferrymead Ave., Grnf.	136	CA69
Ferrymead Dr., Grnf.	136	CA69
Ferrymead Gdns., Grnf.	136	CC68
Ferrymoor, Rich.	177	CH90
Feryby Rd., Grays	171	GH76
Feryngs Clo., Harl.	36	EX11
Watlington Rd.		
Fesants Cft., Harl.	36	EV12
Festing Rd. SW15	159	CX83
Festival Clo., Bex.	186	EX88
Festival Clo., Erith	167	FF80
Betsham Rd.		
Festival Clo., Uxb.	135	BP67
Festival Path, Wok.	226	AT119
Fetcham Common La., Lthd.	230	CB121
Fetcham Pk. Dr., Lthd.	231	CE123
Fetter La. EC4	**274**	**E9**
Fetter La. EC4	141	DN72
Ffinch St. SE8	163	EA80
Fiddicroft Ave., Bans.	218	DB114
Fiddle Bri. La., Hat.	45	CT17
Fiddlers Clo., Green.	169	FV84
Fidler Pl. (Bushey), Wat.	76	CB44
Ashfield Ave.		
Field Clo. E4	101	EB51
Field Clo., Brom.	204	EJ96
Field Clo., Buck.H.	102	EJ48
Field Clo., Chesh.	54	AS28
Field Clo., Chess.	215	CJ106
Field Clo., Guil.	243	BD132
Field Clo., Hayes	155	BQ80
Field Clo., Houns.	155	BV81
Field Clo., Rom.	86	EV41
Field Clo., Ruis.	115	BQ60
Field Way		
Field Clo., St.Alb.	43	CG16
Field Clo., S.Croy.	220	DV114
Field Clo., W.Mol.	196	CB99
Field Ct. WC1	**274**	**C7**
Field Ct., Oxt.	254	EE127
Field End, Barn.	79	CV42
Field End, Couls.	219	DK114
Field End, Nthlt.	136	BX65
Field End, Ruis.	136	BW65
Field End, Twick.	177	CF91
Field End Clo., Wat.	94	BY45
Field End Rd., Pnr.	115	BV57
Field End Rd., Ruis.	116	BW60
Field La., Brent.	157	CJ80
Field La., Gdmg.	258	AT144
The Oval		
Field La., Tedd.	177	CG92
Field Mead NW7	96	CS52
Field Mead NW9	96	CS52
Field Pl., Gdmg.	258	AS144
George Rd.		
Field Pl., N.Mal.	199	CT100
Field Rd. E7	124	EG63
Field Rd. N17	122	DR55
Field Rd. W6	159	CY78
Field Rd., Felt.	175	BV86
Field Rd., Hem.H.	40	BN21
Field Rd., S.Ock.	148	FQ74
Field Rd., Uxb.	113	BD63
Field Rd., Wat.	76	BY44
Field St. WC1	**274**	**B2**
Field St. WC1	141	DM69
Field Vw., Egh.	173	BC92
Field Vw., Felt.	175	BR91
Field Vw. Ri., St.Alb.	60	BY29
Field Vw. Rd., Pot.B.	64	DA33
Field Way NW10	138	CQ66
Twybridge Way		
Field Way, Berk.	38	AY21
Field Way, Croy.	221	EB108
Field Way, Ger.Cr.	90	AX52
Field Way, Grnf.	136	CB67
Field Way, Hem.H.	57	BA27
Field Way, Hodd.	33	EC13
Field Way, Rick.	92	BH46
Field Way, Ruis.	115	BQ60
Field Way, Uxb.	134	BK70
Field Way, Wok.	243	BF125
Fieldcommon La., Walt.	196	BY102
Fieldend Rd. SW16	201	DJ95
Fielders Clo., Enf.	82	DS42
Woodfield Clo.		
Fielders Clo., Har.	116	CC60
Fielders Grn., Guil.	243	BA134
Fieldfare Rd. SE28	146	EW73
Fieldgate La., Mitch.	200	DE97
Fieldgate St. E1	142	DU71
Fieldhouse Rd. SW12	181	DJ88
Fieldhurst, Slou.	153	AZ78
Fieldhurst Clo., Add.	212	BH106
Fielding Ave., Til.	171	GH81
Fielding Ave., Twick.	176	CC90
Fielding Ho. NW6	140	DA69
Fielding Ms. SW13	159	CV79
Castelnau		
Fielding Rd. W4	158	CR76
Fielding Rd. W14	159	CX76
Fielding St. SE17	162	DQ79
Fielding Way, Brwd.	109	GC44
Fieldings, The SE23	182	DW88
Fieldings, The, Horl.	269	DJ147
Fieldings, The, Wok.	226	AT116
Fieldings Rd. (Cheshunt), Wal.Cr.	67	DZ28
Fields Ct., Pot.B.	64	DD33
Fields End La., Hem.H.	39	BD18
Fields Est. E8	142	DU66
Fields Pk. Cres., Rom.	126	EW57
Fieldsend Rd., Sutt.	217	CY106
Fieldside Clo., Orp.	223	EQ105
State Fm. Ave.		
Fieldside Rd., Brom.	183	ED92
Fieldview SW18	180	DD88
Fieldview, Horl.	269	DH147
Stockfield		
Fieldway, Amer.	55	AP41
Fieldway, Dag.	126	EW62
Fieldway, Orp.	205	ER100
Fieldway, Ware	33	EB11
Fieldway Cres. N5	121	DN64
Fiennes Clo., Dag.	126	EW60
Fiennes Way, Sev.	257	FJ127
Fiesta Dr., Dag.	147	FC70
Fife Rd. E16	144	EG71
Fife Rd. N22	99	DP52
Fife Rd. SW14	178	CQ85
Fife Rd., Kings.T.	198	CL96

337

Frank Bailey Wk. E12 125 EN64
Gainsborough Ave.
Frank Burton Clo. SE7 164 EH78
Victoria Way
Frank Dixon Clo. SE21 182 DS88
Frank Dixon Way SE21 182 DS88
Frank Lunnon Clo., B.End 110 AC60
Frank Martin Ct., Wal.Cr. 66 DU30
Frank St. E13 144 EG70
Frank Trowell Ct., Felt. 175 BU88
Frankfurt Rd. SE24 182 DQ85
Frankham St. SE8 163 EA80
Frankland Clo. SE16 162 DW77
Frankland Clo., Rick. 92 BN45
Frankland Clo., Wdf.Grn. 102 EJ50
Frankland Rd. E4 101 EA50
Frankland Rd. SW7 160 DD76
Frankland Rd., Rick. 75 BP44
Franklands Dr., Add. 211 BF108
Franklin Ave., Slou. 131 AP71
Franklin Ave. (Cheshunt), Wal.Cr. 66 DU30
Franklin Clo. N20 98 DC45
Franklin Clo. SE13 163 EB81
John Penn St.
Franklin Clo. SE27 181 DP90
Franklin Clo., Hem.H. 40 BL23
Franklin Clo., Kings.T. 198 CN97
Franklin Clo., St.Alb. 44 CS22
Franklin Cres., Mitch. 201 DJ98
Franklin Ho. NW9 119 CT59
Franklin Pas. SE9 164 EL83
Phineas Pett Rd.
Franklin Rd. SE20 182 DW94
Franklin Rd., Bexh. 166 EY81
Franklin Rd., Grav. 191 GK92
Franklin Rd., Horn. 148 FJ65
Franklin Rd., Wat. 75 BV40
Franklin Sq. W14 159 CZ78
Marchbank Rd.
Franklin St. E3 143 EB69
St. Leonards St.
Franklin St. N15 122 DS58
Franklin Way, Croy. 201 DL102
Franklins Ms., Har. 116 CC61
Franklin's Row SW3 276 E10
Franklin's Row SW3 160 DF78
Franklyn Cres., Wind. 151 AK83
Franklyn Gdns., Ilf. 103 ER51
Franklyn Rd. NW10 139 CT66
Franklyn Rd., Walt. 195 BU100
Franks Ave., N.Mal. 198 CQ98
Franks Fld., Guil. 261 BS144
Franks La. (Horton Kirby), Dart. 208 FN99
Franks Rd., Guil. 242 AU131
Frankswood Ave., Orp. 205 EP99
Frankswood Ave., West Dr. 134 BM72
Franlaw Cres. N13 100 DQ49
Franmil Rd., Horn. 127 FG60
Fransfield Gro. SE26 182 DV90
Frant Clo. SE20 182 DW94
Frant Rd., Th.Hth. 201 DP99
Franthorne Way SE6 183 EB89
Fraser Clo. E6 144 EL72
Linton Gdns.
Fraser Clo., Bex. 187 FC88
Dartford Rd.
Fraser Gdns., Dor. 263 CG135
Fraser Ho., Brent. 158 CM78
Fraser Rd. E17 123 EB57
Fraser Rd. N9 100 DV48
Fraser Rd., Erith 167 FC78
Fraser Rd., Grnf. 137 CH67
Fraser Rd. (Cheshunt), Wal.Cr. 67 DY28
Fraser St. W4 158 CS78
Frating Cres., Wdf.Grn. 102 EH51
Frays Ave., West Dr. 154 BK75
Frays Clo., West Dr. 154 BK76
Frays Lea, Uxb. 134 BJ68
Frays Waye, Uxb. 134 BJ67
Frazer Ave., Ruis. 116 BW64
Frazer Clo., Rom. 127 FF59
Frazier St. SE1 278 D5
Frazier St. SE1 161 DN75
Frean St. SE16 162 DU76
Fred Wigg Twr. E11 124 EF61
Freda Corbett Clo. SE15 162 DU80
Bird in Bush Rd.
Frederic Ms. SW1 276 E5
Frederic St. E17 123 DY57
Frederica Rd. E4 101 ED45
Frederica St. N7 141 DM66
Caledonian Rd.
Frederick Andrews Ct., Grays 170 GD79
Frederick Clo. W2 272 C10
Frederick Clo. W2 140 DE73
Frederick Clo., Sutt. 217 CZ105
Frederick Ct. NW2 119 CY62
Cricklewood La.
Frederick Cres. SW9 161 DP80
Frederick Cres., Enf. 82 DW40
Frederick Gdns., Sutt. 217 CZ106
Frederick Pl. SE18 165 EP78
Frederick Rd. SE17 161 DP78
Chapter Rd.
Frederick Rd., Rain. 147 FD68
Frederick Rd., Sutt. 217 CZ106
Frederick Sq. SE16 143 DY73
Rotherhithe St.
Frederick St. WC1 274 B3
Frederick St. WC1 141 DM69
Frederick Ter. E8 142 DT67
Haggerston Rd.
Frederick's Pl. EC2 275 K9
Fredericks Pl. N12 98 DC49
Frederick's Row EC1 274 F2
Fredora Ave., Hayes 135 BT70
Free Prae Rd., Cher. 194 BG102
Freeborne Gdns., Rain. 147 FG65
Mungo Pk. Rd.
Freedom Clo. E17 123 DY56
Freedom Rd. N17 100 DR54
Freedom St. SW11 160 DF82
Freedown La., Sutt. 218 DB113
Freegrove Rd. N7 121 DL64
Freeland Pk. NW4 97 CY54
Freeland Rd. W5 138 CM73
Freeland Way, Erith 167 FG81
Slade Grn. Rd.
Freelands Ave., S.Croy. 221 DX109
Freelands Gro., Brom. 204 EH95
Freelands Rd., Brom. 204 EH95
Freelands Rd., Cob. 213 BV114
Freeling St. N1 141 DM66
Caledonian Rd.
Freeman Clo., Nthlt. 136 BY66
Freeman Ct., Chesh. 54 AQ30
Barnes Ave.
Freeman Dr., W.Mol. 196 BZ97
Freeman Rd., Grav. 191 GL90
Freeman Rd., Mord. 200 DD99
Freeman Way, Horn. 128 FL58
Freemans Clo., Shep. 195 BS98
Freemans Clo., Slou. 132 AT65
Freemans La., Hayes 135 BS73
Freemantle Ave., Enf. 83 DX43
Freemasons Rd. E16 144 EH71
Freemasons Rd., Croy. 202 DS102
Freesia Clo., Orp. 223 ET106
Briarswood Way
Freethorpe Clo. SE19 202 DS95
Freke Rd. SW11 160 DG83
Fremantle Rd., Belv. 166 FA77
Fremantle Rd., Ilf. 103 EQ54
Fremantle St. SE17 279 M10
Fremantle St. SE17 162 DS78
Fremont St. E9 142 DW67
French Gdns., Cob. 214 BW114
French Horn La., Hat. 45 CV17
French Ordinary Ct. EC3 142 DS73
Crutched Friars
French Pl. E1 275 N4
French Row, St.Alb. 43 CD20
Market Pl.
French St., Sun. 196 BW96
French St., West. 255 ES128
Frenchaye, Add. 212 BJ106
Frenches, The, Red. 250 DG132
Frenches Ct., Red. 250 DG132
Frenches Rd.
Frenches Dr., Red. 250 DG132
The Frenches
Frenches Rd., Red. 250 DG132
Frenchlands Hatch, Lthd. 245 BS127
French's Clo., Ware 33 EB11
French's Wells, Wok. 226 AV117
Frenchum Gdns., Slou. 131 AL73
Frendsbury Rd. SE4 163 DY84
Frensham (Cheshunt), Wal.Cr. 66 DT27
Frensham Clo., Sthl. 136 BZ70
Frensham Ct., Mitch. 200 DD97
Phipps Bri. Rd.
Frensham Dr. SW15 179 CT90
Frensham Dr., Croy. 221 EC108
Frensham Rd. SE9 185 ER89
Frensham Rd., Ken. 219 DP114
Frensham St. SE15 162 DU79
Frensham Way, Epsom 233 CW116
Frere St. SW11 160 DE82
Fresh Wf. Rd., Bark. 145 EP67
Freshborough Ct., Guil. 259 AZ135
Lower Edgeborough Rd.
Freshfield Ave. E8 142 DT66
Middleton Rd.
Freshfield Clo. SE13 163 ED84
Marischal Rd.
Freshfield Dr. N14 99 DH45
Freshfields, Croy. 203 DZ101
Freshfields Ave., Upmin. 128 FP64
Freshford St. SW18 180 DC90
Freshmount Gdns., Epsom 216 CP111
Freshwater Clo. SW17 180 DG93
Freshwater Rd. SW17 180 DG93
Freshwater Rd., Dag. 126 EX60
Freshwaters, Harl. 35 ES14
School La.
Freshwell Ave., Rom. 126 EW56
Freshwood Clo., Beck. 203 EB95
Freshwood Way, Wall. 219 DH109
Freston Gdns., Barn. 80 DF43
Freston Pk. N3 97 CZ54
Freston Rd. W10 139 CX73
Freston Rd. W11 139 CX73
Freta Rd., Bexh. 186 EZ85
Fretherne Rd., Welw.G.C. 29 CX09
Frewin Rd. SW18 180 DD88
Friar Ms. SE27 181 DP90
Prioress Rd.
Friar Rd., Hayes 136 BX70
Friar Rd., Orp. 206 EU99
Friar St. EC4 274 G9
Friars, The, Chig. 103 ES49
Friars, The, Harl. 51 EN17
Friars Ave. N20 98 DE48
Friars Ave. SW15 179 CT90
Friars Ave., Brwd. 109 GA46
Friars Clo. E4 101 EC48
Friars Clo. N2 120 DD56
Friars Clo., Brwd. 109 GA45
Friars Clo., Nthlt. 136 BX69
Broomcroft Ave.
Friars Fld., Berk. 38 AS16
Heron Elm
Friars Gdns. W3 138 CR72
St. Dunstans Ave.
Friars Gate, Guil. 258 AU136
Friars Gate Clo., Wdf.Grn. 102 EG49
Friars La., Bishop's Stortford 37 FH06
Friars La., Rich. 177 CK85
Friars Mead E14 163 EC76
Friars Ms. SE9 185 EN85
Friars Orchard, Lthd. 231 CD121
Friars Pl. La. W3 138 CR73
Friars Ri., Wok. 227 BA118
Friars Rd. E6 144 EK67
Friars Rd., Vir.W. 192 AX98
Friars Stile Pl., Rich. 178 CL86
Friars Stile Rd.
Friars Stile Rd., Rich. 178 CL86
Friars Wk. N14 99 DH45
Friars Wk. SE2 166 EX78
Friars Way W3 138 CR72
Friars Way, Cher. 194 BG99
Friars Way, Kings L. 58 BN30
Friars Way (Bushey), Wat. 76 BZ39
Friars Wd., Croy. 221 DY109
Friarscroft, Brox. 49 EA20
Friary, The, Wind. 172 AW86
Friary Bri., Guil. 258 AW136
Friary Clo. N12 98 DE50
Friary Ct. SW1 277 L3
Friary Ct., Wok. 226 AT118
Friary Dr., Stai. 172 AW86
Friary Est. SE15 162 DU79
Friary La., Wdf.Grn. 102 EG49
Friary Pas., Guil. 258 AW136
Friary St.
Friary Rd. N12 98 DD49
Friary Rd. SE15 162 DU80
Friary Rd. W3 138 CQ72
Friary Rd., Stai. 172 AW87
Friary St., Guil. 258 AW136
Friary Way N12 98 DE49
Friday Hill E4 102 EE47
Friday Hill E. E4 102 EE48
Friday Hill W. E4 102 EE47
Friday Rd., Erith 167 FD78
Friday Rd., Mitch. 180 DF94
Friday St. EC4 275 H9
Friday St. EC4 142 DQ73
Friday St., Dor. 262 BY143
Frideswide Pl. NW5 121 DJ64
Islip St.
Friend St. EC1 274 F2
Friend St. EC1 141 DP69
Friendly Pl. SE13 163 EB81
Lewisham Rd.
Friendly St. SE8 163 EA82
Friendly St. Ms. SE8 163 EA82
Friendly St.
Friends Ave., Wal.Cr. 67 DX31
Friends Rd., Croy. 202 DR104
Friends Rd., Pur. 219 DP112
Friends Wk., Stai. 173 BF92
South St.
Friends Wk., Uxb. 134 BK66
Bakers Rd.
Friendship Wk., Nthlt. 136 BX69
Wayfarer Rd.
Friern Barnet La. N11 98 DF49
Friern Barnet La. N20 98 DC47
Friern Barnet Rd. N11 98 DF50
Friern Ct. N20 98 DD48
Friern Mt. Dr. N20 98 DC45
Friern Pk. N12 98 DC50
Friern Rd. SE22 182 DU87
Friern Watch Ave. N12 98 DC49
Frigate Ms. SE8 163 EA79
Watergate St.
Frimley Ave., Horn. 128 FN60
Frimley Clo. SW19 179 CY89
Frimley Clo., Croy. 221 EC108
Frimley Ct., Sid. 186 EW92
Frimley Cres., Croy. 221 EC108
Frimley Gdns., Mitch. 200 DE97
Frimley Rd., Chess. 215 CK106
Frimley Rd., Hem.H. 39 BE19
Frimley Rd., Ilf. 125 ES62
Frimley Vw., Wind. 151 AK81
Frimley Way E1 143 DX70
Frimley Way, Wall. 219 DL106
Fringewood Clo., Nthwd. 93 BP53
Frinsted Clo., Orp. 206 EX98
Frinsted Rd., Erith 167 FD80
Frinton Clo., Wat. 93 BV47
Frinton Dr., Wdf.Grn. 101 ED52
Frinton Ms., Ilf. 125 EN58
Bramley Cres.
Frinton Rd. E6 144 EK69
Frinton Rd. N15 122 DS58
Frinton Rd. SW17 180 DG93
Frinton Rd., Rom. 104 EZ52
Frinton Rd., Sid. 186 EY89
Friston Path, Chig. 103 ES50
Manford Way
Friston St. SW6 160 DB82
Friswell Pl., Bexh. 166 FA84
Frith Ct. NW7 97 CY52
Frith Knowle, Walt. 213 BV106
Frith La. NW7 97 CY52
Frith Rd. E11 123 EC63
Frith Rd., Croy. 202 DQ103
Frith St. W1 273 M9
Frith St. W1 141 DK72
Fritham Clo., N.Mal. 198 CS100
Frithe, The, Slou. 132 AV72
Friths Dr., Reig. 250 DB131
Frithsden Copse, Berk. 39 AZ15
Frithsden Rd., Berk. 38 AY17
Frithville Gdns. W12 139 CW74
Frithwald Rd., Cher. 193 BF101
Frithwood Ave., Nthwd. 93 BS51
Frizlands La., Dag. 127 FB63
Frobisher Clo., Ken. 236 DR117
Hayes La.
Frobisher Clo., Pnr. 116 BX59
Frobisher Cres., Stai. 174 BL87
Frobisher Gdns., Guil. 243 BA133
Frobisher Gdns., Stai. 174 BL87
Frobisher Cres.
Frobisher Pas. E14 143 EA74
North Colonnade
Frobisher Rd. E6 145 EM72
Frobisher Rd. N8 121 DN56
Frobisher Rd., Erith 167 FF80
Frobisher Rd., St.Alb. 43 CJ22
Frobisher St. SE10 164 EE79
Frobisher Way, Grav. 191 GL92
Frobisher Way, Hat. 44 CR15
Frog La., Guil. 242 AY125
Frog La., Rain. 147 FD71
Froggy La., Uxb. 113 BD61
Froghall La., Chig. 103 ER49
Froghole La., Eden. 255 ER132
Frogley Rd. SE22 162 DT84
Frogmoor La., Rick. 92 BK47
Frogmore SW18 180 DA85
Frogmore, St.Alb. 61 CD27
Frogmore Ave., Hayes 135 BS70
Frogmore Clo., Slou. 151 AN75
Frogmore Clo., Sutt. 199 CX104
Frogmore Dr., Wind. 152 AS81
Frogmore Gdns., Hayes 135 BS70
Frogmore Gdns., Sutt. 217 CY105
Frogmore Mobile Home Pk., St.Alb. 61 CD27
Frogmore Rd., Hem.H. 40 BK23
Durrants Hill Rd.
Frognal NW3 120 DC64
Frognal Ave., Har. 117 CF56
Frognal Ave., Sid. 186 EU92
Frognal Clo. NW3 120 DC64
Frognal Ct. NW3 140 DC65
Frognal Gdns. NW3 120 DC63
Frognal La. NW3 120 DB64
Frognal Par. NW3 140 DC65
Frognal Ct.
Frognal Pl., Sid. 186 EU93
Frognal Ri. NW3 120 DC62
Frognal Way NW3 120 DC63
Froissart Rd. SE9 184 EK85
Frome Rd. N22 121 DP55
Westbury Ave.
Frome Sq., Hem.H. 40 BN15
Waveney
Frome St. N1 142 DQ68
Fromer Rd., H.Wyc. 110 AD59
Fromondes Rd., Sutt. 217 CY106
Front, The, Berk. 39 BB16
Front La., Upmin. 129 FS61
Frostic Wk. E1 142 DU71
Chicksand St.
Froude St. SW8 161 DH82
Frowick Clo., Hat. 45 CV23
Frowyke Cres., Pot.B. 63 CU32
Fruen Rd., Felt. 175 BT87
Fry Clo., Rom. 104 FA50
Fry Rd. E6 144 EK66
Fry Rd. NW10 139 CT67
Fryatt Rd. N17 100 DR52
Fryatt St. E14 144 EE72
Orchard Pl.
Fryent Clo. NW9 118 CN57
Fryent Cres. NW9 118 CS58
Fryent Flds. NW9 118 CS58
Fryent Gro. NW9 118 CS58
Fryent Way NW9 118 CN57
Fryer Clo., Chesh. 54 AR33
Fryern Wd., Cat. 236 DQ124
Frye's Bldgs. N1 141 DN68
Upper St.
Frying Pan All. E1 275 P7
Fryston Ave., Couls. 219 DH114
Fryston Ave., Croy. 202 DU103
Fryth Mead, St.Alb. 42 CB19
Fuchsia St. SE2 166 EV78
Fulbeck Dr. NW9 96 CS53
Fulbeck Way, Har. 94 CC54
Fulbourne Clo., Red. 250 DE132
Dennis Clo.
Fulbourne Rd. E17 101 EC53
Fulbourne St. E1 142 DV71
Durward St.
Fulbrook Ave., Add. 212 BG111
Fulbrook La., S.Ock. 149 FT73
Fulbrook Ms. N19 121 DJ63
Junction Rd.
Fulbrook Rd. N19 121 DJ63
Junction Rd.
Fulbrooks Ave., Wor.Pk. 199 CT102
Fulford Gro., Wat. 93 BV47
Fulford Rd., Cat. 236 DR121
Fulford Rd., Epsom 216 CR108
Fulford St. SE16 162 DV75
Paradise St.
Fulham Bdy. SW6 160 DA80
Fulham Clo., Uxb. 135 BQ70
Uxbridge Rd.
Fulham Ct. SW6 160 DA80
Fulham Rd.
Fulham High St. SW6 159 CY82
Fulham Palace Rd. SW6 159 CX79
Fulham Palace Rd. W6 159 CW78
Fulham Pk. Gdns. SW6 159 CZ82
Fulham Pk. Rd. SW6 159 CZ82
Fulham Rd. SW3 160 DD78
Fulham Rd. SW6 159 CY82
Fulham Rd. SW10 160 DD78
Fulkes Cotts., Lthd. 245 BP128
Fullarton Cres., S.Ock. 149 FT72
Fuller Clo. E2 142 DU70
St. Matthew's Row
Fuller Clo., Orp. 223 ET106
Fuller Gdns., Wat. 75 BV37
Fuller Rd.
Fuller Rd., Dag. 126 EV62
Fuller Rd., Wat. 75 BV37
Fuller St. NW4 119 CW56
Fuller Way, Hayes 155 BT78
Fuller Way, Rick. 74 BN43
Fullers Ave., Surb. 198 CM103
Fullers Ave., Wdf.Grn. 102 EF52
Fullers Clo., Chesh. 54 AP32
Fullers Clo., Rom. 105 FC52
Fullers Clo., Wal.Abb. 68 EF33
Fullers Fm. Rd., Lthd. 245 BP134
Fullers Hill, Amer. 54 AM34
Fullers Hill, Chesh. 54 AM34
Fullers Hill, West. 255 ER126
High St.
Fullers La., Rom. 105 FC52
Fullers Mead, Harl. 52 EW16
Fullers Rd. E18 102 EF53
Fullers Way N., Surb. 198 CM104
Fullers Way S., Chess. 216 CL105
Fullers Wd., Croy. 221 EA106
Fullers Wd. La., Red. 251 DJ134
Fullerton Clo., W.Byf. 212 BM114
Fullerton Dr., W.Byf. 212 BL114
Fullerton Rd. SW18 180 DC85
Fullerton Rd., Cars. 218 DE109
Fullerton Rd., Croy. 202 DT101
Fullerton Rd., W.Byf. 212 BL114
Fullerton Way, W.Byf. 212 BL114
Fullmer Way, Add. 211 BF110
Fullwell Ave., Ilf. 103 EM53
Fullwoods Ms. N1 275 L2
Fulmar Ct., Surb. 198 CM100
Fulmar Cres., Hem.H. 40 BG21
Fulmar Rd., Horn. 147 FG66
Fulmead St. SW6 160 DB81
Fulmer Clo., Hmptn. 176 BY92
Fulmer Common Rd., Iver 133 BA65
Fulmer Common Rd., Slou. 112 AX64
Fulmer Dr., Ger.Cr. 112 AX61
Fulmer La., Ger.Cr. 113 BA62
Fulmer La., Slou. 112 AY62
Fulmer Ri. Est., Slou. 133 AZ65
Fulmer Rd. E16 144 EK71
Fulmer Rd., Ger.Cr. 112 AY59
Fulmer Rd., Slou. 112 AX63
Fulmer Way W13 157 CH76
Fulmer Way, Ger.Cr. 112 AY58
Fulready Rd. E10 123 ED57
Fulstone Clo., Houns. 156 BZ84
Fulthorp Rd. SE3 164 EF82
Fulton Ms. W2 140 DC73
Porchester Ter.
Fulton Rd., Wem. 118 CN62
Fulvens, Guil. 261 BS142
Fulvens Cotts., Guil. 261 BS142
Fulwell Cross, Ilf. 103 ER54
Fulwell Pk. Ave., Twick. 176 CB89
Fulwell Rd., Tedd. 177 CD91
Fulwich Rd., Dart. 188 FM86
Fulwood Ave., Wem. 138 CM68
Fulwood Clo., Hayes 135 BT72
Fulwood Gdns., Twick. 177 CF86
Fulwood Pl. WC1 274 C7
Fulwood Wk. SW19 179 CY88
Furber St. W6 159 CV76
Furham Feild, Pnr. 94 CA52
Furley Rd. SE15 162 DU80
Furlong Clo., Wall. 200 DG102
Furlong Rd. N7 141 DN65
Furlong Rd., Dor. 262 CC137
Furlong Way, Ware 33 DZ09
Furlongs, Hem.H. 40 BG19
Furlough, The, Wok. 227 BA117
Pembroke Rd.
Furmage St. SW18 180 DB87
Furmingers Rd., Orp. 225 FB106
Furneaux Ave. SE27 181 DP92
Furner Clo., Dart. 167 FF83
Furness Clo., Grays 171 GH78
Furness Pl., Wind. 150 AJ82
Furness Row
Furness Rd. NW10 139 CU68
Furness Rd. SW6 160 DB82
Furness Rd., Har. 116 CB59
Furness Rd., Mord. 200 DB101
Furness Row, Wind. 150 AJ82
Furness Sq., Wind. 150 AJ82
Furness Row
Furness Wk., Wind. 150 AJ82
Furness Row
Furness Way, Horn. 127 FG64
Furness Way, Wind. 150 AJ82
Furnival Ave., Slou. 131 AP71
Furnival Clo., Vir.W. 192 AX100
Furnival St. EC4 274 D8
Furnival St. EC4 141 DN72
Furrow La. E9 122 DW64
Furrowfield, Hat. 45 CV16
Cob Mead
Furrows, The, Uxb. 114 BJ57
Furrows, The, Walt. 196 BW103
Furrows Pl., Cat. 236 DT123
Fursby Ave. N3 98 DA51
Furse Ave., St.Alb. 43 CG17
Further Acre NW9 97 CT54
Further Grn. Rd. SE6 184 EE87
Furtherfield, Abb.L. 59 BS32
Furtherfield Clo., Croy. 201 DN100
Furtherground, Hem.H. 40 BL21
Furze Clo., Red. 250 DF133
Furze Clo., Wat. 94 BW50
Furze Fm. Clo., Rom. 104 EY54
Furze Fld., Lthd. 215 CD113
Furze Gro., Tad. 233 CZ121
Furze Hill, Pur. 219 DL111
Furze Hill, Red. 250 DE133
Linkfield La.
Furze Hill, Tad. 233 CZ120
Furze La., Gdmg. 258 AT143
Furze La., Pur. 219 DL111
Furze Rd., Add. 211 BF107
Furze Rd., Hem.H. 39 BE21
Furze Rd., Th.Hth. 202 DQ97
Furze St. E3 143 EA71
Furze Vw., Rick. 73 BC44
Furzebushes La., St.Alb. 60 BY25
Furzedown Dr. SW17 181 DH92
Furzedown Rd. SW17 181 DH92
Furzedown Rd., Sutt. 218 DC111
Furzefield (Cheshunt), Wal.Cr. 66 DV28
Furzefield Clo., Chis. 185 EP93
Furzefield Cres., Reig. 266 DC136
Furzefield Rd. SE3 164 EH80
Furzefield Rd., Beac. 88 AJ52
Furzefield Rd., Reig. 266 DC136
Furzefield Rd., Welw.G.C. 29 CY10
Furzeground Way, Uxb. 135 BQ74
Furzeham Rd., West Dr. 154 BL75
Furzehill Rd., Borwd. 78 CN41
Furzen Clo., Slou. 131 AN69
Furzen Cres., Hat. 45 CT21
Furzewood, Sun. 195 BU95
Fuschia Ct., Wdf.Grn. 102 EE52
Bridle Path
Fusedale Way, S.Ock. 149 FT73
Fuzzens Wk., Wind. 151 AL82
Fyfe Way, Brom. 204 EG96
Fyfield Clo., Brom. 203 ED98
Fyfield Ct. E7 144 EG65
Fyfield Rd. E17 123 ED55
Fyfield Rd. SW9 161 DN83
Fyfield Rd., Enf. 82 DS41
Fyfield Rd., Rain. 147 FF67
Fyfield Rd., Wdf.Grn. 102 EJ52
Fynes St. SW1 277 M8
Fynes St. SW1 161 DK77

G

Gabion Ave., Purf. 169 FR77
Gable Clo. SE26 182 DV91
Lawrie Pk. Ave.
Gable Clo., Abb.L. 59 BS32
Gable Clo., Dart. 187 FG85
Gable Clo., Pnr. 94 CA52
Gable Ct. SE26 182 DV92
Lawrie Pk. Ave.
Gables, The, Bans. 233 CZ117
Gables, The, Hem.H. 40 BK19
Chapel St.
Gables, The, Lthd. 214 CC112
Gables, The, Wem. 118 CM63
Manor Dr.
Gables Ave., Ashf. 174 BM92
Gables Ave., Borwd. 78 CM41
Gables Clo. SE5 162 DS81
Gables Clo. SE12 184 EG88
Gables Clo., Ger.Cr. 90 AY49
Gables Clo., Slou. 152 AU79
Gables Clo., Wok. 227 AZ120
Kingfield Rd.
Gabriel Clo., Felt. 176 BX91
Gabriel Clo., Rom. 105 FC52
Gabriel Spring Rd. (Fawkham Grn.), Long. 209 FR103
Gabriel Spring Rd. (East), Long. 209 FS103
Gabriel St. SE23 183 DX87
Gabrielle Clo., Wem. 118 CM62
Gabrielle Ct. NW3 140 DD65
Gabriels Gdns., Grav. 191 GL92
Gad Clo. E13 144 EH68
Greengate St.
Gadbrook Rd., Bet. 264 CQ140
Gaddesden Ave., Wem. 138 CM65
Gaddesden Cres., Wat. 60 BX34

Gaddesdon Gro., Welw.G.C. 30 DC09
Widford Rd.
Gade Ave., Wat. 75 BS42
Gade Bank, Rick. 75 BR42
Rousebarn La.
Gade Clo., Hayes 135 BV74
Gade Clo., Hem.H. 40 BH17
Gade Clo., Wat. 75 BS42
Gade Twr., Hem.H. 58 BN25
Gade Valley Clo., Kings L. 58 BN28
Gade Vw. Gdns., Kings L. 59 BQ32
Gade Vw. Rd., Hem.H. 40 BK24
Gadebridge La., Hem.H. 40 BH18
Gadebridge Rd., Hem.H. 40 BG18
Gadesden Rd., Epsom 216 CQ107
Gadsbury Clo. NW9 119 CT58
Gadsden Clo., Upmin. 129 FS58
Gadswell Clo., Wat. 76 BX36
Gadwall Clo. E16 144 EH72
Freemasons Rd.
Gadwall Way SE28 165 ER75
Goldfinch Rd.
Gage Rd. E16 144 EE71
Malmesbury Rd.
Gage St. WC1 274 A6
Gainford St. N1 141 DN67
Richmond Ave.
Gainsborough Ave. E12 125 EN64
Gainsborough Ave., Dart. 188 FJ85
Gainsborough Ave., St.Alb. 43 CF19
Gainsborough Ave., Til. 171 GG81
Gainsborough Clo., Beck. 183 EA94
Gainsborough Clo., Esher 197 CE102
Lime Tree Ave.
Gainsborough Ct. N12 98 DB50
Gainsborough Ct. W12 159 CW75
Lime Gro.
Gainsborough Ct., Walt. 213 BU105
Gainsborough Dr., Grav. 190 GD90
Gainsborough Dr., S.Croy. 220 DU113
Gainsborough Gdns. NW3 120 DD62
Gainsborough Gdns. NW11 119 CZ59
Gainsborough Gdns., Edg. 96 CM54
Gainsborough Gdns., Grnf. 117 CE64
Gainsborough Gdns., Islw. 177 CD85
Gainsborough Ms. SE26 182 DV90
Panmure Rd.
Gainsborough Pl., Chig. 103 ET48
Grove La.
Gainsborough Rd. E11 124 EE59
Gainsborough Rd. E15 144 EE69
Gainsborough Rd. N12 98 DB50
Gainsborough Rd. W4 159 CT77
Gainsborough Rd., Dag. 126 EV63
Gainsborough Rd., Epsom 216 CQ110
Gainsborough Rd., Hayes 135 BQ68
Gainsborough Rd., N.Mal. 198 CR100
Gainsborough Rd., Rain. 147 FG67
Gainsborough Rd., Rich. 158 CM82
Gainsborough Rd., Wdf.Grn. 102 EL51
Gainsborough Sq., Bexh. 166 EX83
Regency Way
Gainsford Rd. E17 123 DZ56
Gainsford St. SE1 279 P4
Gainsford St. SE1 162 DT75
Gainswood, Welw.G.C. 29 CY10
Mill Grn. Rd.
Gairloch Rd. SE5 162 DS82
Gaisford St. NW5 141 DJ65
Gaist Ave., Cat. 236 DV122
Gaitskell Rd. SE9 185 EQ88
Galahad Clo., Slou. 151 AN75
Mitchell Clo.
Galahad Rd., Brom. 184 EG90
Galata Rd. SW13 159 CU80
Galatea Sq. SE15 162 DV83
Scylla Rd.
Galbraith St. E14 163 EC76
Galdana Ave., Barn. 80 DC41
Gale Clo., Hmptn. 176 BY93
Stewart Clo.
Gale Clo., Mitch. 200 DD97
Gale Cres., Bans. 234 DA117
Gale St. E3 143 EA71
Gale St., Dag. 126 EW64
Galeborough Ave., Wdf.Grn. 101 ED52
Galen Pl. WC1 274 A7
Galena Rd. W6 159 CV77
Gales Clo., Guil. 243 BD132
Gilliat Dr.
Gales Gdns. E2 142 DV69
Gales Way, Wdf.Grn. 102 EL52
Galesbury Rd. SW18 180 DC86
Galey Grn., S.Ock. 149 FV71
Bovey Way
Galgate Clo. SW19 179 CY88
Gallants Fm. Rd., Barn. 98 DE45
Galleon Boul., Dart. 169 FR84
Galleon Clo. SE16 163 DX75
Kinburn St.
Galleon Rd., Grays 169 FW77
Arterial Rd. W. Thurrock
Galleons La., Slou. 132 AW70
Gallery Gdns., Nthlt. 136 BX68
Gallery Rd. SE21 182 DR88
Galley Grn., Hert. 33 EA13
Galley Hill, Hem.H. 39 BF18
Galley Hill Rd., Grav. 190 FZ85
Galley La., Barn. 79 CT38
Galleyhill Rd., Wal.Abb. 68 EE32
Galleymead Rd., Slou. 153 BF81
Galleywall Rd. SE16 162 DV77
Galleywood Cres., Rom. 105 FD51
Gallia Rd. N5 121 DP64
Galliard Clo. N9 82 DW44
Galliard Rd. N9 100 DU46
Gallions Clo., Bark. 146 EU69
Gallions Rd. E16 145 EP73
Gallions Rd. SE7 164 EH77
Gallon Clo. SE7 164 EJ77
Gallop, The, S.Croy. 220 DV108
Gallop, The, Sutt. 218 DD110
Gallosson Rd. SE18 165 ES77
Galloway Clo., Brox. 67 DZ25
Galloway Path, Croy. 220 DR105
St. Peter's Rd.
Galloway Rd. W12 139 CU74
Gallows Cor., Rom. 106 FJ53
Gallows Hill, Kings L. 59 BQ31
Gallows Hill La., Abb.L. 59 BQ32
Gallus Clo. N21 81 DM44
Gallus Sq. SE3 164 EH83
Gallys Rd., Wind. 151 AK82
Galpins Rd., Th.Hth. 201 DL99
Galsworthy Ave., Rom. 126 EV59
Galsworthy Clo. SE28 146 EV74
Galsworthy Cres. SE3 164 EJ81
Merriman Rd.
Galsworthy Rd. NW2 119 CY63
Galsworthy Rd., Cher. 194 BG101
Galsworthy Rd., Kings.T. 178 CP94
Galsworthy Rd., Til. 171 GJ81
Galsworthy Ter. N16 122 DS62
Hawksley Rd.
Galton St. W10 139 CY69
Galva Clo., Barn. 80 DG42
Galvani Way, Croy. 201 DM102
Ampere Way
Galveston Rd. SW15 179 CZ85
Galvin Rd., Slou. 131 AQ74
Galvins Clo., Guil. 242 AU131
Galway St. EC1 275 J3
Galway St. EC1 142 DQ69
Gambetta St. SW8 161 DH82
Gambia St. SE1 278 G3
Gambles La., Wok. 228 BJ124
Gambole Rd. SW17 180 DE91
Games Rd., Barn. 80 DF41
Gamlen Rd. SW15 159 CX84
Gammon Clo., Hem.H. 40 BN21
Gammons Fm. Clo., Wat. 75 BT36
Gammons La., Brox. 66 DS25
Gammons La., Wat. 75 BS36
Gander Grn. La., Sutt. 199 CY103
Ganders Ash, Wat. 59 BU33
Gandhi Clo. E17 123 EA58
Gane Clo., Wall. 219 DL108
Kingsford Ave.
Gangers Hill, Gdse. 253 DY128
Ganghill, Guil. 243 BA132
Gant Ct., Wal.Abb. 68 EF34
Ganton St. W1 273 K10
Ganton Wk., Wat. 94 BY49
Woodhall La.
Gantshill Cres., Ilf. 125 EN57
Gantshill Cross, Ilf. 125 EN58
Eastern Ave.
Ganymede Pl., Hem.H. 40 BM18
Jupiter Dr.
Gap Rd. SW19 180 DA92
Garage Rd. W3 138 CN72
Garbrand Wk., Epsom 217 CT109
Garbutt Pl. W1 272 G6
Garbutt Rd., Upmin. 128 FQ61
Gard St. EC1 274 G2
Garden Ave., Bexh. 166 FA83
Garden Ave., Hat. 45 CU22
Garden Ave., Mitch. 181 DH94
Garden City, Edg. 96 CN51
Garden Clo. E4 101 EA50
Garden Clo. SE12 184 EH90
Garden Clo. SW15 179 CV87
Garden Clo., Add. 212 BK105
Garden Clo., Ashf. 175 BQ93
Garden Clo., Bans. 234 DA115
Garden Clo., Barn. 79 CV42
Garden Clo., Hmptn. 176 BZ92
Garden Clo., Lthd. 231 CJ124
Garden Clo., Nthlt. 136 BY67
Garden Clo., Ruis. 115 BS61
Garden Clo., St.Alb. 43 CH19
Garden Clo., Wall. 219 DL106
Garden Clo., Wat. 75 BT40
Garden Cotts., Orp. 206 EW96
Main Rd.
Garden Ct. EC4 274 D10
Garden Ct. SE15 162 DT81
Sumner Est.
Garden Ct., Rich. 158 CM81
Lichfield Rd.
Garden Ct., Welw.G.C. 29 CZ08
Tewin Rd.
Garden Ct., W.Mol. 196 CB98
Avern Rd.
Garden End, Amer. 55 AS37
Garden Fld. La., Berk. 39 AZ21
Garden La. SW2 181 DM88
Christchurch Rd.
Garden La., Brom. 184 EH93
Garden Ms. W2 140 DA73
Linden Gdns.
Garden Ms., Slou. 132 AT74
Littledown Rd.
Garden Pl., Dart. 188 FK90
Garden Reach, Ch.St.G. 72 AX41
Garden Rd. NW8 140 DC69
Garden Rd. SE20 202 DW95
Garden Rd., Abb.L. 59 BS31
Garden Rd., Brom. 184 EH94
Garden Rd., Rich. 158 CN83
Garden Rd., Sev. 257 FK122
Garden Rd., Walt. 195 BV100
Garden Row SE1 278 F7
Garden Row SE1 161 DP76
Garden Row, Grav. 191 GF90
Garden St. E1 143 DX71
Garden Ter. SW1 277 M10
Garden Ter. Rd., Harl. 36 EW11
Garden Wk. EC2 275 M3
Garden Wk., Beck. 203 DZ95
Hayne Rd.
Garden Wk., Couls. 235 DH123
Garden Way NW10 138 CQ65
Garden Way, Loug. 85 EN38
Gardeners Clo. N11 98 DG49
Gardeners La. EC4 275 H10
Gardeners Rd., Croy. 201 DP102
Gardeners Wk., Lthd. 246 CB126
Gardenia Rd., Enf. 82 DS44
Gardenia Way, Wdf.Grn. 102 EH50
Harts Gro.
Gardens, The SE22 162 DU84
Gardens, The, Beck. 203 EC95
Gardens, The, Esher 214 CA105
Gardens, The, Felt. 175 BR86
Gardens, The, Har. 116 CC58
Gardens, The, Hat. 63 CY27
Gardens, The, Pnr. 116 BZ58
Gardens, The, Wat. 75 BT40
Gardiner Ave. NW2 119 CW64
Gardiner Clo., Dag. 126 EX63
Hewett Rd.
Gardiner Clo., Orp. 206 EW96
Gardner Clo. E11 124 EH58
Gardner Gro., Felt. 176 BZ89
Gardner Rd. E13 144 EH70
Gardner Rd., Guil. 242 AX134
Gardnor Rd. NW3 120 DD63
Flask Wk.
Garendon Gdns., Mord. 200 DB101
Garendon Rd., Mord. 200 DA101
Gareth Clo., Wor.Pk. 199 CX103
Burnham Dr.
Gareth Gro., Brom. 184 EG91
Garfield Pl., Wind. 151 AR82
Albany Rd.
Garfield Rd. E4 101 ED46
Garfield Rd. E13 144 EF70
Garfield Rd. SW11 160 DG83
Garfield Rd. SW19 180 DC92
Garfield Rd., Add. 212 BJ106
Garfield Rd., Enf. 82 DW42
Garfield Rd., Twick. 177 CG88
York St.
Garfield St., Wat. 75 BV38
Garford St. E14 143 EA73
Garganey Wk. SE28 146 EW73
Gargles Clo., Green. 189 FU85
Cowley Ave.
Garibaldi Rd., Red. 266 DF135
Garibaldi St. SE18 165 ES77
Garland Clo., Hem.H. 40 BK19
Garland Clo., Wal.Cr. 67 DY31
Shortmead Dr.
Garland Rd. SE18 165 ER80
Garland Rd., Stan. 96 CL53
Garland Rd., Ware 33 DY06
Garland Way, Cat. 236 DR122
Garland Way, Horn. 128 FL56
Garlands Ct., Croy. 220 DR105
Chatsworth Rd.
Garlands Rd., Lthd. 231 CH121
Garlands Rd., Red. 266 DF135
Garlic St., Dor. 246 BZ132
Garlichill Rd., Epsom 233 CV117
Garlick Hill EC4 275 J10
Garlick Hill EC4 142 DQ73
Garlies Rd. SE23 183 DY90
Garlinge Rd. NW2 139 CZ65
Garman Clo. N18 100 DR50
Garman Rd. N17 100 DW52
Garnault Ms. EC1 274 E3
Garnault Pl. EC1 274 E3
Garnault Rd., Enf. 82 DT38
Garner Dr., Brox. 67 DY26
Garner Rd. E17 101 EC53
Garner St. E2 142 DU68
Coate St.
Garners Clo., Ger.Cr. 91 AZ51
Garners End, Ger.Cr. 90 AY51
Garners Rd., Ger.Cr. 90 AY51
Garnet Clo., Slou. 151 AN75
Mitchell Clo.
Garnet Rd. NW10 138 CS65
Garnet Rd., Th.Hth. 202 DQ98
Garnet St. E1 142 DW73
Garnet Wk. E6 144 EL71
Kingfisher St.
Garnett Clo. SE9 165 EM83
Garnett Clo., Wat. 76 BX37
Garnett Dr., St.Alb. 60 BZ29
Garnett Rd. NW3 120 DF64
Garnett Way E17 101 DY53
McEntee Ave.
Garnham Clo. N16 122 DT61
Garnham St.
Garnham St. N16 122 DT61
Garnies Clo. SE15 162 DT80
Daniel Gdns.
Garnon Mead, Epp. 70 EX28
Garrad's Rd. SW16 181 DK90
Garrard Clo., Bexh. 166 FA83
Garrard Clo., Chis. 185 EP92
Garrard Rd., Bans. 234 DA116
Garrard Rd., Slou. 131 AL70
Garrard Wk. NW10 138 CS65
Garnet Rd.
Garratt Clo., Croy. 219 DL105
Garratt La. SW17 180 DD91
Garratt La. SW18 180 DB85
Garratt Rd., Edg. 96 CN52
Garratt Ter. SW17 180 DE91
Garratts La., Bans. 233 CZ116
Garratts Rd. (Bushey), Wat. 94 CC45
Garrett Clo. W3 138 CR71
Jenner Ave.
Garrett Clo., Chesh. 54 AR33
Garrett St. EC1 275 J4
Garrick Ave. NW11 119 CY58
Garrick Clo. SW18 160 DC84
Garrick Clo. W5 138 CL70
Garrick Clo., Islw. 157 CG83
Byfield Rd.
Garrick Clo., Rich. 177 CK85
The Grn.
Garrick Clo., Stai. 174 BG94
Garrick Clo., Walt. 213 BV105
Garrick Cres., Croy. 202 DS103
Garrick Dr. NW4 97 CW54
Garrick Dr. SE28 165 ER76
Broadwater Rd.
Garrick Gdns., W.Mol. 196 CA97
Garrick Pk. NW4 97 CX54
Garrick Rd. NW9 119 CT58
Garrick Rd., Grnf. 136 CB70
Garrick Rd., Rich. 158 CN82
Garrick St. WC2 273 P10
Garrick St. WC2 141 DL73
Garrick St., Grav. 191 GH86
Barrack Row
Garrick Way NW4 119 CX56
Garrison Clo. SE18 165 EN80
Red Lion La.
Garrison La., Chess. 215 CK108
Garrison Par., Purf. 168 FN77
Comet Clo.
Garrolds Clo., Swan. 207 FD96
Garron La., S.Ock. 149 FT72
Garry Clo., Rom. 105 FE52
Garry Way, Rom. 105 FE52
Garside Clo. SE28 165 ER76
Goosander Way
Garside Clo., Hmptn. 176 CB93
Garsington Ms. SE4 163 DZ83
Garsmouth Way, Wat. 76 BX36
Garson Gro., Chesh. 54 AN29
Garson La., Stai. 172 AX87
Garson Mead, Esher 214 BZ107
Garson Rd.
Garson Rd., Esher 214 BZ107
Garston Cres., Wat. 60 BW34
Garston Dr., Wat. 60 BW34
Garston La., Ken. 220 DR114
Garston La., Wat. 60 BX34
Garston Pk. Par., Wat. 60 BX34
Garstons, The, Lthd. 246 CA125
Garter Way SE16 163 DX75
Poolmans St.
Garth, The, Abb.L. 59 BR33
Garth, The, Cob. 214 BY113
Garth, The, Hmptn. 176 CB93
Uxbridge Rd.
Garth, The, Har. 118 CM58
Garth Clo. W4 158 CR78
Garth Clo., Kings.T. 178 CM92
Garth Clo., Mord. 199 CX101
Garth Clo., Ruis. 116 BX60
Garth Ct. W4 158 CR78
Garth Rd.
Garth Ms. W5 138 CL70
Greystoke Gdns.
Garth Rd. NW2 119 CZ61
Garth Rd. W4 158 CR79
Garth Rd., Kings.T. 178 CM92
Garth Rd., Mord. 199 CW100
Garth Rd., Sev. 257 FJ128
Garth Rd., S.Ock. 149 FW70
Garth Rd. Ind. Est., Mord. 199 CX101
Garthland Dr., Barn. 79 CV43
Garthorne Rd. SE23 183 DX87
Garthside, Rich. 178 CL92
Garthway N12 98 DE51
Gartlett Rd., Wat. 76 BW41
Gartmoor Gdns. SW19 179 CZ88
Gartmore Rd., Ilf. 125 ET61
Garton Pl. SW18 180 DC86
Gartons Clo., Enf. 82 DW42
Gartons Way SW11 160 DC83
Garvary Rd. E16 144 EH72
Garvin Ave., Beac. 89 AL53
Garvock Dr., Sev. 256 FG126
Garway Rd. W2 140 DB72
Gas Wks. La., Brox. 49 EA19
Gascoigne Gdns., Wdf.Grn. 102 EE52
Gascoigne Pl. E2 275 P2
Gascoigne Pl. E2 142 DT69
Gascoigne Rd., Bark. 145 EQ67
Gascoigne Rd., Croy. 221 EC110
Gascoigne Rd., Wey. 195 BP104
Gascons Gro., Slou. 131 AN70
Gascony Ave. NW6 140 DA66
Gascoyne Clo., Pot.B. 63 CU32
Gascoyne Clo., Rom. 106 FK52
Gascoyne Dr., Dart. 167 FF82
Gascoyne Rd. E9 143 DX66
Gascoyne Way, Hert. 32 DQ09
Gaselee St. E14 143 EC73
Gasholder Pl. SE11 161 DM78
Kennington La.
Gaskarth Rd. SW12 181 DH86
Gaskarth Rd., Edg. 96 CQ53
Gaskell Rd. N6 120 DF58
Gaskell St. SW4 161 DL82
Gaskin St. N1 141 DP67
Gaspar Clo. SW5 160 DB77
Courtfield Gdns.
Gaspar Ms. SW5 160 DB77
Courtfield Gdns.
Gassiot Rd. SW17 180 DF91
Gassiot Way, Sutt. 200 DD104
Gasson Rd., Swans. 190 FY86
Gastein Rd. W6 159 CX79
Gaston Bell Clo., Rich. 158 CM83
Gaston Bri. Rd., Shep. 195 BR100
Gaston Rd., Mitch. 200 DG97
Gaston Way, Shep. 195 BQ99
Gataker St. SE16 162 DV76
Gatcombe Rd. N19 121 DK62
Gatcombe Way, Barn. 80 DF41
Chalk La.
Gate Clo., Borwd. 78 CQ39
Gate End, Nthwd. 93 BU52
Gate Ho. Sq. SE1 142 DQ74
Southwark Bri. Rd.
Gate Ms. SW7 276 C5
Gate Ms. SW7 160 DE75
Gate St. WC2 274 B8
Gatecroft, Hem.H. 40 BM22
Gateforth St. NW8 272 B5
Gateforth St. NW8 140 DE70
Gatehill Rd., Nthwd. 93 BT52
Gatehope Dr., S.Ock. 149 FT72
Gatehouse Clo., Kings.T. 178 CQ94
Gateley Rd. SW9 161 DM83
Gates Grn. Rd., Kes. 222 EH105
Gates Grn. Rd., W.Wick. 204 EF104
Gatesborough St. EC2 275 M4
Gatesden Rd., Lthd. 230 CC123
Gateshead Rd., Borwd. 78 CM40
Gateside Rd. SW17 180 DF90
Gatestone Rd. SE19 182 DS93
Gateway SE17 162 DQ79
Gateway, Wey. 195 BP104
Palace Dr.
Gateway, The, Wok. 211 BB114
Gateway Arc. N1 141 DP68
Islington High St.
Gateway Clo., Nthwd. 93 BQ51
Gateway Ind. Est. NW10 139 CT69
Gateway Ms. E8 122 DT64
Shacklewell La.
Gateways, Guil. 243 BA134
Gateways, The SW3 276 C9
Gatewick Clo., Slou. 132 AW74
Gatfield Gro., Felt. 176 CA89
Gathorne Rd. N22 99 DN54
Gathorne St. E2 143 DX68
Mace St.
Gatley Ave., Epsom 216 CP106
Gatliff Rd. SW1 161 DH78
Gatling Rd. SE2 166 EU78
Gatting Clo., Edg. 96 CQ52
Pavilion Way
Gatting Way, Uxb. 134 BL65
Gatton Bottom, Red. 250 DG127
Gatton Bottom, Reig. 250 DC130
Gatton Clo., Reig. 250 DC131
Gatton Clo., Sutt. 218 DB109
Gatton Pk., Reig. 250 DG128
Gatton Pk. Rd., Red. 250 DD132
Gatton Pk. Rd., Reig. 250 DD132
Gatton Rd. SW17 180 DE91
Gatton Rd., Reig. 250 DC132
Gattons Way, Sid. 186 EZ91
Gatward Clo. N21 81 DP44
Gatward Grn. N9 100 DT47
Gatwick Gate, Craw. 268 DE154
Gatwick Rd. SW18 179 CZ87
Gatwick Rd., Gat. 268 DG154
Gatwick Rd., Grav. 191 GH90
Gatwick Way, Gat. 268 DF151
Gatwick Way, Horn. 128 FM63
Haydock Clo.
Gauden Clo. SW4 161 DK83
Gauden Rd. SW4 161 DK82
Gaumont App., Wat. 75 BV41
Gaumont Ter. W12 159 CW75
Lime Gro.
Gaunt St. SE1 278 G6
Gaunt St. SE1 162 DQ76
Gauntlet Clo., Nthlt. 136 BY66
Gauntlet Cres., Ken. 236 DR120
Gauntlett Ct., Wem. 117 CH64
Gauntlett Rd., Sutt. 218 DD106
Gautrey Rd. SE15 162 DW82
Gautrey Sq. E6 145 EM72
Truesdale Rd.
Gavel St. SE17 279 L8
Gavell Rd., Cob. 213 BU113
Gavenny Path, S.Ock. 149 FT72
Gaverick St. E14 163 EA77
Gaveston Dr., Berk. 38 AV17
Gaveston Rd., Lthd. 231 CG120
Gaveston Rd., Slou. 131 AM69
Gavestone Clo., W.Byf. 212 BM113
Gavestone Cres. SE12 184 EH87
Gavestone Rd. SE12 184 EH87
Gaviller Pl. E5 122 DV63
Clarence Rd.
Gavin St. SE18 165 ES77
Gavina Clo., Mord. 200 DD99
Gaviots Clo., Ger.Cr. 113 AZ60
Gaviots Grn., Ger.Cr. 112 AY60
Gaviots Way, Ger.Cr. 112 AY59
Gawber St. E2 142 DW69
Gawsworth Clo. E15 124 EE64
Ash Rd.
Gawthorne Ave. NW7 97 CY50
Lane App.
Gay Clo. NW2 119 CV64
Gay Gdns., Dag. 127 FC63
Gay Rd. E15 143 ED68
Gay St. SW15 159 CX83
Waterman St.
Gaydon Ho. W2 140 DB71
Gaydon La. NW9 96 CS53
Gayfere Rd., Epsom 217 CU106
Gayfere Rd., Ilf. 125 EM55
Gayfere St. SW1 277 P7
Gayfere St. SW1 161 DL76
Gayford Rd. W12 159 CT75
Gayhurst SE17 162 DR79
Hopwood Rd.
Gayhurst Rd. E8 142 DU66
Gayler Clo., Red. 252 DT133
Gaylor Rd., Nthlt. 116 BZ64
Gaylor Rd., Til. 170 GE81
Gaynes Ct., Upmin. 128 FP63
Gaynes Hill Rd., Wdf.Grn. 102 EL51
Gaynes Pk. Rd., Upmin. 128 FN63
Gaynes Rd., Upmin. 128 FP61
Gaynesford Rd. SE23 183 DX89
Gaynesford Rd., Cars. 218 DF108
Gaysham Ave., Ilf. 125 EN57
Gaysham Hall, Ilf. 125 EP55
Longwood Gdns.
Gayton Clo., Amer. 55 AS35
Gayton Ct., Har. 117 CF58
Gayton Cres. NW3 120 DD63
Gayton Rd. NW3 120 DD63
Gayton Rd. SE2 166 EW76
Florence Rd.
Gayton Rd., Har. 117 CF58
Gayville Rd. SW11 180 DF86
Gaywood Ave. (Cheshunt), Wal.Cr. 67 DX30
Gaywood Clo. SW2 181 DM88
Gaywood Est. SE1 278 G7
Gaywood Rd. E17 123 EA55
Gaywood Rd., Ash. 232 CM118
Gaywood St. SE1 278 G7
Gaza St. SE17 161 DP78
Braganza St.
Gazelda Vill., Wat. 76 BX43
Lower High St.
Gazelle Glade, Grav. 191 GM92
Gean Wk., Hat. 45 CU21
Southdown Rd.
Geariesville Gdns., Ilf. 125 EP56
Geary Clo., Horl. 269 DP150
Geary Dr., Brwd. 108 FW46
Geary Rd. NW10 119 CU64
Geary St. N7 121 DM64
GEC Est., Wem. 117 CK62
Geddes Pl., Bexh. 166 FA84
Market Pl.
Geddes Rd. (Bushey), Wat. 76 CC42
Geddings Rd., Hodd. 49 EB17
Gedeney Rd. N17 100 DQ53
Gedling Pl. SE1 162 DT76
Gee St. EC1 275 H4
Gee St. EC1 142 DQ70
Geere Rd. E15 144 EF67
Gees Ct. W1 272 G9
Geffrye Ct. N1 275 N1
Geffrye Est. N1 142 DS68
Stanway St.
Geffrye St. E2 275 P1
Geffrye St. E2 142 DT68
Geisthorp Ct., Wal.Abb. 68 EG33
Winters Way
Geldart Rd. SE15 162 DV80
Geldeston Rd. E5 122 DU61
Gell Clo., Uxb. 114 BM62
Gellatly Rd. SE14 162 DW82
Gelsthorpe Rd., Rom. 105 FB52
Gemini Gro., Nthlt. 136 BY69
Javelin Way
General Gordon Pl. SE18 165 EP77
General Wolfe Rd. SE10 163 ED81
Generals Wk., The, Enf. 83 DY37
Genesta Rd. SE18 165 EP79
Geneva Clo., Shep. 195 BS96
Geneva Dr. SW9 161 DN84
Geneva Gdns., Rom. 126 EY57
Geneva Rd., Kings.T. 198 CL98
Geneva Rd., Th.Hth. 202 DQ99
Genever Clo. E4 101 EA50
Genista Rd. N18 100 DV50
Genoa Ave. SW15 179 CW85
Genoa Rd. SE20 202 DW95
Genotin Rd., Enf. 82 DR41

Genotin Ter., Enf. 82 DR41
Genotin Rd.
Gentian Row SE13 163 EC81
Sparta St.
Gentlemans Row, Enf. 82 DQ41
Gentry Gdns. E13 144 EG70
Whitwell Rd.
Genyn Rd., Guil. 258 AV135
Geoffrey Ave., Rom. 106 FN51
Geoffrey Clo. SE5 162 DQ82
Geoffrey Gdns. E6 144 EL68
Geoffrey Rd. SE4 163 DZ83
George Avey Cft., Epp. 71 FB26
George Beard Rd. SE8 163 DZ77
George Comberton Wk. E12 125 EN64
Gainsborough Ave.
George Ct. WC2 278 A1
George Cres. N10 98 DG52
George Downing Est. N16 122 DT61
Cazenove Rd.
George V Ave., Pnr. 94 BZ53
George V Clo., Pnr. 116 CA55
George V Ave.
George V Way, Grnf. 137 CH67
George V Way, Rick. 74 BG36
George Gange Way, Har. 117 CE55
High St.
George Grn. Dr., Slou. 133 AZ72
George Grn. Rd., Slou. 132 AX72
George Gro. Rd. SE20 202 DU95
George Inn Yd. SE1 279 K3
George La. E18 102 EG54
George La. SE13 183 EC86
George La., Brom. 204 EH102
George Lansbury Ho. N22 99 DN53
Progress Way
George Loveless Ho. E2 142 DT69
Diss St.
George Lowe Ct. W2 140 DB71
Bourne Ter.
George Ms. NW1 273 K3
George Ms., Enf. 82 DR41
Sydney Rd.
George Pl. N17 122 DS55
Dongola Rd.
George Rd. E4 101 EA51
George Rd., Gdmg. 258 AS144
George Rd., Guil. 242 AX134
George Rd., Kings.T. 178 CP94
George Rd., N.Mal. 199 CT98
George Row SE16 162 DU75
George Sq. SW19 199 CZ97
Mostyn Rd.
George St. E16 144 EF72
George St. W1 272 D8
George St. W1 140 DF72
George St. W7 137 CE74
The Bdy.
George St., Bark. 145 EQ66
George St., Berk. 38 AX19
George St., Chesh. 54 AQ30
Berkhampstead Rd.
George St., Croy. 202 DQ103
George St., Grays 170 GA79
George St., Hem.H. 40 BK19
George St., Hert. 32 DQ09
George St., Houns. 156 BZ82
George St., Rich. 177 CK85
George St., Rom. 127 FF58
George St., St.Alb. 43 CD20
George St., Sthl. 156 BY77
George St., Stai. 173 BF91
George St., Sutt. 218 DB106
George St., Uxb. 134 BK66
George St., Wat. 76 BW42
George Wyver Clo. SW19 179 CY87
Beaumont Rd.
George Yd. EC3 275 L9
George Yd. W1 272 G10
George Yd. W1 140 DG73
Georgelands (Ripley), Wok. 228 BH121
Georges Clo., Orp. 206 EW97
Georges Dr., Brwd. 108 FT43
Georges Dr., H.Wyc. 110 AC56
Georges Mead, Borwd. 77 CK44
George's Rd. N7 121 DM64
Georges Rd., Brom. 205 EM97
Georges Rd., West. 238 EK120
Georges Sq. SW6 159 CZ79
North End Rd.
Georges Ter., Cat. 236 DR122
George's Wd. Rd., Hat. 64 DA26
Georgetown Clo. SE19 182 DR92
St. Kitts Ter.
Georgette Pl. SE10 163 EC80
King George St.
Georgeville Gdns., Ilf. 125 EP56
Georgewood Rd., Hem.H. 58 BM25
Georgia Rd., N.Mal. 198 CQ98
Georgia Rd., Th.Hth. 201 DP95
Georgian Clo., Brom. 204 EH101
Georgian Clo., Stai. 174 BH91
Georgian Clo., Stan. 95 CG52
Georgian Clo., Uxb. 114 BL63
Georgian Ct. SW16 181 DL91
Gleneldon Rd.
Georgian Ct., Wem. 138 CN65
Georgian Way, Har. 117 CD61
Georgiana St. NW1 141 DJ67
Georgina Gdns. E2 142 DT69
Columbia Rd.
Geraint Rd., Brom. 184 EG91
Gerald Ms. SW1 276 G8
Gerald Rd. E16 144 EF70
Gerald Rd. SW1 276 G8
Gerald Rd. SW1 160 DG77
Gerald Rd., Dag. 126 EZ61
Gerald Rd., Grav. 191 GL87
Gerald Sq. SW1 160 DG77
Eccleston St.
Geraldine Rd. SW18 180 DC85
Geraldine Rd. W4 158 CN79
Geraldine St. SE11 278 F7
Geraldine St. SE11 161 DP76
Geralds Gro., Bans. 217 CX114
Gerard Ave., Houns. 176 CA87
Redfern Ave.
Gerard Gdns., Rain. 147 FE68
Gerard Rd. SW13 159 CT81
Gerard Rd., Har. 117 CG58
Gerards Clo. SE16 162 DW78
Gerda Rd. SE9 185 EQ89
Gerdview Dr., Dart. 188 FJ91
Germain St., Chesh. 54 AP32
Germains Clo., Chesh. 54 AP32
Germander Way E15 144 EE69
Gernon Clo., Rain. 148 FK68
Jordans Way
Gernon Rd. E3 143 DY68
Geron Way NW2 119 CV61
Gerpins La., Upmin. 148 FM68
Gerrard Cres., Brwd. 108 FW48
Gerrard Gdns., Pnr. 115 BU57
Gerrard Pl. W1 273 N10
Gerrard Rd. N1 141 DP68
Gerrard St. W1 273 N10
Gerrard St. W1 141 DK73
Gerrards Clo. N14 81 DJ43
Gerrards Cross Rd., Slou. 132 AU66
Gerrards Mead, Bans. 233 CZ117
Garratts La.
Gerridge St. SE1 278 E6
Gerridge St. SE1 161 DN76
Gerry Raffles Sq. E15 143 ED65
Salway Rd.
Gertrude Rd., Belv. 166 FA77
Gertrude St. SW10 160 DC79
Gervase Clo., Wem. 118 CQ62
Gervase Rd., Edg. 96 CQ53
Gervase St. SE15 162 DV80
Gews Cor. (Cheshunt), Wal.Cr. 67 DX29
Ghent St. SE6 183 EA89
Ghent Way E8 142 DT65
Giant Tree Hill (Bushey), Wat. 95 CD46
Gibb Cft., Harl. 51 ES19
Gibbard Ms. SW19 179 CX92
Gibbfield Clo., Rom. 126 EY55
Rose La.
Gibbins Rd. E15 143 EC66
Gibbon Rd. SE15 162 DW82
Gibbon Rd. W3 138 CS73
Gibbon Rd., Kings.T. 198 CL95
Gibbon Wk. SW15 159 CU84
Swinburne Rd.
Gibbons Clo., Borwd. 78 CL39
Gibbons Rd. NW10 138 CS65
Gibbs Ave. SE19 182 DR92
Gibbs Clo. SE19 182 DR92
Gibbs Clo. (Cheshunt), Wal.Cr. 67 DX29
Gibbs Couch, Wat. 94 BX48
Gibbs Grn. W14 159 CZ78
Gibbs Grn., Edg. 96 CQ50
Gibbs Rd. N18 100 DW49
Gibbs Sq. SE19 182 DR92
Gibraltar Clo., Brwd. 107 FW51
Essex Way
Gibraltar Cres., Epsom 216 CS110
Gibraltar Ho., Brwd. 107 FW51
Gibraltar Wk. E2 142 DT69
Gibson Clo. E1 142 DW70
Colebert Ave.
Gibson Clo. N21 81 DN44
Green Dragon La.
Gibson Clo., Chess. 215 CJ107
Gibson Clo., Epp. 71 FC25
Beamish Clo.
Gibson Clo., Grav. 191 GF90
Gibson Clo., Islw. 157 CD83
Gibson Ct., Slou. 153 AZ78
Gibson Gdns. N16 122 DT61
Northwold Rd.
Gibson Pl., Stai. 174 BJ86
Gibson Rd. SE11 278 C9
Gibson Rd. SE11 161 DM77
Gibson Rd., Dag. 126 EW60
Gibson Rd., Sutt. 218 DB106
Gibson Rd., Uxb. 114 BM63
Gibson Sq. N1 141 DN67
Gibson St. SE10 164 EE78
Gibson's Hill SW16 181 DN94
Gidd Hill, Couls. 234 DG116
Gidea Ave., Rom. 127 FG55
Gidea Clo., Rom. 127 FG55
Gidea Clo., S.Ock. 149 FW69
Tyssen Pl.
Gideon Clo., Belv. 167 FB77
Gideon Rd. SW11 160 DG83
Gidian Ct., St.Alb. 61 CD27
Giesbach Rd. N19 121 DJ61
Giffard Rd. N18 100 DS50
Giffard Way, Guil. 242 AU131
Stoughton Rd.
Giffin St. SE8 163 EA80
Gifford Gdns. W7 137 CD71
Gifford Pl., Brwd. 108 FX50
Blackthorn Way
Gifford St. N1 141 DL66
Giffordside, Grays 171 GH78
Gift La. E15 144 EF67
Giggs Hill, Orp. 206 EU96
Giggs Hill Gdns., T.Ditt. 197 CG102
Giggs Hill Rd., T.Ditt. 197 CG101
Gilbert Clo. SE18 165 EM81
Shooter's Hill Rd.
Gilbert Clo., Swans. 189 FX86
Gilbert Gro., Edg. 96 CR53
Gilbert Ho. EC2 142 DQ71
Fore St.
Gilbert Ho. SE8 163 EA79
McMillan St.
Gilbert Pl. WC1 273 P7
Gilbert Rd. SE11 278 E9
Gilbert Rd. SE11 161 DN77
Gilbert Rd. SW19 180 DC94
Gilbert Rd., Belv. 166 FA76
Gilbert Rd., Brom. 184 EG94
Gilbert Rd., Grays 169 FW76
Arterial Rd. W. Thurrock
Gilbert Rd., Pnr. 116 BX56
Gilbert Rd., Rom. 127 FF56
Gilbert Rd., Uxb. 92 BK54
Gilbert St. E15 124 EE63
Gilbert St. W1 272 G9
Gilbert St. W1 140 DG72
Gilbert St., Enf. 82 DW37
Gilbert St., Houns. 156 CC83
High St.
Gilbert Way, Berk. 38 AU19
Gilbey Clo., Uxb. 115 BP63
Gilbey Rd. SW17 180 DE91
Gilbey Wk., H.Wyc. 110 AD59
Stratford Dr.
Gilbeys Yd. NW1 141 DH67
Oval Rd.
Gilbourne Rd. SE18 165 ET79
Gilda Ave., Enf. 83 DY43
Gilda Cres. N16 122 DU60
Gildea St. W1 273 J7
Gilden Clo., Harl. 36 EY11
Gilden Cres. NW5 120 DG64
Gilden Way, Harl. 36 EW12
Gildenhill Rd., Swan. 188 FJ93
Gilders, Saw. 36 EX05
Gilders Rd., Chess. 216 CM108
Gildersome St. SE18 165 EN79
Nightingale Vale
Giles Clo., Rain. 148 FK68
Giles Coppice SE19 182 DT91
Giles Travers Clo., Egh. 193 BC97
Gilfrid Clo., Uxb. 135 BP72
Craig Dr.
Gilhams Ave., Bans. 217 CX112
Gilkes Cres. SE21 182 DS86
Gilkes Pl. SE21 182 DS86
Gill Ave. E16 144 EG72
Gill Cres., Grav. 191 GF90
Gill St. E14 143 DZ73
Gillam Way, Rain. 147 FG65
Gillan Grn. (Bushey), Wat. 94 CC47
Gillender St. E3 143 EC70
Gillender St. E14 143 EC70
Gillespie Rd. N5 121 DN62
Gillett Ave. E6 144 EL68
Gillett Pl. N16 122 DS64
Gillett St.
Gillett Rd., Th.Hth. 202 DR98
Gillett St. N16 122 DS64
Gillfoot NW1 273 K1
Gillfoot NW1 141 DJ68
Gillham Ter. N17 100 DU51
Gilliam Gro., Pur. 219 DN110
Gillian Ave., St.Alb. 42 CC24
Gillian Cres., Rom. 106 FJ54
Gillian Pk. Rd., Sutt. 199 CZ102
Gillian St. SE13 183 EB85
Gilliat Clo., Iver 133 BE72
Dutton Way
Gilliat Dr., Guil. 243 BD132
Gilliat Rd., Slou. 132 AS73
Gilliat's Grn., Rick. 73 BD42
Gillies St. NW5 120 DG64
Gilling Ct. NW3 140 DE65
Gillingham Ms. SW1 277 K8
Gillingham Rd. NW2 119 CY62
Gillingham Row SW1 277 K8
Gillingham St. SW1 277 J8
Gillingham St. SW1 161 DJ77
Gillison Wk. SE16 162 DU76
Tranton Rd.
Gillman Dr. E15 144 EF67
Gillmans Rd., Orp. 206 EV102
Gills Hill, Rad. 77 CF35
Gills Hill La., Rad. 77 CF36
Gills Hollow, Rad. 77 CF36
Gill's Rd., Dart. 209 FS95
Gillum Clo., Barn. 98 DF46
Gilmais, Lthd. 246 CC125
Gilman Cres., Wind. 151 AK83
Gilmore Clo., Slou. 152 AW75
Gilmore Clo., Uxb. 114 BN62
Gilmore Cres., Ashf. 174 BN92
Gilmore Rd. SE13 163 ED84
Gilmour Clo., Wal.Cr. 82 DU35
Gilpin Ave. SW14 158 CR84
Gilpin Clo., Mitch. 200 DE96
Gilpin Cres. N18 100 DT50
Gilpin Cres., Twick. 176 CB87
Gilpin Rd. E5 123 DY63
Gilpin Rd., Ware 33 DY07
Gilpin Way, Hayes 155 BR80
Gilpin's Gallop, Ware 33 EB11
Gilpins Ride, Berk. 38 AX18
Gilroy Clo., Rain. 147 FF65
Gilroy Way, Orp. 206 EV101
Gilsland, Wal.Abb. 84 EE35
Gilsland Rd., Th.Hth. 202 DR98
Gilstead Ho., Bark. 146 EV68
Gilstead Rd. SW6 160 DB82
Gilston Rd. SW10 160 DC78
Gilton Rd. SE6 184 EE90
Giltspur St. EC1 274 G8
Giltspur St. EC1 141 DP72
Gilwell Clo. E4 83 EB42
Antlers Hill
Gilwell La. E4 83 ED42
Gilwell Pk. E4 83 EC41
Gimcrack Hill, Lthd. 231 CH123
Dorking Rd.
Gippeswyck Clo., Pnr. 94 BX53
Uxbridge Rd.
Gipsy Hill SE19 182 DS92
Gipsy La. SW15 159 CU83
Gipsy La., Grays 170 GC79
Gipsy Rd. SE27 182 DQ91
Gipsy Rd., Well. 166 EX81
Gipsy Rd. Gdns. SE27 182 DQ91
Giralda Clo. E16 144 EK71
Fulmer Rd.
Giraud St. E14 143 EB72
Girdlers Rd. W14 159 CX77
Girdlestone Wk. N19 121 DJ61
Girdwood Rd. SW18 179 CY87
Girling Way, Felt. 155 BU83
Gironde Rd. SW6 159 CZ80
Girtin Rd. (Bushey), Wat. 76 CB43
Girton Ave. NW9 118 CN55
Girton Clo., Nthlt. 136 CC65
Girton Ct., Wal.Cr. 67 DY30
Girton Gdns., Croy. 203 EA104
Girton Rd. SE26 183 DX92
Girton Rd., Nthlt. 136 CC65
Girton Vill. W10 139 CX72
Cambridge Gdns.
Girton Way, Rick. 75 BQ43
Gisborne Gdns., Rain. 147 FF69
Gisbourne Clo., Wall. 201 DK104
Streeters La.
Gisburn Rd. N8 121 DM56
Gisburne Ho., Wat. 75 BU37
Gisburne Way, Wat. 75 BU37
Howard Clo.
Gissing Wk. N1 141 DN66
Lofting Rd.
Gittens Clo., Brom. 184 EF91
Durham Hill
Given Wilson Wk. E13 144 EF68
Stride Rd.
Givons Gro., Lthd. 247 CH125
Glacier Way, Wem. 137 CK68
Gladbeck Way, Enf. 81 DP43
Gladding Rd. E12 124 EK63
Glade, The N21 81 DM44
Glade, The SE7 164 EJ80
Glade, The, Brwd. 109 GA46
Glade, The, Brom. 204 EK96
Glade, The, Couls. 235 DN119
Glade, The, Croy. 203 DX99
Glade, The, Enf. 81 DN41
Chase Ridings
Glade, The, Epsom 217 CU106
Glade, The, Ger.Cr. 112 AX60
Glade, The, H.Wyc. 88 AC46
Glade, The, Ilf. 103 EM53
Glade, The, Lthd. 230 CA122
Glade, The, Sev. 257 FH123
Glade, The, Stai. 174 BH94
Glade, The, Sutt. 217 CY109
Glade, The, Tad. 234 DA121
Glade, The, Upmin. 128 FQ64
Glade, The, Welw.G.C. 29 CW07
Glade, The, W.Byf. 211 BE113
Glade, The, W.Wick. 203 EB104
Glade, The, Wdf.Grn. 102 EH48
Glade Clo., Hem.H. 40 BH17
Glade Clo., Surb. 197 CK103
Glade Ct., Ilf. 103 EM53
The Glade
Glade Gdns., Croy. 203 DY101
Glade La., Sthl. 156 CB75
Glade Spur, Tad. 234 DB121
Glades, The, Grav. 191 GK93
Glades, The, Hem.H. 39 BE19
Glades Pl., Brom. 204 EG96
Glades Shop. Cen., The, Brom. 204 EG96
Gladeside N21 99 DM45
Gladeside, Croy. 203 DX101
Gladeside, St.Alb. 43 CK17
Gladeside Clo., Chess. 215 CK108
Leatherhead Rd.
Gladeside Ct., Warl. 236 DV120
Gladesmore Rd. N15 122 DT58
Gladeswood Rd., Belv. 167 FB77
Gladeway, The, Wal.Abb. 67 ED33
Gladiator St. SE23 183 DY87
Glading Ter. N16 122 DT62
Gladioli Clo., Hmptn. 176 CA93
Gresham Rd.
Gladsdale Dr., Pnr. 115 BV56
Gladsmuir Clo., Walt. 196 BW103
Gladsmuir Rd. N19 121 DJ60
Gladsmuir Rd., Barn. 79 CY40
Gladstone Ave. E12 144 EL66
Gladstone Ave. N22 99 DN54
Gladstone Ave., Felt. 175 BU86
Gladstone Ave., Twick. 177 CD87
Gladstone Clo., Ware 33 DX05
High Oak Rd.
Gladstone Ms. NW6 139 CZ66
Cavendish Rd.
Gladstone Ms. SE20 182 DW94
Gladstone Pk. Gdns. NW2 119 CV63
Gladstone Pl. E3 143 DZ68
Roman Rd.
Gladstone Pl., Barn. 79 CX42
Gladstone Rd. SW19 180 DA94
Gladstone Rd. W4 158 CR76
Acton La.
Gladstone Rd., Ash. 231 CK118
Gladstone Rd., Buck.H. 102 EH46
Gladstone Rd., Chesh. 54 AQ31
Gladstone Rd., Croy. 202 DR101
Gladstone Rd., Dart. 188 FM86
Gladstone Rd., Hodd. 49 EB16
Gladstone Rd., Kings.T. 198 CN97
Gladstone Rd., Orp. 223 EQ106
Gladstone Rd., Sthl. 156 BY75
Gladstone Rd., Surb. 197 CK103
Gladstone Rd., Ware 33 DX05
Gladstone Rd., Wat. 76 BW41
Gladstone St. SE1 278 F6
Gladstone St. SE1 161 DP76
Gladstone Ter. SE27 182 DQ91
Gladstone Ter. SW8 161 DH81
Gladstone Way, Har. 117 CE55
Gladstone Way, Slou. 131 AN74
Gladwell Rd. N8 121 DM58
Gladwell Rd., Brom. 184 EG93
Gladwyn Rd. SW15 159 CX83
Gladys Rd. NW6 140 DA66
Glaisher St. SE10 163 EC80
Straightsmouth
Glaisyer Way, Iver 133 BC68
Glamis Clo. (Cheshunt), Wal.Cr. 66 DU29
Glamis Cres., Hayes 155 BQ76
Glamis Dr., Horn. 128 FL60
Glamis Pl. E1 142 DW73
Glamis Rd. E1 142 DW73
Glamis Way, Nthlt. 136 CC65
Glamorgan Clo., Mitch. 201 DL97
Glamorgan Rd., Kings.T. 177 CJ94
Glanfield, Hem.H. 40 BL17
Bathurst Rd.
Glanfield Rd., Beck. 203 DZ98
Glanleam Rd., Stan. 95 CK49
Glanmead, Brwd. 108 FY46
Glanmor Rd., Slou. 132 AV73
Glanthams Clo., Brwd. 109 FZ47
Glanthams Rd., Brwd. 109 FZ47
Glanty, The, Egh. 173 BB91
Glanville Dr., Horn. 128 FM60
Glanville Rd. SW2 181 DL85
Glanville Rd., Brom. 204 EH97
Glasbrook Ave., Twick. 176 BZ88
Glasbrook Rd. SE9 184 EK87
Glaserton Rd. N16 122 DS59
Glasford St. SW17 180 DF93
Glasgow Ho. W9 140 DB68
Glasgow Rd. E13 144 EH68
Glasgow Rd. N18 100 DV50
Aberdeen Rd.
Glasgow Rd., Slou. 131 AN72
Glasgow Ter. SW1 161 DJ78
Glass St. E2 142 DV70
Coventry Rd.
Glass Yd. SE18 165 EN76
Glasse Clo. W13 137 CG73
Glasshill St. SE1 278 G4
Glasshill St. SE1 161 DP75
Glasshouse All. EC4 274 E9
Glasshouse Flds. E1 143 DX73
Glasshouse St. W1 277 L1
Glasshouse St. W1 141 DJ73
Glasshouse Wk. SE11 278 A10
Glasshouse Wk. SE11 161 DL78
Glasshouse Yd. EC1 275 H5
Glasslyn Rd. N8 121 DK57
Glassmill La., Brom. 204 EF96
Glastonbury Ave., Wdf.Grn. 102 EK52
Glastonbury Rd. N9 100 DU46
Glastonbury Rd., Mord. 200 DA101
Glastonbury St. NW6 119 CZ64
Glaucus St. E3 143 EB71
Glazbury Rd. W14 159 CY77
Glazebrook Clo. SE21 182 DR89
Glazebrook Rd., Tedd. 177 CF94
Glean Wk., Hat. 45 CU21
Southdown Rd.
Gleave Clo., St.Alb. 43 CH19
Glebe, The SE3 164 EE83
Glebe, The SW16 181 DK91
Glebe, The, Chis. 205 EQ95
Glebe, The, Horl. 268 DF148
Glebe, The, Kings L. 58 BN29
Glebe, The, Reig. 265 CU141
Glebe, The, Wat. 60 BX33
Glebe, The, West Dr. 154 BM77
Glebe, The, Wor.Pk. 199 CT102
Glebe Ave., Enf. 81 DP41
Glebe Ave., Har. 118 CL55
Glebe Ave., Mitch. 200 DE96
Glebe Ave., Ruis. 135 BV65
Glebe Ave., Uxb. 115 BQ62
Glebe Ave., Wdf.Grn. 102 EG51
Glebe Clo. W4 158 CS78
Glebe St.
Glebe Clo., Ger.Cr. 90 AX52
Glebe Clo., Hat. 46 DF17
Glebe Clo., Hem.H. 40 BL23
Glebe Clo., Lthd. 246 CA126
Glebe Clo., S.Croy. 220 DT111
Glebe Clo., Uxb. 115 BQ63
Glebe Cotts., Guil. 244 BH132
Glebe Cotts., Hat. 46 DF17
Glebe Cotts., Sutt. 218 DB105
Vale Rd.
Glebe Cotts., West. 240 EV123
Glebe Ct. W7 137 CD73
Glebe Ct., Guil. 243 AZ134
Glebe Ct., Mitch. 200 DF97
Glebe Ct., Stan. 95 CJ50
Glebe Rd.
Glebe Cres. NW4 119 CW56
Glebe Cres., Har. 118 CL55
Glebe Gdns., N.Mal. 198 CS101
Glebe Gdns., W.Byf. 212 BK114
Glebe Ho. Dr., Brom. 204 EH102
Glebe Hyrst SE19 182 DT91
Giles Coppice
Glebe Hyrst, S.Croy. 220 DT112
Glebe La., Barn. 79 CU43
Glebe La., Dor. 262 BX143
Glebe La., Har. 118 CL56
Glebe La., Sev. 257 FH126
Glebe Path, Mitch. 200 DE97
Glebe Pl. SW3 160 DE79
Glebe Pl. (Horton Kirby), Dart. 208 FQ98
Glebe Rd. E8 142 DT66
Middleton Rd.
Glebe Rd. N3 98 DC53
Glebe Rd. N8 121 DM56
Glebe Rd. NW10 139 CT65
Glebe Rd. SW13 159 CU82
Glebe Rd., Ash. 231 CK118
Glebe Rd., Brom. 204 EG95
Glebe Rd., Cars. 218 DF107
Glebe Rd., Dag. 147 FB65
Glebe Rd., Dor. 263 CF136
Glebe Rd., Egh. 173 BC93
Glebe Rd., Ger.Cr. 90 AW53
Glebe Rd., Grav. 191 GF88
Glebe Rd., Hayes 135 BT74
Glebe Rd., Hert. 32 DR07
Glebe Rd., Rain. 147 FH69
Glebe Rd., Red. 235 DH124
Glebe Rd., Stai. 174 BH92
Glebe Rd., Stan. 95 CJ50
Glebe Rd., Sutt. 217 CY109
Glebe Rd., Uxb. 134 BJ68
Glebe Rd., Warl. 237 DX117
Glebe Rd., Wind. 172 AV85
Glebe Side, Twick. 177 CF87
Glebe St. W4 158 CS78
Glebe Ter. E3 143 EA69
Bow Rd.
Glebe Way, Amer. 55 AR36
Glebe Way, Erith 167 FE79
Glebe Way, Felt. 176 CA90
Glebe Way, Horn. 128 FL59
Glebe Way, S.Croy. 220 DT112
Glebe Way, W.Wick. 203 EC103
Glebefield, The, Sev. 256 FF123
Amherst Hill
Glebeland, Hat. 45 CW18
St. Ethelreda's Dr.
Glebeland Gdns., Shep. 195 BQ100
Glebelands, Chig. 104 EV48
Glebelands, Dart. 167 FF84
Glebelands, Esher 215 CF109
Glebelands, Harl. 35 ET12
Glebelands, H.Wyc. 88 AC47
Glebelands, W.Mol. 196 CB99
Glebelands Ave. E18 102 EG54
Glebelands Ave., Ilf. 125 ER59
Glebelands Clo. SE5 162 DS83
Grove Hill Rd.
Glebelands Rd., Felt. 175 BU87
Glebeway, Wdf.Grn. 102 EJ50
Gledhow Gdns. SW5 160 DC77
Gledhow Wd., Tad. 234 DB121
Gledstanes Rd. W14 159 CY78
Gledwood Ave., Hayes 135 BT71
Gledwood Cres., Hayes 135 BT71
Gledwood Dr., Hayes 135 BT71
Gledwood Gdns., Hayes 135 BT71
Gleed Ave. (Bushey), Wat. 95 CD47
Gleeson Dr., Orp. 223 ET106
Glegg Pl. SW15 159 CX84
Glen, The, Add. 211 BF106
Glen, The, Brom. 204 EE96
Glen, The, Croy. 203 DX104
Glen, The, Enf. 81 DP42
Glen, The, Hem.H. 40 BM15
Glen, The, Nthwd. 93 BR52
Glen, The, Orp. 205 EM104
Glen, The, Pnr. 115 BV57
Glen, The (Eastcote), Pnr. 116 BY59
Glen, The, Rain. 148 FJ70
Glen, The, Slou. 152 AW77
Glen, The, Sthl. 156 BZ78
Glen, The, Wem. 117 CK63
Glen Albyn Rd. SW19 179 CX89
Glen Ave., Ashf. 174 BN91
Glen Clo., Shep. 194 BN98
Glen Clo., Tad. 233 CY123
Glen Cres., Wdf.Grn. 102 EH51
Glen Faba Rd., Harl. 50 EF17
Glen Gdns., Croy. 201 DP104
Glen Mill, Hmptn. 176 BZ92
Glen Ri., Wdf.Grn. 102 EH51
Glen Rd. E13 144 EJ70

Glen Rd. E17 123 DZ57
Glen Rd., Chess. 198 CL104
Glen Rd. End, Wall. 219 DH109
Glen Ter. E14 163 EC75
Manchester Rd.
Glen Vw., Grav. 191 GJ88
Glen Wk., Islw. 177 CD85
Glen Way, Wat. 75 BS38
Glena Mt., Sutt. 218 DC105
Glenaffric Ave. E14 163 ED77
Glenalla Rd., Ruis. 115 BT59
Glenalmond Rd., Har. 118 CL56
Glenalvon Way SE18 164 EL77
Glenarm Rd. E5 122 DW64
Glenavon Clo., Esher 215 CG107
Glenavon Gdns., Slou. 152 AW77
Glenavon Rd. E15 144 EE66
Glenbarr Clo. SE9 165 EP83
Dumbreck Rd.
Glenbow Rd., Brom. 184 EE93
Glenbrook N., Enf. 81 DM42
Glenbrook Rd. NW6 120 DA64
Glenbrook S., Enf. 81 DM42
Glenbuck Ct., Surb. 197 CK100
Glenbuck Rd.
Glenbuck Rd., Surb. 197 CK100
Glenburnie Rd. SW17 180 DE90
Glencairn Dr. W5 137 CJ70
Glencairn Rd. SW16 181 DL94
Glencairne Clo. E16 144 EK71
Glencoe Ave., Ilf. 125 ER59
Glencoe Dr., Dag. 126 FA63
Glencoe Rd., Hayes 136 BX70
Glencoe Rd. (Bushey), Wat. 76 CA44
Glencoe Rd., Wey. 194 BN104
Glencourse Grn., Wat. 94 BX49
Caldwell Rd.
Glendale, Hem.H. 40 BH20
Glendale, Swan. 207 FF99
Glendale Ave. N22 99 DN52
Glendale Ave., Edg. 96 CN49
Glendale Ave., Rom. 126 EW59
Glendale Clo. SE9 165 EN83
Dumbreck Rd.
Glendale Clo., Brwd. 108 FY46
Glendale Clo., Wok. 226 AW118
Glendale Dr. SW19 179 CZ92
Glendale Dr., Guil. 243 BC131
Glendale Gdns., Wem. 117 CK60
Glendale Ms., Beck. 203 EB95
Glendale Ri., Ken. 235 DP115
Glendale Rd., Erith 167 FC77
Glendale Rd., Grav. 190 GE91
Glendale Wk. (Cheshunt), Wal.Cr. 67 DY30
Glendale Way SE28 146 EW73
Glendall St. SW9 161 DM84
Glendarvon St. SW15 159 CX83
Glendene Ave., Lthd. 245 BS126
Glendevon Clo., Edg. 96 CP48
Tayside Dr.
Glendish Rd. N17 100 DU53
Glendor Gdns. NW7 96 CR49
Glendower Cres., Orp. 206 EU100
Glendower Gdns. SW14 158 CR83
Glendower Rd.
Glendower Pl. SW7 160 DD77
Glendower Rd. E4 101 ED46
Glendower Rd. SW14 158 CR83
Glendown Rd. SE2 166 EU78
Glendun Rd. W3 138 CS73
Gleneagle Ms. SW16 181 DK92
Ambleside Ave.
Gleneagle Rd. SW16 181 DK93
Gleneagles, Stan. 95 CH51
Gleneagles Clo. SE16 162 DV78
Credon Rd.
Gleneagles Clo., Orp. 205 ER102
Gleneagles Clo., Rom. 106 FM52
Gleneagles Clo., Stai. 174 BK86
Gleneagles Clo., Stan. 95 CH51
Gleneagles Clo., Wat. 94 BX49
Gleneagles Grn., Orp. 205 ER102
Tandridge Dr.
Gleneagles Twr., Sthl. 136 CC72
Gleneldon Ms. SW16 181 DL91
Gleneldon Rd. SW16 181 DL91
Glenelg Rd. SW2 181 DL85
Glenesk Rd. SE9 165 EN83
Glenester Clo., Hodd. 33 EA14
Glenfarg Rd. SE6 183 ED88
Glenferrie Rd., St.Alb. 43 CG20
Glenfield Clo., Bet. 264 CP138
Glenfield Cres., Ruis. 115 BR59
Glenfield Rd. SW12 181 DJ88
Glenfield Rd. W13 157 CH75
Glenfield Rd., Ashf. 175 BP93
Glenfield Rd., Bans. 234 DB115
Glenfield Rd., Bet. 264 CP138
Glenfield Ter. W13 137 CH74
Glenfinlas Way SE5 161 DP80
Glenforth St. SE10 164 EF78
Glengall Causeway E14 163 EA76
Westferry Rd.
Glengall Gro. E14 163 EC76
Glengall Rd. NW6 139 CZ67
Glengall Rd. SE15 162 DT78
Glengall Rd., Bexh. 166 EY83
Glengall Rd., Edg. 96 CP48
Glengall Rd., Wdf.Grn. 102 EG51
Glengall Ter. SE15 162 DT79
Glengarnock Ave. E14 163 EC77
Glengarry Rd. SE22 182 DS85
Glenham Dr., Ilf. 125 EP57
Glenhaven Ave., Borwd. 78 CN41
Glenhead Clo. SE9 165 EP83
Dumbreck Rd.
Glenheadon Clo., Lthd. 231 CK123
Glenheadon Ri.
Glenheadon Ri., Lthd. 231 CK123
Glenhill Clo. N3 98 DA54
Glenhouse Rd. SE9 185 EN85
Glenhurst Ave. NW5 120 DG63
Glenhurst Ave., Bex. 186 EZ88
Glenhurst Ave., Ruis. 115 BQ59
Glenhurst Ct. SE19 182 DT92
Glenhurst Ri. SE19 182 DQ94
Glenhurst Rd. N12 98 DD50
Glenhurst Rd., Brent. 157 CJ79
Glenilla Rd. NW3 140 DE65
Glenister Ho., Hayes 135 BV74
Glenister Pk. Rd. SW16 181 DK94
Glenister Rd. SE10 164 EF78
Glenister Rd., Chesh. 54 AQ28
Glenister St. E16 145 EN74
Glenlea Rd. SE9 185 EN85
Glenlion Ct., Wey. 195 BR104
Glenloch Rd. NW3 140 DE65
Glenloch Rd., Enf. 82 DW40
Glenluce Rd. SE3 164 EG79
Glenlyn Ave., St.Alb. 43 CH21
Glenlyon Rd. SE9 185 EN85
Glenmere Ave. NW7 97 CU52
Glenmire Ter., Ware 33 ED11
Glenmore Clo., Add. 194 BH104
Glenmore Gdns., Abb.L. 59 BU32
Stewart Clo.
Glenmore Rd. NW3 140 DE65
Glenmore Rd., Well. 165 ET80
Glenmore Way, Bark. 146 EU69
Glenmount Path SE18 165 EQ78
Raglan Rd.
Glenn Ave., Pur. 219 DP111
Glennie Rd. SE27 181 DN90
Glenny Rd., Bark. 145 EQ65
Glenorchy Clo., Hayes 136 BY71
Glenparke Rd. E7 144 EH65
Glenrosa Gdns., Grav. 191 GM92
Glenrosa St. SW6 160 DC82
Glenrose Ct., Sid. 186 EV92
Glenroy St. W12 139 CW72
Glensdale Rd. SE4 163 DZ83
Glenshee Clo., Nthwd. 93 BQ51
Merrows Clo.
Glenshiel Rd. SE9 185 EN85
Glenside, Chig. 103 EP51
Glenside Cotts., Slou. 152 AT76
Upton Pk.
Glentanner Way SW17 180 DD90
Aboyne Rd.
Glentham Gdns. SW13 159 CV79
Glentham Rd.
Glentham Rd. SW13 159 CU79
Glenthorne Ave., Croy. 202 DV102
Glenthorne Clo., Sutt. 200 DA102
Glenthorne Clo., Uxb. 134 BN69
Uxbridge Rd.
Glenthorne Gdns., Ilf. 125 EN55
Glenthorne Gdns., Sutt. 200 DA102
Glenthorne Ms. W6 159 CV77
Glenthorne Rd.
Glenthorne Rd. E17 123 DY57
Glenthorne Rd. N11 98 DF50
Glenthorne Rd. W6 159 CV77
Glenthorne Rd., Kings.T. 198 CM98
Glenthorpe Rd., Mord. 199 CX99
Glenton Clo., Rom. 105 FE51
Glenton Rd. SE13 164 EE84
Glenton Way, Rom. 105 FE52
Glentrammon Ave., Orp. 223 ET107
Glentrammon Clo., Orp. 223 ET106
Glentrammon Gdns., Orp. 223 ET107
Glentrammon Rd., Orp. 223 ET107
Glentworth St. NW1 272 E5
Glentworth St. NW1 140 DF70
Glenure Rd. SE9 185 EN85
Glenview SE2 166 EX79
Glenview Gdns., Hem.H. 40 BH20
Glenview Rd.
Glenview Rd., Brom. 204 EK96
Glenview Rd., Hem.H. 40 BH20
Glenville Ave., Enf. 82 DQ38
Glenville Gro. SE8 163 DZ80
Glenville Ms. SW18 180 DB87
Glenville Rd., Kings.T. 198 CN95
Glenwood, Brox. 49 DZ19
Glenwood, Dor. 263 CJ138
Glenwood, Welw.G.C. 30 DD10
Glenwood Ave. NW9 118 CS60
Glenwood Ave., Rain. 147 FG70
Glenwood Clo., Har. 117 CF57
Glenwood Dr., Rom. 127 FG57
Glenwood Gdns., Ilf. 125 EN57
Glenwood Gro. NW9 118 CQ60
Glenwood Rd. N15 121 DP57
Glenwood Rd. NW7 96 CS48
Glenwood Rd. SE6 183 DZ88
Glenwood Rd., Epsom 217 CU107
Glenwood Rd., Houns. 157 CD83
Glenwood Way, Croy. 203 DX100
Glenworth Ave. E14 163 ED77
Glenworth Pl., Slou. 131 AQ74
Glevum Clo., St.Alb. 42 BZ22
Gliddon Rd. W14 159 CY77
Glimpsing Grn., Erith 166 EY76
Glisson Rd., Uxb. 134 BN68
Gload Cres., Orp. 206 EX103
Global App. E3 143 EB68
Hancock Rd.
Globe Ct., Hert. 32 DQ07
Grove Wk.
Globe Ind. Estates, Grays 170 GC78
Globe Pond Rd. SE16 143 DY74
Globe Rd. E1 143 DX70
Globe Rd. E2 142 DW69
Globe Rd. E15 124 EF64
Globe Rd., Horn. 127 FG58
Globe Rd., Wdf.Grn. 102 EJ51
Globe Rope Wk. E14 163 EC77
Stebondale St.
Globe St. SE1 279 K5
Globe St. SE1 162 DR75
Globe Ter. E2 142 DW69
Globe Rd.
Globe Yd. W1 273 H9
Glory Clo., H.Wyc. 110 AF56
Glory Mead, Dor. 263 CH139
Glory Mill La., H.Wyc. 110 AE56
Glossop Rd., S.Croy. 220 DR109
Gloster Rd., N.Mal. 198 CS98
Gloster Rd., Wok. 227 BA121
Gloucester Ave. NW1 140 DG66
Gloucester Ave., Grays 170 GC75
Gloucester Ave., Horn. 128 FN56
Gloucester Ave., Sid. 185 ES89
Gloucester Ave., Slou. 131 AQ71
Gloucester Ave., Wal.Cr. 67 DY33
Gloucester Ave., Well. 165 ET84
Gloucester Circ. SE10 163 EC80
Gloucester Clo. NW10 138 CR66
Gloucester Clo., S.Ock. 149 FW69
South Rd.
Gloucester Clo., T.Ditt. 197 CG102
Gloucester Ct. EC3 279 N1
Gloucester Ct., Rich. 158 CN80
Gloucester Ct., Til. 171 GF82
Dock Rd.
Gloucester Ct., Uxb. 114 BG58
Moorfield Rd.
Gloucester Cres. NW1 141 DH67
Gloucester Cres., Stai. 174 BK93
Gloucester Dr. N4 121 DP61
Gloucester Dr. NW11 120 DA56
Gloucester Dr., Stai. 173 BC90
Gloucester Gdns. NW11 119 CZ59
Gloucester Gdns. W2 140 DC72
Bishops Bri. Rd.
Gloucester Gdns., Barn. 80 DG42
Gloucester Gdns., Ilf. 124 EL59
Gloucester Gdns., Sutt. 200 DB103
Gloucester Gate NW1 141 DH68
Gloucester Gate Ms. NW1 141 DH68
Gloucester Gate
Gloucester Gro., Edg. 96 CR53
Gloucester Gro. Est. SE15 162 DS79
Gloucester Ho. N7 121 DL62
Gloucester Ho. NW6 140 DA68
Gloucester Ms. E10 123 EA59
Gloucester Rd.
Gloucester Ms. W2 140 DC72
Gloucester Ms. W. W2 140 DC72
Cleveland Ter.
Gloucester Par., Sid. 186 EU85
Gloucester Pl. NW1 272 D4
Gloucester Pl. NW1 140 DF70
Gloucester Pl. W1 272 E6
Gloucester Pl. W1 140 DF71
Gloucester Pl., Wind. 151 AR82
Gloucester Pl. Ms. W1 272 E7
Gloucester Rd. E10 123 EA59
Gloucester Rd. E11 124 EH57
Gloucester Rd. E12 125 EM62
Gloucester Rd. E17 101 DX54
Gloucester Rd. N17 122 DR55
Gloucester Rd. N18 100 DT50
Gloucester Rd. SW7 160 DC76
Gloucester Rd. W3 158 CQ75
Gloucester Rd. W5 157 CJ75
Gloucester Rd., Barn. 80 DB43
Gloucester Rd., Belv. 166 EZ78
Gloucester Rd., Brwd. 108 FV43
Gloucester Rd., Croy. 202 DR102
Gloucester Rd., Dart. 187 FH87
Gloucester Rd., Enf. 82 DQ38
Gloucester Rd., Felt. 176 BW88
Gloucester Rd., Grav. 191 GJ91
Gloucester Rd., Guil. 242 AT132
Gloucester Rd., Hmptn. 176 CB94
Gloucester Rd., Har. 116 CB57
Gloucester Rd., Houns. 156 BY84
Gloucester Rd., Kings.T. 198 CN96
Gloucester Rd., Red. 250 DF133
Gloucester Rd., Rich. 158 CN80
Gloucester Rd., Rom. 127 FE58
Gloucester Rd., Tedd. 177 CE92
Gloucester Rd., Twick. 176 CC88
Gloucester Sq. E2 142 DU67
Whiston Rd.
Gloucester Sq. W2 272 A9
Gloucester Sq. W2 140 DD72
Gloucester Sq., Wok. 226 AY117
Church St. E.
Gloucester St. SW1 161 DJ78
Gloucester Ter. W2 140 DB72
Gloucester Wk. W8 160 DA75
Gloucester Wk., Wok. 227 AZ117
Church St. E.
Gloucester Way EC1 274 E3
Gloucester Way EC1 141 DN69
Glover Clo. SE2 166 EW77
Abbey Wd. Rd.
Glover Clo., Wal.Cr. 66 DT27
Allwood Rd.
Glover Dr. N18 100 DW51
Glover Rd., Pnr. 116 BX58
Glovers Clo., Hert. 32 DQ11
Glovers Gro., Ruis. 115 BP59
Glovers La., Harl. 52 EY20
Glovers Rd., Reig. 266 DB135
Gloxinia Rd., Grav. 190 GB93
Gloxinia Wk., Hmptn. 176 CA93
The Ave.
Glycena Rd. SW11 160 DF83
Glyn Ave., Barn. 80 DD42
Glyn Clo. SE25 202 DS96
Glyn Clo., Epsom 217 CU109
Glyn Ct. SW16 181 DN90
Glyn Davies Clo., Sev. 241 FE120
London Rd.
Glyn Dr., Sid. 186 EV91
Glyn Rd. E5 123 DX63
Glyn Rd., Enf. 82 DW42
Glyn Rd., Wor.Pk. 199 CX103
Glyn St. SE11 161 DM78
Kennington La.
Glynde Ms. SW3 276 C7
Glynde Rd., Bexh. 166 EX83
Glynde St. SE4 183 DZ86
Glyndebourne Pk., Orp. 205 EP103
Glyndon Rd. SE18 165 EQ77
Glynfield Rd. NW10 138 CS66
Glynne Rd. N22 99 DN54
Glynswood, Ger.Cr. 91 AZ52
Glynwood Dr. SE23 182 DW90
Goat La., Enf. 82 DT38
Goat La., Surb. 197 CH103
Goat Rd., Mitch. 200 DF101
Goat St. SE1 279 P4
Goat Wf., Brent. 158 CL79
Goaters All. SW6 159 CZ80
Dawes Rd.
Goatsfield Rd., West. 238 EJ120
Goatswood La., Rom. 105 FH45
Gobions Ave., Rom. 105 FD52
Gobions Way, Pot.B. 64 DB28
Swanley Bar La.
Goblins Grn., Welw.G.C. 29 CX10
Godalming Ave., Wall. 219 DL106
Godalming Rd. E14 143 EB71
Godbold Rd. E15 144 EE69
Goddard Clo., Shep. 194 BM97
Magdalene Rd.
Goddard Rd., Beck. 203 DX98
Goddards Clo., Hert. 47 DJ19
Goddards Way, Ilf. 125 ER60
Goddington Chase, Orp. 224 EV105
Goddington La., Orp. 206 EU104
Godfrey Ave., Nthlt. 136 BY67
Godfrey Ave., Twick. 177 CD87
Godfrey Hill SE18 164 EL77
Godfrey Rd. SE18 165 EM77
Godfrey St. E15 143 EC68
Abbey La.
Godfrey St. SW3 276 C10
Godfrey St. SW3 160 DE78
Godfrey Way, Houns. 176 BZ87
Goding St. SE11 161 DL78
Godley Rd. SW18 180 DD88
Godley Rd., W.Byf. 212 BM114
Godliman St. EC4 275 H9
Godliman St. EC4 142 DQ72
Godman Rd. SE15 162 DV82
Godman Rd., Grays 171 GG76
Godolphin Clo. N13 99 DP51
Godolphin Clo., Sutt. 217 CZ110
Godolphin Pl. W3 138 CR73
Vyner Rd.
Godolphin Rd. W12 139 CV74
Godolphin Rd., Beac. 89 AQ51
Godolphin Rd., Slou. 131 AR73
Godolphin Rd., Wey. 213 BR107
Godric Cres., Croy. 221 ED110
Godson Rd., Croy. 201 DN104
Godson St. N1 141 DN68
White Lion St.
Godstone Bypass, Gdse. 252 DW129
Godstone Grn., Gdse. 252 DV131
Godstone Grn. Rd., Gdse. 252 DV131
Godstone Hill, Gdse. 252 DV127
Godstone Rd., Cat. 236 DU124
Godstone Rd., Ken. 219 DN112
Godstone Rd., Oxt. 253 EA131
Godstone Rd., Pur. 219 DN112
Godstone Rd., Red. 252 DR133
Godstone Rd., Sutt. 218 DC105
Godstone Rd., Twick. 177 CG86
Godstone Rd., Whyt. 236 DT116
Godstow Rd. SE2 166 EV75
Godwin Clo. E4 83 EC38
Godwin Clo. N1 142 DQ68
Napier Gro.
Godwin Clo., Epsom 216 CQ107
Godwin Ct. NW1 141 DJ68
Crowndale Rd.
Godwin Rd. E7 124 EH63
Godwin Rd., Brom. 204 EJ97
Goffers Rd. SE3 164 EE82
Goffs Cres. (Cheshunt), Wal.Cr. 66 DQ29
Goffs La. (Cheshunt), Wal.Cr. 66 DR29
Goffs Oak Ave. (Cheshunt), Wal.Cr. 65 DP28
Goffs Rd., Ashf. 175 BR93
Gogmore Fm. Clo., Cher. 193 BF101
Gogmore La., Cher. 193 BF101
Goidel Clo., Wall. 219 DK105
Golborne Gdns. W10 139 CZ70
Golborne Rd.
Golborne Ms. W10 139 CY71
Portobello Rd.
Golborne Rd. W10 139 CY71
Gold Clo., Brox. 49 DY21
Baas Hill
Gold Cft., Hem.H. 40 BN22
Gold Hill, Edg. 96 CR51
Gold Hill E., Ger.Cr. 90 AX54
Gold Hill N., Ger.Cr. 90 AW53
Gold Hill W., Ger.Cr. 90 AW54
Gold La., Edg. 96 CR51
Golda Clo., Barn. 79 CX44
Goldace, Grays 170 FZ79
Goldbeaters Gro., Edg. 96 CS51
Goldcliff Clo., Mord. 200 DA101
Goldcrest Clo. E16 144 EK71
Sheerwater Rd.
Goldcrest Clo. SE28 146 EW73
Goldcrest Clo., Horl. 268 DE147
Wither Dale
Goldcrest Ms. W5 137 CK71
Montpelier Ave.
Goldcrest Way, Croy. 221 ED109
Goldcrest Way, Pur. 219 DK110
Goldcrest Way (Bushey), Wat. 94 CC46
Golden Ct., Rich. 177 CK85
George St.
Golden Cres., Hayes 135 BS74
Golden Dell, Welw.G.C. 29 CZ13
Golden La. EC1 275 H5
Golden La. EC1 142 DQ70
Golden La. Est. EC1 275 H5
Golden Manor W7 137 CE73
Golden Oak Clo., Slou. 131 AQ65
Golden Plover Clo. E16 144 EH72
Maplin Rd.
Golden Sq. W1 273 L10
Golden Sq. W1 141 DJ73
Golden Yd. NW3 120 DC63
Heath St.
Golders Clo., Edg. 96 CP50
Golders Gdns. NW11 119 CY59
Golders Grn. Cres. NW11 119 CZ59
Golders Grn. Rd. NW11 119 CY58
Golders Manor Dr. NW11 119 CX58
Golders Pk. Clo. NW11 120 DA60
Golders Ri. NW4 119 CX57
Golders Way NW11 119 CZ59
Goldfinch Clo., Orp. 224 EU106
Goldfinch Gdns., Guil. 243 BD133
Goldfinch Rd. SE28 165 ER76
Goldfinch Rd., S.Croy. 221 DX110
Goldfinch Way, Borwd. 78 CN42
Siskin Clo.
Goldfort Wk., Wok. 226 AS116
Langmans Way
Goldhawk Ms. W12 159 CV75
Devonport Rd.
Goldhawk Rd. W6 159 CT77
Goldhawk Rd. W12 159 CU76
Goldhaze Clo., Wdf.Grn. 102 EK52
Goldhurst Ter. NW6 140 DB66
Golding Clo., Chess. 215 CJ107
Mansfield Rd.
Golding Rd., Sev. 257 FJ122
Golding St. E1 142 DU72
Goldingham Ave., Loug. 85 EQ40
Goldings, The, Wok. 226 AT116
Goldings Cres., Hat. 45 CV17
Goldings Hill, Loug. 85 EM37
Goldings La., Hert. 31 DN06
Goldings Ri., Loug. 85 EN39
Goldings Rd., Loug. 85 EN39
Goldington Clo., Hodd. 33 DZ14
Goldington Cres. NW1 141 DK68
Goldington Cres. Gdns. NW1 141 DK68
Goldington St. NW1 141 DK68
Goldman Clo. E2 142 DU70
Goldney Rd. W9 140 DA70
Goldrings Rd., Lthd. 214 CB113
Goldsborough Cres. E4 101 EB47
Goldsborough Rd. SW8 161 DK81
Goldsdown Clo., Enf. 83 DY40
Goldsdown Rd., Enf. 83 DX40
Goldsel Rd., Swan. 207 FD99
Goldsel Rd. Ind. Est., Swan. 207 FE98
Goldsmid St. SE18 165 ES78
Sladedale Rd.
Goldsmith, Grays 170 FZ79
Goldsmith Ave. E12 144 EL65
Goldsmith Ave. NW9 118 CS57
Goldsmith Ave. W3 138 CR73
Goldsmith Ave., Rom. 126 FA59
Goldsmith Clo. W3 138 CS74
East Acton La.
Goldsmith Clo., Har. 116 CB60
Goldsmith La. NW9 118 CP56
Goldsmith Rd. E10 123 EA60
Goldsmith Rd. E17 101 DX54
Goldsmith Rd. N11 98 DF50
Goldsmith Rd. SE15 162 DU81
Goldsmith Rd. W3 138 CR74
Goldsmith St. EC2 275 J8
Goldsmiths Clo., Wok. 226 AW118
Goldsmith's Row E2 142 DU68
Goldsmith's Sq. E2 142 DU68
Goldstone Clo., Ware 33 DX05
High Oak Rd.
Goldsworth Orchard, Wok. 226 AU118
St. John's Rd.
Goldsworth Pk. Trd. Est., Wok. 226 AU116
Goldsworth Rd., Wok. 226 AW118
Goldsworthy Gdns. SE16 162 DW77
Goldsworthy Way, Slou. 130 AJ72
Goldwell Rd., Th.Hth. 201 DM98
Goldwin Clo. SE14 162 DW81
Goldwing Clo. E16 144 EG72
Golf Clo., Stan. 95 CJ52
Golf Clo. (Bushey), Wat. 76 BX41
Golf Clo., Wok. 211 BE114
Golf Club Dr., Kings.T. 178 CR94
Golf Club Rd., Hat. 64 DA26
Golf Club Rd., Wey. 213 BP109
Golf Club Rd., Wok. 226 AU120
Golf Ho. Rd., Oxt. 254 EJ129
Golf Links Ave., Grav. 191 GH92
Golf Ride, Enf. 81 DN35
Golf Rd. W5 138 CM72
Boileau Rd.
Golf Rd., Brom. 205 EN97
Golf Rd., Ken. 236 DR118
Golf Side, Sutt. 217 CY111
Golf Side, Twick. 177 CD90
Golfe Rd., Ilf. 125 ER62
Golfside Clo. N20 98 DE48
Golfside Clo., N.Mal. 198 CS96
Goliath Clo., Wall. 219 DL108
Avro Way
Gollogly Ter. SE7 164 EJ78
Gombards, St.Alb. 43 CD19
Gombards All., St.Alb. 43 CD20
Worley Rd.
Gomer Gdns., Tedd. 177 CG93
Gomer Pl., Tedd. 177 CG93
Gomm Rd. SE16 162 DW76
Gomms Wd. Clo., Beac. 88 AH51
Gomshall Ave., Wall. 219 DL106
Gomshall Gdns., Ken. 236 DS115
Gomshall La., Guil. 260 BN139
Gomshall Rd., Sutt. 217 CW110
Gondar Gdns. NW6 119 CZ64
Gonnerston, St.Alb. 42 CC19
Kings Rd.
Gonson Pl. SE8 163 EA79
Gonson St. SE8 163 EB79
Gonston Clo. SW19 179 CY89
Boddicott Clo.
Gonville Ave., Rick. 75 BP44
Gonville Cres., Nthlt. 136 CB65
Gonville Rd., Th.Hth. 201 DM99
Gonville St. SW6 159 CY83
Putney Bri. App.
Goodall Rd. E11 123 EC62
Gooden Ct., Har. 117 CE62
Goodenough Clo., Couls. 235 DN120
Goodenough Rd. SW19 179 CZ94
Goodenough Way, Couls. 235 DM120
Goodge Pl. W1 273 L7
Goodge St. W1 273 L7
Goodge St. W1 141 DJ71
Goodhall St. NW10 138 CS69
Goodhart Pl. E14 143 DY73
Goodhart Way, W.Wick. 204 EE101
Goodhew Rd., Croy. 202 DU100
Gooding Clo., N.Mal. 198 CQ98
Goodinge Clo. N7 141 DL65
Goodlake Ct., Uxb. 113 BF59
Goodley Stock Rd., Eden. 255 EP131
Goodley Stock Rd., West. 255 EP128
Goodman Cres. SW2 181 DK89
Goodman Pk., Slou. 132 AW74
Goodman Pl., Stai. 173 BF91
High St.
Goodman Rd. E10 123 EC59
Goodmans Ct., Wem. 117 CK63
Goodman's Flds. E1 142 DU72
Goodman's Stile
Goodman's Stile E1 142 DU72
Goodmans Yd. E1 275 P10
Goodmans Yd. E1 142 DT73
Goodmayes Ave., Ilf. 126 EU60
Goodmayes La., Ilf. 126 EU61
Goodmayes Rd., Ilf. 126 EU60
Goodmead Rd., Orp. 206 EU101
Goodrich Clo., Wat. 75 BU35
Goodrich Rd. SE22 182 DT86
Goods Way NW1 141 DL68
Goodson Rd. NW10 138 CS66
Goodway Gdns. E14 143 ED72
Goodwin Ave., Brwd. 109 GE44
Goodwin Clo. SE16 162 DU76
Goodwin Clo., Mitch. 200 DD97
Goodwin Ct., Wal.Cr. 67 DY28
Goodwin Dr., Sid. 186 EX90
Goodwin Gdns., Croy. 219 DP107
Goodwin Meadows, H.Wyc. 110 AE57
Goodwin Rd. N9 100 DW46
Goodwin Rd. W12 159 CU75
Goodwin Rd., Croy. 219 DP106
Goodwin Rd., Slou. 131 AM69
Goodwin St. N4 121 DN61
Fonthill Rd.
Goodwins Ct. WC2 273 P10
Goodwood Ave., Enf. 82 DW37
Goodwood Ave., Horn. 128 FL63
Goodwood Ave., Wat. 75 BS35
Goodwood Clo., Hodd. 49 EA16
Goodwood Clo., Mord. 200 DA98

Goodwood Clo., Stan. 95 CJ50
Goodwood Cres., Grav. 191 GJ92
Goodwood Dr., Nthlt. 136 CA65
Goodwood Path, Borwd. 78 CN41
Stratfield Rd.
Goodwood Rd. SE14 163 DY80
Goodwood Rd., Red. 250 DF132
Goodwyn Ave. NW7 96 CS50
Goodwyns Rd., Dor. 263 CH139
Goodwyns Vale N10 98 DG53
Goodyers Ave., Rad. 61 CF33
Goodyers Gdns. NW4 119 CX57
Goosander Way SE28 165 ER76
Goose Acre, Chesh. 56 AT30
Goose Acre, Welw.G.C. 29 CZ11
Goose Cft., Hem.H. 39 BF19
Goose Grn., Cob. 229 BU119
Goose Grn., Guil. 261 BQ139
Goose Grn., Slou. 131 AP68
Goose Grn. Clo., Orp. 206 EU96
Goose La., Wok. 226 AV122
Goose Sq. E6 145 EM72
Harper Rd.
Gooseacre La., Har. 117 CK57
Gooseley La. E6 145 EN69
Gooshays Dr., Rom. 106 FL50
Gooshays Gdns., Rom. 106 FL51
Goossens Clo., Sutt. 218 DC106
Turnpike La.
Gophir La. EC4 275 K10
Gopsall St. N1 142 DR67
Goral Mead, Rick. 92 BK46
Gordon Ave. E4 102 EE51
Gordon Ave. SW14 158 CS84
Gordon Ave., Horn. 127 FF61
Gordon Ave., S.Croy. 220 DQ110
Gordon Ave., Stan. 95 CF52
Gordon Ave., Twick. 177 CG85
Gordon Clo. E17 123 EA58
Gordon Clo. N19 121 DJ60
Highgate Hill
Gordon Clo., Cher. 193 BE104
Gordon Clo., St.Alb. 43 CH21
Kitchener Clo.
Gordon Clo., Stai. 174 BH93
Gordon Ct. W12 139 CV72
Gordon Cres., Croy. 202 DS102
Gordon Cres., Hayes 155 BU76
Gordon Dr., Cher. 193 BE104
Gordon Dr., Shep. 195 BR100
Gordon Gdns., Edg. 96 CP54
Gordon Gro. SE5 161 DP82
Gordon Hill, Enf. 82 DQ39
Gordon Ho. Rd. NW5 120 DG63
Gordon Pl. W8 160 DA75
Gordon Pl., Grav. 191 GJ86
East Ter.
Gordon Prom., Grav. 191 GJ86
Gordon Prom. E., Grav. 191 GK86
Canal Rd.
Gordon Rd. E4 102 EE45
Gordon Rd. E11 124 EG58
Gordon Rd. E15 123 EC63
Gordon Rd. E18 102 EH53
Gordon Rd. N3 97 CZ52
Gordon Rd. N9 100 DV47
Gordon Rd. N11 99 DK52
Gordon Rd. SE15 162 DV82
Gordon Rd. W4 158 CP79
Gordon Rd. W5 137 CJ73
Gordon Rd. W13 137 CH73
Gordon Rd., Ashf. 174 BL90
Gordon Rd., Bark. 145 ES67
Gordon Rd., Beck. 203 DZ97
Gordon Rd., Belv. 167 FC77
Gordon Rd., Brwd. 109 GA46
Gordon Rd., Cars. 218 DF107
Gordon Rd., Cat. 236 DR121
Gordon Rd., Chesh. 54 AQ32
Gordon Rd., Dart. 188 FK87
Gordon Rd., Enf. 82 DR39
Gordon Rd., Esher 215 CE108
Gordon Rd., Grav. 190 GE87
Gordon Rd., Grays 170 GE75
Gordon Rd., Har. 117 CE55
Gordon Rd., Houns. 156 CC84
Gordon Rd., Ilf. 125 ER62
Gordon Rd., Kings.T. 198 CM95
Gordon Rd., Red. 250 DG131
Gordon Rd., Rich. 158 CM82
Gordon Rd., Rom. 126 EZ58
Gordon Rd., Sev. 257 FH125
Gordon Rd., Shep. 195 BR100
Gordon Rd., Sid. 185 ES85
Gordon Rd., Sthl. 156 BY77
Gordon Rd., Stai. 173 BC91
Gordon Rd., Surb. 198 CM101
Gordon Rd., Wal.Abb. 67 EA34
Gordon Rd., West Dr. 134 BL73
Gordon Rd., Wind. 151 AM82
Gordon Sq. WC1 273 M4
Gordon Sq. WC1 141 DK70
Gordon St. E13 144 EG69
Grange Rd.
Gordon St. WC1 273 M4
Gordon St. WC1 141 DK70
Gordon Way, Barn. 79 CZ42
Gordon Way, Brom. 204 EG95
Gordon Way, Ch.St.G. 90 AV48
Gordonbrock Rd. SE4 183 EA85
Gordondale Rd. SW19 180 DA89
Gordons Way, Oxt. 253 ED128
Gore Ct. NW9 118 CN57
Gore Hill, Amer. 55 AP43
Gore Rd. E9 142 DW67
Gore Rd. SW20 199 CW96
Gore Rd., Dart. 188 FQ90
Gore Rd., Slou. 130 AH69
Gore St. SW7 160 DC76
Gorefield Pl. NW6 140 DA68
Gorelands La., Ch.St.G. 90 AX46
Gorell Rd., Beac. 89 AP54
Goresbrook Rd., Dag. 146 EV67
Goresbrook Village, Dag. 146 EV67
Goresbrook Rd.
Gorham Dr., St.Alb. 43 CE23
Gorham Pl. W11 139 CY73
Mary Pl.
Gorhambury Dr., St.Alb. 42 BZ19
Goring Clo., Rom. 105 FC53
Goring Gdns., Dag. 126 EW63
Goring Rd. N11 99 DL51
Goring Rd., Dag. 147 FD65
Goring Rd., Stai. 173 BD92
Goring St. EC3 275 N8
Goring St. EC3 142 DS72
Goring Way, Grnf. 136 CC68
Gorings Sq., Stai. 173 BE91
Gorle Clo., Wat. 59 BU34
Gorleston Rd. N15 122 DR57
Gorleston St. W14 159 CY77
Gorman Rd. SE18 165 EM77
Gorringe Ave. (South Darenth), Dart. 209 FR96
Gorringe Pk. Ave., Mitch. 180 DF94
Gorse Clo. E16 144 EG72
Radland Rd.
Gorse Clo., Hat. 45 CT21
Gorse Clo., Tad. 233 CV120
Waterfield
Gorse Ct., Guil. 243 BC132
Kingfisher Dr.
Gorse Hill (Farningham), Dart. 208 FN101
Gorse Hill La., Vir.W. 192 AX98
Gorse Hill Rd., Vir.W. 192 AX98
Gorse La., Wok. 210 AS108
Gorse Mead, Slou. 131 AP74
Gorse Ri. SW17 180 DG92
Gorse Rd., Croy. 203 EA104
Gorse Rd., Orp. 206 EZ102
Gorse Wk., West Dr. 134 BL72
Gorselands Clo., W.Byf. 212 BJ111
Gorseway, Rom. 127 FD61
Gorsewood Rd., Wok. 226 AS119
Gorst Rd. NW10 138 CQ70
Gorst Rd. SW11 180 DF86
Gorsuch Pl. E2 275 P2
Gorsuch St. E2 275 P2
Gorsuch St. E2 142 DT69
Gosberton Rd. SW12 180 DF88
Gosbury Hill, Chess. 216 CL105
Gosden Common, Guil. 258 AY143
Gosden Hill Rd., Guil. 243 BC130
Gosfield Rd., Dag. 126 FA61
Gosfield Rd., Epsom 216 CR112
Gosfield St. W1 273 K6
Gosfield St. W1 141 DJ71
Gosford Gdns., Ilf. 125 EM57
Gosforth La., Wat. 93 BU48
Gosforth Path, Wat. 93 BU48
Gosforth La.
Goshawk Gdns., Hayes 135 BS69
Goslar Way, Wind. 151 AP82
Goslett Yd. WC2 273 N9
Gosling Clo., Grnf. 136 CA69
Gosling Grn., Slou. 152 AY76
Gosling Rd., Slou. 152 AY76
Gosling Way SW9 161 DN81
Gospatrick Rd. N17 100 DQ52
Gospel Oak Est. NW5 120 DF64
Gosport Dr., Horn. 148 FJ65
Gosport Rd. E17 123 DZ57
Gosport Wk. N17 123 DX57
Yarmouth Cres.
Gosport Way SE15 162 DT80
Pentridge St.
Goss Hill, Dart. 188 FJ93
Goss Hill, Swan. 188 FJ93
Gossage Rd. SE18 165 ER78
Ancona Rd.
Gossage Rd., Uxb. 134 BM66
Gossamers, The, Wat. 76 BY35
Gosselin Rd., Hert. 32 DQ07
Gosset St. E2 142 DT69
Gosshill Rd., Chis. 205 EN96
Gossington Clo., Chis. 185 EP91
Beechwood Ri.
Gossoms End, Berk. 38 AU18
Gossoms Ryde, Berk. 38 AU18
Gosterwood St. SE8 163 DY79
Gostling Rd., Twick. 176 CA88
Goston Gdns., Th.Hth. 201 DN97
Goswell Hill, Wind. 151 AR81
Goswell Rd. EC1 274 F1
Goswell Rd. EC1 141 DP68
Goswell Rd., Wind. 151 AR80
Gothic Clo., Dart. 188 FK90
Gothic Ct., Hayes 155 BR79
Sipson La.
Gothic Rd., Twick. 177 CD89
Goudhurst Rd., Brom. 184 EE92
Gouge Ave., Grav. 190 GE88
Gough Rd. E15 124 EF63
Gough Rd., Enf. 82 DV40
Gough Sq. EC4 274 E8
Gough St. WC1 274 C4
Gough St. WC1 141 DM70
Gough Wk. E14 143 EA72
Saracen St.
Gould Clo., Hat. 45 CV24
Gould Ct. SE19 182 DS92
Gould Ct., Guil. 243 BD132
Eustace Rd.
Gould Rd., Felt. 175 BS87
Gould Rd., Twick. 177 CE88
Gould Ter. E8 122 DV64
Kenmure Rd.
Goulds Grn., Uxb. 135 BP72
Goulston St. E1 275 P8
Goulston St. E1 142 DT72
Goulton Rd. E5 122 DV63
Gourley Pl. N15 122 DS57
Gourley St.
Gourley St. N15 122 DS57
Gourock Rd. SE9 185 EN85
Govan St. E2 142 DU67
Whiston Rd.
Government Row, Enf. 83 EA38
Governors Ave., Uxb. 113 BF57
Governors Clo., Amer. 72 AT38
Quill Hall La.
Govett Ave., Shep. 195 BQ99
Govier Clo. E15 144 EE66
Gowan Ave. SW6 159 CY81
Gowan Rd. NW10 139 CV65
Gowar Fld., Pot.B. 63 CU32
Gower, The, Egh. 193 BB97
Gower Clo. SW4 181 DJ86
Abbeville Rd.
Gower Ct. WC1 273 M4
Gower Ms. WC1 273 N7
Gower Ms. WC1 141 DK71
Gower Pl. WC1 273 L4
Gower Pl. WC1 141 DJ70
Gower Rd. E7 144 EG65
Gower Rd., Horl. 268 DE148
Court Lo. Rd.
Gower Rd., Islw. 157 CF79
Gower Rd., Wey. 213 BR107
Gower St. WC1 273 M5
Gower St. WC1 141 DJ70
Gowers, The, Amer. 55 AS36
Gowers, The, Harl. 36 EU13
Gowers La., Grays 171 GF75
Gower's Wk. E1 142 DU72
Gowland Pl., Beck. 203 DZ96
Gowlett Rd. SE15 162 DU83
Gowrie Rd. SW11 160 DG83
Graburn Way, E.Mol. 197 CD97
Grace Ave., Bexh. 166 EZ82
Grace Clo. SE9 184 EK90
Grace Clo., Borwd. 78 CR39
Grace Clo., Edg. 96 CQ52
Pavilion Way
Grace Clo., Ilf. 103 ET51
Grace Ct., Slou. 131 AQ74
Grace Jones Clo. E8 142 DU65
Parkholme Rd.
Grace Path SE26 182 DW91
Silverdale
Grace Rd., Croy. 202 DQ100
Grace St. E3 143 EB69
Gracechurch St. EC3 275 L10
Gracechurch St. EC3 142 DR73
Gracedale Rd. SW16 181 DH92
Gracefield Gdns. SW16 181 DL90
Grace's All. E1 142 DU73
Ensign St.
Graces Ms. SE5 162 DR82
Graces Rd. SE5 162 DS82
Gracious La., Sev. 256 FG130
Gracious La. End, Sev. 256 FF130
Gracious Pond Rd., Wok. 210 AT108
Gradient, The SE26 182 DU91
Graeme Rd., Enf. 82 DR40
Graemesdyke Ave. SW14 158 CP83
Graemesdyke Rd., Berk. 38 AU20
Grafton Clo. W13 137 CG72
Grafton Clo., Houns. 176 BY88
Grafton Clo., Slou. 132 AY72
Grafton Clo., W.Byf. 211 BF113
Madeira Rd.
Grafton Clo., Wor.Pk. 198 CS104
Grafton Ct., Felt. 175 BR88
Loxwood Clo.
Grafton Cres. NW1 141 DH65
Grafton Gdns. N4 122 DQ58
Grafton Gdns., Dag. 126 EY61
Grafton Ho. E3 143 EA69
Wellington Way
Grafton Ms. N1 142 DQ68
Frome St.
Grafton Ms. W1 273 K5
Grafton Pk. Rd., Wor.Pk. 198 CS103
Grafton Pl. NW1 273 M3
Grafton Pl. NW1 141 DK69
Grafton Rd. NW5 120 DG64
Grafton Rd. W3 138 CQ73
Grafton Rd., Croy. 201 DN102
Grafton Rd., Dag. 126 EY60
Grafton Rd., Enf. 81 DM41
Grafton Rd., Har. 116 CC57
Grafton Rd., N.Mal. 198 CS97
Grafton Rd., Wor.Pk. 216 CR105
Grafton Sq. SW4 161 DJ83
Grafton St. W1 277 J1
Grafton St. W1 141 DH73
Grafton Ter. NW5 120 DF64
Grafton Way W1 273 K5
Grafton Way W1 141 DJ70
Grafton Way WC1 273 L5
Grafton Way WC1 141 DJ70
Grafton Way, W.Mol. 196 BZ98
Grafton Yd. NW5 141 DH65
Prince of Wales Rd.
Graftons, The NW2 120 DA62
Hermitage La.
Graham Ave. W13 157 CH75
Graham Ave., Brox. 49 DY20
Graham Ave., Mitch. 200 DG95
Graham Clo., Brwd. 109 GC43
Graham Clo., Croy. 203 EA103
Graham Clo., St.Alb. 43 CD22
Graham Gdns., Surb. 198 CL102
Graham Rd. E8 142 DU65
Graham Rd. E13 144 EG69
Graham Rd. N15 121 DP55
Graham Rd. NW4 119 CV58
Graham Rd. SW19 179 CZ94
Graham Rd. W4 158 CR76
Graham Rd., Bexh. 166 FA84
Graham Rd., Hmptn. 176 CA91
Graham Rd., Har. 117 CE55
Graham Rd., Mitch. 200 DG95
Graham Rd., Pur. 219 DN113
Graham St. N1 274 G1
Graham St. N1 141 DP68
Graham Ter. SW1 276 F9
Graham Ter. SW1 160 DG77
Grahame Pk. Est. NW9 97 CT52
Grahame Pk. Way NW7 97 CT52
Grahame Pk. Way NW9 97 CT54
Grainger Clo., Nthlt. 116 CC64
Lancaster Rd.
Grainger Rd. N22 100 DQ53
Grainger Rd., Islw. 157 CF82
Grainge's Yd., Uxb. 134 BJ66
Cross St.
Gramer Clo. E11 123 ED61
Grampian Clo., Orp. 205 ET100
Cotswold Ri.
Grampian Gdns. NW2 119 CY60
Grampian Way, Hayes 155 BR80
Grampian Way, Slou. 153 BA78
Granard Ave. SW15 179 CV85
Granard Rd. SW12 180 DF87
Granaries, The, Wal.Abb. 68 EE33
Granary, The, Harl. 34 EH14
Granary Clo. N9 100 DW45
Turin Rd.
Granary Clo., Horl. 268 DG146
Waterside
Granary Rd. E1 142 DV70
Selby St.
Granary St. NW1 141 DK67
Granby Bldgs. SE11 278 B9
Granby Pk. Rd. (Cheshunt), Wal.Cr. 66 DT28
Granby Rd. SE9 165 EM82
Granby Rd., Grav. 190 GC86
Granby St. E2 142 DT70
Granby Ter. NW1 273 K1
Granby Ter. NW1 141 DJ68
Grand Ave. EC1 274 G6
Grand Ave. N10 120 DG56
Grand Ave., Surb. 198 CP99
Grand Ave., Wem. 118 CN64
Grand Ave. E., Wem. 138 CN65
Victoria Ave.
Grand Depot Rd. SE18 165 EN78
Grand Dr. SW20 199 CW96
Grand Dr., Sthl. 156 CC75
Grand Par. Ms. SW15 179 CY85
Upper Richmond Rd.
Grand Stand Rd., Epsom 233 CT117
Grand Union Cres. E8 142 DU67
Grand Union Ind. Est. NW10 138 CP68
Grand Union Wk. NW1 141 DH66
Grand Vw. Ave., West. 238 EJ117
Grand Wk. E1 143 DY70
Solebay St.
Granden Rd. SW16 201 DL96
Grandfield Ave., Wat. 75 BT39
Grandis Cotts., Wok. 228 BH122
Grandison Rd. SW11 180 DF85
Grandison Rd., Wor.Pk. 199 CW103
Granfield St. SW11 160 DD81
Grange, The N2 98 DD54
Central Ave.
Grange, The N20 98 DC46
Grange, The SE1 279 P6
Grange, The SE1 162 DT76
Grange, The SW19 179 CX93
Grange, The, Croy. 203 DZ103
Grange, The, Dart. 209 FR95
Grange, The, Walt. 195 BV103
Grange, The, Wem. 138 CN66
Grange, The, Wind. 172 AV85
Grange, The, Wok. 210 AS110
Grange, The, Wor.Pk. 198 CR104
Grange Ave. N12 98 DC50
Grange Ave. N20 97 CY45
Grange Ave. SE25 202 DS96
Grange Ave., Barn. 98 DE46
Grange Ave., Stan. 95 CH54
Grange Ave., Twick. 177 CE89
Grange Ave., Wdf.Grn. 102 EG51
Grange Clo., Brwd. 109 GC50
Grange Clo., Edg. 96 CQ50
Grange Clo., Ger.Cr. 90 AY53
Grange Clo., Grav. 191 GF91
Grange Clo., Guil. 242 AV130
Grange Clo., Hayes 135 BS71
Grange Clo., Hem.H. 40 BN21
Grange Clo., Hert. 31 DP09
Grange Clo., Houns. 156 BZ79
Grange Clo., Lthd. 231 CK120
Grange Clo. (Bletchingley), Red. 252 DR133
Grange Clo. (Merstham), Red. 251 DH128
Grange Clo., Sid. 186 EU90
Grange Clo., Stai. 172 AY86
Grange Clo., W.Mol. 196 CB98
Grange Clo., West. 255 EQ126
Grange Clo., Wdf.Grn. 102 EG52
Grange Ct. E8 142 DT66
Queensbridge Rd.
Grange Ct. WC2 274 C9
Grange Ct., Chig. 103 EQ47
Grange Ct., Loug. 84 EK43
Grange Ct., Nthlt. 136 BW68
Grange Ct., Stai. 174 BG92
Grange Ct., Wal.Abb. 67 EC34
Grange Ct., Walt. 195 BU103
Grange Cres. SE28 146 EW72
Grange Cres., Chig. 103 ER50
Grange Cres., Dart. 188 FP86
Grange Dr., Chis. 184 EL93
Grange Dr., H.Wyc. 110 AD60
Grange Dr., Orp. 224 EW109
Rushmore Hill
Grange Dr., Red. 251 DH128
London Rd. S.
Grange Dr., Wok. 226 AY115
Grange End, Horl. 269 DN148
Grange Fm. Clo., Har. 116 CC61
Grange Flds., Ger.Cr. 90 AY53
Lower Rd.
Grange Gdns. N14 99 DK46
Grange Gdns. NW3 120 DB62
Grange Gdns. SE25 202 DS96
Grange Gdns., Bans. 218 DB113
Grange Gdns., Pnr. 116 BY55
Grange Gdns., Slou. 111 AR64
Grange Gdns., Ware 33 DY07
Grange Gro. N1 142 DQ65
Grange Hill SE25 202 DS96
Grange Hill, Edg. 96 CQ50
Grange Ho., Bark. 145 ER67
St. Margarets
Grange La. SE21 182 DT89
Grange La., Harl. 50 EJ15
Grange La., Wat. 77 CD39
Grange Mans., Epsom 217 CT108
Grange Meadow, Bans. 218 DB113
Grange Ms. SE10 163 ED80
Crooms Hill
Grange Mt., Lthd. 231 CK120
Grange Par., Hayes 135 BT71
Grange Pk. W5 138 CL74
Grange Pk., Wok. 210 AY114
Grange Pk. Ave. N21 82 DQ44
Grange Pk. Pl. SW20 179 CV94
Grange Pk. Rd. E10 123 EB60
Grange Pk. Rd., Th.Hth. 202 DR98
Grange Pl. NW6 140 DA66
Grange Pl., Stai. 194 BJ96
Grange Rd. E10 123 EA60
Grange Rd. E13 144 EF69
Grange Rd. E17 123 DY57
Grange Rd. N6 120 DG58
Grange Rd. N17 100 DU51
Grange Rd. N18 100 DU51
Grange Rd. NW10 139 CV65
Grange Rd. SE1 279 N7
Grange Rd. SE1 162 DS76
Grange Rd. SE19 202 DR96
Grange Rd. SE25 202 DR97
Grange Rd. SW13 159 CU81
Grange Rd. W4 158 CP78
Grange Rd. W5 137 CK74
Grange Rd., Add. 212 BG110
Grange Rd., Borwd. 78 CM43
Grange Rd., Cat. 252 DU125
Grange Rd., Chess. 198 CL104
Grange Rd., Edg. 96 CR51
Grange Rd., Egh. 173 AZ92
Grange Rd., Ger.Cr. 90 AY53
Grange Rd., Grav. 191 GG87
Grange Rd., Grays 170 GB79
Grange Rd., Guil. 242 AV129
Grange Rd. (Greenhill), Har. 117 CG58
Grange Rd. (Roxeth), Har. 117 CD61
Grange Rd., Hayes 135 BS72
Grange Rd., Ilf. 125 EP63
Grange Rd., Kings.T. 198 CL97
Grange Rd., Lthd. 231 CK120
Grange Rd., Orp. 205 EQ103
Grange Rd., Rom. 105 FH52
Grange Rd., Sev. 256 FG127
Grange Rd., S.Croy. 220 DQ110
Grange Rd., S.Ock. 148 FQ74
Grange Rd., Sthl. 156 BY75
Grange Rd., Sutt. 218 DA108
Grange Rd., Th.Hth. 202 DR98
Grange Rd., Walt. 214 BY105
Grange Rd. (Bushey), Wat. 76 BY43
Grange Rd., W.Mol. 196 CB98
Grange Rd., Wok. 210 AY114
Grange St., St.Alb. 43 CD19
Grange Vale, Sutt. 218 DB108
Grange Wk. SE1 279 N6
Grange Wk. SE1 162 DS76
Grange Way N12 98 DB49
Grange Way, Erith 167 FH80
Grange Way, Iver 133 BF72
Grange Yd. SE1 279 P7
Grange Yd. SE1 162 DT76
Grangecliffe Gdns. SE25 202 DS96
Grangecourt Rd. N16 122 DS60
Grangedale Clo., Nthwd. 93 BS53
Grangefields Rd., Guil. 242 AX128
Grangehill Pl. SE9 165 EM83
Westmount Rd.
Grangehill Rd. SE9 165 EM84
Grangemill Rd. SE6 183 EA90
Grangemill Way SE6 183 EA89
Granger Way, Rom. 127 FG58
Grangeview Rd. N20 98 DC46
Grangeway NW6 140 DA66
Messina Ave.
Grangeway, Horl. 269 DN148
Grangeway, Wdf.Grn. 102 EJ49
Grangeway, The N21 81 DP44
Grangeway Gdns., Ilf. 124 EL57
Grangeways Clo., Grav. 191 GF91
Grangewood, Bex. 186 EZ88
Hurst Rd.
Grangewood, Pot.B. 64 DB30
Grangewood, Slou. 132 AW71
Grangewood Ave., Grays 170 GE76
Grangewood Ave., Rain. 148 FJ70
Grangewood Clo., Brwd. 109 GA48
Knight's Way
Grangewood Clo., Pnr. 115 BU57
Grangewood Dr., Sun. 175 BT94
Forest Dr.
Grangewood La., Beck. 183 DZ93
Grangewood St. E6 144 EK67
Granham Gdns. N9 100 DT47
Granite St. SE18 165 ET78
Granleigh Rd. E11 124 EE61
Gransden Ave. E8 142 DV66
Gransden Rd. W12 159 CT75
Wendell Rd.
Grant Ave., Slou. 132 AS72
Grant Clo. N14 99 DJ45
Grant Clo., Shep. 195 BP100
Grant Pl., Croy. 202 DT102
Grant Rd. SW11 160 DD84
Grant Rd., Croy. 202 DT102
Grant Rd., Har. 117 CE55
Grant St. E13 144 EG69
Grant St. N1 141 DN68
Chapel Mkt.
Grant Way, Islw. 157 CG80
Grantbridge St. N1 141 DP68
Grantchester Clo., Har. 117 CF62
Grantham Clo., Edg. 96 CL48
Grantham Gdns., Rom. 126 EZ58
Grantham Gdns., Ware 33 DY05
Grantham Grn., Borwd. 78 CQ43
Grantham Pl. W1 277 H3
Grantham Rd. E12 125 EN63
Grantham Rd. SW9 161 DL83
Grantham Rd. W4 158 CS80
Grantley Clo., Guil. 258 AY141
Grantley Gdns., Guil. 242 AU133
Grantley Rd., Guil. 242 AU133
Grantley Rd., Houns. 156 BW82
Grantley St. E1 143 DX69
Grantock Rd. E17 101 ED53
Granton Ave., Upmin. 128 FM61
Granton Rd. SW16 201 DJ95
Granton Rd., Ilf. 126 EU60
Granton Rd., Sid. 186 EW93
Grants Clo. NW7 97 CW52
Grants La., Oxt. 254 EJ133
Grantully Rd. W9 140 DB69
Grantwood Clo., Red. 267 DH139
Bushfield Dr.
Granville Ave. N9 100 DW48
Granville Ave., Felt. 175 BU89
Granville Ave., Houns. 176 CA85
Granville Ave., Slou. 131 AR71
Granville Clo., Croy. 202 DS103
Granville Clo., W.Byf. 212 BM113
Church Rd.
Granville Clo., Wey. 213 BQ107
Granville Ct. N1 142 DR67
Granville Dene, Hem.H. 57 BA27
Granville Gdns. SW16 201 DM95
Granville Gdns. W5 138 CM74
Granville Gdns., Hodd. 33 EA13
Granville Gro. SE13 163 EC83
Granville Ms., Sid. 186 EU91
Granville Pk. SE13 163 EC83
Granville Pl. (North Finchley) N12 98 DC52
High Rd.
Granville Pl. W1 272 F9
Granville Pl. W1 140 DG72
Granville Pl., Pnr. 116 BX55
Elm Pk. Rd.
Granville Rd. E17 123 EB58
Granville Rd. E18 102 EH54
Granville Rd. N4 121 DM58
Granville Rd. N12 98 DB51
Granville Rd. N13 99 DM51
Russell Rd.
Granville Rd. N22 99 DP53
Granville Rd. NW2 119 CZ61
Granville Rd. NW6 140 DA68
Granville Rd. SW18 179 CZ87
Granville Rd. SW19 180 DA94
Russell Rd.
Granville Rd., Barn. 79 CW42
Granville Rd., Berk. 38 AS17
Granville Rd., Epp. 70 EV29
Granville Rd., Grav. 191 GF88
Granville Rd., Hayes 155 BT77
Granville Rd., Ilf. 125 EP60
Granville Rd., Oxt. 254 EF129
Granville Rd., St.Alb. 43 CF20
Granville Rd., Sev. 256 FG124
Granville Rd., Sid. 186 EU91
Granville Rd., Uxb. 135 BP65

Granville Rd., Wat. 76 BW42
Granville Rd., Well. 166 EW83
Granville Rd., West. 255 EQ126
Granville Rd., Wey. 213 BQ108
Granville Rd., Wok. 227 AZ120
Granville Sq. SE15 162 DS80
Blakes Rd.
Granville Sq. WC1 274 C3
Granville Sq. WC1 141 DM69
Granville St. WC1 274 C3
Granville St. WC1 141 DM69
Grape St. WC2 273 P8
Graphite Sq. SE11 278 B10
Grasdene Rd. SE18 166 EU80
Grasmere Ave. SW15 178 CR91
Grasmere Ave. SW19 200 DA97
Grasmere Ave. W3 138 CR73
Grasmere Ave., Houns. 176 CB86
Grasmere Ave., Orp. 205 EP104
Grasmere Ave., Ruis. 115 BQ59
Grasmere Ave., Slou. 132 AU73
Grasmere Ave., Wem. 117 CJ59
Grasmere Clo., Felt. 175 BT88
Grasmere Clo., Guil. 243 BB133
Grasmere Clo., Hem.H. 41 BP22
Grasmere Clo., Loug. 85 EM40
Grasmere Clo., Wat. 59 BV32
Grasmere Ct. N22 99 DM51
Palmerston Rd.
Grasmere Gdns., Har. 95 CG54
Grasmere Gdns., Ilf. 125 EM57
Grasmere Gdns., Orp. 205 EP104
Grasmere Rd. E13 144 EG68
Grasmere Rd. N10 99 DH53
Grasmere Rd. N17 100 DU51
Grasmere Rd. SE25 202 DV100
Grasmere Rd. SW16 181 DM92
Grasmere Rd., Bexh. 167 FC81
Grasmere Rd., Brom. 204 EF95
Grasmere Rd., Orp. 205 EP104
Grasmere Rd., Pur. 219 DP111
Grasmere Rd., St.Alb. 43 CH22
Grasmere Way, W.Byf. 212 BM112
Grass Pk. N3 97 CZ53
Grass Warren, Welw. 30 DE06
Grassfield Clo., Couls. 235 DJ119
Grassingham End, Ger.Cr. 90 AY52
Grassingham Rd., Ger.Cr. 90 AY52
Grassington Clo., St.Alb. 60 CA30
Grassington Rd., Sid. 186 EU91
Grasslands, Horl. 269 DN148
Broadbridge La.
Grassmere, Horl. 269 DJ147
Grassmere Clo., Egh. 173 BB94
Keswick Rd.
Grassmere Rd., Horn. 128 FM56
Grassmount SE23 182 DV89
Grassmount, Pur. 219 DJ110
Grassway, Wall. 219 DJ105
Grassy Clo., Hem.H. 40 BG19
Grassy La., Sev. 257 FH126
Grasvenor Ave., Barn. 80 DB44
Grately Way SE15 162 DT80
Daniel Gdns.
Gratton Dr., Wind. 151 AL84
Gratton Rd. W14 159 CY76
Gratton Ter. NW2 119 CX62
Gravel Clo., Chig. 104 EU47
Gravel Hill N3 97 CZ54
Gravel Hill, Bexh. 187 FB85
Gravel Hill, Croy. 221 DX107
Gravel Hill, Ger.Cr. 90 AY51
Gravel Hill, Hem.H. 40 BH20
Melsted Rd.
Gravel Hill, Lthd. 231 CG121
Kingston Ave.
Gravel Hill, Loug. 84 EG38
Gravel Hill, Uxb. 114 BK64
Gravel Hill Clo., Bexh. 187 FB85
Gravel Hill Ter., Hem.H. 40 BG21
Gravel La. E1 275 P8
Gravel La., Chig. 85 ET42
Gravel La., Hem.H. 40 BG21
Gravel Path, Berk. 38 AX19
Gravel Path, Hem.H. 40 BG20
Gravel La.
Gravel Pit La. SE9 185 EQ85
Gravel Pit Way, Orp. 206 EU103
Gravel Pits La., Guil. 261 BQ139
Gravel Rd., Brom. 204 EL104
Gravel Rd., Dart. 188 FP94
Gravel Rd., Twick. 177 CE88
Graveley Ave., Borwd. 78 CQ42
Graveley Ct., Hem.H. 41 BQ21
Graveley Dell, Welw.G.C. 30 DB10
Waterford Grn.
Gravelly Hill, Cat. 252 DS128
Gravelly Ride SW19 179 CT91
Gravelwood Clo., Chis. 185 EQ90
Gravely Way, H.Wyc. 88 AF45
Graveney Gro. SE20 182 DW94
Graveney Rd. SW17 180 DE91
Gravesend Rd. W12 139 CU73
Gray Ave., Dag. 126 EZ60
Gray Gdns., Rain. 127 FG64
Gray St. SE1 278 E5
Grayburn Clo., Ch.St.G. 90 AU47
Grayham Cres., N.Mal. 198 CR98
Grayham Rd., N.Mal. 198 CR98
Grayland Clo., Brom. 204 EK95
Graylands, Epp. 85 ER37
Graylands, Wok. 226 AY116
Graylands Clo., Wok. 226 AY116
Grayling Clo. E16 144 EE70
Cranberry La.
Grayling Ct., Berk. 38 AT17
Tortoiseshell Way
Grayling Rd. N16 122 DR61
Grayling Sq. E2 142 DU69
Nelson Gdns.
Graylings, The, Abb.L. 59 BR33
Grays End Clo., Grays 170 GA76
Grays Fm. Rd., Orp. 206 EV95
Gray's Inn WC1 274 C6
Gray's Inn WC1 141 DM71
Gray's Inn Pl. WC1 274 C7
Gray's Inn Rd. WC1 274 A2
Gray's Inn Rd. WC1 141 DL69
Gray's Inn Sq. WC1 274 D6
Grays La., Ashf. 175 BP91
Gray's La., Ash. 232 CM119
Gray's La., Epsom 232 CP121
Shepherds' Wk.
Grays Pk. Rd., Slou. 132 AU68
Grays Pl., Slou. 132 AT74
Grays Rd., Gdmg. 258 AT144
Grays Rd., Slou. 132 AT74
Grays Rd., Uxb. 134 BL67
Grays Rd., West. 239 EP121
Grays Wk., Brwd. 109 GD45
Grays Wk., Chesh. 54 AP29
Grays Wd., Horl. 269 DJ148
Carlton Tye
Gray's Yd. W1 272 G8
Grayscroft Rd. SW16 181 DK94
Graysfield, Welw.G.C. 30 DA12
Grayshott Rd. SW11 160 DG82
Grayswood Gdns. SW20 199 CV96
Farnham Gdns.
Graywood Ct. N12 98 DC52
Grazebrook Rd. N16 122 DR61
Grazeley Clo., Bexh. 187 FC85
Grazeley Ct. SE19 182 DS91
Gipsy Hill
Grazings, The, Hem.H. 40 BM18
Great Acre Ct. SW4 161 DK84
St. Alphonsus Rd.
Great Bell All. EC2 275 K8
Great Benty, West Dr. 154 BL77
Great Bois Wd., Amer. 55 AP36
Bois Ave.
Great Braitch La., Hat. 28 CS13
Great Brays, Harl. 52 EU16
Great Break, Welw.G.C. 30 DB10
Great Brownings SE21 182 DT91
Great Bushey Dr. N20 98 DB46
Great Cambridge Rd. N9 100 DR48
Great Cambridge Rd. N17 100 DR52
Great Cambridge Rd. N18 100 DR49
Great Cambridge Rd., Brox. 67 DY26
Great Cambridge Rd., Enf. 82 DU41
Great Cambridge Rd. (Cheshunt), Wal.Cr. 66 DW32
Great Castle St. W1 273 J8
Great Castle St. W1 141 DH72
Great Cen. Ave., Ruis. 116 BW64
Great Cen. St. NW1 272 D6
Great Cen. St. NW1 140 DF71
Great Cen. Way NW10 118 CQ63
Great Chapel St. W1 273 M8
Great Chapel St. W1 141 DK72
Great Chertsey Rd. W4 158 CQ82
Great Chertsey Rd., Felt. 176 CA90
Great Ch. La. W6 159 CX78
Great College St. SW1 277 P6
Great College St. SW1 161 DL76
Great Conduit, Welw.G.C. 30 DC08
Great Cross Ave. SE10 164 EE80
Great Cullings, Rom. 127 FE61
Great Cumberland Ms. W1 272 D9
Great Cumberland Pl. W1 272 E8
Great Cumberland Pl. W1 140 DF72
Great Dell, Welw.G.C. 29 CX07
Great Dover St. SE1 279 K5
Great Dover St. SE1 162 DR75
Great Eastern Rd. E15 143 ED66
Great Eastern Rd., Brwd. 108 FW49
Great Eastern St. EC2 275 M3
Great Eastern St. EC2 142 DS69
Great Eastern Wk. EC2 275 M7
Great Ellshams, Bans. 234 DA116
Great Elms Rd., Brom. 204 EJ98
Great Elms Rd., Hem.H. 40 BM24
Great Fld. NW9 96 CS53
Great Ganett, Welw.G.C. 30 DB11
Great Gdns. Rd., Horn. 127 FH58
Great George St. SW1 277 N5
Great George St. SW1 161 DK75
Great Goodwin Dr., Guil. 243 BB132
Great Gregories La., Epp. 69 ES33
Great Gro. (Bushey), Wat. 76 CB42
Great Guildford St. SE1 279 H3
Great Guildford St. SE1 142 DQ74
Great Harry Dr. SE9 185 EN90
Great Heath, Hat. 45 CV15
Great Hivings, Chesh. 54 AN27
Great James St. WC1 274 B6
Great James St. WC1 141 DM71
Great Julians, Rick. 74 BN42
Grove Cres.
Great Lake Ct., Horl. 269 DH147
Tanyard Way
Great Ley, Welw.G.C. 29 CY11
Great Leylands, Harl. 52 EU16
Great Marlborough St. W1 273 K9
Great Marlborough St. W1 141 DJ72
Great Maze Pond SE1 279 L4
Great Maze Pond SE1 142 DR74
Great Meadow, Brox. 49 EA22
Great Molewood, Hert. 31 DP06
Great Nelmes Chase, Horn. 128 FM57
Great New St. EC4 274 E8
Great Newport St. WC2 273 N10
Great N. Rd. N2 120 DE56
Great N. Rd. N6 120 DF57
Great N. Rd., Barn. 79 CZ40
Great N. Rd., Hat. 64 DB27
Great N. Rd., Pot.B. 64 DB27
Great N. Rd., Welw. 29 CV05
Great N. Rd., Welw.G.C. 29 CU08
Great N. Way NW4 97 CV53
Great Oaks, Brwd. 109 GB44
Great Oaks, Chig. 103 EQ49
Great Oaks Pk., Guil. 243 BB129
Great Ormond St. WC1 274 A6
Great Ormond St. WC1 141 DL71
Great Owl Rd., Chig. 103 EN48
Great Palmers, Hem.H. 40 BM15
Great Pk., Kings L. 58 BM30
Great Percy St. WC1 274 C2
Great Percy St. WC1 141 DM69
Great Peter St. SW1 277 M7
Great Peter St. SW1 161 DK76
Great Plumtree, Harl. 35 ET13
Great Portland St. W1 273 J6
Great Portland St. W1 141 DH70
Great Pulteney St. W1 273 L10
Great Pulteney St. W1 141 DJ73
Great Quarry, Guil. 258 AX137
Great Queen St. WC2 274 A9
Great Queen St. WC2 141 DL72
Great Queen St., Dart. 188 FM87
Great Rd., Hem.H. 40 BM19
Great Ropers La., Brwd. 107 FU51
Great Russell St. WC1 273 N8
Great Russell St. WC1 141 DK72
Great St. Helens EC3 275 M8
Great St. Thomas Apostle EC4 275 J10
Great Scotland Yd. SW1 277 P2
Great Scotland Yd. SW1 141 DL74
Great Slades, Pot.B. 63 CZ33
Great Smith St. SW1 277 N6
Great Smith St. SW1 161 DK76
Great South-West Rd., Felt. 175 BQ87
Great South-West Rd., Houns. 155 BV83
Great Spilmans SE22 182 DS85
Great Strand NW9 97 CT53
Great Sturgess Rd., Hem.H. 39 BF20
Great Suffolk St. SE1 278 G3
Great Suffolk St. SE1 141 DP74
Great Sutton St. EC1 274 G5
Great Sutton St. EC1 141 DP70
Great Swan All. EC2 275 K8
Great Tattenhams, Epsom 233 CV118
Great Thrift, Orp. 205 EQ98
Great Titchfield St. W1 273 K6
Great Titchfield St. W1 141 DJ71
Great Twr. St. EC3 275 M10
Great Twr. St. EC3 142 DS73
Great Trinity La. EC4 275 J10
Great Turnstile WC1 274 C7
Great Warley St., Brwd. 107 FU53
Great W. Rd. W4 158 CP78
Great W. Rd. W6 159 CU78
Great W. Rd., Brent. 158 CP78
Great W. Rd., Houns. 156 BY82
Great W. Rd., Islw. 157 CD80
Great Western Ind. Pk., Sthl. 156 CB75
Great Western Rd. W9 139 CZ71
Great Western Rd. W11 139 CZ71
Great Whites Rd., Hem.H. 40 BM22
Great Winchester St. EC2 275 L8
Great Winchester St. EC2 142 DR72
Great Windmill St. W1 273 M10
Great Windmill St. W1 141 DK73
Great Woodcote Dr., Pur. 219 DK110
Great Woodcote Pk., Pur. 219 DK110
Great Yd. SE1 279 N4
Greatdown Rd. W7 137 CF70
Greatfield Ave. E6 145 EM70
Greatfield Clo. N19 121 DJ63
Warrender Rd.
Greatfield Clo. SE4 163 EA84
Greatfields Dr., Uxb. 134 BN71
Greatfields Rd., Bark. 145 ER67
Greatford Dr., Guil. 243 BD134
Greatham Rd. (Bushey), Wat. 76 BX41
Greatham Wk. SW15 179 CU88
Bessborough Rd.
Greatheart, Hem.H. 40 BL18
Greathurst End, Lthd. 230 BZ124
Greatness La., Sev. 257 FJ121
Greatness Rd., Sev. 257 FJ121
Greatorex St. E1 142 DU71
Greatwood, Chis. 185 EN94
Greatwood Clo., Cher. 211 BC109
Greaves Clo., Bark. 145 ES66
Norfolk Rd.
Greaves Pl. SW17 180 DE91
Grebe Ave., Hayes 136 BX71
Willow Tree La.
Grebe Clo. E7 124 EF64
Cormorant Rd.
Grebe Clo. E17 101 DY52
Banbury Rd.
Grebe Crest, Grays 169 FU77
Grecian Cres. SE19 181 DP93
Greding Wk., Brwd. 109 GB47
Gredo Ho., Bark. 146 EV69
Greek Ct. W1 273 N9
Greek St. W1 273 N9
Greek St. W1 141 DK72
Greek Yd. WC2 273 P10
Green, The E4 101 EC46
Green, The E11 124 EH58
Green, The E15 144 EE65
Green, The N9 100 DU47
Green, The N14 99 DK48
Green, The N21 99 DN45
Green, The SW14 158 CQ83
Green, The SW19 179 CX92
Green, The W3 138 CS72
Green, The W5 137 CK74
The Gro.
Green, The, Amer. 55 AR38
Batchelors Way
Green, The, Berk. 39 BB17
Green, The, Bexh. 166 FA81
Green, The, Brom. 204 EG101
Green, The, Cars. 218 DG105
Green, The, Cat. 237 EA123
Green, The, Ch.St.G. 90 AW47
High St.
Green, The, Croy. 221 DZ109
Green, The, Epp. 85 ES36
Green, The, Epsom 217 CU112
Green, The, Esher 215 CF107
Green, The, Felt. 175 BV89
Green, The, Hayes 135 BS72
Wood End
Green, The, Hem.H. 57 BA27
Green, The, H.Wyc. 110 AE57
Green, The, Houns. 156 CA79
Heston Rd.
Green, The, Lthd. 231 CD124
Green, The, Mord. 199 CY98
Green, The, N.Mal. 198 CQ97
Green, The (Pratt's Bottom), Orp. 224 EW110
Rushmore Hill
Green, The (St. Paul's Cray), Orp. 186 EV94
The Ave.
Green, The, Rain. 148 FL73
Green, The, Rich. 177 CK85
Green, The (Croxley Grn.), Rick. 74 BM44
Green, The (Sarratt), Rick. 74 BG35
Green, The, Sev. 257 FK122
Green, The, Shep. 195 BS98
Green, The, Sid. 186 EU91
Green, The, Slou. 130 AH70
Green, The (Chalvey), Slou. 151 AR75
Green, The (Datchet), Slou. 152 AV80
Green, The, S.Ock. 149 FW69
Green, The, Sthl. 156 BY76
Green, The, Stai. 172 AY86
Green, The, Sutt. 200 DB104
Green, The, Tad. 233 CY119
Green, The, Til. 171 GL79
Green, The, Twick. 177 CE89
Green, The, Uxb. 115 BQ61
Green, The, Wal.Abb. 67 EC34
Sewardstone Rd.
Green, The (Cheshunt), Wal.Cr. 66 DW28
Green, The, Walt. 213 BS110
Octagon Rd.
Green, The, Warl. 237 DX117
Green, The, Wat. 77 CE39
Green, The, Well. 165 ES84
Green, The, Wem. 117 CG61
Green, The, West Dr. 154 BK76
Green, The, West. 255 ER126
Green, The, Wdf.Grn. 102 EG50
Green Acres, Croy. 202 DT104
Green Acres, Hem.H. 41 BR21
Green Acres, Welw.G.C. 29 CZ12
Green Arbour Ct. EC1 274 F8
Green Ave. NW7 96 CR49
Green Ave. W13 157 CH76
Green Bank E1 142 DV74
Green Bank N12 98 DB49
Green Banks, Upmin. 129 FS60
Green Clo. NW9 118 CQ58
Green Clo. NW11 120 DC59
Green Clo., Brom. 204 EE97
Green Clo., Cars. 200 DF103
Green Clo., Epp. 51 EP24
Green Clo., Felt. 176 BY92
Green Clo., Hat. 63 CY26
Station Rd.
Green Clo., Maid. 130 AH72
Green Clo. (Cheshunt), Wal.Cr. 67 DY31
Green Common La., H.Wyc. 110 AG59
Green Ct. Rd., Swan. 207 FD100
Green Cres., H.Wyc. 110 AC56
Green Cft., Edg. 96 CQ50
Deans La.
Green Cft., Hat. 45 CU15
Talbot Rd.
Green Curve, Bans. 217 CZ114
Green Dale SE22 182 DS85
Green Dale Clo. SE22 182 DS85
Green Dale
Green Dell Way, Hem.H. 41 BQ21
Green Dene, Lthd. 245 BT131
Green Dragon Ct. SE1 279 K2
Green Dragon La. N21 81 DN43
Green Dragon La., Brent. 158 CL78
Green Dragon Yd. E1 142 DU71
Old Montague St.
Green Dr., Slou. 152 AY77
London Rd.
Green Dr., Sthl. 136 CA74
Green Dr., Wok. 227 BF123
Green E. Rd., Beac. 90 AS52
Green End N21 99 DP47
Green End, Chess. 216 CL105
Green End Gdns., Hem.H. 40 BG21
Green End La., Hem.H. 39 BF20
Green End Rd., Hem.H. 40 BG20
Green Gdns., Orp. 223 EQ106
Green Glade, Epp. 85 ES37
Green Glades, Horn. 128 FM58
Green Hill SE18 165 EM78
Green Hill, Buck.H. 102 EJ46
Green Hill, Orp. 223 EM112
Green Hill La., Warl. 237 DY117
Sunny Bank
Green Hill Ter. SE18 165 EM78
Green Hill Way, Croy. 221 DX112
Green Hundred Rd. SE15 162 DU79
Green La. E4 83 ED41
Green La. NW4 119 CX56
Green La. SE9 185 EP88
Green La. SE20 183 DX94
Green La. SW16 181 DM94
Green La. W7 157 CE75
Green La., Add. 194 BG104
Green La., Amer. 55 AS38
Green La. (Chesham Bois), Amer. 55 AR35
Green La., Ash. 231 CJ117
Green La., Brwd. 108 FU46
Greenshaw
Green La. (Pilgrim's Hatch), Brwd. 108 FV43
Green La. (Warley), Brwd. 107 FU52
Green La., Brox. 49 EB23
Green La., Cher. 193 BE103
Green La., Chesh. 56 AV34
Green La., Chess. 216 CL109
Green La., Chig. 103 EQ46
Green La., Chis. 185 EP90
Green La., Cob. 214 BY112
Green La., Couls. 250 DA125
Green La., Dag. 126 EX61
Green La., Edg. 96 CM49
Green La., Egh. 173 BB92
Green La. (Thorpe), Egh. 193 BD95
Green La., Felt. 176 BY92
Green La., Gdmg. 258 AS142
Green La., Guil. 243 BB134
Green La. (Shamley Grn.), Guil. 260 BG144
Green La. (West Clandon), Guil. 244 BG127
Green La., Harl. 52 FA16
Green La., Har. 117 CE62
Green La., Hem.H. 41 BQ21
Green La. (Bovingdon), Hem.H. 57 BA28
Green La., Horl. 269 DM152
Green La., Houns. 155 BV83
Green La., Ilf. 125 EQ61
Green La., Lthd. 231 CK121
Green La. (Fifield), Maid. 150 AC81
Green La., Mord. 200 DA100
Green La., N.Mal. 198 CQ99
Green La., Nthwd. 93 BR52
Green La., Pur. 219 DJ111
Green La., Red. 250 DE132
Green La. (Bletchingley), Red. 252 DS131
Green La. (Outwood), Red. 267 DL141
Green La. (White Bushes), Red. 266 DG139
Green La., Reig. 249 CZ134
Green La., Rick. 74 BM43
Green La., St.Alb. 42 CC17
Green La., Shep. 195 BQ100
Green La., Slou. 130 AJ69
Green La. (Datchet), Slou. 152 AV81
Green La. (Farnham Common), Slou. 111 AP64
Green La., S.Ock. 149 FR69
Green La., Stai. 193 BE95
Green La., Stan. 95 CH49
Green La., Sun. 175 BT94
Green La., Tad. 249 CZ126
Green La., Th.Hth. 201 DP95
Green La., Upmin. 149 FR68
Green La., Uxb. 135 BQ71
Green La., Wal.Abb. 68 EJ34
Green La., Walt. 213 BV107
Green La., Warl. 237 DY116
Green La., Wat. 94 BW46
Green La. (Panshanger), Welw.G.C. 30 DD10
Green La., W.Byf. 212 BM112
Green La., W.Mol. 196 CB99
Green La., Wind. 151 AN82
Green La. (Chobham), Wok. 210 AT110
Green La. (Mayford), Wok. 226 AV121
Copper Beech Clo.
Green La. (Ockham), Wok. 229 BP124
Green La., Wor.Pk. 199 CU102
Green La. Ave., Walt. 214 BW106
Green La. Caravan Pk., Red. 267 DL141
Green La. Clo., Amer. 55 AR36
Green La. Clo., Cher. 193 BE103
Green La. Clo., W.Byf. 212 BM112
Green La. Gdns., Th.Hth. 201 DP96
Green La. W., Wok. 244 BN125
Green Las. N4 121 DP59
Green Las. N8 121 DP55
Green Las. N13 99 DM51
Green Las. N15 121 DP55
Green Las. N16 122 DQ62
Green Las. N21 99 DP47
Green Las., Epsom 216 CS109
Green Las., Hat. 29 CT13
Green Las., Welw.G.C. 29 CT11
Green Lawns, Ruis. 116 BW60
Green Leaf Ave., Wall. 219 DK105
Ferrers Ave.
Green Leas, Sun. 175 BT94
Green Leas, Wal.Abb. 67 ED34
Roundhills
Green Man Gdns. W13 137 CG73
Green Man La. W13 137 CG73
Green Man La., Felt. 155 BU84
Green Man Rd., Ong. 53 FC19
Green Manor Way, Grav. 170 FZ84
Green Mead, Esher 214 BZ107
Winterdown Gdns.
Green Meadow, Pot.B. 64 DA30
Green Moor Link N21 99 DP45
Green N. Rd., Beac. 90 AS51
Green Pk., Stai. 173 BE90
Green Pl., Dart. 187 FE85
Green Pt. E15 144 EE65
Green Pond Clo. E17 123 DY55
Green Pond Rd. E17 123 DY55
Green Ride, Epp. 85 EP35
Green Ride, Loug. 84 EG43
Green Rd. N14 81 DH44
Green Rd. N20 98 DC48
Green Rd., Egh. 193 BA99
Green Sand Rd., Red. 250 DG133
Noke Dr.
Green Shield Ind. Est. E16 144 EG74
Green St. E7 144 EH65
Green St. E13 144 EJ66
Green St. W1 272 E10
Green St. W1 140 DF73
Green St., Enf. 82 DW40
Green St., Hat. 45 CZ20
Green St., Hert. 32 DR09
Green St., Rad. 62 CN34
Green St., Rick. 73 BC41
Green St., Sun. 195 BU95
Green St. Grn. Rd., Dart. 188 FP88
Green Tiles La., Uxb. 113 BF58
Green Vale W5 138 CM72
Green Vale, Bexh. 186 EX85
Green Verges, Stan. 95 CK52
Green Vw., Chess. 216 CM108
Green Vw. Clo., Hem.H. 57 BA29
Green Wk. NW4 119 CX57
Green Wk. SE1 279 M7
Green Wk., Dart. 187 FF85
Green Wk., Hmptn. 176 BZ93
Orpwood Clo.
Green Wk., Ruis. 115 BT60
Green Wk., Sthl. 156 CA78
Green Wk., Wdf.Grn. 102 EL51
Green Wk., The E4 101 EC46
Green Way SE9 184 EK85
Green Way, Brom. 204 EL100
Green Way, Red. 250 DE132
Green Way, Slou. 130 AH68
Green Way, Sun. 195 BU98
Green W. Rd., Beac. 90 AS52
Green Wrythe Cres., Cars. 200 DE102
Green Wrythe La., Cars. 200 DD100
Greenacre, Dart. 188 FL89
Oakfield La.
Greenacre, Wind. 151 AL82
Greenacre, Wok. 226 AS116
Mead Ct.
Greenacre Clo., Barn. 79 CZ38
Greenacre Clo., Swan. 207 FE98
Greenacre Ct., Egh. 172 AW93
Greenacre Gdns. E17 123 EC56
Greenacre Sq. SE16 163 DX75
Fishermans Dr.
Greenacre Wk. N14 99 DL48
Greenacres SE9 185 EN86
Greenacres, Epp. 69 ET28
Greenacres, Lthd. 230 CB124

Greenacres, Oxt. 254 EE127
Greenacres (Bushey), Wat. 95 CD47
Greenacres Ave., Uxb. 114 BM62
Greenacres Clo., Nthlt. 116 BZ64
Eastcote La.
Greenacres Clo., Orp. 223 EQ105
State Fm. Ave.
Greenacres Clo., Rain. 148 FL69
Greenacres Dr., Stan. 95 CH51
Greenall Clo. (Cheshunt), Wal.Cr. 67 DY30
Greenaway Gdns. NW3 120 DB63
Greenbank (Cheshunt), Wal.Cr. 66 DV28
Greenbank Ave., Wem. 117 CG64
Greenbank Clo. E4 101 EC47
Greenbank Clo., Rom. 106 FK48
Greenbank Cres. NW4 119 CY56
Greenbank Rd., Wat. 75 BR36
Greenbanks, Dart. 188 FL89
Greenbanks, St.Alb. 43 CF22
Colindale Ave.
Greenbay Rd. SE7 164 EK80
Greenberry St. NW8 272 B1
Greenberry St. NW8 140 DE68
Greenbrook Ave., Barn. 80 DC39
Greenbury Clo., Rick. 73 BC41
Green St.
Greencoat Pl. SW1 277 L8
Greencoat Pl. SW1 161 DJ77
Greencoat Row SW1 277 L7
Greencourt Ave., Croy. 202 DV103
Greencourt Ave., Edg. 96 CP53
Greencourt Gdns., Croy. 202 DV102
Greencourt Rd., Orp. 205 ER99
Greencrest Pl. NW2 119 CV62
Dollis Hill La.
Greencroft, Guil. 243 BB134
Greencroft Ave., Ruis. 116 BW61
Greencroft Clo. E6 144 EL71
Neatscourt Rd.
Greencroft Gdns. NW6 140 DB66
Greencroft Gdns., Enf. 82 DS41
Greencroft Rd., Houns. 156 BZ81
Greendale Ms., Slou. 132 AU73
St. Pauls Ave.
Greendale Wk., Grav. 190 GE90
Greene Fielde End, Stai. 174 BK94
Berryscroft Rd.
Greene Wk., Berk. 38 AX20
Greenend Rd. W4 158 CS75
Greenfarm Clo., Orp. 223 ET106
Greenfell St. SE10 164 EE76
Greenfern Ave., Slou. 130 AJ72
Greenfield, Hat. 45 CX15
Greenfield, Welw.G.C. 29 CX06
Greenfield Ave., Surb. 198 CP101
Greenfield Ave., Wat. 94 BX47
Greenfield End, Ger.Cr. 91 AZ52
Greenfield Gdns. NW2 119 CY61
Greenfield Gdns., Dag. 146 EX67
Greenfield Gdns., Orp. 205 ER101
Greenfield Link, Couls. 235 DL115
Greenfield Rd. E1 142 DU71
Greenfield Rd. N15 122 DS57
Greenfield Rd., Berk. 38 AW19
Greenfield Rd., Dag. 146 EW66
Greenfield Rd., Dart. 187 FD92
Greenfield St., Wal.Abb. 67 EC34
Greenfield Way, Har. 116 CB55
Greenfields, Loug. 85 EN42
Greenfields (Cuffley), Pot.B. 65 DL30
South Dr.
Greenfields Clo., Brwd. 107 FW51
Essex Way
Greenfields Clo., Horl. 268 DE146
Greenfields Clo., Loug. 85 EN42
Greenfields Rd., Horl. 268 DF146
Greenford Ave. W7 137 CE70
Greenford Ave., Sthl. 136 BZ73
Greenford Gdns., Grnf. 136 CB69
Greenford Rd., Grnf. 136 CC72
Greenford Rd., Har. 117 CF63
Greenford Rd., Sthl. 136 CC72
Greenford Rd., Sutt. 218 DB105
Greengate, Grnf. 137 CH65
Greengate St. E13 144 EH68
Greenhalgh Wk. N2 120 DC56
Greenham Clo. SE1 278 D5
Greenham Clo. SE1 161 DN75
Greenham Cres. E4 101 DZ51
Silver Birch Ave.
Greenham Rd. N10 98 DG54
Greenham Wk., Wok. 226 AW118
Greenhayes Ave., Bans. 218 DA114
Greenhayes Clo., Reig. 250 DC134
Greenhayes Gdns., Bans. 234 DA115
Greenheys Clo., Nthwd. 93 BS53
Greenheys Dr. E18 124 EF55
Greenheys Pl., Wok. 227 AZ118
White Rose La.
Greenhill NW3 120 DD63
Hampstead High St.
Greenhill, Sutt. 200 DC103
Greenhill, Wem. 118 CP61
Greenhill Ave., Cat. 236 DV121
Greenhill Cres., Wat. 75 BS44
Greenhill Gdns., Guil. 243 BC131
Greenhill Gdns., Nthlt. 136 BZ68
Greenhill Gro. E12 124 EL63
Greenhill Pk. NW10 138 CS67
Greenhill Pk., Barn. 80 DB43
Greenhill Rd. NW10 138 CS67
Greenhill Rd., Grav. 191 GF89
Greenhill Rd., Har. 117 CE58
Greenhill Ter., Nthlt. 136 BZ68
Greenhill Way, Har. 117 CE58
Greenhill Way, Wem. 118 CP61
Greenhills, Harl. 51 ES15
Greenhills Clo., Rick. 74 BH43
Greenhill's Rents EC1 274 F6
Greenhills Ter. N1 142 DR65
Baxter Rd.
Greenhithe Clo., Sid. 185 ES87
Greenholm Rd. SE9 185 EP85
Greenhurst La., Oxt. 254 EF132
Greenhurst Rd. SE27 181 DN92
Greening St. SE2 166 EW77
Greenland Cres., Sthl. 156 BW76
Greenland Ms. SE8 163 DX78
Trundleys Rd.
Greenland Pl. NW1 141 DH67
Greenland Rd.
Greenland Quay SE16 163 DX77
Greenland Rd. NW1 141 DH67
Greenland Rd., Barn. 79 CW44
Greenland St. NW1 141 DH67
Camden High St.
Greenlands Rd., Stai. 174 BG91
Greenlands Rd., Wey. 195 BP104
Greenlaw Gdns., N.Mal. 199 CT101
Greenlaw St. SE18 165 EN76
Greenlea Trd. Pk. SW19 200 DD95
Greenleaf Clo. SW2 181 DN87
Tulse Hill
Greenleaf Rd. E6 144 EJ67
Redclyffe Rd.
Greenleaf Rd. E17 123 DZ55
Greenleafe Dr., Ilf. 125 EP55
Greenleaves Ct., Ashf. 175 BP93
Redleaves Ave.
Greenleigh Ave., Orp. 206 EV98
Chipperfield Rd.
Greenman St. N1 142 DQ66
Greenmeads, Wok. 226 AY122
Greenmoor Rd., Enf. 82 DW40
Greeno Cres., Shep. 194 BN99
Greenoak Ri., West. 238 EJ118
Greenoak Way SW19 179 CX91
Greenock Ave., Slou. 131 AN72
Greenock Rd. SW16 201 DK95
Greenock Rd. W3 158 CP76
Greenock Way, Rom. 105 FE52
Greenpark Ct., Wem. 137 CJ66
Bridgewater Rd.
Greens Clo., The, Loug. 85 EN40
Green's Ct. W1 273 M10
Green's End SE18 165 EP77
Greensand Way, Bet. 264 CM136
Old Sch. La.
Greensand Way, Dor. 263 CK136
Punchbowl La.
Greenshank Clo. E17 101 DY52
Banbury Rd.
Greenshaw, Brwd. 108 FV46
Greenside, Bex. 186 EY88
Greenside, Borwd. 78 CN38
Greenside, Dag. 126 EW60
Greenside, Slou. 131 AN71
Greenside, Swan. 207 FD96
Greenside Clo. N20 98 DD47
Greenside Clo. SE6 183 ED89
Penderry Ri.
Greenside Clo., Guil. 243 BC132
Foxglove Gdns.
Greenside Rd. W12 159 CU76
Greenside Rd., Croy. 201 DN101
Greenside Rd., Wey. 195 BP104
Greenside Wk., West. 238 EH118
Kings Rd.
Greenslade Ave., Ash. 232 CP119
Greenstead, Saw. 36 EY06
Greenstead Ave., Wdf.Grn. 102 EJ52
Greenstead Clo., Brwd. 109 GE45
Greenstead Clo., Wdf.Grn. 102 EJ51
Greenstead Gdns.
Greenstead Gdns. SW15 179 CU85
Greenstead Gdns., Wdf.Grn. 102 EJ51
Greensted Rd., Loug. 102 EL45
Greensted Rd., Ong. 71 FG28
Greenstone Ms. E11 124 EG58
Greensward (Bushey), Wat. 76 CB44
Ashfield Ave.
Greenvale, Welw.G.C. 30 DA10
Greenvale Rd. SE9 165 EM84
Greenview Ave., Beck. 203 DY100
Greenview Ave., Croy. 203 DY100
Greenview Ct., Ashf. 174 BM91
Village Way
Greenville Clo., Cob. 214 BY113
Greenway N14 99 DL47
Greenway N20 98 DA47
Greenway SW20 199 CW98
Greenway, Berk. 38 AT19
Greenway, Brwd. 109 GA45
Greenway, Chesh. 54 AP28
Greenway, Chis. 185 EN92
Greenway, Dag. 126 EW61
Greenway, Harl. 50 EL15
Greenway, Har. 118 CL57
Greenway, Hayes 135 BU69
Greenway, Hem.H. 41 BP20
Greenway, Lthd. 230 CB123
Greenway, Pnr. 93 BV54
Greenway, Rom. 106 FP51
Greenway, Wall. 219 DJ105
Greenway, West. 238 EJ120
Greenway, Wdf.Grn. 102 EJ50
Greenway, The NW9 96 CR54
Greenway, The, Enf. 83 DX35
Greenway, The, Epsom 216 CN114
Greenway, The, Ger.Cr. 112 AX55
Greenway, The, Har. 95 CE53
Greenway, The, Houns. 156 BZ84
Greenway, The, Orp. 206 EV100
Greenway, The, Oxt. 254 EH133
Greenway, The, Pnr. 116 BZ58
Greenway, The, Pot.B. 64 DA33
Greenway, The, Rick. 92 BG45
Greenway, The, Slou. 131 AK74
Greenway, The, Uxb. 134 BK68
Greenway, The (Ickenham), Uxb. 115 BP61
Greenway Ave. E17 123 ED56
Greenway Clo. N4 122 DQ61
Greenway Clo. N11 98 DG51
Greenway Clo. N15 122 DT56
Copperfield Dr.
Greenway Clo. N20 98 DA47
Greenway Clo. NW9 96 CR54
Greenway Clo., W.Byf. 212 BG113
Greenway Dr., Stai. 194 BK95
Greenway Gdns. NW9 96 CR54
Greenway Gdns., Croy. 203 DZ104
Greenway Gdns., Grnf. 136 CA69
Greenway Gdns., Har. 95 CE54
Greenway Par., Chesh. 54 AP28
Greenways, Abb.L. 59 BS32
Greenways, Beck. 203 EA96
Greenways, Egh. 172 AY92
Greenways, Esher 215 CE105
Greenways, Hert. 31 DN09
Greenways, Tad. 249 CV125
Greenways (Cheshunt), Wal.Cr. 65 DP29
Greenways, Wok. 227 BA117
Pembroke Rd.
Greenways, The, Twick. 177 CG86
Greenwell St. W1 273 J5
Greenwell St. W1 141 DH70
Greenwich Ch. St. SE10 163 EC79
Greenwich Cres. E6 144 EL71
Swan App.
Greenwich High Rd. SE10 163 EB81
Greenwich Ind. Est. SE7 164 EH77
Greenwich Mkt. SE10 163 EC79
Greenwich Pk. SE10 163 ED80
Greenwich Pk. St. SE10 163 ED78
Greenwich S. St. SE10 163 EB81
Greenwich Vw. Pl. E14 163 EB76
Greenwood, The, Guil. 243 BA134
Greenwood Ave., Dag. 127 FB63
Greenwood Ave., Enf. 83 DY40
Greenwood Ave. (Cheshunt), Wal.Cr. 66 DV31
Greenwood Clo., Add. 211 BF111
Greenwood Clo., Amer. 55 AS38
Greenwood Clo., Beac. 89 AQ51
Farmers Way
Greenwood Clo., Mord. 199 CY98
Greenwood Clo., Orp. 205 ES100
Greenwood Clo., Sid. 186 EU89
Hurst Rd.
Greenwood Clo., T.Ditt. 197 CG102
Greenwood Clo. (Cheshunt), Wal.Cr. 66 DV31
Greenwood Ave.
Greenwood Clo. (Bushey), Wat. 95 CE45
Langmead Dr.
Greenwood Ct. SW1 161 DJ78
Cambridge St.
Greenwood Dr. E4 101 EC50
Avril Way
Greenwood Dr., Red. 266 DG139
Greenwood Dr., Wat. 59 BV34
Greenwood Gdns. N13 99 DP48
Greenwood Gdns., Cat. 252 DU125
Greenwood Gdns., Ilf. 103 EQ52
Greenwood La., Hmptn. 176 CB92
Greenwood Pk., Kings.T. 178 CS94
Greenwood Pl. NW5 121 DH64
Highgate Rd.
Greenwood Rd. E8 142 DU65
Greenwood Rd. E13 144 EF68
Maud Rd.
Greenwood Rd., Bex. 187 FD91
Greenwood Rd., Chig. 104 EV48
Greenwood Rd., Croy. 201 DP101
Greenwood Rd., Islw. 157 CF83
Greenwood Rd., Mitch. 201 DK97
Greenwood Rd., T.Ditt. 197 CG102
Greenwood Rd., Wok. 226 AS120
Greenwood Ter. NW10 138 CR67
Greenwood Way, Sev. 256 FF125
Greenwoods, The, Har. 116 CC61
Sherwood Rd.
Greenyard, Wal.Abb. 67 EC34
Greer Rd., Har. 94 CC53
Greet St. SE1 278 E3
Greet St. SE1 141 DN74
Greg Clo. E10 123 EC58
Essex Rd.
Gregor Ms. SE3 164 EG80
Gregories Fm. La., Beac. 89 AK53
Gregories Rd., Beac. 88 AH53
Gregory Ave., Pot.B. 64 DC33
Gregory Cres. SE9 184 EK87
Gregory Dr., Wind. 172 AV86
Gregory Pl. W8 160 DB75
Gregory Rd., Rom. 126 EX56
Gregory Rd., Slou. 111 AR61
Gregory Rd., Sthl. 156 CA76
Gregson Clo., Borwd. 78 CQ39
Greig Clo. N8 121 DL57
Greig Ter. SE17 161 DP79
Lorrimore Sq.
Grena Gdns., Rich. 158 CM84
Grena Rd., Rich. 158 CM84
Grenaby Ave., Croy. 202 DR101
Grenaby Rd., Croy. 202 DR101
Grenada Rd. SE7 164 EJ80
Grenade St. E14 143 DZ73
Grenadier St. E16 145 EN74
Grenadine Clo., Wal.Cr. 66 DT27
Allwood Rd.
Grendon Clo., Horl. 268 DF146
Grendon Gdns., Wem. 118 CN61
Grendon St. NW8 272 B4
Grendon St. NW8 140 DE70
Grenfell Ave., Horn. 127 FF60
Grenfell Clo., Borwd. 78 CQ39
Denham Way
Grenfell Gdns., Har. 118 CL59
Grenfell Rd. W11 139 CX73
Grenfell Rd., Beac. 89 AL52
Grenfell Rd., Mitch. 180 DF93
Grenfell Twr. W11 139 CX73
Grenfell Wk. W11 139 CX73
Whitchurch Rd.
Grennell Clo., Sutt. 200 DD103
Grennell Rd., Sutt. 200 DC104
Grenoble Gdns. N13 99 DN51
Grenville Ave., Brox. 49 DZ21
Grenville Clo. N3 97 CZ53
Grenville Clo., Slou. 130 AH68
Grenville Clo., Surb. 198 CQ102
Grenville Clo., Wal.Cr. 67 DX32
Grenville Gdns., Wdf.Grn. 102 EJ53
Grenville Ms. SW7 160 DC77
Grenville Ms., Hmptn. 176 CB92
Grenville Pl. NW7 96 CR50
Grenville Pl. SW7 160 DC76
Grenville Rd. N19 121 DL60
Grenville Rd., Croy. 221 EC109
Grenville St. WC1 274 A5
Grenville St. WC1 141 DL70
Gresford Clo., St.Alb. 43 CK20
Gresham Ave. N20 98 DF49
Gresham Ave., Warl. 237 DY118
Gresham Clo., Bex. 186 EY86
Gresham Clo., Brwd. 108 FW48
Gresham Clo., Enf. 82 DQ41
Gresham Clo., Oxt. 254 EF128
Gresham Rd.
Gresham Ct., Berk. 38 AV20
Gresham Dr., Rom. 126 EV57
Gresham Gdns. NW11 119 CY60
Gresham Rd. E6 145 EM68
Gresham Rd. E16 144 EH72
Gresham Rd. NW10 118 CR64
Gresham Rd. SE25 202 DU98
Gresham Rd. SW9 161 DN83
Gresham Rd., Beck. 203 DY96
Gresham Rd., Brwd. 108 FW48
Gresham Rd., Edg. 96 CM51
Gresham Rd., Hmptn. 176 CA93
Gresham Rd., Houns. 156 CC81
Gresham Rd., Oxt. 254 EF128
Gresham Rd., Slou. 131 AN72
Gresham Rd., Stai. 173 BF92
Gresham Rd., Uxb. 134 BN68
Gresham St. EC2 275 J8
Gresham St. EC2 142 DQ72
Gresham Way SW19 180 DA90
Gresley Clo. N15 122 DR56
Clinton Rd.
Gresley Clo., Welw.G.C. 29 CY08
Gresley Ct., Pot.B. 64 DC29
Gresley Rd. N19 121 DJ60
Gresse St. W1 273 M8
Gresse St. W1 141 DK71
Gressenhall Rd. SW18 179 CZ86
Gresswell Clo., Sid. 186 EU90
Greswell St. SW6 159 CX81
Greta Bank, Lthd. 245 BQ126
Gretton Rd. N17 100 DS52
Greville Ave., S.Croy. 221 DX110
Greville Clo., Ash. 232 CL119
Greville Clo., Guil. 242 AS134
Greville Clo., Hat. 45 CV24
Greville Clo., Twick. 177 CH87
Greville Ct., Lthd. 246 CC125
Keswick Rd.
Greville Hall NW6 140 DB68
Greville Ms. NW6 140 DB68
Greville Rd.
Greville Pk. Ave., Ash. 232 CL118
Greville Pk. Rd., Ash. 232 CL118
Greville Pl. NW6 140 DB68
Greville Rd. E17 123 EC56
Greville Rd. NW6 140 DB68
Greville Rd., Rich. 178 CM86
Greville St. EC1 274 E7
Greville St. EC1 141 DN71
Grey Alders, Bans. 217 CW114
High Beeches
Grey Clo. NW11 120 DC58
Grey Eagle St. E1 142 DT71
Grey Twrs. Ave., Horn. 128 FK60
Grey Twrs. Gdns., Horn. 128 FK60
Grey Twrs. Ave.
Greycaine Rd., Wat. 76 BX37
Greycoat Pl. SW1 277 M7
Greycoat Pl. SW1 161 DK76
Greycoat St. SW1 277 M7
Greycoat St. SW1 161 DK76
Greycot Rd., Beck. 183 EA92
Greyfell Clo., Stan. 95 CH50
Coverdale Clo.
Greyfields Clo., Pur. 219 DP113
Greyfriars, Brwd. 109 GB45
Greyfriars Pas. EC1 274 G8
Greyfriars Rd., Wok. 228 BG124
Greygoose Pk., Harl. 51 EN18
Greyhound Hill NW4 119 CU55
Greyhound La. SW16 181 DK93
Greyhound La., Grays 171 GG75
Greyhound La., Pot.B. 63 CU33
Greyhound Rd. N17 122 DS55
Greyhound Rd. NW10 139 CV69
Greyhound Rd. W6 159 CX79
Greyhound Rd. W14 159 CY79
Greyhound Rd., Sutt. 218 DC106
Greyhound Ter. SW16 201 DJ95
Greyhound Way, Dart. 187 FE86
Greys Pk. Clo., Kes. 222 EK106
Greystead Rd. SE23 182 DW87
Greystoke Ave., Pnr. 116 CA55
Greystoke Clo., Berk. 38 AU20
Greystoke Dr., Ruis. 115 BP58
Greystoke Gdns. W5 138 CL70
Greystoke Gdns., Enf. 81 DK42
Greystoke Pk. Ter. W5 137 CK69
Greystoke Pl. EC4 274 D8
Greystoke Rd., Slou. 131 AM71
Greystone Clo., S.Croy. 220 DW111
Greystone Gdns., Har. 117 CJ58
Greystone Gdns., Ilf. 103 EQ54
Greystones Clo., Red. 266 DD136
Hardwick Rd.
Greystones Dr., Reig. 250 DC132
Greyswood St. SW16 181 DH93
Greythorne Rd., Wok. 226 AU118
Grice Ave., West. 222 EH113
Gridiron Pl., Upmin. 128 FP61
Grierson Rd. SE23 183 DX87
Grieves Rd., Grav. 191 GF90
Griffetts Yd., Chesh. 54 AP30
Bellingdon Rd.
Griffin Ave., Upmin. 129 FS58
Griffin Clo. NW10 119 CV64
Griffin Clo., Slou. 151 AQ75
Griffin Manor Way SE28 165 ER76
Griffin Rd. N17 100 DS54
Griffin Rd. SE18 165 ER78
Griffin Wk., Green. 189 FT85
Church Rd.
Griffin Way, Lthd. 246 CA126
Griffin Way, Sun. 195 BU96
Griffins, The, Grays 170 GB75
Griffith Clo., Dag. 126 EW60
Gibson Rd.
Griffiths Clo., Wor.Pk. 199 CV103
Griffiths Rd. SW19 180 DA94
Griffiths Way, St.Alb. 42 CC22
Grifon Rd., Grays 169 FW77
Arterial Rd. W. Thurrock
Griggs App., Ilf. 125 EQ61
Griggs Pl. SE1 279 N6
Griggs Rd. E10 123 EC58
Grilse Clo. N9 100 DV49
Parr Clo.
Grimsby St. E2 142 DU70
Cheshire St.
Grimsdells La., Amer. 55 AR37
Grimsdyke Cres., Barn. 79 CW41
Grimsdyke Rd., Pnr. 94 BY52
Grimsel Path SE5 161 DP80
Laxley Clo.
Grimshaw Clo. N6 120 DG59
Grimshaw Way, Rom. 127 FF57
Grimston Rd. SW6 159 CZ82
Grimston Rd., St.Alb. 43 CF21
Grimstone Clo., Rom. 105 FB51
Grimthorpe Clo., St.Alb. 43 CD17
Grimwade Ave., Croy. 202 DU104
Grimwade Clo. SE15 162 DW83
Grimwade Cres. SE15 162 DW83
Evelina Rd.
Grimwood Rd., Twick. 177 CF87
Grindal St. SE1 278 D5
Grindall Clo., Croy. 219 DP105
Hillside Rd.
Grindcobbe, St.Alb. 43 CD23
Trumpington Dr.
Grindley Gdns., Croy. 202 DT100
Grinling Pl. SE8 163 EA79
Grinstead Rd. SE8 163 DY78
Grisedale Clo., Pur. 220 DR114
Grisedale Gdns., Pur. 220 DS114
Grittleton Ave., Wem. 138 CP65
Grittleton Rd. W9 140 DA70
Grizedale Ter. SE23 182 DV89
Eliot Bank
Grobars Ave., Wok. 226 AW115
Grocer's Hall Ct. EC2 275 K9
Grogan Clo., Hmptn. 176 BZ93
Groom Cres. SW18 180 DD87
Groom Pl. SW1 276 G6
Groom Pl. SW1 160 DG76
Groom Rd., Brox. 67 DZ26
Groom Wk., Guil. 242 AY130
Slyfield Grn.
Groombridge Clo., Walt. 213 BV106
Groombridge Clo., Well. 186 EU85
Groombridge Rd. E9 143 DX66
Groomfield Clo. SW17 180 DG91
Grooms Cotts., Chesh. 56 AV30
Grooms Dr., Pnr. 115 BU57
Grosmont Rd. SE18 165 ET79
Grosse Way SW15 179 CV86
Grosvenor Ave. N5 122 DQ64
Grosvenor Ave. SW14 158 CS83
Grosvenor Ave., Cars. 218 DF107
Grosvenor Ave., Har. 116 CB58
Grosvenor Ave., Hayes 135 BS68
Grosvenor Ave., Kings L. 59 BQ28
Grosvenor Ave., Rich. 178 CL85
Grosvenor Rd.
Grosvenor Clo., Iver 133 BD69
Grosvenor Clo., Loug. 85 EP39
Grosvenor Cotts. SW1 276 F8
Grosvenor Ct. N14 99 DJ45
Grosvenor Ct., Guil. 243 BA132
London Rd.
Grosvenor Ct., Rick. 75 BR43
Mayfare
Grosvenor Ct., Slou. 132 AS72
Stoke Poges La.
Grosvenor Cres. NW9 118 CN56
Grosvenor Cres. SW1 276 G5
Grosvenor Cres. SW1 160 DG75
Grosvenor Cres., Dart. 188 FK85
Grosvenor Cres., Uxb. 135 BP66
Grosvenor Cres. Ms. SW1 276 F5
Grosvenor Cres. Ms. SW1 160 DG75
Grosvenor Dr., Horn. 128 FJ60
Grosvenor Dr., Loug. 85 EP40
Grosvenor Dr., Maid. 130 AC71
Grosvenor Est. SW1 277 N8
Grosvenor Est. SW1 161 DK77
Grosvenor Gdns. E6 144 EK69
Grosvenor Gdns. N10 121 DJ55
Grosvenor Gdns. N14 81 DK42
Grosvenor Gdns. NW2 119 CW64
Grosvenor Gdns. NW11 119 CZ58
Grosvenor Gdns. SW1 277 J7
Grosvenor Gdns. SW1 161 DH76
Grosvenor Gdns. SW14 158 CS83
Grosvenor Gdns., Kings.T. 177 CK93
Grosvenor Gdns., Upmin. 129 FR60
Grosvenor Gdns., Wall. 219 DJ108
Grosvenor Gdns., Wdf.Grn. 102 EG51
Grosvenor Gdns. Ms. E. SW1 277 J6
Grosvenor Gdns. Ms. N. SW1 277 H7
Grosvenor Gdns. Ms. S. SW1 277 J7
Grosvenor Gate W1 276 E1
Grosvenor Hill SW19 179 CY93
Grosvenor Hill W1 273 H10
Grosvenor Hill W1 141 DH73
Grosvenor Pk. SE5 162 DQ80
Grosvenor Pk. Rd. E17 123 EA57
Grosvenor Path, Loug. 85 EP39
Grosvenor Pl. SW1 276 G5
Grosvenor Pl. SW1 160 DG75
Grosvenor Pl., Wey. 195 BR104
Vale Rd.
Grosvenor Ri. E. E17 123 EB57
Grosvenor Rd. E6 144 EK67
Grosvenor Rd. E7 144 EH65
Grosvenor Rd. E10 123 EC60
Grosvenor Rd. E11 124 EG57
Grosvenor Rd. N3 97 CZ52
Grosvenor Rd. N9 100 DV46
Grosvenor Rd. N10 99 DH53
Grosvenor Rd. SE25 202 DU98
Grosvenor Rd. SW1 161 DH79
Grosvenor Rd. W4 158 CP78
Grosvenor Rd. W7 137 CG74
Grosvenor Rd., Belv. 166 FA79
Grosvenor Rd., Bexh. 186 EX85
Grosvenor Rd., Borwd. 78 CN41
Grosvenor Rd., Brent. 157 CK79
Grosvenor Rd., Brox. 49 DZ20
Grosvenor Rd., Dag. 126 EZ60
Grosvenor Rd., Epsom 232 CR119
Grosvenor Rd., Houns. 156 BZ83
Grosvenor Rd., Ilf. 125 EQ62
Grosvenor Rd., Nthwd. 93 BT50
Grosvenor Rd., Orp. 205 ES100
Grosvenor Rd., Rich. 178 CL85
Grosvenor Rd., Rom. 127 FD59
Grosvenor Rd., St.Alb. 43 CE21
Grosvenor Rd., Sthl. 156 BZ76
Grosvenor Rd., Stai. 174 BG94
Grosvenor Rd., Twick. 177 CG87
Grosvenor Rd., Wall. 219 DH107
Grosvenor Rd., Wat. 76 BW41
Grosvenor Rd., W.Wick. 203 EB102
Grosvenor Sq. W1 272 G10
Grosvenor Sq. W1 140 DG73
Grosvenor St. W1 273 H10
Grosvenor St. W1 141 DH73
Grosvenor Ter. SE5 162 DQ79
Grosvenor Ter., Hem.H. 40 BG21
Grosvenor Vale, Ruis. 115 BT61
Grosvenor Way E5 122 DW61
Mount Pleasant Hill
Grosvenor Wf. Rd. E14 163 ED77
Grote's Bldgs. SE3 164 EE82
Grote's Pl. SE3 164 EE82
Groton Rd. SW18 180 DB89
Grotto, The, Ware 33 DX07
Grotto Pas. W1 272 G6
Grotto Rd., Twick. 177 CF89
Grotto Rd., Wey. 195 BP104
Ground La., Hat. 45 CV16
Grove, The E15 144 EE65
Grove, The N3 98 DA53
Grove, The N4 121 DM59

Grove, The N6 120 DG60
Grove, The N8 121 DK57
Grove, The N13 99 DN50
Grove, The N14 81 DJ43
Grove, The NW9 118 CR57
Grove, The NW11 119 CY59
Grove, The W5 137 CK74
Grove, The, Add. 212 BH106
Grove, The, Amer. 55 AR36
Grove, The, Bexh. 166 EX84
Grove, The, Brwd. 108 FT49
Grove, The, Cat. 235 DP121
Grove, The, Chesh. 72 AX36
Grove, The, Couls. 235 DK115
Grove, The, Edg. 96 CP49
Grove, The, Egh. 173 BA92
Grove, The, Enf. 81 DN40
Grove, The, Epsom 216 CS113
Grove, The (Ewell), Epsom 217 CT110
West St.
Grove, The, Esher 196 CB102
Grove, The, Grav. 191 GH87
Grove, The, Grnf. 136 CC72
Grove, The, Hat. 64 DA26
Grove, The, Horl. 269 DH149
Grove, The, Islw. 157 CE81
Grove, The, Pot.B. 64 DD32
Grove, The, Rad. 61 CG34
Grove, The, Sid. 186 EY92
Grove, The, Slou. 152 AU75
Grove, The, Swan. 207 FF97
Grove, The, Swans. 190 FZ85
Grove, The, Tedd. 177 CG91
Grove, The, Twick. 177 CH86
Bridge Rd.
Grove, The, Upmin. 128 FP63
Grove, The, Uxb. 114 BN64
Grove, The, Walt. 195 BV101
Grove, The, W.Wick. 203 EB104
Grove, The, West. 238 EK118
Grove, The, Wok. 227 AZ116
Grove Ave. N3 98 DA52
Grove Ave. N10 99 DJ54
Grove Ave. W7 137 CE72
Grove Ave., Epsom 216 CS113
Grove Ave., Pnr. 116 BY57
Grove Ave., Sutt. 218 DA107
Grove Rd.
Grove Ave., Twick. 177 CF88
Grove Clo. N14 99 DH45
Avenue Rd.
Grove Clo. SE23 183 DY88
Grove Clo., Brom. 204 EG103
Grove Clo., Felt. 176 BY91
Grove Clo., Ger.Cr. 90 AW53
Grove La.
Grove Clo., Kings.T. 198 CM98
Grove Clo., Slou. 152 AU76
Alpha St. S.
Grove Clo., Uxb. 114 BN64
Grove Clo., Wind. 172 AV87
Grove Cor., Lthd. 246 CA126
Lower Shott
Grove Cotts. SW3 160 DE79
Grove Ct. SE3 164 EG81
Grove Ct., E.Mol. 197 CD99
Walton Rd.
Grove Ct., Wal.Abb. 67 EB33
Grove Cres. E18 102 EF54
Grove Cres. NW9 118 CQ56
Grove Cres. SE5 162 DS82
Grove Cres., Felt. 176 BY91
Grove Cres., Kings.T. 198 CL97
Grove Cres., Rick. 74 BN42
Grove Cres., Walt. 195 BV101
Grove Cres. Rd. E15 143 ED65
Grove End E18 102 EF54
Grove Hill
Grove End, Ger.Cr. 90 AW53
Grove End La., Esher 197 CD102
Grove End Rd. NW8 140 DD68
Grove Fm. Ind. Est., Mitch. 200 DF99
Grove Fm. Pk., Nthwd. 93 BR50
Grove Footpath, Surb. 198 CL98
Grove Gdns. E15 144 EE65
Grove Gdns. NW4 119 CU57
Grove Gdns. NW8 272 C3
Grove Gdns., Dag. 127 FC62
Grove Gdns., Enf. 83 DX38
Grove Gdns., Tedd. 177 CG91
Grove Grn. Rd. E11 123 EC62
Grove Hall Ct. NW8 140 DC69
Hall Rd.
Grove Hall Rd., Wat. 76 BY42
Grove Heath Ct., Wok. 228 BJ124
Grove Heath N., Wok. 228 BH122
Grove Heath Rd. (Ripley), Wok. 228 BH123
Grove Hill E18 102 EF54
Grove Hill, Ger.Cr. 90 AW52
Grove Hill, Har. 117 CE59
Grove Hill Rd. SE5 162 DS83
Grove Hill Rd., Har. 117 CE59
Grove Ho. Rd. N8 121 DL56
Grove La. SE5 162 DS82
Grove La., Beac. 89 AL53
Grove La., Chesh. 56 AU27
Grove La., Chig. 103 ET48
Grove La., Couls. 219 DH114
Grove La., Epp. 70 EU30
High St.
Grove La., Ger.Cr. 90 AV53
Grove La., Kings.T. 198 CL98
Grove La., Uxb. 134 BM70
Grove Lea, Hat. 45 CU21
Grove Mkt. Pl. SE9 185 EM86
Grove Mead, Hat. 45 CT18
Grove Meadow, Welw.G.C. 30 DC09
Grove Ms. W6 159 CW76
Grove Ms. W11 139 CZ72
Portobello Rd.
Grove Mill La., Wat. 75 BP37
Grove Pk. E11 124 EH58
Grove Pk. NW9 118 CQ56
Grove Pk. SE5 162 DS82
Grove Pk. Ave. E4 101 EB52
Grove Pk. Bri. W4 158 CQ80
Grove Pk. Gdns. W4 158 CQ80
Grove Pk. Ms. W4 158 CQ80
Grove Pk. Rd. N15 122 DS56
Grove Pk. Rd. SE9 184 EJ90
Grove Pk. Rd. W4 158 CP80
Grove Pk. Rd., Rain. 147 FG67
Grove Pk. Ter. W4 158 CP80
Grove Pas. E2 142 DV68
The Oval
Grove Pas., Tedd. 177 CG92
Grove Path (Cheshunt), Wal.Cr. 66 DU31
Tudor Ave.
Grove Pl. NW3 120 DD63
Christchurch Hill
Grove Pl. W3 138 CQ74
Grove Pl. W5 137 CK74
The Gro.
Grove Pl., Bark. 145 EQ67
Clockhouse Ave.
Grove Pl., Hat. 45 CW24
Dixons Hill Rd.
Grove Pl., Wat. 76 CB39
Hartspring La.
Grove Pl., Wey. 213 BQ106
Princes Rd.
Grove Rd. E3 143 DX67
Grove Rd. E4 101 EC49
Grove Rd. E11 124 EF59
Grove Rd. E17 123 EB58
Grove Rd. E18 102 EF54
Grove Rd. N11 99 DH50
Grove Rd. N12 98 DD50
Grove Rd. N15 122 DS57
Grove Rd. NW2 139 CW65
Grove Rd. SW13 159 CT82
Grove Rd. SW19 180 DC94
Grove Rd. W3 138 CQ74
Grove Rd. W5 137 CK73
Grove Rd., Amer. 72 AT37
Grove Rd., Ash. 232 CM118
Grove Rd., Barn. 80 DE41
Grove Rd., Beac. 89 AK53
Grove Rd., Belv. 166 EZ79
Grove Rd., Bexh. 167 FC84
Grove Rd., Borwd. 78 CN39
Grove Rd., Brent. 157 CJ78
Grove Rd., Cher. 193 BF100
Grove Rd., E.Mol. 197 CD98
Grove Rd., Edg. 96 CN51
Grove Rd., Epsom 216 CS113
Grove Rd., Grav. 190 GB85
Grove Rd., Grays 170 GB79
Grove Rd., Guil. 243 BC134
Grove Rd., Hem.H. 40 BG22
Grove Rd., Horl. 268 DE147
Grove Rd., Houns. 156 CA84
Grove Rd., Islw. 157 CE81
Grove Rd., Mitch. 200 DG97
Grove Rd., Nthwd. 93 BR50
Grove Rd., Oxt. 253 EC134
Southlands La.
Grove Rd., Pnr. 116 BZ57
Grove Rd., Rich. 178 CM86
Grove Rd., Rick. 92 BG47
Grove Rd., Rom. 126 EV59
Grove Rd., St.Alb. 43 CD21
Grove Rd., Sev. 257 FJ121
Grove Rd. (Seal), Sev. 257 FN122
Grove Rd., Shep. 195 BQ100
Grove Rd., Slou. 131 AK68
Grove Rd., Surb. 197 CK99
Grove Rd., Sutt. 218 DA107
Grove Rd., Th.Hth. 201 DN98
Grove Rd., Twick. 177 CD90
Grove Rd., Uxb. 134 BK66
Grove Rd., Ware 33 DZ05
Grove Rd., West. 238 EJ120
Grove Rd., Wind. 151 AQ82
Grove Rd., Wok. 227 AZ116
Grove Rd. W., Enf. 82 DW37
Grove Shaw, Tad. 233 CY124
Grove St. N18 100 DT50
Grove St. SE8 163 DZ77
Grove Ter. NW5 121 DH62
Grove Ter., Tedd. 177 CG91
Grove Vale SE22 162 DS84
Grove Vale, Chis. 185 EN93
Grove Vill. E14 143 EB73
Grove Wk., Hert. 32 DQ07
Grove Way, Esher 196 CC101
Grove Way, Rick. 73 BB43
Grove Way, Uxb. 134 BK66
Grove Wd. Hill, Couls. 219 DJ114
Grovebarns, Stai. 174 BG93
Grovebury Clo., Erith 167 FD79
Grovebury Gdns., St.Alb. 60 CC27
Grovebury Rd. SE2 166 EV75
Grovedale Clo. (Cheshunt), Wal.Cr. 66 DT30
Grovedale Rd. N19 121 DK61
Grovehall Rd. (Bushey), Wat. 76 BY42
Grovehill Rd., Red. 250 DE134
Groveland Ave. SW16 181 DM94
Groveland Ct. EC4 275 J9
Groveland Rd., Beck. 203 DZ97
Groveland Way, N.Mal. 198 CQ99
Grovelands, Hem.H. 41 BQ18
Grovelands, St.Alb. 60 CB27
Grovelands, W.Mol. 196 CA98
Grovelands Clo. SE5 162 DS82
Grovelands Clo., Har. 116 CB62
Grovelands Ct. N14 99 DK45
Grovelands Rd. N13 99 DM49
Grovelands Rd. N15 122 DU58
Grovelands Rd., Orp. 186 EU94
Grovelands Rd., Pur. 219 DL112
Grovelands Way, Grays 170 FZ78
Groveley Rd., Sun. 175 BS92
Grover Clo., Hem.H. 40 BK18
Grover Rd., Wat. 76 BX44
Groves Clo., B.End 110 AC60
Groveside, Lthd. 246 CA127
Groveside Clo. W3 138 CP72
Groveside Clo., Cars. 200 DE103
Groveside Clo., Lthd. 246 CA127
Groveside Rd. E4 102 EE47
Grovestile Waye, Felt. 175 BR87
Groveway SW9 161 DM81
Groveway, Dag. 126 EX63
Groveway, Wem. 118 CQ64
Grovewood, Rich. 158 CM81
Sandycombe Rd.
Grovewood Clo., Rick. 73 BB43
Grovewood Pl., Wdf.Grn. 103 EM51
Manor Rd.
Grubb St., Oxt. 254 EJ128
Grubbs La., Hat. 46 DA22
Grummant Rd. SE15 162 DT81
Grundy St. E14 143 EB72
Gruneisen Rd. N3 98 DB52
Guardian Clo., Horn. 127 FH60
Guards Club Rd., Maid. 130 AC72
Guards Rd., Wind. 150 AJ82
Guards Wk., Wind. 150 AJ82
Guards Rd.
Guardsman Clo., Brwd. 108 FX50
Gubbins La., Rom. 106 FM52
Gubyon Ave. SE24 181 DP85
Guerin Sq. E3 143 DZ69
Malmesbury Rd.
Guernsey Clo., Guil. 243 BA129
Cotts Wd. Dr.
Guernsey Clo., Houns. 156 CA81
Guernsey Fm. Dr., Wok. 226 AX115
Guernsey Gro. SE24 182 DQ87
Guernsey Rd. E11 123 ED60
Guessens Ct., Welw.G.C. 29 CW09
Guessens Gro., Welw.G.C. 29 CW09
Guessens Rd., Welw.G.C. 29 CW09
Guessens Wk., Welw.G.C. 29 CW08
Guibal Rd. SE12 184 EH87
Guild Rd. SE7 164 EK78
Guild Rd., Erith 167 FF80
Guildcroft, Guil. 243 BA134
Guildersfield Rd. SW16 181 DL94
Guildford & Godalming Bypass, Guil. 258 AS137
Guildford Ave., Felt. 175 BT89
Guildford Gdns., Rom. 106 FL51
Guildford Gro. SE10 163 EB81
Guildford La., Guil. 260 BH139
Guildford La., Wok. 226 AX120
Guildford Lo. Dr., Lthd. 245 BT129
Guildford Pk. Ave., Guil. 258 AV135
Guildford Pk. Rd., Guil. 258 AV135
Guildford Rd. E6 145 EM72
Guildford Rd. E17 101 EC53
Guildford Rd. SW8 161 DL81
Guildford Rd., Cher. 193 BE102
Guildford Rd., Croy. 202 DR100
Guildford Rd. (Abinger Hammer), Dor. 261 BS139
Guildford Rd. (Westcott), Dor. 262 CA138
Guildford Rd., Gdmg. 258 AU144
Guildford Rd., Guil. 242 AX127
Guildford Rd., Ilf. 125 ES61
Guildford Rd., Lthd. 247 CE125
Guildford Rd. (Bookham), Lthd. 246 BZ127
Guildford Rd. (East Horsley), Lthd. 245 BT130
Guildford Rd., Rom. 106 FL51
Guildford Rd., St.Alb. 43 CH21
Guildford Rd., Wok. 226 AY119
Guildford Rd. (Mayford), Wok. 226 AX122
Guildford St., Cher. 193 BF102
Guildford St., Stai. 174 BG93
Guildford Way, Wall. 219 DL106
Guildhall Bldgs. EC2 275 K8
Guildhall Yd. EC2 142 DR72
Gresham St.
Guildhouse St. SW1 277 K8
Guildhouse St. SW1 161 DJ77
Guildown Ave. N12 98 DB49
Guildown Ave., Guil. 258 AV137
Guildown Rd., Guil. 258 AV137
Guildsway E17 101 DZ53
Guileshill La., Wok. 228 BL123
Guilford Ave., Surb. 198 CM99
Guilford Pl. WC1 274 B5
Guilford Pl. WC1 141 DM70
Guilford St. WC1 274 A5
Guilford St. WC1 141 DL70
Guilford Vill., Surb. 198 CM100
Alpha Rd.
Guilfords, Harl. 36 EX10
Guilsborough Clo. NW10 138 CS66
Guinevere Gdns., Wal.Cr. 67 DX31
Guinness Bldgs. SE1 279 M7
Guinness Bldgs. SE1 162 DS77
Guinness Clo. E9 143 DY66
Guinness Clo., Hayes 155 BR76
Guinness Ct., Wok. 226 AT118
Iveagh Rd.
Guinness Sq. SE1 279 M8
Guinness Trust Bldgs. SE11 278 F10
Guinness Trust Bldgs. SE11 161 DP78
Guinness Trust Bldgs. SW3 276 D9
Guinness Trust Est. N16 122 DS60
Guinness Trust Est. SW9 161 DP84
Guion Rd. SW6 159 CZ82
Gull Clo., Wall. 219 DL108
Gull Wk., Horn. 147 FH66
Heron Flight Ave.
Gulland Clo. (Bushey), Wat. 76 CC43
Gulland Wk. N1 142 DQ65
Marquess Est.
Gullbrook, Hem.H. 40 BG20
Gullet Wd. Rd., Wat. 75 BU35
Gulliver Clo., Nthlt. 136 BZ67
Gulliver Rd., Sid. 185 ES89
Gulliver St. SE16 163 DZ76
Gulphs, The, Hert. 32 DR09
Gumleigh Rd. W5 157 CJ77
Gumley Gdns., Islw. 157 CG83
Gumley Rd., Grays 169 FX79
Gumping Rd., Orp. 205 EQ102
Gun Hill, Til. 171 GK79
Gun St. E1 275 P7
Gun St. E1 142 DT71
Gundulph Rd., Brom. 204 EJ97
Gunfleet Clo., Grav. 191 GL87
Gunmakers La. E3 143 DY67
Gunn Rd., Swans. 190 FY86
Gunnell Clo. SE26 182 DU91
High Level Dr.
Gunnell Clo., Croy. 202 DU100
Gunner La. SE18 165 EN78
Gunners Gro. E4 101 EC48
Gunners Rd. SW18 180 DD89
Gunnersbury Ave. W3 138 CM74
Gunnersbury Ave. W4 138 CM74
Gunnersbury Ave. W5 138 CM74
Gunnersbury Clo. W4 158 CP78
Grange Rd.
Gunnersbury Ct. W3 158 CP75
Bollo La.
Gunnersbury Cres. W3 158 CN75
Gunnersbury Dr. W5 158 CM75
Gunnersbury Gdns. W3 158 CN75
Gunnersbury La. W3 158 CN76
Gunnersbury Ms. W4 158 CP78
Chiswick High Rd.
Gunnersbury Pk. W3 158 CM77
Gunnersbury Pk. W5 158 CM77
Gunning St. SE18 165 ES77
Gunpowder Sq. EC4 274 E8
Gunpowder Sq. EC4 141 DN72
Gunsite, The, Cob. 214 BW113
Gunstor Rd. N16 122 DS63
Gunter Gro. SW10 160 DC79
Gunter Gro., Edg. 96 CR53
Gunterstone Rd. W14 159 CY77
Gunthorpe St. E1 142 DT71
Gunton Rd. E5 122 DV61
Gunton Rd. SW17 180 DG93
Gunwhale Clo. SE16 143 DX74
Gurdon Rd. SE7 164 EG78
Gurnard Clo., West Dr. 134 BK73
Trout Rd.
Gurnell Gro. W13 137 CF70
Gurnells Rd., Beac. 89 AQ50
Gurney Clo. E15 124 EE64
Gurney Rd.
Gurney Clo. E17 101 DX53
Gurney Clo., Bark. 145 EP65
Gurney Ct. Rd., St.Alb. 43 CF18
Gurney Cres., Croy. 201 DM102
Gurney Dr. N2 120 DC56
Gurney Rd. E15 124 EE64
Gurney Rd., Cars. 200 DG104
Gurney Rd., Nthlt. 135 BV69
Gurney's Clo., Red. 266 DF135
Guthrie St. SW3 276 B10
Gutter La. EC2 275 J8
Gutter La. EC2 142 DQ72
Gutteridge La., Rom. 87 FC44
Stapleford Rd.
Guy Barnett Clo. SE3 164 EG83
Casterbridge Rd.
Guy Rd., Wall. 201 DK104
Guy St. SE1 279 L4
Guy St. SE1 162 DR75
Guyatt Gdns., Mitch. 200 DG96
Ormerod Gdns.
Guyscliff Rd. SE13 183 EC85
Guysfield Clo., Rain. 147 FG67
Guysfield Dr., Rain. 147 FG67
Gwalior Rd. SW15 159 CX83
Felsham Rd.
Gwendolen Ave. SW15 159 CX84
Gwendolen Clo. SW15 179 CX85
Gwendoline Ave. E13 144 EH67
Gwendwr Rd. W14 159 CY78
Gwent Clo., Wat. 60 BX34
Gwillim Clo., Sid. 186 EU85
Gwydor Rd., Beck. 203 DX98
Gwydyr Rd., Brom. 204 EF97
Gwyn Clo. SW6 160 DC80
Gwynn Rd., Grav. 190 GC89
Gwynne Ave., Croy. 203 DX101
Gwynne Clo. W4 158 CS80
Pumping Sta. Rd.
Gwynne Clo., Wind. 151 AL81
Gwynne Pk. Ave., Wdf.Grn. 103 EM51
Gwynne Pl. WC1 274 C3
Gwynne Rd. SW11 160 DD82
Gwynne Vaughan Ave., Guil. 242 AU130
Gwynns Wk., Hert. 32 DS09
Gyfford Wk., Wal.Cr. 66 DV31
Hawthorne Clo.
Gylcote Clo. SE5 162 DR84
Gyles Pk., Stan. 95 CJ52
Gyllyngdune Gdns., Ilf. 125 ET62
Gypsy Clo., Ware 33 DZ11
Gypsy La., Hat. 29 CZ13
Gypsy La., Kings L. 59 BR33
Gypsy La., Slou. 112 AS62
Gypsy La., Ware 33 DZ11
Gypsy Moth Ave., Hat. 44 CS15

H

Ha-Ha Rd. SE18 165 EM79
Haarlem Rd. W14 159 CX76
Haberdasher Pl. N1 275 L2
Haberdasher St. N1 275 L2
Haberdasher St. N1 142 DR69
Habgood Rd., Loug. 84 EL41
Haccombe Rd. SW19 180 DC93
Haydons Rd.
Hackbridge Grn., Wall. 200 DG103
Hackbridge Pk. Gdns., Cars. 200 DG103
Hackbridge Rd., Wall. 200 DG103
Hackett La., Saw. 35 ET05
Hacketts La., Wok. 211 BF114
Hackford Rd. SW9 161 DM81
Hackforth Clo., Barn. 79 CV43
Hackhurst La., Dor. 261 BT139
Hackington Cres., Beck. 183 EA93
Hackney Clo., Borwd. 78 CR43
Hackney Gro. E8 142 DV65
Reading La.
Hackney Rd. E2 275 P2
Hackney Rd. E2 142 DT69
Hacton Dr., Horn. 128 FK63
Hacton La., Horn. 128 FM61
Hacton La., Upmin. 128 FM64
Hadden Rd. SE28 165 ES76
Hadden Way, Grnf. 137 CD65
Haddington Rd., Brom. 183 ED91
Haddo St. SE10 163 EC79
Haddon Clo., Borwd. 78 CN40
Haddon Clo., Enf. 82 DU44
Haddon Clo., Hem.H. 40 BN21
Haddon Clo., N.Mal. 199 CT99
Haddon Clo., Wey. 195 BR104
Haddon Gro., Sid. 185 ET87
Haddon Rd., Orp. 206 EW99
Haddon Rd., Rick. 73 BC43
Haddon Rd., Sutt. 218 DB105
Haddonfield SE8 163 DX77
Hadfield Clo., Sthl. 136 BZ69
Adrienne Ave.
Hadfield Rd., Stai. 174 BK86
Hadleigh Clo. E1 142 DW70
Mantus Rd.
Hadleigh Clo. SW20 199 CZ96
Aylward Rd.
Hadleigh Ct., Brox. 49 DZ22
Hadleigh Dr., Sutt. 218 DB109
Homeland Dr.
Hadleigh Rd. N9 100 DV45
Hadleigh St. E2 142 DW69
Hadleigh Wk. E6 144 EL72
Kirkham Rd.
Hadley Clo. N21 81 DN44
Hadley Clo., Borwd. 78 CM43
Hadley Common, Barn. 80 DA40
Hadley Gdns. W4 158 CR78
Hadley Gdns., Sthl. 156 BZ78
Hadley Gra., Harl. 52 EW15
Hadley Grn., Barn. 79 CZ40
Hadley Grn. Rd., Barn. 79 CZ40
Hadley Grn. W., Barn. 79 CY40
Hadley Gro., Barn. 79 CY40
Hadley Highstone, Barn. 79 CZ39
Hadley Pl., Wey. 212 BN108
Lonsdale Rd.
Hadley Ridge, Barn. 79 CZ41
Hadley Rd. (Hadley Wd.), Barn. 80 DG38
Hadley Rd. (New Barnet), Barn. 80 DB41
Hadley Rd., Belv. 166 EZ77
Hadley Rd., Enf. 81 DL38
Hadley Rd., Mitch. 201 DK98
Hadley St. NW1 141 DH65
Hadley Way N21 81 DN44
Hadley Wd. Ri., Ken. 235 DP115
Hadlow Ct., Slou. 131 AQ73
Hadlow Pl. SE19 182 DU94
Hadlow Rd., Sid. 186 EU91
Hadlow Rd., Well. 166 EW80
Hadlow Way, Grav. 190 GE94
Hadrian Clo., St.Alb. 42 CA22
Hadrian Clo., Stai. 174 BL88
Hadrian Way
Hadrian Clo., Wall. 219 DL108
De Havilland Rd.
Hadrian Est. E2 142 DU68
Hackney Rd.
Hadrian St. SE10 164 EE78
Hadrian Way, Stai. 174 BK87
Hadrians Ride, Enf. 82 DT43
Hadyn Pk. Rd. W12 159 CU75
Hafer Rd. SW11 160 DF84
Hafton Rd. SE6 184 EE88
Hag Hill La., Maid. 130 AG72
Hag Hill Ri., Maid. 130 AG72
Hagden La., Wat. 75 BT43
Haggard Rd., Twick. 177 CG87
Haggerston Rd. E8 142 DT66
Haggerston Rd., Borwd. 78 CL38
Hagsdell La., Hert. 32 DR09
Hagsdell Rd., Hert. 32 DR09
Hague St. E2 142 DU69
Derbyshire St.
Haig Clo., St.Alb. 43 CH21
Kitchener Clo.
Haig Dr., Slou. 151 AP75
Haig Gdns., Grav. 191 GJ87
Haig Rd., Grays 171 GG76
Haig Rd., Stan. 95 CJ50
Haig Rd., Uxb. 135 BP71
Haig Rd., West. 238 EL117
Haig Rd. E. E13 144 EJ69
Haig Rd. W. E13 144 EJ69
Haigh Cres., Red. 267 DH136
Haigville Gdns., Ilf. 125 EP56
Hailes Clo. SW19 180 DC93
North Rd.
Hailey Ave., Hodd. 33 EA13
Hailey La., Hert. 33 DX13
Hailey Rd., Erith 166 FA75
Haileybury Ave., Enf. 82 DT44
Haileybury Rd., Orp. 224 EU105
Hailsham Ave. SW2 181 DM89
Hailsham Clo., Rom. 106 FJ50
Hailsham Clo., Surb. 197 CK101
Hailsham Dr., Har. 117 CD55
Hailsham Gdns., Rom. 106 FJ50
Hailsham Rd. SW17 180 DG93
Hailsham Rd., Rom. 106 FJ50
Hailsham Ter. N18 100 DQ50
Haimo Rd. SE9 184 EK85
Hainault Ct. E17 123 ED56
Hainault Gore, Rom. 126 EY57
Hainault Gro., Chig. 103 EQ49
Hainault Rd. E11 123 EC60
Hainault Rd., Chig. 103 EP48
Hainault Rd., Rom. 105 FC54
Hainault Rd. (Chadwell Heath), Rom. 126 EZ58
Hainault Rd. (Hainault), Rom. 126 EV55
Hainault St. SE9 185 EP88
Hainault St., Ilf. 125 EQ61
Haines Ct., Wey. 213 BR106
St. George's Lo.
Haines Way, Wat. 59 BU34
Hainford Clo. SE4 163 DX84
Haining Clo. W4 158 CN78
Wellesley Rd.
Hainthorpe Rd. SE27 181 DP90
Hainton Clo. E1 142 DV72
Commercial Rd.
Halberd Ms. E5 122 DV61
Knightland Rd.
Halbutt Gdns., Dag. 126 EZ62
Halbutt St., Dag. 126 EZ63
Halcomb St. N1 142 DS67
Halcot Ave., Bexh. 187 FB85
Halcrow St. E1 142 DV71
Newark St.
Halcyon Way, Horn. 128 FM60
Haldan Rd. E4 101 EC51
Haldane Clo. N10 99 DH52
Haldane Gdns., Grav. 190 GC88
Springhead Rd.
Haldane Pl. SW18 180 DB88
Haldane Rd. E6 144 EK69
Haldane Rd. SE28 146 EX73
Haldane Rd. SW6 159 CZ80
Haldane Rd., Sthl. 136 CC73
Haldens, Welw.G.C. 29 CZ06
Haldon Clo., Chig. 103 ES50
Haldon Rd. SW18 179 CZ85
Hale, The E4 101 ED52
Hale, The N17 122 DU55
Hale Clo. E4 101 EC48
Hale Clo., Edg. 96 CQ50
Hale Clo., Orp. 223 EQ105
Hale Dr. NW7 96 CQ51
Hale End, Rom. 105 FH51
Hale End, Wok. 226 AV121
Hook Heath Rd.
Hale End Clo., Ruis. 115 BU58
Hale End Rd. E4 101 ED51
Hale End Rd. E17 101 ED53
Hale End Rd., Wdf.Grn. 101 ED52
Hale Gdns. N17 122 DU55
Hale Gdns. W3 138 CN74
Hale Gro. Gdns. NW7 96 CR50
Hale La. NW7 96 CR50
Hale La., Edg. 96 CP50
Hale La., Sev. 241 FE117
Hale Path SE27 181 DP91
Hale Pit Rd., Lthd. 246 CC126
Hale Rd. E6 144 EL70

Hale Rd. N17 122 DU55
Hale Rd., Hert. 32 DR10
Hale St. E14 143 EB73
Hale St., Stai. 173 BE91
Hale Wk. W7 137 CE71
Benham Rd.
Halefield Rd. N17 100 DU53
Hales Oak, Lthd. 246 CC126
Hales Pk., Hem.H. 41 BQ19
Hales Pk. Clo., Hem.H. 41 BQ19
Hales St. SE8 163 EA80
Deptford High St.
Halesowen Rd., Mord. 200 DB101
Haleswood, Cob. 213 BV114
Haleswood Rd., Hem.H. 41 BP19
Halesworth Clo. E5 122 DW61
Theydon Rd.
Halesworth Clo., Rom. 106 FL52
Halesworth Rd. SE13 163 EB83
Halesworth Rd., Rom. 106 FL51
Haley Rd. NW4 119 CW58
Half Acre, Brent. 157 CK79
Half Acre Rd. W7 137 CE74
Half Moon Ct. EC1 275 H7
Half Moon Cres. N1 141 DM68
Half Moon La. SE24 182 DQ86
Half Moon La., Epp. 69 ET31
Half Moon Meadow, Hem.H. 41 BP15
Half Moon Pas. E1 142 DT72
Braham St.
Half Moon St. W1 277 J2
Half Moon St. W1 141 DH74
Half Moon Yd., St.Alb. 43 CD20
Chequer St.
Halfacre Hill, Ger.Cr. 91 AZ53
Halfhide La. (Cheshunt), Wal.Cr. 67 DX27
Halfhides, Wal.Abb. 67 ED33
Halford Rd. E10 123 ED57
Halford Rd. SW6 160 DA79
Halford Rd., Rich. 178 CL85
Halford Rd., Uxb. 114 BN64
Halfpenny Clo., Guil. 259 BD140
Halfpenny La., Guil. 259 BC136
Halfway Ct., Purf. 168 FN77
Thamley
Halfway Grn., Walt. 195 BV104
Halfway Ho. La., Amer. 54 AL33
Halfway St., Sid. 185 ER87
Haliburton Rd., Twick. 177 CG85
Haliday Wk. N1 142 DR65
Balls Pond Rd.
Halidon Clo. E9 122 DW64
Urswick Rd.
Halidon Ri., Rom. 106 FP51
Halifax Rd., Enf. 82 DQ40
Halifax Rd., Grnf. 136 CB67
Halifax Rd., Rick. 91 BC45
Halifax St. SE26 182 DV91
Halifax Way, Welw.G.C. 30 DE09
Halifield Dr., Belv. 166 EY76
Haling Down Pas., S.Croy. 220 DQ109
Kingsdown Ave.
Haling Gro., S.Croy. 220 DQ108
Haling Pk. Gdns., S.Croy. 219 DP107
Haling Pk. Rd., S.Croy. 219 DP107
Haling Rd., S.Croy. 220 DR107
Halings La., Uxb. 113 BD56
Halkin Arc. SW1 276 F6
Halkin Ms. SW1 276 F6
Halkin Pl. SW1 276 F6
Halkin Pl. SW1 160 DG76
Halkin St. SW1 276 G5
Halkin St. SW1 160 DG75
Halkingcroft, Slou. 152 AW75
Hall, The SE3 164 EG83
Hall Ave. N18 100 DR51
Weir Hall Ave.
Hall Ave., S.Ock. 148 FQ74
Hall Clo. W5 138 CL71
Hall Clo., Gdmg. 258 AS144
Hall Clo., Rick. 92 BG46
Hall Ct., Slou. 152 AV80
Hall Ct., Tedd. 177 CF92
Teddington Pk.
Hall Cres., S.Ock. 168 FQ75
Hall Dene Clo., Guil. 243 BC133
Hall Dr. SE26 182 DW92
Hall Dr. W7 137 CE72
Hall Dr., Uxb. 92 BJ53
Hall Fm. Clo., Stan. 95 CH49
Hall Fm. Dr., Twick. 177 CD87
Hall Gdns. E4 101 DZ49
Hall Gdns., St.Alb. 44 CR23
Hall Gate NW8 140 DC69
Hall Rd.
Hall Grn. La., Brwd. 109 GC45
Hall Gro., Welw.G.C. 30 DB11
Hall Heath Clo., St.Alb. 43 CH18
Hall Hill, Oxt. 253 ED131
Hall Hill, Sev. 257 FP123
Hall La. E4 101 DY50
Hall La. NW4 97 CU53
Hall La., Brwd. 109 FZ44
Hall La., Hayes 155 BR80
Hall La., S.Ock. 149 FW68
Hall La., Upmin. 106 FQ54
Hall Meadow, Slou. 130 AJ68
Hall Oak Wk. NW6 139 CZ65
Maygrove Rd.
Hall Pk., Berk. 38 AY20
Hall Pk. Gate, Berk. 38 AY21
Hall Pk. Hill, Berk. 38 AY21
Hall Pk. Rd., Upmin. 128 FQ64
Hall Pl. W2 140 DD70
Hall Pl., Wok. 227 BA116
Hall Pl. Clo., St.Alb. 43 CE19
Hall Pl. Cres., Bex. 187 FC85
Hall Pl. Dr., Wey. 213 BS106
Hall Pl. Gdns., St.Alb. 43 CE19
Hall Rd. E6 145 EM67
Hall Rd. E15 123 ED63
Hall Rd. NW8 140 DC69
Hall Rd., Dart. 168 FM84
Hall Rd., Grav. 190 GC90
Hall Rd., Hem.H. 41 BP18
Hall Rd., Islw. 177 CD85
Hall Rd., Rom. 126 EW58
Hall Rd. (Gidea Pk.), Rom. 127 FH55
Hall Rd., S.Ock. 168 FQ75
Hall Rd., Wall. 219 DH109
Hall St. EC1 274 G2
Hall St. EC1 141 DP69
Hall St. N12 98 DC50
Hall Ter., Rom. 106 FN52
Hall Ter., S.Ock. 169 FR75
Hall Vw. SE9 184 EK89
Hall Way, Pur. 219 DP113
Downs Ct. Rd.
Hallam Clo., Chis. 185 EM92
Hallam Clo., Wat. 76 BW40
Reeds Cres.
Hallam Gdns., Pnr. 94 BY52
Hallam Ms. W1 273 J6
Hallam Rd. N15 121 DP56
Hallam Rd. SW13 159 CV83
Hallam St. W1 273 J5
Hallam St. W1 141 DH71
Halland Way, Nthwd. 93 BR51
Halley Gdns. SE13 163 ED84
Halley Rd. E7 144 EJ65
Halley Rd. E12 144 EK65
Halley St. E14 143 DY71
Halleys App., Wok. 226 AU118
Halleys Ridge, Hert. 31 DN10
Halleys Wk., Add. 212 BJ108
Hallfield Est. W2 140 DC72
Cleveland Ter.
Hallford Way, Dart. 188 FJ85
Halliards, The, Walt. 195 BU100
Felix Rd.
Halliday Sq., Sthl. 137 CD74
Halliford Clo., Shep. 195 BR98
Halliford Rd., Shep. 195 BS99
Halliford Rd., Sun. 195 BT99
Halliford St. N1 142 DQ66
Halling Hill, Harl. 35 ET13
Hallingbury Ct. E17 123 EB55
Hallington Clo., Wok. 226 AV117
Halliwell Rd. SW2 181 DM86
Halliwick Rd. N10 98 DG53
Hallmark Trd. Est. NW10 118 CQ63
Great Cen. Way
Hallmead Rd., Sutt. 200 DB104
Hallmores, Brox. 49 EA19
Hallowell Ave., Croy. 219 DL105
Hallowell Clo., Mitch. 200 DG97
Hallowell Rd., Nthwd. 93 BS52
Hallowes Cres., Wat. 93 BU48
Hayling Rd.
Hallowfield Way, Mitch. 200 DE97
Church Rd.
Hallside Rd., Enf. 82 DT38
Hallsland Way, Oxt. 254 EF132
Hallsville Rd. E16 144 EF72
Hallswelle Rd. NW11 119 CZ57
Hallwood Cres., Brwd. 108 FY45
Hallywell Cres. E6 145 EM71
Halons Rd. SE9 185 EN87
Halpin Pl. SE17 279 L9
Halsbrook Rd. SE3 164 EJ83
Halsbury Clo., Stan. 95 CH49
Halsbury Rd. W12 139 CU74
Halsbury Rd. E., Nthlt. 116 CC63
Halsbury Rd. W., Nthlt. 116 CB64
Halse Dr., Slou. 111 AM63
Halsend, Hayes 135 BV74
Halsey Ms. SW3 276 D8
Halsey Pk., St.Alb. 62 CM27
Barnet Rd.
Halsey Pl., Wat. 75 BV38
Halsey Rd., Wat. 75 BV41
Halsey St. SW3 276 D8
Halsey St. SW3 160 DF77
Halsford Bri. Ind. Est., Brwd. 108 FW47
Halsham Cres., Bark. 145 ET65
Halsmere Rd. SE5 161 DP81
Halstead Ct. N1 275 L1
Halstead Gdns. N21 100 DR46
Halstead Hill (Cheshunt), Wal.Cr. 66 DS29
Halstead La., Sev. 224 EZ114
Halstead Rd. E11 124 EG57
Halstead Rd. N21 100 DR46
Halstead Rd., Enf. 82 DS42
Halstead Rd., Erith 167 FE81
Halstead Way, Brwd. 109 GC44
Halston Clo. SW11 180 DF86
Halstow Rd. NW10 139 CX69
Halstow Rd. SE10 164 EG78
Halsway, Hayes 135 BU74
Halt Robin La., Belv. 167 FB77
Halt Robin Rd.
Halt Robin Rd., Belv. 166 FA77
Halter Clo., Borwd. 78 CR43
Clydesdale Clo.
Halton Cross St. N1 141 DP67
Halton Rd.
Halton Rd. N1 141 DP66
Halton Rd., Grays 171 GH76
Haltside, Hat. 44 CS19
Halwick Clo., Hem.H. 40 BH21
Anchor La.
Ham, The, Brent. 157 CJ80
Ham Clo., Rich. 177 CJ90
Ham Common, Rich. 177 CK90
Ham Fm. Rd., Rich. 177 CK91
Ham Gate Ave., Rich. 178 CL91
Ham La., Egh. 172 AV91
Ham La., Wind. 152 AW84
Ham Pk. Rd. E7 144 EG66
Ham Pk. Rd. E15 144 EF66
Ham Ridings, Rich. 178 CM92
Ham St., Rich. 177 CH88
Ham Vw., Croy. 203 DY100
Ham Yd. W1 273 M10
Hambalt Rd. SW4 181 DJ85
Hamble Clo., Ruis. 115 BS61
Chichester Ave.
Hamble Clo., Wok. 226 AU117
Hamble Ct., Kings.T. 177 CK94
Hamble La., S.Ock. 149 FT71
Hamble St. SW6 160 DB83
Hamble Wk., Nthlt. 136 CA68
Brabazon Rd.
Hamble Wk., Wok. 226 AU118
Denton Way
Hambleden Pl. SE21 182 DS88
Hambledon Clo., Uxb. 135 BP71
Aldenham Dr.
Hambledon Gdns. SE25 202 DT97
Hambledon Hill, Epsom 232 CQ116
Hambledon Rd. SW18 179 CZ87
Hambledon Vale, Epsom 232 CQ116
Hambledown Rd., Sid. 185 ER87
Hambleton Clo., Wor.Pk. 199 CW103
Cotswold Way
Hamblings Clo., Rad. 62 CL32
Porters Pk. Dr.
Hambridge Way SW2 181 DN87
Hambro Ave., Brom. 204 EG102
Hambro Rd. SW16 181 DK93
Hambro Rd., Brwd. 108 FX47
Hambrook Rd. SE25 202 DV97
Hambrough Rd., Sthl. 136 BY74
Hamburgh Ct., Wal.Cr. 67 DX28
Hamden Cres., Dag. 127 FB62
Hamel Clo., Har. 117 CK55
Hinkler Rd.
Hamelin St. E14 143 EC72
St. Leonards Rd.
Hamels Dr., Hert. 32 DV08
Hamer Clo., Hem.H. 57 BA28
Hyde La.
Hamerton Rd., Grav. 190 GB85
Hameway E6 145 EN70
Hamfield Clo., Oxt. 253 EC127
Hamfrith Rd. E15 144 EF65
Hamhaugh Island, Shep. 194 BN103
Hamilton Ave. N9 100 DU45
Hamilton Ave., Cob. 213 BU113
Hamilton Ave., Hodd. 49 EA15
Hamilton Ave., Ilf. 125 EP56
Hamilton Ave., Rom. 105 FD54
Hamilton Ave., Surb. 198 CN103
Hamilton Ave., Sutt. 199 CY102
Hamilton Ave., Wok. 227 BE115
Hamilton Clo. N17 122 DT55
Hamilton Clo. NW8 140 DD69
Hamilton Clo. SE16 163 DY75
Somerford Way
Hamilton Clo., Barn. 80 DE42
Hamilton Clo., Cher. 193 BF102
Hamilton Clo., Epsom 216 CQ112
Hamilton Clo., Felt. 175 BT92
Hamilton Clo., Guil. 242 AU129
Hamilton Clo., Pot.B. 63 CU33
Hamilton Clo., Pur. 219 DP112
Hamilton Clo., St.Alb. 60 CA31
Hamilton Clo., Stan. 95 CF47
Hamilton Ct. W5 138 CM73
Hamilton Ct. W9 140 DC69
Maida Vale
Hamilton Ct., Hat. 45 CV20
Travellers La.
Hamilton Ct., Lthd. 246 CB125
Eastwick Pk. Ave.
Hamilton Cres. N13 99 DN49
Hamilton Cres., Brwd. 108 FW49
Hamilton Cres., Har. 116 BZ62
Hamilton Cres., Houns. 176 CB85
Hamilton Dr., Guil. 242 AU129
Hamilton Dr., Rom. 106 FL54
Hamilton Gdns. NW8 140 DC69
Hamilton Gdns., Slou. 130 AH69
Hamilton Gordon Ct., Guil. 242 AW133
Langley Clo.
Hamilton La. N5 121 DP63
Hamilton Pk.
Hamilton Mead, Hem.H. 57 BA27
Hamilton Ms. W1 277 H4
Hamilton Pk. N5 121 DP63
Hamilton Pk. W. N5 121 DP63
Hamilton Pl. W1 276 G3
Hamilton Pl. W1 140 DG74
Hamilton Pl., Guil. 242 AU129
Hamilton Pl., Sun. 175 BV94
Hamilton Pl., Tad. 233 CZ122
Beech Dr.
Hamilton Rd. E15 144 EE69
Hamilton Rd. E17 101 DY54
Hamilton Rd. N2 120 DC55
Hamilton Rd. N9 100 DU45
Hamilton Rd. NW10 119 CU64
Hamilton Rd. NW11 119 CX59
Hamilton Rd. SE27 182 DR91
Hamilton Rd. SW19 180 DB94
Hamilton Rd. W4 158 CS75
Hamilton Rd. W5 138 CL73
Hamilton Rd., Barn. 80 DE42
Hamilton Rd., Berk. 38 AV19
Hamilton Rd., Bexh. 166 EY82
Hamilton Rd., Brent. 157 CK79
Hamilton Rd., Felt. 175 BT91
Hamilton Rd., Grays 169 FW78
Arterial Rd. W. Thurrock
Hamilton Rd., Har. 117 CE57
Hamilton Rd., Hayes 135 BV73
Hamilton Rd., Ilf. 125 EP63
Hamilton Rd., Kings L. 59 BQ33
Hamilton Rd., Rom. 127 FH57
Hamilton Rd., St.Alb. 43 CG19
Hamilton Rd., Sid. 186 EU91
Hamilton Rd., Slou. 131 AN72
Hamilton Rd., Sthl. 136 BZ74
Hamilton Rd., Th.Hth. 202 DR97
Hamilton Rd., Twick. 177 CE88
Hamilton Rd., Uxb. 134 BK70
Hamilton Rd., Wat. 93 BV48
Hamilton Sq. SE1 279 L4
Hamilton St. SE8 163 EA79
Deptford High St.
Hamilton St., Wat. 76 BW43
Hamilton Ter. NW8 140 DB68
Hamilton Wk., Erith 167 FF80
Frobisher Rd.
Hamilton Way N3 98 DA51
Hamilton Way N13 99 DP49
Hamilton Way, Wall. 219 DK109
Hamlea Clo. SE12 184 EG85
Hamlet, The SE5 162 DR83
Hamlet, The, Berk. 39 BA16
Hamlet Clo. SE13 164 EE84
Old Rd.
Hamlet Clo., Rom. 104 FA52
Hamlet Gdns. W6 159 CU77
Hamlet Hill, Harl. 50 EF19
Hamlet Rd. SE19 182 DT94
Hamlet Rd., Rom. 104 FA52
Hamlet Sq. NW2 119 CY62
Cricklewood Trd. Est.
Hamlet Sq. NW11 119 CY62
The Vale
Hamlet Way SE1 279 L4
Hamlets Way E3 143 DZ70
Hamlin Cres., Pnr. 116 BW57
Hamlin Rd., Sev. 256 FE121
Hamlyn Clo., Edg. 96 CL48
Hamlyn Gdns. SE19 182 DS94
Hamm Ct., Wey. 194 BM104
Hamm Moor La., Add. 212 BL106
Hammarskjold Rd., Harl. 35 ER13
Hammelton Grn. SW9 161 DP81
Cromwell Rd.
Hammelton Rd., Brom. 204 EF95
Hammer La., Hem.H. 40 BM19
Hammer Par., Wat. 59 BT33
Hammerfield Dr., Dor. 261 BT141
Hammers Gate, St.Alb. 60 CA25
Hammers La. NW7 97 CU50
Hammersmith Bri. SW13 159 CV78
Hammersmith Bri. Rd. W6 159 CW78
Hammersmith Bdy. W6 159 CW77
Hammersmith Flyover W6 159 CW78
Hammersmith Gro. W6 159 CW75
Hammersmith Rd. W6 159 CX77
Hammersmith Rd. W14 159 CX77
Hammersmith Ter. W6 159 CU78
Hammet Clo., Hayes 136 BX71
Willow Tree La.
Hammett St. EC3 275 P10
Hammond Ave., Mitch. 201 DH96
Hammond Clo., Barn. 79 CY43
Hammond Clo., Grnf. 117 CD64
Lilian Board Way
Hammond Clo., Hmptn. 196 CA95
Hammond Clo. (Cheshunt), Wal.Cr. 66 DS26
Hammond Clo., Wok. 226 AW115
Hammond End, Slou. 111 AP63
Hammond Rd., Enf. 82 DV40
Hammond Rd., Sthl. 156 BY76
Hammond Rd., Wok. 226 AW115
Hammond St. NW5 141 DJ65
Hammond Way SE28 146 EV73
Oriole Way
Hammonds Clo., Dag. 126 EW62
Lindsey Rd.
Hammonds La., Brwd. 107 FV51
Hammond's La., Hat. 28 CN12
Hammond's La., St.Alb. 28 CN12
Hammondstreet Rd. (Cheshunt), Wal.Cr. 65 DP25
Hamonde Clo., Edg. 96 CP47
Hampden Ave., Beck. 203 DY96
Hampden Ave., Chesh. 54 AN30
Hampden Clo. NW1 273 N1
Hampden Clo., Epp. 70 FA27
Hampden Clo., Slou. 132 AU69
Hampden Cres., Brwd. 108 FW49
Hampden Cres. (Cheshunt), Wal.Cr. 66 DV31
Hampden Gurney St. W1 272 D9
Hampden Hill, Beac. 88 AH53
Hampden Hill, Ware 33 DZ05
Hampden Hill Clo., Ware 33 DZ05
Hampden Hill
Hampden La. N17 100 DT53
Hampden Pl., St.Alb. 61 CE29
Hampden Rd. N8 121 DN56
Hampden Rd. N10 98 DG52
Hampden Rd. N17 100 DU53
Hampden Rd. N19 121 DK61
Holloway Rd.
Hampden Rd., Beck. 203 DY96
Hampden Rd., Ger.Cr. 90 AX53
Hampden Rd., Grays 170 GB78
Hampden Rd., Har. 94 CC53
Hampden Rd., Kings.T. 198 CN97
Hampden Rd., Rom. 105 FB52
Hampden Rd., Slou. 153 AZ76
Hampden Sq. N14 99 DH46
Osidge La.
Hampden Way N14 99 DH47
Hampden Way, Wat. 75 BS36
Hampermill La., Wat. 93 BT47
Hampshire Ave., Slou. 131 AQ71
Hampshire Clo. N18 100 DV50
Hampshire Hog La. W6 159 CV77
King St.
Hampshire Rd. N22 99 DM52
Hampshire Rd., Horn. 128 FN56
Hampshire St. NW5 141 DK65
Torriano Ave.
Hampson Way SW8 161 DM81
Hampstead Clo. SE28 146 EV74
Hampstead Gdns. NW11 120 DA58
Hampstead Gdns., Rom. 126 EV57
Hampstead Grn. NW3 120 DE64
Hampstead Gro. NW3 120 DC62
Hampstead High St. NW3 120 DC63
Hampstead Hill Gdns. NW3 120 DD63
Hampstead La. N6 120 DD59
Hampstead La. NW3 120 DD60
Hampstead La., Dor. 263 CG137
Hampstead Rd. NW1 273 K1
Hampstead Rd. NW1 141 DJ68
Hampstead Rd., Dor. 263 CG137
Hampstead Sq. NW3 120 DC62
Hampstead Wk. E3 143 DZ67
Parnell Rd.
Hampstead Way NW11 119 CZ57
Hampton Clo. NW6 140 DA69
Hampton Clo. SW20 179 CW94
Hampton Ct. N1 141 DP65
Upper St.
Hampton Ct. Ave., E.Mol. 197 CD99
Hampton Ct. Cres., E.Mol. 197 CD97
Graburn Way
Hampton Ct. Palace, E.Mol. 197 CE97
Hampton Ct. Par., E.Mol. 197 CE98
Creek Rd.
Hampton Ct. Rd., E.Mol. 197 CF97
Hampton Ct. Rd., Hmptn. 196 CC96
Hampton Ct. Rd., Kings.T. 197 CJ96
Hampton Ct. Way, E.Mol. 197 CE100
Hampton Ct. Way, T.Ditt. 197 CE103
Hampton Cres., Grav. 191 GF89
Hampton Fm. Ind. Est., Felt. 176 BY90
Hampton Gdns., Saw. 36 EV08
Hampton Gro., Epsom 217 CT111
Hampton La., Felt. 176 BY91
Hampton Mead, Loug. 85 EP41
Hampton Ri., Har. 118 CL58
Hampton Rd. E4 101 DZ50
Hampton Rd. E7 124 EH64
Hampton Rd. E11 123 ED60
Hampton Rd., Croy. 202 DQ100
Hampton Rd., Hmptn. 177 CD92
Hampton Rd., Ilf. 125 EP63
Hampton Rd., Red. 266 DF139
Hampton Rd., Tedd. 177 CD92
Hampton Rd., Twick. 177 CD90
Hampton Rd., Wor.Pk. 199 CU103
Hampton Rd. E., Felt. 176 BZ90
Hampton Rd. W., Felt. 176 BY89
Hampton St. SE1 278 G9
Hampton St. SE1 162 DQ77
Hampton St. SE17 278 G9
Hampton St. SE17 161 DP77
Hamsey Grn. Gdns., Warl. 236 DV116
Hamsey Way, S.Croy. 236 DV115
Hamshades Clo., Sid. 185 ET90
Hamstel Rd., Harl. 35 EP13
Hanah Ct. SW19 179 CX94
Hanameel St. E16 144 EH74
Hanbury Clo., Slou. 130 AG71
Hanbury Clo. (Cheshunt), Wal.Cr. 67 DX30
Hanbury Clo., Ware 33 DY06
Hanbury Dr. N21 81 DM42
Hanbury Dr., West. 222 EH113
Hanbury La., Hat. 46 DE17
Hanbury Ms. N1 142 DQ67
Mary St.
Hanbury Path, Wok. 211 BD114
Hanbury Rd. N17 100 DV54
Hanbury Rd. W3 158 CP75
Hanbury St. E1 142 DT71
Hanbury Wk., Bex. 187 FE90
Hancock Ct., Borwd. 78 CQ40
Banks Rd.
Hancock Rd. E3 143 EC69
Hancock Rd. SE19 182 DR93
Hand Ct. WC1 274 C7
Hand La., Saw. 36 EW06
Handa Clo., Hem.H. 41 BP23
Handa Wk. N1 142 DR65
Clephane Rd.
Handcroft Rd., Croy. 201 DP101
Handcroft Rd., Hem.H. 40 BM22
Handel Clo., Edg. 96 CM51
Handel Cres., Til. 171 GG80
Handel Pl. NW10 138 CR65
Mitchellbrook Way
Handel St. WC1 273 P4
Handel St. WC1 141 DL70
Handel Way, Edg. 96 CN52
Handen Rd. SE12 184 EE85
Handforth Rd. SW9 161 DN80
Handforth Rd., Ilf. 125 EP62
Winston Way
Handley Rd. E9 142 DW67
Handowe Clo. NW4 119 CU56
Hands Wk. E16 144 EG72
Butchers Rd.
Handside Clo., Welw.G.C. 29 CW09
Handside Clo., Wor.Pk. 199 CX102
Carters Clo.
Handside Grn., Welw.G.C. 29 CW08
Handside La., Welw.G.C. 29 CV11
Handsworth Ave. E4 101 ED51
Handsworth Rd. N17 122 DR55
Handsworth Way, Wat. 93 BU48
Handtrough Way, Bark. 145 EP68
Fresh Wf. Rd.
Hanford Clo. SW18 180 DA88
Hanford Rd., S.Ock. 148 FQ74
Hanford Row SW19 179 CW93
Hangar Ruding, Wat. 94 BZ48
Hanger Clo., Hem.H. 40 BH21
Hanger Grn. W5 138 CN70
Hanger Hill, Wey. 213 BP107
Hanger La. W5 138 CL68
Hanger Vale La. W3 138 CM72
Hanger Vale La. W5 138 CM72
Hanger Vw. Way W3 138 CN72
Hanging Hill La., Brwd. 109 GB48
Hangrove Hill, Orp. 223 EP113
Cudham Rd.
Hankey Pl. SE1 279 L5
Hankey Pl. SE1 162 DR75
Hankins La. NW7 96 CS47
Hanley Clo., Wind. 151 AK81
Hanley Pl., Beck. 183 EA94
Hanley Rd. N4 121 DL60
Hanmer Wk. N7 121 DM61
Newington Barrow Way
Hannah Clo. NW10 118 CQ63
Hannah Clo., Beck. 203 EC97
Hannah Mary Way SE1 162 DU77
Simms Rd.
Hannah Ms., Wall. 219 DJ108
Hannards Way, Chig. 104 EV50
Hannay La. N8 121 DK59
Crouch End Hill
Hannay Wk. SW16 181 DK89
Dingley La.
Hannell Rd. SW6 159 CY80
Hannen Rd. SE27 181 DP90
Norwood High St.
Hannibal Rd. E1 142 DW71
Hannibal Rd., Stai. 174 BK87
Hannibal Way, Croy. 219 DM106
Hannington Rd. SW4 161 DH83
Hanover Ave., Felt. 175 BU88
Hanover Circle, Hayes 135 BQ72
Hanover Clo., Egh. 172 AV93
Hanover Clo., Red. 251 DJ128
Hanover Clo., Rich. 158 CN80
Hanover Clo., Slou. 152 AU76
Hanover Clo., Sutt. 217 CY105
Hanover Ct. W12 139 CU74
Uxbridge Rd.
Hanover Ct., Dor. 263 CF136
Hanover Ct., Guil. 242 AX132
Riverside
Hanover Ct., Hodd. 49 EA16
Jersey Clo.
Hanover Ct., Wok. 226 AY119
Midhope Rd.
Hanover Dr., Chis. 185 EQ91
Hanover Gdns. SE11 161 DN79
Hanover Gdns., Ilf. 103 EQ52
Hanover Gate NW1 272 C3
Hanover Gate NW1 140 DE69
Hanover Grn., Hem.H. 40 BG22
Hanover Mead, Maid. 150 AC76
Hanover Pk. SE15 162 DU81
Hanover Pl. WC2 274 A9
Hanover Rd. N15 122 DT56
Hanover Rd. NW10 139 CW66
Hanover Rd. SW19 180 DC94
Hanover Sq. W1 273 J9
Hanover Sq. W1 141 DH72
Hanover St. W1 273 J9
Hanover St. W1 141 DH72
Hanover St., Croy. 201 DP104
Abbey Rd.
Hanover Ter. NW1 272 C3
Hanover Ter. NW1 140 DE69
Hanover Ter., Islw. 157 CG81
Hanover Ter. Ms. NW1 272 C3
Hanover Wk., Hat. 45 CT21
Hanover Wk., Wey. 195 BS104

Hartsbourne Clo. (Bushey), Wat. 95 CD47
Hartsbourne Rd. (Bushey), Wat. 95 CD47
Hartsbourne Way, Hem.H. 41 BQ21
Hartscroft, Croy. 221 DY109
Hartshill Rd., Grav. 191 GF89
Hartshill Wk., Wok. 226 AV116
Sythwood
Hartshorn All. EC3 275 N9
Hartshorn Gdns. E6 145 EN70
Hartslands Rd., Sev. 257 FJ123
Hartslock Dr. SE2 166 EX75
Hartsmead Rd. SE9 185 EM89
Hartsmoor Ms., Enf. 83 DX37
Ordnance Rd.
Hartspiece Rd., Red. 266 DG136
Hartspring Ind. Est., Wat. 76 CA40
Hartspring La. (Bushey), Wat. 76 CA40
Hartsway, Enf. 82 DW42
Hartswood, Dor. 263 CK139
Wildcroft Dr.
Hartswood Ave., Reig. 266 DA138
Hartswood Clo., Brwd. 108 FY49
Hartswood Grn. (Bushey), Wat. 95 CD47
Hartswood Rd. W12 159 CT75
Hartswood Rd., Brwd. 108 FY49
Hartsworth Clo. E13 144 EF68
Hartville Rd. SE18 165 ES77
Hartwell Clo., H.Wyc. 88 AC45
Hartwell Dr. E4 101 EC51
Hartwell Dr., Beac. 89 AK52
Hartwell St. E8 142 DT65
Dalston La.
Harvard Hill W4 158 CP78
Wolseley Gdns.
Harvard La. W4 158 CP78
Harvard Rd.
Harvard Rd. SE13 183 EC85
Harvard Rd. W4 158 CP78
Harvard Rd., Islw. 157 CE81
Harvard Wk., Horn. 127 FG63
Harvel Clo., Orp. 206 EU97
Harvel Cres. SE2 166 EX78
Harvest Bank Rd., W.Wick. 204 EF104
Harvest Ct., Shep. 194 BN98
Harvest End, Wat. 76 BX36
Harvest Hill, B.End 110 AC61
Harvest La., T.Ditt. 197 CG100
Harvest Mead, Hat. 45 CV17
Harvest Rd., Egh. 172 AX92
Harvest Rd., Felt. 175 BU91
Harvest Rd. (Bushey), Wat. 76 CB42
Harvest Way, Swan. 207 FD101
Harvester Rd., Epsom 216 CR110
Harvesters, St.Alb. 43 CK16
Harvesters Clo., Islw. 177 CD85
Harvestside, Horl. 269 DJ147
Harvey, Grays 170 GB75
Harvey Cen., Harl. 51 EQ15
Harvey Gdns. E11 124 EF60
Harvey Rd.
Harvey Gdns. SE7 164 EJ78
Harvey Gdns., Loug. 85 EP41
Harvey Ho., Brent. 158 CL78
Harvey Orchard, Beac. 88 AJ52
Harvey Pt. E16 144 EH71
Fife Rd.
Harvey Rd. E11 124 EE60
Harvey Rd. N8 121 DM57
Harvey Rd. SE5 162 DR81
Harvey Rd., Guil. 258 AY136
Harvey Rd., Houns. 176 BZ87
Harvey Rd., Ilf. 125 EP64
Harvey Rd., Nthlt. 136 BW66
Harvey Rd., Rick. 74 BN44
Harvey Rd., St.Alb. 61 CJ26
Harvey Rd., Slou. 153 BB76
Harvey Rd., Uxb. 134 BN68
Harvey Rd., Walt. 195 BU101
Harvey St. N1 142 DR67
Harveyfields, Wal.Abb. 67 EC34
Harveys La., Rom. 127 FD61
Harvil Rd. (Harefield), Uxb. 114 BJ56
Harvil Rd. (Ickenham), Uxb. 114 BL60
Harvill Rd., Sid. 186 EX92
Harvington Wk. E8 142 DU66
Wilman Gro.
Harvist Est. N7 121 DN63
Harvist Rd. NW6 139 CX68
Harwater Dr., Loug. 85 EM40
Harwell Clo., Ruis. 115 BR60
Harwell Pas. N2 120 DF56
Harwich La. EC2 275 N6
Harwich La. EC2 142 DS71
Harwich Rd., Slou. 131 AN72
Harwood Ave., Brom. 204 EH96
Harwood Ave., Horn. 128 FL55
Harwood Ave., Mitch. 200 DE97
Harwood Clo. N12 98 DE52
Summerfields Ave.
Harwood Clo., Welw. 30 DE05
Harwood Clo., Welw.G.C. 29 CY05
Harwood Clo., Wem. 117 CK63
Harrowdene Rd.
Harwood Dr., Uxb. 134 BM67
Harwood Gdns., Wind. 172 AV87
Harwood Hall La., Upmin. 148 FP65
Harwood Hill, Welw.G.C. 29 CY06
Harwood Pk., Red. 266 DG143
Harwood Rd. SW6 160 DA80
Harwood Ter. SW6 160 DB81
Harwoods Rd., Wat. 75 BU42
Harwoods Yd. N21 99 DN45
Wades Hill
Hascombe Ter. SE5 162 DR82
Hasedines Rd., Hem.H. 40 BG19
Haselbury Rd. N9 100 DS48
Haselbury Rd. N18 100 DS49
Haseldine Meadows, Hat. 45 CT19
Haseldine Rd., St.Alb. 61 CK26
Haseley End SE23 182 DW87
Tyson Rd.
Haselrigge Rd. SW4 161 DK84
Haseltine Rd. SE26 183 DZ91
Haselwood Dr., Enf. 81 DP42
Haskard Rd., Dag. 126 EX63
Haskell Ho. NW10 138 CR67
Hasker St. SW3 276 C8
Hasker St. SW3 160 DE77
Haslam Ave., Sutt. 199 CY102
Haslam Clo. N1 141 DN66
Haslam Clo., Uxb. 115 BQ61
Haslemere Ave. NW4 119 CX58
Haslemere Ave. SW18 180 DB89
Haslemere Ave. W7 157 CG76
Haslemere Ave. W13 157 CG76
Haslemere Ave., Barn. 98 DF46
Haslemere Ave., Houns. 156 BW82
Haslemere Ave., Mitch. 200 DD96
Haslemere Clo., Hmptn. 176 BZ92
Haslemere Clo., Wall. 219 DL106
Stafford Rd.
Haslemere Est., Harl. 51 EM15
Haslemere Gdns. N3 119 CZ55
Haslemere Heathrow Est., Houns. 155 BV82
Haslemere Rd. N8 121 DK59
Haslemere Rd. N21 99 DP47
Haslemere Rd., Bexh. 166 EZ82
Haslemere Rd., Ilf. 125 ET61
Haslemere Rd., Th.Hth. 201 DP99
Haslemere Rd., Wind. 151 AN81
Hasler Clo. SE28 146 EV73
Haslett Rd., Shep. 195 BS96
Haslewood Ave., Hodd. 49 EA17
Hasluck Gdns., Barn. 80 DB44
Hassard St. E2 142 DT68
Hackney Rd.
Hassendean Rd. SE3 164 EH79
Hassett Rd. E9 143 DX65
Hassock Wd., Kes. 222 EK105
Hassocks Clo. SE26 182 DV90
Hassocks Rd. SW16 201 DJ95
Hassop Rd. NW2 119 CX63
Hassop Wk. SE9 184 EL91
Hasted Clo., Green. 189 FW86
Hasted Rd. SE7 164 EK78
Hastings Ave., Ilf. 125 EQ56
Hastings Clo. SE15 162 DU80
Hastings Clo., Barn. 80 DC42
Leicester Rd.
Hastings Clo., Grays 170 FY79
Argent St.
Hastings Clo., Maid. 150 AC77
Hastings Dr., Surb. 197 CJ100
Seething Wells La.
Hastings Ho. SE18 165 EM77
Cardwell Rd.
Hastings Rd. N11 99 DJ50
Hastings Rd. N17 122 DR55
Hastings Rd. W13 137 CH73
Hastings Rd., Brom. 204 EL102
Hastings Rd., Croy. 202 DT102
Hastings Rd., Rom. 127 FH57
Hastings St. WC1 273 P3
Hastings St. WC1 141 DL69
Hastings Way, Rick. 75 BQ42
Hastings Way (Bushey), Wat. 76 BY42
Hastingwood Rd., Harl. 52 EX20
Hastoe Clo., Hayes 136 BY70
Kingsash Dr.
Hat and Mitre Ct. EC1 274 G5
Hatch, The, Enf. 83 DX39
Hatch, The, Wind. 150 AJ80
Hatch Clo., Add. 194 BH104
Hatch Gdns., Tad. 233 CX120
Hatch Gro., Rom. 126 EY56
Hatch La. E4 101 ED49
Hatch La., Bans. 234 DF115
Rectory La.
Hatch La., Couls. 234 DG115
Hatch La., West Dr. 154 BK80
Hatch La., Wind. 151 AN83
Hatch La., Wok. 229 BP120
Hatch Pl., Kings.T. 178 CM92
Hatch Rd. SW16 201 DL96
Hatch Rd., Brwd. 108 FU43
Hatch Side, Chig. 103 EN50
Hatcham Pk. Ms. SE14 163 DX81
Hatcham Pk. Rd.
Hatcham Pk. Rd. SE14 163 DX81
Hatcham Rd. SE15 162 DW79
Hatchard Rd. N19 121 DK61
Hatchcroft NW4 119 CV55
Hatchett Rd., Felt. 175 BQ88
Hatchgate, Horl. 268 DF149
Hatchgate Gdns., Slou. 131 AK69
Hatching Tan, The, Guil. 242 AX126
Hatchlands Rd., Red. 250 DE134
Hatchwood Clo., Wdf.Grn. 102 EF49
Sunset Ave.
Hatcliffe Clo. SE3 164 EF83
Hatcliffe St. SE10 164 EF78
Woolwich Rd.
Hatfield Ave., Hat. 44 CS15
Hatfield Clo. SE14 163 DX80
Hatfield Clo., Brwd. 109 GD45
Hatfield Clo., Horn. 128 FK64
Hatfield Clo., Ilf. 125 EP55
Hatfield Clo., Mitch. 200 DD98
Hatfield Clo., Sutt. 218 DB109
Moore Way
Hatfield Clo., W.Byf. 212 BH112
Dartnell Ave.
Hatfield Cres., Hem.H. 40 BM16
Hatfield Ho., Hat. 45 CX18
Hatfield Mead, Mord. 200 DA99
Central Rd.
Hatfield Pk., Hat. 45 CV18
Hatfield Rd. E15 124 EE64
Hatfield Rd. W4 158 CR75
Hatfield Rd. W13 137 CG74
Hatfield Rd., Ash. 232 CM119
Hatfield Rd., Dag. 146 EY65
Hatfield Rd., Grays 169 FW78
Arterial Rd. W. Thurrock
Hatfield Rd., Hert. 30 DF12
Hatfield Rd., Pot.B. 64 DC30
Hatfield Rd., St.Alb. 43 CE20
Hatfield Rd., Slou. 152 AU75
Hatfield Rd., Wat. 75 BV39
Hatfields SE1 278 E2
Hatfields SE1 141 DN74
Hatfields, Loug. 85 EP41
Hathaway Clo., Brom. 205 EM102
Hathaway Clo., Ruis. 115 BT63
Stafford Rd.
Hathaway Clo., Stan. 95 CG50
Hathaway Ct., St.Alb. 44 CL20
Hathaway Cres. E12 145 EM65
Hathaway Gdns. W13 137 CF71
Hathaway Gdns., Grays 170 GB76
Hathaway Rd.
Hathaway Gdns., Rom. 126 EX57
Hathaway Rd., Croy. 201 DP101
Hathaway Rd., Grays 170 GB77
Hatherleigh Clo., Chess. 215 CK106
Hatherleigh Clo., Mord. 200 DA98
Hatherleigh Gdns., Pot.B. 64 DD31
Hatherleigh Rd., Ruis. 115 BU61
Hatherleigh Way, Rom. 106 FK53
Hatherley Cres., Sid. 186 EU89
Hatherley Gdns. E6 144 EK68
Hatherley Gdns. N8 121 DL58
Hatherley Gro. W2 140 DB72
Hatherley Ms. E17 123 EA56
Hatherley Rd. E17 123 DZ56
Hatherley Rd., Rich. 158 CM81
Hatherley Rd., Sid. 186 EU91
Hatherley St. SW1 277 L9
Hathern Gdns. SE9 185 EN91
The Knole
Hatherop Rd., Hmptn. 176 BZ94
Hathersham Clo., Horl. 269 DN147
Hathersham La., Horl. 267 DL144
Hatherwood, Lthd. 231 CK121
Hathorne Clo. SE15 162 DV82
Hathway St. SE15 162 DW82
Gibbon Rd.
Hathway Ter. SE14 162 DW82
Gibbon Rd.
Hatley Ave., Ilf. 125 EQ56
Hatley Clo. N11 98 DF50
Hatley Rd. N4 121 DM61
Hatteraick St. SE16 162 DW75
Brunel Rd.
Hatters La., Wat. 75 BR44
Hattersfield Clo., Belv. 166 EZ77
Hatton Ave., Slou. 131 AR70
Hatton Clo. SE18 165 ER80
Hatton Clo., Grav. 190 GE90
Hatton Ct. E5 123 DY63
Gilpin Rd.
Hatton Gdn. EC1 274 E6
Hatton Gdn. EC1 141 DN70
Hatton Gdns., Mitch. 200 DF99
Hatton Grn., Felt. 155 BU84
Hatton Gro., West Dr. 154 BK75
Hatton Ho. E1 142 DU73
Wellclose Sq.
Hatton Pl. EC1 274 E6
Hatton Pl. EC1 141 DN70
Hatton Rd., Croy. 201 DN102
Hatton Rd., Felt. 175 BQ87
Hatton Rd. (Cheshunt), Wal.Cr. 67 DX29
Hatton Row NW8 272 A5
Hatton St. NW8 272 A5
Hatton Wall EC1 274 D6
Hatton Wall EC1 141 DN71
Haunch of Venison Yd. W1 273 H9
Havana Clo., Rom. 127 FE57
Havana Rd. SW19 180 DA89
Havannah St. E14 163 EA75
Havant Rd. E17 123 EC55
Havant Way SE15 162 DT80
Daniel Gdns.
Havelock Pl., Har. 117 CE58
Havelock Rd. N17 100 DU54
Havelock Rd. SW19 180 DC92
Havelock Rd., Belv. 166 EZ77
Havelock Rd., Brom. 204 EJ98
Havelock Rd., Croy. 202 DT103
Havelock Rd., Dart. 187 FH87
Havelock Rd., Grav. 191 GF88
Havelock Rd., Har. 117 CE55
Havelock Rd., Kings L. 58 BM28
Havelock Rd., Sthl. 156 BY76
Havelock St. N1 141 DL67
Havelock St., Ilf. 125 EP61
Havelock Ter. SW8 161 DH80
Havelock Wk. SE23 182 DW88
Haven, The, Grays 171 GG77
Haven, The, Rich. 158 CN83
Haven Clo. SE9 185 EM90
Haven Clo. SW19 179 CX90
Haven Clo., Grav. 191 GF94
Haven Clo., Hat. 45 CT17
Haven Clo., Hayes 135 BS71
Haven Clo., Sid. 186 EW93
Haven Clo., Swan. 207 FF96
Haven Grn. W5 137 CK72
Haven Grn. Ct. W5 137 CK72
Haven La. W5 138 CL72
Haven Pl. W5 137 CK73
The Bdy.
Haven Pl., Grays 170 GC75
Haven Rd., Ashf. 175 BP91
Haven St. NW1 141 DH66
Castlehaven Rd.
Haven Ter. W5 138 CM73
The Bdy.
Havengore Ave., Grav. 191 GL87
Havenhurst Ri., Enf. 81 DN40
Havensfield, Kings L. 58 BH31
Nunfield
Havenwood, Wem. 118 CP62
Havenwood Clo., Brwd. 107 FW51
Wilmot Grn.
Havercroft Clo., St.Alb. 42 CB22
King Harry La.
Haverfield Gdns., Rich. 158 CN80
Haverfield Rd. E3 143 DY69
Haverford Way, Edg. 96 CM53
Haverhill Rd. E4 101 EC46
Haverhill Rd. SW12 181 DJ88
Havering Dr., Rom. 127 FE56
Havering Gdns., Rom. 126 EW57
Havering Rd., Rom. 127 FD55
Havering St. E1 143 DX72
Devonport St.
Havering Way, Bark. 146 EV69
Havers Ave., Walt. 214 BX106
Haversfield Est., Brent. 158 CL78
Haversham Clo., Twick. 177 CK86
Haversham Pl. N6 120 DF61
Merton La.
Haverstock Hill NW3 140 DF65
Haverstock Rd. NW5 120 DG64
Haverstock St. N1 274 G1
Haverstock St. N1 141 DP68
Haverthwaite Rd., Orp. 205 ER103
Havil St. SE5 162 DS80
Havisham Pl. SE19 181 DP93
Haward Rd., Hodd. 49 EC15
Hawarden Gro. SE24 182 DQ87
Hawarden Hill NW2 119 CU62
Hawarden Rd. E17 123 DX56
Hawarden Rd., Cat. 236 DQ121
Hawbridge Rd. E11 123 ED60
Hawes Clo., Nthwd. 93 BT52
Hawes La. E4 83 EC38
Hawes La., W.Wick. 203 EC102
Hawes Rd. N18 100 DV51
Hawes Rd., Brom. 204 EH95
Hawes Rd., Tad. 233 CX120
Hatch Gdns.
Hawes St. N1 141 DP66
Haweswater Dr., Wat. 59 BV34
North Orbital Rd.
Haweswater Ho., Islw. 177 CF85
Hawfield Bank, Orp. 206 EX104
Hawfield Gdns., St.Alb. 61 CD26
Hawgood St. E3 143 EA71
Hawk Clo., Wal.Abb. 68 EG34
Hawkdene E4 83 EB44
Hawke Pk. Rd. N22 121 DP55
Hawke Pl. SE16 163 DX75
Middleton Dr.
Hawke Rd. SE19 182 DS93
Hawkenbury, Harl. 51 EN17
Hawker Clo., Wall. 219 DL108
Kingsford Ave.
Hawkes Clo., Grays 170 GB79
New Rd.
Hawkes Rd., Mitch. 200 DE95
Hawkesbury Rd. SW15 179 CV85
Hawkesfield Rd. SE23 183 DY89
Hawkesley Clo., Twick. 177 CG91
Hawkesworth Clo., Nthwd. 93 BS52
Hawkewood Rd., Sun. 195 BU97
Hawkhirst Rd., Ken. 236 DR115
Hawkhurst, Cob. 214 CA114
Hawkhurst Gdns., Chess. 216 CL105
Hawkhurst Gdns., Rom. 105 FD51
Hawkhurst Rd. SW16 201 DK95
Hawkhurst Way, N.Mal. 198 CR99
Hawkhurst Way, W.Wick. 203 EB103
Hawkinge Wk., Orp. 206 EV97
Farrington Ave.
Hawkinge Way, Horn. 148 FJ65
Hawkins Ave., Grav. 191 GJ91
Hawkins Clo. NW7 96 CR50
Hale La.
Hawkins Clo., Borwd. 78 CQ40
Banks Rd.
Hawkins Clo., Har. 117 CD59
Hawkins Rd., Tedd. 177 CH93
Hawkins Way SE6 183 EA91
Hawkley Gdns. SE27 181 DP89
Hawkridge Clo., Rom. 126 EW58
Hawks Hill, B.End 110 AC61
Hawks Hill, Lthd. 231 CF123
Guildford Rd.
Hawks Hill Clo., Lthd. 231 CF123
Hawks Ms. SE10 163 EC80
Luton Pl.
Hawks Rd., Kings.T. 198 CM96
Hawksbrook La., Beck. 203 EB100
Hawkshaw Clo. SW2 181 DL87
Tierney Rd.
Hawkshead Clo., Brom. 184 EE94
Hawkshead La., Hat. 63 CW28
Hawkshead Rd. NW10 139 CT66
Hawkshead Rd. W4 158 CS75
Hawkshead Rd., Pot.B. 63 CZ28
Hawkshill, St.Alb. 43 CG21
Hawkshill Clo., Esher 214 CA107
Hawkshill Dr., Hem.H. 39 BE23
Hawkshill Rd., Slou. 131 AN69
Hawkshill Way, Esher 214 BZ107
Hawkslade Rd. SE15 183 DX85
Hawksley Rd. N16 122 DR62
Hawksmead Clo., Enf. 83 DX35
Hawksmoor, Rad. 62 CN33
Hawksmoor Clo. E6 144 EL72
Allhallows Rd.
Hawksmoor Clo. SE18 165 ES78
Tewson Rd.
Hawksmoor Grn., Brwd. 109 GD43
Hawksmoor Ms. E1 142 DV73
Cable St.
Hawksmoor St. W6 159 CX79
Hawksmouth E4 101 EB45
Hawkstone Rd. SE16 162 DW77
Hawksview, Cob. 214 BZ113
Hawksway, Stai. 173 BF90
Hawkswell Clo., Wok. 226 AT117
Hawkswell Wk., Wok. 226 AS117
Lockfield Dr.
Hawkswood Gro., Slou. 133 AZ65
Hawkswood La., Ger.Cr. 113 AZ64
Hawkwell Ct. E4 101 EC48
Colvin Gdns.
Hawkwell Wk. N1 142 DQ67
Basire St.
Hawkwood Cres. E4 83 EB44
Hawkwood Dell, Lthd. 246 CA126
Hawkwood La., Chis. 205 EQ95
Hawkwood Mt. E5 122 DV60
Hawkwood Ri., Lthd. 246 CA126
Hawlands Dr., Pnr. 116 BY59
Hawley Clo., Hmptn. 176 BZ93
Hawley Cres. NW1 141 DH66
Hawley Ms. NW1 141 DH66
Hawley St.
Hawley Rd. N18 101 DX50
Hawley Rd. NW1 141 DH66
Hawley Rd., Dart. 188 FL89
Hawley St. NW1 141 DH66
Hawley Way, Ashf. 174 BN92
Haws La., Stai. 174 BG86
Hawstead La., Orp. 224 EZ106
Hawstead Rd. SE6 183 EB86
Hawsted, Buck.H. 102 EH45
Hawthorn Ave. N13 99 DL50
Hawthorn Ave., Brwd. 109 FZ48
Hawthorn Ave., Cars. 218 DG108
Hawthorn Ave., Rain. 147 FH70
Hawthorn Ave., Rich. 158 CL82
Kew Rd.
Hawthorn Ave., Th.Hth. 201 DP95
Hawthorn Cen., Har. 117 CF56
Hawthorn Clo., Abb.L. 59 BU32
Stewart Clo.
Hawthorn Clo., Bans. 217 CY114
Fir Tree Rd.
Hawthorn Clo., Grav. 191 GH87
Hawthorn Clo., Hmptn. 176 CA92
Hawthorn Clo., Hert. 31 DN08
Hawthorn Clo., Houns. 155 BV80
Hawthorn Clo., Orp. 205 ER100
Hawthorn Clo., Red. 266 DG139
Bushfield Dr.
Hawthorn Clo., Wat. 75 BT38
Hawthorn Clo., Wok. 226 AY120
Hawthorn Cotts., Well. 166 EU83
Hook La.
Hawthorn Ct., Rich. 158 CP81
Hawthorn Cres. SW17 180 DG92
Hawthorn Dr., Har. 116 CA58
Hawthorn Dr., Uxb. 134 BJ65
Hawthorn Dr., W.Wick. 222 EE105
Hawthorn Gdns. W5 157 CK76
Hawthorn Gro. SE20 182 DV94
Hawthorn Gro., Barn. 79 CT44
Hawthorn Gro., Enf. 82 DR38
Hawthorn Hatch, Brent. 157 CH80
Hawthorn La., Hem.H. 39 BF19
Hawthorn La., Sev. 256 FF122
Hawthorn La., Slou. 131 AL66
Hawthorn Ms. NW7 97 CY53
Holders Hill Rd.
Hawthorn Pl., Erith 167 FC78
Hawthorn Pl., Hayes 135 BT73
Central Ave.
Hawthorn Pl., H.Wyc. 88 AC47
Hawthorn Rd. N8 121 DK55
Hawthorn Rd. N18 100 DT51
Hawthorn Rd. NW10 139 CU66
Hawthorn Rd., Bexh. 166 EZ84
Hawthorn Rd., Brent. 157 CH80
Hawthorn Rd., Buck.H. 102 EK49
Hawthorn Rd., Dart. 188 FK88
Hawthorn Rd., Hodd. 49 EB15
Hawthorn Rd., Stai. 173 BC91
Hawthorn Rd., Sutt. 218 DE106
Hawthorn Rd., Wall. 219 DH108
Hawthorn Rd., Wok. 226 AX120
Hawthorn Rd. (Send Marsh), Wok. 227 BF124
Hawthorn Wk. W10 139 CY70
Droop St.
Hawthorn Way N9 100 DS47
Hawthorn Way, Add. 212 BJ110
Hawthorn Way, Chesh. 54 AR29
Hawthorn Way, Red. 267 DH136
Hawthorn Way, St.Alb. 42 CA24
Hawthorn Way, Shep. 195 BR98
Hawthorn Way, Stai. 174 BK87
Hawthornden Clo. N12 98 DE52
Fallowfields Dr.
Hawthorndene Clo., Brom. 204 EF103
Hawthorndene Rd., Brom. 204 EF103
Hawthorne Ave., Har. 117 CG58
Hawthorne Ave., Mitch. 200 DD96
Hawthorne Ave., Ruis. 115 BV59
Hawthorne Ave. (Cheshunt), Wal.Cr. 66 DV30
Hawthorne Ave., West. 238 EK115
Hawthorne Clo. N1 142 DS65
Hawthorne Clo., Brom. 205 EM97
Hawthorne Clo., Sutt. 200 DB103
Aultone Way
Hawthorne Clo. (Cheshunt), Wal.Cr. 66 DV31
Hawthorne Ct., Walt. 196 BX103
Ambleside Ave.
Hawthorne Cres., Slou. 132 AS72
Hawthorne Cres., S.Croy. 220 DW111
Hawthorne Cres., West Dr. 154 BM75
Hawthorne Fm. Ave., Nthlt. 136 BY67
Hawthorne Gro. NW9 118 CQ59
Hawthorne Ms., Grnf. 136 CC72
Greenford Rd.
Hawthorne Pl., Epsom 216 CS112
Hawthorne Rd. E17 123 EA55
Hawthorne Rd., Brom. 205 EM97
Hawthorne Rd., Rad. 61 CG34
Hawthorne Way, Guil. 243 BB130
Hawthornes, Hat. 45 CT20
Hazel Gro.
Hawthornes Cen., Har. 117 CF56
Hawthorns, Harl. 51 ET19
Hawthorns, Welw.G.C. 29 CX07
Hawthorns, Wdf.Grn. 102 EG48
Hawthorns, The, Berk. 38 AU18
Hawthorns, The, Epsom 217 CT107
Ewell Bypass
Hawthorns, The, Hem.H. 39 BF24
Hawthorns, The, Loug. 85 EN42
Hawthorns, The, Oxt. 254 EG132
Hawthorns, The, Rick. 91 BD50
Hawthorns, The, Slou. 153 BF81
Hawtrees, Rad. 77 CF35
Hawtrey Ave., Nthlt. 136 BX68
Hawtrey Clo., Slou. 152 AV75
Hawtrey Dr., Ruis. 115 BU59
Hawtrey Rd. NW3 140 DE66
Hawtrey Rd., Wind. 151 AQ82
Haxted Rd., Brom. 204 EH95
North Rd.
Hay Clo. E15 144 EE66
Hay Clo., Borwd. 78 CQ40
Banks Rd.
Hay Currie St. E14 143 EB72
Hay Hill W1 277 J1
Hay Hill W1 141 DH73
Hay La. NW9 118 CQ56
Hay La., Slou. 112 AX63
Hay St. E2 142 DU67
Hayboum Mead, Hem.H. 40 BH21
Hayburn Way, Horn. 127 FF60
Haycroft Clo., Couls. 235 DP118
Caterham Dr.
Haycroft Gdns. NW10 139 CU67
Haycroft Rd. SW2 181 DL85
Haycroft Rd., Surb. 197 CK104
Hayday Rd. E16 144 EG71
Hayden Ct., Add. 212 BH111
Hayden Way, Rom. 105 FC54
Haydens Clo., Orp. 206 EW100
Haydens Pl. W11 139 CZ72
Portobello Rd.
Haydens Rd., Harl. 51 EQ15
Haydn Ave., Pur. 219 DN114
Haydns Ms. W3 138 CQ72
Emanuel Ave.
Haydock Ave., Nthlt. 136 CA65
Haydock Clo., Horn. 128 FM63
Haydock Grn., Nthlt. 136 CA65
Haydock Ave.
Haydon Clo. NW9 118 CQ56
Haydon Clo., Enf. 82 DS44
Mortimer Dr.
Haydon Dr., Pnr. 115 BV56
Haydon Pk. Rd. SW19 180 DA92
Haydon Pl., Guil. 258 AX135
Haydon Rd., Dag. 126 EW61
Haydon Rd., Wat. 76 BY44
Haydon St. EC3 275 P10
Haydon Wk. E1 142 DT73
Mansell St.
Haydon Way SW11 160 DD84
St. John's Hill

Haydons Rd. SW19 180 DB92
Hayes, The, Epsom 232 CR119
Hayes Barton, Wok. 227 BD116
Hayes Chase, W.Wick. 203 ED100
Hayes Clo., Brom. 204 EG103
Hayes Clo., Grays 169 FW79
Hayes Ct. SW2 181 DL88
Hayes Cres. NW11 119 CZ57
Hayes Cres., Sutt. 217 CX105
Hayes Dr., Rain. 147 FH66
Hayes End Clo., Hayes 135 BR70
Hayes End Dr., Hayes 135 BR70
Hayes End Rd., Hayes 135 BR70
Hayes Gdn., Brom. 204 EG103
Hayes Hill, Brom. 204 EE102
Hayes Hill Rd., Brom. 204 EF102
Hayes La., Beck. 203 EC97
Hayes La., Brom. 204 EG99
Hayes La., Ken. 235 DP116
Hayes Mead Rd., Brom. 204 EE102
Hayes Pl. NW1 272 C5
Hayes Rd., Brom. 204 EG98
Hayes Rd., Green. 189 FS87
Hayes Rd., Sthl. 155 BV77
Hayes St., Brom. 204 EH102
Hayes Wk., Brox. 67 DZ25
Landau Way
Hayes Wk., Horl. 269 DN147
Hayes Wk., Pot.B. 64 DB33
Hyde Ave.
Hayes Way, Beck. 203 EC98
Hayes Wd. Ave., Brom. 204 EH102
Hayesford Pk. Dr., Brom. 204 EF99
Hayfield Clo. (Bushey), Wat. 76 CB42
Hayfield Pas. E1 142 DW70
Stepney Grn.
Hayfield Rd., Orp. 206 EU99
Hayfield Yd. E1 142 DW70
Mile End Rd.
Hayfields, Horl. 269 DJ147
Ryelands
Haygarth Pl. SW19 179 CX92
Haygreen Clo., Kings.T. 178 CP93
Kingsnympton Pk.
Hayland Clo. NW9 118 CR56
Hayles St. SE11 278 F8
Hayles St. SE11 161 DP77
Haylett Gdns., Kings.T. 197 CK98
Anglesea Rd.
Hayling Ave., Felt. 175 BU90
Hayling Clo. N16 122 DS64
Pellerin Rd.
Hayling Rd., Wat. 93 BT48
Haymaker Clo., Uxb. 134 BM66
Honey Hill
Hayman Cres., Hayes 135 BR68
Hayman St. N1 141 DP66
Cross St.
Haymarket SW1 277 M1
Haymarket SW1 141 DK73
Haymarket Arc. SW1 277 M1
Haymeads, Welw.G.C. 29 CY06
Haymeads Dr., Esher 214 CC107
Haymer Gdns., Wor.Pk. 199 CU104
Haymerle Rd. SE15 162 DU79
Haymill Clo., Grnf. 137 CF69
Haymill Rd., Slou. 131 AK70
Hayne Rd., Beck. 203 DZ96
Hayne St. EC1 274 G6
Haynes Clo. N11 98 DG48
Brunswick Cres.
Haynes Clo. N17 100 DV52
Haynes Clo. SE3 164 EE83
Haynes Clo., Slou. 153 AZ77
Haynes Clo., Welw.G.C. 30 DA10
Haynes Clo., Wok. 228 BH122
Georgelands
Haynes La. SE19 182 DS93
Haynes Mead, Berk. 38 AU17
Haynes Rd., Grav. 191 GF90
Haynes Rd., Horn. 128 FK57
Haynes Rd., Wem. 138 CL66
Haynt Wk. SW20 199 CY97
Hay's La. SE1 279 M3
Hay's Ms. W1 277 H2
Hay's Ms. W1 141 DH74
Hays Wk., Sutt. 217 CX110
Hayse Hill, Wind. 151 AK81
Haysleigh Gdns. SE20 202 DU96
Haysoms Clo., Rom. 127 FE56
Haystall Clo., Hayes 135 BS68
Hayter Rd. SW2 181 DL85
Hayton Clo. E8 142 DT65
Buttermere Wk.
Haywain, Oxt. 253 ED130
Hayward Clo. SW19 180 DB94
Hayward Clo., Bex. 187 FD85
Hayward Clo., Dart. 187 FD85
Hayward Dr., Dart. 188 FM89
Powder Mill La.
Hayward Gdns. SW15 179 CW86
Hayward Rd. N20 98 DC47
Haywards Clo., Brwd. 109 GE44
Haywards Mead (Eton Wick), Wind. 151 AM78
Hayward's Pl. EC1 274 F5
Haywood Clo., Pnr. 94 BX54
Haywood Ct., Wal.Abb. 68 EF34
Haywood Dr., Hem.H. 39 BF23
Haywood Pk., Rick. 73 BF43
Haywood Ri., Orp. 223 ES105
Haywood Rd., Brom. 204 EK98
Hayworth Clo., Enf. 83 DY40
Green St.
Hazel Ave., Guil. 242 AW130
Hazel Ave., West Dr. 154 BN76
Hazel Bank, Surb. 198 CQ102
Hazel Clo. N13 100 DR48
Hazel Clo. N19 121 DJ61
Hargrave Pk.
Hazel Clo. SE15 162 DU82
Copeland Rd.
Hazel Clo., Brent. 157 CH80
Hazel Clo., Croy. 203 DX102
Primrose La.
Hazel Clo., Egh. 172 AV93
Hazel Clo., Horn. 127 FH62
Hazel Clo., Mitch. 201 DK98
Hazel Clo., Reig. 266 DC136
Hazel Clo., Twick. 176 CC87
Hazel Clo., Wal.Cr. 66 DS26
The Laurels
Hazel Dr., Erith 167 FG81
Hazel Dr., S.Ock. 149 FW69
Brandon Gros. Ave.
Hazel Dr., Wok. 243 BF125
Hazel End, Swan. 207 FE99
Hazel Gdns., Edg. 96 CP49
Hazel Gdns., Grays 170 GE76
Hazel Gdns., Saw. 36 EZ06
Sun St.
Hazel Gro. SE26 183 DX91
Hazel Gro., Enf. 82 DU44
Dimsdale Dr.
Hazel Gro., Hat. 45 CT21
Hazel Gro., Orp. 205 EP103
Hazel Gro., Rom. 126 EY55
Hazel Gro., Stai. 174 BH93
Hazel Gro., Wat. 75 BV35
Cedar Wd. Dr.
Hazel Gro., Welw.G.C. 30 DB08
Hazel Gro., Wem. 138 CL67
Carlyon Rd.
Hazel Gro. Est. SE26 183 DX91
Hazel La., Rich. 178 CL89
Hazel Mead, Barn. 79 CV43
Hazel Mead, Epsom 217 CU110
Hazel Ri., Horn. 128 FJ58
Hazel Rd. E15 124 EE64
Wingfield Rd.
Hazel Rd. NW10 139 CV69
Hazel Rd., Berk. 38 AX20
Hazel Rd., Dart. 188 FK89
Hazel Rd., Erith 167 FG81
Hazel Rd., Reig. 266 DC136
Hazel Rd., St.Alb. 60 CB28
Hazel Rd., W.Byf. 212 BG114
Hazel Tree Rd., Wat. 75 BV37
Hazel Wk., Brom. 205 EN100
Hazel Wk., Dor. 263 CJ139
Lake Vw.
Hazel Way E4 101 DZ51
Hazel Way SE1 279 P8
Hazel Way, Couls. 234 DF119
Hazelwood La.
Hazel Way, Lthd. 230 CC122
Hazelbank Ct., Cher. 194 BJ102
Hazelbank Rd. SE6 183 ED89
Hazelbank Rd., Cher. 194 BJ101
Hazelbourne Rd. SW12 181 DH86
Hazelbrouck Gdns., Ilf. 103 ER52
Hazelbury Ave., Abb.L. 59 BQ32
Hazelbury Clo. SW19 200 DA96
Hazelbury Grn. N9 100 DS48
Hazelbury La. N9 100 DS48
Hazelcroft, Pnr. 94 CB51
Hazelcroft Clo., Uxb. 134 BM66
Hazeldean Rd. NW10 138 CR66
Hazeldell Link, Hem.H. 39 BF21
Hazeldell Rd., Hem.H. 39 BF21
Hazeldene, Add. 212 BJ106
Hazeldene Ct., Ken. 236 DR115
Hazeldene Dr., Pnr. 116 BW55
Hazeldene Gdns., Uxb. 135 BQ67
Hazeldene Rd., Ilf. 126 EV61
Hazeldene Rd., Well. 166 EW82
Hazeldon Rd. SE4 183 DY85
Hazeleigh, Brwd. 109 GB48
Hazeleigh Gdns., Wdf.Grn. 102 EL50
Hazelgreen Clo. N21 99 DP46
Hazelhurst, Beck. 203 ED95
Hazelhurst, Horl. 269 DJ147
Hazelhurst Clo., Guil. 243 BB129
Weybrook Dr.
Hazelhurst Rd. SW17 180 DC91
Hazelhurst Rd., Slou. 130 AJ68
Hazell Cres., Rom. 105 FB53
Hazell Pk., Amer. 55 AR39
Hazell Way, Slou. 132 AT66
Hazells Rd., Grav. 190 GD92
Hazellville Rd. N19 121 DK59
Hazelmere Clo., Felt. 175 BR86
Hazelmere Clo., Lthd. 231 CH119
Hazelmere Clo., Nthlt. 136 BZ68
Hazelmere Dr., Nthlt. 136 BZ68
Hazelmere Gdns., Horn. 127 FH57
Hazelmere Rd. NW6 139 CZ67
Hazelmere Rd., Nthlt. 136 BZ68
Hazelmere Rd., Orp. 205 EQ98
Hazelmere Rd., St.Alb. 43 CJ17
Hazelmere Wk., Nthlt. 136 BZ68
Hazelmere Way, Brom. 204 EG100
Hazels, The, Welw. 30 DE05
Hazeltree La., Nthlt. 136 BY69
Hazelwood, Dor. 263 CH137
South Ter.
Hazelwood, Loug. 84 EK43
Hazelwood Ave., Mord. 200 DB98
Hazelwood Clo. W5 158 CL75
Hazelwood Clo., Chesh. 54 AR29
Hazelwood Clo., Har. 116 CB56
Hazelwood Ct. NW10 118 CS62
Neasden La. N.
Hazelwood Cres. N13 99 DN49
Hazelwood Cft., Surb. 198 CL100
Hazelwood Dr., Pnr. 93 BV54
Hazelwood Dr., St.Alb. 43 CJ18
Hazelwood Gdns., Brwd. 108 FU43
Hazelwood Gro., S.Croy. 220 DV113
Hazelwood La. N13 99 DN49
Hazelwood La., Abb.L. 59 BR31
Hazelwood La., Couls. 234 DE118
Hazelwood Pk. Clo., Chig. 103 ES50
Hazelwood Rd. E17 123 DY57
Hazelwood Rd., Enf. 82 DT44
Hazelwood Rd., Oxt. 254 EH132
Hazelwood Rd., Rick. 75 BQ44
Hazelwood Rd., Sev. 223 ER112
Hazelwood Rd., Wok. 226 AS118
Hazlebury Rd. SW6 160 DB82
Hazledean Rd., Croy. 202 DR103
Hazledene, Wal.Cr. 67 DY32
Hazledene Rd. W4 158 CQ79
Hazlemere Gdns., Wor.Pk. 199 CU102
Hazlemere Rd., H.Wyc. 88 AC45
Hazlemere Rd., Slou. 132 AV74
Hazlewell Rd. SW15 179 CV85
Hazlewood Cres. W10 139 CY70
Hazlitt Ms. W14 159 CY76
Hazlitt Rd.
Hazlitt Rd. W14 159 CY76
Hazon Way, Epsom 216 CQ112
Heacham Ave., Uxb. 115 BQ62
Head St. E1 143 DX72
Headcorn Pl., Th.Hth. 201 DM98
Headcorn Rd.
Headcorn Rd. N17 100 DT52
Headcorn Rd., Brom. 184 EG92
Headcorn Rd., Th.Hth. 201 DM98
Headfort Pl. SW1 276 G5
Headfort Pl. SW1 160 DG75
Headingley Clo., Ilf. 103 ET51
Headingley Clo., Rad. 62 CL32
Headingley Clo. (Cheshunt), Wal.Cr. 66 DT26
Headington Rd. SW18 180 DC89
Headlam Rd. SW4 181 DK86
Headlam St. E1 142 DV70
Headley App., Ilf. 125 EP57
Headley Ave., Wall. 219 DM106
Headley Chase, Brwd. 108 FW49
Headley Clo., Epsom 216 CN107
Headley Common, Brwd. 107 FV52
Warley Gap
Headley Common Rd., Epsom 248 CR126
Headley Common Rd., Tad. 248 CS128
Headley Ct. SE26 182 DW92
Headley Dr., Croy. 221 EB108
Headley Dr., Epsom 233 CV119
Headley Dr., Ilf. 125 EP58
Headley Gro., Tad. 233 CV120
Headley Heath App., Dor. 248 CP130
Ashurst Dr.
Headley Heath App., Tad. 248 CP130
Headley Rd., Dor. 247 CJ129
Headley Rd. (Ashtead Pk.), Epsom 232 CP118
Headley Rd. (Tyrrell's Wd.), Epsom 232 CN122
Headley Rd., Lthd. 231 CJ122
Head's Ms. W11 140 DA72
Artesian Rd.
Headstone Dr., Har. 117 CE55
Headstone Gdns., Har. 116 CC56
Headstone La., Har. 94 CB52
Headstone Rd., Har. 117 CE57
Headway, The, Epsom 217 CT109
Headway Clo., Rich. 177 CJ91
Locksmeade Rd.
Heald St. SE14 163 DZ81
Healey Dr., Orp. 223 ET105
Healey Rd., Wat. 75 BT44
Healey St. NW1 141 DH65
Heanor Ct. E5 123 DX62
Pedro St.
Heards La., Brwd. 109 FZ41
Hearn Ri., Nthlt. 136 BX67
Hearn Rd., Rom. 127 FF58
Hearn St. EC2 275 N5
Hearn St. EC2 142 DS70
Hearne Ct., Ch.St.G. 90 AV48
Gordon Way
Hearne Rd. W4 158 CN79
Hearnes Clo., Beac. 89 AR50
Hearnes Mead, Beac. 89 AR50
Hearn's Bldgs. SE17 279 L9
Hearn's Clo., Orp. 206 EW98
Hearn's Ri., Orp. 206 EX98
Hearn's Rd., Orp. 206 EW98
Hearnville Rd. SW12 180 DG88
Heath, The W7 137 CE74
Lower Boston Rd.
Heath, The, Bishop's Stortford 37 FG05
Heath, The, Cat. 236 DQ124
Heath, The, Rad. 61 CG33
Heath Ave., Bexh. 166 EX79
Heath Ave., St.Alb. 43 CD18
Heath Brow NW3 120 DC62
North End Way
Heath Brow, Hem.H. 40 BJ22
Heath Clo. NW11 120 DB59
Heath Clo. W5 138 CM70
Heath Clo., Bans. 218 DB114
Heath Clo., Guil. 242 AV132
Heath Clo., Hayes 155 BR80
Heath Clo., Hem.H. 40 BJ21
Heath Clo., Orp. 206 EW100
Sussex Rd.
Heath Clo., Pot.B. 64 DB30
Heath Clo., Rom. 127 FG55
Heath Clo., Stai. 174 BJ86
Heath Clo., Vir.W. 192 AX98
Heath Cotts., Pot.B. 64 DB30
Heath Rd.
Heath Ct., Houns. 156 BZ84
Heath Ct., Uxb. 134 BL66
Heath Dr. NW3 120 DB63
Heath Dr. SW20 199 CW98
Heath Dr., Epp. 85 ES36
Heath Dr., Pot.B. 64 DA30
Heath Dr., Rom. 105 FG53
Heath Dr., Sutt. 218 DC109
Heath Dr., Tad. 249 CU125
Heath Dr., Wok. 227 BB122
Heath End Rd., Bex. 187 FE88
Heath Fm. Ct., Wat. 75 BR37
Grove Mill La.
Heath Fm. La., St.Alb. 43 CE18
Heath Gdns., Twick. 177 CF88
Heath Gro. SE20 182 DW94
Maple Rd.
Heath Gro., Sun. 175 BT94
Heath Hill, Dor. 263 CH135
Heath Hurst Rd. NW3 120 DE63
Heath La. SE3 163 ED82
Heath La., Dart. 187 FG89
Heath La., Guil. 260 BL141
Heath La., Hem.H. 40 BJ22
Heath La., Hert. 32 DW13
Heath La. Lwr., Dart. 188 FJ88
Heath La. Upper, Dart. 187 FH88
Heath Mead SW19 179 CX90
Heath Pk. Ct., Rom. 127 FG57
Heath Pk. Rd.
Heath Pk. Dr., Brom. 204 EL97
Heath Pk. Rd., Rom. 127 FG57
Heath Ridge Grn., Cob. 214 CA113
Heath Ri. SW15 179 CX86
Heath Ri., Brom. 204 EF100
Heath Ri., Dor. 262 CC138
Heath Ri., Vir.W. 192 AX98
Heath Ri., Wok. 228 BH123
Heath Rd. SW8 161 DH82
Heath Rd., Beac. 88 AG54
Heath Rd., Bex. 187 FC88
Heath Rd., Cat. 236 DR123
Heath Rd., Dart. 187 FF86
Heath Rd., Grays 171 GG75
Heath Rd., Har. 116 CC59
Heath Rd., Houns. 156 CB84
Heath Rd., Lthd. 214 CC112
Heath Rd., Pot.B. 64 DA30
Heath Rd., Rom. 126 EX59
Heath Rd., St.Alb. 43 CE19
Heath Rd., Th.Hth. 202 DQ97
Heath Rd., Twick. 177 CF88
Heath Rd., Uxb. 135 BQ70
Heath Rd., Wat. 94 BX45
Heath Rd., Wey. 212 BN105
Heath Rd., Wok. 227 AZ115
Heath Side NW3 120 DD63
Heath Side, Orp. 205 EQ102
Heath St. NW3 120 DC62
Heath St., Dart. 188 FK87
Heath Vw. N2 120 DC56
Heath Vw., Lthd. 245 BT125
Heath Vw. Clo. N2 120 DC56
Heath Vw. Gdns., Grays 170 GC75
Heath Vw. Rd., Grays 170 GC75
Heath Vill. SE18 165 ET78
Heath Vill. SW18 180 DC88
Cargill Rd.
Heath Way, Erith 167 FC81
Heatham Pk., Twick. 177 CF87
Heathbourne Rd. (Bushey), Wat. 95 CE46
Heathbridge, Wey. 212 BN108
Heathclose Ave., Dart. 187 FH87
Heathclose Rd., Dart. 187 FG88
Heathcock Ct. WC2 141 DL73
Strand
Heathcote, Tad. 233 CX121
Heathcote Ave., Hat. 45 CU16
Heathcote Ave., Ilf. 103 EM54
Heathcote Gro. E4 101 EC48
Heathcote Rd., Epsom 216 CR114
Heathcote Rd., Twick. 177 CH86
Heathcote St. WC1 274 B4
Heathcote St. WC1 141 DM70
Heathcote Way, West Dr. 134 BK74
Tavistock Rd.
Heathcroft NW11 120 DB60
Heathcroft W5 138 CM70
Heathcroft Ave., Sun. 175 BT94
Heathdale Ave., Houns. 156 BY83
Heathdene, Tad. 233 CY119
Canons La.
Heathdene Dr., Belv. 167 FB77
Heathdene Rd. SW16 181 DM94
Heathdene Rd., Wall. 218 DG108
Heathdown Rd., Wok. 227 BD115
Heathedge SE26 182 DV89
Heathend Rd., Bex. 187 FE88
Heather Ave., Rom. 105 FD54
Heather Clo. E6 145 EP72
Heather Clo. SW8 161 DH83
Heather Clo., Abb.L. 59 BU32
Stewart Clo.
Heather Clo., Add. 212 BH110
Heather Clo., Brwd. 108 FV43
Heather Clo., Guil. 242 AV132
Heather Clo., Hmptn. 196 BZ95
Heather Clo., Islw. 177 CD85
Harvesters Clo.
Heather Clo., Rom. 105 FD53
Heather Clo., Tad. 233 CY122
Heather Clo., Uxb. 134 BM71
Violet Ave.
Heather Clo., Wok. 226 AW115
Heather Dr., Dart. 187 FG87
Heather Dr., Enf. 81 DP40
Chasewood Ave.
Heather Dr., Rom. 105 FD54
Heather End, Swan. 207 FD98
Heather Gdns. NW11 119 CY58
Heather Gdns., Rom. 105 FD54
Heather Gdns., Sutt. 218 DA107
Heather Glen, Rom. 105 FD54
Heather La., Wat. 75 BT35
Heather La., West Dr. 134 BL72
Heather Pk. Dr., Wem. 138 CN66
Heather Pl., Esher 214 CB105
Park Rd.
Heather Ri. (Bushey), Wat. 76 BZ40
Heather Rd. E4 101 DZ51
Silver Birch Ave.
Heather Rd. NW2 119 CT61
Heather Rd. SE12 184 EG89
Heather Rd., Welw.G.C. 29 CW11
Heather Wk. W10 139 CY70
Droop St.
Heather Wk., Edg. 96 CP50
Heather Wk., Twick. 176 CA87
Stephenson Rd.
Heather Wk., Walt. 213 BT110
Octagon Rd.
Heather Way, Hem.H. 40 BK19
Heather Way, Pot.B. 63 CZ32
Heather Way, Rom. 105 FD54
Heather Way, S.Croy. 221 DX109
Heather Way, Stan. 95 CF51
Heather Way, Wok. 210 AS108
Heatherbank SE9 165 EM82
Heatherbank, Chis. 205 EN96
Heatherbank Clo., Dart. 187 FE86
Heatherdale Clo., Kings.T. 178 CP94
Heatherden Grn., Iver 133 BC67
Heatherdene, Lthd. 245 BR125
Heatherdene Clo. N12 98 DC53
Bow La.
Heatherdene Clo., Mitch. 200 DE98
Heatherfields, Add. 212 BH110
Heatherlands, Horl. 269 DH147
Stockfield
Heatherlands, Sun. 175 BU93
Heatherley Dr., Ilf. 124 EL55
Heathers, The, Stai. 174 BM87
Heatherset Gdns. SW16 181 DM94
Heatherside Dr., Vir.W. 192 AU100
Heatherside Gdns., Slou. 111 AR62
Heatherside Rd., Epsom 216 CR108
Heatherside Rd., Sid. 186 EX90
Wren Rd.
Heathersland, Dor. 263 CJ139
Goodwyns Rd.
Heatherton Pk., Amer. 55 AP36
Heathervale Caravan Pk., Add. 212 BJ110
Heathervale Rd., Add. 212 BH110
Heatherwood Clo. E12 124 EJ61
Heatherwood Dr., Hayes 135 BR68
Charville La.
Heathfield E4 101 EC48
Heathfield, Chis. 185 EQ93
Heathfield, Cob. 214 CA114
Heathfield Ave. SW18 180 DD87
Heathfield Rd.
Heathfield Ave., S.Croy. 221 DY109
Heathfield Clo. E16 144 EK71
Heathfield Clo., Kes. 222 EJ106
Heathfield Clo., Pot.B. 64 DB30
Heathfield Clo., Wok. 227 BA118
Heathfield Ct., St.Alb. 43 CE19
Avenue Rd.
Heathfield Dr., Mitch. 200 DE95
Heathfield Dr., Red. 266 DE139
Heathfield Gdns. NW11 119 CX58
Heathfield Gdns. SW18 180 DD86
Heathfield Rd.
Heathfield Gdns. W4 158 CQ78
Heathfield Gdns., Croy. 220 DR105
Coombe Rd.
Heathfield La., Chis. 185 EP93
Heathfield N., Twick. 177 CF87
Heathfield Pk. NW2 139 CW65
Heathfield Pk. Dr., Rom. 126 EV57
Barley La.
Heathfield Ri., Ruis. 115 BQ59
Heathfield Rd. SW18 180 DC86
Heathfield Rd. W3 158 CP75
Heathfield Rd., Bexh. 166 EZ84
Heathfield Rd., Brom. 184 EF94
Heathfield Rd., Croy. 220 DR105
Heathfield Rd., Kes. 222 EJ106
Heathfield Rd., Sev. 256 FF122
Heathfield Rd., Slou. 110 AF63
Heathfield Rd., Walt. 214 BY105
Heathfield Rd. (Bushey), Wat. 76 BY42
Heathfield Rd., Wok. 227 BA118
Heathfield S., Twick. 177 CF87
Heathfield Sq. SW18 180 DD87
Heathfield St. W11 139 CY73
Portland Rd.
Heathfield Ter. SE18 165 ES79
Heathfield Ter. W4 158 CQ78
Heathfield Vale, S.Croy. 221 DX109
Heathfield Way, Ger.Cr. 112 AX58
Heathfields Ct., Houns. 176 BY85
Frampton Rd.
Heathgate NW11 120 DB58
Heathgate, Hert. 32 DV13
Heathland Rd. N16 122 DS60
Heathlands, Tad. 233 CX122
Heathlands Clo., Sun. 195 BT96
Heathlands Clo., Twick. 177 CF88
Heathlands Clo., Wok. 210 AY114
Heathlands Dr., St.Alb. 43 CE18
Heathlands Ri., Dart. 187 FH86
Heathlands Way, Houns. 176 BY85
Frampton Rd.
Heathlee Rd. SE3 164 EF84
Heathlee Rd., Dart. 187 FE86
Heathley End, Chis. 185 EQ93
Heathmans Rd. SW6 159 CZ81
Heathrow, Guil. 261 BQ139
Heathrow Clo., West Dr. 154 BH81
Heathrow International Trd. Est., Houns. 155 BV83
Heathrow W. Business Pk., Slou. 153 BB77
Heaths Clo., Enf. 82 DS40
Heathside, Esher 197 CE104
Heathside, Houns. 176 BZ87
Heathside, St.Alb. 43 CE18
Heathside, Wey. 213 BP106
Heathside Ave., Bexh. 166 EY82
Heathside Clo., Esher 197 CE104
Heathside Clo., Nthwd. 93 BR50
Heathside Ct., Tad. 233 CV123
Heathside Cres., Wok. 227 AZ117
Heathside Gdns., Wok. 227 BA117
Heathside Pk. Rd., Wok. 227 AZ118
Heathside Rd., Nthwd. 93 BR49
Heathside Rd., Wok. 227 AZ118
Heathstan Rd. W12 139 CU72
Heathurst Rd., S.Croy. 220 DS109
Heathview Ave., Dart. 187 FE86
Heathview Ct. SW19 179 CX89
Heathview Cres., Dart. 187 FG87
Heathview Dr. SE2 166 EX79
Heathview Gdns. SW15 179 CW87
Heathview Rd., Th.Hth. 201 DN98
Heathville Rd. N19 121 DL59
Heathwall St. SW11 160 DF83
Heathway SE3 164 EG80
Heathway, Cat. 252 DQ125
Heathway, Croy. 203 DZ104
Heathway, Dag. 126 EZ62
Heathway, Iver 133 BD68
Heathway, Lthd. 229 BT124
Heathway, Wdf.Grn. 102 EJ49
Heathwood Gdns. SE7 164 EL77
Heathwood Gdns., Swan. 207 FC96
Heathwood Wk., Bex. 187 FE88
Heaton Ave., Rom. 105 FH52
Heaton Clo. E4 101 EC48
Friars Clo.
Heaton Clo., Rom. 106 FJ52
Heaton Gra. Rd., Rom. 105 FF54
Heaton Rd. SE15 162 DU83
Heaton Rd., Mitch. 180 DG94
Heaton Way, Rom. 106 FJ52
Heavens Lea, B.End 110 AC61
Heaver Rd. SW11 160 DD83
Wye St.
Heavitree Clo. SE18 165 ER78
Heavitree Rd.
Heavitree Rd. SE18 165 ER78
Heayfield, Welw.G.C. 30 DC08
Hebden Ct. E2 142 DT67
Laburnum St.
Hebden Ter. N17 100 DS51
Commercial Rd.
Hebdon Rd. SW17 180 DE90
Heber Rd. NW2 119 CX64
Heber Rd. SE22 182 DT86
Hebron Rd. W6 159 CV76
Hecham Clo. E17 101 DY54
Heckfield Pl. SW6 160 DA80
Fulham Rd.
Heckford St. E1 143 DX73
The Highway
Hector St. SE18 165 ES77
Heddington Gro. N7 121 DM64
Heddon Clo., Islw. 157 CG84
Heddon Ct. Ave., Barn. 80 DF43
Heddon Rd., Barn. 80 DF43
Heddon St. W1 273 K10
Heddon St. W1 141 DJ73
Hedge Hill, Enf. 81 DP39
Hedge La. N13 99 DP48
Hedge Lea, H.Wyc. 110 AD55
Hedge Pl. Rd., Green. 189 FT86
Hedge Row, Hem.H. 40 BG18
Hedge Wk. SE6 183 EB92
Lushington Rd.
Hedgebrooms, Welw.G.C. 30 DC08
Hedgeley, Ilf. 125 EM56

Hedgemans Rd., Dag. 146 EX66
Hedgemans Way, Dag. 146 EY65
Hedgerley Ct., Wok. 226 AW117
Hedgerley Gdns., Grnf. 136 CC68
Hedgerley Hill, Slou. 111 AR62
Hedgerley La., Beac. 111 AN56
Hedgerley La., Ger.Cr. 112 AV59
Hedgerley La., Slou. 112 AS58
Hedgerow, Ger.Cr. 90 AY54
Hedgerow Wk., Wal.Cr. 67 DX30
Blindman's La.
Hedgerows, Saw. 36 EZ05
Hedgerows, The, Grav. 190 GE89
Hedgers Gro. E9 143 DY65
Hedges, The, St.Alb. 42 CC16
Hedges Clo., Hat. 45 CV17
Hedgeside, Berk. 39 BA16
Hedgeside Rd., Nthwd. 93 BQ50
Hedgeway, Guil. 258 AU136
Hedgewood Gdns., Ilf. 125 EN56
Hedgley St. SE12 184 EF85
Hedingham Clo. N1 142 DQ66
Popham Rd.
Hedingham Clo., Horl. 269 DJ147
Hedingham Rd., Dag. 126 EV64
Hedingham Rd., Grays 169 FW78
Arterial Rd. W. Thurrock
Hedingham Rd., Horn. 128 FN60
Hedley Ave., Grays 169 FW80
Hedley Rd., St.Alb. 43 CH20
Hedley Rd., Twick. 176 CA87
Hedley Row N5 122 DR64
Poets Rd.
Hedley Vw., H.Wyc. 88 AD54
Hedsor Hill, B.End 110 AC61
Hedsor La., H.Wyc. 110 AF60
Hedworth Ave., Wal.Cr. 67 DX33
Heenan Clo., Bark. 145 EQ65
Glenny Rd.
Heene Rd., Enf. 82 DR39
Heeton Ct., Wal.Cr. 67 DX29
Heideck Gdns., Brwd. 109 GB47
Victors Cres.
Heidegger Cres. SW13 159 CV79
Trinity Ch. Rd.
Heigham Rd. E6 144 EL66
Heighams, Harl. 51 EM18
Heighton Gdns., Croy. 219 DP106
Heights, The SE7 164 EJ78
Heights, The, Beck. 183 EC94
Heights, The, Hem.H. 40 BM18
Saturn Way
Heights, The, Loug. 85 EM40
Heights, The, Nthlt. 116 BZ64
Heights, The, Wal.Abb. 68 EH25
Waltham Rd.
Heights, The, Wey. 212 BN110
Heights Clo. SW20 179 CV94
Heights Clo., Bans. 233 CY116
Heiron St. SE17 161 DP79
Helby Rd. SW4 181 DK86
Helder Gro. SE12 184 EF87
Helder St., S.Croy. 220 DR107
Heldmann Clo., Houns. 157 CD84
Helen Ave., Felt. 175 BV87
Helen Clo. N2 120 DC55
Thomas More Way
Helen Clo., Dart. 187 FH87
Helen Clo., W.Mol. 196 CB98
Helen Rd., Horn. 128 FK55
Helen St. SE18 165 EP77
Wilmount St.
Helena Clo., Barn. 80 DD38
Helena Clo., Wall. 219 DL108
Kingsford Ave.
Helena Pl. E9 142 DW67
Fremont St.
Helena Rd. E13 144 EF68
Helena Rd. E17 123 EA57
Helena Rd. NW10 119 CV64
Helena Rd. W5 137 CK71
Helena Rd., Wind. 151 AR82
Helena Sq. SE16 143 DY73
Rotherhithe St.
Helens Gate, Wal.Cr. 67 DZ26
Helen's Pl. E2 142 DW69
Roman Rd.
Helenslea Ave. NW11 119 CZ60
Helford Clo., Ruis. 115 BS61
Chichester Ave.
Helford Wk., Wok. 226 AU118
Helford Way, Upmin. 129 FR58
Helgiford Gdns., Sun. 175 BS94
Helions Rd., Harl. 51 EP15
Helix Gdns. SW2 181 DM86
Helix Rd.
Helix Rd. SW2 181 DM86
Helleborine, Grays 170 FZ78
Hellings St. E1 142 DU74
Wapping High St.
Helme Clo. SW19 179 CZ92
Helmet Row EC1 275 J4
Helmet Row EC1 142 DQ70
Helmsdale, Wok. 226 AV118
Winnington Way
Helmsdale Clo., Hayes 136 BY70
Berrydale Rd.
Helmsdale Clo., Rom. 105 FE52
Helmsdale Rd. SW16 201 DK95
Helmsdale Rd., Rom. 105 FE52
Helmsley Pl. E8 142 DV66
Helsinki Sq. SE16 163 DY76
Finland St.
Helston Clo., Pnr. 94 BZ52
Helston Gro., Hem.H. 40 BK15
Helston La., Wind. 151 AP81
Helston Pl., Abb.L. 59 BT32
Shirley Rd.
Helvellyn Clo., Egh. 173 BB94
Helvetia St. SE6 183 DZ89
Hemans St. SW8 161 DK80
Hemberton Rd. SW9 161 DL83
Hemel Hempstead Rd., Hem.H. 41 BR22
Hemel Hempstead Rd., St.Alb. 42 BW22
Hemel Hempstead Rd. (Redbourn), St.Alb. 41 BQ15
Hemery Rd., Grnf. 117 CD64
Lilian Board Way
Heming Rd., Edg. 96 CP52
Hemingford Rd. N1 141 DM67
Hemingford Rd., Sutt. 217 CW105
Hemingford Rd., Wat. 75 BS36
Hemington Ave. N11 98 DF50
Hemlock Clo., Tad. 233 CY124
Warren Lo. Dr.
Hemlock Rd. W12 139 CT73
Hemmen La., Hayes 135 BT72
Hemming Clo., Hmptn. 196 CA95
Chandler Clo.
Hemming St. E1 142 DU70
Hemming Way, Wat. 75 BU35
Hemmings, The, Berk. 38 AT20
Hemnall St., Epp. 69 ET31
Hemp Wk. SE17 279 L8
Hempshaw Ave., Bans. 234 DF116
Hempson Ave., Slou. 152 AW76
Hempstall, Welw.G.C. 30 DB11
Linces Way
Hempstead Clo., Buck.H. 102 EG47
Hempstead La., Berk. 39 BB17
Hempstead Rd. E17 101 ED54
Hempstead Rd., Hem.H. 57 BA27
Hempstead Rd., Kings L. 58 BM26
Hempstead Rd., Wat. 75 BR36
Hemsby Rd., Chess. 216 CM107
Hemstal Rd. NW6 140 DA66
Hemsted Rd., Erith 167 FE80
Hemswell Dr. NW9 96 CS53
Hemsworth Ct. N1 142 DS68
Hemsworth St.
Hemsworth St. N1 142 DS68
Hemus Pl. SW3 160 DE78
Chelsea Manor St.
Hemwood Rd., Wind. 151 AK83
Hen & Chicken Ct. EC4 141 DN72
Fleet St.
Henbane Path, Rom. 106 FK52
Clematis Clo.
Henbit Clo., Tad. 233 CV119
Henbury Way, Wat. 94 BX48
Henchley Dene, Guil. 243 BD131
Henchman St. W12 139 CT72
Hencroft St. N., Slou. 152 AT75
Osborne St.
Hencroft St. S., Slou. 152 AT76
Osborne St.
Hendale Ave. NW4 119 CU55
Henderson Ave., Guil. 242 AV129
Henderson Clo. NW10 138 CQ65
Henderson Clo., Horn. 127 FH61
St. Leonards Way
Henderson Clo., St.Alb. 42 CC16
Henderson Dr. NW8 140 DD70
Cunningham Pl.
Henderson Dr., Dart. 168 FM84
Henderson Pl., Abb.L. 59 BT27
Henderson Rd. E7 144 EJ65
Henderson Rd. N9 100 DV46
Henderson Rd. SW18 180 DE87
Henderson Rd., Croy. 202 DR100
Henderson Rd., Hayes 135 BU69
Henderson Rd., West. 222 EJ112
Hendham Rd. SW17 180 DE89
Hendon Ave. N3 97 CY53
Hendon Gdns., Rom. 105 FC51
Hendon La. N3 119 CY55
Hendon Pk. Row NW11 119 CZ58
Hendon Rd. N9 100 DU47
Hendon Way NW2 119 CX59
Hendon Way NW4 119 CV58
Hendon Way, Stai. 174 BK86
Hendon Wd. La. NW7 97 CT45
Hendre Rd. SE1 279 N9
Hendren Clo., Grnf. 117 CD64
Dimmock Dr.
Hendrick Ave. SW12 180 DF87
Heneage Cres., Croy. 221 EC110
Heneage La. EC3 275 N9
Heneage St. E1 142 DT71
Henfield Clo. N19 121 DJ60
Henfield Clo., Bex. 186 FA86
Henfield Rd. SW19 199 CZ95
Henfold La., Dor. 264 CL144
Hengelo Gdns., Mitch. 200 DD98
Hengist Rd. SE12 184 EH87
Hengist Rd., Erith 167 FB80
Hengist Way, Brom. 203 ED98
Hengrave Rd. SE23 182 DW87
Hengrove Ct., Bex. 186 EY88
Hurst Rd.
Hengrove Cres., Ashf. 174 BK90
Henhurst Rd., Grav. 191 GL94
Henley Ave., Sutt. 199 CY104
Henley Bank, Guil. 258 AU136
Henley Clo., Grnf. 136 CC68
Henley Clo., Islw. 157 CF81
Henley Ct. N14 99 DJ45
Henley Ct., Wok. 227 BA120
Henley Deane, Grav. 190 GE91
Henley Dr. SE1 162 DT77
Henley Dr., Kings.T. 179 CT94
Henley Gdns., Pnr. 115 BV55
Henley Gdns., Rom. 126 EY57
Henley Rd. E16 165 EM75
Henley Rd. N18 100 DS49
Henley Rd. NW10 139 CW67
Henley Rd., Ilf. 125 EQ63
Henley Rd., Slou. 131 AL72
Henley St. SW11 160 DG82
Henley Way, Felt. 176 BX92
Henlow Pl., Rich. 177 CK89
Sandpits Rd.
Hennel Clo. SE23 182 DW90
Hennessy Ct., Wok. 211 BC114
Devonshire Ave.
Henniker Gdns. E6 144 EK69
Henniker Ms. SW3 160 DD79
Callow St.
Henniker Pt. E15 124 EE64
Henniker Rd. E15 123 ED64
Henning St. SW11 160 DE81
Henningham Rd. N17 100 DR53
Henrietta Ms. WC1 274 A4
Henrietta Pl. W1 273 H8
Henrietta Pl. W1 141 DH72
Henrietta St. E15 123 EC64
Henrietta St. WC2 274 A10
Henrietta St. WC2 141 DL73
Henriques St. E1 142 DU72
Henry Clo., Enf. 82 DS38
Clay Hill
Henry Cooper Way SE9 184 EK90
Henry Darlot Dr. NW7 97 CX50
Henry Dickens Ct. W11 139 CX73
Henry Jackson Rd. SW15 159 CX83
Henry Rd. E6 144 EL68
Henry Rd. N4 122 DQ60
Henry Rd., Barn. 80 DD43
Henry Rd., Slou. 151 AR75
Henry St., Brom. 204 EH95
Henry St., Grays 170 GC79
East Thurrock Rd.
Henry St., Hem.H. 40 BK24
Henry Wells Sq., Hem.H. 40 BL16
Aycliffe Dr.
Henry's Ave., Wdf.Grn. 102 EF50
Henry's Wk., Ilf. 103 ER52
Henryson Rd. SE4 183 EA85
Hensford Gdns. SE26 182 DV91
Wells Pk. Rd.
Henshall St. N1 142 DR65
Henshaw St. SE17 279 K8
Henshaw St. SE17 162 DR77
Henshawe Rd., Dag. 126 EX62
Henshill Pt. E3 143 EB69
Bromley High St.
Henslow Way, Wok. 211 BD114
Henslowe Rd. SE22 182 DU85
Henson Ave. NW2 119 CW64
Henson Clo., Orp. 205 EP103
Henson Path, Har. 117 CK55
Brancker Rd.
Henson Pl., Nthlt. 136 BW67
Henstridge Pl. NW8 140 DE68
Hensworth Rd., Ashf. 174 BK92
Henty Clo. SW11 160 DE80
Henty Wk. SW15 179 CV85
Henville Rd., Brom. 204 EJ95
Henwick Rd. SE9 164 EK83
Henwood Rd. SE16 162 DW76
Gomm Rd.
Henwood Side, Wdf.Grn. 103 EM51
Love La.
Hepburn Gdns., Brom. 204 EE102
Hepburn Ms. SW11 180 DF85
Webbs Rd.
Hepple Clo., Islw. 157 CH82
Hepplestone Clo. SW15 179 CV86
Dover Pk. Dr.
Hepscott Rd. E9 143 EA65
Hepworth Ct., Bark. 126 EU64
Hepworth Gdns., Bark. 126 EU64
Hepworth Rd. SW16 181 DL94
Hepworth Wk. NW3 120 DE64
Haverstock Hill
Hepworth Way, Walt. 195 BT102
Heracles Clo., Wall. 219 DL108
Gull Clo.
Herald Gdns., Wall. 201 DH104
Herald St. E2 142 DV70
Three Colts La.
Herald Wk., Dart. 188 FM85
Temple Hill Sq.
Herald's Ct. SE11 278 F9
Herald's Pl. SE11 278 E8
Herbal Hill EC1 274 E5
Herbal Hill EC1 141 DN70
Herbert Cres. SW1 276 E6
Herbert Cres., Wok. 226 AS118
Herbert Gdns. NW10 139 CV67
Herbert Gdns. W4 158 CP79
Magnolia Rd.
Herbert Gdns., Rom. 126 EX59
Herbert Pl. SE18 165 EP79
Plumstead Common Rd.
Herbert Rd. E12 124 EL63
Herbert Rd. E17 123 DZ59
Herbert Rd. N11 99 DL52
Herbert Rd. N15 122 DT57
Herbert Rd. NW9 119 CU58
Herbert Rd. SE18 165 EN80
Herbert Rd. SW19 179 CZ94
Herbert Rd., Bexh. 166 EY82
Herbert Rd., Brom. 204 EK99
Herbert Rd., Horn. 128 FL59
Herbert Rd., Ilf. 125 ES61
Herbert Rd., Kings.T. 198 CM97
Herbert Rd., Sthl. 136 BZ74
Herbert Rd., Swan. 187 FH93
Herbert Rd., Swans. 190 FZ86
Herbert St. E13 144 EG68
Herbert St. NW5 140 DG65
Herbert St., Hem.H. 40 BK19
St. Mary's Rd.
Herbert Ter. SE18 165 EP79
Herbert Rd.
Herbrand St. WC1 273 P4
Herbrand St. WC1 141 DL70
Hercies Rd., Uxb. 134 BM66
Hercules Pl. N7 121 DL62
Hercules St.
Hercules Rd. SE1 278 C7
Hercules Rd. SE1 161 DM76
Hercules St. N7 121 DL62
Hercules Twr. SE14 163 DY79
Milton Ct. Rd.
Hereford Ave., Barn. 98 DF46
Hereford Clo., Epsom 216 CR113
Hereford Clo., Guil. 242 AT132
Hereford Clo., Stai. 194 BH95
Hereford Copse, Wok. 226 AV119
Hereford Gdns. SE13 184 EE85
Longhurst Rd.
Hereford Gdns., Ilf. 124 EL59
Hereford Gdns., Pnr. 116 BY57
Hereford Gdns., Twick. 176 CC88
Hereford Ho. NW6 140 DA68
Hereford Ms. W2 140 DA72
Hereford Rd.
Hereford Pl. SE14 163 DZ80
Hereford Retreat SE15 162 DU80
Bird in Bush Rd.
Hereford Rd. E11 124 EH57
Hereford Rd. W2 140 DA72
Hereford Rd. W3 138 CP73
Hereford Rd. W5 157 CJ76
Hereford Rd., Felt. 176 BW88
Hereford Sq. SW7 160 DC77
Hereford St. E2 142 DU70
Hereford Way, Chess. 215 CJ106
Herent Dr., Ilf. 124 EL56
Hereward Ave., Pur. 219 DN111
Hereward Clo., Wal.Abb. 67 EC32
Hereward Gdns. N13 99 DN50
Hereward Grn., Loug. 85 EQ39
Hereward Rd. SW17 180 DE91
Herga Ct., Har. 117 CE62
Herga Ct., Wat. 75 BU40
Herga Rd., Har. 117 CF56
Herington Gro., Brwd. 109 GA45
Heriot Ave. E4 101 EA47
Heriot Rd. NW4 119 CW57
Heriot Rd., Cher. 194 BG101
Heriots Clo., Stan. 95 CG49
Heritage Clo., Uxb. 134 BJ70
Heritage Hill, Kes. 222 EJ106
Heritage Lawn, Horl. 269 DJ147
Heritage Vw., Har. 117 CF62
Herkomer Clo. (Bushey), Wat. 76 CB44
Herkomer Rd. (Bushey), Wat. 76 CA43
Herlwyn Ave., Ruis. 115 BS61
Herlwyn Gdns. SW17 180 DF91
Hermes Pt. W9 140 DA70
Harrow Rd.
Hermes St. N1 274 D1
Hermes Wk., Nthlt. 136 CA68
Hotspur Rd.
Hermes Way, Wall. 219 DK108
Hermiston Ave. N8 121 DL57
Hermit Pl. NW6 140 DB67
Belsize Rd.
Hermit Rd. E16 144 EF70
Hermit St. EC1 274 F2
Hermit St. EC1 141 DP69
Hermitage, The SE23 182 DW88
Hermitage, The SW13 159 CT81
Hermitage, The, Felt. 175 BT90
Hermitage, The, Rich. 178 CL85
Hermitage, The, Uxb. 134 BK65
Hermitage Clo. E18 124 EF56
Hermitage Clo., Enf. 81 DP40
Hermitage Clo., Esher 215 CG107
Hermitage Clo., Shep. 194 BN98
Hermitage Clo., Slou. 152 AW76
Hermitage Ct. E18 124 EG56
Hermitage Ct. NW2 120 DA62
Hermitage La.
Hermitage Ct., Pot.B. 64 DC33
Southgate Rd.
Hermitage Gdns. NW2 120 DA62
Hermitage Gdns. SE19 182 DQ94
Hermitage La. N18 100 DR50
Great Cambridge Rd.
Hermitage La. NW2 120 DA62
Hermitage La. SE25 202 DU100
Hermitage La. SW16 181 DM94
Hermitage La., Croy. 202 DU100
Hermitage La., Wind. 151 AN83
Hermitage Path SW16 201 DL95
Hermitage Rd. N4 121 DP59
Hermitage Rd. N15 121 DP59
Hermitage Rd. SE19 182 DQ94
Hermitage Rd., Ken. 236 DQ116
Hermitage Rd., Wok. 226 AS119
Hermitage Row E8 122 DU64
Wayland Ave.
Hermitage St. W2 140 DD71
Harrow Rd.
Hermitage Wk. E18 124 EF56
Hermitage Wall E1 142 DU74
Hermitage Way, Stan. 95 CG53
Hermitage Wds. Cres., Wok. 226 AS119
Hermon Gro., Hayes 135 BU74
Hermon Hill E11 124 EG57
Hermon Hill E18 124 EH55
Herndon Clo., Egh. 173 BA91
High St.
Herndon Rd. SW18 180 DC85
Herne Clo. NW10 118 CR64
North Circular Rd.
Herne Ct., Ch.St.G. 90 AV48
Herne Hill SE24 182 DQ85
Herne Hill Rd. SE24 162 DQ83
Herne Ms. N18 100 DU49
Lyndhurst Rd.
Herne Pl. SE24 181 DP85
Herne Rd., Surb. 197 CK103
Herne Rd. (Bushey), Wat. 76 CB44
Herneshaw, Hat. 45 CT20
Hazel Gro.
Herns La., Welw.G.C. 30 DB08
Herns Way, Welw.G.C. 30 DA07
Heron Clo. E17 101 DZ54
Heron Clo. NW10 138 CS65
Heron Clo., Buck.H. 102 EG46
Heron Clo., Guil. 242 AV131
Heron Clo., Rick. 92 BK47
Heron Clo., Saw. 36 EX06
Heron Clo., Uxb. 134 BK65
Heron Ct., Brom. 204 EJ98
Heron Cres., Sid. 185 ES90
Heron Dale, Add. 212 BK106
Heron Dr., Slou. 153 BB77
Heron Dr., Ware 33 EC12
Heron Elm, Berk. 38 AS16
Heron Flight Ave., Horn. 147 FH66
Heron Hill, Belv. 166 EZ78
Heron Ms., Ilf. 125 EP61
Balfour Rd.
Heron Pl. SE16 143 DY74
Heron Quay E14 143 EA74
Heron Rd. SE24 162 DQ84
Heron Rd., Croy. 202 DS103
Tunstall Rd.
Heron Rd., Twick. 157 CG84
Heron Sq., Rich. 177 CK85
Bridge St.
Heron Wk., Nthwd. 93 BS49
Heron Wk., Wok. 211 BC114
Blackmore Cres.
Heron Way, Grays 169 FV78
Heron Way, Hat. 45 CU19
Heron Way, Upmin. 129 FS60
Herondale, S.Croy. 221 DX109
Herondale Ave. SW18 180 DD88
Heronfield, Egh. 172 AV93
Heronfield, Pot.B. 64 DC30
Herongate Rd. E12 124 EJ61
Herongate Rd., Swan. 187 FE93
Herongate Rd. (Cheshunt), Wal.Cr. 67 DY27
Heronry, The, Walt. 213 BU107
Herons, The E11 124 EF58
Herons Cft., Wey. 213 BR107
Heron's Pl., Islw. 157 CH83
Herons Ri., Barn. 80 DE42
Herons Way, St.Alb. 43 CG24
Herons Wd., Harl. 35 EP13
Herons Wd. Ct., Horl. 269 DH147
Tanyard Way
Heronsforde W13 137 CJ72
Heronsgate, Edg. 96 CN50
Heronsgate Rd., Rick. 73 BB44
Heronslea, Wat. 76 BW36
Heronslea Dr., Stan. 96 CL50
Heronswood, Wal.Abb. 68 EE34
Roundhills
Heronswood Pl., Welw.G.C. 30 DA10
Heronswood Rd., Welw.G.C. 30 DA09
Heronway, Brwd. 109 GB46
Heronway, Wdf.Grn. 102 EJ49
Herrick Rd. N5 122 DQ62
Herrick St. SW1 277 N9
Herrick St. SW1 161 DK77
Herries St. W10 139 CY68
Herringham Rd. SE7 164 EJ76
Herrings La., Cher. 194 BG100
Herrongate Clo., Enf. 82 DT40
Hersant Clo. NW10 139 CU67
Herschel Pk. Dr., Slou. 152 AT75
Herschel St., Slou. 152 AT75
Herschell Rd. SE23 183 DY87
Hersham Bypass, Walt. 213 BV106
Hersham Clo. SW15 179 CU87
Hersham Gdns., Walt. 214 BW105
Hersham Rd., Walt. 195 BU102
Hersham Trd. Est., Walt. 196 BY103
Hertford Ave. SW14 178 CR85
Hertford Clo., Barn. 80 DD41
Hertford Pl. W1 273 K5
Hertford Rd. N1 142 DS67
Hertford Rd. N2 120 DE55
Hertford Rd. N9 100 DU47
Hertford Rd., Bark. 145 EP66
Hertford Rd., Barn. 80 DC41
Hertford Rd., Enf. 82 DW40
Hertford Rd., Hat. 45 CX15
Hertford Rd., Hert. 30 DF08
Hertford Rd. (Hertford Heath), Hert. 32 DW13
Hertford Rd. (Marden Hill), Hert. 30 DG06
Hertford Rd., Hodd. 49 DY15
Hertford Rd., Ilf. 125 ES58
Hertford Rd., Wal.Cr. 83 DY35
Hertford Rd., Ware 32 DW07
Hertford Rd. (Great Amwell), Ware 33 DZ11
Hertford Rd., Welw. 30 DA05
Hertford Rd. (Tewin), Welw. 30 DE05
Hertford Sq., Mitch. 201 DL98
Hertford Way
Hertford St. W1 276 G3
Hertford St. W1 140 DG74
Hertford Wk., Belv. 166 FA78
Hoddesdon Rd.
Hertford Way, Mitch. 201 DL98
Hertingfordbury Rd., Hert. 31 DM10
Hertslet Rd. N7 121 DM62
Hertsmere Rd. E14 143 EA73
Hervey Clo. N3 98 DA53
Hervey Pk. Rd. E17 123 DY56
Hervey Rd. SE3 164 EH81
Hervines Ct., Amer. 55 AQ37
Hervines Rd., Amer. 55 AP37
Hesa Rd., Hayes 135 BU72
Hesiers Hill, Warl. 238 EE117
Hesiers Rd., Warl. 238 EE117
Hesketh Ave., Dart. 188 FP88
Hesketh Pl. W11 139 CY73
Hesketh Rd. E7 124 EG62
Heslop Rd. SW12 180 DF88
Hesper Ms. SW5 160 DB78
Hesperus Cres. E14 163 EB77
Hessel Rd. W13 157 CG75
Hessel St. E1 142 DV72
Hesselyn Dr., Rain. 147 FH66
Hessle Gro., Epsom 217 CT111
Hester Rd. N18 100 DU50
Hester Rd. SW11 160 DE80
Hester Ter., Rich. 158 CN83
Chilton Rd.
Hestercombe Ave. SW6 159 CY82
Heston Ave., Houns. 156 BY79
Heston Gra. La., Houns. 156 BZ79
Heston Ind. Cen., Houns. 156 BW79
Heston Ind. Mall, Houns. 156 BZ80
Heston Rd., Houns. 156 CA79
Heston Rd., Red. 266 DF138
Heston St. SE14 163 EA81
Heston Wk., Red. 266 DF138
Heswell Grn., Wat. 93 BU48
Fairhaven Cres.
Hetchleys, Hem.H. 40 BG17
Hetherington Clo., Slou. 131 AM69
Hetherington Rd. SW4 161 DL84
Hetherington Rd., Shep. 195 BQ96
Hetherington Way, Uxb. 114 BL63
Hethersett Clo., Reig. 250 DC131
Gatton Rd.
Hetley Gdns. SE19 182 DT94
Fox Hill
Hetley Rd. W12 139 CV74
Heton Gdns. NW4 119 CU56
Heusden Way, Ger.Cr. 113 AZ60
Hevelius Clo. SE10 164 EF78
Hever Ct. Rd., Grav. 191 GJ93
Hever Cft. SE9 185 EN91
Hever Gdns., Brom. 205 EN96
Heverham Rd. SE18 165 ES77
Hevers Ave., Horl. 268 DF147
Heversham Rd., Bexh. 166 FA82
Hewens Rd., Hayes 135 BQ70
Hewens Rd., Uxb. 135 BQ70
Hewer St. W10 139 CX71
Hewers Way, Tad. 233 CV120
Hewett Clo., Stan. 95 CH49
Hewett Pl., Swan. 207 FD98
Hewett Rd., Dag. 126 EW64
Hewett St. EC2 275 N5
Hewins Clo., Wal.Abb. 68 EE32
Galleyhill Rd.
Hewish Rd. N18 100 DS49
Hewison St. E3 143 DZ68
Hewitt Ave. N22 99 DP54
Hewitt Clo., Croy. 203 EB104
Oak Ave.
Hewitt Rd. N8 121 DN57
Hewitts Rd., Orp. 224 EZ108
Hewlett Rd. E3 143 DY68
Hexagon, The N6 120 DF60
Hexal Rd. SE6 184 EE90
Hexham Gdns., Islw. 157 CG80
Hexham Rd. SE27 182 DQ89
Hexham Rd., Barn. 80 DB42
Hexham Rd., Mord. 200 DB102
Hextalls La., Red. 252 DR128
Heybourne Rd. N17 100 DV52
Heybridge Ave. SW16 181 DL94
Heybridge Dr., Ilf. 103 ER54
Heybridge Way E10 123 DY59
Heydons Clo., St.Alb. 43 CD18
Heyford Ave. SW8 161 DL80
Heyford Ave. SW20 199 CZ97
Heyford Rd., Mitch. 200 DE96
Heyford Rd., Rad. 77 CF37
Heyford Way, Hat. 45 CW16
St. Albans Rd. W.
Heygate St. SE17 279 H9
Heygate St. SE17 162 DQ77
Heylyn Sq. E3 143 DZ69
Malmesbury Rd.

Heymede, Lthd. 231 CJ123
Heynes Rd., Dag. 126 EW63
Heysham Dr., Wat. 94 BW50
Heysham La. NW3 120 DB62
Heysham Rd. N15 122 DR58
Heythorp St. SW18 179 CZ88
Heythorpe Clo., Wok. 226 AT117
Kenton Way
Heythrop Dr., Uxb. 114 BM63
Woodstock Dr.
Heywood Ave. NW9 96 CS53
Heyworth Rd. E5 122 DV63
Heyworth Rd. E15 124 EF63
Hibbert Ave., Wat. 76 BX38
Hibbert Lo., Ger.Cr. 90 AX54
Gold Hill E.
Hibbert Rd. E17 123 DZ59
Hibbert Rd., Har. 95 CF54
Hibbert St. SW11 160 DC83
Hibberts All., Wind. 151 AR81
Peascod St.
Hibberts Way, Ger.Cr. 112 AY56
North Pk.
Hibbs Clo., Swan. 207 FD96
Hibernia Dr., Grav. 191 GM90
Hibernia Gdns., Houns. 156 CA84
Hibernia Rd., Houns. 156 CA84
Hichisson Rd. SE15 182 DW85
Hickin Clo. SE7 164 EK77
Hickin St. E14 163 EC76
Plevna St.
Hickling Rd., Ilf. 125 EP64
Hickman Ave. E4 101 EC51
Hickman Clo. E16 144 EK71
Hickman Clo., Brox. 49 DY21
Baas Hill
Hickman Rd., Rom. 126 EW59
Hickmans Clo., Gdse. 252 DW132
Hickmore Wk. SW4 161 DJ83
Hickory Clo. N9 100 DU45
Hicks Ave., Grnf. 137 CD68
Hicks Clo. SW11 160 DE83
Hicks St. SE8 163 DY78
Hidalgo Ct., Hem.H. 40 BM18
Hidcote Clo., Wok. 227 BB116
Lavender Rd.
Hidcote Gdns. SW20 199 CV97
Hide E6 145 EN72
Downings
Hide Pl. SW1 277 M9
Hide Pl. SW1 161 DK77
Hide Rd., Har. 116 CC56
Hideaway, The, Abb.L. 59 BT31
College Rd.
Hides, The, Harl. 35 ER14
Hides St. N7 141 DM65
Sheringham Rd.
Higgins Wk., Hmptn. 176 BY93
Abbott Clo.
High, The, Harl. 51 ER15
Cross St.
High Acres, Abb.L. 59 BR32
High Barn La., Dor. 246 BX134
High Barn Rd., Lthd. 246 BX129
High Beech, S.Croy. 220 DS108
High Beech Rd., Loug. 84 EL42
High Beeches, Bans. 217 CW114
High Beeches, Ger.Cr. 112 AX60
High Beeches, Orp. 224 EU107
High Beeches, Sid. 186 EY92
High Beeches Clo., Pur. 219 DK110
Great Woodcote Pk.
High Bois La., Amer. 55 AR35
Bois La.
High Broom Cres., W.Wick. 203 EB101
High Canons, Borwd. 78 CQ37
High Cedar Dr. SW20 179 CV94
High Clandon, Guil. 244 BL133
High Clo., Rick. 74 BJ43
High Coombe Pl., Kings.T. 178 CR94
High Coppice, Amer. 55 AQ39
Station Rd.
High Cross, Wat. 77 CD37
High Cross Cen. N15 122 DU56
High Cross Rd. N17 122 DU55
High Dells, Hat. 45 CT19
High Down La., Sutt. 218 DB111
High Dr., Cat. 237 EA122
High Dr., Lthd. 215 CD114
High Dr., N.Mal. 198 CQ95
High Elms, Chig. 103 ES49
High Elms, Upmin. 129 FS60
High Elms, Wdf.Grn. 102 EG50
High Elms Clo., Nthwd. 93 BR51
High Elms La., Wat. 59 BV31
High Elms Rd., Orp. 223 EN111
High Fld., Bans. 234 DE117
High Firs, Rad. 77 CF35
High Firs, Swan. 207 FE98
High Foleys, Esher 215 CH108
High Gables, Loug. 84 EK43
High Garth, Esher 214 CC107
High Gro. SE18 165 ER80
High Gro., Brom. 204 EJ95
High Gro., St.Alb. 43 CD18
High Gro., Welw.G.C. 29 CW08
High Hill Est. E5 122 DV60
Mount Pleasant La.
High Hill Rd., Warl. 237 EC115
High Holborn WC1 273 P8
High Holborn WC1 141 DL72
High Ho. La., Til. 171 GK77
High Lands, Hat. 45 CW15
High La. W7 137 CD71
High La., Bishop's Stortford 37 FE09
High La., Cat. 237 DZ119
High La., Warl. 237 DZ118
High Lawns, Har. 117 CE62
High Level Dr. SE26 182 DU91
High Mead, Chig. 103 EQ47
High Mead, Har. 117 CE57
High Mead, W.Wick. 203 ED103
High Meadow Clo., Dor. 263 CH137
High Meadow Clo., Pnr. 115 BV56
Daymer Gdns.
High Meadow Cres. NW9 118 CR57
High Meadow Pl., Cher. 193 BF100
Gogmore Fm. Clo.
High Meadows, Chig. 103 ER50
High Meads Rd. E16 144 EK72
Fulmer Rd.
High Mt. NW4 119 CU58
High Oak Rd., Ware 33 DX05
High Oaks, Enf. 81 DM38
High Oaks, St.Alb. 42 CC15
High Oaks Rd., Welw.G.C. 29 CV08
High Pk. Ave., Lthd. 245 BT126
High Pk. Ave., Rich. 158 CN81
High Pk. Rd., Rich. 158 CN81
High Pastures, Bishop's Stortford 37 FD07
High Path SW19 200 DB95
High Path Rd., Guil. 243 BC134
High Pewley, Guil. 258 AY136
High Pine Clo., Wey. 213 BQ106
High Pines, Warl. 236 DW119
High Pt. N6 120 DG59
High Pt. SE9 185 EP90
High Ridge (Cuffley), Pot.B. 65 DL27
High Ridge Clo., Hem.H. 58 BK25
High Ridge Rd., Hem.H. 58 BK25
High Rd. E18 102 EG53
High Rd. N2 98 DD53
High Rd. N11 99 DH50
High Rd. N12 98 DC49
High Rd. N15 122 DT58
High Rd. N17 122 DT55
High Rd. N20 98 DC47
High Rd. N22 99 DM51
High Rd. (Willesden) NW10 139 CT65
High Rd., Brox. 49 DZ23
High Rd., Buck.H. 102 EH48
High Rd., Chig. 103 EN50
High Rd., Couls. 234 DE124
High Rd. (Wilmington), Dart. 188 FJ90
High Rd., Epp. 69 ER32
High Rd. (North Weald Bassett), Epp. 71 FB27
High Rd. (Thornwood), Epp. 70 EV28
High Rd. (Harrow Weald), Har. 95 CE52
High Rd., Hat. 46 DD17
High Rd., Ilf. 125 EQ61
High Rd., Loug. 84 EJ44
High Rd., Pnr. 115 BV57
High Rd., Reig. 250 DC127
High Rd., Rom. 126 EU60
High Rd., Uxb. 134 BJ71
High Rd. (Ickenham), Uxb. 115 BP62
High Rd. (Bushey), Wat. 95 CD46
High Rd. (Leavesden), Wat. 75 BT35
High Rd., Wem. 118 CL64
High Rd., W.Byf. 212 BK112
High Rd., Wdf.Grn. 102 EF51
High Rd. Leyton E10 123 EB58
High Rd. Leyton E15 123 EC63
High Rd. Leytonstone E11 124 EE63
High Rd. Leytonstone E15 124 EE63
High Rd. Turnford, Brox. 67 DY25
High Rd. Wormley (Turnford), Brox. 49 DY24
High Silver, Loug. 84 EK42
High St. E11 124 EG57
High St. E13 144 EG68
High St. E15 143 EC68
High St. E17 123 DY57
High St. N8 121 DL56
High St. N14 99 DK47
High St. NW7 97 CV50
High St. (Harlesden) NW10 139 CT68
High St. SE20 182 DW94
High St. (South Norwood) SE25 202 DT98
High St. SW6 159 CY83
High St. W3 138 CP74
High St. W5 137 CK73
High St., Abb.L. 59 BS31
High St. (Bedmond), Abb.L. 59 BT27
High St., Add. 212 BH105
High St., Amer. 55 AM38
High St., Bans. 234 DA115
High St., Barn. 79 CY41
High St., Beck. 203 EA96
High St., Berk. 38 AW19
High St. (Elstree), Borwd. 77 CK44
High St., Brent. 158 CL79
High St., Brwd. 108 FW47
High St., Brom. 204 EG96
High St., Cars. 218 DF105
High St., Cat. 236 DS123
High St., Ch.St.G. 90 AW48
High St., Chesh. 54 AP31
High St., Chis. 185 EP93
High St., Cob. 213 BV114
High St., Croy. 202 DQ104
High St., Dart. 188 FL87
High St. (Bean), Dart. 189 FV90
High St. (Eynsford), Dart. 208 FL103
High St. (Farningham), Dart. 208 FL100
High St., Dor. 263 CH136
High St., Edg. 96 CN51
High St., Egh. 173 BA92
High St. (Ponders End), Enf. 82 DW42
High St., Epp. 69 ET31
High St., Epsom 216 CR113
High St. (Ewell), Epsom 217 CT109
High St., Esher 214 CB105
High St. (Claygate), Esher 215 CF107
High St., Felt. 175 BT90
High St., Ger.Cr. 90 AY53
High St., Gdse. 252 DV131
High St., Grav. 191 GH86
High St. (Northfleet), Grav. 190 GB86
High St., Grays 170 GA79
High St., Green. 169 FU84
High St., Guil. 258 AX135
High St., Hmptn. 196 CB95
High St., Harl. 36 EW11
High St. (Roydon), Harl. 34 EH14
High St., Har. 95 CE54
High St. (Wealdstone), Har. 117 CE60
High St., Hayes 155 BR79
High St., Hem.H. 40 BK19
High St. (Bovingdon), Hem.H. 57 BA27
High St., Hodd. 49 EA17
High St., Horl. 269 DH148
High St., Horn. 128 FK60
High St., Houns. 156 CB83
High St. (Cranford), Houns. 155 BU80
High St., Ilf. 125 EQ55
High St., Iver 133 BE72
High St., Kings L. 58 BN29
High St., Kings.T. 197 CK97
High St. (Hampton Wick), Kings.T. 197 CJ95
High St., Lthd. 231 CH122
High St. (Bookham), Lthd. 246 CB125
High St. (Oxshott), Lthd. 215 CD113
High St. (Bray), Maid. 150 AC75
High St. (Taplow), Maid. 130 AE70
High St., N.Mal. 198 CS98
High St., Nthwd. 93 BT53
High St., Orp. 206 EU103
High St. (Downe), Orp. 223 EN111
High St. (Farnborough),Orp. 223 EP106
High St. (Green St. Grn.), Orp. 223 ET108
High St. (St. Mary Cray), Orp. 206 EW100
High St., Oxt. 253 ED130
High St. (Limpsfield), Oxt. 254 EG128
High St., Pnr. 116 BY55
High St., Pot.B. 64 DC33
High St., Purf. 168 FN78
London Rd. Purfleet
High St., Pur. 219 DN111
High St., Red. 250 DF134
High St. (Bletchingley), Red. 252 DQ133
High St. (Merstham), Red. 251 DH128
High St. (Nutfield), Red. 251 DM133
High St., Reig. 250 DA134
High St., Rick. 92 BK46
High St., Rom. 127 FE57
High St., Ruis. 115 BS59
High St. (Colney Heath), St.Alb. 44 CP22
High St. (London Colney), St.Alb. 61 CJ25
High St., Sev. 257 FJ126
High St. (Chipstead), Sev. 256 FC122
High St. (Otford), Sev. 241 FF116
High St. (Seal), Sev. 257 FL121
High St. (Shoreham), Sev. 225 FF110
High St., Shep. 195 BP101
High St., Slou. 152 AT75
High St. (Burnham), Slou. 130 AJ69
High St. (Chalvey), Slou. 151 AQ76
High St. (Colnbrook), Slou. 153 BC80
High St. (Datchet), Slou. 152 AV81
High St. (Langley), Slou. 153 AZ78
High St., S.Ock. 148 FQ74
High St., Sthl. 136 BZ74
High St., Stai. 173 BF91
High St. (Stanwell), Stai. 174 BK86
High St. (Wraysbury), Stai. 172 AY86
High St., Sutt. 218 DB105
High St. (Cheam), Sutt. 217 CY107
High St., Swan. 207 FF97
High St., Swans. 190 FZ85
High St., Tad. 233 CW123
High St., Tedd. 177 CF92
High St., T.Ditt. 197 CG101
High St., Th.Hth. 202 DQ98
High St. (Whitton), Twick. 176 CC87
High St., Uxb. 134 BJ66
High St. (Cowley), Uxb. 134 BJ69
High St. (Harefield), Uxb. 92 BJ54
High St., Wal.Cr. 67 DX33
High St. (Cheshunt), Wal.Cr. 67 DX29
High St., Walt. 195 BU102
High St., Ware 33 DX06
High St. (Hunsdon), Ware 34 EK06
High St., Wat. 75 BV41
High St. (Bushey), Wat. 76 BZ44
High St., Wem. 118 CM63
High St., West Dr. 154 BK79
High St. (Yiewsley), West Dr. 134 BK73
High St., W.Mol. 196 CA98
High St., W.Wick. 203 EB102
High St., West. 255 EQ127
High St. (Brasted), West. 240 EV124
High St., Wey. 212 BN105
High St., Wind. 151 AR81
High St. (Eton), Wind. 151 AR79
High St., Wok. 227 AZ117
High St. (Chobham), Wok. 210 AS111
High St. (Horsell), Wok. 226 AV115
High St. (Old Woking), Wok. 227 BA121
High St. (Ripley), Wok. 228 BH122
High St. Colliers Wd. SW19 180 DD94
High St. Grn., Hem.H. 40 BN18
High St. Ms. SW19 179 CY92
High St. N. E6 144 EL66
High St. N. E12 124 EL64
High St. S. E6 145 EM68
High St. Wimbledon SW19 179 CX92
High Timber St. EC4 275 H10
High Timber St. EC4 142 DQ73
High Tor Clo., Brom. 184 EH94
Babbacombe Rd.
High Tree Clo., Add. 211 BF106
High Tree Clo., Saw. 36 EX06
High Tree Ct. W7 137 CE73
High Trees SW2 181 DN88
High Trees, Barn. 80 DE43
High Trees, Croy. 203 DY102
High Trees Clo., Cat. 236 DT123
High Trees Ct., Brwd. 108 FW49
Warley Mt.
High Trees Rd., Reig. 266 DC135
High Vw., Guil. 261 BQ139
High Vw., Hat. 45 CT20
High Vw., Pnr. 116 BW55
High Vw., Rick. 74 BG42
High Vw., Sutt. 217 CZ111
High Vw., Wat. 75 BT44
High Vw. Ave., Grays 170 GC78
High Vw. Clo. SE19 202 DT96
High Vw. Clo., Loug. 84 EJ43
High Vw. Rd. E18 124 EF55
High Vw. Rd., Guil. 258 AS137
High Vw. Rd., Sid. 186 EV91
High Wickfield, Welw.G.C. 30 DC10
Amwell Common
High Worple, Har. 116 BY59
High Wych La., Saw. 36 EU05
High Wych Rd., Saw. 35 ES09
Higham Hill Rd. E17 101 DY53
Higham Mead, Chesh. 54 AQ30
Higham Pl. E17 123 DY55
Higham Rd. N17 122 DR55
Higham Rd., Chesh. 54 AP30
Higham Rd., Wdf.Grn. 102 EG51
Higham Sta. Ave. E4 101 EA51
Higham St. E17 123 DY55
Higham Vw., Epp. 71 FB26
Highams Lo. Business Cen. E17 123 DX55
Highams Pk. Ind. Est. E4 101 EC51
Highbank Way N8 121 DN58
Ridge Rd.
Highbanks Clo., Well. 166 EV80
Highbanks Rd., Pnr. 94 CA51
Highbarns Rd., Hem.H. 58 BN25
Highbarrow Rd., Croy. 202 DU101
Highbridge SE10 163 ED78
Eastney St.
Highbridge Rd., Bark. 145 EP67
Highbridge St., Wal.Abb. 67 EB33
Highbrook Rd. SE3 164 EK83
Highbury Ave., Hodd. 49 EA15
Highbury Ave., Th.Hth. 201 DN96
Highbury Clo., N.Mal. 198 CQ98
Highbury Clo., W.Wick. 203 EB103
Highbury Cor. N5 141 DP65
Highbury Cres. N5 121 DP64
Highbury Est. N5 122 DQ64
Highbury Gdns., Ilf. 125 ES61
Highbury Gra. N5 122 DQ63
Highbury Gro. N5 141 DP65
Highbury Hill N5 121 DN62
Highbury Ms. N7 141 DN65
Holloway Rd.
Highbury New Pk. N5 122 DQ64
Highbury Pk. N5 121 DP63
Highbury Pk. Ms. N5 122 DQ63
Highbury Gra.
Highbury Pl. N5 141 DP65
Highbury Quad. N5 122 DQ62
Highbury Rd. SW19 179 CY92
Highbury Sta. Rd. N1 141 DN65
Highbury Ter. N5 121 DP64
Highbury Ter. Ms. N5 121 DP64
Highclere, Guil. 243 BA132
Highclere Clo., Ken. 236 DQ115
Highclere Ct., St.Alb. 43 CE19
Avenue Rd.
Highclere Dr., Hem.H. 40 BN24
Highclere Rd., N.Mal. 198 CR97
Highclere St. SE26 183 DY91
Highcliffe Dr. SW15 179 CT86
Highcliffe Gdns., Ilf. 124 EL57
Highcombe SE7 164 EH79
Highcombe Clo. SE9 184 EK88
Highcotts La., Guil. 243 BF126
Highcotts La., Wok. 243 BF125
Highcroft NW9 118 CS57
Highcroft Ave., Wem. 138 CN67
Highcroft Ct., Lthd. 230 CA123
Highcroft Gdns. NW11 119 CZ58
Highcroft Rd. N19 121 DL59
Highcroft Rd., Hem.H. 58 BG25
Highcross Rd., Grav. 189 FX92
Highcross Way SW15 179 CU88
Highdaun Dr. SW16 201 DM98
Highdown, Wor.Pk. 198 CS103
Highdown Rd. SW15 179 CV86
Higher Dr., Bans. 217 CX112
Higher Dr., Lthd. 245 BS127
Higher Dr., Pur. 219 DN113
Higher Grn., Epsom 217 CU113
Highfield, Ch.St.G. 90 AX47
Highfield, Felt. 175 BU88
Highfield, Guil. 258 AY142
Highfield, Harl. 52 EU16
Highfield, Kings L. 58 BL28
Highfield Ave. NW9 118 CQ57
Highfield Ave. NW11 119 CX59
Highfield Ave., Erith 167 FB79
Highfield Ave., Grnf. 117 CE64
Highfield Ave., Orp. 223 ET106
Highfield Ave., Pnr. 116 BZ57
Highfield Ave., Wem. 118 CL62
Highfield Clo. N22 99 DN53
Highfield Clo. NW9 118 CQ57
Highfield Clo., Amer. 55 AR37
Highfield Clo., Egh. 172 AW93
Highfield Clo., Lthd. 215 CD111
Highfield Clo., Nthwd. 93 BS53
Highfield Clo., Rom. 105 FC51
Highfield Clo., Surb. 197 CJ102
Highfield Clo., W.Byf. 212 BG113
Highfield Ct. N14 81 DJ44
Highfield Cres., Horn. 128 FM61
Highfield Cres., Nthwd. 93 BS53
Highfield Dr., Brom. 204 EE98
Highfield Dr., Brox. 49 DY21
Highfield Dr., Epsom 217 CT108
Highfield Dr., Uxb. 114 BL62
Highfield Dr., W.Wick. 203 EB103
Highfield Gdns. NW11 119 CY58
Highfield Gdns., Grays 170 GD75
Highfield Grn., Epp. 69 ES31
Highfield Hill SE19 182 DR94
Highfield La., Hem.H. 40 BM18
Highfield La., St.Alb. 43 CJ22
Highfield Link, Rom. 105 FD51
Highfield Pl., Epp. 69 ES31
Highfield Rd. N21 99 DP47
Highfield Rd. NW11 119 CY58
Highfield Rd. W3 138 CP71
Highfield Rd., Berk. 38 AX20
Highfield Rd., Bexh. 186 EZ85
Highfield Rd., Brom. 205 EM98
Highfield Rd., Cat. 236 DU122
Highfield Rd., Cher. 194 BG102
Highfield Rd., Chesh. 54 AP29
Highfield Rd., Chis. 205 ET97
Highfield Rd., Dart. 188 FK87
Highfield Rd., Felt. 175 BU88
Highfield Rd., Hert. 32 DR11
Highfield Rd., Horn. 128 FM61
Highfield Rd., Islw. 157 CF81
Highfield Rd., Nthwd. 93 BS53
Highfield Rd., Pur. 219 DM110
Highfield Rd., Rom. 105 FC52
Highfield Rd., Sun. 195 BT98
Highfield Rd., Surb. 198 CQ101
Highfield Rd., Sutt. 218 DE106
Highfield Rd. (Cheshunt), Wal.Cr. 66 DS26
Highfield Rd., Walt. 195 BU102
Highfield Rd. (Bushey), Wat. 76 BY43
Highfield Rd., W.Byf. 212 BG113
Highfield Rd., West. 238 EJ117
Highfield Rd., Wind. 151 AM83
Highfield Rd., Wdf.Grn. 102 EL52
Highfield Rd. S., Dart. 188 FK87
Highfield Twrs., Rom. 105 FD50
Highfield Way, Horn. 128 FM61
Highfield Way, Pot.B. 64 DB32
Highfield Way, Rick. 74 BG44
Highfields, Ash. 231 CK119
Highfields, Lthd. 231 CD124
Highfields (East Horsley), Lthd. 245 BS128
Highfields (Cuffley), Pot.B. 65 DL28
Highfields, Rad. 77 CF35
Highfields Gro. N6 120 DF60
Highgate Ave. N6 121 DH59
Highgate Clo. N6 120 DG59
Highgate Gro., Saw. 36 EX05
Highgate High St. N6 120 DG60
Highgate Hill N6 121 DH60
Highgate Hill N19 121 DH60
Highgate Rd. NW5 121 DH63
Highgate Wk. SE23 182 DW89
Highgate W. Hill N6 120 DG60
Highgrove, Brwd. 108 FV44
Philip Clo.
Highgrove Clo., Chis. 204 EL95
Highgrove Ct., Beck. 183 EA94
Park Rd.
Highgrove Ms., Cars. 200 DF104
William St.
Highgrove Ms., Grays 170 GC78
Whitehall La.
Highgrove Rd., Dag. 126 EW64
Highgrove Way, Ruis. 115 BU58
Highland Ave. W7 137 CE72
Highland Ave., Brwd. 108 FW46
Highland Ave., Dag. 127 FC62
Highland Ave., Loug. 84 EL44
Highland Cotts., Wall. 219 DH105
Highland Ct. E18 102 EH53
Highland Cft., Beck. 183 EB92
Highland Dr., Hem.H. 41 BP20
Highland Dr. (Bushey), Wat. 94 CC45
Highland Pk., Felt. 175 BT91
Highland Rd. SE19 182 DS93
Highland Rd., Amer. 55 AR39
Highland Rd., Bexh. 186 FA85
Highland Rd., Brom. 204 EF95
Highland Rd., Nthwd. 93 BT54
Highland Rd., Pur. 219 DN114
Highland Rd., Sev. 225 FB110
Highland Rd., Wal.Abb. 50 EE22
Highlands, Ash. 231 CJ119
West Fm. Clo.
Highlands, Wat. 94 BW46
Highlands, The, Edg. 96 CP54
Highlands, The, Lthd. 245 BS125
Highlands, The, Pot.B. 64 DC30
Highlands, The, Rick. 92 BH45
Highlands Ave. W3 138 CQ73
Highlands Ave., Lthd. 231 CJ122
Highlands Clo. N4 121 DL59
Mount Vw. Rd.
Highlands Clo., Ger.Cr. 90 AY52
Highlands Clo., Houns. 156 CB81
Highlands Clo., Lthd. 231 CH122
Highlands End, Ger.Cr. 91 AZ52
Highlands Gdns., Ilf. 125 EM60
Highlands Heath SW15 179 CW87
Highlands Hill, Swan. 207 FG96
Highlands La., Ger.Cr. 91 AZ51
Highlands La., Wok. 226 AY122
Highlands Pk., Lthd. 231 CK123
Highlands Pk., Sev. 257 FL121
Highlands Rd., Barn. 80 DA43
Highlands Rd., Beac. 89 AQ50
Highlands Rd., Lthd. 231 CH122
Highlands Rd., Orp. 206 EV101
Highlands Rd., Reig. 250 DD133
Highlea Clo. NW9 96 CS53
Highlever Rd. W10 139 CW71
Highmead SE18 165 ET80
Highmead Cres., Wem. 138 CM66
Highmoor, Amer. 55 AR39
Highmore Rd. SE3 164 EE80
Highover Pk., Amer. 55 AQ40
Highpoint, Wey. 212 BN106
Highridge Clo., Epsom 232 CS115
Highridge La., Bet. 264 CP140
Highshore Rd. SE15 162 DT82
Highstead Cres., Erith 167 FE80
Highstone Ave. E11 124 EG58
Highview, Cat. 236 DS124
Harestone La.
Highview Ave., Edg. 96 CQ49
Highview Ave., Wall. 219 DM106
Highview Clo., Pot.B. 64 DC33
Highview Gdns.
Highview Cres., Brwd. 109 GC44
Highview Gdns. N3 119 CY56
Highview Gdns. N11 99 DJ50
Highview Gdns., Edg. 96 CQ50
Highview Gdns., Pot.B. 64 DC33
Highview Gdns., St.Alb. 43 CJ15
Highview Gdns., Upmin. 128 FP61
Highview Ho., Rom. 126 EY56
Highview Rd. SE19 182 DR93
Highview Rd. W13 137 CG71
Highway, The E1 142 DU73
Highway, The E14 143 DX73
Highway, The, Orp. 224 EV106
Highway, The, Stan. 95 CF53
Highway, The, Sutt. 218 DC109
Highwold, Couls. 234 DG118
Highwood, Brom. 203 ED97
Highwood Ave. N12 98 DC49
Highwood Ave. (Bushey), Wat. 76 BZ39
Highwood Clo., Brwd. 108 FV45
Highwood Clo., Ken. 236 DQ117
Highwood Clo., Orp. 205 EQ103
Highwood Dr., Orp. 205 EQ103
Highwood Gdns., Ilf. 125 EM57
Highwood Gro. NW7 96 CR50
Highwood Hall La., Hem.H. 59 BQ25
Highwood Hill NW7 97 CT47
Highwood La., Loug. 85 EN43
Highwood Rd. N19 121 DL62

Highwood Rd., Hodd. 33 DZ14
Highwoods, Cat. 252 DS125
Highwoods, Lthd. 231 CJ121
Highworth Rd. N11 99 DK51
Hilary Ave., Mitch. 200 DG97
Hilary Clo. SW6 160 DB80
Hilary Clo., Erith 167 FB81
Hilary Clo., Horn. 128 FK64
Hilary Rd. W12 139 CT72
Hilary Rd., Slou. 152 AY75
Hilbert Rd., Sutt. 199 CX104
Hilborough Way, Orp. 223 ER106
Hilbury Clo., Amer. 55 AQ35
Hilda May Ave., Swan. 207 FD97
Hilda Rd. E6 144 EK66
Hilda Rd. E16 144 EE70
Hilda Ter. SW9 161 DN82
Hilda Vale Clo., Orp. 223 EP105
Hilda Vale Rd., Orp. 223 EN105
Hilden Dr., Erith 167 FH80
Hildenborough Gdns., Brom. 184 EE93
Hildenlea Pl., Brom. 204 EE96
Hildenley Clo., Red. 251 DK128
Malmstone Ave.
Hildens, The, Dor. 262 CB138
Hilders, The, Ash. 232 CP117
Hildreth St. SW12 181 DH88
Hildyard Rd. SW6 160 DA79
Hiley Rd. NW10 139 CW69
Hilfield La., Wat. 76 CB39
Hilfield La. S. (Bushey), Wat. 77 CF44
Hilgay, Guil. 243 AZ134
Hilgay Clo., Guil. 243 AZ134
Hilgrove Rd. NW6 140 DC66
Hiliary Gdns., Stan. 95 CJ54
Hiljon Cres., Ger.Cr. 90 AY53
Hill, The, Cat. 236 DT124
Hill, The, Grav. 190 GC86
Hill, The, Harl. 36 EW11
Hill Ave., Amer. 55 AQ38
Hill Barn, S.Croy. 220 DS111
Hill Brow, Brom. 204 EK95
Hill Brow, Dart. 187 FF86
Hill Brow Clo., Bex. 187 FD91
Hill Clo. NW2 119 CV62
Hill Clo. NW11 120 DA58
Hill Clo., Barn. 79 CW43
Hill Clo., Chis. 185 EP92
Hill Clo., Grav. 190 GE94
Hill Clo., Har. 117 CE62
Hill Clo., H.Wyc. 110 AF56
Hill Clo., Pur. 220 DQ112
Hill Clo., Stan. 95 CH49
Hill Clo., Wok. 226 AX115
Hill Common, Hem.H. 40 BN24
Hill Ct., Gdmg. 258 AS144
Hill Ct., Nthlt. 116 CA64
Hill Cres. N20 98 DB47
Hill Cres., Bex. 187 FC88
Hill Cres., Har. 117 CG57
Hill Cres., Horn. 128 FJ58
Hill Cres., Surb. 198 CM99
Hill Cres., Wor.Pk. 199 CW103
Hill Crest, Pot.B. 64 DC34
Hill Crest, Sev. 256 FG122
Hill Crest, Sid. 186 EU87
Hill Crest Gdns. N3 119 CY56
Hill Dr. NW9 118 CQ60
Hill Dr. SW16 201 DM97
Hill End, Orp. 205 ET103
The App.
Hill End La., St.Alb. 43 CJ23
Hill End Rd., Uxb. 92 BJ52
Hill Fm. App., H.Wyc. 110 AE55
Hill Fm. Ave., Wat. 59 BU33
Hill Fm. Clo., Wat. 59 BU33
Hill Fm. La., Ch.St.G. 90 AT46
Hill Fm. Rd. W10 139 CW71
Hill Fm. Rd., Chesh. 54 AR34
Hill Fm. Rd., Ger.Cr. 90 AY52
Hill Fm. Rd., Maid. 130 AD68
Hill Gro., Rom. 127 FE55
Hill Ho. Ave., Stan. 95 CF52
Hill Ho. Clo. N21 99 DN45
Hill Ho. Clo., Ger.Cr. 90 AY52
Rickmansworth La.
Hill Ho. Dr., Reig. 266 DB136
Hill Ho. Dr., Wey. 212 BN111
Hill Ho. Rd. SW16 181 DM92
Hill Ho. Rd., Dart. 188 FQ87
Hill La., Orp. 207 FB104
Hill La., Ruis. 115 BQ60
Hill La., Tad. 233 CY121
Hill Ley, Hat. 45 CT18
Hill Leys (Cuffley), Pot.B. 65 DL28
Hill Meadow, Amer. 55 AM43
Hill Path SW16 181 DM92
Valley Rd.
Hill Pl., Slou. 131 AP66
Hill Ri. N9 82 DV44
Hill Ri. NW11 120 DB56
Hill Ri. SE23 182 DV88
London Rd.
Hill Ri., Dart. 189 FR92
Hill Ri., Dor. 247 CG134
Hill Ri., Esher 197 CH103
Hill Ri., Ger.Cr. 90 AX54
Hill Ri., Grnf. 136 CC66
Hill Ri., Pot.B. 64 DC34
Hill Ri. (Cuffley), Pot.B. 65 DL28
Hill Ri., Rich. 177 CK85
Hill Ri., Rick. 92 BH45
Hill Ri., Ruis. 115 BQ60
Hill Ri., Slou. 153 BA79
Hill Ri., Upmin. 128 FN61
Hill Ri., Walt. 195 BT101
Hill Ri. Cres., Ger.Cr. 90 AX54
Hill Rd. N10 98 DF53
Hill Rd. NW8 140 DC68
Hill Rd., Brwd. 108 FU48
Hill Rd., Cars. 218 DE107
Hill Rd., Dart. 188 FL89
Hill Rd., Epp. 85 ES38
Hill Rd., Har. 117 CG57
Hill Rd., Hem.H. 39 BE21
Hill Rd., Lthd. 230 CB122
Hill Rd., Mitch. 201 DH95
Hill Rd., Nthwd. 93 BR51
Hill Rd., Pnr. 116 BY58
Hill Rd., Pur. 219 DM112
Hill Rd., Sutt. 218 DB106
Hill Rd., Wem. 117 CH62
Hill St. W1 276 G2
Hill St. W1 140 DG73
Hill St., Rich. 177 CK85
Hill St., St.Alb. 42 CC20
Hill Top NW11 120 DB56
Hill Top, Loug. 85 EN40
Hill Top, Mord. 200 DB100
Hill Top Clo., Loug. 85 EN41
Hill Top Pl., Loug. 85 EN41
Hill Top Clo.
Hill Top Vw., Wdf.Grn. 103 EM51
Hill Vw., Berk. 38 AU17
Hill Vw. Clo., Tad. 233 CW121
Shelvers Way
Hill Vw. Cres., Guil. 242 AT132
Hill Vw. Cres., Orp. 205 ET102
Hill Vw. Dr., Well. 165 ES82
Hill Vw. Gdns. NW9 118 CR57
Hill Vw. Rd., Esher 215 CG108
Hill Vw. Rd., Orp. 205 ET102
Hill Vw. Rd., Stai. 172 AX86
Hill Vw. Rd., Twick. 177 CG86
Hill Vw. Rd., Wok. 227 AZ118
Hill Waye, Ger.Cr. 113 AZ58
Hillars Heath Rd., Couls. 235 DL115
Hillary Ave., Grav. 190 GE90
Hillary Cres., Walt. 196 BW102
Hillary Ri., Barn. 80 DA42
Hillary Rd., Hem.H. 40 BN20
Hillary Rd., Sthl. 156 CA76
Hillbeck Clo. SE15 162 DW80
Hillbeck Way, Grnf. 137 CD67
Hillborne Clo., Hayes 155 BU78
Hillborough Ave., Sev. 257 FK122
Hillborough Clo. SW19 180 DC94
Hillbrook Gdns., Wey. 212 BN108
Hillbrook Rd. SW17 180 DF90
Hillbrow, N.Mal. 199 CT97
Hillbrow Cotts., Gdse. 252 DW132
Hillbrow Ct., Gdse. 252 DW132
Hillbrow Rd., Brom. 184 EE94
Hillbrow Rd., Esher 214 CC105
Hillbury, Hat. 45 CT19
Hillbury Ave., Har. 117 CH57
Hillbury Clo., Warl. 236 DW118
Hillbury Gdns., Warl. 236 DW118
Hillbury Rd. SW17 181 DH90
Hillbury Rd., Warl. 236 DU117
Hillbury Rd., Whyt. 236 DU117
Hillcote Ave. SW16 181 DN94
Hillcourt Ave. N12 98 DB51
Hillcourt Est. N16 122 DR60
Hillcourt Rd. SE22 182 DV86
Hillcrest N6 120 DG59
Hillcrest N21 99 DN45
Hillcrest, Hat. 45 CU18
Hillcrest, St.Alb. 42 CB22
Hillcrest, Wey. 213 BP105
Hillcrest Ave. NW11 119 CY57
Hillcrest Ave., Cher. 211 BE105
Hillcrest Ave., Edg. 96 CP49
Hillcrest Ave., Grays 169 FU79
Hillcrest Ave., Pnr. 116 BX56
Hillcrest Clo. SE26 182 DU91
Hillcrest Clo., Beck. 203 DZ99
Hillcrest Clo., Epsom 233 CT115
Hillcrest Dr., Green. 189 FV85
Riverview Rd.
Hillcrest Gdns. NW2 119 CU62
Hillcrest Gdns., Esher 197 CF104
Hillcrest Par., Couls. 219 DH114
Hillcrest Rd. E17 101 ED54
Hillcrest Rd. E18 102 EF54
Hillcrest Rd. W3 138 CN74
Hillcrest Rd. W5 138 CL71
Hillcrest Rd., Brom. 184 EG91
Hillcrest Rd., Dart. 187 FF87
Hillcrest Rd., Guil. 242 AT133
Hillcrest Rd., Horn. 127 FG59
Hillcrest Rd., Loug. 84 EK44
Hillcrest Rd., Ong. 71 FE30
Hillcrest Rd., Orp. 206 EU103
Hillcrest Rd., Pur. 219 DM110
Hillcrest Rd., Rad. 62 CN33
Hillcrest Rd., West. 238 EK116
Hillcrest Rd., Whyt. 236 DT117
Hillcrest Vw., Beck. 203 DZ100
Hillcrest Way, Epp. 70 EU31
Hillcrest Waye, Ger.Cr. 113 AZ58
Hillcroft, Loug. 85 EN40
Hillcroft Ave., Pnr. 116 BZ58
Hillcroft Ave., Pur. 219 DJ113
Hillcroft Cres. W5 137 CK72
Hillcroft Cres., Ruis. 116 BX62
Hillcroft Cres., Wat. 93 BU46
Hillcroft Cres., Wem. 118 CM63
Hillcroft Rd. E6 145 EP71
Hillcroft Rd., Chesh. 54 AR29
Hillcroft Rd., H.Wyc. 88 AC46
Hillcroome Rd., Sutt. 218 DD107
Hillcross Ave., Mord. 199 CX100
Hilldale Rd., Sutt. 217 CZ105
Hilldeane Rd., Pur. 219 DN109
Hilldene Ave., Rom. 106 FJ51
Hilldene Clo., Rom. 106 FK50
Hilldown Rd. SW16 181 DL94
Hilldown Rd., Brom. 204 EE102
Hilldown Rd., Hem.H. 40 BG18
Hilldrop Cres. N7 121 DK64
Hilldrop Est. N7 121 DK64
Hilldrop La. N7 121 DK64
Hilldrop Rd. N7 121 DK64
Hilldrop Rd., Brom. 184 EG93
Hillend SE18 165 EP81
Hillersdon, Slou. 132 AV71
Hillersdon Ave. SW13 159 CU82
Hillersdon Ave., Edg. 96 CM50
Hillery Clo. SE17 279 L9
Hilley Fld. La., Lthd. 230 CC122
Hillfield, Hat. 45 CV15
Hillfield Ave. N8 121 DL57
Hillfield Ave. NW9 118 CS57
Hillfield Ave., Mord. 200 DE100
Hillfield Ave., Wem. 138 CL66
Hillfield Clo., Guil. 243 BC132
Hillfield Clo., Har. 116 CC56
Hillfield Clo., Red. 250 DG134
Hillfield Ct. NW3 120 DE64
Hillfield Ct., Hem.H. 40 BL20
Hillfield Pk. N10 121 DH55
Hillfield Pk. N21 99 DN47
Hillfield Pk. Ms. N10 121 DH56
Hillfield Rd. NW6 119 CZ64
Hillfield Rd., Ger.Cr. 90 AY52
Hillfield Rd., Hmptn. 176 BZ94
Hillfield Rd., Hem.H. 40 BK20
Hillfield Rd., Red. 250 DG134
Hillfield Rd., Sev. 241 FE120
Hillfield Sq., Ger.Cr. 90 AY52
Hillfoot Ave., Rom. 105 FC53
Hillfoot Rd., Rom. 105 FC53
Hillford Pl., Red. 266 DG140
Hillgate Pl. SW12 181 DH87
Hillgate Pl. W8 140 DA74
Hillgate St. W8 140 DA74
Hillgrove, Ger.Cr. 90 AY53
Hillgrove Business Pk., Wal.Abb. 49 EC22
Nazeing Rd.
Hillhouse, Wal.Abb. 68 EF33
Hillhurst Gdns., Cat. 236 DS120
Hilliard Rd., Nthwd. 93 BT53
Hilliards Ct. E1 142 DV74
Wapping High St.
Hilliards Rd., Uxb. 134 BK72
Hilliards St. E1 142 DW74
Wapping High St.
Hillier Clo., Barn. 80 DB44
Hillier Gdns., Croy. 219 DN106
Crowley Cres.
Hillier Pl., Chess. 215 CJ107
Mansfield Rd.
Hillier Rd. SW11 180 DF86
Hillier Rd., Guil. 243 BA134
Hilliers Ave., Uxb. 134 BN69
Harlington Rd.
Hilliers La., Croy. 201 DL104
Hillingdale, West. 238 EH118
Hillingdon Ave., Sev. 257 FJ121
Hillingdon Ave., Stai. 174 BL88
Hillingdon Hill, Uxb. 134 BL69
Hillingdon Ri., Sev. 257 FK122
Hillingdon Rd., Bexh. 167 FC82
Hillingdon Rd., Grav. 191 GG89
Hillingdon Rd., Uxb. 134 BJ67
Hillingdon Rd., Wat. 59 BU34
Hillingdon St. SE5 161 DP79
Hillingdon St. SE17 161 DP79
Hillington Gdns., Wdf.Grn. 102 EK54
Hillman Clo., Horn. 128 FK55
Hillman Clo., Uxb. 114 BL64
Hillman Dr. W10 139 CW70
Barlby Rd.
Hillman St. E8 142 DV65
Hillmarton Rd. N7 121 DL64
Hillmay Dr., Hem.H. 40 BJ21
Hillmead, Berk. 38 AU20
Hillmead Ct., Maid. 130 AF71
Hillmead Dr. SW9 161 DP84
Hillmont Rd., Esher 197 CE104
Hillmore Gro. SE26 183 DX92
Hillreach SE18 165 EM78
Hillrise Ave., Wat. 76 BX38
Hillrise Rd. N19 121 DL59
Hillrise Rd., Rom. 105 FC51
Hills Chase, Brwd. 108 FW49
Hills La., Nthwd. 93 BS53
Hills Ms. W5 138 CL73
Hills Pl. W1 273 K9
Hills Rd., Buck.H. 102 EH46
Hillsborough Grn., Wat. 93 BU48
Ashburnham Dr.
Hillsborough Rd. SE22 182 DS85
Hillsgrove Clo., Well. 166 EW80
Hadlow Rd.
Hillside NW9 118 CR56
Hillside NW10 138 CQ66
Hillside SW19 179 CX93
Hillside, Bans. 233 CY115
Hillside, Barn. 80 DC43
Hillside, Chesh. 54 AN28
Hillside, Dart. 189 FS92
Hillside (Farningham), Dart. 208 FM101
Hillside, Erith 167 FD77
Valley Rd.
Hillside, Grays 170 GD77
Hillside, Harl. 52 EW17
Hillside, Hat. 45 CU18
Hillside, Hodd. 49 DZ16
Hillside, Slou. 152 AS75
Hillside, Uxb. 114 BJ57
Hillside, Vir.W. 192 AW100
Hillside, Ware 32 DW07
Hillside, Welw.G.C. 30 DB12
Hillside, Wok. 226 AX120
Hillside, The, Orp. 224 EV109
Hillside Ave. N11 98 DF51
Hillside Ave., Borwd. 78 CP42
Hillside Ave., Grav. 191 GK89
Hillside Ave., Pur. 219 DP113
Hillside Ave. (Cheshunt), Wal.Cr. 67 DX31
Hillside Ave., Wem. 118 CM63
Hillside Ave., Wdf.Grn. 102 EJ50
Hillside Clo. NW8 140 DB68
Hillside Clo., Abb.L. 59 BS32
Hillside Clo., Bans. 233 CY116
Hillside Clo., Bet. 264 CN135
Hillside Clo., Ch.St.G. 90 AV48
Hillside Clo., Ger.Cr. 90 AY51
Hillside Clo., Mord. 199 CY98
Hillside Clo., Wdf.Grn. 102 EJ50
Hillside Ct., St.Alb. 43 CE19
Hillside Rd.
Hillside Ct., Swan. 207 FG98
West Vw. Rd.
Hillside Cres., Enf. 82 DR38
Hillside Cres., Har. 116 CC60
Hillside Cres., Nthwd. 93 BU53
Hillside Cres. (Cheshunt), Wal.Cr. 67 DX31
Hillside Cres., Ware 33 EB11
Hillside Cres., Wat. 76 BY44
Pinner Rd.
Hillside Dr., Edg. 96 CN51
Hillside Dr., Grav. 191 GK89
Hillside Est. N15 122 DT58
Hillside Gdns. E17 123 ED55
Hillside Gdns. N6 120 DG58
Hillside Gdns. SW2 181 DN89
Hillside Gdns., Add. 211 BF106
Hillside Gdns., Barn. 79 CY42
Hillside Gdns., Berk. 38 AX20
Hillside Gdns., Bet. 248 CN134
Hillside Gdns., Edg. 96 CM49
Hillside Gdns., Har. 118 CL59
Hillside Gdns., Nthwd. 93 BU52
Hillside Gdns., Wall. 219 DJ108
Hillside Gate, St.Alb. 43 CE19
Hillside Gro. N14 99 DK45
Hillside Gro. NW7 97 CU52
Hillside La., Brom. 204 EG103
Hillside La., Ware 33 EA10
Hillside Pas. SW2 181 DM89
Hillside Ri., Nthwd. 93 BU52
Hillside Rd. N15 122 DS58
Hillside Rd. SW2 181 DM89
Hillside Rd. W5 138 CL71
Hillside Rd., Ash. 232 CM117
Hillside Rd., Brom. 204 EF97
Hillside Rd., Couls. 235 DL118
Hillside Rd., Croy. 219 DP106
Hillside Rd., Dart. 187 FG86
Hillside Rd., Epsom 217 CV110
Hillside Rd., Nthwd. 93 BU52
Hillside Rd., Rad. 77 CH35
Hillside Rd., Rick. 73 BC43
Hillside Rd., St.Alb. 43 CE19
Hillside Rd., Sev. 257 FK123
Hillside Rd., Sthl. 136 CA70
Hillside Rd., Surb. 198 CM98
Hillside Rd., Sutt. 217 CZ108
Hillside Rd. (Bushey), Wat. 76 BY43
Hillside Rd., West. 238 EL119
Hillside Rd., Whyt. 236 DU118
Hillside Ter., Hert. 32 DQ11
Hillside Wk., Brwd. 108 FU48
Hillsleigh Rd. W8 139 CZ74
Hillsmead Way, S.Croy. 220 DU113
Hillspur Clo., Guil. 242 AT133
Hillspur Rd., Guil. 242 AT133
Hillstowe St. E5 122 DW62
Hilltop, Sutt. 199 CZ101
Hilltop Clo., Guil. 242 AT130
Hilltop Clo., Lthd. 231 CJ123
Hilltop Clo. (Cheshunt), Wal.Cr. 66 DT26
Hilltop Gdns. NW4 97 CV53
Great N. Way
Hilltop Gdns., Dart. 188 FM85
Hilltop Gdns., Orp. 205 ES103
Hilltop La., Cat. 251 DN126
Hilltop La., Red. 251 DN126
Hilltop Ri., Lthd. 246 CC126
Hilltop Rd. NW6 140 DA66
Hilltop Rd., Berk. 38 AW20
Hilltop Rd., Grays 169 FV79
Hilltop Rd., Kings L. 59 BR27
Hilltop Rd., Reig. 266 DB136
Hilltop Rd., Whyt. 236 DS117
Hilltop Wk., Cat. 237 DY120
Hilltop Way, Stan. 95 CG48
Hillview SW20 179 CV94
Hillview, Mitch. 201 DL98
Hillview Ave., Har. 118 CL57
Hillview Ave., Horn. 128 FJ58
Hillview Clo., Pnr. 94 BZ51
Hillview Clo., Pur. 219 DP111
Hillview Ct., Wok. 227 AZ118
Hillview Cres., Ilf. 125 EM58
Hillview Dr., Red. 266 DG135
Philanthropic Rd.
Hillview Gdns. NW4 119 CX56
Hillview Gdns., Har. 116 CA55
Hillview Gdns. (Cheshunt), Wal.Cr. 67 DX27
Hillview Rd. NW7 97 CX49
Hillview Rd., Chis. 185 EN92
Hillview Rd., Pnr. 94 BZ52
Hillview Rd., Sutt. 200 DC104
Hillway N6 120 DG60
Hillway NW9 118 CS59
Hillway, Amer. 55 AP41
Hillwood Clo., Brwd. 109 GB46
Hillwood Gro., Brwd. 109 GB46
Hillworth Rd. SW2 181 DN87
Hilly Fld., Harl. 51 ET19
Hilly Flds. Cres. SE4 163 EA83
Hillyard Rd. W7 137 CE71
Hillyard St. SW9 161 DN81
Hillyfield E17 123 DY55
Hillyfields, Loug. 85 EN40
Hillyfields, Welw.G.C. 30 DC08
Hilperton Rd., Slou. 152 AS75
Hilsea St. E5 122 DW63
Hilton Ave. N12 98 DD50
Hilton Clo., Uxb. 134 BH68
Hilton Ct., Horl. 269 DK147
Clarence Way
Hilton Way, S.Croy. 236 DV115
Hilversum Cres. SE22 182 DS85
East Dulwich Gro.
Himalayan Way, Wat. 93 BQ46
Tolpits La.
Himley Rd. SW17 180 DE92
Hinchcliffe Clo., Wall. 219 DM108
Roe Way
Hinchley Clo., Esher 197 CF104
Hinchley Dr., Esher 197 CF104
Hinchley Way, Esher 197 CG104
Hinckler Clo., Wall. 219 DL108
Kingsford Ave.
Hinckley Rd. SE15 162 DU84
Hind Clo., Chig. 103 ET50
Hind Ct. EC4 274 E9
Hind Cres., Erith 167 FD79
Hind Gro. E14 143 EA72
Hind Ter., Grays 169 FX78
Mill La.
Hinde Ms. W1 140 DG72
Marylebone La.
Hinde St. W1 272 G8
Hinde St. W1 140 DG72
Hindes Rd., Har. 117 CD57
Hindhead Clo. N16 122 DS60
East Bank
Hindhead Clo., Uxb. 135 BP71
Aldenham Dr.
Hindhead Gdns., Nthlt. 136 BY67
Hindhead Grn., Wat. 94 BW50
Hindhead Way, Wall. 219 DL106
Hindmans Rd. SE22 182 DU85
Hindmans Way, Dag. 146 EZ70
Hindmarsh Clo. E1 142 DU73
Cable St.
Hindrey Rd. E5 122 DV64
Hindsley's Pl. SE23 182 DW89
Hinkler Rd., Har. 117 CK55
Hinkley Clo., Uxb. 114 BJ56
Hinksey Clo., Slou. 153 BB76
Hinksey Path SE2 166 EX75
Hinstock Rd. SE18 165 EQ79
Hinton Ave., Houns. 156 BX84
Hinton Clo. SE9 184 EL88
Hinton Rd. N18 100 DS49
Hinton Rd. SE24 161 DP83
Hinton Rd., Slou. 131 AL73
Hinton Rd., Uxb. 134 BJ67
Hinton Rd., Wall. 219 DJ107
Hintons, Harl. 51 EM19
Hipley St., Wok. 227 BB121
Hippodrome Ms. W11 139 CY73
Portland Rd.
Hippodrome Pl. W11 139 CY73
Hiroshima Wk. SE7 164 EH76
Hiscocks Ho. NW10 138 CQ66
Hitcham La., Slou. 130 AE69
Hitcham Rd. E17 123 DZ59
Hitcham Rd., Maid. 130 AF72
Hitcham Rd., Slou. 130 AF70
Hitchcock Clo., Shep. 194 BM97
Hitchen Hatch La., Sev. 256 FG124
Hitchens Clo., Hem.H. 39 BF19
Hitchin Clo., Rom. 106 FJ49
Hitchin Sq. E3 143 DY68
Hitchings Way, Reig. 266 DA138
Hithebury Clo., Guil. 258 AW137
Hither Grn. La. SE13 183 EC85
Hither Meadow, Ger.Cr. 90 AY53
Lower Rd.
Hitherbaulk, Welw.G.C. 29 CY11
Hitherbroom Rd., Hayes 135 BU74
Hitherfield Rd. SW16 181 DM89
Hitherfield Rd., Dag. 126 EY61
Hitherlands SW12 181 DH89
Hithermoor Rd., Stai. 174 BG86
Hitherway, Welw.G.C. 29 CX05
Hitherwell Dr., Har. 95 CD53
Hitherwood Clo., Horn. 128 FK63
Swanbourne Dr.
Hitherwood Clo., Reig. 250 DE132
Hitherwood Dr. SE19 182 DT91
Hive Clo. (Bushey), Wat. 95 CD47
Hive La., Grav. 190 GB86
Hive Rd. (Bushey), Wat. 95 CD47
Hivings Hill, Chesh. 54 AN28
Hivings Pk., Chesh. 54 AP28
Hixberry La., St.Alb. 43 CK21
Hoadly Rd. SW16 181 DK90
Hobart Clo. N20 98 DE47
Hobart Clo., Hayes 136 BX70
Hobart Dr., Hayes 136 BX70
Hobart Gdns., Th.Hth. 202 DR97
Hobart La., Hayes 136 BX70
Hobart Pl. SW1 277 H6
Hobart Pl. SW1 161 DH76
Hobart Pl., Rich. 178 CM86
Chisholm Rd.
Hobart Rd., Dag. 126 EX63
Hobart Rd., Hayes 136 BX70
Hobart Rd., Ilf. 103 EQ54
Hobart Rd., Til. 171 GG81
Hobart Rd., Wor.Pk. 199 CV104
Hobart Wk., St.Alb. 43 CF16
Valley Rd.
Hobarts Dr., Uxb. 113 BF58
Hobbans Fm. Chase, Ong. 53 FH23
Hobbayne Rd. W7 137 CD72
Hobbes Wk. SW15 179 CV85
Hobbs Clo., St.Alb. 44 CL21
Hobbs Clo. (Cheshunt), Wal.Cr. 67 DX29
Hobbs Clo., W.Byf. 212 BH113
Hobbs Cross Rd., Epp. 86 EW35
Hobbs Cross Rd., Harl. 36 EY12
Hobbs Grn. N2 120 DC55
Hobbs Hill, Hem.H. 40 BM23
Hobbs Hill Rd., Hem.H. 40 BL24
Hobbs Ms., Ilf. 125 ET61
Ripley Rd.
Hobbs Pl. Est. N1 142 DS67
Pitfield St.
Hobbs Rd. SE27 182 DQ91
Hobbs Way, Welw.G.C. 29 CW10
Hobday St. E14 143 EB71
Hobill Wk., Surb. 198 CM100
Hoblands End, Chis. 185 ES93
Hobletts Rd., Hem.H. 40 BM19
Hobsons Clo., Hodd. 33 DZ14
Hobsons Pl. E1 142 DU71
Hanbury St.
Hobtoe Rd., Harl. 35 EN14
Hobury St. SW10 160 DC79
Hockenden La., Swan. 206 FA97
Hocker St. E2 275 P3
Hockeridge Bottom, Berk. 38 AT21
Hockering Gdns., Wok. 227 BA118
Hockering Rd., Wok. 227 BA118
Hockett Clo. SE8 163 DZ77
Grove St.
Hocklands, Welw.G.C. 30 DC08
Hockley Ave. E6 144 EL68
Hockley Dr., Rom. 105 FH54
Hockley La., Slou. 132 AV67
Hocroft Ave. NW2 119 CZ62
Hocroft Rd. NW2 119 CZ63
Hocroft Wk. NW2 119 CZ62
Hodder Dr., Grnf. 137 CF68
Hoddesdon Bypass, Brox. 49 DX24
Hoddesdon Bypass, Hert. 33 DZ13
Hoddesdon Rd., Belv. 166 FA78
Hoddesdon Rd., Brox. 67 DX26
Hoddesdon Rd., Hodd. 49 DY15
Hoddesdon Rd., Stan. 33 EC11
Hodds Wd. Rd., Chesh. 54 AQ33
Hodford Rd. NW11 119 CZ60
Hodges Way, Wat. 93 BU45
Moor Vw.
Hodgkin Clo. SE28 146 EX73
Fleming Way
Hodgson Gdns., Guil. 243 AZ131
Sutherland Dr.
Hodings Rd., Harl. 35 EP14
Hodnet Gro. SE16 163 DX77
Hawkstone Rd.
Hodsoll Ct., Orp. 206 EX99
Hodson Clo., Har. 116 BZ62
Hodson Cres., Orp. 206 EX99
Hoe, The, Wat. 94 BX47
Hoe La., Dor. 261 BT143
Hoe La., Enf. 82 DU38
Hoe La., Guil. 261 BR144
Hoe La., Rom. 86 EV41
Hoe La., Wal.Abb. 50 EF22
Hoe La., Ware 33 DX09
Hoe Meadow, Beac. 88 AJ51
Hoe St. E17 123 EA57
Hoebrook Clo., Wok. 226 AY121
Bonsey La.
Hoecroft, Wal.Abb. 50 EF22
Hoestock Rd., Saw. 36 EX05
Hofland Rd. W14 159 CX76
Hog Hill Rd., Rom. 104 EZ52
Hogan Ms. W2 140 DD71
Porteus Rd.
Hogan Way E5 122 DU61
Geldeston Rd.
Hogarth Ave., Ashf. 175 BQ93
Hogarth Ave., Brwd. 108 FY48
Hogarth Clo. E16 144 EK71
Hogarth Clo. W5 138 CL71
Hogarth Clo., Slou. 131 AL73
Hogarth Ct. EC3 275 N10
Hogarth Ct. SE19 182 DT91
Fountain Dr.
Hogarth Ct. (Bushey), Wat. 94 CB45
Steeplands

Hogarth Cres. SW19 200 DD95
Hogarth Cres., Croy. 202 DQ101
Hogarth Gdns., Houns. 156 CA80
Hogarth Hill NW11 119 CZ56
Hogarth La. W4 158 CS79
Hogarth Pl. SW5 160 DB77
Hogarth Rd.
Hogarth Reach, Loug. 85 EM43
Hogarth Rd. SW5 160 DB77
Hogarth Rd., Edg. 96 CN54
Hogarth Roundabout W4 158 CS79
Hogarth Way, Hmptn. 196 CC95
Hogback Wd. Rd., Beac. 88 AH51
Hogden La., Dor. 246 BZ134
Hogden La., Lthd. 246 CA129
Hogfair La., Slou. 130 AJ69
Hogg End La., Hem.H. 41 BR17
Hogg End La., St.Alb. 41 BT17
Hogg La., Borwd. 77 CG42
Hogg La., Grays 170 GA76
Hogpits Bottom, Hem.H. 57 BA32
Hogs Back, Guil. 258 AS137
Hogs La., Grav. 190 GD90
Hogscross La., Couls. 234 DF123
Hogshead Pas. E1 142 DV73
Pennington St.
Hogshill La., Cob. 213 BV114
Hogsmill Way, Epsom 216 CQ106
Hogtrough Hill, West. 239 ET120
Hogtrough La., Oxt. 253 EA128
Hogtrough La., Red. 267 DJ135
Holbeach Gdns., Sid. 185 ES86
Holbeach Ms. SW12 181 DH88
Harberson Rd.
Holbeach Rd. SE6 183 EA87
Holbeck La. (Cheshunt), Wal.Cr. 66 DT26
Holbeck Row SE15 162 DU80
Holbein Gate, Nthwd. 93 BS50
Holbein Ms. SW1 276 F10
Holbein Ms. SW1 160 DG78
Holbein Pl. SW1 276 F9
Holbein Pl. SW1 160 DG77
Holberton Gdns. NW10 139 CV69
Holborn EC1 274 D7
Holborn EC1 141 DN71
Holborn Circ. EC1 274 E7
Holborn Clo., St.Alb. 43 CK15
Holborn Pl. WC1 274 B7
Holborn Rd. E13 144 EH70
Holborn Viaduct EC1 274 E7
Holborn Viaduct EC1 141 DN71
Holborn Way, Mitch. 200 DF96
Holbreck Pl., Wok. 227 AZ118
Heathside Rd.
Holbrook Clo. N19 121 DH60
Dartmouth Pk. Hill
Holbrook Clo., Enf. 82 DT39
Holbrook La., Chis. 185 ER94
Holbrook Meadow, Egh. 173 BC93
Pooley Grn. Rd.
Holbrook Rd. E15 144 EF68
Holbrook Way, Brom. 205 EM100
Holbrooke Ct. N7 121 DL62
Holbrooke Pl., Rich. 177 CK85
Hill Ri.
Holburne Clo. SE3 164 EJ81
Holburne Gdns. SE3 164 EK81
Holburne Rd. SE3 164 EJ81
Holcombe Hill NW7 97 CU48
Highwood Hill
Holcombe Rd. N17 122 DT55
Holcombe Rd., Ilf. 125 EN59
Holcombe St. W6 159 CV78
Holcon Ct., Red. 250 DG131
Holcote Clo., Belv. 166 EY76
Blakemore Way
Holcroft Rd. E9 142 DW66
Holdbrook, Wal.Cr. 67 EA34
Holdbrook N., Wal.Cr. 67 DZ34
Holdbrook S., Wal.Cr. 67 DZ34
Queens Way
Holdbrook Way, Rom. 106 FM54
Holden Ave. N12 98 DB50
Holden Ave. NW9 118 CQ60
Holden Clo., Dag. 126 EV62
Holden Clo., Hert. 32 DS08
Holden Gdns., Brwd. 108 FX50
Holden Pt. E15 143 ED65
Waddington Rd.
Holden Rd. N12 98 DB50
Holden St. SW11 160 DG82
Holden Way, Upmin. 129 FR60
Holdenby Rd. SE4 183 DY85
Holdenhurst Ave. N12 98 DB52
Holder Clo. N3 98 DB52
Etchingham Pk. Rd.
Holderness Way SE27 181 DP92
Holdernesse Clo., Islw. 157 CG81
London Rd.
Holdernesse Rd. SW17 180 DF90
Holders Hill Ave. NW4 97 CX54
Holders Hill Circ. NW7 97 CY52
Dollis Rd.
Holders Hill Cres. NW4 97 CX54
Holders Hill Dr. NW4 119 CX55
Holders Hill Gdns. NW4 97 CY54
Holders Hill Rd. NW4 97 CX54
Holders Hill Rd. NW7 97 CY53
Holdgate St. SE7 164 EK76
Westmoor St.
Holdings, The, Hat. 45 CX16
Hole Fm. La., Brwd. 107 FU53
Hole Hill La., Dor. 262 CB136
Holecroft, Wal.Abb. 68 EE34
Holford Pl. WC1 274 C2
Holford Rd. NW3 120 DC62
Holford Rd., Grays 171 GK77
Holford Rd., Guil. 243 BC134
Holford Rd., S.le H. 171 GL75
Holford St. WC1 274 D2
Holford St. WC1 141 DN69
Holgate Ave. SW11 160 DD83
Holgate Gdns., Dag. 146 FA65
Holgate Rd., Dag. 126 FA64
Holland Ave. SW20 199 CT95
Holland Ave., Sutt. 218 DA108
Holland Clo., Barn. 98 DD45
Holland Clo., Brom. 204 EF103
Holland Clo., Red. 250 DF134
Holland Clo., Rom. 127 FC57
Holland Clo., Stan. 95 CH50
Holland Cres., Oxt. 254 EG133
Holland Dr. SE23 183 DY90
Holland Gdns. W14 159 CY76
Holland Gdns., Egh. 193 BF96
Holland Gdns., Wat. 76 BW35
Holland Gro. SW9 161 DN80
Holland La., Oxt. 254 EG133
Holland Pk. W8 159 CZ75
Holland Pk. W11 139 CY74
Holland Pk. Ave. W11 139 CY74
Holland Pk. Ave., Ilf. 125 ES58
Holland Pk. Gdns. W14 159 CY75
Holland Pk. Ms. W11 139 CZ74
Holland Pk. Rd. W14 159 CZ76
Holland Pas. N1 142 DQ67
Basire St.
Holland Pl. W8 160 DB75
Kensington Ch. St.
Holland Rd. E6 145 EM67
Holland Rd. E15 144 EE69
Holland Rd. NW10 139 CU67
Holland Rd. SE25 202 DU99
Holland Rd. W14 159 CX75
Holland Rd., Oxt. 254 EG133
Holland Rd., Wem. 137 CK65
Holland St. SE1 278 G2
Holland St. SE1 141 DP74
Holland St. W8 160 DA75
Holland Vill. Rd. W14 159 CY75
Holland Wk. N19 121 DK60
Duncombe Rd.
Holland Wk. W8 159 CZ75
Holland Wk., Stan. 95 CG50
Holland Way, Brom. 204 EF103
Hollands, The, Felt. 176 BX91
Hollands, The, Wor.Pk. 199 CT102
Hollands Cft., Ware 34 EK06
Hollar Rd. N16 122 DT62
Stoke Newington High St.
Hollen St. W1 273 L8
Hollen St. W1 141 DK72
Holles Clo., Hmptn. 176 CA93
Holles St. W1 273 J8
Holles St. W1 141 DH72
Holley Rd. W3 158 CS75
Hollickwood Ave. N12 98 DF51
Holliday Sq. SW11 160 DD83
Fowler Clo.
Holliday St., Berk. 38 AX19
Hollidge Way, Dag. 147 FB65
Hollier Ct., Hat. 45 CV17
Holliers Way, Hat. 45 CU18
Hollies, The E11 124 EG57
Hollies, The N20 98 DD46
Hollies, The, Grav. 191 GK93
Hollies, The, Har. 117 CG56
Christchurch Ave.
Hollies, The, Hem.H. 57 BA29
Hollies, The, Welw.G.C. 29 CV13
Great N. Rd.
Hollies Ave., Sid. 185 ET89
Hollies Ave., W.Byf. 211 BF113
Hollies Clo. SW16 181 DN93
Hollies Clo., Twick. 177 CF89
Hollies Ct., Add. 212 BJ106
Hollies End NW7 97 CV50
Hollies Rd. W5 157 CJ77
Hollies Way SW12 180 DG87
Bracken Ave.
Hollies Way, Pot.B. 64 DC31
Holligrave Rd., Brom. 204 EG95
Hollingbourne Ave., Bexh. 166 EZ80
Hollingbourne Gdns. W13 137 CH71
Hollingbourne Rd. SE24 182 DQ85
Hollingbourne Twr., Orp. 206 EX102
Hollingsworth Rd., Croy. 220 DV107
Hollington Cres., N.Mal. 199 CT100
Hollington Rd. E6 145 EM69
Hollington Rd. N17 100 DU54
Hollingworth Clo., W.Mol. 196 BZ98
Hollingworth Rd., Orp. 205 EP101
Hollingworth Way, West. 255 ER126
Hollis Pl., Grays 170 GA77
Ward Ave.
Hollisters, Grav. 191 GK91
Hollman Gdns. SW16 181 DP93
Hollow, The, Wdf.Grn. 102 EF49
Hollow Clo., Guil. 258 AV135
Lynwood
Hollow Cotts., Purf. 168 FN78
Hollow Hill La., Iver 133 BB73
Hollow La., Dor. 262 BX140
Hollow La., Vir.W. 192 AW97
Hollow Wk., Rich. 158 CL80
Kew Rd.
Hollow Way La., Amer. 55 AS35
Hollow Way La., Chesh. 72 AT35
Holloway Dr., Vir.W. 192 AY98
Stroude Rd.
Holloway Hill, Cher. 193 BC104
Holloway La., Rick. 73 BB38
Holloway La., West Dr. 154 BK79
Holloway Rd. E6 145 EM69
Holloway Rd. E11 124 EE62
Holloway Rd. N7 121 DM62
Holloway Rd. N19 121 DJ61
Holloway St., Houns. 156 CB83
Holloways La., Hat. 45 CX23
Hollowfield Ave., Grays 170 GD77
Hollowfield Wk., Nthlt. 136 BY65
Hollows, The, Brent. 158 CM79
Kew Bri. Rd.
Holly Ave., Add. 212 BG110
Holly Ave., Stan. 96 CL54
Holly Ave., Walt. 196 BX102
Holly Bank Rd., W.Byf. 212 BG114
Holly Bank Rd., Wok. 226 AV119
Holly Bush Hill NW3 120 DC63
Holly Bush La., Hmptn. 176 BZ94
Holly Bush La., Sev. 257 FJ124
Holly Bush Steps NW3 120 DC63
Heath St.
Holly Bush Vale NW3 120 DC63
Heath St.
Holly Clo. NW10 138 CS66
Holly Clo., Buck.H. 102 EK48
Holly Clo., Cher. 192 AU104
Holly Clo., Egh. 172 AV93
Holly Clo., Felt. 176 BY92
Holly Clo., Hat. 45 CT19
Holly Clo., Slou. 111 AQ63
Holly Clo., Wall. 219 DH108
Holly Clo., Wok. 226 AV119
Holly Cres., Beck. 203 DZ99
Holly Cres., Wind. 151 AK82
Holly Cres., Wdf.Grn. 101 ED52
Holly Cft., Hert. 31 DN08
Holly Cross Rd., Ware 33 DZ07
Holly Dr. E4 101 EB45
Holly Dr., Berk. 38 AX20
Holly Dr., Brent. 157 CG79
New Horizon Ct.
Holly Dr., Pot.B. 64 DB33
Holly Dr., Wind. 172 AS85
Holly Fm. Rd., Sthl. 156 BY78
Holly Fld., Harl. 51 EQ18
Holly Gdns., West Dr. 154 BM75
Holly Grn., Wey. 213 BR105
Holly Gro. NW9 118 CQ59
Holly Gro. SE15 162 DT82
Holly Gro., Pnr. 94 BY53
Holly Gro. (Bushey), Wat. 95 CD45
Holly Gro. Rd., Hert. 31 DH07
Holly Hedge Ter. SE13 183 ED85
Holly Hedges La., Hem.H. 57 BC30
Holly Hedges La., Rick. 57 BD32
Holly Hill N21 81 DM44
Holly Hill NW3 120 DC63
Holly Hill Dr., Bans. 234 DA116
Holly Hill Rd., Belv. 167 FB78
Holly Hill Rd., Erith 167 FC78
Holly Ho., Brwd. 108 FX46
Sawyers Hall La.
Holly La., Bans. 234 DA116
Holly La. E., Bans. 234 DB116
Holly La. W., Bans. 234 DB117
Holly Lea, Guil. 242 AX128
Holly Lo. Gdns. N6 120 DG60
Holly Ms. SW10 160 DC78
Drayton Gdns.
Holly Mt. NW3 120 DC63
Holly Bush Hill
Holly Pk. N3 119 CZ55
Holly Pk. N4 121 DL59
Holly Pk. Est. N4 121 DM59
Blythwood Rd.
Holly Pk. Gdns. N3 120 DA55
Holly Pk. Rd. N11 98 DG50
Holly Pk. Rd. W7 137 CF74
Holly Rd. E11 124 EF59
Holly Rd. W4 158 CR77
Dolman Rd.
Holly Rd., Dart. 188 FK88
Holly Rd., Enf. 83 DX36
Holly Rd., Hmptn. 176 CC93
Holly Rd., Houns. 156 CB84
Holly Rd., Orp. 224 EU108
Holly Rd., Reig. 266 DB136
Holly Rd., Twick. 177 CG88
Holly St. E8 142 DT65
Holly St. Est. E8 142 DT66
Holly Ter. N20 98 DC47
Holly Tree Ave., Swan. 207 FE96
Holly Tree Clo., Chesh. 56 AV31
Holly Tree Rd., Cat. 236 DS122
Elm Gro.
Holly Vw. Clo. NW4 119 CU58
Holly Wk. NW3 120 DC63
Holly Wk., Enf. 82 DQ41
Gentlemans Row
Holly Wk., Rich. 158 CL82
Holly Wk., Welw.G.C. 29 CW05
Holly Way, Mitch. 201 DK98
Hollybank Clo., Hmptn. 176 CA92
Hollyberry La. NW3 120 DC63
Holly Wk.
Hollybrake Clo., Chis. 185 ER94
Hollybush Ave., St.Alb. 42 CA24
Hollybush Clo. E11 124 EG57
Hollybush Clo., Berk. 39 BD16
Hollybush Clo., Har. 95 CE53
Hollybush Clo., Sev. 257 FJ124
Hollybush Clo., Wat. 94 BW45
Hollybush Ct., Sev. 257 FJ124
Hollybush Gdns. E2 142 DV69
Hollybush Hill E11 124 EF59
Hollybush Hill, Slou. 132 AU66
Hollybush La., Amer. 55 AR36
Hollybush La., Hem.H. 39 BF19
Hollybush La., Iver 133 BB72
Hollybush La., Orp. 224 FA107
Hollybush La., Uxb. 113 BC61
Hollybush La., Welw.G.C. 29 CZ12
Hollybush La., Wok. 228 BK119
Hollybush Pl. E2 142 DV69
Bethnal Grn. Rd.
Hollybush Rd., Chesh. 54 AN27
Hollybush Rd., Grav. 191 GJ89
Hollybush Rd., Kings.T. 178 CL92
Hollybush St. E13 144 EH69
Hollybush Wk. SW9 161 DP84
Hollybush Way, Wal.Cr. 66 DU28
Hollycombe, Egh. 172 AW91
Hollycroft Ave. NW3 120 DA62
Hollycroft Ave., Wem. 118 CM61
Hollycroft Clo., West Dr. 154 BN79
Hollycroft Gdns., West Dr. 154 BN79
Hollydale Dr., Brom. 205 EM104
Hollydale Rd. SE15 162 DW81
Hollydell, Hert. 32 DQ11
Hollydene SE15 162 DV81
Hollydown Way E11 123 ED62
Hollyfield, Hat. 45 CU21
Hollyfield Ave. N11 98 DF50
Hollyfield Rd., Surb. 198 CM101
Hollyfields, Brox. 67 DY26
Hollyhedge Rd., Cob. 213 BV114
Hollyhock Clo., Hem.H. 39 BE19
The Ave.
Hollymead, Cars. 200 DF104
Hollymead Rd., Couls. 234 DG118
Hollymeoak Rd., Couls. 235 DH119
Hollymoor La., Epsom 216 CR110
Hollymount Clo. SE10 163 EC81
Hollytree Clo. SW19 179 CX88
Hollytree Clo., Ger.Cr. 90 AY50
Hollywood Ct., Borwd. 78 CM42
Deacon's Hill Rd.
Hollywood Gdns., Hayes 135 BV72
Hollywood Ms. SW10 160 DC79
Hollywood Rd.
Hollywood Rd. E4 101 DY50
Hollywood Rd. SW10 160 DC79
Hollywood Way, Erith 167 FH81
Slade Grn. Rd.
Hollywood Way, Wdf.Grn. 101 ED52
Hollywoods, Croy. 221 DZ109
Holm Clo., Add. 211 BE112
Holm Gro., Uxb. 134 BN66
Holm Oak Clo. SW15 179 CZ86
West Hill
Holm Oak Ms. SW4 181 DL85
King's Ave.
Holm Wk. SE3 164 EG82
Blackheath Pk.
Holman Rd. SW11 160 DD82
Holman Rd., Epsom 216 CQ106
Holmbank Dr., Shep. 195 BS98
Holmbridge Gdns., Enf. 83 DX42
Holmbrook Dr. NW4 119 CX57
Holmbury Ct. SW17 180 DF90
Holmbury Ct. SW19 180 DE94
Cavendish Rd.
Holmbury Dr., Dor. 263 CJ139
Holmbury Gdns., Hayes 135 BT74
Church Rd.
Holmbury Gro., Croy. 221 DZ108
Holmbury Pk., Brom. 184 EL94
Holmbury Vw. E5 122 DV60
Holmbush Rd. SW15 179 CY86
Holmcote Gdns. N5 122 DQ64
Holmcroft, Tad. 249 CV125
Holmcroft Way, Brom. 205 EM99
Holmdale Clo., Borwd. 78 CM40
Holmdale Gdns. NW4 119 CX57
Holmdale Rd. NW6 120 DA64
Holmdale Rd., Chis. 185 EQ92
Holmdale Ter. N15 122 DS59
Holmdene Ave. NW7 97 CU51
Holmdene Ave. SE24 182 DQ85
Holmdene Ave., Har. 116 CB55
Holmdene Clo., Beck. 203 EC96
Holme Chase, Wey. 213 BQ107
Holme Clo., Hat. 45 CT15
Holme Clo. (Cheshunt), Wal.Cr. 67 DY31
Holme Lacey Rd. SE12 184 EF86
Holme Lea, Wat. 60 BW34
Kingsway
Holme Pk., Borwd. 78 CM40
Holme Rd. E6 144 EL67
Holme Rd., Hat. 45 CT15
Holme Rd., Horn. 128 FN60
Holme Way, Stan. 95 CF51
Holmead Rd. SW6 160 DB80
Holmebury Clo. (Bushey), Wat. 95 CE47
Holmedale, Slou. 132 AW73
Holmefield Ct. NW3 140 DE65
Holmes Ave. E17 123 DZ55
Holmes Ave. NW7 97 CY50
Holmes Meadow, Harl. 51 EP21
Holmes Pl. SW10 160 DC79
Fulham Rd.
Holmes Rd. NW5 141 DH65
Holmes Rd. SW19 180 DC94
Holmes Rd., Twick. 177 CF89
Holmes Ter. SE1 278 D4
Holmes Ter. SE1 161 DN75
Holmesdale, Wal.Cr. 82 DW35
Holmesdale Ave. SW14 158 CP83
Holmesdale Clo. SE25 202 DT97
Holmesdale Clo., Guil. 243 BB133
Holmesdale Hill (South Darenth), Dart. 208 FQ95
Holmesdale Rd. N6 121 DH59
Holmesdale Rd. SE25 202 DR99
Holmesdale Rd., Bexh. 166 EX82
Holmesdale Rd., Croy. 202 DR99
Holmesdale Rd. (South Darenth), Dart. 208 FQ95
Holmesdale Rd., Dor. 263 CH140
Holmesdale Rd., Red. 267 DM136
Holmesdale Rd., Reig. 250 DA133
Holmesdale Rd., Rich. 158 CM81
Holmesdale Rd., Tedd. 177 CJ94
Holmesdale Ter., Dor. 263 CH140
Holmesdale Rd.
Holmesley Rd. SE23 183 DY86
Holmethorpe Ave., Red. 251 DH131
Holmethorpe Ind. Est., Red. 251 DH131
Holmewood Gdns. SW2 181 DM87
Holmewood Rd. SE25 202 DS97
Holmewood Rd. SW2 181 DL87
Holmfield Ave. NW4 119 CX57
Holmhurst Rd., Belv. 167 FB78
Holmlea Rd., Slou. 152 AX81
Holmlea Wk., Slou. 152 AW81
Holmleigh Ave., Dart. 168 FJ84
Holmleigh Rd. N16 122 DS60
Holmleigh Rd. Est. N16 122 DT60
Holmleigh Rd.
Holms St. E2 142 DU68
Audrey St.
Holmsdale Clo., Iver 133 BF72
Holmsdale Gro., Bexh. 167 FE82
Holmsdale Rd., Sev. 257 FJ123
Holmshaw Clo. SE26 183 DY91
Holmshill La., Borwd. 78 CS36
Holmside Ri., Wat. 93 BV48
Holmside Rd. SW12 180 DG86
Holmsley Clo., N.Mal. 199 CT100
Holmstall Ave., Edg. 118 CQ55
Holmwood Ave., Brwd. 109 GA43
Holmwood Ave., S.Croy. 220 DT113
Holmwood Clo., Add. 212 BG106
Holmwood Clo., Har. 116 CC55
Holmwood Clo., Lthd. 245 BS128
Holmwood Clo., Nthlt. 136 CB65
Holmwood Clo., Sutt. 217 CX109
Holmwood Gdns. N3 98 DA54
Holmwood Gdns., Wall. 219 DH107
Holmwood Gro. NW7 96 CR50
Holmwood Rd., Chess. 215 CK106
Holmwood Rd., Enf. 83 DX36
Holmwood Rd., Ilf. 125 ES61
Holmwood Rd., Sutt. 217 CW110
Holmwood Vw. Rd., Dor. 263 CH142
Horsham Rd.
Holmwood Vill. SE7 164 EG78
Holne Chase N2 120 DC58
Holne Chase, Mord. 199 CZ100
Holness Rd. E15 144 EF65
Holroyd Clo., Esher 215 CF109
Holroyd Rd. SW15 159 CW84
Holroyd Rd., Esher 215 CF109
Holstein Ave., Wey. 212 BN105
Holstein Way, Erith 166 EX76
Holstock Rd., Ilf. 125 EQ61
Holsworth Clo., Har. 116 CC57
Holsworthy Sq. WC1 274 C5
Holsworthy Way, Chess. 215 CJ106
Holt, The, Hem.H. 40 BL21
Turners Hill
Holt, The, Ilf. 103 EQ51
Holt, The, Wall. 219 DJ105
Holt, The, Welw.G.C. 30 DD10
Holt Clo. N10 120 DG56
Holt Clo. SE28 146 EV73
Holt Clo., Borwd. 78 CM42
Holt Clo., Chig. 103 ET50
Holt Ct. E15 123 EC64
Clays La.
Holt Rd. E16 144 EL74
Holt Rd., Wem. 117 CH62
Holt Way, Chig. 103 ET50
Holton St. E1 143 DX70
Holtsmere Clo., Wat. 76 BW35
Holtspur Ave., H.Wyc. 110 AE56
Holtspur Clo., Beac. 88 AG54
Holtspur La., H.Wyc. 110 AE57
Holtspur Top La., Beac. 88 AG54
Holtspur Way, Beac. 88 AG54
Holtwhite Ave., Enf. 82 DQ40
Holtwhites Hill, Enf. 81 DP39
Holtwood Rd., Lthd. 214 CC114
Holwell Caravan Site, Hat. 30 DE14
Holwell Hyde, Welw.G.C. 30 DC10
Cole Grn. La.
Holwell Hyde La., Welw.G.C. 30 DC12
Holwell La., Hat. 30 DE14
Holwell Pl., Pnr. 116 BY56
Holwell Rd., Welw.G.C. 29 CY10
Holwood Clo., Walt. 196 BW103
Holwood Pk. Ave., Orp. 223 EM105
Holwood Pl. SW4 161 DK84
Holy Cross Hill, Brox. 48 DU24
Holy Wk., Brox. 49 EA19
St. Catherines Rd.
Holybourne Ave. SW15 179 CU87
Holyfield Rd., Wal.Abb. 67 EC29
Holyhead Clo. E3 143 EA69
Holyhead Clo. E6 145 EM71
Valiant Way
Holyoak Rd. SE11 278 F8
Holyoak Rd. SE11 161 DP77
Holyoake Ave., Wok. 226 AW117
Holyoake Ct. SE16 163 DZ75
Bryan Rd.
Holyoake Cres., Wok. 226 AW117
Holyoake Ter., Sev. 256 FG124
Holyoake Wk. N2 120 DC55
Holyoake Wk. W5 137 CJ70
Holyport Rd. SW6 159 CW80
Holyrood Ave., Har. 116 BY63
Holyrood Cres., St.Alb. 43 CD24
Holyrood Gdns., Edg. 118 CP55
Holyrood Gdns., Grays 171 GJ77
Holyrood Rd., Barn. 80 DC44
Holyrood St. SE1 279 M3
Holywell Clo. SE3 164 EG79
Holywell Clo., Stai. 174 BL88
Holywell Hill, St.Alb. 43 CD21
Holywell Ind. Est., Wat. 75 BR44
Holywell La. EC2 275 N4
Holywell La. EC2 142 DS70
Holywell Rd., Wat. 75 BU43
Holywell Row EC2 275 M5
Holywell Row EC2 142 DS70
Holywell Way, Stai. 174 BL88
Home Clo., Brox. 49 DZ24
Home Clo., Cars. 200 DF103
Home Clo., Harl. 35 ET14
Home Clo., Lthd. 231 CD121
Home Clo., Nthlt. 136 BZ69
Home Ct., Felt. 175 BU88
Home Fm. Clo., Bet. 264 CS135
Home Fm. Clo., Epsom 233 CX117
Home Fm. Clo., Esher 214 CB107
Home Fm. Clo., Shep. 195 BS98
Home Fm. Clo., T.Ditt. 197 CF101
Home Fm. Gdns., Walt. 196 BW103
Home Fm. Rd., Rick. 92 BM49
Home Fm. Way, Slou. 132 AW67
Home Fld., Berk. 39 BB16
Home Gdns., Dag. 127 FC62
Home Gdns., Dart. 188 FL86
Home Hill, Swan. 187 FF94
Home Lea, Orp. 223 ET106
Home Ley, Welw.G.C. 29 CY09
Home Mead, Stan. 95 CJ53
Home Mead Clo., Grav. 191 GH87
Home Meadow, Bans. 234 DA116
Holly La.
Home Meadow, Slou. 131 AQ68
Home Meadow, Welw.G.C. 29 CZ09
Home Orchard, Dart. 188 FL86
Home Pk., Oxt. 254 EG131
Home Pk. Mill Link Rd., Kings L. 59 BP31
Home Pk. Rd. SW19 179 CZ91
Home Pk. Wk., Kings.T. 197 CK98
Home Rd. SW11 160 DE82
Home Way, Rick. 91 BF46
Homecroft Gdns., Loug. 85 EP42
Homecroft Rd. N22 99 DP53
Homecroft Rd. SE26 182 DW92
Homedean Rd., Sev. 256 FC122
Homefarm Clo., Cher. 211 BA108
Homefarm Rd. W7 137 CE72
Homefield, Hem.H. 57 BB28
Homefield, Wal.Abb. 68 EG32
Homefield, Walt. 214 BX105
Homefield Ave., Ilf. 125 ES57
Homefield Clo. NW10 138 CQ65
Homefield Clo., Add. 211 BE112
Homefield Clo., Epp. 70 EU30
Homefield Clo., Hayes 136 BX70
Homefield Clo., Horl. 269 DH147
Tanyard Way
Homefield Clo., Lthd. 231 CJ121
Homefield Clo., Orp. 206 EV98
Chipperfield Rd.
Homefield Clo., Swan. 207 FF97
Homefield Gdns. N2 120 DD55
Homefield Gdns., Mitch. 200 DC96
Homefield Gdns., Tad. 233 CW120
Homefield Ms., Beck. 203 EA95
Homefield Pk., Sutt. 218 DB107
Homefield Ri., Orp. 206 EU102
Homefield Rd. SW19 179 CX93
Homefield Rd. W4 159 CT78
Homefield Rd., Brom. 204 EJ95
Homefield Rd., Couls. 235 DP119
Homefield Rd., Edg. 96 CR51
Homefield Rd., Hem.H. 40 BN20
Homefield Rd., Rad. 77 CF37
Homefield Rd., Rick. 73 BC42
Green St.
Homefield Rd., Sev. 256 FE122
Homefield Rd., Walt. 196 BY101
Homefield Rd., Ware 33 DY05
Homefield Rd., Warl. 236 DW119
Homefield Rd. (Bushey), Wat. 76 CA42
Homefield Rd., Wem. 117 CG63
Homefield St. N1 275 M1
Homeland Dr., Sutt. 218 DB109
Homelands, Lthd. 231 CJ121
Homelands Dr. SE19 182 DS94
Homeleigh Ct., Wal.Cr. 66 DV29

Homeleigh Rd. SE15 183 DX85
Homemead SW12 181 DH89
Homemead Rd., Brom. 205 EM99
Homemead Rd., Croy. 202 DW100
Homer Clo., Bexh. 167 FC81
Homer Dr. E14 163 EA77
Homer Rd. E9 143 DY65
Homer Rd., Croy. 203 DX100
Homer Row W1 272 C7
Homer Row W1 140 DE71
Homer St. W1 272 C7
Homer St. W1 140 DE71
Homerfield, Welw.G.C. 29 CW08
Homers Rd., Wind. 151 AK81
Homersham Rd., Kings.T. 198 CN96
Homerswood La., Welw. 29 CU05
Homerton Gro. E9 123 DX64
Homerton High St. E9 122 DW64
Homerton Rd. E9 123 DY64
Homerton Row E9 122 DW64
Homerton Ter. E9 142 DW65
Morning La.
Homesdale Clo. E11 124 EG57
Homesdale Rd., Brom. 204 EJ98
Homesdale Rd., Cat. 236 DR123
Homesdale Rd., Orp. 205 ES101
Homesfield NW11 120 DA57
Homestall Rd. SE22 182 DW85
Homestead, The N11 99 DH49
Homestead, The, Dart. 188 FJ86
Homestead Clo., St.Alb. 60 CC27
Homestead Ct., Welw.G.C. 29 CZ11
Homestead Gdns., Esher 215 CE106
Homestead La., Welw.G.C. 29 CZ12
Homestead Paddock N14 81 DH43
Homestead Pk. NW2 119 CT62
Homestead Rd. SW6 159 CZ80
Homestead Rd., Cat. 236 DR123
Homestead Rd., Dag. 126 EZ61
Homestead Rd., Hat. 45 CU15
Homestead Rd., Orp. 224 EV108
Homestead Rd., Rick. 92 BK45
Park Rd.
Homestead Rd., Stai. 174 BH93
Homestead Way, Croy. 221 EC111
Homesteads, The, Ware 34 EK07
Hunsdon Rd.
Homewaters Ave., Sun. 195 BT95
Homeway, Rom. 106 FP51
Homewillow Clo. N21 81 DP44
Homewood, Slou. 132 AX72
Homewood Ave. (Cuffley), Pot.B. 65 DL27
Homewood Clo., Hmptn. 176 BZ93
Fearnley Cres.
Homewood Cres., Chis. 185 ES93
Homewood La., Pot.B. 65 DJ27
Homewood Rd., St.Alb. 43 CH17
Honduras St. EC1 275 H4
Honey Clo., Dag. 147 FB65
Honey Hill, Uxb. 134 BM66
Honey La. EC2 275 J9
Honey La., Wal.Abb. 68 EE33
Honeybourne Rd. NW6 120 DB64
Honeybourne Way, Orp. 205 ER102
Honeybrook, Wal.Abb. 68 EE33
Honeybrook Rd. SW12 181 DJ87
Honeycrock La., Red. 266 DG141
Honeycroft, Loug. 85 EN42
Honeycroft, Welw.G.C. 29 CW10
Honeycroft Hill, Uxb. 134 BL66
Honeycross Rd., Hem.H. 39 BE21
Honeyden Rd., Sid. 186 EY93
Honeyhill, Harl. 51 ES19
Honeyman Clo. NW6 139 CX66
Honeymeade, Saw. 36 EW08
Honeypot Clo. NW9 118 CM56
Honeypot La. NW9 118 CL55
Honeypot La., Brwd. 108 FU48
Honeypot La., Stan. 118 CL55
Honeypots Rd., Wok. 226 AX122
Honeysett Rd. N17 100 DT54
Reform Row
Honeysuckle Bottom, Lthd. 245 BS134
Honeysuckle Clo., Brwd. 108 FV43
Honeysuckle Clo., Hert. 32 DU09
Honeysuckle Clo., Horl. 269 DJ147
Briars Wd.
Honeysuckle Clo., Iver 133 BC72
Honeysuckle Clo., Rom. 106 FK51
Cloudberry Rd.
Honeysuckle Clo., Sthl. 136 BY73
Lancaster Rd.
Honeysuckle Fld., Chesh. 54 AQ30
Honeysuckle Gdns., Croy. 203 DX102
Primrose La.
Honeysuckle Gdns., Hat. 45 CV19
Honeysuckle La., Dor. 263 CJ139
Treelands
Honeywell Rd. SW11 180 DE86
Honeywood Clo., Pot.B. 64 DD33
Honeywood Rd. NW10 139 CT68
Honeywood Rd., Islw. 157 CG84
Honeywood Wk., Cars. 218 DF105
Honister Clo., Stan. 95 CH53
Honister Gdns., Stan. 95 CH53
Honister Heights, Pur. 220 DR114
Honister Pl., Stan. 95 CH53
Honiton Rd. NW6 139 CZ68
Honiton Rd., Rom. 127 FD58
Honiton Rd., Well. 165 ET82
Honley Rd. SE6 183 EB87
Honnor Rd., Stai. 174 BK94
Honor Oak Pk. SE23 183 DX86
Honor Oak Ri. SE23 182 DW86
Honor Oak Rd. SE23 182 DW88
Hoo, The, Harl. 36 EW10
Hood Ave. N14 81 DH44
Hood Ave. SW14 178 CQ85
Hood Ave., Orp. 206 EV99
Hood Clo., Croy. 201 DP102
Parson's Mead
Hood Ct. EC4 274 E9
Hood Rd. SW20 179 CT94
Hood Rd., Rain. 147 FE68
Hood Wk., Rom. 105 FB53
Hoodcote Gdns. N21 99 DP45
Hook, The, Barn. 80 DD44
Hook Fm. Rd., Brom. 204 EK99
Hook Gate, Enf. 82 DV36
Hook Grn. La., Dart. 187 FF90
Hook Grn. Rd., Grav. 190 FY94
Hook Heath Ave., Wok. 226 AV119
Hook Heath Gdns., Wok. 226 AT121
Hook Heath Rd., Wok. 226 AT121
Hook Hill, S.Croy. 220 DS110
Hook Hill La., Wok. 226 AV121
Hook Hill Pk., Wok. 226 AV121
Hook La., Guil. 260 BN140
Hook La., Pot.B. 64 DF32
Hook La., Rom. 86 EZ44
Hook La., Well. 165 ET84
Hook Ri. N., Surb. 198 CN104
Hook Ri. S., Surb. 198 CN104
Hook Rd., Chess. 215 CK106
Hook Rd., Epsom 216 CQ108
Hook Rd., Surb. 198 CL104
Hook Wk., Edg. 96 CQ51
Hooke Rd., Lthd. 245 BT125
Hookers Rd. E17 123 DX55
Hookfield, Epsom 216 CQ113
Hookfield, Harl. 51 ES17
Hookfields, Grav. 190 GE90
Hooking Grn., Har. 116 CB57
Hooks Clo. SE15 162 DV81
Woods Rd.
Hooks Hall Dr., Dag. 127 FC62
Hooks Way SE22 182 DU88
Dulwich Common
Hookstone Way, Wdf.Grn. 102 EK52
Hookwood Cor., Oxt. 254 EH128
Hookwood La.
Hookwood La., Oxt. 254 EH128
Hookwood Rd., Orp. 224 EW111
Hooley La., Red. 266 DF135
Hoop La. NW11 119 CZ59
Hooper Rd. E16 144 EG72
Hooper St. E1 142 DU73
Hooper's Ct. SW3 276 D5
Hoopers Yd., Sev. 257 FJ126
High St.
Hop Flds., Wok. 226 AY116
Hop Gdns. WC2 141 DL73
St. Martin's La.
Hope Clo. N1 142 DQ65
Wallace Rd.
Hope Clo. SE12 184 EH90
Hope Clo., Sutt. 218 DC106
Hope Clo., Wdf.Grn. 102 EJ51
West Gro.
Hope Grn., Wat. 59 BU33
Hope Pk., Brom. 184 EF94
Hope Rd., Swans. 190 FZ86
High St.
Hope St. SW11 160 DD83
Hope Ter., Grays 169 FX78
Hopedale Rd. SE7 164 EH79
Hopefield Ave. NW6 139 CY68
Hopes Clo., Houns. 156 CA79
Old Cote Dr.
Hopetown St. E1 142 DT71
Brick La.
Hopewell Dr., Grav. 191 GM92
Hopewell St. SE5 162 DR80
Hopewell Yd. SE5 162 DR80
Hopfield Ave., W.Byf. 212 BL112
Hopgarden La., Sev. 256 FG128
Hopgood St. W12 139 CW74
Macfarlane Rd.
Hopground Clo., St.Alb. 43 CG22
Hopkins Clo. N10 98 DG52
Cromwell Rd.
Hopkins Clo., Rom. 128 FJ55
Hopkins St. W1 273 L9
Hopkinsons Pl. NW1 140 DG67
Fitzroy Rd.
Hoppers Rd. N13 99 DN47
Hoppers Rd. N21 99 DN47
Hoppett Rd. E4 102 EE47
Hoppety, The, Tad. 233 CX122
Hopping La. N1 141 DP65
St. Mary's Gro.
Hoppingwood Ave., N.Mal. 198 CS97
Hoppit Rd., Wal.Abb. 67 EB33
Hoppner Rd., Hayes 135 BQ68
Hopton Gdns. SE1 278 G2
Hopton Gdns., N.Mal. 199 CU100
Hopton Rd. SW16 181 DL92
Hopton St. SE1 278 G2
Hopton St. SE1 141 DP74
Hopwood Clo. SW17 180 DC90
Burmester Rd.
Hopwood Rd. SE17 162 DR79
Hopwood Wk. E8 142 DU66
Wilman Gro.
Horace Ave., Rom. 127 FC60
Horace Rd. E7 124 EH63
Horace Rd., Ilf. 125 EQ55
Horace Rd., Kings.T. 198 CM97
Horatio Ct. SE16 142 DW74
Rotherhithe St.
Horatio Pl. SW19 180 DA94
Kingston Rd.
Horatio St. E2 142 DU68
Horatius Way, Croy. 219 DM106
Horbury Cres. W11 140 DA73
Horbury Ms. W11 139 CZ73
Ladbroke Rd.
Horder Rd. SW6 159 CY81
Hordle Gdns., St.Alb. 43 CF21
Hordle Prom. E. SE15 162 DT80
Daniel Gdns.
Hordle Prom. N. SE15 162 DT80
Daniel Gdns.
Hordle Prom. S. SE15 162 DT80
Pentridge St.
Hordle Prom. W. SE15 162 DS80
Diamond St.
Horizon Way SE7 164 EH77
Horksley Gdns., Brwd. 109 GC44
Bannister Dr.
Horley Clo., Bexh. 186 FA85
Horley Lo. La., Red. 266 DF143
Horley Rd. SE9 184 EL91
Horley Rd., Red. 266 DF136
Horley Row, Horl. 268 DF147
Hormead Rd. W9 139 CZ70
Horn Clo., Hert. 32 DQ11
Horn La. SE10 164 EG77
Horn La. W3 138 CQ74
Horn La., Bexh. 167 FC82
Horn La., Wdf.Grn. 102 EG51
Horn Pk. Clo. SE12 184 EH85
Horn Pk. La. SE12 184 EH85
Hornbeam Ave., Upmin. 128 FN63
Hornbeam Clo. SE11 278 D8
Hornbeam Clo., Borwd. 78 CN39
Hornbeam Clo., Brwd. 109 GB48
Hornbeam Clo., Buck.H. 102 EK48
Hornbeam Rd.
Hornbeam Clo., Epp. 85 ER37
Hornbeam Clo., Hert. 31 DP08
Hornbeam Clo., Nthlt. 116 BZ64
Hornbeam Cres., Brent. 157 CH80
Hornbeam Gdns., Slou. 152 AU76
Upton Rd.
Hornbeam Gro. E4 102 EE48
Hornbeam La. E4 84 EE43
Hornbeam La., Bexh. 167 FC82
Hornbeam La., Hat. 46 DE21
Hornbeam La., Hert. 46 DG23
Hornbeam Rd., Buck.H. 102 EK48
Hornbeam Rd., Epp. 85 ER37
Hornbeam Rd., Guil. 242 AW131
Hornbeam Rd., Hayes 136 BW71
Hornbeam Rd., Reig. 266 DB137
Hornbeam Ter., Cars. 200 DE102
Hornbeam Twr. E11 123 ED62
Hollydown Way
Hornbeam Wk., Rich. 178 CM89
Hornbeam Wk., Walt. 213 BT109
Octagon Rd.
Hornbeam Way, Brom. 205 EN100
Hornbeam Way, Wal.Cr. 66 DT29
Hornbeams, St.Alb. 60 BZ30
Hornbeams, The, Harl. 35 EQ13
Hornbeams Ave., Enf. 82 DW35
Hornbeams Ri. N11 98 DG51
Hornbill Clo., Uxb. 134 BK72
Hornblower Clo. SE16 163 DY77
Greenland Quay
Hornbuckle Clo., Har. 117 CD61
Hornby Clo. NW3 140 DD66
Horncastle Clo. SE12 184 EG87
Horncastle Rd. SE12 184 EG87
Hornchurch Clo., Kings.T. 177 CK92
Dukes Ave.
Hornchurch Hill, Whyt. 236 DT117
Hornchurch Rd., Horn. 127 FF60
Horndean Clo. SW15 179 CU88
Bessborough Rd.
Horndon Clo., Rom. 105 FC53
Horndon Grn., Rom. 105 FC53
Horndon Rd., Rom. 105 FC53
Horne Rd., Shep. 194 BM98
Horne Way SW15 159 CW82
Horner La., Mitch. 200 DD96
Hornets, The, Wat. 75 BV42
Hornfair Rd. SE7 164 EJ79
Hornford Way, Rom. 127 FE59
Hornhatch, Guil. 259 BB140
Hornhatch Clo., Guil. 259 BB140
Hornhatch La., Guil. 259 BA140
Hornhill Rd., Ger.Cr. 91 BB50
Hornhill Rd., Rick. 91 BD50
Horniman Dr. SE23 182 DV88
Horning Clo. SE9 184 EL91
Hornminster Glen, Horn. 128 FN61
Horns End, Pnr. 116 BW56
Horns Mill Rd., Hert. 32 DQ12
Horns Rd., Hert. 32 DQ10
Horns Rd., Ilf. 125 ER58
Hornsby La., Grays 171 GG75
Hornsey La. N6 121 DH60
Hornsey La. N19 121 DH60
Hornsey La. Est. N19 121 DK59
Hornsey La.
Hornsey La. Gdns. N6 121 DJ59
Hornsey Pk. Rd. N8 121 DM55
Hornsey Ri. N19 121 DK59
Hornsey Ri. Gdns. N19 121 DK59
Hornsey Rd. N7 121 DM62
Hornsey Rd. N19 121 DL60
Hornsey St. N7 121 DM64
Hornsfield, Welw.G.C. 30 DC08
Hornshay St. SE15 162 DW79
Hornton Pl. W8 160 DB75
Hornton St.
Hornton St. W8 160 DA75
Horsa Clo., Wall. 219 DL108
Kingsford Ave.
Horsa Rd. SE12 184 EJ87
Horsa Rd., Erith 167 FB80
Horse and Dolphin Yd. W1 273 N10
Horse Fair, Kings.T. 197 CK96
Wood St.
Horse Guards Ave. SW1 277 P3
Horse Guards Ave. SW1 141 DL74
Horse Guards Rd. SW1 277 N3
Horse Guards Rd. SW1 141 DK74
Horse Hill, Chesh. 56 AX32
Horse Leaze E6 145 EN72
Horse Ride SW1 277 M3
Horse Ride, Cars. 218 DF112
Horse Ride, Dor. 263 CD144
Wolvens La.
Horse Ride, Lthd. 245 BQ132
Epsom Rd.
Horse Rd. E7 124 EH62
Centre Rd.
Horse Shoe Cres., Nthlt. 136 CA68
Horse Shoe Yd. W1 273 J10
Horse Yd. N1 141 DP67
Essex Rd.
Horsebridges Clo., Dag. 146 EY67
Horsecroft, Bans. 233 CZ117
Lyme Regis Rd.
Horsecroft Clo., Harl. 50 EL16
Horsecroft Clo., Orp. 206 EV102
Horsecroft Rd., Edg. 96 CR52
Horsecroft Rd., Harl. 50 EL16
Horsecroft Rd., Hem.H. 40 BG22
Horseferry Pl. SE10 163 EC79
Horseferry Rd. E14 143 DX73
Horseferry Rd. SW1 277 M7
Horseferry Rd. SW1 161 DK77
Horsehill, Horl. 268 DA146
Horselers, Hem.H. 40 BN23
Horsell Birch, Wok. 226 AV115
Horsell Common, Wok. 210 AV114
Horsell Common Rd., Wok. 210 AW114
Horsell Ct., Cher. 194 BH101
Stepgates
Horsell Moor, Wok. 226 AX117
Horsell Pk., Wok. 226 AX116
Horsell Pk. Clo., Wok. 226 AX116
Horsell Ri., Wok. 226 AX115
Horsell Ri. Clo., Wok. 226 AX115
Horsell Rd. N5 121 DN64
Horsell Rd., Orp. 206 EV95
Horsell Vale, Wok. 226 AY115
Horsell Way, Wok. 226 AW116
Horselydown La. SE1 279 P4
Horselydown La. SE1 162 DT75
Horseman Side, Brwd. 105 FH46
Horsemans Ride, St.Alb. 60 CA25
Horsemoor Clo., Slou. 153 BA77
Parlaunt Rd.
Horsenden Ave., Grnf. 117 CE64
Horsenden Cres., Grnf. 117 CF64
Horsenden La. N., Grnf. 137 CF65
Horsenden La. S., Grnf. 137 CG67
Horseshoe, The, Bans. 233 CZ115
Horseshoe, The, Couls. 219 DK113
Horseshoe, The, Hem.H. 41 BQ22
Horseshoe Clo. E14 163 EC78
Ferry St.
Horseshoe Clo. NW2 119 CV61
Horseshoe Clo., Wal.Abb. 68 EG34
Horseshoe Cres., Beac. 89 AL54
Horseshoe Grn., Sutt. 200 DB103
Aultone Way
Horseshoe Hill, Slou. 110 AJ63
Horseshoe Hill, Wal.Abb. 68 EH33
Horseshoe La. N20 97 CX46
Horseshoe La., Enf. 82 DQ41
Chase Side
Horseshoe La., Wat. 59 BV32
Horseshoe La. E., Guil. 243 BB133
Horseshoe La. W., Guil. 243 BB133
Horseshoe Ridge, Wey. 213 BQ111
Horsfeld Gdns. SE9 184 EL85
Horsfeld Rd. SE9 184 EK85
Horsfield Clo., Dart. 188 FQ87
Horsford Rd. SW2 181 DM85
Horsham Ave. N12 98 DE50
Horsham Rd., Bexh. 186 FA85
Horsham Rd., Dor. 263 CG137
Horsham Rd. (North Holmwood), Dor. 263 CH140
Horsham Rd. (Sutton), Dor. 261 BT142
Horsham Rd., Felt. 175 BQ86
Horsham Rd., Guil. 258 AX142
Horsley Clo., Epsom 216 CR113
Horsley Dr., Croy. 221 EC108
Horsley Dr., Kings.T. 177 CK92
Richmond Rd.
Horsley Rd. E4 101 EC47
Horsley Rd., Brom. 204 EH95
Palace Rd.
Horsley Rd., Cob. 229 BU122
Horsley St. SE17 162 DR79
Horsleys, Rick. 91 BD50
Horsmonden Clo., Orp. 205 ET101
Horsmonden Rd. SE4 183 DZ85
Hortensia Rd. SW10 160 DC80
Horticultural Pl. W4 158 CR78
Heathfield Ter.
Horton Ave. NW2 119 CY63
Horton Bri. Rd., West Dr. 134 BM74
Horton Clo., Maid. 130 AC70
Horton Clo., West Dr. 134 BM74
Horton Gdns., Epsom 216 CQ111
Horton Hill
Horton Hill, Epsom 216 CQ111
Horton Ind. Pk., West Dr. 134 BM74
Horton La., Epsom 216 CP109
Horton Rd. E8 142 DV65
Horton Rd. (Horton Kirby), Dart. 208 FQ98
Horton Rd., Slou. 153 BA82
Horton Rd. (Datchet), Slou. 152 AV80
Horton Rd. (Poyle), Slou. 153 BE83
Horton Rd., Stai. 174 BG85
Horton Rd., West Dr. 134 BL74
Horton St. SE13 163 EB83
Horton Way, Croy. 203 DX99
The Glade
Horton Way (Farningham), Dart. 208 FM101
Hortons Way, West. 255 ER126
Hortus Rd. E4 101 EC47
Hortus Rd., Sthl. 156 BZ75
Horvath Clo., Wey. 213 BR105
Horwood Ct., Wat. 76 BX37
Hosack Rd. SW17 180 DF88
Hoser Ave. SE12 184 EG89
Hosey Common Rd., Eden. 255 EQ133
Hosey Common Rd., West. 255 ER130
Hosey Hill, West. 255 ER127
Hosier La. EC1 274 F7
Hosier La. EC1 141 DP71
Hoskins Clo. E16 144 EJ72
Hoskins Clo., Hayes 155 BT78
Cranford Dr.
Hoskins Rd., Oxt. 254 EE129
Hoskins St. SE10 163 ED78
Hoskins Wk., Oxt. 254 EE129
Station Rd. W.
Hospital Bri. Rd., Twick. 176 CB87
Hospital Hill, Chesh. 54 AQ32
Hospital La., Islw. 177 CF85
Hospital Rd. E9 123 DX64
Homerton Row
Hospital Rd., Houns. 156 CA83
Hospital Rd., Sev. 257 FJ121
Hospital Way SE13 183 ED86
Stainton Rd.
Hotham Clo. (Sutton at Hone), Dart. 188 FN94
Hotham Clo., W.Mol. 196 CA97
Garrick Gdns.
Hotham Rd. SW15 159 CW83
Hotham Rd. SW19 180 DC94
Hotham Rd. Ms. SW19 180 DC94
Haydons Rd.
Hotham St. E15 144 EE67
Hothfield Pl. SE16 162 DW76
Lower Rd.
Hotspur Rd., Nthlt. 136 CA68
Hotspur St. SE11 278 D10
Hotspur St. SE11 161 DN78
Houblon Rd., Rich. 178 CL85
Houblons Hill, Epp. 70 EW31
Houghton Clo. E8 142 DT65
Buttermere Wk.
Houghton Clo., Hmptn. 176 BY93
Houghton Rd. N15 122 DT57
West Grn. Rd.
Houghton St. WC2 274 C9
Houlder Cres., Croy. 219 DP107
Hound Ho. Rd., Guil. 260 BN141
Houndsden Rd. N21 81 DM44
Houndsditch EC3 275 N8
Houndsditch EC3 142 DS72
Houndsfield Rd. N9 100 DV45
Hounslow Ave., Houns. 176 CB85
Hounslow Gdns., Houns. 176 CB85
Hounslow Rd. (Feltham), Felt. 175 BV88
Hounslow Rd. (Hanworth), Felt. 176 BX91
Hounslow Rd., Twick. 176 CB86
House La., St.Alb. 43 CK16
Houseman Way SE5 162 DR80
Hopewell St.
Housewood End, Hem.H. 40 BH17
Houston Pl., Esher 197 CE102
Lime Tree Ave.
Houston Rd. SE23 183 DY89
Hove Ave. E17 123 DZ57
Hove Clo., Brwd. 109 GC47
Hove Gdns., Sutt. 200 DB102
Hoveden Rd. NW2 119 CY64
Hoveton Rd. SE28 146 EW72
How La., Couls. 234 DF119
How Wd., St.Alb. 60 CB28
Howard Agne Clo., Hem.H. 57 BA27
Howard Ave., Bex. 186 EW88
Howard Ave., Epsom 217 CU110
Howard Ave., Slou. 131 AR71
Howard Business Pk., Wal.Abb. 67 ED33
Howard Clo.
Howard Clo. N11 98 DG47
Howard Clo. NW2 119 CY63
Howard Clo. W3 138 CP72
Howard Clo., Ash. 232 CM118
Howard Clo., Hmptn. 176 CC93
Howard Clo., Lthd. 231 CJ123
Windmill Dr.
Howard Clo. (West Horsley), Lthd. 245 BR125
Howard Clo., Loug. 84 EL44
Roding Rd.
Howard Clo., St.Alb. 43 CH22
Howard Clo., Sun. 175 BT93
Catherine Dr.
Howard Clo., Tad. 249 CT125
Howard Clo., Wal.Abb. 67 ED33
Howard Clo., Wat. 75 BU37
Howard Clo. (Bushey), Wat. 95 CE45
Howard Cres., Beac. 89 AQ50
Howard Dr., Borwd. 78 CR42
Howard Gdns., Guil. 243 BA133
Howard Ms. N5 121 DP63
Hamilton Pk.
Howard Pl. SW1 277 K7
Howard Ridge, Guil. 243 BA130
Howard Rd. E6 145 EM68
Howard Rd. E11 124 EE62
Howard Rd. E17 123 EA55
Howard Rd. N15 122 DS58
Howard Rd. N16 122 DR63
Howard Rd. NW2 119 CX63
Howard Rd. SE20 202 DW95
Howard Rd. SE25 202 DU99
Howard Rd., Bark. 145 ER67
Howard Rd., Beac. 89 AQ50
Howard Rd., Brom. 184 EG94
Howard Rd., Chesh. 54 AP28
Howard Rd., Couls. 235 DJ115
Howard Rd., Dart. 188 FN86
Howard Rd., Dor. 263 CG136
Howard Rd. (North Holmwood), Dor. 263 CJ140
Holmesdale Rd.
Howard Rd., Grays 169 FW76
Arterial Rd. W. Thurrock
Howard Rd., Ilf. 125 EP63
Howard Rd., Islw. 157 CF83
Howard Rd., Lthd. 229 BU122
Howard Rd. (Bookham), Lthd. 246 CB127
Howard Rd., N.Mal. 198 CS97
Howard Rd., Reig. 266 DB135
Howard Rd., Sthl. 136 CB72
Howard Rd., Surb. 198 CM100
Howard Rd., Upmin. 128 FQ61
Howard St., T.Ditt. 197 CH101
Howard Wk. N2 120 DC56
Howard Way, Barn. 79 CX43
Sampson Ave.
Howard Way, Harl. 35 ET12
Howards Clo., Pnr. 93 BV54
Howards Clo., Wok. 227 BA120
Howards Crest Clo., Beck. 203 EC96
Howards Dr., Hem.H. 39 BF17
Howards La. SW15 179 CV85
Howards La., Add. 211 BE107
Howards Rd. E13 144 EG69
Howards Rd., Wok. 227 AZ120
Howards Thicket, Ger.Cr. 112 AW61
Howards Wd. Dr., Ger.Cr. 112 AX61
Howardsgate, Welw.G.C. 29 CX08
Howarth Ct. E15 123 EC64
Taylor Ct.
Howarth Rd. SE2 166 EU78
Howberry Clo., Edg. 95 CK51
Howberry Rd., Edg. 95 CK51
Howberry Rd., Stan. 95 CK51
Howberry Rd., Th.Hth. 202 DR95
Howbury La., Erith 167 FG82
Howbury Rd. SE15 162 DW83
Howcroft Cres. N3 98 DA52
Howcroft La., Grnf. 137 CD69
Cowgate Rd.
Howden Clo. SE28 146 EX73
Howden Rd. SE25 202 DT96
Howden St. SE15 162 DU83
Howe Clo., Rad. 62 CL32
King Charles Rd.
Howe Clo., Rom. 104 FA53
Howe Dell, Hat. 45 CV18
Howe Dr., Beac. 89 AK50
Howe Dr., Cat. 236 DR122
Howe Rd., Hem.H. 40 BN22
Howell Clo., Rom. 126 EX57
Howell Hill Clo., Epsom 217 CW111
Howell Hill Gro., Epsom 217 CW110
Howell Wk. SE1 278 G9
Howes Clo. N3 120 DA55
Howfield Grn., Hodd. 33 DZ14
Howgate Rd. SW14 158 CR83
Howick Pl. SW1 277 L7
Howick Pl. SW1 161 DJ76
Howicks Grn., Welw.G.C. 30 DA12
Howie St. SW11 160 DE80
Howitt Rd. NW3 140 DE65
Howland Est. SE16 162 DW76
Lower Rd.
Howland Garth, St.Alb. 42 CC24

Howland Ms. E. W1 273 L6
Howland St. W1 273 K6
Howland St. W1 141 DJ71
Howland Way SE16 163 DY75
Howlands, Welw.G.C. 29 CX12
Howletts La., Ruis. 115 BQ57
Howletts Rd. SE24 182 DQ86
Howley Pl. W2 140 DC71
Howley Rd., Croy. 201 DP104
Hows Clo., Uxb. 134 BJ67
Hows Rd.
Hows Mead, Epp. 53 FD24
Hows Rd., Uxb. 134 BJ67
Hows St. E2 142 DT68
Howsman Rd. SW13 159 CU79
Howson Rd. SE4 163 DY84
Howson Ter., Rich. 178 CL86
Howton Pl. (Bushey), Wat. 95 CD46
Hoxton Mkt. N1 275 M3
Hoxton Sq. N1 275 M3
Hoxton Sq. N1 142 DS69
Hoxton St. N1 142 DS67
Hoy St. E16 144 EF72
Hoy Ter., Grays 169 FX78
Hoylake Cres., Uxb. 114 BN61
Hoylake Gdns., Mitch. 201 DJ97
Hoylake Gdns., Rom. 106 FN52
Hoylake Gdns., Ruis. 115 BV60
Hoylake Gdns., Wat. 94 BX49
Hoylake Rd. W3 138 CS72
Hoyland Clo. SE15 162 DV80
Commercial Way
Hoyle Rd. SW17 180 DE92
Hubbard Dr., Chess. 215 CJ107
Mansfield Rd.
Hubbard Rd. SE27 182 DQ91
Hubbard St. E15 144 EE67
Hubbards Chase, Horn. 128 FN57
Hubbards Clo., Horn. 128 FN57
Hubbard's Hill, Sev. 257 FH130
Hubbards Rd., Rick. 73 BD43
Hubbinet Ind. Est., Rom. 127 FC55
Hubert Day Clo., Beac. 89 AK52
Seeleys Rd.
Hubert Gro. SW9 161 DL83
Hubert Rd. E6 144 EK69
Hubert Rd., Brwd. 108 FV48
Hubert Rd., Rain. 147 FF69
Hubert Rd., Slou. 152 AX76
Hubert Rd. Ind. Est., Brwd. 108 FV48
Hucknall Clo., Rom. 106 FM51
Huddart St. E3 143 DZ71
Huddleston Clo. E2 142 DW68
Huddleston Rd. N7 121 DJ62
Huddlestone Cres., Red. 251 DK128
Huddlestone Rd. E7 124 EF63
Huddlestone Rd. NW2 139 CV65
Hudons Clo., Grays 169 FT78
Motherwell Way
Hudson Ave., Uxb. 113 BF58
Hudson Clo., St.Alb. 43 CD22
Hudson Clo., Wat. 75 BT36
Hudson Ct. SW19 180 DB94
Hudson Ct., Guil. 242 AT133
Cobbett Rd.
Hudson Gdns., Orp. 223 ET107
High St.
Hudson Pl. SE18 165 EQ78
Hudson Rd., Bexh. 166 EZ82
Hudson Rd., Hayes 155 BR79
Hudsons, Tad. 233 CX121
Hudson's Pl. SW1 277 K8
Huggin Ct. EC4 275 J10
Huggin Hill EC4 275 J10
Huggins La., Hat. 45 CW23
Hugh Ms. SW1 277 J9
Hugh Pl. SW1 277 M8
Hugh St. SW1 277 J9
Hugh St. SW1 161 DH77
Hughan Rd. E15 123 ED64
Hughenden Ave., Har. 117 CH57
Hughenden Gdns., Nthlt. 136 BW69
Hughenden Rd., St.Alb. 43 CH17
Hughenden Rd., Slou. 131 AR72
Hughenden Rd., Wor.Pk. 199 CU101
Hughendon Ter. E15 123 EC63
Westdown Rd.
Hughes Rd., Ashf. 175 BQ94
Hughes Rd., Grays 171 GG76
Hughes Rd., Hayes 135 BU73
Hughes Wk., Croy. 202 DQ101
St. Saviours Rd.
Hugh's Twr., Harl. 35 ER14
Hugo Gdns., Rain. 147 FF65
Hugo Rd. N19 121 DJ63
Hugon Rd. SW6 160 DB83
Huguenot Pl. E1 142 DT71
Heneage St.
Huguenot Pl. SW18 180 DC85
Huguenot Sq. SE15 162 DV83
Scylla Rd.
Hull Clo. SE16 163 DX75
Hull Clo., Slou. 151 AQ75
Hull Clo., Sutt. 218 DB110
Yardbridge Clo.
Hull Gro., Harl. 51 EN20
Hull St. EC1 275 H3
Hullbridge Ms. N1 142 DR67
Sherborne St.
Hulletts La., Brwd. 108 FT43
Hulse Ave., Bark. 145 ER65
Hulse Ave., Rom. 105 FB53
Hulsewood Clo., Dart. 187 FH90
Hulton Clo., Lthd. 231 CJ123
Windmill Dr.
Hulverston Clo., Sutt. 218 DB110
Humber Ave., S.Ock. 149 FT72
Humber Dr. W10 139 CW70
Barlby Rd.
Humber Dr., Upmin. 129 FR58
Humber Rd. NW2 119 CV61
Humber Rd. SE3 164 EF79
Humber Rd., Dart. 188 FK85
Humber Way, Slou. 153 BA77
Humberstone Rd. E13 144 EJ69
Humberton Clo. E9 123 DY64
Marsh Hill
Humbolt Clo., Guil. 242 AS134
Humbolt Rd. W6 159 CY79
Hume Ave., Til. 171 GG83
Hume Ter. E16 144 EJ72
Prince Regent La.
Hume Way, Ruis. 115 BU58
Humes Ave. W7 157 CE76
Hummer Rd., Egh. 173 BA91
Humphrey Clo., Ilf. 103 EM53
Humphrey Clo., Lthd. 230 CC122
Humphrey St. SE1 279 P10
Humphrey St. SE1 162 DT78
Humphries Clo., Dag. 126 EZ63
Hundred Acre NW9 97 CT54
Hundred Acres La., Amer. 55 AR40
Hungerdown E4 101 EC46
Hungerford Ave., Slou. 132 AS71
Hungerford Bri. SE1 278 B3
Hungerford Bri. SE1 141 DM74
Hungerford Bri. WC2 278 B3
Hungerford Bri. WC2 141 DM74
Hungerford La. WC2 278 A2
Hungerford Rd. N7 141 DK65
Hungerford Sq., Wey. 213 BR105
Rosslyn Pk.
Hungerford St. E1 142 DV72
Commercial Rd.
Hungry Hill, Wok. 228 BK124
Hungry Hill La.
Hungry Hill La., Wok. 228 BK124
Hunsdon, Welw.G.C. 30 DD09
Hunsdon Clo., Dag. 146 EY65
Hunsdon Dr., Sev. 257 FH123
Hunsdon Rd. SE14 163 DX80
Hunsdon Rd., Ware 33 ED11
Hunsdon Rd. 34 EE11
(Stanstead Abbots), Ware
Hunslett St. E2 142 DW68
Royston St.
Hunston Rd., Mord. 200 DB102
Hunt Clo., St.Alb. 43 CK17
Villiers Cres.
Hunt Rd., Grav. 190 GE90
Hunt Rd., Sthl. 156 CA76
Hunt St. W11 139 CX74
Hunt Way SE22 182 DU88
Dulwich Common
Hunter Ave., Brwd. 109 GA44
Hunter Clo. SE1 279 L7
Hunter Clo. SW12 180 DG88
Balham Pk. Rd.
Hunter Clo., Borwd. 78 CQ43
Hunter Clo., Pot.B. 64 DB33
Hunter Dr., Horn. 128 FJ63
Hunter Ho., Felt. 175 BU88
Hunter Rd. SW20 199 CW95
Hunter Rd., Guil. 258 AY135
Hunter Rd., Ilf. 125 EP64
Hunter Rd., Th.Hth. 202 DR97
Hunter St. WC1 274 A4
Hunter St. WC1 141 DL70
Hunter Wk. E13 144 EG67
Stratford Rd.
Hunter Wk., Borwd. 78 CQ43
Ashley Dr.
Huntercombe Clo., Maid. 130 AH72
Huntercombe La., Slou. 130 AJ71
Huntercombe La. N., 130 AJ72
Maid.
Huntercombe La. S., Maid. 130 AH74
Huntercombe Spur, Slou. 130 AJ73
Huntercrombe Gdns., Wat. 94 BW50
Hunters, The, Beck. 203 EC95
Hunters Clo., Bex. 187 FE90
Hunters Clo., Chesh. 54 AN30
Hunters Clo., Epsom 216 CQ113
Marshalls Clo.
Hunters Clo., Hem.H. 57 BA29
Hunters Ct., Rich. 177 CK85
Friars La.
Hunters Gro., Har. 117 CJ56
Hunters Gro., Hayes 135 BU74
Hunters Gro., Orp. 223 EQ105
State Fm. Ave.
Hunters Gro., Rom. 105 FB50
Hunters Hall Rd., Dag. 126 FA63
Hunters Hill, Ruis. 116 BW62
Hunters La., Wat. 59 BT33
Hunters Meadow SE19 182 DS91
Dulwich Wd. Ave.
Hunters Oak, Hem.H. 41 BP15
Hunters Pk., Berk. 38 AY18
Hunters Reach, Wal.Cr. 66 DT29
Hunters Ride, St.Alb. 60 CA31
Hunters Rd., Chess. 198 CL104
Hunters Sq., Dag. 126 FA63
Hunters Wk., Sev. 224 EY114
Rushmore Hill
Hunters Way, Croy. 220 DS105
Brownlow Rd.
Hunters Way, Enf. 81 DN39
Hunters Way, Welw.G.C. 29 CZ12
Huntersfield Clo., Reig. 250 DB131
Hunting Clo., Esher 214 CA105
Hunting Gate, Hem.H. 40 BL16
Hunting Gate Clo., Enf. 81 DN41
Hunting Gate Dr., Chess. 216 CL108
Hunting Gate Ms., Sutt. 200 DB104
Hunting Gate Ms., Twick. 177 CE88
Colne Rd.
Huntingdon Clo., Brox. 49 DY24
Huntingdon Clo., Mitch. 201 DL98
Huntingdon Gdns. W4 158 CQ80
Huntingdon Gdns., 199 CW104
Wor.Pk.
Huntingdon Rd. N2 120 DE55
Huntingdon Rd. N9 100 DW46
Huntingdon Rd., Red. 250 DF134
Huntingdon Rd., Wok. 226 AT117
Huntingdon St. E16 144 EF72
Huntingdon St. N1 141 DM66
Huntingfield, Croy. 221 DZ108
Huntingfield Rd. SW15 159 CU84
Huntingfield Way, Egh. 173 BD93
Huntings Rd., Dag. 146 FA65
Huntland Clo., Rain. 147 FH71
Huntley Ave., Grav. 190 GB86
Huntley Dr. N3 98 DA51
Huntley St. WC1 273 L5
Huntley St. WC1 141 DJ70
Huntley Way SW20 199 CU96
Huntly Rd. SE25 202 DS98
Hunton Bri. Hill, Kings L. 59 BQ33
Hunton Bri. Ind. Est., 59 BQ33
Kings L.
Hunton St. E1 142 DU71
Hunt's Clo. SE3 164 EG82
Hunt's Ct. WC2 277 N1
Hunts La. E15 143 EC68
Hunts La., Maid. 130 AE68
Hunts Mead, Enf. 83 DX41
Hunts Mead Clo., Chis. 185 EM94
Bullers Wd. Dr.
Hunts Slip Rd. SE21 182 DS90
Huntsman Clo., Warl. 236 DW119
Huntsman Rd., Ilf. 104 EU51
Huntsman St. SE17 279 L9
Huntsman St. SE17 162 DS77
Huntsmans Clo., Felt. 175 BV91
Huntsmans Clo., Lthd. 231 CD124
The Grn.
Huntsmans Dr., Upmin. 128 FQ64
Huntsmill Rd., Hem.H. 39 BE21
Huntsmoor Rd., Epsom 216 CR106
Huntspill St. SW17 180 DC90
Huntswood La., Maid. 130 AE66
Huntsworth La., Slou. 130 AF67
Huntsworth Ms. NW1 272 D5
Hurley Clo., Walt. 195 BV103
Hurley Cres. SE16 163 DX75
Marlow Way
Hurley Gdns., Guil. 243 BA130
Hurley Rd., Grnf. 136 CB72
Hurlfield, Dart. 188 FJ90
Hurlford, Wok. 226 AU117
Hurlingham Ct. SW6 159 CZ83
Hurlingham Gdns. SW6 159 CZ83
Hurlingham Rd. SW6 159 CZ82
Hurlingham Rd., Bexh. 166 EZ80
Hurlingham Sq. SW6 160 DB83
Peterborough Rd.
Hurlock St. N5 121 DP62
Hurlstone Rd. SE25 202 DR99
Hurn Ct. Rd., Houns. 156 BX82
Renfrew Rd.
Hurnford Clo., S.Croy. 220 DS110
Huron Clo., Orp. 223 ET107
High St.
Huron Rd. SW17 180 DG89
Hurren Clo. SE3 164 EE83
Hurricane Way, Abb.L. 59 BU32
Langley La.
Hurricane Way, Epp. 70 FA27
Hurry Clo. E15 144 EE66
Hurst Ave. E4 101 EA49
Hurst Ave. N6 121 DJ58
Hurst Clo. E4 101 EA48
Hurst Clo. NW11 120 DB58
Hurst Clo., Brom. 204 EF102
Hurst Clo., Chess. 216 CN106
Hurst Clo., Nthlt. 136 BZ65
Hurst Clo., Welw.G.C. 30 DC10
Hurst Clo., Wok. 226 AW120
Hurst Cft., Guil. 258 AY137
Hurst Dr., Tad. 249 CU126
Hurst Dr., Wal.Cr. 67 DX34
Hurst Est. SE2 166 EX78
Hurst Grn. Clo., Oxt. 254 EG132
Hurst Grn. Rd., Oxt. 254 EF132
Hurst Gro., Walt. 195 BT102
Hurst La. SE2 166 EX78
Hurst La., E.Mol. 196 CC98
Hurst La., Egh. 193 BA96
Hurst La., Epsom 232 CQ124
Hurst Pk. Ave., Horn. 128 FL63
Newmarket Way
Hurst Pl., Nthwd. 93 BP53
Hurst Ri., Barn. 80 DA41
Hurst Rd. E17 123 EB55
Hurst Rd. N21 99 DN46
Hurst Rd., Bex. 186 EW88
Hurst Rd., Buck.H. 102 EK46
Hurst Rd., Croy. 220 DR106
Hurst Rd., E.Mol. 196 CA97
Hurst Rd., Epsom 216 CR111
Hurst Rd. (Headley), 232 CR123
Epsom
Hurst Rd., Erith 167 FC81
Hurst Rd., Horl. 268 DE147
Hurst Rd., Sid. 186 EU89
Hurst Rd., Slou. 131 AK71
Hurst Rd., Tad. 233 CU123
Hurst Rd., Walt. 196 BW99
Hurst Rd., W.Mol. 196 CA97
Hurst Springs, Bex. 186 EY88
Hurst St. SE24 181 DP86
Hurst Vw. Rd., S.Croy. 220 DS108
Hurst Way, Sev. 257 FJ127
Hurst Way, S.Croy. 220 DS107
Hurst Way, Wok. 211 BE114
Hurstbourne, Esher 215 CF107
Hurstbourne Gdns., Bark. 145 ES65
Hurstbourne Rd. SE23 183 DY88
Hurstcourt Rd., Sutt. 200 DB102
Hurstdene Ave., Brom. 204 EF102
Hurstdene Ave., Stai. 174 BH93
Hurstdene Gdns. N15 122 DS59
Hurstfield, Brom. 204 EG99
Hurstfield Cres., Hayes 135 BS70
Hurstfield Dr., Maid. 130 AH72
Hurstfield Rd., W.Mol. 196 CA97
Hurstlands, Oxt. 254 EG132
Hurstlands Clo., Horn. 128 FJ59
Hurstleigh Clo., Red. 250 DF132
Hurstleigh Dr., Red. 250 DF132
Hurstleigh Gdns., Ilf. 103 EM53
Hurstlings, Welw.G.C. 30 DB10
Hurstmead Ct., Edg. 96 CP49
Hurstway Wk. W11 139 CX73
Whitchurch Rd.
Hurstwood Ave. E18 124 EH56
Hurstwood Ave., Bex. 186 EY88
Hurstwood Ave., Bexh. 167 FE81
Hurstwood Ave., Brwd. 108 FV45
Ongar Rd.
Hurstwood Ave., Erith 167 FE81
Hurstwood Ct., Upmin. 128 FP60
Hurstwood Dr., Brom. 205 EM97
Hurstwood Rd. NW11 119 CY56
Hurtwood Rd., Walt. 196 BZ101
Hurworth Rd., Slou. 152 AW76
Huson Clo. NW3 140 DE66
Husseywell Cres., Brom. 204 EG102
Hutchings Clo., Horn. 128 FL62
Hutchings Rd., Beac. 89 AK50
Hutchings St. E14 163 EA75
Hutchings Wk. NW11 120 DB56
Hutchingsons Rd., Croy. 221 EC111
Hutchins Clo. E15 143 EC66
Gibbins Rd.
Hutchins Way, Horl. 268 DF146
Hutchinson Ter., Wem. 117 CK62
Hutton Clo., Grnf. 117 CD64
Mary Peters Dr.
Hutton Clo., Hert. 31 DN09
Hutton Clo., Wdf.Grn. 102 EH51
Hutton Dr., Brwd. 109 GC45
Hutton Gdns., Har. 94 CC52
Hutton Wk.
Hutton Gate, Brwd. 109 GB45
Hutton Gro. N12 98 DB50
Hutton Ind. Est., Brwd. 109 GE43
Hutton La., Har. 94 CC52
Hutton Rd., Brwd. 109 FZ45
Hutton Row, Edg. 96 CQ52
Pavilion Way
Hutton St. EC4 274 E9
Hutton Village, Brwd. 109 GE44
Hutton Wk., Har. 94 CC52
Huxbear St. SE4 183 DZ85
Huxley Clo., Nthlt. 136 BY67
Huxley Clo., Uxb. 134 BK70
Huxley Dr., Rom. 126 EV59
Huxley Gdns. NW10 138 CM69
Huxley Par. N18 100 DQ50
Huxley Pl. N13 99 DP48
Huxley Rd. E10 123 EC61
Huxley Rd. N18 100 DR49
Huxley Rd., Well. 165 ET83
Huxley Sayze N18 100 DQ50
Huxley St. W10 139 CY69
Hyacinth Clo., Hmptn. 176 CA93
Gresham Rd.
Hyacinth Ct., Pnr. 116 BW55
Tulip Ct.
Hyacinth Dr., Uxb. 134 BL66
Hyacinth Rd. SW15 179 CU88
Hyburn Clo., Hem.H. 41 BP21
Hyburn Clo., St.Alb. 60 BZ30
Hycliffe Gdns., Chig. 103 EQ49
Hyde, The NW9 118 CS56
Hyde, The, Ware 32 DV05
Hyde Ave., Pot.B. 64 DB33
Hyde Clo. E13 144 EG68
Pelly Rd.
Hyde Clo., Ashf. 175 BS93
Hyde Ter.
Hyde Clo., Barn. 79 CZ41
Hyde Ct. N20 98 DD48
Hyde Cres. NW9 118 CS57
Hyde Dr., Orp. 206 EV98
Chipperfield Rd.
Hyde Grn., Beac. 89 AM52
Hyde La. SW11 160 DE81
Battersea Bri. Rd.
Hyde La., Hem.H. 58 BN27
Hyde La. 57 AZ27
(Bovingdon), Hem.H.
Hyde La., St.Alb. 61 CE28
Hyde La., Wok. 228 BN120
Hyde Mead, Wal.Abb. 50 EE23
Hyde Meadows, 57 BA28
Hem.H.
Hyde Pk. SW7 276 B2
Hyde Pk. SW7 140 DE74
Hyde Pk. W1 276 B2
Hyde Pk. W1 140 DE74
Hyde Pk. W2 276 B2
Hyde Pk. W2 140 DE74
Hyde Pk. Ave. N21 100 DQ47
Hyde Pk. Cor. W1 276 G4
Hyde Pk. Cor. W1 160 DG75
Hyde Pk. Cres. W2 272 B9
Hyde Pk. Cres. W2 140 DE72
Hyde Pk. Gdns. N21 100 DQ46
Hyde Pk. Ave.
Hyde Pk. Gdns. W2 272 A10
Hyde Pk. Gdns. W2 140 DD73
Hyde Pk. Gdns. Ms. W2 272 A10
Hyde Pk. Gate SW7 160 DC75
Hyde Pk. Gate Ms. SW7 160 DC75
Hyde Pk. Gate
Hyde Pk. Pl. W2 272 C10
Hyde Pk. Sq. W2 272 B9
Hyde Pk. Sq. W2 140 DE72
Hyde Pk. Sq. Ms. W2 272 B9
Hyde Pk. St. W2 272 B9
Hyde Pk. St. W2 140 DE72
Hyde Rd. N1 142 DS67
Hyde Rd., Bexh. 166 EZ82
Hyde Rd., Rich. 178 CM85
Albert Rd.
Hyde Rd., S.Croy. 220 DR113
Hyde Rd., Wat. 75 BU40
Hyde St. SE8 163 EA79
Deptford High St.
Hyde Ter., Ashf. 175 BS93
Hyde Vale SE10 163 ED81
Hyde Valley, Welw.G.C. 29 CZ11
Hyde Wk., Mord. 200 DA101
Glastonbury Rd.
Hyde Way N9 100 DT47
Hyde Way, Hayes 155 BT77
Hyde Way, Welw.G.C. 29 CY09
Hydefield Clo. N21 100 DR46
Hydefield Ct. N9 100 DS47
Hyder Rd., Grays 171 GJ76
Hyderabad Way E15 144 EE66
Elliot Clo.
Hydes Pl. N1 141 DP66
Compton Ave.
Hydeside Gdns. N9 100 DT47
Hydethorpe Ave. N9 100 DT47
Hydethorpe Rd. SW12 181 DJ88
Hyland Clo., Horn. 127 FH59
Hyland Way, Horn. 127 FH59
Hylands Clo., Epsom 232 CQ115
Hylands Ms., Epsom 232 CQ115
Hylands Rd. E17 101 ED54
Hylands Rd., Epsom 232 CQ115
Hylle Clo., Wind. 151 AL81
Hylton St. SE18 165 ET77
Hyndewood SE23 183 DX90
Hyndman St. SE15 162 DV79
Hynton Rd., Dag. 126 EW61
Hyperion Ct., Hem.H. 40 BM17
Saturn Way
Hyperion Pl., Epsom 216 CR109
Hyperion Wk., Horl. 269 DH150
Hyrons Clo., Amer. 55 AS38
Hyrons La., Amer. 55 AR38
Hyrstdene, S.Croy. 219 DP105
Hyson Rd. SE16 162 DV77
Galleywall Rd.
Hythe, The, Stai. 173 BE92
Hythe Ave., Bexh. 166 EY80
Hythe Clo. N18 100 DU49
Hythe Clo., Orp. 206 EW98
Sandway Rd.
Hythe End Rd., Stai. 173 AZ89
Hythe Fld. Ave., Egh. 173 BD93
Hythe Pk. Rd., Egh. 173 BC92
Hythe Path, Th.Hth. 202 DR97
Buller Rd.
Hythe Rd. NW10 139 CU70
Hythe Rd., Stai. 173 BD92
Hythe Rd., Th.Hth. 202 DR96
Hythe St., Dart. 188 FL86
Hythe St. Lwr., Dart. 188 FL85
Hyver Hill NW7 78 CR44

I

Ian Sq., Enf. 83 DX39
Lansbury Rd.
Ibbetson Path, Loug. 85 EP41
Ibbotson Ave. E16 144 EF72
Ibbott St. E1 142 DW70
Mantus Rd.
Iberian Ave., Wall. 219 DK105
Ibis La. W4 158 CQ81
Ibis Way, Hayes 136 BX71
Willow Tree La.
Ibscott Clo., Dag. 147 FC65
Ibsley Gdns. SW15 179 CU88
Ibsley Way, Barn. 80 DE43
Icehouse Wd., Oxt. 254 EE131
Iceland Rd. E3 143 EA67
Ickburgh Est. E5 122 DV62
Ickburgh Rd.
Ickburgh Rd. E5 122 DV62
Ickenham Clo., Ruis. 115 BR61
Ickenham Rd., Ruis. 115 BQ61
Ickenham Rd., Uxb. 115 BQ61
Ickleton Rd. SE9 184 EL91
Icklingham Gate, Cob. 214 BW112
Icklingham Rd.
Icklingham Rd., Cob. 214 BW112
Icknield Clo., St.Alb. 42 BZ22
Icknield Dr., Ilf. 125 EP57
Ickworth Pk. Rd. E17 123 DY56
Ida Rd. N15 122 DR57
Ida St. E14 143 EC72
Iden Clo., Brom. 204 EE97
Idlecombe Rd. SW17 180 DG93
Idmiston Rd. E15 124 EF64
Idmiston Rd. SE27 182 DQ90
Idmiston Rd., Wor.Pk. 199 CT101
Idmiston Sq., Wor.Pk. 199 CT102
Idol La. EC3 279 M1
Idonia St. SE8 163 EA80
Iffley Clo., Uxb. 134 BK66
Iffley Rd. W6 159 CV76
Ifield Clo., Red. 266 DE136
Pendleton Rd.
Ifield Rd. SW10 160 DB79
Ifield Way, Grav. 191 GK93
Ifold Rd., Red. 266 DG136
Ifor Evans Pl. E1 143 DX70
Mile End Rd.
Ightham Rd., Erith 166 FA80
Ikea Twr. NW10 118 CR64
Ikona Ct., Wey. 213 BQ106
Ilbert St. W10 139 CX69
Ilchester Gdns. W2 140 DB73
Ilchester Pl. W14 159 CZ76
Ilchester Rd., Dag. 126 EV64
Ildersley Gro. SE21 182 DR89
Ilderton Rd. SE15 162 DW80
Ilderton Rd. SE16 162 DV78
Ilex Clo., Egh. 172 AV94
Ilex Clo., Sun. 196 BW96
Oakington Dr.
Ilex Ct., Berk. 38 AV19
Ilex Ho. N4 121 DM59
Ilex Rd. NW10 139 CT65
Ilex Way SW16 181 DN92
Ilford Hill, Ilf. 125 EN62
Ilford La., Ilf. 125 EP62
Ilfracombe Cres., Horn. 128 FJ63
Ilfracombe Gdns., Rom. 126 EV59
Ilfracombe Rd., Brom. 184 EF90
Iliffe St. SE17 278 G10
Iliffe St. SE17 161 DP78
Iliffe Yd. SE17 278 G10
Ilkeston Ct. E5 123 DX63
Overbury St.
Ilkley Clo. SE19 182 DR93
Ilkley Rd. E16 144 EJ71
Ilkley Rd., Wat. 94 BX50
Illingworth, Wind. 151 AL83
Illingworth Clo., Mitch. 200 DD97
Illingworth Way, Enf. 82 DS42
Ilmington Rd., Har. 117 CK58
Ilminster Gdns. SW11 160 DE84
Imber Clo. N14 99 DJ45
Imber Clo., Esher 197 CD102
Ember La.
Imber Ct. Ind. Est., E.Mol. 197 CD100
Imber Gro., Esher 197 CD101
Imber Pk. Rd., Esher 197 CD102
Imber St. N1 142 DR67
Imer Pl., T.Ditt. 197 CF101
Embercourt Rd.
Imperial Ave. N16 122 DT62
Victorian Rd.
Imperial Business & 191 GF86
Retail Pk., Grav.
Imperial Clo., Har. 116 CA58
Imperial College Rd. SW7 160 DD76
Imperial Cres., Wey. 195 BQ104
Churchill Dr.
Imperial Dr., Grav. 191 GM92
Imperial Dr., Har. 116 CA59
Imperial Gdns., Mitch. 201 DH97
Imperial Ms. E6 144 EJ68
Central Pk. Rd.
Imperial Rd. N22 99 DL53
Imperial Rd. SW6 160 DB81
Imperial Rd., Felt. 175 BS87
Imperial Rd., Wind. 151 AN83
Imperial Sq. SW6 160 DB81
Imperial St. E3 143 EC69
Imperial Way, Chis. 185 EQ90
Imperial Way, Croy. 219 DN107
Imperial Way, Har. 118 CL58
Imperial Way, Wat. 76 BW39
Inca Dr. SE9 185 EP87
Ince Rd., Walt. 213 BS108
Inchmery Rd. SE6 183 EB89
Inchwood, Croy. 221 EB105
Indells, Hat. 45 CT19
Independent Pl. E8 122 DT64
Downs Pk. Rd.
Independents Rd. SE3 164 EF83
Blackheath Village
Inderwick Rd. N8 121 DM57
Indescon Ct. E14 163 EA75
India Pl. WC2 141 DM73
Montreal Pl.
India Rd., Slou. 152 AV75
India St. EC3 275 P9
India Way W12 139 CV73
Indus Rd. SE7 164 EJ80
Industry Ter. SW9 161 DN83
Canterbury Cres.
Ingal Rd. E13 144 EG70
Ingate Pl. SW8 161 DH81
Ingatestone Rd. E12 124 EJ60
Ingatestone Rd. SE25 202 DV99
Ingatestone Rd., 102 EH52
Wdf.Grn.
Ingelow Rd. SW8 161 DH82
Ingels Mead, Epp. 69 ET29
Ingersoll Rd. W12 139 CV74
Ingersoll Rd., Enf. 82 DW38

Ingestre Pl. W1 273 L9
Ingestre Rd. E7 124 EG63
Ingestre Rd. NW5 121 DH63
Ingham Clo., S.Croy. 221 DX109
Ingham Rd. NW6 120 DA63
Ingham Rd., S.Croy. 220 DW109
Ingle Clo., Pnr. 116 BZ55
Inglebert St. EC1 274 D2
Ingleboro Dr., Pur. 220 DQ113
Ingleborough St. SW9 161 DN82
Ingleby Clo., Dag. 147 FB65
Ingleby Dr., Har. 117 CD62
Ingleby Gdns., Chig. 104 EV48
Ingleby Rd. N7 121 DL62
Ingleby Rd., Dag. 147 FB65
Ingleby Rd., Grays 171 GH76
Ingleby Rd., Ilf. 125 EP60
Ingleby Way, Chis. 185 EN92
Ingleby Way, Wall. 219 DJ109
Ingledew Rd. SE18 165 ER78
Inglefield, Pot.B. 64 DA30
Ingleglen, Horn. 128 FN59
Ingleglen, Slou. 111 AP64
Inglehurst, Add. 212 BH110
Inglehurst Gdns., Ilf. 125 EM57
Inglemere Rd. SE23 183 DX90
Inglemere Rd., Mitch. 180 DF94
Ingles, Welw.G.C. 29 CX06
Inglesham Wk. E9 143 DZ65
Beanacre Clo.
Ingleside, Slou. 153 BE81
Ingleside Clo., Beck. 183 EA94
Ingleside Gro. SE3 164 EF79
Inglethorpe St. SW6 159 CX81
Ingleton Ave., Well. 186 EU85
Ingleton Rd. N18 100 DU51
Ingleton Rd., Cars. 218 DE109
Ingleton St. SW9 161 DN82
Ingleway N12 98 DD51
Inglewood, Cher. 193 BF104
Inglewood, Croy. 221 DY109
Middlefields
Inglewood, Wok. 226 AV118
Inglewood Clo. E14 163 EA77
Inglewood Clo., Horn. 128 FK63
Inglewood Clo., Ilf. 103 ET51
Inglewood Copse, Brom. 204 EL96
Inglewood Rd. NW6 120 DA64
Inglewood Rd., Bexh. 167 FD84
Inglis Barracks NW7 97 CY50
Inglis Rd. W5 138 CM73
Inglis Rd., Croy. 202 DT102
Inglis St. SE5 161 DP81
Ingoldsby Rd., Grav. 191 GL88
Ingram Ave. NW11 120 DC59
Ingram Clo. SE11 278 C8
Ingram Clo., Stan. 95 CJ50
Ingram Rd. N2 120 DE56
Ingram Rd., Dart. 188 FL88
Ingram Rd., Grays 170 GC77
Ingram Rd., Th.Hth. 202 DQ95
Ingram Way, Grnf. 137 CD67
Ingrams Clo., Walt. 214 BW106
Ingrave Ho., Dag. 146 EV67
Ingrave Rd., Brwd. 108 FX47
Ingrave Rd., Rom. 127 FD56
Ingrave St. SW11 160 DD83
Ingrebourne Gdns., Upmin. 128 FQ60
Ingrebourne Rd., Rain. 147 FH70
Ingress Gdns., Green. 189 FX85
Ingress St. W4 158 CS78
Devonshire Rd.
Ingreway, Rom. 106 FP51
Inholms La., Dor. 263 CH140
Inigo Jones Rd. SE7 164 EL80
Inigo Pl. WC2 273 P10
Inkerman Rd. NW5 141 DH65
Inkerman Rd., St.Alb. 43 CE21
Inkerman Rd. (Eton Wick), Wind. 151 AM77
Inkerman Rd., Wok. 226 AS118
Inkerman Ter., Chesh. 54 AQ33
Inkerman Way, Wok. 226 AS118
Inks Grn. E4 101 EB50
Inman Rd. NW10 138 CS67
Inman Rd. SW18 180 DC87
Inmans Row, Wdf.Grn. 102 EG49
Inner Circle NW1 272 F3
Inner Circle NW1 140 DG69
Inner Pk. Rd. SW19 179 CX88
Inner Ring E., Houns. 155 BP83
Inner Ring W., Houns. 154 BN83
Inner Temple La. EC4 274 D9
Innes Clo. SW20 199 CY96
Innes Ct., Hem.H. 40 BK22
Innes Gdns. SW15 179 CV86
Innes Yd., Croy. 202 DQ104
High St.
Inniskilling Rd. E13 144 EJ68
Inskip Clo. E10 123 EB61
Inskip Dr., Horn. 128 FL60
Inskip Rd., Dag. 126 EX60
Institute Pl. E8 122 DV64
Amhurst Rd.
Institute Rd., Dor. 262 CC137
Guildford Rd.
Institute Rd., Epp. 70 EX29
Institute Rd., Maid. 130 AF72
Instone Clo., Wall. 219 DL108
De Havilland Rd.
Instone Rd., Dart. 188 FK87
Integer Gdns. E11 123 ED59
Forest Rd.
Interchange E. Ind. Est. E5 122 DW60
Theydon Rd.
International Ave., Houns. 156 BW78
International Trd. Est., Sthl. 155 BV76
Inver Clo. E5 122 DW61
Theydon Rd.
Inver Ct. W2 140 DB72
Inverness Ter.
Inveraray Pl. SE18 165 ER79
Old Mill Rd.
Inverclyde Gdns., Rom. 126 EX56
Inveresk Gdns., Wor.Pk. 199 CT104
Inverforth Clo. NW3 120 DC61
North End Way
Inverforth Rd. N11 99 DH50
Inverine Rd. SE7 164 EH78
Invermore Pl. SE18 165 EQ77
Inverness Ave., Enf. 82 DS39
Inverness Dr., Ilf. 103 ES51
Inverness Gdns. W8 140 DB74
Vicarage Gate
Inverness Ms. W2 140 DB73
Inverness Ter.
Inverness Pl. W2 140 DB73
Inverness Rd. N18 100 DV50
Inverness Rd., Houns. 156 BZ84
Inverness Rd., Sthl. 156 BY77
Inverness Rd., Wor.Pk. 199 CX102
Inverness St. NW1 141 DH67
Inverness Ter. W2 140 DB72
Inverton Rd. SE15 163 DX84
Invicta Clo., Chis. 185 EN92
Invicta Gro., Nthlt. 136 BZ69
Invicta Plaza SE1 141 DP74
Southwark St.
Invicta Rd. SE3 164 EG80
Invicta Rd., Dart. 188 FP86
Inville Rd. SE17 162 DR78
Inwen Ct. SE8 163 DY78
Grinstead Rd.
Inwood Ave., Couls. 235 DN120
Inwood Ave., Houns. 156 CC83
Inwood Clo., Croy. 203 DY103
Inwood Ct., Walt. 196 BW103
Inwood Rd., Houns. 156 CB84
Inworth St. SW11 160 DE82
Inworth Wk. N1 142 DQ67
Popham St.
Ion Sq. E2 142 DU68
Hackney Rd.
Iona Clo. SE6 183 EA87
Iona Cres., Slou. 131 AL72
Ionian Way, Hem.H. 40 BM18
Jupiter Dr.
Ipswich Rd. SW17 180 DG93
Ipswich Rd., Slou. 131 AN73
Ireland Clo. E6 145 EM71
Tollgate Rd.
Ireland Pl. N22 99 DL52
Whittington Rd.
Ireland Row E14 143 DZ72
Commercial Rd.
Ireland Yd. EC4 274 G9
Irene Rd. SW6 160 DA81
Irene Rd., Cob. 214 CB114
Irene Rd., Orp. 205 ET101
Ireton Ave., Walt. 195 BS103
Ireton Clo. N10 98 DG52
Cromwell Rd.
Ireton Pl., Grays 170 GA77
Russell Rd.
Ireton St. E3 143 EA70
Tidworth Rd.
Iris Ave., Bex. 186 EY86
Iris Clo. E6 145 EM71
Evelyn Denington Rd.
Iris Clo., Brwd. 108 FV43
Iris Clo., Croy. 203 DX102
Primrose La.
Iris Clo., Surb. 198 CM101
Iris Ct., Pnr. 116 BW55
Iris Cres., Bexh. 166 EZ79
Iris Path, Rom. 106 FJ52
Clematis Clo.
Iris Rd., Epsom 216 CP106
Iris Way E4 101 DZ51
Irkdale Ave., Enf. 82 DT39
Iron Bri. Clo. NW10 118 CS64
Iron Bri. Clo., Sthl. 136 CC74
Iron Bri. Rd., Uxb. 154 BN75
Iron Bri. Rd., West Dr. 154 BN75
Iron Dr., Hert. 32 DV08
Iron Mill La., Dart. 167 FE84
Iron Mill Pl. SW18 180 DB86
Garratt La.
Iron Mill Pl., Dart. 167 FF84
Iron Mill Rd. SW18 180 DB86
Ironmonger La. EC2 275 K9
Ironmonger Pas. EC1 275 J3
Ironmonger Row EC1 275 J3
Ironmonger Row EC1 142 DQ69
Ironmongers Pl. E14 163 EA77
Spindrift Ave.
Irons Bottom, Horl. 268 DA146
Irons Way, Rom. 105 FC52
Ironsbottom, Reig. 265 CZ143
Ironside Clo. SE16 163 DX75
Kinburn St.
Irvine Ave., Har. 117 CG55
Irvine Clo. N20 98 DE47
Irvine Gdns., S.Ock. 149 FT72
Irvine Pl., Vir.W. 192 AY99
Irvine Way, Orp. 205 ET101
Irving Ave., Nthlt. 136 BX67
Irving Gro. SW9 161 DM82
Irving Rd. W14 159 CX76
Irving St. WC2 277 N1
Irving St. WC2 141 DK73
Irving Wk., Swans. 190 FY87
Durrant Way
Irving Way NW9 119 CT57
Irving Way, Swan. 207 FD96
Irwin Ave. SE18 165 ES80
Irwin Gdns. NW10 139 CV67
Irwin Rd., Guil. 258 AU136
Isabel St. SW9 161 DM81
Isabella Clo. N14 99 DJ45
Isabella Dr., Orp. 223 EQ105
Isabella Rd. E9 122 DW64
Isabella St. SE1 278 F3
Isabella St. SE1 141 DP74
Isambard Clo., Uxb. 134 BK70
Isambard Ms. E14 163 EC76
Isambard Pl. SE16 142 DW74
Rotherhithe St.
Isbell Gdns., Rom. 105 FE52
Isbells Dr., Reig. 266 DB136
Isel Way SE22 182 DS85
East Dulwich Gro.
Isenburg Way, Hem.H. 40 BK15
Isham Rd. SW16 201 DL96
Isis Clo. SW15 159 CW84
Isis Clo., Ruis. 115 BQ58
Isis Dr., Upmin. 129 FS58
Isis St. SW18 180 DC89
Isla Rd. SE18 165 EQ79
Island, The, Stai. 173 BA90
Island Clo., Stai. 173 BE91
Island Fm. Ave., W.Mol. 196 BZ99
Island Fm. Rd., W.Mol. 196 BZ99
Island Rd., Mitch. 180 DF94
Island Row E14 143 DY72
Commercial Rd.
Islay Gdns., Houns. 176 BX85
Islay Wk. N1 142 DQ66
Douglas Rd.
Isledon Rd. N7 121 DN62
Islehurst Clo., Chis. 205 EN95
Islet Pk. Dr., Maid. 130 AC68
Islet Pk. Rd., Maid. 130 AC68
Islington Grn. N1 141 DP67
Islington High St. N1 141 DN68
Islington Pk. Ms. N1 141 DN66
Islington Pk. St.
Islington Pk. St. N1 141 DN66
Islip Gdns., Edg. 96 CR52
Islip Gdns., Nthlt. 136 BY66
Islip Manor Rd., Nthlt. 136 BY66
Islip St. NW5 121 DJ64
Ismailia Rd. E7 144 EH66
Ismay Ct., Slou. 132 AS73
Elliman Ave.
Isom Clo. E13 144 EJ70
Belgrave Rd.
Istead Ri., Grav. 191 GF94
Itchingwood Common Rd., Oxt. 254 EJ133
Ivanhoe Clo., Uxb. 134 BK71
Ivanhoe Dr., Har. 117 CG55
Ivanhoe Rd. SE5 162 DT83
Ivanhoe Rd., Houns. 156 BX83
Ivatt Pl. W14 159 CZ78
Ivatt Way N17 121 DP55
Ive Fm. Clo. E10 123 EA61
Ive Fm. La. E10 123 EA61
Iveagh Ave. NW10 138 CN68
Iveagh Clo. E9 143 DX67
Iveagh Clo. NW10 138 CN68
Iveagh Clo., Nthwd. 93 BP53
Iveagh Rd., Guil. 258 AV135
Iveagh Rd., Wok. 226 AT118
Ivedon Rd., Well. 166 EW82
Iveley Rd. SW4 161 DJ82
Iver La., Iver 134 BG72
Iver La., Uxb. 134 BH70
Iver Rd., Brwd. 108 FV44
Iver Rd., Iver 134 BG72
Iverdale Clo., Iver 133 BC73
Ivere Dr., Barn. 80 DB44
Iverhurst Clo., Bexh. 186 EX85
Iverna Ct. W8 160 DA76
Iverna Gdns. W8 160 DA76
Iverna Gdns., Felt. 175 BR85
Ivers Way, Croy. 221 EB108
Iverson Rd. NW6 139 CZ65
Ives Gdns., Rom. 127 FF56
Sims Clo.
Ives Rd. E16 144 EE71
Ives Rd., Hert. 31 DP08
Ives Rd., Slou. 153 AZ76
Ives St. SW3 276 C8
Ives St. SW3 160 DE77
Ivestor Ter. SE23 182 DW87
Ivimey St. E2 142 DU69
Ivinghoe Clo., Enf. 82 DS39
Ivinghoe Clo., St.Alb. 43 CJ15
Highview Gdns.
Ivinghoe Clo., Wat. 76 BX35
Ivinghoe Rd., Dag. 126 EV64
Ivinghoe Rd., Rick. 92 BG45
Ivinghoe Rd. (Bushey), Wat. 95 CD45
Ivins Rd., Beac. 88 AG54
Ivor Clo., Guil. 259 AZ135
Ivor Gro. SE9 185 EP88
Ivor Pl. NW1 272 D5
Ivor Pl. NW1 140 DF70
Ivor St. NW1 141 DJ66
Ivory Clo., Hem.H. 40 BL23
Ivory Sq. SW11 160 DC83
Gartons Way
Ivorydown, Brom. 184 EG91
Ivy Bower Clo., Green. 189 FV85
Riverview Rd.
Ivy Chimneys Rd., Epp. 69 ES32
Ivy Clo., Dart. 188 FN87
Ivy Clo., Grav. 191 GJ90
Ivy Clo., Har. 116 BZ63
Ivy Clo., Pnr. 116 BW59
Ivy Clo., Sun. 196 BW96
Ivy Cotts. E14 143 EB73
Grove Vill.
Ivy Cres. W4 158 CQ77
Bollo La.
Ivy Cres., Slou. 131 AM73
Ivy Gdns. N8 121 DL58
Ivy Gdns., Mitch. 201 DK97
Ivy Ho. La., Berk. 38 AY19
Ivy Ho. La., Sev. 241 FD118
Ivy La., Houns. 156 BZ84
Ivy La., Sev. 240 EY116
Main Rd.
Ivy La., Wok. 227 BB117
Ivy Lea, Rick. 92 BG46
Springwell Ave.
Ivy Mill Clo., Gdse. 252 DV132
Ivy Mill La., Gdse. 252 DU132
Ivy Pl., Surb. 198 CM100
Alpha Rd.
Ivy Rd. E16 144 EG72
Pacific Rd.
Ivy Rd. E17 123 EA58
Ivy Rd. N14 99 DJ45
Ivy Rd. NW2 119 CW63
Ivy Rd. SE4 163 DZ84
Ivy Rd. SW17 180 DE92
Tooting High St.
Ivy Rd., Houns. 156 CB84
Ivy Rd., Surb. 198 CN103
Ivy St. N1 142 DS68
Ivy Ter., Hodd. 49 EC15
Ivy Wk., Dag. 146 EY65
Ivybridge, Brox. 49 EA19
Ivybridge Clo., Twick. 177 CG87
Ivybridge Clo., Uxb. 134 BL69
Ivybridge Est., Islw. 177 CF85
Ivybridge La. WC2 278 A1
Ivychurch Clo. SE20 182 DW94
Laurel Gro.
Ivychurch La. SE17 279 N10
Ivydale Rd. SE15 163 DX83
Ivydale Rd., Cars. 200 DF103
Ivyday Gro. SW16 181 DM90
Ivydene, W.Mol. 196 BZ99
Ivydene Clo., Red. 267 DH139
Ivydene Clo., Sutt. 218 DC105
Ivyhouse Rd., Dag. 146 EX65
Ivyhouse Rd., Uxb. 115 BP63
Ivymount Rd. SE27 181 DN90
Ixworth Pl. SW3 276 B10
Ixworth Pl. SW3 160 DE77
Izane Rd., Bexh. 166 EZ84

J

Jacaranda Clo., N.Mal. 198 CS97
Acacia Gro.
Jack Barnett Way N22 99 DM54
Mayes Rd.
Jack Clow Rd. E15 144 EE68
Manor Rd.
Jack Cornwell St. E12 125 EN63
Jack Dash Way E6 144 EL71
Eisenhower Dr.
Jack Stevens Clo., Harl. 52 EW17
Hillside
Jack Walker Ct. N5 121 DP63
Jackass La., Kes. 222 EH106
Jackass La., Oxt. 253 DZ131
Jackdaws, Welw.G.C. 30 DC09
Jackets La., Nthwd. 93 BP53
Jacketts Fld., Abb.L. 59 BT31
Jacklin Grn., Wdf.Grn. 102 EG49
Jackman Ms. NW10 118 CS62
Jackman St. E8 142 DV67
Jackmans La., Wok. 226 AU119
Jacks La., Uxb. 92 BG52
Jackson Clo., Epsom 216 CR114
Jackson Clo., Green. 189 FU85
Cowley Ave.
Jackson Clo., Uxb. 134 BL66
Jackson Rd.
Jackson Rd. N7 121 DM63
Jackson Rd., Bark. 145 ER67
Jackson Rd., Barn. 80 DD44
Jackson Rd., Brom. 204 EL103
Jackson Rd., Uxb. 134 BL66
Jackson St. SE18 165 EN79
Jackson Way, Sthl. 156 CB75
Jacksons Dr., Wal.Cr. 66 DU28
Jacksons La. N6 120 DG59
Jacksons Pl., Croy. 202 DR102
Cross Rd.
Jacksons Way, Croy. 203 EB104
Oak Ave.
Jacob St. SE1 162 DT75
Jacobs Ave., Rom. 106 FL54
Jacobs Clo., Dag. 127 FB63
Jacobs Clo., Wind. 151 AL81
Jacobs Ho. E13 144 EJ69
Jacobs Ladder, Hat. 45 CW18
The Bdy.
Jacobs La., Dart. 208 FQ97
Jacob's Well Ms. W1 272 G8
Jacob's Well Rd., Guil. 242 AX129
Jacqueline Clo., Nthlt. 136 BZ67
Canford Ave.
Jade Clo. E16 144 EK72
Jade Clo. NW2 119 CX59
Marble Dr.
Jade Clo., Dag. 126 EW60
Jaffe Rd., Ilf. 125 ER60
Jaffray Pl. SE27 181 DP91
Chapel Rd.
Jaffray Rd., Brom. 204 EK98
Jaggard Way SW12 180 DF87
Jagger Ct., Dart. 188 FQ87
Jago Clo. SE18 165 EQ79
Jago Wk. SE5 162 DR80
Lomond Gro.
Jail La. (Biggin Hill), West. 238 EK115
Jamaica Rd. SE1 162 DT75
Jamaica Rd. SE16 162 DU76
Jamaica Rd., Th.Hth. 201 DP100
Jamaica St. E1 142 DW71
James Ave. NW2 119 CW64
James Ave., Dag. 126 EZ60
James Bedford Clo., Pnr. 94 BW54
James Boswell Clo. SW16 181 DN91
Curtis Fld. Rd.
James Clo. E13 144 EG68
Richmond St.
James Clo. NW11 119 CY58
Woodlands
James Clo., Rom. 127 FG57
James Clo. (Bushey), Wat. 76 BY43
Aldenham Rd.
James Collins Clo. W9 139 CZ70
Fermoy Rd.
James Ct. N1 142 DQ66
Morton Rd.
James Dixon Twr. E17 123 DZ59
Beaconsfield Rd.
James Dudson Ct. NW10 138 CQ66
James Gdns. N22 99 DP52
James Hammett Ho. E2 142 DT69
Ravenscroft St.
James Joyce Wk. SE24 161 DP84
Shakespeare Rd.
James La. E10 123 ED59
James La. E11 123 ED58
James Martin Clo., Uxb. 114 BG58
James Newman Ct. SE9 185 EN90
Great Harry Dr.
James Pl. N17 100 DT53
Ruskin Rd.
James Rd., Dart. 187 FF87
James Rd., Guil. 258 AW142
James Sinclair Pt. E13 144 EJ67
James St. W1 272 G8
James St. W1 140 DG72
James St. WC2 274 A10
James St., Bark. 145 EQ66
James St., Enf. 82 DT43
James St., Epp. 69 ET28
James St., Houns. 157 CD83
James St., Wind. 151 AR81
James Ter. SW14 158 CR83
Addington Ct.
James Yd. E4 101 ED51
Larkshall Rd.
Jameson Ct., St.Alb. 43 CF19
Avenue Rd.
Jameson St. W8 140 DA74
James's Cotts., Rich. 158 CN80
Kew Rd.
Jamestown Rd. NW1 141 DH67
Jamieson Ho., Houns. 176 BZ86
Jamnagar Clo., Stai. 173 BF93
Jane St. E1 142 DV72
Commercial Rd.
Janet St. E14 163 EA76
Janeway Pl. SE16 162 DV75
Janeway St.
Janeway St. SE16 162 DU75
Janice Ms., Ilf. 125 EP62
Oakfield Rd.
Janmead, Brwd. 109 GB45
Janoway Hill La., Wok. 226 AW119
Firbank La.
Jansen Wk. SW11 160 DD84
Hope St.
Janson Clo. E15 124 EE64
Janson Rd.
Janson Clo. NW10 118 CS62
Janson Rd. E15 124 EE64
Jansons Rd. N15 122 DS55
Japan Cres. N4 121 DM59
Japan Rd., Rom. 126 EX58
Japonica Clo., Wok. 226 AW118
Jardine Rd. E1 143 DX73
Jarman Clo., Hem.H. 40 BL22
Jarmans Way, Hem.H. 40 BM21
St. Albans Rd.
Jarrah Cotts., Purf. 169 FR79
London Rd. Purfleet
Jarrett Clo. SW2 181 DP88
Jarrow Clo., Mord. 200 DB99
Jarrow Rd. N17 122 DV56
Jarrow Rd. SE16 162 DW77
Jarrow Rd., Rom. 126 EW58
Jarrow Way E9 123 DZ64
Jarvis Cleys (Cheshunt), Wal.Cr. 66 DT26
Roundcroft
Jarvis Clo., Barn. 79 CX43
Jarvis Rd. SE22 162 DS84
Melbourne Gro.
Jarvis Rd., S.Croy. 220 DR107
Jarvis Way, Rom. 106 FL54
Jasmin Clo., Nthwd. 93 BT53
Jasmin Rd., Epsom 216 CP107
Jasmin Way, Hem.H. 39 BE19
The Ave.
Jasmine Clo., Ilf. 125 EP64
Jasmine Clo., Orp. 205 EP103
Jasmine Clo., Red. 266 DG139
Spencer Way
Jasmine Clo., Sthl. 136 BY73
Lancaster Rd.
Jasmine Clo., Wok. 226 AT116
Jasmine Dr., Hert. 32 DU09
Jasmine Gdns., Croy. 203 EA104
Jasmine Gdns., Har. 116 CA61
Jasmine Gdns., Hat. 45 CU16
Jasmine Gro. SE20 202 DV95
Jasmine Ter., West Dr. 154 BN75
Jasmine Way, E.Mol. 197 CE98
Hampton Ct. Way
Jason Clo., Brwd. 108 FT49
Jason Clo., Red. 266 DE139
Jason Clo., Wey. 213 BQ106
Jason Ct. W1 140 DG72
Marylebone La.
Jason Wk. SE9 185 EN91
Jasons Dr., Guil. 243 BC131
Jasons Hill, Chesh. 56 AV30
Jasper Clo., Enf. 82 DW38
Jasper Pas. SE19 182 DT93
Jasper Rd. E16 144 EK72
Jasper Rd. SE19 182 DT93
Jasper Wk. N1 275 K2
Javelin Way, Nthlt. 136 BX69
Jay Gdns., Chis. 185 EM91
Jay Ms. SW7 160 DC75
Jaycroft, Enf. 81 DN39
The Ridgeway
Jays Covert, Couls. 234 DG120
Jebb Ave. SW2 181 DL86
Jebb St. E3 143 EA68
Jedburgh Rd. E13 144 EJ69
Jedburgh St. SW11 160 DG84
Jeddo Rd. W12 159 CT75
Jefferies Ho. NW10 138 CR66
Jefferson Clo. W13 157 CH76
Jefferson Clo., Ilf. 125 EP57
Jefferson Clo., Slou. 153 BA77
Jefferson Wk. SE18 165 EN79
Kempt St.
Jeffreys Pl. NW1 141 DJ66
Jeffreys St.
Jeffreys Rd. SW4 161 DL82
Jeffreys Rd., Enf. 83 DZ41
Jeffreys St. NW1 141 DJ66
Jeffreys Wk. SW4 161 DL82
Jeffries Pas., Guil. 258 AX135
High St.
Jeffries Rd., Lthd. 245 BP131
Jeffries Rd., Ware 33 DY06
Jeffs Clo., Hmptn. 176 CB93
Uxbridge Rd.
Jeffs Rd., Sutt. 217 CZ105
Jeger Ave. E2 142 DT67
Laburnum St.
Jeken Rd. SE9 164 EJ84
Jelf Rd. SW2 181 DN85
Jellicoe Ave., Grav. 191 GJ90
Jellicoe Ave. W., Grav. 191 GJ90
Kitchener Ave.
Jellicoe Clo., Slou. 151 AP75
Jellicoe Gdns., Stan. 95 CF51
Jellicoe Rd. E13 144 EG70
Jutland Rd.
Jellicoe Rd. N17 100 DR52
Jellicoe Rd., Wat. 93 BU45
Moor Vw.
Jengar Clo., Sutt. 218 DB105
Jenkins Ave., St.Alb. 60 BY30
Jenkins La. E6 145 EN68
Jenkins La., Bark. 145 EP68
Jenkins Rd. E13 144 EH70
Jenner Ave. W3 138 CR71
Jenner Ho. SE3 164 EE79
Jenner Pl. SW13 159 CV79
Jenner Rd. N16 122 DT62
Jenner Rd., Guil. 258 AY135
Jennery La., Slou. 130 AJ69
Jennett Rd., Croy. 201 DN104
Jennifer Rd., Brom. 184 EF90
Jennings Clo., Add. 212 BJ109
Woodham La.
Jennings Fld., H.Wyc. 110 AC56
Jennings Rd. SE22 182 DT86
Jennings Rd., St.Alb. 43 CF19
Jennings Way, Barn. 79 CW41
Jennings Way, Hem.H. 40 BL22
Jenningtree Rd., Erith 167 FH80
Jenningtree Way, Belv. 167 FC75
Jenny Hammond Clo. E11 124 EF62
Newcomen Rd.
Jenny Path, Rom. 106 FK52
Jenson Way SE19 182 DT94
Jenton Ave., Bexh. 166 EY81
Jephson Rd. E7 144 EJ66
Jephson St. SE5 162 DR81
Grove La.
Jephtha Rd. SW18 180 DA86
Jeppos La., Mitch. 200 DF98
Jerdan Pl. SW6 160 DA80
Fulham Bdy.
Jeremiah St. E14 143 EB72
Jeremys Grn. N18 100 DV49
Jermyn St. SW1 277 L2
Jermyn St. SW1 141 DJ74
Jerningham Ave., Ilf. 103 EP54
Jerningham Rd. SE14 163 DY82

Jerome Cres. NW8 272 B4
Jerome Cres. NW8 140 DE70
Jerome Dr., St.Alb. 42 CA22
Jerome St. E1 275 P5
Jerounds, Harl. 51 EP17
Jerrard St. N1 275 N1
Jerrard St. SE13 163 EB83
Jersey Ave., Stan. 95 CH54
Jersey Clo., Cher. 193 BF104
Jersey Clo., Guil. 243 BB129
Weybrook Dr.
Jersey Clo., Hodd. 49 EA16
Jersey Dr., Orp. 205 ER100
Jersey La., St.Alb. 43 CH18
Jersey Par., Houns. 156 CB81
Jersey Rd. E11 123 ED60
Jersey Rd. E16 144 EJ72
Prince Regent La.
Jersey Rd. SW17 181 DH93
Jersey Rd. W7 157 CG75
Jersey Rd., Houns. 156 CB81
Jersey Rd., Ilf. 125 EP63
Jersey Rd., Islw. 157 CD80
Jersey Rd., Rain. 147 FG66
Jersey St. E2 142 DV69
Bethnal Grn. Rd.
Jerusalem Pas. EC1 274 F5
Jervis Ave., Enf. 83 DY36
Jervis Ct. W1 273 J9
Jerviston Gdns. SW16 181 DN92
Jesmond Ave., Wem. 138 CM65
Jesmond Clo., Mitch. 201 DH97
Cedars Ave.
Jesmond Rd., Croy. 202 DT101
Jesmond Way, Stan. 96 CL50
Jessam Ave. E5 122 DV60
Jessamine Pl., Dart. 188 FQ87
Jessamine Rd. W7 137 CE74
Jessamine Ter., Swan. 207 FC95
Birchwood Rd.
Jessamy Rd., Wey. 195 BP103
Jesse Rd. E10 123 EC60
Jessel Dr., Loug. 85 EQ39
Jesses La., Guil. 261 BQ144
Jessica Rd. SW18 180 DC86
Jessie Blythe La. N19 121 DL59
Hillrise Rd.
Jessiman Ter., Shep. 194 BN99
Jessop Ave., Sthl. 156 BZ77
Jessop Rd. SE24 161 DP84
Milkwood Rd.
Jessops Way, Croy. 201 DJ100
Jessup Clo. SE18 165 EQ77
Jetstar Way, Nthlt. 136 BY69
Jetty Wk., Grays 170 GA79
Jevington Way SE12 184 EH88
Jewel Rd. E17 123 EA55
Jewels Hill, West. 222 EG112
Jewry St. EC3 275 P9
Jewry St. EC3 142 DT72
Jew's Row SW18 160 DB84
Jews Wk. SE26 182 DV91
Jeymer Ave. NW2 119 CV64
Jeymer Dr., Grnf. 136 CC67
Jeypore Rd. SW18 180 DC87
Jillian Clo., Hmptn. 176 CA94
Jim Bradley Clo. SE18 165 EN77
John Wilson St.
Jim Desormeaux Bungalows, Harl. 35 ES13
School La.
Jinnings, The, Welw.G.C. 30 DA12
Joan Cres. SE9 184 EK87
Joan Gdns., Dag. 126 EY61
Joan Rd., Dag. 126 EY60
Joan St. SE1 278 F3
Joan St. SE1 141 DP74
Jocelyn Rd., Rich. 158 CL83
Jocelyns, Harl. 36 EW11
Jocketts Hill, Hem.H. 39 BF20
Jocketts Rd., Hem.H. 39 BF21
Jockey's Flds. WC1 274 C6
Jockey's Flds. WC1 141 DM71
Jodane St. SE8 163 DZ77
Jodrell Clo., Islw. 157 CG81
London Rd.
Jodrell Rd. E3 143 DZ67
Jodrell Way, Grays 169 FT78
Joel St., Nthwd. 115 BU55
Joel St., Pnr. 115 BU55
Johanna St. SE1 278 D5
John Adam St. WC2 278 A1
John Adam St. WC2 141 DL73
John Aird Ct. W2 140 DC71
Howley Pl.
John Ashby Clo. SW2 181 DL86
John Barnes Wk. E15 144 EF65
Hamfrith Rd.
John Bradshaw Rd. N14 99 DK46
High St.
John Burns Dr., Bark. 145 ES66
John Campbell Rd. N16 122 DS64
John Carpenter St. EC4 274 E10
John Carpenter St. EC4 141 DP73
John Cobb Rd., Wey. 212 BN108
John Cornwall VC Ho. E12 125 EN63
John Ct., Hodd. 33 EA14
Molesworth
John Deed Ind. Est., Mitch. 200 DF100
John Eliot Clo., Wal.Abb. 50 EE21
John Felton Rd. SE16 162 DU75
John Fisher St. E1 142 DU73
John Gooch Dr., Enf. 81 DP39
John Groom's Est., Edg. 96 CQ49
John Islip St. SW1 277 N10
John Islip St. SW1 161 DK78
John Keats Ho. N22 99 DM52
John Maurice Clo. SE17 162 DR77
John McKenna Wk. SE16 162 DU76
Tranton Rd.
John Newton Ct., Well. 166 EV83
Danson La.
John Parker Clo., Dag. 147 FB66
John Parker Sq. SW11 160 DD83
Thomas Baines Rd.
John Penn St. SE13 163 EB81
John Perrin Pl., Har. 118 CL59
John Princes St. W1 273 J8
John Princes St. W1 141 DH72
John Rennie Wk. E1 142 DV74
Wine Clo.
John Roll Way SE16 162 DU76
John Ruskin St. SE5 161 DP80
John Russell Clo., Guil. 242 AU131
John Silkin La. SE8 163 DX78
John Spencer Sq. N1 141 DP65
John St. E15 144 EF67
John St. SE25 202 DU98
John St. WC1 274 C5
John St. WC1 141 DM70
John St., Enf. 82 DT43
John St., Grays 170 GC79
John St., Houns. 156 BY82
John Tate Rd., Hert. 32 DT10
London Rd.
John Taylor Ct., Slou. 131 AQ74
John Trundle Ct. EC2 142 DQ71
Beech St.
John Walsh Twr. E11 124 EF61
John Williams Clo. SE14 163 DX79
Cold Blow La.
John Wilson St. SE18 165 EN76
John Woolley Clo. SE13 163 ED84
Johnby Clo., Enf. 83 DY37
Manly Dixon Dr.
Johns Ave. NW4 119 CW56
Johns Clo., Ashf. 175 BQ91
John's La., Berk. 38 AT21
Johns La., Mord. 200 DC99
John's Ms. WC1 274 C5
John's Ms. WC1 141 DM70
John's Pl. E1 142 DV72
Damien St.
Johns Rd., West. 238 EK120
John's Ter., Croy. 202 DS102
John's Ter., Rom. 106 FP51
Johns Wk., Whyt. 236 DU119
Johnsdale, Oxt. 254 EF129
Johnson Clo. E8 142 DU67
Johnson Clo., Grav. 190 GD90
Johnson Ct., Hem.H. 40 BL22
Johnson Rd., Brom. 204 EK99
Johnson Rd., Croy. 202 DR101
Johnson Rd., Houns. 156 BW80
Johnson St. E1 142 DW73
Cable St.
Johnson St., Sthl. 156 BW76
Johnsons Ave., Sev. 225 FB110
Johnsons Clo., Cars. 200 DE104
Johnson's Ct. EC4 141 DN72
Fleet St.
Johnsons Ct., Sev. 257 FM121
School La.
Johnsons Dr., Hmptn. 196 CC95
Johnson's Pl. SW1 161 DJ78
Johnsons Way NW10 138 CP70
Johnsons Way, Green. 189 FW86
Johnsons Yd., Uxb. 134 BJ66
Redford Way
Johnston Clo. SW9 161 DM81
Hackford Rd.
Johnston Grn., Guil. 242 AU130
Johnston Rd., Wdf.Grn. 102 EG50
Johnston Ter. NW2 119 CX62
Campion Ter.
Johnston Wk., Guil. 242 AU130
Johnstone Rd. E6 145 EM69
Joiner St. SE1 279 L3
Joiner's Arms Yd. SE5 162 DR81
Denmark Hill
Joiners Clo., Chesh. 56 AV30
Joiners Clo., Ger.Cr. 91 AZ52
Joiners La., Ger.Cr. 90 AY53
Joiners Way, Ger.Cr. 90 AY52
Joinville Pl., Add. 212 BK105
Corrie Rd.
Jolliffe Rd., Red. 251 DJ126
Jollys La., Har. 117 CD60
Lower Rd.
Jollys La., Hayes 136 BX71
Jonathan St. SE11 278 B10
Jonathan St. SE11 161 DM78
Jones Rd. E13 144 EH70
Holborn Rd.
Jones Rd. (Cheshunt), Wal.Cr. 65 DP30
Jones St. W1 277 H1
Jones Wk., Rich. 178 CM86
Pyrland Rd.
Jones Way, Slou. 111 AR61
Jonquil Clo., Welw.G.C. 30 DB11
Jonquil Gdns., Hmptn. 176 BZ93
Partridge Rd.
Jonson Clo., Hayes 135 BU71
Jonson Clo., Mitch. 201 DH98
Joram Way SE16 162 DV78
Egan Way
Jordan Clo., Dag. 127 FB63
Muggeridge Rd.
Jordan Clo., Har. 116 BZ62
Hamilton Cres.
Jordan Clo., S.Croy. 220 DT111
Jordan Clo., Wat. 75 BT35
Jordan Rd., Grnf. 137 CH67
Jordans Clo., Guil. 243 BA133
Beatty Ave.
Jordans Clo., Islw. 157 CE81
Jordans Clo., Red. 266 DG139
Spencer Way
Jordans Clo., Stai. 174 BJ87
Jordans La., Beac. 90 AS53
Jordans Rd., Rick. 92 BG45
Jordans Way, Beac. 90 AT51
Jordans Way, Rain. 148 FK68
Jordans Way, St.Alb. 60 BZ30
Joseph Ave. W3 138 CR72
Joseph Locke Way, Esher 196 CA103
Mill Rd.
Joseph Powell Clo. SW12 181 DH86
Hazelbourne Rd.
Joseph Ray Rd. E11 124 EE61
High Rd. Leytonstone
Joseph St. E3 143 DZ70
Josephine Ave. SW2 181 DM85
Josephine Ave., Tad. 249 CZ126
Josephine Clo., Tad. 249 CZ127
Joseph's Rd., Guil. 242 AW133
Joshua St. E14 143 EC72
St. Leonards Rd.
Joslin Rd., Purf. 168 FQ78
Joubert St. SW11 160 DF82
Journeys End, Slou. 132 AS71
Stoke Poges La.
Jowett St. SE15 162 DT80
Joy Rd., Grav. 191 GJ88
Joyce Ave. N18 100 DT50
Joyce Ct., Wal.Abb. 67 ED34
Joyce Dawson Way SE28 146 EU73
Thamesmere Dr.
Joyce Grn. La., Dart. 168 FM84
Joyce Grn. Wk., Dart. 168 FM84
Joyce Page Clo. SE7 164 EK79
Lansdowne La.
Joydens Wd. Rd., Bex. 187 FD91
Joydon Dr., Rom. 126 EV58
Joyes Clo., Rom. 106 FK49
Joyners Clo., Dag. 126 EZ63
Joyners Fld., Harl. 51 EQ19
Jubb Powell Ho. N15 122 DS58
Jubilee Ave. E4 101 EC51
Jubilee Ave., Rom. 127 FB57
Jubilee Ave., St.Alb. 61 CK26
Jubilee Ave., Twick. 176 CC87
Jubilee Ave., Ware 33 DZ05
Jubilee Clo. NW9 118 CR58
Jubilee Clo., Green. 189 FW86
Jubilee Clo., Pnr. 94 BW54
Jubilee Clo., Rom. 127 FB57
Jubilee Clo., Stai. 174 BJ87
Jubilee Ct., Hat. 45 CV15
Jubilee Ct., Stai. 174 BG92
Leacroft
Jubilee Cres. E14 163 EC76
Jubilee Cres. N9 100 DU46
Jubilee Cres., Add. 212 BK106
Jubilee Cres., Grav. 191 GL89
Jubilee Dr., Ruis. 116 BX63
Jubilee Gdns., Sthl. 136 CA72
Jubilee Pl. SW3 276 C10
Jubilee Pl. SW3 160 DE78
Jubilee Ri., Sev. 257 FM121
Jubilee Rd., Grays 169 FV79
Jubilee Rd., Grnf. 137 CH67
Jubilee Rd., Orp. 224 FA107
Jubilee Rd., Sutt. 217 CX108
Jubilee Rd., Wat. 75 BU38
Jubilee St. E1 142 DW72
Jubilee Ter., Bet. 264 CP138
Jubilee Ter., Dor. 263 CH135
Jubilee Way SW19 200 DB95
Jubilee Way, Chess. 216 CN105
Jubilee Way, Felt. 175 BT88
Westmacott Dr.
Jubilee Way, Sid. 186 EU89
Judd St. WC1 273 P3
Judd St. WC1 141 DL69
Jude St. E16 144 EF72
Judeth Gdns., Grav. 191 GL92
Judge Heath La., Hayes 135 BQ72
Judge St., Wat. 75 BV38
Judge Wk., Esher 215 CE107
Judges Hill, Pot.B. 64 DE29
Judith Ave., Rom. 105 FB51
Juer St. SW11 160 DE80
Juglans Rd., Orp. 206 EU102
Julia Gdns., Bark. 146 EX68
Julia St. NW5 120 DG63
Oak Village
Julian Ave. W3 138 CP73
Julian Clo., Barn. 80 DB41
Julian Clo., Wok. 226 AW118
Julian Hill, Har. 117 CE61
Julian Hill, Wey. 212 BN108
Julian Pl. E14 163 EB78
Julian Rd., Orp. 224 EU107
Juliana Clo. N2 120 DB55
East End Rd.
Julians Clo., Sev. 256 FG127
Julians Way, Sev. 256 FG127
Julien Rd. W5 157 CJ77
Julien Rd., Couls. 235 DK115
Juliette Rd. E13 144 EF68
Salmen Rd.
Juliette Way, S.Ock. 168 FM75
Junction App. SE13 163 EC83
Loampit Vale
Junction App. SW11 160 DE83
Junction Ave. W10 139 CW69
Harrow Rd.
Junction Ms. W2 272 B8
Junction Pl. W2 272 A8
Junction Rd. E13 144 EH68
Junction Rd. N9 100 DU46
Junction Rd. N17 122 DU55
Junction Rd. N19 121 DJ63
Junction Rd. W5 157 CK77
Junction Rd., Ashf. 175 BQ92
Junction Rd., Brwd. 108 FW49
Junction Rd., Dart. 188 FK86
Junction Rd., Dor. 263 CG136
Junction Rd., Har. 117 CE58
Junction Rd., Rom. 127 FF56
Junction Rd., S.Croy. 220 DR106
Junction Rd. E., Rom. 126 EY59
Kenneth Rd.
Junction Rd. W., Rom. 126 EY59
Junction Wf. N1 275 H1
Junction Wf. N1 142 DQ68
June Clo., Couls. 219 DH114
June La., Red. 267 DH141
Junewood Clo., Add. 211 BF111
Juniper Ave., St.Alb. 60 CA31
Juniper Clo., Barn. 79 CX43
Sellwood Dr.
Juniper Clo., Brox. 67 DZ25
Juniper Clo., Chess. 216 CM106
Moor La.
Juniper Clo., Guil. 242 AV129
Juniper Clo., Reig. 266 DC136
Juniper Clo., Rick. 92 BK48
Juniper Clo., Wem. 118 CN64
Juniper Clo., West. 238 EL117
Juniper Ct., Slou. 152 AU75
Nixey Clo.
Juniper Cres. NW1 141 DH67
Oval Rd.
Juniper Gdns. SW16 201 DJ95
Leonard Rd.
Juniper Gdns., Sun. 175 BT93
Juniper Gate, Rick. 92 BK47
Stockers Fm. Rd.
Juniper Grn., Hem.H. 39 BE20
Juniper Gro., Wat. 75 BU38
Bay Tree Wk.
Juniper La. E6 144 EL71
Juniper La., H.Wyc. 110 AD56
Juniper Rd., Ilf. 125 EP63
Juniper Rd., Reig. 266 DC136
Juniper St. E1 142 DW73
Juniper Wk., Bet. 264 CQ136
Warrenne Rd.
Juniper Way, Hayes 135 BR73
Juniper Way, Rom. 106 FL53
Juno Rd., Hem.H. 40 BM17
Saturn Way
Juno Way SE14 163 DX79
Jupiter Dr., Hem.H. 40 BM18
Jupiter Way N7 141 DM65
Jupp Rd. E15 143 ED66
Jupp Rd. W. E15 143 EC67
Jurgens Rd., Purf. 169 FR79
London Rd. Purfleet
Justice Wk. SW3 160 DE79
Lawrence St.
Justin Clo., Brent. 157 CK80
Justin Rd. E4 101 DZ51
Jute La., Enf. 83 DY40
Jutland Clo. N19 121 DL60
Sussex Way
Jutland Gdns., Couls. 235 DL120
Goodenough Way
Jutland Pl., Egh. 173 BC92
Mullens Rd.
Jutland Rd. E13 144 EG70
Jutland Rd. SE6 183 EC87
Jutsums Ave., Rom. 127 FB58
Jutsums La., Rom. 127 FB58
Juxon Clo., Har. 94 CB53
Augustine Rd.
Juxon St. SE11 278 C8
Juxon St. SE11 161 DM77

K

Kaduna Clo., Pnr. 115 BV57
Kale Rd., Erith 166 EY75
Kambala Rd. SW11 160 DD83
Kandlewood, Brwd. 109 GB45
Kangley Bri. Rd. SE26 183 DZ91
Karen Clo., Brwd. 108 FW45
Karen Clo., Rain. 147 FE68
Karen Ct. SE4 163 DZ82
Wickham Rd.
Karen Ct., Brom. 204 EF95
Blyth Rd.
Karen Ter. E11 124 EF61
Montague Rd.
Karoline Gdns., Grnf. 137 CD68
Oldfield La. N.
Kashgar Rd. SE18 165 ET77
Kashmir Clo., Add. 212 BK109
Kashmir Rd. SE7 164 EK80
Kassala Rd. SW11 160 DF81
Katella Trd. Est., Bark. 145 ES69
Kates Clo., Barn. 79 CU43
Kates Cft., Welw.G.C. 29 CY13
Katharine St., Croy. 202 DQ104
Katherine Clo., Add. 212 BG107
Katherine Clo., Hem.H. 40 BL23
Katherine Clo., H.Wyc. 88 AC47
Katherine Gdns. SE9 164 EK84
Katherine Gdns., Ilf. 103 EQ52
Katherine Rd. E6 144 EK66
Katherine Rd. E7 144 EJ65
Katherine Rd., Twick. 177 CG88
London Rd.
Katherine Sq. W11 139 CY74
Wilsham St.
Katherines Way, Harl. 51 EN18
Kathleen Ave. W3 138 CQ71
Kathleen Ave., Wem. 138 CL66
Kathleen Rd. SW11 160 DF83
Katrine Sq., Hem.H. 40 BK16
Kavanaghs Rd., Brwd. 108 FU48
Kavanaghs Ter., Brwd. 108 FV48
Kavanaghs Rd.
Kay Rd. SW9 161 DL82
Kay St. E2 142 DU68
Kay St. E15 143 ED66
Kay St., Well. 166 EV81
Kaye Ct., Guil. 242 AW131
Kaye Don Way, Wey. 212 BN111
Kayemoor Rd., Sutt. 218 DE108
Kaywood Clo., Slou. 152 AW76
Kean St. WC2 274 B9
Kean St. WC2 141 DM72
Kearton Clo., Ken. 236 DQ117
Keary Rd., Swans. 190 FY87
Keatley Grn. E4 101 DZ51
Silver Birch Ave.
Keats Ave., Red. 250 DG132
Keats Ave., Rom. 105 FH52
Keats Clo. E11 124 EH57
Nightingale La.
Keats Clo. NW3 120 DE63
Keats Gro.
Keats Clo. SE1 279 P9
Keats Clo. SW19 180 DD93
North Rd.
Keats Clo., Chig. 103 EQ51
Keats Clo., Enf. 83 DX43
Keats Clo., Hayes 135 BU71
Keats Gdns., Til. 171 GH82
Keats Gro. NW3 120 DE63
Keats Ho., Beck. 183 EA93
Keats La., Wind. 151 AR79
Keats Pl. EC2 275 K7
Keats Rd., Belv. 167 FC76
Keats Rd., Well. 165 ES81
Keats Wk., Brwd. 109 GD45
Byron Rd.
Keats Way, Croy. 202 DW100
Keats Way, Grnf. 136 CB71
Keats Way, West Dr. 154 BM77
Keble Clo., Nthlt. 116 CC64
Keble Clo., Wor.Pk. 199 CT102
Keble St. SW17 180 DC91
Keble Ter., Abb.L. 59 BT32
Kechill Gdns., Brom. 204 EG101
Kedelston Ct. E5 123 DX63
Redwald Rd.
Kedleston Dr., Orp. 205 ET100
Kedleston Wk. E2 142 DV69
Middleton St.
Keedonwood Rd., Brom. 184 EE92
Keefield, Harl. 51 EP20
Keel Clo. SE16 143 DX74
Keel Dr., Slou. 151 AP75
Keele Clo., Wat. 76 BW40
Reeds Cres.
Keeler Clo., Wind. 151 AL83
Keeley Rd., Croy. 202 DQ103
Keeley St. WC2 274 B9
Keeley St. WC2 141 DM72
Keeling Rd. SE9 184 EK85
Keely Clo., Barn. 80 DE43
Keemor Clo. SE18 165 EN80
Llanover Rd.
Keens Clo. SW16 181 DK92
Keens La., Guil. 242 AT130
Keens Pk. Rd., Guil. 242 AT130
Keens Rd., Croy. 220 DQ105
Keens Yd. N1 141 DP65
St. Paul's Rd.
Keensacre, Iver 133 BD68
Keep, The SE3 164 EG82
Keep, The, Kings.T. 178 CM93
Keep La. N11 98 DG49
Gardeners Clo.
Keepers Clo., Guil. 243 BD131
Keepers Fm. Clo., Wind. 151 AL82
Keepers Ms., Tedd. 177 CH93
Munster Rd.
Keepers Wk., Vir.W. 192 AX99
Keesey St. SE5 162 DR79
Albany Rd.
Keetons Rd. SE16 162 DV76
Keevil Dr. SW19 179 CX87
Keighley Clo. N7 121 DL64
Penn Rd.
Keighley Rd., Rom. 106 FL52
Keightley Dr. SE9 185 EQ88
Keilder Clo., Uxb. 134 BN68
Charnwood Rd.
Keildon Rd. SW11 160 DF84
Keir, The SW19 179 CW92
West Side Common
Keir Hardie Est. E5 122 DV60
Springfield
Keir Hardie Ho. W6 159 CW79
Lochaline St.
Keir Hardie Way, Bark. 146 EU66
Keir Hardie Way, Hayes 135 BU69
Keith Ave. (Sutton at Hone), Dart. 188 FP93
Keith Connor Clo. SW8 161 DH83
Daley Thompson Way
Keith Gro. W12 159 CU75
Keith Pk. Cres., West. 222 EH113
Keith Pk. Rd., Uxb. 134 BM66
Keith Rd. E17 101 DZ53
Keith Rd., Bark. 145 ER68
Keith Rd., Hayes 155 BS76
Keith Way, Horn. 128 FL59
Keiths Rd., Hem.H. 40 BN21
Kelbrook Rd. SE3 164 EL82
Kelburn Way, Rain. 147 FG69
Dominion Way
Kelby Path SE9 185 EP90
Kelbys, Welw.G.C. 30 DC08
Kelceda Clo. NW2 119 CU61
Kelf Gro., Hayes 135 BT72
Kelfield Gdns. W10 139 CW72
Kell St. SE1 278 G6
Kelland Clo. N8 121 DK57
Palace Rd.
Kelland Rd. E13 144 EG70
Kellaway Rd. SE3 164 EJ82
Keller Cres. E12 124 EK63
Gladding Rd.
Kellerton Rd. SE13 184 EE85
Kellett Rd. SW2 161 DN84
Kelling Gdns., Croy. 201 DP101
Kellino St. SW17 180 DF91
Kellner Rd. SE28 165 ET76
Kelly Clo., Shep. 195 BS96
Kelly Ct., Borwd. 78 CQ40
Banks Rd.
Kelly Rd. NW7 97 CY51
Kelly St. NW1 141 DH65
Kelly Way, Rom. 126 EY57
Kelman Clo. SW4 161 DK82
Kelman Clo., Wal.Cr. 67 DX31
Kelmore Gro. SE22 162 DU84
Kelmscott Clo. E17 101 DZ54
Kelmscott Clo., Wat. 75 BU43
Kelmscott Cres., Wat. 75 BU43
Kelmscott Gdns. W12 159 CU76
Kelmscott Rd. SW11 180 DE85
Kelpatrick Rd., Slou. 131 AK72
Kelross Pas. N5 122 DQ63
Kelross Rd.
Kelross Rd. N5 122 DQ63
Kelsall Clo. SE3 164 EH82
Kelsey Clo., Horl. 268 DF148
Court Lo. Rd.
Kelsey La., Beck. 203 EA97
Kelsey Pk. Ave., Beck. 203 EB96
Kelsey Pk. Rd., Beck. 203 EA96
Kelsey Rd., Orp. 206 EV96
Kelsey Sq., Beck. 203 EA96
High St.
Kelsey St. E2 142 DU70
Kelsey Way, Beck. 203 EA97
Kelshall, Wat. 76 BY36
Kelshall Ct. N4 122 DQ61
Brownswood Rd.
Kelsie Way, Ilf. 103 ES51
Kelso Dr., Grav. 191 GM91
Kelso Pl. W8 160 DB76
Kelso Rd., Cars. 200 DC101
Kelson Ho. E14 163 EC76
Kelston Rd., Ilf. 103 EP54
Kelvedon Ave., Walt. 213 BS108
Kelvedon Clo., Brwd. 109 GE44
Kelvedon Clo., Kings.T. 178 CN93
Kelvedon Rd. SW6 159 CZ80
Kelvedon Wk., Rain. 147 FE67
Ongar Way
Kelvedon Way, Wdf.Grn. 103 EM51
Kelvin Ave. N13 99 DM51
Kelvin Ave., Lthd. 231 CF120
Kelvin Ave., Tedd. 177 CE93
Kelvin Clo., Epsom 216 CN107
Kelvin Cres., Har. 95 CE52
Kelvin Dr., Twick. 177 CH86
Kelvin Gdns., Croy. 201 DL101
Franklin Way
Kelvin Gdns., Sthl. 136 CA72
Kelvin Gro. SE26 182 DV90
Kelvin Gro., Chess. 198 CL104
Kelvin Ind. Est., Grnf. 136 CB66
Kelvin Par., Orp. 205 ES102
Kelvin Rd. N5 121 DP63
Kelvin Rd., Til. 171 GG82
Kelvin Rd., Well. 166 EU83
Kelvinbrook, W.Mol. 196 CB97
Kelvington Clo., Croy. 203 DY101
Kelvington Rd. SE15 183 DX85
Kember St. N1 141 DM66
Carnoustie Dr.
Kemble Clo., Pot.B. 64 DD33
Kemble Clo., Wey. 213 BR105
Kemble Cotts., Add. 194 BG104
Emley Rd.
Kemble Dr., Brom. 204 EL104
Kemble Par., Pot.B. 64 DC32
High St.
Kemble Rd. N17 100 DU53
Kemble Rd. SE23 183 DX88
Kemble Rd., Croy. 201 DN104
Kemble St. WC2 274 B9
Kemble St. WC2 141 DM72
Kembleside Rd., West. 238 EJ118
Kemerton Rd. SE5 162 DQ83
Kemerton Rd., Beck. 203 EB96
Kemerton Rd., Croy. 202 DT101
Kemeys St. E9 123 DY64
Kemishford, Wok. 226 AU123
Kemnal Rd., Chis. 185 EQ94

Kiln Pl. NW5 120 DG63
Kiln Rd., Epp. 70 FA27
Kiln Way, Grays 170 FZ78
Kiln Way, Nthwd. 93 BS51
Kilncroft, Hem.H. 41 BP22
Kilndown, Grav. 191 GJ93
Kilner St. E14 143 EA71
Kilnfield, Welw.G.C. 29 CZ06
Kilnside, Esher 215 CG108
Kilnwood, Sev. 224 EZ113
Kilpatrick Way, Hayes 136 BY71
Kilravock St. W10 139 CY69
Kilross Rd., Felt. 175 BR88
Kilrue La., Walt. 213 BT105
Kilrush Ter., Wok. 227 BA116
Kilsby Wk., Dag. 146 EV65
Rugby Rd.
Kilsha Rd., Walt. 195 BV100
Kilsmore La., Wal.Cr. 67 DX28
Kilvinton Dr., Enf. 82 DR38
Kilworth Ave., Brwd. 109 GA44
Kilworth Clo., Welw.G.C. 30 DB11
Kimbell Gdns. SW6 159 CY81
Kimber Clo., Wind. 151 AM83
Kimber Ct., Guil. 243 BD132
Gilliat Dr.
Kimber Rd. SW18 180 DA87
Kimberley Ave. E6 144 EL68
Kimberley Ave. SE15 162 DV82
Kimberley Ave., Ilf. 125 ER59
Kimberley Ave., Rom. 127 FC58
Kimberley Clo., Horl. 268 DF148
Court Lo. Rd.
Kimberley Clo., Slou. 153 AZ77
Kimberley Dr., Sid. 186 EX89
Kimberley Gdns. N4 121 DP57
Kimberley Gdns., Enf. 82 DT41
Kimberley Gate, Brom. 184 EF94
Oaklands Rd.
Kimberley Pl., Pur. 219 DN111
Brighton Rd.
Kimberley Ride, Cob. 214 CB113
Littleheath La.
Kimberley Rd. E4 102 EE46
Kimberley Rd. E11 123 ED61
Kimberley Rd. E16 144 EF70
Kimberley Rd. E17 101 DZ53
Kimberley Rd. N17 100 DU54
Kimberley Rd. N18 100 DV51
Kimberley Rd. NW6 139 CY67
Kimberley Rd. SW9 161 DL82
Kimberley Rd., Beck. 203 DX96
Kimberley Rd., Croy. 201 DP100
Kimberley Rd., St.Alb. 42 CC19
Kimberley Way E4 102 EE46
Kimbers Dr., Slou. 131 AK69
Kimble Clo., Wat. 75 BS44
Kimble Cres. (Bushey), Wat. 94 CC45
Kimble Rd. SW19 180 DD93
Kimbolton Clo. SE12 184 EF86
Kimbolton Grn., Borwd. 78 CQ42
Kimbolton Row SW3 276 B9
Kimmeridge Gdns. SE9 184 EL91
Kimmeridge Rd. SE9 184 EL91
Kimps Way, Hem.H. 40 BN23
Kimpton Ave., Brwd. 108 FV45
Kimpton Clo., Hem.H. 41 BP15
Kimpton Ind. Est., Sutt. 199 CZ103
Kimpton Pl., Wat. 60 BX34
Kimpton Rd. SE5 162 DR81
Kimpton Rd., Sutt. 199 CZ104
Kimptons Clo., Pot.B. 63 CX33
Kimptons Mead, Pot.B. 63 CX32
Kinburn Dr., Egh. 172 AY92
Kinburn St. SE16 163 DX75
Kincaid Rd. SE15 162 DV80
Kincardine Gdns. W9 139 CZ70
Harrow Rd.
Kinch Gro., Har. 118 CM59
Kincraig Dr., Sev. 256 FG124
Kinder Clo. SE28 146 EX73
Kinder St. E1 142 DV72
Cannon St. Rd.
Kinderscout, Hem.H. 40 BN22
Kindersley Way, Abb.L. 59 BQ31
Kinfauns Ave., Horn. 128 FJ58
Kinfauns Rd. SW2 181 DN89
Kinfauns Rd., Ilf. 126 EU60
King Acre Ct., Stai. 173 BE90
Victoria Rd.
King Alfred Ave. SE6 183 EA91
King Alfred Rd., Rom. 106 FM54
King & Queen Clo. SE9 184 EL91
Beaconsfield Rd.
King & Queen St. SE17 279 J10
King & Queen St. SE17 162 DQ78
King Arthur Clo. SE15 162 DW80
King Arthur Ct., Wal.Cr. 67 DY31
King Charles Cres., Surb. 198 CM101
King Charles Rd., Rad. 62 CL32
King Charles Rd., Surb. 198 CM99
King Charles St. SW1 277 P4
King Charles St. SW1 161 DK75
King Charles Ter. E1 142 DV73
Sovereign Clo.
King Charles Wk. SW19 179 CY88
Princes Way
King David La. E1 142 DW73
King Edward Ave., Dart. 188 FK86
King Edward Ave., Rain. 148 FK68
King Edward Ct., Wind. 151 AR81
King Edward Dr., Chess. 198 CL104
Kelvin Gro.
King Edward Dr., Grays 170 GE75
King Edward Ms. SW13 159 CU81
King Edward Rd. E10 123 EC60
King Edward Rd. E17 123 DY55
King Edward Rd., Barn. 80 DA42
King Edward Rd., Brwd. 108 FW48
King Edward Rd., Green. 169 FU84
King Edward Rd., Rad. 62 CM33
King Edward Rd., Rom. 127 FF58
King Edward Rd., Wal.Cr. 67 DY33
King Edward Rd., Wat. 76 BY44
King Edward VII Ave., Wind. 152 AS80
King Edward St. EC1 275 H8
King Edward St. EC1 142 DQ72
King Edward St., Hem.H. 40 BJ24
King Edward St., Slou. 151 AR75
King Edward Wk. SE1 278 E6
King Edward Wk. SE1 161 DN76
King Edward's Gdns. W3 138 CN74
King Edwards Gro., Tedd. 177 CH93
King Edwards Pl. W3 138 CN74
King Edward's Gdns.
King Edwards Rd. E9 142 DV67
King Edwards Rd. N9 100 DV45
King Edwards Rd., Bark. 145 ER67
King Edward's Rd., Enf. 83 DX42
King Edwards Rd., Ruis. 115 BR60
King Edwards Rd., Ware 33 DY05
King Gdns., Croy. 219 DP106
King George Ave. E16 144 EK72
King George Ave., Ilf. 125 ER57
King George Ave., Walt. 196 BX102
King George Ave. (Bushey), Wat. 76 CB44
King George Clo., Rom. 127 FC55
King George Clo., Sun. 175 BT92
King George V Rd., Amer. 55 AR38
King George Rd., Wal.Abb. 67 EC34
King George Rd., Ware 33 DY05
King George VI Ave., Mitch. 200 DF98
King George VI Ave., West. 238 EK116
King George Sq., Rich. 178 CM86
King George St. SE10 163 EC80
King Georges Ave., Wat. 75 BS42
King Georges Dr., Add. 212 BG110
King Georges Dr., Sthl. 136 BZ71
King Georges Rd., Brwd. 108 FV44
King Harolds Way, Bexh. 166 EX80
King Harry La., St.Alb. 42 CA21
King Harry St., Hem.H. 40 BK21
King Henry Ms., Orp. 223 ET106
Osgood Ave.
King Henry St. N16 122 DS64
King Henry Ter. E1 142 DV73
Sovereign Clo.
King Henry's Dr., Croy. 221 EB109
King Henry's Ms., Enf. 83 EA37
King Henry's Rd. NW3 140 DE66
King Henrys Rd., Kings.T. 198 CP97
King Henry's Wk. N1 142 DS65
King James Ave. (Cuffley), Pot.B. 65 DL29
King James St. SE1 278 G5
King James St. SE1 161 DP75
King John Ct. EC2 275 N4
King John St. E1 143 DX71
King John's Wk. SE9 184 EK88
King Sq. EC1 275 H3
King Stable Ct., Wind. 151 AR80
King Stable St.
King Stable St., Wind. 151 AR80
King Stairs Clo. SE16 162 DV75
Elephant La.
King St. E13 144 EG70
King St. EC2 275 J9
King St. EC2 142 DQ72
King St. N2 120 DD55
King St. N17 100 DT53
King St. SW1 277 L3
King St. SW1 141 DJ74
King St. W3 138 CP74
King St. W6 159 CU77
King St. WC2 273 P10
King St. WC2 141 DL73
King St., Cher. 194 BG102
King St., Chesh. 54 AP32
King St., Grav. 191 GH86
King St., Rich. 177 CK85
King St., Sthl. 156 BY76
King St., Twick. 177 CG88
King St., Wat. 76 BW42
King William IV Gdns. SE20 182 DW93
St. John's Rd.
King William La. SE10 164 EE78
Orlop St.
King William St. EC4 279 L1
King William St. EC4 142 DR73
King William Wk. SE10 163 EC79
Kingaby Gdns., Rain. 147 FG66
Kingcup Clo., Croy. 203 DX102
Primrose La.
Kingdon Rd. NW6 140 DA65
Kingfield Clo., Wok. 227 AZ120
Kingfield Dr., Wok. 227 AZ120
Kingfield Gdns., Wok. 227 AZ119
Kingfield Rd. W5 137 CK70
Kingfield Rd., Wok. 226 AY120
Kingfield St. E14 163 EC77
Kingfisher Clo. SE28 146 EW73
Kingfisher Clo., Brwd. 109 GA45
Kingfisher Clo., Har. 95 CF52
Kingfisher Clo., Nthwd. 93 BP53
Kingfisher Clo., Orp. 206 EX98
Kingfisher Clo., Walt. 214 BY106
Old Esher Rd.
Kingfisher Clo., Ware 33 EC12
Lawrence Ave.
Kingfisher Ct. SW19 179 CY89
Queensmere Rd.
Kingfisher Ct., Wok. 211 BC114
Blackmore Cres.
Kingfisher Dr., Guil. 243 BC132
Kingfisher Dr., Red. 250 DG131
Kingfisher Dr., Rich. 177 CH91
Kingfisher Dr., Stai. 173 BF91
Kingfisher Gdns., S.Croy. 221 DX111
Kingfisher Lure, Kings L. 59 BP29
Kingfisher Lure, Rick. 74 BH42
Kingfisher Rd., Upmin. 129 FT60
Kingfisher Sq. SE8 163 DZ79
Dorking Clo.
Kingfisher St. E6 144 EL71
Kingfisher Wk. NW9 96 CS54
Eagle Dr.
Kingfisher Way NW10 138 CR65
Kingfisher Way, Beck. 203 DX99
Kingham Clo. SW18 180 DC87
Kingham Clo. W11 159 CY75
Kinghorn St. EC1 275 H7
Kinglake Ct., Wok. 226 AS118
Raglan Rd.
Kinglake Est. SE17 279 N10
Kinglake St. SE17 162 DS78
Kingly Ct. W1 273 L10
Kingly St. W1 273 K10
Kingly St. W1 141 DJ73
Kings Arbour, Sthl. 156 BY78
Ringway
Kings Arms Ct. E1 142 DU71
Old Montague St.
Kings Arms Yd. EC2 275 K8
Kings Ave. N10 120 DG55
Kings Ave. N21 99 DP46
King's Ave. SW4 181 DL85
King's Ave. SW12 181 DK88
Kings Ave. W5 137 CK72
Kings Ave., Brom. 184 EF93
Kings Ave., Buck.H. 102 EK47
Kings Ave., Cars. 218 DE108
Kings Ave., Grnf. 136 CB72
Kings Ave., Hem.H. 40 BM24
Kings Ave., Houns. 156 CB81
Kings Ave., N.Mal. 198 CS98
Kings Ave., Red. 250 DE134
Kings Ave., Rom. 126 EZ58
Kings Ave., Sun. 175 BT92
Kings Ave., Wat. 75 BT42
Kings Ave., W.Byf. 212 BK112
Kings Ave., Wdf.Grn. 102 EH51
Kings Bench St. SE1 278 G4
Kings Bench Wk. EC4 274 E9
Kings Chase, Brwd. 108 FW48
Kings Chase, E.Mol. 196 CC97
Kings Clo. E10 123 EB59
Kings Clo. NW4 119 CX56
Kings Clo., Beac. 110 AG55
Holtspur Top La.
Kings Clo., Ch.St.G. 90 AX47
Kings Clo., Dart. 167 FE84
Kings Clo., Kings L. 58 BH31
Kings Clo., Nthwd. 93 BT51
Kings Clo., Stai. 174 BK94
Kings Clo., T.Ditt. 197 CG100
Kings Dr.
Kings Clo., Walt. 195 BV102
King's Clo., Wat. 75 BV42
Lady's Clo.
Kings College Rd. NW3 140 DE66
Kings College Rd., Ruis. 115 BT58
Kings Ct. E13 144 EH67
Kings Ct. W6 159 CU77
King St.
Kings Ct., Berk. 38 AW18
Lower Kings Rd.
Kings Ct., Tad. 233 CW122
Kings Ct., Wem. 118 CP61
Kings Cres. N4 122 DQ62
Kings Cres. Est. N4 122 DQ61
Kings Cross La., Red. 267 DK136
King's Cross Rd. WC1 274 B2
King's Cross Rd. WC1 141 DM69
Kings Dr., Edg. 96 CM49
Kings Dr., Grav. 191 GH90
Kings Dr., Surb. 198 CN101
Kings Dr., Tedd. 177 CD92
Kings Dr., T.Ditt. 197 CH100
Kings Dr., Wem. 118 CP61
Kings Dr., The, Walt. 213 BT109
Kings Fm. Ave., Rich. 158 CN84
Kings Fm. Rd., Rick. 73 BD44
Kings Gdns. NW6 140 DA66
West End La.
Kings Gdns., Ilf. 125 ER60
Kings Gdns., Upmin. 129 FS59
King's Garth Ms. SE23 182 DW89
London Rd.
Kings Grn., Loug. 84 EL41
Kings Gro. SE15 162 DV81
Kings Gro., Rom. 127 FG57
Kings Hall Rd., Beck. 183 DY94
Kings Head Hill E4 101 EB45
Kings Head La., W.Byf. 212 BK111
Kings Head Yd. SE1 279 K3
Kings Highway SE18 165 ES79
Kings Hill, Loug. 84 EL40
Kings Keep, Kings.T. 198 CL98
Beaufort Rd.
Kings La., Egh. 172 AU92
Kings La., Kings L. 58 BG31
Kings La., Sutt. 218 DD107
Kings Langley Bypass, Hem.H. 39 BD22
Kings Langley Bypass, Kings L. 58 BJ25
Kings Lynn Clo., Rom. 106 FK51
Kings Lynn Dr.
Kings Lynn Dr., Rom. 106 FK51
Kings Lynn Path, Rom. 106 FK51
Kings Lynn Dr.
Kings Mead, Horl. 269 DP148
Kings Mead, Red. 267 DL136
Kings Mead Pk., Esher 215 CE108
Kings Meadow, Kings L. 58 BN28
Kings Ms. SW4 181 DL85
King's Ave.
King's Ms. WC1 274 C5
King's Ms. WC1 141 DM70
Kings Ms., Chig. 103 EQ47
Kings Mill La., Red. 267 DJ139
King's Orchard SE9 184 EL86
Kings Paddock, Hmptn. 196 CC95
King's Pas. E11 124 EE59
Kings Pas., Kings.T. 197 CK96
Kings Pl. SE1 279 H5
Kings Pl. W4 158 CQ77
Chiswick High Rd.
Kings Pl., Buck.H. 102 EK47
King's Reach Twr. SE1 278 E2
Kings Ride Gate, Rich. 158 CN84
Kings Rd. E4 101 ED46
Kings Rd. E6 144 EJ67
Kings Rd. E11 124 EE59
King's Rd. N17 100 DT53
Kings Rd. N18 100 DU50
Kings Rd. N22 99 DM53
Kings Rd. NW10 139 CV66
Kings Rd. SE25 202 DU97
King's Rd. SW1 160 DD79
King's Rd. SW3 160 DD79
King's Rd. SW6 160 DB80
King's Rd. SW10 160 DC80
Kings Rd. SW14 158 CR83
Kings Rd. SW19 180 DA93
Kings Rd. W5 137 CK71
Kings Rd., Add. 212 BH110
Kings Rd., Bark. 145 EQ66
North St.
Kings Rd., Barn. 79 CW41
Kings Rd., Berk. 38 AU20
Kings Rd., Brwd. 108 FW47
Kings Rd., Ch.St.G. 90 AW47
Kings Rd., Egh. 173 BA91
Kings Rd., Felt. 176 BW88
Kings Rd., Guil. 242 AX134
Kings Rd. (Shalford), Guil. 258 AY141
Kings Rd., Har. 116 BZ61
Kings Rd., Hert. 32 DU08
Kings Rd., Horl. 268 DG148
Kings Rd., Kings.T. 178 CL94
Kings Rd., Mitch. 200 DG97
Kings Rd., Orp. 223 ET105
Kings Rd., Rich. 178 CM86
Kings Rd., Rom. 127 FG57
Kings Rd., St.Alb. 42 CC20
Kings Rd. (London Colney), St.Alb. 61 CJ26
Kings Rd., Slou. 152 AS76
Kings Rd., Surb. 197 CJ102
Kings Rd., Sutt. 218 DA110
Kings Rd., Tedd. 177 CD92
Kings Rd., Twick. 177 CH86
Kings Rd., Uxb. 134 BK68
Kings Rd., Wal.Cr. 67 DY34
Kings Rd., Walt. 195 BV103
Kings Rd., West Dr. 154 BM75
Kings Rd., West. 238 EH118
Kings Rd., Wind. 151 AR84
Kings Rd., Wok. 227 BA116
King's Scholars' Pas. SW1 277 K7
King's Ter. NW1 141 DJ67
Plender St.
Kings Wk., Grays 170 GA79
Kings Wk., Kings.T. 197 CK95
Kings Wk., S.Croy. 220 DV114
Kings Way, Har. 117 CE56
Kingsand Rd. SE12 184 EG89
Kingsash Dr., Hayes 136 BY70
Kingsbridge Ave. W3 158 CM75
Kingsbridge Circ., Rom. 106 FL52
Kingsbridge Clo., Rom. 106 FL51
Kingsbridge Cres., Sthl. 136 BZ71
Kingsbridge Rd. W10 139 CW72
Kingsbridge Rd., Bark. 145 ER68
Kingsbridge Rd., Mord. 199 CX101
Kingsbridge Rd., Rom. 106 FL51
Kingsbridge Rd., Sthl. 156 BZ77
Kingsbridge Rd., Walt. 195 BV101
Kingsbridge Way, Hayes 135 BS69
Bradenham Rd.
Kingsbrook, Lthd. 231 CG118
Ryebrook Rd.
Kingsbury Ave., St.Alb. 42 CC19
Kingsbury Circle NW9 118 CN57
Kingsbury Cres., Stai. 173 BD91
Kingsbury Dr., Wind. 172 AU87
Kingsbury Rd. N1 142 DS65
Kingsbury Rd. NW9 118 CN57
Kingsbury Ter. N1 142 DS65
Kingsbury Trd. Est. NW9 118 CR58
Kingsclere Clo. SW15 179 CU87
Kingscliffe Gdns. SW19 179 CZ88
Kingscote Rd. W4 158 CR76
Kingscote Rd., Croy. 202 DV101
Kingscote Rd., N.Mal. 198 CR97
Kingscote St. EC4 274 F10
Kingscourt Rd. SW16 181 DK90
Kingscroft, Welw.G.C. 30 DB08
Kingscroft Rd. NW2 139 CZ65
Kingscroft Rd., Bans. 234 DD115
Kingscroft Rd., Lthd. 231 CH120
Kingsdale Gdns. W11 139 CX74
Kingsdale Rd. SE18 165 ET79
Kingsdale Rd. SE20 183 DX94
Kingsdale Rd., Berk. 38 AU20
Kingsdene, Tad. 233 CV121
Kingsdon La., Harl. 52 EW16
Kingsdown Ave. W3 138 CS73
Kingsdown Ave. W13 157 CH75
Kingsdown Ave., S.Croy. 219 DP109
Kingsdown Clo. W10 139 CX72
Kingsdown Clo., Grav. 191 GM88
Farley Rd.
Kingsdown Rd. E11 124 EE62
Kingsdown Rd. N19 121 DL62
Kingsdown Rd., Epsom 217 CU113
Kingsdown Rd., Sutt. 217 CY106
Kingsdown Way, Brom. 204 EG101
Kingsdowne Rd., Surb. 198 CL101
Kingsend, Ruis. 115 BR60
Kingsfield, Guil. 260 BL144
Kingsfield, Hodd. 49 EA15
Kingsfield, Wind. 151 AK81
Kingsfield Ave., Har. 116 CB56
Kingsfield Ct., Wat. 94 BX45
Kingsfield Dr., Enf. 83 DX35
Kingsfield Ho. SE9 184 EK90
Kingsfield Rd., Har. 117 CD59
Kingsfield Rd., Wat. 94 BX45
Kingsfield Ter., Dart. 188 FK86
Priory Rd.
Kingsfield Way, Enf. 83 DX35
Kingsford Ave., Wall. 219 DL108
Kingsford St. NW5 120 DF64
Kingsford Way E6 145 EM71
Tollgate Rd.
Kingsgate, Wem. 118 CQ62
Kingsgate Ave. N3 120 DA55
Kingsgate Clo., Bexh. 166 EY81
Kingsgate Clo., Orp. 206 EW97
Main Rd.
Kingsgate Pl. NW6 140 DA66
Kingsgate Rd. NW6 140 DA66
Kingsgate Rd., Kings.T. 198 CL95
Kingsground SE9 184 EL87
Kingshall Ms. SE13 163 EC83
Lewisham Rd.
Kingshill Ave., Har. 117 CH56
Kingshill Ave., Hayes 135 BS69
Kingshill Ave., Nthlt. 135 BU69
Kingshill Ave., Rom. 105 FC51
Kingshill Ave., St.Alb. 43 CH17
Kingshill Ave., Wor.Pk. 199 CU101
Kingshill Dr., Har. 95 CH54
Kingshill Way, Berk. 38 AU21
Kingshold Rd. E9 142 DW66
Kingsholm Gdns. SE9 164 EK84
Kingshurst Rd. SE12 184 EG87
Kingsland NW8 140 DE67
Broxwood Way
Kingsland, Harl. 51 EQ17
Kingsland, Pot.B. 63 CZ33
Oakroyd Ave.
Kingsland Grn. E8 142 DS65
Kingsland High St. E8 142 DT65
Kingsland Pas. E8 142 DS65
Kingsland Grn.
Kingsland Rd. E2 275 N2
Kingsland Rd. E2 142 DS69
Kingsland Rd. E8 142 DS67
Kingsland Rd. E13 144 EJ69
Kingsland Rd., Hem.H. 40 BG22
Kingslawn Clo. SW15 179 CV85
Howards La.
Kingslea, Lthd. 231 CG120
Kingsleigh Pl., Mitch. 200 DF97
Chatsworth Pl.
Kingsleigh Wk., Brom. 204 EF98
Stamford Dr.
Kingsley Ave. W13 137 CG72
Kingsley Ave., Bans. 234 DA115
Kingsley Ave., Borwd. 78 CM40
Kingsley Ave., Dart. 188 FN85
Kingsley Ave., Egh. 172 AV93
Kingsley Ave., Houns. 156 CC82
Kingsley Ave., Sthl. 136 CA73
Kingsley Ave., Sutt. 218 DD105
Kingsley Ave. (Cheshunt), Wal.Cr. 66 DV29
Kingsley Clo. N2 120 DC57
Kingsley Clo., Dag. 127 FB63
Kingsley Clo., Horl. 268 DF146
Kingsley Rd.
Kingsley Ct., Edg. 96 CP47
Kingsley Ct., Welw.G.C. 29 CZ13
Kingsley Dr., Wor.Pk. 199 CT103
Badgers Copse
Kingsley Flats SE1 162 DS77
Old Kent Rd.
Kingsley Gdns. E4 101 EA50
Kingsley Gdns., Horn. 128 FK56
Kingsley Gro., Reig. 266 DA137
Kingsley Ms. E1 142 DV73
Wapping La.
Kingsley Ms. W8 160 DB76
Stanford Rd.
Kingsley Ms., Chis. 185 EP93
Kingsley Path, Slou. 131 AK70
Wordsworth Rd.
Kingsley Pl. N6 120 DG59
Kingsley Rd. E7 144 EG66
Kingsley Rd. E17 101 EC54
Kingsley Rd. N13 99 DN49
Kingsley Rd. NW6 139 CZ67
Kingsley Rd. SW19 180 DB92
Kingsley Rd., Brwd. 109 GD45
Kingsley Rd., Croy. 201 DN102
Kingsley Rd., Har. 116 CC63
Kingsley Rd., Horl. 268 DF146
Kingsley Rd., Houns. 156 CB81
Kingsley Rd., Ilf. 103 EQ53
Kingsley Rd., Loug. 85 ER41
Kingsley Rd., Orp. 223 ET107
Kingsley Rd., Pnr. 116 BZ56
Kingsley St. SW11 160 DF83
Kingsley Wk., Grays 171 GG77
Kingsley Way N2 120 DC57
Kingsley Wd. Dr. SE9 185 EM90
Kingslyn Cres. SE19 202 DS95
Kingsman Par. SE18 165 EM76
Woolwich Ch. St.
Kingsman St. SE18 165 EM76
Kingsmead, Barn. 80 DA42
Kingsmead (Cuffley), Pot.B. 65 DL28
Kingsmead, Rich. 178 CM86
Kingsmead, St.Alb. 43 CK17
Kingsmead, Saw. 36 EY06
Kingsmead, Wal.Cr. 67 DX28
Kingsmead, West. 238 EK116
Kingsmead Ave. N9 100 DV46
Kingsmead Ave. NW9 118 CR59
Kingsmead Ave., Mitch. 201 DJ97
Kingsmead Ave., Rom. 127 FE58
Kingsmead Ave., Sun. 196 BW96
Kingsmead Ave., Surb. 198 CN103
Kingsmead Ave., Wor.Pk. 199 CV103
Kingsmead Clo., Epsom 216 CR108
Kingsmead Clo., Harl. 50 EH16
Kingsmead Clo., Sid. 186 EU89
Kingsmead Clo., Tedd. 177 CH93
Kingsmead Dr., Nthlt. 136 BZ66
Kingsmead Est. E9 123 DY63
Kingsmead Way
Kingsmead Rd. SW2 181 DN89
Kingsmead Way E9 123 DY63
Kingsmere Clo. SW15 159 CY83
Felsham Rd.
Kingsmere Pk. NW9 118 CP60
Kingsmere Rd. SW19 179 CX89
Kingsmill Ct., Hat. 45 CV20
Travellers La.
Kingsmill Gdns., Dag. 126 EZ64
Kingsmill Rd., Dag. 126 EZ64
Kingsmill Ter. NW8 140 DD68
Kingsmoor Rd., Harl. 51 EP17
Kingsnympton Pk., Kings.T. 178 CP94
Kingspark Ct. E18 124 EG55
Kingsridge SW19 179 CY89
Kingsridge Gdns., Dart. 188 FK86
Kingsthorpe Rd. SE26 183 DX91
Kingston Ave., Felt. 175 BS86
Kingston Ave., Lthd. 231 CH121
Kingston Ave. (East Horsley), Lthd. 245 BS126
Kingston Ave., Sutt. 199 CY104
Kingston Ave., West Dr. 134 BM73
Kingston Bri., Kings.T. 197 CK96
Kingston Bypass SW15 178 CS91
Kingston Bypass SW20 178 CS93
Kingston Bypass, Esher 197 CE103
Kingston Bypass, N.Mal. 199 CU98
Kingston Bypass, Surb. 197 CH104
Kingston Clo., Nthlt. 136 BZ66
Kingston Clo., Rom. 126 EY55
Kingston Clo., Tedd. 177 CH93
Kingston Ct. N4 122 DQ58
Wiltshire Gdns.
Kingston Ct., Grav. 190 GB85
Kingston Cres., Ashf. 174 BJ92
Kingston Cres., Beck. 203 DZ95
Kingston Gdns., Croy. 201 DL104
Wandle Rd.
Kingston Hall Rd., Kings.T. 197 CK97
Kingston Hill, Kings.T. 198 CN95
Kingston Hill Ave., Rom. 126 EY55
Kingston Hill Pl., Kings.T. 178 CQ91
Kingston Ho. Gdns., Lthd. 231 CG121
Upper Fairfield Rd.
Kingston La., Lthd. 244 BM127
Kingston La., Tedd. 177 CG92
Kingston La., Uxb. 134 BL69
Kingston La., West Dr. 154 BM75
Kingston Pk. Est., Kings.T. 178 CP93
Kingston Pl., Har. 95 CF52
Richmond Gdns.
Kingston Ri., Add. 212 BG110
Kingston Rd. N9 100 DU47
Kingston Rd. SW15 179 CU89
Kingston Rd. SW19 199 CY96

Kingston Rd. SW20 199 CW96
Kingston Rd., Ashf. 174 BL93
Kingston Rd., Barn. 80 DD43
Kingston Rd., Epsom 216 CS105
Kingston Rd., Ilf. 125 EP63
Kingston Rd., Kings.T. 198 CP97
Kingston Rd., Lthd. 231 CG121
Kingston Rd., N.Mal. 198 CR98
Kingston Rd., Rom. 127 FF56
Kingston Rd., Sthl. 156 BZ75
Kingston Rd., Stai. 194 BH103
Kingston Rd., Surb. 198 CP103
Kingston Rd., Tedd. 177 CH92
Kingston Rd., Wor.Pk. 198 CQ104
Kingston Sq. SE19 182 DR92
Kingston Vale SW15 178 CR91
Kingstown St. NW1 140 DG67
Kingswater Pl. SW11 160 DE80
Battersea Ch. Rd.
Kingsway N12 98 DC51
Kingsway SW14 158 CP83
Kingsway WC2 274 B8
Kingsway WC2 141 DM72
Kingsway, Croy. 219 DM106
Kingsway, Enf. 82 DV43
Kingsway, Ger.Cr. 112 AY55
Kingsway, Hayes 135 BQ71
Kingsway, Iver 133 BE72
High St.
Kingsway, N.Mal. 199 CW98
Kingsway, Orp. 205 EQ99
Kingsway (Cuffley), Pot.B. 65 DL30
Kingsway, Slou. 131 AP65
Kingsway, Stai. 174 BK88
Kingsway, Wat. 75 BT35
Kingsway, Wem. 118 CL63
Kingsway, W.Wick. 204 EE104
Kingsway, Wok. 226 AX118
Kingsway, Wdf.Grn. 102 EJ50
Kingsway, The, Epsom 216 CS111
Kingsway Ave., S.Croy. 220 DW109
Kingsway Ave., Wok. 226 AX118
Kingsway Business Pk., Hmptn. 196 BZ95
Kingsway Cres., Har. 116 CC56
Kingsway Ind. Est. N18 101 DX51
Kingsway Rd., Sutt. 217 CY107
Kingswear Rd. NW5 121 DH62
Kingswear Rd., Ruis. 115 BU61
Kingswell Ride (Cuffley), Pot.B. 65 DL30
Kingswood Ave. NW6 139 CY67
Kingswood Ave., Belv. 166 EZ77
Kingswood Ave., Brom. 204 EE97
Kingswood Ave., Hmptn. 176 CB93
Kingswood Ave., Houns. 156 BZ81
Kingswood Ave., S.Croy. 236 DV115
Kingswood Ave., Swan. 207 FF98
Kingswood Ave., Th.Hth. 201 DN99
Kingswood Clo. N20 98 DC45
Kingswood Clo. SW8 161 DL80
Kenchester Clo.
Kingswood Clo., Dart. 188 FJ85
Kingswood Clo., Egh. 172 AX91
Kingswood Clo., Enf. 82 DS43
Kingswood Clo., Guil. 243 BC133
Kingswood Clo., N.Mal. 199 CT100
Motspur Pk.
Kingswood Clo., Orp. 205 ER101
Kingswood Clo., Surb. 198 CL101
Kingswood Clo., Wey. 213 BP108
Kingswood Creek, Stai. 172 AX85
Kingswood Dr. SE19 182 DS91
Kingswood Dr., Cars. 200 DF102
Kingswood Dr., Sutt. 218 DB109
Kingswood Est. SE21 182 DS91
Bowen Dr.
Kingswood La., Warl. 236 DW115
Kingswood Pk. N3 97 CZ54
Kingswood Pl. SE13 164 EE84
Kingswood Ri., Egh. 172 AX92
Kingswood Rd. SE20 182 DW93
Kingswood Rd. SW2 181 DL86
Kingswood Rd. SW19 179 CZ94
Kingswood Rd. W4 158 CQ76
Kingswood Rd., Brom. 203 ED98
Kingswood Rd., Ilf. 126 EU60
Kingswood Rd., Sev. 241 FE120
Kingswood Rd., Tad. 233 CV121
Kingswood Rd., Wat. 59 BV34
Kingswood Rd., Wem. 118 CN62
Kingswood Ter. W4 158 CQ76
Kingswood Rd.
Kingswood Way, S.Croy. 220 DW113
Kingswood Way, Wall. 219 DL106
Kingsworth Clo., Beck. 203 DY99
Shirley Cres.
Kingsworthy Clo., Kings.T. 198 CM97
Kingthorpe Rd. NW10 138 CR66
Kingthorpe Ter. NW10 138 CR65
Kingwell Rd., Barn. 80 DD38
Kingwood Rd. SW6 159 CY80
Kinlet Rd. SE18 165 EQ81
Kinloch Dr. NW9 118 CR59
Kinloch St. N7 121 DM62
Hornsey Rd.
Kinloss Gdns. N3 119 CZ55
Kinloss Rd., Cars. 200 DC101
Kinnaird Ave. W4 158 CQ80
Kinnaird Ave., Brom. 184 EF93
Kinnaird Clo., Brom. 184 EF93
Kinnaird Clo., Slou. 130 AJ72
Kinnaird Way, Wdf.Grn. 103 EM51
Kinnear Rd. W12 159 CT75
Kinnersley Manor, Reig. 266 DC142
Reigate Rd.
Kinnersley Wk., Reig. 266 DB139
Castle Dr.
Kinnerton Pl. N. SW1 276 E5
Kinnerton Pl. S. SW1 276 E5
Kinnerton St. SW1 276 F5
Kinnerton St. SW1 160 DG75
Kinnerton Yd. SW1 276 E5
Kinnoul Rd. W6 159 CY79
Kinross Ave., Wor.Pk. 199 CU103
Kinross Clo., Edg. 96 CP47
Tayside Dr.
Kinross Clo., Har. 118 CL57
Kinross Clo., Sun. 175 BT92
Kinross Dr., Sun. 175 BT92
Kinsale Rd. SE15 162 DU83
Kintore Way SE1 279 P8
Kintyre Clo. SW16 201 DM96
Kinveachy Gdns. SE7 164 EL78
Kinver Rd. SE26 182 DW91
Kipings, Tad. 233 CX122
Heathcote
Kipling Ave., Til. 171 GH81
Kipling Dr. SW19 180 DD93
Kipling Est. SE1 279 L5
Kipling Est. SE1 162 DR75
Kipling Pl., Stan. 95 CF51
Uxbridge Rd.
Kipling Rd., Bexh. 166 EY81
Kipling Rd., Dart. 188 FP85
Kipling St. SE1 279 L5
Kipling St. SE1 162 DR75
Kipling Ter. N9 100 DR48
Kipling Twrs., Rom. 105 FH52
Kippington Clo., Sev. 256 FF124
Kippington Dr. SE9 184 EK88
Kippington Rd., Sev. 256 FG124
Kirby Clo., Epsom 217 CT106
Kirby Clo., Ilf. 103 ES51
Kirby Clo., Loug. 102 EL45
Kirby Clo., Nthwd. 93 BT51
Kirby Clo., Rom. 106 FN50
Kirby Est. SE16 162 DV76
Kirby Gro. SE1 279 M4
Kirby Gro. SE1 162 DS75
Kirby Rd., Dart. 188 FQ87
Kirby Rd., Wok. 226 AW117
Kirby St. EC1 274 E6
Kirby Way, Walt. 196 BW100
Kirchen Rd. W13 137 CH73
Kirk Ct., Sev. 256 FG123
Kirk La. SE18 165 EQ79
Kirk Ri., Sutt. 200 DB104
Kirk Rd. E17 123 DZ58
Kirkcaldy Grn., Wat. 94 BW48
Trevose Way
Kirkdale SE26 182 DW91
Kirkdale Rd. E11 124 EE60
Kirkefields, Guil. 242 AU131
Stoughton Rd.
Kirkfield Clo. W13 137 CH74
Broomfield Rd.
Kirkham Rd. E6 144 EL72
Kirkham St. SE18 165 ES79
Kirkland Ave., Ilf. 103 EN55
Kirkland Ave., Wok. 226 AS116
Kirkland Clo., Sid. 185 ES86
Kirkland Wk. E8 142 DT65
Laurel St.
Kirklands, Welw.G.C. 29 CX05
Kirkleas Rd., Surb. 198 CL102
Kirklees Rd., Dag. 126 EW64
Kirklees Rd., Th.Hth. 201 DN99
Kirkley Rd. SW19 200 DA95
Kirkly Clo., S.Croy. 220 DS109
Kirkman Pl. W1 273 M7
Kirkmichael Rd. E14 143 EC72
Dee St.
Kirks Pl. E14 143 DZ71
Rhodeswell Rd.
Kirkside Rd. SE3 164 EG79
Kirkstall Ave. N17 122 DR56
Kirkstall Gdns. SW2 181 DK88
Kirkstall Rd. SW2 181 DK88
Kirkstead Ct. E5 123 DY62
Mandeville St.
Kirksted Rd., Mord. 200 DB102
Kirkstone Way, Brom. 184 EE93
Kirkton Rd. N15 122 DS56
Kirkwall Pl. E2 142 DW69
Kirkwall Spur, Slou. 132 AS71
Kirkwood Rd. SE15 162 DV82
Kirn Rd. W13 137 CH73
Kirchen Rd.
Kirrane Clo., N.Mal. 199 CT99
Woodfield Gdns.
Kirtle Rd., Chesh. 54 AQ31
Kirtley Rd. SE26 183 DY91
Kirtling St. SW8 161 DJ80
Kirton Clo. W4 158 CR77
Dolman Rd.
Kirton Clo., Horn. 148 FJ65
Kirton Gdns. E2 142 DT69
Chambord St.
Kirton Rd. E13 144 EJ68
Kirton Wk., Edg. 96 CQ52
Kirwyn Way SE5 161 DP80
Kitcat Ter. E3 143 EA69
Kitchener Ave., Grav. 191 GJ90
Kitchener Clo., St.Alb. 43 CH21
Kitchener Rd. E7 144 EH65
Kitchener Rd. E17 101 EB53
Kitchener Rd. N2 120 DE55
Kitchener Rd. N17 122 DR55
Kitchener Rd., Dag. 147 FB65
Kitchener Rd., Th.Hth. 202 DR97
Kitcheners Mead, St.Alb. 42 CC20
Kite Fld., Berk. 38 AS16
Kite Yd. SW11 160 DF81
Cambridge Rd.
Kitley Gdns. SE19 202 DT95
Kitsbury Rd., Berk. 38 AV19
Kitsbury Ter., Berk. 38 AV19
Kitsmead La., Cher. 192 AW102
Kitson Rd. SE5 162 DR80
Kitson Rd. SW13 159 CU81
Kitson Way, Harl. 35 EQ14
Kitswell Way, Rad. 61 CF33
Kitten La., Ware 34 EE11
Kitters Grn., Abb.L. 59 BS31
High St.
Kittiwake Clo., S.Croy. 221 DY110
Kittiwake Rd., Nthlt. 136 BX69
Kittiwake Way, Hayes 136 BX71
Willow Tree La.
Kitto Rd. SE14 163 DX82
Kitt's End Rd., Barn. 79 CX36
Kiver Rd. N19 121 DK61
Kiwi Clo., Twick. 177 CH86
Crown Rd.
Klea Ave. SW4 181 DJ86
Knapdale Clo. SE23 182 DV89
Knapmill Rd. SE6 183 EA89
Knapmill Way SE6 183 EB89
Knapp Clo. NW10 138 CS65
Knapp Rd. E3 143 EA70
Knapp Rd., Ashf. 174 BM91
Knapton Ms. SW17 180 DG93
Seely Rd.
Knaresborough Dr. SW18 180 DB88
Strathville Rd.
Knaresborough Pl. SW5 160 DB77
Knatchbull Rd. NW10 138 CR67
Knatchbull Rd. SE5 161 DP82
Knaves Beech, H.Wyc. 88 AD53
Knaves Beech Business Cen., H.Wyc. 88 AC54
Knaves Beech Way, H.Wyc. 88 AC54
Knebworth Ave. E17 101 EA53
Knebworth Path, Borwd. 78 CR42
Knebworth Rd. N16 122 DS63
Nevill Rd.
Knee Hill SE2 166 EW77
Knee Hill Cres. SE2 166 EW77
Knella Grn., Welw.G.C. 30 DA09
Knella Rd., Welw.G.C. 29 CZ10
Kneller Gdns., Islw. 177 CD86
Kneller Rd. SE4 163 DY84
Kneller Rd., N.Mal. 198 CS101
Kneller Rd., Twick. 176 CC86
Knight St., Saw. 36 EY05
Knighten St. E1 142 DU74
Wapping High St.
Knightland Rd. E5 122 DV61
Knighton Clo., Rom. 127 FD58
Knighton Clo., S.Croy. 219 DP108
Knighton Clo., Wdf.Grn. 102 EH49
Knighton Dr., Wdf.Grn. 102 EH49
Knighton La., Buck.H. 102 EH47
Knighton Pk. Rd. SE26 183 DX92
Knighton Rd. E7 124 EG62
Knighton Rd., Red. 266 DG136
Knighton Rd., Rom. 127 FC58
Knighton Rd., Sev. 241 FF116
Knighton St. E1 142 DU74
Sampson St.
Knighton Way La., Uxb. 134 BH65
Knightrider Ct. EC4 142 DQ73
Godliman St.
Knightrider St. EC4 142 DQ73
Godliman St.
Knights Arc. SW1 276 D5
Knights Ave. W5 158 CL75
Knights Clo. E9 122 DW64
Churchill Wk.
Knights Clo., Egh. 173 BD93
Knights Clo., Wind. 151 AK81
Knights Ct., Kings.T. 198 CL97
Knights Ct., Rom. 126 EY58
Knights Hill SE27 181 DP92
Knights Hill Sq. SE27 181 DP91
Knights Hill
Knights La. N9 100 DU48
Knights Manor Way, Dart. 188 FM85
Knights Orchard, Hem.H. 39 BF18
Knights Pk., Kings.T. 198 CL97
Knights Ridge, Orp. 224 EV106
Stirling Dr.
Knights Rd. E16 164 EG75
Knights Rd., Stan. 95 CJ49
Knights Wk. SE11 278 F9
Knights Wk., Rom. 86 EV41
Knight's Way, Brwd. 109 GA48
Knights Way, Ilf. 103 EQ51
Knightsbridge SW1 276 E4
Knightsbridge SW1 160 DF75
Knightsbridge SW7 276 C5
Knightsbridge SW7 160 DE75
Knightsbridge Cres., Stai. 174 BH93
Knightsbridge Gdns., Rom. 127 FD57
Knightsbridge Grn. SW1 276 D5
Knightsbridge Grn. SW1 160 DF75
Knightsbridge Way, Hem.H. 40 BL19
Knightsfield, Welw.G.C. 29 CY06
Knightswood, Wok. 226 AT118
Knightswood Clo., Edg. 96 CQ47
Knightwood Clo., Reig. 266 DA136
Knightwood Cres., N.Mal. 198 CS100
Knipp Hill, Cob. 214 BZ113
Knivet Rd. SW6 160 DA79
Knobfield, Dor. 261 BT143
Knobs Hill Rd. E15 143 EB67
Knockhall Chase, Green. 189 FV85
Knockhall Rd., Green. 189 FV86
Knockholt Clo., Sutt. 218 DB110
Knockholt Main Rd., Sev. 240 EY115
Knockholt Rd. SE9 184 EK85
Knockholt Rd., Sev. 224 EZ113
Knole, The SE9 185 EN91
Knole, The, Grav. 190 GD94
Knole Clo., Croy. 202 DW100
Stockbury Rd.
Knole Gate, Sid. 185 ES90
Woodside Cres.
Knole La., Sev. 257 FJ126
Knole Rd., Dart. 187 FG87
Knole Rd., Sev. 257 FK123
Knole Way, Sev. 257 FJ125
Knoll, The W13 137 CJ71
Knoll, The, Beck. 203 EB95
Knoll, The, Brom. 204 EG102
Knoll, The, Cher. 193 BF102
Guildford Rd.
Knoll, The, Cob. 214 CA113
Knoll, The, Hert. 32 DV08
Knoll, The, Lthd. 231 CJ121
Knoll Ct. SE19 182 DT92
Knoll Cres., Nthwd. 93 BS54
Knoll Dr. N14 98 DG45
Knoll Pk. Rd., Cher. 193 BF102
Guildford Rd.
Knoll Ri., Orp. 205 ET102
Knoll Rd. SW18 180 DC85
Knoll Rd., Bex. 186 FA87
Knoll Rd., Dor. 263 CG138
Knoll Rd., Sid. 186 EV92
Knolles Cres., Hat. 45 CV23
Knollmead, Surb. 198 CQ102
Knolls, The, Epsom 233 CW116
Knolls Clo., Wor.Pk. 199 CV104
Knollys Clo. SW16 181 DN90
Knollys Rd. SW16 181 DM90
Knolton Way, Slou. 132 AV72
Knottisford St. E2 142 DW69
Knottocks Clo., Beac. 89 AK50
Knottocks Dr., Beac. 88 AJ50
Knottocks End, Beac. 89 AK50
Knotts Grn. Ms. E10 123 EB58
Knotts Grn. Rd.
Knotts Grn. Rd. E10 123 EB58
Knotts Pl., Sev. 256 FG124
Knowl Hill, Wok. 227 BB118
Knowl Pk., Borwd. 78 CL43
Knowl Way, Borwd. 78 CM43
Knowland Way, Uxb. 113 BF58
Knowle, The, Hodd. 49 EA18
Knowle, The, Tad. 233 CW121
Knowle Ave., Bexh. 166 EY80
Knowle Clo. SW9 161 DN83
Knowle Gdns., W.Byf. 211 BF113
Madeira Rd.
Knowle Grn., Stai. 174 BG92
Knowle Gro., Vir.W. 192 AW101
Knowle Gro. Clo., Vir.W. 192 AW101
Knowle Hill, Vir.W. 192 AV101
Knowle Pk., Cob. 230 BY115
Knowle Pk. Ave., Stai. 174 BH93
Knowle Rd., Brom. 204 EL103
Knowle Rd., Twick. 177 CE88
Knowles Clo., West Dr. 134 BL74
Knowles Hill Cres. SE13 183 ED85
Knowles Wk. SW4 161 DJ83
Knowlton Grn., Brom. 204 EF99
Knowsley Ave., Sthl. 136 CB74
Knowsley Rd. SW11 160 DF82
Knox Rd. E7 144 EF65
Knox Rd., Guil. 242 AV130
Knox St. W1 272 D6
Knox St. W1 140 DF71
Knoyle St. SE14 163 DY79
Chubworthy St.
Knutsford Ave., Wat. 76 BX38
Kodak Ho., Hem.H. 40 BJ22
Koh-i-noor Ave. (Bushey), Wat. 76 CA44
Kohat Rd. SW19 180 DB92
Koonowla Clo., West. 238 EK115
Kooringa, Warl. 236 DV119
Korda Clo., Shep. 194 BM97
Kossuth St. SE10 164 EE78
Kotree Way SE1 162 DU77
Beatrice Rd.
Kramer Ms. SW5 160 DA78
Kempsford Gdns.
Kreedman Wk. E8 122 DU64
Wayland Ave.
Kreisel Wk., Rich. 158 CM79
Kuala Gdns. SW16 201 DM95
Kuhn Way E7 124 EG64
Forest La.
Kydbrook Clo., Orp. 205 EQ101
Kylemore Clo. E6 144 EK68
Parr Rd.
Kylemore Rd. NW6 140 DA66
Kymberley Rd., Har. 117 CE58
Kyme Rd., Horn. 127 FF58
Kynance Clo., Rom. 106 FJ48
Kynance Gdns., Stan. 95 CJ53
Kynance Ms. SW7 160 DC76
Kynance Pl. SW7 160 DC76
Kynaston Ave. N16 122 DT62
Dynevor Rd.
Kynaston Ave., Th.Hth. 202 DQ99
Kynaston Clo., Har. 95 CD52
Kynaston Cres., Th.Hth. 202 DQ99
Kynaston Rd. N16 122 DS62
Kynaston Rd., Brom. 184 EG92
Kynaston Rd., Enf. 82 DR39
Kynaston Rd., Orp. 206 EV101
Kynaston Rd., Th.Hth. 202 DQ99
Kynaston Wd., Har. 95 CD52
Kynnersley Clo., Cars. 200 DF104
William St.
Kynock Rd. N18 100 DW49
Kyrle Rd. SW11 180 DF86
Kytes Dr., Wat. 60 BX33
Kytes Est., Wat. 60 BX33
Kyverdale Rd. N16 122 DT59

L

La Plata Gro., Brwd. 108 FV48
La Roche Clo., Slou. 152 AW76
La Tourne Gdns., Orp. 205 EQ104
Laburnham Ave., West Dr. 134 BM73
Laburnham Clo., Upmin. 129 FU59
Laburnham Gdns., Upmin. 129 FT59
Laburnum Ave. N9 100 DS47
Laburnum Ave. N17 100 DR52
Laburnum Ave., Dart. 188 FJ88
Laburnum Ave., Horn. 127 FF62
Laburnum Ave., Sutt. 200 DE104
Laburnum Ave., Swan. 207 FC97
Laburnum Clo. E4 101 DZ51
Laburnum Clo. N11 98 DG51
Laburnum Clo. SE15 162 DW80
Clifton Way
Laburnum Clo., Guil. 242 AW131
Laburnum Clo. (Cheshunt), Wal.Cr. 67 DX31
Laburnum Ct. E2 142 DT67
Laburnum St.
Laburnum Ct., Stan. 95 CJ49
Laburnum Cres., Sun. 195 BV95
Batavia Rd.
Laburnum Gdns. N21 100 DQ47
Laburnum Gro.
Laburnum Gdns., Croy. 203 DX102
Primrose La.
Laburnum Gro. N21 100 DQ47
Laburnum Gro. NW9 118 CQ59
Laburnum Gro., Grav. 190 GD87
Laburnum Gro., Houns. 156 BZ84
Laburnum Gro., N.Mal. 198 CR96
Laburnum Gro., Ruis. 115 BR58
Laburnum Gro., St.Alb. 60 CB25
Laburnum Gro., Slou. 153 BB79
Laburnum Gro., S.Ock. 149 FW69
Laburnum Gro., Sthl. 136 BZ70
Laburnum Ho., Dag. 126 FA61
Althorne Way
Laburnum Pl., Egh. 172 AV93
Laburnum Rd. SW19 180 DC94
Laburnum Rd., Cher. 194 BG102
Laburnum Rd., Epp. 70 EW29
Laburnum Rd., Epsom 216 CS113
Laburnum Rd., Hayes 155 BT77
Laburnum Rd., Hodd. 49 EB15
Laburnum Rd., Mitch. 200 DG96
Laburnum Rd., Wok. 226 AX119
Laburnum St. E2 142 DT67
Laburnum Wk., Horn. 128 FJ64
Laburnum Way, Brom. 205 EN101
Laburnum Way, Stai. 174 BM88
Laburnum Way (Cheshunt), Wal.Cr. 65 DP28
Millcrest Rd.
Lacebark Clo., Sid. 185 ET87
Lacey Ave., Couls. 235 DN120
Lacey Clo. N9 100 DU47
Lacey Clo., Egh. 173 BD94
Lacey Dr., Couls. 235 DN120
Lacey Dr., Dag. 126 EV63
Lindsey Rd.
Lacey Dr., Edg. 96 CL49
Lacey Dr., Hmptn. 196 BZ95
Lacey Grn., Couls. 235 DN120
Lacey Wk. E3 143 EA68
Lackford Rd., Couls. 234 DF118
Lackington St. EC2 275 L6
Lackington St. EC2 142 DR71
Lackmore Rd., Enf. 82 DW35
Lacock Clo. SW19 180 DC93
Lacon Rd. SE22 162 DU84
Lacy Rd. SW15 159 CX84
Ladas Rd. SE27 182 DQ91
Ladbroke Cres. W11 139 CY72
Ladbroke Gro.
Ladbroke Gdns. W11 139 CZ73
Ladbroke Gro. W10 139 CX70
Ladbroke Gro. W11 139 CY72
Ladbroke Gro., Red. 250 DG133
Ladbroke Ms. W11 139 CY74
Ladbroke Rd.
Ladbroke Rd. W11 139 CZ74
Ladbroke Rd., Enf. 82 DT44
Ladbroke Rd., Epsom 216 CR114
Ladbroke Rd., Horl. 269 DH146
Ladbroke Rd., Red. 250 DG133
Ladbroke Sq. W11 139 CZ73
Ladbroke Ter. W11 139 CZ73
Ladbroke Wk. W11 139 CZ74
Ladbrook Clo., Pnr. 116 BZ57
Ladbrook Rd. SE25 202 DR97
Ladbrooke Clo., Pot.B. 64 DA32
Strafford Gate
Ladbrooke Cres., Sid. 186 EX90
Ladbrooke Dr., Pot.B. 64 DA32
Ladbrooke Rd., Slou. 151 AQ76
Ladderstile Ride, Kings.T. 178 CQ92
Ladderswood Way N11 99 DJ50
Ladds Way, Swan. 207 FD98
Ladies Gro., St.Alb. 42 CB19
Lady Booth Rd., Kings.T. 198 CL96
Lady Gro., Welw.G.C. 29 CY13
Lady Hay, Wor.Pk. 199 CT103
Lady Margaret Rd. N19 121 DJ63
Lady Margaret Rd. NW5 121 DJ64
Lady Margaret Rd., Sthl. 136 BZ71
Lady Somerset Rd. NW5 121 DH63
Ladybower Ct. E5 123 DY63
Gilpin Rd.
Ladycroft Gdns., Orp. 223 EQ106
Ladycroft Rd. SE13 163 EB83
Ladycroft Wk., Stan. 95 CK53
Ladycroft Way, Orp. 223 EQ106
Ladyday Pl., Slou. 131 AQ74
Glenworth Pl.
Ladyegate Clo., Dor. 263 CK135
Ladyegate Rd., Dor. 263 CJ136
Ladyfield Clo., Loug. 85 EP42
Ladyfields, Grav. 191 GF91
Ladyfields, Loug. 85 EP42
Ladygate La., Ruis. 115 BP58
Ladygrove, Croy. 221 DY109
Ladygrove Dr., Guil. 243 BA129
Ladymead, Guil. 242 AW133
Ladymeadow, Kings L. 58 BK27
Lady's Clo., Wat. 75 BV42
Ladyshot, Harl. 36 EU14
Ladysmith Ave. E6 144 EL68
Ladysmith Ave., Ilf. 125 ER59
Ladysmith Rd. E16 144 EF69
Ladysmith Rd. N17 100 DU54
Ladysmith Rd. N18 100 DV50
Ladysmith Rd. SE9 185 EN86
Ladysmith Rd., Enf. 82 DS41
Ladysmith Rd., Har. 95 CE54
Ladysmith Rd., St.Alb. 43 CD19
Ladythorpe Clo., Add. 212 BH105
Church Rd.
Ladywalk, Rick. 91 BE50
Ladywell Clo. SE4 163 DZ84
Adelaide Ave.
Ladywell Heights SE4 183 DZ86
Crofton Pk. Rd.
Ladywell Prospect, Saw. 36 FA06
Ladywell Rd. SE13 183 EB85
Ladywell St. E15 144 EF67
Plaistow Gro.
Ladywood Ave., Orp. 205 ES99
Ladywood Clo., Rick. 74 BH41
Ladywood Rd., Dart. 189 FS92
Ladywood Rd., Hert. 31 DM09
Ladywood Rd., Surb. 198 CN103
Lafone Ave., Felt. 176 BW88
Alfred Rd.
Lafone St. SE1 279 P4
Lafone St. SE1 162 DT75
Lagado Ms. SE16 143 DX74
Lagger, The, Ch.St.G. 90 AV48
Lagger Clo., Ch.St.G. 90 AV48
Laglands Clo., Reig. 250 DC132
Lagonda Ave., Ilf. 103 ET51
Lagonda Way, Dart. 168 FJ84
Arundel Rd.
Lagoon Rd., Orp. 206 EV99
Laidon Sq., Hem.H. 40 BK16
Laing Clo., Ilf. 103 ER51
Laing Dean, Nthlt. 136 BW67
Laings Ave., Mitch. 200 DF96
Lainlock Pl., Houns. 156 CB81
Spring Gro. Rd.
Lainson St. SW18 180 DA87
Laird Ave., Grays 170 GD75
Laird Ho. SE5 162 DQ80
Redcar St.
Lairdale Clo. SE21 182 DQ88
Lairs Clo. N7 141 DL65
Manger Rd.
Laitwood Rd. SW12 181 DH88
Lake, The (Bushey), Wat. 94 CC46
Lake Ave., Brom. 184 EG93
Lake Ave., Rain. 148 FK68
Lake Ave., Slou. 131 AR73
Lake Clo. SW19 179 CZ92
Lake Rd.
Lake Clo., W.Byf. 212 BK112
Lake Dr. (Bushey), Wat. 94 CC47
Lake End Ct., Maid. 130 AH72
Taplow Rd.
Lake End Rd., Maid. 130 AH73
Lake End Rd., Wind. 150 AH75
Lake Gdns., Dag. 126 FA64
Lake Gdns., Rich. 177 CH89
Lake Gdns., Wall. 201 DH104
Lake Ho. Rd. E11 124 EG62
Lake La., Horl. 267 DJ144
Lake Ri., Grays 169 FU77
Lake Ri., Rom. 105 FF54
Lake Rd. SW19 179 CZ92
Lake Rd., Croy. 203 DZ103
Lake Rd., Rom. 126 EX56
Lake Rd., Vir.W. 192 AV98
Lake Rd., Wal.Abb. 50 EE21

Lake Vw., Dor. 263 CJ139
Lake Vw., Edg. 96 CM50
Lake Vw., Pot.B. 64 DC33
Lake Vw. Rd., Sev. 256 FG123
Lakedale Rd. SE18 165 ES78
Lakefield Rd. N22 99 DP54
Lakefields Clo., Rain. 148 FK68
Lakehall Gdns., Th.Hth. 201 DP99
Lakehall Rd., Th.Hth. 201 DP99
Lakehurst Rd., Epsom 216 CS106
Lakeland Clo., Chig. 104 EV49
Lakeland Clo., Har. 95 CD51
Lakenheath N14 81 DJ43
Laker Pl. SW15 179 CY86
Lakers Ri., Bans. 234 DE116
Lakes Clo., Guil. 259 BB140
Lakes La., Beac. 89 AM54
Lakes Rd., Kes. 222 EJ106
Lakeside N3 98 DB54
Lakeside W13 137 CJ72
Edgehill Rd.
Lakeside, Beck. 203 EB97
Lakeside, Enf. 81 DK42
Lakeside, Rain. 148 FL68
Lakeside, Red. 250 DG132
Kingfisher Dr.
Lakeside, Wall. 201 DH104
Derek Ave.
Lakeside, Wey. 195 BS103
Lakeside, Wok. 226 AS119
Lakeside Ave. SE28 146 EU74
Birchdene Dr.
Lakeside Ave., Ilf. 124 EK56
Lakeside Clo. SE25 202 DU96
Lakeside Clo., Chig. 103 ET49
Lakeside Clo., Ruis. 115 BR56
Lakeside Clo., Sid. 186 EW85
Lakeside Clo., Wok. 226 AS119
Lakeside Ct. N4 121 DP61
Lakeside Ct., Borwd. 78 CN43
Cavendish Cres.
Lakeside Cres., Barn. 80 DF43
Lakeside Cres., Brwd. 108 FX48
Lakeside Cres., Wey. 195 BQ104
Churchill Dr.
Lakeside Dr., Brom. 204 EL104
Lakeside Dr., Esher 214 CC107
Lakeside Dr., Slou. 132 AS67
Lakeside Pl., St.Alb. 61 CK27
Lakeside Rd. N13 99 DM49
Lakeside Rd. W14 159 CX76
Lakeside Rd., Slou. 153 BF80
Lakeside Rd. (Cheshunt), Wal.Cr. 66 DW28
Lakeside Way, Wem. 118 CN63
Lakeswood Rd., Orp. 205 EP99
Lakeview Ct. SW19 179 CY89
Victoria Dr.
Lakeview Rd. SE27 181 DN92
Lakeview Rd., Well. 166 EV84
Lakis Clo. NW3 120 DC63
Flask Wk.
Laleham Ave. NW7 96 CR48
Laleham Ct., Wok. 226 AY116
Laleham Pk., Stai. 194 BJ99
Laleham Reach, Cher. 194 BH96
Laleham Rd. SE6 183 EC87
Laleham Rd., Shep. 194 BL98
Laleham Rd., Stai. 173 BF92
Lalor St. SW6 159 CY82
Lamb Clo., Hat. 45 CV19
Lamb Clo., Til. 171 GJ82
Coleridge Rd.
Lamb Clo., Wat. 60 BW34
Lamb La. E8 142 DV66
Lamb St. E1 275 P6
Lamb St. E1 142 DT71
Lamb Wk. SE1 279 M5
Lamb Yd., Wat. 76 BX43
Lambarde Ave. SE9 185 EN91
Lambarde Dr., Sev. 256 FG123
Lambarde Rd., Sev. 256 FG122
Lambardes Clo., Orp. 224 EW110
Lamberhurst Clo., Orp. 206 EX102
Lamberhurst Rd. SE27 181 DN91
Lamberhurst Rd., Dag. 126 EY60
Lambert Ave., Rich. 158 CN83
Lambert Ave., Slou. 152 AY75
Lambert Clo., West. 238 EK116
Lambert Ct. (Bushey), Wat. 76 BX42
Lambert Jones Ms. EC2 142 DQ71
Beech St.
Lambert Rd. E16 144 EH72
Lambert Rd. N12 98 DC50
Lambert Rd. SW2 181 DL85
Lambert Rd., Bans. 218 DA114
Lambert St. N1 141 DN66
Lambert Wk., Wem. 117 CK62
Clarendon Gdns.
Lambert Way N12 98 DC50
Woodhouse Rd.
Lamberts Pl., Croy. 202 DR102
Lamberts Rd., Surb. 198 CL99
Lambeth Bri. SE1 278 A8
Lambeth Bri. SE1 161 DL77
Lambeth Bri. SW1 278 A8
Lambeth Bri. SW1 161 DL77
Lambeth High St. SE1 278 B8
Lambeth High St. SE1 161 DM77
Lambeth Hill EC4 275 H10
Lambeth Hill EC4 142 DQ73
Lambeth Palace Rd. SE1 278 B7
Lambeth Palace Rd. SE1 161 DM76
Lambeth Rd. SE1 278 D7
Lambeth Rd. SE1 161 DM76
Lambeth Rd. SE11 161 DM76
Lambeth Rd., Croy. 201 DN101
Lambeth Wk. SE11 278 C8
Lambeth Wk. SE11 161 DM77
Lamble St. NW5 120 DG64
Lambley Rd., Dag. 146 EV65
Lambly Hill, Vir.W. 192 AY97
Stroude Rd.
Lambolle Pl. NW3 140 DE65
Lambolle Rd. NW3 140 DE65
Lambourn Chase, Rad. 77 CF36
Lambourn Clo. W7 157 CF75
Lambourn Rd. SW4 161 DH83
Lambourne Ave. SW19 179 CZ91
Lambourne Clo., Chig. 104 EV47
Lambourne Rd.
Lambourne Cres., Chig. 104 EV47
Lambourne Cres., Wok. 211 BD113
Lambourne Dr., Brwd. 109 GE45
Lambourne Dr., Cob. 230 BX115
Lambourne Gdns. E4 101 EA47
Lambourne Gdns., Bark. 145 ET66
Lambourne Rd.
Lambourne Gdns., Enf. 82 DT40
Lambourne Gdns., Horn. 128 FK61
Lambourne Gro., Kings.T. 198 CP96
Kenley Rd.
Lambourne Pl. SE3 164 EH81
Shooter's Hill Rd.
Lambourne Rd. E11 123 ED59
Lambourne Rd., Bark. 145 ES66
Lambourne Rd., Chig. 103 ET49
Lambourne Rd., Ilf. 125 ES61
Lambrook Ter. SW6 159 CY81
Lamb's Bldgs. EC1 275 K5
Lambs Clo. (Cuffley), Pot.B. 65 DM29
Lambs Conduit Pas. WC1 274 B6
Lamb's Conduit St. WC1 274 B5
Lamb's Conduit St. WC1 141 DM70
Lambs La., Rain. 147 FH71
Lambs Meadow, Wdf.Grn. 102 EK54
Lambs Ms. N1 141 DP67
Colebrooke Row
Lamb's Pas. EC1 275 K6
Lamb's Pas. EC1 142 DR71
Lambs Ter. N9 100 DR47
Lambs Wk., Enf. 82 DQ40
Lambscroft Ave. SE9 184 EJ90
Lambscroft Way, Ger.Cr. 90 AY54
Lambton Ave., Wal.Cr. 67 DX32
Lambton Pl. W11 139 CZ72
Westbourne Gro.
Lambton Rd. N19 121 DL60
Lambton Rd. SW20 199 CW95
Lambyn Cft., Horl. 269 DJ147
Lamerock Rd., Brom. 184 EF91
Lamerton Rd., Ilf. 103 EP54
Lamerton St. SE8 163 EA79
Lamford Clo. N17 100 DR52
Lamington St. W6 159 CV77
Lamlash St. SE11 278 F8
Lammas Ave., Mitch. 200 DG96
Lammas Ct., Wind. 151 AQ82
Lammas Dr., Stai. 173 BD91
Lammas Grn. SE26 182 DV90
Lammas La., Esher 214 CA106
Lammas Mead, Brox. 49 DZ23
Lammas Pk. W5 157 CJ75
Lammas Pk. Gdns. W5 137 CJ74
Lammas Pk. Rd. W5 137 CJ74
Lammas Rd. E9 143 DX66
Lammas Rd. E10 123 DY61
Lea Bri. Rd.
Lammas Rd., Rich. 177 CJ91
Lammas Rd., Slou. 131 AK71
Lammas Rd., Wat. 76 BW43
Lammas Way, H.Wyc. 88 AC54
Lammermoor Rd. SW12 181 DH87
Lamont Rd. SW10 160 DC79
Lamont Rd. Pas. SW10 160 DD79
Lamont Rd.
Lamorbey Clo., Sid. 185 ET88
Lamorna Ave., Grav. 191 GK89
Lamorna Clo., Orp. 206 EU101
Lamorna Clo., Rad. 61 CH34
Lamorna Gro., Stan. 95 CK53
Lampard Gro. N16 122 DT60
Lampern Sq. E2 142 DU69
Nelson Gdns.
Lampeter Clo., Wok. 226 AY118
Lampeter Sq. W6 159 CY79
Humbolt Rd.
Lampits, Hodd. 49 EB17
Lamplighter Clo. E1 142 DW70
Cleveland Way
Lamplighters Clo., Dart. 188 FM86
Lamplighters Clo., Wal.Abb. 68 EG34
Lampmead Rd. SE12 184 EF85
Lamport Clo. SE18 165 EM77
Lampton Ave., Houns. 156 CB81
Lampton Ho. Clo. SW19 179 CX91
Lampton Pk. Rd., Houns. 156 CB82
Lampton Rd., Houns. 156 CB82
Lamsey Rd., Hem.H. 40 BK22
Lamson Rd., Rain. 147 FF70
Lanacre Ave. NW9 96 CR53
Lanark Clo. W5 137 CJ71
Lanark Pl. W9 140 DC70
Lanark Rd. W9 140 DB68
Lanark Sq. E14 163 EB76
Lanata Wk., Hayes 136 BX70
Ramulis Dr.
Lanbury Rd. SE15 163 DX84
Lancashire Ct. W1 273 J10
Lancaster Ave. E18 124 EH56
Lancaster Ave. SE27 181 DP89
Lancaster Ave. SW19 179 CX92
Lancaster Ave., Bark. 145 ES66
Lancaster Ave., Barn. 80 DC38
Lancaster Ave., Mitch. 201 DL99
Lancaster Ave., Slou. 131 AQ70
Lancaster Clo. N1 142 DS66
Hertford Rd.
Lancaster Clo. N17 100 DU52
Park La.
Lancaster Clo., Brwd. 108 FU43
Lancaster Clo., Brom. 204 EF98
Lancaster Clo., Egh. 172 AX92
Middle Hill
Lancaster Clo., Kings.T. 177 CK92
Lancaster Cotts., Rich. 178 CL86
Lancaster Pk.
Lancaster Ct. SE27 181 DP89
Lancaster Ct. SW6 159 CZ80
Lancaster Ct. W2 140 DC73
Lancaster Gate
Lancaster Ct., Bans. 217 CZ114
Lancaster Ct., Walt. 195 BU101
Lancaster Dr. E14 143 EC74
Prestons Rd.
Lancaster Dr. NW3 140 DE65
Lancaster Dr., Hem.H. 57 AZ27
Lancaster Dr., Horn. 127 FH64
Lancaster Dr., Loug. 84 EL44
Roding Rd.
Lancaster Gdns. SW19 179 CY92
Lancaster Gdns. W13 157 CH75
Lancaster Gdns., Kings.T. 177 CK92
Lancaster Gate W2 140 DC73
Lancaster Gro. NW3 140 DD65
Lancaster Ms. SW18 180 DB85
East Hill
Lancaster Ms. W2 140 DC73
Lancaster Ms., Rich. 178 CL86
Richmond Hill
Lancaster Pk., Rich. 178 CL85
Lancaster Pl. SW19 179 CX92
Lancaster Rd.
Lancaster Pl. WC2 274 B10
Lancaster Pl. WC2 141 DM73
Lancaster Pl., Houns. 156 BW82
Lancaster Pl., Ilf. 125 EQ64
Staines Rd.
Lancaster Pl., Twick. 177 CG86
Lancaster Rd. E7 144 EG66
Lancaster Rd. E11 124 EE61
Lancaster Rd. E17 101 DX54
Lancaster Rd. N4 121 DM59
Lancaster Rd. N11 99 DK51
Lancaster Rd. N18 100 DT50
Lancaster Rd. NW10 119 CU64
Lancaster Rd. SE25 202 DT96
Lancaster Rd. SW19 179 CX92
Lancaster Rd. W11 139 CY72
Lancaster Rd., Barn. 80 DD43
Lancaster Rd., Enf. 82 DR39
Lancaster Rd., Epp. 70 FA26
Lancaster Rd., Grays 169 FX78
Arterial Rd. W. Thurrock
Lancaster Rd., Har. 116 CA57
Lancaster Rd., Nthlt. 136 CC65
Lancaster Rd., St.Alb. 43 CF18
Lancaster Rd., Sthl. 136 BY73
Lancaster Rd., Uxb. 134 BK65
Lancaster St. SE1 278 G5
Lancaster St. SE1 161 DP75
Lancaster Ter. W2 140 DD73
Lancaster Wk. W2 140 DD74
Lancaster Wk., Hayes 135 BQ72
Lancaster Way, Abb.L. 59 BT31
Lance Rd., Har. 116 CC59
Lancefield St. W10 139 CZ69
Lancell St. N16 122 DS61
Stoke Newington Ch. St.
Lancelot Ave., Wem. 117 CK63
Lancelot Clo., Slou. 151 AN75
Mitchell Clo.
Lancelot Cres., Wem. 117 CK63
Lancelot Gdns., Barn. 98 DG45
Lancelot Pl. SW7 276 D5
Lancelot Pl. SW7 160 DF75
Lancelot Rd., Ilf. 103 ES51
Lancelot Rd., Well. 166 EU84
Lancelot Rd., Wem. 117 CK63
Lancer Sq. W8 160 DB75
Old Ct. Pl.
Lancey Clo. SE7 164 EK77
Cleveley Clo.
Lanchester Rd. N6 120 DF57
Lancing Gdns. N9 100 DT46
Lancing Rd. W13 137 CH73
Drayton Grn. Rd.
Lancing Rd., Croy. 201 DM100
Lancing Rd., Felt. 175 BT89
Lancing Rd., Ilf. 125 ER58
Lancing Rd., Orp. 206 EU103
Lancing Rd., Rom. 106 FL52
Lancing St. NW1 273 M3
Lancing Way, Rick. 75 BP43
Lancresse Clo., Uxb. 134 BK65
Lancresse Ct. N1 142 DS67
Landau Way, Brox. 67 DZ25
Landau Way, Erith 168 FK78
Landcroft Rd. SE22 182 DT85
Landells Rd. SE22 182 DT86
Landen Pk., Horl. 268 DE146
Lander Rd., Grays 170 GD78
Landford Clo., Rick. 92 BL47
Landford Rd. SW15 159 CW83
Landgrove Rd. SW19 180 DA92
Landmann Way SE14 163 DX79
Landmead Rd. (Cheshunt), Wal.Cr. 67 DY29
Landon Pl. SW1 276 D6
Landon Pl. SW1 160 DF76
Landon Wk. E14 143 EB73
Cottage St.
Landon Way, Ashf. 175 BP93
Courtfield Rd.
Landons Clo. E14 143 EC74
Landor Rd. SW9 161 DL83
Landor Wk. W12 159 CU75
Landport Way SE15 162 DT80
Daniel Gdns.
Landra Gdns. N21 81 DP44
Landridge Rd. SW6 159 CZ82
Landrock Rd. N8 121 DL58
Lands End, Borwd. 77 CK44
Landscape Rd., Warl. 236 DV119
Landscape Rd., Wdf.Grn. 102 EH52
Landseer Ave. E12 125 EN64
Landseer Ave., Grav. 190 GD90
Landseer Clo. SW19 200 DC95
Brangwyn Cres.
Landseer Clo., Edg. 96 CN54
Landseer Clo., Horn. 127 FH60
Landseer Rd. N19 121 DL62
Landseer Rd., Enf. 82 DU43
Landseer Rd., N.Mal. 198 CR101
Landseer Rd., Sutt. 218 DA107
Landstead Rd. SE18 165 ER80
Landway, The, Orp. 206 EW97
Lane, The NW8 140 DC68
Marlborough Pl.
Lane, The SE3 164 EG83
Lane, The, Cher. 194 BG97
Lane, The, Vir.W. 192 AY97
Lane App. NW7 97 CY50
Lane Ave., Green. 189 FW86
Lane Clo. NW2 119 CV62
Lane Clo., Add. 212 BH106
Lane End, Bexh. 167 FB83
Lane End, Epsom 216 CP114
Lane End, Harl. 52 EY15
Kiln La.
Lane End, Hat. 45 CT21
Lane Gdns. (Bushey), Wat. 95 CE45
Lane Ms. E12 125 EM62
Colchester Ave.
Lane Wd. Clo., Amer. 72 AT39
Lanefield Wk., Welw.G.C. 29 CW09
Lanercost Clo. SW2 181 DN89
Lanercost Gdns. N14 99 DL45
Lanercost Rd. SW2 181 DN89
Lanes Ave., Grav. 191 GG91
Lanesborough Pl. SW1 276 G4
Laneside, Chis. 185 EP92
Laneside, Edg. 96 CQ50
Laneside Ave., Dag. 126 EZ59
Laneway SW15 179 CV85
Sunnymead Rd.
Lanfranc Rd. E3 143 DY68
Lanfrey Pl. W14 159 CZ78
North End Rd.
Lang Clo., Lthd. 230 CB123
Lang St. E1 142 DW70
Langaller La., Lthd. 230 CB122
Langbourne Ave. N6 120 DG61
Langbourne Way, Esher 215 CG107
Langbrook Rd. SE3 164 EK83
Langcroft Clo., Cars. 200 DF104
Langdale Ave., Mitch. 200 DF97
Langdale Clo. SE17 162 DQ79
Langdale Clo. SW14 158 CP84
Clifford Ave.
Langdale Clo., Dag. 126 EW60
Langdale Clo., Orp. 205 EP104
Grasmere Rd.
Langdale Clo., Wok. 226 AW116
Langdale Ct., Hem.H. 40 BL17
Wharfedale
Langdale Cres., Bexh. 166 FA80
Langdale Dr., Hayes 135 BS68
Langdale Gdns., Grnf. 137 CH69
Langdale Gdns., Horn. 127 FG64
Langdale Gdns., Wal.Cr. 83 DX35
Langdale Rd. SE10 163 EC80
Langdale Rd., Th.Hth. 201 DN98
Langdale St. E1 142 DV72
Burslem St.
Langdale Wk., Grav. 190 GE90
Landseer Ave.
Langdon Ct. NW10 138 CS67
Langdon Cres. E6 145 EN68
Langdon Dr. NW9 118 CQ60
Langdon Pk. Rd. N6 121 DJ59
Langdon Pl. SW14 158 CQ83
Rosemary La.
Langdon Rd. E6 145 EN67
Langdon Rd., Brom. 204 EH97
Langdon Rd., Mord. 200 DC99
Langdon Shaw, Sid. 185 ET92
Langdon Wk., Mord. 200 DC99
Langdon Rd.
Langdon Way SE1 162 DU77
Simms Rd.
Langfield Clo., Wal.Abb. 50 EE22
Langford Clo. E8 122 DU64
Langford Clo. N15 122 DS58
Langford Clo. NW8 140 DC68
Langford Pl.
Langford Ct. NW8 140 DC68
Langford Pl.
Langford Cres., Barn. 80 DF42
Langford Grn. SE5 162 DS83
Langford Grn., Brwd. 109 GC44
Langford Pl. NW8 140 DC68
Langford Pl., Sid. 186 EU90
Langford Rd. SW6 160 DB82
Gilstead Rd.
Langford Rd., Barn. 80 DE42
Langford Rd., Wdf.Grn. 102 EJ51
Langfords, Buck.H. 102 EK47
Langfords Way, Croy. 221 DY111
Langham Clo. N15 121 DP55
Langham Rd.
Langham Clo., St.Alb. 43 CK15
Langham Ct., Horn. 128 FK59
Langham Dene, Ken. 235 DP115
Langham Dr., Rom. 126 EV58
Langham Gdns. N21 81 DN43
Langham Gdns. W13 137 CH73
Langham Gdns., Edg. 96 CQ52
Langham Gdns., Rich. 177 CJ91
Langham Gdns., Wem. 117 CJ61
Langham Ho. Clo., Rich. 177 CK91
Langham Pl. N15 121 DP55
Langham Pl. W1 273 J7
Langham Pl. W1 141 DH71
Langham Pl. W4 158 CS79
Hogarth Roundabout
Langham Pl., Egh. 173 AZ92
Langham Rd. N15 121 DP55
Langham Rd. SW20 199 CW95
Langham Rd., Edg. 96 CQ51
Langham Rd., Tedd. 177 CH92
Langham St. W1 273 J7
Langham St. W1 141 DH71
Langhedge Clo. N18 100 DT51
Langhedge La.
Langhedge La. N18 100 DT50
Langhedge La. Ind. Est. N18 100 DT51
Langholm Clo. SW12 181 DK87
King's Ave.
Langholme (Bushey), Wat. 94 CC46
Langhorne Rd., Dag. 146 FA66
Langland Ct., Nthwd. 93 BQ52
Langland Cres., Stan. 95 CK54
Langland Dr., Pnr. 94 BY52
Langland Gdns. NW3 120 DB64
Langland Gdns., Croy. 203 DZ103
Langlands Dr., Dart. 189 FS92
Langlands Ri., Epsom 216 CQ113
Burnet Gro.
Langler Rd. NW10 139 CW68
Langley Ave., Hem.H. 40 BL23
Langley Ave., Ruis. 115 BV61
Langley Ave., Surb. 197 CK102
Langley Ave., Wor.Pk. 199 CX102
Langley Broom, Slou. 153 AZ78
Langley Business Cen., Slou. 153 BA75
Langley Clo., Epsom 232 CR119
Langley Clo., Guil. 242 AW133
Langley Clo., Rom. 106 FK52
Langley Clo., Wok. 226 AY119
Brooklyn Rd.
Langley Ct. SE9 185 EN86
Langley Ct. WC2 273 P10
Langley Ct., Beck. 203 EB99
Langley Cres. E11 124 EH59
Langley Cres., Dag. 146 EW66
Langley Cres., Edg. 96 CQ48
Langley Cres., Hayes 155 BT80
Langley Cres., Kings L. 58 BN30
Langley Cres., St.Alb. 42 CC18
Langley Dr. E11 124 EH59
Langley Dr. W3 158 CP75
Langley Dr., Brwd. 108 FU48
Langley Gdns., Brom. 204 EJ98
Langley Gdns., Dag. 146 EX66
Langley Gdns., Orp. 205 EP100
Langley Gro., N.Mal. 198 CS96
Langley Hill, Kings L. 58 BM29
Langley Hill Clo., Kings L. 58 BN29
Langley La. SW8 161 DL79
Langley La., Abb.L. 59 BT31
Langley La., Epsom 248 CQ125
Tumber St.
Langley Lo. La., Kings L. 58 BL31
Langley Meadow, Loug. 85 ER40
Langley Oaks Ave., S.Croy. 220 DU110
Langley Pk. NW7 96 CS51
Langley Pk. Rd., Iver 133 BC72
Langley Pk. Rd., Slou. 153 BA75
Langley Pk. Rd., Sutt. 218 DC106
Langley Quay, Slou. 153 BA75
Langley Rd. SW19 199 CZ95
Langley Rd., Abb.L. 59 BS31
Langley Rd., Beck. 203 DY98
Langley Rd., Islw. 157 CF82
Langley Rd., Kings L. 58 BH30
Langley Rd., Slou. 152 AW76
Langley Rd., S.Croy. 221 DX109
Langley Rd., Stai. 173 BF93
Langley Rd., Surb. 198 CL101
Langley Rd., Wat. 75 BT39
Langley Rd., Well. 166 EW79
Langley Row, Barn. 79 CZ39
Langley St. WC2 273 P9
Langley St. WC2 141 DL72
Langley Vale Rd., Epsom 232 CQ120
Langley Wk., Wok. 226 AY119
Midhope Rd.
Langley Way, Wat. 75 BS40
Langley Way, W.Wick. 203 ED102
Langleybury La., Kings L. 75 BP37
Langmans La., Wok. 226 AV118
Langmans Way, Wok. 226 AS116
Langmead Dr. (Bushey), Wat. 95 CD45
Langmead St. SE27 181 DP91
Beadman St.
Langmore Ct., Bexh. 166 EX83
Regency Way
Langport Ct., Walt. 196 BW102
Langridge Ms., Hmptn. 176 BY92
Oak Ave.
Langroyd Rd. SW17 180 DF89
Langshott, Horl. 269 DH146
Langshott Clo., Add. 211 BE111
Langshott La., Horl. 269 DH148
Langside Ave. SW15 159 CU84
Langside Cres. N14 99 DK48
Langston Hughes Clo. SE24 161 DP84
Shakespeare Rd.
Langston Rd., Loug. 85 EQ43
Langthorn Ct. EC2 275 L8
Langthorne Cres., Grays 170 GC77
Langthorne Rd. E11 123 EC62
Langthorne St. SW6 159 CX81
Langton Ave. E6 145 EN69
Langton Ave. N20 98 DC45
Langton Ave., Epsom 217 CT111
Langton Clo. WC1 274 C4
Langton Clo., Add. 194 BH104
Langton Clo., Wok. 226 AT117
Kenton Way
Langton Gro., Nthwd. 93 BQ50
Langton Ri. SE23 182 DV87
Langton Rd. NW2 119 CW62
Langton Rd. SW9 161 DP80
Langton Rd., Har. 94 CC52
Langton Rd., Hodd. 49 DZ17
Langton Rd., W.Mol. 196 CC99
Langton St. SW10 160 DC79
Langton Way SE3 164 EF81
Langton Way, Croy. 202 DS104
Langton Way, Egh. 173 BC93
Langton Way, Grays 171 GJ77
Langton's Meadow, Farn.Com. 131 AQ65
Langtry Rd. NW8 140 DB67
Langtry Rd., Nthlt. 136 BX68
Langtry Wk. NW8 140 DC66
Alexandra Pl.
Langwood Chase, Tedd. 177 CJ93
Langwood Gdns., Wat. 75 BU39
Langworth Clo., Dart. 188 FK90
Langworth Dr., Hayes 135 BU72
Lanhill Rd. W9 140 DA70
Lanier Rd. SE13 183 EC86
Lanigan Dr., Houns. 176 CB85
Lankaster Gdns. N2 98 DD53
Lankers Dr., Har. 116 BZ58
Lankton Clo., Beck. 203 EC95
Lannock Rd., Hayes 135 BS74
Lannoy Rd. SE9 185 EQ88
Lanrick Copse, Berk. 38 AY18
Lanrick Rd. E14 143 ED72
Lanridge Rd. SE2 166 EX76
Lansbury Ave. N18 100 DR50
Lansbury Ave., Bark. 146 EU66
Lansbury Ave., Felt. 175 BV86
Lansbury Ave., Rom. 126 EY57
Lansbury Clo. NW10 118 CQ64
Lansbury Cres., Dart. 188 FN85
Lansbury Dr., Hayes 135 BS68
Lansbury Est. E14 143 EB72
Lansbury Gdns. E14 143 EC72
Lansbury Gdns., Til. 171 GG81
Lansbury Rd., Enf. 83 DX39
Lansbury Way N18 100 DS50
Lansbury Ave.
Lansdell Rd., Mitch. 200 DG96
Lansdown, Guil. 243 BA134
Lansdown Clo., Walt. 196 BW102
St. Johns Dr.
Lansdown Clo., Wok. 226 AT119
Lansdown Pl., Grav. 191 GF88
Lansdown Rd. E7 144 EJ66
Lansdown Rd., Ger.Cr. 90 AX53
Lansdown Rd., Sid. 186 EV90
Lansdowne Ave., Bexh. 166 EW80
Lansdowne Ave., Orp. 205 EP102
Lansdowne Ave., Slou. 132 AS74
Lansdowne Clo. SW20 179 CX94
Lansdowne Clo., Twick. 177 CF88
Lion Rd.
Lansdowne Clo., Wat. 76 BX35
Lansdowne Ct., Slou. 132 AS74
Lansdowne Ct., Wor.Pk. 199 CU103
Lansdowne Cres. W11 139 CZ73
Lansdowne Dr. E8 142 DU65
Lansdowne Gdns. SW8 161 DL81
Lansdowne Grn. SW8 161 DL81
Hartington Rd.
Lansdowne Gro. NW10 118 CS63
Lansdowne Hill SE27 181 DP90
Lansdowne La. SE7 164 EK78
Lansdowne Ms. SE7 164 EK78
Lansdowne Ms. W11 139 CZ74
Lansdowne Rd.
Lansdowne Pl. SE1 279 L6
Lansdowne Pl. SE19 182 DT94
Lansdowne Ri. W11 139 CY73
Lansdowne Rd. E4 101 EA47
Lansdowne Rd. E11 124 EF61
Lansdowne Rd. E17 123 EA58
Lansdowne Rd. E18 124 EG55
Lansdowne Rd. N3 97 CZ52

Lansdowne Rd. N10 99 DJ54
Lansdowne Rd. N17 100 DU53
Lansdowne Rd. SW20 179 CW94
Lansdowne Rd. W11 139 CY73
Lansdowne Rd., Brom. 184 EG94
Lansdowne Rd., Chesh. 54 AQ29
Lansdowne Rd., Croy. 202 DQ103
Lansdowne Rd., Epsom 216 CQ108
Lansdowne Rd., Har. 117 CE59
Lansdowne Rd., Houns. 156 CB83
Lansdowne Rd., Ilf. 125 ET60
Lansdowne Rd., Pur. 219 DN112
Lansdowne Rd., Sev. 257 FK122
Lansdowne Rd., Stai. 174 BH94
Lansdowne Rd., Stan. 95 CJ51
Lansdowne Rd., Til. 171 GF82
Lansdowne Rd., Uxb. 135 BP72
Lansdowne Row W1 277 J2
Lansdowne Sq., Grav. 191 GF86
Lansdowne Ter. WC1 274 A5
Lansdowne Ter. WC1 141 DL70
Lansdowne Wk. W11 139 CZ74
Lansdowne Way SW8 161 DK81
Lansdowne Wd. Clo. SE27 181 DP90
Lansfield Ave. N18 100 DU49
Lant St. SE1 279 H4
Lant St. SE1 162 DQ75
Lantern Clo. SW15 159 CU84
Lantern Clo., Wem. 117 CK64
Lanterns Ct. E14 163 EA75
Lanvanor Rd. SE15 162 DW82
Lapford Clo. W9 139 CZ70
Lapponum Wk., Hayes 136 BX71
Lochan Clo.
Lapse Wd. Wk. SE23 182 DV89
Lapstone Gdns., Har. 117 CJ58
Lapwing Clo., Erith 167 FG80
Slade Grn. Rd.
Lapwing Clo., Hem.H. 40 BL16
Lapwing Clo., S.Croy. 221 DY110
Lapwing Ct., Surb. 198 CN104
Chaffinch Clo.
Lapwing Gro., Guil. 243 BD132
Lapwing Way, Hayes 136 BX71
Willow Tree La.
Lapwings, The, Grav. 191 GK89
Lapworth Clo., Orp. 206 EW103
Lara Clo. SE13 183 EC86
Lara Clo., Chess. 216 CL108
Larbert Rd. SW16 181 DJ94
Larby Pl., Epsom 216 CS110
Larch Ave. W3 138 CS74
Larch Ave., Guil. 242 AW132
Larch Ave., St.Alb. 60 BY30
Larch Clo. E13 144 EJ70
Prince Regent La.
Larch Clo. N11 98 DG52
Larch Clo. N19 121 DJ61
Bredgar Rd.
Larch Clo. SE8 163 DZ79
Clyde St.
Larch Clo. SW12 181 DH88
Larch Clo., H.Wyc. 88 AC45
Larch Clo., Red. 266 DC136
Larch Clo., Slou. 131 AP71
Larch Clo., Tad. 234 DC121
Larch Clo., Wal.Cr. 66 DS27
The Firs
Larch Clo., Warl. 237 DY119
Larch Cres., Epsom 216 CP107
Larch Cres., Hayes 136 BW70
Larch Dr. W4 158 CN78
Gunnersbury Ave.
Larch Grn. NW9 96 CS53
Clayton Fld.
Larch Gro., Sid. 185 ET88
Larch Ms. N19 121 DJ61
Bredgar Rd.
Larch Ri., Berk. 38 AU18
Larch Rd. E10 123 EB61
Oliver Rd.
Larch Rd. NW2 119 CW63
Larch Rd., Dart. 188 FK87
Larch Tree Way, Croy. 203 EA104
Larch Wk., Swan. 207 FD96
Larch Way, Brom. 205 EN101
Larchdene, Orp. 205 EN103
Larches, The N13 100 DQ48
Larches, The, Nthwd. 93 BQ51
Larches, The, St.Alb. 43 CK16
Larches, The, Uxb. 135 BP68
Larches, The, Wat. 76 BY43
Larches, The, Wok. 226 AY116
Larches Ave. SW14 158 CR84
Larches Ave., Enf. 82 DW35
Larchlands, The, H.Wyc. 88 AD46
Larchwood Ave., Rom. 105 FB51
Larchwood Clo., Bans. 233 CY115
Larchwood Clo., Rom. 105 FC51
Larchwood Dr., Egh. 172 AV93
Larchwood Gdns., Brwd. 108 FU44
Larchwood Rd. SE9 185 EP89
Larchwood Rd., Hem.H. 40 BM18
Larcom St. SE17 279 J9
Larcom St. SE17 162 DQ77
Larcombe Clo., Croy. 220 DT105
Larden Rd. W3 138 CS74
Largewood Ave., Surb. 198 CM103
Largo Wk., Erith 167 FE81
Selkirk Dr.
Larissa St. SE17 279 L10
Lark Ave., Stai. 173 BF90
Kestrel Ave.
Lark Ri., Hat. 45 CU20
Lark Ri., Lthd. 245 BS131
Lark Row E2 142 DW67
Lark Way, Cars. 200 DE101
Thornton Rd.
Larkbere Rd. SE26 183 DY91
Larken Dr. (Bushey), Wat. 94 CC46
Larkfield, Cob. 213 BU113
Larkfield Ave., Har. 117 CH55
Larkfield Clo., Brom. 204 EF103
Larkfield Ct., Horl. 269 DN148
Broadbridge La.
Larkfield Rd., Rich. 158 CL84
Larkfield Rd., Sev. 256 FC123
Larkfield Rd., Sid. 185 ET90
Larkfields, Grav. 190 GE90
Larkhall Clo., Walt. 214 BW107
Larkhall Ct., Rom. 105 FC54
Larkhall La. SW4 161 DK82
Larkhall Ri. SW4 161 DJ83
Larkhill Ter. SE18 165 EN80
Larkin Clo., Brwd. 109 GC45
Larkin Clo., Couls. 235 DM117
Stanley Clo.
Larkin Ind. Est., Chesh. 54 AR32
Larkings La., Slou. 132 AV67
Larkins Rd., Gat. 268 DD152
Larks Gro., Bark. 145 ES66
Larks Ri., Chesh. 54 AR33
Larks Wd., Harl. 52 EW17
Larksfield, Egh. 172 AW94
Larksfield Gro., Enf. 82 DV39
Larkshall Cres. E4 101 EC49
Larkshall Rd. E4 101 EC50
Larkspur Clo. E6 144 EL71
Larkspur Clo. N17 100 DR52
Fryatt Rd.
Larkspur Clo., Hem.H. 39 BE19
The Ave.
Larkspur Clo., Orp. 206 EW103
Larkspur Clo., S.Ock. 149 FW69
Larkspur Way, Dor. 263 CK139
Larkspur Way, Epsom 216 CP106
Larkswood Clo., Erith 167 FG81
Larkswood Ct. E4 101 ED50
Larkswood Ri., Pnr. 116 BW56
Larkswood Ri., St.Alb. 43 CJ15
Larkswood Rd. E4 101 EA49
Larkway Clo. NW9 118 CR56
Larmans Rd., Enf. 82 DW36
Larnach Rd. W6 159 CX79
Larne Rd., Ruis. 115 BT59
Larner Rd., Erith 167 FE80
Larpent Ave. SW15 179 CW85
Larsen Dr., Wal.Abb. 67 ED34
Larwood Clo., Grnf. 117 CD64
Las Palmas Est., Shep. 195 BQ101
Lascelles Ave., Har. 117 CD59
Lascelles Clo. E11 123 ED61
Lascelles Clo., Brwd. 108 FU43
Lascelles Rd., Slou. 152 AV76
Lascotts Rd. N22 99 DM51
Lassa Rd. SE9 184 EL85
Lassell St. SE10 163 ED78
Lasseter Pl. SE3 164 EF79
Vanbrugh Hill
Lasswade Rd., Cher. 193 BF101
Lasterton St. E8 142 DV65
Wilton Way
Latchett Rd. E18 102 EH53
Latchford Pl., Chig. 104 EV49
Manford Way
Latching Clo., Rom. 106 FK49
Troopers Dr.
Latchingdon Ct. E17 123 DX56
Latchingdon Gdns., Wdf.Grn. 102 EL51
Latchmere Clo., Rich. 178 CL92
Latchmere La., Kings.T. 178 CM93
Latchmere Pas. SW11 160 DE82
Cabul Rd.
Latchmere Rd. SW11 160 DF82
Latchmere Rd., Kings.T. 178 CL94
Latchmere St. SW11 160 DF82
Latchmoor Ave., Ger.Cr. 112 AX56
Latchmoor Way, Ger.Cr. 112 AX55
Lateward Rd., Brent. 157 CK79
Latham Clo. E6 144 EL72
Oliver Gdns.
Latham Clo., Twick. 177 CG87
Latham Clo., West. 238 EJ116
Latham Ho. E1 143 DX72
Latham Rd., Bexh. 186 FA85
Latham Rd., Twick. 177 CF87
Lathams Way, Croy. 201 DM102
Lathkill Clo., Enf. 100 DT45
Lathom Rd. E6 144 EL66
Latimer SE17 162 DS78
Beaconsfield Rd.
Latimer Ave. E6 145 EM67
Latimer Clo., Amer. 72 AW39
Latimer Clo., Hem.H. 40 BN15
Latimer Clo., Pnr. 94 BW53
Latimer Clo., Wat. 93 BS45
Latimer Clo., Wok. 227 BB116
Latimer Clo., Wor.Pk. 217 CV105
Latimer Dr., Horn. 128 FK62
Latimer Gdns., Pnr. 94 BW53
Latimer Gdns., Welw.G.C. 30 DB09
Panshanger Dr.
Latimer Ms., Chesh. 72 AY36
Latimer Pl. W10 139 CW72
Latimer Rd. E7 124 EH63
Latimer Rd. N15 122 DS58
Latimer Rd. SW19 180 DB93
Latimer Rd. W10 139 CW71
Latimer Rd., Barn. 80 DB41
Latimer Rd., Chesh. 54 AR34
Latimer Rd., Croy. 201 DP104
Abbey Rd.
Latimer Rd., Rick. 73 AZ38
Latimer Rd., Tedd. 177 CF92
Latimer St. E1 143 DX71
Stepney Way
Latimer Way, Beac. 88 AJ49
Latium Clo., St.Alb. 43 CD21
Holywell Hill
Latona Dr., Grav. 191 GM92
Latona Rd. SE15 162 DU79
Lattimore Rd., St.Alb. 43 CE21
Latton Clo., Esher 214 CB105
Latton Clo., Walt. 196 BY101
Latton Common Rd., Harl. 52 EU18
Latton Grn., Harl. 51 ET19
Latton Hall Clo., Harl. 36 EU14
Latton St., Harl. 36 EU14
Latymer Clo., Wey. 213 BQ105
Latymer Ct. W6 159 CX77
Latymer Rd. N9 100 DT47
Latymer Way N9 100 DR47
Laud St. SE11 278 B10
Laud St., Croy. 202 DQ104
Lauder Clo., Nthlt. 136 BX68
Lauderdale Dr., Rich. 177 CK90
Lauderdale Rd. W9 140 DB69
Lauderdale Rd., Kings L. 59 BQ33
Lauderdale Twr. EC2 142 DQ71
Beech St.
Laughton Ct., Borwd. 78 CR40
Banks Rd.
Laughton Rd., Nthlt. 136 BX67
Launcelot Rd., Brom. 184 EG91
Launcelot St. SE1 278 D5
Launceston Clo., Rom. 106 FJ53
Launceston Gdns., Grnf. 137 CJ67
Launceston Pl. W8 160 DC76
Launceston Rd., Grnf. 137 CJ67
Launch St. E14 163 EC76
Launders La., Rain. 148 FM69
Laundress La. N16 122 DU62
Evering Rd.
Laundry La. N1 142 DQ67
Greenman St.
Laundry La., Wal.Abb. 68 EE25
Laundry Rd. W6 159 CY79
Laundry Rd., Guil. 258 AW135
Laura Clo. E11 124 EJ57
Laura Clo., Enf. 82 DS43
Laura Dr., Swan. 187 FG94
Laura Pl. E5 122 DW63
Lauradale Rd. N2 120 DF56
Laureate Way, Hem.H. 40 BG18
Laurel Ave., Egh. 172 AV92
Laurel Ave., Grav. 191 GJ89
Laurel Ave., Pot.B. 63 CZ32
Laurel Ave., Slou. 152 AY75
Laurel Ave., Twick. 177 CF88
Laurel Bank Gdns. SW6 159 CZ82
New Kings Rd.
Laurel Bank Rd., Enf. 82 DQ39
Laurel Clo. N19 121 DJ61
Hargrave Pk.
Laurel Clo. SW17 180 DE92
Laurel Clo., Brwd. 109 GB43
Laurel Clo., Dart. 188 FJ88
Willow Rd.
Laurel Clo., Hem.H. 40 BM19
Laurel Clo., Ilf. 103 EQ51
Laurel Clo., Sid. 186 EU90
Laurel Clo., Slou. 153 BE80
Laurel Clo., Wok. 211 BD113
Laurel Cres., Croy. 203 EA104
Laurel Cres., Rom. 127 FE60
Laurel Cres., Wok. 211 BC113
Laurel Dr. N21 99 DN45
Laurel Dr., Oxt. 254 EF131
Laurel Flds., Pot.B. 63 CZ31
Laurel Gdns. E4 101 EB45
Laurel Gdns. NW7 96 CR48
Laurel Gdns. W7 137 CE74
Laurel Gdns., Houns. 156 BY84
Laurel Gro. SE20 182 DV94
Laurel Gro. SE26 183 DX91
Laurel La., West Dr. 154 BL77
Laurel Lo. La., Barn. 79 CW36
Dancers La.
Laurel Pk., Har. 95 CF52
Laurel Rd. SW13 159 CU82
Laurel Rd. SW20 199 CV95
Laurel Rd., Ger.Cr. 90 AX53
Laurel Rd., Hmptn. 177 CD92
Laurel Rd., St.Alb. 43 CF20
Laurel St. E8 142 DT65
Laurel Vw. N12 98 DB48
Laurel Way E18 124 EF56
Laurel Way N20 98 DA48
Laurels, The, Bans. 233 CZ117
Laurels, The, Berk. 39 BC17
Laurels, The, Cob. 230 BY115
Laurels, The, Dart. 188 FJ90
Laurels, The, Wal.Cr. 66 DS27
Laurels, The, Wey. 195 BR104
Laurels Rd., Iver 133 BD68
Laurelsfield, St.Alb. 42 CB23
Laurence Ms. W12 159 CU75
Askew Rd.
Laurence Pountney Hill EC4 275 K10
Laurence Pountney La. EC4 275 K10
Laurie Gro. SE14 163 DY81
Laurie Rd. W7 137 CE71
Laurie Wk., Rom. 127 FE56
Laurier Rd. NW5 121 DH62
Laurier Rd., Croy. 202 DT101
Lauries Clo., Hem.H. 39 BB22
London Rd.
Laurimel Clo., Stan. 95 CH51
September Way
Laurino Pl. (Bushey), Wat. 94 CC47
Lauriston Rd. E9 143 DX67
Lauriston Rd. SW19 179 CX93
Lausanne Rd. N8 121 DN56
Lausanne Rd. SE15 162 DW81
Lauser Rd., Stai. 174 BJ87
Laustan Clo., Guil. 243 BC134
Lavell St. N16 122 DR63
Lavender Ave. NW9 118 CQ60
Lavender Ave., Brwd. 108 FV43
Lavender Ave., Mitch. 200 DE95
Lavender Ave., Wor.Pk. 199 CW104
Lavender Clo. SW3 160 DD79
Danvers St.
Lavender Clo., Brom. 204 EL100
Turpington La.
Lavender Clo., Cars. 219 DH105
Lavender Clo., Cat. 252 DQ125
Lavender Clo., Couls. 235 DJ119
Lavender Clo., Red. 267 DH139
Lavender Clo., Rom. 106 FK52
Lavender Clo. (Cheshunt), Wal.Cr. 66 DT27
Lavender Ct., W.Mol. 196 CB97
Molesham Way
Lavender Gdns. SW11 160 DF84
Lavender Gdns., Enf. 81 DP39
Lavender Gdns., Har. 95 CE51
Uxbridge Rd.
Lavender Gro. E8 142 DU66
Lavender Gro., Mitch. 200 DE95
Lavender Hill SW11 160 DF84
Lavender Hill, Enf. 81 DN39
Lavender Hill, Swan. 207 FD97
Lavender Ms., Wall. 219 DL107
Cobham Clo.
Lavender Pk. Rd., W.Byf. 212 BG112
Lavender Pl., Ilf. 125 EP64
Lavender Ri., West Dr. 154 BN75
Lavender Rd. SE16 143 DY74
Lavender Rd. SW11 160 DD83
Lavender Rd., Cars. 218 DG105
Lavender Rd., Croy. 201 DM100
Lavender Rd., Enf. 82 DR39
Lavender Rd., Epsom 216 CP106
Lavender Rd., Sutt. 218 DD105
Lavender Rd., Uxb. 134 BM71
Lavender Rd., Wok. 227 BB116
Lavender Sq. E11 124 EE62
Cathall Rd.
Lavender St. E15 144 EE65
Manbey Gro.
Lavender Sweep SW11 160 DF84
Lavender Ter. SW11 160 DE83
Falcon Rd.
Lavender Vale, Wall. 219 DK107
Lavender Wk. SW11 160 DF84
Lavender Wk., Hem.H. 40 BK18
Townsend
Lavender Wk., Mitch. 200 DG97
Lavender Way, Croy. 203 DX100
Lavengro Rd. SE27 182 DQ89
Lavenham Rd. SW18 179 CZ89
Lavernock Rd., Bexh. 166 FA82
Lavers Rd. N16 122 DS62
Laverstoke Gdns. SW15 179 CT87
Laverton Ms. SW5 160 DB77
Laverton Pl.
Laverton Pl. SW5 160 DB77
Lavidge Rd. SE9 184 EL89
Lavina Gro. N1 141 DM68
Wharfdale Rd.
Lavington Rd. W13 137 CH74
Lavington Rd., Croy. 201 DM104
Lavington St. SE1 278 G3
Lavington St. SE1 141 DP74
Lavinia Ave., Wat. 60 BX34
Lavinia Rd., Dart. 188 FM86
Lavrock La., Rick. 92 BM45
Law Ho., Bark. 146 EU68
Law St. SE1 279 L6
Law St. SE1 162 DR76
Lawbrook La., Guil. 261 BQ143
Lawdons Gdns., Croy. 219 DP105
Lawford Ave., Rick. 73 BC44
Lawford Clo., Horn. 128 FJ63
Lawford Clo., Rick. 73 BC44
Lawford Clo., Wall. 219 DL109
Lawford Gdns., Dart. 188 FJ85
Lawford Gdns., Ken. 236 DQ116
Lawford Rd. N1 142 DS66
Lawford Rd. NW5 141 DJ65
Lawford Rd. W4 158 CQ80
Lawkland, Slou. 131 AQ69
Lawless St. E14 143 EB73
Lawley Rd. N14 99 DH45
Lawley St. E5 122 DW63
Lawn, The, Harl. 36 EV12
Lawn, The, Sthl. 156 CA78
Lawn Ave., West Dr. 154 BJ75
Lawn Clo. N9 100 DT45
Lawn Clo., Brom. 184 EH93
Lawn Clo., N.Mal. 198 CS96
Lawn Clo., Ruis. 115 BT62
Lawn Clo., Slou. 152 AW80
Lawn Clo., Swan. 207 FC96
Lawn Cres., Rich. 158 CN82
Lawn Fm. Gro., Rom. 126 EY56
Lawn Gdns. W7 137 CE74
Lawn Ho. Clo. E14 163 EC75
Lawn La. SW8 161 DL79
Lawn La., Hem.H. 40 BK22
Lawn Pk., Sev. 257 FH127
Lawn Pl. SE15 162 DT81
Sumner Est.
Lawn Rd. NW3 120 DF64
Lawn Rd., Beck. 183 DZ94
Lawn Rd., Grav. 190 GC86
Lawn Rd., Guil. 258 AW137
Lawn Rd., Uxb. 134 BJ66
New Windsor St.
Lawn Ter. SE3 164 EE83
Lawn Vale, Pnr. 94 BY54
Lawnfield NW2 139 CX66
Coverdale Rd.
Lawns, The E4 101 EA50
Lawns, The SE3 164 EE83
Lee Ter.
Lawns, The SE19 202 DR95
Lawns, The, Hem.H. 39 BE19
Lawns, The, Pnr. 94 CB52
Lawns, The, St.Alb. 42 CC19
Lawns, The, Sid. 186 EV91
Lawns, The, Sutt. 217 CY108
Lawns, The, Welw.G.C. 29 CX06
Lawns Cres., Grays 170 GD79
Lawns Dr., The, Brox. 49 DZ21
Lawnside SE3 164 EF84
Lawnsway, Rom. 105 FC52
Lawrance Gdns. (Cheshunt), Wal.Cr. 67 DX28
Lawrance Rd., St.Alb. 42 CC16
Lawrence Ave. E12 125 EN63
Lawrence Ave. E17 101 DX53
Lawrence Ave. N13 99 DP49
Lawrence Ave. NW7 96 CS49
Lawrence Ave., N.Mal. 198 CR100
Lawrence Ave., Ware 33 EC11
Lawrence Bldgs. N16 122 DT62
Lawrence Campe Clo. N20 98 DD48
Friern Barnet La.
Lawrence Clo. E3 143 EA69
Lawrence Clo. N15 122 DS55
Lawrence Rd.
Lawrence Clo., Guil. 243 BB129
Ladygrove Dr.
Lawrence Clo., Hert. 31 DL08
Lawrence Ct. NW7 96 CS50
Lawrence Cres., Dag. 127 FB62
Lawrence Cres., Edg. 96 CN54
Lawrence Dr., Uxb. 115 BQ63
Lawrence Est., Houns. 156 BW84
Lawrence Gdns. NW7 97 CT48
Lawrence Gdns., Til. 171 GH80
Lawrence Hill E4 101 EA47
Lawrence Hill Gdns., Dart. 188 FJ86
Lawrence Hill Rd., Dart. 188 FJ86
Lawrence La. EC2 275 J9
Lawrence La., Bet. 249 CV132
Lawrence Moorings, Saw. 36 EZ06
Lawrence Pl. N1 141 DL67
Outram Pl.
Lawrence Rd. E6 144 EL67
Lawrence Rd. E13 144 EH67
Lawrence Rd. N15 122 DS56
Lawrence Rd. N18 100 DV49
Lawrence Rd. SE25 202 DT98
Lawrence Rd. W5 157 CK77
Lawrence Rd., Hmptn. 176 BZ94
Lawrence Rd., Hayes 135 BQ68
Lawrence Rd., Houns. 156 BW84
Lawrence Rd., Pnr. 116 BX58
Lawrence Rd., Rich. 177 CJ91
Lawrence Rd., Rom. 127 FH57
Lawrence Rd., W.Wick. 222 EG105
Lawrence Sq., Grav. 191 GF90
Haynes Rd.
Lawrence St. E16 144 EF71
Lawrence St. NW7 97 CT50
Lawrence St. SW3 160 DE79
Lawrence Way NW10 118 CQ63
Lawrence Way, Slou. 131 AK71
Lawrence Weaver Clo., Mord. 200 DB100
Green La.
Lawrie Pk. Ave. SE26 182 DV92
Lawrie Pk. Cres. SE26 182 DV92
Lawrie Pk. Gdns. SE26 182 DV91
Lawrie Pk. Rd. SE26 182 DV93
Lawson Clo. E16 144 EJ71
Lawson Clo. SW19 179 CX90
Lawson Est. SE1 279 K7
Lawson Gdns., Dart. 188 FK85
Lawson Gdns., Pnr. 115 BV55
Lawson Rd., Dart. 168 FK84
Lawson Rd., Enf. 82 DW39
Lawson Rd., Sthl. 136 BZ70
Lawton Rd. E3 143 DY70
Mile End Rd.
Lawton Rd. E10 123 ED60
Lawton Rd., Barn. 80 DD41
Lawton Rd., Loug. 85 EP40
Laxcon Clo. NW10 118 CQ64
Laxey Rd., Orp. 223 ET107
Laxley Clo. SE5 161 DP80
Laxton Gdns., Red. 251 DK128
Laxton Pl. NW1 273 J4
Layard Rd. SE16 162 DV77
Layard Rd., Enf. 82 DT39
Layard Rd., Th.Hth. 202 DR96
Layard Sq. SE16 162 DV77
Laybrook, St.Alb. 43 CG16
Layburn Cres., Slou. 153 BB79
Laycock St. N1 141 DN65
Layer Gdns. W3 138 CN73
Layfield Clo. NW4 119 CV59
Layfield Cres. NW4 119 CV59
Layfield Rd. NW4 119 CV59
Layhams Rd., Kes. 222 EF106
Layhams Rd., W.Wick. 203 ED104
Layhill, Hem.H. 40 BK18
Laymarsh Clo., Belv. 166 EZ76
Laymead Clo., Nthlt. 136 BY65
Laystall St. EC1 274 D5
Laystall St. EC1 141 DN70
Layters Ave., Ger.Cr. 90 AW54
Layters Ave. S., Ger.Cr. 90 AW54
Layters Clo., Ger.Cr. 90 AW54
Layters End, Ger.Cr. 90 AW54
Layters Grn. La., Ger.Cr. 112 AU55
Layters Way, Ger.Cr. 112 AX56
Layton Ct., Wey. 213 BP105
Castle Vw. Rd.
Layton Cres., Croy. 219 DN106
Layton Rd. N1 141 DN68
Layton Rd., Brent. 157 CK78
Layton Rd., Houns. 156 CB84
Laytons Bldgs. SE1 279 K4
Laytons La., Sun. 195 BT96
Layzell Wk. SE9 184 EK88
Mottingham La.
Lazar Wk. N7 121 DM61
Briset Way
Le Corte Clo., Kings L. 58 BM29
Le May Ave. SE12 184 EH90
Le May Clo., Horl. 268 DG147
Le Personne Rd., Cat. 236 DR122
Lea, The, Egh. 173 BC94
Lea Bri. Rd. E5 122 DV62
Lea Bri. Rd. E10 123 EA59
Lea Bri. Rd. E17 123 ED57
Lea Bushes, Wat. 76 CA35
Lea Clo. (Bushey), Wat. 76 CB43
Lea Cres., Ruis. 115 BT63
Lea Gdns., Wem. 118 CM63
Lea Hall Rd. E10 123 EA60
Lea Mt., Wal.Cr. 66 DS28
Lea Rd., Beck. 203 EA96
Fairfield Rd.
Lea Rd., Enf. 82 DR39
Lea Rd., Grays 171 GG78
Lea Rd., Hodd. 49 EC15
Lea Rd., Sev. 257 FJ127
Lea Rd., Sthl. 156 BY77
Lea Rd., Wal.Abb. 67 EA34
Lea Rd. Trd. Est., Wal.Abb. 67 EA34
Lea Side Ind. Est., Enf. 83 DZ41
Lea Vale, Dart. 167 FD84
Lea Valley Rd. E4 83 DX43
Lea Valley Rd., Enf. 83 DX43
Lea Valley Viaduct E4 101 DX50
Lea Valley Viaduct N18 101 DX50
Lea Vw. Hos. E5 122 DV60
Springfield
Leabank Clo., Har. 117 CE62
Leabank Sq. E9 143 EA65
Leabank Vw. N15 122 DU58
Leabourne Rd. N16 122 DU58
Leach Gro., Lthd. 231 CJ122
Leachcroft, Ger.Cr. 90 AV53
Leacroft, Stai. 174 BG92
Leacroft Ave. SW12 180 DF87
Leacroft Clo., Ken. 236 DQ116
Leacroft Clo., Stai. 174 BH91
Leacroft Clo., West Dr. 134 BL72
Leacroft Rd., Iver 133 BD72
Leadale Ave. E4 101 DZ47
Leadale Rd. N15 122 DU58
Leadale Rd. N16 122 DU58
Leadbeaters Clo. N11 98 DF50
Goldsmith Rd.
Leadenhall Mkt. EC3 275 M9
Leadenhall Pl. EC3 275 M9
Leadenhall St. EC3 275 M9
Leadenhall St. EC3 142 DS72
Leader Ave. E12 125 EN64
Leadings, The, Wem. 118 CQ62
Leaf Clo., Nthwd. 93 BR52
Leaf Clo., T.Ditt. 197 CE99
Leaf Gro. SE27 181 DN92
Leafield Clo. SW16 181 DP93
Leafield Clo., Wok. 226 AV118
Winnington Way
Leafield La., Sid. 186 EZ91
Leafield Rd. SW20 199 CZ97
Leafield Rd., Sutt. 200 DA103
Leaford Cres., Wat. 75 BT37
Leaforis Rd., Wal.Cr. 66 DU28
Leafy Gro., Kes. 222 EJ106
Leafy Oak Rd. SE12 184 EJ91
Leafy Way, Brwd. 109 GD46
Leafy Way, Croy. 202 DT103
Leagrave St. E5 122 DW62
Leahoe Gdns., Hert. 32 DQ10
Leaholme Gdns., Slou. 130 AJ71
Leaholme Way, Ruis. 115 BQ58
Leahurst Rd. SE13 183 ED85
Leake Ct. SE1 278 C4
Leake St. SE1 278 C4
Leake St. SE1 161 DM75
Lealand Rd. N15 122 DT58
Leamington Ave. E17 123 EA57
Leamington Ave., Brom. 184 EJ92
Leamington Ave., Mord. 199 CY98
Leamington Ave., Orp. 223 ES105
Leamington Clo. E12 125 EM64

Leamington Clo., Brom. 184 EJ92
Leamington Clo., Houns. 176 CC85
Leamington Clo., Rom. 106 FN51
Leamington Rd.
Leamington Cres., Har. 116 BY62
Leamington Gdns., Ilf. 125 ET61
Leamington Pk. W3 138 CR71
Leamington Pl., Hayes 135 BT70
Leamington Rd., Rom. 106 FN50
Leamington Rd., Sthl. 156 BX77
Leamington Rd. Vill. W11 139 CZ71
Leamore St. W6 159 CV77
Leamouth Rd. E6 144 EL72
Leamouth Rd. E14 143 ED72
Leander Ct. SE8 163 EA81
Leander Dr., Grav. 191 GM91
Leander Gdns., Wat. 76 BY37
Leander Rd. SW2 181 DM87
Leander Rd., Nthlt. 136 CA68
Leander Rd., Th.Hth. 201 DM98
Leapale La., Guil. 258 AX135
Leapale Rd., Guil. 258 AX135
Learoyd Gdns. E6 145 EN73
Leas, The, Hem.H. 40 BN24
Leas, The, Stai. 174 BG91
Leas, The, Upmin. 129 FR59
Leas, The (Bushey), Wat. 76 BZ39
Leas Clo., Chess. 216 CM108
Leas Dale SE9 185 EN90
Leas Dr., Iver 133 BE72
Leas Grn., Chis. 185 ET93
Leas La., Warl. 237 DX118
Leas Rd., Guil. 258 AW135
Leas Rd., Warl. 237 DX118
Leaside, Hem.H. 41 BQ21
Leaside, Lthd. 230 CA123
Leaside Ave. N10 120 DG55
Leaside Ct., Uxb. 135 BP69
The Larches
Leaside Rd. E5 122 DW60
Leasowes Rd. E10 123 EA60
Leasway, Brwd. 108 FX48
Leasway, Upmin. 128 FQ62
Leathart Clo., Horn. 147 FH66
Dowding Way
Leather Bottle La., Belv. 166 EZ77
St. Augustine's Rd.
Leather Clo., Mitch. 200 DG96
Leather Gdns. E15 144 EE67
Abbey Rd.
Leather La. EC1 274 D6
Leather La. EC1 141 DN70
Leather La., Horn. 128 FK60
North St.
Leatherbottle Grn., Erith 166 EZ76
Leatherdale St. E1 142 DW70
Portelet Rd.
Leatherhead Bypass Rd., Lthd. 231 CH120
Leatherhead Clo. N16 122 DS60
Leatherhead Ind. Est., Lthd. 231 CG121
Station Rd.
Leatherhead Rd., Ash. 231 CK121
Leatherhead Rd., Chess. 215 CJ111
Leatherhead Rd., Lthd. 246 CB126
Leatherhead Rd. (Great Bookham), Lthd. 231 CK121
Leatherhead Rd. (Oxshott), Lthd. 215 CD114
Leathermarket Ct. SE1 162 DS75
Leathermarket St.
Leathermarket St. SE1 279 M5
Leathermarket St. SE1 162 DS75
Leathersellers Clo., Barn. 79 CY42
The Ave.
Leathsail Rd., Har. 116 CB62
Leathwaite Rd. SW11 160 DF84
Leathwell Rd. SE8 163 EB82
Leaveland Clo., Beck. 203 EA98
Leaver Gdns., Grnf. 137 CD68
Leaves Grn. Cres., Kes. 222 EJ111
Leaves Grn. Rd., Kes. 222 EK111
Leavesden Rd., Stan. 95 CG51
Leavesden Rd., Wat. 75 BV38
Leavesden Rd., Wey. 213 BP106
Leaview, Wal.Abb. 67 EB33
Leaway E10 123 DX60
Leazes Ave., Cat. 235 DN124
Lebanon Ave., Felt. 176 BX92
Lebanon Clo., Wat. 75 BR36
Lebanon Ct., Twick. 177 CH87
Lebanon Dr., Cob. 214 CA113
Lebanon Gdns. SW18 180 DA85
Lebanon Gdns., West. 238 EK117
Lebanon Pk., Twick. 177 CH87
Lebanon Rd. SW18 180 DA85
Lebanon Rd., Croy. 202 DS102
Lebrun Sq. SE3 164 EH83
Lechford Rd., Horl. 268 DG149
Lechmere App., Wdf.Grn. 102 EJ54
Lechmere Ave., Chig. 103 EQ49
Lechmere Ave., Wdf.Grn. 102 EK54
Lechmere Rd. NW2 139 CV65
Leckford Rd. SW18 180 DC89
Leckwith Ave., Bexh. 166 EY79
Lecky St. SW7 160 DD78
Leconfield Ave. SW13 159 CT83
Leconfield Rd. N5 122 DR63
Leconfield Wk., Horn. 148 FJ65
Airfield Way
Lectern La., St.Alb. 43 CD24
Leda Ave., Enf. 83 DX38
Leda Rd. SE18 165 EM76
Ledborough La., Beac. 89 AK52
Ledborough Wd., Beac. 89 AL51
Ledbury Est. SE15 162 DV80
Ledbury Ms. N. W11 140 DA73
Ledbury Rd.
Ledbury Ms. W. W11 140 DA73
Ledbury Rd.
Ledbury Pl., Croy. 220 DQ105
Ledbury Rd.
Ledbury Rd. W11 139 CZ72
Ledbury Rd., Croy. 220 DQ105
Ledbury Rd., Reig. 249 CZ133
Ledbury St. SE15 162 DU80
Ledger Clo., Guil. 243 BB132
Ledger Dr., Add. 211 BF107
Ledger La., Maid. 150 AD82
Ledgers Rd., Slou. 151 AR75
Ledgers Rd., Warl. 237 EB119
Ledrington Rd. SE19 182 DU93
Anerley Hill
Ledway Dr., Wem. 118 CM59
Lee Ave., Rom. 126 EY58
Lee Bri. SE13 163 EC83
Lee Ch. St. SE13 164 EE84
Lee Clo. E17 101 DX53
Lee Clo., Hert. 32 DQ11
Lee Clo., Ware 33 EC11
Lee Conservancy Rd. E9 123 DZ64
Lee Fm. Clo., Chesh. 56 AU30
Lee Gdns. Ave., Horn. 128 FN60
Lee Grn. SE12 184 EF85
Lee Grn., Orp. 206 EU99
Lee Grn. La., Epsom 232 CP124
Lee Gro., Chig. 103 EN47
Lee High Rd. SE12 164 EF84
Lee High Rd. SE13 163 ED84
Lee Pk. SE3 164 EF84
Lee Pk. Way N9 101 DY48
Lee Pk. Way N18 101 DX50
Lee Rd. NW7 97 CX52
Lee Rd. SE3 164 EF83
Lee Rd. SW19 200 DB95
Lee Rd., Enf. 82 DU44
Lee Rd., Grnf. 137 CJ67
Lee St. E8 142 DT67
Lee St., Horl. 268 DE148
Lee Ter. SE3 164 EE83
Lee Ter. SE13 164 EE83
Lee Valley Trd. Est. N18 101 DX50
Lee Vw., Enf. 81 DP39
Leech La., Epsom 248 CQ126
Leech La., Lthd. 248 CP126
Leechcroft Ave., Sid. 185 ET85
Leechcroft Ave., Swan. 207 FF97
Leechcroft Rd., Wall. 200 DG104
Leecroft Rd., Barn. 79 CY43
Leeds Clo., Orp. 206 EX103
Leeds Pl. N4 121 DM61
Tollington Pk.
Leeds Rd., Ilf. 125 ER60
Leeds Rd., Slou. 132 AS73
Leeds St. N18 100 DU50
Leefe Way, Pot.B. 65 DK28
Leefern Rd. W12 159 CU75
Leegate SE12 184 EF85
Leegate Clo., Wok. 226 AV116
Sythwood
Leeke St. WC1 274 B2
Leeke St. WC1 141 DM69
Leeland Rd. W13 137 CG74
Leeland Ter. W13 137 CG74
Leeland Way NW10 119 CT63
Leeming Rd., Borwd. 78 CM39
Leerdam Dr. E14 163 EC76
Lees, The, Croy. 203 DZ103
Lees Ave., Nthwd. 93 BT54
Lees Pl. W1 272 F10
Lees Pl. W1 140 DG73
Lees Rd., Uxb. 135 BP70
Leeside, Barn. 79 CY43
Leeside, Pot.B. 64 DD32
Wayside
Leeside Cres. NW11 119 CY58
Leeside Rd. N17 100 DV51
Leeson Rd. SE24 161 DN84
Leesons Hill, Chis. 205 ES97
Leesons Hill, Orp. 206 EU97
Leesons Way, Orp. 205 ET96
Leeward Gdns. SW19 179 CZ92
Leeway SE8 163 DZ78
Leeway Clo., Pnr. 94 BZ52
Woodridings Clo.
Leewood Clo. SE12 184 EF86
Upwood Rd.
Leewood Pl., Swan. 207 FD98
Leewood Way, Lthd. 246 BW127
Lefevre Wk. E3 143 DZ67
Old Ford Rd.
Lefroy Rd. W12 159 CT75
Legard Rd. N5 121 DP62
Legatt Rd. SE9 184 EK85
Leggatt Rd. E15 143 EC68
Leggatts Clo., Wat. 75 BT36
Leggatts Ri., Wat. 75 BU35
Leggatts Way, Wat. 75 BT36
Leggatts Wd. Ave., Wat. 75 BV36
Legge St. SE13 183 EC85
Leggfield Ter., Hem.H. 39 BF20
Leghorn Rd. NW10 139 CT68
Leghorn Rd. SE18 165 ER78
Legion Clo. N1 141 DN66
Legion Ct., Mord. 200 DA100
Legion Rd., Grnf. 136 CC67
Legion Way N12 98 DE52
Downway
Legon Ave., Rom. 127 FC60
Legrace Ave., Houns. 156 BX82
Leicester Ave., Mitch. 201 DL98
Leicester Clo., Wor.Pk. 217 CW105
Leicester Ct. WC2 273 N10
Leicester Gdns., Ilf. 125 ES59
Leicester Pl. WC2 273 N10
Leicester Rd. E11 124 EH57
Leicester Rd. N2 120 DE55
Leicester Rd. NW10 138 CR66
Leicester Rd., Barn. 80 DB43
Leicester Rd., Croy. 202 DS101
Leicester Rd., Til. 171 GF81
Leicester Sq. WC2 277 N1
Leicester Sq. WC2 141 DK73
Leicester St. WC2 273 N10
Leigh Ave., Ilf. 124 EK56
Leigh Clo., Add. 211 BF108
Leigh Clo., N.Mal. 198 CR98
Leigh Common, Welw.G.C. 29 CY11
Leigh Cor., Cob. 214 BW114
Leigh Hill Rd.
Leigh Ct., Borwd. 78 CR40
Banks Rd.
Leigh Ct., Har. 117 CE60
Leigh Ct. Clo., Cob. 214 BW114
Leigh Cres., Croy. 221 EB108
Leigh Dr., Rom. 106 FK49
Leigh Gdns. NW10 139 CW68
Leigh Hill Rd., Cob. 214 BW114
Leigh Hunt Dr. N14 99 DK46
Leigh Hunt St. SE1 279 H4
Leigh Orchard Clo. SW16 181 DM90
Leigh Pk., Slou. 152 AW80
Leigh Pl. EC1 141 DN71
Baldwin's Gdns.
Leigh Pl., Cob. 214 BW114
Leigh Pl., Well. 166 EU82
Leigh Pl. La., Gdse. 253 DY132
Leigh Pl. Rd., Reig. 265 CU140
Leigh Rd. E6 145 EN65
Leigh Rd. E10 123 EC59
Leigh Rd. N5 121 DP63
Leigh Rd., Cob. 213 BV113
Leigh Rd., Grav. 191 GH89
Leigh Rd., Houns. 157 CD84
Leigh Rd., Slou. 131 AP73
Leigh Rodd, Wat. 94 BZ48
Leigh Sq., Wind. 151 AK82
Leigh St. WC1 273 P4
Leigh St. WC1 141 DL70
Leigh Ter., Orp. 206 EV97
Saxville Rd.
Leigham Ave. SW16 181 DL90
Leigham Ct. Rd. SW16 181 DL89
Leigham Dr., Islw. 157 CE80
Leigham Vale SW2 181 DN89
Leigham Vale SW16 181 DM90
Leighton Ave. E12 125 EN64
Leighton Ave., Pnr. 116 BY55
Leighton Buzzard Rd., Hem.H. 40 BJ19
Leighton Clo., Edg. 96 CN54
Leighton Cres. NW5 121 DJ64
Leighton Gro.
Leighton Gdns. NW10 139 CV68
Leighton Gdns., S.Croy. 220 DV113
Leighton Gdns., Til. 171 GG80
Leighton Gro. NW5 121 DJ64
Leighton Pl. NW5 121 DJ64
Leighton Rd. NW5 121 DJ64
Leighton Rd. W13 157 CG75
Leighton Rd., Enf. 82 DT43
Leighton Rd., Har. 95 CD54
Leighton St. E., Croy. 201 DP102
Leighton St. W., Croy. 201 DP102
Leighton Way, Epsom 216 CR114
Leila Parnell Pl. SE7 164 EJ79
Victoria Way
Leinster Ave. SW14 158 CQ83
Leinster Gdns. W2 140 DC72
Leinster Ms. W2 140 DC73
Leinster Pl. W2 140 DC72
Leinster Rd. N10 121 DH56
Leinster Rd. NW6 140 DA69
Stafford Rd.
Leinster Sq. W2 140 DA72
Leinster Ter. W2 140 DC73
Leiston Spur, Slou. 132 AS72
Leisure La., W.Byf. 212 BH112
Leith Clo. NW9 118 CR60
Leith Hill, Orp. 206 EU95
Leith Hill Grn., Orp. 206 EU95
Leith Hill
Leith Hill La., Dor. 262 BY144
Leith Pk. Rd., Grav. 191 GH88
Leith Rd. N22 99 DP53
Leith Rd., Epsom 216 CS112
Leith Vw., Dor. 263 CJ140
Leith Yd. NW6 140 DA67
Quex Rd.
Leithcote Gdns. SW16 181 DM91
Leithcote Path SW16 181 DM90
Lela Ave., Houns. 156 BW82
Lelitia Clo. E8 142 DU67
Pownall Rd.
Leman St. E1 142 DT72
Lemark Clo., Stan. 95 CJ50
Lemmon Rd. SE10 164 EE79
Lemna Rd. E11 124 EE59
Lemonfield Dr., Wat. 60 BY33
Lemonwell Ct. SE9 185 EQ85
Lemsford Clo. N15 122 DU57
Lemsford Ct. N4 122 DQ61
Brownswood Rd.
Lemsford Ct., Borwd. 78 CQ42
Lemsford La., Welw.G.C. 29 CV10
Lemsford Rd., Hat. 45 CT16
Lemsford Rd., St.Alb. 43 CF20
Lemsford Village, Welw.G.C. 29 CT10
Lemsford Village Rd., Welw.G.C. 29 CU10
Lemuel St. SW18 180 DB86
St. Ann's Hill
Lena Gdns. W6 159 CW76
Lena Kennedy Clo. E4 101 EC51
Lenanton Steps E14 163 EA75
Manilla St.
Lendal Ter. SW4 161 DK83
Lenelby Rd., Surb. 198 CN102
Lenham Rd. SE12 164 EF84
Lenham Rd., Bexh. 166 EZ79
Lenham Rd., Sutt. 218 DB105
Lenham Rd., Th.Hth. 202 DR96
Lenmore Ave., Grays 170 GC76
Lennard Ave., W.Wick. 204 EE103
Lennard Clo., W.Wick. 204 EE103
Lennard Rd. SE20 183 DX93
Lennard Rd., Beck. 183 DY94
Lennard Rd., Brom. 205 EM102
Lennard Rd., Croy. 202 DQ102
Lennard Rd., Sev. 241 FE120
Lennard Row, S.Ock. 149 FR74
Lennon Rd. NW2 139 CW65
Lennox Ave., Grav. 191 GF86
Lennox Clo., Rom. 127 FF58
Lennox Gdns. NW10 119 CT63
Lennox Gdns. SW1 276 D7
Lennox Gdns. SW1 160 DF76
Lennox Gdns., Croy. 219 DP105
Lennox Gdns., Ilf. 125 EM60
Lennox Gdns. Ms. SW1 276 D7
Lennox Gdns. Ms. SW1 160 DF76
Lennox Rd. E17 123 DZ58
Lennox Rd. N4 121 DM61
Lennox Rd., Grav. 191 GF86
Lennox Rd. E., Grav. 191 GG87
Lenor Clo., Bexh. 166 EY84
Lens Rd. E7 144 EJ66
Lensbury Clo. (Cheshunt), Wal.Cr. 67 DY28
Ashdown Cres.
Lensbury Way SE2 166 EW76
Lent Grn. La., Slou. 130 AH70
Lent Ri. Rd., Slou. 130 AH69
Lenthall Ave., Grays 170 GA75
Lenthall Pl. SW7 160 DC77
Gloucester Rd.
Lenthall Rd. E8 142 DT66
Lenthall Rd., Loug. 85 ER42
Lenthorp Rd. SE10 164 EF77
Lentmead Rd., Brom. 184 EF90
Lenton Clo., Guil. 261 BR142
Lenton Ri., Rich. 158 CL83
Evelyn Ter.
Lenton St. SE18 165 ER77
Lenville Way SE16 162 DU78
Catlin St.
Leo St. SE15 162 DV80
Leo Yd. EC1 274 G5
Leof Cres. SE6 183 EB92
Leominster Rd., Mord. 200 DC100
Leominster Wk., Mord. 200 DC100
Leonard Ave., Mord. 200 DC99
Leonard Ave., Rom. 127 FD60
Leonard Ave., Sev. 241 FH116
Leonard Ave., Swans. 190 FY87
Leonard Rd. E4 101 EA51
Leonard Rd. E7 124 EG63
Leonard Rd. N9 100 DT48
Leonard Rd. SW16 201 DJ95
Leonard Rd., Sthl. 156 BX76
Leonard Robbins Path SE28 146 EV73
Tawney Rd.
Leonard St. E16 144 EL74
Leonard St. EC2 275 L4
Leonard St. EC2 142 DR70
Leonard Way, Brwd. 108 FS49
Leontine Clo. SE15 162 DU80
Leopards Ct. EC1 274 D6
Leopold Ave. SW19 179 CZ92
Leopold Ms. E9 142 DW67
Fremont St.
Leopold Rd. E17 123 EA57
Leopold Rd. N2 120 DD55
Leopold Rd. N18 100 DW50
Leopold Rd. NW10 138 CS66
Leopold Rd. SW19 179 CZ91
Leopold Rd. W5 138 CM74
Leopold St. E3 143 DZ71
Leopold Ter. SW19 180 DA92
Dora Rd.
Lepe Clo., Brom. 184 EE91
Winlaton Rd.
Leppoc Rd. SW4 181 DK85
Leret Way, Lthd. 231 CG121
Leroy St. SE1 279 M7
Leroy St. SE1 162 DS77
Lerwick Dr., Slou. 132 AS71
Lesbourne Rd., Reig. 266 DB135
Lescombe Clo. SE23 183 DY90
Lescombe Rd. SE23 183 DY90
Lesley Clo., Bex. 187 FB87
Lesley Clo., Grav. 191 GF94
Lesley Clo., Swan. 207 FD97
Leslie Gdns., Sutt. 218 DA107
Leslie Gro., Croy. 202 DR102
Leslie Pk. Rd., Croy. 202 DS102
Leslie Rd. E11 123 EC63
Leslie Rd. E16 144 EH72
Leslie Rd. N2 120 DD55
Leslie Rd., Dor. 247 CK134
Leslie Rd., Wok. 210 AS110
Leslie Smith Sq. SE18 165 EN79
Nightingale Vale
Lesney Fm. Est., Erith 167 FD80
Lesney Pk., Erith 167 FD79
Lesney Pk. Rd., Erith 167 FD79
Lessar Ave. SW4 181 DH85
Lessing St. SE23 183 DY87
Lessingham Ave. SW17 180 DF91
Lessingham Ave., Ilf. 125 EN55
Lessington Ave., Rom. 127 FC58
Lessness Ave., Bexh. 166 EX80
Lessness Pk., Belv. 166 EZ78
Lessness Rd., Belv. 166 FA78
Stapley Rd.
Lessness Rd., Mord. 200 DC100
Lester Ave. E15 144 EE70
Leston Clo., Rain. 147 FG69
Ashwood Ave.
Leswin Pl. N16 122 DT62
Leswin Rd.
Leswin Rd. N16 122 DT62
Letchfield, Chesh. 56 AV31
Letchford Gdns. NW10 139 CU69
Letchford Ms. NW10 139 CU69
Letchford Gdns.
Letchford Rd., Horl. 268 DG149
Letchford Ter., Har. 94 CB53
Letchmore Rd., Rad. 77 CG36
Letchworth Ave., Felt. 175 BT87
Letchworth Clo., Brom. 204 EG99
Letchworth Clo., Wat. 94 BX50
Letchworth Dr., Brom. 204 EG99
Letchworth St. SW17 180 DF91
Lethbridge Clo. SE13 163 EC81
Lett Rd. E15 143 ED66
Letter Box La., Sev. 257 FJ129
Letterstone Rd. SW6 159 CZ80
Varna Rd.
Lettice St. SW6 159 CZ81
Lettsom St. SE5 162 DS82
Lettsom Wk. E13 144 EG68
Stratford Rd.
Leucha Rd. E17 123 DY57
Levana Clo. SW19 179 CY88
Levehurst Way SW4 161 DL82
Leven Clo., Wal.Cr. 67 DX33
Leven Clo., Wat. 94 BX50
Leven Dr., Wal.Cr. 67 DX33
Leven Rd. E14 143 EC71
Leven Way, Hayes 135 BS72
Leven Way, Hem.H. 40 BK16
Levendale Rd. SE23 183 DY89
Lever Sq., Grays 171 GG77
Lever St. EC1 274 G3
Lever St. EC1 141 DP69
Leverett Clo., Croy. 221 ED111
Leveret Clo., Wat. 59 BU34
Leverett St. SW3 276 C8
Leverholme Gdns. SE9 185 EN90
Leverson St. SW16 181 DJ93
Leverstock Grn. Rd., Hem.H. 41 BQ21
Leverstock Grn. Way, Hem.H. 41 BQ20
Leverton Pl. NW5 121 DJ64
Leverton St.
Leverton St. NW5 121 DJ64
Leverton Way, Wal.Abb. 67 EC33
Leveson Rd., Grays 171 GH76
Levett Gdns., Ilf. 125 ET63
Levett Rd., Bark. 145 ES65
Levett Rd., Lthd. 231 CH120
Levine Gdns., Bark. 146 EX68
Levison Way N19 121 DK61
Grovedale Rd.
Levylsdene, Guil. 243 BD134
Lewes Clo., Nthlt. 136 CA65
Lewes Rd. N12 98 DE50
Lewes Rd., Brom. 204 EK96
Lewes Rd., Rom. 106 FK49
Lewes Way, Rick. 75 BQ42
Lewesdon Clo. SW19 179 CX88
Leweston Pl. N16 122 DT59
Lewey Ho. E3 143 DZ70
Lewgars Ave. NW9 118 CQ58
Lewin Rd. SW14 158 CR83
Lewin Rd. SW16 181 DK93
Lewin Rd., Bexh. 186 EY85
Lewins Rd., Epsom 216 CP114
Lewins Rd., Ger.Cr. 112 AX55
Lewins Way, Slou. 131 AM73
Lewis Ave. E17 101 EA53
Lewis Clo. N14 99 DJ45
Orchid Rd.
Lewis Clo., Add. 212 BJ105
Lewis Clo., Brwd. 109 FZ45
Lewis Clo., Uxb. 92 BJ54
Lewis Cres. NW10 118 CQ64
Lewis Gdns. N2 98 DD54
Lewis Gro. SE13 163 EC83
Lewis La., Ger.Cr. 90 AY53
Lewis Rd., Horn. 128 FJ58
Lewis Rd., Mitch. 200 DD96
Lewis Rd., Rich. 177 CK85
Red Lion St.
Lewis Rd., Sid. 186 EW90
Lewis Rd., Sthl. 156 BY75
Lewis Rd., Sutt. 218 DB105
Lewis Rd., Swans. 190 FY86
Lewis Rd., Well. 166 EW83
Lewis St. NW1 141 DH65
Lewis Way, Dag. 147 FB65
Blackborne Rd.
Lewisham High St. SE13 183 EB86
Lewisham Hill SE13 163 EC82
Lewisham Pk. SE13 183 EC85
Lewisham Rd. SE13 163 EB81
Lewisham St. SW1 277 N5
Lewisham Way SE4 163 EA82
Lewisham Way SE14 163 DZ81
Lexden Dr., Rom. 126 EV58
Lexden Rd. W3 138 CP74
Lexden Rd., Mitch. 201 DK98
Lexham Gdns. W8 160 DA77
Lexham Gdns., Amer. 55 AQ37
Lexham Gdns. Ms. W8 160 DB76
Lexham Gdns.
Lexham Ho., Bark. 145 ER67
St. Margarets
Lexham Ms. W8 160 DA77
Lexham Wk. W8 160 DB76
Lexham Gdns.
Lexington Clo., Borwd. 78 CM41
Lexington Ct., Pur. 220 DQ110
Lexington St. W1 273 L10
Lexington St. W1 141 DJ73
Lexington Way, Barn. 79 CX42
Lexington Way, Upmin. 129 FT58
Lexton Gdns. SW12 181 DK88
Ley Hill Rd., Hem.H. 56 AX30
Ley St., Ilf. 125 EP61
Ley Wk., Welw.G.C. 30 DC09
Leyborne Ave. W13 157 CH75
Leyborne Pk., Rich. 158 CN81
Leybourne Ave., W.Byf. 212 BM113
Leybourne Clo., Brom. 204 EG100
Leybourne Clo., W.Byf. 212 BM113
Leybourne Ave.
Leybourne Rd. E11 124 EF60
Leybourne Rd. NW1 141 DH66
Leybourne Rd. NW9 118 CN57
Leybourne Rd., Uxb. 135 BQ67
Leybourne St. NW1 141 DH66
Hawley St.
Leybridge Ct. SE12 184 EG85
Leyburn Clo. E17 123 EC56
Leyburn Cres., Rom. 106 FL52
Leyburn Gdns., Croy. 202 DT103
Leyburn Gro. N18 100 DU51
Leyburn Rd. N18 100 DU51
Leyburn Rd., Rom. 106 FL52
Leycroft Clo., Loug. 85 EN43
Leycroft Gdns., Erith 167 FG81
Leyden St. E1 275 P7
Leydenhatch La., Swan. 207 FC95
Leydon Clo. SE16 143 DX74
Lagado Ms.
Leyes Rd. E16 144 EJ72
Leyfield, Wor.Pk. 198 CS102
Leyhill Clo., Swan. 207 FE99
Leyland Ave., Enf. 83 DY40
Leyland Ave., St.Alb. 43 CD22
Leyland Clo. (Cheshunt), Wal.Cr. 66 DW28
Leyland Gdns., Wdf.Grn. 102 EJ50
Leyland Rd. SE12 184 EF85
Leylands La., Stai. 153 BF84
Leylang Rd. SE14 163 DX80
Leys, The N2 120 DC56
Leys, The, Amer. 55 AP35
Leys, The, Har. 118 CL58
Leys, The, St.Alb. 43 CK17
Leys Ave., Dag. 147 FC67
Leys Clo., Dag. 147 FC66
Leys Clo., Har. 117 CD57
Leys Clo., Uxb. 92 BK53
Leys Gdns., Barn. 80 DG43
Leys Rd., Hem.H. 40 BL22
Leys Rd., Lthd. 215 CD112
Leys Rd. E., Enf. 83 DY39
Leys Rd. W., Enf. 83 DY39
Leysdown, Welw.G.C. 30 DD09
Leysdown Ave., Bexh. 167 FC84
Leysdown Rd. SE9 184 EL89
Leysfield Rd. W12 159 CU76
Leyspring Rd. E11 124 EF60
Leyswood Dr., Ilf. 125 ES57
Leythe Rd. W3 158 CQ75
Leyton Business Cen. E10 123 EA61
Leyton Cross Rd., Dart. 187 FF90
Leyton Gra. E10 123 EB60
Leyton Gra. Est. E10 123 EA60
Leyton Grn. Rd. E10 123 EC58
Leyton Ind. Village E10 123 DX59
Leyton Pk. Rd. E10 123 EC62
Leyton Rd. E15 123 ED64
Leyton Rd. SW19 180 DC94
Leyton Way E11 124 EE59
Leytonstone Rd. E15 144 EE65
Leywick St. E15 144 EE68
Leywood Clo., Amer. 55 AR40
Lezayre Rd., Orp. 223 ET107
Liardet St. SE14 163 DY79
Liberia Rd. N5 141 DP65
Liberty, The, Rom. 127 FE57
Liberty Ave. SW19 200 DC95
Liberty Clo., Hert. 32 DQ12
Liberty Hall Rd., Add. 212 BG106
Liberty La., Add. 212 BG106
Liberty Ms. SW12 181 DH86
Liberty Ri., Add. 212 BG107
Liberty St. SW9 161 DM81
Libra Rd. E3 143 DZ67
Libra Rd. E13 144 EG68
Library Hill, Brwd. 108 FX47
Coptfold Rd.

Library Pl. E1 142 DV73
Cable St.
Library St. SE1 278 F5
Library St. SE1 161 DP75
Library Way, Twick. 176 CC87
Nelson Rd.
Lichfield Clo., Barn. 80 DF41
Chalk La.
Lichfield Gdns., Rich. 158 CL84
Lichfield Gro. N3 98 DA53
Lichfield Rd. E3 143 DY69
Lichfield Rd. E6 144 EK69
Lichfield Rd. N9 100 DU47
Winchester Rd.
Lichfield Rd. NW2 119 CY63
Lichfield Rd., Dag. 126 EV63
Lichfield Rd., Houns. 156 BW83
Lichfield Rd., Nthwd. 115 BU55
Lichfield Rd., Rich. 158 CM81
Lichfield Rd., Wdf.Grn. 102 EE49
Lichfield Sq., Rich. 158 CL84
Lichfield Gdns.
Lichfield Ter., Upmin. 129 FS61
Lichfield Way, Brox. 49 DZ22
Lichfield Way, S.Croy. 221 DX110
Lichlade Clo., Orp. 223 ET105
Lidbury Rd. NW7 97 CY51
Lidcote Gdns. SW9 161 DN82
Liddall Way, West Dr. 134 BM74
Liddell Clo., Har. 117 CK55
Liddell Gdns. NW10 139 CW68
Liddell Pl., Wind. 150 AJ83
Liddell Way
Liddell Rd. NW6 140 DA65
Liddell Sq., Wind. 150 AJ83
Liddell Way
Liddell Way, Wind. 150 AJ83
Lidding Rd., Har. 117 CK57
Liddington Hall Dr., Guil. 242 AS131
Liddington New Rd., Guil. 242 AS131
Liddington Rd. E15 144 EF67
Liddon Rd. E13 144 EH69
Liddon Rd., Brom. 204 EJ97
Liden Clo. E17 123 DZ60
Hitcham Rd.
Lidfield Rd. N16 122 DR63
Lidiard Rd. SW18 180 DC89
Lidlington Pl. NW1 273 L1
Lidlington Pl. NW1 141 DJ68
Lido Sq. N17 100 DR54
Lordship La.
Lidstone Clo., Wok. 226 AV117
Lidyard Rd. N19 121 DJ60
Lieutenant Ellis Way, Wal.Cr. 66 DU29
Liffler Rd. SE18 165 ES78
Lifford St. SW15 159 CX84
Liffords Pl. SW13 159 CT82
Lightcliffe Rd. N13 99 DN49
Lighter Clo. SE16 163 DX77
Plough Way
Lightermans Rd. E14 163 EA75
Lightermans Wk. SW18 160 DA84
Point Pleasant
Lightfoot Rd. N8 121 DL57
Lightley Clo., Wem. 138 CM66
Stanley Ave.
Ligonier St. E2 275 P4
Lila Pl., Swan. 207 FE98
Lilac Ave., Wok. 226 AX120
Lilac Clo. E4 101 DZ51
Lilac Clo., Brwd. 108 FV43
Magnolia Way
Lilac Clo., Guil. 242 AW130
Lilac Clo. (Cheshunt), Wal.Cr. 66 DV31
Greenwood Ave.
Lilac Gdns. W5 157 CK76
Lilac Gdns., Croy. 203 EA104
Lilac Gdns., Hayes 135 BS72
Lilac Gdns., Rom. 127 FE60
Lilac Gdns., Swan. 207 FD97
Lilac Pl. SE11 278 B9
Lilac Pl. SE11 161 DM77
Lilac Pl., West Dr. 134 BM73
Cedar Ave.
Lilac Rd., Hodd. 49 EB15
Lilac St. W12 139 CU73
Lilacs Ave., Enf. 82 DW36
Lilburne Gdns. SE9 184 EL85
Lilburne Rd. SE9 184 EL85
Lilburne Wk. NW10 138 CQ65
Pitfield Way
Lile Cres. W7 137 CE71
Lilestone Est. NW8 140 DD70
Fisherton St.
Lilestone St. NW8 272 B4
Lilestone St. NW8 140 DE70
Lilford Rd. SE5 161 DP82
Lilian Barker Clo. SE12 184 EG85
Lilian Board Way, Grnf. 117 CD64
Lilian Clo. N16 122 DS62
Barbauld Rd.
Lilian Cres., Brwd. 109 GC47
Lilian Gdns., Wdf.Grn. 102 EH53
Lilian Rd. SW16 201 DJ95
Lillechurch Rd., Dag. 146 EV65
Lilleshall Rd., Mord. 200 DD99
Lilley Clo. E1 142 DU74
Hermitage Wall
Lilley Clo., Brwd. 108 FT49
Lilley Dr., Tad. 234 DB122
Lilley La. NW7 96 CR50
Lillian Ave. W3 158 CN75
Lillian Rd. SW13 159 CU79
Lilliard Clo., Hodd. 33 EB13
Lillie Rd. SW6 159 CX79
Lillie Rd., West. 238 EK118
Lillie Yd. SW6 160 DA79
Lillieshall Rd. SW4 161 DH83
Lillington Gdns. Est. SW1 277 L9
Lilliots La., Lthd. 231 CG119
Kingston Rd.
Lilliput Ave., Nthlt. 136 BY67
Lilliput Rd., Rom. 127 FD59
Lily Clo. W14 159 CX77
Gliddon Rd.
Lily Gdns., Wem. 137 CJ68
Lily Pl. EC1 274 E6
Lily Pl. EC1 141 DN71
Lily Rd. E17 123 EA58
Lilyville Rd. SW6 159 CZ81
Limbourne Ave., Dag. 126 EZ59
Limburg Rd. SW11 160 DF84
Lime Ave., Brwd. 109 FZ48
Lime Ave., Grav. 190 GD87
Lime Ave., Upmin. 128 FN63
Lime Ave., West Dr. 134 BM73
Lime Ave., Wind. 152 AT80
Lime Clo. E1 142 DU74
Lime Clo., Brom. 204 EL98
Lime Clo., Buck.H. 102 EK48
Lime Clo., Cars. 200 DF103
Lime Clo., Guil. 244 BH128
Lime Clo., Har. 95 CG54
Lime Clo., Pnr. 115 BT55
Lime Clo., Reig. 266 DB137
Cockshot Hill
Lime Clo., Rom. 127 FC56
Lime Clo., S.Ock. 149 FW69
Lime Clo., Ware 33 DY05
Lime Clo., Wat. 94 BX45
Lime Ct., Mitch. 200 DD96
Lime Cres., Sun. 196 BW96
Lime Gro. N20 97 CZ46
Lime Gro. W12 159 CW75
Lime Gro., Add. 212 BG105
Lime Gro., Guil. 242 AV130
Lime Gro. (Clandon), Guil. 244 BG128
Lime Gro., Hayes 135 BR73
Lime Gro., Ilf. 103 ET51
Lime Gro., N.Mal. 198 CR97
Lime Gro., Orp. 205 EP103
Lime Gro., Ruis. 115 BV58
Lime Gro., Sid. 185 ET86
Lime Gro., Twick. 177 CF86
Lime Gro., Warl. 237 DY118
Lime Gro., Wok. 226 AY121
Lime Meadow Ave., S.Croy. 220 DU113
Lime Pit La., Sev. 241 FC117
Lime Rd., Epp. 69 ET31
Lime Rd., Rich. 158 CM84
St. Mary's Gro.
Lime Rd., Swan. 207 FD97
Lime Row, Erith 166 EZ76
Northwood Pl.
Lime St. E17 123 DY56
Lime St. EC3 275 M10
Lime St. EC3 142 DS73
Lime St. Pas. EC3 275 M10
Lime Ter. W7 137 CE73
Manor Ct. Rd.
Lime Tree Ave., Esher 197 CD102
Lime Tree Ave., T.Ditt. 197 CD102
Lime Tree Clo., Lthd. 230 CA124
Lime Tree Gro., Croy. 203 DZ104
Lime Tree Pl., Mitch. 201 DH95
Lime Tree Pl., St.Alb. 43 CF21
Lime Tree Rd., Houns. 156 CB81
Lime Tree Ter. SE6 183 DZ88
Winterstoke Rd.
Lime Tree Ter., Well. 166 EU83
Hook La.
Lime Tree Wk., Amer. 72 AT39
Lime Tree Wk., Enf. 82 DQ38
Cedar Rd.
Lime Tree Wk., Rick. 74 BH43
Lime Tree Wk., Sev. 257 FH125
Lime Tree Wk., Vir.W. 192 AY98
Stroude Rd.
Lime Tree Wk. (Bushey), Wat. 95 CE46
Lime Tree Wk., W.Wick. 222 EF105
Lime Wk. E15 144 EE67
Church St. N.
Lime Wk., Hem.H. 40 BM22
Lime Wk., Uxb. 114 BJ64
Lime Wks. Rd., Red. 251 DJ126
Limeburner La. EC4 274 F9
Limeburner La. EC4 141 DP72
Limebush Clo., Add. 212 BJ109
Limecroft Clo., Epsom 216 CR108
Limedene Clo., Pnr. 94 BX53
Limeharbour E14 163 EB76
Limehouse Causeway E14 143 DZ73
Limehouse Flds. Est. E14 143 DY71
Limekiln Dr. SE7 164 EH79
Highcombe
Limerick Clo. SW12 181 DJ87
Limerick Gdns., Upmin. 129 FT59
Limerston St. SW10 160 DC79
Limes, The W2 140 DA73
Linden Gdns.
Limes, The, Amer. 55 AP35
Limes, The, Brwd. 109 FZ48
Limes, The, Brom. 204 EL103
Limes, The, Purf. 168 FN78
Tank Hill Rd.
Limes, The, St.Alb. 43 CE18
Limes, The, Welw.G.C. 30 DA11
Limes, The, Wok. 226 AX115
Limes Ave. E11 124 EH56
Limes Ave. N12 98 DC49
Limes Ave. NW7 96 CS51
Limes Ave. NW11 119 CY59
Limes Ave. SE20 182 DV94
Limes Ave. SW13 159 CT82
Limes Ave., Cars. 200 DF102
Limes Ave., Chig. 103 EQ50
Limes Ave., Croy. 201 DN104
Limes Ave., Horl. 269 DH150
Limes Ave., The N11 99 DH50
Limes Clo., Ashf. 174 BN92
Limes Ct., Brwd. 108 FX46
Sawyers Hall La.
Limes Ct., Hodd. 49 EA17
Charlton Way
Limes Gdns. SW18 180 DA86
Limes Gro. SE13 163 EC84
Limes Pl., Croy. 202 DR101
Limes Rd., Beck. 203 EB96
Limes Rd., Croy. 202 DR100
Limes Rd., Egh. 173 AZ92
Limes Rd. (Cheshunt), Wal.Cr. 67 DX32
Limes Rd., Wey. 212 BN105
Limes Row, Orp. 223 EP106
Orchard Rd.
Limes Wk. SE15 162 DV84
Limes Wk. W5 157 CK75
Chestnut Gro.
Limesdale Gdns., Edg. 96 CQ54
Limesfield Rd. SW14 158 CS83
White Hart La.
Limesford Rd. SE15 163 DX84
Limestone Wk., Erith 166 EX76
Alsike Rd.
Limetree Clo. SW2 181 DM88
Limetree Wk. SW17 180 DG92
Church La.
Limeway Ter., Dor. 247 CG134
Limewood Clo. W13 137 CH72
St. Stephens Rd.
Limewood Ct., Ilf. 125 EM57
Beehive La.
Limewood Rd., Erith 167 FC80
Limpsfield Ave. SW19 179 CX89
Limpsfield Ave., Th.Hth. 201 DM99
Limpsfield Rd., S.Croy. 220 DU112
Limpsfield Rd., Warl. 236 DW116
Linacre Ct. W6 159 CX78
Linacre Rd. NW2 139 CV65
Linberry Wk. SE8 163 DY77
Carteret Way
Lince La., Dor. 263 CD137
Guildford Rd.
Linces Way, Welw.G.C. 30 DB11
Linchfield Rd., Slou. 152 AW81
Linchmere Rd. SE12 184 EF87
Lincoln Ave. N14 99 DJ48
Lincoln Ave. SW19 179 CX90
Lincoln Ave., Rom. 127 FD60
Lincoln Ave., Twick. 176 CB89
Lincoln Clo. SE25 202 DU100
Woodside Grn.
Lincoln Clo., Erith 167 FF82
Lincoln Clo., Grnf. 136 CC67
Lincoln Clo., Har. 116 BZ57
Lincoln Clo., Horl. 268 DG149
Suffolk Clo.
Lincoln Clo., Horn. 128 FN57
Lincoln Clo., Welw.G.C. 30 DC08
Lincoln Ct. N16 122 DR59
Lincoln Ct., Berk. 38 AV19
Lincoln Ct., Borwd. 78 CR43
Lincoln Cres., Enf. 82 DS43
Lincoln Dr., Rick. 75 BP44
Lincoln Dr., Wat. 94 BW48
Lincoln Dr., Wok. 227 BE115
Lincoln Gdns., Ilf. 124 EL59
Lincoln Grn. Rd., Orp. 205 ET99
Lincoln Hatch La., Slou. 130 AJ70
Lincoln Ms. NW6 139 CZ67
Willesden La.
Lincoln Ms. SE21 182 DR88
Lincoln Pk., Amer. 55 AS39
Lincoln Rd. E7 144 EK65
Lincoln Rd. E13 144 EH70
Lincoln Rd. E18 102 EG53
Grove Rd.
Lincoln Rd. N2 120 DE55
Lincoln Rd. SE25 202 DV97
Lincoln Rd., Dor. 247 CJ134
Lincoln Rd., Enf. 82 DS42
Lincoln Rd., Erith 167 FF82
Lincoln Rd., Felt. 176 BZ90
Lincoln Rd., Ger.Cr. 90 AY53
Lincoln Rd., Guil. 242 AT132
Lincoln Rd., Har. 116 BZ57
Lincoln Rd., Mitch. 201 DL99
Lincoln Rd., N.Mal. 198 CQ97
Lincoln Rd., Nthwd. 93 BT54
Lincoln Rd., Sid. 186 EV92
Lincoln Rd., Wem. 137 CK65
Lincoln Rd., Wor.Pk. 199 CV102
Lincoln St. E11 124 EE61
Lincoln St. SW3 276 D9
Lincoln St. SW3 160 DF77
Lincoln Wk., Epsom 216 CR110
Hollymoor La.
Lincoln Way, Enf. 82 DV43
Lincoln Way, Rick. 75 BP44
Lincoln Way, Slou. 131 AK73
Lincoln Way, Sun. 195 BS95
Lincolns, The NW7 97 CT48
Lincolns Clo., St.Alb. 43 CJ15
Lincolns Fld., Epp. 69 ET29
Lincoln's Inn WC2 141 DM72
Chancery La.
Lincoln's Inn Flds. WC2 274 B8
Lincoln's Inn Flds. WC2 141 DM72
Lincolnshott, Grav. 190 GA92
Red St.
Lincombe Rd., Brom. 184 EF90
Lind Rd., Sutt. 218 DC106
Lind St. SE8 163 EA82
Lindal Cres., Enf. 81 DL43
Lindal Rd. SE4 183 DZ85
Lindale Clo., Vir.W. 192 AT98
Lindales, The N17 100 DT51
Brantwood Rd.
Lindbergh, Welw.G.C. 30 DC09
Lindbergh Rd., Wall. 219 DL108
Linden Ave. NW10 139 CX68
Linden Ave., Couls. 235 DH116
Chipstead Valley Rd.
Linden Ave., Dart. 188 FJ88
Linden Ave., Enf. 82 DU39
Linden Ave., Houns. 176 CB85
Linden Ave., Ruis. 115 BU60
Linden Ave., Th.Hth. 201 DP98
Linden Ave., Wem. 118 CM64
Linden Chase Rd., Sev. 257 FH122
Linden Clo. N14 81 DJ44
Linden Clo., Add. 212 BG111
Linden Clo., Orp. 224 EU106
Linden Clo., Purf. 168 FQ79
Linden Clo., Ruis. 115 BU60
Linden Clo., Stan. 95 CH50
Linden Clo., Tad. 233 CX120
Fleetwood Clo.
Linden Clo., T.Ditt. 197 CF101
Linden Clo., Wal.Cr. 66 DV30
Linden Ct. W12 139 CW74
Linden Ct., Egh. 172 AV93
Linden Ct., Lthd. 231 CH121
Linden Cres., Grnf. 137 CF65
Linden Cres., Kings.T. 198 CM96
Linden Cres., St.Alb. 43 CJ20
Linden Cres., Wdf.Grn. 102 EH51
Linden Dr., Cat. 236 DQ124
Linden Dr., Ger.Cr. 90 AY54
Woodside Hill
Linden Dr., Slou. 131 AQ67
Linden Gdns. W2 140 DA73
Linden Gdns. W4 158 CS78
Linden Gdns., Enf. 82 DU39
Linden Gdns., Lthd. 231 CJ121
Linden Glade, Hem.H. 40 BH21
Wrensfield
Linden Gro. SE15 162 DV83
Linden Gro. SE26 182 DW93
Linden Gro., N.Mal. 198 CS97
Linden Gro., Tedd. 177 CF92
Waldegrave Rd.
Linden Gro., Walt. 195 BT103
Linden Gro., Warl. 237 DY118
Linden Ho., Slou. 153 BB78
Linden Lawns, Wem. 118 CM63
Linden Lea N2 120 DC57
Linden Lea, Wat. 59 BU33
Linden Leas, W.Wick. 203 ED103
Linden Ms. N1 122 DR64
Newington Grn. Rd.
Linden Ms. W2 140 DA73
Linden Pit Path, Lthd. 231 CH121
Linden Pl., Epsom 216 CS112
East St.
Linden Pl., Lthd. 245 BS126
Station App.
Linden Pl., Mitch. 200 DE98
London Rd.
Linden Ri., Brwd. 108 FX50
Linden Rd. E17 123 DZ57
High St.
Linden Rd. N10 121 DH56
Linden Rd. N11 98 DF47
Linden Rd. N15 122 DQ56
Linden Rd., Guil. 242 AX134
Linden Rd., Hmptn. 176 CA94
Linden Rd., Lthd. 231 CH121
Linden Rd., Wey. 213 BQ109
Linden Sq., Sev. 256 FE122
London Rd.
Linden St., Rom. 127 FD56
Linden Wk. N19 121 DJ61
Hargrave Pk.
Linden Way N14 81 DJ44
Linden Way, Pur. 219 DJ110
Linden Way, Shep. 195 BQ99
Linden Way, Wok. 227 AZ121
St. Martha's Ave.
Linden Way (Send Marsh), Wok. 227 BF124
Lindenfield, Chis. 205 EP96
Lindens, The N12 98 DD50
Lindens, The W4 158 CQ81
Hartington Rd.
Lindens, The, Croy. 221 EC107
Lindens, The, Hem.H. 39 BF23
Lindens, The, Loug. 85 EM43
Lindens Clo., Lthd. 246 BY128
Mount Pleasant
Lindeth Clo., Stan. 95 CJ51
Old Ch. La.
Lindfield Gdns. NW3 120 DC64
Lindfield Gdns., Guil. 243 AZ133
Lindfield Rd. W5 137 CJ70
Lindfield Rd., Croy. 202 DT100
Lindfield Rd., Rom. 106 FL50
Lindfield St. E14 143 EA72
Lindisfarne Clo., Grav. 191 GL89
St. Benedict's Ave.
Lindisfarne Rd. SW20 179 CU94
Lindisfarne Rd., Dag. 126 EW62
Lindisfarne Way E9 123 DY63
Lindley Est. SE15 162 DU80
Bird in Bush Rd.
Lindley Rd. E10 123 EB61
Lindley Rd., Gdse. 252 DW130
Lindley Rd., Walt. 196 BX104
Lindley St. E1 142 DW71
Lindlings, Hem.H. 39 BE21
Lindo Clo., Chesh. 54 AP30
Lindo St. SE15 162 DW82
Selden Rd.
Lindore Rd. SW11 160 DF84
Lindores Rd., Cars. 200 DC101
Lindrop St. SW6 160 DC82
Lindsay Clo., Chess. 216 CL108
Lindsay Clo., Epsom 216 CQ113
Lindsay Clo., Stai. 174 BK85
Lindsay Dr., Har. 118 CL58
Lindsay Dr., Shep. 195 BR100
Lindsay Pl., Wal.Cr. 66 DV30
Lindsay Rd., Add. 212 BG110
Lindsay Rd., Hmptn. 176 CB91
Lindsay Rd., Wor.Pk. 199 CV103
Lindsay Sq. SW1 161 DK78
Lindsell St. SE10 163 EC81
Lindsey Clo., Brwd. 108 FU49
Lindsey Clo., Brom. 204 EK97
Lindsey Clo., Mitch. 201 DL98
Lindsey Gdns., Felt. 175 BR87
Lindsey Ms. N1 142 DQ66
Lindsey Rd., Dag. 126 EW63
Lindsey Rd., Uxb. 114 BG62
Lindsey Smith Ho., Vir.W. 192 AY99
Lindsey St. EC1 274 G6
Lindsey St. EC1 141 DP71
Lindsey St., Epp. 69 ER28
Lindsey Way, Horn. 128 FJ57
Lindum Pl., St.Alb. 42 BZ22
Lindum Rd., Tedd. 177 CJ94
Lindway SE27 181 DP92
Lindwood Clo. E6 144 EL71
Northumberland Rd.
Linfield Clo. NW4 119 CW55
Linfield Clo., Walt. 213 BV106
Linfields, Amer. 72 AW40
Linford Clo., Harl. 51 EP17
Linford End, Harl. 51 EP17
Linford Rd. E17 123 EC55
Linford Rd., Grays 171 GH77
Linford St. SW8 161 DJ81
Ling Rd. E16 144 EG71
Ling Rd., Erith 167 FC79
Lingards Rd. SE13 163 EC84
Lingey Clo., Sid. 185 ET89
Lingfield Ave., Dart. 188 FP87
Lingfield Ave., Kings.T. 198 CL98
Lingfield Ave., Upmin. 128 FM62
Lingfield Clo., Enf. 82 DS44
Lingfield Clo., Nthwd. 93 BS52
Lingfield Cres. SE9 165 ER84
Lingfield Gdns. N9 100 DV45
Lingfield Gdns., Couls. 235 DP119
Lingfield Rd. SW19 179 CX93
Lingfield Rd., Grav. 191 GH89
Lingfield Rd., Wor.Pk. 199 CW104
Lingham St. SW9 161 DL82
Lingholm Way, Barn. 79 CX42
Lingmere Clo., Chig. 103 EQ47
Lingmoor Dr., Wat. 59 BV34
North Orbital Rd.
Lingrove Gdns., Buck.H. 102 EH47
Beech La.
Lings Coppice SE21 182 DR89
Lingwell Rd. SW17 180 DE90
Lingwood Gdns., Islw. 157 CE80
Lingwood Rd. E5 122 DU59
Linhope St. NW1 272 D4
Linhope St. NW1 140 DF70
Link, The SE9 185 EN90
Sandling Ri.
Link, The W3 138 CP72
Link, The, Enf. 83 DY39
Link, The, Nthlt. 116 BZ64
Eastcote La.
Link, The, Pnr. 116 BW59
Link, The, Slou. 132 AV72
Link, The, Wem. 117 CJ60
Nathans Rd.
Link Ave., Wok. 227 BD115
Link Clo., Hat. 45 CV18
Link Dr.
Link Dr., Hat. 45 CV18
Link La., Wall. 219 DK107
Link Rd. N11 98 DG49
Link Rd., Add. 212 BL105
Weybridge Rd.
Link Rd., Dag. 147 FB68
Link Rd., Felt. 175 BT87
Link Rd., Slou. 152 AW80
Link Rd., Wall. 200 DG102
Link Rd. (Bushey), Wat. 76 BX40
Link St. E9 122 DW64
Link Wk., Hat. 45 CV17
Link Way, Brom. 204 EL101
Link Way, Dag. 126 EW63
Link Way, Horn. 128 FL60
Link Way, Pnr. 94 BX53
Link Way, Stai. 174 BH93
Link Way, Uxb. 114 BG58
Link Way, Wok. 227 BC117
Linkfield, Brom. 204 EG100
Linkfield, Welw.G.C. 29 CY13
Linkfield, W.Mol. 196 CB97
Linkfield Cor., Red. 250 DE133
Hatchlands Rd.
Linkfield Gdns., Red. 250 DE134
Hatchlands Rd.
Linkfield La., Red. 250 DE133
Linkfield Rd., Islw. 157 CF82
Linkfield St., Red. 250 DE134
Linklea Clo. NW9 96 CS52
Links, The E17 123 DY56
Links, The (Cheshunt), Wal.Cr. 67 DX26
Links, The, Walt. 195 BU103
Links, The, Welw.G.C. 29 CV09
Applecroft Rd.
Links Ave., Hert. 32 DV08
Links Ave., Mord. 200 DA98
Links Ave., Rom. 127 FH55
Links Brow, Lthd. 231 CE124
Links Clo., Ash. 231 CJ117
Links Dr. N20 98 DA46
Links Dr., Borwd. 78 CM41
Links Dr., Rad. 61 CF33
Links Gdns. SW16 181 DN94
Links Grn. Way, Cob. 214 CA114
Links Pl., Ash. 231 CK117
Links Rd. NW2 119 CT61
Links Rd. SW17 180 DG93
Links Rd. W3 138 CN72
Links Rd., Ashf. 174 BL92
Links Rd., Ash. 231 CJ118
Links Rd., Epsom 217 CU113
Links Rd., Guil. 258 AY144
Links Rd., H.Wyc. 110 AC55
Links Rd., W.Wick. 203 EC102
Links Rd., Wdf.Grn. 102 EG50
Links Side, Enf. 81 DM41
Links Vw. N3 97 CZ52
Links Vw., Dart. 187 FH88
Links Vw., St.Alb. 42 CB18
Links Vw. Ave., Bet. 248 CN134
Links Vw. Clo., Stan. 95 CG51
Links Vw. Rd., Croy. 203 EA104
Links Vw. Rd., Hmptn. 176 CC92
Links Way, Beck. 203 EA100
Links Way, Lthd. 246 BY128
Links Way, Nthwd. 93 BQ52
Links Way, Rick. 75 BQ41
Links Yd. E1 142 DU71
Spelman St.
Linkscroft Ave., Ashf. 175 BP93
Linkside N12 97 CZ51
Linkside, Chig. 103 EQ50
Linkside, N.Mal. 198 CS96
Linkside Clo., Enf. 81 DM41
Linkside Gdns., Enf. 81 DM41
Linksway NW4 97 CX54
Linkswood Rd., Slou. 130 AJ68
Linkway N4 122 DQ59
Linkway SW20 199 CV97
Linkway, Guil. 242 AT133
Linkway, Rich. 177 CH90
Linkway, The, Barn. 80 DB44
Linkway, The, Sutt. 218 DC109
Linkway Rd., Brwd. 108 FT48
Linkwood Wk. NW1 141 DK66
Maiden La.
Linley Cres., Rom. 127 FB55
Linley Rd. N17 100 DS54
Linnell Clo. NW11 120 DB58
Linnell Dr. NW11 120 DB58
Linnell Rd. N18 100 DU50
Fairfield Rd.
Linnell Rd. SE5 162 DS82
Linnell Rd., Red. 266 DG135
Linnet Clo. N9 101 DX46
Linnet Clo. SE28 146 EW73
Linnet Clo., S.Croy. 221 DX110
Linnet Clo. (Bushey), Wat. 94 CC45
Linnet Gro., Guil. 243 BD132
Partridge Way
Linnet Ms. SW12 180 DG87
Linnet Wk., Hat. 45 CU20
Lark Ri.
Linnet Way, Purf. 168 FP78
Linnett Clo. E4 101 EC49
Linnington Ave., Chesh. 56 AU30
Linom Rd. SW4 161 DL84
Linscott Rd. E5 122 DW63
Linsdell Rd., Bark. 145 EQ67
Linsey Clo., Hem.H. 40 BN24
Linsey St. SE16 162 DU77
Linslade Clo., Houns. 176 BY85
Frampton Rd.
Linslade Clo., Pnr. 115 BV55
Linslade Rd., Orp. 224 EU107
Linstead Ct. SE9 185 ES86
Linstead St. NW6 140 DA66
Linstead Way SW18 179 CY87
Linster Gro., Borwd. 78 CQ43
Lintaine Clo. W6 159 CY79
Moylan Rd.
Linthorpe Ave., Wem. 137 CJ65
Linthorpe Rd. N16 122 DS59
Linthorpe Rd., Barn. 80 DE41
Linton Ave., Borwd. 78 CM39
Linton Clo., Mitch. 200 DF101
Middleton Rd.
Linton Clo., Well. 166 EV81
Anthony Rd.
Linton Gdns. E6 144 EL72
Linton Glade, Croy. 221 DY109
Linton Gro. SE27 181 DP92
Linton Rd., Bark. 145 EQ66

Linton St. N1 142 DQ67
Lintons, The, Bark. 145 EQ66
Lintons La., Epsom 216 CS112
Lintott Ct., Stai. 174 BK86
Linver Rd. SW6 159 CZ82
Linwood, Saw. 36 EY05
Linwood Clo. E6 144 EL71
Northumberland Rd.
Linwood Clo. SE5 162 DT82
Linwood Cres., Enf. 82 DU39
Carterhatch La.
Linwood Way SE15 162 DT80
Daniel Gdns.
Linzee Rd. N8 121 DL56
Lion Ave., Twick. 177 CF88
Lion Rd.
Lion Clo. SE4 183 EA86
Lion Clo., Shep. 194 BL97
Lion Ct., Borwd. 78 CQ39
Lion Gate Gdns., Rich. 158 CM83
Lion Grn. Rd., Couls. 235 DK115
Lion La., Red. 250 DF133
Lion Pk. Ave., Chess. 216 CN105
Lion Rd. E6 145 EM71
Lion Rd. N9 100 DU47
Lion Rd., Bexh. 166 EZ84
Lion Rd., Croy. 202 DQ99
Pawson's Rd.
Lion Rd., Twick. 177 CF88
Lion Way, Brent. 157 CK80
Lion Wf. Rd., Islw. 157 CH83
Lion Yd. SW4 161 DK84
Tremadoc Rd.
Lionel Gdns. SE9 184 EK85
Lionel Ms. W10 139 CY71
Telford Rd.
Lionel Rd. SE9 184 EK85
Lionel Rd., Brent. 158 CL76
Lions Clo. SE9 184 EJ90
Liphook Clo., Horn. 127 FF63
Petworth Way
Liphook Cres. SE23 182 DW87
Liphook Rd., Wat. 94 BX49
Lippitts Hill, Loug. 84 EE39
Lipsham Clo., Bans. 218 DD113
Lipton Clo. SE28 146 EW73
Aisher Rd.
Lipton Rd. E1 143 DX72
Bower St.
Lisbon Ave., Twick. 176 CC89
Lisburne Rd. NW3 120 DF63
Lisford St. SE15 162 DT81
Lisgar Ter. W14 159 CZ77
Liskeard Clo., Chis. 185 EQ93
Liskeard Gdns. SE3 164 EG81
Liskeard Lo., Cat. 252 DU126
Lisle Pl., Grays 170 GA76
Lisle St. WC2 273 N10
Lisle St. WC2 141 DK73
Lismore, Hem.H. 41 BQ22
Lismore Circ. NW5 120 DG64
Wellesley Rd.
Lismore Clo., Islw. 157 CG82
Lismore Pk., Slou. 132 AT72
Stoke Rd.
Lismore Rd. N17 122 DR55
Lismore Rd., S.Croy. 220 DS107
Lismore Wk. N1 142 DQ65
Clephane Rd.
Liss Way SE15 162 DT80
Pentridge St.
Lissenden Gdns. NW5 120 DG63
Lissoms Rd., Couls. 234 DG118
Lisson Grn. Est. NW8 272 B3
Lisson Grn. Est. NW8 140 DE69
Lisson Gro. NW1 272 A4
Lisson Gro. NW1 140 DE70
Lisson Gro. NW8 272 A4
Lisson Gro. NW8 140 DD70
Lisson St. NW1 272 B6
Lisson St. NW1 140 DE71
Lister Ave., Rom. 106 FK54
Lister Clo. W3 138 CR71
Lister Clo., Mitch. 200 DE95
Lister Gdns. N18 100 DQ50
Lister Ho. SE3 164 EE79
Lister Ms. N7 121 DM63
Lister Rd. E11 124 EE60
Lister Rd., Til. 171 GG82
Lister St. E13 144 EG69
Sewell St.
Lister Wk. SE28 146 EX73
Haldane Rd.
Liston Rd. N17 100 DU53
Liston Rd. SW4 161 DJ83
Liston Way, Wdf.Grn. 102 EJ52
Listowel Clo. SW9 161 DN80
Mandela St.
Listowel Rd., Dag. 126 FA62
Listria Pk. N16 122 DS61
Litcham Spur, Slou. 131 AR72
Litchfield Ave. E15 144 EE65
Litchfield Ave., Mord. 199 CZ101
Litchfield Gdns. NW10 139 CU65
Litchfield Rd., Sutt. 218 DC105
Litchfield St. WC2 273 N10
Litchfield St. WC2 141 DK73
Litchfield Way NW11 120 DB57
Litchfield Way, Guil. 258 AT136
Lithos Rd. NW3 140 DC65
Little Acre, Beck. 203 EA97
Little Acre, St.Alb. 43 CD17
Little Acres, Ware 33 DX07
Little Albany St. NW1 273 J3
Little Argyll St. W1 273 K9
Little Aston Rd., Rom. 106 FN52
Little Belhus Clo., S.Ock. 149 FU70
Little Benty, West Dr. 154 BK77
Little Birch Clo., Add. 212 BK109
Little Birches, Sid. 185 ES89
Little Boltons, The SW5 160 DB78
Little Boltons, The SW10 160 DB78
Little Bookham St., Lthd. 230 BZ123
Little Bornes SE21 182 DS91
Little Borough, Bet. 264 CN135
Little Brays, Harl. 52 EU16
Little Bri. Rd., Berk. 38 AX19
Little Britain EC1 274 G7
Little Britain EC1 141 DP71
Little Brook Rd., Harl. 34 EJ14
Harlow Rd.
Little Brownings SE23 182 DV89
Little Buntings, Wind. 151 AM83
Little Burrow, Welw.G.C. 29 CX11
Little Bury St. N9 100 DR46
Little Bushey La. (Bushey), Wat. 76 CA41
Little Catherells, Hem.H. 39 BF18
Little Cattins, Harl. 51 EM19
Little Cedars N12 98 DC49
Woodside Ave.
Little Chester St. SW1 277 H6
Little Chester St. SW1 161 DH76
Little College La. EC4 142 DR73
Garlick Hill
Little College St. SW1 277 P6
Little Collins, Red. 267 DP144
Little Common La., Red. 251 DP132
Little Ct., W.Wick. 204 EE103
Little Cranmore La., Lthd. 245 BP128
Little Dean's Yd. SW1 277 P6
Little Dell, Welw.G.C. 29 CX07
Little Dimocks SW12 181 DH89
Little Dormers, Ger.Cr. 113 AZ56
Little Dorrit Ct. SE1 279 J4
Little Dorrit Ct. SE1 162 DQ75
Little Dragons, Loug. 84 EK42
Little Ealing La. W5 157 CJ77
Little Edward St. NW1 273 J2
Little Elms, Hayes 155 BR80
Little Essex St. WC2 274 D10
Little Ferry Rd., Twick. 177 CH88
Ferry Rd.
Little Friday Rd. E4 102 EE47
Little Ganett, Welw.G.C. 30 DB11
Little Gaynes Gdns., Upmin. 128 FP63
Little Gaynes La., Upmin. 128 FM63
Little Gearies, Ilf. 125 EP56
Little George St. SW1 277 P5
Little Gerpins La., Upmin. 148 FM67
Little Gra., Grnf. 137 CG69
Perivale La.
Little Graylings, Abb.L. 59 BS33
Little Grn., Chesh. 54 AN27
Little Grn., Rich. 157 CK84
Little Grn. La., Cher. 193 BE104
Little Grn. La., Rick. 74 BM41
Little Grn. St. NW5 121 DH63
College La.
Little Gregories La., Epp. 85 ER35
Little Gro. (Bushey), Wat. 76 CB42
Little Gro. Fld., Harl. 51 EQ15
Little Halliards, Walt. 195 BU100
Felix Rd.
Little Hardings, Welw.G.C. 30 DC08
Little Hayes, Kings L. 58 BN29
Little Heath SE7 164 EL78
Little Heath, Rom. 126 EV56
Little Heath La., Berk. 39 BB21
Little Heath Rd., Bexh. 166 EY81
Little Heath Rd., Wok. 210 AS109
Little Henleys, Ware 34 EK06
Little Hide, Guil. 243 BB132
Little Hill, Rick. 73 BC44
Little Hivings, Chesh. 54 AN27
Little How Cft., Abb.L. 59 BQ31
Little Ilford La. E12 125 EM63
Little Julians Hill, Sev. 256 FG128
Little Kiln, Gdmg. 258 AS143
Little Lake, Welw.G.C. 30 DB12
Little Ley, Welw.G.C. 29 CY12
Little London, Guil. 260 BL142
Little Marlborough St. W1 273 K9
Little Martins (Bushey), Wat. 76 CB43
Little Mead, Hat. 45 CV15
Little Mead, Wok. 226 AT116
Little Mimms, Hem.H. 40 BK19
Little Moreton Clo., W.Byf. 212 BH112
Dartnell Ave.
Little Moss La., Pnr. 94 BY54
Little Mundells, Welw.G.C. 29 CZ07
Little New St. EC4 274 E8
Little Newport St. WC2 273 N10
Little Newport St. WC2 141 DK73
Little Orchard, Add. 211 BF111
Little Orchard, Hem.H. 40 BN18
High St. Grn.
Little Orchard, Wok. 211 BA114
Little Orchard Clo., Abb.L. 59 BR31
Little Orchard Clo., Pnr. 94 BY54
Barrow Pt. La.
Little Orchard Way, Guil. 258 AY142
Little Oxhey La., Wat. 94 BX50
Little Pk., Hem.H. 57 BA28
Little Pk. Dr., Felt. 176 BX89
Little Pk. Gdns., Enf. 82 DQ41
Little Pastures, Brwd. 108 FT49
Tern Way
Little Pipers Clo. (Cheshunt), Wal.Cr. 65 DP29
Little Plucketts Way, Buck.H. 102 EJ46
Little Port Spur, Slou. 132 AS72
Little Portland St. W1 273 J8
Little Portland St. W1 141 DJ72
Little Potters (Bushey), Wat. 95 CD45
Little Pynchons, Harl. 51 ET18
Little Queen St., Dart. 188 FM87
Little Queens Rd., Tedd. 177 CF93
Little Redlands, Brom. 204 EL96
Little Reeves Ave., Amer. 72 AT39
Little Ridge, Welw.G.C. 30 DA09
Little Rivers, Welw.G.C. 30 DA08
Little Rd., Croy. 202 DS102
Lower Addiscombe Rd.
Little Rd., Hayes 155 BT75
Little Rd., Hem.H. 40 BM19
Little Roke Ave., Ken. 219 DP113
Little Roke Rd., Ken. 220 DQ114
Little Russell St. WC1 273 P7
Little Russell St. WC1 141 DL71
Little Russets, Brwd. 109 GE45
Hutton Village
Little St. James's St. SW1 277 K3
Little St. James's St. SW1 141 DJ74
Little St. Leonards SW14 158 CQ83
Little Sanctuary SW1 277 N5
Little Shardeloes, Amer. 55 AN40
Little Smith St. SW1 277 N6
Little Somerset St. E1 275 P9
Little Spring, Chesh. 54 AP28
Little Strand NW9 97 CT54
Little Stream Clo., Nthwd. 93 BS50
Little St., Guil. 242 AV130
Little Sutton La., Slou. 153 BC78
Little Thistle, Welw.G.C. 30 DC11
Little Thrift, Orp. 205 EQ98
Little Titchfield St. W1 273 K7
Little Trinity La. EC4 275 J10
Little Turnstile WC1 274 B7
Little Wade, Welw.G.C. 29 CZ12
Little Wk., Harl. 51 EQ15
Little Warren Clo., Guil. 259 BB136
Little Widbury, Ware 33 DZ06
Little Widbury La., Ware 33 DZ06
Little Windmill Hill, Kings L. 57 BE32
Little Woodcote La., Cars. 218 DG112
Little Woodcote La., Pur. 218 DG112
Little Woodcote La., Wall. 218 DG112
Little Woodlands, Wind. 151 AM83
Little Youngs, Welw.G.C. 29 CW09
Littlebrook Ave., Slou. 131 AL70
Littlebrook Clo., Croy. 203 DX100
Littlebrook Gdns. (Cheshunt), Wal.Cr. 66 DW30
Littlebrook Manor Way, Dart. 168 FN84
Littlebury Rd. SW4 161 DK83
Littlecombe SE7 164 EH79
Littlecombe Clo. SW15 179 CX86
Littlecote Clo. SW19 179 CX87
Littlecote Pl., Pnr. 94 BZ53
Littlecourt Rd., Sev. 256 FG124
Littlecroft SE9 165 EN83
Littlecroft, Grav. 190 GE94
Littlecroft Rd., Egh. 173 AZ92
Littledale SE2 166 EU79
Littledale, Dart. 188 FQ90
Littledown Rd., Slou. 132 AT74
Littlefield Clo. N19 121 DJ63
Tufnell Pk. Rd.
Littlefield Clo., Kings.T. 198 CL96
Fairfield W.
Littlefield Rd., Edg. 96 CQ52
Littleford La., Guil. 259 BE142
Littlegrove, Barn. 80 DE44
Littleheath La., Cob. 214 BZ114
Littleheath La., Wok. 210 AS109
Littleheath Rd., S.Croy. 220 DV108
Littlehorse La., Ware 33 DX05
Littlejohn Rd. W7 137 CF72
Littlejohn Rd., Orp. 206 EU100
Littlemead, Esher 215 CD105
Littlemede SE9 185 EM90
Littlemoor Rd., Ilf. 125 ER62
Littlemore Rd. SE2 166 EU75
Littlers Clo. SW19 200 DD95
Runnymede
Littlestone Clo., Beck. 183 EA93
Abbey La.
Littleton Ave. E4 102 EF46
Littleton Cres., Har. 117 CF61
Littleton La., Guil. 258 AU139
Littleton La., Reig. 265 CX136
Littleton La., Shep. 194 BK101
Littleton Rd., Ashf. 175 BQ94
Littleton Rd., Har. 117 CF61
Littleton St. SW18 180 DC89
Littlewick Rd., Wok. 210 AW114
Littlewood SE13 183 EC85
Littlewood, Sev. 257 FJ122
Littlewood Clo. W13 157 CH76
Littleworth Ave., Esher 215 CD106
Littleworth Common Rd., Esher 197 CD104
Littleworth La., Esher 215 CD105
Littleworth Pl., Esher 215 CD105
Littleworth Rd., Esher 215 CD106
Littleworth Rd., Slou. 110 AJ63
Litton Ct., H.Wyc. 88 AC53
Livermere Rd. E8 142 DT67
Liverpool Gro. SE17 162 DR78
Liverpool Rd. E10 123 EC58
Liverpool Rd. E16 144 EE71
Liverpool Rd. N1 141 DN66
Liverpool Rd. N7 121 DN64
Liverpool Rd. W5 157 CK75
Liverpool Rd., Kings.T. 178 CN94
Liverpool Rd., St.Alb. 43 CE20
Liverpool Rd., Slou. 131 AP72
Liverpool Rd., Th.Hth. 202 DQ97
Liverpool Rd., Wat. 75 BV43
Liverpool St. EC2 275 M7
Liverpool St. EC2 142 DS71
Livesey Pl. SE15 162 DU79
Peckham Pk. Rd.
Livingston College Twrs. E10 123 EC58
Livingstone Gdns., Grav. 191 GK92
Livingstone Pl. E14 163 EC78
Ferry St.
Livingstone Rd. E15 143 EC67
Livingstone Rd. E17 123 EB58
Livingstone Rd. N13 99 DL51
Livingstone Rd. SW11 160 DD83
Winstanley Rd.
Livingstone Rd., Cat. 236 DR122
Livingstone Rd., Grav. 191 GK92
Livingstone Rd., Houns. 156 CC84
Livingstone Rd., Sthl. 136 BX73
Livingstone Rd., Th.Hth. 202 DQ96
Livingstone Ter., Rain. 147 FE67
Stanley Rd. N.
Livingstone Wk. SW11 160 DD83
Livingstone Wk., Hem.H. 40 BM16
Livonia St. W1 273 L9
Lizard St. EC1 275 J3
Lizard St. EC1 142 DQ69
Lizban St. SE3 164 EH80
Llanbury Clo., Ger.Cr. 90 AY52
Llanelly Rd. NW2 119 CZ61
Llanover Rd. SE18 165 EN79
Llanover Rd., Wem. 117 CK62
Llanthony Rd., Mord. 200 DD100
Llanvanor Rd. NW2 119 CZ61
Llewellyn St. SE16 162 DU75
Chambers St.
Lloyd Ave. SW16 201 DL95
Lloyd Ave., Couls. 218 DG114
Lloyd Baker St. WC1 274 C3
Lloyd Baker St. WC1 141 DM69
Lloyd Ct., Pnr. 116 BX57
Lloyd Pk. Ave., Croy. 220 DT105
Lloyd Rd. E6 145 EM67
Lloyd Rd. E17 123 DX56
Lloyd Rd., Dag. 146 EZ65
Lloyd Rd., Wor.Pk. 199 CW104
Lloyd Sq. WC1 274 D2
Lloyd Sq. WC1 141 DN69
Lloyd St. WC1 274 D2
Lloyd St. WC1 141 DN69
Lloyd's Ave. EC3 275 N9
Lloyd's Ave. EC3 142 DS72
Lloyds Pl. SE3 164 EE82
Lloyd's Row EC1 274 F3
Lloyds Way, Beck. 203 DY99
Loampit Hill SE13 163 EA82
Loampit Vale SE13 163 EB83
Loanda Clo. E8 142 DT67
Clarissa St.
Loates La., Wat. 76 BW41
Loats Rd. SW2 181 DL86
Lobelia Clo. E6 144 EL71
Sorrel Gdns.
Local Board Rd., Wat. 76 BW43
Locarno Rd. W3 138 CQ74
High St.
Locarno Rd., Grnf. 136 CC70
Lochaber Rd. SE13 164 EE84
Lochaline St. W6 159 CW79
Lochan Clo., Hayes 136 BY70
Lochinvar Clo., Slou. 151 AP75
Haig Dr.
Lochinvar St. SW12 181 DH87
Lochmere Clo., Erith 167 FB79
Lochnagar St. E14 143 EC71
Lochnell, Berk. 38 AT17
Lock Ave., Maid. 130 AC69
Lock Chase SE3 164 EE83
Lock Clo., Add. 211 BE112
Lock Clo., Sthl. 156 CC75
Navigator Dr.
Lock Island, Shep. 194 BN103
Lock La., Wok. 228 BH116
Lock Path, Wind. 151 AK79
Lock Rd., Guil. 242 AX131
Lock Rd., Rich. 177 CJ91
Locke Clo., Rain. 147 FF65
Locke Gdns., Slou. 152 AW75
Locke King Clo., Wey. 212 BN108
Locke King Rd., Wey. 212 BN108
Locke Way, Wok. 227 AZ117
Broadway
Lockers Pk. La., Hem.H. 40 BH20
Lockesfield Pl. E14 163 EB78
Lockesley Dr., Orp. 205 ET100
Lockesley Sq., Surb. 197 CK100
Locket Rd., Har. 117 CE55
Lockets Clo., Wind. 151 AL81
Lockfield Ave., Enf. 83 DY40
Lockfield Dr., Wok. 226 AS116
Lockhart Clo. N7 141 DM65
Lockhart Clo., Enf. 82 DV43
Derby Rd.
Lockhart Rd., Cob. 214 BW113
Lockhart St. E3 143 DZ70
Lockhurst St. E5 123 DX63
Lockie Pl. SE25 202 DU97
Lockier Wk., Wem. 117 CK62
Hutchinson Ter.
Lockington Rd. SW8 161 DH81
Lockley Cres., Hat. 45 CV16
Lockmead Rd. N15 122 DU58
Lockmead Rd. SE13 163 EC83
Lockner Holt, Guil. 259 BF141
Locks La., Mitch. 200 DF95
Lockside E14 143 DY73
Northey St.
Locksley Dr., Wok. 226 AT118
Robin Hood Rd.
Locksley Est. E14 143 DZ72
Locksley St. E14 143 DZ71
Locksmeade Rd., Rich. 177 CJ91
Lockswood Clo., Barn. 80 DF42
Langford Rd.
Lockwood Clo. SE26 183 DX91
Lockwood Ind. Pk. N17 122 DV55
Lockwood Path, Wok. 211 BE113
Lockwood Sq. SE16 162 DV76
Lockwood Wk., Rom. 127 FE57
Lockwood Way E17 101 DX54
Lockwood Way, Chess. 216 CN106
Lockyer Est. SE1 279 L4
Lockyer Rd., Purf. 168 FQ79
Lockyer St. SE1 279 L5
Loddiges Rd. E9 142 DW66
Loddon Spur, Slou. 132 AS73
Loder Clo., Wok. 211 BD113
Loder St. SE15 162 DW80
Lodge Ave. SW14 158 CS83
Lodge Ave., Borwd. 78 CM43
Lodge Ave., Croy. 201 DN104
Lodge Ave., Dag. 146 EU67
Lodge Ave., Dart. 188 FJ86
Lodge Ave., Har. 118 CL56
Lodge Ave., Rom. 127 FG57
Lodge Clo. N18 100 DQ50
Lodge Clo., Chig. 104 EU48
Lodge Clo., Cob. 230 BZ116
Lodge Clo., Dor. 263 CJ140
Lodge Clo., Edg. 96 CM51
Lodge Clo., Egh. 172 AX92
Lodge Clo., Epsom 217 CW110
Howell Hill Gro.
Lodge Clo., Hert. 32 DQ07
Lodge Clo., Islw. 157 CH81
Lodge Clo., Lthd. 231 CD122
Lodge Clo., Orp. 206 EV102
Lodge Clo., Slou. 151 AQ75
Lodge Clo., Uxb. 134 BJ70
Lodge Clo., Wall. 200 DG102
Lodge Ct., Horn. 128 FL61
Lodge Cres., Orp. 206 EV102
Lodge Cres., Wal.Cr. 67 DX34
Lodge Dr. N13 99 DN49
Lodge Dr., Hat. 45 CX15
Lodge Dr., Rick. 74 BJ42
Lodge Dr., The, Beac. 89 AL54
Lodge End, Rad. 61 CH34
Lodge End, Rick. 75 BR41
Lodge Fld., Welw.G.C. 29 CY06
Lodge Gdns., Beck. 203 DZ99
Lodge Hall, Harl. 51 ES19
Lodge Hill SE2 166 EV80
Lodge Hill, Ilf. 124 EL56
Lodge Hill, Pur. 235 DN115
Lodge Hill, Well. 166 EV80
Lodge La. N12 98 DC50
Lodge La., Bex. 186 EX86
Lodge La., Ch.St.G. 73 AZ43
Lodge La., Croy. 221 EA107
Lodge La., Dor. 264 CL144
Lodge La., Grays 170 GC76
Lodge La., Red. 266 DE143
Lodge La., Rom. 104 FA52
Lodge La., Wal.Abb. 83 ED35
Lodge La., West. 255 EQ127
Lodge Pl., Sutt. 218 DB106
Lodge Rd. NW4 119 CW56
Lodge Rd. NW8 272 A3
Lodge Rd. NW8 140 DD69
Lodge Rd., Brom. 184 EH94
Lodge Rd., Croy. 201 DP100
Lodge Rd., Epp. 69 EN34
Lodge Rd., Lthd. 230 CC122
Lodge Rd., Sutt. 218 DB106
Throwley Way
Lodge Rd., Wall. 219 DH106
Lodge Vill., Wdf.Grn. 102 EF52
Lodge Way, Ashf. 174 BL89
Lodge Way, Shep. 195 BQ96
Lodge Way, Wind. 151 AL83
Lodgebottom Rd., Lthd. 248 CN127
Lodgehill Pk. Clo., Har. 116 CB61
Lodore Gdns. NW9 118 CS57
Lodore Grn., Uxb. 114 BL62
Lodore St. E14 143 EC72
Loewen Rd., Grays 171 GG76
Lofthouse Pl., Chess. 215 CJ107
Mansfield Rd.
Loftie St. SE16 162 DU75
Lofting Rd. N1 141 DM66
Loftus Rd. W12 139 CV74
Logan Clo., Enf. 83 DX39
Logan Clo., Houns. 156 BZ83
Logan Ms. W8 160 DA77
Logan Pl. W8 160 DA77
Logan Rd. N9 100 DV47
Logan Rd., Wem. 118 CL61
Loggetts, The SE21 182 DR90
Logmore La., Dor. 262 CB138
Logs Hill, Chis. 184 EL94
Logs Hill Clo., Chis. 204 EL95
Lois Dr., Shep. 195 BP99
Lolesworth Clo. E1 142 DT71
Commercial St.
Lollard St. SE11 278 C8
Lollard St. SE11 161 DN77
Lollards Clo., Amer. 55 AQ37
Lollesworth La., Lthd. 245 BQ126
Loman Path, S.Ock. 149 FT72
Loman St. SE1 278 G4
Loman St. SE1 161 DP75
Lomas Clo., Croy. 221 EC108
Lomas Ct. E8 142 DT66
Lomas St. E1 142 DU71
Lombard Ave., Enf. 82 DW39
Lombard Ave., Ilf. 125 ES60
Lombard Business Pk. SW19 200 DB96
Lombard Ct. EC3 275 L10
Lombard La. EC4 274 E9
Lombard Rd. N11 99 DH50
Lombard Rd. SW11 160 DD82
Lombard Rd. SW19 200 DB96
Lombard St. EC3 275 L9
Lombard St. EC3 142 DR72
Lombard St., Dart. 208 FQ99
Lombard Wall SE7 164 EH76
Lombards, The, Horn. 128 FM59
Lombardy Clo., Hem.H. 41 BR21
Lombardy Clo., Wok. 226 AT117
Nethercote Ave.
Lombardy Dr., Berk. 38 AX20
Lombardy Pl. W2 140 DB73
Bark Pl.
Lombardy Way, Borwd. 78 CL39
Lomond Clo. N15 122 DS57
Lomond Clo., Wem. 138 CM66
Lomond Gdns., S.Croy. 221 DY108
Lomond Gro. SE5 162 DR80
Lomond Ho. SE5 162 DR81
Lomond Gro.
Lomond Rd., Hem.H. 40 BK16
Loncin Mead Ave., Add. 212 BJ109
Loncroft Rd. SE5 162 DS79
Londesborough Rd. N16 122 DS63
London Bri. EC4 279 L2
London Bri. EC4 142 DR73
London Bri. SE1 279 L2
London Bri. SE1 142 DR74
London Bri. St. SE1 279 L3
London Bri. St. SE1 142 DR74
London Bri. Wk. SE1 279 L2
London City Airport E16 144 EL74
London Colney Bypass, St.Alb. 61 CK25
London Colney Ind. Est., St.Alb. 62 CL27
London End, Beac. 89 AM54
London Flds. E8 142 DV66
London Flds. E. Side E8 142 DV66
London Flds. W. Side E8 142 DU66
London Hollow, H.Wyc. 88 AD54
London Ind. Pk. E6 145 EP71
London La. E8 142 DV66
London La., Brom. 184 EF94
London La., Guil. 260 BN138
London La., Lthd. 245 BU131
London Ms. W2 272 A9
London Rd. E13 144 EG68
London Rd. SE1 278 F6
London Rd. SE1 161 DP76
London Rd. SE23 182 DV88
London Rd. SW16 201 DM95
London Rd. SW17 180 DF94
London Rd., Amer. 55 AQ40
London Rd., Ashf. 174 BJ90
London Rd., Bark. 145 EP66
London Rd., Beac. 89 AM54
London Rd., Berk. 38 AX20
London Rd., Borwd. 78 CQ36
London Rd., Brent. 157 CF82
London Rd., Brwd. 108 FT49
London Rd., Brom. 184 EF94
London Rd., Cat. 236 DR123
London Rd., Ch.St.G. 90 AW47
London Rd., Croy. 201 DP102
London Rd., Dart. 188 FP87
London Rd. (Crayford), Dart. 187 FD85
London Rd. (Farningham), Dart. 208 FL100
London Rd., Dor. 247 CH133
London Rd., Egh. 192 AW95
London Rd., Enf. 82 DR42
London Rd., Epp. 52 EV23
London Rd., Epsom 217 CU108
London Rd., Felt. 174 BH90
London Rd., Gat. 268 DF150
London Rd., Grav. 190 GD86
London Rd., Grays 169 FW79
London Rd., Green. 189 FT86
London Rd., Guil. 258 AY135

Lower Boston Rd. W7 137 CE74
Lower Bri. Rd., Red. 250 DF134
Lower Britwell Rd., Slou. 131 AK70
Lower Broad St., Dag. 146 FA67
Lower Bury La., Epp. 69 ES31
Lower Camden, Chis. 185 EM94
Lower Ch. Hill, Green. 189 FS85
Church Hill
Lower Ch. St., Croy. 201 DP103
Waddon New Rd.
Lower Cippenham La., Slou. 131 AL74
Lower Clabdens, Ware 33 DZ06
Lower Clapton Rd. E5 122 DW64
Lower Clarendon Wk. W11 139 CY72
Lancaster Rd.
Lower Common S. SW15 159 CV83
Lower Cookham Rd., Maid. 130 AC67
Lower Coombe St., Croy. 220 DQ105
Lower Ct. Rd., Epsom 216 CQ111
Lower Cft., Swan. 207 FF98
Lower Dagnall St., St.Alb. 42 CC20
Lower Downs Rd. SW20 199 CX95
Lower Drayton Pl., Croy. 201 DP103
Drayton Rd.
Lower Dr., Beac. 89 AK50
Lower Dunnymans, Bans. 217 CZ114
Basing Rd.
Lower Edgeborough Rd., Guil. 259 AZ135
Lower Emms, Hem.H. 41 BP15
Lower Fm. Rd., Lthd. 229 BV124
Lower George St., Rich. 177 CK85
George St.
Lower Gravel Rd., Brom. 204 EL102
Lower Grn., Welw. 30 DE05
Lower Grn. Rd., Esher 196 CB103
Lower Grn. W., Mitch. 200 DE97
Lower Grosvenor Pl. SW1 277 H6
Lower Grosvenor Pl. SW1 161 DH76
Lower Gro. Rd., Rich. 178 CM86
Lower Hall La. E4 101 DY50
Lower Ham Rd., Kings.T. 177 CK93
Lower Hampton Rd., Sun. 196 BW97
Lower Hatfield Rd., Hert. 47 DK15
Lower High St., Wat. 76 BW42
Lower Higham Rd., Grav. 191 GM88
Lower Hill Rd., Epsom 216 CP112
Lower James St. W1 273 L10
Lower John St. W1 273 L10
Lower Kenwood Ave., Enf. 81 DK43
Lower Kings Rd., Berk. 38 AW19
Lower Lea Crossing E14 144 EE73
Lower Lees Rd., Slou. 131 AN69
Lower Maidstone Rd. N11 99 DJ51
Telford Rd.
Lower Mall W6 159 CV78
Lower Mardyke Ave., Rain. 147 FC68
Lower Marsh SE1 278 D5
Lower Marsh SE1 161 DM75
Lower Marsh La., Kings.T. 198 CM98
Lower Mead, Iver 133 BD69
Lower Meadow, Harl. 51 ES19
Lower Meadow, Wal.Cr. 67 DX27
Lower Merton Ri. NW3 140 DE66
Lower Morden La., Mord. 199 CX100
Lower Mortlake Rd., Rich. 158 CL84
Lower Noke Clo., Brwd. 106 FM47
Lower Northfield, Bans. 217 CZ114
Lower Paddock Rd., Wat. 76 BY44
Lower Pk. Rd. N11 99 DJ50
Lower Pk. Rd., Belv. 166 FA76
Lower Pk. Rd., Couls. 234 DE118
Lower Pk. Rd., Loug. 84 EK43
Lower Paxton Rd., St.Alb. 43 CE21
Lower Peryers, Lthd. 245 BS128
Lower Plantation, Rick. 74 BJ41
Lower Queens Rd., Buck.H. 102 EK47
Lower Range Rd., Grav. 191 GL87
Lower Richmond Rd. SW14 158 CP83
Lower Richmond Rd. SW15 159 CV83
Lower Richmond Rd., Rich. 158 CN83
Lower Riding, Beac. 88 AH53
Lower Rd. SE8 163 DX77
Lower Rd. SE16 162 DW76
Lower Rd., Belv. 167 FB76
Lower Rd., Brwd. 109 GD41
Lower Rd., Erith 167 FD77
Lower Rd., Ger.Cr. 90 AY53
Lower Rd., Grav. 170 GA84
Lower Rd., Har. 117 CD60
Lower Rd., Hem.H. 58 BN25
Lower Rd., Ken. 219 DP113
Lower Rd., Lthd. 231 CD123
Lower Rd., Loug. 85 EN39
Lower Rd., Orp. 206 EV100
Lower Rd., Red. 266 DD136
Lower Rd., Rick. 73 BC42
Lower Rd., Sutt. 218 DC105
Lower Rd., Swan. 187 FF94
Lower Rd., Til. 171 GG84
Lower Rd., Uxb. 113 BC59
Lower Rd., Ware 33 DZ08
Lower Robert St. WC2 278 A1
Lower Sales, Hem.H. 39 BF21
Lower Sandfields, Wok. 227 BD124
Lower Sawley Wd., Bans. 217 CZ114
Upper Sawley Wd.
Lower Shott, Lthd. 246 CA126
Lower Shott (Cheshunt), Wal.Cr. 66 DT26
Lower Sloane St. SW1 276 F9
Lower Sloane St. SW1 160 DG77
Lower Sq., Islw. 157 CH83
Lower Sta. Rd. (Crayford), Dart. 187 FE86
Lower Strand NW9 97 CT54
Lower St., Guil. 260 BN139
Lower Sunbury Rd., Hmptn. 196 BZ96
Lower Swaines, Epp. 69 ES30
Lower Sydenham Ind. Est. SE26 183 DZ92
Lower Tail, Wat. 94 BY48
Lower Talbot Wk. W11 139 CY72
Lancaster Rd.
Lower Teddington Rd., Kings.T. 177 CK94
Lower Ter. NW3 120 DC62
Lower Thames St. EC3 279 L1
Lower Thames St. EC3 142 DR73
Lower Tub (Bushey), Wat. 95 CD45
Lower Wd. Rd., Esher 215 CG107
Lower Yott, Hem.H. 40 BM21
Lowerfield, Welw.G.C. 30 DA10
Lowestoft Clo. E5 122 DW61
Theydon Rd.
Lowestoft Dr., Slou. 130 AJ72
Lowestoft Rd., Wat. 75 BV39
Loweswater Clo., Wat. 59 BV34
North Orbital Rd.
Loweswater Clo., Wem. 117 CK61
Lowfield, Saw. 36 EX06
Lowfield Heath Ind. Est., Craw. 268 DD154
Lowfield La., Hodd. 49 EA17
Lowfield Rd. NW6 140 DA66
Lowfield Rd. W3 138 CQ72
Lowfield St., Dart. 188 FL89
Lowick Rd., Har. 117 CE56
Lowlands, Hat. 45 CW15
Lowlands Dr., Stai. 174 BK85
Lowlands Gdns., Rom. 127 FB58
Lowlands Rd., Har. 117 CE58
Lowlands Rd., Pnr. 116 BW58
Lowlands Rd., S.Ock. 148 FP74
Lowman Rd. N7 121 DM63
Lowndes Ave., Chesh. 54 AP30
Lowndes Clo. SW1 276 G7
Lowndes Clo. SW1 160 DG76
Lowndes Pl. SW1 276 F7
Lowndes Pl. SW1 160 DG76
Lowndes Sq. SW1 276 E5
Lowndes Sq. SW1 160 DF75
Lowndes St. SW1 276 E6
Lowndes St. SW1 160 DF76
Lowood Ct. SE19 182 DT92
Lowood St. E1 142 DV73
Dellow St.
Lowry Cres., Mitch. 200 DE96
Lowshoe La., Rom. 104 FA53
Lowson Gro., Wat. 94 BY45
Lowswood Clo., Nthwd. 93 BQ53
Lowth Rd. SE5 162 DQ82
Lowther Clo., Borwd. 78 CM43
Lowther Dr., Enf. 81 DL42
Lowther Gdns. SW7 160 DD75
Prince Consort Rd.
Lowther Hill SE23 183 DY87
Lowther Rd. E17 101 DY54
Lowther Rd. N7 121 DN64
Mackenzie Rd.
Lowther Rd. SW13 159 CT81
Lowther Rd., Kings.T. 198 CM95
Lowther Rd., Stan. 118 CM55
Lowthorpe, Wok. 226 AU118
Shilburn Way
Loxford Ave. E6 144 EK68
Loxford La., Ilf. 125 EQ64
Loxford Rd., Bark. 145 EP65
Loxford Rd., Cat. 252 DT125
Loxford Way, Cat. 252 DT125
Loxham Rd. E4 101 EA52
Loxham St. WC1 274 A3
Loxley Clo. SE26 183 DX92
Loxley Rd. SW18 180 DD88
Loxley Rd., Berk. 38 AS17
Loxley Rd., Hmptn. 176 BZ91
Loxton Rd. SE23 183 DX88
Loxwood Clo., Felt. 175 BR88
Loxwood Clo., Orp. 206 EX103
Loxwood Rd. N17 122 DS55
Lubbock Rd., Chis. 185 EM94
Lubbock St. SE14 162 DW80
Lucan Dr., Stai. 174 BK94
Lucan Pl. SW3 276 B9
Lucan Pl. SW3 160 DE77
Lucan Rd., Barn. 79 CY41
Lucas Ave. E13 144 EH67
Lucas Ave., Har. 116 CA61
Lucas Ct., Har. 116 CA60
Lucas Ct., Wal.Abb. 68 EF33
Lucas Rd. SE20 182 DW93
Lucas Rd., Grays 170 GA76
Lucas Sq. NW11 120 DA58
Hampstead Way
Lucas St. SE8 163 EA81
Lucerne Clo. N13 99 DL48
Lucerne Clo., Wok. 226 AY119
Claremont Ave.
Lucerne Ct., Erith 166 EY76
Middle Way
Lucerne Gro. E17 123 ED56
Lucerne Ms. W8 140 DA74
Kensington Mall
Lucerne Rd. N5 121 DP63
Lucerne Rd., Orp. 205 ET102
Lucerne Rd., Th.Hth. 201 DP99
Lucerne Way, Rom. 106 FK51
Lucey Rd. SE16 162 DU76
Lucey Way SE16 162 DU76
Linsey St.
Lucie Ave., Ashf. 175 BP93
Lucien Rd. SW17 180 DG91
Lucien Rd. SW19 180 DB89
Lucknow St. SE18 165 ES80
Lucks Hill, Hem.H. 39 BE20
Lucorn Clo. SE12 184 EF86
Lucton Ms., Loug. 85 EF42
Homecroft Gdns.
Luctons Ave., Buck.H. 102 EJ46
Lucy Cres. W3 138 CQ71
Lucy Gdns., Dag. 126 EY62
Grafton Rd.
Luddesdon Rd., Erith 166 FA79
Luddington Ave., Vir.W. 193 AZ96
Ludford Clo. NW9 96 CS54
Ludford Clo., Croy. 219 DP105
Warrington Rd.
Ludgate Bdy. EC4 274 F9
Ludgate Bdy. EC4 141 DP72
Ludgate Circ. EC4 274 F9
Ludgate Hill EC4 274 F9
Ludgate Hill EC4 141 DP72
Ludgate Sq. EC4 274 G9
Ludham Clo. SE28 146 EW72
Rollesby Way
Ludlow Clo., Brom. 204 EG97
Ludlow Clo., Har. 116 BZ63
Ludlow Mead, Wat. 93 BV48
Ludlow Pl., Grays 170 GB76
Ludlow Rd. W5 137 CJ70
Ludlow Rd., Felt. 175 BU91
Ludlow Rd., Guil. 258 AV135
Ludlow St. EC1 275 H4
Ludlow Way N2 120 DC56
Ludlow Way, Rick. 75 BQ42
Ludovick Wk. SW15 158 CS84
Ludwick Clo., Welw.G.C. 29 CZ11
Ludwick Way
Ludwick Grn., Welw.G.C. 29 CZ10
Ludwick Ms. SE14 163 DY80
Ludwick Way, Welw.G.C. 29 CZ09
Luff Clo., Wind. 151 AL83
Luffield Rd. SE2 166 EV76
Luffman Rd. SE12 184 EH90
Lugard Rd. SE15 162 DV82
Lugg App. E12 125 EN62
Romford Rd.
Luke Ho. E1 142 DV72
Luke St. EC2 275 M4
Luke St. EC2 142 DS70
Lukin Cres. E4 101 ED48
Lukin St. E1 142 DW72
Lukintone Clo., Loug. 84 EL44
Roding Rd.
Lullarook Clo., West. 238 EJ116
Lullingstone Ave., Swan. 207 FF97
Lullingstone Clo., Orp. 186 EV94
Lullingstone Cres.
Lullingstone Cres., Orp. 186 EU94
Lullingstone La. (Eynsford), Dart. 208 FJ104
Lullingstone Rd., Belv. 166 EZ79
Lullington Garth N12 97 CZ50
Lullington Garth, Borwd. 78 CP43
Lullington Garth, Brom. 184 EE94
Lullington Rd. SE20 182 DU94
Lullington Rd., Dag. 146 EY66
Lulot Gdns. N19 121 DH61
Dartmouth Pk. Hill
Lulworth SE17 279 K10
Lulworth Ave., Houns. 156 CB80
Lulworth Ave. (Cheshunt), Wal.Cr. 65 DP29
Lulworth Ave., Wem. 117 CJ59
Lulworth Clo., Har. 116 BZ62
Lulworth Cres., Mitch. 200 DE96
Lulworth Dr., Pnr. 116 BX59
Lulworth Dr., Rom. 105 FB50
Lulworth Gdns., Har. 116 BY61
Lulworth Rd. SE9 184 EL89
Lulworth Rd. SE15 162 DV82
Lulworth Rd., Well. 165 ET82
Lulworth Waye, Hayes 135 BV72
Lumbards, Welw.G.C. 30 DA06
Lumen Rd., Wem. 117 CK61
Lumley Clo., Belv. 166 FA79
Lumley Ct. WC2 278 A1
Lumley Ct., Horl. 268 DG147
Lumley Gdns., Sutt. 217 CY106
Lumley Rd., Horl. 268 DG147
Lumley Rd., Sutt. 217 CY107
Lumley St. W1 272 G9
Lumley St. W1 140 DG72
Luna Rd., Th.Hth. 202 DQ97
Lunar Clo., West. 238 EK116
Lunar Ho., Croy. 202 DQ102
Lundin Wk., Wat. 94 BX49
Woodhall La.
Lundy Dr., Hayes 155 BS77
Lundy Wk. N1 142 DQ65
Marquess Est.
Lunedale Rd., Dart. 188 FP89
Lunedale Wk., Dart. 188 FP88
Lunedale Rd.
Lunghurst Rd., Cat. 237 DZ120
Lunham Rd. SE19 182 DS93
Lupin Clo. SW2 181 DP89
Palace Rd.
Lupin Clo., Croy. 203 DX102
Primrose La.
Lupin Clo., West Dr. 154 BK78
Magnolia St.
Luppit Clo., Brwd. 109 GA46
Lupton Clo. SE12 184 EH91
Lupton St. NW5 121 DJ63
Lupus St. SW1 161 DH78
Luralda Gdns. E14 163 EC78
Saunders Ness Rd.
Lurgan Ave. W6 159 CX79
Lurline Gdns. SW11 160 DG81
Luscombe Ct., Brom. 204 EE96
Luscombe Way SW8 161 DL80
Lushes Ct., Loug. 85 EP43
Lushes Rd.
Lushes Rd., Loug. 85 EP43
Lushington Dr., Cob. 213 BV114
Lushington Rd. NW10 139 CV68
Lushington Rd. SE6 183 EB92
Lushington Ter. E8 122 DU64
Wayland Ave.
Lusted Hall La., West. 238 EJ120
Lusted Rd., Sev. 241 FE120
Lusteds Clo., Dor. 263 CJ139
Glory Mead
Luther Clo., Edg. 96 CQ47
Luther King Clo. E17 123 DY58
Luther King Rd., Harl. 51 ER15
Luther Rd., Tedd. 177 CF92
Luton Pl. SE10 163 EC80
Luton Rd. E17 123 DZ55
Luton Rd., Sid. 186 EW90
Luton St. NW8 272 A5
Luton St. NW8 140 DD70
Lutton Ter. NW3 120 DD63
Flask Wk.
Luttrell Ave. SW15 179 CV85
Lutwyche Rd. SE6 183 DZ89
Luxborough La., Chig. 102 EL48
Luxborough St. W1 272 F5
Luxborough St. W1 140 DG71
Luxemburg Gdns. W6 159 CX77
Luxfield Rd. SE9 184 EL88
Luxford St. SE16 163 DX77
Luxmore Gdns. SE4 163 DZ81
Luxmore St.
Luxmore St. SE4 163 DZ81
Luxor St. SE5 162 DQ83
Luxted Rd., Orp. 223 EN112
Lyal Rd. E3 143 DY68
Lyall Ave. SE21 182 DS90
Lyall Ms. SW1 276 F7
Lyall Ms. SW1 160 DG76
Lyall Ms. W. SW1 276 F7
Lyall St. SW1 276 F7
Lyall St. SW1 160 DG76
Lycaste Clo., St.Alb. 43 CG21
Lycett Pl. W12 159 CU75
Becklow Rd.
Lych Gate, Wat. 60 BX33
Lych Gate Rd., Orp. 206 EU102
Lych Gate Wk., Hayes 135 BT73
Lych Way, Wok. 226 AX116
Lyconby Gdns., Croy. 203 DY101
Lycrome La., Chesh. 54 AR28
Lycrome Rd., Chesh. 54 AR28
Lydd Clo., Sid. 185 ES90
Lydd Rd., Bexh. 166 EZ80
Lydden Ct. SE9 185 ES86
Lydden Gro. SW18 180 DB87
Lydden Rd. SW18 180 DB87
Lydeard Rd. E6 145 EM66
Lydele Clo., Wok. 227 AZ115
Lydford Ave., Slou. 131 AR70
Lydford Clo. N16 122 DS64
Pellerin Rd.
Lydford Rd. N15 122 DR57
Lydford Rd. NW2 139 CW65
Lydford Rd. W9 139 CZ70
Lydhurst Ave. SW2 181 DM89
Lydia Ms., Hat. 45 CW24
Lydia Rd., Erith 167 FF79
Lydney Clo. SE15 162 DS80
Blakes Rd.
Lydney Clo. SW19 179 CY89
Princes Way
Lydon Rd. SW4 161 DJ83
Lydsey Clo., Slou. 131 AN69
Lydstep Rd., Chis. 185 EN91
Lye, The, Tad. 233 CW122
Lye Grn. Rd., Chesh. 54 AR30
Lye La., St.Alb. 60 CA28
Lyell Pl. E., Wind. 150 AJ83
Lyell Pl. W., Wind. 150 AJ83
Lyell Pl. E.
Lyell Wk. E., Wind. 150 AJ83
Lyell Pl. E.
Lyell Wk. W., Wind. 150 AJ83
Lyell Pl. E.
Lyfield, Lthd. 214 CB114
Lyford Rd. SW18 180 DD87
Lygean Ave., Ware 33 DY06
Lygon Pl. SW1 277 H7
Lyham Clo. SW2 181 DL86
Lyham Rd. SW2 181 DL85
Lyle Clo., Mitch. 200 DG101
Wolseley Rd.
Lyle Pk., Sev. 257 FH123
Lymbourne Clo., Sutt. 218 DA110
Lymden Gdns., Reig. 266 DB135
Lyme Fm. Rd. SE12 164 EG84
Lyme Gro. E9 142 DW66
St. Thomas's Sq.
Lyme Regis Rd., Bans. 233 CZ117
Lyme Rd., Well. 166 EV81
Lyme St. NW1 141 DJ66
Lyme Ter. NW1 141 DJ66
Royal College St.
Lymer Ave. SE19 182 DT92
Lymescote Gdns., Sutt. 200 DA103
Lyminge Clo., Sid. 185 ET91
Lyminge Gdns. SW18 180 DE88
Lymington Ave. N22 99 DN54
Lymington Clo. E6 145 EM71
Valiant Way
Lymington Clo. SW16 201 DK96
Lymington Dr., Ruis. 115 BR61
Lymington Gdns., Epsom 217 CT106
Lymington Rd. NW6 140 DB65
Lymington Rd., Dag. 126 EX60
Lympstone Gdns. SE15 162 DU80
Lyn Ms. E3 143 DZ69
Tredegar Sq.
Lynbridge Gdns. N13 99 DP49
Lynbrook Clo. SE15 162 DS80
Blakes Rd.
Lynbrook Clo., Rain. 147 FD68
Lynceley Gra., Epp. 70 EU29
Lynch, The, Hodd. 49 EB17
Lynch, The, Uxb. 134 BJ67
New Windsor St.
Lynch Clo., Uxb. 134 BJ66
New Windsor St.
Lynch Hill La., Slou. 131 AL70
Lynch Wk. SE8 163 DZ79
Prince St.
Lynchen Clo., Houns. 155 BU81
The Ave.
Lyncott Cres. SW4 161 DH84
Lyncroft Ave., Pnr. 116 BY57
Lyncroft Gdns. NW6 120 DA64
Lyncroft Gdns. W13 157 CJ75
Lyncroft Gdns., Epsom 217 CT109
Lyncroft Gdns., Houns. 176 CC85
Lyndale NW2 119 CZ63
Lyndale Ave. NW2 119 CZ62
Lyndale Clo. SE3 164 EF79
Lyndale Ct., W.Byf. 212 BG113
Parvis Rd.
Lyndale Rd., Red. 250 DF131
Lynden Way, Swan. 207 FC97
Lyndhurst Ave. N12 98 DF51
Lyndhurst Ave. NW7 96 CS51
Lyndhurst Ave. SW16 201 DK96
Lyndhurst Ave., Pnr. 93 BV53
Lyndhurst Ave., Sthl. 136 CB74
Lyndhurst Ave., Sun. 195 BU97
Lyndhurst Ave., Surb. 198 CP102
Lyndhurst Ave., Twick. 176 BZ88
Lyndhurst Clo. NW10 118 CR62
Lyndhurst Clo., Bexh. 167 FB83
Lyndhurst Clo., Croy. 202 DT104
Lyndhurst Clo., Orp. 223 EP105
Lyndhurst Clo., Wok. 226 AX115
Lyndhurst Dr. E10 123 EC59
Lyndhurst Dr., Horn. 128 FJ60
Lyndhurst Dr., N.Mal. 198 CS100
Lyndhurst Dr., Sev. 256 FE124
Lyndhurst Gdns. N3 97 CY53
Lyndhurst Gdns. NW3 120 DD64
Lyndhurst Gdns., Bark. 145 ES65
Lyndhurst Gdns., Enf. 82 DS42
Lyndhurst Gdns., Ilf. 125 ER58
Lyndhurst Gdns., Pnr. 93 BV53
Lyndhurst Gro. SE15 162 DS82
Lyndhurst Ri., Chig. 103 EN49
Lyndhurst Rd. E4 101 EC52
Lyndhurst Rd. N18 100 DU49
Lyndhurst Rd. N22 99 DM51
Lyndhurst Rd. NW3 120 DD64
Lyndhurst Rd., Bexh. 167 FB83
Lyndhurst Rd., Chesh. 54 AP28
Lyndhurst Rd., Couls. 234 DG116
Lyndhurst Rd., Grnf. 136 CB70
Lyndhurst Rd., Reig. 266 DA137
Lyndhurst Rd., Th.Hth. 201 DN98
Lyndhurst Sq. SE15 162 DT81
Lyndhurst Ter. NW3 120 DD64
Lyndhurst Way SE15 162 DT81
Lyndhurst Way, Brwd. 109 GC45
Lyndhurst Way, Cher. 193 BE104
Lyndhurst Way, Sutt. 218 DA108
Lyndon Ave., Pnr. 94 BY51
Lyndon Ave., Sid. 185 ET85
Lyndon Ave., Wall. 200 DG104
Lyndon Rd., Belv. 166 FA77
Lyndwood Dr., Wind. 172 AU86
Lyne Clo., Vir.W. 193 AZ100
Lyne Cres. E17 101 DZ53
Lyne Crossing Rd., Cher. 193 BA100
Lyne La., Cher. 193 BA100
Lyne La., Egh. 193 BA98
Lyne La., Vir.W. 193 BA100
Lyne Rd., Vir.W. 192 AX100
Lyne Way, Hem.H. 39 BF18
Lynegrove Ave., Ashf. 175 BQ92
Lyneham Wk. E5 123 DY64
Ashenden Rd.
Lyneham Wk., Pnr. 115 BT55
Fore St.
Lynett Rd., Dag. 126 EX61
Lynette Ave. SW4 181 DH86
Lynford Clo., Edg. 96 CQ53
Lynford Gdns., Edg. 96 CP48
Lynford Gdns., Ilf. 125 ET61
Lynhurst Cres., Uxb. 135 BQ66
Lynhurst Rd., Uxb. 135 BQ66
Lynmere Rd., Well. 166 EV82
Lynmouth Ave., Enf. 82 DT44
Lynmouth Ave., Mord. 199 CX101
Lynmouth Dr., Ruis. 115 BV61
Lynmouth Gdns., Grnf. 137 CH67
Lynmouth Gdns., Houns. 156 BX81
Lynmouth Ri., Orp. 206 EV98
Lynmouth Rd. E17 123 DY58
Lynmouth Rd. N2 120 DF56
Lynmouth Rd. N16 122 DT60
Lynmouth Rd., Grnf. 137 CH67
Lynn Clo., Ashf. 175 BR92
Goffs Rd.
Lynn Clo., Har. 95 CD54
Lynn Ms. E11 124 EE61
Lynn Rd.
Lynn Rd. E11 124 EE61
Lynn Rd. SW12 181 DH87
Lynn Rd., Ilf. 125 ER59
Lynn St., Enf. 82 DR39
Lynn Wk., Reig. 266 DB137
Lynne Clo., Orp. 223 ET107
Lynne Clo., S.Croy. 220 DW111
Lynne Wk., Esher 214 CC106
Lynne Way NW10 138 CS65
Lynne Way, Nthlt. 136 BX68
Lynross Clo., Rom. 106 FM54
Lynscott Way, S.Croy. 219 DP109
Lynsted Clo., Bexh. 187 FB85
Lynsted Clo., Brom. 204 EJ96
Lynsted Ct., Beck. 203 DY96
Churchfields Rd.
Lynsted Gdns. SE9 164 EK83
Lynton Ave. N12 98 DD49
Lynton Ave. NW9 119 CT56
Lynton Ave. W13 137 CG72
Lynton Ave., Orp. 206 EV98
Lynton Ave., Rom. 104 FA53
Lynton Ave., St.Alb. 43 CJ21
Lynton Clo. NW10 118 CS64
Great Cen. Way
Lynton Clo., Chess. 216 CL105
Lynton Clo., Islw. 157 CF84
Lynton Cres., Ilf. 125 EP58
Lynton Crest, Pot.B. 64 DA32
Strafford Gate
Lynton Est. SE1 162 DU77
Lynton Rd.
Lynton Gdns. N11 99 DK51
Lynton Gdns., Enf. 100 DS45
Lynton Mead N20 98 DA48
Lynton Par., Wal.Cr. 67 DX30
Turners Hill
Lynton Rd. E4 101 EB50
Lynton Rd. N8 121 DK57
Lynton Rd. NW6 139 CZ67
Lynton Rd. SE1 162 DT77
Lynton Rd. W3 138 CN73
Lynton Rd., Chesh. 54 AP28
Lynton Rd., Croy. 201 DN100
Lynton Rd., Grav. 191 GG88
Lynton Rd., Har. 116 BY61
Lynton Rd., N.Mal. 198 CR99
Lynton Rd. S., Grav. 191 GG88
Lynton Wk., Hayes 135 BS69
Exmouth Rd.
Lynwood, Guil. 258 AV135
Lynwood Ave., Couls. 235 DH115
Lynwood Ave., Egh. 172 AY93
Lynwood Ave., Epsom 217 CT114
Lynwood Ave., Slou. 152 AX76
Lynwood Clo. E18 102 EJ53
Gordon Rd.
Lynwood Clo., Har. 116 BY62
Lynwood Clo., Rom. 105 FB51
Lynwood Clo., Wok. 211 BD113
Lynwood Dr., Nthwd. 93 BS53
Lynwood Dr., Rom. 105 FB51
Lynwood Dr., Wor.Pk. 199 CU103
Lynwood Gdns., Croy. 219 DM105
Lynwood Gdns., Sthl. 136 BZ71
Lynwood Gro. N21 99 DN46
Lynwood Gro., Orp. 205 ES101
Lynwood Heights, Rick. 74 BH43
Lynwood Rd. SW17 180 DF90
Lynwood Rd. W5 138 CL70
Lynwood Rd., Epsom 217 CT114
Lynwood Rd., Red. 250 DG132
Lynwood Rd., T.Ditt. 197 CF103
Lynx Hill, Lthd. 245 BS128
Lyon Business Pk., Bark. 145 ES68
Lyon Meade, Stan. 95 CJ53
Lyon Pk. Ave., Wem. 138 CL65
Lyon Rd. SW19 200 DC95
Lyon Rd., Har. 117 CF58
Lyon Rd., Rom. 127 FF59
Lyon Rd., Walt. 196 BY103
Lyon St. N1 141 DM66
Caledonian Rd.

Lyon Way, Grnf. 137 CE67
Lyon Way, St.Alb. 44 CN20
Lyons Ct., Dor. 263 CH136
High St.
Lyons Dr., Guil. 242 AU129
Lyons Pl. NW8 140 DD70
Lyons Wk. W14 159 CY77
Lyonsdene, Tad. 249 CZ127
Smithy La.
Lyonsdown Ave., Barn. 80 DC44
Lyonsdown Rd., Barn. 80 DB44
Lyoth Rd., Orp. 205 EQ103
Lyric Dr., Grnf. 136 CB70
Lyric Rd. SW13 159 CT81
Lys Hill Gdns., Hert. 31 DP07
Lysander Clo., Hem.H. 57 AZ27
Lancaster Dr.
Lysander Gdns., Surb. 198 CM100
Ewell Rd.
Lysander Gro. N19 121 DK60
Lysander Rd., Croy. 219 DM107
Lysander Rd., Ruis. 115 BR61
Lysander Way, Abb.L. 59 BU32
Langley La.
Lysander Way, Orp. 205 EQ104
Lysander Way, Welw.G.C. 30 DD08
Lysia St. SW6 159 CX80
Lysias Rd. SW12 181 DH86
Lysons Wk. SW15 179 CU85
Swinburne Rd.
Lytchet Rd., Brom. 184 EH94
Lytchet Way, Enf. 82 DW39
Lytchgate Clo., S.Croy. 220 DS108
Lytcott Dr., W.Mol. 196 BZ97
Freeman Dr.
Lytcott Gro. SE22 182 DT85
Lyte St. E2 142 DW68
Bishops Way
Lytham Ave., Wat. 94 BX50
Lytham Gro. W5 138 CM69
Lytham St. SE17 162 DR78
Lyttelton Clo. NW3 140 DE66
Hawtrey Rd.
Lyttelton Rd. E10 123 EB62
Lyttelton Rd. N2 120 DC57
Lyttleton Rd. N8 121 DN55
Lytton Ave. N13 99 DN47
Lytton Ave., Enf. 83 DY38
Lytton Clo. N2 120 DC58
Lytton Clo., Loug. 85 ER41
Lytton Clo., Nthlt. 136 BZ66
Lytton Gdns., Wall. 219 DK105
Lytton Gdns., Welw.G.C. 29 CX09
Lytton Gro. SW15 179 CX85
Lytton Rd. E11 124 EE59
Lytton Rd., Barn. 80 DC42
Lytton Rd., Grays 171 GG77
Lytton Rd., Pnr. 94 BY52
Lytton Rd., Rom. 127 FH57
Lytton Rd., Wok. 227 BB116
Lytton Strachey Path SE28 146 EV73
Titmuss Ave.
Lyttons Way, Hodd. 33 EA14
Lyveden Rd. SE3 164 EH80
Lyveden Rd. SW17 180 DE93
Lywood Clo., Tad. 233 CW122

M

Mabbotts, Tad. 233 CX121
Mabbutt Clo., St.Alb. 60 BY30
Mabel Rd., Swan. 187 FG93
Mabel St., Wok. 226 AX117
Maberley Cres. SE19 182 DU94
Maberley Rd. SE19 202 DT95
Maberley Rd., Beck. 203 DX97
Mabeys Wk., Saw. 36 EV06
Mabledon Pl. WC1 273 N3
Mabledon Pl. WC1 141 DK69
Mablethorpe Rd. SW6 159 CY80
Mabley St. E9 123 DY64
Macaret Clo. N20 98 DC45
Macarthur Ter. SE7 164 EK79
Macaulay Ave., Esher 197 CE103
Macaulay Ct. SW4 161 DH83
Macaulay Rd. E6 144 EK68
Macaulay Rd. SW4 161 DH83
Macaulay Rd., Cat. 236 DS122
Macaulay Sq. SW4 161 DH84
Macaulay Way SE28 146 EV73
Booth Clo.
Macauley Ms. SE13 163 EC81
Macbean St. SE18 165 EP76
Macbeth St. W6 159 CV78
Macclesfield Bri. NW1 140 DE68
Macclesfield Rd. EC1 275 H2
Macclesfield Rd. EC1 142 DQ69
Macclesfield Rd. SE25 202 DV99
Macclesfield St. W1 273 N10
Macdonald Ave., Dag. 127 FB62
Macdonald Ave., Horn. 128 FL55
Macdonald Clo., Amer. 55 AR35
Macdonald Rd. E7 124 EG63
Macdonald Rd. E17 101 EC54
Macdonald Rd. N11 98 DF50
Macdonald Rd. N19 121 DJ61
Macdonald Way, Horn. 128 FL56
Macdonnell Gdns., Wat. 75 BT35
High Rd.
Macduff Rd. SW11 160 DG81
Mace Clo. E1 142 DV74
Kennet St.
Mace Ct., Grays 170 GE79
Mace La., Sev. 223 ER113
Mace St. E2 143 DX68
Macers Ct., Brox. 49 DZ24
Macers La., Brox. 49 DZ24
MacFarlane La., Islw. 157 CF79
Macfarlane Rd. W12 139 CW74
Macfarren Pl. NW1 272 G5
Macgregor Rd. E16 144 EJ71
Machell Rd. SE15 162 DW83
Mackay Rd. SW4 161 DH83
Mackennal St. NW8 140 DE68
Mackenzie Mall, Slou. 152 AT75
High St.
Mackenzie Rd. N7 141 DM65
Mackenzie Rd., Beck. 202 DW96
Mackenzie St., Slou. 132 AT74
Mackenzie Wk. E14 143 EA74
South Colonnade
Mackenzie Way, Grav. 191 GK93
Mackeson Rd. NW3 120 DF63
Mackie Rd. SW2 181 DN87
Mackies Hill, Guil. 261 BR144
Mackintosh La. E9 123 DX64
Homerton High St.
Macklin St. WC2 274 A8
Macklin St. WC2 141 DL72
Mackrells, Red. 266 DC137
Mackrow Wk. E14 143 EC73
Robin Hood La.
Macks Rd. SE16 162 DU77
Mackworth St. NW1 273 K2
Mackworth St. NW1 141 DJ69
Maclaren Ms. SW15 159 CW84
Clarendon Dr.
Maclean Rd. SE23 183 DY86
Maclennan Ave., Rain. 148 FK69
Macleod Clo., Grays 170 GD77
Macleod St. SE17 162 DQ78
Maclise Rd. W14 159 CY76
Macmillan Gdns., Dart. 168 FN84
Keyes Rd.
Macoma Rd. SE18 165 ER79
Macoma Ter. SE18 165 ER79
Macon Way, Upmin. 129 FS59
Maconochies Rd. E14 163 EB78
Macquarie Way E14 163 EB77
Macready Pl. N7 121 DL63
Warlters Rd.
Macroom Rd. W9 139 CZ69
Mada Rd., Orp. 205 EP103
Madan Rd., West. 255 ER125
Madans Wk., Epsom 232 CR115
Maddams St. E3 143 EB70
Madden Clo., Swans. 189 FX86
Maddison Clo., Tedd. 177 CF93
Maddock Way SE17 161 DP79
Cooks Rd.
Maddocks Clo., Sid. 186 EX92
Maddox La., Lthd. 230 BY123
Maddox Pk., Lthd. 230 BY123
Maddox Rd., Harl. 35 ES14
Maddox Rd., Hem.H. 41 BP20
Maddox St. W1 273 J10
Maddox St. W1 141 DH73
Madeira Ave., Brom. 184 EE94
Madeira Clo., W.Byf. 212 BG113
Brantwood Gdns.
Madeira Cres., W.Byf. 212 BG113
Brantwood Gdns.
Madeira Gro., Wdf.Grn. 102 EJ51
Madeira Rd. E11 123 ED60
Madeira Rd. N13 99 DP49
Madeira Rd. SW16 181 DL92
Madeira Rd., Mitch. 200 DF98
Madeira Rd., W.Byf. 211 BF113
Madeira Wk., Brwd. 108 FY48
Madeira Wk., Reig. 250 DD133
Madeira Wk., Wind. 151 AR81
Madeley Clo., Amer. 55 AR36
Madeley Rd. W5 138 CL72
Madeline Rd. SE20 182 DU94
Madells, Epp. 69 ET31
Madge Gill Way E6 144 EL67
Ron Leighton Way
Madgeways Clo., Ware 33 DZ10
Madgeways La., Ware 33 DZ10
Madison Cres., Bexh. 166 EW80
Madison Gdns., Bexh. 166 EW80
Madison Gdns., Brom. 204 EF97
Madison Way, Sev. 256 FF123
Madras Pl. N7 141 DN65
Madras Rd., Ilf. 125 EP63
Madresfield Ct., Rad. 62 CL32
Porters Pk. Dr.
Madrid Rd. SW13 159 CU81
Madrid Rd., Guil. 258 AV135
Madrigal La. SE5 161 DP80
Madron St. SE17 279 N10
Madron St. SE17 162 DS78
Maesmaur Rd., West. 238 EK121
Mafeking Ave. E6 144 EL68
Mafeking Ave., Brent. 158 CL79
Mafeking Ave., Ilf. 125 ER59
Mafeking Rd. E16 144 EF70
Mafeking Rd. N17 100 DU54
Mafeking Rd., Enf. 82 DT41
Mafeking Rd., Stai. 173 BB89
Mag Ct., Beac. 111 AM55
Magazine Pl., Lthd. 231 CH122
Magdala Ave. N19 121 DH61
Magdala Rd., Islw. 157 CG83
Magdala Rd., S.Croy. 220 DR108
Napier Rd.
Magdalen Clo., W.Byf. 212 BL114
Magdalen Cres., W.Byf. 212 BL114
Magdalen Gdns., Brwd. 109 GE44
Magdalen Gro., Orp. 224 EV105
Magdalen Pas. E1 142 DT73
Prescot St.
Magdalen Rd. SW18 180 DC88
Magdalen St. SE1 279 M3
Magdalen St. SE1 142 DS74
Magdalene Clo. SE15 162 DV82
Heaton Rd.
Magdalene Gdns. E6 145 EN70
Magdalene Rd., Shep. 194 BM97
Magee St. SE11 161 DN79
Maggie Blake's Cause 279 P3
SE1
Magna Carta La., Stai. 172 AX88
Magna Rd., Egh. 172 AV93
Magnaville Rd. 95 CE45
(Bushey), Wat.
Magnet Rd., Grays 169 FW79
Magnet Rd., Wem. 117 CK61
Magnin Clo. E8 142 DU67
Wilde Clo.
Magnolia Ave., Abb.L. 59 BU32
Stewart Clo.
Magnolia Clo., Hert. 32 DU09
Magnolia Clo., Kings.T. 178 CP93
Magnolia Clo., St.Alb. 61 CD27
Magnolia Ct., Har. 118 CM59
Magnolia Ct., Horl. 268 DG148
Magnolia Ct., Rich. 158 CP81
West Hall Rd.
Magnolia Dr., West. 238 EK116
Magnolia Gdns. E10 123 EB61
Oliver Rd.
Magnolia Gdns., Slou. 152 AW76
Magnolia Pl. SW4 181 DL85
Magnolia Pl. W5 138 CL71
Montpelier Rd.
Magnolia Rd. W4 158 CP79
Magnolia St., West Dr. 154 BK77
Magnolia Way, Brwd. 108 FV43
Magnolia Way, Dor. 263 CK139
Magnolia Way, Epsom 216 CQ106
Magnum Clo., Rain. 148 FJ70
Magpie All. EC4 274 E9
Magpie Clo. E7 124 EF64
Magpie Clo. NW9 96 CS54
Eagle Dr.
Magpie Clo., Couls. 235 DJ118
Magpie Clo., Enf. 82 DU39
Magpie Hall Clo., Brom. 204 EL100
Magpie Hall La., Brom. 204 EL101
Magpie Hall Rd. 95 CE47
(Bushey), Wat.
Magpie La., Amer. 89 AM45
Magpie La., Brwd. 107 FW54
Magpie Wk., Hat. 45 CU20
Lark Ri.
Magpie Way, Slou. 131 AL70
Pemberton Rd.
Magpies, The, Epp. 51 EP24
Magri Wk. E1 142 DW71
Ashfield St.
Maguire Dr., Rich. 177 CJ91
Maguire St. SE1 162 DT75
Mahatma Gandhi Ho., 118 CM64
Wem.
Mahlon Ave., Ruis. 115 BV64
Mahogany Clo. SE16 143 DY74
Mahon Clo., Enf. 82 DT39
Maida Ave. E4 101 EB45
Maida Ave. W2 140 DC71
Maida Rd., Belv. 166 FA76
Maida Vale W9 140 DB68
Maida Vale Rd., Dart. 187 FG85
Maida Way E4 101 EB45
Maiden Erlegh Ave., Bex. 186 EY88
Maiden La. NW1 141 DK66
Maiden La. SE1 279 J2
Maiden La. WC2 274 A10
Maiden La. WC2 141 DL73
Maiden La., Dart. 167 FG83
Maiden Rd. E15 144 EE66
Maidenhead Rd., Wind. 151 AK80
Maidenhead St., Hert. 32 DR09
Maidenshaw Rd., Epsom 216 CR112
Maidenstone Hill SE10 163 EC81
Maids of Honour Row, 177 CK85
Rich.
The Grn.
Maidstone Ave., Rom. 105 FC54
Maidstone Bldgs. SE1 279 K3
Maidstone Ho. E14 143 EB72
Carmen St.
Maidstone Rd. N11 99 DJ51
Maidstone Rd., Grays 170 GA79
Maidstone Rd., Sev. 256 FE122
Maidstone Rd. 257 FN121
(Seal), Sev.
Maidstone Rd., Sid. 186 EX93
Maidstone Rd., Swan. 207 FC95
Maidstone St. E2 142 DU68
Audrey St.
Main Ave., Enf. 82 DT43
Main Ave., Nthwd. 93 BQ48
Main Dr., Ger.Cr. 112 AW57
Main Dr., Iver 153 BE77
Main Dr., Wem. 117 CK62
Main Par., Rick. 73 BC42
Whitelands Ave.
Main Rd. 208 FM100
(Farningham), Dart.
Main Rd. 188 FP93
(Sutton at Hone), Dart.
Main Rd., Eden. 255 EQ134
Main Rd., Kes. 222 EJ112
Main Rd., Long. 209 FX96
Main Rd., Orp. 206 EW98
Main Rd., Rom. 127 FF56
Main Rd. (Knockholt), Sev. 239 ET119
Main Rd. (Sundridge), Sev. 240 EX124
Main Rd., Sid. 185 ES90
Main Rd., Swan. 187 FF94
Main Rd. (Crockenhill), 207 FC100
Swan.
Main Rd., West. 222 EJ114
Main St., Felt. 176 BX92
Mainridge Rd., Chis. 185 EN91
Maisemore St. SE15 162 DU80
Peckham Pk. Rd.
Maisie Webster Clo., Stai. 174 BK87
Lauser Rd.
Maitland Clo. SE10 163 EB80
Maitland Clo., Houns. 156 BZ83
Maitland Clo., W.Byf. 212 BG113
Maitland Pk. Est. NW3 140 DF65
Maitland Pk. Rd. NW3 140 DF65
Maitland Pk. Vill. NW3 140 DF65
Maitland Pl. E5 122 DV63
Clarence Rd.
Maitland Rd. E15 144 EF65
Maitland Rd. SE26 183 DX93
Maize Row E14 143 DZ73
Commercial Rd.
Maizecroft, Horl. 269 DJ147
Oatlands
Maizey Ct., Brwd. 108 FU43
Danes Way
Majendie Rd. SE18 165 ER78
Majestic Way, Mitch. 200 DF96
Major Rd. E15 123 ED64
Major Rd. SE16 162 DU76
Jamaica Rd.
Majors Fm. Rd., Slou. 152 AX80
Makepeace Ave. N6 120 DG61
Makepeace Rd. E11 124 EG56
Hermon Hill
Makepeace Rd., Nthlt. 136 BY67
Makins St. SW3 276 C9
Makins St. SW3 160 DE77
Malabar St. E14 163 EA75
Malacca Fm., Guil. 244 BH128
Malam Gdns. E14 143 EB73
Wades Pl.
Malan Clo., West. 238 EL117
Malan Sq., Rain. 147 FH65
Malbrook Rd. SW15 159 CV84
Malcolm Ct., Stan. 95 CJ50
Malcolm Cres. NW4 119 CU58
Malcolm Dr., Surb. 197 CK102
Malcolm Gdns., Horl. 268 DD150
Malcolm Pl. E2 142 DW70
Malcolm Rd. E1 142 DW70
Malcolm Rd. SE20 182 DW94
Malcolm Rd. SE25 202 DU100
Malcolm Rd. SW19 179 CY93
Malcolm Rd., Couls. 235 DK115
Malcolm Rd., Uxb. 114 BM63
Malcolm Way E11 124 EG57
Malden Ave. SE25 202 DV97
Malden Ave., Grnf. 117 CE64
Malden Clo., Amer. 72 AT38
Quill Hall La.
Malden Cres. NW1 140 DG65
Malden Grn. Ave., 199 CT102
Wor.Pk.
Malden Hill, N.Mal. 199 CT97
Malden Hill Gdns., N.Mal. 199 CT97
Malden Pk., N.Mal. 199 CT100
Malden Pl. NW5 120 DG64
Grafton Ter.
Malden Rd. NW5 120 DF64
Malden Rd., Borwd. 78 CN41
Malden Rd., N.Mal. 198 CS99
Malden Rd., Sutt. 217 CW105
Malden Rd., Wat. 75 BU40
Malden Rd., Wor.Pk. 199 CT101
Malden Way, N.Mal. 198 CR100
Maldon Clo. E15 123 ED64
David St.
Maldon Clo. N1 142 DQ67
Maldon Clo. SE5 162 DS83
Maldon Rd. N9 100 DT48
Maldon Rd. W3 138 CQ73
Maldon Rd., Rom. 127 FC59
Maldon Rd., Wall. 219 DH106
Maldon Wk., Wdf.Grn. 102 EJ51
Malet Clo., Egh. 173 BD93
Malet Pl. WC1 273 M5
Malet Pl. WC1 141 DK70
Malet St. WC1 273 M5
Malet St. WC1 141 DK70
Maley Ave. SE27 181 DP89
Malford Ct. E18 102 EG54
Malford Gro. E18 124 EF56
Malfort Rd. SE5 162 DS83
Malham Rd. SE23 183 DX88
Malins Clo., Barn. 79 CV43
Malkin Dr., Beac. 88 AJ52
Mall, The E15 143 ED66
Broadway
Mall, The N14 99 DL48
Mall, The SW1 277 L4
Mall, The SW1 141 DJ74
Mall, The SW14 178 CQ85
Mall, The W5 138 CL73
Mall, The, Brom. 204 EG97
High St.
Mall, The, Croy. 202 DQ102
Poplar Wk.
Mall, The, Har. 118 CM58
Mall, The, Horn. 127 FH60
Landseer Clo.
Mall, The, St.Alb. 60 CC27
Mall, The, Surb. 197 CK99
Mall Rd. W6 159 CV78
Mallams Ms. SW9 161 DP83
St. James's Cres.
Mallard Clo. E9 143 DZ65
Mallard Clo., Barn. 80 DD44
The Hook
Mallard Clo., Dart. 188 FM85
Mallard Clo., Red. 250 DG131
Mallard Clo., Twick. 176 CA87
Stephenson Rd.
Mallard Clo., Upmin. 129 FT59
Mallard Dr., Slou. 131 AM73
Mallard Path SE28 165 ER76
Tom Cribb Rd.
Mallard Pl., Twick. 177 CH90
Mallard Rd., S.Croy. 221 DX110
Mallard Wk. SE28 165 ER76
Goosander Way
Mallard Wk., Beck. 203 DX99
Mallard Wk., Sid. 186 EW93
Cray Rd.
Mallard Way NW9 118 CQ59
Mallard Way, Brwd. 109 GB45
Mallard Way, Nthwd. 93 BQ52
Mallard Way, Wall. 219 DJ109
Mallard Way, Wat. 76 BY36
Mallards, The, Stai. 194 BH96
Thames Side
Mallards Reach, Wey. 195 BR103
Mallards Ri., Harl. 52 EX15
Mallards Rd., Wdf.Grn. 102 EH52
Mallet Dr., Nthlt. 116 BZ64
Mallet Rd. SE13 183 ED86
Malling Clo., Croy. 202 DW100
Malling Gdns., Mord. 200 DC100
Malling Way, Brom. 204 EF101
Mallinson Clo., Horn. 128 FJ64
Mallinson Rd. SW11 180 DE85
Mallinson Rd., Croy. 201 DK104
Mallion Ct., Wal.Abb. 68 EF33
Mallord St. SW3 160 DD79
Mallory Clo. SE4 163 DY84
Mallory Gdns., Barn. 98 DG45
Mallory St. NW8 272 B5
Mallory St. NW8 140 DE70
Mallow Clo., Croy. 203 DX102
Marigold Way
Mallow Clo., Grav. 190 GE91
Mallow Clo., Tad. 233 CV119
Henbit Clo.
Mallow Ct., Grays 170 GD79
Mallow Cft., Hat. 45 CV19
Oxlease Dr.
Mallow Mead NW7 97 CY52
Mallow St. EC1 275 K4
Mallow Wk., Wal.Cr. 66 DR28
St. James Rd.
Mallows, The, Uxb. 115 BP62
Mallows Grn., Harl. 51 EN20
Mallys Pl., Dart. 208 FQ95
Malm Clo., Rick. 92 BK47
Malmains Clo., Beck. 203 ED98
Malmains Way, Beck. 203 EC98
Malmesbury Clo., Pnr. 115 BT56
Malmesbury Rd. E3 143 DZ69
Malmesbury Rd. E16 144 EE71
Malmesbury Rd. E18 102 EF53
Malmesbury Rd., Mord. 200 DC101
Malmesbury Ter. E16 144 EF71
Malmescroft, Hem.H. 41 BQ22
Malmsdale, Welw.G.C. 29 CX05
Malmstone Ave., Red. 251 DJ128
Malpas Dr., Pnr. 116 BX57
Malpas Rd. E8 142 DV65
Malpas Rd. SE4 163 DZ82
Malpas Rd., Dag. 146 EX65
Malpas Rd., Grays 171 GJ76
Malpas Rd., Slou. 132 AV73
Malt Hill, Egh. 172 AY92
Malt Ho. Clo., Wind. 172 AV87
Malt La., Rad. 77 CG35
Newlands Ave.
Malt St. SE1 162 DU79
Malta Rd. E10 123 EA60
Malta Rd., Til. 171 GF82
Malta St. EC1 274 G4
Maltby Clo., Orp. 206 EU102
Vinson Clo.
Maltby Dr., Enf. 82 DV38
Maltby Rd., Chess. 216 CN107
Maltby St. SE1 279 P5
Maltby St. SE1 162 DT76
Malthouse Dr. W4 158 CS80
Pumping Sta. Rd.
Malthouse Dr., Felt. 176 BX92
Malthouse Pas. SW13 158 CS82
The Ter.
Malthouse Pl., Rad. 61 CG34
Malthouse Sq., Beac. 111 AM55
Malthus Path SE28 146 EW74
Owen Clo.
Malting Ho. E14 143 DZ73
Oak La.
Malting Way, Islw. 157 CF82
St. John's Rd.
Maltings, The, Harl. 36 EW11
Maltings, The, Kings L. 59 BQ33
Maltings, The, Orp. 205 ET102
Maltings, The, Oxt. 254 EF131
Maltings, The, St.Alb. 43 CD20
Chequer St.
Maltings, The, W.Byf. 212 BM113
Maltings Clo. SW13 158 CS82
Cleveland Gdns.
Maltings Dr., Epp. 70 EU29
Palmers Hill
Maltings La., Epp. 70 EU29
Maltings Ms., Amer. 55 AP40
Maltings Ms., Sid. 186 EU90
Station Rd.
Maltings Pl. SW6 160 DB81
Maltmans La., Ger.Cr. 112 AW55
Malton Ave., Slou. 131 AP72
Malton Ms. SE18 165 ES79
Malton St.
Malton Ms. W10 139 CY72
Cambridge Gdns.
Malton Rd. W10 139 CY72
St. Marks Rd.
Malton St. SE18 165 ES79
Maltravers St. WC2 274 C10
Malus Clo., Add. 211 BF108
Malus Clo., Hem.H. 40 BN19
Malus Dr., Add. 211 BF107
Malva Clo. SW18 180 DB85
St. Ann's Hill
Malvern Ave. E4 101 ED52
Malvern Ave., Bexh. 166 EY80
Malvern Ave., Har. 116 BY62
Malvern Clo. SE20 202 DU96
Derwent Rd.
Malvern Clo. W10 139 CZ71
Malvern Clo., Cher. 211 BC107
Malvern Clo., Hat. 45 CT17
Malvern Clo., Mitch. 201 DJ97
Malvern Clo., St.Alb. 43 CJ16
Malvern Clo., Surb. 198 CL102
Malvern Clo., Uxb. 114 BN61
Malvern Ct. SE14 162 DW80
Avonley Rd.
Malvern Ct. SW7 276 A8
Malvern Ct. SW7 160 DD77
Malvern Ct., Slou. 153 BA79
Hill Ri.
Malvern Dr., Felt. 176 BX92
Malvern Dr., Ilf. 125 ET63
Malvern Dr., Wdf.Grn. 102 EJ50
Malvern Gdns. NW2 119 CY61
Malvern Gdns. NW6 139 CZ68
Malvern Gdns., Har. 118 CL56
Malvern Gdns., Loug. 85 EM44
Malvern Ms. NW6 140 DA69
Malvern Rd.
Malvern Pl. NW6 139 CZ69
Malvern Rd. E6 144 EL67
Malvern Rd. E8 142 DU66
Malvern Rd. E11 124 EE61
Malvern Rd. N8 121 DM55
Malvern Rd. N17 122 DU55
Malvern Rd. NW6 140 DA69
Malvern Rd., Enf. 83 DY36
Malvern Rd., Grays 170 GD77
Malvern Rd., Hmptn. 176 CA94
Malvern Rd., Hayes 155 BS80
Malvern Rd., Horn. 127 FG58
Malvern Rd., Orp. 224 EV105
Malvern Rd., Surb. 198 CL103
Malvern Rd., Th.Hth. 201 DN98
Malvern Ter. N1 141 DN67
Malvern Ter. N9 100 DT46
Malvern Way W13 137 CH71
Templewood
Malvern Way, Hem.H. 40 BM18
Malvern Way, Rick. 75 BP43
Malvina Ave., Grav. 191 GH89
Malwood Rd. SW12 181 DH86
Malyons, The, Shep. 195 BR100
Gordon Rd.
Malyons Rd. SE13 183 EB86
Malyons Rd., Swan. 187 FF94
Malyons Ter. SE13 183 EB85
Managers St. E14 143 EC74
Prestons Rd.
Manan Clo., Hem.H. 41 BQ22
Manaton Clo. SE15 162 DV83
Manaton Cres., Sthl. 136 CA72
Manbey Gro. E15 144 EE65
Manbey Pk. Rd. E15 144 EE65
Manbey Rd. E15 144 EE65
Manbey St. E15 144 EE65
Manborough Ave. E6 145 EM69
Manbre Rd. W6 159 CW79
Manchester Dr. W10 139 CY70
Manchester Gro. E14 163 EC78
Manchester Ms. W1 272 F7
Manchester Rd. E14 163 EC78
Manchester Rd. N15 122 DR58
Manchester Rd., Th.Hth. 202 DQ97
Manchester Row, Dart. 187 FE85
Manchester Sq. W1 272 F8
Manchester Sq. W1 140 DG72
Manchester St. W1 272 F7
Manchester St. W1 140 DG71
Manchester Way, Dag. 127 FB63
Manchuria Rd. SW11 180 DG86
Manciple St. SE1 279 L5
Manciple St. SE1 162 DR75
Mandalay Rd. SW4 181 DJ85
Mandarin St. E14 143 EA73
Salter St.
Mandarin Way, Hayes 136 BX71
Willow Tree La.
Mandela Avenue-First 35 ES13
Ave., Harl.
Mandela Clo. NW10 138 CQ66
Mandela Rd. E16 144 EG72
Mandela St. NW1 141 DJ67
Mandela St. SW9 161 DN80
Mandela Way SE1 279 N8
Mandela Way SE1 162 DS77

Mandelyns, Berk. 38 AS16
Mandeville Clo. SE3 164 EF80
Vanbrugh Pk.
Mandeville Clo. SW20 199 CY95
Mandeville Clo., Brox. 49 DZ20
Mandeville Clo., Guil. 242 AU131
Mandeville Clo., Harl. 52 EW17
Mandeville Clo., Hert. 32 DQ12
Mandeville Clo., Wat. 75 BT38
Mandeville Ct. E4 101 DY49
Mandeville Ct., Egh. 173 BA91
Mandeville Dr., St.Alb. 43 CD23
Mandeville Dr., Surb. 197 CK102
Mandeville Pl. W1 272 G8
Mandeville Pl. W1 140 DG72
Mandeville Ri., Welw.G.C. 29 CX07
Mandeville Rd. N14 99 DH47
Mandeville Rd., Enf. 83 DY36
Mandeville Rd., Hert. 32 DQ12
Mandeville Rd., Islw. 157 CG82
Mandeville Rd., Nthlt. 136 BZ66
Mandeville Rd., Pot.B. 64 DC32
Mandeville Rd., Shep. 194 BN99
Mandeville St. E5 123 DY62
Mandeville Wk., Brwd. 109 GE44
Kelvedon Clo.
Mandrake Rd. SW17 180 DF89
Mandrake Way E15 144 EE66
Elliot Clo.
Mandrell Rd. SW2 181 DL85
Manette St. W1 273 N9
Manette St. W1 141 DK72
Manfield Clo., Slou. 131 AN69
Manford Clo., Chig. 104 EU49
Manford Cross, Chig. 104 EU50
Manford Way, Chig. 103 ES49
Manfred Rd. SW15 179 CZ85
Manger Rd. N7 141 DL65
Mangles Rd., Guil. 242 AX132
Mangold Way, Erith 166 EY76
Mangrove Dr., Hert. 32 DS11
Mangrove La., Hert. 32 DS11
Mangrove Rd., Hert. 32 DS10
Manhattan Ct., Nthlt. 136 BX69
Manilla St. E14 163 EA75
Manister Rd. SE2 166 EU76
Manitoba Ct. SE16 162 DW75
Renforth St.
Manitoba Gdns., Orp. 223 ET107
High St.
Manley Ct. N16 122 DT62
Stoke Newington High St.
Manley Rd., Hem.H. 40 BL19
Knightsbridge Way
Manley St. NW1 140 DG67
Manly Dixon Dr., Enf. 83 DY37
Mannamead, Epsom 232 CS119
Mannamead Clo., Epsom 232 CS119
Mannamead
Mannicotts, Welw.G.C. 29 CV09
Mannin Rd., Rom. 126 EV59
Manning Gdns., Har. 117 CK59
Manning Pl., Rich. 178 CM86
Grove Rd.
Manning Rd. E17 123 DY57
Southcote Rd.
Manning Rd., Dag. 146 FA65
Manning Rd., Orp. 206 EX99
Manning St., S.Ock. 148 FQ74
Manningford Clo. EC1 274 F2
Manningtree Clo. SW19 179 CY88
Manningtree Rd., Ruis. 115 BV63
Manningtree St. E1 142 DU72
White Ch. La.
Mannock Dr., Loug. 85 EQ40
Mannock Rd. N22 121 DP55
Mannock Rd., Dart. 168 FM83
Barnwell Rd.
Manns Clo., Islw. 177 CF85
Manns Rd., Edg. 96 CN51
Manoel Rd., Twick. 176 CC89
Manor Ave. SE4 163 DZ82
Manor Ave., Cat. 236 DS124
Manor Ave., Hem.H. 40 BK23
Manor Ave., Horn. 128 FJ57
Manor Ave., Houns. 156 BX83
Manor Ave., Nthlt. 136 BZ66
Manor Chase, Wey. 213 BP106
Manor Clo. E17 101 DY54
Manor Rd.
Manor Clo. NW7 96 CR50
Manor Dr.
Manor Clo. NW9 118 CP57
Manor Clo. SE28 146 EW73
Manor Clo., Barn. 79 CY42
Manor Clo., Berk. 38 AW19
Manor Clo., Dag. 147 FD65
Manor Clo. (Crayford), Dart. 167 FD84
Manor Clo. (Wilmington), Dart. 187 FG90
Manor Clo., Hat. 45 CT15
Manor Clo., Hert. 32 DR07
Manor Clo., Horl. 268 DF148
Manor Clo., Lthd. 245 BS128
Manor Clo., Rom. 127 FG57
Manor Rd.
Manor Clo., Ruis. 115 BT60
Manor Clo., S.Ock. 148 FQ74
Manor Clo., Warl. 237 DY117
Manor Clo., Wok. 227 BF116
Manor Clo., Wor.Pk. 198 CS102
Manor Clo. S., S.Ock. 148 FQ74
Manor Clo.
Manor Cotts., Nthwd. 93 BT53
Manor Cotts. App. N2 98 DC54
Manor Ct. N2 120 DF57
Manor Ct. SW6 160 DB81
Bagley's La.
Manor Ct., Enf. 82 DV36
Manor Rd.
Manor Ct., Rad. 77 CF37
Common La.
Manor Ct., Twick. 176 CC89
Manor Ct., Wem. 118 CL64
Manor Ct., Wey. 213 BP105
Manor Ct. Rd. W7 137 CE73
Manor Cres., Beac. 89 AR50
Manor Cres., Guil. 242 AV132
Manor Cres., Horn. 128 FJ57
Manor Cres., Surb. 198 CN100
Manor Cres., W.Byf. 212 BM113
Manor Dr. N14 99 DH45
Manor Dr. N20 98 DE48
Manor Dr. NW7 96 CR50
Manor Dr., Add. 212 BG110
Manor Dr., Amer. 55 AP36
Manor Dr., Epsom 216 CS107
Manor Dr., Esher 197 CF104
Manor Dr., Felt. 176 BX92
Manor Dr., Horl. 268 DF148
Manor Dr., St.Alb. 60 CA27
Manor Dr., Sun. 195 BU96
Manor Dr., Surb. 198 CM100
Manor Dr., Wem. 118 CM63
Manor Dr., The, Wor.Pk. 198 CS102
Manor Dr. N., N.Mal. 198 CR100
Manor Dr. N., Wor.Pk. 198 CS102
Manor Est. SE16 162 DV77
Manor Fm. 208 FM101
(Farningham), Dart.
Manor Fm. Ave., Shep. 195 BP100
Manor Fm. Clo., Wind. 151 AM83
Manor Fm. Dr. E4 102 EE48
Manor Fm. Est., Stai. 172 AW86
Manor Fm. La., Egh. 173 BA92
Manor Fm. Rd., Enf. 82 DV36
Manor Fm. Rd., Th.Hth. 201 DN96
Manor Fm. Rd., Wem. 137 CK67
Manor Fm. Way, Beac. 89 AR51
Orchard Rd.
Manor Flds. SW15 179 CX86
Manor Gdns. N7 121 DL62
Manor Gdns. SW20 199 CZ96
Manor Gdns. W3 158 CN77
Manor Gdns., Gdmg. 258 AS144
Farncombe St.
Manor Gdns., Guil. 242 AV132
Manor Gdns., Hmptn. 176 CB94
Manor Gdns., H.Wyc. 110 AE58
Manor Gdns., Lthd. 246 BX128
Manor Gdns., Rich. 158 CM84
Manor Gdns., Ruis. 116 BW64
Manor Gdns., S.Croy. 220 DT107
Manor Gdns., Sun. 195 BU95
Manor Gate, Nthlt. 136 BY66
Manor Grn. Rd., Epsom 216 CP113
Manor Gro. SE15 162 DW79
Manor Gro., Beck. 203 EB96
Manor Gro., Maid. 150 AD80
Manor Gro., Rich. 158 CN84
Manor Hall Ave. NW4 97 CW54
Manor Hall Dr. NW4 97 CX54
Manor Hatch, Harl. 52 EU17
Manor Hatch Clo., Harl. 52 EV16
Tumbler Rd.
Manor Ho. Ct., Epsom 216 CQ113
Manor Ho. Ct., Shep. 195 BP101
Manor Ho. Dr. NW6 139 CX66
Manor Ho. Dr., Nthwd. 93 BP52
Ducks Hill Rd.
Manor Ho. Gdns., Abb.L. 59 BR31
Manor Ho. La., Slou. 152 AV80
Horton Rd.
Manor Ho. Way, Islw. 157 CH83
Manor La. SE12 184 EE86
Manor La. SE13 184 EE85
Manor La., Felt. 175 BU89
High St.
Manor La., Ger.Cr. 112 AX59
Manor La., Hayes 155 BR79
Manor La. 209 FW101
(Fawkham), Long.
Manor La., Sev. 209 FW103
Manor La., Sun. 195 BU96
Manor La., Sutt. 218 DC106
Manor La., Tad. 250 DA129
Manor La. Ter. SE13 164 EE84
Manor Leaze, Egh. 173 BB92
Manor Lo., Guil. 242 AV132
Manor Ms. NW6 140 DA68
Cambridge Ave.
Manor Ms. SE4 163 DZ82
Manor Mt. SE23 182 DW88
Manor Par. NW10 139 CT68
Station Rd.
Manor Par., Hat. 45 CT15
Green Las.
Manor Pk. SE13 183 ED85
Manor Pk., Chis. 205 ER96
Manor Pk., Rich. 158 CM84
Manor Pk. Clo., W.Wick. 203 EB102
Manor Pk. Cres., Edg. 96 CN51
Manor Pk. Dr., Har. 116 CB55
Manor Pk. Gdns., Edg. 96 CN50
Manor Pk. Par. SE13 163 ED84
Lee High Rd.
Manor Pk. Rd. E12 124 EK63
Manor Pk. Rd. N2 120 DC55
Manor Pk. Rd. NW10 139 CT67
Manor Pk. Rd., Chis. 205 EQ95
Manor Pk. Rd., Sutt. 218 DC106
Manor Pk. Rd., W.Wick. 203 EB102
Manor Pl. SE17 279 H10
Manor Pl. SE17 161 DP78
Manor Pl., Chis. 205 ER96
Manor Pl., Dart. 188 FL88
Highfield Rd. S.
Manor Pl., Felt. 175 BU88
Manor Pl., Mitch. 201 DJ97
Manor Pl., Stai. 174 BH92
Manor Pl., Sutt. 218 DB106
Manor Pl., Walt. 195 BT101
Manor Rd.
Manor Rd. E10 123 EA59
Manor Rd. E15 144 EE68
Manor Rd. E16 144 EE70
Manor Rd. E17 101 DY54
Manor Rd. N16 122 DR61
Manor Rd. N17 100 DU53
Manor Rd. N22 99 DL51
Manor Rd. SE25 202 DU98
Manor Rd. SW20 199 CZ96
Manor Rd. W13 137 CG73
Manor Rd., Ashf. 174 BM92
Manor Rd., Bark. 145 ET65
Manor Rd., Barn. 79 CY43
Manor Rd., Beac. 89 AR50
Manor Rd., Beck. 203 EA96
Manor Rd., Bex. 187 FB88
Manor Rd., Chesh. 54 AP29
Lansdowne Rd.
Manor Rd., Chig. 103 EN51
Manor Rd., Dag. 147 FC65
Manor Rd., Dart. 167 FE84
Manor Rd., E.Mol. 197 CD98
Manor Rd., Enf. 82 DQ40
Manor Rd., Erith 167 FF79
Manor Rd., Grav. 191 GH86
Manor Rd., Grays 170 GC79
Manor Rd. 169 FW79
(West Thurrock), Grays
Manor Rd., Guil. 242 AV131
Manor Rd., Harl. 36 EW10
Manor Rd., Har. 117 CG58
Manor Rd., Hat. 28 CR14
Manor Rd., Hayes 135 BU72
Manor Rd., Hodd. 49 EA16
Manor Rd., Loug. 84 EH44
Manor Rd. 84 EH39
(High Beach), Loug.
Manor Rd., Mitch. 201 DJ98
Manor Rd., Pot.B. 63 CZ31
Manor Rd., Red. 251 DJ129
Manor Rd., Reig. 249 CZ132
Manor Rd., Rich. 158 CM83
Manor Rd., Rom. 127 FG57
Manor Rd. 126 EX58
(Chadwell Heath), Rom.
Manor Rd. 104 EW47
(Lambourne End), Rom.
Manor Rd., Ruis. 115 BR60
Manor Rd., St.Alb. 43 CE19
Manor Rd. 61 CJ26
(London Colney), St.Alb.
Manor Rd., Sev. 240 EX124
Manor Rd., Sid. 186 EU90
Manor Rd., Sutt. 217 CZ108
Manor Rd., Swans. 189 FX86
Manor Rd., Tedd. 177 CG92
Manor Rd., Til. 171 GG82
Manor Rd., Twick. 176 CC89
Manor Rd., Wall. 219 DH105
Manor Rd., Wal.Abb. 67 ED33
Manor Rd., Walt. 195 BT101
Manor Rd., Wat. 75 BU39
Manor Rd., W.Wick. 203 EB103
Manor Rd., West. 238 EL120
Manor Rd., Wind. 151 AL82
Manor Rd., Wok. 226 AW116
Manor Rd. 227 BF123
(Send Marsh), Wok.
Manor Rd., Wdf.Grn. 103 EM51
Manor Rd. N., Esher 197 CF104
Manor Rd. N., T.Ditt. 197 CG103
Manor Rd. N., Wall. 219 DH105
Manor Rd. S., Esher 215 CE105
Manor Sq., Dag. 126 EW61
Manor St., Berk. 38 AW19
Manor Vale, Brent. 157 CJ78
Manor Vw. N3 98 DB54
Manor Wk., Wey. 213 BP106
Manor Way E4 101 ED49
Manor Way NW9 118 CS56
Manor Way SE3 164 EF84
Manor Way, Amer. 55 AM44
Manor Way, Bans. 234 DF116
Manor Way, Beck. 203 EA96
Manor Way, Bex. 186 FA88
Manor Way, Bexh. 167 FD83
Manor Way, Borwd. 78 CQ40
Manor Way, Brwd. 108 FU48
Manor Way, Brom. 204 EL100
Manor Way, Chesh. 54 AR30
Manor Way, Egh. 173 AZ93
Manor Way, Grays 170 GB80
Manor Way, Grays 170 GD80
(Little Thurrock Marshes)
Manor Way, Guil. 258 AS137
Manor Way, Har. 116 CB56
Manor Way, Lthd. 230 CC115
Manor Way, Mitch. 201 DJ97
Manor Way, Orp. 205 EQ99
Manor Way, Pot.B. 64 DA30
Manor Way, Pur. 219 DL112
Manor Way, Rain. 147 FE72
Manor Way, Rick. 74 BN42
Manor Way, Ruis. 115 BS59
Manor Way, S.Croy. 220 DS107
Manor Way, Sthl. 156 BX77
Manor Way, Swans. 169 FX84
Manor Way, Til. 170 GC80
Manor Way 67 DY31
(Cheshunt), Wal.Cr.
Russells Ride
Manor Way, Wok. 227 BB121
Manor Way, Wor.Pk. 198 CS102
Manor Way, The, Wall. 219 DH105
Manor Way Ind. Est., Grays 170 GC80
Manor Waye, Uxb. 134 BK67
Manor Wd. Rd., Pur. 219 DL113
Manorbrook SE3 164 EG84
Manorcrofts Rd., Egh. 173 BA93
Manordene Clo., T.Ditt. 197 CG102
Manordene Rd. SE28 146 EW72
Manorfield Clo. N19 121 DJ63
Tufnell Pk. Rd.
Manorfields Clo., Chis. 205 ET97
Manorgate Rd., Kings.T. 198 CN95
Manorhall Gdns. E10 123 EA60
Manorhouse La., Lthd. 246 BY126
Manorside, Barn. 79 CY42
Manorside Clo. SE2 166 EW77
Manorville Rd., Hem.H. 40 BJ24
Manorway, Enf. 100 DS45
Manorway, Wdf.Grn. 102 EJ50
Manpreet Ct. E12 125 EM64
Morris Ave.
Manresa Rd. SW3 160 DE78
Mansard Beeches SW17 180 DG92
Mansard Clo., Horn. 127 FG61
Mansard Clo., Pnr. 116 BX55
Mansards, The, St.Alb. 43 CE19
Avenue Rd.
Manscroft Rd., Hem.H. 40 BH18
Manse Clo., Hayes 155 BR79
Manse Rd. N16 122 DT62
Manse Way, Swan. 207 FG98
Mansel Clo., Guil. 242 AV129
Mansel Clo., Slou. 132 AV71
Mansel Gro. E17 101 EA53
Mansel Rd. SW19 179 CY93
Mansell Clo., Wind. 151 AL82
Mansell Rd. W3 158 CR75
Mansell Rd., Grnf. 136 CB71
Mansell St. E1 142 DT72
Mansell Way, Cat. 236 DR122
Manser Rd., Rain. 147 FE69
Mansergh Clo. SE18 164 EL80
Mansfield, Saw. 36 EU06
Mansfield Ave. N15 122 DR56
Mansfield Ave., Barn. 80 DF44
Mansfield Ave., Ruis. 115 BV60
Mansfield Clo. N9 82 DU44
Mansfield Clo., Orp. 206 EX101
Mansfield Clo., Wey. 213 BP106
Mansfield Dr., Hayes 135 BS70
Mansfield Dr., Red. 251 DK128
Mansfield Gdns., Hert. 32 DQ07
Mansfield Gdns., Horn. 128 FK61
Mansfield Hill E4 101 EB46
Mansfield Ms. W1 273 H7
Mansfield Pl. NW3 120 DC63
New End
Mansfield Rd. E11 124 EH58
Mansfield Rd. E17 123 DZ56
Mansfield Rd. NW3 120 DF64
Mansfield Rd. W3 138 CP70
Mansfield Rd., Chess. 215 CJ106
Mansfield Rd., Ilf. 125 EN61
Mansfield Rd., S.Croy. 220 DR107
Mansfield Rd., Swan. 187 FE93
Mansfield St. W1 273 H7
Mansfield St. W1 141 DH71
Mansford St. E2 142 DU68
Manship Rd., Mitch. 180 DG94
Mansion Gdns. NW3 120 DB62
Mansion Ho. EC4 275 K9
Mansion Ho. Pl. EC4 275 K9
Mansion La., Iver 133 BC74
Manson Ms. SW7 160 DC77
Manson Pl. SW7 160 DD77
Manstead Gdns., Rain. 147 FH72
Mansted Gdns., Rom. 126 EW59
Manston Ave., Sthl. 156 CA77
Manston Clo. SE20 202 DW95
Garden Rd.
Manston Clo. 66 DW30
(Cheshunt), Wal.Cr.
Manston Gro., Kings.T. 177 CK92
Richmond Rd.
Manston Rd., Guil. 243 BA130
Manston Rd., Harl. 51 ES15
Manston Way, Horn. 147 FH65
Manstone Rd. NW2 119 CY64
Manthorp Rd. SE18 165 EQ78
Mantilla Rd. SW17 180 DG91
Mantle Rd. SE4 163 DY83
Mantle Way E15 144 EE66
Romford Rd.
Mantlet Clo. SW16 181 DJ94
Manton Ave. W7 157 CF75
Manton Clo., Hayes 135 BS73
Manton Rd. SE2 166 EU77
Mantua St. SW11 160 DD83
Mantus Clo. E1 142 DW70
Mantus Rd.
Mantus Rd. E1 142 DW70
Manus Way N20 98 DC47
Blakeney Clo.
Manville Gdns. SW17 181 DH89
Manville Rd. SW17 180 DG89
Manwood Rd. SE4 183 DZ85
Manwood St. E16 145 EM74
Manygate La., Shep. 195 BQ101
Manygates SW12 181 DH89
Maori Rd., Guil. 243 AZ134
Mape St. E2 142 DV70
Mapesbury Rd. NW2 139 CY66
Mapeshill Pl. NW2 139 CW65
Willesden La.
Maple Ave. E4 101 DZ50
Maple Ave. W3 138 CS74
Maple Ave., Har. 116 CB61
Maple Ave., St.Alb. 42 CC16
Maple Ave., Upmin. 128 FP62
Maple Ave., West Dr. 134 BL73
Maple Clo. N16 122 DU58
Maple Clo. SW4 181 DK86
Maple Clo., Brwd. 109 FZ48
Cherry Ave.
Maple Clo., Buck.H. 102 EK48
Maple Clo., Epp. 85 ER37
Loughton La.
Maple Clo., Hmptn. 176 BZ93
Maple Clo., Hat. 45 CU19
Elm Dr.
Maple Clo., Hayes 136 BX69
Maple Clo., Horn. 127 FH62
Maple Clo., Ilf. 103 ES50
Maple Clo., Mitch. 201 DH95
Maple Clo., Orp. 205 ER99
Maple Clo., Ruis. 115 BV58
Maple Clo., Swan. 207 FE96
Maple Clo. (Bushey), Wat. 76 BY40
Maple Clo., Whyt. 236 DT117
Maple Ct., Egh. 172 AV93
Ashwood Rd.
Maple Ct., N.Mal. 198 CR97
Maple Ct., Ware 33 ED11
Maple Cres., Sid. 186 EU86
Maple Cres., Slou. 132 AV73
Maple Cross Ind. Est., Rick. 91 BF49
Maple Gdns., Edg. 96 CS52
Maple Gdns., Stai. 174 BL89
Maple Gate, Loug. 85 EN40
Maple Grn., Hem.H. 39 BE18
Maple Gro. NW9 118 CQ59
Maple Gro. W5 157 CJ76
Maple Gro., Brent. 157 CH80
Maple Gro., Guil. 242 AX132
Maple Gro., Sthl. 136 BZ71
Maple Gro., Wat. 75 BU39
Maple Gro., Welw.G.C. 29 CZ06
Maple Gro., Wok. 226 AY121
Maple Hill, Hem.H. 56 AX30
Ley Hill Rd.
Maple Ind. Est., Felt. 175 BU90
Maple Leaf Clo., Abb.L. 59 BU32
Stewart Clo.
Maple Leaf Clo., West. 238 EK116
Main Rd.
Maple Leaf Dr., Sid. 185 ET88
Maple Leaf Sq. SE16 163 DX75
St. Elmos Rd.
Maple Lo. Clo., Rick. 91 BE49
Maple Ms. NW6 140 DB68
Kilburn Pk. Rd.
Maple Ms. SW16 181 DM92
Maple Pl. W1 273 L5
Maple Pl., Bans. 233 CX115
Maple Pl., West Dr. 134 BM73
Maple Ave.
Maple Rd. E11 124 EE58
Maple Rd. SE20 202 DV95
Maple Rd., Ash. 231 CK119
Maple Rd., Dart. 188 FJ88
Maple Rd., Grav. 191 GJ91
Maple Rd., Grays 170 GC79
Maple Rd., Hayes 136 BW69
Maple Rd., Red. 266 DF138
Maple Rd., Surb. 197 CK100
Maple Rd., Whyt. 236 DT117
Maple Rd., Wok. 228 BG124
Maple Springs, Wal.Abb. 68 EG33
Maple St. W1 273 K6
Maple St. W1 141 DJ71
Maple St., Rom. 127 FC56
Maple Wk. W10 139 CX70
Droop St.
Maple Wk., Sutt. 218 DB110
Maple Way, Couls. 235 DH121
Maple Way, Felt. 175 BU90
Maplecourt Wk., Wind. 151 AN77
Common Rd.
Maplecroft Clo. E6 144 EL72
Allhallows Rd.
Maplecroft La., Wal.Abb. 50 EE21
Mapledale Ave., Croy. 202 DU103
Mapledene, Chis. 185 EQ92
Kemnal Rd.
Mapledene Rd. E8 142 DU66
Maplefield, St.Alb. 60 CB29
Maplefield La., Ch.St.G. 72 AV41
Maplehurst, Lthd. 231 CD123
Maplehurst Clo., Kings.T. 198 CL98
Mapleleafe Gdns., Ilf. 125 EP55
Maples, The, Bans. 218 DB114
Maples, The, Cher. 211 BC107
Maples, The, Harl. 51 EP20
Maples Pl. E1 142 DV71
Raven Row
Maplescombe La. 208 FN104
(Farningham), Dart.
Maplestead Rd. SW2 181 DM87
Maplestead Rd., Dag. 146 EV67
Maplethorpe Rd., Th.Hth. 201 DN98
Mapleton Clo., Brom. 204 EG100
Mapleton Cres. SW18 180 DB86
Mapleton Cres., Enf. 82 DW38
Mapleton Rd. E4 101 EC48
Mapleton Rd. SW18 180 DA86
Mapleton Rd., Eden. 255 ET133
Mapleton Rd., Enf. 82 DV40
Mapleton Rd., West. 255 ES131
Maplin Clo. N21 81 DM44
Maplin Pk., Slou. 153 BB75
Maplin Rd. E16 144 EG72
Maplin St. E3 143 DZ69
Mapperley Dr., Wdf.Grn. 102 EE52
Forest Dr.
Mar Rd., S.Ock. 149 FW70
Maran Way, Erith 166 EX75
Marban Rd. W9 139 CZ69
Marbeck Clo., Wind. 151 AK81
Marble Arch W1 272 D10
Marble Arch W1 140 DF73
Marble Clo. W3 138 CP74
Marble Dr. NW2 119 CX60
Marble Hill Clo., Twick. 177 CH87
Marble Hill Gdns., Twick. 177 CH87
Marble Quay E1 142 DU74
Marbles Way, Tad. 233 CX119
Marbrook Ct. SE12 184 EJ90
Marcellina Way, Orp. 205 ES104
Marcet Rd., Dart. 188 FJ85
March Rd., Twick. 177 CG87
March Rd., Wey. 212 BN106
Marchant Rd. E11 123 ED61
Marchant St. SE14 163 DY79
Sanford St.
Marchbank Rd. W14 159 CZ79
Marchmant Clo., Horn. 128 FJ62
Marchmont Gdns., Rich. 178 CM85
Marchmont Rd.
Marchmont Grn., Hem.H. 40 BK18
Paston Rd.
Marchmont Rd., Rich. 178 CM85
Marchmont Rd., Wall. 219 DJ108
Marchmont St. WC1 273 P4
Marchmont St. WC1 141 DL70
Marchside Clo., Houns. 156 BX81
Springwell Rd.
Marchwood Clo. SE5 162 DS80
Marchwood Cres. W5 137 CJ72
Marcia Rd. SE1 279 N9
Marcia Rd. SE1 162 DS77
Marcilly Rd. SW18 180 DD85
Marco Rd. W6 159 CV76
Marcon Pl. E8 122 DV64
Marconi Rd. E10 123 EA60
Marconi Rd., Grav. 190 GD90
Marconi Way, Sthl. 136 CB72
Marcourt Lawns W5 138 CL70
Marcus Ct. E15 144 EE67
Marcus Garvey Way SE24 161 DN84
Marcus Rd., Dart. 187 FG87
Marcus St. E15 144 EE67
Marcus St. SW18 180 DB86
Marcus Ter. SW18 180 DB86
Mardale Dr. NW9 118 CR57
Mardell Rd., Croy. 203 DX99
Marden Ave., Brom. 204 EF100
Marden Clo., Chig. 104 EV47
Marden Cres., Bex. 187 FC85
Marden Cres., Croy. 201 DM100
Marden Pk., Cat. 253 DZ125
Marden Rd. N17 122 DS55
Marden Rd., Croy. 201 DM100
Marden Rd., Rom. 127 FE58
Kingsmead Ave.
Marden Sq. SE16 162 DV76
Marder Rd. W13 157 CG75
Mardon St. E14 143 DY71
Mardyke Rd., Harl. 36 EU13
Mare St. E8 142 DV67
Marechal Niel Ave., Sid. 185 ER90
Mares Fld., Croy. 202 DS104
Mareschal Rd., Guil. 258 AW136
Marescroft Rd., Slou. 131 AL70
Maresfield Gdns. NW3 120 DC64
Marfleet Clo., Cars. 200 DE103
Marford Rd., St.Alb. 28 CN07
Marford Rd., Welw.G.C. 28 CR09
Margaret Ave. E4 83 EB44
Margaret Ave., Brwd. 109 FZ45
Margaret Ave., St.Alb. 43 CD18
Margaret Bondfield Ave., Bark. 146 EU66
Margaret Bldgs. N16 122 DT60
Margaret Rd.
Margaret Clo., Abb.L. 59 BT32
Margaret Clo., Epp. 70 EU29
Margaret Rd.
Margaret Clo., Pot.B. 64 DC33
Margaret Clo., Rom. 127 FH57
Margaret Rd.
Margaret Clo., Stai. 174 BK93
Charles Rd.
Margaret Clo., Wal.Abb. 67 EC33
Margaret Ct. W1 273 K8
Margaret Dr., Horn. 128 FM60
Margaret Gardner Dr. SE9 185 EM89
Margaret Rd. N16 122 DT60
Margaret Rd., Barn. 80 DD42
Margaret Rd., Bex. 186 EX86
Margaret Rd., Epp. 70 EU29
Margaret Rd., Guil. 258 AW135

Maryland Pk. E15 124 EE64
Maryland Pt. E15 144 EE65
Leytonstone Rd.
Maryland Rd. E15 123 ED64
Maryland Rd. N22 99 DM51
Maryland Rd., Th.Hth. 201 DP95
Maryland Sq. E15 124 EE64
Maryland St. E15 123 ED64
Maryland Wk. N1 142 DQ67
Popham St.
Maryland Way, Sun. 195 BU96
Marylands Rd. W9 140 DA70
Marylebone Flyover NW1 272 B7
Marylebone Flyover W2 272 A7
Marylebone High St. W1 272 G6
Marylebone High St. W1 140 DG71
Marylebone La. W1 272 G7
Marylebone La. W1 140 DG72
Marylebone Ms. W1 273 H7
Marylebone Ms. W1 141 DH71
Marylebone Pas. W1 273 L8
Marylebone Rd. NW1 272 E6
Marylebone Rd. NW1 140 DE71
Marylebone St. W1 272 G7
Marylebone St. W1 140 DG71
Marylee Way SE11 278 C10
Marylee Way SE11 161 DM77
Maryon Gro. SE7 164 EL77
Maryon Ms. NW3 120 DE63
South End Rd.
Maryon Rd. SE7 164 EL77
Maryon Rd. SE18 164 EL77
Mary's Clo. N17 100 DT53
Kemble Rd.
Mary's Ter., Twick. 177 CG87
Maryside, Slou. 152 AY75
Masbro Rd. W14 159 CX76
Mascalls Ct. SE7 164 EJ79
Victoria Way
Mascalls Gdns., Brwd. 108 FT49
Mascalls La., Brwd. 108 FT49
Mascalls Rd. SE7 164 EJ79
Mascotte Rd. SW15 159 CX84
Mascotts Clo. NW2 119 CV62
Masefield Ave., Borwd. 78 CP43
Masefield Ave., Sthl. 136 CA73
Masefield Ave., Stan. 95 CF50
Masefield Clo., Chesh. 54 AP28
Masefield Clo., Erith 167 FF81
Masefield Clo., Rom. 106 FJ53
Masefield Ct., Brwd. 108 FW49
Masefield Cres. N14 81 DJ43
Masefield Cres., Rom. 106 FJ53
Masefield Dr., Upmin. 128 FQ59
Masefield Gdns. E6 145 EN70
Masefield La., Hayes 135 BV70
Masefield Rd., Dart. 188 FP85
Masefield Rd., Grav. 190 GD90
Masefield Rd., Grays 170 GE75
Masefield Rd., Hmptn. 176 BZ91
Wordsworth Rd.
Masefield Vw., Orp. 205 EQ104
Masefield Way, Stai. 174 BM88
Mashie Rd. W3 138 CS72
Mashiters Hill, Rom. 105 FD54
Mashiters Wk., Rom. 127 FE55
Maskall Clo. SW2 181 DN88
Maskani Wk. SW16 181 DJ94
Bates Cres.
Maskell Rd. SW17 180 DC90
Maskelyne Clo. SW11 160 DE81
Mason Bradbear Ct. N1 142 DR65
St. Paul's Rd.
Mason Clo. E16 144 EG73
Mason Clo. SE16 162 DU78
Stevenson Cres.
Mason Clo. SW20 199 CX95
Mason Clo., Bexh. 167 FB83
Mason Clo., Borwd. 78 CQ40
Banks Rd.
Mason Clo., Hmptn. 196 BZ95
Mason Ct., Slou. 131 AL73
Mason Dr., Rom. 106 FL54
Whitmore Ave.
Mason Rd., Wdf.Grn. 102 EE49
Mason St. SE17 279 L8
Mason St. SE17 162 DR77
Mason Way, Wal.Abb. 68 EE33
Masonic Hall Rd., Cher. 193 BF100
Masons Arms Ms. W1 273 J10
Masons Ave. EC2 275 K8
Masons Ave., Croy. 202 DQ104
Masons Ave., Har. 117 CF56
Mason's Bri. Rd., Red. 267 DH139
Masons Ct., Wem. 118 CN61
Masons Grn. La. W3 138 CN70
Dukes Rd.
Masons Hill SE18 165 EP77
Masons Hill, Brom. 204 EG97
Masons Paddock, Dor. 247 CG134
Mason's Pl. EC1 275 H2
Mason's Pl. EC1 142 DQ69
Masons Pl., Mitch. 200 DF95
Masons Rd., Enf. 82 DV36
Masons Rd., Hem.H. 41 BP19
Masons Rd., Slou. 131 AL73
Mason's Yd. SW1 277 L2
Mason's Yd. SW19 179 CX92
High St. Wimbledon
Massetts Rd., Horl. 268 DF149
Massey Clo. N11 99 DH50
Grove Rd.
Massie Rd. E8 142 DU65
Graham Rd.
Massinger St. SE17 279 M9
Massingham St. E1 143 DX70
Masson Ave., Ruis. 136 BW65
Mast Ho. Ter. E14 163 EA77
Master Clo., Oxt. 254 EE129
Church La.
Master Gunner Pl. SE18 164 EL80
Masterman Ho. SE5 162 DR80
Lomond Gro.
Masterman Rd. E6 144 EL69
Masters St. E1 143 DX71
Masthead Clo., Dart. 168 FQ84
Mastmaker Rd. E14 163 EA75
Maswell Pk. Cres., Houns. 176 CC85
Maswell Pk. Rd., Houns. 176 CB85
Matcham Rd. E11 124 EE62
Matching Rd., Bishop's Stortford 37 FH05
Matching Rd. (Old Harlow), Harl. 37 FB11
Matching Rd., Ong. 53 FH17
Matchless Dr. SE18 165 EN80
Red Lion La.
Matfield Clo., Brom. 204 EG99
Matfield Rd., Belv. 166 FA79
Matham Gro. SE22 162 DT84
Matham Rd., E.Mol. 197 CD99
Matheson Rd. W14 159 CZ77
Mathews Pk. Ave. E15 144 EF65
Mathias Clo., Epsom 216 CQ113
Mathisen Way, Slou. 153 BE81
Mathon Ct., Guil. 243 AZ134
Cross Las.
Matilda St. N1 141 DM67
Matlock Clo. SE24 162 DQ84
Matlock Clo., Barn. 79 CX44
Chesterfield Rd.
Matlock Ct. SE5 162 DR84
Denmark Hill Est.
Matlock Cres., Sutt. 217 CY105
Matlock Cres., Wat. 94 BW48
Matlock Gdns., Horn. 128 FL62
Matlock Gdns., Sutt. 217 CY105
Matlock Pl., Sutt. 217 CY105
Matlock Rd. E10 123 EC58
Matlock Rd., Cat. 236 DS121
Matlock St. E14 143 DY72
Matlock Way, N.Mal. 198 CR95
Matrimony Pl. SW8 161 DJ82
Wandsworth Rd.
Matson Ct., Wdf.Grn. 102 EE52
Bridle Path
Matthew Arnold Clo., Cob. 213 BU114
Matthew Clo. W10 139 CX70
Matthew Ct., Mitch. 201 DK99
Matthew Parker St. SW1 277 N5
Matthew Parker St. SW1 161 DK75
Matthew Rd., Red. 250 DF133
Matthew St., Reig. 266 DA138
Matthews Ave. E6 145 EN68
Matthews Clo. (Havering-atte-Bower), Rom. 106 FM53
Oak Rd.
Matthews Gdns., Croy. 221 ED111
Matthews Rd., Grnf. 117 CD64
Matthews St. SW11 160 DF82
Matthews Yd. WC2 273 P9
Matthias Rd. N16 122 DR64
Mattingley Way SE15 162 DT80
Daniel Gdns.
Mattison Rd. N4 121 DN58
Mattock La. W5 137 CJ74
Mattock La. W13 137 CH74
Maud Cashmore Way SE18 165 EM76
Leda Rd.
Maud Gdns. E13 144 EF67
Maud Gdns., Bark. 145 ET68
Maud Rd. E10 123 EC62
Maud Rd. E13 144 EF68
Maud St. E16 144 EF71
Maude Cres., Wat. 75 BV37
Maude Rd. E17 123 DY57
Maude Rd. SE5 162 DS81
Maude Rd., Beac. 89 AN54
Maude Rd., Swan. 187 FG93
Maude Ter. E17 123 DY56
Maudlin's Grn. E1 142 DU74
Marble Quay
Maudslay Rd. SE9 165 EM83
Maudsley Ho., Brent. 158 CL78
Mauleverer Rd. SW2 181 DL85
Maundeby Wk. NW10 138 CS65
Neasden La.
Maunder Rd. W7 137 CE74
Maunsel St. SW1 277 M8
Maunsel St. SW1 161 DK77
Maurice Ave. N22 99 DP54
Maurice Ave., Cat. 236 DR122
Maurice Brown Clo. NW7 97 CX50
Maurice St. W12 139 CV72
Maurice Wk. NW11 120 DC56
Maurier Clo., Nthlt. 136 BW67
Mauritius Rd. SE10 164 EE77
Maury Rd. N16 122 DU61
Mavelstone Clo., Brom. 204 EL95
Mavelstone Rd., Brom. 204 EK95
Maverton Rd. E3 143 EA67
Mavis Ave., Epsom 216 CS106
Mavis Clo., Epsom 216 CS106
Mavis Gro., Horn. 128 FL61
Mavis Wk. E6 144 EL71
Tollgate Rd.
Mawbey Est. SE1 162 DT78
Mawbey Pl. SE1 162 DT78
Mawbey Rd. SE1 162 DT78
Old Kent Rd.
Mawbey Rd., Cher. 211 BD107
Mawbey St. SW8 161 DL80
Mawney Clo., Rom. 105 FB54
Mawney Rd., Rom. 105 FB54
Mawson Clo. SW20 199 CY96
Mawson La. W4 159 CT79
Great W. Rd.
Maxey Gdns., Dag. 126 EY63
Maxey Rd. SE18 165 EQ77
Maxey Rd., Dag. 126 EY64
Maxfield Clo. N20 98 DC45
Maxilla Gdns. W10 139 CX72
Cambridge Gdns.
Maxilla Wk. W10 139 CX72
Kingsdown Clo.
Maxim Rd. N21 81 DN44
Maxim Rd., Dart. 187 FE85
Maxim Rd., Erith 167 FE77
Maximfeldt Rd., Erith 167 FE78
Maxted Clo., Hem.H. 41 BQ18
Maxted Pk., Har. 117 CE59
Maxted Rd. SE15 162 DT83
Maxted Rd., Hem.H. 41 BP17
Maxwell Clo., Croy. 201 DL101
Franklin Way
Maxwell Clo., Rick. 92 BG47
Maxwell Dr., W.Byf. 212 BJ111
Maxwell Gdns., Orp. 205 ET104
Maxwell Ri., Wat. 94 BY45
Maxwell Rd. SW6 160 DB80
Maxwell Rd., Ashf. 175 BQ93
Maxwell Rd., Beac. 89 AK52
Maxwell Rd., Borwd. 78 CP41
Maxwell Rd., Nthwd. 93 BR52
Maxwell Rd., St.Alb. 43 CH21
Maxwell Rd., Well. 166 EU83
Maxwell Rd., West Dr. 154 BM77
Maxwelton Ave. NW7 96 CR50
Maxwelton Clo. NW7 96 CR50
May Ave., Grav. 191 GF88
Dover Rd. E.
May Ave., Orp. 206 EV99
May Clo., Chess. 216 CM107
May Clo., St.Alb. 43 CD18
May Cotts., Wat. 76 BW43
Watford Fld. Rd.
May Ct. SW19 200 DB95
May Ct., Grays 170 GE79
Medlar Rd.
May Gdns., Wem. 137 CJ69
May Rd. E4 101 EA51
May Rd. E13 144 EG68
May Rd., Dart. 188 FM91
May Rd., Twick. 177 CE88
May St. W14 159 CZ78
North End Rd.
May Tree La., Stan. 95 CF52
May Wk. E13 144 EH68
Queens Rd. W.
Maya Rd. N2 120 DC56
Mayall Rd. SE24 181 DP85
Maybank Ave. E18 102 EH54
Maybank Ave., Horn. 128 FJ64
Maybank Ave., Wem. 117 CF64
Maybank Gdns., Pnr. 115 BU57
Maybank Lo., Horn. 128 FJ64
Maybank Rd. E18 102 EH53
Maybells Commercial Est., Bark. 146 EX68
Mayberry Pl., Surb. 198 CM101
Maybourne Clo. SE26 182 DV92
Maybourne Ri., Wok. 226 AX124
Maybrick Rd., Horn. 128 FJ57
Maybrook Meadow Est., Bark. 126 EU64
Maybury Ave., Dart. 188 FQ88
Maybury Ave. (Cheshunt), Wal.Cr. 66 DV28
Maybury Clo., Loug. 85 EP42
Homecroft Gdns.
Maybury Clo., Orp. 205 EP99
Maybury Clo., Slou. 131 AK72
Maybury Clo., Tad. 233 CY119
Ballards Grn.
Maybury Gdns. NW10 139 CV65
Maybury Hill, Wok. 227 BB116
Maybury Ms. N6 121 DJ59
Maybury Rd. E13 144 EJ70
Maybury Rd., Bark. 145 ET68
Maybury Rd., Wok. 227 AZ117
Maybury St. SW17 180 DE92
Maybush Rd., Horn. 128 FL59
Maychurch Clo., Stan. 95 CK52
Maycock Gro., Nthwd. 93 BT51
Maycroft, Pnr. 93 BV54
Maycroft Ave., Grays 170 GD78
Maycroft Gdns., Grays 170 GD78
Maycroft Rd. (Cheshunt), Wal.Cr. 66 DS26
Maycross Ave., Mord. 199 CZ97
Mayday Gdns. SE3 164 EL82
Mayday Rd., Th.Hth. 201 DP100
Maydwell Lo., Borwd. 78 CM40
Mayell Clo., Lthd. 231 CJ123
Mayerne Rd. SE9 184 EK85
Mayes Clo., Swan. 207 FG98
Mayes Clo., Warl. 237 DX118
Mayes Rd. N22 99 DM54
Mayesbrook Rd., Bark. 145 ET67
Mayesbrook Rd., Dag. 126 EV62
Mayesbrook Rd., Ilf. 126 EU62
Mayesford Rd., Rom. 126 EW59
Mayeswood Rd. SE12 184 EJ90
Mayfair Ave., Bexh. 166 EX81
Mayfair Ave., Ilf. 125 EM61
Mayfair Ave., Rom. 126 EX58
Mayfair Ave., Twick. 176 CC87
Mayfair Ave., Wor.Pk. 199 CT102
Mayfair Clo., Beck. 203 EB95
Mayfair Clo., St.Alb. 43 CJ15
Mayfair Clo., Surb. 198 CL102
Mayfair Gdns. N17 100 DQ51
Mayfair Gdns., Wdf.Grn. 102 EG52
Mayfair Ms. NW1 140 DF66
Regents Pk. Rd.
Mayfair Pl. W1 277 J2
Mayfair Pl. W1 141 DH74
Mayfair Rd., Dart. 188 FK85
Mayfair Ter. N14 99 DK45
Mayfare, Rick. 75 BR43
Mayfield, Bexh. 166 EZ83
Mayfield, Wal.Abb. 67 ED34
Roundhills
Mayfield, Welw.G.C. 29 CW05
Mayfield Ave. N12 98 DC49
Mayfield Ave. N14 99 DJ47
Mayfield Ave. W4 158 CS77
Mayfield Ave. W13 157 CH76
Mayfield Ave., Add. 212 BH110
Mayfield Ave., Ger.Cr. 112 AX56
Mayfield Ave., Har. 117 CH57
Mayfield Ave., Orp. 205 ET101
Mayfield Ave., Wdf.Grn. 102 EG51
Mayfield Clo. E8 142 DT65
Forest Rd.
Mayfield Clo. SW4 181 DK85
Mayfield Clo., Add. 212 BJ110
Mayfield Clo., Ashf. 175 BP93
Mayfield Clo., Harl. 36 EZ11
Mayfield Clo., Red. 266 DG140
Brookfield Clo.
Mayfield Clo., T.Ditt. 197 CH102
Mayfield Clo., Uxb. 135 BP69
Mayfield Clo., Walt. 213 BU105
Mayfield Cres. N9 82 DV44
Mayfield Cres., Th.Hth. 201 DM98
Mayfield Dr., Pnr. 116 BZ56
Mayfield Gdns. NW4 119 CX58
Mayfield Gdns. W7 137 CD72
Mayfield Gdns., Brwd. 108 FV46
Mayfield Gdns., Stai. 173 BF93
Mayfield Gdns., Walt. 213 BU105
Mayfield Rd. E4 101 EC47
Mayfield Rd. E8 142 DT66
Mayfield Rd. E13 144 EF70
Mayfield Rd. E17 101 DY54
Mayfield Rd. N8 121 DM57
Mayfield Rd. SW19 199 CZ95
Mayfield Rd. W3 138 CP73
Mayfield Rd. W12 158 CS75
Mayfield Rd., Belv. 167 FC77
Mayfield Rd., Brom. 204 EL99
Mayfield Rd., Dag. 126 EW60
Mayfield Rd., Enf. 83 DX40
Mayfield Rd., Grav. 191 GF87
Mayfield Rd., H.Wyc. 110 AE57
Mayfield Rd., S.Croy. 220 DR109
Mayfield Rd., Sutt. 218 DD107
Mayfield Rd., Th.Hth. 201 DM98
Mayfield Rd., Walt. 213 BU105
Mayfield Rd., Wey. 212 BM106
Mayfields, Grays 170 GC75
Mayfields, Swans. 190 FY86
Madden Clo.
Mayfields, Wem. 118 CN61
Mayfields Clo., Wem. 118 CN61
Mayflower Ave., Hem.H. 40 BK20
Mayflower Clo. SE16 163 DX77
Greenland Quay
Mayflower Clo., Hert. 31 DL11
Mayflower Clo., S.Ock. 149 FW70
Mayflower Clo., Wal.Abb. 50 EE22
Mayflower Ct. SE16 162 DW75
St. Marychurch St.
Mayflower Path, Brwd. 107 FW51
Eagle Way
Mayflower Rd. SW9 161 DL83
Mayflower Rd., Grays 169 FW78
Arterial Rd. W. Thurrock
Mayflower Rd., St.Alb. 60 CB27
Mayflower St. SE16 162 DW75
St. Marychurch St.
Mayflower Way, Beac. 110 AG55
Mayflower Way, Slou. 111 AR63
Mayfly Clo., Pnr. 116 BW59
Mayfly Gdns., Nthlt. 136 BX69
Ruislip Rd.
Mayford Clo. SW12 180 DF87
Mayford Clo., Beck. 203 DX97
Mayford Clo., Wok. 226 AX122
Mayford Rd. SW12 180 DF87
Maygood St. N1 141 DM68
Maygoods Clo., Uxb. 134 BK71
Maygoods Grn., Uxb. 134 BK71
Worcester Rd.
Maygoods La., Uxb. 134 BK71
Maygoods Vw., Uxb. 134 BJ71
Benbow Waye
Maygreen Cres., Horn. 127 FG59
Maygrove Rd. NW6 139 CZ65
Mayhall La., Amer. 55 AP35
Mayhew Clo. E4 101 EA48
Mayhill Rd. SE7 164 EH79
Mayhill Rd., Barn. 79 CY43
Maylands Ave., Hem.H. 41 BP17
Maylands Ave., Horn. 127 FH63
Maylands Dr., Sid. 186 EX90
Maylands Dr., Uxb. 134 BK65
Maylands Rd., Wat. 94 BW49
Maylands Way, Rom. 106 FQ51
Maylins Dr., Saw. 36 EX05
Maynard Clo. N15 122 DS56
Brunswick Rd.
Maynard Clo. SW6 160 DB80
Cambria St.
Maynard Clo., Erith 167 FF80
Maynard Ct., Wal.Abb. 68 EF34
Maynard Dr., St.Alb. 43 CD23
Maynard Path E17 123 EC57
Maynard Rd.
Maynard Pl., Pot.B. 65 DM29
Maynard Rd. E17 123 EC57
Maynard Rd., Hem.H. 40 BK21
Maynards, Horn. 128 FL59
Maynards Quay E1 142 DW73
Garnet St.
Mayne Ave., St.Alb. 42 BZ22
Maynooth Gdns., Cars. 200 DF101
Middleton Rd.
Mayo Clo. (Cheshunt), Wal.Cr. 66 DV28
Mayo Rd. NW10 138 CS65
Mayo Rd., Croy. 202 DR99
Mayo Rd., Walt. 195 BT101
Mayola Rd. E5 122 DW63
Mayor's La., Dart. 188 FJ92
Mayow Rd. SE23 183 DX90
Mayow Rd. SE26 183 DX91
Mayplace Ave., Dart. 167 FG84
Mayplace Clo., Bexh. 167 FB83
Mayplace La. SE18 165 EP80
Mayplace Rd. E., Bexh. 167 FB83
Mayplace Rd. E., Dart. 167 FE84
Mayplace Rd. W., Bexh. 166 FA84
Maypole Cres., Erith 168 FK79
Maypole Cres., Ilf. 103 ER52
Maypole Dr., Chig. 104 EU48
Maypole Rd., Grav. 191 GM88
Damigos Rd.
Maypole Rd., Maid. 130 AG71
Maypole Rd., Orp. 224 EZ106
Mayroyd Ave., Surb. 198 CN103
Mays Clo., Wey. 212 BM110
Eyston Dr.
Mays Ct. WC2 277 P1
Mays Gro., Wok. 227 BD123
Mays Hill Rd., Brom. 204 EE96
Mays La. E4 101 ED47
Mays La., Barn. 97 CU45
Mays Rd., Tedd. 177 CD92
Maysfield Rd., Wok. 227 BD123
Maysoule Rd. SW11 160 DD84
Mayswood Gdns., Dag. 147 FC65
Maythorne Clo., Wat. 75 BS42
Mayton St. N7 121 DM62
Maytree Clo., Edg. 96 CQ48
Maytree Clo., Guil. 242 AW131
Maytree Clo., Rain. 147 FE68
Maytree Cres., Wat. 75 BT35
Maytree Wk. SW2 181 DN89
Maytrees, Rad. 77 CG37
Mayville Est. N16 122 DS64
King Henry St.
Mayville Rd. E11 124 EE61
Mayville Rd., Ilf. 125 EP64
Maywater Clo., S.Croy. 220 DR111
Maywin Dr., Horn. 128 FM60
Maywood Clo., Beck. 183 EB94
Maze Hill SE3 164 EE80
Maze Hill SE10 164 EE79
Maze Rd., Rich. 158 CN80
Mazenod Ave. NW6 140 DA66
McAdam Clo., Hodd. 49 EA15
McAdam Dr., Enf. 81 DP40
Rowantree Rd.
McAuley Clo. SE1 278 D6
McAuley Clo. SE1 161 DN76
McAuley Clo. SE9 185 EP85
McAuliffe Dr., Slou. 111 AM63
McCall Clo. SW4 161 DL82
Jeffreys Rd.
McCall Cres. SE7 164 EL78
McCarthy Rd., Felt. 176 BX92
McCoid Way SE1 279 H5
McCrone Ms. NW3 140 DD65
Belsize La.
McCudden Rd., Dart. 168 FM83
Cornwall Rd.
McCullum Rd. E3 143 DZ67
McDermott Clo. SW11 160 DE83
McDermott Rd. SE15 162 DU83
McDonald Ct., Hat. 45 CU20
McDonough Clo., Chess. 216 CL105
McDowall Rd. SE5 162 DQ81
McDowell Clo. E16 144 EF71
McEntee Ave. E17 101 DY53
McEwan Way E15 143 ED67
McGrath Rd. E15 124 EF64
McGredy (Cheshunt), Wal.Cr. 66 DV29
McGregor Rd. W11 139 CZ71
McIntosh Clo., Rom. 127 FE55
McIntosh Clo., Wall. 219 DL108
McIntosh Rd., Rom. 127 FE55
McKay Rd. SW20 179 CV94
McKay Trd. Est., Slou. 153 BE82
McKellar Clo. (Bushey), Wat. 94 CC47
McKenzie Rd., Brox. 49 DZ20
McKerrell Rd. SE15 162 DU81
McLeod Rd. SE2 166 EU77
McLeod's Ms. SW7 160 DB77
McMillan Clo., Grav. 191 GJ91
Hawthorn Clo.
McMillan St. SE8 163 EA79
McNeil Rd. SE5 162 DS82
McNicol Dr. NW10 138 CQ68
Abbey Rd.
McRae La., Mitch. 200 DF101
Middleton Rd.
Mead, The N2 98 DC54
Mead, The W13 137 CH71
Mead, The, Ash. 232 CL119
Mead, The, Beac. 89 AL53
Mead, The, Beck. 203 EC95
Mead, The, Stan. 95 CJ53
Mead, The, Uxb. 114 BN61
Mead, The, Wall. 219 DK107
Mead, The (Cheshunt), Wal.Cr. 66 DW29
Mead, The, Wat. 94 BY47
Mead, The, W.Wick. 203 ED102
Mead Ave., Red. 266 DG142
Mead Ave., Slou. 153 BB75
Mead Business Pk., Hert. 32 DS08
Mead Clo., Egh. 173 BB93
Mead Clo., Grays 170 GB75
Mead Clo., Har. 95 CD53
Mead Clo., Loug. 85 EP40
Mead Clo., Red. 250 DG131
Mead Clo., Rom. 105 FG54
Mead Clo., Slou. 153 BB75
Mead Clo., Swan. 207 FG99
Mead Clo., Uxb. 114 BG61
Mead Ct. NW9 118 CQ57
Mead Ct., Egh. 173 BC93
Pooley Grn. Rd.
Mead Ct., Wal.Abb. 67 EB34
Mead Ct., Wok. 226 AS116
Mead Cres. E4 101 EC49
Mead Cres., Dart. 188 FK88
Beech Rd.
Mead Cres., Lthd. 246 CA125
Mead Cres., Sutt. 218 DE105
Mead End, Ash. 232 CM117
Mead Gro., Rom. 126 EX55
Mead Ho. Rd., Hayes 135 BR70
Mead La., Cher. 194 BJ102
Mead La., Hert. 32 DS08
Mead La. Caravan Pk., Cher. 194 BJ102
Mead Pk. Est., Harl. 35 ET11
Mead Path SW17 180 DC91
Mead Pl. E9 142 DW65
Mead Pl., Croy. 201 DP102
Mead Pl., Rick. 92 BH46
Mead Plat NW10 138 CQ65
Mead Rd., Cat. 236 DT123
Mead Rd., Chis. 185 EQ93
Mead Rd., Dart. 188 FK88
Mead Rd., Edg. 96 CN51
Mead Rd., Grav. 191 GH89
Mead Rd., Rad. 62 CN33
Mead Rd., Rich. 177 CJ90
Mead Rd., Uxb. 134 BK65
Mead Rd., Walt. 214 BY105
Mead Row SE1 278 D6
Mead Wk., Slou. 153 BB75
Mead Way, Brom. 204 EE100
Mead Way, Couls. 235 DL118
Mead Way, Croy. 203 DY103
Mead Way, Slou. 131 AK71
Mead Way (Bushey), Wat. 76 BY40
Meadcroft Rd. SE11 161 DP79
Meade Clo. W4 158 CN79
Meade Ct., Tad. 233 CU124
Meades, The, Wey. 213 BR107
Meades La., Chesh. 54 AP32
Meadfield, Edg. 96 CP47
Meadfield Ave., Slou. 153 BA75
Meadfield Grn., Edg. 96 CP47
Meadfield Rd., Slou. 153 BA76
Meadfoot Rd. SW16 181 DJ94
Meadgate Ave., Wdf.Grn. 102 EL50
Meadgate Rd., Brox. 49 EC20
Meadhurst Rd., Cher. 194 BH102
Meadlands Dr., Rich. 177 CK89
Meadow, The, Chis. 185 EQ93
Meadow, The, Hert. 33 DY13
Meadow Ave., Croy. 203 DX100
Meadow Bank N21 81 DM44
Meadow Bungalows, Guil. 259 BB140
Hornhatch
Meadow Clo. E4 101 EB46
Mount Echo Ave.
Meadow Clo. E9 143 DZ65
Eastway
Meadow Clo. SE6 183 EA92
Meadow Clo. SW20 199 CW98
Meadow Clo., Barn. 79 CZ44
Meadow Clo., Bexh. 186 EZ85
Oaklands Rd.
Meadow Clo., Chesh. 54 AN27
Little Hivings
Meadow Clo., Chis. 185 EP92
Meadow Clo., Enf. 83 DY38
Meadow Clo., Esher 197 CF104
Meadow Clo., Gdmg. 258 AS144
Meadow Clo., Hat. 45 CX24
Meadow Clo., Hert. 32 DT08
Tamworth Rd.
Meadow Clo., Houns. 176 CA86
Meadow Clo., Nthlt. 136 CA68
Meadow Clo., Pur. 219 DK113
Meadow Clo., Rich. 178 CL88
Meadow Clo., Ruis. 115 BT58
Meadow Clo., St.Alb. 43 CJ17
Meadow Clo. (Bricket Wd.), St.Alb. 60 CA29
Meadow Clo. (London Colney), St.Alb. 61 CK27

This index reads in the sequence: Street Name / Postal District or Post Town / Map Page Number / Grid Reference

Meadow Clo., Sev. 256 FG123
Meadow Clo., Sutt. 200 DB103
Aultone Way
Meadow Clo., Walt. 214 BZ105
Meadow Clo., Wind. 172 AW86
Meadow Cotts., Beac. 89 AL54
Meadow Ct., Epsom 216 CQ113
Meadow Ct., Harl. 51 ES19
Lodge Hall
Meadow Ct., Stai. 173 BE90
Moor La.
Meadow Cft., Hat. 45 CT18
Meadow Dell, Hat. 45 CT18
Meadow Dr. N10 120 DG55
Meadow Dr. NW4 97 CW54
Meadow Dr., Amer. 55 AS37
Meadow Dr., Wok. 227 BF123
Meadow Gdns., Edg. 96 CP51
Meadow Gdns., Stai. 173 BD92
Meadow Garth NW10 138 CQ65
Meadow Grn., 29 CW09
Welw.G.C.
Meadow Hill, N.Mal. 198 CS100
Meadow Hill, Pur. 219 DJ113
Meadow La., Beac. 89 AM53
Meadow La., Cars. 200 DE103
Meadow La., Lthd. 230 CC121
Meadow La. 151 AQ80
(Eton), Wind.
Meadow Ms. SW8 161 DM79
Meadow Pl. SW8 161 DL80
Meadow Pl. W4 158 CS80
Edensor Rd.
Meadow Ri., Couls. 219 DK113
Meadow Rd. SW8 161 DM80
Meadow Rd. SW19 180 DC94
Meadow Rd., Ashf. 175 BR92
Meadow Rd., Ash. 232 CL117
Meadow Rd., Bark. 145 ET66
Meadow Rd., Berk. 38 AU17
Meadow Rd., Borwd. 78 CP40
Meadow Rd., Brom. 204 EE95
Meadow Rd., Dag. 146 EZ65
Meadow Rd., Epp. 69 ET29
Meadow Rd., Esher 215 CE106
Meadow Rd., Felt. 176 BY89
Meadow Rd., Grav. 191 GG89
Meadow Rd., Guil. 243 BA130
Meadow Rd., Hem.H. 40 BN24
Meadow Rd., Loug. 84 EL43
Meadow Rd., Pnr. 116 BX56
Meadow Rd., Rom. 127 FC60
Meadow Rd., Slou. 152 AY76
Meadow Rd., Sthl. 136 BZ73
Meadow Rd., Sutt. 218 DE106
Meadow Rd., Vir.W. 192 AS99
Meadow Rd., Wat. 59 BU34
Meadow Rd. 76 CB43
(Bushey), Wat.
Meadow Row SE1 279 H7
Meadow Row SE1 162 DQ76
Meadow Stile, Croy. 202 DQ104
High St.
Meadow Vw., Ch.St.G. 90 AU48
Meadow Vw., Har. 117 CE60
Meadow Vw., Orp. 206 EW97
Meadow Vw., Sid. 186 EW87
Meadow Vw., Stai. 173 BF85
Hithermoor Rd.
Meadow Vw. Rd., Hayes 135 BQ70
Meadow Vw. Rd., 201 DP99
Th.Hth.
Meadow Wk. E18 124 EG56
Meadow Wk., Dag. 146 EZ65
Meadow Wk., Dart. 188 FJ91
Meadow Wk., Epsom 216 CS107
Meadow Wk., H.Wyc. 88 AC46
Meadow Wk., Tad. 233 CV124
Meadow Wk., Wall. 201 DH104
Meadow Way NW9 118 CR57
Meadow Way, Abb.L. 59 BT27
Meadow Way, Add. 212 BH105
Meadow Way, Chess. 216 CL106
Meadow Way, Chig. 103 EQ48
Meadow Way, Dart. 188 FQ87
Meadow Way, Hem.H. 39 BF23
Meadow Way, Kings L. 58 BN30
Meadow Way 230 CB123
(Bookham), Lthd.
Meadow Way 245 BR125
(West Horsley), Lthd.
Meadow Way 150 AF75
(Dorney Reach), Maid.
Meadow Way 150 AD81
(Fifield), Maid.
Meadow Way, Orp. 205 EN104
Meadow Way, Pot.B. 64 DA34
Meadow Way, Reig. 266 DB138
Meadow Way, Rick. 92 BJ45
Meadow Way, Ruis. 115 BV58
Meadow Way, Saw. 36 FA06
Meadow Way, Tad. 233 CY117
Meadow Way, Upmin. 128 FQ62
Meadow Way, Wem. 117 CK63
Meadow Way, Wind. 172 AV86
Meadow Waye, Houns. 156 BY79
Meadowbank NW3 140 DF66
Meadowbank SE3 164 EF83
Meadowbank, Kings L. 58 BN30
Meadowbank, Lthd. 245 BS127
Meadowbank, Surb. 198 CM100
Meadowbank, Wat. 94 BW45
Meadowbank Clo. SW6 160 CW80
Meadowbank Clo., Barn. 78 CR44
Barnet Rd.
Meadowbank Gdns., 155 BU81
Houns.
Meadowbank Rd. NW9 118 CR59
Meadowbanks, Barn. 79 CU43
Barnet Rd.
Meadowbrook, Oxt. 253 EC130
Meadowbrook Clo., 153 BF81
Slou.
Meadowbrook Rd., Dor. 263 CG135
Meadowcot La., Amer. 55 AM44
Meadowcourt Rd. SE3 164 EF84
Meadowcroft, Brom. 205 EM97
Meadowcroft, Ger.Cr. 90 AX54
Meadowcroft, St.Alb. 43 CG23
Meadowcroft 76 CB44
(Bushey), Wat.
Meadowcroft Clo., Horl. 269 DJ151
Meadowcroft Rd. N13 99 DN47
Meadowcross, Wal.Abb. 68 EE34
Meadowlands, Cob. 213 BU113
Meadowlands, Guil. 244 BH130
Meadowlands, Horn. 128 FL59
Meadowlands, Oxt. 254 EG134

Meadowlands Pk., Add. 194 BL104
Meadowlea Clo., West Dr. 154 BK79
Holloway La.
Meadows, The, Amer. 55 AS39
Meadows, The, Guil. 258 AW137
Meadows, The, Hem.H. 39 BE19
Meadows, The, Orp. 224 EW107
Parkfield La.
Meadows, The, Saw. 36 FA05
Meadows, The, Sev. 224 EZ113
Meadows, The, Warl. 237 DX117
Farleigh Rd.
Meadows, The, 30 DC09
Welw.G.C.
Meadows Clo. E10 123 EA61
Meadows End, Sun. 195 BU95
Meadows Leigh Clo., Wey. 195 BQ104
Meadowside SE9 164 EJ84
Meadowside, Beac. 90 AT52
Meadowside, Dart. 188 FK88
Meadowside, Horl. 269 DH147
Stockfield
Meadowside, Lthd. 230 CA123
Meadowside, Walt. 196 BW103
Meadowside Rd., Sutt. 217 CY109
Meadowside Rd., 128 FQ64
Upmin.
Meadowsweet Clo. E16 144 EK71
Monarch Dr.
Meadowview Rd. SE6 183 EA91
Meadowview Rd., Bex. 186 EY86
Meadowview Rd., Epsom 216 CS109
Meads, The, Berk. 38 AS17
Meads, The, Edg. 96 CR51
Meads, The, St.Alb. 60 BZ29
Meads, The, Sutt. 199 CY104
Meads, The, Upmin. 129 FS61
Meads, The, Uxb. 134 BL70
Meads La., Ilf. 125 ES59
Meads Rd. N22 99 DP54
Meads Rd., Enf. 83 DY39
Meads Rd., Guil. 243 BA134
Meadsway, Brwd. 107 FV51
Meadvale Rd. W5 137 CH70
Meadvale Rd., Croy. 202 DT101
Meadview Rd., Ware 33 DX07
Meadway N14 99 DK47
Meadway NW11 120 DB58
Meadway SW20 199 CW98
Meadway, Ashf. 174 BN91
Meadway, Barn. 79 CZ42
Meadway, Beck. 203 EC95
Meadway, Berk. 38 AY18
Meadway, Enf. 82 DW37
Meadway, Epsom 214 CQ113
Meadway, Esher 214 CB105
Meadway, Grays 170 GD77
Meadway, Guil. 243 BC129
Meadway, Hodd. 49 EA19
Meadway, Ilf. 125 ES63
Meadway (Bookham), 246 BY128
Lthd.
Meadway (Oxshott), 215 CD114
Lthd.
Meadway, Rom. 105 FG54
Meadway, Ruis. 115 . BR58
Meadway, St.Alb. 44 CR23
Meadway, Sev. 224 EZ113
Meadway, Stai. 174 BG94
Meadway, Surb. 198 CQ102
Meadway, Twick. 177 CD88
Meadway, Warl. 236 DW116
Meadway, Welw.G.C. 29 CZ11
Meadway, The SE3 163 ED82
Heath La.
Meadway, The, Buck.H. 102 EK46
Meadway, The, Horl. 269 DJ148
Meadway, The, Loug. 85 EM44
Meadway, The, Orp. 224 EV106
Meadway, The 65 DM28
(Cuffley), Pot.B.
Meadway, The, Sev. 256 FF122
Meadway Clo. NW11 120 DB58
Meadway Clo., Barn. 80 DA42
Meadway Clo., Pnr. 94 CB51
Highbanks Rd.
Meadway Clo., Stai. 173 BF94
Meadway Ct. NW11 120 DB58
Meadway Dr., Add. 212 BJ108
Meadway Dr., Wok. 226 AW116
Meadway Gdns., Ruis. 115 BR58
Meadway Gate NW11 120 DA58
Meadway Pk., Ger.Cr. 112 AX60
Meaford Way SE20 182 DV94
Meakin Est. SE1 279 M6
Meakin Est. SE1 162 DS76
Meanley Rd. E12 124 EL63
Meard St. W1 273 M9
Meard St. W1 141 DK72
Meare Clo., Tad. 233 CW123
Meare Est., H.Wyc. 110 AD55
Meath Clo., Orp. 206 EV99
Meath Grn. Ave., Horl. 268 DF146
Meath Grn. La., Horl. 266 DE143
Meath Rd. E15 144 EF68
Meath Rd., Ilf. 125 EQ62
Meath St. SW11 161 DH81
Meautys, St.Alb. 42 BZ22
Mechanics Path SE8 163 EA80
Deptford High St.
Mecklenburgh Pl. WC1 274 B4
Mecklenburgh Pl. WC1 141 DM70
Mecklenburgh Sq. WC1 274 B4
Mecklenburgh Sq. WC1 141 DM70
Mecklenburgh Sq. WC1 274 B4
Mecklenburgh St. WC1 141 DM69
Medburn St. NW1 141 DK68
Medbury Rd., Grav. 191 GM88
Medcalf Rd., Enf. 83 DZ37
Medcroft Gdns. SW14 158 CQ84
Mede Clo., Stai. 172 AX88
Mede Fld., Lthd. 231 CD124
Medebourne Clo. SE3 164 EG83
Medena Rd. E8 142 DU65
Dalston La.
Medesenge Way N13 99 DP51
Medfield St. SW15 179 CU87
Medhurst Clo. E3 143 DY68
Arbery Rd.
Medhurst Clo., Wok. 210 AT109
Medhurst Cres., Grav. 191 GL90
Medhurst Gdns., Grav. 191 GM90
Medhurst Rd. E3 143 DY68
Arbery Rd.
Median Rd. E5 122 DW64
Medick Ct., Grays 170 GE79
Medina Ave., Esher 197 CE104
Medina Gro. N7 121 DN62
Medina Rd.

Medina Rd. N7 121 DN62
Medina Rd., Grays 170 GD77
Medlake Rd., Egh. 173 BC93
Medland Clo., Wall. 200 DG102
Medlar Clo., Guil. 242 AW132
Medlar Clo., Nthlt. 136 BY68
Parkfield La.
Medlar Ct., Slou. 132 AW74
Medlar Rd., Grays 170 GD79
Medlar St. SE5 162 DQ81
Medley Rd. NW6 140 DA66
Medman Clo., Uxb. 134 BJ68
Chiltern Vw. Rd.
Medora Rd. SW2 181 DM87
Medora Rd., Rom. 127 FD56
Medow Mead, Rad. 61 CF33
Medusa Rd. SE6 183 EB86
Medway Bldgs. E3 143 DY68
Medway Rd.
Medway Clo., Croy. 202 DW100
Medway Clo., Ilf. 125 EQ64
Loxford La.
Medway Clo., Wat. 60 BW34
Medway Dr., Grnf. 137 CF68
Medway Gdns., Wem. 117 CG63
Medway Ms. E3 143 DY68
Medway Rd.
Medway Par., Grnf. 137 CF68
Medway Rd. E3 143 DY68
Medway Rd., Dart. 167 FG83
Medway Rd., Hem.H. 40 BM15
Medway St. SW1 277 N7
Medway St. SW1 161 DK76
Medwick Ms., Hem.H. 41 BP15
Hunters Oak
Medwin St. SW4 161 DM84
Meerbrook Rd. SE3 164 EJ83
Meeson Rd. E15 144 EF67
Meeson St. E5 123 DY63
Meesons La., Grays 170 FZ77
Meeting Flds. Path E9 142 DW65
Morning La.
Meeting Ho. La. SE15 162 DV81
Meetinghouse All. E1 142 DV74
Wapping La.
Megg La., Kings L. 58 BH29
Mehetabel Rd. E9 142 DW65
Meister Clo., Ilf. 125 ER60
Melancholy Wk., Rich. 177 CJ89
Melanda Clo., Chis. 185 EM92
Melanie Clo., Bexh. 166 EY81
Melba Gdns., Til. 171 GG80
Melba Way SE13 163 EB81
Melbourne Ave. N13 99 DM51
Melbourne Ave. W13 137 CG74
Melbourne Ave., Pnr. 116 CB55
Melbourne Ave., Slou. 131 AQ72
Melbourne Clo., Orp. 205 ES101
Melbourne Clo., St.Alb. 43 CF16
Melbourne Clo., Uxb. 114 BN63
Melbourne Clo., Wall. 219 DJ106
Melbourne Ct. E5 123 DY63
Daubeney Rd.
Melbourne Ct. N10 99 DH52
Sydney Rd.
Melbourne Ct. SE20 182 DU94
Melbourne Ct., Welw.G.C. 29 CV10
Melbourne Gdns., Rom. 126 EY57
Melbourne Gro. SE22 162 DS84
Melbourne Ho., Hayes 136 BW70
Melbourne Ms. SE6 183 EC87
Melbourne Ms. SW9 161 DN81
Melbourne Pl. WC2 274 C9
Melbourne Pl. WC2 141 DM73
Melbourne Rd. E6 145 EM67
Melbourne Rd. E10 123 EB59
Melbourne Rd. E17 123 DY56
Melbourne Rd. SW19 200 DA95
Melbourne Rd., Ilf. 125 EP60
Melbourne Rd., Tedd. 177 CJ93
Melbourne Rd., Til. 170 GE81
Melbourne Rd., Wall. 219 DH106
Melbourne Rd. 76 CB43
(Bushey), Wat.
Melbourne Sq. SW9 161 DN81
Melbourne Ms.
Melbourne Ter. SW6 160 DB80
Waterford Rd.
Melbourne Way, Enf. 82 DT44
Melbury Ave., Sthl. 156 CB76
Melbury Clo., Cher. 194 BG101
Melbury Clo., Chis. 184 EL93
Melbury Clo., Esher 215 CH107
Melbury Clo., W.Byf. 212 BG114
Melbury Ct. W8 159 CZ76
Melbury Dr. SE5 162 DS80
Sedgmoor Pl.
Melbury Gdns. SW20 199 CV95
Melbury Rd. W14 159 CZ76
Melbury Rd., Har. 118 CM57
Melbury Ter. NW1 272 C5
Melbury Ter. NW1 140 DE70
Melcombe Gdns., Har. 118 CM58
Melcombe Pl. NW1 272 D6
Melcombe Pl. NW1 140 DF71
Melcombe St. NW1 272 E5
Melcombe St. NW1 140 DF70
Meldon Clo. SW6 160 DB81
Bagley's La.
Meldone Clo., Surb. 198 CP101
Raeburn Ave.
Meldrum Clo., Orp. 206 EW100
Killewarren Way
Meldrum Rd., Ilf. 126 EU61
Melfield Gdns. SE6 183 EB91
Melford Ave., Bark. 145 ES65
Melford Clo., Chess. 216 CN106
Moor La.
Melford Rd. E6 145 EM70
Melford Rd. E11 124 EE61
Melford Rd. E17 123 DY56
Melford Rd. SE22 182 DU87
Melford Rd., Ilf. 125 ER61
Melford Rd., Til. 171 GG82
Melfort Ave., Th.Hth. 201 DP97
Melfort Rd., Th.Hth. 201 DP97
Melgund Rd. N5 121 DN64
Melina Clo., Hayes 135 BR71
Middleton Rd.
Melina Pl. NW8 140 DD69
Melina Rd. W12 159 CV75
Melior Pl. SE1 279 M4
Melior St. SE1 279 M4
Melior St. SE1 162 DS75
Meliot Rd. SE6 183 ED89
Melksham Clo., Rom. 106 FM52
Melksham Dr., Rom. 106 FM52
Melksham Gdns.

Melksham Gdns., Rom. 106 FL52
Melksham Grn., Rom. 106 FM52
Melksham Gdns.
Mell St. SE10 164 EE78
Trafalgar Rd.
Meller Clo., Croy. 201 DL104
Melling Dr., Enf. 82 DU39
Carterhatch La.
Melling St. SE18 165 ES79
Mellings, The, Hem.H. 41 BP15
Mellish Clo., Bark. 145 ET67
Mellish Gdns., Wdf.Grn. 102 EG50
Harts Gro.
Mellish St. E14 163 EA76
Mellison Rd. SW17 180 DE92
Mellitus St. W12 139 CT72
Mellor Clo., Walt. 196 BZ101
Mellow La. E., Hayes 135 BQ69
Mellow La. W., Uxb. 135 BQ69
Mellows Rd., Ilf. 125 EM55
Mellows Rd., Wall. 219 DK106
Mells Cres. SE9 185 EM91
Melody La. N5 121 DP64
Melody Rd. SW18 180 DC85
Melody Rd., West. 238 EJ118
Melon Pl. W8 160 DB75
Kensington Ch. St.
Melon Rd. E11 124 EE62
Cathall Rd.
Melon Rd. SE15 162 DU81
Melrose Ave. N22 99 DP53
Melrose Ave. NW2 119 CV64
Melrose Ave. SW16 201 DM97
Melrose Ave. SW19 179 CZ89
Melrose Ave., Borwd. 78 CP43
Melrose Ave., Grnf. 136 CB68
Melrose Ave., Mitch. 181 DH94
Melrose Ave., Pot.B. 64 DB32
Melrose Ave., Twick. 176 CB87
Melrose Clo. SE12 184 EG88
Melrose Clo., Grnf. 136 CB68
Melrose Clo., Hayes 135 BU71
Melrose Cres., Orp. 223 ER105
Melrose Dr., Sthl. 136 CA74
Melrose Gdns. W6 159 CW76
Melrose Gdns., Edg. 96 CP54
Melrose Gdns., N.Mal. 198 CR97
Melrose Gdns., Walt. 214 BW106
Melrose Pl., Wat. 75 BT38
Wentworth Clo.
Melrose Rd. SW13 159 CT82
Melrose Rd. SW18 179 CZ86
Melrose Rd. SW19 200 DA96
Melrose Rd. W3 158 CQ76
Stanley Rd.
Melrose Rd., Couls. 235 DH115
Melrose Rd., Pnr. 116 BZ56
Melrose Rd., West. 238 EJ116
Melrose Rd., Wey. 212 BN106
Melrose Ter. W6 159 CW75
Melsa Rd., Mord. 200 DC100
Melsted Rd., Hem.H. 40 BH20
Melstock Ave., Upmin. 128 FQ63
Meltham Way SE16 162 DV78
Egan Way
Melthorne Dr., Ruis. 116 BW62
Melthorpe Gdns. SE3 164 EK81
Melton Clo., Ruis. 116 BW60
Melton Ct. SW7 276 A9
Melton Ct. SW7 160 DD77
Melton Ct., Sutt. 218 DC108
Melton Flds., Epsom 216 CR109
Melton Gdns., Rom. 127 FF59
Melton Pl., Epsom 216 CR109
Melton Rd., Red. 251 DJ130
Melton St. NW1 273 L3
Melton St. NW1 141 DJ69
Melville Ave. SW20 179 CU94
Melville Ave., Grnf. 117 CF64
Melville Ave., S.Croy. 220 DT106
Melville Clo., Uxb. 115 BR62
Melville Gdns. N13 99 DN50
Melville Rd. E17 123 DZ55
Melville Rd. NW10 138 CR66
Melville Rd. SW13 159 CU81
Melville Rd., Rain. 147 FG70
Melville Rd., Rom. 105 FB52
Melville Rd., Sid. 186 EW89
Melville Vill. Rd. W3 138 CR74
High St.
Melvin Rd. SE20 202 DW95
Melvinshaw, Lthd. 231 CJ121
Melvyn Clo. 65 DP28
(Cheshunt), Wal.Cr.
Melyn Clo. N7 121 DJ63
Anson Rd.
Memel Ct. EC1 275 H5
Memel St. EC1 275 H5
Memess Path SE18 165 EN79
Engineer Clo.
Memorial Ave. E15 144 EE69
Memorial Clo., Houns. 156 BZ79
Mendip Clo. SE26 182 DW91
Mendip Clo. SW19 179 CY89
Queensmere Rd.
Mendip Clo., Hayes 155 BR80
Mendip Clo., St.Alb. 43 CJ15
Mendip Clo., Slou. 153 BA78
Mendip Clo., Wor.Pk. 199 CW103
Cotswold Way
Mendip Dr. NW2 119 CY61
Mendip Rd. SW11 160 DC83
Mendip Rd., Bexh. 167 FE81
Mendip Rd., Horn. 127 FG59
Mendip Rd., Ilf. 125 ES57
Mendip Rd. (Bushey), 76 CC44
Wat.
Mendip Way, Hem.H. 40 BL17
Mendlesham, Welw.G.C. 30 DE09
Mendora Rd. SW6 159 CY80
Mendoza Clo., Horn. 128 FL57
Menelik Rd. NW2 119 CY63
Menlo Gdns. SE19 182 DR94
Menotti St. E2 142 DU70
Dunbridge St.
Menthone Pl., Horn. 128 FK59
Mentmore Clo., Har. 117 CJ58
Mentmore Rd., St.Alb. 43 CD22
Mentmore Ter. E8 142 DV66
Meon Clo., Tad. 233 CV122
Meon Ct., Islw. 157 CE82
Meon Rd. W3 158 CQ75
Meopham Rd., Mitch. 201 DJ95
Mepham Cres., Har. 94 CC52
Mepham Gdns., Har. 94 CC52
Mepham St. SE1 278 D3
Mepham St. SE1 141 DM74
Mera Dr., Bexh. 166 FA84
Merantun Way SW19 200 DC95
Merbury Clo. SE13 183 ED85

Merbury Rd. SE28 165 ES75
Mercator Rd. SE13 163 ED84
Mercer Clo., T.Ditt. 197 CE101
Mercer Pl., Pnr. 94 BW54
Cross Way
Mercer St. WC2 273 P9
Mercer St. WC2 141 DL72
Mercer Wk., Uxb. 134 BJ66
High St.
Merceron St. E1 142 DV70
Mercers, Harl. 51 EN17
Mercers, Hem.H. 40 BL18
Mercers Clo. SE10 164 EF77
Mercers Pl. W6 159 CW77
Mercers Rd. N19 121 DK62
Merchant St. E3 143 DZ69
Merchiston Rd. SE6 183 ED89
Merchland Rd. SE9 185 EQ88
Mercia Gro. SE13 163 EC84
Mercia Wk., Wok. 227 AZ117
Church St. W.
Mercian Way, Slou. 131 AK74
Mercier Rd. SW15 179 CY85
Mercury Cen. Ind. Est., 175 BU85
Felt.
Mercury Gdns., Rom. 127 FE56
Mercury Wk., Hem.H. 40 BM17
Mercury Way SE14 163 DX79
Mercy Ter. SE13 163 EB84
Mere Clo. SW15 179 CX87
Mere End, Croy. 203 DX101
Mere Rd., Shep. 195 BP100
Mere Rd., Slou. 152 AT76
Mere Rd., Tad. 233 CV124
Mere Rd., Wey. 195 BR104
Mere Side, Orp. 205 EN103
Merebank La., Croy. 219 DM106
Meredith Ave. NW2 119 CW64
Meredith Clo., Pnr. 94 BX52
Meredith Rd., Grays 171 GG77
Meredith St. E13 144 EG69
Meredith St. EC1 274 F3
Meredyth Rd. SW13 159 CU82
Merefield, Saw. 36 EY06
Merefield Gdns., Tad. 233 CX119
Mereside Pl., Vir.W. 192 AX99
Beechmont Ave.
Meretone Clo. SE4 163 DY84
Merevale Cres., Mord. 200 DC100
Mereway Rd., Twick. 177 CD88
Merewood Clo., Brom. 205 EN96
Merewood Rd., Bexh. 167 FC82
Mereworth Clo., Brom. 204 EF99
Mereworth Dr. SE18 165 EP80
Merganser Gdns. SE28 165 ER76
Avocet Ms.
Meriden Clo., Brom. 184 EK94
Meriden Clo., Ilf. 103 EQ53
Meriden Way, Wat. 76 BY36
Meridian Gate E14 163 EC75
Meridian Gro., Horl. 269 DJ147
Wheatfield Way
Meridian Pl. E14 163 EC75
Meridian Rd. SE7 164 EK80
Meridian Trd. Est. SE7 164 EH77
Commercial Rd.
Meridian Wk. N17 100 DS51
Meridian Way N9 101 DX47
Meridian Way N18 100 DW51
Meridian Way, Enf. 83 DX44
Meridian Way, Ware 33 EB10
Merifield Rd. SE9 164 EJ84
Merino Clo. E11 124 EJ56
Merino Pl., Sid. 186 EU86
Blackfen Rd.
Merivale Rd. SW15 159 CY84
Merivale Rd., Har. 116 CC59
Merland Clo., Tad. 233 CW120
Merland Grn., Tad. 233 CW120
Merland Ri.
Merland Ri., Epsom 233 CW119
Merland Ri., Tad. 233 CW120
Merle Ave., Uxb. 92 BH54
Merlewood, Sev. 257 FH123
Merlewood Clo., Cat. 236 DR120
Merlewood Dr., Chis. 205 EM95
Merley Ct. NW9 118 CQ60
Merlin Clo., Croy. 220 DS105
Minster Dr.
Merlin Clo., Ilf. 104 EW50
Merlin Clo., Mitch. 200 DE97
Miles Rd.
Merlin Clo., Nthlt. 136 BW69
Merlin Clo., Rom. 105 FD51
Merlin Clo., Slou. 153 BB79
Merlin Clo., Wal.Abb. 68 EG34
Merlin Ct., Wok. 211 BC114
Blackmore Cres.
Merlin Cres., Edg. 96 CM53
Merlin Gdns., Brom. 184 EG90
Merlin Gdns., Rom. 105 FD51
Merlin Gro., Beck. 203 DZ98
Merlin Gro., Ilf. 103 EP51
Merlin Rd. E12 124 EK61
Merlin Rd., Rom. 105 FD51
Merlin Rd., Well. 166 EU84
Merlin Rd. N., Well. 166 EU84
Merlin St. WC1 274 D3
Merlin Way, Epp. 70 FA25
Merling Clo., Chess. 215 CK106
Mansfield Rd.
Merlins Ave., Har. 116 BZ62
Mermagen Dr., Rain. 147 FH66
Mermaid Ct. SE1 279 K4
Mermaid Ct. SE1 162 DR75
Mermaid Ct. SE16 143 DZ74
Mermers Gdns., Grav. 191 GM91
Merredene Rd. SW2 181 DM86
Merrick Rd., Sthl. 156 BZ75
Merrick Sq. SE1 279 K6
Merrick Sq. SE1 162 DQ76
Merridene N21 81 DP44
Merrielands Cres., Dag. 146 EZ67
Merrilands Rd., Wor.Pk. 199 CW102
Merrilees Rd., Sid. 185 ES88
Merrilyn Clo., Esher 215 CG107
Merriman Rd. SE3 164 EJ81
Merrington Rd. SW6 160 DA79
Merrion Ave., Stan. 95 CK50
Merrion Wk. SE17 162 DR78
Dawes St.
Merritt Gdns., Chess. 215 CJ107
Mansfield Rd.
Merritt Rd. SE4 183 DZ85
Merritt Wk., Hat. 45 CV23

Mil–Mon This index reads in the sequence: Street Name / Postal District or Post Town / Map Page Number / Grid Reference

Millford, Wok. 226 AV117
Millgrove St. SW11 160 DG81
Millharbour E14 163 EB76
Millhaven Clo., Rom. 126 EV58
Millhedge Clo., Cob. 230 BY116
Millhoo Ct., Wal.Abb. 68 EF34
Millhouse La., Abb.L. 59 BU27
Millhouse Pl. SE27 181 DP91
Millicent Rd. E10 123 DZ60
Milligan St. E14 143 DZ73
Three Colt St.
Milliners Ct., Loug. 85 EN40
The Cft.
Milling Rd., Edg. 96 CR52
Millington Rd., Hayes 155 BS76
Millman Ms. WC1 274 B5
Millman Ms. WC1 141 DM70
Millman St. WC1 274 B5
Millman St. WC1 141 DM70
Millmark Gro. SE14 163 DY82
Millmarsh La., Enf. 83 DY40
Millmead, Guil. 258 AW136
Millmead, W.Byf. 212 BM112
Millmead Ter., Guil. 258 AW136
Millpond Ct., Add. 212 BL106
Millpond Est. SE16 162 DV75
West La.
Mills Clo., Uxb. 134 BN68
Mills Ct. EC2 275 M4
Mills Gro. E14 143 EC71
Dewberry St.
Mills Gro. NW4 119 CX55
Mills Rd., Walt. 214 BW106
Mills Row W4 158 CR77
Bridge St.
Mills Spur, Wind. 172 AV87
Mills Way, Brwd. 109 GC46
Millshot Dr., Amer. 55 AQ40
Millside, B.End 110 AC60
Millside, Cars. 200 DF103
Millside Ind. Est., Dart. 168 FK84
Millside Pl., Islw. 157 CH82
Millsmead Way, Loug. 85 EM40
Millson Clo. N20 98 DD47
Millstead Clo., Tad. 233 CV122
Millstone Clo. 208 FQ96
(Sutton at Hone), Dart.
Millstone Ms., Dart. 208 FQ95
Millstone Clo.
Millstream Clo. N13 99 DN50
Millstream La., Slou. 131 AL74
Millstream Rd. SE1 279 P5
Millstream Rd. SE1 162 DT75
Millthorn Clo., Rick. 74 BM43
Millview Clo., Reig. 250 DD132
Millwall Dock Rd. E14 163 EA76
Millwards, Hat. 45 CV21
Millway NW7 96 CS50
Millway, Reig. 250 DD134
Millway Gdns., Nthlt. 136 BZ65
Millwell Cres., Chig. 103 ER50
Millwood Rd., Houns. 176 CC85
Millwood Rd., Orp. 206 EW97
Millwood St. W10 139 CY71
St. Charles Sq.
Milman Clo., Pnr. 116 BX55
Milman Rd. NW6 139 CX68
Milman's St. SW10 160 DD79
Milne Feild, Pnr. 94 CA52
Milne Gdns. SE9 184 EL85
Milne Pk. E., Croy. 221 ED111
Milne Pk. W., Croy. 221 ED111
Milne Way, Uxb. 92 BH53
Milner App., Cat. 236 DU121
Milner Clo., Cat. 236 DU121
Milner Clo., Wat. 59 BV34
Milner Ct. 76 CB44
(Bushey), Wat.
Milner Dr., Cob. 214 BZ112
Milner Dr., Twick. 177 CD87
Milner Pl. N1 141 DN67
Milner Pl., Cars. 218 DG105
High St.
Milner Rd. E15 144 EE69
Milner Rd. SW19 200 DB95
Milner Rd., Cat. 236 DU122
Milner Rd., Dag. 126 EW61
Milner Rd., Kings.T. 197 CK97
Milner Rd., Mord. 200 DD99
Milner Rd., Slou. 130 AG71
Milner Rd., Th.Hth. 202 DR97
Milner Sq. N1 141 DP66
Milner St. SW3 276 D8
Milner St. SW3 160 DF77
Milnthorpe Rd. W4 158 CR79
Milo Rd. SE22 182 DT86
Milroy Ave., Grav. 190 GE89
Milroy Wk. SE1 278 F2
Milson Rd. W14 159 CX76
Milstream Way, H.Wyc. 110 AD55
Milton Ave. E6 144 EK66
Milton Ave. N6 121 DJ59
Milton Ave. NW9 118 CQ55
Milton Ave. NW10 138 CQ67
Milton Ave., Barn. 79 CZ43
Milton Ave., Croy. 202 DR101
Milton Ave., Dor. 263 CD137
Milton Ave., Ger.Cr. 112 AX56
Milton Ave., Grav. 191 GJ88
Milton Ave., Horn. 127 FF61
Milton Ave., Sev. 225 FB110
Milton Ave., Sutt. 200 DD104
Milton Clo. N2 120 DC57
Milton Clo. SE1 279 P9
Milton Clo. SE1 162 DT77
Milton Clo., Hayes 135 BU72
Milton Clo., Slou. 153 BA83
Milton Clo., Sutt. 200 DD104
Milton Ct. EC2 275 K6
Milton Ct., Uxb. 115 BP62
Milton Ct., Wal.Abb. 67 EC34
Milton Ct. Rd. SE14 163 DY79
Milton Cres., Ilf. 125 EQ59
Milton Dene, Hem.H. 41 BP15
Milton Dr., Borwd. 78 CP43
Milton Dr., Shep. 194 BL98
Milton Flds., Ch.St.G. 90 AV48
Milton Gdn. Est. N16 122 DS64
Milton Gro.
Milton Gdns., Epsom 216 CS114
Milton Gdns., Stai. 174 BM88
Milton Gdns., Til. 171 GH81
Milton Gro. N11 99 DJ50
Milton Gro. N16 122 DR63
Milton Hall Rd., Grav. 191 GK88
Milton Hill, Ch.St.G. 90 AV48
Milton Flds.
Milton Lawns, Amer. 55 AR36
Milton Pk. N6 121 DJ59
Milton Pl. N7 121 DN64
George's Rd.
Milton Pl., Grav. 191 GJ86
Milton Rd. E17 123 EA56
Milton Rd. N6 121 DJ59
Milton Rd. N15 121 DP56
Milton Rd. NW7 97 CU50
Milton Rd. NW9 119 CU59
West Hendon Bdy.
Milton Rd. SE24 181 DP86
Milton Rd. SW14 158 CR83
Milton Rd. SW19 180 DC93
Milton Rd. W3 138 CR74
Milton Rd. W7 137 CF73
Milton Rd., Add. 212 BG107
Milton Rd., Belv. 166 FA77
Milton Rd., Brwd. 108 FW49
Milton Rd., Cat. 236 DR121
Milton Rd., Chesh. 54 AP29
Milton Rd., Croy. 202 DR102
Milton Rd., Egh. 173 AZ92
Milton Rd., Grav. 191 GH86
Milton Rd., Grays 170 GB78
Milton Rd., Hmptn. 176 CA94
Milton Rd., Har. 117 CE56
Milton Rd., Mitch. 180 DG94
Milton Rd., Rom. 127 FG58
Milton Rd., Sev. 256 FE121
Milton Rd., Slou. 131 AR70
Milton Rd., Sutt. 200 DA104
Milton Rd., Swans. 190 FY86
Milton Rd., Uxb. 114 BN63
Milton Rd., Wall. 219 DJ107
Milton Rd., Walt. 196 BX104
Milton Rd., Ware 33 DX05
Milton Rd., Well. 165 ET81
Milton St. EC2 275 K6
Milton St. EC2 142 DR71
Milton St., Dor. 263 CD137
Milton St., Swans. 189 FX86
Milton St., Wal.Abb. 67 EC34
Milton St., Wat. 75 BV38
Milton Way, Lthd. 246 CC125
Milton Way, West Dr. 154 BM77
Miltoncourt La., Dor. 263 CF136
Milverton Dr., Uxb. 115 BQ63
Milverton Gdns., Ilf. 125 ET61
Milverton Rd. NW6 139 CW66
Milverton St. SE11 161 DN78
Milverton Way SE9 185 EN91
Milward St. E1 142 DV71
Stepney Way
Milward Wk. SE18 165 EN79
Spearman St.
Milwards, Harl. 51 EP19
Mimas Rd., Hem.H. 40 BM17
Saturn Way
Mimms Hall Rd., Pot.B. 63 CX31
Mimms La., Pot.B. 62 CQ33
Mimms La., Rad. 62 CN33
Mimosa Clo., Brwd. 108 FV43
Mimosa Clo., Orp. 206 EW104
Berrylands
Mimosa Clo., Rom. 106 FJ52
Mimosa Rd., Hayes 136 BW71
Mimosa St. SW6 159 CZ81
Mimran Rd., Hert. 31 DP10
Mina Ave., Slou. 152 AX75
Mina Rd. SE17 162 DS78
Mina Rd. SW19 200 DA95
Minard Rd. SE6 184 EE87
Minchen Rd., Harl. 35 ET13
Minchenden Cres. N14 99 DJ48
Minchin Clo., Lthd. 231 CG122
Mincing La. EC3 275 M10
Mincing La. EC3 142 DS73
Mincing La., Wok. 210 AT108
Minden Rd. SE20 202 DV95
Minden Rd., Sutt. 199 CZ103
Minehead Rd. SW16 181 DM92
Minehead Rd., Har. 116 CA62
Minera Ms. SW1 276 G8
Minera Ms. SW1 160 DG77
Mineral St. SE18 165 ES77
Minerva Clo. SW9 161 DN80
Minerva Clo., Sid. 185 ES90
Minerva Dr., Wat. 75 BS36
Minerva Rd. E4 101 EB52
Minerva Rd. NW10 138 CQ69
Minerva Rd., Kings.T. 198 CM96
Minerva St. E2 142 DV68
Minerva Way, Beac. 89 AM54
Minet Ave. NW10 138 CS68
Minet Dr., Hayes 135 BU74
Minet Gdns. NW10 138 CS68
Minet Gdns., Hayes 135 BU74
Minet Rd. SW9 161 DP82
Minford Gdns. W14 159 CX75
Ming St. E14 143 EA73
Mingard Wk. N7 121 DM61
Hornsey Rd.
Minims, The, Hat. 45 CU16
Wellfield Rd.
Ministry Way SE9 185 EM89
Miniver Pl. EC4 142 DQ73
Garlick Hill
Mink Ct., Houns. 156 BW82
Minniecroft Rd., Slou. 130 AH69
Minniedale, Surb. 198 CM99
Minnow St. SE17 162 DS77
East St.
Minnow Wk. SE17 279 N9
Minorca Rd., Wey. 212 BN105
Minories EC3 275 P9
Minories EC3 142 DT72
Minshull Pl., Beck. 183 EA94
Minshull St. SW8 161 DK81
Wandsworth Rd.
Minson Rd. E9 143 DX67
Minstead Gdns. SW15 179 CT87
Minstead Way, N.Mal. 198 CS100
Minster Ave., Sutt. 200 DA103
Leafield Rd.
Minster Clo., Hat. 45 CU20
Minster Ct. EC3 142 DR73
Mincing La.
Minster Dr., Croy. 220 DS105
Minster Gdns., W.Mol. 196 BZ99
Molesey Ave.
Minster Pavement EC3 142 DR73
Mincing La.
Minster Rd. NW2 119 CY64
Minster Rd., Brom. 184 EH94
Minster Wk. N8 121 DL56
Lightfoot Rd.
Minster Way, Horn. 128 FM60
Minster Way, Slou. 153 AZ75
Minsterley Ave., 195 BS98
Shep.
Minstrel Clo., Hem.H. 40 BH19
Laureate Way
Minstrel Gdns., Surb. 198 CM99
Mint Clo., Uxb. 135 BP69
Pole Hill Rd.
Mint Gdns., Dor. 263 CG135
Church St.
Mint Rd., Bans. 234 DC116
Mint Rd., Wall. 219 DH105
Mint St. SE1 279 H4
Mint Wk., Croy. 202 DQ104
High St.
Mint Wk., Warl. 237 DX117
Mint Wk., Wok. 226 AS117
Staveley Way
Mintern Clo. N13 99 DP48
Mintern St. N1 142 DR68
Minterne Ave., Sthl. 156 CA77
Minterne Rd., Har. 118 CM57
Minterne Way, Hayes 136 BW72
Minton La., Harl. 52 EW15
Church Langley Way
Minton Ms. NW6 140 DB65
Lymington Rd.
Minton Ri., Maid. 130 AH72
Mirabel Rd. SW6 159 CZ80
Mirador Cres., Slou. 132 AV73
Miramar Way, Horn. 128 FK64
Miranda Clo. E1 142 DW71
Sidney St.
Miranda Ct. W3 138 CM72
Queens Dr.
Miranda Rd. N19 121 DJ60
Mirfield St. SE7 164 EK76
Miriam Rd. SE18 165 ES78
Mirrie La., Uxb. 113 BC57
Mirror Path SE9 184 EJ90
Lambscroft Ave.
Misbourne Ave., Ger.Cr. 90 AX50
Misbourne Clo., Ger.Cr. 90 AY50
Misbourne Ct., Slou. 153 BA77
High St.
Misbourne Rd., Uxb. 134 BN67
Misbourne Vale, Ger.Cr. 90 AX50
Miskin Rd., Dart. 188 FJ87
Miskin Way, Grav. 191 GK93
Missden Dr., Hem.H. 41 BQ22
Missenden Clo., Felt. 175 BT88
Westmacott Dr.
Missenden Gdns., 200 DC100
Mord.
Missenden Gdns., Slou. 130 AJ72
Huntercombe La.
Missenden Rd., Chesh. 54 AL32
Mission Gro. E17 123 DY57
Mission Pl. SE15 162 DU81
Mission Sq., Brent. 158 CL79
Netley Rd.
Mistletoe Clo., Croy. 203 DX102
Marigold Way
Mistley Rd., Harl. 36 EU13
Misty's Fld., Walt. 196 BW102
Mitali Pas. E1 142 DU72
Back Ch. La.
Mitcham Gdn. Vill., 200 DG99
Mitch.
Mitcham Ind. Est., 200 DG95
Mitch.
Mitcham La. SW16 181 DH93
Mitcham Pk., Mitch. 200 DE98
Mitcham Rd. E6 144 EL69
Mitcham Rd. SW17 180 DF92
Mitcham Rd., Croy. 201 DL100
Mitcham Rd., Ilf. 125 ET59
Mitchell Ave., Grav. 190 GD89
Mitchell Clo. SE2 166 EW77
Mitchell Clo., Abb.L. 59 BU32
Langley La.
Mitchell Clo., Belv. 167 FC76
Mitchell Clo., Dart. 188 FL89
Mitchell Clo., Hem.H. 57 AZ27
Lancaster Dr.
Mitchell Clo., Rain. 148 FJ68
Briscoe Rd.
Mitchell Clo., St.Alb. 43 CD24
Mitchell Clo., Slou. 151 AN75
Mitchell Clo., Welw.G.C. 30 DC09
Mitchell Rd. N13 99 DP50
Mitchell Rd., Orp. 223 ET105
Mitchell St. EC1 275 H4
Mitchell St. EC1 142 DQ70
Mitchell Wk. E6 144 EL71
Oliver Gdns.
Mitchell Wk., Amer. 55 AS38
Mitchell Wk., Swans. 190 FY87
Mitchell Way NW10 138 CQ65
Mitchell Way, Brom. 204 EG95
Mitchellbrook Way NW10 138 CR65
Mitchells Clo., Guil. 258 AY140
Station Rd.
Mitchison Rd. N1 142 DR65
Mitchley Ave., Pur. 220 DQ113
Mitchley Ave., S.Croy. 220 DS113
Mitchley Gro., S.Croy. 220 DU113
Mitchley Hill, S.Croy. 220 DS113
Mitchley Rd. N17 122 DU55
Mitchley Vw., S.Croy. 220 DU113
Mitford Clo., Chess. 215 CK106
Mansfield Rd.
Mitford Rd. N19 121 DL61
Mitre, The E14 143 DZ73
Three Colt St.
Mitre Ave. E17 123 DZ55
Greenleaf Rd.
Mitre Clo., Brom. 204 EF96
Beckenham La.
Mitre Clo., Shep. 195 BR100
Gordon Dr.
Mitre Clo., Sutt. 218 DC108
Mitre Ct. EC2 275 J8
Mitre Ct. EC4 274 E9
Mitre Rd. E15 144 EE68
Mitre Rd. SE1 278 E4
Mitre Rd. SE1 161 DN75
Mitre Sq. EC3 275 N9
Mitre St. EC3 275 N9
Mitre St. EC3 142 DS72
Mitre Way NW10 139 CV70
Mixbury Gro., Wey. 213 BR107
Mixnams La., Cher. 193 BF97
Mizen Clo., Cob. 214 BX114
Mizen Way, Cob. 230 BW115
Moat, The, N.Mal. 198 CS95
Moat, The, Ong. 71 FF29
Moat Clo., Orp. 223 ET107
Moat Clo. 76 CB43
(Bushey), Wat.
Moat Ct., Ash. 232 CL117
Moat Cres. N3 120 DB55
Moat Cft., Well. 166 EW83
Moat Dr. E13 144 EJ68
Boundary Rd.
Moat Dr., Har. 116 CC56
Moat Dr., Ruis. 115 BS59
Moat Dr., Slou. 132 AW71
Moat Fm. Rd., Nthlt. 136 BZ65
Moat La., Erith 167 FG81
Moat Pl. SW9 161 DM83
Moat Pl. W3 138 CP72
Moat Pl., Uxb. 114 BH63
Moatfield Rd. 76 CB43
(Bushey), Wat.
Moats La., Red. 267 DN140
Moatside, Enf. 82 DW42
Moatside, Felt. 176 BW91
Moatview Ct. 76 CB43
(Bushey), Wat.
Palmer Ave.
Moatwood Grn., 29 CY10
Welw.G.C.
Moberley Rd. SW4 181 DK87
Modbury Gdns. NW5 140 DG65
Queens Cres.
Modder Pl. SW15 159 CX84
Cardinal Pl.
Model Cotts. SW14 158 CQ84
Upper Richmond Rd. W.
Model Fm. Clo. SE9 184 EL90
Modling Ho. E2 143 DX69
Mace St.
Moelwyn Hughes Ct. N7 121 DK64
Hilldrop Cres.
Moelyn Ms., Har. 117 CG57
Moffat Gdns., Mitch. 200 DD97
Moffat Rd. N13 99 DL51
Moffat Rd. SW17 180 DE91
Moffat Rd., Th.Hth. 202 DQ96
Moffats Clo., Hat. 64 DA26
Moffats La., Hat. 63 CY27
Mogador Cotts., Tad. 249 CX128
Mogador Rd.
Mogador Rd., Tad. 249 CY128
Mogden La., Islw. 177 CE85
Mohmmad Khan Rd. E11 124 EF60
Harvey Rd.
Moiety Rd. E14 163 EA75
Moir Clo., S.Croy. 220 DU109
Moira Clo. N17 100 DS54
Moira Rd. SE9 165 EM84
Moland Mead SE16 163 DX78
Crane Mead
Molash Rd., Orp. 206 EX98
Molasses Row SW11 160 DC83
Cinnamon Row
Mole Abbey Gdns., W.Mol. 196 CA97
New Rd.
Mole Business Pk., Lthd. 231 CG121
Mole Ct., Epsom 216 CQ105
Mole Rd., Lthd. 231 CD121
Mole Rd., Walt. 214 BX106
Mole Valley Pl., Ash. 231 CK119
Molember Ct., E.Mol. 197 CE99
Molember Rd., E.Mol. 197 CD99
Moles Hill, Lthd. 215 CD111
Molescroft SE9 185 EQ90
Molesey Ave., W.Mol. 196 BZ99
Molesey Clo., Walt. 214 BX105
Molesey Dr., Sutt. 199 CY103
Molesey Pk. Ave., 196 CB99
W.Mol.
Molesey Pk. Clo., E.Mol. 196 CC99
Molesey Pk. Rd., E.Mol. 196 CB99
Molesey Pk. Rd., 196 CB99
W.Mol.
Molesey Rd., Walt. 196 BY101
Molesey Rd., W.Mol. 196 BY99
Molesford Rd. SW6 160 DA81
Molesham Clo., W.Mol. 196 CB97
Molesham Way, W.Mol. 196 CB97
Molesworth, Hodd. 33 EA13
Molesworth Rd., Cob. 213 BU113
Molesworth St. SE13 163 EC84
Molewood Rd., Hert. 31 DP08
Molineaux Pl., Tedd. 177 CG92
Mollands La., S.Ock. 149 FW70
Mollison Ave., Enf. 83 DY43
Mollison Dr., Wall. 219 DK108
Mollison Ri., Grav. 191 GL92
Michael Gdns.
Mollison Way, Edg. 96 CM54
Molloy Ct., Wok. 227 BA116
Molly Huggins Clo. SW12 181 DJ87
Molteno Rd., Wat. 75 BU39
Molyneaux Ave., 57 AZ27
Hem.H.
Molyneux Rd., Gdmg. 258 AT144
Molyneux Rd., Wey. 212 BN106
Molyneux St. W1 272 C7
Molyneux St. W1 140 DE71
Momples Rd., Harl. 36 EV13
Mona Rd. SE15 162 DW82
Mona St. E16 144 EF71
Monahan Ave., Pur. 219 DM112
Monarch Clo., Felt. 175 BS87
Monarch Clo., Til. 171 GH82
Monarch Clo., W.Wick. 222 EF105
Monarch Dr. E16 144 EK71
Monarch Ms. E17 123 EB58
Granville Rd.
Monarch Ms. SW16 181 DN92
Monarch Pl., Buck.H. 102 EJ47
Princes Rd.
Monarch Rd., Belv. 166 FA76
Monarchs Way, Ruis. 115 BR60
Monarchs Way, Wal.Cr. 67 DY33
Monastery Gdns., Enf. 82 DR40
Monaveen Gdns., 196 CA97
W.Mol.
Monck St. SW1 277 N7
Monck St. SW1 161 DK76
Monclar Rd. SE5 162 DR84
Moncorvo Clo. SW7 276 B5
Moncrieff Clo. E6 144 EL72
Linton Gdns.
Moncrieff St. SE15 162 DU82
Mondial Way, Hayes 155 BQ80
Monega Rd. E7 144 EJ65
Monega Rd. E12 144 EK65
Money Ave., Cat. 236 DR122
Money Hill Rd., Rick. 92 BJ45
Money Hole La., 30 DE08
Welw.G.C.
Money La., West Dr. 154 BK76
Money Rd., Cat. 236 DR122
Moneyhill Par., Rick. 92 BH46
Uxbridge Rd.
Monfitchet E6 145 EP72
Warwall
Mongers La., Epsom 217 CT110
Monica Clo., Wat. 76 BW40
Monier Rd. E3 143 EA66
Monivea Rd., Beck. 183 DZ94
Monk Dr. E16 144 EG72
Monk Pas. E16 144 EG73
Monk Dr.
Monk St. SE18 165 EN77
Monkchester Clo., Loug. 85 EN39
Monkey Island La., 150 AE78
Maid.
Monkfrith Ave. N14 81 DH44
Monkfrith Clo. N14 99 DH45
Monkfrith Way N14 98 DG45
Monkhams Ave., 102 EG50
Wdf.Grn.
Monkhams Dr., 102 EH50
Wdf.Grn.
Monkhams La., Buck.H. 102 EH48
Monkhams La., 102 EG50
Wdf.Grn.
Monkleigh Rd., Mord. 199 CY97
Monks Ave., Barn. 80 DC44
Monks Ave., W.Mol. 196 BZ99
Monks Chase, Brwd. 109 GC50
Monks Clo. SE2 166 EX77
Monks Clo., Brox. 49 EA20
Monks Clo., Enf. 82 DQ40
Monks Clo., Har. 116 CB61
Monks Clo., Ruis. 116 BX63
Monks Clo., St.Alb. 43 CE22
Monks Cres., Add. 212 BH106
Monks Cres., Walt. 195 BV102
Monks Dr. W3 138 CN71
Monks Grn., Lthd. 230 CC121
Monks Horton Way, 43 CH19
St.Alb.
Monks Orchard, Dart. 188 FJ89
Monks Orchard Rd., 203 EA102
Beck.
Monks Pk., Wem. 138 CP65
Monks Pk. Gdns., Wem. 138 CP66
Monks Pl., Cat. 236 DU122
Tillingdown Hill
Monks Ri., Welw.G.C. 29 CX05
Monks Rd., Bans. 234 DA116
Monks Rd., Enf. 82 DQ40
Monks Rd., Vir.W. 192 AX98
Monks Rd., Wind. 151 AK82
Monks Wk., Grav. 190 GA93
Monk's Wk., Reig. 250 DB134
Monks Way NW11 119 CZ56
Hurstwood Rd.
Monks Way, Beck. 203 EA100
Monks Way, Orp. 205 EQ102
Monks Way, Stai. 174 BK94
Monks Way, West Dr. 154 BL79
Harmondsworth La.
Monksbury, Harl. 51 ET18
Monksdene Gdns., Sutt. 200 DB104
Monksfield Way, Slou. 131 AN70
Monksgrove, Loug. 85 EN43
Monksmead, Borwd. 78 CQ42
Monkswell Ct. N10 98 DG53
Pembroke Rd.
Monkswell La., Couls. 234 DB124
Monkswick Rd., Harl. 35 ET13
Monkswood, Welw.G.C. 29 CW05
Monkswood Ave., 67 ED33
Wal.Abb.
Monkswood Gdns., 78 CR43
Borwd.
Monkswood Gdns., Ilf. 125 EN55
Monkton Rd., Well. 165 ET82
Monkton St. SE11 278 E8
Monkton St. SE11 161 DN77
Monkville Ave. NW11 119 CZ56
Monkwell Sq. EC2 275 J7
Monmouth Ave. E18 124 EH55
Monmouth Ave., 177 CJ94
Kings.T.
Monmouth Clo. W4 158 CR76
Beaumont Rd.
Monmouth Clo., Mitch. 201 DL98
Recreation Way
Monmouth Clo., Well. 166 EU84
Monmouth Gro. W5 158 CL77
Sterling Pl.
Monmouth Pl. W2 140 DA72
Monmouth Rd.
Monmouth Rd. E6 145 EM69
Monmouth Rd. N9 100 DV47
Monmouth Rd. W2 140 DA72
Monmouth Rd., Dag. 126 EZ64
Monmouth Rd., Hayes 155 BS77
Monmouth Rd., Wat. 75 BV41
Monmouth St. WC2 273 P10
Monmouth St. WC2 141 DL72
Monnery Rd. N19 121 DJ62
Monnow Grn., S.Ock. 148 FQ73
Monnow Rd.
Monnow Rd. SE1 162 DU78
Monnow Rd., S.Ock. 148 FQ73
Mono La., Felt. 175 BV89
Monoux Gro. E17 101 EA53
Monro Dr., Guil. 242 AU131
Stoughton Rd.
Monro Gdns., Har. 95 CE52
Monroe Cres., Enf. 82 DV39
Monroe Dr. SW14 178 CP85
Mons Wk., Egh. 173 BC92
Mons Way, Brom. 204 EL100
Monsal Ct. E5 123 DX63
Redwald Rd.
Monsell Gdns., Stai. 173 BE92
Monsell Rd. N4 121 DP62
Monson Rd. NW10 139 CU68
Monson Rd. SE14 163 DX80
Monson Rd., Brox. 49 DZ20
Monson Rd., Red. 250 DF131
Montacute Rd. SE6 183 DZ87
Montacute Rd., Croy. 221 EC109
Montacute Rd., Mord. 200 DC100
Montacute Rd. 95 CE45
(Bushey), Wat.
Montagu Cres. N18 100 DV49
Montagu Gdns. N18 100 DV49
Montagu Gdns., Wall. 219 DJ105
Montagu Mans. W1 272 E6
Montagu Ms. N. W1 272 E7
Montagu Ms. N. W1 140 DF71
Montagu Ms. S. W1 272 E8
Montagu Ms. W. W1 272 E8
Montagu Pl. W1 272 D7
Montagu Pl. W1 140 DF71
Montagu Rd. N9 100 DW48
Montagu Rd. N18 100 DV50
Montagu Rd. NW4 119 CU58
Montagu Rd. Ind. Est. N18 100 DW49

Montagu Row W1 272 E7
Montagu Sq. W1 272 E7
Montagu Sq. W1 140 DF71
Montagu St. W1 272 E8
Montagu St. W1 140 DF72
Montague Ave. SE4 163 DZ84
Montague Ave. W7 137 CF74
Montague Ave., S.Croy. 220 DS112
Montague Clo. SE1 279 K2
Montague Clo. SE1 142 DR74
Montague Clo., Walt. 195 BU101
Montague Dr., Cat. 236 DQ122
Drake Ave.
Montague Gdns. W3 138 CN73
Montague Pl. WC1 273 N6
Montague Pl. WC1 141 DK71
Montague Rd. E8 122 DU64
Montague Rd. E11 124 EF62
Montague Rd. N8 121 DM57
Montague Rd. N15 122 DU56
Montague Rd. SW19 180 DB94
Montague Rd. W7 157 CF75
Montague Rd. W13 137 CH72
Montague Rd., Berk. 38 AV19
Montague Rd., Croy. 201 DP102
Montague Rd., Houns. 156 CB83
Montague Rd., Rich. 178 CL86
Montague Rd., Slou. 132 AT73
Montague Rd. (Datchet), Slou. 152 AV81
Montague Rd., Sthl. 156 BY77
Montague Rd., Uxb. 134 BK66
Montague Sq. SE15 162 DW80
Clifton Way
Montague St. EC1 275 H7
Montague St. EC1 142 DQ71
Montague St. WC1 273 P6
Montague St. WC1 141 DL71
Montague Waye, Sthl. 156 BY76
Montalt Rd., Wdf.Grn. 102 EF50
Montana Clo., S.Croy. 220 DQ110
Montana Rd. SW17 180 DG91
Montana Rd. SW20 199 CW95
Montayne Rd. (Cheshunt), Wal.Cr. 67 DX32
Montbelle Rd. SE9 185 EP90
Montcalm Clo., Brom. 204 EG100
Montcalm Clo., Hayes 135 BV69
Ayles Rd.
Montcalm Rd. SE7 164 EK80
Montclare St. E2 275 P4
Monteagle Ave., Bark. 145 EQ65
Monteagle Way E5 122 DU62
Rendlesham Rd.
Monteagle Way SE15 162 DV83
Montefiore St. SW8 161 DH82
Montego Clo. SE24 181 DN85
Railton Rd.
Monteith Rd. E3 143 DZ67
Montem La., Slou. 131 AR74
Montem Rd. SE23 183 DZ87
Montem Rd., N.Mal. 198 CS98
Montem St. N4 121 DM60
Thorpedale Rd.
Montenotte Rd. N8 121 DJ57
Monterey Clo., Bex. 187 FC89
Montesole Ct., Pnr. 94 BW54
Pinner Hill Rd.
Montford Pl. SE11 161 DN78
Montford Rd., Sun. 195 BU98
Montfort Gdns., Ilf. 103 EQ51
Montfort Pl. SW19 179 CX88
Montfort Ri., Red. 266 DF142
Montgolfier Wk., Nthlt. 136 BY69
Jetstar Way
Montgomerie Clo., Berk. 38 AU17
Mortain Dr.
Montgomerie Dr., Guil. 242 AU129
Montgomery Ave., Esher 197 CE104
Montgomery Ave., Hem.H. 40 BN19
Montgomery Clo., Grays 170 GC75
Montgomery Clo., Mitch. 201 DL98
Montgomery Clo., Sid. 185 ET86
Montgomery Cres., Rom. 106 FJ50
Montgomery Dr. (Cheshunt), Wal.Cr. 67 DY28
Montgomery Rd. W4 158 CQ77
Montgomery Rd. (South Darenth), Dart. 209 FR95
Montgomery Rd., Edg. 96 CM51
Montgomery Rd., Wok. 226 AY118
Montholme Rd. SW11 180 DF86
Monthope Rd. E1 142 DU71
Casson St.
Montolieu Gdns. SW15 179 CV85
Montpelier Ave. W5 137 CJ71
Montpelier Ave., Bex. 186 EX87
Montpelier Clo., Uxb. 134 BN67
Montpelier Gdns. E6 144 EK69
Montpelier Gdns., Rom. 126 EW59
Montpelier Gro. NW5 121 DJ64
Montpelier Ms. SW7 276 C6
Montpelier Pl. SW7 276 C6
Montpelier Pl. SW7 160 DE76
Montpelier Ri. NW11 119 CY59
Montpelier Ri., Wem. 117 CK60
Montpelier Rd. N3 98 DC53
Montpelier Rd. SE15 162 DV81
Montpelier Rd. W5 137 CK71
Montpelier Rd., Pur. 219 DP110
Montpelier Rd., Sutt. 218 DC105
Montpelier Row SE3 164 EF82
Montpelier Row, Twick. 177 CH87
Montpelier Sq. SW7 276 C6
Montpelier Sq. SW7 160 DE75
Montpelier St. SW7 276 C5
Montpelier St. SW7 160 DE76
Montpelier Ter. SW7 276 C5
Montpelier Vale SE3 164 EF82
Montpelier Wk. SW7 276 B6
Montpelier Wk. SW7 160 DE76
Montpelier Way NW11 119 CY59
Montrave Rd. SE20 182 DW94
Montreal Pl. WC2 274 B10
Montreal Pl. WC2 141 DM73
Montreal Rd., Ilf. 125 EQ59
Montreal Rd., Sev. 256 FE123
Montreal Rd., Til. 171 GG83
Montrell Rd. SW2 181 DL88
Montrose Ave. NW6 139 CY68
Montrose Ave., Edg. 96 CQ54
Montrose Ave., Rom. 106 FJ54
Montrose Ave., Sid. 186 EU87
Montrose Ave., Slou. 131 AP72
Montrose Ave. (Datchet), Slou. 152 AW80
Montrose Ave., Twick. 176 CB87
Montrose Ave., Well. 165 ER83
Montrose Clo., Ashf. 175 BQ93
Montrose Clo., Well. 165 ET83
Montrose Clo., Wdf.Grn. 102 EG49
Montrose Ct. SW7 276 A5
Montrose Ct. SW7 160 DD75
Montrose Cres. N12 98 DC51
Montrose Cres., Wem. 138 CL65
Montrose Gdns., Lthd. 215 CD112
Montrose Gdns., Mitch. 200 DF97
Montrose Gdns., Sutt. 200 DA103
Montrose Pl. SW1 276 G5
Montrose Pl. SW1 160 DG75
Montrose Rd., Felt. 175 BR87
Montrose Rd., Har. 95 CE54
Montrose Wk., Wey. 195 BP104
Montrose Way SE23 183 DX88
Montrose Way, Slou. 152 AX81
Montrouge Cres., Epsom 233 CW116
Montserrat Ave., Wdf.Grn. 101 ED52
Montserrat Clo. SE19 182 DR92
Montserrat Rd. SW15 159 CY84
Monument Bri. Ind. Est., Wok. 227 BB115
Monument Gdns. SE13 183 EC85
Monument Grn., Wey. 213 BP105
Monument Hill, Wey. 213 BP105
Monument La., Ger.Cr. 90 AY51
Monument Rd., Wey. 213 BP105
Monument Rd., Wok. 211 BA114
Monument St. EC3 275 L10
Monument St. EC3 142 DR73
Monument Way N17 122 DT55
Monument Way E., Wok. 227 BB115
Monument Way W., Wok. 227 BA115
Monza St. E1 142 DW73
Moodkee St. SE16 162 DW76
Moody St. E1 143 DX69
Moon La., Barn. 79 CZ41
Moon St. N1 141 DP67
Moor End, Maid. 150 AC78
Moor End Rd., Hem.H. 40 BJ21
Waterhouse St.
Moor Hall Rd., Harl. 36 EZ11
Moor La. EC2 275 K7
Moor La. EC2 142 DR71
Moor La., Chess. 216 CL105
Moor La., Rick. 92 BM46
Moor La. (Sarratt), Rick. 73 BE36
Moor La., Stai. 173 BD89
Moor La., Upmin. 129 FS60
Moor La., West Dr. 154 BJ79
Moor La., Wok. 226 AY122
Moor La. Crossing, Wat. 93 BQ46
Moor Mead Rd., Twick. 177 CG86
Moor Pk. Est., Nthwd. 93 BQ49
Moor Pk. Gdns., Kings.T. 178 CS94
Moor Pk. Ind. Cen., Wat. 93 BQ45
Moor Pk. Rd., Nthwd. 93 BQ50
Moor Pl. EC2 275 K7
Moor Rd., Chesh. 54 AQ32
Moor Rd., Sev. 241 FH120
Moor St. W1 273 N9
Moor Twr., Harl. 51 ET16
Moor Vw., Wat. 93 BU45
Moorcroft Gdns., Brom. 204 EL99
Southborough Rd.
Moorcroft La., Uxb. 134 BN71
Moorcroft Rd. SW16 181 DL90
Moorcroft Way, Pnr. 116 BY57
Moordown SE18 165 EN81
Moore Ave., Grays 170 FY78
Moore Ave., Til. 171 GH82
Moore Clo. SW14 158 CQ83
Little St. Leonards
Moore Clo., Add. 212 BH106
Moore Clo., Mitch. 201 DH96
Moore Clo., Slou. 151 AP75
Moore Clo., Wall. 219 DL109
Brabazon Ave.
Moore Cres., Dag. 146 EV67
Moore Gro. Cres., Egh. 172 AY94
Moore Pk. Rd. SW6 160 DB80
Moore Rd. SE19 182 DQ93
Moore Rd., Berk. 38 AT17
Moore Rd., Swans. 190 FY86
Moore St. SW3 276 D8
Moore St. SW3 160 DF77
Moore Wk. E7 124 EG63
Stracey Rd.
Moore Way SE22 182 DU88
Lordship La.
Moore Way, Sutt. 218 DA109
Moorefield Rd. N17 122 DT55
Moorehead Way SE3 164 EH83
Mooreland Rd., Brom. 184 EF94
Moorend, Welw.G.C. 30 DA12
Moores La. (Eton Wick), Wind. 151 AM77
Moores Pl., Brwd. 108 FX47
Moores Rd., Dor. 263 CH135
Moorey Clo. E15 144 EF67
Stephen's Rd.
Moorfield, Harl. 51 EQ20
Moorfield Ave. W5 137 CK70
Moorfield Rd., Chess. 216 CL106
Moorfield Rd., Enf. 82 DW39
Moorfield Rd., Guil. 242 AX130
Moorfield Rd., Orp. 206 EU101
Moorfield Rd., Uxb. 134 BK72
Moorfield Rd. (Harefield), Uxb. 114 BG59
Moorfields EC2 275 K7
Moorfields EC2 142 DR71
Moorfields Clo., Stai. 193 BE95
Moorfields Highwalk EC2 142 DR71
Fore St.
Moorgate EC2 275 K7
Moorgate EC2 142 DR71
Moorgate Pl. EC2 275 K8
Moorhall Rd., Uxb. 114 BH58
Moorhayes Dr., Stai. 194 BJ97
Moorhen Clo., Erith 167 FG80
Slade Grn. Rd.
Moorholme, Wok. 226 AY119
Oak Bank
Moorhouse Rd. W2 140 DA72
Moorhouse Rd., Har. 117 CK55
Moorhouse Rd., Oxt. 255 EM131
Moorhurst Ave. (Cheshunt), Wal.Cr. 65 DN29
Moorings, The SE28 146 EV73
Titmuss Ave.
Moorland Clo., Rom. 105 FB53
Moorland Clo., Twick. 176 CA87
Telford Rd.
Moorland Rd. SW9 161 DP84
Moorland Rd., Hem.H. 40 BG22
Moorland Rd., West Dr. 154 BJ79
Moorlands, Welw.G.C. 30 DA12
Moorlands, The, Wok. 227 AZ121
Moorlands Ave. NW7 97 CV51
Moorlands Est. SW9 161 DN84
Moorlands Reach, Saw. 36 EZ06
Sun St.
Moormead Dr., Epsom 216 CS106
Moormede Cres., Stai. 173 BF91
Moors, The, Welw.G.C. 30 DA08
Moors Wk., Welw.G.C. 30 DB08
Moorside, Hem.H. 40 BH23
Stratford Way
Moorside, H.Wyc. 110 AE55
Moorside, Welw.G.C. 30 DA12
Moorside Rd., Brom. 184 EE90
Moorsom Way, Couls. 235 DK117
Moortown Rd., Wat. 94 BW49
Moot Ct. NW9 118 CN57
Mora Rd. NW2 119 CW63
Mora St. EC1 275 J3
Mora St. EC1 142 DQ69
Morant Gdns., Rom. 105 FB50
Morant Pl. N22 99 DM53
Commerce Rd.
Morant Rd., Grays 171 GH76
Morant St. E14 143 EA73
Morants Ct. Rd., Sev. 241 FC118
Morat St. SW9 161 DM81
Moravian Pl. SW10 160 DD79
Milman's St.
Moravian St. E2 142 DW69
Moray Ave., Hayes 135 BT74
Moray Clo., Rom. 105 FE52
Moray Dr., Slou. 132 AU72
Moray Ms. N7 121 DM61
Durham Rd.
Moray Rd. N4 121 DM61
Moray Way, Rom. 105 FD52
Morcote Clo., Guil. 258 AY141
Mordaunt Gdns., Dag. 146 EY66
Mordaunt Ho. NW10 138 CR67
Mordaunt Rd. NW10 138 CR67
Mordaunt St. SW9 161 DM83
Morden Clo. SE13 163 EC82
Morden Clo., Tad. 233 CX120
Marbles Way
Morden Ct., Mord. 200 DB98
Morden Gdns., Grnf. 117 CF64
Morden Gdns., Mitch. 200 DD98
Morden Hall Rd., Mord. 200 DB97
Morden Hill SE13 163 EC82
Morden La. SE13 163 EC81
Morden Rd. SE3 164 EG82
Morden Rd. SW19 200 DB95
Morden Rd., Mitch. 200 DC98
Morden Rd., Rom. 126 EY59
Morden Rd. Ms. SE3 164 EG82
Morden St. SE13 163 EB81
Morden Way, Sutt. 200 DA101
Morden Wf. Rd. SE10 164 EE76
Mordon Rd., Ilf. 125 ET59
Mordred Rd. SE6 184 EE89
More Circle, Gdmg. 258 AS144
More Clo. E16 144 EF72
More Clo. W14 159 CX77
More Clo., Pur. 219 DN111
More La., Esher 196 CB103
More Rd., Gdmg. 258 AS144
Moreau Wk., Slou. 132 AY72
Alan Way
Morecambe Clo. E1 143 DX71
Morecambe Clo., Horn. 127 FH64
Morecambe Gdns., Stan. 95 CK49
Morecambe St. SE17 279 J9
Morecambe St. SE17 162 DQ77
Morecambe Ter. N18 100 DR49
Morecoombe Clo., Kings.T. 178 CP94
Moree Way N18 100 DU49
Morel Ct., Sev. 257 FH122
Bradbourne Rd.
Moreland Ave., Grays 170 GC75
Moreland Ave., Slou. 153 BC80
Moreland Clo., Slou. 153 BC80
Moreland Ave.
Moreland Dr., Ger.Cr. 113 AZ58
Moreland St. EC1 274 G2
Moreland St. EC1 141 DP69
Moreland Way E4 101 EB48
Morella Clo., Vir.W. 192 AX98
Morella Rd. SW12 180 DF87
Morello Ave., Uxb. 135 BP71
Morello Clo., Swan. 207 FD98
Morello Dr., Slou. 133 AZ74
Moremead, Wal.Abb. 67 ED33
Moremead Rd. SE6 183 DZ91
Morena St. SE6 183 EB87
Moresby Ave., Surb. 198 CP101
Moresby Rd. E5 122 DV60
Moresby Wk. SW8 161 DH82
Moretaine Rd., Ashf. 174 BK90
Hengrove Cres.
Moreton Ave., Islw. 157 CE81
Moreton Clo. E5 122 DW61
Moreton Clo. N15 122 DR58
Moreton Clo. NW7 97 CW51
Moreton Clo., Swan. 207 FE96
Bonney Way
Moreton Clo. (Cheshunt), Wal.Cr. 66 DV27
Moreton Gdns., Wdf.Grn. 102 EL50
Moreton Ind. Est., Swan. 207 FG98
Moreton Pl. SW1 277 L10
Moreton Pl. SW1 161 DJ78
Moreton Rd. N15 122 DR58
Moreton Rd., Ong. 53 FG24
Moreton Rd., S.Croy. 220 DR106
Moreton Rd., Wor.Pk. 199 CU103
Moreton St. SW1 277 L10
Moreton St. SW1 161 DJ78
Moreton Ter. SW1 277 L10
Moreton Ter. SW1 161 DJ78
Moreton Ter. Ms. N. SW1 277 L10
Moreton Ter. Ms. S. SW1 277 L10
Moreton Twr. W3 138 CP74
Moreton Way, Slou. 131 AK74
Morewood Clo., Sev. 256 FF123
Morford Clo., Ruis. 115 BV59
Morford Way, Ruis. 115 BV59
Morgan Ave. E17 123 ED56
Morgan Clo., Dag. 146 FA66
Morgan Clo., Nthwd. 93 BT50
Morgan Cres., Epp. 85 ER36
Morgan Dr., Green. 189 FS87
Morgan Rd. N7 121 DN64
Morgan Rd. W10 139 CZ71
Morgan Rd., Brom. 184 EG94
Morgan St. E3 143 DY69
Morgan St. E16 144 EF71
Morgan Way, Rain. 148 FJ69
Morgan Way, Wdf.Grn. 102 EL51
Morgans Clo., Hert. 32 DR11
Morgans La. SE1 279 M3
Morgans La. SE1 142 DS74
Morgans La., Hayes 135 BR71
Morgans Rd., Hert. 32 DR11
Moriatri Clo. N7 121 DL63
Morice Rd., Hodd. 49 DZ15
Morie St. SW18 160 DB84
Morieux Rd. E10 123 DZ60
Moring Rd. SW17 180 DG91
Morkyns Wk. SE21 182 DS90
Morland Ave., Croy. 202 DS102
Morland Ave., Dart. 187 FH85
Morland Clo. NW11 120 DB60
Morland Clo., Hmptn. 176 BZ92
Morland Clo., Mitch. 200 DE97
Morland Gdns. NW10 138 CR66
Morland Gdns., Sthl. 136 CB74
Morland Ms. N1 141 DN66
Lofting Rd.
Morland Rd. E17 123 DX57
Morland Rd. SE20 183 DX93
Morland Rd., Croy. 202 DS102
Morland Rd., Dag. 146 FA66
Morland Rd., Har. 118 CL57
Morland Rd., Ilf. 125 EP61
Morland Rd., Sutt. 218 DC106
Morland Way (Cheshunt), Wal.Cr. 67 DY28
Morley Ave. E4 101 ED52
Morley Ave. N18 100 DU49
Morley Ave. N22 99 DN54
Morley Clo., Orp. 205 EP103
Morley Clo., Ruis. 116 BW61
Morley Clo., Slou. 153 AZ75
Morley Cres., Edg. 96 CQ47
Morley Cres. E., Stan. 95 CJ54
Morley Cres. W., Stan. 117 CJ55
Morley Gro., Harl. 35 EQ13
Morley Hill, Enf. 82 DR38
Morley Rd. E10 123 EC60
Morley Rd. E15 144 EF68
Morley Rd. SE13 163 EC84
Morley Rd., Bark. 145 ER67
Morley Rd., Chis. 205 EQ95
Morley Rd., Rom. 126 EY57
Morley Rd., S.Croy. 220 DT110
Morley Rd., Sutt. 199 CZ102
Morley Rd., Twick. 177 CK86
Morley Sq., Grays 171 GG77
Morley St. SE1 278 E6
Morley St. SE1 161 DN76
Morna Rd. SE5 162 DQ82
Morning La. E9 142 DW65
Morning Ri., Rick. 74 BK41
Morningside Rd., Wor.Pk. 199 CV103
Mornington Ave. W14 159 CZ77
Mornington Ave., Brom. 204 EJ97
Mornington Ave., Ilf. 125 EN59
Mornington Clo., West. 238 EK117
Mornington Clo., Wdf.Grn. 102 EG49
Mornington Ct., Bex. 187 FC88
Mornington Cres. NW1 141 DJ68
Mornington Cres., Houns. 155 BV81
Mornington Gro. E3 143 EA69
Mornington Ms. SE5 162 DQ81
Mornington Pl. NW1 141 DH68
Mornington Ter.
Mornington Rd. E4 101 ED45
Mornington Rd. E11 124 EF60
Mornington Rd. SE8 163 DZ80
Mornington Rd., Ashf. 175 BQ92
Mornington Rd., Grnf. 136 CB71
Mornington Rd., Loug. 85 EQ41
Mornington Rd., Rad. 61 CH34
Mornington Rd., Wdf.Grn. 102 EF49
Mornington St. NW1 141 DH68
Mornington Ter. NW1 141 DH68
Mornington Wk., Rich. 177 CJ91
Morningtons, Harl. 51 EQ19
Morocco St. SE1 279 M5
Morocco St. SE1 162 DS75
Morpeth Ave., Borwd. 78 CM38
Morpeth Clo., Hem.H. 40 BL21
Old Crabtree La.
Morpeth Gro. E9 143 DX67
Morpeth Rd. E9 142 DW67
Morpeth St. E2 143 DX69
Morpeth Ter. SW1 277 K7
Morpeth Ter. SW1 161 DJ76
Morpeth Wk. N17 100 DV52
West Rd.
Morrab Gdns., Ilf. 125 ET62
Morrell Clo., Barn. 80 DC41
Galdana Ave.
Morrell Ct., Welw.G.C. 29 CZ08
Brownfields
Morrice Clo., Slou. 153 BA77
Morris Ave. E12 125 EM64
Morris Clo., Croy. 203 DY100
Morris Clo., Ger.Cr. 91 AZ53
Morris Clo., Orp. 205 ES104
Morris Ct. E4 101 EB48
Flaxen Rd.
Morris Ct., Wal.Abb. 68 EF34
Morris Gdns. SW18 180 DA87
Morris Gdns., Dart. 188 FN85
Morris Pl. N4 121 DN61
Morris Rd. E14 143 EB71
Morris Rd. E15 123 ED63
Morris Rd., Dag. 126 EZ61
Morris Rd., Islw. 157 CF83
Morris Rd., Red. 267 DL136
Morris Rd., Rom. 105 FH52
Morris St. E1 142 DV72
Morris Way, St.Alb. 61 CK26
Morrish Rd. SW2 181 DL87
Morrison Ave. N17 122 DS55
Morrison Rd., Bark. 146 EY68
Morrison Rd., Hayes 135 BV69
Morrison St. SW11 160 DG83
Morriston Clo., Wat. 94 BW50
Morse Clo. E13 144 EG69
Morse Clo., Uxb. 92 BJ54
Morshead Rd. W9 140 DA69
Morson Rd., Enf. 83 DY44
Morston Clo., Tad. 233 CV120
Waterfield
Morston Gdns. SE9 185 EM91
Mortain Dr., Berk. 38 AT17
Morten Clo. SW4 181 DK86
Morten Gdns., Uxb. 114 BG59
Mortens Wd., Amer. 55 AS40
Morteyne Rd. N17 100 DR53
Mortgramit Sq. SE18 165 EN76
Powis St.
Mortham St. E15 144 EE67
Mortimer Clo. NW2 119 CZ62
Mortimer Clo. SW16 181 DK89
Mortimer Clo. (Bushey), Wat. 76 CB44
Ashfield Ave.
Mortimer Cres. NW6 140 DB67
Mortimer Cres., Wor.Pk. 198 CR104
Mortimer Dr., Enf. 82 DS43
Mortimer Est. NW6 140 DB67
Mortimer Gate, Wal.Cr. 67 DZ27
Mortimer Mkt. WC1 273 L5
Mortimer Pl. NW6 140 DB67
Mortimer Rd. E6 145 EM69
Mortimer Rd. N1 142 DS66
Mortimer Rd. NW10 139 CW69
Mortimer Rd. W13 137 CJ72
Mortimer Rd., Erith 167 FD79
Mortimer Rd., Mitch. 200 DF95
Mortimer Rd., Orp. 206 EU102
Mortimer Rd., Slou. 152 AX76
Mortimer Rd., West. 222 EJ112
Mortimer Sq. W11 139 CX73
St. Anns Rd.
Mortimer St. W1 273 K8
Mortimer St. W1 141 DJ72
Mortimer Ter. NW5 121 DH63
Gordon Ho. Rd.
Mortlake Clo., Croy. 201 DL104
Richmond Rd.
Mortlake Dr., Mitch. 200 DE95
Mortlake High St. SW14 158 CR83
Mortlake Rd. E16 144 EH72
Mortlake Rd., Ilf. 125 EQ63
Mortlake Rd., Rich. 158 CN80
Mortlake Ter., Rich. 158 CN80
Kew Rd.
Mortlock Clo. SE15 162 DV81
Cossall Wk.
Morton, Tad. 233 CX121
Morton Clo., Wok. 226 AX115
Morton Cres. N14 99 DK49
Morton Dr., Slou. 111 AL64
Morton Gdns., Wall. 219 DJ106
Morton Ms. SW5 160 DB77
Earls Ct. Gdns.
Morton Pl. SE1 278 D7
Morton Rd. E15 144 EF66
Morton Rd. N1 142 DQ66
Morton Rd., Mord. 200 DD99
Morton Rd., Wok. 226 AX115
Morton Way N14 99 DJ48
Morval Rd. SW2 181 DN85
Morvale Clo., Belv. 166 EZ77
Morven Clo., Pot.B. 64 DC31
Morven Rd. SW17 180 DF90
Morville St. E3 143 EA68
Morwell St. WC1 273 N7
Mosbach Gdns., Brwd. 109 GB47
Moscow Pl. W2 140 DB73
Moscow Rd.
Moscow Rd. W2 140 DB73
Moselle Ave. N22 99 DN54
Moselle Clo. N8 121 DM55
Miles Rd.
Moselle Ho. N17 100 DT52
Moselle Pl. N17 100 DT52
High Rd.
Moselle Rd., West. 238 EL118
Moselle St. N17 100 DT52
Mosford Clo., Horl. 268 DF146
Mospey Cres., Epsom 233 CT115
Moss Bank, Grays 170 FZ77
Moss Clo. E1 142 DU71
Old Montague St.
Moss Clo., Pnr. 94 BZ54
Moss Clo., Rick. 92 BK47
Moss Gdns., Felt. 175 BU89
Rose Gdns.
Moss Gdns., S.Croy. 221 DX108
Warren Ave.
Moss Grn., Welw.G.C. 29 CY11
Moss Hall Cres. N12 98 DB51
Moss Hall Gro. N12 98 DB51
Moss La., Pnr. 94 BY53
Moss La., Rom. 127 FF58
Wheatsheaf Rd.
Moss Rd., Dag. 146 FA66
Moss Rd., S.Ock. 149 FW71
Moss Rd., Wat. 59 BV34
Moss Side, St.Alb. 60 BZ30
Moss Way, Beac. 88 AJ50
Mossborough Clo. N12 98 DB51
Mossbury Rd. SW11 160 DE83
Mossdown Clo., Belv. 166 FA77
Mossendew Clo., Uxb. 92 BK53
Mossfield, Cob. 213 BU113
Mossford Ct., Ilf. 125 EP55
Mossford Grn., Ilf. 125 EP55
Mossford La., Ilf. 103 EP54
Mossford St. E3 143 DZ70
Mossington Gdns. SE16 162 DW77
Abbeyfield Rd.
Mosslea Rd. SE20 182 DW93
Mosslea Rd., Brom. 204 EK99
Mosslea Rd., Orp. 205 EQ104
Mosslea Rd., Whyt. 236 DT116
Mossop St. SW3 276 C8
Mossop St. SW3 160 DE77
Mossville Gdns., Mord. 199 CZ97
Moston Clo., Hayes 155 BT78
Fuller Way
Mostyn Ave., Wem. 118 CM64
Mostyn Gdns. NW10 139 CX69
Mostyn Gro. E3 143 EA68
Mostyn Rd. SW9 161 DN81
Mostyn Rd. SW19 199 CZ95
Mostyn Rd., Edg. 96 CR52
Mostyn Rd. (Bushey), Wat. 76 CC43
Mostyn Ter., Red. 266 DG135
Mosul Way, Brom. 204 EL100
Mosyer Dr., Orp. 206 EX103
Motcomb St. SW1 276 E6
Motcomb St. SW1 160 DG76
Mothers Sq. E5 122 DV63
Clarence Rd.

Motherwell Way, Grays 169 FU78
Motley Ave. EC2 142 DS70
Scrutton St.
Motley St. SW8 161 DJ82
St. Rule St.
Motspur Pk., N.Mal. 199 CT100
Mott St. E4 83 ED38
Mott St., Loug. 84 EE39
Mottingham Gdns. SE9 184 EK88
Mottingham La. SE9 184 EJ88
Mottingham La. SE12 184 EJ88
Mottingham Rd. N9 83 DX44
Mottingham Rd. SE9 184 EL89
Mottisfont Rd. SE2 166 EU76
Motts Hill La., Tad. 233 CU123
Mouchotte Clo., West. 222 EH112
Moulins Rd. E9 142 DW66
Moultain Hill, Swan. 207 FG98
Moulton Ave., Houns. 156 BY82
Moultrie Way, Upmin. 129 FS59
Mound, The SE9 185 EN90
Moundfield Rd. N16 122 DU58
Mount, The N20 98 DC47
Mount, The NW3 120 DC63
Heath St.
Mount, The, Brwd. 108 FW48
Mount, The, Couls. 234 DG115
Mount, The (Ewell), Epsom 217 CT110
Mount, The, Esher 214 CA107
Mount, The, Guil. 258 AV137
Mount, The, Lthd. 231 CE123
Mount, The, N.Mal. 199 CT97
Mount, The, Pot.B. 64 DB30
Mount, The, Rick. 74 BJ44
Mount, The, Rom. 106 FJ48
Mount, The, Tad. 249 CZ126
Mount, The, Vir.W. 192 AX100
Mount, The (Cheshunt), Wal.Cr. 66 DR26
Mount, The, Warl. 236 DU119
Mount, The, Wem. 118 CP61
Mount, The, Wey. 195 BS103
Mount, The, Wok. 226 AX118
Mount, The (St. John's), Wok. 226 AU119
Mount, The, Wor.Pk. 217 CV105
Mount Adon Pk. SE22 182 DU87
Mount Angelus Rd. SW15 179 CT87
Laverstoke Gdns.
Mount Ararat Rd., Rich. 178 CL85
Mount Ash Rd. SE26 182 DV90
Mount Ave. E4 101 EA48
Mount Ave. W5 137 CJ71
Mount Ave., Brwd. 109 GA44
Mount Ave., Cat. 236 DQ124
Mount Ave., Rom. 106 FQ51
Mount Ave., Sthl. 136 CA72
Mount Clo. W5 137 CJ71
Mount Clo., Barn. 80 DG42
Mount Clo., Brom. 204 EL95
Mount Clo., Cars. 218 DG109
Mount Clo., Hem.H. 39 BF20
Mount Clo., Ken. 236 DR116
Mount Clo., Lthd. 231 CE123
Mount Clo., Sev. 256 FF123
Mount Clo., Slou. 111 AQ63
Mount Clo., Wok. 226 AV121
Mount Clo., The, Vir.W. 192 AX100
Mount Cor., Felt. 176 BX89
Mount Ct. SW15 159 CY83
Weimar St.
Mount Ct., W.Wick. 204 EE103
Mount Cres., Brwd. 108 FX49
Mount Culver Ave., Sid. 186 EX93
Mount Dr., Bexh. 186 EY85
Mount Dr., Har. 116 BZ57
Mount Dr., St.Alb. 61 CD25
Mount Dr., Wem. 118 CQ61
Mount Dr., The, Reig. 250 DC132
Mount Echo Ave. E4 101 EB47
Mount Echo Dr. E4 101 EB46
Mount Ephraim La. SW16 181 DK90
Mount Ephraim Rd. SW16 181 DK90
Mount Est., The E5 122 DV61
Mount Pleasant La.
Mount Felix, Walt. 195 BT102
Mount Gdns. SE26 182 DV90
Mount Grace Rd., Pot.B. 64 DA31
Mount Gro., Edg. 96 CQ48
Mount Harry Rd., Sev. 256 FG123
Mount Hermon Clo., Wok. 226 AY118
York Rd.
Mount Hermon Rd., Wok. 226 AX119
Mount Hill La., Ger.Cr. 112 AV60
Mount La., Uxb. 113 BD61
Mount Lee, Egh. 173 AZ92
Mount Ms., Hmptn. 196 CB95
Mount Mills EC1 274 G3
Mount Nod Rd. SW16 181 DM90
Mount Nugent, Chesh. 54 AN27
Mount Pk., Cars. 218 DG109
Mount Pk. Ave., Har. 117 CD61
Mount Pk. Ave., S.Croy. 219 DP109
Mount Pk. Cres. W5 137 CK72
Mount Pk. Rd. W5 137 CK71
Mount Pk. Rd., Har. 117 CD62
Mount Pk. Rd., Pnr. 115 BU57
Mount Pl., Guil. 258 AW136
The Mt.
Mount Pleasant SE27 182 DQ92
Mount Pleasant WC1 274 D5
Mount Pleasant WC1 141 DN70
Mount Pleasant, Barn. 80 DE42
Mount Pleasant, Epsom 217 CT110
Mount Pleasant, Guil. 258 AW136
Mount Pleasant, Hert. 32 DW11
Mount Pleasant (Effingham), Lthd. 246 BY128
Mount Pleasant (West Horsley), Lthd. 245 BP129
Mount Pleasant, Ruis. 116 BW61
Mount Pleasant, St.Alb. 42 CB19
Mount Pleasant, Uxb. 92 BG53
Mount Pleasant, Wem. 138 CL67
Mount Pleasant, West. 238 EK117
Mount Pleasant, Wey. 194 BN104
Mount Pleasant Ave., Brwd. 109 GE44
Mount Pleasant Clo., Hat. 45 CW15
Mount Pleasant Cres. N4 121 DM59
Mount Pleasant Hill E5 122 DV61
Mount Pleasant La. E5 122 DV61
Mount Pleasant La., Hat. 29 CW14
Mount Pleasant La., St.Alb. 60 BY30
Mount Pleasant Rd. E17 101 DY54
Mount Pleasant Rd. N17 100 DS53
Mount Pleasant Rd. NW10 139 CW66
Mount Pleasant Rd. SE13 183 EC86
Mount Pleasant Rd. W5 137 CJ70
Mount Pleasant Rd., Cat. 236 DU123
Mount Pleasant Rd., Chig. 103 ER49
Mount Pleasant Rd., Dart. 188 FM86
Mount Pleasant Rd., N.Mal. 198 CQ97
Mount Pleasant Rd., Rom. 105 FD51
Mount Pleasant Vill. N4 121 DM59
Mount Pleasant Wk., Bex. 187 FC85
Mount Ri., Red. 266 DD136
Mount Rd. NW2 119 CV62
Mount Rd. NW4 119 CU58
Mount Rd. SE19 182 DR93
Mount Rd. SW19 180 DA89
Mount Rd., Barn. 80 DE43
Mount Rd., Bexh. 186 EX85
Mount Rd., Chess. 216 CM106
Mount Rd., Dag. 126 EZ60
Mount Rd., Dart. 187 FF86
Mount Rd., Epp. 70 EW32
Mount Rd., Felt. 176 BY90
Mount Rd., Hayes 155 BT75
Mount Rd., Hert. 31 DN10
Mount Rd., Ilf. 125 EP64
Mount Rd., Mitch. 200 DD96
Mount Rd., N.Mal. 198 CR97
Mount Rd., Wok. 226 AV121
Mount Rd. (Chobham), Wok. 210 AV112
Mount Row W1 277 H1
Mount Row W1 141 DH73
Mount Sorrel, Hert. 32 DT09
Mount Sq., The NW3 120 DC62
Heath St.
Mount Stewart Ave., Har. 117 CK58
Mount St. W1 276 F1
Mount St. W1 140 DG73
Mount St., Dor. 263 CG136
Mount Ter. E1 142 DV71
New Rd.
Mount Vernon NW3 120 DC63
Mount Vw. NW7 96 CR48
Mount Vw. W5 137 CK70
Mount Vw., Enf. 81 DM38
Mount Vw., Rick. 92 BH46
Mount Vw., St.Alb. 62 CL27
Mount Vw. Rd. E4 101 EC45
Mount Vw. Rd. N4 121 DL59
Mount Vw. Rd. NW9 118 CR57
Mount Vill. SE27 181 DP90
Mount Way, Cars. 218 DG109
Mountacre Clo. SE26 182 DT91
Mountague Pl. E14 143 EC73
Mountain Ct. (Eynsford), Dart. 208 FL103
Pollyhaugh
Mountbatten Clo. SE18 165 ES79
Mountbatten Clo. SE19 182 DS92
Mountbatten Clo., St.Alb. 43 CH23
Mountbatten Clo., Slou. 152 AU75
Mountbatten Ct. SE16 142 DW74
Rotherhithe St.
Mountbatten Ct., Buck.H. 102 EK47
Mountbatten Ms. SW18 180 DC88
Inman Rd.
Mountbatten Sq., Wind. 151 AQ81
Alma Rd.
Mountbel Rd., Stan. 95 CG53
Mountcombe Clo., Surb. 198 CL101
Mountearl Gdns. SW16 181 DM90
Mountfield Rd. E6 145 EN68
Mountfield Rd. N3 119 CZ55
Mountfield Rd. W5 137 CK72
Mountfield Rd., Hem.H. 40 BL20
Mountfield Way, Orp. 206 EW98
Mountford St. E1 142 DU72
Adler St.
Mountfort Cres. N1 141 DN66
Barnsbury Sq.
Mountfort Ter. N1 141 DN66
Barnsbury Sq.
Mountgrove Rd. N5 121 DP62
Mounthurst Rd., Brom. 204 EF101
Mountington Pk. Clo., Har. 117 CK58
Mountjoy Clo. SE2 166 EV75
Mountjoy Ho. EC2 142 DQ71
The Barbican
Mountnessing Bypass, Brwd. 109 GD41
Mounts Pond Rd. SE3 163 ED82
Mounts Rd., Green. 189 FV85
Mountsfield Clo. SE6 183 ED87
Stainton Rd.
Mountsfield Clo., Stai. 174 BG85
Mountsfield Ct. SE13 183 ED86
Mountside, Felt. 176 BY90
Mountside, Guil. 258 AV136
Mountside, Stan. 95 CF53
Mountview, Nthwd. 93 BT51
Mountview Clo., Red. 266 DE136
Pendleton Rd.
Mountview Ct. N8 121 DP56
Green Las.
Mountview Ct., Wat. 76 CB43
Moatfield Rd.
Mountview Dr., Red. 250 DE134
Pendleton Rd.
Mountview Rd., Esher 215 CH108
Mountview Rd., Orp. 206 EU101
Mountview Rd. (Cheshunt), Wal.Cr. 66 DS26
Mountway, Pot.B. 64 DA30
Mountway, Welw.G.C. 29 CZ12
Mountway Clo., Welw.G.C. 29 CZ12
Mountwood, W.Mol. 196 CA97
Mountwood Clo., S.Croy. 220 DV110
Movers La., Bark. 145 ER67
Mowatt Clo. N19 121 DK60
Mowbray Ave., W.Byf. 212 BL113
Mowbray Cres., Egh. 173 BA92
Mowbray Gdns., Dor. 247 CH134
Mowbray Rd. NW6 139 CY66
Mowbray Rd. SE19 202 DT95
Mowbray Rd., Barn. 80 DC42
Mowbray Rd., Edg. 96 CN49
Mowbray Rd., Harl. 35 ET13
Mowbray Rd., Rich. 177 CJ90
Mowbrays Clo., Rom. 105 FC53
Mowbrays Rd., Rom. 105 FC54
Mowbrey Gdns., Loug. 85 EQ39
Mowlem St. E2 142 DV68
Mowlem Trd. Est. N17 100 DW52
Mowll St. SW9 161 DN80
Moxon Clo. E13 144 EF68
Whitelegg Rd.
Moxon St. W1 272 F7
Moxon St. W1 140 DG71
Moxon St., Barn. 79 CZ41
Moye Clo. E2 142 DU67
Dove Row
Moyers Rd. E10 123 EC59
Moylan Rd. W6 159 CY79
Moyne Ct., Wok. 226 AT118
Iveagh Rd.
Moyne Pl. NW10 138 CN68
Moys Clo., Croy. 201 DL100
Mitcham Rd.
Moyser Rd. SW16 181 DH92
Mozart St. W10 139 CZ69
Mozart Ter. SW1 276 G9
Muchelney Rd., Mord. 200 DC100
Muckhatch La., Egh. 193 BB97
Muckingford Rd., Til. 171 GL77
Mud La. W5 137 CK71
Muddy La., Slou. 132 AS71
Mudlarks Way SE7 164 EH76
Mudlarks Way SE10 164 EF76
Muggeridge Rd., Dag. 127 FB63
Muir Rd. E5 122 DU63
Muir St. E16 145 EM74
Newland St.
Muirdown Ave. SW14 158 CR84
Muirfield W3 138 CS72
Muirfield Clo. SE16 162 DV78
Credon Rd.
Muirfield Clo., Wat. 94 BW50
Muirfield Cres. E14 163 EB76
Millharbour
Muirfield Grn., Wat. 94 BW49
Muirfield Rd., Wat. 93 BV49
Muirfield Rd., Wok. 226 AU118
Muirkirk Rd. SE6 183 EC88
Mulberry Ave., Stai. 174 BL88
Mulberry Ave., Wind. 152 AT82
Mulberry Clo. E4 101 EA47
Mulberry Clo. N8 121 DL57
Hermiston Ave.
Mulberry Clo. NW3 120 DD63
Hampstead High St.
Mulberry Clo. NW4 119 CW55
Mulberry Clo. SE7 164 EK79
Mulberry Clo. SE22 182 DU86
Mulberry Clo. SW16 181 DJ91
Mulberry Clo., Amer. 72 AT39
Mulberry Clo., Barn. 80 DD42
Mulberry Clo., Brox. 49 DZ24
Mulberry Clo., Nthlt. 136 BY68
Parkfield Ave.
Mulberry Clo., Rom. 127 FH56
Mulberry Clo., St.Alb. 60 CB28
Mulberry Clo., Wey. 195 BP104
Mulberry Clo., Wok. 210 AY114
Mulberry Ct., Bark. 145 ET66
Westrow Dr.
Mulberry Ct., Beac. 89 AM54
Mulberry Ct., Guil. 243 BD131
Gilliat Dr.
Mulberry Cres., Brent. 157 CH80
Mulberry Cres., West Dr. 154 BN75
Mulberry Dr., Purf. 168 FM77
Mulberry Dr., Slou. 152 AY78
Mulberry Grn., Harl. 36 EX11
Mulberry Hill, Brwd. 109 FZ45
Mulberry La., Croy. 202 DT102
Mulberry Ms., Wall. 219 DJ107
Ross Rd.
Mulberry Par., West Dr. 154 BN76
Mulberry Pl. W6 159 CU78
Chiswick Mall
Mulberry Rd. E8 142 DT66
Middleton Rd.
Mulberry Rd., Grav. 190 GE90
Mulberry St. E1 142 DU72
Adler St.
Mulberry Trees, Shep. 195 BR101
Mulberry Wk. SW3 160 DD79
Mulberry Way E18 102 EH54
Mulberry Way, Belv. 167 FC75
Mulberry Way, Ilf. 125 EQ56
Mulgrave Rd. NW10 119 CT63
Mulgrave Rd. SW6 159 CZ79
Mulgrave Rd. W5 137 CK70
Mulgrave Rd., Croy. 202 DR104
Mulgrave Rd., Har. 117 CG61
Mulgrave Rd., Sutt. 217 CZ108
Mulgrave Way, Wok. 226 AS118
Mulholland Clo., Mitch. 201 DH96
Mulkern Rd. N19 121 DK60
Mull Wk. N1 142 DQ65
Clephane Rd.
Mullards Clo., Mitch. 200 DG102
New Rd.
Mullein Ct., Grays 170 GD79
Mullens Rd., Egh. 173 BB92
Muller Rd. SW4 181 DK86
Mullet Gdns. E2 142 DU68
St. Peter's Clo.
Mullins Path SW14 158 CR83
Mullion Clo., Har. 94 CB53
Mullion Wk., Wat. 94 BX49
Ormskirk Rd.
Mulready St. NW8 272 B5
Multi Way W3 158 CS75
Valetta Rd.
Multon Rd. SW18 180 DD87
Mulvaney Way SE1 279 L5
Mulvaney Way SE1 162 DR75
Mumford Ct. EC2 275 J8
Mumford Rd. SE24 181 DP85
Railton Rd.
Mumfords La., Ger.Cr. 112 AU55
Muncaster Clo., Ashf. 174 BN91
Muncaster Rd. SW11 180 DF85
Muncaster Rd., Ashf. 175 BP92
Muncies Ms. SE6 183 EC89
Mund St. W14 159 CZ78
Mundania Rd. SE22 182 DV86
Munday Rd. E16 144 EG72
Mundells, Wal.Cr. 66 DU27
Mundells, Welw.G.C. 29 CZ07
Mundells Ct., Welw.G.C. 29 CZ07
Munden Dr., Wat. 76 BY37
Colne Way
Munden Gro., Wat. 76 BW38
Munden St. W14 159 CY77
Munden Vw., Wat. 76 BX36
Mundesley Clo., Wat. 94 BW49
Mundesley Spur, Slou. 132 AS72
Mundford Rd. E5 122 DW61
Mundon Gdns., Ilf. 125 ER60
Mundy St. N1 275 N2
Mundy St. N1 142 DS69
Munford Dr., Swans. 190 FY87
Mungo Pk. Clo. (Bushey), Wat. 94 CC47
Mungo Pk. Rd., Grav. 191 GK92
Mungo Pk. Rd., Rain. 147 FG65
Mungo Pk. Way, Orp. 206 EW100
Munnery Way, Orp. 205 EN103
Munnings Gdns., Islw. 177 CD85
Munro Dr. N11 99 DJ51
Munro Ms. W10 139 CY71
Munro Rd. (Bushey), Wat. 76 CB43
Munro Ter. SW10 160 DD79
Munslow Gdns., Sutt. 218 DD105
Benhill Rd.
Munstead Vw., Guil. 258 AV138
Munster Ave., Houns. 156 BY84
Munster Ct., Tedd. 177 CJ93
Munster Gdns. N13 99 DP49
Munster Ms. SW6 159 CY80
Munster Rd.
Munster Rd. SW6 159 CY80
Munster Rd., Tedd. 177 CH93
Munster Sq. NW1 273 J3
Munster Sq. NW1 141 DH69
Munton Rd. SE17 279 J8
Munton Rd. SE17 162 DQ77
Murchison Ave., Bex. 186 EX88
Murchison Rd. E10 123 EC61
Murchison Rd., Hodd. 33 EB14
Murdoch Clo., Stai. 174 BG92
Murdock Clo. E16 144 EF72
Rogers Rd.
Murdock St. SE15 162 DV79
Murfett Clo. SW19 179 CY89
Murfitt Way, Upmin. 128 FN63
Muriel Ave., Wat. 76 BW43
Muriel St. N1 141 DM67
Murillo Rd. SE13 163 ED84
Murphy St. SE1 278 D5
Murphy St. SE1 161 DN75
Murray Ave., Brom. 204 EH97
Murray Ave., Houns. 176 CB85
Murray Cres., Pnr. 94 BX53
Murray Grn., Wok. 211 BC114
Bunyard Dr.
Murray Gro. N1 275 J1
Murray Gro. N1 142 DQ68
Murray Ms. NW1 141 DK66
Murray Rd. SW19 179 CX93
Murray Rd. W5 157 CK77
Murray Rd., Berk. 38 AV18
Murray Rd., Cher. 211 BC107
Murray Rd., Nthwd. 93 BS53
Murray Rd., Orp. 206 EV97
Murray Rd., Rich. 177 CH89
Murray Sq. E16 144 EG72
Murray St. NW1 141 DK66
Murray Ter. NW3 120 DD63
Flask Wk.
Murray Ter. W5 157 CK77
Murray Rd.
Murrays La., W.Byf. 212 BK114
Murrells Wk., Lthd. 230 CA123
Murreys, The, Ash. 231 CK118
Murreys Ct., Ash. 231 CK118
Mursell Est. SW8 161 DM81
Murthering La., Rom. 105 FF45
Murton Ct., St.Alb. 43 CE19
Murtwell Dr., Chig. 103 EQ51
Musard Rd. W6 159 CY79
Musbury St. E1 142 DW72
Muscal W6 159 CY79
Muscatel Pl. SE5 162 DS81
Dalwood St.
Muschamp Rd. SE15 162 DT83
Muschamp Rd., Cars. 200 DE103
Muscovy St. EC3 279 N1
Museum Pas. E2 142 DV69
Victoria Pk. Sq.
Museum St. WC1 273 P7
Museum St. WC1 141 DL71
Musgrave Clo., Barn. 80 DC39
Musgrave Clo., Wal.Cr. 66 DT27
Allwood Rd.
Musgrave Cres. SW6 160 DA80
Musgrave Rd., Islw. 157 CF81
Musgrove Rd. SE14 163 DX81
Musjid Rd. SW11 160 DD82
Kambala Rd.
Musk Hill, Hem.H. 39 BE21
Muskalls Clo. (Cheshunt), Wal.Cr. 66 DU27
Muskham Rd., Harl. 36 EU12
Musleigh Manor, Ware 33 DZ06
Musley Hill, Ware 33 DY05
Musley La., Ware 33 DY05
Musquash Way, Houns. 156 BW82
Mussenden La. (Horton Kirby), Dart. 208 FQ99
Mussenden La. (Fawkham), Long. 209 FT101
Mustard Mill Rd., Stai. 173 BE91
Muston Rd. E5 122 DV61
Mustow Pl. SW6 159 CZ82
Munster Rd.
Muswell Ave. N10 99 DH53
Muswell Hill N10 121 DH55
Muswell Hill Bdy. N10 121 DH55
Muswell Hill Pl. N10 121 DH56
Muswell Hill Rd. N6 120 DG58
Muswell Hill Rd. N10 120 DG58
Muswell Ms. N10 121 DH55
Muswell Rd.
Muswell Rd. N10 121 DH55
Mutchetts Clo., Wat. 60 BY33
Mutrix Rd. NW6 140 DA67
Mutton La., Pot.B. 63 CW31
Mutton Pl. NW1 141 DH65
Harmood St.
Muybridge Rd., N.Mal. 198 CQ96
Myatt Rd. SW9 161 DP81
Myatt's Flds. N. SW9 161 DN81
Eythorne Rd.
Myatt's Flds. S. SW9 161 DN82
Mycenae Rd. SE3 164 EG80
Myddelton Ave., Enf. 82 DS38
Myddelton Clo., Enf. 82 DT39
Myddelton Ave.
Myddelton Gdns. N21 99 DP45
Myddelton Pk. N20 98 DD48
Myddelton Pas. EC1 274 E2
Myddelton Rd. N8 121 DL56
Myddelton Sq. EC1 274 E2
Myddelton Sq. EC1 141 DN69
Myddelton St. EC1 274 E3
Myddelton St. EC1 141 DN69
Myddleton Ms. N22 99 DL52
Whittington Rd.
Myddleton Path (Cheshunt), Wal.Cr. 66 DV31
Hawthorne Clo.
Myddleton Rd. N22 99 DL52
Myddleton Rd., Uxb. 134 BJ67
Myddleton Rd., Ware 33 DX07
Myers Dr., Slou. 111 AP64
Stewart's Dr.
Myers La. SE14 163 DX79
Mygrove Clo., Rain. 148 FK68
Mygrove Gdns., Rain. 148 FK68
Mygrove Rd., Rain. 148 FK68
Myles Ct., Wal.Cr. 66 DQ29
Mylis Clo. SE26 182 DV91
Mylius Clo. SE14 162 DW81
Kender St.
Mylne Clo., Wal.Cr. 66 DW27
Brookfield La.
Mylne St. EC1 274 D2
Mylne St. EC1 141 DN68
Mylor Clo., Wok. 210 AY114
Mymms Dr., Hat. 64 DA26
Mynchen Clo., Beac. 89 AK49
Mynchen End, Beac. 89 AK49
Mynchen Rd., Beac. 89 AK50
Mynns Clo., Epsom 216 CP114
Myra St. SE2 166 EU77
Myrdle St. E1 142 DU71
Myrke, The, Slou. 152 AT77
Myrna Clo. SW19 180 DE94
Myron Pl. SE13 163 EC83
Myrtle Ave., Felt. 155 BS84
Myrtle Ave., Ruis. 115 BU59
Myrtle Clo., Barn. 98 DF46
Myrtle Clo., Erith 167 FE81
Myrtle Clo., Slou. 153 BE81
Myrtle Clo., Uxb. 134 BM71
Violet Ave.
Myrtle Clo., West Dr. 154 BM76
Myrtle Cres., Slou. 132 AT73
Myrtle Gdns. W7 137 CE74
Myrtle Grn., Hem.H. 39 BE20
Newlands Rd.
Myrtle Gro., Enf. 82 DR38
Myrtle Gro., N.Mal. 198 CQ96
Myrtle Gro., S.Ock. 168 FQ75
Myrtle Pl., Dart. 189 FR87
Myrtle Rd. E6 144 EL67
Myrtle Rd. E17 123 DY58
Myrtle Rd. N13 100 DQ48
Myrtle Rd. W3 138 CQ74
Myrtle Rd., Brwd. 108 FW48
Myrtle Rd., Croy. 203 EA104
Myrtle Rd., Dart. 188 FK88
Myrtle Rd., Dor. 263 CG135
Myrtle Rd., Hmptn. 176 CC93
Myrtle Rd., Houns. 156 CC82
Myrtle Rd., Ilf. 125 EP61
Myrtle Rd., Rom. 106 FJ51
Myrtle Rd., Sutt. 218 DC106
Myrtle Wk. N1 275 M1
Myrtle Wk. N1 142 DS68
Myrtleberry Clo. E8 142 DT65
Beechwood Rd.
Myrtledene Rd. SE2 166 EU78
Myrtleside Clo., Nthwd. 93 BR52
Mysore Rd. SW11 160 DF83
Myth Clo., Upmin. 129 FR58
Myton Rd. SE21 182 DR90

N

Nadine St. SE7 164 EJ78
Nafferton Ri., Loug. 84 EK43
Nagasaki Wk. SE7 164 EJ76
Nagle Clo. E17 101 ED54
Nag's Head Ct. EC1 275 J5
Nags Head La., Brwd. 107 FS51
Nags Head La., Upmin. 106 FQ54
Nags Head La., Well. 166 EV83
Nags Head Rd., Enf. 82 DW42
Nailsworth Cres., Red. 251 DK129
Nailzee Clo., Ger.Cr. 112 AY59
Nairn Ct., Til. 171 GF82
Dock Rd.
Nairn Grn., Wat. 93 BU48
Nairn Rd., Ruis. 136 BW65
Nairn St. E14 143 EC71
Nairne Gro. SE24 182 DR85
Naish Ct. N1 141 DL67
Nalders Rd., Chesh. 54 AR30
Nallhead Rd., Felt. 176 BW92
Namton Dr., Th.Hth. 201 DM98
Nan Clark's La. NW7 97 CT47
Nancy Downs, Wat. 94 BW45
Nankin St. E14 143 EA72
Nansen Rd. SW11 160 DG84
Nansen Rd., Grav. 191 GK92
Nant Rd. NW2 119 CZ61
Nant St. E2 142 DV69
Cambridge Heath Rd.
Nantes Clo. SW18 160 DC84
Nantes Pas. E1 275 P6
Naoroji St. WC1 274 D3
Nap, The, Kings L. 58 BN29
Napier Ave. E14 163 EA78
Napier Ave. SW6 159 CZ83
Napier Clo. SE8 163 DZ80
Amersham Vale
Napier Clo. W14 159 CZ76
Napier Rd.
Napier Clo., Horn. 127 FH60
St. Leonards Way
Napier Clo., St.Alb. 61 CK25
Napier Clo., West Dr. 154 BM76
Napier Ct. SW6 159 CZ83
Ranelagh Gdns.
Napier Ct. (Cheshunt), Wal.Cr. 66 DV28
Flamstead End Rd.
Napier Dr. (Bushey), Wat. 76 BY42
Napier Gdns., Guil. 243 BB133
Napier Gro. N1 142 DQ68
Napier Ho., Rain. 147 FF69

Napier Pl. W14 159 CZ76
Napier Rd. E6 145 EN67
Napier Rd. E11 124 EE63
Napier Rd. E15 144 EE68
Napier Rd. N17 122 DS55
Napier Rd. NW10 139 CV69
Napier Rd. SE25 202 DV98
Napier Rd. W14 159 CY76
Napier Rd., Ashf. 175 BR94
Napier Rd., Belv. 166 EZ77
Napier Rd., Brom. 204 EH98
Napier Rd., Enf. 83 DX43
Napier Rd., Grav. 191 GF88
Napier Rd., Houns. 154 BK81
Napier Rd., Islw. 157 CG84
Napier Rd., S.Croy. 220 DR108
Napier Rd., Wem. 117 CK64
Napier Ter. N1 141 DP65
Napoleon Rd. E5 122 DV62
Napoleon Rd., Twick. 177 CH87
Napsbury Ave., St.Alb. 61 CJ26
Napsbury La., St.Alb. 43 CG23
Napton Clo., Hayes 136 BY70
Kingsash Dr.
Narbonne Ave. SW4 181 DJ85
Narboro Ct., Rom. 127 FG57
Manor Rd.
Narborough Clo., Uxb. 115 BQ61
Aylsham Dr.
Narborough St. SW6 160 DB82
Narcissus Rd. NW6 120 DA64
Narcot La., Ch.St.G. 90 AU48
Narcot La., Ger.Cr. 90 AW52
Narcot Rd., Ch.St.G. 90 AU48
Narcot Way, Ch.St.G. 90 AU49
Nare Rd., S.Ock. 148 FQ73
Naresby Fold, Stan. 95 CJ51
Narford Rd. E5 122 DU62
Narrow La., Warl. 236 DV119
Narrow St. E14 143 DY73
Narrow Way, Brom. 204 EL100
Nascot Pl., Wat. 75 BV40
Stamford Rd.
Nascot Rd., Wat. 75 BV40
Nascot St. W12 139 CW72
Nascot St., Wat. 75 BV40
Nascot Wd. Rd., Wat. 75 BT37
Naseby Clo. NW6 140 DC66
Fairfax Rd.
Naseby Clo., Islw. 157 CE81
Naseby Ct., Walt. 196 BW103
Clements Rd.
Naseby Rd. SE19 182 DR93
Naseby Rd., Dag. 126 FA62
Naseby Rd., Ilf. 103 EM53
Nash Clo., Borwd. 78 CM42
Nash Clo., Hat. 45 CX23
Nash Cft., Grav. 190 GE91
Nash Dr., Red. 250 DF132
Nash Gdns., Red. 250 DF132
Nash Grn., Brom. 184 EG93
Nash Grn., Hem.H. 58 BM25
Nash La., Kes. 222 EG108
Nash Pl. E14 143 EB74
South Colonnade
Nash Rd. N9 100 DW47
Nash Rd. SE4 163 DY84
Nash Rd., Rom. 126 EX56
Nash Rd., Slou. 153 AZ77
Nash St. NW1 273 J2
Nashdom La., Slou. 130 AF66
Nashleigh Hill, Chesh. 54 AQ29
Nash's Yd., Uxb. 134 BK66
Bakers Rd.
Nasmyth St. W6 159 CV76
Nassau Path SE28 146 EW74
Disraeli Clo.
Nassau Rd. SW13 159 CT81
Nassau St. W1 273 K7
Nassau St. W1 141 DJ71
Nassington Rd. NW3 120 DE63
Natal Rd. N11 99 DL51
Natal Rd. SW16 181 DK93
Natal Rd., Ilf. 125 EP63
Natal Rd., Th.Hth. 202 DR97
Natalie Clo., Felt. 175 BR87
Natalie Ms., Twick. 176 CC90
Sixth Cross Rd.
Nathan Clo., Upmin. 129 FS60
Nathan Way SE28 165 ES76
Nathaniel Clo. E1 142 DT71
Thrawl St.
Nathans Rd., Wem. 117 CJ60
Nation Way E4 101 EC46
The Ridgeway
Natwoke Clo., Beac. 89 AK50
Naunton Way, Horn. 128 FK62
Latimer Dr.
Naval Row E14 143 EC73
Naval Wk., Brom. 204 EG97
High St.
Navarino Gro. E8 142 DU65
Navarino Rd. E8 142 DU65
Navarre Gdns., Rom. 105 FB50
Navarre Rd. E6 144 EL68
Navarre St. E2 275 P4
Navarre St. E2 142 DT70
Navenby Wk. E3 143 EA70
Rounton Rd.
Navestock Clo. E4 101 EC48
Mapleton Rd.
Navestock Cres., Wdf.Grn. 102 EJ53
Navestock Ho., Bark. 146 EV68
Navigator Dr., Sthl. 156 CC75
Navy St. SW4 161 DK83
Naylor Gro., Enf. 83 DX43
South St.
Naylor Rd. N20 98 DC47
Naylor Rd. SE15 162 DV80
Nazareth Gdns. SE15 162 DV82
Gordon Rd.
Nazeing Common Rd., Wal.Abb. 50 EH24
Nazeing New Rd., Brox. 49 EA21
Nazeing Rd., Wal.Abb. 49 EC22
Nazeing Wk., Rain. 147 FE67
Ongar Way
Nazrul St. E2 275 P2
Nazrul St. E2 142 DT69
Neagle Clo., Borwd. 78 CQ39
Balcon Way
Neal Ave., Sthl. 136 BZ69
Neal Clo., Ger.Cr. 113 BB60
Neal Clo., Nthwd. 93 BU53
Neal Ct., Hert. 32 DQ09
Neal Ct., Wal.Abb. 68 EF33
Neal St. WC2 273 P9
Neal St. WC2 141 DL72
Neal St., Wat. 76 BW43
Nealden St. SW9 161 DM83
Neale Clo. N2 120 DC55
Neal's Yd. WC2 273 P9
Near Acre NW9 97 CT53
Neasden Clo. NW10 118 CS64
Neasden La. NW10 118 CS62
Neasden La. N. NW10 118 CR62
Neasden Underpass NW10 118 CR62
Neasham Rd., Dag. 126 EV64
Neate St. SE5 162 DS79
Neath Gdns., Mord. 200 DC100
Neathouse Pl. SW1 277 K8
Neats Acre, Ruis. 115 BR59
Neatscourt Rd. E6 144 EK71
Neave Cres., Rom. 106 FJ53
Neb Cor. Rd., Oxt. 253 EC131
Nebraska St. SE1 279 K5
Neckinger SE16 162 DT76
Neckinger Est. SE16 162 DT76
Neckinger St. SE1 162 DT75
Nectarine Way SE13 163 EB82
Necton Rd., St.Alb. 28 CL07
Needham Clo., Wind. 151 AL81
Needham Rd. W11 140 DA72
Westbourne Gro.
Needham Ter. NW2 119 CX62
Needleman St. SE16 163 DX75
Needles Bank, Gdse. 252 DV131
Neela Clo., Uxb. 115 BP63
Neeld Cres. NW4 119 CV57
Neeld Cres., Wem. 118 CN64
Neil Clo., Ashf. 175 BQ92
Neil Wates Cres. SW2 181 DN88
Maskall Clo.
Nelgarde Rd. SE6 183 EA87
Nell Gwynn Clo., Rad. 62 CL32
Nell Gwynne Ave., Shep. 195 BR100
Nella Rd. W6 159 CX79
Nelldale Rd. SE16 162 DW77
Nellgrove Rd., Uxb. 135 BP70
Nello James Gdns. SE27 182 DR91
Nelmes Clo., Horn. 128 FM57
Nelmes Cres., Horn. 128 FL57
Nelmes Rd., Horn. 128 FL59
Nelmes Way, Horn. 128 FK56
Nelson Ave., St.Alb. 43 CH23
Nelson Clo., Brwd. 108 FX50
Nelson Clo., Croy. 201 DP102
Nelson Clo., Felt. 175 BT88
Westmacott Dr.
Nelson Clo., Rom. 105 FB53
Nelson Clo., Slou. 152 AX77
Nelson Clo., Uxb. 135 BP69
Nelson Clo., Walt. 195 BV102
Nelson Clo., West. 238 EL117
Nelson Ct. SE16 142 DW74
Brunel Rd.
Nelson Gdns. E2 142 DU69
Nelson Gdns., Guil. 243 BA133
Nelson Gdns., Houns. 176 CA86
Nelson Gro. Rd. SW19 200 DB95
Nelson La., Uxb. 135 BP69
Nelson Rd.
Nelson Mandela Clo. N10 98 DG54
Nelson Mandela Rd. SE3 164 EJ83
Nelson Pas. EC1 275 J3
Nelson Pas. EC1 142 DQ69
Nelson Pl. N1 274 G1
Nelson Pl. N1 141 DP68
Nelson Pl., Sid. 186 EU91
Nelson Rd. E4 101 EA51
Nelson Rd. E11 124 EG56
Nelson Rd. N8 121 DM57
Nelson Rd. N9 100 DV47
Nelson Rd. N15 122 DS56
Nelson Rd. SE10 163 EC79
Nelson Rd. SW19 180 DB94
Nelson Rd., Ashf. 174 BL92
Nelson Rd., Belv. 166 EZ78
Nelson Rd., Brom. 204 EJ98
Nelson Rd., Cat. 236 DR123
Nelson Rd., Dart. 188 FJ86
Nelson Rd., Enf. 83 DX44
Nelson Rd., Grav. 191 GF89
Nelson Rd., Har. 117 CD60
Nelson Rd., Houns. 176 CA86
Nelson Rd. (Heathrow), Houns. 154 BM81
Nelson Rd., N.Mal. 198 CR99
Nelson Rd., Rain. 147 FF68
Nelson Rd., Sid. 186 EU91
Nelson Rd., S.Ock. 149 FW68
Nelson Rd., Stan. 95 CJ51
Nelson Rd., Twick. 176 CB87
Nelson Rd., Uxb. 135 BP69
Nelson Rd., Wind. 151 AM83
Nelson Sq. SE1 278 F4
Nelson Sq. SE1 161 DP75
Nelson St. E1 142 DV72
Nelson St. E6 145 EM68
Nelson St. E16 144 EF73
Huntingdon St.
Nelson St., Hert. 31 DP08
Nelson Ter. N1 274 G1
Nelson Ter. N1 141 DP68
Nelson Trd. Est. SW19 200 DB95
Nelson Wk. SE16 143 DY74
Rotherhithe St.
Nelson's Row SW4 161 DK84
Nelsons Yd. NW1 141 DJ68
Mornington Cres.
Nelwyn Ave., Horn. 128 FM57
Nemoure Rd. W3 138 CQ73
Nene Gdns., Felt. 176 BZ89
Nene Rd., Houns. 155 BP81
Nepaul Rd. SW11 160 DE82
Afghan Rd.
Nepean St. SW15 179 CU86
Neptune Dr., Hem.H. 40 BL18
Neptune Rd., Har. 117 CD58
Neptune Rd. (Heathrow), Houns. 155 BR81
Neptune St. SE16 162 DW76
Nesbit Rd. SE9 164 EK84
Nesbitt Clo. SE3 164 EE83
Hurren Clo.
Nesbitt Sq. SE19 182 DS94
Coxwell Rd.
Nesbitts All., Barn. 79 CZ41
Bath Pl.
Nesham St. E1 142 DU74
Ness Rd., Erith 168 FK79
Ness St. SE16 162 DU76
Spa Rd.
Nesta Rd., Wdf.Grn. 102 EE51
Nestles Ave., Hayes 155 BT76
Neston Rd., Wat. 76 BW37
Nestor Ave. N21 81 DP44
Nethan Dr., S.Ock. 148 FQ73
Nether Clo. N3 98 DA52
Nether Mt., Guil. 258 AV136
Nether St. N3 98 DA53
Nether St. N12 98 DB51
Netheravon Rd. W7 137 CF74
Netheravon Rd. N. W4 159 CT77
Netheravon Rd. S. W4 159 CT78
Netherbury Rd. W5 157 CK76
Netherby Gdns., Enf. 81 DL42
Netherby Pk., Wey. 213 BR106
Netherby Rd. SE23 182 DW87
Nethercote Ave., Wok. 226 AT117
Nethercourt Ave. N3 98 DA51
Netherfield Gdns., Bark. 145 ER65
Netherfield La., Ware 33 ED12
Netherfield Rd. N12 98 DB50
Netherfield Rd. SW17 180 DG90
Netherford Rd. SW4 161 DJ82
Netherhall Gdns. NW3 140 DC65
Netherhall Rd., Harl. 50 EF17
Netherhall Way NW3 120 DC64
Netherhall Gdns.
Netherlands, The, Couls. 235 DJ119
Netherlands Rd., Barn. 80 DD44
Netherleigh Clo. N6 121 DH60
Hornsey La.
Netherleigh Pk., Red. 267 DL137
Nethern Ct. Rd., Cat. 237 EA123
Netherne La., Couls. 235 DJ123
Netherne La., Red. 235 DJ123
Netherpark Dr., Rom. 105 FF54
Netherton Gro. SW10 160 DC79
Netherton Rd. N15 122 DR58
Seven Sisters Rd.
Netherton Rd., Twick. 177 CG85
Netherway, St.Alb. 42 CA23
Netherwood N2 98 DD54
Netherwood Pl. W14 159 CX76
Netherwood Rd.
Netherwood Rd. W14 159 CX76
Netherwood Rd., Beac. 89 AK50
Netherwood St. NW6 139 CZ66
Netley Clo., Croy. 221 EC108
Netley Clo., Sutt. 217 CX106
Netley Dr., Walt. 196 BZ101
Netley Gdns., Mord. 200 DC101
Netley Rd. E17 123 DZ57
Netley Rd., Brent. 158 CL79
Netley Rd. (Heathrow), Houns. 155 BR81
Netley Rd., Ilf. 125 ER57
Netley Rd., Mord. 200 DC101
Netley St. NW1 273 K3
Netteswell Orchard, Harl. 35 ER14
Netteswell Rd., Harl. 35 ES13
Netteswell Twr., Harl. 35 ER14
Nettlecombe Clo., Sutt. 218 DB109
Nettlecroft, Hem.H. 40 BH21
Nettlecroft, Welw.G.C. 30 DB08
Nettleden Ave., Wem. 138 CN65
Nettleden Rd., Berk. 39 AZ17
Nettlefold Pl. SE27 181 DP90
Nettles Ter., Guil. 242 AX134
Nettlestead Clo., Beck. 183 DZ94
Copers Cope Rd.
Nettleton Rd. SE14 163 DX81
Nettleton Rd., Houns. 155 BP81
Nettleton Rd., Uxb. 114 BM63
Nettlewood Rd. SW16 181 DK94
Neuchatel Rd. SE6 183 DZ89
Nevada Clo., N.Mal. 198 CQ98
Georgia Rd.
Nevada St. SE10 163 EC79
Nevell Rd., Grays 171 GH76
Nevern Pl. SW5 160 DA77
Nevern Rd. SW5 160 DA77
Nevern Sq. SW5 160 DA77
Nevill Clo. W3 158 CQ75
Acton La.
Nevill Gro., Wat. 75 BV39
Nevill Rd. N16 122 DS63
Nevill Way, Loug. 102 EL45
Valley Hill
Neville Ave., N.Mal. 198 CR95
Neville Clo. E11 124 EF62
Neville Clo. NW1 273 N1
Neville Clo. NW6 139 CZ68
Neville Clo. SE15 162 DU80
Neville Clo., Bans. 218 DB114
Neville Clo., Esher 214 BZ107
Neville Clo., Houns. 156 CB82
Neville Clo., Pot.B. 63 CZ31
Neville Clo., Sid. 185 ET91
Neville Clo., Slou. 132 AT65
Neville Ct., Slou. 130 AJ69
Dropmore Rd.
Neville Dr. N2 120 DC58
Neville Gdns., Dag. 126 EX62
Neville Gill Clo. SW18 180 DB86
Neville Pl. N22 99 DM53
Neville Rd. E7 144 EG66
Neville Rd. NW6 139 CZ68
Neville Rd. W5 137 CK70
Neville Rd., Croy. 202 DR101
Neville Rd., Dag. 126 EX61
Neville Rd., Ilf. 103 EQ53
Neville Rd., Kings.T. 198 CN96
Neville Rd., Rich. 177 CJ89
Neville St. SW7 160 DD78
Neville Ter. SW7 160 DD78
Neville Wk., Cars. 200 DE101
Green Wrythe La.
Nevilles Ct. NW2 119 CU62
Nevin Dr. E4 101 EB46
Nevis Clo., Rom. 105 FE51
Nevis Rd. SW17 180 DG89
New Ash Clo. N2 120 DD55
Oakridge Dr.
New Barn La., Beac. 90 AS49
New Barn La., Sev. 239 EQ116
New Barn La., West. 239 EQ118
New Barn La., Whyt. 236 DS116
New Barn Rd., Grav. 190 GC92
New Barn Rd., Swan. 207 FE95
New Barn St. E13 144 EG70
New Barnes Ave., St.Alb. 43 CG23
New Barns Ave., Mitch. 201 DK98
New Barns Way, Chig. 103 EP48
New Battlebridge La., Red. 251 DH130
New Berry La., Walt. 214 BX106
New Bond St. W1 273 H9
New Bond St. W1 141 DH72
New Brent St. NW4 119 CW57
New Bri. St. EC4 274 F9
New Bri. St. EC4 141 DP72
New Broad St. EC2 275 M7
New Bdy. W5 137 CJ73
New Bdy., Hmptn. 177 CD92
Hampton Rd.
New Burlington Ms. W1 273 K10
New Burlington Pl. W1 273 K10
New Burlington St. W1 273 K10
New Burlington St. W1 141 DJ73
New Butt La. SE8 163 EA80
New Butt La. N. SE8 163 EA80
Reginald Rd.
New Causeway, Reig. 266 DB137
New Cavendish St. W1 272 G7
New Cavendish St. W1 140 DG71
New Change EC4 275 H9
New Change EC4 142 DQ72
New Chapel Sq., Felt. 175 BV88
New Charles St. EC1 274 G2
New Ch. Rd. SE5 162 DR80
New City Rd. E13 144 EJ69
New Clo. SW19 200 DC97
New Clo., Felt. 176 BY92
New College Ms. N1 141 DN66
Islington Pk. St.
New Compton St. WC2 273 N9
New Compton St. WC2 141 DK72
New Coppice, Wok. 226 AT119
Hermitage Wds. Cres.
New Ct. EC4 274 D10
New Ct., Add. 194 BJ104
New Covent Gdn. Mkt. SW8 161 DK80
New Coventry St. W1 277 N1
New Crane Pl. E1 142 DW74
Garnet St.
New Cross Rd. SE14 162 DW80
New Cross Rd., Guil. 242 AU132
New End NW3 120 DC63
New End Sq. NW3 120 DD63
New England St., St.Alb. 42 CC20
New Fm. Ave., Brom. 204 EG98
New Fm. Dr., Rom. 86 EW41
New Fm. La., Nthwd. 93 BS53
New Fetter La. EC4 274 E8
New Fetter La. EC4 141 DN72
New Ford Rd., Wal.Cr. 67 DZ34
New Forest La., Chig. 103 EN51
New Gdn. Dr., West Dr. 154 BL75
Drayton Gdns.
New Globe Wk. SE1 279 H2
New Globe Wk. SE1 142 DQ74
New Goulston St. E1 275 P8
New Grns. Ave., St.Alb. 43 CD15
New Hall Dr., Rom. 106 FL53
New Haw Rd., Add. 212 BJ106
New Heston Rd., Houns. 156 BZ80
New Horizon Ct., Brent. 157 CG79
New Ho. La., Epp. 71 FC25
New Ho. La., Grav. 191 GF90
New Ho. La., Red. 267 DK142
New Ho. Pk., St.Alb. 43 CG23
New Inn Bdy. EC2 275 N4
New Inn La., Guil. 243 BB130
New Inn Pas. WC2 274 C9
New Inn St. EC2 275 N4
New Inn Yd. EC2 275 N4
New Inn Yd. EC2 142 DS70
New James Ct. SE15 162 DV83
Nunhead La.
New Kent Rd. SE1 279 H7
New Kent Rd. SE1 162 DQ76
New Kent Rd., St.Alb. 43 CD20
New King St. SE8 163 EA79
New Kings Rd. SW6 159 CZ82
New La., Guil. 227 AZ124
New La., Wok. 226 AY122
New Lo. Dr., Oxt. 254 EF128
New London St. EC3 275 N10
New Lydenburgh St. SE7 164 EJ76
New Mill Rd., Orp. 206 EW95
New Mt. St. E15 143 ED66
New N. Pl. EC2 275 M5
New N. Rd. N1 142 DQ66
New N. Rd., Ilf. 103 ER52
New N. Rd., Reig. 249 CZ134
New N. St. WC1 274 B6
New N. St. WC1 141 DM71
New Oak Rd. N2 98 DC54
New Orleans Wk. N19 121 DK59
New Oxford St. WC1 273 N8
New Oxford St. WC1 141 DK72
New Par., Ashf. 174 BM91
Church Rd.
New Par., Rick. 73 BC42
Whitelands Ave.
New Pk. Ave. N13 100 DQ48
New Pk. Clo., Ntht. 136 BY65
New Pk. Ct. SW2 181 DL87
New Pk. Dr., Hem.H. 41 BP19
New Pk. Par. SW2 181 DL86
Doverfield Rd.
New Pk. Rd. SW2 181 DK88
New Pk. Rd., Ashf. 175 BQ92
New Pk. Rd., Hert. 47 DK24
New Pk. Rd., Uxb. 92 BJ53
New Peachey La., Uxb. 134 BK72
New Pl. Gdns., Upmin. 129 FR61
New Pl. Sq. SE16 162 DV76
New Plaistow Rd. E15 144 EE67
New Pond Rd., Gdmg. 258 AS142
New Printing Ho. Sq. WC1 141 DM70
Gray's Inn Rd.
New Priory Ct. NW6 140 DA66
Mazenod Ave.
New Quebec St. W1 272 E9
New Quebec St. W1 140 DF72
New Ride SW7 276 B4
New River Ave., Ware 33 EB11
New River Clo., Hodd. 49 EB16
New River Ct. (Cheshunt), Wal.Cr. 66 DV30
Pengelly Clo.
New River Cres. N13 99 DP49
New Rd. E1 142 DV71
New Rd. E4 101 EB49
New Rd. N8 121 DL57
New Rd. N9 100 DU48
New Rd. N17 100 DT53
New Rd. N22 100 DQ53
New Rd. NW7 97 CY52
New Rd. (Barnet Gate) NW7 97 CT45
New Rd. SE2 166 EX77
New Rd., Amer. 55 AS37
New Rd. (Coleshill), Amer. 55 AM42
New Rd., Berk. 38 AX18
New Rd. (Northchurch), Berk. 38 AS17
New Rd., Borwd. 77 CK44
New Rd., Brent. 157 CK78
New Rd., Brwd. 108 FX47
New Rd., Brox. 49 DZ19
New Rd., Ch.St.G. 72 AY41
New Rd., Dag. 146 FA67
New Rd. (South Darenth), Dart. 208 FQ96
New Rd., Dor. 263 CJ137
Deepdene Ave.
New Rd., Epp. 70 FA32
New Rd., Esher 196 CC104
New Rd. (Claygate), Esher 215 CF110
New Rd., Felt. 175 BR86
New Rd. (East Bedfont), Felt. 175 BV88
New Rd. (Hanworth), Felt. 176 BY92
New Rd., Grav. 191 GH86
New Rd., Grays 170 GA79
New Rd. (Manor Way), Grays 170 GB79
New Rd., Guil. 244 BL131
New Rd. (Albury), Guil. 260 BK139
New Rd. (Chilworth), Guil. 259 BB141
New Rd. (Gomshall), Guil. 261 BQ139
New Rd. (Wonersh), Guil. 259 BB143
New Rd., Harl. 36 EX11
New Rd., Har. 117 CF63
New Rd., Hayes 155 BQ80
New Rd., Hert. 32 DQ07
New Rd., Horl. 269 DP148
New Rd., Houns. 156 CB84
Station Rd.
New Rd., Ilf. 125 ES61
New Rd., Kings L. 57 BF30
New Rd., Kings.T. 178 CN94
New Rd., Lthd. 215 CF110
New Rd., Mitch. 200 DG102
New Rd., Orp. 206 EU101
New Rd. (Limpsfield), Oxt. 254 EH130
New Rd., Pot.B. 63 CU33
New Rd., Rad. 77 CE36
New Rd. (Shenley), Rad. 62 CN34
New Rd., Rain. 147 FC68
New Rd., Rich. 177 CJ91
New Rd., Rick. 74 BN43
New Rd. (Church End), Rick. 73 BF39
New Rd., Rom. 86 EX44
New Rd., Sev. 240 EX124
New Rd., Shep. 194 BN97
New Rd. (Datchet), Slou. 152 AX81
New Rd. (Langley), Slou. 153 BA76
New Rd., Stai. 173 BC92
New Rd., Swan. 207 FF97
New Rd. (Hextable), Swan. 187 FF94
New Rd., Tad. 233 CW123
New Rd., Uxb. 135 BQ70
New Rd., Ware 33 DX06
New Rd., Wat. 76 BW42
New Rd. (Letchmore Heath), Wat. 77 CE39
New Rd., Well. 166 EV82
New Rd. (Stanborough), Welw.G.C. 29 CU12
New Rd., W.Mol. 196 CA97
New Rd., Wey. 213 BQ106
New Rd. Hill, Kes. 222 EL109
New Rd. Hill, Orp. 222 EL109
New Row WC2 273 P10
New Row WC2 141 DL73
New Spring Gdns. Wk. SE11 161 DL78
Goding St.
New Sq. E6 145 EM72
Porter Rd.
New Sq. WC2 274 C8
New Sq. WC2 141 DM72
New Sq., Felt. 175 BQ88
New Sq., Slou. 152 AT75
New Sq. Pas. WC2 141 DM72
New Sq.
New St. EC2 275 N7
New St. EC2 142 DS71
New St., Berk. 38 AX19
New St., Stai. 174 BG91
New St., Wat. 76 BW42
New St., West. 255 EQ127
New St. Hill, Brom. 184 EH92
New St. Sq. EC4 274 E8
New Swan Yd., Grav. 191 GH86
Bank St.
New Trinity Rd. N2 120 DD55
New Turnstile WC1 274 B7
New Union Clo. E14 163 EC76
New Union St. EC2 275 K7
New Union St. EC2 142 DR71
New Wanstead E11 124 EF58
New Way La., Harl. 53 FB16
New Way Rd. NW9 118 CS56
New Wf. Rd. N1 141 DL68
New Wickham La., Egh. 173 BA94
New Windsor St., Uxb. 134 BJ66
New Wd., Welw.G.C. 30 DC08
New Years La., Orp. 239 ET115
New Years La., Sev. 239 ET115
New Zealand Ave., Walt. 195 BT102
New Zealand Way W12 139 CV73
India Way
New Zealand Way, Rain. 147 FF69
Newall Rd., Houns. 155 BQ81
Newark Clo., Guil. 243 BB129
Dairyman's Wk.
Newark Clo., Wok. 228 BG121
Newark Cotts., Wok. 228 BG121
Newark Ct., Walt. 196 BW102
St. Johns Dr.
Newark Cres. NW10 138 CR69
Newark Grn., Borwd. 78 CR41
Newark Knok E6 145 EN72
Newark La., Wok. 227 BF118
Newark Rd., S.Croy. 220 DR107
Newark St. E1 142 DV71
Newark Way NW4 119 CU56
Newberries Ave., Rad. 77 CH35
Newberry Cres., Wind. 151 AK82
Newbery Rd., Erith 167 FF81
Newbery Way, Slou. 151 AR75
Newbiggin Path, Wat. 94 BW49
Newbolt Ave., Sutt. 217 CW106

Newbolt Rd., Stan. 95 CF50
Newborough Grn., N.Mal. 198 CR98
Newburgh Rd. W3 138 CQ74
Newburgh St. W1 273 K9
Newburgh St. W1 141 DJ72
Newburn St. SE11 161 DM78
Newbury Ave., Enf. 83 DZ38
Newbury Clo., Nthlt. 136 BZ65
Newbury Clo., Rom. 106 FK51
Newbury Gdns., Epsom 217 CT105
Newbury Gdns., Rom. 106 FK51
Newbury Gdns., Upmin. 128 FM62
Newbury Ho. N22 99 DL53
Newbury Ms. NW5 140 DG65
Malden Rd.
Newbury Rd. E4 101 EC51
Newbury Rd., Brom. 204 EG97
Newbury Rd., Houns. 154 BM81
Newbury Rd., Ilf. 125 ES58
Newbury Rd., Rom. 106 FK50
Newbury St. EC1 275 H6
Newbury Wk., Rom. 106 FK50
Newbury Way, Nthlt. 136 BZ65
Newby Clo., Enf. 82 DS40
Newby Pl. E14 143 EC73
Newby St. SW8 161 DH83
Newcastle Ave., Ilf. 104 EU51
Newcastle Clo. EC4 274 F8
Newcastle Pl. W2 272 A7
Newcastle Pl. W2 140 DD71
Newcastle Row EC1 274 E5
Newchurch Rd., Slou. 131 AM71
Newcombe Gdns. SW16 181 DL91
Newcombe Pk. NW7 96 CS50
Newcombe Pk., Wem. 138 CM67
Newcombe Ri., West Dr. 134 BL72
Newcombe Rd., Rad. 62 CN34
Newcombe St. W8 140 DA74
Kensington Pl.
Newcome Path, Rad. 62 CN34
Newcombe Rd.
Newcomen Rd. E11 124 EF62
Newcomen Rd. SW11 160 DD83
Newcomen St. SE1 279 K4
Newcomen St. SE1 162 DR75
Newcourt, Uxb. 134 BJ71
Newcourt St. NW8 272 B1
Newcourt St. NW8 140 DE68
Newcroft Clo., Uxb. 134 BM71
Newdales Clo. N9 100 DU47
Balham Rd.
Newdene Ave., Nthlt. 136 BX68
Newdigate Grn., Uxb. 92 BK53
Newdigate Rd., Uxb. 92 BJ53
Newdigate Rd. E., Uxb. 92 BK53
Newell Rd., Hem.H. 40 BL23
Newell St. E14 143 DZ72
Newenham Rd., Lthd. 246 CA126
Newent Clo. SE15 162 DS80
Newent Clo., Cars. 200 DF102
Newfield Clo., Hmptn. 196 CA95
Percy Rd.
Newfield La., Hem.H. 40 BL20
Newfield Ri. NW2 119 CV62
Newfields, Welw.G.C. 29 CV10
Newford Clo., Hem.H. 41 BP19
Newgale Gdns., Edg. 96 CM53
Newgate, Croy. 202 DQ102
Newgate Clo., Felt. 176 BY89
Newgate Clo., St.Alb. 43 CK17
Newgate St. E4 102 EF48
Newgate St. EC1 274 G8
Newgate St. EC1 141 DP72
Newgate St., Hert. 47 DK21
Newgate St. Village, Hert. 65 DL25
Newgatestreet Rd. (Cheshunt), Wal.Cr. 65 DP25
Newhall Clo., Hem.H. 57 BA27
Newhall Ct., Wal.Abb. 68 EF33
Newham Way E6 145 EN70
Newham Way E16 144 EF71
Newhams Clo., Brom. 205 EM97
Newhams Row SE1 279 N5
Newhaven Clo., Hayes 155 BT77
Newhaven Cres., Ashf. 175 BR92
Newhaven Gdns. SE9 164 EK84
Newhaven La. E16 144 EF70
Newhaven Rd. SE25 202 DR99
Newhaven Spur, Slou. 131 AP70
Newhouse Ave., Rom. 126 EX55
Newhouse Clo., N.Mal. 198 CS101
Newhouse Cres., Wat. 59 BV32
Newhouse Rd., Hem.H. 57 BA26
Newhouse Wk., Mord. 200 DC101
Newick Clo., Bex. 187 FB86
Newick Rd. E5 122 DV62
Newing Grn., Brom. 184 EK94
Newington Barrow Way N7 121 DM62
Newington Butts SE1 278 G9
Newington Butts SE1 161 DP77
Newington Butts SE11 278 G9
Newington Butts SE11 161 DP77
Newington Causeway SE1 278 G7
Newington Causeway SE1 161 DP76
Newington Grn. N1 122 DR64
Newington Grn. N16 122 DR64
Newington Grn. Rd. N1 142 DR65
Newington Way N7 121 DM61
Hornsey Rd.
Newland Clo., Pnr. 94 BY51
Newland Clo., St.Alb. 43 CG23
Newland Ct., Wem. 118 CN61
Forty Ave.
Newland Dr., Enf. 82 DV39
Newland Gdns. W13 157 CG75
Newland Rd. N8 121 DL55
Newland St. E16 144 EL74
Newlands, Hat. 45 CW16
Newlands, The, Wall. 219 DJ108
Newlands Ave., Rad. 61 CF34
Newlands Ave., T.Ditt. 197 CE102
Newlands Ave., Wok. 227 AZ121
Newlands Clo., Brwd. 109 GD45
Newlands Clo., Edg. 96 CL48
Newlands Clo., Horl. 268 DF146
Newlands Clo., Sthl. 156 BY78
Newlands Clo., Walt. 214 BY105
Newlands Clo., Wem. 137 CJ65
Newlands Cor., Guil. 260 BG136
Shere Rd.
Newlands Ct. SE9 185 EN86
Newlands Dr., Slou. 153 BE83
Newlands Mobile Home Pk., Abb.L. 59 BT26
Newlands Pk. SE26 183 DX92
Newlands Pl., Barn. 79 CX43
Newlands Quay E1 142 DW73
Newlands Rd. SW16 201 DL96
Newlands Rd., Hem.H. 39 BE19
Newlands Rd., Wdf.Grn. 102 EF47
Newlands Wk., Wat. 60 BX33
Trevellance Way
Newlands Way, Chess. 215 CJ106
Newlands Way, Pot.B. 64 DB30
Newlands Wd., Croy. 221 DZ109
Newling Clo. E6 145 EM72
Porter Rd.
Newlyn Clo., St.Alb. 60 BY30
Newlyn Clo., Uxb. 134 BN71
Newlyn Gdns., Har. 116 BZ59
Newlyn Rd. N17 100 DT53
Newlyn Rd. NW2 119 CW60
Tilling Rd.
Newlyn Rd., Barn. 79 CZ42
Newlyn Rd., Well. 165 ET82
Newman Clo., Horn. 128 FL57
Newman Pas. W1 273 L7
Newman Rd. E13 144 EH69
Newman Rd. E17 123 DX57
Southcote Rd.
Newman Rd., Brom. 204 EG95
Newman Rd., Croy. 201 DM102
Newman Rd., Hayes 135 BV73
Newman St. W1 273 L7
Newman St. W1 141 DJ71
Newman Yd. W1 273 L8
Newmans Clo., Loug. 85 EP41
Newman's Ct. EC3 275 L9
Newmans Dr., Brwd. 109 GC45
Newmans La., Loug. 85 EN41
Newmans La., Surb. 197 CK100
Newmans Rd., Grav. 191 GF89
Newman's Row WC2 274 C7
Newmans Way, Barn. 80 DC39
Newmarket Ave., Nthlt. 116 CB64
Newmarket Grn. SE9 184 EK87
Middle Pk. Ave.
Newmarket Way, Horn. 128 FL63
Newminster Rd., Mord. 200 DC100
Newnes Path SW15 159 CV84
Putney Pk. La.
Newnham Ave., Ruis. 116 BW60
Newnham Clo., Loug. 84 EK44
Newnham Clo., Nthlt. 116 CC64
Newnham Clo., Slou. 132 AU74
Newnham Clo., Th.Hth. 202 DQ96
Newnham Gdns., Nthlt. 136 CC65
Newnham Ms. N22 99 DM53
Newnham Rd.
Newnham Pl., Grays 171 GG77
Newnham Rd. N22 99 DM53
Newnham Ter. SE1 278 D6
Newnham Way, Har. 118 CL57
Newnhams Clo., Brom. 205 EM97
Newnton Clo. N4 122 DR59
Newpiece, Loug. 85 EP41
Newport Ave. E13 144 EH70
Palmer Rd.
Newport Clo., Enf. 83 DY37
Newport Ct. WC2 273 N10
Newport Mead, Wat. 94 BX49
Kilmarnock Rd.
Newport Pl. WC2 273 N10
Newport Pl. WC2 141 DK73
Newport Rd. E10 123 EC61
Newport Rd. E17 123 DY56
Newport Rd. SW13 159 CU81
Newport Rd., Hayes 135 BR71
Uxbridge Rd.
Newport Rd., Houns. 154 BN81
Newport Rd., Slou. 131 AL70
Newport St. SE11 278 B9
Newport St. SE11 161 DM77
Newports, Saw. 36 EW06
Newports, Swan. 207 FD101
Newquay Cres., Har. 116 BY61
Newquay Gdns., Wat. 93 BV47
Fulford Gro.
Newquay Rd. SE6 183 EB89
Newry Rd., Twick. 177 CG85
Newsam Ave. N15 122 DR57
Newsham Rd., Wok. 226 AT117
Newstead, Hat. 45 CT21
Newstead Ave., Orp. 205 ER104
Newstead Clo. N12 98 DE52
Summerfields Ave.
Newstead Ri., Cat. 252 DV126
Newstead Rd. SE12 184 EF87
Newstead Wk., Cars. 200 DC101
Newstead Way SW19 179 CX91
Newteswell Dr., Wal.Abb. 67 ED32
Newton Abbot Rd., Grav. 191 GF89
Newton Ave. N10 98 DG53
Newton Ave. W3 158 CQ75
Newton Clo., Hodd. 33 EB13
Newton Clo., Slou. 153 AZ75
Newton Ct., Wind. 172 AU86
Newton Cres., Borwd. 78 CQ42
Newton Dr., Saw. 36 EX06
Newton Gro. W4 158 CS77
Newton La., Wind. 172 AV86
Newton Rd. E15 123 ED64
Newton Rd. N15 122 DT57
Newton Rd. NW2 119 CW62
Newton Rd. SW19 179 CY94
Newton Rd. W2 140 DB72
Newton Rd., Chig. 104 EV50
Newton Rd., Har. 95 CE54
Newton Rd., Islw. 157 CF82
Newton Rd., Pur. 219 DJ112
Newton Rd., Til. 171 GG82
Newton Rd., Well. 166 EU83
Newton Rd., Wem. 138 CM66
Newton St. WC2 274 A8
Newton St. WC2 141 DL72
Newton Wk., Edg. 96 CP53
North Rd.
Newton Way N18 100 DQ50
Newton Wd. Rd., Ash. 232 CM116
Newtons Clo., Rain. 147 FF66
Newtons Ct., Dart. 169 FR84
Newtons Yd. SW18 180 DB85
Wandsworth High St.
Newtown Rd., Uxb. 134 BH65
Newtown St. SW11 161 DH81
Strasburg Rd.
Newyears Grn. La., Uxb. 114 BL58
Niagara Ave. W5 157 CJ77
Niagara Clo. N1 142 DR68
Cropley St.
Niagara Clo. (Cheshunt), Wal.Cr. 67 DX29
Nibthwaite Rd., Har. 117 CE57
Nichol Clo. N14 99 DK46
Nichol La., Brom. 184 EG94
Nicholas Clo., Grnf. 136 CB68
Nicholas Clo., St.Alb. 43 CD17
Nicholas Clo., S.Ock. 149 FW69
Nicholas Clo., Wat. 75 BV37
Nicholas Dr., Sev. 257 FH126
Nicholas Gdns. W5 157 CK75
Nicholas Gdns., Wok. 227 BE116
Nicholas La. EC4 275 L10
Nicholas La., Hert. 32 DQ09
Old Cross
Nicholas Rd. E1 142 DW70
Nicholas Rd., Borwd. 78 CM44
Nicholas Rd., Croy. 219 DL105
Nicholas Rd., Dag. 126 EZ61
Nicholas Wk., Grays 171 GH75
Godman Rd.
Nicholas Way, Hem.H. 40 BM18
Nicholas Way, Nthwd. 93 BQ53
Nicholay Rd. N19 121 DK61
Fairbridge Rd.
Nicholes Rd., Houns. 156 CA84
Nicholl Rd., Epp. 69 ET31
Nicholl St. E2 142 DU67
Nicholls Ave., Uxb. 134 BN70
Nicholls Fld., Harl. 52 EU16
Nicholls Wk., Wind. 150 AJ83
Nichollsfield Wk. N7 121 DM64
Hillmarton Rd.
Nichols Clo., Chess. 215 CJ107
Mansfield Rd.
Nichols Grn. W5 138 CL71
Montpelier Rd.
Nicholson Dr. (Bushey), Wat. 94 CC46
Nicholson Ms., Egh. 173 BA92
Nicholson Wk.
Nicholson Rd., Croy. 202 DT102
Nicholson St. SE1 278 F3
Nicholson St. SE1 141 DP74
Nicholson Wk., Egh. 173 BA92
Nicholson Way, Sev. 257 FK122
Nickelby Clo. SE28 146 EW72
Nickelby Clo., Uxb. 135 BP72
Dickens Ave.
Nicol Clo., Ger.Cr. 90 AX53
Nicol Clo., Twick. 177 CH86
Cassilis Rd.
Nicol End, Ger.Cr. 90 AW53
Nicol Rd., Ger.Cr. 90 AW53
Nicola Clo., Har. 95 CD54
Nicola Clo., S.Croy. 220 DQ107
Nicola Ms., Ilf. 103 EP52
Nicoll Pl. NW4 119 CV58
Nicoll Rd. NW10 138 CS67
Nicoll Way, Borwd. 78 CR43
Nicolson Rd., Orp. 206 EX101
Nicosia Rd. SW18 180 DE87
Nidderdale, Hem.H. 40 BM17
Wharfedale
Niederwald Rd. SE26 183 DY91
Nield Rd., Hayes 155 BT75
Nigel Clo., Nthlt. 136 BY67
Church Rd.
Nigel Ms., Ilf. 125 EP63
Nigel Playfair Ave. W6 159 CV77
King St.
Nigel Rd. E7 124 EJ64
Nigel Rd. SE15 162 DU83
Nigeria Rd. SE7 164 EJ80
Nightingale, St.Alb. 43 CJ23
Nightingale Ave. E4 102 EE50
Nightingale Ave., Lthd. 229 BR124
Nightingale Ave., Upmin. 129 FT60
Nightingale Clo. E4 102 EE49
Nightingale Clo. W4 158 CQ79
Grove Pk. Ter.
Nightingale Clo., Cars. 200 DG103
Nightingale Clo., Cob. 214 BX111
Nightingale Clo., Grav. 190 GE91
Nightingale Clo., Pnr. 116 BW57
Nightingale Clo., Rad. 77 CF36
Nightingale Clo., Red. 252 DS134
Nightingale Cres., Lthd. 245 BQ125
Nightingale Dr., Epsom 216 CP107
Nightingale Est. E5 122 DU62
Nightingale Gro. SE13 183 ED85
Nightingale Gro., Dart. 168 FN84
Keyes Rd.
Nightingale La. E11 124 EH57
Nightingale La. N6 120 DE59
Nightingale La. N8 121 DL56
Nightingale La. SW4 181 DH86
Nightingale La. SW12 180 DF87
Nightingale La., Brom. 204 EJ96
Nightingale La., Rich. 178 CL87
Nightingale La., St.Alb. 43 CJ24
Nightingale La., Sev. 256 FB130
Nightingale Pk., Slou. 131 AM66
Nightingale Pl. SE18 165 EN79
Nightingale Pl. SW10 160 DC79
Fulham Rd.
Nightingale Pl., Rick. 92 BK45
Nightingale Rd. E5 122 DV62
Nightingale Rd. N9 82 DW44
Nightingale Rd. N22 99 DL53
Nightingale Rd. NW10 139 CT68
Nightingale Rd. W7 137 CF74
Nightingale Rd., Cars. 200 DF104
Nightingale Rd., Chesh. 54 AP29
Nightingale Rd., Esher 214 BZ106
Nightingale Rd., Guil. 242 AX134
Nightingale Rd., Hmptn. 176 CA92
Nightingale Rd., Lthd. 245 BT125
Nightingale Rd., Orp. 205 EQ100
Nightingale Rd., Rick. 92 BJ45
Nightingale Rd., S.Croy. 221 DX111
Nightingale Rd., Walt. 195 BV101
Nightingale Rd. (Bushey), Wat. 76 CA43
Nightingale Rd., W.Mol. 196 CB99
Nightingale Sq. SW12 180 DG87
Nightingale Vale SE18 165 EN79
Nightingale Wk. SW4 181 DH86
Nightingale Way E6 144 EL71
Nightingale Way, Swan. 207 FE97
Nightingale Way, Uxb. 113 BF59
Nightingales, Wal.Abb. 68 EE34
Roundhills
Nightingales, The, Stai. 174 BM87
Nightingales La., Ch.St.G. 90 AX46
Nile Path SE18 165 EN79
Jackson St.
Nile Rd. E13 144 EJ68
Nile St. N1 275 J2
Nile St. N1 142 DR69
Nile Ter. SE15 162 DT78
Nimbus Rd., Epsom 216 CR110
Nimegen Way SE22 182 DS85
East Dulwich Gro.
Nimmo Dr. (Bushey), Wat. 95 CD45
Nimrod Clo., Nthlt. 136 BX69
Britannia Clo.
Nimrod Pas. N1 142 DS65
Tottenham Rd.
Nimrod Rd. SW16 181 DH93
Nimrod Rd., Houns. 154 BN81
Northern Perimeter Rd.
Nine Acres Clo. E12 124 EL64
Nine Ashes, Ware 34 EK08
Acorn St.
Nine Elms Ave., Uxb. 134 BK71
Nine Elms Clo., Felt. 175 BT88
Westmacott Dr.
Nine Elms Clo., Uxb. 134 BK72
Nine Elms Gro., Grav. 191 GG87
Nine Elms La. SW8 161 DJ80
Nine Stiles Clo., Uxb. 134 BH65
Nineacres Way, Couls. 235 DL116
Ninefields, Wal.Abb. 68 EF33
Ninehams Clo., Cat. 236 DR120
Ninehams Gdns., Cat. 236 DR120
Ninehams Rd., Cat. 236 DR121
Ninehams Rd., West. 238 EJ121
Nineteenth Rd., Mitch. 201 DL98
Ninhams Wd., Orp. 223 EN105
Ninian Rd., Hem.H. 40 BL15
Ninnings Rd., Ger.Cr. 91 AZ52
Ninnings Way, Ger.Cr. 91 AZ52
Ninth Ave., Hayes 135 BU73
Nisbet Ho. E9 123 DX64
Homerton High St.
Nita Rd., Brwd. 108 FW50
Nithdale Rd. SE18 165 EP80
Nithsdale Gro., Uxb. 115 BQ62
Tweeddale Gro.
Niton Clo., Barn. 79 CX44
Niton Rd., Rich. 158 CN83
Niton St. SW6 159 CX80
Niven Clo., Borwd. 78 CQ39
Nixey Clo., Slou. 152 AU75
Noak Hill Rd., Rom. 106 FJ49
Nobel Dr., Hayes 155 BR80
Nobel Rd. N18 100 DW49
Noble St. EC2 275 H8
Noble St. EC2 142 DQ72
Noble St., Walt. 195 BV104
Nobles Way, Egh. 172 AY93
Noel Pk. Rd. N22 99 DN54
Noel Rd. E6 144 EL70
Noel Rd. N1 141 DP68
Noel Rd. W3 138 CN72
Noel Sq., Dag. 126 EW63
Noel St. W1 273 L9
Noel St. W1 141 DJ72
Noel Ter. SE23 182 DW89
Dartmouth Rd.
Noke Dr., Red. 250 DG133
Noke La., St.Alb. 60 BY26
Noke Side, St.Alb. 60 CA27
Nokes, The, Hem.H. 40 BG18
Nolan Way E5 122 DU63
Nolton Pl., Edg. 96 CM53
Nonsuch Clo., Ilf. 103 EP51
Nonsuch Ct. Ave., Epsom 217 CV110
Nonsuch Wk., Sutt. 217 CW110
Noons Cor. Rd., Dor. 262 BZ143
Nora Gdns. NW4 119 CX56
Norbiton Ave., Kings.T. 198 CN95
Norbiton Common Rd., Kings.T. 198 CP97
Norbiton Rd. E14 143 DZ72
Norbreck Gdns. NW10 138 CM69
Lytham Gro.
Norbreck Par. NW10 138 CM69
Lytham Gro.
Norbroke St. W12 139 CT73
Norburn St. W10 139 CY71
Chesterton Rd.
Norbury Ave. SW16 201 DM95
Norbury Ave., Houns. 157 CD84
Norbury Ave., Th.Hth. 201 DN96
Norbury Ave., Wat. 76 BW39
Norbury Clo. SW16 201 DN95
Norbury Ct. Rd. SW16 201 DL97
Norbury Cres. SW16 201 DM95
Norbury Cross SW16 201 DL97
Norbury Gdns., Rom. 126 EX57
Norbury Gro. NW7 96 CS48
Norbury Hill SW16 181 DN94
Norbury Pk., Dor. 247 CF127
Norbury Ri. SW16 201 DL97
Norbury Rd. E4 101 EA50
Norbury Rd., Reig. 249 CZ134
Norbury Rd., Th.Hth. 202 DQ96
Norbury Way, Lthd. 246 CC125
Norcombe Gdns., Har. 117 CJ58
Norcott Clo., Hayes 136 BW70
Willow Tree La.
Norcott Rd. N16 122 DU61
Norcroft Gdns. SE22 182 DU87
Norcutt Rd., Twick. 177 CE88
Nordenfeldt Rd., Erith 167 FD78
Nordmann Pl., S.Ock. 149 FX70
Norelands Dr., Slou. 130 AJ68
Norfield Rd., Dart. 187 FC91
Norfolk Ave. N13 99 DP51
Norfolk Ave. N15 122 DT58
Norfolk Ave., Slou. 131 AQ71
Norfolk Ave., S.Croy. 220 DT110
Norfolk Ave., Wat. 76 BW38
Norfolk Clo. N2 120 DE55
Park Rd.
Norfolk Clo. N13 99 DP51
Norfolk Clo., Barn. 80 DG42
Norfolk Clo., Dart. 188 FN86
Norfolk Clo., Horl. 268 DG149
Suffolk Clo.
Norfolk Clo., Twick. 177 CH86
Cassilis Rd.
Norfolk Cres. W2 272 B8
Norfolk Cres. W2 140 DE72
Norfolk Cres., Sid. 185 ES87
Norfolk Fm. Clo., Wok. 227 BD116
Norfolk Fm. Rd., Wok. 227 BD115
Norfolk Gdns., Bexh. 166 EZ81
Norfolk Gdns., Borwd. 78 CR42
Norfolk Ho. SE3 164 EE79
Norfolk Ho. Rd. SW16 181 DK90
Norfolk La., Dor. 263 CH142
Norfolk Pl. W2 272 A8
Norfolk Pl. W2 140 DD72
Norfolk Pl., Well. 166 EU82
Norfolk Rd. E6 145 EM67
Norfolk Rd. E17 101 DX54
Norfolk Rd. NW8 140 DD67
Norfolk Rd. NW10 138 CS66
Norfolk Rd. SW19 180 DE94
Norfolk Rd., Bark. 145 ES66
Norfolk Rd., Barn. 80 DA41
Norfolk Rd., Dag. 127 FB64
Norfolk Rd., Dor. 263 CG136
Norfolk Rd. (South Holmwood), Dor. 263 CJ144
Norfolk Rd., Enf. 82 DV44
Norfolk Rd., Esher 215 CE106
Norfolk Rd., Felt. 176 BW88
Norfolk Rd., Grav. 191 GK86
Norfolk Rd., Har. 116 CB57
Norfolk Rd., Ilf. 125 ES60
Norfolk Rd., Rick. 92 BL46
Norfolk Rd., Rom. 127 FC58
Norfolk Rd., Th.Hth. 202 DQ97
Norfolk Rd., Upmin. 128 FN62
Norfolk Rd., Uxb. 134 BK65
Norfolk Row SE1 278 B8
Norfolk Row SE1 161 DM76
Norfolk Sq. W2 272 A9
Norfolk Sq. W2 140 DD72
Norfolk Sq. Ms. W2 272 A9
Norfolk St. E7 124 EG64
Norfolk Ter. W6 159 CY78
Field Rd.
Norgrove Pk., Ger.Cr. 112 AY56
Norgrove St. SW12 180 DG88
Norheads La., Warl. 238 EG119
Norheads La., West. 238 EH117
Norhyrst Ave. SE25 202 DT97
Nork Gdns., Bans. 217 CY114
Nork Ri., Bans. 233 CX115
Nork Way, Bans. 217 CY114
Norland Pl. W11 139 CY74
Norland Rd. W11 139 CX74
Norland Sq. W11 139 CY74
Norlands Cres., Chis. 205 EP95
Norlands Gate, Chis. 205 EP95
Norlands Cres.
Norlands La., Egh. 193 BE97
Norley Vale SW15 179 CU88
Norlington Rd. E10 123 EC60
Norlington Rd. E11 123 ED60
Norman Ave. N22 99 DP53
Norman Ave., Epsom 217 CT112
Norman Ave., Felt. 176 BY89
Norman Ave., S.Croy. 220 DQ110
Norman Ave., Sthl. 136 BY73
Norman Ave., Twick. 177 CH87
Norman Clo., Orp. 205 EQ104
Norman Clo., Rom. 105 FB54
Norman Clo., Wal.Abb. 67 ED33
Norman Ct., Ilf. 125 ER59
Norman Ct., Pot.B. 64 DC30
Norman Cres., Brwd. 109 GA48
Norman Cres., Houns. 156 BX80
Norman Cres., Pnr. 94 BW53
Norman Gro. E3 143 DY68
Norman Rd. E6 145 EM70
Norman Rd. E11 123 ED61
Norman Rd. N15 122 DT57
Norman Rd. SE10 163 EB80
Norman Rd. SW19 180 DC94
Norman Rd., Ashf. 175 BR93
Norman Rd., Belv. 167 FB76
Norman Rd., Dart. 188 FL88
Norman Rd., Horn. 127 FG59
Norman Rd., Ilf. 125 EP64
Norman Rd., Sutt. 218 DA106
Norman Rd., Th.Hth. 201 DP99
Norman St. EC1 275 H3
Norman Way N14 99 DL47
Norman Way W3 138 CP71
Normanby Clo. SW15 179 CZ85
Manfred Rd.
Normanby Rd. NW10 119 CT63
Normand Gdns. W14 159 CY79
Greyhound Rd.
Normand Ms. W14 159 CY79
Normand Rd.
Normand Rd. W14 159 CZ79
Normandy Ave., Barn. 79 CZ43
Normandy Dr., Berk. 38 AV17
Normandy Dr., Hayes 135 BQ72
Normandy Rd. SW9 161 DN81
Normandy Rd., St.Alb. 43 CD18
Normandy Ter. E16 144 EH72
Normandy Wk., Egh. 173 BC92
Mullens Rd.
Normandy Way, Erith 167 FE81
Normanhurst, Ashf. 174 BN92
Normanhurst, Brwd. 109 GC44
Normanhurst Ave., Bexh. 166 EX81
Normanhurst Dr., Twick. 177 CH85
St. Margarets Rd.
Normanhurst Rd. SW2 181 DM89
Normanhurst Rd., Orp. 206 EV96
Normanhurst Rd., Walt. 196 BX103
Normans, The, Slou. 132 AV72
Norman's Bldgs. EC1 142 DQ69
Ironmonger Row
Normans Clo. NW10 138 CR65
Normans Clo., Grav. 191 GG87
Normans Clo., Uxb. 134 BM71
Normans Mead NW10 138 CR65
Normansfield Ave., Tedd. 177 CJ94
Normansfield Clo. (Bushey), Wat. 94 CB45
Normanshire Ave. E4 101 EC49
Normanshire Dr.
Normanshire Dr. E4 101 EA49
Normanton Ave. SW19 180 DA89
Normanton Pk. E4 102 EE48
Normanton Rd., S.Croy. 220 DS106
Normanton St. SE23 183 DX89
Normington Clo. SW16 181 DN92
Norrels Dr., Lthd. 245 BT126
Norrels Ride, Lthd. 245 BT125
Norrice Lea N2 120 DD57
Norris Gro., Brox. 49 DY20
Norris La., Hodd. 49 EA16
Norris Ri., Hodd. 49 DZ16
Norris Rd., Hodd. 49 EA17
Norris Rd., Stai. 173 BF91
Norris St. SW1 277 M1
Norris Way, Dart. 167 FF83
Norroy Rd. SW15 159 CX84
Norrys Clo., Barn. 80 DF42
Norrys Rd., Barn. 80 DF42
Norseman Clo., Ilf. 126 EV60
Norseman Way, Grnf. 136 CB67
Olympic Way

Norstead Pl. SW15 179 CU89
Norsted La., Orp. 224 EU112
North Access Rd. E17 123 DX58
North Acre NW9 96 CS53
North Acre, Bans. 233 CZ116
North Acton Rd. NW10 138 CR68
North App., Nthwd. 93 BQ47
North App., Wat. 75 BT35
North Audley St. W1 272 F9
North Audley St. W1 140 DG73
North Ave. N18 100 DU49
North Ave. W13 137 CH71
North Ave., Brwd. 106 FQ45
North Ave., Cars. 218 DG108
North Ave., Har. 116 CB58
North Ave., Hayes 135 BU73
North Ave., Rad. 62 CL32
North Ave., Rich. 157 CK81
Sandycombe Rd.
North Ave., Sthl. 136 BZ73
North Ave., Walt. 213 BS109
North Bank NW8 272 B3
North Bank NW8 140 DE69
North Barn, Brox. 49 EA21
North Birkbeck Rd. E11 123 ED62
North Branch Ave. W10 139 CW69
Harrow Rd.
North Burnham Clo., Slou. 130 AH68
Wyndham Cres.
North Carriage Dr. W2 272 B10
North Carriage Dr. W2 140 DE73
North Circular Rd. E4 101 DZ52
North Circular Rd. E18 102 EH53
North Circular Rd. N3 119 CZ56
North Circular Rd. N12 98 DD53
North Circular Rd. N13 99 DN50
North Circular Rd. NW2 118 CS62
North Circular Rd. NW10 118 CS63
North Circular Rd. NW11 119 CX58
North Clo., Barn. 79 CW43
North Clo., Bexh. 166 EX84
North Clo., Chig. 104 EU50
North Clo., Dag. 146 FA67
North Clo., Dor. 263 CJ140
North Clo., Felt. 175 BR86
North Rd.
North Clo., Mord. 199 CY98
North Clo., St.Alb. 60 CB25
North Clo., Wind. 151 AM81
North Colonnade E14 143 EA74
North Common, Wey. 213 BP105
North Common Rd. W5 138 CL73
North Common Rd., Uxb. 114 BK64
North Cotts., St.Alb. 61 CG25
North Countess Rd. E17 101 DZ54
North Ct. W1 273 L6
North Ct., Rick. 92 BG46
Hall Clo.
North Cray Rd., Bex. 186 FA89
North Cray Rd., Sid. 186 EY93
North Cres. E16 143 ED70
Cody Rd.
North Cres. N3 97 CZ54
North Cres. WC1 273 M6
North Cross Rd. SE22 182 DT85
North Cross Rd., Ilf. 125 EQ56
North Dene NW7 96 CR48
North Dene, Houns. 156 CB81
North Down, S.Croy. 220 DS111
North Downs Cres., Croy. 221 EB110
North Downs Rd., Croy. 221 EB109
North Downs Way, Bet. 248 CQ132
North Downs Way, Dor. 261 BU137
North Downs Way, Guil. 258 AT138
North Downs Way (Albury), Guil. 260 BJ136
North Downs Way, Oxt. 254 EE126
North Downs Way, Sev. 241 FD118
North Downs Way, Tad. 248 CQ132
North Downs Way, West. 239 ER121
North Dr. SW16 181 DJ91
North Dr., Beac. 110 AG55
North Dr., Houns. 156 CC82
North Dr., Orp. 223 ES105
North Dr., Rom. 128 FJ55
North Dr., Ruis. 115 BS59
North Dr., Slou. 132 AS69
North Dr., Vir.W. 192 AS100
North End NW3 120 DC61
North End, Buck.H. 102 EJ45
North End, Croy. 202 DQ103
North End Ave. NW3 120 DC61
North End Cres. W14 159 CZ77
North End Ho. W14 159 CY77
North End La., Orp. 223 EN111
North End Par. W14 159 CY77
North End Rd.
North End Rd. NW11 120 DA60
North End Rd. SW6 159 CZ79
North End Rd. W14 159 CY77
North End Rd., Wem. 118 CN62
North End Way NW3 120 DC61
North Eyot Gdns. W6 159 CT78
St. Peter's Sq.
North Feltham Trd. Est., Felt. 175 BV85
North Flockton St. SE16 162 DU75
Chambers St.
North Gdns. SW19 180 DD94
North Gate, Harl. 35 EQ14
North Glade, The, Bex. 186 EZ87
Camden Rd.
North Gower St. NW1 273 L3
North Gower St. NW1 141 DJ69
North Grn. NW9 96 CS52
Clayton Fld.
North Grn., Slou. 132 AS73
North Gro. N6 120 DG59
North Gro. N15 122 DR57
North Gro., Cher. 193 BF100
North Gro., Harl. 52 EU16
North Hatton Rd. (Heathrow), Houns. 155 BR81
North Hill N6 120 DF58
North Hill, Rick. 73 BD40
North Hill Ave. N6 120 DF58
North Hill Dr., Rom. 106 FK48
North Hill Grn., Rom. 106 FK49
Preston Rd.
North Hyde Gdns., Hayes 155 BU77
North Hyde La., Houns. 156 BY79
North Hyde La., Sthl. 156 BX78
North Hyde Rd., Hayes 155 BS76
North Kent Ave., Grav. 190 GC86
North La., Tedd. 177 CF93
North Lo. Clo. SW15 179 CX85
Westleigh Ave.
North Mall N9 100 DV47
St. Martins Rd.
North Mead, Red. 250 DF131
North Ms. WC1 274 C5
North Ms. WC1 141 DM70
North Moors, Guil. 242 AY129
North Orbital Rd., Rick. 91 BE50
North Orbital Rd., St.Alb. 60 BY30
North Orbital Rd., Uxb. 113 BF55
North Orbital Rd., Wat. 59 BV34
North Orbital Trd. Est., St.Alb. 43 CG24
North Par., Chess. 216 CL106
North Pk. SE9 185 EN86
North Pk., Ger.Cr. 112 AY55
North Pk. La., Gdse. 252 DU131
North Pk. Rd., Iver 153 BD76
North Pas. SW18 180 DA85
North Peckham Est. SE15 162 DS80
North Perimeter Rd., Uxb. 134 BL69
Kingston La.
North Pl., Guil. 258 AX135
North Pl., Mitch. 180 DF94
North Pl., Tedd. 177 CF93
North Pl., Wal.Abb. 67 EB33
Highbridge St.
North Pl. Ind. Est., Harl. 36 EU10
North Pole La., Kes. 222 EF107
North Pole Rd. W10 139 CW71
North Ride W2 276 B1
North Ride W2 140 DE74
North Riding, St.Alb. 60 BZ30
North Rd. N6 120 DG59
North Rd. N7 141 DL65
North Rd. N9 100 DV46
North Rd. SE18 165 ES77
North Rd. SW19 180 DC93
North Rd. W5 157 CK76
North Rd., Amer. 55 AQ36
North Rd., Belv. 167 FB76
North Rd., Berk. 38 AV19
North Rd., Brent. 158 CL79
North Rd., Brwd. 108 FW46
North Rd., Brom. 204 EH95
North Rd., Dart. 187 FF87
North Rd., Edg. 96 CP53
North Rd., Felt. 175 BR86
North Rd., Guil. 242 AV131
North Rd., Hayes 135 BR71
North Rd., Hert. 31 DN05
North Rd., Hodd. 49 EA16
North Rd., Ilf. 125 ES61
North Rd., Purf. 168 FQ77
North Rd., Reig. 265 CZ137
North Rd., Rich. 158 CN83
North Rd., Rick. 73 BD43
North Rd., Rom. 126 EY57
North Rd. (Havering-atte-Bower), Rom. 105 FE48
North Rd., S.Ock. 149 FW66
North Rd., Sthl. 136 CA72
North Rd., Surb. 197 CK100
North Rd., Wal.Cr. 67 DY33
North Rd., Walt. 214 BW106
North Rd., West Dr. 154 BM76
North Rd., W.Wick. 203 EB102
North Rd., Wok. 227 BA116
North Rd. Ave., Brwd. 108 FW46
North Rd. Ave., Hert. 31 DN08
North Rd. Gdns., Hert. 31 DP09
North Row W1 272 E10
North Row W1 140 DF73
North Service Rd., Brwd. 108 FW47
North Several SE3 163 ED82
Orchard Dr.
North Sq. N9 100 DV47
St. Martins Rd.
North Sq. NW11 120 DA57
North Sta. App., Red. 267 DM136
North St. E13 144 EH68
North St. NW4 119 CW57
North St. SW4 161 DJ83
North St., Bark. 145 EP65
North St., Bexh. 166 FA84
North St., Brom. 204 EG95
North St., Cars. 200 DF104
North St., Dart. 188 FK87
North St., Dor. 263 CG136
North St. (Westcott), Dor. 262 CC137
Guildford Rd.
North St., Egh. 173 AZ92
North St., Gdmg. 258 AT144
Station Rd.
North St., Grav. 191 GH87
North St., Guil. 258 AX135
North St., Horn. 128 FK59
North St., Islw. 157 CG83
North St., Lthd. 231 CG121
North St., Red. 250 DF133
North St., Rom. 127 FD55
North St., Wal.Abb. 50 EE22
North St. Pas. E13 144 EH68
North St.
North Tenter St. E1 142 DT72
North Ter. SW3 276 B7
North Ter., Wind. 151 AR80
The Long Wk.
North Verbena Gdns. W6 159 CU78
St. Peter's Sq.
North Vw. SW19 179 CW92
North Vw. W5 137 CJ70
North Vw., Ilf. 104 EU52
North Vw., Pnr. 116 BW59
North Vw. Ave., Til. 171 GG81
North Vw. Cres. NW10 119 CT63
North Vw. Cres., Epsom 233 CV117
North Vw. Dr., Wdf.Grn. 102 EK54
North Vw. Rd. N8 121 DK55
North Vw. Rd., Sev. 257 FJ121
Seal Rd.
North Vill. NW1 141 DK65
North Wk. W2 140 DC73
Bayswater Rd.
North Wk., Croy. 221 EB107
North Way N9 101 DX47
North Way N11 99 DJ51
North Way NW9 118 CP55
North Way, Mord. 199 CY97
North Way, Pnr. 116 BW55
North Way, Uxb. 134 BL66
North Weald Ind. Est., Epp. 70 FA26
North Western Ave., Wat. 75 BR35
North Wf. Rd. W2 140 DD71
North Woolwich Rd. E16 144 EG74
North Worple Way SW14 158 CR83
Northall Rd., Bexh. 167 FC82
Northallerton Way, Rom. 106 FK50
Northampton Ave., Slou. 131 AQ72
Northampton Gro. N1 142 DR65
Northampton Pk.
Northampton Pk. N1 142 DQ65
Northampton Rd. EC1 274 E4
Northampton Rd. EC1 141 DN70
Northampton Rd., Croy. 202 DU103
Northampton Rd., Enf. 83 DY42
Northampton Sq. EC1 274 F3
Northampton Sq. EC1 141 DP69
Northampton St. N1 142 DQ66
Northanger Rd. SW16 181 DL93
Northaw Clo., Hem.H. 41 BP15
Northaw Pk., Pot.B. 64 DF32
Northaw Rd. E. (Cuffley), Pot.B. 65 DK31
Northaw Rd. W., Pot.B. 64 DG30
Northbank Rd. E17 101 EC54
Northborough Rd. SW16 201 DK97
Northborough Rd., Slou. 131 AN70
Northbourne, Brom. 204 EG101
Northbourne, Gdmg. 258 AT143
Furze La.
Northbourne Rd. SW4 161 DK84
Northbridge Rd., Berk. 38 AT17
Northbrook Dr., Nthwd. 93 BS53
Northbrook Rd. N22 99 DL52
Northbrook Rd. SE13 183 ED85
Northbrook Rd., Barn. 79 CY44
Northbrook Rd., Croy. 202 DR99
Northbrook Rd., Ilf. 125 EN61
Northbrooks, Harl. 51 EQ15
Northburgh St. EC1 274 G5
Northburgh St. EC1 141 DP70
Northchurch SE17 279 L10
Northchurch La., Berk. 38 AS21
Northchurch Rd. N1 142 DR66
Northchurch Rd., Wem. 138 CN65
Northchurch Ter. N1 142 DS66
Northcliffe Clo., Wor.Pk. 198 CS104
Northcliffe Dr. N20 97 CZ46
Northcote, Add. 212 BK105
Northcote Ave. W5 138 CL73
Northcote Ave., Islw. 177 CG85
Northcote Ave., Sthl. 136 BY73
Northcote Ave., Surb. 198 CN101
Northcote Clo., Lthd. 245 BQ125
Northcote Cres., Lthd. 245 BQ125
Northcote Pk., Lthd. 214 CC114
Northcote Rd. E17 123 DY56
Northcote Rd. NW10 138 CS66
Northcote Rd. SW11 180 DE85
Northcote Rd., Croy. 202 DR100
Northcote Rd., Grav. 191 GF88
Northcote Rd., Lthd. 245 BQ125
Northcote Rd., N.Mal. 198 CR97
Northcote Rd., Sid. 185 ES91
Northcote Rd., Twick. 177 CG85
Northcott Ave. N22 99 DL53
Northcotts, Abb.L. 59 BR33
Long Elms
Northcourt, Rick. 92 BG46
Springwell Ave.
Northcroft, H.Wyc. 110 AE56
Northcroft, Slou. 131 AP70
Northcroft Clo., Egh. 172 AV92
Northcroft Gdns., Egh. 172 AV92
Northcroft Rd.
Northcroft Rd. W13 157 CH75
Northcroft Rd., Egh. 172 AV92
Northcroft Rd., Epsom 216 CR108
Northcroft Ter. W13 157 CH75
Northcroft Rd.
Northcroft Vill., Egh. 172 AV92
Northdene, Chig. 103 ER50
Northdene Gdns. N15 122 DT58
Northdown Clo., Ruis. 115 BT62
Northdown Gdns., Ilf. 125 ES57
Northdown La., Guil. 258 AY137
Northdown Rd., Cat. 237 EA123
Northdown Rd., Ger.Cr. 90 AY51
Northdown Rd., Hat. 45 CU21
Northdown Rd., Horn. 127 FH59
Northdown Rd., Long. 209 FX96
Northdown Rd., Sutt. 218 DA110
Northdown Rd., Well. 166 EV82
Northdown St. N1 141 DL68
Northend, Brwd. 108 FW50
Northend, Hem.H. 41 BP22
Northend Clo., H.Wyc. 110 AC56
Northend Rd., Dart. 167 FF81
Northend Rd., Erith 167 FF81
Northern Ave. N9 100 DS47
Northern Perimeter Rd., Houns. 154 BK81
Northern Relief Rd., Bark. 145 EP66
Northern Rd. E13 144 EH68
Northern Rd., Slou. 131 AR70
Northern Service Rd., Barn. 79 CY41
Northern Wds., H.Wyc. 110 AC56
Northernhay Wk., Mord. 199 CY98
Northey Ave., Sutt. 217 CX110
Northey St. E14 143 DY73
Northfield, Guil. 258 AY142
Northfield, Hat. 45 CV15
Longmead
Northfield, Loug. 84 EK42
Northfield Ave. W5 137 CH74
Northfield Ave. W13 137 CH74
Northfield Ave., Orp. 206 EW100
Northfield Ave., Pnr. 116 BX56
Northfield Clo., Brom. 204 EL95
Northfield Clo., Hayes 155 BT76
Northfield Ct., Stai. 194 BH95
Northfield Cres., Sutt. 217 CY105
Northfield Gdns., Dag. 126 EZ63
Northfield Rd.
Northfield Gdns., Wat. 76 BW37
Northfield Pk., Hayes 155 BS76
Northfield Path, Dag. 126 EZ63
Connor Rd.
Northfield Pl., Wey. 213 BP108
Northfield Rd. E6 145 EM66
Northfield Rd. N16 122 DS59
Northfield Rd. W13 157 CH75
Northfield Rd., Barn. 80 DE41
Northfield Rd., Borwd. 78 CP39
Northfield Rd., Cob. 213 BV113
Portsmouth Rd.
Northfield Rd., Dag. 126 EZ63
Northfield Rd., Enf. 82 DV43
Northfield Rd., Houns. 156 BX80
Northfield Rd., Stai. 194 BH95
Northfield Rd., Wal.Cr. 67 DY32
Northfield Rd. (Eton Wick), Wind. 151 AM77
Northfields SW18 160 DA84
Northfields, Ash. 232 CL119
Northfields, Grays 170 GC77
Northfields Ind. Est., Wem. 138 CN67
Northfields Rd. W3 138 CP71
Northfleet Bypass, Grav. 190 GD88
Northfleet Grn. Rd., Grav. 190 GC92
Northfleet Ind. Est., Grav. 190 FZ85
Northgate, Gat. 268 DF151
Northgate, Nthwd. 93 BQ52
Northgate Dr. NW9 118 CS58
Northgate Path, Borwd. 78 CM38
Northiam N12 98 DA49
Northiam St. E9 142 DV67
Northington St. WC1 274 C5
Northington St. WC1 141 DM70
Northlands, Pot.B. 64 DD31
Northlands Ave., Orp. 223 ES105
Northlands St. SE5 162 DQ82
Northmead Rd., Slou. 131 AM70
Northolm, Edg. 96 CR49
Northolme Clo., Grays 170 GC76
Premier Ave.
Northolme Gdns., Edg. 96 CN53
Northolme Ri., Orp. 205 ES103
Northolme Rd. N5 122 DQ63
Northolt Ave., Ruis. 115 BV64
Northolt Gdns., Grnf. 117 CF64
Northolt Ind. Est., Nthlt. 136 CB66
Northolt Rd., Har. 116 CB63
Northolt Rd., Houns. 154 BK81
Northolt Way, Horn. 128 FJ64
Northover, Brom. 184 EF90
Northport St. N1 142 DR67
Northridge Rd., Grav. 191 GJ90
Northridge Way, Hem.H. 40 BG21
Northrop Rd., Houns. 155 BS82
Northside Rd., Brom. 204 EG95
Mitchell Way
Northspur Rd., Sutt. 200 DA104
Northstead Rd. SW2 181 DN89
Northumberland All. EC3 275 N9
Northumberland All. EC3 142 DS72
Northumberland Ave. E12 124 EJ60
Northumberland Ave. WC2 277 P2
Northumberland Ave. WC2 141 DL74
Northumberland Ave., Enf. 82 DV39
Northumberland Ave., Horn. 128 FJ57
Northumberland Ave., Islw. 157 CF81
Northumberland Ave., Well. 165 ER84
Northumberland Clo., Erith 167 FC80
Northumberland Clo., Stai. 174 BL86
Northumberland Cres., Felt. 175 BS86
Northumberland Gdns. N9 100 DT48
Northumberland Gdns., Islw. 157 CG80
Northumberland Ave.
Northumberland Gdns., Mitch. 201 DK99
Northumberland Gro. N17 100 DV52
Northumberland Pk. N17 100 DT52
Northumberland Pk., Erith 167 FC80
Northumberland Pl. W2 140 DA72
Northumberland Pl., Rich. 177 CK86
Northumberland Rd. E6 144 EL72
Northumberland Rd. E17 123 EA59
Northumberland Rd., Barn. 80 DC44
Northumberland Rd., Grav. 191 GF94
Northumberland Rd., Har. 116 BZ57
Northumberland Rd., S.le H. 171 GM75
Northumberland Row, Twick. 177 CE88
Colne Rd.
Northumberland St. WC2 277 P2
Northumberland St. WC2 141 DL74
Northumberland Way, Erith 167 FC81
Northumbria St. E14 143 EA72
Northview, Swan. 207 FE96
Northway NW7 97 CU52
Northway NW11 120 DB57
Northway, Guil. 242 AU132
Northway, Rick. 92 BK45
Northway, Wall. 219 DJ105
Northway, Welw.G.C. 29 CZ06
Nursery Hill
Northway Circ. NW7 96 CR49
Northway Cres. NW7 96 CR49
Northway Rd. SE5 162 DQ83
Northway Rd., Croy. 202 DT100
Northweald La., Kings.T. 177 CK92
Dukes Ave.
Northwest Pl. N1 141 DN68
Chapel Mkt.
Northwick Ave., Har. 117 CG58
Northwick Circle, Har. 117 CJ58
Northwick Clo. NW8 140 DD70
Northwick Ter.
Northwick Pk. Rd., Har. 117 CF58
Northwick Rd., Wat. 94 BW49
Northwick Rd., Wem. 137 CK67
Northwick Ter. NW8 140 DD70
Northwick Wk., Har. 117 CF59
Peterborough Rd.
Northwold Dr., Pnr. 116 BW55
Cuckoo Hill
Northwold Est. E5 122 DU61
Northwold Rd. E5 122 DU61
Northwold Rd. N16 122 DT61
Northwood, Grays 171 GH75
Northwood, Welw.G.C. 30 DD09
Northwood Ave., Horn. 127 FG63
Northwood Ave., Pur. 219 DN112
Northwood Clo., Wal.Cr. 66 DT27
Northwood Gdns. N12 98 DD50
Northwood Gdns., Grnf. 117 CF64
Northwood Gdns., Ilf. 125 EN56
Northwood Hall N6 121 DJ59
Northwood Ho. SE27 182 DR91
Northwood Pl., Erith 166 EZ76
Northwood Rd. N6 121 DH59
Northwood Rd. SE23 183 DZ88
Northwood Rd., Cars. 218 DG107
Northwood Rd., Houns. 154 BK81
Northwood Rd., Th.Hth. 201 DP96
Northwood Rd., Uxb. 92 BJ53
Northwood Way SE19 182 DR93
Roman Ri.
Northwood Way, Nthwd. 93 BU53
Northwood Way, Uxb. 92 BK53
Nortoft Rd., Ger.Cr. 91 AZ51
Norton Ave., Surb. 198 CP101
Norton Clo. E4 101 EA50
Norton Clo., Borwd. 78 CN39
Norton Clo., Enf. 82 DV40
Brick La.
Norton Folgate E1 275 N6
Norton Folgate E1 142 DS71
Norton Gdns. SW16 201 DL96
Norton La., Cob. 229 BT119
Norton Rd. E10 123 DZ60
Norton Rd., Dag. 147 FD65
Norton Rd., Uxb. 134 BK69
Norton Rd., Wem. 137 CK65
Norton Way, West. 255 ER126
Norval Rd., Wem. 117 CH61
Norway Dr., Slou. 132 AV71
Norway Gate SE16 163 DY76
Norway Pl. E14 143 DZ72
East India Dock Rd.
Norway St. SE10 163 EB79
Norway Wk., Rain. 148 FJ70
The Glen
Norwich Ho. E14 143 EB72
Cordelia St.
Norwich Ms., Ilf. 126 EU60
Ashgrove Rd.
Norwich Pl., Bexh. 166 FA84
Norwich Rd. E7 124 EG64
Norwich Rd., Dag. 146 FA68
Norwich Rd., Grnf. 136 CB67
Norwich Rd., Nthwd. 115 BT55
Norwich Rd., Th.Hth. 202 DQ97
Norwich St. EC4 274 D8
Norwich St. EC4 141 DN72
Norwich Wk., Edg. 96 CQ52
Norwich Way, Rick. 75 BP41
Norwick La., Har. 117 CF59
Norwood Ave., Rom. 127 FD59
Norwood Ave., Wem. 138 CM67
Norwood Clo., Hert. 31 DM08
Norwood Clo., Lthd. 246 BY128
Norwood Clo., Sthl. 156 CA77
Norwood Ct., Amer. 55 AP40
Norwood Cres., Houns. 155 BQ81
Norwood Dr., Har. 116 BZ58
Norwood Fm. La., Cob. 213 BU111
Norwood Gdns., Hayes 136 BW70
Norwood Gdns., Sthl. 156 BZ77
Norwood Grn. Rd., Sthl. 156 CA77
Norwood High St. SE27 181 DP90
Norwood La., Iver 133 BD70
Norwood Pk. Rd. SE27 182 DQ92
Norwood Rd. SE24 181 DP88
Norwood Rd. SE27 181 DP89
Norwood Rd., Lthd. 246 BY128
Norwood Rd., Sthl. 156 BZ77
Norwood Ter., Sthl. 156 CB77
Tentelow La.
Nota Ms. N3 98 DB53
Station Rd.
Notley End, Egh. 172 AW94
Notley St. SE5 162 DR80
Notre Dame Est. SW4 161 DJ84
Notson Rd. SE25 202 DV98
Belfast Rd.
Notting Barn Rd. W10 139 CX70
Notting Hill Gate W11 140 DA74
Nottingdale Sq. W11 139 CY74
Wilsham St.
Nottingham Ave. E16 144 EJ71
Nottingham Clo., Wat. 59 BU33
Nottingham Clo., Wok. 226 AT118
Nottingham Ct. WC2 273 P9
Nottingham Pl. W1 272 F5
Nottingham Pl. W1 140 DG71
Nottingham Rd. E10 123 EC58
Nottingham Rd. SW17 180 DF88
Nottingham Rd., Islw. 157 CF82
Nottingham Rd., Rick. 91 BC45
Nottingham Rd., S.Croy. 220 DQ105
Nottingham St. W1 272 F6
Nottingham St. W1 140 DG71
Nottingham Ter. NW1 272 F5
Nova Ms., Sutt. 199 CY101
Nova Rd., Croy. 201 DP102
Novar Clo., Orp. 205 ET101
Novar Rd. SE9 185 EQ88
Novello St. SW6 160 DA81
Novello Way, Borwd. 78 CQ39
Denham Way
Nowell Rd. SW13 159 CU79
Nower, The, Sev. 239 ET119
Nower Hill, Pnr. 116 BZ56
Nower Rd., Dor. 263 CG136
Noyna Rd. SW17 180 DF90
Nuding Clo. SE13 163 EA83
Nuffield Rd., Swan. 187 FG93
Nugent Rd. N19 121 DL60
Nugent Rd. SE25 202 DT97
Nugent Ter. NW8 140 DC68
Nugents Ct., Pnr. 94 BY53
St. Thomas' Dr.
Nugents Pk., Pnr. 94 BY53
Nun Ct. EC2 275 K8
Nunappleton Way, Oxt. 254 EG132
Nuneaton Rd., Dag. 146 EX66
Nunfield, Kings L. 58 BH31
Nunhead Cres. SE15 162 DV83
Nunhead Est. SE15 162 DV83
Nunhead La.
Nunhead Grn. SE15 162 DV83
Nunhead Grn., Uxb. 113 BF58
Nunhead Gro. SE15 162 DV83
Nunhead La. SE15 162 DV83
Nunhead Pas. SE15 162 DU83
Peckham Rye
Nunnery Clo., St.Alb. 43 CE22
Nunnery Stables, St.Alb. 43 CD22
Nunnington Clo. SE9 184 EL90
Nunns Rd., Enf. 82 DQ40
Nunns Way, Grays 170 GD77

Nuns La., St.Alb. 43 CE24
Nuns Wk., Vir.W. 192 AX99
Nunsbury Dr., Brox. 67 DY25
Nupton Dr., Barn. 79 CW44
Nurseries Rd., St.Alb. 28 CL08
Nursery, The, Erith 167 FF80
Nursery Ave. N3 98 DC54
Nursery Ave., Bexh. 166 EZ83
Nursery Ave., Croy. 203 DX103
Nursery Clo. SE4 163 DZ82
Nursery Clo. SW15 159 CX84
Nursery Clo., Add. 211 BF110
Nursery Clo., Amer. 55 AS39
Nursery Clo., Croy. 203 DX103
Nursery Clo., Dart. 188 FQ87
Nursery Clo., Enf. 83 DX39
Nursery Clo., Epsom 216 CS110
Nursery Clo., Felt. 175 BV87
Nursery Clo., H.Wyc. 88 AC47
Nursery Clo., Orp. 205 ET101
Nursery Clo., Rom. 126 EX58
Nursery Clo., Sev. 257 FJ122
Nursery Clo., S.Ock. 149 FW70
Nursery Clo., Swan. 207 FC96
Nursery Clo., Tad. 249 CV125
Nursery Clo., Wok. 226 AW116
Nursery Clo., Wdf.Grn. 102 EH50
Nursery Ct. N17 100 DT52
Nursery St.
Nursery Dr., Maid. 130 AH72
Nursery Flds., Saw. 36 EX05
Nursery Gdns., Chis. 185 EP93
Willow Gro.
Nursery Gdns., Enf. 83 DX39
Nursery Gdns., Guil. 259 BB140
Nursery Gdns., Stai. 174 BH94
Nursery Gdns., Sun. 195 BT96
Nursery Gdns., Ware 33 DY06
Nursery Gdns., Welw.G.C. 29 CY06
Nursery Hill, Welw.G.C. 29 CY06
Nursery La. E2 142 DT67
Laburnum St.
Nursery La. E7 144 EG65
Nursery La. W10 139 CW71
Nursery La., H.Wyc. 88 AC47
Nursery La., Horl. 268 DD149
Nursery La., Slou. 132 AW74
Nursery Pl., Sev. 256 FD122
Nursery Rd. E9 142 DW65
Morning La.
Nursery Rd. N2 98 DD53
Nursery Rd. N14 99 DJ45
Nursery Rd. SW9 161 DM84
Nursery Rd. (Merton) SW19 200 DB96
Nursery Rd. (Wimbledon) SW19 179 CY94
Worple Rd.
Nursery Rd., Brox. 67 DY25
Nursery Rd., Gdmg. 258 AT144
Nursery Rd., Hodd. 33 EB14
Nursery Rd., Loug. 84 EJ43
Nursery Rd. (High Beach), Loug. 84 EH39
Nursery Rd., Pnr. 116 BW55
Nursery Rd., Sun. 195 BS96
Nursery Rd., Sutt. 218 DC105
Nursery Rd., Tad. 249 CV125
Nursery Rd., Th.Hth. 202 DR98
Nursery Rd., Wal.Abb. 49 ED22
Nursery Row SE17 162 DR77
Orb St.
Nursery Row, Barn. 79 CY41
St. Albans Rd.
Nursery St. N17 100 DT52
Nursery Wk. NW4 119 CV55
Nursery Wk., Rom. 127 FD59
Nursery Way, Stai. 172 AX86
Nursery Waye, Uxb. 134 BK67
Nurserymans Rd. N11 98 DG49
Nurstead Rd., Erith 166 FA80
Nut Gro., Welw.G.C. 29 CX06
Nut Tree Clo., Orp. 206 EX104
Nutberry Ave., Grays 170 GA75
Nutberry Clo., Grays 170 GA75
Long La.
Nutbourne St. W10 139 CY69
Nutbrook St. SE15 162 DU83
Nutbrowne Rd., Dag. 146 EZ67
Nutcombe La., Dor. 263 CF136
Nutcroft Gro., Lthd. 231 CE121
Nutcroft Rd. SE15 162 DV80
Nutfield, Welw.G.C. 30 DA06
Nutfield Clo. N18 100 DU51
Nutfield Clo., Cars. 200 DE104
Nutfield Gdns., Ilf. 125 ET61
Nutfield Gdns., Nthlt. 136 BW68
Nutfield Marsh Rd., Red. 251 DK131
Nutfield Rd. E15 123 EC63
Nutfield Rd. NW2 119 CU61
Nutfield Rd. SE22 182 DT85
Nutfield Rd., Couls. 234 DG116
Nutfield Rd., Red. 250 DG134
Nutfield Rd. (South Merstham), Red. 251 DJ129
Nutfield Rd., Th.Hth. 201 DP98
Nutfield Way, Orp. 205 EN103
Nutford Pl. W1 272 C8
Nutford Pl. W1 140 DE72
Nuthatch Clo., Stai. 174 BM88
Nuthatch Gdns. SE28 165 ER75
Nuthatch Gdns., Reig. 266 DC138
Rushetts Rd.
Nuthurst Ave. SW2 181 DM89
Nutkins Way, Chesh. 54 AQ29
Nutley Clo., Swan. 207 FF95
Nutley Ct., Reig. 249 CZ134
Nutley La.
Nutley La., Reig. 249 CZ133
Nutley Ter. NW3 140 DC65
Nutmead Clo., Bex. 187 FC88
Nutmeg Clo. E16 144 EE70
Cranberry La.
Nutmeg La. E14 143 ED72
Nutt Gro., Edg. 95 CK47
Nutt St. SE15 162 DT80
Nuttall St. N1 142 DS68
Nutter La. E11 124 EJ58
Nuttfield Clo., Rick. 75 BP44
Nutty La., Shep. 195 BQ97
Nutwell St. SW17 180 DE92
Nutwood Ave., Bet. 264 CQ135
Nutwood Clo., Bet. 264 CQ135
Nuxley Rd., Belv. 166 EZ79
Nyanza St. SE18 165 ER79
Nye Bevan Est. E5 123 DX62
Nye Way, Hem.H. 57 BA28
Nyefield Pk., Tad. 249 CU126
Nylands Ave., Rich. 158 CN81
Nymans Gdns. SW20 199 CV97
Hidcote Gdns.
Nynehead St. SE14 163 DY80
Nyon Gro. SE6 183 DZ89
Nyssa Clo., Wdf.Grn. 103 EM51
Gwynne Pk. Ave.
Nyth Clo., Upmin. 129 FR58
Nyton Clo. N19 121 DL60
Courtauld Rd.

O

Oak Apple Ct. SE12 184 EG89
Oak Ave. N8 121 DL56
Oak Ave. N10 99 DH52
Oak Ave. N17 100 DR52
Oak Ave., Croy. 203 EA102
Oak Ave., Egh. 173 BC94
Oak Ave., Enf. 81 DM39
Oak Ave., Hmptn. 176 BY92
Oak Ave., Houns. 156 BY80
Oak Ave., St.Alb. 60 CA30
Oak Ave., Sev. 257 FH128
Oak Ave., Upmin. 128 FP62
Oak Ave., Uxb. 115 BP61
Oak Ave., West Dr. 154 BN76
Oak Bank, Croy. 221 EC107
Oak Bank, Wok. 226 AY119
Oak Clo. N14 99 DH45
Oak Clo., Dart. 167 FE84
Oak Clo., Gdmg. 258 AS143
Oak Clo., Hem.H. 40 BM24
Great Elms Rd.
Oak Clo., Sutt. 200 DC103
Oak Clo., Wal.Abb. 67 ED34
Oak Cottage Clo. SE6 184 EF88
Oak Cres. E16 144 EE71
Oak Dene W13 137 CH71
The Dene
Oak Dr., Berk. 38 AX20
Oak Dr., Saw. 36 EW07
Oak Dr., Tad. 248 CP130
Oak End, Harl. 51 ET17
Oak End Dr., Iver 133 BC68
Glaisyer Way
Oak End Way, Add. 211 BE112
Oak End Way, Ger.Cr. 113 AZ57
Oak Gdns., Croy. 203 EA103
Oak Gdns., Edg. 96 CQ54
Oak Glade, Epp. 70 EX29
Coopersale Common
Oak Glade, Nthwd. 93 BP53
Oak Glen, Horn. 128 FL55
Oak Gra. Rd., Guil. 244 BG129
Oak Grn., Abb.L. 59 BS31
Oak Grn. Way, Abb.L. 59 BS32
Oak Grn.
Oak Gro. NW2 119 CX63
Oak Gro., Hat. 45 CT18
Oak Gro., Hert. 32 DS11
Oak Gro., Ruis. 115 BV59
Oak Gro., Sun. 175 BV94
Oak Gro., W.Wick. 203 EC103
Oak Gro. Rd. SE20 202 DW96
Oak Hill, Epsom 232 CR116
Oak Hill, Guil. 243 BC129
Oak Hill, Wdf.Grn. 101 ED52
Oak Hill Clo., Wdf.Grn. 101 ED52
Oak Hill Ct. SW19 179 CX94
Oak Hill Cres., Wdf.Grn. 101 ED52
Oak Hill Gdns., Wdf.Grn. 102 EE53
Oak Hill Pk. NW3 120 DB63
Oak Hill Pk. Ms. NW3 120 DC63
Oak Hill Rd., Rom. 105 FD45
Oak Hill Rd., Sev. 256 FG124
Oak Hill Way NW3 120 DC63
Oak La. E14 143 DZ73
Oak La. N2 98 DD54
Oak La. N11 99 DK51
Oak La., Egh. 172 AW90
Oak La., Islw. 157 CE84
Oak La. (Cuffley), Pot.B. 65 DM28
Oak La., Sev. 256 FF129
Oak La., Twick. 177 CG87
Oak La., Wind. 151 AN81
Oak La., Wok. 227 BC116
Beaufort Rd.
Oak La., Wdf.Grn. 102 EF49
Oak Leaf Clo., Epsom 216 CQ112
Oak Lo. Ave., Chig. 103 ER50
Oak Lo. Clo., Stan. 95 CJ50
Dennis La.
Oak Lo. Clo., Walt. 214 BW106
Oak Lo. Dr., Red. 266 DG142
Oak Lo. Dr., W.Wick. 203 EB101
Oak Lo. La., West. 255 ER125
Oak Manor Dr., Wem. 118 CM64
Oakington Manor Dr.
Oak Pk., W.Byf. 211 BE113
Oak Pk. Gdns. SW19 179 CX87
Oak Path (Bushey), Wat. 76 CB44
Ashfield Ave.
Oak Piece, Epp. 71 FC25
Oak Pl. SW18 180 DB85
East Hill
Oak Ridge, Dor. 263 CH139
Oak Ri., Buck.H. 102 EK48
Oak Rd. W5 137 CK73
The Bdy.
Oak Rd., Cat. 236 DS122
Oak Rd., Cob. 230 BX115
Oak Rd., Epp. 69 ET30
Oak Rd. (Northumberland Heath), Erith 167 FC80
Oak Rd. (Slade Grn.), Erith 167 FG81
Oak Rd., Grav. 191 GJ90
Oak Rd., Grays 170 GC79
Oak Rd., Green. 189 FS86
Oak Rd., Lthd. 231 CG119
Oak Rd., N.Mal. 198 CR96
Oak Rd., Orp. 224 EU108
Oak Rd., Reig. 250 DB133
Oak Rd., Rom. 106 FM53
Oak Rd., West. 255 ER125
Oak Row SW16 201 DJ96
Oak Side, Uxb. 134 BH65
Oak St., Hem.H. 40 BM24
Great Elms Rd.
Oak St., Rom. 127 FC57
Oak Stubbs La., Maid. 150 AF75
Oak Tree Clo. W5 137 CJ72
Pinewood Gro.
Oak Tree Clo., Abb.L. 59 BR32
Broomfield Ri.
Oak Tree Clo. (Burpham), Guil. 243 BC129
Oak Tree Clo. (Stringers Common), Guil. 242 AX128
Oak Tree Clo., Hat. 45 CU17
Oak Tree Clo., Hert. 32 DW12
Oak Tree Clo., Loug. 85 EQ39
Colebrook La.
Oak Tree Clo., Stan. 95 CH52
Oak Tree Clo., Vir.W. 192 AX100
Oak Tree Ct., Borwd. 77 CK44
Barnet La.
Oak Tree Dell NW9 118 CQ57
Oak Tree Dr. N20 98 DB46
Oak Tree Dr., Egh. 172 AW92
Oak Tree Dr., Guil. 242 AW130
Oak Tree Gdns., Brom. 184 EH92
Oak Tree Rd. NW8 272 A3
Oak Tree Rd. NW8 140 DE69
Oak Village NW5 120 DG63
Oak Wk., Saw. 36 EX07
Oak Way N14 99 DH45
Oak Way W3 138 CS74
Oak Way, Ash. 232 CN116
Oak Way, Croy. 203 DX100
Oak Way, Felt. 175 BS88
Oak Way, Reig. 250 DD134
Oakapple Clo., S.Croy. 220 DV114
Oakbank, Brwd. 109 GE43
Oakbank, Lthd. 230 CC123
Oakbank Ave., Walt. 196 BZ101
Oakbank Gro. SE24 162 DQ84
Oakbrook Clo., Brom. 184 EH91
Oakbury Rd. SW6 160 DB82
Oakcombe Clo., N.Mal. 198 CS95
Traps La.
Oakcroft Clo., Pnr. 93 BV54
Oakcroft Clo., W.Byf. 211 BF114
Oakcroft Rd. SE13 163 ED82
Oakcroft Rd., Chess. 216 CM105
Oakcroft Rd., W.Byf. 211 BF114
Oakcroft Vill., Chess. 216 CM105
Oakdale N14 99 DH46
Oakdale, Welw.G.C. 29 CX05
Oakdale Ave., Har. 118 CL57
Oakdale Ave., Nthwd. 93 BU54
Oakdale Clo., Wat. 94 BW49
Oakdale Ct. E4 101 EC50
Larkshall Rd.
Oakdale Gdns. E4 101 EC50
Larkshall Rd.
Oakdale La., Eden. 255 EQ133
Oakdale Rd. E7 144 EH66
Oakdale Rd. E11 123 ED61
Oakdale Rd. E18 102 EH54
Oakdale Rd. N4 122 DQ58
Oakdale Rd. SE15 162 DW83
Oakdale Rd. SW16 181 DL92
Oakdale Rd., Epsom 216 CR109
Oakdale Rd., Wat. 94 BW48
Oakdale Rd., Wey. 194 BN104
Oakdale Way, Mitch. 200 DG101
Wolseley Rd.
Oakden St. SE11 278 E8
Oakden St. SE11 161 DN77
Oakdene SE15 162 DV81
Carlton Gro.
Oakdene, Beac. 89 AL52
Wilton Rd.
Oakdene, Tad. 233 CY120
Oakdene (Cheshunt), Wal.Cr. 67 DY30
Oakdene, Wok. 210 AT110
Oakdene Ave., Chis. 185 EN92
Oakdene Ave., Erith 167 FC79
Oakdene Ave., T.Ditt. 197 CG102
Oakdene Clo., Bet. 264 CQ136
Oakdene Clo., Horn. 127 FH58
Oakdene Clo., Lthd. 246 CC127
Oakdene Clo., Pnr. 94 BZ52
Oakdene Dr., Surb. 198 CQ101
Oakdene Ms., Sutt. 199 CZ102
Oakdene Pk. N3 97 CZ52
Oakdene Rd., Bet. 264 CP136
Oakdene Rd., Cob. 213 BV114
Oakdene Rd., Guil. 258 AW142
Oakdene Rd., Hem.H. 40 BM24
Oakdene Rd., Lthd. 230 BZ124
Oakdene Rd., Orp. 205 ET99
Oakdene Rd., Red. 250 DE134
Oakdene Rd., Sev. 256 FG122
Oakdene Rd., Uxb. 135 BP68
Oakdene Rd., Wat. 75 BV36
Oakdene Way, St.Alb. 43 CJ20
Oake Ct. SW15 179 CY85
Oaken Coppice, Ash. 232 CN119
Oaken Dr., Esher 215 CF107
Oaken Gro., Welw.G.C. 29 CY11
Oaken La., Esher 215 CE105
Oakenshaw Clo., Surb. 198 CL101
Oakes Clo. E6 145 EM72
Savage Gdns.
Oakeshott Ave. N6 120 DG61
Oakey La. SE1 278 D6
Oakfield E4 101 EB50
Oakfield, Rick. 91 BF45
Oakfield, Wok. 226 AS116
Oakfield Ave., Har. 117 CH55
Oakfield Ave., Slou. 131 AP74
Oakfield Clo., N.Mal. 199 CT99
Blakes La.
Oakfield Clo., Pot.B. 63 CZ31
Oakfield Clo., Wey. 213 BQ105
Oakfield Ct. N8 121 DL59
Oakfield Ct. NW2 119 CX59
Hendon Way
Oakfield Dr., Reig. 250 DA132
Oakfield Gdns. N18 100 DS49
Oakfield Gdns. SE19 182 DT92
Oakfield Gdns., Beck. 203 EA99
Oakfield Gdns., Cars. 200 DE102
Oakfield Gdns., Grnf. 137 CD70
Oakfield Glade, Wey. 213 BQ105
Oakfield La., Bex. 187 FE89
Oakfield La., Dart. 187 FG89
Oakfield La., Kes. 222 EJ105
Oakfield Pk. Rd., Dart. 188 FK89
Oakfield Pl., Dart. 188 FK89
Oakfield Rd. E6 144 EL67
Oakfield Rd. E17 101 DY54
Oakfield Rd. N3 98 DB53
Oakfield Rd. N4 121 DN58
Oakfield Rd. N14 99 DL48
Oakfield Rd. SE20 202 DV95
Oakfield Rd. SW19 179 CX90
Oakfield Rd., Ashf. 175 BP91
Oakfield Rd., Ash. 231 CK117
Oakfield Rd., Cob. 213 BV113
Oakfield Rd., Croy. 202 DQ102
Oakfield Rd., Ilf. 125 EP61
Oakfield Rd., Orp. 206 EU101
Goodmead Rd.
Oakfield St. SW10 160 DC79
Oakfields, Guil. 242 AS133
Oakfields, Sev. 257 FH126
Oakfields, Walt. 195 BU102
Oakfields, W.Byf. 212 BH114
Oakfields Rd. NW11 119 CY58
Oakford Rd. NW5 121 DJ63
Oakhall Dr., Sun. 175 BT92
Oakhall Rd. E11 124 EH58
Oakham Clo. SE6 183 DZ89
Rutland Wk.
Oakham Clo., Barn. 80 DF41
Chalk La.
Oakham Dr., Brom. 204 EF98
Oakhampton Rd. NW7 97 CX52
Oakhill, Esher 215 CG107
Oakhill, Surb. 198 CL101
Oakhill Ave. NW3 120 DB63
Oakhill Ave., Pnr. 94 BY54
Oakhill Clo., Ash. 231 CJ118
Oakhill Ct. E11 124 EH58
Eastern Ave.
Oakhill Ct. SW19 179 CX94
Edge Hill
Oakhill Cres., Surb. 198 CL101
Oakhill Dr., Surb. 198 CL101
Oakhill Gdns., Wey. 195 BS103
Oatlands Dr.
Oakhill Gro., Surb. 198 CL100
Oakhill Path, Surb. 198 CL100
Glenbuck Rd.
Oakhill Pl. SW15 180 DA85
Oakhill Rd.
Oakhill Rd. SW15 179 CZ85
Oakhill Rd. SW16 201 DL95
Oakhill Rd., Add. 211 BF107
Oakhill Rd., Ash. 231 CJ118
Oakhill Rd., Beck. 203 EC96
Oakhill Rd., Orp. 205 ET102
Oakhill Rd., Purf. 168 FP78
Oakhill Rd., Reig. 266 DB135
Oakhill Rd., Rick. 91 BD49
Oakhill Rd., Surb. 198 CL100
Oakhill Rd., Sutt. 200 DB104
Oakhouse Rd., Bexh. 186 FA85
Oakhurst, Wok. 210 AS109
Oakhurst Ave., Barn. 98 DE45
Oakhurst Ave., Bexh. 166 EY80
Oakhurst Clo. E17 124 EE56
Oakhurst Clo., Ilf. 103 EQ53
Oakhurst Clo., Tedd. 177 CE92
Oakhurst Gdns. E4 102 EF46
Oakhurst Gdns. E17 124 EE56
Oakhurst Gdns., Bexh. 166 EY80
Oakhurst Gro. SE22 162 DU84
Oakhurst Ri., Cars. 218 DE110
Oakhurst Rd., Enf. 83 DX36
Oakhurst Rd., Epsom 216 CQ107
Oakington, Welw.G.C. 30 DD09
Oakington Ave., Amer. 72 AY39
Oakington Ave., Har. 116 CA59
Oakington Ave., Hayes 155 BR77
Oakington Ave., Wem. 118 CM62
Oakington Dr., Sun. 196 BW96
Oakington Manor Dr., Wem. 118 CN64
Oakington Rd. W9 140 DA70
Oakington Way N8 121 DL58
Oakland Gdns., Brwd. 109 GC43
Oakland Gro., Brox. 49 DY24
Oakland Pl., Buck.H. 102 EG47
Whitehall La.
Oakland Way, Epsom 216 CR107
Oaklands N21 99 DM47
Oaklands, Berk. 38 AU19
Oaklands, Horl. 269 DJ147
Oaklands, Ken. 220 DQ114
Oaklands, Lthd. 231 CD124
Oaklands, Twick. 176 CC87
Oaklands Ave. N9 82 DV44
Oaklands Ave., Esher 197 CD102
Oaklands Ave., Hat. 63 CY26
Oaklands Ave., Islw. 157 CF79
Oaklands Ave., Rom. 127 FE55
Oaklands Ave., Sid. 185 ET87
Oaklands Ave., Th.Hth. 201 DN98
Oaklands Ave., Wat. 93 BV46
Oaklands Ave., W.Wick. 203 EB104
Oaklands Clo., Bexh. 186 EZ85
Oaklands Clo., Chess. 215 CJ105
Oaklands Clo., Guil. 258 AY142
Oaklands Clo., Orp. 205 ES100
Oaklands Ct., Add. 194 BH104
Oaklands Ct., Wat. 75 BT39
Oaklands Ct., Wem. 117 CK64
Oaklands Dr., Harl. 52 EW16
Oaklands Dr., Red. 267 DH136
Oaklands Dr., S.Ock. 149 FW71
Oaklands Est. SW4 181 DJ86
Oaklands Gdns., Ken. 220 DQ114
Oaklands Gate, Nthwd. 93 BS51
Green La.
Oaklands Gro. W12 139 CU74
Oaklands La., Barn. 79 CV42
Oaklands La., St.Alb. 44 CL18
Oaklands La., West. 222 EH113
Oaklands Pk. Ave., Ilf. 125 ER61
High Rd.
Oaklands Pl. SW4 161 DJ84
St. Alphonsus Rd.
Oaklands Rd. N20 97 CZ45
Oaklands Rd. NW2 119 CX63
Oaklands Rd. SW14 158 CR83
Oaklands Rd. W7 157 CF75
Oaklands Rd., Bexh. 166 EZ84
Oaklands Rd., Brom. 184 EE94
Oaklands Rd., Dart. 188 FP88
Oaklands Rd., Grav. 191 GF91
Oaklands Rd. (Cheshunt), Wal.Cr. 66 DS26
Oaklands Way, Tad. 233 CW122
Oaklands Way, Wall. 219 DK108
Oaklawn Rd., Lthd. 231 CE118
Oaklea Pas., Kings.T. 197 CK97
Oakleafe Gdns., Ilf. 125 EP55
Oakleigh Ave. N20 98 DD47
Oakleigh Ave., Edg. 96 CP54
Oakleigh Ave., Surb. 198 CN102
Oakleigh Clo. N20 98 DF48
Oakleigh Clo., Swan. 207 FE97
Oakleigh Ct., Barn. 80 DE44
Church Hill Rd.
Oakleigh Ct., Edg. 96 CQ54
Oakleigh Cres. N20 98 DE47
Oakleigh Dr., Rick. 75 BQ44
Oakleigh Gdns. N20 98 DC46
Oakleigh Gdns., Edg. 96 CM50
Oakleigh Gdns., Orp. 223 ES105
Oakleigh Ms. N20 98 DC47
Oakleigh Rd. N.
Oakleigh Pk. Ave., Chis. 205 EN96
Oakleigh Pk. N. N20 98 DD46
Oakleigh Pk. S. N20 98 DE45
Oakleigh Ri., Epp. 70 EU32
Bower Hill
Oakleigh Rd., Pnr. 94 BZ51
Oakleigh Rd., Uxb. 135 BQ66
Oakleigh Rd. N. N20 98 DE47
Oakleigh Rd. S. N11 98 DG48
Oakleigh Way, Mitch. 201 DH95
Oakleigh Way, Surb. 198 CN102
Oakley Ave. W5 138 CN73
Oakley Ave., Bark. 145 ET66
Oakley Ave., Croy. 219 DM105
Oakley Clo. E4 101 EC48
Mapleton Rd.
Oakley Clo. E6 144 EL72
Northumberland Rd.
Oakley Clo. W7 137 CE73
Oakley Clo., Add. 212 BK105
Oakley Clo., Grays 169 FW79
Oakley Clo., Islw. 157 CD81
Oakley Ct., Mitch. 200 DG102
London Rd.
Oakley Cres. EC1 274 G1
Oakley Cres., Slou. 132 AS73
Oakley Dell, Guil. 243 BC132
Oakley Dr. SE9 185 ER88
Oakley Dr., Brom. 204 EL104
Oakley Dr., Rom. 106 FN50
Oakley Gdns. N8 121 DM57
Oakley Gdns. SW3 160 DE79
Oakley Gdns., Bans. 234 DB115
Oakley Grn. Rd., Wind. 150 AG82
Oakley Pk., Bex. 186 EW87
Oakley Pl. SE1 162 DT78
Oakley Rd. N1 142 DR66
Oakley Rd. SE25 202 DV99
Oakley Rd., Brom. 204 EL104
Oakley Rd., Har. 117 CE58
Oakley Rd., Warl. 236 DU118
Oakley Sq. NW1 141 DJ68
Oakley St. SW3 160 DE79
Oakley Wk. W6 159 CX79
Greyhound Rd.
Oakley Yd. E2 142 DT70
Bacon St.
Oaklodge Way NW7 97 CT51
Flower La.
Oakmead Ave., Brom. 204 EG100
Oakmead Gdns., Edg. 96 CR49
Oakmead Grn., Epsom 232 CQ115
Oakmead Pl., Mitch. 200 DE95
Oakmead Rd. SW12 180 DG88
Oakmead Rd., Croy. 202 DW100
Oakmeade, Pnr. 94 CA51
Oakmere Ave., Pot.B. 64 DC33
Oakmere Clo., Pot.B. 64 DD31
Oakmere La., Pot.B. 64 DC32
Oakmere Rd. SE2 166 EU79
Oakmoor Way, Chig. 103 ES50
Oakmount Pl., Orp. 205 ER102
Oakridge, St.Alb. 60 BZ29
Oakridge Ave., Rad. 61 CF34
Oakridge Dr. N2 120 DD55
Oakridge La., Brom. 183 ED92
Downham Way
Oakridge La., Wat. 77 CD35
Oakridge Rd., Brom. 183 ED91
Oakroyd Ave., Pot.B. 63 CZ33
Oakroyd Clo., Pot.B. 63 CZ33
Oaks, The N12 98 DB49
Oaks, The SE18 165 EQ78
Oaks, The, Berk. 38 AU19
Oaks, The, Epsom 217 CT114
Oaks, The, Hayes 135 BQ68
Charville La.
Oaks, The, Ruis. 115 BS59
Oaks, The, Stai. 173 BF91
Moormede Cres.
Oaks, The, Swan. 207 FE96
Oaks, The, Wat. 94 BW46
Oaks, The, W.Byf. 212 BG114
Oaks, The, Wdf.Grn. 102 EE52
Oaks Ave. SE19 182 DS92
Oaks Ave., Felt. 176 BY89
Oaks Ave., Rom. 105 FC54
Oaks Ave., Wor.Pk. 199 CV104
Oaks Clo., Lthd. 231 CG121
Oaks Clo., Rad. 77 CF35
Oaks Gro. E4 102 EE47
Oaks La., Croy. 202 DW104
Oaks La., Dor. 263 CH143
Oaks La., Ilf. 125 ES57
Oaks Rd., Croy. 220 DV106
Oaks Rd., Ken. 219 DP114
Oaks Rd., Reig. 250 DD133
Oaks Rd., Stai. 174 BK86
Oaks Rd., Wok. 226 AY117
Oaks Track, Cars. 218 DF111
Oaks Track, Wall. 219 DH110
Oaks Way, Cars. 218 DF108
Oaks Way, Epsom 233 CV119
Epsom La. N.
Oaks Way, Ken. 220 DQ114
Oaks Way, Surb. 197 CK103
Oaksford Ave. SE26 182 DV90
Oakshade Rd., Brom. 183 ED91
Oakshade Rd., Lthd. 214 CC114
Oakshaw, Oxt. 253 ED127
Oakshaw Rd. SW18 180 DB87
Oakside, Uxb. 134 BH65
Oakside Ct., Horl. 269 DJ147
Oakside La.
Oakside La., Horl. 269 DJ147
Oakthorpe Rd. N13 99 DN50
Oaktree Ave. N13 99 DP48
Oaktree Clo., Brwd. 109 FZ49
Hawthorn Ave.
Oaktree Clo., Wal.Cr. 65 DP28
Oaktree Garth, Welw.G.C. 29 CY10
Oakview Clo., Wal.Cr. 66 DV28
Oakview Gdns. N2 120 DD56
Oakview Gro., Croy. 203 DY102
Oakview Rd. SE6 183 EB92
Oakway SW20 199 CW98
Oakway, Amer. 55 AP35
Oakway, Brom. 203 ED96
Oakway, Wok. 226 AS119
Oakway Clo., Bex. 186 EY86
Oakways SE9 185 EP86
Oakwood, Berk. 38 AT20
Oakwood, Guil. 242 AU129
Oakwood, Wall. 219 DH109

Oakwood, Wal.Abb.	83	ED35
Roundhills		
Oakwood Ave. N14	99	DK45
Oakwood Ave., Beck.	203	EC96
Oakwood Ave., Borwd.	78	CP42
Oakwood Ave., Brwd.	109	GE44
Oakwood Ave., Brom.	204	EH97
Oakwood Ave., Mitch.	200	DD96
Oakwood Ave., Pur.	219	DP112
Oakwood Ave., Sthl.	136	CA73
Oakwood Chase, Horn.	128	FM58
Oakwood Clo. N14	81	DJ44
Oakwood Clo., Chis.	185	EM93
Oakwood Clo., Dart.	188	FP88
Oakwood Clo., Lthd.	245	BS127
Oakwood Clo., Red.	250	DG134
Oakwood Clo. (South Nutfield), Red.	267	DM136
The Ave.		
Oakwood Clo., Wdf.Grn.	102	EL51
Green Wk.		
Oakwood Ct. W14	159	CZ76
Oakwood Cres. N21	81	DL44
Oakwood Cres., Grnf.	137	CG65
Oakwood Dr. SE19	182	DR93
Oakwood Dr., Bexh.	167	FD84
Oakwood Dr., Edg.	96	CQ51
Oakwood Dr., Lthd.	245	BS127
Oakwood Dr., St.Alb.	43	CJ19
Oakwood Dr., Sev.	257	FH123
Hitchen Hatch La.		
Oakwood Gdns., Ilf.	125	ET61
Oakwood Gdns., Orp.	205	EQ103
Oakwood Gdns., Sutt.	200	DA103
Oakwood Hill, Loug.	85	EM44
Oakwood Hill Ind. Est. (Oakwood Hill), Loug.	85	EP43
Oakwood La. W14	159	CZ76
Oakwood Pk. Rd. N14	99	DK45
Oakwood Pl., Croy.	201	DN100
Oakwood Rd. NW11	120	DA56
Oakwood Rd. SW20	199	CU95
Oakwood Rd., Croy.	201	DN100
Oakwood Rd., Horl.	268	DG147
Oakwood Rd., Orp.	205	EQ103
Oakwood Rd., Pnr.	93	BV54
Oakwood Rd., Red.	251	DN129
Oakwood Rd., St.Alb.	60	BY29
Oakwood Rd., Vir.W.	192	AW99
Oakwood Rd., Wok.	226	AS119
Oakwood Vw. N14	81	DK43
Oakworth Rd. W10	139	CW71
Oast Ho. Clo., Stai.	172	AY87
Oast Rd., Oxt.	254	EF131
Oasthouse Way, Orp.	206	EV98
Oat La. EC2	**275**	**J8**
Oat La. EC2	142	DQ72
Oates Clo., Brom.	203	ED97
Oates Rd., Rom.	105	FB50
Oatfield Rd., Orp.	205	ET102
Oatfield Rd., Tad.	233	CV121
Oatland Ri. E17	101	DY54
Oatlands, Horl.	269	DH147
Oatlands Ave., Wey.	213	BQ106
Oatlands Chase, Wey.	195	BS104
Oatlands Clo., Wey.	213	BQ105
Oatlands Dr., Slou.	131	AR72
Oatlands Dr., Wey.	195	BR104
Oatlands Grn., Wey.	195	BR104
Oatlands Dr.		
Oatlands Mere, Wey.	195	BR104
Oatlands Rd., Enf.	82	DW39
Oatlands Rd., Tad.	233	CY119
Oban Ct., Slou.	151	AR75
Montem La.		
Oban Ho., Bark.	145	ER68
Wheelers Cross		
Oban Rd. E13	144	EJ69
Oban Rd. SE25	202	DR98
Oban St. E14	143	ED72
Obelisk Ride, Egh.	172	AS93
Oberon Clo., Borwd.	78	CQ39
Denham Way		
Oberon Way, Shep.	194	BL97
Oberstein Rd. SW11	160	DD84
Oborne Clo. SE24	181	DP85
Observatory Gdns. W8	160	DA75
Observatory Rd. SW14	158	CQ84
Observatory Wk., Red.	250	DF134
Lower Bri. Rd.		
Occupation La. SE18	165	EP81
Occupation La. W5	157	CK77
Occupation Rd. SE17	**279**	**H10**
Occupation Rd. SE17	162	DQ78
Occupation Rd. W13	157	CH75
Occupation Rd., Wat.	75	BV43
Ocean Est. E1	143	DX70
Ocean St. E1	143	DX71
Ockenden Clo., Wok.	227	AZ118
Ockenden Rd.		
Ockenden Gdns., Wok.	227	AZ118
Ockenden Rd.		
Ockenden Rd., Wok.	227	AZ118
Ockendon Rd. N1	142	DR65
Ockendon Rd., Upmin.	128	FQ64
Ockham Dr., Lthd.	229	BR124
Ockham Dr., Orp.	186	EU94
Ockham La., Cob.	229	BR120
Ockham La., Wok.	228	BN121
Ockham Rd. N., Lthd.	229	BQ123
Ockham Rd. N., Wok.	228	BL120
Ockham Rd. S., Lthd.	245	BS126
Ockley Ct., Guil.	243	BB129
Cotts Wd. Dr.		
Ockley Rd. SW16	181	DL91
Ockley Rd., Croy.	201	DM101
Ockleys Mead, Gdse.	252	DW130
Octagon Arc. EC2	**275**	**M7**
Octagon Rd., Walt.	213	BS109
Octavia Clo., Mitch.	200	DE99
Octavia Rd., Islw.	157	CF83
Octavia St. SW11	160	DE81
Octavia Way SE28	146	EV73
Booth Clo.		
Octavia Way, Stai.	174	BG93
Octavius St. SE8	163	EA80
Odard Rd., W.Mol.	196	CA98
Down St.		
Oddesey Rd., Borwd.	78	CP39
Odencroft, Slou.	131	AN69
Odessa Rd. E7	124	EF63
Odessa Rd. NW10	139	CU68
Odessa St. SE16	163	DZ75
Odger St. SW11	160	DF82
Odhams Wk. WC2	**273**	**P9**
Odyssey Business Pk., Ruis.	115	BV64
Offa Rd., St.Alb.	42	CC20
Offas Mead E9	123	DY63
Lindisfarne Way		
Offenbach Ho. E2	143	DX68
Mace St.		
Offenham Rd. SE9	185	EM91
Offerton Rd. SW4	161	DJ83
Offham Slope N12	97	CZ50
Offley Rd. SW9	161	DN80
Offord Clo. N17	100	DU52
Offord Rd. N1	141	DM66
Offord St. N1	141	DM66
Ogard Rd., Hodd.	49	EC15
Ogilby St. SE18	165	EM77
Oglander Rd. SE15	162	DT84
Ogle St. W1	**273**	**K6**
Ogle St. W1	141	DJ71
Oglethorpe Rd., Dag.	126	EZ62
Ohio Rd. E13	144	EF70
Oil Mill La. W6	159	CU78
Okeburn Rd. SW17	180	DG92
Okehampton Clo. N12	98	DD50
Okehampton Cres., Well.	166	EV81
Okehampton Rd. NW10	139	CW67
Okehampton Rd., Rom.	106	FJ51
Okehampton Sq., Rom.	106	FJ51
Okemore Gdns., Orp.	206	EW98
Olaf St. W11	139	CX73
Old Acre, Wok.	212	BG114
Old Ave., W.Byf.	211	BE113
Old Ave., Wey.	213	BQ108
Old Ave. Clo., W.Byf.	211	BE113
Old Bailey EC4	**274**	**G9**
Old Bailey EC4	141	DP72
Old Bakery Ms., Guil.	260	BH139
Old Barn Clo., Sutt.	217	CY108
Old Barn La., Pur.	236	DT116
Old Barn La., Rick.	74	BM43
Old Barn Rd., Epsom	232	CQ117
Old Barn Way, Bexh.	167	FD83
Old Barrack Yd. SW1	**276**	**F5**
Old Barrowfield E15	144	EE67
New Plaistow Rd.		
Old Bethnal Grn. Rd. E2	142	DU69
Old Bexley La., Bex.	187	FD89
Old Bexley La., Dart.	187	FF88
Old Bond St. W1	**277**	**K1**
Old Bond St. W1	141	DJ73
Old Brewers Yd. WC2	**273**	**P9**
Old Brewery Ms. NW3	120	DD63
Hampstead High St.		
Old Bri. Clo., Nthlt.	136	CA68
Old Bri. St., Kings.T.	197	CK96
Old Broad St. EC2	**275**	**L9**
Old Broad St. EC2	142	DR72
Old Bromley Rd., Brom.	183	ED92
Old Brompton Rd. SW5	160	DB78
Old Brompton Rd. SW7	160	DB78
Old Bldgs. WC2	**274**	**D8**
Old Burlington St. W1	**273**	**K10**
Old Burlington St. W1	141	DJ73
Old Carriageway, The, Sev.	256	FC122
Old Castle St. E1	**275**	**P8**
Old Castle St. E1	142	DT72
Old Cavendish St. W1	**273**	**H8**
Old Cavendish St. W1	141	DH72
Old Change Ct. EC4	142	DQ72
Carter La.		
Old Chapel Rd., Swan.	207	FC101
Old Charlton Rd., Shep.	195	BQ99
Old Chelsea Ms. SW3	160	DD79
Danvers St.		
Old Chertsey Rd., Wok.	210	AV110
Old Chestnut Ave., Esher	214	CA107
Old Ch. La. NW9	118	CR61
Old Ch. La., Brwd.	109	GE42
Old Ch. La., Grnf.	137	CG69
Perivale La.		
Old Ch. La., Stan.	95	CH50
Old Ch. Path, Esher	214	CB105
High St.		
Old Ch. Rd. E1	143	DX72
Old Ch. Rd. E4	101	EA49
Old Ch. St. SW3	160	DD78
Old Claygate La., Esher	215	CG107
Old Clem Sq. SE18	165	EN79
Kempt St.		
Old Coach Rd., Cher.	193	BD99
Old Common Rd., Cob.	213	BU112
Old Compton St. W1	**273**	**M10**
Old Compton St. W1	141	DK73
Old Cote Dr., Houns.	156	CA79
Old Ct., Ash.	232	CL119
Old Ct. Grn., Berk.	39	BC17
Hempstead La.		
Old Ct. Pl. W8	160	DB75
Old Ct. Rd., Guil.	258	AU135
Old Crabtree La., Hem.H.	40	BL21
Old Cross, Hert.	32	DQ09
Old Dartford Rd. (Farningham), Dart.	208	FM100
Old Dean, Hem.H.	57	BA28
Old Deer Pk. Gdns., Rich.	158	CL83
Old Devonshire Rd. SW12	181	DH87
Old Dock App. Rd., Grays	170	GE77
Old Dock Clo., Rich.	158	CN79
Watcombe Cotts.		
Old Dover Rd. SE3	164	EG80
Old Dr., The, Welw.G.C.	29	CV10
Old Epsom Rd., Guil.	244	BK131
Old Esher Clo., Walt.	214	BX106
Old Esher Rd.		
Old Esher Rd., Walt.	214	BX106
Old Farleigh Rd., S.Croy.	220	DW110
Old Farleigh Rd., Warl.	237	DY117
Old Fm. Ave. N14	99	DJ45
Old Fm. Ave., Sid.	185	ER88
Old Fm. Clo., Beac.	88	AJ50
Old Fm. Clo., Houns.	156	BZ84
Old Fm. Gdns., Swan.	207	FF97
Old Fm. Pas., Hmptn.	196	CC95
Old Fm. Rd. N2	98	DD53
Old Fm. Rd., Guil.	242	AX131
Old Fm. Rd., Hmptn.	176	BZ93
Old Fm. Rd., West Dr.	154	BK75
Old Fm. Rd. E., Sid.	186	EU89
Old Fm. Rd. W., Sid.	185	ET89
Old Farmhouse Dr., Lthd.	231	CD115
Old Ferry Dr., Stai.	172	AW86
Old Fld. Clo., Amer.	72	AY39
Old Fish St. Hill EC4	**275**	**H10**
Old Fishery La., Hem.H.	39	BF22
Old Fives Ct., Slou.	130	AH69
Old Fleet La. EC4	**274**	**F8**
Old Fold Clo., Barn.	79	CZ39
Old Fold La.		
Old Fold La., Barn.	79	CZ39
Old Fold Vw., Barn.	79	CW41
Old Ford Rd. E2	142	DW68
Old Ford Rd. E3	143	DX68
Old Forge Clo., Stan.	95	CG49
Old Forge Clo., Wat.	59	BU33
Old Forge Clo., Welw.G.C.	29	CZ05
Old Forge Cres., Shep.	195	BP100
Old Forge Ms. W12	159	CV75
Goodwin Rd.		
Old Forge Rd., Enf.	82	DT38
Old Forge Way, Sid.	186	EV91
Old Fox Clo., Cat.	235	DP121
Old Fox Footpath, S.Croy.	220	DS108
Essenden Rd.		
Old French Horn La., Hat.	45	CW17
Old Gannon Clo., Nthwd.	93	BQ50
Old Gdn., The, Sev.	256	FD123
Old Gdn. Ct., St.Alb.	42	CC20
Old Gloucester St. WC1	**274**	**A6**
Old Gloucester St. WC1	141	DL71
Old Hall Clo., Pnr.	94	BY53
Old Hall Dr., Pnr.	94	BY53
Old Hall Ri., Harl.	52	EY15
Church Langley Way		
Old Hall St., Hert.	32	DR09
Old Harpenden Rd., St.Alb.	43	CE17
Old Harrow La., West.	239	EQ119
Old Hatch Manor, Ruis.	115	BT59
Old Herns La., Welw.G.C.	30	DC07
Herns La.		
Old Hertford Rd., Hat.	45	CW16
Old Highway, Hodd.	33	EB14
Old Hill, Chis.	205	EN95
Old Hill, Orp.	223	ER107
Old Hill, Wok.	226	AX120
Old Homesdale Rd., Brom.	204	EJ98
Old Hospital Clo. SW12	180	DF88
St. James's Dr.		
Old Ho. Clo. SW19	179	CY92
Old Ho. Clo., Epsom	217	CT110
Old Ho. Ct., Hem.H.	40	BM20
Old Ho. Rd.		
Old Ho. Gdns., Twick.	177	CJ86
Old Ho. La., Harl.	50	EK18
Old Ho. La., Kings L.	74	BL35
Old Ho. La., Wal.Abb.	50	EF23
Old Ho. Rd., Hem.H.	40	BM20
Old Jamaica Rd. SE16	162	DU76
Old James St. SE15	162	DV83
Old Jewry EC2	**275**	**K9**
Old Jewry EC2	142	DR72
Old Kent Rd. SE1	**279**	**M8**
Old Kent Rd. SE1	162	DS77
Old Kent Rd. SE15	162	DV79
Old Kenton La. NW9	118	CP57
Old Kiln La., Bet.	264	CQ135
Old Kiln Rd. (Tylers Grn.), H.Wyc.	88	AC45
Old Kingston Rd., Wor.Pk.	198	CQ104
Old La., Cob.	229	BP117
Old La., West.	238	EK121
Old La. Gdns., Cob.	229	BT122
Old Leys, Hat.	45	CU21
Old Lo. La., Ken.	235	DN116
Old Lo. La., Pur.	219	DM113
Old Lo. Pl., Twick.	177	CH86
St. Margarets Rd.		
Old Lo. Way, Stan.	95	CG50
Old London Rd., Dor.	247	CJ127
Old London Rd., Epsom	233	CU118
Old London Rd., Harl.	36	EW12
Old London Rd., Hert.	32	DS09
Old London Rd., Lthd.	245	BU126
Old London Rd., St.Alb.	43	CD21
Old London Rd., Sev.	224	EY109
Old London Rd. (Knockholt Pound), Sev.	240	EY115
Old Long Gro., Beac.	89	AQ51
Old Maidstone Rd., Sid.	186	EZ94
Old Malden La., Wor.Pk.	198	CR104
Old Malt Way, Wok.	226	AX117
Old Manor Dr., Grav.	191	GJ88
Parrock Rd.		
Old Manor Dr., Islw.	176	CC86
Old Manor Gdns., Guil.	259	BC140
Old Manor La., Guil.	259	BC140
Old Manor Way, Bexh.	167	FD82
Old Manor Way, Chis.	185	EM92
Old Manor Yd. SW5	160	DB77
Earls Ct. Rd.		
Old Marsh La., Maid.	150	AF75
Old Marylebone Rd. NW1	**272**	**C7**
Old Marylebone Rd. NW1	140	DE71
Old Mead, Ger.Cr.	90	AY51
Old Meadow Clo., Berk.	38	AU21
Old Merrow St., Guil.	243	BC131
Old Ms., Har.	117	CE57
Hindes Rd.		
Old Mill Clo. (Eynsford), Dart.	208	FL102
Old Mill Ct. E18	124	EJ55
Old Mill Gdns., Berk.	38	AX20
London Rd.		
Old Mill La. W6	159	CU78
Old Mill La., Maid.	150	AC75
Old Mill La., Red.	251	DH128
Old Mill La., Uxb.	134	BH71
Old Mill Pl., Rom.	127	FD58
Old Mill Rd. SE18	165	ER79
Old Mill Rd., Kings L.	59	BQ34
Old Mill Rd., Uxb.	114	BG62
Old Mitre Ct. EC4	141	DN72
Fleet St.		
Old Montague St. E1	142	DU71
Old Moor La., H.Wyc.	110	AE55
Watery La.		
Old Nazeing Rd., Brox.	49	EA21
Old Nichol St. E2	**275**	**P4**
Old Nichol St. E2	142	DT70
Old N. St. WC1	**274**	**B6**
Old Nursery Ct., Slou.	111	AQ61
Old Oak Ave., Couls.	234	DE119
Old Oak Common La. NW10	138	CS70
Old Oak Common La. W3	138	CS71
Old Oak La. NW10	139	CT69
Old Oak Rd. W3	139	CT73
Old Oaks, Wal.Abb.	68	EE32
Old Orchard, Harl.	51	ER17
Old Orchard, St.Alb.	60	CC26
Old Orchard, Sun.	196	BW96
Old Orchard, W.Byf.	212	BM112
Old Orchard, The NW3	120	DF63
Nassington Rd.		
Old Orchard Clo., Barn.	80	DD38
Parklands Clo.		
Old Orchard Clo., Uxb.	134	BN72
Stockley Rd.		
Old Orchard Ms., Berk.	38	AW20
Old Otford Rd., Sev.	241	FH117
Old Palace, The, Hat.	45	CX18
Old Palace La., Rich.	177	CJ85
Old Palace Rd., Croy.	201	DP104
Old Palace Rd., Guil.	258	AU135
Old Palace Rd., Wey.	195	BP104
Old Palace Ter., Rich.	177	CK85
King St.		
Old Palace Yd. SW1	**277**	**P6**
Old Palace Yd. SW1	161	DL76
Old Palace Yd., Rich.	177	CK85
Old Paradise St. SE11	**278**	**B8**
Old Paradise St. SE11	161	DM77
Old Pk. Ave. SW12	180	DG86
Old Pk. Ave., Enf.	82	DQ42
Old Pk. Gro., Enf.	82	DQ42
Old Pk. La. W1	**276**	**G3**
Old Pk. La. W1	140	DG74
Old Pk. Ms., Houns.	156	BZ80
Old Pk. Ride, Wal.Cr.	65	DP31
Old Pk. Ridings N21	81	DP44
Old Pk. Rd. N13	99	DM49
Old Pk. Rd. SE2	166	EU78
Old Pk. Rd., Enf.	81	DP41
Old Pk. Rd. S., Enf.	81	DP42
Old Pk. Vw., Enf.	81	DN41
Old Parkbury La., St.Alb.	61	CF29
Old Parvis Rd., W.Byf.	212	BJ112
Old Perry St., Chis.	185	ES93
Old Perry St., Grav.	190	GE89
Old Polhill, Sev.	239	ET115
Old Portsmouth Rd., Gdmg.	258	AV143
Old Portsmouth Rd., Guil.	258	AV143
Old Pottery Clo., Reig.	266	DB136
Old Pound Clo., Islw.	157	CG81
London Rd.		
Old Pye St. SW1	**277**	**M6**
Old Pye St. SW1	161	DK76
Old Quebec St. W1	**272**	**E9**
Old Quebec St. W1	140	DF72
Old Queen St. SW1	**277**	**N5**
Old Queen St. SW1	161	DK75
Old Rectory Clo., Tad.	233	CU124
Old Rectory Dr., Hat.	45	CV18
Old Rectory Gdns., Edg.	96	CN51
Old Rectory La., Lthd.	245	BS126
Old Rectory La., Uxb.	113	BE59
Old Rectory Rd., Ong.	71	FH34
Old Redding, Har.	94	CB50
Old Redstone Dr., Red.	266	DG135
Philanthropic Rd.		
Old Reigate Rd., Bet.	248	CP134
Old Reigate Rd., Dor.	248	CL134
Old Rd. SE13	164	EE84
Old Rd., Add.	211	BF108
Old Rd., Bet.	248	CR134
Old Rd., Dart.	187	FD85
Old Rd., Enf.	82	DW39
Old Rd., Harl.	36	EW09
Old Rd. E., Grav.	191	GH88
Old Rd. W., Grav.	191	GF88
Old Rope Wk., Sun.	195	BV97
The Ave.		
Old Royal Free Pl. N1	141	DN67
Liverpool Rd.		
Old Royal Free Sq. N1	141	DN67
Liverpool Rd.		
Old Ruislip Rd., Nthlt.	136	BW68
Old Savill's Cotts., Chig.	103	EQ49
The Chase		
Old Sch. Clo. SW19	200	DA96
Old Sch. Clo., Beck.	203	DX96
Old Sch. Ct., Stai.	172	AY87
Old Sch. La., Bet.	264	CN138
Old Sch. Ms., Wey.	213	BR105
Old Sch. Pl., Wok.	226	AY121
Old Schools La., Epsom	217	CT109
Old Seacoal La. EC4	**274**	**F9**
Old Shire La., Ger.Cr.	91	BA46
Old Shire La., Rick.	73	BB44
Old Shire La., Wal.Abb.	84	EG35
Old Slade La., Iver	153	BE76
Old Sopwell Gdns., St.Alb.	43	CE22
Old S. Clo., Pnr.	94	BX53
Old S. Lambeth Rd. SW8	161	DL80
Old Sq. WC2	**274**	**C8**
Old Sq. WC2	141	DM72
Old Sta. App., Lthd.	231	CG121
Old Sta. Rd., Hayes	155	BT76
Old Sta. Rd., Loug.	84	EL43
Old Sta. Way, H.Wyc.	110	AE58
Old Stockley Rd., West Dr.	155	BP75
Old St. E13	144	EH68
Old St. EC1	**275**	**H5**
Old St. EC1	142	DQ70
Old Swan Yd., Cars.	218	DF105
Old Tilburstow Rd., Gdse.	252	DW134
Old Town SW4	161	DJ83
Old Town, Croy.	201	DP104
Old Town Clo., Beac.	89	AL54
Old Town Hall Arts Cen., Hem.H.	40	BJ19
Old Tram Yd. SE18	165	ES77
Lakedale Rd.		
Old Tye Ave., West.	238	EL116
Old Uxbridge Rd., Rick.	91	BE50
Old Vicarage Way, H.Wyc.	110	AE59
Old Wk., The, Sev.	241	FH117
Old Watery La., H.Wyc.	110	AE55
Old Watford Rd., St.Alb.	60	BY30
Old Watling St., Grav.	191	GG92
Old Westhall Clo., Warl.	236	DW119
Old Woking Rd., W.Byf.	211	BF113
Old Woking Rd., Wok.	227	BB118
Old Woolwich Rd. SE10	163	ED78
Old York Rd. SW18	180	DB85
Oldacre Ms. SW12	181	DH87
Balham Gro.		
Oldberry Rd., Edg.	96	CR51
Oldborough Rd., Wem.	117	CJ61
Oldbury Clo., Cher.	193	BE101
Oldbury Rd.		
Oldbury Clo., Orp.	206	EX98
Oldbury Gro., Beac.	89	AK50
Oldbury Pl. W1	**272**	**G6**
Oldbury Pl. W1	140	DG71
Oldbury Rd., Cher.	193	BE101
Oldbury Rd., Enf.	82	DU40
Oldchurch Gdns., Rom.	127	FD59
Oldchurch Ri., Rom.	127	FD59
Oldchurch Rd., Rom.	127	FE58
Olden La., Pur.	219	DN112
Oldfield Circ., Nthlt.	136	CC65
The Fairway		
Oldfield Clo., Brom.	205	EM98
Oldfield Clo., Grnf.	117	CE64
Oldfield Clo., Horl.	268	DF150
Oldfield Rd.		
Oldfield Clo., Stan.	95	CG50
Oldfield Clo. (Cheshunt), Wal.Cr.	67	DY28
Oldfield Dr. (Cheshunt), Wal.Cr.	67	DY28
Oldfield Fm. Gdns., Grnf.	137	CD67
Oldfield Gdns., Ash.	231	CK119
Oldfield Gro. SE16	163	DX77
Oldfield La. N., Grnf.	137	CD68
Oldfield La. S., Grnf.	136	CC69
Oldfield Ms. N6	121	DJ59
Oldfield Pk., Brom.	205	EN98
Oldfield Rd. N16	122	DS62
Oldfield Rd. NW10	139	CT66
Oldfield Rd. SW19	179	CY93
Oldfield Rd. W3	159	CT75
Valetta Rd.		
Oldfield Rd., Bexh.	166	EY82
Oldfield Rd., Brom.	204	EL98
Oldfield Rd., Hmptn.	196	BZ95
Oldfield Rd., Hem.H.	39	BE21
Oldfield Rd., Horl.	268	DF150
Oldfield Rd., St.Alb.	61	CK25
Oldfields Rd., Sutt.	199	CZ104
Oldforge Rd., H.Wyc.	88	AC53
Oldham Ter. W3	138	CQ74
Oldhill St. N16	122	DU60
Oldhouse Cft., Harl.	35	ES13
Oldridge Rd. SW12	180	DG87
Olds App., Wat.	93	BP46
Olds Clo., Wat.	93	BP46
Oldstead Rd., Brom.	183	ED91
Oldway La., Slou.	131	AK74
Oleander Clo., Orp.	223	ER106
O'Leary Sq. E1	142	DW71
Oley Pl. E1	143	DX71
Redman's Rd.		
Olinda Rd. N16	122	DT58
Oliphant St. W10	139	CX69
Olive Rd. E13	144	EJ69
Olive Rd. NW2	119	CW63
Olive Rd. SW19	180	DC94
Norman Rd.		
Olive Rd. W5	157	CK76
Olive Rd., Dart.	188	FK88
Olive St., Rom.	127	FD57
Oliver Ave. SE25	202	DT97
Oliver Clo. W4	158	CP79
Oliver Clo., Add.	212	BG105
Oliver Clo., Grays	169	FT80
Oliver Clo., Hem.H.	40	BL24
Oliver Clo., St.Alb.	61	CD27
Oliver Cres. (Farningham), Dart.	208	FM101
Oliver Gdns. E6	144	EL72
Oliver Goldsmith Est. SE15	162	DU81
Goldsmith Rd.		
Oliver Gro. SE25	202	DT98
Oliver Ri., Hem.H.	40	BL24
Oliver Rd. E10	123	EB61
Oliver Rd. E17	123	EC57
Oliver Rd., Brwd.	109	GA43
Oliver Rd., Grays	169	FT81
Oliver Rd., Hem.H.	40	BL24
Oliver Rd., N.Mal.	198	CQ96
Oliver Rd., Rain.	147	FF67
Oliver Rd., Sutt.	218	DD105
Oliver Rd., Swan.	207	FD97
Olivers Clo., Berk.	39	BC16
Olivers Yd. EC1	**275**	**L4**
Olivette St. SW15	159	CX83
Felsham Rd.		
Olivia Gdns., Uxb.	92	BJ53
Ollards Gro., Loug.	84	EK42
Olleberrie La., Rick.	57	BD32
Ollerton Grn. E3	143	DZ67
Ollerton Rd. N11	99	DK50
Olley Clo., Wall.	219	DL107
Ollgar Clo. W12	139	CT74
Olliffe St. E14	163	EC76
Olmar St. SE1	162	DU79
Olney Rd. SE17	161	DP79
Olron Cres., Bexh.	186	EX85
Olven Rd. SE18	165	EQ79
Olveston Wk., Cars.	200	DD100
Olwen Ms., Pnr.	94	BX54
Olyffe Ave., Well.	166	EU81
Olyffe Dr., Beck.	203	EC95
Olympia Ms. W2	140	DB73
Queensway		
Olympia Way W14	159	CY76
Olympic Way, Grnf.	136	CB67
Olympic Way, Wem.	118	CN62
Olympus Sq. E5	122	DU63
Nolan Way		
Oman Ave. NW2	119	CV63
O'Meara St. SE1	**279**	**J3**
O'Meara St. SE1	142	DQ74
Omega Clo. E14	163	EB76
Tiller Rd.		
Omega Ct., Ware	33	DX06
Crib St.		
Omega Pl. N1	**274**	**A1**
Omega Rd., Wok.	227	BA115
Omega St. SE14	163	EA81
Omega Way, Egh.	193	BC95
Crabtree Rd.		
Ommaney Rd. SE14	163	DX81
Omnibus Way E17	101	EA54
Chingford Rd.		
On The Hill, Wat.	94	BY47
Ondine Rd. SE15	162	DT84
One Pin La., Slou.	111	AQ63
One Tree Clo. SE23	182	DW86
One Tree Hill Rd., Guil.	259	BB135
One Tree La., Beac.	89	AL52
Onega Gate SE16	163	DY76
O'Neill Path SE18	165	EN79
Kempt St.		
Ongar Clo., Add.	211	BF107
Ongar Clo., Rom.	126	EW57
Ongar Hill, Add.	211	BF107
Ongar Pl., Add.	212	BG107

Ongar Rd. SW6 160 DA79
Ongar Rd., Add. 212 BG106
Ongar Rd., Brwd. 108 FV45
Ongar Rd., Rom. 86 EV41
Ongar Way, Rain. 147 FE67
Onra Rd. E17 123 EA59
Onslow Ave., Rich. 178 CL85
Onslow Ave., Sutt. 217 CZ110
Onslow Clo. E4 101 ED47
Onslow Clo., Hat. 45 CV18
Onslow Clo., T.Ditt. 197 CE102
Onslow Clo., Wok. 227 BA117
Onslow Cres.
Onslow Cres., Chis. 205 EP95
Onslow Cres., Wok. 227 BA117
Onslow Dr., Sid. 186 EX90
Onslow Gdns. E18 124 EH55
Onslow Gdns. N10 121 DH57
Onslow Gdns. N21 81 DN43
Onslow Gdns. SW7 160 DD78
Onslow Gdns., S.Croy. 220 DU112
Onslow Gdns., T.Ditt. 197 CE102
Onslow Gdns., Wall. 219 DJ107
Onslow Ms., Cher. 194 BG100
Onslow Ms. E. SW7 160 DD77
Cranley Pl.
Onslow Ms. W. SW7 160 DD77
Cranley Pl.
Onslow Rd., Croy. 201 DN102
Onslow Rd., Guil. 242 AX134
Onslow Rd., N.Mal. 199 CU98
Onslow Rd., Rich. 178 CL85
Onslow Rd., Walt. 213 BT105
Onslow Sq. SW7 276 A9
Onslow Sq. SW7 160 DD77
Onslow St. EC1 274 E5
Onslow St., Guil. 258 AW136
Onslow Way, T.Ditt. 197 CE102
Onslow Way, Wok. 227 BF115
Ontario Clo., Horl. 269 DN149
Ontario St. SE1 278 G7
Ontario Way E14 143 EA74
Hertsmere Rd.
Opal Clo. E16 144 EK72
Opal Ct., Slou. 132 AV70
Wexham St.
Opal Ms. NW6 139 CZ67
Priory Pk. Rd.
Opal Ms., Ilf. 125 EP61
Ley St.
Opal St. SE11 278 F10
Opal St. SE11 161 DP77
Opendale Rd., Slou. 130 AH71
Openshaw Rd. SE2 166 EV77
Openview SW18 180 DC88
Ophelia Gdns. NW2 119 CY62
The Vale
Ophir Ter. SE15 162 DU81
Opossum Way, Houns. 156 BW82
Oppenheim Rd. SE13 163 EC82
Oppidans Ms. NW3 140 DF66
Meadowbank
Oppidans Rd. NW3 140 DF66
Orange Ct. E1 142 DU74
Hermitage Wall
Orange Ct. La., Orp. 223 EM109
Orange Gro. E11 124 EE62
Cathall Rd.
Orange Hill Rd., Edg. 96 CQ52
Orange Pl. SE16 162 DW76
Lower Rd.
Orange St. WC2 277 N1
Orange St. WC2 141 DK73
Orange Tree Hill 105 FD50
(Havering-atte-Bower), Rom.
Orange Yd. W1 273 N9
Orangery, The, Rich. 177 CJ89
Orangery La. SE9 185 EM85
Oratory La. SW3 276 A10
Orb St. SE17 279 K9
Orb St. SE17 162 DR77
Orbain Rd. SW6 159 CY80
Orbel St. SW11 160 DE81
Orbital Cres., Wat. 75 BT35
Orbital One, Dart. 188 FP89
Orchard, The N14 81 DH43
Orchard, The N21 82 DR44
Orchard, The NW11 120 DA57
Orchard, The SE3 163 ED82
Orchard, The W4 158 CR77
Orchard, The W5 137 CK71
Orchard, The, Bans. 234 DA115
The Horseshoe
Orchard, The, Dor. 263 CJ140
Orchard, The, Epsom 217 CT108
Orchard, The, Houns. 156 CC82
Orchard, The, Kings L. 58 BN29
Orchard, The, Sev. 256 FE121
Milton Rd.
Orchard, The, Swan. 207 FD96
Orchard, The, Vir.W. 192 AY99
Orchard, The, 29 CX07
Welw.G.C.
Orchard, The, Wey. 213 BP105
Orchard, The, Wok. 226 AY122
Orchard Ave. N3 120 DA55
Orchard Ave. N14 81 DJ44
Orchard Ave. N20 98 DD47
Orchard Ave., Add. 211 BF111
Orchard Ave., Ashf. 175 BQ93
Orchard Ave., Belv. 166 EY79
Orchard Ave., Berk. 38 AU19
Orchard Ave., Brwd. 109 FZ48
Orchard Ave., Croy. 203 DY103
Orchard Ave., Dart. 187 FH87
Orchard Ave., Felt. 175 BR85
Orchard Ave., Grav. 191 GH92
Orchard Ave., Houns. 156 BY80
Orchard Ave., Mitch. 200 DG102
Orchard Ave., N.Mal. 198 CS96
Orchard Ave., Rain. 148 FJ70
Orchard Ave., Slou. 131 AK71
Orchard Ave., Sthl. 136 BY74
Orchard Ave., T.Ditt. 197 CG102
Orchard Ave., Wat. 59 BV31
Orchard Ave., Wind. 151 AN81
Orchard Bungalow 131 AM66
Caravan Site, Slou.
Orchard Clo. E4 101 EA49
Chingford Mt. Rd.
Orchard Clo. E11 124 EH56
Orchard Clo. N1 142 DQ66
Morton Rd.
Orchard Clo. NW2 119 CU62
Orchard Clo. SE23 182 DW86
Brenchley Gdns.
Orchard Clo. SW20 199 CW98
Grand Dr.
Orchard Clo. W10 139 CY71
Orchard Clo., Ashf. 175 BQ93
Orchard Clo., Bans. 218 DB114
Orchard Clo., Beac. 89 AK52
Seeleys Rd.
Orchard Clo., Bexh. 166 EY81
Orchard Clo., 37 FC07
Bishop's Stortford
Orchard Clo., Borwd. 78 CM42
Orchard Clo., Edg. 96 CL51
Orchard Clo., Egh. 173 BB92
Orchard Clo., Epsom 216 CP107
Orchard Clo., Guil. 243 BB134
Orchard Clo., Hem.H. 40 BM18
Orchard Clo., Hert. 47 DJ19
Orchard Clo., Horl. 268 DF147
Orchard Clo. 229 BT124
(Effingham), Lthd.
Orchard Clo. 231 CD122
(Fetcham), Lthd.
Orchard Clo., Nthlt. 116 CC64
Orchard Clo. 65 DL28
(Cuffley), Pot.B.
Orchard Clo., Rad. 77 CE37
Orchard Clo., Rick. 73 BD42
Orchard Clo., Ruis. 115 BQ59
Orchard Clo., St.Alb. 43 CF21
Orchard Clo., S.Ock. 149 FW70
Orchard Clo., Surb. 197 CH101
Orchard Clo., Uxb. 134 BH65
Orchard Clo., Walt. 195 BV101
Garden Rd.
Orchard Clo., Ware 33 DX05
Orchard Clo. 33 EC11
(Stanstead Abbots), Ware
Orchard Clo., Wat. 75 BT40
Orchard Clo. 95 CD46
(Bushey), Wat.
Orchard Clo., Wem. 138 CL67
Orchard Clo., Wok. 227 BB116
Orchard Ct., Hem.H. 57 BA27
Apple Cotts.
Orchard Ct., Islw. 157 CD81
Orchard Ct., Twick. 177 CD89
Orchard Ct., Wor.Pk. 199 CU102
Orchard Cres., Edg. 96 CQ50
Orchard Cres., Enf. 82 DT39
Orchard Cft., Harl. 36 EU13
Orchard Dr. SE3 164 EE82
Orchard Dr., Ash. 231 CK120
Orchard Dr., Edg. 96 CM50
Orchard Dr., Epp. 85 ES36
Orchard Dr., Grays 170 GA75
Orchard Dr. 110 AD59
(Wooburn), H.Wyc.
Orchard Dr., Rick. 73 BC41
Orchard Dr., St.Alb. 60 CB27
Orchard Dr., Uxb. 134 BK70
Orchard Dr., Wat. 75 BT39
Orchard Dr., Wok. 226 AY115
Orchard End, Cat. 236 DS122
Town End
Orchard End, Lthd. 230 CC124
Orchard End, Wey. 195 BS103
Orchard End Ave., 72 AT39
Amer.
Orchard End Clo., Amer. 72 AT39
Orchard Fld. Rd., Gdmg. 258 AT144
Orchard Gdns., Chess. 216 CL105
Orchard Gdns., Epsom 216 CQ114
Orchard Gdns., Lthd. 246 BY128
Orchard Gdns., Sutt. 218 DA106
Orchard Gdns., Wal.Abb. 67 EC34
Orchard Gate NW9 118 CS56
Orchard Gate, Esher 197 CD102
Orchard Gate, Grnf. 117 CH64
Orchard Gate, Slou. 111 AQ64
Orchard Grn., Orp. 205 ES103
Orchard Gro. SE20 182 DU94
Orchard Gro., Croy. 203 DY101
Orchard Gro., Edg. 96 CN53
Orchard Gro., Ger.Cr. 90 AW53
Orchard Gro., Har. 118 CM57
Orchard Gro., Orp. 205 ET103
Orchard Hill SE13 163 EB82
Coldbath St.
Orchard Hill, Cars. 218 DF106
Orchard Hill, Dart. 187 FE85
Orchard Ho. La., St.Alb. 43 CD21
Orchard La. SW20 199 CV95
Durham Rd.
Orchard La., Amer. 55 AR38
Orchard La., Brwd. 108 FT43
Orchard La., E.Mol. 197 CD100
Orchard La., Harl. 36 EY11
Orchard La., Wdf.Grn. 102 EJ49
Orchard Lea Clo., Wok. 227 BE115
Orchard Leigh, Chesh. 56 AT28
Orchard Leigh, Lthd. 231 CH122
Orchard Mains, Wok. 226 AW119
Orchard Mead, Hat. 45 CT18
Days Mead
Orchard Ms. N1 142 DR66
Southgate Gro.
Orchard Ms., Beac. 89 AQ50
Orchard Rd.
Orchard Path, Slou. 133 BA72
Orchard Pl. E14 144 EE73
Orchard Pl. N17 100 DT52
Orchard Pl., Sev. 240 EY124
Orchard Ri., Croy. 203 DY102
Orchard Ri., Kings.T. 198 CQ95
Orchard Ri., Pnr. 115 BT55
Orchard Ri., Rich. 158 CP84
Orchard Ri. E., Sid. 185 ES85
Orchard Ri. W., Sid. 185 ES85
Orchard Rd. N6 121 DH59
Orchard Rd. SE3 164 EE82
Eliot Pl.
Orchard Rd. SE18 165 ER77
Orchard Rd., Barn. 79 CY42
Orchard Rd., Beac. 89 AM54
Orchard Rd. 89 AQ50
(Seer Grn.), Beac.
Orchard Rd., Belv. 166 FA77
Orchard Rd., Brent. 157 CJ79
Orchard Rd., Brom. 204 EJ95
Orchard Rd., Ch.St.G. 90 AW47
Orchard Rd., Chess. 216 CL105
Orchard Rd., Dag. 146 FA67
Orchard Rd., Dor. 263 CH137
Orchard Rd., Enf. 82 DW43
Orchard Rd., Grav. 190 GC89
Orchard Rd., Guil. 258 AT136
Orchard Rd. 243 BB130
(Burpham), Guil.
Orchard Rd. 258 AY140
(Shalford), Guil.
Orchard Rd. 260 BN139
(Shere), Guil.
Orchard Rd., Hmptn. 176 BZ94
Orchard Rd., Hayes 135 BT73
Orchard Rd., Houns. 176 BZ85
Orchard Rd., Kings.T. 198 CL96
Orchard Rd., Mitch. 200 DG102
Orchard Rd. 223 EP106
(Farnborough), Orp.
Orchard Rd. 224 EW110
(Pratt's Bottom), Orp.
Orchard Rd., Reig. 250 DB134
Orchard Rd., Rich. 158 CN83
Orchard Rd., Rom. 105 FB54
Orchard Rd. 241 FF116
(Otford), Sev.
Orchard Rd. 256 FE122
(Riverhead), Sev.
Orchard Rd., Sid. 185 ES91
Orchard Rd., S.Croy. 220 DV114
Orchard Rd., S.Ock. 149 FW70
Orchard Rd., Sun. 175 BV94
Hanworth Rd.
Orchard Rd., Sutt. 218 DA105
Orchard Rd., Swans. 190 FY85
Orchard Rd., Twick. 177 CG85
Orchard Rd., Well. 166 EV83
Orchard Rd., Wind. 172 AV86
Orchard Sq. W14 159 CZ78
Sun Rd.
Orchard Sq., Brox. 49 DZ24
Orchard St. E17 123 DY56
Orchard St. W1 272 F9
Orchard St. W1 140 DG72
Orchard St., Dart. 188 FL86
Orchard St., Hem.H. 40 BJ24
Orchard St., St.Alb. 42 CC21
Orchard Ter., Enf. 82 DU44
Great Cambridge Rd.
Orchard Vw., Uxb. 134 BK70
Orchard Way, Add. 212 BH106
Orchard Way, Ashf. 174 BM89
Orchard Way, Beck. 203 DY99
Orchard Way, Chig. 104 EU48
Orchard Way, Croy. 203 DY102
Orchard Way, Dart. 188 FK90
Orchard Way, Dor. 263 CH137
Orchard Way, Enf. 82 DS41
Orchard Way, Esher 214 CC107
Orchard Way, Hem.H. 57 BA28
Orchard Way, Oxt. 254 EG133
Orchard Way, Pot.B. 64 DB28
Orchard Way, Reig. 266 DB138
Orchard Way, Rick. 92 BG45
Orchard Way, Slou. 132 AY74
Orchard Way, Sutt. 218 DD105
Orchard Way, Tad. 249 CZ126
Orchard Way 65 DP27
(Cheshunt), Wal.Cr.
Orchard Way, Wok. 243 BC125
Orchard Waye, Uxb. 134 BK68
Orchardleigh Ave., Enf. 82 DW40
Orchardmede N21 82 DR44
Orchards, The, Epp. 70 EU32
Orchards, The, Hert. 32 DQ06
Orchards, The, Saw. 36 EY05
Orchards Business 267 DH143
Cen., Red.
Orchardson St. NW8 140 DD70
Orchardville, Slou. 130 AH70
Orchehill Ave., Ger.Cr. 112 AX56
Orchehill Ct., Ger.Cr. 112 AY57
Orchehill Ri., Ger.Cr. 112 AY57
Orchid Clo. E6 144 EL71
Orchid Clo., Rom. 86 EV41
Orchid Clo., Sthl. 136 BY73
Lancaster Rd.
Orchid Ct., Egh. 173 BB91
Albany Pl.
Orchid Rd. N14 99 DJ45
Orchid St. W12 139 CU73
Orchis Gro., Grays 170 FZ78
Orchis Way, Rom. 106 FM51
Orde Hall St. WC1 274 B6
Orde Hall St. WC1 141 DM71
Ordell Rd. E3 143 DZ68
Ordnance Clo., Felt. 175 BU90
Ordnance Cres. SE10 164 EE75
Ordnance Hill NW8 140 DD67
Ordnance Ms. NW8 140 DD68
St. Ann's Ter.
Ordnance Rd. E16 144 EF71
Ordnance Rd. SE18 165 EN79
Ordnance Rd., Enf. 83 DX37
Ordnance Rd., Grav. 191 GJ86
Oregano Dr. E14 143 ED72
Oregano Way, Guil. 242 AU129
Oregon Ave. E12 125 EM63
Oregon Clo., N.Mal. 198 CQ98
Georgia Rd.
Oregon Sq., Orp. 205 ER102
Orestan La., Lthd. 245 BV127
Orestes Ms. NW6 120 DA64
Aldred Rd.
Oreston Rd., Rain. 148 FK69
Orewell Gdns., Reig. 266 DB136
Orford Ct. SE27 181 DP89
Orford Gdns., Twick. 177 CF89
Orford Rd. E17 123 EA57
Orford Rd. E18 124 EH55
Orford Rd. SE6 183 EB90
Bromley Rd.
Organ Hall Rd., Borwd. 77 CK39
Organ La. E4 101 EC47
Oriel Clo., Mitch. 201 DK98
Oriel Ct. NW3 120 DC63
Heath St.
Oriel Gdns., Ilf. 125 EM55
Oriel Pl. NW3 120 DC63
Heath St.
Oriel Rd. E9 143 DX65
Oriel Way, Nthlt. 136 CB66
Orient Ind. Pk. E10 123 EA61
Orient St. SE11 278 F8
Orient Way E5 123 DX62
Oriental Clo., Wok. 227 BA117
Oriental Rd.
Oriental Rd. E16 144 EK74
Oriental Rd., Wok. 227 AZ117
Oriental St. E14 143 EA73
Morant St.
Oriole Way SE28 146 EV73
Orion Way, Nthwd. 93 BT49
Orissa Rd. SE18 165 ES78
Orkney St. SW11 160 DG82
Orlando Gdns., Epsom 216 CR110
Orlando Rd. SW4 161 DJ83
Orleans Clo., Esher 197 CD103
Orleans Rd. SE19 182 DR93
Orleans Rd., Twick. 177 CH87
Orleston Ms. N7 141 DN65
Orleston Rd. N7 141 DN65
Orlestone Gdns., Orp. 224 EY106
Orley Fm. Rd., Har. 117 CE62
Orlop St. SE10 164 EE78
Ormanton Rd. SE26 182 DU91
Orme Ct. W2 140 DB73
Orme Ct. Ms. W2 140 DB73
Orme La.
Orme La. W2 140 DB73
Orme Rd., Kings.T. 198 CP96
Orme Sq. W2 140 DB73
Bayswater Rd.
Ormeley Rd. SW12 181 DH87
Ormerod Gdns., Mitch. 200 DG96
Ormesby Clo. SE28 146 EX73
Wroxham Rd.
Ormesby Dr., Pot.B. 63 CX32
Ormesby Way, Har. 118 CM58
Ormiston Gro. W12 139 CV74
Ormiston Rd. SE10 164 EG78
Ormond Ave., Hmptn. 196 CB95
Ormond Ave., Rich. 177 CK85
Ormond Rd.
Ormond Clo. WC1 274 A6
Ormond Clo., Rom. 106 FK54
Chadwick Dr.
Ormond Cres., Hmptn. 196 CB95
Ormond Dr., Hmptn. 176 CB94
Ormond Ms. WC1 274 A5
Ormond Rd. N19 121 DL60
Ormond Rd., Rich. 177 CK85
Ormond Yd. SW1 277 L2
Ormonde Ave., 216 CR109
Epsom
Ormonde Ave., Orp. 205 EQ103
Ormonde Gate SW3 160 DF78
Ormonde Pl. SW1 276 F9
Ormonde Ri., Buck.H. 102 EJ46
Ormonde Rd. SW14 158 CQ83
Ormonde Rd., Nthwd. 93 BR49
Ormonde Rd., Wok. 226 AW116
Ormonde Ter. NW8 140 DF67
Ormsby Gdns., Grnf. 136 CC68
Ormsby Pl. N16 122 DT62
Victorian Gro.
Ormsby Pt. SE18 165 EP77
Troy Ct.
Ormsby St. E2 275 P1
Ormsby St. E2 142 DT68
Ormside St. SE15 162 DW79
Ormside Way, Red. 251 DH130
Ormskirk Rd., Wat. 94 BX49
Ornan Rd. NW3 120 DE64
Oronsay, Hem.H. 41 BP22
Northend
Oronsay Wk. N1 142 DQ65
Marquess Est.
Orpen Wk. N16 122 DS62
Orphanage Rd., Wat. 76 BW40
Orpheus St. SE5 162 DR81
Orpin Rd., Red. 251 DH130
Orpington Bypass, Orp. 224 EX106
Orpington Bypass, Sev. 224 EZ109
Orpington Gdns. N18 100 DS48
Orpington Rd. N21 99 DN46
Orpington Rd., Chis. 205 ES97
Orpwood Clo., Hmptn. 176 BZ93
Orsett Heath Cres., 171 GG76
Grays
Orsett Rd., Grays 170 GA78
Orsett St. SE11 278 C10
Orsett St. SE11 161 DM78
Orsett Ter. W2 140 DB72
Orsett Ter., Wdf.Grn. 102 EJ52
Orsman Rd. N1 142 DS67
Orton Clo., St.Alb. 43 CH16
Orton St. E1 142 DU74
Hermitage Wall
Orville Rd. SW11 160 DD82
Orwell Clo., Rain. 147 FD71
Orwell Clo., Wind. 151 AR83
Orwell Ct. N5 122 DQ63
Orwell Rd. E13 144 EJ67
Osbaldeston Rd. N16 122 DU61
Osbert St. SW1 277 M9
Osberton Rd. SE12 184 EG85
Osborn Clo. E8 142 DU67
Osborn Gdns. NW7 97 CX52
Osborn La. SE23 183 DY87
Osborn St. E1 142 DT71
Osborn Ter. SE3 164 EF84
Lee Rd.
Osborn Way, Welw.G.C. 29 CX10
Osborne Ave., Stai. 174 BL87
Osborne Clo., Barn. 80 DF41
Chalk La.
Osborne Clo., Beck. 203 DY98
Osborne Clo., Felt. 176 BX92
Osborne Clo., Horn. 127 FH58
Osborne Ct., Pot.B. 64 DB30
Osborne Gdns., Pot.B. 64 DB30
Osborne Gdns., Th.Hth. 202 DQ96
Osborne Gro. E17 123 DZ56
Osborne Gro. N4 121 DN60
Osborne Ms. E17 123 DZ56
Osborne Gro.
Osborne Ms., Wind. 151 AQ82
Osborne Pl., Sutt. 218 DD106
Osborne Rd. E7 124 EH64
Osborne Rd. E9 143 DZ65
Osborne Rd. E10 123 EB62
Osborne Rd. N4 121 DN60
Osborne Rd. N13 99 DN48
Osborne Rd. NW2 139 CV65
Osborne Rd. W3 158 CP75
Osborne Rd., Belv. 166 EZ78
Osborne Rd., Brwd. 108 FU44
Osborne Rd., Brox. 49 EA19
Osborne Rd., Buck.H. 102 EH46
Osborne Rd., Dag. 126 EZ64
Osborne Rd., Egh. 173 AZ93
Osborne Rd., Enf. 83 DY40
Osborne Rd., Horn. 127 FH58
Osborne Rd., Houns. 156 BZ83
Osborne Rd., Kings.T. 178 CL94
Osborne Rd., Pot.B. 64 DB30
Osborne Rd., Red. 250 DG131
Osborne Rd., Sthl. 136 CC72
Osborne Rd., Th.Hth. 202 DQ96
Osborne Rd., Uxb. 134 BJ66
Oxford Rd.
Osborne Rd., Wal.Cr. 67 DY27
Osborne Rd., Walt. 195 BU102
Osborne Rd., Wat. 76 BW38
Osborne Rd., Wind. 151 AQ82
Osborne Sq., Dag. 126 EZ63
Osborne St., Slou. 152 AT75
Osborne Ter. SW17 180 DG92
Church La.
Osbourne Ave., Kings L. 58 BM28
Osbourne Rd., Dart. 188 FP86
Oscar St. SE8 163 EA81
Oseney Cres. NW5 141 DJ65
Osgood Ave., Orp. 223 ET106
Osgood Gdns., Orp. 223 ET106
O'Shea Gro. E3 143 DZ67
Osidge La. N14 98 DG46
Osier Ms. W4 158 CS80
Pumping Sta. Rd.
Osier Pl., Egh. 173 BC93
Pooley Grn. Rd.
Osier St. E1 142 DW70
Osier Way E10 123 EB62
Osier Way, Bans. 217 CY114
Osier Way, Mitch. 200 DE99
Osiers Rd. SW18 160 DA84
Oslac Rd. SE6 183 EB92
Oslo Ct. NW8 272 B1
Oslo Sq. SE16 163 DY76
Norway Gate
Osman Clo. N15 122 DR58
Tewkesbury Rd.
Osman Rd. N9 100 DU48
Osman Rd. W6 159 CW76
Batoum Gdns.
Osmond Clo., Har. 116 CC61
Osmond Gdns., Wall. 219 DJ106
Osmund St. W12 139 CT72
Braybrook St.
Osnaburgh St. NW1 273 J4
Osnaburgh St. NW1 141 DH70
Osnaburgh Ter. NW1 273 J4
Osney Wk., Cars. 200 DD100
Osney Way, Grav. 191 GM89
Osprey Clo. E6 144 EL71
Dove App.
Osprey Clo. E11 124 EG56
Osprey Clo. E17 101 DY52
Osprey Clo., Wat. 60 BY34
Osprey Clo., West Dr. 154 BK75
Osprey Ct., Wal.Abb. 68 EG34
Farthingale La.
Osprey Gdns., S.Croy. 221 DX110
Osprey Ms., Enf. 82 DV43
Osprey Rd., Wal.Abb. 68 EG34
Farthingale La.
Ospringe Clo. SE20 182 DW94
Ospringe Ct. SE9 185 ER86
Ospringe Rd. NW5 121 DJ63
Osram Pl. NW2 119 CZ62
Ridge Rd.
Osram Rd., Wem. 117 CK62
Osric Path N1 275 M1
Ossian Ms. N4 121 DM59
Ossian Rd.
Ossian Rd. N4 121 DM59
Ossington Bldgs. W1 272 F6
Ossington Clo. W2 140 DB73
Ossington St.
Ossington St. W2 140 DB73
Ossory Rd. SE1 162 DU79
Ossulston St. NW1 273 M1
Ossulston St. NW1 141 DK68
Ossulton Pl. N2 120 DC55
East End Rd.
Ossulton Way N2 120 DC56
Ostade Rd. SW2 181 DM87
Osten Ms. SW7 160 DB76
McLeod's Ms.
Oster St., St.Alb. 42 CC19
Oster Ter. E17 123 DX57
Southcote Rd.
Osterberg Rd., Dart. 168 FM84
Osterley Ave., Islw. 157 CD80
Osterley Clo., Orp. 206 EU95
Leith Hill
Osterley Ct., Islw. 157 CD81
Osterley Cres., Islw. 157 CE81
Osterley Gdns., Th.Hth. 202 DQ96
Osterley Ho. E14 143 EB72
Giraud St.
Osterley La., Islw. 156 CC78
Osterley La., Sthl. 156 CA78
Osterley Pk., Islw. 157 CD78
Osterley Pk. Rd., Sthl. 156 BZ76
Osterley Pk. Vw. Rd. W7 157 CE75
Osterley Rd. N16 122 DS63
Osterley Rd., Islw. 157 CE80
Osterley Views, Sthl. 136 CC74
West Pk. Rd.
Ostliffe Rd. N13 99 DP50
Oswald Clo., Lthd. 230 CC122
Oswald Rd., Lthd. 230 CC122
Oswald Rd., St.Alb. 43 CE21
Oswald Rd., Sthl. 136 BY74
Oswald St. E5 123 DX62
Oswald Ter. NW2 119 CW62
Temple Rd.
Oswalds Mead E9 123 DY63
Lindisfarne Way
Osward, Croy. 221 DZ109
Osward Pl. N9 100 DV47
Osward Rd. SW17 180 DF89
Oswell Ho. E1 142 DV74
Penang St.
Oswin St. SE11 278 G8
Oswin St. SE11 161 DP77
Oswyth Rd. SE5 162 DS82
Otford Clo. SE20 202 DW95
Otford Clo., Bex. 187 FB86
Southwold Rd.
Otford Clo., Brom. 205 EN97
Otford Cres. SE4 183 DZ86
Otford La., Sev. 224 EZ112
Otford Rd., Sev. 241 FH118
Othello Clo. SE11 278 F10
Otis St. E3 143 EC69
Otley App., Ilf. 125 EP58
Otley Dr., Ilf. 125 EP58
Otley Rd. E16 144 EJ72
Otley Ter. E5 123 DX62
Otley Way, Wat. 94 BW48
Otlinge Clo., Orp. 206 EX98
Ottawa Gdns., Dag. 147 FD66
Ottawa Rd., Til. 171 GG82
Ottaway St. E5 122 DU62
Stellman Clo.
Ottenden Clo., Orp. 223 ES105
Southfleet Rd.
Otter Clo., Cher. 211 BB107
Otter Gdns., Hat. 45 CV19
Otter Rd., Grnf. 136 CC70
Otterbourne Rd. E4 101 ED48
Otterbourne Rd., Croy. 201 DP103
Otterburn Gdns., Islw. 157 CG80
Otterburn Ho. SE5 162 DQ80
Sultan St.
Otterburn St. SW17 180 DF93
Otterden St. SE6 183 EA91

Otterfield Rd., West Dr. 134 BL73
Ottermead La., Cher. 211 BC107
Otterspool La., Wat. 76 BY38
Otterspool Way, Wat. 76 BZ38
Otto Clo. SE26 182 DV90
Otto St. SE17 161 DP79
Ottoman Ter., Wat. 76 BW41
Ebury Rd.
Ottways Ave., Ash. 231 CK119
Ottways La., Ash. 231 CK120
Otway Gdns., Wat. 77 CE44
Caldecote Gdns.
Otways Clo., Pot.B. 64 DB32
Oulton Clo. E5 122 DW61
Mundford Rd.
Oulton Clo. SE28 146 EW72
Rollesby Way
Oulton Cres., Bark. 145 ET65
Oulton Cres., Pot.B. 63 CX32
Oulton Rd. N15 122 DR57
Oulton Way, Wat. 94 BY49
Oundle Ave. 76 CC44
(Bushey), Wat.
Ousden Clo. 67 DY30
(Cheshunt), Wal.Cr.
Ousden Dr. 67 DY30
(Cheshunt), Wal.Cr.
Ouseley Rd. SW12 180 DF88
Ouseley Rd., Stai. 172 AW87
Ouseley Rd., Wind. 172 AW87
Outdowns, Lthd. 245 BV129
Outer Circle NW1 272 F5
Outer Circle NW1 140 DG70
Outfield Rd., Ger.Cr. 90 AX52
Outgate Rd. NW10 139 CT66
Outlook Dr., Ch.St.G. 90 AX48
Outram Pl. N1 141 DL67
Outram Pl., Wey. 213 BQ106
Outram Rd. E6 144 EL67
Outram Rd. N22 99 DK53
Outram Rd., Croy. 202 DT103
Outwich St. EC3 275 N8
Outwich St. EC3 142 DS72
Outwood La., Couls. 234 DE120
Outwood La., Tad. 234 DB122
Oval, The E2 142 DV68
Oval, The, Bans. 218 DA114
Oval, The, Brox. 67 DY25
Oval, The, Gdmg. 258 AT144
Oval, The, Guil. 258 AU135
Oval, The, Sid. 186 EU87
Oval Gdns., Grays 170 GC76
Oval Pl. SW8 161 DM80
Oval Rd. NW1 141 DH67
Oval Rd., Croy. 202 DR103
Oval Rd. N., Dag. 147 FB67
Oval Rd. S., Dag. 147 FB68
Oval Way SE11 161 DM78
Oval Way, Ger.Cr. 112 AY56
Ovenden Rd., Sev. 240 EX120
Over The Misbourne, 113 BA58
Ger.Cr.
Over The Misbourne, 113 BB58
Uxb.
Overbrae, Beck. 183 EA93
Overbrook, Lthd. 245 BP129
Overbrook Wk., Edg. 96 CN52
Overbury Ave., Beck. 203 EB97
Overbury Cres., Croy. 221 EC110
Overbury Rd. N15 122 DR58
Overbury St. E5 123 DX63
Overcliff Rd. SE13 163 EA83
Overcliff Rd., Grays 170 GD78
Overcliffe, Grav. 191 GF86
Overcourt Clo., Sid. 186 EV86
Overdale, Ash. 232 CL116
Overdale, Dor. 263 CK135
Overdale, Red. 252 DQ133
Overdale Ave., N.Mal. 198 CQ96
Overdale Rd. W5 157 CJ76
Overdale Rd., Chesh. 54 AP28
Overdown Rd. SE6 183 EA91
Overhill, Warl. 236 DW119
Overhill Rd. SE22 182 DU87
Overhill Rd., Pur. 219 DN109
Overhill Way, Beck. 203 EC99
Overlea Rd. E5 122 DU59
Overlord Clo., Brox. 49 DY21
Baas Hill
Overmead, Sid. 185 ER87
Overmead, Swan. 207 FE99
Oversley Ho. W2 140 DA71
Overstand Clo., Beck. 203 EA99
Overstone Gdns., Croy. 203 DZ101
Overstone Rd. W6 159 CW76
Overstream, Rick. 74 BH42
Overthorpe Clo., Wok. 226 AS117
Overton Clo. NW10 138 CQ65
Overton Clo., Islw. 157 CF81
Avenue Rd.
Overton Ct. E11 124 EG59
Overton Dr. E11 124 EG59
Overton Dr., Rom. 126 EW59
Overton Rd. E10 123 DY60
Overton Rd. N14 81 DL43
Overton Rd. SE2 166 EW76
Overton Rd. SW9 161 DN82
Overton Rd., Sutt. 218 DA107
Overton Rd. E. SE2 166 EX76
Overtons Yd., Croy. 202 DQ104
Overy St., Dart. 188 FL86
Ovesdon Ave., Har. 116 BZ60
Oveton Way, Lthd. 246 CA126
Ovett Clo. SE19 182 DS93
Ovex Clo. E14 163 EC75
Ovington Ct., Wok. 226 AT116
Roundthorn Way
Ovington Gdns. SW3 276 C7
Ovington Gdns. SW3 160 DE76
Ovington Ms. SW3 276 C7
Ovington Ms. SW3 160 DE76
Ovington Sq. SW3 276 C7
Ovington Sq. SW3 160 DE76
Ovington St. SW3 276 C7
Ovington St. SW3 160 DE77
Owen Clo. SE28 146 EW74
Owen Clo., Hayes 135 BV69
Owen Gdns., 102 EL51
Wdf.Grn.
Owen Pl., Lthd. 231 CH122
Church Rd.
Owen Rd. N13 100 DQ49
Owen Rd., Hayes 135 BV69
Owen St. EC1 274 E1
Owen Wk. SE20 182 DU94
Sycamore Gro.
Owen Waters Ho., Ilf. 103 EN53
Owen Way NW10 118 CQ64
Owenite St. SE2 166 EV77
Owen's Ct. EC1 274 F2
Owens Row EC1 274 F2
Owens Way SE23 183 DY87
Owens Way, Rick. 74 BN43
Owgan Clo. SE5 162 DR80
Benhill Rd.
Owl Clo., S.Croy. 221 DX110
Owlets Hall Clo., Horn. 128 FM55
Prospect Rd.
Owlsears Clo., Beac. 89 AK51
Ownstead Gdns., 220 DT111
S.Croy.
Ownstead Hill, Croy. 221 EC110
Ox La., Epsom 217 CU109
Church St.
Oxberry Ave. SW6 159 CY82
Oxdowne Clo., Cob. 214 CB114
Oxenden Dr., Hodd. 49 EA18
Oxenden Wd. Rd., Orp. 224 EW108
Oxendon St. SW1 277 M1
Oxendon St. SW1 141 DK73
Oxenford St. SE15 162 DT83
Oxenholme NW1 273 L1
Oxenholme NW1 141 DJ68
Oxenpark Ave., Wem. 118 CL60
Oxestalls Rd. SE8 163 DY78
Oxfield Clo., Berk. 38 AU20
Oxford Ave. SW20 199 CY96
Oxford Ave., Grays 171 GG77
Oxford Ave., Hayes 155 BT80
Oxford Ave., Horn. 128 FN56
Oxford Ave., Houns. 156 CA78
Oxford Ave., St.Alb. 43 CJ21
Oxford Ave., Slou. 131 AM71
Oxford Ave. 130 AH68
(Burnham), Slou.
Oxford Circ. Ave. W1 273 K9
Oxford Clo. N9 100 DV47
Oxford Clo., Ashf. 175 BQ94
Oxford Clo., Grav. 191 GM89
Oxford Clo., Mitch. 201 DJ97
Oxford Clo. 66 DW29
(Cheshunt), Wal.Cr.
Oxford Ct. EC4 275 K10
Oxford Ct. W3 138 CN72
Queens Dr.
Oxford Ct., Brwd. 108 FX49
Oxford Ct., Felt. 176 BX91
Oxford Way
Oxford Cres., N.Mal. 198 CR100
Oxford Dr., Ruis. 116 BW61
Oxford Gdns. N20 98 DD46
Oxford Gdns. N21 100 DQ45
Oxford Gdns. W4 158 CN78
Oxford Gdns. W10 139 CX72
Oxford Gdns., Uxb. 114 BG62
Oxford Rd.
Oxford Gate W6 159 CX77
Oxford La., Guil. 258 AX136
Sydenham Rd.
Oxford Ms., Bex. 186 FA87
Bexley High St.
Oxford Rd. E15 143 ED65
Oxford Rd. N4 121 DN60
Oxford Rd. N9 100 DV47
Oxford Rd. NW6 140 DA68
Oxford Rd. SE19 182 DR93
Oxford Rd. SW15 159 CY84
Oxford Rd. W5 137 CK73
Oxford Rd., Beac. 111 AP55
Oxford Rd. 88 AE54
(Holtspur), Beac.
Oxford Rd., Cars. 218 DE107
Oxford Rd., Enf. 82 DV43
Oxford Rd., Ger.Cr. 112 AT56
Oxford Rd., Guil. 258 AX136
Oxford Rd., Har. 116 CC58
Oxford Rd. 117 CF55
(Wealdstone), Har.
Oxford Rd., H.Wyc. 88 AE54
Oxford Rd., Ilf. 125 EQ64
Oxford Rd., Red. 250 DE133
Oxford Rd., Rom. 106 FM51
Oxford Rd., Sid. 186 EV92
Oxford Rd., Tedd. 177 CD92
Oxford Rd., Uxb. 134 BJ65
Oxford Rd., Wall. 219 DJ106
Oxford Rd., Wind. 151 AQ81
Oxford Rd., Wdf.Grn. 102 EK50
Oxford Rd. E., Wind. 151 AQ81
Oxford Rd. N. W4 158 CP78
Oxford Rd. S. W4 158 CN78
Oxford Sq. W2 272 C9
Oxford Sq. W2 140 DE72
Oxford St. W1 272 F9
Oxford St. W1 140 DG72
Oxford St., Wat. 75 BV43
Oxford Ter., Guil. 258 AX136
Pewley Hill
Oxford Wk., Sthl. 136 BZ74
Oxford Way, Felt. 176 BX91
Oxgate Gdns. NW2 119 CV62
Oxgate La. NW2 119 CV61
Oxhawth Cres., Brom. 205 EN99
Oxhey Ave., Wat. 94 BX45
Oxhey Dr., Nthwd. 93 BV49
Oxhey Dr., Wat. 94 BW48
Oxhey Dr. S., Nthwd. 93 BV50
Oxhey La., Pnr. 94 CA50
Oxhey La., Wat. 94 BY46
Oxhey Ridge Clo., 93 BU50
Nthwd.
Oxhey Rd., Wat. 76 BW44
Oxleas E6 145 EP72
Oxleas Clo., Well. 165 ER82
Oxlease Dr., Hat. 45 CV19
Oxleay Ct., Har. 116 CA60
Oxleay Rd., Har. 116 CA60
Oxleigh Clo., N.Mal. 198 CS99
Oxley Clo. SE1 162 DT78
Oxley Clo., Rom. 106 FJ54
Oxleys, The, Harl. 36 EY11
Oxleys Rd. NW2 119 CV62
Oxleys Rd., Wal.Abb. 68 EG33
Oxlip Clo., Croy. 203 DX102
Marigold Way
Oxlow La., Dag. 126 EZ63
Oxonian St. SE22 162 DT84
Oxshott Ri., Cob. 214 BX113
Oxshott Rd., Lthd. 231 CE116
Oxshott Way, Cob. 230 BY115
Oxted Clo., Mitch. 200 DD97
Oxted Rd., Gdse. 252 DW130
Oxtoby Way SW16 201 DK95
Oyster Catchers Clo. E16 144 EH72
Freemasons Rd.
Oyster La., W.Byf. 212 BK110
Oyster Row E1 142 DW72
Lukin St.
Oysterfields, St.Alb. 42 CB19
Ozolins Way E16 144 EG72

P

Pablo Neruda Clo. SE24 161 DP84
Shakespeare Rd.
Pace Pl. E1 142 DV72
Bigland St.
Paceheath Clo., Rom. 105 FD51
Pachesham Dr., Lthd. 231 CF116
Oxshott Rd.
Pachesham Pk., Lthd. 231 CF117
Pacific Clo., Felt. 175 BT88
Westmacott Dr.
Pacific Rd. E16 144 EG72
Packet Boat La., Uxb. 134 BH72
Packham Clo., Orp. 206 EW104
Berrylands
Packham Rd., Grav. 191 GF91
Packhorse Clo., St.Alb. 43 CJ17
Packhorse La., Borwd. 78 CS37
Buckettsland La.
Packhorse La., Pot.B. 62 CR32
Packhorse Rd., Ger.Cr. 112 AY55
Packhorse Rd., Sev. 256 FC123
Packington Rd. W3 158 CQ76
Packington Sq. N1 142 DQ67
Packington St. N1 141 DP67
Packmores Rd. SE9 185 ER85
Padbrook, Oxt. 254 EG129
Padbury SE17 162 DS78
Bagshot St.
Padbury Clo., Felt. 175 BR88
Padbury Ct. E2 142 DT69
Brick La.
Padcroft Rd., West Dr. 134 BK74
Paddenswick Rd. W6 159 CU76
Paddick Clo., Hodd. 49 DZ16
Paddington Clo., Hayes 136 BX70
Paddington Grn. W2 272 A6
Paddington Grn. W2 140 DD71
Paddington St. W1 272 F6
Paddington St. W1 140 DG71
Paddock, The, Brox. 49 EA20
Paddock, The, Dor. 262 CB137
Paddock, The, Ger.Cr. 90 AY50
Paddock, The, Guil. 243 BD133
Paddock, The, Hat. 45 CU16
Paddock, The, Slou. 152 AV81
Paddock, The, Uxb. 115 BP63
Paddock, The, West. 255 EQ126
Paddock Clo. SE3 164 EG83
Paddock Clo. SE26 183 DX91
Paddock Clo. 208 FQ95
(South Darenth), Dart.
Paddock Clo., Nthlt. 136 CA68
Paddock Clo., Orp. 223 EP105
State Fm. Ave.
Paddock Clo., Oxt. 254 EF131
Paddock Clo., Ware 34 EK06
Paddock Clo., Wor.Pk. 198 CS102
Paddock Gdns. SE19 182 DS93
Westow St.
Paddock Mead, Harl. 51 EQ20
Paddock Rd. NW2 119 CU62
Paddock Rd., Bexh. 166 EY84
Paddock Rd., Ruis. 116 BX62
Paddock Wk., Warl. 236 DV119
Paddock Way, Chis. 185 ER94
Paddock Way, Hem.H. 39 BE20
Paddock Way, Oxt. 254 EF131
Paddock Way, Wok. 211 BB114
Paddocks, The, Add. 212 BH110
Paddocks, The, Barn. 80 DF41
Paddocks, The, Lthd. 246 CB126
Leatherhead Rd.
Paddocks, The, Rick. 73 BF42
Paddocks, The, Rom. 87 FF44
Murthering La.
Paddocks, The, Sev. 257 FK124
Seal Hollow Rd.
Paddocks, The, Vir.W. 192 AY100
Paddocks, The, 30 DB08
Welw.G.C.
Paddocks, The, Wem. 118 CP61
Paddocks, The, Wey. 195 BS104
Paddocks Clo., Ash. 232 CL118
Paddocks Clo., Cob. 214 BW114
Paddocks Clo., Har. 116 CB63
Paddocks Clo., Orp. 206 EX103
Paddocks Mead, Wok. 226 AS116
Paddocks Rd., Guil. 243 BA130
Paddocks Way, Ash. 232 CL118
Paddocks Way, Cher. 194 BH102
Padfield Rd. SE5 162 DQ83
Padnall Rd., Rom. 126 EX55
Padstow Clo., Slou. 152 AY76
Padstow Rd., Enf. 81 DP40
Padstow Wk., Felt. 175 BT88
Westmacott Dr.
Padua Rd. SE20 202 DW95
Pagden St. SW8 161 DH81
Page Clo., Dag. 126 EY64
Page Clo., Dart. 189 FW90
Page Clo., Hmptn. 176 BY93
Page Clo., Har. 118 CM58
Page Cres., Croy. 219 DN106
Page Cres., Erith 167 FF80
Page Grn. Rd. N15 122 DU57
Page Grn. Ter. N15 122 DT57
Page Heath La., Brom. 204 EK97
Page Heath Vill., Brom. 204 EK97
Page Hill, Ware 32 DW05
Page Meadow NW7 97 CU52
Page Rd., Felt. 175 BR86
Page Rd., Hert. 32 DU09
Page St. NW7 97 CU51
Page St. SW1 277 N8
Page St. SW1 161 DK77
Pageant Ave. NW9 96 CS53
Pageant Clo., Til. 171 GJ81
Pageant Rd., St.Alb. 43 CD21
Pageant Wk., Croy. 202 DS104
Pageantmaster Ct. EC4 274 F9
Pagehurst Rd., Croy. 202 DV101
Pages Cft., Berk. 38 AU17
Pages Hill N10 98 DG54
Pages La. N10 98 DG54
Pages La., Rom. 106 FP54
Pages La., Uxb. 134 BJ65
Pages Wk. SE1 279 M8
Pages Wk. SE1 162 DS77
Pages Yd. W4 158 CS79
Church St.
Paget Ave., Sutt. 200 DD104
Paget Clo., Hmptn. 177 CD91
Paget Gdns., Chis. 205 EP95
Paget La., Islw. 157 CD83
Paget Pl., Kings.T. 178 CQ93
Paget Pl., T.Ditt. 197 CG102
Brooklands Rd.
Paget Ri. SE18 165 EN79
Paget Rd. N16 122 DR60
Paget Rd., Ilf. 125 EP63
Paget Rd., Slou. 153 AZ77
Paget Rd., Uxb. 135 BQ70
Paget St. EC1 274 F2
Paget Ter. SE18 165 EN79
Pagette Way, Grays 170 GA77
Pagitts Gro., Barn. 80 DB39
Paglesfield, Brwd. 109 GC44
Pagnell St. SE14 163 DZ80
Pagoda Ave., Rich. 158 CM83
Pagoda Gdns. SE3 163 ED82
Paignton Rd. N15 122 DS58
Paignton Rd., Ruis. 115 BU62
Paines Brook Rd., Rom. 106 FM51
Paines Brook Way
Paines Brook Way, 106 FM51
Rom.
Paines Clo., Pnr. 94 BY54
Paines La., Pnr. 94 BY53
Pains Clo., Mitch. 201 DH96
Pains Hill, Oxt. 254 EJ132
Painsthorpe Rd. N16 122 DS62
Oldfield Rd.
Painters Ash La., Grav. 190 GD90
Painters La., Enf. 83 DY35
Painters Rd., Ilf. 125 ET55
Paisley Rd. N22 99 DP53
Paisley Rd., Cars. 200 DD102
Pakeman St. N7 121 DM62
Pakenham Clo. SW12 180 DG88
Balham Pk. Rd.
Pakenham St. WC1 274 C3
Pakenham St. WC1 141 DM69
Pakes Way, Epp. 85 ES37
Palace Ave. W8 140 DB74
Palace Clo., Kings L. 58 BM30
Palace Ct. NW3 120 DB64
Palace Ct. W2 140 DB73
Palace Ct., Brom. 204 EH95
Palace Gro.
Palace Ct., Har. 118 CL58
Palace Ct. Gdns. N10 121 DJ55
Palace Dr., Wey. 195 BP104
Palace Gdn. Ms. W8 140 DA74
Palace Gdns., Buck.H. 102 EK46
Palace Gdns., Enf. 82 DR42
Sydney Rd.
Palace Gdns. Ter. W8 140 DA74
Palace Gate W8 160 DC75
Palace Gates Rd. N22 99 DK54
Palace Grn. W8 160 DB75
Palace Grn., Croy. 221 DZ108
Palace Gro. SE19 182 DT94
Palace Gro., Brom. 204 EH95
Palace Ms. E17 123 DZ56
Palace Ms. SW1 276 G9
Palace Ms. SW6 159 CZ80
Hartismere Rd.
Palace Pl. SW1 277 K6
Palace Rd. N8 121 DK57
Palace Rd. N11 99 DK52
Palace Rd. SE19 182 DT94
Palace Rd. SW2 181 DM88
Palace Rd., Brom. 204 EH95
Palace Rd., E.Mol. 197 CD97
Palace Rd., Kings.T. 197 CK98
Palace Rd., Ruis. 116 BY63
Palace Rd., West. 239 EN121
Chestnut Ave.
Palace Rd. Est. SW2 181 DM88
Palace Sq. SE19 182 DT94
Palace St. SW1 277 K6
Palace St. SW1 161 DJ76
Palace Vw. SE12 184 EG89
Palace Vw., Brom. 204 EH97
Palace Vw., Croy. 221 DZ105
Palace Vw. Rd. E4 101 EB50
Palace Way, Wey. 195 BP104
Palace Dr.
Palamos Rd. E10 123 EA60
Palatine Ave. N16 122 DT63
Stoke Newington Rd.
Palatine Rd. N16 122 DS63
Palermo Rd. NW10 139 CU68
Palestine Gro. SW19 200 DD95
Palewell Clo., Orp. 206 EV96
Palewell Common Dr. 178 CR85
SW14
Palewell Pk. SW14 178 CR85
Paley Gdns., Loug. 85 EP41
Palfrey Clo., St.Alb. 43 CD18
Palfrey Pl. SW8 161 DM80
Palgrave Ave., Sthl. 136 CA73
Palgrave Rd. W12 159 CT76
Palissy St. E2 275 P3
Pall Mall SW1 277 L3
Pall Mall SW1 141 DJ74
Pall Mall E. SW1 277 N2
Pall Mall E. SW1 141 DK74
Pall Mall Pl. SW1 277 L3
Pallant Way, Orp. 205 EN104
Pallas Rd., Hem.H. 40 BM18
Pallet Way SE18 164 EL81
Palliser Dr., Rain. 147 FG71
Ellis Ave.
Palliser Rd. W14 159 CY78
Palliser Rd., Ch.St.G. 90 AV48
Palm Ave., Sid. 186 EX93
Palm Clo. E10 123 EB61
Oliver Rd.
Palm Gro. W5 158 CL76
Palm Gro., Guil. 242 AW130
Palm Rd., Rom. 127 FC57
Palmar Cres., Bexh. 166 FA83
Palmar Rd., Bexh. 166 FA82
Palmarsh Clo., Orp. 206 EX98
Wotton Grn.
Palmeira Rd., Bexh. 166 EX83
Palmer Ave., Grav. 191 GK92
Palmer Ave., Sutt. 217 CW105
Palmer Ave. 76 CB43
(Bushey), Wat.
Palmer Clo., Hert. 32 DQ07
Palmer Clo., Horl. 268 DF146
Palmer Clo., Houns. 156 CA81
Palmer Clo., Red. 266 DG135
Palmer Clo., W.Wick. 203 ED104
Palmer Cres., Cher. 211 BD107
Palmer Cres., Kings.T. 198 CL97
Palmer Gdns., Barn. 79 CX43
Palmer Pl. N7 121 DN64
Palmer Rd. E13 144 EH70
Palmer Rd., Dag. 126 EX60
Palmer Rd., Hert. 32 DR07
Palmer St. SW1 277 M6
Palmer St. SW1 161 DK76
Palmers Ave., Grays 170 GC78
Palmers Dr., Grays 170 GC77
Palmers Gro., Wal.Abb. 50 EF22
Palmers Gro., W.Mol. 196 CA98
Palmers Hill, Epp. 70 EU29
Palmers La., Enf. 82 DW39
Palmer's Lo., Guil. 258 AU135
Old Palace Rd.
Palmers Moor La., Iver 134 BG70
Palmers Orchard, Sev. 225 FF111
Palmers Pas. SW14 158 CQ83
Palmers Rd.
Palmers Rd. E2 143 DX68
Palmers Rd. N11 99 DJ50
Palmers Rd. SW14 158 CQ83
Palmers Rd. SW16 201 DM96
Palmers Rd., Borwd. 78 CP39
Palmers Way 67 DY29
(Cheshunt), Wal.Cr.
Palmersfield Rd., Bans. 218 DA114
Palmerston Ave., Slou. 152 AV76
Palmerston Clo., 29 CW09
Welw.G.C.
Palmerston Clo., Wok. 211 BA114
Palmerston Cres. N13 99 DM50
Palmerston Cres. SE18 165 EQ79
Palmerston Gdns., Grays 169 FX78
Palmerston Gro. SW19 180 DA94
Palmerston Rd. E7 124 EH64
Palmerston Rd. E17 123 DZ55
Palmerston Rd. N22 99 DM52
Palmerston Rd. NW6 139 CZ66
Palmerston Rd. SW14 158 CQ84
Palmerston Rd. SW19 180 DA94
Palmerston Rd. W3 158 CQ76
Palmerston Rd., Buck.H. 102 EH47
Palmerston Rd., Cars. 218 DF105
Palmerston Rd., Grays 169 FX79
Palmerston Rd., Har. 117 CE55
Palmerston Rd., Orp. 223 EQ105
Palmerston Rd., Rain. 148 FJ68
Palmerston Rd., Sutt. 218 DC105
Vernon Rd.
Palmerston Rd., Th.Hth. 202 DR99
Palmerston Rd., Twick. 177 CE86
Palmerston Way SW8 161 DH80
Bradmead
Pamela Ave., Hem.H. 40 BM23
Pamela Gdns., Pnr. 115 BV57
Pamela Wk. E8 142 DU67
Marlborough Ave.
Pampisford Rd., Pur. 219 DN111
Pampisford Rd., S.Croy. 220 DQ107
Pams Way, Epsom 216 CR106
Pancake La., Hem.H. 41 BR21
Pancras La. EC4 275 J9
Pancras Rd. NW1 273 P1
Pancras Rd. NW1 141 DK68
Pancroft, Rom. 86 EV41
Pandora Rd. NW6 140 DA65
Panel Rd., Ware 33 DZ05
Panfield Ms., Ilf. 125 EN58
Cranbrook Rd.
Panfield Rd. SE2 166 EU76
Pangbourne Ave. W10 139 CW71
Pangbourne Dr., Stan. 95 CK50
Pankhurst Clo. SE14 163 DX80
Briant St.
Pankhurst Clo., Islw. 157 CF82
St. John's Rd.
Pankhurst Rd., Walt. 196 BW101
Panmuir Rd. SW20 199 CV95
Panmure Clo. N5 121 DP63
Panmure Rd. SE26 182 DV90
Pannard Pl., Sthl. 136 CB73
Pannells Clo., Cher. 193 BF102
Guildford Rd.
Pannells Ct., Guil. 258 AX135
Panshanger Dr., 30 DB09
Welw.G.C.
Panshanger La., Hert. 30 DF09
Pansy Gdns. W12 139 CU73
Panters, Swan. 187 FF94
Pantile Rd., Wey. 213 BR105
Pantile Row, Slou. 153 BA77
Pantile Wk., Uxb. 134 BJ66
High St.
Pantiles, The NW11 119 CZ57
Willifield Way
Pantiles, The, Bexh. 166 EZ80
Pantiles, The, Brom. 204 EL97
Pantiles, The 95 CD45
(Bushey), Wat.
Pantiles Clo. N13 99 DP50
Princes Ave.
Pantiles Clo., Wok. 226 AV118
Panton St. SW1 277 M1
Panxworth Rd., Hem.H. 40 BL22
Panyer All. EC4 275 H8
Paper Ms., Dor. 263 CH135
Papercourt La., Wok. 227 BF122
Papermill Clo., Cars. 218 DG105
Mill La.
Papillons Wk. SE3 164 EG83
Papworth Gdns. N7 121 DM64
Liverpool Rd.
Papworth Way SW2 181 DN87
Parade, The SW11 160 DF80
Parade, The, Brwd. 108 FW48
Parade, The, Dart. 187 FF85
Crayford Way
Parade, The, Epsom 216 CR113
Parade, The, Esher 215 CE107
Parade, The, Rom. 106 FP51
Parade, The, S.Ock. 168 FQ75
Parade, The, Sun. 175 BT94
Parade, The, Vir.W. 192 AX100
Parade, The, Wat. 75 BV41
High St.
Parade, The 94 BY48
(Carpenders Pk.), Wat.
Parade, The, Wind. 151 AK81
Parade Ms. SE27 181 DP89
Norwood Rd.
Paradise Clo. 66 DV28
(Cheshunt), Wal.Cr.
Paradise Pas. N7 141 DN65
Sheringham Rd.
Paradise Pl. SE18 164 EL77
Woodhill
Paradise Rd. SW4 161 DL82
Paradise Rd., Rich. 178 CL85
Paradise Rd., Wal.Abb. 67 EC34
Paradise Row E2 142 DV69
Bethnal Grn. Rd.

Paradise St. SE16 162 DV75
Paradise Wk. SW3 160 DF79
Paradise Wd. La., Hem.H. 40 BK21
Paragon, The SE3 164 EF82
Paragon Clo. E16 144 EG72
Pacific Rd.
Paragon Gro., Surb. 198 CM100
Paragon Ms. SE1 279 L8
Paragon Pl. SE3 164 EF82
Paragon Pl., Surb. 198 CM100
Berrylands Rd.
Paragon Rd. E9 142 DW65
Parbury Ri., Chess. 216 CL107
Parbury Rd. SE23 183 DY86
Parchment Clo., Amer. 55 AS37
Parchmore Rd., Th.Hth. 201 DP96
Parchmore Way, Th.Hth. 201 DP96
Pardon St. EC1 274 G4
Pardoner St. SE1 279 L6
Pardoner St. SE1 162 DR76
Pares Clo., Wok. 226 AX116
Parfett St. E1 142 DU71
Parfitt Clo. NW3 120 DC61
North End
Parfour Dr., Ken. 236 DQ116
Parfrey St. W6 159 CW79
Parham Dr., Ilf. 125 EP58
Parham Way N10 99 DJ54
Rosebery Rd.
Paringdon Rd., Harl. 51 EP19
Paris Gdns. SE1 278 F2
Paris Gdns. SE1 141 DP74
Parish Clo., Horn. 127 FH61
St. Leonards Way
Parish Gate Dr., Sid. 185 ES86
Parish La. SE20 183 DX93
Parish La., Slou. 111 AP61
Parish Ms. SE20 183 DX94
Parish Wf. Pl. SE18 164 EL77
Woodhill
Park, The N6 120 DG58
Park, The NW11 120 DB60
Park, The SE19 182 DS94
Park, The SE23 182 DV88
Park Hill
Park, The W5 137 CK74
Park, The, Cars. 218 DF106
Park, The, Lthd. 230 CA123
Park, The, St.Alb. 43 CG18
Park, The, Sid. 186 EU91
Park App., Well. 166 EV84
Park Ave. E6 145 EN67
Park Ave. E15 144 EE65
Park Ave. N3 98 DB53
Park Ave. N13 99 DN48
Park Ave. N18 100 DU49
Park Ave. N22 99 DL54
Park Ave. NW2 139 CV65
Park Ave. NW10 138 CM68
Park Ave. NW11 120 DB60
Park Ave. SW14 158 CR84
Park Ave., Bark. 145 EQ65
Park Ave., Barn. 80 DC43
Park Ave., Brwd. 109 GC46
Park Ave., Brom. 184 EF94
Park Ave., Cars. 218 DG107
Park Ave., Cat. 236 DS124
Park Ave., Chis. 205 ES97
Park Ave., Egh. 173 BC93
Park Ave., Enf. 82 DR43
Park Ave., Grav. 191 GJ88
Park Ave. (Perry St.), Grav. 190 GE88
Park Ave., Grays 169 FU79
Park Ave., Harl. 52 EW18
Park Ave., Houns. 176 CB86
Park Ave., Ilf. 125 EN60
Park Ave., Mitch. 181 DH94
Park Ave., Orp. 206 EU103
Park Ave. (Farnborough), Orp. 205 EM104
Park Ave., Pot.B. 64 DC34
Park Ave., Rad. 61 CH34
Park Ave., Red. 266 DF142
Park Ave., Rick. 74 BG43
Park Ave., Ruis. 115 BR58
Park Ave., St.Alb. 43 CG19
Park Ave., Sthl. 156 BZ75
Park Ave., Stai. 173 BF93
Park Ave. (Sunnymeads), Stai. 172 AX85
Park Ave., Upmin. 129 FS59
Park Ave., Wat. 75 BU41
Park Ave. (Bushey), Wat. 76 BX41
Park Ave., W.Wick. 203 EC103
Park Ave., Wdf.Grn. 102 EH50
Park Ave. E., Epsom 217 CU107
Park Ave. Ms., Mitch. 181 DH94
Park Ave.
Park Ave. N. N8 121 DK55
Park Ave. N. NW10 119 CV64
Park Ave. Rd. N17 100 DV52
Park Ave. S. N8 121 DK56
Park Ave. W., Epsom 217 CU107
Park Barn Dr., Guil. 242 AS132
Park Barn E., Guil. 242 AT133
Park Boul., Rom. 105 FF53
Park Chase, Guil. 242 AY134
Park Chase, Wem. 118 CM63
Park Clo. E9 142 DW67
Skipworth Rd.
Park Clo. NW2 119 CV62
Park Clo. NW10 138 CM69
Park Clo. SW1 276 D5
Park Clo. W4 158 CR78
Park Clo. W14 159 CZ76
Park Clo., Add. 212 BH110
Park Clo., Bushey 264 CP138
Park Clo., Cars. 218 DF107
Park Clo., Epp. 70 FA27
Park Clo., Esher 214 BZ107
Park Clo., Hmptn. 196 CC95
Park Clo., Har. 95 CE53
Park Clo., Hat. 63 CZ26
Park Clo. (Brookmans Pk.), Hat. 45 CW17
Park Clo., Houns. 176 CC85
Park Clo., Lthd. 231 CD124
Park Clo., Rick. 93 BP49
Park Clo., Walt. 195 BT103
Park Clo. (Bushey), Wat. 76 BX41
Park Clo., Wind. 151 AR82
Park Copse, Dor. 263 CK136
Park Cor., Wind. 151 AL83
Park Cor. Dr., Lthd. 245 BS128
Park Cor. Rd., Grav. 190 FZ90
Park Ct. SE26 182 DV93
Park Ct., Harl. 35 ER13
Park Ct., Kings.T. 197 CJ95
Park Ct., N.Mal. 198 CR98
Park Ct., Wem. 118 CL64
Park Ct., W.Byf. 212 BG113
Park Ct., Wok. 227 AZ118
Park Dr.
Park Cres. N3 98 DB52
Park Cres. W1 273 H5
Park Cres. W1 141 DH70
Park Cres., Borwd. 78 CM41
Park Cres., Enf. 82 DR42
Park Cres., Erith 167 FC79
Park Cres., Har. 95 CE53
Park Cres., Horn. 127 FG59
Park Cres., Twick. 177 CD88
Park Cres. Ms. E. W1 273 J5
Park Cres. Ms. W. W1 273 H5
Park Cres. Rd., Erith 167 FD79
Park Cft., Edg. 96 CQ53
Park Dale N11 99 DK51
Bounds Grn. Rd.
Park Dr. N21 82 DQ44
Park Dr. NW11 120 DB60
Park Dr. SE7 164 EL79
Park Dr. SW14 158 CR84
Park Dr. W3 158 CN76
Park Dr., Bishop's Stortford 37 FH05
Chelmsford Rd.
Park Dr., Dag. 127 FC62
Park Dr., Har. 116 CA59
Park Dr. (Harrow Weald), Har. 95 CE51
Park Dr., Pot.B. 64 DA31
Park Dr., Rom. 127 FD56
Park Dr., Upmin. 128 FP63
Park Dr., Wey. 213 BP106
Park Dr., Wok. 227 AZ118
Park Dr. Clo. SE7 164 EL78
Park End NW3 120 DE63
South Hill Pk.
Park End, Brom. 204 EF95
Park End Rd., Rom. 127 FE56
Park Fm. Clo. N2 120 DC55
Park Fm. Clo., Pnr. 115 BV57
Field End Rd.
Park Fm. Rd., Brom. 204 EK95
Park Fm. Rd., Kings.T. 178 CL94
Park Fm. Rd., Upmin. 128 FM64
Park Flds., Harl. 50 EG15
Park Gdn. Pl. W2 272 A9
Park Gdns. NW9 118 CP55
Park Gdns., Erith 167 FD77
Park Gdns., Kings.T. 178 CM92
Park Gate N2 120 DD55
Park Gate N21 99 DM45
Park Gate W5 137 CK71
Mount Ave.
Park Gate Clo., Kings.T. 178 CP93
Warboys App.
Park Gra. Gdns., Sev. 257 FJ127
Solefields Rd.
Park Grn., Lthd. 230 CA124
Park Gro. E15 144 EG67
Park Gro. N11 99 DK52
Park Gro., Bexh. 167 FC84
Park Gro., Brom. 204 EH95
Park Gro., Ch.St.G. 72 AX41
Park Gro., Edg. 96 CM50
Park Gro. Rd. E11 124 EE61
Park Hall Rd. N2 120 DE56
Park Hall Rd. SE21 182 DR90
Park Hall Rd., Reig. 250 DA132
Park Hill SE23 182 DV89
Park Hill SW4 181 DK85
Park Hill W5 137 CK71
Park Hill, Brom. 204 EL98
Park Hill, Cars. 218 DE107
Park Hill, Harl. 36 EV12
Park Hill, Loug. 84 EK43
Park Hill, Rich. 178 CM86
Park Hill Clo., Cars. 218 DE106
Park Hill Ct. SW17 180 DF90
Beeches Rd.
Park Hill Ri., Croy. 202 DS103
Park Hill Rd., Brom. 204 EE96
Park Hill Rd., Croy. 202 DS103
Park Hill Rd., Hem.H. 40 BH20
Park Hill Rd., Sid. 185 ES90
Park Hill Rd., Wall. 219 DH107
Park Horsley, Lthd. 245 BU129
Park Ho. N21 99 DM45
Park Ho. Dr., Reig. 265 CZ136
Park Ho. Gdns., Twick. 177 CJ86
Park Ind. Est., St.Alb. 61 CE27
Park La. E15 143 ED67
High St.
Park La. N9 100 DS48
Park La. N17 100 DT52
Park La. N18 100 DS49
Sheldon Rd.
Park La. W1 272 E10
Park La. W1 140 DF73
Park La., Ash. 232 CM118
Park La., Bans. 234 DD118
Park La., Beac. 89 AM54
Park La., Brox. 49 DY19
Park La. (Wormley), Brox. 48 DV22
Park La., Cars. 218 DG105
Park La., Couls. 235 DK121
Park La., Croy. 202 DR104
Park La., Guil. 243 BC131
Park La., Harl. 35 ER13
Park La., Har. 116 CB62
Park La., Hayes 135 BS71
Park La., Hem.H. 40 BK21
Park La., Horn. 127 FF58
Park La. (Elm Pk.), Horn. 147 FH65
Park La., Houns. 155 BU80
Park La., Reig. 265 CY135
Park La., Rich. 157 CK84
Park La. (Chadwell Heath), Rom. 126 EX58
Park La., St.Alb. 44 CP23
Park La., Sev. 257 FJ124
Park La. (Seal), Sev. 257 FN121
Park La., Slou. 152 AV76
Park La. (Burnham), Slou. 111 AL64
Park La. (Horton), Slou. 153 BA83
Park La., S.Ock. 149 FR73
Park La., Stan. 95 CG48
Park La., Sutt. 217 CY107
Park La., Swan. 208 FJ96
Park La., Tedd. 177 CF93
Park La., Uxb. 92 BG53
Park La., Wal.Cr. 66 DW33
Park La. (Cheshunt), Wal.Cr. 66 DU26
Park La., Wem. 118 CL64
Park La. Clo. N17 100 DU52
Park La. E., Reig. 265 CZ137
Park La. Paradise (Cheshunt), Wal.Cr. 66 DU25
Park Lawn Ave., Horl. 268 DF146
Park Lawn Rd., Wey. 213 BQ105
Park Lawns, Wem. 118 CM63
Park Ley Rd., Cat. 237 DX120
Park Mead, Harl. 35 EP14
Park Mead, Har. 116 CB62
Park Mead, Sid. 186 EV85
Park Meadow, Hat. 45 CW17
Park Ms. SE24 182 DQ86
Croxted Rd.
Park Ms., Chis. 185 EP93
Park Rd.
Park Ms., E.Mol. 196 CC98
Park Ms., Hmptn. 176 CC92
Park Rd.
Park Ms., Hat. 45 CW16
Park Nook Gdns., Enf. 82 DR37
Park Par. NW10 139 CT68
Park Pl. E14 143 EA74
Park Pl. SW1 277 K3
Park Pl. SW1 141 DJ74
Park Pl. W3 158 CN77
Park Pl. W5 137 CK74
Park Pl., Amer. 72 AT38
Park Pl., Grav. 191 GJ86
Park Pl., Hmptn. 176 CC93
Park Pl., St.Alb. 61 CD27
Park Pl., Sev. 256 FD123
Park Pl., Wem. 118 CM63
Park Pl. Vill. W2 140 DC71
Park Ridings N8 121 DN55
Park Ri. SE23 183 DY88
Park Ri., Berk. 38 AS17
Park Ri., Har. 95 CE53
Park Ri., Lthd. 231 CH121
Park Ri. Clo., Lthd. 231 CH121
Park Ri. Rd. SE23 183 DY88
Park Rd. E6 144 EJ67
Park Rd. E10 123 EA60
Park Rd. E12 124 EH60
Park Rd. E15 144 EG67
Park Rd. E17 123 DZ57
Park Rd. N2 120 DD55
Park Rd. N8 121 DJ56
Park Rd. N11 99 DK52
Park Rd. N14 99 DK45
Park Rd. N15 121 DP56
Park Rd. N18 100 DT49
Park Rd. NW1 272 D4
Park Rd. NW1 140 DF70
Park Rd. NW4 119 CU59
Park Rd. NW8 272 B2
Park Rd. NW8 140 DE69
Park Rd. NW9 118 CR59
Park Rd. NW10 138 CS67
Park Rd. SE25 202 DS98
Park Rd. SW19 180 DD94
Park Rd. W4 158 CQ80
Park Rd. W7 137 CF73
Park Rd., Amer. 72 AT37
Park Rd., Ashf. 175 BP92
Park Rd., Ash. 232 CL118
Park Rd., Bans. 234 DB115
Park Rd., Barn. 79 CZ42
Park Rd. (New Barnet), Barn. 80 DD42
Park Rd., Beck. 183 DZ94
Park Rd., Brwd. 108 FV46
Park Rd., Brom. 204 EH95
Park Rd., Cat. 236 DS123
Park Rd., Chesh. 54 AP31
Park Rd., Chis. 185 EP93
Park Rd., Dart. 188 FN87
Park Rd., E.Mol. 196 CC98
Park Rd., Egh. 173 BA91
Park Rd., Enf. 83 DY36
Park Rd., Esher 214 CB105
Park Rd., Felt. 176 BX91
Park Rd., Grav. 191 GH88
Park Rd., Grays 170 GB78
Park Rd., Guil. 242 AX134
Park Rd. (Albury), Guil. 260 BL140
Park Rd., Hmptn. 176 CB91
Park Rd., Hayes 135 BS71
Park Rd., Hem.H. 40 BJ22
Park Rd., Hert. 32 DS09
Park Rd., Hodd. 49 EA17
Park Rd., Houns. 176 CB85
Park Rd., Ilf. 125 ER62
Park Rd., Islw. 157 CH81
Park Rd., Ken. 235 DP115
Park Rd., Kings.T. 178 CM92
Park Rd. (Hampton Wick), Kings.T. 197 CJ95
Park Rd., N.Mal. 198 CR98
Park Rd., Orp. 206 EW99
Park Rd., Oxt. 254 EF128
Park Rd., Pot.B. 64 DG30
Park Rd., Rad. 77 CG35
Park Rd., Red. 250 DF132
Park Rd., Rich. 178 CM86
Park Rd., Rick. 92 BK45
Park Rd., Shep. 194 BN102
Park Rd., Slou. 131 AQ68
Park Rd., Stai. 174 BH86
Park Rd., Sun. 175 BV94
Park Rd., Surb. 198 CM100
Park Rd., Sutt. 217 CY107
Park Rd., Swan. 207 FF98
Park Rd., Swans. 190 FY86
Park Rd., Tedd. 177 CF94
Park Rd., Twick. 177 CJ86
Park Rd., Uxb. 134 BL66
Park Rd., Wall. 219 DH106
Park Rd. (Hackbridge), Wall. 201 DH103
Park Rd., Wal.Cr. 67 DX33
Park Rd., Ware 32 DV05
Park Rd., Warl. 222 EE114
Park Rd., Wat. 75 BV39
Park Rd. (Bushey), Wat. 76 CA44
Park Rd., Wem. 138 CL65
Park Rd., Wok. 227 AZ117
Park Rd. E. W3 158 CP75
Park Rd. E., Uxb. 134 BK68
Hillingdon Rd.
Park Rd. N. W3 158 CP75
Park Rd. N. W4 158 CR78
Park Rd. W., Kings.T. 197 CJ95
Park Row SE10 163 ED79
Park Royal Rd. NW10 138 CQ70
Park Royal Rd. W3 138 CQ70
Park Side, Add. 212 BH111
Park Side, Sutt. 217 CY107
Park Sq., Esher 214 CB105
Park Rd.
Park Sq. E. NW1 273 H4
Park Sq. E. NW1 141 DH70
Park Sq. Ms. NW1 273 H5
Park Sq. Ms. NW1 141 DH70
Park Sq. W. NW1 273 H4
Park Sq. W. NW1 141 DH70
Park St. SE1 279 H2
Park St. SE1 142 DQ74
Park St. W1 272 F10
Park St. W1 140 DG73
Park St., Berk. 38 AV18
Park St., Croy. 202 DQ103
Park St., Guil. 258 AW136
Park St., Hat. 45 CW17
Park St., St.Alb. 61 CD26
Park St., Slou. 152 AT76
Park St. (Colnbrook), Slou. 153 BD80
Park St., Tedd. 177 CE93
Park St., Wind. 151 AR81
Park St. La., St.Alb. 60 CB30
Park Ter., Green. 189 FV85
Park Ter. (Sundridge), Sev. 240 EX124
Main Rd.
Park Ter., Wor.Pk. 199 CU102
Park Vw. N21 99 DM45
Park Vw. W3 138 CQ71
Park Vw., Hat. 45 CW16
Park Vw., Hodd. 49 EA18
Park Vw., Horl. 268 DG148
Brighton Rd.
Park Vw., Lthd. 246 CA125
Park Vw., N.Mal. 199 CT97
Park Vw., Pnr. 94 BZ53
Park Vw., Pot.B. 64 DC33
Park Vw., S.Ock. 149 FR74
Park Vw., Wem. 118 CP64
Park Vw. Clo., St.Alb. 43 CG21
Cell Barnes La.
Park Vw. Ct., Ilf. 125 ES58
Brancaster Rd.
Park Vw. Ct., Wok. 227 AZ119
Park Vw. Cres. N11 99 DH49
Park Vw. Est. E2 143 DX68
Sewardstone Rd.
Park Vw. Gdns. NW4 119 CX58
Park Vw. Gdns., Bark. 145 ES68
River Rd.
Park Vw. Gdns., Grays 170 GB78
Park Vw. Gdns., Ilf. 125 EM56
Woodford Ave.
Park Vw. Rd. N3 98 DB53
Park Vw. Rd. N17 122 DU55
Park Vw. Rd. NW10 119 CT63
Park Vw. Rd. W5 138 CL71
Park Vw. Rd., Berk. 38 AV19
Park Vw. Rd., Cat. 237 DY122
Park Vw. Rd., Pnr. 93 BV52
Park Vw. Rd., Red. 266 DG141
Park Vw. Rd., Sthl. 136 CA74
Park Vw. Rd., Uxb. 134 BN72
Stockley Rd.
Park Vw. Rd., Well. 166 EV83
Park Village E. NW1 141 DH68
Park Village W. NW1 141 DH68
Park Vill., Rom. 126 EX58
Park Vista SE10 163 ED79
Park Wk. N6 120 DG59
North Rd.
Park Wk. SW10 160 DC79
Park Wk., Ash. 232 CM119
Rectory La.
Park Way N20 98 DF49
Park Way NW11 119 CY57
Park Way, Bex. 187 FE90
Park Way, Brwd. 109 FZ46
Park Way, Edg. 96 CP53
Park Way, Enf. 81 DN40
Park Way, Felt. 175 BV87
Park Way, Horl. 268 DG148
Park Way, Ilf. 125 ET62
Park Way, Lthd. 230 CA123
Park Way, Rick. 92 BJ46
Park Way, Ruis. 115 BU60
Park Way, W.Mol. 196 CB97
Park W. W2 272 A9
Park W. Pl. W2 272 C8
Park Wks. Rd., Red. 251 DM133
Parkcroft Rd. SE12 184 EF87
Parkdale Cres., Wor.Pk. 198 CR104
Parkdale Rd. SE18 165 ES78
Parke Rd. SW13 159 CU81
Parke Rd., Sun. 195 BU98
Parker Ave., Hert. 32 DR07
Parker Ave., Til. 171 GJ81
Parker Clo. E16 144 EL74
Parker Ms. WC2 274 A8
Parker Rd., Croy. 220 DQ105
Parker Rd., Grays 170 FZ78
Parker St. E16 144 EL74
Parker St. WC2 274 A8
Parker St. WC2 141 DL72
Parker St., Wat. 75 BV39
Parkers Clo., Ash. 232 CL119
Parkers Hill, Ash. 232 CL119
Parkers La., Ash. 232 CL119
Parkers Row SE1 162 DT75
Jamaica Rd.
Parkes Rd., Chig. 103 ES50
Parkfield, Rick. 73 BF42
Parkfield, Sev. 257 FM123
Parkfield Ave. SW14 158 CS84
Parkfield Ave., Amer. 55 AR37
Parkfield Ave., Felt. 175 BU90
Parkfield Ave., Har. 94 CC54
Parkfield Ave., Nthlt. 136 BX68
Parkfield Ave., Uxb. 135 BP69
Parkfield Clo., Edg. 96 CP51
Parkfield Clo., Nthlt. 136 BY68
Parkfield Cres., Felt. 175 BU90
Parkfield Cres., Har. 94 CC54
Parkfield Cres., Ruis. 116 BY62
Parkfield Dr., Nthlt. 136 BX68
Parkfield Gdns., Har. 116 CB55
Parkfield Rd. NW10 139 CU66
Parkfield Rd. SE14 163 DZ81
Parkfield Rd., Felt. 175 BU90
Parkfield Rd., Har. 116 CC62
Parkfield Rd., Nthlt. 136 BY68
Parkfield Rd., Uxb. 115 BP61
Parkfield St. N1 141 DN68
Parkfield Way, Brom. 205 EM100
Parkfields SW15 159 CW84
Parkfields, Croy. 203 DZ102
Parkfields, Lthd. 215 CD111
Parkfields, Welw.G.C. 29 CX09
Parkfields Ave. NW9 118 CR60
Parkfields Ave. SW20 199 CV96
Parkfields Clo., Cars. 218 DG105
Devonshire Rd.
Parkfields Rd., Kings.T. 178 CM92
Parkgate SE3 164 EF83
Parkgate, Slou. 130 AJ70
Parkgate Ave., Barn. 80 DC39
Parkgate Cres., Barn. 80 DC39
Parkgate Gdns. SW14 178 CR85
Parkgate Rd. SW11 160 DE80
Parkgate Rd., Orp. 225 FB105
Parkgate Rd., Reig. 266 DB135
Parkgate Rd., Wall. 218 DG106
Parkgate Rd., Wat. 76 BW37
Parkham Ct., Brom. 204 EE96
Parkham St. SW11 160 DD81
Parkhill Clo., Horn. 128 FJ62
Parkhill Rd. E4 101 EC46
Parkhill Rd. NW3 120 DF64
Parkhill Rd., Bex. 186 EZ87
Parkhill Rd., Epsom 217 CT111
Parkhill Wk. NW3 120 DF64
Parkholme Rd. E8 142 DU65
Parkhouse St. SE5 162 DR80
Parkhurst, Epsom 216 CQ110
Parkhurst Gdns., Bex. 186 FA87
Parkhurst Gro., Horl. 268 DE147
Parkhurst Rd. E12 125 EN63
Parkhurst Rd. E17 123 DY56
Parkhurst Rd. N7 121 DL63
Parkhurst Rd. N11 98 DG49
Parkhurst Rd. N17 100 DU54
Parkhurst Rd. N22 99 DM51
Parkhurst Rd., Bex. 186 FA87
Parkhurst Rd., Guil. 242 AU133
Parkhurst Rd., Hert. 31 DP08
Parkhurst Rd., Horl. 268 DE147
Parkhurst Rd., Sutt. 218 DD105
Parkland Ave., Rom. 127 FE55
Parkland Ave., Slou. 152 AX77
Parkland Ave., Upmin. 128 FP64
Parkland Clo., Chig. 103 EQ48
Parkland Clo., Hodd. 33 EB14
Parkland Clo., Sev. 257 FJ129
Parkland Dr., St.Alb. 42 CA21
Parkland Gdns. SW19 179 CX88
Parkland Gro., Ashf. 174 BN91
Parkland Rd. N22 99 DM54
Parkland Rd., Ashf. 174 BN91
Parkland Rd., Wdf.Grn. 102 EG52
Parkland Wk. N4 121 DN59
Parkland Wk. N6 121 DJ59
Parkland Wk. N10 121 DH56
Parklands N6 121 DH59
Parklands, Add. 212 BJ106
Parklands, Chig. 103 EQ48
Parklands, Epp. 70 EX29
Parklands, Lthd. 230 CA123
Parklands, Oxt. 254 EE131
Parklands, Surb. 198 CM99
Parklands, Wal.Abb. 67 EC33
Parklands Clo. SW14 178 CQ85
Parklands Clo., Barn. 80 DD38
Parklands Ct., Houns. 156 BX82
Parklands Dr. N3 119 CY55
Parklands Pl., Guil. 243 BB134
Parklands Rd. SW16 181 DH92
Parklands Way, Wor.Pk. 198 CS103
Parklawn Ave., Epsom 216 CP113
Parklea Clo. NW9 96 CS53
Parkleigh Rd. SW19 200 DB96
Parkleys, Rich. 177 CK91
Parkmead SW15 179 CV86
Parkmead, Loug. 85 EN43
Parkmead Gdns. NW7 97 CT51
Parkmore Clo., Wdf.Grn. 102 EG49
Parkpale La., Bet. 264 CN139
Parkshot, Rich. 158 CL84
Parkside N3 98 DB53
Parkside NW2 119 CU62
Parkside NW7 97 CU51
Parkside SE3 164 EF80
Parkside SW19 179 CX91
Parkside, Buck.H. 102 EH47
Parkside, Ger.Cr. 113 AZ56
Lower Rd.
Parkside, Grays 170 GD76
Parkside, Hmptn. 177 CD92
Parkside, Pot.B. 64 DC32
High St.
Parkside, Sev. 224 EZ113
Parkside, Sid. 186 EV89
Parkside, Wal.Cr. 67 DY34
Parkside, Wat. 76 BW44
Parkside Ave. SW19 179 CX92
Parkside Ave., Bexh. 167 FD82
Parkside Ave., Brom. 204 EL98
Parkside Ave., Rom. 127 FD55
Parkside Ave., Til. 171 GH82
Parkside Clo. SE20 182 DW94
Parkside Clo., Lthd. 245 BT125
Parkside Ct., Wey. 212 BN105
Parkside Cres. N7 121 DN62
Isledon Rd.
Parkside Cres., Surb. 198 CQ100
Parkside Cross, Bexh. 167 FE82
Parkside Dr., Edg. 96 CN48
Parkside Dr., Wat. 75 BS40
Parkside Est. E9 142 DW67
Rutland Rd.
Parkside Gdns. SW19 179 CX91
Parkside Gdns., Barn. 98 DF46
Parkside Gdns., Couls. 235 DH117
Parkside Ho., Dag. 127 FC62
Parkside Pl., Lthd. 245 BT125
Parkside Rd. SW11 160 DG81
Parkside Rd., Belv. 167 FB77
Parkside Rd., Houns. 176 CB85
Parkside Rd., Nthwd. 93 BT50
Parkside Ter. N18 100 DR49
Great Cambridge Rd.
Parkside Way, Har. 116 CB56
Parkstead Rd. SW15 179 CU85
Parkstone Ave. N18 100 DT50
Parkstone Ave., Horn. 128 FK58
Parkstone Rd. E17 123 EC55
Parkstone Rd. SE15 162 DU82
Rye La.
Parkthorne Clo., Har. 116 CB58
Parkthorne Dr., Har. 116 CA58
Parkthorne Rd. SW12 181 DK87
Parkview, St.Alb. 43 CG21
Parkview Chase, Slou. 131 AL72
Parkview Ct. SW18 180 DA86
Broomhill Rd.

Pembroke Clo. SW1 160 DG75
Pembroke Clo., Bans. 234 DB117
Pembroke Clo., Brox. 49 DY23
Pembroke Clo., Erith 167 FD77
Pembroke Clo., Horn. 128 FM56
Pembroke Dr. (Cheshunt), Wal.Cr. 65 DP29
Pembroke Gdns. W8 159 CZ77
Pembroke Gdns., Dag. 127 FB62
Pembroke Gdns., Wok. 227 BA118
Pembroke Gdns. Clo. W8 159 CZ76
Pembroke Ms. E3 143 DY69
Morgan St.
Pembroke Ms. N10 98 DG53
Pembroke Rd.
Pembroke Ms. W8 160 DA76
Earls Wk.
Pembroke Ms., Sev. 257 FH125
Pembroke Rd.
Pembroke Pl. W8 160 DA76
Pembroke Pl. (Sutton at Hone), Dart. 208 FP95
Pembroke Pl., Edg. 96 CN52
Pembroke Pl., Islw. 157 CE82
Clifton Rd.
Pembroke Rd. E6 145 EM71
Pembroke Rd. E17 123 EB57
Pembroke Rd. N8 121 DL56
Pembroke Rd. N10 98 DG53
Pembroke Rd. N13 100 DQ48
Pembroke Rd. N15 122 DT57
Pembroke Rd. SE25 202 DS98
Pembroke Rd. W8 160 DA77
Pembroke Rd., Brom. 204 EJ96
Pembroke Rd., Erith 167 FC78
Pembroke Rd., Grnf. 136 CB69
Pembroke Rd., Ilf. 125 ET60
Pembroke Rd., Mitch. 200 DG96
Pembroke Rd., Nthwd. 93 BQ48
Pembroke Rd., Ruis. 115 BS60
Pembroke Rd., Sev. 257 FH125
Pembroke Rd., Wem. 117 CK62
Pembroke Rd., Wok. 227 BA118
Pembroke Sq. W8 160 DA76
Pembroke St. N1 141 DL66
Pembroke Studios W8 159 CZ76
Pembroke Vill. W8 160 DA77
Pembroke Vill., Rich. 157 CK84
Pembroke Wk. W8 160 DA77
Pembroke Way, Hayes 155 BQ76
Pembury Ave., Wor.Pk. 199 CU102
Pembury Clo., Brom. 204 EF101
Pembury Clo., Couls. 218 DG114
Pembury Ct., Hayes 155 BR79
Pembury Cres., Sid. 186 EY90
Pembury Pl. E5 122 DV64
Pembury Rd. E5 122 DV64
Pembury Rd. N17 100 DT53
Pembury Rd. SE25 202 DU98
Pembury Rd., Bexh. 166 EY80
Pemdevon Rd., Croy. 201 DN101
Pemell Clo. E1 142 DW70
Colebert Ave.
Pemerich Clo., Hayes 155 BT78
Pempath Pl., Wem. 117 CK61
Pemsel Ct., Hem.H. 40 BK22
Crabtree La.
Penally Pl. N1 142 DR67
Shepperton Rd.
Penang St. E1 142 DV74
Penarth St. SE15 162 DW79
Penates, Esher 215 CD105
Penberth Rd. SE6 183 EC88
Penbury Rd., Sthl. 156 BZ77
Pencombe Ms. W11 139 CZ73
Denbigh Rd.
Pencraig Way SE15 162 DV79
Pencroft Dr., Dart. 188 FJ87
Shepherds La.
Penda Rd., Erith 167 FB80
Pendarves Rd. SW20 199 CW95
Penda's Mead E9 123 DY63
Lindisfarne Way
Pendell Ave., Hayes 155 BT80
Pendell Rd., Red. 251 DP131
Pendennis Clo., W.Byf. 212 BG114
Pendennis Rd. N17 122 DR55
Pendennis Rd. SW16 181 DL91
Pendennis Rd., Orp. 206 EW103
Pendennis Rd., Sev. 257 FH123
Penderel Rd., Houns. 176 CA85
Penderry Ri. SE6 183 ED89
Penderyn Way N7 121 DK63
Pendle Rd. SW16 181 DH93
Pendlestone Rd. E17 123 EB57
Pendleton Clo., Red. 266 DF136
Church Rd.
Pendleton Rd., Red. 266 DC137
Pendleton Rd., Reig. 266 DC137
Pendragon Rd., Brom. 184 EF90
Pendragon Wk. NW9 118 CS58
Pendrell Rd. SE4 163 DY82
Pendrell St. SE18 165 ER79
Pendula Dr., Hayes 136 BX70
Pendulum Ms. E8 122 DT64
Birkbeck Rd.
Penerley Rd. SE6 183 EB88
Penerley Rd., Rain. 147 FH71
Penfold Clo., Croy. 201 DN104
Epsom Rd.
Penfold La., Bex. 186 EX88
Carisbrooke Ave.
Penfold Pl. NW1 272 B6
Penfold Pl. NW1 140 DE71
Penfold Rd. N9 101 DX46
Penfold St. NW1 272 A5
Penfold St. NW1 140 DD70
Penfold St. NW8 272 A5
Penfold St. NW8 140 DD70
Penford Gdns. SE9 164 EK83
Penford St. SE5 161 DP82
Pengarth Rd., Bex. 186 EX85
Penge Ho. SW11 160 DD83
Wye St.
Penge La. SE20 182 DW94
Penge Rd. E13 144 EJ67
Penge Rd. SE20 202 DU97
Penge Rd. SE25 202 DU97
Pengelly Clo. (Cheshunt), Wal.Cr. 66 DV30
Penhall Rd. SE7 164 EK77
Penhill Rd., Bex. 186 EW86
Penhurst, Wok. 211 AZ114
Penhurst Rd., Ilf. 103 EP52
Penifather La., Grnf. 137 CD69
Peninsular Clo., Felt. 175 BR86
Penistone Rd. SW16 181 DL94
Penistone Wk., Rom. 106 FJ51
Okehampton Rd.
Penketh Dr., Har. 117 CD62
Penlow Rd., Harl. 51 EQ18
Penman Clo., St.Alb. 60 CA27
Penmon Rd. SE2 166 EU76
Penn Ave., Chesh. 54 AN30
Penn Bottom, H.Wyc. 88 AG45
Penn Clo., Grnf. 136 CB68
Penn Clo., Har. 117 CJ56
Penn Clo., Rick. 73 BD44
Penn Clo., Uxb. 134 BK70
Penn Dr., Uxb. 113 BF58
Penn Gdns., Chis. 205 EP96
Penn Gdns., Rom. 104 FA52
Penn Gaskell La., Ger.Cr. 91 AZ50
Penn La., Bex. 186 EX86
Penn Meadow, Slou. 132 AT67
Penn Pl., Rick. 92 BK45
Northway
Penn Rd. N7 121 DL64
Penn Rd., Beac. 88 AJ48
Penn Rd., Ger.Cr. 90 AX53
Penn Rd., Rick. 91 BF46
Penn Rd., St.Alb. 60 CC27
Penn Rd., Slou. 131 AR70
Penn Rd. (Datchet), Slou. 152 AX81
Penn Rd., Wat. 75 BV39
Penn St. N1 142 DR67
Penn Way, Rick. 73 BD44
Pennack Rd. SE15 162 DT79
Pennant Ms. W8 160 DB77
Pennant Ter. E17 101 DZ54
Pennard Rd. W12 159 CW75
Pennards, The, Sun. 196 BW96
Penne Clo., Rad. 61 CF34
Goodyers Ave.
Penner Clo. SW19 179 CY89
Victoria Dr.
Pennethorne Clo. E9 142 DW67
Victoria Pk. Rd.
Pennethorne Rd. SE15 162 DV80
Penney Clo., Dart. 188 FK87
Pennine Dr. NW2 119 CX61
Pennine La. NW2 119 CY61
Pennine Dr.
Pennine Rd., Slou. 131 AN71
Pennine Way, Bexh. 167 FE81
Pennine Way, Grav. 190 GE90
Pennine Way, Hayes 155 BR80
Pennine Way, Hem.H. 40 BM17
Pennings Ave., Guil. 242 AT132
Pennington Clo. SE27 182 DR91
Hamilton Rd.
Pennington Clo., Rom. 104 FA51
Pennington Dr. N21 81 DM43
Worlds End La.
Pennington Dr., Wey. 195 BS104
Pennington Rd., Beac. 110 AH55
Pennington Rd., Ger.Cr. 90 AX52
Pennington St. E1 142 DU73
Pennington Way SE12 184 EJ89
Penningtons, The, Amer. 55 AS37
Pennis La. (Fawkham), Long. 209 FW100
Penniston Clo. N17 100 DQ54
Westbury Ave.
Penny Clo., Rain. 147 FH69
Penny La., Shep. 195 BS101
Walton Bri. Rd.
Penny Ms. SW12 181 DH87
Caistor Rd.
Penny Rd. NW10 138 CP69
Pennycroft, Croy. 221 DY109
Pennyfield, Cob. 213 BU113
Pennyfields E14 143 EA73
Pennyfields, Brwd. 108 FW49
Pennylets Grn., Slou. 132 AT66
Pennymead, Harl. 36 EU14
Pennymead Dr., Lthd. 245 BT127
Pennymead Ri., Lthd. 245 BT127
Pennymoor Wk. W9 139 CZ69
Ashmore Rd.
Pennyroyal Ave. E6 145 EN72
Pennys La., Saw. 35 ER05
Penpoll Rd. E8 142 DV65
Penpool La., Well. 166 EV83
Penrhyn Ave. E17 101 DZ53
Penrhyn Cres. E17 101 EA53
Penrhyn Cres. SW14 158 CQ84
Penrhyn Gro. E17 101 EA53
Penrhyn Rd., Kings.T. 198 CL98
Penrith Clo. SW15 179 CY85
Penrith Clo., Beck. 203 EB95
Albemarle Rd.
Penrith Clo., Reig. 250 DE133
Penrith Clo., Uxb. 134 BK66
Chippendale Waye
Penrith Cres., Rain. 127 FG64
Penrith Pl. SE27 181 DP89
Harpenden Rd.
Penrith Rd. N15 122 DR57
Penrith Rd., Ilf. 103 ET51
Penrith Rd., N.Mal. 198 CR98
Penrith Rd., Rom. 106 FN51
Penrith Rd., Th.Hth. 202 DQ96
Penrith St. SW16 181 DJ93
Penrose Ave., Wat. 94 BX47
Penrose Ct., Hem.H. 40 BL16
Penrose Gro. SE17 162 DQ78
Penrose Ho. SE17 162 DQ78
Penrose St.
Penrose Rd., Lthd. 230 CC122
Penrose St. SE17 162 DQ78
Penry St. SE1 279 N9
Penryn St. NW1 141 DK68
Pensbury Pl. SW8 161 DJ82
Pensbury St. SW8 161 DJ82
Penscroft Gdns., Borwd. 78 CR42
Pensford Ave., Rich. 158 CN82
Penshurst, Harl. 36 EV12
Penshurst Ave., Sid. 186 EU86
Penshurst Clo., Ger.Cr. 90 AX54
Penshurst Gdns., Edg. 96 CP50
Penshurst Grn., Brom. 204 EF99
Penshurst Rd. E9 143 DX66
Penshurst Rd. N17 100 DT52
Penshurst Rd., Bexh. 166 EZ81
Penshurst Rd., Pot.B. 64 DD31
Penshurst Rd., Th.Hth. 201 DP99
Penshurst Wk., Brom. 204 EF99
Hayesford Pk. Dr.
Penshurst Way, Orp. 206 EW98
Star La.
Penshurst Way, Sutt. 218 DA108
Pensons La., Ong. 71 FG28
Penstemon Clo. N3 98 DA53
Nether St.
Penstock Footpath N22 121 DL55
Pentavia Retail Pk. NW7 97 CT52
Bunns La.
Pentelowe Gdns., Felt. 175 BU86
Pentire Clo., Upmin. 129 FS58
Pentire Rd. E17 101 ED53
Pentland, Hem.H. 40 BM17
Mendip Way
Pentland Ave., Edg. 96 CP47
Pentland Ave., Shep. 194 BN99
Pentland Clo. NW11 119 CY61
Pentland Gdns. SW18 180 DC86
St. Ann's Hill
Pentland Pl., Nthlt. 136 BY67
Pentland Rd., Slou. 131 AN71
Pentland Rd. (Bushey), Wat. 76 CC44
Pentland St. SW18 180 DC86
Pentland Way, Uxb. 115 BQ62
Pentlands Clo., Mitch. 201 DH97
Pentley Clo., Welw.G.C. 29 CX06
Pentley Pk., Welw.G.C. 29 CX07
Pentlow St. SW15 159 CW83
Pentlow Way, Buck.H. 102 EL45
Pentney Rd. E4 101 ED46
Pentney Rd. SW12 181 DJ88
Pentney Rd. SW19 199 CY95
Midmoor Rd.
Penton Ave., Stai. 173 BF94
Penton Dr. (Cheshunt), Wal.Cr. 67 DX29
Penton Gro. N1 274 D1
Penton Hall Dr., Stai. 194 BG95
Penton Hook Rd., Stai. 174 BG94
Penton Pk. Est., Cher. 194 BH97
Penton Pl. SE17 278 G10
Penton Pl. SE17 161 DP78
Penton Ri. WC1 274 C2
Penton Ri. WC1 141 DM69
Penton Rd., Stai. 173 BF94
Penton St. N1 274 D1
Penton St. N1 141 DN68
Pentonville Rd. N1 274 B1
Pentonville Rd. N1 141 DM68
Pentrich Ave., Enf. 82 DU38
Pentridge St. SE15 162 DT80
Pentyre Ave. N18 100 DR50
Penwerris Ave., Islw. 156 CC80
Penwith Rd. SW18 180 DA89
Penwith Wk., Wok. 226 AX119
Wych Hill Pk.
Penwood End, Wok. 226 AV121
Penwortham Rd. SW16 181 DH93
Penwortham Rd., S.Croy. 220 DQ110
Penylan Pl., Edg. 96 CN52
Penywern Rd. SW5 160 DA78
Penzance Clo., Uxb. 92 BK53
Penzance Gdns., Rom. 106 FN51
Penzance Pl. W11 139 CY74
Penzance Rd., Rom. 106 FN51
Penzance Spur, Slou. 131 AP70
Penzance St. W11 139 CY74
Peony Clo., Brwd. 108 FV44
Peony Ct., Wdf.Grn. 102 EE52
Bridle Path
Peony Gdns. W12 139 CU73
Peplins Clo., Hat. 63 CY26
Peplins Way, Hat. 63 CY25
Peploe Rd. NW6 139 CX68
Peplow Clo., West Dr. 134 BK74
Tavistock Rd.
Pepper All., Loug. 84 EF40
Pepper Clo. E6 145 EM71
Pepper Clo., Cat. 252 DS125
Harestone La.
Pepper Hill, Grav. 190 GC90
Pepper Hill, Ware 33 DZ10
Pepper St. E14 163 EB76
Pepper St. SE1 279 H4
Pepperhill La., Grav. 190 GC90
Peppermead Sq. SE13 183 EB85
Ladywell Rd.
Peppermint Clo., Croy. 201 DL101
Peppermint Pl. E11 124 EE62
Cathall Rd.
Peppie Clo. N16 122 DS61
Bouverie Rd.
Pepys Clo., Ash. 232 CN117
Pepys Clo., Dart. 168 FN84
Keyes Rd.
Pepys Clo., Grav. 190 GD90
Pepys Clo., Slou. 153 BB79
Pepys Clo., Til. 171 GJ81
Pepys Clo., Uxb. 115 BP63
Pepys Cres., Barn. 79 CW43
Pepys Ri., Orp. 205 ET102
Pepys Rd. SE14 163 DX81
Pepys Rd. SW20 199 CW96
Pepys St. EC3 275 N10
Pepys St. EC3 142 DS73
Perceval Ave. NW3 120 DE64
Perch St. E8 122 DT63
Percheron Clo., Islw. 157 CF83
St. John's Rd.
Percheron Rd., Borwd. 78 CR44
Percival Ct. N17 100 DT52
High Rd.
Percival Ct., Nthlt. 116 CA64
Percival Gdns., Rom. 126 EW58
Percival Rd. SW14 158 CQ84
Percival Rd., Enf. 82 DT42
Percival Rd., Felt. 175 BT89
Percival Rd., Horn. 128 FJ58
Percival Rd., Orp. 205 EP103
Percival St. EC1 274 F4
Percival St. EC1 141 DP70
Percival Way, Epsom 216 CQ105
Percy Ave., Ashf. 174 BN92
Percy Bryant Rd., Sun. 175 BS94
Percy Bush Rd., West Dr. 154 BM76
Porters Way
Percy Circ. WC1 274 C2
Percy Circ. WC1 141 DM69
Percy Gdns., Enf. 83 DX43
Percy Gdns., Hayes 135 BS69
Percy Gdns., Islw. 157 CG83
Percy Gdns., Wor.Pk. 198 CS102
Percy Ms. W1 273 M7
Percy Pas. W1 273 L7
Percy Pl., Slou. 152 AV81
Percy Rd. E11 124 EE59
Percy Rd. E16 144 EE71
Percy Rd. N12 98 DC50
Percy Rd. N21 100 DQ45
Percy Rd. NW6 140 DA69
Stafford Rd.
Percy Rd. SE20 203 DX95
Percy Rd. SE25 202 DU99
Percy Rd. W12 159 CU75
Percy Rd., Bexh. 166 EY82
Percy Rd., Guil. 242 AV132
Percy Rd., Hmptn. 176 CA94
Percy Rd., Ilf. 126 EU59
Percy Rd., Islw. 157 CG84
Percy Rd., Mitch. 200 DG101
Percy Rd., Rom. 127 FB55
Percy Rd., Twick. 176 CB88
Percy Rd., Wat. 75 BV42
Percy St. W1 273 M7
Percy St. W1 141 DK71
Percy St., Grays 170 GC79
Percy Ter., Ch.St.G. 90 AU48
Sycamore Rd.
Percy Way, Twick. 176 CC88
Percy Yd. WC1 274 C2
Peregrin Rd., Wal.Abb. 68 EG34
Peregrine Clo. NW10 118 CR64
Peregrine Clo., Wat. 60 BY34
Peregrine Ct. SW16 181 DM91
Leithcote Gdns.
Peregrine Ct., Well. 165 ET81
Peregrine Gdns., Croy. 203 DY103
Peregrine Ho. EC1 274 G2
Peregrine Ho. EC1 141 DP69
Peregrine Rd., Ilf. 104 EV50
Peregrine Rd., Sun. 195 BT96
Peregrine Wk., Horn. 147 FH65
Heron Flight Ave.
Peregrine Way SW19 179 CW94
Perham Rd. W14 159 CY78
Perham Way, St.Alb. 61 CK26
Peridot St. E6 144 EL71
Perifield SE21 182 DQ88
Perimeade Rd., Grnf. 137 CJ68
Perimeter Rd. E., Gat. 268 DG154
Perimeter Rd. N., Gat. 268 DD151
Perimeter Rd. S., Gat. 268 DC154
Periton Rd. SE9 164 EK84
Perivale Gdns. W13 137 CH70
Bellevue Rd.
Perivale Gdns., Wat. 59 BV34
Perivale Gra., Grnf. 137 CG69
Perivale Ind. Pk., Grnf. 137 CG67
Perivale La., Grnf. 137 CG69
Perivale New Business Cen., Grnf. 137 CH68
Perkins Clo., Green. 189 FT85
Perkins Clo., Wem. 117 CH64
Perkins Ct., Ashf. 174 BM92
Perkin's Rents SW1 277 M6
Perkin's Rents SW1 161 DK76
Perkins Rd., Ilf. 125 ER57
Perkins Sq. SE1 279 J2
Perks Clo. SE3 164 EE83
Hurren Clo.
Perleybrooke La., Wok. 226 AU117
Bampton Way
Perpins Rd. SE9 185 ER86
Perram Clo., Brox. 67 DY26
Perran Rd. SW2 181 DP89
Christchurch Rd.
Perran Wk., Brent. 158 CL78
Burford Rd.
Perren St. NW5 141 DH65
Ryland Rd.
Perrers Rd. W6 159 CV77
Perrin Clo., Ashf. 174 BM92
Fordbridge Rd.
Perrin Rd., Wem. 117 CG63
Perrins Ct. NW3 120 DC63
Hampstead High St.
Perrins La. NW3 120 DC63
Perrin's Wk. NW3 120 DC63
Perrior Rd., Gdmg. 258 AS144
Perriors Clo. (Cheshunt), Wal.Cr. 66 DU27
Perrott St. SE18 165 EQ77
Plumstead Rd.
Perry Ave. W3 138 CR72
Perry Clo., Rain. 147 FD68
Lowen Rd.
Perry Clo., Uxb. 135 BQ72
Harlington Rd.
Perry Ct. N15 122 DS58
Albert Rd.
Perry Cft., Wind. 151 AL83
Perry Gdns. N9 100 DS48
Deansway
Perry Garth, Nthlt. 136 BW67
Perry Gro., Dart. 168 FN84
Perry Hall Clo., Orp. 206 EU101
Perry Hall Rd., Orp. 205 ET100
Perry Hill SE6 183 DZ90
Perry Hill, Guil. 242 AS128
Perry Hill, Wal.Abb. 50 EF23
Perry How, Wor.Pk. 199 CT102
Perry Mead, Enf. 81 DP40
Perry Mead (Bushey), Wat. 94 CB45
Perry Oaks Dr. (Heathrow), Houns. 154 BH82
Perry Ri. SE23 183 DY90
Perry Rd., Dag. 146 EZ70
Chequers La.
Perry Rd., Harl. 51 EQ18
Perry Spring, Harl. 52 EX17
Perry St., Chis. 185 ER93
Perry St., Dart. 167 FE84
Perry St., Grav. 190 GE88
Perry St. Gdns., Chis. 185 ES93
Old Perry St.
Perry Vale SE23 182 DW90
Perry Way, S.Ock. 148 FQ73
Perryfield Way NW9 119 CT58
Perryfield Way, Rich. 177 CH89
Perryfields Way, Slou. 130 AH70
St. Peter's Clo.
Perrylands La., Horl. 269 DM149
Perryman Ho., Bark. 145 EQ67
Perryman Way, Slou. 131 AM69
Perrymans Fm. Rd., Ilf. 125 ER58
Perrymead St. SW6 160 DA81
Perryn Rd. SE16 162 DV76
Drummond Rd.
Perryn Rd. W3 138 CR74
Perrys La., Sev. 224 EV113
Perrys Pl. W1 273 M8
Perrysfield Rd. (Cheshunt), Wal.Cr. 67 DY26
Perrywood Business Pk., Red. 267 DH142
Persant Rd. SE6 184 EE90
Perseverance Pl. SW9 161 DN80
Mandela St.
Perseverance Pl., Rich. 158 CL83
Shaftesbury Rd.
Persfield Clo., Epsom 217 CT110
Pershore Clo., Ilf. 125 EP57
Pershore Gro., Cars. 200 DD100
Pert Clo. N10 99 DH51
Perth Ave. NW9 118 CR59
Perth Ave., Hayes 136 BW70
Perth Ave., Slou. 131 AP72
Perth Clo. SW20 199 CU96
Perth Rd. E10 123 DY60
Perth Rd. E13 144 EH68
Perth Rd. N4 121 DN60
Perth Rd. N22 99 DP53
Perth Rd., Bark. 145 ER67
Perth Rd., Beck. 203 EC96
Perth Rd., Ilf. 125 EN58
Perth Ter., Ilf. 125 EQ59
Perwell Ave., Har. 116 BZ60
Perwell Ct., Har. 116 BZ60
Pescot Hill, Hem.H. 40 BH18
Peter Ave. NW10 139 CV66
Peter Ave., Oxt. 253 ED129
Peter Ms., Slou. 153 BA78
Grampian Way
Peter St. W1 273 M10
Peter St. W1 141 DK73
Peter St., Grav. 191 GH87
William St.
Peterboat Clo. SE10 164 EE77
Tunnel Ave.
Peterborough Ave., Upmin. 129 FS60
Peterborough Gdns., Ilf. 124 EL59
Peterborough Ms. SW6 160 DA82
Peterborough Rd. E10 123 EC57
Peterborough Rd. SW6 160 DA82
Peterborough Rd., Cars. 200 DE100
Peterborough Rd., Guil. 242 AT132
Peterborough Rd., Har. 117 CE60
Peterborough Vill. SW6 160 DB81
Peterchurch Ho. SE15 162 DV79
Commercial Way
Petergate SW11 160 DC84
Peterhead Ms., Slou. 153 BA78
Peterhill Clo., Ger.Cr. 90 AY50
Peterlee Ct., Hem.H. 40 BM16
Peters Ave., St.Alb. 61 CJ26
Peters Clo., Dag. 126 EX60
Peters Clo., Stan. 95 CK51
Peters Clo., Well. 165 ES82
Peters Hill EC4 275 H9
Peter's La. EC1 274 F6
Peters Path SE26 182 DV91
Peters Pl., Berk. 38 AS17
Peters Wd. Hill, Ware 33 DX07
Petersfield Ave., Rom. 106 FL51
Petersfield Ave., Slou. 132 AU74
Petersfield Ave., Stai. 174 BJ92
Petersfield Clo. N18 100 DQ50
Petersfield Clo., Rom. 106 FN51
Petersfield Cres., Couls. 235 DL115
Petersfield Ri. SW15 179 CV88
Petersfield Rd. W3 158 CQ75
Petersham Ave., W.Byf. 212 BL112
Petersham Clo., Rich. 177 CK89
Petersham Clo., Sutt. 217 CZ106
Petersham Clo., W.Byf. 212 BL112
Petersham Dr., Orp. 205 ET96
Petersham Gdns., Orp. 205 ET96
Petersham La. SW7 160 DC76
Petersham Ms. SW7 160 DC76
Petersham Pl. SW7 160 DC76
Petersham Rd., Rich. 177 CK86
Peterstone Rd. SE2 166 EV76
Peterstow Clo. SW19 179 CY89
Peterswood, Harl. 51 ER19
Parnall Rd.
Peterwood Way, Croy. 201 DM103
Petherton Rd. N5 122 DQ64
Petley Rd. W6 159 CW79
Peto Pl. NW1 273 J4
Peto Pl. NW1 141 DH70
Peto St. N. E16 144 EF73
Victoria Dock Rd.
Petridge Rd., Red. 266 DF139
Petrie Clo. NW2 139 CY65
Pett Clo., Horn. 127 FH61
St. Leonards Way
Pett St. SE18 164 EL77
Petten Clo., Orp. 206 EX102
Petten Gro., Orp. 206 EW102
Petters Rd., Ash. 232 CM116
Petticoat Sq. E1 275 P8
Pettits Boul., Rom. 105 FE53
Pettits Clo., Rom. 105 FE54
Pettits La., Rom. 105 FE54
Pettits La. N., Rom. 105 FD53
Pettits Pl., Dag. 126 FA64
Pettits Rd., Dag. 126 FA64
Pettiward Clo. SW15 159 CW84
Pettley Gdns., Rom. 127 FD57
Pettman Cres. SE28 165 ER76
Petts Hill, Nthlt. 116 CB64
Petts La., Shep. 194 BN98
Petts Wd. Rd., Orp. 205 EQ99
Pettsgrove Ave., Wem. 117 CJ64
Petty France SW1 277 L6
Petty France SW1 161 DJ76
Petworth Clo., Couls. 235 DJ119
Petworth Clo., Nthlt. 136 BZ66
Petworth Ct., Wind. 151 AP81
Petworth Gdns. SW20 199 CV97
Hidcote Gdns.
Petworth Gdns., Uxb. 135 BQ67
Petworth Rd. N12 98 DE50
Petworth Rd., Bexh. 186 FA85
Petworth St. SW11 160 DE81
Petworth Way, Horn. 127 FF63
Petyt Pl. SW3 160 DE79
Old Ch. St.
Petyward SW3 276 C9
Petyward SW3 160 DE77
Pevel Ho., Dag. 126 FA61
Pevensey Ave. N11 99 DK50
Pevensey Ave., Enf. 82 DR40
Pevensey Clo., Islw. 156 CC80
Pevensey Rd. E7 124 EF63
Pevensey Rd. SW17 180 DD91
Pevensey Rd., Felt. 176 BY88
Pevensey Rd., Slou. 131 AN71
Peverel E6 145 EN72
Downings
Peveret Clo. N11 99 DH50
Woodland Rd.
Peveril Dr., Tedd. 177 CD92
Pewley Bank, Guil. 258 AY136
Pewley Hill, Guil. 258 AX136
Pewley Pt., Guil. 258 AY136
Pewley Way, Guil. 258 AY136
Pewsey Clo. E4 101 EA50
Peyton Pl. SE10 163 EC80

Peytons Cotts., Red. 251 DM132
Nutfield Marsh Rd.
Pharaoh Clo., Mitch. 200 DF101
Middleton Rd.
Pharaoh's Island, Shep. 194 BM103
Pheasant Clo. E16 144 EG72
Maplin Rd.
Pheasant Clo., Berk. 38 AW20
Pheasant Clo., Pur. 219 DP113
Pheasant Hill, Ch.St.G. 90 AW47
Pheasant Ri., Chesh. 54 AR33
Pheasant Wk., Ger.Cr. 90 AX49
Pheasants Way, Rick. 92 BH45
Phelips Rd., Harl. 51 EN20
Phelp St. SE17 162 DR79
Phelps Way, Hayes 155 BT77
Phene St. SW3 160 DE79
Phil Brown Pl. SW8 161 DH82
Heath Rd.
Philan Way, Rom. 105 FD51
Philanthropic Rd., Red. 266 DG135
Philbeach Gdns. SW5 160 DA78
Philchurch Pl. E1 142 DU72
Ellen St.
Philip Ave., Rom. 127 FD60
Philip Clo., Brwd. 108 FW44
Philip Clo., Rom. 127 FD60
Philip Ave.
Philip Gdns., Croy. 203 DZ103
Philip La. N15 122 DR56
Philip Rd. SE15 162 DU83
Peckham Rye
Philip Rd., Rain. 147 FE69
Philip Rd., Stai. 174 BK93
Philip St. E13 144 EG70
Philip Wk. SE15 162 DV83
Philipot Path SE9 185 EM86
Court Yd.
Philippa Gdns. SE9 184 EK85
Philippa Way, Grays 171 GH77
Philips Clo., Mitch. 200 DG102
Culvers Ave.
Phillida Rd., Rom. 106 FN54
Phillimore Gdns. NW10 139 CW67
Phillimore Gdns. W8 160 DA75
Phillimore Gdns. Clo. W8 160 DA76
Phillimore Gdns.
Phillimore Pl. W8 160 DA75
Phillimore Pl., Rad. 77 CE36
Phillimore Wk. W8 160 DA76
Phillip Ave., Swan. 207 FD98
Phillip Dr., H.Wyc. 110 AC56
Phillipers, Wat. 76 BX36
Phillipp St. N1 142 DS67
Phillips Clo., Dart. 187 FH86
Phillips Hatch, Guil. 259 BC143
Philpot La. EC3 275 M10
Philpot La., Wok. 210 AV113
Philpot Path, Ilf. 125 EQ62
Sunnyside Rd.
Philpot Sq. SW6 160 DB83
Peterborough Rd.
Philpot St. E1 142 DV72
Philpots Clo., West Dr. 134 BK73
Phineas Pett Rd. SE9 164 EL83
Phipp St. EC2 275 M4
Phipp St. EC2 142 DS70
Phipps Bri. Rd. SW19 200 DC96
Phipps Bri. Rd., Mitch. 200 DC96
Phipps Hatch La., Enf. 82 DQ38
Phipp's Ms. SW1 277 H7
Phipps Rd., Slou. 131 AL71
Phoebe Rd., Hem.H. 40 BM17
Phoebeth Rd. SE4 183 EA85
Phoenix Clo. E8 142 DT67
Stean St.
Phoenix Clo., Nthwd. 93 BT49
Phoenix Clo., W.Wick. 203 ED103
Phoenix Ct., Guil. 258 AX136
High St.
Phoenix Dr., Kes. 204 EK104
Phoenix Pk., Brent. 157 CK78
Phoenix Pl. WC1 274 C4
Phoenix Pl. WC1 141 DM70
Phoenix Pl., Dart. 188 FK87
Phoenix Rd. NW1 273 M2
Phoenix Rd. NW1 141 DK69
Phoenix Rd. SE20 182 DW93
Phoenix St. WC2 273 N9
Phoenix Way, Houns. 156 BW79
Phygtle, The, Ger.Cr. 90 AY51
Phyllis Ave., N.Mal. 199 CV99
Physic Pl. SW3 160 DF79
Royal Hospital Rd.
Piazza, The WC2 141 DL73
Covent Gdn.
Picardy Manorway, Belv. 167 FB76
Picardy Rd., Belv. 166 FA78
Picardy St., Belv. 166 FA76
Piccadilly W1 277 J3
Piccadilly W1 141 DH74
Piccadilly Arc. SW1 277 K2
Piccadilly Circ. W1 277 M1
Piccadilly Circ. W1 141 DJ73
Piccadilly Pl. W1 277 L1
Piccards, The, Guil. 258 AW138
Chestnut Ave.
Piccotts End La., Hem.H. 40 BJ17
Piccotts End Rd., Hem.H. 40 BH16
Pick Hill, Wal.Abb. 68 EF32
Pickard St. EC1 274 G2
Pickering Ave. E6 145 EN68
Pickering Gdns., Croy. 202 DT100
Pickering Ms. W2 140 DB72
Bishops Bri. Rd.
Pickering Pl. SW1 277 L3
Pickering St. N1 141 DP67
Essex Rd.
Pickets Clo. (Bushey), Wat. 95 CD46
Pickets St. SW12 181 DH87
Pickett Cft., Stan. 95 CK53
Picketts, Welw.G.C. 29 CX06
Picketts La., Red. 267 DJ144
Picketts Lock La. N9 100 DW47
Pickford Clo., Bexh. 166 EY82
Pickford Dr., Slou. 133 AZ74
Pickford La., Bexh. 166 EY82
Pickford Rd., Bexh. 166 EY84
Pickford Rd., St.Alb. 43 CH20
Pickford Wf. N1 275 H1
Pickford Wf. N1 142 DQ68
Pickhurst Grn., Brom. 204 EF101
Pickhurst La., Brom. 204 EF101
Pickhurst La., W.Wick. 204 EE99
Pickhurst Mead, Brom. 204 EF101
Pickhurst Pk., Brom. 204 EE99
Pickhurst Ri., W.Wick. 203 EC101
Pickins Piece, Slou. 153 BA82
Pickle Herring St. SE1 142 DS74
Tooley St.
Pickmoss La., Sev. 241 FH116
Pickwick Clo., Houns. 176 BY85
Dorney Way
Pickwick Ct. SE9 184 EL88
West Pk.
Pickwick Gdns., Grav. 190 GD90
Pickwick Ms. N18 100 DS50
Pickwick Pl., Har. 117 CE59
Pickwick Rd. SE21 182 DR87
Pickwick St. SE1 279 H5
Pickwick Way, Chis. 185 EQ93
Pickworth Clo. SW8 161 DL80
Kenchester Clo.
Picquets Way, Bans. 233 CZ117
Picton Pl. W1 272 G9
Picton St. SE5 162 DR80
Piedmont Rd. SE18 165 ER78
Pield Heath Ave., Uxb. 134 BN70
Pield Heath Rd., Uxb. 134 BL70
Pier Head E1 142 DV74
Wapping High St.
Pier Par. E16 165 EN75
Pier Rd.
Pier Rd. E16 165 EN75
Pier Rd., Erith 167 FE79
Pier Rd., Felt. 175 BV85
Pier Rd., Grav. 191 GF86
Pier Rd., Green. 169 FV84
Pier St. E14 163 EC77
Pier Ter. SW18 160 DC84
Jew's Row
Pier Wk., Grays 170 GA79
Columbia Wf. Rd.
Pier Way SE28 165 ER76
Piercing Hill, Epp. 85 ER35
Piermont Grn. SE22 182 DV85
Piermont Pl., Brom. 204 EL96
Piermont Rd. SE22 182 DV85
Pierrepoint Arc. N1 141 DP68
Islington High St.
Pierrepoint Rd. W3 138 CP73
Pierrepoint Row N1 141 DP68
Islington High St.
Pierson Rd., Wind. 151 AK82
Pigeon La., Hmptn. 176 CA91
Pigeonhouse La., Couls. 250 DC125
Piggotts End, Amer. 55 AP40
Piggotts Orchard, Amer. 55 AP40
Piggs Cor., Grays 170 GC76
Piggy La., Rick. 73 BB44
Bullsland La.
Pigott St. E14 143 EA72
Pike Clo., Brom. 184 EH92
Pike La., Upmin. 129 FT64
Pike Rd. NW7 96 CR49
Ellesmere Ave.
Pike Way, Epp. 70 FA27
Pikes End, Pnr. 115 BV56
Pikes Hill, Epsom 216 CS113
Pikestone Clo., Hayes 136 BY70
Berrydale Rd.
Pilgrim Clo., Mord. 200 DB101
Canterbury Rd.
Pilgrim Clo., St.Alb. 60 CC27
Pilgrim Hill SE27 182 DQ91
Pilgrim Hill, Orp. 206 EX96
Pilgrim St. EC4 274 F9
Pilgrim St. EC4 141 DP72
Pilgrimage St. SE1 279 K5
Pilgrimage St. SE1 162 DR75
Pilgrims Clo. N13 99 DM49
Pilgrims Clo., Brwd. 108 FT43
Pilgrims Clo., Dor. 247 CG131
Pilgrims Clo., Guil. 260 BN139
Pilgrims Clo., Nthlt. 116 CC64
Pilgrims Clo., Wat. 60 BX33
Kytes Dr.
Pilgrims Ct. SE3 164 EG81
Pilgrim's La. NW3 120 DD63
Pilgrims La., Cat. 251 DM125
Pilgrims La., Oxt. 254 EH125
Pilgrims La., West. 238 EL123
Pilgrims Pl. NW3 120 DD63
Hampstead High St.
Pilgrims Pl., Reig. 250 DA132
Pilgrims Ri., Barn. 80 DE43
Pilgrims Rd., Swans. 170 FY84
Pilgrims Vw., Green. 189 FW86
Pilgrims Way E6 144 EL67
Ron Leighton Way
Pilgrims Way N19 121 DK60
Pilgrims' Way, Bet. 248 CQ133
Chalkpit La.
Pilgrims Way, Dart. 188 FN88
Pilgrims' Way, Dor. 261 BT139
Pilgrims Way (Westhumble), Dor. 247 CH131
Pilgrims Way, Guil. 258 AX138
Pilgrims' Way (Albury), Guil. 259 BF138
Pilgrims Way (Shere), Guil. 260 BN139
Pilgrims' Way, Reig. 249 CZ133
Pilgrims Way (Sundridge), Sev. 240 EV121
Pilgrims Way, S.Croy. 220 DT107
Bench Fld.
Pilgrim's Way, Wem. 118 CP60
Pilgrims Way, West. 239 EM123
Pilgrims Way W., Sev. 241 FD116
Pilkington Rd. SE15 162 DV82
Pilkington Rd., Orp. 205 EQ103
Pilkingtons, Harl. 52 EX15
Church Langley Way
Pilot Ind. Est. NW10 138 CR70
Pilots Pl., Grav. 191 GJ86
East Ter.
Pilsdon Clo. SW19 179 CX88
Inner Pk. Rd.
Piltdown Rd., Wat. 94 BX49
Pimlico Rd. SW1 276 F10
Pimlico Rd. SW1 160 DG78
Pimlico Wk. N1 275 M2
Pimms Clo., Guil. 243 BA130
Pimpernel Way, Rom. 106 FK51
Pinceybrook Rd., Harl. 51 EQ19
Pinchbeck Rd., Orp. 223 ET107
Pinchfield, Rick. 91 BD50
Pinchin St. E1 142 DU73
Pincott La., Lthd. 245 BP129
Pincott Pl. SE4 163 DX83
Billingford Clo.
Pincott Rd. SW19 180 DC94
Pincott Rd., Bexh. 186 FA85
Pindar Rd., Hodd. 49 EC16
Pindar St. EC2 275 M6
Pindar St. EC2 142 DS71
Pindock Ms. W9 140 DB70
Warwick Ave.
Pine Ave. E15 123 ED64
Pine Ave., Grav. 191 GK88
Pine Ave., W.Wick. 203 EB102
Pine Clo. E10 123 EB61
Oliver Rd.
Pine Clo. N14 99 DJ45
Pine Clo. N19 121 DJ61
Hargrave Pk.
Pine Clo. SE20 182 DW94
Graveney Gro.
Pine Clo., Add. 212 BH111
Pine Clo., Berk. 38 AV19
Pine Clo., Ken. 236 DR117
Pine Clo., Stan. 95 CH49
Pine Clo., Swan. 207 FF98
Pine Clo. (Cheshunt), Wal.Cr. 67 DX28
Pine Clo., Wok. 226 AW117
Pine Coombe, Croy. 221 DX105
Pine Ct., Upmin. 128 FN63
Pine Cres., Brwd. 109 GD42
Pine Cres., Cars. 218 DD111
Pine Cft., Rom. 128 FJ56
Pine Dean, Lthd. 246 CB125
Pine Gdns., Horl. 268 DF149
Pine Gdns., Ruis. 115 BV60
Pine Gdns., Surb. 198 CN100
Pine Glade, Orp. 223 EM105
Pine Gro. N4 121 DL61
Pine Gro. N20 97 CZ46
Pine Gro. SW19 179 CZ92
Pine Gro., Hat. 64 DB25
Pine Gro., St.Alb. 60 BZ30
Pine Gro. (Bushey), Wat. 76 BZ40
Pine Gro., Wey. 213 BP106
Pine Gro. Ms., Wey. 213 BQ106
Pine Hill, Epsom 232 CR115
Pine Martin Clo. NW2 119 CW62
Pine Pl., Bans. 217 CX114
Pine Pl., Hayes 135 BT70
Pine Ridge, Cars. 218 DG109
Pine Rd. N11 98 DG47
Pine Rd. NW2 119 CW63
Pine Rd., Wok. 226 AW120
Pine St. EC1 274 D4
Pine St. EC1 141 DN70
Pine Tree Clo., Hem.H. 40 BK19
Christchurch Rd.
Pine Tree Clo., Houns. 155 BV81
Pine Tree Hill, Wok. 227 BD116
Pine Trees Dr., Uxb. 114 BL63
Pine Vw. Clo., Guil. 259 BF140
Pine Vw. Manor, Epp. 70 EU30
Pine Wk., Bans. 234 DF117
Pine Wk., Cars. 218 DD110
Pine Wk., Cat. 236 DS122
Pine Wk., Cob. 214 BX114
Pine Wk. (East Horsley), Lthd. 245 BT128
Pine Wk., Surb. 198 CN100
Pine Wk. E., Cars. 218 DD111
Pine Wk. W., Cars. 218 DD111
Pine Way, Egh. 172 AV93
Ashwood Rd.
Pine Wd., Sun. 195 BU95
Pineapple Ct. SW1 277 K6
Pineapple Rd., Amer. 72 AT39
Pinecrest Gdns., Orp. 223 EP105
Pinecroft, Brwd. 109 GB45
London Rd.
Pinecroft, Hem.H. 40 BM24
Pinecroft, Rom. 128 FJ56
Brentwood Rd.
Pinecroft Cres., Barn. 79 CY42
Hillside Gdns.
Pinedene SE15 162 DV81
Meeting Ho. La.
Pinefield Clo. E14 143 EA73
Pinehurst, Sev. 257 FL121
Pinehurst Clo., Abb.L. 59 BS32
Pinehurst Clo., Tad. 234 DA122
Pinehurst Wk., Orp. 205 ES102
Andover Rd.
Pinelands Clo. SE3 164 EF80
St. John's Pk.
Pinemartins Clo. NW2 119 CW62
Gladstone Pk. Gdns.
Pineneedle La., Sev. 257 FH123
Pines, The N14 81 DJ43
Pines, The, Borwd. 78 CM40
Anthony Rd.
Pines, The, Dor. 263 CH137
Pines, The, Hem.H. 39 BF24
Pines, The, Pur. 220 DQ113
Pines, The, Sun. 195 BU97
Pines, The, Wok. 211 AZ114
Woodham Rd.
Pines, The, Wdf.Grn. 102 EG48
Pines Ave., Enf. 82 DV36
Pines Clo., Amer. 55 AP36
Pines Clo., Nthwd. 93 BS51
Pines Rd., Brom. 204 EL96
Pinetree Clo., Ger.Cr. 90 AW52
Pinewalk (Bookham), Lthd. 246 CB125
Pinewood, Welw.G.C. 29 CY11
Pinewood Ave., Add. 212 BJ109
Pinewood Ave., Pnr. 94 CB51
Pinewood Ave., Rain. 147 FH70
Pinewood Ave., Sev. 257 FK121
Pinewood Ave., Sid. 185 ES88
Pinewood Ave., Uxb. 134 BM72
Pinewood Clo., Borwd. 78 CR39
Pinewood Clo., Croy. 203 DY104
Pinewood Clo., Ger.Cr. 112 AY59
Dukes Wd. Ave.
Pinewood Clo., Harl. 52 EW16
Pinewood Clo., Iver 133 BC66
Pinewood Clo., Orp. 205 ER102
Pinewood Clo., Pnr. 94 CB51
Pinewood Clo., St.Alb. 43 CJ20
Pinewood Clo., Wat. 75 BU39
Langwood Gdns.
Pinewood Clo., Wok. 227 BA115
Pinewood Dr., Orp. 223 ES106
Pinewood Dr., Pot.B. 63 CZ31
Pinewood Dr., Stai. 174 BG92
Cotswold Clo.
Pinewood Gdns., Hem.H. 40 BH20
Pinewood Grn., Iver 133 BC66
Pinewood Gro. W5 137 CJ72
Pinewood Gro., Add. 212 BH110
Pinewood Pk., Add. 212 BH111
Pinewood Ride, Iver 133 BB65
Pinewood Ride, Slou. 133 BA65
Fulmer Common Rd.
Pinewood Rd. SE2 166 EX79
Pinewood Rd., Brom. 204 EG98
Pinewood Rd., Felt. 175 BV90
Pinewood Rd., Iver 133 BA65
Pinewood Rd. (Havering-atte-Bower), Rom. 105 FD49
Pinewood Rd., Vir.W. 192 AU98
Pinewood Way, Brwd. 109 GD43
Pinfold Rd. SW16 181 DL91
Pinfold Rd. (Bushey), Wat. 76 BZ40
Pinglestone Clo., West Dr. 154 BL80
Pink La., Slou. 130 AH68
Pinkcoat Clo., Felt. 175 BV90
Tanglewood Way
Pinkerton Pl. SW16 181 DK91
Riggindale Rd.
Pinkham Way N11 98 DG52
Pinkneys Ct., Maid. 130 AG72
Pinks Hill, Swan. 207 FE99
Pinkwell Ave., Hayes 155 BR77
Pinkwell La., Hayes 155 BQ77
Pinley Gdns., Dag. 146 EV67
Stamford Rd.
Pinn Clo., Uxb. 134 BK72
High Rd.
Pinn Way, Ruis. 115 BR59
Pinnacle Hill, Bexh. 167 FB84
Pinnacle Hill N., Bexh. 167 FB83
Pinnacles, Wal.Abb. 68 EE34
Pinnacles Ind. Est., Harl. 51 EM16
Pinnate Pl., Welw.G.C. 29 CY13
Pinnell Pl. SE9 164 EK84
Pinnell Rd. SE9 164 EK84
Pinner Ct., Pnr. 116 CA56
Pinner Grn., Pnr. 94 BW54
Pinner Gro., Pnr. 116 BY56
Pinner Hill, Pnr. 93 BV52
Pinner Hill Rd., Pnr. 94 BW53
Pinner Pk. Ave., Har. 116 CB55
Pinner Pk. Gdns., Har. 94 CC54
Pinner Rd., Har. 116 CB57
Pinner Rd., Nthwd. 93 BT53
Pinner Rd., Pnr. 116 BZ56
Pinner Rd., Wat. 76 BX44
Pinner Vw., Har. 116 CC56
Pinnocks Ave., Grav. 191 GH88
Pinstone Way, Ger.Cr. 113 BB61
Pintail Clo. E6 144 EL71
Swan App.
Pintail Rd., Wdf.Grn. 102 EH52
Pintail Way, Hayes 136 BX71
Willow Tree La.
Pinto Clo., Borwd. 78 CR44
Percheron Rd.
Pinto Way SE3 164 EH84
Pioneer Pl., Croy. 221 EA109
Featherbed La.
Pioneer Way W12 139 CV72
Du Cane Rd.
Piper Clo. N7 121 DM64
Piper Rd., Kings.T. 198 CN97
Pipers Clo., Cob. 230 BX115
Pipers Clo., Slou. 130 AJ69
Pipers End, Hert. 31 DJ13
Pipers End, Vir.W. 192 AX97
Piper's Gdns., Croy. 203 DY101
Pipers Grn. NW9 118 CQ57
Pipers Grn. La., Edg. 96 CL48
Pipewell Rd., Cars. 200 DE100
Pippbrook Gdns., Dor. 263 CH135
London Rd.
Pippens, Welw.G.C. 29 CY06
Pippin Clo. NW2 119 CV62
Pippin Clo., Croy. 203 DZ102
Pippins, The, Slou. 133 AZ74
Pickford Dr.
Pippins Clo., West Dr. 154 BK76
Pippins Ct., Ashf. 175 BP93
Piquet Rd. SE20 202 DW96
Pirbright Cres., Croy. 221 EC107
Pirbright Rd. SW18 179 CZ88
Pirie Clo. SE5 162 DR83
Denmark Hill
Pirie St. E16 144 EH74
Pirrip Clo., Grav. 191 GM89
Pirton Clo., St.Alb. 43 CJ15
Pishiobury Dr., Saw. 36 EW07
Pishiobury Ms., Saw. 36 EX08
Pit Fm. Rd., Guil. 243 BA134
Pitcairn Clo., Rom. 126 FA56
Pitcairn Rd., Mitch. 180 DF94
Pitch Pond Clo., Beac. 88 AH50
Pitchfont La., Oxt. 238 EF124
Pitchford St. E15 143 ED66
Pitfield Cres. SE28 146 EU74
Pitfield Est. N1 275 M2
Pitfield St. N1 275 M3
Pitfield St. N1 142 DS69
Pitfield Way NW10 138 CQ65
Pitfield Way, Enf. 82 DW39
Pitfold Clo. SE12 184 EG86
Pitfold Rd. SE12 184 EG86
Pitlake, Croy. 201 DP103
Pitman St. SE5 162 DQ80
Pitman's Fld., Harl. 35 ET14
Pitsea Pl. E1 143 DX72
Pitsea St.
Pitsea St. E1 143 DX72
Pitsfield, Welw.G.C. 29 CX06
Pitshanger La. W5 137 CH70
Pitshanger Pk. W13 137 CG70
Pitson Clo., Add. 212 BK105
Pitstone Clo., St.Alb. 43 CJ15
Highview Gdns.
Pitt Cres. SW19 180 DB91
Pitt Pl., Epsom 216 CS114
Pitt Rd., Epsom 216 CS114
Pitt Rd., Orp. 223 EQ105
Pitt Rd., Th.Hth. 202 DQ99
Pitt St. SE15 162 DT80
Pitt St. W8 160 DA75
Pittman Clo., Brwd. 109 GC50
Pittman Gdns., Ilf. 125 EQ64
Pitt's Head Ms. W1 276 G3
Pitt's Head Ms. W1 140 DG74
Pitts Rd., Slou. 131 AQ74
Pittsmead Ave., Brom. 204 EG101
Pittville Gdns. SE25 202 DU97
Pittwood, Brwd. 109 GA46
Pitwood Grn., Tad. 233 CW120
Pix Fm. La., Hem.H. 39 BB21
Pixfield Ct., Brom. 204 EF96
Beckenham La.
Pixham La., Dor. 247 CJ133
Pixholme Gro., Dor. 247 CJ134
Pixies Hill Cres., Hem.H. 39 BF22
Pixies Hill Rd., Hem.H. 39 BF21
Pixley St. E14 143 DZ72
Pixton Way, Croy. 221 DY109
Place Fm. Ave., Orp. 205 ER102
Place Fm. Rd., Red. 252 DR130
Placehouse La., Couls. 235 DM119
Placket Way, Slou. 131 AK74
Plain, The, Epp. 70 EV29
Plaistow Gro. E15 144 EF67
Plaistow Gro., Brom. 184 EH94
Plaistow La., Brom. 184 EG94
Plaistow Pk. Rd. E13 144 EH68
Plaistow Rd. E13 144 EF67
Plaistow Rd. E15 144 EF67
Plaitford Clo., Rick. 92 BL47
Plane Ave., Grav. 190 GD87
Plane St. SE26 182 DV90
Plane Tree Cres., Felt. 175 BV90
Plane Tree Wk. SE19 182 DS93
Central Hill
Planes, The, Cher. 194 BJ101
Plantaganet Pl., Wal.Abb. 67 EB33
Plantagenet Clo., Wor.Pk. 216 CR105
Plantagenet Gdns., Rom. 126 EX59
Broomfield Rd.
Plantagenet Pl., Rom. 126 EX59
Broomfield Rd.
Plantagenet Rd., Barn. 80 DC42
Plantain Gdns. E11 124 EE62
Hollydown Way
Plantain Pl. SE1 279 K4
Plantation, The SE3 164 EG82
Plantation Dr., Orp. 206 EX102
Plantation La., Warl. 237 DX119
Plantation Rd., Amer. 55 AS37
Plantation Rd., Erith 167 FG81
Plantation Rd., Swan. 187 FG94
Plantation Wk., Hem.H. 40 BG17
Plantation Way, Amer. 55 AS37
Plantation Wf. SW11 160 DC83
Plasel Ct. E13 144 EG67
Plashet Rd.
Plashet Gdns., Brwd. 109 GA49
Plashet Gro. E6 144 EJ67
Plashet Rd. E13 144 EG67
Plashets, Bishop's Stortford 37 FC06
Plassy Rd. SE6 183 EB87
Platford Grn., Horn. 128 FL55
Platina St. EC2 275 L4
Plato Rd. SW2 161 DL84
Platt, The SW15 159 CX83
Platt Meadow, Guil. 243 BD131
Eustace Rd.
Platt St. NW1 141 DK68
Platts Ave., Wat. 75 BV41
Platt's Eyot, Hmptn. 196 CA96
Platt's La. NW3 120 DA63
Platts Rd., Enf. 82 DW39
Plawsfield Rd., Beck. 203 DX95
Plaxtol Clo., Brom. 204 EJ95
Plaxtol Rd., Erith 166 FA79
Playfair St. W6 159 CW78
Winslow Rd.
Playfield Ave., Rom. 105 FC53
Playfield Cres. SE22 182 DT85
Playfield Rd., Edg. 96 CQ54
Playford Rd. N4 121 DM61
Playgreen Way SE6 183 EA90
Playground Clo., Beck. 203 DX96
Churchfields Rd.
Playhouse Yd. EC4 274 F9
Plaza W., Houns. 156 CB81
Pleasance, The SW15 159 CV84
Pleasance Rd. SW15 179 CV85
Pleasance Rd., Orp. 206 EV96
Pleasant Gro., Croy. 203 DZ104
Pleasant Pl. N1 141 DP66
Pleasant Pl., Rick. 91 BE52
Pleasant Pl., Walt. 214 BW107
Pleasant Ri., Hat. 45 CW15
Pleasant Rd., Kings.T. 198 CQ97
Pleasant Row NW1 141 DH67
Camden High St.
Pleasant Vw., Erith 167 FE78
Pleasant Vw. Pl., Orp. 223 EP106
High St.
Pleasant Way, Wem. 137 CJ68
Pleasure Pit Rd., Ash. 232 CP118
Plender St. NW1 141 DJ67
Plender St. Est. NW1 141 DJ67
Plender St.
Pleshey Rd. N7 121 DK63
Plesman Way, Wall. 219 DL109
Plevna Cres. N15 122 DS58
Plevna Rd. N9 100 DU48
Plevna Rd., Hmptn. 196 CB95
Plevna St. E14 163 EC76
Pleydell Ave. SE19 182 DT94
Pleydell Ave. W6 159 CT77
Pleydell Ct. EC4 141 DN72
Fleet St.
Pleydell Est. EC1 142 DQ69
Radnor St.
Pleydell St. EC4 274 E9
Plimsoll Clo. E14 143 EB72
Grundy St.
Plimsoll Rd. N4 121 DN62
Plough Ct. EC3 275 L10
Plough Fm. Clo., Ruis. 115 BR58
Bury St.
Plough Hill (Cuffley), Pot.B. 65 DL28
Plough La. SE22 182 DT86
Plough La. SW17 180 DC91
Plough La. SW19 180 DB92
Plough La., Berk. 39 BB16
Plough La., Cob. 229 BU117
Plough La., Pur. 219 DM109
Plough La., Rick. 57 BF33
Plough La., Slou. 132 AV67
Plough La., Uxb. 92 BJ51
Plough La., Wall. 219 DL105
Plough La. Clo., Wall. 219 DL106
Plough Lees La., Slou. 132 AS73
Plough Ms. SW11 160 DD84
Plough Ter.
Plough Pl. EC4 274 E8
Plough Ri., Upmin. 129 FS59
Plough Rd. SW11 160 DD83
Plough Rd., Epsom 216 CR109
Plough Rd., Horl. 269 DP148
Plough St. E1 142 DT72
Leman St.
Plough Ter. SW11 160 DD84
Plough Way SE16 163 DX77
Plough Yd. EC2 275 N5
Plough Yd. EC2 142 DS70
Ploughmans Clo. NW1 141 DK67
Crofters Way

Plo–Poy This index reads in the sequence: Street Name / Postal District or Post Town / Map Page Number / Grid Reference

Ploughmans End, Islw. 177 CD85
Ploughmans End, Welw.G.C. 30 DC10
Plover Clo., Berk. 38 AW20
Plover Clo., Stai. 173 BF90
Waters Dr.
Plover Gdns., Upmin. 129 FT60
Plover Way SE16 163 DY76
Plover Way, Hayes 136 BX71
Willow Tree La.
Plowden Bldgs. EC4 141 DN72
Middle Temple La.
Plowman Clo. N18 100 DR50
Plowman Way, Dag. 126 EW60
Ployters Rd., Harl. 51 EQ18
Plum Garth, Brent. 157 CK77
Plum La. SE18 165 EP80
Plumbers Row E1 142 DU71
Plumbridge St. SE10 163 EC81
Blackheath Hill
Plummer La., Mitch. 200 DF96
Plummer Rd. SW4 181 DK87
Plumpton Ave., Horn. 128 FL63
Plumpton Clo., Nthlt. 136 CA65
Plumpton Rd., Hodd. 49 EC15
Plumpton Way, Cars. 200 DE104
Plumstead Common Rd. SE18 165 EP79
Plumstead High St. SE18 165 ER77
Plumstead Rd. SE18 165 EP77
Plumtree Clo., Dag. 147 FC65
Plumtree Clo., Wall. 219 DK108
Plumtree Ct. EC4 274 F8
Plumtree Mead, Loug. 85 EN41
Pluto Ri., Hem.H. 40 BL18
Plymouth Dr., Sev. 257 FJ124
Plymouth Ho., Rain. 147 FF69
Plymouth Pk., Sev. 257 FJ124
Plymouth Rd. E16 144 EG71
Plymouth Rd., Brom. 204 EH95
Plymouth Rd., Slou. 131 AL71
Plymouth Wf. E14 163 ED77
Plympton Ave. NW6 139 CZ66
Plympton Clo., Belv. 166 EY76
Halifield Dr.
Plympton Pl. NW8 272 B5
Plympton Rd. NW6 139 CZ66
Plympton St. NW8 272 B5
Plympton St. NW8 140 DE70
Plymstock Rd., Well. 166 EW80
Pocketsdell La., Hem.H. 56 AX28
Pocklington Clo. NW9 96 CS54
Pocock Ave., West Dr. 154 BM76
Porters Way
Pocock St. SE1 278 F4
Pocock St. SE1 161 DP75
Pococks La. (Eton), Wind. 152 AS78
Podmore Rd. SW18 160 DC84
Poets Chase, Hem.H. 40 BH18
Laureate Way
Poets Rd. N5 122 DR64
Poets Way, Har. 117 CE56
Blawith Rd.
Point, The, Ruis. 115 BU63
Bedford Rd.
Point Clo. SE10 163 EC81
Point Hill
Point Hill SE10 163 EC80
Point of Thomas Path E1 142 DW73
Glamis Rd.
Point Pl., Wem. 138 CP66
Point Pleasant SW18 160 DA84
Pointalls Clo. N3 98 DC54
Pointer Clo. SE28 146 EX72
Pointers, The, Ash. 232 CL120
Stag Leys
Pointers Clo. E14 163 EB78
Pointers Hill, Dor. 262 CC138
Pointers Rd., Cob. 229 BQ116
Poland St. W1 273 L8
Poland St. W1 141 DJ72
Polayn Garth, Welw.G.C. 29 CW08
Pole Cat All., Brom. 204 EF103
Pole Hanger La., Hem.H. 39 BE18
Pole Hill Rd. E4 101 EC45
Pole Hill Rd., Uxb. 135 BP70
Pole La., Ong. 53 FE17
Polebrook Rd. SE3 164 EJ83
Polecroft La. SE6 183 DZ89
Polehamptons, The, Hmptn. 176 CC94
High St.
Poles Hill, Chesh. 54 AN29
Poles Hill, Rick. 57 BE33
Polesden Gdns. SW20 199 CV96
Polesden Lacey, Dor. 246 CB130
Polesden La., Wok. 227 BF122
Polesden Rd., Lthd. 246 CB129
Polesden Vw., Lthd. 246 CB127
Polesteeple Hill, West. 238 EK117
Polesworth Ho. W2 140 DA71
Polesworth Rd., Dag. 146 EX66
Polhill, Sev. 225 FC114
Police Sta. La. (Bushey), Wat. 94 CB45
Sparrows Herne
Police Sta. Rd., Walt. 214 BW107
Pollard Ave., Uxb. 113 BF58
Pollard Clo. E16 144 EG73
Pollard Clo. N7 121 DM63
Pollard Clo., Chig. 104 EU50
Pollard Clo., Wind. 172 AV85
Pollard Hatch, Harl. 51 EP18
Pollard Rd. N20 98 DE47
Pollard Rd., Mord. 200 DD99
Pollard Rd., Wok. 227 BB116
Pollard Row E2 142 DU69
Pollard St. E2 142 DU69
Pollard Wk., Sid. 186 EW93
Evry Rd.
Pollards, Rick. 91 BD50
Pollards Clo., Loug. 84 EJ43
Pollards Clo. (Cheshunt), Wal.Cr. 66 DQ29
Pollards Cres. SW16 201 DL97
Pollards Hill E. SW16 201 DM97
Pollards Hill N. SW16 201 DL97
Pollards Hill S. SW16 201 DL97
Pollards Hill W. SW16 201 DL97
Pollards Oak Cres., Oxt. 254 EG132
Pollards Oak Rd., Oxt. 254 EG132
Pollards Wd. Hill, Oxt. 254 EH130
Pollards Wd. Rd. SW16 201 DL96
Pollards Wd. Rd., Oxt. 254 EH131
Pollen St. W1 273 K9
Pollicot Clo., St.Alb. 43 CJ15
Pollitt Dr. NW8 272 A4
Pollyhaugh (Eynsford), Dart. 208 FK104
Polperro Clo., Orp. 205 ET100
Cotswold Ri.
Polsted Rd. SE6 183 DZ87
Polthorne Est. SE18 165 EQ77
Polthorne Gro.
Polthorne Gro. SE18 165 EQ77
Poltimore Rd., Guil. 258 AU136
Polworth Rd. SW16 181 DL92
Polygon, The SW4 161 DJ84
Old Town
Polygon Rd. NW1 273 M1
Polygon Rd. NW1 141 DK68
Polytechnic St. SE18 165 EN77
Pomell Way E1 142 DT72
Commercial St.
Pomeroy Clo., Amer. 55 AR39
Pomeroy Cres., Wat. 75 BV36
Pomeroy St. SE14 162 DW81
Pomfret Rd. SE5 161 DP83
Flaxman Rd.
Pompadour Clo., Brwd. 108 FW50
Queen St.
Pond Clo. SE3 164 EF82
Pond Clo., Ash. 232 CL117
Pond Clo., Uxb. 92 BJ54
Pond Clo., Walt. 213 BT107
Pond Cottage La., W.Wick. 203 EA102
Pond Cotts. SE21 182 DS88
Pond Cft., Hat. 45 CT18
Pond Cft., Welw.G.C. 29 CY10
Pond Fld., Welw.G.C. 30 DA06
Pond Fld. End, Loug. 102 EJ45
Pond Grn., Ruis. 115 BS61
Pond Hill Gdns., Sutt. 217 CY107
Pond La., Ger.Cr. 90 AV53
Pond La., Guil. 261 BQ144
Pond Mead SE21 182 DR86
Pond Meadow, Guil. 242 AS134
Pond Pk. Rd., Chesh. 54 AP29
Pond Piece, Lthd. 214 CB113
Pond Pl. SW3 276 B9
Pond Pl. SW3 160 DE77
Pond Rd. E15 144 EE68
Pond Rd. SE3 164 EF82
Pond Rd., Egh. 173 BC93
Pond Rd., Hem.H. 58 BN25
Pond Rd., Wok. 226 AU120
Pond Sq. N6 120 DG60
South Gro.
Pond St. NW3 120 DE64
Pond Wk., Upmin. 129 FS61
Pond Way, Tedd. 177 CJ93
Holmesdale Rd.
Ponder St. N7 141 DM66
Ponders End Ind. Est., Enf. 83 DZ42
Pondfield Cres., St.Alb. 43 CH16
Pondfield La., Brwd. 109 GA49
Pondfield Rd., Brom. 204 EE102
Pondfield Rd., Dag. 127 FB64
Pondfield Rd., Gdmg. 258 AT144
Pondfield Rd., Ken. 235 DP117
Pondfield Rd., Orp. 205 EP104
Ponds, The, Wey. 213 BS107
Ellesmere Rd.
Ponds La., Guil. 260 BL142
Pondside Clo., Hayes 155 BR80
Providence La.
Pondwicks, Amer. 55 AP39
Pondwicks Clo., St.Alb. 42 CC21
Pondwood Ri., Orp. 205 ES101
Ponler St. E1 142 DV72
Ponsard Rd. NW10 139 CV69
Ponsbourne Ho., Hert. 47 DL23
Ponsford St. E9 122 DW64
Ponsonby Pl. SW1 277 N10
Ponsonby Pl. SW1 161 DK78
Ponsonby Rd. SW15 179 CV87
Ponsonby Ter. SW1 277 N10
Ponsonby Ter. SW1 161 DK78
Pont St. SW1 276 D7
Pont St. SW1 160 DF76
Pont St. Ms. SW1 276 D7
Pont St. Ms. SW1 160 DF76
Pontefract Rd., Brom. 184 EF92
Ponton Rd. SW8 161 DK79
Pontosie Clo., Sev. 256 FF122
Pontypool Pl. SE1 278 F4
Pontypool Wk., Rom. 106 FJ51
Saddleworth Rd.
Pony Chase, Cob. 214 BZ113
Pool Clo., Beck. 183 EA92
Pool Clo., W.Mol. 196 BZ99
Pool Gro., Croy. 221 DY112
Pool La., Slou. 132 AS73
Pool Rd., Har. 117 CD59
Pool Rd., W.Mol. 196 BZ99
Poole Clo., Ruis. 115 BS61
Chichester Ave.
Poole Ct. Rd., Houns. 156 BY82
Vicarage Fm. Rd.
Poole Rd. E9 143 DX65
Poole Rd., Epsom 216 CR107
Poole Rd., Horn. 128 FM59
Poole Rd., Wok. 226 AY117
Poole St. N1 142 DR67
Poole Way, Hayes 135 BR69
Pooles Bldgs. EC1 274 D5
Pooles La. SW10 160 DC80
Lots Rd.
Pooles La., Dag. 146 EY68
Pooles Pk. N4 121 DN61
Seven Sisters Rd.
Pooley Ave., Egh. 173 BB92
Pooley Grn. Clo., Egh. 173 BC92
Pooley Grn. Rd., Egh. 173 BB92
Pooleys La., Hat. 45 CV23
Poolmans Rd., Wind. 151 AK83
Poolmans St. SE16 163 DX75
Poolsford Rd. NW9 118 CS56
Poonah St. E1 142 DW72
Hardinge St.
Pootings Rd., Eden. 255 ER134
Pope Clo. SW19 180 DD93
Shelley Way
Pope Clo., Felt. 175 BT88
Pope Rd., Brom. 204 EK99
Pope St. SE1 279 N5
Pope St. SE1 162 DS75
Popes Ave., Twick. 177 CE89
Popes Clo., Amer. 72 AT37
Popes Clo., Slou. 153 BB80
Popes Dr. N3 98 DA53
Popes Gro., Croy. 203 DZ104
Popes Gro., Twick. 177 CE89
Pope's Head All. EC3 142 DR72
Cornhill
Popes La. W5 157 CK76
Popes La., Oxt. 254 EE134
Popes La., Wat. 75 BV37
Popes Rd. SW9 161 DN83
Popes Rd., Abb.L. 59 BS31
Popham Clo., Felt. 176 BZ90
Popham Rd. N1 142 DQ67
Popham St. N1 142 DQ67
Poplar Ave., Amer. 72 AT39
Poplar Ave., Grav. 191 GJ91
Poplar Ave., Lthd. 231 CH122
Poplar Ave., Mitch. 200 DF95
Poplar Ave., Orp. 205 EP103
Poplar Ave., Sthl. 156 CB76
Poplar Ave., West Dr. 134 BM73
Poplar Bath St. E14 143 EB73
Lawless St.
Poplar Clo., Chesh. 54 AQ28
Poplar Clo., Pnr. 94 BX53
Poplar Clo., Slou. 153 BE81
Poplar Ct. SW19 180 DA92
Poplar Cres., Epsom 216 CQ107
Poplar Dr., Bans. 217 CY114
Poplar Dr., Brwd. 109 GC44
Poplar Fm. Clo., Epsom 216 CQ107
Poplar Gdns., N.Mal. 198 CR96
Poplar Gro. N11 98 DG51
Poplar Gro. W6 159 CW75
Poplar Gro., N.Mal. 198 CR97
Poplar Gro., Wem. 118 CQ62
Poplar Gro., Wok. 226 AY119
Poplar High St. E14 143 EB73
Poplar Mt., Belv. 167 FB77
Poplar Pl. SE28 146 EW73
Poplar Pl. W2 140 DB73
Poplar Pl., Hayes 135 BU73
Central Ave.
Poplar Rd. SE24 162 DQ84
Poplar Rd. SW19 200 DA96
Poplar Rd., Ashf. 175 BQ93
Poplar Rd., Guil. 258 AY141
Poplar Rd., Lthd. 231 CH122
Poplar Rd., Sutt. 199 CZ102
Poplar Rd., Uxb. 114 BJ64
Poplar Rd. S. SW19 200 DA97
Poplar Row, Epp. 85 ES37
Poplar Shaw, Wal.Abb. 68 EF33
Poplar St., Rom. 127 FC56
Poplar Vw., Wem. 117 CK61
Magnet Rd.
Poplar Wk. SE24 162 DQ84
Poplar Wk., Cat. 236 DS123
Park Rd.
Poplar Wk., Croy. 202 DQ103
Poplar Way, Felt. 175 BU90
Poplar Way, Ilf. 125 EQ56
Poplars, Welw.G.C. 30 DB08
Poplars, The N14 81 DH43
Poplars, The, Hem.H. 40 BH21
Poplars, The, Rom. 86 EV41
Hoe La.
Poplars, The, St.Alb. 43 CH24
Poplars Ave. NW10 139 CW65
Poplars Ave., Hat. 44 CR18
Poplars Clo., Hat. 44 CQ18
Poplars Clo., Ruis. 115 BS60
Poplars Clo., Wat. 59 BV32
Poplars Rd. E17 123 EB58
Poppins Ct. EC4 274 F9
Poppleton Rd. E11 124 EE58
Poppy Clo., Brwd. 108 FV43
Poppy Clo., Hem.H. 39 BE19
Poppy Clo., Wall. 200 DG102
Poppy La., Croy. 202 DW101
Poppyfields, Welw.G.C. 30 DC09
Porch Way N20 98 DF48
Porchester Clo., Horn. 128 FL58
Porchester Gdns. W2 140 DB73
Porchester Gdns. Ms. W2 140 DB72
Porchester Gdns.
Porchester Mead, Beck. 183 EA93
Porchester Ms. W2 140 DB72
Porchester Sq.
Porchester Pl. W2 272 C9
Porchester Pl. W2 140 DE72
Porchester Rd. W2 140 DB71
Porchester Rd., Kings.T. 198 CP96
Porchester Sq. W2 140 DB72
Porchester Ter. W2 140 DC73
Porchester Ter. N. W2 140 DB72
Porchfield Clo., Grav. 191 GJ89
Whitehill Rd.
Porchfield Clo., Sutt. 218 DB110
Porcupine Clo. SE9 184 EL89
Porden Rd. SW2 161 DM84
Porlock Ave., Har. 116 CC60
Porlock Rd. W10 139 CX70
Ladbroke Gro.
Porlock Rd., Enf. 100 DT45
Porlock St. SE1 279 L4
Porlock St. SE1 162 DR75
Porridge Pot All., Guil. 258 AW136
Buryfields
Porrington Clo., Chis. 205 EN95
Port Ave., Green. 189 FV86
Port Cres. E13 144 EH70
Jenkins Rd.
Port Hill, Hert. 32 DQ09
Port Hill, Orp. 224 EV112
Port Vale, Hert. 31 DP08
Portal Clo. SE27 181 DN90
Portal Clo., Ruis. 115 BU63
Portal Clo., Uxb. 134 BL66
Portbury Clo. SE15 162 DU81
Clayton Rd.
Portchester Clo. SE5 162 DR84
Portcullis Lo. Rd., Enf. 82 DR41
Portelet Rd. E1 143 DX69
Porten Rd. W14 159 CY76
Porter Clo., Grays 169 FW79
Porter Rd. E6 145 EM72
Porter St. SE1 279 J2
Porter St. W1 272 E6
Porters Ave., Dag. 146 EV65
Porters Clo., Brwd. 108 FU46
Greenshaw
Porters Pk. Dr., Rad. 62 CL32
Porters Wk. E1 142 DV73
Pennington St.
Porters Way, West Dr. 154 BM76
Porters Wd., St.Alb. 43 CE16
Portersfield Rd., Enf. 82 DS42
Porteus Rd. W2 140 DC71
Portgate Clo. W9 139 CZ70
Porthcawe Rd. SE26 183 DY91
Porthkerry Ave., Well. 166 EU84
Portia Way E3 143 DZ70
Portinscale Rd. SW15 179 CY85
Portland Ave. N16 122 DT59
Portland Ave., Grav. 191 GH89
Portland Ave., N.Mal. 199 CT101
Portland Ave., Sid. 186 EU86
Portland Clo., Rom. 126 EY57
Portland Clo., Slou. 131 AK70
Portland Cres. SE9 184 EL89
Portland Cres., Felt. 175 BR91
Portland Cres., Grnf. 136 CB70
Portland Cres., Stan. 95 CK54
Portland Dr., Enf. 82 DS38
Clay Hill
Portland Dr., Red. 251 DK129
Portland Dr. (Cheshunt), Wal.Cr. 66 DU31
Portland Gdns. N4 121 DP58
Portland Gdns., Rom. 126 EX57
Portland Gro. SW8 161 DM81
Portland Heights, Nthwd. 93 BT49
Portland Ms. W1 273 L9
Portland Pl. W1 273 H5
Portland Pl. W1 141 DH71
Portland Pl., Epsom 216 CS112
Portland Pl., Hert. 32 DW11
Portland Ri. N4 121 DP60
Portland Ri. Est. N4 122 DQ60
Portland Rd. N15 122 DT56
Portland Rd. SE9 184 EL89
Portland Rd. SE25 202 DU98
Portland Rd. W11 139 CY73
Portland Rd., Ashf. 174 BL90
Portland Rd., Brom. 184 EJ91
Portland Rd., Dor. 263 CG135
Portland Rd., Grav. 191 GH88
Portland Rd., Hayes 135 BS69
Portland Rd., Kings.T. 198 CL97
Portland Rd., Mitch. 200 DE96
Portland Rd., Sthl. 156 BZ76
Portland Sq. E1 142 DV74
Watts St.
Portland St. SE17 279 K10
Portland St. SE17 162 DR78
Portland St., St.Alb. 42 CC20
Portland Ter., Rich. 157 CK84
Portland Wk. SE17 162 DR79
Portland St.
Portley La., Cat. 236 DS121
Portley Wd. Rd., Whyt. 236 DT121
Portman Ave. SW14 158 CR83
Portman Clo. W1 272 E8
Portman Clo. W1 140 DF72
Portman Clo., Bex. 187 FE88
Portman Clo., Bexh. 166 EX83
Queen Anne's Gate
Portman Clo., St.Alb. 43 CJ15
Portman Dr., Wdf.Grn. 102 EK55
Portman Gdns. NW9 96 CR54
Portman Gdns., Uxb. 134 BN66
Portman Gate NW1 272 C5
Portman Ho., St.Alb. 43 CD17
Portman Ms. S. W1 272 F9
Portman Ms. S. W1 140 DG72
Portman Pl. E2 142 DW69
Portman Rd., Kings.T. 198 CM96
Portman Sq. W1 272 F8
Portman Sq. W1 140 DG72
Portman St. W1 272 F9
Portman St. W1 140 DG72
Portmeadow Wk. SE2 166 EX75
Portmeers Clo. E17 123 DZ58
Lennox Rd.
Portmore Gdns., Rom. 104 FA50
Portmore Pk. Rd., Wey. 212 BN105
Portmore Quays, Wey. 212 BM105
Bridge Rd.
Portmore Way, Wey. 194 BN104
Portnall Dr., Vir.W. 192 AT99
Portnall Ri., Vir.W. 192 AT99
Portnall Rd. W9 139 CZ68
Portnall Rd., Vir.W. 192 AT99
Portnalls Clo., Couls. 235 DH116
Portnalls Ri., Couls. 235 DH116
Portnalls Rd., Couls. 235 DH118
Portnoi Clo., Rom. 105 FD54
Portobello Clo., Chesh. 54 AN29
Portobello Ct. W11 139 CZ73
Westbourne Gro.
Portobello Ms. W11 140 DA73
Portobello Rd.
Portobello Rd. W10 139 CY71
Portobello Rd. W11 139 CZ72
Porton Ct., Surb. 197 CJ100
Portpool La. EC1 274 D6
Portpool La. EC1 141 DN71
Portree Clo. N22 99 DM52
Nightingale Rd.
Portree St. E14 143 ED72
Portsdown, Edg. 96 CN50
Rectory La.
Portsdown Ave. NW11 119 CZ58
Portsdown Ms. NW11 119 CZ58
Portsea Ms. W2 272 C9
Portsea Pl. W2 272 C9
Portsea Rd., Til. 171 GJ81
Portslade Rd. SW8 161 DJ82
Portsmouth Ave., T.Ditt. 197 CG101
Portsmouth Ct., Slou. 132 AS73
Portsmouth Rd. SW15 179 CV87
Portsmouth Rd., Cob. 229 BQ115
Portsmouth Rd., Esher 214 BZ108
Portsmouth Rd., Guil. 258 AV141
Portsmouth Rd., Kings.T. 197 CK98
Portsmouth Rd., Surb. 197 CJ100
Portsmouth Rd., T.Ditt. 197 CE103
Portsmouth Rd., Wok. 228 BM119
Portsmouth St. WC2 274 B9
Portsoken St. E1 275 P10
Portsoken St. E1 142 DT73
Portswood Pl. SW15 179 CT87
Danebury Ave.
Portugal Gdns., Twick. 176 CC89
Fulwell Pk. Ave.
Portugal Rd., Wok. 227 AZ116
Portugal St. WC2 274 B9
Portugal St. WC2 141 DM72
Portway E15 144 EF67
Portway, Epsom 217 CU110
Portway Cres., Epsom 217 CU109
Portway Gdns. SE18 164 EK80
Shooter's Hill Rd.
Post Ho. La., Lthd. 246 CA125
Post La., Twick. 177 CD88
Post Meadow, Iver 133 BD69
Post Office App. E7 124 EH64
Post Office Ct. EC3 275 L9
Post Office La., Beac. 89 AK52
Post Office La., Slou. 132 AX72
Post Office Rd., Harl. 35 ER14
Post Office Way SW8 161 DK80
Post Wd. Rd., Ware 33 DY08
Postern Grn., Enf. 81 DN40
Postfield, Welw.G.C. 30 DA06
Postmill Clo., Croy. 203 DX104
Postway Ms., Ilf. 125 EP62
Clements Rd.
Postwood Grn., Hert. 32 DW12
Potier St. SE1 279 L7
Potier St. SE1 162 DR76
Potkiln La., Beac. 111 AQ55
Pott St. E2 142 DV69
Potten End Hill, Berk. 39 BD16
Potten End Hill, Hem.H. 39 BE15
Potter Clo., Mitch. 201 DH96
Potter St., Harl. 52 EW16
Potter St., Nthwd. 93 BU53
Potter St., Pnr. 93 BV53
Potter St. Hill, Pnr. 93 BV51
Potterne Clo. SW19 179 CX87
Castlecombe Dr.
Potters Clo., Croy. 203 DY102
Potters Clo., Loug. 84 EL40
Potters Cross, Iver 133 BE69
Potters Fld., Harl. 52 EX17
Potters Fld., St.Alb. 43 CE16
Potters Flds. SE1 142 DS74
Tooley St.
Potters Gro., N.Mal. 198 CQ98
Potters Heights Clo., Pnr. 93 BV52
Potters La. SW16 181 DK93
Potters La., Barn. 80 DA42
Potters La., Borwd. 78 CQ39
Potters La., Wok. 227 BB123
Potters Rd. SW6 160 DC82
Townmead Rd.
Potters Rd., Barn. 80 DB42
Potters Way, Reig. 266 DC138
Pottery La. W11 139 CY73
Portland Rd.
Pottery Rd., Bex. 187 FC89
Pottery Rd., Brent. 158 CL79
Pottery St. SE16 162 DV75
Pouchen End La., Hem.H. 39 BD17
Poulcott, Stai. 172 AY86
Poulett Gdns., Twick. 177 CF88
Poulett Rd. E6 145 EM68
Poulner Way SE15 162 DT80
Daniel Gdns.
Poulters Wd., Kes. 222 EK106
Poultney Clo., Rad. 62 CL32
King Charles Rd.
Poulton Ave., Sutt. 200 DD104
Poulton Clo. E8 122 DV64
Spurstowe Ter.
Poultry EC2 275 K9
Poultry EC2 142 DR72
Pound, The, Slou. 130 AJ70
Hogfair La.
Pound Clo., Orp. 205 ER103
Pound Clo., Surb. 197 CJ102
Pound Clo., Wal.Abb. 50 EE23
Pound Ct., Ash. 232 CM118
Pound Ct. Dr., Orp. 205 ER103
Pound Cres., Lthd. 231 CD121
Pound Fld., Guil. 242 AX133
Pound Fld., Wat. 75 BT35
Ashfields
Pound La. NW10 139 CU65
Pound La., Epsom 216 CQ112
Pound La., Rad. 62 CM33
Pound La., Sev. 240 EX115
Pound La. (Knockholt Pound), Sev. 257 FJ124
Pound Pk. Rd. SE7 164 EK77
Pound Pl. SE9 185 EN86
Pound Pl., Guil. 259 AZ140
Pound Pl. Clo., Guil. 259 AZ140
Pound Rd., Bans. 233 CZ117
Pound Rd., Cher. 194 BH101
Pound St., Cars. 218 DF106
Pound Way, Chis. 185 EQ94
Royal Par.
Poundfield Gdns., Wok. 227 BC120
Poundfield Rd., Loug. 85 EN43
Poundwell, Welw.G.C. 30 DA10
Pounsley Rd., Sev. 256 FE121
Pountney Rd. SW11 160 DG83
Poverest Rd., Orp. 205 ET99
Povey Cross Rd., Horl. 268 DD150
Powder Mill La., Dart. 188 FL89
Powder Mill La., Twick. 176 BZ87
Powdermill La., Wal.Abb. 67 EB33
Powdermill Way, Wal.Abb. 67 EB32
Powell Clo., Chess. 215 CK106
Mansfield Rd.
Powell Clo., Edg. 96 CM51
Powell Clo., Guil. 258 AT136
Powell Clo., Horl. 268 DE147
Baden Dr.
Powell Clo., Wall. 219 DK108
Hermes Way
Powell Gdns., Dag. 126 FA63
Powell Rd. E5 122 DV62
Powell Rd., Buck.H. 102 EJ45
Powells Clo., Dor. 263 CJ139
Goodwyns Rd.
Powell's Wk. W4 158 CS79
Power Rd. W4 158 CN77
Powers Ct., Twick. 177 CK87
Powerscroft Rd. E5 122 DW63
Powerscroft Rd., Sid. 186 EW93
Powis Ct., Pot.B. 64 DC34
Powis Gdns. NW11 119 CZ59
Powis Gdns. W11 139 CZ72
Powis Ms. W11 139 CZ72
Westbourne Pk. Rd.
Powis Pl. WC1 274 A5
Powis Pl. WC1 141 DL70
Powis Rd. E3 143 EB69
Powis Sq. W11 139 CZ72
Powis St. SE18 165 EN76
Powis Ter. W11 139 CZ72
Powlett Pl. NW1 141 DH65
Harmood St.
Pownall Gdns., Houns. 156 CB84
Pownall Rd. E8 142 DU67
Pownall Rd., Houns. 156 CB84
Powster Rd., Brom. 184 EH92
Powys Clo., Bexh. 166 EX79
Powys La. N13 99 DL49
Powys La. N14 99 DL49
Poyle Ind. Est., Slou. 153 BE82
Poyle La., Slou. 130 AH67
Poyle Rd., Guil. 258 AY136
Poyle Rd., Slou. 153 BE83
Poyle Ter., Guil. 258 AX136
Sydenham Rd.

Poynder Rd., Til. 171 GH81
Poynders Ct. SW4 181 DJ86
Poynders Rd.
Poynders Gdns. SW4 181 DJ87
Poynders Hill, Hem.H. 41 BQ21
Poynders Rd. SW4 181 DJ86
Poynes Rd., Horl. 268 DE146
Poynings, The, Iver 153 BF77
Poynings Clo., Orp. 206 EW103
Poynings Rd. N19 121 DJ62
Poynings Way N12 98 DA50
Poynings Way, Rom. 106 FL53
Arlington Gdns.
Poyntell Cres., Chis. 205 ER95
Poynter Rd., Enf. 82 DU43
Poynton Rd. N17 100 DU54
Poyntz Rd. SW11 160 DF82
Poyser St. E2 142 DV68
Prae, The, Wok. 227 BF118
Prae Clo., St.Alb. 42 CB20
Praed Ms. W2 272 A8
Praed St. W2 272 A8
Praed St. W2 140 DD72
Praetorian Ct., St.Alb. 42 CC23
Pragel St. E13 144 EH68
Pragnell Rd. SE12 184 EH89
Prague Pl. SW2 181 DL85
Prah Rd. N4 121 DN61
Prairie Clo., Add. 194 BH104
Prairie Rd., Add. 194 BH104
Prairie St. SW8 160 DG82
Pratt Ms. NW1 141 DJ67
Pratt St.
Pratt St. NW1 141 DJ67
Pratt Wk. SE11 278 C8
Pratt Wk. SE11 161 DM77
Pratts La., Walt. 214 BX105
Molesey Rd.
Pratts Pas., Kings.T. 198 CL96
Eden St.
Prayle Gro. NW2 119 CX60
Prebend Gdns. W4 159 CT77
Prebend Gdns. W6 159 CT77
Prebend St. N1 142 DQ67
Precinct, The, W.Mol. 196 CB97
Victoria Ave.
Precinct Rd., Hayes 135 BU73
Precincts, The, Mord. 200 DB100
Green La.
Precincts, The, Slou. 130 AH70
Premier Ave., Grays 170 GC75
Premier Cor. W9 139 CZ68
Kilburn La.
Premier Pl. SW15 159 CY84
Putney High St.
Premiere Pl. E14 143 EA73
Garford St.
Prendergast Rd. SE3 164 EE83
Prentice Pl., Harl. 52 EW17
Prentis Rd. SW16 181 DK91
Prentiss Ct. SE7 164 EK77
Presburg Rd., N.Mal. 198 CS99
Prescelly Pl., Edg. 96 CM53
Prescot Rd., Slou. 153 BE82
Prescot St. E1 142 DT73
Prescott Ave., Orp. 205 EP100
Prescott Clo. SW16 181 DL94
Prescott Clo., Horn. 127 FH60
St. Leonards Way
Prescott Grn., Loug. 85 EQ41
Prescott Ho. SE17 161 DP79
Hillingdon St.
Prescott Pl. SW4 161 DK83
Prescott Rd. (Cheshunt), Wal.Cr. 67 DY27
Presdale Dr., Ware 33 DX07
Presentation Ms. SW2 181 DM88
Palace Rd.
President Dr. E1 142 DV74
Waterman Way
President St. EC1 275 H2
Press Rd. NW10 118 CR62
Press Rd., Uxb. 134 BK65
Prestage Way E14 143 EC73
Ditchburn St.
Prestbury Ct., Wok. 226 AU118
Muirfield Rd.
Prestbury Cres., Bans. 234 DF116
Prestbury Rd. E7 144 EJ66
Prestbury Sq. SE9 185 EM91
Prested Rd. SW11 160 DE84
St. John's Hill
Preston Ave. E4 101 ED51
Preston Clo. SE1 279 M8
Preston Clo., Ash. 231 CJ116
Preston Clo., Twick. 177 CE90
Preston Ct., Walt. 196 BW102
St. Johns Dr.
Preston Dr. E11 124 EJ57
Preston Dr., Bexh. 166 EX81
Preston Dr., Epsom 216 CS107
Preston Gdns. NW10 138 CS65
Church Rd.
Preston Gdns., Enf. 83 DY37
Preston Gdns., Ilf. 124 EL58
Preston Gro., Ash. 231 CJ117
Preston Hill, Chesh. 54 AR29
Preston Hill, Har. 118 CL59
Preston La., Tad. 233 CV121
Preston Pl. NW2 139 CU65
Preston Pl., Rich. 178 CL85
Preston Rd. E11 124 EE58
Preston Rd. SE19 181 DP93
Preston Rd. SW20 179 CT94
Preston Rd., Grav. 190 GE88
Preston Rd., Har. 118 CL59
Preston Rd., Rom. 106 FK49
Preston Rd., Shep. 194 BN99
Preston Rd., Slou. 132 AW73
Preston Rd., Wem. 118 CL61
Preston Waye, Har. 118 CL60
Prestons Rd. E14 163 EC75
Prestons Rd., Brom. 204 EG104
Prestwick Clo., Sthl. 156 BY78
Ringway
Prestwick Rd., Wat. 94 BW46
Prestwood, Slou. 132 AV72
Prestwood Ave., Har. 117 CH56
Prestwood Clo. SE18 166 EU80
Prestwood Clo., Har. 117 CH56
Prestwood Dr., Rom. 105 FC50
Prestwood Gdns., Croy. 202 DQ101
Prestwood St. N1 275 J1
Pretoria Ave. E17 123 DY56
Pretoria Clo. N17 100 DT52
Pretoria Rd.
Pretoria Cres. E4 101 EC46
Pretoria Rd. E4 101 EC46
Pretoria Rd. E11 123 ED60
Pretoria Rd. E16 144 EF70
Pretoria Rd. N17 100 DT52
Pretoria Rd. SW16 181 DH93
Pretoria Rd., Cher. 193 BF102
Pretoria Rd., Ilf. 125 EP64
Pretoria Rd., Rom. 127 FC56
Pretoria Rd., Wat. 75 BU42
Pretoria Rd. N. N18 100 DT51
Prevost Rd. N11 98 DG47
Prey Heath, Wok. 226 AV123
Prey Heath Clo., Wok. 226 AW124
Prey Heath Rd., Wok. 226 AV124
Price Clo. NW7 97 CY51
Price Clo. SW17 180 DF90
Price Rd., Croy. 219 DP105
Price Way, Hmptn. 176 BY93
Victors Dr.
Prices La., Reig. 266 DA137
Price's Yd. N1 141 DM67
Matilda St.
Pricklers Hill, Barn. 80 DB44
Prickley Wd., Brom. 204 EF102
Priddy's Yd., Croy. 202 DQ103
Crown Hill
Prideaux Pl. W3 138 CR73
Friars Pl. La.
Prideaux Pl. WC1 274 C2
Prideaux Pl. WC1 141 DM69
Prideaux Rd. SW9 161 DL83
Pridham Rd., Th.Hth. 202 DR98
Priest Ct. EC2 275 H8
Priest Hill, Egh. 172 AW90
Priest Hill, Wind. 172 AW88
Priest Pk. Ave., Har. 116 CA61
Priestfield Rd. SE23 183 DY90
Priestlands Pk. Rd., Sid. 185 ET90
Priestley Clo. N16 122 DT59
Ravensdale Rd.
Priestley Gdns., Rom. 126 EV58
Priestley Rd., Mitch. 200 DG96
Priestley Way E17 123 DX55
Priestley Way NW2 119 CU60
Priestly Gdns., Wok. 227 BA120
Priests Ave., Rom. 105 FD54
Priests Bri. SW14 158 CS83
Priests Bri. SW15 158 CS83
Priests Fld., Brwd. 109 GC50
Priests La., Brwd. 108 FY47
Prima Rd. SW9 161 DN80
Primley La., Bishop's Stortford 37 FC06
Primrose Ave., Enf. 82 DR39
Primrose Ave., Horl. 269 DH149
Primrose Ave., Rom. 126 EU59
Primrose Clo. SE6 183 EC92
Primrose Clo., Har. 116 BZ62
Primrose Clo., Hat. 45 CV19
Primrose Clo., Hem.H. 39 BE21
Primrose Clo., Wall. 201 DH101
Primrose Dr., Hert. 32 DV09
Primrose Fld., Harl. 51 ET18
Primrose Gdns. NW3 140 DE65
Primrose Gdns., Ruis. 116 BW64
Primrose Gdns. (Bushey), Wat. 94 CB45
Primrose Glen, Horn. 128 FL56
Primrose Hill EC4 274 E9
Primrose Hill, Brwd. 108 FW48
Primrose Hill, Kings L. 59 BP28
Primrose Hill Ct. NW3 140 DF66
Primrose Hill Rd. NW3 140 DF66
Primrose Hill Studios NW1 140 DG67
Fitzroy Rd.
Primrose La., Croy. 202 DW102
Primrose Ms. NW1 140 DF66
Sharpleshall St.
Primrose Ms. SE3 164 EF81
Langton Way
Primrose Path (Cheshunt), Wal.Cr. 66 DU31
Primrose Rd. E10 123 EB60
Primrose Rd. E18 102 EH54
Primrose Rd., Walt. 214 BW106
Primrose St. EC2 275 M6
Primrose St. EC2 142 DS71
Primrose Wk., Epsom 217 CT108
Kingston Rd.
Primrose Way, Wem. 137 CK68
Primula St. W12 139 CU72
Prince Albert Rd. NW1 272 C1
Prince Albert Rd. NW1 140 DF68
Prince Albert Rd. NW8 272 C1
Prince Albert Rd. NW8 140 DE69
Prince Albert Sq., Red. 266 DF139
Prince Alberts Wk., Wind. 152 AU81
Prince Arthur Ms. NW3 120 DC63
Perrins La.
Prince Arthur Rd. NW3 120 DC64
Prince Charles Ave. (South Darenth), Dart. 209 FR96
Prince Charles Dr. NW4 119 CW59
Prince Charles Rd. SE3 164 EF82
Prince Charles Way, Wall. 201 DH104
Prince Consort Cotts., Wind. 151 AR82
Prince Consort Dr., Chis. 205 ER95
Prince Consort Rd. SW7 160 DC76
Prince Edward Rd. E9 143 DZ65
Prince Edward St., Berk. 38 AW19
Prince George Ave. N14 81 DJ42
Prince George Duke of Kent Ct., Chis. 185 ER94
Holbrook La.
Prince George Rd. N16 122 DS63
Prince George's Ave. SW20 199 CW96
Prince George's Rd. SW19 200 DD95
Prince Henry Rd. SE7 164 EK80
Prince Imperial Rd. SE18 165 EM81
Prince Imperial Rd., Chis. 185 EP94
Prince John Rd. SE9 184 EL85
Prince of Orange La. SE10 163 EC80
Greenwich High Rd.
Prince of Wales Clo. NW4 119 CV56
Church Ter.
Prince of Wales Dr. SW8 161 DH80
Prince of Wales Dr. SW11 160 DE81
Prince of Wales Footpath, Enf. 83 DX37
St. Stephens Rd.
Prince of Wales Gate SW7 276 B5
Prince of Wales Gate SW7 160 DE75
Prince of Wales Pas. NW1 273 K3
Prince of Wales Rd. E16 144 EJ72
Prince of Wales Rd. NW5 140 DG65
Prince of Wales Rd. SE3 164 EF81
Prince of Wales Rd., Red. 267 DN143
Prince of Wales Rd., Sutt. 200 DD103
Prince of Wales Ter. W4 158 CS78
Prince of Wales Ter. W8 160 DB75
Kensington Rd.
Prince Pk., Hem.H. 40 BG21
Prince Regent Ct. SE16 143 DY74
Rotherhithe St.
Prince Regent La. E13 144 EH69
Prince Regent La. E16 144 EJ71
Prince Regent Rd., Houns. 156 CC83
Prince Rd. SE25 202 DS99
Prince Rupert Rd. SE9 165 EM84
Prince St. SE8 163 DZ79
Prince St., Wat. 76 BW41
Princedale Rd. W11 139 CY74
Princelet St. E1 142 DT71
Prince's Arc. SW1 277 L2
Princes Ave. N3 98 DA53
Princes Ave. N10 121 DH55
Princes Ave. N13 99 DN50
Princes Ave. N22 99 DK53
Princes Ave. NW9 118 CN56
Princes Ave. W3 158 CN76
Princes Ave., Cars. 218 DF108
Princes Ave., Dart. 188 FP88
Princes Ave., Enf. 83 DY36
Princes Ave., Grnf. 136 CB72
Princes Ave., Orp. 205 ES99
Princes Ave., S.Croy. 236 DV115
Princes Ave., Surb. 198 CN102
Princes Ave., Wat. 75 BT43
Princes Ave., Wdf.Grn. 102 EH49
Princes Clo. N4 121 DP60
Portland Ri.
Princes Clo. NW9 118 CN56
Princes Clo. SW4 161 DJ83
Old Town
Princes Clo., Berk. 38 AU17
Princes Clo., Edg. 96 CN50
Princes Clo., Epp. 71 FC25
Princes Clo., Sid. 186 EX90
Princes Clo., S.Croy. 236 DV115
Princes Clo., Tedd. 177 CD91
Princes Clo., Wind. 151 AM78
Princes Ct. E1 142 DV73
Princes Ct., Hem.H. 40 BH23
Roughdown Rd.
Princes Ct., Wem. 118 CL64
Princes Dr., Har. 117 CE55
Prince's Dr., Lthd. 215 CE112
Princes Gdns. SW7 276 A6
Princes Gdns. SW7 160 DD76
Princes Gdns. W3 138 CN71
Princes Gdns. W5 137 CJ70
Princes Gate SW7 276 A5
Princes Gate SW7 160 DE75
Princes Gate Ct. SW7 276 A5
Princes Gate Ms. SW7 276 A6
Princes Gate Ms. SW7 160 DD76
Princes La. N10 121 DH55
Princes Ms. W2 140 DA73
Hereford Rd.
Princes Par., Pot.B. 64 DC32
High St.
Princes Pk., Rain. 147 FG66
Princes Pk. Ave. NW11 119 CY58
Princes Pk. Ave., Hayes 135 BR73
Princes Pk. Circle, Hayes 135 BR73
Princes Pk. Clo., Hayes 135 BR73
Princes Pk. La., Hayes 135 BR73
Princes Pk. Par., Hayes 135 BR73
Princes Pk. La.
Princes Pl. SW1 277 L2
Princes Pl. W11 139 CY74
Princes Plain, Brom. 204 EL101
Princes Ri. SE13 163 EC82
Princes Rd. N18 100 DW49
Princes Rd. SE20 183 DX93
Princes Rd. SW14 158 CR83
Princes Rd. SW19 180 DA93
Princes Rd. W13 137 CH74
Broomfield Rd.
Princes Rd., Ashf. 174 BM92
Princes Rd., B.End 110 AC60
Princes Rd., Buck.H. 102 EJ47
Princes Rd., Dart. 187 FG86
Princes Rd., Egh. 173 AZ93
Princes Rd., Felt. 175 BT89
Princes Rd., Grav. 191 GJ91
Princes Rd., Ilf. 125 ER56
Princes Rd., Kings.T. 198 CN95
Princes Rd., Red. 266 DF136
Princes Rd., Rich. 178 CM85
Princes Rd. (Kew), Rich. 158 CM81
Princes Rd., Rom. 127 FG57
Princes Rd., Tedd. 177 CD91
Princes Rd., Wey. 213 BP106
Princes Sq. W2 140 DB73
Princes St. EC2 275 K9
Princes St. EC2 142 DR72
Princes St. N17 100 DS51
Queen St.
Princes St. W1 273 J9
Princes St. W1 141 DH72
Princes St., Bexh. 166 EZ84
Princes St., Grav. 191 GH86
Princes St., Rich. 178 CL85
Sheen Rd.
Princes St., Slou. 152 AV75
Princes St., Sutt. 218 DD105
Princes St., Ware 33 DX05
Princes Ter. E13 144 EH67
Princes Vw., Dart. 188 FN88
Princes Way SW19 179 CX87
Princes Way, Brwd. 109 GA46
Princes Way, Buck.H. 102 EJ47
Princes Way, Croy. 219 DM106
Princes Way, Ruis. 116 BY63
Princes Way, W.Wick. 222 EF105
Princes Yd. W11 139 CY74
Princedale Rd.
Princesfield Rd., Wal.Abb. 68 EH33
Princess Ave., Wem. 118 CL61
Princess Ave., Wind. 151 AP83
Princess Ct. SE16 163 DZ76
Princess Cres. N4 121 DP61
Princess Gdns., Wok. 227 BB116
Princess La., Ruis. 115 BS60
Princess Mary's Rd., Add. 212 BJ105
Princess May Rd. N16 122 DS63
Princess Ms. NW3 140 DD65
Belsize Cres.
Princess Par., Orp. 205 EN104
Crofton Rd.
Princess Rd. NW1 140 DG67
Princess Rd. NW6 140 DA68
Princess Rd., Croy. 202 DQ100
Princess Rd., Swan. 187 FG93
Princess Rd., Wok. 227 BB116
Princess St. SE1 278 G7
Princess St. SE1 161 DP76
Princess Way, Red. 250 DG133
Princesses Wk., Rich. 158 CL80
Kew Rd.
Princethorpe Ho. W2 140 DB71
Princethorpe Rd. SE26 183 DX91
Princeton Ct. SW15 159 CX83
Felsham Rd.
Princeton St. WC1 274 B7
Princeton St. WC1 141 DM71
Pringle Gdns. SW16 181 DJ91
Print Village SE15 162 DT82
Chadwick Rd.
Printer St. EC4 274 E8
Printers Way, Harl. 36 EU10
Printing Ho. Yd. E2 275 N3
Printinghouse La., Hayes 155 BS75
Priolo Rd. SE7 164 EJ78
Prior Ave., Sutt. 218 DE108
Prior Bolton St. N1 141 DP65
Prior Chase, Grays 170 FZ77
Prior Gro., Chesh. 54 AQ30
Prior Rd., Ilf. 125 EN62
Prior St. SE10 163 EC80
Prioress Rd. SE27 181 DP90
Prioress St. SE1 279 L7
Prioress St. SE1 162 DR76
Priors, The, Ash. 231 CK119
Priors Clo., Hert. 32 DV12
Priors Clo., Slou. 152 AU76
Priors Ct., Wok. 226 AU118
Priors Cft. E17 101 DY54
Priors Cft., Wok. 227 BA120
Priors Fld., Nthlt. 136 BY65
Arnold Rd.
Priors Gdns., Ruis. 116 BW64
Priors Mead, Enf. 82 DS39
Priors Mead, Lthd. 246 CC125
Priors Pk., Horn. 128 FJ62
Priors Rd., Wind. 151 AK83
Priors Wd. Rd., Hert. 32 DW12
Priorsford Ave., Orp. 206 EU98
Priory, The SE3 164 EF84
Priory, The, Gdse. 252 DV131
Priory Ave. E4 101 DZ48
Priory Ave. E17 123 EA57
Priory Ave. N8 121 DK56
Priory Ave. W4 158 CS77
Priory Ave., Harl. 36 EW10
Priory Ave., Orp. 205 ER100
Priory Ave., Sutt. 217 CX105
Priory Ave., Uxb. 114 BJ56
Priory Ave., Wem. 117 CF63
Priory Clo. E4 101 DZ48
Priory Clo. E18 102 EG53
Priory Clo. N3 97 CZ53
Church Cres.
Priory Clo. N14 81 DH43
Priory Clo. N20 97 CZ45
Priory Clo. SW19 200 DB95
High Path
Priory Clo., Beck. 203 DY97
Priory Clo., Brwd. 108 FU43
Priory Clo., Brox. 49 DY24
High Rd. Turnford
Priory Clo., Chis. 205 EM95
Priory Clo., Dart. 188 FJ85
Priory Clo., Dor. 263 CG138
Priory Clo., Hmptn. 196 BZ95
Priory Gdns.
Priory Clo., Hayes 135 BV73
Priory Clo., Hodd. 49 EA18
Priory Clo., Horl. 268 DF147
Priory Clo., Ruis. 115 BT60
Priory Clo., Stan. 95 CF48
Priory Clo., Sun. 175 BU94
Priory Clo. (Denham), Uxb. 114 BG62
Priory Clo. (Harefield), Uxb. 114 BH56
Priory Clo., Walt. 195 BU104
Priory Clo. (Sudbury), Wem. 117 CF63
Priory Clo., Wok. 211 BD113
Priory Ct. E17 123 DZ55
Priory Ct. EC4 141 DP72
Pilgrim St.
Priory Ct. SW8 161 DK81
Priory Ct., Berk. 38 AW19
Priory Ct., Guil. 258 AW137
Portsmouth Rd.
Priory Ct., Harl. 52 EV18
Southern Way
Priory Ct. (Bushey), Wat. 94 CC46
Sparrows Herne
Priory Ct. Est. E17 101 DZ54
Priory Cres. SE19 182 DQ94
Priory Cres., Sutt. 217 CX105
Priory Cres., Wem. 117 CG62
Priory Dr. SE2 166 EX78
Priory Dr., Reig. 266 DA136
Priory Dr., Stan. 95 CF48
Priory Fld. Dr., Edg. 96 CP49
Priory Flds. (Farningham), Dart. 208 FM103
Priory Gdns. N6 121 DH58
Priory Gdns. SW13 159 CT83
Priory Gdns. W4 158 CS77
Priory Gdns. W5 138 CL69
Hanger La.
Priory Gdns., Berk. 38 AW19
Priory Gdns., Dart. 188 FK85
Priory Gdns., Hmptn. 176 BZ94
Priory Gdns., Uxb. 114 BJ56
Priory Gdns., Wem. 117 CG63
Priory Gate, Wal.Cr. 67 DZ27
Priory Grn., Stai. 174 BH92
Priory Grn. Est. N1 141 DM68
Priory Gro. SW8 161 DL81
Priory Gro., Rom. 106 FL48
Priory Hill, Dart. 188 FK85
Priory Hill, Wem. 117 CG63
Priory La. SW15 178 CS86
Priory La. (Farningham), Dart. 208 FM102
Priory La., Rich. 158 CN80
Forest Rd.
Priory La., W.Mol. 196 CA98
Priory Ms. SW8 161 DL81
Priory Ms., Stai. 174 BH92
Chestnut Manor Clo.
Priory Pk. SE3 164 EF83
Priory Pk. Rd. NW6 139 CZ67
Priory Pk. Rd., Wem. 117 CG63
Priory Path, Rom. 106 FL48
Priory Pl., Dart. 188 FK86
Priory Pl., Walt. 195 BU104
Priory Rd. E6 144 EK67
Priory Rd. N8 121 DJ56
Priory Rd. NW6 140 DB67
Priory Rd. SW19 180 DD94
Priory Rd. W4 158 CR76
Priory Rd., Bark. 145 ER66
Priory Rd., Chess. 198 CL104
Priory Rd., Croy. 201 DN101
Priory Rd., Dart. 188 FK86
Priory Rd., Ger.Cr. 112 AX55
Priory Rd., Hmptn. 176 BZ94
Priory Rd., Houns. 176 CC85
Priory Rd., Loug. 84 EL42
Priory Rd., Reig. 266 DA136
Priory Rd., Rich. 158 CN80
Priory Rd., Rom. 106 FL48
Priory Rd., Slou. 130 AJ71
Priory Rd., Sutt. 217 CX105
Priory St. E3 143 EB69
St. Leonards St.
Priory St., Hert. 32 DR09
Priory St., Ware 32 DW06
Priory Ter. NW6 140 DB67
Priory Ter., Sun. 175 BU94
Priory Clo.
Priory Vw. (Bushey), Wat. 95 CE45
Priory Wk. SW10 160 DC78
Priory Wk., St.Alb. 43 CE23
Priory Way, Ger.Cr. 112 AX55
Priory Way, Har. 116 CB56
Priory Way, Slou. 152 AV80
Priory Way, Sthl. 156 BX76
Western Rd.
Priory Way, West Dr. 154 BL79
Pritchard's Rd. E2 142 DU68
Priter Rd. SE16 162 DU76
Priter Way SE16 162 DU76
Dockley Rd.
Private Rd., Enf. 82 DR43
Probert Rd. SW2 181 DN85
Probyn Rd. SW2 181 DP89
Procter St. WC1 274 B7
Procter St. WC1 141 DM71
Proctor Gdns., Lthd. 246 CB125
Proctors Clo., Felt. 175 BU88
Profumo Rd., Walt. 214 BX106
Progress Business Pk., The, Croy. 201 DM103
Progress Way N22 99 DN53
Progress Way, Croy. 201 DM103
Progress Way, Enf. 82 DU43
Promenade, The W4 158 CS81
Promenade App. Rd. W4 158 CS80
Promenade de Verdun, Pur. 219 DK111
Prospect Clo. SE26 182 DV91
Prospect Clo., Belv. 166 FA77
Prospect Clo., Houns. 156 BZ81
Prospect Clo., Ruis. 116 BX59
Prospect Cotts. SW18 160 DA84
Point Pleasant
Prospect Cres., Twick. 176 CC86
Prospect Gro., Grav. 191 GK87
Prospect Hill E17 123 EB56
Prospect La., Egh. 172 AU92
Prospect Pl. E1 142 DW74
Prospect Pl. N2 120 DD56
Prospect Pl. N17 100 DS53
Church Rd.
Prospect Pl. NW2 119 CZ62
Ridge Rd.
Prospect Pl. NW3 120 DC63
Holly Wk.
Prospect Pl., Brom. 204 EH97
Prospect Pl., Dart. 188 FL86
Prospect Pl., Epsom 216 CS113
Clayton Rd.
Prospect Pl., Grav. 191 GK87
Prospect Pl., Grays 170 GB79
Prospect Pl., Rom. 105 FC54
Prospect Pl., Stai. 173 BF92
Prospect Ring N2 120 DD55
Prospect Rd. NW2 119 CZ62
Ridge Rd.
Prospect Rd., Barn. 80 DA43
Prospect Rd., Horn. 128 FM55
Prospect Rd., St.Alb. 43 CD22
Prospect Rd., Sev. 257 FJ123
Prospect Rd., Surb. 197 CJ100
Prospect Rd. (Cheshunt), Wal.Cr. 66 DW29
Prospect Rd., Wdf.Grn. 102 EJ51
Prospect St. SE16 162 DV75
Jamaica Rd.
Prospect Vale SE18 164 EL77
Prospect Way, Brwd. 109 GE42
Prospero Rd. N19 121 DJ60
Prossers, Tad. 233 CX121
Croffets
Prothero Gdns. NW4 119 CV57
Prothero Ho. NW10 138 CR66
Prothero Rd. SW6 159 CY80
Prout Gro. NW10 118 CS63
Prout Rd. E5 122 DV62
Provence St. N1 142 DQ68
St. Peters St.
Providence Ct. W1 272 G10
Providence Ct. W1 140 DG73
Providence La., Hayes 155 BR80
Providence Pl. N1 141 DP67
Upper St.
Providence Pl., Epsom 216 CS112
Providence Pl., Rom. 104 EZ54
Providence Pl., Wok. 212 BG114
Providence Rd., West Dr. 134 BL74
Providence Row N1 274 B1
Providence St. N1 142 DQ68
St. Peters St.
Providence St., Green. 189 FU85
Providence Yd. E2 142 DU69
Ezra St.
Provident Ind. Est., Hayes 155 BU75
Provost Est. N1 275 K2
Provost Est. N1 142 DR68
Provost Rd. NW3 140 DF66
Provost St. N1 275 K1
Provost St. N1 142 DR68
Prowse Ave. (Bushey), Wat. 94 CC47

Prowse Pl. NW1 141 DH66
Bonny St.
Pruden Clo. N14 99 DJ47
Prudent Pas. EC2 275 K8
Prune Hill, Egh. 172 AX94
Prusom St. E1 142 DV74
Pryford Wds. Rd., Wok. 227 BE115
Pryor Clo., Abb.L. 59 BT32
Pryors, The NW3 120 DD62
Puck La., Wal.Abb. 67 ED29
Puddenhole Cotts., Bet. 248 CN133
Pudding La. EC3 279 L1
Pudding La. EC3 142 DR73
Pudding La., Chig. 85 ES44
Pudding La., Hem.H. 40 BG18
Pudding La., Sev. 257 FN121
Church St.
Pudding Mill La. E15 143 EB67
Puddle Dock EC4 274 G10
Puddledock La., Dart. 187 FE92
Puddledock La., West. 255 ET133
Puers La., Beac. 90 AS51
Puffin Clo., Beck. 203 DX99
Pulborough Rd. SW18 179 CZ87
Pulborough Way, Houns. 156 BW84
Pulford Rd. N15 122 DR58
Pulham Ave. N2 120 DC56
Pulham Ave., Brox. 49 DY21
Baas Hill
Puller Rd., Barn. 79 CY40
Puller Rd., Hem.H. 40 BG21
Pulleyns Ave. E6 144 EL69
Pulleys Clo., Hem.H. 39 BF19
Pulleys La., Hem.H. 39 BF19
Pullfields, Chesh. 54 AN30
Pullman Ct. SW2 181 DL88
Pullman Gdns. SW15 179 CW86
Pullman Pl. SE9 184 EL85
Sherard Rd.
Pulpit Clo., Chesh. 54 AN29
Pulross Rd. SW9 161 DM83
Pulteney Clo. E3 143 DZ67
Pulteney Rd. E18 124 EH55
Pulteney Ter. N1 141 DM67
Pulton Pl. SW6 160 DA80
Puma Ct. E1 275 P6
Pump All., Brent. 157 CK80
Pump Clo., Nthlt. 136 CA68
Union Rd.
Pump Ct. EC4 274 D9
Pump Hill, Loug. 85 EM40
Pump La. SE14 162 DW80
Pump La., Chesh. 54 AS32
Pump La., Epp. 51 EP24
Pump La., Hayes 155 BT75
Pump La., Orp. 225 FB106
Pump Pail N., Croy. 202 DQ104
Old Town
Pump Pail S., Croy. 202 DQ104
Southbridge Rd.
Pumping Sta. Rd. W4 158 CS80
Pumpkin Hill, Slou. 131 AL65
Punch Bowl, Chesh. 54 AQ32
Red Lion St.
Punch Bowl La., Hem.H. 41 BR17
Punch Bowl La., St.Alb. 41 BT16
Punchbowl La., Dor. 263 CK135
Pundersons Gdns. E2 142 DV69
Purbeck Ave., N.Mal. 199 CT100
Purbeck Clo., Red. 251 DK128
Purbeck Dr. NW2 119 CX61
Purbeck Dr., Wok. 211 AZ114
Purbeck Rd., Horn. 127 FG59
Purberry Gro., Epsom 217 CT110
Purbrock Ave., Wat. 75 BV36
Purbrook Clo., Red. 251 DK128
Purbrook Est. SE1 279 N5
Purbrook St. SE1 279 N6
Purcell Clo., Borwd. 77 CK39
Purcell Cres. SW6 159 CX80
Purcell Ms. NW10 138 CS66
Suffolk Rd.
Purcell Rd., Grnf. 136 CB71
Purcell St. N1 142 DS68
Purcells Ave., Edg. 96 CN50
Purcells Clo., Ash. 232 CM118
Albert Rd.
Purchese St. NW1 141 DK68
Purdy St. E3 143 EB70
Purelake Ms. SE13 163 ED83
Marischal Rd.
Purfleet Bypass, Purf. 168 FP77
Purfleet Deep Wf., Purf. 168 FQ80
Purfleet Rd., S.Ock. 168 FN75
Purford Grn., Harl. 52 EU16
Purkiss Rd., Hert. 32 DQ12
Purland Clo., Dag. 126 EZ60
Purland Rd. SE28 165 ET75
Purleigh Ave., Wdf.Grn. 102 EL51
Purley Ave. NW2 119 CY61
Purley Bury Ave., Pur. 220 DQ111
Purley Bury Clo., Pur. 220 DQ111
Purley Clo., Ilf. 103 EN54
Purley Downs Rd., Pur. 220 DQ110
Purley Downs Rd., S.Croy. 220 DQ110
Purley Hill, Pur. 219 DP112
Purley Knoll, Pur. 219 DM111
Purley Oaks Rd., S.Croy. 220 DR109
Purley Pk. Rd., Pur. 219 DP110
Purley Pl. N1 141 DP66
Islington Pk. St.
Purley Ri., Pur. 219 DM112
Purley Rd. N9 100 DR48
Purley Rd., Pur. 219 DN111
Purley Rd., S.Croy. 220 DR108
Purley Vale, Pur. 219 DP113
Purley Way, Croy. 201 DM101
Purley Way, Pur. 219 DN111
Purlieu Way, Epp. 85 ES35
Purlings Rd. (Bushey), Wat. 76 CB43
Purneys Rd. SE9 164 EK84
Purrett Rd. SE18 165 ET78
Purser's Cross Rd. SW6 159 CZ81
Pursers La., Guil. 261 BR142
Pursewardens Clo. W13 137 CJ74
Pursley Gdns., Borwd. 78 CN38
Pursley Rd. NW7 97 CV52
Purton Ct., Slou. 131 AQ66
Purton La., Slou. 131 AQ66
Purves Rd. NW10 139 CV68
Puteaux Ho. E2 143 DX68
Mace St.
Putney Bri. SW6 159 CY83
Putney Bri. SW15 159 CY83
Putney Bri. App. SW6 159 CY83
Putney Bri. Rd. SW15 159 CY84
Putney Bri. Rd. SW18 180 DA85
Putney Common SW15 159 CW83
Putney Heath SW15 179 CV87
Putney Heath La. SW15 179 CX86
Putney High St. SW15 159 CX84
Putney Hill SW15 179 CX86
Putney Pk. Ave. SW15 159 CU84
Putney Pk. La. SW15 159 CV84
Putney Rd., Enf. 83 DX36
Puttenham Clo., Wat. 94 BX47
Putters Cft., Hem.H. 40 BM15
Puttocks Clo., Hat. 45 CW23
Puttocks Dr., Hat. 45 CW23
Pycroft Rd., Cher. 193 BE101
Pycroft Way N9 100 DU48
Pyebush La., Beac. 111 AN56
Pyecombe Cor. N12 97 CZ49
Pyenest Rd., Harl. 51 EP18
Pyghtle, The, Uxb. 114 BG59
Savay La.
Pylbrook Rd., Sutt. 200 DA104
Pyle Hill, Wok. 226 AX124
Pylon Way, Croy. 201 DL102
Pym Clo., Barn. 80 DD43
Pym Pl., Grays 170 GA77
Pymers Mead SE21 182 DQ88
Pymmes Clo. N13 99 DM50
Pymmes Clo. N17 100 DV53
Pymmes Gdns. N. N9 100 DT48
Pymmes Gdns. S. N9 100 DT48
Pymmes Grn. Rd. N11 99 DH49
Pymmes Rd. N13 99 DL51
Pymms Brook Dr., Barn. 80 DE42
Pynchester Clo., Uxb. 114 BN61
Pyne Rd., Surb. 198 CN102
Pyne Ter. SW19 179 CX88
Windlesham Gro.
Pynest Grn. La., Wal.Abb. 84 EG38
Pynham Clo. SE2 166 EV76
Pynnacles Clo., Stan. 95 CH50
Pypers Hatch, Harl. 35 ET14
Pyrcroft La., Wey. 213 BP106
Pyrcroft Rd., Cher. 193 BF101
Pyrford Common Rd., Wok. 227 BE116
Pyrford Ct., Wok. 227 BE117
Pyrford Heath, Wok. 227 BF116
Pyrford Lock, Wok. 228 BJ116
Pyrford Rd., W.Byf. 212 BG113
Pyrford Rd., Wok. 228 BH116
Pyrford Wds. Clo., Wok. 227 BF115
Pyrford Wds. Rd., Wok. 227 BE115
Pyrland Rd. N5 122 DR64
Pyrland Rd., Rich. 178 CM86
Pyrles Grn., Loug. 85 EP39
Pyrles La., Loug. 85 EP40
Pyrmont Gro. SE27 181 DP90
Pyrmont Rd. W4 158 CN79
Pyrmont Rd., Ilf. 125 EQ61
High Rd.
Pytchley Cres. SE19 182 DQ93
Pytchley Rd. SE22 162 DS83
Pytt Fld., Harl. 52 EV16

Q

Quadrangle, The, Guil. 258 AU135
The Oval
Quadrangle, The, Welw.G.C. 29 CW08
Quadrant, The SE24 182 DQ85
Herne Hill
Quadrant, The SW20 199 CY95
Quadrant, The, Bexh. 166 EX80
Quadrant, The, Purf. 168 FQ77
Quadrant, The, Rich. 158 CL84
Quadrant, The, St.Alb. 43 CH17
Quadrant, The, Sutt. 218 DC107
Quadrant Arc. W1 277 L1
Quadrant Arc., Rom. 127 FE57
Quadrant Gro. NW5 120 DF64
Quadrant Rd., Rich. 157 CK84
Quadrant Rd., Th.Hth. 201 DP98
Quaggy Wk. SE3 164 EG84
Quail Gdns., S.Croy. 221 DY110
Quainton St. NW10 118 CR62
Quaker Clo., Sev. 257 FK123
Quaker La., Sthl. 156 CA76
Quaker La., Wal.Abb. 67 EC34
Quaker St. E1 275 P5
Quaker St. E1 142 DT70
Quakers Course NW9 97 CT53
Quakers Hall La., Sev. 257 FJ122
Quakers La., Islw. 157 CG81
Quakers La., Pot.B. 64 DB30
Quakers Wk. N21 82 DR44
Quality Ct. WC2 274 D8
Quality St., Red. 251 DH128
Quantock Clo., Hayes 155 BR80
Quantock Clo., St.Alb. 43 CJ16
Quantock Clo., Slou. 153 BA78
Quantock Dr., Wor.Pk. 199 CW103
Cotswold Way
Quantock Gdns. NW2 119 CX61
Quantock Rd., Bexh. 167 FE82
Cumbrian Ave.
Quantocks, Hem.H. 40 BM17
Quarles Clo., Rom. 104 FA52
Quarley Way SE15 162 DT80
Daniel Gdns.
Quarr Rd., Cars. 200 DD100
Quarrendon Rd., Amer. 55 AR40
Quarrendon St. SW6 160 DA82
Quarry, The, Bet. 248 CS132
Station Rd.
Quarry Clo., Oxt. 254 EE130
Quarry Cotts., Sev. 256 FG123
Quarry Hill, Grays 170 GA78
Quarry Hill, Sev. 257 FK123
Quarry Hill Pk., Reig. 250 DC131
Quarry Ms., Purf. 168 FN77
Fanns Ri.
Quarry Pk. Rd., Sutt. 217 CZ107
Quarry Ri., Sutt. 217 CZ107
Quarry Rd. SW18 180 DC86
Quarry Rd., Gdse. 252 DW128
Quarry Rd., Oxt. 254 EE130
Quarry Spring, Harl. 52 EU15
Quarry St., Guil. 258 AX136
Quarter Mile La. E10 123 EB63
Quarterdeck, The E14 163 EA75
Quartermaine Ave., Wok. 227 AZ122
Quartermass Clo., Hem.H. 40 BG19
Quartermass Rd.
Quartermass Rd., Hem.H. 40 BG19
Quaves Rd., Slou. 152 AV76
Quay La., Green. 169 FV84
Quay W., Tedd. 177 CH92
Quebec Ave., West. 255 ER126
Quebec Clo., Horl. 269 DN148
Alberta Dr.
Quebec Ms. W1 272 E9
Quebec Rd., Hayes 136 BW73
Quebec Rd., Ilf. 125 EP59
Quebec Rd., Til. 171 GG82
Quebec Sq., West. 255 ER126
Quebec Way SE16 163 DX75
Queen Adelaide Rd. SE20 182 DW93
Queen Alexandra's Ct. SW19 179 CZ92
Queen Anne Ave. N15 122 DT57
Suffield Rd.
Queen Anne Ave., Brom. 204 EF97
Queen Anne Clo., Esher 215 CE108
Queen Anne Ms. W1 273 J7
Queen Anne Rd. E9 143 DX65
Queen Anne St. W1 273 H8
Queen Anne St. W1 141 DH71
Queen Anne Ter. E1 142 DV73
Sovereign Clo.
Queen Anne's Clo., Twick. 177 CD90
Queen Anne's Gdns. W4 158 CS76
Queen Annes Gdns. W5 158 CL75
Queen Annes Gdns., Enf. 82 DS44
Queen Annes Gdns., Lthd. 231 CH121
Upper Fairfield Rd.
Queen Anne's Gdns., Mitch. 200 DF97
Queen Anne's Gate SW1 277 M5
Queen Anne's Gate SW1 161 DK75
Queen Anne's Gate, Bexh. 166 EX83
Queen Anne's Gro. W4 158 CS76
Queen Annes Gro. W5 158 CL75
Queen Annes Gro., Enf. 100 DR45
Queen Annes Pl., Enf. 82 DS44
Queen Annes Rd., Wind. 151 AQ84
Queen Annes Ter., Lthd. 231 CH121
Upper Fairfield Rd.
Queen Anne's Wk. WC1 274 A5
Queen Caroline Est. W6 159 CW78
Queen Caroline St. W6 159 CW78
Queen Charlotte St., Wind. 151 AR81
High St.
Queen Eleanor's Rd., Guil. 258 AT135
Queen Elizabeth Gdns., Mord. 200 DA98
Queen Elizabeth Pl., Til. 171 GG84
Queen Elizabeth Rd. E17 123 DY55
Queen Elizabeth Rd., Kings.T. 198 CM96
Queen Elizabeth II Bri., Dart. 169 FR82
Queen Elizabeth II Bri., Grays 169 FR82
Queen Elizabeth St. SE1 279 P4
Queen Elizabeth St. SE1 162 DT75
Queen Elizabeth Wk. SW13 159 CU81
Queen Elizabeth Wk., Wall. 219 DK105
Queen Elizabeth Wk., Wind. 152 AS82
Queen Elizabeth Way, Wok. 227 AZ119
Queen Elizabeths Clo. N16 122 DR61
Queen Elizabeths Dr. N14 99 DK46
Queen Elizabeth's Dr., Croy. 221 ED110
Queen Elizabeth's Gdns., Croy. 221 ED110
Queen Elizabeth's Dr.
Queen Elizabeths Wk. N16 122 DR61
Queen Margaret's Gro. N1 122 DS64
Queen Mary Ave., Mord. 199 CX99
Queen Mary Clo., Rom. 127 FF58
Queen Mary Clo., Wok. 227 BC116
Queen Mary Rd. SE19 181 DP93
Queen Mary Rd., Shep. 195 BQ96
Queen Mary's Ave., Cars. 218 DF108
Queen Marys Ave., Wat. 75 BS42
Queen Marys Dr., Add. 211 BF110
Queen Mother's Dr., Uxb. 113 BF58
Queen of Denmark Ct. SE16 163 DZ76
Queen Sq. WC1 274 A6
Queen Sq. WC1 141 DL70
Queen Sq. Pl. WC1 274 A5
Queen St. EC4 275 J10
Queen St. EC4 142 DQ73
Queen St. N17 100 DS51
Queen St. W1 277 H2
Queen St. W1 141 DH74
Queen St., Bexh. 166 EZ83
Queen St., Brwd. 108 FW50
Queen St., Cher. 194 BG102
Queen St., Croy. 202 DQ104
Church Rd.
Queen St., Erith 167 FE79
Queen St., Grav. 191 GH86
Queen St., Guil. 261 BQ139
Queen St., Kings L. 58 BG31
Queen St., Rom. 127 FD58
Queen St., St.Alb. 42 CC20
Queen St. Pl. EC4 279 J1
Queen Victoria Ave., Wem. 137 CK66
Queen Victoria St. EC4 274 G10
Queen Victoria St. EC4 141 DP73
Queen Victoria Ter. E1 142 DV73
Sovereign Clo.
Queen Victoria's Wk., Wind. 152 AS80
Queenborough Gdns., Chis. 185 ER93
Queenborough Gdns., Ilf. 125 EN56
Queendale Ct., Wok. 226 AT116
Roundthorn Way
Queenhill Rd., S.Croy. 220 DV110
Queenhithe EC4 275 J10
Queenhithe EC4 142 DQ73
Queenhythe Rd., Guil. 242 AX128
Queens Acre, Sutt. 217 CX108
Queens Acre, Wind. 151 AR84
Queens All., Epp. 69 ET31
Hemnall St.
Queens Ave. N3 98 DC52
Queens Ave. N10 120 DG55
Queens Ave. N20 98 DD47
Queen's Ave. N21 99 DP46
Queens Ave., Felt. 176 BW91
Queens Ave., Grnf. 136 CB72
Queens Ave., Stan. 117 CH55
Queens Ave., Wat. 75 BT42
Queens Ave., W.Byf. 212 BK112
Queens Ave., Wdf.Grn. 102 EH50
Queen's Circ. SW8 161 DH80
Queenstown Rd.
Queens Clo., Edg. 96 CN50
Queens Clo., Tad. 233 CU124
Queens Clo., Wall. 219 DH106
Queens Rd.
Queens Clo., Wind. 172 AU85
Queens Club Gdns. W14 159 CY79
Queens Ct. SE23 182 DW89
Queens Ct., Brox. 49 DZ24
Queens Ct., Rich. 178 CM86
Queens Ct., St.Alb. 43 CH20
Hatfield Rd.
Queens Ct., Slou. 132 AT73
Queens Ct., Wey. 213 BR106
Queens Ct. Ride, Cob. 213 BU113
Queens Cres. NW5 140 DG65
Queens Cres., Rich. 178 CM85
Queens Cres., St.Alb. 43 CH17
Queens Dr. E10 123 EA59
Queens Dr. N4 121 DP61
Queens Dr. W3 138 CM72
Queens Dr., Abb.L. 59 BT32
Queens Dr., Guil. 242 AU131
Queens Dr., Lthd. 214 CC111
Queen's Dr., Slou. 133 AZ66
Queens Dr., Surb. 198 CN101
Queens Dr., T.Ditt. 197 CG101
Queens Dr., Wal.Cr. 67 EA34
Queens Dr., The, Rick. 91 BF45
Queen's Elm Sq. SW3 160 DD78
Old Ch. St.
Queens Gdns. NW4 119 CW57
Queens Gdns. W2 140 DC72
Queens Gdns. W5 137 CJ71
Queens Gdns., Dart. 188 FP88
Queen's Gdns., Houns. 156 BY81
Queens Gdns., Rain. 147 FD68
Queens Gdns., Upmin. 129 FT58
Queen's Gate SW7 160 DC76
Queens Gate, Gat. 268 DG152
Queen's Gate Gdns. SW7 160 DC76
Queens Gate Gdns. SW15 159 CV84
Upper Richmond Rd.
Queen's Gate Ms. SW7 160 DC76
Queen's Gate Pl. SW7 160 DC76
Queen's Gate Pl. Ms. SW7 160 DC76
Queen's Gate Ter. SW7 160 DC76
Queen's Gro. NW8 140 DD67
Queen's Gro. Ms. NW8 140 DD67
Queen's Gro.
Queens Gro. Rd. E4 101 ED46
Queen's Head St. N1 141 DP67
Queens Head Wk., Brox. 49 DY23
High Rd. Wormley
Queens Head Yd. SE1 279 K3
Queens Ho., Tedd. 177 CF93
Queens La. N10 121 DH55
Queens La., Ashf. 174 BM91
Clarendon Rd.
Queens Mkt. E13 144 EJ67
Green St.
Queens Ms. W2 140 DB73
Salem Rd.
Queens Par. N11 98 DF50
Colney Hatch La.
Queens Par. W5 138 CM72
Queens Pk. Ct. W10 139 CX69
Queens Pk. Gdns., Felt. 175 BU90
Vernon Rd.
Queens Pk. Rd., Cat. 236 DS123
Queens Pk. Rd., Rom. 106 FM53
Queens Pas., Chis. 185 EP93
High St.
Queens Pl., Mord. 200 DA98
Queens Pl., Wat. 76 BW41
Queen's Prom., Kings.T. 197 CK97
Portsmouth Rd.
Queens Reach, E.Mol. 197 CE98
Queens Ride SW13 159 CU83
Queens Ride SW15 159 CW83
Queen's Ride, Rich. 178 CP88
Queens Ri., Rich. 178 CM86
Queens Rd. E11 123 ED59
Queens Rd. E13 144 EH67
Queen's Rd. E17 123 DZ58
Queens Rd. N3 98 DC53
Queens Rd. N9 100 DV48
Queen's Rd. N11 99 DL52
Queens Rd. NW4 119 CW57
Queens Rd. SE14 162 DV81
Queens Rd. SE15 162 DV81
Queens Rd. SW14 158 CR83
Queens Rd. SW19 179 CZ93
Queens Rd. W5 138 CL72
Queens Rd., Bark. 145 EQ65
Queens Rd., Barn. 79 CX41
Queens Rd., Beck. 203 DY96
Queens Rd., Berk. 38 AU18
Queens Rd., Brwd. 108 FW48
Queens Rd., Brom. 204 EG96
Queens Rd., Buck.H. 102 EH47
Queens Rd., Chesh. 54 AQ30
Queens Rd., Chis. 185 EP93
Queen's Rd., Croy. 201 DP100
Queens Rd., Egh. 173 AZ93
Queens Rd., Enf. 82 DS42
Queens Rd., Epp. 71 FB26
Queen's Rd., Erith 167 FE79
Queens Rd., Felt. 175 BV88
Queens Rd., Grav. 191 GJ90
Queens Rd., Guil. 242 AX134
Queens Rd., Hmptn. 176 CB91
Queens Rd., Hayes 135 BS72
Queens Rd., Hert. 32 DR11
Queens Rd., Horl. 268 DG148
Queen's Rd., Houns. 156 CB83
Queens Rd., Ilf. 145 EQ65
Queens Rd., Kings.T. 178 CN94
Queens Rd., Loug. 84 EL41
Queens Rd., Mitch. 200 DD96
Queens Rd., Mord. 200 DA98
Queens Rd., N.Mal. 199 CT98
Queens Rd., Rich. 178 CM86
Queens Rd., Slou. 132 AT73
Queens Rd. (Datchet), Slou. 152 AV80
Queens Rd., Sthl. 156 BX75
Queens Rd., Sutt. 218 DA110
Queens Rd., Tedd. 177 CE93
Queens Rd., T.Ditt. 197 CF99
Queens Rd., Twick. 177 CF87
Queens Rd., Uxb. 134 BJ69
Queens Rd., Wall. 219 DH106
Queens Rd., Wal.Cr. 67 DY34
Queens Rd., Walt. 213 BS106
Queens Rd., Ware 33 DZ05
Queens Rd., Wat. 76 BW42
Queen's Rd., Well. 166 EV82
Queens Rd., West Dr. 154 BM75
Queens Rd., Wey. 213 BP105
Queens Rd., Wind. 151 AQ82
Queens Rd. (Eton Wick), Wind. 151 AM78
Queens Rd. W. E13 144 EG68
Queen's Row SE17 162 DR79
Queen's Sq., The, Hem.H. 40 BM20
Queens Ter. E13 144 EH67
Queen's Ter. NW8 140 DD67
Queens Ter., Islw. 157 CG84
Queens Ter. Cotts. W7 157 CE75
Boston Rd.
Queens Wk. E4 101 ED46
The Grn. Wk.
Queens Wk. NW9 118 CQ61
Queen's Wk. SW1 277 K3
Queen's Wk. SW1 141 DJ74
Queens Wk. W5 137 CJ70
Queens Wk., Ashf. 174 BK91
Queens Wk., Har. 117 CE56
Queens Wk., Ruis. 116 BX62
Queen's Wk., The SE1 142 DR74
London Bri.
Queens Way NW4 119 CW57
Queens Way, Felt. 176 BW91
Queens Way, Rad. 62 CL32
Queens Way, Wal.Cr. 67 DZ34
Queens Well Ave. N20 98 DE49
Queen's Wd. Rd. N10 121 DH58
Queens Yd. WC1 273 L5
Queensberry Ms. W. SW7 160 DD77
Queen's Gate
Queensberry Pl. SW7 160 DD77
Queensberry Way SW7 160 DD77
Harrington Rd.
Queensborough Ms. W2 140 DC73
Porchester Ter.
Queensborough Pas. W2 140 DC73
Porchester Ter.
Queensborough S. Bldgs. W2 140 DC73
Porchester Ter.
Queensborough Studios W2 140 DC73
Porchester Ter.
Queensborough Ter. W2 140 DB73
Queensbridge Pk., Islw. 177 CE85
Queensbridge Rd. E2 142 DT67
Queensbridge Rd. E8 142 DT66
Queensbury Circle Par., Har. 118 CL55
Streatfield Rd.
Queensbury Pl., Rich. 177 CK85
Friars La.
Queensbury Rd. NW9 118 CR59
Queensbury Rd., Wem. 138 CM68
Queensbury Sta. Par., Edg. 118 CM55
Queensbury St. N1 142 DQ66
Queenscourt, Wem. 118 CL63
Queenscroft Rd. SE9 184 EK86
Queensdale Cres. W11 139 CX74
Queensdale Pl. W11 139 CY74
Queensdale Rd. W11 139 CX74
Queensdale Wk. W11 139 CY74
Queensdown Rd. E5 122 DV63
Queensferry Wk. N17 123 DX56
Jarrow Rd.
Queensgate, Cob. 214 BX112
Queensgate Gdns., Chis. 205 ER95
Queensgate Pl. NW6 140 DA66
Queensland Ave. N18 100 DQ51
Queensland Ave. SW19 200 DB95
Queensland Pl. N7 121 DN63
Queensland Rd.
Queensland Rd. N7 121 DN63
Queensmead NW8 140 DD67
Queensmead, Lthd. 214 CC111
Stokesheath Rd.
Queensmead, Slou. 152 AV81
Queensmead Ave., Epsom 217 CV110
Queensmead Rd., Brom. 204 EF96
Queensmere, Slou. 152 AT75
High St.
Queensmere Clo. SW19 179 CX89
Queensmere Rd. SW19 179 CX89
Queensmere Rd., Slou. 152 AU75
Wellington St.
Queensmill Rd. SW6 159 CX80
Queensthorpe Rd. SE26 183 DX91
Queenstown Gdns., Rain. 147 FF69
Queenstown Ms. SW8 161 DH82
Queenstown Rd.
Queenstown Rd. SW8 161 DH79
Queensville Rd. SW12 181 DK87
Queensway W2 140 DB72
Queensway, Croy. 219 DM107
Queensway, Enf. 82 DV42
Queensway, Hat. 45 CU17
Queensway, Hem.H. 40 BK19
Queensway, Orp. 205 EQ99
Queensway, Red. 250 DF133
Queensway, Sun. 195 BV96
Queensway, W.Wick. 204 EE104
Queensway, The, Ger.Cr. 112 AX56
Queensway N., Walt. 214 BW105
Robinsway
Queensway S., Walt. 214 BW106
Trenchard Clo.
Queenswood Ave. E17 101 EC53
Queenswood Ave., Brwd. 109 GD42
Queenswood Ave., Hmptn. 176 CB93
Queenswood Ave., Houns. 156 BZ82

Queenswood Ave., Th.Hth. 201 DN99
Queenswood Ave., Wall. 219 DK105
Queenswood Cres., Wat. 59 BU33
Queenswood Gdns. E11 124 EH60
Queenswood Pk. N3 97 CY54
Queenswood Rd. SE23 183 DX90
Queenswood Rd., Sid. 185 ET85
Quemerford Rd. N7 121 DM64
Quendell Wk., Hem.H. 40 BL20
Bencroft Rd.
Quendon Dr., Wal.Abb. 67 ED33
Quennel Way, Brwd. 109 GC45
Quennell Clo., Ash. 232 CL119
Parkers La.
Quentin Pl. SE13 164 EE83
Quentin Rd. SE13 164 EE83
Quentin Way, Vir.W. 192 AV98
Quernmore Clo., Brom. 184 EG93
Quernmore Rd. N4 121 DN58
Quernmore Rd., Brom. 184 EG93
Querrin St. SW6 160 DC82
Quex Ms. NW6 140 DA67
Quex Rd.
Quex Rd. NW6 140 DA67
Quick Pl. N1 141 DP67
Essex Rd.
Quick Rd. W4 158 CS78
Quick St. N1 274 G1
Quick St. N1 141 DP68
Quick St. Ms. N1 141 DP68
Quick St.
Quickbeams, Welw.G.C. 30 DA06
Quickberry Pl., Amer. 55 AQ39
Quickley La., Rick. 73 BB44
Quickley Ri., Rick. 73 BC44
Quickmoor La., Kings L. 58 BH33
Quicks Rd. SW19 180 DB94
Quickswood NW3 140 DE66
King Henry's Rd.
Quickwood Clo., Rick. 74 BG44
Quiet Clo., Add. 212 BG105
Quiet Nook, Kes. 204 EK104
Croydon Rd.
Quill Hall La., Amer. 55 AS37
Quill La. SW15 159 CX84
Quill St. N4 121 DN62
St. Thomas's Rd.
Quill St. W5 138 CL69
Quillot, The, Walt. 213 BT106
Quilp St. SE1 279 H4
Quilter Gdns., Orp. 206 EW102
Tintagel Rd.
Quilter Rd., Orp. 206 EW102
Quilter St. E2 142 DU69
Quilter St. SE18 165 ET78
Speranza St.
Quinbrookes, Slou. 132 AW72
Quince Tree Clo., S.Ock. 149 FW70
Quinces Cft., Hem.H. 40 BG18
Quincy Rd., Egh. 173 BA92
Quinta Dr., Barn. 79 CV43
Quintin Ave. SW20 199 CZ95
Quintin Clo., Pnr. 115 BV57
Eastcote High Rd.
Quinton Clo., Beck. 203 EC97
Quinton Clo., Houns. 155 BV80
Quinton Clo., Wall. 219 DH105
Quinton Rd., T.Ditt. 197 CG102
Quinton St. SW18 180 DC89
Quintrell Clo., Wok. 226 AV117
Sythwood
Quixley St. E14 143 ED73
Quorn Rd. SE22 162 DS84

R

Raans Rd., Amer. 72 AT38
Rabbit La., Walt. 213 BU108
Rabbit Row W8 140 DA74
Kensington Mall
Rabbits Rd. E12 124 EL63
Rabbits Rd. (South Darenth), Dart. 209 FR96
Rabies Heath Rd., Gdse. 252 DU134
Rabies Heath Rd., Red. 252 DS133
Rabournmead Dr., Nthlt. 116 BY64
Raby Rd., N.Mal. 198 CR98
Raby St. E14 143 DY72
Salmon La.
Raccoon Way, Houns. 156 BW82
Rachel Pt. E5 122 DU63
Muir Rd.
Rachels Way, Chesh. 54 AR34
Cresswell Rd.
Rackham Ms. SW16 181 DJ93
Westcote Rd.
Racks Ct., Guil. 258 AX136
Racton Rd. SW6 160 DA79
Rad La., Dor. 261 BS142
Horsham Rd.
Rad La., Guil. 261 BR142
Radbourne Ave. W5 157 CJ77
Radbourne Clo. E5 123 DX63
Overbury St.
Radbourne Cres. E17 101 ED54
Radbourne Rd. SW12 181 DJ87
Radburn Clo., Harl. 52 EU19
Radcliffe Ave. NW10 139 CU68
Radcliffe Ave., Enf. 82 DQ39
Radcliffe Gdns., Cars. 218 DE108
Radcliffe Ms., Hmptn. 176 CC92
Taylor Clo.
Radcliffe Path SW8 161 DJ82
St. Rule St.
Radcliffe Rd. N21 99 DP46
Radcliffe Rd., Croy. 202 DT103
Radcliffe Rd., Har. 95 CG54
Radcliffe Sq. SW15 179 CX86
Radcliffe Way, Nthlt. 136 BX69
Radcot Ave., Slou. 153 BB76
Radcot Pt. SE23 183 DX90
Radcot St. SE11 161 DN78
Methley St.
Raddington Rd. W10 139 CY71
Radfield Way, Sid. 185 ER87
Radford Rd. SE13 183 EC85
Radford Way, Bark. 145 ET69
Radipole Rd. SW6 159 CZ81
Radland Rd. E16 144 EF72
Radlet Ave. SE26 182 DV90
Radlett Clo. E7 144 EF65
Radlett La., Rad. 77 CK35
Radlett Pk. Rd., Rad. 61 CG34
Radlett Pl. NW8 140 DE67
Radlett Rd., St.Alb. 61 CE28
Radlett Rd., Wat. 76 BW41
Radlett Rd. (Aldenham), Wat. 76 CB39
Radley Ave., Ilf. 125 ET63
Radley Clo., Felt. 175 BT88
Westmacott Dr.
Radley Ct. SE16 163 DX75
Thame Rd.
Radley Gdns., Har. 118 CL56
Radley Ms. W8 160 DA76
Radley Rd. N17 100 DS54
Radley's La. E18 102 EG54
Radleys Mead, Dag. 147 FB65
Radlix Rd. E10 123 EA60
Radnor Ave., Har. 117 CE57
Radnor Ave., Well. 186 EV85
Radnor Clo., Chis. 185 ES93
Homewood Cres.
Radnor Clo., Mitch. 201 DL98
Radnor Cres. SE18 166 EU80
Radnor Cres., Ilf. 125 EM57
Radnor Gdns., Enf. 82 DS39
Radnor Gdns., Twick. 177 CF89
Radnor Gro., Uxb. 134 BN68
Charnwood Rd.
Radnor La., Dor. 261 BU144
Radnor Ms. W2 272 A9
Radnor Pl. W2 272 B9
Radnor Pl. W2 140 DE72
Radnor Rd. NW6 139 CY67
Radnor Rd. SE15 162 DU80
Radnor Rd., Har. 117 CD57
Radnor Rd., Twick. 177 CF88
Radnor Rd., Wey. 194 BN104
Radnor St. EC1 275 J3
Radnor St. EC1 142 DQ69
Radnor Ter. W14 159 CZ77
Radnor Wk. E14 163 EA77
Copeland Dr.
Radnor Wk. SW3 160 DE78
Radnor Wk., Croy. 203 DY100
Radnor Way NW10 138 CP70
Radnor Way, Slou. 152 AY77
Radolphs, Tad. 233 CX122
Heathcote
Radstock Ave., Har. 117 CG55
Radstock St. SW11 160 DE80
Radstock Way, Red. 251 DK128
Radstone Ct., Wok. 227 AZ118
Radwell Path, Borwd. 78 CL39
Cromwell Rd.
Raebarn Gdns., Barn. 79 CV43
Raeburn Ave., Dart. 187 FH85
Raeburn Ave., Surb. 198 CP102
Raeburn Clo. NW11 120 DC58
Raeburn Clo., Kings.T. 177 CK94
Raeburn Rd., Edg. 96 CN54
Raeburn Rd., Hayes 135 BR68
Raeburn Rd., Sid. 185 ES86
Raeburn St. SW2 161 DL84
Raeside Clo., Beac. 89 AQ50
Rafford Way, Brom. 204 EH96
Raft Rd. SW18 160 DA84
North Pas.
Rag Hill Clo., West. 238 EL121
Rag Hill Rd., West. 238 EK121
Ragged Hall La., St.Alb. 42 BX24
Raggleswood, Chis. 205 EN95
Raglan Ave., Wal.Cr. 67 DX34
Raglan Clo., Houns. 176 BY85
Vickers Way
Raglan Clo., Reig. 250 DC132
Raglan Ct. SE12 184 EG85
Raglan Ct., S.Croy. 219 DP106
Raglan Ct., Wem. 118 CM63
Raglan Gdns., Wat. 93 BV46
Raglan Rd. E17 123 EC57
Raglan Rd. SE18 165 EQ78
Raglan Rd., Belv. 166 EZ78
Raglan Rd., Brom. 204 EJ98
Raglan Rd., Enf. 100 DS45
Raglan Rd., Reig. 250 DB131
Raglan Rd., Wok. 226 AS118
Raglan St. NW5 141 DH65
Raglan Ter., Har. 116 CB63
Raglan Way, Nthlt. 136 CC65
Ragley Clo. W3 158 CQ75
Avenue Rd.
Rags La. (Cheshunt), Wal.Cr. 66 DS28
Ragstone Rd., Slou. 151 AR76
Rahn Rd., Epp. 70 EU31
Raider Clo., Rom. 104 FA53
Raikes Hollow, Dor. 261 BV142
Raikes La., Dor. 261 BV143
Railey Ms. NW5 121 DJ64
Railpit La., Warl. 238 EE115
Railshead Rd., Islw. 157 CH84
Railton Rd. SE24 161 DN84
Railway App. N4 121 DN58
Wightman Rd.
Railway App. SE1 279 L3
Railway App. SE1 142 DR74
Railway App., Har. 117 CF56
Railway App., Hert. 32 DQ09
Railway App., Twick. 177 CG87
Railway App., Wall. 219 DH107
Railway Ave. SE16 162 DW75
Railway Cotts., Hat. 44 CS19
Ellenbrook La.
Railway Cotts., Wat. 75 BV40
St. Albans Rd.
Railway Ms. E3 143 EA69
Wellington Way
Railway Ms. W10 139 CY72
Ladbroke Gro.
Railway Pas., Tedd. 177 CG93
Victoria Rd.
Railway Pl. SW19 179 CZ93
Hartfield Rd.
Railway Pl., Belv. 166 FA76
Railway Pl., Hert. 32 DS09
Railway Ri. SE22 162 DS84
Grove Vale
Railway Rd., Tedd. 177 CF91
Railway Rd., Wal.Cr. 67 DY33
Railway Side SW13 158 CS83
Railway Sq., Brwd. 108 FW48
Fairfield Rd.
Railway St. N1 274 A1
Railway St. N1 141 DL68
Railway St., Grav. 190 GA85
Railway St., Hert. 32 DR09
Railway St., Rom. 126 EW60
Railway Ter. SE13 183 EB85
Ladywell Rd.
Railway Ter., Felt. 175 BU88
Railway Ter., Hem.H. 58 BN27
Railway Ter., Slou. 132 AT74
Railway Ter., Stai. 173 BD92
Railway Ter., West. 255 ER125
Rainborough Clo. NW10 138 CQ65
Rainbow Ave. E14 163 EB78
Rainbow Ct., Wat. 76 BW44
Oxhey Rd.
Rainbow Ct., Wok. 226 AS116
Langmans Way
Rainbow Ind. Est., West Dr. 134 BK73
Rainbow Rd., Grays 169 FW77
Arterial Rd. W. Thurrock
Rainbow Rd., Harl. 37 FE12
Rainbow St. SE5 162 DS80
Raine St. E1 142 DV74
Rainer Clo. (Cheshunt), Wal.Cr. 67 DX29
Rainham Clo. SE9 185 ER86
Rainham Clo. SW11 180 DE86
Rainham Rd. NW10 139 CW69
Rainham Rd., Rain. 147 FG69
Rainham Rd. N., Dag. 126 FA61
Rainham Rd. S., Dag. 127 FB63
Rainhill Way E3 143 EA69
Rainsborough Ave. SE8 163 DY77
Rainsford Clo., Stan. 95 CJ50
Rainsford Rd. NW10 138 CP68
Rainsford St. W2 272 B8
Rainsford Way, Horn. 127 FG60
Rainton Rd. SE7 164 EG78
Rainville Rd. W6 159 CW79
Raisins Hill, Pnr. 116 BW55
Raith Ave. N14 99 DK48
Raleana Rd. E14 143 EC74
Raleigh Ave., Hayes 135 BV71
Raleigh Ave., Wall. 219 DK105
Raleigh Clo. NW4 119 CW57
Raleigh Clo., Erith 167 FF79
Raleigh Clo., Pnr. 116 BX59
Raleigh Clo., Ruis. 115 BT61
Raleigh Clo., Slou. 131 AN74
Raleigh Ct. SE16 143 DX74
Rotherhithe St.
Raleigh Ct., Stai. 174 BG91
Raleigh Ct., Wall. 219 DH107
Raleigh Dr. N20 98 DE48
Raleigh Dr., Esher 215 CD106
Raleigh Dr., Horl. 269 DN148
Raleigh Dr., Surb. 198 CQ102
Raleigh Gdns. SW2 181 DM86
Brixton Hill
Raleigh Gdns., Mitch. 200 DF97
Raleigh Ms. N1 141 DP67
Queen's Head St.
Raleigh Ms., Orp. 223 ET106
Osgood Ave.
Raleigh Rd. N8 121 DN56
Raleigh Rd. SE20 183 DX94
Raleigh Rd., Enf. 82 DR42
Raleigh Rd., Felt. 175 BT90
Raleigh Rd., Rich. 158 CM83
Raleigh Rd., Sthl. 156 BY78
Raleigh St. N1 141 DP67
Raleigh Way N14 99 DK46
Raleigh Way, Felt. 176 BW91
Ralliwood Rd., Ash. 232 CN119
Ralph Ct. W2 140 DB72
Queensway
Ralph Perring Ct., Beck. 203 EA98
Ralston St. SW3 160 DF78
Tedworth Sq.
Ralston Way, Wat. 94 BX47
Ram Gorse, Harl. 35 EP13
Ram Pas., Kings.T. 197 CK96
High St.
Ram Pl. E9 142 DW65
Chatham Pl.
Ram St. SW18 180 DB85
Rama Clo. SW16 181 DL94
Rama Ct., Har. 117 CE61
Ramac Ind. Est. SE7 164 EG77
Ramac Way SE7 164 EH78
Rambler Clo. SW16 181 DJ91
Rambler Clo., Maid. 130 AH72
Rambler La., Slou. 152 AW76
Ramblers Way, Welw.G.C. 30 DC10
Rambling Way, Berk. 39 BC16
Rame Clo. SW17 180 DG92
Church La.
Ramilles Clo. SW2 181 DL86
Ramillies Pl. W1 273 K9
Ramillies Pl. W1 141 DJ72
Ramillies Rd. NW7 96 CS47
Ramillies Rd. W4 158 CR77
Ramillies Rd., Sid. 186 EV86
Ramillies St. W1 273 K9
Ramney Dr., Enf. 83 DY36
Ramornie Clo., Walt. 214 BZ106
Rampart St. E1 142 DV72
Commercial Rd.
Ramparts, The, St.Alb. 42 CB21
Rampayne St. SW1 277 M10
Rampayne St. SW1 161 DK78
Rampton Clo. E4 101 EA48
Rams Gro., Rom. 126 EY56
Ramsay Clo., Brox. 49 DY21
Ramsay Gdns., Rom. 106 FJ53
Ramsay Pl., Har. 117 CE60
Ramsay Rd. E7 124 EE63
Ramsay Rd. W3 158 CQ76
Ramsbury Rd., St.Alb. 43 CE21
Ramscote La., Chesh. 54 AN25
Ramscroft Clo. N9 100 DS45
Ramsdale Rd. SW17 180 DG92
Ramsden Clo., Orp. 206 EW102
Ramsden Dr., Rom. 104 FA52
Ramsden Rd. N11 98 DF50
Ramsden Rd. SW12 180 DG86
Ramsden Rd., Erith 167 FD80
Ramsden Rd., Orp. 206 EV101
Ramsey Clo. NW9 119 CT58
West Hendon Bdy.
Ramsey Clo., Grnf. 117 CD64
Ramsey Clo., Hat. 64 DD27
Ramsey Clo., Horl. 268 DF148
Ramsey Clo., St.Alb. 43 CG22
Ramsey Ct., Slou. 131 AK70
Lower Britwell Rd.
Ramsey Ho., Wem. 138 CL65
Ramsey Lo. Ct., St.Alb. 43 CE19
Hillside Rd.
Ramsey Rd., Th.Hth. 201 DM100
Ramsey St. E2 142 DU70
Ramsey Wk. N1 142 DR65
Marquess Est.
Ramsey Way N14 99 DJ45
Ramsgate St. E8 142 DT65
Dalston La.
Ramsgill App., Ilf. 125 ET56
Ramsgill Dr., Ilf. 125 ET57
Ramson Ri., Hem.H. 39 BE21
Ramulis Dr., Hayes 136 BX70
Ramus Wd. Ave., Orp. 223 ES106
Rancliffe Gdns. SE9 164 EL84
Rancliffe Rd. E6 144 EL68
Randal Cres., Reig. 266 DA136
Randall Ave. NW2 118 CS61
Randall Clo. SW11 160 DE81
Randall Clo., Erith 167 FC79
Randall Clo., Slou. 153 AZ78
Randall Dr., Horn. 128 FJ63
Randall Pl. SE10 163 EC80
Randall Rd. SE11 278 B9
Randall Rd. SE11 161 DM78
Randall Row SE11 278 B9
Randalls Cres., Lthd. 231 CG120
Randalls Dr., Brwd. 109 GE44
Randalls Pk. Ave., Lthd. 231 CG120
Randalls Pk. Dr., Lthd. 231 CG121
Randalls Rd.
Randalls Ride, Hem.H. 40 BL18
Randalls Rd., Lthd. 231 CE119
Randalls Way, Lthd. 231 CG121
Randell's Rd. N1 141 DL67
Randle Rd., Rich. 177 CJ91
Randles La., Sev. 240 EX115
Randlesdown Rd. SE6 183 EA91
Randolph App. E16 144 EJ72
Baxter Rd.
Randolph Ave. W9 140 DB68
Randolph Clo., Bexh. 167 FC83
Randolph Clo., Cob. 230 CA115
Randolph Clo., Kings.T. 178 CQ92
Randolph Clo., Wok. 226 AS117
Creston Ave.
Randolph Cres. W9 140 DC70
Randolph Gdns. NW6 140 DB68
Randolph Gro., Rom. 126 EW57
Donald Dr.
Randolph Ho., Croy. 202 DQ102
Randolph Ms. W9 140 DC70
Randolph Rd. E17 123 EB57
Randolph Rd. W9 140 DC70
Randolph Rd., Epsom 217 CT114
Randolph Rd., Slou. 152 AY77
Randolph Rd., Sthl. 156 BZ75
Randolph St. NW1 141 DJ66
Randolph's La., West. 255 EP126
Randon Clo., Har. 94 CB54
Ranelagh Ave. SW6 159 CZ83
Ranelagh Ave. SW13 159 CU82
Ranelagh Bri. W2 140 DB71
Gloucester Ter.
Ranelagh Clo., Edg. 96 CN49
Ranelagh Dr., Edg. 96 CN49
Ranelagh Dr., Twick. 157 CH84
Ranelagh Gdns. E11 124 EJ57
Ranelagh Gdns. SW6 159 CZ83
Ranelagh Gdns. W4 158 CQ80
Grove Pk. Gdns.
Ranelagh Gdns. W6 159 CT76
Ranelagh Gdns., Grav. 191 GF87
Ranelagh Gdns., Ilf. 125 EM60
Ranelagh Gro. SW1 276 G10
Ranelagh Gro. SW1 160 DG78
Ranelagh Ms. W5 157 CK75
Ranelagh Rd.
Ranelagh Pl., N.Mal. 198 CS99
Rodney Rd.
Ranelagh Rd. E6 145 EN67
Ranelagh Rd. E11 124 EE63
Ranelagh Rd. E15 144 EE67
Ranelagh Rd. N17 122 DS55
Ranelagh Rd. N22 99 DM53
Ranelagh Rd. NW10 139 CT68
Ranelagh Rd. SW1 161 DJ78
Lupus St.
Ranelagh Rd. W5 157 CK75
Ranelagh Rd., Hem.H. 41 BP20
Ranelagh Rd., Red. 250 DE134
Ranelagh Rd., Sthl. 136 BX74
Ranelagh Rd., Wem. 137 CK65
Ranfurly Rd., Sutt. 200 DA103
Range Rd., Grav. 191 GL87
Range Way, Shep. 194 BN101
Rangefield Rd., Brom. 184 EE92
Rangemoor Rd. N15 122 DT57
Ranger Wk., Add. 212 BH106
Monks Cres.
Rangers Rd. E4 102 EE45
Rangers Rd., Loug. 102 EG45
Rangers Sq. SE10 163 ED81
Rangeworth Pl., Sid. 185 ET90
Priestlands Pk. Rd.
Rangoon St. EC3 142 DT72
Northumberland All.
Rank Ho., Harl. 51 EQ15
Rankin Clo. NW9 118 CS55
Ranleigh Gdns., Bexh. 166 EZ80
Ranmere St. SW12 181 DH88
Ormeley Rd.
Ranmoor Clo., Har. 117 CD56
Ranmoor Gdns., Har. 117 CD56
Ranmore Ave., Croy. 202 DT104
Ranmore Clo., Red. 250 DG131
Ranmore Common, Dor. 246 CA133
Ranmore Common Rd., Dor. 245 BU134
Ranmore Common Rd., Lthd. 245 BU134
Ranmore Path, Orp. 206 EU98
Ranmore Rd., Dor. 246 CC134
Ranmore Rd., Sutt. 217 CX109
Rannoch Clo., Edg. 96 CP47
Rannoch Rd. W6 159 CW79
Rannoch Wk., Hem.H. 40 BK16
Rannock Ave. NW9 118 CR59
Ranskill Rd., Borwd. 78 CN39
Ransom Clo., Wat. 94 BW45
Ransom Rd. SE7 164 EJ78
Harvey Gdns.
Ransom Wk. SE7 164 EJ78
Woolwich Rd.
Ranston Clo., Uxb. 113 BF58
Nightingale Way
Ranston St. NW1 272 B6
Rant Meadow, Hem.H. 40 BN22
Ranulf Rd. NW2 119 CZ63
Ranwell Clo. E3 143 DZ67
Beale Rd.
Ranwell St. E3 143 DZ67
Ranworth Ave., Hodd. 33 EB13
Ranworth Clo., Erith 167 FE82
Ranworth Clo., Hem.H. 40 BK22
Panxworth Rd.
Ranworth Rd. N9 100 DW47
Ranyard Clo., Chess. 198 CM104
Raphael Ave., Rom. 105 FF54
Raphael Ave., Til. 171 GG80
Raphael Clo., Rad. 62 CL32
King Charles Rd.
Raphael Dr., Wat. 76 BW40
Raphael Rd., Grav. 191 GK87
Raphael St. SW7 276 D5
Raphael St. SW7 160 DF75
Rapier Clo., Purf. 168 FM77
Rasehill Clo., Rick. 74 BJ43
Rashleigh St. SW8 161 DH82
Peardon St.
Rashleigh Way (Horton Kirby), Dart. 208 FQ98
Rasper Rd. N20 98 DC47
Rastell Ave. SW2 181 DK89
Ratcliff Rd. E7 124 EJ64
Ratcliffe Clo. SE12 184 EG87
Ratcliffe Clo., Uxb. 134 BK69
Ratcliffe Cross St. E1 143 DX72
Ratcliffe La. E14 143 DY72
Ratcliffe Orchard E1 143 DX73
Rathbone Mkt. E16 144 EF71
Barking Rd.
Rathbone Pl. W1 273 M7
Rathbone Pl. W1 141 DK71
Rathbone Pt. E5 122 DU63
Nolan Way
Rathbone St. E16 144 EF71
Rathbone St. W1 273 L7
Rathbone St. W1 141 DJ71
Rathcoole Ave. N8 121 DM57
Rathcoole Gdns. N8 121 DM57
Rathfern Rd. SE6 183 DZ88
Rathgar Ave. W13 137 CH74
Rathgar Clo. N3 97 CZ54
Rathgar Clo., Red. 266 DG139
Rathgar Rd. SW9 161 DP83
Coldharbour La.
Rathlin, Hem.H. 41 BP22
Rathlin Wk. N1 142 DQ65
Marquess Est.
Rathmell Dr. SW4 181 DK86
Rathmore Rd. SE7 164 EH78
Rathmore Rd., Grav. 191 GH87
Rathwell Path, Borwd. 78 CL39
Cromwell Rd.
Rats La., Loug. 84 EH38
Rattray Rd. SW2 161 DN84
Ratty's La., Hodd. 49 ED17
Raul Rd. SE15 162 DU81
Ravel Gdns., S.Ock. 148 FQ72
Ravel Rd., S.Ock. 148 FQ72
Raveley St. NW5 121 DJ63
Raven Clo. NW9 96 CS54
Eagle Dr.
Raven Clo., Rick. 92 BK45
Raven Ct. E5 122 DU62
Stellman Clo.
Raven Ct., Hat. 45 CU19
Raven Rd. E18 102 EJ54
Raven Row E1 142 DV71
Ravencroft, Grays 171 GH75
Alexandra Clo.
Ravendale Rd., Sun. 195 BT96
Ravenet St. SW11 161 DH81
Strasburg Rd.
Ravenfield, Egh. 172 AW93
Ravenfield Rd. SW17 180 DF90
Ravenfield Rd., Welw.G.C. 29 CZ09
Ludwick Way
Ravenhill Rd. E13 144 EJ68
Ravenna Rd. SW15 179 CX85
Ravenor Pk. Rd., Grnf. 136 CB69
Ravens Clo., Brom. 204 EF96
Ravens Clo., Enf. 82 DS40
Ravens Clo., Red. 250 DF133
Ravens La., Berk. 38 AX19
Ravens Ms. SE12 184 EG85
Ravens Way
Ravens Way SE12 184 EG85
Ravens Wf., Berk. 38 AX19
Ravensbourne Ave., Brom. 183 ED94
Ravensbourne Ave., Stai. 174 BL88
Ravensbourne Cres., Rom. 128 FM55
Ravensbourne Gdns. W13 137 CH71
Ravensbourne Gdns., Ilf. 103 EN53
Ravensbourne Pk. SE6 183 EA87
Ravensbourne Pk. Cres. SE6 183 DZ87
Ravensbourne Pl. SE13 163 EB82
Ravensbourne Rd. SE6 183 DZ88
Ravensbourne Rd., Brom. 204 EG97
Ravensbourne Rd., Dart. 167 FG83
Ravensbourne Rd., Twick. 177 CJ86
Ravensbury Ave., Mord. 200 DC99
Ravensbury Gro., Mitch. 200 DD98
Ravensbury La., Mitch. 200 DD98
Ravensbury Path, Mitch. 200 DD98
Ravensbury Rd. SW18 180 DA89
Ravensbury Rd., Orp. 205 ET97
Ravensbury Ter. SW18 180 DB88
Ravenscar Rd., Brom. 184 EE91
Ravenscar Rd., Surb. 198 CM103
Ravenscourt, Sun. 195 BT95
Ravenscourt Ave. W6 159 CU77
Ravenscourt Clo., Horn. 128 FL62
Ravenscourt Dr.
Ravenscourt Clo., Ruis. 115 BQ59
Ravenscourt Dr., Horn. 128 FL62
Ravenscourt Gdns. W6 159 CU77
Ravenscourt Gro., Horn. 128 FL61
Ravenscourt Pk. W6 159 CU76
Ravenscourt Pl. W6 159 CV77
Ravenscourt Rd. W6 159 CV77
Ravenscourt Rd., Orp. 206 EU97
Ravenscourt Sq. W6 159 CU76
Ravenscraig Rd. N11 99 DH49
Ravenscroft, Wat. 60 BY34
Ravenscroft Ave. NW11 119 CZ59
Ravenscroft Ave., Wem. 118 CL60
Ravenscroft Clo. E16 144 EG71
Ravenscroft Cres. SE9 185 EM90
Ravenscroft Pk., Barn. 79 CX42
Ravenscroft Rd. E16 144 EG71
Ravenscroft Rd. W4 158 CQ77
Ravenscroft Rd., Beck. 202 DW96
Ravenscroft Rd., Wey. 213 BQ111
Ravenscroft St. E2 142 DT68
Ravensdale Ave. N12 98 DC49
Ravensdale Gdns. SE19 182 DR94
Ravensdale Ms., Stai. 174 BH93

Regina Clo., Barn. 79 CX41
Regina Rd. N4 121 DM60
Regina Rd. SE25 202 DU97
Regina Rd. W13 137 CG74
Regina Rd., Sthl. 156 BY77
Regina Ter. W13 137 CH74
Reginald Rd. E7 144 EG65
Reginald Rd. SE8 163 EA80
Reginald Rd., Nthwd. 93 BT53
Reginald Rd., Rom. 106 FN53
Reginald Sq. SE8 163 EA80
Regis Rd. NW5 121 DH64
Regnart Bldgs. NW1 273 L4
Reid Ave., Cat. 236 DR121
Reid Clo., Pnr. 115 BU56
Reidhaven Rd. SE18 165 ES77
Reigate Ave., Sutt. 200 DA103
Reigate Heath, Reig. 265 CX135
Reigate Hill, Reig. 250 DA133
Reigate Hill Clo., Reig. 250 DA131
Reigate Rd., Bet. 248 CN133
Reigate Rd., Brom. 184 EF90
Reigate Rd., Dor. 263 CJ135
Reigate Rd., Epsom 217 CU110
Reigate Rd., Horl. 268 DC146
Reigate Rd., Ilf. 125 ET61
Reigate Rd., Lthd. 231 CJ122
Reigate Rd., Red. 250 DD134
Reigate Rd., Reig. 250 DB134
Reigate Rd. (Sidlow Bri.), Reig. 266 DB141
Reigate Rd., Tad. 233 CY119
Reigate Way, Wall. 219 DL106
Reighton Rd. E5 122 DU62
Relay Rd. W12 139 CW74
Relf Rd. SE15 162 DU83
Relko Ct., Epsom 216 CR111
Relko Gdns., Sutt. 218 DD106
Relton Ms. SW7 276 C6
Rembrandt Clo. E14 163 ED76
Rembrandt Clo. SW1 276 F9
Rembrandt Dr., Grav. 190 GD90
Rembrandt Rd. SE13 164 EE84
Rembrandt Rd., Edg. 96 CN54
Rembrandt Way, Walt. 195 BV103
Remington Rd. E6 144 EL72
Remington Rd. N15 122 DR58
Remington St. N1 274 G1
Remington St. N1 141 DP68
Remnant St. WC2 274 B8
Rempstone Ms. N1 142 DR68
Mintern St.
Remus Rd. E3 143 EA66
Monier Rd.
Rendle Clo., Croy. 202 DT99
Rendle Clo., Ware 32 DV05
Rendlesham Ave., Rad. 77 CF37
Rendlesham Rd. E5 122 DU63
Rendlesham Rd., Enf. 81 DP39
Rendlesham Way, Rick. 73 BC44
Renforth St. SE16 162 DW75
Renfree Way, Shep. 194 BM101
Renfrew Clo. E6 145 EN73
Renfrew Rd. SE11 278 F8
Renfrew Rd. SE11 161 DP77
Renfrew Rd., Houns. 156 BX82
Renfrew Rd., Kings.T. 178 CP94
Renmans, The, Ash. 232 CM116
Renmuir St. SW17 180 DF93
Rennell St. SE13 163 EC83
Lewisham High St.
Rennels Way, Islw. 157 CE82
St. John's Rd.
Renness Rd. E17 123 DY55
Rennets Clo. SE9 185 ES85
Rennets Wd. Rd. SE9 185 ER85
Rennie Clo., Ashf. 174 BK90
Rennie Est. SE16 162 DV77
Rennie St. SE1 278 F2
Rennie St. SE1 141 DP74
Rennie Ter., Red. 266 DG135
Rennison Clo., Wal.Cr. 66 DT27
Allwood Rd.
Renown Clo., Croy. 201 DP102
Renown Clo., Rom. 104 FA53
Rensburg Rd. E17 123 DX57
Renshaw Clo., Belv. 166 EZ79
Grove Rd.
Renters Ave. NW4 119 CW58
Renton Dr., Orp. 206 EX101
Renwick Ind. Est., Bark. 146 EV68
Renwick Rd.
Renwick Rd., Bark. 146 EV70
Repens Way, Hayes 136 BX70
Stipularis Dr.
Rephidim St. SE1 279 L7
Replingham Rd. SW18 179 CZ88
Reporton Rd. SW6 159 CY81
Repository Rd. SE18 165 EM79
Repton Ave., Hayes 155 BR77
Repton Ave., Rom. 127 FG55
Repton Ave., Wem. 117 CJ63
Repton Clo., Cars. 218 DE106
Repton Ct. E5 123 DY62
Repton Ct., Beck. 203 EB95
Repton Dr., Rom. 127 FG56
Repton Gdns., Rom. 127 FG55
Repton Grn., St.Alb. 43 CD17
Repton Gro., Ilf. 103 EM53
Repton Pl., Amer. 72 AU39
Repton Rd., Har. 118 CM56
Repton Rd., Orp. 206 EU104
Repton St. E14 143 DY72
Repton Way, Rick. 74 BN43
Repulse Clo., Rom. 105 FB53
Reservoir Rd. N14 81 DJ43
Reservoir Rd. SE4 163 DY82
Reservoir Rd., Ruis. 115 BQ57
Resolution Wk. SE18 165 EM76
Venus Rd.
Reson Way, Hem.H. 40 BH21
Restell Clo. SE3 164 EE79
Reston Clo., Borwd. 78 CN38
Reston Path, Borwd. 78 CN38
Reston Clo.
Reston Pl. SW7 160 DC75
Hyde Pk. Gate
Restons Cres. SE9 185 ER86
Restormel Clo., Houns. 176 CA85
Retcar Clo. N19 121 DH61
Dartmouth Pk. Hill
Retcar Pl. N19 121 DH61
Dartmouth Pk. Hill
Retford Clo., Borwd. 78 CN38
The Campions
Retford Clo., Rom. 106 FN51
Retford Path, Rom. 106 FN51
Retford Rd., Rom. 106 FM51
Retford St. N1 275 N1
Retingham Way E4 101 EB47
Retreat, The NW9 118 CR57
Retreat, The SW14 158 CS83
South Worple Way
Retreat, The, Abb.L. 59 BQ31
Abbots Rd.
Retreat, The, Add. 212 BK106
Retreat, The, Amer. 72 AY39
Retreat, The, Brwd. 108 FV46
Costead Manor Rd.
Retreat, The (Hutton), Brwd. 109 GB44
Retreat, The, Egh. 172 AX92
Retreat, The, Grays 170 GB79
Retreat, The, Har. 116 CA59
Retreat, The, Maid. 150 AD80
Retreat, The, Orp. 224 EV107
Retreat, The, Surb. 198 CM100
Retreat, The, Th.Hth. 202 DR98
Retreat, The, Wor.Pk. 199 CV103
Retreat Clo., Har. 117 CJ57
Retreat Pl. E9 142 DW65
Retreat Rd., Rich. 177 CK85
Retreat Way, Chig. 104 EV48
Reubens Rd., Brwd. 109 GB44
Reunion Row E1 142 DV73
Pennington St.
Revel Rd., H.Wyc. 110 AD55
Reveley Sq. SE16 163 DY75
Howland Way
Revell Clo., Lthd. 230 CB122
Revell Dr., Lthd. 230 CB122
Revell Ri. SE18 165 ET79
Revell Rd., Kings.T. 198 CP96
Revell Rd., Sutt. 217 CZ107
Revelon Rd. SE4 163 DY83
Revels Clo., Hert. 32 DR07
Revels Rd., Hert. 32 DR07
Revelstoke Rd. SW18 179 CZ89
Reventlow Rd. SE9 185 EQ88
Reverdy Rd. SE1 162 DU77
Reverend Clo., Har. 116 CB62
Revesby Rd., Cars. 200 DD100
Review Rd. NW2 119 CT61
Review Rd., Dag. 147 FB67
Rewell St. SW6 160 DC80
Rewley Rd., Cars. 200 DD100
Rex Ave., Ashf. 174 BN93
Rex Clo., Rom. 105 FB52
Rex Pl. W1 276 G1
Reydon Ave. E11 124 EJ58
Reynard Clo. SE4 163 DY83
Foxwell St.
Reynard Clo., Brom. 205 EM97
Reynard Dr. SE19 182 DT94
Reynard Way, Hert. 32 DV09
Reynards Way, St.Alb. 60 BZ30
Reynardson Rd. N17 100 DQ52
Reynold Wk., Chesh. 54 AN27
Hivings Hill
Reynolds Ave. E12 125 EN64
Reynolds Ave., Chess. 216 CL108
Reynolds Ave., Rom. 126 EW59
Reynolds Clo. NW11 120 DB59
Reynolds Clo. SW19 200 DD95
Reynolds Clo., Cars. 200 DF102
Reynolds Clo., Hem.H. 40 BG19
Reynolds Ct. E11 124 EF62
Cobbold Rd.
Reynolds Dr., Edg. 118 CM55
Reynolds Pl. SE3 164 EH80
Reynolds Pl., Rich. 178 CM86
Cambrian Rd.
Reynolds Rd. SE15 182 DW85
Reynolds Rd. W4 158 CQ76
Reynolds Rd., Beac. 88 AJ52
Reynolds Rd., Hayes 136 BW70
Reynolds Rd., N.Mal. 198 CR101
Reynolds Way, Croy. 220 DS105
Rheidol Ms. N1 142 DQ68
Rheidol Ter.
Rheidol Ter. N1 142 DQ67
Rheingold Way, Wall. 219 DL109
Rheola Clo. N17 100 DT53
Rhoda St. E2 142 DT70
Brick La.
Rhodes Ave. N22 99 DJ53
Rhodes Clo., Egh. 173 BC92
Mullens Rd.
Rhodes Moorhouse Ct., Mord. 200 DA100
Rhodes St. N7 121 DM64
Mackenzie Rd.
Rhodes Way, Wat. 76 BX40
Rhodesia Rd. E11 123 ED61
Rhodesia Rd. SW9 161 DL82
Rhodeswell Rd. E14 143 DY71
Rhododendron Ride, Egh. 172 AT93
Rhododendron Ride, Slou. 133 AZ69
Rhodrons Ave., Chess. 216 CL106
Rhondda Gro. E3 143 DY69
Rhyl Rd., Grnf. 137 CF68
Rhyl St. NW5 140 DG65
Rhys Ave. N11 99 DK52
Rialto Rd., Mitch. 200 DG96
Rib Vale, Hert. 32 DR06
Ribble Clo., Wdf.Grn. 102 EJ51
Prospect Rd.
Ribbledale, St.Alb. 62 CM27
Ribblesdale, Dor. 263 CH138
Roman Rd.
Ribblesdale, Hem.H. 40 BL17
Ribblesdale Ave., Nthlt. 136 CB65
Ribblesdale Rd. N8 121 DM56
Ribblesdale Rd. SW16 181 DH93
Ribblesdale Rd., Dart. 188 FQ88
Ribbon Dance Ms. SE5 162 DR81
Camberwell Gro.
Ribchester Ave., Grnf. 137 CF69
Ribston Clo., Brom. 205 EM102
Ribston Clo., Rad. 62 CL32
Porters Pk. Dr.
Ricardo Path SE28 146 EW74
Byron Clo.
Ricardo Rd., Wind. 172 AV86
Meadow Way
Ricardo St. E14 143 EB72
Ricards Rd. SW19 179 CZ92
Rice Clo., Hem.H. 40 BM19
Ricebridge La., Reig. 265 CU137
Rich La. SW5 160 DB78
Warwick Rd.
Rich St. E14 143 DZ73
Richard Clo. SE18 164 EL77
Richard Foster Clo. E17 123 DZ59
Richard Stagg Clo., St.Alb. 43 CJ22
Richard St. E1 142 DV72
Commercial Rd.
Richards Ave., Rom. 127 FC57
Richards Clo., Har. 117 CG57
Richards Clo., Hayes 155 BR79
Richards Clo., Uxb. 134 BN67
Richards Clo. (Bushey), Wat. 95 CD45
Richards Pl. E17 123 EA55
Richards Pl. SW3 276 C8
Richards Rd., Cob. 214 CB114
Richardson Clo. E8 142 DT67
Clarissa St.
Richardson Clo., Green. 189 FT85
Richardson Clo., St.Alb. 62 CL27
Richardson Pl., St.Alb. 44 CP22
Richardson Rd. E15 144 EE68
Richardson's Ms. W1 273 K5
Richbell Clo., Ash. 231 CK118
Richbell Pl. WC1 274 B6
Richborne Ter. SW8 161 DM80
Richborough Clo., Orp. 206 EX98
Richborough Rd. NW2 119 CY63
Riches Rd., Ilf. 125 EQ61
Richfield Rd. (Bushey), Wat. 94 CC45
Richford Rd. E15 144 EF67
Richford St. W6 159 CW75
Richings Way, Iver 153 BE76
Richland Ave., Couls. 218 DG114
Richlands Ave., Epsom 217 CU105
Richmer Rd., Erith 167 FG80
Richmond Ave. E4 101 ED50
Richmond Ave. N1 141 DM67
Richmond Ave. NW10 139 CW65
Richmond Ave. SW20 199 CY95
Richmond Ave., Felt. 175 BS86
Richmond Ave., Uxb. 135 BP65
Richmond Bri., Rich. 177 CK85
Richmond Bri., Twick. 177 CK86
Richmond Bldgs. W1 273 M9
Richmond Clo. E17 123 DZ58
Richmond Clo., Amer. 72 AT38
Quill Hall La.
Richmond Clo., Epsom 216 CS114
Richmond Clo., Lthd. 230 CC124
Richmond Clo. (Cheshunt), Wal.Cr. 66 DW29
Richmond Clo., West. 238 EH119
Richmond Ct., Brox. 49 DZ20
Richmond Ct., Hat. 45 CV20
Travellers La.
Richmond Ct., Pot.B. 64 DC31
Richmond Cres. E4 101 ED50
Richmond Cres. N1 141 DM67
Richmond Cres. N9 100 DU46
Richmond Cres., Slou. 132 AU74
Richmond Cres., Stai. 173 BF92
Richmond Dr., Grav. 191 GL89
Jubilee Cres.
Richmond Dr., Shep. 195 BQ100
Richmond Dr., Wat. 75 BS40
Richmond Gdns. NW4 119 CU57
Richmond Gdns., Har. 95 CF52
Richmond Grn., Croy. 201 DL104
Richmond Gro. N1 141 DP66
Richmond Gro., Surb. 198 CM100
Alpha Rd.
Richmond Hill, Rich. 178 CL86
Richmond Hill Ct., Rich. 178 CL86
Richmond Ms. W1 273 M9
Richmond Ms., Tedd. 177 CF93
Broad St.
Richmond Pk., Kings.T. 178 CN88
Richmond Pk., Rich. 178 CN88
Richmond Pk. Rd. SW14 178 CQ85
Richmond Pk. Rd., Kings.T. 198 CL95
Richmond Pl. SE18 165 EQ77
Richmond Rd. E4 101 ED46
Richmond Rd. E7 124 EH64
Richmond Rd. E8 142 DT66
Richmond Rd. E11 123 ED61
Richmond Rd. N2 98 DC54
Richmond Rd. N11 99 DL51
Richmond Rd. N15 122 DS58
Richmond Rd. SW20 199 CV95
Richmond Rd. W5 158 CL75
Richmond Rd., Barn. 80 DB43
Richmond Rd., Couls. 235 DH115
Richmond Rd., Croy. 201 DL104
Richmond Rd., Grays 170 GC79
Richmond Rd., Ilf. 125 EQ62
Richmond Rd., Islw. 157 CG83
Richmond Rd., Kings.T. 177 CK92
Richmond Rd., Pot.B. 64 DC31
Richmond Rd., Rom. 127 FF58
Richmond Rd., Stai. 173 BF92
Richmond Rd., Th.Hth. 201 DP97
Richmond Rd., Twick. 177 CG88
Richmond St. E13 144 EG68
Richmond Ter. SW1 277 P4
Richmond Ter. SW1 161 DL75
Richmond Ter. Ms. SW1 161 DL75
Parliament St.
Richmond Wk., St.Alb. 43 CK16
Richmond Way E11 124 EG61
Richmond Way W12 159 CX75
Richmond Way W14 159 CX75
Richmond Way, Lthd. 230 CB124
Richmond Way, Rick. 75 BQ42
Richmount Gdns. SE3 164 EG83
Rick Roberts Way E15 143 EC67
High St.
Rickard Clo. NW4 119 CU56
Rickard Clo. SW2 181 DN88
Rickard Clo., West Dr. 154 BK76
Rickards Clo., Surb. 198 CL102
Rickett St. SW6 160 DA79
Ricketts Hill Rd., West. 238 EK121
Rickfield Clo., Hat. 45 CU20
Rickman Cres., Add. 194 BH104
Rickman Hill, Couls. 235 DH117
Rickman Hill Rd., Couls. 235 DH118
Rickman St. E1 142 DW69
Mantus Rd.
Rickmans La., Slou. 112 AS64
Rickmansworth Bypass, Rick. 73 BF42
Rickmansworth La., Ger.Cr. 90 AY52
Rickmansworth Rd., Amer. 55 AQ37
Rickmansworth Rd., Nthwd. 93 BP50
Rickmansworth Rd., Pnr. 93 BV54
Rickmansworth Rd., Rick. 73 BE41
Rickmansworth Rd., Uxb. 92 BJ53
Rickmansworth Rd., Wat. 75 BS42
Ricksons La., Lthd. 245 BP127
Rickthorne Rd. N19 121 DL61
Landseer Rd.
Rickwood, Horl. 269 DH147
Woodhayes
Rickyard Path SE9 164 EL84
Ridding La., Grnf. 117 CF64
Riddings, The, Cat. 252 DT125
Riddings La., Harl. 51 ET19
Riddlesdown Ave., Pur. 220 DQ111
Riddlesdown Rd., Pur. 220 DQ110
Riddons Rd. SE12 184 EJ90
Ride, The, Brent. 157 CH78
Ride, The, Enf. 82 DW41
Rideout St. SE18 165 EM77
Rider Clo., Sid. 185 ES86
Riders Way, Gdse. 252 DW131
Ridgdale St. E3 143 EA68
Ridge, The, Bex. 186 EZ87
Ridge, The, Cat. 253 EB126
Ridge, The, Couls. 219 DL114
Ridge, The, Epsom 232 CQ118
Ridge, The, Lthd. 231 CD124
Ridge, The, Orp. 205 ER103
Ridge, The, Pur. 219 DJ110
Ridge, The, Surb. 198 CN99
Ridge, The, Twick. 177 CD87
Ridge, The, Wok. 227 BB117
Ridge Ave. N21 100 DQ45
Ridge Ave., Dart. 187 FF86
Ridge Clo. NW4 97 CX54
Ridge Clo. NW9 118 CR56
Ridge Clo., Bet. 264 CP138
Ridge Clo., Wok. 226 AV121
Ridge Crest, Enf. 81 DM39
Ridge Grn., Red. 267 DL137
Ridge Grn. Clo., Red. 267 DL137
Ridge Hill NW11 119 CY60
Ridge La., Wat. 75 BS38
Ridge Langley, S.Croy. 220 DU109
Ridge Lea, Hem.H. 39 BF20
Ridge Pk., Pur. 219 DK110
Ridge Rd. N8 121 DM58
Ridge Rd. N21 100 DQ46
Ridge Rd. NW2 119 CZ62
Ridge Rd., Mitch. 181 DH94
Ridge Rd., Sutt. 199 CY102
Ridge St., Wat. 75 BV38
Ridge Way SE19 182 DS93
Central Hill
Ridge Way, Dart. 187 FF86
Ridge Way, Felt. 176 BY90
Ridge Way, Iver 133 BE73
Ridge Way, Rick. 92 BH45
Ridge Way, The, S.Croy. 220 DS109
Ridgebank, Slou. 131 AM73
Ridgebrook Rd. SE3 164 EJ83
Ridgecroft Clo., Bex. 187 FC88
Ridgefield, Wat. 75 BS37
Ridgegate Clo., Reig. 250 DD132
Ridgehurst Ave., Wat. 59 BT34
Ridgelands, Lthd. 231 CD124
Ridgemead Rd., Egh. 172 AU90
Ridgemont Gdns., Edg. 96 CQ49
Ridgemount, Guil. 258 AV135
Ridgemount, Wey. 195 BS103
Ridgemount Ave., Couls. 235 DH117
Ridgemount Ave., Croy. 203 DX103
Ridgemount Clo. SE20 182 DV94
Anerley Pk.
Ridgemount End, Ger.Cr. 90 AY50
Ridgemount Gdns., Enf. 81 DP41
Ridges, The, Guil. 258 AW139
Ridgeview, St.Alb. 62 CM28
Ridgeview Clo., Barn. 79 CX44
Ridgeview Rd. N20 98 DB48
Ridgeway, Berk. 38 AT19
Ridgeway, Brwd. 109 GB46
Ridgeway, Brom. 204 EG103
Ridgeway, Dart. 189 FS92
Ridgeway, Epsom 216 CQ112
Ridgeway, Grays 170 GE77
Ridgeway, Welw.G.C. 30 DB09
Ridgeway, Wok. 226 AX115
Ridgeway, Wdf.Grn. 102 EJ49
Ridgeway, The E4 101 EB47
Ridgeway, The N3 98 DB52
Ridgeway, The N11 98 DF49
Ridgeway, The N14 99 DL47
Ridgeway, The NW7 97 CU48
Ridgeway, The NW9 118 CS56
Ridgeway, The NW11 119 CZ60
Ridgeway, The W3 158 CN76
Ridgeway, The, Amer. 55 AR40
Ridgeway, The, Croy. 201 DM104
Ridgeway, The, Enf. 81 DN39
Ridgeway, The, Ger.Cr. 112 AY55
Ridgeway, The, Guil. 259 BA135
Ridgeway, The, Har. 116 BZ57
Ridgeway, The (Kenton), Har. 117 CJ58
Ridgeway, The, Hert. 31 DM08
Ridgeway, The, Horl. 268 DG150
Ridgeway, The, Lthd. 214 CC114
Ridgeway, The (Oxshott), Lthd. 231 CD123
Ridgeway, The, Pot.B. 64 DD34
Ridgeway, The (Cuffley), Pot.B. 64 DE28
Ridgeway, The, Rad. 77 CF37
Ridgeway, The (Gidea Pk.), Rom. 127 FG56
Ridgeway, The (Harold Wd.), Rom. 106 FM53
Ridgeway, The, Ruis. 115 BU59
Ridgeway, The, St.Alb. 43 CG17
Ridgeway, The, Stan. 95 CJ51
Ridgeway, The, Sutt. 218 DD107
Ridgeway, The, Wat. 75 BS37
Ridgeway Ave., Barn. 80 DF44
Ridgeway Ave., Grav. 191 GH90
Ridgeway Clo., Chesh. 54 AP28
Ridgeway Clo., Dor. 263 CG138
Ridgeway Clo., Hem.H. 58 BM26
London Rd.
Ridgeway Clo., Lthd. 214 CC114
Ridgeway Clo., Wok. 226 AX115
Ridgeway Ct., Red. 250 DF134
Ridgeway Rd.
Ridgeway Cres., Orp. 205 ES104
Ridgeway Cres. Gdns., Orp. 205 ES103
Ridgeway Dr., Brom. 184 EH92
Ridgeway Dr., Dor. 263 CG139
Ridgeway E., Sid. 185 ET85
Ridgeway Gdns. N6 121 DJ59
Ridgeway Gdns., Ilf. 124 EL57
Ridgeway Gdns., Wok. 226 AX115
Ridgeway Ind. Est., Iver 133 BF73
Ridgeway Rd. SW9 161 DP83
Ridgeway Rd., Chesh. 54 AN28
Ridgeway Rd., Dor. 263 CG138
Ridgeway Rd., Islw. 157 CE80
Ridgeway Rd., Red. 250 DE134
Ridgeway Rd. N., Islw. 157 CE79
Ridgeway Wk., Nthlt. 136 BY65
Fortunes Mead
Ridgeway W., Sid. 185 ES85
Ridgewell Clo. N1 142 DQ67
Basire St.
Ridgewell Clo. SE26 183 DZ91
Kangley Bri. Rd.
Ridgewell Clo., Dag. 147 FB67
Ridgmont Rd., St.Alb. 43 CE21
Ridgmount Gdns. WC1 273 M6
Ridgmount Pl. WC1 273 M6
Ridgmount Rd. SW18 180 DB85
Ridgmount St. WC1 273 M6
Ridgway SW19 179 CW94
Ridgway, Wok. 228 BG115
Ridgway Gdns. SW19 179 CX94
Ridgway Pl. SW19 179 CY93
Ridgway Rd., Wok. 227 BF115
Ridgwell Rd. E16 144 EJ71
Riding, The NW11 119 CZ59
Golders Grn. Rd.
Riding, The, Wok. 211 BB114
Riding Ct. Rd., Slou. 152 AW80
Riding Hill, S.Croy. 220 DU113
Riding Ho. St. W1 273 J7
Riding Ho. St. W1 141 DJ71
Riding La., Beac. 88 AF53
Ridings, The W5 138 CM70
Ridings, The, Add. 211 BE107
Ridings, The, Amer. 55 AR35
Ridings, The, Ash. 231 CK117
Ridings, The, Chesh. 72 AX36
Ridings, The, Chig. 104 EV49
Manford Way
Ridings, The, Cob. 214 CA112
Ridings, The, Epsom 232 CS115
Ridings, The (Ewell), Epsom 217 CT109
Chessington Rd.
Ridings, The, Hert. 31 DN10
Ridings, The, Iver 153 BF77
Ridings, The, Lthd. 245 BS125
Ridings, The, Reig. 250 DD132
Ridings, The, Sun. 195 BU95
Ridings, The, Surb. 198 CN99
Ridings, The, Tad. 233 CZ120
Ridings, The, West. 238 EL117
Ridings, The, Wok. 228 BG123
Ridings Ave. N21 81 DP42
Ridings Clo. N6 121 DJ59
Hornsey La. Gdns.
Ridings La., Wok. 229 BP123
Ridlands Gro., Oxt. 254 EL130
Ridlands La., Oxt. 254 EK130
Ridlands Ri., Oxt. 254 EL130
Ridler Rd., Enf. 82 DS38
Ridley Ave. W13 157 CH76
Ridley Clo., Rom. 105 FH53
Ridley Rd. E7 124 EJ63
Ridley Rd. E8 122 DT64
Ridley Rd. NW10 139 CU68
Ridley Rd. SW19 180 DB94
Ridley Rd., Brom. 204 EF97
Ridley Rd., Warl. 236 DW118
Ridley Rd., Well. 166 EV81
Ridley Several SE3 164 EH82
Blackheath Pk.
Ridsdale Rd. SE20 202 DV95
Ridsdale Rd., Wok. 226 AV117
Riefield Rd. SE9 165 EQ84
Riesco Dr., Croy. 220 DW107
Riffel Rd. NW2 119 CW64
Riffhams, Brwd. 109 GB48
Rifle Butts All., Epsom 217 CT114
Rifle Pl. SE11 161 DN79
Stannary St.
Rifle Pl. W11 139 CX74
Rifle St. E14 143 EB71
Rigault Rd. SW6 159 CY82
Rigby Clo., Croy. 201 DN104
Rigby Gdns., Grays 171 GH77
Rigby La., Hayes 155 BQ75
Rigby Ms., Ilf. 125 EP61
Cranbrook Rd.
Rigden St. E14 143 EB72
Rigeley Rd. NW10 139 CU69
Rigg App. E10 123 DX60
Rigge Pl. SW4 161 DK84
Rigger Row SW11 160 DC83
Cinnamon Row
Riggindale Rd. SW16 181 DK91
Riley Rd. SE1 279 P6
Riley Rd. SE1 162 DT76
Riley Rd., Enf. 82 DW38
Riley St. SW10 160 DD80
Rinaldo Rd. SW12 181 DH87
Ring, The W2 272 B10
Ring, The W2 140 DD73
Ring Clo., Brom. 184 EH94
Garden Rd.
Ring Rd. W12 139 CW73
Wood La.
Ringcroft St. N7 121 DN64
Ringers Rd., Brom. 204 EG97
Ringford Rd. SW18 179 CZ85
Ringlewell Clo., Enf. 82 DV40
Central Ave.
Ringley Ave., Horl. 268 DG148
Ringley Pk. Ave., Reig. 250 DD134
Ringley Pk. Rd., Reig. 250 DC134
Ringmer Ave. SW6 159 CY81
Ringmer Gdns. N19 121 DL61
Sussex Way
Ringmer Pl. N21 82 DR43
Ringmer Way, Brom. 205 EM99
Ringmore Dr., Guil. 243 BC131
Ringmore Ri. SE23 182 DV87
Ringmore Rd., Walt. 196 BW104
Ringshall Rd., Orp. 206 EU97
Ringslade Rd. N22 99 DM54
Ringstead Rd. SE6 183 EB87
Ringstead Rd., Sutt. 218 DD105
Ringway N11 99 DJ51
Ringway, Sthl. 156 BX78
Ringway Rd., St.Alb. 60 CB27
Ringwold Clo., Beck. 183 DY94
Ringwood Ave. N2 98 DF54
Ringwood Ave., Croy. 201 DL101
Ringwood Ave., Horn. 128 FK61
Ringwood Ave., Orp. 224 EW110
Ringwood Ave., Red. 250 DF131
Ringwood Clo., Pnr. 116 BW55

Ringwood Gdns. E14 163 EA77
Ringwood Gdns. SW15 179 CU89
Ringwood Rd. E17 123 DZ58
Ringwood Way N21 99 DP46
Ringwood Way, Hmptn. 176 CA91
Ripley Ave., Egh. 172 AY93
Ripley Clo., Brom. 205 EM99
Ringmer Way
Ripley Clo., Croy. 221 EC107
Ripley Clo., Slou. 152 AY77
Ripley Gdns. SW14 158 CR83
Ripley Gdns., Sutt. 218 DC105
Ripley La., Lthd. 244 BN126
Ripley La., Wok. 228 BL123
Ripley Ms. E11 124 EE59
Wadley Rd.
Ripley Rd. E16 144 EJ72
Ripley Rd., Belv. 166 FA77
Ripley Rd., Enf. 82 DQ39
Ripley Rd., Guil. 244 BK128
Ripley Rd., Hmptn. 176 CA94
Ripley Rd., Ilf. 125 ET61
Ripley Rd., Wok. 244 BJ126
Ripley Vw., Loug. 85 EP38
Ripley Vill. W5 137 CJ72
Castlebar Rd.
Ripley Way, Hem.H. 39 BE19
Ripley Way (Cheshunt), Wal.Cr. 66 DV30
Riplington Ct. SW15 179 CU87
Longwood Dr.
Ripon Clo., Guil. 242 AT131
Ripon Clo., Nthlt. 116 CA64
Ripon Gdns., Chess. 215 CK106
Ripon Gdns., Ilf. 124 EL59
Ripon Rd. N9 100 DV45
Ripon Rd. N17 122 DR55
Ripon Rd. SE18 165 EP79
Ripon Way, Borwd. 78 CQ43
Ripon Way, St.Alb. 43 CK16
Rippersley Rd., Well. 166 EU81
Ripple Rd., Bark. 145 ER67
Ripple Rd., Dag. 146 EX67
Rippleside Ind. Est., Bark. 146 EV68
Ripplevale Gro. N1 141 DM66
Rippolson Rd. SE18 165 ET78
Ripston Rd., Ashf. 175 BR92
Risborough Dr., Wor.Pk. 199 CU101
Risborough St. SE1 278 G4
Risdon St. SE16 162 DW75
Renforth St.
Rise, The E11 124 EG57
Rise, The N13 99 DN49
Rise, The NW7 97 CT51
Rise, The NW10 118 CR63
Rise, The, Amer. 55 AQ39
Rise, The, Bex. 186 EW87
Rise, The, Borwd. 78 CM43
Rise, The, Buck.H. 102 EK45
Rise, The, Dart. 167 FF84
Rise, The, Edg. 96 CP50
Rise, The, Epsom 217 CT110
Rise, The, Grav. 191 GL91
Rise, The, Grnf. 117 CG64
Rise, The, Lthd. 245 BS126
Rise, The, St.Alb. 61 CD25
Rise, The, Sev. 257 FJ129
Rise, The, Sid. 186 EW87
Rise, The, S.Croy. 220 DW109
Rise, The, Tad. 233 CW121
Rise, The, Uxb. 134 BM68
Rise Cotts., Ware 34 EK05
Widford Rd.
Rise Pk. Boul., Rom. 105 FF53
Beauly Way
Rise Pk. Par., Rom. 105 FE54
Pettits La. N.
Risebridge Chase, Rom. 105 FF52
Risebridge Rd., Rom. 105 FF54
Risedale Clo., Hem.H. 40 BL23
Risedale Hill
Risedale Hill, Hem.H. 40 BL23
Risedale Rd., Bexh. 167 FB83
Risedale Rd., Hem.H. 40 BL23
Riseldine Rd. SE23 183 DY86
Riseway, Brwd. 108 FY48
Rising Hill Clo., Nthwd. 93 BQ51
Ducks Hill Rd.
Rising Sun Ct. EC1 274 G7
Risinghill St. N1 141 DM68
Risingholme Clo., Har. 95 CE53
Risingholme Clo. (Bushey), Wat. 94 CB45
Risingholme Rd., Har. 95 CE54
Risings, The E17 123 ED56
Risley Ave. N17 100 DQ53
Rita Rd. SW8 161 DL79
Ritches Rd. N15 122 DQ57
Ritchie Rd., Croy. 202 DV100
Ritchie St. N1 141 DN68
Ritchings Ave. E17 123 DY56
Ritcroft Clo., Hem.H. 41 BP21
Ritcroft Dr., Hem.H. 41 BP21
Ritcroft St., Hem.H. 41 BP21
Ritherdon Rd. SW17 180 DG89
Ritson Rd. E8 142 DU65
Ritter St. SE18 165 EN79
Ritz Ct., Pot.B. 64 DA31
Rivaz Pl. E9 142 DW65
Rivenhall End, Welw.G.C. 30 DC09
Rivenhall Gdns. E18 124 EF56
River Ave. N13 99 DP48
River Ave., Hodd. 49 EB16
River Ave., T.Ditt. 197 CG101
River Bank N21 100 DQ45
River Bank, E.Mol. 197 CE97
River Bank, T.Ditt. 197 CF99
River Bank, W.Mol. 196 BZ97
River Barge Clo. E14 163 EC75
Stewart St.
River Brent Business Pk. W7 157 CE76
Trumpers Way
River Clo. E11 124 EJ58
River Clo., Rain. 147 FH71
River Clo., Ruis. 115 BT58
River Clo., Surb. 197 CK99
Catherine Rd.
River Clo., Wal.Cr. 67 EA34
River Crane Wk., Felt. 176 BY88
Pevensey Rd.
River Crane Wk., Twick. 177 CG86
Hill Vw. Rd.
River Dr., Upmin. 128 FQ58
River Front, Enf. 82 DR41
River Gdns., Cars. 200 DG104
River Gdns., Felt. 155 BV84
River Gdns., Maid. 150 AD75
River Gro. Pk., Beck. 203 DZ95
River Hill, Cob. 229 BV115
River Island Clo., Lthd. 231 CD121
River La., Lthd. 231 CD121
River La., Rich. 177 CK88
River Meads, Ware 33 EC11
River Meads Ave., Twick. 176 CA90
River Pk., Hem.H. 40 BG22
River Pk. Ave., Stai. 173 BD91
River Pk. Gdns., Brom. 183 ED94
River Pk. Rd. N22 99 DM54
River Pl. N1 142 DQ66
River Reach, Tedd. 177 CJ92
River Rd., Bark. 145 ES68
River Rd., Brwd. 108 FS49
River Rd., Buck.H. 102 EL46
River Rd., Maid. 130 AC73
River Rd., Stai. 193 BF95
River Rd. Business Pk., Bark. 145 ET69
River St. EC1 274 D2
River St. EC1 141 DN69
River St., Ware 33 DY06
River St., Wind. 151 AR80
River Ter. W6 159 CW78
Crisp Rd.
River Vw., Enf. 82 DQ41
Chase Side
River Vw., Grays 171 GF77
River Vw., Welw.G.C. 29 CZ05
River Vw. Gdns., Twick. 177 CF89
River Wk., Uxb. 114 BJ64
River Wk., Walt. 195 BU100
River Way SE10 164 EF76
River Way, Epsom 216 CR107
River Way, Harl. 36 EU10
River Way, Loug. 85 EM44
River Way, Twick. 176 CB89
River Wey Navigation, Guil. 242 AX132
River Wey Navigation, Wok. 227 BC122
Riverbank, Stai. 173 BF93
Riverbank Way, Brent. 157 CJ79
Rivercourt Rd. W6 159 CV77
Riverdale SE13 163 EC83
Lewisham High St.
Riverdale Dr. SW18 180 DB88
Strathville Rd.
Riverdale Dr., Wok. 227 AZ121
Riverdale Gdns., Twick. 177 CJ86
Riverdale Rd. SE18 165 ET78
Riverdale Rd., Bex. 186 EY87
Riverdale Rd., Erith 167 FB78
Riverdale Rd., Felt. 176 BZ91
Riverdale Rd., Twick. 177 CJ86
Riverdene, Edg. 96 CQ48
Riverdene Rd., Ilf. 125 EN62
Riverfield Rd., Stai. 173 BF93
Riverhead Clo. E17 101 DX54
Riverhead Dr., Sutt. 218 DB110
Sevenoaks Clo.
Riverhill, Sev. 257 FL130
Riverholme Dr., Epsom 216 CR109
Rivermead, E.Mol. 196 CC96
Winchilsea Cres.
Rivermead, W.Byf. 212 BM113
Rivermead Clo., Add. 212 BJ108
Rivermead Clo., Tedd. 177 CH92
Rivermead Ct. SW6 159 CZ83
Rivermill, Harl. 35 EQ13
Rivermount, Walt. 195 BT101
Rivermount Gdns., Guil. 258 AW137
Rivernook Clo., Walt. 196 BW99
Riverpark, Berk. 38 AU18
Riversdale, Grav. 190 GE89
Riversdale Rd. N5 121 DP62
Riversdale Rd., Rom. 105 FB52
Riversdale Rd., T.Ditt. 197 CG99
Riversdell Clo., Cher. 193 BF101
Riversend Rd., Hem.H. 40 BJ23
Riversfield Rd., Enf. 82 DS41
Riverside NW4 119 CV59
Riverside SE7 164 EH76
Anchor & Hope La.
Riverside, Cher. 194 BG97
Riverside (Eynsford), Dart. 208 FK103
Riverside, Dor. 247 CK134
Riverside (Runnymede), Egh. 173 BA90
Windsor Rd.
Riverside, Guil. 242 AX132
Riverside, Horl. 268 DG150
Riverside, Stai. 193 BF95
Riverside (Wraysbury), Stai. 172 AW87
Riverside, Twick. 177 CH88
Riverside, The, E.Mol. 197 CD97
Graburn Way
Riverside Ave., Brox. 49 EA22
Riverside Ave., E.Mol. 197 CD99
Riverside Clo. E5 122 DW60
Riverside Clo. W7 137 CE70
Riverside Clo., Kings L. 59 BP29
Riverside Clo., Kings.T. 197 CK98
Riverside Clo., Orp. 206 EW96
Riverside Clo., St.Alb. 43 CE21
Riverside Rd.
Riverside Clo., Stai. 193 BF95
Riverside Clo., Wall. 201 DH104
Riverside Ct. E4 83 EB44
Chelwood Clo.
Riverside Ct. SW8 161 DK79
Riverside Ct., Harl. 36 EW09
Cambridge Rd.
Riverside Ct., St.Alb. 43 CE22
Riverside Dr. NW11 119 CY58
Riverside Dr. W4 158 CR80
Riverside Dr., Esher 214 CA105
Riverside Dr., Guil. 259 BA144
Riverside Dr., Mitch. 200 DE99
Riverside Dr., Rich. 177 CH89
Riverside Dr., Rick. 92 BK46
Riverside Dr., Stai. 193 BF95
Riverside Dr. (Egham Hythe), Stai. 173 BE92
Riverside Gdns. N3 119 CY55
Hendon La.
Riverside Gdns. W6 159 CV78
Riverside Gdns., Berk. 38 AU18
Riverside Gdns., Enf. 82 DQ40
Riverside Gdns., Wem. 138 CL68
Riverside Gdns., Wok. 227 BB121
Riverside Ind. Est. SE10 164 EF76
River Way
Riverside Ind. Est., Bark. 146 EU69
Riverside Ind. Est., Enf. 83 DY44
Morson Rd.
Riverside Ms., Croy. 201 DL104
Bridle Path
Riverside Path (Cheshunt), Wal.Cr. 67 DY29
Church La.
Riverside Pl., Stai. 174 BK86
Riverside Rd. E15 143 EC68
Riverside Rd. N15 122 DU58
Riverside Rd. SW17 180 DB91
Riverside Rd., St.Alb. 43 CE21
Riverside Rd., Sid. 186 EY90
Riverside Rd., Stai. 173 BF94
Riverside Rd. (Stanwell), Stai. 174 BK85
Riverside Rd., Walt. 214 BX105
Riverside Rd., Wat. 75 BV44
Riverside Wk. SE1 278 C2
Riverside Wk. SE1 141 DN74
Riverside Wk., Bex. 186 EX87
Riverside Wk., Islw. 157 CE83
Riverside Wk., Kings.T. 197 CK96
High St.
Riverside Way, Dart. 188 FL85
Riverside Way, St.Alb. 61 CD31
Riverside Way, Uxb. 134 BH67
Riversmead, Hodd. 49 EA18
Riversmeet, Hert. 31 DP10
Riverton Clo. W9 139 CZ69
Riverview Gdns. SW13 159 CV79
Riverview Gro. W4 158 CP79
Riverview Pk. SE6 183 EA88
Riverview Rd. W4 158 CP79
Riverview Rd., Epsom 216 CR106
Riverview Rd., Green. 189 FU85
Riverway N13 99 DN49
Riverway, Stai. 194 BH95
Riverway Est., Guil. 258 AV142
Riverwood La., Chis. 205 ER95
Rivett Drake Rd., Guil. 242 AU130
Rivey Clo., W.Byf. 211 BF114
Rivington Ave., Wdf.Grn. 102 EK54
Rivington Ct. NW10 139 CU67
Rivington Cres. NW7 97 CT52
Rivington Pl. EC2 275 N3
Rivington St. EC2 275 M3
Rivington St. EC2 142 DS69
Rivington Wk. E8 142 DU67
Wilde Clo.
Rivulet Rd. N17 100 DQ52
Rixon Clo., Slou. 132 AY72
Rixon Ho. SE18 165 EP79
Barnfield Rd.
Rixon St. N7 121 DN62
Tollington Rd.
Rixsen Rd. E12 124 EL64
Roach Rd. E3 143 EA66
Roads Pl. N19 121 DL61
Hornsey Rd.
Roakes Ave., Add. 194 BH103
Roan St. SE10 163 EB80
Roasthill La., Wind. 151 AK79
Boveney Rd.
Robarts Clo., Pnr. 115 BV57
Field End Rd.
Robb Rd., Stan. 95 CG51
Robbs Clo., Hem.H. 40 BG18
Robe End, Hem.H. 39 BF18
Robert Adam St. W1 272 F8
Robert Adam St. W1 140 DG72
Robert Ave., St.Alb. 42 CB24
Robert Clo. W9 140 DC70
Randolph Ave.
Robert Clo., Chig. 103 ET50
Robert Clo., Pot.B. 63 CY33
Robert Clo., Walt. 213 BV106
Robert Dashwood Way SE17 279 H9
Robert Dashwood Way SE17 162 DQ77
Robert Gentry Ho. W14 159 CY78
Comeragh Rd.
Robert Keen Clo. SE15 162 DU81
Cicely Rd.
Robert Lowe Clo. SE14 163 DX80
Robert Owen Ho. SW6 159 CX81
Robert Rd., Slou. 111 AR61
Robert St. E16 145 EP74
Robert St. NW1 273 J3
Robert St. NW1 141 DH69
Robert St. SE18 165 ER78
Robert St. WC2 278 A1
Roberta St. E2 142 DU69
Roberton Dr., Brom. 204 EJ95
Roberts Clo. SE9 185 ER88
Roberts Clo., Orp. 206 EW99
Sholden Gdns.
Roberts Clo., Pnr. 115 BV57
Field End Rd.
Roberts Clo., Rom. 105 FH53
Roberts Clo., Stai. 174 BJ86
Roberts Clo., Sutt. 217 CX108
Roberts Clo., West Dr. 134 BL74
Roberts La., Ger.Cr. 91 BA50
Roberts Ms. SW1 276 F7
Robert's Pl. EC1 274 E4
Roberts Rd. E17 101 EB53
Roberts Rd. NW7 97 CY51
Roberts Rd., Belv. 166 FA78
Roberts Rd., Wat. 76 BW43
Tucker St.
Roberts St., Croy. 202 DQ104
High St.
Roberts Way, Egh. 172 AW94
Roberts Way, Hat. 45 CT19
Roberts Wd. Dr., Ger.Cr. 91 AZ50
Robertsbridge Rd., Cars. 200 DC102
Robertson Clo., Brox. 67 DY26
Robertson Ct., Wok. 226 AS118
Raglan Rd.
Robertson Rd. E15 143 EC67
Robertson St. SW8 161 DH83
Robeson St. E3 143 DZ71
Ackroyd Dr.
Robeson Way, Borwd. 78 CQ39
Denham Way
Robin Clo. NW7 96 CS48
Robin Clo., Add. 212 BK106
Bois Hall Rd.
Robin Clo., Hmptn. 176 BY92
Robin Clo., Rom. 105 FD52
Robin Clo., Ware 33 EC12
Robin Ct. SE16 162 DU77
Robin Cres. E6 144 EL71
Robin Gdns., Red. 250 DG132
Robin Gro. N6 120 DG61
Robin Gro., Brent. 157 CJ79
Robin Gro., Har. 118 CM58
Robin Hill, Berk. 38 AW20
Robin Hill Dr., Chis. 184 EL93
Robin Hood Clo., Slou. 131 AM74
Robin Hood Clo., Wok. 226 AT118
Robin Hood Cres., Wok. 226 AS117
Robin Hood Dr., Har. 95 CF52
Robin Hood Dr. (Bushey), Wat. 76 BZ39
Robin Hood Grn., Orp. 206 EU99
Robin Hood La. E14 143 EC72
Robin Hood La. SW15 178 CS91
Robin Hood La., Bexh. 186 EY85
Robin Hood La., Guil. 227 AZ124
Robin Hood La., Hat. 45 CU17
Robin Hood La., Sutt. 218 DA106
Robin Hood Meadow, Hem.H. 40 BM15
Robin Hood Rd. SW19 179 CV92
Robin Hood Rd., Brwd. 108 FV45
Robin Hood Rd., Wok. 226 AS117
Robin Hood Way SW15 178 CS91
Robin Hood Way SW20 178 CS91
Robin Hood Way, Grnf. 137 CF65
Robin Mead, Welw.G.C. 30 DA06
Robin Way, Guil. 242 AV130
Robin Way, Orp. 206 EV97
Robin Way (Cuffley), Pot.B. 65 DL28
Robin Way, Stai. 173 BF90
Robin Willis Way, Wind. 172 AU86
St. Lukes Rd.
Robina Clo., Bexh. 166 EX84
Robina Clo., Nthwd. 93 BT53
Robinhood Clo., Mitch. 201 DJ98
Robinhood La., Mitch. 201 DJ97
Robinia Ave., Grav. 190 GD87
Robinia Clo., Chig. 103 ES50
Robinia Cres. E10 123 EB61
Oliver Rd.
Robins Clo., Uxb. 134 BJ71
Newcourt
Robins Ct. SE12 184 EJ90
Robins Gro., W.Wick. 204 EG104
Robins La., Epp. 85 EQ36
Robins Nest Hill, Hert. 47 DJ19
Robins Orchard, Ger.Cr. 90 AY51
Robins Rd., Hem.H. 40 BN22
Robins Way, Hat. 45 CT21
Robinscroft Ms. SE10 163 EB81
Sparta St.
Robinsfield, Hem.H. 40 BG20
Robinson Ave. (Cheshunt), Wal.Cr. 65 DP28
Robinson Clo., Horn. 147 FH66
Robinson Cres. (Bushey), Wat. 94 CC46
Robinson Rd. E2 142 DW68
Robinson Rd. SW17 180 DE93
Robinson Rd., Dag. 126 FA63
Robinson St. SW3 160 DF79
Christchurch St.
Robinsons Clo. W13 137 CG71
Robinsway, Wal.Abb. 68 EE34
Roundhills
Robinsway, Walt. 214 BW105
Robinswood Clo., Beac. 88 AJ50
Robinwood Gro., Uxb. 134 BM70
Robinwood Pl. SW15 178 CR91
Roborough Wk., Horn. 148 FJ65
Coltishall Rd.
Robsart St. SW9 161 DM82
Robson Ave. NW10 139 CU67
Robson Clo. E6 144 EL72
Linton Gdns.
Robson Clo., Enf. 81 DP40
Robson Clo., Ger.Cr. 90 AY50
Robson Rd. SE27 181 DP90
Robsons Clo., Wal.Cr. 66 DW29
Robyns Cft., Grav. 190 GE90
Robyns Way, Sev. 256 FF122
Roch Ave., Edg. 96 CM54
Rochdale Rd. E17 123 EA59
Rochdale Rd. SE2 166 EV78
Rochdale Way SE8 163 EA80
Idonia St.
Roche Rd. SW16 201 DL95
Roche Wk., Cars. 200 DD100
Rochelle Clo. SW11 160 DD84
Rochelle St. E2 275 P3
Rochemont Wk. E8 142 DT67
Pownall Rd.
Rochester Ave. E13 144 EJ67
Rochester Ave., Brom. 204 EH96
Rochester Ave., Felt. 175 BT89
Rochester Clo. SW16 181 DL94
Rochester Clo., Enf. 82 DS39
Rochester Clo., Sid. 186 EV86
Rochester Dr., Bex. 186 EZ86
Rochester Dr., Pnr. 116 BX57
Rochester Dr., Wat. 60 BW34
Rochester Gdns., Cat. 236 DS122
Rochester Gdns., Croy. 202 DS104
Rochester Gdns., Ilf. 125 EM59
Rochester Ms. NW1 141 DJ66
Rochester Pl. NW1 141 DJ65
Rochester Rd. NW1 141 DJ65
Rochester Rd., Cars. 218 DF105
Rochester Rd., Dart. 188 FN87
Rochester Rd., Grav. 191 GL87
Rochester Rd., Nthwd. 115 BT55
Rochester Rd., Stai. 173 BD92
Rochester Row SW1 277 L8
Rochester Row SW1 161 DJ77
Rochester Sq. NW1 141 DJ66
Rochester St. SW1 277 M7
Rochester St. SW1 161 DK76
Rochester Ter. NW1 141 DJ65
Rochester Wk. SE1 279 K2
Rochester Wk., Reig. 266 DB139
Castle Dr.
Rochester Way SE3 164 EJ82
Rochester Way SE9 165 EM83
Rochester Way, Dart. 187 FD87
Rochester Way, Rick. 75 BP42
Rochester Way Relief Rd. SE3 164 EH81
Rochester Way Relief Rd. SE9 164 EJ84
Rochford Ave., Brwd. 109 GA43
Rochford Ave., Loug. 85 EQ41
Rochford Ave., Rom. 126 EW57
Rochford Ave., Wal.Abb. 67 ED34
Rochford Clo. E6 144 EK68
Boleyn Rd.
Rochford Clo., Brox. 67 DY26
Rochford Clo., Horn. 147 FH65
Rochford Grn., Loug. 85 EQ41
Rochford St. NW5 120 DF64
Rochford Wk. E8 142 DU66
Wilman Gro.
Rochford Way, Croy. 201 DL100
Rochford Way, Maid. 130 AG72
Rochfords Gdns., Slou. 132 AW74
Rock Ave. SW14 158 CR83
South Worple Way
Rock Gdns., Dag. 127 FB64
Rockwell Rd.
Rock Gro. Way SE16 162 DV77
Blue Anchor La.
Rock Hill SE26 182 DT91
Rock Hill, Orp. 224 FA107
Rock St. N4 121 DN61
Rockall Ct., Slou. 153 BB76
Rockbourne Rd. SE23 183 DX88
Rockchase Gdns., Horn. 128 FL58
Rockcliffe Ave., Kings L. 58 BN30
Rockdale Rd., Sev. 257 FH126
Rockells Pl. SE22 182 DV86
Rockfield Clo., Oxt. 254 EF131
Rockfield Rd., Oxt. 254 EF129
Rockford Ave., Grnf. 137 CG68
Rockhall Rd. NW2 119 CX63
Rockhampton Clo. SE27 181 DN91
Rockhampton Rd.
Rockhampton Rd. SE27 181 DN91
Rockhampton Rd., S.Croy. 220 DS107
Rockingham Ave., Horn. 127 FH58
Rockingham Clo. SW15 159 CT84
Rockingham Clo., Uxb. 134 BJ67
Rockingham Est. SE1 279 H7
Rockingham Est. SE1 162 DQ76
Rockingham Par., Uxb. 134 BJ66
Rockingham Rd., Uxb. 134 BH67
Rockingham St. SE1 279 H7
Rockingham St. SE1 162 DQ76
Rockland Rd. SW15 159 CY84
Rocklands Dr., Stan. 95 CH54
Rockleigh Ct., Brwd. 109 GA45
Hutton Rd.
Rockley Rd. W14 159 CX75
Rockmount Rd. SE18 165 ET78
Rockmount Rd. SE19 182 DR93
Rocks La. SW13 159 CU83
Rockshaw Rd., Red. 251 DJ127
Rockware Ave., Grnf. 137 CD67
Rockways, Barn. 79 CT44
Rockwell Gdns. SE19 182 DS91
Rockwell Rd., Dag. 127 FB64
Rockwood Pl. W12 159 CW75
Shepherds Bush Grn.
Rocky La., Reig. 250 DF128
Rocliffe St. N1 274 G1
Rocmoale Way SE8 163 EA80
Octavius St.
Rocombe Cres. SE23 182 DW87
Rocque La. SE3 164 EF83
Rodborough Rd. NW11 120 DA60
Roden Clo., Harl. 36 EZ11
Roden Ct. N6 121 DK59
Hornsey La.
Roden Gdns., Croy. 202 DS100
Roden St. N7 121 DM62
Roden St., Ilf. 125 EN62
Rodenhurst Rd. SW4 181 DJ86
Roderick Rd. NW3 120 DF63
Rodgers Clo., Borwd. 77 CK44
Roding Ave., Wdf.Grn. 102 EL51
Roding Gdns., Loug. 84 EL44
Roding Rd.
Roding La., Buck.H. 102 EK46
Roding La., Chig. 103 EP47
Roding La. N., Wdf.Grn. 102 EL51
Roding La. S., Ilf. 124 EK56
Roding La. S., Wdf.Grn. 124 EK55
Roding Ms. E1 142 DU74
Kennet St.
Roding Rd. E5 123 DY63
Roding Rd. E6 145 EP71
Roding Rd., Loug. 84 EL43
Roding Trd. Est., Bark. 145 EP66
Roding Vw., Buck.H. 102 EK46
Roding Way, Rain. 148 FK68
Rodings, The, Upmin. 129 FR58
Rodings, The, Wdf.Grn. 102 EJ51
Rodings Row, Barn. 79 CY43
Leecroft Rd.
Rodmarton St. W1 272 E7
Rodmarton St. W1 140 DF71
Rodmell Clo., Hayes 136 BY70
Rodmell Slope N12 97 CZ50
Rodmere St. SE10 164 EE78
Trafalgar Rd.
Rodmill La. SW2 181 DL87
Rodney Ave., St.Alb. 43 CG22
Rodney Clo., Croy. 201 DP102
Rodney Clo., N.Mal. 198 CS99
Rodney Clo., Pnr. 116 BY59
Rodney Clo., Walt. 196 BW102
Rodney Rd.
Rodney Ct. W9 140 DC70
Maida Vale
Rodney Cres., Hodd. 49 EA15
Rodney Gdns., Pnr. 115 BV57
Rodney Gdns., W.Wick. 222 EG105
Rodney Grn., Walt. 196 BW103
Rodney Pl. E17 101 DY54
Rodney Pl. SE17 279 J8
Rodney Pl. SE17 162 DQ77
Rodney Pl. SW19 200 DC95
Rodney Rd. E11 124 EH56
Rodney Rd. SE17 279 J8
Rodney Rd. SE17 162 DQ77
Rodney Rd., Mitch. 200 DE96
Rodney Rd., N.Mal. 198 CS99
Rodney Rd., Twick. 176 CA86
Rodney Rd., Walt. 196 BW103
Rodney St. N1 141 DM68
Rodney Way, Guil. 243 BA133
Rodney Way, Rom. 104 FA53
Rodney Way, Slou. 153 BE81
Rodona Rd., Wey. 213 BR111
Rodway Rd. SW15 179 CU87
Rodway Rd., Brom. 204 EH95
Rodwell Clo., Ruis. 116 BW60
Rodwell Ct., Add. 212 BJ105
Garfield Rd.
Rodwell Pl., Edg. 96 CN51
Whitchurch La.
Rodwell Rd. SE22 182 DT86
Roe End NW9 118 CQ56
Roe Grn. NW9 118 CQ57
Roe Grn. Clo., Hat. 44 CS19
Roe Grn. La., Hat. 45 CT18
Roe Hill Clo., Hat. 45 CT19

Roe La. NW9 118 CP56
Roe Way, Wall. 219 DL108
Roebourne Way E16 165 EN75
Roebuck Clo., Ash. 232 CL120
Roebuck Clo., Felt. 175 BV91
Roebuck Clo., Reig. 250 DA134
Roebuck Grn., Slou. 131 AL74
Roebuck La. N17 100 DT51
High Rd.
Roebuck La., Buck.H. 102 EJ45
Roebuck Rd., Chess. 216 CN106
Roebuck Rd., Ilf. 104 EV50
Roedean Ave., Enf. 82 DW39
Roedean Clo., Enf. 82 DW39
Roedean Clo., Orp. 224 EV105
Roedean Cres. SW15 178 CS86
Roefields Clo., Hem.H. 40 BG24
Roehampton Clo. SW15 159 CU84
Roehampton Clo., Grav. 191 GL87
Roehampton Dr., Chis. 185 EQ93
Roehampton Gate SW15 178 CS86
Roehampton High St. SW15 179 CU87
Roehampton La. SW15 159 CU84
Roehampton Vale SW15 179 CT90
Roehyde Way, Hat. 44 CS20
Roestock Gdns., St.Alb. 44 CS22
Roestock La., St.Alb. 44 CR23
Rofant Rd., Nthwd. 93 BS51
Roffes La., Cat. 236 DR124
Roffey Clo., Horl. 268 DF148
Court Lo. Rd.
Roffey Clo., Pur. 235 DP116
Roffey St. E14 163 EC75
Roffords, Wok. 226 AV117
Rogate Ho. E5 122 DU62
Muir Rd.
Roger St. WC1 274 C5
Roger St. WC1 141 DM70
Rogers Clo., Cat. 236 DV122
Tillingdown Hill
Rogers Clo., Couls. 235 DP118
Rogers Ct., Swan. 207 FG98
Rogers Gdns., Dag. 126 FA64
Rogers La., Slou. 132 AT67
Rogers La., Warl. 237 DZ118
Rogers Mead, Gdse. 252 DV132
Ivy Mill La.
Rogers Rd. E16 144 EF72
Rogers Rd. SW17 180 DD91
Rogers Rd., Dag. 126 FA64
Rogers Rd., Grays 170 GC77
Rogers Ruff, Nthwd. 93 BQ53
Rogers Wk. N12 98 DB48
Brook Meadow
Rojack Rd. SE23 183 DX88
Roke Clo., Ken. 220 DQ114
Roke Lo. Rd., Ken. 219 DP113
Roke Rd., Ken. 236 DQ115
Rokeby Ct., Wok. 226 AT117
Rokeby Gdns., Wdf.Grn. 102 EG53
Rokeby Pl. SW20 179 CV94
Rokeby Rd. SE4 163 DZ82
Rokeby St. E15 143 ED67
Roker Pk. Ave., Uxb. 114 BL63
Rokesby Clo., Well. 165 ER82
Rokesby Pl., Wem. 117 CK64
Rokesby Rd., Slou. 131 AM69
Rokesly Ave. N8 121 DL57
Rokewood Ms., Ware 33 DX05
Roland Gdns. SW7 160 DC78
Roland Gdns., Felt. 176 BZ90
Roland Ms. E1 143 DX71
Stepney Grn.
Roland Rd. E17 123 ED56
Roland St., St.Alb. 43 CG20
Roland Way SE17 162 DR78
Roland Way SW7 160 DC78
Roland Gdns.
Roland Way, Wor.Pk. 199 CT103
Roles Gro., Rom. 126 EX56
Rolfe Clo., Barn. 80 DE42
Rolfe Clo., Beac. 89 AL54
Rolinsden Way, Kes. 222 EK105
Roll Gdns., Ilf. 125 EN57
Rollesby Rd., Chess. 216 CN107
Rollesby Way SE28 146 EW73
Rolleston Ave., Orp. 205 EP100
Rolleston Clo., Orp. 205 EP101
Rolleston Rd., S.Croy. 220 DR108
Rollins St. SE15 162 DW79
Rollit Cres., Houns. 176 CA85
Rollit St. N7 121 DM64
Hornsey Rd.
Rollo Rd., Swan. 187 FF94
Rolls Bldgs. EC4 274 D8
Rolls Pk. Ave. E4 101 EA51
Rolls Pk. Rd. E4 101 EB50
Rolls Pas. EC4 274 D8
Rolls Rd. SE1 162 DT78
Rollscourt Ave. SE24 182 DQ85
Rollswood, Welw.G.C. 29 CY12
Rolt St. SE8 163 DY79
Rolvenden Gdns., Brom. 184 EK94
Rolvenden Pl. N17 100 DU53
Manor Rd.
Rom Cres., Rom. 127 FF59
Rom Valley Way, Rom. 127 FE58
Roma Read Clo. SW15 179 CV87
Bessborough Rd.
Roma Rd. E17 123 DY55
Roman Clo. W3 158 CP75
Avenue Gdns.
Roman Clo., Felt. 176 BW85
Roman Clo., Rain. 147 FD68
Roman Clo., Uxb. 92 BG53
Roman Gdns., Kings L. 59 BP30
Roman Ms., Hodd. 49 EA16
North Rd.
Roman Ri. SE19 182 DR93
Roman Rd. E2 142 DW69
Roman Rd. E3 143 DY68
Roman Rd. E6 144 EK70
Roman Rd. N10 99 DH52
Roman Rd. NW2 119 CW62
Edgware Rd.
Roman Rd. W4 159 CT77
Roman Rd., Brwd. 109 GC41
Roman Rd., Dor. 263 CG138
Roman Rd., Grav. 190 GC90
Roman Rd., Hert. 32 DV14
Roman Rd., Ilf. 145 EP65
Roman Sq. SE28 146 EU74
Roman St., Hodd. 49 EA16
Roman Vale, Harl. 36 EW10
Roman Vill. Rd. (South Darenth), Dart. 188 FQ92
Roman Way N7 141 DM65
Roman Way SE15 162 DW80
Clifton Way
Roman Way, Croy. 201 DP103
Roman Way, Dart. 187 FE85
Roman Way, Enf. 82 DT43
Roman Way, Slou. 131 AP71
Roman Way Ind. Est. N1 141 DM66
Offord St.
Romanhurst Ave., Brom. 204 EE98
Romanhurst Gdns., Brom. 204 EE98
Romans End, St.Alb. 42 CC22
Romans Way, Wok. 228 BG115
Romany Gdns. E17 101 DY53
McEntee Ave.
Romany Gdns., Sutt. 200 DA101
Romany Ri., Orp. 205 EQ102
Romberg Rd. SW17 180 DG90
Romborough Gdns. SE13 183 EC85
Romborough Way SE13 183 EC85
Romeland, Borwd. 77 CK44
Romeland, Wal.Abb. 67 EC33
Romeland Hill, St.Alb. 42 CC20
Romero Clo. SW9 161 DM83
Stockwell Rd.
Romero Sq. SE3 164 EJ84
Romeyn Rd. SW16 181 DM90
Romford Rd. E7 124 EH64
Romford Rd. E12 124 EL63
Romford Rd. E15 144 EE65
Romford Rd., Chig. 104 EU48
Romford Rd., Rom. 104 EY52
Romford Rd., S.Ock. 148 FQ69
Romford St. E1 142 DU71
Romilly Dr., Wat. 94 BY49
Romilly Rd. N4 121 DP61
Romilly St. W1 273 M10
Romilly St. W1 141 DK73
Rommany Rd. SE27 182 DR91
Romney Chase, Horn. 128 FM58
Romney Clo. N17 100 DV53
Romney Clo. NW11 120 DC60
Romney Clo. SE14 162 DW80
Kender St.
Romney Clo., Ashf. 175 BQ92
Romney Clo., Chess. 216 CL105
Romney Clo., Har. 116 CA59
Romney Dr., Brom. 184 EK94
Romney Dr., Har. 116 CA59
Romney Gdns., Bexh. 166 EZ81
Romney Lock Rd., Wind. 151 AR80
Romney Ms. W1 272 F6
Romney Rd. SE10 163 EC79
Romney Rd., Grav. 190 GE90
Romney Rd., Hayes 135 BR68
Romney Rd., N.Mal. 198 CR100
Romney Row NW2 119 CX61
Brent Ter.
Romney St. SW1 277 P7
Romney St. SW1 161 DL76
Romola Rd. SE24 181 DP88
Romsey Clo., Orp. 223 EP105
Romsey Clo., Slou. 153 AZ76
Romsey Dr., Slou. 111 AR62
Romsey Gdns., Dag. 146 EX67
Romsey Rd. W13 137 CG73
Romsey Rd., Dag. 146 EX67
Ron Leighton Way E6 144 EL67
Rona Rd. NW3 120 DG63
Rona Wk. N1 142 DR65
Marquess Est.
Ronald Ave. E15 144 EE69
Ronald Clo., Beck. 203 DZ98
Ronald Rd., Beac. 89 AM53
Ronald Rd., Rom. 106 FN53
Ronald St. E1 142 DW72
Devonport St.
Ronalds Rd. N5 121 DN64
Ronalds Rd., Brom. 204 EG95
Ronaldsay Spur, Slou. 132 AS71
Ronaldstone Rd., Sid. 185 ES86
Ronart St., Har. 117 CF55
Stuart Rd.
Rondu Rd. NW2 119 CY64
Ronelean Rd., Surb. 198 CM104
Roneo Cor., Horn. 127 FF60
Hornchurch Rd.
Roneo Link, Horn. 127 FF60
Ronfearn Ave., Orp. 206 EX99
Ronneby Clo., Wey. 195 BS104
Ronson Way, Lthd. 231 CG121
Randalls Rd.
Ronver Rd. SE12 184 EG88
Baring Rd.
Rood La. EC3 275 M10
Rood La. EC3 142 DS73
Rook Clo., Horn. 147 FG66
Rook La., Cat. 235 DM124
Rook Rd., H.Wyc. 110 AD59
Rook Wk. E6 144 EL72
Allhallows Rd.
Rookdean, Sev. 256 FC122
Rooke Way SE10 164 EF78
Rookeries Clo., Felt. 175 BV90
Rookery, The, Dor. 262 CA138
Rookery, The, Grays 169 FU79
Rookery Clo. NW9 119 CT57
Rookery Clo., Lthd. 231 CE124
Rookery Ct., Grays 169 FU79
Rookery Cres., Dag. 147 FB66
Rookery Dr., Chis. 205 EN95
Rookery Dr., Dor. 262 CA138
Rookery Gdns., Orp. 206 EW99
Rookery Hill, Ash. 232 CN118
Rookery Hill, Red. 269 DN145
Rookery La., Brom. 204 EK100
Rookery La., Grays 170 GE78
Rookery La., Horl. 269 DN146
Rookery Rd. SW4 161 DJ84
Rookery Rd., Orp. 223 EM110
Rookery Rd., Stai. 174 BH92
Rookery Vw., Grays 170 GD78
Rookery Way NW9 119 CT57
Rookery Way, Tad. 249 CZ127
Rookes All., Hert. 32 DR09
Gascoyne Way
Rookesley Rd., Orp. 206 EX101
Rookfield Ave. N10 121 DJ56
Rookfield Clo. N10 121 DJ56
Cranmore Way
Rookley Clo., Sutt. 218 DB110
Rooks Clo., Welw.G.C. 29 CX10
Longcroft La.
Rooks Hill, Rick. 74 BK42
Rooks Hill, Welw.G.C. 29 CW10
Rooksmead Rd., Sun. 195 BT96
Rookstone Rd. SW17 180 DF92
Rookwood Ave., Loug. 85 EQ41
Rookwood Ave., N.Mal. 199 CU98
Rookwood Ave., Wall. 219 DK105
Rookwood Clo., Grays 170 GB77
Rookwood Clo., Red. 251 DH129
Rookwood Ct., Guil. 258 AW137
Rookwood Gdns. E4 102 EF46
Whitehall Rd.
Rookwood Gdns., Loug. 85 EQ41
Rookwood Ho., Bark. 145 ER68
St. Marys
Rookwood Rd. N16 122 DT59
Roosevelt Way, Dag. 147 FD65
Rootes Dr. W10 139 CX70
Barlby Rd.
Roothill La., Bet. 264 CN140
Rope St. SE16 163 DY76
Rope Wk., Sun. 196 BW97
Rope Wk. Gdns. E1 142 DU72
Commercial Rd.
Rope Yd. Rails SE18 165 EP76
Ropemaker Rd. SE16 163 DY75
Ropemaker St. EC2 275 K6
Ropemaker St. EC2 142 DR71
Ropemakers Flds. E14 143 DZ73
Narrow St.
Roper La. SE1 279 N5
Roper St. SE9 185 EM86
Roper Way, Mitch. 200 DG96
Ropers Ave. E4 101 EB50
Ropers Wk. SW2 181 DN87
Brockwell Pk. Gdns.
Ropery St. E3 143 DZ70
Ropley St. E2 142 DU68
Rosa Alba Ms. N5 122 DQ63
Kelross Rd.
Rosa Ave., Ashf. 174 BN91
Rosaline Rd. SW6 159 CY80
Rosamund St. SE26 182 DV90
Rosary, The, Egh. 193 BE96
Rosary Clo., Houns. 156 BY82
Rosary Ct., Pot.B. 64 DB30
Rosary Gdns. SW7 160 DC77
Rosary Gdns., Ashf. 175 BP91
Rosaville Rd. SW6 159 CZ80
Roscoe St. EC1 275 J5
Roscoff Clo., Edg. 96 CQ53
Rose All. SE1 279 J2
Rose All. SE1 142 DQ74
Rose & Crown Ct. EC2 275 H8
Rose & Crown Yd. SW1 277 L2
Rose Ave. E18 102 EH54
Rose Ave., Grav. 191 GL88
Rose Ave., Mitch. 200 DF95
Rose Ave., Mord. 200 DC99
Rose Bank, Brwd. 108 FX48
Rose Bank Cotts., Wok. 226 AY122
Rose Bates Dr. NW9 118 CN56
Rose Bushes, Epsom 233 CV116
Rose Ct. E1 142 DS71
Sandy's Row
Rose Ct. SE26 182 DV89
Rose Ct., Pnr. 116 BW55
Nursery Rd.
Rose Ct., Wal.Cr. 66 DU27
Rose Dale, Orp. 205 EP103
Rose Dr., Chesh. 54 AR33
Rose End, Wor.Pk. 199 CX102
Rose Gdn. Clo., Edg. 96 CL51
Rose Gdns. W5 157 CK76
Rose Gdns., Felt. 175 BU89
Rose Gdns., Sthl. 136 CA70
Rose Gdns., Stai. 174 BK87
Diamedes Ave.
Rose Gdns., Wat. 75 BU43
Rose Glen NW9 118 CR56
Rose Glen, Rom. 127 FE60
Rose Hill, Dor. 263 CG137
Rose Hill, Slou. 130 AG67
Rose Hill, Sutt. 200 DB104
Rose La., Rom. 126 EX55
Rose La., Wok. 228 BJ121
Rose Lawn (Bushey), Wat. 94 CC46
Rose St. WC2 273 P10
Rose St., Grav. 190 GB86
Rose Vale, Hodd. 49 EA17
Rose Valley, Brwd. 108 FW48
Rose Vill., Dart. 188 FP87
Rose Wk., Pur. 219 DK111
Rose Wk., St.Alb. 43 CJ18
Rose Wk., Slou. 131 AP71
Birch Gro.
Rose Wk., Surb. 198 CP99
Rose Wk., W.Wick. 203 EC103
Rose Wk., The, Rad. 77 CH37
Rose Way SE12 184 EG85
Roseacre, Oxt. 254 EG134
Roseacre Clo. W13 137 CH71
Middlefielde
Roseacre Clo., Horn. 128 FM60
Roseacre Clo., Shep. 194 BN99
Roseacre Gdns., Guil. 259 BF140
Roseacre Gdns., Welw.G.C. 30 DD09
Roseacre Rd., Well. 166 EV83
Roseary Clo., West Dr. 154 BK77
Rosebank SE20 182 DV94
Rosebank, Epsom 216 CQ114
Rosebank, Wal.Abb. 68 EE33
Rosebank Ave., Horn. 128 FJ64
Rosebank Ave., Wem. 117 CF63
Rosebank Clo. N12 98 DE50
Rosebank Clo., Tedd. 177 CG93
Rosebank Gdns. E3 143 DZ68
Rosebank Gro. E17 123 DZ55
Rosebank Rd. E17 123 EB58
Rosebank Rd. W7 157 CE75
Rosebank Vill. E17 123 EA56
Rosebank Vill. E17 123 DY57
High St.
Rosebank Wk. NW1 141 DK66
Maiden La.
Rosebank Wk. SE18 164 EL77
Woodhill
Rosebank Way W3 138 CR72
Roseberry Clo., Upmin. 129 FT58
Roseberry Ct., Wat. 75 BU39
Grandfield Ave.
Roseberry Gdns. N4 121 DP58
Roseberry Gdns., Dart. 188 FJ87
Roseberry Gdns., Orp. 205 ES104
Roseberry Gdns., Upmin. 129 FS58
Roseberry Pl. E8 142 DT65
Roseberry St. SE16 162 DV77
Rosebery Ave. E12 144 EL65
Rosebery Ave. EC1 274 D4
Rosebery Ave. EC1 141 DN70
Rosebery Ave. N17 100 DU54
Rosebery Ave., Epsom 216 CS114
Rosebery Ave., Har. 116 BY63
Rosebery Ave., N.Mal. 199 CT96
Rosebery Ave., Sid. 185 ES87
Rosebery Ave., Th.Hth. 202 DQ96
Rosebery Clo., Mord. 199 CX100
Rosebery Ct. EC1 141 DN70
Rosebery Ave.
Rosebery Ct., Grav. 191 GF88
Churchill Rd.
Rosebery Cres., Wok. 227 AZ121
Rosebery Gdns. N8 121 DL57
Rosebery Gdns. W13 137 CG72
Rosebery Gdns., Sutt. 218 DB105
Rosebery Ms. N10 99 DJ54
Rosebery Ms. SW2 181 DL86
Rosebery Rd.
Rosebery Rd. N9 100 DU48
Rosebery Rd. N10 99 DJ54
Rosebery Rd. SW2 181 DL86
Rosebery Rd., Epsom 232 CR119
Rosebery Rd., Grays 170 FY79
Rosebery Rd., Houns. 176 CC85
Rosebery Rd., Kings.T. 198 CP96
Rosebery Rd., Sutt. 217 CZ107
Rosebery Rd. (Bushey), Wat. 94 CB45
Rosebery Sq. EC1 274 D5
Rosebery Sq., Kings.T. 198 CP96
Rosebine Ave., Twick. 177 CD87
Rosebriar Clo., Wok. 228 BG116
Rosebriar Wk., Wat. 75 BT36
Rosebriars, Cat. 236 DS120
Salmons La. W.
Rosebriars, Esher 214 CC106
Esher Pk. Ave.
Rosebury Rd. SW6 160 DB82
Rosebury Vale, Ruis. 115 BU61
Rosecourt Rd., Croy. 201 DM100
Rosecroft Ave. NW3 120 DA62
Rosecroft Clo., Orp. 206 EW100
Rosecroft Clo., West. 239 EM118
Lotus Rd.
Rosecroft Dr., Wat. 75 BS36
Rosecroft Gdns. NW2 119 CU62
Rosecroft Gdns., Twick. 177 CD88
Rosecroft Rd., Sthl. 136 CA70
Rosecroft Wk., Pnr. 116 BX57
Rosecroft Wk., Wem. 117 CK64
Rosedale, Ash. 231 CJ118
Rosedale, Cat. 236 DS123
Rosedale, Welw.G.C. 29 CZ05
Rosedale Ave., Hayes 135 BR71
Rosedale Ave. (Cheshunt), Wal.Cr. 66 DT29
Rosedale Clo. SE2 166 EV76
Finchale Rd.
Rosedale Clo. W7 157 CF75
Boston Rd.
Rosedale Clo., Dart. 188 FP87
Rosedale Clo., St.Alb. 60 BY30
Rosedale Clo., Stan. 95 CH51
Rosedale Ct. N5 121 DP63
Panmure Clo.
Rosedale Gdns., Dag. 146 EV66
Rosedale Rd. E7 124 EJ64
Rosedale Rd., Dag. 146 EV66
Rosedale Rd., Epsom 217 CU106
Rosedale Rd., Grays 170 GD78
Rosedale Rd., Rich. 158 CL84
Rosedale Rd., Rom. 105 FC54
Rosedale Way (Cheshunt), Wal.Cr. 66 DU27
Rosedene NW6 139 CX67
Rosedene Ave. SW16 181 DM90
Rosedene Ave., Croy. 201 DL101
Rosedene Ave., Grnf. 136 CA69
Rosedene Ave., Mord. 200 DA99
Rosedene Ct., Dart. 188 FJ87
Shepherds La.
Rosedene Ct., Ruis. 115 BS60
Rosedene Gdns., Ilf. 125 EN56
Rosedene Ter. E10 123 EB61
Rosedew Rd. W6 159 CX79
Rosefield, Sev. 256 FG124
Rosefield Clo., Cars. 218 DE106
Alma Rd.
Rosefield Gdns. E14 143 EA73
Rosefield Gdns., Cher. 211 BD107
Rosefield Rd., Stai. 174 BG91
Roseford Ct. W12 159 CX75
Shepherds Bush Grn.
Rosehart Ms. W11 140 DA72
Westbourne Gro.
Rosehatch Ave., Rom. 126 EX55
Roseheath, Hem.H. 39 BF19
Roseheath Rd., Houns. 176 BZ85
Rosehill, Esher 215 CG107
Rosehill, Hmptn. 196 CA95
Rosehill Ave., Sutt. 200 DC102
Rosehill Ave., Wok. 226 AW116
Rosehill Clo., Hodd. 49 DZ17
Rosehill Ct., Slou. 152 AU76
Yew Tree Rd.
Rosehill Fm. Meadow, Bans. 234 DB115
The Tracery
Rosehill Gdns., Abb.L. 59 BQ32
Rosehill Gdns., Grnf. 117 CF64
Rosehill Gdns., Sutt. 200 DB103
Rosehill Pk. W., Sutt. 200 DB102
Rosehill Rd. SW18 180 DC86
Rosehill Rd., West. 238 EJ117
Roseland Clo. N17 100 DR52
Cavell Rd.
Roselands Ave., Hodd. 49 DZ15
Roseleigh Ave. N5 121 DP63
Roseleigh Clo., Twick. 177 CK86
Roseley Cotts., Harl. 35 EP11
Rosemary Ave. N3 98 DB54
Rosemary Ave. N9 100 DV46
Rosemary Ave., Enf. 82 DR39
Rosemary Ave., Houns. 156 BX82
Rosemary Ave., Rom. 127 FF55
Rosemary Ave., W.Mol. 196 CA97
Rosemary Clo., Croy. 201 DL101
Therapia La.
Rosemary Clo., Harl. 36 EW11
Rosemary Clo., Oxt. 254 EG133
Rosemary Clo., S.Ock. 149 FW69
Rosemary Clo., Uxb. 134 BN71
Rosemary Ct., Horl. 268 DE147
Rosemary Cres., Guil. 242 AT130
Rosemary Dr. E14 143 ED72
Rosemary Dr., Ilf. 124 EK57
Rosemary Gdns. SW14 158 CQ83
Rosemary La.
Rosemary Gdns., Chess. 216 CL105
Rosemary Gdns., Dag. 126 EZ60
Rosemary La. SW14 158 CQ83
Rosemary La., Egh. 193 BB97
Rosemary La., Horl. 269 DH149
Rosemary Pl. N1 142 DR67
Shepperton Rd.
Rosemary Rd. SE15 162 DT80
Rosemary Rd. SW17 180 DC90
Rosemary Rd., Well. 165 ET81
Rosemary St. N1 142 DR67
Shepperton Rd.
Rosemead NW9 119 CT59
Rosemead, Cher. 194 BH101
Rosemead, Pot.B. 64 DC30
Rosemead Ave., Felt. 175 BT89
Rosemead Ave., Mitch. 201 DJ96
Rosemead Ave., Wem. 118 CL64
Rosemead Clo., Red. 266 DD136
Cronks Hill Rd.
Rosemead Gdns., Brwd. 109 GD42
Rosemont Ave. N12 98 DC51
Rosemont Rd. NW3 140 DC65
Rosemont Rd. W3 138 CP73
Rosemont Rd., Kings.T. 198 CQ97
Rosemont Rd., N.Mal. 198 CQ97
Rosemont Rd., Rich. 178 CL86
Rosemont Rd., Wem. 138 CL67
Rosemoor St. SW3 276 D9
Rosemoor St. SW3 160 DF77
Rosemount, Harl. 51 EP18
Rosemount Ave., W.Byf. 212 BG113
Rosemount Clo., Wdf.Grn. 103 EM51
Chapelmount Rd.
Rosemount Dr., Brom. 205 EM98
Rosemount Rd. W13 137 CG72
Rosenau Cres. SW11 160 DE81
Rosenau Rd. SW11 160 DE81
Rosendale Rd. SE21 182 DQ87
Rosendale Rd. SE24 182 DQ87
Roseneath Ave. N21 99 DP46
Roseneath Clo., Orp. 224 EW108
Roseneath Rd. SW11 180 DG86
Roseneath Wk., Enf. 82 DR42
Rosens Wk., Edg. 96 CP48
Rosenthal Rd. SE6 183 EB86
Rosenthorpe Rd. SE15 183 DX85
Roserton St. E14 163 EC75
Rosery, The, Croy. 203 DX100
Roses, The, Wdf.Grn. 102 EF52
Roses La., Wind. 151 AK82
Rosethorn Clo. SW12 181 DK87
Rosetrees, Guil. 259 BA135
Rosetta Clo. SW8 161 DL80
Kenchester Clo.
Roseveare Rd. SE12 184 EJ91
Roseville Ave., Houns. 176 CA85
Roseville Rd., Hayes 155 BU78
Rosevine Rd. SW20 199 CW95
Rosewarne Clo., Wok. 226 AU118
Muirfield Rd.
Roseway SE21 182 DR86
Rosewood, Dart. 187 FE91
Rosewood, Esher 197 CG103
Manor Rd. N.
Rosewood, Sutt. 218 DC110
Bawtree Clo.
Rosewood, Wok. 227 BA119
Rosewood Ave., Grnf. 117 CG64
Rosewood Ave., Horn. 127 FG64
Rosewood Clo., Sid. 186 EW90
Rosewood Ct., Brom. 204 EJ95
Rosewood Ct., Hem.H. 39 BE19
The Shrubbery
Rosewood Ct., Rom. 126 EW57
Tendring Way
Rosewood Dr., Enf. 81 DN35
Rosewood Dr., Shep. 194 BM99
Rosewood Gdns. SE13 163 EC82
Lewisham Rd.
Rosewood Gro., Sutt. 200 DC103
Rosewood Sq. W12 139 CU72
Primula St.
Rosewood Ter. SE20 182 DW94
Laurel Gro.
Rosewood Way, Slou. 111 AQ64
Rosher Clo. E15 143 ED66
Rosherville Way, Grav. 190 GE87
Rosina St. E9 123 DX64
Roskell Rd. SW15 159 CX83
Rosken Dr., Slou. 131 AP68
Roslin Rd. W3 158 CP76
Roslin Way, Brom. 184 EG92
Roslyn Clo., Brox. 49 DY21
Roslyn Clo., Mitch. 200 DD96
Roslyn Ct., Wok. 226 AU118
St. John's Rd.
Roslyn Gdns., Rom. 105 FE54
Roslyn Rd. N15 122 DR57
Rosmead Rd. W11 139 CY73
Rosoman Pl. EC1 274 E4
Rosoman St. EC1 274 E3
Rosoman St. EC1 141 DN69
Ross Ave. NW7 97 CY50
Ross Ave., Dag. 126 EZ61
Ross Clo., Har. 94 CC52
Ross Clo., Hat. 45 CU15
Homestead Rd.
Ross Clo., Hayes 155 BR76
Ross Ct. SW15 179 CX87
Ross Cres., Wat. 75 BU35
Ross Par., Wall. 219 DH107
Ross Rd. SE25 202 DR97
Ross Rd., Cob. 214 BW113
Ross Rd., Dart. 187 FG86
Ross Rd., Twick. 176 CB88
Ross Rd., Wall. 219 DJ106
Ross Way SE9 164 EL83
Ross Way, Nthwd. 93 BT49
Rossall Clo., Horn. 127 FG58
Rossall Cres. NW10 138 CM69
Rossdale, Sutt. 218 DE106
Rossdale Dr. N9 82 DW44
Rossdale Dr. NW9 118 CQ60
Rossdale Rd. SW15 159 CW84
Rosse Ms. SE3 164 EH81
Rossendale St. E5 122 DV61
Rossendale Way NW1 141 DJ67
Rossetti Gdns., Couls. 235 DM117
Stanley Clo.
Rossetti Rd. SE16 162 DV78
Rossgate, Hem.H. 40 BG18
Galley Hill
Rossignol Gdns., Cars. 200 DG103
Rossindel Rd., Houns. 176 CA85
Rossington Ave., Borwd. 78 CL38
Rossington St. E5 122 DU61
Rossiter Clo., Slou. 152 AY77
Rossiter Flds., Barn. 79 CY44

Rushmere La., Hem.H. 56 AX27
Rushmere Pl. SW19 179 CX92
Marryat Rd.
Rushmoor Clo., Guil. 242 AT131
Rushmoor Clo., Pnr. 115 BV56
Rushmoor Clo., Rick. 92 BK47
Rushmore Clo., Brom. 204 EL97
Rushmore Hill, Orp. 224 EW109
Rushmore Hill, Sev. 224 EX112
Rushmore Rd. E5 122 DW63
Rusholme Ave., Dag. 126 FA62
Rusholme Gro. SE19 182 DS92
Rusholme Rd. SW15 179 CX86
Rushout Ave., Har. 117 CH58
Rushton Ave., Wat. 75 BU35
Rushton Gro., Harl. 52 EX15
Church Langley Way
Rushton St. N1 142 DR68
Rushworth Ave. NW4 119 CU55
Rushworth Gdns.
Rushworth Gdns. NW4 119 CU55
Rushworth Rd., Reig. 250 DA133
Rushworth St. SE1 278 G4
Rushworth St. SE1 161 DP75
Rushy Meadow La., Cars. 200 DE103
Ruskin Ave. E12 144 EL65
Ruskin Ave., Felt. 175 BT86
Ruskin Ave., Rich. 158 CN80
Ruskin Ave., Upmin. 128 FQ59
Ruskin Ave., Wal.Abb. 68 EE34
Ruskin Ave., Well. 166 EU82
Ruskin Clo. NW11 120 DB58
Ruskin Clo. (Cheshunt), Wal.Cr. 66 DS26
Ruskin Dr., Orp. 205 ES104
Ruskin Dr., Well. 166 EU83
Ruskin Dr., Wor.Pk. 199 CV103
Ruskin Gdns. W5 137 CK70
Ruskin Gdns., Har. 118 CM56
Ruskin Gdns., Rom. 105 FH52
Ruskin Gro., Dart. 188 FN85
Ruskin Gro., Well. 166 EU82
Ruskin Pk. Ho. SE5 162 DR83
Ruskin Rd. N17 100 DT53
Ruskin Rd., Belv. 166 FA77
Ruskin Rd., Cars. 218 DF106
Ruskin Rd., Croy. 201 DP103
Ruskin Rd., Grays 171 GG77
Ruskin Rd., Islw. 157 CF83
Ruskin Rd., Sthl. 136 BY73
Ruskin Rd., Stai. 173 BF94
Ruskin Wk. N9 100 DU47
Durham Rd.
Ruskin Wk. SE24 182 DQ85
Ruskin Wk., Brom. 204 EL100
Ruskin Way SW19 200 DD95
Rusland Ave., Orp. 205 ER104
Rusland Pk. Rd., Har. 117 CE56
Rusper Clo. NW2 119 CW62
Rusper Clo., Stan. 95 CJ49
Rusper Rd. N22 99 DP54
Rusper Rd., Dag. 146 EW65
Russelcroft Rd., Welw.G.C. 29 CW08
Russell Ave. N22 99 DN54
Russell Ave., St.Alb. 43 CD20
Russell Clo. NW10 138 CQ66
Russell Clo. SE7 164 EJ80
Russell Clo. W4 158 CS80
Pumping Sta. Rd.
Russell Clo., Amer. 72 AX39
Russell Clo., Beck. 203 EB97
Russell Clo., Bexh. 166 FA84
Russell Clo., Brwd. 108 FV45
Russell Clo., Dart. 167 FG83
Russell Clo., Nthwd. 93 BQ50
Russell Clo., Ruis. 116 BW61
Russell Clo., Tad. 249 CU125
Russell Clo., Wok. 226 AW115
Russell Ct. SW1 277 L3
Russell Ct., Chesh. 54 AR29
Russell Ct., Lthd. 231 CH122
Russell Ct., St.Alb. 60 CA30
Russell Cres., Wat. 75 BT35
High Rd.
Russell Dr., Stai. 174 BK86
Russell Gdns. N20 98 DE47
Russell Gdns. NW11 119 CY58
Russell Gdns. W14 159 CY76
Russell Gdns., Rich. 177 CJ89
Russell Gdns., West Dr. 154 BN78
Russell Gdns. Ms. W14 159 CY75
Russell Grn. Clo., Pur. 219 DN110
Russell Gro. NW7 96 CS50
Russell Gro. SW9 161 DN81
Russell Hill, Pur. 219 DM110
Russell Hill Pl., Pur. 219 DN111
Purley Way
Russell Hill Rd., Pur. 219 DN110
Russell Kerr Clo. W4 158 CQ80
Burlington La.
Russell La. N20 98 DE47
Russell La., Wat. 75 BR36
Russell Mead, Har. 95 CF52
Russell Pl. NW3 120 DE64
Aspern Gro.
Russell Pl. SE16 163 DY76
Onega Gate
Russell Pl. (Sutton at Hone), Dart. 208 FN95
Russell Pl., Hem.H. 40 BH23
Russell Rd. E4 101 DZ49
Russell Rd. E10 123 EB58
Russell Rd. E16 144 EG72
Russell Rd. E17 123 DZ55
Russell Rd. N8 121 DK58
Russell Rd. N13 99 DM51
Russell Rd. N15 122 DS57
Russell Rd. N20 98 DE47
Russell Rd. NW9 119 CT58
Russell Rd. SW19 180 DA94
Russell Rd. W14 159 CY76
Russell Rd., Buck.H. 102 EH46
Russell Rd., Enf. 82 DT38
Russell Rd., Grav. 191 GK86
Russell Rd., Grays 170 GA77
Russell Rd., Mitch. 200 DE97
Russell Rd., Nthlt. 116 CC64
Russell Rd., Nthwd. 93 BQ48
Russell Rd., Shep. 195 BP101
Russell Rd., Til. 170 GE81
Russell Rd., Twick. 177 CF86
Russell Rd., Walt. 195 BU100
Russell Rd., Wok. 226 AW115
Russell Sq. WC1 273 P5
Russell Sq. WC1 141 DL70
Russell Sq., Long. 209 FX97
Cavendish Sq.
Russell St. WC2 274 A10
Russell St. WC2 141 DL73
Russell St., Hert. 32 DQ09
Russell St., Wind. 151 AR81
Russell Wk., Rich. 178 CM86
Park Hill
Russell Way, Sutt. 218 DA106
Russells, Tad. 233 CX122
Russells Cres., Horl. 268 DG149
Russell's Footpath SW16 181 DL92
Russells Ride (Cheshunt), Wal.Cr. 67 DY30
Russet Clo., Horl. 269 DJ148
Carlton Tye
Russet Clo., Stai. 173 BF86
Russet Clo., Uxb. 135 BQ70
Uxbridge Rd.
Russet Clo., Walt. 196 BX104
Russet Cres. N7 121 DM64
Stock Orchard Cres.
Russet Dr., Croy. 203 DY102
Russet Dr., Rad. 62 CL32
Porters Pk. Dr.
Russet Way, Dor. 263 CK140
Russets, The, Ger.Cr. 90 AX54
Austenwood Clo.
Russets Clo. E4 101 ED49
Larkshall Rd.
Russett Clo., Orp. 224 EV106
Russett Clo., Wal.Cr. 66 DS26
Appleby St.
Russett Ct., Cat. 252 DU125
Russett Hill, Ger.Cr. 112 AY55
Russett Way SE13 163 EB82
Conington Rd.
Russett Way, Swan. 207 FD96
Russett Wd., Welw.G.C. 30 DD10
Russetts, The, Horn. 128 FL56
Russetts Clo., Wok. 227 AZ115
Orchard Dr.
Russia Ct. EC2 275 J9
Russia Dock Rd. SE16 143 DY74
Russia La. E2 142 DW68
Russia Row EC2 275 J9
Russia Wk. SE16 163 DX75
Archangel St.
Russington Rd., Shep. 195 BR100
Rust Sq. SE5 162 DR80
Rusthall Ave. W4 158 CR77
Rusthall Clo., Croy. 202 DW100
Rustic Ave. SW16 181 DH94
Rustic Clo., Upmin. 129 FS60
Rustic Pl., Wem. 117 CK63
Rustic Wk. E16 144 EH72
Lambert Rd.
Rustington Wk., Mord. 199 CZ101
Ruston Ave., Surb. 198 CP101
Ruston Gdns. N14 80 DG44
Farm La.
Ruston Ms. W11 139 CY72
St. Marks Rd.
Ruston St. E3 143 DZ67
Rutford Rd. SW16 181 DL92
Ruth Clo., Stan. 118 CM56
Ruthen Clo., Epsom 216 CP114
Rutherford Clo., Borwd. 78 CQ40
Studio Way
Rutherford Clo., Sutt. 218 DD107
Rutherford Clo., Wind. 151 AM81
Rutherford St. SW1 277 M8
Rutherford St. SW1 161 DK77
Rutherford Twr., Sthl. 136 CB72
Rutherford Way (Bushey), Wat. 95 CD46
Rutherford Way, Wem. 118 CN62
Rutherglen Rd. SE2 166 EU79
Rutherwick Clo., Horl. 268 DF148
Rutherwick Ri., Couls. 235 DL117
Rutherwick Twr., Horl. 268 DF148
Rutherwyk Rd., Cher. 193 BE101
Rutherwyke Clo., Epsom 217 CU107
Ruthin Clo. NW9 118 CS58
Ruthin Rd. SE3 164 EG79
Ruthven Ave., Wal.Cr. 67 DX33
Ruthven St. E9 143 DX67
Lauriston Rd.
Rutland App., Horn. 128 FN57
Rutland Ave., Sid. 186 EU87
Rutland Ave., Slou. 131 AQ71
Rutland Clo. SW14 158 CP83
Rutland Clo. SW19 180 DE94
Rutland Rd.
Rutland Clo., Bex. 186 EX88
Rutland Clo., Chess. 216 CM107
Rutland Clo., Dart. 188 FK87
Rutland Clo., Epsom 216 CR110
Rutland Clo., Red. 250 DF133
Rutland Ct., Enf. 82 DV43
Rutland Dr., Horn. 128 FN57
Rutland Dr., Mord. 199 CZ100
Rutland Dr., Rich. 177 CK88
Rutland Gdns. N4 121 DP58
Rutland Gdns. SW7 276 C5
Rutland Gdns. SW7 160 DE75
Rutland Gdns. W13 137 CG71
Rutland Gdns., Croy. 220 DS105
Rutland Gdns., Dag. 126 EW64
Rutland Gdns., Hem.H. 40 BM19
Rutland Gdns. Ms. SW7 276 C5
Rutland Gate SW7 276 C5
Rutland Gate SW7 160 DE75
Rutland Gate, Belv. 167 FB78
Rutland Gate, Brom. 204 EF98
Rutland Gate Ms. SW7 276 B5
Rutland Gro. W6 159 CV78
Rutland Ms. NW8 140 DB67
Boundary Rd.
Rutland Ms. E. SW7 276 B6
Rutland Ms. S. SW7 276 B6
Rutland Pk. NW2 139 CW65
Rutland Pk. SE6 183 DZ89
Rutland Pl. EC1 274 G6
Rutland Pl. (Bushey), Wat. 95 CD46
The Rutts
Rutland Rd. E7 144 EK66
Rutland Rd. E9 142 DW67
Rutland Rd. E11 124 EH57
Rutland Rd. E17 123 EA58
Rutland Rd. SW19 180 DE94
Rutland Rd., Har. 116 CC58
Rutland Rd., Hayes 155 BR77
Rutland Rd., Ilf. 125 EP63
Rutland Rd., Sthl. 136 CA70
Rutland Rd., Twick. 177 CD89
Rutland St. SW7 276 C6
Rutland St. SW7 160 DE76
Rutland Wk. SE6 183 DZ89
Rutland Way, Orp. 206 EW100
Rutley Clo. SE17 161 DP79
Royal Rd.
Rutley Clo., Rom. 106 FK54
Pasteur Dr.
Rutlish Rd. SW19 200 DA95
Rutson Rd., W.Byf. 212 BM114
Rutter Gdns., Mitch. 200 DD98
Rutters Clo., West Dr. 154 BN75
Rutts, The (Bushey), Wat. 95 CD46
Rutts Ter. SE14 163 DX81
Ruvigny Gdns. SW15 159 CX83
Ruxbury Rd., Cher. 193 BC100
Ruxley Clo., Epsom 216 CP106
Ruxley Clo., Sid. 186 EY93
Ruxley Cor. Ind. Est., Sid. 186 EX93
Ruxley Cres., Esher 215 CH107
Ruxley La., Epsom 216 CP107
Ruxley Ms., Epsom 216 CP106
Ruxley Ridge, Esher 215 CG108
Ruxton Clo., Swan. 207 FE97
Ryall Clo., St.Alb. 60 BY29
Ryalls Ct. N20 98 DF48
Ryan Clo. SE3 164 EJ84
Ryan Clo., Ruis. 115 BV60
Ryan Dr., Brent. 157 CG79
Ryan Way, Wat. 76 BW39
Ryarsh Cres., Orp. 223 ES105
Rycott Path SE22 182 DU87
Lordship La.
Rycroft La., Sev. 256 FE130
Rycroft Way N17 122 DT55
Ryculff Sq. SE3 164 EF82
Rydal Clo. NW4 97 CX53
Rydal Clo., Pur. 220 DR113
Rydal Ct., Wat. 59 BV32
Grasmere Clo.
Rydal Cres., Grnf. 137 CH69
Rydal Dr., Bexh. 166 EZ82
Rydal Dr., W.Wick. 204 EE103
Rydal Gdns. NW9 118 CS57
Rydal Gdns. SW15 178 CS92
Rydal Gdns., Houns. 176 CB86
Rydal Gdns., Wem. 117 CJ60
Rydal Rd. SW16 181 DK91
Rydal Way, Egh. 173 BB94
Rydal Way, Enf. 82 DW44
Rydal Way, Ruis. 116 BW63
Ryde, The, Hat. 45 CW15
Ryde, The, Stai. 194 BH95
Ryde Clo., Wok. 228 BJ121
Ryde Heron, Wok. 226 AS117
Robin Hood Rd.
Ryde Pl., Twick. 177 CJ86
Ryde Vale Rd. SW12 181 DH89
Rydens Ave., Walt. 195 BV103
Rydens Clo., Walt. 196 BW103
Rydens Gro., Walt. 214 BX105
Rydens Pk., Walt. 196 BX103
Rydens Rd.
Rydens Rd., Walt. 195 BV104
Rydens Way, Wok. 227 BA120
Ryder Ave., Hat. 44 CS20
Ryder Clo., Brom. 184 EH92
Ryder Clo., Hem.H. 57 BA28
Ryder Clo., Hert. 32 DV08
Ryder Clo. (Bushey), Wat. 76 CB44
Ryder Ct. SW1 277 L2
Ryder Dr. SE16 162 DV78
Credon Rd.
Ryder Gdns., Rain. 147 FF65
Ryder Ms. E9 122 DW64
Homerton High St.
Ryder St. SW1 277 L2
Ryder St. SW1 141 DJ74
Ryder Yd. SW1 277 L2
Ryders Ter. NW8 140 DC68
Blenheim Ter.
Rydes Ave., Guil. 242 AT131
Rydes Clo., Wok. 227 BC120
Rydes Hill Cres., Guil. 242 AT130
Rydes Hill Rd., Guil. 242 AT132
Rydings, Wind. 151 AM83
Rydon St. N1 142 DQ67
St. Paul St.
Rydons Clo. SE9 164 EL83
Rydon's La., Couls. 236 DQ120
Rydons Pk., Walt. 195 BT102
Rydon's Wd. Clo., Couls. 236 DQ120
Rydston Clo. N7 141 DM66
Sutterton St.
Rye, The N14 99 DJ45
Rye Clo., Bex. 187 FB86
Rye Clo., Guil. 242 AS132
Rye Clo., Horn. 128 FJ64
Rye Cres., Orp. 206 EW102
Rye Fld., Orp. 206 EX103
Rye Hill Est. SE15 162 DW84
Rye Hill Pk. SE15 162 DW84
Rye Hill Rd., Epp. 52 EU22
Rye Hill Rd., Harl. 51 ER20
Rye La. SE15 162 DU82
Rye La., Sev. 241 FE120
Rye Pas. SE15 162 DU83
Rye Rd. SE15 163 DX84
Rye Rd., Hodd. 49 EB15
Rye Wk. SW15 179 CX85
Chartfield Ave.
Rye Way, Edg. 96 CM51
Canons Dr.
Ryebridge Clo., Lthd. 231 CG118
Ryebrook Rd., Lthd. 231 CG118
Ryecotes Mead SE21 182 DS88
Ryecroft, Grav. 191 GL92
Ryecroft, Harl. 51 EP15
Ryecroft, Hat. 45 CT20
Hazel Gro.
Ryecroft, Wind. 151 AM83
Ryecroft Ave., Ilf. 103 EP54
Ryecroft Ave., Twick. 176 CB87
Ryecroft Clo., Hem.H. 41 BQ21
Poynders Hill
Ryecroft Ct., St.Alb. 44 CM20
Ryecroft Cres., Barn. 79 CV43
Ryecroft Rd. SE13 183 EC85
Ryecroft Rd. SW16 181 DN93
Ryecroft Rd., Chesh. 54 AN32
Ryecroft Rd., Orp. 205 ER100
Ryecroft Rd., Sev. 241 FG116
Ryecroft St. SW6 160 DB81
Ryedale SE22 182 DV86
Ryefield Ave., Uxb. 135 BP66
Ryefield Clo., Hodd. 33 EB13
Ryefield Path SW15 179 CU88
Ryefield Rd. SE19 182 DQ93
Ryeland Clo., West Dr. 134 BL72
Ryelands, Horl. 269 DJ147
Ryelands, Welw.G.C. 29 CZ12
Ryelands Clo., Cat. 236 DS121
Ryelands Ct., Lthd. 231 CG118
Ryelands Cres. SE12 184 EJ86
Ryelands Pl., Wey. 195 BS104
Ryfold Rd. SW19 180 DA90
Ryhope Rd. N11 99 DH49
Rykhill, Grays 171 GH76
Ryland Clo., Felt. 175 BT91
Ryland Ho., Croy. 202 DQ104
Ryland Rd. NW5 141 DH65
Rylandes Rd. NW2 119 CU62
Rylandes Rd., S.Croy. 220 DV109
Rylett Cres. W12 159 CT75
Rylett Rd. W12 159 CT76
Rylston Rd. N13 100 DR48
Rylston Rd. SW6 159 CZ79
Rymer Rd., Croy. 202 DS101
Rymer St. SE24 181 DP86
Rymill Clo., Hem.H. 57 BA28
Rymill St. E16 145 EN74
Rysbrack St. SW3 276 D6
Rysbrack St. SW3 160 DF76
Rysted La., West. 255 EQ126
Rythe Ct., T.Ditt. 197 CG101
Rythe Rd., Esher 215 CD106
Ryvers Rd., Slou. 153 AZ76

S

Sabah Ct., Ashf. 174 BN91
Sabbarton St. E16 144 EF72
Victoria Dock Rd.
Sabella Ct. E3 143 DZ68
Mostyn Gro.
Sabina Rd., Grays 171 GJ77
Sabine Rd. SW11 160 DF83
Sable Clo., Houns. 156 BW83
Sable St. N1 141 DP66
Canonbury Rd.
Sach Rd. E5 122 DV61
Sackville Ave., Brom. 204 EG102
Sackville Clo., Har. 117 CD62
Sackville Clo., Sev. 257 FH122
Sackville Ct., Rom. 106 FL53
Sackville Cres.
Sackville Cres., Rom. 106 FL53
Sackville Est. SW16 181 DL90
Sackville Gdns., Ilf. 125 EM60
Sackville Rd., Dart. 188 FK89
Sackville Rd., Sutt. 218 DA108
Sackville St. W1 277 L1
Sackville St. W1 141 DJ73
Sackville Way SE22 182 DU88
Dulwich Common
Sacombe Rd., Hem.H. 39 BF18
Saddington St., Grav. 191 GH87
Saddle Yd. W1 141 DH74
Hay's Ms.
Saddlebrook Pk., Sun. 175 BS94
Cadbury Rd.
Saddlers Clo., Borwd. 78 CR44
Farriers Way
Saddlers Clo., Pnr. 94 CA51
Saddlers Mead, Harl. 52 EU16
Saddlers Ms., Wem. 117 CF63
The Boltons
Saddler's Pk. (Eynsford), Dart. 208 FK104
Saddlers Way, Epsom 232 CR119
Saddlescombe Way N12 98 DA50
Saddleworth Rd., Rom. 106 FJ51
Saddleworth Sq., Rom. 106 FJ51
Sadler Clo., Mitch. 200 DF96
Sadlers Clo., Guil. 243 BD133
Sadlers Ride, W.Mol. 196 CB97
Sadlers Way, Hert. 31 DN09
Sadlier Rd., St.Alb. 43 CE22
Saffron Ave. E14 143 ED73
Saffron Clo. NW11 119 CZ57
Saffron Clo., Croy. 201 DL101
Therapia La.
Saffron Clo., Hodd. 49 DZ16
Saffron Clo., Slou. 152 AV81
Saffron Hill EC1 274 E6
Saffron Hill EC1 141 DN70
Saffron La., Hem.H. 40 BH19
Saffron Platt, Guil. 242 AU130
Saffron Rd., Grays 169 FW77
Arterial Rd. W. Thurrock
Saffron Rd., Rom. 105 FC54
Saffron St. EC1 274 E6
Saffron Way, Surb. 197 CK102
Sage Clo. E6 145 EM71
Tollgate Rd.
Sage St. E1 142 DW73
Cable St.
Sage Way WC1 274 B3
Saigasso Clo. E16 144 EK72
Royal Rd.
Sail St. SE11 278 C8
Sail St. SE11 161 DM77
Sainfoin Rd. SW17 180 DG89
Sainsbury Rd. SE19 182 DS92
St. Agatha's Dr., Kings.T. 178 CM93
St. Agathas Gro., Cars. 200 DF102
St. Agnells Ct., Hem.H. 40 BN16
St. Agnells La., Hem.H. 40 BM15
St. Agnes Clo. E9 142 DW67
Gore Rd.
St. Agnes Pl. SE11 161 DP79
St. Agnes Well EC1 142 DR70
Old St.
St. Aidan's Rd. SE22 182 DV86
St. Aidans Rd. W13 157 CH75
St. Aidan's Way, Grav. 191 GK90
St. Albans Ave. E6 145 EM69
St. Alban's Ave. W4 158 CR76
St. Albans Ave., Felt. 176 BX92
St. Albans Ave., Upmin. 129 FS60
St. Albans Ave., Wey. 194 BN104
St. Albans Clo. NW11 120 DA60
St. Albans Clo., Grav. 191 GK90
St. Albans Cres. N22 99 DN53
St. Alban's Cres., Wdf.Grn. 102 EG52
St. Albans Gdns., Grav. 191 GK90
St. Alban's Gdns., Tedd. 177 CG92
St. Albans Gro. W8 160 DB76
St. Alban's Gro., Cars. 200 DE101
St. Albans Hill, Hem.H. 40 BL23
St. Albans La. NW11 120 DA60
West Heath Dr.
St. Albans La., Abb.L. 59 BT26
St. Alban's Pl. N1 141 DP67
St. Albans Rd. NW5 120 DG62
St. Albans Rd. NW10 138 CS67
St. Albans Rd., Barn. 79 CW35
St. Albans Rd., Dart. 188 FM87
St. Albans Rd., Epp. 70 EX29
St. Albans Rd., Hem.H. 40 BK22
St. Albans Rd., Ilf. 125 ET60
St. Alban's Rd., Kings.T. 178 CL93
St. Albans Rd. (Dancers Hill), Pot.B. 79 CV35
St. Albans Rd. (South Mimms), Pot.B. 62 CS30
St. Albans Rd., Rad. 62 CN28
St. Albans Rd., Reig. 250 DA133
St. Albans Rd., St.Alb. 43 CF17
St. Albans Rd. (London Colney), St.Alb. 62 CN28
St. Alban's Rd., Sutt. 217 CZ105
St. Albans Rd., Wat. 75 BV40
St. Alban's Rd., Wdf.Grn. 102 EG52
St. Albans Rd. E., Hat. 45 CV17
St. Albans Rd. W., Hat. 44 CQ18
St. Albans Rd. W. (Roe Grn.), Hat. 45 CT17
St. Albans St. SW1 277 M1
St. Alban's St., Wind. 151 AR81
St. Albans Ter. W6 159 CY79
Margravine Rd.
St. Albans Twr. E4 101 DZ51
St. Alfege Pas. SE10 163 EC79
St. Alfege Rd. SE7 164 EK79
St. Alphage Gdns. EC2 275 J7
St. Alphage Highwalk EC2 142 DR71
London Wall
St. Alphage Wk., Edg. 96 CQ54
St. Alphege Rd. N9 100 DW45
St. Alphonsus Rd. SW4 161 DK84
St. Amunds Clo. SE6 183 EA91
St. Andrew Ms., Hert. 32 DQ09
St. Andrew St.
St. Andrew St. EC4 274 E7
St. Andrew St. EC4 141 DN71
St. Andrew St., Hert. 32 DQ09
St. Andrews Ave., Horn. 127 FF64
St. Andrews Ave., Wem. 117 CG63
St. Andrews Ave., Wind. 151 AM82
St. Andrew's Clo. N12 98 DC49
Woodside Ave.
St. Andrews Clo. NW2 119 CV62
St. Andrews Clo. SE16 162 DV78
Credon Rd.
St. Andrews Clo., Epp. 53 FD24
St. Andrew's Clo., Islw. 157 CD81
St. Andrews Clo., Reig. 266 DB135
St. Marys Rd.
St. Andrews Clo., Ruis. 116 BX61
St. Andrew's Clo., Shep. 195 BR98
St. Andrews Clo., Stai. 172 AY87
St. Andrews Clo., Stan. 95 CJ54
St. Andrews Clo., Wind. 172 AU86
St. Andrews Clo., Wok. 226 AW117
St. Mary's Rd.
St. Andrew's Ct. SW18 180 DC89
Waynflete St.
St. Andrews Ct., Wat. 75 BV39
St. Andrews Cres., Wind. 151 AM82
St. Andrews Dr., Orp. 206 EV100
St. Andrews Dr., Stan. 95 CJ53
St. Andrews Gdns., Cob. 214 BW113
Brunswick Gro.
St. Andrew's Gro. N16 122 DR60
St. Andrew's Hill EC4 274 G10
St. Andrew's Hill EC4 141 DP73
St. Andrew's Ms. N16 122 DS60
Dunsmure Rd.
St. Andrews Ms. SE3 164 EG80
Mycenae Rd.
St. Andrews Pl. NW1 273 J4
St. Andrews Pl., Brwd. 109 FZ47
St. Andrews Rd. E11 124 EE58
St. Andrews Rd. E13 144 EH69
St. Andrews Rd. E17 101 DX54
St. Andrews Rd. N9 100 DW45
St. Andrews Rd. NW9 118 CR60
St. Andrews Rd. NW10 139 CV65
St. Andrews Rd. NW11 119 CZ58
St. Andrews Rd. W3 138 CS72
St. Andrews Rd. W7 157 CE75
Church Rd.
St. Andrews Rd. W14 159 CY79
St. Andrews Rd., Cars. 200 DE104
St. Andrews Rd., Couls. 235 DH116
St. Andrews Rd., Croy. 220 DQ105
Lower Coombe St.
St. Andrews Rd., Enf. 82 DR41
St. Andrew's Rd., Grav. 191 GH87
St. Andrews Rd., Hem.H. 40 BJ24
West Valley Rd.
St. Andrews Rd., Ilf. 125 EM59
St. Andrews Rd., Rom. 127 FD58
St. Andrews Rd., Sid. 186 EX90
St. Andrew's Rd., Surb. 197 CK100
St. Andrews Rd., Til. 170 GE81
St. Andrews Rd., Uxb. 134 BL67
St. Andrews Rd., Wat. 94 BX48
Bridlington Rd.
St. Andrews Sq. W11 139 CY72
St. Marks Rd.
St. Andrew's Sq., Surb. 197 CK100
St. Andrews Twr., Sthl. 136 CC73
St. Andrews Wk., Cob. 229 BV115
St. Andrews Way E3 143 EB70
St. Andrews Way, Oxt. 255 EM130
St. Andrews Way, Slou. 131 AK73
St. Anna Rd., Barn. 79 CX43
Sampson Ave.
St. Annes Ave., Stai. 174 BK87
St. Anne's Clo. N6 120 DG62
Highgate W. Hill
St. Annes Clo. (Cheshunt), Wal.Cr. 66 DU28
St. Anne's Clo., Wat. 94 BW49
St. Anne's Ct. W1 273 M9
St. Anne's Dr., Red. 250 DG133
St. Annes Gdns. NW10 138 CM69
St. Anne's Ho. N16 122 DS60
St. Anne's Mt., Red. 250 DG133
St. Annes Pk., Brox. 49 EA20
Friarscroft
St. Annes Pas. E14 143 DZ72
Newell St.
St. Annes Ri., Red. 250 DG133
St. Annes Rd. E11 123 ED61
St. Annes Rd., Cher. 193 BE100
St. Annes Rd., St.Alb. 61 CK27

St. Anne's Rd., Uxb. 114 BJ55
St. Anne's Rd., Wem. 117 CK64
St. Anne's Row E14 143 DZ72
St. Anne's St. E14 143 DZ72
Commercial Rd.
St. Anne's Way, Red. 250 DG133
St. Anne's Dr.
St. Ann's, Bark. 145 EQ67
St. Anns Clo., Cher. 193 BF100
St. Ann's Cres. SW18 180 DB86
St. Ann's Gdns. NW5 140 DG65
Queens Cres.
St. Ann's Hill SW18 180 DB85
St. Anns Hill Rd., Cher. 193 BC100
St. Ann's La. SW1 277 N6
St. Ann's Pk. Rd. SW18 180 DC86
St. Ann's Pas. SW13 158 CS83
Cross St.
St. Anns Rd. N9 100 DT47
St. Ann's Rd. N15 121 DP57
St. Ann's Rd. SW13 159 CT82
St. Anns Rd. W11 139 CX73
St. Ann's Rd., Bark. 145 EQ67
Axe St.
St. Anns Rd., Cher. 193 BF100
St. Ann's Rd., Har. 117 CE58
St. Ann's St. SW1 277 N6
St. Ann's St. SW1 161 DK76
St. Ann's Ter. NW8 140 DD68
St. Anns Vill. W11 139 CX74
St. Anns Way, S.Croy. 219 DP107
St. Anselm's Pl. W1 273 H9
St. Anselms Rd., Hayes 155 BT75
St. Anthonys Ave., Hem.H. 41 BP22
St. Anthonys Ave., Wdf.Grn. 102 EJ51
St. Anthonys Clo. E1 142 DU74
Thomas More St.
St. Anthonys Clo. SW17 180 DE89
College Gdns.
St. Anthony's Way, Felt. 155 BT84
St. Antony's Rd. E7 144 EH66
St. Arvans Clo., Croy. 202 DS104
St. Asaph Rd. SE4 163 DX83
St. Aubyn's Ave. SW19 179 CZ92
St. Aubyns Ave., Houns. 176 CA85
St. Aubyns Clo., Orp. 205 ET104
St. Aubyns Gdns., Orp. 205 ET103
St. Aubyn's Rd. SE19 182 DT93
St. Audrey Ave., Bexh. 166 FA82
St. Audreys Clo., Hat. 45 CV21
St. Audreys Grn., Welw.G.C. 29 CZ10
St. Augustine Rd., Grays 171 GH77
St. Augustine's Ave. W5 138 CL68
St. Augustines Ave., Brom. 204 EL99
St. Augustine's Ave., S.Croy. 220 DQ107
St. Augustines Ave., Wem. 118 CL62
St. Augustines Clo., Brox. 49 DZ20
St. Augustines Dr., Brox. 49 DZ19
St. Augustine's Path N5 121 DP64
St. Augustine's Rd. NW1 141 DK66
St. Augustine's Rd., Belv. 166 EZ77
St. Austell Clo., Edg. 96 CM54
St. Austell Rd. SE13 163 EC82
St. Awdry's Rd., Bark. 145 ER66
St. Awdry's Wk., Bark. 145 EQ66
Station Par.
St. Barnabas Clo., Beck. 203 EC96
St. Barnabas Ct., Har. 94 CC53
St. Barnabas Rd. E17 123 EA58
St. Barnabas Rd., Mitch. 180 DG94
St. Barnabas Rd., Sutt. 218 DD106
St. Barnabas Rd., Wdf.Grn. 102 EH53
St. Barnabas St. SW1 276 G10
St. Barnabas St. SW1 160 DG78
St. Barnabas Ter. E9 123 DX64
St. Barnabas Vill. SW8 161 DL81
St. Bartholomews Clo. SE26 182 DV91
St. Bartholomews Ct., Guil. 259 AZ136
Warren Rd.
St. Bartholomew's Rd. E6 145 EM68
St. Bejamins Dr., Orp. 224 EW109
St. Benedict's Ave., Grav. 191 GL89
St. Benedict's Clo. SW17 180 DG92
Church La.
St. Benet's Clo. SW17 180 DE89
College Gdns.
St. Benet's Gro., Cars. 200 DC101
St. Benet's Pl. EC3 275 L10
St. Bernards, Croy. 202 DS104
St. Bernard's Clo. SE27 182 DR91
St. Gothard Rd.
St. Bernard's Rd. E6 144 EK67
St. Bernards Rd., St.Alb. 43 CE19
St. Bernards Rd., Slou. 152 AW76
St. Blaise Ave., Brom. 204 EH96
St. Botolph Rd., Grav. 190 GD90
St. Botolph Row EC3 275 P9
St. Botolph St. EC3 275 P8
St. Botolph St. EC3 142 DT72
St. Botolph's Ave., Sev. 256 FG124
St. Botolph's Rd., Sev. 256 FG124
St. Brelades Clo., Dor. 263 CG138
St. Brelades Pl., St.Alb. 43 CK16
Harvesters
St. Bride St. EC4 274 F8
St. Bride St. EC4 141 DP72
St. Bride's Ave. EC4 141 DP72
New Bri. St.
St. Brides Ave., Edg. 96 CM53
St. Brides Clo., Erith 166 EX75
St. Katherines Rd.
St. Bride's Pas. EC4 274 F9
St. Catherines, Wok. 226 AW119
St. Catherines Clo. SW17 180 DE89
College Gdns.
St. Catherines Cross, Red. 252 DS134
St. Catherines Dr. SE14 163 DX82
Kitto Rd.
St. Catherines Dr., Guil. 258 AV138
St. Catherines Fm. Ct., Ruis. 115 BQ58
St. Catherines Hill, Guil. 258 AW138
Portsmouth Rd.
St. Catherine's Ms. SW3 276 D8
St. Catherines Pk., Guil. 259 AZ136
Warren Rd.
St. Catherines Rd. E4 101 EA47
St. Catherines Rd., Brox. 49 EA19
St. Catherines Rd., Ruis. 115 BR57
St. Cecilia Rd., Grays 171 GH77
St. Chads Clo., Surb. 197 CJ101
St. Chad's Dr., Grav. 191 GL90
St. Chad's Gdns., Rom. 126 EY59
St. Chad's Pl. WC1 274 A2
St. Chad's Pl. WC1 141 DL69
St. Chad's Rd., Rom. 126 EY58
St. Chad's Rd., Til. 171 GG82
St. Chad's St. WC1 274 A2
St. Chad's St. WC1 141 DL69
St. Charles Ct., Wey. 212 BN106
St. Charles Pl. W10 139 CY71
Chesterton Rd.
St. Charles Pl., Wey. 212 BN106
St. Charles Rd., Brwd. 108 FV46
St. Charles Sq. W10 139 CY71
St. Christopher Rd., Uxb. 134 BK71
St. Christopher's Clo., Islw. 157 CE81
St. Christopher's Dr., Hayes 135 BV73
Coldharbour La.
St. Christophers Gdns., Th.Hth. 201 DN97
St. Christophers Ms., Wall. 219 DJ106
St. Christopher's Pl. W1 272 G8
St. Clair Clo., Oxt. 253 EC130
St. Clair Clo., Reig. 250 DC134
St. Clair Dr., Wor.Pk. 199 CV104
St. Clair Rd. E13 144 EH68
St. Claire Clo., Ilf. 103 EM54
St. Clair's Rd., Croy. 202 DT103
St. Clare St. EC3 275 P9
St. Clement Clo., Uxb. 134 BK72
St. Clements Ave., Grays 169 FU79
St. Clements Clo., Grav. 191 GF90
Coldharbour Rd.
St. Clements Ct. N7 141 DN65
Arundel Sq.
St. Clements Ct., Purf. 168 FN77
Thamley
St. Clements Heights SE26 182 DU90
St. Clement's La. WC2 274 C9
St. Clements Rd., Grays 169 FW80
St. Clements St. N1 141 DN65
St. Clements St. N7 141 DN65
St. Cloud Rd. SE27 182 DQ91
St. Columba's Clo., Grav. 191 GL90
St. Crispins Clo. NW3 120 DE63
St. Crispins Clo., Sthl. 136 BZ72
St. Crispins Way, Cher. 211 BC109
St. Cross Ct., Hodd. 49 EA19
St. Cross St. EC1 274 E6
St. Cross St. EC1 141 DN71
St. Cuthberts Clo., Egh. 172 AX93
Harvest Rd.
St. Cuthberts Gdns., Pnr. 94 BZ52
Westfield Pk.
St. Cuthberts Rd. N13 99 DN51
Fairbrook Rd.
St. Cuthberts Rd. NW2 139 CZ65
St. Cuthberts Rd., Hodd. 33 EC14
St. Cyprian's St. SW17 180 DF91
St. David Clo., Uxb. 134 BK71
St. Davids, Couls. 235 DM117
St. Davids Clo., Hem.H. 41 BR21
St. Davids Clo., Iver 133 BD67
St. David's Clo., Reig. 250 DC133
St. Davids Clo., Wem. 118 CQ62
St. David's Clo., W.Wick. 203 EB101
St. David's Ct. E17 123 EC55
St. David's Cres., Grav. 191 GK91
St. David's Dr., Brox. 49 DZ19
St. Davids Dr., Edg. 96 CM53
St. Davids Pl. NW4 119 CV59
St. Davids Rd., Swan. 187 FF93
St. Denis Rd. SE27 182 DR91
St. Dionis Rd. SW6 159 CZ82
St. Donatts Rd. SE14 163 DZ81
St. Dunstan's All. EC3 279 M1
St. Dunstans Ave. W3 138 CR73
St. Dunstans Clo., Hayes 155 BT77
St. Dunstan's Ct. EC4 141 DN72
Fleet St.
St. Dunstan's Dr., Grav. 191 GL91
St. Dunstans Gdns. W3 138 CR73
St. Dunstans Ave.
St. Dunstan's Hill EC3 279 M1
St. Dunstan's Hill EC3 142 DS73
St. Dunstan's Hill, Sutt. 217 CY106
St. Dunstan's La. EC3 279 M1
St. Dunstan's La., Beck. 203 EC100
St. Dunstan's Rd. E7 144 EJ65
St. Dunstans Rd. SE25 202 DT98
St. Dunstans Rd. W6 159 CX78
St. Dunstans Rd. W7 157 CE75
St. Dunstan's Rd., Felt. 175 BT90
St. Dunstans Rd., Houns. 155 BV82
St. Dunstans Rd., Ware 34 EK07
St. Edmunds, Berk. 38 AW20
St. Edmunds Ave., Ruis. 115 BR58
St. Edmunds Clo. NW8 140 DF67
St. Edmunds Ter.
St. Edmunds Clo. SW17 180 DE89
College Gdns.
St. Edmunds Clo., Erith 166 EX75
St. Katherines Rd.
St. Edmunds Dr., Stan. 95 CG53
St. Edmund's La., Twick. 176 CB87
St. Edmunds Rd. N9 100 DU45
St. Edmunds Rd., Dart. 168 FM84
St. Edmunds Rd., Ilf. 125 EM58
St. Edmunds Ter. NW8 140 DE68
St. Edmunds Way, Harl. 36 EW11
St. Edwards Clo. NW11 120 DA58
St. Edwards Clo., Croy. 221 ED111
St. Edwards Way, Rom. 127 FD57
St. Egberts Way E4 101 EC46
St. Elmo Clo., Slou. 131 AR70
St. Elmo Cres.
St. Elmo Cres., Slou. 131 AR70
St. Elmo Rd. W12 139 CT74
St. Elmos Rd. SE16 163 DX75
St. Erkenwald Ms., Bark. 145 ER67
St. Erkenwald Rd.
St. Erkenwald Rd., Bark. 145 ER67
St. Ermin's Hill SW1 277 M6
St. Ervans Rd. W10 139 CZ71
St. Ethelreda's Dr., Hat. 45 CW18
St. Fabian Twr. E4 101 DZ51
St. Faiths Clo., Enf. 82 DQ39
St. Faith's Rd. SE21 181 DP88
St. Fidelis Rd., Erith 167 FD77
St. Fillans Rd. SE6 183 EC88
St. Francis Ave., Grav. 191 GL91
St. Francis Clo., Orp. 205 ES100
St. Francis Clo., Pot.B. 64 DC33
St. Francis Clo., Wat. 93 BV46
St. Francis Rd. SE22 162 DS84
St. Francis Rd., Erith 167 FD77
West St.
St. Francis Rd., Uxb. 113 BF58
St. Francis Twr. E4 101 DZ51
St. Francis Way, Grays 171 GJ77
St. Gabriel's Clo. E11 124 EH60
St. Gabriels Rd. NW2 119 CX64
St. George St. W1 273 J10
St. George St. W1 141 DH73
St. Georges Ave. E7 144 EH66
St. Georges Ave. N7 121 DK63
St. Georges Ave. NW9 118 CQ56
St. George's Ave. W5 157 CK75
St. Georges Ave., Grays 170 GC77
St. Georges Ave., Horn. 128 FM59
St. Georges Ave., Sthl. 136 BZ73
St. George's Ave., Wey. 213 BP107
St. Georges Circ. SE1 278 F6
St. Georges Circ. SE1 161 DP76
St. Georges Clo. NW11 119 CZ58
St. George's Clo. SW8 161 DJ81
Patmore Est.
St. Georges Clo., Horl. 269 DH148
St. Georges Clo., Wem. 117 CG62
St. George's Clo., Wey. 213 BQ106
St. Georges Clo., Wind. 151 AL81
St. Georges Ct. E6 145 EM70
St. Georges Ct. EC4 274 F8
St. Georges Ct. SW7 160 DC76
Gloucester Rd.
St. Georges Cres., Grav. 191 GK91
St. George's Cres., Slou. 131 AK73
St. George's Dr. SW1 277 J9
St. George's Dr. SW1 161 DH77
St. George's Dr., Uxb. 114 BM62
St. Georges Dr., Wat. 94 BY48
St. George's Est., Amer. 72 AU39
St. Georges Flds. W2 272 C9
St. Georges Flds. W2 140 DE72
St. Georges Gdns., Epsom 217 CT114
Lynwood Rd.
St. George's Gdns., Surb. 198 CP103
Hamilton Ave.
St. Georges Gro. SW17 180 DD90
St. Georges Gro. Est. SW17 180 DD90
St. Georges Ind. Est. N17 99 DP52
St. Georges La. EC3 275 L10
St. George's Lo., Wey. 213 BR106
St. Georges Ms. NW1 140 DF66
Regents Pk. Rd.
St. Georges Pl., Twick. 177 CG88
Church St.
St. Georges Rd. E7 144 EH65
St. Georges Rd. E10 123 EC62
St. Georges Rd. N9 100 DU48
St. Georges Rd. N13 99 DM48
St. Georges Rd. NW11 119 CZ58
St. Georges Rd. SE1 278 E6
St. Georges Rd. SE1 161 DN76
St. George's Rd. SW19 179 CZ94
St. Georges Rd. W4 158 CR75
St. Georges Rd. W7 137 CF74
St. Georges Rd., Add. 212 BJ105
St. George's Rd., Beck. 203 EB95
St. Georges Rd., Brom. 205 EM96
St. Georges Rd., Dag. 126 EY64
St. Georges Rd., Enf. 82 DT38
St. George's Rd., Felt. 176 BX91
St. Georges Rd., Hem.H. 40 BJ24
St. Georges Rd., Ilf. 125 EM59
St. George's Rd., Kings.T. 178 CN94
St. George's Rd., Mitch. 201 DH97
St. Georges Rd., Orp. 205 ER100
St. Georges Rd., Red. 267 DK142
St. Georges Rd., Rich. 158 CM83
St. George's Rd., Sev. 257 FH122
St. George's Rd., Sid. 186 EX93
St. Georges Rd., Swan. 207 FF98
St. Georges Rd., Twick. 177 CH85
St. Georges Rd., Wall. 219 DH106
St. Georges Rd., Wat. 75 BV38
St. George's Rd., Wey. 213 BR107
St. Georges Rd. W., Brom. 204 EL95
St. Georges Sq. E7 144 EH66
St. Georges Sq. E14 143 DY73
St. Georges Sq. SE8 163 DZ77
St. George's Sq. SW1 161 DK78
St. George's Sq., N.Mal. 198 CS97
High St.
St. George's Sq. Ms. SW1 161 DK78
St. Georges Ter. NW1 140 DF66
Regents Pk. Rd.
St. Georges Wk., Croy. 202 DQ104
St. Georges Way SE15 162 DS79
St. Gerards Clo. SW4 181 DJ85
St. German's Pl. SE3 164 EG81
St. Germans Rd. SE23 183 DY88
St. Giles Ave., Dag. 147 FB66
St. Giles Ave., Pot.B. 63 CV32
St. Giles Ave., Uxb. 115 BQ63
St. Giles Clo., Dag. 147 FB66
St. Giles Ave.
St. Giles Clo., Orp. 223 ER106
St. Giles High St. WC2 273 N8
St. Giles High St. WC2 141 DK72
St. Giles Pas. WC2 273 N9
St. Giles Rd. SE5 162 DS80
St. Gilles Ho. E2 143 DX68
Mace St.
St. Gothard Rd. SE27 182 DR91
St. Gregory Clo., Ruis. 116 BW63
St. Gregorys Cres., Grav. 191 GL89
St. Helena Rd. SE16 163 DX77
St. Helena St. WC1 274 D3
St. Helens Clo., Uxb. 134 BK71
St. Helens Ct., Epp. 70 EU30
Hemnall St.
St. Helens Ct., Rain. 147 FG70
St. Helens Cres. SW16 201 DM95
St. Helens Rd.
St. Helens Gdns. W10 139 CX71
St. Helens Pl. EC3 275 M8
St. Helens Rd. SW16 201 DM95
St. Helen's Rd. W13 137 CH74
Dane Rd.
St. Helens Rd., Erith 166 EX75
St. Helens Rd., Ilf. 125 EM58
St. Helier Ave., Mord. 200 DC101
St. Heliers Ave., Houns. 176 CA85
St. Heliers Rd. E10 123 EC58
St. Heliers Rd., St.Alb. 43 CH15
St. Hildas Ave., Ashf. 174 BL92
St. Hildas Clo. NW6 139 CX67
St. Hildas Clo. SW17 180 DE89
St. Hildas Clo., Horl. 269 DH148
St. Hilda's Rd. SW13 159 CV79
St. Hilda's Way, Grav. 191 GK91
St. Huberts Clo., Ger.Cr. 112 AY61
St. Huberts La., Ger.Cr. 113 AZ61
St. Hughe's Clo. SW17 180 DE89
College Gdns.
St. Hughs Rd. SE20 202 DV95
Ridsdale Rd.
St. Ives Clo., Rom. 106 FM52
Barnsley Rd.
St. Ivians Dr., Rom. 127 FG55
St. James Ave. E2 142 DW68
St. James Ave. N20 98 DE48
St. James Ave. W13 137 CG74
St. James Ave., Epsom 217 CT111
St. James Ave., Sutt. 218 DA106
St. James Clo. N20 98 DE48
St. James Clo. SE18 165 EQ78
Congleton Gro.
St. James Clo., Barn. 80 DD42
Park Rd.
St. James Clo., Epsom 216 CS114
Heathcote Rd.
St. James Clo., N.Mal. 199 CT99
St. James Clo., Ruis. 116 BW61
St. James Clo., Wok. 226 AU118
St. James Gdns. W11 139 CY74
St. James Gdns., Wem. 137 CK66
St. James Gate NW1 141 DK66
St. Paul's Cres.
St. James Gro. SW11 160 DF82
Reform St.
St. James La., Green. 189 FS88
St. James Ms. E14 163 EC76
St. James Ms., Wey. 213 BP105
St. James Pl., Dart. 188 FK86
Spital St.
St. James Pl., Slou. 130 AJ72
Greenfern Ave.
St. James Rd. E15 124 EF64
St. James Rd. N9 100 DV47
Queens Rd.
St. James Rd., Cars. 200 DE104
St. James Rd., Kings.T. 197 CK96
St. James Rd., Mitch. 180 DG94
St. James Rd., Pur. 219 DP113
St. James Rd., Sev. 257 FH122
St. James Rd., Surb. 197 CK100
St. James Rd., Sutt. 218 DA106
St. James Rd. (Cheshunt), Wal.Cr. 66 DQ28
St. James Rd., Wat. 75 BV43
St. James St. W6 159 CW78
St. James Wk. EC1 274 F4
St. James Wk. EC1 141 DP70
St. James Wk. SE15 162 DT80
Commercial Way
St. James Wk., Iver 153 BE75
St. James Way, Sid. 186 EY92
St. James's SE14 163 DY81
St. James's Ave., Beck. 203 DY97
St. James's Ave., Grav. 191 GG87
St. James's Ave., Hmptn. 176 CC92
St. James's Clo. SW17 180 DF89
St. James's Dr.
St. James's Cotts., Rich. 177 CK85
Paradise Rd.
St. James's Ct. SW1 277 L6
St. James's Ct. SW1 161 DJ76
St. James's Cres. SW9 161 DN83
St. James's Dr. SW12 180 DF88
St. James's Dr. SW17 180 DF88
St. James's La. N10 121 DH56
St. James's Mkt. SW1 277 M1
St. James's Ms. E17 123 DY57
St. James's St.
St. James's Palace SW1 277 L3
St. James's Palace SW1 141 DJ74
St. James's Pk. SW1 277 M6
St. James's Pk. SW1 161 DJ75
St. James's Pk., Croy. 202 DQ101
St. James's Pas. EC3 275 N9
St. James's Pl. SW1 277 K3
St. James's Pl. SW1 141 DJ74
St. James's Rd. SE1 162 DU78
St. James's Rd. SE16 162 DU76
St. James's Rd., Brwd. 108 FW48
St. James's Rd., Croy. 201 DP101
St. James's Rd., Grav. 191 GG86
St. James's Rd., Hmptn. 176 CB92
St. James's Row EC1 274 F4
St. James's Sq. SW1 277 L2
St. James's Sq. SW1 141 DK74
St. James's St. E17 123 DY57
St. James's St. SW1 277 K2
St. James's St. SW1 141 DJ74
St. James's St., Grav. 191 GG86
St. James's Ter. NW8 140 DF68
Prince Albert Rd.
St. James's Ter. Ms. NW8 140 DF67
St. Jeromes Gro., Hayes 135 BQ72
St. Joans Rd. N9 100 DT46
St. John Fisher Rd., Erith 166 EX76
St. John St. EC1 274 F2
St. John St. EC1 141 DN68
St. Johns, Dor. 263 CH140
St. John's, Red. 266 DE136
Church Rd.
St. Johns Ave. N11 98 DF50
St. John's Ave. NW10 139 CT67
St. John's Ave. SW15 179 CX85
St. Johns Ave., Brwd. 108 FX49
St. Johns Ave., Epsom 217 CT112
St. John's Ave., Harl. 36 EW11
St. Johns Ave., Lthd. 231 CH121
St. John's Ch. Rd. E9 122 DW64
St. John's Ch. Rd., Dor. 262 BZ139
Coast Hill
St. Johns Clo. N14 81 DJ44
Chase Rd.
St. John's Clo. SW6 160 DA80
Dawes Rd.
St. John's Clo., Guil. 258 AU135
St. John's Rd.
St. Johns Clo., Lthd. 231 CJ120
St. John's Clo., Pot.B. 64 DC33
St. Johns Clo., Rain. 147 FG66
St. John's Clo., Uxb. 134 BH67
St. John's Clo., Wem. 118 CL64
St. John's Cotts. SE20 182 DW94
Maple Rd.
St. Johns Cotts., Rich. 158 CL84
Kew Foot Rd.
St. Johns Ct., Buck.H. 102 EH46
St. Johns Ct., Egh. 173 BA92
St. John's Ct., Islw. 157 CF82
St. Johns Ct., Nthwd. 93 BS53
Murray Rd.
St. Johns Ct., St.Alb. 43 CH19
St. John's Cres. SW9 161 DN83
St. Johns Dr. SW18 180 DB88
St. Johns Dr., Walt. 196 BW102
St. Johns Dr., Wind. 151 AN82
St. John's Est. N1 275 L1
St. John's Est. N1 142 DR68
St. John's Est. SE1 279 P5
St. John's Gdns. W11 139 CY73
St. Johns Gro. N19 121 DJ61
St. Johns Gro. SW13 159 CT82
Terrace Gdns.
St. Johns Gro., Rich. 158 CL84
Kew Foot Rd.
St. John's Hill SW11 160 DD84
St. Johns Hill, Couls. 235 DN117
Canon's Hill
St. Johns Hill, Pur. 235 DN116
St. John's Hill, Sev. 257 FJ123
St. John's Hill Gro. SW11 160 DD84
St. Johns Hill Rd., Wok. 226 AU119
St. John's La. EC1 274 F5
St. John's La. EC1 141 DP70
St. John's La., Ware 33 EA09
St. John's Lye, Wok. 226 AT119
St. John's Ms. W11 140 DA72
Ledbury Rd.
St. Johns Ms., Wok. 226 AU119
St. John's Rd.
St. Johns Par., Sid. 186 EU91
Church Rd.
St. John's Pk. SE3 164 EF80
St. Johns Pas. SE23 182 DW88
Davids Rd.
St. John's Pas. SW19 179 CY93
Ridgway Pl.
St. John's Path EC1 274 F5
St. Johns Pathway SE23 182 DW88
Devonshire Rd.
St. John's Pl. EC1 274 F5
St. Johns Ri., Wok. 226 AV119
St. John's Rd. E4 101 EB48
St. Johns Rd. E6 144 EL67
St. Johns Rd. E16 144 EG72
St. John's Rd. E17 101 EB54
St. John's Rd. N15 122 DS58
St. Johns Rd. NW11 119 CZ58
St. John's Rd. SE20 182 DW94
St. Johns Rd. SW11 160 DE84
St. John's Rd. SW19 179 CY93
St. John's Rd., Bark. 145 ES67
St. John's Rd., Cars. 200 DE104
St. John's Rd., Croy. 201 DP104
Sylverdale Rd.
St. John's Rd., Dart. 188 FQ87
St. John's Rd., Dor. 262 CC137
St. Johns Rd., E.Mol. 197 CD98
St. Johns Rd., Epp. 69 ET30
St. Johns Rd., Erith 167 FD78
St. John's Rd., Felt. 176 BY91
St. Johns Rd., Grav. 191 GK87
St. Johns Rd., Grays 171 GH78
St. John's Rd., Guil. 258 AT135
St. Johns Rd., Har. 117 CF58
St. Johns Rd., Hem.H. 40 BG22
St. Johns Rd., Ilf. 125 ER59
St. John's Rd., Islw. 157 CE82
St. Johns Rd., Kings.T. 197 CJ96
St. Johns Rd., Lthd. 231 CJ121
St. Johns Rd., Loug. 85 EM40
St. John's Rd., N.Mal. 198 CQ97
St. Johns Rd., Orp. 205 ER100
St. John's Rd., Red. 266 DF136
St. Johns Rd., Rich. 158 CL84
St. Johns Rd., Rom. 105 FC50
St. Johns Rd., Sev. 257 FH121
St. John's Rd., Sid. 186 EV91
St. Johns Rd., Slou. 132 AU73
St. Johns Rd., Sthl. 156 BY76
St. Johns Rd., Sutt. 200 DA103
St. Johns Rd., Uxb. 134 BH67
St. Johns Rd., Wat. 75 BV40
St. Johns Rd., Well. 166 EV83
St. John's Rd., Wem. 118 CL64
St. Johns Rd., Wind. 151 AN82
St. John's Rd., Wok. 226 AU119
St. John's Sq. EC1 274 F5
St. John's St., Hert. 32 DR09
St. Johns Ter. E7 144 EH65
St. Johns Ter. SE18 165 EQ79
St. Johns Ter. SW15 178 CR91
Kingston Vale
St. Johns Ter. W10 139 CX70
Harrow Rd.
St. Johns Ter., Enf. 82 DR37
St. John's Ter., Red. 266 DF136
St. John's Ter. Rd.
St. John's Ter. Rd., Red. 266 DF136
St. Johns Vale SE8 163 EA82
St. Johns Vill. N19 121 DK61
St. John's Vill. W8 160 DB76
St. Mary's Pl.
St. Johns Way N19 121 DJ61
St. Johns Well Ct., Berk. 38 AV18
St. Johns Well La., Berk. 38 AV18
St. John's Wd. Ct. NW8 272 A3
St. John's Wd. High St. NW8 272 A1
St. John's Wd. High St. NW8 140 DD68
St. John's Wd. Pk. NW8 140 DD67
St. John's Wd. Rd. NW8 140 DD70
St. John's Wd. Ter. NW8 140 DD68
St. Josephs Clo. W10 139 CY71
Bevington Rd.
St. Joseph's Clo., Orp. 223 ET105
St. Joseph's Ct. SE7 164 EH79
St. Josephs Dr., Sthl. 136 BY74
St. Joseph's Gro. NW4 119 CV56
St. Josephs Rd. N9 100 DV45
St. Joseph's Rd., Wal.Cr. 67 DY33

St. Thomas Clo., Wok. 226 AW117
St. Mary's Rd.
St. Thomas Ct., Bex. 186 FA87
St. Thomas Dr., Guil. 244 BL131
The St.
St. Thomas Dr., Orp. 205 EQ102
St. Thomas' Dr., Pnr. 94 BY53
St. Thomas Gdns., Ilf. 145 EQ65
St. Thomas Pl. NW1 141 DK66
Maiden La.
St. Thomas Rd. E16 144 EG72
St. Thomas Rd. N14 99 DK45
St. Thomas Rd., Belv. 167 FC75
St. Thomas Rd., Brwd. 108 FX47
St. Thomas Rd., Grav. 191 GF89
St. Thomas St. SE1 279 L3
St. Thomas St. SE1 142 DR74
St. Thomas Wk., Slou. 153 BD80
St. Thomas's Ave., Grav. 191 GH88
St. Thomas's Clo., Wal.Abb. 68 EH33
St. Thomas's Gdns. NW5 140 DG65
Queens Cres.
St. Thomas's Ms., Guil. 259 AZ136
Warren Rd.
St. Thomas's Pl. E9 142 DW66
St. Thomas's Rd. N4 121 DN61
St. Thomas's Rd. NW10 138 CS67
St. Thomas's Rd. W4 158 CQ79
St. Thomas's Sq. E9 142 DW66
St. Thomas's Way SW6 159 CZ80
St. Timothy's Ms., Brom. 204 EH95
Wharton Rd.
St. Ursula Gro., Pnr. 116 BX57
St. Ursula Rd., Sthl. 136 CA72
St. Vincent Clo. SE27 181 DP92
St. Vincent Dr., St.Alb. 43 CG23
St. Vincent Rd., Twick. 176 CC86
St. Vincent Rd., Walt. 195 BV104
St. Vincent St. W1 272 G7
St. Vincents Ave., Dart. 188 FM85
St. Vincents Rd., Dart. 188 FN86
St. Vincents Way, Pot.B. 64 DC33
St. Wilfrids Clo., Barn. 80 DD43
East Barnet Rd.
St. Wilfrids Rd., Barn. 80 DD43
East Barnet Rd.
St. Winefride's Ave. E12 125 EM64
St. Winifreds, Ken. 236 DQ115
St. Winifreds Clo., Chig. 103 EQ50
St. Winifreds Rd., Tedd. 177 CH93
St. Winifred's Rd., West. 239 EM118
St. Yon Ct., St.Alb. 44 CL20
Saints Clo. SE27 181 DP91
Wolfington Rd.
Saints Dr. E7 124 EK64
Saints La., Rick. 92 BN45
Saints Wk., Grays 171 GJ77
Sakins Cft., Harl. 51 ET18
Saladin Dr., Purf. 168 FN77
Salamanca Pl. SE1 278 B9
Salamanca St. SE1 278 B9
Salamanca St. SE1 161 DM77
Salamander Clo., Kings.T. 177 CK92
Dukes Ave.
Salamander Quay, Uxb. 92 BG52
Coppermill La.
Salamons Way, Rain. 147 FE72
Salbrook Rd., Red. 266 DG142
Salcombe Dr., Mord. 199 CX102
Salcombe Dr., Rom. 126 EZ58
Salcombe Gdns. NW7 97 CW51
Salcombe Pk., Loug. 84 EK43
High Rd.
Salcombe Rd. E17 123 DZ59
Salcombe Rd. N16 122 DS64
Salcombe Rd., Ashf. 174 BL91
Salcombe Way, Hayes 135 BS69
Portland Rd.
Salcombe Way, Ruis. 115 BU61
Salcot Cres., Croy. 221 EC110
Salcote Rd., Grav. 191 GL92
Salcott Rd. SW11 180 DE85
Salcott Rd., Croy. 201 DL104
Sale Pl. W2 272 B7
Sale Pl. W2 140 DE72
Sale St. E2 142 DU70
Salehurst Clo., Har. 118 CL57
Salehurst Rd. SE4 183 DZ86
Salem Pl., Croy. 202 DQ104
Salem Pl., Grav. 190 GD87
Shepherd St.
Salem Rd. W2 140 DB73
Salford Rd. SW2 181 DK88
Salfords Ind. Est., Red. 267 DH143
Salfords Way, Red. 266 DG142
Salhouse Clo. SE28 146 EW72
Rollesby Way
Salisbury Ave. N3 119 CZ55
Salisbury Ave., Bark. 145 ER66
Salisbury Ave., St.Alb. 43 CH19
Salisbury Ave., Slou. 131 AQ70
Salisbury Ave., Sutt. 217 CZ107
Salisbury Ave., Swan. 207 FG98
Salisbury Clo. SE17 279 K8
Salisbury Clo., Amer. 55 AS39
Salisbury Clo., Pot.B. 64 DC32
Salisbury Clo., Upmin. 129 FT61
Canterbury Ave.
Salisbury Clo., Wor.Pk. 199 CT104
Salisbury Ct. EC4 274 E9
Salisbury Ct. EC4 141 DP72
Salisbury Cres. (Cheshunt), Wal.Cr. 67 DX32
Salisbury Gdns. SW19 179 CY94
Salisbury Gdns., Buck.H. 102 EK47
Salisbury Gdns., Welw.G.C. 29 CZ10
Salisbury Hall Gdns. E4 101 EA51
Salisbury Ho. E14 143 EB72
Hobday St.
Salisbury Ms. SW6 159 CZ80
Dawes Rd.
Salisbury Pl. SW9 161 DP80
Salisbury Pl. W1 272 D6
Salisbury Pl. W1 140 DF71
Salisbury Pl., W.Byf. 212 BJ111
Dartnell Pk. Rd.
Salisbury Plaza, Hat. 45 CT16
Lemsford Rd.
Salisbury Rd. E4 101 EA48
Salisbury Rd. E7 144 EG65
Salisbury Rd. E10 123 EC61
Salisbury Rd. E12 124 EK64
Salisbury Rd. E17 123 EC57
Salisbury Rd. N4 121 DP57
Salisbury Rd. N9 100 DU48
Salisbury Rd. N22 99 DP53
Salisbury Rd. SE25 202 DU100
Salisbury Rd. SW19 179 CY94
Salisbury Rd. W13 157 CG75
Salisbury Rd., Bans. 218 DB114
Salisbury Rd., Barn. 79 CY41
Salisbury Rd., Bex. 186 FA88
Salisbury Rd., Brom. 204 EL99
Salisbury Rd., Cars. 218 DF107
Salisbury Rd., Dag. 147 FB65
Salisbury Rd., Dart. 188 FQ88
Salisbury Rd., Enf. 83 DZ37
Salisbury Rd., Felt. 176 BW88
Salisbury Rd., Gdse. 252 DW131
Salisbury Rd., Grav. 191 GF88
Salisbury Rd., Grays 170 GC79
Salisbury Rd., Har. 117 CD57
Salisbury Rd., Hodd. 49 EC15
Salisbury Rd., Houns. 156 BW83
Salisbury Rd. (Heathrow), Houns. 175 BQ85
Salisbury Rd., Ilf. 125 ES61
Salisbury Rd., N.Mal. 198 CR97
Salisbury Rd., Pnr. 115 BU56
Salisbury Rd., Rich. 158 CL84
Salisbury Rd., Rom. 127 FH57
Salisbury Rd., Sthl. 156 BY77
Salisbury Rd., Uxb. 134 BH68
Salisbury Rd., Wat. 75 BV38
Salisbury Rd., Welw.G.C. 29 CZ10
Salisbury Rd., Wok. 226 AY119
Salisbury Rd., Wor.Pk. 216 CR105
Salisbury Sq. EC4 274 E9
Salisbury Sq., Hat. 45 CW17
Park St.
Salisbury St. NW8 272 B5
Salisbury St. NW8 140 DE70
Salisbury St. W3 158 CQ75
Salisbury Ter. SE15 162 DW83
Salisbury Wk. N19 121 DJ61
Salix Clo., Sun. 175 BV94
Oak Gro.
Salix Rd., Grays 170 GD79
Salliesfield, Twick. 177 CD86
Salmen Rd. E13 144 EF68
Salmon Clo., Welw.G.C. 30 DA06
Rowans
Salmon La. E14 143 DY72
Salmon Meadow Footpath, Hem.H. 40 BK24
London Rd.
Salmon Rd., Belv. 166 FA78
Salmon St. E14 143 DZ72
Salmon La.
Salmon St. NW9 118 CP60
Salmond Clo., Stan. 95 CG51
Robb Rd.
Salmons La., Cat. 236 DS120
Salmons La., Whyt. 236 DS120
Salmons La. W., Cat. 236 DS120
Salmons Rd. N9 100 DU46
Salmons Rd., Chess. 215 CK107
Salmons Rd., Lthd. 245 BV129
Salomons Rd. E13 144 EJ71
Chalk Rd.
Salop Rd. E17 123 DX58
Salt Box Hill, West. 222 EH113
Salt Box Rd., Guil. 242 AT129
Salt Hill Ave., Slou. 131 AQ74
Salt Hill Dr., Slou. 131 AQ74
Salt Hill Way, Slou. 131 AQ74
Saltash Clo., Sutt. 217 CZ105
Saltash Rd., Ilf. 103 ER52
Saltash Rd., Well. 166 EW81
Saltcoats Rd. W4 158 CS75
Saltcroft Clo., Wem. 118 CP60
Salter Rd. SE16 143 DX74
Salter St. E14 143 EA73
Salter St. NW10 139 CU69
Salterford Rd. SW17 180 DG93
Salters Clo., Berk. 38 AT17
Salters Gdns., Wat. 75 BU39
Salters Hall Ct. EC4 275 K10
Salters Hill SE19 182 DR92
Salters Rd. E17 123 ED56
Salters Rd. W10 139 CX70
Salterton Rd. N7 121 DL62
Saltford Clo., Erith 167 FE78
Salthill Clo., Uxb. 114 BL64
Saltley Clo. E6 144 EL72
Dunnock Rd.
Saltoun Rd. SW2 161 DN84
Saltram Clo. N15 122 DT56
Saltram Cres. W9 139 CZ69
Saltwell St. E14 143 EA73
Saltwood Clo., Orp. 224 EW105
Saltwood Gro. SE17 162 DR78
Merrow St.
Salusbury Rd. NW6 139 CY67
Salvia Gdns., Grnf. 137 CG68
Selborne Gdns.
Salvin Rd. SW15 159 CX83
Salway Clo., Wdf.Grn. 102 EF52
Salway Pl. E15 144 EE65
Broadway
Salway Rd. E15 143 ED65
Salwey Cres., Brox. 49 DZ20
Sam Bartram Clo. SE7 164 EJ78
Samantha Clo. E17 123 DZ59
Samantha Ms. (Havering-atte-Bower), Rom. 105 FE48
Sambruck Ms. SE6 183 EB89
Inchmery Rd.
Samels Ct. W6 159 CU78
South Black Lion La.
Samford St. NW8 272 B5
Samford St. NW8 140 DE70
Samian Gate, St.Alb. 42 BZ22
Mayne Ave.
Samos Rd. SE20 202 DV96
Samphire Ct., Grays 170 GE80
Salix Rd.
Sampleoak La., Guil. 259 BE140
Sampson Ave., Barn. 79 CX43
Sampson Clo., Belv. 166 EX76
Carrill Way
Sampson St. E1 142 DU74
Sampsons Ct., Shep. 195 BQ99
Linden Way
Samson St. E13 144 EJ68
Samuel Clo. E8 142 DT67
Pownall Rd.
Samuel Clo. SE14 163 DX79
Samuel Clo. SE18 164 EL77
Samuel Johnson Clo. SW16 181 DN91
Curtis Fld. Rd.
Samuel Lewis Trust Dws. E8 122 DU63
Amhurst Rd.
Samuel Lewis Trust Dws. N1 141 DN66
Liverpool Rd.
Samuel Lewis Trust Dws. SW3 276 B9
Samuel Lewis Trust Dws. SW6 160 DA80
Samuel St. SE18 165 EM77
Sancroft Clo. NW2 119 CV62
Sancroft Rd., Har. 95 CF54
Sancroft St. SE11 278 C10
Sancroft St. SE11 161 DM78
Sanctuary, The SW1 277 N6
Sanctuary, The, Bex. 186 EX86
Sanctuary, The, Mord. 200 DB100
Sanctuary Clo., Dart. 188 FJ86
Sanctuary Clo., Uxb. 92 BJ52
Sanctuary Rd., Houns. 174 BN86
Sanctuary St. SE1 279 J5
Sandal Rd. N18 100 DU50
Sandal Rd., N.Mal. 198 CR99
Sandal St. E15 144 EE67
Sandale Clo. N16 122 DR62
Stoke Newington Ch. St.
Sandall Clo. W5 138 CL70
Sandall Rd. NW5 141 DJ65
Sandall Rd. W5 138 CL70
Sandalls Spring, Hem.H. 39 BF18
Sandalwood, Guil. 258 AV135
Sandalwood Clo. E1 143 DY70
Solebay St.
Sandalwood Rd., Felt. 175 BV90
Sanday Clo., Hem.H. 41 BP22
Sandbach Pl. SE18 165 EQ78
Sandbanks, Felt. 175 BS88
Sandbanks Hill, Dart. 189 FV93
Sandbourne Ave. SW19 200 DB96
Sandbourne Rd. SE4 163 DY82
Sandbrook Clo. NW7 96 CR51
Sandbrook Rd. N16 122 DS62
Sandby Grn. SE9 164 EL83
Sandcliff Rd., Erith 167 FD77
Sandcroft Clo. N13 99 DP51
St. Pauls Ri.
Sandcross La., Reig. 265 CZ137
Sandell St. SE1 278 D4
Sandells Ave., Ashf. 175 BQ91
Sandels Way, Beac. 89 AK51
Sandelswood End, Beac. 89 AK50
Sanders Clo., Hmptn. 176 CC92
Sanders Clo., Hem.H. 40 BM24
Great Elms Rd.
Sanders Clo., St.Alb. 61 CK27
Sanders La. NW7 97 CW52
Sanders Rd., Hem.H. 40 BM23
Great Elms Rd.
Sanders Way N19 121 DK60
Sussex Way
Sandersfield Gdns., Bans. 234 DA115
Sandersfield Rd., Bans. 234 DB115
Sanderson Ave., Sev. 224 FA110
Sanderson Clo. NW5 121 DH63
Sanderson Rd., Uxb. 134 BJ65
Sanderstead Ave. NW2 119 CY62
Sanderstead Clo. SW12 181 DJ87
Atkins Rd.
Sanderstead Ct. Ave., S.Croy. 220 DU113
Sanderstead Hill, S.Croy. 220 DS111
Sanderstead Rd. E10 123 DY60
Sanderstead Rd., Orp. 206 EV100
Sanderstead Rd., S.Croy. 220 DR108
Sandes Pl., Lthd. 231 CG118
Sandfield, Hat. 45 CV21
Sandfield Gdns., Th.Hth. 201 DP97
Sandfield Ind. Est., Hmptn. 196 BZ95
Sandfield Pas., Th.Hth. 202 DQ97
Sandfield Rd., St.Alb. 43 CG20
Sandfield Rd., Th.Hth. 201 DP97
Sandfield Ter., Guil. 258 AX135
Sandfields, Wok. 227 BD124
Sandford Ave. N22 100 DQ53
Sandford Ave., Loug. 85 EP41
Sandford Clo. E6 145 EM70
Sandford Ct. N16 122 DS60
Bethune Rd.
Sandford Rd. E6 144 EL69
Sandford Rd., Bexh. 166 EY84
Sandford Rd., Brom. 204 EG97
Sandford St. SW6 160 DB80
King's Rd.
Sandgate Clo., Rom. 127 FC59
Sandgate La. SW18 180 DE88
Sandgate Rd., Well. 166 EW80
Sandgate St. SE15 162 DV79
Sandham Pt. SE18 165 EP77
Troy Ct.
Sandhills, Wall. 219 DK105
Sandhills La., Vir.W. 192 AY99
Sandhills Meadow, Shep. 195 BQ101
Sandhills Rd., Reig. 266 DA136
Sandhurst Ave., Har. 116 CB58
Sandhurst Ave., Surb. 198 CP101
Sandhurst Clo. NW9 118 CN55
Sandhurst Clo., S.Croy. 220 DS109
Sandhurst Dr., Ilf. 125 ET63
Sandhurst Rd. N9 82 DW44
Sandhurst Rd. NW9 118 CN55
Sandhurst Rd. SE6 183 ED88
Sandhurst Rd., Bex. 186 EX85
Sandhurst Rd., Orp. 206 EU104
Sandhurst Rd., Sid. 185 ET90
Sandhurst Rd., Til. 171 GJ82
Sandhurst Way, S.Croy. 220 DS108
Sandiford Rd., Sutt. 199 CZ103
Sandiland Cres., Brom. 204 EF103
Sandilands, Croy. 202 DU103
Sandilands, Sev. 256 FD122
Sandilands Rd. SW6 160 DB81
Sandison St. SE15 162 DT83
Sandland St. WC1 274 C7
Sandland St. WC1 141 DM71
Sandlands Gro., Tad. 233 CU123
Sandlands Rd., Tad. 233 CU123
Sandlers End, Slou. 131 AP70
Sandlewood Ave., Cher. 193 BE104
Sandling Ri. SE9 185 EN90
Sandlings, The N22 99 DN54
Sandmere Clo., Hem.H. 40 BN21
St. Albans Rd.
Sandmere Rd. SW4 161 DL84
Sandon Clo., Esher 197 CD101
Sandon Rd. (Cheshunt), Wal.Cr. 66 DW30
Sandow Cres., Hayes 155 BT76
Sandown Ave., Dag. 147 FC65
Sandown Ave., Esher 214 CC106
Sandown Ave., Horn. 128 FK61
Sandown Clo., Houns. 155 BU81
Sandown Dr., Cars. 218 DG109
Sandown Gate, Esher 197 CD104
Sandown Ind. Pk., Esher 196 CA103
Sandown Rd. SE25 202 DV99
Sandown Rd., Couls. 234 DG116
Sandown Rd., Esher 214 CC105
Sandown Rd., Grav. 191 GJ93
Sandown Rd., Slou. 131 AM71
Sandown Rd., Wat. 76 BW38
Sandown Way, Nthlt. 136 BY65
Sandpiper Clo. E17 101 DY52
Banbury Rd.
Sandpiper Clo. SE16 163 DZ75
Rotherhithe St.
Sandpiper Rd., S.Croy. 221 DX111
Sandpiper Way, Orp. 206 EX98
Sandpipers, The, Grav. 191 GK89
Sandpit Hall Rd., Wok. 210 AU112
Sandpit La., Brwd. 108 FT46
Sandpit La., St.Alb. 43 CE19
Sandpit Pl. SE7 164 EL78
Sandpit Rd., Brom. 184 EE92
Sandpit Rd., Dart. 168 FJ84
Sandpit Rd., Red. 266 DE135
Sandpit Rd., Welw.G.C. 29 CY11
Sandpits La., H.Wyc. 88 AC48
Sandpits Rd., Croy. 221 DX105
Sandpits Rd., Rich. 177 CK89
Sandra Clo. N22 100 DQ53
New Rd.
Sandra Clo., Houns. 176 CB85
Sandridge Clo., Har. 117 CE56
Sandridge Ct. N4 122 DQ62
Queens Dr.
Sandridge Rd., St.Alb. 43 CE18
Sandridge St. N19 121 DJ61
Sandridgebury La., St.Alb. 43 CE16
Sandringham Ave. SW20 199 CY95
Sandringham Ave., Harl. 50 EL15
Sandringham Clo. SW19 179 CX88
Sandringham Clo., Enf. 82 DS40
Sandringham Clo., Ilf. 125 EQ55
Sandringham Gdns.
Sandringham Clo., Wok. 228 BG116
Engliff La.
Sandringham Ct. W9 140 DC69
Maida Vale
Sandringham Ct., Slou. 131 AK72
Sandringham Cres., Har. 116 CA61
Sandringham Cres., St.Alb. 43 CG16
Sandringham Dr., Ashf. 174 BK91
Sandringham Dr., Well. 165 ES82
Sandringham Gdns. N8 121 DL58
Sandringham Gdns. N12 98 DC51
Sandringham Gdns., Houns. 155 BU81
Sandringham Gdns., Ilf. 125 EQ55
Sandringham Ms. W5 137 CK73
High St.
Sandringham Rd. E7 124 EJ64
Sandringham Rd. E8 122 DT64
Sandringham Rd. E10 123 ED58
Sandringham Rd. N22 122 DQ55
Sandringham Rd. NW2 139 CV65
Sandringham Rd. NW11 119 CY59
Sandringham Rd., Bark. 145 ET65
Sandringham Rd., Brwd. 108 FV43
Sandringham Rd., Brom. 184 EG92
Sandringham Rd., Houns. 174 BK85
Sandringham Rd., Nthlt. 136 CA66
Sandringham Rd., Pot.B. 64 DB30
Sandringham Rd., Th.Hth. 202 DQ99
Sandringham Rd., Wat. 76 BW37
Sandringham Rd., Wor.Pk. 199 CU104
Sandringham Way, Wal.Cr. 66 DW34
Sandrock Pl., Croy. 221 DX105
Sandrock Rd. SE13 163 EA83
Sandrock Rd., Dor. 262 CB138
Sandroyd Way, Cob. 214 CA113
Adeyfield Rd.
Sand's End La. SW6 160 DB81
Sands Fm. Dr., Slou. 130 AJ70
Sands Way, Wdf.Grn. 103 EM51
Sandstone Pl. N19 121 DH61
Dartmouth Pk. Hill
Sandstone Rd. SE12 184 EH89
Sandtoft Rd. SE7 164 EH79
Sandway Path, Orp. 206 EW98
Okemore Gdns.
Sandway Rd., Orp. 206 EW98
Sandwell Cres. NW6 140 DA65
Sandwich St. WC1 273 P3
Sandwich St. WC1 141 DL69
Sandy Bank Rd., Grav. 191 GH88
Sandy Bury, Orp. 205 ER104
Sandy Clo., Hert. 31 DP09
Sandy Clo., Wok. 227 BB117
Sandy La.
Sandy Dr., Cob. 214 CA111
Sandy Dr., Felt. 175 BS88
Sandy Hill Ave. SE18 165 EP78
Sandy Hill Rd. SE18 165 EP78
Sandy Hill Rd., Wall. 219 DJ109
Sandy La., Bet. 264 CS135
Sandy La., Cob. 214 BZ112
Sandy La., Dart. 189 FW89
Sandy La. (Chadwell St. Mary), Grays 171 GJ78
Sandy La. (West Thurrock), Grays 169 FV79
London Rd.
Sandy La., Guil. 258 AU139
Sandy La. (Albury Heath), Guil. 260 BJ141
Sandy La. (Shere), Guil. 260 BN139
Sandy La., Har. 118 CM58
Sandy La., Kings.T. 197 CH95
Sandy La., Lthd. 214 CB111
Sandy La., Mitch. 200 DG95
Sandy La., Nthwd. 93 BT47
Sandy La., Orp. 206 EU101
Sandy La. (St. Paul's Cray), Orp. 206 EW96
Sandy La., Oxt. 253 EC129
Sandy La. (Limpsfield), Oxt. 254 EH127
Sandy La. (Bletchingley), Red. 251 DP132
Sandy La. (Nutfield), Red. 267 DK135
Sandy La., Reig. 265 CW135
Sandy La., Rich. 177 CJ89
Sandy La., Sev. 257 FJ123
Sandy La., Sid. 186 EX94
Sandy La., S.Ock. 148 FM73
Sandy La., Sutt. 217 CY108
Sandy La., Tad. 234 DA123
Sandy La., Tedd. 177 CG94
Sandy La., Vir.W. 193 AZ99
Sandy La., Walt. 195 BV100
Sandy La. (Bushey), Wat. 76 CC41
Sandy La., West. 255 ER125
Sandy La., Wok. 227 BC116
Sandy La. (Chobham), Wok. 228 BG116
Sandy La. (Send), Wok. 227 BC123
Sandy La. Est., Rich. 177 CK89
Sandy La. N., Wall. 219 DK107
Sandy La. S., Wall. 219 DK107
Sandy Lo. La., Nthwd. 93 BR47
Sandy Lo. Rd., Rick. 93 BP47
Sandy Lo. Way, Nthwd. 93 BS50
Sandy Mead, Maid. 150 AC78
Sandy Ridge, Chis. 185 EN93
Sandy Ri., Ger.Cr. 90 AY53
Sandy Rd. NW3 120 DB61
Sandy Rd., Add. 212 BG107
Sandy Way, Cob. 214 CA112
Sandy Way, Croy. 203 DZ104
Sandy Way, Walt. 195 BT102
Sandy Way, Wok. 227 BC117
Sandycombe Rd., Felt. 175 BU88
Sandycombe Rd., Rich. 158 CN83
Sandycombe Rd., Twick. 177 CJ86
Sandycroft SE2 166 EU79
Sandycroft, Epsom 217 CW110
Sandycroft Rd., Amer. 72 AV39
Sandyhill Rd., Ilf. 125 EP63
Sandymount Ave., Stan. 95 CJ50
Sandy's Row E1 275 N7
Sandy's Row E1 142 DS71
Sanfoin End, Hem.H. 40 BN18
Sanford La. N16 122 DT61
Stoke Newington High St.
Sanford St. SE14 163 DY79
Sanford Ter. N16 122 DT61
Sanford Wk. N16 122 DT61
Sanford Ter.
Sanford Wk. SE14 163 DY79
Cold Blow La.
Sanger Ave., Chess. 216 CL106
Sanger Dr., Wok. 227 BC123
Sangers Dr., Horl. 268 DF148
Sangers Wk., Horl. 268 DF148
Sangers Dr.
Sangley Rd. SE6 183 EB87
Sangley Rd. SE25 202 DS98
Sangora Rd. SW11 160 DD84
Sans Wk. EC1 274 E4
Sans Wk. EC1 141 DN70
Sansom Rd. E11 124 EF61
Sansom St. SE5 162 DR80
Santers La., Pot.B. 63 CY33
Santley St. SW4 161 DL84
Santos Rd. SW18 180 DA85
Santway, The, Stan. 95 CE50
Sanway Clo., W.Byf. 212 BL114
Sanway Rd., W.Byf. 212 BL114
Sapho Pk., Grav. 191 GM91
Saphora Clo., Orp. 223 ER106
Oleander Clo.
Sappers Clo., Saw. 36 EZ05
Sapphire Clo. E6 145 EN72
Sapphire Clo., Dag. 126 EW60
Sapphire Rd. SE8 163 DY78
Sappho Ct., Wok. 226 AS116
Langmans Way
Sara Ct., Beck. 203 EB95
Albemarle Rd.
Sara Pk., Grav. 191 GL91
Saracen Clo., Croy. 202 DR100
Saracen Est., Hem.H. 41 BP18
Saracen St. E14 143 EA72
Saracens Head, Hem.H. 40 BN19
Saracen's Head Yd. EC3 275 P9
Sarah Ho. SW15 159 CT84
Arabella Dr.
Sarah St. N1 275 N2
Saratoga Rd. E5 122 DW63
Sardinia St. WC2 274 B9
Sarel Way, Horl. 269 DH146
Sargeant Clo., Uxb. 134 BK69
Ratcliffe Clo.
Sarita Clo., Har. 95 CD54
Sarjant Path SW19 179 CX89
Queensmere Rd.
Sark Clo., Houns. 156 CA80
Sark Wk. E16 144 EH72
Sarnesfield Ho. SE15 162 DV79
Pencraig Way
Sarnesfield Rd., Enf. 82 DR41
Church St.
Sarratt La., Rick. 74 BH40
Sarratt Rd., Rick. 74 BH37
Sarre Ave., Horn. 148 FJ65
Sarre Rd. NW2 119 CZ64
Sarre Rd., Orp. 206 EW99
Sarsby Dr., Stai. 173 BA89
Feathers La.
Sarsen Ave., Houns. 156 BZ82
Sarsfeld Rd. SW12 180 DF89
Sarsfield Rd., Grnf. 137 CH68
Sartor Rd. SE15 163 DX84
Sarum Grn., Wey. 195 BS104
Sarum Pl., Hem.H. 40 BL16
Satanita Clo. E16 144 EK72
Fulmer Rd.
Satchell Mead NW9 97 CT53
Satchwell Rd. E2 142 DU69
Bethnal Grn. Rd.
Satchwell St. E2 142 DU69
Turin St.

Selwyn Cres., Well. 166 EV83
Selwyn Dr., Hat. 44 CR18
Selwyn Pl., Orp. 206 EV97
Saxville Rd.
Selwyn Rd. E3 143 DZ68
Selwyn Rd. E13 144 EH67
Selwyn Rd. NW10 138 CR66
Selwyn Rd., N.Mal. 198 CR99
Selwyn Rd., Til. 171 GF82
Dock Rd.
Semaphore Rd., Guil. 258 AY136
Semley Gate E9 143 DZ65
Eastway
Semley Pl. SW1 276 G9
Semley Pl. SW1 160 DG77
Semley Rd. SW16 201 DL96
Semper Clo., Wok. 226 AS117
Semper Rd., Grays 171 GJ75
Semphill Rd., Hem.H. 40 BL23
Senate St. SE15 162 DW82
Senator Wk. SE28 165 ER76
Broadwater Rd.
Send Barns La., Wok. 227 BD124
Send Clo., Wok. 227 BC123
Send Hill Rd., Wok. 243 BC125
Send Marsh Rd., Wok. 227 BE123
Send Par. Clo., Wok. 227 BC123
Send Rd.
Send Rd., Wok. 227 BB122
Seneca Rd., Th.Hth. 202 DQ98
Senga Rd., Wall. 200 DG102
Senhouse Rd., Sutt. 199 CX104
Senior St. W2 140 DB71
Senlac Rd. SE12 184 EH88
Sennen Rd., Enf. 100 DT45
Sennen Wk. SE9 184 EL90
Nunnington Clo.
Senrab St. E1 143 DX72
Sentinel Clo., Nthlt. 136 BY70
Sentinel Sq. NW4 119 CW56
Brent St.
Sentis Ct., Nthwd. 93 BS51
Carew Rd.
September Way, Stan. 95 CH51
Sequoia Clo. (Bushey), Wat. 95 CD46
Giant Tree Hill
Sequoia Gdns., Orp. 205 ET101
Sequoia Pk., Pnr. 94 CB51
Serbin Clo. E10 123 EC59
Sergeants Grn. La., Wal.Abb. 68 EJ33
Sergehill La., Abb.L. 59 BT27
Serjeants Inn EC4 274 E9
Serle St. WC2 274 C8
Serle St. WC2 141 DM72
Sermed Ct., Slou. 132 AW74
Sermon Dr., Swan. 207 FC97
Sermon La. EC4 142 DQ72
Carter La.
Serpentine Ct., Sev. 257 FK122
Serpentine Grn., Red. 251 DK129
Malmstone Ave.
Serpentine Rd. W2 276 D3
Serpentine Rd. W2 140 DF74
Serpentine Rd., Sev. 257 FJ123
Service Rd., The, Pot.B. 64 DA32
Servden Dr., Brom. 204 EK95
Setchell Rd. SE1 279 P8
Setchell Way SE1 279 P8
Seth St. SE16 162 DW75
Swan Rd.
Seton Gdns., Dag. 146 EW66
Settle Pt. E13 144 EG68
London Rd.
Settle Rd. E13 144 EG68
London Rd.
Settle Rd., Rom. 106 FN49
Settles St. E1 142 DU71
Settrington Rd. SW6 160 DB82
Seven Acres, Cars. 200 DE103
Seven Acres, Nthwd. 93 BU51
Seven Acres, Swan. 207 FD100
Seven Arches Rd., Brwd. 108 FX47
Seven Clo., Cars. 200 DE103
Seven Hills Clo., Walt. 213 BS109
Seven Hills Rd., Cob. 213 BS110
Seven Hills Rd., Iver 133 BB65
Seven Hills Rd., Walt. 213 BS110
Seven Hills Rd. S., Cob. 213 BS113
Seven Kings Rd., Ilf. 125 ET60
Seven Sisters Rd. N4 122 DQ59
Seven Sisters Rd. N7 121 DM62
Seven Sisters Rd. N15 122 DR58
Sevenoaks Bypass, Sev. 256 FC123
Sevenoaks Clo., Bexh. 167 FB84
Sevenoaks Clo., Rom. 106 FJ49
Sevenoaks Clo., Sutt. 218 DA110
Sevenoaks Ct., Nthwd. 93 BQ52
Sevenoaks Ho. SE25 202 DU97
Sevenoaks Rd. SE4 183 DY86
Sevenoaks Rd., Orp. 223 ET105
Sevenoaks Rd. (Green St. Grn.), Orp. 223 ET108
Sevenoaks Rd. (Otford), Sev. 241 FH116
Sevenoaks Way, Orp. 206 EW98
Sevenoaks Way, Sid. 186 EW94
Seventh Ave. E12 125 EM63
Seventh Ave., Hayes 135 BT74
Severalls Ave., Chesh. 54 AQ30
Severn Ave., Rom. 127 FH55
Severn Cres., Slou. 153 BB78
Severn Dr., Enf. 82 DU38
Severn Dr., Esher 197 CG103
Severn Dr., Upmin. 129 FR58
Severn Dr., Walt. 196 BX103
Severn Rd., S.Ock. 148 FQ72
Severn Way NW10 119 CT64
Severn Way, Wat. 60 BW34
Severnake Clo. E14 163 EA77
Severnmead, Hem.H. 40 BL17
Severns Fld., Epp. 70 EU29
Severnvale, St.Alb. 62 CM27
Thamesdale
Severus Rd. SW11 160 DE84
Seville Ms. N1 142 DS66
Ufton Rd.
Seville St. SW1 276 E5
Seville St. SW1 160 DF75
Sevington Rd. NW4 119 CV58
Sevington St. W9 140 DB70
Seward Rd. W7 157 CG75
Seward Rd., Beck. 203 DX96
Seward St. EC1 274 G3
Seward St. EC1 141 DP70
Sewardstone Gdns. E4 83 EB43
Sewardstone Rd. E2 142 DW68
Sewardstone Rd. E4 101 EB45
Sewardstone Rd., Wal.Abb. 83 ED38
Sewardstone St., Wal.Abb. 67 EC34
Sewdley St. E5 123 DX63
Sewell Clo., St.Alb. 44 CL20
Sewell Harris Clo., Harl. 35 ET13
Sewell Rd. SE2 166 EU75
Sewell St. E13 144 EG69
Sewells, Welw.G.C. 29 CY05
Sextant Ave. E14 163 ED77
Sexton Clo., Rain. 147 FF67
Blake Clo.
Sexton Rd., Til. 171 GF81
Seymer Rd., Rom. 127 FD55
Seymour Ave. N17 100 DU54
Seymour Ave., Cat. 236 DQ122
Fairbourne La.
Seymour Ave., Epsom 217 CV109
Seymour Ave., Mord. 199 CX101
Seymour Clo., E.Mol. 196 CC99
Seymour Clo., Loug. 84 EL44
Roding Rd.
Seymour Clo., Pnr. 94 BZ53
Seymour Ct. E4 102 EF47
Seymour Cres., Hem.H. 40 BL20
Seymour Dr., Brom. 205 EM102
Seymour Gdns. SE4 163 DY83
Seymour Gdns., Felt. 176 BW91
Seymour Gdns., Ilf. 125 EM60
Seymour Gdns., Ruis. 116 BX60
Seymour Gdns., Surb. 198 CM99
Seymour Gdns., Twick. 177 CH87
Seymour Ms. W1 272 F8
Seymour Ms. W1 140 DG72
Seymour Ms., Saw. 36 EX08
Seymour Pl. SE25 202 DV98
Seymour Pl. W1 272 C6
Seymour Pl. W1 140 DE71
Seymour Rd. E4 101 EB46
Seymour Rd. E6 144 EK68
Seymour Rd. E10 123 DZ60
Seymour Rd. N3 98 DB52
Seymour Rd. N8 121 DP57
Seymour Rd. N9 100 DV47
Seymour Rd. SW18 179 CZ87
Seymour Rd. SW19 179 CX90
Seymour Rd. W4 158 CQ77
Seymour Rd., Berk. 38 AS17
Seymour Rd., Cars. 218 DG106
Seymour Rd., Ch.St.G. 90 AW49
Seymour Rd., E.Mol. 196 CC99
Seymour Rd., Grav. 191 GF88
Seymour Rd., Hmptn. 176 CC92
Seymour Rd., Kings.T. 197 CK95
Seymour Rd., Mitch. 200 DG101
Seymour Rd., St.Alb. 43 CE17
Seymour Rd., Slou. 151 AR75
Seymour Rd., Til. 171 GF81
Seymour Rd., W.Mol. 196 CC99
Seymour St. W1 272 D9
Seymour St. W1 140 DF72
Seymour St. W2 272 D9
Seymour St. W2 140 DF72
Seymour Ter. SE20 202 DV95
Seymour Vill. SE20 202 DV95
Seymour Wk. SW10 160 DC79
Seymour Wk., Swans. 190 FY87
Seymour Way, Sun. 175 BS94
Seymours, Harl. 51 EM18
Seymours, The, Loug. 85 EN39
Seyssel St. E14 163 EC77
Shaa Rd. W3 138 CR73
Shacklands Rd., Sev. 225 FB111
Shackleford Rd., Wok. 227 BA121
Shacklegate La., Tedd. 177 CE91
Shackleton Clo. SE23 182 DV89
Shackleton Rd., Slou. 132 AT73
Shackleton Rd., Sthl. 136 BZ73
Shackleton Wk., Guil. 242 AT134
Humbolt Clo.
Shackleton Way, Abb.L. 59 BU32
Langley La.
Shackleton Way, Welw.G.C. 30 DD09
Shacklewell Grn. E8 122 DT63
Shacklewell La.
Shacklewell La. E8 122 DT64
Shacklewell Rd. N16 122 DT63
Shacklewell Row E8 122 DT63
Shacklewell St. E2 142 DT69
Shad Thames SE1 279 P3
Shad Thames SE1 162 DT75
Shadbolt Clo., Wor.Pk. 199 CT103
Shadwell Dr., Nthlt. 136 BZ69
Shadwell Gdns. E1 142 DW72
Martha St.
Shadwell Pierhead E1 142 DW73
Glamis Rd.
Shadwell Pl. E1 142 DW73
Sutton St.
Shady Bush Clo. (Bushey), Wat. 94 CC45
Richfield Rd.
Shady La., Wat. 75 BV40
Shaef Way, Tedd. 177 CG94
Shafter Rd., Dag. 147 FC65
Shaftesbury, Loug. 84 EK41
Shaftesbury Ave. W1 273 M10
Shaftesbury Ave. W1 141 DK73
Shaftesbury Ave. WC2 277 M1
Shaftesbury Ave. WC2 141 DK73
Shaftesbury Ave., Barn. 80 DC41
Shaftesbury Ave., Enf. 83 DX40
Shaftesbury Ave., Felt. 175 BU86
Shaftesbury Ave., Har. 116 CB60
Shaftesbury Ave. (Kenton), Har. 117 CK57
Shaftesbury Ave., Sthl. 156 CA77
Shaftesbury Circle, Har. 116 CC60
Shaftesbury Ave.
Shaftesbury Ct. N1 142 DR68
Shaftesbury St.
Shaftesbury Cres., Stai. 174 BK94
Shaftesbury Gdns. NW10 138 CS70
Shaftesbury La., Dart. 168 FP84
Shaftesbury Ms. SW4 181 DJ85
Clapham Common S. Side
Shaftesbury Ms. W8 160 DA76
Stratford Rd.
Shaftesbury Pt. E13 144 EH68
High St.
Shaftesbury Rd. E4 101 ED46
Shaftesbury Rd. E7 144 EJ66
Shaftesbury Rd. E10 123 EA60
Shaftesbury Rd. E17 123 EB58
Shaftesbury Rd. N18 100 DS51
Shaftesbury Rd. N19 121 DL60
Shaftesbury Rd., Beck. 203 DZ96
Shaftesbury Rd., Cars. 200 DD101
Shaftesbury Rd., Epp. 69 ET29
Shaftesbury Rd., Rich. 158 CL83
Shaftesbury Rd., Rom. 127 FF58
Shaftesbury Rd., Wat. 76 BW41
Shaftesbury Rd., Wok. 227 BA117
Shaftesbury St. N1 275 J1
Shaftesbury St. N1 142 DQ68
Shaftesbury Way, Twick. 177 CD90
Shaftesbury Waye, Hayes 136 BW71
Shaftesburys, The, Bark. 145 EQ68
Shafto Ms. SW1 276 D7
Shafton Rd. E9 143 DX67
Shaftsbury Rd., Beck. 203 DZ96
Shaftsbury Way, Kings L. 59 BQ28
Shaggy Calf La., Slou. 132 AU73
Shakespeare Ave. N11 99 DJ50
Shakespeare Ave. NW10 138 CR67
Shakespeare Ave., Felt. 175 BU86
Shakespeare Ave., Hayes 135 BU72
Shakespeare Ave., Til. 171 GH82
Shakespeare Cres. E12 145 EM65
Shakespeare Cres. NW10 138 CR67
Shakespeare Dr., Har. 118 CM58
Shakespeare Gdns. N2 120 DF56
Shakespeare Ho. N14 99 DK47
High St.
Shakespeare Rd. E17 101 DX54
Shakespeare Rd. N3 98 DA53
Popes Dr.
Shakespeare Rd. NW7 97 CT49
Shakespeare Rd. SE24 181 DP85
Shakespeare Rd. W3 138 CQ74
Shakespeare Rd. W7 137 CF73
Shakespeare Rd., Add. 212 BK105
Shakespeare Rd., Bexh. 166 EY81
Shakespeare Rd., Dart. 168 FN84
Shakespeare Rd., Rom. 127 FF58
Shakespeare Sq., Ilf. 103 EQ51
Shakespeare St., Wat. 75 BV38
Shakespeare Twr. EC2 142 DQ71
Beech St.
Shakespeare Way, Felt. 176 BW91
Shakspeare Ms. N16 122 DS64
Shakspeare Wk.
Shakspeare Wk. N16 122 DS63
Shalcomb St. SW10 160 DC79
Shalcross Dr. (Cheshunt), Wal.Cr. 67 DZ30
Shaldon Dr., Mord. 199 CY99
Shaldon Dr., Ruis. 116 BW62
Shaldon Rd., Edg. 96 CM54
Shaldon Way, Walt. 196 BW104
Shale Grn., Red. 251 DK129
Bletchingley Rd.
Shalfleet Dr. W10 139 CX73
Shalford Clo., Orp. 223 EQ105
Shalford Rd., Guil. 258 AX138
Shalimar Gdns. W3 138 CQ73
Shalimar Rd. W3 138 CQ73
Hereford Rd.
Shallcross Cres., Hat. 45 CU21
Shallons Rd. SE9 185 EP91
Shalston Vill., Surb. 198 CM100
Shalstone Rd. SW14 158 CP83
Shamrock Clo., Lthd. 231 CD121
Shamrock Rd., Croy. 201 DM100
Shamrock Rd., Grav. 191 GL87
Shamrock St. SW4 161 DK83
Shamrock Way N14 99 DH46
Shand St. SE1 279 N4
Shand St. SE1 162 DS75
Shandon Rd. SW4 181 DJ86
Shandy St. E1 143 DX71
Shanklin Clo., Wal.Cr. 66 DT29
Hornbeam Way
Shanklin Gdns., Wat. 94 BW49
Shanklin Rd. N8 121 DK57
Shanklin Rd. N15 122 DU56
Shanklin Way SE15 162 DT80
Pentridge St.
Shannon Clo. NW2 119 CX62
Shannon Clo., Sthl. 156 BX78
Shannon Gro. SW9 161 DM84
Shannon Pl. NW8 140 DE68
Allitsen Rd.
Shannon Way, Beck. 183 EB93
Shannon Way, S.Ock. 148 FQ73
Shantock Hall La., Hem.H. 56 AY29
Shantock La., Hem.H. 56 AX30
Shap Cres., Cars. 200 DF102
Shap St. E2 142 DT67
Shapland Way N13 99 DM50
Shardcroft Ave. SE24 181 DP85
Shardeloes Rd. SE14 163 DZ82
Sharland Clo., Th.Hth. 201 DN100
Dunheved Rd. N.
Sharland Rd., Grav. 191 GJ89
Sharman Ct., Sid. 186 EU91
Sharnbrooke Clo., Well. 166 EW83
Sharney Ave., Slou. 153 BB76
Sharon Clo., Epsom 216 CQ113
Sharon Clo., Lthd. 230 CA124
Sharon Clo., Surb. 197 CJ102
Sharon Gdns. E9 142 DW67
Sharon Rd. W4 158 CR78
Sharon Rd., Enf. 83 DY40
Sharp Way, Dart. 168 FM83
Sharpcroft, Hem.H. 40 BK18
Sharpe Clo. W7 137 CF71
Templeman Rd.
Sharpecroft, Harl. 51 EQ15
Haydens Rd.
Sharpes La., Hem.H. 39 BB22
Sharpleshall St. NW1 140 DF66
Sharpness Clo., Hayes 136 BY71
Sharps La., Ruis. 115 BR60
Sharratt St. SE15 162 DW79
Sharsted St. SE17 161 DP78
Shavers Pl. SW1 277 M1
Shaw Ave., Bark. 146 EY68
Shaw Clo. SE28 146 EV74
Shaw Clo., Cher. 211 BC107
Shaw Clo., Epsom 217 CT111
Shaw Clo., Horn. 127 FH60
St. Leonards Way
Shaw Clo., S.Croy. 220 DT112
Shaw Clo. (Cheshunt), Wal.Cr. 66 DW28
Shaw Clo. (Bushey), Wat. 95 CE47
Shaw Ct., Wind. 172 AU85
Shaw Cres., Brwd. 109 GD42
Shaw Cres., S.Croy. 220 DT112
Shaw Cres., Til. 171 GH81
Shaw Dr., Walt. 196 BW101
Shaw Gdns., Bark. 146 EY68
Shaw Rd., Brom. 184 EF90
Shaw Rd., Enf. 83 DX39
Shaw Rd., West. 238 EJ120
Shaw Sq. E17 101 DY53
Shaw Way, Wall. 219 DL108
Shawbridge, Harl. 51 EQ18
Shawbrooke Rd. SE9 184 EJ85
Shawbury Rd. SE22 182 DT85
Shawfield Ct., West Dr. 154 BL76
Shawfield Pk., Brom. 204 EK96
Shawfield St. SW3 160 DE78
Shawford Ct. SW15 179 CU87
Shawford Rd., Epsom 216 CR107
Shawley Cres., Epsom 233 CW118
Shawley Way, Epsom 233 CV118
Shaws, The, Welw.G.C. 30 DC10
Shaws Cotts. SE23 183 DY90
Shaxton Cres., Croy. 221 EC109
Shearing Dr., Cars. 200 DC101
Stavordale Rd.
Shearling Way N7 141 DL65
Shearman Rd. SE3 164 EF84
Shearsmith Ho. E1 142 DU73
Cable St.
Shearwater Way, Hayes 136 BX71
Willow Tree La.
Shearwood Cres., Dart. 167 FF83
Sheath's La., Lthd. 214 CB113
Sheaveshill Ave. NW9 118 CS56
Sheehy Way, Slou. 132 AV73
Sheen Common Dr., Rich. 158 CN84
Sheen Ct., Rich. 158 CN84
Sheen Rd.
Sheen Ct. Rd., Rich. 158 CN84
Sheen Gate Gdns. SW14 158 CQ84
Sheen Gro. N1 141 DN67
Richmond Ave.
Sheen La. SW14 178 CQ85
Sheen Pk., Rich. 158 CL84
Sheen Rd., Orp. 205 ET98
Sheen Rd., Rich. 178 CL85
Sheen Way, Wall. 219 DM106
Sheen Wd. SW14 178 CQ85
Sheendale Rd., Rich. 158 CM84
Sheenewood SE26 182 DV92
Sheep La. E8 142 DV67
Sheep Wk., Epsom 232 CR122
Sheep Wk., Reig. 249 CY131
Sheep Wk., Shep. 194 BM101
Sheep Wk. Ms. SW19 179 CY93
Sheepbarn La., Warl. 222 EF112
Sheepcot Dr., Wat. 60 BW34
Sheepcot La., Wat. 59 BU33
Sheepcote, Welw.G.C. 30 DA12
Sheepcote Clo., Beac. 88 AJ51
Sheepcote Clo., Houns. 155 BU80
Sheepcote Gdns., Uxb. 114 BG58
Sheepcote La. SW11 160 DF82
Sheepcote La., H.Wyc. 110 AG61
Sheepcote La., Orp. 206 EZ100
Sheepcote La., St.Alb. 28 CL07
Sheepcote La., Slou. 110 AF62
Sheepcote La., Swan. 206 FA98
Sheepcote Rd., Har. 117 CF58
Sheepcote Rd., Hem.H. 40 BM20
Sheepcote Rd., Wind. 151 AL82
Sheepcote Rd. (Eton Wick), Wind. 151 AN78
Sheepcotes Rd., Rom. 126 EX56
Sheepfold La., Amer. 55 AR39
Sheepfold Rd., Guil. 242 AT131
Sheephouse Grn., Dor. 262 BZ140
Sheephouse La., Dor. 262 BZ139
Sheephouse Rd., Hem.H. 40 BM22
Sheephouse Way, N.Mal. 198 CR102
Sheeplands Ave., Guil. 243 BC132
Sheepwalk La., Lthd. 245 BT134
Sheering Dr., Harl. 36 EX11
Sheering Lwr. Rd., Harl. 36 EZ09
Sheering Lwr. Rd., Saw. 36 EZ08
Sheering Mill La., Saw. 36 EZ05
Sheering Rd., Harl. 36 EZ10
Sheerwater Ave., Add. 211 BE112
Sheerwater Business Cen., Wok. 211 BC114
Sheerwater Rd. E16 144 EK71
Sheerwater Rd., Add. 211 BE112
Sheerwater Rd., W.Byf. 211 BE113
Sheerwater Rd., Wok. 211 BE112
Sheet St., Wind. 151 AR82
Sheethanger La., Hem.H. 40 BG24
Sheffield Dr., Rom. 106 FN50
Sheffield Gdns., Rom. 106 FN50
Sheffield Rd., Slou. 131 AQ72
Sheffield Sq. E3 143 DZ69
Malmesbury Rd.
Sheffield St. WC2 274 B9
Sheffield Ter. W8 140 DA74
Shefton Ri., Nthwd. 93 BU52
Sheila Clo., Rom. 105 FB52
Sheila Rd., Rom. 105 FB52
Sheilings, The, Horn. 128 FM57
Shelbourne Clo., Pnr. 116 BZ55
Shelbourne Rd. N17 100 DV54
Shelburne Rd. N7 121 DM63
Shelbury Clo., Sid. 186 EU90
Shelbury Rd. SE22 182 DV85
Sheldon Ave. N6 120 DE59
Sheldon Ave., Ilf. 103 EP54
Sheldon Clo. SE12 184 EH85
Sheldon Clo. SE20 202 DV95
Sheldon Clo., Harl. 52 EY15
Church Langley Way
Sheldon Clo., Reig. 266 DB135
Sheldon Clo. (Cheshunt), Wal.Cr. 66 DS26
Sheldon Ct., Guil. 259 AZ135
Lower Edgeborough Rd.
Sheldon Rd. N18 100 DS49
Sheldon Rd. NW2 119 CX63
Sheldon Rd., Bexh. 166 EZ81
Sheldon Rd., Dag. 146 EY66
Sheldon St., Croy. 202 DQ104
Wandle Rd.
Sheldrake Clo. E16 145 EM74
Newland St.
Sheldrake Pl. W8 160 DA75
Sheldrick Clo. SW19 200 DD96
Sheldwich Ter., Brom. 204 EL100
Turpington La.
Shelford Pl. N16 122 DR62
Stoke Newington Ch. St.
Shelford Ri. SE19 182 DT94
Shelford Rd., Barn. 79 CW44
Shelgate Rd. SW11 180 DE85
Shell Clo., Brom. 204 EL100
Shell Rd. SE13 163 EB83
Shellbank La., Dart. 189 FU93
Shellduck Clo. NW9 96 CS54
Swan Dr.
Shelley Ave. E12 144 EL65
Shelley Ave., Grnf. 137 CD69
Shelley Ave., Horn. 127 FF61
Shelley Clo., Bans. 233 CX115
Shelley Clo., Couls. 235 DM117
Stanley Clo.
Shelley Clo., Edg. 96 CN49
Shelley Clo., Grnf. 137 CD69
Shelley Clo., Hayes 135 BU71
Shelley Clo., H.Wyc. 110 AE55
Watery La.
Shelley Clo., Nthwd. 93 BT50
Shelley Clo., Orp. 205 ES104
Shelley Clo., Slou. 153 AZ78
Shelley Cres., Houns. 156 BX81
Shelley Cres., Sthl. 136 BZ72
Shelley Dr., Well. 165 ES81
Shelley Gdns., Wem. 117 CJ61
Shelley Gro., Loug. 85 EM42
Shelley Pl., Til. 171 GH81
Kipling Ave.
Shelley Rd., Brwd. 109 GD45
Shelley Rd., Chesh. 54 AP29
Shelley Way SW19 180 DD93
Shelleys La., Sev. 239 ET116
Shellfield Clo., Stai. 174 BG85
Shellgrove Est. N16 122 DS64
Shellness Rd. E5 122 DV64
Shellwood Dr., Dor. 263 CJ140
Shellwood Rd. SW11 160 DF82
Shellwood Rd., Reig. 264 CQ141
Shelmerdine Clo. E3 143 EA71
Shelson Ave., Felt. 175 BT90
Shelton Ave., Warl. 236 DW117
Shelton Clo., Guil. 242 AU129
Shelton Clo., Warl. 236 DW117
Shelton Ct., Slou. 152 AW76
London Rd.
Shelton Rd. SW19 200 DA95
Shelton St. WC2 273 P9
Shelton St. WC2 141 DL72
Shelvers Grn., Tad. 233 CW121
Shelvers Hill, Tad. 233 CW121
Ashurst Rd.
Shelvers Spur, Tad. 233 CW121
Shelvers Way, Tad. 233 CW121
Shenden Clo., Sev. 257 FJ128
Shenden Way, Sev. 257 FJ128
Shenfield Clo., Couls. 235 DJ119
Woodfield Clo.
Shenfield Cres., Brwd. 108 FY47
Shenfield Gdns., Brwd. 109 GB44
Shenfield Grn., Brwd. 109 GA45
Hutton Rd.
Shenfield Ho. SE18 164 EK80
Shooter's Hill Rd.
Shenfield Pl., Brwd. 108 FY45
Shenfield Rd., Brwd. 108 FX47
Shenfield Rd., Wdf.Grn. 102 EH52
Shenfield St. N1 275 N1
Shenfield St. N1 142 DS68
Shenley Ave., Ruis. 115 BT61
Shenley Hill, Rad. 77 CG35
Shenley La., St.Alb. 61 CG25
Shenley Rd. SE5 162 DS81
Shenley Rd., Borwd. 78 CN42
Shenley Rd., Dart. 188 FN87
Shenley Rd., Hem.H. 40 BN15
Shenley Rd., Houns. 156 BY81
Shenley Rd., Rad. 61 CH34
Shenleybury Cotts., Rad. 62 CL31
Shenstone Clo., Dart. 167 FD84
Shenstone Dr., Slou. 131 AK70
Shenstone Gdns., Rom. 106 FJ53
Shenstone Hill, Berk. 38 AY18
Shepcot Ho. N14 81 DJ44
Shepherd Mkt. W1 277 H3
Shepherd St. W1 277 H3
Shepherd St., Grav. 190 GD87
Shepherdess Pl. N1 275 J2
Shepherdess Wk. N1 275 J1
Shepherdess Wk. N1 142 DQ68
Shepherds Bush Grn. W12 159 CW75
Shepherds Bush Mkt. W12 159 CW75
Uxbridge Rd.
Shepherds Bush Pl. W12 159 CX75
Shepherds Bush Rd. W6 159 CW77
Shepherds Clo. N6 121 DH58
Shepherds Clo., Beac. 89 AM54
Shepherds La.
Shepherds Clo., Lthd. 231 CK124
Shepherds Clo., Orp. 205 ET104
Stapleton Rd.
Shepherds Clo., Rom. 126 EX57
Shepherds Clo., Shep. 195 BP100
Shepherds Clo. (Cowley), Uxb. 134 BJ70
High St.
Shepherds Ct. W12 159 CX75
Shepherds Bush Grn.
Shepherds Ct., Hert. 32 DQ06
Shepherds Grn., Chis. 185 ER94
Shepherds Grn., Hem.H. 39 BE21
Shepherds Hill N6 121 DH58
Shepherds Hill, Guil. 242 AU132
Shepherds Hill, Red. 251 DJ126
Shepherds Hill, Rom. 106 FN54
Shepherds La. E9 143 DX65
Shepherds La., Beac. 89 AM54
Shepherds La., Brwd. 108 FS45
Shepherds La., Dart. 187 FG88
Shepherds La., Guil. 242 AT131
Shepherds La., Rick. 73 BD44
Shepherds Path, Nthlt. 136 BY65
Fortunes Mead
Shepherds Pl. W1 272 F10
Shepherds Rd., Wat. 75 BT41
Shepherds Wk. NW2 119 CU61
Shepherds Wk. NW3 120 DD63
Shepherds' Wk., Epsom 232 CP121
Shepherds Wk. (Bushey), Wat. 95 CD47
Shepherds Way, Chesh. 54 AR33
Shepherds Way, Guil. 258 AY138

403

Sil–Sou This index reads in the sequence: Street Name / Postal District or Post Town / Map Page Number / Grid Reference

Silvermere Rd. SE6 183 EB86
Silversmiths Way, Wok. 226 AW118
Silverst Clo., Nthlt. 136 CB65
Silverstead La., West. 239 ER121
Silverston Way, Stan. 95 CJ51
Silverstone Clo., Red. 250 DF132
Goodwood Rd.
Silverthorn Dr., Hem.H. 41 BP24
Silverthorn Gdns. E4 101 EA47
Silverthorne Rd. SW8 161 DH82
Silverton Rd. W6 159 CX79
Silvertown Way E16 144 EE72
Silvertree La., Grnf. 137 CD69
Cowgate Rd.
Silverwood Clo., Beck. 183 EA94
Silverwood Clo., Croy. 221 EA109
Silverwood Clo., Nthwd. 93 BQ53
Silverwood Cotts., Guil. 260 BM138
Shere Rd.
Silvester Rd. SE22 182 DT85
Silvester St. SE1 279 K5
Silvesters, Harl. 51 EM17
Silwood Est. SE16 162 DW77
Millender Wk.
Silwood St. SE16 162 DW77
Simla Clo. SE14 163 DY79
Chubworthy St.
Simla Ho. SE1 279 L5
Simmil Rd., Esher 215 CE106
Simmonds Ri., Hem.H. 40 BK22
Simmons Clo. N20 98 DE46
Simmons Clo., Chess. 215 CJ107
Mansfield Rd.
Simmons Clo., Slou. 153 BA77
Common Rd.
Simmons La. E4 101 ED47
Simmons Pl., Stai. 173 BE92
Chertsey La.
Simmons Rd. SE18 165 EP78
Simmons Way N20 98 DE47
Simms Clo., Cars. 200 DE103
Simms Rd. SE1 162 DU77
Simnel Rd. SE12 184 EH87
Simon Clo. W11 139 CZ73
Portobello Rd.
Simon Dean, Hem.H. 57 BA27
Simonds Rd. E10 123 EA61
Simone Clo., Brom. 204 EK95
Simone Dr., Ken. 236 DQ116
Simons Clo., Cher. 211 BC107
Simons Wk. E15 123 ED64
Waddington St.
Simons Wk., Egh. 172 AW94
Simplemarsh Ct., Add. 212 BH105
Simplemarsh Rd.
Simplemarsh Rd., Add. 212 BG105
Simpson Dr. W3 138 CR72
Simpson Rd., Houns. 176 BZ86
Simpson Rd., Rain. 147 FF65
Simpson Rd., Rich. 177 CJ91
Simpson St. SW11 160 DE82
Simpsons Grn., Slou. 131 AM69
Rokesby Rd.
Simpsons Rd. E14 143 EB73
Simpsons Rd., Brom. 204 EG97
Sims Clo., Rom. 127 FF56
Sims Wk. SE3 164 EF84
Lee Rd.
Sinclair Ct., Beck. 183 EA94
Sinclair Dr., Sutt. 218 DB109
Sinclair Gdns. W14 159 CX75
Sinclair Gro. NW11 119 CX58
Sinclair Rd. E4 101 DY50
Sinclair Rd. W14 159 CX75
Sinclair Way, Dart. 189 FR91
Sinclare Clo., Enf. 82 DT39
Sincots Rd., Red. 250 DF134
Lower Bri. Rd.
Sinderby Clo., Borwd. 78 CL39
Singapore Rd. W13 137 CG74
Singer St. EC2 275 L3
Single St., West. 239 EP115
Singles Cross La., Sev. 224 EW114
Singleton Clo. SW17 180 DF94
Singleton Clo., Croy. 202 DQ101
St. Saviours Rd.
Singleton Clo., Horn. 127 FF63
Carfax Rd.
Singleton Rd., Dag. 126 EZ64
Singleton Scarp N12 98 DA50
Singlewell Rd., Grav. 191 GH90
Singret Pl. 134 BJ70
(Cowley), Uxb.
High St.
Sinnott Rd. E17 101 DX53
Sion Rd., Twick. 177 CH87
Sipson Clo., West Dr. 154 BN79
Sipson La., Hayes 155 BQ79
Sipson La., West Dr. 154 BN79
Sipson Rd., West Dr. 154 BN78
Sipson Way, West Dr. 154 BN81
Sir Alexander Clo. W3 139 CT74
Sir Alexander Rd. W3 139 CT74
Sir Cyril Black Way 180 DA94
SW19
Sir Francis Way, Brwd. 108 FV47
Sir Henry Peeks Dr., 131 AN65
Slou.
Sir Thomas More Est. 160 DD79
SW3
Beaufort St.
Sirdar Rd. N22 121 DP55
Sirdar Rd. W11 139 CX73
Sirdar Rd., Mitch. 180 DG93
Grenfell Rd.
Sirdar Strand, Grav. 191 GM92
Sirinham Pt. SW8 161 DM79
Sirus Rd., Nthwd. 93 BU50
Sise La. EC4 275 K9
Siskin Clo., Borwd. 78 CN42
Siskin Clo., Wat. 76 BY42
Sisley Rd., Bark. 145 ES67
Sispara Gdns. SW18 179 CZ86
Sissinghurst Rd., Croy. 202 DU101
Sister Mabel's Way SE15 162 DU80
Radnor Rd.
Sisters Ave. SW11 160 DF83
Sistova Rd. SW12 181 DH88
Sisulu Pl. SW9 161 DN83
Sittingbourne Ave., Enf. 82 DR44
Sitwell Gro., Stan. 95 CF50
Sivill Ho. E2 142 DT69
Siviter Rd., Dag. 147 FB66
Siviter Way, Dag. 147 FB66
Siward Rd. N17 100 DR53
Siward Rd. SW17 180 DC90
Siward Rd., Brom. 204 EH97
Six Acres, Hem.H. 40 BN23
Six Acres Est. N4 121 DN61
Six Bells La., Sev. 257 FJ126
Sixth Ave. E12 125 EM63
Sixth Ave. W10 139 CY69
Sixth Ave., Hayes 135 BT74
Sixth Ave., Wat. 76 BX35
Sixth Cross Rd., Twick. 176 CC90
Skardu Rd. NW2 119 CY64
Skarnings Ct., Wal.Abb. 68 EG33
Skeena Hill SW18 179 CY87
Skeet Hill La., Orp. 206 EX102
Skeffington Rd. E6 145 EM67
Skelbrook St. SW18 180 DB89
Skeleton Clo., Beac. 110 AG55
Skelgill Rd. SW15 159 CZ84
Skelley Rd. E15 144 EF66
Skelton Clo. E8 142 DT65
Buttermere Wk.
Skelton Rd. E7 144 EG65
Skeltons La. E10 123 EB59
Skelwith Rd. W6 159 CW79
Skenfrith Ho. SE15 162 DV79
Commercial Way
Skerne Rd., Kings.T. 197 CK95
Skerries Ct., Slou. 153 BA77
Blacksmith Row
Sketchley Gdns. SE16 163 DX78
Sketty Rd., Enf. 82 DS41
Skibbs La., Orp. 224 EY106
Skid Hill La., Warl. 222 EF113
Skidmore Way, Rick. 92 BL46
Skiers St. E15 144 EE67
Skiffington Clo. SW2 181 DN88
Skillet Hill, Wal.Abb. 84 EH35
Skimpans Clo., Hat. 45 CX24
Skinner Ct. E2 142 DV68
Parmiter St.
Skinner Pl. SW1 276 F9
Skinner St. EC1 274 E3
Skinner St. EC1 141 DN69
Skinners La. EC4 275 J10
Skinners La., Ash. 231 CK118
Skinners La., Houns. 156 CB81
Skinner's Row SE10 163 EB81
Blackheath Rd.
Skinney La., Dart. 208 FQ97
Skip La., Uxb. 114 BL60
Skippers Clo., Green. 189 FV85
Skipsey Ave. E6 145 EM69
Skipton Dr., Hayes 155 BQ76
Skipton Way, Horl. 269 DH145
Skipworth Rd. E9 142 DW67
Skomer Wk. N1 142 DQ65
Clephane Rd.
Sky Peals Rd., 101 ED52
Wdf.Grn.
Skydmore Path, Slou. 131 AM69
Umberville Way
Skylark Rd., Uxb. 113 BC60
Skyport Dr., West Dr. 154 BK80
Skys Wd. Rd., St.Alb. 43 CH16
Slackesbury Hatch, 51 EP15
Harl.
Slade, The SE18 165 ES79
Slade Ct., Cher. 211 BD107
Slade Ct., Rad. 77 CG35
Slade End, Epp. 85 ES36
Slade Gdns., Erith 167 FF81
Slade Grn. Rd., Erith 167 FG80
Slade Ho., Houns. 176 BZ86
Slade Oak La., Ger.Cr. 113 BB55
Slade Oak La., Uxb. 113 BC57
Slade Rd., Cher. 211 BD107
Slade Twr. E10 123 EA61
Slade Wk. SE17 161 DP79
Heiron St.
Sladebrook Rd. SE3 164 EK83
Sladedale Rd. SE18 165 ES78
Sladen Pl. E5 122 DV63
Clarence Rd.
Slades Clo., Enf. 81 DN41
Slades Dr., Chis. 185 EQ90
Slades Gdns., Enf. 81 DN40
Slades Hill, Enf. 81 DN41
Slades Ri., Enf. 81 DN41
Slagrove Pl. SE13 183 EB85
Ladywell Rd.
Slaidburn St. SW10 160 DC79
Slaithwaite Rd. SE13 163 EC84
Slaney Pl. N7 121 DN64
Hornsey Rd.
Slaney Rd., Rom. 127 FE57
Slapleys, Wok. 226 AX120
Slater Clo. SE18 165 EN78
Woolwich New Rd.
Slattery Rd., Felt. 176 BW88
Sleaford Grn., Wat. 94 BX48
Sleaford St. SW8 161 DJ80
Sleapcross Gdns., 44 CP21
St.Alb.
Sleapshyde La., St.Alb. 44 CP21
Sleddale, Hem.H. 40 BL17
Sledmore Ct., Felt. 175 BS88
Kilross Rd.
Sleepers Fm. Rd., Grays 171 GH75
Sleets End, Hem.H. 40 BH18
Slewins Clo., Horn. 128 FJ57
Slewins La., Horn. 128 FJ57
Slievemore Clo. SW4 161 DK83
Voltaire Rd.
Slimmons Dr., St.Alb. 43 CG16
Slines New Rd., Cat. 237 DX120
Slines Oak Rd., Cat. 237 EA123
Slines Oak Rd., Warl. 237 EA119
Slingsby Pl. WC2 273 P10
Slip, The, West. 255 EQ126
Slipe La., Brox. 49 DZ24
Slippers Hill, Hem.H. 40 BK19
Slippers Pl. SE16 162 DV76
Slipshatch Rd., Reig. 265 CX138
Slipshoe St., Reig. 249 CZ134
West St.
Sloane Ave. SW3 276 C9
Sloane Ave. SW3 160 DE77
Sloane Ct. E. SW3 276 F10
Sloane Ct. W. SW3 276 F10
Sloane Ct. W. SW3 160 DG78
Sloane Gdns. SW1 276 F9
Sloane Gdns. SW1 160 DG77
Sloane Gdns., Orp. 205 EQ104
Partridge Dr.
Sloane Sq. SW1 276 E9
Sloane Sq. SW1 160 DF77
Sloane St. SW1 276 E6
Sloane St. SW1 160 DF75
Sloane Ter. SW1 276 E8
Sloane Ter. SW1 160 DF77
Sloane Wk., Croy. 203 DZ100
Sloansway, Welw.G.C. 30 DA06
Slocock Hill, Wok. 226 AW117
Slocum Clo. SE28 146 EW73
Woodpecker Rd.
Slough La. NW9 118 CQ57
Slough La., Bet. 249 CU133
Slough La., Epp. 53 FC24
Slough La., Epsom 248 CQ125
Slough Rd., Iver 133 BC69
Slough Rd., Slou. 152 AU78
Slough Rd. 151 AR78
(Eton), Wind.
Slough Trd. Est., Slou. 131 AP72
Sly St. E1 142 DV72
Cannon St. Rd.
Slyfield Ct., Guil. 242 AY130
Slyfield Grn.
Slyfield Grn., Guil. 242 AY130
Slyted Ind. Est., Guil. 242 AY130
Small Acre, Hem.H. 39 BF20
Small Grains 209 FV104
(Fawkham), Long.
Smallberry Ave., Islw. 157 CF82
Smallbrook Ms. W2 140 DD72
Craven Rd.
Smallcroft, Welw.G.C. 30 DB08
Smalley Clo. N16 122 DT62
Smalley Rd. Est. N16 122 DT62
Smalley Clo.
Smallfield Rd., Horl. 269 DH148
Smallford La., St.Alb. 44 CP21
Smallford Trail, St.Alb. 43 CE20
Smallholdings Rd., 217 CW114
Epsom
Smallmead, Horl. 269 DH148
Small's Hill Rd., Reig. 265 CU141
Smallwood Clo., St.Alb. 28 CL08
Smallwood Rd. SW17 180 DD91
Smardale Rd. SW18 180 DC85
Alma Rd.
Smarden Clo., Belv. 166 FA78
Essenden Rd.
Smarden Gro. SE9 185 EM91
Smart Clo., Rom. 105 FH53
Smart St. E2 143 DX69
Smarts Grn. 66 DT26
(Cheshunt), Wal.Cr.
Smarts Heath La., Wok. 226 AU123
Smarts Heath Rd., Wok. 226 AT123
Smarts La., Loug. 84 EK42
Smarts Pl. N18 100 DU50
Fore St.
Smart's Pl. WC2 274 A8
Smarts Rd., Grav. 191 GH90
Smeaton Clo., Chess. 215 CK107
Mansfield Rd.
Smeaton Clo., Wal.Abb. 68 EE32
Smeaton Rd. SW18 180 DA87
Smeaton Rd., Wdf.Grn. 103 EM50
Smeaton St. E1 142 DV74
Smedley St. SW4 161 DK82
Smedley St. SW8 161 DK82
Smeed Rd. E3 143 EA66
Smiles Pl. SE13 163 EC82
Smith Clo. SE16 143 DX74
Smith Rd., Reig. 265 CZ137
Smith Sq. SW1 277 P7
Smith Sq. SW1 161 DL76
Smith St. SW3 276 D10
Smith St. SW3 160 DF78
Smith St., Surb. 198 CM100
Smith St., Wat. 76 BW42
Smith Ter. SW3 160 DF78
Smitham Bottom La., 219 DJ111
Pur.
Smitham Downs Rd., 219 DK113
Pur.
Smithbarn Clo., Horl. 269 DH147
Tanyard Way
Smithers, The, Bet. 264 CP136
Smithfield, Hem.H. 40 BK18
Smithfield St. EC1 274 F7
Smithies Ct. E15 123 EC64
Clays La.
Smithies Rd. SE2 166 EV77
Smith's Ct. W1 273 L10
Smiths Cres., St.Alb. 44 CQ21
Smiths Fm. Est., Nthlt. 136 CA68
Smiths La., Eden. 255 EQ133
Smiths La. 66 DR26
(Cheshunt), Wal.Cr.
Smiths La., Wind. 151 AL82
Smiths Yd. SW18 180 DC89
Summerley St.
Smith's Yd., Croy. 202 DQ104
St. Georges Wk.
Smithson Rd. N17 100 DR53
Smithwood Clo. SW19 179 CY88
Smithy Clo., Tad. 249 CZ126
Smithy La., Tad. 249 CZ127
Smithy St. E1 142 DW71
Smock Wk., Croy. 202 DQ100
Smoke La., Reig. 266 DB136
Smokehouse Yd. EC1 274 G6
Smug Oak Business Pk., 60 CB30
St.Alb.
Smug Oak La., St.Alb. 60 CB30
Smugglers Wk., Green. 189 FV85
Smugglers Way SW18 160 DB84
Smyrks Rd. SE17 162 DS78
Smyrna Rd. NW6 140 DA66
Smythe Rd. 208 FN95
(Sutton at Hone), Dart.
Smythe St. E14 143 EB73
Snag La., Sev. 223 ER112
Snakely Clo., H.Wyc. 88 AC54
Snakes La., Barn. 81 DJ41
Snakes La. E., Wdf.Grn. 102 EJ51
Snakes La. W., Wdf.Grn. 102 EG51
Snape Spur, Slou. 132 AS72
Snaresbrook Dr., Stan. 95 CK49
Snaresbrook Rd. E11 124 EE56
Snarsgate St. W10 139 CW71
Snatts Hill, Oxt. 254 EF129
Sneath Ave. NW11 119 CZ59
Snelgar Rd., Wok. 226 AY118
Snelling Ave., Grav. 190 GE89
Snellings Rd., Walt. 214 BW106
Snells La., Amer. 72 AV39
Snells Pk. N18 100 DT51
Snells Wd. Ct., Amer. 72 AW40
Sneyd Rd. NW2 119 CW63
Snipe Clo., Erith 167 FG80
Slade Grn. Rd.
Snodland Clo., Orp. 223 EN110
Mill La.
Snow Hill EC1 274 F7
Snow Hill EC1 141 DP71
Snow Hill Ct. EC1 274 G8
Snowbury Rd. SW6 160 DB82
Snowden Ave., Uxb. 135 BP68
Snowden St. EC2 275 M5
Snowden St. EC2 142 DS70
Snowdon Clo., Wind. 151 AK83
Snowdon Cres., Hayes 155 BQ76
Snowdon Dr. NW9 118 CS58
Snowdown Clo. SE20 203 DX95
Snowdrop Clo., Hmptn. 176 CA93
Gresham Rd.
Snowdrop Path, Rom. 106 FK52
Snowerhill Rd., Bet. 264 CS136
Snowhill Cotts., Chesh. 38 AT24
Snowman Ho. NW6 140 DB66
Snowsfields SE1 279 L4
Snowsfields SE1 162 DR75
Snowshill Rd. E12 124 EL64
Snowy Fielder Waye, 157 CH82
Islw.
Soames St. SE15 162 DT83
Soames Wk., N.Mal. 198 CS95
Socket La., Brom. 204 EH100
Soham Rd., Enf. 83 DZ37
Soho Cres., H.Wyc. 110 AD59
Soho Mills Ind. Est., 110 AD59
H.Wyc.
Soho Sq. W1 273 M8
Soho Sq. W1 141 DK72
Soho St. W1 273 M8
Sojourner Truth Clo. E8 142 DV65
Richmond Rd.
Solander Gdns. E1 142 DV73
Dellow St.
Sole Fm. Ave., Lthd. 246 BZ125
Sole Fm. Clo., Lthd. 230 BZ124
Sole Fm. Rd., Lthd. 246 BZ125
Solebay St. E1 143 DY70
Solecote, Lthd. 246 CA125
Solefields Rd., Sev. 257 FH128
Solent Rd. NW6 120 DA64
Solent Rd., Houns. 174 BM86
Soleoak Dr., Sev. 257 FH127
Solesbridge Clo., Rick. 73 BF41
Solesbridge La.
Solesbridge La., Rick. 73 BF41
Soley Ms. WC1 274 D2
Solna Ave. SW15 179 CW85
Solna Rd. N21 100 DR46
Solomons Hill, Rick. 92 BK45
Northway
Solomon's Pas. SE15 162 DV84
Soloms Ct. Rd., Bans. 234 DD117
Solon New Rd. SW4 161 DL84
Solon New Rd. Est. SW4 161 DL84
Solon New Rd.
Solon Rd. SW2 161 DL84
Solway, Hem.H. 40 BM18
Solway Clo. E8 142 DT65
Buttermere Wk.
Solway Clo., Houns. 156 BY83
Solway Rd. N22 99 DP53
Solway Rd. SE22 162 DU84
Somaford Gro., Barn. 80 DD44
Somali Rd. NW2 119 CZ64
Somerby Clo., Brox. 49 EA21
Somerby Rd., Bark. 145 ER66
Somercoates Clo., Barn. 80 DE41
Somerden Rd., Orp. 206 EX101
Somerfield Clo., Tad. 233 CY119
Somerfield Rd. N4 121 DP61
Somerford Clo., Pnr. 115 BU56
Somerford Gro. N16 122 DT63
Somerford Gro. N17 100 DU52
Somerford Gro. Est. N16 122 DT63
Somerford Gro.
Somerford St. E1 142 DV70
Somerford Way SE16 163 DY75
Somerhill Ave., Sid. 186 EV87
Somerhill Rd., Well. 166 EV82
Someries Rd., Hem.H. 39 BF18
Somerleyton Pas. SW9 161 DP84
Somerleyton Rd. SW9 161 DN84
Somers Clo. NW1 141 DK68
Platt St.
Somers Clo., Reig. 250 DA133
Somers Cres. W2 272 B9
Somers Cres. W2 140 DE72
Somers Ms. W2 272 B9
Somers Pl. SW2 181 DM87
Somers Rd. E17 123 DZ56
Somers Rd. SW2 181 DM86
Somers Rd., Hat. 45 CW24
Somers Rd., Reig. 249 CZ133
Somers Sq., Hat. 45 CW23
Somers Way 94 CC45
(Bushey), Wat.
Somersby Gdns., Ilf. 125 EM57
Somerset Ave. SW20 199 CV96
Somerset Ave., Chess. 215 CK105
Somerset Ave., Well. 185 ET85
Somerset Clo. N17 100 DR54
Lordship La.
Somerset Clo., Epsom 216 CR109
Somerset Clo., N.Mal. 198 CS100
Somerset Clo., Walt. 213 BV106
Queens Rd.
Somerset Clo., Wdf.Grn. 102 EG53
Somerset Est. SW11 160 DD81
Somerset Gdns. N6 120 DG59
Somerset Gdns. SE13 163 EB82
Somerset Gdns. SW16 201 DM97
Somerset Gdns., Horn. 128 FN60
Somerset Gdns., Tedd. 177 CE92
Somerset Rd. E17 123 EA57
Somerset Rd. N17 122 DT55
Somerset Rd. N18 100 DT50
Somerset Rd. NW4 119 CW56
Somerset Rd. SW19 179 CX90
Somerset Rd. W4 158 CR76
Somerset Rd. W13 137 CH74
Somerset Rd., Barn. 80 DB43
Somerset Rd., Brent. 157 CK79
Somerset Rd., Dart. 187 FH86
Somerset Rd., Enf. 83 EA38
Somerset Rd., Har. 116 CC58
Somerset Rd., Kings.T. 198 CM96
Somerset Rd., Orp. 206 EU101
Somerset Rd., Red. 266 DD136
Somerset Rd., Sthl. 136 BZ72
Somerset Rd., Tedd. 177 CE92
Somerset Sq. W14 159 CY75
Somerset Way, Iver 153 BF75
Somerset Waye, Houns. 156 BY80
Somersham, Welw.G.C. 30 DD09
Somersham Rd., Bexh. 166 EY82
Somerswey, Guil. 258 AY142
Somerton Ave., Rich. 158 CP83
Somerton Clo., Pur. 235 DN115
Somerton Rd. NW2 119 CX62
Somerton Rd. SE15 162 DV84
Somertons Clo., Guil. 242 AU131
Somertrees Ave. SE12 184 EH89
Somervell Rd., Har. 116 BZ64
Somerville Rd. SE20 183 DX94
Somerville Rd., Cob. 214 CA114
Somerville Rd., Dart. 188 FM86
Somerville Rd., Rom. 126 EW58
Somerville Rd. 151 AQ78
(Eton), Wind.
Sonderburg Rd. N7 121 DM62
Seven Sisters Rd.
Sondes Pl. Dr., Dor. 263 CF136
Sondes St. SE17 162 DR79
Sonia Clo., Wat. 94 BW45
Sonia Ct., Har. 117 CF58
Sonia Gdns. N12 98 DC49
Woodside Ave.
Sonia Gdns. NW10 119 CT63
Sonia Gdns., Houns. 156 CA80
Sonnet Wk., West. 238 EH118
Kings Rd.
Sonnets, The, Hem.H. 40 BH19
Laureate Way
Sonning Gdns., Hmptn. 176 BY93
Sonning Rd. SE25 202 DU100
Soothouse Spring, 43 CF16
St.Alb.
Soper Clo. E4 101 DZ50
Sopers Rd. 65 DM29
(Cuffley), Pot.B.
Sophia Clo. N7 141 DM65
Mackenzie Rd.
Sophia Rd. E10 123 EB60
Sophia Rd. E16 144 EH72
Sophia Sq. SE16 143 DY73
Rotherhithe St.
Sopwell La., St.Alb. 43 CD21
Sopwith Ave., Chess. 216 CL106
Sopwith Clo., Kings.T. 178 CM92
Park Rd.
Sopwith Clo., West. 238 EK116
Sopwith Dr., W.Byf. 212 BL112
Sopwith Dr., Wey. 212 BL111
Sopwith Rd., Houns. 156 BW80
Sopwith Way SW8 161 DH80
Queenstown Rd.
Sopwith Way, Kings.T. 198 CL95
Sorbie Clo., Wey. 213 BR107
Sorrel Bank, Croy. 221 DY110
Sorrel Clo. SE28 146 EU74
Sorrel Ct., Grays 170 GD79
Salix Rd.
Sorrel Gdns. E6 144 EL71
Sorrel La. E14 143 ED72
Sorrel Wk., Rom. 127 FF55
Sorrel Way, Grav. 190 GE91
Sorrell Clo. SE14 163 DY80
Southerngate Way
Sorrento Rd., Sutt. 200 DA104
Sospel Ct., Slou. 131 AQ68
Sotheby Rd. N5 122 DQ62
Sotheran Clo. E8 142 DU67
Sotheron Rd. SW6 160 DB80
Sotheron Rd., Wat. 76 BW41
Soudan Rd. SW11 160 DF81
Souldern Rd. W14 159 CX76
Souldern St., Wat. 75 BV43
Sounds Lo., Swan. 207 FC100
South Access Rd. E17 123 DY59
South Acre NW9 97 CT54
South Africa Rd. W12 139 CV74
South Albert Rd., Reig. 249 CZ133
South App., Nthwd. 93 BR48
South Audley St. W1 276 G1
South Audley St. W1 140 DG73
South Ave. E4 101 EB45
South Ave., Cars. 218 DG108
South Ave., Egh. 173 BC93
South Ave., Rich. 157 CK81
Sandycombe Rd.
South Ave., Sthl. 136 BZ73
South Ave., Walt. 213 BS110
South Ave. Gdns., Sthl. 136 BZ73
South Bank, Chis. 185 EQ90
South Bank, Surb. 198 CL100
South Bank, West. 255 ER126
South Bank Rd., Berk. 38 AT17
South Bank Ter., Surb. 198 CL100
South Birkbeck Rd. E11 123 ED62
South Black Lion La. W6 159 CU78
South Bolton Gdns. SW5 160 DB78
South Border, The, Pur. 219 DK111
South Carriage Dr. SW1 160 DE75
South Carriage Dr. SW7 276 B4
South Carriage Dr. SW7 160 DE75
South Clo. N6 121 DH58
South Clo., Barn. 79 CZ41
South Clo., Bexh. 166 EX84
South Clo., Dag. 146 FA67
South Clo., Mord. 200 DB100
Green La.
South Clo., Pnr. 116 BZ59
South Clo., St.Alb. 60 CB25
South Clo., Slou. 131 AK73
St. George's Cres.
South Clo., Twick. 176 CA90
South Clo., West Dr. 154 BM76
South Clo., Wok. 226 AW116
South Clo. Grn., Red. 251 DH129
South Colonnade E14 143 EA74
South Common Rd., 134 BL65
Uxb.
South Cottage Dr., Rick. 73 BF43
South Cottage Gdns., 73 BF43
Rick.
South Countess Rd. E17 123 DZ55
South Cres. E16 143 ED70
Cody Rd.
South Cres. WC1 273 M7
South Cres. WC1 141 DK71
South Cft., Egh. 172 AV92
Bond St.
South Cross Rd., Ilf. 125 EQ57
South Croxted Rd. SE21 182 DR90
South Dene NW7 96 CR48
South Dr., Bans. 218 DE113
South Dr., Beac. 110 AH55
South Dr., Brwd. 108 FX49
South Dr., Couls. 235 DK115
South Dr., Dor. 263 CJ136
South Dr., Orp. 223 ES106
South Dr. 65 DL30
(Cuffley), Pot.B.
South Dr., Rom. 128 FJ55
South Dr., Ruis. 115 BS60
South Dr., St.Alb. 43 CK20
South Dr., Sutt. 217 CY110
South Dr., Vir.W. 192 AU102
South Ealing Rd. W5 157 CK75
South Eastern Ave. N9 100 DT48

South Eaton Pl. SW1 276 **G8**
South Eaton Pl. SW1 160 DG77
South Eden Pk. Rd., Beck. 203 EB100
South Edwardes Sq. W8 159 CZ76
South End W8 160 DB76
St. Albans Gro.
South End, Croy. 220 DQ105
South End, Lthd. 246 CB126
South End Clo. NW3 120 DE63
South End Rd. NW3 120 DE63
South End Rd., Horn. 147 FH65
South End Rd., Rain. 147 FG68
South End Row W8 160 DB76
South Esk Rd. E7 144 EJ65
South Gdns. SW19 180 DD94
South Gate, Harl. 51 ER15
South Gate Ave., Felt. 175 BR91
South Gipsy Rd., Well. 166 EX83
South Glade, The, Bex. 186 EZ88
Camden Rd.
South Grn. NW9 96 CS53
Clayton Fld.
South Grn., Slou. 132 AS73
South Gro. E17 123 DZ57
South Gro. N6 120 DG60
South Gro. N15 122 DR57
South Gro., Cher. 193 BF100
South Gro. Ho. N6 120 DG60
Highgate W. Hill
South Hall Clo., Dart. 208 FM101
South Hall Dr., Rain. 147 FH71
South Hill, Chis. 185 EM93
South Hill, Guil. 258 AX136
South Hill Ave., Har. 116 CC62
South Hill Gro., Har. 117 CE63
South Hill Pk. NW3 120 DE63
South Hill Pk. Gdns. NW3 120 DE63
South Hill Rd., Brom. 204 EE97
South Hill Rd., Grav. 191 GH88
South Hill Rd., Hem.H. 40 BJ20
South Huxley N18 100 DR50
South Island Pl. SW9 161 DM80
South Kensington Sta. Arc. SW7 160 DD77
Pelham St.
South Kent Ave., Grav. 190 GC87
South Lambeth Pl. SW8 161 DL79
South Lambeth Rd. SW8 161 DL79
South La., Kings.T. 197 CK97
South La., N.Mal. 198 CR98
South La. W., N.Mal. 198 CR98
South Ley, Welw.G.C. 29 CY12
South Lo. Ave., Mitch. 201 DL98
South Lo. Cres., Enf. 81 DK42
South Lo. Dr. N14 81 DK42
South Mall N9 100 DU48
Plevna Rd.
South Mead NW9 97 CT53
South Mead, Epsom 216 CS108
South Mead, Red. 250 DF131
South Meadow La., Wind. 151 AQ79
South Meadows, Wem. 118 CL64
South Molton La. W1 273 **H9**
South Molton La. W1 141 DH72
South Molton Rd. E16 144 EG72
South Molton St. W1 273 **H9**
South Molton St. W1 141 DH72
South Mundells, Welw.G.C. 29 CZ08
South Norwood Hill SE25 202 DS95
South Oak Rd. SW16 181 DM91
South Par. SW3 276 **A10**
South Par. SW3 160 DD78
South Par. W4 158 CR77
South Par., Wal.Abb. 67 EC33
Sun St.
South Pk. SW6 160 DA82
South Pk., Ger.Cr. 113 AZ57
South Pk., Sev. 257 FH125
South Pk. Ave., Rick. 73 BF43
South Pk. Cres. SE6 184 EF88
South Pk. Cres., Ger.Cr. 112 AY56
South Pk. Cres., Ilf. 125 ER62
South Pk. Dr., Bark. 125 ES62
South Pk. Dr., Ger.Cr. 112 AY56
South Pk. Dr., Ilf. 125 ES61
South Pk. Gdns., Berk. 38 AV17
South Pk. Gro., N.Mal. 198 CQ98
South Pk. Hill Rd., S.Croy. 220 DR106
South Pk. Ms. SW6 160 DB83
South Pk. Rd. SW19 180 DA93
South Pk. Rd., Ilf. 125 ER62
South Pk. Ter., Ilf. 125 ES62
South Pk. Vw., Ger.Cr. 113 AZ56
South Pk. Way, Ruis. 136 BW65
South Path, Wind. 151 AQ81
South Penge Pk. Est. SE20 202 DV96
South Perimeter Rd., Uxb. 134 BL69
Kingston La.
South Pier Rd., Gat. 269 DH152
South Pl. EC2 275 **L7**
South Pl. EC2 142 DR71
South Pl., Enf. 82 DW43
South Pl., Harl. 36 EU12
South Rd.
South Pl., Surb. 198 CM101
South Pl. Ms. EC2 275 **L7**
South Ridge, Wey. 213 BP110
South Riding, St.Alb. 60 CA30
South Ri., Cars. 218 DE109
South Ri. Way SE18 165 ER78
Elmley St.
South Rd. N9 100 DU46
South Rd. SE23 183 DX89
South Rd. SW19 180 DC93
South Rd. W5 157 CK77
South Rd., Amer. 55 AQ36
South Rd., Edg. 96 CP53
South Rd., Egh. 172 AW93
South Rd., Erith 167 FF80
South Rd., Felt. 176 BX92
South Rd., Guil. 242 AV132
South Rd., Hmptn. 176 BY93
South Rd., Harl. 36 EU12
South Rd., Reig. 266 DB135
South Rd., Rick. 73 BC43
South Rd. (Chadwell Heath), Rom. 126 EY58
South Rd. (Little Heath), Rom. 126 EV57
South Rd., S.Ock. 149 FW70
South Rd., Sthl. 156 BZ75
South Rd., Twick. 177 CD90
South Rd., West Dr. 154 BN76
South Rd., Wey. 213 BQ106
South Rd. (St. George's Hill), Wey. 212 BN110
South Rd., Wok. 210 AX114
South Row SE3 164 EF82
South Sea St. SE16 163 DZ76
South Side W6 159 CT76
South Spur, Slou. 153 BC75
South Sq. NW11 120 DB58
South Sq. WC1 274 **D7**
South Sta. App., Red. 267 DL136
South St. W1 276 **G2**
South St. W1 140 DG74
South St., Brwd. 108 FW47
South St., Brom. 204 EG96
South St., Dor. 263 CG137
South St., Enf. 82 DW43
South St., Epsom 216 CR113
South St., Grav. 191 GH87
South St., Hert. 32 DR09
South St., Islw. 157 CG83
South St., Rain. 147 FC68
South St., Rom. 127 FE57
South St., Stai. 173 BF92
South St., Ware 33 EC11
South Tenter St. E1 142 DT73
South Ter. SW7 276 **B8**
South Ter. SW7 160 DE77
South Ter., Dor. 263 CH137
South Ter., Surb. 198 CL100
South Vale SE19 182 DS93
South Vale, Har. 117 CE63
South Vw., Brom. 204 EH96
South Vw. Ave., Til. 171 GG81
South Vw. Ct., Wok. 226 AY118
Constitution Hill
South Vw. Dr. E18 124 EH55
South Vw. Dr., Upmin. 128 FN62
South Vw. Rd. N8 121 DK55
South Vw. Rd., Ash. 231 CK119
South Vw. Rd., Dart. 188 FK90
South Vw. Rd., Ger.Cr. 112 AX56
South Vw. Rd., Grays 169 FW79
South Vw. Rd., Loug. 85 EM44
South Vw. Rd., Pnr. 93 BV51
South Vill. NW1 141 DK65
South Wk., Hayes 135 BR71
Middleton Rd.
South Wk., Reig. 250 DB134
Church St.
South Wk., W.Wick. 204 EE104
South Way N9 100 DW47
South Way N11 99 DJ51
Ringway
South Way, Abb.L. 59 BR33
South Way, Beac. 110 AG55
South Way, Brom. 204 EG101
South Way, Cars. 218 DD110
South Way, Croy. 203 DY104
South Way, Har. 116 CA56
South Way, Purf. 169 FS76
South Way, Wem. 118 CN64
South Weald Dr., Wal.Abb. 67 ED33
South Weald Rd., Brwd. 108 FU48
South W. India Dock Entrance E14 163 EC75
South Western Rd., Twick. 177 CG86
South Wf. Rd. W2 140 DD72
South Woodford to Barking Relief Rd. E11 124 EJ55
South Woodford to Barking Relief Rd. E12 125 EN63
South Woodford to Barking Relief Rd. E18 124 EJ55
South Woodford to Barking Relief Rd., Bark. 125 EN63
South Woodford to Barking Relief Rd., Ilf. 124 EJ55
South Worple Ave. SW14 158 CS83
South Worple Way
South Worple Way SW14 158 CR83
Southacre Way, Pnr. 94 BW53
Southall Clo., Ware 33 DX05
Southall La., Houns. 155 BV79
Southall Pl. SE1 279 **K5**
Southall Pl. SE1 162 DR75
Southall Way, Brwd. 108 FT49
Southam St. W10 139 CY70
Southampton Bldgs. WC2 274 **D7**
Southampton Gdns., Mitch. 201 DL99
Southampton Pl. WC1 274 **A7**
Southampton Pl. WC1 141 DL71
Southampton Rd. NW5 120 DF64
Southampton Rd., Houns. 174 BL86
Southampton Row WC1 274 **A6**
Southampton Row WC1 141 DL71
Southampton St. WC2 274 **A10**
Southampton St. WC2 141 DL73
Southampton Way SE5 162 DR80
Southbank, T.Ditt. 197 CH101
Southborough Clo., Surb. 197 CK102
Southborough La., Brom. 204 EL99
Southborough Rd. E9 143 DX66
Southborough Rd., Brom. 204 EL97
Southborough Rd., Surb. 198 CL102
Southbourne, Brom. 204 EG101
Southbourne Ave. NW9 96 CQ54
Southbourne Clo., Pnr. 116 BY59
Southbourne Cres. NW4 119 CY56
Southbourne Gdns. SE12 184 EH85
Southbourne Gdns., Ilf. 125 EQ64
Southbourne Gdns., Ruis. 115 BV60
Southbridge Pl., Croy. 220 DQ105
Southbridge Rd., Croy. 220 DQ105
Southbridge Way, Sthl. 156 BY75
Southbrook, Saw. 36 EY06
Southbrook Dr. (Cheshunt), Wal.Cr. 67 DX28
Southbrook Ms. SE12 184 EF86
Southbrook Rd. SE12 184 EF86
Southbrook Rd. SW16 201 DL95
Southbury Ave., Enf. 82 DU43
Southbury Clo., Horn. 128 FK64
Southbury Rd., Enf. 82 DR41
Southchurch Rd. E6 145 EM68
Southcliffe Dr., Ger.Cr. 90 AY50
Southcombe St. W14 159 CY77
Southcote, Wok. 226 AX115
Southcote Ave., Felt. 175 BT89
Southcote Ave., Surb. 198 CP101
Southcote Ri., Ruis. 115 BR59
Southcote Rd. E17 123 DX57
Southcote Rd. N19 121 DJ63
Southcote Rd. SE25 202 DV99
Southcote Rd., Red. 251 DJ129
Southcote Rd., S.Croy. 220 DS110
Southcroft, Slou. 131 AP70
Southcroft Ave., Well. 165 ES83
Southcroft Ave., W.Wick. 203 EC103
Southcroft Rd. SW16 181 DH93
Southcroft Rd. SW17 180 DG93
Southcroft Rd., Orp. 205 ES104
Southdale, Chig. 103 ER51
Southdean Gdns. SW19 179 CZ89
Southdene, Sev. 224 EZ113
Southdown Ave. W7 157 CG76
Southdown Ct., Hat. 45 CU21
Southdown Cres., Har. 116 CC60
Southdown Cres., Ilf. 125 ES57
Southdown Dr. SW20 179 CX94
Crescent Rd.
Southdown Rd. SW20 199 CX95
Southdown Rd., Cars. 218 DG109
Southdown Rd., Cat. 237 DZ122
Southdown Rd., Hat. 45 CU21
Southdown Rd., Horn. 127 FH59
Southdown Rd., Walt. 214 BY105
Southdowns (South Darenth), Dart. 209 FR96
Skinney La.
Southend Arterial Rd., Brwd. 129 FW57
Southend Arterial Rd., Horn. 128 FL55
Southend Arterial Rd., Rom. 106 FK54
Southend Arterial Rd., Upmin. 128 FP56
Southend Clo. SE9 185 EP86
Southend Cres. SE9 185 EP86
Southend La. SE6 183 EA91
Southend La. SE26 183 DZ91
Southend La., Wal.Abb. 68 EH34
Southend Rd. E4 101 DZ51
Southend Rd. E6 145 EM66
Southend Rd. E17 101 ED53
Southend Rd. E18 102 EF54
Southend Rd., Beck. 183 EA94
Southend Rd., Grays 170 GC77
Southend Rd., Wdf.Grn. 102 EJ54
Southerland Clo., Wey. 213 BQ105
Southern Ave. SE25 202 DT97
Southern Ave., Felt. 175 BU88
Southern Ave., Red. 266 DG142
Southern Dr., Loug. 85 EM44
Southern Gro. E3 143 DZ69
Southern Lo., Harl. 51 EQ18
Southern Perimeter Rd., Houns. 174 BJ85
Southern Pl., Swan. 207 FD98
Southern Rd. E13 144 EH68
Southern Rd. N2 120 DF56
Southern Row W10 139 CY70
Southern St. N1 141 DM68
Southern Way, Harl. 51 EN18
Southern Way, Rom. 126 FA58
Southerngate Way SE14 163 DY80
Southernhay, Loug. 84 EK42
Southerns La., Couls. 234 DD124
Southernwood Clo., Hem.H. 40 BN19
Southerton Rd. W6 159 CW76
Southey Rd. N15 122 DS57
Southey Rd. SW9 161 DN81
Southey Rd. SW19 180 DA94
Southey St. SE20 183 DX94
Southey Wk., Til. 171 GH81
Southfield, Barn. 79 CX44
Southfield, Welw.G.C. 29 CX11
Southfield Ave., Wat. 76 BW38
Southfield Clo., Uxb. 134 BN69
Southfield Clo., Wind. 150 AJ76
Southfield Cotts. W7 157 CF75
Oaklands Rd.
Southfield Gdns., Slou. 130 AH71
Southfield Gdns., Twick. 177 CF91
Southfield Pk., Har. 116 CB56
Southfield Pl., Wey. 213 BP108
Southfield Rd. N17 100 DS54
Southfield Rd. W4 158 CR75
Southfield Rd., Chis. 205 ET97
Southfield Rd., Enf. 82 DV44
Southfield Rd., Hodd. 49 EA16
Southfield Rd., Wal.Cr. 67 DY32
Southfield Way, St.Alb. 43 CK17
Southfields NW4 119 CV55
Southfields, E.Mol. 197 CE100
Southfields, Swan. 187 FE94
Claremont Rd.
Southfields Ave., Ashf. 175 BP93
Southfields Ct. SW19 179 CY88
Southfields Pas. SW18 180 DA86
Southfields Rd.
Southfields Rd. SW18 180 DA86
Southfields Rd., Cat. 237 EB124
Southfleet Rd., Dart. 189 FW91
Southfleet Rd., Grav. 191 GF89
Southfleet Rd., Orp. 205 ES104
Southfleet Rd., Swans. 190 FZ87
Southgate, Purf. 168 FQ77
Southgate Ave., Felt. 175 BR91
Southgate Circ. N14 99 DK46
The Bourne
Southgate Gro. N1 142 DR66
Southgate Rd. N1 142 DR67
Southgate Rd., Barn. 80 DD35
Southgate Rd., Pot.B. 64 DC33
Southholme Clo. SE19 202 DT95
Southill La., Pnr. 115 BV56
Southill Rd., Chis. 184 EL93
Southill St. E14 143 EB72
Chrisp St.
Southland Rd. SE18 165 ET80
Southland Way, Houns. 177 CD85
Southlands Ave., Horl. 268 DG147
Southlands Ave., Orp. 223 ER105
Southlands Clo., Couls. 235 DM117
Southlands Gro., Brom. 204 EL97
Southlands La., Oxt. 253 EB134
Southlands Rd., Brom. 204 EJ99
Southlands Rd., Uxb. 113 BF62
Southlea, Wind. 152 AU84
Southlea Rd., Slou. 152 AV81
Southly Clo., Sutt. 200 DA104
Southmead Cres. (Cheshunt), Wal.Cr. 67 DY30
Southmead Rd. SW19 179 CY88
Southmont Rd., Esher 197 CE103
Southmoor Way E9 143 DZ65
Southold Ri. SE9 185 EM90
Southolm St. SW11 161 DH81
Southover N12 98 DA48
Southover, Brom. 184 EG92
Southport Rd. SE18 165 ER77
Southridge Pl. SW20 179 CX94
Southsea Ave., Wat. 75 BU42
Southsea Rd., Kings.T. 198 CL98
Southside, Ger.Cr. 112 AX55
Southside Common SW19 179 CW93
Southspring, Sid. 185 ER87
Southvale Rd. SE3 164 EE82
Southview Ave. NW10 119 CT64
Southview Clo. SW17 180 DG92
Rectory La.
Southview Clo., Bex. 186 EZ86
Southview Clo., Swan. 207 FG98
Southview Clo. (Cheshunt), Wal.Cr. 66 DS26
Southview Cres., Ilf. 125 EP58
Southview Gdns., Wall. 219 DJ108
Southview Rd., Brom. 183 ED91
Southview Rd., Cat. 237 EB124
Southview Rd., Warl. 236 DV119
Southviews, S.Croy. 221 DX109
Southville SW8 161 DK81
Southville Clo., Epsom 216 CR109
Southville Clo., Felt. 175 BS88
Southville Cres., Felt. 175 BS88
Southville Rd., Felt. 175 BS88
Southville Rd., T.Ditt. 197 CG101
Southwark Bri. EC4 279 **J1**
Southwark Bri. EC4 142 DQ74
Southwark Bri. SE1 279 **J1**
Southwark Bri. SE1 142 DQ74
Southwark Bri. Rd. SE1 279 **H5**
Southwark Bri. Rd. SE1 161 DP76
Southwark Gro. SE1 279 **H3**
Southwark Pk. Est. SE16 162 DV77
Southwark Pk. Rd. SE16 162 DT77
Southwark Pl., Brom. 205 EM97
St. Georges Rd.
Southwark St. SE1 278 **G2**
Southwark St. SE1 141 DP74
Southwater Clo. E14 143 DZ72
Southwater Clo., Beck. 183 EB94
Southway N20 98 DA47
Southway NW7 97 CU52
Southway NW11 120 DB57
Southway SW20 199 CW98
Southway, Guil. 242 AS134
Southway, Hat. 45 CU22
Southway, Wall. 219 DJ105
Southway Ct., Guil. 242 AS134
Southwell Ave., Nthlt. 136 CA65
Southwell Gdns. SW7 160 DC77
Southwell Gro. Rd. E11 124 EE61
Southwell Rd. SE5 162 DQ83
Southwell Rd., Croy. 201 DN100
Southwell Rd., Har. 117 CK58
Southwest Rd. E11 123 ED60
Southwick Ms. W2 272 **A8**
Southwick Pl. W2 272 **B9**
Southwick Pl. W2 140 DE72
Southwick St. W2 272 **B8**
Southwick St. W2 140 DE72
Southwold Dr., Bark. 126 EU64
Southwold Rd. E5 122 DV61
Southwold Rd., Bex. 187 FB86
Southwold Rd., Wat. 76 BW38
Southwold Spur, Slou. 153 BC75
Southwood Ave. N6 121 DH59
Southwood Ave., Cher. 211 BC108
Southwood Ave., Couls. 235 DJ115
Southwood Ave., Kings.T. 198 CQ95
Southwood Clo., Brom. 205 EM98
Southwood Clo., Wor.Pk. 199 CX102
Carters Clo.
Southwood Dr., Surb. 198 CQ101
Southwood Gdns., Esher 197 CG104
Southwood Gdns., Ilf. 125 EP56
Southwood La. N6 120 DG59
Southwood Lawn Rd. N6 120 DG59
Southwood Rd. SE9 185 EP89
Southwood Rd. SE28 146 EV74
Southwood Smith St. N1 141 DN67
Barford St.
Soval Ct., Nthwd. 93 BR52
Sovereign Clo. E1 142 DV73
Sovereign Clo. W5 137 CJ71
Sovereign Clo., Ruis. 115 BS60
Sovereign Ct., Brom. 205 EM99
Sovereign Cres. SE16 143 DY74
Rotherhithe St.
Sovereign Gro., Wem. 117 CK62
Sovereign Ms. E2 142 DT68
Pearson St.
Sovereign Pk. NW10 138 CP70
Sovereign Pl., Kings L. 58 BN29
Sowerby Clo. SE9 184 EL85
Sowrey Ave., Rain. 147 FF65
Soyer Ct., Wok. 226 AS118
Raglan Rd.
Spa Clo. SE25 202 DS95
Spa Dr., Epsom 216 CN114
Spa Grn. Est. EC1 274 **E2**
Spa Hill SE19 202 DR95
Spa Rd. SE16 279 **P7**
Spa Rd. SE16 162 DT76
Space Waye, Felt. 175 BU85
Spackmans Way, Slou. 151 AQ76
Spafield St. EC1 274 **D4**
Spalding Rd. NW4 119 CW58
Spalding Rd. SW17 181 DH92
Spalt Clo., Brwd. 109 GB47
Spanby Rd. E3 143 EA70
Spaniards Clo. NW11 120 DD60
Spaniards End NW3 120 DC60
Spaniards Rd. NW3 120 DC62
Spanish Pl. W1 272 **G8**
Spanish Pl. W1 140 DG72
Spanish Rd. SW18 180 DC85
Spareleaze Hill, Loug. 84 EL43
Sparepenny La. (Eynsford), Dart. 208 FK103
Sparkbridge Rd., Har. 117 CE56
Sparks Clo. W3 138 CR72
Joseph Ave.
Sparks Clo., Dag. 126 EX61
Green La.
Sparks Clo., Hmptn. 176 BY93
Victors Dr.
Sparrow Clo., Hmptn. 176 BY93
Sparrow Dr., Orp. 205 EQ102
Sparrow Fm. Dr., Felt. 176 BW86
Sparrow Fm. Rd., Epsom 217 CU105
Sparrow Grn., Dag. 127 FB62
Sparrows Herne (Bushey), Wat. 94 CB45
Sparrows La. SE9 185 EQ87
Sparrows Mead, Red. 250 DG131
Sparrows Way (Bushey), Wat. 94 CC46
Sparrows Herne
Sparrowswick Ride, St.Alb. 42 CC15
Sparsholt Rd. N19 121 DM60
Sparsholt Rd., Bark. 145 ES67
Sparta St. SE10 163 EC81
Spear Ms. SW5 160 DA77
Spearman St. SE18 165 EN79
Spearpoint Gdns., Ilf. 125 ET56
Spears Rd. N19 121 DL60
Speart La., Houns. 156 BY80
Spedan Clo. NW3 120 DB62
Speed Ho. EC2 142 DR71
Silk St.
Speedgate Hill (Fawkham), Long. 209 FU103
Speedwell Clo., Guil. 243 BC131
Speedwell Clo., Hem.H. 39 BE21
Campion Rd.
Speedwell Ct., Grays 170 GE80
Speedwell St. SE8 163 EA80
Comet St.
Speedy Pl. WC1 273 **P3**
Speer Rd., T.Ditt. 197 CF101
Speke Ho. SE5 162 DQ80
Speke Rd., Th.Hth. 202 DR96
Spekehill SE9 185 EM90
Speldhurst Clo., Brom. 204 EG99
Speldhurst Rd. E9 143 DX66
Speldhurst Rd. W4 158 CR76
Spellbrook Wk. N1 142 DQ67
Basire St.
Spelman St. E1 142 DU71
Spelthorne Gro., Sun. 175 BT94
Spelthorne La., Ashf. 195 BQ95
Spence Ave., W.Byf. 212 BL114
Spence Clo. SE16 163 DZ75
Vaughan St.
Spencer Ave. N13 99 DM51
Spencer Ave., Hayes 135 BU71
Spencer Ave. (Cheshunt), Wal.Cr. 66 DS26
Spencer Clo. N3 98 DA54
Spencer Clo. NW10 138 CM69
Spencer Clo., Epsom 232 CS119
Spencer Clo., Orp. 205 ES103
Spencer Clo., Uxb. 134 BJ69
Spencer Clo., Wok. 211 BC113
Spencer Clo., Wdf.Grn. 102 EJ50
Spencer Ct. NW8 140 DC68
Marlborough Pl.
Spencer Dr. N2 120 DC58
Spencer Gdns. SE9 185 EM85
Spencer Gdns. SW14 178 CQ85
Spencer Gdns., Egh. 172 AX92
Spencer Gate, St.Alb. 43 CE18
Spencer Hill SW19 179 CY93
Spencer Hill Rd. SW19 179 CY94
Spencer Ms. W6 159 CY79
Greyhound Rd.
Spencer Pk. SW18 180 DD85
Spencer Pas. E2 142 DV68
Pritchard's Rd.
Spencer Pl. N1 141 DP66
Canonbury La.
Spencer Pl., Croy. 202 DR101
Gloucester Rd.
Spencer Ri. NW5 121 DH63
Spencer Rd. E6 144 EK67
Spencer Rd. E17 101 EC54
Spencer Rd. N8 121 DM57
Spencer Rd. N11 99 DH49
Spencer Rd. N17 100 DU53
Spencer Rd. SW18 160 DD84
Spencer Rd. SW20 199 CV95
Spencer Rd. W3 138 CQ74
Spencer Rd. W4 158 CQ80
Spencer Rd., Brom. 184 EF94
Spencer Rd., Cat. 236 DR121
Spencer Rd., Cob. 229 BV115
Spencer Rd., E.Mol. 197 CD98
Spencer Rd., Har. 95 CE54
Spencer Rd., Ilf. 125 ET60
Spencer Rd., Islw. 156 CC81
Spencer Rd., Mitch. 200 DG97
Spencer Rd. (Beddington), Mitch. 200 DG101
Spencer Rd., Rain. 147 FD69
Spencer Rd., Slou. 153 AZ76
Spencer Rd., S.Croy. 220 DS106
Spencer Rd., Twick. 177 CE90
Spencer Rd., Wem. 117 CJ61
Spencer St. EC1 274 **F3**
Spencer St. EC1 141 DP69
Spencer St., Grav. 191 GG87
Spencer St., Hert. 32 DS08
Spencer St., St.Alb. 43 CD20
Spencer St., Sthl. 156 BX75
Spencer Wk. NW3 120 DC63
Hampstead High St.
Spencer Wk. SW15 159 CX84
Spencer Wk., Rick. 74 BJ43
Spencer Wk., Til. 171 GG82
Spencer Way, Hem.H. 40 BG17
Fennycroft Rd.
Spencer Way, Red. 266 DG139
Spencers Cft., Harl. 52 EV17
Spenser Ave., Wey. 212 BN109
Spenser Cres., Upmin. 128 FQ59
Spenser Gro. N16 122 DS63
Spenser Rd. SE24 181 DN85
Spenser St. SW1 277 **L6**
Spenser St. SW1 161 DJ76
Spensley Wk. N16 122 DR62
Clissold Rd.
Speranza St. SE18 165 ET78
Sperling Rd. N17 100 DS54
Spert St. E14 143 DY73
Spey St. E14 143 EC71
Spey Way, Rom. 105 FE52
Speyside N14 81 DJ44
Spezia Rd. NW10 139 CU68
Sphere Ind. Est., St.Alb. 43 CG21
Spicer Clo. SW9 161 DP82
Spicer Clo., Walt. 196 BW100
Spicer St., St.Alb. 42 CC20

Standard Rd., Bexh. 166 EY84
Standard Rd., Enf. 83 DY37
Standard Rd., Houns. 156 BY83
Standard Rd., Orp. 223 EN110
Standen Ave., Horn. 128 FK62
Standen Rd. SW18 179 CZ87
Standfield, Abb.L. 59 BS31
Standfield Gdns., Dag. 146 FA65
Standfield Rd.
Standfield Rd., Dag. 126 FA64
Standingford, Harl. 51 EP20
Phelips Rd.
Standish Rd. W6 159 CU77
Standlake Pt. SE23 183 DX90
Standring Ri., Hem.H. 40 BH23
Stane Clo. SW19 200 DB95
Hayward Clo.
Stane St., Dor. 247 CK128
Stane St., Lthd. 232 CM124
Reigate Rd.
Stane Way SE18 164 EL80
Stane Way, Epsom 217 CU110
Stanfield Rd. E3 143 DY68
Stanford Clo., Hmptn. 176 BZ93
Stanford Clo., Rom. 127 FB58
Stanford Clo., Ruis. 115 BQ58
Stanford Clo., Wdf.Grn. 102 EL50
Stanford Ct., Wal.Abb. 68 EG33
Stanford Gdns., S.Ock. 149 FS74
Stanford Ho., Bark. 146 EV68
Stanford Pl. SE17 279 M9
Stanford Rd. N11 98 DF50
Stanford Rd. SW16 201 DK96
Stanford Rd. W8 160 DB76
Stanford Rd., Grays 170 GD76
Stanford St. SW1 277 M9
Stanford Way SW16 201 DK96
Stangate Cres., Borwd. 78 CR43
Stangate Gdns., Stan. 95 CH49
Stanger Rd. SE25 202 DU98
Stanham Pl., Dart. 167 FG84
Crayford Way
Stanham Rd., Dart. 188 FJ85
Stanhope Ave. N3 119 CZ55
Stanhope Ave., Brom. 204 EF102
Stanhope Ave., Har. 95 CD53
Stanhope Clo. SE16 163 DX75
Middleton Dr.
Stanhope Gdns. N4 121 DP58
Stanhope Gdns. N6 121 DH58
Stanhope Gdns. NW7 97 CT50
Stanhope Gdns. SW7 160 DC77
Stanhope Gdns., Dag. 126 EZ62
Stanhope Rd.
Stanhope Gdns., Ilf. 125 EM60
Stanhope Gate W1 276 G2
Stanhope Gate W1 140 DG74
Stanhope Gro., Beck. 203 DZ99
Stanhope Heath, Stai. 174 BJ86
Stanhope Ms. E. SW7 160 DC77
Stanhope Ms. S. SW7 160 DC77
Gloucester Rd.
Stanhope Ms. W. SW7 160 DC77
Stanhope Par. NW1 273 K2
Stanhope Pk. Rd., Grnf. 136 CC70
Stanhope Pl. W2 272 D9
Stanhope Pl. W2 140 DF73
Stanhope Rd. E17 123 EB57
Stanhope Rd. N6 121 DJ58
Stanhope Rd. N12 98 DC50
Stanhope Rd., Barn. 79 CW43
Stanhope Rd., Bexh. 166 EY82
Stanhope Rd., Cars. 218 DG108
Stanhope Rd., Croy. 202 DS104
Stanhope Rd., Dag. 126 EZ61
Stanhope Rd., Grnf. 136 CC71
Stanhope Rd., Rain. 147 FG68
Stanhope Rd., St.Alb. 43 CF20
Stanhope Rd., Sid. 186 EU91
Stanhope Rd., Slou. 131 AK72
Stanhope Rd., Swans. 190 FZ85
Stanhope Rd., Wal.Cr. 67 DY33
Stanhope Row W1 277 H3
Stanhope St. NW1 273 K2
Stanhope St. NW1 141 DJ69
Stanhope Ter. W2 272 A10
Stanhope Ter. W2 140 DD73
Stanhope Way, Sev. 256 FD122
Stanhope Way, Stai. 174 BJ86
Stanhopes, Oxt. 254 EH128
Stanier Clo. W14 159 CZ78
Aisgill Ave.
Stanier Ri., Berk. 38 AT16
Staniland Dr., Wey. 212 BM111
Eyston Dr.
Stanlake Ms. W12 139 CW74
Stanlake Rd. W12 139 CW74
Stanlake Vill. W12 139 CW74
Stanley Ave., Bark. 145 ET68
Stanley Ave., Beck. 203 EC96
Stanley Ave., Chesh. 54 AP31
Stanley Ave., Dag. 126 EZ60
Stanley Ave., Grnf. 136 CC67
Stanley Ave., N.Mal. 199 CU99
Stanley Ave., Rom. 127 FG56
Stanley Ave., St.Alb. 60 CA25
Stanley Ave., Wem. 138 CL66
Stanley Clo. SW8 161 DM79
Stanley Clo., Couls. 235 DM117
Stanley Clo., Green. 189 FS85
Stanley Clo., Horn. 128 FJ61
Stanley Rd.
Stanley Clo., Rom. 127 FG56
Stanley Clo., Uxb. 134 BK67
Stanley Clo., Wem. 138 CL66
Stanley Cotts., Slou. 132 AT74
Stanley Cres. W11 139 CZ73
Stanley Cres., Grav. 191 GK92
Stanley Dr., Hat. 45 CV20
Travellers La.
Stanley Gdns. NW2 119 CW64
Stanley Gdns. W3 158 CS75
Stanley Gdns. W11 139 CZ73
Stanley Gdns., Borwd. 78 CL39
Stanley Gdns., Mitch. 180 DG93
Ashbourne Rd.
Stanley Gdns., S.Croy. 220 DU112
Stanley Gdns., Wall. 219 DJ107
Stanley Gdns., Walt. 214 BW107
Stanley Gdns. Ms. W11 139 CZ73
Stanley Cres.
Stanley Gdns. Rd., Tedd. 177 CE92
Stanley Grn. E., Slou. 153 AZ77
Stanley Grn. W., Slou. 153 AZ77
Stanley Gro. SW8 160 DG82
Stanley Gro., Croy. 201 DN100
Stanley Hill, Amer. 55 AR40
Stanley Hill Ave., Amer. 55 AR39
Stanley Pk. Dr., Wem. 138 CM67
Stanley Pk. Rd., Cars. 218 DE108
Stanley Pk. Rd., Wall. 219 DH107
Stanley Pas. NW1 273 P1
Stanley Rd. E4 101 ED46
Stanley Rd. E10 123 EB58
Stanley Rd. E12 124 EL64
Stanley Rd. E15 143 ED67
Stanley Rd. E18 102 EF53
Stanley Rd. N2 120 DD55
Stanley Rd. N9 100 DT46
Stanley Rd. N10 99 DH52
Stanley Rd. N11 99 DK51
Stanley Rd. N15 121 DP56
Stanley Rd. NW9 119 CU59
West Hendon Bdy.
Stanley Rd. SW14 158 CP84
Stanley Rd. SW19 180 DA94
Stanley Rd. W3 158 CQ76
Stanley Rd., Ashf. 174 BL92
Stanley Rd., Brom. 204 EH98
Stanley Rd., Cars. 218 DG108
Stanley Rd., Croy. 201 DN101
Stanley Rd., Enf. 82 DS41
Stanley Rd., Grav. 190 GE89
Stanley Rd., Grays 170 GB78
Stanley Rd., Har. 116 CC61
Stanley Rd., Hert. 32 DS10
Stanley Rd., Horn. 128 FJ61
Stanley Rd., Houns. 156 CC84
Stanley Rd., Ilf. 125 ER61
Stanley Rd., Mitch. 180 DG94
Stanley Rd., Mord. 200 DA98
Stanley Rd., Nthwd. 93 BU53
Stanley Rd., Orp. 206 EU102
Stanley Rd., Sid. 186 EU90
Stanley Rd., Sthl. 136 BY73
Stanley Rd., Sutt. 218 DB107
Stanley Rd., Swans. 190 FZ86
Stanley Rd., Tedd. 177 CE91
Stanley Rd., Twick. 177 CD90
Stanley Rd., Wat. 76 BW41
Stanley Rd., Wem. 138 CM65
Stanley Rd., Wok. 227 AZ116
Stanley Rd. N., Rain. 147 FE67
Stanley Rd. S., Rain. 147 FF68
Stanley Sq., Cars. 218 DF109
Stanley St. SE8 163 DZ80
Stanley Ter. N19 121 DL61
Stanley Way, Orp. 206 EV99
Stanley Wd., Amer. 55 AS40
Stanley Hill
Stanleycroft Clo., Islw. 157 CE81
Stanmer St. SW11 160 DE81
Stanmore Gdns., Rich. 158 CM83
Stanmore Gdns., Sutt. 200 DC104
Stanmore Hill, Stan. 95 CG48
Stanmore Pl. NW1 141 DH67
Arlington Rd.
Stanmore Rd. E11 124 EF60
Stanmore Rd. N15 121 DP56
Stanmore Rd., Belv. 167 FC77
Stanmore Rd., Rich. 158 CM83
Stanmore Rd., Wat. 75 BV39
Stanmore St. N1 141 DM67
Caledonian Rd.
Stanmore Ter., Beck. 203 EA96
Stanmore Way, Loug. 85 EN39
Stanmount Rd., St.Alb. 60 CA25
Stannard Ms. E8 142 DU65
Stannard Rd.
Stannard Rd. E8 142 DU65
Stannary Pl. SE11 161 DN78
Stannary St.
Stannary St. SE11 161 DN79
Stannet Way, Wall. 219 DJ105
Bute Rd.
Stannington Path, Borwd. 78 CN39
Warenford Way
Stansfeld Rd. E6 144 EK71
Stansfield Rd. SW9 161 DM83
Stansfield Rd., Houns. 155 BV82
Stansgate Rd., Dag. 126 FA61
Stanstead Clo., Brom. 204 EF99
Stanstead Dr., Hodd. 49 EB15
Stanstead Gro. SE6 183 DZ88
Catford Hill
Stanstead Manor, Sutt. 218 DA107
Stanstead Rd. E11 124 EH57
Stanstead Rd. SE6 183 DZ88
Catford Hill
Stanstead Rd. SE23 183 DX88
Stanstead Rd., Cat. 252 DR127
Stanstead Rd., Hert. 32 DT08
Stanstead Rd., Hodd. 49 EB16
Stanstead Rd., Houns. 174 BM86
Stanstead Rd., Ware 32 DW09
Stansted Clo., Horn. 147 FH65
Stansted Cres., Bex. 186 EX88
Stanswood Gdns. SE5 162 DS80
Sedgmoor Pl.
Stanthorpe Clo. SW16 181 DL92
Stanthorpe Rd. SW16 181 DL92
Stanton Ave., Tedd. 177 CE92
Stanton Clo., Epsom 216 CP106
Stanton Clo., Orp. 206 EW101
Stanton Clo., St.Alb. 43 CK16
Stanton Clo., Wor.Pk. 199 CX102
Stanton Rd. SE26 183 DZ91
Stanton Way
Stanton Rd. SW13 159 CT82
Stanton Rd. SW20 199 CX95
Stanton Rd., Croy. 202 DQ101
Stanton Sq. SE26 183 DZ91
Stanton Way
Stanton St. SE15 162 DU81
Stanton Way SE26 183 DZ91
Stanton Way, Slou. 152 AY77
Stantons, Harl. 51 EN15
Stantons Wf., Guil. 259 BA144
Station Rd.
Stanway Clo., Chig. 103 ES50
Stanway Ct. N1 142 DS68
Hoxton St.
Stanway Gdns. W3 138 CN74
Stanway Gdns., Edg. 96 CQ51
Stanway Rd., Wal.Abb. 68 EG33
Stanway St. N1 142 DS68
Stanwell Clo., Stai. 174 BK86
Stanwell Gdns., Stai. 174 BK86
Stanwell Moor Rd., Stai. 174 BH90
Stanwell Moor Rd., West Dr. 154 BH81
Stanwell New Rd., Stai. 174 BH90
Stanwell Rd., Ashf. 174 BL89
Stanwell Rd., Felt. 175 BQ87
Stanwell Rd., Slou. 153 BA83
Stanwick Rd. W14 159 CZ77
Stanworth St. SE1 279 P5
Stanworth St. SE1 162 DT75
Stanwyck Dr., Chig. 103 EQ50
Stanwyck Gdns., Rom. 105 FH50
Stapenhill Rd., Wem. 117 CH62
Staple Clo., Bex. 187 FD90
Staple Hill Rd., Wok. 210 AS105
Staple Inn Bldgs. WC1 274 D7
Staple La., Guil. 244 BK132
Staple St. SE1 279 L5
Staple St. SE1 162 DR75
Staple Tye, Harl. 51 ER18
Parnall Rd.
Staplefield Clo. SW2 181 DL88
Staplefield Clo., Pnr. 94 BY52
Stapleford, Welw.G.C. 30 DD09
Stapleford Ave., Ilf. 125 ES57
Stapleford Clo. E4 101 EC48
Stapleford Clo. SW19 179 CY87
Beaumont Rd.
Stapleford Clo., Kings.T. 198 CN97
Stapleford Ct., Sev. 256 FF123
Stapleford Gdns., Rom. 104 FA51
Stapleford Rd., Rom. 87 FB43
Stapleford Rd., Wem. 137 CK66
Stapleford Tawney, Ong. 71 FC32
Stapleford Tawney, Rom. 87 FC35
Stapleford Way, Bark. 146 EV69
Staplehurst Clo., Reig. 266 DC138
Staplehurst Rd. SE13 184 EE85
Staplehurst Rd., Cars. 218 DE108
Staplehurst Rd., Reig. 266 DC138
Staples Clo. SE16 143 DY74
Staples Cor. NW2 119 CV60
Staples Cor. Business Pk. NW2 119 CU60
Staples Rd., Loug. 84 EK41
Stapleton Clo., Pot.B. 64 DE31
Stapleton Cres., Rain. 147 FG65
Stapleton Gdns., Croy. 219 DN106
Stapleton Hall Rd. N4 121 DM60
Stapleton Rd. SW17 180 DG90
Stapleton Rd., Bexh. 166 EZ80
Stapleton Rd., Borwd. 78 CN38
Stapleton Rd., Orp. 205 ET104
Stapley Rd., Belv. 166 FA78
Stapley Rd., St.Alb. 43 CD19
Stapylton Rd., Barn. 79 CY41
Star & Garter Hill, Rich. 178 CL88
Star Hill, Dart. 187 FE85
Star Hill, Wok. 226 AW119
Star Hill Rd., Sev. 240 EZ115
Star Home Ct., Ware 33 DY06
Star La. E16 144 EE70
Star La., Couls. 234 DG122
Star La., Epp. 70 EU30
Star La., Orp. 206 EW98
Star Path, Nthlt. 136 CA68
Brabazon Rd.
Star Rd. W14 159 CZ79
Star Rd., Islw. 157 CD82
Star Rd., Uxb. 135 BP70
Star St. E16 144 EF71
Star St. W2 272 A8
Star St. W2 140 DE72
Star St., Ware 33 DY06
Star Yd. WC2 274 D8
Starboard Ave., Green. 189 FV86
Starboard Way E14 163 EA76
Starch Ho. La., Ilf. 103 ER54
Starcross St. NW1 273 L3
Starcross St. NW1 141 DJ69
Starfield Rd. W12 159 CU75
Starkleigh Way SE16 162 DV78
Egan Way
Starling Clo., Buck.H. 102 EG46
Starling Clo., Pnr. 116 BW55
Starling La. (Cuffley), Pot.B. 65 DM28
Starling Ms. SE28 165 ER75
Whinchat Rd.
Starling Wk., Hmptn. 176 BY93
Oak Ave.
Starlings, The, Lthd. 214 CC113
Starrock La., Couls. 234 DF120
Starrock Rd., Couls. 235 DH119
Starts Clo., Orp. 205 EN104
Starts Hill Ave., Orp. 223 EP105
Starts Hill Rd., Orp. 205 EN104
Starveall Clo., West Dr. 154 BM76
Porters Way
Starwood Clo., W.Byf. 212 BJ111
Starwood Ct., Slou. 152 AW76
London Rd.
State Fm. Ave., Orp. 223 EP105
Staten Gdns., Twick. 177 CF88
Lion Rd.
Statham Gro. N16 122 DQ63
Green Las.
Statham Gro. N18 100 DS50
Tanners End La.
Station App. E7 124 EH63
Woodford Rd.
Station App. (Snaresbrook) E11 124 EG57
High St.
Station App. N11 99 DH50
Station App. (Woodside Pk.) N12 98 DB49
Holden Rd.
Station App. (Stoke Newington) N16 122 DT61
Stamford Hill
Station App. NW10 139 CT69
Station Rd.
Station App. SE3 164 EH83
Kidbrooke Pk. Rd.
Station App. (Mottingham) SE9 185 EM88
Station App. (Lower Sydenham) SE26 183 DZ92
Worsley Bri. Rd.
Station App. (Sydenham) SE26 182 DW91
Sydenham Rd.
Station App. SW6 159 CY83
Station App. SW16 181 DK92
Station App. W7 137 CE74
Station App., Amer. 55 AQ38
Station App. (Little Chalfont), Amer. 72 AX39
Chalfont Sta. Rd.
Station App., Ashf. 174 BM91
Station App., Bex. 186 FA87
Bexley High St.
Station App., Bexh. 166 EY82
Avenue Rd.
Station App. (Barnehurst), Bexh. 167 FC82
Station App., Brom. 204 EG102
Station App., Buck.H. 102 EK49
Cherry Tree Ri.
Station App., Chis. 205 EN95
Station App. (Elmstead Wds.), Chis. 184 EL93
Station App., Couls. 235 DK115
Station App. (Chipstead), Couls. 234 DF118
Station App., Dart. 188 FL86
Station App. (Crayford), Dart. 187 FF86
Station App., Dor. 247 CJ134
Station App. (Theydon Bois), Epp. 85 ES36
Coppice Row
Station App., Epsom 216 CR113
Station App. (Ewell E.), Epsom 217 CV110
Station App. (Ewell W.), Epsom 217 CT109
Chessington Rd.
Station App. (Stoneleigh), Epsom 217 CT106
Station App. (Hinchley Wd.), Esher 197 CF104
Station App., Ger.Cr. 112 AY57
Station App., Grays 170 GA79
Station App., Grnf. 137 CD66
Station App., Guil. 258 AY135
Station App., Hmptn. 196 CA95
Milton Rd.
Station App., Harl. 36 EW10
Station App., Har. 117 CE59
Station App., Hayes 155 BT75
Station App., Hem.H. 40 BG23
Station App., Horl. 269 DH148
Station App., Ilf. 125 ER55
Station App., Kings.T. 198 CN96
Station App., Lthd. 231 CG121
Station App. (East Horsley), Lthd. 245 BS126
Station App. (Oxshott), Lthd. 214 CC113
Station App., Loug. 84 EL43
Station App. (Debden), Loug. 85 EQ42
Station App., Nthwd. 93 BS52
Station App., Orp. 205 ET103
Station App. (Chelsfield), Orp. 224 EV106
Station App. (St. Mary Cray), Orp. 206 EV98
Station App., Oxt. 254 EE129
Station App., Pnr. 116 BY56
Station App. (Hatch End), Pnr. 94 CA52
Uxbridge Rd.
Station App., Pot.B. 63 CZ32
Wyllyotts Pl.
Station App., Pur. 219 DN111
Whytecliffe Rd. S.
Station App., Rad. 77 CG35
Shenley Hill
Station App., Rich. 158 CN81
Station App., Rick. 73 BC42
Station App., Ruis. 115 BV64
Station App., Shep. 195 BQ99
Station App., Sid. 186 EU89
Station App., S.Croy. 220 DR109
Sanderstead Rd.
Station App., Stai. 174 BG91
Station App., Sun. 195 BU95
Station App. (Belmont), Sutt. 218 DB110
Brighton Rd.
Station App. (Cheam), Sutt. 217 CY108
Station App., Swan. 207 FE98
Station App., Upmin. 128 FQ61
Station App. (Denham Golf Club), Uxb. 113 BD59
Middle Rd.
Station App., Vir.W. 192 AX98
Station App., Wal.Cr. 67 DY34
Station App. (Cheshunt), Wal.Cr. 67 DZ30
Station App., Wat. 75 BT41
Cassiobury Pk. Ave.
Station App. (Carpenders Pk.), Wat. 94 BX48
Prestwick Rd.
Station App., Well. 166 EU82
Station App., Wem. 137 CH65
Station App., W.Byf. 212 BG112
Station App., West Dr. 134 BL74
High St.
Station App., Wey. 212 BN107
Station App., Whyt. 236 DU118
Station App., Wok. 227 AZ118
Station App. Rd. W4 158 CQ80
Station App. Rd., Gat. 269 DH152
London Rd.
Station App. Rd., Tad. 233 CW122
Station App. Rd., Til. 171 GG84
Station App. W., Red. 266 DF136
Earlswood Rd.
Station Ave. SW9 161 DP83
Coldharbour La.
Station Ave., Cat. 236 DU124
Station Ave., Epsom 216 CS109
Station Ave., N.Mal. 198 CS97
Station Ave., Rich. 158 CN81
Station Ave., Walt. 213 BT105
Station Clo. N3 98 DA53
Station Clo., Hmptn. 196 CB95
Station Clo., Hat. 63 CY26
Station Rd.
Station Clo., Pot.B. 63 CZ31
Station Cres. N15 122 DR56
Station Cres. SE3 164 EG78
Station Cres., Ashf. 174 BK90
Station Cres., Wem. 137 CH65
Station Est., Beck. 203 DX98
Elmers End Rd.
Station Est. Rd., Felt. 175 BV88
Station Footpath, Kings L. 59 BP30
Station Gdns. W4 158 CQ80
Station Gro., Wem. 138 CL65
Station Hill, Brom. 204 EG103
Station Ho. Ms. N9 100 DU49
Fore St.
Station La., Horn. 128 FK62
Station Par. E11 124 EG57
Station Par. N14 99 DK46
High St.
Station Par. NW2 139 CW65
Station Par. SW12 180 DG88
Balham High Rd.
Station Par. W3 138 CN72
Station Par., Bark. 145 EQ66
Station Par., Couls. 234 DF118
Station App.
Station Par., Horn. 127 FH63
Rosewood Ave.
Station Par., Lthd. 245 BS126
Ockham Rd. S.
Station Par., Rich. 158 CN81
Station Ave.
Station Par., Sev. 256 FG124
London Rd.
Station Par., Uxb. 114 BG59
Station Par., Vir.W. 192 AX98
Station Pas. E18 102 EH54
Maybank Rd.
Station Pas. SE15 162 DW79
Asylum Rd.
Station Path E8 142 DV65
Amhurst Rd.
Station Path, Stai. 173 BF91
Station Pl. N4 121 DN61
Seven Sisters Rd.
Station Pl., Gdmg. 258 AT144
Summers Rd.
Station Ri. SE27 181 DP89
Norwood Rd.
Station Rd. (Chingford) E4 101 ED46
Station Rd. E7 124 EG63
Station Rd. E10 123 EC62
Station Rd. E12 124 EK63
Station Rd. E17 123 DY58
Station Rd. N3 98 DA53
Station Rd. N11 99 DH50
Station Rd. N17 122 DU55
Hale Rd.
Station Rd. N19 121 DJ62
Station Rd. N21 99 DP46
Station Rd. N22 99 DL54
Station Rd. NW4 119 CU58
Station Rd. NW7 96 CS50
Station Rd. NW10 139 CT68
Station Rd. SE20 182 DW93
Station Rd. (Norwood Junct.) SE25 202 DT98
Station Rd. SW13 159 CT82
Station Rd. SW19 200 DC95
Station Rd. W5 138 CM72
Station Rd. (Hanwell) W7 137 CE74
Station Rd., Add. 212 BJ105
Station Rd., Amer. 55 AQ38
Station Rd., Ashf. 174 BM91
Station App.
Station Rd., Barn. 80 DB43
Station Rd., Beac. 89 AK52
Station Rd., Belv. 166 FA76
Station Rd., Berk. 38 AW18
Station Rd., Bet. 248 CS131
Station Rd., Bexh. 166 EY83
Station Rd., Borwd. 78 CN42
Station Rd., Brom. 204 EG95
Station Rd. (Shortlands), Brom. 204 EE96
Station Rd., Brox. 49 DZ20
Station Rd., Cars. 218 DF105
Station Rd., Cat. 237 DY122
Station Rd., Cher. 193 BF102
Station Rd., Chesh. 54 AQ31
Station Rd., Chess. 216 CL106
Station Rd., Chig. 103 EP48
Station Rd., Cob. 230 BY117
Station Rd. (East Croydon), Croy. 202 DR103
Station Rd. (West Croydon), Croy. 202 DQ102
Station Rd. (Crayford), Dart. 187 FF86
Station Rd. (Eynsford), Dart. 208 FK104
Station Rd. (South Darenth), Dart. 208 FP96
Station Rd., Dor. 263 CG135
Station Rd., Edg. 96 CN51
Station Rd., Egh. 173 BA92
Station Rd., Enf. 82 DQ41
Station Rd., Epp. 69 ET30
Station Rd. (North Weald), Epp. 71 FB27
Station Rd., Esher 197 CD103
Station Rd. (Claygate), Esher 215 CD106
Station Rd., Ger.Cr. 112 AY57
Station Rd., Gdmg. 258 AT144
Station Rd. (Betsham), Grav. 190 FZ91
Station Rd. (Northfleet), Grav. 190 GB86
Station Rd., Green. 189 FU85
Station Rd., Guil. 258 AY140
Station Rd. (Gomshall), Guil. 261 BQ138
Station Rd., Hmptn. 196 CA95
Station Rd., Harl. 36 EW11
Station Rd., Har. 117 CF56
Station Rd. (North Harrow), Har. 116 CB57
Station Rd., Hat. 45 CW24
Station Rd., Hayes 155 BS77
Station Rd., Hem.H. 40 BH22
Station Rd., Hert. 30 DG12
Station Rd., H.Wyc. 88 AC53
Station Rd., Horl. 269 DH148
Station Rd., Houns. 156 CB84
Station Rd., Ilf. 125 EP62
Station Rd. (Barkingside), Ilf. 125 ER55
Station Rd., Ken. 220 DQ114
Station Rd., Kings L. 59 BP29
Station Rd., Kings.T. 198 CN95
Station Rd. (Hampton Wick), Kings.T. 197 CK95
Station Rd., Lthd. 231 CG121
Station Rd., Loug. 84 EL42
Station Rd., Maid. 130 AF72
Station Rd. (Motspur Pk.), N.Mal. 199 CV99
Station Rd., Orp. 205 ET103
Station Rd. (St. Mary Cray), Orp. 206 EW98
Station Rd. (Cuffley), Pot.B. 65 DL29
Station Rd., Rad. 77 CG35
Station Rd., Red. 250 DE133

Station Rd. (Merstham), Red. 251 DJ128
Station Rd., Rick. 92 BK45
Station Rd. (Chadwell Heath), Rom. 126 EX60
Station Rd. (Gidea Pk.), Rom. 127 FH56
Station Rd. (Harold Wd.), Rom. 106 FM53
Station Rd. (Bricket Wd.), St.Alb. 60 CA31
Station Rd. (Colney Heath), St.Alb. 44 CP19
Station Rd. (Dunton Grn.), Sev. 241 FE120
Station Rd. (Halstead), Sev. 224 EZ110
Station Rd. (Otford), Sev. 241 FH116
Station Rd. (Shoreham), Sev. 225 FG111
Station Rd., Shep. 195 BQ99
Station Rd., Sid. 186 EU91
Station Rd., Slou. 131 AL72
Station Rd. (Langley), Slou. 153 BA76
Station Rd. (Wraysbury), Stai. 173 AZ86
Station Rd., Sun. 175 BU94
Station Rd. (Belmont), Sutt. 218 DA110
Station Rd., Swan. 207 FE98
Station Rd., Tedd. 177 CF92
Station Rd., T.Ditt. 197 CF101
Station Rd., Twick. 177 CF88
Station Rd., Upmin. 128 FQ61
Station Rd., Uxb. 134 BJ70
Station Rd., Wal.Cr. 67 EA34
Station Rd., Ware 33 DX06
Station Rd., Wat. 75 BV40
Station Rd., W.Byf. 212 BG112
Station Rd., West Dr. 134 BK74
Station Rd., W.Wick. 203 EC103
Station Rd., West. 240 EV123
Station Rd., Whyt. 236 DT118
Station Rd., Wok. 210 AT111
Station Rd. E., Oxt. 254 EE128
Station Rd. N., Belv. 167 FB76
Station Rd. N., Egh. 173 BA92
Station Rd. N., Red. 251 DJ128
Station Rd. S., Red. 251 DJ128
Station Rd. W., Oxt. 254 EE129
Station Row, Guil. 258 AY140
Station Sq. (Petts Wd.), Orp. 205 EQ99
Station Sq. (St. Mary Cray), Orp. 206 EV98
Station St. E15 143 ED66
Station St. E16 145 EP74
Station St., Ware 33 EA11
Station Ter. NW10 139 CX68
Station Ter. SE5 162 DQ81
Station Vw., Grnf. 137 CD67
Station Way SE15 162 DU82
Rye La.
Station Way (Roding Valley), Buck.H. 102 EJ49
Station Way (Epsom), Epsom 216 CR113
High St.
Station Way (Claygate), Esher 215 CE107
Station Way, St.Alb. 43 CF20
Station Way (Cheam), Sutt. 217 CY107
Station Way, Welw.G.C. 29 CX08
Station Yd., Twick. 177 CG87
Stationers Hall Ct. EC4 141 DP72
Ludgate Hill
Staunton Rd., Kings.T. 178 CL93
Staunton Rd., Slou. 131 AR71
Staunton St. SE8 163 DZ79
Stave Yd. Rd. SE16 143 DY74
Staveley Clo. E9 122 DW64
Churchill Wk.
Staveley Clo. N7 121 DL63
Penn Rd.
Staveley Clo. SE15 162 DV81
Asylum Rd.
Staveley Gdns. W4 158 CR81
Staveley Rd. W4 158 CQ79
Staveley Rd., Ashf. 175 BR93
Staveley Way, Wok. 226 AS117
Staverton Rd. NW2 139 CW66
Staverton Rd., Horn. 128 FK58
Stavordale Rd. N5 121 DP63
Stavordale Rd., Cars. 200 DC102
Stayne End, Vir.W. 192 AU98
Stayner's Rd. E1 143 DX70
Stayton Rd., Sutt. 200 DA104
Stead St. SE17 279 K9
Stead St. SE17 162 DR77
Steadfast Rd., Kings.T. 197 CK95
Steam Fm. La., Felt. 155 BT84
Stean St. E8 142 DT67
Stebbing Way, Bark. 146 EU68
Stebondale St. E14 163 EC78
Stedham Pl. WC1 273 P8
Stedman Clo., Bex. 187 FE90
Stedman Clo., Uxb. 114 BN62
Steed Clo., Horn. 127 FH61
St. Leonards Way
Steedman St. SE17 279 H9
Steeds Rd. N10 98 DF53
Steeds Way, Loug. 84 EL41
Steele Ave., Green. 189 FT85
Steele Rd. E11 124 EE63
Steele Rd. N17 122 DS55
Steele Rd. NW10 138 CQ68
Steele Rd. W4 158 CQ76
Steele Rd., Islw. 157 CG84
Steeles Ms. N. NW3 140 DF65
Steeles Rd.
Steeles Ms. S. NW3 140 DF65
Steeles Rd.
Steeles Rd. NW3 140 DF65
Steel's La. E1 142 DW72
Devonport St.
Steels La., Lthd. 214 CB114
Steen Way SE22 182 DS85
East Dulwich Gro.
Steep Clo., Orp. 223 ET107
Steep Hill SW16 181 DK90
Steep Hill, Croy. 220 DS105
Steeplands (Bushey), Wat. 94 CB45
Steeple Clo. SW6 159 CY82
Steeple Clo. SW19 179 CY92
Steeple Ct. E1 142 DV70
Coventry Rd.
Steeple Gdns., Add. 212 BH106
Weatherall Clo.
Steeple Heights Dr., West. 238 EK117
Steeple Wk. N1 142 DQ67
Basire St.
Steeplestone Clo. N18 100 DQ50
Steer Pl., Red. 266 DG143
Bonehurst Rd.
Steerforth St. SW18 180 DC89
Steers Mead, Mitch. 200 DF95
Steers Way SE16 163 DY75
Stella Rd. SW17 180 DF93
Stellar Ho. N17 100 DU51
Stelling Rd., Erith 167 FD80
Stellman Clo. E5 122 DU62
Stembridge Rd. SE20 202 DV96
Stents La., Cob. 230 BZ120
Stents La., Lthd. 230 BZ120
Cobham Rd.
Stepbridge Path, Wok. 226 AX117
Goldsworth Rd.
Stepgates, Cher. 194 BH101
Stepgates Clo., Cher. 194 BH101
Stephan Clo. E8 142 DU67
Stephen Ave., Rain. 147 FG65
Stephen Clo., Egh. 173 BC93
Stephen Clo., Orp. 205 ES104
Stephen Ms. W1 273 M7
Stephen Rd., Bexh. 167 FC83
Stephen St. W1 273 M7
Stephen St. W1 141 DK71
Stephendale Rd. SW6 160 DB83
Stephens Clo., Rom. 106 FJ50
Stephen's Rd. E15 144 EE67
Stephenson Ave., Til. 171 GG81
Stephenson Dr., Wind. 151 AP80
Stephenson Rd. W7 137 CF72
Stephenson Rd., Twick. 176 CA87
Stephenson St. E16 144 EE70
Stephenson St. NW10 138 CS69
Stephenson Way NW1 273 L4
Stephenson Way NW1 141 DJ70
Stephenson Way, Wat. 76 BX41
Stepney Causeway E1 143 DX72
Stepney Grn. E1 142 DW71
Stepney High St. E1 143 DX71
Stepney Way E1 142 DV71
Sterling Ave., Edg. 96 CM49
Sterling Ave., Wal.Cr. 67 DX34
Sterling Gdns. SE14 163 DY79
Sterling Ind. Est., Dag. 127 FB63
Sterling Pl. W5 158 CL77
Sterling Rd., Enf. 82 DR39
Sterling St. SW7 276 C5
Sterling Way N18 100 DR49
Sterndale Rd. W14 159 CX76
Sterndale Rd., Dart. 188 FM87
Sterne St. W12 159 CX75
Sternhall La. SE15 162 DU83
Sternhold Ave. SW2 181 DK89
Sterry Cres., Dag. 126 FA64
Alibon Rd.
Sterry Dr., Epsom 216 CS105
Sterry Dr., T.Ditt. 197 CE100
Sterry Gdns., Dag. 146 FA65
Sterry Rd., Bark. 145 ET67
Sterry Rd., Dag. 126 FA63
Sterry St. SE1 279 K5
Sterry St. SE1 162 DR75
Steucers La. SE23 183 DY88
Steve Biko La. SE6 183 EA91
Steve Biko Rd. N7 121 DN62
Tollington Rd.
Steve Biko Way, Houns. 156 CA83
Stevedale Rd., Well. 166 EW82
Stevedore St. E1 142 DV74
Stevenage Cres., Borwd. 78 CL39
Stevenage Ri., Hem.H. 40 BM16
Stevenage Rd. E6 145 EN65
Stevenage Rd. SW6 159 CX80
Stevens Ave. E9 142 DW65
Stevens Clo., Beck. 183 EA93
Stevens Clo., Bex. 187 FD91
Steven's Clo., Dart. 188 FQ92
Stevens Clo., Epsom 216 CS113
Upper High St.
Stevens Clo., Hmptn. 176 BY93
Stevens Clo., Pnr. 116 BW57
Bridle Rd.
Stevens Grn. (Bushey), Wat. 94 CC46
Stevens La., Esher 215 CG108
Stevens Rd., Dag. 126 EV62
Stevens St. SE1 279 N6
Stevens Way, Chig. 103 ES49
Stevenson Clo., Erith 167 FH80
Stevenson Cres. SE16 162 DU78
Stevenson Rd., Slou. 111 AR61
Steventon Rd. W12 139 CT73
Stew La. EC4 142 DQ73
High Timber St.
Steward Clo. (Cheshunt), Wal.Cr. 67 DY30
Steward St. E1 275 N6
Steward St. E1 142 DS71
Stewards Clo., Epp. 70 EU32
Stewards Grn. La., Epp. 70 EV32
Stewards Grn. Rd., Epp. 70 EU33
Stewards Wk., Rom. 127 FE57
Stewart, Tad. 233 CX121
Stewart Ave., Shep. 194 BN98
Stewart Ave., Slou. 132 AT71
Stewart Ave., Upmin. 128 FP62
Stewart Clo. NW9 118 CQ58
Stewart Clo., Abb.L. 59 BT31
Stewart Clo., Chis. 185 EP92
Stewart Clo., Hmptn. 176 BY93
Stewart Clo., Maid. 150 AD81
Stewart Clo., Wok. 226 AT117
Nethercote Ave.
Stewart Rainbird Ho. E12 125 EN64
Stewart Rd. E15 123 EC63
Stewart St. E14 163 EC75
Stewart's Dr., Slou. 111 AP63
Stewart's Gro. SW3 276 B10
Stewart's Gro. SW3 160 DE78
Stewart's Rd. SW8 161 DJ80
Stewartsby Clo. N18 100 DQ50
Steyne Rd. W3 138 CP74
Steyning Clo., Ken. 235 DP116
Steyning Gro. SE9 185 EM91
Steyning Way, Houns. 156 BW84
Steynings Way N12 98 DA50
Steynton Ave., Bex. 186 EX89
Stickland Rd., Belv. 166 FA77
Picardy Rd.
Stickleton Clo., Grnf. 136 CB69
Stifford Hill, S.Ock. 149 FW73
Stifford Rd., S.Ock. 149 FS74
Stile Hall Gdns. W4 158 CN78
Stile Path, Sun. 195 BU97
Stile Rd., Slou. 152 AX76
Stilecroft, Harl. 52 EU17
Stilecroft Gdns., Wem. 117 CH62
Stiles Clo., Brom. 205 EM100
Stiles Clo., Erith 167 FB78
Riverdale Rd.
Stillingfleet Rd. SW13 159 CU79
Stillington St. SW1 277 L8
Stillington St. SW1 161 DJ77
Stillness Rd. SE23 183 DY86
Stilton Cres. NW10 138 CQ66
Stilton Path, Borwd. 78 CN38
Brampton Ter.
Stipularis Dr., Hayes 136 BX70
Stirling Clo. SW16 201 DJ95
Stirling Clo., Bans. 233 CZ117
Stirling Clo., Rain. 147 FH69
Stirling Clo., Uxb. 134 BJ69
Ferndale Cres.
Stirling Clo., Wind. 151 AK82
Stirling Dr., Orp. 224 EV106
Stirling Gro., Houns. 156 CC82
Kingsley Rd.
Stirling Rd. E13 144 EH68
Stirling Rd. E17 123 DY55
Stirling Rd. N17 100 DU53
Stirling Rd. N22 99 DP53
Stirling Rd. SW9 161 DL82
Stirling Rd. W3 158 CP76
Stirling Rd., Har. 117 CF55
Stirling Rd., Hayes 135 BV73
Stirling Rd., Houns. 174 BM86
Stirling Rd., Slou. 131 AN71
Stirling Rd., Twick. 176 CA87
Stirling Rd. Path E17 123 DY55
Stirling Wk., N.Mal. 198 CQ99
Green La.
Stirling Wk., Surb. 198 CP100
Stirling Way, Abb.L. 59 BU32
Langley La.
Stirling Way, Borwd. 78 CR44
Stirling Way, Croy. 201 DL101
Stirling Way, Welw.G.C. 30 DE09
Stites Hill Rd., Cat. 235 DP120
Stiven Cres., Har. 116 BZ62
Stoats Nest Rd., Couls. 219 DL114
Stoats Nest Village, Couls. 235 DL115
Stock Hill, West. 238 EK116
Stock La., Dart. 188 FJ90
Stock Orchard Cres. N7 121 DM64
Stock Orchard St. N7 121 DM64
Stock St. E13 144 EG68
Stockbreach Clo., Hat. 45 CU17
Stockbreach Rd., Hat. 45 CU17
Stockbury Rd., Croy. 202 DW100
Stockdale Rd., Dag. 126 EZ61
Stockdales Rd. (Eton Wick), Wind. 151 AM77
Stockdove Way, Grnf. 137 CF69
Stockers Fm. Rd., Rick. 92 BK48
Stockers La., Wok. 227 AZ120
Stockfield, Horl. 269 DH147
Stockfield Ave., Hodd. 49 EA15
Stockfield Rd. SW16 181 DM90
Stockfield Rd., Esher 215 CE106
Stockhams Clo., S.Croy. 220 DR111
Stockham's Clo., S.Croy. 220 DR110
Beech Ave.
Stockholm Rd. SE16 162 DW78
Stockholm Way E1 142 DU74
Thomas More St.
Stockhurst Clo. SW15 159 CW82
Stocking La. (Bayford), Hert. 47 DN18
Stockings La. (Little Berkhamsted), Hert. 47 DK18
Stockingswater La., Enf. 83 DY41
Stockland Rd., Rom. 127 FD58
Stockley Clo., West Dr. 155 BP75
Stockley Fm. Rd., West Dr. 155 BP76
Stockley Rd.
Stockley Pk. Business Pk., Uxb. 135 BP74
Stockley Rd., Uxb. 134 BN72
Stockley Rd., West Dr. 135 BP74
Stockport Rd. SW16 201 DK95
Stockport Rd., Rick. 91 BC45
Stocks Clo., Horl. 269 DH149
Limes Ave.
Stocks Pl. E14 143 DZ73
Grenade St.
Stocksfield Rd. E17 123 EC55
Stockton Gdns. N17 100 DQ52
Stockton Rd.
Stockton Gdns. NW7 96 CS48
Stockton Rd. N17 100 DQ52
Stockton Rd. N18 100 DU51
Stockton Rd., Reig. 266 DA137
Stockwell Ave. SW9 161 DM83
Stockwell Clo., Brom. 204 EH96
Stockwell Clo. (Cheshunt), Wal.Cr. 66 DU27
Stockwell Gdns. SW9 161 DM81
Stockwell Gdns. Est. SW9 161 DL82
Stockwell Grn. SW9 161 DM82
Stockwell La. SW9 161 DM82
Stockwell La. (Cheshunt), Wal.Cr. 66 DV28
Stockwell Ms. SW9 161 DM82
Stockwell Rd.
Stockwell Pk. Cres. SW9 161 DM82
Stockwell Pk. Est. SW9 161 DM82
Stockwell Pk. Rd. SW9 161 DM81
Stockwell Pk. Wk. SW9 161 DM83
Stockwell Rd. SW9 161 DM82
Stockwell St. SE10 163 EC79
Stockwell Ter. SW9 161 DM81
Stockwells, Maid. 130 AD70
Stocton Clo., Guil. 242 AW133
Stocton Rd., Guil. 242 AW133
Stodart Rd. SE20 202 DW95
Stofield Gdns. SE9 184 EK90
Aldersgrove Ave.
Stoford Clo. SW19 179 CY87
Stoke Ave., Ilf. 104 EU51
Stoke Clo., Cob. 230 BZ116
Stoke Common Rd., Slou. 112 AU63
Stoke Ct. Dr., Slou. 132 AS67
Stoke Flds., Guil. 258 AX135
York Rd.
Stoke Gdns., Slou. 132 AS74
Stoke Grn., Slou. 132 AU70
Stoke Gro., Guil. 242 AX134
York Rd.
Stoke Ms., Guil. 258 AX135
Stoke Rd.
Stoke Newington Ch. St. N16 122 DR62
Stoke Newington Common N16 122 DT62
Stoke Newington High St. N16 122 DT62
Stoke Newington Rd. N16 122 DT64
Stoke Pk. Ave., Slou. 131 AQ69
Stoke Pl. NW10 139 CT69
Stoke Pl. Conference Cen., Slou. 132 AU70
Stoke Poges La., Slou. 132 AS74
Stoke Rd., Cob. 230 BW115
Stoke Rd., Guil. 242 AX133
Stoke Rd., Kings.T. 178 CQ94
Stoke Rd., Rain. 148 FK68
Stoke Rd., Slou. 132 AT74
Stoke Rd., Walt. 196 BW104
Stoke Wd., Slou. 112 AT63
Stokenchurch St. SW6 160 DB81
Stokers Clo., Horl. 268 DE151
Stokes Ridings, Tad. 233 CX123
Stokes Rd. E6 144 EL70
Stokes Rd., Croy. 203 DX100
Stokesay, Slou. 132 AT73
Stokesby Rd., Chess. 216 CM107
Stokesheath Rd., Lthd. 214 CC111
Stokesley Ri., H.Wyc. 110 AE55
Wootton Way
Stokesley St. W12 139 CT72
Stoll Clo. NW2 119 CW62
Stomp Rd., Slou. 130 AH71
Stompond La., Walt. 195 BU103
Stoms Path SE6 183 EA92
Sedgehill Rd.
Stonard Rd. N13 99 DN48
Stonard Rd., Dag. 126 EV64
Stonards Hill, Epp. 70 EU29
Stonards Hill, Loug. 85 EM44
Stondon Pk. SE23 183 DY86
Stondon Wk. E6 144 EK68
Arragon Rd.
Stone Bldgs. WC2 274 C7
Stone Bldgs. WC2 141 DM72
Stone Clo. SW4 161 DJ82
Larkhall Ri.
Stone Clo., Dag. 126 EZ61
Stone Clo., West Dr. 134 BM74
Stone Cres., Felt. 175 BT87
Stone Cross, Harl. 35 ER14
Post Office Rd.
Stone Hall Gdns. W8 160 DB76
St. Mary's Gate
Stone Hall Pl. W8 160 DB76
St. Mary's Gate
Stone Hall Rd. N21 99 DM45
Stone Ho. Ct. EC3 275 N8
Stone Ness Rd., Grays 169 FV79
Stone Pk. Ave., Beck. 203 EA98
Stone Pl., Wor.Pk. 199 CU103
Stone Pl. Rd., Green. 189 FS85
Stone Rd., Brom. 204 EF99
Stone St., Croy. 219 DN106
Stone St., Grav. 191 GH86
Stonebanks, Walt. 195 BU101
Stonebridge Common E8 142 DT66
Mayfield Rd.
Stonebridge Fld., Wind. 151 AP78
Broken Furlong
Stonebridge Flds., Guil. 258 AX141
Stonebridge Pk. NW10 138 CR66
Stonebridge Rd. N15 122 DT57
Stonebridge Rd., Grav. 190 GA85
Stonebridge Way, Wem. 138 CP65
Stonebridge Wf., Guil. 258 AX141
Stonechat Sq. E6 144 EL71
Peridot St.
Stonecot Clo., Sutt. 199 CY102
Stonecot Hill, Sutt. 199 CY102
Stonecourt Clo., Horl. 269 DJ148
Stonecroft Ave., Iver 133 BE72
Stonecroft Clo., Barn. 79 CV42
Barnet Rd.
Stonecroft Rd., Erith 167 FC80
Stonecroft Way, Croy. 201 DL101
Stonecrop Rd., Guil. 243 BC132
Kingfisher Dr.
Stonecross, St.Alb. 43 CE19
Stonecross Clo., St.Alb. 43 CE19
Stonecross
Stonecross Rd., Hat. 45 CV16
Stonecutter Ct. EC4 141 DP72
Stonecutter St.
Stonecutter St. EC4 274 F8
Stonecutter St. EC4 141 DP72
Stonefield Clo., Bexh. 166 FA83
Stonefield Clo., Ruis. 116 BY64
Stonefield St. N1 141 DN67
Stonefield Way SE7 164 EK80
Greenbay Rd.
Stonefield Way, Ruis. 116 BY63
Stonegate Clo., Orp. 206 EW97
Main Rd.
Stonegrove, Edg. 96 CL49
Stonegrove Est., Edg. 96 CL49
Stonegrove Gdns., Edg. 96 CL50
Stonehall Ave., Ilf. 124 EL58
Stoneham Rd. N11 99 DJ50
Stonehill Clo. SW14 178 CR85
Stonehill Clo., Lthd. 246 CA125
Stonehill Grn. Rd., Dart. 187 FC94
Birchwood Rd.
Stonehill Rd. SW14 178 CQ85
Stonehill Rd. W4 158 CN78
Wellesley Rd.
Stonehill Rd., Cher. 210 AY107
Stonehill Rd., Wok. 210 AW108
Stonehill Wds. Caravan Pk., Sid. 187 FB93
Stonehills, Welw.G.C. 29 CX08
Stonehills Ct. SE21 182 DS90
Stonehorse Rd., Enf. 82 DW43
Stonehouse Gdns., Cat. 252 DS125
Stonehouse La., Purf. 169 FS79
Stonehouse La., Sev. 224 EX109
Stonehouse Rd., Sev. 224 EW110
Stoneings La., Sev. 239 ET118
Stonelea Rd., Hem.H. 40 BM23
Stoneleigh Ave., Enf. 82 DV38
Stoneleigh Ave., Wor.Pk. 199 CU104
Stoneleigh Clo., Wal.Cr. 67 DX33
Stoneleigh Cres., Epsom 217 CT106
Stoneleigh Dr., Hodd. 33 EB14
Stoneleigh Pk., Wey. 213 BQ106
Stoneleigh Pk. Ave., Croy. 203 DX100
Stoneleigh Pk. Rd., Epsom 217 CT107
Stoneleigh Pl. W11 139 CX73
Stoneleigh Rd. N17 122 DT55
Stoneleigh Rd., Cars. 200 DE101
Stoneleigh Rd., Ilf. 124 EL55
Stoneleigh Rd., Oxt. 254 EL130
Stoneleigh St. W11 139 CX73
Stoneleigh Ter. N19 121 DH61
Dartmouth Pk. Hill
Stonells Rd. SW11 180 DF85
Chatham Rd.
Stonenest St. N4 121 DM60
Stones All., Wat. 75 BV42
Exchange Rd.
Stones Cross Rd., Swan. 207 FC99
Stones End St. SE1 279 H5
Stones End St. SE1 162 DQ75
Stones La., Dor. 262 CC137
Stones Rd., Epsom 216 CS112
Stoneswood Rd., Oxt. 254 EH130
Stonewood, Dart. 189 FW90
Stonewood Rd., Erith 167 FE78
Stoney All. SE18 165 EN82
Stoney Brook, Guil. 242 AS133
Stoney Cft., Hem.H. 40 BG20
Stoney Cft., Welw.G.C. 30 DA08
Stoney Gro., Chesh. 54 AR30
Stoney La. E1 275 P8
Stoney La. SE19 182 DT93
Church Rd.
Stoney La., Hem.H. 57 BB27
Stoney La., Kings L. 57 BE30
Stoney La., Slou. 131 AN67
Stoney Meade, Slou. 131 AP74
Weekes Dr.
Stoney St. SE1 279 K2
Stoney St. SE1 142 DR74
Stoneyard La. E14 143 EB73
Poplar High St.
Stoneycroft, Hem.H. 40 BG20
Long Chaulden
Stoneycroft Clo. SE12 184 EF87
Stoneycroft Rd., Wdf.Grn. 102 EL51
Stoneydeep, Tedd. 177 CG91
Twickenham Rd.
Stoneydown E17 123 DY56
Stoneydown Ave. E17 123 DY56
Stoneyfield Rd., Couls. 235 DM117
Stoneyfields Gdns., Edg. 96 CQ49
Stoneyfields La., Edg. 96 CQ50
Stoneylands Ct., Egh. 173 AZ92
Stoneylands Rd., Egh. 173 AZ92
Stonhouse St. SW4 161 DK83
Stonny Cft., Ash. 232 CM117
Stonor Rd. W14 159 CZ77
Stony La., Amer. 72 AY38
Stony Path, Loug. 85 EM39
Stony Wd., Harl. 51 ES16
Stonycroft Clo., Enf. 83 DY40
Brimsdown Ave.
Stonyrock La., Dor. 246 BY134
Stonyshotts, Wal.Abb. 68 EE34
Stoop Ct., W.Byf. 212 BH112
Stopford Rd. E13 144 EG67
Stopford Rd. SE17 161 DP78
Store Gdns., Brwd. 109 GD43
Store Rd. E16 165 EN75
Store St. E15 123 ED64
Store St. WC1 273 M7
Store St. WC1 141 DK71
Storers Quay E14 163 ED77
Storey Rd. E17 123 DZ56
Storey Rd. N6 120 DF58
Storey St. E16 145 EN74
Storey St., Hem.H. 40 BK24
Storey's Gate SW1 277 N5
Storey's Gate SW1 161 DK75
Stories Ms. SE5 162 DS82
Stories Rd. SE5 162 DS83
Stork Rd. E7 144 EF65
Storks Rd. SE16 162 DU76
Storksmead Rd., Edg. 96 CS52
Stormont Rd. N6 120 DF59
Stormont Rd. SW11 160 DG83
Stormont Way, Chess. 215 CJ106
Stormount Dr., Hayes 155 BQ75
Stornaway Strand, Grav. 191 GM91
Stornoway, Hem.H. 41 BP22
Storr Gdns., Brwd. 109 GD43
Storrington Rd., Croy. 202 DT102
Stort Mill, Harl. 36 EV09
Stort Twr., Harl. 35 ET13
Stortford Rd., Hodd. 49 EB16
Story St. N1 141 DM66
Carnoustie Dr.
Stothard Pl. EC2 142 DS71
Bishopsgate
Stothard St. E1 142 DW70
Colebert Ave.
Stoughton Ave., Sutt. 217 CX106
Stoughton Clo. SE11 278 C9
Stoughton Clo. SW15 179 CU88
Bessborough Rd.
Stoughton Rd., Guil. 242 AU131
Stour Ave., Sthl. 156 CA76
Stour Clo., Kes. 222 EJ105
Stour Clo., Slou. 151 AP76
Stour Rd. E3 143 EA66
Stour Rd., Dag. 126 FA61
Stour Rd., Dart. 167 FG83
Stour Rd., Grays 171 GG78
Stour Way, Upmin. 129 FS58
Stourcliffe St. W1 272 D9
Stourcliffe St. W1 140 DF72
Stourhead Clo. SW19 179 CX87
Castlecombe Dr.
Stourhead Gdns. SW20 199 CU97
Stourton Ave., Felt. 176 BZ91
Stovell Rd., Wind. 151 AP80
Stow, The, Harl. 35 ET13
Stow Cres. E17 101 DY52
Stowage SE8 163 EA79
Stowe Ct., Dart. 188 FQ87
Stowe Cres., Ruis. 115 BP58
Stowe Gdns. N9 100 DT46
Latymer Rd.
Stowe Pl. N15 122 DS55
Stowe Rd. W12 159 CV75
Stowe Rd., Orp. 224 EV105

Stowe Rd., Slou. 131 AL73
Stowell Ave., Croy. 221 ED109
Stowting Rd., Orp. 223 ES105
Stox Mead, Har. 95 CD53
Stracey Rd. E7 124 EG63
Stracey Rd. NW10 138 CR67
Strachan Pl. SW19 179 CW93
Woodhayes Rd.
Stradbroke Dr., Chig. 103 EN51
Stradbroke Gro., Buck.H. 102 EK46
Stradbroke Gro., Ilf. 124 EL55
Stradbroke Pk., Chig. 103 EP51
Stradbroke Rd. N5 122 DQ63
Stradella Rd. SE24 182 DQ86
Strafford Ave., Ilf. 103 EN54
Strafford Clo., Pot.B. 64 DA32
Strafford Gate
Strafford Gate, Pot.B. 64 DA32
Strafford Rd. W3 158 CQ75
Strafford Rd., Barn. 79 CY41
Strafford Rd., Houns. 156 BZ83
Strafford Rd., Twick. 177 CG87
Strafford St. E14 163 EA75
Strahan Rd. E3 143 DY69
Straight, The, Sthl. 156 BX75
Straight Bit, H.Wyc. 110 AC55
Straight Rd., Rom. 105 FH50
Straight Rd., Wind. 172 AU85
Straightsmouth SE10 163 EC80
Strait Rd. E6 144 EL73
Straker's Rd. SE15 162 DV84
Strand WC2 277 P1
Strand WC2 141 DL73
Strand Clo., Epsom 232 CR119
Strand La. WC2 274 C10
Strand on the Grn. W4 158 CN79
Strand Pl. N18 100 DS49
Silver St.
Strand Sch. App. W4 158 CN79
Strandfield Clo. SE18 165 ES78
Strangeways, Wat. 75 BS36
Strangways Ter. W14 159 CZ76
Melbury Rd.
Stranraer Gdns., Slou. 132 AS74
Lansdowne Ave.
Stranraer Rd., Houns. 174 BL86
Stranraer Way N1 141 DL66
Strasburg Rd. SW11 161 DH81
Stratfield Dr., Brox. 49 DY19
Stratfield Pk. Clo. N21 99 DP45
Stratfield Rd., Borwd. 78 CM41
Stratfield Rd., Slou. 152 AU75
Stratford Ave. W8 160 DA76
Stratford Rd.
Stratford Ave., Uxb. 134 BM68
Stratford Cen., The E15 143 ED66
Broadway
Stratford Clo., Bark. 146 EU66
Stratford Clo., Dag. 147 FC66
Stratford Clo., Slou. 131 AK70
Stratford Ct., N.Mal. 198 CR98
Kingston Rd.
Stratford Dr., H.Wyc. 110 AD59
Stratford Gro. SW15 159 CX84
Stratford Ho. Ave., Brom. 204 EL97
Southborough Rd.
Stratford Mkt. E15 143 ED67
Bridge Rd.
Stratford Pl. W1 273 H9
Stratford Pl. W1 141 DH72
Stratford Rd. E13 144 EF67
Stratford Rd. W3 158 CQ75
Bollo Bri. Rd.
Stratford Rd. W8 160 DA76
Stratford Rd., Hayes 135 BV70
Stratford Rd., Houns. 175 BP86
Stratford Rd., Sthl. 156 BY77
Stratford Rd., Th.Hth. 201 DN98
Stratford Rd., Wat. 75 BU40
Stratford Vill. NW1 141 DJ66
Stratford Way, Hem.H. 40 BH23
Stratford Way, St.Alb. 60 BZ29
Stratford Way, Wat. 75 BT40
Strath Ter. SW11 160 DE84
Strathan Clo. SW18 179 CY86
Strathaven Rd. SE12 184 EH86
Strathblaine Rd. SW11 180 DD85
Strathbrook Rd. SW16 181 DM94
Strathcona Ave., Lthd. 246 BY128
Strathcona Clo., H.Wyc. 110 AC56
Strathcona Rd., Wem. 117 CK61
Strathcona Way, H.Wyc. 110 AC56
Strathdale SW16 181 DM92
Strathdon Dr. SW17 180 DD90
Strathearn Ave., Hayes 155 BT80
Strathearn Ave., Twick. 176 CB88
Strathearn Pl. W2 272 B10
Strathearn Pl. W2 140 DE73
Strathearn Rd. SW19 180 DA92
Strathearn Rd., Sutt. 218 DA106
Stratheden Par. SE3 164 EG80
Stratheden Rd.
Stratheden Rd. SE3 164 EG81
Strathfield Gdns., Bark. 145 ER65
Strathleven Rd. SW2 161 DL84
Strathmore Clo., Cat. 236 DS121
Strathmore Gdns. N3 98 DB53
Strathmore Gdns. W8 140 DA74
Palace Gdns. Ter.
Strathmore Gdns., Edg. 96 CP54
Strathmore Gdns., Horn. 127 FF60
Strathmore Rd. SW19 180 DA90
Strathmore Rd., Croy. 202 DQ101
Strathmore Rd., Tedd. 177 CE91
Strathnairn St. SE1 162 DU77
Strathray Gdns. NW3 140 DE65
Strathville Rd. SW18 180 DA89
Strathyre Ave. SW16 201 DN97
Stratton Ave., Enf. 82 DR37
Stratton Ave., Wall. 219 DK109
Stratton Chase Dr., Ch.St.G. 90 AU46
Stratton Clo. SW19 200 DA96
Stratton Clo., Bexh. 166 EY83
Stratton Clo., Edg. 96 CM51
Stratton Clo., Houns. 156 BZ81
Stratton Clo., Walt. 196 BW102
St. Johns Dr.
Stratton Dr., Bark. 125 ET64
Stratton Gdns., Sthl. 136 BZ72
Stratton Rd. SW19 200 DA96
Stratton Rd., Beac. 88 AH53
Stratton Rd., Bexh. 166 EY83
Stratton Rd., Rom. 106 FN50
Stratton Rd., Sun. 195 BT96
Stratton St. W1 277 J2
Stratton St. W1 141 DH74
Stratton Ter., West. 255 EQ127
High St.
Stratton Wk., Rom. 106 FN50
Strattondale St. E14 163 EC76
Strauss Rd. W4 158 CR75
Strawberry Fld., Hat. 45 CU21
Strawberry Flds., Swan. 207 FE95
Strawberry Hill, Twick. 177 CF90
Strawberry Hill Clo., Twick. 177 CF91
Strawberry Hill Rd., Twick. 177 CF90
Strawberry La., Cars. 200 DF104
Strawberry Vale N2 98 DD53
Strawberry Vale, Twick. 177 CF90
Strawfields, Welw.G.C. 30 DB08
Strawmead, Hat. 45 CV16
Crop Common
Strayfield Rd., Enf. 81 DP37
Streakes Fld. Rd. NW2 119 CU61
Stream Clo., W.Byf. 212 BK112
Stream La., Edg. 96 CP50
Streamay, Belv. 166 EZ79
Streamdale SE2 166 EU79
Streamside Clo. N9 100 DT46
Streamside Clo., Brom. 204 EG98
Streatfield Ave. E6 145 EM67
Streatfield Rd., Har. 118 CL55
Streatham Clo. SW16 181 DL90
Streatham Common N. SW16 181 DL92
Streatham Common S. SW16 181 DL93
Streatham Ct. SW16 181 DL90
Streatham High Rd. SW16 181 DL92
Streatham Hill SW2 181 DL89
Streatham Pl. SW2 181 DL87
Streatham Rd. SW16 200 DG95
Streatham Rd., Mitch. 200 DG95
Streatham St. WC1 273 P8
Streatham Vale SW16 201 DJ95
Streathbourne Rd. SW17 180 DG89
Streatley Pl. NW3 120 DC63
New End Sq.
Streatley Rd. NW6 139 CZ66
Street, The, Ash. 232 CM118
Street, The, Bet. 248 CS134
Street, The, Bishop's Stortford 37 FC07
Street, The, Dart. 208 FQ98
Street, The (Albury), Guil. 260 BJ139
Street, The (East Clandon), Guil. 244 BK131
Street, The (Shalford), Guil. 258 AX139
Street, The (West Clandon), Guil. 244 BG128
Street, The (Wonersh), Guil. 259 BA144
Street, The, Kings L. 58 BG31
Street, The, Lthd. 231 CD121
Street, The (Effingham), Lthd. 246 BX127
Street, The (West Horsley), Lthd. 245 BP130
Streeters La., Wall. 201 DK104
Streetfield Ms. SE3 164 EG83
Streimer Rd. E15 143 EC68
Strelley Way W3 138 CS73
Stretton Pl., Amer. 72 AT38
Quill Hall La.
Stretton Rd., Croy. 202 DS101
Stretton Rd., Rich. 177 CJ89
Stretton Way, Borwd. 78 CL38
Strickland Ave., Dart. 168 FM83
Strickland Rd., Belv. 166 FA77
Strickland Row SW18 180 DD87
Strickland St. SE8 163 EA81
Strickland Way, Orp. 223 ET105
Stride Rd. E13 144 EF68
Stringers Ave., Guil. 242 AW128
Stringer's Common, Guil. 242 AW129
Stringhams Copse, Wok. 227 BF124
Stripling Way, Wat. 93 BU45
Moor Vw.
Strode Clo. N10 98 DG52
Pembroke Rd.
Strode Rd. E7 124 EG63
Strode Rd. N17 100 DS54
Strode Rd. NW10 139 CU65
Strode Rd. SW6 159 CY80
Strode St., Egh. 173 BA91
Strodes College La., Egh. 173 AZ92
High St.
Strodes Cres., Stai. 174 BJ92
Stroma Clo., Hem.H. 41 BQ22
Stroma Ct., Slou. 131 AK73
Lincoln Way
Strone Rd. E7 144 EJ65
Strone Rd. E12 144 EK65
Strone Way, Hayes 136 BY70
Strongbow Cres. SE9 185 EM85
Strongbow Rd. SE9 185 EM85
Strongbridge Clo., Har. 116 CA60
Stronsa Rd. W12 159 CT75
Stronsay Clo., Hem.H. 41 BQ22
Northend
Strood Ave., Rom. 127 FD60
Stroud Clo., Wind. 151 AK83
Stroud Cres. SW15 179 CU90
Stroud Fld., Nthlt. 136 BY65
Stroud Gate, Har. 116 CB63
Stroud Grn. Gdns., Croy. 202 DW101
Stroud Grn. Rd. N4 121 DM60
Stroud Grn. Way, Croy. 202 DV101
Stroud Rd. SE25 202 DU100
Stroud Rd. SW19 180 DA90
Stroud Way, Ashf. 175 BP93
Courtfield Rd.
Stroude Rd., Egh. 193 BA96
Stroude Rd., Vir.W. 192 AY98
Stroudes Clo., Wor.Pk. 198 CS101
Stroudley Wk. E3 143 EB69
Stroudwater Pk., Wey. 213 BP107
Strouts Pl. E2 275 P2
Strutton Grd. SW1 277 M6
Strutton Grd. SW1 161 DK76
Struttons Ave., Grav. 191 GF89
Strype St. E1 275 P7
Stuart Ave. NW9 119 CU59
Stuart Ave. W5 138 CM74
Stuart Ave., Brom. 204 EG102
Stuart Ave., Har. 116 BZ62
Stuart Ave., Walt. 195 BV102
Stuart Clo., Brwd. 108 FV43
Stuart Clo., Swan. 187 FF94
Stuart Clo., Uxb. 134 BN65
Stuart Clo., Wind. 151 AM82
Stuart Ct. (Elstree), Borwd. 77 CK44
High St.
Stuart Cres. N22 99 DM53
Stuart Cres., Croy. 221 DZ105
Stuart Cres., Hayes 135 BQ72
Stuart Cres., Reig. 266 DA137
Stuart Evans Clo., Well. 166 EW83
Stuart Gro., Tedd. 177 CE92
Stuart Mantle Way, Erith 167 FD80
Stuart Pl., Mitch. 200 DF95
Stuart Rd. NW6 140 DA69
Stuart Rd. SE15 162 DW84
Stuart Rd. SW19 180 DA90
Stuart Rd. W3 138 CQ74
Stuart Rd., Bark. 145 ET66
Stuart Rd., Barn. 98 DE45
Stuart Rd., Grav. 191 GG86
Stuart Rd., Grays 170 GB78
Stuart Rd., Har. 117 CF55
Stuart Rd., Reig. 266 DA137
Stuart Rd., Rich. 177 CH89
Stuart Rd., Th.Hth. 202 DQ98
Stuart Rd., Warl. 236 DV120
Stuart Rd., Well. 166 EV81
Stuart Twr. W9 140 DC69
Stuart Way, Stai. 174 BH93
Stuart Way, Vir.W. 192 AU97
Stuart Way (Cheshunt), Wal.Cr. 66 DV31
Stuart Way, Wind. 151 AL82
Stuarts Clo., Hem.H. 40 BK22
Marriots Way
Stubbers La., Upmin. 149 FR65
Stubbings Hall La., Wal.Abb. 67 EB28
Stubbs Dr. SE16 162 DV78
Stubbs End Clo., Amer. 55 AS37
Stubbs Hill, Sev. 224 EW113
Stubbs La., Tad. 249 CZ128
Stubbs Pt. E13 144 EG70
Stubbs Way SW19 200 DD95
Brangwyn Cres.
Stubbs Wd., Amer. 55 AS36
Stubs Clo., Dor. 263 CJ138
Stubs Hill
Stubs Hill, Dor. 263 CJ138
Stucley Pl. NW1 141 DH66
Hawley Cres.
Stucley Rd., Houns. 156 CC80
Stud Grn., Wat. 59 BV32
Studd St. N1 141 DP67
Studdridge St. SW6 160 DA82
Studholme Ct. NW3 120 DA63
Studholme St. SE15 162 DV80
Studio Ct., Borwd. 78 CQ40
Studio Way
Studio Pl. SW1 276 E5
Studio Way, Borwd. 78 CQ40
Studios, The (Bushey), Wat. 76 CA44
Studios Rd., Shep. 194 BM97
Studland SE17 279 K10
Studland Clo., Sid. 185 ET90
Studland Rd. SE26 183 DX92
Studland Rd. W7 137 CD72
Studland Rd., Kings.T. 178 CL93
Studland Rd., W.Byf. 212 BM113
Studland St. W6 159 CV77
Studley Ave. E4 101 ED52
Studley Clo. E5 123 DY64
Studley Ct., Sid. 186 EV92
Studley Dr., Ilf. 124 EK58
Studley Est. SW4 161 DL81
Studley Gra. Rd. W7 157 CE75
Studley Rd. E7 144 EH65
Studley Rd. SW4 161 DL81
Studley Rd., Dag. 146 EX66
Stukeley Rd. E7 144 EH66
Stukeley St. WC2 274 A8
Stukeley St. WC2 141 DL72
Stumps Hill La., Beck. 183 EA93
Stumps La., Whyt. 236 DS117
Stumpwell La., H.Wyc. 88 AE48
Sturdy Rd. SE15 162 DV82
Sturge Ave. E17 101 EB53
Sturge St. SE1 279 H4
Sturgeon Rd. SE17 161 DP78
Sturges Fld., Chis. 185 ER93
Sturgess Ave. NW4 119 CU59
Sturlas Way, Wal.Cr. 67 DX33
Sturmer Way N7 121 DM64
Stock Orchard Cres.
Sturminster Clo., Hayes 136 BW72
Lulworth Waye
Sturrock Clo. N15 122 DR56
Sturry St. E14 143 EB72
Sturt Ct., Guil. 243 BC132
Ashbury Cres.
Sturt St. N1 275 J1
Sturt St. N1 142 DQ68
Sturts La., Tad. 249 CT127
Stutfield St. E1 142 DU72
Stychens Clo., Red. 252 DQ133
Stychens La., Red. 252 DQ132
Stylecroft Rd., Ch.St.G. 90 AX47
Styles End, Lthd. 246 CB127
Styles Gdns. SW9 161 DP83
Styles Way, Beck. 203 EC98
Styventon Pl., Cher. 193 BF101
Succombs Hill, Warl. 236 DV120
Succombs Hill, Whyt. 236 DV120
Succombs Pl., Warl. 236 DV120
Sudbourne Rd. SW2 181 DL85
Sudbrook Gdns., Rich. 178 CL90
Sudbrook La., Rich. 178 CL88
Sudbrooke Rd. SW12 180 DF86
Sudbury E6 145 EN72
Newark Knok
Sudbury Ave., Wem. 117 CJ64
Sudbury Ct. E5 123 DY63
Sudbury Ct. Dr., Har. 117 CF62
Sudbury Ct. Rd., Har. 117 CF62
Sudbury Cres., Brom. 184 EG93
Sudbury Cres., Wem. 117 CH64
Sudbury Cft., Wem. 117 CF63
Sudbury Gdns., Croy. 220 DS105
Langton Way
Sudbury Heights Ave., Grnf. 117 CF64
Sudbury Hill, Har. 117 CE61
Sudbury Hill Clo., Wem. 117 CF63
Sudbury Meadows, Wem. 117 CJ62
Sudbury Rd., Bark. 125 ET64
Sudeley St. N1 274 G1
Sudeley St. N1 141 DP68
Sudicamps Ct., Wal.Abb. 68 EG33
Sudlow Rd. SW18 180 DA85
Sudrey St. SE1 279 H5
Suez Ave., Grnf. 137 CF68
Suez Rd., Enf. 83 DY42
Suffield Clo., S.Croy. 221 DX112
Suffield Rd. E4 101 EB48
Suffield Rd. N15 122 DT57
Suffield Rd. SE20 202 DW96
Suffolk Clo., Borwd. 78 CR43
Clydesdale Clo.
Suffolk Clo., Horl. 268 DG149
Suffolk Clo., St.Alb. 61 CJ25
Suffolk Clo., Slou. 131 AL72
Suffolk Ct. E10 123 EA59
Suffolk Ct., Ilf. 125 ES58
Suffolk Dr., Guil. 243 BB129
Suffolk La. EC4 275 K10
Suffolk Pk. Rd. E17 123 DY56
Suffolk Pl. SW1 277 N2
Suffolk Rd. E13 144 EG69
Suffolk Rd. N15 122 DR58
Suffolk Rd. NW10 138 CS66
Suffolk Rd. SE25 202 DT98
Suffolk Rd. SW13 159 CT80
Suffolk Rd., Bark. 145 ER66
Suffolk Rd., Dag. 127 FC64
Suffolk Rd., Dart. 188 FL86
Suffolk Rd., Enf. 82 DV43
Suffolk Rd., Grav. 191 GK86
Suffolk Rd., Har. 116 BZ58
Suffolk Rd., Ilf. 125 ES58
Suffolk Rd., Pot.B. 63 CY32
Suffolk Rd., Sid. 186 EW93
Suffolk Rd., Wor.Pk. 199 CT103
Suffolk St. E7 124 EG64
Suffolk St. SW1 277 N1
Suffolk Way, Horn. 128 FN56
Suffolk Way, Sev. 257 FJ125
Sugar Bakers Ct. EC3 275 N9
Sugar Ho. La. E15 143 EC68
Sugar La., Berk. 39 AZ22
Sugar La., Hem.H. 39 BB22
Sugar Loaf Wk. E2 142 DW69
Victoria Pk. Sq.
Sugden Rd. SW11 160 DG83
Sugden Rd., T.Ditt. 197 CH102
Sugden Way, Bark. 145 ET68
Sulgrave Gdns. W6 159 CW75
Sulgrave Rd.
Sulgrave Rd. W6 159 CW76
Sulina Rd. SW2 181 DL87
Sulivan Ct. SW6 160 DA82
Sulivan Rd. SW6 160 DA83
Sullivan Ave. E16 144 EK71
Sullivan Clo. SW11 160 DE83
Sullivan Clo., Dart. 187 FH86
Sullivan Clo., W.Mol. 196 CA97
Victoria Ave.
Sullivan Cres., Uxb. 92 BK54
Sullivan Rd. SE11 278 E8
Sullivan Rd. SE11 161 DN77
Sullivan Rd., Til. 171 GG81
Sullivan Way, Borwd. 77 CJ44
Sullivans Reach, Walt. 195 BT101
Sultan Rd. E11 124 EH56
Sultan St. SE5 162 DQ80
Sultan St., Beck. 203 DX96
Sumatra Rd. NW6 120 DA64
Sumburgh Rd. SW12 180 DG86
Sumburgh Spur, Slou. 132 AS71
Summer Ave., E.Mol. 197 CE99
Summer Clo., Lthd. 231 CD124
Summer Ct., Hem.H. 40 BK18
Townsend
Summer Gdns., E.Mol. 197 CE99
Summer Gro., Borwd. 77 CK44
Summer Hill, Borwd. 78 CN43
Summer Hill, Chis. 205 EN96
Summer Hill Vill., Chis. 205 EN95
Summer Ho. Rd. N16 122 DS61
Stoke Newington Ch. St.
Summer Rd., E.Mol. 197 CE99
Summer Rd., T.Ditt. 197 CF99
Summer St. EC1 274 D5
Summer Trees, Sun. 195 BV95
The Ave.
Summercourt Rd. E1 142 DW72
Summerdale, Welw.G.C. 29 CX05
Summerdene Clo. SW16 181 DJ94
Bates Cres.
Summerfield, Ash. 231 CK119
Summerfield, Hat. 45 CU21
Summerfield Ave. NW6 139 CY68
Summerfield Clo., Add. 211 BF106
Spinney Hill
Summerfield Clo., St.Alb. 61 CJ26
Summerfield La., Surb. 197 CK103
Summerfield Pl., Cher. 211 BD107
Crawshaw Rd.
Summerfield Rd. W5 137 CH70
Summerfield Rd., Loug. 84 EK44
Summerfield Rd., Wat. 75 BU35
Summerfield St. SE12 184 EF87
Summerfields Ave. N12 98 DE52
Summerhayes Clo., Wok. 210 AY114
Summerhays, Cob. 214 BX113
Summerhill Clo., Orp. 205 ES104
Summerhill Ct., St.Alb. 43 CF19
Avenue Rd.
Summerhill Gro., Enf. 82 DS44
Summerhill Rd. N15 122 DR56
Summerhill Rd., Dart. 188 FK87
Summerhill Way, Mitch. 200 DG95
Summerhouse Ave., Houns. 156 BY81
Summerhouse Dr., Bex. 187 FD91
Summerhouse Dr., Dart. 187 FD92
Summerhouse La., Uxb. 92 BG52
Summerhouse La., Wat. 76 CC40
Summerhouse La., West Dr. 154 BK79
Summerhouse La. Ind. Est., Uxb. 92 BG51
Summerhouse Way, Abb.L. 59 BT30
Summerland Gdns. N10 121 DH55
Summerlands Ave. W3 138 CQ73
Summerlands Rd., St.Alb. 43 CJ16
Summerlay Clo., Tad. 233 CY120
Summerlea, Slou. 131 AP74
Summerlee Ave. N2 120 DF56
Summerlee Gdns. N2 120 DF56
Summerley St. SW18 180 DB89
Summerly Ave., Reig. 250 DA133
Burnham Dr.
Summers Clo., Sutt. 218 DA108
Overton Rd.
Summers Clo., Wem. 118 CP60
Summers Clo., Wey. 212 BN111
Summers La. N12 98 DD52
Summers Rd., Gdmg. 258 AT144
Summers Rd., Slou. 130 AJ69
Summers Row N12 98 DE51
Summersbury Dr., Guil. 258 AY142
Summersby Rd. N6 121 DH58
Summerstown SW17 180 DC90
Summerswood Clo., Ken. 236 DR116
Longwood Rd.
Summerswood La., Borwd. 78 CS35
Summerton Way SE28 146 EX73
Summerville Gdns., Sutt. 217 CZ107
Summerwood Rd., Islw. 177 CF85
Summit, The, Loug. 85 EM39
Summit Ave. NW9 118 CR57
Summit Clo. N14 99 DJ47
Summit Clo. NW9 118 CR56
Summit Clo., Edg. 96 CN52
Summit Ct. NW2 119 CY64
Summit Dr., Wdf.Grn. 102 EK54
Summit Est. N16 122 DU59
Summit Pl., Wey. 212 BN108
Caenshill Rd.
Summit Rd. E17 123 EB56
Summit Rd., Nthlt. 136 CA66
Summit Rd., Pot.B. 63 CY30
Summit Way N14 99 DH47
Summit Way SE19 182 DS94
Sumner Ave. SE15 162 DT81
Sumner Rd.
Sumner Clo., Orp. 223 EQ105
Sumner Est. SE15 162 DT80
Sumner Gdns., Croy. 201 DN102
Sumner Pl. SW7 276 A9
Sumner Pl. SW7 160 DD77
Sumner Pl., Add. 212 BG106
Sumner Pl. Ms. SW7 276 A9
Sumner Rd. SE15 162 DT80
Sumner Rd., Croy. 201 DN102
Sumner Rd., Har. 116 CC59
Sumner Rd. S., Croy. 201 DN102
Sumner St. SE1 278 G2
Sumner St. SE1 141 DP74
Sumners Fm. Clo., Harl. 51 EN20
Sumpter Clo. NW3 140 DC65
Sumpter Yd., St.Alb. 43 CD20
Sun Ct. EC3 275 L9
Sun Ct., Erith 167 FF82
Sun Hill (Fawkham), Long. 209 FU103
Sun Hill, Wok. 226 AV121
Sun La. SE3 164 EH80
Sun La., Grav. 191 GJ89
Sun Pas. SE16 162 DU76
Frean St.
Sun Pas., Wind. 151 AR81
Peascod St.
Sun Ray Ave., Brwd. 109 GE44
Sun Rd. W14 159 CZ78
Sun Rd., Swans. 190 FZ86
Sun Sq., Hem.H. 40 BK19
High St.
Sun St. EC2 275 L6
Sun St. EC2 142 DR71
Sun St., Saw. 36 EZ06
Sun St., Wal.Abb. 67 EC33
Sun St. Pas. EC2 275 M7
Sunbeam Cres. W10 139 CW70
Barlby Rd.
Sunbeam Rd. NW10 138 CR70
Sunbury Ave. NW7 96 CR50
Sunbury Ave. SW14 158 CR84
Sunbury Ct., Sun. 196 BX96
Sunbury Ct. Island, Sun. 196 BX96
Sunbury Ct. Rd., Sun. 196 BW96
Sunbury Cres., Felt. 175 BT91
Ryland Clo.
Sunbury Gdns. NW7 96 CR50
Sunbury La. SW11 160 DD81
Sunbury La., Walt. 195 BU100
Sunbury Rd., Felt. 175 BT90
Sunbury Rd., Sutt. 199 CX104
Sunbury Rd. (Eton), Wind. 151 AR79
Sunbury St. SE18 165 EM76
Sunbury Way, Felt. 176 BW92
Suncroft Pl. SE26 182 DW90
Sundale Ave., S.Croy. 220 DW110
Sunderland Ave., St.Alb. 43 CG19
Sunderland Ct. SE22 182 DU87
Sunderland Rd. SE23 183 DX88
Sunderland Rd. W5 157 CK76
Sunderland Ter. W2 140 DB72
Sunderland Way E12 124 EK61
Sundew Ave. W12 139 CU73
Sundew Ct., Grays 170 GD79
Salix Rd.
Sundew Rd., Hem.H. 39 BE21
Sundial Ave. SE25 202 DT97
Sundon Cres., Vir.W. 192 AV99
Sundorne Rd. SE7 164 EH78
Sundown Ave., S.Croy. 220 DT111
Sundown Rd., Ashf. 175 BQ92
Sundra Wk. E1 143 DX70
Beaumont Gro.
Sundridge Ave., Brom. 204 EK96
Sundridge Ave., Chis. 184 EL94
Sundridge Ave., Well. 165 ER82
Sundridge Clo., Dart. 188 FN86
Sundridge Ho., Brom. 184 EH92
Burnt Ash La.
Sundridge La., Sev. 240 EV117
Sundridge Pl., Croy. 202 DU102
Inglis Rd.
Sundridge Rd., Croy. 202 DT101
Sundridge Rd., Sev. 240 FA120
Sundridge Rd., Wok. 227 BA119
Sunfields Pl. SE3 164 EH80
Sunflower Way, Rom. 106 FK53
Sunkist Way, Wall. 219 DL109
Sunland Ave., Bexh. 166 EY84
Sunleigh Rd., Wem. 138 CL67
Sunley Gdns., Grnf. 137 CG67
Sunmead Clo., Lthd. 231 CF122
Sunmead Rd., Hem.H. 40 BK18
Sunmead Rd., Sun. 195 BU97

Sunna Gdns., Sun. 195 BV96
Sunning Hill, Grav. 190 GE89
Sunningdale N14 99 DK50
Wilmer Way
Sunningdale Ave. W3 138 CS73
Sunningdale Ave., Bark. 145 ER67
Sunningdale Ave., Felt. 176 BY89
Sunningdale Ave., Rain. 147 FH70
Sunningdale Ave., Ruis. 116 BW60
Sunningdale Clo. E6 145 EM69
Ascot Rd.
Sunningdale Clo. SE16 162 DV78
Credon Rd.
Sunningdale Clo., Stan. 95 CG52
Sunningdale Clo., Surb. 198 CL103
Culsac Rd.
Sunningdale Gdns. NW9 118 CQ57
Sunningdale Gdns. W8 160 DA76
Lexham Ms.
Sunningdale Ms., Welw.G.C. 29 CY05
Sunningdale Rd., Brom. 204 EL98
Sunningdale Rd., Rain. 147 FG66
Sunningdale Rd., Sutt. 217 CZ105
Sunningfields Cres. NW4 97 CV54
Sunningfields Rd. NW4 119 CV55
Sunninghill Rd. SE13 163 EB82
Sunnings La., Upmin. 128 FQ64
Sunningvale Ave., West. 238 EJ115
Sunningvale Clo., West. 238 EK116
Sunny Bank SE25 202 DU97
Sunny Bank, Warl. 237 DY117
Sunny Cres. NW10 138 CQ66
Sunny Cft., Harl. 51 ET18
Sunny Gdns. Par. NW4 97 CW54
Great N. Way
Sunny Gdns. Rd. NW4 97 CV54
Sunny Hill NW4 119 CV55
Sunny Nook Gdns., S.Croy. 220 DR107
Selsdon Rd.
Sunny Ri., Cat. 236 DR124
Sunny Rd., The, Enf. 83 DX39
Sunny Side, Walt. 196 BW99
Sunny Vw. NW9 118 CR57
Sunny Way N12 98 DE52
Sunnybank, Epsom 232 CQ116
Sunnybank Rd., Pot.B. 64 DA33
Sunnybank Vill., Red. 252 DT132
Sunnycroft Gdns., Upmin. 129 FT59
Sunnycroft Rd. SE25 202 DU97
Sunnycroft Rd., Houns. 156 CB82
Sunnycroft Rd., Sthl. 136 CA71
Sunnydale, Orp. 205 EN103
Sunnydale Gdns. NW7 96 CR51
Sunnydale Rd. SE12 184 EH85
Sunnydell, St.Alb. 60 CB26
Sunnydene Ave. E4 101 ED50
Sunnydene Ave., Ruis. 115 BU60
Sunnydene Clo., Rom. 106 FM52
Sunnydene Gdns., Wem. 137 CJ65
Sunnydene Rd., Pur. 219 DP113
Sunnydene St. SE26 183 DY91
Sunnyfield NW7 97 CT49
Sunnyfield, Hat. 45 CX15
Sunnyfield Rd., Chis. 206 EU97
Sunnyhill Rd. SW16 181 DL91
Sunnyhill Rd., Hem.H. 40 BH20
Sunnyhill Rd., Rick. 91 BD51
Sunnyhurst Clo., Sutt. 200 DA104
Sunnymead Ave., Mitch. 201 DJ97
Sunnymead Rd. NW9 118 CR59
Sunnymead Rd. SW15 179 CV85
Sunnymede, Chig. 104 EV47
Sunnymede Ave., Cars. 218 DD111
Sunnymede Ave., Chesh. 54 AS28
Sunnymede Ave., Epsom 216 CS109
Sunnymede Dr., Ilf. 125 EP57
Sunnyside NW2 119 CZ62
Sunnyside SW19 179 CY93
Sunnyside, Wal.Abb. 50 EF22
Sunnyside Cotts., Chesh. 38 AT24
Two Dells La.
Sunnyside Dr. E4 101 EC45
Sunnyside Gdns., Upmin. 128 FQ61
Sunnyside Pas. SW19 179 CY93
Sunnyside Pl. SW19 179 CY93
Sunnyside
Sunnyside Rd. E10 123 EA60
Sunnyside Rd. N19 121 DK59
Sunnyside Rd. W5 137 CK74
Sunnyside Rd., Chesh. 54 AP30
Sunnyside Rd., Epp. 69 ET32
Sunnyside Rd., Ilf. 125 EQ62
Sunnyside Rd., Tedd. 177 CD91
Sunnyside Rd. E. N9 100 DU48
Sunnyside Rd. N. N9 100 DT48
Sunnyside Rd. S. N9 100 DT48
Sunray Ave. SE24 162 DR84
Sunray Ave., Brom. 204 EL100
Sunray Ave., Surb. 198 CP103
Sunray Ave., West Dr. 154 BK75
Sunrise Ave., Horn. 128 FJ61
Sunrise Clo., Felt. 176 BZ90
Exeter Rd.
Sunrise Cres., Hem.H. 40 BM23
Sunset Ave. E4 101 EB46
Sunset Ave., Wdf.Grn. 102 EF49
Sunset Clo., Erith 167 FH81
Slade Grn. Rd.
Sunset Dr. (Havering-atte-Bower), Rom. 105 FH50
Sunset Gdns. SE25 202 DT96
Sunset Rd. SE5 162 DQ84
Sunset Rd. SE28 146 EU74
Birchdene Dr.
Sunset Vw., Barn. 79 CY40
Sunshine Way, Mitch. 200 DF96
Sunstone Gro., Red. 251 DL129
Sunwell Clo. SE15 162 DV81
Cossall Wk.
Superior Dr., Orp. 223 ET107
High St.
Surbiton Ct., Surb. 197 CJ100
Surbiton Cres., Kings.T. 198 CL99
Surbiton Hall Clo., Kings.T. 198 CL98
Surbiton Hill Pk., Surb. 198 CM99
Surbiton Hill Rd., Surb. 198 CL98
Surbiton Par., Surb. 198 CL100
St. Mark's Hill
Surbiton Rd., Kings.T. 197 CK98
Surlingham Clo. SE28 146 EX73
Surly Hall Wk., Wind. 151 AM81
Surma Clo. E1 142 DV70
Selby St.
Surman Cres., Brwd. 109 GC45
Surr St. N7 121 DL64
Surrendale Pl. W9 140 DA70
Surrey Ave., Slou. 131 AQ71
Surrey Canal Rd. SE14 163 DX79
Surrey Canal Rd. SE15 162 DW79
Surrey Cres. W4 158 CN78
Surrey Dr., Horn. 128 FN56
Surrey Gdns. N4 122 DQ58
Surrey Gdns., Lthd. 229 BU122
Surrey Gro. SE17 162 DS78
Surrey Sq.
Surrey Gro., Sutt. 200 DD104
Surrey Hills, Tad. 248 CP130
Surrey Hills Ave., Tad. 248 CQ130
Surrey La. SW11 160 DE81
Surrey La. Est. SW11 160 DE81
Surrey Lo. SE1 278 D7
Surrey Ms. SE27 182 DS91
Hamilton Rd.
Surrey Mt. SE23 182 DV88
Surrey Quays Rd. SE16 162 DW76
Surrey Rd. SE15 183 DX85
Surrey Rd., Bark. 145 ES66
Surrey Rd., Dag. 127 FB64
Surrey Rd., Har. 116 CC57
Surrey Rd., W.Wick. 203 EB102
Surrey Row SE1 278 F4
Surrey Row SE1 161 DP75
Surrey Sq. SE17 279 M10
Surrey Sq. SE17 162 DS78
Surrey St. E13 144 EH69
Surrey St. WC2 274 C10
Surrey St. WC2 141 DM73
Surrey St., Croy. 202 DQ103
Surrey Ter. SE17 279 N10
Surrey Ter. SE17 162 DS77
Surrey Water Rd. SE16 143 DX74
Surridge Clo., Rain. 148 FJ69
Surridge Gdns. SE19 182 DR93
Hancock Rd.
Susan Clo., Rom. 127 FC55
Susan Rd. SE3 164 EH82
Susan Wd., Chis. 205 EN95
Susannah St. E14 143 EB72
Sussex Ave., Islw. 157 CE83
Sussex Ave., Rom. 106 FM52
Sussex Border Path, Horl. 268 DA152
Sussex Clo. N19 121 DL61
Cornwallis Rd.
Sussex Clo., Ch.St.G. 90 AV47
Sussex Clo., Hodd. 49 EA16
Roman St.
Sussex Clo., Ilf. 125 EM58
Sussex Clo., N.Mal. 198 CS98
Sussex Clo., Reig. 250 DD134
Sussex Clo., Slou. 152 AV75
Sussex Clo., Twick. 177 CH86
Westmorland Clo.
Sussex Cres., Nthlt. 136 CA65
Sussex Gdns. N4 122 DQ57
Sussex Gdns. N6 120 DF57
Great N. Rd.
Sussex Gdns. W2 140 DD72
Sussex Gdns., Chess. 215 CK107
Sussex Keep, Slou. 152 AV75
Sussex Clo.
Sussex Ms. E. W2 272 A9
Sussex Ms. W. W2 272 A10
Sussex Pl. NW1 272 D3
Sussex Pl. NW1 140 DF70
Sussex Pl. W2 272 A9
Sussex Pl. W2 140 DD72
Sussex Pl. W6 159 CW78
Sussex Pl., Erith 167 FB80
Sussex Pl., N.Mal. 198 CS98
Sussex Pl., Slou. 152 AV75
Sussex Ring N12 98 DA50
Sussex Rd. E6 145 EN67
Sussex Rd., Brwd. 108 FV49
Sussex Rd., Cars. 218 DF107
Sussex Rd., Dart. 188 FN87
Sussex Rd., Erith 167 FB80
Sussex Rd., Har. 116 CC57
Sussex Rd., Mitch. 201 DL99
Lincoln Rd.
Sussex Rd., N.Mal. 198 CS98
Sussex Rd., Orp. 206 EW100
Sussex Rd., Sid. 186 EV92
Sussex Rd., S.Croy. 220 DR107
Sussex Rd., Sthl. 156 BX76
Sussex Rd., Uxb. 115 BQ63
Sussex Rd., Wat. 75 BU37
Sussex Rd., W.Wick. 203 EB102
Sussex Sq. W2 272 A10
Sussex Sq. W2 140 DD73
Sussex St. E13 144 EH69
Sussex St. SW1 161 DH78
Sussex Wk. SW9 161 DP84
Sussex Way N7 121 DL61
Sussex Way N19 121 DL60
Sussex Way, Barn. 81 DH43
Sussex Way, Uxb. 113 BF57
Sutcliffe Clo. NW11 120 DB57
Sutcliffe Clo. (Bushey), Wat. 76 CC42
Sutcliffe Ho., Hayes 135 BU72
Sutcliffe Rd. SE18 165 ES79
Sutcliffe Rd., Well. 166 EW82
Sutherland Ave. W9 140 DA70
Sutherland Ave. W13 137 CH72
Sutherland Ave., Guil. 242 AX128
Sutherland Ave., Hayes 155 BU77
Sutherland Ave., Orp. 205 ET100
Sutherland Ave. (Cuffley), Pot.B. 65 DK28
Sutherland Ave., Sun. 195 BT96
Sutherland Ave., Well. 165 ES84
Sutherland Ave., West. 238 EK117
Sutherland Clo., Barn. 79 CY42
Sutherland Clo., Green. 189 FU85
Cowley Ave.
Sutherland Ct. NW9 118 CP56
Sutherland Ct., Welw.G.C. 29 CZ08
Sutherland Dr. SW19 200 DD95
Willow Vw.
Sutherland Dr., Guil. 243 AZ131
Sutherland Gdns. SW14 158 CS83
Sutherland Gdns., Sun. 195 BT96
Sutherland Ave.
Sutherland Gdns., Wor.Pk. 199 CV101
Sutherland Gro. SW18 179 CY86
Sutherland Gro., Tedd. 177 CE92
Sutherland Pl. W2 140 DA72
Sutherland Pt. E5 122 DV63
Tiger Way
Sutherland Rd. E17 101 DX54
Sutherland Rd. N9 100 DU46
Sutherland Rd. N17 100 DU52
Sutherland Rd. W4 158 CS79
Sutherland Rd. W13 137 CG72
Sutherland Rd., Belv. 166 FA76
Sutherland Rd., Croy. 201 DN101
Sutherland Rd., Enf. 83 DX43
Sutherland Rd., Sthl. 136 BZ72
Sutherland Rd. Path E17 123 DX55
Sutherland Row SW1 277 J10
Sutherland Row SW1 161 DH78
Sutherland Sq. SE17 162 DQ78
Sutherland St. SW1 277 H10
Sutherland St. SW1 161 DH78
Sutherland Wk. SE17 162 DQ78
Sutherland Way (Cuffley), Pot.B. 65 DK28
Sutlej Rd. SE7 164 EJ80
Sutterton St. N7 141 DM65
Sutton Arc., Sutt. 218 DB106
Throwley Way
Sutton Ave., Slou. 152 AW75
Sutton Ave., Wok. 226 AS119
Sutton Clo., Beck. 203 EB95
Albemarle Rd.
Sutton Clo., Brox. 49 DY20
Sutton Clo., Loug. 102 EL45
Sutton Clo., Pnr. 115 BU57
Sutton Common Rd., Sutt. 199 CZ101
Sutton Ct. W4 158 CQ79
Sutton Ct. Rd. E13 144 EJ69
Sutton Ct. Rd. W4 158 CQ80
Sutton Ct. Rd., Sutt. 218 DC107
Sutton Ct. Rd., Uxb. 135 BP67
Sutton Cres., Barn. 79 CX43
Sutton Dene, Houns. 156 CB81
Sutton Est. SW3 276 C10
Sutton Est. SW3 160 DE78
Sutton Est. W10 139 CW71
Sutton Est., The N1 141 DP66
Sutton Gdns., Bark. 145 ES67
Sutton Rd.
Sutton Gdns., Croy. 202 DT99
Sutton Gdns., Red. 251 DK129
Sutton Grn., Bark. 145 ES67
Sutton Rd.
Sutton Grn. Rd., Guil. 242 AY126
Sutton Gro., Sutt. 218 DD105
Sutton Hall Rd., Houns. 156 CA80
Sutton Ho., Hem.H. 40 BL16
Sutton La., Bans. 234 DB115
Sutton La., Dor. 261 BV143
Sutton La., Houns. 156 BZ83
Sutton La., Slou. 153 BB79
Sutton La., Sutt. 218 DB111
Sutton La. N. W4 158 CQ78
Sutton La. S. W4 158 CQ79
Sutton Pk., Guil. 243 AZ127
Sutton Pk. Rd., Sutt. 218 DB107
Sutton Path, Borwd. 78 CN40
Stratfield Rd.
Sutton Pl. E9 122 DW64
Sutton Pl., Dor. 261 BT143
Sutton Pl., Slou. 153 BB79
Sutton Rd. E13 144 EF70
Sutton Rd. E17 101 DX53
Sutton Rd. N10 98 DG53
Sutton Rd., Bark. 145 ES68
Sutton Rd., Houns. 156 CA81
Sutton Rd., St.Alb. 43 CH21
Sutton Rd., Wat. 76 BW41
Sutton Row W1 273 N8
Sutton Row W1 141 DK72
Sutton Sq. E9 122 DW64
Urswick Rd.
Sutton Sq., Houns. 156 BZ81
Sutton St. E1 142 DW73
Sutton Way W10 139 CW71
Sutton Way, Houns. 156 BZ81
Suttons Ave., Horn. 128 FJ62
Suttons Gdns., Horn. 128 FK62
Suttons La., Horn. 128 FK64
Sutton's Way EC1 275 J5
Swabey Rd., Slou. 153 BA77
Swaby Rd. SW18 180 DC88
Swaffham Way N22 99 DP52
White Hart La.
Swaffield Rd. SW18 180 DB87
Swaffield Rd., Sev. 257 FJ122
Swain Clo. SW16 181 DH93
Swain Rd., Th.Hth. 202 DQ99
Swains Clo., West Dr. 154 BL75
Swains La. N6 120 DG60
Swains Rd. SW17 180 DF94
Swainson Rd. W3 159 CT75
Swaisland Dr., Dart. 187 FF85
Swaisland Rd., Dart. 187 FH85
Swakeleys Dr., Uxb. 114 BM63
Swakeleys Rd., Uxb. 114 BL63
Swale Clo., S.Ock. 148 FQ72
Swale Rd., Dart. 167 FG83
Swaledale Rd., Dart. 188 FQ88
Swallands Rd. SE6 183 EA90
Swallow Clo. SE14 163 DX81
Swallow Clo., Erith 167 FE81
Colyers La.
Swallow Clo., Green. 189 FT85
Swallow Clo., Rick. 92 BJ45
Swallow Clo., Stai. 173 BF91
Swallow Clo. (Bushey), Wat. 94 CC46
Swallow Ct., Hert. 32 DQ09
Swallow Dr. NW10 138 CR65
Kingfisher Way
Swallow Dr., Nthlt. 136 CA68
Swallow End, Welw.G.C. 29 CZ09
Swallow Gdns., Hat. 45 CU20
Swallow La., Dor. 263 CH142
Swallow La., St.Alb. 43 CH23
Swallow Oaks, Abb.L. 59 BT31
Swallow Pas. W1 273 J9
Swallow Pl. W1 273 J9
Swallow St. E6 144 EL71
Swallow St. W1 277 L1
Swallow St., Iver 133 BD69
Swallow Wk., Horn. 147 FH65
Heron Flight Ave.
Swallowdale, Iver 133 BD69
Swallowdale, S.Croy. 221 DX109
Swallowdale La., Hem.H. 40 BN17
Swallowfield, Egh. 172 AV93
Heronfield
Swallowfield Rd. SE7 164 EH78
Swallowfield Way, Hayes 155 BR75
Swallowfields, Grav. 190 GE90
Hillary Ave.
Swallowfields, Welw.G.C. 29 CZ09
Swallows, Harl. 36 EW11
Station Rd.
Swallows, The, Welw.G.C. 29 CZ05
Swan & Pike Rd., Enf. 83 EA38
Swan App. E6 144 EL71
Swan Ave., Upmin. 129 FT60
Swan Clo. E17 101 DY53
Banbury Rd.
Swan Clo., Chesh. 54 AP27
Swan Clo., Croy. 202 DS101
Swan Clo., Felt. 176 BY91
Swan Clo., Orp. 206 EU97
Swan Ct. SW3 160 DE78
Flood St.
Swan Ct., Guil. 242 AX132
Swan Dr. NW9 96 CS54
Swan La. EC4 279 K1
Swan La. N20 98 DC48
Swan La., Dart. 187 FF87
Swan La., Guil. 258 AX135
Swan La., Loug. 102 EJ45
Swan Mead SE1 279 M7
Swan Mead SE1 162 DS76
Swan Ms. SW9 161 DM81
Swan Mill Gdns., Dor. 247 CJ134
Swan Pas. E1 142 DT73
Cartwright St.
Swan Pl. SW13 159 CT82
Swan Rd. SE16 162 DW75
Swan Rd. SE18 164 EK76
Swan Rd., Felt. 176 BY92
Swan Rd., Iver 133 BF72
Swan Rd., Sthl. 136 CB72
Swan Rd., West Dr. 154 BK75
Swan St. SE1 279 J6
Swan St. SE1 162 DQ76
Swan St., Islw. 157 CH83
Swan Ter., Wind. 151 AP80
Mill La.
Swan Wk. SW3 160 DF79
Swan Wk., Rom. 127 FE57
Swan Wk., Shep. 195 BS101
Walton Bri. Rd.
Swan Way, Enf. 83 DX40
Swan Yd. N1 141 DP65
Highbury Sta. Rd.
Swan Yd., Grav. 191 GH86
Queen St.
Swanage Rd. E4 101 EC52
Swanage Rd. SW18 180 DC86
Swanage Waye, Hayes 136 BW72
Swanbourne Dr., Horn. 128 FJ64
Swanbridge Rd., Bexh. 166 FA81
Swandon Way SW18 160 DB84
Swanfield Rd., Wal.Cr. 67 DY33
Swanfield St. E2 275 P3
Swanfield St. E2 142 DT69
Swanhill, Welw.G.C. 30 DA06
Swanland Rd., Hat. 63 CV25
Swanland Rd., Pot.B. 63 CV33
Swanley Bar La., Pot.B. 64 DB28
Swanley Bypass, Sid. 207 FC96
Swanley Bypass, Swan. 207 FC96
Swanley Cres., Pot.B. 64 DB29
Swanley La., Swan. 207 FF97
Swanley Rd., Well. 166 EW81
Swanley Village Rd., Swan. 207 FH95
Swanns Meadow, Lthd. 246 CA126
Swans Clo., St.Alb. 44 CL21
Swanscombe Rd. W4 158 CS78
Swanscombe Rd. W11 139 CX74
Swanscombe St., Swans. 190 FY87
Swansea Rd., Enf. 82 DW42
Swanshope, Loug. 85 EP40
Swansland Gdns. E17 101 DY53
McEntee Ave.
Swanston Path, Wat. 94 BW48
Swanton Gdns. SW19 179 CX88
Swanton Rd., Erith 167 FB80
Swanwick Clo. SW15 179 CT87
Swanworth La., Dor. 247 CH128
Sward Rd., Orp. 206 EU100
Swaton Rd. E3 143 EA70
Swaylands Rd., Belv. 166 FA79
Swaynes La., Guil. 243 BE134
Swaynesland Rd., Eden. 255 EM134
Swaythling Clo. N18 100 DV49
Sweden Gate SE16 163 DY76
Swedenborg Gdns. E1 142 DU73
Sweeney Cres. SE1 162 DT75
Sweeps Ditch Clo., Stai. 194 BG95
Sweeps La., Egh. 173 AZ92
Sweeps La., Orp. 206 EX99
Sweet Briar, Welw.G.C. 30 DA11
Sweet Briar Grn. N9 100 DT48
Sweet Briar Gro. N9 100 DT48
Sweet Briar La., Epsom 216 CR114
Madans Wk.
Sweet Briar Wk. N18 100 DT49
Sweet La., Guil. 261 BR143
Sweetbriar Clo., Hem.H. 40 BG17
Sweetcroft La., Uxb. 134 BM66
Sweetmans Ave., Pnr. 116 BX55
Sweets Way N20 98 DD47
Swete St. E13 144 EG68
Swetenham Wk. SE18 165 EQ78
Sandbach Pl.
Sweyn Pl. SE3 164 EG82
Sweyne Rd., Swans. 190 FY86
Sweyns, Harl. 52 EX17
Swievelands Rd., West. 238 EH119
Swift Clo. E17 101 DY52
Banbury Rd.
Swift Clo., Har. 116 CB61
Swift Clo., Hayes 135 BT72
Church Rd.
Swift Clo., Upmin. 129 FS60
Swift Clo., Ware 33 EC12
Swift Rd., Felt. 176 BX91
Swift Rd., Sthl. 156 BZ76
Swift St. SW6 159 CZ81
Swiftfields, Welw.G.C. 29 CZ08
Swiftsden Way, Brom. 184 EE93
Swinbrook Rd. W10 139 CY71
Swinburne Ct. SE5 162 DR84
Basingdon Way
Swinburne Cres., Croy. 202 DW100
Swinburne Gdns., Til. 171 GH82
Swinburne Rd. SW15 159 CU84
Swinderby Rd., Wem. 138 CL65
Swindon Clo., Ilf. 125 ES61
Salisbury Rd.
Swindon Clo., Rom. 106 FM50
Swindon Gdns., Rom. 106 FM50
Swindon La., Rom. 106 FM50
Swindon Rd., Houns. 175 BQ86
Southern Perimeter Rd.
Swindon St. W12 139 CV74
Swinfield Clo., Felt. 176 BY91
Swinford Gdns. SW9 161 DP83
Swing Gate La., Berk. 38 AX21
Swingate La. SE18 165 ES80
Swinnerton St. E9 123 DY64
Swinton Clo., Wem. 118 CP60
Swinton Pl. WC1 274 B2
Swinton Pl. WC1 141 DM69
Swinton St. WC1 274 B2
Swinton St. WC1 141 DM69
Swires Shaw, Kes. 222 EK105
Swiss Ave., Wat. 75 BS42
Swiss Clo., Wat. 75 BS41
Swiss Ter. NW6 140 DD66
Swithland Gdns. SE9 185 EN91
Sword Clo., Brox. 49 DY21
Baas Hill
Swyncombe Ave. W5 157 CH77
Swynford Gdns. NW4 119 CU56
Handowe Clo.
Sybil Ms. N4 121 DP58
Lothair Rd. N.
Sybil Phoenix Clo. SE8 163 DX78
Sybil Thorndike Ho. N1 142 DQ65
Clephane Rd.
Sybourn St. E17 123 DZ59
Sycamore App., Rick. 75 BQ43
Sycamore Ave. W5 157 CK76
Sycamore Ave., Hat. 45 CU19
Sycamore Ave., Hayes 135 BS73
Sycamore Ave., Sid. 185 ET86
Sycamore Ave., Upmin. 128 FN62
Sycamore Clo. E16 144 EE70
Clarence Rd.
Sycamore Clo. N9 100 DU49
Pycroft Way
Sycamore Clo. SE9 184 EL89
Sycamore Clo. W3 138 CS74
Bromyard Ave.
Sycamore Clo., Amer. 55 AR37
Sycamore Clo., Barn. 80 DD44
Sycamore Clo., Cars. 218 DF105
Sycamore Clo., Ch.St.G. 90 AU48
Sycamore Clo., Felt. 175 BU90
Sycamore Clo., Grav. 191 GK87
Sycamore Clo., Lthd. 231 CE123
Sycamore Clo., Nthlt. 136 BY67
Sycamore Clo., Wal.Cr. 66 DS27
Sycamore Clo., Wat. 75 BV35
Sycamore Clo. (Bushey), Wat. 76 BY40
Sycamore Clo., West Dr. 134 BM73
Whitethorn Ave.
Sycamore Dean, Chesh. 54 AR28
Sycamore Dr., Brwd. 108 FW46
Copperfield Gdns.
Sycamore Dr., St.Alb. 61 CD27
Sycamore Dr., Swan. 207 FE97
Sycamore Fld., Harl. 51 EN19
Broadley Rd.
Sycamore Gdns. W6 159 CV75
Sycamore Gdns., Mitch. 200 DD96
Sycamore Gro. NW9 118 CQ59
Sycamore Gro. SE6 183 EC86
Sycamore Gro. SE20 182 DU94
Sycamore Gro., N.Mal. 198 CR97
Sycamore Hill N11 98 DG51
Sycamore Ms. SW4 161 DJ83
Orlando Rd.
Sycamore Ri., Bans. 217 CX114
Sycamore Ri., Berk. 38 AX20
Sycamore Ri., Ch.St.G. 90 AU48
Sycamore Rd. SW19 179 CW93
Sycamore Rd., Amer. 55 AQ37
Sycamore Rd., Ch.St.G. 90 AU48
Sycamore Rd., Dart. 188 FK87
Sycamore Rd., Guil. 242 AX134
Sycamore Rd., Rick. 75 BQ43
Sycamore Rd., Tedd. 177 CJ93
Sycamore St. EC1 275 H5
Sycamore Wk. W10 139 CY70
Fifth Ave.
Sycamore Wk., Egh. 172 AV93
Sycamore Wk., Ilf. 125 EQ56
Civic Way
Sycamore Wk., Reig. 266 DC136
Sycamore Wk., Slou. 132 AY72
Sycamore Way, S.Ock. 149 FX70
Sycamore Way, Th.Hth. 201 DN99
Grove Rd.
Sycamores, The, Hem.H. 39 BF23
Sycamores, The, Rad. 61 CH34
Sycamores, The, S.Ock. 149 FR74
Dacre Ave.
Sydenham Ave. SE26 182 DV92
Sydenham Clo., Rom. 127 FF56
Sydenham Cotts. SE12 184 EJ89
Sydenham Hill SE23 182 DV88
Sydenham Hill SE26 182 DT91
Sydenham Hill Est. SE26 182 DU90
Sydenham Pk. SE26 182 DW90
Sydenham Pk. Rd. SE26 182 DW90
Sydenham Ri. SE23 182 DV89
Sydenham Rd. SE26 183 DX92
Sydenham Rd., Croy. 202 DQ102
Sydenham Rd., Guil. 258 AX136
Sydmons Ct. SE23 182 DW87
Sydner Ms. N16 122 DT63
Sydner Rd.
Sydner Rd. N16 122 DT63
Sydney Ave., Pur. 219 DM112
Sydney Clo. SW3 276 A9
Sydney Clo. SW3 160 DD77
Sydney Cres., Ashf. 175 BP93
Sydney Gro. NW4 119 CW57
Sydney Gro., Slou. 131 AQ72
Sydney Ms. SW3 276 A9
Sydney Pl. SW7 276 A9
Sydney Pl. SW7 160 DD77
Sydney Pl., Guil. 259 AZ135
Sydney Rd. E11 124 EH58
Mansfield Rd.
Sydney Rd. N8 121 DN56
Sydney Rd. N10 98 DG53
Sydney Rd. SE2 166 EW76
Sydney Rd. SW20 199 CX96

Sydney Rd. W13 137 CG74
Sydney Rd., Bexh. 166 EX84
Sydney Rd., Enf. 82 DR41
Sydney Rd., Felt. 175 BU88
Sydney Rd., Guil. 259 AZ135
Sydney Rd., Ilf. 103 EQ54
Sydney Rd., Rich. 158 CL84
Sydney Rd., Sid. 185 ES91
Sydney Rd., Sutt. 218 DA105
Sydney Rd., Tedd. 177 CF92
Sydney Rd., Til. 171 GG82
Sydney Rd., Wat. 75 BS43
Sydney Rd., Wdf.Grn. 102 EG49
Sydney St. SW3 276 B10
Sydney St. SW3 160 DE78
Sykecluan, Iver 153 BE75
Sykeings, Iver 153 BE76
Sykes Dr., Stai. 174 BH92
Sykes Rd., Slou. 131 AP72
Sylvan Ave. N3 98 DA54
Sylvan Ave. N22 99 DM52
Sylvan Ave. NW7 97 CT51
Sylvan Ave., Horn. 128 FL58
Sylvan Ave., Rom. 126 EZ58
Sylvan Clo., Grays 170 FY77
Warren La.
Sylvan Clo., Hem.H. 40 BN21
Sylvan Clo., Oxt. 254 EH129
Sylvan Clo., S.Croy. 220 DV110
Sylvan Clo., Wok. 227 BB117
Sylvan Est. SE19 202 DT95
Sylvan Gdns., Surb. 197 CK101
Sylvan Gro. NW2 119 CX63
Sylvan Gro. SE15 162 DV79
Sylvan Hill SE19 202 DS95
Sylvan Rd. E7 144 EG65
Sylvan Rd. E11 124 EG57
Sylvan Rd. E17 123 EA57
Sylvan Rd. SE19 202 DT95
Sylvan Wk., Brom. 205 EM97
Sylvan Way, Chig. 104 EV48
Sylvan Way, Dag. 126 EV62
Sylvan Way, Red. 266 DG135
Sylvan Way, W.Wick. 222 EE105
Sylvana Clo., Uxb. 134 BM67
Sylvandale, Welw.G.C. 30 DC10
Sylverdale Rd., Croy. 201 DP104
Sylverdale Rd., Pur. 219 DP113
Sylvester Ave., Chis. 185 EM93
Sylvester Gdns., Ilf. 104 EV50
Sylvester Path E8 142 DV65
Sylvester Rd.
Sylvester Rd. E8 142 DV65
Sylvester Rd. E17 123 DZ59
Sylvester Rd. N2 98 DC54
Sylvester Rd., Wem. 117 CJ64
Sylvestrus Clo., Kings.T. 198 CN95
Sylvia Ave., Brwd. 109 GC47
Sylvia Ave., Pnr. 94 BY51
Sylvia Gdns., Wem. 138 CP66
Symes Ms. NW1 141 DJ68
Camden High St.
Symons St. SW3 276 E9
Symons St. SW3 160 DF77
Syon Gate Way, Brent. 157 CG80
Syon La., Islw. 157 CF79
Syon Pk. Gdns., Islw. 157 CF80
Syon Vista, Rich. 157 CK81
Kew Rd.
Syracuse Ave., Rain. 148 FL69
Syringa Ct., Grays 170 GD80
Sythwood, Wok. 226 AV117

T

Tabard Gdn. Est. SE1 279 L5
Tabard Gdn. Est. SE1 162 DR75
Tabard St. SE1 279 K5
Tabard St. SE1 162 DR75
Tabarin Way, Epsom 233 CW116
Tabernacle Ave. E13 144 EG70
Barking Rd.
Tabernacle St. EC2 275 L5
Tabernacle St. EC2 142 DR70
Tableer Ave. SW4 181 DJ85
Tabley Rd. N7 121 DL63
Tabor Gdns., Sutt. 217 CZ107
Tabor Gro. SW19 179 CY94
Tabor Rd. W6 159 CV76
Tabrums Way, Upmin. 129 FS59
Tachbrook Est. SW1 161 DK78
Tachbrook Ms. SW1 277 K8
Tachbrook Rd., Felt. 175 BT87
Tachbrook Rd., Sthl. 156 BX77
Tachbrook Rd., Uxb. 134 BJ68
Tachbrook St. SW1 277 L9
Tachbrook St. SW1 161 DJ77
Tack Ms. SE4 163 EA83
Tadema Rd. SW10 160 DC80
Tadlows Clo., Upmin. 128 FP64
Tadmor Clo., Sun. 195 BT98
Tadmor St. W12 139 CX74
Tadorne Rd., Tad. 233 CW121
Tadworth Ave., N.Mal. 199 CT99
Tadworth Clo., Tad. 233 CX122
Tadworth Par., Horn. 127 FH63
Maylands Ave.
Tadworth Rd. NW2 119 CU61
Tadworth St., Tad. 233 CW123
Taeping St. E14 163 EB77
Taffy's How, Mitch. 200 DE97
Taft Way E3 143 EB69
St. Leonards St.
Tagg's Island, Hmptn. 197 CD96
Tailworth St. E1 142 DU71
Chicksand St.
Tait Rd., Croy. 202 DS101
Takeley Clo., Rom. 105 FD54
Takeley Clo., Wal.Abb. 67 ED33
Talacre Rd. NW5 140 DG65
Talbot Ave. N2 120 DD55
Talbot Ave., Slou. 153 AZ76
Talbot Ave., Wat. 94 BY45
Talbot Clo. N15 122 DT56
Talbot Clo., Reig. 266 DB135
Talbot Ct. EC3 275 L10
Talbot Ct., Hem.H. 40 BK22
Crabtree La.
Talbot Cres. NW4 119 CU57
Talbot Gdns., Ilf. 126 EU61
Talbot Ho. E14 143 EB72
Giraud St.
Talbot Pl. SE3 164 EE82
Talbot Pl., Slou. 152 AW81
Talbot Rd. E6 145 EN68
Talbot Rd. E7 124 EG63
Talbot Rd. N6 120 DG58
Talbot Rd. N15 122 DT56
Talbot Rd. N22 99 DJ54
Talbot Rd. W2 140 DA72
Talbot Rd. W11 139 CZ72
Talbot Rd. W13 137 CG73
Talbot Rd., Ashf. 174 BK92
Talbot Rd., Brom. 204 EH98
Masons Hill
Talbot Rd., Cars. 218 DG106
Talbot Rd., Dag. 146 EZ65
Talbot Rd., Har. 95 CF54
Talbot Rd., Hat. 45 CU15
Talbot Rd., Islw. 157 CG84
Talbot Rd., Rick. 92 BL46
Talbot Rd., Sthl. 156 BY77
Talbot Rd., Th.Hth. 202 DR98
Talbot Rd., Twick. 177 CE88
Talbot Rd., Wem. 117 CK64
Talbot Sq. W2 272 A9
Talbot Sq. W2 140 DD72
Talbot St., Hert. 32 DS09
Talbot Wk. NW10 138 CS65
Garnet Rd.
Talbot Wk. W11 139 CY72
Lancaster Rd.
Talbot Yd. SE1 279 K3
Talbrook, Brwd. 108 FT48
Taleworth Clo., Ash. 231 CK120
Taleworth Rd.
Taleworth Pk., Ash. 231 CK120
Taleworth Rd., Ash. 231 CK119
Talfourd Pl. SE15 162 DT81
Talfourd Rd. SE15 162 DT81
Talgarth Rd. W6 159 CX78
Talgarth Rd. W14 159 CX78
Talgarth Wk. NW9 118 CS57
Talisman Clo., Ilf. 126 EV60
Talisman Sq. SE26 182 DU91
Talisman Way, Epsom 233 CW116
Talisman Way, Wem. 118 CM62
Forty Ave.
Tall Elms Clo., Brom. 204 EF99
Tall Oaks, Amer. 55 AR37
Tall Trees SW16 201 DM97
Tall Trees, Slou. 153 BE81
Tall Trees Clo., Horn. 128 FK58
Tallack Clo., Har. 95 CE52
College Hill Rd.
Tallack Rd. E10 123 DZ60
Tallents Clo. (Sutton at Hone), Dart. 188 FP94
Tallis Gro. SE7 164 EH79
Tallis St. EC4 274 E10
Tallis St. EC4 141 DN73
Tallis Vw. NW10 138 CR65
Mitchellbrook Way
Tallis Way, Borwd. 77 CK39
Tallon Rd., Brwd. 109 GE43
Tally Ho Cor. N12 98 DC50
Tally Rd., Oxt. 254 EL131
Talma Gdns., Twick. 177 CE86
Talma Rd. SW2 161 DN84
Talmage Clo. SE23 182 DW87
Tyson Rd.
Talman Gro., Stan. 95 CK51
Talus Clo., Purf. 169 FR77
Brimfield Rd.
Talwin St. E3 143 EB69
Tamar Clo., Upmin. 129 FS58
Tamar Dr., S.Ock. 148 FQ72
Tamar Grn., Hem.H. 40 BM15
Tamar Sq., Wdf.Grn. 102 EH51
Tamar St. SE7 164 EL76
Tamar Way N17 122 DT55
Tamar Way, Slou. 153 BB78
Tamarind Clo., Guil. 242 AU129
Tamarind Yd. E1 142 DU74
Asher Way
Tamarisk Clo., St.Alb. 43 CD16
New Grns. Ave.
Tamarisk Clo., S.Ock. 149 FW70
Tamarisk Rd., S.Ock. 149 FW69
Tamarisk Sq. W12 139 CT73
Tamarisk Way, Slou. 151 AN75
Tamesis Gdns., Wor.Pk. 198 CS103
Tamesis Strand, Grav. 191 GL92
Tamian Est., Houns. 156 BW84
Tamian Way, Houns. 156 BW84
Tamworth Ave., Wdf.Grn. 102 EE51
Tamworth Gdns., Pnr. 93 BV54
Tamworth La., Mitch. 200 DG96
Tamworth Pk., Mitch. 201 DH98
Tamworth Pl., Croy. 202 DQ103
Tamworth Rd., Croy. 201 DP103
Tamworth Rd., Hert. 32 DT08
Tamworth St. SW6 160 DA79
Tancred Rd. N4 121 DP58
Tandridge Ct., Cat. 236 DU122
Tandridge Dr., Orp. 205 ER102
Tandridge Gdns., S.Croy. 220 DT113
Tandridge Hill La., Gdse. 253 DZ128
Tandridge La., Oxt. 253 EA131
Tandridge Pl., Orp. 205 ER101
Tandridge Dr.
Tandridge Rd., Warl. 237 DX119
Tanfield Ave. NW2 119 CT63
Tanfield Rd., Croy. 220 DQ105
Tangent Rd., Rom. 106 FK53
Tangier La. (Eton), Wind. 151 AR79
Tangier Rd., Guil. 259 BA135
Tangier Rd., Rich. 158 CP84
Tangier Way, Tad. 233 CY117
Tangier Wd., Tad. 233 CY118
Tanglebury Clo., Brom. 204 EL98
Tangles Clo., Uxb. 134 BN69
Tanglewood Clo., Cher. 192 AV104
Tanglewood Clo., Croy. 202 DW104
Tanglewood Clo., Stan. 95 CE47
Tanglewood Clo., Wok. 227 BD116
Tanglewood Way, Felt. 175 BV90
Tangley Gro. SW15 179 CT87
Tangley La., Guil. 242 AT130
Tangley Pk. Rd., Hmptn. 176 BZ92
Tanglyn Ave., Shep. 194 BN99
Tangmere Cres., Horn. 147 FH65
Tangmere Gdns., Nthlt. 136 BW68
Tangmere Gro., Kings.T. 177 CK92
Richmond Rd.
Tangmere Way NW9 96 CS54
Tanhouse Rd., Oxt. 253 ED132
Tanhurst Wk. SE2 166 EX76
Alsike Rd.
Tank Hill Rd., Purf. 168 FN78
Tank La., Purf. 168 FN77
Tankerton Rd., Surb. 198 CM103
Tankerton St. WC1 274 A3
Tankerville Rd. SW16 181 DK94
Tankridge Rd. NW2 119 CV61
Tanner St. SE1 279 N5
Tanner St. SE1 162 DS75
Tanner St., Bark. 145 EQ65
Tanners Clo., St.Alb. 42 CC19
Oysterfields
Tanners Clo., Walt. 195 BV100
Tanners Cres., Hert. 32 DQ11
Tanners Dean, Lthd. 231 CJ122
Tanners End La. N18 100 DS49
Tanners Hill SE8 163 DZ81
Tanners Hill, Abb.L. 59 BT31
Tanners La., Ilf. 125 EQ55
Tanners Meadow, Bet. 264 CP138
Tanners Way, Ware 34 EJ06
Tanners Wd. Clo., Abb.L. 59 BS32
Tanners Wd. La.
Tanners Wd. La., Abb.L. 59 BS32
Tannersfield, Guil. 258 AY142
Tannery, The, Red. 250 DE134
Oakdene Rd.
Tannery Clo., Beck. 203 DX99
Tannery Clo., Dag. 127 FB62
Tannery La., Guil. 258 AY144
Tannery La., Wok. 227 BD123
Tannington Ter. N5 121 DN62
Gillespie Rd.
Tannsfeld Rd. SE26 183 DX92
Tannsfield Dr., Hem.H. 40 BM18
Tannsmore Clo., Hem.H. 40 BM18
Tansley Clo. N7 121 DK64
Hilldrop Rd.
Tanswell Est. SE1 278 E5
Tanswell St. SE1 278 D5
Tansy Clo. E6 145 EN72
Tansy Clo., Guil. 243 BC132
Tansy Clo., Rom. 106 FL51
Tansycroft, Welw.G.C. 30 DB08
Tant Ave. E16 144 EF72
Tantallon Rd. SW12 180 DG88
Tantony Gro., Rom. 126 EX55
Tanworth Clo., Nthwd. 93 BQ51
Tanyard La., Bex. 186 FA87
Bexley High St.
Tanyard Way, Horl. 269 DH146
Tanys Dell, Harl. 36 EU12
Tanza Rd. NW3 120 DF63
Tapestry Clo., Sutt. 218 DB108
Taplow NW3 140 DD66
Taplow SE17 162 DR78
Taplow Common Rd., Slou. 130 AF65
Taplow Rd. N13 100 DQ49
Taplow Rd., Maid. 130 AG71
Taplow St. N1 275 J1
Taplow St. N1 142 DQ68
Tapners Rd., Reig. 265 CT139
Tapp St. E1 142 DV70
Tappesfield Rd. SE15 162 DW83
Tapster St., Barn. 79 CZ41
Taransay, Hem.H. 41 BP22
Tarbay La., Wind. 150 AH82
Tarbert Rd. SE22 182 DS85
Tarbert Wk. E1 142 DW73
Juniper St.
Target Clo., Felt. 175 BS86
Tarham Clo., Horl. 268 DE146
Tariff Cres. SE8 163 DZ77
Enterprize Way
Tariff Rd. N17 100 DU51
Tarleton Gdns. SE23 182 DV88
Tarling Clo., Sid. 186 EV90
Tarling Rd. E16 144 EF72
Tarling Rd. N2 98 DC54
Tarling St. E1 142 DV72
Tarling St. Est. E1 142 DW72
Tarmac Way, West Dr. 154 BH80
Tarn St. SE1 279 H7
Tarnbank, Enf. 81 DL43
Tarnwood Pk. SE9 185 EM87
Tarnworth Rd., Rom. 106 FN50
Tarpan Way, Brox. 67 DZ26
Tarquin Ho. SE26 182 DU91
Tarragon Clo. SE14 163 DY80
Southerngate Way
Tarragon Dr., Guil. 242 AU129
Tarragon Gdns. SE14 163 DY80
Southerngate Way
Tarragon Gro. SE26 183 DX93
Tarrant Pl. W1 272 D7
Tarrington Clo. SW16 181 DK90
Tarry La. SE8 163 DY77
Tartar Rd., Cob. 214 BW113
Tarver Rd. SE17 161 DP78
Tarves Way SE10 163 EB80
Tash Pl. N11 99 DH50
Woodland Rd.
Tasker Clo., Hayes 155 BQ80
Tasker Ho., Bark. 145 ER68
Dovehouse Mead
Tasker Rd. NW3 120 DF64
Tasker Rd., Grays 171 GH76
Tasman Rd. SW9 161 DL83
Tasman Wk. E16 144 EK72
Royal Rd.
Tasmania Ter. N18 100 DQ51
Tasso Rd. W6 159 CY79
Tatam Rd. NW10 138 CR66
Tate Clo., Lthd. 231 CJ123
Windmill Dr.
Tate Rd. E16 145 EM74
Newland St.
Tate Rd., Ger.Cr. 91 AZ50
Tate Rd., Sutt. 218 DA106
Tatnell Rd. SE23 183 DY86
Tatsfield App. Rd., West. 238 EH123
Tatsfield Ave., Wal.Abb. 49 ED23
Tatsfield La., West. 238 EL121
Tattenham Cor. Rd., Epsom 232 CS117
Tattenham Cres., Epsom 233 CU118
Tattenham Gro., Epsom 233 CV118
Tattenham Way, Tad. 233 CX118
Tattersall Clo. SE9 184 EL85
Tattle Hill, Hert. 31 DL05
Tatton Cres. N16 122 DT59
Clapton Common
Tatum St. SE17 279 L9
Tatum St. SE17 162 DR77
Tauber Clo., Borwd. 77 CK43
Allum La.
Taunton Ave. SW20 199 CV96
Taunton Ave., Cat. 236 DT123
Taunton Ave., Houns. 156 CC82
Taunton Clo., Bexh. 167 FD82
Taunton Clo., Ilf. 103 ET51
Taunton Clo., Sutt. 200 DA102
Taunton Ct. N17 100 DS52
Taunton Dr. N2 98 DC54
Oak La.
Taunton Dr., Enf. 81 DN41
Taunton La., Couls. 235 DN119
Taunton Ms. NW1 272 D5
Taunton Pl. NW1 272 D4
Taunton Pl. NW1 140 DF70
Taunton Rd. SE12 184 EE85
Taunton Rd., Grav. 190 GA85
Taunton Rd., Grnf. 136 CB67
Taunton Rd., Rom. 106 FJ49
Taunton Vale, Grav. 191 GK89
Taunton Way, Stan. 96 CL54
Tavern La. SW9 161 DN82
Taverner Sq. N5 122 DQ63
Highbury Gra.
Taverners, Hem.H. 40 BL18
Taverners Clo. W11 139 CY74
Addison Ave.
Taverners Way E4 102 EE46
Douglas Rd.
Taverners Way, Hodd. 49 EA17
Tavistock Ave. E17 123 DX55
Tavistock Ave., Grnf. 137 CG68
Tavistock Ave., St.Alb. 43 CD23
Tavistock Clo. N16 122 DS64
Crossway
Tavistock Clo., Pot.B. 64 DD31
Tavistock Clo., Rom. 106 FK53
Tavistock Clo., St.Alb. 43 CD23
Tavistock Clo., Stai. 174 BK94
Tavistock Cres. W11 139 CZ71
Tavistock Cres., Mitch. 201 DL98
Tavistock Gdns., Ilf. 125 ES63
Tavistock Gate, Croy. 202 DR102
Tavistock Gro., Croy. 202 DR101
Tavistock Ms. E18 124 EG56
Avon Way
Tavistock Ms. W11 139 CZ72
Lancaster Rd.
Tavistock Pl. E18 124 EG55
Avon Way
Tavistock Pl. N14 99 DH45
Chase Side
Tavistock Pl. WC1 273 P4
Tavistock Pl. WC1 141 DL70
Tavistock Rd. E7 124 EF63
Tavistock Rd. E15 144 EF65
Tavistock Rd. E18 124 EG55
Tavistock Rd. N4 122 DR58
Tavistock Rd. NW10 139 CT68
Tavistock Rd. W11 139 CZ72
Tavistock Rd., Brom. 204 EF98
Tavistock Rd., Cars. 200 DD102
Tavistock Rd., Croy. 202 DR102
Tavistock Rd., Edg. 96 CN53
Tavistock Rd., Uxb. 115 BQ64
Tavistock Rd., Wat. 76 BX39
Tavistock Rd., Well. 166 EW81
Tavistock Rd., West Dr. 134 BK74
Tavistock Sq. WC1 273 N4
Tavistock Sq. WC1 141 DK70
Tavistock St. WC2 274 A10
Tavistock St. WC2 141 DL73
Tavistock Ter. N19 121 DK62
Tavistock Wk., Cars. 200 DD102
Tavistock Rd.
Taviton St. WC1 273 M4
Taviton St. WC1 141 DK70
Tavy Bri. SE2 166 EW76
Tavy Clo. SE11 278 E10
Tawney Common, Epp. 70 FA32
Tawney Rd. SE28 146 EV73
Tawneys Rd., Harl. 51 ES16
Tawny Ave., Upmin. 128 FP64
Tawny Clo. W13 137 CH74
Tawny Clo., Felt. 175 BU90
Chervil Clo.
Tawny Way SE16 163 DX77
Tay Way, Rom. 105 FF53
Tayben Ave., Twick. 177 CE86
Taybridge Rd. SW11 160 DG83
Tayburn Clo. E14 143 EC72
Tayfield Clo., Uxb. 115 BQ62
Tayles Hill, Epsom 217 CT110
Taylifers, Harl. 51 EN20
Taylor Ave., Rich. 158 CP82
Taylor Clo. N17 100 DU52
Taylor Clo., Hmptn. 176 CC92
Taylor Clo., Orp. 223 ET105
Taylor Clo., Rom. 104 FA52
Taylor Clo., St.Alb. 43 CG15
Taylor Ct. E15 123 EC64
Taylor Rd., Ash. 231 CK117
Taylor Rd., Mitch. 180 DE94
Taylor Rd., Wall. 219 DH106
Taylors Ave., Hodd. 49 EA18
Taylors Bldgs. SE18 165 EP77
Spray St.
Taylors Clo., Sid. 185 ET91
Taylors Grn. W3 138 CS72
Long Dr.
Taylors La. NW10 138 CS66
Taylors La. SE26 182 DV91
Taylors La., Barn. 79 CZ39
Taylors Rd., Chesh. 54 AR29
Taymount Ri. SE23 182 DW89
Taynton Dr., Red. 251 DK129
Tayport Clo. N1 141 DL66
Tayside Dr., Edg. 96 CP48
Taywood Rd., Nthlt. 136 BZ69
Invicta Gro.
Teak Clo. SE16 143 DY74
Teal Clo. E16 144 EK71
Fulmer Rd.
Teal Clo., S.Croy. 221 DX111
Teal Dr., Nthwd. 93 BQ52
Teale St. E2 142 DU68
Tealing Dr., Epsom 216 CR105
Teardrop Ind. Est., Swan. 207 FH99
Teasel Clo., Croy. 203 DX102
Teasel Way E15 144 EE69
Teazle Wd. Hill, Lthd. 231 CE117
Oaklawn Rd.
Teazlewood Pk., Lthd. 231 CG117
Tebworth Rd. N17 100 DT52
Teck Clo., Islw. 157 CG82
Twickenham Rd.
Tedder Clo., Chess. 215 CJ107
Tedder Clo., Ruis. 115 BV64
West End Rd.
Tedder Clo., Uxb. 134 BM66
Tedder Rd., Hem.H. 40 BN19
Tedder Rd., S.Croy. 220 DW108
Teddington Clo., Epsom 216 CR110
Teddington Lock, Tedd. 177 CG91
Teddington Pk., Tedd. 177 CF92
Teddington Pk. Rd., Tedd. 177 CF91
Tedworth Gdns. SW3 160 DF78
Tedworth Sq.
Tedworth Sq. SW3 160 DF78
Tee, The W3 138 CS72
Tees Ave., Grnf. 137 CE68
Tees Clo., Upmin. 129 FR58
Tees Dr., Rom. 106 FK48
Teesdale, Hem.H. 40 BL17
Teesdale Ave., Islw. 157 CG81
Teesdale Clo. E2 142 DU68
Teesdale Gdns. SE25 202 DS96
Grange Hill
Teesdale Gdns., Islw. 157 CG81
Teesdale Rd. E11 124 EF58
Teesdale Rd., Dart. 188 FQ88
Teesdale Rd., Slou. 131 AM70
Teesdale St. E2 142 DV68
Teesdale Yd. E2 142 DV68
Teesdale St.
Teeswater Ct., Erith 166 EX76
Middle Way
Teevan Clo., Croy. 202 DU101
Teevan Rd., Croy. 202 DU102
Teggs La., Wok. 227 BF116
Teignmouth Clo. SW4 161 DK84
Teignmouth Clo., Edg. 96 CM54
Teignmouth Gdns., Grnf. 137 CF68
Teignmouth Rd. NW2 119 CX64
Teignmouth Rd., Well. 166 EW82
Telcote Way, Ruis. 116 BW59
Woodlands Ave.
Telegraph Hill NW3 120 DB62
Telegraph La., Esher 215 CF107
Telegraph Ms., Ilf. 126 EU60
Telegraph Rd. SW15 179 CV87
Telegraph St. EC2 275 K8
Telegraph Track, Wall. 219 DH110
Telemann Sq. SE3 164 EH83
Telephone Pl. SW6 159 CZ79
Lillie Rd.
Telfer Clo. W3 158 CQ75
Church Rd.
Telferscot Rd. SW12 181 DK88
Telford Ave. SW2 181 DK88
Telford Clo. SE19 182 DT93
St. Aubyn's Rd.
Telford Clo. W3 158 CQ75
Church Rd.
Telford Clo., Wat. 76 BX35
Telford Ct., Guil. 258 AY135
Clandon Rd.
Telford Ct., St.Alb. 43 CE21
Telford Dr., Slou. 151 AN75
Telford Dr., Walt. 196 BW101
Telford Rd. N11 99 DJ51
Telford Rd. NW9 119 CU58
West Hendon Bdy.
Telford Rd. SE9 185 ER89
Telford Rd. W10 139 CY71
Telford Rd., St.Alb. 61 CJ27
Telford Rd., Sthl. 136 CB73
Telford Rd., Twick. 176 CA87
Telford Ter. SW1 161 DJ79
Telford Way W3 138 CS71
Telford Way, Hayes 136 BY71
Telfords Yd. E1 142 DU73
The Highway
Telham Rd. E6 145 EN68
Tell Gro. SE22 162 DT84
Tellisford, Esher 214 CB105
Tellson Ave. SE18 164 EK81
Telscombe Clo., Orp. 205 ES103
Telston La., Sev. 241 FF117
Temeraire St. SE16 162 DW75
Albion St.
Temperance St., St.Alb. 42 CC20
Temperley Rd. SW12 180 DG87
Tempest Ave., Pot.B. 64 DD32
Tempest Rd., Egh. 173 BC93
Tempest Way, Rain. 147 FG65
Templar Dr. SE28 146 EX72
Templar Dr., Grav. 191 GG92
Templar Ho. NW2 139 CZ65
Shoot Up Hill
Templar Pl., Hmptn. 176 CA94
Templar St. SE5 161 DP82
Templars Ave. NW11 119 CZ58
Templars Cres. N3 98 DA54
Templars Dr., Har. 95 CD51
Temple EC4 274 D10
Temple EC4 141 DN73
Temple Ave. EC4 274 E10
Temple Ave. EC4 141 DN73
Temple Ave. N20 98 DD45
Temple Ave., Croy. 203 DZ103
Temple Ave., Dag. 126 FA60
Temple Bank, Harl. 36 EV09
Temple Bar Rd., Wok. 226 AT119
Temple Clo. E11 124 EE59
Wadley Rd.
Temple Clo. N3 97 CZ54
Cyprus Rd.
Temple Clo. SE28 165 EQ76
Temple Clo. (Cheshunt), Wal.Cr. 66 DU31
Temple Clo., Wat. 75 BT40
Temple Ct., Hert. 32 DR06
Temple Ct., Pot.B. 63 CY31
Mimms Hall Rd.
Temple Cft., Ashf. 175 BR93
Temple Flds. Ind. Area, Harl. 36 EU11
Temple Fortune Hill NW11 120 DA57
Temple Fortune La. NW11 119 CZ57
Temple Gdns. NW11 119 CZ58
Temple Gdns., Dag. 126 EX62
Temple Gdns., Rick. 93 BP49
Temple Gdns., Stai. 193 BF95
Temple Gro. NW11 120 DA58
Temple Gro., Enf. 81 DP41
Temple Hill, Dart. 188 FM86
Temple Hill Sq., Dart. 188 FM85
Temple La. EC4 274 E9
Temple Mead, Harl. 50 EH15
Temple Mead, Hem.H. 40 BK18
Temple Mead Clo., Stan. 95 CH51
Temple Mill La. E15 123 EA63
Temple Pk., Uxb. 134 BN69

Temple Pl. WC2 274 C10
Temple Pl. WC2 141 DM73
Temple Rd. E6 144 EL67
Temple Rd. N8 121 DM56
Temple Rd. NW2 119 CW63
Temple Rd. W4 158 CQ76
Temple Rd. W5 157 CK76
Temple Rd., Croy. 220 DR105
Temple Rd., Epsom 216 CR111
Temple Rd., Houns. 156 CB84
Temple Rd., Rich. 158 CM82
Temple Rd., West. 238 EK117
Temple Rd., Wind. 151 AQ82
Temple Sheen SW14 158 CP84
Temple Sheen Rd. SW14 158 CP84
Temple St. E2 142 DV68
Temple Vw., St.Alb. 42 CC18
Temple Way, Slou. 111 AQ64
Temple Way, Sutt. 200 DD104
Temple W. Ms. SE11 278 F7
Temple W. Ms. SE11 161 DP76
Temple Wd. Dr., Red. 250 DF131
Monson Rd.
Templecombe Ms., Wok. 227 BA116
Dorchester Ct.
Templecombe Rd. E9 142 DW67
Templecombe Way, Mord. 199 CY99
Templedene Ave., Stai. 174 BH94
Templefield Clo., Add. 212 BH107
Templefields, Hert. 32 DR06
Templehof Ave. NW2 119 CW59
Templeman Clo., Pur. 235 DP116
Croftleigh Ave.
Templeman Rd. W7 137 CF71
Templemead Clo. W3 138 CS72
Templemere, Wey. 195 BR104
Templepan La., Rick. 74 BL37
Templer Ave., Grays 171 GG77
Templeton Ave. E4 101 EA49
Templeton Clo. N16 122 DS64
Truman's Rd.
Templeton Clo. SE19 202 DR95
Templeton Pl. SW5 160 DA77
Templeton Rd. N15 122 DR58
Templewood W13 137 CH71
Templewood, Welw.G.C. 29 CX06
Templewood Ave. NW3 120 DB62
Templewood Gdns. NW3 120 DB62
Templewood La., Slou. 111 AQ64
Templewood Pk., Slou. 112 AT63
Templewood La.
Tempsford, Welw.G.C. 30 DD09
Tempsford Ave., Borwd. 78 CR42
Tempsford Clo., Enf. 82 DQ41
Gladbeck Way
Temsford Clo., Har. 94 CC54
Ten Acre, Wok. 226 AU118
Abercorn Way
Ten Acre La., Egh. 193 BC96
Ten Acres, Lthd. 231 CD124
Ten Acres Clo., Lthd. 231 CD124
Tenbury Clo. E7 124 EK64
Romford Rd.
Tenbury Ct. SW2 181 DK88
Tenby Ave., Har. 95 CH54
Tenby Clo. N15 122 DT56
Hanover Rd.
Tenby Clo., Rom. 126 EY58
Tenby Gdns., Nthlt. 136 CA65
Tenby Rd. E17 123 DY57
Tenby Rd., Edg. 96 CM53
Tenby Rd., Enf. 82 DW41
Tenby Rd., Rom. 126 EY58
Tenby Rd., Well. 166 EX81
Tench St. E1 142 DV74
Tenchleys La., Oxt. 254 EK131
Tenda Rd. SE16 162 DV77
Roseberry St.
Tendring Rd., Harl. 51 EQ17
Tendring Way, Rom. 126 EW57
Tenham Ave. SW2 181 DK89
Tenison Ct. W1 273 K10
Tenison Way SE1 278 C3
Tenison Way SE1 141 DM74
Tennand Clo. (Cheshunt), Wal.Cr. 66 DT26
Tenniel Clo. W2 140 DC72
Porchester Gdns.
Tennis Ct. La., E.Mol. 197 CF97
Hampton Ct. Way
Tennis St. SE1 279 K4
Tennis St. SE1 162 DR75
Tennison Ave., Borwd. 78 CP43
Tennison Clo., Couls. 235 DP120
Tennison Rd. SE25 202 DT98
Tenniswood Rd., Enf. 82 DS39
Tennyson Ave. E11 124 EG59
Tennyson Ave. E12 144 EL66
Tennyson Ave. NW9 118 CQ55
Tennyson Ave., Grays 170 GB76
Tennyson Ave., N.Mal. 199 CV99
Tennyson Ave., Twick. 177 CF88
Tennyson Ave., Wal.Abb. 68 EE34
Tennyson Clo., Enf. 83 DX43
Tennyson Clo., Felt. 175 BT86
Tennyson Clo., Well. 165 ET81
Tennyson Rd. E10 123 EB60
Tennyson Rd. E15 144 EE66
Tennyson Rd. E17 123 DZ58
Tennyson Rd. NW6 139 CZ67
Tennyson Rd. NW7 97 CU50
Tennyson Rd. SE20 183 DX94
Tennyson Rd. SW19 180 DC93
Tennyson Rd. W7 137 CF73
Tennyson Rd., Add. 212 BL105
Tennyson Rd., Ashf. 174 BL92
Tennyson Rd., Brwd. 109 GC45
Tennyson Rd., Dart. 188 FN85
Tennyson Rd., Houns. 156 CC82
Tennyson Rd., Rom. 106 FJ52
Tennyson Rd., St.Alb. 60 CA26
Tennyson Rd., Well. 165 ET81
Tennyson St. SW8 161 DH82
Tennyson Wk., Grav. 190 GD90
Tennyson Wk., Til. 171 GH82
Tennyson Way, Horn. 127 FG61
Tennyson Way, Slou. 131 AL70
Wordsworth Rd.
Tensing Ave., Grav. 190 GE90
Tensing Rd., Sthl. 156 CA76
Tent Peg La., Orp. 205 EQ99
Tent St. E1 142 DV70
Tentelow La., Sthl. 156 CA78
Tenter Grd. E1 275 P7
Tenter Pas. E1 142 DT72
Mansell St.
Tenterden Clo. NW4 119 CX55
Tenterden Clo. SE9 185 EM91
Tenterden Dr. NW4 119 CX55
Tenterden Gdns. NW4 119 CX55
Tenterden Gdns., Croy. 202 DU101
Tenterden Gro. NW4 119 CX55
Tenterden Rd. N17 100 DT52
Tenterden Rd., Croy. 202 DU101
Tenterden Rd., Dag. 126 EZ61
Tenterden St. W1 273 J9
Tenterden St. W1 141 DH72
Tenzing Rd., Hem.H. 40 BN20
Terborch Way SE22 182 DS85
East Dulwich Gro.
Tercel Path, Chig. 104 EV49
Terence Clo., Grav. 191 GM89
Teresa Gdns., Wal.Cr. 66 DW34
Teresa Ms. E17 123 EA56
Teresa Wk. N10 121 DH57
Connaught Gdns.
Terling Clo. E11 124 EF62
Terling Rd., Dag. 126 FA61
Terling Wk. N1 142 DQ67
Britannia Row
Terlings, The, Brwd. 108 FU48
Terminus Ho., Harl. 35 ER14
Terminus Pl. SW1 277 J7
Terminus Pl. SW1 161 DH76
Terminus St., Harl. 35 ER14
Tern Gdns., Upmin. 129 FS60
Tern Way, Brwd. 108 FS49
Terrace, The E4 102 EE48
Chingdale Rd.
Terrace, The N3 97 CZ54
Hendon La.
Terrace, The NW6 140 DA67
Terrace, The SW13 158 CS82
Terrace, The, Add. 212 BL106
Terrace, The, Dor. 263 CJ137
Deepdene Wd.
Terrace, The, Grav. 191 GH86
Terrace, The, Har. 117 CH60
Terrace, The, Maid. 150 AC76
Terrace, The, Sev. 256 FD122
Terrace, The, Wdf.Grn. 102 EG51
Broadmead Rd.
Terrace Gdns. SW13 159 CT82
Terrace Gdns., Wat. 75 BV40
St. Albans Rd.
Terrace La., Rich. 178 CL86
Terrace Rd. E9 142 DW66
Terrace Rd. E13 144 EG67
Terrace Rd., Walt. 195 BU101
Terrace St., Grav. 191 GH86
Terrace Wk., Dag. 126 EY64
Terraces, The, Dart. 188 FQ87
Terrapin Rd. SW17 181 DH90
Terretts Pl. N1 141 DP66
Upper St.
Terrick Rd. N22 99 DL53
Terrick St. W12 139 CV72
Terrilands, Pnr. 116 BZ55
Terront Rd. N15 122 DQ57
Tessa Sanderson Pl. SW8 161 DH83
Heath Rd.
Tessa Sanderson Way, Grnf. 117 CD64
Lilian Board Way
Testard Rd., Guil. 258 AW136
Testers Clo., Oxt. 254 EH132
Testerton Wk. W11 139 CX73
Whitchurch Rd.
Testwood Rd., Wind. 151 AK81
Tetbury Pl. N1 141 DP67
Upper St.
Tetcott Rd. SW10 160 DC80
Tetherdown N10 120 DG55
Tethys Rd., Hem.H. 40 BM17
Tetterby Way SE16 162 DU78
Catlin St.
Tetty Way, Brom. 204 EG96
Teversham La. SW8 161 DL81
Teviot Ave., S.Ock. 148 FQ72
Teviot Clo., Guil. 242 AU131
Stoughton Rd.
Teviot Clo., Well. 166 EV81
Teviot St. E14 143 EC71
Tewin Clo., St.Alb. 43 CJ16
Tewin Ct., Welw.G.C. 29 CZ09
Tewin Rd., Hem.H. 41 BQ20
Tewin Rd., Welw.G.C. 29 CZ09
Tewkesbury Ave. SE23 182 DV87
Tewkesbury Ave., Pnr. 116 BY57
Tewkesbury Clo. N15 122 DR58
Tewkesbury Rd.
Tewkesbury Clo., Loug. 84 EL44
Roding Rd.
Tewkesbury Clo., W.Byf. 212 BK111
Tewkesbury Gdns. NW9 118 CP55
Tewkesbury Rd. N15 122 DR58
Tewkesbury Rd. W13 137 CG73
Tewkesbury Rd., Cars. 200 DD102
Tewkesbury Ter. N11 99 DJ51
Tewson Rd. SE18 165 ES77
Teynham Ave., Enf. 82 DR44
Teynham Grn., Brom. 204 EG99
Teynton Ter. N17 100 DQ53
Thackeray Ave. N17 100 DU54
Thackeray Ave., Til. 171 GH81
Thackeray Clo. SW19 179 CX94
Thackeray Clo., Har. 116 CA60
Thackeray Clo., Islw. 157 CG82
Twickenham Rd.
Thackeray Clo., Uxb. 135 BP72
Dickens Ave.
Thackeray Dr., Ilf. 126 EU59
Thackeray Dr., Rom. 126 EU59
Thackeray Rd. E6 144 EK68
Thackeray Rd. SW8 161 DH82
Thackeray St. W8 160 DB75
Thackrah Clo. N2 98 DC54
Thakeham Clo. SE26 182 DV92
Thalia Clo. SE10 163 ED79
Feathers Pl.
Thalmassing Clo., Brwd. 109 GB47
Thame Rd. SE16 163 DX75
Thames Ave. SW10 160 DC81
Thames Ave., Cher. 194 BG97
Thames Ave., Dag. 146 FA70
Thames Ave., Grnf. 137 CF68
Thames Ave., Hem.H. 40 BM15
Thames Ave., Wind. 151 AR80
Thames Bank SW14 158 CQ82
Thames Circle E14 163 EA77
Westferry Rd.
Thames Clo., Cher. 194 BH101
Thames Clo., Hmptn. 196 CB96
Thames Clo., Rain. 147 FH72
Thames Ct., W.Mol. 196 CB96
Thames Dr., Grays 171 GG78
Thames Dr., Ruis. 115 BQ58
Thames Gate, Dart. 168 FN84
St. Edmunds Rd.
Thames Mead, Walt. 195 BU101
Thames Mead, Wind. 151 AL81
Thames Meadow, Shep. 195 BR102
Thames Meadow, W.Mol. 196 CA96
Thames Pl. SW15 159 CX83
Thames Rd. E16 144 EK74
Thames Rd. W4 158 CN79
Thames Rd., Bark. 145 ES69
Thames Rd., Dart. 167 FF82
Thames Rd., Grays 170 GB80
Thames Rd., Slou. 153 BA77
Thames Rd. Ind. Est. E16 144 EK74
Thames Side, Cher. 194 BJ99
Thames Side, Kings.T. 197 CK95
Thames Side, Stai. 194 BH96
Thames Side, Tedd. 177 CK94
Thames Side, Wind. 151 AR80
Thames St. SE10 163 EB79
Thames St., Hmptn. 196 CB95
Thames St., Kings.T. 197 CK96
Thames St., Stai. 173 BE91
Thames St., Sun. 195 BU98
Thames St., Walt. 195 BT101
Thames St., Wey. 195 BP103
Thames St., Wind. 151 AR81
Thames Vw., Grays 171 GG78
Thames Vill. W4 158 CQ81
Thames Way, Grav. 190 GC88
Thamesbank Pl. SE28 146 EW72
Thamesdale, St.Alb. 62 CM27
Thamesfield Ct., Shep. 195 BQ101
Thamesgate Clo., Rich. 177 CH91
Locksmeade Rd.
Thameshill Ave., Rom. 105 FC54
Thameside, Tedd. 177 CJ94
Thameside Ind. Est. E16 164 EL75
Thameside Wk. SE28 146 EV72
Thamesmead, Walt. 195 BU101
Thamesmead Spine Rd., Belv. 167 FC75
Thamesmere Dr. SE28 146 EU73
Thamesvale Clo., Houns. 156 CA82
Thamley, Purf. 168 FN77
Thane Vill. N7 121 DM62
Thane Wks. N7 121 DM61
Thane Vill.
Thanescroft Gdns., Croy. 202 DS104
Thanet Dr., Kes. 204 EK104
Phoenix Dr.
Thanet Pl., Croy. 220 DQ105
Thanet Rd., Bex. 186 FA87
Thanet Rd., Erith 167 FE80
Thanet St. WC1 273 P3
Thanet St. WC1 141 DL69
Thanington Ct. SE9 185 ES86
Thant Clo. E10 123 EB62
Tharp Rd., Wall. 219 DK106
Thatcham Gdns. N20 98 DC45
Thatcher Clo., West Dr. 154 BL75
Classon Clo.
Thatchers Clo., Horl. 269 DH146
Wheatfield Way
Thatchers Clo., Loug. 85 EQ40
Thatchers Cft., Hem.H. 40 BL16
Marlborough Ri.
Thatchers Way, Islw. 177 CD85
Thatches Gro., Rom. 126 EY56
Thavies Inn EC1 274 E8
Thaxted Grn., Brwd. 109 GC43
Thaxted Pl. SW20 179 CX94
Thaxted Rd. SE9 185 EQ89
Thaxted Rd., Buck.H. 102 EK45
Thaxted Wk., Rain. 147 FF67
Ongar Way
Thaxted Way, Wal.Abb. 67 ED33
Thaxton Rd. W14 159 CZ79
Thayer St. W1 272 G7
Thayer St. W1 140 DG71
Thayers Fm. Rd., Beck. 203 DY95
Thaynesfield, Pot.B. 64 DD31
Theatre St. SW11 160 DF83
Theberton St. N1 141 DN67
Theed St. SE1 278 E3
Theed St. SE1 141 DN74
Thele Ave., Ware 33 ED11
Thelma Clo., Grav. 191 GM92
Thelma Gdns. SE3 164 EK81
Thelma Gdns., Felt. 176 BY90
Thelma Gro., Tedd. 177 CG93
Theobald Cres., Har. 94 CB53
Theobald Rd. E17 123 DZ59
Theobald Rd., Croy. 201 DP103
Theobald St. SE1 279 K7
Theobald St., Borwd. 78 CL39
Theobald St., Rad. 77 CH36
Theobalds Ave. N12 98 DC49
Theobalds Ave., Grays 170 GC78
Theobalds Clo. (Cuffley), Pot.B. 65 DM30
Theobalds Ct. N4 122 DQ61
Queens Dr.
Theobalds La. (Cheshunt), Wal.Cr. 66 DW32
Theobalds Pk. Rd., Enf. 81 DP35
Theobald's Rd. WC1 274 B6
Theobald's Rd. WC1 141 DM71
Theobalds Rd. (Cuffley), Pot.B. 65 DL30
Theodore Rd. SE13 183 ED86
Thepps Clo., Red. 267 DM137
Therapia La., Croy. 201 DK101
Therapia Rd. SE22 182 DW86
Theresa Rd. W6 159 CU77
Theresas Wk., S.Croy. 220 DR110
Sanderstead Rd.
Therfield Ct. N4 122 DQ61
Brownswood Rd.
Therfield Rd., St.Alb. 43 CD16
Thermopylae Gate E14 163 EB77
Theseus Wk. N1 274 G1
Thesiger Rd. SE20 183 DX94
Thessaly Rd. SW8 161 DJ80
Thetford Clo. N13 99 DP51
Thetford Gdns., Dag. 146 EX66
Thetford Rd., Ashf. 174 BL91
Thetford Rd., Dag. 146 EX66
Thetford Rd., N.Mal. 198 CR100
Thetis Ter., Rich. 158 CN79
Theydon Bower, Epp. 70 EU31
Theydon Ct., Wal.Abb. 68 EG33
Theydon Gdns., Rain. 147 FE66
Theydon Gate, Epp. 85 ES37
Coppice Row
Theydon Gro., Epp. 70 EU30
Theydon Gro., Wdf.Grn. 102 EJ51
Theydon Pk. Rd., Epp. 85 ES39
Theydon Pl., Epp. 69 ET31
Theydon Rd. E5 122 DW61
Theydon Rd., Epp. 69 ER34
Theydon St. E17 123 DZ59
Thicket, The, West Dr. 134 BL72
Thicket Cres., Sutt. 218 DC105
Thicket Gro. SE20 182 DU94
Anerley Rd.
Thicket Gro., Dag. 146 EW65
Thicket Rd. SE20 182 DU94
Thicket Rd., Sutt. 218 DC105
Thicketts, Sev. 257 FJ123
Thickthorne La., Stai. 174 BJ94
Berryscroft Rd.
Thieves La., Hert. 31 DM10
Thieves La., Ware 32 DW08
Third Ave. E12 124 EL63
Third Ave. E13 144 EG69
Third Ave. E17 123 EA57
Third Ave. W3 139 CT74
Third Ave. W10 139 CY69
Third Ave., Dag. 147 FB67
Third Ave., Enf. 82 DT43
Third Ave., Grays 171 GF79
Third Ave., Harl. 51 EM16
Third Ave., Hayes 135 BT74
Third Ave., Rom. 126 EW58
Third Ave., Wat. 76 BX35
Third Ave., Wem. 117 CK61
Third Clo., W.Mol. 196 CB98
Third Cres., Slou. 131 AQ71
Third Cross Rd., Twick. 177 CD89
Third Way, Wem. 118 CP63
Thirkleby Clo., Slou. 131 AQ74
Thirleby Rd. SW1 277 L7
Thirleby Rd. SW1 161 DJ76
Thirleby Rd., Edg. 96 CR53
Thirlmere Ave., Grnf. 137 CJ69
Thirlmere Ave., Slou. 130 AJ71
Thirlmere Clo., Egh. 173 BB94
Keswick Rd.
Thirlmere Dr., St.Alb. 43 CH22
Thirlmere Gdns., Nthwd. 93 BP50
Thirlmere Gdns., Wem. 117 CJ60
Thirlmere Ho., Islw. 177 CF85
Thirlmere Ri., Brom. 184 EF93
Thirlmere Rd. N10 99 DH53
Thirlmere Rd. SW16 181 DK91
Thirlmere Rd., Bexh. 167 FC82
Thirlstane, St.Alb. 43 CF19
Thirsk Clo., Nthlt. 136 CA65
Thirsk Rd. SE25 202 DR98
Thirsk Rd. SW11 160 DG83
Thirsk Rd., Borwd. 78 CN37
Thirsk Rd., Mitch. 180 DG94
Thirza Rd., Dart. 188 FM86
Thistle Clo., Hem.H. 39 BE21
Thistle Gro. SW10 160 DC78
Thistle Gro., Welw.G.C. 30 DC11
Thistle Mead, Loug. 85 EN41
Thistle Rd., Grav. 191 GL87
Thistle Wd. Cres., Croy. 221 ED112
Thistlebrook SE2 166 EW76
Thistlecroft, Hem.H. 40 BH21
Thistlecroft Gdns., Stan. 95 CK53
Thistlecroft Rd., Walt. 214 BW105
Thistledene, T.Ditt. 197 CE100
Thistledene, W.Byf. 211 BF113
Thistledene Ave., Har. 116 BY62
Thistledene Ave., Rom. 105 FB50
Thistledown, Grav. 191 GK93
Thistlemead, Chis. 205 EP96
Thistles, The, Hem.H. 40 BH19
Thistlewaite Rd. E5 122 DV62
Thistlewood Clo. N7 121 DM61
Thistleworth Clo., Islw. 157 CD80
Thistley Clo. N12 98 DE52
Summerfields Ave.
Thomas Ave., Cat. 236 DQ121
Thomas Baines Rd. SW11 160 DD83
Thomas Clo., Brwd. 108 FY48
Thomas Darby Ct. W11 139 CY72
Thomas Dinwiddy Rd. SE12 184 EJ89
Thomas Doyle St. SE1 278 G6
Thomas Doyle St. SE1 161 DP76
Thomas Dr., Grav. 191 GK89
Thomas Hardy Ho. N22 99 DM52
Thomas La. SE6 183 EA87
Thomas More Ho. EC2 142 DQ71
The Barbican
Thomas More St. E1 142 DU73
Thomas More Way N2 120 DC55
Thomas Pl. W8 160 DB76
St. Mary's Pl.
Thomas Rd. E14 143 DZ72
Thomas Rd., H.Wyc. 110 AD59
Thomas Rochford Way, Wal.Cr. 67 DY26
Thomas Sims Ct., Horn. 127 FH64
Thomas St. SE18 165 EP77
Thomas Wall Clo., Sutt. 218 DB106
Clarence Rd.
Thomas à Beckett Clo., Wem. 117 CF63
Thompkins La., Slou. 131 AM66
Thompson Ave., Rich. 158 CN83
Thompson Clo., Ilf. 125 EQ61
High Rd.
Thompson Clo., Slou. 153 BA77
Thompson Rd. SE22 182 DT86
Thompson Rd., Dag. 126 EZ62
Thompson Rd., Uxb. 134 BL66
Thompson Way, Rick. 92 BG45
Thompson's Ave. SE5 162 DQ80
Thompsons Clo., Wal.Cr. 66 DT29
Goffs La.
Thompson's La., Loug. 84 EF38
Thomson Cres., Croy. 201 DN102
Thomson Rd., Har. 117 CE55
Thong La., Grav. 191 GM91
Thorburn Sq. SE1 162 DU77
Thorburn Way SW19 200 DD95
Willow Vw.
Thoresby St. N1 275 J2
Thoresby St. N1 142 DQ69
Thorkhill Gdns., T.Ditt. 197 CG102
Thorkhill Rd., T.Ditt. 197 CG102
Thorley Clo., W.Byf. 212 BG114
Thorley Gdns., Wok. 212 BG114
Thorn Ave. (Bushey), Wat. 94 CC46
Thorn Bank, Guil. 258 AU136
Thorn Clo., Brom. 205 EN100
Thorn Clo., Nthlt. 136 BZ69
Thorn Dr., Slou. 132 AY72
Thorn Hill Clo., Amer. 55 AP40
Thorn Ho., Beck. 203 DY95
Thorn La., Rain. 148 FK68
Thorn Ter. SE15 162 DW83
Nunhead Gro.
Thornaby Gdns. N18 100 DU51
Thornaby Pl., H.Wyc. 110 AE55
Wootton Way
Thornash Clo., Wok. 226 AW115
Thornash Rd., Wok. 226 AW115
Thornash Way, Wok. 226 AW115
Thornbank Clo., Stai. 174 BG85
Thornbridge Rd., Iver 133 BC67
Thornbury Ave., Islw. 157 CD80
Thornbury Clo. N16 122 DS64
Truman's Rd.
Thornbury Clo., Hodd. 33 EB13
Thornbury Gdns., Borwd. 78 CQ41
Thornbury Rd. SW2 181 DL86
Thornbury Rd., Islw. 157 CD80
Thornbury Sq. N6 121 DJ60
Thornby Rd. E5 122 DW62
Thorncliffe Rd. SW2 181 DL86
Thorncliffe Rd., Sthl. 156 BZ78
Thorncombe Rd. SE22 182 DS85
Thorncroft, Egh. 172 AW94
Thorncroft, Hem.H. 41 BP22
Thorncroft, Horn. 127 FH58
Thorncroft Clo., Couls. 235 DN120
Waddington Ave.
Thorncroft Dr., Lthd. 231 CH123
Thorncroft Rd., Sutt. 218 DB105
Thorncroft St. SW8 161 DL80
Thorndales, Brwd. 108 FX49
Thorndean St. SW18 180 DC89
Thorndene Ave. N11 98 DG46
Thorndike, Slou. 131 AN71
Thorndike Ave., Nthlt. 136 BX67
Thorndike Clo. SW10 160 DC80
Thorndike St. SW1 277 M9
Thorndike St. SW1 161 DK77
Thorndon Clo., Orp. 205 ET96
Thorndon Gdns., Epsom 216 CS106
Thorndon Gate, Brwd. 109 GC50
Thorndon Rd., Orp. 205 ET96
Thorndyke Ct., Pnr. 94 BZ52
Westfield Pk.
Thorne Clo. E11 124 EE63
Thorne Clo. E16 144 EF72
Thorne Clo., Ashf. 175 BQ94
Thorne Clo., Erith 167 FC79
Thorne Pas. SW13 158 CS82
Thorne Rd. SW8 161 DL80
Thorne St. E16 144 EF72
Rogers Rd.
Thorne St. SW13 158 CS83
Thorneloe Gdns., Croy. 219 DN106
Thornes Clo., Beck. 203 EC97
Thornet Wd. Rd., Brom. 205 EN97
Thorney Cres. SW11 160 DD80
Thorney Hedge Rd. W4 158 CP77
Thorney La. N., Iver 133 BF72
Thorney La. S., Iver 153 BF75
Thorney Mill Rd., Iver 154 BG76
Thorney St. SW1 277 P8
Thorney St. SW1 161 DL77
Thorneycroft Clo., Walt. 196 BW100
Thornfield Ave. NW7 97 CY53
Thornfield Rd. W12 159 CV75
Thornfield Rd., Bans. 234 DA117
Thornford Rd. SE13 183 EC85
Thorngate Rd. W9 140 DA70
Thorngrove Rd. E13 144 EH67
Thornham Gro. E15 123 ED64
Thornham St. SE10 163 EB79
Thornhaugh Ms. WC1 273 N5
Thornhaugh St. WC1 273 N6
Thornhaugh St. WC1 141 DK71
Thornhill, Epp. 71 FC26
Thornhill Ave. SE18 165 ES80
Thornhill Ave., Surb. 198 CL103
Thornhill Bri. Wf. N1 141 DM67
Caledonian Rd.
Thornhill Cres. N1 141 DM66
Thornhill Gdns. E10 123 EB61
Thornhill Gdns., Bark. 145 ES66
Thornhill Gro. N1 141 DM66
Lofting Rd.
Thornhill Ho. N1 141 DN66
Thornhill Rd.
Thornhill Rd. E10 123 EB61
Thornhill Rd. N1 141 DN66
Thornhill Rd., Croy. 202 DQ101
Thornhill Rd., Nthwd. 93 BQ49
Thornhill Rd., Surb. 198 CL103
Thornhill Rd., Uxb. 114 BM63
Thornhill Sq. N1 141 DM66
Thornhill Way, Shep. 194 BN99
Thornlaw Rd. SE27 181 DN91
Thornleas Pl., Lthd. 245 BS126
Station App.
Thornley Clo. N17 100 DU52
Thornley Dr., Har. 116 CB61
Thornley Pl. SE10 164 EE78
Caradoc St.
Thornridge, Brwd. 108 FV45
Thorns, The, Reig. 250 DC131
Thorns Meadow, West. 240 EW123
Thornsbeach Rd. SE6 183 EC88
Thornsett Pl. SE20 202 DV96
Thornsett Rd. SE20 202 DV96
Thornsett Rd. SW18 180 DB88
Thornside, Edg. 96 CN51
High St.
Thornton Ave. SW2 181 DK88
Thornton Ave. W4 158 CS77
Thornton Ave., Croy. 201 DM100
Thornton Ave., West Dr. 154 BM76
Thornton Clo., Guil. 242 AU130
Thornton Clo., Horl. 268 DE148
Thornton Clo., West Dr. 154 BM76
Thornton Ct. SW20 199 CX99
Thornton Cres., Couls. 235 DN119
Thornton Dene, Beck. 203 EA96
Thornton Gdns. SW12 181 DK88
Thornton Gro., Pnr. 94 CA51
Thornton Hill SW19 179 CY94
Thornton Pl. W1 272 D6
Thornton Pl. W1 140 DF71

Thornton Pl., Horl. 268 DE147
Thornton Rd. E11 123 ED61
Thornton Rd. N18 100 DW48
Thornton Rd. SW12 181 DK87
Thornton Rd. SW14 158 CR83
Thornton Rd. SW19 179 CX93
Thornton Rd., Barn. 79 CY41
Thornton Rd., Belv. 167 FB77
Thornton Rd., Brom. 184 EG92
Thornton Rd., Cars. 200 DD102
Thornton Rd., Croy. 201 DM101
Thornton Rd., Ilf. 125 EP63
Thornton Rd., Pot.B. 64 DC30
Thornton Rd., Th.Hth. 201 DN99
Thornton Rd. E. SW19 179 CX93
Thornton Rd.
Thornton Row, Th.Hth. 201 DN99
London Rd.
Thornton St. SW9 161 DN82
Thornton St., Hert. 32 DR09
Thornton St., St.Alb. 42 CC19
Thornton Wk., Horl. 268 DE148
Thornton Pl.
Thornton Way NW11 120 DB57
Thorntons Fm. Ave., Rom. 127 FC60
Thorntree Rd. SE7 164 EK78
Thornville St. SE8 163 EA81
Thornwood Clo. E18 102 EH54
Thornwood Rd. SE13 184 EE85
Thornwood Rd., Epp. 70 EV29
Thorogood Gdns. E15 124 EE64
Thorogood Way, Rain. 147 FE67
Thorold Clo., S.Croy. 221 DX110
Thorold Rd. N22 99 DL52
Thorold Rd., Ilf. 125 EP61
Thoroughfare, The, Tad. 249 CU125
Chequers La.
Thorparch Rd. SW8 161 DK81
Thorpe Bypass, Egh. 193 BB96
Thorpe Clo. W10 139 CY72
Cambridge Gdns.
Thorpe Clo., Croy. 221 EC111
Thorpe Clo., Orp. 205 ES103
Thorpe Cres. E17 101 DZ54
Thorpe Cres., Wat. 94 BW45
Thorpe Hall Rd. E17 101 EC53
Thorpe Ind. Pk., Egh. 193 BC95
Thorpe Lea Rd., Egh. 173 BB93
Thorpe Lo., Horn. 128 FK58
Thorpe Rd. E6 145 EM67
Thorpe Rd. E7 124 EF63
Thorpe Rd. E17 101 EC54
Thorpe Rd. N15 122 DS58
Thorpe Rd., Bark. 145 ER66
Thorpe Rd., Cher. 193 BD99
Thorpe Rd., Kings.T. 178 CL94
Thorpe Rd., St.Alb. 43 CD21
Thorpe Rd., Stai. 173 BD93
Thorpebank Rd. W12 139 CU74
Thorpedale Gdns., Ilf. 125 EN56
Thorpedale Rd. N4 121 DL61
Thorpefield Clo., St.Alb. 43 CK17
Thorpes Clo., Guil. 242 AU131
Thorpeside Clo., Stai. 193 BE96
Thorpewood Ave. SE26 182 DV89
Thorpland Ave., Uxb. 115 BQ62
Thorsden Clo., Wok. 226 AY119
Thorsden Ct., Wok. 226 AY118
Guildford Rd.
Thorsden Way SE19 182 DS91
Oaks Ave.
Thorverton Rd. NW2 119 CY62
Thoydon Rd. E3 143 DY68
Thrale Rd. SW16 181 DJ91
Thrale St. SE1 279 J3
Thrale St. SE1 142 DQ74
Thrasher Clo. E8 142 DT67
Stean St.
Thrawl St. E1 142 DT71
Threadneedle St. EC2 275 L9
Threadneedle St. EC2 142 DR72
Three Arch Rd., Red. 266 DF138
Three Cherrytrees La., Hem.H. 41 BP16
Three Clo. La., Berk. 38 AW20
Three Colt St. E14 143 DZ72
Three Colts Cor. E2 142 DU70
Weaver St.
Three Colts La. E2 142 DV70
Three Cors., Bexh. 167 FB82
Three Cors., Hem.H. 40 BN22
Three Cups Yd. WC1 274 C7
Three Forest Way, Epp. 51 EM22
Three Forest Way, Harl. 34 EG14
Three Forest Way (Mark Hall N.), Harl. 36 EU10
Three Forest Way, Wal.Abb. 51 EM21
Three Forest Way, Ware 35 EM12
Three Forests Way, Chig. 104 EW48
Three Gates, Guil. 243 BC132
Three Gates Rd. (Fawkham), Long. 209 FT104
Three Horseshoes Rd., Harl. 51 EP17
Three Kings Rd., Mitch. 200 DG97
Three Kings Yd. W1 273 H10
Three Kings Yd. W1 141 DH73
Three Mill La. E3 143 EC69
Three Oak La. SE1 279 P4
Three Oaks Clo., Uxb. 114 BM62
Three Pears Rd., Guil. 243 BE134
Threehouseholds, Ch.St.G. 90 AT49
Threshers Bush, Harl. 36 FA14
Threshers Pl. W11 139 CY73
Thriffwood SE26 182 DW90
Thrift, The, Dart. 189 FW90
Thrift Fm. La., Borwd. 78 CQ40
Thrift Grn., Brwd. 109 GA48
Knight's Way
Thrift La., Sev. 239 ER116
Cudham La. S.
Thrift Vale, Guil. 243 BD131
Thriftfield, Hem.H. 40 BK18
Thrifts Mead, Epp. 85 ES37
Thrigby Rd., Chess. 216 CM107
Throckmorton Rd. E16 144 EH72
Throgmorton Ave. EC2 275 L8
Throgmorton Ave. EC2 142 DR72
Throgmorton St. EC2 275 L8
Throgmorton St. EC2 142 DR72
Throwley Clo. SE2 166 EW76
Throwley Rd., Sutt. 218 DB106
Throwley Way, Sutt. 218 DB105
Thrums, The, Wat. 75 BV37
Thrupp Clo., Mitch. 201 DH96
Thrupps Ave., Walt. 214 BX106
Thrupps La., Walt. 214 BX106
Thrush Ave., Hat. 45 CU20
Thrush Grn., Har. 116 CA56
Thrush Grn., Rick. 92 BJ45
Thrush La. (Cuffley), Pot.B. 65 DL28
Thrush St. SE17 279 H10
Thruxton Way SE15 162 DT80
Daniel Gdns.
Thumbswood, Welw.G.C. 30 DA12
Thumpers, Hem.H. 40 BL18
Thundercourt, Ware 33 DX05
Thunderer Rd., Dag. 146 EY70
Hindmans Way
Thundridge Clo., Welw.G.C. 30 DB10
Amwell Common
Thurbarn Rd. SE6 183 EB92
Thurgood Rd., Hodd. 49 EA15
Thurland Rd. SE16 162 DU76
Thurlby Clo., Har. 117 CG58
Gayton Rd.
Thurlby Clo., Wdf.Grn. 103 EM50
Thurlby Rd. SE27 181 DN91
Thurlby Rd., Wem. 137 CK65
Thurleigh Ave. SW12 180 DG86
Thurleigh Rd. SW12 180 DF87
Thurleston Ave., Mord. 199 CY99
Thurlestone Ave. N12 98 DF51
Thurlestone Ave., Ilf. 125 ET63
Thurlestone Rd. SE27 181 DN90
Thurloe Clo. SW7 276 B8
Thurloe Clo. SW7 160 DE77
Thurloe Gdns., Rom. 127 FF58
Thurloe Pl. SW7 276 A8
Thurloe Pl. SW7 160 DD77
Thurloe Pl. Ms. SW7 276 A8
Thurloe Sq. SW7 276 B8
Thurloe Sq. SW7 160 DE77
Thurloe St. SW7 276 A8
Thurloe St. SW7 160 DD77
Thurloe Wk., Grays 170 GA76
Thurlow Clo. E4 101 EB51
Higham Sta. Ave.
Thurlow Gdns., Ilf. 103 ER51
Thurlow Gdns., Wem. 117 CK64
Thurlow Hill SE21 182 DQ88
Thurlow Pk. Rd. SE21 181 DP88
Thurlow Rd. NW3 120 DD64
Thurlow Rd. W7 157 CG75
Thurlow St. SE17 279 L10
Thurlow St. SE17 162 DR78
Thurlow Ter. NW5 120 DG64
Thurlston Rd., Ruis. 115 BU62
Thurlstone Clo., Shep. 195 BQ100
Thurlton Ct., Wok. 226 AY116
Chobham Rd.
Thurnby Ct., Twick. 177 CE90
Thurnham Way, Tad. 233 CW120
Thurrock Lakeside, Grays 169 FV77
Thurrock Pk. Ind. Est., Til. 170 GD80
Thurrock Pk. Way, Til. 170 GD80
Thursby Rd., Wok. 226 AU118
Thursland Rd., Sid. 186 EY92
Thursley Cres., Croy. 221 EC108
Thursley Gdns. SW19 179 CX89
Thursley Rd. SE9 185 EM90
Thurso Clo., Rom. 106 FP51
Thurso St. SW17 180 DD91
Thurstan Rd. SW20 179 CV94
Thurstans, Harl. 51 EQ20
Thurston Rd. SE13 163 EB82
Thurston Rd., Slou. 132 AS72
Thurston Rd., Sthl. 136 BZ72
Thurtle Rd. E2 142 DT67
Thwaite Clo., Erith 167 FC79
Thyer Clo., Orp. 223 EQ105
Isabella Dr.
Thyra Gro. N12 98 DB51
Tibbatts Rd. E3 143 EB70
Tibbenham Wk. E13 144 EF68
Whitelegg Rd.
Tibberton Sq. N1 142 DQ66
Popham Rd.
Tibbets Clo. SW19 179 CX88
Tibbets Cor. SW19 179 CX87
Tibbet's Ride SW15 179 CX87
Tibbles Clo., Wat. 76 BY35
Tibbs Hill Rd., Abb.L. 59 BT30
Tiber Gdns. N1 141 DM67
Treaty St.
Ticehurst Clo., Orp. 186 EU94
Grovelands Rd.
Ticehurst Rd. SE23 183 DY89
Tichborne Wd., Rick. 91 BD50
Tichmarsh, Epsom 216 CQ110
Tickenhall Dr., Harl. 52 EX15
Tickford Clo. SE2 166 EW75
Ampleforth Rd.
Tidal Basin Rd. E16 144 EF73
Tidenham Gdns., Croy. 202 DS104
Tideswell Rd. SW15 159 CW84
Tideswell Rd., Croy. 203 EA104
Tideway Clo., Rich. 177 CH91
Locksmeade Rd.
Tidey St. E3 143 EA71
Tidford Rd., Well. 165 ET82
Tidworth Rd. E3 143 EA70
Tidy's La., Epp. 70 EV29
Tiepigs La., Brom. 204 EF102
Tiepigs La., W.Wick. 204 EE103
Tierney Rd. SW2 181 DL87
Tiger La., Brom. 204 EH98
Tiger Way E5 122 DV63
Tilbrook Rd. SE3 164 EJ83
Tilburstow Hill Rd., Gdse. 252 DW132
Tilbury Clo. SE15 162 DT80
Willowbrook Rd.
Tilbury Clo., Orp. 206 EV96
Tilbury Docks, Til. 170 GE84
Tilbury Gdns., Til. 171 GG84
Tilbury Hotel Rd., Til. 171 GG84
Tilbury Mead, Harl. 52 EU17
Tilbury Rd. E6 145 EM68
Tilbury Rd. E10 123 EC59
Tildesley Rd. SW15 179 CW86
Tile Fm. Rd., Orp. 205 ER104
Tile Kiln Clo., Hem.H. 41 BP21
Tile Kiln Cres., Hem.H. 41 BP21
Tile Kiln La. N6 121 DJ60
Winchester Rd.
Tile Kiln La. N13 100 DQ50
Tile Kiln La., Bex. 187 FC89
Tile Kiln La., Hem.H. 41 BP21
Tile Kiln La., Uxb. 115 BP59
Tile Yd. E14 143 DZ72
Commercial Rd.
Tilecroft, Welw.G.C. 29 CX05
Tilegate Rd., Harl. 51 ET17
Tilegate Rd., Ong. 53 FC19
Tilehost, Guil. 242 AU130
Tilehouse Clo., Borwd. 78 CM41
Tilehouse La., Ger.Cr. 91 BE53
Tilehouse La., Rick. 91 BE53
Tilehouse La., Uxb. 113 BE55
Tilehouse Rd., Guil. 258 AY138
Tilehouse Way, Uxb. 113 BF59
Tilehurst La., Dor. 263 CK137
Tilehurst Rd. SW18 180 DD88
Tilehurst Rd., Sutt. 217 CY106
Tilekiln Clo., Wal.Cr. 66 DT29
Goffs La.
Tiler's Way, Reig. 266 DC138
Tileyard Rd. N7 141 DL66
Tilford Ave., Croy. 221 EC108
Tilford Gdns. SW19 179 CX88
Tilia Rd. E5 122 DV63
Clarence Rd.
Tilia Wk. SW9 161 DP84
Moorland Rd.
Till Ave. (Farningham), Dart. 208 FM102
Tiller Rd. E14 163 EA76
Tillett Clo. NW10 138 CQ65
Tillett Sq. SE16 163 DY75
Howland Way
Tillett Way E2 142 DU69
Gosset St.
Tilley La., Epsom 232 CQ123
Tillgate Common, Red. 252 DQ133
Tilling Rd. NW2 119 CW60
Tilling Way, Wem. 117 CK63
Tillingbourne Gdns. N3 119 CZ55
Tillingbourne Grn., Orp. 205 ET98
Tillingbourne Rd., Guil. 258 AY140
Tillingbourne Way N3 119 CZ55
Tillingbourne Gdns.
Tillingdown Hill, Cat. 236 DU122
Tillingdown La., Cat. 252 DV125
Tillingham Ct., Wal.Abb. 68 EG33
Tillingham Way N12 98 DA49
Tillman St. E1 142 DV72
Bigland St.
Tilloch St. N1 141 DM66
Carnoustie Dr.
Tillotson Rd. N9 100 DT47
Tillotson Rd., Har. 94 CB52
Tillotson Rd., Ilf. 125 EN59
Tillwicks Rd., Harl. 51 ET16
Tilly's La., Stai. 173 BF91
Tilmans Mead (Farningham), Dart. 208 FM101
Tilney Ct. EC1 275 J4
Tilney Dr., Buck.H. 102 EG47
Tilney Gdns. N1 142 DR65
Mitchison Rd.
Tilney Rd., Dag. 146 EZ65
Tilney Rd., Sthl. 156 BW77
Tilney St. W1 276 G2
Tilney St. W1 140 DG74
Tilson Gdns. SW2 181 DL87
Tilson Ho. SW2 181 DL87
Tilson Gdns.
Tilson Rd. N17 100 DU53
Tilstone Ave. (Eton Wick), Wind. 151 AL78
Tilstone Clo. (Eton Wick), Wind. 151 AL78
Tilsworth Rd., Beac. 88 AJ54
Tilsworth Wk., St.Alb. 43 CJ15
Sandringham Cres.
Tilt Clo., Cob. 230 BY116
Tilt Meadow, Cob. 230 BY116
Tilt Rd., Cob. 230 BW115
Tilt Yd. App. SE9 185 EM86
Tilthams Cor. Rd., Gdmg. 258 AV143
Tilthams Grn., Gdmg. 258 AV143
Tilton St. SW6 159 CY79
Tiltwood, The W3 138 CQ73
Acacia Rd.
Timber Clo., Chis. 205 EN96
Timber Clo., Lthd. 246 CC126
Timber Clo., Wok. 211 BF114
Hacketts La.
Timber Hill Rd., Cat. 236 DU124
Timber La., Cat. 236 DU124
Timber Hill Rd.
Timber Mill Way SW4 161 DK83
Timber Orchard, Hert. 31 DN05
Timber Pond Rd. SE16 143 DX74
Timber Ridge, Rick. 74 BJ42
Timber Slip Dr., Wall. 219 DK109
Timber St. EC1 275 H4
Timbercroft, Epsom 216 CS105
Timbercroft, Welw.G.C. 29 CZ06
Timbercroft La. SE18 165 ES79
Timberdene NW4 97 CX54
Timberdene Ave., Ilf. 103 EQ53
Timberham Fm. Rd., Gat. 268 DD151
Timberham Way, Horl. 268 DE151
Timberhill, Ash. 232 CL119
Ottways La.
Timberland Rd. E1 142 DV72
Timberling Gdns., S.Croy. 220 DR109
Sanderstead Rd.
Timbertop Rd., West. 238 EJ118
Timberwharf Rd. N16 122 DU58
Timberwood, Slou. 111 AR62
Time Sq. E8 122 DT64
Colvestone Cres.
Times Sq., Sutt. 218 DB106
High St.
Timothy Clo. SW4 181 DJ85
Elms Rd.
Timothy Clo., Bexh. 186 EY85
Timothy Rd. E3 143 DZ71
Timperley Gdns., Red. 250 DE132
Timplings Row, Hem.H. 40 BH18
Timsbury Wk. SW15 179 CU88
Timsway, Stai. 173 BF92
Tindal St. SW9 161 DP81
Tindale Clo., S.Croy. 220 DR111
Tindall Clo., Rom. 106 FM54
Tinderbox All. SW14 158 CR83
Tine Rd., Chig. 103 ES50
Tinkers La., Wind. 151 AK82
Tinniswood Clo. N5 121 DN64
Drayton Pk.
Tinsey Clo., Egh. 173 BB92
Tinsley Rd. E1 142 DW71
Tintagel Clo., Epsom 217 CT114
Tintagel Clo., Hem.H. 40 BK15
Tintagel Cres. SE22 162 DT84
Tintagel Dr., Stan. 95 CK49
Tintagel Gdns. SE22 162 DT84
Oxonian St.
Tintagel Rd., Orp. 206 EW103
Tintagel Way, Wok. 227 BA116
Tintells La., Lthd. 245 BP128
Tintern Ave. NW9 118 CP55
Tintern Clo. SW15 179 CY85
Tintern Clo. SW19 180 DC94
Tintern Clo., Slou. 151 AQ76
Tintern Gdns. N14 99 DL45
Tintern Path NW9 118 CS58
Ruthin Clo.
Tintern Rd. N22 100 DQ53
Tintern Rd., Cars. 200 DD102
Tintern St. SW4 161 DL84
Tintern Way, Har. 116 CB60
Tinto Rd. E16 144 EG70
Tinwell Ms., Borwd. 78 CQ43
Cranes Way
Tinworth St. SE11 278 A10
Tinworth St. SE11 161 DL78
Tippendell La., St.Alb. 60 CA25
Tippetts Clo., Enf. 82 DQ39
Tipthorpe Rd. SW11 160 DG83
Tipton Cotts., Add. 212 BG105
Oliver Clo.
Tipton Dr., Croy. 220 DS105
Tiptree Clo. E4 101 EC48
Tiptree Clo., Horn. 128 FN60
Tiptree Cres., Ilf. 125 EN55
Tiptree Dr., Enf. 82 DR42
Tiptree Est., Ilf. 125 EN55
Tiptree Rd., Ruis. 115 BV63
Tiree Clo., Hem.H. 41 BP22
Tirlemont Rd., S.Croy. 220 DQ108
Tirrell Rd., Croy. 202 DQ100
Tisbury Ct. W1 273 M10
Tisbury Rd. SW16 201 DL96
Tisdall Pl. SE17 279 L9
Tisdall Pl. SE17 162 DR77
Titan Rd., Grays 170 GA78
Titan Rd., Hem.H. 40 BM17
Titchborne Row W2 272 C9
Titchfield Rd. NW8 140 DF67
Titchfield Rd., Cars. 200 DD102
Titchfield Rd., Enf. 83 DY37
Titchfield Wk., Cars. 200 DD101
Titchfield Rd.
Titchwell Rd. SW18 180 DD87
Tite Hill, Egh. 172 AX92
Tite St. SW3 160 DF79
Tithe Barn Clo., Kings.T. 198 CM95
Tithe Barn Clo., St.Alb. 42 CC23
Tithe Barn Ct., Abb.L. 59 BT29
Tithe Barn Dr., Maid. 150 AD78
Tithe Barn Est., St.Alb. 42 CC24
Tithe Barn Way, Nthlt. 135 BV68
Tithe Clo. NW7 97 CU53
Tithe Clo., Maid. 150 AC78
Tithe Ct., Slou. 153 BA77
Tithe Fm. Ave., Har. 116 CA62
Tithe Fm. Clo., Har. 116 CA62
Tithe La., Stai. 173 BA86
Tithe Meadow, Vir.W. 192 AX100
Tithe Meadows, Wat. 75 BR44
Tithe Wk. NW7 97 CU53
Tithebarns La., Wok. 244 BG126
Tithelands, Harl. 51 EN18
Tithepit Shaw La., Warl. 236 DV117
Titian Ave. (Bushey), Wat. 95 CE45
Titley Clo. E4 101 EA50
Titmus Clo., Uxb. 135 BQ72
Titmuss Ave. SE28 146 EV73
Titmuss St. W12 159 CV75
Titsey Hill, Oxt. 238 EF123
Titsey Rd., Oxt. 254 EG128
Tiverton Ave., Ilf. 125 EN55
Tiverton Dr. SE9 185 EQ88
Tiverton Gro., Rom. 106 FN50
Tiverton Rd. N15 122 DR58
Tiverton Rd. N18 100 DS50
Tiverton Rd. NW10 139 CX67
Tiverton Rd., Edg. 96 CM54
Tiverton Rd., Houns. 156 CC82
Tiverton Rd., Pot.B. 64 DD31
Tiverton Rd., Ruis. 115 BU62
Tiverton Rd., Th.Hth. 201 DN99
Willett Rd.
Tiverton Rd., Wem. 138 CL68
Tiverton St. SE1 279 H7
Tiverton St. SE1 162 DQ76
Tiverton Way, Chess. 215 CJ106
Tivoli Ct. SE16 163 DZ75
Tivoli Gdns. SE18 164 EL77
Tivoli Rd. N8 121 DK57
Tivoli Rd. SE27 182 DQ92
Tivoli Rd., Houns. 156 BY84
Tobacco Quay E1 142 DV73
Wapping La.
Tobago St. E14 163 EA75
Manilla St.
Tobin Clo. NW3 140 DE66
Toby La. E1 143 DY70
Tockley Rd., Slou. 130 AH69
Todd Clo., Rain. 148 FK70
Toddbrook, Harl. 51 EP16
Harberts Rd.
Todds Clo., Horl. 268 DE146
Todds Wk. N7 121 DM61
Andover Rd.
Toft Ave., Grays 170 GD77
Token Yd. SW15 159 CY84
Montserrat Rd.
Tokenhouse Yd. EC2 275 K8
Tokyngton Ave., Wem. 138 CN65
Toland Sq. SW15 179 CU85
Tolcarne Dr., Pnr. 93 BU54
Toley Ave., Wem. 118 CL59
Tollbridge Clo. W10 139 CY70
Kensal Rd.
Tolldene Clo., Wok. 226 AS117
Robin Hood Rd.
Tollers La., Couls. 235 DM119
Tollesbury Gdns., Ilf. 125 ER55
Tollet St. E1 143 DX70
Tollgate, Guil. 243 BD133
Tollgate Ave., Red. 266 DF139
Tollgate Clo., Rick. 73 BF41
Tollgate Dr. SE21 182 DS89
Tollgate Gdns. NW6 140 DB68
Tollgate Rd. E6 144 EK71
Tollgate Rd. E16 144 EJ71
Tollgate Rd., Dart. 189 FR87
Tollgate Rd., Dor. 263 CH139
Tollgate Rd., St.Alb. 44 CR23
Tollgate Rd., Wal.Cr. 83 DX35
Tollhouse La., Wall. 219 DJ109
Tollhouse Way N19 121 DJ61
Tollington Pk. N4 121 DM61
Tollington Pl. N4 121 DM61
Tollington Rd. N7 121 DM63
Tollington Way N7 121 DL62
Tollpit End, Hem.H. 40 BG17
Tolmers Ave. (Cuffley), Pot.B. 65 DL28
Tolmers Gdns. (Cuffley), Pot.B. 65 DM29
Tolmers Ms., Hert. 65 DL25
Tolmers Pk., Hert. 65 DL25
Tolmers Rd. (Cuffley), Pot.B. 65 DK27
Tolmers Sq. NW1 273 L4
Tolpits Clo., Wat. 75 BT43
Tolpits La., Wat. 93 BQ46
Tolpuddle St. N1 141 DN68
Tolsford Rd. E5 122 DV64
Tolson Rd., Islw. 157 CG83
Tolvaddon, Wok. 226 AU117
Cardingham
Tolverne Rd. SW20 199 CW95
Tolworth Clo., Surb. 198 CP102
Tolworth Gdns., Rom. 126 EX57
Tolworth Pk. Rd., Surb. 198 CM103
Tolworth Ri. N., Surb. 198 CQ101
Elmbridge Ave.
Tolworth Ri. S., Surb. 198 CQ102
Warren Dr. S.
Tolworth Rd., Surb. 198 CL103
Tom Coombs Clo. SE9 164 EL84
Well Hall Rd.
Tom Cribb Rd. SE28 165 EQ76
Tom Gros. Clo. E15 123 ED64
Maryland St.
Tom Hood Clo. E15 123 ED64
Maryland St.
Tom Mann Clo., Bark. 145 ES67
Tom Nolan Clo. E15 144 EE68
Manor Rd.
Tom Smith Clo. SE10 164 EE79
Maze Hill
Tom Thumbs Arch E3 143 EA68
Malmesbury Rd.
Tomahawk Gdns., Nthlt. 136 BX69
Javelin Way
Tomkins Clo., Borwd. 78 CL39
Tallis Way
Tomkyns La., Upmin. 107 FR54
Tomlin Clo., Epsom 216 CR111
Hook Rd.
Tomlin Rd., Slou. 131 AL70
Tomlins Gro. E3 143 EA69
Tomlins Orchard, Bark. 145 EQ67
Tomlins Ter. E14 143 DZ71
Rhodeswell Rd.
Tomlins Wk. N7 121 DM61
Briset Way
Tomlinson Clo. E2 142 DT69
Tomlinson Clo. W4 158 CP78
Oxford Rd. N.
Tomlyns Clo., Brwd. 109 GE44
Tompion St. EC1 274 F3
Toms Cft., Hem.H. 40 BL21
Toms Fld., Hat. 44 CS19
Toms La., Abb.L. 59 BS27
Toms La., Kings L. 59 BP29
Tomswood Hill, Ilf. 103 EP52
Tomswood Rd., Chig. 103 EN51
Tonbridge Clo., Bans. 218 DF114
Tonbridge Cres., Har. 118 CL56
Tonbridge Ho. SE25 202 DU97
Tonbridge Rd., Rom. 106 FK52
Tonbridge Rd., Sev. 257 FJ126
Tonbridge Rd., W.Mol. 196 BY98
Tonbridge St. WC1 273 P2
Tonbridge St. WC1 141 DL69
Tonbridge Wk. WC1 273 P2
Tonfield Rd., Sutt. 199 CZ102
Tonge Clo., Beck. 203 EA99
Tonsley Hill SW18 180 DB85
Tonsley Pl. SW18 180 DB85
Tonsley Rd. SW18 180 DB85
Tonsley St. SW18 180 DB85
Tonstall Rd., Epsom 216 CR110
Tonstall Rd., Mitch. 200 DG96
Tony Cannell Ms. E3 143 DZ69
Maplin St.
Tooke Clo., Pnr. 94 BY53
Took's Ct. EC4 274 D8
Tooley St. SE1 279 L2
Tooley St. SE1 142 DS74
Tooley St., Grav. 190 GD87
Toorack Rd., Har. 95 CD54
Toot Hill Rd., Ong. 71 FF30
Tooting Bec Gdns. SW16 181 DK91
Tooting Bec Rd. SW16 181 DH91
Tooting Bec Rd. SW17 180 DG90
Tooting Gro. SW17 180 DE92
Tooting High St. SW17 180 DE93
Tootswood Rd., Brom. 204 EE99
Tooveys Mill Clo., Kings L. 58 BN28
Top Dartford Rd., Swan. 187 FF94
Top Ho. Ri. E4 101 EC45
Parkhill Rd.
Top Pk., Beck. 204 EE99
Top Pk., Ger.Cr. 112 AW58
Topaz Clo., Slou. 131 AP74
Pearl Gdns.
Topaz Wk. NW2 119 CX59
Marble Dr.
Topcliffe Dr., Orp. 223 ER106
Topham Sq. N17 100 DQ53
Topham St. EC1 274 D4
Topiary Sq., Rich. 158 CM83
Topland Rd., Ger.Cr. 90 AX52
Toplands Ave., S.Ock. 148 FP74
Topley St. SE9 164 EK84
Topp Wk. NW2 119 CW61
Topsfield Clo. N8 121 DK57
Wolseley Rd.
Topsfield Par. N8 121 DL57
Tottenham La.
Topsfield Rd. N8 121 DL57
Topsham Rd. SW17 180 DF90
Tor Gdns. W8 160 DA75
Tor La., Wey. 213 BQ111
Tor Rd., Well. 166 EW81
Torbay Rd. NW6 139 CZ66
Torbay Rd., Har. 116 BY61
Torbay St. NW1 141 DH66
Hawley Rd.
Torbitt Way, Ilf. 125 ET57
Aldborough Rd. N.

Torbridge Clo., Edg. 96 CL52
Torbrook Clo., Bex. 186 EY86
Torcross Dr. SE23 182 DW89
Torcross Rd., Ruis. 115 BV62
Torin Ct., Egh. 172 AW92
Torland Dr., Lthd. 215 CD114
Tormead Clo., Sutt. 218 DA107
Tormead Rd., Guil. 243 AZ134
Tormount Rd. SE18 165 ES79
Toronto Ave. E12 125 EM63
Toronto Dr., Horl. 269 DN148
Toronto Rd. E11 123 ED63
Toronto Rd., Ilf. 125 EP60
Toronto Rd., Til. 171 GG82
Torquay Gdns., Ilf. 124 EK56
Torquay Spur, Slou. 131 AP69
Torquay St. W2 140 DB71
Harrow Rd.
Torr Rd. SE20 183 DX94
Torrance Clo., Horn. 127 FH60
Torre Wk., Cars. 200 DE102
Torrens Clo., Guil. 242 AU131
Stoughton Rd.
Torrens Rd. E15 144 EF65
Torrens Rd. SW2 181 DM85
Torrens Sq. E15 144 EF65
Torrens St. EC1 274 E1
Torrens St. EC1 141 DN68
Torrens Wk., Grav. 191 GL92
Torriano Ave. NW5 121 DK64
Torriano Cotts. NW5 121 DJ64
Torriano Ave.
Torriano Ms. NW5 121 DK64
Torriano Ave.
Torridge Gdns. SE15 162 DW84
Torridge Rd., Slou. 153 BB79
Torridge Rd., Th.Hth. 201 DP99
Torridge Wk., Hem.H. 40 BM15
The Dee
Torridon Clo., Wok. 226 AV117
Torridon Rd. SE6 183 ED87
Torridon Rd. SE13 184 EE87
Torrington Ave. N12 98 DD50
Torrington Clo. N12 98 DD49
Torrington Clo., Esher 215 CE107
Torrington Dr., Har. 116 CB63
Torrington Dr., Loug. 85 EQ42
Torrington Dr., Pot.B. 64 DD32
Torrington Gdns. N11 99 DJ51
Torrington Gdns., Grnf. 137 CJ67
Torrington Gdns., Loug. 85 EQ42
Torrington Gro. N12 98 DE50
Torrington Pk. N12 98 DC50
Torrington Pl. E1 142 DU74
Torrington Pl. WC1 273 L6
Torrington Pl. WC1 141 DK71
Torrington Rd. E18 124 EG55
Torrington Rd., Berk. 38 AV19
Torrington Rd., Dag. 126 EZ60
Torrington Rd., Esher 215 CE107
Torrington Rd., Grnf. 137 CJ67
Torrington Rd., Ruis. 115 BT62
Torrington Sq. WC1 273 N5
Torrington Sq. WC1 141 DK70
Torrington Sq., Croy. 202 DR101
Tavistock Gro.
Torrington Way, Mord. 200 DA101
Tortoiseshell Way, Berk. 38 AT17
Torver Rd., Har. 117 CE56
Torver Way, Orp. 205 ER103
Torwood Clo., Berk. 38 AT19
Torwood La., Whyt. 236 DT120
Torwood Rd. SW15 179 CU85
Torworth Rd., Borwd. 78 CM38
Tothill St. SW1 277 M5
Tothill St. SW1 161 DK75
Totnes Rd., Well. 166 EV80
Totnes Wk. N2 120 DD56
Tottenhall Rd. N13 99 DN51
Tottenham Ct. Rd. W1 273 L5
Tottenham Ct. Rd. W1 141 DJ70
Tottenham Grn. E. N15 122 DT56
Tottenham La. N8 121 DL57
Tottenham Ms. W1 273 L6
Tottenham Rd. N1 142 DS65
Tottenham St. W1 273 L7
Tottenham St. W1 141 DJ71
Totterdown St. SW17 180 DF91
Totteridge Common N20 97 CU47
Totteridge Grn. N20 98 DA47
Totteridge La. N20 98 DA47
Totteridge Rd., Enf. 83 DX37
Totteridge Village N20 97 CY46
Totternhoe Clo., Har. 117 CJ57
Totton Rd., Th.Hth. 201 DN97
Toulmin Dr., St.Alb. 42 CC16
Toulmin St. SE1 279 H5
Toulmin St. SE1 162 DQ75
Toulon St. SE5 162 DQ80
Tournay Rd. SW6 159 CZ80
Toussaint Wk. SE16 162 DU76
John Roll Way
Tovey Ave., Hodd. 49 EA15
Tovey Clo., St.Alb. 61 CK26
Tovey Clo., Wal.Abb. 50 EE23
Tovil Clo. SE20 202 DV96
Towcester Rd. E3 143 EB70
Tower Bri. E1 279 P3
Tower Bri. E1 142 DT74
Tower Bri. SE1 279 P3
Tower Bri. SE1 142 DT74
Tower Bri. App. E1 279 P2
Tower Bri. App. E1 142 DT74
Tower Bri. Rd. SE1 279 M7
Tower Bri. Rd. SE1 162 DS76
Tower Clo. NW3 120 DD64
Lyndhurst Rd.
Tower Clo. SE20 182 DV94
Tower Clo., Berk. 38 AU20
Tower Clo., Epp. 53 FD24
Tower Clo., Grav. 191 GL92
Tower Clo., H.Wyc. 110 AC56
Tower Clo., Horl. 268 DF148
Rutherwick Clo.
Tower Clo., Ilf. 103 EP51
Tower Clo., Orp. 205 ET103
Tower Clo., Wok. 226 AX117
Tower Ct. WC2 273 P9
Tower Ct., Brwd. 108 FV47
Tower Cft. 208 FL103
(Eynsford), Dart.
High St.
Tower Gdns. Rd. N17 100 DQ53
Tower Gro., Wey. 195 BS103
Tower Hamlets Rd. E7 124 EF63
Tower Hamlets Rd. E17 123 EA55
Tower Hill EC3 279 P1
Tower Hill EC3 142 DS73
Tower Hill, Brwd. 108 FW47
Tower Hill, Dor. 263 CH138
Tower Hill, Guil. 261 BQ140
Tower Hill, Kings L. 57 BE29
Tower Hill La., Guil. 261 BQ140
Tower Hill
Tower Hill La., St.Alb. 28 CM10
Tower Hill Ri., Guil. 261 BQ140
Tower Hill
Tower Hill Rd., Dor. 263 CH138
Tower Hill Ter. EC3 142 DS73
Byward St.
Tower La., Guil. 261 BQ140
Tower La., Wem. 117 CK62
Main Dr.
Tower Ms. E17 123 EA56
Tower Pier EC3 279 N2
Tower Pier EC3 142 DS73
Tower Pl. EC3 279 N1
Tower Pt., Enf. 82 DR42
Tower Ri., Rich. 158 CL83
Jocelyn Rd.
Tower Rd. NW10 139 CU66
Tower Rd., Amer. 55 AN43
Tower Rd., Belv. 167 FC77
Tower Rd., Bexh. 166 FA84
Tower Rd., Dart. 188 FJ87
Tower Rd., Epp. 69 ES30
Tower Rd., Orp. 205 ET103
Tower Rd., Tad. 233 CW123
Tower Rd., Twick. 177 CF90
Tower Rd., Ware 33 DY05
Tower Royal EC4 275 J10
Tower St. WC2 273 N9
Tower St. WC2 141 DK72
Tower St., Hert. 32 DQ07
Tower Ter. N22 99 DM54
Mayes Rd.
Tower Vw., Croy. 203 DX101
Towers, The, Ken. 236 DQ115
Towers Ave., Uxb. 135 BQ69
Towers Pl., Rich. 178 CL85
Eton St.
Towers Rd., Grays 170 GC78
Towers Rd., Hem.H. 40 BL19
Towers Rd., Pnr. 94 BY52
Towers Rd., Sthl. 136 CA70
Towers Wk., Wey. 213 BP107
Towers Wd., Dart. 209 FR95
Towfield Rd., Felt. 176 BZ89
Towing Path, Guil. 242 AW132
Towing Path Wk. N1 141 DK67
York Way
Town, The, Enf. 82 DR41
Town Bri. Ct., Chesh. 54 AP32
Water Meadow
Town Cen., Hat. 45 CU17
Queensway
Town Ct. Path N4 122 DQ60
Town End, Cat. 236 DS122
Town End Clo., Cat. 236 DS122
Town Fld. La., Ch.St.G. 90 AW48
Town Fld. Way, Islw. 157 CG82
Twickenham Rd.
Town Flds., Hat. 45 CU17
Town Hall App. N16 122 DS63
Milton Gro.
Town Hall App. Rd. N15 122 DT56
Town Hall Ave. W4 158 CR78
Town Hall Rd. SW11 160 DF83
Town La., H.Wyc. 110 AD59
Town La., Stai. 174 BK86
Town Meadow, Brent. 157 CK80
Town Path, Egh. 173 BA92
High St.
Town Quay, Bark. 145 EP67
Town Rd. N9 100 DV47
Town Sq., Erith 167 FE79
Pier Rd.
Town Tree Rd., Ashf. 174 BN92
Towncourt Cres., Orp. 205 EQ99
Towncourt La., Orp. 205 ER100
Towney Mead, Nthlt. 136 BZ68
Townfield, Chesh. 54 AP32
Townfield, Rick. 92 BJ45
Townfield Cor., Grav. 191 GJ88
Townfield Rd., Dor. 263 CG137
Townfield Rd., Hayes 135 BT74
Townfield Sq., Hayes 135 BT73
Towngate, Cob. 230 BY115
Townholm Cres. W7 157 CF76
Townley Ct. E15 144 EF65
Townley Rd. SE22 182 DS85
Townley Rd., Bexh. 186 EZ86
Townley St. SE17 279 K10
Townmead, Red. 252 DR133
Townmead Rd. SW6 160 DB83
Townmead Rd., Rich. 158 CP82
Townmead Rd., 67 EC34
Wal.Abb.
Townsend, Hem.H. 40 BK18
Townsend Ave. N14 99 DK49
Townsend Ave., St.Alb. 43 CE19
Townsend Dr., St.Alb. 43 CD17
Townsend Ind. Est. 138 CQ68
NW10
Townsend La. NW9 118 CR59
Townsend La., Wok. 227 BB121
St. Peters Rd.
Townsend Rd. N15 122 DT57
Townsend Rd., Ashf. 174 BL92
Townsend Rd., Chesh. 54 AP30
Townsend Rd., Sthl. 136 BY74
Townsend St. SE17 279 M8
Townsend St. SE17 162 DR77
Townsend Way, Nthwd. 93 BT52
Townsend Yd. N6 120 DG60
Townshend Clo., Sid. 186 EV93
Townshend Est. NW8 140 DE68
Townshend Rd. NW8 140 DE67
Townshend Rd., Chis. 185 EP92
Townshend Rd., Rich. 158 CM84
Townshend St., Hert. 32 DS09
Townshend Ter., Rich. 158 CM84
Townshott Clo., Lthd. 246 CA125
Townslow La., Wok. 228 BK116
Townson Ave., Nthlt. 135 BU69
Townson Way, Nthlt. 135 BU68
Townson Ave.
Towpath, Shep. 194 BM102
Dockett Eddy La.
Towpath Way, Croy. 202 DT100
Towton Rd. SE27 182 DQ89
Toynbec Clo., Chis. 185 EP91
Beechwood Ri.
Toynbee Rd. SW20 199 CY95
Toynbee St. E1 275 P7
Toynbee St. E1 142 DT71
Toyne Way N6 120 DF58
Gaskell Rd.
Tozer Wk., Wind. 151 AK83
Tinkers La.
Tracery, The, Bans. 234 DB115
Tracey Ave. NW2 119 CW64
Tracious Clo., Wok. 226 AV116
Sythwood
Tracious La., Wok. 226 AV116
Tracy Ct., Stan. 95 CJ52
Tracyes Rd., Harl. 52 EV17
Trade Clo. N13 99 DN49
Green Las.
Trader Rd. E6 145 EP72
Ferndale St.
Tradescant Rd. SW8 161 DL80
Trading Est. Rd. NW10 138 CQ70
Trafalgar Ave. N17 100 DS51
Trafalgar Ave. SE15 162 DT78
Trafalgar Ave., Brox. 49 DZ21
Trafalgar Ave., Wor.Pk. 199 CX102
Trafalgar Business Cen., 145 ET70
Bark.
Trafalgar Clo. SE16 163 DY77
Greenland Quay
Trafalgar Ct., Cob. 213 BU113
Trafalgar Dr., Walt. 195 BU104
Trafalgar Gdns. E1 143 DX71
Trafalgar Gro. SE10 163 ED79
Trafalgar Pl. E11 124 EG56
Trafalgar Pl. N18 100 DU50
Trafalgar Rd. SE10 163 ED79
Trafalgar Rd. SW19 180 DB94
Trafalgar Rd., Dart. 188 FL89
Trafalgar Rd., Grav. 191 GG87
Trafalgar Rd., Rain. 147 FF68
Trafalgar Rd., Twick. 177 CD89
Trafalgar Sq. SW1 277 N2
Trafalgar Sq. SW1 141 DK74
Trafalgar Sq. WC2 277 N2
Trafalgar Sq. WC2 141 DK74
Trafalgar St. SE17 279 K10
Trafalgar St. SE17 162 DR78
Trafalgar Ter., Har. 117 CE60
Nelson Rd.
Trafalgar Way E14 143 EC74
Trafalgar Way, Croy. 201 DM103
Trafford Clo. E15 123 EB64
Trafford Clo., Ilf. 103 ET51
Trafford Clo., Rad. 62 CL32
Trafford Rd., Th.Hth. 201 DM99
Tramway Ave. E15 144 EE66
Tramway Ave. N9 100 DV45
Tramway Path, Mitch. 200 DE98
London Rd.
Tranby Pl. E9 123 DX64
Homerton High St.
Tranley Ms. NW3 120 DE63
Fleet Rd.
Tranmere Rd. N9 100 DT45
Tranmere Rd. SW18 180 DC88
Tranmere Rd., Twick. 176 CB87
Tranquil Dale, Bet. 249 CT132
Tranquil Pas. SE3 164 EF82
Tranquil Vale
Tranquil Ri., Erith 167 FE78
West St.
Tranquil Vale SE3 164 EE82
Transay Wk. N1 142 DR65
Marquess Rd.
Transept St. NW1 272 C7
Transept St. NW1 140 DE71
Transmere Clo., Orp. 205 EQ100
Transmere Rd., Orp. 205 EQ100
Transom Clo. SE16 163 DX77
Plough Way
Transom Sq. E14 163 EB77
Transport Ave., Brent. 157 CG78
Tranton Rd. SE16 162 DU76
Trapps La., Chesh. 54 AR32
Traps Hill, Loug. 85 EM41
Traps La., N.Mal. 198 CS95
Trapstyle Rd., Ware 32 DU05
Trasher Mead, Dor. 263 CJ139
Travellers Clo., Hat. 45 CW23
Travellers La., Hat. 45 CU19
Travellers La. 45 CV21
(North Mymms), Hat.
Travellers Way, 156 BW82
Houns.
Travers Clo. E17 101 DX53
Travers Rd. N7 121 DN62
Travic Rd., Slou. 131 AM69
Travis Ct., Slou. 131 AP69
Treachers Clo., Chesh. 54 AP31
Treacy Clo. 94 CC47
(Bushey), Wat.
Treadgold St. W11 139 CX73
Treadway St. E2 142 DV68
Treadwell Rd., Epsom 233 CT115
Treaty Rd., Houns. 156 CB83
Hanworth Rd.
Treaty St. N1 141 DM67
Trebble Rd., Swans. 190 FY86
Trebeck St. W1 277 H2
Trebellan Dr., Hem.H. 40 BM19
Trebovir Rd. SW5 160 DA78
Treby St. E3 143 DZ70
Trecastle Way N7 121 DK63
Carleton Rd.
Tredegar Ms. E3 143 DZ69
Tredegar Ter.
Tredegar Rd. E3 143 DZ68
Tredegar Rd. N11 99 DK52
Tredegar Rd., Dart. 187 FG89
Tredegar Sq. E3 143 DZ69
Tredegar Ter. E3 143 DZ69
Trederwen Rd. E8 142 DU67
Tredown Rd. SE26 182 DW92
Tredwell Clo., Brom. 204 EL98
Tredwell Rd. SE27 181 DP91
Tree Clo., Rich. 177 CK88
Tree Rd. E16 144 EJ72
Tree Tops, Brwd. 108 FW46
Treebourne Rd., West. 238 EJ117
Treebys Ave., Guil. 242 AX128
Treelands, Dor. 263 CJ139
Treen Ave. SW13 158 CS83
Treeside Clo., West Dr. 154 BK77
Treetops, Grav. 191 GH92
Treetops, Whyt. 236 DU118
Treetops Clo. SE2 166 EY78
Treetops Clo., Nthwd. 93 BR50
Treeview Clo. SE19 202 DS95
Treewall Gdns., Brom. 184 EH91
Treeway, Reig. 250 DB131
Trefgarne Rd., Dag. 126 FA61
Trefil Wk. N7 121 DL63
Trefoil Rd. SW18 180 DC85
Trefusis Wk., Wat. 75 BS39
Tregaron Ave. N8 121 DL58
Tregaron Gdns., N.Mal. 198 CS98
Avenue Rd.
Tregarth Pl., Wok. 226 AT117
Tregarthen Pl., Lthd. 231 CJ121
Tregarvon Rd. SW11 160 DG84
Tregelles Rd., Hodd. 33 EA14
Tregenna Ave., Har. 116 BZ63
Tregenna Clo. N14 81 DJ43
Tregenna Ct., Har. 116 CA63
Trego Rd. E9 143 EA66
Tregothnan Rd. SW9 161 DL83
Tregunter Rd. SW10 160 DC79
Trehearn Rd., Ilf. 103 ER52
Trehern Rd. SW14 158 CR83
Treherne Ct. SW9 161 DN81
Eythorne Rd.
Treherne Ct. SW17 180 DG91
Trehurst St. E5 123 DY64
Trelawn Clo., Cher. 211 BC108
Trelawn Rd. E10 123 EC62
Trelawn Rd. SW2 181 DN85
Trelawney Ave., Slou. 152 AX76
Trelawney Clo. E17 123 EB56
Orford Rd.
Trelawney Est. E9 142 DW65
Trelawney Gro., Wey. 212 BN107
Trelawney Rd., Ilf. 103 ER52
Trellick Twr. W10 139 CZ70
Trellis Sq. E3 143 DZ69
Malmesbury Rd.
Treloar Gdns. SE19 182 DR93
Hancock Rd.
Tremadoc Rd. SW4 161 DK84
Tremaine Clo. SE4 163 EA82
Tremaine Gro., Hem.H. 40 BL16
Tremaine Rd. SE20 202 DV96
Trematon Pl., Tedd. 177 CJ94
Tremlett Gro. N19 121 DJ62
Tremlett Ms. N19 121 DJ62
Tremlett Gro.
Trenance, Wok. 226 AU117
Cardingham
Trenance Gdns., Ilf. 126 EU62
Trench Yd. Ct., Mord. 200 DB100
Green La.
Trenchard Ave., Ruis. 115 BV63
Trenchard Clo., Stan. 95 CG51
Trenchard Clo., Walt. 214 BW106
Trenchard Ct., Mord. 200 DB100
Trenchard St. SE10 163 ED78
Trenches La., Slou. 133 BA73
Trenchold St. SW8 161 DL79
Trenham Dr., Warl. 236 DW116
Trenholme Clo. SE20 182 DV94
Trenholme Ct., Cat. 236 DU122
Trenholme Rd. SE20 182 DV94
Trenholme Ter. SE20 182 DV94
Trenmar Gdns. NW10 139 CV69
Trent Ave. W5 157 CJ76
Trent Ave., Upmin. 129 FR58
Trent Clo., Rad. 62 CL32
Trent Gdns. N14 81 DH44
Trent Rd. SW2 181 DM85
Trent Rd., Buck.H. 102 EH46
Trent Rd., Slou. 153 BB79
Trent Way, Hayes 135 BS69
Trent Way, Wor.Pk. 199 CW104
Trentbridge Clo., Ilf. 103 ET51
Trentham Cres., Wok. 227 BA121
Trentham Dr., Orp. 206 EU98
Trentham Rd., Red. 266 DG136
Trentham St. SW18 180 DA88
Trentwood Side, Enf. 81 DM41
Treport St. SW18 180 DB87
Tresco Clo., Brom. 184 EE93
Tresco Gdns., Ilf. 126 EU61
Tresco Rd. SE15 162 DV84
Tresco Rd., Berk. 38 AT18
Trescoe Gdns., Har. 116 BY59
Trescoe Gdns., Rom. 105 FC50
Tresham Cres. NW8 272 B4
Tresham Cres. NW8 140 DE70
Tresham Rd., Bark. 145 ET66
Tresham Wk. E9 122 DW64
Churchill Wk.
Tresilian Ave. N21 81 DM43
Tresilian Sq., Hem.H. 40 BM15
The Dee
Tresillian Way, Wok. 226 AU116
Tressell Clo. N1 141 DP66
Sebbon St.
Tressillian Cres. SE4 163 EA83
Tressillian Rd. SE4 163 DZ84
Tresta Wk., Wok. 226 AU115
Trestis Clo., Hayes 136 BY71
Jollys La.
Treston Ct., Stai. 173 BF92
Treswell Rd., Dag. 146 EY67
Tretawn Gdns. NW7 96 CS49
Tretawn Pk. NW7 96 CS49
Trevanion Rd. W14 159 CY77
Treve Ave., Har. 116 CC59
Trevelga Way, Hem.H. 40 BL16
Trevellance Way, Wat. 60 BW33
Trevelyan Ave. E12 125 EM63
Trevelyan Clo., Dart. 168 FM84
Trevelyan Cres., Har. 117 CK59
Trevelyan Gdns. NW10 139 CW67
Trevelyan Rd. E15 124 EF63
Trevelyan Rd. SW17 180 DE92
Trevelyan Way, Berk. 38 AV17
Trevereux Hill, Oxt. 255 EM131
Treveris St. SE1 278 G3
Treverton St. W10 139 CY70
Treville St. SW15 179 CV87
Treviso Rd. SE23 183 DX89
Farren Rd.
Trevithick Clo., Felt. 175 BT88
Westmacott Dr.
Trevithick Dr., Dart. 168 FM84
Trevithick St. SE8 163 EA79
Trevone Gdns., Pnr. 116 BY58
Trevor Clo., Barn. 80 DD44
Trevor Clo., Brom. 204 EF101
Trevor Clo., Har. 95 CF52
Kenton La.
Trevor Clo., Islw. 177 CF85
Trevor Clo., Nthlt. 136 BW68
Trevor Cres., Ruis. 115 BT63
Trevor Gdns., Edg. 96 CR53
Trevor Gdns., Nthlt. 136 BW68
Trevor Pl. SW7 276 C5
Trevor Pl. SW7 160 DE75
Trevor Rd. SW19 179 CY94
Trevor Rd., Edg. 96 CR53
Trevor Rd., Hayes 155 BS75
Trevor Rd., Wdf.Grn. 102 EG52
Trevor Sq. SW7 276 D5
Trevor Sq. SW7 160 DE76
Trevor St. SW7 276 C5
Trevor St. SW7 160 DE75
Trevose Ave., W.Byf. 211 BF114
Trevose Rd. E17 101 ED53
Trevose Way, Wat. 94 BW48
Trewarden Ave., Iver 133 BD68
Bangors Rd. N.
Trewenna Dr., Chess. 215 CK106
Trewenna Dr., Pot.B. 64 DD32
Trewince Rd. SW20 199 CW95
Trewint St. SW18 180 DC89
Trewsbury Rd. SE26 183 DX92
Triandra Way, Hayes 136 BX71
Triangle, The EC1 141 DP70
Goswell Rd.
Triangle, The N13 99 DN49
Triangle, The, Bark. 145 EQ65
Tanner St.
Triangle, The, Hmptn. 196 CC95
High St.
Triangle, The, Kings.T. 198 CQ96
Kenley Rd.
Triangle, The, Wok. 226 AW118
St. John's Rd.
Triangle Ct. E16 144 EK71
Tollgate Rd.
Triangle Pas., Barn. 80 DC42
Station Rd.
Triangle Pl. SW4 161 DK84
Triangle Rd. E8 142 DV67
Trident Gdns., Nthlt. 136 BX69
Jetstar Way
Trident Ind. Est., Hodd. 49 EB17
Trident Ind. Est., Slou. 153 BE83
Trident Rd., Wat. 59 BT34
Trident St. SE16 163 DX77
Trident Wk. SE16 163 DX77
Greenland Quay
Trident Way, Sthl. 155 BV76
Trig La. EC4 275 H10
Trigg's Clo., Wok. 226 AX119
Trigg's La., Wok. 226 AX118
Trigo Ct., Epsom 216 CR111
Blakeney Clo.
Trigon Rd. SW8 161 DM80
Trilby Rd. SE23 183 DX89
Trimmer Wk., Brent. 158 CL79
Netley Rd.
Trinder Gdns. N19 121 DL60
Trinder Rd.
Trinder Rd. N19 121 DL60
Trinder Rd., Barn. 79 CW43
Trindles Rd., Red. 267 DM136
Tring Ave. W5 138 CM74
Tring Ave., Sthl. 136 BZ72
Tring Ave., Wem. 138 CN65
Tring Clo., Ilf. 125 ER57
Tring Clo., Rom. 106 FM49
Tring Gdns., Rom. 106 FL49
Tring Grn., Rom. 106 FL49
Tring Gdns.
Tring Wk., Rom. 106 FL49
Tring Gdns.
Tringham Clo., Cher. 211 BC106
Trinidad Gdns., Dag. 147 FD66
Trinidad St. E14 143 DZ73
Trinity Ave. N2 120 DD55
Trinity Ave., Enf. 82 DT44
Trinity Ch. Pas. SW13 159 CV79
Trinity Ch. Rd. SW13 159 CV79
Trinity Ch. Sq. SE1 279 J6
Trinity Ch. Sq. SE1 162 DQ76
Trinity Chyd., Guil. 258 AX136
High St.
Trinity Clo. E8 122 DV64
Dalston La.
Trinity Clo. E11 124 EE61
Trinity Clo. NW3 120 DD63
Hampstead High St.
Trinity Clo. SE13 163 ED84
Wisteria Rd.
Trinity Clo., Brom. 204 EL102
Trinity Clo., Hert. 32 DW12
Trinity Clo., Houns. 156 BY84
Trinity Clo., Nthwd. 93 BS51
Trinity Clo., S.Croy. 220 DS109
Trinity Clo., Stai. 174 BJ86
Trinity Cotts., Rich. 158 CM83
Trinity Rd.
Trinity Ct. N1 142 DS66
Downham Rd.
Trinity Ct. SE7 164 EK77
Charlton La.
Trinity Cres. SW17 180 DF89
Trinity Gdns. SW9 161 DM84
Trinity Gro. SE10 163 EC81
Trinity Gro., Hert. 32 DQ07
Trinity Hall Clo., Wat. 76 BW40
Trinity La., Wal.Cr. 67 DY32
Trinity Ms. SE20 202 DV95
Croydon Rd.
Trinity Ms. W10 139 CX72
Cambridge Gdns.
Trinity Ms., Hem.H. 41 BR21
Pancake La.
Trinity Path SE26 182 DW90
Sydenham Pk.
Trinity Pl., Bexh. 166 EZ84
Trinity Pl., Wind. 151 AQ82
Trinity Ri. SW2 181 DN88
Trinity Rd. N2 120 DD55
Trinity Rd. N22 99 DL52
Whittington Rd.
Trinity Rd. SW17 180 DF89
Trinity Rd. SW18 180 DD85
Trinity Rd. SW19 180 DA93
Trinity Rd., Grav. 191 GJ87
Trinity Rd., Hert. 32 DW12
Trinity Rd., Ilf. 125 EQ55
Trinity Rd., Rich. 158 CM83
Trinity Rd., Sthl. 136 BY74
Trinity Rd., Ware 33 DY05
Trinity Sq. EC3 279 N1
Trinity Sq. EC3 142 DS73
Trinity St. E16 144 EG71
Vincent St.
Trinity St. SE1 279 J5
Trinity St. SE1 162 DQ75
Trinity St., Enf. 82 DQ40
Trinity Wk. NW3 140 DC65
Trinity Wk., Hem.H. 41 BR21
Pancake La.
Trinity Way E4 101 DZ51
Trinity Way W3 138 CS73
Trio Pl. SE1 279 J5
Tripps Hill, Ch.St.G. 90 AU48
Tripps Hill Clo., Ch.St.G. 90 AU48
Tripton Rd., Harl. 51 ES16
Tristan Sq. SE3 164 EE83

Tristram Clo. E17 123 ED55
Tristram Rd., Brom. 184 EF91
Triton Sq. NW1 273 K4
Triton Sq. NW1 141 DJ70
Triton Way, Hem.H. 40 BM18
Tritton Ave., Croy. 219 DL105
Tritton Rd. SE21 182 DR90
Trittons, Tad. 233 CW121
Triumph Clo., Hayes 155 BQ81
Triumph Ho., Bark. 146 EU69
Triumph Rd. E6 145 EM72
Trivett Clo., Green. 189 FU85
Trodd's La., Guil. 243 BD133
Trojan Ct. NW6 139 CY66
Willesden La.
Trojan Way, Croy. 201 DM104
Trolling Down Hill, Dart. 188 FQ89
Troon St. E1 143 DY72
White Horse Rd.
Troopers Dr., Rom. 106 FK49
Trosley Ave., Grav. 191 GH89
Trosley Rd., Belv. 166 FA79
Trossachs Rd. SE22 182 DS85
Trothy Rd. SE1 162 DU77
Monnow Rd.
Trotsworth Ave., Vir.W. 192 AY98
Trotsworth Ct., Vir.W. 192 AX98
Trott Rd. N10 98 DF52
Trott St. SW11 160 DD81
Trotters Bottom, Barn. 79 CU37
Trotters Gap, Ware 33 ED11
Trotters La., Wok. 210 AV112
Trotters Rd., Harl. 52 EU17
Trotts La., West. 255 EQ127
Trotwood, Chig. 103 ER51
Trotwood Clo., Brwd. 108 FY46
Middleton Rd.
Troughton Rd. SE7 164 EH78
Trout La., West Dr. 134 BH73
Trout Ri., Rick. 74 BH41
Trout Rd., West Dr. 134 BK74
Troutbeck Clo., Slou. 132 AU73
St. Pauls Ave.
Troutbeck Rd. SE14 163 DY81
Troutstream Way, Rick. 74 BH42
Trouville Rd. SW4 181 DJ86
Trowbridge Est. E9 143 DZ65
Trowbridge Rd. E9 143 DZ65
Trowbridge Rd., Rom. 106 FK51
Trowers Way, Red. 251 DH131
Trowley Ri., Abb.L. 59 BS31
Trowlock Ave., Tedd. 177 CJ93
Trowlock Island, Tedd. 177 CJ92
Trowlock Way, Tedd. 177 CK93
Troy Clo., Tad. 233 CV120
Troy Ct. SE18 165 EP77
Troy Rd. SE19 182 DR93
Troy Town SE15 162 DU83
Truesdale Dr., Uxb. 114 BJ56
Truesdale Rd. E6 145 EM72
Trulock Ct. N17 100 DU52
Trulock Rd. N17 100 DU52
Truman Clo., Edg. 96 CP52
Pavilion Way
Truman's Rd. N16 122 DS64
Trump St. EC2 275 J9
Trumper Way, Uxb. 134 BJ67
Trumpers Way W7 157 CE75
Trumpetshill Rd., Reig. 265 CU135
Trumpington Dr., St.Alb. 43 CD23
Trumpington Rd. E7 124 EF63
Trumps Mill La., Vir.W. 193 AZ100
Trumpsgreen Ave., Vir.W. 192 AX100
Trumpsgreen Clo., Vir.W. 192 AY99
Trumpsgreen Rd.
Trumpsgreen Rd., Vir.W. 192 AW102
Trundle St. SE1 279 H4
Trundlers Way (Bushey), Wat. 95 CE46
Trundleys Rd. SE8 163 DX78
Trundleys Ter. SE8 163 DX77
Trunks All., Swan. 207 FB96
Trunley Heath Rd., Guil. 258 AW144
Truro Gdns., Ilf. 124 EL59
Truro Rd. E17 123 DZ56
Truro Rd. N22 99 DL52
Truro Rd., Grav. 191 GK90
Truro St. NW5 140 DG65
Truro Wk., Rom. 106 FJ51
Saddleworth Rd.
Truro Way, Hayes 135 BS69
Portland Rd.
Truslove Rd. SE27 181 DN92
Trussley Rd. W6 159 CW76
Trust Rd., Wal.Cr. 67 DY34
Trust Wk. SE21 181 DP88
Peabody Hill
Trustees Way, Uxb. 113 BF57
Trustons Gdns., Horn. 127 FG59
Tryfan Clo., Ilf. 124 EK57
Tryon St. SW3 276 D10
Tryon St. SW3 160 DF78
Trystings Clo., Esher 215 CG107
Tuam Rd. SE18 165 ER79
Tubbenden Clo., Orp. 205 ES103
Tubbenden Dr., Orp. 223 ER105
Tubbenden La., Orp. 223 ER105
Tubbenden La. S., Orp. 223 ER106
Tubbs Rd. NW10 139 CT68
Tubs Hill Par., Sev. 256 FG124
Tubwell Rd., Slou. 132 AV67
Tuck Rd., Rain. 147 FG65
Tucker Rd., Cher. 211 BD107
Tucker St., Wat. 76 BW43
Tuckey Gro., Wok. 227 BF124
Tudor Ave., Hmptn. 176 CA93
Tudor Ave., Rom. 127 FG55
Tudor Ave. (Cheshunt), Wal.Cr. 66 DU31
Tudor Ave., Wat. 76 BX38
Tudor Ave., Wor.Pk. 199 CV104
Tudor Circle, Gdmg. 258 AS144
Tudor Clo. N6 121 DJ59
Tudor Clo. NW3 120 DE64
Tudor Clo. NW7 97 CU51
Tudor Clo. NW9 118 CQ61
Tudor Clo. SW2 181 DM86
Elm Pk.
Tudor Clo., Ashf. 174 BL91
Tudor Clo., Bans. 233 CY115
Tudor Clo., Brwd. 109 FZ44
Tudor Clo., Chess. 216 CL106
Tudor Clo., Chig. 103 EN49
Tudor Clo., Chis. 205 EM95
Tudor Clo., Cob. 214 BZ113
Tudor Clo., Couls. 235 DN118
Tudor Clo., Dart. 187 FH86
Tudor Clo., Grav. 190 GE88
Vale Rd.
Tudor Clo., Hat. 45 CT21
Tudor Clo., Horl. 269 DP148
Tudor Clo., Lthd. 230 CA124
Tudor Clo., Pnr. 115 BU57
Tudor Clo., S.Croy. 236 DV115
Tudor Clo., Sutt. 217 CY107
Tudor Clo., Wall. 219 DJ108
Tudor Clo. (Cheshunt), Wal.Cr. 66 DV31
Tudor Clo., Ware 34 EK07
Tudor Clo., Wdf.Grn. 102 EH50
Tudor Ct. E17 123 DZ59
Tudor Ct., Borwd. 78 CL40
Tudor Ct., Felt. 176 BW91
Tudor Ct., Swan. 207 FC101
Tudor Ct. N., Wem. 118 CN64
Tudor Ct. S., Wem. 118 CN64
Tudor Cres., Enf. 82 DQ39
Tudor Cres., Ilf. 103 EP51
Tudor Dr., H.Wyc. 110 AD55
Tudor Dr., Kings.T. 177 CK92
Tudor Dr., Mord. 199 CX100
Tudor Dr., Rom. 127 FG56
Tudor Dr., Walt. 196 BX102
Tudor Dr., Wat. 76 BX38
Tudor Est. NW10 138 CP69
Tudor Gdns. NW9 118 CQ61
Tudor Gdns. SW13 158 CS83
Treen Ave.
Tudor Gdns. W3 138 CN71
Tudor Gdns., Rom. 127 FG56
Tudor Gdns., Slou. 130 AJ72
Tudor Gdns., Twick. 177 CF88
Tudor Gdns., Upmin. 128 FQ61
Tudor Gdns., W.Wick. 203 EC104
Tudor Gro. E9 142 DW66
Tudor Gro. N20 98 DE48
Church Cres.
Tudor La., Wind. 172 AW87
Tudor Manor Gdns., Wat. 60 BX32
Tudor Par., Rick. 92 BG45
Berry La.
Tudor Pk., Amer. 55 AR37
Tudor Pl. W1 273 M8
Tudor Pl., Mitch. 180 DE94
Tudor Ri., Brox. 49 DY21
Tudor Rd. E4 101 EB51
Tudor Rd. E6 144 EJ67
Tudor Rd. E9 142 DV67
Tudor Rd. N9 100 DV45
Tudor Rd. SE19 182 DT94
Tudor Rd. SE25 202 DV99
Tudor Rd., Ashf. 175 BR93
Tudor Rd., Bark. 145 ET67
Tudor Rd., Barn. 80 DA41
Tudor Rd., Beck. 203 EB97
Tudor Rd., Gdmg. 258 AS144
Tudor Rd., Hmptn. 176 CA94
Tudor Rd., Har. 95 CD54
Tudor Rd., Hayes 135 BR72
Tudor Rd., Houns. 157 CD84
Tudor Rd., Kings.T. 178 CN94
Tudor Rd., Pnr. 94 BW54
Tudor Rd., St.Alb. 43 CE16
Tudor Rd. (Wheathampstead), St.Alb. 28 CL07
Tudor Rd., Sthl. 136 BY73
Tudor Sq., Hayes 135 BR71
Tudor St. EC4 274 E10
Tudor St. EC4 141 DN73
Tudor Wk., Bex. 186 EY86
Tudor Wk., Lthd. 231 CF120
Tudor Wk., Wat. 76 BX37
Tudor Wk., Wey. 195 BP104
West Palace Gdns.
Tudor Way N14 99 DK46
Tudor Way W3 158 CN75
Tudor Way, Hert. 31 DN08
Tudor Way, Orp. 205 ER100
Tudor Way, Rick. 92 BG46
Tudor Way, Uxb. 134 BN65
Tudor Way, Wal.Abb. 67 ED33
Tudor Way, Wind. 151 AL81
Tudor Well Clo., Stan. 95 CH50
Tudors, The, Reig. 250 DC131
Tudorwalk, Grays 170 GA76
Thurloe Wk.
Tudway Rd. SE3 164 EH83
Tufnail Rd., Dart. 188 FM86
Tufnell Pk. Rd. N7 121 DK63
Tufnell Pk. Rd. N19 121 DJ63
Tufter Rd., Chig. 103 ET50
Tufton Gdns., W.Mol. 196 CB96
Tufton Rd. E4 101 EA49
Tufton St. SW1 277 P7
Tufton St. SW1 161 DK76
Tugboat St. SE28 165 ES75
Goldfinch Rd.
Tugela Rd., Croy. 202 DR100
Tugela St. SE6 183 DZ89
Tugmutton Clo., Orp. 223 EP105
Acorn Way
Tuilerie St. E2 142 DU68
Hackney Rd.
Tulip Clo. E6 145 EM71
Tollgate Rd.
Tulip Clo., Brwd. 108 FV43
Poppy Clo.
Tulip Clo., Croy. 203 DX102
Tulip Clo., Hmptn. 176 BZ93
Partridge Rd.
Tulip Clo., Rom. 106 FK51
Cloudberry Rd.
Tulip Ct., Pnr. 116 BW55
Tull St., Mitch. 200 DF101
Middleton Rd.
Tulse Clo., Beck. 203 EC97
Tulse Hill SW2 181 DN86
Tulse Hill Est. SW2 181 DN86
Tulsemere Rd. SE27 182 DQ89
Tulyar Clo., Tad. 233 CV120
Tumber St., Epsom 248 CQ125
Tumbler Rd., Harl. 52 EU16
Tumblewood Rd., Bans. 233 CY116
Tumbling Bay, Walt. 195 BU100
Tummons Gdns. SE25 202 DS96
Tun Yd. SW8 161 DH82
Peardon St.
Tuncombe Rd. N18 100 DS49
Tunfield Rd., Hodd. 33 EB14
Tunis Rd. W12 139 CV74
Tunley Grn. E14 143 DZ71
Burdett Rd.
Tunley Rd. NW10 138 CS67
Tunley Rd. SW17 180 DG88
Tunmarsh La. E13 144 EH69
Tunmers End, Ger.Cr. 90 AW53
Tunnan Leys E6 145 EN72
Horse Leaze
Tunnel Ave. SE10 163 ED75
Tunnel Gdns. N11 99 DJ52
Tunnel Rd. SE16 162 DW75
St. Marychurch St.
Tunnel Rd., Reig. 250 DA133
Church St.
Tunnel Wd. Clo., Wat. 75 BT37
Tunnel Wd. Rd., Wat. 75 BT37
Tunnmeade, Harl. 36 EU14
Tuns La., Slou. 151 AQ76
Tunsgate, Guil. 258 AX136
Castle St.
Tunstall Ave., Ilf. 104 EU51
Tunstall Clo., Orp. 223 ES105
Tunstall Rd. SW9 161 DM84
Tunstall Rd., Croy. 202 DS102
Tunstall Wk., Brent. 158 CL79
Ealing Rd.
Tunstock Way, Belv. 166 EY76
Tunworth Clo. NW9 118 CQ58
Tunworth Cres. SW15 179 CT86
Tupelo Rd. E10 123 EB61
Oliver Rd.
Tupwood Ct., Cat. 252 DU125
Tupwood La., Cat. 252 DU125
Tupwood Scrubbs Rd., Cat. 252 DU128
Turenne Clo. SW18 160 DC84
Turfhouse La., Wok. 210 AS109
Turin Rd. N9 100 DW45
Turin St. E2 142 DU69
Turkey Oak Clo. SE19 202 DS95
Turkey St., Enf. 82 DU36
Turks Clo., Uxb. 134 BN69
Harlington Rd.
Turk's Head Yd. EC1 274 F6
Turks Row SW3 276 E10
Turks Row SW3 160 DF78
Turle Rd. N4 121 DM60
Turle Rd. SW16 201 DL96
Turlewray Clo. N4 121 DM60
Turley Clo. E15 144 EE67
Turmore Dale, Welw.G.C. 29 CW10
Turnagain La. EC4 274 F8
Turnagain La., Dart. 187 FG90
Turnage Rd., Dag. 126 EY60
Turnberry Clo. SE16 162 DV78
Credon Rd.
Turnberry Ct., Wat. 94 BW48
Turnberry Dr., St.Alb. 60 BY30
Turnberry Quay E14 163 EB76
Pepper St.
Turnberry Way, Orp. 205 ER102
Turnbull Clo., Green. 189 FS87
Turnchapel Ms. SW4 161 DH83
Cedars Rd.
Turner Ave. N15 122 DS56
Turner Ave., Mitch. 200 DF95
Turner Ave., Twick. 176 CC90
Turner Clo. NW11 120 DB58
Turner Clo., Hayes 135 BQ68
Charville La.
Turner Ct., Dart. 188 FJ85
Wilmot Rd.
Turner Dr. NW11 120 DB58
Turner Rd. E17 123 EC55
Turner Rd., Dart. 189 FV90
Turner Rd., Edg. 96 CL54
Turner Rd., N.Mal. 198 CR101
Turner Rd., Slou. 152 AW75
Turner Rd. (Bushey), Wat. 76 CC42
Turner Rd., West. 222 EJ112
Turner St. E1 142 DV71
Turner St. E16 144 EF72
Turners Clo., Stai. 174 BH92
Turners Gdns., Sev. 257 FJ128
Turners Hill, Hem.H. 40 BL20
Turners Hill (Cheshunt), Wal.Cr. 67 DX30
Turners La., Walt. 213 BV107
Turners Meadow Way, Beck. 203 DZ95
Turners Rd. E3 143 DZ71
Turners Way, Croy. 201 DN103
Turners Wd. NW11 120 DC60
Turners Wd. Dr., Ch.St.G. 90 AX48
Turneville Rd. W14 159 CZ79
Turney Rd. SE21 182 DQ87
Turneys Orchard, Rick. 73 BD43
Turnham Clo., Guil. 258 AW138
Portsmouth Rd.
Turnham Grn. Ter. W4 158 CS77
Turnham Grn. Ter. Ms. W4 158 CS77
Turnham Grn. Ter.
Turnham Rd. SE4 183 DY85
Turnmill St. EC1 274 E5
Turnmill St. EC1 141 DN70
Turnoak Ave., Wok. 226 AY120
Turnoak La., Wok. 226 AY119
Wych Hill La.
Turnoak Pk., Wind. 151 AL83
Turnpike Clo. SE8 163 DZ80
Amersham Vale
Turnpike Dr., Orp. 224 EW109
Turnpike Grn., Hem.H. 40 BM16
Turnpike Ho. EC1 274 G3
Turnpike La. N8 121 DM56
Turnpike La., Sutt. 218 DC106
Turnpike La., Til. 171 GK78
Turnpike La., Uxb. 134 BL69
Turnpike Link, Croy. 202 DS103
Turnpike Way, Islw. 157 CG81
London Rd.
Turnpin La. SE10 163 EC79
Turnstone Clo. E13 144 EG69
Turnstone Clo. NW9 96 CS54
Kestrel Clo.
Turnstone Clo., S.Croy. 221 DY110
Turnstone Clo., Uxb. 115 BP64
Long La.
Turnstones, The, Grav. 191 GK89
Turnstones, The, Wat. 76 BY36
Turp Ave., Grays 170 GC75
Turpentine La. SW1 161 DH78
Sutherland St.
Turpin Ave., Rom. 104 FA51
Turpin La., Erith 167 FG80
Turpin Rd., Felt. 175 BT86
Staines Rd.
Turpin Way N19 121 DK61
Elthorne Rd.
Turpin Way, Wall. 219 DH108
Turpington Clo., Brom. 204 EL100
Turpington La., Brom. 204 EL101
Turpins Clo., Hert. 31 DM09
Turpins La., Wdf.Grn. 103 EM50
Turquand St. SE17 279 J9
Turret Gro. SW4 161 DJ83
Turton Rd., Wem. 118 CL64
Turton Way, Slou. 151 AR76
Turville Ct., Lthd. 246 CB125
Proctor Gdns.
Turville St. E2 142 DT70
Old Nichol St.
Tuscan Rd. SE18 165 ER78
Tuskar St. SE10 164 EE78
Tustin Est. SE15 162 DW79
Tuttlebee La., Buck.H. 102 EG47
Tuxford Clo., Borwd. 78 CL38
Twankhams All., Epp. 70 EU30
Hemnall St.
Tweed Clo., Berk. 38 AV18
Tweed Glen, Rom. 105 FD52
Tweed Grn., Rom. 105 FD52
Tweed La., Bet. 264 CP139
Tweed Rd., Slou. 153 BB79
Tweed Way, Rom. 105 FD52
Tweedale Ct. E15 123 EC64
Tweeddale Gro., Uxb. 115 BQ62
Tweeddale Rd., Cars. 200 DD102
Tweedmouth Rd. E13 144 EH68
Tweedy Rd., Brom. 204 EG95
Tweenways, Chesh. 54 AR30
Tweezer's All. WC2 274 D10
Twelve Acre Clo., Lthd. 230 BZ124
Twelve Acres, Welw.G.C. 29 CY11
Twelvetrees Cres. E3 143 EC70
Twentyman Clo., Wdf.Grn. 102 EG50
Twickenham Bri., Rich. 177 CJ85
Twickenham Bri., Twick. 177 CJ85
Twickenham Clo., Croy. 201 DM104
Twickenham Gdns., Grnf. 117 CG64
Twickenham Gdns., Har. 95 CE52
Twickenham Rd. E11 123 ED61
Twickenham Rd., Felt. 176 BZ90
Twickenham Rd., Islw. 177 CG85
Twickenham Rd., Rich. 177 CJ85
Twickenham Rd., Tedd. 177 CG91
Twickenham Trd. Est., Twick. 177 CF86
Twigg Clo., Erith 167 FE80
Twilley St. SW18 180 DB87
Twinches La., Slou. 131 AP74
Twine Ct. E1 142 DW73
Twineham Grn. N12 98 DA49
Tillingham Way
Twining Ave., Twick. 176 CC90
Twinn Rd. NW7 97 CY51
Twinoaks, Cob. 214 CA113
Twisden Rd. NW5 121 DH63
Twisleton Ct., Dart. 188 FK86
Priory Hill
Twitchells La., Beac. 90 AT51
Twitton La., Sev. 241 FD115
Twitton Meadows, Sev. 241 FE116
Two Acres, Welw.G.C. 29 CZ11
Two Dells La., Chesh. 38 AT24
Two Waters Rd., Hem.H. 40 BJ24
Twybridge Way NW10 138 CQ66
Twyford Abbey Rd. NW10 138 CM69
Twyford Ave. N2 120 DF55
Twyford Ave. W3 138 CN73
Twyford Cres. W3 138 CN74
Twyford Pl. WC2 274 B8
Twyford Rd., Cars. 200 DD102
Twyford Rd., Har. 116 CB60
Twyford Rd., Ilf. 125 EQ64
Twyford Rd., St.Alb. 43 CJ16
Twyford St. N1 141 DM67
Twyner Clo., Horl. 269 DK147
Twysdens Ter., Hat. 45 CW24
Dellsome La.
Tyas Rd. E16 144 EF70
Tybenham Rd. SW19 199 CZ97
Tyberry Rd., Enf. 82 DV41
Tyburn La., Har. 117 CE59
Tyburn Way W1 272 E10
Tyburns, The, Brwd. 109 GC47
Tycehurst Hill, Loug. 85 EM42
Tychbourne Dr., Guil. 243 BC131
Tydcombe Rd., Warl. 236 DW119
Tye Grn. Village, Harl. 51 ET18
Tye La., Epsom 248 CR126
Headley Common Rd.
Tye La., Orp. 223 EQ106
Tye La., Tad. 249 CT128
Dorking Rd.
Tyers Est. SE1 279 M4
Tyers Est. SE1 162 DS75
Tyers Gate SE1 279 M5
Tyers St. SE11 161 DM78
Tyers Ter. SE11 161 DM78
Tyeshurst Clo. SE2 166 EY78
Tyfield Clo. (Cheshunt), Wal.Cr. 66 DW30
Tykeswater La., Borwd. 77 CJ40
Tyle Grn., Horn. 128 FL56
Tyle Pl., Wind. 172 AU85
Tylecroft Rd. SW16 201 DL96
Tylehost, Guil. 242 AU130
Tylehurst Gdns., Ilf. 125 EQ64
Tyler Clo. E2 142 DT68
Tyler Gdns., Add. 212 BJ105
Tyler Gro., Dart. 168 FM84
Spielman Rd.
Tyler St. SE10 164 EE78
Tylers Causeway, Hert. 47 DH23
Tylers Clo., Gdse. 252 DV130
Tylers Clo., Kings L. 58 BL28
Tylers Clo., Loug. 102 EL45
Tyler's Ct. W1 273 M9
Tylers Cres., Horn. 128 FJ64
Tylers Gate, Har. 118 CL58
Tylers Grn. Rd., Swan. 207 FC100
Tylers Hill Rd., Chesh. 56 AT30
Tylers Path, Cars. 218 DF105
Rochester Rd.
Tylers Rd., Harl. 50 EJ19
Tylers Way, Wat. 77 CE43
Tylersfield, Abb.L. 59 BT31
Tylney Ave. SE19 182 DT92
Tylney Cft., Harl. 51 EQ17
Tylney Rd. E7 124 EJ63
Tylney Rd., Brom. 204 EK96
Tylsworth Clo., Amer. 55 AR38
King George V Rd.
Tynan Clo., Felt. 175 BU88
Sandycombe Rd.
Tyndale Clo., Dart. 189 FR88
Tyndale Ct. E14 163 EB78
Tyndale La. N1 141 DP66
Upper St.
Tyndale Ter. N1 141 DP66
Canonbury La.
Tyndall Rd. E10 123 EC61
Tyndall Rd., Well. 165 ET83
Tyne Clo., Upmin. 129 FR58
Tyne Gdns., S.Ock. 148 FQ73
Tyne St. E1 142 DT72
Old Castle St.
Tynedale, St.Alb. 62 CM27
Thamesdale
Tynedale Rd., Bet. 264 CP138
Tyneham Rd. SW11 160 DG82
Tynemouth Clo. E6 145 EP72
Warwall
Tynemouth Dr., Enf. 82 DU38
Tynemouth Rd. N15 122 DT56
Tynemouth Rd. SE18 165 ET78
Riverdale Rd.
Tynemouth Rd., Mitch. 180 DG94
Tynemouth St. SW6 160 DC82
Tynley Gro., Guil. 242 AX128
Type St. E2 143 DX68
Typelden Clo., Hem.H. 40 BK18
Tyrawley Rd. SW6 160 DB81
Tyrell Clo., Har. 117 CE63
Tyrell Ct., Cars. 218 DF105
Tyrell Gdns., Wind. 151 AM83
Tyrell Ri., Brwd. 108 FW50
Tyrell Sq., Mitch. 200 DE95
Tyrells Clo., Upmin. 128 FP61
Tyrols Rd. SE23 183 DX88
Wastdale Rd.
Tyron Way, Sid. 185 ES91
Tyrone Rd. E6 145 EM68
Tyrrel Way NW9 119 CT59
Tyrrell Ave., Well. 186 EU85
Tyrrell Rd. SE22 162 DU84
Tyrrells Hall Clo., Grays 170 GD79
Tyrrells Wd. Dr., Lthd. 231 CH123
Tyrwhitt Ave., Guil. 242 AV130
Tyrwhitt Rd. SE4 163 EA83
Tysea Clo., Harl. 51 ET18
Tysea Hill, Rom. 105 FF45
Tysea Rd., Harl. 51 ET18
Tysoe Ave., Enf. 83 DZ36
Tysoe St. EC1 274 D3
Tyson Rd. SE23 182 DW87
Tyssen Pas. E8 142 DT65
Tyssen St.
Tyssen Pl., S.Ock. 149 FW69
Tyssen Rd. N16 122 DT62
Tyssen St. E8 142 DT65
Tyssen St. N1 275 N1
Tythebarn Clo., Guil. 243 BB129
Dairyman's Wk.
Tytherton Rd. N19 121 DK62
Tyttenhanger Grn., St.Alb. 43 CK23

U

Uamvar St. E14 143 EB71
Uckfield Gro., Mitch. 200 DG95
Uckfield Rd., Enf. 83 DX37
Udall Gdns., Rom. 104 FA51
Udall St. SW1 277 L9
Udney Pk. Rd., Tedd. 177 CG92
Uffington Rd. NW10 139 CU67
Uffington Rd. SE27 181 DN91
Ufford Clo., Har. 94 CB52
Ufford Rd.
Ufford Rd., Har. 94 CB52
Ufford St. SE1 278 E4
Ufford St. SE1 161 DN75
Ufton Gro. N1 142 DR66
Ufton Rd. N1 142 DR66
Uhura Sq. N16 122 DS62
Victorian Gro.
Ujima Ct. SW16 181 DL91
Sunnyhill Rd.
Ullathorne Rd. SW16 181 DJ91
Ulleswater Rd. N14 99 DL49
Ullin St. E14 143 EC71
St. Leonards Rd.
Ullswater Business Pk., The, Couls. 235 DL116
Ullswater Clo. SW15 178 CR91
Ullswater Clo., Brom. 184 EE94
Ullswater Clo., Hayes 135 BS68
Ullswater Clo., Slou. 130 AJ71
Buttermere Ave.
Ullswater Ct., Har. 116 CA59
Oakington Ave.
Ullswater Cres. SW15 178 CR91
Ullswater Cres., Couls. 235 DL116
Ullswater Rd. SE27 181 DP89
Ullswater Rd. SW13 159 CU80
Ullswater Rd., Hem.H. 41 BQ22
Ullswater Way, Horn. 127 FG64
Ulstan Clo., Cat. 237 EA123
Ulster Gdns. N13 100 DQ49
Ulster Pl. NW1 273 H5
Ulster Ter. NW1 273 H4
Ulundi Rd. SE3 164 EE79
Ulva Rd. SW15 179 CX85
Ravenna Rd.
Ulverscroft Rd. SE22 182 DT85
Ulverston Rd. E17 101 ED54
Ulverstone Rd. SE27 181 DP89
Ulwin Ave., W.Byf. 212 BL113
Ulysses Rd. NW6 119 CZ64
Umberston St. E1 142 DU72
Hessel St.
Umberville Way, Slou. 131 AM69
Umbria St. SW15 179 CU86
Umfreville Rd. N4 121 DP58
Underacres Clo., Hem.H. 40 BN19
Undercliff Rd. SE13 163 EA83
Underhill, Barn. 80 DA43
Underhill Pk. Rd., Reig. 250 DA131
Underhill Pas. NW1 141 DH67
Camden High St.
Underhill Rd. SE22 182 DU85
Underhill St. NW1 141 DH67
Camden High St.
Underne Ave. N14 99 DH47
Underriver Ho. Rd., Sev. 257 FP130
Undershaft EC3 275 M9

Und–Van This index reads in the sequence: Street Name / Postal District or Post Town / Map Page Number / Grid Reference

Undershaft EC3 142 DS72
Undershaw Rd., Brom. 184 EF90
Underwood, Croy. 221 EC106
Underwood, The SE9 185 EM89
Underwood Rd. E1 142 DU70
Underwood Rd. E4 101 EB50
Underwood Rd., Cat. 252 DS126
Underwood Rd., Wdf.Grn. 102 EJ52
Underwood Row N1 275 J2
Underwood Row N1 142 DQ69
Underwood St. N1 275 J2
Underwood St. N1 142 DQ69
Undine Rd. E14 163 EB77
Undine St. SW17 180 DF92
Uneeda Dr., Grnf. 137 CD67
Unicorn Wk., Green. 189 FT85
Union Cotts. E15 144 EE66
Welfare Rd.
Union Ct. EC2 275 M8
Union Ct., Rich. 178 CL85
Eton St.
Union Dr. E1 143 DY70
Solebay St.
Union Grn., Hem.H. 40 BK19
Union Gro. SW8 161 DK82
Union Rd. N11 99 DK51
Union Rd. SW4 161 DK82
Union Rd. SW8 161 DK82
Union Rd., Brom. 204 EK99
Union Rd., Croy. 202 DQ101
Union Rd., Nthlt. 136 CA68
Union Rd., Wem. 138 CL65
Union Sq. N1 142 DQ67
Union St. E15 143 EC67
Union St. SE1 278 G3
Union St. SE1 141 DP74
Union St., Barn. 79 CY42
Union St., Kings.T. 197 CK96
Union Wk. E2 275 N2
Unity Clo. NW10 139 CU65
Unity Clo. SE19 182 DQ92
Unity Clo., Croy. 221 EB109
Castle Hill Ave.
Unity Rd., Enf. 82 DW37
Unity Way SE18 164 EK76
Unity Wf. SE1 162 DT75
Mill St.
University Clo. NW7 97 CT52
University Clo., Wat. 76 CA42
University Gdns., Bex. 186 EZ87
Upton Rd. S.
University Pl., Erith 167 FB80
Belmont Rd.
University Rd. SW19 180 DD93
University St. WC1 273 L5
University St. WC1 141 DJ70
University Way, Dart. 168 FJ84
(Dartford Northern Bypass)
Unstead La., Guil. 258 AW144
Unstead Wd., Guil. 258 AW142
Unwin Ave., Felt. 175 BR85
Unwin Clo. SE15 162 DU79
Unwin Rd. SW7 160 DD76
Imperial College Rd.
Unwin Rd., Islw. 157 CE83
Upbrook Ms. W2 140 DC72
Chilworth St.
Upcerne Rd. SW10 160 DC80
Upchurch Clo. SE20 182 DV94
Upcroft, Wind. 151 AP83
Upcroft Ave., Edg. 96 CQ50
Updale Clo., Pot.B. 63 CY33
Updale Rd., Sid. 185 ET91
Upfield, Croy. 202 DV103
Upfield, Horl. 268 DG149
Upfield Clo., Horl. 268 DG150
Upfield Rd. W7 137 CF70
Upfolds Grn., Guil. 243 BC130
Upgrove Manor Way SW2 181 DN87
Trinity Ri.
Uphall Rd., Ilf. 125 EP64
Upham Pk. Rd. W4 158 CS77
Uphill Dr. NW7 96 CS50
Uphill Dr. NW9 118 CQ57
Uphill Gro. NW7 96 CS49
Uphill Rd. NW7 96 CS49
Upland Ave., Chesh. 54 AP28
Upland Ct. Rd., Rom. 106 FM54
Upland Dr., Hat. 64 DB25
Upland Ms. SE22 182 DU85
Upland Rd.
Upland Rd. E13 144 EF70
Sutton Rd.
Upland Rd. SE22 182 DU85
Upland Rd., Bexh. 166 EZ83
Upland Rd., Cat. 237 EA120
Upland Rd., Epp. 69 ER25
Upland Rd., S.Croy. 220 DR106
Upland Rd., Sutt. 218 DD107
Upland Way, Epsom 233 CW118
Uplands, Ash. 231 CK120
Uplands, Beck. 203 EA96
Uplands, Rick. 74 BM44
Uplands, Ware 33 DZ05
Uplands, Welw.G.C. 29 CW05
Uplands, The, Ger.Cr. 112 AY60
Uplands, The, Loug. 85 EM41
Uplands, The, Ruis. 115 BU60
Uplands, The, St.Alb. 60 BY30
Uplands Ave. E17 101 DX54
Blackhorse La.
Uplands Business Pk. E17 123 DX55
Uplands Clo. SW14 178 CP85
Monroe Dr.
Uplands Clo., Ger.Cr. 112 AY60
Uplands Clo., Sev. 256 FF123
Uplands Dr., Lthd. 215 CD113
Uplands End, Wdf.Grn. 102 EL52
Uplands Pk. Rd., Enf. 81 DN41
Uplands Rd. N8 121 DM57
Uplands Rd., Barn. 98 DG46
Uplands Rd., Brwd. 108 FY50
Uplands Rd., Ken. 236 DQ116
Uplands Rd., Orp. 206 EV102
Uplands Rd., Rom. 126 EX55
Uplands Rd., Wdf.Grn. 102 EL52
Uplands Way N21 81 DN43
Uplands Way, Sev. 256 FF123
Upminster Rd., Horn. 128 FM61
Upminster Rd., Upmin. 128 FN61
Upminster Rd. N., Rain. 148 FJ70
Upminster Rd. S., Rain. 147 FG70
Upney Clo., Horn. 128 FJ64
Tylers Cres.
Upney La., Bark. 145 ES65
Upnor Way SE17 279 N10
Uppark Dr., Ilf. 125 EQ58
Upper Abbey Rd., Belv. 166 EZ77
Upper Addison Gdns. W14 159 CY75
Upper Ashlyns Rd., Berk. 38 AV20
Upper Bardsey Wk. N1 142 DQ65
Marquess Est.
Upper Barn, Hem.H. 40 BM23
Upper Belgrave St. SW1 276 G6
Upper Belgrave St. SW1 160 DG76
Upper Belmont Rd., Chesh. 54 AP28
Upper Berkeley St. W1 272 D9
Upper Berkeley St. W1 140 DF72
Upper Beulah Hill SE19 202 DS95
Upper Bray Rd., Maid. 150 AC77
Upper Brentwood Rd., Rom. 128 FJ56
Upper Bri. Rd., Red. 250 DE134
Upper Brighton Rd., Surb. 197 CK100
Upper Brockley Rd. SE4 163 DZ82
Upper Brook St. W1 276 F1
Upper Brook St. W1 140 DG73
Upper Butts, Brent. 157 CJ79
Upper Caldy Wk. N1 142 DQ65
Marquess Est.
Upper Camelford Wk. W11 139 CY72
Lancaster Rd.
Upper Cavendish Ave. N3 120 DA55
Upper Cheyne Row SW3 160 DE79
Upper Ch. Hill, Green. 189 FS85
Upper Clabdens, Ware 33 DZ06
Upper Clapton Rd. E5 122 DV60
Upper Clarendon Wk. W11 139 CY72
Lancaster Rd.
Upper Cor. Clo., Ch.St.G. 90 AV47
Upper Cornsland, Brwd. 108 FX48
Upper Ct. Rd., Cat. 237 EA123
Upper Ct. Rd., Epsom 216 CQ111
Upper Culver Rd., St.Alb. 43 CE18
Upper Dagnall St., St.Alb. 43 CD20
Upper Dengie Wk. N1 142 DQ67
Popham Rd.
Upper Dr., Beac. 89 AK50
Upper Dr., West. 238 EJ118
Upper Dunnymans, Bans. 217 CZ114
Basing Rd.
Upper Edgeborough Rd., Guil. 259 AZ135
Upper Elmers End Rd., Beck. 203 DY98
Upper Fairfield Rd., Lthd. 231 CH121
Upper Fm. Rd., W.Mol. 196 BZ98
Upper Fosters NW4 119 CW57
New Brent St.
Upper George St., Chesh. 54 AQ30
Frances St.
Upper Gladstone Rd., Chesh. 54 AQ30
Upper Grn. E., Mitch. 200 DF96
Upper Grn. W., Mitch. 200 DF97
London Rd.
Upper Grenfell Wk. W11 139 CX73
Whitchurch Rd.
Upper Grosvenor St. W1 276 F1
Upper Grosvenor St. W1 140 DG73
Upper Grotto Rd., Twick. 177 CF89
Upper Grd. SE1 278 D2
Upper Grd. SE1 141 DN74
Upper Gro. SE25 202 DS98
Upper Gro. Rd., Belv. 166 EZ79
Upper Guildown Rd., Guil. 258 AV137
Upper Gulland Wk. N1 142 DQ65
Marquess Est.
Upper Hall Pk., Berk. 38 AX20
Upper Halliford Bypass, Shep. 195 BS99
Upper Halliford Rd., Shep. 195 BS98
Upper Ham Rd., Rich. 177 CK91
Upper Handa Wk. N1 142 DR65
Marquess Est.
Upper Harley St. NW1 272 G5
Upper Harley St. NW1 140 DG70
Upper Hawkwell Wk. N1 142 DQ67
Popham Rd.
Upper Heath Rd., St.Alb. 43 CF18
Upper High St., Epsom 216 CS113
Upper Highway, Abb.L. 59 BR33
Upper Highway, Kings L. 59 BQ32
Upper Hill Ri., Rick. 74 BH44
Upper Hitch, Wat. 94 BY46
Upper Holly Hill Rd., Belv. 167 FB78
Upper Hook, Harl. 51 ES17
Upper James St. W1 273 L10
Upper John St. W1 273 L10
Upper Lattimore Rd., St.Alb. 43 CE20
Upper Lees Rd., Slou. 131 AP69
Upper Lismore Wk. N1 142 DQ65
Marquess Est.
Upper Mall W6 159 CU78
Upper Manor Rd., Gdmg. 258 AS144
Upper Marlborough Rd., St.Alb. 43 CE20
Upper Marsh SE1 278 C6
Upper Marsh SE1 161 DM75
Upper Marsh La., Hodd. 49 EA18
Upper Mealines, Harl. 52 EU18
Upper Montagu St. W1 272 D6
Upper Montagu St. W1 140 DF71
Upper Mulgrave Rd., Sutt. 217 CY108
Upper N. St. E14 143 EA71
Upper Paddock Rd., Wat. 76 BY44
Upper Palace Rd., E.Mol. 196 CC97
Upper Pk., Harl. 35 EP14
Upper Pk., Loug. 84 EK42
Upper Pk. Rd. N11 99 DH50
Upper Pk. Rd. NW3 140 DF65
Upper Pk. Rd., Belv. 167 FB77
Upper Pk. Rd., Brom. 204 EH95
Upper Pk. Rd., Kings.T. 178 CN93
Upper Phillimore Gdns. W8 160 DA75
Upper Pines, Bans. 234 DF117
Upper Rainham Rd., Horn. 127 FF60
Upper Ramsey Wk. N1 142 DR65
Marquess Est.
Upper Rawreth Wk. N1 142 DQ67
Popham Rd.
Upper Richmond Rd. SW15 159 CT84
Upper Richmond Rd. W. SW14 158 CR84
Upper Richmond Rd. W., Rich. 158 CN84
Upper Riding, Beac. 88 AG54
Upper Rd. E13 144 EG69
Upper Rd., Uxb. 113 BD59
Upper Rd., Wall. 219 DK106
Upper Rose Hill, Dor. 263 CH137
Upper Ryle, Brwd. 108 FW45
Upper St. Martin's La. WC2 273 P10
Upper St. Martin's La. WC2 141 DL73
Upper Sales, Hem.H. 39 BF21
Upper Sawley Wd., Bans. 217 CZ114
Upper Selsdon Rd., S.Croy. 220 DS108
Upper Sheppey Wk. N1 142 DQ66
Marquess Est.
Upper Sheridan Rd., Belv. 166 FA77
Coleman Rd.
Upper Shirley Rd., Croy. 202 DW103
Upper Shot, Welw.G.C. 30 DA08
Upper Shott (Cheshunt), Wal.Cr. 66 DT26
Upper Sq., Islw. 157 CG83
North St.
Upper Sta. Rd., Rad. 77 CG35
Upper Stonyfield, Harl. 51 EP15
Upper St. N1 141 DP65
Upper St., Guil. 260 BM139
Upper Sunbury Rd., Hmptn. 196 BY95
Upper Sutton La., Houns. 156 CA80
Upper Swaines, Epp. 69 ET30
Upper Tachbrook St. SW1 277 L8
Upper Tachbrook St. SW1 161 DJ77
Upper Tail, Wat. 94 BY48
Upper Talbot Wk. W11 139 CY72
Lancaster Rd.
Upper Teddington Rd., Kings.T. 177 CJ94
Upper Ter. NW3 120 DC62
Upper Thames St. EC4 274 G10
Upper Thames St. EC4 142 DQ73
Upper Tollington Pk. N4 121 DN59
Upper Tooting Pk. SW17 180 DF89
Upper Tooting Rd. SW17 180 DF91
Upper Town Rd., Grnf. 136 CB70
Upper Tulse Hill SW2 181 DM87
Upper Vernon Rd., Sutt. 218 DD106
Upper Wk., Vir.W. 192 AY99
Christchurch Rd.
Upper Walthamstow Rd., E17 123 ED56
Upper W. St., Reig. 249 CZ134
Upper Wickham La., Well. 166 EV83
Upper Wimpole St. W1 272 G6
Upper Wimpole St. W1 140 DG71
Upper Woburn Pl. WC1 273 N3
Upper Woburn Pl. WC1 141 DK69
Upper Woodcote Village, Pur. 219 DK113
Upperfield Rd., Welw.G.C. 29 CZ10
Upperton Rd., Guil. 258 AW135
Upperton Rd., Sid. 185 ET92
Upperton Rd. E. E13 144 EJ69
Inniskilling Rd.
Upperton Rd. W. E13 144 EJ69
Uppingham Ave., Stan. 95 CH53
Upsdell Ave. N13 99 DN51
Upshire Rd., Wal.Abb. 68 EF32
Upshott La., Wok. 227 BF117
Upstall St. SE5 161 DP81
Upton, Wok. 226 AV117
Upton Ave. E7 144 EG66
Upton Ave., St.Alb. 43 CD19
Upton Clo., Bex. 186 EZ86
Upton Clo., St.Alb. 61 CD25
Upton Clo., Slou. 152 AT76
Upton Ct. SE20 182 DW94
Blean Gro.
Upton Ct. Rd., Slou. 152 AU76
Upton Dene, Sutt. 218 DB108
Upton Gdns., Har. 117 CH57
Upton La. E7 144 EH65
Upton Lo. Clo. (Bushey), Wat. 94 CC45
Upton Pk., Slou. 152 AS76
Upton Pk. Rd. E7 144 EH66
Upton Rd. N18 100 DU50
Upton Rd. SE18 165 EQ79
Upton Rd., Bex. 186 EZ86
Upton Rd., Bexh. 166 EY84
Upton Rd., Houns. 156 CA83
Upton Rd., Slou. 152 AU76
Upton Rd., Th.Hth. 202 DR96
Upton Rd., Wat. 75 BV42
Upton Rd. S., Bex. 186 EZ86
Upway N12 98 DE52
Upway, Ger.Cr. 91 AZ52
Upwood Rd. SE12 184 EG86
Upwood Rd. SW16 201 DL95
Uranus Rd., Hem.H. 40 BM18
Urban Ave., Horn. 128 FJ62
Urlwin St. SE5 162 DQ79
Urlwin Wk. SW9 161 DN81
Urmston Dr. SW19 179 CY88
Ursula Ms. N4 121 DP60
Portland Ri.
Ursula St. SW11 160 DE81
Urswick Gdns., Dag. 146 EY66
Urswick Rd.
Urswick Rd. E9 122 DW64
Urswick Rd., Dag. 146 EX66
Usborne Ms. SW8 161 DM80
Usher Rd. E3 143 DZ68
Usk Rd. SW11 160 DC84
Usk Rd., S.Ock. 148 FQ71
Usk St. E2 143 DX69
Utopia Village NW1 140 DG67
Chalcot Rd.
Uvedale Clo., Croy. 221 ED111
Uvedale Cres.
Uvedale Cres., Croy. 221 ED111
Uvedale Rd., Dag. 126 FA62
Uvedale Rd., Enf. 82 DR43
Uvedale Rd., Oxt. 254 EF129
Uverdale Rd. SW10 160 DC80
Uxbridge Gdns., Felt. 176 BX89
Marlborough Rd.
Uxbridge Ind. Est., Uxb. 134 BH69
Uxbridge Rd. W3 138 CN74
Uxbridge Rd. W5 138 CM73
Uxbridge Rd. W7 137 CF74
Uxbridge Rd. W12 139 CU74
Uxbridge Rd. W13 137 CH74
Uxbridge Rd., Felt. 176 BW88
Uxbridge Rd., Hmptn. 176 CA91
Uxbridge Rd., Har. 95 CD52
Uxbridge Rd., Hayes 135 BT72
Uxbridge Rd., Iver 132 AY71
Uxbridge Rd., Kings.T. 197 CK98
Uxbridge Rd., Pnr. 94 BW54
Uxbridge Rd., Rick. 91 BF47
Uxbridge Rd., Slou. 152 AU75
Uxbridge Rd., Sthl. 136 CA74
Uxbridge Rd., Stan. 95 CF51
Uxbridge Rd., Uxb. 135 BP69
Uxbridge St. W8 140 DA74
Uxendon Cres., Wem. 118 CL60
Uxendon Hill, Wem. 118 CM60

V

Vache La., Ch.St.G. 90 AW47
Vaillant Rd., Wey. 213 BQ105
Valan Leas, Brom. 204 EE97
Valance Ave. E4 102 EE46
Vale, The N10 98 DG53
Vale, The N14 99 DK45
Vale, The NW11 119 CX62
Vale, The SW3 160 DD79
Vale, The W3 138 CR74
Vale, The, Brwd. 108 FW46
Vale, The, Chesh. 54 AQ26
Vale, The, Couls. 219 DK114
Vale, The, Croy. 203 DX103
Vale, The, Felt. 175 BV86
Vale, The, Ger.Cr. 90 AX53
Vale, The, Houns. 156 BY79
Vale, The, Ruis. 116 BW63
Vale, The, Sun. 175 BU93
Ashridge Way
Vale, The, Wdf.Grn. 102 EG52
Vale Ave., Borwd. 78 CP43
Vale Border, Croy. 221 DX111
Vale Clo. N2 120 DF55
Church Vale
Vale Clo. W9 140 DC69
Maida Vale
Vale Clo., Brwd. 108 FT43
Vale Clo., Ger.Cr. 90 AX53
Vale Clo., Orp. 223 EN105
Vale Clo., Wey. 195 BR104
Vale Clo., Wok. 226 AY116
The Larches
Vale Cotts. SW15 178 CR91
Kingston Vale
Vale Ct. W9 140 DC69
Maida Vale
Vale Ct., Wey. 195 BR104
Vale Cres. SW15 178 CS90
Vale Cft., Esher 215 CE109
Vale Cft., Pnr. 116 BY57
Vale Dr., Barn. 79 CZ42
Vale End SE22 162 DS84
Grove Vale
Vale Fm. Rd., Wok. 226 AX117
Vale Gro. N4 122 DQ59
Vale Gro. W3 138 CR74
The Vale
Vale Gro., Slou. 152 AS76
Vale Ind. Pk., Wat. 93 BP46
Vale La. W3 138 CN71
Vale of Health NW3 120 DD62
East Heath Rd.
Vale Par. SW15 178 CR91
Kingston Vale
Vale Ri. NW11 119 CZ60
Vale Ri., Chesh. 54 AQ28
Vale Rd. E7 144 EH65
Vale Rd. N4 122 DQ59
Vale Rd., Brom. 205 EN96
Vale Rd., Chesh. 54 AQ28
Vale Rd., Dart. 187 FH88
Vale Rd., Epsom 217 CT105
Vale Rd., Esher 215 CE109
Vale Rd., Grav. 190 GD87
Vale Rd., Mitch. 201 DK97
Vale Rd., Sutt. 218 DB105
Vale Rd. (Bushey), Wat. 76 BY43
Vale Rd., Wey. 195 BR104
Vale Rd., Wind. 151 AM80
Vale Rd., Wor.Pk. 199 CT104
Vale Rd. N., Surb. 198 CL103
Vale Rd. S., Surb. 198 CL103
Vale Row N5 121 DP62
Gillespie Rd.
Vale Royal N7 141 DL66
Vale St. SE27 182 DR90
Vale Ter. N4 122 DQ58
Valence Ave., Dag. 126 EX60
Valence Circ., Dag. 126 EX62
Valence Dr. (Cheshunt), Wal.Cr. 66 DU28
Valence Rd., Erith 167 FD80
Valence Wd. Rd., Dag. 126 EX62
Valencia Rd., Stan. 95 CJ49
Valency Clo., Nthwd. 93 BT49
Valentia Pl. SW9 161 DN84
Brixton Sta. Rd.
Valentine Ave., Bex. 186 EY89
Valentine Ct. SE23 183 DX89
Valentine Pl. SE1 278 F4
Valentine Pl. SE1 161 DP75
Valentine Rd. E9 143 DX65
Valentine Rd., Har. 116 CC62
Valentine Row SE1 278 F5
Valentine Way, Ch.St.G. 90 AX48
Valentines Rd., Ilf. 125 EP60
Valentines Way, Rom. 127 FD61
Valentyne Clo., Croy. 222 EE111
Warbank Cres.
Valerian Way E15 144 EE69
Valerie Clo., St.Alb. 43 CH20
Valerie Ct. (Bushey), Wat. 94 CC45
Valeside, Hert. 31 DN10
Valeswood Rd., Brom. 184 EF92
Valetta Gro. E13 144 EG68
Valetta Rd. W3 158 CS75
Valette St. E9 142 DV65
Valiant Clo., Nthlt. 136 BX69
Ruislip Rd.
Valiant Clo., Rom. 104 FA54
Valiant Ho. SE7 164 EJ78
Valiant Path NW9 96 CS52
Blundell Rd.
Valiant Way E6 145 EM71
Vallance Rd. E1 142 DU70
Vallance Rd. E2 142 DU69
Vallance Rd. N22 99 DJ54
Vallentin Rd. E17 123 EC56
Valley, The, Guil. 258 AW138
Portsmouth Rd.
Valley Ave. N12 98 DD49
Valley Clo., Dart. 187 FF86
Valley Clo., Hert. 32 DR09
Valley Clo., Loug. 85 EM44
Valley Clo., Pnr. 93 BV54
Alandale Dr.
Valley Clo., Wal.Abb. 67 EC32
Valley Clo., Ware 32 DV05
Valley Ct., Ken. 220 DQ114
Hayes La.
Valley Dr. NW9 118 CN58
Valley Dr., Grav. 191 GK89
Valley Dr., Sev. 257 FH125
Valley Flds. Cres., Enf. 81 DN40
Valley Gdns. SW19 180 DD94
Valley Gdns., Wem. 138 CM66
Valley Grn., The, Welw.G.C. 29 CW08
Valley Gro. SE7 164 EJ78
Valley Hill, Loug. 102 EL45
Valley Link Est., Enf. 83 DY44
Valley Ms., Twick. 177 CG89
Cross Deep
Valley Ri., Wat. 59 BV33
Valley Rd. SW16 181 DM92
Valley Rd., Belv. 167 FB77
Valley Rd., Berk. 38 AT17
Valley Rd., Brom. 204 EE96
Valley Rd., Dart. 187 FF86
Valley Rd., Erith 167 FD77
Valley Rd., Ken. 220 DR114
Valley Rd. (Fawkham), Long. 209 FV103
Valley Rd., Orp. 206 EV95
Valley Rd., Rick. 74 BG43
Valley Rd., St.Alb. 43 CE16
Valley Rd., Uxb. 134 BL68
Valley Rd., Welw.G.C. 29 CV10
Valley Side E4 101 EA47
Valley Side Par. E4 101 EA47
Valley Side
Valley Vw., Barn. 79 CY44
Valley Vw., Chesh. 54 AN32
Valley Vw., Green. 189 FV86
Valley Vw. (Cheshunt), Wal.Cr. 66 DQ28
Valley Vw., West. 238 EJ118
Valley Vw. Gdns., Ken. 236 DS115
Godstone Rd.
Valley Wk., Croy. 202 DW103
Valley Wk., Rick. 75 BQ43
Valley Way, Ger.Cr. 112 AW58
Valleyfield Rd. SW16 181 DM92
Valleyside, Hem.H. 39 BF20
Valliere Rd. NW10 139 CU69
Valliers Wd. Rd., Sid. 185 ER88
Vallis Way W13 137 CG71
Vallis Way, Chess. 215 CK105
Valmar Rd. SE5 162 DQ81
Valnay St. SW17 180 DF92
Valognes Ave. E17 101 DY53
Valonia Gdns. SW18 179 CZ86
Vambery Rd. SE18 165 EQ79
Van Dyck Ave., N.Mal. 198 CR101
Vanbrough Cres., Nthlt. 136 BW67
Vanbrugh Clo. E16 144 EK71
Fulmer Rd.
Vanbrugh Dr., Walt. 196 BW101
Vanbrugh Flds. SE3 164 EF79
Vanbrugh Hill SE3 164 EF79
Vanbrugh Hill SE10 164 EF79
Vanbrugh Pk. SE3 164 EF80
Vanbrugh Pk. Rd. SE3 164 EF80
Vanbrugh Pk. Rd. W. SE3 164 EF80
Vanbrugh Rd. W4 158 CR76
Vanbrugh Ter. SE3 164 EF81
Vanburgh Clo., Orp. 205 ES102
Vancouver Clo., Epsom 216 CQ111
Horton Hill
Vancouver Ct., Horl. 269 DN148
Vancouver Rd. SE23 183 DY89
Vancouver Rd., Edg. 96 CP53
Vancouver Rd., Hayes 135 BV70
Vancouver Rd., Rich. 177 CJ91
Vanda Cres., St.Alb. 43 CF21
Vanderbilt Rd. SW18 180 DB88
Vandome Clo. E16 144 EH72
Vandon Pas. SW1 277 L6
Vandon St. SW1 277 L6
Vandon St. SW1 161 DJ76
Vandy St. EC2 275 M5
Vandyke Clo. SW15 179 CX86
Vandyke Clo., Red. 250 DF131
Vandyke Cross SE9 184 EL85
Vane Clo. NW3 120 DD63
Vane Clo., Har. 118 CM58
Vane St. SW1 277 L8
Vanessa Clo., Belv. 166 FA78
Vanessa Wk., Grav. 191 GM92
Vanessa Way, Bex. 187 FD90
Vanguard Clo., Croy. 201 DP102
Vanguard Clo., Rom. 105 FB54
Vanguard St. SE8 163 EA81
Vanguard Way, Cat. 237 EB121
Slines Oak Rd.
Vanguard Way, Wall. 219 DL108
Vanguard Way, Warl. 237 EC120
Croydon Rd.
Vanners Par., W.Byf. 212 BL113
Brewery La.
Vanoc Gdns., Brom. 184 EG91
Vanquisher Wk., Grav. 191 GM90
Vansittart Ind. Est., Wind. 151 AQ81
Vansittart Rd. E7 124 EF63
Vansittart Rd., Wind. 151 AP81
Vansittart St. SE14 163 DY80
Vanston Pl. SW6 160 DA80

Vant Rd. SW17 180 DF92
Vantage Rd., Slou. 131 AP74
Summerlea
Vantorts Clo., Saw. 36 EY05
Vantorts Rd., Saw. 36 EY06
Varcoe Rd. SE16 162 DV78
Varden Clo. W3 138 CR72
Varden St. E1 142 DV72
Vardens Rd. SW11 160 DD84
Vardon Clo. N3 97 CY53
Claremont Pk.
Varley Par. NW9 118 CS56
Varley Rd. E16 144 EH72
Varley Way, Mitch. 200 DD96
Varna Rd. SW6 159 CY80
Varna Rd., Hmptn. 196 CB95
Varndell St. NW1 273 K2
Varndell St. NW1 141 DJ69
Varney Clo., Hem.H. 39 BF20
Varney Clo. 66 DU27
(Cheshunt), Wal.Cr.
Varney Rd., Hem.H. 39 BF20
Varsity Dr., Twick. 177 CE85
Varsity Row SW14 158 CQ82
William's La.
Vartry Rd. N15 122 DR58
Vassall Rd. SW9 161 DN80
Vauban Est. SE16 162 DT76
Vauban St. SE16 162 DT76
Vaughan Ave. NW4 119 CU57
Vaughan Ave. W6 159 CT77
Vaughan Ave., Horn. 128 FK63
Vaughan Clo., Hmptn. 176 BY93
Oak Ave.
Vaughan Gdns., Ilf. 125 EM59
Vaughan Gdns. 151 AM77
(Eton Wick), Wind.
Eton Wick Rd.
Vaughan Rd. E15 144 EF65
Vaughan Rd. SE5 162 DQ83
Vaughan Rd., Har. 116 CC59
Vaughan Rd., T.Ditt. 197 CH101
Vaughan Rd., Well. 165 ET82
Vaughan St. SE16 163 DZ75
Vaughan Way E1 142 DU73
Vaughan Way, Dor. 263 CG136
Vaughan Way, Slou. 131 AL70
Vaughan Williams Clo. 163 EA80
SE8
Watson's St.
Vaux Cres., Walt. 213 BV107
Vauxhall Bri. SE1 161 DL78
Vauxhall Bri. SW1 161 DL78
Vauxhall Bri. Rd. SW1 277 L8
Vauxhall Bri. Rd. SW1 161 DJ76
Vauxhall Clo., Grav. 191 GF87
Vauxhall Gdns., S.Croy. 220 DQ107
Vauxhall Gdns. Est. 161 DM78
SE11
Vauxhall Gro. SW8 161 DM79
Vauxhall Pl., Dart. 188 FL87
Vauxhall Rd., Hem.H. 40 BN20
Vauxhall St. SE11 161 DM78
Vauxhall Wk. SE11 278 B10
Vauxhall Wk. SE11 161 DM78
Vawdrey Clo. E1 142 DW70
Veals Mead, Mitch. 200 DE95
Vectis Gdns. SW17 181 DH93
Vectis Rd.
Vectis Rd. SW17 181 DH93
Veda Rd. SE13 163 EA84
Vega Cres., Nthwd. 93 BT50
Vega Rd. 94 CC45
(Bushey), Wat.
Vegal Cres., Egh. 172 AW92
Velde Way SE22 182 DS85
East Dulwich Gro.
Velizy Ave., Harl. 35 ER14
Velletri Ho. E2 143 DX68
Mace St.
Vellicoe Rd. E13 144 EG70
Jutland Rd.
Vellum Dr., Cars. 200 DG104
Venables Clo., Dag. 127 FB63
Venables St. NW8 272 A5
Venables St. NW8 140 DD70
Vencourt Pl. W6 159 CU77
Venetia Rd. N4 121 DP58
Venetia Rd. W5 157 CK75
Venetian Rd. SE5 162 DQ82
Venette Clo., Rain. 147 FH71
Venn St. SW4 161 DJ84
Venner Rd. SE26 182 DW93
Venners Clo., Bexh. 167 FE82
Ventnor Ave., Stan. 95 CH53
Ventnor Dr. N20 98 DB48
Ventnor Gdns., Bark. 145 ES65
Ventnor Rd. SE14 163 DX80
Ventnor Rd., Sutt. 218 DB108
Venton Clo., Wok. 226 AV117
Ventura Pk., St.Alb. 61 CF29
Venture Clo., Bex. 186 EY87
Venue St. E14 143 EC71
Venus Hill, Hem.H. 57 AZ31
Venus Rd. SE18 165 EM76
Veny Cres., Horn. 128 FK64
Ver Rd., St.Alb. 42 CC20
Vera Ave. N21 81 DN43
Vera Ct., Wat. 94 BX45
Vera Lynn Clo. E7 124 EG63
Dames Rd.
Vera Rd. SW6 159 CY81
Verbena Clo. E16 144 EF70
Cranberry La.
Verbena Clo., S.Ock. 149 FW72
Verbena Clo., West Dr. 154 BK78
Magnolia St.
Verbena Gdns. W6 159 CU78
Verdant La. SE6 184 EE88
Verdayne Ave., Croy. 203 DX102
Verdayne Gdns., Warl. 236 DW116
Vererders Rd., Chig. 104 EU50
Verdun Rd. SE18 166 EU79
Verdun Rd. SW13 159 CU79
Verdure Clo., Wat. 60 BY32
Vere Rd., Loug. 85 EQ42
Vere St. W1 273 H9
Vere St. W1 141 DH72
Vereker Dr., Sun. 195 BU97
Vereker Rd. W14 159 CY78
Verity Clo. W11 139 CY72
Veritys, Hat. 45 CU18
Vermont Clo., Enf. 81 DP42
Waverley Rd.
Vermont Rd. SE19 182 DR93
Vermont Rd. SW18 180 DB86
Vermont Rd., Slou. 131 AM70
Vermont Rd., Sutt. 200 DB104
Verney Clo., Berk. 38 AT18
Verney Gdns., Dag. 126 EY63
Verney Rd. SE16 162 DU79
Verney Rd., Dag. 126 EY63
Verney Rd., Slou. 153 BA77
Verney St. NW10 118 CR62
Verney Way SE16 162 DV78
Vernham Rd. SE18 165 EQ79
Vernon Ave. E12 125 EM63
Vernon Ave. SW20 199 CX96
Vernon Ave., Enf. 83 DY36
Vernon Ave., 102 EH52
Wdf.Grn.
Vernon Clo., Cher. 211 BD107
Vernon Clo., Epsom 216 CQ107
Vernon Clo., Orp. 206 EV97
Vernon Clo., St.Alb. 43 CE21
Vernon Ct., Stan. 95 CH53
Vernon Dr.
Vernon Cres., Barn. 80 DG44
Vernon Cres., Brwd. 109 GA48
Vernon Dr., Stan. 95 CG53
Vernon Dr., Uxb. 92 BJ53
Vernon Ms. E17 123 DZ56
Vernon Rd.
Vernon Ms. W14 159 CY77
Vernon St.
Vernon Pl. WC1 274 A7
Vernon Pl. WC1 141 DL71
Vernon Ri. WC1 274 C2
Vernon Ri. WC1 141 DM69
Vernon Ri., Grnf. 117 CD64
Vernon Rd. E3 143 DZ68
Vernon Rd. E11 124 EE60
Vernon Rd. E15 144 EE66
Vernon Rd. E17 123 DZ56
Vernon Rd. N8 121 DN55
Vernon Rd. SW14 158 CR83
Vernon Rd., Felt. 175 BU90
Vernon Rd., Ilf. 125 ET60
Vernon Rd., Rom. 105 FC50
Vernon Rd., Sutt. 218 DC106
Vernon Rd., Swans. 190 FZ86
Vernon Rd. 76 BY43
(Bushey), Wat.
Vernon Sq. WC1 274 C2
Vernon St. W14 159 CY77
Vernon Wk., Tad. 233 CX120
Vernon Way, Cat. 236 DQ122
Wellington Rd.
Vernon Way, Guil. 242 AT133
Vernon Yd. W11 139 CZ73
Portobello Rd.
Veroan Rd., Bexh. 166 EY82
Verona Clo., Uxb. 134 BJ71
Verona Dr., Surb. 198 CL103
Verona Gdns., Grav. 191 GL91
Verona Rd. E7 144 EG66
Upton La.
Veronica Clo., Rom. 106 FJ52
Veronica Gdns. SW16 201 DJ95
Veronica Rd. SW17 181 DH90
Veronique Gdns., Ilf. 125 EQ57
Verran Rd. SW12 181 DH87
Balham Gro.
Versailles Rd. SE20 182 DU94
Verulam Ave. E17 123 DZ58
Verulam Ave., Pur. 219 DJ112
Verulam Bldgs. WC1 274 C6
Verulam Clo., 29 CZ09
Welw.G.C.
Verulam Pas., Wat. 75 BV40
Station Rd.
Verulam Rd., Grnf. 136 CA70
Verulam Rd., St.Alb. 42 CB19
Verulam St. WC1 274 D6
Verwood Dr., Barn. 80 DF41
Chalk La.
Verwood Rd., Har. 94 CC54
Veryan, Wok. 226 AU117
Vesey Path E14 143 EB72
East India Dock Rd.
Vespan Rd. W12 159 CU75
Vesta Ave., St.Alb. 42 CC23
Vesta Rd. SE4 163 DY82
Vesta Rd., Hem.H. 40 BM18
Saturn Way
Vestris Rd. SE23 183 DX89
Vestry Ms. SE5 162 DS81
Vestry Rd. E17 123 EB56
Vestry Rd. SE5 162 DS81
Vestry St. N1 275 K2
Vestry St. N1 142 DR69
Vevers Rd., Reig. 266 DB137
Vevey St. SE6 183 DZ89
Vexil Clo., Purf. 169 FR77
Veysey Clo., Hem.H. 40 BH22
Anchor La.
Veysey Gdns., Dag. 126 FA62
Oglethorpe Rd.
Viaduct, The E18 102 EG54
Viaduct Pl. E2 142 DV69
Viaduct St.
Viaduct Rd., Ware 33 DY06
Viaduct St. E2 142 DV69
Viaduct Way, Welw.G.C. 29 CZ05
Vian Ave., Enf. 83 DY35
Vian St. SE13 163 EB83
Vibart Gdns. SW2 181 DM87
Vibart Wk. N1 141 DL67
Outram Pl.
Vicarage Ave. SE3 164 EG80
Vicarage Ave., Egh. 173 BB92
Vicarage Causeway, 32 DV11
Hert.
Vicarage Clo., Beac. 89 AR52
Bayne Hill
Vicarage Clo., Brwd. 108 FS49
Vicarage Clo., Erith 167 FC79
Vicarage Clo., Hem.H. 40 BJ22
Vicarage Clo., Lthd. 246 CA125
Vicarage Clo., Nthlt. 136 BZ67
Vicarage Clo., Pot.B. 64 DG30
Vicarage Clo., Ruis. 115 BR59
Vicarage Clo., St.Alb. 42 CC23
Vicarage Clo., Tad. 233 CY124
Vicarage Ct. W8 160 DB75
Vicarage Gate
Vicarage Ct., Egh. 173 BB93
Vicarage Ct., Felt. 175 BQ87
Vicarage Cres. SW11 160 DD81
Vicarage Cres., Egh. 173 BB92
Vicarage Dr. SW14 178 CR85
Vicarage Dr., Bark. 145 EQ66
Vicarage Dr., Beck. 203 EA95
Vicarage Dr., Grav. 190 GC86
Vicarage Dr., Maid. 150 AC75
Vicarage Fm. Rd., 156 BY82
Houns.
Vicarage Flds., Walt. 196 BW100
Vicarage Gdns. SW14 178 CQ85
Vicarage Rd.
Vicarage Gdns. W8 140 DA74
Vicarage Gate
Vicarage Gdns., Berk. 39 BB16
Vicarage Gdns., Mitch. 200 DE97
Vicarage Gate W8 140 DB74
Vicarage Gate, Guil. 258 AU136
Vicarage Gate Ms., Tad. 233 CY124
Warren Lo. Dr.
Vicarage Gro. SE5 162 DR81
Vicarage Hill, West. 255 ER127
Vicarage La. E6 145 EM69
Vicarage La. E15 144 EE66
Vicarage La., Chig. 103 EQ47
Vicarage La., Epp. 52 FA24
Vicarage La., Epsom 217 CU109
Vicarage La., Hem.H. 57 BA26
Vicarage La., Horl. 268 DF147
Vicarage La., Ilf. 125 ER60
Vicarage La., Kings L. 58 BM29
Vicarage La., Lthd. 231 CH122
Vicarage La., Sev. 241 FD119
London Rd.
Vicarage La. 194 BH97
(Laleham), Stai.
Vicarage La. 172 AY88
(Wraysbury), Stai.
Vicarage La., Wok. 243 BC126
Vicarage Ms., Tad. 233 CY124
Vicarage Pk. SE18 165 EQ78
Vicarage Path N8 121 DL59
Oakfield Ct.
Vicarage Pl., Slou. 152 AU76
Vicarage Rd. E10 123 EA59
Vicarage Rd. E15 144 EF66
Vicarage Rd. N17 100 DU52
Vicarage Rd. NW4 119 CU58
Vicarage Rd. SE18 165 EQ78
Vicarage Rd. SW14 178 CR85
Vicarage Rd., Berk. 39 BA16
Vicarage Rd., Bex. 187 FB88
Vicarage Rd., Croy. 201 DN104
Vicarage Rd., Dag. 147 FB66
Vicarage Rd., Egh. 173 BA92
Vicarage Rd., Epp. 70 EW29
Vicarage Rd., Horn. 127 FG60
Vicarage Rd., Kings.T. 197 CK96
Vicarage Rd. 197 CJ95
(Hampton Wick), Kings.T.
Vicarage Rd., Stai. 173 BE90
Vicarage Rd., Sun. 175 BT92
Vicarage Rd., Sutt. 218 DB105
Vicarage Rd., Tedd. 177 CG92
Vicarage Rd., Twick. 177 CE89
Vicarage Rd. 176 CC86
(Whitton), Twick.
Vicarage Rd., Ware 33 DY06
Vicarage Rd., Wat. 75 BU43
Vicarage Rd., Wok. 227 AZ121
Vicarage Rd., Wdf.Grn. 102 EL52
Vicarage Sq., Grays 170 GA79
Vicarage Wk., Maid. 150 AC75
Vicarage Wk., Reig. 250 DB134
Chartway
Vicarage Way NW10 118 CR62
Vicarage Way, Ger.Cr. 113 AZ58
Vicarage Way, Har. 116 CA59
Vicarage Way, Slou. 153 BC80
Vicarage Wd., Harl. 35 ET14
Vicars Bri. Clo., Wem. 138 CL68
Vicars Clo. E9 142 DW67
Victoria Pk. Rd.
Vicars Clo. E15 144 EG67
Vicars Clo., Enf. 82 DS40
Vicars Hill SE13 163 EB84
Vicars Moor La. N21 99 DN45
Vicars Oak Rd. SE19 182 DS93
Vicars Rd. NW5 120 DG64
Vicars Wk., Dag. 126 EV62
Viceroy Clo. N2 120 DE56
Market Pl.
Viceroy Ct. NW8 140 DE68
Prince Albert Rd.
Viceroy Par. N2 120 DE55
High Rd.
Viceroy Rd. SW8 161 DL81
Vickers Dr. N., Wey. 212 BL110
Vickers Dr. S., Wey. 212 BL111
Vickers Rd., Erith 167 FD78
Vickers Way, Houns. 176 BY85
Victor App., Horn. 128 FK60
Abbs Cross Gdns.
Victor Clo., Horn. 128 FK60
Victor Ct., Horn. 128 FK60
Victor Ct., Rain. 147 FD68
Askwith Rd.
Victor Gdns., Horn. 128 FK60
Victor Gro., Wem. 138 CL66
Victor Rd. NW10 139 CV68
Victor Rd. SE20 183 DX94
Victor Rd., Har. 116 CC55
Victor Rd., Tedd. 177 CE91
Victor Rd., Wind. 151 AQ83
Victor Smith Ct., St.Alb. 60 CA31
Victor Vill. N9 100 DR48
Victor Wk. NW9 96 CS54
Booth Rd.
Victor Wk., Horn. 128 FK60
Abbs Cross Gdns.
Victoria Ave. E6 144 EK67
Victoria Ave. EC2 275 N7
Victoria Ave. N3 97 CZ53
Victoria Ave., Barn. 80 DD42
Victoria Rd.
Victoria Ave., Grav. 191 GH87
Sheppy Pl.
Victoria Ave., Grays 170 GC75
Victoria Ave., Houns. 176 BZ85
Victoria Ave., Rom. 105 FB51
Victoria Ave., S.Croy. 220 DQ110
Victoria Ave., Surb. 197 CK100
Victoria Ave., Uxb. 135 BP65
Victoria Ave., Wall. 200 DG104
Victoria Ave., Wem. 138 CP65
Victoria Ave., W.Mol. 196 CA97
Victoria Clo., Barn. 80 DD42
Victoria Clo., Grays 170 GC75
Victoria Clo., Hayes 135 BR72
Commonwealth Ave.
Victoria Clo., Horl. 268 DG148
Victoria Clo., Rick. 92 BK45
Victoria Clo., Wal.Cr. 67 DX30
Victoria Clo., W.Mol. 196 CA97
Victoria Ave.
Victoria Clo., Wey. 195 BR104
Victoria Cotts., Rich. 158 CM81
Victoria Ct., Wem. 138 CN65
Victoria Cres. N15 122 DS57
Victoria Cres. SE19 182 DS93
Victoria Cres. SW19 179 CZ94
Victoria Cres., Iver 134 BG73
Victoria Dock Rd. E16 144 EG73
Victoria Dr. SW19 179 CX87
Victoria Dr. 209 FR96
(South Darenth), Dart.
Victoria Dr., Slou. 131 AL65
Victoria Embk. EC4 278 C1
Victoria Embk. EC4 141 DN73
Victoria Embk. SW1 278 A4
Victoria Embk. SW1 161 DL75
Victoria Embk. WC2 278 C1
Victoria Embk. WC2 141 DM73
Victoria Gdns. W11 140 DA74
Victoria Gdns., 156 BY81
Houns.
Victoria Gdns., West. 238 EJ115
Victoria Gro. N12 98 DD50
Victoria Gro. W8 160 DC76
Victoria Gro. Ms. W2 140 DB73
Ossington St.
Victoria Hill Rd., Swan. 207 FF95
Victoria Ind. Est. NW10 138 CS69
Victoria Ind. Est., Dart. 188 FK85
Victoria La., Barn. 79 CZ42
Victoria La., Hayes 155 BQ78
Victoria Ms. NW6 140 DA67
Victoria Ms. SW4 161 DH84
Victoria Ri.
Victoria Pk. E9 143 DY67
Victoria Pk. Rd. E9 142 DW67
Victoria Pk. Sq. E2 142 DW69
Victoria Pas. NW8 140 DD70
Cunningham Pl.
Victoria Pas., Wat. 75 BV42
Addiscombe Rd.
Victoria Pl., Epsom 216 CS112
Victoria Pl., Rich. 177 CK85
Victoria Pt. E13 144 EG68
Victoria Rd.
Victoria Ri. SW4 161 DH83
Victoria Rd. E4 102 EE46
Victoria Rd. E11 124 EE63
Thorne Clo.
Victoria Rd. E13 144 EG68
Victoria Rd. E17 101 EC54
Victoria Rd. E18 102 EH54
Victoria Rd. N4 121 DM59
Victoria Rd. N9 100 DT48
Victoria Rd. N15 122 DU56
Victoria Rd. N18 100 DT49
Victoria Rd. N22 99 DJ53
Victoria Rd. NW4 119 CW56
Victoria Rd. NW6 139 CZ68
Victoria Rd. NW7 97 CT50
Victoria Rd. NW10 138 CS70
Victoria Rd. SW14 158 CR83
Victoria Rd. W3 138 CR71
Victoria Rd. W5 137 CH71
Victoria Rd. W8 160 DC75
Victoria Rd., Add. 212 BK105
Victoria Rd., Bark. 145 EP65
Victoria Rd., Barn. 80 DD42
Victoria Rd., Berk. 38 AX20
Victoria Rd., Bexh. 166 FA84
Victoria Rd., Brwd. 108 FW49
Victoria Rd., Brom. 204 EK99
Victoria Rd., Buck.H. 102 EK47
Victoria Rd., Chesh. 54 AQ31
Victoria Rd., Chis. 185 EN92
Victoria Rd., Couls. 235 DK115
Victoria Rd., Dag. 127 FB64
Victoria Rd., Dart. 188 FK85
Victoria Rd., Erith 167 FE79
Victoria Rd., Felt. 175 BV88
Victoria Rd., Grav. 191 GF88
Victoria Rd., Guil. 242 AY134
Victoria Rd., Horl. 268 DG148
Victoria Rd., Kings.T. 198 CM96
Victoria Rd., Mitch. 180 DE94
Victoria Rd., Red. 266 DG135
Victoria Rd., Rom. 127 FE58
Victoria Rd., Ruis. 115 BU60
Victoria Rd., Sev. 257 FH125
Victoria Rd., Sid. 185 ET90
Victoria Rd., Slou. 132 AV74
Victoria Rd. 131 AQ65
(Farnham Common), Slou.
Victoria Rd., Sthl. 156 BZ76
Victoria Rd., Stai. 173 BE90
Victoria Rd., Surb. 197 CK100
Victoria Rd., Sutt. 218 DD106
Victoria Rd., Tedd. 177 CG93
Victoria Rd., Twick. 177 CH87
Victoria Rd., Uxb. 134 BJ66
New Windsor St.
Victoria Rd., Wal.Abb. 67 EC34
Victoria Rd., Wat. 75 BV38
Victoria Rd. 94 CB46
(Bushey), Wat.
Victoria Rd., Wey. 195 BR104
Victoria Rd. 151 AM78
(Eton Wick), Wind.
Victoria Rd., Wok. 226 AY117
Victoria Sq. SW1 277 J6
Victoria Sta. SW1 277 J8
Victoria Sta. SW1 161 DH77
Victoria Steps, Brent. 158 CM79
Kew Bri. Rd.
Victoria St. E15 144 EE66
Victoria St. SW1 277 K7
Victoria St. SW1 161 DJ76
Victoria St., Belv. 166 EZ78
Victoria St., Egh. 172 AW93
Victoria St., St.Alb. 43 CD20
Victoria St., Slou. 152 AT75
Victoria St., Wind. 151 AR81
Victoria Ter. N4 121 DN60
Victoria Ter. NW10 138 CS69
Old Oak La.
Victoria Ter., Dor. 263 CG136
South St.
Victoria Ter., Har. 117 CE60
Victoria Vill., Rich. 158 CM83
Victoria Way SE7 164 EH78
Victoria Way, Wey. 195 BR104
Victoria Way, Wok. 226 AY117
Victorian Gro. N16 122 DS63
Victorian Rd. N16 122 DS62
Victors Cres., Brwd. 109 GB47
Victors Dr., Hmptn. 176 BY93
Victors Way, Barn. 79 CZ41
Victory Ave., Mord. 200 DC99
Victory Business Cen., 157 CF84
Islw.
Victory Pk. Rd., Add. 194 BJ104
Victory Pl. SE17 279 J8
Victory Pl. SE17 162 DQ77
Victory Pl. SE19 182 DS93
Westow St.
Victory Rd. E11 124 EG56
Hermon Hill
Victory Rd. SW19 180 DC94
Victory Rd., Berk. 38 AU18
Gossoms End
Victory Rd., Cher. 194 BG102
Victory Rd., Grays 169 FW78
Arterial Rd. W. Thurrock
Victory Rd., Rain. 147 FG68
Victory Wk. SE8 163 EA81
Ship St.
Victory Way SE16 163 DY75
Victory Way, Houns. 156 BW78
Victory Way, Rom. 105 FB54
Vidler Clo., Chess. 215 CJ107
Mansfield Rd.
Vienna Clo., Ilf. 102 EL54
Coburg Gdns.
View, The SE2 166 EY78
View Clo. N6 120 DF59
View Clo., Chig. 103 ER50
View Clo., Har. 117 CD56
View Clo., West. 238 EJ116
View Rd. N6 120 DF59
View Rd., Pot.B. 64 DC32
Viewfield Clo., Har. 118 CL59
Viewfield Rd. SW18 179 CZ86
Viewfield Rd., Bex. 186 EW88
Viewland Rd. SE18 165 ET78
Viewlands Ave., West. 239 ES120
Viga Rd. N21 81 DN44
Vigerons Way, Grays 171 GH77
Viggory La., Wok. 226 AW115
Vigilant Clo. SE26 182 DU91
Vigilant Way, Grav. 191 GL91
Vignoles Rd., Rom. 126 FA59
Vigo St. W1 277 K1
Vigo St. W1 141 DJ73
Vigors Cft., Hat. 45 CT19
Viking Clo. E3 143 DY68
Selwyn Rd.
Viking Ct. SW6 160 DA79
Viking Gdns. E6 144 EL71
Eisenhower Dr.
Viking Pl. E10 123 DZ60
Viking Rd., Grav. 190 GC90
Viking Rd., Sthl. 136 BY73
Viking Way, Brwd. 108 FV45
Viking Way, Erith 167 FC76
Viking Way, Rain. 147 FG70
Villa Ct., Dart. 188 FL89
Greenbanks
Villa Rd. SW9 161 DN83
Villa St. SE17 162 DR78
Villacourt Rd. SE18 166 EU80
Village, The SE7 164 EJ79
Village Arc. E4 101 ED46
Station Rd.
Village Clo. E4 101 EC50
Village Clo. NW3 120 DE64
Ornan Rd.
Village Clo., Wey. 195 BR104
Oatlands Dr.
Village Gdns., Epsom 217 CT110
Village Grn. Ave., West. 238 EL117
Village Grn. Rd., Dart. 167 FG84
Village Grn. Way, West. 238 EL117
Main Rd.
Village Heights, 102 EF50
Wdf.Grn.
Village La., Slou. 111 AR60
Village Ms. NW9 118 CR61
Village Pk. Clo., Enf. 82 DS44
Village Rd.
Village Rd. N3 97 CY54
Village Rd., Amer. 89 AM45
Village Rd., Egh. 193 BC97
Village Rd., Enf. 100 DR45
Village Rd., Uxb. 113 BF61
Village Rd., Wind. 150 AH76
Village Row, Sutt. 218 DA108
Village Way NW10 118 CR63
Village Way SE21 182 DR86
Village Way, Amer. 72 AX40
Village Way, Ashf. 174 BM91
Village Way, Beck. 203 EA97
Village Way, Pnr. 116 BY59
Village Way, S.Croy. 220 DU113
Village Way E., Har. 116 CA59
Villas Rd. SE18 165 EQ77
Villier St., Uxb. 134 BK68
Villiers, The, Wey. 213 BR107
Villiers Ave., Surb. 198 CM99
Villiers Ave., Twick. 176 BZ88
Villiers Clo. E10 123 EA61
Villiers Clo., Surb. 198 CM98
Villiers Ct. N20 98 DC45
Buckingham Ave.
Villiers Cres., St.Alb. 43 CK17
Villiers Gro., Sutt. 217 CX109
Villiers Path, Surb. 198 CL99
Villiers Rd. NW2 139 CU65
Villiers Rd., Beck. 203 DX96
Villiers Rd., Islw. 157 CE82
Villiers Rd., Kings.T. 198 CM98
Villiers Rd., Slou. 131 AR71
Villiers Rd., Sthl. 136 BZ74
Villiers Rd., Wat. 76 BY44
Villiers St. WC2 278 A2
Villiers St. WC2 141 DL74
Villiers St., Hert. 32 DS09
Vincam Clo., Twick. 176 CA87
Vince St. EC1 275 L3
Vince St. EC1 142 DR69
Vincent Ave., Cars. 218 DD111
Vincent Ave., Croy. 221 DX112
Vincent Ave., Surb. 198 CP102
Vincent Clo. SE16 163 DY75
Vincent Clo., Barn. 80 DB41
Vincent Clo., Brom. 204 EH98
Vincent Clo., Cher. 193 BE101
Vincent Clo., Couls. 234 DF120
Vincent Clo., Esher 196 CB104
Vincent Clo., Ilf. 103 EQ51
Vincent Clo., Lthd. 230 CB123
Vincent Clo., Sid. 185 ES88
Vincent Clo. 67 DY28
(Cheshunt), Wal.Cr.
Vincent Clo., West Dr. 154 BN79
Vincent Dr., Dor. 263 CG137
Vincent Dr., Shep. 195 BS97
Vincent Gdns. NW2 119 CT62
Vincent Grn., Couls. 234 DF120
High Rd.
Vincent La., Dor. 263 CG136
Vincent Ms. E3 143 EA68
Fairfield Rd.

Vincent Rd. E4 101 ED51
Vincent Rd. N15 122 DQ56
Vincent Rd. N22 99 DN54
Vincent Rd. SE18 165 EP77
Vincent Rd. W3 158 CQ76
Vincent Rd., Cher. 193 BE101
Vincent Rd., Cob. 230 BY116
Vincent Rd., Couls. 235 DJ116
Vincent Rd., Croy. 202 DS101
Vincent Rd., Dag. 146 EY66
Vincent Rd., Dor. 263 CG136
Vincent Rd., Houns. 156 BX82
Vincent Rd., Islw. 157 CD81
Vincent Rd., Kings.T. 198 CN97
Vincent Rd., Rain. 148 FJ70
Vincent Rd., Wem. 138 CM66
Vincent Row, Hmptn. 176 CC93
Vincent Sq. SW1 277 M8
Vincent Sq. SW1 161 DJ77
Vincent Sq., West. 222 EJ113
Vincent St. E16 144 EF71
Vincent St. SW1 277 M8
Vincent St. SW1 161 DK77
Vincent Ter. N1 141 DP68
Vincents Dr., Dor. 263 CG137
Nower Rd.
Vincents Path, Nthlt. 136 BY65
Arnold Rd.
Vincents Wk., Dor. 263 CG136
Arundel Rd.
Vincenzo Clo., Hat. 45 CW23
Vine, The, Sev. 257 FJ124
Vine Ave., Sev. 257 FH124
Vine Clo., Stai. 174 BG85
Vine Clo., Surb. 198 CM100
Vine Clo., Sutt. 200 DC104
Vine Clo., Welw.G.C. 29 CY07
Vine Clo., West Dr. 154 BN77
Vine Ct. E1 142 DU71
Whitechapel Rd.
Vine Ct., Har. 118 CL58
Vine Ct. Rd., Sev. 257 FJ124
Vine Gdns., Ilf. 125 EQ64
Vine Gate, Slou. 131 AQ65
Parsonage La.
Vine Gro., Harl. 35 ER10
Eastwick Rd.
Vine Gro., Uxb. 134 BN66
Vine Hill EC1 274 D5
Vine La. SE1 279 N3
Vine La., Uxb. 134 BM67
Vine Pl. W5 138 CL74
The Common
Vine Pl., Houns. 156 CB84
Vine Rd. E15 144 EF66
Vine Rd. SW13 159 CT83
Vine Rd., E.Mol. 196 CC98
Vine Rd., Orp. 223 ET107
Vine Rd., Slou. 132 AT65
Vine Sq. W14 159 CZ78
Vine St. EC3 275 P9
Vine St. W1 277 L1
Vine St., Rom. 127 FC56
Vine St., Uxb. 134 BK67
Vine St. Bri. EC1 274 E5
Vine St. Bri. EC1 141 DN70
Vine Way, Brwd. 108 FW46
Vine Yd. SE1 279 J5
Vinegar All. E17 123 EB56
Vinegar St. E1 142 DV74
Reardon St.
Vinegar Yd. SE1 279 M4
Viner Clo., Walt. 196 BW100
Vineries, The N14 81 DJ43
Vineries, The, Enf. 82 DS41
Vineries Bank NW7 97 CV50
Vineries Clo., Dag. 146 FA65
Heathway
Vineries Clo., West Dr. 154 BN79
Vines Ave. N3 98 DB53
Viney Bank, Croy. 221 DZ109
Viney Rd. SE13 163 EB83
Vineyard, The, Rich. 178 CL85
Vineyard, The, Ware 33 EA05
Vineyard, The, Welw.G.C. 29 CX07
Vineyard Ave. NW7 97 CY52
Vineyard Clo. SE6 183 EA88
Vineyard Gro. N3 98 DB54
Squires La.
Vineyard Hill Rd. SW19 179 CZ91
Vineyard Pas., Rich. 178 CL85
Paradise Rd.
Vineyard Path SW14 158 CR83
Vineyard Rd., Felt. 175 BU90
Vineyard Row, Kings.T. 197 CJ95
Vineyard Wk. EC1 274 D4
Vineyards Hill, Pot.B. 64 DF30
Vineyards Rd., Pot.B. 64 DF30
Vining St. SW9 161 DN84
Vinlake Ave., Uxb. 114 BM62
Vinson Clo., Orp. 206 EU102
Vintry Ms. E17 123 EA56
Cleveland Pk. Cres.
Viola Ave. SE2 166 EV77
Viola Ave., Felt. 176 BW86
Viola Ave., Stai. 174 BL88
Viola Clo., S.Ock. 149 FW69
Viola Sq. W12 139 CT73
Violet Ave., Enf. 82 DR38
Violet Ave., Uxb. 134 BM71
Violet Clo., Wall. 200 DG102
Violet Gdns., Croy. 219 DP106
Violet Hill NW8 140 DC68
Violet La., Croy. 219 DP107
Violet Rd. E3 143 EB70
Violet Rd. E17 123 EA58
Violet Rd. E18 102 EH54
Violet St. E2 142 DV70
Three Colts La.
Violet Way, Rick. 74 BJ42
Virgil Dr., Brox. 49 DZ23
Virgil Pl. W1 272 D7
Virgil St. SE1 278 C6
Virgil St. SE1 161 DM76
Virginia Ave., Vir.W. 192 AW99
Virginia Beeches, Vir.W. 192 AW97
Virginia Clo., Ash. 231 CK118
Skinners La.
Virginia Clo., N.Mal. 198 CQ98
Willow Rd.
Virginia Clo., Wey. 213 BQ107
Virginia Dr., Vir.W. 192 AW99
Virginia Gdns., Ilf. 103 EQ54
Virginia Rd. E2 275 P3
Virginia Rd. E2 142 DT69
Virginia Rd., Th.Hth. 201 DP95
Virginia St. E1 142 DU73
Virginia Wk. SW2 181 DM86
Beechdale Rd.
Virginia Wk., Grav. 191 GK93
Viscount Dr. E6 145 EM71
Viscount Gdns., W.Byf. 212 BL112
Viscount Gro., Nthlt. 136 BX69
Wayfarer Rd.
Viscount Rd., Stai. 174 BL88
Viscount St. EC1 275 H6
Viscount Way, Houns. 155 BS84
Vista, The SE9 184 EK86
Vista, The, Sid. 185 ET92
Langdon Shaw
Vista Ave., Enf. 83 DX40
Vista Dr., Ilf. 124 EK57
Vista Way, Har. 118 CL58
Viveash Clo., Hayes 155 BT76
Vivian Ave. NW4 119 CU57
Vivian Ave., Wem. 118 CN64
Vivian Clo., Wat. 93 BU46
Vivian Gdns., Wat. 93 BU46
Vivian Gdns., Wem. 118 CN64
Vivian Rd. E3 143 DY68
Vivian Sq. SE15 162 DV83
Scylla Rd.
Vivian Way N2 120 DD57
Vivien Clo., Chess. 216 CL108
Vivienne Clo., Twick. 177 CK86
Vixen Dr., Hert. 32 DU09
Voce Rd. SE18 165 ER80
Voewood Clo., N.Mal. 199 CT100
Vogan Clo., Reig. 266 DB137
Volta Way, Croy. 201 DM102
Voltaire Rd. SW4 161 DK83
Voltaire Way, Hayes 135 BS73
Judge Heath La.
Voluntary Pl. E11 124 EG58
Vorley Rd. N19 121 DJ61
Voss Ct. SW16 181 DL93
Voss St. E2 142 DU69
Vulcan Clo., Wall. 219 DM108
De Havilland Rd.
Vulcan Gate, Enf. 81 DN41
Vulcan Rd. SE4 163 DZ82
Vulcan Sq. E14 163 EA77
Britannia Rd.
Vulcan Ter. SE4 163 DZ82
Vulcan Way N7 141 DM65
Vulcan Way, Croy. 221 ED110
Vyne, The, Bexh. 167 FB83
Vyner Rd. W3 138 CR73
Vyner St. E2 142 DV67
Vyners Way, Uxb. 114 BN64
Vyse Clo., Barn. 79 CW42

W

Wacketts (Cheshunt), Wal.Cr. 66 DU27
Longfield La.
Wadding St. SE17 279 K9
Wadding St. SE17 162 DR77
Waddington Ave., Couls. 235 DN120
Waddington Clo., Couls. 235 DP119
Waddington Clo., Enf. 82 DS42
Waddington Rd. E15 123 ED64
Waddington Rd., St.Alb. 43 CD20
Waddington St. E15 143 ED65
Waddington Way SE19 182 DQ94
Waddon Clo., Croy. 201 DN104
Waddon Ct. Rd., Croy. 219 DN105
Waddon Marsh Way, Croy. 201 DM102
Waddon New Rd., Croy. 201 DP104
Waddon Pk. Ave., Croy. 201 DN104
Waddon Rd., Croy. 201 DN104
Waddon Way, Croy. 219 DN107
Wade, The, Welw.G.C. 29 CZ12
Wade Ave., Orp. 206 EX101
Wade Dr., Slou. 131 AN74
Wade Rd. E16 144 EJ72
Leyes Rd.
Wades, The, Hat. 45 CU21
Wades Gro. N21 99 DN45
Wades Hill N21 81 DN44
Wades La., Tedd. 177 CG92
High St.
Wades Ms. N21 99 DN45
Wades Hill
Wades Pl. E14 143 EB73
Wadesmill Rd., Hert. 32 DQ06
Wadeson St. E2 142 DV68
Wadeville Ave., Rom. 126 EZ58
Wadeville Clo., Belv. 166 FA78
Wadham Ave. E17 101 EB52
Wadham Clo., Shep. 195 BQ101
Wadham Gdns. NW3 140 DE66
Wadham Gdns., Grnf. 137 CD65
Wadham Rd. E17 101 EB53
Wadham Rd. SW15 159 CY84
Wadham Rd., Abb.L. 59 BT31
Lancaster Way
Wadhurst Clo. SE20 202 DV96
Wadhurst Rd. SW8 161 DJ81
Wadhurst Rd. W4 158 CR76
Wadley Clo., Hem.H. 40 BM21
White Hart Dr.
Wadley Rd. E11 124 EE59
Wadsworth Clo., Enf. 83 DX43
Falcon Rd.
Wadsworth Clo., Grnf. 137 CJ68
Wadsworth Rd., Grnf. 137 CH68
Wager St. E3 143 DZ70
Waggon Clo., Guil. 242 AS133
Waggon Ms. N14 99 DJ46
Chase Side
Waggon Rd., Barn. 80 DC37
Waghorn Rd. E13 144 EJ67
Waghorn Rd., Har. 117 CK55
Waghorn St. SE15 162 DU83
Wagner St. SE15 162 DW80
Wagon Rd., Barn. 80 DA35
Wagon Way, Rick. 74 BJ41
Wagtail Clo. NW9 96 CS54
Swan Dr.
Wagtail Gdns., S.Croy. 221 DY110
Waid Clo., Dart. 188 FM86
Waights Ct., Kings.T. 198 CL95
Wain Clo., Pot.B. 64 DB29
Wainfleet Ave., Rom. 105 FC54
Wainford Clo. SW19 179 CX88
Windlesham Gro.
Wainwright Ave., Brwd. 109 GD44
Wainwright Gro., Islw. 157 CD84
Waite Davies Rd. SE12 184 EF87
Waite St. SE15 162 DT79
Waithman St. EC4 274 F9
Wake Rd., Loug. 84 EJ38
Wakefield Clo., W.Byf. 212 BL112
Wakefield Cres., Slou. 132 AT65
Wakefield Gdns. SE19 182 DS94
Wakefield Gdns., Ilf. 124 EL58
Wakefield Ms. WC1 274 A3
Wakefield Rd. N11 99 DK50
Wakefield Rd. N15 122 DT57
Wakefield Rd., Green. 189 FW85
Wakefield Rd., Rich. 177 CK85
Wakefield St. E6 144 EK67
Wakefield St. N18 100 DU50
Wakefield St. WC1 274 A3
Wakefield St. WC1 141 DL69
Wakefield Wk., Wal.Cr. 67 DY31
Wakeham St. N1 142 DR65
Wakehams Hill, Pnr. 116 BZ55
Wakehurst Path, Wok. 211 BC114
Bunyard Dr.
Wakehurst Rd. SW11 180 DE85
Wakelin Rd. E15 144 EE68
Wakeling Rd. W7 137 CF71
Templeman Rd.
Wakeling St. E14 143 DY72
Wakely Clo., West. 238 EJ118
Wakeman Rd. NW10 139 CW69
Wakemans Hill Ave. NW9 118 CR57
Wakerfield Clo., Horn. 128 FM57
Wakering Rd., Bark. 145 EQ65
Wakerley Clo. E6 145 EM72
Truesdale Rd.
Wakley St. EC1 274 F2
Wakley St. EC1 141 DP69
Walberswick St. SW8 161 DL80
Walbrook EC4 275 K10
Walbrook EC4 142 DR73
Walbrook Ho. N9 100 DW47
Walburgh St. E1 142 DV72
Bigland St.
Walburton Rd., Pur. 219 DJ113
Walcorde Ave. SE17 279 J9
Walcot Rd., Enf. 83 DZ40
Walcot Sq. SE11 278 E8
Walcot Sq. SE11 161 DN77
Walcott St. SW1 277 L8
Waldair Ct. E16 165 EP75
Barge Ho. Rd.
Waldeck Gro. SE27 181 DP90
Waldeck Rd. N15 121 DP56
Waldeck Rd. SW14 158 CQ83
Lower Richmond Rd.
Waldeck Rd. W4 158 CN79
Waldeck Rd. W13 137 CH72
Waldeck Rd., Dart. 188 FM86
Waldeck Ter. SW14 158 CQ83
Lower Richmond Rd.
Waldegrave Ave., Tedd. 177 CF92
Waldegrave Rd.
Waldegrave Gdns., Twick. 177 CF89
Waldegrave Gdns., Upmin. 128 FP60
Waldegrave Pk., Twick. 177 CF91
Waldegrave Rd. N8 121 DN55
Waldegrave Rd. SE19 182 DT94
Waldegrave Rd. W5 138 CM73
Waldegrave Rd., Brom. 204 EL98
Waldegrave Rd., Dag. 126 EW61
Waldegrave Rd., Tedd. 177 CF91
Waldegrave Rd., Twick. 177 CF91
Waldegrove, Croy. 202 DT104
Waldemar Ave. SW6 159 CY81
Waldemar Ave. W13 137 CJ74
Waldemar Rd. SW19 180 DA92
Walden Ave. N13 100 DQ49
Walden Ave., Chis. 185 EM91
Walden Ave., Rain. 147 FD69
Walden Clo., Belv. 166 EZ78
Walden Gdns., Th.Hth. 201 DM98
Walden Pl., Welw.G.C. 29 CX07
Walden Rd. N17 100 DR53
Walden Rd., Chis. 185 EM93
Walden Rd., Horn. 128 FK58
Walden Rd., Welw.G.C. 29 CX07
Walden St. E1 142 DV72
Walden Way NW7 97 CX51
Walden Way, Horn. 128 FK58
Walden Way, Ilf. 103 ES52
Waldenhurst Rd., Orp. 206 EX101
Waldens Clo., Orp. 206 EX101
Waldens Pk. Rd., Wok. 226 AW116
Waldens Rd., Orp. 206 EY101
Waldens Rd., Wok. 226 AX117
Waldenshaw Rd. SE23 182 DW88
Waldo Clo. SW4 181 DJ85
Waldo Pl., Mitch. 180 DE94
Waldo Rd. NW10 139 CU69
Waldo Rd., Brom. 204 EK97
Waldorf Clo., S.Croy. 219 DP109
Waldram Cres. SE23 182 DW88
Waldram Pk. Rd. SE23 183 DX88
Waldram Pl. SE23 182 DW88
Waldrist Way, Erith 166 EZ75
Waldron Gdns., Brom. 203 ED97
Waldron Ms. SW3 160 DD79
Old Ch. St.
Waldron Rd. SW18 180 DC90
Waldron Rd., Har. 117 CE60
Waldronhyrst, S.Croy. 219 DP105
Waldrons, The, Croy. 219 DP105
Waldrons, The, Oxt. 254 EF131
Waldrons Path, S.Croy. 220 DQ105
Bramley Hill
Waleran Clo., Stan. 95 CF51
Chenduit Way
Waleran Flats SE1 162 DS77
Old Kent Rd.
Walerand Rd. SE13 163 EC82
Wales Ave., Cars. 218 DE106
Wales Fm. Rd. W3 138 CR71
Waley St. E1 143 DY71
Walfield Ave. N20 98 DB45
Walford Rd. N16 122 DS63
Walford Rd., Dor. 263 CH140
Walford Rd., Uxb. 134 BJ68
Walfrey Gdns., Dag. 146 EY66
Walham Gro. SW6 160 DA80
Walham Ri. SW19 179 CY93
Walham Yd. SW6 160 DA80
Walham Gro.
Walk, The, Horn. 128 FM61
Walk, The, Oxt. 253 EA133
Walk, The, Pot.B. 64 DA32
Walk, The, Sun. 175 BT94
Walk, The (Eton Wick), Wind. 151 AN78
Walkden Rd., Chis. 185 EN92
Walker Clo. N11 99 DJ49
Walker Clo. SE18 165 EQ77
Walker Clo. W7 137 CE74
Walker Clo., Dart. 167 FF83
Walker Clo., Hmptn. 176 BZ93
Fearnley Cres.
Walkers Ct. E8 142 DU65
Wilton Way
Walkers Ct. W1 273 M10
Walkers Pl. SW15 159 CY83
Felsham Rd.
Walkerscroft Mead SE21 182 DQ88
Walkfield Dr., Epsom 233 CV117
Walkford Way SE15 162 DT80
Daniel Gdns.
Walkley Rd., Dart. 187 FH85
Walks, The N2 120 DD55
Walkwood End, Beac. 88 AJ54
Walkwood Ri., Beac. 110 AJ55
Wall End Rd. E6 145 EN66
Wall St. N1 142 DR65
Wallace Clo. SE28 146 EX73
Haldane Rd.
Wallace Clo., Horn. 127 FH60
Wallace Clo., Shep. 195 BR98
Wallace Clo., Uxb. 134 BL68
Grays Rd.
Wallace Cres., Cars. 218 DF106
Wallace Flds., Epsom 217 CT112
Wallace Gdns., Swans. 190 FY86
Milton St.
Wallace Rd. N1 142 DQ65
Wallace Rd., Grays 170 GA76
Wallace Wk., Add. 212 BJ105
Wallace Way N19 121 DK61
Giesbach Rd.
Wallasey Cres., Uxb. 114 BN61
Wallbutton Rd. SE4 163 DY82
Wallcote Ave. NW2 119 CX60
Walled Gdn., The, Bet. 264 CR135
Walled Gdn., The, Tad. 233 CX122
Heathcote
Wallenger Ave., Rom. 127 FH55
Waller Dr., Nthwd. 93 BU54
Waller La., Cat. 236 DT123
Waller Rd. SE14 163 DX81
Waller Rd., Beac. 89 AM53
Wallers Clo., Dag. 146 EY67
Wallers Clo., Wdf.Grn. 103 EM51
Waller's Hoppit, Loug. 84 EL40
Wallers Way, Hodd. 33 EB14
Wallfield All., Hert. 32 DQ10
Wallflower St. W12 139 CT73
Wallgrave Rd. SW5 160 DB77
Wallhouse Rd., Erith 167 FH80
Wallingford Ave. W10 139 CX71
Wallingford Rd., Uxb. 134 BH68
Wallingford Wk., St.Alb. 43 CD23
Wallington Clo., Ruis. 115 BQ58
Wallington Rd., Chesh. 54 AP30
Wallington Rd., Ilf. 125 ET59
Wallington Sq., Wall. 219 DH107
Woodcote Rd.
Wallis All. SE1 279 J5
Wallis Clo. SW11 160 DD83
Wallis Clo., Dart. 187 FG90
Wallis Ct., Slou. 152 AU76
Nixey Clo.
Wallis Ms., Lthd. 231 CG122
Guildford Rd.
Wallis Pk., Grav. 190 GB85
Wallis Rd. E9 143 DZ65
Wallis Rd., Sthl. 136 CB72
Walliss Cotts. SW2 181 DL87
Wallorton Gdns. SW14 158 CR84
Wallside EC2 142 DQ71
Wood St.
Wallwood Rd. E11 123 ED60
Wallwood St. E14 143 DZ71
Walm La. NW2 139 CW65
Walmar Clo., Barn. 80 DD39
Walmer Clo. E4 101 EB47
Walmer Clo., Orp. 223 ER105
Tubbenden La. S.
Walmer Clo., Rom. 105 FB54
Walmer Gdns. W13 157 CG75
Walmer Ho. N9 100 DT46
Walmer Pl. W1 272 D6
Walmer Rd. W10 139 CW72
Latimer Rd.
Walmer Rd. W11 139 CY73
Walmer St. W1 272 D6
Walmer Ter. SE18 165 EQ77
Walmgate Rd., Grnf. 137 CH67
Walmington Fold N12 98 DA51
Walney Wk. N1 142 DQ65
St. Paul's Rd.
Walnut Ave., West Dr. 154 BN76
Walnut Clo. SE8 163 DZ79
Clyde St.
Walnut Clo., Cars. 218 DF106
Walnut Clo., Epsom 233 CT115
Walnut Clo., Hayes 135 BS73
Walnut Clo., Ilf. 125 EQ56
Civic Way
Walnut Clo., St.Alb. 60 CB27
Walnut Ct. W5 158 CL75
Walnut Ct., Welw.G.C. 29 CY12
Walnut Dr., Tad. 233 CY124
Warren Lo. Dr.
Walnut Flds., Epsom 217 CT109
Walnut Gdns. E15 124 EE63
Burgess Rd.
Walnut Grn. (Bushey), Wat. 76 BZ40
Walnut Gro., Bans. 217 CX114
Walnut Gro., Enf. 82 DR43
Walnut Gro., Hem.H. 40 BK20
Walnut Gro., Welw.G.C. 29 CY12
Walnut Ms., Sutt. 218 DC108
Walnut Rd. E10 123 EB61
Oliver Rd.
Walnut Tree Ave., Dart. 188 FL89
Walnut Tree Ave., Mitch. 200 DE97
Dearn Gdns.
Walnut Tree Clo. SW13 159 CT81
Walnut Tree Clo., Bans. 217 CY112
Walnut Tree Clo., Chis. 205 EQ95
Walnut Tree Clo., Guil. 242 AW134
Walnut Tree Clo., Hodd. 49 EA17
Walnut Tree Clo. (Cheshunt), Wal.Cr. 67 DX31
Walnut Tree Cotts. SW19 179 CY91
Church Rd.
Walnut Tree La., W.Byf. 212 BK112
Walnut Tree Pk., Guil. 242 AW134
Walnut Tree Rd. SE10 164 EE78
Walnut Tree Rd., Brent. 158 CL79
Walnut Tree Rd., Dag. 126 EX61
Walnut Tree Rd., Erith 167 FE78
Walnut Tree Rd., Houns. 156 BZ79
Walnut Tree Rd., Shep. 195 BQ96
Walnut Tree Wk. SE11 278 D8
Walnut Tree Wk. SE11 161 DN77
Walnut Tree Wk., Ware 33 DX08
Walnut Way, Buck.H. 102 EK48
Walnut Way, Ruis. 136 BW65
Walnut Way, Swan. 207 FD96
Walnuts, The, Orp. 206 EU102
High St.
Walnuts Rd., Orp. 206 EU102
Walpole Ave., Couls. 234 DF119
Walpole Ave., Rich. 158 CM82
Walpole Clo. W13 157 CJ75
Walpole Clo., Grays 170 GC77
Palmers Dr.
Walpole Clo., Pnr. 94 CA51
Walpole Cres., Tedd. 177 CF92
Walpole Gdns. W4 158 CQ78
Walpole Gdns., Twick. 177 CE89
Walpole Ms. NW8 140 DD67
Queen's Gro.
Walpole Ms. SW19 180 DD93
Walpole Rd.
Walpole Pk. W5 137 CJ74
Walpole Pk., Wey. 212 BN108
Walpole Pl. SE18 165 EP77
Anglesea Rd.
Walpole Pl., Tedd. 177 CF92
Walpole Rd. E6 144 EJ66
Walpole Rd. E17 123 DY56
Walpole Rd. E18 102 EF53
Walpole Rd. (Downhills Way) N17 122 DQ55
Walpole Rd. (Lordship La.) N17 100 DQ54
Walpole Rd. SW19 180 DD93
Walpole Rd., Brom. 204 EK99
Walpole Rd., Croy. 202 DR103
Walpole Rd., Slou. 131 AK72
Walpole Rd., Surb. 198 CL101
Walpole Rd., Tedd. 177 CF92
Walpole Rd., Twick. 177 CE89
Walpole Rd., Wind. 172 AV87
Walpole St. SW3 276 D10
Walpole St. SW3 160 DF78
Walrond Ave., Wem. 118 CL64
Walsh Cres., Croy. 222 EE112
Walsham Clo. N16 122 DU59
Braydon Rd.
Walsham Clo. SE28 146 EX73
Walsham Rd. SE14 163 DX82
Walsham Rd., Felt. 175 BV87
Walshford Way, Borwd. 78 CN38
Walsingham Clo., Hat. 45 CT17
Walsingham Gdns., Epsom 216 CS105
Walsingham Pk., Chis. 205 ER96
Walsingham Rd. E5 122 DU62
Walsingham Rd. W13 137 CG74
Walsingham Rd., Croy. 221 EC110
Walsingham Rd., Enf. 82 DR42
Walsingham Rd., Mitch. 200 DF99
Walsingham Rd., Orp. 206 EV95
Walsingham Wk., Belv. 166 FA79
Walsingham Way, St.Alb. 61 CJ27
Walt Whitman Clo. SE24 161 DP84
Shakespeare Rd.
Walter Savill Twr. E17 123 EA59
Colchester Rd.
Walter St. E2 143 DX69
Walter St., Kings.T. 198 CL95
Sopwith Way
Walter Ter. E1 143 DX72
Walter Wk., Edg. 96 CQ51
Walters Ho. SE17 161 DP79
Otto St.
Walters Rd. SE25 202 DS98
Walters Rd., Enf. 82 DW43
Walters Way SE23 183 DX86
Walters Yd., Brom. 204 EG96
Waltersmead, Ash. 232 CL117
Walterton Rd. W9 139 CZ70
Waltham Ave. NW9 118 CN58
Waltham Ave., Guil. 242 AV131
Waltham Ave., Hayes 155 BQ76
Waltham Clo., Brwd. 109 GC44
Bannister Dr.
Waltham Clo., Dart. 187 FG86
Waltham Clo., Orp. 206 EX102
Waltham Dr., Edg. 96 CN54
Waltham Gdns., Enf. 82 DW36
Waltham Pk. Way E17 101 EA53
Waltham Rd., Cars. 200 DD101
Waltham Rd., Cat. 236 DV122
Waltham Rd., Sthl. 156 BY76
Waltham Rd., Wal.Abb. 68 EE26
Waltham Rd., Wdf.Grn. 102 EL51
Waltham Way E4 101 DZ49
Walthamstow Ave. E4 101 DY50
Walthamstow Business Cen. E17 101 EC54
Waltheof Ave. N17 100 DR53
Waltheof Gdns. N17 100 DR53
Walton Ave., Har. 116 BZ64
Walton Ave., N.Mal. 199 CT98
Walton Ave., Sutt. 199 CY104
Walton Bri., Shep. 195 BS101
Walton Bri. Rd., Shep. 195 BR100
Walton Clo. E5 123 DX62
Orient Way
Walton Clo. NW2 119 CV61
Walton Clo. SW8 161 DL80
Walton Clo., Har. 117 CD56
Walton Ct., Wok. 227 BA116
Walton Cres., Har. 116 BZ63
Walton Dr. NW10 138 CR65
Mitchellbrook Way
Walton Dr., Har. 117 CD56
Walton Gdns. W3 138 CP71
Walton Gdns., Brwd. 109 GC43
Walton Gdns., Felt. 175 BT91
Walton Gdns., Wal.Abb. 67 EB33
Walton Gdns., Wem. 118 CL61
Walton Grn., Croy. 221 EB109
Walton La., Shep. 195 BR101
Walton La., Slou. 131 AL69
Walton La., Wey. 195 BP103
Walton Pk., Walt. 196 BX103
Walton Pk. La., Walt. 196 BX103
Walton Pl. SW3 276 D6
Walton Pl. SW3 160 DF76
Walton Rd. E12 125 EN63
Walton Rd. E13 144 EJ68
Walton Rd. N15 122 DT56
Walton Rd., E.Mol. 196 BY98

Waterloo Pl., Rich. 178 CL85
Sheen Rd.
Waterloo Rd. E6 144 EJ66
Waterloo Rd. E7 124 EF64
Wellington Rd.
Waterloo Rd. E10 123 EA59
Waterloo Rd. NW2 119 CU60
Waterloo Rd. SE1 278 D4
Waterloo Rd. SE1 141 DN74
Waterloo Rd., Brwd. 108 FW46
Waterloo Rd., Epsom 216 CR112
Waterloo Rd., Ilf. 103 EQ54
Waterloo Rd., Rom. 127 FE58
Waterloo Rd., Sutt. 218 DD106
Waterloo Rd., Uxb. 134 BJ67
Waterloo St., Grav. 191 GJ87
Waterloo Ter. N1 141 DP66
Waterlow Ct. NW11 120 DB59
Heath Clo.
Waterlow Rd. N19 121 DJ60
Waterlow Rd., Reig. 266 DC135
Waterman Clo., Wat. 75 BV44
Waterman St. SW15 159 CX83
Waterman Way E1 142 DV74
Waterman's Clo., Kings.T. 178 CL94
Woodside Rd.
Watermans Wk. SE16 143 DY74
Redriff Rd.
Watermans Way, Epp. 70 FA27
Watermark Way, Hert. 32 DT10
London Rd.
Watermead, Felt. 175 BS88
Watermead, Tad. 233 CV121
Watermead, Wok. 226 AT116
Watermead La., Cars. 200 DF101
Middleton Rd.
Watermead Rd. SE6 183 EB91
Watermead Way N17 122 DU55
Watermeadow La. SW6 160 DC82
Townmead Rd.
Watermen's Sq. SE20 182 DW94
Watermill Clo., Rich. 177 CJ90
Watermill La. N18 100 DS50
Watermill La., Hert. 32 DR06
Watermill La. N., Hert. 32 DQ06
Watermill Way SW19 200 DC95
Watermill Way, Felt. 176 BZ89
Watermint Quay N16 122 DU58
Waterperry La., Wok. 210 AT110
Waters Dr., Rick. 92 BL46
Waters Dr., Stai. 173 BF90
Waters Gdns., Dag. 126 FA64
Sterry Rd.
Waters Rd. SE6 184 EE90
Waters Rd., Kings.T. 198 CP96
Waters Sq., Kings.T. 198 CP97
Watersedge, Epsom 216 CQ105
Watersfield Way, Edg. 95 CK52
Waterside, Beck. 203 EA95
Rectory Rd.
Waterside, Berk. 38 AX19
Holliday St.
Waterside, Chesh. 54 AQ32
Waterside, Dart. 187 FE85
Waterside, H.Wyc. 110 AE56
Waterside, Horl. 268 DG146
Waterside, Kings L. 58 BN29
Waterside, St.Alb. 62 CL27
Waterside, Uxb. 134 BJ71
Waterside, Welw.G.C. 30 DA07
Waterside Clo. SE16 162 DU75
Bevington St.
Waterside Clo., Bark. 126 EU63
Waterside Clo., Nthlt. 136 BZ69
Waterside Clo., Rom. 106 FN52
Waterside Clo., Surb. 198 CL103
Culsac Rd.
Waterside Dr., Slou. 153 AZ75
Waterside Dr., Walt. 195 BU99
Waterside Ms., Guil. 242 AW132
Waterside Pl. NW1 140 DG67
Princess Rd.
Waterside Pl., Saw. 36 FA05
Waterside Pt. SW11 160 DE80
Waterside Rd., Guil. 242 AX131
Waterside Rd., Sthl. 156 CA76
Waterside Trd. Cen. W7 157 CE76
Trumpers Way
Waterside Way SW17 180 DC91
Waterside Way, Wok. 226 AV118
Winnington Way
Watersmeet, Harl. 51 EP19
Watersmeet Clo., Guil. 243 BA129
Cotts Wd. Dr.
Watersmeet Way SE28 146 EW72
Waterson Rd., Grays 171 GH77
Waterson St. E2 275 N2
Waterson St. E2 142 DS69
Watersplash Clo., Kings.T. 198 CL97
Watersplash La., Hayes 155 BU77
North Hyde Rd.
Watersplash La., Houns. 155 BV78
Watersplash Rd., Shep. 194 BN99
Waterton Ave., Grav. 191 GL87
Waterview Ho. E14 143 DY71
Carr St.
Waterway Rd., Lthd. 231 CG122
Waterworks Cotts., Brox. 49 DY22
Waterworks La. E5 123 DX61
Waterworks Rd. SW2 181 DM86
Waterworks Yd., Croy. 202 DQ104
Surrey St.
Watery La. SW20 199 CZ96
Watery La., Cher. 193 BD101
Watery La., Hat. 44 CS19
Watery La., H.Wyc. 110 AE55
Watery La., Nthlt. 136 BW68
Watery La., St.Alb. 61 CK28
Watery La., Sid. 186 EV93
Wates Way, Brwd. 108 FX46
Wates Way, Mitch. 200 DF100
Wateville Rd. N17 100 DQ53
Watford Bypass, Borwd. 95 CG45
Watford Clo. SW11 160 DE81
Petworth St.
Watford Clo., Guil. 243 AZ134
Watford Clo., Harl. 36 EW12
Watford Fld. Rd., Wat. 76 BW43
Watford Heath, Wat. 94 BX45
Watford Rd. E16 144 EG71
Watford Rd., Borwd. 77 CJ44
Watford Rd., Har. 117 CG59
Watford Rd., Kings L. 58 BN30
Watford Rd., Nthwd. 93 BT52
Watford Rd., Rad. 77 CE35
Watford Rd., Rick. 74 BM44
Watford Rd., St.Alb. 60 CA27
Watford Rd., Wem. 117 CG61
Watford Way NW4 119 CU56
Watford Way NW7 96 CS49
Wathen Rd., Dor. 263 CH135
Watkin Rd., Wem. 118 CP62
Watkinson Rd. N7 141 DM65
Watling Ave., Edg. 96 CQ53
Watling Clo., Hem.H. 40 BL17
Watling Ct. EC4 275 J9
Watling Ct., Borwd. 77 CK44
Watling Fm. Clo., Stan. 95 CJ45
Watford Bypass
Watling Gdns. NW2 139 CY65
Watling Knoll, Rad. 61 CF33
Watling St. EC4 275 H9
Watling St. EC4 142 DQ72
Watling St., Bexh. 167 FB84
Watling St., Borwd. 77 CK41
Watling St., Dart. 189 FR88
Watling St., Grav. 191 GG92
Watling St., Rad. 61 CF32
Watling St., St.Alb. 61 CE30
Watling St. Caravan Site (Travellers), St.Alb. 60 CC25
Watling Vw., St.Alb. 42 CC23
Watlings Clo., Croy. 203 DY100
Watlington Gro. SE26 183 DY92
Watlington Rd., Harl. 36 EX11
Watney Mkt. E1 142 DV72
Commercial Rd.
Watney Rd. SW14 158 CQ83
Watney St. E1 142 DV72
Watneys Rd., Mitch. 201 DK99
Watson Ave. E6 145 EN66
Watson Ave., Sutt. 199 CY104
Watson Clo. N16 122 DR64
Matthias Rd.
Watson Clo. SW19 180 DE93
Watson Clo., Grays 169 FU81
Watson Gdns., Rom. 106 FK54
Watson Rd., Dor. 262 CC137
Watson St. E13 144 EH68
Watsons Ave., St.Alb. 43 CF17
Watsons Ms. W1 272 C7
Watsons Rd. N22 99 DM53
Watson's St. SE8 163 EA80
Watsons Wk., St.Alb. 43 CE21
Watsons Yd. NW2 119 CT61
North Circular Rd.
Wattendon Rd., Ken. 235 DP116
Wattisfield Rd. E5 122 DW62
Wattleton Rd., Beac. 110 AJ55
Watts Bri. Rd., Erith 167 FF79
Reddy Rd.
Watts Clo. N15 122 DS57
Seaford Rd.
Watts Clo., Tad. 233 CX122
Watts La.
Watts Cres., Purf. 168 FQ77
Watts Fm. Par., Wok. 210 AT110
Barnmead
Watts Gro. E3 143 EB71
Watts La., Chis. 205 EP95
Watts La., Tad. 233 CX122
Watts La., Tedd. 177 CG92
Watts Mead, Tad. 233 CX122
Watts Rd., T.Ditt. 197 CG101
Watts St. E1 142 DV74
Watts Way SW7 276 A6
Wauthier Clo. N13 99 DP50
Wavel Ms. N8 121 DK56
Wavel Ms. NW6 140 DB66
Acol Rd.
Wavel Pl. SE26 182 DT91
Sydenham Hill
Wavell Clo. (Cheshunt), Wal.Cr. 67 DY27
Wavell Dr., Sid. 185 ES86
Wavell Gdns., Slou. 131 AM69
Wavell Rd., Beac. 89 AP54
Wavendene Ave., Egh. 173 BB94
Wavendon Ave. W4 158 CR78
Waveney, Hem.H. 40 BM15
Waveney Ave. SE15 162 DV84
Waveney Clo. E1 142 DU74
Kennet St.
Waverley Ave. E4 101 DZ49
Waverley Ave. E17 123 ED55
Waverley Ave., Ken. 236 DS116
Waverley Ave., Surb. 198 CP100
Waverley Ave., Sutt. 200 DB103
Waverley Ave., Twick. 176 BZ88
Waverley Ave., Wem. 118 CM64
Waverley Clo. E18 102 EJ53
Waverley Clo., Brom. 204 EK99
Waverley Clo., Hayes 155 BR77
Waverley Ct., Wok. 226 AY117
Waverley Cres. SE18 165 ER79
Waverley Cres., Rom. 106 FJ52
Waverley Dr., Cher. 193 BD104
Waverley Dr., Vir.W. 192 AU97
Waverley Gdns. E6 144 EL71
Oliver Gdns.
Waverley Gdns. NW10 138 CM68
Waverley Gdns., Bark. 145 ES68
Waverley Gdns., Grays 170 GA75
Waverley Gdns., Ilf. 103 EQ54
Waverley Gdns., Nthwd. 93 BU53
Waverley Gro. N3 119 CX55
Waverley Ind. Pk., Har. 117 CD55
Waverley Pl. N4 121 DP61
Adolphus Rd.
Waverley Pl. NW8 140 DD68
Waverley Pl., Lthd. 231 CH122
Church Rd.
Waverley Rd. E17 123 EC55
Waverley Rd. E18 102 EJ53
Waverley Rd. N8 121 DL58
Waverley Rd. N17 100 DV52
Waverley Rd. SE18 165 EQ78
Waverley Rd. SE25 202 DV98
Waverley Rd., Cob. 214 CB114
Waverley Rd., Enf. 81 DP42
Waverley Rd., Epsom 217 CU107
Waverley Rd., Har. 116 BY60
Waverley Rd., Lthd. 214 CB114
Waverley Rd., Rain. 147 FH69
Waverley Rd., St.Alb. 42 CC18
Waverley Rd., Slou. 131 AQ71
Waverley Rd., Sthl. 136 CA73
Waverley Rd., Wey. 212 BN106
Waverley Vill. N17 100 DT54
Waverley Wk. W2 140 DA71
Waverley Way, Cars. 218 DE107
Waverton Ho. E3 143 DZ67
Waverton Rd. SW18 180 DC87
Waverton St. W1 277 H2
Waverton St. W1 140 DG74
Wavertree Ct. SW2 181 DM88
Streatham Hill
Wavertree Rd. E18 102 EG54
Wavertree Rd. SW2 181 DL88
Waxlow Cres., Sthl. 136 CA72
Waxlow Rd. NW10 138 CQ68
Waxwell Clo., Pnr. 94 BX54
Waxwell La., Pnr. 94 BX54
Waxwell Ter. SE1 278 C5
Way, The, Reig. 250 DD133
Way Volante, Grav. 191 GL91
Waybourne Gro., Ruis. 115 BQ58
Waycross Rd., Upmin. 129 FS59
Waye Ave., Houns. 155 BU81
Wayfarer Rd., Nthlt. 136 BX69
Wayfarers Pk., Berk. 38 AT19
Wayfaring Grn., Grays 170 FZ78
Curling La.
Wayfield Link SE9 185 ER86
Wayford St. SW11 160 DE82
Wayland Ave. E8 122 DU64
Waylands, Swan. 207 FF98
Waylands Clo., Sev. 240 EY115
Knockholt Main Rd.
Waylands Mead, Beck. 203 EB95
Wayleave, The SE28 146 EV73
Oriole Way
Waylett Pl. SE27 181 DP90
Waylett Pl., Wem. 117 CK62
Wayman Ct. E8 142 DV65
Wayne Clo., Orp. 205 ET104
Wayneflete Twr. Ave., Esher 196 CA104
Waynflete Ave., Croy. 201 DP104
Waynflete Sq. W10 139 CX72
Waynflete St. SW18 180 DC89
Wayre St., Harl. 36 EW11
Wayside NW11 119 CY60
Wayside SW14 178 CQ85
Wayside, Kings L. 58 BH30
Wayside, Pot.B. 64 DD33
Wayside, Rad. 62 CL32
Porters Pk. Dr.
Wayside, The, Hem.H. 41 BQ21
Wayside Ave., Horn. 128 FK61
Wayside Ave. (Bushey), Wat. 77 CD44
Wayside Clo. N14 81 DJ44
Wayside Clo., Rom. 127 FF55
Wayside Commercial Est., Bark. 146 EU68
Wayside Ct., Twick. 177 CJ86
Wayside Ct., Wem. 118 CN62
Oakington Ave.
Wayside Ct., Wok. 226 AS116
Langmans Way
Wayside Gdns. SE9 185 EM91
Wayside Gro.
Wayside Gdns., Dag. 126 FA64
Wayside Gdns., Ger.Cr. 112 AX59
Wayside Gro. SE9 185 EM91
Wayside Ms., Ilf. 125 EN57
Gaysham Ave.
Wayville Rd., Dart. 188 FP87
Weald, The, Chis. 185 EM93
Weald Bri. Rd., Epp. 53 FD24
Weald Clo. SE16 162 DV78
Stevenson Cres.
Weald Clo., Brwd. 108 FU48
Weald Clo., Brom. 204 EL103
Weald Clo., Grav. 190 GE94
Weald Clo., Guil. 258 AY140
Station Rd.
Weald Hall La., Epp. 70 EW25
Weald La., Har. 95 CD54
Weald Pk. Way, Brwd. 108 FS47
Weald Ri., Har. 95 CF52
Weald Rd., Brwd. 106 FM46
Weald Rd., Sev. 257 FH129
Weald Rd., Uxb. 134 BN68
Weald Sq. E5 122 DV61
Rossington St.
Weald Way, Cat. 252 DS128
Weald Way, Hayes 135 BS69
Weald Way, Reig. 266 DC138
Weald Way, Rom. 127 FB58
Wealdstone Rd., Sutt. 199 CZ103
Wealdwood Gdns., Pnr. 94 CB51
Highbanks Rd.
Weale Rd. E4 101 ED48
Weall Grn., Wat. 59 BV32
Wear Pl. E2 142 DV69
Weardale Ave., Dart. 188 FQ89
Weardale Gdns., Enf. 82 DR39
Weardale Rd. SE13 163 ED84
Wearside Rd. SE13 183 EB85
Weasdale Ct., Wok. 226 AT116
Roundthorn Way
Weatherall Clo., Add. 212 BH106
Weatherhill Clo., Horl. 269 DM148
Weatherhill Common, Horl. 269 DM147
Weatherhill Rd., Horl. 269 DM148
Weatherley Clo. E3 143 DZ71
Weaver Clo. E6 145 EP72
Ferndale St.
Weaver St. E1 142 DU70
Weaver Wk. SE27 182 DQ91
Weavers Clo., Grav. 191 GG88
Weavers Clo., Islw. 157 CE84
Weavers La., Sev. 257 FJ121
Weavers Orchard, Grav. 190 GA93
Weavers Ter. SW6 160 DA79
Micklethwaite Rd.
Weavers Way NW1 141 DK66
Webb Clo., Chesh. 54 AP30
Webb Clo., Slou. 152 AX77
Webb Est. E5 122 DU59
Webb Gdns. E13 144 EG70
Kelland Rd.
Webb Pl. NW10 139 CT69
Old Oak La.
Webb Rd. SE3 164 EF79
Webb St. SE1 279 M7
Webb St. SE1 162 DS76
Webber Clo., Borwd. 77 CK44
Rodgers Clo.
Webber Clo., Erith 167 FH80
Webber Row SE1 278 E5
Webber Row SE1 161 DN75
Webber St. SE1 278 F5
Webber St. SE1 161 DN75
Webb's All., Sev. 257 FJ125
Webbs Rd. SW11 160 DF84
Webbs Rd., Hayes 135 BV69
Webbscroft Rd., Dag. 127 FB63
Webster Clo., Horn. 128 FK62
Latimer Dr.
Webster Clo., Lthd. 214 CB114
Webster Clo., Wal.Abb. 68 EG33
Webster Gdns. W5 137 CK74
Webster Rd. E11 123 EC62
Webster Rd. SE16 162 DU76
Websters Clo., Wok. 226 AV120
Wedderburn Rd. NW3 120 DD64
Wedderburn Rd., Bark. 145 ER67
Wedgewood Clo., Epp. 70 EU30
Wedgewood Clo., Nthwd. 93 BQ52
Wedgewood Dr., Harl. 52 EY15
Kiln La.
Wedgewood Wk. NW6 120 DB64
Lymington Rd.
Wedgewood Way SE19 182 DQ94
Wedgewoods, West. 238 EJ121
Westmore Rd.
Wedgwood Ms. W1 273 N9
Wedhey, Harl. 51 EQ15
Wedlake Clo., Horn. 128 FL60
Wedlake St. W10 139 CY70
Kensal Rd.
Wedmore Ave., Ilf. 103 EN53
Wedmore Gdns. N19 121 DK61
Wedmore Ms. N19 121 DK62
Wedmore St.
Wedmore Rd., Grnf. 137 CD69
Wedmore St. N19 121 DK62
Wednesbury Gdns., Rom. 106 FM52
Wednesbury Grn., Rom. 106 FM52
Wednesbury Gdns.
Wednesbury Rd., Rom. 106 FM52
Weech Rd. NW6 120 DA63
Weedington Rd. NW5 120 DG64
Weedon Clo., Ger.Cr. 90 AV53
Weedon La., Amer. 55 AN36
Weekes Dr., Slou. 131 AP74
Weekley Sq. SW11 160 DD83
Thomas Baines Rd.
Weigall Rd. SE12 164 EG84
Weighouse St. W1 272 G9
Weighouse St. W1 140 DG72
Weighton Rd. SE20 202 DV96
Weighton Rd., Har. 95 CD53
Weihurst Gdns., Sutt. 218 DD106
Weimar St. SW15 159 CY83
Weind, The, Epp. 85 ES36
Weir Est. SW12 181 DJ87
Weir Hall Ave. N18 100 DR51
Weir Hall Gdns. N18 100 DR50
Weir Hall Rd. N17 100 DR51
Weir Hall Rd. N18 100 DR50
Weir Pl., Stai. 193 BE95
Weir Rd. SW12 181 DJ87
Weir Rd. SW19 180 DB90
Weir Rd., Bex. 187 FB87
Weir Rd., Cher. 194 BH101
Weir Rd., Walt. 195 BU100
Weirdale Ave. N20 98 DF47
Weir's Pas. NW1 273 N2
Weir's Pas. NW1 141 DK69
Weiss Rd. SW15 159 CX83
Welbeck Ave., Brom. 184 EG91
Welbeck Ave., Hayes 135 BV70
Welbeck Ave., Sid. 186 EU88
Welbeck Clo. N12 98 DD50
Torrington Pk.
Welbeck Clo., Borwd. 78 CN41
Welbeck Clo., Epsom 217 CU108
Welbeck Clo., N.Mal. 199 CT99
Welbeck Rd. E6 144 EK69
Welbeck Rd., Barn. 80 DD44
Welbeck Rd., Cars. 200 DE102
Welbeck Rd., Har. 116 CB60
Welbeck Rd., Sutt. 200 DD103
Welbeck St. W1 272 G7
Welbeck St. W1 140 DG71
Welbeck Wk., Cars. 200 DE102
Welbeck Rd.
Welbeck Way W1 273 H8
Welbeck Way W1 141 DH72
Welby St. SE5 161 DP81
Welch Pl., Pnr. 94 BW53
Welclose St., St.Alb. 42 CC20
Welcomes Rd., Ken. 236 DQ116
Welcote Dr., Nthwd. 93 BR51
Weld Pl. N11 99 DH50
Welden, Slou. 132 AW72
Welders La., Beac. 90 AT52
Welders La., Ger.Cr. 90 AV52
Weldon Clo., Ruis. 135 BV65
Weldon Dr., W.Mol. 196 BZ98
Weldon Way, Red. 251 DK129
Welfare Rd. E15 144 EE66
Welford Clo. E5 123 DX62
Denton Way
Welford Pl. SW19 179 CY91
Welham Clo., Hat. 45 CW24
Welham Ct., Hat. 45 CW24
Dixons Hill Rd.
Welham Manor, Hat. 45 CW24
Welham Rd. SW16 181 DH93
Welham Rd. SW17 180 DG92
Welhouse Rd., Cars. 200 DE102
Well App., Barn. 79 CW43
Well Clo. SW16 181 DM91
Well Clo., Ruis. 116 BY62
Parkfield Cres.
Well Clo., Wok. 226 AW117
Well Cottage Clo. E11 124 EJ59
Well Ct. EC4 275 J9
Well Ct. SW16 181 DM91
Well Cft., Hem.H. 40 BH19
Gadebridge Rd.
Well End Rd., Borwd. 78 CQ37
Well Fm. Rd., Whyt. 236 DU119
Well Garth, Welw.G.C. 29 CY10
Well Gro. N20 98 DC45
Well Hall Par. SE9 165 EM84
Well Hall Rd.
Well Hall Rd. SE9 164 EL83
Well Hill, Orp. 225 FB107
Well Hill La., Orp. 225 FB108
Well Hill Rd., Sev. 225 FC107
Well La. SW14 178 CQ85
Well La., Brwd. 108 FT41
Well La., Harl. 35 EN14
Well La., Wok. 226 AW117
Well Pas. NW3 120 DD62
Well Path, Wok. 226 AW117
Well La.
Well Rd. NW3 120 DD62
Well Rd., Barn. 79 CW43
Well Rd., Pot.B. 64 DB28
Well Row, Hert. 47 DM17
Well St. E9 142 DW66
Well St. E15 144 EE65
Well Wk. NW3 120 DD63
Well Way, Epsom 232 CN115
Wellacre Rd., Har. 117 CH58
Wellan Clo., Sid. 186 EV85
Welland Clo., Slou. 153 BB79
Welland Gdns., Grnf. 137 CF68
Welland Ms. E1 142 DU74
Kennet St.
Welland St. SE10 163 EC79
Wellands, Hat. 45 CU16
Wellands Clo., Brom. 205 EM96
Wellbank, Maid. 130 AE70
Rectory Rd.
Wellbrook Rd., Orp. 223 EN105
Wellbury Ter., Hem.H. 41 BQ20
Wellclose Sq. E1 142 DU73
Wellclose St. E1 142 DU73
The Highway
Wellcome Ave., Dart. 168 FM84
Wellcome Chemical Wks., Dart. 188 FM85
Wellcroft Clo., Welw.G.C. 30 DA11
Wellcroft Rd., Slou. 131 AP74
Wellcroft Rd., Welw.G.C. 30 DA10
Welldon Cres., Har. 117 CE58
Wellen Ri., Hem.H. 40 BL23
Weller Clo., Amer. 55 AS37
Weller Rd., Amer. 55 AS37
Weller St. SE1 279 H4
Wellers Clo., West. 255 EQ127
Weller's Ct. N1 273 P1
Wellers Gro. (Cheshunt), Wal.Cr. 66 DU28
Wellesford Clo., Bans. 233 CZ117
Wellesley, Harl. 51 EN20
Wellesley Ave. W6 159 CV76
Wellesley Ave., Iver 153 BF76
Wellesley Ave., Nthwd. 93 BT50
Wellesley Ct. W9 140 DC69
Maida Vale
Wellesley Ct. Rd., Croy. 202 DR103
Wellesley Cres., Pot.B. 63 CY33
Wellesley Cres., Twick. 177 CE89
Wellesley Gro., Croy. 202 DR103
Wellesley Pk. Ms., Enf. 81 DP40
Wellesley Path, Slou. 152 AU75
Wellesley Rd.
Wellesley Pl. NW1 273 M3
Wellesley Rd. E11 124 EG57
Wellesley Rd. E17 123 EA58
Wellesley Rd. N22 99 DN54
Wellesley Rd. NW5 120 DG64
Wellesley Rd. W4 158 CN78
Wellesley Rd., Brwd. 108 FW46
Wellesley Rd., Croy. 202 DQ102
Wellesley Rd., Har. 117 CE57
Wellesley Rd., Ilf. 125 EP61
Wellesley Rd., Slou. 152 AU75
Wellesley Rd., Sutt. 218 DC107
Wellesley Rd., Twick. 177 CD90
Wellesley St. E1 143 DX71
Wellesley Ter. N1 275 J2
Wellesley Ter. N1 142 DQ69
Welley Ave., Stai. 152 AY84
Welley Rd., Stai. 172 AX85
Wellfield Ave. N10 121 DH55
Wellfield Clo., Hat. 45 CU17
Wellfield Rd. SW16 181 DL91
Wellfield Rd., Hat. 45 CU16
Wellfield Wk. SW16 181 DM92
Wellfields Rd., Loug. 85 EN41
Wellfit St. SE24 161 DP83
Hinton Rd.
Wellgarth, Grnf. 137 CH65
Wellgarth Rd. NW11 120 DB60
Wellhouse La., Barn. 79 CW42
Wellhouse La., Bet. 264 CQ138
Wellhouse Rd., Beck. 203 DZ98
Welling High St., Well. 166 EU83
Welling Way SE9 165 ER83
Welling Way, Well. 165 ES83
Wellings Ho., Hayes 135 BV74
Wellington Ave. E4 101 EA47
Wellington Ave. N9 100 DV48
Wellington Ave. N15 122 DT58
Wellington Ave., Houns. 176 CA85
Wellington Ave., Pnr. 94 BZ53
Wellington Ave., Sid. 186 EU86
Wellington Ave., Vir.W. 192 AV99
Wellington Ave., Wor.Pk. 199 CW104
Wellington Bldgs. SW1 161 DH78
Ebury Bri. Rd.
Wellington Clo. SE14 163 DX81
Rutts Ter.
Wellington Clo. W11 140 DA72
Ledbury Rd.
Wellington Clo., Dag. 147 FC66
Wellington Clo., Walt. 195 BT102
Hepworth Way
Wellington Cotts, Lthd. 245 BS129
Wellington Ct. NW8 140 DD68
Wellington Rd.
Wellington Ct., Stai. 174 BL87
Wellington Cres., N.Mal. 198 CQ97
Wellington Dr., Dag. 147 FC66
Wellington Dr., Pur. 219 DM110
Wellington Dr., Welw.G.C. 30 DC09
Wellington Gdns. SE7 164 EJ78
Wellington Gdns., Twick. 177 CD91
Wellington Hill, Loug. 84 EH37
Wellington Ms. SE7 164 EJ79
Wellington Gdns.
Wellington Ms. SE22 162 DU84
Peckham Rye
Wellington Pk. Ind. Est. NW2 119 CU60
Wellington Pas. E11 124 EG57
Wellington Rd.
Wellington Pl. N2 120 DE57
Great N. Rd.
Wellington Pl. NW8 272 A2
Wellington Pl. NW8 140 DD69
Wellington Pl., Brwd. 108 FW50
Wellington Pl., Brox. 48 DW23
Church La.
Wellington Rd. E6 145 EM67
Wellington Rd. E7 124 EF63
Wellington Rd. E10 123 DY60
Wellington Rd. E11 124 EG57
Wellington Rd. E17 123 DY55
Wellington Rd. NW8 140 DD68
Wellington Rd. NW10 139 CX69
Wellington Rd. SW19 180 DA89
Wellington Rd. W5 157 CJ76
Wellington Rd., Ashf. 174 BL92

Westcombe Hill SE3 164 EG79
Westcombe Hill SE10 164 EG78
Westcombe Lo. Dr., Hayes 135 BR71
Westcombe Pk. Rd. SE3 164 EE79
Westcoombe Ave. SW20 199 CT95
Westcote Ri., Ruis. 115 BQ59
Westcote Rd. SW16 181 DJ92
Westcott, Welw.G.C. 30 DD08
Westcott Ave., Grav. 191 GG90
Westcott Clo. N15 122 DT58
Ermine Rd.
Westcott Clo., Brom. 204 EL99
Ringmer Way
Westcott Clo., Croy. 221 EB109
Castle Hill Ave.
Westcott Cres. W7 137 CE72
Westcott Rd. SE17 161 DP79
Westcott Rd., Dor. 263 CE137
Westcott St., Dor. 262 CB137
Westcott Way, Sutt. 217 CW110
Westcott Way, Uxb. 134 BJ68
Westcourt, Sun. 195 BV96
Westcroft, Slou. 131 AP70
Westcroft Clo. NW2 119 CY63
Westcroft Clo., Enf. 82 DW38
Westcroft Ct., Brox. 49 EA19
Westcroft Gdns., Mord. 199 CZ97
Westcroft Rd., Cars. 218 DG105
Westcroft Rd., Wall. 218 DG105
Westcroft Sq. W6 159 CU77
Westcroft Way NW2 119 CY63
Westdale Pas. SE18 165 EP79
Westdale Rd.
Westdale Rd. SE18 165 EP79
Westdean Ave. SE12 184 EH88
Westdean Clo. SW18 180 DB85
Westdown Rd. E15 123 EC63
Westdown Rd. SE6 183 EA87
Wested La., Swan. 207 FG101
Westel Ho. W5 137 CJ73
Westerdale, Hem.H. 40 BL17
Westerdale Rd. SE10 164 EG78
Westerfield Rd. N15 122 DT57
Westerfolds Clo., Wok. 227 BC116
Westergate Rd. SE2 166 EY79
Westerham Ave. N9 100 DR48
Westerham Clo., Add. 212 BJ107
Westerham Clo., Sutt. 218 DA110
Westerham Dr., Sid. 186 EV86
Westerham Hill, West. 239 EN120
Westerham Rd. E10 123 EB58
Westerham Rd., Kes. 222 EK108
Westerham Rd., Oxt. 254 EF129
Westerham Rd., Sev. 256 FC123
Westerham Rd., West. 255 EM128
Westerley Cres. SE26 183 DZ92
Westerly Ware, Rich. 158 CN79
Kew Grn.
Western Ave. NW11 119 CX58
Western Ave. W3 138 CN70
Western Ave. W5 138 CM70
Western Ave., Brwd. 108 FW46
Western Ave., Cher. 194 BG97
Western Ave., Dag. 147 FC65
Western Ave., Egh. 193 BB97
Western Ave., Epp. 69 ET32
Western Ave., Grays 169 FT79
Western Ave., Grnf. 137 CE68
Western Ave., Nthlt. 136 BZ67
Western Ave., Rom. 106 FJ54
Western Ave., Ruis. 135 BQ65
Western Ave. (Denham), Uxb. 114 BJ63
Western Ave. (Ickenham), Uxb. 114 BK63
Western Clo., Cher. 194 BG97
Western Ave.
Western Ct. N3 98 DA51
Huntley Dr.
Western Cross Clo., Green. 189 FW86
Johnsons Way
Western Dr., H.Wyc. 110 AE58
Western Dr., Shep. 195 BR100
Western Gdns. W5 138 CN73
Western Gdns., Brwd. 108 FW47
Western Gateway E16 144 EG73
Western Ho. W5 138 CL69
Western La. SW12 180 DG87
Western Ms. W9 139 CZ70
Great Western Rd.
Western Par., Reig. 266 DB137
Prices La.
Western Pathway, Horn. 148 FJ65
Western Perimeter Rd., Houns. 154 BH83
Western Pl. SE16 162 DW75
Canon Beck Rd.
Western Rd. E13 144 EJ67
Western Rd. E17 123 EC57
Western Rd. N2 120 DF56
Western Rd. N22 99 DM54
Western Rd. NW10 138 CQ70
Western Rd. SW9 161 DN83
Western Rd. SW19 200 DD95
Western Rd. W5 137 CK73
Western Rd., Brwd. 108 FW47
Western Rd., Epp. 69 ES32
Western Rd., Mitch. 200 DE95
Western Rd., Rom. 127 FE57
Western Rd., Sthl. 156 BW77
Western Rd., Sutt. 218 DA106
Western Rd., Wal.Abb. 50 EE22
Western Ter. W6 159 CU78
Chiswick Mall
Western Trd. Est. NW10 138 CP70
Western Vw., Hayes 155 BT75
Station Rd.
Western Way SE28 165 ER76
Western Way, Barn. 80 DA44
Westernville Gdns., Ilf. 125 EQ59
Westferry Circ. E14 143 EA74
Westferry Rd. E14 163 EA75
Westfield, Ash. 232 CM118
Westfield, Dor. 261 BT143
Westfield, Harl. 51 ES16
Westfield, Hat. 46 DA23
Westfield, Loug. 84 EJ43
Westfield, Reig. 250 DB131
Westfield, Sev. 257 FJ122
Westfield, Welw.G.C. 30 DA08
Westfield Ave., S.Croy. 220 DR113
Westfield Ave., Wat. 76 BW37
Westfield Ave., Wok. 226 AY121
Westfield Clo. NW9 118 CQ55
Westfield Clo. SW10 160 DC80
Lots Rd.
Westfield Clo., Enf. 83 DY41
Westfield Clo., Grav. 191 GJ93
Westfield Clo., Sutt. 217 CZ105
Westfield Clo., Wal.Cr. 67 DY31
Westfield Common, Wok. 226 AY122
Westfield Ct., St.Alb. 43 CK17
Westfield Dr., Har. 117 CK56
Westfield Dr., Lthd. 230 CA122
Westfield Gdns., Har. 117 CK56
Westfield Gro., Wok. 226 AY120
Westfield La., Har. 117 CK56
Westfield La., Slou. 132 AX72
Westfield Par., Add. 212 BK110
Westfield Pk., Pnr. 94 BZ52
Westfield Rd. NW7 96 CR48
Westfield Rd. W13 137 CG74
Westfield Rd., Beac. 88 AJ54
Westfield Rd., Beck. 203 DZ96
Westfield Rd., Berk. 38 AS17
Westfield Rd., Bexh. 167 FC82
Westfield Rd., Croy. 201 DP103
Westfield Rd., Dag. 126 EY63
Westfield Rd., Guil. 242 AY130
Westfield Rd., Hert. 32 DQ07
Westfield Rd., Hodd. 49 DZ16
Westfield Rd., Mitch. 200 DF96
Westfield Rd., Slou. 131 AP70
Westfield Rd., Surb. 197 CK99
Westfield Rd., Sutt. 217 CZ105
Westfield Rd., Walt. 196 BY101
Westfield Rd., Wok. 226 AX122
Westfield St. SE18 164 EK76
Westfield Wk., Wal.Cr. 67 DZ31
Westfield Clo.
Westfield Way E1 143 DY70
Mile End Rd.
Westfield Way, Ruis. 115 BS62
Westfield Way, Wok. 226 AY122
Westfields SW13 159 CT83
Westfields, St.Alb. 42 CA22
Westfields Ave. SW13 158 CS83
Westfields Rd. W3 138 CP71
Westgate Clo., Epsom 232 CR115
Chalk La.
Westgate Ct., Wal.Cr. 83 DX35
Holmesdale
Westgate Cres., Slou. 131 AM73
Westgate Rd. SE25 202 DV98
Westgate Rd., Beck. 203 EC95
Westgate Rd., Dart. 188 FK86
Westgate St. E8 142 DV67
Westgate Ter. SW10 160 DB78
Westglade Ct., Har. 117 CK57
Westgrove La. SE10 163 EC81
Westhall Pk., Warl. 236 DW119
Westhall Rd., Warl. 236 DU118
Westhay Gdns. SW14 178 CP85
Westhill Clo., Grav. 191 GH88
Leith Pk. Rd.
Westhill Rd., Hodd. 49 DZ16
Westholm NW11 120 DB56
Westholme, Orp. 205 ES101
Westholme Gdns., Ruis. 115 BU60
Westhorne Ave. SE9 184 EK85
Westhorne Ave. SE12 184 EH86
Westhorpe Gdns. NW4 119 CW55
Westhorpe Rd. SW15 159 CW83
Westhumble St., Dor. 247 CH131
Westhurst Dr., Chis. 185 EP92
Westlake Clo. N13 99 DN48
Westlake Clo., Hayes 136 BY70
Lochan Clo.
Westlake Rd., Wem. 117 CK61
Westland Ave., Horn. 128 FL60
Westland Clo., Stai. 174 BL86
Westland Dr., Brom. 204 EF103
Westland Dr., Hat. 63 CY26
Westland Pl. N1 275 K2
Westland Pl. N1 142 DR69
Westland Rd., Wat. 75 BV40
Westlands Ave., Slou. 130 AJ72
Westlands Clo., Hayes 155 BU77
Granville Rd.
Westlands Clo., Slou. 130 AJ72
Westlands Ave.
Westlands Ct., Epsom 232 CQ115
Westlands Est., Hayes 155 BS76
Westlands Ter. SW12 181 DJ86
Gaskarth Rd.
Westlands Way, Oxt. 253 ED127
Westlea Ave., Wat. 76 BY36
Westlea Clo., Brox. 49 DZ24
Westlea Rd. W7 157 CG76
Westlea Rd., Brox. 49 DZ23
Westleas, Horl. 268 DE146
Westlees Clo., Dor. 263 CK139
Wildcroft Dr.
Westleigh Ave. SW15 179 CV85
Westleigh Ave., Couls. 234 DG116
Westleigh Dr., Brom. 204 EL95
Westleigh Gdns., Edg. 96 CN53
Westlinks, Wem. 137 CK69
Alperton La.
Westly Wd., Welw.G.C. 30 DA08
Westlyn Clo., Rain. 148 FJ69
Westmacott Dr., Felt. 175 BT87
Westmead SW15 179 CV87
Westmead, Wind. 151 AP83
Westmead, Wok. 226 AV117
Westmead Cor., Cars. 218 DE105
Colston Ave.
Westmead Dr., Red. 266 DG142
Westmead Rd., Sutt. 218 DD105
Westmeade Clo. (Cheshunt), Wal.Cr. 66 DV29
Westmede, Chig. 103 EQ51
Westmere Dr. NW7 96 CR48
Westmill Ct. N4 122 DQ61
Brownswood Rd.
Westminster Ave., Th.Hth. 201 DP96
Westminster Bri. SE1 278 A5
Westminster Bri. SE1 161 DM75
Westminster Bri. SW1 278 A5
Westminster Bri. SW1 161 DL75
Westminster Bri. Rd. SE1 278 C5
Westminster Bri. Rd. SE1 161 DM75
Westminster Cathedral Piazza SW1 277 K7
Westminster Clo., Felt. 175 BT88
Westmacott Dr.
Westminster Clo., Ilf. 103 ER54
Westminster Clo., Tedd. 177 CG92
Westminster Ct., St.Alb. 42 CC22
Westminster Dr. N13 99 DL50
Westminster Gdns. E4 102 EE46
Westminster Gdns., Bark. 145 ES68
Westminster Gdns., Ilf. 103 EQ54
Westminster Rd. N9 100 DV46
Westminster Rd. W7 137 CE74
Westminster Rd., Sutt. 200 DD103
Westmoat Clo., Beck. 183 EC94
Westmont Rd., Esher 197 CE103
Westmoor Gdns., Enf. 83 DX40
Westmoor Rd., Enf. 83 DX40
Westmoor St. SE7 164 EK76
Westmore Grn., West. 238 EJ121
Westmore Rd., West. 238 EJ121
Westmoreland Ave., Horn. 128 FJ57
Westmoreland Ave., Well. 165 ES83
Westmoreland Bldgs. EC1 142 DQ71
Bartholomew Clo.
Westmoreland Dr., Sutt. 218 DB109
Westmoreland Pl. SW1 161 DH78
Westmoreland Pl. W5 137 CK71
Mount Ave.
Westmoreland Rd. NW9 118 CM55
Westmoreland Rd. SE17 162 DR79
Westmoreland Rd. SW13 159 CT81
Westmoreland Rd., Brom. 204 EE99
Westmoreland St. W1 272 G7
Westmoreland St. W1 140 DG71
Westmoreland Ter. SW1 161 DH78
Westmoreland Wk. SE17 162 DR79
Westmoreland Rd.
Westmorland Clo. E12 124 EK61
Westmorland Clo., Epsom 216 CS110
Westmorland Clo., Twick. 177 CH86
Westmorland Rd. E17 123 EA58
Westmorland Rd., Har. 116 CB57
Westmorland Ter. SE20 182 DV94
Hawthorn Gro.
Westmorland Way, Mitch. 201 DK98
Westmount Ave., Amer. 55 AQ39
Westmount Rd. SE9 165 EM82
Westoe Rd. N9 100 DV47
Weston Ave., Add. 212 BG105
Weston Ave., Grays 169 FT78
Weston Ave., T.Ditt. 197 CE101
Weston Ave., W.Mol. 196 BY97
Weston Clo., Brwd. 109 GC45
Weston Clo., Couls. 235 DM120
Weston Clo., Pot.B. 63 CZ32
Mutton La.
Weston Ct. N4 122 DQ62
Queens Dr.
Weston Dr., Stan. 95 CH53
Weston Gdns., Islw. 157 CD81
Weston Gdns., Wok. 227 BE116
Weston Grn., Dag. 126 EZ63
Weston Grn., T.Ditt. 197 CE102
Weston Grn. Rd., Esher 197 CD102
Weston Grn. Rd., T.Ditt. 197 CE102
Weston Gro., Brom. 184 EF94
Weston Lea, Lthd. 245 BR125
Weston Pk. N8 121 DL58
Weston Pk., Kings.T. 198 CL96
Fairfield W.
Weston Pk., T.Ditt. 197 CE102
Weston Pk. Clo., T.Ditt. 197 CE102
Weston Pk.
Weston Ri. WC1 274 C1
Weston Ri. WC1 141 DM69
Weston Rd. W4 158 CQ76
Weston Rd., Brom. 184 EF94
Weston Rd., Dag. 126 EY63
Weston Rd., Enf. 82 DR39
Weston Rd., Epsom 216 CS111
Kiln La.
Weston Rd., Guil. 242 AU133
Weston Rd., Slou. 131 AM71
Weston Rd., T.Ditt. 197 CE102
Weston St. SE1 279 L4
Weston St. SE1 162 DR75
Weston Wk. E8 142 DV66
Mare St.
Weston Way, Wok. 227 BE116
Weston Yd., Guil. 260 BJ139
Westonfields, Guil. 260 BJ139
Westover Clo., Sutt. 218 DB109
Westover Hill NW3 120 DA61
Westover Rd. SW18 180 DC87
Westow Hill SE19 182 DS93
Westow St. SE19 182 DS93
Westpoint Trd. Est. W3 138 CN70
Westpole Ave., Barn. 80 DG42
Westport Rd. E13 144 EH70
Westport St. E1 143 DX72
Westray, Hem.H. 41 BQ22
Westridge Clo., Hem.H. 39 BF20
Westrow SW15 179 CW86
Westrow Dr., Bark. 145 ET66
Westrow Gdns., Ilf. 125 ET61
Westside NW4 97 CV54
Westvale Ms. W3 158 CS75
Westview, Hat. 45 CU16
Westview Clo. NW10 119 CT64
Westview Clo. W7 137 CE72
Westview Clo. W10 139 CW72
Westview Clo., Rain. 148 FJ69
Westview Clo., Red. 266 DE136
Pendleton Rd.
Westview Cres. N9 100 DS45
Westview Dr., Wdf.Grn. 102 EK54
Westview Rd., Warl. 236 DV119
Westville Rd. W12 159 CU75
Westville Rd., T.Ditt. 197 CG102
Westward Ho, Guil. 243 AZ132
Westward Rd. E4 101 DY50
Westward Way, Har. 118 CL58
Westway NW7 97 CU52
Westway SW20 199 CV97
Westway W2 140 DA71
Westway W9 140 DA71
Westway W10 139 CY72
Westway W12 139 CT73
Westway, Cat. 236 DR122
Westway, Guil. 242 AT132
Westway, Orp. 205 ER99
Westway Clo. SW20 199 CV97
Westway Gdns., Red. 251 DH131
Westways, Epsom 217 CT105
Westways, West. 255 EQ126
Westwell Clo., Orp. 206 EX102
Westwell Rd. SW16 181 DL93
Westwell Rd. App. SW16 181 DL93
Westwell Rd.
Westwick Clo., Hem.H. 41 BR21
Pancake La.
Westwick Gdns. W14 159 CX75
Westwick Gdns., Houns. 155 BV82
Westwick Pl., Wat. 60 BW34
Westwick Row, Hem.H. 41 BR20
Westwood Ave. SE19 202 DQ95
Westwood Ave., Add. 211 BF112
Westwood Ave., Brwd. 108 FU49
Westwood Ave., Har. 116 CB63
Westwood Clo., Amer. 72 AX39
Westwood Clo., Brom. 204 EK97
Westwood Clo., Esher 196 CC104
Westwood Clo., Pot.B. 64 DA30
Westwood Clo., Ruis. 115 BP58
Westwood Ct., Guil. 242 AT133
Hillcrest Rd.
Westwood Dr., Amer. 72 AX39
Westwood Gdns. SW13 159 CT83
Westwood Hill SE26 182 DU92
Westwood La., Sid. 186 EU85
Westwood La., Well. 165 ET83
Westwood Pk. SE23 182 DV87
Westwood Rd. E16 144 EH74
Westwood Rd. SW13 159 CT83
Westwood Rd., Couls. 235 DK118
Westwood Rd., Grav. 189 FX94
Westwood Rd., Ilf. 125 ET60
Westwood Way, Sev. 256 FF122
Wetheral Dr., Stan. 95 CJ53
Wetherby Clo., Nthlt. 136 CB65
Wetherby Gdns. SW5 160 DC77
Wetherby Ms. SW5 160 DB78
Bolton Gdns.
Wetherby Pl. SW7 160 DC77
Wetherby Rd., Borwd. 78 CL39
Wetherby Rd., Enf. 82 DQ39
Wetherby Way, Chess. 216 CL108
Wetherden St. E17 123 DZ59
Wethered Dr., Slou. 130 AH71
Wetherell Rd. E9 143 DX67
Wetherill Rd. N10 98 DG53
Wettern Clo., S.Croy. 220 DS110
Purley Oaks Rd.
Wetton Pl., Egh. 173 AZ92
High St.
Wexfenne Gdns., Wok. 228 BH116
Wexford Rd. SW12 180 DF87
Wexham Pk. La., Slou. 132 AW70
Wexham Rd., Slou. 152 AU75
Wexham St., Slou. 132 AV70
Wexham Wds., Slou. 132 AW71
Wey Ave., Cher. 194 BG97
Wey Barton, W.Byf. 212 BM113
Wey Clo., W.Byf. 212 BH113
Broadoaks Cres.
Wey Ct., Add. 212 BK109
Wey Ct., Epsom 216 CQ105
Wey La., Chesh. 54 AP32
Wey Manor Rd., Add. 212 BK109
Wey Meadows, Wey. 212 BL106
Wey Rd., Wey. 194 BM104
Wey Vw. Ct., Guil. 258 AW135
Walnut Tree Clo.
Weybank, Wok. 228 BL116
Weybourne Pl., S.Croy. 220 DR110
Weybourne St. SW18 180 DC89
Weybridge Business Pk., Add. 212 BL105
Weybridge Pk., Wey. 212 BN106
Weybridge Pt. SW11 160 DF82
Weybridge Rd., Add. 194 BK104
Weybridge Rd., Th.Hth. 201 DN98
Weybridge Rd., Wey. 194 BK104
Weybrook Dr., Guil. 243 BB129
Weydown Clo. SW19 179 CY88
Weydown Clo., Guil. 242 AU129
Weydown La., Guil. 242 AU129
Cumberland Ave.
Weyhill Rd. E1 142 DU72
Commercial Rd.
Weylands Clo., Walt. 196 BZ102
Weylands Pk., Wey. 213 BS107
Ellesmere Rd.
Weylea Ave., Guil. 243 BA131
Weylond Rd., Dag. 126 EY62
Weyman Rd. SE3 164 EJ81
Weymead Clo., Cher. 194 BJ102
Weymede, W.Byf. 212 BM112
Weymouth Ave. NW7 96 CS50
Weymouth Ave. W5 157 CJ76
Weymouth Clo. E6 145 EP72
Warwall
Weymouth Ct., Sutt. 218 DA108
Weymouth Ms. W1 273 H6
Weymouth Ms. W1 141 DH71
Weymouth Rd., Hayes 135 BS69
Weymouth St. W1 272 G7
Weymouth St. W1 140 DG71
Weymouth St., Hem.H. 40 BK24
Weymouth Ter. E2 142 DT68
Weymouth Wk., Stan. 95 CG51
Weyside Clo., W.Byf. 212 BM112
Weyside Gdns., Guil. 242 AW132
Weyside Rd., Guil. 242 AW133
Weystone Rd., Add. 212 BM105
Weybridge Rd.
Whadcote St. N4 121 DN61
Seven Sisters Rd.
Whalebone Ave., Rom. 126 EZ58
Whalebone Ct. EC2 275 L8
Whalebone Gro., Rom. 126 EZ58
Whalebone La. E15 144 EE66
West Ham La.
Whalebone La. N., Rom. 104 EY54
Whalebone La. S., Dag. 126 EZ59
Whalebone La. S., Rom. 126 EZ58
Whaley Rd., Pot.B. 64 DC33
Wharf La., Rick. 92 BL46
Wharf La., Twick. 177 CG88
Wharf La. (Ripley), Wok. 228 BK119
Mill La.
Wharf La. (Send), Wok. 227 BC123
Wharf Pl. E2 142 DU67
Wharf Rd. E15 143 ED67
Wharf Rd. N1 275 H1
Wharf Rd. N1 142 DQ68
Wharf Rd., Brwd. 108 FW48
Wharf Rd., Brox. 49 DZ23
Wharf Rd., Enf. 83 DY44
Wharf Rd., Grav. 191 GL86
Wharf Rd., Grays 170 FZ79
Wharf Rd., Guil. 242 AW134
Wharf Rd., Hem.H. 40 BH22
Wharf Rd., Stai. 172 AW87
Wharf Rd. Ind. Est., Enf. 83 DY44
Wharf Rd. S., Grays 170 FZ79
Wharf St. E16 144 EE71
Wharfdale Ct. E5 123 DX63
Rushmore Rd.
Wharfdale Rd. N1 141 DL68
Wharfedale, Hem.H. 40 BL17
Wharfedale Gdns., Th.Hth. 201 DM98
Wharfedale Rd., Dart. 188 FQ88
Wharfedale St. SW10 160 DB78
Coleherne Rd.
Wharfside Rd. E16 144 EE71
Wharley Hook, Harl. 51 ET18
Wharncliffe Dr., Sthl. 137 CD74
Wharncliffe Gdns. SE25 202 DS96
Wharncliffe Rd. SE25 202 DS96
Wharton Clo. NW10 138 CS65
Wharton Rd., Brom. 204 EH95
Wharton St. WC1 274 C3
Wharton St. WC1 141 DM69
Whateley Rd. SE20 183 DX94
Whateley Rd. SE22 182 DT85
Whateley Rd., Guil. 242 AV130
Whatley Ave. SW20 199 CX97
Whatman Rd. SE23 183 DX87
Whatmore Clo., Stai. 174 BG86
Wheat Clo., St.Alb. 43 CG16
Wheat Knoll, Ken. 236 DQ116
Wheat Leys, St.Alb. 43 CJ18
Wheatash Rd., Add. 194 BH103
Wheatbarn, Welw.G.C. 30 DB08
Wheatbutts, The (Eton Wick), Wind. 151 AM77
Wheatcroft (Cheshunt), Wal.Cr. 66 DV28
Wheatfield, Hat. 45 CV17
Crop Common
Wheatfield, Hem.H. 40 BK18
Wheatfield Way, Horl. 269 DH147
Wheatfield Way, Kings.T. 198 CL96
Wheatfields E6 145 EP72
Oxleas
Wheatfields, Enf. 83 DY40
Wheatfields, Harl. 36 EX09
Wheathill Rd. SE20 202 DV96
Wheatland Rd., Slou. 152 AW76
Wheatlands, Houns. 156 CA79
Wheatlands Rd. SW17 180 DG90
Stapleton Rd.
Wheatley Clo. NW4 97 CU54
Wheatley Clo., Green. 189 FU85
Steele Ave.
Wheatley Clo., Saw. 36 EW06
Wheatley Clo., Welw.G.C. 30 DA11
Wheatley Cres., Hayes 135 BU73
Wheatley Gdns. N9 100 DS47
Wheatley Rd., Islw. 157 CF83
Wheatley Rd., Welw.G.C. 30 DA10
Wheatley St. W1 272 G7
Wheatley Ter. Rd., Erith 167 FF79
Wheatley Way, Ger.Cr. 90 AY51
Wheatsheaf Clo., Cher. 211 BD107
Wheatsheaf Clo., Nthlt. 116 BY64
Wheatsheaf Clo., Wok. 226 AY116
Wheatsheaf Hill (Halstead), Sev. 224 EZ109
Wheatsheaf La. SW6 159 CW80
Wheatsheaf La. SW8 161 DL80
Wheatsheaf La., Stai. 173 BF94
Wheatsheaf Rd., Rom. 127 FF58
Wheatsheaf Rd., Ware 34 EK05
Wheatsheaf Ter. SW6 159 CZ80
Bishops Rd.
Wheatstone Clo., Mitch. 200 DE95
Wheatstone Rd. W10 139 CY71
Wheel Fm. Dr., Dag. 127 FC62
Wheeler Ave., H.Wyc. 88 AC47
Wheeler Ave., Oxt. 253 ED129
Wheeler Gdns. N1 141 DL67
Outram Pl.
Wheelers, Epp. 69 ET29
Wheelers Clo., Wal.Abb. 50 EE22
Wheelers Cross, Bark. 145 ER68
Wheelers Dr., Ruis. 115 BQ58
Wallington Clo.
Wheelers Fm. Gdns., Epp. 71 FB26
Wheelers La., Bet. 264 CP136
Wheelers La., Epsom 216 CP114
Wheelers La., Hem.H. 40 BL22
Wheelers La., Horl. 269 DN149
Wheelers Orchard, Ger.Cr. 90 AY51
Wheelwright Clo. (Bushey), Wat. 76 CB44
Ashfield Ave.
Wheelwright St. N7 141 DM66
Whelan Way, Wall. 201 DK104
Wheler St. E1 275 P5
Wheler St. E1 142 DT70
Whellock Rd. W4 158 CS76
Whenman Ave., Bex. 187 FC89
Whernside Clo. SE28 146 EW73
Wherwell Rd., Guil. 258 AW136
Whetstone Clo. N20 98 DD47
Oakleigh Rd. N.
Whetstone Pk. WC2 274 B8
Whetstone Rd. SE3 164 EJ82
Whewell Rd. N19 121 DL61
Whichcote Gdns., Chesh. 54 AR33
Pheasant Ri.
Whichcote St. SE1 278 B3
Whichert Clo., Beac. 88 AJ49
Whidborne Clo. SE8 163 EA82
Cliff Ter.
Whidborne St. WC1 274 A3
Whidborne St. WC1 141 DL69
Whielden Gate, Amer. 55 AL43
Whielden Grn., Amer. 55 AP40
Whielden La., Amer. 55 AL43
Whielden St., Amer. 55 AN41
Whiffins Orchard, Epp. 70 EX29
Whimbrel Clo. SE28 146 EW73
Whimbrel Way, Hayes 136 BX71
Willow Tree La.
Whinchat Rd. SE28 165 ER76
Whinfell Clo. SW16 181 DK92
Whinfell Way, Grav. 191 GM91
Whinneys Rd., H.Wyc. 88 AC52
Whinyates Rd. SE9 164 EL83
Whipley Clo., Guil. 243 BB129
Weybrook Dr.
Whippendell Clo., Orp. 206 EV95
Whippendell Hill, Kings L. 58 BJ30
Whippendell Rd., Wat. 75 BS43
Whippendell Way, Orp. 206 EV95
Whipps Cross Rd. E11 123 ED57
Whiskin St. EC1 274 F3
Whiskin St. EC1 141 DP69
Whisper Wd., Rick. 74 BH41

Whisperwood Clo., Har. 95 CE52
Whistler Gdns., Edg. 96 CM54
Whistler St. N5 121 DP64
Whistler Wk. SW10 160 DD80
World's End Est.
Whistlers Ave. SW11 160 DD80
Whiston Rd. E2 142 DT68
Whit Hern Ct., Wal.Cr. 66 DW30
College Rd.
Whitakers Way, Loug. 85 EM39
Whitbread Clo. N17 100 DU53
Whitbread Rd. SE4 163 DY84
Whitburn Rd. SE13 163 EB84
Whitby Ave. NW10 138 CP69
Whitby Clo., Green. 189 FU85
Whitby Clo., West. 238 EH119
Whitby Gdns. NW9 118 CN55
Whitby Gdns., Sutt. 200 DD103
Whitby Rd. SE18 165 EM77
Whitby Rd., Har. 116 CC62
Whitby Rd., Ruis. 115 BV62
Whitby Rd., Slou. 131 AQ73
Whitby Rd., Sutt. 200 DD103
Whitby St. E1 275 P4
Whitcher Clo. SE14 163 DY79
Chubworthy St.
Whitcher Pl. NW1 141 DJ66
Rochester Rd.
Whitchurch Ave., Edg. 96 CM52
Whitchurch Clo., Edg. 96 CM51
Whitchurch Gdns., Edg. 96 CM51
Whitchurch La., Edg. 95 CK52
Whitchurch Rd. W11 139 CX73
Whitchurch Rd., Rom. 106 FK49
Whitcomb Ct. WC2 141 DK73
Whitcomb St.
Whitcomb St. WC2 277 N1
Whitcomb St. WC2 141 DK73
White Acre NW9 96 CS54
White Adder Way E14 163 EB77
Spindrift Ave.
White Ave., Grav. 191 GF90
White Beam Way, Tad. 233 CU121
White Beams, St.Alb. 60 CB28
White Bear Pl. NW3 120 DD63
New End Sq.
White Butts Rd., Ruis. 116 BX62
White Ch. La. E1 142 DU72
White Ch. Pas. E1 142 DU72
White Ch. La.
White City Clo. W12 139 CW73
White City Est. W12 139 CV73
White City Rd. W12 139 CV73
White Clo., Slou. 131 AR74
White Conduit St. N1 141 DN68
Chapel Mkt.
White Craig Clo., Pnr. 94 CA50
White Down Rd., Dor. 261 BV139
White Friars, Sev. 256 FG127
White Gdns., Dag. 146 FA65
Sterry Rd.
White Gate Gdns., Har. 95 CF52
White Hall, Rom. 86 EV41
Market Pl.
White Hart Clo., Ch.St.G. 90 AU48
White Hart Clo., Sev. 257 FJ128
White Hart Ct. EC2 142 DS72
Bishopsgate
White Hart Ct., Wok. 228 BJ121
White Hart Dr., Hem.H. 40 BM21
White Hart La. N17 100 DQ52
White Hart La. N22 99 DN53
White Hart La. NW10 139 CT65
Church Rd.
White Hart La. SW13 158 CS82
White Hart La., Rom. 104 FA53
White Hart Meadows, Beac. 89 AL54
White Hart Meadows, Wok. 228 BJ121
White Hart Rd. SE18 165 ES77
White Hart Rd., Hem.H. 40 BN21
White Hart Rd., Slou. 151 AR76
White Hart Row, Cher. 194 BG101
Heriot Rd.
White Hart Slip, Brom. 204 EG96
White Hart St. SE11 278 E10
White Hart St. SE11 161 DN78
White Hart Wd., Sev. 257 FJ129
White Hart Yd. SE1 279 K3
White Heart Ave., Uxb. 135 BQ71
White Hedge Dr., St.Alb. 42 CC19
White Heron Ms., Tedd. 177 CF93
Park La.
White Hill, Chesh. 54 AQ31
White Hill, Couls. 234 DC124
White Hill, Hem.H. 39 BF21
White Hill, Rick. 92 BM51
White Hill, S.Croy. 220 DR109
St. Marys Rd.
White Hill, Welw. 29 CU05
White Hill Clo., Chesh. 54 AQ30
White Hill Rd., Berk. 38 AV21
White Hill Rd., Chesh. 56 AX26
White Hill Rd., Hem.H. 56 AY27
White Horse Dr., Epsom 216 CQ114
White Horse Hill, Chis. 185 EM91
White Horse La. E1 143 DX70
White Horse La., St.Alb. 61 CK26
White Horse La., Wok. 228 BJ121
White Horse Ms. SE1 278 E6
White Horse Rd. E1 143 DY72
White Horse Rd. E6 145 EM69
White Horse Rd., Wind. 151 AK83
White Horse St. W1 277 J3
White Horse St. W1 141 DH74
White Ho. Dr., Guil. 243 BB134
White Ho. Dr., Stan. 95 CJ49
White Ho. La., Guil. 242 AX129
Jacob's Well Rd.
White Ho. Rd., Sev. 256 FF130
White Kennet St. E1 275 N8
White Knights Rd., Wey. 213 BQ108
White Knobs Way, Cat. 252 DU125
Godstone Rd.
White La., Guil. 259 BC136
White La., Oxt. 238 EH124
White La., Warl. 238 EH123
White Lion Clo., Amer. 72 AU39
White Lion Ct. EC3 275 M9
White Lion Hill EC4 274 G10
White Lion Hill EC4 141 DP73
White Lion Hos., Hat. 45 CU17
Robin Hood La.
White Lion Rd., Amer. 72 AT38
White Lion Sq., Hat. 45 CU17
Robin Hood La.
White Lion St. N1 274 D1
White Lion St. N1 141 DN68
White Lion St., Hem.H. 40 BK24
White Lion Wk., Guil. 258 AX136
High St.
White Lion Yd. W1 273 H10
White Lo. SE19 181 DP94
White Lo. Clo. N2 120 DD58
White Lo. Clo., Sev. 257 FH123
Hitchen Hatch La.
White Lo. Clo., Sutt. 218 DC108
White Lo. Gdns., Red. 266 DG142
White Lyon Ct. EC2 142 DQ70
Fann St.
White Lyons Rd., Brwd. 108 FW47
White Oak Dr., Beck. 203 EC96
White Orchards N20 97 CZ45
White Orchards, Stan. 95 CG50
White Post Fld., Saw. 36 EX05
White Post Hill (Farningham), Dart. 208 FN101
White Post La. E9 143 DZ66
White Post La. SE13 163 EA83
White Post St. SE15 162 DW80
White Rd. E15 144 EE66
White Rd., Bet. 248 CN133
White Rd., Tad. 248 CN133
White Rose La., Wok. 227 AZ118
White Shack La., Rick. 74 BM37
White St., Sthl. 156 BX75
White Stubbs La., Brox. 48 DS22
White Stubbs La., Hert. 47 DK21
White Swan Ms. W4 158 CS79
Bennett St.
White Way, Lthd. 246 CB126
White Wd. Rd., Berk. 38 AU19
Whiteadder Way E14 163 EB77
Taeping St.
Whitear Wk. E15 143 ED65
Whitebarn La., Dag. 146 FA67
Whitebeam Ave., Brom. 205 EN101
Whitebeam Clo. SW9 161 DM80
Clapham Rd.
Whitebeam Clo., Wal.Cr. 66 DS26
The Laurels
Whitebeam Dr., Reig. 266 DB137
Whitebeam Dr., S.Ock. 149 FW69
Brandon Gros. Ave.
Whitebeam Twr. E17 123 DY55
Whitebeams, Hat. 45 CU21
Whiteberry Rd., Dor. 262 CB143
Whitebridge Clo., Felt. 175 BT86
Whitebroom Rd., Hem.H. 39 BE18
Whitechapel High St. E1 142 DT72
Whitechapel Rd. E1 142 DU71
Whitecote Rd., Sthl. 136 CC72
Whitecroft, Horl. 269 DH147
Woodhayes
Whitecroft, St.Alb. 43 CH23
Whitecroft, Swan. 207 FE96
Whitecroft Clo., Beck. 203 ED98
Whitecroft Way, Beck. 203 EC99
Whitecross Pl. EC2 275 L6
Whitecross St. EC1 275 J4
Whitecross St. EC1 142 DQ70
Whitecross St. EC2 275 J6
Whitecross St. EC2 142 DQ71
Whitefield Ave. NW2 119 CW59
Whitefield Ave., Pur. 235 DN116
Whitefield Clo. SW15 179 CY86
Whitefield Clo., Orp. 206 EW97
Whitefields Rd. (Cheshunt), Wal.Cr. 66 DW28
Whitefoot La., Brom. 183 EC91
Whitefoot Ter., Brom. 184 EE90
Whiteford Rd., Slou. 132 AS71
Whitefriars Ave., Har. 95 CE54
Whitefriars Dr., Har. 95 CD54
Whitefriars Ave.
Whitefriars St. EC4 274 E9
Whitefriars St. EC4 141 DN72
Whitegate Way, Tad. 233 CV120
Whitegates, Whyt. 236 DU119
Court Bushes Rd.
Whitegates, Wok. 227 AZ120
Loop Rd.
Whitegates Clo., Rick. 74 BN42
Whitehall SW1 277 P2
Whitehall SW1 141 DL74
Whitehall Clo., Chig. 104 EU47
Whitehall Clo., Uxb. 134 BJ67
Whitehall Clo., Wal.Abb. 50 EE22
Whitehall Ct. SW1 278 A3
Whitehall Ct. SW1 141 DL74
Whitehall Cres., Chess. 215 CK106
Whitehall Est., Harl. 50 EL16
Whitehall Fm. La., Vir.W. 192 AY97
Whitehall Gdns. E4 101 ED46
Whitehall Gdns. SW1 277 P3
Whitehall Gdns. W3 138 CN74
Whitehall Gdns. W4 158 CP79
Whitehall La., Buck.H. 102 EG47
Whitehall La., Egh. 173 AZ94
Whitehall La., Erith 167 FF82
Whitehall La., Grays 170 GC78
Whitehall La., Reig. 265 CZ138
Whitehall La., Stai. 173 BA86
Whitehall Pk. N19 121 DJ60
Whitehall Pk. Rd. W4 158 CP79
Whitehall Pl. E7 124 EG64
Station Rd.
Whitehall Pl. SW1 277 P3
Whitehall Pl. SW1 141 DL74
Whitehall Pl., Wall. 219 DH105
Bernard Rd.
Whitehall Rd. E4 102 EE47
Whitehall Rd. W7 157 CG75
Whitehall Rd., Brom. 204 EK99
Whitehall Rd., Grays 170 GC77
Whitehall Rd., Har. 117 CE59
Whitehall Rd., Th.Hth. 201 DN100
Whitehall Rd., Uxb. 134 BK67
Whitehall Rd., Wdf.Grn. 102 EF47
Whitehall St. N17 100 DT52
Whitehands Clo., Hodd. 49 DZ17
Whitehart Rd., Orp. 206 EU101
Whitehaven, Slou. 132 AT73
Whitehaven Clo., Brom. 204 EG98
Whitehaven St. NW8 272 B5
Whitehead Clo. N18 100 DR50
Whitehead Clo. SW18 180 DC87
Whitehead Clo., Dart. 188 FJ90
Whitehead's Gro. SW3 276 C10
Whitehead's Gro. SW3 160 DE78
Whiteheath Ave., Ruis. 115 BQ59
Whitehill, Berk. 38 AW18
Whitehill Clo., Berk. 38 AX18
Whitehill
Whitehill Ct., Berk. 38 AX18
Whitehill
Whitehill La., Grav. 191 GJ89
Whitehill La., Red. 252 DR127
Whitehill La., Wok. 229 BQ123
Whitehill Par., Grav. 191 GJ90
Whitehill Pl., Vir.W. 192 AY99
Sandhills La.
Whitehill Rd., Dart. 187 FG85
Whitehill Rd., Grav. 191 GJ89
Whitehill Rd. (Hook Grn.), Grav. 189 FX94
Whitehill Rd., Long. 209 FX96
Whitehills Rd., Loug. 85 EN41
Whitehorn Gdns., Croy. 202 DV103
Whitehorse La. SE25 202 DR98
Whitehorse Rd., Croy. 202 DQ101
Whitehorse Rd., Th.Hth. 202 DR98
Whitehouse Ave., Borwd. 78 CP41
Whitehouse Clo., Ger.Cr. 90 AY52
Whitehouse Clo., H.Wyc. 88 AE54
Whitehouse La., Abb.L. 59 BV26
Whitehouse La., Enf. 82 DQ39
Brigadier Hill
Whitehouse La., H.Wyc. 88 AE54
Whitehouse Way N14 99 DH47
Whitehouse Way, Iver 133 BD69
Whitelands Ave., Rick. 73 BB41
Whitelands Way, Rom. 106 FK53
Whiteleaf Rd., Hem.H. 40 BJ23
Whiteledges W13 137 CJ72
Whitelegg Rd. E13 144 EF68
Whiteley, Wind. 151 AL80
Whiteley Rd. SE19 182 DR92
Whiteleys Cotts. W14 159 CZ77
Whiteleys Way, Felt. 176 CA90
Whitemore Rd., Guil. 242 AX130
Whiteoak Gdns., Sid. 185 ET87
Whiteoaks, Bans. 218 DB113
Whiteoaks La., Grnf. 137 CD68
Whitepit La., H.Wyc. 110 AC56
Whitepost Hill, Red. 250 DE134
Whites Ave., Ilf. 125 ES58
Whites Clo., Green. 189 FW86
Whites Dr., Brom. 204 EF101
Whites Grds. SE1 279 N5
Whites Grds. SE1 162 DS75
Whites Grds. Est. SE1 279 N4
Whites La., Slou. 152 AV79
White's Row E1 275 P7
White's Row E1 142 DT71
White's Sq. SW4 161 DK84
Nelson's Row
Whitestile Rd., Brent. 157 CJ78
Whitestone La. NW3 120 DC62
Heath St.
Whitestone Wk. NW3 120 DC62
North End Way
Whitestone Wk., Hem.H. 40 BG17
Fennycroft Rd.
Whitethorn, Welw.G.C. 30 DB10
Whitethorn Ave., Couls. 234 DG115
Whitethorn Ave., West Dr. 134 BL73
Whitethorn Gdns., Enf. 82 DR43
Whitethorn Gdns., Horn. 128 FJ58
Whitethorn Pl., West Dr. 134 BM74
Whitethorn Ave.
Whitethorn St. E3 143 EA70
Whitewaits, Harl. 35 ES14
Whiteways Ct., Stai. 174 BH94
Pavilion Gdns.
Whitewebbs La., Enf. 82 DS35
Whitewebbs Rd.
Whitewebbs Rd., Enf. 81 DP35
Whitewebbs Way, Orp. 205 ET95
Whitewood Cotts., West. 238 EJ120
Whitfield Clo., Guil. 242 AU131
Stoughton Rd.
Whitfield Pl. W1 273 K5
Whitfield Rd. E6 144 EJ66
Whitfield Rd. SE3 163 ED81
Whitfield Rd., Bexh. 166 EZ80
Whitfield St. W1 273 K5
Whitfield St. W1 141 DJ70
Whitfield Way, Rick. 91 BF46
Whitford Gdns., Mitch. 200 DF97
Whitgift Ave., S.Croy. 219 DP106
Whitgift St. SE11 278 B8
Whitgift St. SE11 161 DM77
Whitgift St., Croy. 202 DQ104
High St.
Whiting Ave., Bark. 145 EP66
Whitings, Ilf. 125 ER57
Whitings Rd., Barn. 79 CW43
Whitings Way E6 145 EN71
Whitland Rd., Cars. 200 DD102
Whitlars Dr., Kings L. 58 BM28
Whitley Clo., Abb.L. 59 BU32
Langley La.
Whitley Clo., Stai. 174 BL86
Whitley Rd. N17 100 DS54
Whitley Rd., Hodd. 49 EB15
Whitlock Dr. SW19 179 CY87
Whitman Rd. E3 143 DY70
Whitmead Clo., S.Croy. 220 DS107
Whitmoor Common, Guil. 242 AV127
Whitmoor La., Guil. 242 AX126
Whitmore Ave., Rom. 106 FL54
Whitmore Clo. N11 99 DH50
Whitmore Est. N1 142 DS68
Nuttall St.
Whitmore Gdns. NW10 139 CW68
Whitmore Rd. N1 142 DS67
Whitmore Rd., Beck. 203 DZ97
Whitmore Rd., Har. 116 CC59
Whitmores Clo., Epsom 232 CQ115
Whitnell Way SW15 179 CW85
Whitney Ave., Ilf. 124 EK56
Whitney Rd. E10 123 EA59
Whitney Wk., Sid. 186 EY93
Whitstable Clo., Beck. 203 DZ95
Whitstable Clo., Ruis. 115 BS61
Chichester Ave.
Whitstable Ho. W10 139 CX72
Silchester Rd.
Whitta Rd. E12 124 EK63
Whittaker Ave., Rich. 177 CK85
Hill St.
Whittaker Rd. E6 144 EK66
Whittaker Rd., Slou. 131 AK70
Whittaker Rd., Sutt. 199 CZ104
Whittaker St. SW1 276 F9
Whittaker St. SW1 160 DG77
Whittaker Way SE1 162 DU77
Lynton Rd.
Whittell Gdns. SE26 182 DW90
Whittenham Clo., Slou. 132 AU74
Whittingstall Rd. SW6 159 CZ81
Whittingstall Rd., Hodd. 49 EB15
Whittington Ave. EC3 275 M9
Whittington Ave., Hayes 135 BT71
Whittington Ct. N2 120 DF57
Whittington Rd. N22 99 DL52
Whittington Rd., Brwd. 109 GC44
Whittington Way, Pnr. 116 BY57
Whittle Clo., Sthl. 136 CB72
Whittle Parkway, Slou. 131 AK72
Whittle Rd., Houns. 156 BW80
Whittlebury Clo., Cars. 218 DF108
Whittlesea Clo., Har. 94 CC52
Whittlesea Rd.
Whittlesea Path, Har. 94 CC53
Whittlesea Rd., Har. 94 CC53
Whittlesey St. SE1 278 E3
Whitton Ave. E., Grnf. 117 CE64
Whitton Ave. W., Grnf. 117 CD64
Whitton Ave. W., Nthlt. 116 CB64
Whitton Clo., Grnf. 137 CH65
Whitton Dene, Houns. 176 CB85
Whitton Dene, Islw. 177 CD85
Whitton Dr., Grnf. 137 CG65
Whitton Manor Rd., Islw. 176 CC85
Whitton Rd., Houns. 156 CB84
Whitton Rd., Twick. 177 CE86
Whitton Wk. E3 143 EA69
Whitton Waye, Houns. 176 CA86
Whitwell Rd. E13 144 EG69
Whitwell Rd., Wat. 76 BX35
Whitworth Pl. SE18 165 EP77
Whitworth Rd. SE18 165 EN79
Whitworth Rd. SE25 202 DS97
Whitworth St. SE10 164 EE78
Whopshott Ave., Wok. 226 AW116
Whopshott Clo., Wok. 226 AW116
Whopshott Dr., Wok. 226 AW116
Whorlton Rd. SE15 162 DV83
Whybridge Clo., Rain. 147 FE67
Whymark Ave. N22 121 DN55
Whytebeam Vw., Whyt. 236 DT118
Regents Clo.
Whytecliffe Rd. N., Pur. 219 DP111
Whytecliffe Rd. S., Pur. 219 DN111
Whytecroft, Houns. 156 BX80
Whyteleafe Hill, Whyt. 236 DS120
Whyteleafe Rd., Cat. 236 DS122
Whyteville Rd. E7 144 EH65
Whichling Clo., Orp. 206 EX102
Wick, The, Hert. 31 DP06
Wick La. E3 143 DZ66
Wick La., Egh. 172 AT92
Wick Rd. E9 143 DX65
Wick Rd., Egh. 192 AU95
Wick Rd., Tedd. 177 CH94
Wick Sq. E9 143 DZ65
Eastway
Wick Way, St.Alb. 43 CH17
Marshalswick La.
Wickenden Rd., Sev. 257 FJ122
Wicker St. E1 142 DV72
Burslem St.
Wickers Oake SE19 182 DT91
Wickersley Rd. SW11 160 DG82
Wicket, The, Croy. 221 EA106
Wicket Rd., Grnf. 137 CG69
Wickets, The, Ashf. 174 BL91
Woodthorpe Rd.
Wickets Way, Ilf. 103 ET51
Wickford Clo., Rom. 106 FM50
Wickford Dr.
Wickford Dr., Rom. 106 FM50
Wickford St. E1 142 DW70
Wickford Way E17 123 DX56
Wickham Ave., Croy. 203 DY103
Wickham Ave., Sutt. 217 CW106
Wickham Chase, W.Wick. 203 ED102
Wickham Clo., Enf. 82 DV41
Wickham Clo., Horl. 268 DF147
Wickham Clo., N.Mal. 199 CT99
Wickham Clo., Uxb. 92 BK53
Wickham Ct., St.Alb. 43 CH18
Wickham Ct. Rd., W.Wick. 203 EC103
Wickham Cres., W.Wick. 203 EC103
Wickham Fld., Sev. 241 FF116
Wickham Gdns. SE4 163 DZ83
Wickham Ho. E1 142 DW71
Jamaica St.
Wickham La. SE2 166 EU78
Wickham La., Egh. 173 BA94
Wickham La., Well. 166 EU78
Wickham Ms. SE4 163 DZ82
Wickham Rd. E4 101 EC52
Wickham Rd. SE4 163 DZ83
Wickham Rd., Beck. 203 EB96
Wickham Rd., Croy. 202 DW103
Wickham Rd., Grays 171 GJ75
Wickham Rd., Har. 95 CD54
Wickham St. SE11 278 B10
Wickham St. SE11 161 DM78
Wickham St., Well. 165 ES82
Wickham Way, Beck. 203 EC98
Wicklands Rd. (Hunsdon), Ware 34 EK07
Wickliffe Ave. N3 97 CY54
Wickliffe Gdns., Wem. 118 CP61
Wicklow St. WC1 274 B2
Wicklow St. WC1 141 DM69
Wicks Clo. SE9 184 EK91
Wicksteed Clo., Bex. 187 FD90
Wicksteed Ho., Brent. 158 CM78
Wickwood St. SE5 161 DP82
Wid Clo., Brwd. 109 GD43
Widbury Gdns., Ware 33 DZ06
Widbury Hill, Ware 33 DZ06
Widdecombe Ave., Har. 116 BY61
Widdenham Rd. N7 121 DM63
Widdin St. E15 143 ED66
Wide Way, Mitch. 201 DK97
Widecombe Clo., Rom. 106 FK53
Widecombe Gdns., Ilf. 124 EL56
Widecombe Rd. SE9 184 EL90
Widecombe Way N2 120 DD57
Widecroft Rd., Iver 133 BE72
Widegate St. E1 275 N7
Widenham Clo., Pnr. 116 BW57
Bridle Rd.
Widford Rd. (Hunsdon), Ware 34 EK05
Widford Rd., Welw.G.C. 30 DB09
Widgeon Clo. E16 144 EH72
Maplin Rd.
Widgeon Way, Wat. 76 BY37
Widley Rd. W9 140 DA69
Widmoor, H.Wyc. 110 AE60
Widmore Dr., Hem.H. 40 BN18
Widmore Lo. Rd., Brom. 204 EK96
Widmore Rd., Brom. 204 EG96
Widmore Rd., Uxb. 135 BP70
Widworthy Hayes, Brwd. 109 GB46
Wieland Rd., Nthwd. 93 BU52
Wigan Ho. E5 122 DV60
Warwick Gro.
Wigeon Path SE28 165 ER76
Wigeon Way, Hayes 136 BX71
Willow Tree La.
Wiggenhall Rd., Wat. 75 BV43
Wiggie La., Red. 250 DG132
Wiggington Ave., Wem. 138 CP65
Wiggins Mead NW9 97 CT52
Wigham Ho., Bark. 145 EQ66
Wightman Rd. N4 121 DN56
Wightman Rd. N8 121 DN56
Wigley Bush La., Brwd. 108 FS47
Wigley Rd., Felt. 176 BX89
Wigmore Pl. W1 273 H8
Wigmore Pl. W1 141 DH72
Wigmore Rd., Cars. 200 DD103
Wigmore St. W1 272 F9
Wigmore St. W1 140 DG72
Wigmore Wk., Cars. 200 DD103
Wigmore Rd.
Wigmores N., Welw.G.C. 29 CX08
Wigmores S., Welw.G.C. 29 CX09
Wigram Rd. E11 124 EJ58
Wigram Sq. E17 101 ED54
Wigston Clo. N18 100 DS50
Wigston Rd. E13 144 EH70
Wigton Gdns., Stan. 96 CL53
Wigton Pl. SE11 161 DN78
Milverton St.
Wigton Rd. E17 101 DZ53
Wigton Rd., Rom. 106 FL49
Wigton Way, Rom. 106 FL49
Wilberforce Rd. N4 121 DP61
Wilberforce Rd. NW9 119 CU58
Wilberforce Way SW19 179 CX93
Wilberforce Way, Grav. 191 GK92
Wilbraham Pl. SW1 276 E8
Wilbraham Pl. SW1 160 DF77
Wilbury Ave., Sutt. 217 CZ110
Wilbury Rd., Wok. 226 AX117
Wilbury Way N18 100 DR50
Wilby Ms. W11 139 CZ73
Wilcot Ave., Wat. 94 BY45
Wilcox Clo. SW8 161 DL80
Wilcox Clo., Borwd. 78 CQ39
Wilcox Gdns., Shep. 194 BM97
Wilcox Pl. SW1 277 L7
Wilcox Rd. SW8 161 DL80
Wilcox Rd., Sutt. 218 DB105
Wilcox Rd., Tedd. 177 CD91
Wild Acres, W.Byf. 212 BJ111
Wild Ct. WC2 274 B8
Wild Ct. WC2 141 DM72
Wild Goose Dr. SE14 162 DW81
Wild Grn. N., Slou. 153 BA77
Verney Rd.
Wild Grn. S., Slou. 153 BA77
Swabey Rd.
Wild Hatch NW11 120 DA58
Wild Oaks Clo., Nthwd. 93 BT51
Wild St. WC2 274 A9
Wild St. WC2 141 DL72
Wildbank Ct., Wok. 227 AZ118
White Rose La.
Wildcroft Dr., Dor. 263 CK139
Wildcroft Gdns., Edg. 95 CK51
Wildcroft Rd. SW15 179 CW87
Wilde Clo. E8 142 DU67
Wilde Clo., Til. 171 GJ82
Coleridge Rd.
Wilde Pl. N13 99 DP51
Medesenge Way
Wilde Pl. SW18 180 DD87
Heathfield Rd.
Wilder Clo., Ruis. 115 BV60
Wilderness, The, Berk. 38 AW19
Wilderness, The, Hmptn. 176 CB91
Park Rd.
Wilderness Rd., Chis. 185 EP94
Wilderness Rd., Guil. 258 AT135
Wilderness Rd., Oxt. 254 EE130
Wildernesse Ave., Sev. 257 FL122
Wildernesse Mt., Sev. 257 FK122
Wilders Clo., Wok. 226 AW118
Wilderton Rd. N16 122 DS59
Wildfell Rd. SE6 183 EB87
Wildhill Rd., Hat. 45 CY23
Wild's Rents SE1 279 M6
Wild's Rents SE1 162 DS76
Wildwood NW3 120 DC60
Wildwood, Nthwd. 93 BR51
Wildwood Ave., St.Alb. 60 BZ30
Wildwood Clo. SE12 184 EF87
Wildwood Clo., Lthd. 245 BT125
Wildwood Clo., Wok. 227 BF115
Wildwood Ct., Ken. 236 DR115
Wildwood Gro. NW3 120 DC60
North End Way
Wildwood Ri. NW11 120 DC60
Wildwood Rd. NW11 120 DB58
Wilford Clo., Enf. 82 DR41
Wilford Clo., Nthwd. 93 BR52
Wilford Rd., Slou. 152 AY77
Wilfred Ave., Rain. 147 FG71
Wilfred Owen Clo. SW19 180 DC93
Tennyson Rd.
Wilfred St. SW1 277 K6
Wilfred St. SW1 161 DJ76
Wilfred St., Grav. 191 GH86
Wilfred St., Wok. 226 AX118
Wilfrid Gdns. W3 138 CQ71
Wilhelmina Ave., Couls. 235 DJ119
Wilkes Rd., Brent. 158 CL79
Albany Rd.
Wilkes Rd., Brwd. 109 GD43
Wilkes St. E1 142 DT71
Wilkie Way SE22 182 DU88
Lordship La.
Wilkin St. NW5 141 DH65
Wilkin St. Ms. NW5 141 DH65
Wilkin St.
Wilkins Clo., Hayes 155 BT78

Wilkins Clo., Mitch. 200 DE95
Wilkins Grn. La., Hat. 44 CR19
Wilkins Grn. La., St.Alb. 44 CP20
Wilkins Gro., Welw.G.C. 29 CX10
Longcroft La.
Wilkins Way, West. 240 EV124
Wilkinson Clo., Dart. 168 FM84
Henderson Dr.
Wilkinson Rd. E16 144 EJ72
Wilkinson St. SW8 161 DM80
Wilkinson Way W4 158 CR75
Southfield Rd.
Wilks Ave., Dart. 188 FM89
Powder Mill La.
Wilks Gdns., Croy. 203 DY102
Wilks Pl. N1 275 N1
Will Crooks Gdns. SE9 164 EJ84
Willan Rd. N17 100 DR54
Willan Wall E16 144 EF73
Victoria Dock Rd.
Willard St. SW8 161 DH83
Willcocks Clo., Chess. 198 CL104
Willcott Rd. W3 138 CP74
Willen Fld. Rd. NW10 138 CQ68
Abbey Rd.
Willenhall Ave., Barn. 80 DC44
Willenhall Dr., Hayes 135 BS73
Willenhall Rd. SE18 165 EP78
Willersley Ave., Orp. 205 ER104
Willersley Ave., Sid. 185 ET88
Willersley Clo., Sid. 185 ET88
Willes Rd. NW5 141 DH65
Willesden La. NW2 139 CW65
Willesden La. NW6 139 CZ67
Willet Way SE16 162 DV78
Egan Way
Willett Clo., Nthlt. 136 BW69
Broomcroft Ave.
Willett Clo., Orp. 205 ES100
Willett Pl., Th.Hth. 201 DN99
Willett Rd.
Willett Rd., Th.Hth. 201 DN99
Willett Way, Orp. 205 ER99
Willetts La., Uxb. 113 BF63
Willey Broom La., Cat. 251 DN125
Willey Fm. La., Cat. 252 DQ126
Willey La., Cat. 252 DR125
William Barefoot Dr. SE9 185 EM91
William Bonney Est. SW4 161 DK84
William Booth Rd. SE20 202 DU95
William Carey Way, Har. 117 CE58
William Clo., Rom. 105 FC53
William Clo., Sthl. 156 CC75
Windmill Ave.
William Cory Prom., Erith 167 FE78
Erith High St.
William Ct., Hem.H. 40 BK24
King Edward St.
William Covell Clo., Enf. 81 DM38
William Dunbar Ho. NW6 139 CZ68
William Ellis Clo., Wind. 172 AU85
William Ellis Way SE16 162 DU76
St. James's Rd.
William Evelyn Ct., Dor. 262 BZ139
William IV St. WC2 277 P1
William IV St. WC2 141 DL73
William Gdns. SW15 179 CV85
William Guy Gdns. E3 143 EB69
Talwin St.
William Margrie Clo. SE15 162 DU82
Moncrieff St.
William Ms. SW1 276 E5
William Morley Clo. E6 144 EK67
William Morris Clo. E17 123 DZ55
William Morris Way SW6 160 DC83
Townmead Rd.
William Moulder Ct., Chesh. 54 AP28
William Nash Ct., Orp. 206 EW97
Brantwood Way
William Pl. E3 143 DZ68
Roman Rd.
William Rd. NW1 273 K3
William Rd. NW1 141 DJ69
William Rd. SW19 179 CY94
William Rd., Cat. 236 DR122
William Rd., Guil. 242 AW134
William Rd., Sutt. 218 DC106
William Russell Ct., Wok. 226 AS118
Raglan Rd.
William Saville Ho. NW6 139 CZ68
William Sq. SE16 143 DY73
Rotherhithe St.
William St. E10 123 EB58
William St. N17 100 DT52
William St. SW1 276 E5
William St. SW1 160 DF75
William St., Bark. 145 EQ66
William St., Berk. 38 AX19
William St., Cars. 220 DE104
William St., Grav. 191 GH87
William St., Grays 170 GB79
William St., Slou. 132 AT74
William St. (Bushey), Wat. 76 BX41
William St., Wind. 151 AR81
William Swayne Pl., Guil. 258 AY135
Station App.
Williams Ave. E17 101 DZ53
Williams Bldgs. E2 142 DW70
Williams Clo. N8 121 DK58
Coolhurst Rd.
Williams Clo., Add. 212 BH106
Monks Cres.
Williams Gro. N22 99 DN53
William's La. SW14 158 CQ83
Williams La., Mord. 200 DC99
Williams Rd. W13 137 CG73
Williams Rd., Sthl. 156 BY77
Williams Ter., Croy. 219 DN107
Williams Wk., Guil. 242 AV130
Grange Rd.
Williams Way, Rad. 77 CH35
Williamson Clo. SE10 164 EF77
Lenthorp Rd.
Williamson Rd. N4 121 DP58
Williamson St. N7 121 DL63
Williamson Way NW7 97 CY51
Williamson Way, Rick. 92 BG46
Willifield Way NW11 119 CZ56
Willingale Clo., Brwd. 109 GE44
Fairview Ave.
Willingale Clo., Loug. 85 EQ40
Willingale Rd.
Willingale Clo., Wdf.Grn. 102 EJ51
Willingale Rd., Loug. 85 EQ39
Willingdon Rd. N22 99 DP54
Willinghall Clo., Wal.Abb. 67 ED32
Willingham Clo. NW5 121 DJ64
Leighton Rd.
Willingham Ter. NW5 121 DJ64
Leighton Rd.
Willingham Way, Kings.T. 198 CN97
Willington Ct. E5 123 DY62
Mandeville St.
Willington Rd. SW9 161 DL83
Willis Ave., Sutt. 218 DE108
Willis Clo., Epsom 216 CP114
Willis Rd. E15 144 EF68
Willis Rd., Croy. 202 DQ101
Willis Rd., Erith 167 FC77
Willis St. E14 143 EB72
Willmore End SW19 200 DB95
Willoughby Ave., Croy. 219 DM105
Willoughby Clo., Brox. 49 DY21
Willoughby Dr., Rain. 147 FE66
Willoughby Gro. N17 100 DV52
Willoughby Ho. EC2 142 DR71
Moor La.
Willoughby La. N17 100 DV51
Willoughby Pk. Rd. N17 100 DV52
Willoughby Pas. E14 143 EA74
West India Ave.
Willoughby Rd. N8 121 DN55
Willoughby Rd. NW3 120 DD63
Willoughby Rd., Kings.T. 198 CM95
Willoughby Rd., Slou. 153 BA76
Willoughby Rd., Twick. 177 CK86
Willoughby St. WC1 273 P7
Willoughby Way SE7 164 EH77
Willoughbys, The SW14 158 CS83
Upper Richmond Rd.
Willow Ave. SW13 159 CT82
Willow Ave., Sid. 186 EU86
Willow Ave., Swan. 207 FF97
Willow Ave., Uxb. 114 BJ64
Willow Ave., West Dr. 134 BM73
Willow Bank SW6 159 CY83
Willow Bank, Rich. 177 CH90
Willow Bank, Wok. 226 AY122
Willow Brean, Horl. 268 DE146
Willow Bri. Rd. N1 142 DQ65
Willow Clo. W5 137 CK71
Willow Clo., Add. 211 BF111
Willow Clo., Bex. 186 EZ86
Willow Clo., Brent. 157 CJ79
Willow Clo., Brwd. 109 GB44
Willow Clo., Brom. 205 EM99
Willow Clo., Buck.H. 102 EK48
Willow Clo., Erith 167 FG81
Willow Rd.
Willow Clo., H.Wyc. 110 AC57
Willow Clo., Horn. 127 FH62
Willow Clo., Orp. 206 EV101
Willow Clo., Slou. 153 BC80
Willow Clo., Th.Hth. 201 DN100
Willow Clo. (Cheshunt), Wal.Cr. 66 DS26
Willow Cotts., Mitch. 201 DJ97
Willow Cotts., Rich. 158 CN79
Cambridge Cotts.
Willow Ct. EC2 142 DS70
Willow St.
Willow Ct., Edg. 96 CL49
Willow Ct., Horl. 269 DH145
Willow Ct., St.Alb. 61 CK26
Willow Cres., St.Alb. 43 CJ20
Willow Cres. E., Uxb. 114 BJ64
Willow Cres. W., Uxb. 114 BJ64
Willow Dene, Pnr. 94 BX54
Willow Dene (Bushey), Wat. 95 CE45
Willow Dr., Barn. 79 CY42
Willow Dr., Wok. 228 BG124
Willow Edge, Kings L. 58 BN29
Willow End N20 98 DA47
Willow End, Nthwd. 93 BU51
Willow End, Surb. 198 CL102
Willow Fm. La. SW15 159 CV83
Queens Ride
Willow Gdns., Houns. 156 CA81
Willow Gdns., Ruis. 115 BT61
Willow Grn. NW9 96 CS53
Clayton Fld.
Willow Grn., Borwd. 78 CR43
Ashley Dr.
Willow Grn., Dor. 263 CH140
Holmesdale Rd.
Willow Gro. E13 144 EG68
Libra Rd.
Willow Gro., Chis. 185 EN93
Willow Gro., Ruis. 115 BT61
Willow La., Amer. 72 AT41
Willow La., Guil. 243 BA133
Boxgrove Rd.
Willow La., Mitch. 200 DF100
Willow La., Wat. 75 BU43
Willow La. Ind. Est., Mitch. 200 DF100
Willow Mead, Chig. 104 EU48
Willow Mead, Saw. 36 EY06
Willow Mt., Croy. 202 DS104
Langton Way
Willow Pk., Sev. 241 FF117
Willow Pk., Slou. 132 AU66
Willow Path, Wal.Abb. 68 EF34
Mason Way
Willow Pl. SW1 277 L8
Willow Pl. SW1 161 DJ77
Willow Pl., Wind. 151 AQ79
Willow Rd. NW3 120 DD63
Willow Rd. W5 158 CL75
Willow Rd., Dart. 188 FJ88
Willow Rd., Enf. 82 DS41
Willow Rd., Erith 167 FG81
Willow Rd., Gdmg. 258 AT143
Willow Rd., N.Mal. 198 CQ98
Willow Rd., Red. 266 DC137
Willow Rd., Rom. 126 EY58
Willow Rd., Slou. 153 BE82
Willow Rd., Wall. 219 DH108
Willow Side, St.Alb. 62 CL27
Willow St. E4 101 ED45
Willow St. EC2 275 M4
Willow St. EC2 142 DS70
Willow St., Rom. 127 FC56
Willow Tree Clo. E3 143 DZ67
Birdsfield La.
Willow Tree Clo. SW18 180 DB88
Cargill Rd.
Willow Tree Clo., Hayes 136 BW70
Willow Tree Clo., Uxb. 115 BQ62
Willow Tree La., Hayes 136 BW70
Willow Tree Wk., Brom. 204 EH95
Willow Vale W12 139 CU74
Willow Vale, Chis. 185 EP93
Willow Vale, Lthd. 230 CB123
Willow Vw. SW19 200 DD95
Willow Wk. E17 123 DZ57
Willow Wk. N2 98 DD54
Central Ave.
Willow Wk. N15 121 DP56
Willow Wk. N21 81 DM44
Willow Wk. SE1 279 N8
Willow Wk. SE1 162 DS77
Willow Wk., Cher. 194 BG101
Willow Wk., Dart. 188 FK85
Francis Rd.
Willow Wk., Egh. 172 AW92
Willow Wk., Orp. 205 EP104
Willow Wk., Red. 267 DH136
Ash Dr.
Willow Wk., Sutt. 199 CZ104
Willow Wk., Tad. 248 CQ130
Oak Dr.
Willow Wk., Upmin. 129 FS60
Willow Way N3 98 DB52
Willow Way SE26 182 DV90
Willow Way W11 139 CX74
Freston Rd.
Willow Way, Epsom 216 CR107
Willow Way, Gdse. 252 DU132
Willow Way, Guil. 242 AV130
Willow Way, Hat. 45 CT21
Willow Way, Hem.H. 40 BH18
Willow Way, Pot.B. 64 DB33
Willow Way, Rad. 77 CE36
Willow Way, Rom. 106 FP51
Willow Way, St.Alb. 60 CA27
Willow Way, Sun. 195 BU98
Willow Way, Tad. 248 CP130
Oak Dr.
Willow Way, Twick. 176 CB89
Willow Way, Wem. 117 CG62
Willow Way, W.Byf. 212 BJ111
Willow Way, Wok. 226 AX121
Willow Wd. Cres. SE25 202 DS100
Willowbank Gdns., Tad. 233 CV122
The Ave.
Willowbrook (Eton), Wind. 151 AR77
Willowbrook Rd. SE15 162 DT79
Willowbrook Rd., Sthl. 156 CA76
Willowbrook Rd., Stai. 174 BL89
Willowcourt Ave., Har. 117 CH57
Willowdene N6 120 DF59
Denewood Rd.
Willowdene, Brwd. 108 FT43
Willowdene, Wal.Cr. 67 DY27
Willowdene Clo., Twick. 176 CC87
Willowdene Ct., Brwd. 108 FW49
Willowfield, Harl. 51 ER17
Willowhayne Dr., Walt. 195 BV101
Willowhayne Gdns., Wor.Pk. 199 CW104
Willowherb Wk., Rom. 106 FJ52
Clematis Clo.
Willowmead, Hert. 31 DP10
Willowmead, Stai. 194 BH95
Northfield Rd.
Willowmead Clo. W5 137 CK71
Willowmead Clo., Wok. 226 AU116
Willowmere, Esher 214 CC105
Willows, The, Amer. 55 AP35
Willows, The, Buck.H. 102 EK48
Willows, The, Esher 215 CE107
Albany Cres.
Willows, The, Grays 170 GD79
Willows, The, Rick. 92 BG47
Uxbridge Rd.
Willows, The, St.Alb. 43 CH24
Willows, The, Wat. 93 BV45
Brookside Rd.
Willows, The, W.Byf. 212 BL113
Willows, The, Wey. 194 BN104
Willows Ave., Mord. 200 DB99
Willows Clo., Pnr. 94 BW54
Willows Path, Epsom 216 CP114
Willows Path, Wind. 150 AJ81
Willrose Cres. SE2 166 EV78
Wills Cres., Houns. 176 CB86
Wills Gro. NW7 97 CU50
Willson Rd., Egh. 172 AV92
Wilman Gro. E8 142 DU66
Wilmar Clo., Hayes 135 BR70
Wilmar Clo., Uxb. 134 BK66
Wilmar Gdns., W.Wick. 203 EB102
Wilmcote Ho. W2 140 DA71
Wilmer Clo., Kings.T. 178 CM92
Wilmer Cres., Kings.T. 178 CM92
Wilmer Gdns. N1 142 DS67
Wilmer Lea Clo. E15 143 EC66
Wilmer Pl. N16 122 DT61
Stoke Newington Ch. St.
Wilmer Way N14 99 DK50
Wilmerhatch La., Epsom 232 CP118
Wilmington Ave. W4 158 CR80
Wilmington Ave., Orp. 206 EW103
Wilmington Ct. Rd., Dart. 187 FG90
Wilmington Gdns., Bark. 145 ER65
Wilmington Sq. WC1 274 D3
Wilmington Sq. WC1 141 DN69
Wilmington St. WC1 274 D3
Wilmot Clo. N2 98 DC54
Wilmot Clo. SE15 162 DU80
Wilmot Grn., Brwd. 107 FW51
Wilmot Pl. NW1 141 DJ66
Wilmot Pl. W7 137 CE74
Boston Rd.
Wilmot Rd. E10 123 EB61
Wilmot Rd. N17 122 DR55
Wilmot Rd., Cars. 218 DF106
Wilmot Rd., Dart. 187 FG85
Wilmot Rd., Pur. 219 DN112
Wilmot Rd., Slou. 130 AH69
Wilmot St. E2 142 DV70
Wilmot Way, Bans. 218 DA114
Wilmots Clo., Reig. 250 DC133
Wilmount St. SE18 165 EP77
Wilna Rd. SW18 180 DC87
Wilsham St. W11 139 CX74
Wilshaw St. SE14 163 EA81
Wilshere Ave., St.Alb. 42 CC23
Wilsman Rd., S.Ock. 149 FW68
Wilsmere Dr., Har. 95 CE52
Wilsmere Dr., Nthlt. 136 BY65
Wilson Ave., Mitch. 180 DE94
Wilson Clo., Wem. 118 CM59
Wilson Clo., West Dr. 154 BK79
Hatch La.
Wilson Dr., Cher. 211 BB106
Wilson Dr., Wem. 118 CM59
Wilson Gdns., Har. 116 CC59
Wilson Gro. SE16 162 DV75
Wilson La., Dart. 209 FT96
Wilson Rd. E6 144 EK69
Wilson Rd. SE5 162 DS81
Wilson Rd., Chess. 216 CM107
Wilson Rd., Ilf. 125 EM59
Wilson St. E17 123 EC57
Wilson St. EC2 275 L6
Wilson St. EC2 142 DR71
Wilson St. N21 99 DN45
Wilson Way, Wok. 226 AX116
Wilsons, Tad. 233 CX121
Heathcote
Wilsons Pl. E14 143 DZ72
Salmon La.
Wilsons Rd. W6 159 CX78
Wilstone Clo., Hayes 136 BY70
Kingsash Dr.
Wilstone Dr., St.Alb. 43 CJ15
Wilthorne Gdns., Dag. 147 FB66
Acre Rd.
Wilton Ave. W4 158 CS78
Wilton Clo., West Dr. 154 BK79
Hatch La.
Wilton Cres. SW1 276 F5
Wilton Cres. SW1 160 DG75
Wilton Cres. SW19 199 CZ95
Wilton Cres., Beac. 89 AL52
Wilton Cres., Hert. 32 DQ12
Wilton Cres., Wind. 151 AK84
Wilton Dr., Rom. 105 FC52
Wilton Gdns., Walt. 196 BX102
Wilton Gdns., W.Mol. 196 CA97
Wilton Gro. SW19 199 CZ95
Wilton Gro., N.Mal. 199 CT100
Wilton La., Beac. 89 AR52
Wilton Ms. SW1 276 G6
Wilton Ms. SW1 160 DG76
Wilton Par., Felt. 175 BU89
Highfield Rd.
Wilton Pk. Ct. SE18 165 EN81
Prince Imperial Rd.
Wilton Pl. SW1 276 F5
Wilton Pl. SW1 160 DG75
Wilton Pl., Add. 212 BK108
Wilton Rd. N10 98 DG54
Wilton Rd. SE2 166 EW77
Wilton Rd. SW1 277 J7
Wilton Rd. SW1 161 DJ77
Wilton Rd. SW19 180 DE94
Wilton Rd., Barn. 80 DF42
Wilton Rd., Beac. 89 AL51
Wilton Rd., Houns. 156 BX83
Wilton Rd., Ilf. 125 EP62
Ilford La.
Wilton Rd., Red. 266 DF135
Wilton Row SW1 276 F5
Wilton Row SW1 160 DG75
Wilton Sq. N1 142 DR67
Wilton St. SW1 277 H6
Wilton St. SW1 161 DH76
Wilton Ter. SW1 276 F6
Wilton Ter. SW1 160 DG76
Wilton Vill. N1 142 DR67
Wilton Way E8 142 DU65
Wilton Way, Hert. 32 DQ11
Wiltshire Ave., Horn. 128 FM56
Wiltshire Ave., Slou. 131 AQ70
Wiltshire Clo. NW7 97 CT50
Watford Way
Wiltshire Clo. SW3 276 D9
Wiltshire Clo., Dart. 189 FR87
Wiltshire Gdns. N4 122 DQ58
Wiltshire Gdns., Twick. 176 CC88
Wiltshire La., Pnr. 115 BT55
Wiltshire Rd. SW9 161 DN83
Wiltshire Rd., Orp. 206 EU101
Wiltshire Rd., Th.Hth. 201 DN97
Wiltshire Row N1 142 DR67
Wilverley Cres., N.Mal. 198 CS100
Wimbart Rd. SW2 181 DM87
Wimbledon Bri. SW19 179 CZ93
Wimbledon Common SW19 179 CT91
Wimbledon Hill Rd. SW19 179 CY93
Wimbledon Pk. SW19 179 CZ89
Wimbledon Pk. Est. SW19 179 CZ88
Wimbledon Pk. Rd. SW18 179 CZ88
Wimbledon Pk. Rd. SW19 179 CY89
Wimbledon Pk. Side SW19 179 CX89
Wimbledon Rd. SW17 180 DC91
Wimbledon Sta. SW19 179 CZ93
The Bdy.
Wimbolt St. E2 142 DU69
Wimborne Ave., Hayes 135 BV72
Wimborne Ave., Orp. 205 ET98
Wimborne Ave., Sthl. 156 CA77
Wimborne Clo. SE12 184 EF85
Wimborne Clo., Buck.H. 102 EJ47
Wimborne Clo., Epsom 216 CS113
Wimborne Clo., Saw. 36 EX05
Wimborne Clo., Wor.Pk. 199 CW102
Wimborne Dr. NW9 118 CN55
Wimborne Dr., Pnr. 116 BX59
Wimborne Gdns. W13 137 CH71
Wimborne Gro., Wat. 75 BS37
Wimborne Rd. N9 100 DU47
Wimborne Rd. N17 100 DS54
Wimborne Way, Beck. 203 DX98
Wimbourne Ave., Red. 266 DF139
Wimbourne Ct. N1 142 DR68
Wimbourne St.
Wimbourne St. N1 142 DR68
Wimbrel Clo., S.Croy. 220 DR111
Wimpole Clo., Brom. 204 EJ98
Stanley Rd.
Wimpole Clo., Kings.T. 198 CM96
Wimpole Ms. W1 273 H6
Wimpole Ms. W1 141 DH71
Wimpole Rd., West Dr. 134 BK74
Wimpole St. W1 273 H7
Wimpole St. W1 141 DH72
Wimshurst Clo., Croy. 201 DL102
Franklin Way
Winans Wk. SW9 161 DN82
Wincanton Cres., Nthlt. 116 CA64
Wincanton Gdns., Ilf. 125 EP55
Wincanton Rd. SW18 179 CZ87
Wincanton Rd., Rom. 106 FK48
Winch Dells, Hem.H. 40 BN23
Winchcomb Gdns. SE9 164 EK83
Winchcombe Rd., Cars. 200 DD103
Winchelsea Ave., Bexh. 166 EZ80
Winchelsea Clo. SW15 179 CX85
Winchelsea Rd. E7 124 EG63
Winchelsea Rd. N17 122 DS55
Winchelsea Rd. NW10 138 CR67
Winchelsey Ri., S.Croy. 220 DT107
Winchendon Rd. SW6 159 CZ80
Winchendon Rd., Tedd. 177 CD91
Winchester Ave. NW6 139 CY67
Winchester Ave. NW9 118 CM55
Winchester Ave., Houns. 156 BZ79
Winchester Ave., Upmin. 129 FT60
Winchester Clo. E6 144 EL72
Boultwood Rd.
Winchester Clo. SE17 278 G9
Winchester Clo. SE17 161 DP77
Winchester Clo., Amer. 55 AS39
Lincoln Pk.
Winchester Clo., Brom. 204 EF97
Winchester Clo., Enf. 82 DS43
Winchester Clo., Esher 214 CA105
Winchester Clo., Kings.T. 178 CP94
Winchester Clo., Slou. 153 BE81
Winchester Cres., Grav. 191 GK90
Winchester Cres., H.Wyc. 88 AC53
Winchester Dr., Pnr. 116 BX57
Winchester Gro., Sev. 257 FH123
Winchester Ho. SE18 164 EK80
Shooter's Hill Rd.
Winchester Ms. NW3 140 DD66
Winchester Rd.
Winchester Pk., Brom. 204 EF97
Winchester Pl. E8 122 DT64
Kingsland High St.
Winchester Pl. N6 121 DH60
Cromwell Ave.
Winchester Pl. W3 158 CQ75
Avenue Rd.
Winchester Rd. E4 101 EC52
Winchester Rd. N6 121 DH59
Winchester Rd. N9 100 DU47
Winchester Rd. NW3 140 DD66
Winchester Rd., Bexh. 166 EX82
Winchester Rd., Brom. 204 EF97
Winchester Rd., Felt. 176 BZ90
Winchester Rd., Har. 118 CL56
Winchester Rd., Hayes 155 BS80
Winchester Rd., Ilf. 125 ER62
Winchester Rd., Nthwd. 93 BT54
Winchester Rd., Orp. 224 EW105
Winchester Rd., Twick. 177 CH87
Winchester Rd., Walt. 195 BU102
Winchester Sq. SE1 279 K2
Winchester St. SW1 277 J10
Winchester St. SW1 161 DH78
Winchester St. W3 158 CQ75
Winchester Wk. SE1 279 K2
Winchester Wk. SE1 142 DR74
Winchester Way, Rick. 75 BP43
Winchet Wk., Croy. 202 DW100
Medway Clo.
Winchfield Clo., Har. 117 CJ58
Winchfield Rd. SE26 183 DY92
Winchfield Way, Rick. 92 BJ45
Winchilsea Cres., W.Mol. 196 CC96
Winchmore Hill Rd. N14 99 DK46
Winchmore Hill Rd. N21 99 DM45
Winchstone Clo., Shep. 194 BM98
Winckley Clo., Har. 118 CM57
Wincott St. SE11 278 E9
Wincott St. SE11 161 DN77
Wincrofts Dr. SE9 165 ER84
Wind Hill, Ong. 53 FF20
Windborough Rd., Cars. 218 DG108
Windermere Ave. N3 120 DA55
Windermere Ave. NW6 139 CY67
Windermere Ave. SW19 200 DB97
Windermere Ave., Har. 117 CJ59
Windermere Ave., Horn. 127 FG64
Windermere Ave., Ruis. 116 BW59
Windermere Ave., St.Alb. 43 CH22
Windermere Ave., Wem. 117 CJ59
Windermere Clo., Dart. 187 FH88
Windermere Clo., Egh. 173 BB94
Derwent Rd.
Windermere Clo., Felt. 175 BT88
Windermere Clo., Hem.H. 41 BQ21
Windermere Clo., Orp. 205 EP104
Windermere Clo., Rick. 73 BD43
Copmans Wick
Windermere Clo., Stai. 174 BL88
Viola Ave.
Windermere Ct. SW13 159 CT79
Windermere Ct., Ken. 235 DP115
Windermere Gdns., Ilf. 124 EL57
Windermere Gro., Wem. 117 CJ60
Windermere Ave.
Windermere Ho., Islw. 177 CF85
Windermere Rd. N10 99 DH53
Windermere Rd. N19 121 DJ61
Holloway Rd.
Windermere Rd. SW15 178 CS91
Windermere Rd. SW16 201 DJ95
Windermere Rd. W5 157 CJ76
Windermere Rd., Bexh. 167 FC82
Windermere Rd., Couls. 235 DL115
Windermere Rd., Croy. 202 DT102
Windermere Rd., Sthl. 136 BZ71
Windermere Rd., W.Wick. 204 EE103
Windermere Way, Reig. 250 DE133
Windermere Way, West Dr. 134 BM74
Providence Rd.
Winders Rd. SW11 160 DE82
Windfield, Lthd. 231 CH121
Windfield Clo. SE26 183 DX91
Windgates, Guil. 243 BC131
Tychbourne Dr.
Windham Ave., Croy. 221 ED110
Windham Rd., Rich. 158 CM83
Windhill, Welw.G.C. 30 DA08
Windhover Way, Grav. 191 GL91
Winding Shot, Hem.H. 40 BG19
Winding Way, Dag. 126 EW62

Winding Way, Har. 117 CE63
Windings, The, S.Croy. 220 DT111
Windlass Pl. SE8 163 DY77
Windlesham Gro. SW19 179 CX88
Windley Clo. SE23 182 DW89
Windmere Way, Slou. 130 AJ71
Windmill Ave., Epsom 217 CT111
Windmill Ave., St.Alb. 43 CJ16
Windmill Ave., Sthl. 156 CC75
Windmill Clo. SE1 162 DU77
Beatrice Rd.
Windmill Clo. SE13 163 EC82
Windmill Clo., Cat. 236 DQ121
Windmill Clo., Epsom 217 CT112
Windmill Clo., Horl. 269 DH148
Windmill Clo., Sun. 175 BS94
Windmill Clo., Surb. 197 CJ102
Windmill Clo., Upmin. 128 FN61
Windmill Clo., Wal.Abb. 68 EE34
Windmill Clo., Wind. 151 AP82
Windmill Ct. NW2 139 CY65
Windmill Dr. SW4 181 DH85
Windmill Dr., Kes. 222 EJ105
Windmill Dr., Lthd. 231 CJ123
Windmill Dr., Reig. 250 DD132
Windmill Dr., Rick. 74 BM44
Windmill End, Epsom 217 CT112
Windmill Fld., Ware 33 DX07
Windmill Flds., Harl. 36 EZ11
Windmill Gdns., Enf. 81 DN41
Windmill Grn., Shep. 195 BS101
Windmill Gro., Croy. 202 DQ100
Windmill Hill NW3 120 DC62
Windmill Hill, Amer. 89 AM45
Windmill Hill, Enf. 81 DP41
Windmill Hill, Kings L. 57 BF32
Windmill Hill, Ruis. 115 BT59
Windmill La. E15 143 ED65
Windmill La., Barn. 79 CT44
Windmill La., Epsom 217 CT112
Windmill La., Grnf. 136 CC71
Windmill La., Islw. 157 CE77
Windmill La., Sthl. 156 CC75
Windmill La., Surb. 197 CH100
Windmill La. 67 DY30
(Cheshunt), Wal.Cr.
Windmill La. 95 CD46
(Bushey), Wat.
Windmill Ms. W4 158 CS77
Chiswick Common Rd.
Windmill Pas. W4 158 CS77
Chiswick Common Rd.
Windmill Ri., Kings.T. 178 CP94
Windmill Rd. N18 100 DR49
Windmill Rd. SW18 180 DD86
Windmill Rd. SW19 179 CW90
Windmill Rd. W4 158 CS77
Windmill Rd. W5 157 CJ77
Windmill Rd., Brent. 157 CK78
Windmill Rd., Croy. 202 DQ101
Windmill Rd., Ger.Cr. 90 AX52
Windmill Rd., Hmptn. 176 CB92
Windmill Rd., Hem.H. 40 BL20
Windmill Rd., Mitch. 201 DJ99
Windmill Rd., Sev. 257 FH130
Windmill Rd., Slou. 131 AR74
Windmill Rd. 112 AX64
(Fulmer), Slou.
Windmill Rd., Sun. 195 BS95
Windmill Rd. W., Sun. 195 BS96
Windmill Row SE11 161 DN78
Windmill St. W1 273 M7
Windmill St. W1 141 DK71
Windmill St., Grav. 191 GH87
Windmill St. 95 CE46
(Bushey), Wat.
Windmill Wk. SE1 278 E3
Windmill Wk. SE1 141 DN74
Windmill Way, Reig. 250 DD132
Windmill Way, Ruis. 115 BT60
Windmill Wd., Amer. 55 AN37
Windmore Ave., Pot.B. 63 CW31
Windover Ave. NW9 118 CR56
Windridge Clo., St.Alb. 42 CA22
Windridge Rd., St.Alb. 42 BX24
Windrose Clo. SE16 163 DX75
Windrush Ave., Slou. 153 BB76
Windrush Clo. SW11 160 DD84
Maysoule Rd.
Windrush Clo. W4 158 CQ81
Windrush Clo., Uxb. 114 BM63
Windrush La. SE23 183 DX90
Winds End Clo., Hem.H. 40 BN18
Winds Ridge, Wok. 243 BC125
Windsock Clo. SE16 163 DX77
Plough Way
Windsor & Eton Relief 151 AP81
Rd., Wind.
Windsor Ave. E17 101 DY54
Windsor Ave. SW19 200 DC95
Windsor Ave., Edg. 96 CP49
Windsor Ave., Grays 170 GB75
Windsor Ave., N.Mal. 198 CQ99
Windsor Ave., Sutt. 199 CY104
Windsor Ave., Uxb. 135 BP67
Windsor Ave., W.Mol. 196 CA97
Windsor Castle, Wind. 152 AS80
Windsor Cen., The SE27 182 DQ91
Advance Rd.
Windsor Clo. N3 97 CY54
Windsor Clo. SE27 182 DQ91
Windsor Clo., Borwd. 78 CN39
Warenford Way
Windsor Clo., Brent. 157 CH79
Amalgamated Dr.
Windsor Clo., Chis. 185 EP92
Windsor Clo., Guil. 258 AT136
Windsor Clo., Har. 116 CA62
Windsor Clo., Hem.H. 40 BL21
Old Crabtree La.
Windsor Clo. 57 BA28
(Bovingdon), Hem.H.
Windsor Clo., 93 BU54
Nthwd.
Windsor Clo. 66 DU30
(Cheshunt), Wal.Cr.
Windsor Ct. N14 99 DJ45
Windsor Ct., Sun. 175 BU93
Windsor Rd.
Windsor Ct. Rd., Wok. 210 AS109
Windsor Cres., Har. 116 CA62
Windsor Cres., Wem. 118 CP62
Windsor Dr., Ashf. 174 BK91
Windsor Dr., Barn. 80 DF44
Windsor Dr., Dart. 187 FG86
Windsor Dr., Hert. 31 DM09
Windsor Dr., Orp. 224 EU107
Windsor End, Beac. 111 AM55
Windsor Gdns. W9 140 DA71
Windsor Gdns., Croy. 201 DL104
Richmond Rd.
Windsor Gdns., Hayes 155 BR76
Windsor Gro. SE27 182 DQ91
Windsor Hill, H.Wyc. 110 AE58
Windsor La., Slou. 130 AJ70
Windsor Pk. Rd., Hayes 155 BT80
Windsor Pl. SW1 277 L7
Windsor Pl., Cher. 194 BG100
Windsor St.
Windsor Rd. E4 101 EB49
Chivers Rd.
Windsor Rd. E7 124 EH64
Windsor Rd. E10 123 EB61
Windsor Rd. E11 124 EG60
Windsor Rd. N3 97 CY54
Windsor Rd. N7 121 DL62
Windsor Rd. N13 99 DN48
Windsor Rd. N17 100 DU54
Windsor Rd. NW2 139 CV65
Windsor Rd. W5 138 CL73
Windsor Rd., Barn. 79 CX44
Windsor Rd., Beac. 111 AN57
Windsor Rd., Bexh. 166 EY84
Windsor Rd., Brwd. 108 FV44
Windsor Rd., Chesh. 54 AP28
Windsor Rd., Dag. 126 EY62
Windsor Rd., Egh. 172 AW88
Windsor Rd., Enf. 83 DX36
Windsor Rd., Ger.Cr. 112 AW60
Windsor Rd., Grav. 191 GH90
Windsor Rd., Har. 95 CD53
Windsor Rd., Horn. 128 FJ59
Windsor Rd., Houns. 155 BV82
Windsor Rd., Ilf. 125 EP63
Windsor Rd., Kings.T. 178 CL94
Windsor Rd., Maid. 150 AE79
Windsor Rd., Rich. 158 CM82
Windsor Rd., Slou. 152 AS76
Windsor Rd. 152 AU80
(Datchet), Slou.
Windsor Rd. 112 AU62
(Fulmer), Slou.
Windsor Rd., Sthl. 156 BZ76
Windsor Rd., Stai. 172 AY86
Windsor Rd., Sun. 175 BU93
Windsor Rd., Tedd. 177 CD92
Windsor Rd., Th.Hth. 201 DP96
Windsor Rd., Wat. 76 BW38
Windsor Rd., Wind. 150 AE79
Windsor Rd. 151 AR79
(Eton), Wind.
Windsor Rd., Wok. 210 AS109
Windsor Rd., Wor.Pk. 199 CU103
Windsor St. N1 141 DP67
Windsor St., Cher. 194 BG100
Windsor St., Uxb. 134 BJ66
Windsor Ter. N1 275 J2
Windsor Ter. N1 142 DQ69
Windsor Wk. SE5 162 DR82
Windsor Wk., Walt. 196 BX102
King George Ave.
Windsor Wk., Wey. 213 BP106
Windsor Way W14 159 CX77
Windsor Way, Rick. 92 BG46
Windsor Way, Wok. 227 BC116
Windsor Wf. E9 143 DZ65
Eastway
Windsor Wd., Wal.Abb. 68 EE33
Monkswood Ave.
Windsors, The, Buck.H. 102 EL47
Windspoint Dr. SE15 162 DV79
Ethnard Rd.
Windus Rd. N16 122 DT60
Windus Wk. N16 122 DT60
Alkham Rd.
Windward Clo., Enf. 83 DX35
Bullsmoor La.
Windy Hill, Brwd. 109 GC46
Windy Ridge, Brom. 204 EL95
Windycroft Clo., Pur. 219 DK113
Windyridge Clo. SW19 179 CX92
Wine Clo. E1 142 DW73
Wine Office Ct. EC4 274 E9
Winern Glebe, W.Byf. 212 BK113
Winford Dr., Brox. 49 DZ22
Winford Ho. E3 143 DZ66
Jodrell Rd.
Winforton St. SE10 163 EC81
Winfrith Rd. SW18 180 DC87
Wing Way, Brwd. 108 FW46
Geary Dr.
Wingate Cres., Croy. 201 DK100
Wingate Rd. W6 159 CV76
Wingate Rd., Ilf. 125 EP64
Wingate Rd., Sid. 186 EW93
Wingate Trd. Est. N17 100 DT52
Wingate Way, St.Alb. 43 CG21
Wingfield, Grays 170 FZ78
Wingfield Bank, Grav. 190 GC89
Hall Rd.
Wingfield Clo., Add. 212 BH110
Wingfield Clo., Brwd. 109 GA48
Pondfield La.
Wingfield Gdns., 129 FS58
Upmin.
Wingfield Ms. SE15 162 DU83
Wingfield St.
Wingfield Rd. E15 124 EE63
Wingfield Rd. E17 123 EB57
Wingfield Rd., Grav. 191 GH87
Wingfield Rd., Kings.T. 178 CN93
Wingfield St. SE15 162 DU83
Wingfield Way, Ruis. 135 BV65
Wingford Rd. SW2 181 DL86
Wingletye La., Horn. 128 FM61
Wingmore Rd. SE24 162 DQ83
Wingrave Cres., Brwd. 108 FS49
Wingrave Rd. W6 159 CW79
Wingrove Rd. SE6 184 EE89
Wings Clo., Sutt. 218 DA105
Winifred Ave., Horn. 128 FK63
Winifred Gro. SW11 160 DF84
Winifred Rd. SW19 200 DA95
Winifred Rd., Couls. 234 DG116
Winifred Rd., Dag. 126 EY61
Winifred Rd., Dart. 187 FH85
Winifred Rd., Erith 167 FE78
Winifred Rd., Hmptn. 176 CA91
Winifred Rd., Hem.H. 40 BK24
Winifred St. E16 145 EM74
Winifred Ter. E13 144 EG68
Victoria Rd.
Winifred Ter., Enf. 100 DT45
Great Cambridge Rd.
Winkers Clo., Ger.Cr. 91 AZ53
Winkers La., Ger.Cr. 91 AZ53
Winkfield Rd. E13 144 EH68
Winkfield Rd. N22 99 DN53
Winkley St. E2 142 DV68
Winkwell, Hem.H. 39 BD22
Winkworth Pl., Bans. 217 CZ114
Bolters La.
Winkworth Rd., Bans. 218 DA114
Winlaton Rd., Brom. 183 ED91
Winmill Rd., Dag. 126 EZ62
Winn Common Rd. SE18 165 ES79
Winn Rd. SE12 184 EH88
Winnards, Wok. 226 AV118
Abercorn Way
Winnett St. W1 273 M10
Winnings Wk., Nthlt. 136 BY65
Arnold Rd.
Winnington Clo. N2 120 DD58
Winnington Rd. N2 120 DD60
Winnington Rd., Enf. 82 DW38
Winnington Way, Wok. 226 AV118
Winnipeg Dr., Orp. 223 ET107
High St.
Winnock Rd., West Dr. 134 BK74
Winns Ave. E17 123 DY55
Winns Ms. N15 122 DS56
Grove Pk. Rd.
Winns Ter. E17 101 EA54
Winsbeach E17 101 ED54
Winscombe Cres. W5 137 CK70
Winscombe St. N19 121 DH61
Winscombe Way, Stan. 95 CG50
Winsford Rd. SE6 183 DZ90
Winsford Ter. N18 100 DR50
Winsham Gro. SW11 180 DG85
Winslade Rd. SW2 181 DL85
Winslade Way SE6 183 EB87
Rushey Grn.
Winsland Ms. W2 140 DD72
London St.
Winsland St. W2 140 DD72
Winsley St. W1 273 K8
Winsley St. W1 141 DJ72
Winslow SE17 162 DS78
Kinglake St.
Winslow Clo. NW10 118 CS62
Neasden La. N.
Winslow Clo., Pnr. 115 BV58
Winslow Gro. E4 102 EE47
Winslow Rd. W6 159 CW79
Winslow Way, Felt. 176 BX90
Winslow Way, Walt. 196 BW104
Winsor Ter. E6 145 EN71
Winstanley Clo., Cob. 213 BV114
Winstanley Est. SW11 160 DD83
Winstanley Rd. SW11 160 DD83
Winstead Gdns., Dag. 127 FC64
Winston Ave. NW9 118 CS59
Winston Clo., Green. 189 FT85
Winston Clo., Har. 95 CF51
Winston Clo., Rom. 127 FB56
Winston Ct., Har. 94 CB52
Winston Dr., Cob. 230 BY116
Winston Gdns., Berk. 38 AT19
Winston Rd. N16 122 DR63
Winston Wk. W4 158 CR77
Acton La.
Winston Way, Ilf. 125 EP62
Winston Way, Pot.B. 64 DA33
Winston Way, Wok. 227 BB120
Winstone Clo., Amer. 54 AP34
Winstre Rd., Borwd. 78 CN39
Winter Ave. E6 144 EL67
Winter Box Wk., Rich. 158 CM84
Winterborne Ave., Orp. 205 ER104
Winterbourne Gro., 213 BQ107
Wey.
Winterbourne Rd. SE6 183 DZ88
Winterbourne Rd., Dag. 126 EW61
Winterbourne Rd., 201 DN98
Th.Hth.
Winterbrook Rd. SE24 182 DQ86
Winterdown Gdns., 214 BZ107
Esher
Winterdown Rd., Esher 214 BZ107
Winterfold Clo. SW19 179 CY89
Wintergreen Clo. E6 144 EL71
Yarrow Cres.
Winterhill Way, Guil. 243 BB130
Winters Cft., Grav. 191 GK93
Winters Rd., T.Ditt. 197 CH101
Winters Way, Wal.Abb. 68 EG33
Winterscroft Rd., Hodd. 49 DZ16
Wintersells Rd., W.Byf. 212 BK110
Winterstoke Gdns. NW7 97 CU50
Winterstoke Rd. SE6 183 DZ88
Winterton Ho. E1 142 DV72
Winterton Pl. SW10 160 DC79
Park Wk.
Winterwell Rd. SW2 181 DL85
Winthorpe Rd. SW15 159 CY84
Winthrop St. E1 142 DV71
Winthrop Wk., Wem. 118 CL62
Everard Way
Winton App., Rick. 75 BQ43
Winton Ave. N11 99 DJ52
Winton Clo. N9 101 DX45
Winton Cres., Rick. 75 BP43
Winton Dr., Rick. 75 BP44
Winton Dr. 67 DY29
(Cheshunt), Wal.Cr.
Winton Gdns., Edg. 96 CM52
Winton Rd., Orp. 223 EP105
Winton Rd., Ware 33 DZ06
Winton Way SW16 181 DN92
Wintoun Path, Slou. 131 AL70
Winvale, Slou. 152 AS76
Winwood, Slou. 132 AW72
Wireless Rd., West. 238 EK115
Wisbeach Rd., Croy. 202 DR99
Wisborough Rd., 220 DT109
S.Croy.
Wisdons Clo., Dag. 127 FB60
Wise La. NW7 97 CU50
Wise La., West Dr. 154 BK76
Wise Rd. E15 143 ED67
Wiseman Ct. SE19 182 DT92
Wiseman Rd. E10 123 EA61
Wisemans Gdns., Saw. 36 EW06
High Wych Rd.
Wise's La., Hat. 63 CW27
Wiseton Rd. SW17 180 DE88
Wishart Rd. SE3 164 EK82
Wishbone Way, Wok. 226 AT116
Wishford Ct., Ash. 232 CM118
The Marld
Wisley Common, Wok. 228 BM117
Wisley La., Wok. 228 BJ116
Wisley Rd. SW11 180 DG85
Wisley Rd., Orp. 186 EU94
Wissants, Harl. 51 EP19
Wisteria Clo., Brwd. 108 FV43
Wisteria Clo., Ilf. 125 EP64
Lavender Pl.
Wisteria Clo., Orp. 205 EP103
Wisteria Gdns., Swan. 207 FD96
Wisteria Rd. SE13 163 ED84
Wistlea Cres., St.Alb. 44 CP22
Witan St. E2 142 DV69
Witches La., Sev. 256 FD123
Witchford, Welw.G.C. 30 DD09
Witham Clo., Loug. 84 EL44
Witham Rd. SE20 202 DW97
Witham Rd. W13 137 CG74
Witham Rd., Dag. 126 FA64
Witham Rd., Islw. 157 CD81
Witham Rd., Rom. 127 FH57
Withens Clo., Orp. 206 EW98
Wither Dale, Horl. 268 DE147
Witherby Clo., Croy. 220 DS106
Witherfield Way SE16 162 DV78
Egan Way
Witheridge La., H.Wyc. 88 AF48
Witherings, The, Horn. 128 FL57
Witherington Rd. N5 121 DN64
Withers Clo., Chess. 215 CJ107
Mansfield Rd.
Withers Mead NW9 97 CT53
Witherston Way SE9 185 EN89
Withey Clo., Wind. 151 AL81
Withey Meadows, Horl. 268 DD150
Witheygate Ave., Stai. 174 BH93
Withies, The, Lthd. 231 CH121
Withies, The, Wok. 226 AS117
Robin Hood Rd.
Withy La., Ruis. 115 BQ57
Withy Mead E4 101 ED48
Withybed Cor., Tad. 233 CV123
Withycombe Rd. SW19 179 CX87
Withycroft, Slou. 132 AY72
Witley Cres., Croy. 221 EC107
Witley Gdns., Sthl. 156 BZ77
Witley Rd. N19 121 DJ61
Holloway Rd.
Witney Clo., Pnr. 94 BZ51
Witney Clo., Uxb. 114 BM63
Witney Path SE23 183 DX90
Inglemere Rd.
Wittenham Way E4 101 ED48
Wittering Clo., Kings.T. 177 CK92
Richmond Rd.
Wittering Wk., Horn. 148 FJ65
Pembrey Way
Wittersham Rd., Brom. 184 EF92
Wivenhoe Clo. SE15 162 DV83
Wivenhoe Ct., Houns. 156 BZ84
Wivenhoe Rd., Bark. 146 EU68
Wiverton Rd. SE26 182 DW93
Wix Hill, Lthd. 245 BP130
Wix Rd., Dag. 146 EX67
Wixs La. SW4 161 DH83
Woburn Ave., Epp. 85 ES37
Woburn Ave., Horn. 127 FG63
Woburn Ave., Pur. 219 DN111
High St.
Woburn Clo. SW19 180 DC93
Tintern Clo.
Woburn Clo. 76 CC43
(Bushey), Wat.
Woburn Hill, Add. 194 BJ103
Woburn Pl. WC1 273 N4
Woburn Pl. WC1 141 DK70
Woburn Rd., Cars. 200 DE102
Woburn Rd., Croy. 202 DQ102
Woburn Sq. WC1 273 N5
Woburn Sq. WC1 141 DK70
Woburn Wk. WC1 273 N3
Wodeland Ave., Guil. 258 AV136
Woffington Clo., 197 CJ95
Kings.T.
Wokindon Rd., Grays 171 GH76
Woking Business Pk., 227 BB115
Wok.
Woking Clo. SW15 159 CT84
Woking Rd., Guil. 242 AW128
Wold, The, Cat. 237 EA122
Woldham Pl., Brom. 204 EJ98
Woldham Rd.
Woldham Rd., Brom. 204 EJ98
Woldingham Rd., Cat. 236 DV120
Wolds Dr., Orp. 223 EN105
Wolf La., Wind. 151 AK83
Wolfe Clo., Brom. 204 EG100
Wolfe Clo., Hayes 135 BV69
Ayles Rd.
Wolfe Cres. SE7 164 EK78
Wolfe Cres. SE16 163 DX75
Wolferton Rd. E12 125 EM63
Wolffe Gdns. E15 144 EF65
Wolffram Clo. SE13 184 EE85
Wolfington Rd. SE27 181 DP91
Wolfs Hill, Oxt. 254 EG131
Wolf's Row, Oxt. 254 EH130
Wolfs Wd., Oxt. 254 EG132
Wolftencroft Clo. SW11 160 DD83
Wollaston Clo. SE1 279 H8
Wolmer Clo., Edg. 96 CP49
Wolmer Gdns., Edg. 96 CN48
Wolseley Ave. SW19 180 DA89
Wolseley Gdns. W4 158 CP79
Wolseley Rd. E7 144 EH66
Wolseley Rd. N8 121 DK58
Wolseley Rd. N22 99 DM53
Wolseley Rd. W4 158 CQ77
Wolseley Rd., Har. 117 CE55
Wolseley Rd., Mitch. 200 DG101
Wolseley Rd., Rom. 127 FD59
Wolseley St. SE1 162 DU75
Wolsey Ave. E6 145 EN69
Wolsey Ave. E17 123 DZ55
Wolsey Ave., T.Ditt. 197 CF99
Aragon Ave.
Wolsey Ave. 66 DT29
(Cheshunt), Wal.Cr.
Wolsey Clo. SW20 179 CV94
Wolsey Clo., Houns. 156 CC84
Wolsey Clo., Kings.T. 198 CP95
Wolsey Clo., Sthl. 156 CC76
Wolsey Clo., Wor.Pk. 217 CU105
Wolsey Cres., Croy. 221 EC109
Wolsey Cres., Mord. 199 CY101
Wolsey Dr., Kings.T. 178 CL92
Wolsey Dr., Walt. 196 BX102
Wolsey Gdns., Ilf. 103 EP51
Wolsey Gro., Edg. 96 CR52
Wolsey Gro., Esher 214 CB105
Wolsey Ms. NW5 141 DJ65
Wolsey Ms., Orp. 223 ET106
Osgood Ave.
Wolsey Pk., Wat. 93 BR45
Wolsey Rd. N1 122 DR64
Wolsey Rd., Ashf. 174 BL91
Wolsey Rd., E.Mol. 197 CD98
Wolsey Rd., Enf. 82 DV40
Wolsey Rd., Esher 214 CB105
Wolsey Rd., Hmptn. 176 CB93
Wolsey Rd., Hem.H. 40 BK21
Wolsey Rd., Nthwd. 93 BQ47
Wolsey Rd., Sun. 175 BT94
Wolsey St. E1 142 DW71
Sidney St.
Wolsey Wk., Wok. 226 AY117
Church St. W.
Wolsey Way, Chess. 216 CN106
Wolsley Clo., Dart. 187 FE85
Wolstan Clo., Uxb. 114 BG62
Lindsey Rd.
Wolstonbury N12 98 DA50
Wolvens La., Dor. 262 CA140
Wolvercote Rd. SE2 166 EX75
Wolverley St. E2 142 DV69
Bethnal Grn. Rd.
Wolverton SE17 279 M10
Wolverton Ave., 198 CN95
Kings.T.
Wolverton Clo., Horl. 268 DF150
Wolverton Gdns. W5 138 CM73
Wolverton Gdns. W6 159 CX77
Wolverton Gdns., Horl. 268 DF149
Wolverton Rd., Stan. 95 CH51
Wolverton Way N14 81 DJ43
Wolves La. N13 99 DN51
Wolves La. N22 99 DN52
Wombwell Gdns., Grav. 190 GE89
Womersley Rd. N8 121 DM58
Wonersh Common, 259 BB141
Guil.
Wonersh Common Rd., 259 BB142
Guil.
Wonersh Way, Sutt. 217 CX109
Wonford Clo., Kings.T. 198 CS95
Wonford Clo., Tad. 249 CU126
Wonham La., Bet. 264 CS135
Wonham Way, Guil. 261 BR139
Wontford Rd., Pur. 235 DN115
Wontner Clo. N1 142 DQ66
Greenman St.
Wontner Rd. SW17 180 DF89
Wooburn Common, 110 AF59
H.Wyc.
Wooburn Common Rd., 110 AG59
H.Wyc.
Wooburn Gra., H.Wyc. 110 AD60
Wooburn Grn. La., 110 AG56
Beac.
Wooburn Manor Pk., 110 AE58
H.Wyc.
Wooburn Ms., H.Wyc. 110 AE58
Wooburn Town, H.Wyc. 110 AD59
Wood Ave., Purf. 168 FQ77
Wood Clo. E2 142 DU70
Wood Clo. NW9 118 CR59
Wood Clo., Bex. 187 FE90
Wood Clo., Har. 117 CD59
Wood Clo., Hat. 45 CV18
Wood Clo., Red. 266 DG143
Wood Clo., Wind. 151 AQ84
Wood Common, Hat. 45 CV15
Wood Cres., Hem.H. 40 BK21
Wood Dr., Chis. 184 EL93
Wood Dr., Sev. 256 FF126
Wood End, Hayes 135 BS72
Wood End, St.Alb. 60 CC28
Wood End Ave., Har. 116 CB63
Wood End Clo., Hem.H. 41 BQ19
Wood End Clo., Nthlt. 117 CD64
Wood End Clo., Slou. 111 AR62
Wood End Gdns., Nthlt. 116 CC64
Wood End Grn. Rd., 135 BR71
Hayes
Wood End La., Nthlt. 136 CB65
Wood End Rd., Har. 117 CD63
Wood End Way, Nthlt. 116 CC64
Wood Fm. Rd., Hem.H. 40 BL20
Wood Grn. Way 67 DY31
(Cheshunt), Wal.Cr.
Holme Clo.
Wood Ho. La., Brox. 48 DT21
Wood La. N6 121 DH58
Wood La. NW9 118 CR59
Wood La. W12 139 CW72
Wood La., Cat. 236 DR124
Wood La., Dag. 126 EW63
Wood La., Dart. 189 FR91
Wood La., Horn. 127 FG64
Wood La., Islw. 157 CE79
Wood La., Iver 133 BC69
Wood La., Ruis. 115 BR60
Wood La., Slou. 151 AM76
Wood La., Stan. 95 CG48
Wood La., Tad. 233 CZ117
Brighton Rd.
Wood La., Ware 33 EA05
Wood La., Wey. 213 BQ109
Wood La., Wdf.Grn. 102 EF49
Wood La. Clo., Iver 133 BB69
Wood La. End, Hem.H. 40 BN19
Wood Lo. Gdns., Brom. 184 EL94
Wood Lo. La., W.Wick. 203 EC104
Wood Meads, Epp. 70 EU29
Wood Pt. E16 144 EG71
Fife Rd.
Wood Pond Clo., Beac. 89 AQ51
Wood Retreat SE18 165 ER80
Clothworkers Rd.
Wood Ride, Barn. 80 DD39
Wood Ride, Orp. 205 ER98
Wood Riding, Wok. 227 BF115
Pyrford Wds. Rd.
Wood Ri., Guil. 242 AS132
Wood Rd., Gdmg. 258 AT144
Wood Rd., Shep. 194 BN98
Wood Rd., West. 238 EJ118
Wood St. E16 144 EH73
Ethel Rd.
Wood St. E17 123 EC55
Wood St. EC2 275 J9
Wood St. EC2 142 DQ72
Wood St. W4 158 CS78
Wood St., Barn. 79 CW42
Wood St., Grays 170 GC79
Wood St., Kings.T. 198 CL95
Wood St., Mitch. 200 DG101
Wood St., Red. 251 DJ129
Wood St., Swan. 208 FJ95
Wood Vale N10 121 DJ57
Wood Vale SE23 182 DV88
Wood Vale, Hat. 45 CV18
Wood Vale Est. SE23 182 DW86
Wood Vw., Hem.H. 40 BH18

Wood Vw. 65 DL27
(Cuffley), Pot.B.
Wood Wk., Rick. 73 BE40
Wood Way, Beac. 88 AF54
Wood Way, Orp. 205 EN103
Wood Wf. SE10 163 EB79
Thames St.
Woodall Clo. E14 143 EB73
Lawless St.
Woodall Rd., Enf. 83 DX44
Woodbank Ave., Ger.Cr. 112 AX58
Woodbank Dr., Ch.St.G. 90 AX48
Turners Wd. Dr.
Woodbank Rd., Brom. 184 EF90
Woodbastwick Rd. SE26 183 DX92
Woodberry Ave. N21 99 DN47
Woodberry Ave., Har. 116 CB56
Woodberry Clo., Sun. 175 BU93
Ashridge Way
Woodberry Cres. N10 121 DH55
Woodberry Down N4 122 DQ59
Woodberry Down, Epp. 70 EU29
Woodberry Down Est. 122 DQ59
N4
Woodberry Gdns. N12 98 DC51
Woodberry Gro. N4 122 DQ59
Woodberry Gro. N12 98 DC51
Woodberry Gro., Bex. 187 FD90
Woodberry Way E4 101 EC46
Woodberry Way N12 98 DC51
Woodbine Clo., Harl. 51 EQ17
Linford End
Woodbine Clo., Twick. 177 CD89
Woodbine Clo., 84 EJ35
Wal.Abb.
Woodbine Gro. SE20 182 DV94
Woodbine Gro., Enf. 82 DR38
Woodbine La., Wor.Pk. 199 CV104
Woodbine Pl. E11 124 EG58
Woodbine Rd., Sid. 185 ES88
Woodbine Ter. E9 142 DW65
Morning La.
Woodbines Ave., 197 CK97
Kings.T.
Woodborough Rd. SW15 159 CV84
Woodbourne Ave. SW16 181 DK90
Woodbourne Clo. SW16 181 DL90
Woodbourne Ave.
Woodbourne Dr., Esher 215 CF107
Woodbourne Gdns., 219 DH108
Wall.
Woodbridge Ave., Lthd. 231 CG118
Woodbridge Clo. N7 121 DM61
Woodbridge Clo. NW2 119 CU62
Woodbridge Clo., Rom. 106 FK49
Woodbridge Ct., 102 EL52
Wdf.Grn.
Woodbridge Gro., Lthd. 231 CG118
Woodbridge Hill, Guil. 242 AV133
Woodbridge Hill Gdns., 242 AU133
Guil.
Woodbridge La., Rom. 106 FK48
Woodbridge Meadows, 242 AW133
Guil.
Woodbridge Rd., Bark. 125 ET64
Woodbridge Rd., Guil. 242 AV133
Woodbridge St. EC1 274 F4
Woodbridge St. EC1 141 DP70
Woodbrook Gdns., 68 EE33
Wal.Abb.
Woodbrook Rd. SE2 166 EU79
Woodburn Clo. NW4 119 CX57
Woodburn Clo., Uxb. 135 BP70
Aldenham Dr.
Woodbury, B.End 110 AC59
Eastern Dr.
Woodbury Clo. E11 124 EH56
Woodbury Clo., Croy. 202 DT103
Woodbury Clo., West. 239 EM118
Woodbury Dr., Sutt. 218 DC110
Woodbury Hill, Loug. 84 EL41
Woodbury Hollow, 84 EL40
Loug.
Woodbury Pk. Rd. W13 137 CH70
Woodbury Rd. E17 123 EB56
Woodbury Rd., West. 239 EM118
Woodbury St. SW17 180 DE92
Woodchester Pk., Beac. 88 AJ49
Woodchester Sq. W2 140 DB71
Woodchurch Clo., Sid. 185 ER90
Woodchurch Dr., Brom. 184 EK94
Woodchurch Rd. NW6 140 DA66
Woodclyffe Dr., Chis. 205 EN96
Woodcock Ct., Har. 118 CL59
Woodcock Dell Ave., 117 CK59
Har.
Woodcock Hill, Har. 117 CJ57
Woodcock Hill, Rick. 92 BL50
Woodcock Hill, St.Alb. 28 CN14
Woodcock Hill Trd. Est., 92 BL49
Rick.
Woodcocks E16 144 EJ71
Tollgate Rd.
Woodcombe Cres. SE23 182 DW88
Woodcote, Guil. 258 AV138
Woodcote, Horl. 269 DJ147
The Fieldings
Woodcote Ave. NW7 97 CW51
Woodcote Ave., Horn. 127 FG63
Woodcote Ave., Th.Hth. 201 DP98
Woodcote Ave., Wall. 219 DH109
Woodcote Clo., Enf. 82 DW44
Woodcote Clo., Epsom 216 CR114
Woodcote Clo., Kings.T. 178 CM92
Woodcote Clo. 66 DW30
(Cheshunt), Wal.Cr.
Woodcote Dr., Orp. 205 ER102
Woodcote Dr., Pur. 219 DK110
Woodcote End, Epsom 232 CR115
Woodcote Grn., Wall. 219 DJ109
Woodcote Grn. Rd., 232 CQ116
Epsom
Woodcote Gro., Cars. 219 DH112
Woodcote Gro. Rd., 235 DK115
Couls.
Woodcote Hurst, Epsom 232 CQ116
Woodcote La., Pur. 219 DK111
Woodcote Ms., Wall. 219 DH107
Woodcote Pk. Ave., Pur. 219 DJ112
Woodcote Pk. Rd., Epsom 232 CQ116
Woodcote Pl. SE27 181 DP92
Woodcote Rd. E11 124 EG59
Woodcote Rd., Epsom 216 CR114
Woodcote Rd., Wall. 219 DH107
Woodcote Side, Epsom 232 CP115
Woodcote Valley Rd., 219 DK113
Pur.
Woodcrest Rd., Pur. 219 DL113
Woodcrest Wk., Reig. 250 DE132
Woodcroft N21 99 DM46
Woodcroft SE9 185 EM90
Woodcroft, Grnf. 137 CG65
Woodcroft, Harl. 51 EQ17
Woodcroft Ave. NW7 96 CS52
Woodcroft Ave., Stan. 95 CF53
Woodcroft Ave., Ware 33 ED11
Woodcroft Cres., Uxb. 135 BP67
Woodcroft Rd., Chesh. 54 AR28
Woodcroft Rd., Th.Hth. 201 DP99
Woodcutters Ave., 170 GC75
Grays
Woodedge Clo. E4 102 EF46
Woodend SE19 182 DQ93
Woodend, Esher 196 CC103
Woodend, Lthd. 247 CJ125
Woodend, Sutt. 200 DC103
Woodend, The, Wall. 219 DH109
Woodend Clo., Wok. 226 AU119
Woodend Gdns., Enf. 81 DL42
Woodend Pk., Cob. 230 BX115
Woodend Rd. E17 101 EC54
Wooder Gdns. E7 124 EG63
Wooderson Clo. SE25 202 DS98
Woodfall Ave., Barn. 79 CZ43
Woodfall Dr., Dart. 167 FE84
Woodfall Rd. N4 121 DN60
Woodfall St. SW3 160 DF78
Woodfarrs SE5 162 DR84
Woodfield, Ash. 231 CK117
Woodfield Ave. NW9 118 CS56
Woodfield Ave. SW16 181 DK90
Woodfield Ave. W5 137 CJ70
Woodfield Ave., Cars. 218 DG107
Woodfield Ave., Grav. 191 GH88
Woodfield Ave., Nthwd. 93 BS49
Woodfield Ave., Wem. 117 CJ62
Woodfield Clo. SE19 182 DQ94
Woodfield Clo., Ash. 231 CK117
Woodfield Clo., Couls. 235 DJ119
Woodfield Clo., Enf. 82 DS42
Woodfield Clo., Red. 250 DE133
Woodfield Cres. W5 137 CK70
Woodfield Dr., Barn. 98 DG46
Woodfield Dr., Hem.H. 41 BR22
Woodfield Dr., Rom. 127 FG56
Woodfield Gdns. W9 139 CZ71
Woodfield Rd.
Woodfield Gdns., 41 BR22
Hem.H.
Woodfield Gdns., 199 CT99
N.Mal.
Woodfield Gro. SW16 181 DK90
Woodfield Hill, Couls. 235 DH119
Woodfield La. SW16 181 DK90
Woodfield La., Ash. 232 CL117
Woodfield La., Hat. 46 DD23
Woodfield La., Hert. 46 DD23
Woodfield Pk., Amer. 55 AN37
Woodfield Pl. W9 139 CZ70
Woodfield Ri. 95 CD45
(Bushey), Wat.
Woodfield Rd. W5 137 CJ70
Woodfield Rd. W9 139 CZ71
Woodfield Rd., Ash. 231 CK117
Woodfield Rd., Houns. 155 BV82
Woodfield Rd., Rad. 77 CG36
Woodfield Rd., T.Ditt. 197 CF103
Woodfield Rd., 29 CZ09
Welw.G.C.
Woodfield Ter., Epp. 70 EW25
High Rd.
Woodfield Ter., Uxb. 92 BH54
Woodfield Way N11 99 DK52
Woodfield Way, Horn. 128 FK60
Woodfield Way, Red. 250 DE132
Woodfield Way, St.Alb. 43 CJ17
Woodfields, Sev. 256 FD122
Woodfields, The, 220 DT111
S.Croy.
Woodfines, The, Horn. 128 FK58
Woodford Ave., Ilf. 124 EL55
Woodford Bri. Rd., Ilf. 124 EK55
Woodford Ct. W12 159 CX75
Shepherds Bush Grn.
Woodford Ct., Wal.Abb. 68 EG33
Woodford Cres., Pnr. 93 BV54
Woodford New Rd. E17 124 EE56
Woodford New Rd. E18 102 EE54
Woodford New Rd., 102 EF52
Wdf.Grn.
Woodford Pl., Wem. 118 CL60
Woodford Rd. E7 124 EH63
Woodford Rd. E18 124 EG56
Woodford Rd., Wat. 75 BV40
Woodford Trd. Est., 102 EK54
Wdf.Grn.
Woodford Way, Slou. 131 AN69
Woodgate, Wat. 59 BV33
Woodgate Ave., Chess. 215 CK106
Woodgate Cres., Nthwd. 93 BU51
Woodgate Dr. SW16 181 DK94
Streatham Vale
Woodgavil, Bans. 233 CZ116
Woodger Clo., Guil. 243 BC132
Kingfisher Dr.
Woodger Rd. W12 159 CW75
Goldhawk Rd.
Woodgers Gro., Swan. 207 FF96
Woodget Clo. E6 144 EL72
Remington Rd.
Woodgrange Ave. N12 98 DD51
Woodgrange Ave. W5 138 CN74
Woodgrange Ave., Enf. 82 DU44
Woodgrange Ave., Har. 117 CJ57
Woodgrange Clo., Har. 117 CK57
Woodgrange Gdns., Enf. 82 DU44
Woodgrange Rd. E7 124 EH64
Woodgrange Ter., Enf. 82 DU44
Great Cambridge Rd.
Woodgreen Rd., 68 EH33
Wal.Abb.
Woodhall Ave. SE21 182 DT90
Woodhall Ave., Pnr. 94 BY54
Woodhall Clo., Hert. 32 DQ07
Woodhall Clo., Uxb. 114 BK64
Woodhall Ct., 29 CY10
Welw.G.C.
Woodhall Cres., Horn. 128 FM59
Woodhall Dr. SE21 182 DT90
Woodhall Dr., Pnr. 94 BX53
Woodhall Gate, Pnr. 94 BX52
Woodhall La., Hem.H. 40 BL19
Woodhall La., Rad. 78 CL35
Woodhall La., Wat. 94 BX48
Woodhall La., 29 CY10
Welw.G.C.
Woodhall Par., 29 CZ11
Welw.G.C.
Woodhall Rd., Pnr. 94 BX52
Woodham Ct. E18 124 EF56
Woodham La., Add. 212 BG110
Woodham La., Wok. 211 BB114
Woodham Pk. Rd., Add. 211 BF109
Woodham Pk. Way, 211 BF111
Add.
Woodham Ri., Wok. 211 AZ114
Woodham Rd. SE6 183 EC90
Woodham Rd., Wok. 211 AZ114
Woodham Waye, Wok. 211 BB114
Woodhatch Clo. E6 144 EL72
Remington Rd.
Woodhatch Rd., Red. 266 DC137
Woodhatch Rd., Reig. 266 DB137
Woodhatch Spinney, 235 DL116
Couls.
Woodhaven Gdns., Ilf. 125 EQ55
Brandville Gdns.
Woodhaw, Egh. 173 BB91
Woodhayes, Horl. 269 DH147
Woodhayes Rd. SW19 179 CW94
Woodhead Dr., Orp. 205 ES103
Sherlies Ave.
Woodheyes Rd. NW10 118 CR64
Woodhill SE18 164 EL77
Woodhill, Harl. 51 ES19
Woodhill, Wok. 243 BD126
Woodhill Ave., Ger.Cr. 113 AZ58
Woodhill Cres., Har. 117 CK58
Woodhouse Ave., Grnf. 137 CF68
Woodhouse Clo., Grnf. 137 CF68
Woodhouse Clo., Hayes 155 BS76
Woodhouse Eaves, 93 BU50
Nthwd.
Woodhouse Gro. E12 144 EL65
Woodhouse La., Dor. 261 BU143
Woodhouse Rd. E11 124 EF62
Woodhouse Rd. N12 98 DC51
Woodhurst Ave., Orp. 205 EQ100
Woodhurst Ave., Wat. 60 BX34
Woodhurst Dr., Uxb. 113 BF57
Woodhurst La., Oxt. 254 EE131
Woodhurst Pk., Oxt. 254 EE130
Woodhurst Rd. SE2 166 EU78
Woodhurst Rd. W3 138 CQ73
Woodhyrst Gdns., Ken. 235 DP115
Firs Rd.
Wooding Gro., Harl. 51 EP15
Woodington Clo. SE9 185 EN86
Woodison St. E3 143 DY70
Woodknoll Dr., Chis. 205 EM95
Woodland Ave., Brwd. 109 GC43
Woodland Ave., Hem.H. 40 BH21
Woodland Ave., Slou. 131 AR73
Woodland Ave., Wind. 151 AM84
Woodland Clo. NW9 118 CQ58
Woodland Clo. SE19 182 DS93
Woodland Hill
Woodland Clo., Brwd. 109 GC43
Woodland Clo., Epsom 216 CS107
Woodland Clo., Hem.H. 40 BH21
Woodland Clo., Lthd. 245 BT127
Woodland Clo., Uxb. 115 BP61
Woodland Clo., Wey. 213 BR105
Woodland Gro.
Woodland Clo., 102 EH48
Wdf.Grn.
Woodland Ct., Oxt. 253 ED128
Woodland Cres. SE10 164 EE79
Woodland Dr., Lthd. 245 BT127
Woodland Dr., St.Alb. 43 CJ19
Woodland Dr., Wat. 75 BT39
Woodland Gdns. N10 121 DH57
Woodland Gdns., Islw. 157 CE83
Woodland Gdns., 220 DW111
S.Croy.
Woodland Gro. SE10 164 EE78
Woodland Gro., Epp. 70 EU31
Woodland Gro., Wey. 213 BR105
Woodland Hill SE19 182 DS93
Woodland La., Rick. 73 BD41
Woodland Mt., Hert. 32 DT09
Woodland Pl., Hem.H. 40 BH21
Woodland Pl., Rick. 73 BF42
Dog Kennel La.
Woodland Ri. N10 121 DH56
Woodland Ri., Grnf. 137 CG65
Woodland Ri., Oxt. 254 EE130
Woodland Ri., Sev. 257 FL123
Woodland Ri., 29 CW07
Welw.G.C.
Woodland Rd. E4 101 EC46
Woodland Rd. N11 99 DH50
Woodland Rd. SE19 182 DT92
Woodland Rd., Hert. 32 DW12
Woodland Rd., Loug. 84 EL41
Woodland Rd., Rick. 91 BD50
Woodland Rd., Th.Hth. 201 DN98
Woodland St. E8 142 DT65
Dalston La.
Woodland Ter. SE7 164 EL77
Woodland Ter. SE18 164 EL77
Woodland Vw., Chesh. 54 AR33
Woodland Vw., Gdmg. 258 AS142
Woodland Wk. NW3 120 DE64
Aspern Gro.
Woodland Wk. SE10 164 EE78
Woodland Gro.
Woodland Wk., Brom. 184 EE91
Woodland Way N21 99 DN47
Woodland Way NW7 96 CS51
Woodland Way SE2 166 EX77
Woodland Way, Cat. 252 DS128
Woodland Way, Croy. 203 DY102
Woodland Way, Epp. 85 ER35
Woodland Way, Green. 169 FU84
Woodland Way, Mitch. 180 DG94
Woodland Way, Mord. 199 CZ98
Woodland Way, Orp. 205 EQ98
Woodland Way, Pur. 219 DN113
Woodland Way, Surb. 198 CP103
Woodland Way, Tad. 233 CY122
Woodland Way 65 DP28
(Cheshunt), Wal.Cr.
Woodland Way, 221 EB105
W.Wick.
Woodland Way, Wey. 213 BR106
Woodland Way, 102 EH48
Wdf.Grn.
Woodlands NW11 119 CY58
Woodlands SW20 199 CW98
Woodlands, Har. 116 CA56
Woodlands, Hat. 64 DB26
Woodlands, Horl. 269 DJ147
Woodlands, Rad. 61 CG34
Woodlands, St.Alb. 60 CC27
Woodlands, Wok. 226 AY118
Constitution Hill
Woodlands, The N14 99 DH46
Woodlands, The SE13 183 ED87
Woodlands, The SE19 182 DQ94
Woodlands, The, Amer. 55 AQ35
Woodlands, The, Esher 196 CC103
Woodlands, The, 113 AZ57
Ger.Cr.
Woodlands, The, 41 BP19
Hem.H.
Woodlands, The, Horl. 269 DP148
Woodlands, The, Islw. 157 CF82
Woodlands, The, Orp. 224 EV107
Woodlands, The, Wall. 219 DH109
Woodlands Ave. E11 124 EG60
Woodlands Ave. N3 98 DC52
Woodlands Ave. W3 138 CP74
Woodlands Ave., Berk. 38 AW20
Woodlands Ave., Horn. 128 FK57
Woodlands Ave., N.Mal. 198 CQ95
Woodlands Ave., Red. 266 DF135
Woodlands Ave., Rom. 126 EY58
Woodlands Ave., Ruis. 116 BW59
Woodlands Ave., Sid. 185 ES88
Woodlands Ave., W.Byf. 211 BF113
Woodlands Ave., 199 CT103
Wor.Pk.
Woodlands Clo. NW11 119 CY57
Woodlands Clo., Borwd. 78 CP42
Woodlands Clo., Brom. 205 EM96
Woodlands Clo., Cher. 211 BB110
Woodlands Clo., Esher 215 CF108
Woodlands Clo., Ger.Cr. 113 BA58
Woodlands Clo., Grays 170 GE76
Woodlands Clo., Hodd. 49 EA18
Woodlands Clo., Swan. 207 FF97
Woodlands Ct., Wok. 226 AY119
Constitution Hill
Woodlands Dr., Beac. 88 AJ51
Woodlands Dr., Hodd. 49 EA19
Woodlands Dr., Kings L. 59 BQ28
Woodlands Dr., Stan. 95 CF51
Woodlands Dr., Sun. 196 BW96
Woodlands Glade, 88 AJ51
Beac.
Woodlands Glade, Slou. 111 AR62
Woodlands Gro., Couls. 234 DG117
Woodlands Gro., Islw. 157 CE82
Woodlands Hill, Beac. 111 AL58
Woodlands La., Cob. 230 BY117
Woodlands Par., Ashf. 175 BQ93
Woodlands Pk., Add. 211 BF106
Woodlands Pk., Bex. 187 FC91
Woodlands Pk., Guil. 243 BB133
Woodlands Pk., Tad. 248 CP131
Woodlands Pk., Wok. 211 BC114
Blackmore Cres.
Woodlands Pk. Rd. N15 121 DP57
Woodlands Pk. Rd. SE10 164 EE79
Woodlands Ri., Swan. 207 FF96
Woodlands Rd. E11 124 EE61
Woodlands Rd. E17 123 EC55
Woodlands Rd. N9 100 DW46
Woodlands Rd. SW13 159 CT83
Woodlands Rd., Bexh. 166 EY83
Woodlands Rd., Brom. 204 EL96
Woodlands Rd., Enf. 82 DR38
Woodlands Rd., Epsom 232 CN115
Woodlands Rd., Guil. 242 AX130
Woodlands Rd., Har. 117 CF57
Woodlands Rd., Hem.H. 58 BN27
Woodlands Rd., Hert. 32 DT09
Woodlands Rd., Ilf. 125 EQ62
Woodlands Rd., Islw. 157 CD83
Woodlands Rd., Lthd. 231 CD117
Woodlands Rd. 246 BY128
(Effingham), Lthd.
Woodlands Rd., Orp. 224 EU107
Woodlands Rd., Red. 266 DF136
Woodlands Rd., Rom. 127 FF55
Woodlands Rd. 106 FN53
(Harold Wd.), Rom.
Fitzilian Ave.
Woodlands Rd., Sthl. 136 BX74
Woodlands Rd., Surb. 197 CK101
Woodlands Rd., Vir.W. 192 AW98
Woodlands Rd. 76 BY43
(Bushey), Wat.
Woodlands Rd., W.Byf. 211 BF114
Woodlands Rd. E., 192 AW98
Vir.W.
Woodlands Rd. W., 192 AW98
Vir.W.
Woodlands St. SE13 183 ED87
Woodlands Vw., Dor. 263 CH142
Woodlands Vw., Sev. 224 FA110
Woodlands Way SW15 179 CZ85
Oakhill Rd.
Woodlands Way, Ash. 232 CN116
Woodlands Way, Tad. 248 CQ130
Woodlawn Clo. SW15 179 CZ85
Woodlawn Cres., Twick. 176 CB89
Woodlawn Dr., Felt. 176 BX89
Woodlawn Gro., Wok. 227 AZ115
Woodlawn Rd. SW6 159 CX80
Woodlea Dr., Brom. 204 EE99
Woodlea Gro., Nthwd. 93 BQ51
Woodlea Rd. N16 122 DS62
Woodleigh Ave. N12 98 DE51
Woodleigh Gdns. SW16 181 DL90
Woodley Clo. SW17 180 DF94
Arnold Rd.
Woodley Hill, Chesh. 54 AR34
Woodley La., Cars. 200 DE104
Woodley Rd., Orp. 206 EW103
Woodley Rd., Ware 33 DZ05
Woodman La. E4 84 EE43
Woodman Path, Chig. 103 ES51
Woodman Rd., Brwd. 108 FW50
Woodman Rd., Couls. 235 DJ115
Woodman Rd., Hem.H. 40 BL22
Woodman St. E16 145 EN74
Woodmancote Gdns., 212 BG113
W.Byf.
Woodmans Gro. NW10 119 CT64
Woodmans Ms. W12 139 CW71
Wood La.
Woodman's Yd., Wat. 76 BX42
Woodmansterne La., 234 DB115
Bans.
Woodmansterne La., 218 DF112
Cars.
Woodmansterne La., 219 DH111
Wall.
Woodmansterne Rd. 181 DJ94
SW16
Woodmansterne Rd., 218 DF112
Cars.
Woodmansterne Rd., 235 DJ115
Couls.
Woodmansterne St., 234 DE115
Bans.
Woodmere SE9 185 EM87
Woodmere Ave., Croy. 202 DW101
Woodmere Ave., Wat. 76 BX38
Woodmere Clo. SW11 160 DG83
Lavender Hill
Woodmere Clo., Croy. 203 DX101
Woodmere Gdns., Croy. 202 DW101
Woodmere Way, Beck. 203 ED99
Woodmill Ms., Hodd. 49 EB15
Whittingstall Rd.
Woodmount, Swan. 207 FC101
Woodnook Rd. SW16 181 DH92
Woodpecker Clo. N9 82 DV44
Woodpecker Clo., Cob. 214 BY112
Woodpecker Clo., Har. 95 CF53
Kenton La.
Woodpecker Clo., Hat. 45 CT21
Woodpecker Clo. 94 CC46
(Bushey), Wat.
Woodpecker Mt., Croy. 221 DY109
Woodpecker Rd. SE14 163 DY79
Woodpecker Rd. SE28 146 EW73
Woodpecker Way, Wok. 226 AX123
Woodplace Clo., Couls. 235 DJ119
Woodplace La., Couls. 235 DJ118
Woodquest Ave. SE24 182 DQ85
Woodredon Clo., Harl. 50 EH16
Epping Rd.
Woodredon Fm. La., 68 EK33
Wal.Abb.
Woodridden Hill, 84 EJ35
Wal.Abb.
Woodridge Clo., Enf. 81 DN39
Woodridge Way, 93 BS51
Nthwd.
Woodridings Ave., Pnr. 94 BZ53
Woodridings Clo., Pnr. 94 BZ52
Woodriffe Rd. E11 123 ED59
Woodrise, Pnr. 115 BU57
Woodrow SE18 165 EM77
Woodrow Ave., Hayes 135 BT71
Woodrow Clo., Grnf. 137 CH66
Woodrow Ct. N17 100 DV52
Heybourne Rd.
Woodroyd Ave., Horl. 268 DF149
Woodroyd Gdns., Horl. 268 DF150
Woodruff Ave., Guil. 243 BA131
Woodrush Clo. SE14 163 DY80
Southerngate Way
Woodrush Way, Rom. 126 EX56
Woods, The, Nthwd. 93 BU50
Woods, The, Rad. 61 CH34
Woods, The, Uxb. 115 BP63
Woods Ave., Hat. 45 CU20
Woods Clo. SE19 182 DS93
Woodland Hill
Woods Dr., Slou. 111 AM64
Woods Ms. W1 272 F10
Woods Ms. W1 140 DG73
Woods Pl. SE1 279 N7
Woods Rd. SE15 162 DV81
Woodseer St. E1 142 DT71
Woodsford SE17 162 DR78
Portland St.
Woodsford Sq. W14 159 CY75
Woodshire Rd., Dag. 127 FB62
Woodshore Clo., Vir.W. 192 AV100
Woodshots Meadow, 75 BR43
Wat.
Woodside NW11 120 DA57
Woodside SW19 179 CZ93
Woodside, Borwd. 78 CM42
Woodside, Buck.H. 102 EJ47
Woodside, Epp. 70 EW26
Woodside, Hert. 32 DW12
Woodside, Lthd. 230 CB122
Woodside 245 BQ126
(West Horsley), Lthd.
Woodside, Orp. 224 EU106
Woodside, Tad. 249 CZ128
Woodside 66 DU31
(Cheshunt), Wal.Cr.
Woodside, Walt. 195 BU102
Ashley Rd.
Woodside, Wat. 75 BU36
Woodside Ave. N6 120 DF57
Woodside Ave. N10 120 DF57
Woodside Ave. N12 98 DC49
Woodside Ave. SE25 202 DV100
Woodside Ave., Amer. 55 AR36
Woodside Ave., Beac. 88 AJ52
Woodside Ave., Chis. 185 EQ92
Woodside Ave., Esher 197 CE101
Woodside Ave., H.Wyc. 110 AC57
Woodside Ave., Walt. 213 BV105
Woodside Ave., Wem. 138 CL67
Woodside Clo., Amer. 55 AQ37
Woodside Clo., Beac. 88 AJ52
Woodside Clo., Bexh. 167 FD84
Woodside Clo., Brwd. 109 GD43
Woodside Clo., Cat. 236 DS124
Woodside Clo., Ger.Cr. 90 AY54
Woodside Clo., Rain. 148 FJ70
Woodside Clo., Stan. 95 CH50
Woodside Clo., Surb. 198 CQ102
Woodside Clo., Wem. 138 CL67
Woodside Ct. N12 98 DC49
Woodside Ave.
Woodside Ct. Rd., Croy. 202 DU101
Woodside Cres., Horl. 269 DN148
Woodside Cres., Sid. 185 ES90
Woodside Dr., Dart. 187 FF91
Woodside End, Wem. 138 CL67
Woodside Gdns. E4 101 EB50
Woodside Gdns. N17 100 DS54
Woodside Gra. Rd. N12 98 DB49
Woodside Grn. SE25 202 DU100
Woodside Gro. N12 98 DC48
Woodside Hill, Ger.Cr. 90 AY54
Woodside La. N12 98 DB48
Woodside La., Bex. 186 EX86
Woodside La., Hat. 45 CZ21
Woodside Pk. SE25 202 DU99
Woodside Pk. Ave. E17 123 ED56
Woodside Pk. Rd. N12 98 DB49
Woodside Pl., Wem. 138 CL67
Woodside Rd. E13 144 EJ70
Woodside Rd. N22 99 DM52
Woodside Rd. SE25 202 DV100
Woodside Rd., Abb.L. 59 BV31
Woodside Rd., Amer. 55 AR37
Woodside Rd., Beac. 88 AJ52
Woodside Rd., Bexh. 167 FD84
Woodside Rd., Brom. 204 EL99
Woodside Rd., Cob. 214 CA113
Woodside Rd., Guil. 242 AT133
Woodside Rd., Kings.T. 178 CL94

This index reads in the sequence: Street Name / Postal District or Post Town / Map Page Number / Grid Reference

Name	Page	Grid
Yateley St. SE18	164	EK76
Yates Ct. NW2	139	CX65
Yattendon Rd., Horl.	269	DH148
Yeading Ave., Har.	116	BY61
Yeading Fork, Hayes	136	BW71
Yeading Gdns., Hayes	135	BV71
Yeading La., Hayes	135	BV72
Yeading La., Nthlt.	136	BW69
Yeames Clo. W13	137	CG72
Yeate St. N1	142	DR66
Yeatman Rd. N6	120	DF58
Yeats Clo. SE13	163	ED82
Eliot Pk.		
Yeats Clo., Red.	266	DC137
Yeldham Rd. W6	159	CX78
Yellow Hammer Ct. NW9	96	CS54
Eagle Dr.		
Yellowpine Way, Chig.	104	EV49
Yelverton Clo., Rom.	106	FK53
Yelverton Rd. SW11	160	DD82
Yenston Clo., Mord.	200	DA100
Yeo St. E3	143	EB71
Yeoman Clo. E6	145	EP72
Ferndale Rd.		
Yeoman Clo. SE27	181	DP90
Yeoman Rd., Nthlt.	136	BY66
Yeoman St. SE8	163	DY77
Yeoman Way, Red.	267	DH139
Yeomanry Clo., Epsom	217	CT112
Dirdene Gdns.		
Yeomans Acre, Ruis.	115	BU58
Yeomans Meadow, Sev.	256	FG126
Yeoman's Ms., Islw.	177	CE85
Queensbridge Pk.		
Yeoman's Row SW3	**276**	**C7**
Yeoman's Row SW3	160	DE76
Yeomans Way, Enf.	82	DW40
Yeomans Yd. E1	142	DT73
Chamber St.		
Yeomen Way, Ilf.	103	EQ51
Yeoveney Clo., Stai.	173	BD89
Yeovil Clo., Orp.	205	ES103
Yeovil Rd., Slou.	131	AL71
Yeovilton Pl., Kings.T.	177	CK92
Dukes Ave.		
Yerbury Rd. N19	121	DK62
Yester Dr., Chis.	184	EL94
Yester Pk., Chis.	185	EM94
Yester Rd., Chis.	184	EL94
Yevele Way, Horn.	128	FL59
Yew Ave., West Dr.	134	BL73
Yew Clo., Buck.H.	102	EK47
Yew Clo., Wal.Cr.	66	DS72
Yew Gro. NW2	119	CX63
Yew Gro., Welw.G.C.	30	DC10
Yew Pl., Wey.	195	BT104
Yew Tree Bottom Rd., Epsom	233	CV116
Yew Tree Clo. N21	99	DN45
Yew Tree Clo., Beac.	89	AM54
Yew Tree Clo., Brwd.	109	GB44
Yew Tree Clo., Chesh.	56	AU30
Botley Rd.		
Yew Tree Clo., Couls.	234	DF119
Yew Tree Clo., Hem.H.	40	BG22
Fishery Rd.		
Yew Tree Clo., Horl.	268	DG146
Yew Tree Clo., Sev.	256	FD123
Yew Tree Clo., Well.	166	EU81
Yew Tree Clo., Wor.Pk.	198	CS102
Yew Tree Ct., Borwd.	77	CK44
Barnet La.		
Yew Tree Dr., Cat.	252	DT125
Yew Tree Dr., Guil.	242	AV130
Yew Tree Dr., Hem.H.	57	BB28
Yew Tree Gdns., Rom.	127	FD57
Yew Tree Gdns. (Chadwell Heath), Rom.	126	EY57
Yew Tree Rd. W12	139	CT73
Yew Tree Rd., Dor.	247	CG134
Yew Tree Rd., Slou.	152	AU76
Yew Tree Rd., Uxb.	134	BM67
Yew Tree Wk., Houns.	176	BZ85
Yew Tree Wk., Lthd.	246	BX127
Yew Tree Wk., Maid.	110	AC64
Yew Tree Wk., Pur.	220	DQ110
Yew Tree Way, Croy.	221	DY110
Yew Trees, Egh.	193	BC97
Yew Trees, Shep.	194	BM98
Laleham Rd.		
Yew Wk., Har.	117	CE60
Yew Wk., Hodd.	49	EA18
Yewbank Clo., Ken.	236	DR115
Yewdale Clo., Brom.	184	EG93
Yewdells Clo., Bet.	249	CU133
Yewfield Rd. NW10	139	CT65
Yewlands, Hodd.	49	EA18
Yewlands, Saw.	36	EY06
Yewlands Clo., Bans.	234	DB115
Yewlands Dr., Hodd.	49	EA18
High St.		
Yews, The, Ashf.	175	BP91
Yews, The, Grav.	191	GK89
Yews Ave., Enf.	82	DV36
Yewtree Clo. N22	99	DJ53
Yewtree Clo., Har.	116	CB56
Yewtree Clo., E.St.Alb.	60	CB27
Yewtree Gdns., Epsom	232	CP115
Yewtree Rd., Beck.	203	DZ97
Yoakley Rd. N16	122	DS61
Yoke Clo. N7	141	DL65
Ewe Clo.		
Yolande Gdns. SE9	184	EL85
Yonge Pk. N4	121	DN62
York Ave. SW14	178	CQ85
York Ave. W7	137	CE74
York Ave., Hayes	135	BQ71
York Ave., Sid.	185	ES89
York Ave., Slou.	131	AQ72
York Ave., Stan.	95	CH53
York Ave., Wind.	151	AP82
York Bri. NW1	**272**	**F4**
York Bri. NW1	140	DG70
York Bldgs. WC2	**278**	**A1**
York Clo. E6	145	EM72
Boultwood Rd.		
York Clo. W7	137	CE74
York Ave.		
York Clo., Amer.	72	AT39
York Clo., Brwd.	109	FZ45
York Clo., Kings L.	58	BN29
York Clo., Mord.	200	DB98
York Clo., W.Byf.	212	BL112
York Cres., Borwd.	78	CR40
York Cres., Loug.	84	EL41
York Gdns., Walt.	196	BX103
York Gate N14	99	DL45
York Gate NW1	**272**	**F5**
York Gate NW1	140	DG70
York Gate, Cat.	236	DR122
York Gro. SE15	162	DW81
York Hill SE27	181	DP90
York Hill, Loug.	84	EL41
York Hill Est. SE27	181	DP90
York Ho., Wem.	118	CM63
York Ho. Pl. W8	160	DB75
York Ms. NW5	121	DH64
Kentish Town Rd.		
York Ms., Ilf.	125	EN62
York Rd.		
York Par., Brent.	157	CK78
York Pl. SW11	160	DC83
York Pl. WC2	**278**	**A1**
York Pl., Dag.	147	FC65
York Pl., Grays	170	GA79
York Pl., Ilf.	125	EN61
York Rd.		
York Ri. NW5	121	DH62
York Ri., Orp.	205	ES102
York Rd. E4	101	EA50
York Rd. E7	144	EG65
York Rd. E10	123	EC62
York Rd. E17	123	DX57
York Rd. N11	99	DK51
York Rd. N18	100	DV51
York Rd. N21	100	DR45
York Rd. SE1	**278**	**C4**
York Rd. SE1	161	DM75
York Rd. SW11	160	DC84
York Rd. SW18	160	DC84
York Rd. SW19	180	DC93
York Rd. W3	138	CQ72
York Rd. W5	157	CJ76
York Rd., Barn.	80	DC43
York Rd., Brent.	157	CK78
York Rd., Brwd.	109	FZ45
York Rd., Croy.	201	DN101
York Rd., Dart.	188	FM87
York Rd., Grav.	191	GJ90
York Rd., Epp.	70	FA27
York Rd. (Northfleet), Grav.	190	GD87
York Rd., Guil.	258	AX135
York Rd., Houns.	156	CB83
York Rd., Ilf.	125	EN62
York Rd., Kings.T.	178	CM94
York Rd., Nthwd.	93	BU54
York Rd., Rain.	147	FD66
York Rd., Rich.	178	CM85
Albert Rd.		
York Rd., St.Alb.	43	CF19
York Rd., S.Croy.	221	DX110
York Rd., Sutt.	218	DA107
York Rd., Tedd.	177	CE91
York Rd., Uxb.	134	BK66
York Rd., Wal.Cr.	67	DY34
York Rd., Wat.	76	BW43
York Rd., W.Byf.	212	BK112
York Rd., West.	238	EH119
York Rd., Wind.	151	AP82
York Rd., Wok.	226	AX119
York Sq. E14	143	DY72
York St. W1	**272**	**D7**
York St. W1	140	DF71
York St., Bark.	145	EQ67
Abbey Rd.		
York St., Mitch.	200	DG101
York St., Twick.	177	CG88
York Ter., Enf.	82	DQ38
York Ter. E. NW1	**272**	**G5**
York Ter. E. NW1	140	DG70
York Ter. W. NW1	**272**	**F5**
York Ter. W. NW1	140	DG70
York Way N1	141	DL67
York Way N7	141	DK65
York Way N20	98	DF48
York Way, Borwd.	78	CR40
York Way, Chess.	216	CL108
York Way, Felt.	176	BZ90
York Way, Hem.H.	40	BL21
Old Crabtree La.		
York Way, Wat.	76	BX36
York Way Ct. N1	141	DL67
York Way Est. N7	141	DL65
York Way		
Yorke Gdns., Reig.	250	DA133
Yorke Rd., Reig.	249	CZ133
Yorke Rd., Rick.	74	BN44
Yorkes, Harl.	51	ET17
Yorkland Ave., Well.	165	ET83
Yorkshire Clo. N16	122	DS62
Yorkshire Gdns. N18	100	DV50
Yorkshire Grey Pl. NW3	120	DC63
Heath St.		
Yorkshire Grey Yd. WC1	**274**	**B7**
Yorkshire Rd. E14	143	DY72
Yorkshire Rd., Mitch.	201	DL99
Yorkton St. E2	142	DU68
Young Rd. E16	144	EJ72
Young St. W8	160	DB75
Young St., Lthd.	247	CE125
Youngfield Rd., Hem.H.	39	BF19
Youngmans Clo., Enf.	82	DQ39
Young's Bldgs. EC1	**275**	**J4**
Youngs Ri., Welw.G.C.	29	CV09
Youngs Rd., Ilf.	125	ER57
Youngstroat La., Wok.	210	AY110
Yoxley App., Ilf.	125	EQ58
Yoxley Dr., Ilf.	125	EQ58
Yukon Rd. SW12	181	DH87
Yule Clo., St.Alb.	60	BZ30
Yuletide Clo. NW10	138	CS66
Yunus Khan Clo. E17	123	EA57

Z

Name	Page	Grid
Zampa Rd. SE16	162	DW78
Zander Ct. E2	142	DU68
St. Peter's Clo.		
Zangwill Rd. SE3	164	EK81
Zealand Ave., West Dr.	154	BK80
Zealand Rd. E3	143	DY68
Zelah Rd., Orp.	206	EV101
Zennor Rd. SW12	181	DJ88
Zenoria St. SE22	162	DT84
Zermatt Rd., Th.Hth.	202	DQ98
Zetland St. E14	143	EB71
Zig Zag Rd., Dor.	247	CJ130
Zig Zag Rd., Tad.	247	CK132
Zig-Zag Rd., Ken.	236	DQ116
Zion Pl., Grav.	191	GH87
Zion Pl., Th.Hth.	202	DR98
Zion Rd., Th.Hth.	202	DR98
Zion St., Sev.	257	FM121
Church Rd.		
Zoar St. SE1	**279**	**H2**
Zoffany St. N19	121	DK61

The following is a comprehensive listing of all the railway stations which appear in this atlas. Bold references can be found within the Central London enlarged scale section (pages 272-279).

The following is a comprehensive listing of all London Regional Transport Stations which appear in this atlas. Bold references can be found within the Central London enlarged scale section (pages 272-279). A London Underground map can be found on page 431. Restricted line services are indicated by brackets.

London Undergound Line Abbreviations

Bak.	Bakerloo	Dist.	District	Met.	Metropolitan
Cen.	Central	E.L.	East London	North.	Northern
Circ.	Circle	H. & C.	Hammersmith & City	Picc.	Piccadilly
D.L.R.	Docklands Light Railway	Jub.	Jubilee	Vic.	Victoria

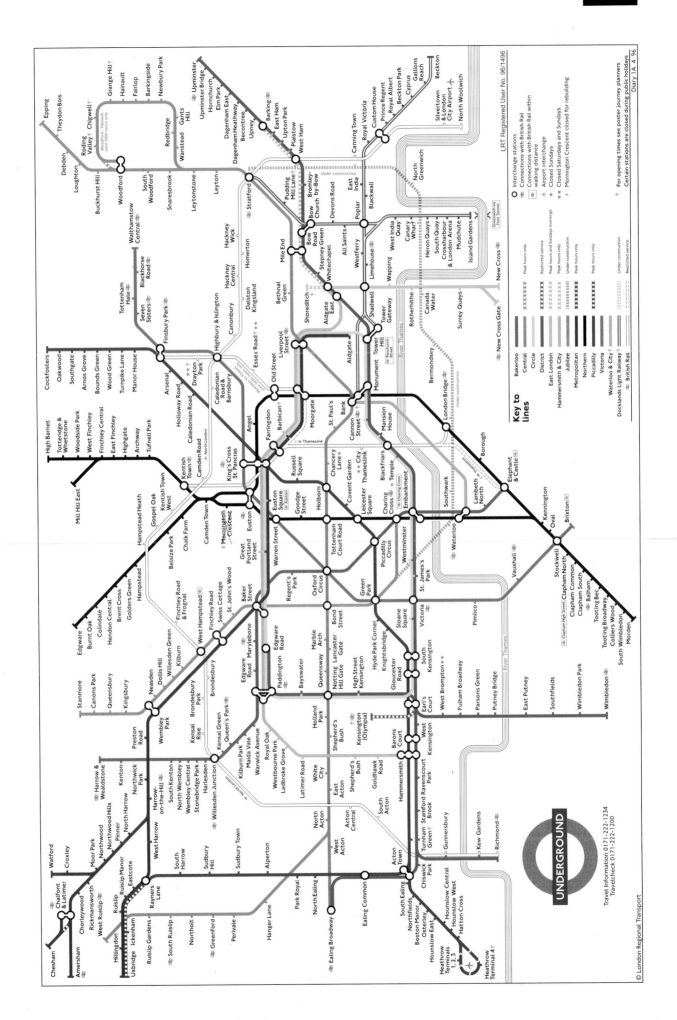

AYLESBURY VALE

D A C O R U M

ST.

WELWYN

ALBANS

HATFIELD

28 29 30

38 39 40 41 42 43 44 45 46

54 56 57 58 59 60 61 62 63 64

CHILTERN

WYCOMBE

55 72 73 74 75 76 77 78 79 80

THREE
RIVERS

WATFORD

HERTSMERE

88 89 90 91 92 93 94 95 96 97 98

BARNET

HARROW

110 111 112 113 114 115 116 117 118 119 120

SOUTH BUCKS

HILLINGDON

BRENT

CAMDE

130 131 132 133 134 135 136 137 138 139 140

SLOUGH

EALING

KENSINGTON &
CHELSEA

HAMMERSMITH &
FULHAM

WESTMIN

150 151 152 153 154 155 156 157 158 159 160

WINDSOR & MAIDENHEAD

HOUNSLOW

RICHMOND
UPON THAMES

WANDSWORTH

WOKINGHAM

172 173 174 175 176 177 178 179 180

SPELTHORNE

BRACKNELL
FOREST

192 193 194 195 196 197 198 199 200

RUNNYMEDE

KINGSTON

UPON THAMES

MERTON

SUTTON

210 211 212 213 214 215 216 217 218

SURREY HEATH

ELMBRIDGE

EPSOM
& EWELL

HART

226 227 228 229 230 231 232 233 234

WOKING

RUSHMOOR

REIGATE &

242 243 244 245 246 247 248 249 250

BANSTEAD

GUILDFORD

258 259 260 261 262 263 264 265 266

EAST
HANTS

MOLE VALLEY

268

W A V E R L E Y

CRAWL